SUPPLEMENT OF BASIC DOCUMENTS TO

INTERNATIONAL ENVIRONMENTAL LAW AND WORLD ORDER

A PROBLEM-ORIENTED COURSEBOOK

Second Edition

By

Lakshman D. Guruswamy
Professor of Law
The University of Tulsa

Sir Geoffrey W. R. Palmer, PC, KCMG, AC
Professor of Law
Victoria University of Wellington

Burns H. Weston
Bessie Dutton Murray Professor of Law
The University of Iowa

Jonathan C. Carlson
Professor of Law
The University of Iowa

AMERICAN CASEBOOK SERIES®

ST. PAUL, MINN., 1999

610 Opperman Drive
P.O. Box 64526
St. Paul, MN 55164–0526
1–800–328–9352

ISBN 0–314–23102–1

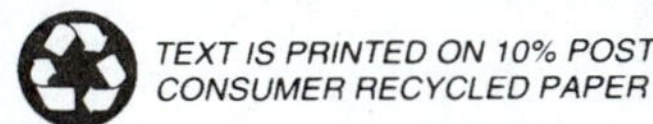

Preface

This collection, like its predecessor, has been assembled, with due regard for space limitations, to serve primarily as a documentary supplement to our coursebook, *International Environmental Law and World Order—A Problem-Oriented Coursebook* (2nd ed., West Group, 1999). Therefore, a fair number of the instruments contained in these pages (*e.g.*, Agenda 21), particularly if they are not principally environmental instruments (*e.g.*, the Helsinki Final Act, the GATT, etc.), are not reprinted in full and contain only those provisions that are pertinent to our pedagogical purposes. Nevertheless, we have tried to be as thorough as space would allow. To persons outside the classroom who are engaged in research or otherwise working in the international environmental law field—international civil servants and diplomats, governmental officials, non-governmental (citizen action) organizations, practicing lawyers, and others—we thus recommend this volume as a convenient quick and easy general reference.

As may be quickly ascertained from the Table of Contents, the majority of the instruments that follow are organized around the same themes to which our coursebook is dedicated, namely, the conceptually divisible components of our otherwise indivisible global environment: the atmosphere, the hydrosphere, the lithosphere, and the biosphere. The remainder—the "constitutive/organic" and the "miscellaneous"—reflect the truism that international environmental law, while clearly deserving of distinctive treatment in its own right, is nonetheless an interdependent function of the larger world order of which it is a part.

Three additional features merit special mention.

First, to help demonstrate the timing and evolution of international environmental law, we present the instruments that give partial expression to its existence in each topical area in chronological order.

Second, in Section 8, we have summarized and excerpted most of the leading international adjudicative and arbitral decisions, several of them pre-dating World War II, that have helped to lay the foundations of the emerging, modern-day customary international law of global environmental protection: the *Case Relating to the Territorial Jurisdiction of the International Commission of the River Oder*, the *Diversion of Water from the Meuse Case*, the *Lake Lanoux Arbitration*, the *Trail Smelter Arbitration*, the *Corfu Channel Case*, and the *Nuclear Tests Cases*. The first three involve disputes arising out of the use of shared water resources and therefore are grouped together.

Third, in the Appendix, we have detailed the status, usually as of at least 1 January 1999, of the instruments contained in this volume.[1] In so doing, we have sought to contribute to the knowledge that is needed to assess the extent to which, if at all, any given instrument "counts as law."

1. Anyone seeking to know the status of these or other environmentally pertinent instruments beginning after 1 January 1999 is encouraged to consult B. Weston, ed., *International Law and World Order: Basic Documents* (1994), particularly Volume V thereof.

Each of these features, we believe, adds significantly to the utility of this volume both within and beyond the classroom.

Finally, while not wanting to imply in any way any dissatisfaction with those who have helped us and to whom we extend our sincere thanks in the Acknowledgments, we recognize that there always is room for improvement. Accordingly, we will welcome any and all suggestions for improvements should our effort warrant future editions.

LAKSHMAN D. GURUSWAMY
Tulsa, Oklahoma

SIR GEOFFREY W. R. PALMER
Wellington, New Zealand

BURNS H. WESTON
Iowa City, Iowa

JONATHAN C. CARLSON
Iowa City, Iowa

February 1999

Acknowledgments

Inasmuch as this *Supplement of Basic Documents to International Environmental Law and World Order* builds upon a prior edition, we continue to remain indebted to those who helped so graciously to assist in the preparation of the first edition. Their names are recorded therein and we thank them again.

This second edition would not have been possible without the good humor and able assistance of Jason Aamodt (Rearch Fellow, the National Energy-Environment Law and Policy Institute at the University of Tulsa) and our research assistants at the University of Iowa: Yasir S. Aleemuddin, Matthew T. Cronin, Du Guangming, Ryan Maas, Edwin M. Rodriguez, and Dimiter L. Vutov. We also wish to express our sincere appreciation and gratitude to Grace Newby and Mary E. Sleichter, who put many hours of effort toward all aspects of the endeavor, without which this would be a poorer volume in every respect. Errors, of course, are our responsibility alone.

L.D.G.
G.W.R.P.
B.H.W.
J.C.C.

February 1999

Table of Abbreviations

The following abbreviations are used in the headnotes and footnotes to the instruments included in this documentary supplement.

A	United Nations General Assembly
Add.	Addendum
A.J.I.L.	American Journal of International Law
Alb.	Albania
AMR/SCM	Document of the Session of the Special Consultative Meeting on Antarctic Mineral Resources
App.	Appendix
ASEAN	Association of South-East Asian Nations
ATSCM	Special Consultative Meeting of Antarctic Treaty Parties
Belg.	Belgium
Can.	Canada
CE	Council of Europe
CONF, Conf	Conference
C.M.L.R.	Common Market Law Reports
Czech.	Czechoslovakia
Den.	Denmark
Doc.	Document
E	United Nations Economic and Social Council
ECE	Economic Commission for Europe
EEC	European Economic Community
EU	European Union
FAO	Food and Agriculture Organisation of the United Nations
FCCC	Framework Convention on Climate Change
Fr.	France
G.A., GA	United Nations General Assembly
G.A.T.T., GATT	General Agreement on Tariffs and Trade
Ger.	Germany
IAEA	International Atomic Energy Agency
IAEA INFCIRC	International Atomic Energy Agency Information Circular
IAEA Leg. Ser.	International Atomic Energy Agency Legal Series
I.C.J.	Reports of Judgments, Advisory Opinions and Orders of the International Court of Justice
I.L.A., ILA	International Law Association, Reports of Annual Conferences of the International Law Association
I.L.C., ILC	International Law Commission
I.L.M.	International Legal Materials
IMCO	Inter-Governmental Maritime Consultative Organisation
IMO	International Maritime Organisation

Mtg.	Meeting
Neth.	Netherlands
N.Z.	New Zealand
No.	Number
O.A.S. Off. Rec.	Organisation of American States Official Records
O.A.S.T.S.	Organisation of American States Treaty Series
OAU	Organisation of African Unity
OEA/Ser.	Organizacion Estados Americanos Series (Organisation of American States Series)
O.E.C.D., OECD	Organisation for Economic Co-operation and Development
Off.	Official
O.J.E.C.	Official Journal of the European Communities
P.C.I.J.	Permanent Court of International Justice: Reports
Pt., pt.	Part
RES, Res.	Resolution
Rev.	Revision, Revised
S	United Nations Security Council
Ser.	Series
Sess.	Session
Stat.	U.S. Statutes at Large
Supp.	Supplement
T.I.A.S.	U.S. Treaties and Other International Acts Series
U.K.	United Kingdom
U.N., UN	United Nations
UNEP	United Nations Environment Programme
U.N.G.A., UNGA	United Nations General Assembly
U.N. GAOR	United Nations General Assembly Official Record
U.N.J.Y.B.	United Nations Juridical Yearbook
U.N.R.I.A.A.	United Nations Reports of International Arbitral Awards
UNSC	United Nations Security Council
U.N.T.S.	United Nations Treaty Series
U.S.	United States
U.S.T.	U.S. Treaties
Weston	International Law and World Order: Basic Documents (Burns H. Weston ed., 7 vols, 1994—)
WCED	World Commission on Environment and Development
W.T.O., WTO	World Trade Organization
Y.B.I.L.C.	Yearbook of the International Law Commission
Y.B.U.N.	Yearbook of the United Nations

Table of Contents

Page

SUPPLEMENT OF BASIC DOCUMENTS TO

INTERNATIONAL ENVIRONMENTAL LAW AND WORLD ORDER

A PROBLEM-ORIENTED COURSEBOOK

SECOND EDITION

*

1. Constitutive/Organic

A. General

1.1 Constitution of the United States of America. *Arts. I, II, III, V & Amendment X*

ARTICLE I

* * *

SECTION 8. The Congress shall have Power To lay and collect Taxes, Duties, Imposts and Excises, to pay the Debts and provide for the common Defence and general Welfare of the United States; but all Duties, Imposts and Excises shall be uniform throughout the United States;

To borrow Money on the credit of the United States;

To regulate Commerce with foreign Nations, and among the several States, and with the Indian Tribes;

To establish an uniform Rule of Naturalization, and uniform Laws on the subject of Bankruptcies throughout the United States;

To coin Money, regulate the Value thereof, and of foreign Coin, and fix the Standard of Weights and Measures;

To provide for the Punishment of counterfeiting the Securities and current Coin of the United States;

To establish Post Offices and post Roads;

To promote the Progress of Science and useful Arts, by securing for limited Times to Authors and Inventors the exclusive Right to their respective Writings and Discoveries;

To constitute Tribunals inferior to the supreme Court;

To define and punish Piracies and Felonies committed on the high Seas, and Offences against the Law of Nations;

To declare War, grant Letters of Marque and Reprisal, and make Rules concerning Captures on Land and Water;

To raise and support Armies, but no Appropriation of Money to that Use shall be for a longer Term than two Years;

To provide and maintain a Navy;

To make Rules for the Government and Regulation of the land and naval Forces;

To provide for calling forth the Militia to execute the Laws of the Union, suppress Insurrections and repel Invasions;

To provide for organizing, arming, and disciplining, the Militia, and for governing such Part of them as may be employed in the Service of the United States, reserving to the States respectively, the Appointment of the Officers, and the Authority of training the Militia according to the discipline prescribed by Congress;

To exercise exclusive Legislation in all Cases whatsoever, over such District (not exceeding ten Miles square) as may, by Cession of particular States, and the Acceptance of Congress, become the Seat of the Government of the United States, and to exercise like Authority over all Places purchased by the Consent of the Legislature of the State in which the Same shall be, for the Erection of Forts, Magazines, Arsenals, dock–Yards, and other needful Buildings;—And

To make all Laws which shall be necessary and proper for carrying into Execution the foregoing Powers, and all other Powers vested by this Constitution in the Government of the United States, or in any Department or Officer thereof.

SECTION 9. The Migration or Importation of such Persons as any of the States now existing shall think proper to admit, shall not be prohibited by the Congress prior to the Year one thousand eight hundred and eight, but a Tax or duty may be imposed on such Importation, not exceeding ten dollars for each Person.

The Privilege of the Writ of Habeas Corpus shall not be suspended, unless when in Cases of Rebellion or Invasion the public Safety may require it.

No Bill of Attainder or ex post facto Law shall be passed.

No Capitation, or other direct, Tax shall be laid, unless in Proportion to the Census or Enumeration herein before directed to be taken.

No Tax or Duty shall be laid on Articles exported from any State.

No Preference shall be given by any Regulation of Commerce or Revenue to the Ports of one State over those of another; nor shall Vessels bound to, or from, one State, be obliged to enter, clear or pay Duties in another.

No Money shall be drawn from the Treasury, but in Consequence of Appropriations made by Law; and a regular Statement and Account of the Receipts and Expenditures of all public Money shall be published from time to time.

No Title of Nobility shall be granted by the United States: And no Person holding any Office of Profit or Trust under them, shall, without the Consent of the Congress, accept of any present, Emolument, Office, or Title, of any kind whatever, from any King, Prince or foreign State.

SECTION 10. No State shall enter into any Treaty, Alliance, or Confederation; grant Letters of Marque and Reprisal; coin Money; emit Bills of Credit; make any Thing but gold and silver Coin a Tender in Payment of Debts; pass any Bill of Attainder, ex post facto Law, or Law impairing the Obligation of Contracts, or grant any Title of Nobility.

No State shall, without the Consent of the Congress, lay any Imposts or Duties on Imports or Exports, except what may be absolutely necessary for executing its inspection Laws: and the net Produce of all Duties and Imposts, laid by any State on Imports or Exports, shall be for the Use of the Treasury of the United States; and all such Laws shall be subject to the Revision and Control of the Congress.

No State shall, without the Consent of Congress, lay any Duty of Tonnage, keep Troops, or Ships of War in time of Peace, enter into any Agreement or Compact with another State, or with a foreign Power, or engage in War, unless actually invaded, or in such imminent Danger as will not admit of delay.

ARTICLE II

SECTION 1. The executive Power shall be vested in a President of the United States of America. He shall hold his Office during the Term of four Years[.]

* * *

SECTION 2. The President shall be Commander in Chief of the Army and Navy of the United States, and of the Militia of the several States, when called into the actual Service of the United States; he may require the Opinion, in writing, of the principal Officer in each of the executive Departments, upon any Subject relating to the Duties of their respective Offices, and he shall have Power to grant Reprieves and Pardons for Offences against the United States, except in Cases of Impeachment.

He shall have Power, by and with the Advice and Consent of the Senate, to make Treaties, provided two thirds of the Senators present concur; and he shall nominate, and by and with the Advice and Consent of the Senate, shall appoint Ambassadors, other public Ministers and Consuls, Judges of the supreme Court, and all other Officers of the United States, whose Appointments are not herein otherwise provided for, and which shall be established by Law: but the Congress may by Law vest the Appointment of such inferior Officers, as they think proper, in the President alone, in the Courts of Law, or in the Heads of Departments.

The President shall have Power to fill up all Vacancies that may happen during the Recess of the Senate, by granting Commissions which shall expire at the End of their next Session.

SECTION 3. He shall * * * receive Ambassadors and other public Ministers.

* * *

ARTICLE III

SECTION 1. The judicial Power of the United States, shall be vested in one supreme Court, and in such inferior Courts as the Congress may from time to time ordain and establish. * * *

SECTION 2. The judicial Power shall extend to all Cases, in Law and Equity, arising under this Constitution, the Laws of the United States, and Treaties made, or which shall be made, under their Authority;—to all Cases affecting Ambassadors, other public ministers and Consuls;—to all Cases of admiralty and maritime Jurisdiction;—to Controversies to which the United States shall be a Party;—to Controversies between two or more States;—between a State and Citizens of another State;—between Citizens of different States;—between Citizens of the same State claiming Lands under Grants of different States, and between a State, or the Citizens thereof, and foreign States, Citizens or Subjects.

In all Cases affecting Ambassadors, other public Ministers and Consuls, and those in which a State shall be Party, the supreme Court shall have original Jurisdiction. In all the other Cases before mentioned, the supreme Court shall have appellate Jurisdiction, both as to Law and Fact, with such Exceptions, and under such Regulations as the Congress shall make.

* * *

SECTION 3. Treason against the United States, shall consist only in levying War against them, or in adhering to their Enemies, giving them Aid and Comfort. No Person shall be convicted of Treason unless on the Testimony of two Witnesses to the same overt Act, or on Confession in open Court.

The Congress shall have Power to declare the Punishment of Treason, but no Attainder of Treason shall work Corruption of Blood, or Forfeiture except during the Life of the Person attainted.

* * *

ARTICLE VI

This Constitution, and the Laws of the United States which shall be made in Pursuance thereof; and all Treaties made, or which shall be made, under the Authority of the United States, shall be the supreme Law of the Land; and the Judges in every

State shall be bound thereby, any Thing in the Constitution or Laws of any State to the Contrary notwithstanding.

* * *

AMENDMENT X

The powers not delegated to the United States by the Constitution, nor prohibited by it to the States, are reserved to the States respectively, or to the people.

* * *

1.2 Constitution of the International Labour Organization (Without Annex, but as Revised Through 9 October 1946). Concluded at Versailles, 28 June 1919. Entered into force, 10 January 1920. 15 U.N.T.S. 35, 49 Stat. 2712 & 3480, T.I.A.S. No. 1868, T.S. No. 874: *Arts. 1, 2, 22, 24–34, 37*

Preamble

Whereas universal and lasting peace can be established only if it is based upon social justice;

And whereas conditions of labour exist involving such injustice, hardship and privation to large numbers of people as to produce unrest so great that the peace and harmony of the world are imperilled; and an improvement of those conditions is urgently required; as, for example, by the regulation of the hours of work, including the establishment of a maximum working day and week, the regulation of the labour supply, the prevention of unemployment, the provision of an adequate living wage, the protection of the worker against sickness, disease and injury arising out of his employment, the protection of children, young persons and women, provision for old age and injury, protection of the interests of workers when employed in countries other than their own, recognition of the principle of equal remuneration for work of equal value, recognition of the principle of freedom of association, the organisation of vocational and technical education and other measures;

Whereas also the failure of any nation to adopt humane conditions of labour is an obstacle in the way of other nations which desire to improve the conditions in their own countries;

The High Contracting Parties, moved by sentiments of justice and humanity as well as by the desire to secure the permanent peace of the world, and with a view to attaining the objectives set forth in this Preamble, agree to the following Constitution of the International Labour Organisation:

Chapter I—Organisation

Article 1

1. A permanent organisation is hereby established for the promotion of the objects set forth in the Preamble to this Constitution and in the Declaration concerning the aims and purposes of the International Labour Organisation adopted at Philadelphia on 10 May 1944 the text of which is annexed to this Constitution.

2. The Members of the International Labour Organisation shall be the States which were Members of the Organisation on 1 November 1945, and such other States as may become Members in pursuance of the provisions of paragraphs 3 and 4 of this article.

3. Any original member of the United Nations and any State admitted to membership of the United Nations by a decision of the General Assembly in accordance with the provisions of the Charter may become a Member of the International Labour Organisation by communicating to the Director–General of the International Labour Office its formal acceptance of the obligations of the Constitution of the International Labour Organisation.

4. The General Conference of the International Labour Organisation may also admit Members to the Organisation by a vote concurred in by two-thirds of the delegates attending the session, including two-thirds of the Government delegates present and voting. Such admission shall take effect on the communication to the Director–General of the International Labour Office by the government of the new Member of its formal acceptance of the obligations of the Constitution of the Organisation.

5. No Member of the International Labour Organisation may withdraw from the Organisation without giving notice of its intention so to do to the Director–General of the International Labour Office. Such notice shall take effect two years after the date of its reception by the Director–General, subject to the Member having at that time fulfilled all financial obligations arising out of its membership. When a Member has ratified any international labour Convention, such withdrawal shall not affect the continued validity for the period provided for in the Convention of all obligations arising thereunder or relating thereto.

6. In the event of any State having ceased to be a Member of the Organisation, its readmission to membership shall be governed by the provisions of paragraph 3 or paragraph 4 of this article as the case may be.

Article 2

The permanent organisation shall consist of—

(a) a General Conference of representatives of the Members;

(b) a Governing Body composed as described in article 7; and

(c) an International Labour Office controlled by the Governing Body.

* * *

Article 22

Each of the Members agrees to make an annual report to the International Labour Office on the measures which it has taken to give effect to the provisions of Conventions to which it is a party. These reports shall be made in such form and shall contain such particulars as the Governing Body may request.

* * *

Article 24

In the event of any representation being made to the International Labour Office by an industrial association of employers or of workers that any of the Members has failed to secure in any respect the effective observance within its jurisdiction of any Convention to which it is a party, the Governing Body may communicate this representation to the government against which it is made, and may invite that government to make such statement on the subject as it may think fit.

Article 25

If no statement is received within a reasonable time from the government in question, or if the statement when received is not deemed to be satisfactory by the Governing Body, the latter shall have the right to publish the representation and the statement, if any, made in reply to it.

Article 26

1. Any of the Members shall have the right to file a complaint with the International Labour Office if it is not satisfied that any other Member is securing the effective observance of any Convention which both have ratified in accordance with the foregoing articles.

2. The Governing Body may, if it thinks fit, before referring such a complaint to a Commission of Inquiry, as hereinafter provided for, communicate with the government in question in the manner described in article 24.

3. If the Governing Body does not think it necessary to communicate the complaint to the government in question, or if, when it has made such communication,

no statement in reply has been received within a reasonable time which the Governing Body considers to be satisfactory, the Governing Body may appoint a Commission of Inquiry to consider the complaint and to report thereon.

4. The Governing Body may adopt the same procedure either of its own motion or on receipt of a complaint from a delegate to the Conference.

5. When any matter arising out of article 25 or 26 is being considered by the Governing Body, the government in question shall, if not already represented thereon, be entitled to send a representative to take part in the proceedings of the Governing Body while the matter is under consideration. Adequate notice of the date on which the matter will be considered shall be given to the government in question.

Article 27

The Members agree that, in the event of the reference of a complaint to a Commission of Inquiry under article 26, they will each, whether directly concerned in the complaint or not, place at the disposal of the Commission all the information in their possession which bears upon the subject-matter of the complaint.

Article 28

When the Commission of Inquiry has fully considered the complaint, it shall prepare a report embodying its findings on all questions of fact relevant to determining the issue between the parties and containing such recommendations as it may think proper as to the steps which should be taken to meet the complaint and the time within which they should be taken.

Article 29

1. The Director–General of the International Labour Office shall communicate the report of the Commission of Inquiry to the Governing Body and to each of the governments concerned in the complaint, and shall cause it to be published.

2. Each of these governments shall within three months inform the Director–General of the International Labour Office whether or not it accepts the recommendations contained in the report of the Commission; and if not, whether it proposes to refer the complaint to the International Court of Justice.

Article 30

In the event of any Member failing to take the action required by paragraphs 5*(b)*, 6*(b)* or 7*(b)*(i) of article 19 with regard to a Convention or Recommendation, any other Member shall be entitled to refer the matter to the Governing Body. In the event of the Governing Body finding that there has been such a failure, it shall report the matter to the Conference.

Article 31

The decision of the International Court of Justice in regard to a complaint or matter which has been referred to it in pursuance of article 29 shall be final.

Article 32

The International Court of Justice may affirm, vary or reverse any of the findings or recommendations of the Commission of Inquiry, if any.

Article 33

In the event of any Member failing to carry out within the time specified the recommendations, if any, contained in the report of the Commission of Inquiry, or in the decision of the International Court of Justice, as the case may be, the Governing

Body may recommend to the Conference such action as it may deem wise and expedient to secure compliance therewith.

Article 34

The defaulting government may at any time inform the Governing Body that it has taken the steps necessary to comply with the recommendations of the Commission of Inquiry or with those in the decision of the International Court of Justice, as the case may be, and may request it to constitute a Commission of Inquiry to verify its contention. In this case the provisions of articles 27, 28, 29, 31 and 32 shall apply, and if the report of the Commission of Inquiry or the decision of the International Court of Justice is in favour of the defaulting government, the Governing Body shall forthwith recommend the discontinuance of any action taken in pursuance of article 33.

* * *

Article 37

1. Any question or dispute relating to the interpretation of this Constitution or of any subsequent Convention concluded by the Members in pursuance of the provisions of this Constitution shall be referred for decision to the International Court of Justice.

2. Notwithstanding the provisions of paragraph 1 of this article the Governing Body may make and submit to the Conference for approval rules providing for the appointment of a tribunal for the expeditious determination of any dispute or question relating to the interpretation of a Convention which may be referred thereto by the Governing Body or in accordance with the terms of the Convention. Any applicable judgement or advisory opinion of the International Court of Justice shall be binding upon any tribunal established in virtue of this paragraph. Any award made by such a tribunal shall be circulated to the Members of the Organisation and any observations which they may make thereon shall be brought before the Conference.

* * *

1.3 Charter of the United Nations (as Amended). Concluded at San Francisco, 26 June 1945. Entered into force, 24 October 1945. 1 U.N.T.S. XVI, 1976 Y.B.U.N. 1043, 59 Stat. 1031, T.S. No. 993, *reprinted in* 1 Weston I.A.1

WE THE PEOPLES OF THE UNITED NATIONS DETERMINED

to save succeeding generations from the scourge of war, which twice in our life-time has brought untold sorrow to mankind, and

to reaffirm faith in fundamental human rights, in the dignity and worth of the human person, in the equal rights of men and women and of nations large and small, and

to establish conditions under which justice and respect for the obligations arising from treaties and other sources of international law can be maintained, and

to promote social progress and better standards of life in larger freedom,

AND FOR THESE ENDS

to practice tolerance and live together in peace with one another as good neighbours, and

to unite our strength to maintain international peace and security, and

to ensure, by the acceptance of principles and the institution of methods, that armed force shall not be used, save in the common interest, and

to employ international machinery for the promotion of the economic and social advancement of all peoples,

HAVE RESOLVED TO COMBINE OUR EFFORTS TO ACCOMPLISH THESE AIMS

Accordingly, our respective Governments, through representatives assembled in the city of San Francisco, who have exhibited their full powers found to be in good and due form, have agreed to the present Charter of the United Nations and do hereby establish an international organization to be known as the United Nations.

Chapter I. PURPOSES AND PRINCIPLES

Article 1

The Purposes of the United Nations are:

1. To maintain international peace and security, and to that end: to take effective collective measures for the prevention and removal of threats to the peace, and for the suppression of acts of aggression or other breaches of the peace, and to bring about by peaceful means, and in conformity with the principles of justice and international law, adjustment or settlement of international disputes or situations which might lead to a breach of the peace;

2. To develop friendly relations among nations based on respect for the principle of equal rights and self-determination of peoples, and to take other appropriate measures to strengthen universal peace;

3. To achieve international co-operation in solving international problems of an economic, social, cultural, or humanitarian character, and in promoting and encouraging respect for human rights and for fundamental freedoms for all without distinction as to race, sex, language, or religion; and

4. To be a centre for harmonizing the actions of nations in the attainment of these common ends.

Article 2

The Organization and its Members, in pursuit of the Purposes stated in Article 1, shall act in accordance with the following Principles.

1. The Organization is based on the principle of the sovereign equality of all its Members.

2. All Members, in order to ensure to all of them the rights and benefits resulting from membership, shall fulfil in good faith the obligations assumed by them in accordance with the present Charter.

3. All Members shall settle their international disputes by peaceful means in such a manner that international peace and security, and justice, are not endangered.

4. All Members shall refrain in their international relations from the threat or use of force against the territorial integrity or political independence of any state, or in any other manner inconsistent with the Purposes of the United Nations.

5. All Members shall give the United Nations every assistance in any action it takes in accordance with the present Charter, and shall refrain from giving assistance to any state against which the United Nations is taking preventive or enforcement action.

6. The Organization shall ensure that states which are not Members of the United Nations act in accordance with these Principles so far as may be necessary for the maintenance of international peace and security.

7. Nothing contained in the present Charter shall authorize the United Nations to intervene in matters which are essentially within the domestic jurisdiction of any state or shall require the Members to submit such matters to settlement under the present Charter; but this principle shall not prejudice the application of enforcement measures under Chapter VII.

Chapter II. MEMBERSHIP

Article 3

The original Members of the United Nations shall be the states which, having participated in the United Nations Conference on International Organization at San Francisco, or having previously signed the Declaration by United Nations of 1 January 1942, sign the present Charter and ratify it in accordance with Article 110.

Article 4

1. Membership in the United Nations is open to all other peace-loving states which accept the obligations contained in the present Charter and, in the judgment of the Organization, are able and willing to carry out these obligations.

2. The admission of any such state to membership in the United Nations will be effected by a decision of the General Assembly upon the recommendation of the Security Council.

Article 5

A Member of the United Nations against which preventive or enforcement action has been taken by the Security Council may be suspended from the exercise of the rights and privileges of membership by the General Assembly upon the recommendation of the Security Council. The exercise of these rights and privileges may be restored by the Security Council.

Article 6

A Member of the United Nations which has persistently violated the Principles contained in the present Charter may be expelled from the Organization by the General Assembly upon the recommendation of the Security Council.

Chapter III. ORGANS

Article 7

1. There are established as the principal organs of the United Nations: a General Assembly, a Security Council, an Economic and Social Council, a Trusteeship Council, an International Court of Justice, and a Secretariat.

2. Such subsidiary organs as may be found necessary may be established in accordance with the present Charter.

Article 8

The United Nations shall place no restrictions on the eligibility of men and women to participate in any capacity and under conditions of equality in its principal and subsidiary organs.

Chapter IV. THE GENERAL ASSEMBLY

Composition

Article 9

1. The General Assembly shall consist of all the Members of the United Nations.

2. Each Member shall have not more than five representatives in the General Assembly.

Function and powers

Article 10

The General Assembly may discuss any questions or any matters within the scope of the present Charter or relating to the powers and functions of any organs provided for in the present Charter, and, except as provided in Article 12, may make recommendations to the Members of the United Nations or to the Security Council or to both on any such questions or matters.

Article 11

1. The General Assembly may consider the general principles of co-operation in the maintenance of international peace and security, including the principles governing disarmament and the regulation of armaments, and may make recommendations with regard to such principles to the Members or to the Security Council or to both.

2. The General Assembly may discuss any questions relating to the maintenance of international peace and security brought before it by any Member of the United Nations, or by the Security Council, or by a state which is not a Member of the United Nations in accordance with Article 35, paragraph 2, and, except as provided in Article 12, may make recommendations with regard to any such questions to the state or states concerned or to the Security Council or to both. Any such question on which action is necessary shall be referred to the Security Council by the General Assembly either before or after discussion.

3. The General Assembly may call the attention of the Security Council to situations which are likely to endanger international peace and security.

4. The powers of the General Assembly set forth in this Article shall not limit the general scope of Article 10.

Article 12

1. While the Security Council is exercising in respect of any dispute or situation the functions assigned to it in the present Charter, the General Assembly shall not

make any recommendation with regard to that dispute or situation unless the Security Council so requests.

2. The Secretary–General, with the consent of the Security Council, shall notify the General Assembly at each session of any matters relative to the maintenance of international peace and security which are being dealt with by the Security Council and shall similarly notify the General Assembly, or the Members of the United Nations if the General Assembly is not in session, immediately the Security Council ceases to deal with such matters.

Article 13

1. The General Assembly shall initiate studies and make recommendations for the purpose of:

a. Promoting international co-operation in the political field and encouraging the progressive development of international law and its codification;

b. Promoting international co-operation in the economic, social, cultural, educational, and health fields, and assisting in the realization of human rights and fundamental freedoms for all without distinction as to race, sex, language, or religion.

2. The further responsibilities, functions and powers of the General Assembly with respect to matters mentioned in paragraph 1(b) above are set forth in Chapters IX and X.

Article 14

Subject to the provisions of Article 12, the General Assembly may recommend measures for the peaceful adjustment of any situation, regardless of origin, which it deems likely to impair the general welfare or friendly relations among nations, including situations resulting from a violation of the provisions of the present Charter setting forth the Purposes and Principles of the United Nations.

Article 15

1. The General Assembly shall receive and consider annual and special reports from the Security Council; these reports shall include an account of the measures that the Security Council has decided upon or taken to maintain international peace and security.

2. The General Assembly shall receive and consider reports from the other organs of the United Nations.

Article 16

The General Assembly shall perform such functions with respect to the international trusteeship system as are assigned to it under Chapters XII and XIII, including the approval of the trusteeship agreements for areas not designated as strategic.

Article 17

1. The General Assembly shall consider and approve the budget of the Organization.

2. The expenses of the Organization shall be borne by the Members as apportioned by the General Assembly.

3. The General Assembly shall consider and approve any financial and budgetary arrangements with specialized agencies referred to in Article 57 and shall examine the administrative budgets of such specialized agencies with a view to making recommendations to the agencies concerned.

Voting

Article 18

1. Each member of the General Assembly shall have one vote.

2. Decisions of the General Assembly on important questions shall be made by a two-thirds majority of the members present and voting. These questions shall include: recommendations with respect to the maintenance of international peace and security, the election of the non-permanent members of the Security Council, the election of members of the Economic and Social Council, the election of the members of the Trusteeship Council in accordance with paragraph 1(c) of Article 86, the admission of new Members to the United Nations, the suspension of the rights and privileges of membership, the expulsion of Members, questions relating to the operation of the trusteeship system, and budgetary questions.

3. Decisions on other questions, including the determination of additional categories of questions to be decided by a two-thirds majority, shall be made by a majority of the members present and voting.

Article 19

A Member of the United Nations which is in arrears in the payment of its financial contributions to the Organization shall have no vote in the General Assembly if the amount of its arrears equals or exceeds the amount of the contributions due from it for the preceding two full years. The General Assembly may, nevertheless, permit such a member to vote if it is satisfied that the failure to pay is due to conditions beyond the control of the Member.

Procedure

Article 20

The General Assembly shall meet in regular annual sessions and in such special sessions as occasion may require. Special sessions shall be convoked by the Secretary-General at the request of the Security Council or of a majority of the Members of the United Nations.

Article 21

The General Assembly shall adopt its own rules of procedure. It shall elect its President for each session.

Article 22

The General Assembly may establish such subsidiary organs as it deems necessary for the performance of its functions.

CHAPTER V. THE SECURITY COUNCIL

Composition

Article 23[a]

1. The Security Council shall consist of fifteen Members of the United Nations. The Republic of China, France, the Union of Soviet Socialist Republics, the United Kingdom of Great Britain and Northern Ireland, and the United States of America shall be permanent members of the Security Council. The General Assembly shall elect ten other Members of the United Nations to be non-permanent members of the Security Council, due regard being specially paid, in the first instance to contribution

a. Amended text of Article 23, which entered into force on 31 August 1965.

of Members of the United Nations to the maintenance of international peace and security and to the other purposes of the Organization, and also to equitable geographical distribution.

2. The non-permanent members of the Security Council shall be elected for a term of two years. In the first election of the non-permanent members after the increase of the membership of the Security Council from eleven to fifteen, two of the four additional members shall be chosen for a term of one year. A retiring member shall not be eligible for immediate re-election.

3. Each member of the Security Council shall have one representative.

Functions and powers

Article 24

1. In order to ensure prompt and effective action by the United Nations, its Members confer on the Security Council primary responsibility for the maintenance of international peace and security, and agree that in carrying out its duties under this responsibility the Security Council acts on their behalf.

2. In discharging these duties the Security Council shall act in accordance with the Purposes and Principles of the United Nations. The specific powers granted to the Security Council for the discharge of these duties are laid down in Chapters VI, VII, VIII, and XII.

3. The Security Council shall submit annual and, when necessary, special reports to the General Assembly for its consideration.

Article 25

The members of the United Nations agree to accept and carry out the decisions of the Security Council in accordance with the present Charter.

Article 26

In order to promote the establishment and maintenance of international peace and security with the least diversion for armaments of the world's human and economic resources, the Security Council shall be responsible for formulating, with the assistance of the Military Staff Committee referred to in Article 47, plans to be submitted to the Members of the United Nations for the establishment of a system for the regulation of armaments.

Voting

Article 27[b]

1. Each member of the Security Council shall have one vote.

2. Decisions of the Security Council on procedural matters shall be made by an affirmative vote of nine members.

3. Decisions of the Security Council on all other matters shall be made by an affirmative vote of nine members including the concurring votes of the permanent members; provided that, in decisions under Chapter VI, and under paragraph 3 of Article 52, a party to a dispute shall abstain from voting.

Procedure

Article 28

1. The Security Council shall be so organized as to be able to function continuously. Each member of the Security Council shall for this purpose be represented at all times at the seat of the Organization.

b. Amended text of Article 27, which entered into force on 31 August 1965.

2. The Security Council shall hold periodic meetings at which each of its members may, if it so desires, be represented by a member of the government or by some other specially designated representative.

3. The Security Council may hold meetings at such places other than the seat of the Organization as in its judgment will best facilitate its work.

Article 29

The Security Council may establish such subsidiary organs as it deems necessary for the performance of its functions.

Article 30

The Security Council shall adopt its own rules of procedure, including the method of selecting its President.

Article 31

Any Member of the United Nations which is not a member of the Security Council may participate, without vote, in the discussion of any question brought before the Security Council whenever the latter considers that the interests of that Member are specially affected.

Article 32

Any Member of the United Nations which is not a member of the Security Council or any state which is not a Member of the United Nations, if it is a party to a dispute under consideration by the Security Council, shall be invited to participate, without vote, in the discussion relating to the dispute. The Security Council shall lay down such conditions as it deems just for the participation of a state which is not a Member of the United Nations.

Chapter VI. PACIFIC SETTLEMENT OF DISPUTES

Article 33

1. The parties to any dispute, the continuance of which is likely to endanger the maintenance of international peace and security, shall, first of all, seek a solution by negotiation, enquiry, mediation, conciliation, arbitration, judicial settlement, resort to regional agencies or arrangements, or other peaceful means of their own choice.

2. The Security Council shall, when it deems necessary, call upon the parties to settle their dispute by such means.

Article 34

The Security Council may investigate any dispute, or any situation which might lead to international friction or give rise to a dispute, in order to determine whether the continuance of the dispute or situation is likely to endanger the maintenance of international peace and security.

Article 35

1. Any Member of the United Nations may bring any dispute, or any situation of the nature referred to in Article 34, to the attention of the Security Council or of the General Assembly.

2. A state which is not a Member of the United Nations may bring to the attention of the Security Council or of the General Assembly any dispute to which it is a party if it accepts in advance, for the purposes of the dispute, the obligations of pacific settlement provided in the present Charter.

3. The proceedings of the General Assembly in respect of matters brought to its attention under this Article will be subject to the provisions of Articles 11 and 12.

Article 36

1. The Security Council may, at any stage of a dispute of the nature referred to in Article 33 or of a situation of like nature, recommend appropriate procedures or methods of adjustment.

2. The Security Council should take into consideration any procedures for the settlement of the dispute which have already been adopted by the parties.

3. In making recommendations under this Article the Security Council should also take into consideration that legal disputes should as a general rule be referred by the parties to the International Court of Justice in accordance with the provisions of the Statute of the Court.

Article 37

1. Should the parties to a dispute of the nature referred to in Article 33 fail to settle it by the means indicated in that Article, they shall refer it to the Security Council.

2. If the Security Council deems that the continuance of the dispute is in fact likely to endanger the maintenance of international peace and security, it shall decide whether to take action under Article 36 or to recommend such terms of settlement as it may consider appropriate.

Article 38

Without prejudice to the provisions of Articles 33 to 37, the Security Council may, if all the parties to any dispute so request, make recommendations to the parties with a view to a pacific settlement of the dispute.

CHAPTER VII. ACTION WITH RESPECT TO THREATS TO THE PEACE, BREACHES OF THE PEACE, AND ACTS OF AGGRESSION

Article 39

The Security Council shall determine the existence of any threat to the peace, breach of the peace, or act of aggression and shall make recommendations, or decide what measures shall be taken in accordance with Articles 41 and 42, to maintain or restore international peace and security.

Article 40

In order to prevent an aggravation of the situation, the Security Council may, before making the recommendations or deciding upon the measures provided for in Article 39, call upon the parties concerned to comply with such provisional measures as it deems necessary or desirable. Such provisional measures shall be without prejudice to the rights, claims, or position of the parties concerned. The Security Council shall duly take account of failure to comply with such provisional measures.

Article 41

The Security Council may decide what measures not involving the use of armed force are to be employed to give effect to its decisions, and it may call upon the Members of the United Nations to apply such measures. These may include complete or partial interruption of economic relations and of rail, sea, air, postal, telegraphic, radio, and other means of communication, and the severance of diplomatic relations.

Article 42

Should the Security Council consider that measures provided for in Article 41 would be inadequate or have proved to be inadequate, it may take such action by air, sea, or land forces as may be necessary to maintain or restore international peace and security. Such action may include demonstrations, blockade, and other operations by air, sea, or land forces of Members of the United Nations.

Article 43

1. All Members of the United Nations, in order to contribute to the maintenance of international peace and security, undertake to make available to the Security Council, on its call and in accordance with a special agreement or agreements, armed forces, assistance, and facilities, including rights of passage, necessary for the purpose of maintaining international peace and security.

2. Such agreement or agreements shall govern the numbers and types of forces, their degree of readiness and general location, and the nature of the facilities and assistance to be provided.

3. The agreement or agreements shall be negotiated as soon as possible on the initiative of the Security Council. They shall be concluded between the Security Council and Members or between the Security Council and groups of members and shall be subject to ratification by the signatory states in accordance with their respective constitutional processes.

Article 44

When the Security Council has decided to use force it shall, before calling upon a Member not represented on it to provide armed forces in fulfilment of the obligations assumed under Article 43, invite that Member, if the Member so desires, to participate in the decisions of the Security Council concerning the employment of contingents of that Member's armed forces.

Article 45

In order to enable the United Nations to take urgent military measures, Members shall hold immediately available national air-force contingents for combined international enforcement action. The strength and degree of readiness of these continents and plans for their combined action shall be determined, within the limits laid down in the special agreement or agreements referred to in Article 43, by the Security Council with the assistance of the Military Staff Committee.

Article 46

Plans for the application of armed force shall be made by the Security Council with the assistance of the Military Staff Committee.

Article 47

1. There shall be established a Military Staff Committee to advise and assist the Security Council on all questions relating to the Security Council's military requirements for the maintenance of international peace and security, the employment and command of forces placed at its disposal, the regulation of armaments, and possible disarmament.

2. The Military Staff Committee shall consist of the Chiefs of Staff of the permanent members of the Security Council or their representatives. Any Member of the United Nations not permanently represented on the Committee shall be invited by the Committee to be associated with it when the efficient discharge of the Committee's responsibilities requires the participation of that Member in its work.

3. The Military Staff Committee shall be responsible under the Security Council for the strategic direction of any armed forces placed at the disposal of the Security Council. Questions relating to the command of such forces shall be worked out subsequently.

4. The Military Staff Committee, with the authorization of the Security Council and after consultation with appropriate regional agencies, may establish regional subcommittees.

Article 48

1. The action required to carry out the decisions of the Security Council for the maintenance of international peace and security shall be taken by all the Members of the United Nations or by some of them, as the Security Council may determine.

2. Such decisions shall be carried out by the Members of the United Nations directly and through their action in the appropriate international agencies of which they are members.

Article 49

The Members of the United Nations shall join in affording mutual assistance in carrying out the measures decided upon by the Security Council.

Article 50

If preventive or enforcement measures against any state are taken by the Security Council, any other state, whether a Member of the United Nations or not, which finds itself confronted with special economic problems arising from the carrying out of those measures shall have the right to consult the Security Council with regard to a solution of those problems.

Article 51

Nothing in the present Charter shall impair the inherent right of individual or collective self-defence if an armed attack occurs against a Member of the United Nations, until the Security Council has taken measures necessary to maintain international peace and security. Measures taken by Members in the exercise of this right of self-defence shall be immediately reported to the Security Council and shall not in any way affect the authority and responsibility of the Security Council under the present Charter to take at any time such action as it deems necessary in order to maintain or restore international peace and security.

CHAPTER VIII. REGIONAL ARRANGEMENTS

Article 52

1. Nothing in the present Charter precludes the existence of regional arrangements or agencies for dealing with such matters relating to the maintenance of international peace and security as are appropriate for regional action, provided that such arrangements or agencies and their activities are consistent with the Purposes and Principles of the United Nations.

2. The Members of the United Nations entering into such arrangements or constituting such agencies shall make every effort to achieve pacific settlement of local disputes through such regional arrangements or by such regional agencies before referring them to the Security Council.

3. The Security Council shall encourage the development of pacific settlement of local disputes through such regional arrangements or by such regional agencies either on the initiative of the states concerned or by reference from the Security Council.

4. This Article in no way impairs the application of Articles 34 and 35.

Article 53

1. The Security Council shall, where appropriate, utilize such regional arrangements or agencies for enforcement action under its authority. But no enforcement action shall be taken under regional arrangements or by regional agencies without the authorization of the Security Council, with the exception of measures against any enemy state, as defined in paragraph 2 of this Article, provided for pursuant to Article 107 or in regional arrangements directed against renewal of aggressive policy on the part of any such state, until such time as the Organization may, on request of the Governments concerned, be charged with the responsibility for preventing further aggression by such a state.

2. The term enemy state as used in paragraph 1 of this Article applies to any state which during the Second World War has been an enemy of any signatory of the present Charter.

Article 54

The Security Council shall at all times be kept fully informed of activities undertaken or in contemplation under regional arrangements or by regional agencies for the maintenance of international peace and security.

Chapter IX. INTERNATIONAL ECONOMIC AND SOCIAL CO-OPERATION

Article 55

With a view to the creation of conditions of stability and well-being which are necessary for peaceful and friendly relations among nations based on respect for the principle of equal rights and self-determination of peoples, the United Nations shall promote:

a. higher standards of living, full employment, and conditions of economic and social progress and development.

b. solutions of international economic, social, health, and related problems; and international cultural and educational co-operation; and

c. universal respect for, and observance of, human rights and fundamental freedoms for all without distinction as to race, sex, language, or religion.

Article 56

All Members pledge themselves to take joint and separate action in co-operation with the Organization for the achievement of the purposes set forth in Article 55.

Article 57

1. The various specialized agencies, established by intergovernmental agreement and having wide international responsibilities, as defined in their basic instruments, in economic, social, cultural, educational, health, and related fields, shall be brought into relationship with the United Nations in accordance with the provisions of Article 63.

2. Such agencies thus brought into relationship with the United Nations are hereinafter referred to as specialized agencies.

Article 58

The Organization shall make recommendations for the co-ordination of the policies and activities of the specialized agencies.

Article 59

The Organization shall, where appropriate, initiate negotiations among the states concerned for the creation of any new specialized agencies required for the accomplishment of the purposes set forth in Article 55.

Article 60

Responsibility for the discharge of functions of the Organization set forth in this Chapter shall be vested in the General Assembly and, under the authority of the General Assembly, in the Economic and Social Council, which shall have for this purpose the powers set forth in Chapter X.

CHAPTER X. THE ECONOMIC AND SOCIAL COUNCIL

Composition

Article 61[c]

1. The Economic and Social Council shall consist of fifty-four Members of the United Nations elected by the General Assembly.

2. Subject to the provisions of paragraph 3, eighteen members of the Economic and Social Council shall be elected each year for a term of three years. A retiring member shall be eligible for immediate re-election.

3. At the first election after the increase in the membership of the Economic and Social Council from twenty-seven to fifty-four members, in addition to the members elected in place of the nine members whose terms of office expires at the end of that year, twenty-seven additional members shall be elected. Of these twenty-seven additional members, the term of office of nine members so elected shall expire at the end of one year, and of nine other members at the end of two years, in accordance with arrangements made by the General Assembly.

4. Each member of the Economic and Social Council shall have one representative.

Functions and powers

Article 62

1. The Economic and Social Council may make or initiate studies and reports with respect to international economic, social, cultural, educational, health, and related matters and may make recommendations with respect to any such matters of the General Assembly, to the Members of the United Nations, and to the specialized agencies concerned.

2. It may make recommendations for the purpose of promoting respect for, and observance of, human rights and fundamental freedoms for all.

3. It may prepare draft conventions for submission to the General Assembly, with respect to matters falling within its competence.

4. It may call, in accordance with the rules prescribed by the United Nations, international conferences on matters falling within its competence.

Article 63

1. The Economic and Social Council may enter into agreements with any of the agencies referred to in Article 57, defining the terms on which the agency concerned shall be brought into relationship with the United Nations. Such agreements shall be subject to approval by the General Assembly.

2. It may co-ordinate the activities of the specialized agencies through consultation with and recommendations to such agencies and through recommendations to the General Assembly and to the Members of the United Nations.

c. Amended text of Article 61, which entered into force on 24 September 1973.

Article 64

1. The Economic and Social Council may take appropriate steps to obtain regular reports from the specialized agencies. It may make arrangements with the Members of the United Nations and with the specialized agencies to obtain reports on the steps taken to give effect to its own recommendations and to recommendations on matters falling within its competence made by the General Assembly.

2. It may communicate its observations on these reports to the General Assembly.

Article 65

The Economic and Social Council may furnish information to the Security Council and shall assist the Security Council upon its request.

Article 66

1. The Economic and Social Council shall perform such functions as fall within its competence in connexion with the carrying out of the recommendations of the General Assembly.

2. It may, with the approval of the General Assembly, perform services at the request of Members of the United Nations and at the request of specialized agencies.

3. It shall perform such other functions as are specified elsewhere in the present Charter or as may be assigned to it by the General Assembly.

Voting

Article 67

1. Each member of the Economic and Social Council shall have one vote.

2. Decisions of the Economic and Social Council shall be made by a majority of the members present and voting.

Procedure

Article 68

The Economic and Social Council shall set up commissions in economic and social fields and for the promotion of human rights, and such other commissions as may be required for the performance of its functions.

Article 69

The Economic and Social Council shall invite any Member of the United Nations to participate, without vote, in its deliberations on any matter of particular concern to that Member.

Article 70

The Economic and Social Council may make arrangements for representatives of the specialized agencies to participate, without vote, in its deliberations and in those of the commissions established by it, and for its representatives to participate in the deliberations of the specialized agencies.

Article 71

The Economic and Social Council may make suitable arrangements for consultation with non-governmental organizations which are concerned with matters within its competence. Such arrangements may be made with international organizations and, where appropriate, with national organizations after consultation with the Member of the United Nations concerned.

Article 72

1. The Economic and Social Council shall adopt its own rules of procedure, including the method of selecting its President.

2. The Economic and Social Council shall meet as required in accordance with its rules, which shall include provision for the convening of meetings on the request of a majority of its members.

Chapter XI. DECLARATION REGARDING NON–SELF–GOVERNING TERRITORIES

Article 73

Members of the United Nations which have or assume responsibilities for the administration of territories whose peoples have not yet attained a full measure of self-government recognize the principle that the interests of the inhabitants of these territories are paramount, and accept as a sacred trust the obligation to promote to the utmost, within the system of international peace and security established by the present Charter, the well-being of the inhabitants of these territories, and, to this end:

a. to ensure, with due respect for the culture of the peoples concerned, their political, economic, social, and educational advancement, their just treatment, and their protection against abuses;

b. to develop self-government, to take due account of the political aspirations of the peoples, and to assist them in the progressive development of their free political institutions, according to the particular circumstances of each territory and its peoples and their varying stages of advancement;

c. to further international peace and security;

d. to promote constructive measures of development, to encourage research, and to cooperate with one another and, when and where appropriate, with specialized international bodies with a view to the practical achievement of the social, economic, and scientific purposes set forth in this Article; and

e. to transmit regularly to the Secretary–General for information purposes, subject to such limitation as security and constitutional considerations may require, statistical and other information of a technical nature relating to economic, social, and educational conditions in the territories for which they are respectively responsible other than those territories to which Chapters XII and XIII apply.

Article 74

Members of the United Nations also agree that their policy in respect of the territories to which this Chapter applies, no less than in respect of their metropolitan areas, must be based on the general principle of good-neighbourliness, due account being taken of the interests and well-being of the rest of the world, in social, economic, and commercial matters.

Chapter XII. INTERNATIONAL TRUSTEESHIP SYSTEM

Article 75

The United Nations shall establish under its authority an international trusteeship system for the administration and supervision of such territories as may be placed thereunder by subsequent individual agreements. These territories are hereinafter referred to as trust territories.

Article 76

The basic objectives of the trusteeship system, in accordance with the Purposes of the United Nations laid down in Article 1 of the present Charter, shall be:

a. to further international peace and security;

b. to promote the political, economic, social, and educational advancement of the inhabitants of the trust territories, and their progressive development towards self-government or independence as may be appropriate to the particular circumstances of each territory and its peoples and the freely expressed wishes of the peoples concerned, and as may be provided by the terms of each trusteeship agreement;

c. to encourage respect for human rights and for fundamental freedoms for all without distinction as to race, sex, language, or religion, and to encourage recognition of the interdependence of the peoples of the world; and

d. to ensure equal treatment in social, economic, and commercial matters for all Members of the United nations and their nationals, and also equal treatment for the latter in the administration of justice, without prejudice to the attainment of the foregoing objectives and subject to the provisions of Article 80.

Article 77

1. The trusteeship system shall apply to such territories in the following categories as may be placed thereunder by means of trusteeship agreements:

a. territories now held under mandate;

b. territories which may be detached from enemy states as a result of the Second World War; and

c. territories voluntarily placed under the system by states responsible for their administration.

2. It will be a matter for subsequent agreement as to which territories in the foregoing categories will be brought under the trusteeship system and upon what terms.

Article 78

The trusteeship system shall not apply to territories which have become Members of the United Nations, relationship among which shall be based on respect for the principle of sovereign equality.

Article 79

The terms of trusteeship for each territory to be placed under the trusteeship system, including any alteration or amendment, shall be agreed upon by the states directly concerned, including the mandatory power in the case of territories held under mandate by a Member of the United Nations, and shall be approved as provided for in Articles 83 and 85.

Article 80

1. Except as may be agreed upon in individual trusteeship agreements, made under Articles 77, 79, and 81, placing each territory under the trusteeship system, and until such agreements have been concluded, nothing in this Chapter shall be construed in or of itself to alter in any manner the rights whatsoever of any states or any peoples or the terms of existing international instruments to which Members of the United Nations may respectively be parties.

2. Paragraph 1 of this Article shall not be interpreted as giving grounds for delay or postponement of the negotiation and conclusion of agreements for placing mandated and other territories under the trusteeship system as provided for in Article 77.

Article 81

The trusteeship agreement shall in each case include the terms under which the trust territory will be administered and designate the authority which will exercise the administration of the trust territory. Such authority, hereinafter called the administering authority, may be one or more states or the organization itself.

Article 82

There may be designated, in any trusteeship agreement, a strategic area or areas which may include part or all of the trust territory to which the agreement applies, without prejudice to any special agreement or agreements made under Article 43.

Article 83

1. All functions of the United Nations relating to strategic areas, including the approval of the terms of the trusteeship agreements and of their alterations or amendment, shall be exercised by the Security Council.

2. The basic objectives set forth in Article 76 shall be applicable to the people of each strategic area.

3. The Security Council shall, subject to the provisions of the trusteeship agreements and without prejudice to security considerations, avail itself of the assistance of the Trusteeship Council to perform those functions of the United Nations under the trusteeship system relating to political, economic, social, and educational matters in the strategic areas.

Article 84

It shall be the duty of the administering authority to ensure that the trust territory shall play its part in the maintenance of international peace and security. To this end the administering authority may make use of volunteer forces, facilities, and assistance from the trust territory in carrying out the obligations towards the Security Council undertaken in this regard by the administering authority, as well as for local defence and the maintenance of law and order within the trust territory.

Article 85

1. The functions of the United Nations with regard to trusteeship agreements for all areas not designated as strategic, including the approval of the terms of the trusteeship agreements and of their alteration or amendment, shall be exercised by the General Assembly.

2. The Trusteeship Council, operating under the authority of the General Assembly, shall assist the General Assembly in carrying out these functions.

Chapter XIII. THE TRUSTEESHIP COUNCIL

Composition

Article 86

1. The Trusteeship Council shall consist of the following Members of the United Nations:

a. those Members administering trust territories;

b. such of those Members mentioned by name in Article 23 as are not administering trust territories; and

c. as many other Members elected for three-year terms by the General Assembly as may be necessary to ensure that the total number of members of the Trusteeship Council is equally divided between those Members of the United Nations which administer trust territories and those which do not.

2. Each member of the Trusteeship Council shall designate one specially qualified person to represent it therein.

Functions and powers

Article 87

The General Assembly and, under its authority, the Trusteeship Council, in carrying out their functions, may:

a. consider reports submitted by the administering authority;

b. accept petitions and examine them in consultation with the administering authority;

c. provide for periodic visits to the respective trust territories at times agreed upon with the administering authority; and

d. take these and other actions in conformity with the terms of the trusteeship agreements.

Article 88

The Trusteeship Council shall formulate a questionnaire on the political, economic, social, and educational advancement of the inhabitants of each trust territory, and the administering authority for each trust territory within the competence of the General Assembly shall make an annual report to the General Assembly upon the basis of such questionnaire.

Voting

Article 89

1. Each member of the Trusteeship Council shall have one vote.

2. Decisions of the Trusteeship Council shall be made by a majority of the members present and voting.

Procedure

Article 90

1. The Trusteeship Council shall adopt its own rules of procedure, including the method of selecting its President.

2. The Trusteeship Council shall meet as required in accordance with its rules, which shall include provision for the convening of meetings on the request of a majority of its members.

Article 91

The Trusteeship Council shall, when appropriate, avail itself of the assistance of the Economic and Social Council and of the specialized agencies in regard to matters with which they are respectively concerned.

CHAPTER XIV. THE INTERNATIONAL COURT OF JUSTICE

Article 92

The International Court of Justice shall be principle judicial organ of the United Nations. It shall function in accordance with the annexed Statute, which is based upon the Statute of the Permanent Court of International Justice and forms an integral part of the present Charter.

Article 93

1. All Members of the United Nations are ipso facto parties to the Statute of the International Court of Justice.

2. A state which is not a Member of the United Nations may become a party to the Statute of the International Court of Justice on conditions to be determined in each case by the General Assembly upon the recommendation of the Security Council.

Article 94

1. Each Member of the United Nations undertakes to comply with the decision of the International Court of Justice in any case to which it is a party.

2. If any party to a case fails to perform the obligations incumbent upon it under a judgment rendered by the Court, the other party may have recourse to the Security Council, which may, if it deems necessary, make recommendations or decide upon measures to be taken to give effect to the judgment.

Article 95

Nothing in the present Charter shall prevent members of the United Nations from entrusting the solution of their differences to other tribunals by virtue of agreements already in existence or which may be concluded in the future.

Article 96

1. The General Assembly or the Security Council may request the International Court of Justice to give an advisory opinion on any legal question.

2. Other organs of the United Nations and specialized agencies, which may at any time be so authorized by the General Assembly, may also request advisory opinions of the Court on legal questions arising within the scope of their activities.

CHAPTER XV. THE SECRETARIAT

Article 97

The Secretariat shall comprise a Secretary–General and such staff as the Organization may require. The Secretary–General shall be appointed by the General Assembly upon the recommendation of the Security Council. He shall be the chief administrative officer of the Organization.

Article 98

The Secretary–General shall act in that capacity in all meetings of the General Assembly, of the Security Council, of the Economic and Social Council, and of the Trusteeship Council, and shall perform such other functions as are entrusted to him by these organs. The Secretary–General shall make an annual report to the General Assembly on the work of the Organization.

Article 99

The Secretary–General may bring to the attention of the Security Council any matter which in his opinion may threaten the maintenance of international peace and security.

Article 100

1. In the performance of their duties the Secretary–General and the staff shall not seek or receive instructions from any government or from any other authority external to the Organization. They shall refrain from any action which might reflect on their position as international officials responsible only to the Organization.

2. Each Member of the United Nations undertakes to respect the exclusively international character of the responsibilities of the Secretary–General and the staff and not to seek to influence them in the discharge of their responsibilities.

Article 101

1. The staff shall be appointed by the Secretary–General under regulations established by the General Assembly.

2. Appropriate staffs shall be permanently assigned to the Economic and Social Council, the Trusteeship Council, and, as required, to other organs of the United Nations. These staffs shall form a part of the Secretariat.

3. The paramount consideration in the employment of the staff and in the determination of the conditions of service shall be the necessity of securing the highest standards of efficiency, competence, and integrity. Due regard shall be paid to the importance of recruiting the staff on as wide a geographical basis as possible.

Chapter XVI. MISCELLANEOUS PROVISIONS

Article 102

1. Every treaty and every international agreement entered into by any Member of the United Nations after the present Charter comes into force shall as soon as possible be registered with the Secretariat and published by it.

2. No party to any such treaty or international agreement which has not been registered in accordance with the provisions of paragraph 1 of this Article may invoke that treaty or agreement before an organ of the United Nations.

Article 103

In the event of a conflict between the obligations of the Members of the United Nations under the present Charter and their obligations under any other international agreement, their obligations under the present Charter shall prevail.

Article 104

The Organization shall enjoy in the territory of each of its Members such legal capacity as may be necessary for the exercise of its functions and the fulfilment of its purposes.

Article 105

1. The Organization shall enjoy in the territory of each of its Members such privileges and immunities as are necessary for the fulfilment of its purposes.

2. Representatives of the Members of the United Nations and officials of the Organization shall similarly enjoy such privileges and immunities as are necessary for the independent exercise of their functions in connexion with the Organization.

3. The General Assembly may make recommendations with a view to determining the details of the application of paragraphs 1 and 2 of this Article or may propose conventions to the Members of the United Nations for this purpose.

CHAPTER XVII. TRANSITIONAL SECURITY ARRANGEMENTS

Article 106

Pending the coming into force of such special agreements referred to in Article 43 as in the opinion of the Security Council enable it to begin the exercise of its responsibilities under Article 42, the parties to the Four–Nation Declaration, signed at Moscow, 30 October 1943, and France, shall, in accordance with the provisions of paragraph 5 of that Declaration, consult with one another and as occasion requires with other Members of the United Nations with a view to such joint action on behalf of the Organization as may be necessary for the purpose of maintaining international peace and security.

Article 107

Nothing in the present Charter shall invalidate or preclude action, in relation to any state which during the Second World War has been an enemy of any signatory to the present Charter, taken or authorized as a result of that war by the Governments having responsibility for such action.

CHAPTER XVIII. AMENDMENTS

Article 108

Amendments to the present Charter shall come into force for all Members of the United Nations when they have been adopted by a vote of two thirds of the members of the General Assembly and ratified in accordance with their respective constitutional processes by two thirds of the Members of the United Nations, including all the permanent members of the Security Council.

Article 109[d]

1. A General Conference of the Members of the United Nations for the purpose of reviewing the present Charter may be held at a date and place to be fixed by a two-thirds vote of the members of the General Assembly and by a vote of any nine members of the Security Council. Each Member of the United Nations shall have one vote in the conference.

2. Any alteration of the present Charter recommended by a two-thirds vote of the conference shall take effect when ratified in accordance with their respective constitutional processes by two thirds of the Members of the United Nations including all the permanent members of the Security Council.

3. If such a conference has not been held before the tenth annual session of the General Assembly following the coming into force of the present Charter, the proposal to call such a conference shall be placed on the agenda of that session of the General Assembly, and the conference shall be held if so decided by a majority vote of the members of the General Assembly and by a vote of any seven members of the Security Council.

CHAPTER XIX. RATIFICATION AND SIGNATURE

Article 110

1. The present Charter shall be ratified by the signatory states in accordance with their respective constitutional processes.

2. The ratifications shall be deposited with the Government of the United States of America, which shall notify all the signatory states of each deposit as well as the Secretary–General of the Organization when he has been appointed.

d. Amended text of Article 109, which entered into force on 12 June 1968.

3. The present Charter shall come into force upon the deposit of ratifications by the Republic of China, France, the Union of Soviet Socialist Republics, the United Kingdom of Great Britain and Northern Ireland, and the United States of America, and by a majority of the other signatory states. A protocol of the ratifications deposited shall thereupon be drawn up by the Government of the United States of America which shall communicate copies thereof to all the signatory states.

4. The states signatory to the present Charter which ratify it after it has come into force will become original Members of the United Nations on the date of the deposit of their respective ratifications.

Article 111

The present Charter, of which the Chinese, French, Russian, English, and Spanish texts are equally authentic, shall remain deposited in the archives of the Government of the United States of America. Duly certified copies thereof shall be transmitted by that Government to the Governments of the other signatory states.

1.4 Statute of the International Court of Justice. **Concluded at San Francisco, 26 June 1945. Entered into force, 24 October 1945. 1976 Y.B.U.N. 1052, 59 Stat. 1031, T.S. No. 993; *reprinted in* 1 Weston I.A.2**

Article 1

THE INTERNATIONAL COURT OF JUSTICE established by the Charter of the United Nations as the principal judicial organ of the United Nations shall be constituted and shall function in accordance with the provisions of the present Statute.

Chapter I. ORGANIZATION OF THE COURT

Article 2

The Court shall be composed of a body of independent judges, elected regardless of their nationality from among persons of high moral character, who possess the qualifications required in their respective countries for appointment to the highest judicial offices, or are jurisconsults of recognized competence in international law.

Article 3

1. The Court shall consist of fifteen members, no two of whom may be nationals of the same state.

2. A person who for the purposes of membership in the Court could be regarded as a national of more than one state shall be deemed to be a national of the one in which he ordinary exercises civil and political rights.

Article 4

1. The members of the Court shall be elected by the General Assembly and by the Security Council from a list of persons nominated by the national groups in the Permanent Court of Arbitration, in accordance with the following provisions.

2. In the case of Members of the United Nations not represented in the Permanent Court of Arbitration, candidates shall be nominated by national groups appointed for this purpose by their governments under the same conditions as those prescribed for members of the Permanent Court of Arbitration by Article 44 of the Convention of the Hague of 1907 for the pacific settlement of international disputes.

3. The conditions under which a state which is a party to the present Statute but is not a Member of the United Nations may participate in electing the members of the Court shall, in the absence of a special agreement, be laid down by the General Assembly upon recommendation of the Security Council.

Article 5

1. At least three months before the date of the election, the Secretary–General of the United Nations shall address a written request to the members of the Permanent Court of Arbitration belonging to the states which are parties to the present Statute, and to the members of the national groups appointed under Article 4, paragraph 2, inviting them to undertake, within a given time, by national groups, the nomination of persons in a position to accept the duties of a member of the Court.

2. No group may nominate more than four persons, not more than two of whom shall be of their own nationality. In no case may the number of candidates nominated by a group be more than double the number of seats to be filled.

Article 6

Before making these nominations, each national group is recommended to consult its highest court of justice, its legal faculties and schools of law, and its national academies and national sections of international academies devoted to the study of law.

Article 7

1. The Secretary–General shall prepare a list in alphabetical order of all the persons thus nominated. Save as provided in Article 12, paragraph 2, these shall be the only persons eligible.

2. The Secretary–General shall submit this list to the General Assembly and to the Security Council.

Article 8

The General Assembly and the Security Council shall proceed independently of one another to elect the members of the Court.

Article 9

At every election, the electors shall bear in mind not only that the persons to be elected should individually possess the qualifications required, but also that in the body as a whole the representation of the main forms of civilization and of the principal legal systems of the world should be assured.

Article 10

1. Those candidates who obtain an absolute majority of votes in the General Assembly and in the Security Council shall be considered as elected.

2. Any vote of the Security Council, whether for the election of judges or for the appointment of members of the conference envisaged in Article 12, shall be taken without any distinction between permanent and non-permanent members of the Security Council.

3. In the event of more than one national of the same state obtaining an absolute majority of the votes both of the General Assembly and of the Security Council, the eldest of these only shall be considered as elected.

Article 11

If, after the first meeting held for the purpose of the election, one or more seats remain to be filled, a second and, if necessary, a third meeting shall take place.

Article 12

1. If, after the third meeting, one or more seats still remain unfilled, a joint conference consisting of six members, three appointed by the General Assembly and three by the Security Council, may be formed at any time at the request of either the General Assembly or the Security Council, for the purpose of choosing by the vote of an absolute majority one name for each seat still vacant, to submit to the General Assembly and the Security Council for their respective acceptance.

2. If the joint conference is unanimously agreed upon any person who fulfils the required conditions, he may be included in its list, even though he was not included in the list of nominations referred to in Article 7.

3. If the joint conference is satisfied that it will not be successful in procuring an election, those members of the Court who have already been elected shall, within a period to be fixed by the Security Council, proceed to fill the vacant seats by selection from among those candidates who have obtained votes either in the General Assembly or in the Security Council.

4. In the event of an equality of votes among the judges, the eldest judge shall have a casting vote.

Article 13

1. The members of the Court shall be elected for nine years and may be re-elected; provided, however, that of the judges elected at the first election, the terms of five judges shall expire at the end of three years and the terms of five more judges shall expire at the end of six years.

2. The judges whose terms are to expire at the end of the above-mentioned initial periods of three and six years shall be chosen by lot to be drawn by the Secretary–General immediately after the first election has been completed.

3. The members of the Court shall continue to discharge their duties until their places have been filled. Though replaced, they shall finish any cases which they may have begun.

4. In the case of the resignation of a member of the Court, the resignation shall be addressed to the President of the Court for transmission to the Secretary–General. This last notification makes the place vacant.

Article 14

Vacancies shall be filled by the same methods as that laid down for the first election, subject to the following provision: the Secretary–General shall, within one month of the occurrence of the vacancy, proceed to issue the invitations provided for in Article 5, and the date of the election shall be fixed by the Security Council.

Article 15

A member of the Court elected to replace a member whose term of office has not expired shall hold office for the remainder of his predecessor's term.

Article 16

1. No member of the Court may exercise any political or administrative function, or engage in any other occupation of a professional nature.

2. Any doubt on this point shall be settled by the decision of the Court.

Article 17

1. No member of the Court may act as agent, counsel, or advocate in any case.

2. No member may participate in the decision of any case in which he has previously taken part as agent, counsel, or advocate for one of the parties, or as a member of a national or international court, or of a commission of enquiry, or in any other capacity.

3. Any doubt on this point shall be settled by the decision of the Court.

Article 18

1. No member of the Court can be dismissed unless, in the unanimous opinion of the other members, he has ceased to fulfil the required conditions.

2. Formal notification thereof shall be made to the Secretary–General by the Registrar.

3. This notification makes the place vacant.

Article 19

The members of the Court, when engaged on the business of the Court, shall enjoy diplomatic privileges and immunities.

Article 20

Every member of the Court shall, before taking up his duties, make a solemn declaration in open court that he will exercise his powers impartially and conscientiously.

Article 21

1. The Court shall elect its President and Vice–President for three years; they may be re-elected.

2. The Court shall appoint its Registrar and may provide for the appointment of such other officers as may be necessary.

Article 22

1. The seat of the Court shall be established at The Hague. This, however, shall not prevent the Court from sitting and exercising its functions elsewhere whenever the Court considers it desirable.

2. The President and the Registrar shall reside at the seat of the Court.

Article 23

1. The Court shall remain permanently in session, except during the judicial vacations, the dates and duration which shall be fixed by the Court.

2. Members of the Court are entitled to periodic leave, the dates and duration of which shall be fixed by the Court, having in mind the distance between The Hague and the home of each judge.

3. Members of the Court shall be bound, unless they are on leave or prevented from attending by illness or other serious reasons duly explained to the President, to hold themselves permanently at the disposal of the Court.

Article 24

1. If, for some special reason, a member of the Court considers that he should not take part in the decision of a particular case, he shall so inform the President.

2. If the President considers that for some special reason one of the members of the Court should not sit in a particular case, he shall give him notice accordingly.

3. If in any such case the member of the Court and the President disagree, the matter shall be settled by the decision of the Court.

Article 25

1. The full Court shall sit except when it is expressly provided otherwise in the present Statute.

2. Subject to the condition that the number of judges available to constitute the Court is not thereby reduced below eleven, the Rules of the Court may provide for allowing one or more judges, according to circumstances and in rotation, to be dispensed from sitting.

3. A quorum of nine judges shall suffice to constitute the Court.

Article 26

1. The Court may from time to time form one or more chambers, composed of three or more judges as the Court may determine, for dealing with particular categories of cases; for example, labour cases and cases relating to transit and communications.

2. The Court may at any time form a chamber for dealing with a particular case. The number of judges to constitute such a chamber shall be determined by the Court with the approval of the parties.

3. Cases shall be heard and determined by the chambers provided for in this Article if the parties so request.

Article 27

A judgment given by any of the chambers provided for in Articles 26 and 29 shall be considered as rendered by the Court.

Article 28

The chambers provided for in Articles 26 and 29 may, with the consent of the parties, sit and exercise their functions elsewhere than at The Hague.

Article 29

With a view to the speedy dispatch of business, the Court shall form annually a chamber composed of five judges which, at the request of the parties, may hear and determine cases by summary procedure. In addition, two judges shall be selected for the purpose of replacing judges who find it impossible to sit.

Article 30

1. The Court shall frame rules for carrying out its functions. In particular, it shall lay down rules of procedure.

2. The Rules of the Court may provide for assessors to sit with the Court or with any of its chambers, without the right to vote.

Article 31

1. Judges of the nationality of each of the parties shall retain their right to sit in the case before the Court.

2. If the Court includes upon the Bench a judge of the nationality of one of the parties, any other party may choose a person to sit as judge. Such person shall be chosen preferably from among those persons who have been nominated as candidates as provided in Articles 4 and 5.

3. If the Court includes upon the Bench no judge of the nationality of the parties, each of these parties may proceed to choose a judge as provided in paragraph 2 of this Article.

4. The provisions of this Article shall apply to the case of Articles 26 and 29. In such cases, the President shall request one or, if necessary, two of the members of the Court forming the chamber to give place to the members of the Court of the nationality of the parties concerned, and, failing such, or if they are unable to be present, to the judges specially chosen by the parties.

5. Should there be several parties in the same interest, they shall, for the purpose of the preceding provisions, be reckoned as one party only. Any doubt upon this point shall be settled by the decision of the Court.

6. Judges chosen as laid down in paragraphs 2, 3, and 4 of this Article shall fulfil the conditions required by Articles 2, 17 (paragraph 2), 20, and 24 of the present Statute. They shall take part in the decision on terms of complete equality with their colleagues.

Article 32

1. Each member of the Court shall receive an annual salary.

2. The President shall receive a special annual allowance.

3. The Vice–President shall receive a special allowance for every day on which he acts as President.

4. The judges chosen under Article 31, other than members of the Court, shall receive compensation for each day on which they exercise their functions.

5. These salaries, allowances, and compensation shall be fixed by the General Assembly. They may not be decreased during the term of office.

6. The salary of the Registrar shall be fixed by the General Assembly on the proposal of the Court.

7. Regulations made by the General Assembly shall fix the conditions under which retirement pensions may be given to members of the Court and to the Registrar, and the conditions under which members of the Court and the Registrar shall have their travelling expenses refunded.

8. The above salaries, allowances, and compensation shall be free of all taxation.

Article 33

The expenses of the Court shall be borne by the United Nations in such a manner as shall be decided by the General Assembly.

Chapter II. COMPETENCE OF THE COURT

Article 34

1. Only states may be parties in cases before the Court.

2. The Court, subject to and in conformity with its Rules, may request of public international organizations information relevant to cases before it, and shall receive such information presented by such organizations on their own initiative.

3. Whenever the construction of the constituent instrument of a public international organization or of an international convention adopted thereunder is in question in a case before the Court, the Registrar shall so notify the public international organization concerned and shall communicate to it copies of all the written proceedings.

Article 35

1. The Court shall be open to the states parties to the present Statute.

2. The conditions under which the Court shall be open to other states shall, subject to the special provisions contained in treaties in force, be laid down by the Secretary Council, but in no case shall such conditions place the parties in a position of inequality before the Court.

3. When a state which is not a Member of the United Nations is a party to a case, the Court shall fix the amount which that party is to contribute towards the expenses of the Court. This provision shall not apply it such state is bearing a share of the expenses of the Court.

Article 36

1. The jurisdiction of the Court comprises all cases which the parties refer to it and all matters specially provided for in the Charter of the United Nations or in treaties and conventions in force.

2. The states parties to the present Statute may at any time declare that they recognize as compulsory *ipso facto* and without special agreement, in relation to any other state accepting the same obligation, the jurisdiction of the Court in all legal disputes concerning:

a. the interpretation of a treaty;

b. any question of international law;

c. the existence of any fact which, if established, would constitute a breach of an international obligation;

d. the nature or extent of the reparation to be made for the breach of an international obligation.

3. The declarations referred to above may be made unconditionally or on condition of reciprocity on the part of several or certain states, or for a certain time.

4. Such declarations shall be deposited with the Secretary–General of the United Nations, who shall transmit copies thereof to the parties to the Statute and to the Registrar of the Court.

5. Declarations made under Article 36 of the Statute of the Permanent Court of International Justice and which are still in force shall be deemed, as between the parties to the present Statute, to be acceptances of the compulsory jurisdiction of the International Court of Justice for the period which they still have to run and in accordance with their terms.

6. In the event of a dispute as to whether the Court has jurisdiction, the matter shall be settled by the decision of the Court.

Article 37

Wherever a treaty or convention in force provides for reference of a matter to a tribunal to have been instituted by the League of Nations, or to the Permanent Court of International Justice, the matter shall, as between the parties to the present Statute, be referred to the International Court of Justice.

Article 38

1. The Court, whose function is to decide in accordance with international law such disputes as are submitted to it, shall apply:

a. international conventions, whether general or particular, establishing rules expressly recognized by the contesting states;

b. international custom, as evidence of a general practice accepted as law;

c. the general principles of law recognized by civilized nations;

d. subject to the provisions of Article 59, judicial decisions and the teachings of the most highly qualified publicists of the various nations, as subsidiary means for the determination of rules of law.

2. This provision shall not prejudice the power of the Court to decide a case *ex aequo et bono*, if the parties agree thereto.

CHAPTER III. PROCEDURE

Article 39

1. The official languages of the Court shall be French and English. If the parties agree that the case shall be conducted in French, the judgment shall be delivered in French. If the parties agree that the case shall be conducted in English, the judgment shall be delivered in English.

2. In the absence of an agreement as to which language shall be employed, each party may, in the pleadings, use the language which it prefers; the decision of the Court shall be given in French and English. In this case the Court shall at the same time determine which of the two texts shall be considered as authoritative.

3. The Court shall, at the request of any party, authorize a language other than French or English to be used by that party.

Article 40

1. Cases are brought before the Court, as the case may be, either by the notification of the special agreement or by a written application addressed to the Registrar. In either case the subject of the dispute and the parties shall be indicated.

2. The Registrar shall forthwith communicate the application to all concerned.

3. He shall also notify the Members of the United Nations through the Secretary–General, and also any other states entitled to appear before the Court.

Article 41

1. The Court shall have the power to indicate, if it considers that circumstances so require, any provisional measures which ought to be taken to preserve the respective rights of either party.

2. Pending the final decision, notice of the measures suggested shall forthwith be given to the parties and to the Security Council.

Article 42

1. The parties shall be represented by agents.

2. They may have the assistance of counsel or advocates before the Court.

3. The agents, counsel, and advocates of parties before the Court shall enjoy the privileges and immunities necessary to the independent exercise of their duties.

Article 43

1. The procedure shall consist of two parts: written and oral.

2. The written proceedings shall consist of the communication to the Court and to the parties of memorials, counter-memorials and, if necessary, replies; also all papers and documents in support.

3. These communications shall be made through the Registrar, in the order and within the time fixed by the Court.

4. A certified copy of every document produced by one party shall be communicated to the other party.

5. The oral proceedings shall consist of the hearing by the Court of witnesses, experts, agents, counsel, and advocates.

Article 44

1. For the service of all notices upon persons other than the agents, counsel, and advocates, the Court shall apply direct to the government of the state upon whose territory the notice has to be served.

2. The same provision shall apply whenever steps are to be taken to procure evidence on the spot.

Article 45

The hearing shall be under the control of the President or, if he is unable to preside, of the Vice–President; if neither is able to preside, the senior judge present shall preside.

Article 46

The hearing in Court shall be public, unless the Court shall decide otherwise, or unless the parties demand that the public be not admitted.

Article 47

1. Minutes shall be made at each hearing and signed by the Registrar and the President.

2. These minutes alone shall be authentic.

Article 48

The Court shall make orders for the conduct of the case, shall decide the form and time in which each party must conclude its arguments, and make all arrangements connected with the taking of evidence.

Article 49

The Court may, even before the hearing begins, call upon the agents to produce any document or to supply any explanations. Formal note shall be taken of any refusal.

Article 50

The Court may, at any time, entrust any individual, body, bureau, commission, or other organization that it may select, with the task of carrying out an enquiry or giving an expert opinion.

Article 51

During the hearing any relevant questions are to be put to the witnesses and experts under the conditions laid down by the Court in the rules of procedure referred to in Article 30.

Article 52

After the Court has received the proofs and evidence within the time specified for the purpose, it may refuse to accept any further oral or written evidence that one party may desire to present unless the other side consents.

Article 53

1. Whenever one of the parties does not appear before the Court, or fails to defend its case, the other party may call upon the Court to decide in favour of its claim.

2. The Court must, before doing so, satisfy itself, not only that it has jurisdiction in accordance with Articles 36 and 37, but also that the claim is well founded in fact and law.

Article 54

1. When, subject to the control of the Court, the agents, counsel, and advocates have completed their presentation of the case, the President shall declare the hearing closed.

2. The Court shall withdraw to consider the judgment.

3. The deliberation of the Court shall take place in private and remain secret.

Article 55

1. All questions shall be decided by a majority of the judges present.

2. In the event of an equality of votes, the President or the judge who acts in his place shall have a casting vote.

Article 56

1. The judgment shall state the reasons on which it is based.

2. It shall contain the names of the judges who have taken part in the decision.

Article 57

If the judgment does not represent in whole or in part the unanimous opinion of the judges, any judge shall be entitled to deliver a separate opinion.

Article 58

The judgment shall be signed by the President and by the Registrar. It shall be read in open court, due notice having been given to the agents.

Article 59

The decision of the Court has no binding force except between the parties and in respect of that particular case.

Article 60

The judgment is final and without appeal. In the event of dispute as to the meaning or scope of the judgment, the Court shall construe it upon the request of any party.

Article 61

1. An application for revision of a judgment may be made only when it is based upon the discovery of some fact of such a nature as to be a decisive factor, which fact was, when the judgment was given, unknown to the Court and also to the party claiming revision, always provided that such ignorance was not due to negligence.

2. The proceedings for revision shall be opened by a judgment of the Court expressly recording the existence of the new fact, recognizing that it has such a character as to lay the case open to revision, and declaring the application admissible on this ground.

3. The Court may require previous compliance with the terms of the judgment before it admits proceedings in revision.

4. The application for revision must be made at latest within six months of the discovery of the new fact.

5. No application for revision may be made after the lapse of ten years from the date of the judgment.

Article 62

1. Should a state consider that it has an interest of a legal nature which may be affected by the decision in the case, it may submit a request to the Court to be permitted to intervene.

2. It shall be for the Court to decide upon this request.

Article 63

1. Whenever the construction of a convention to which states other than those concerned in the case are parties is in question, the Registrar shall notify all such states forthwith.

2. Every state so notified has the right to intervene in the proceedings; but if it uses this right, the construction given by the judgement will be equally binding upon it.

Article 64

Unless otherwise decided by the Court, each party shall bear its own costs.

Chapter IV. ADVISORY OPINIONS

Article 65

1. The Court may give an advisory opinion on any legal question at the request of whatever body may be authorized by or in accordance with the Charter of the United Nations to make such a request.

2. Questions upon which the advisory opinion of the Court is asked shall be laid before the Court by means of a written request containing an exact statement of the question upon which an opinion is required, and accompanied by all documents likely to throw light upon the question.

Article 66

1. The Registrar shall forthwith give notice of the request for an advisory opinion to all states entitled to appear before the Court.

2. The Registrar shall also, by means of a special and direct communication, notify any state entitled to appear before the Court or international organization considered by the Court, or, should it not be sitting, by the President, as likely to be able to furnish information on the question, that the Court will be prepared to receive, within a time limit to be fixed by the President, written statements, or to hear, at a public sitting to be held for the purpose, oral statements relating to the question.

3. Should any such state entitled to appear before the Court have failed to receive the special communication referred to in paragraph 2 of this Article, such state may express a desire to submit a written statement or to be heard; and the Court will decide.

4. States and organizations having presented written or oral statements or both shall be permitted to comment on the statements made by other states or organizations in the form, to the extent, and within the time limits which the Court, or, should it not be sitting, the President, shall decide in each particular case. Accordingly, the Registrar shall in due time communicate any such written statements to states and organizations having submitted similar statements.

Article 67

The Court shall deliver its advisory opinions in open court, notice having been given to the Secretary–General and to the representatives of Members of the United Nations, of other states and of international organizations immediately concerned.

Article 68

In the exercise of its advisory functions the Court shall further be guided by the provisions of the present Statute which apply in contentious cases to the extent to which it recognizes them to be applicable.

Chapter V. AMENDMENT

Article 69

Amendments to the present Statute shall be effected by the same procedure as is provided by the Charter of the United Nations for amendments to that Charter, subject however to any provisions which the General Assembly upon recommendation of the Security Council may adopt concerning the participation of states which are parties to the present Statute but are not Members of the United Nations.

Article 70

The Court shall have power to propose such amendments to the present Statute as it may deem necessary, through written communications to the Secretary–General, for consideration in conformity with the provisions of Article 69.

1.5 Statute of the International Atomic Energy Agency (IAEA) (as Amended). Concluded at New York, 26 October 1956. Entered into force, 29 July 1957. 276 U.N.T.S. 3, T.I.A.S. NO. 3873, 8 T.S. No. 1093; 471 U.N.T.S. 334, T.I.A.S. No. 5284, 14 T.S. NO. 135; T.I.A.S. No. 7668, 24 T.S. No. 1637; *reprinted in* 5 Weston V.A.3: *Arts. I, II, III, XI, XII*

Art. I. *Establishment of the agency*

The parties hereto establish an International Atomic Energy Agency (hereinafter referred to as "the Agency") upon the terms and conditions hereinafter set forth.

Art. II. *Objectives*

The agency shall seek to accelerate and enlarge the contribution of atomic energy to peace, health and prosperity throughout the world. It shall ensure, so far as it is able, that assistance provided by it or at its request or under its supervision or control is not used in such a way as to further any military purpose.

Art. III. *Functions*

(A) The agency is authorized:

1. To encourage and assist research on, and development and practical application, of atomic energy for peaceful uses throughout the world; and, if requested to do so, to act as an intermediary for the purposes of securing the performance of services or the supplying of materials, equipment, or facilities by one member of the agency for another; and to perform any operation or service useful in research on, or development or practical application of, atomic energy for peaceful purposes;

2. To make provision, in accordance with this statute, for materials, services, equipment, and facilities to meet the needs of research on, and development and practical application of, atomic energy for peaceful purposes, including the production of electric power, with due consideration for the needs of the under-developed areas of the world;

3. To foster the exchange of scientific and technical information on peaceful uses of atomic energy;

4. To encourage the exchange and training of scientists and experts in the field of peaceful uses of atomic energy;

5. To establish and administer safeguards designed to ensure that special fissionable and other materials, services, equipment, facilities and information made available by the agency or at its request or under its supervision or control are not used in such a way as to further any military purpose; and to apply safeguards, at the request of the parties, to any bilateral or multilateral arrangement, or, at the request of a state, to any of that state's activities in the field of atomic energy;

6. To establish or adopt, in consultation and, where appropriate, in collaboration with the competent organs of the United Nations and with the specialized agencies concerned, standards of safety for protection of health and minimization of danger to life and property (including such standards for labor conditions), and to provide for the application of these standards to its own operations as well as to the operations making use of materials, services, equipment, facilities and information made available by the agency or at its request or under its control or supervision; and to provide for the application of these standards, at the request of the parties, to operations under any bilateral or multilateral arrangement, or, at the request of a state, to any of that state's activities in the field of atomic energy;

7. To acquire or establish any facilities, plant and equipment useful in carrying out its authorized functions, whenever the facilities, plant and equipment otherwise available to it in the area concerned are inadequate or available only on terms it deems unsatisfactory.

(B) In carrying out its functions, the agency shall:

1. Conduct its activities in accordance with the purposes and principles of the United Nations to promote peace and international cooperation, and in conformity with policies of the United Nations furthering the establishment of safeguarded world-wide disarmament and in conformity with any international agreements entered into pursuant to such policies;

2. Establish control over the use of special fissionable materials received by the agency, in order to ensure that these materials are used only for peaceful purposes;

3. Allocate its resources in such a manner as to secure efficient utilization and the greatest possible general benefit in all areas of the world, bearing in mind the special needs of the underdeveloped areas of the world;

4. Submit reports on its activities annually to the General Assembly of the United Nations and, when appropriate, to the Security Council: if in connection with the activities of the agency there should arise questions that are within the competence of the Security Council, the agency shall notify the Security Council, as the organ bearing the main responsibility for the maintenance of international peace and security, and may also take the measures open to it under this statute, including those provided in paragraph C of Article XII;

5. Submit reports to the Economic and Social Council and other organs of the United Nations on matters within the competence of these organs.

(C) In carrying out its functions, the agency shall not make assistance to members subject to any political, economic, military, or other conditions incompatible with the provisions of this statute.

(D) Subject to the provisions of this statute and to the terms of agreements concluded between a state or a group of states and the agency which shall be in accordance with the provisions of the statute, the activities of the agency shall be carried out with due observance of the sovereign rights of states.

* * *

Art. XI. *Agency projects*

(A) Any member or group of members of the agency desiring to set up any project for research on, or development or practical application of, atomic energy for peaceful purposes may request the assistance of the agency in securing special fissionable and other materials, services, equipment and facilities necessary for this purpose. Any such request shall be accompanied by an explanation of the purpose and extent of the project and shall be considered by the Board of Governors.

(B) Upon request, the agency may also assist any member or group of members to make arrangements to secure necessary financing from outside sources to carry out such projects. In extending this assistance, the agency will not be required to provide any guarantees or to assume any financial responsibilities for the project.

(C) The agency may arrange for the supplying of any materials, services, equipment, and facilities necessary for the project by one or more members or may itself undertake to provide any or all of these directly, taking into consideration the wishes of the member or members making the request.

(D) For the purpose of considering the request, the agency may send into the territory of the member or group of members making the request a person or persons qualified to examine the project. For this purpose the agency may, with the approval of the member or group of members making the request, use members of its own staff or employ suitably qualified nationals of any member.

(E) Before approving a project under this Article, the Board of Governors shall give due consideration to:

1. The usefulness of the project, including its scientific and technical feasibility;

2. The adequacy of plans, funds, and technical personnel to assure the effective execution of the project;

3. The adequacy of proposed health and safety standards for handling and storing materials and for operating facilities;

4. The inability of the member or group of members making the request to secure the necessary finances, materials, facilities, equipment, and services;

5. The equitable distribution of materials and other resources available to the agency;

6. The special needs of the under-developed areas of the world; and

7. Such other matters as may be relevant.

(F) Upon approving a project, the agency shall enter into an agreement with the member or group of members submitting the project, which agreement shall:

1. Provide for allocation to the project of any required special fissionable or other materials;

2. Provide for transfer of special fissionable materials from their then place of custody, whether the materials be in custody of the agency or of the member making them available for use in agency projects, to the member or group of members submitting the project, under conditions which ensure the safety of any shipment required and meet applicable health and safety standards;

3. Set forth the terms and conditions, including charges, on which any materials, services, equipment and facilities are to be provided by the agency itself, and, if any such materials, services, equipment and facilities are to be provided by a member, the terms and conditions as arranged for by the member or group of members submitting the project and the supplying member;

4. Include undertakings by the member or group of members submitting the project (*a*) that the assistance provided shall not be used in such a way as to further any military purpose; and (*b*) that the project shall be subject to the safeguards provided for in Article XII, the relevant safeguards being specified in the agreement;

5. Make appropriate provision regarding the rights and interests of the agency and the member or members concerned in any inventions or discoveries, or any patents therein, arising from the project;

6. Make appropriate provision regarding settlement of disputes;

7. Include such other provisions as may be appropriate.

(G) The provisions of this Article shall also apply where appropriate to a request for materials, services, facilities, or equipment in connection with an existing project.

Art. XII. *Agency safeguards*

(A) With respect to any agency project or other arrangement where the agency is requested by the parties concerned to apply safeguards, the agency shall have the following rights and responsibilities to the extent relevant to the project or arrangement:

1. To examine the design of specialized equipment and facilities, including nuclear reactors, and to approve it only from the viewpoint of assuring that it will not further any military purpose, that it complies with applicable health and safety standards, and that it will permit effective application of the safeguards provided for in this Article;

2. To require the observance of any health and safety measures prescribed by the agency;

3. To require the maintenance and production of operating records to assist in ensuring accountability for source and special fissionable materials used or produced in the project or arrangement;

4. To call for and receive progress reports;

5. To approve the means to be used for the chemical processing of irradiated materials solely to ensure that this chemical processing will not lend itself to diversion of materials for military purposes and will comply with applicable health and safety standards; to require that special fissionable materials recovered or produced as a by-product be used for peaceful purposes under continuing agency safeguards for research or in reactors, existing or under construction, specified by the member or members concerned; and to require deposit with the agency of any excess of any special fissionable materials recovered or produced as a by-product over what is needed for the above stated uses in order to prevent stock-piling of these materials, provided that thereafter at the request of the member or members concerned special fissionable materials so deposited with the agency shall be returned promptly to the member or members concerned for use under the same provisions as stated above;

6. To send into the territory of the recipient state or states inspectors, designated by the agency after consultation with the state or states concerned, who shall have access at all times to all places and data and to any person who by reason of his occupation deals with materials, equipment, or facilities which are required by this statute to be safeguarded, as necessary to account for source and special fissionable materials supplied and fissionable products and to determine whether there is compliance with the undertaking against use in furtherance of any military purpose referred to in sub-Paragraph F–4 of Article XI, with the health and safety measures referred to in sub-Paragraph A–2 of this Article, and with any other conditions prescribed in the agreement between the agency and the state or states concerned. Inspectors designated by the agency shall be accompanied by representatives of the authorities of the state concerned, if that state so requests, provided that the inspectors shall not thereby be delayed or otherwise impeded in the exercise of their functions;

7. In the event of non-compliance and failure by the recipient state or states to take requested corrective steps within a reasonable time, to suspend or terminate assistance and withdraw any materials and equipment made available by the agency or a member in furtherance of the project.

(B) The agency shall, as necessary, establish a staff of inspectors. The staff of inspectors shall have the responsibility of examining all operations conducted by the agency itself to determine whether the agency is complying with the health and safety measures prescribed by it for application to projects subject to its approval, supervision or control, and whether the agency is taking adequate measures to prevent the source and special fissionable materials in its custody or used or produced in its own operations from being used in furtherance of any military purpose. The agency shall take remedial action forthwith to correct any non-compliance or failure to take adequate measures.

(C) The staff of inspectors shall also have the responsibility of obtaining and verifying the accounting referred to in sub-Paragraph A–6 of this Article and of determining whether there is compliance with the undertaking referred to in sub-Paragraph F–4 in Article XI, with the measures referred to in sub-Paragraph A–2 of this Article, and with all other conditions of the project prescribed in the agreement between the agency and the state or states concerned. The inspectors shall report any non-compliance to the director general who shall thereupon transmit the report to the board of governors. The board shall call upon the recipient state or states to remedy forthwith any non-compliance which it finds to have occurred. The board shall report the non-compliance to all members and to the Security Council and General Assembly of the United Nations. In the event of failure of the recipient state or states to take fully corrective action within a reasonable time, the board may take one or both of the following measures: direct curtailment or suspension of assistance being provided by the agency or by a member, and call for the return of materials and equipment made available to the recipient member or group of members. The agency may also, in accordance with Article XIV, suspend any non-complying member from the exercise of the privileges and rights of membership.

1.6 EUROPEAN UNION: CONSOLIDATED VERSION OF THE TREATY ESTABLISHING THE EUROPEAN COMMUNITY. Concluded at Rome, 25 March 1957. Entered into force, 1 January 1958. Amended by the Treaty on European Union, concluded at Maastricht, 7 Feb 1992, entered into force, 1 November 1993, and the Treaty of Amsterdam, concluded at Amsterdam, 2 October 1997, not in force as of 1 January 1999. *Reprinted in* 37 I.L.M. 56 (1998) & 1 Weston I.B.7 (Rome) and 1 Weston I.B.13a (Maastricht): *Art. 1–3, 7, 10, 12, 94–5, 174–76, 211, 220–22, 226–228, 232, 234, 249*

PART ONE
PRINCIPLES

Article 1 (ex Article 1)

By this Treaty, the HIGH CONTRACTING PARTIES establish among themselves a EUROPEAN COMMUNITY.

Article 2 (ex Article 2)

The Community shall have as its task, by establishing a Common Market and an economic and monetary union and by implementing common policies or activities referred to in Articles 3 and 4, to promote throughout the Community a harmonious, balanced and sustained development of economic activities, a high level of employment and of social protection, equality between men and women, sustainable and non-inflationary growth, a high degree of competitiveness and convergence of economic performance, a high level of protection and improvement of the quality of the environment, the raising of the standard of living and quality of life, and economic and social cohesion and solidarity among Member States. It shall be the aim of the Community, by establishing a Common Market and progressively approximating the economic policies of Member States, to promote throughout the Community a harmonious development of economic activities, a continuous and balanced expansion, an increased stability, an accelerated raising of the standard of living and closer relations between its Member States.

Article 3 (ex Article 3)

For the purposes set out in Article 2, the activities of the Community shall include, as provided in this Treaty and in accordance with the timetable set out therein:

(a) the prohibition, as between Member States, of customs duties and of quantitative restrictions on the import and export of goods, as well as of all other measures with equivalent effect;

(b) a common commercial policy;

(c) an internal market characterised by the abolition, as between Member States, of obstacles to the free movement of goods, persons, services and capital;

(d) measures concerning the entry and movement of persons as provided for in Title IV;

(e) a common policy in the sphere of agricultural and fisheries;

(f) a common policy in the sphere of transport;

(g) a system ensuring that competition in the internal market shall not be distorted;

(h) the approximation of the laws of Member States to the extent required for the functioning of the common market;

(i) the promotion of coordination between employment policies of the Member States with a view to enhancing their effectiveness by developing a coordinated strategy for employment;

(j) a policy in the social sphere comprising a European Social Fund;

(k) the strengthening of economic and social cohesion;

(*l*) a policy in the sphere of the environment;

(m) the strengthening of the competitiveness of Community industry;

(n) the promotion of research and technological development;

(*o*) encouragement for the establishment and development of trans-European networks;

(p) a contribution to the attainment of a high level of health protection;

(q) a contribution to education and training of quality and to the flowering of the cultures of the Member States;

(r) a policy in the sphere of development cooperation;

(s) the association of the overseas countries and territories in order to increase trade and promote jointly economic and social development;

(t) a contribution to the strengthening of consumer protection;

(u) measures in the spheres of energy, civil protection and tourism.

2. In all the activities referred to in this Article, the Community shall aim to eliminate inequalities, and to promote equality, between men and women.

Article 7 (ex Article 4)

1. The tasks entrusted to the Community shall be carried out by the following institutions:

—a European Parliament,

—a Council,

—a Commission,

—a Court of Justice,

—a Court of Auditors.

Each of these institutions shall act within the limits of the powers conferred upon it by this Treaty.

2. The Council and the Commission shall be assisted by an Economic and Social Committee acting in an advisory capacity.

Article 10 (ex Article 5)

Member States shall take all appropriate measures, whether general or particular, to ensure fulfilment of the obligations arising out of this Treaty or resulting from action taken by the institutions of the Community. They shall facilitate the achievement of the Community's tasks. They shall abstain from any measure which could jeopardise the attainment of the objectives of this Treaty.

Article 12 (ex Article 6)

Within the scope of application of this Treaty, and without prejudice to any special provisions contained therein, any discrimination on grounds of nationality shall be prohibited.

The Council, acting in accordance with the procedure referred to in Article 251, may adopt rules designed to prohibit such discrimination.

* * *

Article 94 (ex Article 100)

The Council shall, acting unanimously on a proposal from the Commission and after consulting the European Parliament and the Economic and Social Committee, issue directives for the approximation of such laws, regulations or administrative provisions of the Member States as directly affect the establishment or functioning of the common market.

Article 95 (ex Article 100a)

1. By way of derogation from Article 100 and save where otherwise provided in this Treaty, the following provisions shall apply for the achievement of the objectives set out in Article 14. The Council shall, acting in accordance with the procedure referred to in Article 251 and after consulting the Economic and Social Committee, adopt the measures for the approximation of the provisions laid down by law, regulation or administrative action in Member States which have as their object the establishment and functioning of the internal market.

2. Paragraph 1 shall not apply to fiscal provisions, to those relating to the free movement of persons nor to those relating to the rights and interests of employed persons.

3. The Commission, in its proposals envisaged in paragraph 1 concerning health, safety, environmental protection and consumer protection, will take as a base a high level of protection, taking into account in particular of any new development based on scientific facts. Within their respective powers, the European Parliament and the Council will also seek to achieve this objective.

4. If, after the adoption by the Council or by the Commission of a harmonization measure, a Member State deems it necessary to maintain national provisions on grounds of major needs referred to in Article 30, or relating to protection of the environment or the working environment, it shall notify the Commission of these provisions as well as the grounds for maintaining them.

5. Moreover, without prejudice to paragraph 4, if, after the adoption by the Council or by the Commission of a harmonisation measure, a Member State deems it necessary to introduce national provisions based on new scientific evidence relating to the protection of the environment or the working environment on grounds of a problem specific to that Member State arising after the adoption of the harmonisation measure, it shall notify the Commission of the envisaged provisions as well as the grounds for introducing them.

* * *

Title XIX (ex Title XVI)

ENVIRONMENT

Article 174 (ex Article 130r)

1. Community policy on the environment shall contribute to pursuit of the following objectives:

—preserving, protecting and improving the quality of the environment;

—protecting human health;

—prudent and rational utilisation of natural resources;

—promoting measures at international level to deal with regional or worldwide environmental problems.

2. Community policy on the environment shall aim at a high level of protection taking into account the diversity of situations in the various regions of the Community. It shall be based on the precautionary principle and on the principles that preventive action should be taken, that environmental damage should as a priority be rectified at source and that the polluter should pay.

In this context, harmonization measures answering these requirements shall include, where appropriate, a safeguard clause allowing Member States to take provisional measures, for non-economic environmental reasons, subject to a Community inspection procedure.

3. In preparing its policy on the environment, the Community shall take account of:

—available scientific and technical data;

—environmental conditions in the various regions of the Community;

—the potential benefits and costs of action or lack of action;

—the economic and social development of the Community as a whole and the balanced development of its regions.

4. Within their respective spheres of competence, the Community and the Member States shall cooperate with third countries and with the competent international organizations. The arrangements for Community cooperation may be the subject of agreements between the Community and the third parties concerned, which shall be negotiated and concluded in accordance with Article 300.

The previous subparagraph shall be without prejudice to Member States' competence to negotiate in international bodies and to conclude international agreements.

Article 175 (ex Article 130s)

1. The Council, acting in accordance with the procedure referred to in Article 251 and after consulting the Economic and Social Committee and the Committee of the Regions, shall decide what action is to be taken by the Community in order to achieve the objectives referred to in Article 174.

2. By way of derogation from the decision-making procedure provided for in paragraph 1 and without prejudice to Article 95, the Council, acting unanimously on a proposal from the Commission and after consulting the European Parliament, the Economic and Social Committee and the Committee of the Regions, shall adopt:

—provisions primarily of a fiscal nature;

—measures concerning town and country planning, land use with the exception of waste management and measures of a general nature, and management of water resources;

—measures significantly affecting a Member State's choice between different energy sources and the general structure of its energy supply.

The Council may, under the conditions laid down in the preceding subparagraph, define those matters referred to in this paragraph on which decisions are to be taken by a qualified majority.

3. In other areas, general action programmes setting out priority objectives to be attained shall be adopted by the Council, acting in accordance with the procedure referred to in Article 251 and after consulting the Economic and Social Committee and the Committee of the Regions.

The Council, acting under the terms of paragraph 1 or paragraph 2 according to the case, shall adopt the measures necessary for the implementation of these programmes.

4. Without prejudice to certain measures of a Community nature, the Member States shall finance and implement the environment policy.

5. Without prejudice to the principle that the polluter should pay, if a measure based on the provisions of paragraph 1 involves costs deemed disproportionate for the public authorities of a Member State, the Council shall, in the act adopting that measure, lay down appropriate provisions in the form of:

—temporary derogations, and/or

—financial support from the Cohesion Fund pursuant to Article 161.

Article 176 (ex Article 130t)

The protective measures adopted pursuant to Article 175 shall not prevent any Member State from maintaining or introducing more stringent protective measures. Such measures must be compatible with this Treaty. They shall be notified to the Commission.

* * *

PART FIVE

INSTITUTIONS OF THE COMMUNITY

Title I

Provisions Governing the Institutions

Section 3: The Commission

Article 211 (ex Article 155)

In order to ensure the proper functioning and development of the common market, the Commission shall:

- ensure that the provisions of this Treaty and the measures taken by the institutions pursuant thereto are applied;
- formulate recommendations or deliver opinions on matters dealt with in this Treaty, if it expressly so provides or if the Commission considers it necessary;
- have its own power of decision and participate in the shaping of measures taken by the Council and by the European Parliament in the manner provided for in this Treaty;
- exercise the powers conferred on it by the Council for the implementation of the rules laid down by the latter.

Section 4: The Court of Justice

Article 220 (ex Article 164)

The Court of Justice shall ensure that in the interpretation and application of this Treaty the law is observed.

Article 221 (ex Article 165)

The Court of Justice shall consist of 15 Judges.

The Court of Justice shall sit in plenary session. It may, however, form chambers, each consisting of three, five or seven Judges, either to undertake certain preparatory inquiries or to adjudicate on particular categories of cases in accordance with rules laid down for these purposes.

The Court of Justice shall sit in plenary session when a Member State or a Community institution that is a party to the proceedings so requests.

Should the Court of Justice so request, the Council may, acting unanimously, increase the number of Judges and make the necessary adjustments to the second and third paragraphs of this Article and to the second paragraph of Article 223.

Article 222 (ex Article 166)

The Court of Justice shall be assisted by eight Advocates–General. However, a ninth Advocate–General shall be appointed as from 1 January 1995 until 6 October 2000.

It shall be the duty of the Advocate–General, acting with complete impartiality and independence, to make, in open court, reasoned submissions on cases brought before the Court of Justice, in order to assist the Court in the performance of the task assigned to it in Article 220.

Should the Court of Justice so request, the Council may, acting unanimously, increase the number of Advocates–General and make the necessary adjustments to the third paragraph of Article 223.

* * *

Article 226 (ex Article 169)

If the Commission considers that a Member State has failed to fulfil an obligation under this Treaty, it shall deliver a reasoned opinion on the matter after giving the State concerned the opportunity to submit its observations.

If the State concerned does not comply with the opinion within the period laid down by the Commission, the latter may bring the matter before the Court of Justice.

Article 227 (ex Article 170)

A Member State which considers that another Member State has failed to fulfil an obligation under this Treaty may bring the matter before the Court of Justice.

Before a Member State brings an action against another Member State for an alleged infringement of an obligation under this Treaty, it shall bring the matter before the Commission.

The Commission shall deliver a reasoned opinion after each of the States concerned has been given the opportunity to submit its own case and its observations on the other party's case both orally and in writing.

If the Commission has not delivered an opinion within three months of the date on which the matter was brought before it, the absence of such opinion shall not prevent the matter from being brought before the Court of Justice.

Article 228 (ex Article 171)

1. If the Court of Justice finds that a Member State has failed to fulfil an obligation under this Treaty, the State shall be required to take the necessary measures to comply with the judgment of the Court of Justice.

2. If the Commission considers that the Member State concerned has not taken such measures it shall, after giving that State the opportunity to submit its observations, issue a reasoned opinion specifying the points on which the Member State concerned has not complied with the judgment of the Court of Justice.

If the Member State concerned fails to take the necessary measures to comply with the Court's judgment within the time-limit laid down by the Commission, the latter may bring the case before the Court of Justice. In so doing it shall specify the amount of the lump sum or penalty payment to be paid by the Member State concerned which it considers appropriate in the circumstances.

If the Court of Justice finds that the Member State concerned has not complied with its judgment it may impose a lump sum or penalty payment on it.

This procedure shall be without prejudice to Article 227.

* * *

Article 232 (ex Article 175)

Should the European Parliament, the Council or the Commission, in infringement of this Treaty, fail to act, the Member States and the other institutions of the Community may bring an action before the Court of Justice to have the infringement established.

The action shall be admissible only if the institution concerned has first been called upon to act. If, within two months of being so called upon, the institution concerned has not defined its position, the action may be brought within a further period of two months.

Any natural or legal person may, under the conditions laid down in the preceding paragraphs, complain to the Court of Justice that an institution of the Community has failed to address to that person any act other than a recommendation or an opinion.

The Court of Justice shall have jurisdiction, under the same conditions, in actions or proceedings brought by the ECB in the areas falling within the latter's field of competence and in actions or proceedings brought against the latter.

* * *

Article 234 (ex Article 177)

The Court of Justice shall have jurisdiction to give preliminary rulings concerning:

(a) the interpretation of this Treaty;

(b) the validity and interpretation of acts of the institutions of the Community and of the ECB;

(c) the interpretation of the statutes of bodies established by an act of the Council, where those statutes so provide.

Where such a question is raised before any court or tribunal of a Member State, that court or tribunal may, if it considers that a decision on the question is necessary to enable it to give judgment, request the Court of Justice to give a ruling thereon.

Where any such question is raised in a case pending before a court or tribunal of a Member State against whose decisions there is no judicial remedy under national law, that court or tribunal shall bring the matter before the Court of Justice.

Chapter 2: Provisions Common to Several Institutions

Article 249 (ex Article 189)

In order to carry out their task and in accordance with the provisions of this Treaty, the European Parliament acting jointly with the Council, the Council and the Commission shall make regulations and issue directives, take decisions, make recommendations or deliver opinions.

A regulation shall have general application. It shall be binding in its entirety and directly applicable in all Member States.

A directive shall be binding, as to the result to be achieved, upon each Member State to which it is addressed, but shall leave to the national authorities the choice of form and methods.

A decision shall be binding in its entirety upon those to whom it is addressed.

Recommendations and opinions shall have no binding force.

1.7 Vienna Convention on the Law of Treaties (With Annex). Concluded at Vienna, 23 May 1969. Entered into force, 27 January 1988. 1155 U.N.T.S. 331; *reprinted in* 1 Weston I.E.1

The States Parties to the present Convention,

Considering the fundamental role of treaties in the history of international relations,

Recognizing the ever-increasing importance of treaties as a source of international law and as a means of developing peaceful co-operation among nations, whatever their constitutional and social systems,

Noting that the principles of free consent and of good faith and the *pacta sunt servanda* rule are universally recognized,

Affirming that disputes concerning treaties, like other international disputes, should be settled by peaceful means and in conformity with the principles of justice and international law,

Recalling the determination of the peoples of the United Nations to establish conditions under which justice and respect for the obligations arising from treaties can be maintained,

Having in mind the principles of international law embodied in the Charter of the United Nations, such as the principles of the equal rights and self-determination of peoples, of the sovereign equality and independence of all States, of noninterference in the domestic affairs of States, of the prohibition of the threat or use of force and of universal respect for, and observance of, human rights and fundamental freedoms for all,

Believing that the codification and progressive development of the law of treaties achieved in the present Convention will promote the purposes of the United Nations set forth in the Charter, namely, the maintenance of international peace and security, the development of friendly relations and the achievement of co-operation among nations,

Affirming that the rules of customary international law will continue to govern questions not regulated by the provisions of the present Convention,

Have agreed as follows:

PART I. INTRODUCTION

Article 1. Scope of the Present Convention

The present Convention applies to treaties between States

Article 2. Use of Terms

1. For the purposes of the present Convention:

(*a*) "Treaty" means an international agreement concluded between States in written form and governed by international law, whether embodied in a single instrument or in two or more related instruments and whatever its particular designation;

(*b*) "Ratification", "acceptance", "approval" and "accession" means in each case the international act so named whereby a State establishes on the international plane its consent to be bound by a treaty;

(*c*) "Full powers" means a document emanating from the competent authority of a State designating a person or persons to represent the State for negotiating, adopting or authenticating the text of a treaty, for expressing the consent of the State to be bound by a treaty, or for accomplishing any other act with respect to a treaty;

(*d*) "Reservation" means a unilateral statement, however phrased or named, made by a State, when signing, ratifying, accepting, approving or acceding to a treaty, whereby it purports to exclude or to modify the legal effect of certain provisions of the treaty in their application to that State;

(*e*) "Negotiating State" means a State which took part in the drawing up and adoption of the text of the treaty;

(*f*) "Contracting State" means a State which has consented to be bound by the treaty, whether or not the treaty has entered into force;

(*g*) "Party" means a State which has consented to be bound by the treaty and for which the treaty is in force;

(*h*) "Third State" means a State not a party to the treaty;

(*i*) "International organization" means an intergovernmental organization.

2. The provisions of paragraph 1 regarding the use of terms in the present Convention are without prejudice to the use of those terms or to the meanings which may be given to them in the internal law of any State.

Article 3. International Agreements Not Within the Scope of the Present Convention

The fact that the present Convention does not apply to international agreements concluded between States and other subjects of international law or between such other subjects of international law, or to international agreements not in written form, shall not affect:

(*a*) The legal force of such agreements;

(*b*) The application to them of any of the rules set forth in the present Convention to which they would be subject under international law independently of the Convention;

(*c*) The application of the Convention to the relations of States as between themselves under international agreements to which other subjects of international law are also parties.

Article 4. Non-Retroactivity of the Present Convention

Without prejudice to the application of any rules set forth in the present Convention to which treaties would be subject under international law independently of the Convention, the Convention applies only to treaties which are concluded by States after the entry into force of the present Convention with regard to such States.

Article 5. Treaties Constituting International Organizations and Treaties Adopted Within an International Organization

The present Convention applies to any treaty which is the constituent instrument of an international organization and to any treaty adopted within an international organization without prejudice to any relevant rules of the organizations.

PART II. CONCLUSION AND ENTRY INTO FORCE OF TREATIES

Section 1. Conclusion of Treaties

Article 6. Capacity of States to Conclude Treaties

Every State possesses capacity to conclude treaties.

Article 7. FULL POWERS

1. A person is considered as representing a State for the purpose of adopting or authenticating the text of a treaty or for the purpose of expressing the consent of the State to be bound by a treaty if:

(*a*) He produces appropriate full powers; or

(*b*) It appears from the practice of the States concerned or from other circumstances that their intention was to consider that person as representing the State for such purposes and to dispense with full powers.

2. In virtue of their functions and without having to produce full powers, the following are considered as representing their State:

(*a*) Heads of State, Heads of Government and Ministers for Foreign Affairs, for the purpose of performing all acts relating to the conclusion of a treaty;

(*b*) Heads of diplomatic missions, for the purpose of adopting the text of a treaty between the accrediting State and the State to which they are accredited;

(*c*) Representatives accredited by States to an international conference or to an international organization or one of its organs, for the purpose of adopting the text of a treaty in that conference, organization or organ.

Article 8. SUBSEQUENT CONFIRMATION OF AN ACT PERFORMED WITHOUT AUTHORIZATION

An act relating to the conclusion of a treaty performed by a person who cannot be considered under Article 7 as authorized to represent a State for that purpose is without legal effect unless afterwards confirmed by that State.

Article 9. ADOPTION OF THE TEXT

1. The adoption of the text of a treaty takes place by the consent of all the States participating in its drawing up except as provided in paragraph 2.

2. The adoption of the text of a treaty at an international conference takes place by the vote of two thirds of the States present and voting, unless by the same majority they shall decide to apply a different rule.

Article 10. AUTHENTICATION OF THE TEXT

The text of a treaty is established as authentic and definitive:

(*a*) By such procedure as may be provided for in the text or agreed upon by the States participating in its drawing up; or

(*b*) Failing such procedure, by the signature, signature ad referendum or initialling by the representatives of those States of the text of the treaty or of the Final Act of a conference incorporating the text.

Article 11. MEANS OF EXPRESSING CONSENT TO BE BOUND BY A TREATY

The consent of a State to be bound by a treaty may be expressed by signature, exchange of instruments constituting a treaty, ratification, acceptance, approval or accession, or by any other means if so agreed.

Article 12. CONSENT TO BE BOUND BY A TREATY EXPRESSED BY SIGNATURE

1. The consent of a State to be bound by a treaty is expressed by the signature of its representative when:

(*a*) The treaty provides that signature shall have that effect;

(*b*) It is otherwise established that the negotiating States were agreed that signature should have that effect; or (*c*) The intention of the state to give that effect to the signature appears from the full powers of its representative or was expressed during the negotiation.

2. For the purposes of paragraph 1:

(*a*) The initialling of a text constitutes a signature of the treaty when it is established that the negotiating States so agreed;

(*b*) The signature *ad referendum* of a treaty by a representative, if confirmed by his State, constitutes a full signature of the treaty.

Article 13. CONSENT TO BE BOUND BY A TREATY EXPRESSED BY AN EXCHANGE OF INSTRUMENTS CONSTITUTING A TREATY

The consent of States to be bound by a treaty constituted by instruments exchanged between them is expressed by that exchange when:

(*a*) The instruments provide that their exchange shall have that effect; or

(*b*) It is otherwise established that those States were agreed that the exchange of instruments shall have that effect.

Article 14. CONSENT TO BE BOUND BY A TREATY EXPRESSED BY RATIFICATION, ACCEPTANCE OR APPROVAL

1. The consent of a State to be bound by a treaty is expressed by ratification when:

(*a*) The treaty provides for such consent to be expressed by means of ratification;

(*b*) It is otherwise established that the negotiating States were agreed that ratification should be required;

(*c*) The representative of the State has signed the treaty subject to ratification; or

(*d*) The intention of the State to sign the treaty subject to ratification appears from the full powers of its representative or was expressed during the negotiation.

2. The consent of a State to be bound by a treaty is expressed by acceptance or approval under conditions similar to those which apply to ratification.

Article 15. CONSENT TO BE BOUND BY A TREATY EXPRESSED BY ACCESSION

The consent of a State to be bound by a treaty is expressed by accession when:

(*a*) The treaty provides that such consent may be expressed by that State by means of accession;

(*b*) It is otherwise established that the negotiating States were agreed that such consent may be expressed by that State by means of accession; or

(*c*) All the parties have subsequently agreed that such consent may be expressed by that State by means of accession.

Article 16. EXCHANGE OR DEPOSIT OF INSTRUMENTS OF RATIFICATION, ACCEPTANCE, APPROVAL OR ACCESSION

Unless the treaty otherwise provides, instruments of ratification, acceptance, approval or accession establish the consent of a State to be bound by a treaty upon:

(*a*) Their exchange between the contracting States;

(*b*) Their deposit with the depositary; or

(*c*) Their notification to the contracting States or to the depositary, if so agreed.

Article 17. CONSENT TO BE BOUND BY PART OF A TREATY AND CHOICE OF DIFFERING PROVISIONS

1. Without prejudice to Articles 19 to 23, the consent of a State to be bound by part of a treaty is effective only if the treaty so permits or the other contracting States so agree.

2. The consent of a State to be bound by a treaty which permits a choice between differing provisions is effective only if it is made clear to which of the provisions the consent relates.

Article 18. OBLIGATION NOT TO DEFEAT THE OBJECT AND PURPOSE OF A TREATY PRIOR TO ITS ENTRY INTO FORCE

A State is obliged to refrain from acts which would defeat the object and purpose of a treaty when:

(*a*) It has signed the treaty or has exchanged instruments constituting the treaty subject to ratification, acceptance or approval, until it shall have made its intention clear not to become a party to the treaty; or

(*b*) It has expressed its consent to be bound by the treaty, pending the entry into force of the treaty and provided that such entry into force is not unduly delayed.

SECTION 2. RESERVATIONS

Article 19. FORMULATION OF RESERVATIONS

A State may, when signing, ratifying, accepting, approving or acceding to a treaty, formulate a reservation unless:

(*a*) The reservation is prohibited by the treaty;

(*b*) The treaty provides that only specified reservations, which do not include the reservation in question, may be made; or

(*c*) In cases not falling under sub-paragraphs (*a*) and (*b*), the reservation is incompatible with the object and purpose of the treaty.

Article 20. ACCEPTANCE OF AND OBJECTION TO RESERVATIONS

1. A reservation expressly authorized by a treaty does not require any subsequent acceptance by the other contracting States unless the treaty so provides.

2. When it appears from the limited number of the negotiating States and the object and purpose of a treaty that the application of the treaty in its entirety between all the parties is an essential condition of the consent of each one to be bound by the treaty, a reservation requires acceptance by all the parties;

3. When a treaty is a constituent instrument of an international organization and unless it otherwise provides, a reservation requires the acceptance of the competent organ of that organization.

4. In cases not falling under the preceding paragraphs and unless the treaty otherwise provides:

(*a*) Acceptance by another contracting State of a reservation constitutes the reserving State a party to the treaty in relation to that other State if or when the treaty is in force for those States;

(*b*) An objection by another contracting State to a reservation does not preclude the entry into force of the treaty as between the objecting and reserving States unless a contrary intention is definitely expressed by the objecting State;

(c) An act expressing a State's consent to be bound by the treaty and containing a reservation is effective as soon as at least one other contracting State has accepted the reservation.

5. For the purposes of paragraphs 2 and 4 and unless the treaty otherwise provides, a reservation is considered to have been accepted by a State if it shall have raised no objection to the reservation by the end of a period of twelve months after it was notified of the reservation or by the date on which it expressed its consent to be bound by the treaty, whichever is later.

Article 21. LEGAL EFFECTS OF RESERVATIONS AND OF OBJECTIVES TO RESERVATIONS

1. A reservation established with regard to another party in accordance with Articles 19, 20 and 23:

(*a*) Modifies for the reserving State in its relations with that other party the provisions of the treaty to which the reservation relates to the extent of the reservation; and

(*b*) Modifies those provisions to the same extent for that other party in its relations with the reserving State.

2. The reservation does not modify the provisions of the treaty for the other parties to the treaty *inter se.*

3. When a State objecting to a reservation has not opposed the entry into force of the treaty between itself and the reserving State, the provisions to which the reservation relates do not apply as between the two States to the extent of the reservation.

Article 22. WITHDRAWAL OF RESERVATIONS AND OF OBJECTIVES TO RESERVATIONS

1. Unless the treaty otherwise provides, a reservation may be withdrawn at any time and the consent of a State which has accepted the reservation is not required for its withdrawal.

2. Unless the treaty otherwise provides, an objection to a reservation may be withdrawn at any time.

3. Unless the treaty otherwise provides, or it is otherwise agreed:

(*a*) The withdrawal of a reservation becomes operative in relation to another contracting State only when notice of it has been received by that State;

(*b*) The withdrawal of an objection to a reservation becomes operative only when notice of it has been received by the State which formulated the reservation.

Article 23. PROCEDURE REGARDING RESERVATIONS

1. A reservation, an express acceptance of a reservation and an objection to a reservation must be formulated in writing and communicated to the contracting States and other States entitled to become parties to the treaty.

2. If formulated when signing the treaty subject to ratification, acceptance or approval, a reservation must be formally confirmed by the reserving State when expressing its consent to be bound by the treaty. In such a case the reservation shall be considered as having been made on the date of its confirmation.

3. An express acceptance of, or an objection to, a reservation made previously to confirmation of the reservation does not itself require confirmation.

4. The withdrawal of a reservation or of an objection to a reservation must be formulated in writing.

SECTION 3. ENTRY INTO FORCE PROVISIONAL APPLICATION OF TREATIES

Article 24. ENTRY INTO FORCE

1. A treaty enters into force in such manner and upon such date as it may provide or as the negotiating States may agree.

2. Failing any such provision or agreement, a treaty enters into force as soon as consent to be bound by the treaty has been established for all the negotiating States.

3. When the consent of a State to be bound by a treaty is established on a date after the treaty has come into force, the treaty enters into force for that State on that date, unless the treaty otherwise provides.

4. The provisions of a treaty regulating the authentication of its text, the establishment of the consent of States to be bound by the treaty, the manner or date of its entry into force, reservations, the functions of the depositary and other matters arising necessarily before the entry into force of the treaty apply from the time of the adoption of its text.

Article 25. PROVISIONAL APPLICATION

1. A treaty or a part of a treaty is applied provisionally pending its entry into force if:

(*a*) The treaty itself so provides; or

(*b*) The negotiating States have in some other manner so agreed.

2. Unless the treaty between provides or the negotiating States have otherwise agreed, the provisional application of a treaty or a part of a treaty with respect to a State shall be terminated if that State notifies the other States between which the treaty is being applied provisionally of its intention not to become a party to the treaty.

PART III. OBSERVANCE, APPLICATION AND INTERPRETATION OF TREATIES

SECTION 1. OBSERVANCE OF TREATIES

Article 26. "PACTA SUNT SERVANDA"

Every treaty in force is binding upon the parties to it and must be performed by them in good faith.

Article 27. INTERNAL LAW AND OBSERVANCE OF TREATIES

A party may not invoke the provisions of its internal law as justification for its failure to perform a treaty. This rule is without prejudice to Article 46.

SECTION 2. APPLICATION OF TREATIES

Article 28. NON-RETROACTIVITY OF TREATIES

Unless a different intention appears from the treaty or is otherwise established, its provisions do not bind a party in relation to any act or fact which took place or any situation which ceased to exist before the date of the entry into force of the treaty with respect to that party.

Article 29. TERRITORIAL SCOPE OF TREATIES

Unless a different intention appears from the treaty or is otherwise established, a treaty is binding upon each party in respect of its entire territory.

Article 30. APPLICATION OF SUCCESSIVE TREATIES RELATING TO THE SAME SUBJECT-MATTER

1. Subject to Article 103 of the Charter of the United Nations, the rights and obligations of States parties to successive treaties relating to the same subject-matter shall be determined in accordance with the following paragraphs.

2. When a treaty specifies that it is subject to, or that it is not to be considered as incompatible with, an earlier or later treaty, the provisions of that other treaty prevail.

3. When all the parties to the earlier treaty are parties also to the later treaty but the earlier treaty is not terminated or suspended in operation under Article 59, the earlier treaty applies only to the extent that its provisions are compatible with those of the later treaty.

4. When the parties to the later treaty do not include all the parties to the earlier one:

(*a*) As between States parties to both treaties the same rule applies as in paragraph 3;

(*b*) As between a State party to both treaties and a State party to only one of the treaties, the treaty to which both States are parties governs their mutual rights and obligations.

5. Paragraph 4 is without prejudice to Article 41, or to any question of the termination or suspension of the operation of a treaty under Article 60 or to any question of responsibility which may arise for a State from the conclusion or application of a treaty the provisions of which are incompatible with its obligations towards another State under another treaty.

SECTION 3. INTERPRETATION OF TREATIES

Article 31. GENERAL RULE OF INTERPRETATION

1. A treaty shall be interpreted in good faith in accordance with the ordinary meaning to be given to the terms of the treaty in their context and in the light of its object and purpose.

2. The context for the purpose of the interpretation of a treaty shall comprise, in addition to the text, including its preamble and annexes:

(*a*) Any agreement relating to the treaty which was made between all the parties in connexion with the conclusion of the treaty;

(*b*) Any instrument which was made by one or more parties in connexion with the conclusion of the treaty and accepted by the other parties as an instrument related to the treaty.

3. There shall be taken into account, together with the context:

(*a*) Any subsequent agreement between the parties regarding the interpretation of the treaty or the application of its provisions;

(*b*) Any subsequent practice in the application of the treaty which establishes the agreement of the parties regarding its interpretation;

(*c*) Any relevant rules of international law applicable in the relations between the parties.

4. A special meaning shall be given to a term if it is established that the parties so intended.

Article 32. SUPPLEMENTARY MEANS OF INTERPRETATION

Recourse may be had to supplementary means of interpretation, including the preparatory work of the treaty and the circumstances of its conclusion, in order to confirm the meaning resulting from the application of Article 31, or to determine the meaning when the interpretation according to Article 31:

(*a*) Leaves the meaning ambiguous or obscure; or

(*b*) Leads to a result which is manifestly absurd or unreasonable.

Article 33. INTERPRETATION OF TREATIES AUTHENTICATED IN TWO OR MORE LANGUAGES

1. When a treaty has been authenticated in two or more languages, the text is equally authoritative in each language, unless the treaty provides or the parties agree that, in case of divergence, a particular text shall prevail.

2. A version of the treaty in a language other than one of those in which the text was authenticated shall be considered an authentic text only if the treaty so provides or the parties so agree.

3. The terms of the treaty are presumed to have the same meaning in each authentic text.

4. Except where a particular text prevails in accordance with paragraph 1, when a comparison of the authentic texts discloses a difference of meaning which the application of Articles 31 and 32 does not remove, the meaning which best reconciles the texts, having regard to the object and purpose of the treaty, shall be adopted.

SECTION 4. TREATIES AND THIRD STATES

Article 34. GENERAL RULE REGARDING THIRD STATES

A treaty does not create either obligations or rights for a third State without its consent.

Article 35. TREATIES PROVIDING FOR OBLIGATIONS FOR THIRD STATES

An obligation arises for a third State from a provision of a treaty if the parties to the treaty intend the provision to be the means of establishing the obligation and the third State expressly accepts that obligation in writing.

Article 36. TREATIES PROVIDING FOR RIGHTS FOR THIRD STATES

1. A right arises for a third State from a provision of a treaty if the parties to the treaty intend the provision to accord that right either to the third State, or to a group of States to which it belongs, or to all States, and the third State assents thereto. Its assent shall be presumed so long as the contrary is not indicated, unless the treaty otherwise provides.

2. A State exercising a right in accordance with paragraph 1 shall comply with the conditions for its exercise provided for in the treaty or established in conformity with the treaty.

Article 37. REVOCATION OR MODIFICATION OF OBLIGATIONS OR RIGHTS OF THIRD STATES

1. When an obligation has arisen for a third State in conformity with Article 35, the obligation may be revoked or modified only with the consent of the parties to the treaty and of the third State, unless it is established that they had otherwise agreed.

2. When a right has arisen for a third State in conformity with Article 36, the right may not be revoked or modified by the parties if it is established that the right was intended not to be revocable or subject to modification without the consent of the third State.

Article 38. RULES IN A TREATY BECOMING BINDING ON THIRD STATES THROUGH INTERNATIONAL CUSTOM

Nothing in Articles 34 to 37 precludes a rule set forth in a treaty from becoming binding upon a third State as a customary rule of international law, recognized as such.

PART IV. AMENDMENT AND MODIFICATION OF TREATIES

Article 39. General Rule Regarding the Amendment of Treaties

A treaty may be amended by agreement between the parties. The rules laid down in Part II apply to such an agreement except in so far as the treaty may otherwise provide.

Article 40. Amendment of Multilateral Treaties

1. Unless the treaty otherwise provides, the amendment of multilateral treaties shall be governed by the following paragraphs.

2. Any proposal to amend a multilateral treaty as between all the parties must be notified to all the contracting States, each one of which shall have the right to take part in:

(*a*) The decision as to the action to be taken in regard to such proposal;

(*b*) The negotiation and conclusion of any agreement for the amendment of the treaty.

3. Every State entitled to become a party to the treaty shall also be entitled to become a party to the treaty as amended.

4. The amending agreement does not bind any State already a party to the treaty which does not become a party to the amending agreement; Article 30, paragraph 4(b), applies in relation to such State.

5. Any State which becomes a party to the treaty after the entry into force of the amending agreement shall, failing an expression of a different intention by that State:

(*a*) be considered as a party to the treaty as amended; and

(*b*) be considered as a party to the unamended treaty in relation to any party to the treaty not bound by the amending agreement.

Article 41. Agreements to Modify Multilateral Treaties Between Certain of the Parties Only

1. Two or more of the parties to a multilateral treaty may conclude an agreement to modify the treaty as between themselves alone if:

(*a*) The possibility of such a modification is provided for by the treaty; or

(*b*) The modification in question is not prohibited by the treaty and:

(i) Does not affect the enjoyment by the other parties of their rights under the treaty or the performance of their obligations;

(ii) Does not relate to a provision, derogation from which is incompatible with the effective execution of the object and purpose of the treaty as a whole.

2. Unless in a case falling under paragraph 1(a) the treaty otherwise provides, the parties in question shall notify the other parties of their intention to conclude the agreement and of the modification to the treaty for which it provides.

PART V. INVALIDITY, TERMINATION AND SUSPENSION OF THE OPERATION OF TREATIES

Section 1. General Provisions

Article 42. Validity and Continuance in Force of Treaties

1. The validity of a treaty or of the consent of a State to be bound by a treaty may be impeached only through the application of the present Convention.

2. The termination of a treaty, its denunciation or the withdrawal of a party, may take place only as a result of the application of the provisions of the treaty or of

the present Convention. The same rule applies to suspension of the operation of a treaty.

Article 43. Obligations Imposed by International Law Independently of a Treaty

The invalidity, termination or denunciation of a treaty, the withdrawal of a party from it, or the suspension of its operation, as a result of the application of the present Convention or of the provisions of the treaty, shall not in any way impair the duty of any State to fulfil any obligation embodied in the treaty to which it would be subject under international law independently of the treaty.

Article 44. Separability of Treaty Provisions

1. A right of a party, provided for in a treaty or arising under Article 56, to denounce, withdraw from or suspend the operation of the treaty may be exercised only with respect to the whole treaty unless the treaty otherwise provides or the parties otherwise agree.

2. A ground for invalidating, terminating, withdrawing from or suspending the operation of a treaty recognized in the present Convention may be invoked only with respect to the whole treaty except as provided in the following paragraphs or in Article 60.

3. If the ground relates solely to particular clauses, it may be invoked only with respect to those clauses where:

(*a*) The said clauses are separable from the remainder of the treaty with regard to their application;

(*b*) It appears from the treaty or is otherwise established that acceptance of those clauses was not an essential basis of the consent of the other party or parties to be bound by the treaty as a whole; and

(*c*) Continued performance of the remainder of the treaty would not be unjust.

4. In cases falling under Articles 49 and 50 the State entitled to invoke the fraud or corruption may do so with respect either to the whole treaty or, subject to paragraph 3, to the particular clauses alone.

5. In cases falling under Articles 51, 52 and 53, no separation of the provisions of the treaty is permitted.

Article 45. Loss of a Right to Invoke a Ground for Invalidating, Terminating, Withdrawing from or Suspending the Operation of a Treaty

A State may no longer invoke a ground for invalidating, terminating, withdrawing from or suspending the operation of a treaty under Articles 46 to 50 or Articles 60 and 62 if, after becoming aware of the facts:

(*a*) It shall have expressly agreed that the treaty is valid or remains in force or continues in operation, as the case may be; or

(*b*) It must by reason of its conduct be considered as having acquiesced in the validity of the treaty or in its maintenance in force or in operation, as the case may be.

Section 2. Invalidity of Treaties

Article 46. Provisions of Internal Law Regarding Competence to Conclude Treaties

1. A State may not invoke the fact that its consent to be bound by a treaty has been expressed in violation of a provision of its internal law regarding competence to conclude treaties as invalidating its consent unless that violation was manifest and concerned a rule of its internal law of fundamental importance.

2. A violation is manifest if it would be objectively evident to any State conducting itself in the matter in accordance with normal practice and in good faith.

Article 47. SPECIFIC RESTRICTIONS ON AUTHORITY TO EXPRESS THE CONSENT OF A STATE

If the authority of a representative to express the consent of a State to be bound by a particular treaty has been made subject to a specific restriction, his omission to observe the restriction may not be invoked as invalidating the consent expressed by him unless the restriction was notified to the other negotiating States prior to his expressing such consent.

Article 48. ERROR

1. A State may invoke an error in a treaty as invalidating its consent to be bound by the treaty if the error relates to a fact or situation which was assumed by that State to exist at the time when the treaty was concluded and formed an essential basis of its consent to be bound by the treaty.

2. Paragraph 1 shall not apply if the State in question contributed by its own conduct to the error or if the circumstances were such as to put that State on notice of a possible error.

3. An error relating only to the wording of the text of a treaty does not affect its validity; Article 79 then applies.

Article 49. FRAUD

If a State has been induced to conclude a treaty by the fraudulent conduct of another negotiating State, the State may invoke the fraud as invalidating its consent to be bound by the treaty.

Article 50. CORRUPTION OF A REPRESENTATIVE OF A STATE

If the expression of a State's consent to be bound by a treaty has been procured through the corruption of its representative directly or indirectly by another negotiating State, the State may invoke such corruption as invalidating its consent to be bound by the treaty

Article 51. COERCION OF A REPRESENTATIVE OF A STATE

The expression of a State's consent to be bound by a treaty which has been procured by the coercion of its representative through acts or threats directed against him shall be without any legal effect.

Article 52. COERCION OF A STATE BY THE THREAT OR USE OF FORCE

A treaty is void if its conclusion has been procured by the threat or use of force in violation of the principles of international law embodied in the Charter of the United Nations.

Article 53. TREATIES CONFLICTING WITH A PEREMPTORY NORM OF GENERAL INTERNATIONAL LAW ("JUS COGENS")

A treaty is void if, at the time of its conclusion, it conflicts with a peremptory norm of general international law. For the purposes of the present Convention, a peremptory norm of general international law is a norm accepted and recognized by the international community of States as a whole as a norm from which no derogation is permitted and which can be modified only by a subsequent norm of general international law having the same character.

Section 3. Termination and Suspension of the Operation of Treaties

Article 54. Termination of or Withdrawal from a Treaty Under its Provisions or by Consent of the Parties

The termination of a treaty or the withdrawal of a party may take place:

(*a*) In conformity with the provisions of the treaty; or

(*b*) At any time by consent of all the parties after consultation with the other contracting States.

Article 55. Reduction of the Parties to a Multilateral Treaty Below the Number Necessary for its Entry into Force

Unless the treaty otherwise provides a multilateral treaty does not terminate by reason only of the fact that the number of the parties falls below the number necessary for its entry into force.

Article 56. Denunciation of or Withdrawal from a Treaty Containing no Provision Regarding Termination, Denunciation or Withdrawal

1. A treaty which contains no provision regarding its termination and which does not provide for denunciation or withdrawal is not subject to denunciation or withdrawal unless:

(*a*) It is established that the parties intended to admit the possibility of denunciation or withdrawal; or

(*b*) A right of denunciation or withdrawal may be implied by the nature of the treaty.

2. A party shall give no less than twelve months' notice of its intention to denounce or withdraw from a treaty under paragraph 1.

Article 57. Suspension of the Operation of a Treaty Under its Provisions or by consent of the parties

The operation of a treaty in regard to all the parties or to a particular party may be suspended:

(*a*) In conformity with the provisions of the treaty; or

(*b*) At any time by consent of all the parties after consultation with the other contracting States.

Article 58. Suspension of the Operation of a Multilateral Treaty by Agreement Between Certain of the Parties Only

1. Two or more parties to a multilateral treaty may conclude an agreement to suspend the operation of provisions of the treaty, temporarily and as between themselves alone, if:

(*a*) The possibility of such a suspension is provided for by the treaty; or

(*b*) The suspension in question is not prohibited by the treaty and:

(i) Does not affect the enjoyment by the other parties of their rights under the treaty or the performance of their obligations;

(ii) Is not incompatible with the object and purpose of the treaty.

2. Unless in a case falling under paragraph 1(*a*) the treaty otherwise provides, the parties in question shall notify the other parties of their intention to conclude the agreement and of those provisions of the treaty the operation of which they intend to suspend.

Article 59. Termination or Suspension of the Operation of a Treaty Implied by Conclusion of a Later Treaty

1. A treaty shall be considered as terminated if all the parties to it conclude a later treaty relating to the same subject-matter and:

(*a*) It appears from the later treaty or is otherwise established that the parties intended that the matter should be governed by that treaty; or

(*b*) The provisions of the later treaty are so far incompatible with those of the earlier one that the two treaties are not capable of being applied at the same time.

2. The earlier treaty shall be considered as only suspended in operation if it appears from the later treaty or is otherwise established that such was the intention of the parties.

Article 60. Termination or Suspension of the Operation of a Treaty as a Consequence of its Breach

1. A material breach of a bilateral treaty by one of the parties entitles the other to invoke the breach as a ground for terminating the treaty or suspending its operation in whole or in part.

2. A material breach of a multilateral treaty by one of the parties entitles:

(*a*) The other parties by unanimous agreement to suspend the operation of the treaty in whole or in part or to terminate it either:

(i) In the relations between themselves and the defaulting State, or

(ii) As between all the parties;

(*b*) A party specially affected by the breach to invoke it as a ground for suspending the operation of the treaty in whole or in part in the relations between itself and the defaulting State;

(*c*) Any party other than the defaulting State to invoke the breach as a ground for suspending the operation of the treaty in whole or in part with respect to itself if the treaty is of such a character that a material breach of its provisions by one party radically changes the position of every party with respect to the further performance of its obligations under the treaty.

3. A material breach of a treaty, for the purposes of this Article, consists in:

(*a*) A repudiation of the treaty not sanctioned by the present Convention; or

(*b*) The violation of a provision essential to the accomplishment of the object or purpose of the treaty.

4. The foregoing paragraphs are without prejudice to any provision in the treaty applicable in the event of a breach.

5. Paragraphs 1 to 3 do not apply to provisions relating to the protection of the human person contained in treaties of a humanitarian character, in particular to provisions prohibiting any form of reprisals against persons protected by such treaties.

Article 61. Supervening Impossibility of Performance

1. A party may invoke the impossibility of performing a treaty as a ground for terminating or withdrawing from it if the impossibility results from the permanent disappearance or destruction of an object indispensable for the execution of the treaty. If the impossibility is temporary, it may be invoked only as a ground for suspending the operation of the treaty.

2. Impossibility of performance may not be invoked by a party as a ground for terminating, withdrawing from or suspending the operation of a treaty if the impossi-

bility is the result of a breach by that party either of an obligation under the treaty or of any other international obligation owed to any other party to the treaty.

Article 62. FUNDAMENTAL CHANGE OF CIRCUMSTANCES

1. A fundamental change of circumstances which has occurred with regard to those existing at the time of the conclusion of a treaty, and which was not foreseen by the parties, may not be invoked as a ground for terminating or withdrawing from the treaty unless:

(*a*) The existence of those circumstances constituted an essential basis of the consent of the parties to be bound by the treaty; and

(*b*) The effect of the change is radically to transform the extent of obligations still to be performed under the treaty.

2. A fundamental change of circumstances may not be invoked as a ground for terminating or withdrawing from a treaty:

(*a*) If the treaty establishes a boundary; or

(*b*) If the fundamental change is the result of a breach by the party invoking it either of an obligation under the treaty or of any other international obligation owed to any other party to the treaty.

3. If, under the foregoing paragraphs, a party may invoke a fundamental change of circumstances as a ground for terminating or withdrawing from a treaty it may also invoke the change as a ground for suspending the operation of the treaty.

Article 63. SEVERANCE OF DIPLOMATIC OR CONSULAR RELATIONS

The severance of diplomatic or consular relations between parties to a treaty does not affect the legal relations established between them by the treaty except in so far as the existence of diplomatic or consular relations is indispensable for the application of the treaty.

Article 64. EMERGENCE OF A NEW PEREMPTORY NORM OF GENERAL INTERNATIONAL LAW ("JUS COGENS")

If a new peremptory norm of general international law emerges, any existing treaty which is in conflict with that norm becomes void and terminates.

SECTION 4. PROCEDURE

Article 65. PROCEDURE TO BE FOLLOWED WITH RESPECT TO INVALIDITY, TERMINATION, WITHDRAWAL FROM OR SUSPENSION OF THE OPERATION OF A TREATY

1. A party which, under the provisions of the present Convention, invokes either a defect in its consent to be bound by a treaty or a ground for impeaching the validity of a treaty, terminating it, withdrawing from it or suspending its operation, must notify the other parties of its claim. The notification shall indicate the measure proposed to be taken with respect to the treaty and the reasons therefore.

2. If, after the expiry of a period which, except in cases of special urgency, shall not be less than three months after the receipt of the notification, no party has raised any objection, the party making the notification may carry out in the manner provided in Article 67 the measure which it has proposed.

3. If, however, objection has been raised by any other party, the parties shall seek a solution through the means indicated in Article 33 of the Charter of the United Nations.

4. Nothing in the foregoing paragraphs shall affect the rights or obligations of the parties under any provisions in force binding the parties with regard to the settlement of disputes.

5. Without prejudice to Article 45, the fact that a State has not previously made the notification prescribed in paragraph 1 shall not prevent it from making such notification in answer to another party claiming performance of the treaty or alleging its violation.

Article 66. PROCEDURES FOR JUDICIAL SETTLEMENT, ARBITRATION AND CONCILIATION

If, under paragraph 3 of Article 65, no solution has been reached within a period of twelve months following the date on which the objection was raised, the following procedures shall be followed:

(*a*) Any one of the parties to a dispute concerning the application or the interpretation of Articles 53 to 64 may, by a written application, submit it to the International Court of Justice for a decision unless the parties by common consent agree to submit the dispute to arbitration;

(*b*) Any one of the parties to a dispute concerning the application or the interpretation of any of the other Articles in Part V of the present Convention may set in motion the procedure specified in the Annex to the Convention by submitting a request to that effect to the Secretary–General of the United Nations.

Article 67. INSTRUMENTS FOR DECLARING INVALID, TERMINATING, WITHDRAWING FROM OR SUSPENDING THE OPERATION OF A TREATY

1. The notification provided for under Article 65, paragraph 1 must be made in writing.

2. Any act declaring invalid, terminating, withdrawing from or suspending the operation of a treaty pursuant to the provisions of the treaty or of paragraphs 2 or 3 of Article 65 shall be carried out through an instrument communicated to the other parties. If the instrument is not signed by the Head of State, Head of Government or Minister for Foreign Affair, the representative of the State communicating it may be called upon to produce full powers.

Article 68. REVOCATION OF NOTIFICATIONS AND INSTRUMENTS PROVIDED FOR IN ARTICLES 65 AND 67

A notification or instrument provided for in Articles 65 or 67 may be revoked at any time before it takes effect.

SECTION 5. CONSEQUENCES OF THE INVALIDITY, TERMINATION OR SUSPENSION OF THE OPERATION OF A TREATY

Article 69. CONSEQUENCES OF THE INVALIDITY OF A TREATY

1. A treaty the invalidity of which is established under the present Convention is void. The provisions of a void treaty have no legal force.

2. If acts have nevertheless been performed in reliance on such a treaty:

(*a*) Each party may require any other party to establish as far as possible in their mutual relations the position that would have existed if the acts had not been performed;

(*b*) Acts performed in good faith before the invalidity was invoked are not rendered unlawful by reason only of the invalidity of the treaty.

3. In cases falling under Articles 49, 50, 51 or 52, paragraph 2 does not apply with respect to the party to which the fraud, the act of corruption or the coercion is imputable.

4. In the case of the invalidity of a particular State's consent to be bound by a multilateral treaty, the foregoing rules apply in the relations between that State and the parties to the treaty.

Article 70. CONSEQUENCES OF THE TERMINATION OF A TREATY

1. Unless the treaty otherwise provides or the parties otherwise agree, the termination of a treaty under its provisions or in accordance with the present Convention:

(*a*) Releases the parties from any obligation further to perform the treaty;

(*b*) Does not affect any right, obligation or legal situation of the parties created through the execution of the treaty prior to its termination.

2. If a State denounces or withdraws from a multilateral treaty, paragraph 1 applies in the relations between that State and each of the other parties to the treaty from the date when such denunciation or withdrawal takes effect.

Article 71. CONSEQUENCES OF THE INVALIDITY OF A TREATY WHICH CONFLICTS WITH A PEREMPTORY NORM OF GENERAL INTERNATIONAL LAW

1. In the case of a treaty which is void under Article 53 the parties shall:

(*a*) Eliminate as far as possible the consequences of any act performed in reliance on any provision which conflicts with the peremptory norm of general international law; and

(*b*) Bring their mutual relations into conformity with the peremptory norm of general international law.

2. In the case of a treaty which becomes void and terminates under Article 64, the termination of the treaty:

(*a*) Releases the parties from any obligation further to perform the treaty;

(*b*) Does not affect any right, obligation or legal situation of the parties created through the execution of the treaty prior to its termination, provided that those rights, obligations or situations may thereafter be maintained only to the extent that their maintenance is not in itself in conflict with the new peremptory norm of general international law.

Article 72. CONSEQUENCES OF THE SUSPENSION OF THE OPERATION OF A TREATY

1. Unless the treaty otherwise provides or the parties otherwise agree, the suspension of the operation of a treaty under its provisions or in accordance with the present Convention:

(*a*) Release the parties between which the operation of the treaty is suspended from the obligation to perform the treaty in mutual relations during the period of the suspension;

(*b*) Does not otherwise affect the legal relations between the parties established by the treaty.

2. During the period of the suspension the parties shall refrain from acts tending to obstruct the resumption of the operation of the treaty.

PART VI. MISCELLANEOUS PROVISIONS

Article 73. CASES OF STATE SUCCESSION, STATE RESPONSIBILITY AND OUTBREAK OF HOSTILITIES

The provisions of the present Convention shall not prejudge any question that may arise in regard to a treaty from a succession of States or from the international responsibility of a State or from the outbreak of hostilities between States.

Article 74. Diplomatic and Consular Relations and the Conclusion of Treaties

The severance or absence of diplomatic or consular relations between two or more States does not prevent the conclusion of treaties between those States. The conclusion of a treaty does not in itself affect the situation in regard to diplomatic or consular relations.

Article 75. Case of an Aggressor State

The provisions of the present Convention are without prejudice to any obligation in relation to a treaty which may arise for an aggressor State in consequence of measures taken in conformity with the Charter of the United Nations with reference to that State's aggression.

PART VII. DEPOSITARIES, NOTIFICATIONS, CORRECTIONS AND REGISTRATION

Article 76. Depositaries of Treaties

1. The designation of the depositary of a treaty may be made by the negotiating States, either in the treaty itself or in some other manner. The depositary may be one or more States, an international organization or the chief administrative officer of the organization.

2. The functions of the depositary of a treaty are international in character and the depositary is under an obligation to act impartially in their performance. In particular, the fact that a treaty has not entered into force between certain of the parties or that a difference has appeared between a State and a depositary with regard to the performance of the latter's functions shall not affect that obligation.

Article 77. Functions of Depositaries

1. The functions of a depositary, unless otherwise provided in the treaty or agreed by the contracting States, comprise in particular:

(*a*) Keeping custody of the original text of the treaty and of any full powers delivered to the depositary;

(*b*) Preparing certified copies of the original text and preparing any further text of the treaty in such additional languages as may be required by the treaty and transmitting them to the parties and to the States entitled to become parties to the treaty;

(*c*) Receiving any signatures to the treaty and receiving and keeping custody of any instruments, notifications and communications relating to it;

(*d*) Examining whether the signature or any instrument, notification or communication relating to the treaty is in due and proper form and, if need be, bringing the matter to the attention of the State in question;

(*e*) Informing the parties and the States entitled to become parties to the treaty of acts, notifications and communications relating to the treaty;

(*f*) Informing the States entitled to become parties to the treaty when the number of signatures or of instruments of ratification, acceptance, approval or accession required for the entry into force of the treaty has been received or deposited;

(*g*) Registering the treaty with the Secretariat of the United Nations;

(*h*) Performing the functions specified in other provisions of the present Convention.

2. In the event of any difference appearing between a State and the depositary as to the performance of the latter's functions, the depositary shall bring the question to

the attention of the signatory States and the contracting States or, where appropriate, of the competent organ of the international organization concerned.

Article 78. NOTIFICATIONS AND COMMUNICATIONS

Except as the treaty or the present Convention otherwise provides, any notification or communication to be made by any State under the present Convention shall:

(*a*) If there is no depositary, be transmitted direct to the States for which it is intended, or if there is a depositary, to the latter;

(*b*) Be considered as having been made by the State in question only upon its receipt by the State to which it was transmitted or, as the case may be, upon its receipt by the depositary;

(*c*) If transmitted to a depositary, be considered as received by the State for which it was intended only when the latter State has been informed by the depositary in accordance with Article 77, paragraph 1(e).

Article 79. CORRECTION OF ERRORS IN TEXTS OR IN CERTIFIED COPIES OF TREATIES

1. Where, after the authentication of the text of a treaty, the signatory States and the contracting States are agreed that it contains an error, the error shall, unless they decide upon some other means of correction, be corrected:

(*a*) By having the appropriate correction made in the text and causing the correction to be initialled by duly authorized representatives;

(*b*) By executing or exchanging an instrument or instruments setting out the correction which it has been agreed to make; or

(*c*) By executing a corrected text of the whole treaty by the same procedure as in the case of the original text.

2. Where the treaty is one for which there is a depositary, the latter shall notify the signatory States and the contracting States of the error and of the proposal to correct it and shall specify an appropriate time-limit within which objection to the proposed correction may be raised. If, on the expiry of the time-limit:

(*a*) No objection has been raised, the depositary shall make and initial the correction in the text and shall execute a *process-verbal* of the rectification of the text and communicate a copy of it to the parties and to the States entitled to become parties to the treaty;

(*b*) An objection has been raised, the depositary shall communicate the objection to the signatory States and to the contracting States.

3. The rules in paragraphs 1 and 2 apply also where the text has been authenticated in two or more languages and it appears that there is a lack of concordance which the signatory States and the contracting States agree should be corrected.

4. The corrected text replaces the defective text *ab initio,* unless the signatory States and the contracting States otherwise decide.

5. The correction of the text of a treaty that has been registered shall be notified to the Secretariat of the United Nations.

6. Where an error is discovered in a certified copy of a treaty, the depositary shall execute a *process-verbal* specifying the rectification and communicate a copy of it to the signatory States and to the contracting States.

Article 80. REGISTRATION AND PUBLICATION OF TREATIES

1. Treaties shall, after their entry into force, be transmitted to the Secretariat of the United Nations for registration or filing and recording, as the case may be, and for publication.

2. The designation of a depositary shall constitute authorization for it to perform the acts specified in the preceding paragraph.

PART VIII. FINAL PROVISIONS

Article 81. Signature

The present Convention shall be open for signature by all States Members of the United Nations or of any of the specialized agencies or of the International Atomic Energy Agency or parties to the Statute of the International Court of Justice, and by any other State invited by the General Assembly of the United Nations to become a party to the Convention, as follows: until 30 November 1969, at the Federal Ministry for Foreign Affairs of the Republic of Austria, and subsequently, until 30 April 1970, at United Nations Headquarters, New York.

Article 82. Ratification

The present Convention is subject to ratification. The instruments of ratification shall be deposited with the Secretary–General of the United Nations.

Article 83. Accession

The present Convention shall remain open for accession by any State belonging to any of the categories mentioned in Article 81. The instruments of accession shall be deposited with the Secretary–General of the United Nations.

Article 84. Entry into Force

1. The present Convention shall enter into force on the thirtieth day following the date of deposit of the thirty-fifth instrument of ratification or accession.

2. For each State ratifying or acceding to the Convention after the deposit of the thirty-fifth instrument of ratification or accession, the Convention shall enter into force on the thirtieth day after deposit by such State of its instrument of ratification or accession.

Article 85. Authentic Texts

The original of the present Convention, of which the Chinese, English, French, Russian and Spanish texts are equally authentic, shall be deposited with the Secretary–General of the United Nations.

ANNEX

1. A list of conciliators consisting of qualified jurists shall be drawn up and maintained by the Secretary–General of the United Nations. To this end, every State which is a Member of the United Nations or a party to the present Convention shall be invited to nominate two conciliators, and the names of the persons so nominated shall constitute the list. The term of a conciliator, including that of any conciliator nominated to fill a casual vacancy, shall be five years and may be renewed. A conciliator whose term expires shall continue to fulfil any function for which he shall have been chosen under the following paragraph.

2. When a request has been made to the Secretary–General under Article 66, the Secretary–General shall bring the dispute before a conciliation commission constituted as follows:

The State or States constituting one of the parties to the dispute shall appoint:

(*a*) One conciliator of the nationality of that State or of one of those States, who may or may not be chosen from the list referred to in paragraph 1; and (*b*) One conciliator not of the nationality of that State or of any of those States, who shall be chosen from the list.

The State or States constituting the other party to the dispute shall appoint two conciliators in the same way. The four conciliators chosen by the parties shall be appointed within sixty days following the date on which the Secretary–General receives the request.

The four conciliators shall, within sixty days following the date of the last of their own appointments, appoint a fifth conciliator chosen from the list, who shall be chairman.

If the appointment of the chairman or of any of the other conciliators has not been made within the period prescribed above for such appointment, it shall be made by the Secretary–General within sixty days following the expiry of that period. The appointment of the chairman may be made by the Secretary–General either from the list or from the membership of the International Law Commission. Any of the periods within which appointments must be made may be extended by agreement between the parties to the dispute.

Any vacancy shall be filled in the manner prescribed for the initial appointment.

3. The Conciliation Commission shall decide its own procedure. The Commission, with the consent of the parties to the dispute, may invite any party to the treaty to submit to it its views orally or in writing. Decisions and recommendations of the Commission shall be made by a majority vote of the five members.

4. The Commission may draw the attention of the parties to the dispute to any measures which might facilitate an amicable settlement.

5. The Commission shall hear the parties, examine the claims and objections, and make proposals to the parties with a view to reaching an amicable settlement of the dispute.

1.8 Declaration on Principles of International Law Concerning Friendly Relations and Co-operation Among States in Accordance With the Charter of the United Nations. Adopted by the U.N. General Assembly, 24 October 1970. G.A.Res. 2625, U.N. GAOR, 25th Sess., Supp. No. 28, at 121, U.N.Doc. A/8028 (1971); *reprinted in* 9 I.L.M. 1292 (1970) & 1 Weston I.D.7

THE GENERAL ASSEMBLY,

Reaffirming in the terms of the Charter that the maintenance of international peace and security and the development of friendly relations and co-operation between nations are among the fundamental purposes of the United Nations,

Recalling that the peoples of the United Nations are determined to practise tolerance and live together in peace with one another as good neighbours,

Bearing in mind the importance of maintaining and strengthening international peace and founded upon freedom, equality, justice and respect for fundamental human rights and of developing friendly relations among nations irrespective of their political, economic and social systems or the levels of their development,

Bearing in mind also the paramount importance of the Charter of the United Nations in the promotion of the rule of law among nations,

Considering that the faithful observance of the principles of international law concerning friendly relations and co-operation among States, and fulfilment in good faith of the obligation assumed by States, in accordance with the Charter, is of the greatest importance for the maintenance of international peace and security, and for the implementation of the other purposes of the United Nations,

Noting that the great political, economic and social changes and scientific progress which have taken place in the world since the adoption of the Charter of the United Nations give increased importance to these principles and to the need for their more effective application in the conduct of States wherever carried on,

Recalling the established principle that outer space, including the Moon and other celestial bodies, is not subject to national appropriation by claim of sovereignty by means of use or occupation or by any other means, and mindful of the fact that consideration is being given in the United Nations to the question of establishing other appropriate provisions similarly inspired,

Convinced that the strict observance by States of the obligation not to intervene in the affairs of any other State is an essential condition to ensure that nations live together in peace with one another since the practice of any form of intervention not only violates the spirit and letter of the Charter of the United Nations but also leads to the creation of situations which threaten international peace and security,

Recalling the duty of States to refrain in their international relations from military, political, economic or any other form of coercion aimed against the political independence or territorial integrity of any State,

Considering it essential that all States shall refrain in their international relations from the threat or use of force against the territorial integrity or political independence of any State, or in any other manner inconsistent with the purposes of the United Nations,

Considering it equally essential that all States shall settle their international disputes by peaceful means in accordance with the Charter,

Reaffirming, in accordance with the Charter, the basic importance of sovereign equality and stressing that the purposes of the United Nations can be implemented only if States enjoy sovereign equality and comply fully with the requirements of this principle in their international relations,

Convinced that the subjection of peoples to alien subjugation, domination and exploitation constitutes a major obstacle to the promotion of international peace and security,

Convinced that the principle of equal rights and self-determination of peoples constitutes a significant contribution to contemporary international law, and that its effective application is of paramount importance for the promotion of friendly relations among States, based on respect for the principle of sovereign equality,

Convinced in consequence that any attempt aimed at the partial or total disruption of the national unity and territorial integrity of a State or country or at its political independence is incompatible with the purposes and principles of the Charter,

Considering the provisions of the Charter as a whole and taking into account the role of relevant resolutions adopted by the competent organs of the United Nations relating to the content of the principles,

Considering that the progressive development and codification of the following principles:

(*a*) The principle that States shall refrain in their international relations from the threat or use of force against the territorial integrity or political independence of any State, or in any other manner inconsistent with the purposes of the United Nations,

(*b*) The principle that States shall settle their international disputes by peaceful means in such a manner that international peace and security and justice are not endangered,

(*c*) The duty not to intervene in matters within the domestic jurisdiction of any State, in accordance with the Charter,

(*d*) The duty of States to co-operate with one another in accordance with the Charter,

(*e*) The principle of equal rights and self-determination of peoples,

(*f*) The principle of sovereign equality of States,

(*g*) The principle that States shall fulfil in good faith the obligations assumed by them in accordance with the Charter, so as to secure their more effective application within the international community would promote the realization of the purposes of the United Nations,

Having considered the principles of international law relating to friendly relations and cooperation among States,

1. *Solemnly proclaims* the following principles:

The principle that States shall refrain in their international relations from the threat or use of force against the territorial integrity or political independence of any State, or in any other manner inconsistent with the purposes of the United Nations,

Every State has the duty to refrain in its international relations from the threat or use of force against the territorial integrity or political independence of any State, or in any other manner inconsistent with the purposes of the United Nations. Such a threat or use of force constitutes a violation of international law and the Charter of the United Nations and shall never be employed as a means of settling international issues.

A war of aggression constitutes a crime against the peace, for which there is responsibility under international law.

In accordance with the purposes and principles of the United Nations, States have the duty to refrain from propaganda for wars of aggression.

Every State has the duty to refrain from the threat or use of force to violate the existing international boundaries of another State or as a means of solving international disputes, including territorial disputes and problems concerning frontiers of States.

Every State likewise has the duty to refrain from the threat or use of force to violate international lines of demarcation, such as armistice lines, established by or pursuant to an international agreement to which it is a party or which it is otherwise bound to respect. Nothing in the foregoing shall be construed as prejudicing the positions of the parties concerned with regard to the status and effects of such lines under their special regimes or as affecting their temporary character.

States have a duty to refrain from acts of reprisal involving the use of force.

Every State has the duty to refrain from any forcible action which deprives peoples referred to in the elaboration of the principle of equal rights and self-determination of their right to self-determination and freedom and independence.

Every State has the duty to refrain from organizing or encouraging the organization of irregular forces or armed bands, including mercenaries, for incursion into the territory of another state.

Every State has the duty to refrain from organizing, instigating, assisting or participating in acts of civil strife or terrorist acts in another State or acquiescing in organized activities within its territory directed towards the commission of such acts, when the acts referred to in the present paragraph involve a threat or use of force.

The territory of a State shall not be the object of military occupation resulting from the use of force in contravention of the provisions of the Charter. The territory of a State shall not be the object of acquisition by another State resulting from the threat or use of force. No territorial acquisition resulting from the threat or use of force shall be recognized as legal. Nothing in the foregoing shall be construed as affecting:

(*a*) Provisions of the Charter or any international agreement prior to the Charter regime and valid under international law; or

(*b*) The powers of the Security Council under the Charter.

All States shall pursue in good faith negotiations for the early conclusion of a universal treaty on general and complete disarmament under effective international control and strive to adopt appropriate measures to reduce international tensions and strengthen confidence among States.

All States shall comply in good faith with their obligations under the generally recognized principles and rules of international law with respect to the maintenance of international peace and security, and shall endeavour to make the United Nations security system based upon the Charter more effective.

Nothing in the foregoing paragraphs shall be construed as enlarging or diminishing in any way the scope of the provisions of the Charter concerning cases in which the use of force is lawful.

The principle that States shall settle their international disputes by peaceful means in such a manner that international peace and security and justice are not endangered

Every State shall settle its international disputes with other States by peaceful means, in such a manner that international peace and security, and justice, are not endangered.

States shall accordingly seek early and just settlement of their international disputes by negotiation, inquiry, mediation, conciliation, arbitration, judicial settlement, resort to regional agencies or arrangements or other peaceful means of their choice. In seeking such a settlement, the parties shall agree upon such peaceful means as may be appropriate to the circumstances and nature of the dispute.

The parties to a dispute have the duty, in the event of failure to reach a solution by any one of the above peaceful means, to continue to seek a settlement of the dispute by other peaceful means agreed upon by them.

States parties to an international dispute, as well as other States, shall refrain from any action which may aggravate the situation so as to endanger the maintenance of international peace and security, and shall act in accordance with the purposes and principles of the United Nations.

International disputes shall be settled on the basis of the sovereign equality of States and in accordance with the principle of free choice of means. Recourse to, or acceptance of, a settlement procedure freely agreed to by States with regard to existing or future disputes to which they are parties shall not be regarded as incompatible with sovereign equality.

Nothing in the foregoing paragraphs prejudices or derogates from the applicable provisions of the Charter, in particular those relating to the pacific settlement of international disputes.

The principle concerning the duty not to intervene in matters within the domestic jurisdiction of any State, in accordance with the Charter

No State or group of States has the right to intervene, directly or indirectly, for any reason whatever, in the internal or external affairs of any other State. Consequently, armed intervention and all other forms of interference or attempted threats against the personality of the State or against its political, economic and cultural elements, are in violation of international law.

No State may use or encourage the use of economic, political or any other type of measures to coerce another State in order to obtain from it the subordination of the exercise of its sovereign rights and to secure from it advantages of any kind. Also, no State shall organize, assist, foment, finance, incite or tolerate subversive, terrorist or armed activities directed towards the violent overthrow of the regime of another State, or interfere in civil strife in another State.

The use of force to deprive peoples of their national identity constitutes a violation of their inalienable rights and of the principle of non-intervention.

Every State has an inalienable right to choose its political, economic, social and cultural systems, without interference in any form by another State.

Nothing in the foregoing paragraphs shall be construed as affecting the relevant provisions of the Charter relating to the maintenance of international peace and security.

The duty of States to co-operate with one another in accordance with the Charter

States have the duty to co-operate with one another, irrespective of the differences in their political, economic and social systems, in the various spheres of international relations, in order to maintain international peace and security and to promote international economic stability and progress, the general welfare of nations and international co-operation free from discrimination based on such differences.

To this end:

(a) States shall co-operate with other States in the maintenance of international peace and security;

(b) States shall co-operate in the promotion of universal respect for and observance of human rights and financial freedoms for all, and in the elimination of all forms of racial discrimination and all forms of religious intolerance;

(c) States shall conduct their international relations in the economic, social, cultural, technical and trade fields in accordance with the principles of sovereign equality and non-intervention;

(d) States Members of the United Nations have the duty to take joint and separate action in co-operation with the United Nations in accordance with the relevant provisions of the Charter.

States should co-operate in the economic, social and cultural fields as well as in the field of science and technology and for the promotion of international cultural and educational progress. States should co-operate in the promotion of economic growth throughout the world, especially that of the developing countries.

The principle of equal rights and self-determination of peoples

By virtue of the principle of equal rights and self-determination of peoples enshrined in the Charter, all peoples have the right freely to determine, without external interference, their political status and to pursue their economic, social and cultural development, and every State has the duty to respect this right in accordance with the provisions of the Charter.

Every State has the duty to promote, through joint and separate action, the realization of the principle of equal rights and self-determination of peoples, in accordance with the provisions of the Charter, and to render assistance to the United Nations in carrying out the responsibilities entrusted to it by the Charter regarding the implementation of the principle in order:

(*a*) To promote friendly relations and co-operation among States; and

(*b*) To bring a speedy end to colonialism, having due regard to the freely expressed will of the peoples concerned;

and bearing in mind that subjection of peoples to alien subjugation, domination and exploitation constitutes a violation of the principle, as well as a denial of fundamental human rights, and is contrary to the Charter of the United Nations.

Every State has the duty to promote through joint and separate action universal respect for and observance of human rights and fundamental freedoms in accordance with the Charter.

The establishment of a sovereign and independent State, the free association or integration with an independent State or the emergence into any other political status freely determined by a people constitute modes of implementing the right of self-determination by that peoples.

Every State has the duty to refrain from any forcible action which deprives peoples referred to above in the elaboration of the present principle of their right to self-determination and freedom and independence. In their actions against and resistance to such forcible action in pursuit of the exercise of their right to self-determination such peoples are entitled to seek and to receive support in accordance with the purposes and principles of the Charter of the United Nations.

The territory of a colony or other non-self-governing territory has, under the Charter of the United Nations, a status separate and distinct from the territory of the State administering it; and status separate and distinct from the territory of the State administering it; and such separate and distinct status under the Charter shall exist until the people of the colony or non-self-governing territory have exercised their right of self-determination in accordance with the Charter, and particularly its purposes and principles.

Nothing in the foregoing paragraphs shall be construed as authorizing or encouraging any action which would dismember or impair, totally or in part, the territorial integrity or political unity of sovereign and independent States conducting themselves in compliance with the principle of equal rights and self-determination of peoples as described above and thus possessed of a government representing the whole people belonging to the territory without distinction as to race, creed or colour.

Every State shall refrain from any action aimed at the partial or total disruption of the national unity and territorial integrity of any State or country.

The principle of sovereign equality of States

All States enjoy sovereign equality. They have equal right and duties and are equal members of the international community, notwithstanding differences of an economic, social, political or other nature.

In particular, sovereign equality includes the following elements:

(*a*) States are juridically equal;

(*b*) Each State enjoys the rights inherent in full sovereignty;

(*c*) Each State has the duty to respect the personality of other States;

(*d*) The territorial integrity and political independence of the State are inviolable;

(*e*) Each State has the right freely to choose and develop its political, social, economic and cultural systems;

(*f*) Each State has the duty to comply fully and in good faith with its international obligations and to live in peace with other States.

The principle that States shall fulfil in good faith the obligations assumed by them in accordance with the Charter

Every State has the duty to fulfil in good faith the obligations assumed by it in accordance with the Charter of the United Nations.

Every State has the duty to fulfil in good faith its obligations under the generally recognized principles and rules of international law.

Every State has the duty to fulfil in good faith its obligations under international agreements valid under the generally recognized principles and rules of international law.

Where obligations arising under international agreements are in conflict with the obligations of Members of the United Nations under the Charter of the United Nations, the obligations under the Charter shall prevail.

General part

2. *Declares* that:

In their interpretation and application the above principles are interrelated and each principle should be construed in the context of the other principles,

Nothing in this Declaration shall be construed as prejudicing in any manner the provisions of the Charter or the rights and duties of Member States under the Charter or the rights of peoples under the Charter taking into account the elaboration of these rights in this Declaration,

3. *Declares further* that:

The principles of the Charter which are embodied in this Declaration constitute basic principles of international law, and consequently appeals to all States to be guided by these principles in their international conduct and to develop their mutual relations on the basis of their strict observance.

1.9 International Law Commission Draft Articles on International Liability for Injurious Consequences Arising Out of Acts Not Prohibited by International Law. Adopted by the International Law Commission, 30 May 1989. Report of the International Law Commission on the Work of Its Forty-First Session. U.N. GAOR, 44th Sess., Supp. No. 10, at 222, U.N. Doc. A/44/10 (1989); *reprinted in* 1 Weston I.G.2

"CHAPTER I

GENERAL PROVISIONS

"Article 1

Scope of the present Articles

The present Articles shall apply with respect to activities carried out in the territory of a State or in other places under its jurisdiction as recognized by international law or, in the absence of such jurisdiction, under its control, when the physical consequences of such activities cause, or create an appreciable risk of causing, transboundary harm throughout the process.

"Article 2

Use of terms

For the purposes of the present Articles:

(a) 'Risk' means the risk occasioned by the use of things whose physical properties, considered either intrinsically or in relation to the place, environment or way in which they are used, make them likely to cause transboundary harm throughout the process, notwithstanding any precautions which might be taken in their regard.

'Appreciable risk' means the risk which may be identified through a simple examination of the activity and the substances involved, in relation to the place, environment or way in which they are used, and includes both the low probability of very considerable (disastrous) transboundary harm and the high probability of minor appreciable harm.

(b) 'Activities involving risk' means the activities referred to in the preceding paragraph, in which harm is contingent, and 'activities with harmful effects' means those causing appreciable transboundary harm throughout the process.

(c) 'Transboundary harm' means the effect which arises as a physical consequence of the activities referred to in Article 1 and which, in the territory or in places under the jurisdiction or control of another State, is appreciably detrimental to persons or objects, to the use or enjoyment of areas or to the environment, whether or not the States concerned have a common border. Under the regime of these Articles, 'transboundary harm' always refers to 'appreciable harm'.

(d) 'State of origin' means the State in whose territory or in places under whose jurisdiction or control the activities referred to in Article 1 take place.

(e) 'Affected State' means the State in whose territory or under whose jurisdiction persons or objects, the use or enjoyment of areas, or the environment, are or may be appreciably affected.

"Article 3

Assignment of obligations

The State of origin shall have the obligations established by the present Articles, provided that it knew or had means of knowing that an activity referred to in Article 1 was being, or was about to be, carried out in its territory or in other places under its jurisdiction or control.

Unless there is evidence to the contrary, it shall be presumed that the State of origin has the knowledge or the means of knowing referred to in the preceding paragraph.

"Article 4

Relationship between the present Articles and other international agreements

Where States Parties to the present Articles are also parties to another international agreement concerning activities referred to in Article 1, in relations between such States the present Articles shall apply, subject to that other international agreement.

"Article 5[1]

Absence of effect upon other rules of international law

[The fact that the present Articles do not specify circumstances in which the occurrence of transboundary harm arises from a wrongful act or omission of the State of origin shall be without prejudice to the operation of any other rule of international law.]

[The present Articles are without prejudice to the operation of any other rule of international law establishing liability for transboundary harm resulting from a wrongful act.]

"CHAPTER II

PRINCIPLES

"Article 6

Freedom of action and the limits thereto

The sovereign freedom of States to carry out or permit human activities in their territory or in other places under their jurisdiction or control must be compatible with the protection of the rights emanating from the sovereignty of other States.

"Article 7

Co-operation

States shall co-operate in good faith among themselves, and request the assistance of any international organizations that might be able to help them, in trying to prevent any activities referred to in Article 1 carried out in their territory or in other places under their jurisdiction or control from causing transboundary harm. If such harm occurs, the State of origin shall cooperate with the affected State in minimizing its effects. In the event of harm caused by an accident, the affected State shall, if possible, also cooperate with the State of origin with regard to any harmful effects which may have arisen in the territory of the State of origin or in other places under its jurisdiction or control.

"Article 8

Prevention

States of origin shall take appropriate measures to prevent or, where necessary, minimize the risk of transboundary harm. To that end they shall, in so far as they are

1. The Special Rapporteur proposed two alternatives for Article 5.

able, use the best practicable, available means with regard to activities referred to in Article 1.

"Article 9

Reparation

To the extent compatible with the present Articles, the State of origin shall make reparation for appreciable harm caused by an activity referred to in Article 1. Such reparation shall be decided by negotiation between the State of origin and the affected State or States and shall be guided, in principle, by the criteria set forth in these Articles, bearing in mind in particular that reparation should seek to restore the balance of interests affected by the harm."

"CHAPTER III

NOTIFICATION, INFORMATION AND WARNING BY THE AFFECTED STATE

"Article 10

Assessment, notification and information

If a State has reason to believe that an activity referred to in Article 1 is being, or is about to be, carried out in its territory or in other places under its jurisdiction or control, it shall:

(a) Review that activity to assess its potential transboundary effects and, if it finds that the activity may cause, or create the risk of causing, transboundary harm, determine the nature of the harm or risk to which it gives rise;

(b) Give the affected State or States timely notification of the conclusions of the aforesaid review;

(c) Accompany such notification by available technical data and information in order to enable the notified States to assess the potential effects of the activity in question;

(d) Inform them of the measures which it is attempting to take to comply with Article 8 and, if it deems appropriate, those which might serve as a basis for a legal regime between the parties governing such activity.

"Article 11

Procedure for protecting national security or industrial secrets

If the State of origin invokes reasons of national security or the protection of industrial secrets in order not to reveal some information which it would otherwise have had to transmit to the affected State:

(a) It shall inform the affected State that it is withholding some information and shall indicate which of the two reasons mentioned above it is invoking for that purpose;

(b) If possible, it shall transmit to the affected State any information which does not affect the areas of reservation invoked, especially information on the type of risk or harm it considers foreseeable and the measures it proposes for establishing a regime to govern the activity in question.

"Article 12

Warning by the presumed affected State

If a State has serious reason to believe that it is, or may be, affected by an activity referred to in Article 1 and that activity is being carried out in the territory or in other places under the jurisdiction or control of another State, it may request that State to apply the provisions of Article 10. The request shall be accompanied by a technical, documented explanation setting forth the reasons for such belief.

"Article 13

Period for reply to notification. Obligation of the State of origin

Unless otherwise agreed, the notifying State shall allow the notified State or States a period of six months within which to study and evaluate the potential effects of the activity and to communicate their findings to it. During such period, the notifying State shall co-operate with the notified State or States by providing them, on request, with any additional data and information that is available and necessary for a better evaluation of the effects of the activity.

"Article 14

Reply to notification

The State which has been notified shall communicate its findings to the notifying State as early as possible, informing the notifying State of whether it accepts the measures proposed by that State and transmitting to that State any measures that it might itself propose in order to supplement or replace such proposed measures, together with a documented technical explanation setting forth the reasons for such findings.

"Article 15

Absence of reply to notification

If, within the period referred to in Article 13, the notifying State receives no communication under Article 14, it may consider that the preventive measures and, where appropriate, the legal regime which it proposed at the time of the notification are acceptable for the activity in question.

If it did not propose any measure for the establishment of a legal regime, the regime imposed by the present Articles shall apply.

"Article 16

Obligation to negotiate

[Beginning identical in both formulations]

If the notifying State and the notified State or States disagree on:

(a) The nature of the activity or its effects; or

(b) The legal regime for such activity:

Alternative (A): They shall hold consultations without delay with a view to establishing the facts with certainty in the case of paragraph (a), and with a view to reaching agreement on the matter in question in the case of paragraph (b);

Alternative (B): They shall, unless otherwise agreed, establish fact-finding machinery, in accordance with the provisions laid down in the annex to the present Articles, to determine the likely transboundary effects of the activity.

The report of that fact-finding machinery shall be of an advisory nature and shall not be binding on the States concerned.

Once the report has been completed, the States concerned shall hold consultations with a view to negotiating a suitable legal regime for the activity.

[End identical in both formulations]

Such consultations and negotiations shall be conducted on the basis of the principle of good faith and the principle that each State must show reasonable regard for the rights and legitimate interests of the other State or States.

"Article 17

Absence of reply to the notification under Article 12

If the State notified under the provisions of Article 12 does not give any reply within six months of receiving the warning, the presumed affected State may consider that the activity referred to in the notification has the characteristics attributed to it therein in which case the activity shall be subject to the regime laid down in the present Articles."

1.10 INTERNATIONAL LAW COMMISSION DRAFT ARTICLES ON STATE RESPONSIBILITY. Adopted by the International Law Commission on 12 July 1996. Report of the International Law Commission on the Work of Its Forty-eighth Session. U.N.Doc. A/51/10 and Corr. 1, Pp. 125–151; *reprinted in* 37 I.L.M. 440 (1998)

STATE RESPONSIBILITY

PART ONE

ORIGIN OF INTERNATIONAL RESPONSIBILITY

Chapter I. General Principles

Article 1. Responsibility of a State for its internationally wrongful acts

Every internationally wrongful act of a State entails the international responsibility of that State.

Article 2. Possibility that every State may be held to have committed an internationally wrongful act

Every State is subject to the possibility of being held to have committed an internationally wrongful act entailing its international responsibility.

Article 3. Elements of an internationally wrongful act of a State

There is an internationally wrongful act of a State when:

a) conduct consisting of an action or omission is attributable to the State under international law; and

b) that conduct constitutes a breach of an international obligation of the State.

Article 4. Characterization of an act of a State as internationally wrongful

An act of a State may only be characterized as internationally wrongful by international law. Such characterization cannot be affected by the characterization of the same act as lawful by internal law.

Chapter II. The "Act of the State" Under International Law

Article 5. Attribution to the State of the conduct of its organs

For the purposes of the present Articles, conduct of any State organ having that status under the internal law of that State shall be considered as an act of the State concerned under international law, provided that organ was acting in that capacity in the case in question.

Article 6. Irrelevance of the position of the organ in the organization of the State

The conduct of an organ of the State shall be considered as an act of that State under international law, whether that organ belongs to the constituent, legislative, executive, judicial or other power, whether its functions are of an international or an internal character, and whether it holds a superior or a subordinate position in the organization of the State.

Article 7. Attribution to the State of the conduct of other entities empowered to exercise elements of the government authority

1. The conduct of an organ of a territorial governmental entity within a State shall also be considered as an act of that State under international law, provided that organ was acting in that capacity in the case in question.

2. The conduct of an organ of an entity which is not part of the formal structure of the State or of a territorial governmental entity, but which is empowered by the internal law of that State to exercise elements of the governmental authority, shall also be considered as an act of the State under international law, provided that organ was acting in that capacity in the case in question.

Article 8. Attribution to the State of the conduct of persons acting in fact on behalf of the State

The conduct of a person or group of persons shall also be considered as an act of the State under international law if:

a) it is established that such person or group of persons was in fact acting on behalf of that State; or

b) such person or group of persons was in fact exercising elements of the governmental authority in the absence of the official authorities and in circumstances which justified the exercise of those elements of authority.

Article 9. Attribution to the State of the conduct of organs placed at its disposal by another State or by an international organization

The conduct of an organ which has been placed at the disposal of a State by another State or by an international organization shall be considered as an act of the former State under international law, if that organ was acting in the exercise of elements of the governmental authority of the State at whose disposal it has been placed.

Article 10. Attribution to the State of Conduct of Organs Acting Outside their Competence or Contrary to Instructions Concerning their Activity

The conduct of an organ of a State, of a territorial governmental entity or of an entity empowered to exercise elements of the governmental authority, such organ having acted in that capacity, shall be considered as an act of the State under international law even if, in the particular case, the organ exceeded its competence according to internal law or contravened instructions concerning its activity.

Article 11. Conduct of persons not acting on behalf of the State

1. The conduct of a person or a group of persons not acting on behalf of the State shall not be considered as an act of the State under international law.

2. Paragraph 1 is without prejudice to the attribution to the State of any other conduct which is related to that of the persons or groups of persons referred to in that paragraph and which is to be considered as an act of the State by virtue of Articles 5 to 10.

Article 12. Conduct of organs of another State

1. The conduct of an organ of a State acting in that capacity which takes place in the territory of another State or in any other territory under its jurisdiction shall not be considered as an act of the latter State under international law.

2. Paragraph 1 is without prejudice to the attribution to a State of any other conduct which is related to that referred to in that paragraph and which is to be considered as an act of that State by virtue of Articles 5 to 10.

Article 13. Conduct of organs of an international organization

The conduct of an organ of an international organization acting in that capacity shall not be considered as an act of a State under international law by reason only of the fact that such conduct has taken place in the territory of that State or in any other territory under its jurisdiction.

Article 14. Conduct of organs of an insurrectional movement

1. The conduct of an organ of an insurrectional movement which is established in the territory of a State or in any other territory under its administration shall not be considered as an act of that State under international law.

2. Paragraph 1 is without prejudice to the attribution to a State of any other conduct which is related to that of the organ of the insurrectional movement and which is to be considered as an act of that Sate by virtue of Articles 5 to 10.

3. Similarly, paragraph 1 is without prejudice to the attribution of the conduct of the organ of the insurrectional movement to that movement in any case in which such attribution may be made under international law.

Article 15. Attribution to the State of the act of an insurrectional movement which becomes the new government of a State or which results in the formation of a new State

1. The act of an insurrectional movement which becomes the new government of a State shall be considered as an act of that State. However, such attribution shall be without prejudice to the attribution to that State of conduct which would have been previously considered as an act of the State by virtue of Articles 5 to 10.

2. The act of an insurrectional movement whose action results in the formation of a new State in part of the territory of a pre-existing State or in a territory under its administration shall be considered as an act of the new State.

Chapter III. Breach of an International Obligation

Article 16. Existence of a breach of an international obligation

There is a breach of an international obligation by a State when an act of that State is not in conformity with what is required of it by that obligation.

Article 17. Irrelevance of the origin of the international obligation breached

1. An act of a State which constitutes a breach of an international obligation is an internationally wrongful act regardless of the origin, whether customary, conventional or other, of that obligation.

2. The origin of the international obligation breached by a State does not affect the international responsibility arising from the internationally wrongful act of that State.

Article 18. Requirement that the international obligation be in force for the State

1. An act of the State which is not in conformity with what is required of it by an international obligation constitutes a breach of that obligation only if the act was performed at the time when the obligation was in force for that State.

2. However, an act of the State which, at the time when it was performed, was not in conformity with what was required of it by an international obligation in force for that State, ceases to be considered an internationally wrongful act if, subsequently, such an act has become compulsory by virtue of a peremptory norm of general international law.

3. If an act of the State which is not in conformity with what is required of it by an international obligation has a continuing character, there is a breach of that obligation only in respect of the period during which the act continues while the obligation is in force for that State.

4. If an act of the State which is not in conformity with what is required of it by an international obligation is composed of a series of actions or omissions in respect of separate cases, there is a breach of that obligation if such an act may be considered to be constituted by the actions or omissions occurring within the period during which the obligation is in force for that State.

5. If an act of the State which is not in conformity with what is required of it by an international obligation is a complex act constituted by actions or omissions by the same or different organs of the State in respect of the same case, there is a breach of that obligation if the complex act not in conformity with it begins with an action or omission occurring within the period during which the obligation is in force for that State, even if that act is completed after that period.

Article 19. International crimes and international delicts

1. An act of a State which constitutes a breach of an international obligation is an internationally wrongful act, regardless of the subject-matter of the obligation breached.

2. An internationally wrongful act which results from the breach by a State of an international obligation so essential for the protection of fundamental interests of the international community that its breach is recognized as a crime by that community as a whole constitutes an international crime.

3. Subject to paragraph 2, and on the basis of the rules of international law in force, an international crime may result, inter alia, from:

a) a serious breach of an international obligation of essential importance for the maintenance of international peace and security, such as that prohibiting aggression;

b) a serious breach of an international obligation of essential importance for safeguarding the right of self-determination of peoples, such as that prohibiting the establishment or maintenance by force of colonial domination;

c) a serious breach on a widespread scale of an international obligation of essential importance for safeguarding the human being, such as those prohibiting slavery, genocide and apartheid;

d) a serious breach of an international obligation of essential importance for the safeguarding and preservation of the human environment, such as those prohibiting massive pollution of the atmosphere or of the seas.

4. Any internationally wrongful act which is not an international crime in accordance with paragraph 2 constitutes an international delict.

Article 20. Breach of an international obligation requiring the adoption of a particular course of conduct

There is a breach by a State of an international obligation requiring it to adopt a particular course of conduct when the conduct of that State is not in conformity with that required of it by that obligation.

Article 21. Breach of an international obligation requiring the achievement of a specified result

1. There is a breach by a State of an international obligation requiring it to achieve, by means of its own choice, a specified result if, by the conduct adopted, the State does not achieve the result required of it by that obligation.

2. When the conduct of the State has created a situation not in conformity with the result required of it by an international obligation, but the obligation allows that this or an equivalent result may nevertheless be achieved by subsequent conduct of the State, there is a breach of the obligation only if the State also fails by its subsequent conduct to achieve the result required of it by that obligation.

Article 22. Exhaustion of local remedies

When the conduct of a State has created a situation not in conformity with the result required of it by an international obligation concerning the treatment to be accorded to aliens, whether natural or juridical persons, but the obligation allows that this or an equivalent result may nevertheless be achieved by subsequent conduct of the State, there is a breach of the obligation only if the aliens concerned have exhausted the effective local remedies available to them without obtaining the treatment called for by the obligation or, where that is not possible, an equivalent treatment.

Article 23. Breach of an international obligation to prevent a given event

When the result required of a State by an international obligation is the prevention, by means of its own choice, of the occurrence of a given event, there is a breach of that obligation only if, by the conduct adopted, the State does not achieve that result.

Article 24. Moment and duration of the breach of an international obligation by an act of the State not extending in time

The breach of an international obligation by an act of the State not extending in time occurs at the moment when that act is performed. The time of commission of the breach does not extend beyond that moment, even if the effects of the act of the State continue subsequently.

Article 25. Moment and duration of the breach of an international obligation by an act of the State extending in time

1. The breach of an international obligation by an act of the State having a continuing character occurs at the moment when that act begins. Nevertheless, the time of commission of the breach extends over the entire period during which the act continues and remains not in conformity with the international obligation.

2. The breach of an international obligation by an act of the State, composed of a series of actions or omissions in respect of separate cases, occurs at the moment when that action or omission of the series is accomplished which establishes the existence of the composite act. Nevertheless, the time of commission of the breach extends over the entire period from the first of the actions or omissions constituting the composite act not in conformity with the international obligation and so long as such actions or omissions are repeated.

3. The breach of an international obligation by a complex act of the State, consisting of a succession of actions or omissions by the same or different organs of the State in respect of the same case, occurs at the moment when the last constituent element of that complex act is accomplished. Nevertheless, the time of commission of the breach extends over the entire period between the action or omission which initiated the breach and that which completed it.

Article 26. Moment and duration of the breach of an international obligation to prevent a given event

The breach of an international obligation requiring a State to prevent a given event occurs when the event begins. Nevertheless, the time of commission of the breach extends over the entire period during which the event continues.

Chapter IV. Implication of a State in the Internationally Wrongful Act of Another State

Article 27. Aid or assistance by a State to another State for the commission of an internationally wrongful act

Aid or assistance by a State to another State, if it is established that it is rendered for the commission of an internationally wrongful act carried out by the latter, itself constitutes an internationally wrongful act, even if, taken alone, such aid or assistance would not constitute the breach of an international obligation.

Article 28. Responsibility of a State for an internationally wrongful act of another State

1. An internationally wrongful act committed by a State in a field of activity in which that State is subject to the power of direction or control of another State entails the international responsibility of that other State.

2. An internationally wrongful act committed by a State as the result of coercion exerted by another State to secure the commission of that act entails the international responsibility of that other State.

3. Paragraphs 1 and 2 are without prejudice to the international responsibility, under the other provisions of the present Articles, of the State which has committed the internationally wrongful act.

Chapter V. Circumstances Precluding Wrongfulness

Article 29. Consent

1. The consent validly given by a State to the commission by another State of a specified act not in conformity with an obligation of the latter State towards the former State precludes the wrongfulness of the act in relation to that State to the extent that the act remains within the limits of that consent.

2. Paragraph 1 does not apply if the obligation arises out of a peremptory norm of general international law. For the purposes of the present Articles, a peremptory norm of general international law is a norm accepted and recognized by the international community of States as a whole as a norm from which no derogation is permitted and which can be modified only by a subsequent norm of general international law having the same character.

Article 30. Countermeasures in respect of an internationally wrongful act

The wrongfulness of an act of a State not in conformity with an obligation of that State towards another State is precluded if the act constitutes a measure legitimate under international law against that other State, in consequence of an internationally wrongful act of that other State.

Article 31. Force majeure and fortuitous event

1. The wrongfulness of an act of a State not in conformity with an international obligation of that State is precluded if the act was due to an irresistible force or to an unforeseen external event beyond its control which made it materially impossible for the State to act in conformity with that obligation or to know that its conduct was not in conformity with that obligation.

2. Paragraph 1 shall not apply if the State in question has contributed to the occurrence of the situation of material impossibility.

Article 32. Distress

1. The wrongfulness of an act of a State not in conformity with an international obligation of that State is precluded if the author of the conduct which constitutes the act of that State had no other means, in a situation of extreme distress, of saving his life or that of persons entrusted to his care.

2. Paragraph 1 shall not apply if the State in question has contributed to the occurrence of the situation of extreme distress or if the conduct in question was likely to create a comparable or greater peril.

Article 33. State of necessity

1. A state of necessity may not be invoked by a State as a ground for precluding the wrongfulness of an act of that State not in conformity with an international obligation of the State unless:

a) the act was the only means of safeguarding an essential interest of the State against a grave and imminent peril; and

b) the act did not seriously impair an essential interest of the State towards which the obligation existed.

2. In any case, a state of necessity may not be invoked by a State as a ground for precluding wrongfulness:

a) if the international obligation with which the act of the State is not in conformity arises out of a peremptory norm of general international law; or

b) if the international obligation with which the act of the State is not in conformity is laid down by a treaty which, explicitly or implicitly, excludes the possibility of invoking the state of necessity with respect to that obligation; or

c) if the State in question has contributed to the occurrence of the state of necessity.

Article 34. Self-defence

The wrongfulness of an act of a State not in conformity with an international obligation of that State is precluded if the act constitutes a lawful measure of self-defence taken in conformity with the Charter of the United Nations.

Article 35. Reservation as to compensation for damage

Preclusion of the wrongfulness of an act of a State by virtue of the provisions of Articles 29, 31, 32 or 33 does not prejudge any question that may arise in regard to compensation for damage caused by that act. Part Two—Content, forms and degrees of international responsibility

PART TWO

CONTENT, FORMS AND DEGREES OF INTERNATIONAL RESPONSIBILITY

Chapter I. General Principles

Article 36. Consequences of an internationally wrongful act

1. The international responsibility of a State which, in accordance with the provisions of Part One, arises from an internationally wrongful act committed by that State, entails legal consequences as set out in this Part.

2. The legal consequences referred to in paragraph 1 are without prejudice to the continued duty of the State which has committed the internationally wrongful act to perform the obligation it has breached.

Article 37. Lex specialis

The provisions of this Part do not apply where and to the extent that the legal consequences of an internationally wrongful act of a State have been determined by other rules of international law relating specifically to that act.

Article 38. Customary international law

The rules of customary international law shall continue to govern the legal consequences of an internationally wrongful act of a State not set out in the provisions of this Part.

Article 39. Relationship to the Charter of the United Nations

The legal consequences of an internationally wrongful act of a State set out in the provisions of this Part are subject, as appropriate, to the provisions and procedure of the Charter of the United Nations relating to the maintenance of international peace and security.

Article 40. Meaning of injured State

1. For the purposes of the present Articles, "injured State" means any State a right of which is infringed by the act of another State, if that act constitutes, in accordance with Part One, an internationally wrongful act of that State.

2. In particular, "injured State" means:

a) if the right infringed by the act of a State arises from a bilateral treaty, the other State party to the treaty;

b) if the right infringed by the act of a State arises from a judgement or other binding dispute settlement decision of an international court or tribunal, the other State or States parties to the dispute and entitled to the benefit of that right;

c) if the right infringed by the act of a State arises from a binding decision of an international organ other than an international court or tribunal, the State or States which, in accordance with the constituent instrument of the international organization concerned, are entitled to the benefit of that right;

d) if the right infringed by the act of a State arises from a treaty provision for a third State, that third State;

e) if the right infringed by the act of a State arises from a multilateral treaty or from a rule of customary international law, any other State party to the multilateral treaty or bound by the relevant rule of customary international law, if it is established that:

the right has been created or is established in its favour;

the infringement of the right by the act of a State necessarily affects the enjoyment of the rights or the performance of the obligations of the other States parties to the multilateral treaty or bound by the rule of customary international law; or

the right has been created or is established for the protection of human rights and fundamental freedoms;

f) if the right infringed by the act of a State arises from a multilateral treaty, any other State party to the multilateral treaty, if it is established that the right has been expressly stipulated in that treaty for the protection of the collective interests of the States parties thereto.

3. In addition, "injured State" means, if the internationally wrongful act constitutes an international crime, all other States.

Chapter II. Right of the Injured State and Obligations of the State Which Has Committed an Internationally Wrongful Act

Article 41. Cessation of wrongful conduct

A State whose conduct constitutes an internationally wrongful act having a continuing character is under the obligation to cease that conduct, without prejudice to the responsibility it has already incurred.

Article 42. Reparation

1. The injured State is entitled to obtain from the State which has committed an internationally wrongful act full reparation in the form of restitution in kind, compen-

sation, satisfaction and assurances and guarantees of non-repetition, either singly or in combination.

2. In the determination of reparation, account shall be taken of the negligence or the wilful act or omission of:

a) the injured State; or

b) a national of that State on whose behalf the claim is brought;

which contributed to the damage.

3. In no case shall reparation result in depriving the population of a State of its own means of subsistence.

4. The State which has committed the internationally wrongful act may not invoke the provisions of its internal law as justification for the failure to provide full reparation.

Article 43. Restitution in kind

The injured State is entitled to obtain from the State which has committed an internationally wrongful act restitution in kind, that is, the re-establishment of the situation which existed before the wrongful act was committed, provided and to the extent that restitution in kind:

a) is not materially impossible;

b) would not involve a breach of an obligation arising from a peremptory norm of general international law;

c) would not involve a burden out of all proportion to the benefit which the injured State would gain from obtaining restitution in kind instead of compensation; or

d) would not seriously jeopardize the political independence or economic stability of the State which has committed the internationally wrongful act, whereas the injured State would not be similarly affected if it did not obtain restitution in kind.

Article 44. Compensation

1. The injured State is entitled to obtain from the State which has committed an internationally wrongful act compensation for the damage caused by that act, if and to the extent that the damage is not made good by restitution in kind.

2. For the purposes of the present Article, compensation covers any economically assessable damage sustained by the injured State, and may include interest and, where appropriate, loss of profits.

Article 45. Satisfaction

1. The injured State is entitled to obtain from the State which has committed an internationally wrongful act satisfaction for the damage, in particular moral damage, caused by that act, if and to the extent necessary to provide full reparation.

2. Satisfaction may take the form of one or more of the following:

a) an apology;

b) nominal damages;

c) in cases of gross infringement of the rights of the injured State, damages reflecting the gravity of the infringement;

d) in cases where the internationally wrongful act arose from the serious misconduct of officials or from criminal conduct of officials or private parties, disciplinary action against, or punishment of, those responsible.

3. The right of the injured State to obtain satisfaction does not justify demands which would impair the dignity of the State which has committed the internationally wrongful act.

Article 46. Assurances and guarantees of non-repetition

The injured State is entitled, where appropriate, to obtain from the State which has committed an internationally wrongful act assurances or guarantees of non-repetition of the wrongful act.

Chapter III. Countermeasures

Article 47. Countermeasures by an injured State

1. For the purposes of the present Articles, the taking of countermeasures means that an injured State does not comply with one or more of its obligations towards a State which has committed an internationally wrongful act in order to induce it to comply with its obligations under Articles 41 to 46, as long as it has not complied with those obligations and as necessary in the light of its response to the demands of the injured State that it do so.

2. The taking of countermeasures is subject to the conditions and restrictions set out in Articles 48 to 50.

3. Where a countermeasure against a State which has committed an internationally wrongful act involves a breach of an obligation towards a third State, such a breach cannot be justified under this chapter as against the third State.

Article 48. Conditions relating to resort to countermeasures

1. Prior to taking countermeasures, an injured State shall fulfil its obligation to negotiate provided for in Article 54. This obligation is without prejudice to the taking by that State of interim measures of protection which are necessary to preserve its rights and which otherwise comply with the requirements of this Chapter.

2. An injured State taking countermeasures shall fulfil the obligations in relation to dispute settlement arising under Part Three or any other binding dispute settlement procedure in force between the injured State and the State which has committed the internationally wrongful act.

3. Provided that the internationally wrongful act has ceased, the injured State shall suspend countermeasures when and to the extent that the dispute settlement procedure referred to in paragraph 2 is being implemented in good faith by the State which has committed the internationally wrongful act and the dispute is submitted to a tribunal which has the authority to issue orders binding on the parties.

4. The obligation to suspend countermeasures ends in case of failure by the State which has committed the internationally wrongful act to honour a request or order emanating from the dispute settlement procedure.

Article 49. Proportionality

Countermeasures taken by an injured State shall not be out of proportion to the degree of gravity of the internationally wrongful act and the effects thereof on the injured State.

Article 50. Prohibited countermeasures

An injured State shall not resort by way of countermeasures to:

a) the threat or use of force as prohibited by the Charter of the United Nations;

b) extreme economic or political coercion designed to endanger the territorial integrity or political independence of the State which has committed the internationally wrongful act;

c) any conduct which infringes the inviolability of diplomatic or consular agents, premises, archives and documents;

d) any conduct which derogates from basic human rights; or

e) any other conduct in contravention of a peremptory norm of general international law.

Chapter IV. International Crimes

Article 51. Consequences of an international crime

An international crime entails all the legal consequences of any other internationally wrongful act and, in addition, such further consequences as are set out in Articles 52 and 53.

Article 52. Specific consequences

Where an internationally wrongful act of a State is an international crime:

a) an injured State's entitlement to obtain restitution in kind is not subject to the limitations set out in subparagraphs (c) and (d) of Article 43;

b) an injured State's entitlement to obtain satisfaction is not subject to the restriction in paragraph 3 of Article 45.

Article 53. Obligations for all States

An international crime committed by a State entails an obligation for every other State:

a) not to recognize as lawful the situation created by the crime;

b) not to render aid or assistance to the State which has committed the crime in maintaining the situation so created;

c) to cooperate with other States in carrying out the obligations under subparagraphs (a) and (b); and

d) to cooperate with other States in the application of measures designed to eliminate the consequences of the crime.

PART THREE

SETTLEMENT OF DISPUTES

Article 54. Negotiation

If a dispute regarding the interpretation or application of the present Articles arises between two or more States Parties to the present Articles, they shall, upon the request of any of them, seek to settle it amicably by negotiation.

Article 55. Good offices and mediation

Any State Party to the present Articles, not being a party to the dispute may, at the request of any party to the dispute or upon its own initiative, tender its good offices or offer to mediate with a view to facilitating an amicable settlement of the dispute.

Article 56. Conciliation

If, three months after the first request for negotiations, the dispute has not been settled by agreement and no mode of binding third party settlement has been instituted, any party to the dispute may submit it to conciliation in conformity with the procedure set out in annex I to the present Articles.

Article 57. Task of the Conciliation Commission

1. The task of the Conciliation Commission shall be to elucidate the questions in dispute, to collect with that object all necessary information by means of inquiry or otherwise and to endeavour to bring the parties to the dispute to a settlement.

2. To that end, the parties shall provide the Commission with a statement of their position regarding the dispute and of the facts upon which that position is based. In addition, they shall provide the Commission with any further information or evidence as the Commission may request and shall assist the Commission in any independent fact-finding it may wish to undertake, including fact-finding within the territory of any party to the dispute, except where exceptional reasons make this impractical. In that event, that party shall give the Commission an explanation of those exceptional reasons.

3. The Commission may, at its discretion, make preliminary proposals to any or all of the parties, without prejudice to its later recommendations.

4. The recommendations to the parties shall be embodied in a report to be presented not later than three months from the formal constitution of the Commission, and the Commission may specify the period within which the parties are to respond to those recommendations.

5. If the response by the parties to the Commission's recommendations does not lead to the settlement of the dispute, the Commission may submit to them a final report containing its own evaluation of the dispute and its recommendations for settlement.

Article 58. Arbitration

1. Failing a reference of the dispute to the Conciliation Commission provided for in Article 56 or failing an agreed settlement within six months following the report of the Commission, the parties to the dispute may, by agreement, submit the dispute to an arbitral tribunal to be constituted in conformity with annex II to the present Articles.

2. In cases, however, where the dispute arises between States Parties to the present Articles, one of which has taken countermeasures against the other, the State against which they are taken is entitled at any time unilaterally to submit the dispute to an arbitral tribunal to be constituted in conformity with annex II to the present Articles.

Article 59. Terms of reference of the Arbitral Tribunal

1. The Arbitral Tribunal, which shall decide with binding effect any issues of fact or law which may be in dispute between the parties and are relevant under any of the provisions of the present Articles, shall operate under the rules laid down or referred to in annex II to the present Articles and shall submit its decision to the parties within six months from the date of completion of the parties' written and oral pleadings and submissions.

2. The Tribunal shall be entitled to resort to any fact-finding it deems necessary for the determination of the facts of the case.

Article 60. Validity of an arbitral award

1. If the validity of an arbitral award is challenged by either party to the dispute, and if within three months of the date of the challenge the parties have not agreed on another tribunal, the International Court of Justice shall be competent, upon the

timely request of any party, to confirm the validity of the award or declare its total or partial nullity.

2. Any issue in dispute left unresolved by the nullification of the award may, at the request of any party, be submitted to a new arbitration before an arbitral tribunal to be constituted in conformity with annex II to the present Articles.

ANNEX I

THE CONCILIATION COMMISSION

1. A list of conciliators consisting of qualified jurists shall be drawn up and maintained by the Secretary–General of the United Nations. To this end, every State which is a Member of the United Nations or a Party to the present Articles shall be invited to nominate two conciliators, and the names of the persons so nominated shall constitute the list. The term of a conciliator, including that of any conciliator nominated to fill a casual vacancy, shall be five years and may be renewed. A conciliator whose term expires shall continue to fulfil any function for which he shall have been chosen under paragraph 2.

2. A party may submit a dispute to conciliation under Article 56 by a request to the Secretary–General who shall establish a Conciliation Commission to be constituted as follows:

a) The State or States constituting one of the parties to the dispute shall appoint:

one conciliator of the nationality of that State or of one of those States, who may or may not be chosen from the list referred to in paragraph 1; and

one conciliator not of the nationality of that State or of any of those States, who shall be chosen from the list.

b) The State or States constituting the other party to the dispute shall appoint two conciliators in the same way.

c) The four conciliators appointed by the parties shall be appointed within 60 days following the date on which the Secretary–General receives the request.

d) The four conciliators shall, within 60 days following the date of the last of their own appointments, appoint a fifth conciliator chosen from the list, who shall be chairman.

e) If the appointment of the chairman or of any of the other conciliators has not been made within the period prescribed above for such appointment, it shall be made from the list by the Secretary–General within 60 days following the expiry of that period. Any of the periods within which appointments must be made may be extended by agreement between the parties.

f) Any vacancy shall be filled in the manner prescribed for the initial appointment.

3. The failure of a party or parties to participate in the conciliation procedure shall not constitute a bar to the proceedings.

4. A disagreement as to whether a Commission acting under this Annex has competence shall be decided by the Commission.

5. The Commission shall determine its own procedure. Decisions of the Commission shall be made by a majority vote of the five members.

6. In disputes involving more than two parties having separate interests, or where there is disagreement as to whether they are of the same interest, the parties shall apply paragraph 2 in so far as possible.

ANNEX II

THE ARBITRAL TRIBUNAL

1. The Arbitral Tribunal referred to in Articles 58 and 60, paragraph 2 shall consist of five members. The parties to the dispute shall each appoint one member, who may be chosen from among their respective nationals. The three other arbitrators including the Chairman shall be chosen by common agreement from among the nationals of third States.

2. If the appointment of the members of the Tribunal is not made within a period of three months from the date on which one of the parties requested the other party to constitute an arbitral tribunal, the necessary appointments shall be made by the President of the International Court of Justice. If the President is prevented from acting or is a national of one of the parties, the appointments shall be made by the Vice–President. If the Vice–President is prevented from acting or is a national of one of the parties, the appointments shall be made by the most senior member of the Court who is not a national of either party. The members so appointed shall be of different nationalities and, except in the case of appointments made because of failure by either party to appoint a member, may not be nationals of, in the service of or ordinarily resident in the territory of a party.

3. Any vacancy which may occur as a result of death, resignation or any other cause shall be filled within the shortest possible time in the manner prescribed for the initial appointment.

4. Following the establishment of the Tribunal, the parties shall draw up an agreement specifying the subject-matter of the dispute, unless they have done so before.

5. Failing the conclusion of an agreement within a period of three months from the date on which the Tribunal was constituted, the subject-matter of the dispute shall be determined by the Tribunal on the basis of the application submitted to it.

6. The failure of a party or parties to participate in the arbitration procedure shall not constitute a bar to the proceedings.

7. Unless the parties otherwise agree, the Tribunal shall determine its own procedure. Decisions of the Tribunal shall be made by a majority vote of the five members.

B. Environmental

1.11 Resolution on Permanent Sovereignty Over Natural Resources. Adopted by the U.N. General Assembly, 14 December 1962. G.A.Res. 1803, U.N.GAOR, 17th Sess., Supp. No. 17, at 15, U.N.Doc. A/5217 (1963), 16 U.N.Y.B. 503; *reprinted in* 2 I.L.M. 223 (1963) & 5 Weston V.B.1

The General Assembly,

Recalling its resolutions 523(VI) of 12 January 1952 and 626(VII) of 21 December 1952,

Bearing in mind its resolution 1314(XIII) of 12 December 1958, by which it established the Commission on Permanent Sovereignty over Natural Resources and instructed it to conduct a full survey of the status of permanent sovereignty over natural wealth and resources as a basic constituent of the right to self-determination, with recommendations, where necessary, for its strengthening, and decided further that, in the conduct of the full survey of the status of the permanent sovereignty of peoples and nations over their natural wealth and resources, due regard should be paid to the rights and duties of States under international law and to the importance of encouraging international co-operation in the economic development of developing countries,

Bearing in mind its resolution 1515(XV) of 15 December 1960, in which it recommended that the sovereign right of every State to dispose of its wealth and its natural resources should be respected,

Considering that any measure in this respect must be based on the recognition of the inalienable right of all States freely to dispose of their natural wealth and resources in accordance with their national interests, and on respect for the economic independence of States,

Considering that nothing in paragraph 4 below in any way prejudices the position of any Member State on any aspect of the question of the rights and obligations of successor States and Governments in respect of property acquired before the accession to complete sovereignty of countries formerly under colonial rule,

Noting that the subject of succession of States and Governments is being examined as a matter of priority by the International Law Commission,

Considering that it is desirable to promote international co-operation for the economic development of developing countries, and that economic and financial agreements between the developed and the developing countries must be based on the principles of equality and of the right of peoples and nations to self-determination,

Considering that the provision of economic and technical assistance, loans and increased foreign investment must not be subject to conditions which conflict with the interests of the recipient State,

Considering the benefits to be derived from exchanges of technical and scientific information likely to promote the development and use of such resources and wealth, and the important part which the United Nations and other international organizations are called upon to play in that connexion,

Attaching particular importance to the question of promoting the economic development of developing countries and securing their economic independence,

Noting that the creation and strengthening of the inalienable sovereignty of States over their natural wealth and resources reinforces their economic independence,

Desiring that there should be further consideration by the United Nations of the subject of permanent sovereignty over natural resources in the spirit of international co-operation in the field of economic development, particularly that of the developing countries,

I

Declares that:

1. The right of peoples and nations to permanent sovereignty over their natural wealth and resources must be exercised in the interest of their national development and of the well-being of the people of the State concerned.

2. The exploration, development and disposition of such resources, as well as the import of the foreign capital required for these purposes, should be in conformity with the rules and conditions which the peoples and nations freely consider to be necessary or desirable with regard to the authorization, restriction or prohibition of such activities.

3. In cases where authorization is granted, the capital imported and the earnings on that capital shall be governed by the terms thereof, by the national legislation in force, and by international law. The profits derived must be shared in the proportions freely agreed upon, in each case, between the investors and the recipient State, due care being taken to ensure that there is no impairment, for any reason, of that State's sovereignty over its natural wealth and resources.

4. Nationalization, expropriation or requisitioning shall be based on grounds or reasons of public utility, security or the national interest which are recognized as overriding purely individual or private interests, both domestic and foreign. In such cases the owner shall be paid appropriate compensation, in accordance with the rules in force in the State taking such measures in the exercise of its sovereignty and in accordance with international law. In any case where the question of compensation gives rise to a controversy, the national jurisdiction of the State taking such measures shall be exhausted. However, upon agreement by sovereign States and other parties concerned, settlement of the dispute should be made through arbitration or international adjudication.

5. The free and beneficial exercise of the sovereignty of peoples and nations over their natural resources must be furthered by the mutual respect of States based on their sovereign equality.

6. International co-operation for the economic development of developing countries, whether in the form of public or private capital investments, exchange of goods and services, technical assistance, or exchange of scientific information, shall be such as to further their independent national development and shall be based upon respect for their sovereignty over their natural wealth and resources.

7. Violation of the rights of peoples and nations to sovereignty over their natural wealth and resources is contrary to the spirit and principles of the Charter of the United Nations and hinders the development of international co-operation and the maintenance of peace.

8. Foreign investment agreements freely entered into by or between sovereign States shall be observed in good faith: States and international organizations shall strictly and conscientiously respect the sovereignty of peoples and nations over their natural wealth and resources in accordance with the Charter and the principles set forth in the present resolution.

II

Welcomes the decision of the International Law Commission to speed up its work on the codification of the topic of responsibility of States for the consideration of the General Assembly;

III

Requests the Secretary–General to continue the study of the various aspects of permanent sovereignty over natural resources, taking into account the desire of Member States to ensure the protection of their sovereign rights while encouraging international co-operation in the field of economic development, and to report to the Economic and Social Council and to the General Assembly, if possible at its eighteenth session.

1.12 Stockholm Declaration of the United Nations Conference on the Human Environment. Adopted by the U.N. Conference on the Human Environment at Stockholm, 16 June 1972. ***Report of the Un Conference on the Human Environment, Stockholm, 5–16 June 1972,*** **U.N.Doc. A/CONF.48/14/Rev. 1 at 3 (1973), U.N.Doc. A/CONF.48/14 at 2–65, and Corr. 1 (1972);** ***reprinted in*** **11 I.L.M. 1416 (1972) & 5 Weston V.B.3**

The United Nations Conference on the Human Environment.

Having Met at Stockholm from 5 to 16 June 1972.

Having Considered the need for a common outlook and for common principles to inspire and guide the peoples of the world in the preservation and enhancement of the human environment.

I

Proclaims That:

1. Man is both creature and moulder of his environment, which gives him physical sustenance and affords him the opportunity for intellectual, moral, social and spiritual growth. In the long and tortuous evolution of the human race on this planet a stage has been reached when, through the rapid acceleration of science and technology, man has acquired the power to transform his environment in countless ways and on an unprecedented scale. Both aspects of man's environment, the natural and the man-made, are essential to his well-being and to the enjoyment of basic human rights—even the right to life itself.

2. The protection and improvement of the human environment is a major issue which affects the well-being of peoples and economic development throughout the world; it is the urgent desire of the peoples of the whole world and the duty of all Governments.

3. Man has constantly to sum up experience and go on discovering, inventing, creating and advancing. In our time, man's capability to transform his surroundings, if used wisely, can bring to all peoples the benefits of development and the opportunity to enhance the quality of life. Wrongly or heedlessly applied, the same power can do incalculable harm to human beings and the human environment. We see around us growing evidence of man-made harm in many regions of the earth: dangerous levels of pollution in water, air, earth and living beings; major and undesirable disturbances to the ecological balance of the biosphere; destruction and depletion of irreplaceable resources; and gross deficiencies harmful to the physical, mental and social health of man, in the man-made environment, particularly in the living and working environment.

4. In the developing countries most of the environmental problems are caused by under-development. Millions continue to live far below the minimum levels required for a decent human existence, deprived of adequate food and clothing, shelter and education, health and sanitation. Therefore, the developing countries must direct their efforts to development, bearing in mind their priorities and the need to safeguard and improve the environment. For the same purpose, the industrialized countries should make efforts to reduce the gap between themselves and the developing countries. In the industrialized countries, environmental problems are generally related to industrialization and technological development.

5. The natural growth of population continuously presents problems on the preservation of the environment, and adequate policies and measures should be adopted, as appropriate, to face these problems. Of all things in the world, people are the most precious. It is the people that propel social progress, create social wealth, develop science and technology and, through their hard work, continuously transform

the human environment. Along with social progress and the advance of production, science and technology, the capability of man to improve the environment increases with each passing day.

6. A point has been reached in history when we must shape our actions throughout the world with a more prudent care for their environmental consequences. Through ignorance or indifference we can do massive and irreversible harm to the earthly environment on which our life and well-being depend. Conversely, through fuller knowledge and wiser action, we can achieve for ourselves and our posterity a better life in an environment more in keeping with human needs and hopes. There are broad vistas for the enhancement of environmental quality and the creation of a good life. What is needed is an enthusiastic but calm state of mind and intense but orderly work. For the purpose of attaining freedom in the world of nature, man must use knowledge to build, in collaboration with nature, a better environment. To defend and improve the human environment for present and future generations has become an imperative goal for mankind—a goal to be pursued together with, and in harmony with, the established and fundamental goals of peace and of world-wide economic and social development.

7. To achieve this environmental goal will demand the acceptance of responsibility by citizens and communities and by enterprises and institutions at every level, all sharing equitably in common efforts. Individuals in all walks of life as well as organizations in many fields, by their values and the sum of their actions, will shape the world environment of the future. Local and national governments will bear the greatest burden for large-scale environmental policy and action within their jurisdictions. International co-operation is also needed in order to raise resources to support the developing countries in carrying out their responsibilities in this field. A growing class of environmental problems, because they are regional or global in extent or because they affect the common international realm, will require extensive co-operation among nations and action by international organizations in the common interest. The Conference calls upon Governments and peoples to exert common efforts for the preservation and improvement of the human environment, for the benefit of all the people and for their posterity.

II

Principles

STATES THE COMMON CONVICTION THAT:

Principle 1

Man has the fundamental right to freedom, equality and adequate conditions of life, in an environment of a quality that permits a life of dignity and well-being, and he bears a solemn responsibility to protect and improve the environment for present and future generations. In this respect, policies promoting or perpetuating apartheid, racial segregation, discrimination, colonial and other forms of oppression and foreign domination stand condemned and must be eliminated.

Principle 2

The natural resources of the earth including the air, water, land, flora and fauna and especially representative samples of natural ecosystems must be safeguarded for the benefit of present and future generations through careful planning or management, as appropriate.

Principle 3

The capacity of the earth to produce vital renewable resources must be maintained and, wherever practicable, restored or improved.

Principle 4

Man has a special responsibility to safeguard and wisely manage the heritage of wildlife and its habitat which are now gravely imperilled by a combination of adverse factors. Nature conservation including wildlife must therefore receive importance in planning for economic development.

Principle 5

The non-renewable resources of the earth must be employed in such a way as to guard against the danger of their future exhaustion and to ensure that benefits from such employment are shared by all mankind.

Principle 6

The discharge of toxic substances or of other substances and the release of heat, in such quantities or concentrations as to exceed the capacity of the environment to render them harmless, must be halted in order to ensure that serious or irreversible damage is not inflicted upon ecosystems. The just struggle of the peoples of all countries against pollution should be supported.

Principle 7

States shall take all possible steps to prevent pollution of the seas by substances that are liable to create hazards to human health, to harm living resources and marine life, to damage amenities or to interfere with other legitimate uses of the sea.

Principle 8

Economic and social development is essential for ensuring a favourable living and working environment for man and for creating conditions on earth that are necessary for the improvement of the quality of life.

Principle 9

Environmental deficiencies generated by the conditions of underdevelopment and natural disasters pose grave problems and can best be remedied by accelerated development through the transfer of substantial quantities of financial and technological assistance as a supplement to the domestic effort of the developing countries and such timely assistance as may be required.

Principle 10

For the developing countries, stability of prices and adequate earnings for primary commodities and raw material are essential to environmental management since economic factors as well as ecological processes must be taken into account.

Principle 11

The environmental policies of all States should enhance and not adversely affect the present or future development potential of developing countries, nor should they hamper the attainment of better living conditions for all, and appropriate steps should be taken by States and international organizations with a view to reaching agreement on meeting the possible national and international economic consequences resulting from the application of environmental measures.

Principle 12

Resources should be made available to preserve and improve the environment, taking into account the circumstances and particular requirements of developing countries and any costs which may emanate from their incorporating environmental safeguards into their development planning and the need for making available to them, upon their request, additional international technical and financial assistance for this purpose.

Principle 13

In order to achieve a more rational management of resources and thus to improve the environment, State should adopt an integrated and co-ordinated approach to their development planning so as to ensure that development is compatible with the need to protect and improve the human environment for the benefit for their population.

Principle 14

Rational planning constitutes an essential tool for reconciling any conflict between the needs of development and the need to protect and improve the environment.

Principle 15

Planning must be applied to human settlements and urbanization with a view to avoiding adverse effects on the environment and obtaining maximum social, economic and environmental benefits for all. In this respect projects which are designed for colonialist and racist domination must be abandoned.

Principle 16

Demographic policies, which are without prejudice to basic human rights and which are deemed appropriate by Governments concerned, should be applied in those regions where the rate of population growth or excessive population concentrations are likely to have adverse effects on the environment or development, or where low population density may prevent improvement of the human environment and impede development.

Principle 17

Appropriate national institutions must be entrusted with the task of planning, managing or controlling the environmental resources of States with the view to enhancing environmental quality.

Principle 18

Science and technology, as part of their contribution to economic and social development, must be applied to the identification, avoidance and control of environmental risks and the solution of environmental problems and for the common good of mankind.

Principle 19

Education in environmental matters, for the younger generation as well as adults, giving due consideration to the underprivileged, is essential in order to broaden the basis for an enlightened opinion and responsible conduct by individuals, enterprises and communities in protecting and improving the environment in its full human dimension. It is also essential that mass media of communications avoid contributing to the deterioration of the environment, but, on the contrary, disseminate information of an educational nature, on the need to protect and improve the environment in order to enable man to develop in every respect.

Principle 20

Scientific research and development in the context of environmental problems, both national and multinational, must be promoted in all countries, especially the developing countries. In this connection, the free flow of up-to-date scientific information and transfer of experience must be supported and assisted, to facilitate the solution of environmental problems; environmental technologies should be made available to developing countries on terms which would encourage their wide dissemination without constituting an economic burden on the developing countries.

Principle 21

States have, in accordance with the Charter of the United Nations and the principles of international law, the sovereign right to exploit their own resources pursuant to their own environmental policies, and the responsibility to ensure that activities within their jurisdiction or control do not cause damage to the environment of other States or of areas beyond the limits of national jurisdiction.

Principle 22

States shall co-operate to develop further the international law regarding liability and compensation for the victims of pollution and other environmental damage caused by activities within the jurisdiction or control of such States to areas beyond their jurisdiction.

Principle 23

Without prejudice to such criteria as may be agreed upon by the international community, or to standards which will have to be determined nationally, it will be essential in all cases to consider the systems of values prevailing in each country, and the extent of the applicability of standards which are valid for the most advanced countries but which may be inappropriate and of unwarranted social cost for the developing countries.

Principle 24

International matters concerning the protection and improvement of the environment should be handled in a co-operative spirit by all countries, big or small, on an equal footing. Co-operation through multilateral or bilateral arrangements or other appropriate means is essential to effectively control, prevent, reduce and eliminate adverse environmental effects resulting from activities conducted in all spheres, in such a way that due account is taken of the sovereignty and interests of all States.

Principle 25

States shall ensure that international organizations play a co-ordinated, efficient and dynamic role for the protection and improvement of the environment.

Principle 26

Man and his environment must be spared the effects of nuclear weapons and all other means of mass destruction. States must strive to reach prompt agreement, in the relevant international organs, on the elimination and complete destruction of such weapons.

1.13 RESOLUTION ON THE INSTITUTIONAL AND FINANCIAL ARRANGEMENT FOR INTERNATIONAL ENVIRONMENT COOPERATION (ESTABLISHING THE UNITED NATIONS ENVIRONMENT PROGRAM, UNEP). Adopted by the U.N. General Assembly, 15 December 1972. G.A.Res. 2997, U.N. GAOR, 27th Sess., Supp. 30, at 42, U.N.Doc. A/8370 (1973); *reprinted in* 13 I.L.M. 234 (1974) & 5 Weston V.A.4

I

Governing Council of the United Nations Environment Programme

1. *Decides* to establish a Governing–Council of the United Nations Environment Programme, composed of fifty-eight members elected by the General Assembly for three-year terms on the following basis:

(*a*) Sixteen seats for African States;

(*b*) Thirteen seats for Asian States;

(*c*) Six seats for Eastern European States;

(*d*) Ten seats for Latin American States;

(*e*) Thirteen seats for Western European and other States;

2. *Decides* that the Governing Council shall have the following main functions and responsibilities:

(*a*) To promote international co-operation in the field of the environment and to recommend, as appropriate, policies to this end;

(*b*) To provide general policy guidance for the direction and co-ordination of environmental programmes within the United Nations system;

(*c*) To receive and review the periodic reports of the Executive Director, referred to in section II, paragraph 2, below, on the implementation of environmental programmes within the United Nations system;

(*d*) To keep under review the world environmental situation in order to ensure that emerging environmental problems of wide international significance receive appropriate and adequate consideration by Governments;

(*e*) To promote the contribution of the relevant international scientific and other professional communities to the acquisition, assessment and exchange of environmental knowledge and information and, as appropriate, to the technical aspects of the formulation and implementation of environmental programmes within the United Nations system;

(*f*) To maintain under continuing review the impact of national and international environmental policies and measures on developing countries, as well as the problem of additional costs that may be incurred by developing countries in the implementation of environmental programmes and projects, and to ensure that such programmes and projects shall be compatible with the development plans and priorities of those countries;

(*g*) To review and approve annually the programme of utilization of resources of the Environment Fund referred to in section III below;

3. *Decides* that the Governing Council shall report annually to the General Assembly through the Economic and Social Council, which will transmit to the Assembly such comments on the report as it may deem necessary, particularly with regard to questions of co-ordination and to the relationship of environmental policies and programmes within the United Nations system to over-all economic and social policies and priorities;

II

Environment secretariat

1. *Decides* that a small secretariat shall be established in the United Nations to serve as a focal point for environmental action and co-ordination within the United Nations system in such a way as to ensure a high degree of effective management;

2. *Decides* that the environment secretariat shall be headed by the Executive Director of the United Nations Environment Programme, who shall be elected by the General Assembly on the nomination of the Secretary–General for a term of four years and who shall be entrusted, *inter alia,* with the following responsibilities:

(*a*) To provide substantive support to the Governing Council of the United Nations Environment Programme;

(*b*) To co-ordinate, under the guidance of the Governing Council, environmental programmes within the United Nations system to keep their implementation under review and to assess their effectiveness;

(*c*) To advise, as appropriate and under the guidance of the Governing Council, intergovernmental bodies of the United Nations system on the formulation and implementation of environmental programmes;

(*d*) To secure the effective co-operation of, and contribution from, the relevant scientific and other professional communities in all parts of the world;

(*e*) To provide, at the request of all parties concerned, advisory services for the promotion of international co-operation in the field of the environment;

(*f*) To submit to the Governing Council, on his own initiative or upon request, proposals embodying medium-range and long-range planning for United Nations programmes in the field of the environment;

(*g*) To bring to the attention of the Governing Council any matter which he deems to require consideration by it;

(*h*) To administer, under the authority and policy guidance of the Governing Council, the Environment Fund referred to in section III below;

(*i*) To report on environmental matters to the Governing Council;

(*j*) To perform such other functions as may be entrusted to him by the Governing Council;

3. *Decides* that the costs of servicing the Governing Council and providing the small secretariat referred to in paragraph 1 above shall be borne by the regular budget of the United Nations and that operational programme costs, programme support and administrative costs of the Environment Fund established under section III below shall be borne by the Fund;

III

Environment Fund

1. *Decides* that, in order to provide for additional financing for environmental programmes, a voluntary fund shall be established, with effect from 1 January 1973, in accordance with existing United Nations financial procedures;

2. *Decides* that, in order to enable the Governing Council of the United Nations Environment Programme to fulfil its policy-guidance role for the direction and co-ordination of environmental activities, the Environment Fund shall finance wholly or partly the costs of the new environmental initiatives undertaken within the United Nations system—which will include the initiatives envisaged in the Action Plan for the Human Environment adopted by the United Nations Conference on the Human Environment, with particular attention to integrated projects, and such other environ-

mental activities as may be decided upon by the Governing Council—and that the Governing Council shall review these initiatives with a view to taking appropriate decisions as to their continued financing;

3. *Decides* that the Environment Fund shall be used for financing such programmes of general interest as regional and global monitoring, assessment and data-collecting systems, including, as appropriate, costs for national counterparts; the improvement of environmental quality management; environmental research; information exchange and dissemination; public education and training; assistance for national, regional and global environmental institutions; the promotion of environmental research and studies for the development of industrial and other technologies best suited to a policy of economic growth compatible with adequate environmental safeguards; and such other programmes as the Governing Council may decide upon, and that in the implementation of such programmes due account should be taken of the special needs of the developing countries;

4. *Decides* that, in order to ensure that the development priorities of developing countries shall not be adversely affected, adequate measures shall be taken to provide additional financial resources on terms compatible with the economic situation of the recipient developing country, and that, to this end, the Executive Director, in co-operation with competent organizations, shall keep this problem under continuing review;

5. *Decides* that the Environment Fund, in pursuance of the objectives stated in paragraphs 2 and 3 above, shall be directed to the need for effective co-ordination in the implementation of international environmental programmes of the organizations in the United Nations system and other international organizations;

6. *Decides* that, in the implementation of programmes to be financed by the Environment Fund, organizations outside the United Nations system, particularly those in the countries and regions concerned, shall also be utilized as appropriate, in accordance with the procedures established by the Governing Council, and that such organizations are invited to support the United Nations environmental programmes by complementary initiatives and contributions;

7. *Decides* that the Governing Council shall formulate such general procedures as are necessary to govern the operations of the Environment Fund.

IV

Environment Co-ordination Board

1. *Decides* that, in order to provide for the most efficient co-ordination of United Nations environmental programmes, an Environment Co-ordination Board, under the chairmanship of the Executive Director, shall be established under the auspices and within the framework of the Administrative Committee on Co-ordination;

2. *Further decides* that the Environment Co-ordination Board shall meet periodically for the purpose of ensuring co-operation and co-ordination among all bodies concerned in the implementation of environmental programmes and that it shall report annually to the Governing Council of the United Nations Environment Programme;

3. *Invites* the organizations of the United Nations system to adopt the measures that may be required to undertake concerted and co-ordinated programmes with regard to international environmental problems, taking into account existing procedures for prior consultation, particularly on programme and budgetary matters;

4. *Invites* the regional economic commissions and the United Nations Economic and Social Office at Beirut, in co-operation where necessary with other appropriate regional bodies, to intensify further their efforts directed towards contributing to the

implementation of environmental programmes in view of the particular need for the rapid development of regional co-operation in this field;

5. *Also invites* other intergovernmental and those non-governmental organizations that have an interest in the field of the environment to lend their full support and collaboration to the United Nations with a view to achieving the largest possible degree of co-operation and co-ordination;

6. *Calls upon* Governments to ensure that appropriate national institutions shall be entrusted with the task of the co-ordination of environmental action, both national and international;

7. *Decides* to review as appropriate, at its thirty-first session, the above institutional arrangements, bearing in mind, *inter alia,* the responsibilities of the Economic and Social Council under the Charter of the United Nations.

1.14 Resolution on Co-operation in the Field of the Environment Concerning Natural Resources Shared by Two or More States. Adopted by the U.N. General Assembly, 13 December 1973. G.A.Res. 3129, U.N. GAOR, 28th Sess., Supp. No. 30, at 48, U.N. Doc A/RES/3129 (1973); *reprinted in* 13 I.L.M. 232 (1974) & 5 Weston V.B.5

The General Assembly,

Reaffirming principles 21, 22 and 24 of the Declaration of the United Nations Conference on the Human Environment, held at Stockholm from 5 to 16 June 1972,

Recalling its resolutions 2995 (XXVII), 2996 (XXVII) and 2997 (XXVII) of 15 December 1972 relating to co-operation between States in the field of the environment, to international responsibility of States in regard to the environment and to the establishment of the Governing Council of the United Nations Environment Programme, respectively,

Reaffirming the duty of the international community to adopt measures to protect and improve the environment, and particularly the need for continuous international collaboration to that end,

Convinced of the need to pursue, in the field of the environment, the elaboration of international norms conducive to the achievement of those purposes,

Taking note with satisfaction of the important Economic Declaration adopted by the Fourth Conference of Heads of State or Government of Non–Aligned Countries, held at Algiers from 5 to 9 September 1973,

Conscious of the importance and urgency of safeguarding the conservation and exploitation of the natural resources shared by two or more States, by means of an effective system of co-operation, as indicated in the above-mentioned Economic Declaration of Algiers,

1. *Considers* that it is necessary to ensure effective co-operation between countries through the establishment of adequate international standards for the conservation and harmonious exploitation of natural resources common to two or more States in the context of the normal relations existing between them;

2. *Considers further* that co-operation between countries sharing such natural resources and interested in their exploitation must be developed on the basis of a system of information and prior consultation within the framework of the normal relations existing between them;

3. *Requests* the Governing Council of the United Nations Environment Programme, in keeping with its function of promoting international co-operation according to the mandate conferred upon it by the General Assembly, to take duly into account the preceding paragraphs and to report on measures adopted for their implementation;

4. *Urges* Member States, within the framework of their mutual relations, to take fully into account the provisions of the present resolution.

1.15 RESOLUTION ON PERMANENT SOVEREIGNTY OVER NATURAL RESOURCES. Adopted by the U.N. General Assembly, 17 December 1973. G.A.Res. 3171, U.N.GAOR, 28th Sess., Supp. No. 30, at 52, U.N.Doc. A/9030 (1974); *reprinted in* 13 I.L.M. 238 (1974) & 5 Weston V.B.6

The General Assembly,

Reiterating that the inalienable right of each State to the full exercise of national sovereignty over its natural resources has been repeatedly recognized by the international community in numerous resolutions of various organs of the United Nations,

Reiterating also that an intrinsic condition of the exercise of the sovereignty of every State is that it be exercised fully and effectively over all the natural resources of the State, whether found on land or in the sea,

Reaffirming the inviolable principle that every country has the right to adopt the economic and social system which it deems most favourable to its development,

Recalling its resolutions 1803 (XVII) of 14 December 1962, 2158 (XXI) of 25 November 1966, 2386 (XXIII) of 19 November 1968, 2625 (XXV) of 24 October 1970, 2692 (XXV) of 11 December 1970 and 3016 (XXVII) of 18 December 1972, and Security Council resolution 330 (1973) of 21 March 1973, which relate to permanent sovereignty over natural resources,

Recalling, in particular, the Declaration on Principles of International Law concerning Friendly Relations and Co-operation among States in accordance with the Charter of the United Nations, which proclaims that no State may use or encourage the use of economic, political or any other type of measures to coerce another State in order to obtain from it the subordination of the exercise of its sovereign rights and to secure from it advantages of any kind,

Considering that the full exercise by each State of sovereignty over its natural resources is an essential condition for achieving the objectives and targets of the Second United Nations Development Decade, and that this exercise requires that action by States aimed at achieving a better utilization and use of those resources must cover all stages, from exploration to marketing,

Taking note of section VII of the Economic Declaration adopted by the Fourth Conference of Heads of State or Government of Non–Aligned Countries, held at Algiers from 5 to 9 September 1973,

Taking note also of the report of the Secretary–General on permanent sovereignty over natural resources,

1. *Strongly reaffirms* the inalienable rights of States to permanent sovereignty over all their natural resources, on land within their international boundaries as well as those in the sea-bed and the subsoil thereof within their national jurisdiction and in the superjacent waters;

2. *Supports resolutely* the efforts of the developing countries and of the peoples of the territories under colonial and racial domination and foreign occupation in their struggle to regain effective control over their natural resources;

3. *Affirms* that the application of the principle of nationalization carried out by States, as an expression of their sovereignty in order to safeguard their natural resources, implies that each State is entitled to determine the amount of possible compensation and the mode of payment, and that any disputes which might arise should be settled in accordance with the national legislation of each State carrying out such measures;

4. *Deplores* acts of States which use force, armed aggression, economic coercion or any other illegal or improper means in resolving disputes concerning the exercise of the sovereign rights mentioned in paragraphs 1 to 3 above;

5. *Re-emphasizes* that actions, measures or legislative regulations by States aimed at coercing, directly or indirectly, other States or peoples engaged in the reorganization of their internal structure or in the exercise of their sovereign rights over their natural resources, both on land and in their coastal waters, are in violation of the Charter of the United Nations and of the Declaration contained in General Assembly resolution 2625 (XXV) and contradict the targets, objectives and policy measures of the International Development Strategy for the Second United Nations Development Decade, and that to persist therein could constitute a threat to international peace and security;

6. *Emphasizes* the duty of all States to refrain in their international relations from military, political, economic or any other form of coercion aimed against the territorial integrity of any State and the exercise of its national jurisdiction;

7. *Recognizes* that, as stressed in Economic and Social Council resolution 1737 (LIV) of 4 May 1973, one of the most effective ways in which the developing countries can protect their natural resources is to establish, promote or strengthen machinery for co-operation among them which has as its main purpose to concert pricing policies, to improve conditions of access to markets, to co-ordinate production policies and, thus, to guarantee the full exercise of sovereignty by developing countries over their natural resources;

8. *Requests* the Economic and Social Council, at its fifty-sixth session, to consider the report of the Secretary–General mentioned in the last preambular paragraph above and requests the Secretary–General to prepare a supplement to that report, in the light of the discussions that are to take place at the fifty-sixth session of the Council and of any other relevant developments, and to submit that supplementary report to the General Assembly at its twenty-ninth session.

1.16 CONVENTION ON THE PROTECTION OF THE ENVIRONMENT BETWEEN DENMARK, FINLAND, NORWAY AND SWEDEN (With Protocol). Concluded at Stockholm, 9 February 1974. Entered into force, 5 October 1976. 1092 U.N.T.S. 279; *reprinted in* 13 I.L.M. 591 (1974) & 5 Weston V.C.1

* * *

Article 1. For the purpose of this Convention, environmentally harmful activities shall mean the discharge from the soil or from buildings or installations of solid or liquid waste, gas or any other substance into watercourses, lakes or the sea and the use of land, the sea-bed, buildings or installations in any other way which entails, or may entail environmental nuisance by water pollution or any other effect on water conditions, sand drift, air pollution, noise, vibration, changes in temperature, ionizing radiation, light, etc.

The Convention shall not apply insofar as environmentally harmful activities are regulated by a special agreement between two or more of the Contracting States.

Article 2. In considering the permissibility of environmentally harmful activities, the nuisance which such activities entail or may entail in another Contracting State shall be equated with a nuisance in the State where the activities are carried out.

Article 3. Any person who is affected or may be affected by a nuisance caused by environmentally harmful activities in another Contracting State shall have the right to bring before the appropriate Court of Administrative Authority of that State the question of the permissibility of such activities, including the question of measures to prevent damage, and to appeal against the decision of the Court or the Administrative Authority to the same extent and on the same terms as a legal entity of the State in which the activities are being carried out.

The provisions of the first paragraph of this Article shall be equally applicable in the case of proceedings concerning compensation for damage caused by environmentally harmful activities. The question of compensation shall not be judged by rules which are less favourable to the injured Party than the rules of compensation of the State in which the activities are being carried out.

Article 4. Each State shall appoint a special authority (supervisory authority) to be entrusted with the task of safeguarding general environmental interests insofar as regards nuisances arising out of environmentally harmful activities in another Contracting State.

For the purpose of safeguarding such interests, the supervisory authority shall have the right to institute proceedings before or be heard by the competent Court or Administrative Authority of another Contracting State regarding the permissibility of the environmentally harmful activities if an authority or other representative of general environmental interests in that State can institute proceedings or be heard in matters of this kind, as well as the right to appeal against the decision of the Court or the Administrative Authority in accordance with the procedures and rules of appeal applicable to such cases in the State concerned.

Article 5. If the Court or the Administrative Authority examining the permissibility of environmentally harmful activities (examining authority) finds that the activities entail or may entail nuisance of significance in another Contracting State, the examining authority shall, if proclamation or publication is required in cases of that nature, send as soon as possible a copy of the documents of the case to the supervisory authority of the other State, and afford it the opportunity of giving its opinion. Notification of the date and place of a meeting or inspection shall, where appropriate, be given well in advance to the supervisory authority which, moreover, shall be kept informed of any developments that may be of interest to it.

Article 6. Upon the request of the supervisory authority, the examining authority shall, in so far as compatible with the procedural rules of the State in which the activities are being carried out, require the applicant for a permit to carry out environmentally harmful activities to submit such additional particulars, drawings and technical specifications as the examining authority deems necessary for evaluating the effects in the other State.

Article 7. The supervisory authority, if it finds it necessary on account of public or private interests, shall publish communications from the examining authority in the local newspaper or in some other suitable manner. The supervisory authority shall also institute such investigations of the effects in its own State as it deems necessary.

Article 8. Each State shall defray the cost of the activities of its supervisory authority.

Article 9. If, in a particular case, the supervisory authority has informed the appropriate Court of Administrative authority of the State in which the activities are being carried out that in the case concerned the duties of the supervisory authority shall be discharged by another authority, the provisions of this Convention relating to supervisory activities shall, where appropriate, apply to that authority.

Article 10. If necessary for determining the damage caused in another State by environmentally harmful activities, the supervisory authority of that other State shall upon request of the examining authority of the State in which the activities are being carried out make arrangements for on-site inspection. The examining authority or an expert appointed by it may be present at such an inspection.

Where necessary, more detailed instructions concerning inspections such as referred to in the preceding paragraph shall be drawn up in consultation between the countries concerned.

Article 11. Where the permissibility of environmentally harmful activities which entail or may entail considerable nuisance in another Contracting State is being examined by the Government or by the appropriate Minister or Ministry of the State in which the activities are being carried out, consultations shall take place between the States concerned if the Government of the former State so requests.

Article 12. In cases such as those referred to in Article 11, the Government of each State concerned may demand that an opinion be given by a Commission which, unless otherwise agreed, shall consist of a chairman from another Contracting State to be appointed jointly by the Parties and three members from each of the States concerned. Where such a Commission has been appointed, the case cannot be decided upon until the Commission has given its opinion.

Each State shall remunerate the members it has appointed. Fees or other remuneration of the Chairman as well as any other costs incidental to the activities of the Commission which are not manifestly the responsibility of one or the other State shall be equally shared by the States concerned.

Article 13. This Convention shall also apply to the continental shelf areas of the Contracting States.

Article 14. This Convention shall enter into force six months from the date on which all the Contracting States have notified the Swedish Ministry for Foreign Affairs that the constitutional measures necessary for the entry into force of the Convention have been implemented. The Swedish Ministry for Foreign Affairs shall notify the other Contracting States of the receipt of such communications.

Article 15. Actions or cases relevant to this Convention, which are pending before a Court or an Administrative Authority on the date when this Convention enters into force, shall be dealt with and judged according to provisions previously in force.

Article 16. Any Contracting State wishing to denounce this Convention shall give notice of its intention in writing to the Swedish Government, which shall forthwith inform the other Contracting States of the denunciation and of the date on which notice was received.

The denunciation shall take effect 12 months from the date on which the Swedish Government received such notification or on such later date as may be indicated in the notice of denunciation.

This Convention shall be deposited with the Swedish Ministry for Foreign Affairs, which shall send certified copies thereof to the Government of each Contracting State.

PROTOCOL

In connection with the signing today of the Nordic Environmental Protection Convention the duly authorized signatories agreed that the following comments on its application shall be appended to the Convention.

In the applications of Article 1 discharge from the soil, or from buildings or installations of solid or liquid waste, gases or other substances into watercourses, lakes or the sea shall be regarded as environmentally harmful activities only if the discharge entails or may entail a nuisance to the surroundings.

The right established in Article 3 for anyone who suffers injury as a result of environmentally harmful activities in a neighbouring State to institute proceedings for compensation before a court or administrative authority of that State shall, in principle, be regarded as including the right to demand the purchase of his real property.

Article 5 shall be regarded as applying also to application for permits where such applications are referred to certain authorities and organizations for their opinion but not in conjunction with proclamation or publication procedures.

The Contracting States shall require officials of the supervisory authority to observe professional secrecy as regards trade secrets, operational devices or business conditions of which they have become cognizant in dealing with cases concerning environmentally harmful activities in another State.

1.17 Final Act of the Conference on Security and Co-operation in Europe. Adopted by the Conference on Security and Co-operation in Europe at Helsinki, 1 August 1975. *Reprinted in* 14 I.L.M. 1292 (1975) & 1 Weston I.D.9: *Co-operation in the Field of Economics, of Science and Technology and of the Environment*

* * *

Motivated by the political will, in the interest of peoples, to improve and intensify their relations and to contribute in Europe to peace, security, justice and co-operation as well as to rapprochement among themselves and with the other States of the world,

Determined, in consequence, to give full effect to the results of the Conference and to assure, among their States and throughout Europe, the benefits deriving from those results and thus to broaden, deepen and make continuing and lasting the process of detente.

The High Representatives of the participating States have solemnly adopted the following:

* * *

CO-OPERATION IN THE FIELD OF ECONOMICS, OF SCIENCE AND TECHNOLOGY AND OF THE ENVIRONMENT

The participating States,

Convinced that their efforts to develop co-operation in the fields of trade, industry, science and technology, the environment and other areas of economic activity contribute to the reinforcement of peace and security in Europe and in the world as a whole,

Recognizing that co-operation in these fields would promote economic and social progress and the improvement of the conditions of life,

Aware of the diversity of their economic and social systems,

Reaffirming their will to intensify such co-operation between one another, irrespective of their systems,

Recognizing that such co-operation, with due regard for the different levels of economic development, can be developed, on the basis of equality and mutual satisfaction of the partners, and of reciprocity permitting, as a whole, an equitable distribution of advantages and obligations of comparable scale, with respect for bilateral and multilateral agreements,

Taking into account the interests of the developing countries throughout the world, including those among the participating countries as long as they are developing from the economic point of view; reaffirming their will to co-operate for the achievement of the aims and objectives established by the appropriate bodies of the United Nations in the pertinent documents concerning development, it being understood that each participating State maintains the positions it has taken on them; giving special attention to the least developed countries,

Convinced that the growing world-wide, economic interdependence calls for increasing common and effective efforts towards the solution of major world economic problems such as food, energy, commodities, monetary and financial problems, and therefore emphasizes the need for promoting stable and equitable international economic relations, thus contributing to the continuous and diversified economic development of all countries,

Having taken into account the work already undertaken by relevant international organizations and wishing to take advantage of the possibilities offered by these organizations, in particular by the United Nations Economic Commission for Europe, for giving effect to the provisions of the final documents of the Conference,

Considering that the guidelines and concrete recommendations contained in the following texts are aimed at promoting further development of their mutual economic relations, and convinced that their co-operation in this field should take place in full respect for the principles guiding relations among participating States as set forth in the relevant document,

Have adopted the following:

* * *

5. Environment

The participating States,

Affirming that the protection and improvement of the environment, as well as the protection of nature and the rational utilization of its resources in the interests of present and future generations, is one of the tasks of major importance to the well-being of peoples and the economic development of all countries and the many environmental problems, particularly in Europe, can be solved effectively only through close international co-operation,

Acknowledging that each of the participating States, in accordance with the principles of international law, ought to ensure, in a spirit of co-operation, that activities carried out on its territory do not cause degradation of the environment in another State or in areas lying beyond the limits of national jurisdiction,

Considering that the success of any environmental policy presupposes that all population groups and social forces, aware of their responsibilities, help to protect and improve the environment, which necessitates continued and thorough educative action, particularly with regard to youth,

Affirming that experience has shown that economic development and technological progress must be compatible with the protection of the environment and the preservation of historical and cultural values; that damage to the environment is best avoided by preventive measures; and that the ecological balance must be preserved in the exploitation and management of natural resources,

Aims of co-operation

Agree to the following aims of co-operation, in particular:

—to study, with a view to their solution, those environmental problems which, by their nature, are of a multilateral, bilateral, regional or sub-regional dimension; as well as to encourage the development of an interdisciplinary approach to environmental problems;

—to increase the effectiveness of national and international measures for the protection of the environment, by the comparison and, if appropriate, the harmonization of methods of gathering and analyzing facts, by improving the knowledge of pollution phenomena and rational utilization of natural resources, by the exchange of information, by the harmonization of definitions and the adoption, as far as possible, of a common terminology in the field of the environment;

—to take the necessary measures to bring environmental policies closer together and, where appropriate and possible, to harmonize them;

—to encourage, where possible and appropriate, national and international efforts by their interested organizations, enterprises and firms in the development, production and improvement of equipment designed for monitoring, protecting and enhancing the environment.

Fields of co-operation

To attain these aims, the participating States will make use of every suitable opportunity to co-operate in the field of environment and, in particular, within the areas described below as examples:

Control of air pollution

Desulphurization of fossil fuels and exhaust gases; pollution control of heavy metals, pArticles, aerosols, nitrogen oxides, in particular those emitted by transport, power stations, and other industrial plants; systems and methods of observation and control of air pollution and its effects, including long-range transport of air pollutants;

Water pollution control and fresh water utilization

Prevention and control of water pollution, in particular of transboundary rivers and international lakes; techniques for the improvement of the quality of water and further development of ways and means for industrial and municipal sewage effluent purification; methods of assessment of fresh water resources and the improvement of their utilization, in particular by developing methods of production which are less polluting and lead to less consumption of fresh water;

Protection of the marine environment

Protection of the marine environment of participating States, and especially the Mediterranean Sea, from pollutants emanating from land-based sources and those from ships and other vessels, notably the harmful substances listed in Annexes I and II to the London Convention on the Prevention of Marine Pollution by the Dumping of Wastes and Other Matters; problems of maintaining marine ecological balances and food chains, in particular such problems as may arise from the exploration and exploitation of biological and mineral resources of the seas and the seabed;

Land utilization and soils

Problems associated with more effective use of lands, including land amelioration, reclamation and recultivation; control of soil pollution, water and air erosion, as well as other forms of soil degradation; maintaining and increasing the productivity of soils with due regard for the possible negative effects of the application of chemical fertilizers and pesticides;

Nature conservation and nature reserves

Protection of nature and nature reserves; conservation and maintenance of existing genetic resources, especially rare animal and plant species; conservation of natural ecological systems; establishment of nature reserves and other protected landscapes and areas, including their use for research, tourism, recreation and other purposes;

Improvement of environmental conditions in areas of human settlement

Environmental conditions associated with transport, housing, working areas, urban development and planning, water supply and sewage disposal systems; assessment of harmful effects of noise, and noise control methods; collection, treatment and utilization of wastes, including the recovery and recycling of materials; research on substitutes for non-biodegradable substances;

Fundamental research, monitoring, forecasting and assessment of environmental changes

Study of changes in climate, landscapes and ecological balances under the impact of both natural factors and human activities; forecasting of possible genetic changes in flora and fauna as a result of environmental pollution; harmonization of statistical data, development of scientific concepts and systems of monitoring networks, standardized methods of observation, measurement and assessment of changes in the biosphere; assessment of the effects of environmental pollution levels and degradation of the environment upon human health; study and development of criteria and standards for various environmental pollutants and regulation regarding production and use of various products;

Legal and administrative measures

Legal and administrative measures for the protection of the environment including procedures for establishing environmental impact assessments.

Forms and methods of co-operation

The participating States declare that problems relating to the protection and improvement of the environment will be solved on both a bilateral and multilateral, including regional and sub-regional, basis, making full use of existing patterns and forms of co-operation. They will develop co-operation in the field of the environment in particular by taking into consideration the Stockholm Declaration on the Human Environment, relevant resolutions of the United Nations General Assembly and the United Nations Economic Commission for Europe Prague symposium on environmental problems.

The participating States are resolved that co-operation in the field of the environment will be implemented in particular through:

—exchanges of scientific and technical information, documentation and research results, including information on the means of determining the possible effects on the environment of technical and economic activities;

—organization of conferences, symposia and meetings of experts;

—exchanges of scientists, specialists and trainees;

—joint preparation and implementation of programmes and projects for the study and solution of various problems of environmental protection;

—harmonization, where appropriate and necessary, of environmental protection standards and norms, in particular with the object of avoiding possible difficulties in trade which may arise from efforts to resolve ecological problems of production processes and which relate to the achievement of certain environmental qualities in manufactured products:

—consultations on various aspects of environmental protection, as agreed upon among countries concerned, especially in connection with problems which could have international consequences.

The participating States will further develop such co-operation by:

—promoting the progressive development, codification and implementation of international law as one means of preserving and enhancing the human environment, including principles and practices, as accepted by them, relating to pollution and other environmental damage caused by activities within the jurisdiction or control of their States affecting other countries and regions;

—supporting and promoting the implementation of relevant international Conventions to which they are parties, in particular those designed to prevent and combat marine and fresh water pollution, recommending States to ratify Conventions which have already been signed, as well as considering possibilities of accepting other appropriate Conventions to which they are not parties at present;

—advocating the inclusion, where appropriate and possible, of the various areas of co-operation into the programmes of work of the United Nations Economic Commission for Europe, supporting such co-operation within the framework of the Commission and of the United Nations Environment Programme, and taking into account the work of other competent international organizations of which they are members;

—making wider use in all types of co-operation, of information already available for national and international sources, including internationally agreed criteria, and utilizing the possibilities and capabilities of various competent international organizations.

The participating States agree on the following recommendations on specific measures:

—to develop through international co-operation an extensive programme for the monitoring and evaluation of the long-range transport of air pollutants, starting with sulphur dioxide and with possible extension to other pollutants, and to this end to take into account basic elements of a co-operation programme which were identified by the experts who met in Oslo in December 1974 at the invitation of the Norwegian Institute of Air Research;

—to advocate that within the framework of the United Nations Economic Commission for Europe a study be carried out of procedures and relevant experience relating to the activities of Governments in developing the capabilities of their countries to predict adequately environmental consequences of economic activities and technological development.

1.18 DRAFT PRINCIPLES OF CONDUCT IN THE FIELD OF THE ENVIRONMENT FOR GUIDANCE OF STATES IN THE CONSERVATION AND HARMONIOUS UTILIZATION OF NATURAL RESOURCES SHARED BY TWO OR MORE STATES. Approved by the U.N. Environment Programme Governing Council, 19 May 1978. U.N.Doc. UNEP/IG12/2 (1978); *reprinted in* 17 I.L.M. 1097 (1978) & 5 Weston V.B.8

Principle 1

It is necessary for States to co-operate in the field of the environment concerning the conservation and harmonious utilization of natural resources shared by two or more States. Accordingly, it is necessary that consistent with the concept of equitable utilization of shared natural resources, States co-operate with a view to controlling, preventing, reducing or eliminating adverse environmental effects which may result from the utilization of such resources. Such co-operation is to take place on an equal footing and taking into account the sovereignty, rights and interests of the States concerned.

Principle 2

In order to ensure effective international co-operation in the field of the environment concerning the conservation and harmonious utilization of natural resources shared by two or more States, States sharing such natural resources should endeavor to conclude bilateral or multilateral agreements between or among themselves in order to secure specific regulation of their conduct in this respect, applying as necessary the present principles in a legally binding manner or should endeavor to enter into other arrangements, as appropriate, for this purpose. In entering into such agreements or arrangements, States should consider the establishment of institutional structures, such as joint international commissions, for consultations on environmental problems relating to the protection and use of shared natural resources.

Principle 3

1. States have, in accordance with the Charter of the United Nations and the principles of international law, the sovereign right to exploit their own resources pursuant to their own environmental policies, and the responsibility to ensure that activities within their jurisdiction or control do not cause damage to the environment of other States or of areas beyond the limits of national jurisdiction.

2. The principles set forth in paragraph 1, as well as the other principles contained in this document, apply to shared natural resources.

3. Accordingly, it is necessary for each State to avoid to the maximum extent possible and to reduce to the minimum extent possible the adverse environmental effects beyond its jurisdiction of the utilization of a shared natural resource so as to protect the environment, in particular when such utilization might:

(*a*) cause damage to the environment which could have repercussions on the utilization of the resource by another sharing State;

(*b*) threaten the conservation of a shared renewable resource;

(*c*) endanger the health of the population of another State.

Without prejudice to the generality of the above principle, it should be interpreted, taking into account, where appropriate, the practical capabilities of States sharing the natural resource.

Principle 4

States should make environmental assessments before engaging in any activity with respect to a shared natural resource which may create a risk of significantly[1] affecting the environment of another State or States sharing that resource.

Principle 5

States sharing a natural resource should, to the extent practicable, exchange information and engage in consultations on a regular basis on its environmental aspects.

Principle 6

1. It is necessary for every State sharing a natural resource with one or more other States:

(*a*) to notify in advance the other State or States of the pertinent details of plans to initiate, or make a change in, the conservation or utilization of the resource which can reasonably be expected to affect significantly the environment in the territory of the other State or States; and

(*b*) upon request of the other State or States, to enter into consultations concerning the above-mentioned plans; and

(*c*) to provide, upon request to that effect by the other State or States, specific additional pertinent information concerning such plans; and

(*d*) if there has been no advance notification as envisaged in sub-paragraph (a) above, to enter into consultations about such plans upon request of the other State or States.

2. In cases where the transmission of certain information is prevented by national legislation or international conventions, the State or States withholding such information shall nevertheless, on the basis, in particular, of the principle of good faith and in the spirit of good neighbourliness, co-operate with the other interested State or States with the aim of finding a satisfactory solution.

Principle 7

Exchange of information, notification, consultations and other forms of co-operation regarding shared natural resources are carried out on the basis of the principle of good faith and in the spirit of good neighbourliness and in such a way as to avoid any unreasonable delays either in the forms of co-operation or in carrying out development or conservation projects.

Principle 8

When it would be useful to clarify environmental problems relating to a shared natural resource, States should engage in joint scientific studies and assessments, with a view to facilitating the finding of appropriate and satisfactory solutions to such problems on the basis of agreed data.

Principle 9

1. States have a duty urgently to inform other States which may be affected:

(*a*) Of any emergency situation arising from the utilization of a shared natural resource which might cause sudden harmful effects on their environment;

(*b*) Of any sudden grave natural events related to a shared natural resource which may affect the environment of such States.

2. States should also, when appropriate, inform the competent international organizations of any such situation or event.

1. See "Definition" following Principle 15.

3. States concerned should co-operate, in particular by means of agreed contingency plans, when appropriate, and mutual assistance, in order to avert grave situations, and to eliminate, reduce or correct, as far as possible, the effects of such situations or events.

Principle 10

States sharing a natural resource should, when appropriate, consider the possibility of jointly seeking the services of any competent international organization in clarifying the environmental problems relating to the conservation or utilization of such natural resource.

Principle 11

1. The relevant provisions of the Charter of the United Nations and of the Declaration of Principles of International Law concerning Friendly Relations and Co-operation among States in accordance with the Charter of the United Nations apply to the settlement of environmental disputes arising out of the conservation or utilization of shared natural resources.

2. In case negotiations or other non-binding means have failed to settle a dispute within a reasonable time, it is necessary for States to submit the dispute to an appropriate settlement procedure which is mutually agreed by them, preferably in advance. The procedure should be speedy, effective and binding.

3. It is necessary for the States parties to such a dispute to refrain from any action which may aggravate the situation with respect to the environment to the extent of creating an obstacle to the amicable settlement of the dispute.

Principle 12

1. States are responsible for the fulfillment of their international obligations in the field of the environment concerning the conservation and utilization of shared natural resources. They are subject to liability in accordance with applicable international law for environmental damage resulting from violations of these obligations caused to areas beyond their jurisdiction.

2. States should co-operate to develop further international law regarding liability and compensation for the victims of environmental damage arising out of the utilization of a shared natural resource and caused to areas beyond their jurisdiction.

Principle 13

It is necessary for States, when considering, under their domestic environmental policy, the permissibility of domestic activities, to take into account the potential adverse environmental effects arising out of the utilization of shared natural resources, without discrimination as to whether the effects would occur within their jurisdiction or outside it.

Principle 14

States should endeavour, in accordance with their legal systems and, where appropriate, on a basis agreed by them, to provide persons in other States who have been or may be adversely affected by environmental damage resulting from the utilization of shared natural resources with equivalent access to and treatment in the same administrative and judicial proceedings, and make available to them the same remedies as are available to persons within their own jurisdictions who have been or may be similarly affected.

Principle 15

The present principles should be interpreted and applied in such a way as to enhance and not to affect adversely development and the interests of all countries, and in particular of the developing countries.

DEFINITION

In the present text, the expression "significantly affect" refers to any appreciable effects on a shared natural resource and excludes "*de minimis*" effects.

1.19 Resolution on Historical Responsibility of States for the Preservation of Nature for Present and Future Generations. Adopted by the U.N. General Assembly, 30 October 1980. G.A.Res. 35/48, U.N. GAOR, 35th Sess, Supp. No. 48, at 15, U.N.Doc A/35/48 (1981); *reprinted in* 5 Weston V.B.9

The General Assembly,

Having considered the item entitled "Historical responsibility of States for the preservation of nature for present and future generations",

Conscious of the disastrous consequences which a war involving the use of nuclear weapons and other weapons of mass destruction would have on man and his environment,

Noting that the continuation of the arms race, including the testing of various types of weapons, especially nuclear weapons, and the accumulation of toxic chemicals are adversely affecting the human environment and damaging the vegetable and animal world,

Bearing in mind that the arms race is diverting material and intellectual resources from the solution of the urgent problems of preserving nature,

Attaching great importance to the development of planned, constructive international co-operation in solving the problems of preserving nature,

Recognizing that the prospects for solving problems so universal as the preservation of nature are closely linked to the strengthening and development of international detente and the creation of conditions which would banish war from the life of mankind,

Noting with satisfaction the drafting and signature in recent years of a number of international agreements designed to preserve the environment,

Determined to preserve nature as a prerequisite for the normal life of man,

1. *Proclaims* the historical responsibility of States for the preservation of nature for present and future generations;

2. *Draws the attention* of States to the fact that the continuing arms race has pernicious effects on the environment and reduces the prospects for the necessary international co-operation in preserving nature on our planet;

3. *Calls upon* States, in the interests of present and future generations, to demonstrate due concern and take the measures, including legislative measures, necessary for preserving nature, and also to promote international co-operation in this field;

4. *Requests* the Secretary–General, with the co-operation of the United Nations Environment Programme, to prepare a report on the pernicious effects of the arms race on nature and to seek the views of States on possible measures to be taken at the international level for the preservation of nature;

5. *Decides* to include in the provisional agenda of its thirty-sixth session an item entitled "Historical responsibility of States for the preservation of nature for present and future generations: report of the Secretary–General".

1.20 ILA Rules on International Law Applicable to Transfrontier Pollution. Adopted at Montreal, 4 September 1982. 60 I.L.A. 158 (1983); *reprinted in* 5 Weston V.B.10

Article 1 (Applicability)

The following rules of international law concerning transfrontier pollution are applicable except as may be otherwise provided by convention, agreement or binding custom among the States concerned.

Article 2 (Definition)

(1) "Pollution" means any introduction by man, directly or indirectly, of substance or energy into the environment resulting in deleterious effects of such a nature as to endanger human health, harm living resources, ecosystems and material property and impair amenities or interfere with other legitimate uses of the environment.

(2) "Transfrontier pollution" means pollution of which the physical origin is wholly or in part situated within the territory of one State and which has deleterious effects in the territory of another State.

Article 3 (Prevention and Abatement)

(1) Without prejudice to the operation of the rules relating to the reasonable and equitable utilisation of shared natural resources States are in their legitimate activities under an obligation to prevent, abate and control transfrontier pollution to such an extent that no substantial injury is caused in the territory of another State.

(2) Furthermore States shall limit new and increased transfrontier pollution to the lowest level that may be reached by measures practicable and reasonable under the circumstances.

(3) States should endeavour to reduce existing transfrontier pollution, below the requirements of paragraph 1 of this Article, to the lowest level that may be reached by measures practicable and reasonable under the circumstances.

Article 4 (Highly Dangerous Substances)

Notwithstanding the provisions in Article 3 States shall refrain from causing transfrontier pollution by discharging into the environment substances generally considered as being highly dangerous to human health. If such substances are already being discharged, States shall eliminate the polluting discharge within a reasonable time.

Article 5 (Prior Notice)

(1) States planning to carry out activities which might entail a significant risk of transfrontier pollution shall give early notice to States likely to be affected. In particular they shall on their own initiative or upon request of the potentially affected States, communicate such pertinent information as will permit the recipient to make an assessment of the probable effects of the planned activities.

(2) In order to appraise whether a planned activity implies a significant risk of transfrontier pollution, States should make environmental assessment before carrying out such activities.

Article 6 (Consultations)

(1) Upon request of a potentially affected State, the State furnishing the information should enter into consultations on transfrontier pollution problems connected with the planned activities and pursue such consultations in good faith and over a reasonable period of time.

(2) States are under an obligation to enter into consultations whenever transfrontier pollution problems arise in connection with the equitable utilization of a shared natural resource as envisaged in Art. 5.

Article 7 (Emergency Situations)

When as a result of an emergency situation or of other circumstances activities already carried out in the territory of a State cause or might cause a sudden increase in the existing level of transfrontier pollution the State of origin is under a duty:

(a) to promptly warn the affected or potentially affected States;

(b) to provide them with such pertinent information as will enable them to minimize the transfrontier pollution damage;

(c) to inform them of the steps taken to abate the cause of the increased transfrontier pollution level.

1.21 World Charter for Nature. Adopted by the U.N. General Assembly, 28 October 1982. G.A. Res. 37/7 (Annex), U.N. GAOR, 37th Sess., Supp. No. 51, at 17, U.N. Doc. A/37/51; *reprinted in* 22 I.L.M. 455 (1983) & 5 Weston V.B.11

The General Assembly,

Reaffirming the fundamental purposes of the United Nations, in particular the maintenance of international peace and security, the development of friendly relations among nations and the achievement of international cooperation in solving international problems of an economic, social, cultural, technical, intellectual or humanitarian character,

Aware that:

(*a*) Mankind is a part of nature and life depends on the uninterrupted functioning of natural systems which ensure the supply of energy and nutrients,

(*b*) Civilization is rooted in nature, which has shaped human culture and influenced all artistic and scientific achievement, and living in harmony with nature gives man the best opportunities for the development of his creativity, and for rest and recreation,

Convinced that:

(*a*) Every form of life is unique, warranting respect regardless of its worth to man, and, to accord other organisms such recognition, man must be guided by a moral code of action,

(*b*) Man can alter nature and exhaust natural resources by his action or its consequences and, therefore, must fully recognize the urgency of maintaining the stability and quality of nature and of conserving natural resources,

Persuaded that:

(*a*) Lasting benefits from nature depend upon the maintenance of essential ecological processes and life support systems, and upon the diversity of life forms, which are jeopardized through excessive exploitation and habitat destruction by man,

(*b*) The degradation of natural systems owing to excessive consumption and misuse of natural resources, as well as to failure to establish an appropriate economic order among peoples and among States, leads to the breakdown of the economic, social and political framework of civilization,

(*c*) Competition for scarce resources creates conflicts, whereas the conservation of nature and natural resources contributes to justice and the maintenance of peace and cannot be achieved until mankind learns to live in peace and to forsake war and armaments,

Reaffirming that man must acquire the knowledge to maintain and enhance his ability to use natural resources in a manner which ensures the preservation of the species and ecosystems for the benefit of present and future generations,

Firmly convinced of the need for appropriate measures, at the national and international, individual and collective, and private and public levels, to protect nature and promote international co-operation in this field,

Adopts, to these ends, the present World Charter for Nature, which proclaims the following principles of conservation by which all human conduct affecting nature is to be guided and judged.

I. General Principles

1. Nature shall be respected and its essential processes shall not be impaired.

2. The genetic viability on the earth shall not be compromised; the population levels of all life forms, wild and domesticated, must be at least sufficient for their survival, and to this end necessary habitats shall be safeguarded.

3. All areas of the earth, both land and sea, shall be subject to these principles of conservation; special protection shall be given to unique areas, to representative samples of all the different types of ecosystems and to the habitats of rare or endangered species.

4. Ecosystems and organisms, as well as the land, marine and atmospheric resources that are utilized by man, shall be managed to achieve and maintain optimum sustainable productivity, but not in such a way as to endanger the integrity of those other ecosystems or species with which they coexist.

5. Nature shall be secured against degradation caused by warfare or other hostile activities.

II. Functions

6. In the decision-making process it shall be recognized that man's needs can be met only by ensuring the proper functioning of natural systems and by respecting the principles set forth in the present Charter.

7. In the planning and implementation of social and economic development activities, due account shall be taken of the fact that the conservation of nature is an integral part of those activities.

8. In formulating long-term plans for economic development, population growth and the improvement of standards of living, due account shall be taken of the long-term capacity of natural systems to ensure the subsistence and settlement of the populations concerned, recognizing that this capacity may be enhanced through science and technology.

9. The allocation of areas of the earth to various uses shall be planned, and due account shall be taken of the physical constraints, the biological productivity and diversity and the natural beauty of the areas concerned.

10. Natural resources shall not be wasted, but used with a restraint appropriate to the principles set forth in the present Charter, in accordance with the following rules:

(*a*) Living resources shall not be utilized in excess of their natural capacity for regeneration;

(*b*) The productivity of soils shall be maintained or enhanced through measures which safeguard their long-term fertility and the process of organic decomposition, and prevent erosion and all other forms of degradation;

(*c*) Resources, including water, which are not consumed as they are used shall be reused or recycled;

(*d*) Non-renewable resources which are consumed as they are used shall be exploited with restraint, taking into account their abundance, the rational possibilities of converting them for consumption, and the compatibility of their exploitation with the functioning of natural systems.

11. Activities which might have an impact on nature shall be controlled, and the best available technologies that minimize significant risks to nature or other adverse effects shall be used; in particular:

(*a*) Activities which are likely to cause irreversible damage to nature shall be avoided;

(*b*) Activities which are likely to pose a significant risk to nature shall be preceded by an exhaustive examination; their proponents shall demonstrate that expected benefits outweigh potential damage to nature, and where potential adverse effects are not fully understood, the activities should not proceed.

(*c*) Activities which may disturb nature shall be preceded by assessment of their consequences, and environmental impact studies of development projects shall be conducted sufficiently in advance, and if they are to be undertaken, such activities shall be planned and carried out so as to minimize potential adverse effects;

(*d*) Agriculture, grazing, forestry and fisheries practices shall be adapted to the natural characteristics and constraints of given areas;

(*e*) Areas degraded by human activities shall be rehabilitated for purposes in accord with their natural potential and compatible with the well-being of affected populations.

12. Discharge of pollutants into natural systems shall be avoided and:

(*a*) Where this is not feasible, such pollutants shall be treated at the source, using the best practicable means available;

(*b*) Special precautions shall be taken to prevent discharge of radioactive or toxic wastes.

13. Measures intended to prevent, control or limit natural disasters, infestations and diseases shall be specifically directed to the causes of these scourges and shall avoid adverse side-effects on nature.

III. Implementation

14. The principles set forth in the present Charter shall be reflected in the law and practice of each State, as well as at the international level.

15. Knowledge of nature shall be broadly disseminated by all possible means, particularly by ecological education as an integral part of general education.

16. All planning shall include, among its essential elements, the formulation of strategies for the conservation of nature, the establishment of inventories of ecosystems and assessments of the effects on nature of proposed policies and activities; all of these elements shall be disclosed to the public by appropriate means in time to permit effective consultation and participation.

17. Funds, programmes and administrative structures necessary to achieve the objective of the conservation of nature shall be provided.

18. Constant efforts shall be made to increase knowledge of nature by scientific research and to disseminate such knowledge unimpeded by restrictions of any kind.

19. The status of natural processes, ecosystems and species shall be closely monitored to enable early detection of degradation or threat, ensure timely intervention and facilitate the evaluation of conservation policies and methods.

20. Military activities damaging to nature shall be avoided.

21. States and, to the extent they are able, other public authorities, international organizations, individuals, groups and corporations shall:

(*a*) Co-operate in the task of conserving nature through common activities and other relevant actions, including information exchange and consultations;

(*b*) Establish standards for products and manufacturing processes that may have adverse effects on nature, as well as agreed methodologies for assessing these effects;

(*c*) Implement the applicable international legal provisions for the conservation of nature and the protection of the environment;

(*d*) Ensure that activities within their jurisdictions or control do not cause damage to the natural systems located within other States or in the areas beyond the limits of national jurisdiction;

(*e*) Safeguard and conserve nature in areas beyond national jurisdiction.

22. Taking fully into account the sovereignty of States over their natural resources, each State shall give effect to the provisions of the present Charter through its competent organs and in co-operation with other States.

23. All persons, in accordance with their national legislation, shall have the opportunity to participate, individually or with others, in the formulation of decisions of direct concern to their environment, and shall have access to means of redress when their environment has suffered damage or degradation.

24. Each person has a duty to act in accordance with the provisions of the present Charter; acting individually, in association with others or through participation in the political process, each person shall strive to ensure that the objectives and requirements of the present Charter are met.

1.22 Legal Principles for Environmental Protection and Sustainable Development. Adopted by the Experts Group on Environmental Law of the World Commission on Environment and Development (WCED), 18–20 June 1986. U.N.Doc. WCED/86/23/Add. 1 (1986); *reprinted in* 5 Weston V.B.12

USE OF TERMS

For the purposes of the present text:

(a) "use of a natural resource" means any human conduct, which, directly or indirectly, takes advantage of the benefits of a natural resource in the form of preservation, exploitation, consumption or otherwise of the natural resource, in so far as it does not result in an environmental interference as defined in Paragraph (f);

(b) "interference with the use of a natural resource" means any impairment, directly or indirectly, by man of the use of a natural resource in so far as it does not constitute an environmental interference as defined in Paragraph (f);

(c) "transboundary natural resource" means a natural resource which physically crosses the boundary between an area under the national jurisdiction of a State and an area under the national jurisdiction of another State or an area beyond the limits of national jurisdiction to the extent that its use in an area under the national jurisdiction of one State may affect its use in an area under the national jurisdiction of another State or in an area beyond the limits of national jurisdiction or vice versa;

(d) "transboundary interference with the use of a transboundary natural resource" means an interference with the use of a natural resource of which the physical origin is wholly or in part located outside the area under national jurisdiction of a State or outside the area beyond the limits of national jurisdiction in which the use takes place;

(e) "international natural resource" means a natural resource physically within an area beyond the limits of national jurisdiction to the extent that the origin and effects of any impairment of the use of the natural resource remain within the area beyond the limits of national jurisdiction;

(f) "environmental interference" means any impairment of human health, living resources, ecosystems, material property, amenities or other legitimate uses of a natural resource or the environment caused, directly or indirectly, by man through polluting substances, ionizing radiation, noise, explosions, vibration or other forms of energy, plants, animals, diseases, flooding, sand-drift or other similar means;

(g) "transboundary environmental interference" means an environmental interference of which the physical origin is wholly or in part located either outside the area under national jurisdiction of a State in which the effects caused by the interference occur, or outside the area beyond the limits of national jurisdiction in which the effects caused by the interference occur;

(h) "international environmental interference" means an environmental interference of which the physical origin and the effects are located within an area beyond the limits of national jurisdiction;

(i) "conservation" means the management of human use of a natural resource or the environment in such a manner that it may yield the greatest sustainable benefit to present generations while maintaining its potential to meet the needs and aspirations of future generations. It embraces preservation, maintenance, sustainable utilization, restoration and enhancement of a natural resource or the environment.

GENERAL PRINCIPLES CONCERNING NATURAL RESOURCES AND ENVIRONMENTAL INTERFERENCES

Article 1

Fundamental human right

All human beings have the fundamental right to an environment adequate for their health and well-being.

Article 2

Conservation for present and future generations

States shall ensure that the environment and natural resources are conserved and used for the benefit of present and future generations.

Article 3

Ecosystems, related ecological processes, biological diversity, and sustainability

States shall:

(a) maintain ecosystems and related ecological processes essential for the functioning of the biosphere in all its diversity, in particular those important for food production, health and other aspects of human survival and sustainable development;

(b) maintain maximum biological diversity by ensuring the survival and promoting the conservation in their natural habitat of all species of fauna and flora, in particular those which are rare, endemic or endangered;

(c) observe in the exploitation of living natural resources and ecosystems, the principle of optimum sustainable yield.

Article 4

Environmental standards and monitoring

States shall:

(a) establish specific environmental standards, in particular environmental quality standards, emission standards, technological standards and product standards aimed at preventing or abating interferences with natural resources or the environment;

(b) establish systems for the collection and dissemination of data and regular observation of natural resources and the environment in order to permit adequate planning of the use of natural resources and the environment, to permit early detection of interferences with natural resources or the environment and ensure timely intervention, and to facilitate the evaluation of conservation policies and methods.

Article 5

Assessment of planned activities

States planning to carry out or permit activities which may significantly affect a natural resource or the environment shall make or require an assessment of their effects before carrying out or permitting the planned activities.

Article 6

Timely information, access and due process

States shall inform all persons in a timely manner of activities which may significantly affect their use of a natural resource or their environment and shall grant the concerned persons access to and due process in administrative and judicial proceedings.

Article 7

Planning and implementation of development activities

1. States shall ensure that the conservation of natural resources and the environment is treated as an integral part of the planning and implementation of development activities. Particular attention shall be paid to environmental problems arising in developing countries and to the need to incorporate environmental considerations in all development assistance programmes.

2. States shall make available to other States, and especially to developing countries, upon their request and under agreed terms scientific and technical information and expertise, results of research programmes, training opportunities and specialized equipment and facilities which are needed by such other States to promote rational use of natural resources, and the environment or to prevent or abate interference with natural resources or the environment, in particular in cases of environmental emergencies.

Article 8

General obligation to co-operate

States shall co-operate in good faith with other States or through competent international organizations in the implementation of the provisions of the preceding Articles.

PRINCIPLES SPECIFICALLY CONCERNING TRANSBOUNDARY NATURAL RESOURCES AND ENVIRONMENTAL INTERFERENCES

Article 9

Reasonable and equitable use of transboundary natural resources

States shall use transboundary natural resources in a reasonable and equitable manner.

Article 10

Prevention and abatement of a transboundary environmental interference

States shall, without prejudice to the principles laid down in Articles 11 and 12, prevent or abate any transboundary environmental interference or a significant risk thereof which causes substantial harm—i.e. harm which is not minor or insignificant.

Article 11

Liability for transboundary environmental interferences resulting from lawful activities

1. If one or more activities create a significant risk of substantial harm as a result of a transboundary environmental interference, and if the overall technical and socio-economic cost or loss of benefits involved in preventing or reducing such risk far exceeds in the long run the advantage which such prevention or reduction would entail, the State which carried out or permitted the activities shall ensure that compensation is provided should substantial harm occur in an area under national jurisdiction of another State or in an area beyond the limits of national jurisdiction.

2. A State shall ensure that compensation is provided for substantial harm caused by transboundary environmental interferences resulting from activities carried

out or permitted by that State notwithstanding that the activities were not initially known to cause such interferences.

Article 12

Transboundary environmental interferences involving substantial harm far less than cost of prevention

1. If a State is planning to carry out or permit an activity which will entail a transboundary environmental interference causing harm which is substantial but far less than the overall technical and socio-economic cost or loss of benefits involved in preventing or reducing such interference, such State shall enter into negotiations with the affected State on the equitable conditions, both technical and financial, under which the activity could be carried out.

2. In the event of a failure to reach a solution on the basis of equitable principles within a period of 18 months after the beginning of the negotiations or within any other period of time agreed upon by the States concerned, the dispute shall at the request of any of the States concerned, and under the conditions set forth in Paragraphs 3 and 4 of Article 22, be submitted to conciliation or thereafter to arbitration or judicial settlement in order to reach a solution on the basis of equitable principles.

Article 13

Non-discrimination between domestic and transboundary environmental interferences

Without prejudice to the principles laid down in Articles 10, 11 and 12 when calling for a more stringent approach, States shall, when considering under their domestic policy or law the permissibility of an environmental interference or a significant risk thereof, take into account the detrimental effects which are or may be caused by the environmental interference without discrimination as to whether the effects would occur inside or outside the area under their national jurisdiction.

Article 14

General obligation to co-operate on transboundary environmental problems

1. States shall co-operate in good faith with the other States concerned in maintaining or attaining for each of them a reasonable and equitable use of a transboundary natural resource or in preventing or abating a transboundary environmental interference or significant risk thereof.

2. The co-operation shall, as much as possible, be aimed at arriving at an optimal use of the transboundary natural resource or at maximizing the effectiveness of measures to prevent or abate a transboundary environmental interference.

Article 15

Exchange of information

States shall provide the other States concerned upon their request and in a timely manner with all relevant and reasonably available data concerning a transboundary natural resource, including the uses made of such a resource and transboundary interferences with them, or concerning a transboundary environmental interference.

Article 16

Prior notice of planned activities, environmental impact assessments

1. States planning to carry out or permit activities which may entail a transboundary interference or a significant risk thereof with the reasonable and equitable use of

a transboundary natural resource or which may entail a transboundary environmental interference or a significant risk thereof causing substantial harm in an area under national jurisdiction of another State or in an area beyond the limits of national jurisdiction shall give timely notice to the States concerned. In particular, they shall on their own initiative or upon request of the other States concerned provide such relevant information as will permit those other States to make an assessment of the probable effects of the planned activities.

2. When a State has reasonable grounds for believing that planned activities may have the effects referred to in Paragraph 1, it shall make an assessment of those effects before carrying out or permitting the planned activities.

Article 17

Consultations

Consultations shall be held in good faith, upon request, at an early stage between, on the one hand, States whose reasonable and equitable use of a transboundary natural resource is or may be affected by a transboundary interference or whose environmental interests are or may be affected by a transboundary environmental interference and, on the other hand, States in whose area under national jurisdiction or under whose jurisdiction such a transboundary interference originates or may originate in connection with activities carried on or contemplated therein or thereunder.

Article 18

Co-operative arrangements for environmental assessment and protection

In order to maintain or attain a reasonable and equitable use of a transboundary natural resource or to prevent or abate transboundary environmental interferences or significant risks thereof the States concerned shall, inter alia:

(a) establish co-ordinated or unified systems for the collection and dissemination of data relating to the transboundary natural resource or for regular observation of transboundary environmental interferences;

(b) co-ordinate and, where appropriate, jointly undertake scientific or technical studies to that effect;

(c) establish by common agreement specific environmental standards, in particular environmental quality standards and emission standards;

(d) jointly establish or resort to an institutional mechanism or other appropriate arrangement.

Article 19

Emergency situations

1. In the case of an emergency situation or other change of circumstances suddenly giving rise to a transboundary interference or a significant risk thereof with the reasonable and equitable use of a transboundary natural resource or to a transboundary environmental interference or a significant risk thereof, causing substantial harm in an area under national jurisdiction of another State or in an area beyond the limits of national jurisdiction, the State in whose area under national jurisdiction or under whose jurisdiction the interference originates shall promptly warn the other States concerned, provide them with such pertinent information as will enable them to minimize the transboundary environmental interference, inform them of steps taken to abate the cause of the transboundary environmental interference, and co-operate with those States in order to prevent or minimize the harmful effects of such an emergency situation or other change of circumstances.

2. States shall develop contingency plans in order to prevent or minimize the harmful effects of an emergency situation or other change of circumstances referred to in Paragraph 1.

Article 20

Non-intergovernmental proceedings

States shall provide remedies for persons who have been or may be detrimentally affected by a transboundary interference with their use of a transboundary natural resource or by a transboundary environmental interference. In particular, States of origin shall grant those persons equal access as well as due process and equal treatment in the same administrative and judicial proceedings as are available to persons within their own jurisdiction who have been or may be similarly affected.

Article 21

1. A State is responsible under international law for a breach of an international obligation relating to the use of a natural resource or the prevention or abatement of an environmental interference.

2. In particular, it shall:

(a) cease the internationally wrongful act;

(b) as far as possible, re-establish the situation which would have existed if the internationally wrongful act had not taken place;

(c) provide compensation for the harm which results from the internationally wrongful act;

(d) where appropriate, give satisfaction for the internationally wrongful act.

PEACEFUL SETTLEMENT OF DISPUTES

Article 22

1. States, when they cannot avoid international disputes concerning the use of a natural resource or concerning an environmental interference in accordance with the preceding Articles, shall settle such disputes by peaceful means in such a manner that international peace and security, and justice, are not endangered.

2. States shall accordingly seek a settlement of such disputes by negotiation, good offices, enquiry, mediation, conciliation, arbitration, judicial settlement, resort to appropriate bodies or arrangements, whether global or regional, or by any other peaceful means of their own choice.

3. In the event of a failure to reach a solution by another non-binding peaceful means within a period of 18 months after the dispute has arisen or within any other period of time agreed upon by the States concerned, the dispute shall be submitted to conciliation at the request of any of the States concerned, unless it is agreed to proceed with an already agreed peaceful means or to submit the dispute to another binding or non-binding means of peaceful settlement.

4. In the event that the conciliation envisaged in Paragraph 3, or any other non-binding means of peaceful settlement resorted to in lieu thereof, does not lead to a solution of the dispute, the dispute shall be submitted to arbitration or judicial settlement at the request of any of the States concerned, unless it is agreed to submit the dispute to another means of peaceful settlement.

1.23 Restatement (Third) of the Foreign Relations Law of the United States. Adopted by the American Law Institute, 14 May 1987: *§§ 601–604 (with comments)*

§ 601. State Obligations with Respect to Environment of Other States and the Common Environment

(1) A state is obligated to take such measures as may be necessary, to the extent practicable under the circumstances, to ensure that activities within its jurisdiction or control

(a) conform to generally accepted international rules and standards for the prevention, reduction, and control of injury to the environment of another state or of areas beyond the limits of national jurisdiction; and

(b) are conducted so as not to cause significant injury to the environment of another state or of areas beyond the limits of national jurisdiction.

(2) A state is responsible to all other states

(a) for any violation of its obligations under Subsection (1)(a), and

(b) for any significant injury, resulting from such violation, to the environment of areas beyond the limits of national jurisdiction.

(3) A state is responsible for any significant injury, resulting from a violation of its obligations under Subsection (1), to the environment of another state or to its property, or to persons or property within that state's territory or under its jurisdiction or control.

Comment:

a. Application of general principles of state responsibility. This Part applies to environmental questions the general principles of international law relating to the responsibility of states for injury to another state or its property or to persons within its territory or their property, or for injury to interests common to all states. A state is responsible under Subsections (2) and (3) for breach of any of its obligations under Subsection (1). It is responsible under Subsection (2) to all states, and any state may request that it abate a threat of pollution and make arrangements to prevent future violations. Under Subsection (3), it is responsible to an injured state for any significant injury and is required to make reparation for the injury. The conditions of responsibility and the remedies available may differ with the circumstances and with the interests affected. See Comment *d* and § 602; see also the general principles in § 711 and §§ 901–902.

b. "Generally accepted international rules and standards." This phrase is adopted from the law of the sea; see § 502, Comment *c*. The obligation under Subsection (1)(a) refers to both general rules of customary international law (see, *e.g.*, the *Trail Smelter* case, Reporters' Note 1) and those derived from international conventions, and from standards adopted by international organizations pursuant to such conventions, that deal with a specific subject, such as oil pollution or radioactive wastes. See Reporters' Notes 3–7 and § 603, Reporters' Notes 4 and 5; see also § 102, Comments *f* and *g*, and § 103, Comment *c*. A state is also obligated to comply with an environmental rule or standard that has been accepted by both it and an injured state, even if that rule or standard has not been generally accepted.

Where an international rule or standard has been violated, any state can object to the violation; where a state has been injured in consequence of such violation, it is entitled to damages or other appropriate relief from the responsible state; where there is a threat of injury, the threatened state, or any state acting on behalf of threatened common interests, is entitled to have the dangerous activity terminated. See § 602.

c. "Activities within its jurisdiction" and "significant injury." An activity is considered to be within a state's jurisdiction under this section if the state may exercise jurisdiction to prescribe law with respect to that activity under §§ 402–403. The phrase "activities within its jurisdiction or control" includes activities in a state's territory, on the coastal waters that are under its jurisdiction, Part V, as well as activities on ships flying its flag or on installations on the high seas operating under its authority. See § 502(1)(b) and Comment *c* thereto, § 514, Comment *i* and § 521, Comment *c*. International law does not address internal pollution, but a state is responsible under this section if pollution within its jurisdiction causes significant injuries beyond its borders. "Significant injury" is not defined but references to "significant" impact on the environment are common in both international law and United States law. The word "significant" excludes minor incidents causing minimal damage. In special circumstances, the significance of injury to another state is balanced against the importance of the activity to the state causing the injury. See Reporters' Note 3.

d. Conditions of responsibility. A state is responsible under Subsections (2) and (3) for both its own activities and those of individuals or private or public corporations under its jurisdiction. The state may be responsible, for instance, for not enacting necessary legislation, for not enforcing its laws against persons acting in its territory or against its vessels, or for not preventing or terminating an illegal activity, or for not punishing the person responsible for it. In the case of ships flying its flags, a state is responsible for injury due to the state's own defaults under Subsection (1) but is not responsible for injury due to fault of the operators of the ship. In both cases, a state is responsible only if it has not taken "such measures as may be necessary" to comply with applicable international standards and to avoid causing injury outside its territory, as required by Subsection (1). In general, the applicable international rules and standards do not hold a state responsible when it has taken the necessary and practicable measures; some international agreements provide also for responsibility regardless of fault in case of a discharge of highly dangerous (radioactive, toxic, etc.) substances, or an abnormally dangerous activity (*e.g.*, launching of space satellites). See also the principles applicable to weather modification, Comment *f*. In all cases, however, some defenses may be available to the state; *e.g.*, that it had acted pursuant to a binding decision of the Security Council of the United Nations, or that injury was due to the failure of the injured state to exercise reasonable care to avoid the threatened harm. Compare Restatement, Second, Torts §§ 519, 520, and 524. A state is not responsible for injury due to a natural disaster such as an eruption of a volcano, unless such disaster was triggered or aggravated by a human act, such as nuclear explosion in a volcano's vicinity. But a state is responsible if after a natural disaster has occurred it does not take necessary and practicable steps to prevent or reduce injury to other states.

Under Subsections (2)(b) and (3), responsibility of a state for a significant injury entails payment of appropriate damages if the complaining state proves the existence of a causal link between an activity within the jurisdiction of the responsible state and the injury to the complaining state. Determination of responsibility raises special difficulties in cases of long-range pollution where the link between multiple activities in some distant states and the pollution in the injured state might be difficult to prove. Where more than one state contributes to the pollution causing significant injury, the liability will be apportioned among the states, taking into account, where appropriate, the contribution to the injury of the injured state itself.

A state is responsible under this section for environmental harm proximately caused by activity under its own jurisdiction, not for activity by another state. For instance, a state is not responsible under this section merely because it encourages activities in another state, such as plant eradication programs, that inflict environmental injury in that state or in a third state. Similarly, if a group of states imposes economic sanctions on state *A* depriving it of oil supplies and requiring state *A* to use coal, which results in an increase in air pollution in state *B*, the boycotting states are not responsible under principles of international environmental law for injury resulting to state *B*.

Although there has been no authoritative consideration of the issue, international environmental law has apparently not extended responsibility beyond the state directly responsible for the activities causing injury, under principles analogous to "product liability" which apply in some national legal systems. Thus, under this section, state *A* is responsible for a radioactive emission from a nuclear reactor operated in its territory that causes injury to state *B*, but there is no recognized responsibility to *B* by state *C* in which the defective reactor was manufactured or from which it was sold to state *A*. There may, however, be such responsibility pursuant to an international agreement between state *A* and state *C*, and in special circumstances under general principles of state responsibility. See, *e.g.*, §§ 207, 711, and 901. Also, there may be liability by the manufacturer or seller of the defective reactor, whether it is a state or a private person, under principles of national law applicable to the transaction. Compare, for example, Restatement, Second, Torts §§ 388–408.

Under this section, a state is obligated to take all necessary precautionary measures where an activity is contemplated that poses a substantial risk of a significant transfrontier environmental injury; if the activity has already taken place, the state is obligated to take all necessary measures to prevent or reduce pollution beyond its borders. Similarly, where a violation of international environmental rules and standards has already occurred, the violating state is obligated to take promptly all necessary preventive or remedial measures, even if no injury has yet taken place.

For the remedies for breach of obligations under this section, see § 602.

e. Obligation to notify and consult. Under Subsection 1(a), a state has an obligation to warn another state promptly of any situation that may cause significant pollution damage in that state. A state has also an obligation to consult with another state if a proposed activity within its jurisdiction or control poses a substantial risk of significant injury to the environment of the other state, but it need not permit such consultations to delay the proposed activity unduly.

f. Weather modification. Weather modification programs are normally used either to prevent injuries to the environment (*e.g.*, by a storm) or to obtain some benefit (*e.g.*, by causing rain during a drought). A state's weather modification programs have sometimes caused injury to another state, *e.g.*, by bringing it excessive rain or by depriving it of rain, or, by changing the direction of a storm, causing injury to that state's ships at sea, to its shore, or to the marine environment. Under international law, a state engaged in weather modification activities is responsible for any significant injuries if causation can be proved, even if the injury was neither intended nor due to negligence, and even if the state took all necessary measures to prevent or reduce injury. Compare the rule as to abnormally dangerous activities, Comment *d*.

* * *

§ 602. Remedies for Violation of Environmental Obligations

(1) A state responsible to another state for violation of § 601 is subject to general interstate remedies (§ 902) to prevent, reduce, or terminate the activity threatening or causing the violation, and to pay reparation for injury caused.

(2) Where pollution originating in a state has caused significant injury to persons outside that state, or has created a significant risk of such injury,

the state of origin is obligated to accord to the person injured or exposed to such risk access to the same judicial or administrative remedies as are available in similar circumstances to persons within the state.

Comment:

a. International law remedies. The remedies referred to in Subsection (1) usually begin with a protest against the violation, accompanied by a demand that the offending state terminate the violation, desist from further violations, and make reparation for past violations. If the matter is not resolved by diplomatic negotiations, the aggrieved state may resort to agreed third-party procedures, such as conciliation, mediation, arbitration, or adjudication. Some neighboring states have established international joint commissions to deal with transboundary problems, including pollution, but usually such commissions can only make recommendations. Strictly limited and reasonable measures of "self help" may be permitted in special circumstances. See § 905. Remedies under international law are to the injured state; whether that state is obligated to pay any reparation received over to any injured person in its territory is a matter of its domestic law. See § 902, Comments *i* and *l*.

Remedies under this section are available for injury to a state's environmental interests within its territory as well as to interests beyond its territory, such as injury to its fishing interests on the high seas; it may pursue remedies, not only for injury to state interests but also to those of its political subdivisions or of its inhabitants or nationals. A state may also pursue appropriate remedies for injury to the common interest in the global commons, such as the high seas.

Even where reparations for past injuries are not appropriate or feasible, a state may demand that violations be discontinued.

b. Local remedies. A state responsible for transfrontier pollution can fulfill its obligation to inhabitants of other states who suffered injuries by giving them access to its tribunals for adjudication of their claims. If such local remedies are available, the person who suffered injuries must exhaust these remedies before the state of which he is a national can bring an international claim on his behalf under Subsection (1). See § 703, Comment *d*; § 713, Comments *b* and *f*; § 902, Comment *k*. The two states, however, may agree at any time to settle the claim or include it in a lump-sum settlement. See § 902, Comment *i*.

Subsection (2) applies the principle of non-discrimination against foreign nationals (§ 711, Comment *f*). This principle requires that a state in which pollution originates avoid discrimination in the enforcement of applicable international rules and standards, as well as give to foreign victims the benefit of its own rules and standards for the protection of the environment, even if they are stricter than the international rules or standards. Subsection (2) applies the principle of nondiscrimination also to remedies. A state must provide the same procedures, and apply the same substantive law and the same measures of compensation, to persons outside its territory as are available to persons injured within its territory. Thus, a state applying the "polluter-pays" principle should apply it to all pollution originating within the state, whether it causes injury at home or abroad. If a state applies the principle of strict liability, a victim of transfrontier pollution will be entitled to the benefit of that principle. On the other hand, if the state makes liability conditional on fault or negligence, the foreign victim can be required to meet that condition even if in the place of injury fault or negligence is not a necessary element for liability. Similarly, if a state's law imposes an obligation to reduce pollution to the lowest level that is attainable by the application of the most advanced technology that is economically feasible, this requirement applies equally to pollution at home and abroad.

When environmental injury in one state results from private activity in another state, a remedy may sometimes be available in the courts of the victim state, or even of a third state, and if the victim has received satisfaction by such a remedy the interstate remedy would abate.

c. *Availability of private remedies under state law.* Under the law of many states, pollution damage is considered a local tort; suit for damages lies only in the state where the injury occurred, not in the state where the pollution originated. If personal jurisdiction over the person responsible for the pollution can be obtained in the state where the injury occurred, a suit for compensation or for an injunction would lie, but such suit might not be possible if the alleged polluter has no business or property in that state. Even if a suit there is brought under a long-arm statute and results in a default judgment, the judgment might not be enforceable in the polluter's home state. See § 421(2)(j) and § 481, Reporters' Note 4.

* * *

§ 603. State Responsibility for Marine Pollution

(1) A state is obligated

(a) to adopt laws and regulations to prevent, reduce, and control any significant pollution of the marine environment that are no less effective than generally accepted international rules and standards; and

(b) to ensure compliance with the laws and regulations adopted pursuant to clause (a) by ships flying its flag, and, in case of a violation, to impose adequate penalties on the owner or captain of the ship.

(2) A state is obligated to take, individually and jointly with other states, such measures as may be necessary, to the extent practicable under the circumstances, to prevent, reduce, and control pollution causing or threatening to cause significant injury to the marine environment.

Source Note:

This section is based on Articles 194, 207–12, 217, and 220 of the 1982 Convention on the Law of the Sea.

Comment:

a. *State responsibility for marine pollution.* This section applies the principles of § 601 to marine pollution. In fulfilling their obligations under this section, states must use "the best practicable means at their disposal and in accordance with their capabilities," and must "endeavour to harmonize their policies in this connection." LOS Convention, Article 194(1). In taking measures to prevent, reduce, or control pollution, states are obligated to implement any pertinent international rules and standards, and to refrain from unjustifiable interference with activities carried out by other states in exercise of their rights and in pursuance of their duties in conformity with international law. Articles 194(4) and 213–22.

The measures to be taken must "minimize to the fullest possible extent" the release of toxic, harmful, or noxious substances from land-based sources (such as rivers, estuaries, pipelines, and sewers), from or through the atmosphere, or by dumping of waste. Articles 194(3), 207, 210, and 212. In order to limit pollution from ships, all states must take measures for preventing accidents and dealing with emergencies, ensuring the safety of operations at sea, and preventing harmful discharges, whether intentional or unintentional. Navigational routing systems should also be designed to minimize the danger of accidents. Articles 194(3)(b) and 211(1). For the obligations of flag states, see Comment *b*; for the obligations of states engaged in sea-bed mining, see Comment *c*.

Under the principles of § 601(2) and (3), a state is responsible for injuries caused by pollution resulting from a violation of its obligations under this section to a coast or coastal waters of another state or to the marine areas beyond the limits of national jurisdiction, *i.e.,* areas of the sea not included in internal waters, the territorial sea, or the exclusive economic zone of a state, or in the archipelagic waters of an archipelagic state. See Article 86. State responsibility extends to injuries such as those caused by pollution, *e.g.,* by: toxic or noxious substances flowing down-river into the sea and moving into the coastal waters of a neighboring state; sewage drifting from the coastal waters of one state to the coast of another state; toxic or noxious substances dumped, or garbage or fuel discharged, by ships flying the flag of one state and landing on the coast of another state; or oil spills, mineral tailings, or other discharges from installations for exploration and exploitation of oil or polymetallic nodules that contaminate the high seas or are moved by currents to the waters or coast of another state.

b. Obligations of flag state. The flag state has the primary obligation to ensure that its ships respect generally accepted international anti-pollution rules and standards established through the competent international organization or general diplomatic conference, and that they comply with the state's laws and regulations implementing such rules and standards. A flag state is obligated to prohibit its ships from sailing unless they have complied with such international rules and standards, and have also met standards set by the state's own laws, especially those relating to design, construction, equipment, and manning of ships; to require its ships to carry on board certificates of compliance with the international rules; and to inspect its ships periodically to verify that their condition conforms to the certificates they carry. Other states must accept the certificates issued by the flag state as evidence of the condition of the ship, unless there are clear grounds for believing that the condition of the ship does not correspond substantially to the certificates. Article 217(1)–(3).

The flag state is obligated to provide for penalties for pollution by its vessels adequate in severity to discourage violations. Article 217(8). For further enforcement obligations of the flag state, see § 604, Comment *c.*

c. Obligations of sea-bed mining states. States are obligated to adopt laws, regulations, and other measures for preventing, reducing, and controlling pollution of the marine environment arising from or in connection with their exploration and exploitation of the sea-bed and subsoil, or from artificial islands, installations, and structures under their jurisdiction that are operating in the marine environment. Such laws, regulations, and measures must be no less effective than international rules, standards, and recommended practices and procedures. Articles 194(3)(c) and (d) and 208.

d. Protection of fragile ecosystems. States are obligated to take measures necessary to protect and preserve rare or fragile ecosystems, and the habitat of depleted, threatened, or endangered species and other forms of marine life. Where the area to be protected forms part of a state's exclusive economic zone, the competent international organization may authorize that state to implement special international rules and standards applicable to such zones. Articles 194(5) and 211(6).

A coastal state also has the right to adopt and enforce nondiscriminatory laws and regulations for the prevention, reduction, and control of marine pollution from vessels in ice-covered areas within the limits of its exclusive economic zone, where particularly severe climatic conditions and the presence of ice for most of the year create obstructions or exceptional hazards to navigation, and where pollution of the marine environment could cause major harm to, or irreversible disturbance of, the ecological balance. The coastal state is obligated to base such laws and regulations on the best available scientific evidence and to have due regard to navigation. Article 234.

e. Obligation to notify. When a state becomes aware that the marine environment has been injured or is in imminent danger of being injured, it is obligated immediately to notify other states likely to be affected by such injuries as well as the competent global or regional international organization. Article 198.

f. Joint action in emergencies. States in an area affected by a maritime pollution disaster are obligated to cooperate in eliminating the effects of pollution and in preventing or minimizing injury. To be able to deal better with such emergencies, neighboring states are obligated to develop and be ready to put into operation contingency plans for responding to pollution incidents affecting the marine environment in their vicinity. Article 199.

g. Pollution by aircraft. States are responsible under this section for pollution of the marine environment by aircraft of their registry, *e.g.*, by noxious emissions. States are obligated to adopt laws and regulations to prevent, reduce, and control such pollution, taking into account internationally agreed rules, standards, and recommended practices and procedures adopted by the International Civil Aviation Organization, but must not prejudice thereby the safety of air navigation. Article 212.

* * *

§ 604. Remedies for Marine Pollution

(1) A state responsible to another state for a violation of the principles of § 603 is subject to general interstate remedies (§ 902) to prevent, reduce, or terminate the activity threatening or causing pollution, and to pay reparation for injury caused.

(2) A state is obligated to ensure that a remedy is available, in accordance with its legal system, to provide prompt and adequate compensation or other relief for an injury to private interests caused by pollution of the marine environment resulting from a violation of § 603.

(3) In addition to remedies that may be available to it under Subsection (1):

(a) a coastal state may detain, and institute proceedings against, a foreign ship:

(i) navigating in its territorial sea, for a violation therein of antipollution laws that the coastal state adopted in accordance with applicable international rules and standards; or

(ii) navigating in its territorial sea or its exclusive economic zone, for a violation in that zone of applicable international antipollution rules and standards that resulted in a discharge causing or threatening a major injury to the coastal state;

(b) a port state may institute proceedings against a foreign ship that has voluntarily come into that state's port,

(i) for a violation of the port state's antipollution laws adopted in accordance with applicable international rules and standards, if the violation had occurred in the port state's territorial sea or exclusive economic zone; or

(ii) for a discharge in violation of applicable international antipollution rules and standards that had occurred beyond the limits of national jurisdiction of any state; and

(c) a port state is obligated to investigate, as far as practicable, whether a foreign ship that has voluntarily come into that state's port was responsible for a discharge in violation of applicable international antipollution rules and standards,

(i) at the request of another state, where the discharge was alleged to have occurred in waters subject to that state's jurisdiction, or to have caused or threatened damage to that state; or

(ii) at the request of the flag state, irrespective of where the violation was alleged to have occurred.

Source Note:

This section is based on Articles 211, 217–18, 220, and 228 of the 1982 Convention on the Law of the Sea.

Comment:

a. Ordinary remedies between states. Subsection (1) states that ordinary international remedies are available for violations of obligations under § 603 as for violations of other obligations under international environmental law (§ 602), or of international obligations generally (§ 902). A state is responsible for a violation of international antipollution rules and standards, resulting from an act or omission by state officials or public vessels, or by ships, aircraft, platforms, or other structures at sea, or by natural or juridical persons, that are under the state's jurisdiction.

Interstate remedies may include claims for reparation for injury to the state or its political subdivisions, or injury to its nationals or inhabitants when they are not afforded reparation by domestic remedy in the offending state. See Subsection (2) and Comment *b*. The obligations of states in respect of the common environment are *erga omnes* and any state may pursue remedies for violations that inflict significant injury on that environment (for instance, to obtain termination of the wrongful conduct). See also Comment *c*.

b. Remedies for private injury. Under Subsection (2), when a natural or juridical person for whose acts a state is responsible under § 601 has caused injury to interests of a private person who is not the state's own national or resident, the state must provide to the injured person access to domestic remedies so that prompt and adequate compensation or preventive or injunctive relief may be obtained. See LOS Convention, Article 235. Where the injury results from a violation by a private ship or installation, the owner is presumably liable under domestic law, and the responsibility of the state is invoked only where adequate reparation is not obtained from the person responsible by domestic remedies. If complex patterns of ownership and agency make it difficult to determine who was legally liable under domestic law for the violation causing the injury, the state is responsible for ensuring that the injured person is compensated.

c. Enforcement by flag states. In addition to the remedies set forth in Comments *a* and *b*, if a ship has committed a violation of applicable international rules and standards, the flag state is obligated to investigate immediately and to institute appropriate proceedings, irrespective of the place of the violation or injury. See LOS Convention, Article 217. The state that is the victim of a violation by a ship (or, in case of pollution of the common environment, any state) may complain to the flag state and request that the guilty persons be punished and be enjoined from further pollution (see Articles 217(6) and 235); if dissatisfied with action taken by the flag state, it may invoke against the flag state the remedies available under international law. Subsection (1) and Comment *a*. In addition, if the flag state has repeatedly disregarded its obligations to enforce effectively the applicable international rules and standards in respect of violations committed by its ships, a port state where proceedings against a ship have been instituted under Subsection (3)(b) or (c) may continue such proceedings and impose penalties, regardless of a request of the flag state that the proceedings be transferred to it. See Comment *e*; LOS Convention, Article 228(1).

d. Enforcement by coastal states. The authority of the coastal state to bring proceedings against an offending foreign vessel (Subsection 3(a)) varies according to where the vessel is located and where the violation occurred. The coastal state has jurisdiction to prescribe, adjudicate, and enforce with respect to acts of pollution committed in its ports. The coastal state can also institute proceedings against a ship voluntarily in port, or against its crew, for a violation of its laws that occurred within its territorial sea or exclusive economic zone, provided that its laws were adopted in accordance with applicable international rules and standards. An offshore terminal is assimilated to a port for these purposes. LOS Convention, Article 220(1).

Where there are clear grounds for believing that a foreign ship, while passing through the territorial sea of the coastal state, violated laws and regulations of that state adopted in accordance with applicable international rules and standards, the coastal state may, subject to certain procedural safeguards (see Article 226), undertake physical inspection of the vessel in the territorial sea in order to ascertain the facts relating to the violation. Where evidence so warrants, the coastal state may institute proceedings against the ship, in accordance with its laws, and may detain the ship pending such proceedings. Article 220(2); see also Articles 19(2)(h), 21(1)(f), and 27.

When a violation of applicable international antipollution rules and standards is committed in the exclusive economic zone of the coastal state, and the ship is still in the zone or in the territorial sea of the coastal state, that state can take various steps, depending on the gravity of the violation. Where there are clear grounds for believing that a violation has occurred, the coastal state may require the ship to identify itself and its port of registry, indicate its last and its next port of call, and provide other relevant information needed to establish whether a violation has occurred. When there are clear grounds for believing that the violation resulted in "a substantial discharge causing or threatening significant pollution of the marine environment," and the ship either refuses to give information or the information supplied is manifestly at variance with the facts, the coastal state is entitled to proceed with a physical inspection. Only if there is "clear objective evidence" that the ship committed the violation and that the discharge is causing or threatens to cause "major damage to the coastline or related interests of the coastal state, or to any resources of its territorial sea or exclusive economic zone," is that state entitled to institute proceedings in accordance with its laws, and to detain the ship. Article 220(3)–(6).

To ensure that a ship is not unduly detained, appropriate procedures must be established, either through the competent international organization or by special agreement, for bonding or other appropriate financial security. If the ship makes the necessary arrangements, the coastal state is obligated to allow the vessel to proceed. Only monetary penalties may be imposed, unless the violation was committed in the territorial sea and the act of pollution was willful and serious, in which case the vessel may be confiscated and the person responsible may be tried and punished. Articles 220(7) and 230.

The principle of sovereign immunity protects warships, warplanes, and other government ships and aircraft on noncommercial service against coastal state proceedings, but the flag state is obligated to ensure that such ships or aircraft act in a manner consistent, as far as is reasonable and practicable, with applicable international rules and standards. Article 236.

e. Enforcement by port states. The jurisdiction of the port state with respect to a foreign ship voluntarily in its port or offshore terminal includes authority for the state to investigate and, where the evidence warrants, to institute proceedings with respect to any discharge from that ship that occurred on the high seas. The port state may also institute proceedings if an unlawful discharge outside its coastal waters caused or is likely to cause pollution within those waters. If the discharge occurred in the coastal waters of another state, the port state is obligated to institute proceedings, as far as practicable, when requested by that state. In addition, under Subsection (3)(c), the port state is obligated to conduct an investigation, as far as practicable, when so requested by the flag state, or by a state damaged or threatened by the discharge. LOS Convention, Article 218(1)–(4).

The records of the investigation carried out by a port state must be transmitted to the state that asked for the investigation if it so requests. The state in whose coastal waters the violation took place, but not the state where the injury occurred, is entitled to have the proceedings transferred to it. Once the records, the evidence, and the bonds (or other financial security) are transmitted to the requesting state, the proceedings in the port state must be suspended. Article 218(4).

The flag state is entitled to have penal proceedings against its ship in a foreign state suspended as soon as the flag state has itself instituted proceedings against the ship. However, the state that has instituted the proceedings need not suspend them (1) if the violation was committed in its territorial sea; (2) if the coastal state suffered major damage; or (3) if the flag state "has repeatedly disregarded its obligations to enforce effectively the applicable international rules and standards in respect of violations committed by its vessels." A proceeding that is suspended is to be terminated upon completion of proceedings in the flag state. Article 228(1). If the coastal state is dissatisfied with the action taken by the flag state after the case has been transferred, it may protest both to the flag state and to the competent international organization; and if the lack of enforcement recurs, the coastal state may refuse to suspend proceedings on a future occasion.

f. Liability for wrongful enforcement measures. If a state has taken measures against a foreign ship that were unlawful or exceeded those reasonably required in the light of available information, it is obligated to pay the flag state for any injury or loss attributable to such measures. It must provide for recourse in its courts for private actions in respect of such injury or loss. LOS Convention, Article 232.

1.24 DECLARATION OF THE HAGUE. Concluded at the Hague, 11 March 1989. U.N.Doc. A/44/340–E/1989/120 (Annex) (1989); *reprinted in* 28 I.L.M. 1308 (1989) & 5 Weston V.E.13

The right to live is the right from which all other rights stem. Guaranteeing this right is the paramount duty of those in charge of all States throughout the world.

Today, the very conditions of life on our planet are threatened by the severe attacks to which the earth's atmosphere is subjected.

Authoritative scientific studies have shown the existence and scope of considerable dangers linked in particular to the warming of the atmosphere and to the deterioration of the ozone layer. The latter has already led to action, under the 1985 Vienna Convention for the Protection of the Ozone Layer and the 1987 Montreal Protocol, while the former is being addressed by the Intergovernmental Panel on Climatic Change established by UNEP and WMO, which has just begun its work. In addition the UN General Assembly adopted Resolution 43/53 on the Protection of the Global Climate in 1988, recognizing climate change as a common concern of mankind.

According to present scientific knowledge, the consequences of these phenomena may well jeopardize ecological systems as well as the most vital interests of mankind at large.

Because the problem is planet-wide in scope, solutions can only be devised on a global level. Because of the nature of the dangers involved, remedies to be sought involve not only the fundamental duty to preserve the ecosystem, but also the right to live in dignity in a viable global environment, and the consequent duty of the community of nations vis-à-vis present and future generations to do all that can be done to preserve the quality of the atmosphere.

Therefore we consider that, faced with a problem the solution to which has three salient features, namely that it is vital, urgent and global, we are in a situation that calls not only for implementation of existing principles but also for a new approach, through the development of new principles of international law including new and more effective decision-making and enforcement mechanisms.

What is needed here are regulatory, supportive and adjustment measures that take into account the participation and potential contribution of countries which have reached different levels of development. Most of the emissions that affect the atmosphere at present originate in the industrialized nations. And it is in these same nations that the room for change is greatest, and these nations are also those which have the greatest resources to deal with this problem effectively.

The international community and especially the industrialized nations have special obligations to assist developing countries which will be very negatively affected by changes in the atmosphere although the responsibility of many of them for the process may only be marginal today.

Financial institutions and development agencies, be they international or domestic, must coordinate their activities in order to promote sustainable development.

Without prejudice to the international obligations of each State, the signatories acknowledge and will promote the following principles:

(*a*) The principle of developing, within the framework of the United Nations, new institutional authority, either by strengthening existing institutions or by creating a new institution, which, in the context of the preservation of the earth's atmosphere, shall be responsible for combating any further global warming of the atmosphere and shall involve such decision-making procedures as may be effective even if, on occasion, unanimous agreement has not been achieved;

(*b*) The principle that this institutional authority undertake or commission the necessary studies, be granted appropriate information upon request, ensure the circulation and exchange of scientific and technological information—including facilitation of access to the technology needed—, develop instruments and define standards to enhance or guarantee the protection of the atmosphere and monitor compliance herewith;

(*c*) The principle of appropriate measures to promote the effective implementation of and compliance with the decisions of the new institutional authority, decisions which will be subject to control by the International Court of Justice;

(*d*) The principle that countries to which decisions taken to protect the atmosphere shall prove to be an abnormal or special burden, in view, inter alia, of the level of their development and actual responsibility for the deterioration of the atmosphere, shall receive fair and equitable assistance to compensate them for bearing such burden. To this end mechanisms will have to be developed;

(*e*) The negotiation of the necessary legal instruments to provide an effective and coherent foundation, institutionally and financially, for the aforementioned principles.

The Heads of State and Government or their representatives, who have expressed their endorsement of this Declaration by placing their signatures under it, stress their resolve to promote the principles thus defined by:

— furthering the development of their initiative within the United Nations and in close coordination and collaboration with existing agencies set up under the auspices of the United Nations;

— inviting all States of the world and the international organisations competent in this field to join in developing, taking into account studies by the IPCC, the framework conventions and other legal instruments necessary to establish institutional authority and to implement the other principles stated above to protect the atmosphere and to counter climate change, particularly global warming;

— urging all States of the world and the international organisations competent in this field to sign and ratify conventions relating to the protection of nature and the environment;

— calling upon all States of the world to endorse the present declaration.

The original of this Declaration, drawn up in French and English, will be transmitted to the Government of the Kingdom of the Netherlands, which will retain it in its archives. Each of the participating States will receive from the Government of the Kingdom of the Netherlands a true copy of this Declaration.

The Prime Minister of the Netherlands is requested to transmit the text of this Declaration, which is not eligible for registration under Article 102 of the Charter of the United Nations, to all members of the United Nations.

1.25 The Langkawi Declaration on Environment. Adopted by the Commonwealth Heads of Government at Langkawi (Malaysia), 21 October 1989. *Reprinted in* 5 A.J.I.L. 589 (1990) & 5 Weston V.C.9

We, the Heads of Government of the Commonwealth, representing a quarter of the world's population and a broad cross-section of global interests, are deeply concerned at the serious deterioration in the environment and the threat this poses to the well-being of present and future generations. Any delay in taking action to halt this progressive deterioration will result in permanent and irreversible damage.

2. The current threat to the environment, which is a common concern of all mankind, stems essentially from past neglect in managing the natural environment and resources. The environment has been degraded by decades of industrial and other forms of pollution, including unsafe disposal of toxic wastes, the burning of fossil fuels, nuclear testing and non-sustainable practices in agriculture, fishery and forestry.

3. The main environment problems facing the world are the greenhouse effect (which may lead to severe climatic changes that could induce floods, droughts and rising sea levels), the depletion of the ozone layer, acid rain, marine pollution, land degradation and the extinction of numerous animal and plant species. Some developing countries also face distinct environmental problems arising from poverty and population pressure. In addition, some islands and low-lying areas of other countries, are threatened by the prospect of rising sea level.

4. Many environmental problems transcend national boundaries and interests, necessitating a co-ordinated global effort. This is particularly true in areas outside national jurisdiction, and where there is transboundary pollution on land and in the oceans, atmosphere and outer space.

5. The need to protect the environment should be viewed in a balanced perspective and due emphasis be accorded to promoting economic growth and sustainable development, including eradication of poverty, meeting basic needs, and enhancing the quality of life. The responsibility for ensuring a better environment should be equitably shared and the ability of developing countries to respond be taken into account.

6. To achieve sustainable development, economic growth is a compelling necessity. Sustainable development implies the incorporation of environmental concerns into economic planning and policies. Environmental concerns should not be used to introduce a new form of conditionality in aid and development financing, nor as a pretext for creating unjustified barriers to trade.

7. The success of global and national environmental programmes requires mutually reinforcing strategies and the participation and commitment of all levels of society—government, individuals and organisations, industry and the scientific community.

8. Recognising that our shared environment binds all countries to a common future, we, the Heads of Government of the Commonwealth, resolved to act collectively and individually, commit ourselves to the following programme of action:

— advance policies and programmes which help achieve sustainable development, including the development of new and better techniques in integrating the environmental dimension in economic decision-making;

— strengthen and support the development of international funding mechanisms and appropriate decision-making procedures to respond to environmental protection needs which will include assisting developing countries to obtain access to and transfer of needed environmental technologies and which should take account of proposals for an international environment fund/Planet Protection Fund;

— support the work of the UNEP/WMO Intergovernmental Panel on Climate Change (IPCC);

— call for the early conclusion of an international convention to protect and conserve the global climate and, in this context, applaud the efforts of member governments to advance the negotiation of a framework convention under UN auspices;

— support the findings and recommendations of the Commonwealth Expert Group's Report on Climate Change as a basis for achievable action to develop strategies for adapting to climate change and for reducing greenhouse gas emissions, as well as making an important contribution to the work of the IPCC;

— support measures to improve energy conservation and energy efficiency;

— promote the reduction and eventual phase-out of substances depleting the ozone layer;

— promote afforestation and agricultural practices in developed and developing countries to arrest the increase in atmospheric carbon dioxide and halt the deterioration of land and water resources;

— strengthen efforts by developing countries in sustainable forest management and their manufacture and export of higher value-added forest products and, in this regard, support the activities of the International Tropical Timber Organisation and the Food and Agriculture Organisation's Tropical Forestry Action Plan, as well as take note of the recommendations of the 13th Commonwealth Forestry Conference;

— support activities related to the conservation of biological diversity and genetic resources, including the conservation of significant areas of virgin forest and other protected natural habitats;

— support low-lying and island countries in their efforts to protect themselves and their vulnerable natural marine ecosystems from the effects of sea level rise;

— discourage and restrict non-sustainable fishing practices and seek to ban tangle net and pelagic drift net fishing;

— support efforts to prevent marine pollution including curbing ocean dumping of toxic wastes;

— strengthen international action to ensure the safe management and disposal of hazardous wastes and to reduce transboundary movements, particularly to prevent dumping in developing countries;

— participate in relevant international agreements relating to the environment and promote new and innovated instruments which will attract widespread support for protecting the global environment; and

— strengthen national, regional and international institutions responsible for environmental protection as well as the promotion of active programmes on environmental education to heighten public awareness and support.

9. We, the Heads of Government of the Commonwealth, resolve to take immediate and positive actions on the basis of the above programme. In this regard, we pledge our full support for the convening of the 1992 UN Conference on Environment and Development.

10. We call on the international community to join us in the endeavour.

1.26 AFRICAN, CARIBBEAN AND PACIFIC STATES—EUROPEAN ECONOMIC COMMUNITY CONVENTION (LOMÉ IV) (Without Protocols). Concluded at Lomé (Togo), 15 December 1989. Entered into force, 1 September 1991. 1990 E.C. 120; *reprinted in* 29 I.L.M. 783 (1990) & 4 Weston IV.B.12: *Arts. 33–41 (Title I) and Annex VIII*

TITLE I

Environment

Article 33

In the framework of this Convention, the protection and the enhancement of the environment and natural resources, the halting of the deterioration of land and forests, the restoration of ecological balances, the preservation of natural resources and their rational exploitation are basic objectives that the ACP States concerned shall strive to achieve with Community support, with a view to bringing an immediate improvement in the living conditions of their populations and to safeguarding those of future generations.

Article 34

The ACP States and the Community recognize that the existence of some ACP States is under threat as a result of a rapid deterioration of the environment that hinders any development efforts, in particular those aimed at achieving the priority objectives of food self-sufficiency and food security.

For many ACP States, efforts to halt this deterioration of the environment and conserve natural resources are imperative and call for the preparation and implementation of coherent modes of development that have due regard for ecological balances.

Article 35

The dimension of the environmental problem and of the means to be deployed mean that operations will have to be carried out in the context of overall, long-term policies, drawn up and implemented by the ACP States at national, regional and international levels with international support.

To this end, the Parties agree to give priority in their activities to:

— a preventive approach aimed at avoiding harmful effects on the environment as a result of any programme or operation;

— a systematic approach that will ensure ecological viability at all stages, from identification to implementation;

— a trans-sectoral approach that takes into account not only the direct but also the indirect consequences of the operations undertaken.

Article 36

The protection of the environment and natural resources requires a comprehensive approach embracing the social and cultural dimensions.

In order to ensure that this specific dimension shall be taken into account, attention shall be given to incorporating suitable educational, training, information and research schemes in projects and programmes.

Article 37

Cooperation instruments appropriate to environmental needs shall be designed and implemented.

Where necessary, both qualitative and quantitative criteria may be used. Jointly approved check-lists shall be used to help estimate the environmental viability of proposed operations, whatever their scale. Environmental impact assessment will be carried out as appropriate in the case of large-scale projects and those posing a significant threat to the environment.

For the proper integration of environmental considerations, physical inventories, where possible translated into accounting terms, shall be drawn up.

The implementation of these instruments has to ensure that, should an adverse environmental impact be foreseen, the necessary corrective measures are formulated in the early stage of the preparation of the proposed project or programme so that it can go ahead in accordance with the planned timetable though improved in terms of environmental and natural resource protection.

Article 38

The Parties, desirous of bringing real protection and effective management to the environment and natural resources, consider that the areas of ACP–EEC cooperation covered in Part Two of this Convention shall be systematically examined and appraised in this light.

In this spirit the Community shall support efforts made by the ACP States at national, regional and international levels and also operations mounted by intergovernmental and nongovernmental organizations in furtherance of national and intergovernmental policies and priorities.

Article 39

1. The Contracting Parties undertake, for their part, to make every effort to ensure that international movements of hazardous waste and radioactive waste are generally controlled, and they emphasize the importance of efficient international cooperation in this area.

With this in view, the Community shall prohibit all direct or indirect export of such waste to the ACP States while at the same time the ACP States shall prohibit the direct or indirect import into their territory of such waste from the Community or from any other country, without prejudice to specific international undertakings to which the Contracting Parties have subscribed or may subscribe in the future in these two areas within the competent international fora.

These provisions do not prevent a Member State to which an ACP State has chosen to export waste for processing from returning the processed waste to the ACP State of origin.

The Contracting Parties shall expedite adoption of the necessary internal legislation and administrative regulations to implement this undertaking. At the request of one of the Parties, consultations may be held if delays are encountered. At the conclusion of such consultations each Party may take appropriate steps in the light of the situation.

2. The Parties undertake to monitor strictly the implementation of the prohibition measures referred to in the second paragraph of paragraph 1. Should difficulties arise in this respect, consultations may be held subject to the same conditions as those provided for in the second paragraph of paragraph 1 and with the same effect.

3. The term "hazardous waste" within the meaning of this Article shall cover categories of products listed in Annexes 1 and 2 to the Basle Convention on the Control of Transboundary Movements of Hazardous Wastes and their Disposal.

As regards radioactive waste, the applicable definitions and thresholds shall be those which will be laid down in the framework of the IAEA. In the meantime, the said definitions and thresholds shall be those specified in the declaration in Annex VIII to this Convention.

* * *

Article 40

At the request of the ACP States, the Community shall provide available technical information on pesticides and other chemical products with a view to helping them develop or reinforce a suitable and safe use of these products. Where necessary and in accordance with the provisions for development finance cooperation, technical assistance can be given in order to ensure conditions of safety at all stages, from production to disposal of such products.

Article 41

The Parties recognize the value of exchanging views, using existing consultation mechanisms under this Convention, on major ecological hazards, whether on a planetary scale (such as the greenhouse effect, the deterioration of the ozone layer, tropical forests, etc.), or of a more specific scope resulting from the application of industrial technology. Such consultations may be requested by either Party, insofar as these hazards may in practice affect the Contracting Parties, and will be aimed at assessing the scope for joint action to be undertaken within the terms of this Convention. If necessary, the consultations will also provide for an exchange of views prior to discussions conducted on these subjects in the appropriate international fora.

* * *

ANNEX VIII

Joint declaration on Article 39 on movements of hazardous waste or radioactive waste

Keenly aware of the specific risks attaching to radioactive waste, the Contracting Parties will refrain from any practice of discharging such waste which would encroach upon the sovereignty of States or threaten the environment or public health in other countries. They attach the greatest importance to developing international cooperation to protect the environment and public health against such risks. They accordingly affirm their determination to play an active part in the work being done in the IAEA to produce an internationally approved code of good practice.

Until such time as a more precise definition is formulated in that framework, the term "radioactive waste" will be taken to mean any material for which no further use is envisaged and which contains or is contaminated by radionuclides of which the levels of radioactivity or the concentrations exceed the limits which the Community has set itself for protecting its own population in Article 4(a) and (b) of Directive 80/836 EURATOM, as last amended by Directive 84/467/EURATOM. As regards levels or radioactivity, these limits range from 5×10^3 becquerel for nuclides of very high radiotoxicity to 5×10^6 becquerel for those of low radiotoxicity. As regards concentrations, these limits are 100 $Bq.g^{-1}$ and 500 $Bq.g^{-1}$ for solid natural radioactive substances.

1.27 Convention on Environmental Impact Assessment in a Transboundary Context. Adopted at Espoo (Finland), 25 February 1991. Entered into force, 10 September 1997. *Reprinted in* 30 I.L.M. 800 (1991) & 5 Weston V.B.15

The Parties to this Convention,

Aware of the interrelationship between economic activities and their environmental consequences,

Affirming the need to ensure environmentally sound and sustainable development,

Determined to enhance international co-operation in assessing environmental impact, in particular in a transboundary context,

Mindful of the need and importance to develop anticipatory policies and of preventing, mitigating and monitoring significant adverse environmental impact in general and more specifically in a transboundary context,

Recalling the relevant provisions of the Charter of the United Nations, the Declaration of the Stockholm Conference on the Human Environment, the Final Act of the Conference on Security and Co-operation in Europe (CSCE) and the Concluding Documents of the Madrid and Vienna Meetings of Representatives of the Participating States of the CSCE,

Commending the ongoing activities of States to ensure that, through their national legal and administrative provisions and their national policies, environmental impact assessment is carried out,

Conscious of the need to give explicit consideration to environmental factors at an early stage in the decision-making process by applying environmental impact assessment, at all appropriate administrative levels, as a necessary tool to improve the quality of information presented to decision makers so that environmentally sound decisions can be made paying careful attention to minimizing significant adverse impact, particularly in a transboundary context,

Mindful of the efforts of international organizations to promote the use of environmental impact assessment both at the national and international levels, and taking into account work on environmental impact assessment carried out under the auspices of the United Nations Economic Commission for Europe, in particular results achieved by the Seminar on Environmental Impact Assessment (September 1987, Warsaw, Poland) as well as noting the Goals and Principles on environmental impact assessment adopted by the Governing Council of the United Nations Environment Programme, and the Ministerial Declaration on Sustainable Development (May 1990, Bergen, Norway),

Have agreed as follows:

Article 1

Definitions

For the purposes of this Convention;

(i) "Parties" means, unless the text otherwise indicates, the Contracting Parties to this Convention;

(ii) "Party of origin" means the Contracting Party or Parties to this Convention under whose jurisdiction a proposed activity is envisaged to take place;

(iii) "Affected Party" means the Contracting Party or Parties to this Convention likely to be affected by the transboundary impact of a proposed activity;

(iv) "Concerned Parties" means the Party of origin and the affected Party of an environmental impact assessment pursuant to this Convention;

(v) "Proposed activity" means any activity or any major change to an activity subject to a decision of a competent authority in accordance with an applicable national procedure;

(vi) "Environmental impact assessment" means a national procedure for evaluating the likely impact of a proposed activity on the environment;

(vii) "Impact" means any effect caused by a proposed activity on the environment including human health and safety, flora, fauna, soil, air, water, climate, landscape and historical monuments or other physical structures or the interaction among these factors; it also includes effects on cultural heritage or socio-economic conditions resulting from alterations to those factors;

(viii) "Transboundary impact" means any impact, not exclusively of a global nature, within an area under the jurisdiction of a Party caused by a proposed activity the physical origin of which is situated wholly or in part within the area under the jurisdiction of another Party;

* * *

(ix) "Competent authority" means the national authority or authorities designated by a Party as responsible for performing the tasks covered by this Convention and/or the authority or authorities entrusted by a Party with decision-making powers regarding a proposed activity;

(x) "The Public" means one or more natural or legal persons.

Article 2

General Provisions

1. The Parties shall, either individually or jointly, take all appropriate and effective measures to prevent, reduce and control significant adverse transboundary environmental impact from proposed activities.

2. Each Party shall take the necessary legal, administrative or other measures to implement the provisions of this Convention, including, with respect to proposed activities listed in Appendix I that are likely to cause significant adverse transboundary impact, the establishment of an environmental impact assessment procedure that permits public participation and preparation of the environmental impact assessment documentation described in Appendix II.

3. The Party of origin shall ensure that in accordance with the provisions of this Convention an environmental impact assessment is undertaken prior to a decision to authorize or undertake a proposed activity listed in Appendix I that is likely to cause a significant adverse transboundary impact.

4. The Party of origin shall, consistent with the provisions of this Convention, ensure that affected Parties are notified of a proposed activity listed in Appendix I that is likely to cause a significant adverse transboundary impact.

5. Concerned Parties shall, at the initiative of any such Party, enter into discussions on whether one or more proposed activities not listed in Appendix I is or are likely to cause a significant adverse transboundary impact and thus should be treated as if it or they were so listed. Where those Parties so agree, the activity or activities shall be thus treated. General guidance for identifying criteria to determine significant adverse impact is set forth in Appendix III.

6. The Party of origin shall provide, in accordance with the provisions of this Convention, an opportunity to the public in the areas likely to be affected to

participate in relevant environmental impact assessment procedures regarding proposed activities and shall ensure that the opportunity provided to the public of the affected Party is equivalent to that provided to the public of the Party of origin.

7. Environmental impact assessments as required by this Convention shall, as a minimum requirement, be undertaken at the project level of the proposed activity. To the extent appropriate, the Parties shall endeavour to apply the principles of environmental impact assessment to policies, plans and programmes.

8. The provisions of this Convention shall not affect the right of Parties to implement national laws, regulations, administrative provisions or accepted legal practices protecting information the supply of which would be prejudicial to industrial and commercial secrecy or national security.

9. The provisions of this Convention shall not affect the right of particular Parties to implement, by bilateral or multilateral agreement where appropriate, more stringent measures than those of this Convention.

10. The provisions of this Convention shall not prejudice any obligations of the Parties under international law with regard to activities having or likely to have a transboundary impact.

Article 3

Notification

1. For a proposed activity listed in Appendix I that is likely to cause a significant adverse transboundary impact, the Party of origin shall, for the purposes of ensuring adequate and effective consultations under Article 5, notify any Party which it considers may be an affected Party as early as possible and no later than when informing its own public about that proposed activity.

2. This notification shall contain, *inter alia:*

(a) Information on the proposed activity, including any available information on its possible transboundary impact;

(b) The nature of the possible decision; and

(c) An indication of a reasonable time within which a response under paragraph 3 of this Article is required, taking into account the nature of the proposed activity;

and may include the information set out in paragraph 5 of this Article.

3. The affected Party shall respond to the Party of origin within the time specified in the notification, acknowledging receipt of the notification, and shall indicate whether it intends to participate in the environmental impact assessment procedure.

4. If the affected Party indicates that it does not intend to participate in the environmental impact assessment procedure, or if it does not respond within the time specified in the notification, the provisions in paragraphs 5, 6, 7 and 8 of this Article and in Articles 4 to 7 will not apply. In such circumstances the right of a Party of origin to determine whether to carry out an environmental impact assessment on the basis of its national law and practice is not prejudiced.

5. Upon receipt of a response from the affected Party indicating its desire to participate in the environmental impact assessment procedure, the Party of origin shall, if it has not already done so, provide to the affected Party:

(a) Relevant information regarding the environmental impact assessment procedure, including an indication of the time schedule for transmittal of comments; and

(b) Relevant information on the proposed activity and its possible significant adverse transboundary impact.

6. An affected Party shall, at the request of the Party of origin, provide the latter with reasonably obtainable information relating to the potentially affected environment under the jurisdiction of the affected Party, where such information is necessary for the preparation of the environmental impact assessment documentation. The information shall be furnished promptly and, as appropriate, through a joint body where one exists.

7. When a Party considers that it would be affected by a significant adverse transboundary impact of a proposed activity listed in Appendix I, and when no notification has taken place in accordance with paragraph 1 of this Article, the concerned Parties shall, at the request of the affected Party, exchange sufficient information for the purposes of holding discussions on whether there is likely to be a significant adverse transboundary impact. If those Parties agree that there is likely to be a significant adverse transboundary impact, the provisions of this Convention shall apply accordingly. If those Parties cannot agree whether there is likely to be a significant adverse transboundary impact, any such Party may submit that question to an inquiry commission in accordance with the provisions of Appendix IV to advise on the likelihood of significant adverse transboundary impact, unless they agree on another method of settling this question.

8. The concerned Parties shall ensure that the public of the affected Party in the areas likely to be affected be informed of, and be provided with possibilities for making comments or objections on the proposed activity, and for the transmittal of these comments or objections to the competent authority of the Party of origin, either directly to this authority or, where appropriate, through the Party of origin.

Article 4

Preparation of the Environmental Impact Assessment Documentation

1. The environmental impact assessment documentation to be submitted to the competent authority of the Party of origin shall contain, at a minimum, the information described in Appendix II.

2. The Party of origin shall furnish the affected Party, as appropriate through a joint body where one exists, with the environmental impact assessment documentation. The concerned Parties shall arrange for distribution of the documentation to the authorities and the public of the affected Party in the areas likely to be affected and for the submission of comments to the competent authority of the Party of origin, either directly to this authority or, where appropriate, through the Party of origin within a reasonable time before the final decision is taken on the proposed activity.

Article 5

Consultations on the Basis of the Environmental Impact Assessment Documentation

The Party of origin shall, after completion of the environmental impact assessment documentation, without undue delay enter into consultations with the affected Party concerning, *inter alia,* the potential transboundary impact of the proposed activity and measures to reduce or eliminate its impact. Consultations may relate to:

(a) Possible alternatives to the proposed activity, including the no-action alternative and possible measures to mitigate significant adverse transboundary impact and to monitor the effects of such measures at the expense of the Party of origin;

(b) Other forms of possible mutual assistance in reducing any significant adverse transboundary impact of the proposed activity; and

(c) Any other appropriate matters relating to the proposed activity.

The Parties shall agree, at the commencement of such consultations, on a reasonable time-frame for the duration of the consultation period. Any such consultations may be conducted through an appropriate joint body, where one exists.

Article 6

Final Decision

1. The Parties shall ensure that, in the final decision on the proposed activity, due account is taken of the outcome of the environmental impact assessment, including the environmental impact assessment documentation, as well as the comments thereon received pursuant to Article 3, paragraph 8 and Article 4, paragraph 2, and the outcome of the consultations as referred to in Article 5.

2. The Party of origin shall provide to the affected Party the final decision on the proposed activity along with the reasons and considerations on which it was based.

3. If additional information on the significant transboundary impact of a proposed activity, which was not available at the time a decision was made with respect to that activity and which could have materially affected the decision, becomes available to a concerned Party before work on that activity commences, that Party shall immediately inform the other concerned Party or Parties. If one of the concerned Parties so requests, consultations shall be held as to whether the decision needs to be revised.

Article 7

Post–Project Analysis

1. The concerned Parties, at the request of any such Party, shall determine whether, and if so to what extent, a post-project analysis shall be carried out, taking into account the likely significant adverse transboundary impact of the activity for which an environmental impact assessment has been undertaken pursuant to this Convention. Any post-project analysis undertaken shall include, in particular, the surveillance of the activity and the determination of any adverse transboundary impact. Such surveillance and determination may be undertaken with a view to achieving the objectives listed in Appendix V.

2. When, as a result of post-project analysis, the Party of origin or the affected Party has reasonable grounds for concluding that there is a significant adverse transboundary impact or factors have been discovered which may result in such an impact, it shall immediately inform the other Party. The concerned Parties shall then consult on necessary measures to reduce or eliminate the impact.

Article 8

Bilateral and Multilateral Co-operation

The Parties may continue existing or enter into new bilateral or multilateral agreements or other arrangements in order to implement their obligations under this Convention. Such agreements or other arrangements may be based on the elements listed in Appendix VI.

Article 9

Research Programmes

The Parties shall give special consideration to the setting up, or intensification of specific research programmes aimed at:

(a) Improving existing qualitative and quantitative methods for assessing the impacts of proposed activities;

(b) Achieving a better understanding of cause-effect relationships and their role in integrated environmental management;

(c) Analysing and monitoring the efficient implementation of decisions on proposed activities with the intention of minimizing or preventing impacts;

(d) Developing methods to stimulate creative approaches in the search for environmentally sound alternatives to proposed activities, production and consumption patterns;

(e) Developing methodologies for the application of the principles of environmental impact assessment at the macro-economic level.

The results of the programmes listed above shall be exchanged by the Parties.

Article 10

Status of the Appendices

The Appendices attached to this Convention form an integral part of the Convention.

Article 11

Meeting of Parties

1. The Parties shall meet, so far as possible, in connection with the annual sessions of the Senior Advisers to ECE Governments on Environmental and Water Problems. The first meeting of the Parties shall be convened not later than one year after the date of the entry into force of this Convention. Thereafter, meetings of the Parties shall be held at such other times as may be deemed necessary by a meeting of the Parties, or at the written request of any Party, provided that, within six months of the request being communicated to them by the secretariat, it is supported by at least one third of the Parties.

2. The Parties shall keep under continuous review the implementation of this Convention, and, with this purpose in mind, shall:

(a) Review the policies and methodological approaches to environmental impact assessment by the Parties with a view to further improving environmental impact assessment procedures in a transboundary context;

(b) Exchange information regarding experience gained in concluding and implementing bilateral and multilateral agreements or other arrangements regarding the use of environmental impact assessment in a transboundary context to which one or more of the Parties are party;

(c) Seek, where appropriate, the services of competent international bodies and scientific committees in methodological and technical aspects pertinent to the achievement of the purposes of this Convention;

(d) At their first meeting, consider and by consensus adopt rules of procedure for their meetings;

(e) Consider and, where necessary, adopt proposals for amendments to this Convention;

(f) Consider and undertake any additional action that may be required for the achievement of the purposes of this Convention.

Article 12

Right to vote

1. Each Party to this Convention shall have one vote.

2. Except as provided for in paragraph 1 of this Article, regional economic integration organizations, in matters within their competence, shall exercise their right to vote with a number of votes equal to the number of their member States which are Parties to this Convention. Such organizations shall not exercise their right to vote if their member States exercise theirs, and vice versa.

Article 13

Secretariat

The Executive Secretary of the Economic Commission for Europe shall carry out the following secretariat functions:

(a) The convening and preparing of meetings of the Parties;

(b) The transmission of reports and other information received in accordance with the provisions of this Convention to the Parties; and

(c) The performance of other functions as may be provided for in this Convention or as may be determined by the Parties.

Article 14

Amendments to the Convention

1. Any Party may propose amendments to this Convention.

2. Proposed amendments shall be submitted in writing to the secretariat, which shall communicate them to all Parties. The proposed amendments shall be discussed at the next meeting of the Parties, provided these proposals have been circulated by the secretariat to the Parties at least ninety days in advance.

3. The Parties shall make every effort to reach agreement on any proposed amendment to this Convention by consensus. If all efforts at consensus have been exhausted, and no agreement reached, the amendment shall as a last resort be adopted by a three-fourths majority vote of the Parties present and voting at the meeting.

4. Amendments to this Convention adopted in accordance with paragraph 3 of this Article shall be submitted by the Depositary to all Parties for ratification, approval or acceptance. They shall enter into force for Parties having ratified, approved or accepted them on the ninetieth day after the receipt by the Depositary of notification of their ratification, approval or acceptance by at least three-fourths of these Parties. Thereafter they shall enter into force for any other Party on the ninetieth day after that Party deposits its instrument of ratification, approval or acceptance of the amendments.

5. For the purpose of this Article, "Parties present and voting" means Parties present and casting an affirmative or negative vote.

6. The voting procedure set forth in paragraph 3 of this Article is not intended to constitute a precedent for future agreements negotiated within the Economic Commission for Europe.

Article 15

Settlement of Disputes

1. If a dispute arises between two or more Parties about the interpretation or application of this Convention, they shall seek a solution by negotiation or by any other method of dispute settlement acceptable to the parties to the dispute.

2. When signing, ratifying, accepting, approving or acceding to this Convention, or at any time thereafter, a Party may declare in writing to the Depositary that for a dispute not resolved in accordance with paragraph 1 of this Article, it accepts one or both of the following means of dispute settlement as compulsory in relation to any Party accepting the same obligation:

(a) Submission of the dispute to the International Court of Justice;

(b) Arbitration in accordance with the procedure set out in Appendix VII.

3. If the parties to the dispute have accepted both means of dispute settlement referred to in paragraph 2 of this Article, the dispute may be submitted only to the International Court of Justice, unless the parties agree otherwise.

Article 16

Signature

This Convention shall be open for signature at Espoo (Finland) from 25 February to 1 March 1991 and thereafter at United Nations Headquarters in New York until 2 September 1991 by State members of the Economic Commission for Europe as well as States having consultative status with the Economic Commission for Europe pursuant to paragraph 8 of the Economic and Social Council resolution 36(IV) of 28 March 1947, and by regional economic integration organizations constituted by sovereign States members of the Economic Commission for Europe to which their member States have transferred competence in respect of matters governed by this Convention, including the competence to enter into treaties in respect of these matters.

Article 17

Ratification, Acceptance, Approval and Accession

1. This Convention shall be subject to ratification, acceptance or approval by signatory States and regional economic integration organizations.

2. This Convention shall be open for accession as from 3 September 1991 by the States and organizations referred to in Article 16.

3. The instruments of ratification, acceptance, approval or accession shall be deposited with the Secretary–General of the United Nations, who shall perform the functions of Depositary.

4. Any organization referred to in Article 16 which becomes a Party to this Convention without any of its member States being a Party shall be bound by all the obligations under this Convention. In the case of such organizations, one or more of whose member States is a Party to this Convention, the organization and its member States shall decide on their respective responsibilities for the performance of their obligations under this Convention. In such cases, the organization and the member States shall not be entitled to exercise rights under this Convention concurrently.

5. In their instruments of ratification, acceptance, approval or accession, the regional economic integration organizations referred to in Article 16 shall declare the extent of their competence with respect to the matters governed by this Convention. These organizations shall also inform the Depositary of any relevant modification to the extent of their competence.

Article 18

Entry into Force

1. This Convention shall enter into force on the ninetieth day after the date of deposit of the sixteenth instrument of ratification, acceptance, approval or accession.

2. For the purposes of paragraph 1 of this Article, any instrument deposited by a regional economic integration organization shall not be counted as additional to those deposited by States members of such an organization.

3. For each State or organization referred to in Article 16 which ratifies, accepts or approves this Convention or accedes thereto after the deposit of the sixteenth instrument of ratification, acceptance, approval or accession, this Convention shall enter into force on the ninetieth day after the date of deposit by such State or organization of its instrument of ratification, acceptance, approval or accession.

Article 19

Withdrawal

At any time after four years from the date on which this Convention has come into force with respect to a Party, that Party may withdraw from this Convention by giving written notification to the Depositary. Any such withdrawal shall take effect on the nineteenth day after the date of its receipt by the Depositary. Any such withdrawal shall not affect the application of Articles 3 to 6 of this Convention to a proposed activity in respect of which a notification has been made pursuant to Article 3, paragraph 1, or a request has been made pursuant to Article 3, paragraph 7, before such withdrawal took effect.

Article 20

Authentic Texts

The original of this Convention, of which the English, French and Russian texts are equally authentic, shall be deposited with the Secretary-General of the United Nations.

1.28 Arctic Environmental Protection Strategy (AEPS). Adopted by the eight Arctic countries, 14 June 1991. *Reprinted in* 30 I.L.M. 1624 (1991)

PREFACE

In September 1989, on the initiative of the government of Finland, officials from the eight Arctic countries met in Rovaniemi, Finland to discuss cooperative measures to protect the Arctic environment. They agreed to work towards a meeting of circumpolar Ministers responsible for Arctic environmental issues. The September 1989 meeting was followed by preparatory meetings in Yellowknife, Canada in April 1990; Kiruna, Sweden in January 1991; and, Rovaniemi, Finland in June 1991.

In addition to the numerous technical and scientific reports prepared under this initiative, the Arctic Environmental Protection Strategy was developed. This Strategy represents the culmination of the cooperative efforts of the eight Arctic countries:

Canada
Denmark
Finland
Iceland
Norway
Sweden
Union of Soviet Socialist Republics
United States of America.

The eight Arctic countries were assisted in the preparation of the Strategy by the following observers:

Inuit Circumpolar Conference
Nordic Saami Council
USSR Association of Small Peoples of the North
Federal Republic of Germany
Poland
United Kingdom
United Nations Economic Commission for Europe
United Nations Environment Program
International Arctic Science Committee

1. INTRODUCTION

There is a growing national and international appreciation of the importance of Arctic ecosystems and an increasing knowledge of global pollution and resulting environmental threats. The Arctic is highly sensitive to pollution and much of its human population and culture is directly dependent on the health of the region's ecosystems. Limited sunlight, ice cover that inhibits energy penetration, low mean and extreme temperatures, low species diversity and biological productivity and long-lived organisms with high lipid levels all contribute to the sensitivity of the Arctic ecosystem and cause it to be easily damaged. This vulnerability of the Arctic to pollution requires that action be taken now, or degradation may become irreversible.

The governments of the Arctic countries have become increasingly aware of the need for, and their responsibility to combat these threats to the Arctic ecosystem. On the initiative of Finland, the eight Arctic countries of USSR, USA, Sweden, Norway, Iceland, Finland, Denmark and Canada have met to prepare a strategy to protect the Arctic environment. The Arctic countries realize that the pollution problems of today do not respect national boundaries and that no state alone will be able to act effectively against environmental threats to the Arctic. They have also been moved by the international call for action expressed by the World Commission on Environment and Development as well as the concerns of the indigenous peoples living in the Arctic region. The Arctic countries with the participation of Arctic indigenous peoples have prepared this environmental protection Strategy. The Strategy builds on the initiatives already taken nationally and by indigenous peoples to protect the Arctic environment.

It is recognized that this Strategy, and its implementation, must incorporate the knowledge and culture of indigenous peoples. It is understood that the cultures and the continued existence of the indigenous peoples have been built on the sound stewardship of nature and its resources.

The use of natural resources is an important activity of Arctic nations. Therefore, this Strategy should allow for sustainable economic development in the north so that such development does not have unacceptable ecological or cultural impacts. The Strategy must also rely on the best scientific and technological advice that countries are able to produce and share.

Arctic ecosystems are influenced and in some cases threatened by factors occurring also outside the Arctic. In turn, the Arctic also exerts an important influence on the global environment. The implementation of an Arctic Environmental Protection Strategy will therefore benefit both the Arctic countries and the world at large. The Strategy is also designed to guide development in a way that will safeguard the Arctic environment for future generations and in a manner that is compatible with nature.

The Arctic countries are committed to international cooperation to ensure the protection of the Arctic environment and its sustainable and equitable development, while protecting the cultures of indigenous peoples.

Only through careful stewardship by Arctic countries and Arctic peoples can environmental damage and degradation be prevented. These are the challenges which must be taken up in order to secure our common future.

The Strategy is comprised of a number of component parts, beginning with a statement of objectives. These objectives establish the broad direction in which the eight-Arctic countries are intending to move. The objectives are accompanied by statements of principle which are designed to guide the actions of Arctic countries individually and collectively, as they move toward achievement of the objectives. The Strategy also describes the problems and priorities which the eight Arctic countries agree need to be addressed at this time.

Tools, whether legal, scientific or administrative, are also reviewed in order to define appropriate mechanisms for implementation of the Strategy. This is particularly relevant to that section of the Strategy which defines the specific actions that the eight countries will undertake jointly or individually to deal with priority issues and pollution problems. The implementation of the Strategy will be carried out through national legislation and in accordance with international law, including customary international law as reflected in the 1982 United Nations Convention on the Law of the Sea.

Finally, the Strategy outlines plans for future cooperation towards the implementation of the Strategy.

2. OBJECTIVES AND PRINCIPLES

2.1 Objectives

The objectives of the Arctic Environmental Protection Strategy are:

i) To protect the Arctic ecosystem including humans;

ii) To provide for the protection, enhancement and restoration of environmental quality and the sustainable utilization of natural resources, including their use by local populations and indigenous peoples in the Arctic;

iii) To recognize and, to the extent possible, seek to accommodate the traditional and cultural needs, values and practices of the indigenous peoples as determined by themselves, related to the protection of the Arctic environment;

iv) To review regularly the state of the Arctic environment;

v) To identify, reduce, and, as a final goal, eliminate pollution.

2.2 *Principles*:

The Arctic Environmental Protection Strategy and its implementation by the eight Arctic countries will be guided by the following principles:

i) Management, planning and development activities shall provide for the conservation, sustainable utilization and protection of Arctic ecosystems and natural resources for the benefit and enjoyment of present and future generations, including indigenous peoples;

ii) Use and management of natural resources shall be based on an approach which considers the value and interdependent nature of ecosystem components;

iii) Management, planning and development activities which may significantly affect the Arctic ecosystems shall:

a) be based on informed assessments of their possible impacts on the Arctic environment, including cumulative impacts;

b) provide for the maintenance of the regions's ecological systems and biodiversity;

c) respect the Arctic's significance for and influence on the global climate;

d) be compatible with the sustainable utilization of Arctic ecosystems;

e) take into account the results of scientific investigations and the traditional knowledge of indigenous peoples;

vi) Information and knowledge concerning Arctic ecosystems and resource use will be developed and shared to support planning and should precede, accompany and follow development activities;

vii) Consideration of the health, social, economic and cultural needs and values of indigenous peoples shall be incorporated into management, planning and development activities;

viii) Development of a network of protected areas shall be encouraged and promoted with due regard for the needs of indigenous peoples;

ix) International cooperation to protect the Arctic environment shall be supported and promoted.

x) Mutual cooperation in fulfilling national and international responsibilities in the Arctic consistent with this Strategy, including the use, transfer and/or trade, of the most effective and appropriate technology to protect the environment, shall be promoted and developed.

3. PROBLEMS AND PRIORITIES

At the first meeting in 1989 of the eight Arctic countries there was early recognition that many of the environmental problems that individual nations had been addressing, were in fact shared amongst the eight. To begin with, six specific pollution issues were identified as requiring attention. These issues were associated with persistent organic contaminants, oil, heavy metals, noise, radioactivity, and acidification.

State of the Environment Reports were prepared on each of these topics and have been published separately. It was also agreed that these will be updated as necessary.

It was recognized that the ability to completely understand these issues was restricted by the lack of a comprehensive scientific data base and coordinated monitoring program on the state of Arctic ecosystems. Furthermore, the potential impact of these specific pollutants on Arctic flora and fauna underlined the need to consider establishing a mechanism to facilitate a cooperative approach to their conservation. Other environmental problems including the depletion of the ozone layer and global warming were not addressed because they were already being considered in other fora. It was also determined that since the Arctic environment is particularly vulnerable to accidental discharges and uncontrolled releases of pollutants, enhanced mechanisms to address environmental emergencies in the Arctic were needed.

3.1 Persistent Organic Contaminants

The use and production of persistent organic contaminants (e.g. polychlorinated biphenyls (PCBs), DDT, hexachlorocyclohexane (HCH), chlordane and toxaphene has been stopped or restricted in some countries, however, many are still widely manufactured and used on a global basis. They are hazardous environmental contaminants due to their high stability and persistence in the environment, potential for bioaccumulation and high chronic toxicity, and the large quantities which have been released into the environment.

Although there are no major sources of these contaminants in the Arctic, they, nevertheless, reach the Arctic environment via long-range transport by rivers, the atmosphere and ocean currents from more industrialized centres, particularly Asia, Europe and North America. Due to the highly lipophilic nature of most chlorinated organic contaminants, they become concentrated in the fatty tissues of species in the Arctic food chain. The highest levels of contaminants are therefore detected in the blubber and fat tissue of animals at the top of the food chain (e.g. polar bears, whales and seals). This is of particular concern in the Arctic because of the high level of consumption of lipid-rich wildlife foods by residents, resulting in a pathway of these contaminants to humans.

The presence of chlorinated organic contaminants has been reported in human populations throughout the world. The level of PCBs in breast milk samples collected from Inuit women in northern Quebec, was approximately five times higher than that of Caucasian women living in southern Quebec, Canada.

The variable and generally sparse database on chlorinated organic contaminants in the Arctic prohibits for the most part, the determination of any spatial or temporal trends. In Canadian studies, chlordane compound residue levels in polar bear fat have been reported to be four times higher in 1984 than in 1969, while levels of DDT did not change and other chlorinated contaminants measures were twice as high.

Concentrations of chlorinated organic contaminants in the Arctic ecosystem are generally lower than in heavily polluted areas such as the Great Lakes, or the Baltic Sea. There are, however, some exceptions—the more volatile compounds (e.g. HCB, toxaphene) are often detected in the Arctic at concentrations similar to those in source regions.

Little is known about the potential effects of chlorinated organic contaminants on the ecosystem. However, there is evidence that a broad spectrum of contaminants is reaching the Arctic and there is sufficient toxicological data as well as field data to make reasonable extrapolations with regard to ecosystem consequences in the Arctic. Chronic effects of chlorinated organic contamination observed in other regions (e.g. reproductive failure, bill and foot abnormalities, cancer) are of the most significance. The lower concentrations detected in the Arctic do not diminish the potential significance of their effects on ecosystem health.

3.2 Oil Pollution

The Arctic is one of the areas Most vulnerable to adverse impacts from chronic and acute oil pollution. This is due to physical environmental conditions such as low temperature, periods with little or no light, ice cover etc. Low temperatures lead to reduced evaporation of the more volatile, toxic oil components. Dark, cold winters in the Arctic lead to reduced ultraviolet radiation and biological decomposition of oil. In areas of drift ice, oil dispersal caused by wave action is also reduced. Oil in iced areas will be trapped between ice floes or under the ice, and only partly transported to the ice surface. These factors result in a generally slower decomposition of oil in the Arctic than in temperate regions. The period in which a particular oil spill can be harmful to wildlife is thus comparatively longer in the Arctic.

The marginal ice zone is particularly vulnerable to oil pollution. A large part of the primary production in the Arctic, is found in this zone, which makes it extremely important for the whole Arctic ecosystem. Although there is no evidence that an oil spill reduces primary productivity to a significant degree, direct effects on marine life can be devastating, especially in the marginal ice zones.

Feathers and fur contaminated by oil quickly lose their insulating properties, and the oil will often cause skin inflammation. Both will lead to a negative energy balance of the affected animal. Ingested oil, in particular unweathered oil with a high content of volatile substances, can cause serious intoxication of birds and mammals. No studies indicate that any of these species tend to avoid oil spills.

The amount of information available on oil spills in the Arctic, and probably the accuracy of the estimated quantities, varies considerably. Information on continuous discharges is scarce, and estimates of indirect oil transport (atmosphere, ocean currents, and rivers) have not been available. Order of magnitude calculations show that river transport is the main contribution of oil pollution to the Arctic (estimated at 200,000 metric tons per annum).

The highest risk of oil spills is connected with transportation activities and production of oil as well as to a lesser degree, exploration activities. Their occurrence will depend on the level of activity in the Arctic, the technical standards of the activity and the preventative measures taken.

The physical constraints caused by Arctic conditions imply particular technological challenges regarding oil spill clean up. Effective methods and techniques for containing and cleaning up oil spills from water and ice are currently limited.

The available information on ambient oil pollution in the Arctic is scarce. More information is needed, obtained with standardized methodologies in order to have comparable data for the whole region, with special emphasis on fluvial inputs and concentrations in surface marine waters.

3.3 Heavy Metals

Levels of heavy metals have been found in the air, precipitation, ocean waters, soils, rivers, lakes and bottom sediments of the Arctic as well as in marine, freshwater and terrestrial biota. These levels occur as a result of natural phenomena as well as from regional sources and global transport.

Heavy metal concentrations in air and precipitation are mainly due to long-range atmospheric transport from industrial centers resulting in a deposition of heavy metals on vegetation, snow, and the sea which generally decreases from south to north. To a lesser extent discharges from local mining operations and the methylation of inorganic mercury often associated with large scale impoundments of water in previously vegetated areas (i.e. hydroelectric developments), also account for elevated heavy metal concentrations. Canadian and Finnish studies indicate methyl mercury levels in fish rise measurably after the flooding of new reservoirs, depending upon the amount of organic material present.

The temporal trends of long-range heavy metal pollution of the Arctic particularly mercury, cadmium, lead, arsenic and nickel have been determined by analyzing ice cores from glaciers. There has been an increasing trend since the middle of the 19th century and a sharp increase in the 20th century. Recent analyses of vegetation seem to indicate that a decrease may now be occurring.

The concentrations of heavy metals in lakes and rivers are generally higher than in Arctic sea water. A decrease in pH caused by acid precipitation increases the dissolution rates of heavy metals which may increase the rate of accumulation in the biota.

In the Arctic marine environment the concentrations of heavy metals in water are low compared to more southerly latitudes. However, the concentrations in biota increase in the food chain, and in the top level predators such as seals and whales the concentrations, especially of cadmium, increase to levels much higher than observed in other areas. For example, in some Canadian studies, cadmium levels in narwhal kidney were among the highest ever reported in marine mammals. This build-up is probably due to naturally occurring phenomena, but such occurrences make increases in the concentrations of heavy metals in the Arctic marine environment as a result of industrial sources more problematic than elsewhere.

The high concentrations of heavy metals in marine mammals and some bird species constitute a problem in districts where tissues from such animals constitute a significant part of the diet. Thus increased concentrations of mercury have been found in Greenlanders from hunting districts. Elevated levels of mercury have also been found in the Native populations of Northern Quebec, Canada.

3.4 Noise

The waters of the Arctic region are a unique noise environment mainly due to the presence of ice. The ambient noise is strongly influenced by the dynamic processes of ice formation, melt, deformation and movement. This situation is different from ice free waters. In periods where ice cracking and wind noise are absent, areas covered by shore-fast ice are among the quietest underwater environments.

Human activities create noise types and levels, which may disturb marine mammals, or mask the "natural" sounds of importance to those mammals. Some types of noise may affect fish as well as marine mammals. There are a number of serious gaps in our knowledge of the effects of underwater noise on marine mammals, including the inability to assess the effect of repeated noise exposure on stocks.

There is considerable evidence that most types of disturbance do not cause mortality. However, some noisy activities, including low level overflights by aircraft, near seals and walrus at haul out sites can cause mortality through stampedes or abandonment.

Many marine mammals seem able to adapt to or at least tolerate many types of disturbances or increased noise levels. However the scarcity of direct evidence of serious consequences from disturbances does not necessarily mean that marine mammals are not stressed or affected in some other way. Noise from human activities may cause short-term or long-term behavioral reactions and temporary displacement of various marine mammals. The biological significance of most of these reactions is unknown.

Moving sound sources, notably boats and aircraft, seem to be more disturbing than stationary sources, e.g. dredges and drillships. The effects on fish and wildlife of cumulative exposure to noise are largely unknown.

3.5 Radioactivity

There have been two major causes of radioactive contamination affecting the Arctic region: atmospheric nuclear-weapons testing during the 1950s and 1960s and the accident at the Chernobyl nuclear power plant in 1986. Of greatest concern are the long-lived radionuclides, including Strontium–90 (29 year half-life) and Cesium–137 (30 year half-life). Studies have shown that these fallout derived radionuclides are efficiently retained by surface vegetation, especially lichen, in this nutrient-poor environment and are biologically recycled in Arctic ecosystems. As a result those indigenous peoples and local populations consuming as their main food caribou or reindeer meat with elevated levels of radiocesium, may have accumulated higher levels.

Other radioactive threats to the environment exist, e. g. accidental discharges which are of a biological significance associated with nuclear power sources and transport, storage and disposal of radioactive waste.

When considering the total radiation dose, attention should be given to the radiation from man-made sources and to natural radiation.

A number of bilateral and multilateral arrangements, including those with the International Atomic Energy Agency (IAEA), address issues related to exchange of information, early notification of radiation release, emergency preparedness and response to nuclear accidents and transboundary movement of radioactive materials.

3.6 Acidification

The most important acidifying substances are sulphur and nitrogen compounds emitted mainly by vehicles, industrial activities and coal and oil based power plants. Long-range transport is the most important factor influencing the air quality in the Arctic, especially in winter. The sulphur and nitrogen emission from industrial activities in the Arctic is also a considerable factor. Until now, little emphasis has been placed on the effects of acid deposition on Arctic ecosystems. Furthermore, knowledge derived from studies in temperate zones is not directly relevant to the Arctic.

One of the most well known examples of a problem associated with acidity in the Arctic is the Arctic haze phenomenon produced from acid pollutant aerosols. Arctic haze has been under intense study and much is known about its nature, distribution and composition. Acidification is evolving into a prominent environmental problem around certain northern industrial centers. In northern Fennoscandia, in the northwestern parts of the Soviet Union and in the eastern parts of Canada, natural factors increase the sensitivity to acidification and anthropogenic impacts have extended through the whole area.

The interaction between acidic deposition and the soils of different ecosystems is an important component of the acidification process. A continuous excessive acid load leads to the mobilization of aluminum and heavy metals.

The combined effects of acid deposition and the stresses already induced by the harsh climate increase the possibility of vegetation damage in the Arctic.

Critical loads, rates of acidification, and conditions influencing cold climate environments need more detailed regional monitoring and research. In general, northern ecosystems are under greater stress than temperate ecosystems.

4. INTERNATIONAL MECHANISMS FOR THE PROTECTION OF THE ARCTIC ENVIRONMENT

Before determining the specific actions required to protect the Arctic environment, a review of existing and proposed international and bilateral agreements and policy declarations pertaining to the Arctic environment has been completed. This review has revealed the existence of a number of mechanisms that may be employed to protect the Arctic environment, and provides a useful tool for the implementation of the Strategy. The List of Major International Instruments and Policy Declarations Pertaining to the Arctic Environment has been distributed and will be periodically updated. Through the more specific studies of the six priority areas, some important gaps have been identified.

4.1 Persistent Organic Contaminants

International legal instruments which currently control air pollution are not specifically directed at limiting the emission of persistent organic contaminants and related contaminants. Work is underway within the UN ECE Convention on Long-Range Transboundary Air Pollution (LRTAP) to review the problem and identify specific control actions. Any new international legal instrument would need to target contaminant reductions in the industrialized areas of Asia, Europe and North America. Consequently, proper management and protection of the Arctic ecosystem from the effects of these contaminants will require cooperation through effective bilateral and multilateral agreements among both circumpolar and non-circumpolar nations.

4.2 Oil Pollution

The main international instruments relevant inter alia to oil pollution in the Arctic are:

i) the 1969 International Convention on Civil Liability for Oil Pollution Damage (CLC Convention);

ii) the 1969 International Convention relating to Intervention on the High Seas in Cases of Oil Pollution Casualties (Convention on Intervention);

iii) the 1971 International Convention on the Establishment of an International Fund for Compensation for Oil Pollution Damage (Fund Convention);

iv) the 1972 Convention on the Prevention of Marine Pollution by Dumping of Wastes and Other Matter (London Dumping Convention);

v) the 1974 Convention on the Prevention of Marine Pollution from Land-Based Sources (Paris Convention);

vi) the International Convention for the Prevention of Pollution from Ships (MARPOL 1973/78); and

vii) the 1982 United Nations Convention on the Law of the Sea (UNCLOS) (not yet in force);

viii) the International Convention on Oil Pollution Preparedness, Response and Cooperation, 1990 (not yet in force).

Certain issues with respect to oil pollution in the Arctic are insufficiently covered by the existing international agreements and conventions. For example, some instruments are limited in their application and only partially apply to the Arctic region. There is a need to consider the possibility of extending the geographic scope of these instruments. The provisions of the various instruments also need to be further assessed to determine their adequacy under Arctic conditions taking into account the particularly vulnerable nature of the region.

Strict standards in the transportation of oil in the Arctic are needed. Such standards should be developed under the framework of the International Maritime Organization (IMO). Arctic countries should consider becoming parties to or applying the relevant principles of the various existing conventions and agreements on oil pollution management.

4.3 Heavy Metals

There are few multilateral conventions and bilateral agreements which deal with heavy metal inputs in the environment.

The UN ECE LRTAP Convention is one of the major international conventions which limits harmful atmospheric emissions. Work is currently underway within this forum to identify and decide upon specific control actions to deal with heavy metals.

Control of discharges of heavy metals to the marine environment are governed by both the 1972 Convention for the Prevention of Marine Pollution by Dumping from

Ships and Aircraft (Oslo Convention) and the 1974 Convention on the Prevention of Marine Pollution from [Oslo and Paris Conventions at 11 I.L.M. 262 (1972) & 13 I.L.M. 352 (1974] Land-based Sources (Paris Convention). The UNCLOS provides opportunities for controlling the discharge of harmful substances e.g. heavy metals. There are only a few bilateral arrangements between the Arctic countries controlling these substances.

4.4 Noise

Existing legal instruments do not address the effects of noise on the Arctic ecosystem. There may be a need for Arctic countries to agree on the adoption of procedures to ensure that in the planning and conduct of activities in the Arctic, measures are taken to facilitate the adequate monitoring of the potential disturbance from noise including the verification of predicted effects and the identification of any unforseen effects. Such evaluations should ensure that environmental protection measures are given due consideration.

4.5 Radioactivity

The 1986 International Atomic Energy Agency (IAEA) Convention on Early Notification of a Nuclear Accident, provides an adequate mechanism for cooperation and exchange of information applicable in the Arctic region. In addition, there are a number of bilateral and multilateral agreements in existence which provide for such events as the early notification of accidental radioactive discharges (e.g. between Finland and other Nordic countries, Finland and the USSR, 1987). [IAEA Convention at 25 I.L.M. 1369 (1986)]

With respect to emergency preparedness and assistance, the IAEA Convention on Assistance in the Case of a Nuclear Accident or Radiological Emergency was established to facilitate prompt international assistance when requested in the event of a nuclear accident. Additionally, a number of bilateral and multilateral agreements have been concluded between the Arctic countries that both supplement and provide greater precision to the IAEA arrangements. These should be examined to ensure that the specific environmental conditions of the Arctic are addressed.

Furthermore, consideration should be given to practical mechanisms between national authorities to implement the coordination of emergency measures within the existing international legal framework of the IAEA.

4.6 Acidification

The Arctic is exposed to the long range transport of acidifying substances from various sources. A number of control measures have been introduced at the United Nations Economic Commission for Europe (ECE) and bilaterally. Although, in general, these measures do not contain provisions relating specifically to the Arctic region, they do refer to emission sources that affect the Arctic.

Arctic acidification is a complex phenomenon resulting from a wide range of different types of activities also conducted outside the Arctic itself. The extent of acidification in the Arctic is still uncertain, although there is recognition of problems such as Arctic haze and forest devastation and other large-scale acidification effects and regional damage in certain Arctic areas. There is however, insufficient knowledge of the critical loads, to allow for agreement on common standards. The lack of comparable data also presents problems. Consequently, improved monitoring and research directed at the rate and nature of acidification processes under Arctic conditions are needed.

Under both the 1985 and 1988 protocols to the UN ECE LRTAP Convention for the Reduction of Sulphur and Nitrogen Oxide Emissions or their Transboundary Fluxes, the Cooperative Program for Monitoring and Evaluation of the Long–Range Transmission of Air Pollutants in Europe (EMEP) is to report annually to the LRTAP Executive Body its calculations of budgets, transboundary fluxes and deposition of sulphur and nitrogen oxides. EMEPs geographical scope is currently limited to Europe but it is suggested that EMEP might be utilized for collecting data on Arctic acidification in cooperation with the Arctic Monitoring and Assessment Program (AMAP). Arctic countries should consider becoming parties to all the relevant agreements in this field. This is particularly relevant for those countries in the northern hemisphere where there are major sources of sulphur and nitrogen emissions.

[LRTAP and 1985 and 1988 Protocols at 18 I.L.M. 1442 (1979), 24 I.L.M. 484 (1985) and 28 I.L.M. 212 (1989)]

5. ACTIONS

The eight Arctic countries agree to proceed cooperatively with the following action plan. These commitments will begin the process of addressing the serious environmental issues identified and assessed through the preparation of specific state of environment reports. These issues will require regular updates for evaluation by the eight Arctic countries on the progress being made, and to advise on possible new courses of action.

5.1 Persistent Organic Contaminants

i) In order to further define the likely sources, pathways, sinks and effects of these pollutants, and to expand the data base to cover all the component parts of the Arctic environment, the eight Arctic countries will undertake cooperative monitoring (AMAP) and research related to the problem of persistent organic contaminants in the Arctic ecosystem.

ii) The Arctic countries will consider the feasibility of developing national inventories on the production, use, and emissions of persistent organic contaminants (e.g. pesticides) to be collected, and made available and summarized in the state of the Arctic environment reports.

iii) The Arctic countries will also address the problem of persistent organic contaminants under existing or proposed international agreements and will review other mechanisms to advance this issue in other international fora.

iv) In order to achieve an early reduction in the movement of persistent organic contaminants into the Arctic environment, the eight Arctic countries will support the process now under way within the UN ECE LRTAP Convention to further define the problem and to develop proposals for international action on the control of these substances under the Convention. Those Arctic countries which are partners to the Paris and Helsinki Conventions will actively support ongoing inventory and assessment work under those conventions.

v) The Arctic countries agree to implement measures to reduce and/or control the use of the following polluting substances: chlordane, DDT, toxaphene and PCBs. Those Arctic countries which have not already done so, also recognize that the elimination of the problem of persistent organic contaminants in the Arctic may also require controls on the production of these substances.

vi) The Arctic countries will review the situation with regard to other persistent organic contaminants with a view to establishing priorities and timetables for a program of emission elimination or control in cooperation with other international fora.

5.2 Oil Pollution

i) In order to achieve better documentation of the level of oil pollution in the Arctic environment, the initiation of monitoring of hydrocarbons as a part of the AMAP, will play a important role.

ii) There is also a need to consider establishment of a reporting system on discharges and spills, with regard to provide adequate documentation on the pollution threat, in the Arctic.

iii) The elements agreed upon in Section 8, Protection of the Arctic Marine Environment and Section 9, Emergency Prevention, Preparedness and Response will comprise the basis for further cooperation in preventing and combatting oil pollution.

iv) The Arctic countries agree to take measures as soon as possible to adhere to the strictest relevant international standards, within the conventions, to which the countries are parties, regarding discharges irrespective of origin.

v) The Arctic countries agree to undertake joint actions in relevant international fora to further strengthen recognition of the particularly sensitive character of ice-covered parts of the Arctic Ocean.

5.3 *Heavy Metals*

i) An improved understanding of the dynamics of heavy metals in the Arctic ecosystem is required. The countries will undertake a program of coordinated monitoring (AMAP) and research to identify sources, pathways and sinks of heavy metals; spatial and temporal trends; and, ecological effects with special emphasis on human health effects.

ii) The eight Arctic countries agree to implement measures to control conditions that lead to the release of heavy metals by industrial activities including as appropriate the implementation of best available technology and other concerted actions in accordance with appropriate international agreements (e.g. UN ECE LRTAP Convention).

5.4 *Noise*

i) The effects of noise associated with Arctic marine and terrestrial projects should be evaluated as part of the project planning and approval processes, and if significant adverse noise effects on the specific components of Arctic ecosystems are predicted, then measures should be implemented to avoid or mitigate the impact.

ii) Efforts should be made to improve the knowledge on marine mammal auditory function, communication and behavior and the current noise exposure assessment techniques. For specific project evaluations, site-specific data should be addressed before and during the evaluation. This includes determining how much exposure migrating stocks are encountering throughout the year.

5.5 *Radioactivity*

i) AMAP should address radioactivity. Common standards and techniques for monitoring and analysis, consistent with IAEA standards and technology should be developed.

ii) Future monitoring and health assessments should consider the effects from exposure to radiation from man-made sources together with natural or background radiation.

iii) Further consideration should be given to the development of more specific measures, consistent within the international legal framework of IAEA procedures, for cooperation amongst Arctic countries to deal with emergencies caused by the accidental release of radioactive substances and to provide mutual assistance in the harsh Arctic environment.

iv) All relevant data concerning previous studies and measurements should be collated in the existing relevant data bases of which information should be exchanged between the governments and institutions concerned.

5.6 Acidification

i) Regional Arctic research programs should be developed to assess the current loadings and potential effects of acid deposition on representative sensitive Arctic ecosystems. Special attention should be given to those regions or ecosystems for which existing data or assessments suggest that there is or is likely to be an acidification problem.

ii) Consideration should be given to expanding deposition monitoring programs, within the framework of AMAP and existing networks such as the ECE/EMEP deposition monitoring network, to encompass measurement of acid deposition in the Arctic. Emphasis should also be placed on measuring dry deposition.

iii) Emphasis should be placed on defining critical loads and setting target loads for sensitive Arctic ecosystems. In the event that these target loads are being exceeded, steps should be taken to reduce those emissions contributing to the problem, in accordance with international agreements such as the ECE LRTAP Convention. Reduction of emissions of sulphur and nitrogen should be sought by, inter alia, implementing the use of the best available technology.

6. ARCTIC MONITORING AND ASSESSMENT PROGRAM

The eight Arctic countries recognize that the Arctic region represents one of the relatively pristine areas on earth. It is therefore of great importance to preserve and to protect the Arctic.

Measurements in the Arctic indicate that pollutants originating from anthropogenic activities in the mid-latitudes are transported to the Arctic by atmospheric processes, ocean currents and rivers, and that pollutants are deposited and accumulated in the Arctic environment and its ecosystems.

Exploitation of natural resources, and concomitant urban and industrial expansion within the Arctic region, also contribute to the degradation of the Arctic environment and affect the living conditions for the people of the region.

Distinguishing human-induced changes from changes caused by natural phenomena in the Arctic will require monitoring of selected key indicators of the Arctic Environment. Therefore, the eight Arctic countries have agreed to promote development of an Arctic Monitoring and Assessment Program (AMAP) in order to understand and document these changes and so that the monitoring results may be used to anticipate adverse biological, chemical and physical changes to the ecosystem and to prevent, minimize and mitigate these adverse effects.

The primary objective of the AMAP is the measurement of the levels of anthropogenic pollutants and the assessment of their effects in relevant component parts of the Arctic environment. The assessments should be presented in status reports to relevant fora as a basis for necessary steps to be taken to reduce the pollution.

Two of the most significant threats to the present Arctic environment may come from climate change, induced by global warming, and the effects of stratospheric ozone depletion. Programs to detect and determine the causes and effects of climate change and ozone depletion are to a large extent being developed by other international groupings and in other fora.

It is important for AMAP to be aware of these programs and to develop links with them from an Arctic perspective in order to encourage and facilitate an Arctic component in climate programs. Data obtained for assessing climate change will provide important inputs to the AMAP dataset. In turn, AMAP data will be relevant to climate change programs in the Arctic.

The pollution data available from the Arctic region are with a few exceptions based on research programs performed within limited subject areas by national programs and not supported by bilateral or international cooperation. There is an urgent need for cooperation among local and regional efforts and global programs in order to obtain better documentation on the environmental situation in the Arctic especially with regard to long-range air and marine pollution.

From the outset, the AMAP should as far as possible be based on existing programs. The program should be initiated in a step by step fashion as indicated in the proposal for the AMAP.

6.1 Actions

i) Distinguishing human-induced changes from changes caused by natural phenomena in the Arctic will require estimates and regular reporting by the Arctic countries of contaminant emissions and discharges, including accidental discharges, as well as transport and deposition. In addition monitoring of deposition and selected key indicators of the Arctic biological environment, are required. The eight Arctic countries should therefore agree to establish an Arctic Monitoring and Assessment Program (AMAP) to fulfill these monitoring objectives.

ii) The AMAP should be implemented through the establishment of an Arctic Monitoring and Assessment Task Force and a small secretariat, established by the Government of Norway.

iii) AMAP should as far as possible build upon existing, programs. Thus, one of the important tasks of the AMAP will be to review and coordinate existing national programs, establish a data directory, and to develop these programs when appropriate in an international framework.

iv) As an initial priority, the AMAP should focus on persistent organic contaminants and on selected heavy metals and radionuclides, and ultimately to monitor ecological indicators to provide a basis for assessments of the status of Arctic ecosystems.

v) The eight Arctic countries will receive regular State of the Arctic Environment Reports summarizing the results of the AMAP.

As a result of these actions, the Arctic Monitoring and Assessment Program will provide information for:

i) integrated assessment reports on status and trends in the condition of Arctic ecosystems;

ii) identifying possible causes for changing conditions;

iii) detecting emerging problems, their possible causes, and the potential risk to Arctic ecosystems including indigenous peoples and other Arctic residents; and

iv) recommending actions required to reduce risks to Arctic ecosystems.

7. PROTECTION OF THE ARCTIC MARINE ENVIRONMENT

The eight Arctic Countries recognize their particular interests and responsibilities as neighbouring countries in the Arctic, and emphasize the need to take preventive measures directly or through competent international organizations, consistent in particular with the 1982 United Nations Convention on the Law of the Sea regarding marine pollution in the Arctic, irrespective of origin.

To this end the Arctic countries agree to:

i) Apply the principles concerning the protection and preservation of the Marine Environment as reflected in the 1982 United Nations Convention on the Law of the Sea, and, in accordance with the continuing development of international environmental law, to further strengthen rules in order to protect the Arctic;

ii) Take measures as soon as possible to adhere to the strictest relevant international standards within the conventions, to which the countries are parties, regarding discharges irrespective of origin;

iii) Undertake joint actions in relevant international fora to further strengthen recognition of the particularly sensitive character of ice-covered parts of the Arctic Ocean;

iv) Review, in accordance with the general aims of this environmental Strategy, the relevance to the Arctic of international instruments connected with the protection of the marine environment, with the aim that all Arctic countries accede, where appropriate, to the instruments, or apply the principles and regulations embodied therein;

v) Jointly support the appropriate initiatives of international organizations in developing mandatory standards in order to improve the protection against accidental pollution affecting the marine environment, and actively ensure application of such standards;

vi) Carry out studies of pollution in the monitoring activities within AMAP,

8. EMERGENCY PREVENTION, PREPAREDNESS AND RESPONSE

At the same time as the Arctic is exhibiting signs of serious contamination from pollutants carried via long range transport from mid latitudes, there has been an increase in development activities and shipping within the Arctic. These activities can have serious environmental consequences in the Arctic as a result of accidents leading, inter alia, to spills and discharges of oil and other harmful substances. The vulnerability of the Arctic ecosystem to these sudden intrusions will be variable. Some limited mapping of areas sensitive to oil spills has been conducted but more remains to be done. The relative hazard/risk associated with different activities is also not well documented, nor is the geographic distribution of high risk activities.

There are a number of bilateral, regional and global arrangements which presently exist to deal with accidental pollution, such as the 1983 Canada-Denmark Agreement for Cooperating relating to the Marine Environment, the 1971 Agreement between Denmark, Finland, Norway and Sweden on Cooperation on Oil Pollution and the 1990 International Convention on Oil Pollution Preparedness, Response and Cooperation. There are other multilateral conventions related to nuclear accidents or radiological emergencies supplemented by bilateral agreements on the exchange of information and reporting relative to nuclear plants and events. [1983 Canada–Denmark Agreement at 23 I.L.M. 269 (1984); 1990 Preparedness Convention at 30 I.L.M. 733 (1991)]

The UN ECE has started work on an international convention, on the prevention and control of the transboundary effects of industrial accidents. A part of the work is the establishment or reinforcement of regional and subregional mechanisms for response, assistance and exchange of information on environmental emergencies.

8.1 Actions

The Arctic countries agree to the following framework for taking early cooperative action on emergency prevention, preparedness and response in the Arctic. They will take steps to review existing bilateral and multilateral arrangements in order to evaluate the adequacy of the geographical coverage of the Arctic regions by cooperative agreements. They will also take steps to convene a meeting of experts to consider and recommend the necessary system of cooperation, which could include, inter alia, the following elements:

i) Actions to respond to significant accidental pollution from any source;

ii) Coordination and harmonization of preventive policies, strategies and measures;

iii) Establishment of a system for early notification in the event of significant accidental pollution or an imminent threat of such pollution;

iv) Assessment of the risks for significant accidental pollution and of the adverse effects in such cases so as to enable the parties to take the necessary preventive, preparedness and response measures;

v) Inclusion of studies on effects of accidental pollution in conjunction with the monitoring activities of AMAP;

vi) Cooperation in the conduct of research into and development of methods and technologies for prevention of, preparedness for and response to significant accidental pollution in the Arctic;

vii) Cooperation in developing a system for exchange of information on research and new developments regarding methods and technologies on response in the Arctic;

viii) Exchange of information on legislative and administrative measures as well as policies;

ix) Measures for providing information to the public and public participation; and

x) Further enhance regional bilateral and multilateral cooperation in the Arctic regarding prevention, preparedness and response by developing, as appropriate, contingency plans, training programs, as well as other measures to facilitate assistance to the parties, in particular mutual assistance for efficient emergency response in the event of significant accidental pollution, or the imminent threat of such pollution.

9. CONSERVATION OF ARCTIC FLORA AND FAUNA

The health of Arctic flora and fauna is a key concern of the Arctic countries. These flora and fauna assume special significance in this region since they are an essential factor helping to define the culture and survival of the people living there. Although isolated geographically from the industrialized temperate regions of the globe, it has now been amply demonstrated that this has not excluded Arctic flora and fauna from the negative consequences of human activities in mid latitudes. The impacts on the Arctic have escalated over the past several decades and both scientific and traditional knowledge have been pointing to the danger signals. Many of these concerns are enumerated in the six Arctic state of the Environment reports. They confirm that Arctic flora, fauna and their habitats are being threatened by large scale economic development projects; long range transport of pollutants; and degradation of habitats.

The problems facing Arctic flora, fauna and habitats are not confined to any one country but are circumpolar in nature. Furthermore, because of the uniqueness of Arctic ecosystems, strategies to deal with these problems will differ from those of other regions.

Several multilateral and bilateral agreements which pertain to the conservation of Arctic flora and fauna and their habitats are currently in existence. Most however, have been designed to be universally applicable to, or to apply to, a wider geographical area than the Arctic. Only the Agreement on Conservation of Polar Bears and some individual provisions in other agreements provide a specific Arctic focus.

The eight Arctic countries should therefore seek to create a distinct forum for scientists, indigenous peoples and conservation managers engaged in Arctic flora, fauna and habitat related activities to exchange data and information on issues such as shared species and habitats and to collaborate, as appropriate, for more effective research, sustainable utilization and conservation.

9.1 Actions

The eight Arctic countries are mindful of the need to conserve Arctic flora and fauna and their habitats in their natural diversity, and protect these resources from the pollution threats described in this Arctic Environmental Protection Strategy. They recognize the special relationship and importance of Arctic flora and fauna and their habitats to indigenous peoples. The countries also recognize the benefits to be gained from sharing scientific and management information, traditional knowledge, and other data with respect to Arctic flora and fauna and their habitats. With due regard to existing international cooperation, and in an effort to improve research and information aimed at protecting these resources and their habitats from pollution and environmental degradation, they have reached the following understanding:

i) The eight Arctic countries will cooperate for the conservation of Arctic flora and fauna, their diversity, and their habitats. Such cooperation shall include, inter alia, exchanges of research and management information and data, and coordination of research, on the following:

a) Arctic species, their health and habitats;

b) the laws, regulations and practices of the parties with respect to the conservation and management of such species; and

c) the importance and relationship to, and use of, such species by indigenous peoples and the unique contribution of indigenous peoples to the stewardship of nature and its resources;

ii) Each country will provide to the other countries, as appropriate, such information, publications, and/or documents as may be agreed under the terms of the Strategy;

iii) The eight Arctic countries will seek to develop other forms of cooperation, including exchanges of experts, of traditional knowledge, and of other data, as well as engaging in joint projects, bilateral or multilateral meetings, symposia and joint publications, to meet the intent of this Strategy;

iv) The eight Arctic countries will each seek to develop more effective laws, regulations and practices for the conservation of Arctic flora and fauna, their diversity, and their habitats in close cooperation with Arctic indigenous peoples;

v) The eight Arctic countries agree to establish a mechanism for furthering the following aims in close cooperation with Arctic indigenous peoples:

a) Promoting and facilitating exchanges of information and personnel as provided for in this Strategy;

b) Making recommendations with respect to the priorities, the orientation and the nature of research and monitoring programs of the Arctic countries;

c) Proposing strategies for enhanced conservation of Arctic species and their habitats; and

d) Regularly compiling and disseminating information on activities regarding the conservation of Arctic flora and fauna.

vi) The eight Arctic countries will consult, as deemed appropriate with the International Arctic Science Committee and other bodies on any matter that falls within the scope of this Strategy;

vii) By October 1991 each Country will identify to the others its national agency designated to coordinate the cooperation envisaged by this section;

viii) The Countries agree that the terms and conditions of the cooperation and exchanges provided for in this section will be subject to the laws and regulations of the Countries;

ix) Each country will make its best efforts to provide resources adequate to carry out its responsibilities under this section. It is understood that the ability of each country to carry out activities is subject to the availability of funds, and that countries will seek to ensure long-term funding for necessary projects.

10. FURTHER COOPERATION

Continuity and further cooperation are essential for increasing the protection of the Arctic environment. In order to ensure this continuity and cooperation, the eight Arctic countries agree to hold regular Meetings on the Arctic Environment.

The date and venue of the next meeting will be agreed upon at the preceding meeting. Decisions on the agenda and participation of observers will be made and communicated to interested parties in advance of the meeting.

The decision to invite observers should be based on a pragmatic and functional evaluation of their involvement in and contribution to Arctic environmental questions.

In order to facilitate the participation of Arctic indigenous peoples the following organizations will be invited as observers: the Inuit Circumpolar Conference, the Nordic Saami Council and the U.S.S.R. Association of Small Peoples of the North.

The Meetings on the Arctic Environment shall serve to:

i) identify and coordinate actions to implement and further develop the Arctic Environmental Protection Strategy;

ii) initiate cooperation in new fields relevant to the environmental protection of the Arctic;

iii) make necessary recommendations in order to protect the Arctic environment;

iv) improve existing environmental regimes relevant to the Arctic; and

v) assess and report on progress on actions agreed upon.

1.29 Rio Declaration on Environment and Development. Adopted by the U.N. Conference on Environment and Development (UNCED) at Rio De Janeiro, 13 June 1992. U.N.Doc. A/CONF.151/26 (vol. I) (1992); *reprinted in* 31 I.L.M. 874 (1992) & 5 Weston V.B.16

The United Nations Conference on Environment and Development,

Having met at Rio de Janeiro from 3 to 14 June 1992,

Reaffirming the Declaration of the United Nations Conference on the Human Environment, adopted at Stockholm on 16 June 1972, and seeking to build upon it,

With the goal of establishing a new and equitable global partnership through the creation of new levels of cooperation among States, key sectors of societies and people,

Working towards international agreements which respect the interests of all and protect the integrity of the global environmental and developmental system,

Recognizing the integral and interdependent nature of the Earth, our home,

Proclaims that:

Principle 1

Human beings are at the centre of concerns for sustainable development. They are entitled to a healthy and productive life in harmony with nature.

Principle 2

States have, in accordance with the Charter of the United Nations and the principles of international law, the sovereign right to exploit their own resources pursuant to their own environmental and developmental policies, and the responsibility to ensure that activities within their jurisdiction or control do not cause damage to the environment of other States or of areas beyond the limits of national jurisdiction.

Principle 3

The right to development must be fulfilled so as to equitably meet developmental and environmental needs of present and future generations.

Principle 4

In order to achieve sustainable development, environmental protection shall constitute an integral part of the development process and cannot be considered in isolation from it.

Principle 5

All States and all people shall cooperate in the essential task of eradicating poverty as an indispensable requirement for sustainable development, in order to decrease the disparities in standards of living and better meet the needs of the majority of the people of the world.

Principle 6

The special situation and needs of developing countries, particularly the least developed and those most environmentally vulnerable, shall be given special priority. International actions in the field of environment and development should also address the interests and needs of all countries.

Principle 7

States shall cooperate in a spirit of global partnership to conserve, protect and restore the health and integrity of the Earth's ecosystem. In view of the different contributions to global environmental degradation, States have common but differentiated responsibilities. The developed countries acknowledge the responsibility that they bear in the international pursuit of sustainable development in view of the pressures their societies place on the global environment and of the technologies and financial resources they command.

Principle 8

To achieve sustainable development and a higher quality of life for all people, States should reduce and eliminate unsustainable patterns of production and consumption and promote appropriate demographic policies.

Principle 9

States should cooperate to strengthen endogenous capacity-building for sustainable development by improving scientific understanding through exchanges of scientific and technological knowledge, and by enhancing the development, adaptation, diffusion and transfer of technologies, including new and innovative technologies.

Principle 10

Environmental issues are best handled with the participation of all concerned citizens, at the relevant level. At the national level, each individual shall have appropriate access to information concerning the environment that is held by public authorities, including information on hazardous materials and activities in their communities, and the opportunity to participate in decision-making processes. States shall facilitate and encourage public awareness and participation by making information widely available. Effective access to judicial and administrative proceedings, including redress and remedy, shall be provided.

Principle 11

States shall enact effective environmental legislation. Environmental standards, management objectives and priorities should reflect the environmental and developmental context to which they apply. Standards applied by some countries may be inappropriate and of unwarranted economic and social cost to other countries, in particular developing countries.

Principle 12

States should cooperate to promote a supportive and open international economic system that would lead to economic growth and sustainable development in all countries, to better address the problems of environmental degradation. Trade policy measures for environmental purposes should not constitute a means of arbitrary or unjustifiable discrimination or a disguised restriction on international trade. Unilateral actions to deal with environmental challenges outside the jurisdiction of the importing country should be avoided. Environmental measures addressing transboundary or global environmental problems should, as far as possible, be based on an international consensus.

Principle 13

States shall develop national law regarding liability and compensation for the victims of pollution and other environmental damage. States shall also cooperate in an expeditious and more determined manner to develop further international law regarding liability and compensation for adverse effects of environmental damage caused by activities within their jurisdiction or control to areas beyond their jurisdiction.

Principle 14

States should effectively cooperate to discourage or prevent the relocation and transfer to other States of any activities and substances that cause severe environmental degradation or are found to be harmful to human health.

Principle 15

In order to protect the environment, the precautionary approach shall be widely applied by States according to their capabilities. Where there are threats of serious or irreversible damage, lack of full scientific certainty shall not be used as a reason for postponing cost-effective measures to prevent environmental degradation.

Principle 16

National authorities should endeavor to promote the internalization of environmental costs and the use of economic instruments, taking into account the approach that the polluter should, in principle, bear the cost of pollution, with due regard to the public interest and without distorting international trade and investment.

Principle 17

Environmental impact assessment, as a national instrument, shall be undertaken for proposed activities that are likely to have a significant adverse impact on the environment and are subject to a decision of a competent national authority.

Principle 18

States shall immediately notify other States of any natural disasters or other emergencies that are likely to produce sudden harmful effects on the environment of those States. Every effort shall be made by the international community to help States so afflicted.

Principle 19

States shall provide prior and timely notification and relevant information to potentially affected States on activities that may have a significant adverse transboundary environmental effect and shall consult with those States at an early stage and in good faith.

Principle 20

Women have a vital role in environmental management and development. Their full participation is therefore essential to achieve sustainable development.

Principle 21

The creativity, ideals and courage of the youth of the world should be mobilized to forge a global partnership in order to achieve sustainable development and ensure a better future for all.

Principle 22

Indigenous people and their communities and other local communities have a vital role in environmental management and development because of their knowledge and traditional practices. States should recognize and duly support their identity, culture and interests and enable their effective participation in the achievement of sustainable development.

Principle 23

The environment and natural resources of people under oppression, domination and occupation shall be protected.

Principle 24

Warfare is inherently destructive of sustainable development. States shall therefore respect international law providing protection for the environment in times of armed conflict and cooperate in its further development, as necessary.

Principle 25

Peace, development and environmental protection are interdependent and indivisible.

Principle 26

States shall resolve all their environmental disputes peacefully and by appropriate means in accordance with the Charter of the United Nations.

Principle 27

States and people shall cooperate in good faith and in a spirit of partnership in the fulfilment of the principles embodied in this Declaration and in the further development of international law in the field of sustainable development.

1.30 AGENDA 21. Approved by the U.N. Conference on Environment and Development (UNCED) at Rio De Janeiro, 13 June 1992. U.N. Doc. A/CONF. 151/26 (vols. I, II, & III) (1992); *reprinted in* 5 Weston V.B.17: *Table of Contents & Chs. 5, 15, 17, 20, 33, 38.*

Agenda 21 was adopted by the U.N. Conference on Environment and Development (UNCED) at Rio de Janeiro, 13 June 1992. The complete text is too lengthy for publication in this volume. The following table of contents provides a summary of its provisions. The full text may be found in the above-cited source.

Chapter **Paragraphs**

* * *

Chapter 5

DEMOGRAPHIC DYNAMICS AND SUSTAINABILITY

5.1. This chapter contains the following programme areas:

(a) Developing and disseminating knowledge concerning the links between demographic trends and factors and sustainable development;

(b) Formulating integrated national policies for environment and development, taking into account demographic trends and factors;

(c) Implementing integrated, environment and development programmes at the local level, taking into account demographic trends and factors.

PROGRAMME AREAS

A. *Developing and disseminating knowledge concerning the links between demographic trends and factors and sustainable development*

Basis for action

5.2. Demographic trends and factors and sustainable development have a synergistic relationship.

5.3. The growth of world population and production combined with unsustainable consumption patterns places increasingly severe stress on the life-supporting capacities of our planet. These interactive processes affect the use of land, water, air, energy and other resources. Rapidly growing cities, unless well-managed, face major environmental problems. The increase in both the number and size of cities calls for greater attention to issues of local government and municipal management. The human dimensions are key elements to consider in this intricate set of relationships and they should be adequately taken into consideration in comprehensive policies for sustainable development. Such policies should address the linkages of demographic trends and factors, resource use, appropriate technology dissemination, and development. Population policy should also recognize the role played by human beings in environmental and development concerns. There is a need to increase awareness of this issue among decision makers at all levels and to provide both better information on which to base national and international policies and a framework against which to interpret this information.

5.4. There is a need to develop strategies to mitigate both the adverse impact on the environment of human activities and the adverse impact of environmental change on human populations. The world's population is expected to exceed 8 billion by the year 2020. Sixty per cent of the world's population already live in coastal areas, while 65 per cent of cities with populations above 2.5 million are located along the world coasts; several of them are already at or below the present sea level.

Objectives

5.5. The following objectives should be achieved as soon as practicable:

(a) To incorporate demographic trends and factors in the global analysis of environment and development issues;

(b) To develop a better understanding of the relationships among demographic dynamics, technology, cultural behaviour, natural resources and life support systems;

(c) To assess human vulnerability in ecologically sensitive areas and centres of population to determine the priorities for action at all levels, taking full account of community defined needs.

Activities

Research on the interaction between demographic trends and factors and sustainable development

5.6. Relevant international, regional and national institutions should consider undertaking the following activities:

(a) Identifying the interactions between demographic processes, natural resources and life support systems, bearing in mind regional and subregional variations deriving from, *inter alia,* different levels of development;

(b) Integrating demographic trends and factors into the ongoing study of environmental change, using the expertise of international, regional and national research networks and of local communities, first, to study the human dimensions of environmental change and, second, to identify vulnerable areas;

(c) Identifying priority areas for action and developing strategies and programmes to mitigate the adverse impact of environmental change on human populations, and vice versa.

Means of implementation

(a) *Financing and cost evaluation*

5.7. The Conference secretariat has estimated the average total annual cost (1993–2000) of implementing the activities of this programme to be about $10 million from the international community on grant or concessional terms. These are indicative and order-of-magnitude estimates only and have not been reviewed by Governments. Actual costs and financial terms, including any that are non-concessional, will depend upon, *inter alia,* the specific strategies and programmes Governments decide upon for implementation.

(b) *Strengthening research programmes that integrate population, environment and development*

5.8. In order to integrate demographic analysis into a broader social science perspective on environment and development, interdisciplinary research should be increased. International institutions and networks of experts should enhance their scientific capacity, taking full account of community experience and knowledge, and should disseminate the experience gained in multidisciplinary approaches and in linking theory to action.

5.9. Better modelling capabilities should be developed, identifying the range of possible outcomes of current human activities, especially the interrelated impact of demographic trends and factors, per capita resource use and wealth distribution, as well as the major migration flows that may be expected with increasing climatic events and cumulative environmental change that may destroy people's local livelihoods.

(c) *Developing information and public awareness*

5.10. Socio-demographic information should be developed in a suitable format for interfacing with physical, biological and socio-economic data. Compatible spatial and temporal scales, cross-country and time-series information, as well as global behavioural indicators should be developed, learning from local communities' perceptions and attitudes.

5.11. Awareness should be increased at all levels concerning the need to optimize the sustainable use of resources through efficient resource management, taking into account the development needs of the populations of developing countries.

5.12. Awareness should be increased of the fundamental linkages between improving the status of women and demographic dynamics, particularly through women's access to education, primary and reproductive health care programmes, economic independence and their effective, equitable participation in all levels of decision-making.

5.13. Results of research concerned with sustainable development issues should be disseminated through technical reports, scientific journals, the media, workshops, forums or other means so that the information can be used by decision makers at all levels and increase public awareness.

(d) *Developing and/or enhancing institutional capacity and collaboration*

5.14. Collaboration and exchange of information should be increased between research institutions and international, regional and national agencies and all other sectors (including the private sector, local communities, non-governmental organizations and scientific institutions) from both the industrialized and developing countries, as appropriate.

5.15. Efforts should be intensified to enhance the capacities of national and local governments, the private sector and non-governmental organizations in developing countries to meet the growing needs for improved management of rapidly growing urban areas.

B. *Formulating integrated national policies for environment and development, taking into account demographic trends and factors*

Basis for action

5.16. Existing plans for sustainable development have generally recognized demographic trends and factors as elements that have a critical influence on consumption patterns, production, lifestyles and long-term sustainability. But in future, more attention will have to be given to these issues in general policy formulation and the design of development plans. To do this, all countries will have to improve their own capacities to assess the environment and development implications of their demographic trends and factors. They will also need to formulate and implement policies and action programmes where appropriate. Policies should be designed to address the consequences of population growth built into population momentum, while at the same time incorporating measures to bring about demographic transition. They should combine environmental concerns and population issues within a holistic view of development whose primary goals include the alleviation of poverty; secure livelihoods; good health; quality of life; improvement of the status and income of women and their access to schooling and professional training, as well as fulfilment of their personal aspirations; and empowerment of individuals and communities. Recognizing that large increases in the size and number of cities will occur in developing countries under any likely population scenario, greater attention should be given to preparing for the needs, in particular of women and children, for improved municipal management and local government.

Objective

5.17. Full integration of population concerns into national planning, policy and decision-making processes should continue. Population policies and programmes should be considered, with full recognition of women's rights.

Activities

5.18. Governments and other relevant actors could, *inter alia,* undertake the following activities, with appropriate assistance from aid agencies, and report on their status of implementation to the International Conference on Population and Development to be held in 1994, especially to its committee on population and environment.

(a) *Assessing the implications of national demographic trends and factors*

5.19. The relationships between demographic trends and factors and environmental change and between environmental degradation and the components of demographic change should be analysed.

5.20. Research should be conducted on how environmental factors interact with socio-economic factors as a cause of migration.

5.21. Vulnerable population groups (such as rural landless workers, ethnic minorities, refugees, migrants, displaced people, women heads of household) whose changes in demographic structure may have specific impacts on sustainable development should be identified.

5.22. An assessment should be made of the implications of the age structure of the population on resource demand and dependency burdens, ranging from educational expenses for the young to health care and support for the elderly, and on household income generation.

5.23. An assessment should also be made of national population carrying capacity in the context of satisfaction of human needs and sustainable development, and special attention should be given to critical resources, such as water and land, and environmental factors, such as ecosystem health and biodiversity.

5.24. The impact of national demographic trends and factors on the traditional livelihoods of indigenous groups and local communities, including changes in traditional land use because of internal population pressures, should be studied.

(b) *Building and strengthening a national information base*

5.25. National databases on demographic trends and factors and environment should be built and/or strengthened, disaggregating data by ecological region (ecosystem approach), and population/environment profiles should be established by region.

5.26. Methodologies and instruments should be developed to identify areas where sustainability is, or may be, threatened by the environmental effects of demographic trends and factors, incorporating both current and projected demographic data linked to natural environmental processes.

5.27. Case-studies of local level responses by different groups to demographic dynamics should be developed, particularly in areas subject to environmental stress and in deteriorating urban centres.

5.28. Population data should be disaggregated by, *inter alia,* sex and age in order to take into account the implications of the gender division of labour for the use and management of natural resources.

(c) *Incorporating demographic features into policies and plans*

5.29. In formulating human settlements policies, account should be taken of resource needs, waste production and ecosystem health.

5.30. The direct and induced effects of demographic changes on environment and development programmes should, where appropriate, be integrated, and the impact on demographic features assessed.

5.31. National population policy goals and programmes that are consistent with national environment and development plans for sustainability and in keeping with the freedom, dignity and personally held values of individuals should be established and implemented.

5.32. Appropriate socio-economic policies for the young and the elderly, both in terms of family and state support systems, should be developed.

5.33. Policies and programmes should be developed for handling the various types of migrations that result from or induce environmental disruptions, with special attention to women and vulnerable groups.

5.34. Demographic concerns, including concerns for environmental migrants and displaced people, should be incorporated in the programmes for sustainable development of relevant international and regional institutions.

5.35. National reviews should be conducted and the integration of population policies in national development and environment strategies should be monitored nationally.

Means of implementation

(a) *Financing and cost evaluation*

5.36. The Conference secretariat has estimated the average total annual cost (1993–2000) of implementing the activities of this programme to be about $90 million from the international community on grant or concessional terms. These are indicative and order-of-magnitude estimates only and have not been reviewed by Governments. Actual costs and financial terms, including any that are non-concessional, will depend upon, *inter alia,* the specific strategies and programmes Governments decide upon for implementation.

(b) *Raising awareness of demographic and sustainable development interactions*

5.37. Understanding of the interactions between demographic trends and factors and sustainable development should be increased in all sectors of society. Stress should be placed on local and national action. Demographic and sustainable development education should be coordinated and integrated in both the formal and non-formal education sectors. Particular attention should be given to population literacy programmes, notably for women. Special emphasis should be placed on the linkage between these programmes, primary environmental care and the provision of primary health care and services.

(c) *Strengthening institutions*

5.38. The capacity of national, regional and local structures to deal with issues relating to demographic trends and factors and sustainable development should be enhanced. This would involve strengthening the relevant bodies responsible for population issues to enable them to elaborate policies consistent with the national prospects for sustainable development. Cooperation among government, national research institutions, non-governmental organizations and local communities in assessing problems and evaluating policies should also be enhanced.

5.39. The capacity of the relevant United Nations organs, organizations and bodies, international and regional intergovernmental bodies, non-governmental organizations and local communities should, as appropriate, be enhanced to help countries develop sustainable development policies on request and, as appropriate, provide assistance to environmental migrants and displaced people.

5.40. Inter-agency support for national sustainable development policies and programmes should be improved through better coordination of population and environment activities.

(d) *Promoting human resource development*

5.41. The international and regional scientific institutions should assist Governments, upon request, to include concerns regarding the population/environment interactions at the global, ecosystem and micro-levels in the training of demographers and population and environment specialists. Training should include research on linkages and ways to design integrated strategies.

C. *Implementing integrated environment and development programmes at the local level, taking into account demographic trends and factors*

Basis for action

5.42. Population programmes are more effective when implemented together with appropriate cross-sectoral policies. To attain sustainability at the local level, a new framework is needed that integrates demographic trends and factors with such factors as ecosystem health, technology and human settlements, and with socio-economic structures and access to resources. Population programmes should be consistent with socio-economic and environmental planning. Integrated sustainable development programmes should closely correlate action on demographic trends and factors with resource management activities and development goals that meet the needs of the people concerned.

Objective

5.43. Population programmes should be implemented along with natural resource management and development programmes at the local level that will ensure sustainable use of natural resources, improve the quality of life of the people and enhance environmental quality.

Activities

5.44. Governments and local communities, including community-based women's organizations and national non-governmental organizations, consistent with national plans, objectives, strategies and priorities, could, *inter alia*, undertake the activities set out below with the assistance and cooperation of international organizations, as appropriate. Governments could share their experience in the implementation of Agenda 21 at the International Conference on Population and Development, to be held in 1994, especially its committee on population and environment.

(a) *Developing a framework for action*

5.45. An effective consultative process should be established and implemented with concerned groups of society where the formulation and decision-making of all components of the programmes are based on a nationwide consultative process drawing on community meetings, regional workshops and national seminars, as appropriate. This process should ensure that views of women and men on needs, perspective and constraints are equally well reflected in the design of programmes, and that solutions are rooted in specific experience. The poor and underprivileged should be priority groups in this process.

5.46. Nationally determined policies for integrated and multifaceted programmes, with special attention to women, to the poorest people living in critical areas and to other vulnerable groups should be implemented, ensuring the involvement of groups with a special potential to act as agents for change and sustainable development. Special emphasis should be placed on those programmes that achieve multiple objectives, encouraging sustainable economic development, and mitigating adverse impacts of demographic trends and factors, and avoiding long-term environmental damage. Food security, access to secure tenure, basic shelter, and essential infrastructure, education, family welfare, women's reproductive health, family credit schemes, reforestation programmes, primary environmental care, women's employment should, as appropriate, be included among other factors.

5.47. An analytical framework should be developed to identify complementary elements of sustainable development policies as well as the national mechanisms to monitor and evaluate their effects on population dynamics.

5.48. Special attention should be given to the critical role of women in population/environment programmes and in achieving sustainable development. Projects should take advantage of opportunities to link social, economic and environmental gains for women and their families. Empowerment of women is essential and should be assured through education, training and policies to accord and improve women's rights and access to assets, human and civil rights, labour-saving measures, job opportunities and participation in decision-making. Population/environment programmes must enable women to mobilize themselves to alleviate their burden and improve their capacity to participate in and benefit from socio-economic development. Specific measures should be undertaken to close the gap between female and male illiteracy rates.

(b) *Supporting programmes that promote changes in demographic trends and factors towards sustainability*

5.49. Reproductive health programmes and services, should, as appropriate, be developed and enhanced to reduce maternal and infant mortality from all causes and enable women and men to fulfil their personal aspirations in terms of family size, in a way in keeping with their freedom and dignity and personally held values.

5.50. Governments should take active steps to implement, as a matter of urgency, in accordance with country-specific conditions and legal systems, measures to ensure that women and men have the same right to decide freely and responsibly on the number and spacing of their children, to have access to the information, education and means, as appropriate, to enable them to exercise this right in keeping with their freedom, dignity and personally held values taking into account ethical and cultural considerations.

5.51. Governments should take active steps to implement programmes to establish and strengthen preventive and curative health facilities that include women-centred, women-managed, safe and effective reproductive health care and affordable, accessible services, as appropriate, for the responsible planning of family size, in keeping with freedom, dignity and personally held values and taking into account ethical and cultural considerations. Programmes should focus on providing comprehensive health care, including pre-natal care, education and information on health and responsible parenthood and should provide the opportunity for all women to breast-feed fully, at least during the first four months post-partum. Programmes should fully support women's productive and reproductive roles and well being, with special attention to the need for providing equal and improved health care for all children and the need to reduce the risk of maternal and child mortality and sickness.

5.52. Consistent with national priorities, culturally based information and education programmes that transmit reproductive health messages to men and women that are easily understood should be developed.

(c) *Creating appropriate institutional conditions*

5.53. Constituencies and institutional conditions to facilitate the implementation of demographic activities should, as appropriate, be fostered. This requires support and commitment from political, indigenous, religious and traditional authorities, the private sector and the national scientific community. In developing these appropriate institutional conditions, countries should closely involve established national machinery for women.

5.54. Population assistance should be coordinated with bilateral and multilateral donors to ensure that population needs and requirements of all developing countries are addressed, fully respecting the overall coordinating responsibility and the choice and strategies of the recipient countries.

5.55. Coordination should be improved at local and international levels. Working practices should be enhanced in order to make optimum use of resources, draw on collective experience and improve the implementation of programmes. UNFPA and other relevant agencies should strengthen the coordination of international cooperation activities with recipient and donor countries in order to ensure that adequate funding is available to respond to growing needs.

5.56. Proposals should be developed for local, national and international population/environment programmes in line with specific needs for achieving sustainability. Where appropriate, institutional changes must be implemented so that old-age security does not entirely depend on input from family members.

Means of implementation

(a) *Financing and cost evaluation*

5.57. The Conference secretariat has estimated the average total annual cost (1993–2000) of implementing the activities of this programme to be about $7 billion, including about $3.5 billion from the international community on grant or concessional terms. These are indicative and order-of-magnitude estimates only and have not been reviewed by Governments. Actual costs and financial terms, including any that are non-concessional, will depend upon, *inter alia,* the specific strategies and programmes Governments decide upon for implementation.

(b) *Research*

5.58. Research should be undertaken with a view to developing specific action programmes; it will be necessary to establish priorities between proposed areas of research.

5.59. Socio-demographic research should be conducted on how populations respond to a changing environment.

5.60. Understanding of socio-cultural and political factors that can positively influence acceptance of appropriate population policy instruments should be improved.

5.61. Surveys of changes in needs for appropriate services relating to responsible planning of family size, reflecting variations among different socio-economic groups and variations in different geographical regions should be undertaken.

(c) *Human resource development and capacity-building*

5.62. The areas of human resource development and capacity-building, with particular attention to the education and training of women, are areas of critical importance and are a very high priority in the implementation of population programmes.

5.63. Workshops to help programme and projects managers to link population programmes to other development and environmental goals should be conducted.

5.64. Educational materials, including guides/workbooks for planners and decision makers and other actors of population/environment/development programmes, should be developed.

5.65. Cooperation should be developed between Governments, scientific institutions and non-governmental organizations within the region, and similar institutions outside the region. Cooperation with local organizations should be fostered in order to raise awareness, engage in demonstration projects and report on the experience gained.

5.66. The recommendations contained in this chapter should in no way prejudice discussions at the International Conference on Population and Development in 1994, which will be the appropriate forum for dealing with population and development issues, taking into account the recommendations of the International Conference on Population, held in Mexico City in 1984, and the Forward-looking Strategies for the Advancement of Women, adopted by the World Conference to Review and Appraise the Achievements of the United Decade for Women: Equality, Development and Peace, held in Nairobi in 1985.

* * *

Chapter 15
CONSERVATION OF BIOLOGICAL DIVERSITY
INTRODUCTION

15.1. The objectives and activities in this chapter of Agenda 21 are intended to improve the conservation of biological diversity and the sustainable use of biological resources, as well as to support the Convention on Biological Diversity.

15.2. Our planet's essential goods and services depend on the variety and variability of genes, species, populations and ecosystems. Biological resources feed and clothe us and provide housing, medicines and spiritual nourishment. The natural ecosystems of forests, savannahs, pastures and rangelands, deserts, tundras, rivers, lakes and seas contain most of the Earth's biodiversity. Farmers' fields and gardens are also of great importance as repositories, while gene banks, botanical gardens, zoos and other germplasm repositories make a small but significant contribution. The current decline in biodiversity is largely the result of human activity and represents a serious threat to human development.

PROGRAMME AREA

Conservation of biological diversity

Basis for action

15.3. Despite mounting efforts over the past 20 years, the loss of the world's biological diversity, mainly from habitat destruction, over-harvesting, pollution and the inappropriate introduction of foreign plants and animals, has continued. Biological resources constitute a capital asset with great potential for yielding sustainable benefits. Urgent and decisive action is needed to conserve and maintain genes, species and ecosystems, with a view to the sustainable management and use of biological resources. Capacities for the assessment, study and systematic observation and evaluation of biodiversity need to be reinforced at national and international levels. Effective national action and international cooperation is required for the *in situ* protection of ecosystems, for the *ex situ* conservation of biological and genetic resources and for the enhancement of ecosystem functions. The participation and support of local communities are elements essential to the success of such an approach. Recent advances in biotechnology have pointed up the likely potential for agriculture, health and welfare and for the environmental purposes of the genetic material contained in plants, animals and micro-organisms. At the same time, it is particularly important in this context to stress that States have the sovereign right to exploit their own biological resources pursuant to their environmental policies, as well as the responsibility to conserve their biodiversity and use their biological resources sustainably, and to ensure that activities within their jurisdiction or control do not cause damage to the biological diversity of other States or of areas beyond the limits of national jurisdiction.

Objectives

15.4. Governments at the appropriate level, with the cooperation of the relevant United Nations bodies and regional, intergovernmental and non-governmental organizations, the private sector and financial institutions, and taking into consideration indigenous people and their communities, as well as social and economic factors, should:

(a) Press for the early entry into force of the Convention on Biological Diversity, with the widest possible participation;

(b) Develop national strategies for the conservation of biological diversity and the sustainable use of biological resources;

(c) Integrate strategies for the conservation of biological diversity and the sustainable use of biological resources into national development strategies and/or plans;

(d) Take appropriate measures for the fair and equitable sharing of benefits derived from research and development and use of biological and genetic resources, including biotechnology, between the sources of those resources and those who use them;

(e) Carry out country studies, as appropriate, on the conservation of biological diversity and the sustainable use of biological resources, including analyses of relevant costs and benefits, with particular reference to socio-economic aspects;

(f) Produce regularly updated world reports on biodiversity based upon national assessments;

(g) Recognize and foster the traditional methods and the knowledge of indigenous people and their communities, emphasizing the particular role of women, relevant to the conservation of biological diversity and the sustainable use of biological resources, and ensure the opportunity for the participation of those groups in the economic and commercial benefits derived from the use of such traditional methods and knowledge;

(h) Implement mechanisms for the improvement, generation, development and sustainable use of biotechnology and its safe transfer, particularly to developing countries, taking account the potential contribution of biotechnology to the conservation of biological diversity and the sustainable use of biological resources;

(i) Promote broader international and regional cooperation in furthering scientific and economic understanding of the importance of biodiversity and its functions in ecosystems;

(j) Develop measures and arrangements to implement the rights of countries of origin of genetic resources or countries providing genetic resources, as defined in the Convention on Biological Diversity, particularly developing countries, to benefit from the biotechnological development and the commercial utilization of products derived from such resources.

Activities

(a) *Management-related activities*

15.5. Governments at the appropriate levels, consistent with national policies and practices, with the cooperation of the relevant United Nations bodies and, as appropriate, intergovernmental organizations and, with the support of indigenous people and their communities, non-governmental organizations and other groups, including the business and scientific communities, and consistent with the requirements of international law, should, as appropriate:

(a) Develop new or strengthen existing strategies, plans or programmes of action for the conservation of biological diversity and the sustainable use of biological resources, taking account of education and training needs;

(b) Integrate strategies for the conservation of biological diversity and the sustainable use of biological and genetic resources into relevant sectoral or cross-sectoral plans, programmes and policies, with particular reference to the special importance of terrestrial and aquatic biological and genetic resources for food and agriculture;

(c) Undertake country studies or use other methods to identify components of biological diversity important for its conservation and for the sustainable use of biological resources, ascribe values to biological and genetic resources, identify processes and activities with significant impacts upon biological diversity, evaluate the potential economic implications of the conservation of biological diversity and the sustainable use of biological and genetic resources, and suggest priority action;

(d) Take effective economic, social and other appropriate incentive measures to encourage the conservation of biological diversity and the sustainable use of biological resources, including the promotion of sustainable production systems, such as traditional methods of agriculture, agroforestry, forestry, range and wildlife management, which use, maintain or increase biodiversity;

(e) Subject to national legislation, take action to respect, record, protect and promote the wider application of the knowledge, innovations and practices of indigenous and local communities embodying traditional lifestyles for the conservation of biological diversity and the sustainable use of biological resources, with a view to the fair and equitable sharing of the benefits arising, and promote mechanisms to involve those communities, including women, in the conservation and management of ecosystems;

(f) Undertake long-term research into the importance of biodiversity for the functioning of ecosystems and the role of ecosystems in producing goods, environmental services and other values supporting sustainable development, with particular reference to the biology and reproductive capacities of key terrestrial and aquatic species, including native, cultivated and cultured species; new observation and inventory techniques; ecological conditions necessary for biodiversity conservation and continued evolution; and social behaviour and nutrition habits dependent on natural ecosystems, where women play key roles. The work should be undertaken with the widest possible participation, especially of indigenous people and their communities, including women;

(g) Take action where necessary for the conservation of biological diversity through the *in situ* conservation of ecosystems and natural habitats, as well as primitive cultivars and their wild relatives, and the maintenance and recovery of viable populations of species in their natural surroundings, and implement *ex situ* measures, preferably in the source country. *In situ* measures should include the reinforcement of terrestrial, marine and aquatic protected area systems and embrace, *inter alia,* vulnerable freshwater and other wetlands and coastal ecosystems, such as estuaries, coral reefs and mangroves;

(h) Promote the rehabilitation and restoration of damaged ecosystems and the recovery of threatened and endangered species;

(i) Develop policies to encourage the conservation of biodiversity and the sustainable use of biological and genetic resources on private lands;

(j) Promote environmentally sound and sustainable development in areas adjacent to protected areas with a view to furthering protection of these areas;

(k) Introduce appropriate environmental impact assessment procedures for proposed projects likely to have significant impacts upon biological diversity, providing for suitable information to be made widely available and for public participation, where appropriate, and encourage the assessment of the impacts of relevant policies and programmes on biological diversity;

(*l*) Promote, where appropriate, the establishment and strengthening of national inventory, regulation or management and control systems related to biological resources, at the appropriate level;

(m) Take measures to encourage a greater understanding and appreciation of the value of biological diversity, as manifested both in its component parts and in the ecosystem services provided.

(b) *Data and information*

15.6. Governments at the appropriate level, consistent with national policies and practices, with the cooperation of the relevant United Nations bodies and, as appropriate, intergovernmental organizations, and with the support of indigenous people and their communities, non-governmental organizations and other groups, including the business and scientific communities, and consistent with the requirements of international law, should, as appropriate:

(a) Regularly collate, evaluate and exchange information on the conservation of biological diversity and the sustainable use of biological resources;

(b) Develop methodologies with a view to undertaking systematic sampling and evaluation on a national basis of the components of biological diversity identified by means of country studies;

(c) Initiate or further develop methodologies and begin or continue work on surveys at the appropriate level on the status of ecosystems and establish baseline information on biological and genetic resources, including those in terrestrial, aquatic, coastal and marine ecosystems, as well as inventories undertaken with the participation of local and indigenous people and their communities;

(d) Identify and evaluate the potential economic and social implications and benefits of the conservation and sustainable use of terrestrial and aquatic species in each country, building upon the results of country studies;

(e) Undertake the updating, analysis and interpretation of data derived from the identification, sampling and evaluation activities described above;

(f) Collect, assess and make available relevant and reliable information in a timely manner and in a form suitable for decision-making at all levels, with the full support and participation of local and indigenous people and their communities.

(c) *International and regional cooperation and coordination*

15.7. Governments at the appropriate level, with the cooperation of the relevant United Nations bodies and, as appropriate, intergovernmental organizations, and, with the support of indigenous people and their communities, non-governmental organizations and other groups, including the business and scientific communities, and consistent with the requirements of international law, should, as appropriate:

(a) Consider the establishment or strengthening of national or international capabilities and networks for the exchange of data and information of relevance to the conservation of biological diversity and the sustainable use of biological and genetic resources;

(b) Produce regularly updated world reports on biodiversity based upon national assessments in all countries;

(c) Promote technical and scientific cooperation in the field of conservation of biological diversity and the sustainable use of biological and genetic resources. Special attention should be given to the development and strengthening of national capabilities by means of human resource development and institution-building, including the transfer of technology and/or development of research and management facilities, such as herbaria, museums, gene banks, and laboratories, related to the conservation of biodiversity;

(d) Without prejudice to the relevant provisions of the Convention on Biological Diversity, facilitate for this chapter the transfer of technologies relevant to the conservation of biological diversity and the sustainable use of biological resources or technologies that make use of genetic resources and cause no significant damage to the environment, in conformity with chapter 34, and recognizing that technology includes biotechnology;

(e) Promote cooperation between the parties to relevant international conventions and action plans with the aim of strengthening and coordinating efforts to conserve biological diversity and the sustainable use of biological resources;

(f) Strengthen support for international and regional instruments, programmes and action plans concerned with the conservation of biological diversity and the sustainable use of biological resources;

(g) Promote improved international coordination of measures for the effective conservation and management of endangered/non-pest migratory species, including appropriate levels of support for the establishment and management of protected areas in transboundary locations;

(h) Promote national efforts with respect to surveys, data collection, sampling and evaluation, and the maintenance of gene banks.

Means of implementation

(a) *Financing and cost evaluation*

15.8. The Conference secretariat has estimated the average total annual cost (1993–2000) of implementing the activities of this chapter to be about $3.5 billion, including about $1.75 billion from the international community on grant or concessional terms. These are indicative and order-of-magnitude estimates only and have not been reviewed by Governments. Actual costs and financial terms, including any that are non-concessional, will depend upon, *inter alia,* the specific strategies and programmes Governments decide upon for implementation.

(b) *Scientific and technological means*

15.9. Specific aspects to be addressed include the need to develop:

(a) Efficient methodologies for baseline surveys and inventories, as well as for the systematic sampling and evaluation of biological resources;

(b) Methods and technologies for the conservation of biological diversity and the sustainable use of biological resources;

(c) Improved and diversified methods for *ex situ* conservation with a view to the long-term conservation of genetic resources of importance for research and development.

(c) *Human resource development*

15.10. There is a need, where appropriate, to:

(a) Increase the number and/or make more efficient use of trained personnel in scientific and technological fields relevant to the conservation of biological diversity and the sustainable use of biological resources;

(b) Maintain or establish programmes for scientific and technical education and training of managers and professionals, especially in developing countries, on measures for the identification, conservation of biological diversity and the sustainable use of biological resources;

(c) Promote and encourage understanding of the importance of the measures required for the conservation of biological diversity and the sustainable use of biological resources at all policy-making and decision-making levels in Governments, business enterprises and lending institutions, and promote and encourage the inclusion of these topics in educational programmes.

(d) *Capacity-building*

15.11. There is a need, where appropriate, to:

(a) Strengthen existing institutions and/or establish new ones responsible for the conservation of biological diversity and to consider the development of mechanisms such as national biodiversity institutes or centres;

(b) Continue to build capacity for the conservation of biological diversity and the sustainable use of biological resources in all relevant sectors;

(c) Build capacity, especially within Governments, business enterprises and bilateral and multilateral development agencies, for integrating biodiversity concerns, potential benefits and opportunity cost calculations into project design, implementation and evaluation processes, as well as for evaluating the impact on biological diversity of proposed development projects;

(d) Enhance the capacity of governmental and private institutions, at the appropriate level, responsible for protected area planning and management to undertake intersectoral coordination and planning with other governmental institutions, non-governmental organizations and, where appropriate, indigenous people and their communities.

* * *

Chapter 17

PROTECTION OF THE OCEANS, ALL KINDS OF SEAS, INCLUDING ENCLOSED AND SEMI-ENCLOSED AREAS, AND COASTAL AREAS AND THE PROTECTION, RATIONAL USE AND DEVELOPMENT OF THEIR LIVING RESOURCES

INTRODUCTION

17.1. The marine environment—including the oceans and all seas and adjacent coastal areas—forms an integrated whole that is an essential component of the global life-support system and a positive asset that presents opportunities for sustainable development. International law, as reflected in the provisions of the United Nations Convention on the Law of the Sea, referred to in this chapter of Agenda 21, sets forth rights and obligations of States and provides the international basis upon which to pursue the protection and sustainable development of the marine and coastal environment and its resources. This requires new approaches to marine and coastal area management and development at the national, subregional, regional and global levels, approaches that are integrated in content and are precautionary and anticipatory in ambit, as reflected in the following programme areas:

(a) Integrated management and sustainable development of coastal areas, including exclusive economic zones;

(b) Marine environmental protection;

(c) Sustainable use and conservation of marine living resources of the high seas;

(d) Sustainable use and conservation of marine living resources under national jurisdiction;

(e) Addressing critical uncertainties for the management of the marine environment and climate change;

(f) Strengthening international, including regional, cooperation and coordination;

(g) Sustainable development of small islands.

17.2. The implementation by developing countries of the activities set forth below shall be commensurate with their individual technological and financial capacities and priorities in allocating resources for development needs and ultimately depends on the technology transfer and financial resources required and made available to them.

PROGRAMME AREAS

A. *Integrated management and sustainable development of coastal and marine areas, including exclusive economic zones*

Basis for action

17.3. The coastal area contains diverse and productive habitats important for human settlements, development and local subsistence. More than half the world's population lives within 60 km of the shoreline, and this could rise to three quarters by the year 2020. Many of the world's poor are crowded in coastal areas. Coastal resources are vital for many local communities and indigenous people. The exclusive economic zone (EEZ) is also an important marine area where the States manage the development and conservation of natural resources for the benefit of their people. For small island States or countries, these are the areas most available for development activities.

17.4. Despite national, subregional, regional and global efforts, current approaches to the management of marine and coastal resources have not always proved capable of achieving sustainable development, and coastal resources and the coastal environment are being rapidly degraded and eroded in many parts of the world.

Objectives

17.5. Coastal States commit themselves to integrated management and sustainable development of coastal areas and the marine environment under their national jurisdiction. To this end, it is necessary to, *inter alia:*

(a) Provide for an integrated policy and decision-making process, including all involved sectors, to promote compatibility and a balance of uses;

(b) Identify existing and projected uses of coastal areas and their interactions;

(c) Concentrate on well-defined issues concerning coastal management;

(d) Apply preventive and precautionary approaches in project planning and implementation, including prior assessment and systematic observation of the impacts of major projects;

(e) Promote the development and application of methods, such as national resource and environmental accounting, that reflect changes in value resulting from uses of coastal and marine areas, including pollution, marine erosion, loss of resources and habitat destruction;

(f) Provide access, as far as possible, for concerned individuals, groups and organizations to relevant information and opportunities for consultation and participation in planning and decision-making at appropriate levels.

Activities

(a) *Management-related activities*

17.6. Each coastal State should consider establishing, or where necessary, strengthening, appropriate coordinating mechanisms (such as a high-level policy planning body) for integrated management and sustainable development of coastal and marine areas and their resources, at both the local and national levels. Such mechanisms should include consultation, as appropriate, with the academic and private sectors, non-governmental organizations, local communities, resource user groups, and indigenous people. Such national coordinating mechanisms could provide, *inter alia,* for:

(a) Preparation and implementation of land and water use and siting policies;

(b) Implementation of integrated coastal and marine management and sustainable development plans and programmes at appropriate levels;

(c) Preparation of coastal profiles identifying critical areas, including eroded zones, physical processes, development patterns, user conflicts and specific priorities for management;

(d) Prior environmental impact assessment, systematic observation and follow-up of major projects, including the systematic incorporation of results in decision-making;

(e) Contingency plans for human induced and natural disasters, including likely effects of potential climate change and sealevel rise, as well as contingency plans for degradation and pollution of anthropogenic origin, including spills of oil and other materials;

(f) Improvement of coastal human settlements, especially in housing, drinking water and treatment and disposal of sewage, solid wastes and industrial effluents;

(g) Periodic assessment of the impacts of external factors and phenomena to ensure that the objectives of integrated management and sustainable development of coastal areas and the marine environment are met;

(h) Conservation and restoration of altered critical habitats;

(i) Integration of sectoral programmes on sustainable development for settlements, agriculture, tourism, fishing, ports and industries affecting the coastal area;

(j) Infrastructure adaptation and alternative employment;

(k) Human resource development and training;

(*l*) Public education, awareness and information programmes;

(m) Promoting environmentally sound technology and sustainable practices;

(n) Development and simultaneous implementation of environmental quality criteria.

17.7. Coastal States, with the support of international organizations, upon request, should undertake measures to maintain biological diversity and productivity of marine species and habitats under national jurisdiction. *Inter alia,* these measures might include: surveys of marine biodiversity, inventories of endangered species and critical coastal and marine habitats; establishment and management of protected areas; and support of scientific research and dissemination of its results.

(b) *Data and information*

17.8. Coastal States, where necessary, should improve their capacity to collect, analyse, assess and use information for sustainable use of resources, including environmental impacts of activities affecting the coastal and marine areas. Information for management purposes should receive priority support in view of the intensity and magnitude of the changes occurring in the coastal and marine areas. To this end, it is necessary to, *inter alia:*

(a) Develop and maintain databases for assessment and management of coastal areas and all seas and their resources;

(b) Develop socio-economic and environmental indicators;

(c) Conduct regular environmental assessment of the state of the environment of coastal and marine areas;

(d) Prepare and maintain profiles of coastal area resources, activities, uses, habitats and protected areas based on the criteria of sustainable development;

(e) Exchange information and data.

17.9. Cooperation with developing countries, and, where applicable, subregional and regional mechanisms, should be strengthened to improve their capacities to achieve the above.

(c) *International and regional cooperation and coordination*

17.10. The role of international cooperation and coordination on a bilateral basis and, where applicable, within a subregional, interregional, regional or global framework, is to support and supplement national efforts of coastal States to promote integrated management and sustainable development of coastal and marine areas.

17.11. States should cooperate, as appropriate, in the preparation of national guidelines for integrated coastal zone management and development, drawing on existing experience. A global conference to exchange experience in the field could be held before 1994.

Means of implementation

(a) *Financing and cost evaluation*

17.12. The Conference secretariat has estimated the average total annual cost (1993–2000) of implementing the activities of this programme to be about $6 billion, including about $50 million from the international community on grant or concessional terms. These are indicative and order-of-magnitude estimates only and have not been reviewed by Governments. Actual costs and financial terms, including any that are non-concessional, will depend upon, *inter alia,* the specific strategies and programmes Governments decide upon for implementation.

(b) *Scientific and technological means*

17.13. States should cooperate in the development of necessary coastal systematic observation, research and information management systems. They should provide access to and transfer environmentally safe technologies and methodologies for sustainable development of coastal and marine areas to developing countries. They should also develop technologies and endogenous scientific and technological capacities.

17.14. International organizations, whether subregional, regional or global, as appropriate, should support coastal States, upon request, in these efforts, as indicated above, devoting special attention to developing countries.

(c) *Human resource development*

17.15. Coastal States should promote and facilitate the organization of education and training in integrated coastal and marine management and sustainable development for scientists, technologists, managers (including community-based managers) and users, leaders, indigenous peoples, fisherfolk, women and youth, among others. Management and development, as well as environmental protection concerns and local planning issues, should be incorporated in educational curricula and public awareness campaigns, with due regard to traditional ecological knowledge and socio-cultural values.

17.16. International organizations, whether subregional, regional or global, as appropriate, should support coastal States, upon request, in the areas indicated above, devoting special attention to developing countries.

(d) *Capacity-building*

17.17. Full cooperation should be extended, upon request, to coastal States in their capacity-building efforts and, where appropriate, capacity-building should be included in bilateral and multilateral development cooperation. Coastal States may consider, *inter alia:*

(a) Ensuring capacity-building at the local level;

(b) Consulting on coastal and marine issues with local administrations, the business community, the academic sector, resource user groups and the general public;

(c) Coordinating sectoral programmes while building capacity;

(d) Identifying existing and potential capabilities, facilities and needs for human resource development and scientific and technological infrastructure;

(e) Developing scientific and technological means and research;

(f) Promoting and facilitating human resource development and education;

(g) Supporting "centres of excellence" in integrated coastal and marine resource management;

(h) Supporting pilot demonstration programmes and projects in integrated coastal and marine management.

B. *Marine environmental protection*

Basis for action

17.18. Degradation of the marine environment can result from a wide range of sources. Land-based sources contribute 70 per cent of marine pollution, while maritime transport and dumping-at-sea activities contribute 10 per cent each. The contaminants that pose the greatest threat to the marine environment are, in variable order of importance and depending on differing national or regional situations, sewage, nutrients, synthetic organic compounds, sediments, litter and plastics, metals, radionucleides, oil/hydrocarbons and polycyclic aromatic hydrocarbons (PAHs). Many of the polluting substances originating from land-based sources are of particular concern to the marine environment since they exhibit at the same time toxicity, persistence and bioaccumulation in the food chain. There is currently no global scheme to address marine pollution from land-based sources.

17.19. Degradation of the marine environment can also result from a wide range of activities on land. Human settlements, land use, construction of coastal infrastructure, agriculture, forestry, urban development, tourism and industry can affect the marine environment. Coastal erosion and siltation are of particular concern.

17.20. Marine pollution is also caused by shipping and sea-based activities. Approximately 600,000 tons of oil enter the oceans each year as a result of normal shipping operations, accidents and illegal discharges. With respect to offshore oil and gas activities, currently machinery space discharges are regulated internationally and six regional conventions to control platform discharges have been under consideration. The nature and extent of environmental impacts from offshore oil exploration and production activities generally account for a very small proportion of marine pollution.

17.21. A precautionary and anticipatory rather than a reactive approach is necessary to prevent the degradation of the marine environment. This requires, *inter alia,* the adoption of precautionary measures, environmental impact assessments, clean production techniques, recycling, waste audits and minimization, construction and/or improvement of sewage treatment facilities, quality management criteria for the proper handling of hazardous substances, and a comprehensive approach to damaging impacts from air, land and water. Any management framework must include the improvement of coastal human settlements and the integrated management and development of coastal areas.

Objectives

17.22. States, in accordance with the provisions of the United Nations Convention on the Law of the Sea on protection and preservation of the marine environment, commit themselves, in accordance with their policies, priorities and resources, to prevent, reduce and control degradation of the marine environment so as to maintain and improve its life-support and productive capacities. To this end, it is necessary to:

(a) Apply preventive, precautionary and anticipatory approaches so as to avoid degradation of the marine environment, as well as to reduce the risk of long-term or irreversible adverse effects upon it;

(b) Ensure prior assessment of activities that may have significant adverse impacts upon the marine environment;

(c) Integrate protection of the marine environment into relevant general environmental, social and economic development policies;

(d) Develop economic incentives, where appropriate, to apply clean technologies and other means consistent with the internalization of environmental costs, such as the polluter pays principle, so as to avoid degradation of the marine environment;

(e) Improve the living standards of coastal populations, particularly in developing countries, so as to contribute to reducing the degradation of the coastal and marine environment.

17.23. States agree that provision of additional financial resources, through appropriate international mechanisms, as well as access to cleaner technologies and relevant research, would be necessary to support action by developing countries to implement this commitment.

Activities

(a) *Management-related activities*

Prevention, reduction and control of degradation of the marine environment from land-based activities

17.24. In carrying out their commitment to deal with degradation of the marine environment from land-based activities, States should take action at the national level and, where appropriate, at the regional and subregional levels, in concert with action to implement programme area A, and should take account of the Montreal Guidelines for the Protection of the Marine Environment from Land–Based Sources.

17.25. To this end, States, with the support of the relevant international environmental, scientific, technical and financial organizations, should cooperate, *inter alia,* to:

(a) Consider updating, strengthening and extending the Montreal Guidelines, as appropriate;

(b) Assess the effectiveness of existing regional agreements and action plans, where appropriate, with a view to identifying means of strengthening action, where necessary, to prevent, reduce and control marine degradation caused by land-based activities;

(c) Initiate and promote the development of new regional agreements, where appropriate;

(d) Develop means of providing guidance on technologies to deal with the major types of pollution of the marine environment from land-based sources, according to the best scientific evidence;

(e) Develop policy guidance for relevant global funding mechanisms;

(f) Identify additional steps requiring international cooperation.

17.26. The UNEP Governing Council is invited to convene, as soon as practicable, an intergovernmental meeting on protection of the marine environment from land-based activities.

17.27. As concerns sewage, priority actions to be considered by States may include:

(a) Incorporating sewage concerns when formulating or reviewing coastal development plans, including human settlement plans;

(b) Building and maintaining sewage treatment facilities in accordance with national policies and capacities and international cooperation available;

(c) Locating coastal outfalls so as to maintain an acceptable level of environmental quality and to avoid exposing shell fisheries, water intakes and bathing areas to pathogens;

(d) Promoting environmentally sound co-treatments of domestic and compatible industrial effluents, with the introduction, where practicable, of controls on the entry of effluents that are not compatible with the system;

(e) Promoting primary treatment of municipal sewage discharged to rivers, estuaries and the sea, or other solutions appropriate to specific sites;

(f) Establishing and improving local, national, subregional and regional, as necessary, regulatory and monitoring programmes to control effluent discharge, using minimum sewage effluent guidelines and water quality criteria and giving due consideration to the characteristics of receiving bodies and the volume and type of pollutants.

17.28. As concerns other sources of pollution, priority actions to be considered by States may include:

(a) Establishing or improving, as necessary, regulatory and monitoring programmes to control effluent discharges and emissions, including the development and application of control and recycling technologies;

(b) Promoting risk and environmental impact assessments to help ensure an acceptable level of environmental quality;

(c) Promoting assessment and cooperation at the regional level, where appropriate, with respect to the input of point source pollutants from new installations;

(d) Eliminating the emission or discharge of organohalogen compounds that threaten to accumulate to dangerous levels in the marine environment;

(e) Reducing the emission or discharge of other synthetic organic compounds that threaten to accumulate to dangerous levels in the marine environment;

(f) Promoting controls over anthropogenic inputs of nitrogen and phosphorus that enter coastal waters where such problems as eutrophication threaten the marine environment or its resources;

(g) Cooperating with developing countries, through financial and technological support, to maximize the best practicable control and reduction of substances and wastes that are toxic, persistent or liable to bio-accumulate and to establish environmentally sound land-based waste disposal alternatives to sea dumping;

(h) Cooperating in the development and implementation of environmentally sound land-use techniques and practices to reduce run-off to water-courses and estuaries which would cause pollution or degradation of the marine environment;

(i) Promoting the use of environmentally less harmful pesticides and fertilizers and alternative methods for pest control, and considering the prohibition of those found to be environmentally unsound;

(j) Adopting new initiatives at national, subregional and regional levels for controlling the input of non-point source pollutants, which require broad changes in sewage and waste management, agricultural practices, mining, construction and transportation.

17.29. As concerns physical destruction of coastal and marine areas causing degradation of the marine environment, priority actions should include control and prevention of coastal erosion and siltation due to anthropogenic factors related to, *inter alia,* land-use and construction techniques and practices. Watershed management practices should be promoted so as to prevent, control and reduce degradation of the marine environment.

Prevention, reduction and control of degradation of the marine environment from sea-based activities

17.30. States, acting individually, bilaterally, regionally or multilaterally and within the framework of IMO and other relevant international organizations, whether subregional, regional or global, as appropriate, should assess the need for additional measures to address degradation of the marine environment:

(a) From shipping, by:

(i) Supporting wider ratification and implementation of relevant shipping conventions and protocols;

(ii) Facilitating the processes in (i), providing support to individual States upon request to help them overcome the obstacles identified by them;

(iii) Cooperating in monitoring marine pollution from ships, especially from illegal discharges (e.g., aerial surveillance), and enforcing MARPOL discharge, provisions more rigorously;

(iv) Assessing the state of pollution caused by ships in particularly sensitive areas identified by IMO and taking action to implement applicable measures, where necessary, within such areas to ensure compliance with generally accepted international regulations;

(v) Taking action to ensure respect of areas designated by coastal States, within their exclusive economic zones, consistent with international law, in order to protect and preserve rare or fragile ecosystems, such as coral reefs and mangroves;

(vi) Considering the adoption of appropriate rules on ballast water discharge to prevent the spread of non-indigenous organisms;

(vii) Promoting navigational safety by adequate charting of coasts and ship-routing, as appropriate;

(viii) Assessing the need for stricter international regulations to further reduce the risk of accidents and pollution from cargo ships (including bulk carriers);

(ix) Encouraging IMO and IAEA to work together to complete consideration of a code on the carriage of irradiated nuclear fuel in flasks on board ships;

(x) Revising and updating the IMO Code of Safety for Nuclear Merchant Ships and considering how best to implement a revised code;

(xi) Supporting the ongoing activity within IMO regarding development of appropriate measures for reducing air pollution from ships;

(xii) Supporting the ongoing activity within IMO regarding the development of an international regime governing the transportation of hazardous and noxious substances carried by ships and further considering whether the compensation funds similar to the ones established under the Fund Convention would be appropriate in respect of pollution damage caused by substances other than oil;

(b) From dumping, by:

(i) Supporting wider ratification, implementation and participation in relevant Conventions on dumping at sea, including early conclusion of a future strategy for the London Dumping Convention;

(ii) Encouraging the London Dumping Convention parties to take appropriate steps to stop ocean dumping and incineration of hazardous substances;

(c) From offshore oil and gas platforms, by assessing existing regulatory measures to address discharges, emissions and safety and assessing the need for additional measures;

(d) From ports, by facilitating establishment of port reception facilities for the collection of oily and chemical residues and garbage from ships, especially in MARPOL special areas, and promoting the establishment of smaller scale facilities in marinas and fishing harbours.

17.31. IMO and as appropriate, other competent United Nations organizations, when requested by the States concerned, should assess, where appropriate, the state of marine pollution in areas of congested shipping, such as heavily used international straits, with a view to ensuring compliance with generally accepted international regulations, particularly those related to illegal discharges from ships, in accordance with the provisions of Part III of the United Nations Convention on the Law of the Sea.

17.32. States should take measures to reduce water pollution caused by organotin compounds used in anti-fouling paints.

17.33. States should consider ratifying the Convention on Oil Pollution Preparedness, Response and Cooperation, which addresses, *inter alia,* the development of contingency plans on the national and international level, as appropriate, including provision of oil-spill response material and training of personnel, including its possible extension to chemical spill response.

17.34. States should intensify international cooperation to strengthen or establish, where necessary, regional oil/chemical-spill response centres and/or, as appropriate, mechanisms in cooperation with relevant subregional, regional or global intergovernmental organizations and, where appropriate, industry-based organizations.

(b) *Data and information*

17.35. States should, as appropriate, and in accordance with the means at their disposal and with due regard for their technical and scientific capacity and resources, make systematic observations on the state of the marine environment. To this end, States should, as appropriate, consider:

(a) Establishing systematic observation systems to measure marine environmental quality, including causes and effects of marine degradation, as a basis for management;

(b) Regularly exchanging information on marine degradation caused by land-based and sea-based activities and on actions to prevent, control and reduce such degradation;

(c) Supporting and expanding international programmes for systematic observations such as the mussel watch programme, building on existing facilities with special attention to developing countries;

(d) Establishing a clearing-house on marine pollution control information, including processes and technologies to address marine pollution control and to support their transfer to developing countries and other countries with demonstrated needs;

(e) Establishing a global profile and database providing information on the sources, types, amounts and effects of pollutants reaching the marine environment from land-based activities in coastal areas and sea-based sources;

(f) Allocating adequate funding for capacity-building and training programmes to ensure the full participation of developing countries, in particular, in any international scheme under the organs and organizations of the United Nations system for the collection, analysis and use of data and information.

Means of implementation

(a) *Financing and cost evaluation*

17.36. The Conference secretariat has estimated the average total annual cost (1993–2000) of implementing the activities of this programme to be about $200 million from the international community on grant or concessional terms. These are indicative and order-of-magnitude estimates only and have not been reviewed by Governments. Actual costs and financial terms, including any that are non-concessional, will depend upon, *inter alia,* the specific strategies and programmes Governments decide upon for implementation.

(b) *Scientific and technological means*

17.37. National, subregional and regional action programmes will, where appropriate, require technology transfer, in conformity with Chapter 34, and financial resources, particularly where developing countries are concerned, including:

(a) Assistance to industries in identifying and adopting clean production or cost-effective pollution control technologies;

(b) Planning development and application of low-cost and low-maintenance sewage installation and treatment technologies for developing countries;

(c) Equipment of laboratories to observe systematically human and other impacts on the marine environment;

(d) Identification of appropriate oil-and chemical-spill control materials, including low-cost locally available materials and techniques, suitable for pollution emergencies in developing countries;

(e) Study of the use of persistent organohalogens that are liable to accumulate in the marine environment to identify those that cannot be adequately controlled and to provide a basis for a decision on a time schedule for phasing them out as soon as practicable;

(f) Establishment of a clearing-house for information on marine pollution control, including processes and technologies to address marine pollution control, and support for their transfer to developing and other countries with demonstrated needs.

(c) *Human resource development*

17.38. States individually or in cooperation with each other and with the support of international organizations, whether subregional, regional or global, as appropriate, should:

(a) Provide training for critical personnel required for the adequate protection of the marine environment as identified by training needs' surveys at the national, regional or subregional levels;

(b) Promote the introduction of marine environmental protection topics into the curriculum of marine studies programmes;

(c) Establish training courses for oil-and chemical-spill response personnel, in cooperation, where appropriate, with the oil and chemical industries;

(d) Conduct workshops on environmental aspects of port operations and development;

(e) Strengthen and provide secure financing for new and existing specialized international centres of professional maritime education;

(f) States should, through bilateral and multilateral cooperation, support and supplement the national efforts of developing countries as regards human resource development in relation to prevention and reduction of degradation of the marine environment.

(d) *Capacity-building*

17.39. National planning and coordinating bodies should be given the capacity and authority to review all land-based activities and sources of pollution for their impacts on the marine environment and to propose appropriate control measures.

17.40. Research facilities should be strengthened or, where appropriate, developed in developing countries for systematic observation of marine pollution, environmental impact assessment and development of control recommendations and should be managed and staffed by local experts.

17.41. Special arrangements will be needed to provide adequate financial and technical resources to assist developing countries in preventing and solving problems associated with activities that threaten the marine environment.

17.42. An international funding mechanism should be created for the application of appropriate sewage treatment technologies and building sewage treatment facilities, including grants or concessional loans from international agencies and appropriate regional funds, replenished at least in part on a revolving basis by user fees.

17.43. In carrying out these programme activities, particular attention needs to be given to the problems of developing countries that would bear an unequal burden because of their lack of facilities, expertise or technical capacities.

C. *Sustainable use and conservation of marine living resources of the high seas*

Basis for action

17.44. Over the last decade, fisheries on the high seas have considerably expanded and currently represent approximately 5 per cent of total world landings. The provisions of the United Nations Convention on the Law of the Sea on the marine living resources of the high seas sets forth rights and obligations of States with respect to conservation and utilization of those resources.

17.45. However, management of high seas fisheries, including the adoption, monitoring and enforcement of effective conservation measures, is inadequate in many areas and some resources are overutilized. There are problems of unregulated fishing, overcapitalization, excessive fleet size, vessel reflagging to escape controls, insufficiently selective gear, unreliable databases and lack of sufficient cooperation between States. Action by States whose nationals and vessels fish on the high seas, as well as cooperation at the bilateral, subregional, regional and global levels, is essential particularly for highly migratory species and straddling stocks. Such action and cooperation should address inadequacies in fishing practices, as well as in biological knowledge, fisheries statistics and improvement of systems for handling data. Emphasis should also be on multi-species management and other approaches that take into account the relationships among species, especially in addressing depleted species, but also in identifying the potential of underutilized or unutilized populations.

Objectives

17.46. States commit themselves to the conservation and sustainable use of marine living resources on the high seas. To this end, it is necessary to:

(a) Develop and increase the potential of marine living resources to meet human nutritional needs, as well as social, economic and development goals;

(b) Maintain or restore populations of marine species at levels that can produce the maximum sustainable yield as qualified by relevant environmental and economic factors, taking into consideration relationships among species;

(c) Promote the development and use of selective fishing gear and practices that minimize waste in the catch of target species and minimize by-catch of non-target species;

(d) Ensure effective monitoring and enforcement with respect to fishing activities;

(e) Protect and restore endangered marine species;

(f) Preserve habitats and other ecologically sensitive areas;

(g) Promote scientific research with respect to the marine living resources in the high seas.

17.47. Nothing in paragraph 17.46 above restricts the right of a State or the competence of an international organization, as appropriate, to prohibit, limit or regulate the exploitation of marine mammals on the high seas more strictly than provided for in that paragraph. States shall cooperate with a view to the conservation of marine mammals and, in the case of cetaceans, shall in particular work through the appropriate international organizations for their conservation, management and study.

17.48. The ability of developing countries to fulfil the above objectives is dependent upon their capabilities, including the financial, scientific and technological means at their disposal. Adequate financial, scientific and technological cooperation should be provided to support action by them to implement these objectives.

Activities

(a) Management-related Activities

17.49 States should take effective action, including bilateral and multilateral cooperation, where appropriate at the subregional, regional and global levels, to ensure that high seas fisheries are managed in accordance with the provisions of the United Nations Convention on the Law of the Sea. In particular, they should:

(a) Give full effect to these provisions with regard to fisheries populations whose ranges lie both within and beyond exclusive economic zones (straddling stocks);

(b) Give full effect to these provisions with regard to highly migratory species;

(c) Negotiate, where appropriate, international agreements for the effective management and conservation of fishery stocks;

(d) Define and identify appropriate management units;

* * *

17.51. States should ensure that fishing activities by vessels flying their flags on the high seas take place in a manner so as to minimize incidental catches.

17.52. States should take effective action consistent with international law to monitor and control fishing activities by vessels flying their flags on the high seas to ensure compliance with applicable conservation and management rules, including full, detailed, accurate and timely reporting of catches and effort.

* * *

17.55. States should fully implement General Assembly resolution 46/215 on large-scale pelagic drift-net fishing.

* * *

(c) International and regional cooperation and coordination

17.58. States, through bilateral and multilateral cooperation and within the framework of subregional and regional fisheries bodies, as appropriate, and with the support of other international intergovernmental agencies, should assess high seas resource potentials and develop profiles of all stocks (target and non-target).

17.59. States should, where and as appropriate, ensure adequate coordination and cooperation in enclosed and semi-enclosed seas and between subregional, regional and global intergovernmental fisheries bodies.

17.60. Effective cooperation within existing subregional, regional or global fisheries bodies should be encouraged. Where such organizations do not exist, States should, as appropriate, cooperate to establish such organizations.

17.61. States with an interest in a high seas fishery regulated by an existing subregional and/or regional high seas fisheries organization of which they are not members should be encouraged to join that organization, where appropriate.

* * *

Chapter 20

ENVIRONMENTALLY SOUND MANAGEMENT OF HAZARDOUS WASTES, INCLUDING PREVENTION OF ILLEGAL INTERNATIONAL TRAFFIC IN HAZARDOUS WASTES

INTRODUCTION

20.1. Effective control of the generation, storage, treatment, recycling and reuse, transport, recovery and disposal of hazardous wastes is of paramount importance for proper health, environmental protection and natural resource management, and sustainable development. This will require the active cooperation and participation of the international community, Governments and industry. Industry, as referred to in this paper, shall include large industrial enterprises, including transnational corporations and domestic industry.

20.2. Prevention of the generation of hazardous wastes and the rehabilitation of contaminated sites are the key elements, and both require knowledge, experienced people, facilities, financial resources and technical and scientific capacities.

20.3. The activities outlined in the present chapter are very closely related to, and have implications for, many of the programme areas described in other chapters, so that an overall integrated approach to hazardous waste management is necessary.

20.4. There is international concern that part of the international movement of hazardous wastes is being carried out in contravention of existing national legislation and international instruments to the detriment of the environment and public health of all countries, particularly developing countries.

20.5. In section I of resolution 44/226 of 22 December 1989, the General Assembly requested each regional commission, within existing resources, to contribute to the prevention of the illegal traffic in toxic and dangerous products and wastes by monitoring and making regional assessments of that illegal traffic and its environmental and health implications. The Assembly also requested the regional commissions to interact among themselves and cooperate with the United Nations Environment Programme (UNEP), with a view to maintaining efficient and coordinated monitoring and assessment of the illegal traffic in toxic and dangerous products and wastes.

Overall objective

20.6. Within the framework of integrated life-cycle management, the overall objective is to prevent to the extent possible, and minimize, the generation of hazardous wastes, as well as to manage those wastes in such a way that they do not cause harm to health and the environment.

Overall targets

20.7. The overall targets are:

(a) Preventing or minimizing the generation of hazardous wastes as part of an overall integrated cleaner production approach; eliminating or reducing to a minimum transboundary movements of hazardous wastes, consistent with the environmentally sound and efficient management of those wastes; and ensuring that environmentally sound hazardous waste management options are pursued to the maximum extent possible within the country of origin (the self-sufficiency principle). The transboundary movements that take place should be on environmental and economic grounds and based upon agreements between the States concerned;

(b) Ratification of the Basel Convention on the Control of Transboundary Movements of Hazardous Wastes and their Disposal and the expeditious elaboration of related protocols, such as the protocol on liability and compensation, mechanisms and guidelines to facilitate the implementation of the Basel Convention;

(c) Ratification and full implementation by the countries concerned of the Bamako Convention on the Ban on the Import into Africa and the Control of Transboundary Movement of Hazardous Wastes within Africa and the expeditious elaboration of a protocol on liability and compensation;

(d) Elimination of the export of hazardous wastes to countries that, individually or through international agreements, prohibits the import of such wastes, such as, the contracting parties to the Bamako Convention, the fourth Lomé Convention or other relevant conventions, where such prohibition is provided for.

20.8. The following programme areas are included in this chapter:

(a) Promoting the prevention and minimization of hazardous waste;

(b) Promoting and strengthening institutional capacities in hazardous waste management;

(c) Promoting and strengthening international cooperation in the management of transboundary movements of hazardous wastes;

(d) Preventing illegal international traffic in hazardous wastes.

PROGRAMME AREAS

A. *Promoting the prevention and minimization of hazardous waste*

Basis for action

20.9. Human health and environmental quality are undergoing continuous degradation by the increasing amount of hazardous wastes being produced. There are increasing direct and indirect costs to society and to individual citizens in connection with the generation, handling and disposal of such wastes. It is therefore crucial to enhance knowledge and information on the economics of prevention and management of hazardous wastes, including the impact in relation to the employment and environmental benefits, in order to ensure that the necessary capital investment is made available in development programmes through economic incentives. One of the first priorities in hazardous waste management is minimization, as part of a broader approach to changing industrial processes and consumer patterns through pollution prevention and cleaner production strategies.

20.10. Among the most important factors in these strategies is the recovery of hazardous wastes and their transformation into useful material. Technology application, modification and development of new low-waste technologies are therefore currently a central focus of hazardous waste minimization.

Objectives

20.11. The objectives of this programme area are:

(a) To reduce the generation of hazardous wastes, to the extent feasible, as part of an integrated cleaner production approach;

(b) To optimize the use of materials by utilizing, where practicable and environmentally sound, the residues from production processes;

(c) To enhance knowledge and information on the economics of prevention and management of hazardous wastes.

20.12. To achieve those objectives, and thereby reduce the impact and cost of industrial development, countries that can afford to adopt the requisite technologies without detriment to their development should establish policies that include:

(a) Integration of cleaner production approaches and hazardous waste minimization in all planning, and the adoption of specific goals;

(b) Promotion of the use of regulatory and market mechanisms;

(c) Establishment of an intermediate goal for the stabilization of the quantity of hazardous waste generated;

(d) Establishment of long-term programmes and policies including targets where appropriate for reducing the amount of hazardous waste produced per unit of manufacture;

(e) Achievement of a qualitative improvement of waste streams, mainly through activities aimed at reducing their hazardous characteristics;

(f) Facilitation of the establishment of cost-effective policies and approaches to hazardous waste prevention and management, taking into consideration the state of development of each country.

Activities

(a) *Management-related activities*

20.13. The following activities should be undertaken:

(a) Governments should establish or modify standards or purchasing specifications to avoid discrimination against recycled materials, provided that those materials are environmentally sound;

(b) Governments, according to their possibilities and with the help of multilateral cooperation, should provide economic or regulatory incentives, where appropriate, to stimulate industrial innovation towards cleaner production methods, to encourage industry to invest in preventive and/or recycling technologies so as to ensure environmentally sound management of all hazardous wastes, including recyclable wastes, and to encourage waste minimization investments;

(c) Governments should intensify research and development activities on cost-effective alternatives for processes and substances that currently result in the generation of hazardous wastes that pose particular problems for environmentally sound disposal or treatment, the possibility of ultimate phase-out of those substances that present an unreasonable or otherwise unmanageable risk and are toxic, persistent and bio-accumulative to be considered as soon as practicable. Emphasis should be given to alternatives that could be economically accessible to developing countries;

(d) Governments, according to their capacities and available resources and with the cooperation of the United Nations and other relevant organizations and industries, as appropriate, should support the establishment of domestic facilities to handle hazardous wastes of domestic origin;

(e) Governments of developed countries should promote the transfer of environmentally sound technologies and know-how on clean technologies and low-waste production to developing countries in conformity with chapter 34, which will bring about changes to sustain innovation. Governments should cooperate with industry to develop guidelines and codes of conduct, where appropriate, leading to cleaner production through sectoral trade industry associations;

(f) Governments should encourage industry to treat, recycle, reuse and dispose of wastes at the source of generation, or as close as possible thereto, whenever hazardous waste generation is unavoidable and when it is both economically and environmentally efficient for industry to do so;

(g) Governments should encourage technology assessments, for example through the use of technology assessment centres;

(h) Governments should promote cleaner production through the establishment of centres providing training and information on environmentally sound technologies;

(i) Industry should establish environmental management systems, including environmental auditing of its production or distribution sites, in order to identify where the installation of cleaner production methods is needed;

(j) A relevant and competent United Nations organization should take the lead, in cooperation with other organizations, to develop guidelines for estimating the costs and benefits of various approaches to the adoption of cleaner production and waste minimization and environmentally sound management of hazardous wastes, including rehabilitation of contaminated sites, taking into account, where appropriate, the report of the 1991 Nairobi meeting of government-designated experts on an international strategy and an action programme, including technical guidelines for the environmentally sound management of hazardous wastes, in particular in the context of the work of the Basel Convention, being developed under the UNEP secretariat;

(k) Governments should establish regulations that lay down the ultimate responsibility of industries for environmentally sound disposal of the hazardous wastes their activities generate.

(b) *Data and information*

20.14. The following activities should be undertaken:

(a) Governments, assisted by international organizations, should establish mechanisms for assessing the value of existing information systems;

(b) Governments should establish nationwide and regional information collection and dissemination clearing-houses and networks that are easy for Government institutions and industry and other non-governmental organizations to access and use;

(c) International organizations, through the UNEP Cleaner Production programme and ICPIC, should extend and strengthen existing systems for collection of cleaner production information;

(d) All United Nations organs and organizations should promote the use and dissemination of information collected through the Cleaner Production network;

(e) OECD should, in cooperation with other organizations, undertake a comprehensive survey of, and disseminate information on, experiences of member countries in adopting economic regulatory schemes and incentive mechanisms for hazardous waste management and for the use of clean technologies that prevent such waste from being generated;

(f) Governments should encourage industries to be transparent in their operations and provide relevant information to the communities that might be affected by the generation, management and disposal of hazardous wastes.

(c) *International and regional cooperation and coordination*

20.15. International/regional cooperation should encourage the ratification by States of the Basel and Bamako Conventions and promote the implementation of those Conventions. Regional cooperation will be necessary for the development of similar conventions in regions other than Africa, if so required. In addition there is a need for effective coordination of international regional and national policies and instruments. Another activity proposed is cooperating in monitoring the effects of the management of hazardous wastes.

Means of implementation

(a) *Financing and cost evaluation*

20.16. The Conference secretariat has estimated the average total annual cost (1993–2000) of implementing the activities of this programme to be about $750 million from the international community on grant or concessional terms. These are indicative and order-of-magnitude estimates only and have not been reviewed by Governments. Actual costs and financial terms, including any that are non-concessional, will depend upon, *inter alia,* the specific strategies and programmes Governments decide upon for implementation.

(b) *Scientific and technological means*

20.17. The following activities related to technology development and research should be undertaken:

(a) Governments, according to their capacities and available resources and with the cooperation of the United Nations and other relevant organizations, and industries, as appropriate, should significantly increase financial support for cleaner technology research and development programmes, including the use of biotechnologies;

(b) States, with the cooperation of international organizations where appropriate, should encourage industry to promote and undertake research into the phase-out of the processes that pose the greatest environmental risk based on hazardous wastes generated;

(c) States should encourage industry to develop schemes to integrate the cleaner production approach into design of products and management practices;

(d) States should encourage industry to exercise environmentally responsible care through hazardous waste reduction and by ensuring the environmentally sound reuse, recycling and recovery of hazardous wastes, as well as their final disposal.

(c) *Human resource development*

20.18. The following activities should be undertaken:

(a) Governments, international organizations and industry should encourage industrial training programmes, incorporating hazardous waste prevention and minimization techniques and launching demonstration projects at the local level to develop "success stories" in cleaner production;

(b) Industry should integrate cleaner production principles and case examples into training programmes and establish demonstration projects/networks by sector/country;

(c) All sectors of society should develop cleaner production awareness campaigns and promote dialogue and partnership with industry and other actors.

(d) *Capacity-building*

20.19. The following activities should be undertaken:

(a) Governments of developing countries, in cooperation with industry and with the cooperation of appropriate international organizations, should develop inventories of hazardous waste production, in order to identify their needs with respect to technology transfer and implementation of measures for the sound management of hazardous wastes and their disposal;

(b) Governments should include in national planning and legislation an integrated approach to environmental protection, driven by prevention and source reduction criteria, taking into account the "polluter pays" principle, and adopt programmes for hazardous waste reduction, including targets and adequate environmental control;

(c) Governments should work with industry on sector-by-sector cleaner production and hazardous waste minimization campaigns, as well as on the reduction of such wastes and other emissions;

(d) Governments should take the lead in establishing and strengthening, as appropriate, national procedures for environmental impact assessment, taking into account the cradle-to-grave approach to the management of hazardous wastes, in order to identify options for minimizing the generation of hazardous wastes, through safer handling, storage, disposal and destruction;

(e) Governments, in collaboration with industry and appropriate international organizations, should develop procedures for monitoring the application of the cradle to grave approach, including environmental audits;

(f) Bilateral and multilateral development assistance agencies should substantially increase funding for cleaner technology transfer to developing countries, including small-and medium-sized enterprises.

B. *Promoting and strengthening institutional capacities in hazardous waste management*

Basis for action

20.20. Many countries lack the national capacity to handle and manage hazardous wastes. This is primarily due to inadequate infrastructure, deficiencies in regulatory frameworks, insufficient education and training programmes and lack of coordination between the different ministries and institutions involved in various aspects of waste management. In addition, there is a lack of knowledge about environmental contamination and pollution and the associated health risk from the exposure of populations, especially women and children, and ecosystems to hazardous wastes; assessment of risks; and the characteristics of wastes. Steps need to be taken immediately to identify populations at high risk and to take remedial measures, where necessary. One of the main priorities in ensuring environmentally sound management of hazardous wastes is to provide awareness, education and training programmes covering all levels of society. There is also a need to undertake research programmes to understand the nature of hazardous wastes, to identify their potential environmental effects and to develop technologies to safely handle those wastes. Finally, there is a need to strengthen the capacities of institutions that are responsible for the management of hazardous wastes.

Objectives

20.21. The objectives in this programme area are:

(a) To adopt appropriate coordinating, legislative and regulatory measures at the national level for the environmentally sound management of hazardous wastes, including the implementation of international and regional conventions;

(b) To establish public awareness and information programmes on hazardous waste issues and to ensure that basic education and training programmes are provided for industry and government workers in all countries;

(c) To establish comprehensive research programmes on hazardous wastes in countries;

(d) To strengthen service industries to enable them to handle hazardous wastes, and to build up international networking;

(e) To develop endogenous capacities in all developing countries to educate and train staff at all levels in environmentally sound hazardous waste handling and monitoring and in environmentally sound management;

(f) To promote human exposure assessment with respect to hazardous waste sites and identify the remedial measures required;

(g) To facilitate the assessment of impacts and risks of hazardous wastes on human health and the environment by establishing appropriate procedures, methodologies, criteria and/or effluent-related guidelines and standards;

(h) To improve knowledge regarding the effects of hazardous wastes on human health and the environment;

(i) To make information available to Governments and to the general public on the effects of hazardous wastes, including infectious wastes, on human health and the environment.

Activities

(a) *Management-related activities*

20.22. The following activities should be undertaken:

(a) Governments should establish and maintain inventories, including computerized inventories, of hazardous wastes and their treatment/disposal sites, as well as of contaminated sites that require rehabilitation, and assess exposure and risk to human health and the environment; they should also identify the measures required to clean up the disposal sites. Industry should make the necessary information available;

(b) Governments, industry and international organizations should collaborate in developing guidelines and easy-to-implement methods for the characterization and classification of hazardous wastes;

(c) Governments should carry out exposure and health assessments of populations residing near uncontrolled hazardous waste sites and initiate remedial measures;

(d) International organizations should develop improved health-based criteria, taking into account national decision-making processes, and assist in the preparation of practical technical guidelines for the prevention, minimization and safe handling and disposal of hazardous wastes;

(e) Governments of developing countries should encourage interdisciplinary and intersectoral groups, in cooperation with international organizations and agencies, to implement training and research activities related to evaluation, prevention and control of hazardous waste health risks. Such groups should serve as models to develop similar regional programmes;

(f) Governments, according to their capacities and available resources and with the cooperation of the United Nations and other relevant organizations as appropriate, should encourage as far as possible the establishment of combined treatment/disposal facilities for hazardous wastes in small-and medium-sized industries;

(g) Governments should promote identification and clean-up of sites of hazardous wastes in collaboration with industry and international organizations. Technologies, expertise and financing should be available for this purpose, as far as possible and when appropriate with the application of the "polluter pays" principle;

(h) Governments should ascertain that their military establishments conform to their nationally applicable environmental norms in the treatment and disposal of hazardous wastes.

(b) *Data and information*

20.23. The following activities should be undertaken:

(a) Governments, international and regional organizations and industry should facilitate and expand the dissemination of technical and scientific information dealing with the various health aspects of hazardous wastes, and promote its application;

(b) Governments should establish notification systems and registries of exposed populations and of adverse health effects and databases on risk assessments of hazardous wastes;

(c) Governments should endeavour to collect information on those who generate or dispose/recycle hazardous wastes and provide such information to the individuals and institutions concerned.

(c) *International and regional cooperation and coordination*

20.24. Governments, according to their capacities and available resources and with the cooperation of the United Nations and other relevant organizations, as appropriate, should:

(a) Promote and support the integration and operation, at the regional and local levels as appropriate, of institutional and interdisciplinary groups that collaborate, according to their capabilities, in activities oriented towards strengthening risk assessment, risk management and risk reduction with respect to hazardous wastes;

(b) Support capacity-building and technological development and research in developing countries in connection with human resource development, with particular support to be given to consolidating networks;

(c) Encourage self-sufficiency in hazardous waste disposal in the country of origin to the extent environmentally sound and feasible. The transboundary movements that take place should be on environmental and economic grounds and based upon agreements between all States concerned.

Means of implementation

(a) *Financing and cost evaluation*

20.25. The Conference secretariat has estimated the average total annual cost (1993–2000) of implementing the activities of this programme to be about $18.5 billion on a global basis with about $3.5 billion related to developing countries, including about $500 million from the international community on grant or concessional terms. These are indicative and order-of-magnitude estimates only and have not been reviewed by Governments. Actual costs and financial terms, including any that are non-concessional, will depend upon, *inter alia,* the specific strategies and programmes Governments decide upon for implementation.

(b) *Scientific and technological means*

20.26. The following activities should be undertaken:

(a) Governments, according to their capacities and available resources and with the cooperation of the United Nations and other relevant organizations and industry as appropriate, should increase support for hazardous waste research management in developing countries;

(b) Governments, in collaboration with international organizations, should conduct research on the health effects of hazardous wastes in developing countries, including the long-term effects on children and women;

(c) Governments should conduct research aimed at the needs of small-and medium-sized industries;

(d) Governments and international organizations in cooperation with industry should expand technological research on environmentally sound hazardous waste handling, storage, transport, treatment and disposal and on hazardous waste assessment, management and remediation;

(e) International organizations should identify relevant and improved technologies for handling, storage, treatment and disposal of hazardous wastes.

(c) *Human resource development*

20.27. Governments, according to their capacities and available resources and with the cooperation of the United Nations and other relevant organizations and industry as appropriate, should:

(a) Increase public awareness and information on hazardous waste issues and promote the development and dissemination of hazardous wastes information that the general public can understand;

(b) Increase participation in hazardous waste management programmes by the general public, particularly women, including participation at grass-roots levels;

(c) Develop training and education programmes for men and women in industry and Government aimed at specific real-life problems, for example, planning and implementing hazardous waste minimization programmes, conducting hazardous materials audits and establishing appropriate regulatory programmes;

(d) Promote the training of labour, industrial management and government regulatory staff in developing countries on technologies to minimize and manage hazardous wastes in an environmentally sound manner.

20.28. The following activities should also be undertaken:

(a) Governments, according to their capacities and available resources and with the cooperation of the United Nations, other organizations and non-governmental organizations, should collaborate in developing and disseminating educational materials concerning hazardous wastes and their effects on environment and human health, for use in schools, by women's groups and by the general public;

(b) Governments, according to their capacities and available resources and with the cooperation of the United Nations and other organizations, should establish or strengthen programmes for the environmentally sound management of hazardous wastes in accordance with, as appropriate, health and environmental standards, and extend surveillance systems for the purpose of identifying adverse effects on populations and the environment of exposure to hazardous wastes;

(c) International organizations should provide assistance to member States in assessing the health and environmental risks resulting from exposure to hazardous wastes, and in identifying their priorities for controlling the various categories or classes of wastes;

(d) Governments, according to their capacities and available resources and with the cooperation of the United Nations and other relevant organizations, should promote centres of excellence for training in hazardous waste management, building on appropriate national institutions and encouraging international cooperation, *inter alia,* through institutional links between developed and developing countries.

(d) *Capacity-building*

20.29. Wherever they operate, transnational corporations and other large-scale enterprises should be encouraged to introduce policies and make commitments to adopt standards of operation with reference to hazardous waste generation and disposal that are equivalent to or no less stringent than standards in the country of origin, and Governments are invited to make efforts to establish regulations requiring environmentally sound management of hazardous wastes.

20.30. International organizations should provide assistance to member States in assessing the health and environmental risks resulting from exposure to hazardous wastes and in identifying their priorities for controlling the various categories or classes of wastes.

20.31. Governments, according to their capacities and available resources and with the cooperation of the United Nations and other relevant organizations and industries, should:

(a) Support national institutions in dealing with hazardous wastes from the regulatory monitoring and enforcement perspectives, with such support including enabling of those institutions to implement international conventions;

(b) Develop industry-based institutions for dealing with hazardous wastes and service industries for handling hazardous wastes;

(c) Adopt technical guidelines for the environmentally sound management of hazardous wastes and support the implementation of regional and international conventions;

(d) Develop and expand international networking among professionals working in the area of hazardous wastes and maintain an information flow among countries;

(e) Assess the feasibility of establishing and operating national, subregional and regional hazardous wastes treatment centres. Such centres could be used for education and training, as well as for facilitation and promotion of the transfer of technologies for the environmentally sound management of hazardous wastes;

(f) Identify and strengthen relevant academic/research institutions or centres for excellence to enable them to carry out education and training activities in the environmentally sound management of hazardous wastes;

(g) Develop a programme for the establishment of national capacities and capabilities to educate and train staff at various levels in hazardous wastes management;

(h) Conduct environmental audits of existing industries to improve in-plant regimes for the management of hazardous wastes.

C. *Promoting and strengthening international cooperation in the management of transboundary movements of hazardous wastes Basis for action*

20.32. In order to promote and strengthen international cooperation in the management, including control and monitoring, of transboundary movements of hazardous wastes, a precautionary approach should be applied. There is a need to harmonize the procedures and criteria used in various international and legal instruments. There is also a need to develop or harmonize existing criteria for identifying wastes dangerous to the environment and to build monitoring capacities.

Objectives

20.33. The objectives of this programme area are:

(a) To facilitate and strengthen international cooperation in the environmentally sound management of hazardous wastes, including control and monitoring of transboundary movements of such wastes, including wastes for recovery, by using internationally adopted criteria to identify and classify hazardous wastes and to harmonize relevant international legal instruments;

(b) To adopt a ban on or prohibit, as appropriate, the export of hazardous wastes to countries that do not have the capacity to deal with those wastes in an environmentally sound way or that have banned the import of such wastes;

(c) To promote the development of control procedures for the transboundary movement of hazardous wastes destined for recovery operations under the Basel Convention that encourage environmentally and economically sound recycling options.

Activities

(a) *Management-related activities*

Strengthening and harmonizing criteria and regulations

20.34. Governments, according to their capacities and available resources and with the cooperation of [the] United Nations and other relevant organizations, as appropriate, should:

(a) Incorporate the notification procedure called for in the Basel Convention and relevant regional conventions, as well as in their annexes, into national legislation;

(b) Formulate, where appropriate, regional agreements such as the Bamako Convention regulating the transboundary movement of hazardous wastes;

(c) Help promote the compatibility and complementarity of such regional agreements with international conventions and protocols;

(d) Strengthen national and regional capacities and capabilities to monitor and control the transboundary movement of hazardous wastes;

(e) Promote the development of clear criteria and guidelines, within the framework of the Basel Convention and regional conventions, as appropriate, for environmentally and economically sound operation in resource recovery, recycling reclamation, direct use or alternative uses and for determination of acceptable recovery practices, including recovery levels where feasible and appropriate, with a view to preventing abuses and false presentation in the above operations;

(f) Consider setting up, at national and regional levels, as appropriate, systems for monitoring and surveillance of the transboundary movements of hazardous wastes;

(g) Develop guidelines for the assessment of environmentally sound treatment of hazardous wastes;

(h) Develop guidelines for the identification of hazardous wastes at the national level, taking into account existing internationally—and, where appropriate, regionally—agreed criteria and prepare a list of hazard profiles for the hazardous wastes listed in national legislation;

(i) Develop and use appropriate methods for testing, characterizing and classifying hazardous wastes and adopt or adapt safety standards and principles for managing hazardous wastes in an environmentally sound way.

Implementing existing agreements

20.35. Governments are urged to ratify the Basel Convention and the Bamako Convention, as applicable, and to pursue the expeditious elaboration of related protocols, such as protocols on liability and compensation, and of mechanisms and guidelines to facilitate the implementation of the Conventions.

Means of implementation

(a) *Financing and cost evaluation*

20.36. Because this programme area covers a relatively new field of operation and because of the lack so far of adequate studies on costing of activities under this programme, no cost estimate is available at present. However, the costs for some of the activities related to capacity-building that are presented under this programme could be considered to have been covered under the costing of programme area B above.

20.37. The interim secretariat for the Basel Convention should undertake studies in order to arrive at a reasonable cost estimate for activities to be undertaken initially until the year 2000.

(b) *Capacity-building*

20.38. Governments, according to their capacities and available resources and with the cooperation of [the] United Nations and other relevant organizations, as appropriate, should:

(a) Elaborate or adopt policies for the environmentally sound management of hazardous wastes, taking into account existing international instruments;

(b) Make recommendations to the appropriate forums or establish or adapt norms, including the equitable implementation of the polluter pays principle, and regulatory measures to comply with obligations and principles of the Basel Convention, the Bamako Convention and other relevant existing or future agreements, including protocols, as appropriate, for setting appropriate rules and procedures in the field of liability and compensation for damage resulting from the transboundary movement and disposal of hazardous wastes;

(c) Implement policies for the implementation of a ban or prohibition, as appropriate, of exports of hazardous wastes to countries that do not have the capacity to deal with those wastes in an environmentally sound way or that have banned the import of such wastes;

(d) Study, in the context of the Basel Convention and relevant regional conventions, the feasibility of providing temporary financial assistance in the case of an emergency situation, in order to minimize damage from accidents arising from transboundary movements of hazardous wastes or during the disposal of those wastes.

D. *Preventing illegal international traffic in hazardous wastes*

Basis for action

20.39. The prevention of illegal traffic in hazardous wastes will benefit the environment and public health in all countries, particularly developing countries. It will also help to make the Basel Convention and regional international instruments, such as the Bamako Convention and the fourth Lomé Convention, more effective by promoting compliance with the controls established in those agreements. Article IX of the Basel Convention specifically addresses the issue of illegal shipments of hazardous wastes. Illegal traffic of hazardous wastes may cause serious threats to human health and the environment and impose a special and abnormal burden on the countries that receive such shipments.

20.40. Effective prevention requires action through effective monitoring and the enforcement and imposition of appropriate penalties.

Objectives

20.41. The objectives of this programme area are:

(a) To reinforce national capacities to detect and halt any illegal attempt to introduce hazardous wastes into the territory of any State in contravention of national legislation and relevant international legal instruments;

(b) To assist all countries, particularly developing countries, in obtaining all appropriate information concerning illegal traffic in hazardous wastes;

(c) To cooperate, within the framework of the Basel Convention, in assisting countries that suffer the consequences of illegal traffic.

Activities

(a) *Management-related activities*

20.42. Governments, according to their capacities and available resources and with the cooperation of the United Nations and other relevant organizations, as appropriate, should:

(a) Adopt, where necessary, and implement legislation to prevent the illegal import and export of hazardous wastes;

(b) Develop appropriate national enforcement programmes to monitor compliance with such legislation, detect and deter violations through appropriate penalties and give special attention to those who are known to have conducted illegal traffic in hazardous wastes and to hazardous wastes that are particularly susceptible to illegal traffic.

(b) *Data and information*

20.43. Governments should develop as appropriate, an information network and alert system to assist in detecting illegal traffic in hazardous wastes. Local communities and others could be involved in the operation of such a network and system.

20.44. Governments should cooperate in the exchange of information on illegal transboundary movements of hazardous wastes and should make such information available to appropriate United Nations bodies such as UNEP and the regional commissions.

(c) *International and regional cooperation*

20.45. The regional commissions, in cooperation with and relying upon expert support and advice from UNEP and other relevant bodies of the United Nations system, taking full account of the Basel Convention, shall continue to monitor and assess the illegal traffic in hazardous wastes, including its environmental, economic and health implications, on a continuing basis, drawing upon the results and experience gained in the joint UNEP/ESCAP preliminary assessment of illegal traffic.

20.46. Countries and international organizations, as appropriate, should cooperate to strengthen the institutional and regulatory capacities, in particular of developing countries, in order to prevent the illegal import and export of hazardous wastes.

* * *

SECTION IV. MEANS OF IMPLEMENTATION

Chapter 33

FINANCIAL RESOURCES AND MECHANISMS

INTRODUCTION

33.1. The General Assembly, in resolution 44/228 of 22 December 1989, *inter alia,* decided that the United Nations Conference on Environment and Development should:

Identify ways and means of providing new and additional financial resources, particularly to developing countries, for environmentally sound development programmes and projects in accordance with national development objectives, priorities and plans and to consider ways of effectively monitoring the provision of such new and additional financial resources, particularly to developing countries, so as to enable the international community to take further appropriate action on the basis of accurate and reliable data;

Identify ways and means of providing additional financial resources for measures directed towards solving major environmental problems of global concern and especially of supporting those countries, in particular developing countries, for which the implementation of such measures would entail a special or abnormal burden, owing, in particular, to their lack of financial resources, expertise or technical capacity;

Consider various funding mechanisms, including voluntary ones, and examine the possibility of a special international fund and other innovative approaches, with a view to ensuring, on a favourable basis, the most effective and expeditious transfer of environmentally sound technologies to developing countries;

Quantify the financial requirements for the successful implementation of Conference decisions and recommendations and identify possible sources, including innovative ones, of additional resources.

33.2. This chapter deals with the financing of the implementation of Agenda 21, which reflects a global consensus integrating environmental considerations into an accelerated development process. For each of the other chapters, the secretariat of the Conference has provided indicative estimates of the total costs of implementation for developing countries and the requirements for grant or other concessional financing needed from the international community. These reflect the need for a substantially increased effort, both by countries themselves and by the international community.

BASIS FOR ACTION

33.3. Economic growth, social development and poverty eradication are the first and overriding priorities in developing countries and are themselves essential to meeting national and global sustainability objectives. In the light of the global benefits to be realized by the implementation of Agenda 21 as a whole, the provision to developing countries of effective means, *inter alia,* financial resources and technology, without which it will be difficult for them to fully implement their commitments, will serve the common interests of developed and developing countries and of humankind in general, including future generations.

33.4. The cost of inaction could outweigh the financial costs of implementing Agenda 21. Inaction will narrow the choices of future generations.

33.5. For dealing with environmental issues, special efforts will be required. Global and local environmental issues are interrelated. The United Nations Framework Convention on Climate Change and the Convention on Biological Diversity address two of the most important global issues.

33.6. Economic conditions, both domestic and international, that encourage free trade and access to markets will help make economic growth and environmental protection mutually supportive for all countries, particularly for developing countries and countries undergoing the process of transition to a market economy (see chapter 2 for a fuller discussion of these issues).

33.7. International cooperation for sustainable development should also be strengthened in order to support and complement the efforts of developing countries, particularly the least developed countries.

33.8. All countries should assess how to translate Agenda 21 into national policies and programmes through a process that will integrate environment and development considerations. National and local priorities should be established by means that include public participation and community involvement, promoting equal opportunity for men and women.

33.9. For an evolving partnership among all countries of the world, including, in particular, between developed and developing countries, sustainable development strategies and enhanced and predictable levels of funding in support of longer term objectives are required. For that purpose, developing countries should articulate their own priority actions and needs for support and developed countries should commit themselves to addressing these priorities. In this respect, consultative groups and round tables and other nationally based mechanisms can play a facilitative role.

33.10. The implementation of the huge sustainable development programmes of Agenda 21 will require the provision to developing countries of substantial new and additional financial resources. Grant or concessional financing should be provided according to sound and equitable criteria and indicators. The progressive implementation of Agenda 21 should be matched by the provision of such necessary financial resources. The initial phase will be accelerated by substantial early commitments of concessional funding.

OBJECTIVES

33.11. The objectives are as follows:

(a) To establish measures concerning financial resources and mechanisms for the implementation of Agenda 21;

(b) To provide new and additional financial resources that are both adequate and predictable;

(c) To seek full use and continuing qualitative improvement of funding mechanisms to be utilized for the implementation of Agenda 21.

ACTIVITIES

33.12. Fundamentally, the activities of this chapter are related to the implementation of all the other chapters of Agenda 21.

MEANS OF IMPLEMENTATION

33.13. In general, the financing for the implementation of Agenda 21 will come from a country's own public and private sectors. For developing countries, particularly the least developed countries, ODA is a main source of external funding, and substantial new and additional funding for sustainable development and implementation of Agenda 21 will be required. Developed countries reaffirm their commitments to reach the accepted United Nations target of 0.7 per cent of GNP for ODA and, to the extent that they have not yet achieved that target, agree to augment their aid programmes in order to reach that target as soon as possible and to ensure prompt and effective implementation of Agenda 21. Some countries have agreed to reach the target by the year 2000. It was decided that the Commission on Sustainable Development would regularly review and monitor progress towards this target. This review process should systematically combine the monitoring of the implementation of Agenda 21 with a review of the financial resources available. Those countries that have already reached the target are to be commended and encouraged to continue to contribute to the common effort to make available the substantial additional resources that have to be mobilized. Other developed countries, in line with their support for reform efforts in developing countries, agree to make their best efforts to increase their level of ODA. In this context, the importance of equitable burden-sharing among developed countries is recognized. Other countries, including those undergoing the process of transition to a market economy, may voluntarily augment the contributions of the developed countries.

33.14. Funding for Agenda 21 and other outcomes of the Conference should be provided in a way that maximizes the availability of new and additional resources and uses all available funding sources and mechanisms. These include, among others:

(a) The multilateral development banks and funds:

(i) *The International Development Association (IDA).* Among the various issues and options that IDA deputies will examine in connection with the forthcoming tenth replenishment of IDA, the statement made by the President of the World Bank at the United Nations Conference on Environment and Development should be given special consideration in order to help the poorest countries meet their sustainable development objectives as contained in Agenda 21;

(ii) *Regional and subregional development banks.* The regional and subregional development banks and funds should play an increased and more effective role in providing resources on concessional or other favourable terms needed to implement Agenda 21;

(iii) *The Global Environment Facility,* managed jointly by the World Bank, UNDP and UNEP, whose additional grant and concessional funding is designed to achieve global environmental benefits, should cover the agreed incremental costs of relevant activities under Agenda 21, in particular for developing countries. Therefore, it should be restructured so as to, *inter alia:*

Encourage universal participation;

Have sufficient flexibility to expand its scope and coverage to relevant programme areas of Agenda 21, with global environmental benefits, as agreed;

Ensure a governance that is transparent and democratic in nature, including in terms of decision-making and operations, by guaranteeing a balanced and equitable representation of the interests of developing countries and giving due weight to the funding efforts of donor countries;

Ensure new and additional financial resources on grant and concessional terms, in particular to developing countries;

Ensure predictability in the flow of funds by contributions from developed countries, taking into account the importance of equitable burden-sharing;

Ensure access to and disbursement of the funds under mutually agreed criteria without introducing new forms of conditionality;

(b) *The relevant specialized agencies, other United Nations bodies and other international organizations,* which have designated roles to play in supporting national Governments in implementing Agenda 21;

(c) *Multilateral institutions for capacity-building and technical cooperation.* Necessary financial resources should be provided to UNDP to use its network of field offices and its broad mandate and experience in the field of technical cooperation for facilitating capacity-building at the country level, making full use of the expertise of the specialized agencies and other United Nations bodies within their respective areas of competence, in particular UNEP and including the multilateral and regional development banks;

(d) *Bilateral assistance programmes.* These programmes will need to be strengthened in order to promote sustainable development;

(e) *Debt relief.* It is important to achieve durable solutions to the debt problems of low-and middle-income developing countries in order to provide them with the needed means for sustainable development. Measures to address the continuing debt problems of low-and middle-income countries should be kept under review. All creditors in the Paris Club should promptly implement the agreement of December 1991 to provide debt relief for the poorest heavily indebted countries pursuing structural adjustment; debt relief measures should be kept under review so as to address the continuing difficulties of those countries;

(f) *Private funding.* Voluntary contributions through non-governmental channels, which have been running at about 10 per cent of ODA, might be increased.

33.15. *Investment.* Mobilization of higher levels of foreign direct investment and technology transfers should be encouraged through national policies that promote investment and through joint ventures and other modalities.

33.16. *Innovative financing.* New ways of generating new public and private financial resources should be explored, in particular:

(a) Various forms of debt relief, apart from official or Paris Club debt, including greater use of debt swaps;

(b) The use of economic and fiscal incentives and mechanisms;

(c) The feasibility of tradeable permits;

(d) New schemes for fund-raising and voluntary contributions through private channels, including non-governmental organizations;

(e) The reallocation of resources at present committed to military purposes.

33.17. A supportive international and domestic economic climate conducive to sustained economic growth and development is important, particularly for developing countries, in order to achieve sustainability.

33.18. The secretariat of the Conference has estimated the average annual costs (1993–2000) of implementing in developing countries the activities in Agenda 21 to be over $600 billion, including about $125 billion on grant or concessional terms from the international community. These are indicative and order-of-magnitude estimates only, and have not been reviewed by Governments. Actual costs will depend upon, *inter alia,* the specific strategies and programmes Governments decide upon for implementation.

33.19. Developed countries and others in a position to do so should make initial financial commitments to give effect to the decisions of the Conference. They should report on such plans and commitments to the United Nations General Assembly at its forty-seventh session, in 1992.

33.20. Developing countries should also begin to draw up national plans for sustainable development to give effect to the decisions of the Conference.

33.21. Review and monitoring of the financing of Agenda 21 is essential. Questions related to the effective follow-up of the Conference are discussed in chapter 38 (International institutional arrangements). It will be important to review on a regular basis the adequacy of funding and mechanisms, including efforts to reach agreed objectives of the present chapter, including targets where applicable.

Chapter 38

INSTITUTIONAL STRUCTURE

A) General Assembly

38.9. The General Assembly, as the highest intergovernmental mechanism, is the principal policy-making and appraisal organ on matters relating to the follow-up of the Conference. The Assembly would organize a regular review of the implementation of Agenda 21. In fulfilling this task, the Assembly could consider the timing, format and organizational aspects of such a review. In particular, the Assembly could consider holding a special session not later than 1997 for the overall review and appraisal of Agenda 21, with adequate preparations at a high level.

B) Economic and Social Council

38.10. The Economic and Social Council, in the context of its role under the Charter *vis-à-vis* the General Assembly and the ongoing restructuring and revitalization of the United Nations in the economic, social and related fields, would assist the General Assembly by overseeing system-wide coordination in the implementation of Agenda 21 and making recommendations in this regard. In addition, the Council would undertake the task of directing system-wide coordination and integration of environmental and developmental aspects of United Nations policies and programmes and would make appropriate recommendations to the General Assembly, specialized agencies concerned and Member States. Appropriate steps should be taken to obtain regular reports from specialized agencies on their plans and programmes related to the implementation of Agenda 21, pursuant to Article 64 of the Charter of the United Nations. The Economic and Social Council should organize a periodic review of the work of the Commission on Sustainable Development envisaged in paragraph 38.11, as well as of system-wide activities to integrate environment and development, making full use of its high-level and coordination segments.

C) Commission on Sustainable Development

38.11. In order to ensure the effective follow-up of the Conference, as well as to enhance international cooperation and rationalize the intergovernmental decisionmaking capacity for the integration of environment and development issues and to examine the progress in the implementation of Agenda 21 at the national, regional and international levels, a high-level Commission on Sustainable Development should be established in accordance with Article 68 of the Charter of the United Nations. This Commission would report to the Economic and Social Council in the context of the Council's role under the Charter *vis-à-vis* the General Assembly. It would consist of representatives of States elected as members with due regard to equitable geographical distribution. Representatives of non-member States of the Commission would have observer status. The Commission should provide for the active involvement of organs, programmes and organizations of the United Nations system, international financial institutions and other relevant intergovernmental organizations, and encourage the participation of non-governmental organizations, including industry and the business and scientific communities. The first meeting of the Commission should be convened no later than 1993. The Commission should be supported by the secretariat envisaged in paragraph 38.19. Meanwhile the Secretary-General of the United Nations is requested to ensure adequate interim administrative secretariat arrangements.

38.12. The General Assembly, at its forty-seventh session, should determine specific organizational modalities for the work of this Commission, such as its membership, its relationship with other intergovernmental United Nations bodies dealing with matters related to environment and development, and the frequency, duration and venue of its meetings. These modalities should take into account the ongoing process of revitalization and restructuring of the work of the United Nations in the economic, social and related fields, in particular measures recommended by the General Assembly in resolutions 45/264 of 13 May 1991 and 46/235 of 13 April 1992 and other relevant Assembly resolutions. In this respect, the Secretary–General of the United Nations, with the assistance of the Secretary–General of the United Nations Conference on Environment and Development, is requested to prepare for the Assembly a report with appropriate recommendations and proposals.

38.13. The Commission on Sustainable Development should have the following functions:

(a) To monitor progress in the implementation of Agenda 21 and activities related to the integration of environmental and developmental goals throughout the United Nations system through analysis and evaluation of reports from all relevant organs, organizations, programmes and institutions of the United Nations system dealing with various issues of environment and development, including those related to finance;

(b) To consider information provided by Governments, including, for example, information in the form of periodic communications or national reports regarding the activities they undertake to implement Agenda 21, the problems they face, such as problems related to financial resources and technology transfer, and other environment and development issues they find relevant;

(c) To review the progress in the implementation of the commitments contained in Agenda 21, including those related to provision of financial resources and transfer of technology;

(d) To receive and analyse relevant input from competent non-governmental organizations, including the scientific and private sectors, in the context of the overall implementation of Agenda 21;

(e) To enhance the dialogue, within the framework of the United Nations, with non-governmental organizations and the independent sector, as well as other entities outside the United Nations system;

(f) To consider, where appropriate, information regarding the progress made in the implementation of environmental conventions, which could be made available by the relevant Conferences of Parties;

(g) To provide appropriate recommendations to the General Assembly through the Economic and Social Council on the basis of an integrated consideration of the reports and issues related to the implementation of Agenda 21;

(h) To consider, at an appropriate time, the results of the review to be conducted expeditiously by the Secretary–General of all recommendations of the Conference for capacity-building programmes, information networks, task forces and other mechanisms to support the integration of environment and development at regional and subregional levels.

38.14. Within the intergovernmental framework, consideration should be given to allowing non-governmental organizations, including those related to major groups, particularly women's groups, committed to the implementation of Agenda 21 to have relevant information available to them, including information, reports and other data produced within the United Nations system.

D) The Secretary–General

38.15. Strong and effective leadership on the part of the Secretary–General is crucial, since he/she would be the focal point of the institutional arrangements within the United Nations system for the successful follow-up to the Conference and for the implementation of Agenda 21.

* * *

H) Organs, Programmes and Organizations of the United Nations System

38.20. In the follow-up to the Conference, in particular the implementation of Agenda 21, all relevant organs, programmes and organizations of the United Nations system will have an important role within their respective areas of expertise and mandates in supporting and supplementing national efforts. Coordination and mutual complementarity of their efforts to promote integration of environment and development can be enhanced by encouraging countries to maintain consistent positions in the various governing bodies.

1) United Nations Environment Programme

38.21. In the follow-up to the Conference, there will be a need for an enhanced and strengthened role for UNEP and its Governing Council. The Governing Council should, within its mandate, continue to play its role with regard to policy guidance and coordination in the field of the environment, taking into account the development perspective.

38.22. Priority areas on which UNEP should concentrate include the following:

(a) Strengthening its catalytic role in stimulating and promoting environmental activities and considerations throughout the United Nations system;

(b) Promoting international cooperation in the field of environment and recommending, as appropriate, policies to this end;

(c) Developing and promoting the use of such techniques as natural resource accounting and environmental economics;

(d) Environmental monitoring and assessment, through both improved participation by the United Nations system agencies in the Earthwatch programme and expanded relations with private scientific and non-governmental research institutes; and strengthening and making operational its early-warning function;

(e) Coordination and promotion of relevant scientific research with a view to providing a consolidated basis for decision-making;

(f) Dissemination of environmental information and data to Governments and to organs, programmes and organizations of the United Nations system;

(g) Raising general awareness and action in the area of environmental protection through collaboration with the general public, non-governmental entities and intergovernmental institutions;

(h) Further development of international environmental law, in particular conventions and guidelines, promotion of its implementation, and coordinating functions arising from an increasing number of international legal agreements, *inter alia,* the functioning of the secretariats of the conventions, taking into account the need for the most efficient use of resources, including possible co-location of secretariats established in the future;

(i) Further development and promotion of the widest possible use of environmental impact assessments, including activities carried out under the auspices of specialized agencies of the United Nations system, and in connection with every significant economic development project or activity;

(j) Facilitation of information exchange on environmentally sound technologies, including legal aspects, and provision of training;

(k) Promotion of subregional and regional cooperation and support to relevant initiatives and programmes for environmental protection, including playing a major contributing and coordinating role in the regional mechanisms in the field of environment identified for the follow-up to the Conference;

(l) Provision of technical, legal and institutional advice to Governments, upon request, in establishing and enhancing their national legal and institutional frameworks, in particular, in cooperation with UNDP capacity-building efforts;

(m) Support to Governments, upon request, and development agencies and organs in the integration of environmental aspects into their development policies and programmes, in particular through provision of environmental, technical and policy advice during programme formulation and implementation;

(n) Further developing assessment and assistance in cases of environmental emergencies.

38.23. In order to perform all of these functions, while retaining its role as the principal body within the United Nations system in the field of environment and taking into account the development aspects of environmental questions, UNEP would require access to greater expertise and provision of adequate financial resources and it would require closer cooperation and collaboration with development organs and other relevant organs of the United Nations system. Furthermore, the regional offices of UNEP should be strengthened without weakening its headquarters in Nairobi, and UNEP should take steps to reinforce and intensify its liaison and interaction with UNDP and the World Bank.

2) United Nations Development Programme

38.24. UNDP, like UNEP, also has a crucial role in the follow-up to the United Nations Conference on Environment and Development. Through its network of field offices it would foster the United Nations system's collective thrust in support of the implementation of Agenda 21, at the country, regional, interregional and global levels, drawing on the expertise of the specialized agencies and other United Nations organizations and bodies involved in operational activities. The role of the resident representative/resident coordinator of UNDP needs to be strengthened in order to coordinate the field-level activities of the United Nations operational activities.

38.25. Its role should include the following:

(a) Acting as the lead agency in organizing United Nations system efforts towards capacity-building at the local, national and regional levels;

(b) Mobilizing donor resources on behalf of Governments for capacity-building in recipient countries and, where appropriate, through the use of the UNDP donor round-table mechanisms;

(c) Strengthening its own programmes in support of follow-up to the Conference without prejudice to the fifth programming cycle;

(d) Assisting recipient countries, upon request, in the establishment and strengthening of national coordination mechanisms and networks related to activities for the follow-up to the Conference;

(e) Assisting recipient countries, upon request, in coordinating the mobilization of domestic financial resources;

(f) Promoting and strengthening the role and involvement of women, youth and other major groups in recipient countries in the implementation of Agenda 21.

3) United Nations Conference on Trade and Development

38.26. UNCTAD should play an important role in the implementation of Agenda 21 as extended at its eighth session, taking into account the importance of the interrelationships between development, international trade and the environment and in accordance with its mandate in the area of sustainable development.

* * *

1.31 Resolution on Institutional Arrangement to Follow up the United Nations Conference on Environment and Development. Adopted by the U.N. General Assembly, 22 December 1992. U.N. Doc.A/47/191; *reprinted in* 32 I.L.M. 238 (1993) & 5 Weston V.A.7

The General Assembly,

Welcoming the adoption by the United Nations Conference on Environment and Development of Agenda 21, in particular chapter 38, entitled "International institutional arrangements", which contains a set of important recommendations on institutional arrangements to follow up the Conference,

Stressing the overall objective of the integration of environment and development issues at the national, subregional, regional and international levels, including the United Nations system institutional arrangements, and the specific objectives recommended by the Conference in paragraph 38.8 of Agenda 21,

Taking note of the report of the Secretary–General, prepared with the assistance of the Secretary–General of the United Nations Conference on Environment and Development, on institutional arrangements to follow up the Conference, as well as the recommendations and proposals contained therein,

1. *Endorses* the recommendations on international institutional arrangements to follow up the United Nations Conference on Environment and Development as contained in chapter 38 of Agenda 21, particularly those on the establishment of a high-level Commission on Sustainable Development;

Commission on Sustainable Development

2. *Requests* the Economic and Social Council, at its organizational session for 1993, to set up a high-level Commission on Sustainable Development as a functional commission of the Council in accordance with Article 68 of the Charter of the United Nations in order to ensure the effective follow-up of the Conference, as well as to enhance international cooperation and rationalize the intergovernmental decision-making capacity for the integration of environment and development issues and to examine the progress of the implementation of Agenda 21 at the national, regional and international levels, fully guided by the principles of the Rio Declaration on Environment and Development and all other aspects of the Conference, in order to achieve sustainable development in all countries;

3. *Recommends* that the Commission shall have the following functions, as agreed in paragraphs 38.13, 33.13 and 33.21 of Agenda 21:

(a) To monitor progress in the implementation of Agenda 21 and activities related to the integration of environmental and developmental goals throughout the United Nations system through analysis and evaluation of reports from all relevant organs, organizations, programmes and institutions of the United Nations system dealing with various issues of environment and development, including those related to finance;

(b) To consider information provided by Governments, including, for example, in the form of periodic communications or national reports regarding the activities they undertake to implement Agenda 21, the problems they face, such as problems related to financial resources and technology transfer, and other environment and development issues they find relevant;

(c) To review the progress in the implementation of the commitments contained in Agenda 21, including those related to the provision of financial resources and transfer of technology;

(d) To review and monitor regularly progress towards the United Nations target of 0.7 per cent of the gross national product of developed countries for official development assistance. This review process should systematically combine the monitoring of the implementation of Agenda 21 with the review of financial resources available;

(e) To review on a regular basis the adequacy of funding and mechanisms, including efforts to reach agreed objectives of chapter 33 of Agenda 21, including targets where applicable;

(f) To receive and analyse relevant input from competent non-governmental organizations, including the scientific and the private sector, in the context of the overall implementation of Agenda 21;

(g) To enhance the dialogue, within the framework of the United Nations, with non-governmental organizations and the independent sector, as well as other entities outside the United Nations system;

(h) To consider, where appropriate, information regarding the progress made in the implementation of environmental conventions, which could be made available by the relevant Conferences of Parties;

(i) To provide appropriate recommendations to the General Assembly, through the Economic and Social Council, on the basis of an integrated consideration of the reports and issues related to the implementation of Agenda 21;

(j) To consider, at an appropriate time, the results of the review to be conducted expeditiously by the Secretary–General of all recommendations of the Conference for capacity-building programmes, information networks, task forces and other mechanisms to support the integration of environment and development at regional and subregional levels;

4. *Also recommends* that the Commission shall:

(a) Promote the incorporation of the principles of the Rio Declaration on Environment and Development in the implementation of Agenda 21;

(b) Promote the incorporation of the Non-legally Binding Authoritative Statement of Principles for a Global Consensus on the Management, Conservation and Sustainable Development of All Types of Forests in the implementation of Agenda 21, in particular in the context of the review of the implementation of chapter 11 thereof;

(c) Keep under review the implementation of Agenda 21, recognizing that it is a dynamic programme that could evolve over time, taking into account the agreement to review Agenda 21 in 1997, and make recommendations, as appropriate, on the need for new cooperative arrangements related to sustainable development to the Economic and Social Council and, through it, to the General Assembly;

5. *Decides* that the Commission, in the fulfilment of its functions, will also:

(a) Monitor progress in promoting, facilitating and financing, as appropriate, the access to and the transfer of environmentally sound technologies and corresponding know-how, in particular to developing countries, on favourable terms, including on concessional and preferential terms, as mutually agreed, taking into account the need to protect intellectual property rights as well as the special needs of developing countries for the implementation of Agenda 21;

(b) Consider issues related to the provision of financial resources from all available funding sources and mechanisms, as contained in paragraphs 33.13 to 33.16 of Agenda 21;

6. *Recommends* that the Commission consist of representatives of 53 States elected by the Economic and Social Council from among the Member States of the United Nations and its specialized agencies for three-year terms, with due regard to

equitable geographical distribution. The regional allocation of seats could be the same as in the Commission on Science and Technology for Development, as decided in Economic and Social Council decision 1992/222 of 29 May 1992. Representation should be at a high level, including ministerial participation. Other Member States of the United Nations and its specialized agencies, as well as other observers of the United Nations, may participate in the Commission in the capacity of observer, in accordance with established practice;

7. *Also recommends* that the Commission should:

(a) Provide for representatives of various parts of the United Nations system and other intergovernmental organizations, including international financial institutions, the General Agreement on Tariffs and Trade, regional development banks, subregional financial institutions, relevant regional and subregional economic and technical cooperation organizations and regional economic integration organizations, to assist and advise the Commission in the performance of its functions within their respective areas of expertise and mandates, and participate actively in its deliberations; and provide for the European Economic Community, within its areas of competence, to participate—as will be appropriately defined in the rules of procedure of the Commission on Sustainable Development—fully, without the right to vote;

(b) Provide for non-governmental organizations, including those related to major groups as well as industry and the scientific and business communities, to participate effectively in its work and contribute within their areas of competence to its deliberations;

8. *Requests* the Secretary–General, in the light of paragraph 7 above, to submit, for the consideration of the the Economic and Social Council at its organizational session for 1993, his proposals on the rules of procedure of the Commission, including those related to participation of relevant intergovernmental and non-governmental organizations, as recommended by the United Nations Conference on Environment and Development, taking into account the following:

(a) The procedures, while ensuring the intergovernmental nature of the Commission, should allow its members to benefit from the expertise and competence of relevant intergovernmental and non-governmental organizations;

(b) The procedures should permit relevant intergovernmental organizations inside and outside the United Nations system, including multilateral financial institutions, to appoint special representatives to the Commission;

(c) The rules of procedure of the Economic and Social Council and the rules of procedure of its functional commissions;

(d) The rules of procedure of the United Nations Conference on Environment and Development;

(e) Decisions 1/1 and 2/1 of the Preparatory Committee for the United Nations Conference on Environment and Development;

(f) Paragraphs 38.11 and 38.44 of Agenda 21;

9. *Recommends* that the Commission on Sustainable Development shall meet once a year for a period of two to three weeks. The first substantive session of the Commission will be held in New York in 1993, without prejudice to the venue of its future sessions;

10. *Requests* the Committee on Conferences to consider the need for readjusting the calendar of meetings in order to take account of the interrelationship between the work of the Commission and the work of other relevant United Nations intergovernmental subsidiary organs, in order to ensure timely reporting to the Economic and Social Council;

11. *Recommends* that in 1993, as a transitional measure, the Commission hold a short organizational session in New York. At that session, the Commission will elect the Bureau of the Commission, consisting of a chairperson, three vice-chairpersons and a rapporteur, coming from each of the regional groups, decide on the agenda of its first substantive session and consider all other organizational issues as may be necessary. The agenda of the organizational session of the Commission shall be decided on by the Economic and Social Council at its organizational session of 1993;

12. *Also recommends* that the Commission, at its first substantive session, adopt a multi-year thematic programme of its work that will provide a framework to assess progress achieved in the implementation of Agenda 21 and ensure an integrated approach to all of its environment and development components as well as linkages between sectoral and cross-sectoral issues. This programme could be of clusters that would integrate in an effective manner related sectoral and cross-sectoral components of Agenda 21 in such a way as to allow the Commission to review the progress of the implementation of the entire Agenda 21 by 1997. This programme of work could be adjusted, as the need may arise, at the future sessions of the Commission;

13. *Requests* the Secretary–General to submit his proposals for such a programme of work during the organizational session of the Commission;

14. *Recommends* that in order to carry out its functions and implement its work programme effectively the Commission consider organizing its work on the following lines:

(a) Financial resources, mechanisms, transfer of technology, capacity-building and other cross-sectoral issues;

(b) Review of implementation of Agenda 21 at the international level, as well as at the regional and national levels, including the means of implementation, in accordance with paragraph 12 above and the functions of the Commission, taking into account, where appropriate, information regarding the progress in the implementation of relevant environmental conventions;

(c) A high-level meeting, with ministerial participation, to have an integrated overview of the implementation of Agenda 21, to consider emerging policy issues and to provide necessary political impetus to the implementation of decisions of the United Nations Conference on Environment and Development and commitments contained therein.

Review and consideration of implementation of Agenda 21 should be in an integrated manner;

15. *Requests* the Secretary–General to provide for each session of the Commission, in accordance with the programme of work mentioned in paragraph 12 above and in accordance with its organizational modalities, analytical reports containing information on relevant activities to implement Agenda 21, progress achieved and emerging issues to be addressed;

16. *Also requests* the Secretary–General to prepare, for the first substantive session of the Commission, reports containing information and proposals, as appropriate, on the following issues:

(a) Initial financial commitments, financial flows and arrangements to give effect to the decisions of the Conference from all available funding sources and mechanisms;

(b) Progress achieved in facilitating and promoting transfer of environmentally sound technologies, cooperation and capacity-building;

(c) Progress in the incorporation of recommendations of the United Nations Conference on Environment and Development in the activities of international organizations and measures undertaken by the Administrative Committee on

Coordination to ensure that sustainable development principles are incorporated into programmes and processes within the United Nations system;

(d) Ways in which, upon request, the United Nations system and bilateral donors are assisting countries, particularly developing countries, in the preparation of national reports and national Agenda 21 action plans;

(e) Urgent and major emerging issues that may be addressed in the course of the high-level meeting;

17. *Decides* that organizational modalities for the Commission should be reviewed in the context of the overall review and appraisal of Agenda 21 during the special session of the General Assembly and adjusted, as may be required, to improve its effectiveness;

Relationship with other United Nations intergovernmental bodies

18. *Recommends* that the Commission, in discharging its functions, submit its consolidated recommendations to the Economic and Social Council and, through it, to the General Assembly, to be considered by the Council and the Assembly in accordance with their respective responsibilities as defined in the Charter of the United Nations and the relevant provisions of paragraphs 38.9 and 38.10 of Agenda 21;

19. *Also recommends* that the Commission actively interact with other intergovernmental United Nations bodies dealing with matters related to environment and development;

20. *Emphasizes* that the ongoing restructuring and revitalization of the United Nations in the economic, social and related fields should take into account the organizational modalities for the Commission on Sustainable Development, with a view to optimizing the work of the Commission and other intergovernmental United Nations bodies dealing with matters related to environment and development;

Coordination within the United Nations system

21. *Requests* all United Nations specialized agencies and related organizations of the United Nations system to strengthen and adjust their activities, programmes and medium-term plans, as appropriate, in line with Agenda 21, in particular regarding projects for promoting sustainable development, in accordance with paragraph 38.28 of Agenda 21, and make their reports on steps they have taken to give effect to this recommendation available to the Commission on Sustainable Development and the Economic and Social Council in 1993 or, at the latest, in 1994, in accordance with Article 64 of the Charter of the United Nations;

22. *Invites* all relevant governing bodies to ensure that the tasks assigned to them are carried out effectively, including the elaboration and publication on a regular basis of reports on the activities of the organs, programmes and organizations for which they are responsible, and that continuous reviews are undertaken of their policies, programmes, budgets and activities;

23. *Invites* the World Bank and other international, regional and subregional financial and development institutions, including the Global Environment Facility, to submit regularly to the Commission on Sustainable Development reports containing information on their experience, activities and plans to implement Agenda 21;

24. *Requests* the Secretary-General to submit to the Commission on Sustainable Development, at its substantive session of 1993, recommendations and proposals for improving coordination of programmes related to development data that exist within the United Nations system, taking into account provisions of paragraph 40.13 of Agenda 21, *inter alia,* regarding "Development Watch";

United Nations Environment Programme, United Nations Development Programme, United Nations Conference on Trade and Development and United Nations Sudano–Sahelian Office

25. *Requests* the Governing Councils of the United Nations Environment Programme, the United Nations Development Programme and the Trade and Development Board to examine the relevant provisions of chapter 38 of Agenda 21 at their next sessions and submit reports on their specific plans to implement Agenda 21 to the General Assembly at its forty-eighth session, through the Commission on Sustainable Development and the Economic and Social Council;

26. *Takes note* of the work of the United Nations Centre on Urgent Environmental Assistance, established by the Governing Council of the United Nations Environment Programme on an experimental basis, and invites the Governing Council to report to the General Assembly at its forty-eighth session on the experience gained within the Centre;

Regional commissions

27. *Requests* United Nations regional commissions to examine the relevant provisions of chapter 38 of Agenda 21 at their next sessions and submit reports on their specific plans to implement Agenda 21;

28. *Requests* the Economic and Social Council to decide on the arrangements required so that the reports of regional commissions with the conclusions related to such a review be made available to the Commission on Sustainable Development in 1993, or at the latest in 1994;

High-level Advisory Board

29. *Endorses* the view of the Secretary–General that the High-level Advisory Board should consist of eminent persons broadly representative of all regions of the world, with recognized expertise on the broad spectrum of issues to be dealt with by the Commission on Sustainable Development, drawn from relevant scientific disciplines, industry, finance and other major non-governmental constituencies, as well as various disciplines related to environment and development, and that due account should also be given to gender balance;

30. *Decides* that the main task of this Board is to give broad consideration to issues related to implementation of Agenda 21, taking into account the thematic multi-year programme of work of the Commission on Sustainable Development, and provide expert advice in that regard to the Secretary–General and, through him to the Commission, the Economic and Social Council and the General Assembly;

31. *Takes note* of the views of the Secretary–General regarding the functions of the Board and of the Committee for Development Planning, and requests the Secretary–General to submit appropriate proposals to the Economic and Social Council at its organizational session for 1993, including the possibility of organizing expert rosters;

Secretariat support arrangements

32. *Takes note* of the decision of the Secretary–General to establish at the Under–Secretary–General level a new Department for Policy Coordination and Sustainable Development and in this context calls upon the Secretary–General to establish a clearly identifiable, highly qualified and competent secretariat support structure to provide support for the Commission on Sustainable Development, the Inter–Agency Committee on Sustainable Development and the High–Level Advisory Board, taking into account gender balance at all levels, the paramount importance of securing the highest standards of efficiency, competence and integrity, and the importance of recruiting the staff on as wide a geographical basis as possible in accordance with Articles 8 and 101 of the Charter of the United Nations and the following criteria:

(a) It should draw on the expertise gained and the working methods and organizational structures developed during the preparatory process for the United Nations Conference on Environment and Development;

(b) It should work closely with United Nations and other expert bodies in the field of sustainable development and should cooperate closely and cooperatively with the economic and social entities of the Secretariat and the secretariats of relevant organs, organizations and bodies of the United Nations system, including the secretariats of international financial institutions, and it should provide for effective liaison with relevant non-governmental organizations, including those related to major groups, in particular non-governmental organizations from developing countries;

(c) The secretariat, which will be located in New York, should ensure easy access to all countries to its services; effective interaction with secretariats of other international organizations, financial institutions and relevant conventions whose secretariats have been established definitely or on an interim basis and should have a relevant office at Geneva to establish close links with activities related to follow-up of legal instruments, signed at or mandated by the United Nations Conference on Environment and Development, and to liaise with agencies in the fields of environment and development. The secretariat should also have a liaison office at Nairobi, on the basis of arrangements of the United Nations Conference on Environment and Development;

(d) It should be headed by a high-level official designated by the Secretary–General to work closely and directly with him and with assured access to him, as well as with the heads of relevant organizations of the United Nations system, including the multilateral financial and trade organizations, dealing with the implementation of Agenda 21;

(e) It should be funded from the United Nations regular budget and depend to the maximum extent possible upon existing budgetary resources;

(f) It should be supplemented or reinforced, as appropriate, by secondments from other relevant bodies and agencies of the United Nations system, especially the United Nations Environment Programme, the United Nations Development Programme and the World Bank, taking into account the need to ensure that the work programmes of those organizations are not negatively affected, and national Governments, as well as by appropriate specialists on limited-term contracts from outside the United Nations in such areas as may be required;

(g) It should take into account relevant resolutions and decisions of the General Assembly and the Economic and Social Council regarding women in the United Nations Secretariat;

(h) Sustainable development should be integrated and coordinated with other economic, social and environmental activities of the Secretariat. Organizational decisions should be consistent with consensus resolutions in the context of the restructuring and revitalization of the United Nations in the economic, social and related fields;

33. *Requests* the Secretary–General to make the necessary interim secretariat arrangements to ensure adequate preparations and support for the first session of the Commission on Sustainable Development and the work of the Inter–Agency Committee on Sustainable Development;

34. *Also requests* the Secretary–General to report to the General Assembly at its forty-eighth session on the implementation of the present resolution.

1.32 NUUK Declaration on Environment and Development in the Arctic. Adopted by the Ministers of the Arctic Countries, at Nuuk, Greenland, 16 September 1993. 1993 WL 645202 (Intl.Envtl.L.)

We, the Ministers of the Arctic Countries,

Recognizing the special role and responsibilities of the Arctic Countries with respect to the protection of the Arctic environment,

Acknowledging that the Arctic environment consists of ecosystems with unique features and resources which are especially slow to recover from the impact of human activities, and as such, require special protective measures,

Further acknowledging that the indigenous peoples who have been permanent residents of the Arctic for millenia, are at risk from environmental degradation,

Determined individually and jointly, to conserve and protect the Arctic environment for the benefit of present and future generations, as well as for the global environment,

Noting that in order to achieve sustainable development, environmental protection shall constitute an integral part of the development process and cannot be considered in isolation from it,

Recognizing the importance of applying the results of the United Nations Conference on Environment and Development to the Arctic region,

Welcoming the efforts of the eight Arctic Countries to implement, through the Arctic Environmental Protection Strategy, relevant provisions of the Rio Declaration, Agenda 21 and the Forest Principles, efforts which include the Arctic Monitoring and Assessment Program (AMAP), and the Working Groups on the Conservation of Arctic Flora and Fauna (CAFF), Emergency Prevention, Preparedness and Response, and the Protection of the Arctic Marine Environment,

Affirming Principle 2 of the Rio Declaration on Environment and Development which affirms that States have, in accordance with the Charter of the United Nations and the principles of international law, the sovereign right to exploit their own resources pursuant to their own environmental and developmental policies, and the responsibility to ensure that activities within their jurisdiction or control do not cause damage to the environment of other States or of areas beyond the limits of national jurisdiction,

Further affirming Principle 22 of the Rio Declaration, which states that: "indigenous people and their communities.... have a vital role in environmental management and development because of their knowledge and traditional practices. States should recognize and duly support their identity, culture and interests and enable their effective participation in the achievement of sustainable development."

hereby make the following Declaration.

1. We reaffirm our commitment to the protection of the Arctic Environment as a priority and to the implementation of the Arctic Environmental Protection Strategy.

2. We adopt the report of the Second Ministerial Conference of the Arctic Environmental Protection Strategy, and endorse its provisions to implement the Strategy, in particular:

—seeking resources to enable each country to fully participate in the program activities under the Arctic Environmental Protection Strategy;

—endeavouring to support, through these resources, joint projects in order to ensure that each country is able to participate in the activities of the Arctic Monitoring and Assessment Program (AMAP), including the completion of national implementation plans and the comprehensive assessment of results;

—establishing a working group to assess the need for further action or instruments to prevent pollution of the Arctic marine environment and to evaluate the need for action in appropriate international fora to obtain international recognition of the particularly sensitive character of the ice-covered sea areas of the Arctic;

—reaffirming the commitment to sustainable development, including the sustainable use of renewable resources by indigenous peoples, and to that end agreeing to establish a Task Force for this purpose.

—underlining the necessity of a notification system and improved cooperation for mutual aid in case of accidents in the Arctic area:

—reaffirming that management, planning and development activities shall provide for the conservation, sustainable use and protection of Arctic flora and fauna for the benefit and enjoyment of present and future generations, including local populations and indigenous peoples.

3. We will cooperate to conserve, protect and, as appropriate, restore the ecosystems of the Arctic. We will in particular cooperate to strengthen the knowledge base and to develop information and monitoring systems for the Arctic region.

4. We recognize that effective domestic environmental legislation is a prerequisite to the protection of the environment. As Ministers we shall promote legislation required for the protection of the Arctic environment.

5. We support the achievements of the United Nations Conference on Environment and Development, and state our beliefs that the Principles of the Rio Declaration on Environment and Development have particular relevance with respect to sustainable development in the Arctic.

6. We believe that decisions relating to Arctic activities must be made in a transparent fashion and therefore undertake to facilitate, through national rules and legislation, appropriate access to information concerning such decisions, to participation in such decisions and to judicial and administrative proceedings.

7. We recognize the special role of the indigenous peoples in environmental management and development in the Arctic, and of the significance of their knowledge and traditional practices, and will promote their effective participation in the achievement of sustainable development in the Arctic.

8. We believe that development in the Arctic must incorporate the application of precautionary approaches to development with environmental implications, including prior assessment and systematic observation of the impacts of such development. Therefore we shall maintain, as appropriate, or put into place as quickly as possible, an internationally transparent domestic process for the environmental impact assessment of proposed activities that are likely to have a significant adverse impact on the Arctic environment and are subject to decisions by competent national authorities. To this end we support the implementation of the provisions of the Convention on Environmental Impact Assessment in a Transboundary Context.

9. We underline the importance of prior and timely notification and consultation regarding activities that may have significant adverse transboundary environmental effects, including preparedness for natural disasters and other emergencies that are likely to produce sudden harmful effects on the Arctic environment or its peoples.

10. We recognize the need for effective application of existing legal instruments relevant to protection of the Arctic environment, and will cooperate in the future development of such instruments, as needed. We support the early ratification of the United Nations Conventions on Biological Diversity and Climate Change.

11. We undertake to consider the development of regional instruments concerned with the protection of the Arctic environment.

In witness whereof we have signed the present Declaration.

1.33 Agreement Between the Government of the United States of America and the Government of the Russian Federation on Cooperation in the Field of Protection of the Environment and Natural Resources. Signed at Washington, 23 June 1994. Entered into force, 23 June 1994. State Dept. No. 94–160. 1994 WL 449099 (Treaty)

The Government of the United States of America and the Government of the Russian Federation, hereinafter referred to as the Parties;

Determined to develop cooperation in the field of protection of the environment and natural resources, taking into account mutual interests and the experience obtained from implementation of the Agreement between the Government of the United States of America and the Government of the Russian Federation on Cooperation in the Field of Environmental Protection of May 23, 1972;

Recognizing that many important environmental problems are global in nature and require the cooperation of all countries and peoples to resolve;

Attaching great significance to the protection and enhancement of the environment and to its preservation from the damage resulting from pollution and overuse;

Bearing in mind that sustainable economic and social development for the benefit of present and future generations already now requires effective measures to be taken for the protection and enhancement of the environment;

Considering the readiness of the Parties to cooperate to enable the Russian Federation better to take into account environmental issues and the rational and sustainable use of natural resources in the transition to a market economy and thereafter;

Desiring to facilitate the establishment of long-term cooperation between interested organizations in the two countries in the field of protection of the environment and natural resources;

Have agreed as follows:

Article I

1. The Parties shall assist in the development of cooperation in the field of protection of the environment and natural resources on national, regional and global levels. Their activity shall focus on studying harmful impacts on the environment and jointly developing measures to improve the condition of the environment and to solve problems of the protection and rational and sustainable use of natural resources, including work on the areas of pollution prevention and remediation and preservation and conservation of natural resources.

2. The Parties shall work together to develop mutually agreed-upon policies in the field of protection of the environment and natural resources on a bilateral, regional and global basis.

3. The Parties shall develop cooperation in the field of protection of the environment and natural resources on a basis of equality, reciprocity and mutual benefit.

Article II

Cooperation may be implemented in the following main areas of mutual interest:

1. atmosphere, and water and soil resources;

2. environmental aspects of agricultural production;

3. preservation, conservation and management of natural and cultural resources in the context of their relationship to the environment, including the organization of preserves and other specially protected areas;

4. marine and coastal areas and resources;

5. arctic and subarctic areas and resources;

6. environmental impact assessment;

7. global environmental issues, including climate change, depletion of the ozone layer and conservation and restoration of the biological diversity of local, regional and global ecological systems, including forest ecosystems;

8. the impact of environmental factors on human health and the condition of flora and fauna;

9. application of digital mapping and GIS (geographic information systems) technologies and use of sensor technology in addressing environmental issues;

10. energy-saving measures and creation of alternative energy sources;

11. legal and administrative measures relating to the protection of the environment, including legislation, enforcement and access to the administrative and judicial systems;

12. participation of the public, including non-governmental organizations, in environmental decision making;

13. education in the field of environmental protection and natural resources;

14. economics and the management of environmental issues and the use of natural resources;

15. the role of the military in the field of protection of the environment and natural resources;

16. environmental emergencies;

17. earthquake prediction and assessment of seismic risks;

18. environmental monitoring; and

19. any other area of cooperation agreed by the Parties.

Article III

Cooperation between the Parties may be implemented by the following means:

1. joint scientific and technical projects;

2. exchange of scientific and technical information, documentation and research results, including exchange of information on the condition of the environment;

3. exchange of experience in the area of environmental management;

4. organizing and convening bilateral meetings, symposia and workshops, and publication of reports, Articles, and monographs;

5. exchange of delegations, scientists, experts, research scholars and specialists;

6. participation of specialists of the Parties in international conferences, symposia and exhibitions on protection of the environment and ecology held in the two countries; and

7. any other means of cooperation agreed by the Parties.

Article IV

The Parties shall duly encourage and facilitate the establishment and development of direct contacts and cooperation between governmental, public, and private institutions and organizations of the two countries, and encourage and facilitate the conclusion, where required, of separate agreements and contracts necessary to implement activities under this Agreement.

Article V

1. To implement this Agreement, a Joint U.S.—Russian Committee on Cooperation in the Field of Protection of the Environment and Natural Resources, hereinafter, the "Joint Committee", shall be established. As a rule, the Joint Committee shall meet once a year, alternately in Washington and Moscow. The Joint Committee shall review specific measures and programs of cooperation, coordinate the activities of organizations involved in implementation of these programs, and, as appropriate, make proposals to the Parties on the subject matter of this Agreement.

2. Each Party shall name a government agency, which agency shall designate a co-chair of the Joint Committee. In the period between sessions of the Joint Committee, the co-chairs will maintain contact between the American and Russian sections, coordinate the implementation of the pertinent programs of cooperation, update individual sections of these programs and coordinate the activity of organizations participating in cooperation in accordance with this Agreement.

Article VI

1. Scientific and technological information of a non-proprietary nature resulting from cooperation under this Agreement, other than information which is not disclosed for national security, commercial or industrial reasons, shall be made available, unless otherwise agreed, to the world scientific community through customary channels and in accordance with normal procedures of the participating agencies and entities.

2. The treatment of intellectual property created or furnished in the course of cooperative activities under this Agreement, unless agreed otherwise by the Parties in writing, is provided for in the Annex, which is an integral part of this Agreement.

Article VII

1. This Agreement shall enter into force upon signature and shall remain in force for five years, after which it will be extended for successive five-year periods, unless one of the Parties notifies the other of the termination thereof not later than six months before the Agreement's expiration.

2. Termination of this Agreement shall not affect the implementation of activities under this Agreement that are not fully completed upon the termination hereof.

Article VIII

This Agreement supersedes, as between the United States of America and the Russian Federation, the Agreement between the Government of the United States of America and the Government of the Union of Soviet Socialist Republics on Cooperation in the Field of Environmental Protection of May 23, 1972. The Parties may agree that an institutional structure developed under that Agreement may continue without being reconstituted.

Article IX

All activities under this Agreement shall be conducted in accordance with applicable laws, regulations and procedures of the United States of America and the Russian Federation and shall be subject to the availability of resources.

Done at Washington, this twenty-third day of June, 1994, in duplicate, in the English and Russian languages, both texts being equally authentic.

ANNEX

INTELLECTUAL PROPERTY

Pursuant to Article 6 of this Agreement:

The Parties shall ensure adequate and effective protection of intellectual property created or furnished under this Agreement and relevant implementing arrangements.

The Parties agree to notify one another in a timely fashion of any inventions or copyrighted works arising under this Agreement and to seek protection for such intellectual property in a timely fashion. Rights to such intellectual property shall be allocated as provided in this Annex.

I. SCOPE

A. This Annex is applicable to all cooperative activities undertaken pursuant to this Agreement, except as otherwise specifically agreed to by the Parties or their designees.

B. For purposes of this Agreement, "intellectual property" shall have the meaning found in Article 2 of the Convention Establishing the World Intellectual Property Organization, done at Stockholm, July 14, 1967.

C. This Annex addresses the allocation of rights, interests, and royalties between the Parties. Each Party shall ensure that the other Party can obtain the rights to intellectual property allocated in accordance with the Annex, by obtaining those rights from its own participants through contracts or other legal means, if necessary. This Annex does not otherwise alter or prejudice the allocation between a Party and its nationals, which shall be determined by that Party's laws and practices.

D. Disputes concerning intellectual property arising under this Agreement should be resolved through discussions between the concerned participating institutions or, if necessary, the Parties or their designees. Upon mutual agreement of the Parties, a dispute shall be submitted to an arbitral tribunal for binding arbitration in accordance with the applicable rules of international law. Unless the Parties or their designees agree otherwise in writing, the arbitration rules of the UNCITRAL shall govern.

E. Termination or expiration of this Agreement shall not affect rights or obligations under this Annex.

II. ALLOCATION OF RIGHTS

A. Each Party shall be entitled to a non-exclusive, irrevocable, royalty-free license in all countries to translate, reproduce, and publicly distribute scientific and technical journal Articles, reports, and books directly arising from cooperation under this Agreement. All publicly distributed copies of a copyrighted work prepared under this provision shall indicate the names of the authors of the work unless an author explicitly declines to be named.

B. Rights to all forms of intellectual property, other than those rights described in Part A of Section II above, shall be allocated as follows:

1. Researchers and scientists visiting in furtherance of their education shall receive intellectual property rights under the existing rules of the host institution. In addition, each visiting researcher named as an inventor or author shall have the right to national treatment regarding awards, benefits or other compensation, including royalties, in accordance with the existing rules of the host institution.

2. (a) For intellectual property created by the participants during joint research, for example, when the Parties, participating institutions, or participating personnel have agreed in advance on the scope of work, each Party shall be entitled to obtain all rights and interests in its own territory. The allocation of rights and interests in third countries will be determined in implementing arrangements. The rights to intellectual property shall be allocated with due regard for the economic, scientific and technological contributions from each Party to the creation of intellectual property. If research is not designated as "joint research" in the relevant implementing arrangement, rights to intellectual property arising from the research shall be allocated in accordance with Part B, paragraph 1 of Section II. In addition, each person named as an inventor or

author shall have the right to national treatment regarding awards, benefits and other compensation, including royalties, in accordance with the existing rules of the host institution;

(b) Notwithstanding Part B, paragraph 2(a) of Section II, if a type of intellectual property is available under the laws of one Party but not the other Party, the Party whose laws provide for this type of protection shall be entitled to all rights and interests in all countries which provide rights to such intellectual property. Persons named as inventors or authors of the property shall nonetheless be entitled to national treatment in regard to awards, benefits, or other compensations, including royalties, in accordance with the rules as provided in Part B, paragraph 2(a) of Section II.

III. BUSINESS CONFIDENTIAL INFORMATION

In the event that information identified in a timely fashion as business-confidential is furnished or created under the Agreement, each Party and its participants shall protect such information in accordance with applicable laws, regulations, and administrative practice. Information may be identified as "business-confidential" if a person having the information may derive an economic benefit from it or may obtain a competitive advantage over those who do not have it, the information is not generally known or publicly available from other sources, and the owner has not previously made the information available without imposing in a timely manner an obligation to keep it confidential.

1.34 AGREEMENT BETWEEN THE GOVERNMENT OF THE UNITED STATES OF AMERICA AND THE GOVERNMENT OF THE RUSSIAN FEDERATION ON COOPERATION IN THE PREVENTION OF POLLUTION OF THE ENVIRONMENT IN THE ARCTIC. Signed at Moscow, 16 December 1994. Entered into force, 16 December 1994. State Dept. No. 95–28, 1994 WL 761204 (Treaty)

The Government of the United States of America and the Government of the Russian Federation (hereinafter referred to as the Parties),

Recognizing the sensitivity of the Arctic environment and our mutual commitment to protect the Arctic environment and to promote the social and economic interests of local, especially indigenous populations, including their traditional way of life;

Concerned over the potential threats posed by contaminants in the Arctic region to the health of the indigenous and local populations of the region as well as to its flora and fauna;

Convinced that cooperation and sharing of experience between the Parties will contribute to understanding and effective response to any such threat both on a national basis and within broader international efforts to protect the Arctic environment;

Desiring to build upon the results of the American–Russian Summit held in Vancouver, April 3–4, 1993;

Noting the particular importance of relevant provisions of Part XII of the United Nations Convention on the Law of the Sea of 1982; the provisions of the Convention on the Prevention of Marine Pollution by Dumping of Wastes and Other Matter of 1972; and the provisions of the Arctic Environmental Protection Strategy of 1991;

Have agreed as follows:

Article 1

The Parties shall cooperate in the prevention, reduction and control of pollution in the Arctic marine and terrestrial environment resulting from the accidental or intentional introduction of contaminants into that environment.

To this end the Parties shall cooperate in research, monitoring, assessment and other activities, bilaterally and in the appropriate multilateral fora.

Article 2

1. The Parties shall cooperate in the conduct of scientific research, monitoring, and assessment activities to determine the potential impacts of contaminants in the Arctic environment, including, inter alia:

1) the pathways by which such contaminants reach and are dispersed within the Arctic environment;

2) the effects of such contaminants, including rates of bio-accumulation, upon Arctic flora and fauna, including fish populations; and

3) the effects of such contaminants upon human health in the Arctic environment, especially upon local and indigenous populations.

2. The Parties further shall cooperate in the monitoring and assessment of levels of hazardous contamination in the Arctic environment, including, inter alia:

1) exchange of data and information on the effects of disposal and release of such contaminants introduced directly or indirectly into the Arctic environment;

2) determination of the level, chemical composition, and patterns of such contamination caused by releases from sites at which materials have been stored, processed or disposed; and

3) determination of the amount, concentrations and dynamics of transport of such contaminants introduced into the marine zone, including through rivers and other watercourses, natural or artificial, and via ice transport and ice rafted sediment.

3. The Parties shall consult with regard to technical solutions for the elimination of radioactive and other types of contamination impacts.

4. The Parties shall cooperate in the conduct of joint scientific research to predict ecological impacts of the existing disposals of radioactive waste and consult with regard to technical solutions for the elimination of disposals in places where ecological safety is not insured.

5. Cooperation between the Parties in scientific research and monitoring referred to in this Article shall take place bilaterally, and within the appropriate international, including regional, mechanisms, in particular the Arctic Monitoring and Assessment Program of the Arctic Environmental Protection Strategy of 1991 and the International Arctic Seas Assessment Program of 1993 the International Atomic Energy Agency.

Article 3

1. Each Party shall facilitate joint activities under Article 2 in areas that are under its jurisdiction in accordance with international law and that are or are believed to be contaminated, under such reasonable conditions as it may establish.

2. The Parties shall ensure that the data and information resulting from such research and monitoring are exchanged and made freely available on a reciprocal basis.

Article 4

The Parties shall promote the development of specific measures to give effect to this Agreement, including:

1) programs for the exchange of scientists, students and experts;

2) organization of seminars and meetings of experts;

3) organization of joint research activities, including marine scientific research cruises;

4) development of Geographic Information Systems, data bases and inventories on Arctic environmental data;

5) cooperation in emergency preparedness exercises and prompt exchange of information concerning major accidental releases of contaminants into the Arctic environment; and

6) exchange of information on technologies and assessment methodologies applicable within the framework of this Agreement and on relevant environmental protection legislation and regulations.

Article 5

Activities under this Agreement, including specific projects and programs, shall be carried out by responsible agencies of each Party in accordance with the Agreement Between the Government of the Union of Soviet Socialist Republics and the Government of the United States on Cooperation in Ocean Studies of 1990 and the Agreement between the Government of the United States and the Government of the Russian Federation on Cooperation in the Field of Protection of the Environment and National Resources of 1994 and under the overall coordination of the United States-Russian Commission on Economic and Technological Cooperation or under any other coordinating body as may be agreed by the Parties.

Article 6

1. All activities undertaken pursuant to this Agreement shall be conducted in accordance with the applicable laws, regulations, and procedures in both countries and shall be subject to the availability of funds and personnel.

2. Scientific and technological information resulting from cooperation under this Agreement, other than information which is not disclosed for national security, commercial or industrial reasons, shall be made freely available, unless otherwise agreed.

3. Issues of intellectual property created or furnished in the course of joint activities under this Agreement shall be governed by Annex II of the Agreement between the Government of the United States of America and the Government of the Russian Federation on Science and Technology Cooperation, signed at Moscow December 16, 1993.

Article 7

The Parties shall resolve by consultation any differences as to the interpretation or application of this Agreement.

Article 8

1. This Agreement shall enter into force upon signature and remain in force for a period of five years, and may be extended for additional five year periods upon written agreement of the Parties.

2. Either Party may terminate this Agreement by so notifying the other Party in writing. Such termination shall be effective six months from such written notification.

IN WITNESS WHEREOF, the undersigned, being duly authorized by their respective Governments, have signed this Agreement.

DONE at Moscow, in duplicate, this sixteenth day of December 1994, in the English and Russian languages, each text being equally authentic.

1.35 Memorandum of Understanding Between the Government of the United States of America and the Government of the Russian Federation on Cooperation in Natural and Man-made Technological Emergency Prevention and Response. Signed at Moscow, 16 July 1996. Entered into force, 16 July 1996. State Dept. No. 96–143, 1996 WL 516876 (Treaty)

The Government of the United States of America and the Government of the Russian Federation, (hereinafter referred to as "the Parties"),

Recognizing:

The need for cooperation in man-made technological emergency and natural disaster prevention, mitigation, response, and recovery;

That cooperation in the areas of natural and man-made technological emergency preparedness, prevention, response, recovery and mitigation can promote the well-being and security of both nations;

The usefulness to the Parties of scientific and technical information exchanges, emergency simulations, and joint training exercises on natural and man-made technological emergency prevention and response;

The need for improved mechanisms of communication and cooperation between the Parties during times of natural and man-made technological emergencies in their two countries;

The importance of consultation and cooperation between the Parties in responding to natural and man-made technological emergencies in other nations, and the necessity of expanding the existing relevant collaboration under the United States–Russian Federation Agreement on Cooperation in the Field of Protection of the Environment and Natural Resources of June 23, 1994, and within the framework of the U.S.-Russian Joint Commission on Economic and Technological Cooperation (the Gore–Chernomyrdin Commission); and the role of international organizations such as the United Nations, World Bank, and NATO, as well as the Arctic Environmental Protection Strategy, International Atomic Energy Agency, other international bodies, and non-governmental organizations in natural and man-made technological emergency prevention and response;

Have agreed as follows:

Article I

The Parties will cooperate in emergency preparedness, response, recovery and mitigation of natural and man-made technological disasters not occurring within the context of international or internal military or civilian conflict. To this end, the Parties may cooperate in the following areas of mutual interest:

1. Development of techniques and methods for increasing the Parties' capabilities in emergency preparedness, response, recovery and mitigation of natural and man-made technological disasters, including:

— monitoring of dangerous environmental, industrial, and natural phenomena;

— forecasting of natural and man-made technological emergencies and disasters;

— assessment of disaster effects and response needs; and development of contingency plans.

2. Establishment of formal mechanisms for timely and direct communication of:

— information on natural and man-made technological emergencies or disasters occurring on their territories;

— requests for, and offers of, assistance between the Parties;

— possible joint responses to natural and man-made technological emergencies or disasters in third countries; and,

— information from the Department of Humanitarian Affairs of the United Nations, the Civil Emergency Planning Directorate of NATO, the Emergency Prevention, Preparedness, and Response Working Group of the Arctic Environmental Protection Strategy, and other relevant international bodies.

3. Consideration of international and non-governmental organizations in the Parties' capabilities for emergency preparedness, response, recovery, and mitigation of natural and man-made technological emergencies.

Cooperation in the above areas will be based on principles of equality, reciprocity, and mutual benefit and will be aimed at solving common problems and improving the Parties' emergency preparedness and relief operations in cases of natural and man-made technological disasters.

Article II

Cooperation under this Memorandum may involve:

— Exchanges of specialists, researchers, information, technology, and assessment methodologies;

— Joint conferences, seminars, workshops, as well as joint planning and development of research and demonstration projects;

— Development of Geographic Information Systems, data bases, and inventories applicable to the subject matter of this Memorandum.

— Publication of printed materials, reports, and case studies;

— Creation of communication links between government agencies of the Parties; and

— Such other natural and man-made technological emergency related activities as may be mutually agreed by the Executive Agents designated by the Parties pursuant to Article V of this Memorandum.

Article III

The Parties will encourage, as appropriate, cooperation by government agencies and ministries other than those named by the Parties as Executive Agents, and by interested international and non-governmental organizations involved in the areas applicable to this Memorandum.

Article IV

To implement this Memorandum, the Parties will establish a Joint Committee on Cooperation in Natural and Man-made Technological Emergency Prevention and Response (hereinafter referred to as "the Joint Committee").

The Executive Agents will establish procedures for the operation of the Joint Committee and will establish sub-units thereof by mutual agreement. The Joint Committee will plan and coordinate cooperative activities under this Memorandum and review progress of such activities. The Joint Committee will meet at least annually.

Meetings of the Joint Committee will be held alternately in the United States and in the Russian Federation, unless otherwise agreed by the Executive Agents.

Article V

With a view to coordinating efforts to implement this Memorandum, each Party will designate one or more Executive Agents. The Executive Agent for the Russian Federation will be the Ministry for Civil Defense, Emergencies, and Elimination of Consequences of Natural Disasters (EMERCOM of Russia). The Executive Agent for the United States of America will be the Federal Emergency Management Agency (FEMA). The Office of U.S. Foreign Disaster Assistance of the Agency for International Development (OFDA) will act on behalf of the U.S. Executive Agent on matters concerning international humanitarian assistance.

The Executive Agents will facilitate the conduct of cooperative activities, including organizing and determining the membership of the Joint Committee.

The Executive Agents will develop cooperative action plans and other appropriate activities in implementation of this Memorandum.

Each Party will notify the other Party without delay should an Executive Agent cease to have authority to function in that capacity; a Party will, as soon as possible, but no later than sixty (60) days from the date of such notification, advise the other of the identity of the successor Executive Agent.

Article VI

All cooperative activities under this Memorandum, including exchanges of information, exchanges of specialists, training and exercises, and implementation of other cooperative activities, will be conducted in accordance with the respective national laws and regulations of the Parties' states and will be subject to the availability to each Party of appropriated or necessary funds, resources, and personnel.

Article VII

In accordance with international law and with the laws of both states, each Party shall, for the purpose of cooperative activities under this Memorandum, facilitate access to areas that are under its jurisdiction, as well as to relevant institutions, organizations, and sources of information under such reasonable conditions as the Party may establish.

Article VIII

Information derived pursuant to activities under this Memorandum, with the exception of information that is not disclosable under the applicable laws and regulations of either state, will be made available to the world community through customary channels and the normal practices and regulations of the Parties, except when otherwise agreed in writing by the Executive Agents.

Article IX

This Memorandum shall not affect the cooperation of the United States of America or the Russian Federation with other States and international organizations, nor shall it affect ongoing cooperative activities between United States and Russian Federation government agencies.

Article X

This Memorandum will remain in force for a period of ten years, and may be extended for additional ten year periods upon written agreement of the Parties.

This Memorandum may be amended by mutual agreement of the Parties. Either Party may terminate this Memorandum upon six months, written notice to the other Party.

Expiration or termination of this Memorandum will not affect the validity or duration of any activity initiated prior to termination but not completed at the time of expiration or termination.

This Memorandum supersedes, as between the United States of American and the Russian Federation, the Memorandum of Understanding between the Government of the United States of America and the Government of the Union of Soviet Socialist Republics on Cooperation in Natural and Man Made Emergency Prevention and Response of July 30, 1991.

1.36 Joint Communique and Declaration on the Establishment of the Arctic Council. Signed at Ottawa, 19 September 1996. *Reprinted in* 35 I.L.M. 1382 & 1 Weston I.B.1A

JOINT COMMUNIQUE

Ministers and Senior Representatives of the Governments of Canada, Denmark, Finland, Iceland, Norway, the Russian Federation, Sweden and the United States of America met in Ottawa, Canada, on September 19, 1996, and signed the Declaration on the Establishment of the Arctic Council.

This inaugural meeting was attended by the leaders and senior representatives of three international Arctic indigenous organizations—the Inuit Circumpolar Conference, the Saami Council, and the Association of Indigenous Minorities of the North, Siberia, and the Far East of the Russian Federation, as Permanent Participants in the Council.

Also present at the signing ceremony were the Standing Committee of Parliamentarians of the Arctic Region; the Nordic Council of Ministers; the Nordic Council Finnish Secretariat; the non-Arctic States of Great Britain, Germany, Japan, Poland and the Netherlands; the International Union for Circumpolar Health; the International Arctic Science Committee; the United Nations Environment Programme; the International Union for the Conservation of Nature; the Advisory Committee on Protection of the Sea; and the World Wildlife Fund.

Ministers viewed the establishment of this new intergovernmental forum as an important milestone in their commitment to enhance cooperation in the circumpolar North. The Council will provide a mechanism for addressing the common concerns and challenges faced by their governments and the people of the Arctic. To this end, Ministers referred particularly to the protection of the Arctic environment and sustainable development as a means of improving the economic, social and cultural well-being in the North.

Ministers noted that the indigenous people of the Arctic have played an important role in the negotiations to create the Arctic Council. The Declaration provides for their full consultation and involvement in the Arctic Council. To this end, the Inuit Circumpolar Conference, the Saami Council, and the Association of the Indigenous Minorities of the North, Siberia, and the Far East of the Russian Federation, are named as Permanent Participants in the Arctic Council. Provision is also made for additional organizations representing Arctic indigenous people to become Permanent Participants.

Ministers acknowledged the significant work accomplished under the Arctic Environmental Protection Strategy (AEPS), whose existing programs will be integrated within the Council. They agreed to complete the integration process by the time of the final AEPS Ministerial meeting being held in Norway in 1997.

The Ministers recognized the contribution of international science to the knowledge and understanding of the Arctic region and noted the role that scientific cooperation, through the International Arctic Science Committee and other organizations, is playing in developing a truly circumpolar cooperation.

Ministers welcomed the attendance of the Standing Committee of the Parliamentarians of the Arctic Region and looked forward to its future participation in the meetings of the Council. They also recognized the need for providing the opportunity to non-Arctic countries, governmental and non-governmental organizations with Arctic interests to participate actively, as Observers, in the work of the Council, and to draw on their experience.

Ministers set the initial priority tasks for the start-up of the Council as follows:

— developing, for adoption by the Council, rules of procedure;

— developing, for adoption by the Council, terms of reference for a sustainable development program as a basis for collaborative projects; and

— ensuring an effective transition of the AEPS into the Arctic Council, to be completed at the time of the 1997 AEPS Ministerial meeting in Norway.

Ministers expressed their appreciation to Canada for hosting the inauguration of the Arctic Council, and welcomed Canada's offer to host the first meeting of the Council in 1998.

DECLARATION

The representatives of the Governments of Canada, Denmark, Finland, Iceland, Norway, the Russian Federation, Sweden and the United States of America (hereinafter referred to as the Arctic States) meeting in Ottawa;

Affirming our commitment to the well-being of the inhabitants of the Arctic, including recognition of the special relationship and unique contributions to the Arctic of indigenous people and their communities;

Affirming our commitment to sustainable development in the Arctic region, including economic and social development, improved health conditions and cultural well-being;

Affirming concurrently our commitment to the protection of the Arctic environment, including the health of Arctic ecosystems, maintenance of biodiversity in the Arctic region and conservation and sustainable use of natural resources;

Recognizing the contributions of the Arctic Environmental Protection Strategy to these commitments;

Recognizing the traditional knowledge of the indigenous people of the Arctic and their communities and taking note of its importance and that of Arctic science and research to the collective understanding of the circumpolar Arctic;

Desiring further to provide a means for promoting cooperative activities to address Arctic issues requiring circumpolar cooperation, and to ensure full consultation with and the full involvement of indigenous people and their communities and other inhabitants of the Arctic in such activities;

Recognizing the valuable contribution and support of the Inuit Circumpolar Conference, Saami Council, and the Association of the Indigenous Minorities of the North, Siberia, and the Far East of the Russian Federation in the development of the Arctic Council;

Desiring to provide for regular intergovernmental consideration of and consultation on Arctic issues.

Hereby declare:

1. The Arctic Council is established as a high level forum to:

(a) provide a means for promoting cooperation, coordination and interaction among the Arctic States, with the involvement of the Arctic indigenous communities and other Arctic inhabitants on common Arctic issues,[1] in particular issues of sustainable development and environmental protection in the Arctic.

(b) oversee and coordinate the programs established under the AEPS on the Arctic Monitoring and Assessment Program (AMAP); Conservation of Arctic Flora and Fauna (CAFF); Protection of the Arctic Marine Environment (PAME); and Emergency Prevention, Preparedness and Response (EPPR).

(c) adopt terms of reference for, and oversee and coordinate a sustainable development program.

1. The Arctic Council should not deal with matters related to military security.

(d) disseminate information, encourage education and promote interest in Arctic-related issues.

2. Members of the Arctic Council are: Canada, Denmark, Finland, Iceland, Norway, the Russian Federation, Sweden and the United States of America (the Arctic States).

The Inuit Circumpolar Conference, the Saami Council and the Association of Indigenous Minorities of the North, Siberia and the Far East of the Russian Federation are Permanent Participants in the Arctic Council. Permanent participation equally is open to other Arctic organizations of indigenous peoples[2] with majority Arctic indigenous constituency, representing:

(a) a single indigenous people resident in more than one Arctic State; or

(b) more than one Arctic indigenous people resident in a single Arctic state.

The determination that such an organization has met this criterion is to be made by decision of the Council. The number of Permanent Participants should at any time be less than the number of members.

The category of Permanent Participation is created to provide for active participation and full consultation with the Arctic indigenous representatives within the Arctic Council.

3. Observer status in the Arctic Council is open to:

(a) non-Arctic states;

(b) inter-governmental and inter-parliamentary organizations, global and regional; and

(c) non-governmental organizations that the Council determines can contribute to its work.

4. The Council should normally meet on a biennial basis, with meetings of senior officials taking place more frequently, to provide for liaison and co-ordination. Each Arctic State should designate a focal point on matters related to the Arctic Council.

5. Responsibility for hosting meetings of the Arctic Council, including provision of secretariat support functions, should rotate sequentially among the Arctic States.

6. The Arctic Council, as its first order of business, should adopt rules of procedure for its meetings and those of its working groups.

7. Decisions of the Arctic Council are to be by consensus of the Members.

8. The Indigenous Peoples' Secretariat established under AEPS is to continue under the framework of the Arctic Council.

9. The Arctic Council should regularly review the priorities and financing of its programs and associated structures.

* * *

2. The use of the term "peoples" in this Declaration shall not be construed as having any implications as regard the rights which may attach to the term under international law.

1.37 Declaration Among the Royal Ministry of Defence of the Kingdom of Norway, the Ministry of Defence of the Russian Federation, and the Department of Defense of the United States of America, on Arctic Military Environmental Cooperation (AMEC). Signed at Bergen, 26 September 1996

The Royal Ministry of Defence of the Kingdom of Norway, the Ministry of Defence of the Russian Federation, and the Department of Defense of the United States of America, hereinafter referred to as the Parties,

Recognizing the need to ensure the conservation and sustainable use of the Arctic environment, including through the Arctic Military Environmental Cooperation program, hereinafter referred to as AMEC,

Understanding that some aspects of military activities, in particular radioactive and chemical contamination issues, may have negative impacts on the Arctic environment,

Underscoring the vital importance of cooperation between military organizations to prevent and solve environmental problems in the Arctic caused by their activities,

Considering cooperation between military organizations as a valuable contribution to the established framework for international environmental cooperation in the Arctic.

Expressing a common desire of the Parties to contribute to the realization of specific projects to protect the Arctic environment,

Taking into account

— the Memorandum between the Department of Defense of the United States of America and the Ministry of Defence of the Russian Federation on Cooperation in Environmental Protection Issues of 30 June 1995;

— the Agreement between the Royal Ministry of Defence of the Kingdom of Norway and the Ministry of Defence of the Russian Federation on Cooperation on Defence–Related Environmental Issues of 15 December 1995;

— the Agreement between the Government of the United States of America and the Government of the Russian Federation on Cooperation in the Prevention of Pollution of the Environment in the Arctic of 16 December 1994; and

— the Agreement between the Department of Defense of the United States of America and the Royal Ministry of Defence of the Kingdom of Norway for Cooperation on Environmental Protection in Defense Matters of 19 May 1994,

Hereby declare:

Article I

This Declaration establishes a framework for contacts and cooperation among the Parties on military environmental issues in the Arctic, and does not pertain to matters beyond the competencies of the Parties.

Article II

Contacts and cooperation under this Declaration are based on reciprocal rights and obligations in accordance with the laws of the Kingdom of Norway, the laws of the Russian Federation and the laws of the United States of America, and the international obligations of the Parties.

Article III

Cooperation between the Parties may include the following:

Discussing the principles, directions, and methods for the repair and protection of the environment with regard to military activities in the Arctic;

Studying the processes of the movement of contamination and evaluating its environmental impact in the Arctic in connection with military activities;

Reviewing the methods, technologies, and organization of the work to prevent contamination and carry out clean-up efforts in Arctic conditions, as well as the disposal of military arms and equipment;

Examining methods of emergency response simulation;

Reviewing and prioritizing technical and other projects, consistent with the laws of the Kingdom of Norway, the laws of the Russian Federation and the laws of the United States of America. for the repair and protection of the Arctic environment with regard to military activities; and

Undertaking other activities upon written mutual agreement of the Parties.

Article IV

Cooperation between the Parties may take the following forms:

Meetings of ad-hoc tripartite working groups on specific topics;

Conferences, seminars, and workshops;

Exchanges of visits and delegations;

Communication of AMEC's achievements and concerns regarding work on military environmental problems in the Arctic through appropriate media;

Exchange of information on results of environmental monitoring studies in the Arctic and work plans designed to eliminate or reduce the negative impact on the Arctic environment;

Surveys of the sources of contamination in the Arctic associated with military activities; and

Research work and technology exchange, upon mutual agreement of the Parties.

Article V

In principle, each Party will pay its own costs for participation in AMEC activities. All activities undertaken pursuant to this Declaration are subject to availability of funds.

For delegations conducting visits to promote activities under this Declaration, the visiting Parties will cover travel expenses to and from the host country, expenses for room and board within the host country, as well as travel allowance and insurance costs. The host party will, to the extent practicable, cover travel expenses within the host country.

Each specific AMEC project conducted under this Declaration may be supported by all three Parties in the form of direct financing, the supply of materiel and equipment, or other forms of payment, to the extent permitted by the laws of the Kingdom of Norway, the laws of the Russian Federation and the laws of the United States of America. Financial arrangements for each specific AMEC project-shall be governed by subsequent, written mutual agreements of the Parties.

To the extent permitted by the laws and regulations applicable to the host party, the host party will be responsible for the other costs associated with organizing events in accordance with this Declaration. Other arrangements may be agreed upon, in writing, on a case by case basis.

Article VI

A Steering Group with representatives from the three countries is created to organize the AMEC Program work. The Steering Group is led by leaders of the environmental organizations, who select and affirm the priority projects on military environmental issues in the Arctic.

Each year, the Parties will prepare proposals for cooperation in the fields referred to in Articles III and IV of this Declaration. On the basis of these proposals, the AMEC Steering Group shall develop a work plan to implement the AMEC program. Due account will be taken of related activities in other fora in order to avoid duplication of effort.

Not less than once a year, the AMEC Steering Group will inform the Parties about the work being conducted.

The AMEC Steering Group will prepare proposals to implement Articles III and IV, including standard operating procedures, for consideration by the Parties and will oversee implementation of the approved program and report to the Parties no less frequently than annually.

The AMEC Steering Group is composed of representatives appointed by the Parties to discuss issues as directed by the Parties at times and locations approved by the Parties. The Steering Group currently consists of representatives from the environmental organizations of the Parties.

Article VII

Ministry of Defense organizations of any other country may participate in activities conducted under this Declaration, subject to the written approval of all the Parties. Requests for such participation shall be directed to the AMEC Steering Group.

Article VIII

Information obtained within the framework of AMEC will be protected and exchanged in accordance with the laws of the Kingdom of Norway, the laws of the Russian Federation and the laws of the United States of America in this respect. Any disagreement as to the interpretation or implementation of this Declaration shall be resolved by consultation between the Parties and shall not be referred to any third party.

Signed at Bergen on the 26 September 1996, in three copies in the Norwegian, Russian, and English languages, each being equally authentic.

23 September 1996

Arctic Military Environmental Cooperation

Summary of Initial Projects

AMEC 1.1—Development of a prototype container for interim storage of spent nuclear fuel

This project will support the design and construction of a safe interim storage container for damaged and undamaged naval nuclear fuel. Additionally, appropriate training in the use of this container and in monitoring and handling of radioactive waste will be provided to training Russian Navy personnel.

Projected Timeline: 27 Months

AMEC 1.2—Development of technology for treatment of liquid radioactive waste.

A joint experts group will evaluate newly developed Russian sorption materials for use in processing liquid radioactive waste from military and industrial sources. If the technology proves a significant improvement over existing systems, development of this technology will be initiated.

Projected Timeline: 6 months

AMEC 1.3—Review and implementation of technology for solid radioactive waste volume reduction.

This project will attempt to characterize the solid radioactive waste stream associated with the Russian military; review applicable technologies for volume induction of this waste; and then implement the most promising technology.

Projected Timeline: 26 Months

AMEC 1.4—Review of technologies and procedures for interim storage of solid radioactive waste, and development of a storage facility.

A need exists for additional interim storage for solid radioactive waste in the Northern fleet. This project will characterize the solid radioactive waste problem and assess existing storage facilities and equipment. Further requirements for storage will be also be evaluated and will be assessed with respect to currently planned storage expansion and to new technologies and storage strategies. The final stage of this project will be the implementation of the selected storage expansion option.

Projected Timeline: 18 Months

AMEC 2.1—Remediation of hazardous waste sites on military bases.

This project will focus on the,selection of proper and effective methods of dealing with hazardous material spills,in the Arctic environment. The first stage of this project will include discussion of the main types of hazardous materials; of national regulatory standards; and remediation technologies appropriate to the Arctic region. The second portion of this project will involve the selection of a site at a Russian military facility and the application of the selected technology in a pilot project.

Projected Timeline: 36 Months

AMEC 2.2—Review and implementation of clean ship technologies.

Timeline: This project will examine technologies for the collection and comprehensive processing of Naval ship waste. This project will be implemented in several stages: assessment of the waste problem on board Russian Naval vessels; evaluation of suitability of existing clean ship technologies and strategies for ship waste processing; and assistance in the implementation of the appropriate technologies.

Projected Timeline: 27 Months

1.38 Nairobi Declaration and Governing Council Decision on the Role, Mandate and Governance of the United Nations Environment Programme. Adopted by the Governing Council of the United Nations Environmental Programme, 7 February 1997. U.N. Doc. GC19/1/1997 (1997)

A. Nairobi Declaration on the Role and Mandate of the United Nations Environmental Programme

We, the ministers and heads of delegation attending the nineteenth session of the Governing Council of the United Nations Environment Programme, held in Nairobi from 27 January to 7 February 1997,

Recalling the goal of the Rio Declaration on Environment and Development, which is to establish a new and equitable global partnership through the creation of new levels of cooperation among States, key sectors of society and people,

Reiterating our commitment to the implementation of the Rio Declaration, Agenda 21, and the Non-legally Binding Authoritative Statement of Principles for a Global Consensus on the Management, Conservation and Sustainable Development of All Types of Forests, adopted by the United Nations Conference on Environment and Development, as well as other environmental conventions agreed upon in the Rio process,

Recognizing the progress made in the implementation of the Rio agreements,

Deeply concerned, nevertheless, at the continuing deterioration of the global environment, including the worsening trends in environmental pollution and the degradation of natural resources, as reflected in the Global Environment Outlook report of the United Nations Environment Programme,

Aware of the rapid changes currently taking place in the world and the increasing complexity and fragmentation of the institutional responses to them, as well as the far-reaching significance of the concept of sustainable development which encompasses economic, social and environmental dimensions, supported by capacity-building, transfer of technology and financial resources to developing countries, in particular least developed countries,

Convinced that a strong, effective and revitalized United Nations Environment Programme is essential to assist the international community in its efforts to reverse environmentally unsustainable trends,

Aware that the special session of the General Assembly for the purpose of an overall review and appraisal of the implementation of Agenda 21 offers a unique opportunity to review and appraise the follow-up to the United Nations Conference on Environment and Development and to confirm the revitalized role of the United Nations Environment Programme,

Determined to assist the General Assembly in this important task, and guided by the principles agreed in the Rio Declaration on Environment and Development,

Declare:

1. That the United Nations Environment Programme has been and should continue to be the principal United Nations body in the field of the environment and that we, the ministers of the environment and heads of delegation attending the nineteenth session of the Governing Council, are determined to play a stronger role in the implementation of the goals and objectives of the United Nations Environment Programme;

2. That the role of the United Nations Environment Programme is to be the leading global environmental authority that sets the global environmental agenda, that promotes the coherent implementation of the environmental dimension of sustainable

development within the United Nations system and that serves as an authoritative advocate for the global environment;

3. That to this end, we reaffirm the continuing relevance of the mandate of the United Nations Environment Programme deriving from General Assembly resolution 2997 (XXVII) of 15 December 1972 and further elaborated by Agenda 21. The core elements of the focused mandate of the revitalized United Nations Environment Programme should be the following:

(a) To analyse the state of the global environment and assess global and regional environmental trends, provide policy advice, early warning information on environmental threats, and to catalyse and promote international cooperation and action, based on the best scientific and technical capabilities available;

(b) To further the development of its international environmental law aiming at sustainable development, including the development of coherent interlinkages among existing international environmental conventions;

(c) To advance the implementation of agreed international norms and policies, to monitor and foster compliance with environmental principles and international agreements and stimulate cooperative action to respond to emerging environmental challenges;

(d) To strengthen its role in the coordination of environmental activities in the United Nations system in the field of the environment, as well as its role as an Implementing Agency of the Global Environment Facility, based on its comparative advantage and scientific and technical expertise;

(e) To promote greater awareness and facilitate effective cooperation among all sectors of society and actors involved in the implementation of the international environmental agenda, and to serve as an effective link between the scientific community and policy makers at the national and international levels;

(f) To provide policy and advisory services in key areas of institution-building to Governments and other relevant institutions;

4. That, for the effective discharge of its focused mandate and to ensure the implementation of the global environmental agenda, we have decided to improve the governance structure of United Nations Environment Programme. In doing so, we have been guided by the following considerations:

(a) The United Nations Environment Programme should serve as the world forum for the ministers and the highest-level government officials in charge of environmental matters in the policy and decision-making processes of the United Nations Environment Programme;

(b) Regionalization and decentralization should be strengthened through the increased involvement and participation of regional ministerial and other relevant forums in the United Nations Environment Programme process, complementary to the central coordinating role of the Programme's headquarters in Nairobi;

(c) The participation of major groups should be increased;

(d) A cost-effective and politically influential intersessional mechanism should be designed;

5. That, in order to operationalize its mandate, the revitalized United Nations Environment Programme needs adequate, stable and predictable financial resources and, in this regard, we recognize the interrelationship between excellence, relevance and cost-effectiveness in programme delivery, confidence in the organization and a consequent increase in the competitive ability of the Programme to attract funding;

6. That ways must be sought to assure financial stability for the implementation of the global environmental agenda. In this regard, the predictability and early

notification of expected contributions to the Environment Fund would facilitate an effective planning and programming process;

7. That we reaffirm the central importance of the Environment Fund as the principal source of financing for the implementation of the programme of the United Nations Environment Programme;

8. That we are convinced that the expeditious implementation of our decisions and the principles contained in this Declaration, adopted in the year of the twenty-fifth anniversary of the founding of the United Nations Environment Programme, will revitalize and strengthen the organization and place it at the forefront of international efforts to protect the global environment for present and future generations and in the pursuit of sustainable development;

9. That we request the President of the Governing Council to present this Declaration to the high-level segment of the fifth session of the Commission on Sustainable Development and to the special session of the General Assembly for the purpose of an overall review and appraisal of the implementation of Agenda 21.

B. Governance of the United Nations Environment Programme

The Governing Council,

Recalling United Nations General Assembly resolution 2997 (XXVII) of 15 December 1972 on institutional and financial arrangements for international environmental cooperation, including the mandate of the Governing Council of the United Nations Environment Programme,

Recalling also its decision 18/2 of 26 May 1995 on the review of the governing structures of the United Nations Environment Programme,

Reaffirming the importance for the United Nations Environment Programme to continue to be the leading global environmental authority that sets the global environmental agenda, and to promote the coherent implementation of the environmental dimension of sustainable development within the United Nations system,

Conscious of the need to improve the governance of the United Nations Environment Programme to enable it to fulfil its mandate as strengthened by chapter 38 of Agenda 21, and further enhanced by the Nairobi Declaration on the Role and Mandate of the United Nations Environment Programme adopted by the Governing Council in its decision 19/1 A of 7 February 1997,

Emphasizing the importance of democratic, efficient, transparent and representative governing structures of the United Nations Environment Programme, with a complementary, specific and distinct role and mandate for each of their components,

Recognizing the need for properly mandated subsidiary bodies that can act during the inter-sessional period for and on behalf of the Governing Council within their respective mandates and the framework of the decisions adopted by the Council,

Recognizing also the need to ensure adequate and predictable funding for the United Nations Environment Programme,

Decides

1. To establish a High-level Committee of Ministers and Officials as a subsidiary organ of the Governing Council, with the following mandate:

(a) To consider the international environmental agenda and to make reform and policy recommendations to the Governing Council;

(b) To provide guidance and advice to the Executive Director on emerging environmental issues between sessions of the Governing Council to enable the United Nations Environment Progamme to make a timely response;

(c) To enhance the collaboration and cooperation of the United Nations Environment Programme with other relevant multilateral bodies as well as with the environmental conventions and their secretariats;

(d) To support the Executive Director in mobilizing adequate and predictable financial resources for the United Nations Environment Programme for the implementation of the global environmental agenda approved by the Governing Council;

2. That the High-level Committee of Ministers and Officials shall consist of 36 members, elected by the Governing Council from among Members of the United Nations and members of its specialized agencies, for a period of two years, taking into account the principle of equitable regional representation as reflected in the composition of the Governing Council. The President of the Governing Council and the Chairman of the Committee of Permanent Representatives shall be invited to attend the meetings. No member State shall serve on the Committee for more than two consecutive terms;

3. That the European Community and other regional intergovernmental economic organizations may attend the meetings of the Committee;

4. That the High-level Committee of Ministers and Officials shall elect from amongst its members a Chairperson, three Vice–Chairpersons and a Rapporteur;

5. That the High-level Committee of Ministers and Officials shall meet at least once a year in Nairobi. Meetings of the Committee may be convened elsewhere by its Chairperson, in consultation with its Bureau, in connection with major international environmental meetings;

6. That the report of the meetings of the High-level Committee of Ministers and Officials shall be made immediately available to all members of the United Nations Environment Programme;

7. That, with a view to strengthening the Committee of Permanent Representatives, as a subsidiary organ of the Governing Council, it shall have henceforth the following mandate:

(a) Within the policy and budgetary framework provided by the Governing Council, to review, monitor and assess the implementation of decisions of the Council on administrative, budgetary and programme matters;

(b) To review the draft programme of work and budget during their preparation by the secretariat;

(c) To review reports requested of the secretariat by the Governing Council on the effectiveness, efficiency and transparency of the functions and work of the secretariat and to make recommendations thereon to the Governing Council;

(d) To prepare draft decisions for consideration by the Governing Council based on inputs from the secretariat and on the results of the functions specified above;

8. That the Committee of Permanent Representatives shall consist of the representatives of all States Members of the United Nations and members of its specialized agencies, and the European Community, accredited to the United Nations Environment Programme, whether based in Nairobi or outside;

9. That the Committee of Permanent Representatives shall elect a Bureau composed of a Chairperson, three Vice–Chairpersons and a Rapporteur, for a period of two years, taking into account the principles of rotation and equitable geographical representation;

10. That the Committee of Permanent Representatives shall hold four regular meetings a year. Extraordinary meetings may be also convened by its Chairperson,

after consultation with the other members of the Bureau or at the request of at least five members of the Committee. The Committee of Permanent Representatives may establish subcommittees, working groups and task forces as deemed appropriate to carry out its mandate;

11. That the High-level Committee of Ministers and Officials and the Committee of Permanent Representatives shall be accountable to the Governing Council and will submit reports on their work at each session of the Governing Council;

12. That, save as otherwise provided in this decision, the rules of procedure of the Governing Council, including rule 63 shall apply, mutatis mutandis, to the High-level Committee of Ministers and Officials until it adopts its own rules of procedure. The proceedings of the Committee of Permanent Representatives will be conducted in English;

13. That the secretariat shall provide documentation and information related to the meetings of the High-level Committee of Ministers and Officials and the Committee of Permanent Representatives, four weeks in advance of the meeting in question;

14. That an appropriate budget shall be allocated by the Governing Council for these two subsidiary organs. The financial implications of the present decision shall not be borne by the Environment Fund and should be within the financial provisions currently available for meetings of the Governing Council;

15. To invite Members of the United Nations and members of its specialized agencies to consider providing financial assistance to facilitate the participation of developing countries and in particular the least developed among them, as well as countries with economies in transition, and to establish a trust fund to this end;

16. That this governance structure shall be reviewed by the Governing Council at its twenty-first session, with a view to assessing its effectiveness taking into account any relevant results of the reform process of the United Nations system.

1.39 Agreement Between the Government of the Kingdom of Norway and the Government of the Russian Federation on Environmental Cooperation in Connection With the Dismantling of Russian Nuclear Powered Submarines Withdrawn From the [Russian] Navy's Service in the Northern Region, and the Enhancement of Nuclear and Radiation Safety. Done at Moscow, 26 May 1998. Entered into force, 26 May 1998

The Government of the Kingdom of Norway and the Government of the Russian Federation, hereinafter referred to as the "Parties";

Considering the Declaration of 26 March 1996 on the foundations of relations between the Kingdom of Norway and the Russian Federation, the Agreement of 3 September 1992 between the Government of the Kingdom of Norway and the Government of the Russian Federation on environmental cooperation, the Agreement of 10 January 1993 between the Government of the Kingdom of Norway and the Government of the Russian Federation on early notification in case of a nuclear accident and exchange of information on nuclear facilities, the Agreement of 15 December 1995 between the Ministry of Defence of the Kingdom of Norway and the Ministry of Defence of the Russian Federation on defense-related environmental cooperation, the Memorandum of 4 October 1995 on Norwegian–Russian cooperation in the area of nuclear safety, the Vienna Convention of 21 May 1963 on Civil Liability for Nuclear Damage;

Emphasizing that each state has the obligation to ensure that activities within its jurisdiction or control do not cause environmental damage in other states or in areas outside of national jurisdiction;

Reaffirming their commitment to the protection and preservation of the environment in areas adjacent to the Norwegian–Russian border, on the basis of the principles and priorities of the Declaration of 14 June 1991 on the protection of the Arctic environment, the Declaration of 11 January 1993 on Cooperation in the Barents Euro–Arctic region, the Action Programme for the environment adopted by the Barents Euro–Arctic Council on 15 June 1994, and the Declaration of 19 September 1996 on the establishment of the Arctic Council,

Have agreed as follows:

Article 1

1. The Norwegian Party shall render free technical assistance to the Russian Party in the form of delivery of equipment, technology transfer, provision of financial means and services in order to contribute to an early, environmentally safe and cost-effective dismantling of Russian nuclear powered submarines withdrawn from the Navy's service in the northern region, including the management of spent nuclear fuel and radioactive waste which is formed thereby, and to enhance nuclear and radiation safety at nuclear power plants ant other nuclear facilities.

2. The free technical assistance from the Norwegian Party in accordance with this Agreement is provided on agreement between the Parties within the framework of the Storting's budget appropriations.

3. The Russian Party shall use the free technical assistance provided by the Norwegian Party exclusively for the purposes listed in paragraph 1 of this Article.

Article 2

1. The Parties shall cooperate in order to promote the realization of the following projects:

Emptying and decommissioning of the storage facility for spent nuclear fuel from Russian nuclear powered submarines in Andreyev Bay (Murmansk oblast), and the development of methods for the management of this fuel;

–Establishment of an interim storage facility for spent nuclear fuel from ships' reactors at the production association "Mayak" (Chelyabinsk oblast);

Design, construction and commissioning of a temporary storage facility for solid waste at Andreyev Bay (Murmansk oblast);

–Design, construction and commissioning of a specialized self-propelled vessel for the transport of containers with spent nuclear fuel;

Construction and commissioning of four specialized railway cars for the transport of containers with spent nuclear fuel;

Modernization and commissioning of an interim storage facility for liquid radioactive waste at the "Zvezdochka" shipyard (Severodvinsk, Arkhangelsk oblast);

Delivery of a mobile facility for treatment of liquid radioactive waste (Murmansk);

Dismantling of the floating technical base "Lepse" (Murmansk);

Modernization of the facility for treatment of liquid radioactive waste at the repair and technical enterprise "Atomflot" (Murmansk);

Enhancement of operational safety at the Kola nuclear power plant (Polyarnye, Zori).

2. If the Parties so agree, other projects may also be added to those listed in paragraph 1 of this Article.

Article 3

1. A joint Norwegian–Russian commission, hereinafter referred to as the "Commission", shall be established to coordinate and control the implementation of this Agreement.

2. The Commission shall take and recommend any measures it deems necessary for an effective implementation of the cooperation within the framework of this Agreement, including approval of projects and cooperation programmes proposed by involved organizations of the Parties.

3. The meetings of the Commission shall be held at regular intervals, but at least once a year, alternately in Norway and the Russian Federation, unless otherwise agreed.

4. The competent authorities for the purpose of this Agreement are: for the Norwegian Party—the Royal Norwegian, Ministry of Foreign Affairs; for the Russian Party—the Ministry of the Russian Federation for Atomic Energy.

5. The implementation of projects as foreseen in Article 2 shall be based on individual agreements for each project, hereinafter referred to as "project agreements" or "contracts", to be concluded between Norwegian and Russian organizations.

6. The cooperation shall be carried out on the basis of the national legislation of the Parties, as well as conventions to which both Parties have acceded and internationally recognized principles and recommendations for nuclear and radiation safety and environmental protection.

7. The project agreements or contracts shall be endorsed by the competent authorities of the Parties.

Article 4

1. The Norwegian Party shall according to established procedures deliver equipment, materials and other goods, transfer technology and provide financial means add

services to Russian recipients or customers within the framework of this Agreement in accordance with the provisions of each project agreement or contract.

2. The Russian recipients or customers shall receive the equipment, materials and other goods which are provided by the Norwegian Party according to the procedures established in the Russian Federation, and undertakes to use the equipment, materials and goods solely for the purposes specified in Article 1, Paragraph 1.

3. The Russian Party shall ensure that the free technical assistance provided by the Norwegian Party is used for the implementation of projects listed in Article 2 of this Agreement.

4. The design, construction, delivery and commissioning of technical means and objects financed by funds provided by the Norwegian Party shall be conducted in accordance with the legislation, norms and regulations of the Russian Federation. The procedure for execution of the work shall be prescribed by the project agreements or contracts.

5. Training of Russian personnel for the qualified operation of equipment which is delivered shall be foreseen by the respective project agreements or contracts.

6. The Parties shall mutually provide effective protection of intellectual and industrial property rights in accordance with the national legislation of the Parties, and in accordance with international agreements to which they are a party. The recipient or customer and the contractor may agree on additional terms in each project agreement or contract.

Article 5

1. Equipment and materials which are imported into the territory of the Russian Federation as as free technical assistance for the implementation of this Agreement, and which are financed by funds provided by the Norwegian Party, shall be exempt from taxes, customs duties and other fees in accordance with the legislation of the Russian Federation.

2. Exemption in accordance with paragraph 1 of this Article shall be granted on terms not less favourable than those accorded to technical assistance provided free of charge by any third party.

Article 6

1. Any disagreement concerning the interpretation of individual provisions of this Agreement, or its implementation, shall be resolved through consultations between the Parties. Consultations shall take place not later than three months after one of the Parties has so requested.

2. In case of any divergence between this Agreement and the provisions of project agreements or contracts which are concluded within the framework af this Agreement, the provisions of this Agreement shall prevail.

3. The Parties may conclude additional agreements on any question that might arise in the course of the implementation of this Agreement.

4. The provisions of this Agreement may be amended on written agreement between the Parties.

Article 7

1. At the request of one of the Parties, the Parties shall hold meetings and consultations in order to examine the implementation of the project agreements or contracts.

2. The Norwegian Party is accorded the right to verify and control that equipment, technology and financial means provided free of charge to the Russian Party as

technical assistance is used in accordance with the terms of this Agreement. The procedure for verification and control shall be established in the project agreements, contracts or in separate agreements.

3. Each Party shall declare which data and information are to be considered confidential in connection with the implementation of the projects listed in Article 2 of this Agreement. Confidential data and information, relating to concrete projects within the framework of this Agreement, shall not be made public, or disclosed to any individual or legal person who does not participate directly in the implementation of this Agreement, without the written permission of the Party that has provided such information.

Article 8

1. The provisions of this Agreement shall not affect the rights and obligations of the Parties under international agreements they have previously concluded, or their membership in international organizations.

2. The Parties will facilitate the involvement of third parties in financing and /or practical implementation of projects listed in Article 2 of this Agreement.

Article 9

1. With the exception of claims for damage or injury against individuals arising from their premeditated actions, the Russian Party shall bring no claims or legal proceedings against the Norwegian Party and its personnel or contractors, subcontractors, consultants, suppliers of equipment or services at any tier and their personnel, for indirect, direct or consequential damage to property owned by the Russian Federation. This paragraph shall not apply to legal actions brought by the Russian Party to enforce the provisions of contracts to which it or a Russian national is a party.

2. With the exception of claims for damage or injury against individuals arising from their premeditated actions, the Russian Party shall provide for the adequate legal defence of, indemnify, and shall bring no claims or legal proceedings against, the Norwegian Party and its personnel, contractors, subcontractors, consultants, suppliers of equipment or services at any tier and their personnel in connection with third party claims in any court or forum arising from activities undertaken pursuant to this Agreement for injury, loss or damage occurring within or outside the territory of the Russian Federation that results from a nuclear incident occurring within the territory of the Russian Federation.

3. Without prejudice to paragraphs1 and 2 of this Article nothing in this Article shall be interpreted to prevent legal proceedings or claims against nationals of the Russian Federation or permanent residents on the territory of the Russian Federation.

4. The provisions of this Article shall not prevent indemnification by the Parties for damage in accordance with their national laws.

5. Nothing in this Article shall be construed as acknowledging the jurisdiction of any court or forum outside of the Russian Federation over third party claims, for which paragraph 2 of this Article applies, except as provided for in paragraph 9 of this Article and in any other case where the Russian Federation has pledged itself to acknowledge and execute a legal decision on the basis of provisions of international agreements.

6. Nothing in this Article shall be construed as waiving the immunity of the Kingdom of Norway or the Russian Federation with respect to potential third-party claims that may be brought against either of the Parties.

7. The provisions of this Article shall—if so requested by the contractor—be incorporated into the project agreements or contracts by the issue, by or on behalf of the Russian Party, of an indemnity confirmation letter to the contractor.

8. In case a nuclear incident has occurred which may lead to the fulfilment of the obligation to compensate damage, the Parties shall hold consultations upon request by one of the Parties.

9. As regards its obligations in this Article to the contractors, subcontractors, consultants, suppliers of equipment or services at any tier and their personnel, the Russian Party undertakes to have any conflict, controversy or claim arising out of or in relation to this Article, if not settled amicably within three months, referred to and finally resolved by arbitration in accordance with the UNCITRAL Arbitration Rules. The national legislation of the Parties shall not be applied for the resolution of any conflict, controversy or claim.

10. Any payments related to the indemnification in paragraph 2 of this Article shall be made promptly and in a convertible currency.

11. The obligations concerning liability for nuclear damage undertaken by the Russian Party in accordance with the present Article shall be valid for objects which are the subject of cooperation under this Agreement, and shall remain in effect regardless of any subsequent transfer of ownership of these objects, termination of this Agreement or the expiry of its validity.

Article 10

1. This Agreement shall enter into force on signature and shall remain in force for a period of five years. The Agreement shall be extended for additional five-year periods on written agreement between the Parties at the expiry of each five-year period.

2. Each Party may inform in writing the other Party of its intention to denounce this Agreement at any time. The Agreement shall cease to have effect six months after written notice of denunciation has been received from either of the Parties through diplomatic channels.

3. At the expiry of the validity of this Agreement the Parties shall consult each other concerning the conclusion of projects started during this period when the Agreement was in effect.

Done in the city of Moscow, this 26th day of May 1998 in duplicate, in the Norwegian, Russian and English languages, all three texts being equally authentic. In case of any divergences of interpretation of the texts in Norwegian and Russian, the text in English shall prevail.

2. Global Commons: Antarctica

2.1 Antarctic Treaty.[a] Concluded at Washington, 1 December 1959. Entered into force, 23 June 1961. 402 U.N.T.S. 71, 12 U.S.T. 794, T.I.A.S. No. 4780; *reprinted in* 19 I.L.M. 860 (1980) & 5 Weston V.D.1

The Governments of Argentina, Australia, Belgium, Chile, the French Republic, Japan, New Zealand, Norway, the Union of South Africa, the Union of Soviet Socialist Republics, the United Kingdom of Great Britain and Northern Ireland, and the United States of America,

Recognizing that it is in the interest of all mankind that Antarctica shall continue forever to be used exclusively for peaceful purposes and shall not become the scene or object of international discord;

Acknowledging the substantial contributions to scientific knowledge resulting from international cooperation in scientific investigation in Antarctica;

Convinced that the establishment of a firm foundation for the continuation and development of such cooperation on the basis of freedom of scientific investigation in Antarctica as applied during the International Geophysical Year accords with the interests of science and the progress of all mankind;

Convinced also that a treaty ensuring the use of Antarctica for peaceful purposes only and the continuance of international harmony in Antarctica will further the purposes and principles embodied in the Charter of the United Nations;

Have agreed as follows:

Article I

1. Antarctica shall be used for peaceful purposes only. There shall be prohibited, *inter alia,* any measures of a military nature, such as the establishment of military bases and fortifications, the carrying out of military maneuvers, as well as the testing of any type of weapons.

2. The present Treaty shall not prevent the use of military personnel or equipment for scientific research or for any other peaceful purpose.

Article II

Freedom of scientific investigation in Antarctica and cooperation toward that end, as applied during the International Geophysical Year, shall continue, subject to the provisions of the present Treaty.

Article III

1. In order to promote international cooperation in scientific investigation in Antarctica, as provided for in Article II of the present Treaty, the Contracting Parties agree that, to the greatest extent feasible and practicable:

(*a*) information regarding plans for scientific programs in Antarctica shall be exchanged to permit maximum economy and efficiency of operations;

(*b*) scientific personnel shall be exchanged in Antarctica between expeditions and stations;

a. *See also* Basic Document 2.9, *infra.*

(*c*) scientific observations and results from Antarctica shall be exchanged and made freely available.

2. In implementing this Article, every encouragement shall be given to the establishment of cooperative working relations with those Specialized Agencies of the United Nations and other international organizations having a scientific or technical interest in Antarctica.

Article IV

1. Nothing contained in the present Treaty shall be interpreted as:

(*a*) a renunciation by any Contracting Party of previously asserted rights of or claims to territorial sovereignty in Antarctica;

(*b*) a renunciation or diminution by any Contracting Party of any basis of claim to territorial sovereignty in Antarctica which it may have whether as a result of its activities or those of its nationals in Antarctica, or otherwise;

(*c*) prejudicing the position of any Contracting Party as regards its recognition or non-recognition of any other State's right of or claim or basis of claim to territorial sovereignty in Antarctica.

2. No acts or activities taking place while the present Treaty is in force shall constitute a basis for asserting, supporting or denying a claim to territorial sovereignty in Antarctica or create any rights of sovereignty in Antarctica. No new claim, or enlargement of an existing claim, to territorial sovereignty in Antarctica shall be asserted while the present Treaty is in force.

Article V

1. Any nuclear explosions in Antarctica and the disposal there of radioactive waste material shall be prohibited.

2. In the event of the conclusion of international agreements concerning the use of nuclear energy, including nuclear explosions and the disposal of radioactive waste material, to which all of the Contracting Parties whose representatives are entitled to participate in the meetings provided for under Article IX are parties, the rules established under such agreements shall apply in Antarctica.

Article VI

The provisions of the present Treaty shall apply to the area south of 60E South Latitude, including all ice shelves, but nothing in the present Treaty shall prejudice or in any way affect the rights, or the exercise of the rights, of any State under international law with regard to the high seas within that area.

Article VII

1. In order to promote the objectives and ensure the observance of the provisions of the present Treaty, each Contracting Party whose representatives are entitled to participate in the meetings referred to in Article IX of the Treaty shall have the right to designate observers to carry out any inspection provided for by the present Article. Observers shall be nationals of the Contracting Parties which designate them. The names of observers shall be communicated to every other Contracting Party having the right to designate observers, and like notice shall be given of the termination of their appointment.

2. Each observer designated in accordance with the provisions of paragraph 1 of this Article shall have complete freedom of access at any time to any or all areas of Antarctica.

3. All areas of Antarctica, including all stations, installations and equipment within those areas, and all ships and aircraft at points of discharging or embarking cargoes or personnel in Antarctica, shall be open at all times to inspection by any observers designated in accordance with paragraph 1 of this Article.

4. Aerial observation may be carried out at any time over any or all areas of Antarctica by any of the Contracting Parties having the right to designate observers.

5. Each Contracting Party shall, at the time when the present Treaty enters into force for it, inform the other Contracting Parties, and thereafter shall give them notice in advance, of

(*a*) all expeditions to and within Antarctica, on the part of its ships or nationals, and all expeditions to Antarctica organized in or proceeding from its territory;

(*b*) all stations in Antarctica occupied by its nationals; and

(*c*) any military personnel or equipment intended to be introduced by it into Antarctica subject to the conditions prescribed in paragraph 2 of Article I of the present Treaty.

Article VIII

1. In order to facilitate the exercise of their functions under the present Treaty, and without prejudice to the respective positions of the Contracting Parties relating to jurisdiction over all other persons in Antarctica, observers designated under paragraph 1 of Article VII and scientific personnel exchanged under subparagraph 1(*b*) of Article III of the Treaty, and members of the staffs accompanying any such persons, shall be subject only to the jurisdiction of the Contracting Party of which they are nationals in respect of all acts or omissions occurring while they are in Antarctica for the purpose of exercising their functions.

2. Without prejudice to the provisions of paragraph 1 of this Article, and pending the adoption of measures in pursuance of subparagraph 1(*e*) of Article IX, the Contracting Parties concerned in any case of dispute with regard to the exercise of jurisdiction in Antarctica shall immediately consult together with a view to reaching a mutually acceptable solution.

Article IX

1. Representatives of the Contracting Parties named in the preamble to the present Treaty shall meet at the City of Canberra within two months after the date of entry into force of the Treaty, and thereafter at suitable intervals and places, for the purpose of exchanging information, consulting together on matters of common interest pertaining to Antarctica, and formulating and considering, and recommending to their Governments, measures in furtherance of the principles and objectives of the Treaty, including measures regarding:

(*a*) use of Antarctica for peaceful purposes only;

(*b*) facilitation of scientific research in Antarctica;

(*c*) facilitation of international scientific cooperation in Antarctica;

(*d*) facilitation of the exercise of the rights of inspection provided for in Article VII of the Treaty;

(*e*) questions relating to the exercise of jurisdiction in Antarctica;

(*f*) preservation and conservation of living resources in Antarctica.

2. Each Contracting Party which has become a party to the present Treaty by accession under Article XIII shall be entitled to appoint representatives to participate in the meetings referred to in paragraph 1 of the present Article, during such time as

that Contracting Party demonstrates its interest in Antarctica by conducting substantial scientific research activity there, such as the establishment of a scientific station or the despatch of a scientific expedition.

3. Reports from the observers referred to in Article VII of the present Treaty shall be transmitted to the representatives of the Contracting Parties participating in the meetings referred to in paragraph 1 of the present Article.

4. The measures referred to in paragraph 1 of this Article shall become effective when approved by all the Contracting Parties whose representatives were entitled to participate in the meetings held to consider those measures.

5. Any or all of the rights established in the present Treaty may be exercised as from the date of entry into force of the Treaty whether or not any measures facilitating the exercise of such rights have been proposed, considered or approved as provided in this Article.

Article X

Each of the Contracting Parties undertakes to exert appropriate efforts, consistent with the Charter of the United Nations, to the end that no one engages in any activity in Antarctica contrary to the principles or purposes of the present Treaty.

Article XI

1. If any dispute arises between two or more of the Contracting Parties concerning the interpretation or application of the present Treaty, those Contracting Parties shall consult among themselves with a view to having the dispute resolved by negotiation, inquiry, mediation, conciliation, arbitration, judicial settlement or other peaceful means of their own choice.

2. Any dispute of this character not so resolved shall, with the consent, in each case, of all parties to the dispute, be referred to the International Court of Justice for settlement; but failure to reach agreement on reference to the International Court shall not absolve parties to the dispute from the responsibility of continuing to seek to resolve it by any of the various peaceful means referred to in paragraph 1 of this Article.

Article XII

1. (*a*) The present Treaty may be modified or amended at any time by unanimous agreement of the Contracting Parties whose representatives are entitled to participate in the meetings provided for under Article IX. Any such modification or amendment shall enter into force when the depositary Government has received notice from all such Contracting Parties that they have ratified it.

(*b*) Such modification or amendment shall thereafter enter into force as to any other Contracting Party when notice of ratification by it has been received by the depositary Government. Any such Contracting Party from which no notice of ratification is received within a period of two years from the date of entry into force of the modification or amendment in accordance with the provisions of subparagraph 1 (*a*) of this Article shall be deemed to have withdrawn from the present Treaty on the date of the expiration of such period.

2. (*a*) If after the expiration of thirty years from the date of entry into force of the present Treaty, any of the Contracting Parties whose representatives are entitled to participate in the meetings provided for under Article IX so requests by a communication addressed to the depositary Government, a Conference of all the Contracting Parties shall be held as soon as practicable to review the operation of the Treaty.

(*b*) Any modification or amendment to the present Treaty which is approved at such a Conference by a majority of the Contracting Parties there represented, including a majority of those whose representatives are entitled to participate in the meetings provided for under Article IX, shall be communicated by the depositary Government to all the Contracting Parties immediately after the termination of the Conference and shall enter into force in accordance with the provisions of paragraph 1 of the present Article.

(*c*) If any such modification or amendment has not entered into force in accordance with the provisions of subparagraph 1 (*a*) of this Article within a period of two years after the date of its communication to all the Contracting Parties, any Contracting Party may at any time after the expiration of that period give notice to the depositary Government of its withdrawal from the present Treaty; and such withdrawal shall take effect two years after the receipt of the notice by the depositary Government.

Article XIII

1. The present Treaty shall be subject to ratification by the signatory States. It shall be open for accession by any State which is a Member of the United Nations, or by any other State which may be invited to accede to the Treaty with the consent of all the Contracting Parties whose representatives are entitled to participate in the meetings provided for under Article IX of the Treaty.

2. Ratification of or accession to the present Treaty shall be effected by each State in accordance with its constitutional processes.

3. Instruments of ratification and instruments of accession shall be deposited with the Government of the United States of America, hereby designated as the depositary Government.

4. The depositary Government shall inform all signatory and acceding States of the date of each deposit of an instrument of ratification or accession, and the date of entry into force of the Treaty and of any modification or amendment thereto.

5. Upon the deposit of instruments of ratification by all the signatory States, the present Treaty shall enter into force for those States and for States which have deposited instruments of accession. Thereafter the Treaty shall enter into force for any acceding State upon the deposit of its instrument of accession.

6. The present Treaty shall be registered by the depositary Government pursuant to Article 102 of the Charter of the United Nations.

Article XIV

The present Treaty, done in the English, French, Russian and Spanish languages, each version being equally authentic, shall be deposited in the archives of the Government of the United States of America, which shall transmit duly certified copies thereof to the Governments of the signatory and acceding States.

2.2 CERTAIN RECOMMENDATIONS OF THIRD ANTARCTIC TREATY CONSULTATIVE MEETING, ANNEX: AGREED MEASURES FOR THE CONSERVATION OF ANTARCTIC FAUNA AND FLORA. Concluded at Brussels, 13 June 1964. 17 U.S.T. 992, T.I.A.S. No. 6058; *reprinted in* 5 Weston V.D.2

The Representatives, taking into consideration Article IX of the Antarctic Treaty, and recalling Recommendation I–VIII of the First Consultative Meeting and Recommendation II–II of the Second Consultative Meeting, recommend to their Governments that they approve as soon as possible and implement without delay the annexed "Agreed Measures for the Conservation of Antarctic Fauna and Flora".

Preamble

The Governments participating in the Third Consultative Meeting under Article IX of the Antarctic Treaty,

Desiring to implement the principles and purposes of the Antarctic Treaty;

Recognising the scientific importance of the study of Antarctic fauna and flora, their adaptation to their rigorous environment, and their interrelationship with that environment;

Considering the unique nature of these fauna and flora, their circumpolar range, and particularly their defencelessness and susceptibility to extermination;

Desiring by further international collaboration within the framework of the Antarctic Treaty to promote and achieve the objectives of protection, scientific study, and rational use of these fauna and flora; and

Having particular regard to the conservation principles developed by the Scientific Committee on Antarctic Research (SCAR) of the International Council of Scientific Unions;

Hereby consider the Treaty Area as a Special Conservation Area and have agreed on the following measures:

Article I

1. These Agreed Measures shall apply to the same area to which the Antarctic Treaty is applicable (hereinafter referred to as the Treaty Area) namely the area south of 60E South Latitude, including all ice shelves.

However, nothing in these Agreed Measures shall prejudice or in any way affect the rights, or the exercise of the rights, of any State under international law with regard to the high seas within the Treaty Area, or restrict the implementation of the provisions of the Antarctic Treaty with respect to inspection.

2. The Annexes to these Agreed Measures shall form an integral part thereof, and all references to the Agreed Measures shall be considered to include the Annexes.

Article II

For the purposes of these Agreed Measures:

a) "Native mammal" means any member, at any stage of its life cycle, of any species belonging to the Class Mammalia indigenous to the Antarctic or occurring there through natural agencies of dispersal, excepting whales;

b) "native bird" means any member, at any stage of its life cycle (including eggs), of any species of the Class Aves indigenous to the Antarctic or occurring there through natural agencies of dispersal;

c) "native plant" means any kind of vegetation at any stage of its life cycle (including seeds), indigenous to the Antarctic or occurring there through natural agencies of dispersal;

d) "appropriate authority" means any person authorised by a Participating Government to issue permits under these Agreed Measures;

e) "permit" means a formal permission in writing issued by an appropriate authority;

f) "participating government" means any Government for which these Agreed Measures have become effective in accordance with Article XIII of these Agreed Measures.

Article III

Each Participating Government shall take appropriate action to carry out these Agreed Measures.

Article IV

The Participating Governments shall prepare and circulate to members of expeditions and stations information to ensure understanding and observance of the provisions of these Agreed Measures, setting forth in particular prohibited activities, and providing lists of specially protected species and specially protected areas.

Article V

The provisions of these Agreed Measures shall not apply in cases of extreme emergency involving possible loss of human life or involving the safety of ships or aircraft.

Article VI

1. Each Participating Government shall prohibit within the Treaty Area the killing, wounding, capturing or molesting of any native mammal or native bird, or any attempt at any such act, except in accordance with a permit.

2. Such permits shall be drawn in terms as specific as possible and issued only for the following purposes:

a) to provide indispensable food for men or dogs in the Treaty Area in limited quantities, and in conformity with the purposes and principles of these Agreed Measures;

b) to provide specimens for scientific study or scientific information;

c) to provide specimens for museums, zoological gardens, or other educational or cultural institutions or uses.

3. Permits for Specially Protected Areas shall be issued only in accordance with the provisions of Article VIII.

4. Participating Governments shall limit the issue of such permits so as to ensure as far as possible that:

a) no more native mammals or birds are killed or taken in any year than can normally be replaced by natural reproduction in the following breeding season;

b) the variety of species and the balance of the natural ecological systems existing within the Treaty Area are maintained.

5. The species of native mammals and birds listed in Annex A of these Measures shall be designated "Specially Protected Species", and shall be accorded special protection by Participating Governments.

6. A Participating Government shall not authorise an appropriate authority to issue a permit with respect to a Specially Protected Species except in accordance with paragraph 7 of this Article.

7. A permit may be issued under this Article with respect to a Specially Protected Species, provided that:

a) it is issued for a compelling scientific purpose, and;

b) the actions permitted thereunder will not jeopardise the existing natural ecological system or the survival of that species.

Article VII

1. Each Participating Government shall take appropriate measures to minimize harmful interference within the Treaty Area with the normal living conditions of any native mammal or bird, or any attempt at such harmful interference, except as permitted under Article VI.

2. The following acts and activities shall be considered as harmful interference:

a) allowing dogs to run free;

b) flying helicopters or other aircraft in a manner which would unnecessarily disturb bird and seal concentrations, or landing close to such concentrations (e.g. within 200 metres);

c) driving vehicles unnecessarily close to concentrations of birds and seals (e.g. within 200 metres);

d) use of explosives close to concentrations of birds and seals;

e) discharge of firearms close to bird and seal concentrations (e.g. within 300 metres);

f) any disturbance of bird and seal colonies during the breeding period by persistent attention from persons on foot.

However, the above activities, with the exception of those mentioned in a) and e) may be permitted to the minimum extent necessary for the establishment, supply and operation of stations.

3. Each Participating Government shall take all reasonable steps towards the alleviation of pollution of the waters adjacent to the coast and ice shelves.

Article VIII

1. The areas of outstanding scientific interest listed in Annex B shall be designated "Specially Protected Areas" and shall be accorded special protection by the Participating Governments in order to preserve their unique natural ecological system.

2. In addition to the prohibitions and measures of protection dealt with in other Articles of these Agreed Measures, the Participating Governments shall in Specially Protected Areas further prohibit:

a) the collection of any native plant, except in accordance with a permit;

b) the driving of any vehicle.

3. A permit issued under Article VI shall not have effect within a Specially Protected Area except in accordance with paragraph 4 of the present Article.

4. A permit shall have effect within a Specially Protected Area provided that:

a) it was issued for a compelling scientific purpose which cannot be served elsewhere; and

b) the actions permitted thereunder will not jeopardise the natural ecological system existing in that Area.

Article IX

1. Each Participating Government shall prohibit the bringing into the Treaty Area of any species of animal or plant not indigenous to that Area, except in accordance with a permit.

2. Permits under paragraph 1 of this Article shall be drawn in terms as specific as possible and shall be issued to allow the importation only of the animals and plants listed in Annex C. When any such animal or plant might cause harmful interference with the natural system if left unsupervised within the Treaty Area, such permits shall require that it be kept under controlled conditions and, after it has served its purpose, it shall be removed from the Treaty Area or destroyed.

3. Nothing in paragraphs 1 and 2 of this Article shall apply to the importation of food into the Treaty Area so long as animals and plants used for this purpose are kept under controlled conditions.

4. Each Participating Government undertakes to ensure that all reasonable precautions shall be taken to prevent the accidental introduction of parasites and diseases into the Treaty Area. In particular, the precautions listed in Annex D shall be taken.

Article X

Each Participating Government undertakes to exert appropriate efforts, consistent with the Charter of the United Nations, to the end that no one engages in any activity in the Treaty Area contrary to the principles or purposes of these Agreed Measures.

Article XI

Each Participating Government whose expeditions use ships sailing under flags of nationalities other than its own shall, as far as feasible, arrange with the owners of such ships that the crews of these ships observe these Agreed Measures.

Article XII

1. The Participating Governments may make such arrangements as may be necessary for the discussion of such matters as:

a) the collection and exchange of records (including records of permits) and statistics concerning the numbers of each species of native mammal and bird killed or captured annually in the Treaty Area;

b) the obtaining and exchange of information as to the status of native mammals and birds in the Treaty Area, and the extent to which any species needs protection;

c) the number of native mammals or birds which should be permitted to be harvested for food, scientific study, or other uses in the various regions;

d) the establishment of a common form in which this information shall be submitted by Participating Governments in accordance with paragraph 2 of this Article.

2. Each Participating Government shall inform the other Governments in writing before the end of November of each year of the steps taken and information collected in the preceding period of July 1st to June 30th relating to the implementation of these Agreed Measures. Governments exchanging information under paragraph 5 of Article VII of the Antarctic Treaty may at the same time transmit the information relating to the implementation of these Agreed Measures.

Article XIII

1. After the receipt by the Government designated in Recommendation I–XIV (5) of notification of approval by all Governments whose representatives are entitled to participate in meetings provided for under Article IX of the Antarctic Treaty, these Agreed Measures shall become effective for those Governments.

2. Thereafter any other Contracting Party to the Antarctic Treaty may, in consonance with the purposes of Recommendation III–VII, accept these Agreed Measures by notifying the designated Government of its intention to apply the Agreed Measures and to be bound by them. The Agreed Measures shall become effective with regard to such Governments on the date of receipt of such notification.

3. The designated Government shall inform the Governments referred to in paragraph 1 of this Article of each notification of approval, the effective date of these Agreed Measures and of each notification of acceptance. The designated Government shall also inform any Government which has accepted these Agreed Measures of each subsequent notification of acceptance.

Article XIV

1. These Agreed Measures may be amended at any time by unanimous agreement of the Governments whose Representatives are entitled to participate in meetings under Article IX of the Antarctic Treaty.

2. The Annexes, in particular, may be amended as necessary through diplomatic channels.

3. An amendment proposed through diplomatic channels shall be submitted in writing to the designated Government which shall communicate it to the Governments referred to in paragraph 1. of the present Article for approval; at the same time, it shall be communicated to the other Participating Governments.

4. Any amendment shall become effective on the date on which notifications of approval have been received by the designated Government from all of the Governments referred to in paragraph 1. of this article.

5. The designated Government shall notify those same Governments of the date of receipt of each approval communicated to it and the date on which the amendment will become effective for them.

6. Such amendment shall become effective on that same date for all other Participating Governments, except those which before the expiry of two months after that date notify the designated Government that they do not accept it.

ANNEXES TO THESE AGREED MEASURES

Annex A

Specially protected species

. . . .

. . . .

Annex B

Specially protected areas

. . . .

. . . .

Annex C

Importation of animals and plants

The following animals and plants may be imported into the Treaty Area in accordance with permits issued under Article IX (2) of these Agreed Measures:

a) sledge dogs;

b) domestic animals and plants;

c) laboratory animals and plants.

Annex D

Precautions to prevent accidental introduction of parasites and diseases into the Treaty Area

The following precautions shall be taken:

1. *Dogs:* All dogs imported into the Treaty Area shall be inoculated against the following diseases:

a) distemper;

b) contagious canine hepatitis;

c) rabies

d) leptospirosis (*L. canicola* and *L. icterohaemorrhagicae*).

Each dog shall be inoculated at least two months before the time of its arrival in the Treaty Area.

2. *Poultry:* Notwithstanding the provisions of Article IX (3) of these Agreed Measures, no living poultry shall be brought into the Treaty Area after July 1st 1966.

2.3 Convention for the Conservation of Antarctic Seals (With Annex). Concluded at London, 11 February 1972. Entered into force, 11 March 1978. 29 U.S.T. 441, T.I.A.S. No. 8826; *reprinted in* 11 I.L.M. 251 (1972) & 5 Weston V.D.3

The Contracting Parties,

Recalling the Agreed Measures for the Conservation of Antarctic Fauna and Flora, adopted under the Antarctic Treaty signed at Washington on 1 December 1959;

Recognizing the general concern about the vulnerability of Antarctic seals to commercial exploitation and the consequent need for effective conservation measures;

Recognizing that the stocks of Antarctic seals are an important living resource in the marine environment which requires an international agreement for its effective conservation;

Recognizing that this resource should not be depleted by over-exploitation, and hence that any harvesting should be regulated so as not to exceed the levels of the optimum sustainable yield;

Recognizing that in order to improve scientific knowledge and so place exploitation on a rational basis, every effort should be made both to encourage biological and other research on Antarctic seal populations and to gain information from such research and from the statistics of future sealing operations, so that further suitable regulations may be formulated;

Noting that the Scientific Committee on Antarctic Research of the International Council of Scientific Unions (SCAR) is willing to carry out the tasks requested of it in this Convention;

Desiring to promote and achieve the objectives of protection, scientific study and rational use of Antarctic seals, and to maintain a satisfactory balance within the ecological system,

Have agreed as follows:

Article 1

Scope

1. This Convention applies to the seas south of 60E South Latitude, in respect of which the Contracting Parties affirm the provisions of Article IV of the Antarctic Treaty.

2. This Convention may be applicable to any or all of the following species:

   Southern elephant seal *Mirounga leonina,*

   Leopard seal *Hydrurga leptonyx,*

   Weddell seal *Leptonychotes weddelli,*

   Crabeater seal *Lobodon carcinophagus,*

   Ross seal *Ommatophoca rossi,*

   Southern fur seals *Arctocephalus* sp.

3. The Annex to this Convention forms an integral part thereof.

Article 2

Implementation

1. The Contracting Parties agree that the species of seals enumerated in Article 1 shall not be killed or captured within the Convention area by their nationals or vessels under their respective flags except in accordance with the provisions of this Convention.

2. Each Contracting Party shall adopt for its nationals and for vessels under its flag such laws, regulations and other measures, including a permit system as appropriate, as may be necessary to implement this Convention.

Article 3

Annexed Measures

1. This Convention includes an Annex specifying measures which the Contracting Parties hereby adopt. Contracting Parties may from time to time in the future adopt other measures with respect to the conservation, scientific study and rational and humane use of seal resources, prescribing *inter alia:*

(a) permissible catch;

(b) protected and unprotected species;

(c) open and closed seasons;

(d) open and closed areas, including the designation of reserves;

(e) the designation of special areas where there shall be no disturbance of seals;

(f) limits relating to sex, size, or age for each species;

(g) restrictions relating to time of day and duration, limitations of effort and methods of sealing;

(h) types and specifications of gear and apparatus and appliances which may be used;

(i) catch returns and other statistical and biological records;

(j) procedures for facilitating the review and assessment of scientific information;

(k) other regulatory measures including an effective system of inspection.

2. The measures adopted under paragraph 1 of this Article shall be based upon the best scientific and technical evidence available.

3. The Annex may from time to time be amended in accordance with the procedures provided for in Article 9.

Article 4

Special Permits

1. Notwithstanding the provisions of this Convention, any Contracting Party may issue permits to kill or capture seals in limited quantities and in conformity with the objectives and principles of this Convention for the following purposes:

(a) to provide indispensable food for men or dogs;

(b) to provide for scientific research; or

(c) to provide specimens for museums, educational or cultural institutions.

2. Each Contracting Party shall, as soon as possible, inform the other Contracting Parties and SCAR of the purpose and content of all permits issued under paragraph 1 of this Article and subsequently of the numbers of seals killed or captured under these permits.

Article 5

Exchange of Information and Scientific Advice

1. Each Contracting Party shall provide to the other Contracting Parties and to SCAR the information specified in the Annex within the period indicated therein.

2. Each Contracting Party shall also provide to the other Contracting Parties and to SCAR before 31 October each year information on any steps it has taken in accordance with Article 2 of this Convention during the preceding period 1 July to 30 June.

3. Contracting Parties which have no information to report under the two preceding paragraphs shall indicate this formally before 31 October each year.

4. SCAR is invited:

(a) to assess information received pursuant to this Article; encourage exchange of scientific data and information among the Contracting Parties; recommend programmes for scientific research; recommend statistical and biological data to be collected by sealing expeditions within the Convention area; and suggest amendments to the Annex; and

(b) to report on the basis of the statistical, biological and other evidence available when the harvest of any species of seal in the Convention area is having a significantly harmful effect on the total stocks of such species or on the ecological system in any particular locality.

5. SCAR is invited to notify the Depositary which shall report to the Contracting Parties when SCAR estimates in any sealing season that the permissible catch limits for any species are likely to be exceeded and, in that case, to provide an estimate of the date upon which the permissible catch limits will be reached. Each Contracting Party shall then take appropriate measures to prevent its nationals and vessels under its flag from killing or capturing seals of that species after the estimated date until the Contracting Parties decide otherwise.

6. SCAR may if necessary seek the technical assistance of the Food and Agriculture Organization of the United Nations in making its assessments.

7. Notwithstanding the provisions of paragraph 1 of Article 1 the Contracting Parties shall, in accordance with their internal law, report to each other and to SCAR, for consideration statistics relating to the Antarctic seals listed in paragraph 2 of Article 1 which have been killed or captured by their nationals and vessels under their respective flags in the area of floating sea ice north of 60E South Latitude.

Article 6

Consultations Between Contracting Parties

1. At any time after commercial sealing has begun a Contracting Party may propose through the Depositary that a meeting of Contracting Parties be convened with a view to:

(a) establishing by a two-third majority of the Contracting Parties, including the concurring votes of all States signatory to this Convention present at the meeting, an effective system of control, including inspection, over the implementation of the provisions of this Convention;

(b) establishing a commission to perform such functions under this Convention as the Contracting Parties may deem necessary; or

(c) considering other proposals, including:

(i) the provision of independent scientific advice;

(ii) the establishment, by a two-thirds majority, of a scientific advisory committee which may be assigned some or all of the functions requested of SCAR under this Convention, if commercial sealing reaches significant proportions;

(iii) the carrying out of scientific programmes with the participation of the Contracting Parties; and

(iv) the provision of further regulatory measures, including moratoria.

2. If one-third of the Contracting Parties indicate agreement the Depositary shall convene such a meeting, as soon as possible.

3. A meeting shall be held at the request of any Contracting Party, if SCAR reports that the harvest of any species of Antarctic seal in the area to which this Convention applies is having a significantly harmful effect on the total stocks or the ecological system in any particular locality.

Article 7

Review of Operations

The Contracting Parties shall meet within five years after the entry into force of this Convention and at least every five years thereafter to review the operation of the Convention.

Article 8

Amendments to the Convention

1. This Convention may be amended at any time. The text of any amendment proposed by a Contracting Party shall be submitted to the Depositary, which shall transmit it to all the Contracting Parties.

2. If one third of the Contracting Parties request a meeting to discuss the proposed amendment the Depositary shall call such a meeting.

3. An amendment shall enter into force when the Depositary has received instruments of ratification or acceptance thereof from all the Contracting Parties.

Article 9

Amendments to the Annex

1. Any Contracting Party may propose amendments to the Annex to this Convention. The text of any such proposed amendment shall be submitted to the Depositary which shall transmit it to all Contracting Parties.

2. Each such proposed amendment shall become effective for all Contracting Parties six months after the date appearing on the notification from the Depositary to the Contracting Parties, if within 120 days of the notification date, no objection has been received and two-thirds of the Contracting Parties have notified the Depositary in writing of their approval.

3. If an objection is received from any Contracting Party within 120 days of the notification date, the matter shall be considered by the Contracting Parties at their next meeting. If unanimity on the matter is not reached at the meeting, the Contracting Parties shall notify the Depositary within 120 days from the date of closure of the meeting of their approval or rejection of the original amendment or of any new amendment proposed by the meeting. If, by the end of this period, two-thirds of the Contracting Parties have approved such amendment, it shall become effective six months from the date of the closure of the meeting for those Contracting Parties which have by then notified their approval.

4. Any Contracting Party which has objected to a proposed amendment may at any time withdraw that objection, and the proposed amendment shall become effective with respect to such Party immediately if the amendment is already in effect, or at such time as it becomes effective under the terms of this Article.

5. The Depositary shall notify each Contracting Party immediately upon receipt of each approval or objection, of each withdrawal of objection, and of the entry into force of any amendment.

6. Any State which becomes a party to this Convention after an amendment to the Annex has entered into force shall be bound by the Annex as so amended. Any State which becomes a Party to this Convention during the period when a proposed amendment is pending may approve or object to such an amendment within the time limits applicable to other Contracting Parties.

Article 10

Signature

This Convention shall be open for signature at London from 1 June to 31 December 1972 by States participating in the Conference on the Conservation of Antarctic Seals held at London from 3 to 11 February 1972.

Article 11

Ratification

This Convention is subject to ratification or acceptance. Instruments of ratification or acceptance shall be deposited with the Government of the United Kingdom of Great Britain and Northern Ireland, hereby designated as the Depositary.

Article 12

Accession

The Convention shall be open for accession by any State which may be invited to accede to this Convention with the consent of all the Contracting Parties.

Article 13

Entry into Force

1. This Convention shall enter into force on the thirtieth day following the date of deposit of the seventh instrument of ratification or acceptance.

2. Thereafter this Convention shall enter into force for each ratifying, accepting or acceding State on the thirtieth day after deposit by such State of its instrument of ratification, acceptance or accession.

Article 14

Withdrawal

Any Contracting Party may withdraw from this Convention on 30 June of any year by giving notice on or before 1 January of the same year to the Depositary which upon receipt of such a notice shall at once communicate it to the other Contracting Parties. Any other Contracting Party may, in like manner, within one month of the receipt of a copy of such a notice from the Depositary, give notice of withdrawal, so that the Convention shall cease to be in force on 30 June of the same year with respect to the Contracting Party giving such notice.

Article 15

Notification by the Depositary

The Depositary shall notify all signatory and acceding States of the following:

(a) signatures of this Convention, the deposit of instruments of ratification, acceptance or accession and notices of withdrawal;

(b) the date of entry into force of this Convention and of any amendments to it or its Annex.

Article 16

Certified Copies and Registration

1. This Convention, done in the English, French, Russian and Spanish languages, each version being equally authentic, shall be deposited in the archives of the Government of the United Kingdom of Great Britain and Northern Ireland, which shall transmit duly certified copies thereof to all signatory and acceding States.

2. This Convention shall be registered by the Depositary pursuant to Article 102 of the Charter of the United Nations.

ANNEX

1. *Permissible Catch*

The Contracting Parties shall in any one year, which shall run from 1 July to 30 June inclusive, restrict the total number of seals of each species killed or captured to the numbers specified below. These numbers are subject to review in the light of scientific assessments.

(a) in the case of Crabeater seals *Lobodon carcinophague* 175,000

(b) in the case of Leopard seals *Hydrurga leptonyx* 12,000

(c) in the case of Weddell seals *Leptonychotes weddelli,* 5,000

2. *Protected Species*

(a) It is forbidden to kill or capture Ross seals *Ommatophoca rossi,* Southern elephant seals *Mirounga leonina,* or fur seals of the genus *Arctocephalus.*

(b) In order to protect the adult breeding stock during the period when it is most concentrated and vulnerable, it is forbidden to kill or capture any Weddell seal *Leptonychotes weddelli* one year old or older between 1 September and 31 January inclusive.

3. *Closed Season and Sealing Season*

The period between 1 March and 31 August inclusive is a Closed Season, during which the killing or capturing of seals is forbidden. The period 1 September to the last day in February constitutes a Sealing Season.

4. *Sealing Zones*

Each of the sealing zones listed in this paragraph shall be closed in numerical sequence to all sealing operations for the seal species listed in paragraph 1 of this Annex for the period 1 September to the last day of February inclusive. Such closures shall begin with the same zone as is closed under paragraph 2 of Annex B to Annex 1 of the Report of the Fifth Antarctic Treaty Consultative Meeting at the moment the Convention enters into force. Upon the expiration of each closed period, the affected zone shall reopen.

Zone 1—between 60E and 120E West Longitude

Zone 2—between 0E and 60E West Longitude, together with that part of the Weddell Sea lying westward of 60E West Longitude

Zone 3—between 0E and 70E East Longitude

Zone 4—between 70E and 130E East Longitude

Zone 5—between 130E East Longitude and 170E West Longitude

Zone 6—between 120E and 170E West Longitude.

5. *Seal Reserves*

It is forbidden to kill or capture seals in the following reserves, which are seal breeding areas or the site of long-term scientific research:

(a) The area around the South Orkmov Islands between 60E 20N and 60E 56N South Latitude and 44E 05N and 46E 25N West Longitude.

(b) The area of the southwestern Ross Sea south of 76E South Latitude and west of 170E East Longitude.

(c) The area of Edisto Inlet south and west of a line drawn between Cape Hallet at 72E 19N South Latitude, 170E 18N East Longitude, and Helm Point, at 72E 11N South Latitude, 72E 11N South Latitude, 170E 00N East Longitude.

6. *Exchange of Information*

(a) Contracting Parties shall provide before 31 October each year to other Contracting Parties and to SCAR a summary of statistical information on all seals killed or captured by their respective flags in the Convention areas, in respect of the preceding period 1 July to 30 June. This information shall include by zones and months:

(i) The gross and nett [sic] tonnage, brake horse-power, number of crew, and number of days' operation of vessels under the flag of the Contracting Party:

(ii) The number of adult individuals and pups of each species taken. When specifically requested, this information shall be provided in respect of each ship, together with its daily position at noon each operating day and the catch on that day.

(b) When an industry has started, reports of the number of seals of each species killed or captured in each zone shall be made to SCAR in the form and at the intervals (not shorter than once a week) requested by that body.

(c) Contracting Parties shall provide to SCAR biological information concerning in particular

(i) Sex

(ii) Reproductive condition

(iii) Age

SCAR may request additional information or material with the approval of the Contracting Parties.

(d) Contracting Parties shall provide to other Contracting Parties and to SCAR at least 30 days in advance of departure from their home ports, information on proposed sealing expenditures.

7. *Sealing Methods*

(a) SCAR is invited to report on methods of sealing and to make recommendations with a view to ensuring that the killing or capturing of seals is quick, painless and efficient. Contracting Parties, as appropriate, shall adopt rules for their nationals and vessels under their respective flags engaged in the killing and capturing of seals, giving due consideration to the views of SCAR.

(b) In the light of the available scientific and technical data, Contracting Parties agree to take appropriate steps to ensure that their nationals and vessels under their respective flags refrain from killing, or capturing seals in the water, except in limited quantities to provide for scientific research in conformity with the objectives and principles of this Convention. Such research shall include studies as to the effectiveness of methods of sealing from the viewpoint of the management and humane and rational utilization of the Antarctic seal resources for conservation purposes. The undertaking and the results of any such scientific research programme shall be communicated to SCAR and the Depositary which shall transmit them to the Contracting Parties.

2.4 CONVENTION ON THE CONSERVATION OF ANTARCTIC MARINE LIVING RESOURCES (CCAMLR) (Without Annex). Concluded at Canberra, 20 May 1980. Entered into force, 7 April 1982. L252 O.J.E.C. 27 (1981), T.I.A.S. No. 10240; *reprinted in* 19 I.L.M. 841 (1980) & 5 Weston V.D.4

THE CONTRACTING PARTIES,

RECOGNIZING the importance of safeguarding the environment and protecting the integrity of the ecosystem of the seas surrounding Antarctica;

NOTING the concentration of marine living resources found in Antarctic waters and the increased interest in the possibilities offered by the utilization of these resources as a source of protein;

CONSCIOUS of the urgency of ensuring the conservation of Antarctic marine living resources;

CONSIDERING that it is essential to increase knowledge of the Antarctic marine ecosystem and its components so as to be able to base decisions on harvesting on sound scientific information;

BELIEVING that the conservation of Antarctic marine living resources calls for international cooperation with due regard for the provisions of the Antarctic Treaty and with the active involvement of all States engaged in research or harvesting activities in Antarctic waters;

RECOGNIZING the prime responsibilities of the Antarctic Treaty Consultative Parties for the protection and preservation of the Antarctic environment and, in particular, their responsibilities under Article IX, paragraph 1(f) of the Antarctic Treaty in respect of the preservation and conservation of living resources in Antarctica;

RECALLING the action already taken by the Antarctic Treaty Consultative Parties including, in particular, the agreed measures for the conservation of Antarctic fauna and flora, as well as the provisions of the Convention for the conservation of Antarctic seals;

BEARING in mind the concern regarding the conservation of Antarctic marine living resources expressed by the consultative parties at the ninth consultative meeting of the Antarctic Treaty and the importance of the provisions of recommendations IX–2 which led to the establishment of the present convention;

BELIEVING that it is in the interest of all mankind to preserve the waters surrounding the Antarctic continent for peaceful purposes only and to prevent their becoming the scene or object of international discord;

RECOGNIZING, in the light of the foregoing, that it is desirable to establish suitable machinery for recommending, promoting, deciding upon and coordinating the measures and scientific studies needed to ensure the conservation of Antarctic marine living organisms,

HAVE AGREED AS FOLLOWS:

Article I

1. This Convention applies to the Antarctic marine living resources of the area south of 60E South latitude and to the Antarctic marine living resources of the area between that latitude and the Antarctic Convergence which form part of the Antarctic marine ecosystem.

2. Antarctic marine living resources means the populations of fin fish, molluscs, crustaceans and all other species of living organisms, including birds, found south of the Antarctic Convergence.

3. The Antarctic marine ecosystem means the complex of relationships of Antarctic marine living resources with each other and with their physical environment.

4. The Antarctic Convergence shall be deemed to be a line joining the following points along parallels of latitude and meridians of longitude:

50ES, 0E; 50ES, 30EE; 45ES, 30EE; 45ES, 80EE; 55ES, 80EE; 55ES, 150EE; 60ES, 150EE; 60ES, 50EW; 50ES, 50EW; 50ES, 0E.

Article II

1. The objective of this Convention is the Conservation of Antarctic marine living resources.

2. For the purposes of this Convention, the term "conservation" includes rational use.

3. Any harvesting and associated activities in the area to which this Convention applies shall be conducted in accordance with the provisions of this Convention and with the following principles of conservation:

(*a*) prevention of decrease in the size of any harvested population to levels below those which ensure its stable recruitment. For this purpose its size should not be allowed to fall below a level close to that which ensures the greatest net annual increment;

(*b*) maintenance of the ecological relationships between harvested, dependent and related populations of Antarctic marine living resources and the restoration of depleted populations to the levels defined in sub-paragraph (a) above;

and

(*c*) prevention of changes or minimization of the risk of changes in the marine ecosystem which are not potentially reversible over two or three decades, taking into account the state of available knowledge of the direct and indirect impact of harvesting, the effect of the introduction of alien species, the effects of associated activities on the marine ecosystem and of the effects of environmental changes, with the aim of making possible the sustained conservation of Antarctic marine living resources.

Article III

The Contracting Parties, whether or not they are Parties to the Antarctic Treaty, agree that they will not engage in any activities in the Antarctic Treaty area contrary to the principles and purposes of that Treaty and that, in their relations with each other, they are bound by the obligations contained in Articles I and V of the Antarctic Treaty.

Article IV

1. With respect to the Antarctic Treaty area, all Contracting Parties, whether or not they are Parties to the Antarctic Treaty, are bound by Articles IV and VI of the Antarctic Treaty in their relations with each other.

2. Nothing in this Convention and no acts or activities taking place while the present Convention is in force shall:

(*a*) constitute a basis for asserting, supporting or denying a claim to territorial sovereignty in the Antarctic Treaty area or create any rights of sovereignty in the Antarctic Treaty area;

(*b*) be interpreted as a renunciation or diminution by any Contracting Party of, or as prejudicing, any right or claim or basis of claim to exercise coastal state jurisdiction under international law within the area to which this Convention applies;

(*c*) be interpreted as prejudicing the position of any Contracting Party as regards its recognition or non-recognition of any such right, claim or basis of claim;

(*d*) affect the provision of Article IV, paragraph 2, of the Antarctic Treaty that no new claim, or enlargement of an existing claim, to territorial sovereignty in Antarctica shall be asserted while the Antarctic Treaty is in force.

Article V

1. The Contracting Parties which are not Parties to the Antarctic Treaty acknowledge the special obligations and responsibilities of the Antarctic Treaty Consultative Parties for the protection and preservation of the environment of the Antarctic Treaty area.

2. The Contracting Parties which are not Parties to the Antarctic Treaty agree that, in their activities in the Antarctic Treaty area, they will observe as and when appropriate the Agreed Measures for the Conservation of Antarctic Fauna and Flora and such other measures as have been recommended by the Antarctic Treaty Consultative Parties in fulfilment of their responsibility for the protection of the Antarctic environment from all forms of harmful human interference.

3. For the purposes of this Convention, "Antarctic Treaty Consultative Parties" means the Contracting Parties to the Antarctic Treaty whose Representatives participate in meetings under Article IX of the Antarctic Treaty.

Article VI

Nothing in this Convention shall derogate from the rights and obligations of Contracting Parties under the International Convention for the Regulation of Whaling and the Convention for the Conservation of Antarctic Seals.

Article VII

1. The Contracting Parties hereby establish and agree to maintain the Commission for the Conservation of Antarctic Marine Living Resources (hereinafter referred to as "the Commission").

2. Membership in the Commission shall be as follows:

(*a*) each Contracting Party which participated in the meeting at which this Convention was adopted shall be a Member of the Commission;

(*b*) each State Party which has acceded to this Convention pursuant to Article XXIX shall be entitled to be a Member of the Commission during such time as that acceding party is engaged in research or harvesting activities in relation to the marine living resources to which this Convention applies;

(*c*) each regional economic integration organization which has acceded to this Convention pursuant to Article XXIX shall be entitled to be a Member of the Commission during such time as its States members are so entitled;

(*d*) a Contracting Party seeking to participate in the work of the Commission pursuant to sub-paragraphs (b) and (c) above shall notify the Depositary of the basis upon which it seeks to become a Member of the Commission and of its willingness to accept conservation measures in force. The Depositary shall communicate to each Member of the Commission such notification and accompanying information. Within two months of receipt of such communication from the Depositary, any Member of the Commission may request that a special meeting of the Commission be held to consider the matter. Upon receipt of such request, the Depositary shall call such a meeting. If there is no request for a meeting, the

Contracting Party submitting the notification shall be deemed to have satisfied the requirements for Commission Membership.

3. Each Member of the Commission shall be represented by one representative who may be accompanied by alternate representatives and advisers.

Article VIII

The Commission shall have legal personality and shall enjoy in the territory of each of the States Parties such legal capacity as may be necessary to perform its function and achieve the purposes of this Convention. The privileges and immunities to be enjoyed by the Commission and its staff in the territory of a State Party shall be determined by agreement between the Commission and the State Party concerned.

Article IX

1. The function of the Commission shall be to give effect to the objective and principles set out in Article II of this Convention. To this end, it shall:

(*a*) facilitate research into and comprehensive studies of Antarctic marine living resources and of the Antarctic marine ecosystem;

(*b*) compile data on the status of and changes in population of Antarctic marine living resources and on factors affecting the distribution, abundance and productivity of harvested species and dependent or related species or populations;

(*c*) ensure the acquisition of catch and effort statistics on harvested populations;

(*d*) analyse, disseminate and publish the information referred to in subparagraphs (b) and (c) above and the reports of the Scientific Committee;

(*e*) identify conservation needs and analyse the effectiveness of conservation measures;

(*f*) formulate, adopt and revise conservation measures on the basis of the best scientific evidence available, subject to the provisions of paragraph 5 of this Article;

(*g*) implement the system of observation and inspection established under Article XXIV of this Convention;

(*h*) carry out such other activities as are necessary to fulfil the objective of this Convention.

2. The conservation measures referred to in paragraph 1(f) above include the following:

(*a*) the designation of the quantity of any species which may be harvested in the area to which this Convention applies;

(*b*) the designation of regions and sub-regions based on the distribution of populations of Antarctic marine living resources;

(*c*) the designation of the quantity which may be harvested from the populations of regions and sub-regions;

(*d*) the designation of protected species;

(*e*) the designation of the size, age and, as appropriate, sex of species which may be harvested;

(*f*) the designation of open and closed seasons for harvesting;

(*g*) the designation of the opening and closing of areas, regions or sub-regions for purposes of scientific study or conservation, including special areas for protection and scientific study;

(*h*) regulation of the effort employed and methods of harvesting, including fishing gear, with a view, inter alia, to avoiding undue concentration of harvesting in any region or sub-region;

(*i*) the taking of such other conservation measures as the Commission considers necessary for the fulfilment of the objective of this Convention, including measures concerning the effects of harvesting and associated activities on components of the marine ecosystem other than the harvested populations.

3. The Commission shall publish and maintain a record of all conservation measures in force.

4. In exercising its functions under paragraph 1 above, the Commission shall take full account of the recommendations and advice of the Scientific Committee.

5. The Commission shall take full account of any relevant measures or regulations established or recommended by the Consultative Meetings pursuant to Article IX of the Antarctic Treaty or by existing fisheries commissions responsible for species which may enter the area to which this Convention applies, in order that there shall be no inconsistency between the rights and obligations of a Contracting Party under such regulations or measures and conservation measures which may be adopted by the Commission.

6. Conservation measures adopted by the Commission in accordance with this Convention shall be implemented by Members of the Commission in the following manner:

(*a*) the Commission shall notify conservation measures to all Members of the Commission;

(*b*) conservation measures shall become binding upon all Members of the Commission 180 days after such notification, except as provided in subparagraphs (c) and (d) below;

(*c*) if a Member of the Commission, within ninety days following the notification specified in sub-paragraph (a), notifies the Commission that it is unable to accept the conservation measure, in whole or in part, the measure shall not, to the extent stated, be binding upon that Member of the Commission;

(*d*) in the event that any Member of the Commission invokes the procedure set forth in sub-paragraph (c) above, the Commission shall meet at the request of any Member of the Commission to review the conservation measure. At the time of such meeting and within thirty days following the meeting, any Member of the Commission shall have the right to declare that it is no longer able to accept the conservation measure, in which case the Member shall no longer be bound by such measure.

Article X

1. The Commission shall draw the attention of any State which is not a Party to this Convention to any activity undertaken by its nationals or vessels which, in the opinion of the Commission, affects the implementation of the objective of this Convention.

2. The Commission shall draw the attention of all Contracting Parties to any activity which, in the opinion of the Commission, affects the implementation by a Contracting Party of the objective of this Convention or the compliance by that Contracting Party with its obligations under this Convention.

Article XI

The Commission shall seek to cooperate with Contracting Parties which may exercise jurisdiction in marine areas adjacent to the area to which this Convention applies in respect of the conservation of any stock or stocks of associated species which occur both within those areas and the area to which this Convention applies, with a view to harmonizing the conservation measures adopted in respect of such stocks.

Article XII

1. Decisions of the Commission on matters of substance shall be taken by consensus. The question of whether a matter is one of substance shall be treated as a matter of substance.

2. Decisions on matters other than those referred to in paragraph 1 above shall be taken by a simple majority of the Members of the Commission present and voting.

3. In Commission consideration of any item requiring a decision, it shall be made clear whether a regional economic integration organization will participate in the taking of the decision and, if so, whether any of its member States will also participate. The number of Contracting Parties so participating shall not exceed the number of member States of the regional economic integration organization which are Members of the Commission.

4. In the taking of decisions pursuant to this Article, a regional economic integration organization shall have only one vote.

Article XIII

1. The headquarters of the Commission shall be established at Hobart, Tasmania, Australia.

2. The Commission shall hold a regular annual meeting. Other meetings shall also be held at the request of one-third of its members and as otherwise provided in this Convention. The first meeting of the Commission shall be held within three months of the entry into force of this Convention, provided that among the Contracting Parties there are at least two States conducting harvesting activities within the area to which this Convention applies. The first meeting shall, in any event, be held within one year of the entry into force of this Convention. The Depositary shall consult with the signatory States regarding the first Commission meeting, taking into account that a broad representation of such States is necessary for the effective operation of the Commission.

3. The Depositary shall convene the first meeting of the Commission at the headquarters of the Commission. Thereafter, meetings of the Commission shall be held at its headquarters, unless it decides otherwise.

4. The Commission shall elect from among its members a Chairman and Vice–Chairman, each of whom shall serve for a term of two years and shall be eligible for re-election for one additional term. The first Chairman shall, however, be elected for an initial term of three years. The Chairman and Vice–Chairman shall not be representatives of the same Contracting Party.

5. The Commission shall adopt and amend as necessary the rules of procedure for the conduct of its meetings, except with respect to the matters dealt with in Article XII of this Convention.

6. The Commission may establish such subsidiary bodies as are necessary for the performance of its functions.

Article XIV

1. The Contracting Parties hereby establish the Scientific Committee for the Conservation of Antarctic Marine Living Resources (hereinafter referred to as "the Scientific Committee") which shall be a consultative body to the Commission. The

Scientific Committee shall normally meet at the headquarters of the Commission unless the Scientific Committee decides otherwise.

2. Each Member of the Commission shall be a member of the Scientific Committee and shall appoint a representative with suitable scientific qualifications who may be accompanied by other experts and advisers.

3. The Scientific Committee may seek the advice of other scientists and experts as may be required on an ad hoc basis.

Article XV

1. The Scientific Committee shall provide a forum for consultation and cooperation concerning the collection, study and exchange of information with respect to the marine living resources to which this Convention applies. It shall encourage and promote cooperation in the field of scientific research in order to extend knowledge of the marine living resources of the Antarctic marine ecosystem.

2. The Scientific Committee shall conduct such activities as the Commission may direct in pursuance of the objective of this Convention and shall:

(*a*) establish criteria and methods to be used for determinations concerning the conservation measures referred to in Article IX of this Convention;

(*b*) regularly assess the status and trends of the populations of Antarctic marine living resources;

(*c*) analyse data concerning the direct and indirect effects of harvesting on the populations of Antarctic marine living resources;

(*d*) assess the effects of proposed changes in the methods or levels of harvesting and proposed conservation measures;

(*e*) transmit assessments, analyses, reports and recommendations to the Commission as requested or on its own initiative regarding measures and research to implement the objective of this Convention;

(*f*) formulate proposals for the conduct of international and national programs of research into Antarctic marine living resources.

3. In carrying out its functions, the Scientific Committee shall have regard to the work of other relevant technical and scientific organizations and to the scientific activities conducted within the framework of the Antarctic Treaty.

Article XVI

1. The first meeting of the Scientific Committee shall be held within three months of the first meeting of the Commission. The Scientific Committee shall meet thereafter as often as may be necessary to fulfil its functions.

2. The Scientific Committee shall adopt and amend as necessary its rules of procedure. The rules and any amendments thereto shall be approved by the Commission. The rules shall include procedures for the presentation of minority reports.

3. The Scientific Committee may establish, with the approval of the Commission, such subsidiary bodies as are necessary for the performance of its functions.

Article XVII

1. The Commission shall appoint an Executive Secretary to serve the Commission and Scientific Committee according to such procedures and on such terms and conditions as the Commission may determine. His term of office shall be for four years and he shall be eligible for reappointment.

2. The Commission shall authorize such staff establishment for the Secretariat as may be necessary and the Executive Secretary shall appoint, direct and supervise

such staff according to such rules and procedures and on such terms and conditions as the Commission may determine.

3. The Executive Secretary and Secretariat shall perform the functions entrusted to them by the Commission.

Article XVIII

The official languages of the Commission and of the Scientific Committee shall be English, French, Russian and Spanish.

Article XIX

1. At each annual meeting, the Commission shall adopt by consensus its budget and the budget of the Scientific Committee.

2. A draft budget for the Commission and the Scientific Committee and any subsidiary bodies shall be prepared by the Executive Secretary and submitted to the Members of the Commission at least sixty days before the annual meeting of the Commission.

3. Each Member of the Commission shall contribute to the budget. Until the expiration of five years after the entry into force of this Convention, the contribution of each Member of the Commission shall be equal. Thereafter the contribution shall be determined in accordance with two criteria: the amount harvested and an equal sharing among all Members of the Commission. The Commission shall determine by consensus the proportion in which these two criteria shall apply.

4. The financial activities of the Commission and Scientific Committee shall be conducted in accordance with financial regulations adopted by the Commission and shall be subject to an annual audit by external auditors selected by the Commission.

5. Each Member of the Commission shall meet its own expenses arising from attendance at meetings of the Commission and of the Scientific Committee.

6. A Member of the Commission that fails to pay its contributions for two consecutive years shall not, during the period of its default, have the right to participate in the taking of decisions in the Commission.

Article XX

1. The Members of the Commission shall, to the greatest extent possible, provide annually to the Commission and to the Scientific Committee such statistical, biological and other data and information as the Commission and Scientific Committee may require in the exercise of their functions.

2. The Members of the Commission shall provide, in the manner and at such intervals as may be prescribed, information about their harvesting activities, including fishing areas and vessels, so as to enable reliable catch and effort statistics to be compiled.

3. The Members of the Commission shall provide to the Commission at such intervals as may be prescribed information on steps taken to implement the conservation measures adopted by the Commission.

4. The Members of the Commission agree that in any of their harvesting activities, advantage shall be taken of opportunities to collect data needed to assess the impact of harvesting.

Article XXI

1. Each Contracting Party shall take appropriate measures within its competence to ensure compliance with the provisions of this Convention and with conservation

measures adopted by the Commission to which the Party is bound in accordance with Article IX of this Convention.

2. Each Contracting Party shall transmit to the Commission information on measures taken pursuant to paragraph 1 above, including the imposition of sanctions for any violation.

Article XXII

1. Each Contracting Party undertakes to exert appropriate efforts, consistent with the Charter of the United Nations, to the end that no one engages in any activity contrary to the objective of this Convention.

2. Each Contracting Party shall notify the Commission of any such activity which comes to its attention.

Article XXIII

1. The Commission and the Scientific Committee shall co-operate with the Antarctic Treaty Consultative Parties on matters falling within the competence of the latter.

2. The Commission and the Scientific Committee shall co-operate, as appropriate, with the Food and Agriculture Organization of the United Nations and with other Specialised Agencies.

3. The Commission and the Scientific Committee shall seek to develop co-operative working relationships, as appropriate, with inter-governmental and non-governmental organizations which could contribute to their work, including the Scientific Committee on Antarctic Research, the Scientific Committee on Oceanic Research and the International Whaling Commission.

4. The Commission may enter into agreements with the organizations referred to in this Article and with other organizations as may be appropriate. The Commission and the Scientific Committee may invite such organizations to send observers to their meetings and to meetings of their subsidiary bodies.

Article XXIV

1. In order to promote the objective and ensure observance of the provisions of this Convention, the Contracting Parties agree that a system of observation and inspection shall be established.

2. The system of observation and inspection shall be elaborated by the Commission on the basis of the following principles:

(*a*) Contracting Parties shall cooperate with each other to ensure the effective implementation of the system of observation and inspection, taking account of the existing international practice. This system shall include, inter alia, procedures for boarding and inspection by observers and inspectors designated by the Members of the Commission and procedures for flag state prosecution and sanctions on the basis of evidence resulting from such boarding and inspections. A report of such prosecutions and sanctions imposed shall be included in the information referred to in Article XXI of this Convention;

(*b*) in order to verify compliance with measures adopted under this Convention, observation and inspection shall be carried out on board vessels engaged in scientific research or harvesting of marine living resources in the area to which this Convention applies, through observers and inspectors designated by the Members of the Commission and operating under terms and conditions to be established by the Commission;

(*c*) designated observers and inspectors shall remain subject to the jurisdiction of the Contracting Party of which they are nationals. They shall report to the Member of the Commission by which they have been designated which in turn shall report to the Commission.

3. Pending the establishment of the system of observation and inspection, the Members of the Commission shall seek to establish interim arrangements to designate observers and inspectors and such designated observers and inspectors shall be entitled to carry out inspections in accordance with the principles set out in paragraph 2 above.

Article XXV

1. If any dispute arises between two or more of the Contracting Parties concerning the interpretation or application of this Convention, those Contracting Parties shall consult among themselves with a view to having the dispute resolved by negotiation, inquiry, mediation, conciliation, arbitration, judicial settlement or other peaceful means of their own choice.

2. Any dispute of this character not so resolved shall, with the consent in each case of all Parties to the dispute, be referred for settlement to the International Court of Justice or to arbitration; but failure to reach agreement on reference to the International Court or to arbitration shall not absolve Parties to the dispute from the responsibility of continuing to seek to resolve it by any of the various peaceful means referred to in paragraph 1 above.

3. In cases where the dispute is referred to arbitration, the arbitral tribunal shall be constituted as provided in the Annex to this Convention.

Article XXVI

1. This Convention shall be open for signature at Canberra from 1 August to 31 December 1980 by the States participating in the Conference on the Conservation of Antarctic Marine Living Resources held at Canberra from 7 to 20 May 1980.

2. The States which so sign will be the original signatory States of the Convention.

Article XXVII

1. This Convention is subject to ratification, acceptance or approval by signatory States.

2. Instruments of ratification, acceptance or approval shall be deposited with the Government of Australia, hereby designated as the Depositary.

Article XXVIII

1. This Convention shall enter into force on the thirtieth day following the date of deposit of the eighth instrument of ratification, acceptance or approval by States referred to in paragraph 1 of Article XXVI of this Convention.

2. With respect to each State or regional economic integration organization which subsequent to the date of entry into force of this Convention deposits an instrument of ratification, acceptance, approval or accession, the Convention shall enter into force on the thirtieth day following such deposit.

Article XXIX

1. This Convention shall be open for accession by any State interested in research or harvesting activities in relation to the marine living resources to which this Convention applies.

2. This Convention shall be open for accession by regional economic integration organizations constituted by sovereign States which include among their members one or more States Members of the Commission and to which the States members of the organization have transferred, in whole or in part, competences with regard to the matters covered by this Convention. The accession of such regional economic integration organizations shall be the subject of consultations among Members of the Commission.

Article XXX

1. This Convention may be amended at any time.

2. If one-third of the Members of the Commission request a meeting to discuss a proposed amendment the Depositary shall call such a meeting.

3. An amendment shall enter into force when the Depositary has received instruments of ratification, acceptance or approval thereof from all the Members of the Commission.

4. Such amendment shall thereafter enter into force as to any other Contracting Party when notice of ratification, acceptance or approval by it has been received by the Depositary. Any such Contracting Party from which no such notice has been received within a period of one year from the date of entry into force of the amendment in accordance with paragraph 3 above shall be deemed to have withdrawn from this Convention.

Article XXXI

1. Any Contracting Party may withdraw from this Convention on 30 June of any year, by giving written notice not later than 1 January of the same year to the Depositary, which, upon receipt of such a notice, shall communicate it forthwith to the other Contracting Parties.

2. Any other Contracting Party may, within sixty days of the receipt of a copy of such a notice from the Depositary, give written notice of withdrawal to the Depositary in which case the Convention shall cease to be in force on 30 June of the same year with respect to the Contracting Party giving such notice.

3. Withdrawal from this Convention by any Member of the Commission shall not affect its financial obligations under this Convention.

Article XXXII

The Depositary shall notify all Contracting Parties of the following:

(*a*) signatures of this Convention and the deposit of instruments of ratification, acceptance, approval or accession;

(*b*) the date of entry into force of this Convention and of any amendment thereto.

Article XXXIII

1. This Convention, of which the English, French, Russian and Spanish texts are equally authentic, shall be deposited with the Government of Australia which shall transmit duly certified copies thereof to all signatory and acceding Parties.

2. This Convention shall be registered by the Depositary pursuant to Article 102 of the Charter of the United Nations.

2.5 Resolution on the Question of Antarctica. Adopted by the UN General Assembly, 15 December 1983. G.A.Res. 38/77, U.N. GAOR, 38th Sess., Supp. No. 47, at 69, U.N.Doc. A/38/69 (1983)

The General Assembly,

Having considered the item entitled "Question of Antarctica",

Conscious of the increasing international awareness of and interest in Antarctica,

Bearing in mind the Antarctic Treaty and the significance of the system it has developed,

Taking into account the debate on this item at its thirty-eighth session,

Convinced of the advantages of a better knowledge of Antarctica,

Affirming the conviction that, in the interest of all mankind, Antarctica should continue forever to be used exclusively for peaceful purposes and that it should not become the scene or object of international discord,

Recalling the relevant paragraphs of the Economic Declaration adopted by the Seventh Conference of Heads of State or Government of the Non–Aligned Countries, held at New Delhi from 7 to 12 March 1983,

1. *Requests* the Secretary–General to prepare a comprehensive, factual and objective study on all aspects of Antarctica, taking fully into account the Antarctica Treaty system and other relevant factors;

2. *Also requests* the Secretary–General to seek the views of all Member States in the preparation of the study;

3. *Requests* those States conducting scientific research in Antarctica, other interested States, the relevant specialized agencies, organs, organizations and bodies of the United Nations system and relevant international organizations having scientific or technical information on Antarctica to lend the Secretary–General whatever assistance he may request for the purpose of carrying out the study;

4. *Requests* the Secretary–General to report to the General Assembly at its thirty-ninth session;

5. *Decides* to include in the provisional agenda of its thirty-ninth session the item entitled "Question of Antarctica".

2.6 Resolution on the Question of Antarctica. Adopted by the UN General Assembly, 17 December 1984. G.A. Res. 39/152, U.N. GAOR, 39th Sess., Supp. No. 51, at 94, U.N. Doc. A/39/51 (1984)

The General Assembly,

Recalling its resolution 38/77 of 15 December 1983,

Having considered the item entitled "Question of Antarctica",

Taking note of the study on the question of Antarctica,

Conscious of the increasing international awareness of and interest in Antarctica,

Bearing in mind the Antarctic Treaty and the significance of the system it has developed,

Taking into account the debate on this item at its thirty-ninth session,

Convinced of the advantages of a better knowledge of Antarctica,

Affirming the conviction that, in the interest of all mankind, Antarctica should continue forever to be used exclusively for peaceful purposes and that it should not become the scene or object of international discord,

Recalling the relevant paragraphs of the Economic Declaration adopted at the Seventh Conference of Heads of State or Government of Non–Aligned Countries, held at New Delhi from 7 to 12 March 1983,

1. *Expresses its appreciation* to the Secretary–General for the study on the question of Antarctica;

2. *Decides* to include in the provisional agenda of its fortieth session the item entitled "Question of Antarctica".

2.7 CONVENTION ON THE REGULATION OF ANTARCTIC MINERAL RESOURCE ACTIVITIES (CRAMRA) (Without Annex for Arbitral Tribunal). Concluded at Wellington, 2 June 1988. Not yet in force. Doc AMR/SCM/88/78; *reprinted in* 27 I.L.M. 859 (1988) & 5 Weston V.D.5

CHAPTER I: GENERAL PROVISIONS

Article 1
Definitions

For the purposes of this Convention:

1. "Antarctic Treaty" means the Antarctic Treaty done at Washington on 1 December 1959.

2. "Antarctic Treaty Consultative Parties" means the Contracting Parties to the Antarctic Treaty entitled to appoint representatives to participate in the meetings referred to in Article IX of that Treaty.

3. "Antarctic Treaty area" means the area to which the provisions of the Antarctic Treaty apply in accordance with Article VI of that Treaty.

4. "Convention for the Conservation of Antarctic Seals" means the Convention done at London on 1 June 1972.

5. "Convention on the Conservation of Antarctic Marine Living Resources" means the Convention done at Canberra on 20 May 1980.

6. "Mineral resources" means all non-living natural non-renewable resources, including fossil fuels, metallic and non-metallic minerals.

7. "Antarctic mineral resource activities" means prospecting, exploration or development, but does not include scientific research activities within the meaning of Article III of the Antarctic Treaty.

8. "Prospecting" means activities, including logistic support, aimed at identifying areas of mineral resource potential for possible exploration and development, including geological, geochemical and geophysical investigations and field observations, the use of remote sensing techniques and collection of surface, seafloor and sub-ice samples. Such activities do not include dredging and excavations, except for the purpose of obtaining small-scale samples, or drilling, except shallow drilling into rock and sediment to depths not exceeding 25 metres, or such other depth as the Commission may determine for particular circumstances.

9. "Exploration" means activities, including logistic support, aimed at identifying and evaluating specific mineral resource occurrences or deposits, including exploratory drilling, dredging and other surface or subsurface excavations required to determine the nature and size of mineral resource deposits and the feasibility of their development, but excluding pilot projects or commercial production.

10. "Development" means activities, including logistic support, which take place following exploration and are aimed at or associated with exploitation of specific mineral resource deposits, including pilot projects, processing, storage and transport activities.

11. "Operator" means:

(*a*) a Party; or

(*b*) an agency or instrumentality of a Party; or

(*c*) a juridical person established under the law of a Party or;

(*d*) a joint venture consisting exclusively of any combination of any of the foregoing, which is undertaking Antarctic mineral resource activities and for which there is a Sponsoring State.

12. "Sponsoring State" means the Party with which an Operator has a substantial and genuine link, through being:

(*a*) in the case of a Party, that Party;

(*b*) in the case of an agency or instrumentality of a Party, that Party;

(*c*) in the case of a juridical person other than an agency or instrumentality of a Party, the Party:

(i) under whose law that juridical person is established and to whose law it is subject, without prejudice to any other law which might be applicable, and

(ii) in whose territory the management of that juridical person is located, and

(iii) to whose effective control that juridical person is subject;

(*d*) in the case of a joint venture not constituting a juridical person:

(i) where the managing member of the joint venture is a Party or an agency or instrumentality of a Party, that Party; or

(ii) in any other cases, where in relation to a Party the managing member of the joint venture satisfies the requirements of subparagraph (c) above, that Party.

13. "Managing member of the joint venture" means that member which the participating members in the joint venture have by agreement designated as having responsibility for central management of the joint venture, including the functions of organising and supervising the activities to be undertaken, and controlling the financial resources involved.

14. "Effective control" means the ability of the Sponsoring State to ensure the availability of substantial resources of the Operator for purposes connected with the implementation of this Convention, through the location of such resources in the territory of the Sponsoring State or otherwise.

15. "Damage to the Antarctic environment or dependent or associated ecosystems" means any impact on the living or non-living components of that environment or those ecosystems, including harm to atmospheric, marine or terrestrial life, beyond that which is negligible or which has been assessed and judged to be acceptable pursuant to this Convention.

16. "Commission" means the Antarctic Mineral Resources Commission established pursuant to Article 18.

17. "Regulatory Committee" means an Antarctic Mineral Resources Regulatory Committee established pursuant to Article 39.

18. "Advisory Committee" means the Scientific, Technical and Environmental Advisory Committee established pursuant to Article 13.

19. "Special Meeting of Parties" means the Meeting referred to in Article 28.

20. "Arbitral Tribunal" means an Arbitral Tribunal constituted as provided for in the Annex, which forms an integral part of this Convention.

Article 2

Objectives and General Principles

1. This Convention is an integral part of the Antarctic Treaty system, comprising the Antarctic Treaty, the measures in effect under that Treaty, and its associated

separate legal instruments, the prime purpose of which is to ensure that Antarctica shall continue forever to be used exclusively for peaceful purposes and shall not become the scene or object of international discord. The Parties provide through this Convention, the principles it establishes, the rules it prescribes, the institutions it creates and the decisions adopted pursuant to it, a means for:

(*a*) assessing the possible impact on the environment of Antarctic mineral resource activities;

(*b*) determining whether Antarctic mineral resource activities are acceptable;

(*c*) governing the conduct of such Antarctic mineral resource activities as may be found acceptable; and

(*d*) ensuring that any Antarctic mineral resource activities are undertaken in strict conformity with this Convention.

2. In implementing this Convention, the Parties shall ensure that Antarctic mineral resource activities, should they occur, take place in a manner consistent with all the components of the Antarctic Treaty system and the obligations flowing therefrom.

3. In relation to Antarctic mineral resource activities, should they occur, the Parties acknowledge the special responsibility of the Antarctic Treaty Consultative Parties for the protection of the environment and the need to:

(*a*) protect the Antarctic environment and dependent and associated ecosystems;

(*b*) respect Antarctica's significance for, and influence on, the global environment;

(*c*) respect other legitimate uses of Antarctica;

(*d*) respect Antarctica's scientific value and aesthetic and wilderness qualities;

(*e*) ensure the safety of operations in Antarctica;

(*f*) promote opportunities for fair and effective participation of all Parties; and

(*g*) take into account the interests of the international community as a whole.

Article 3

Prohibition of Antarctic Mineral Resource Activities Outside This Convention

No Antarctic mineral resource activities shall be conducted except in accordance with this Convention and measures in effect pursuant to it and, in the case of exploration or development, with a Management Scheme approved pursuant to Article 48 or 54.

Article 4

Principles Concerning Judgments on Antarctic Mineral Resource Activities

1. Decisions about Antarctic mineral resource activities shall be based upon information adequate to enable informed judgments to be made about their possible impacts and no such activities shall take place unless this information is available for decisions relevant to those activities.

2. No Antarctic mineral resource activity shall take place until it is judged, based upon assessment of its possible impacts on the Antarctic environment and on dependent and on associated ecosystems, that the activity in question would not cause:

(*a*) significant adverse effects on air and water quality;

(*b*) significant changes in atmospheric, terrestrial or marine environments;

(*c*) significant change in the distribution, abundance or productivity of populations of species of fauna or flora;

(*d*) further jeopardy to endangered or threatened species or populations of such species; or

(*e*) degradation of, or substantial risk to, areas of special biological, scientific, historic, aesthetic or wilderness significance.

3. No Antarctic mineral resource activity shall take place until it is judged, based upon assessment of its possible impacts, that the activity in question would not cause significant adverse effects on global or regional climate or weather patterns.

4. No Antarctic mineral resource activity shall take place until it is judged that:

(*a*) technology and procedures are available to provide for safe operations and compliance with paragraphs 2 and 3 above;

(*b*) there exists the capacity to monitor key environmental parameters and ecosystem components so as to identify any adverse effects of such activity and to provide for the modification of operating procedures as may be necessary in the light of the results of monitoring or increased knowledge of the Antarctic environment or dependent or associated ecosystems; and

(*c*) there exists the capacity to respond effectively to accidents, particularly those with potential environmental effects.

5. The judgments referred to in paragraphs 2, 3 and 4 above shall take into account the cumulative impacts of possible Antarctic mineral resource activities both by themselves and in combination with other such activities and other uses of Antarctica.

Article 5

Area of Application

1. This Convention shall, subject to paragraphs 2, 3 and 4 below, apply to the Antarctic Treaty area.

2. Without prejudice to the responsibilities of the Antarctic Treaty Consultative Parties under the Antarctic Treaty and measures pursuant to it, the Parties agree that this Convention shall regulate Antarctic mineral resource activities which take place on the continent of Antarctica and all Antarctic islands, including all ice shelves, south of 60E south latitude and in the seabed and subsoil of adjacent offshore areas up to the deep seabed.

3. For the purposes of this Convention "deep seabed" means the seabed and subsoil beyond the geographic extent of the continental shelf as the term continental shelf is defined in accordance with international law.

4. Nothing in this Article shall be construed as limiting the application of other Articles of this Convention in so far as they relate to possible impacts outside the area referred to in paragraphs 1 and 2 above, including impacts on dependent or on associated ecosystems.

Article 6

Cooperation and International Participation

In the implementation of this Convention cooperation within its framework shall be promoted and encouragement given to international participation in Antarctic mineral resource activities by interested Parties which are Antarctic Treaty Consultative Parties and by other interested Parties, in particular, developing countries in either category. Such participation may be realised through the Parties themselves and their Operators.

Article 7

Compliance with This Convention

1. Each Party shall take appropriate measures within its competence to ensure compliance with this Convention and any measures in effect pursuant to it.

2. If a Party is prevented by the exercise of jurisdiction by another Party from ensuring compliance in accordance with paragraph 1 above, it shall not, to the extent that it is so prevented, bear responsibility for that failure to ensure compliance.

3. If any jurisdictional dispute related to compliance with this Convention or any measure in effect pursuant to it arises between two or more Parties, the Parties concerned shall immediately consult together with a view to reaching a mutually acceptable solution.

4. Each Party shall notify the Executive Secretary, for circulation to all other Parties, of the measures taken pursuant to paragraph 1 above.

5. Each Party shall exert appropriate efforts, consistent with the Charter of the United Nations, to the end that no one engages in any Antarctic mineral resource activities contrary to the objectives and principles of this Convention.

6. Each Party may, whenever it deems it necessary, draw the attention of the Commission to any activity which in its opinion affects the implementation of the objectives and principles of this Convention.

7. The Commission shall draw the attention of all Parties to any activity which, in the opinion of the Commission, affects the implementation of the objectives and principles of this Convention or the compliance by any Party with its obligations under this Convention and any measures in effect pursuant to it.

8. The Commission shall draw the attention of any State which is not a Party to this Convention to any activity undertaken by that State, its agencies or instrumentalities, natural or juridical persons, ships, aircraft or other means of transportation which, in the opinion of the Commission, affects the implementation of the objectives and principles of this Convention. The Commission shall inform all Parties accordingly.

9. Nothing in this Article shall affect the operation of Article 12(7) of this Convention or Article VIII of the Antarctic Treaty.

Article 8

Response Action and Liability

1. An Operator undertaking any Antarctic mineral resource activity shall take necessary and timely response action, including prevention, containment, clean up and removal measures, if the activity results in or threatens to result in damage to the Antarctic environment or dependent or associated ecosystems. The Operator, through its Sponsoring State, shall notify the Executive Secretary, for circulation to the relevant institutions of this Convention and to all Parties, of action taken pursuant to this paragraph.

2. An Operator shall be strictly liable for:

(*a*) damage to the Antarctic environment or dependent or associated ecosystems arising from its Antarctic mineral resource activities, including payment in the event that there has been no restoration to the *status quo ante;*

(*b*) loss of or impairment to an established use, as referred to in Article 15, or loss of or impairment to an established use of dependent or associated ecosystems, arising directly out of damage described in subparagraph (a) above;

(*c*) loss of or damage to property of a third party or loss of life or personal injury of a third party arising directly out of damage described in subparagraph (a) above; and

(*d*) reimbursement of reasonable costs by whomsoever incurred relating to necessary response action, including prevention, containment, clean up and removal measures, and action taken to restore the *status quo ante* where Antarctic mineral resource activities undertaken by that Operator result in or threaten to result in damage to the Antarctic environment or dependent or associated ecosystems.

3. (*a*) Damage of the kind referred to in paragraph 2 above which would not have occurred or continued if the Sponsoring State had carried out its obligations under this Convention with respect to its Operator shall, in accordance with international law, entail liability of that Sponsoring State. Such liability shall be limited to that portion of liability not satisfied by the Operator or otherwise.

(*b*) Nothing in subparagraph (a) above shall affect the application of the rules of international law applicable in the event that damage not referred to in that subparagraph would not have occurred or continued if the Sponsoring State had carried out its obligations under this Convention with respect to its Operator.

4. An Operator shall not be liable pursuant to paragraph 2 above if it proves that the damage has been caused directly by, and to the extent that it has been caused directly by:

(*a*) an event constituting in the circumstances of Antarctica a natural disaster of an exceptional character which could not reasonably have been foreseen; or

(*b*) armed conflict, should it occur notwithstanding the Antarctic Treaty, or an act of terrorism directed against the activities of the Operator, against which no reasonable precautionary measures could have been effective.

5. Liability of an Operator for any loss of life, personal injury or loss of or damage to property other than that governed by this Article shall be regulated by applicable law and procedures.

6. If an Operator proves that damage has been caused totally or in part by an intentional or grossly negligent act or omission of the party seeking redress, that Operator may be relieved totally or in part from its obligation to pay compensation in respect of the damage suffered by such party.

7. (*a*) Further rules and procedures in respect of the provisions on liability set out in this Article shall be elaborated through a separate Protocol which shall be adopted by consensus by the members of the Commission and shall enter into force according to the procedure provided for in Article 62 for the entry into force of this Convention.

(*b*) Such rules and procedures shall be designed to enhance the protection of the Antarctic environment and dependent and associated ecosystems.

(*c*) Such rules and procedures:

(i) may contain provisions for appropriate limits on liability, where such limits can be justified:

(ii) without prejudice to Article 57, shall prescribe means and mechanisms such as a claims tribunal or other fora by which claims against Operators pursuant to this Article may be assessed and adjudicated:

(iii) shall ensure that a means is provided to assist with immediate response action, and to satisfy liability under paragraph 2 above in the event, *inter alia,* that an Operator liable is financially incapable of meeting its obligation in full that it exceeds any relevant limits of liability, that there is a defence to liability or that the loss or damage is of undetermined origin.

Unless it is determined during the elaboration of the Protocol that there are other effective means of meeting these objectives, the Protocol shall establish a Fund or Funds and make provision in respect of such Fund or Funds, *inter alia,* for the following:

—financing by Operators or on industry wide bases;

—ensuring the permanent liquidity and mandatory supplementation thereof in the event of insufficiency;

—reimbursement of costs of response action, by whomsoever incurred.

8. Nothing in paragraphs 4, 6 and 7 above or in the Protocol adopted pursuant to paragraph 7 shall affect in any way the provisions of paragraph 1 above.

9. No application for an exploration or development permit shall be made until the Protocol provided for in paragraph 7 above is in force for the Party lodging such application.

10. Each Party, pending the entry into force for it of the Protocol provided for in paragraph 7 above, shall ensure, consistently with Article 7 and in accordance with its legal system, that recourse is available in its national courts for adjudicating liability claims pursuant to paragraphs 2, 4 and 6 above against Operators which are engaged in prospecting. Such recourse shall include the adjudication of claims against any Operator it has sponsored. Each Party shall also ensure, in accordance with its legal system, that the Commission has the right to appear as a party in its national courts to pursue relevant liability claims under paragraph 2(a) above.

11. Nothing in this Article or in the Protocol provided for in paragraph 7 above shall be construed so as to:

(*a*) preclude the application of existing rules on liability, and the development in accordance with international law of further such rules, which may have application to either States or Operators; or

(*b*) affect the right of an Operator incurring liability pursuant to this Article to seek redress from another party which caused or contributed to the damage in question.

12. When compensation has been paid other than under this Convention liability under this Convention shall be offset by the amount of such payment.

Article 9

Protection of Legal Positions under the Antarctic Treaty

Nothing in this Convention and no acts or activities taking place while this Convention is in force shall:

(*a*) constitute a basis for asserting, supporting or denying a claim to territorial sovereignty in the Antarctic Treaty area or create any rights of sovereignty in the Antarctic Treaty area;

(*b*) be interpreted as a renunciation or diminution by any Party of, or as prejudicing, any right or claim or basis of claim to territorial sovereignty in Antarctica or to exercise coastal state jurisdiction under international law;

(*c*) be interpreted as prejudicing the position of any Party as regards its recognition or non-recognition of any such right, claim or basis of claim; or (*d*) affect the provision of Article IV(2) of the Antarctic Treaty that no new claim, or enlargement of an existing claim, to territorial sovereignty in Antarctica shall be asserted while the Antarctic Treaty is in force.

Article 10

Consistency with the Other Components of the Antarctic Treaty System

1. Each Party shall ensure that Antarctic mineral resource activities take place in a manner consistent with the components of the Antarctic Treaty system, including the Antarctic Treaty, the Convention for the Conservation of Antarctic Seals and the Convention on the Conservation of Antarctic Marine Living Resources and the measures in effect pursuant to those instruments.

2. The Commission shall consult and cooperate with the Antarctic Treaty Consultative Parties, the Contracting Parties to the Convention for the Conservation of Antarctic Seals, and the Commission for the Conservation of Antarctic Marine Living Resources with a view to ensuring the achievement of the objectives and principles of this Convention and avoiding any interference with the achievement of the objectives and principles of the Antarctic Treaty, the Convention for the Conservation of Antarctic Seals or the Convention on the Conservation of Antarctic Marine Living Resources, or inconsistency between the measures in effect pursuant to those instruments and measures in effect pursuant to this Convention.

Article 11

Inspection under the Antarctic Treaty

All stations, installations and equipment, in the Antarctic Treaty area, relating to Antarctic mineral resource activities, as well as ships and aircraft supporting such activities at points of discharging or embarking cargoes or personnel at such stations and installations, shall be open at all times to inspection by observers designated under Article VII of the Antarctic Treaty for the purposes of that Treaty.

Article 12

Inspection under This Convention

1. In order to promote the objectives and principles and to ensure the observance of this Convention and measures in effect pursuant to it, all stations, installations and equipment relating to Antarctic mineral resource activities in the area in which these activities are regulated by this Convention, as well as ships and aircraft supporting such activities at points of discharging or embarking cargoes or personnel anywhere in that area shall be open at all times to inspection by:

(*a*) observers designated by any member of the Commission who shall be nationals of that member; and

(*b*) observers designated by the Commission or relevant Regulatory Committees.

2. Aerial inspection may be carried out at any time over the area in which Antarctic mineral resource activities are regulated by this Convention.

3. The Commission shall maintain an up-to-date list of observers designated pursuant to paragraph 1(a) and (b) above.

4. Reports from the observers shall be transmitted to the Commission and to any Regulatory Committee having competence in the area where the inspection has been carried out.

5. Observers shall avoid interference with the safe and normal operations of stations, installations and equipment visited and shall respect measures adopted by the Commission to protect confidentiality of data and information.

6. Inspections undertaken pursuant to paragraph 1(a) and (b) above shall be compatible and reinforce each other and shall not impose an undue burden on the operation of stations, installations and equipment visited.

7. In order to facilitate the exercise of their functions under this Convention, and without prejudice to the respective positions of the Parties relating to jurisdiction over all other persons in the area in which Antarctic mineral resource activities are regulated by this Convention, observers designated under this Article shall be subject only to the jurisdiction of the Party of which they are nationals in respect of all acts or omissions occurring while they are in that area for the purpose of exercising their functions.

8. No exploration or development shall take place in an area identified pursuant to Article 41 until effective provision has been made for inspection in that area.

Article 13
Protected Areas

1. Antarctic mineral resource activities shall be prohibited in any area designated as a Specially Protected Area or a Site of Special Scientific Interest under Article IX(1) of the Antarctic Treaty. Such activities shall also be prohibited in any other area designated as a protected area in accordance with Article IX(1) of the Antarctic Treaty, except to the extent that the relevant measure provides otherwise pending any designation becoming effective in accordance with Article IX(4) of the Antarctic Treaty, no Antarctic mineral resource activities shall take place in any such area which would prejudice the purpose for which it was designated.

2. The Commission shall also prohibit or restrict Antarctic mineral resource activities in any area which, for historic, ecological, environmental, scientific or other reasons, it has designated as a protected area.

3. In exercising its powers under paragraph 2 above or under Article 41 the Commission shall consider whether to restrict or prohibit Antarctic mineral resource activities in any area, in addition to those referred to in paragraph 1 above, protected or set aside pursuant to provisions of other components of the Antarctic Treaty system, to ensure the purposes which they are designated.

4. In relation to any area in which Antarctic mineral resource activities are prohibited or restricted in accordance with paragraph 1, 2 or 3 above, the Commission shall consider whether, for the purposes of Article 4(2)(e), it would be prudent, additionally, to prohibit or restrict Antarctic mineral resource activities in adjacent areas for the purpose of creating a buffer zone.

5. The Commission shall give effect to Article 10(2) in acting pursuant to paragraphs 2, 3 and 4 above.

6. The Commission shall, where appropriate, bring any decisions it takes pursuant to this Article to the attention of the Antarctic Treaty Consultative Parties, the Contracting Parties to the Convention for the Conservation of Antarctic Seals, the Commission for the Conservation of Antarctic Marine Living Resources and the Scientific Committee on Antarctic Research.

Article 14
Non-Discrimination

In the implementation of this Convention there shall be no discrimination against any Party or its Operators.

Article 15

Respect for Other Uses of Antarctica

1. Decisions about Antarctic mineral resource activities shall take into account the need to respect other established uses of Antarctica, including:

(*a*) the operation of stations and their associated installations, support facilities and equipment in Antarctica;

(*b*) scientific investigation in Antarctic and cooperation therein;

(*c*) the conservation, including national use, of Antarctic marine living resources;

(*d*) tourism;

(*e*) the preservation of historic monuments; and

(*f*) navigation and aviation, that are consistent with the Antarctic Treaty system.

2. Antarctic mineral resource activities shall be conducted so as to respect any uses of Antarctica as referred to in paragraph 1 above.

Article 16

Availability and Confidentiality of Data and Information

Data and information obtained from Antarctic mineral resource activities shall, to the greatest extent practicable and feasible, be made freely available, provided that:

(*a*) as regards data and information of commercial value deriving from prospecting, they may be retained by the Operator in accordance with Article 37;

(*b*) as regards data and information deriving from exploration or development, the Commission shall adopt measures relating, as appropriate, to their release and to ensure the confidentiality of data and information of commercial value.

Article 17

Notifications and Provisional Exercise of Functions of the Executive Secretary

1. Where in this Convention there is a reference to the provision of information, a notification or a report to any institution provided for in this Convention and that institution has not been established, the information, notification or report shall be provided to the Executive Secretary who shall circulate it as required.

2. Where in this Convention a function is assigned to the Executive Secretary and no Executive Secretary has been appointed under Article 33, that function shall be performed by the Depositary.

CHAPTER II: INSTITUTIONS

Article 18

Commission

1. There is hereby established the Antarctic Mineral Resources Commission.

2. Membership of the Commission shall be as follows:

(*a*) each Party which was an Antarctic Treaty Consultative Party on the date when this Convention was opened for signature; and

(*b*) each other Party during such time as it is actively engaged in substantial scientific, technical or environmental research in the area to which this Convention applies directly relevant to decisions about Antarctic mineral resource activities, particularly the assessments and judgments called for in Article 4; and

(*c*) each other Party sponsoring Antarctic mineral resource exploration or development during such time as the relevant Management Scheme is in force.

3. A Party seeking to participate in the work of the Commission pursuant to subparagraph (b) or (c) above shall notify the Depositary of the basis upon which it seeks to become a member of the Commission. In the case of a Party which is not an Antarctic Treaty Consultative Party, such notification shall include a declaration of intent to abide by recommendations pursuant to Article IX(1) of the Antarctic Treaty. The Depositary shall communicate to each member of the Commission such notification and accompanying information.

4. The Commission shall consider the notification at its next meeting. In the event that a Party referred to in paragraph 2(b) above submitting a notification pursuant to paragraph 3 above is an Antarctic Treaty Consultative Party, it shall be deemed to have satisfied the requirements for Commission membership unless more than one-third of the members of the Commission object at the meeting at which such notification is considered. Any other Party submitting a notification shall be deemed to have satisfied the requirements for Commission membership if no member of the Commission objects at the meeting at which such notification is considered.

5. Each member of the Commission shall be represented by one representative who may be accompanied by alternate representatives and advisers.

6. Observer status in the Commission shall be open to any Party and to any Contracting Party to the Antarctic Treaty which is not a Party to this Convention.

Article 19

Commission Meetings

1. (*a*) The first meeting of the Commission, held for the purpose of taking organizational, financial and other decisions necessary for the effective functioning of this Convention and its institutions, shall be convened within six months of the entry into force of this Convention.

(*b*) After the Commission has held the meeting or meetings necessary to take the decisions referred to in subparagraph (a) above, the Commission shall not hold further meetings except in accordance with paragraph 2 or 3 below.

2. Meetings of the Commission shall be held within two months of:

(*a*) receipt of a notification pursuant to Article 39;

(*b*) a request by at least six members of the Commission; or

(*c*) a request by a member of a Regulatory Committee in accordance with Article 49(1).

3. The Commission may establish a regular schedule of meetings if it determines that it is necessary for the effective functioning of this Convention.

4. Unless the Commission decides otherwise, its meetings shall be convened by the Executive Secretary

5. Each member of the Commission shall be represented by one representative who may be accompanied by alternate representatives and advisers.

6. Observer status in the Commission shall be open to any Party and to any Contracting Party to the Antarctic Treaty which is not a Party to this Convention.

Article 20

Commission Procedure

1. The Commission shall elect from among its members a Chairman and two Vice–Chairmen, each of whom shall be a representative of a different Party.

2. (*a*) Until such time as the Commission has established a regular schedule of meetings in accordance with Article 19(3), the Chairman and Vice–Chairmen shall be elected to serve for a period of two years, provided that if no meeting is held during that period they shall continue to serve until the conclusion of the first meeting held thereafter.

(*b*) When a regular schedule of meetings has been established, the Chairman and Vice–Chairmen shall be elected to serve for a period of two years.

3. The Commission shall adopt its rules of procedure. Such rules may include provisions concerning the number of terms of office which the Chairman and Vice–Chairmen may serve and for the rotation of such offices.

4. The Commission may establish such subsidiary bodies as are necessary for the performance of its functions.

5. The Commission may decide to establish a permanent headquarters which shall be in New Zealand.

6. The Commission shall have legal personality and shall enjoy in the territory of each Party such legal capacity as may be necessary to perform its functions and achieve the objectives of this Convention.

7. The privileges and immunities to be enjoyed by the Commission, the Secretariat and representatives attending meetings in the territory of a Party shall be determined by agreement between the Commission and the Party concerned.

Article 21

Functions of the Commission

1. The functions of the Commission shall be:

(*a*) to facilitate and promote the collection and exchange of scientific, technical and other information and research projects necessary to predict, detect and assess the possible environmental impact of Antarctic mineral resource activities, including the monitoring of key environmental parameters and ecosystem components;

(*b*) to designate areas in which Antarctic mineral resource activities shall be prohibited or restricted in accordance with Article 13, and to perform the related functions assigned to it in that Article;

(*c*) to adopt measures for the protection of the Antarctic environment and dependent and associated ecosystems and for the promotion of safe and effective exploration and development techniques and, as it may deem appropriate, to make available a handbook of such measures;

(*d*) to determine, in accordance with Article 41, whether or not to identify an area for possible exploration and development, and to perform the related functions assigned to it in Article 42;

(*e*) to adopt measures relating to prospecting applicable to all relevant Operators:

(i) to determine for particular circumstances maximum drilling depths in accordance with Article 1(8);

(ii) to restrict or prohibit prospecting consistently with Articles 13, 37 and 38;

(*f*) to ensure the effective application of Articles 12(4), 37(7) and (8), 38(2) and 39(2), which require the submission to the Commission of information, notifications and reports;

(*g*) to give advance public notice of matters upon which it is requesting the advice of the Advisory Committee;

(*h*) to adopt measures relating to the availability and confidentiality of data and information, including measures pursuant to Article 16;

(*i*) to elaborate the principle of non-discrimination set forth in Article 14;

(*j*) to adopt measures with respect to maximum block sizes;

(*k*) to perform the functions assigned to it in Article 29;

(*l*) to review action by Regulatory Committees in accordance with Article 49;

(*m*) to adopt measures in accordance with Articles 6 and 41(1)(d) related to the promotion of cooperation and to participation in Antarctic mineral resource activities;

(*n*) to adopt general measures pursuant to Article 51(6);

(*o*) to take decisions on budgetary matters and adopt financial regulations in accordance with Article 35;

(*p*) to adopt measures regarding fees payable in connection with notifications submitted pursuant to Articles 37 and 39 and applications lodged pursuant to Articles 44 and 53, the purpose of which fees shall be to cover the administrative costs of handling such notifications and applications;

(*q*) to adopt measures regarding levies payable by Operators engaged in exploration and development, the principal purpose of which levies shall be to cover the costs of the institutions of this Convention;

(*r*) to determine in accordance with Article 35(7) the disposition of revenues, if any, accruing to the Commission which are surplus to the requirements for financing the budget pursuant to Article 35;

(*s*) to perform the functions assigned to it in Article 7(7) and (8);

(*t*) to perform the functions relating to inspection assigned to it in Article 12;

(*u*) to consider monitoring reports received pursuant to Article 52;

(*v*) to perform the functions relating to dispute settlement assigned to it in Article 59;

(*w*) to perform the functions relating to consultation and cooperation assigned to it in Article 10(2) and 34;

(*x*) to keep under review the conduct of Antarctic mineral resource activities with a view to safeguarding the protection of the Antarctic environment in the interest of all mankind; and

(*y*) to perform such other functions as are provided for elsewhere in this Convention.

2. In performing its functions the Commission shall seek and take full account of the views of the Advisory Committee provided in accordance with Article 26.

3. Each measure adopted by the Commission shall specify the date on which it comes into effect.

4. The Commission shall, subject to Article 16 and measures in effect pursuant to it and paragraph 1(h) above, ensure that a publicly available record of its meetings and decisions and of information, notifications and reports submitted to it is maintained.

Article 22

Decision Making in the Commission

1. The Commission shall take decisions on matters of substance by a three-quarters majority of the members present and voting. When a question arises as to whether a matter is one of substance or not, that matter shall be treated as one of substance unless otherwise decided by a three-quarters majority of the members present and voting.

2. Notwithstanding paragraph 1 above, consensus shall be required for the following:

(*a*) the adoption of the budget and decisions on budgetary and related matters pursuant to Article 22(1)(p), (q) and (r) and Article 35(1), (2), (3), (4) and (5);

(*b*) decisions taken pursuant to Article 21(1)(i);

(*c*) decisions taken pursuant to Article 41(2).

3. Decisions on matters of procedure shall be taken by a simple majority of the members present and voting.

4. Nothing in this Article shall be interpreted as preventing the Commission, in taking decisions on matters of substance, from endeavouring to reach a consensus.

5. For the purposes of this Article, consensus means the absence of a formal objection. If, with respect to any decision covered by paragraph 2(c) above, the Chairman of the Commission determines that there would be such an objection he shall consult the members of the Commission. If, as a result of these consultations, the Chairman determines that an objection would remain, he shall convene those members most directly interested for the purpose of seeking to reconcile the differences and producing a generally acceptable proposal.

Article 23

Advisory Committee

1. There is hereby established the Scientific, Technical and Environmental Advisory Committee.

2. Membership of the Advisory Committee shall be open to all Parties.

3. Each member of the advisory Committee shall be represented by one representative with suitable scientific, technical or environmental competence who may be accompanied by alternate representatives and by experts and advisers.

4. Observer status in the Advisory Committee shall be open to any Contracting Party to the Antarctic Treaty or to the Convention on the Conservation of Antarctic Marine Living Resources which is not a Party to this Convention.

Article 24

Advisory Committee Meetings

1. Unless the Commission decides otherwise, the Advisory Committee shall be convened for its first meeting within six months of the first meeting of the Commission. It shall meet thereafter as necessary to fulfill its functions on the basis of a schedule established by the Commission.

2. Meetings of the Advisory Committee, in addition to those scheduled pursuant to paragraph 1 above, shall be convened at the request of at least six members of the Commission or pursuant to Article 40(1).

3. Unless the Commission decides otherwise, the meetings of the Advisory Committee shall be convened by the Executive Secretary.

Article 25

Advisory Committee Procedure

1. The Advisory Committee shall elect from among its members a Chairman and two Vice–Chairmen, each of whom shall be a representative of a different Party.

2. (*a*) Until such time as the Commission has established a schedule of meetings in accordance with Article 24(1), the Chairman and Vice–Chairmen shall be elected to serve for a period of two years, provided that if no meeting is held during that period they shall continue to serve until the conclusion of the first meeting held thereafter.

(*b*) When a schedule of meetings has been established, the Chairman and Vice–Chairmen shall be elected to serve for a period of two years.

3. The Advisory Committee shall give advance public notice of its meetings and of matters to be considered at each meeting so as to permit the receipt and consideration of views on such matters from international organizations having an interest in them. For this purpose the Advisory Committee may, subject to review by the Commission, establish procedures for the transmission of relevant information to these organizations.

4. The Advisory Committee shall, by a two-thirds majority of the members present and voting, adopt its rules of procedure. Such rules may include provisions concerning the number of terms of office which the Chairman and Vice–Chairmen may serve and for the rotation of such offices. The rules of procedure and any amendments thereto shall be subject to approval by the Commission.

5. The Advisory Committee may establish such subcommittees, subject to budgetary approval, as may be necessary for the performance of its functions.

Article 26

Functions of the Advisory Committee

1. The Advisory Committee shall advise the Commission and Regulatory Committees, as required by this Convention, or as requested by them, on the scientific, technical and environmental aspects of Antarctic mineral resources activities. It shall provide a forum for consultation and cooperation concerning the collection, exchange and evaluation of information related to the scientific, technical and environmental aspects of Antarctic mineral resource activities.

2. It shall provide advice to:

(*a*) the Commission relating to its functions under Articles 21(1)(a) to (f), (u) and 35(7)(a) (in matters relating to scientific research) as well as on the implementation of Article 4; and

(*b*) Regulatory Committees with respect to:

(i) the implementation of Article 4;

(ii) scientific, technical and environmental aspects of Articles 43(3) and (5), 45, 47, 51, 52 and 54;

(iii) data to be collected and reported in accordance with Articles 47 and 52; and

(iv) the scientific, technical and environmental implications of reports and reported data provided in accordance with Articles 47 and 53.

3. It shall provide advice to the Commission and to Regulatory Committees on:

(*a*) criteria in respect of the judgments required under Article 4(2) and (3) for the purposes of Article 4(1);

(*b*) types of data and information required to carry out its functions, and how they should be collected reported and archived;

(*c*) scientific research which would contribute to the base of data and information required in subparagraph (b) above;

(*d*) effective procedures and systems for data and information analysis, evaluation, presentation and dissemination to facilitate the judgments referred to in Article 4; and

(*e*) possibilities for scientific, technical and environmental cooperation amongst interested Parties which are developing countries and other Parties.

4. The Advisory Committee, in providing advice on decisions to be taken in accordance with Articles 41, 43, 45 and 54 shall, in each case, undertake a comprehensive environmental and technical assessment of the proposed actions. Such assessments shall be based on all information, and any amplifications thereof, available to the Advisory Committee, including the information provided pursuant to Articles 39(2)(e), 44(2)(b)(iii) and 53(2)(b). The assessments of the Advisory Committee shall, in each case, address the nature and scope of the decisions to be taken and shall include consideration, as appropriate, of, *inter alia:*

(*a*) the adequacy of existing information to enable informed judgments to be made;

(*b*) the nature, extent, duration and intensity of likely direct environmental impacts resulting from the proposed activity;

(*c*) possible indirect impacts;

(*d*) means and alternatives by which such direct or indirect impacts might be reduced, including environmental consequences of the alternative of not proceeding;

(*e*) cumulative impacts of the proposed activity in the light of existing or planned activities;

(*f*) capacity to respond effectively to accidents with potential environmental effects;

(*g*) the environmental significance of unavoidable impacts; and

(*h*) the probabilities of accidents and their environmental consequences.

5. In preparing its advice the Advisory Committee may seek information and advice from other scientists and experts or scientific organizations as may be required on an *ad hoc* basis.

6. The Advisory Committee shall, with a view to promoting international participation in Antarctic mineral resource activities as provided for in Article 6, provide advice concerning the availability to interested developing country Parties and other Parties, of the information referred to in paragraph 3 above, of training programmes related to scientific, technical and environmental matters bearing on Antarctic mineral resource activities, and of opportunities for cooperation among Parties in these programmes.

Article 27

Reporting by the Advisory Committee

The Advisory Committee shall present a report on each of its meetings to the Commission and to any relevant Regulatory Committee. The report shall cover all matters considered at the meeting and shall reflect the conclusions reached and all the views expressed by members of the Advisory Committee. The report shall be circulated by the Executive Secretary to all Parties, and to observers attending the meeting, and shall thereupon be made publicly available.

Article 28

Special Meeting of Parties

1. A Special Meeting of Parties shall, as required, be convened in accordance with Article 40(2) and shall have the functions, in relation to the identification of an area for possible exploration and development, specified in Article 40(3).

2. Membership of a Special Meeting of Parties shall be open to all Parties, each of which shall be represented by one representative who may be accompanied by alternate representative who may be accompanied by alternate representatives and advisers.

3. Observer status at a Special Meeting of Parties shall be open to any Contracting Party to the Antarctic Treaty which is not a Party to this Convention.

4. Each Special Meeting of Parties shall elect from among its members a Chairman and Vice–Chairman, each of whom shall serve for the duration of that meeting. The Chairman and Vice–Chairman shall not be representatives of the same Party.

5. The Special Meeting of Parties shall, by a two-thirds majority of the members present and voting, adopt its rules of procedure. Until such time as this has been done the Special Meeting of Parties shall apply provisional rules of procedure drawn up by the Commission.

6. Unless the Commission decides otherwise, a Special Meeting of Parties shall be convened by the Executive Secretary and shall be held at the same venue as the meeting of the Commission convened to consider the identification of an area for possible exploration and development.

Article 29

Regulatory Committees

1. An Antarctic Mineral Resources Regulatory Committee shall be established for each area identified by the Commission pursuant to Article 41.

2. Subject to paragraph 6 below, each Regulatory Committee shall consist of 10 members. Membership shall be determined by the Commission in accordance with this Article and, taking into account Article 9, shall include:

(*a*) the member, if any, or if there are more than one, those members of the Commission identified by reference to Article 9(b) which assert rights or claims in the identified area;

(*b*) the two members of the Commission also identified by reference to Article 9(b) which assert a basis of claim in Antarctica;

(*c*) other members of the Commission determined in accordance with this Article so that the Regulatory Committee shall, subject to paragraph 6 below, consist, in total, of 10 members;

(i) four members identified by reference to Article 9(b) which assert rights or claims, including the member or members, if any, referred to in subparagraph (a) above; and

(ii) six members which do not assert rights or claims as described in Article 9(b), including the two members referred to in subparagraph (b) above.

3. Upon the identification of an area in accordance with Article 41(2), the Chairman of the Commission shall, as soon as possible and in any event within 90

days, make a recommendation to the Commission concerning the membership of the Regulatory Committee. To this end the Chairman shall consult, as appropriate, with the Chairman of the Advisory Committee and all members of the Commission. Such recommendation shall comply with the requirements of paragraphs 2 and 4 of this Article and shall ensure:

(*a*) the inclusion of members of the Commission which, whether through prospecting, scientific research or otherwise, have contributed substantial scientific, technical or environmental information relevant to the identification of the area by the Commission pursuant to Article 41;

(*b*) adequate and equitable representation of developing country members of the Commission, having regard to the overall balance between developed and developing country members of the Commission, including at least three developing country members of the Commission;

(*c*) that account is taken of the value of a rotation of membership of Regulatory Committees as a further means of ensuring equitable representation of members of the Commission.

4. (*a*) When there are one or more members of the Regulatory Committee referred to in paragraph 2(a) above, the Chairman of the Commission shall make the recommendation in respect of paragraph 2(c)(i) above upon the nomination, if any, of such member or members which shall take into account paragraph 3 above, in particular subparagraph (b) of that paragraph.

(*b*) in making the recommendation in respect of paragraph 2(c)(ii) above, the Chairman of the Commission shall give full weight to the views (which shall take into account paragraph 3 above) which may be presented on behalf of those members of the Commission which do not assert rights of or claims to territorial sovereignty in Antarctica and, with reference to the requirements of paragraph 3(b) above, to the views which may be presented on behalf of the developing countries among them.

5. The recommendation of the Chairman of the Commission shall be deemed to have been approved by the Commission if it does not decide otherwise at the same meeting as the recommendation is submitted. In taking any decision in accordance with this Article the Commission shall ensure that the requirements of paragraphs 2 and 3 above are complied with and that the nomination, if any, referred to in paragraph 4(a) above is given effect.

6. (*a*) If a member of the Commission which has sponsored prospecting in the identified area and submitted the notification pursuant to Article 39 upon which the Commission based its identification of the area pursuant to Article 41, is not a member of the Regulatory Committee by virtue of paragraphs 2 and 3 above, that member of the Commission shall be a member of the Regulatory Committee until such time as an application for an exploration permit is lodged pursuant to Article 44.

(*b*) If a Party lodging an application for an exploration permit pursuant to Article 44 is not a member of the Regulatory Committee by virtue of paragraphs 2 and 3 above, that Party shall be a member of the Regulatory Committee for its consideration of that application. Should such application result in approval of a Management Scheme pursuant to Article 48, the Party in question shall remain a member of the Regulatory Committee during such time as that Management Scheme is in force with the right to take part in decisions on matters affecting that Management Scheme.

7. Nothing in this Article shall be interpreted as affecting Article IV of the Antarctic Treaty.

Article 30

Regulatory Committee Procedure

1. The first meeting of each Regulatory Committee shall be convened by the Executive Secretary in accordance with Article 43(1). Each Regulatory Committee shall meet thereafter when and where necessary to fulfill its functions.

2. Each member of a Regulatory Committee shall be represented by one representative who may be accompanied by alternate representatives and advisers.

3. Each Regulatory Committee shall elect from among its members a Chairman and Vice–Chairman. The Chairman and Vice–Chairman shall not be representatives of the same Party.

4. Any Party may attend meetings of a Regulatory Committee as an observer.

5. Each Regulatory Committee shall adopt its rules of procedure. Such rules may include provisions concerning the period and number of terms of office which the Chairman and Vice–Chairman may serve and for the rotation of such offices.

Article 31

Functions of Regulatory Committees

1. The Functions of each Regulatory Committee shall be:

(*a*) to undertake the preparatory work provided for in Article 43;

(*b*) to consider application for exploration and development permits in accordance with Articles 45, 46 and 54;

(*c*) to approve Management Schemes and issue exploration and development permits in accordance with Articles 47, 48 and 54;

(*d*) to monitor exploration and development activities in accordance with Article 52;

(*e*) to perform the functions assigned to it in Article 51;

(*f*) to perform the functions relating to inspection assigned to it in Article 12;

(*g*) to perform the functions relating to dispute settlement assigned to it in Article 47(r); and

(*h*) to perform such other functions as are provided for elsewhere in this Convention.

2. In performing its functions each Regulatory Committee shall seek and take full account of the views of the Advisory Committee provided in accordance with Article 26.

3. Each Regulatory Committee shall, subject to Article 16 and measures in effect pursuant to it and Article 21(1)(h), ensure that a publicly available record of its decisions, and of Management Scheme in force, is maintained.

Article 32

Decision Making in Regulatory Committees

1. Decisions by a Regulatory Committee pursuant to Articles 48 and 54(5) shall be taken by a two-thirds majority of the members present and voting, which majority shall include a simple majority of those members present and voting referred to in Article 29(2)(*c*)(i) and also a simple majority of those members present and voting referred to in Article 29(2)(*c*)(ii).

2. Decisions by a Regulatory Committee pursuant to Article 43(3) and (5) shall be taken by a two-thirds majority of the members present and voting, which majority

shall include at least half of those members present and voting referred to in Article 29(2)(c)(i) and also at least half of those members present and voting referred to in Article 29(2)(c)(ii).

3. Decisions on all other matters of substance shall be taken by a two-thirds majority of the members present and voting. When a question arises as to whether a matter is one of substance or not, that matter shall be treated as one of substance unless otherwise decided by a two-thirds majority of the members present and voting.

4. Decisions on matters of procedure shall be taken by a simple majority of the members present and voting.

5. Nothing in this Article shall be interpreted as preventing a Regulatory Committee, in taking decisions on matters of substance, from endeavoring to reach a consensus.

Article 33

Secretariat

1. The Commission may establish a Secretariat to serve the Commission, Regulatory Committees, the Advisory Committee, the Special Meeting of Parties and any subsidiary bodies established.

2. The Commission may appoint an Executive Secretary, who shall be the head of the Secretariat, according to such procedures and on such terms and conditions as the Commission may determine. The Executive Secretary shall serve for a four year term and may be reappointed.

3. The Commission may, with due regard to the need for efficiency and economy, authorize such staff establishment for the Secretariat as may be necessary. The Executive Secretary shall appoint, direct and supervise the staff according to such rules and procedures and on such terms and conditions as the Commission may determine.

4. The Secretariat shall perform the functions specified in this Convention and, subject to the approved budget, the tasks entrusted to it by the Commission, Regulatory Committees, the Advisory Committee and the Special Meeting of Parties.

Article 34

Cooperation with International Organizations

1. The Commission and, as appropriate, the Advisory Committee shall cooperate with the Antarctic Treaty Consultative Parties, the Contracting Parties to the Convention for the Conservation of Antarctic Seals, the Commission for the Conservation of Antarctic Marine Living Resources, and the Scientific Committee on Antarctic Research.

2. The Commission shall cooperate with the United Nations, its relevant Specialized Agencies, and, as appropriate, any international organization which may have competence in respect of mineral resources in areas adjacent to those covered by this Convention.

3. The Commission shall also, as appropriate, cooperate with the International Union for the Conservation of Nature and Natural Resources, and with other relevant international organizations, including non-governmental organizations, having a scientific, technical or environmental interest in Antarctica.

4. The Commission may, as appropriate, accord observer status in the Commission and in the Advisory Committee to such relevant international organizations, including non-governmental organizations, as might assist in the work of the institution in question. Observer status at a Special Meeting of Parties shall be open to such

organizations as have been accorded observer status in the Commission or the Advisory Committee.

5. The Commission may enter into agreements with the organizations referred to in this Article.

Article 35

Financial Provisions

1. The Commission shall adopt a budget, on an annual or other appropriate basis, for:

(*a*) its activities and the activities of Regulatory Committees, the Advisory Committee, the Special Meeting of Parties, any subsidiary bodies established and the Secretariat; and

(*b*) the progressive reimbursement of any contributions paid under paragraphs 5 and 6 below whenever revenues under paragraph 4 below exceed expenditure.

2. The first draft budget shall be submitted by the Depositary at least 90 days before the first meeting of the Commission. At that meeting the Commission shall adopt its first budget and decide upon arrangements for the preparation of subsequent budgets.

3. The Commission shall adopt financial regulations.

4. Subject to paragraph 5 below, the budget shall be financed, *inter alia,* by:

(*a*) fees prescribed pursuant, to Articles 21(1)(p) and 43(2)(b);

(*b*) levies on Operators, subject to any measures adopted by the Commission in accordance with Article 21(1)(q), pursuant to Article 47(k)(i); and

(*c*) such other financial payments by Operators pursuant to Article 47(k)(ii) as may be required to be paid to the institutions of this Convention.

5. If the budget is not fully financed by revenues in accordance with paragraph 4 above, and subject to reimbursement in accordance with paragraph 1(b) above, the budget shall, to the extent of any shortfall and subject to paragraph 6 below, be financed by contributions from the members of the Commission. To this end, the Commission shall adopt as soon as possible a method of equitable sharing of contributions to the budget. The budget shall, in the meantime, to the extent of any shortfall, be financed by equal contributions from each member of the Commission.

6. In adopting the method of contributions referred to in paragraph 5 above the Commission shall consider the extent to which members of and observers at institutions of this Convention may be called upon to contribute to the cost of those institutions.

7. The Commission, in determining the disposition of revenues accruing to it, which are surplus to the requirements for financing the budget pursuant to this Article, shall:

(*a*) promote scientific research in Antarctica, particularly that related to the Antarctic environment and Antarctic resources, and a wide spread of participation in such research by all Parties, in particular developing country Parties;

(*b*) ensure that the interests of the members of Regulatory Committees having the most direct interest in the matter in relation to the areas in question are respected in any disposition of that surplus.

8. The finances of the Commission, Regulatory Committees, the Advisory Committee, the Special Meeting of Parties, any subsidiary bodies established and the Secretariat shall accord with the financial regulations adopted by the Commission and shall be subject to an annual audit by external auditors selected by the Commission.

9. Each member of the Commission, Regulatory Committees, the Advisory Committee, the Special Meeting of Parties and any subsidiary bodies established, as well as any observer at a meeting of any of the institutions of this Convention, shall meet its own expenses arising from attendance at meetings.

10. A member of the Commission that fails to pay its contribution for two consecutive years shall not, during the period of its continuing subsequent default, have the right to participate in the taking of decisions in any of the institutions of this Convention. If it continues to be in default for a further two consecutive years, Commission shall decide what further action should be taken, which may include loss by that member of the right to participate in meetings of the institutions of this Convention. Such member shall resume the full enjoyment of its rights upon payment of the outstanding contributions.

11. Nothing in this Article shall be construed as prejudicing the position of any member of a Regulatory Committee on the outcome of consideration by the Regulatory Committee of terms and conditions in a Management Scheme pursuant to Article 47(k)(ii).

Article 36

Official and Working Languages

The official and working languages of the Commission, Regulatory Committees, the Advisory Committee, the Special Meeting of Parties and any meeting convened under Article 64 shall be English, French, Russian and Spanish.

CHAPTER III: PROSPECTING

Article 37

Prospecting

1. Prospecting shall not confer upon any Operator any right to Antarctic mineral resources.

2. Prospecting shall at all times be conducted in compliance with this Convention and with measures in effect pursuant to this Convention, but shall not require authorization by the institutions of this Convention.

3. (*a*) The Sponsoring State shall ensure that its Operators undertaking prospecting maintain the necessary financial and technical means to comply with Article 8(1), and, to the extent that any such Operator fails to take response action as required in Article 8(1), shall ensure that this is undertaken.

(*b*) The Sponsoring State shall also ensure that its Operators undertaking prospecting maintain financial capacity, commensurate with the nature and level of the activity undertaken and the risks involved, to comply with Article 8(2).

4. In cases where more than one Operator is engaged in prospecting in the same general area, the Sponsoring State or States shall ensure that those cooperators conduct their activities with due regard to each others' rights.

5. Where an Operator wishes to conduct prospecting in an area identified under Article 41 in which another Operator has been authorized to undertake exploration or development, the Sponsoring State shall ensure that such prospecting is carried out subject to the rights of any authorized Operator and any requirements to protect its rights specified by the relevant Regulatory Committee.

6. Each Operator shall ensure upon cessation of prospecting the removal of all installations and equipment and site rehabilitation. On the request of the Sponsoring State, the Commission may waive the obligation to remove installations and equipment.

7. The Sponsoring State shall notify the Commission at least nine months in advance of the commencement of planned prospecting. The notification shall be accompanied by such fees as may be established by the Commission in accordance with Article 21(1)(p) and shall:

(*a*) identify, by reference to coordinates of latitude and longitude or identifiable geographic features, the general area in which the prospecting is to take place;

(*b*) broadly identify the mineral resource or resources which are to be the subject of the prospecting;

(*c*) describe the prospecting, including the methods to be used, and the general programme of work to be undertaken and its expected duration;

(*d*) provide an assessment of the possible environmental and other impacts of the prospecting, taking into account possible cumulative impacts as referred to in Article 4(5);

(*e*) describe the measures, including monitoring programmes, to be adopted to avoid harmful environmental consequences or undue interference with other established uses of Antarctica, and outline the measures to be put into effect in the event of any accident and contingency plans for evacuation in an emergency;

(*f*) provide details on the Operator and certify that it:

(i) has a substantial and genuine link with the Sponsoring State as defined in Article 1(12); and

(ii) is financially and technically qualified to carry out the proposed prospecting in accordance with this Convention; and

(*g*) provide such further information as may be required by measures adopted by the Commission.

8. The Sponsoring State shall subsequently provide to the Commission:

(*a*) notification of any changes to the information referred to in paragraph 7 above;

(*b*) notification of the cessation of prospecting, including removal of any installations and equipment as well as site rehabilitation; and

(*c*) a general annual report on the prospecting undertaken by the Operator.

9. Notifications and reports submitted pursuant to this Article shall be circulated by the Executive Secretary without delay to all Parties and observers attending Commission meetings.

10. Paragraphs 7, 8 and 9 above shall not be interpreted as requiring the disclosure of data and information of commercial value.

11. The Sponsoring State shall ensure that basic data and information of commercial value generated by prospecting are maintained in archives and may at any time release part of or all such data and information, on conditions which it shall establish, for scientific or environmental purposes.

12. The Sponsoring State shall ensure that basic data and information, other than interpretative data, generated by prospecting are made readily available when such data and information are not, or are no longer, of commercial value and, in any event, no later than 10 years after the year the data and information were collected, unless it certifies to the Commission that the data and information continue to have commercial value. It shall review at regular intervals whether such data and information may be released and shall report the results of such reviews to the Commission.

13. The Commission may adopt measures consistent with this Article relating to the release of data and information of commercial value including requirements for

certifications, the frequency of reviews and maximum time limits for extensions of the protection of such data and information.

Article 38

Consideration of Prospecting by the Commission

1. If a member of the Commission considers that a notification submitted in accordance with Article 37(7) or (8), or ongoing prospecting, causes concern as to consistency with this Convention or measures in effect pursuant thereto, that member may request the Sponsoring State to provide a clarification. If that member considers that an adequate response is not forthcoming from the Sponsoring State within a reasonable time, the member may request that the Commission be convened in accordance with Article 19(2)(b) to consider the question and take appropriate action.

2. If measures applicable to all relevant Operators are adopted by the Commission following a request made in accordance with paragraph 1 above, Sponsoring States that have submitted notifications in accordance with Article 37(7) or (8), and Sponsoring States whose Operators are conducting prospecting, shall ensure that the plans and activities of their Operators are modified to the extent necessary to conform with those measures within such time limit as the Commission may prescribe, and shall notify the Commission accordingly.

CHAPTER IV: EXPLORATION

Article 39

Requests for Identification of an Area for Possible Exploration and Development

1. Any Party may submit to the Executive Secretary a notification requesting that the Commission identify an area for possible exploration and development of a particular mineral resource or resources.

2. Any such notification shall be accompanied by such fees as may be established by the Commission in accordance with Article 21(1)(p) and shall contain:

(*a*) a precise delineation, including coordinates, of the area proposed for identification;

(*b*) specification of the resource or resources for which the area would be identified and any relevant data and information, excluding data and information of commercial value, concerning that resource or those resources, including a geological description of the proposed area;

(*c*) a detailed description of the physical and environmental characteristics of the proposed area;

(*d*) a description of the likely scale of exploration and development for the resource or resources involved in the proposed area and of the methods which could be employed in such exploration and development;

(*e*) a detailed assessment of the environmental and other impacts of possible exploration and development for the resource or resources involved, taking into account Articles 15 and 26(4); and

(*f*) such other information as may be required pursuant to measures adopted by the Commission.

3. A notification under paragraph 1 above shall be referred promptly by the Executive Secretary to all Parties and shall be circulated to observers attending the meeting of the Commission to be convened pursuant to Article 19(2)(a).

Article 40

Action by the Advisory Committee and Special Meeting of Parties

1. The Advisory Committee shall meet as soon as possible after the meeting of the Commission convened pursuant to Article 19(2)(a) has commenced. The Advisory Committee shall provide advice to the Commission on the notification submitted pursuant to Article 39(1). The Commission may prescribe a time limit for the provision of such advice.

2. A Special Meeting of Parties shall meet as soon as possible after circulation of the report of the Advisory Committee and in any event not later than two months after that report has been circulated.

3. The Special Meeting of Parties shall consider whether identification of an area by the Commission in accordance with the request contained in the notification would be consistent with this Convention, and shall report thereon to the Commission as soon as possible and in any event not later than 21 days from the commencement of the meeting.

4. The report of the Special Meeting of Parties to the Commission shall reflect the conclusions reached and all the views expressed by Parties participating in the meeting.

Article 41

Action by the Commission

1. The Commission shall, as soon as possible after receipt of the report of the Special Meeting of Parties, consider whether or not it will identify an area as requested. Taking full account of the views and giving special weight to the conclusions of the Special Meeting of Parties, and taking full account of the views and the conclusions of the Advisory Committee, the Commission shall determine whether such identification would be consistent with this Convention. For this purpose:

(*a*) the Commission shall ensure that an area to be identified shall be such that, taking into account all factors relevant to such identification, including the physical, geological, environmental and other characteristics of such area, it forms a coherent unit for the purposes of resource management. The Commission shall thus consider whether an area to be identified should include all or part of that which was requested in the notification and, subject to the necessary assessments having been made, adjacent areas not covered by that notification;

(*b*) the Commission shall consider whether there are, within an area requested or to be identified, any areas in which exploration and development are or should be prohibited or restricted in accordance with Article 13;

(*c*) the Commission shall specify the mineral resource or resources for which the area would be identified;

(*d*) the Commission shall give effect to Article 6, by elaborating opportunities for joint ventures or different forms of participation, up to a defined level, including procedures for offering such participation, in possible exploration and development, within the area, by interested Parties which are Antarctic Treaty Consultative Parties and by other interested Parties, in particular, developing countries in either category;

(*e*) the Commission shall prescribe any additional associated conditions necessary to ensure that an area to be identified is consistent with other provisions of this Convention and may prescribe general guidelines relating to the operational requirements for exploration and development in an area to be identified including measures establishing maximum block sizes and advice concerning related support activities; and (*f*) the Commission shall give effect to the requirement in Article 59 to establish additional procedures for the settlement of disputes.

2. After it has completed its consideration in accordance with paragraph 1 above, the Commission shall identify an area for possible exploration and development if there is a consensus of Commission members that such identification is consistent with this Convention.

Article 42

Revision in the Scope of an Identified Area

1. If, after an area has been identified in accordance with Article 41, a Party requests identification of an area, all or part of which is contained within the boundaries of the area already identified but in respect of a mineral resource or resources different from any resource in respect of which the area has already been identified, the request shall be dealt with in accordance with Articles 39, 40 and 41. Should the Commission identify an area in respect of such different mineral resource or resources, it shall have regard, in addition to the requirements of Article 41(1)(a), to the desirability of specifying the boundaries of the area in such a way that it can be assigned to the Regulatory Committee with competence for the area already identified.

2. In the light of increased knowledge bearing on the effective management of the area, and after seeking the views of the Advisory Committee and the relevant Regulatory Committee, the Commission may amend the boundaries of any area it has identified. In making any such amendment the Commission shall ensure that authorized exploration and development in the area are not adversely affected. Unless there are compelling reasons for doing so, the Commission shall not amend the boundaries of an area it has identified in such a way as to involve a change in the composition of the relevant Regulatory Committee.

Article 43

Preparatory Work by Regulatory Committees

1. As soon as possible after the identification of an area pursuant to Article 41, the relevant Regulatory Committee established in accordance with Article 29 shall be convened.

2. The Regulatory Committee shall:

(*a*) subject to any measures adopted by the Commission pursuant to Article 21(1)(j) relating to maximum block sizes, divide its area of competence into blocks in respect of which applications for exploration and development may be submitted and make provision for a limit in appropriate circumstances on the number of blocks to be accorded to any Party;

(*b*) subject to any measures adopted by the Commission pursuant to Article 21(1)(p), establish fees to be paid with any application for an exploration or development permit lodged pursuant to Article 44 or 53;

(*c*) establish periods within which applications for exploration and development may be lodged, all applications received within each such period being considered as simultaneous;

(*d*) establish procedures for the handling of applications; and

(*e*) determine a method of resolving competing applications which are not resolved in accordance with Article 45(4)(a), which method shall, provided that all other requirements of this Convention are satisfied and consistently with measures adopted pursuant to Article 41(1)(d), include priority for the application with the broadest participation among interested Parties which are Antarctic Treaty

Consultative Parties and other interested Parties, in particular, developing countries in either category.

3. The Regulatory Committee shall adopt guidelines which are consistent with, and which taken together with, the provisions of this Convention and measures of general applicability adopted by the Commission, as well as associated conditions and general guidelines adopted by the Commission when identifying the area, shall, by addressing the relevant items in Article 47, identify the general requirements for exploration and development in its area of competence.

4. Upon adoption of guidelines under paragraph 3 above the Executive Secretary shall, without delay, inform all members of the Commission of the decisions taken by the Regulatory Committee pursuant to paragraphs 2 and 3 above and shall make them publicly available together with relevant measures, associated conditions and general guidelines adopted by the Commission.

5. The Regulatory Committee may from time to time revise guidelines adopted under paragraph 3 above, taking into account any views of the Commission.

6. In performing its functions under paragraphs 3 and 5 above, the Regulatory Committee shall seek and take full account of the views of the Advisory Committee provided in accordance with Article 26.

Article 44
Application for an Exploration Permit

1. Following completion of the work undertaken pursuant to Article 43, any Party, on behalf of an Operator for which it is the Sponsoring State, may lodge with the Regulatory Committee an application for an exploration permit within the periods established by the Regulatory Committee pursuant to Article 43(2)(c).

2. An application shall be accompanied by the fees established by the Regulatory Committee in accordance with Article 43(2)(b) and shall contain:

(*a*) a detailed description of the Operator, including its managerial structure, financial composition and resources and technical expertise, and, in the case of an Operator being a joint venture, the inclusion of a detailed description of the degree to which Parties are involved in the Operator through, *inter alia,* juridical persons with which Parties have substantial and genuine links, so that each component of the joint venture can be easily attributed to a Party or Parties for the purposes of identifying the level of Antarctic mineral resource activities thereof, which description of substantial and genuine links shall include a description of equity sharing;

(*b*) a detailed description of the proposed exploration activities and a description in as much detail as possible of proposed development activities, including:

(i) an identification of the mineral resource or resources and the block to which the application applies;

(ii) a detailed explanation of how the proposed activities conform with the general requirements referred to in Article 43(3);

(iii) a detailed assessment of the environmental and other impacts of the proposed activities, taking into account Articles 15 and 26(4); and

(iv) a description of the capacity to respond effectively to accidents, especially those with potential environmental effects;

(*c*) a certification by the Sponsoring State of the capacity of the Operator to comply with the general requirements referred to in Article 43(3);

(*d*) a certification by the Sponsoring State of the technical competence and financial capacity of the Operator and that the Operator has a substantial and genuine link with it as defined in Article 1(12);

(*e*) a description of the manner in which the application complies with any measures adopted by the Commission pursuant to Article 41(1)(d), and

(*f*) such further information as may be required by the Regulatory Committee or in measures adopted by the Commission.

Article 45
Examination of Applications

1. The Regulatory Committee shall meet as soon as possible after an application has been lodged pursuant to Article 44, for the purpose of elaborating a Management Scheme. In performing this function it shall:

(*a*) determine whether the application contains sufficient or adequate information pursuant to Article 44(2). To this end, it may at any time seek further information from the Sponsoring State consistent with Article 44(2);

(*b*) consider the exploration and development activities, proposed in the application, and such elaborations, revisions or adaptations as necessary:

(i) to ensure their consistency with this Convention as well as measures in effect pursuant thereto and the general requirements referred to in Article 43(3); and

(ii) to prescribe the specific terms and conditions of a Management Scheme in accordance with Article 47.

2. At any time during the process of consideration described above, the Regulatory Committee may decline the application if it considers that the activities proposed therein cannot be elaborated, revised or adapted to ensure consistency with this Convention as well as measures in effect pursuant thereto and the general requirements referred to in Article 43(3).

3. In performing its functions under this Article, the Regulatory Committee shall seek and take full account of the views of the Advisory Committee. To that end the Regulatory Committee shall refer to the Advisory Committee all parts of the application which are necessary for it to provide advice pursuant to Article 26, together with any other relevant information.

4. If two or more applications meeting the requirements of Article 44(2) are lodged in respect of the same block:

(*a*) the competing applicants shall be invited by the Regulatory Committee to resolve the competition amongst themselves, by means of their own choice within a prescribed period;

(*b*) if the competition is not resolved pursuant to subparagraph (a) above it shall be resolved by the Regulatory Committee in accordance with the method determined by it pursuant to Article 43(2)(e).

Article 46
Management Scheme

In performing its functions under Article 45, including the preparation of a Management Scheme, and under Article 54, the Regulatory Committee shall have recourse to the Sponsoring State and the member or members, if any, referred to in Article 29(2)(a) and, as may be required, one or two additional members of the Regulatory Committee.

Article 47
Scope of the Management Scheme

The Management Scheme shall prescribe the specific terms and conditions for exploration and development of the mineral resource or resources concerned within the relevant block. Such terms and conditions shall be consistent with the general requirements referred to in Article 43(3), and shall cover, *inter alia:*

(*a*) duration of exploration and development permits;

(*b*) measures and procedures for the protection of the Antarctic environment and dependent and associated ecosystems, including methods, activities and undertakings by the Operator to minimize environmental risks and damage;

(*c*) provision for necessary and timely response action, including prevention, containment and clean up and removal measures, for restoration to the *status quo ante,* and for contingency plans, resources and equipment to enable such action to be taken;

(*d*) procedures for the implementation of different stages of exploration and development;

(*e*) performance requirements;

(*f*) technical and safety specifications, including standards and procedures to ensure safe operations;

(*g*) monitoring and inspection;

(*h*) liability;

(*i*) procedures for the development of mineral deposits which extend outside the area covered by a permit;

(*j*) resource conservation requirements;

(*k*) financial obligations of the Operator including:

(i) levies in accordance with measures adopted pursuant to Article 21(1)(q);

(ii) payments in the nature of and similar to taxes, royalties or payments in kind;

(*l*) financial guarantees and insurance;

(*m*) assignment and relinquishment;

(*n*) suspension and modification of the Management Scheme, or cancellation of the Management Scheme, exploration or development permit, and the imposition of monetary penalties, in accordance with Article 51;

(*o*) procedures for agreed modifications;

(*p*) enforcement of the Management Scheme;

(*q*) applicable law to the extent necessary;

(*r*) effective additional procedures for the settlement of disputes;

(*s*) provisions to avoid and to resolve conflict with other legitimate uses of Antarctica;

(*t*) data and information collection, reporting and notification requirements;

(*u*) confidentiality; and

(*v*) removal of installations and equipment, as well as site rehabilitation.

Article 48

Approval of the Management Scheme

A Management Scheme prepared in accordance with Articles 45, 46 and 47 shall be subject to approval pursuant to Article 32. Such approval shall constitute authorization for the issue without delay of an exploration permit by the Regulatory Committee. The exploration permit shall accord exclusive rights to the Operator to explore and, subject to Articles 53 and 54, to develop the mineral resource or resources which are the subject of the Management Scheme exclusively in accordance with the terms and conditions of the Management Scheme.

Article 49
Review

1. Any member of the Commission, or any member of a Regulatory Committee, may within one month of a decision by that Regulatory Committee to approve a Management Scheme or issue a development permit, request that the Commission be convened in accordance with Article 19(2)(b) or (c), as the case may be, to review the decision of the Regulatory Committee for consistency with the decision taken by the Commission to identify the area pursuant to Article 41 and any measures in effect relevant to that decision.

2. The Commission shall complete its consideration within three months of a request made pursuant to paragraph 1 above. In performing its functions the Commission shall not assume the functions of the Regulatory Committee, nor shall it substitute its discretion for that of the Regulatory Committee.

3. Should the Commission determine that a decision to approve a Management Scheme or issue a development permit is inconsistent with the decision taken by the Commission to identify the area pursuant to Article 41 and any measures in effect relevant to that decision, it may request that Regulatory Committee to reconsider its decision.

Article 50
Rights of Authorized Operators

1. No Management Scheme shall be suspended or modified and no Management Scheme, exploration or development permit shall be cancelled without the consent of the Sponsoring State except pursuant to Article 51, or Article 54 or the Management Scheme itself.

2. Each Operator authorized to conduct activities pursuant to a Management Scheme shall exercise its rights with due regard to the rights of other Operators undertaking exploration or development in the same identified area.

Article 51
Suspension, Modification or Cancellation of the Management Scheme and Monetary Penalties

1. If a Regulatory Committee determines that exploration or development authorised pursuant to a Management Scheme has resulted or is about to result in impacts on the Antarctic environment or dependent or associated ecosystems beyond those judged acceptable pursuant to this Convention, it shall suspend the relevant activities and as soon as possible modify the Management Scheme so as to avoid such impacts. If such impacts cannot be avoided by the modification of the Management Scheme, the Regulatory Committee shall suspend it, or cancel it and the exploration or development permit.

2. In performing its functions under paragraph 1 above a Regulatory Committee shall, unless emergency action is required, seek and take into account the views of the Advisory Committee.

3. If a Regulatory Committee determines that an Operator has failed to comply with this Convention or with measures in effect pursuant to it or a Management Scheme applicable to that Operator, the Regulatory Committee may do all or any of the following:

(*a*) modify the Management Scheme;

(*b*) suspend the Management Scheme;

(*c*) cancel the Management Scheme and the exploration or development permit; and

(*d*) impose a monetary penalty.

4. Sanctions determined pursuant to paragraph 3(a) to (d) above shall be proportionate to the seriousness of the failure to comply.

5. A Regulatory Committee shall cancel a Management Scheme and the exploration or development permit if an Operator ceases to have a substantial and genuine link with the Sponsoring State as defined in Article 1(12).

6. The Commission shall adopt general measures, which may include mitigation, relating to action by Regulatory Committees pursuant to paragraphs 1 and 3 above and, as appropriate, to the consequences of such action. No application pursuant to Article 44 may be lodged until such measures have come into effect.

Article 52

Monitoring in Relation to Management Schemes

1. Each Regulatory Committee shall monitor the compliance of Operators with Management Schemes within its area of competence.

2. Each Regulatory Committee, taking into account the advice of the Advisory Committee, shall monitor and assess the effects on the Antarctic environment and on dependent and on associated ecosystems of Antarctic mineral resource activities within its area of competence, particularly by reference to key environmental parameters and ecosystem components.

3. Each Regulatory Committee shall, as appropriate, inform the Commission and the Advisory Committee in a timely fashion of monitoring under this Article.

CHAPTER V: DEVELOPMENT

Article 53

Application for a Development Permit

1. At any time during the period in which an approved Management Scheme and exploration permit are in force for an Operator, the Sponsoring State may, on behalf of that Operator, lodge with the Regulatory Committee an application for a development permit.

2. An application shall be accompanied by the fees established by the Regulatory Committee in accordance with Article 43(2)(b) and shall contain:

(*a*) an updated description of the planned development identifying any modifications proposed to the approved Management Scheme and any additional measures to be taken, consequent upon such modifications, to ensure consistency with this Convention, including any measures in effect pursuant thereto and the general requirements referred to in Article 43(3);

(*b*) a detailed assessment of the environmental and other impacts of the planned development, taking into account Articles 15 and 26(4);

(*c*) a recertification by the Sponsoring State of the technical competence and financial capacity of the Operator and that the Operator has a substantial and genuine link with it as defined in Article 1(12);

(*d*) a recertification by the Sponsoring State of the capacity of the Operator to comply with the general requirements referred to in Article 43(3);

(*e*) updated information in relation to all other matters specified in Article 44(2); and

(*f*) such further information as may be required by the Regulatory Committee or in measures adopted by the Commission.

Article 54

Examination of Applications and Issue of Development Permits

1. The Regulatory Committee shall meet as soon as possible after an application has been lodged pursuant to Article 53.

2. The Regulatory Committee shall determine whether the application contains sufficient or adequate information pursuant to Article 53(2). In performing this function it may at any time seek further information from the Sponsoring State consistent with Article 53(2).

3. The Regulatory Committee shall consider whether:

(*a*) the application reveals modifications to the planned development previously envisaged;

(*b*) the planned development would cause previously unforeseen impacts on the Antarctic environment or dependent or associated ecosystems, either as a result of any modifications referred to in subparagraph (a) above or in the light of increased knowledge.

4. The Regulatory Committee shall consider any modifications to the Management Scheme necessary in the light of paragraph 3 above to ensure that the development activities proposed would be undertaken consistently with this Convention as well as measures in effect pursuant thereto and the general requirements referred to in Article 43(3). However, the financial obligations specified in the approved Management Scheme may not be revised without the consent of the Sponsoring State, unless provided for in the Management Scheme itself.

5. If the Regulatory Committee in accordance with Article 32 approves modifications under paragraph 4 above, or if it does not consider that such modifications are necessary, the Regulatory Committee shall issue without delay a development permit.

6. In performing its functions under this Article, the Regulatory Committee shall seek and take full account of the views of the Advisory Committee. To that end the Regulatory Committee shall refer to the Advisory Committee all parts of the application which are necessary for it to provide advice pursuant to Article 26, together with any other relevant information.

CHAPTER VI: DISPUTES SETTLEMENT

Article 55

Disputes Between Two or More Parties

Articles 56, 57 and 58 apply to disputes between two or more Parties.

Article 56

Choice of Procedure

1. Each Party, when signing, ratifying, accepting, approving or acceding to this Convention, or at any time thereafter, may choose, by written declaration, one or both of the following means for the settlement of disputes concerning the interpretation or application of this Convention:

(*a*) the International Court of Justice;

(*b*) the Arbitral Tribunal.

2. A declaration made under paragraph 1 above shall not affect the operation of Article 57(1), (3), (4) and (5).

3. A Party that has not made a declaration under paragraph 1 above or in respect of which a declaration is no longer in force shall be deemed to have accepted the competence of the Arbitral Tribunal.

4. If the parties to a dispute have accepted the same means for the settlement of a dispute, the dispute may be submitted only to that procedure, unless the parties otherwise agree.

5. If the parties to a dispute have not accepted the same means for the settlement of a dispute, or if they have both accepted both means, the dispute may be submitted only to the Arbitral Tribunal, unless the parties otherwise agree.

6. A declaration made under paragraph 1 above shall remain in force until it expires in accordance with its terms or until 3 months after written notice of revocation has been deposited with the Depositary.

7. A new declaration, a notice of revocation or the expiry of a declaration shall not in any way affect proceedings pending before the International Court of Justice or the Arbitral Tribunal, unless the parties to the dispute otherwise agree.

8. Declarations and notices referred to in this Article shall be deposited with the Depositary who shall transmit copies thereof to all Parties.

Article 57

Procedure for Dispute Settlement

1. If a dispute arises concerning the interpretation or application of this Convention, the parties to the dispute shall, at the request of any one of them, consult among themselves as soon as possible with a view to having the dispute resolved by negotiation, enquiry, mediation, conciliation, arbitration, judicial settlement or other peaceful means of their choice.

2. If the parties to a dispute concerning the interpretation or application of this Convention have not agreed on a means for resolving it within 12 months of the request for consultation pursuant to paragraph 1 above, the dispute shall be referred, at the request of any party to the dispute, for settlement in accordance with the procedure determined by the operation of Article 56(4) and (5).

3. If a dispute concerning the interpretation or application of this Convention relates to a measure in effect pursuant to this Convention or a Management Scheme and the parties to such a dispute:

(*a*) have not agreed on a means for resolving the dispute within 6 months of the request for consultation pursuant to paragraph 1 above, the dispute shall be referred, at the request of any party to the dispute, for discussion in the institution which adopted the instrument in question;

(*b*) have not agreed on a means for resolving the dispute within 12 months of the request for consultation pursuant to paragraph 1 above, the dispute shall be referred for settlement, at the request of any party to the dispute, to the Arbitral Tribunal.

4. The Arbitral Tribunal shall not be competent to decide or otherwise rule upon any matter within the scope of Article 9. In addition, nothing in this Convention shall be interpreted as conferring competence or jurisdiction on the International Court of Justice or any other tribunal established for the purpose of settling disputes between Parties to decide or otherwise rule upon any matter within the scope of Article 9.

5. The Arbitral Tribunal shall not be competent with regard to the exercise by an institution of its discretionary powers in accordance with this Convention; in no case

shall the Arbitral Tribunal substitute its discretion for that of an institution. In addition, nothing in this Convention shall be interpreted as conferring competence or jurisdiction on the International Court of Justice or any other tribunal established for the purpose of settling disputes between Parties with regard to the exercise by an institution of its discretionary powers or to substitute its discretion for that of an institution.

Article 58

Exclusion of Categories of Disputes

1. Any Party, when signing, ratifying, accepting, approving or acceding to this Convention, or at any time thereafter, may, by written declaration, exclude the operation of Article 57(2) or (3) without its consent with respect to a category or categories of disputes specified in the declaration. Such declaration may not cover disputes concerning the interpretation or application of:

(*a*) any provision of this Convention or of any measure in effect pursuant to it relating to the protection of the Antarctic environment or dependent or associated ecosystems;

(*b*) Article 7(1);

(*c*) Article 8;

(*d*) Article 12;

(*e*) Article 14;

(*f*) Article 15; or

(*g*) Article 37.

2. Nothing in paragraph 1 above or in any declaration made under it shall affect the operation of Article 57(1), (4) and (5).

3. A declaration made under paragraph 1 above shall remain in force until it expires in accordance with its terms or until 3 months after written notice of revocation has been deposited with the Depositary.

4. A new declaration, a notice of revocation or the expiry of a declaration shall not in any way affect proceedings pending before the International Court of Justice or the Arbitral Tribunal, unless the parties to the dispute otherwise agree.

5. Declarations and notices referred to in this Article shall be deposited with the Depositary who shall transmit copies thereof to all Parties.

6. A Party which, by declaration made under paragraph 1 above, has excluded specific category or categories of disputes from the operation of Article 57(2) or (3) without its consent shall not be entitled to submit any dispute falling within that category or those categories for settlement pursuant to Article 57(2) or (3), as the case may be, without the consent of the other party or parties to the dispute.

Article 59

Additional Dispute Settlement Procedures

1. The Commission, in conjunction with its responsibilities pursuant to Article 41(1), shall establish additional procedures for third-party settlement, by the Arbitral Tribunal or through other similar procedures, of disputes which may arise if it is alleged that a violation of this Convention has occurred by virtue of:

(*a*) a decision to decline a Management Scheme;

(*b*) a decision to decline the issue of a development permit; or (*c*) a decision to suspend, modify or cancel a Management Scheme or to impose monetary penalties.

2. Such procedures shall:

(*a*) permit, as appropriate, Parties and Operators under their sponsorship, but not both in respect of any particular dispute, to initiate proceedings against a Regulatory Committee;

(*b*) require disputes to which they relate to be referred in the first instance to the relevant Regulatory Committee for consideration;

(*c*) incorporate the rules in Article 57(4) and (5).

CHAPTER VII: FINAL CLAUSES

Article 60
Signature

This Convention shall be open for signature at Wellington from 25 November 1988 to 25 November 1989 by States which participated in the final session of the Fourth Special Antarctic Treaty Consultative Meeting.

Article 61
Ratification, Acceptance, Approval or Accession

1. This Convention is subject to ratification, acceptance or approval by Signatory States.

2. After 25 November 1989 this Convention shall be open for accession by any State which is a Contracting Party to the Antarctic Treaty.

3. Instruments of ratification, acceptance, approval or accession shall be deposited with the Government of New Zealand, hereby designated as the Depositary.

Article 62
Entry Into Force

1. This Convention shall enter into force on the thirtieth day following the date of deposit of instruments of ratification, acceptance, approval or accession by 16 Antarctic Treaty Consultative Parties which participated as such in the final session of the Fourth Special Antarctic Treaty Consultative Meeting, provided that number includes all the States necessary in order to establish all of the institutions of the Convention in respect of every area of Antarctica, including 5 developing countries and 11 developed countries.

2. For each State which, subsequent to the date of entry into force of this Convention, deposits an instrument of ratification, acceptance, approval or accession, the Convention shall enter into force on the thirtieth by following such deposit.

Article 63
Reservations, Declarations and Statements

1. Reservations to this Convention shall not be permitted. This does not preclude a State, when signing, ratifying, accepting, approving or acceding to this Convention, from making declarations or statements, however phrased or named, with a view, *inter alia,* to the harmonization of its laws and regulations with this Convention, provided that such declarations or statements do not purport to exclude or to modify the legal effect of this Convention in its application to that State.

2. The provisions of this Article are without prejudice to the right to make written declarations in accordance with Article 58.

Article 64

Amendment

1. This Convention shall not be subject to amendment until after the expiry of 10 years from the date of its entry into force. Thereafter, any Party may, by written communication addressed to the Depositary, propose a specific amendment to this Convention and request the convening of a meeting to consider such proposed amendment.

2. The Depositary shall circulate such communication to all Parties. If within 12 months of the date of circulation of the communication at least one-third of the Parties reply favorably to the request, the Depositary shall convene the meeting.

3. The adoption of an amendment considered at such a meeting shall require the affirmative votes of two-thirds of the Parties present and voting including the concurrent votes of the members of the Commission attending the meeting.

4. The adoption of any amendment relating to the Special Meeting of Parties or to the Advisory Committee shall require the affirmative votes of three-quarters of the Parties present and voting, including the concurrent votes of the members of the Commission attending the meeting.

5. An amendment shall enter into force for those Parties having deposited instruments of ratification, acceptance or approval thereof 30 days after the Depositary has received such instruments of ratification, acceptance or approval from all the members of the Commission.

6. Such amendment shall thereafter enter into force for any other Party 30 days after the Depositary has received its instrument of ratification, acceptance or approval thereof.

7. An amendment that has entered into force pursuant to this Article shall be without prejudice to the provisions of any Management Scheme approved before the date on which the amendment entered into force.

Article 65

Withdrawal

1. Any Party may withdraw from this Convention by giving to the Depositary notice in writing of its intention to withdraw. Withdrawal shall take effect two years after the date of receipt of such notice by the Depositary.

2. Any Party which ceases to be a Contracting Party to the Antarctic Treaty shall be deemed to have withdrawn from this Convention on the date that it ceases to be a Contracting Party to the Antarctic Treaty.

3. Where an amendment has entered into force pursuant to Article 64(5), any Party from which no instrument of ratification, acceptance or approval of the amendment has been received by the Depositary within a period of two years from the date of the entry into force of the amendment shall be deemed to have withdrawn from this Convention on the date of the expiration of a further two year period.

4. Subject to paragraph 5 and 6 below, the rights and obligations of any Operator pursuant to this Convention shall cease at the time its Sponsoring State withdraws or is deemed to have withdrawn from this Convention.

5. Such Sponsoring State shall ensure that the obligations of its Operators have been discharged no later than the date on which its withdrawal takes effect.

6. Withdrawal from this Convention by any Party shall not affect its financial or other obligations under this Convention pending on the date withdrawal takes effect. Any dispute settlement procedure in which that Party is involved and which has been

commenced prior to that date shall continue to its conclusion unless agreed otherwise by the parties to the dispute.

Article 66

Notifications by the Depositary

The Depositary shall notify all Contracting Parties to the Antarctic Treaty of the following:

(*a*) signatures of this Convention and the deposit of instruments of ratification, acceptance, approval or accession;

(*b*) the deposit of instruments of ratification, acceptance or approval of any amendment adopted pursuant to Article 64;

(*c*) the date of entry into force of this Convention and of any amendment thereto;

(*d*) the deposit of declarations and notices pursuant to Articles 56 and 58;

(*e*) notifications pursuant to Article 18; and

(*f*) the withdrawal of a Party pursuant to Article 65.

Article 67

Authentic Texts, Certified Copies and Registration with the United Nations

1. This Convention of which the Chinese, English, French, Russian and Spanish texts are equally authentic shall be deposited with the Government of New Zealand which shall transmit duly certified copies thereof to all Signatory and Acceding States.

2. The Depositary shall also transmit duly certified copies to all Signatory and Acceding States of the text of this Convention in any additional language of a Signatory or Acceding State which submits such text to the Depositary.

3. This Convention shall be registered by the Depositary pursuant to Article 102 of the Charter of the United Nations.

2.8 RESOLUTION ON THE QUESTION OF ANTARCTICA. Adopted by the UN General Assembly, 15 December 1989. G.A. Res. 44/124, U.N. GAOR, 44th Sess., Supp. No. 49, at 91, U.N. Doc. A/44/49 (1989)

A

The General Assembly,

Recalling its resolution 43/83 B of 7 December 1988,

Having considered the item entitled "Question of Antarctica",

Noting with regret that the racist *apartheid* régime of South Africa, which has been suspended from participation in the General Assembly of the United Nations, has continued to participate in the meetings of the Antarctic Treaty Consultative Parties,

Recalling the resolution adopted by the Council of Ministers of the Organization of African Unity at its fiftieth ordinary session, held at Addis Ababa from 17 to 22 July 1989,

Recalling also the final document on Antarctica adopted by the Ninth Conference of Heads of State or Government of Non–Aligned Countries, held at Belgrade from 4 to 7 September 1989,

Recalling further that the Antarctic Treaty is, by its terms, intended to further the purposes and principles embodied in the Charter of the United Nations,

Noting that the policy of *apartheid* practised by the racist minority régime of South Africa, which has been universally condemned, constitutes a threat to regional and international peace and security,

1. *Views with concern* the continuing participation of the *apartheid* régime of South Africa in the meetings of the Antarctic Treaty Consultative Parties;

2. *Appeals once again* to the Antarctic Treaty Consultative Parties to take urgent measures to exclude the racist *apartheid* régime of South Africa from participation in the meetings of the Consultative Parties at the earliest possible date;

3. *Invites* the States parties to the Antarctic Treaty to inform the Secretary–General of the actions taken regarding the provisions of the present resolution;

4. *Requests* the Secretary–General to submit a report in this regard to the General Assembly at its forty-fifth session;

5. *Decides* to include in the provisional agenda of its forty-fifth session the item entitled "Question of Antarctica".

B

The General Assembly,

Having considered the item entitled "Question of Antarctica",

Recalling its resolutions 38/77 of 15 December 1983, 39/152 of 17 December 1984, 40/156 A and B of 16 December 1985, 41/88 A and B of 4 December 1986, 42/46 A and B of 30 November 1987 and 43/83 A and B of 7 December 1988,

Recalling also the relevant paragraphs of the Political Declaration adopted by the Eighth Conference of Heads of State or Government of Non–Aligned Countries, held at Harare from 1 to 6 September 1986, and the resolution on Antarctica adopted by the Council of Ministers of the Organization of African Unity at its forty-second ordinary session, held at Addis Ababa from 10 to 17 July 1985, as well as the relevant paragraphs of the decision of the Council of Ministers of the League of Arab States meeting at Tunis on 17 and 18 September 1986 and resolution 25/5–P(IS) adopted by the Fifth Islamic Summit Conference of the Organization of the Islamic Conference, held at Kuwait from 26 to 29 January 1987, the final document on Antarctica adopted by the Ninth Conference of Heads of State or Government of Non–Aligned Countries, held at Belgrade from 4 to 7 September 1989 and the communiqué issued by Commonwealth Heads of Government at Kuala Lumpur on 24 October 1989,

Taking into account the debates on this item held since its thirty-eighth session,

Welcoming the increasing awareness of and interest in Antarctica shown by the international community,

Convinced of the advantages to the whole of mankind of a better knowledge of Antarctica,

Affirming its conviction that, in the interest of all mankind, Antarctica should continue forever to be used exclusively for peaceful purposes and that it should not become the scene or object of international discord,

Reaffirming the principle that the international community is entitled to information covering all aspects of Antarctica and that the United Nations should be made the repository for all such information in accordance with General Assembly resolutions 41/88 A, 42/46 B and 43/83 A,

Conscious of the particular significance of Antarctica to the international community in terms, *inter alia,* of international peace and security, environment, its effects on global climatic conditions, economy and scientific research,

Conscious also of the interrelationship between Antarctica and the physical, chemical and biological processes that regulate the total Earth system,

Reaffirming that the management and use of Antarctica should be conducted in accordance with the purposes and principles of the Charter of the United Nations and in the interest of maintaining international peace and security and of promoting international co-operation for the benefit of mankind as a whole,

Affirming the necessity of ensuring, in the interest of all mankind, comprehensive environmental protection and conservation of the Antarctic environment and its dependent and associated ecosystems through negotiations with the full participation of all members of the international community,

Conscious of the environmental degradation that prospecting and mining in and around Antarctica would pose to the Antarctic and global environment and ecosystems,

Convinced of the need to prevent or minimize any impact of human activity resulting from the large number of scientific stations and expeditions in Antarctica on the environment and its dependent and associated ecosystems,

Taking into account all aspects pertaining to all areas covered by the Antarctic Treaty system,

Taking note with appreciation of the reports of the Secretary–General on the question of Antarctica,

1. *Expresses its regret* that, despite the numerous resolutions in which it has called upon the Antarctic Treaty Consultative Parties to invite the Secretary–General or his representative to their meetings, including their consultative meetings, the Secretary–General was not invited to the Preparatory Meeting of the XVth Antarctic Treaty Consultative Meeting or to the XVth Consultative Meeting, held in Paris from 9 to 13 May and from 9 to 20 October 1989, respectively;

2. *Reiterates its call* upon the Antarctic Treaty Consultative Parties to invite the Secretary–General or his representative to all meetings of the Treaty parties, including their consultative meetings;

3. *Requests* the Secretary–General to submit a report on his evaluations thereon to the General Assembly at its forty-fifth session;

4. *Expresses the conviction* that, in view of the significant impact that Antarctica exerts on the global environment and ecosystems, any régime to be established for the protection and conservation of the Antarctic environment and its dependent and associated ecosystems, in order to be for the benefit of mankind as a whole and in order to gain the universal acceptability necessary to ensure full compliance and enforcement, must be negotiated with the full participation of all members of the international community;

5. *Urges* all members of the international community to support all efforts to ban prospecting and mining in and around Antarctica and to ensure that all activities are carried out exclusively for the purpose of peaceful scientific investigation and that all such activities ensure the maintenance of international peace and security in Antarctica and the protection of its environment and are for the benefit of all mankind;

6. *Expresses its conviction* that the establishment, through negotiations with the full participation of all members of the international community, of Antarctica as a nature reserve or a world park would ensure the protection and conservation of its environment and its dependent and associated ecosystems for the benefit of all mankind;

7. *Also expresses its conviction,* in view of the large number of scientific stations and expeditions, that international scientific research should be enhanced through the establishment of international stations devoted to scientific investigations of global significance, regulated by stringent environmental safeguards, so as to avoid or minimize any adverse impact of human activities on the Antarctic environment and its dependent and associated ecosystems;

8. *Urges* all States Members of the United Nations to co-operate with the Secretary–General and to continue consultations on all aspects relating to Antarctica;

9. *Decides* to include in the provisional agenda of its forty-fifth session the item entitled "Question of Antarctica".

2.9 Protocol on Environmental Protection to the Antarctic Treaty (With Annexes I & III Only).[b] Concluded at Madrid, 4 October 1991. Entered into force, 14 January 1998. XI ATSCM/2; *reprinted in* 30 I.L.M. 1461 (1991) & 5 Weston V.D.6

PREAMBLE

The States Parties to this Protocol to the Antarctic Treaty, hereinafter referred to as the Parties,

Convinced of the need to enhance the protection of the Antarctic environment and dependent and associated ecosystems;

Convinced of the need to strengthen the Antarctic Treaty system so as to ensure that Antarctica shall continue forever to be used exclusively for peaceful purposes and shall not become the scene or object of international discord;

Bearing in mind the special legal and political status of Antarctica and the special responsibility of the Antarctic Treaty Consultative Parties to ensure that all activities in Antarctica are consistent with the purposes and principles of the Antarctic Treaty;

Recalling the designation of Antarctica as a Special Conservation Area and other measures adopted under the Antarctic Treaty system to protect the Antarctic environment and dependent and associated ecosystems;

Acknowledging further the unique opportunities Antarctica offers for scientific monitoring of and research on processes of global as well as regional importance;

Reaffirming the conservation principles of the Convention on the Conservation of Antarctic Marine Living Resources;[c]

Convinced that the development of a comprehensive regime for the protection of the Antarctic environment and dependent and associated ecosystems is in the interest of mankind as a whole;

Desiring to supplement the Antarctic Treaty to this end;

Have agreed as follows:

ARTICLE 1

DEFINITIONS

For the purposes of this Protocol:

(a) "The Antarctic Treaty" means the Antarctic Treaty done at Washington on 1 December 1959;

(b) "Antarctic Treaty area" means the area to which the provisions of the Antarctic Treaty apply in accordance with Article VI of that Treaty;

(c) "Antarctic Treaty Consultative Meetings" means the meetings referred to in Article IX of the Antarctic Treaty;

(d) "Antarctic Treaty Consultative Parties" means the Contracting Parties to the Antarctic Treaty entitled to appoint representatives to participate in the meetings referred to in Article IX of that Treaty;

(e) "Antarctic Treaty system" means the Antarctic Treaty, the measures in effect under that Treaty, its associated separate international instruments in force and the measures in effect under those instruments;

(f) "Arbitral Tribunal" means the Arbitral Tribunal established in accordance with the Schedule to this Protocol, which forms an integral part thereof;

b. *See also* Basic Document 2.1, *supra*.

c. *See* Basic Document 2.4, *supra*.

(g) "Committee" means the Committee for Environmental Protection established in accordance with Article 11.

ARTICLE 2

OBJECTIVE AND DESIGNATION

The Parties commit themselves to the comprehensive protection of the Antarctic environment and dependent and associated ecosystems and hereby designate Antarctica as a natural reserve, devoted to peace and science.

ARTICLE 3

ENVIRONMENTAL PRINCIPLES

1. The protection of the Antarctic environment and dependent and associated ecosystems and the intrinsic value of Antarctica, including its wilderness and aesthetic values and its value as an area for the conduct of scientific research, in particular research essential to understanding the global environment, shall be fundamental considerations in the planning and conduct of all activities in the Antarctic Treaty area.

2. To this end:

(a) activities in the Antarctic Treaty area shall be planned and conducted so as to limit adverse impacts on the Antarctic environment and dependent and associated ecosystems;

(b) activities in the Antarctic Treaty area shall be planned and conducted so as to avoid:

(i) adverse effects on climate or weather patterns;

(ii) significant adverse effects on air or water quality;

(iii) significant changes in the atmospheric, terrestrial (including aquatic), glacial or marine environments;

(iv) detrimental changes in the distribution, abundance or productivity of species or populations of species of fauna and flora;

(v) further jeopardy to endangered or threatened species or populations of such species; or

(vi) degradation of, or substantial risk to, areas of biological, scientific, historic, aesthetic or wilderness significance;

(c) activities in the Antarctic Treaty area shall be planned and conducted on the basis of information sufficient to allow prior assessments of, and informed judgments about, their possible impacts on the Antarctic environment and dependent and associated ecosystems and on the value of Antarctica for the conduct of scientific research; such judgments shall take full account of:

(i) the scope of the activity, including its area, duration and intensity;

(ii) the cumulative impacts of the activity, both by itself and in combination with other activities in the Antarctic Treaty area;

(iii) whether the activity will detrimentally affect any other activity in the Antarctic Treaty area;

(iv) whether technology and procedures are available to provide for environmentally safe operations;

(v) whether there exists the capacity to monitor key environmental parameters and ecosystem components so as to identify and provide early warning of any adverse effects of the activity and to provide for such modification of operating procedures as may be necessary in the light of the results of monitoring or increased knowledge of the Antarctic environment and dependent and associated ecosystems; and

(vi) whether there exists the capacity to respond promptly and effectively to accidents, particularly those with potential environmental effects;

(d) regular and effective monitoring shall take place to allow assessment of the impacts of ongoing activities, including the verification of predicted impacts;

(e) regular and effective monitoring shall take place to facilitate early detection of the possible unforeseen effects of activities carried on both within and outside the Antarctic Treaty area on the Antarctic environment and dependent and associated ecosystems.

3. Activities shall be planned and conducted in the Antarctic Treaty area so as to accord priority to scientific research and to preserve the value of Antarctica as an area for the conduct of such research, including research essential to understanding the global environment.

4. Activities undertaken in the Antarctic Treaty area pursuant to scientific research programmes, tourism and all other governmental and non-governmental activities in the Antarctic Treaty area for which advance notice is required in accordance with Article VII(5) of the Antarctic Treaty, including associated logistic support activities, shall:

(a) take place in a manner consistent with the principles in this Article; and

(b) be modified, suspended or cancelled if they result in or threaten to result in impacts upon the Antarctic environment or dependent or associated ecosystems inconsistent with those principles.

ARTICLE 4

RELATIONSHIP WITH THE OTHER COMPONENTS OF THE ANTARCTIC TREATY SYSTEM

1. This Protocol shall supplement the Antarctic Treaty and shall neither modify nor amend that Treaty.

2. Nothing in this Protocol shall derogate from the rights and obligations of the Parties to this Protocol under the other international instruments in force within the Antarctic Treaty system.

ARTICLE 5

CONSISTENCY WITH THE OTHER COMPONENTS OF THE ANTARCTIC TREATY SYSTEM

The Parties shall consult and co-operate with the Contracting Parties to the other international instruments in force within the Antarctic Treaty system and their respective institutions with a view to ensuring the achievement of the objectives and principles of this Protocol and avoiding any interference with the achievement of the objectives and principles of those instruments or any inconsistency between the implementation of those instruments and of this Protocol.

ARTICLE 6

CO-OPERATION

1. The Parties shall co-operate in the planning and conduct of activities in the Antarctic Treaty area. To this end, each Party shall endeavour to:

(a) promote co-operative programmes of scientific, technical and educational value, concerning the protection of the Antarctic environment and dependent and associated ecosystems;

(b) provide appropriate assistance to other Parties in the preparation of environmental impact assessments;

(c) provide to other Parties upon request information relevant to any potential environmental risk and assistance to minimize the effects of accidents which may damage the Antarctic environment or dependent and associated ecosystems;

(d) consult with other Parties with regard to the choice of sites for prospective stations and other facilities so as to avoid the cumulative impacts caused by their excessive concentration in any location;

(e) where appropriate, undertake joint expeditions and share the use of stations and other facilities; and

(f) carry out such steps as may be agreed upon at Antarctic Treaty Consultative Meetings.

2. Each Party undertakes, to the extent possible, to share information that may be helpful to other Parties in planning and conducting their activities in the Antarctic Treaty area, with a view to the protection of the Antarctic environment and dependent and associated ecosystems.

3. The Parties shall co-operate with those Parties which may exercise jurisdiction in areas adjacent to the Antarctic Treaty area with a view to ensuring that activities in the Antarctic Treaty area do not have adverse environmental impacts on those areas.

ARTICLE 7

PROHIBITION OF MINERAL RESOURCE ACTIVITIES

Any activity relating to mineral resources, other than scientific research, shall be prohibited.

ARTICLE 8

ENVIRONMENTAL IMPACT ASSESSMENT

1. Proposed activities referred to in paragraph 2 below shall be subject to the procedures set out in Annex I for prior assessment of the impacts of those activities on the Antarctic environment or on dependent or associated ecosystems according to whether those activities are identified as having:

(a) less than a minor or transitory impact;

(b) a minor or transitory impact; or

(c) more than a minor or transitory impact.

2. Each Party shall ensure that the assessment procedures set out in Annex I are applied in the planning processes leading to decisions about any activities undertaken in the Antarctic Treaty area pursuant to scientific research programmes, tourism and all other governmental and non-governmental activities in the Antarctic Treaty area for which advance notice is required under Article VII(5) of the Antarctic Treaty, including associated logistic support activities.

3. The assessment procedures set out in Annex I shall apply to any change in an activity whether the change arises from an increase or decrease in the intensity of an existing activity, from the addition of an activity, the decommissioning of a facility, or otherwise.

4. Where activities are planned jointly by more than one Party, the Parties involved shall nominate one of their number to coordinate the implementation of the environmental impact assessment procedures set out in Annex I.

ARTICLE 9

ANNEXES

1. The Annexes to this Protocol shall form an integral part thereof.

2. Annexes, additional to Annexes I–IV, may be adopted and become effective in accordance with Article IX of the Antarctic Treaty.

3. Amendments and modifications to Annexes may be adopted and become effective in accordance with Article IX of the Antarctic Treaty, provided that any Annex may itself make provision for amendments and modifications to become effective on an accelerated basis.

4. Annexes and any amendments and modifications thereto which have become effective in accordance with paragraphs 2 and 3 above shall, unless an Annex itself provides otherwise in respect of the entry into effect of any amendment or modification thereto, become effective for a Contracting Party to the Antarctic Treaty which is not an Antarctic Treaty Consultative Party, or which was not an Antarctic Treaty Consultative Party at the time of the adoption, when notice of approval of that Contracting Party has been received by the Depositary.

5. Annexes shall, except to the extent that an Annex provides otherwise, be subject to the procedures for dispute settlement set out in Articles 18 to 20.

ARTICLE 10

ANTARCTIC TREATY CONSULTATIVE MEETINGS

1. Antarctic Treaty Consultative Meetings shall, drawing upon the best scientific and technical advice available:

(a) define, in accordance with the provisions of this Protocol, the general policy for the comprehensive protection of the Antarctic environment and dependent and associated ecosystems; and

(b) adopt measures under Article IX of the Antarctic Treaty for the implementation of this Protocol.

2. Antarctic Treaty Consultative Meetings shall review the work of the Committee and shall draw fully upon its advice and recommendations in carrying out the tasks referred to in paragraph 1 above, as well as upon the advice of the Scientific Committee on Antarctic Research.

ARTICLE 11

COMMITTEE FOR ENVIRONMENTAL PROTECTION

1. There is hereby established the Committee for Environmental Protection.

2. Each Party shall be entitled to be a member of the Committee and to appoint a representative who may be accompanied by experts and advisers.

3. Observer status in the Committee shall be open to any Contracting Party to the Antarctic Treaty which is not a Party to this Protocol.

4. The Committee shall invite the President of the Scientific Committee on Antarctic Research and the Chairman of the Scientific Committee for the Conservation of Antarctic Marine Living Resources to participate as observers at its sessions. The Committee may also, with the approval of the Antarctic Treaty Consultative Meeting,

invite such other relevant scientific, environmental and technical organisations which can contribute to its work to participate as observers at its sessions.

5. The Committee shall present a report on each of its sessions to the Antarctic Treaty Consultative Meeting. The report shall cover all matters considered at the session and shall reflect the views expressed. The report shall be circulated to the Parties and to observers attending the session, and shall thereupon be made publicly available.

6. The Committee shall adopt its rules of procedure which shall be subject to approval by the Antarctic Treaty Consultative Meeting.

ARTICLE 12

FUNCTIONS OF THE COMMITTEE

1. The functions of the Committee shall be to provide advice and formulate recommendations to the Parties in connection with the implementation of this Protocol, including the operation of its Annexes, for consideration at Antarctic Treaty Consultative Meetings, and to perform such other functions as may be referred to it by the Antarctic Treaty Consultative Meetings. In particular, it shall provide advice on:

(a) the effectiveness of measures taken pursuant to this Protocol;

(b) the need to update, strengthen or otherwise improve such measures;

(c) the need for additional measures, including the need for additional Annexes, where appropriate;

(d) the application and implementation of the environmental impact assessment procedures set out in Article 8 and Annex I;

(e) means of minimising or mitigating environmental impacts of activities in the Antarctic Treaty area;

(f) procedures for situations requiring urgent action, including response action in environmental emergencies;

(g) the operation and further elaboration of the Antarctic Protected Area system;

(h) inspection procedures, including formats for inspection reports and checklists for the conduct of inspections;

(i) the collection, archiving, exchange and evaluation of information related to environmental protection;

(j) the state of the Antarctic environment; and

(k) the need for scientific research, including environmental monitoring, related to the implementation of this Protocol.

2. In carrying out its functions, the Committee shall, as appropriate, consult with the Scientific Committee on Antarctic Research, the Scientific Committee for the Conservation of Antarctic Marine Living Resources and other relevant scientific, environmental and technical organizations.

ARTICLE 13

COMPLIANCE WITH THIS PROTOCOL

1. Each Party shall take appropriate measures within its competence, including the adoption of laws and regulations, administrative actions and enforcement measures, to ensure compliance with this Protocol.

2. Each Party shall exert appropriate efforts, consistent with the Charter of the United Nations, to the end that no one engages in any activity contrary to this Protocol.

3. Each Party shall notify all other Parties of the measures it takes pursuant to paragraphs 1 and 2 above.

4. Each Party shall draw the attention of all other Parties to any activity which in its opinion affects the implementation of the objectives and principles of this Protocol.

5. The Antarctic Treaty Consultative Meetings shall draw the attention of any State which is not a Party to this Protocol to any activity undertaken by that State, its agencies, instrumentalities, natural or juridical persons, ships, aircraft or other means of transport which affects the implementation of the objectives and principles of this Protocol.

ARTICLE 14

INSPECTION

1. In order to promote the protection of the Antarctic environment and dependent and associated ecosystems, and to ensure compliance with this Protocol, the Antarctic Treaty Consultative Parties shall arrange, individually or collectively, for inspections by observers to be made in accordance with Article VII of the Antarctic Treaty.

2. Observers are:

(a) observers designated by any Antarctic Treaty Consultative Party who shall be nationals of that Party; and

(b) any observers designated at Antarctic Treaty Consultative Meetings to carry out inspections under procedures to be established by an Antarctic Treaty Consultative Meeting.

3. Parties shall co-operate fully with observers undertaking inspections, and shall ensure that during inspections, observers are given access to all parts of stations, installations, equipment, ships and aircraft open to inspection under Article VII(3) of the Antarctic Treaty, as well as to all records maintained thereon which are called for pursuant to this Protocol.

4. Reports of inspections shall be sent to the Parties whose stations, installations, equipment, ships or aircraft are covered by the reports. After those Parties have been given the opportunity to comment, the reports and any comments thereon shall be circulated to all the Parties and to the Committee, considered at the next Antarctic Treaty Consultative Meeting, and thereafter made publicly available.

ARTICLE 15

EMERGENCY RESPONSE ACTION

1. In order to respond to environmental emergencies in the Antarctic Treaty area, each Party agrees to:

(a) provide for prompt and effective response action to such emergencies which might arise in the performance of scientific research programmes, tourism and all other governmental and nongovernmental activities in the Antarctic Treaty area for which advance notice is required under Article VII(5) of the Antarctic Treaty, including associated logistic support activities; and

(b) establish contingency plans for response to incidents with potential adverse effects on the Antarctic environment or dependent and associated ecosystems.

2. To this end, the Parties shall:

(a) co-operate in the formulation and implementation of such contingency plans; and

(b) establish procedures for immediate notification of, and co-operative response to, environmental emergencies.

3. In the implementation of this Article, the Parties shall draw upon the advice of the appropriate international organisations.

ARTICLE 16

LIABILITY

Consistent with the objectives of this Protocol for the comprehensive protection of the Antarctic environment and dependent and associated ecosystems, the Parties undertake to elaborate rules and procedures relating to liability for damage arising from activities taking place in the Antarctic Treaty area and covered by this Protocol. Those rules and procedures shall be included in one or more Annexes to be adopted in accordance with Article 9(2).

ARTICLE 17

ANNUAL REPORT BY PARTIES

1. Each Party shall report annually on the steps taken to implement this Protocol. Such reports shall include notifications made in accordance with Article 13(3), contingency plans established in accordance with Article 15 and any other notifications and information called for pursuant to this Protocol for which there is no other provision concerning the circulation and exchange of information.

2. Reports made in accordance with paragraph 1 above shall be circulated to all Parties and to the Committee, considered at the next Antarctic Treaty Consultative Meeting, and made publicly available.

ARTICLE 18

DISPUTE SETTLEMENT

If a dispute arises concerning the interpretation or application of this Protocol, the parties to the dispute shall, at the request of any one of them, consult among themselves as soon as possible with a view to having the dispute resolved by negotiation, inquiry, mediation, conciliation, arbitration, judicial settlement or other peaceful means to which the parties to the dispute agree.

ARTICLE 19

CHOICE OF DISPUTE SETTLEMENT PROCEDURE

1. Each Party, when signing, ratifying, accepting, approving or acceding to this Protocol, or at any time thereafter, may choose, by written declaration, one or both of the following means for the settlement of disputes concerning the interpretation or application of Articles 7, 8 and 15 and, except to the extent that an Annex provides otherwise, the provisions of any Annex and, insofar as it relates to these Articles and provisions, Article 13:

(a) the International Court of Justice;

(b) the Arbitral Tribunal.

2. A declaration made under paragraph 1 above shall not affect the operation of Article 18 and Article 20(2).

3. A Party which has not made a declaration under paragraph 1 above or in respect of which a declaration is no longer in force shall be deemed to have accepted the competence of the Arbitral Tribunal.

4. If the parties to a dispute have accepted the same means for the settlement of a dispute, the dispute may be submitted only to that procedure, unless the parties otherwise agree.

5. If the parties to a dispute have not accepted the same means for the settlement of a dispute, or if they have both accepted both means, the dispute may be submitted only to the Arbitral Tribunal, unless the parties otherwise agree.

6. A declaration made under paragraph 1 above shall remain in force until it expires in accordance with its terms or until three months after written notice of revocation has been deposited with the Depositary.

7. A new declaration, a notice of revocation or the expiry of a declaration shall not in any way affect proceedings pending before the International Court of Justice or the Arbitral Tribunal, unless the parties to the dispute otherwise agree.

8. Declarations and notices referred to in this Article shall be deposited with the Depositary who shall transmit copies thereof to all Parties.

ARTICLE 20

DISPUTE SETTLEMENT PROCEDURE

1. If the parties to a dispute concerning the interpretation or application of Articles 7, 8 or 15 or, except to the extent that an Annex provides otherwise, the provisions of any Annex or, insofar as it relates to these Articles and provisions, Article 13, have not agreed on a means for resolving it within 12 months of the request for consultation pursuant to Article 18, the dispute shall be referred, at the request of any party to the dispute, for settlement in accordance with the procedure determined by Article 19(4) and (5).

2. The Arbitral Tribunal shall not be competent to decide or rule upon any matter within the scope of Article IV of the Antarctic Treaty. In addition, nothing in this Protocol shall be interpreted as conferring competence or jurisdiction on the International Court of Justice or any other tribunal established for the purpose of settling disputes between Parties to decide or otherwise rule upon any matter within the scope of Article IV of the Antarctic Treaty.

ARTICLE 21

SIGNATURE

This Protocol shall be open for signature at Madrid on the 4th of October 1991 and thereafter at Washington until the 3rd of October 1992 by any State which is a Contracting Party to the Antarctic Treaty.

ARTICLE 22

RATIFICATION, ACCEPTANCE, APPROVAL OR ACCESSION

1. This Protocol is subject to ratification, acceptance or approval by signatory States.

2. After the 3rd of October 1992 this Protocol shall be open for accession by any State which is a Contracting Party to the Antarctic Treaty.

3. Instruments of ratification, acceptance, approval or accession shall be deposited with the Government of the United States of America, hereby designated as the Depositary.

4. After the date on which this Protocol has entered into force, the Antarctic Treaty Consultative Parties shall not act upon a notification regarding the entitlement of a Contracting Party to the Antarctic Treaty to appoint representatives to participate in Antarctic Treaty Consultative Meetings in accordance with Article IX(2) of the Antarctic Treaty unless that Contracting Party has first ratified, accepted, approved or acceded to this Protocol.

ARTICLE 23

ENTRY INTO FORCE

1. This Protocol shall enter into force on the thirtieth day following the date of deposit of instruments of ratification, acceptance, approval or accession by all States which are Antarctic Treaty Consultative Parties at the date on which this Protocol is adopted.

2. For each Contracting Party to the Antarctic Treaty which, subsequent to the date of entry into force of this Protocol, deposits an instrument of ratification, acceptance, approval or accession, this Protocol shall enter into force on the thirtieth day following such deposit.

ARTICLE 24

RESERVATIONS

Reservations to this Protocol shall not be permitted.

ARTICLE 25

MODIFICATION OR AMENDMENT

1. Without prejudice to the provisions of Article 9, this Protocol may be modified or amended at any time in accordance with the procedures set forth in Article XII(1)(a) and (b) of the Antarctic Treaty.

2. If, after the expiration of 50 years from the date of entry into force of this Protocol, any of the Antarctic Treaty Consultative Parties so requests by a communication addressed to the Depositary, a conference shall be held as soon as practicable to review the operation of this Protocol.

3. A modification or amendment proposed at any Review Conference called pursuant to paragraph 2 above shall be adopted by a majority of the Parties, including 3/4 of the States which are Antarctic Treaty Consultative Parties at the time of adoption of this Protocol.

4. A modification or amendment adopted pursuant to paragraph 3 above shall enter into force upon ratification, acceptance, approval or accession by 3/4 of the Antarctic Treaty Consultative Parties, including ratification, acceptance, approval or accession by all States which are Antarctic Treaty Consultative Parties at the time of adoption of this Protocol.

5. (a) With respect to Article 7, the prohibition on Antarctic mineral resource activities contained therein shall continue unless there is in force a binding legal regime on Antarctic mineral resource activities that includes an agreed means for determining whether, and, if so, under which conditions, any such activities would be acceptable. This regime shall fully safeguard the interests of all States referred to in Article IV of the Antarctic Treaty and apply the principles thereof. Therefore, if a modification or amendment to Article 7 is proposed at a Review Conference referred to in paragraph 2 above, it shall include such a binding legal regime.

(b) If any such modification or amendment has not entered into force within 3 years of the date of its adoption, any Party may at any time thereafter notify the

Depositary of its withdrawal from this Protocol, and such withdrawal shall take effect 2 years after receipt of the notification by the Depositary.

ARTICLE 26

NOTIFICATIONS BY THE DEPOSITARY

The Depositary shall notify all Contracting Parties to the Antarctic Treaty of the following:

(a) signatures of this Protocol and the deposit of instruments of ratification, acceptance, approval or accession;

(b) the date of entry into force of this Protocol and any additional Annex thereto;

(c) the date of entry into force of any amendment or modification to this Protocol;

(d) the deposit of declarations and notices pursuant to Article 19; and

(e) any notification received pursuant to Article 25(5)(b)

ARTICLE 27

AUTHENTIC TEXTS AND REGISTRATION WITH THE UNITED NATIONS

1. This Protocol, done in the English, French, Russian and Spanish languages, each version being equally authentic, shall be deposited in the archives of the Government of the United States of America, which shall transmit duly certified copies thereof to all Contracting Parties to the Antarctic Treaty.

2. This Protocol shall be registered by the Depositary pursuant to Article 102 of the Charter of the United Nations.

* * *

Annex I to the Protocol on Environmental Protection to the Antarctic Treaty

ENVIRONMENTAL IMPACT ASSESSMENT

ARTICLE 1

Preliminary Stage

1. The environmental impacts of proposed activities referred to in Article 8 of the Protocol shall, before their commencement, be considered in accordance with appropriate national procedures.

2. If an activity is determined as having less than a minor or transitory impact, the activity may proceed forthwith.

ARTICLE 2

Initial Environmental Evaluation

1. Unless it has been determined that an activity will have less than a minor or transitory impact, or unless a Comprehensive Environmental Evaluation is being prepared in accordance with Article 3, an Initial Environmental Evaluation shall be prepared. It shall contain sufficient detail to assess whether a proposed activity may have more than a minor or transitory impact and shall include:

(a) a description of the proposed activity, including its purpose, location, duration, and intensity; and

(b) consideration of alternatives to the proposed activity and any impacts that the activity may have, including consideration of cumulative impacts in the light of existing and known planned activities.

2. If an Initial Environmental Evaluation indicates that a proposed activity is likely to have no more than a minor or transitory impact, the activity may proceed, provided that appropriate procedures, which may include monitoring, are put in place to assess and verify the impact of the activity.

ARTICLE 3

Comprehensive Environmental Evaluation

1. If an Initial Environmental Evaluation indicates or if it is otherwise determined that a proposed activity is likely to have more than a minor or transitory impact, a Comprehensive Environmental Evaluation shall be prepared.

2. A Comprehensive Environmental Evaluation shall include:

(a) a description of the proposed activity including its purpose, location, duration and intensity, and possible alternatives to the activity, including the alternatives of not proceeding, and the consequences of those alternatives;

(b) a description of the initial environmental reference state with which predicted changes are to be compared and a prediction of the future environmental reference state in the absence of the proposed activity;

(c) a description of the methods and data used to forecast the impacts of the proposed activity;

(d) estimation of the nature, extent, duration, and intensity of the likely direct impacts of the proposed activity;

(e) consideration of possible indirect or second order impacts of the proposed activity;

(f) consideration of cumulative impacts of the proposed activity in the light of existing activities and other known planned activities;

(g) identification of measures, including monitoring programmes, that could be taken to minimise or mitigate impacts of the proposed activity and to detect unforeseen impacts and that could provide early warning of any adverse effects of the activity as well as to deal promptly and effectively with accidents;

(h) identification of unavoidable impacts of the proposed activity;

(i) consideration of the effects of the proposed activity on the conduct of scientific research and on other existing uses and values;

(j) an identification of gaps in knowledge and uncertainties encountered in compiling the information required under this paragraph;

(k) a non-technical summary of the information provided under this paragraph; and

(*l*) the name and address of the person or organization which prepared the Comprehensive Environmental Evaluation and the address to which comments thereon should be directed.

3. The draft Comprehensive Environmental Evaluation shall be made publicly available and shall be circulated to all Parties, which shall also make it publicly available, for comment. A period of 90 days shall be allowed for the receipt of comments.

4. The draft Comprehensive Environmental Evaluation shall be forwarded to the Committee at the same time as it is circulated to the Parties, and at least 120 days

before the next Antarctic Treaty Consultative Meeting, for consideration as appropriate.

5. No final decision shall be taken to proceed with the proposed activity in the Antarctic Treaty area unless there has been an opportunity for consideration of the draft Comprehensive Environmental Evaluation by the Antarctic Treaty Consultative Meeting on the advice of the Committee, provided that no decision to proceed with a proposed activity shall be delayed through the operation of this paragraph for longer than 15 months from the date of circulation of the draft Comprehensive Environmental Evaluation.

6. A final Comprehensive Environmental Evaluation shall address and shall include or summarise comments received on the draft Comprehensive Environmental Evaluation. The final Comprehensive Environmental Evaluation, notice of any decisions relating thereto, and any evaluation of the significance of the predicted impacts in relation to the advantages of the proposed activity, shall be circulated to all Parties, which shall also make them publicly available, at least 60 days before the commencement of the proposed activity in the Antarctic Treaty area.

ARTICLE 4

Decisions to Be Based on Comprehensive Environmental Evaluations

Any decision on whether a proposed activity, to which Article 3 applies, should proceed, and, if so, whether in its original or in a modified form, shall be based on the Comprehensive Environmental Evaluation as well as other relevant considerations.

ARTICLE 5

Monitoring

1. Procedures shall be put in place, including appropriate monitoring of key environmental indicators, to assess and verify the impact of any activity that proceeds following the completion of a Comprehensive Environmental Evaluation.

2. The procedures referred to in paragraph 1 above and in Article 2(2) shall be designed to provide a regular and verifiable record of the impacts of the activity in order, *inter alia,* to:

(a) enable assessments to be made of the extent to which such impacts are consistent with the Protocol; and

(b) provide information useful for minimising or mitigating impacts, and, where appropriate, information on the need for suspension, cancellation or modification of the activity.

ARTICLE 6

Circulation of Information

1. The following information shall be circulated to the Parties, forwarded to the Committee and made publicly available:

(a) a description of the procedures referred to in Article 1;

(b) an annual list of any Initial Environmental Evaluations prepared in accordance with Article 2 and any decisions taken in consequence thereof;

(c) significant information obtained, and any action taken in consequence thereof, from procedures put in place in accordance with Articles 2(2) and 5; and

(d) information referred to in Article 3(6).

2. Any Initial Environmental Evaluation prepared in accordance with Article 2 shall be made available on request.

ARTICLE 7

Cases of Emergency

1. This Annex shall not apply in cases of emergency relating to the safety of human life or of ships, aircraft, or equipment and facilities of high value, or the protection of the environment, which require an activity to be undertaken without completion of the procedures set out in this Annex.

2. Notice of activities undertaken in cases of emergency, which would otherwise have required preparation of a Comprehensive Environmental Evaluation, shall be circulated immediately to all Parties and to the Committee and a full explanation of the activities carried out shall be provided within 90 days of those activities.

ARTICLE 8

Amendment or Modification

1. This Annex may be amended or modified by a measure adopted in accordance with Article IX(1) of the Antarctic Treaty. Unless the measure specifies otherwise, the amendment or modification shall be deemed to have been approved, and shall become effective, one year after the close of the Antarctic Treaty Consultative Meeting at which it was adopted, unless one or more of the Antarctic Treaty Consultative Parties notifies the Depositary, within that period, that it wishes an extension of that period or that it is unable to approve the measure.

2. Any amendment or modification of this Annex which becomes effective in accordance with paragraph 1 above shall thereafter become effective as to any other Party when notice of approval by it has been received by the Depositary.

* * *

Annex III to the Protocol on Environmental Protection to the Antarctic Treaty

WASTE DISPOSAL AND WASTE MANAGEMENT

ARTICLE 1

General Obligations

1. This Annex shall apply to activities undertaken in the Antarctic Treaty area pursuant to scientific research programmes, tourism and all other governmental and non-governmental activities in the Antarctic Treaty area for which advance notice is required under Article VII (5) of the Antarctic Treaty, including associated logistic support activities.

2. The amount of wastes produced or disposed of in the Antarctic Treaty area shall be reduced as far as practicable so as to minimise impact on the Antarctic environment and to minimise interference with the natural values of Antarctica, with scientific research and with other uses of Antarctica which are consistent with the Antarctic Treaty.

3. Waste storage, disposal and removal from the Antarctic Treaty area, as well as recycling and source reduction, shall be essential considerations in the planning and conduct of activities in the Antarctic Treaty area.

4. Wastes removed from the Antarctic Treaty area shall, to the maximum extent practicable, be returned to the country from which the activities generating the waste were organized or to any other country in which arrangements have been made for the disposal of such wastes in accordance with relevant international agreements.

5. Past and present waste disposal sites on land and abandoned work sites of Antarctic activities shall be cleaned up by the generator of such wastes and the user of such sites. This obligation shall not be interpreted as requiring:

(a) the removal of any structure designated as a historic site or monument; or

(b) the removal of any structure or waste material in circumstances where the removal by any practical option would result in greater adverse environmental impact than leaving the structure or waste material in its existing location.

ARTICLE 2

Waste Disposal by Removal From the Antarctic Treaty Area

1. The following wastes, if generated after entry into force of this Annex, shall be removed from the Antarctic Treaty area by the generator of such wastes:

(a) radio-active materials;

(b) electrical batteries;

(c) fuel, both liquid and solid;

(d) wastes containing harmful levels of heavy metals or acutely toxic or harmful persistent compounds;

(e) poly-vinyl chloride (PVC), polyurethane foam, polystyrene foam, rubber and lubricating oils, treated timbers and other products which contain additives that could produce harmful emissions if incinerated;

(f) all other plastic wastes, except low density polyethylene containers (such as bags for storing wastes), provided that such containers shall be incinerated in accordance with Article 3(1);

(g) fuel drums; and

(h) other solid, non-combustible wastes;

provided that the obligation to remove drums and solid non-combustible wastes contained in subparagraphs (g) and (h) above shall not apply in circumstances where the removal of such wastes by any practical option would result in greater adverse environmental impact than leaving them in their existing locations.

2. Liquid wastes which are not covered by paragraph 1 above and sewage and domestic liquid wastes, shall, to the maximum extent practicable, be removed from the Antarctic Treaty area by the generator of such wastes.

3. The following wastes shall be removed from the Antarctic Treaty area by the generator of such wastes, unless incinerated, autoclaved or otherwise treated to be made sterile:

(a) residues of carcasses of imported animals;

(b) laboratory culture of micro-organisms and plant pathogens; and

(c) introduced avian products.

ARTICLE 3

Waste Disposal by Incineration

1. Subject to paragraph 2 below, combustible wastes, other than those referred to in Article 2(1), which are not removed from the Antarctic Treaty area shall be burnt in incinerators which to the maximum extent practicable reduce harmful emissions. Any emissions standards and equipment guidelines which may be recommended by, inter alia, the Committee and the Scientific Committee on Antarctic Research shall be taken into account. The solid residue of such incineration shall be removed from the Antarctic Treaty area.

2. All open burning of wastes shall be phased out as soon as practicable, but no later than the end of the 1998/1999 season. Pending the completion of such phase-out, when it is necessary to dispose of wastes by open burning, allowance shall be made for the wind direction and speed and the type of wastes to be burnt to limit particulate deposition and to avoid such deposition over areas of special biological, scientific, historic, aesthetic or wilderness significance including, in particular, areas accorded protection under the Antarctic Treaty.

ARTICLE 4

Other Waste Disposal on Land

1. Wastes not removed or disposed of in accordance with Articles 2 and 3 shall not be disposed of onto ice-free areas or into fresh water systems.

2. Sewage, domestic liquid wastes and other liquid wastes not removed from the Antarctic Treaty area in accordance with Article 2, shall, to the maximum extent practicable, not be disposed of onto sea ice, ice shelves or the grounded ice-sheet, provided that such wastes which are generated by stations located inland on ice shelves or on the grounded ice-sheet may be disposed of in deep ice pits where such disposal is the only practicable option. Such pits shall not be located on known ice-flow lines which terminate at ice-free areas or in areas of high ablation.

3. Wastes generated at field camps shall, to the maximum extent practicable, be removed by the generator of such wastes to supporting stations or ships for disposal in accordance with this Annex.

ARTICLE 5

Disposal of Waste in the Sea

1. Sewage and domestic liquid wastes may be discharged directly into the sea, taking into account the assimilative capacity of the receiving marine environment and provided that:

(a) such discharge is located, wherever practicable, where conditions exist for initial dilution and rapid dispersal; and

(b) large quantities of such wastes (generated in a station where the average weekly occupancy over the austral summer is approximately 30 individuals or more) shall be treated at least by maceration.

2. The by-product of sewage treatment by the Rotary Biological Contactor process or similar processes may be disposed of into the sea provided that such disposal does not adversely affect the local environment, and provided also that any such disposal at sea shall be in accordance with Annex IV to the Protocol.

ARTICLE 6

Storage of Waste

All wastes to be removed from the Antarctic Treaty area, or otherwise disposed of, shall be stored in such a way as to prevent their dispersal into the environment.

ARTICLE 7

Prohibited Products

No polychlorinated biphenyls (PCBs), non-sterile soil, polystyrene beads, chips or similar forms of packaging, or pesticides (other than those required for scientific, medical or hygiene purposes) shall be introduced onto land or ice shelves or into water in the Antarctic Treaty area.

ARTICLE 8

Waste Management Planning

1. Each Party which itself conducts activities in the Antarctic Treaty area shall, in respect of those activities, establish a waste disposal classification system as a basis for recording wastes and to facilitate studies aimed at evaluating the environmental impacts of scientific activity and associated logistic support. To that end, wastes produced shall be classified as:

(a) sewage and domestic liquid wastes (Group 1);

(b) other liquid wastes and chemicals, including fuels and lubricants (Group 2);

(c) solids to be combusted (Group 3);

(d) other solid wastes (Group 4); and

(e) radioactive material (Group 5).

2. In order to reduce further the impact of waste on the Antarctic environment, each such Party shall prepare and annually review and update its waste management plans (including waste reduction, storage and disposal), specifying for each fixed site, for field camps generally, and for each ship (other than small boats that are part of the operations of fixed sites or of ships and taking into account existing management plans for ships):

(a) programmes for cleaning up existing waste disposal sites and abandoned work sites;

(b) current and planned waste management arrangements, including final disposal;

(c) current and planned arrangements for analysing the environmental effects of waste and waste management; and

(d) other efforts to minimise any environmental effects of wastes and waste management.

3. Each such Party shall, as far as is practicable, also prepare an inventory of locations of past activities (such as traverses, fuel depots, field bases, crashed aircraft) before the information is lost, so that such locations can be taken into account in planning future scientific programmes (such as snow chemistry, pollutants in lichens or ice core drilling).

ARTICLE 9

Circulation and Review of Waste Management Plans

1. The waste management plans prepared in accordance with Article 8, reports on their implementation, and the inventories referred to in Article 8(3), shall be included in the annual exchanges of information in accordance with Articles III and VII of the Antarctic Treaty and related Recommendations under Article IX of the Antarctic Treaty.

2. Each Party shall send copies of its waste management plans, and reports on their implementation and review, to the Committee.

3. The Committee may review waste management plans and reports thereon and may offer comments, including suggestions for minimising impacts and modifications and improvement to the plans, for the consideration of the Parties.

4. The Parties may exchange information and provide advice on, inter alia, available low waste technologies, reconversion of existing installations, special requirements for effluents, and appropriate disposal and discharge methods.

ARTICLE 10

Management Practices

Each Party shall:

(a) designate a waste management official to develop and monitor waste management plans; in the field, this responsibility shall be delegated to an appropriate person at each site;

(b) ensure that members of its expeditions receive training designed to limit the impact of its operations on the Antarctic environment and to inform them of requirements of this Annex; and

(c) discourage the use of poly-vinyl chloride (PVC) products and ensure that its expeditions to the Antarctic Treaty area are advised of any PVC products they may introduce into that area in order that these products may be removed subsequently in accordance with this Annex.

ARTICLE 11

Review

This Annex shall be subject to regular review in order to ensure that it is updated to reflect improvement in waste disposal technology and procedures and to ensure thereby maximum protection of the Antarctic environment.

ARTICLE 12

Cases of Emergency

1. This Annex shall not apply in cases of emergency relating to the safety of human life or of ships, aircraft or equipment and facilities of high value or the protection of the environment.

2. Notice of activities undertaken in cases of emergency shall be circulated immediately to all Parties and to the Committee.

ARTICLE 13

Amendment or Modification

1. This Annex may be amended or modified by a measure adopted in accordance with Article IX(1) of the Antarctic Treaty. Unless the measure specifies otherwise, the amendment or modification shall be deemed to have been approved, and shall become effective, one year after the close of the Antarctic Treaty Consultative Meeting at which it was adopted, unless one or more of the Antarctic Treaty Consultative Parties notifies the Depositary, within that time period, that it wishes an extension of that period or that it is unable to approve the amendment.

2. Any amendment or modification of this Annex which becomes effective in accordance with paragraph 1 above shall thereafter become effective as to any other Party when notice of approval by it has been received by the Depositary.

3. Atmosphere/Space

3.1 Convention on Third Party Liability in the Field of Nuclear Energy (as Amended Through 1964). Concluded at Paris, 29 July 1960. Entered into force, 1 April 1968. 956 U.N.T.S. 251; *reprinted in* 5 Weston V.J.1

THE GOVERNMENTS of the Federal Republic of Germany, the Republic of Austria, the Kingdom of Belgium, the Kingdom of Denmark, Spain, the French Republic, the Kingdom of Greece, the Italian Republic, the Grand Duchy of Luxembourg, the Kingdom of Norway, the Kingdom of the Netherlands, the Portuguese Republic, the United Kingdom of Great Britain and Northern Ireland, the Kingdom of Sweden, the Swiss Confederation and the Turkish Republic;

CONSIDERING that the OECD Nuclear Energy Agency, established within the framework of the Organisation for Economic Co-operation and Development (hereinafter referred to as the "Organisation"), is charged with encouraging the elaboration and harmonization of legislation relating to nuclear energy in participating countries, in particular with regard to third party liability and insurance against atomic risks;

DESIROUS of ensuring adequate and equitable compensation for persons who suffer damage caused by nuclear incidents whilst taking the necessary steps to ensure that the development of the production and uses of nuclear energy for peaceful purposes is not thereby hindered;

CONVINCED of the need for unifying the basic rules applying in the various countries to the liability incurred for such damage, whilst leaving these countries free to take, on a national basis, any additional measures which they deem appropriate;

Article 1

(*a*) For the purposes of this Convention:

(i) "A nuclear incident" means any occurrence or succession of occurrences having the same origin which causes damage, provided that such occurrence or succession of occurrences, or any of the damage caused, arises out of or results either from the radioactive properties, or a combination of radioactive properties with toxic, explosive, or other hazardous properties of nuclear fuel or radioactive products or waste or with any of them, or from ionizing radiations emitted by any other source of radiation inside a nuclear installation.

(ii) "Nuclear installation" means reactors other than those comprised in any means of transport; factories for the manufacture or processing of nuclear substances; factories for the separation of isotopes of nuclear fuel; factories for the reprocessing of irradiated nuclear fuel; facilities for the storage of nuclear substances other than storage incidental to the carriage of such substances; and such other installations in which there are nuclear fuel or radioactive products or waste as the Steering Committee for Nuclear Energy of the Organisation (hereinafter referred to as the "Steering Committee") shall from time to time determine; any Contracting Party may determine that two or more nuclear installations of one operator which are located on the same site shall, together with any other premises on that site where radioactive material is held, be treated as a single nuclear installation.

(iii) "Nuclear fuel" means fissionable material in the form of uranium metal, alloy, or chemical compound (including natural uranium), plutonium metal, alloy, or chemical compound, and such other fissionable material as the Steering Committee shall from time to time determine.

(iv) "Radioactive products or waste" means any radioactive material produced in or made radioactive by exposure to the radiation incidental to the process of producing or utilizing nuclear fuel, but does not include (1) nuclear fuel, or (2) radioisotopes outside a nuclear installation which have reached the final stage of fabrication so as to be usable for any industrial, commercial, agricultural, medical, scientific or educational purpose.

(v) "Nuclear substances" means nuclear fuel (other than natural uranium and other than depleted uranium) and radioactive products or waste.

(vi) "Operator" in relation to a nuclear installation means the person designated or recognized by the competent public authority as the operator of that installation.

(*b*) The Steering Committee may, if in its view the small extent of the risks involved so warrants, exclude any nuclear installation, nuclear fuel, or nuclear substances from the application of this Convention.

Article 2

This Convention does not apply to nuclear incidents occurring in the territory of non-Contracting States or to damage suffered in such territory, unless otherwise provided by the legislation of the Contracting Party in whose territory the nuclear installation of the operator liable is situated, and except in regard to rights referred to in article 6(*e*).

Article 3

(*a*) The operator of a nuclear installation shall be liable, in accordance with this Convention, for:

(i) damage to or loss of life of any person; and

(ii) damage to or loss of any property other than

1. the nuclear installation itself and any other nuclear installation, including a nuclear installation under construction, on the site where that installation is located; and

2. any property on that same site which is used or to be used in connection with any such installation, upon proof that such damage or loss (hereinafter referred to as "damage") was caused by a nuclear incident in such installation or involving nuclear substances coming from such installation, except as otherwise provided for in Article 4.

(*b*) Where the damage or loss is caused jointly by a nuclear incident and by an incident other than a nuclear incident, that part of the damage or loss which is caused by such other incident shall, to the extent that it is not reasonably separable from the damage or loss caused by the nuclear incident, be considered to be damage caused by the nuclear incident. Where the damage or loss is caused jointly by a nuclear incident and by an emission of ionizing radiation not covered by this Convention, nothing in this Convention shall limit or otherwise affect the liability of any person in connection with that emission of ionizing radiation.

Article 4

In the case of carriage of nuclear substances, including storage incidental thereto, without prejudice to article 2:

(*a*) The operator of a nuclear installation shall be liable, in accordance with this Convention, for damage upon proof that it was caused by a nuclear incident outside that installation and involving nuclear substances in the course of carriage therefrom, only if the incident occurs:

(i) before liability with regard to nuclear incidents involving the nuclear substances has been assumed, pursuant to the express terms of a contract in writing, by the operator of another nuclear installation;

(ii) in the absence of such express terms, before the operator of another nuclear installation has taken charge of the nuclear substances; or

(iii) where the nuclear substances are intended to be used in a reactor comprised in a means of transport, before the person duly authorized to operate that reactor has taken charge of the nuclear substances; but

(iv) where the nuclear substances have been sent to a person within the territory of a non-Contracting State, before they have been unloaded from the means of transport by which they have arrived in the territory of that non-Contracting State.

(*b*) The operator of a nuclear installation shall be liable, in accordance with this Convention, for damage upon proof that it was caused by a nuclear incident outside that installation and involving nuclear substances in the course of carriage thereto, only if the incident occurs:

(i) after liability with regard to nuclear incidents involving the nuclear substances has been assumed by him, pursuant to the express terms of a contract in writing, from the operator of another nuclear installation;

(ii) in the absence of such express terms, after he has taken charge of the nuclear substances; or

(iii) after he has taken charge of the nuclear substances from a person operating a reactor comprised in a means of transport; but

(iv) where the nuclear substances have, with the written consent of the operator, been sent from a person within the territory of a non-Contracting State, after they have been loaded on the means of transport by which they are to be carried from the territory of that State.

(*c*) The operator liable in accordance with this Convention shall provide the carrier with a certificate issued by or on behalf of the insurer or other financial guarantor furnishing the security required pursuant to Article 10. However, a Contracting Party may exclude this obligation in relation to carriage which takes place wholly within its own territory. The certificate shall state the name and address of that operator and the amount, type and duration of the security, and these statements may not be disputed by the person by whom or on whose behalf the certificate was issued. The certificate shall also indicate the nuclear substances and the carriage in respect of which the security applies and shall include a statement by the competent public authority that the person named is an operator within the meaning of this Convention.

(*d*) A Contracting Party may provide by legislation that, under such terms as may be contained therein and upon fulfilment of the requirements of article 10(*a*), a carrier may, at his request and with the consent of an operator of a nuclear installation situated in its territory, by decision of the competent public authority, be liable in accordance with this Convention in place of that operator. In such case for all the purposes of this Convention the carrier shall be considered, in respect of nuclear incidents occurring in the course of carriage of nuclear substances, as an operator of a nuclear installation on the territory of the Contracting Party whose legislation so provides.

Article 5

(*a*) If the nuclear fuel or radioactive products or waste involved in a nuclear incident have been in more than one nuclear installation and are in a nuclear installation at the time damage is caused, no operator of any nuclear installation in which they have previously been shall be liable for the damage.

(*b*) Where, however, damage is caused by a nuclear incident occurring in a nuclear installation and involving only nuclear substances stored therein incidentally to their carriage, the operator of the nuclear installation shall not be liable where another operator or person is liable pursuant to article 4.

(*c*) If the nuclear fuel or radioactive products or waste involved in a nuclear incident have been in more than one nuclear installation and are not in a nuclear installation at the time damage is caused, no operator other than the operator of the last nuclear installation in which they were before the damage was caused or an operator who has subsequently taken them in charge, or has assumed liability therefor pursuant to the express terms of a contract in writing shall be liable for the damage.

(*d*) If damage gives rise to liability of more than one operator in accordance with this Convention, the liability of these operators shall be joint and several: provided that where such liability arises as a result of damage caused by a nuclear incident involving nuclear substances in the course of carriage in one and the same means of transport, or, in the case of storage incidental to the carriage, in one and the same nuclear installation, the maximum total amount for which such operators shall be liable shall be the highest amount established with respect to any of them pursuant to article 7 and provided that in no case shall any one operator be required, in respect of a nuclear incident, to pay more than the amount established with respect to him pursuant to article 7.

Article 6

(*a*) The right to compensation for damage caused by a nuclear incident may be exercised only against an operator liable for the damage in accordance with this Convention, or, if a direct right of action against the insurer or other financial guarantor furnishing the security required pursuant to article 10 is given by national law, against the insurer or other financial guarantor.

(*b*) Except as otherwise provided in this article, no other person shall be liable for damage caused by a nuclear incident, but this provision shall not affect the application of any international agreement in the field of transport in force or open for signature, ratification or accession at the date of this Convention.

(*c*)(i) Nothing in this Convention shall affect the liability:

1. of any individual for damage caused by a nuclear incident for which the operator, by virtue of article 3(*a*)(ii)(1) and (2) or Article 9, is not liable under this Convention and which results from an act or omission of that individual done with intent to cause damage;

2. of a person duly authorized to operate a reactor comprised in a means of transport for damage caused by a nuclear incident when an operator is not liable for such damage pursuant to article 4(*a*)(iii) or (*b*)(iii).

(ii) The operator shall incur no liability outside this Convention for damage caused by a nuclear incident.

(*d*) Any person who has paid compensation in respect of damage caused by a nuclear incident under any international agreement referred to in paragraph (*b*) of this article or under any legislation of a non-Contracting State shall, up to the amount which he has paid, acquire by subrogation the rights under this Convention of the person suffering damage whom he has so compensated.

(*e*) Any person who has his principal place of business in the territory of a Contracting Party or who is the servant of such a person and who has paid compensation in respect of damage caused by a nuclear incident occurring in the territory of a non-Contracting State or in respect of damage suffered in such territory shall, up to the amount which he has paid, acquire the rights which the person so compensated would have had against the operator but for the provisions of article 2.

(*f*) The operator shall have a right of recourse only:

(i) if the damage caused by a nuclear incident results from an act or omission done with intent to cause damage, against the individual acting or omitting to act with such intent;

(ii) if and to the extent that it is so provided expressly by contract.

(*g*) If the operator has a right of recourse to any extent pursuant to paragraph (*f*) of this article against any person, that person shall not, to that extent, have a right against the operator under paragraphs (*d*) or (*e*) of this article.

(*h*) Where provisions of national or public health insurance, social security, workmen's compensation or occupational disease compensation systems include compensation for damage caused by a nuclear incident, rights of beneficiaries of such systems and rights of recourse by virtue of such systems shall be determined by the law of the Contracting Party or by the regulations of the inter-Governmental organization which has established such systems.

Article 7

(*a*) The aggregate of compensation required to be paid in respect of damage caused by a nuclear incident shall not exceed the maximum liability established in accordance with this article.

(*b*) The maximum liability of the operator in respect of damage caused by a nuclear incident shall be 15,000,000 Special Drawing Rights as defined by the International Monetary Fund and used by it for its own operations and transactions (hereinafter referred to as "Special Drawing Rights"). However,

(i) any Contracting Party, taking into account the possibilities for the operator of obtaining the insurance or other financial security required pursuant to Article 10, may establish by legislation a greater or lesser amount;

(ii) any Contracting Party, having regard to the nature of the nuclear installation or the nuclear substances involved and to the likely consequences of an incident originating therefrom, may establish a lower amount;

provided that in no event shall any amounts so established be less than 5,000,000 Special Drawing Rights. The sums mentioned above may be converted into national currency in round figures.

(*c*) Compensation for damage caused to the means of transport on which the nuclear substances involved were at the time of the nuclear incident shall not have the effect of reducing the liability of the operator in respect of other damage to an amount less than either 5,000,000 Special Drawing Rights, or any higher amount established by the legislation of a Contracting Party.

(*d*) The amount of liability of operators of nuclear installations in the territory of a Contracting Party established in accordance with paragraph (*b*) of this article as well as the provisions of any legislation of a Contracting Party pursuant to paragraph (*c*) of this article shall apply to the liability of such operators wherever the nuclear incident occurs.

(*e*) A Contracting Party may subject the transit of nuclear substances through its territory to the condition that the maximum amount of liability of the foreign operator concerned be increased, if it considers that such amount does not adequately cover the risks of a nuclear incident in the course of the transit: provided that the maximum amount thus increased shall not exceed the maximum amount of liability of operators of nuclear installations situated in its territory.

(*f*) The provisions of paragraph (*e*) of this article shall not apply:

(i) to carriage by sea where, under international law, there is a right of entry in cases of urgent distress into the ports of such Contracting Party or a right of innocent passage through its territory; or

(ii) to carriage by air where, by agreement or under international law there is a right to fly over or land on the territory of such Contracting Party.

(*g*) Any interest and costs awarded by a court in actions for compensation under this Convention shall not be considered to be compensation for the purposes of this Convention and shall be payable by the operator in addition to any sum for which he is liable in accordance with this article.

Article 8

(*a*) The right of compensation under this Convention shall be extinguished if an action is not brought within ten years from the date of the nuclear incident. National legislation may, however, establish a period longer than ten years if measures have been taken by the Contracting Party in whose territory the nuclear installation of the operator liable is situated to cover the liability of that operator in respect of any actions for compensation begun after the expiry of the period of ten years and during such longer period: provided that such extension of the extinction period shall in no case affect the right of compensation under this Convention of any person who has brought an action in respect of loss of life or personal injury against the operator before the expiry of the period of ten years.

(*b*) In the case of damage caused by a nuclear incident involving nuclear fuel or radioactive products or waste which, at the time of the incident have been stolen, lost, jettisoned or abandoned and have not yet been recovered, the period established pursuant to paragraph (*a*) of this article shall be computed from the date of that nuclear incident, but the period shall in no case exceed twenty years from the date of the theft, loss, jettison or abandonment.

(*c*) National legislation may establish a period of not less than two years for the extinction of the right or as a period of limitation either from the date at which the person suffering damage has knowledge or from the date at which he ought reasonably to have known of both the damage and the operator liable: provided that the period established pursuant to paragraphs (*a*) and (*b*) of this article shall not be exceeded.

(*d*) Where the provisions of article 13(*c*)(ii) are applicable, the right of compensation shall not, however, be extinguished if, within the time provided for in paragraphs (*a*), (*b*) and (*c*) of this Article.

(i) prior to the determination by the Tribunal referred to in article 17, an action has been brought before any of the courts from which the Tribunal can choose; if the Tribunal determines that the competent court is a court other than that before which such action has already been brought, it may fix a date by which such action has to be brought before the competent court so determined; or

(ii) a request has been made to a Contracting Party concerned to initiate a determination by the Tribunal of the competent court pursuant to article 13(*c*)(ii) and an action is brought subsequent to such determination within such time as may be fixed by the Tribunal.

(*e*) Unless national law provides to the contrary, any person suffering damage caused by a nuclear incident who has brought an action for compensation within the period provided for in this article may amend his claim in respect of any aggravation of the damage after the expiry of such period provided that final judgment has not been entered by the competent court.

Article 9

The operator shall not be liable for damage caused by a nuclear incident directly due to an act of armed conflict, hostilities, civil war, insurrection or, except in so far as the legislation of the Contracting Party in whose territory his nuclear installation is situated may provide to the contrary, a grave natural disaster of an exceptional character.

Article 10

(*a*) To cover the liability under this Convention, the operator shall be required to have and maintain insurance or other financial security of the amount established pursuant to article 7 and of such type and terms as the competent public authority shall specify.

(*b*) No insurer or other financial guarantor shall suspend or cancel the insurance or other financial security provided for in paragraph (*a*) of this article without giving notice in writing of at least two months to the competent public authority or in so far as such insurance or other financial security relates to the carriage of nuclear substances, during the period of the carriage in question.

(*c*) The sums provided as insurance, reinsurance, or other financial security may be drawn upon only for compensation for damage caused by a nuclear incident.

Article 11

The nature, form and extent of the compensation, within the limits of this Convention, as well as the equitable distribution thereof, shall be governed by national law.

Article 12

Compensation payable under this Convention, insurance and reinsurance premiums, sums provided as insurance, reinsurance, or other financial security required pursuant to article 10, and interest and costs referred to in article 7(*g*), shall be freely transferable between the monetary areas of the Contracting Parties.

Article 13

(*a*) Except as otherwise provided in this article, jurisdiction over actions under articles 3, 4, 6(*a*) and 6(*e*) shall lie only with the courts of the Contracting Party in whose territory the nuclear incident occurred.

(*b*) Where a nuclear incident occurs outside the territory of the Contracting Parties, or where the place of the nuclear incident cannot be determined with certainty, jurisdiction over such actions shall lie with the courts of the Contracting Party in whose territory the nuclear installation of the operator liable is situated.

(*c*) Where jurisdiction would lie with the courts of more than one Contracting Party by virtue of paragraphs (*a*) or (*b*) of this article, jurisdiction shall lie,

(i) if the nuclear incident occurred partly outside the territory of any Contracting Party and partly in the territory of a single Contracting Party, with the courts of that Contracting Party; and

(ii) in any other case, with the courts of the Contracting Party determined, at the request of a Contracting Party concerned, by the Tribunal referred to in article 17 as being the most closely related to the case in question.

(*d*) Judgments entered by the competent court under this article after trial, or by default, shall, when they have become enforceable under the law applied by that court, become enforceable in the territory of any of the other Contracting Parties as soon as the formalities required by the Contracting Party concerned have been complied with. The merits of the case shall not be the subject of further proceedings. The foregoing provisions shall not apply to interim judgements.

(*e*) If an action is brought against a Contracting Party under this Convention, such Contracting Party may not, except in respect of measures of execution, invoke any jurisdictional immunities before the court competent in accordance with this article.

Article 14

(*a*) This Convention shall be applied without any discrimination based upon nationality, domicile, or residence.

(*b*) "National law" and "national legislation" mean the national law or the national legislation of the court having jurisdiction under this Convention over claims arising out of a nuclear incident, and that law or legislation shall apply to all matters both substantive and procedural not specifically governed by this Convention.

(*c*) That law and legislation shall be applied without any discrimination based upon nationality, domicile, or residence.

Article 15

(*a*) Any Contracting Party may take such measures as it deems necessary to provide for an increase in the amount of compensation specified in this Convention.

(*b*) In so far as compensation for damage involves public funds and is in excess of the 5,000,000 Special Drawing Rights referred to in Article 7, any such measure in whatever form may be applied under conditions which may derogate from the provisions of this Convention.

Article 16

Decisions taken by the Steering Committee under article 1(*a*)(ii), 1(*a*)(iii) and 1(*b*) shall be adopted by mutual agreement of the members representing the Contracting Parties.

Article 17

Any dispute arising between two or more Contracting Parties concerning the interpretation or application of this Convention shall be examined by the Steering Committee and in the absence of friendly settlement shall, upon the request of a Contracting Party concerned, be submitted to the Tribunal established by the Convention of 20th December, 1957, on the Establishment of a Security Control in the Field of Nuclear Energy.

Article 18

(*a*) Reservations to one or more of the provisions of this Convention may be made at any time prior to ratification of or accession to this Convention or prior to the time of notification under article 23 in respect of any territory or territories mentioned in the notification, and shall be admissible only if the terms of these reservations have been expressly accepted by the signatories.

(*b*) Such acceptance shall not be required from a signatory which has not itself ratified this Convention within a period of twelve months after the date of notification to it of such reservation by the Secretary–General of the Organisation in accordance with article 24.

(c) Any reservation admitted in accordance with this article may be withdrawn at any time by notification addressed to the Secretary–General of the Organisation.

Article 19

(a) This Convention shall be ratified. Instruments of ratification shall be deposited with the Secretary–General of the Organisation.

(b) This Convention shall come into force upon the deposit of instruments of ratification by not less than five of the signatories. For each Signatory ratifying thereafter, this Convention shall come into force upon the deposit of its instrument of ratification.

Article 20

Amendments to this Convention shall be adopted by mutual agreement of all the Contracting Parties. They shall come into force when ratified or confirmed by two-thirds of the Contracting Parties. For each Contracting Party ratifying or confirming thereafter, they shall come into force at the date of such ratification or confirmation.

Article 21

(a) The Government of any Member or Associate country of the Organisation which is not a signatory to this Convention may accede thereto by notification addressed to the Secretary–General of the Organisation.

(b) The Government of any other country which is not a signatory to this Convention may accede thereto by notification addressed to the Secretary–General of the Organisation and with the unanimous assent of the Contracting Parties. Such accession shall take effect from the date of such assent.

Article 22

(a) This Convention shall remain in effect for a period of ten years as from the date of its coming into force. Any Contracting Party may, by giving twelve months' notice to the Secretary–General of the Organisation, terminate the application of this Convention to itself at the end of the period of ten years.

(b) This Convention shall, after the period of ten years, remain in force for a period of five years for such Contracting Parties as have not terminated its application in accordance with paragraph *(a)* of this article, and thereafter for successive periods of five years for such Contracting Parties as have not terminated its application at the end of one of such periods of five years by giving twelve months' notice to that effect to the Secretary–General of the Organisation.

(c) A conference shall be convened by the Secretary–General of the Organisation in order to consider revisions to this Convention after a period of five years as from the date of its coming into force or, at any other time, at the request of a Contracting Party, within six months from the date of such request.

Article 23

(a) This Convention shall apply to the metropolitan territories of the Contracting Parties.

(b) Any signatory or Contracting Party may, at the time of signature or ratification of or accession to this Convention or at any later time, notify the Secretary–General of the Organisation that this Convention shall apply to those of its territories, including the territories for whose international relations it is responsible, to which this Convention is not applicable in accordance with paragraph *(a)* of this article and which are mentioned in the notification. Any such notification may in respect of any

territory or territories mentioned therein be withdrawn by giving twelve months' notice to that effect to the Secretary–General of the Organisation.

(c) Any territories of a Contracting Party, including the territories for whose international relations it is responsible, to which this Convention does not apply shall be regarded for the purposes of this Convention as being a territory of a non-Contracting State.

Article 24

The Secretary–General of the Organisation shall give notice to all Signatories and acceding Governments of the receipt of any instrument of ratification, accession, withdrawal, notification under article 23, and decisions of the Steering Committee under article 1*(a)* (ii), 1*(a)* (iii) and 1*(b)*. He shall also notify them of the date on which this Convention comes into force, the text of any amendment thereto and of the date on which such amendment comes into force, and any reservation made in accordance with article 18.

3.2 Convention Supplementary to the 1960 Convention on Third Party Liability in the Field of Nuclear Energy (With Annex and as Amended Through 1964). Concluded at Brussels, 31 January 1963. Entered into force, 4 December 1974. *Reprinted in* 2 I.L.M. 685 (1963) & 5 Weston V.J.2

* * *

Article 1

The system instituted by this Convention is supplementary to that of the Paris Convention, shall be subject to the provisions of the Paris Convention, and shall be applied in accordance with the following Articles.

Article 2

(a) The system of this Convention shall apply to damage caused by nuclear incidents, other than those occurring entirely in the territory of a State which is not a Party to this Convention:

(i) for which an operator of a nuclear installation, used for peaceful purposes, situated in the territory of a Contracting Party to this Convention (hereinafter referred to as a "Contracting Party"), and which appears on the list established and kept up to date in accordance with the terms of Article 13, is liable under the Paris Convention, and

(ii) suffered

(1) in the territory of a Contracting Party; or

(2) on or over the high seas on board a ship or aircraft registered in the territory of a Contracting Party; or

(3) on or over the high seas by a national of a Contracting Party, provided that, in the case of damage to a ship or an aircraft, the ship or aircraft is registered in the territory of a Contracting Party;

provided that the courts of a Contracting Party have jurisdiction pursuant to the Paris Convention.

(b) Any Signatory or acceding Government may, at the time of signature of or accession to this Convention or on the deposit of its instrument of ratification, declare that, for the purposes of the application of paragraph (a)(ii)(3) of this Article, individuals or certain categories thereof, considered under its law as having their habitual residence in its territory, are assimilated to its own nationals.

(c) In this Article, the expression "a national of a Contracting Party" shall include a Contracting Party or any of its constituent sub-divisions, or a partnership, or any public or private body whether corporate or not established in the territory of a Contracting Party.

Article 3

(a) Under the conditions established by this Convention, the Contracting Parties undertake that compensation in respect of the damage referred to in Article 2 shall be provided up to the amount of 300 million Special Drawing Rights per incident.

(b) Such compensation shall be provided:

(i) up to an amount of at least 5 million Special Drawing Rights, out of funds provided by insurance or other financial security, such amount to be established by the legislation of the Contracting Party in whose territory the nuclear installation of the operator liable is situated;

(ii) between this amount and 175 million Special Drawing Rights, out of public funds to be made available by the Contracting Party in whose territory the nuclear installation of the operator liable is situated;

(iii) between 175 million and 300 million Special Drawing Rights, out of public funds to be made available by the Contracting Parties according to the formula for contributions specified in Article 12.

(c) For this purpose, each Contracting Party shall either:

(i) establish the maximum liability of the operator, pursuant to Article 7 of the Paris Convention, at 300 million Special Drawing Rights, and provide that such liability shall be covered by all the funds referred to in paragraph (b) of this Article; or

(ii) establish the maximum liability of the operator at an amount at least equal to that established pursuant to paragraph (b)(i) of this Article and provide that, in excess of such amount and up to 300 million Special Drawing Rights, the public funds referred to in paragraph (b)(ii) and (iii) of this Article shall be made available by some means other than as cover for the liability of the operator, provided that the rules of substance and procedure laid down in this Convention are not thereby affected.

(d) The obligation of the operator to pay compensation, interest or costs out of public funds made available pursuant to paragraphs (b)(ii) and (iii), and (f) of this Article shall only be enforceable against the operator as and when such funds are in fact made available.

(e) The Contracting Parties, in carrying out this Convention, undertake not to make use of the right provided for in Article 15(b) of the Paris Convention to apply special conditions:

(i) in respect of compensation for damage provided out of the funds referred to in paragraph (b)(i) of this Article;

(ii) other than those laid down in this Convention in respect of compensation for damage provided out of the public funds referred to in paragraph (b)(ii) and (iii) of this Article.

(f) The interest and costs referred to in Article 7(g) of the Paris Convention are payable in addition to the amounts referred to in paragraph (b) of this Article and shall be borne in so far as they are awarded in respect of compensation payable out of the funds referred to in:

(i) paragraph (b)(i) of this Article, by the operator liable;

(ii) paragraph (b)(ii) of this Article, by the Contracting Party in whose territory the nuclear installation of that operator is situated;

(iii) paragraph (b)(iii) of this Article, by the Contracting Parties together.

(g) For the purposes of this Convention, "Special Drawing Right" means the Special Drawing Right as it is defined by the International Monetary Fund. The amounts mentioned in this Convention shall be converted into the national currency of a Contracting Party in accordance with the value of that currency at the date of the incident, unless another date is fixed for a given incident by agreement between the Contracting Parties. The equivalent in Special Drawings Rights of the national currency of a Contracting Party shall be calculated in accordance with the method of valuation applied at the date in question by the International Monetary Fund for its own operations and transactions.

Article 4

(a) If a nuclear incident causes damage which gives rise to liability of more than one operator, the aggregate liability provided for in Article 5(d) of the Paris Convention shall not, to the extent that public funds have to be made available pursuant to Article 3(b)(ii) and (iii), exceed 300 million Special Drawing Rights.

(b) The total amount of the public funds made available pursuant to Article 3 (b)(ii) and (iii) shall not, in such event, exceed the difference between 300 million Special Drawing Rights and the sum of the amounts established with respect to such operators pursuant to Article 3(b)(i) or, in the case of an operator whose nuclear installation is situated in the territory of a State which is not a Party to this Convention, the amount established pursuant to Article 7 of the Paris Convention. If more than one Contracting Party is required to make available public funds pursuant to Article 3(b)(ii), such funds shall be made available by them in proportion to the number of nuclear installations situated in their respective territories, which are involved in the nuclear incident and of which the operators are liable.

Article 5

(a) Where the operator liable has a right of recourse pursuant to Article 6(f) of the Paris Convention, the Contracting Party in whose territory the nuclear installation of that operator is situated shall take such legislative measures as are necessary to enable both that Contracting Party and the other Contracting Parties to benefit from this recourse to the extent that public funds have been made available pursuant to Article 3(b)(ii) and (iii), and (f).

(b) Such legislation may provide for the recovery of public funds made available pursuant to Article 3(b)(ii) and (iii), and (f) from such operator if the damage results from fault on his part.

Article 6

In calculating the public funds to be made available pursuant to this Convention, account shall be taken only of those rights to compensation exercised within ten years from the date of the nuclear incident. In the case of damage caused by a nuclear incident involving nuclear fuel or radioactive products or waste which, at the time of the incident have been stolen, lost, jettisoned, or abandoned and have not yet been recovered such period shall not in any case exceed twenty years from the date of the theft, loss, jettison or abandonment. It shall also be extended in the cases and under the conditions laid down in Article 8(d) of the Paris Convention. Amendments made to claims after the expiry of this period, under the conditions laid down in Article 8(e) of the Paris Convention, shall also be taken into account.

Article 7

Where a Contracting Party makes use of the right provided for in Article 8(c) of the Paris Convention, the period which it establishes shall be a period of prescription of three years either from the date at which the person suffering damage has knowledge or from the date at which he ought reasonably to have known of both the damage and the operator liable.

Article 8

Any person who is entitled to benefit from the provisions of this Convention shall have the right to full compensation in accordance with national law for damage suffered, provided that, where the amount of damage exceeds or is likely to exceed:

(i) 300 million Special Drawing Rights; or

(ii) if there is aggregate liability under Article 5(d) of the Paris Convention and a higher sum results therefrom, such higher sum;

any Contracting Party may establish equitable criteria for apportionment. Such criteria shall be applied whatever the origin of the funds and, subject to the provisions of Article 2, without discrimination based on the nationality, domicile or residence of the person suffering the damage.

Article 9

(a) The system of disbursements by which the public funds required under Article 3(b)(ii) and (iii), and (f) are to be made available shall be that of the Contracting Party whose courts have jurisdiction.

(b) Each Contracting Party shall ensure that persons suffering damage may enforce their rights to compensation without having to bring separate proceedings according to the origin of the funds provided for such compensation.

(c) No Contracting Party shall be required to make available the public funds referred to in Article 3(b)(ii) and (iii) so long as any of the funds referred to in Article 3(b)(i) remain available.

Article 10

(a) The Contracting Party whose courts have jurisdiction shall be required to inform the other Contracting Parties of a nuclear incident and its circumstances as soon as it appears that the damage caused by such incident exceeds, or is likely to exceed, 175 million Special Drawing Rights. The Contracting Parties shall without delay make all the necessary arrangements to settle the procedure for their relations in this connection.

(b) Only the Contracting Party whose courts have jurisdiction shall be entitled to request the other Contracting Parties to make available the public funds required under Article 3(b)(iii) and (f) and shall have exclusive competence to disburse such funds.

(c) Such Contracting Party shall, when the occasion arises, exercise the right of recourse provided for in Article 5 on behalf of the other Contracting Parties who have made available public funds pursuant to Article 3(b)(iii) and (f).

(d) Settlements effected in respect of the payment of compensation out of the public funds referred to in Article 8(b)(ii) and (iii) in accordance with the conditions established by national legislation shall be recognized by the other Contracting Parties, and judgements entered by the competent courts in respect of such compensation shall become enforceable in the territory of the other Contracting Parties in accordance with the provisions of Article 13(d) of the Paris Convention.

Article 11

(a) If the courts having jurisdiction are those of a Contracting Party other than the Contracting Party in whose territory the nuclear installation of the operator liable is situated, the public funds required under Article 3(b)(ii) and (f) shall be made available by the first-named Contracting Party. The Contracting Party in whose territory the nuclear installation of the operator liable is situated shall reimburse to the other Contracting Party the sums paid. These two Contracting Parties shall agree on the procedure for reimbursement.

(b) In adopting all legislative, regulatory or administrative provisions, after the nuclear incident has occurred, concerning the nature, form and extent of the compensation, the procedure for making available the public funds required under Article 3(b)(ii) and, if necessary, the criteria for the apportionment of such funds, the Contracting Party whose courts have jurisdiction shall consult the Contracting Party in whose territory the nuclear installation of the operator liable is situated. It shall further take all measures necessary to enable the latter to intervene in proceedings and to participate in any settlement concerning compensation.

Article 12

(a) The formula for contributions according to which the Contracting Parties shall make available the public funds referred to in Article 3(b)(iii) shall be determined as follows:

(i) as to 50%, on the basis of the ratio between the gross national product at current prices of each Contracting Party and the total of the gross national products at current prices of all Contracting Parties as shown by the official statistics published by the Organisation for Economic Co-operation and Development for the year preceding the year in which the nuclear incident occurs;

(ii) as to 50%, on the basis of the ratio between the thermal power of the reactors situated in the territory of each Contracting Party and the total thermal power of the reactors situated in the territories of all the Contracting Parties. This calculation shall be made on the basis of the thermal power of the reactors shown at the date of the nuclear incident in the list referred to in Article 2(a)(i): provided that a reactor shall only be taken into consideration for the purposes of this calculation as from the date when it first reaches criticality.

(b) For the purposes of this Convention, "thermal power" means

(i) before the issue of a final operating licence, the planned thermal power;

(ii) after the issue of such licence, the thermal power authorized by the competent national authorities.

Article 13

(a) Each Contracting Party shall ensure that all nuclear installations used for peaceful purposes situated in its territory, and falling within the definition in Article 1 of the Paris Convention, appear in the list referred to in Article 2(a)(i).

(b) For this purpose, each Signatory or acceding Government shall, on the deposit of its instrument of ratification or accession, communicate to the Belgian Government full particulars of such installations.

(c) Such particulars shall indicate:

(i) in the case of all installations not yet completed, the expected date on which the risk of a nuclear incident will exist;

(ii) and further, in the case of reactors, the expected date on which they will first reach criticality, and also their thermal power.

(d) Each Contracting Party shall also communicate to the Belgian Government the exact date of the existence of the risk of a nuclear incident and, in the case of reactors, the date on which they first reached criticality.

(e) Each Contracting Party shall also communicate to the Belgian Government all modifications to be made to the list. Where such modifications include the addition of a nuclear installation, the communication must be made at least three months before the expected date on which the risk of a nuclear incident will exist.

(f) If a Contracting Party is of the opinion that the particulars, or any modification to be made to the list, communicated by another Contracting Party do not comply with the provisions of Article 2(a)(i) and of this Article, it may raise objections thereto only by addressing them to the Belgian Government within three months from the date on which it has received notice pursuant to paragraph (h) of this Article.

(g) If a Contracting Party is of the opinion that a communication required in accordance with this Article has not been made within the time prescribed in this Article, it may raise objections only by addressing them to the Belgian Government within three months from the date on which it knew of the facts which, in its opinion, ought to have been communicated.

(h) The Belgian Government shall give notice as soon as possible to each Contracting Party of the communications and objections which it has received pursuant to this Article.

(i) The list referred to in Article 2(a)(i) shall consist of all the particulars and modifications referred to in paragraphs (b), (c), (d) and (e) of this Article, it being understood that objections submitted pursuant to paragraphs (f) and (g) of this Article shall have effect retrospective to the date on which they were raised, if they are sustained.

(j) The Belgian Government shall supply any Contracting Party on demand with an up-to-date statement of the nuclear installations covered by this Convention and the details supplied in respect of them pursuant to this Article.

Article 14

(a) Except insofar as this Convention otherwise provides, each Contracting Party may exercise the powers vested in it by virtue of the Paris Convention, and any provisions made thereunder may be invoked against the other Contracting Parties in order that the public funds referred to in Article 3(b)(ii) and (iii) be made available.

(b) Any such provisions made by a Contracting Party pursuant to Articles 2 and 9 of the Paris Convention as a result of which the public funds referred to in Article 3(b)(ii) and (iii) are required to be made available may not be invoked against any other Contracting Party unless it has consented thereto.

(c) Nothing in this Convention shall prevent a Contracting Party from making provisions outside the scope of the Paris Convention and of this Convention, provided that such provisions shall not involve any further obligation on the part of the other Contracting Parties insofar as their public funds are concerned.

Article 15

(a) Any Contracting Party may conclude an agreement with a State which is not a Party to this Convention concerning compensation out of public funds for damage caused by a nuclear incident.

(b) To the extent that the conditions for payment of compensation under any such agreement are not more favourable than those which result from the measures adopted by the Contracting Party concerned for the application of the Paris Convention and of this Convention, the amount of damage caused by a nuclear incident covered by this Convention and for which compensation is payable by virtue of such an agreement may be taken into consideration, where the proviso to Article 8 applies, in calculating the total amount of damage caused by that incident.

(c) The provisions of paragraphs (a) and (b) of this Article shall in no case affect the obligations under Article 3(b)(ii) and (iii) of those Contracting Parties which have not given their consent to such agreement.

(d) Any Contracting Party intending to conclude such an agreement shall notify the other Contracting Parties of its intention. Agreements concluded shall be notified to the Belgian Government.

Article 16

(a) The Contracting Parties shall consult each other upon all problems of common interest raised by the application of this Convention and of the Paris Convention, especially Articles 20 and 22(c) of the latter Convention.

(b) They shall consult each other on the desirability of revising this Convention after a period of five years from the date of its coming into force, and at any other time upon the request of a Contracting Party.

Article 17

Any dispute arising between two or more Contracting Parties concerning the interpretation or application of this Convention shall, upon the request of a Contracting Party concerned, be submitted to the European Nuclear Energy Tribunal established by the Convention of 20th December 1957 on the Establishment of a Security Control in the Field of Nuclear Energy.

Article 18

(a) Reservations to one or more of the provisions of this Convention may be made at any time prior to ratification of this Convention if the terms of these reservations have been expressly accepted by all Signatories or, at the time of accession or of the application of the provisions of Articles 21 and 24, if the terms of these reservations have been expressly accepted by all Signatories and acceding Governments.

(b) Such acceptance shall not be required from a Signatory which has not itself ratified this Convention within a period of twelve months after the date of notification to it of such reservation by the Belgian Government in accordance with Article 25.

(c) Any reservation accepted in accordance with the provisions of paragraph (a) of this Article may be withdrawn at any time by notification addressed to the Belgian Government.

Article 19

No State may become or continue to be a Contracting Party to this Convention unless it is a Contracting Party to the Paris Convention.

Article 20

(a) The Annex to this Convention shall form an integral part thereof.

(b) This Convention shall be ratified. Instruments of ratification shall be deposited with the Belgian Government.

(c) This Convention shall come into force three months after the deposit of the sixth instrument of ratification.

(d) For each Signatory ratifying this Convention after the deposit of the sixth instrument of ratification, it shall come into force three months after the date of the deposit of its instrument of ratification.

Article 21

Amendments to this Convention shall be adopted by agreement among all the Contracting Parties. They shall come into force on the date when all Contracting Parties have ratified or confirmed them.

Article 22

(a) After the coming into force of this Convention, any Contracting Party to the Paris Convention which has not signed this Convention may request accession to this Convention by notification addressed to the Belgian Government.

(b) Such accession shall require the unanimous assent of the Contracting Parties.

(c) Once such assent has been given, the Contracting Party to the Paris Convention requesting accession shall deposit its instrument of accession with the Belgian Government.

(d) The accession shall take effect three months from the date of deposit of the instrument of accession.

Article 23

(a) This Convention shall remain in force until the expiry of the Paris Convention.

(b) Any Contracting Party may, by giving twelve months' notice to the Belgian Government, terminate the application of this Convention to itself after the end of the period of ten years specified in Article 22(a) of the Paris Convention. Within six months after receipt of such notice, any other Contracting Party may, by notice to the Belgian Government, terminate the application of this Convention to itself as from the date when it ceases to have effect in respect of the Contracting Party which first gave notice.

(c) The expiry of this Convention or the withdrawal of a Contracting Party shall not terminate the obligations assumed by each Contracting Party under this Convention to pay compensation for damage caused by nuclear incidents occurring before the date of such expiry or withdrawal.

(d) The Contracting Parties shall, in good time, consult each other on what measures should be taken after the expiry of this Convention or the withdrawal of one or more of the Contracting Parties, to provide compensation comparable to that accorded by this Convention for damage caused by nuclear incidents occurring after the date of such expiry or withdrawal and for which the operator of a nuclear installation in operation before such date within the territories of the Contracting Parties is liable.

Article 24

(a) This Convention shall apply to the metropolitan territories of the Contracting Parties.

(b) Any Contracting Party desiring the application of this Convention to one or more of the territories in respect of which, pursuant to Article 23 of the Paris Convention, it has given notification of application of that Convention, shall address a request to the Belgian Government.

(c) The application of this Convention to any such territory shall require the unanimous assent of the Contracting Parties.

(d) Once such assent has been given, the Contracting Party concerned shall address to the Belgian Government a notification which shall take effect as from the date of its receipt.

(e) Such notification may, as regards any territory mentioned therein, be withdrawn by the Contracting Party which has made it by giving twelve months' notice to that effect to the Belgian Government.

(f) If the Paris Convention ceases to apply to any such territory, this Convention shall also cease to apply thereto.

Article 25

The Belgian Government shall notify all Signatories and acceding Governments of the receipt of any instrument of ratification, accession or withdrawal, and shall also notify them of the date on which this Convention comes into force, the text of any amendment thereto and the date on which such amendment comes into force, any reservations made in accordance with Article 18, and all notifications which it has received.

ANNEX

THE GOVERNMENTS OF THE CONTRACTING PARTIES declare that compensation for damage caused by a nuclear incident not covered by the Supplementary Convention solely by reason of the fact that the relevant nuclear installation, on account of its utilization, is not on the list referred to in Article 2 of the Supplementary Convention, (including the case where such installation is considered by one or more but not all of the Governments to be outside the Paris Convention):

— shall be provided without discrimination among the nationals of the Contracting Parties to the Supplementary Convention; and

— shall not be limited to less than 300 million Special Drawing Rights.

In addition, if they have not already done so, they shall endeavor to make the rules for compensation of persons suffering damage caused by such incidents as similar as possible to those established in respect of nuclear incidents occurring in connection with nuclear installations covered by the Supplementary Convention.

3.3 TREATY ON PRINCIPLES GOVERNING THE ACTIVITIES OF STATES IN THE EXPLORATION AND USE OF OUTER SPACE, INCLUDING THE MOON AND OTHER CELESTIAL BODIES.[a] Concluded at London, Moscow, and Washington, 27 January 1967. Entered into force, 10 October 1967. 610 U.N.T.S. 205; *reprinted in* 6 I.L.M. 386 (1967) & 5 Weston V.E.21

Article I

The exploration and use of outer space, including the moon and other celestial bodies, shall be carried out for the benefit and in the interests of all countries, irrespective of their degree of economic or scientific development, and shall be the province of all mankind.

Outer space, including the moon and other celestial bodies, shall be free for exploration and use by all States without discrimination of any kind, on a basis of equality and in accordance with international law, and there shall be free access to all areas of celestial bodies.

There shall be freedom of scientific investigation in outer space, including the moon and other celestial bodies, and States shall facilitate and encourage international co-operation in such investigation.

Article II

Outer space, including the moon and other celestial bodies, is not subject to national appropriation by claim of sovereignty, by means of use or occupation, or by any other means.

Article III

States Parties to the Treaty shall carry on activities in the exploration and use of outer space, including the moon and other celestial bodies, in accordance with international law, including the Charter of the United Nations, in the interest of maintaining international peace and security and promoting international co-operation and understanding.

Article IV

States Parties to the Treaty undertake not to place in orbit around the earth any objects carrying nuclear weapons or any other kinds of weapons of mass destruction, instal such weapons on celestial bodies, or station such weapons in outer space in any other manner.

The moon and other celestial bodies shall be used by all States Parties to the Treaty exclusively for peaceful purposes. The establishment of military bases, installations and fortifications, the testing of any type of weapons and the conduct of military manoeuvres on celestial bodies shall be forbidden. The use of military personnel for scientific research or for any other peaceful purposes shall not be prohibited. The use of any equipment or facility necessary for peaceful exploration of the moon and other celestial bodies shall also not be prohibited.

Article V

States Parties to the Treaty shall regard astronauts as envoys of mankind in outer space and shall render to them all possible assistance in the event of accident, distress, or emergency landing on the territory of another State Party or on the high seas. When astronauts make such a landing, they shall be safely and promptly returned to the State of registry of their space vehicle.

a. Also known as "the Outer Space Treaty."

In carrying on activities in outer space and on celestial bodies, the astronauts of one State Party shall render all possible assistance to the astronauts of other States Parties.

States Parties to the Treaty shall immediately inform the other States Parties to the Treaty or the Secretary-General of the United Nations of any phenomena they discover in outer space, including the moon and other celestial bodies, which could constitute a danger to the life or health of astronauts.

Article VI

States Parties to the Treaty shall bear international responsibility for national activities in outer space, including the moon and other celestial bodies, whether such activities are carried on by governmental agencies or by non-governmental entities, and for assuring that national activities are carried out in conformity with the provisions set forth in the present Treaty. The activities of non-governmental entities in outer space, including the moon and other celestial bodies, shall require authorization and continuing supervision by the appropriate State Party to the Treaty. When activities are carried on in outer space, including the moon and other celestial bodies, by an international organization, responsibility for compliance with this Treaty shall be borne both by the international organization and by the States Parties to the Treaty participating in such organization.

Article VII

Each State Party to the Treaty that launches or procures the launching of an object into outer space, including the moon and other celestial bodies, and each State Party from whose territory or facility an object is launched, is internationally liable for damage to another State Party to the Treaty or to its natural or juridical persons by such object or its component parts on the Earth, in air space or in outer space, including the moon and other celestial bodies.

Article VIII

A State Party to the Treaty on whose registry an object launched into outer space is carried shall retain jurisdiction and control over such object, and over any personnel thereof, while in outer space or on a celestial body. Ownership of objects launched into outer space, including objects landed or constructed on a celestial body, and of their component parts, is not affected by their presence in outer space or on a celestial body or by their return to the Earth. Such objects or component parts found beyond the limits of the State Party to the Treaty on whose registry they are carried shall be returned to that State Party, which shall, upon request, furnish identifying data prior to their return.

Article IX

In the exploration and use of outer space, including the moon and other celestial bodies, States Parties to the Treaty shall be guided by the principle of co-operation and mutual assistance and shall conduct all their activities in outer space, including the moon and other celestial bodies, with due regard to the corresponding interests of all other States Parties to the Treaty. States Parties to the Treaty shall pursue studies of outer space, including the moon and other celestial bodies, and conduct exploration of them so as to avoid their harmful contamination and also adverse changes in the environment of the Earth resulting from the introduction of extraterrestrial matter and, where necessary, shall adopt appropriate measures for this purpose. If a State Party to the Treaty has reason to believe that an activity or experiment planned by it or its nationals in outer space, including the moon and other celestial bodies, would cause potentially harmful interference with activities of other States Parties in the peaceful exploration and use of outer space, including the moon and other celestial bodies, it shall undertake appropriate international consultations before proceeding with any such activity or experiment. A State Party to the Treaty which has reason to believe that an activity or experiment planned by another State Party in outer space, including the moon and other celestial bodies, would cause potentially harmful interference with activities in the peaceful exploration and use of outer space, including the moon and other celestial bodies, may request consultation concerning the activity or experiment.

Article X

In order to promote international co-operation in the exploration and use of outer space, including the moon and other celestial bodies, in conformity with the purposes of this Treaty, the States Parties to the Treaty shall consider on a basis of equality any requests by other States Parties to the Treaty to be afforded an opportunity to observe the flight of space objects launched by those States.

The nature of such an opportunity for observation and the conditions under which it could be afforded shall be determined by agreement between the States concerned.

Article XI

In order to promote international co-operation in the peaceful exploration and use of outer space, States Parties to the Treaty conducting activities in outer space, including the moon and other celestial bodies, agree to inform the Secretary–General of the United Nations as well as the public and the international scientific community, to the greatest extent feasible and practicable, of the nature, conduct, locations and results of such activities. On receiving the said information, the Secretary–General of the United Nations should be prepared to disseminate it immediately and effectively.

Article XII

All stations, installations, equipment and space vehicles on the moon and other celestial bodies shall be open to representatives of other States Parties to the Treaty on a basis of reciprocity. Such representatives shall give reasonable advance notice of a projected visit, in order that appropriate consultations may be held and that maximum precautions may be taken to assure safety and to avoid interference with normal operations in the facility to be visited.

Article XIII

The provisions of this Treaty shall apply to the activities of States Parties to the Treaty in the exploration and use of outer space, including the moon and other celestial bodies, whether such activities are carried on by a single State Party to the Treaty or jointly with other States, including cases where they are carried on within the framework of international inter-governmental organizations.

Any practical questions arising in connexion with activities carried on by international inter-governmental organizations in the exploration and use of outer space, including the moon and other celestial bodies, shall be resolved by the States Parties to the Treaty either with the appropriate international organization or with one or more States members of that international organization, which are Parties to this Treaty.

Article XIV

1. This Treaty shall be open to all States for signature. Any State which does not sign this Treaty before its entry into force in accordance with paragraph 3 of this Article may accede to it at any time.

2. This Treaty shall be subject to ratification by signatory States. Instruments of ratification and instruments of accession shall be deposited with the Governments of the United Kingdom of Great Britain and Northern Ireland, the Union of Soviet

Socialist Republics and the United States of America, which are hereby designated the Depositary Governments.

3. This Treaty shall enter into force upon the deposit of instruments of ratification by five Governments including the Governments designated as Depositary Governments under this Treaty.

4. For States whose instruments of ratification or accession are deposited subsequent to the entry into force of this Treaty, it shall enter into force on the date of the deposit of their instruments of ratification or accession.

5. The Depositary Governments shall promptly inform all signatory and acceding States of the date of each signature, the date of deposit of each instrument of ratification of and accession to this Treaty, the date of its entry into force and other notices.

6. This Treaty shall be registered by the Depositary Governments pursuant to Article 102 of the Charter of the United Nations.

Article XV

Any State Party to the Treaty may propose amendments to this Treaty. Amendments shall enter into force for each State Party to the Treaty accepting the amendments upon their acceptance by a majority of the States Parties to the Treaty and thereafter for each remaining State Party to the Treaty on the date of acceptance by it.

Article XVI

Any State Party to the Treaty may give notice of its withdrawal from the Treaty one year after its entry into force by written notification to the Depositary Governments. Such withdrawal shall take effect one year from the date of receipt of this notification.

Article XVII

This Treaty, of which the English, Russian, French, Spanish and Chinese texts are equally authentic, shall be deposited in the archives of the Depositary Governments. Duly certified copies of this Treaty shall be transmitted by the Depositary Governments to the Governments of the signatory and acceding States.

3.4 Council of Europe Committee of Ministers Resolution on Air Pollution in Frontier Areas. Adopted 26 March 1971. C/E Res. 71(5), 19 E.Y.B. 263

The Committee of Ministers,

Having regard to the Declaration of Principles on Air Pollution Control (Resolution (68) 4) and specially to Title II, Chapter 7 concerning pollution in frontier areas;

Considering that it is in the common interest to prevent so far as possible the occurrence of problems caused by transfrontier air pollution;

Considering that the comments of the inhabitants of regions beyond the frontier should be examined in the same spirit as those made by the inhabitants of the country where the pollution plant is situated or planned,

Recommends that governments of member States of the Council of Europe ensure for the inhabitants of regions beyond their frontiers the same protection against air pollution in frontier areas as is provided for their own inhabitants.

To this end they should in particular ensure that the competent authorities should inform each other in good time about any project for installations liable to pollute the atmosphere beyond the frontier.

The competent authorities beyond the frontier should be able to make their comments on such projects. These comments should be given the same consideration and treatment as if they had been made by the inhabitants of the country where the plant is situated or proposed.

3.5 Convention on International Liability for Damage Caused by Space Objects. Concluded at Washington, London, and Moscow, 29 March 1972. Entered into force, 1 September 1972. 961 U.N.T.S. 187, 24 U.S.T. 2389, T.I.A.S. No. 7762; *reprinted in* 5 Weston V.J.4

Article I. For the purposes of this Convention:

(*a*) The term "damage" means loss of life, personal injury or other impairment of health; or loss of or damage to property of States or of persons, natural or juridical, or property of international intergovernmental organisations;

(*b*) The term "launching" includes attempted launching;

(*c*) The term "launching State" means:

(i) a state which launches or procures the launching of a space object;

(ii) a State from whose territory or facility a space object is launched;

(*d*) The term "space object" includes component parts of a space object as well as its launch vehicle and parts thereof.

Article II. A launching State shall be absolutely liable to pay compensation for damage caused by its space object on the surface of the earth or to aircraft in flight.

Article III. In the event of damage being caused elsewhere than on the surface of the earth to a space object of one launching State or to persons or property on board such a space object by a space object of another launching State, the latter shall be liable only if the damage is due to its fault or the fault of persons for whom it is responsible.

Article IV. 1. In the event of damage being caused elsewhere than on the surface of the earth to a space object of one launching State or to persons or property on board such a space object by a space object of another launching State, and of damage thereby being caused to a third State or to its natural or juridical persons, the first two States shall be jointly and severally liable to the third State, to the extent indicated by the following:

(*a*) If the damage has been caused to the third State on the surface of the earth or to aircraft in flight, their liability to the third State shall be absolute;

(*b*) If the damage has been caused to a space object of the third State or to persons or property on board that space object elsewhere than on the surface of the earth, their liability to the third State shall be based on the fault of either of the first two States or on the fault of persons for whom either is responsible.

2. In all cases of joint and several liability referred to in paragraph 1 of this Article, the burden of compensation for the damage shall be apportioned between the first two States in accordance with the extent to which they were at fault; if the extent of the fault of each of these States cannot be established, the burden of compensation shall be apportioned equally between them. Such apportionment shall be without prejudice to the right of the third State to seek the entire compensation due under this Convention from any or all of the launching States which are jointly and severally liable.

Article V. 1. Whenever two or more States jointly launch a space object, they shall be jointly and severally liable for any damage caused.

2. A launching State which has paid compensation for damage shall have the right to present a claim for indemnification to other participants in the joint launching. The participants in a joint launching may conclude agreements regarding the apportioning among themselves of the financial obligation in respect of which they are jointly and severally liable. Such agreements shall be without prejudice to the right of a State sustaining damage to seek the entire compensation due under this Convention from any or all of the launching States which are jointly and severally liable.

3. A State from whose territory or facility a space object is launched shall be regarded as a participant in a joint launching.

Article VI. 1. Subject to the provisions of paragraph 2 of this Article, exoneration from absolute liability shall be granted to the extent that a launching State establishes that the damage has resulted either wholly or partially from gross negligence or from an act or omission done with intent to cause damage on the part of a claimant State or of natural or juridical persons it represents.

2. No exoneration whatever shall be granted in cases where the damage has resulted from activities conducted by a launching State which are not in conformity with international law including, in particular, the Charter of the United Nations and the Treaty on Principles Governing the Activities of States in the Exploration and Use of Outer Space, including the Moon and Other Celestial Bodies.

Article VII. The provisions of this Convention shall not apply to damage caused by a space object of a launching State to:

(*a*) nationals of that launching State;

(*b*) foreign nationals during such time as they are participating in the operation of that space object from the time of its launching or at any stage thereafter until its descent, or during such time as they are in the immediate vicinity of a planned launching or recovery area as the result of an invitation by that launching State.

Article VIII. 1. A State which suffers damage, or whose natural or juridical persons suffer damage, may present to a launching State a claim for compensation for such damage.

2. If the State of nationality has not presented a claim, another State may, in respect of damage sustained in its territory by any natural or juridical person, present a claim to a launching State.

3. If neither the State of nationality nor the State in whose territory the damage was sustained has presented a claim or notified its intention of presenting a claim, another State may, in respect of damage sustained by its permanent residents, present a claim to a launching State.

Article IX. A claim for compensation for damage shall be presented to a launching State through diplomatic channels. If a State does not maintain diplomatic relations with the launching State concerned, it may request another State to present its claim to that launching State or otherwise represent its interests under this Convention. It may also present its claim through the Secretary–General of the United Nations, provided the claimant State and the launching State are both Members of the United Nations.

Article X. 1. A claim for compensation for damage may be presented to a launching State not later than one year following the date of the occurrence of the damage or the identification of the launching State which is liable.

2. If, however, a State does not know of the occurrence of the damage or has not been able to identify the launching State which is liable, it may present a claim within one year following the date on which it learned of the aforementioned facts; however, this period shall in no event exceed one year following the date on which the State could reasonably be expected to have learned of the facts through the exercise of due diligence.

3. The time-limits specified in paragraphs 1 and 2 of this Article shall apply even if the full extent of the damage may not be known. In this event, however, the claimant State shall be entitled to revise the claim and submit additional documentation after the expiration of such time-limits until one year after the full extent of the damage is known.

Article XI. 1. Presentation of a claim to a launching State for compensation for damage under this Convention shall not require the prior exhaustion of any local remedies which may be available to a claimant State or to natural or juridical persons it represents.

2. Nothing in this Convention shall prevent a State, or natural or juridical persons it might represent, from pursuing a claim in the courts or administrative tribunals or agencies of a launching State. A State shall not, however, be entitled to present a claim under this Convention in respect of the same damage for which a claim is being pursued in the courts or administrative tribunals or agencies of a launching State or under another international agreement which is binding on the States concerned.

Article XII. The compensation which the launching State shall be liable to pay for damage under this Convention shall be determined in accordance with international law and the principles of justice and equity, in order to provide such reparation in respect of the damage as will restore the person, natural or juridical, State or international organisation on whose behalf the claim is presented to the condition which would have existed if the damage had not occurred.

Article XIII. Unless the claimant State and the State from which compensation is due under this Convention agree on another form of compensation, the compensation shall be paid in the currency of the claimant State or, if that State so requests, in the currency of the State from which compensation is due.

Article XIV. If no settlement of a claim is arrived at through diplomatic negotiations as provided for in Article IX, within one year from the date on which the claimant State notifies the launching State that it has submitted the documentation of its claim, the parties concerned shall establish a Claims Commission at the request of either party.

Article XV. 1. The Claims Commission shall be composed of three members: one appointed by the claimant State, one appointed by the launching State and the third member, the Chairman, to be chosen by both parties jointly. Each party shall make its appointment within two months of the request for the establishment of the Claims Commission.

2. If no agreement is reached on the choice of the Chairman within four months of the request for the establishment of the Commission, either party may request the Secretary–General of the United Nations to appoint the Chairman within a further period of two months.

Article XVI. 1. If one of the parties does not make its appointment within the stipulated period, the Chairman shall, at the request of the other party, constitute a single-member Claims Commission.

2. Any vacancy which may arise in the Commission for whatever reason shall be filled by the same procedure adopted for the original appointment.

3. The Commission shall determine its own procedure.

4. The Commission shall determine the place or places where it shall sit and all other administrative matters.

5. Except in the case of decisions and awards by a single-member Commission, all decisions and awards of the Commission shall be by majority vote.

Article XVII. No increase in the membership of the Claims Commission shall take place by reason of two or more claimant States or launching States being joined in any one proceeding before the Commission. The claimant States so joined shall collectively appoint one member of the Commission in the same manner and subject to the same conditions as would be the case for a single claimant State. When two or more launching States are so joined, they shall collectively appoint one member of the

Commission in the same way. If the claimant States or the launching States do not make the appointment within the stipulated period, the Chairman shall constitute a single-member Commission.

Article XVIII. The Claims Commission shall decide the merits of the claim for compensation and determine the amount of compensation payable, if any.

Article XIX. 1. The Claims Commission shall act in accordance with the provisions of Article XII.

2. The decision of the Commission shall be final and binding if the parties have so agreed; otherwise the Commission shall render a final and recommendatory award, which the parties shall consider in good faith. The Commission shall state the reasons for its decision or award.

3. The Commission shall give its decision or award as promptly as possible and no later than one year from the date of its establishment, unless an extension of this period is found necessary by the Commission.

4. The Commission shall make its decision or award public. It shall deliver a certified copy of its decision or award to each of the parties and to the Secretary-General of the United Nations.

Article XX. The expenses in regard to the Claims Commission shall be borne equally by the parties, unless otherwise decided by the Commission.

Article XXI. If the damage caused by a space object presents a large-scale danger to human life or seriously interferes with the living conditions of the population or the functioning of vital centres, the States Parties, and in particular the launching State, shall examine the possibility of rendering appropriate and rapid assistance to the State which has suffered the damage, when it so requests. However, nothing in this Article shall affect the rights or obligations of the States Parties under this Convention.

Article XXII. 1. In this Convention, with the exception of Articles XXIV to XXVII, references to States shall be deemed to apply to any international intergovernmental organisation which conducts space activities if the organisation declares its acceptance of the rights and obligations provided for in this Convention and if a majority of the States members of the organisation are States Parties to this Convention and to the Treaty on Principles Governing the Activities of States in the Exploration and Use of Outer Space, including the Moon and Other Celestial Bodies.

2. States members of any such organisation which are States Parties to this Convention shall take all appropriate steps to ensure that the organisation makes a declaration in accordance with the preceding paragraph.

3. If an international intergovernmental organisation is liable for damage by virtue of the provisions of this Convention, that organisation and those of its members which are States Parties to this Convention shall be jointly and severally liable; provided, however, that:

(*a*) any claim for compensation in respect of such damage shall be first presented to the organisation;

(*b*) only where the organisation has not paid, within a period of six months, any sum agreed or determined to be due as compensation for such damage, may the claimant State invoke the liability of the members which are States Parties to this Convention for the payment of that sum.

4. Any claim, pursuant to the provisions of this Convention, for compensation in respect of damage caused to an organisation which has made a declaration in accordance with paragraph 1 of this Article shall be presented by a State member of the organisation which is a State Party to this Convention.

Article XXIII. 1. The provisions of this Convention shall not affect other international agreements in force in so far as relations between the States Parties to such agreements are concerned.

2. No provision of this Convention shall prevent States from concluding international agreements reaffirming, supplementing or extending its provisions.

Article XXIV. 1. This Convention shall be open to all States for signature. Any State which does not sign this Convention before its entry into force in accordance with paragraph 3 of this Article may accede to it at any time.

2. This Convention shall be subject to ratification by signatory States. Instruments of ratification and instruments of accession shall be deposited with the Governments of the United Kingdom of Great Britain and Northern Ireland, the Union of Soviet Socialist Republics and the United States of America, which are hereby designated the Depositary Governments.

3. This Convention shall enter into force on the deposit of the fifth instrument of ratification.

4. For States whose instruments of ratification or accession are deposited subsequent to the entry into force of this Convention, it shall enter into force on the date of the deposit of their instruments of ratification or accession.

5. The Depositary Governments shall promptly inform all signatory and acceding States of the date of each signature, the date of deposit of each instrument of ratification of and accession to this Convention, the date of its entry into force and other notices.

6. This Convention shall be registered by the Depositary Governments pursuant to Article 102 of the Charter of the United Nations.

Article XXV. Any State Party to this Convention may propose amendments to this Convention. Amendments shall enter into force for each State Party to the Convention accepting the amendments upon their acceptance by a majority of the States Parties to the Convention and thereafter for each remaining State Party on the date of acceptance by it.

Article XXVI. Ten years after the entry into force of this Convention, the question of the review of this Convention shall be included in the provisional agenda of the United Nations General Assembly in order to consider, in the light of past application of the Convention, whether it requires revision. However, at any time after the Convention has been in force for five years, and at the request of one third of the States Parties to the Convention, and with the concurrence of the majority of the States Parties, a conference of the States Parties shall be convened to review this Convention.

Article XXVII. Any State Party to this Convention may give notice of its withdrawal from the Convention one year after its entry into force by written notification to the Depositary Governments. Such withdrawal shall take effect one year from the date of receipt of this notification.

Article XXVIII. This Convention, of which the English, Russian, French, Spanish and Chinese texts are equally authentic, shall be deposited in the archives of the Depositary Governments. Duly certified copies of this Convention shall be transmitted by the Depositary Governments to the Governments of the signatory and acceding States.

3.6 OECD Council Recommendation on Principles Concerning Transfrontier Pollution (With Annex). Adopted 14 November 1974. 1974 O.E.C.D. C224, O.E.C.D. 142; *reprinted in* 14 I.L.M. 242 (1975) & 5 Weston V.E.1

The Council,

Having regard to Article 5(b) of the Convention on the Organization for Economic Co-operation and Development of 14th December, 1960;

Considering that the protection and improvement of the environment are common objectives of Member countries;

Considering that the common interests of countries concerned by transfrontier pollution should induce them to co-operate more closely in a spirit of international solidarity and to initiate concerted action for preventing and controlling transfrontier pollution;

Having regard to the Recommendations of the United Nations Conference on the Human Environment held in Stockholm in June 1972 and in particular those Principles of the Declaration on the Human Environment which are relevant to transfrontier pollution;

On the proposal of the Environment Committee;

I. RECOMMENDS that, without prejudice to future developments in international law and international co-operation in relation to transfrontier pollution, Member countries should be guided in their environmental policy by the principles concerning transfrontier pollution contained in this Recommendation and its Annex, which is an integral part of this Recommendation.

II. INSTRUCTS the Environment Committee to prepare without delay, taking account of the work undertaken by other international organizations, a programme of work designed to elaborate further these principles and to facilitate their practical implementation.

III. RECOMMENDS Member countries to co-operate in developing international law applicable to transfrontier pollution.

IV. INSTRUCTS the Environment Committee, within the framework of its mandate, to examine or investigate further, as the case may be, the issues related to the Principles of the Stockholm Declaration regarding responsibility and liability, taking into account the work undertaken by other international organizations, to submit a first report to the Council on its work by 1st March, 1976 and to seek to formulate as soon as possible Draft Recommendations.

V. INSTRUCTS the Environment Committee to investigate further the issues concerning equal right of hearing, to formulate as soon as possible Draft Recommendations and to report to the Council on its work by 1st July, 1975.

Annex

Some Principles Concerning Transfrontier Pollution

Title A—Introduction

This Annex sets forth some principles designed to facilitate the development of harmonized environmental policies with a view to solving transfrontier pollution problems. Their implementation should be based on a fair balance of rights and obligations among countries concerned by transfrontier pollution.

These principles should subsequently be supplemented and developed in the light of work undertaken by the OECD or other appropriate international organizations.

For the purpose of these principles, pollution means the introduction by man, directly or indirectly, of substances or energy into the environment resulting in deleterious effects of such a nature as to endanger human health, harm living resources and ecosystems, and impair or interfere with amenities and other legitimate uses of the environment.

Unless otherwise specified, these principles deal with pollution originating in one country and having effects within other countries.

Title B—International solidarity

1. Countries should define a concerted long-term policy for the protection and improvement of the environment in zones liable to be affected by transfrontier pollution.

Without prejudice to their rights and obligations under international law and in accordance with their responsibility under Principle 21 of the Stockholm Declaration, countries should seek, as far as possible, an equitable balance of their rights and obligations as regards the zones concerned by transfrontier pollution.

In implementing this concerted policy, countries should among other things:

(*a*) take account of:

— levels of existing pollution and the present quality of the environment concerned;

— the nature and quantities of pollutants;

— the assimilative capacity of the environment, as established by mutual agreement by the countries concerned, taking into account the particular characteristics and use of the affected zone;

— activities at the source of pollution and activities and uses sensitive to such pollution;

— the situation, prospective use and development of the zones concerned from a socio-economic stand-point;

(*b*) define:

— environmental quality objectives and corresponding protective measures:

(*c*) promote:

— guidelines for a land-use planning policy consistent with the requirements both of environmental protection and socio-economic development;

(*d*) draw up and maintain up to date:

(i) list of particularly dangerous substances regarding which efforts should be made to eliminate polluting discharges, if necessary by stages, and

(ii) lists of substances regarding which polluting discharges should be subject to very strict control.

2. Pending the definition of such concerted long-term policies countries should, individually and jointly, take all appropriate measures to prevent and control transfrontier pollution, and harmonize as far as possible their relevant policies.

3. Countries should endeavour to prevent any increase in transfrontier pollution, including that stemming from new or additional substances and activities, and to reduce, and as far as possible eliminate any transfrontier pollution existing between them within time limits to be specified.

Title C—Principle of non-discrimination

4. Countries should initially base their action on the principle of nondiscrimination, whereby:

(*a*) polluters causing transfrontier pollution should be subject to legal or statutory provisions no less severe than those which would apply for any equivalent pollution occurring within their country, under comparable conditions and in comparable zones, taking into account, when appropriate, the special nature and environmental needs of the zone affected;

(*b*) in particular, without prejudice to quality objectives or standards applying to transfrontier pollution mutually agreed upon by the countries concerned, the levels of transfrontier pollution entering into the zones liable to be affected by such pollution should not exceed those considered acceptable under comparable conditions and in comparable zones inside the country in which it originates, taking into account, when appropriate, the special state of the environment in the affected country;

(*c*) any country whenever it applies the Polluter–Pays Principle should apply it to all polluters within this country without making any difference according to whether pollution affects this country or another country;

(*d*) persons affected by transfrontier pollution should be granted no less favourable treatment than persons affected by a similar pollution in the country from which such transfrontier pollution originates.

Title D—Principle of equal right of hearing

5. Countries should make every effort to introduce, where not already in existence, a system affording equal right of hearing, according to which:

(*a*) whenever a project, a new activity or a course of conduct may create a significant risk of transfrontier pollution and is investigated by public authorities, those who may be affected by such pollution should have the same rights of standing in judicial or administrative proceedings in the country where it originates as those of that country;

(*b*) whenever transfrontier pollution gives rise to damage in a country, those who are affected by such pollution should have the same rights of standing in judicial or administrative proceedings in the country where such pollution originates as those of that country, and they should be extended procedural rights equivalent to the rights extended to those of that country.

Title E—Principle of information and consultation

6. Prior to the initiation in a country of works or undertakings which might create a significant risk of transfrontier pollution, this country should provide early information to other countries which are or may be affected. It should provide these countries with relevant information and data, the transmission of which is not prohibited by legislative provisions or prescriptions or applicable international conventions, and should invite their comments.

7. Countries should enter into consultation on an existing or foreseeable transfrontier pollution problem at the request of a country which is or may be directly affected and should diligently pursue such consultations on this particular problem over a reasonable period of time.

8. Countries should refrain from carrying out projects or activities which might create a significant risk of transfrontier pollution without first informing the countries which are or may be affected and, except in cases of extreme urgency, providing a reasonable amount of time in the light of circumstances for diligent consultation. Such consultations held in the best spirit of co-operation and good neighbourliness should not enable a country to unreasonably delay or to impede the activities or projects on which consultations are taking place.

Title F—Warning systems and incidents

9. Countries should promptly warn other potentially affected countries of any situation which may cause any sudden increase in the level of pollution in areas

outside the country of origin of pollution, and take all appropriate steps to reduce the effects of any such sudden increase.

10. Countries should assist each other, wherever necessary, in order to prevent incidents which may result in transfrontier pollution, and to minimise, and if possible eliminate, the effects of such incidents, and should develop contingency plans to this end.

Title G—Exchange of scientific information, monitoring measures and research

11. Countries concerned should exchange all relevant scientific information and data on transfrontier pollution, when not prohibited by legislative provisions or prescriptions or by applicable international conventions. They should develop and adopt pollution measurement methods providing results which are compatible.

12. They should, when appropriate, co-operate in scientific and technical research programmes inter alio for identifying the origin and pathways of transfrontier pollution, any damage caused and the best methods of pollution prevention and control, and should share all information and data thus obtained.

They should, where necessary, consider setting up jointly, in zones affected by transfrontier pollution, a permanent monitoring system or network for assessing the levels of pollution and the effectiveness of measures taken by them to reduce pollution.

Title H—Institutions

13. Countries concerned by a particular problem of transfrontier pollution should consider the advantages of co-operation, by setting up international commissions or other bodies, or by strengthening existing institutions, in order to deal more effectively with particular aspects of such problems.

Such institutions could be authorised to collect any data needed for a proper evaluation of the problem and its causes, and make to the countries concerned practical proposals for concerted efforts to combat transfrontier pollution. With the consent of the States concerned, they could also carry out any necessary additional investigations into the origin and degree of pollution, review the effectiveness of any pollution prevention and control measures which have been taken, and publish reports of their findings.

Title I—Disputes

14. Should negotiations and other means of diplomatically settling disputes concerning transfrontier pollution fail, countries should have the opportunity to submit such a dispute to a procedure of legal settlement which is prompt, effective and binding.

Title J—International agreements

15. Countries should endeavour to conclude, where necessary, bilateral or multilateral agreements for the abatement of transfrontier pollution in accordance with the above principles, to bring promptly into force any agreements which may already have been signed.

16. When negotiating new bilateral or multilateral agreements countries should, while taking into account the principles set out above, strive for the application of efficient pollution prevention and control measures in accordance with the Polluter–Pays Principle.

Such agreements could, inter alia, include provisions for practical procedures promoting the prompt and equitable compensation of persons affected by transfrontier pollution, and could also contain procedures facilitating the provision of information and consultation.

3.7 OECD Council Recommendation for the Implementation of a Regime of Equal Right of Access and Non-discrimination in Relation to Transfrontier Pollution (With Annex). Adopted 17 May 1977. 1977 O.E.C.D. C(77)28, O.E.C.D. 150; *reprinted in* 16 I.L.M. 977 (1977) & 5 Weston V.E.2

The Council,

Having regard to Article 5(b) of the Convention on the Organisation for Economic Co-operation and Development of 14th December, 1960;

Having regard to the Declaration on the Human Environment adopted in Stockholm in June 1972 and in particular Principles 21, 22, 23 and 24 of that Declaration;

Having regard to the Recommendations of the Council of 14th November, 1974, on Principles concerning Transfrontier Pollution and of 11th May, 1976, on Equal Right of Access in relation to Transfrontier Pollution (C(74)224 and C(76)55(Final) and without prejudice to such Recommendations;

Having regard to the Report by the Secretary–General of 18th March, 1977 on the Implementation of a Regime of Equal Right of Access and Non-discrimination in relation to Transfrontier Pollution;

Considering that the protection and improvement of the environment are common objectives of Member countries;

Conscious that pollution originating in the area within the national jurisdiction of a State may have effects on the environment outside this jurisdiction;

Considering that the implementation of a regime of equal right of access and non-discrimination among Member countries should lead to improved protection of the environment without prejudice to other channels available for the solution of transfrontier problems;

On the proposal of the Environment Committee;

RECOMMENDS that Member Countries, in regard to each other, take into account the principles concerning transfrontier pollution set forth in the Annex to this Recommendation, which is an integral part of it, in their domestic legislation, possibly on the basis of reciprocity, notably regarding individual rights, and in bilateral or multilateral international agreements.

ANNEX

Introduction

This Annex sets out a number of principles intended to promote the implementation between Member countries of a regime of equal right of access and non-discrimination in matters of transfrontier pollution, while maintaining a fair balance of rights and obligations between Countries concerned by such pollution.

These principles do not prejudice any more favourable measures for the protection of the environment and of persons whose property, rights or interests are or could be affected by pollution the origin of which is situated within the area under the jurisdiction of a Member country.

For the purposes of this Recommendation:

a) "Pollution" means any introduction by man, directly or indirectly, of substance or energy into the environment resulting in deleterious effects of such a nature as to endanger human health, harm living resources and eco-systems, impair amenities or interfere with other legitimate uses of the environment;

b) "Domestic pollution" means any intentional or unintentional pollution, the physical origin of which is situated wholly within the area under the national jurisdiction of one Country and which has effects within that area only.

c) "Transfrontier pollution" means any intentional or unintentional pollution whose physical origin is subject to, and situated wholly or in part within the area under, the national jurisdiction of one Country and which has effects in the area under the national jurisdiction of another Country;

d) "Country" means any Member country which participates in this Recommendation;

e) "Country of origin" means any Country within which, and subject to the jurisdiction of which, transfrontier pollution originates or could originate in connection with activities carried on or contemplated in that Country;

f) "Exposed Country" means any Country affected by transfrontier pollution or exposed to a significant risk of transfrontier pollution;

g) "Countries concerned" means any Country of origin of transfrontier pollution and any Country exposed to such pollution;

h) "Regions concerned by transfrontier pollution" means any region of origin of transfrontier pollution in the Country of origin and any regions of the Country of origin and of any exposed Country where such pollution produces or might produce its effects;

i) "Persons" means any natural or legal person, either private or public;

j) "Regime of environmental protection" means any set of statutory and administrative measures related to the protection of the environment, including those concerning the property, rights or interests of persons.

Title A. PRINCIPLES TO FACILITATE THE SOLUTION AT INTER-STATE LEVEL OF TRANSFRONTIER POLLUTION PROBLEMS

1. When preparing and giving effect to their policies affecting the environment, Countries should, consistent with their obligations and rights as regards the protection of the environment, take fully into consideration the effects of such policies on the environment of exposed Countries so as to protect such environment against transfrontier pollution.

2. With a view to improved protection of the environment, Countries should attempt by common agreement to:

a) make their environmental policies mutually compatible, particularly those bearing on regions concerned by transfrontier pollution;

b) bring closer together quality objectives and environmental standards adopted by Countries, apply them systematically to cases of transfrontier pollution and, where necessary, improve those already in force;

c) work out additional rules of conduct of States to be applied in matters of transfrontier pollution.

3. a) Pending the implementation of the objectives laid down in paragraph 2, and without prejudice to more favourable measures taken in accordance with paragraphs 1 and 2 above, each Country should ensure that its regime of environmental protection does not discriminate between pollution originating from it which affects or is likely to affect the area under its national jurisdiction and pollution originating from it which affects or is likely to affect an exposed Country.

b) Thus, transfrontier pollution problems should be treated by the Country of origin in an equivalent way to similar domestic pollution problems occurring under comparable conditions in the Country of origin.

c) In the event of difficulties arising between Countries concerned because the situations resulting from transfrontier pollution and domestic pollution are manifestly not comparable, for example as a result of unco-ordinated land use policies in regions concerned by transfrontier pollution, those countries should strive to arrive at a mutually agreed arrangement which ensures to the largest extent possible the application of the principle referred to in sub-paragraph (a) of this paragraph.

Title B. LEGAL PROTECTION OF PERSONS

4. a) Countries of origin should ensure that any person who has suffered transfrontier pollution damage or is exposed to a significant risk of transfrontier pollution, shall at least receive equivalent treatment to that afforded in the Country of origin in cases of domestic pollution and in comparable circumstances, to persons of equivalent condition or status.

b) From a procedural standpoint, this treatment includes the right to take part in, or have resort to, all administrative and judicial procedures existing within the Country of origin, in order to prevent domestic pollution, to have it abated and/or to obtain compensation for the damage caused.

5. Where in spite of the existence of a liability ceiling instituted by an international agreement, there exists in a Country a system of additional compensation financed or administered by the public authorities, then such Country should not be required in the absence of reciprocal arrangements to grant entitlement to such additional compensation to victims of transfrontier pollution, but it should in advance inform the exposed Countries of the particular situation.

6. a) Where the domestic law of Countries permits private non profit legal persons that are resident within their own territories, such as environmental defence associations, to commence proceedings to safeguard environmental interests which it is their aim to protect, those Countries should grant the same right for comparable matters to similar legal persons resident in exposed Countries, provided that the latter satisfy the conditions laid down for the former in the Country of origin.

b) When some of the conditions concerning matters of form laid down in the Country of origin cannot reasonably be imposed on legal persons resident in an exposed Country, these latter should be entitled to commence proceedings in the Country of origin if they satisfy comparable conditions.

7. When the law of a Country of origin permits a public authority to participate in administrative or judicial proceedings in order to safeguard general environmental interests, the Country of origin should consider, if its legal system allows it, providing, by means of international agreement if it deems it necessary, competent public authorities of exposed Countries with access to such proceedings.

Title C. EXCHANGE OF INFORMATION AND CONSULTATION

8. a) The Country of origin, on its own initiative or at the request of an exposed Country, should communicate to the latter appropriate information concerning it in matters of transfrontier pollution or significant risk of such pollution (and enter into consultations with it)

b) In order to enable a Country of origin to implement adequately the principles set out in Title A of this Recommendation, each exposed Country should, on its own initiative or at the request of the Country of origin, supply appropriate information of mutual concern.

c) Each Country should designate one or more authorities entitled to receive directly information communicated under subparagraphs (a) and (b) of this paragraph.

9. a) Countries of origin should take any appropriate measures to provide persons exposed to a significant risk of transfrontier pollution with sufficient information to enable them to exercise in a timely manner the rights referred to in this Recommendation. As far as possible, such information should be equivalent to that provided in the Country of origin in cases of comparable domestic pollution.

b) Exposed Countries should designate one or more authorities which will have the duty to receive and the responsibility to disseminate such information within limits of time compatible with the exercise of existing procedures in the Country of origin.

10. Countries should encourage and facilitate regular contacts between representatives designated by them at regional and/or local levels in order to examine such transfrontier pollution matters as may arise.

3.8 Convention on Long-range Transboundary Air Pollution (LRTAP) (Without Protocols).[b] Concluded at Geneva, 13 November 1979. Entered into force, 16 March 1983. 1302 U.N.T.S. 217, T.I.A.S. No. 10541; *reprinted in* 18 I.L.M. 1442 (1979) & 5 Weston V.E.3

The Parties to the present Convention,

Determined to promote relations and co-operation in the field of environmental protection,

Aware of the significance of the activities of the United Nations Economic Commission for Europe in strengthening such relations and co-operation, particularly in the field of air pollution including long-range transport of air pollutants,

Recognizing the contribution of the Economic Commission for Europe to the multilateral implementation of the pertinent provisions of the Final Act of the Conference on Security and Co-operation in Europe,

Cognizant of the references in the chapter on environment of the Final Act of the Conference on Security and Co-operation in Europe calling for co-operation to control air pollution and its effects, including long-range transport of air pollutants, and to the development through international co-operation of an extensive programme for the monitoring and evaluation of long-range transport of air pollutants, starting with sulphur dioxide and with possible extension to other pollutants,

Considering the pertinent provisions of the Declaration of the United Nations Conference on the Human Environment, and in particular principle 21, which expresses the common conviction that States have, in accordance with the Charter of the United Nations and the principles of international law, the sovereign right to exploit their own resources pursuant to their own environmental policies, and the responsibility to ensure that activities within their jurisdiction or control do not cause damage to the environment of other States or of areas beyond the limits of natural jurisdiction,

Recognizing the existence of possible adverse effects, in the short and long term, of air pollution including transboundary air pollution,

Concerned that a rise in the level of emissions of air pollutants within the region as forecast may increase such adverse effects,

Recognizing the need to study the implications of the long-range transport of air pollutants and the need to seek solutions for the problems identified,

Affirming their willingness to reinforce active international co-operation to develop appropriate national policies and by means of exchange of information, consultation, research and monitoring, to co-ordinate national action for combating air pollution including long-range transboundary air pollution,

Have agreed as follows:

DEFINITIONS

Article 1

For the purposes of the present Convention:

(a) "*air pollution*" means the introduction by man, directly or indirectly, of substances or energy into the air resulting in deleterious effects of such a nature as to endanger human health, harm living resources and ecosystems and material property and impair or interfere with amenities and other legitimate uses of the environment, and "air pollutants" shall be construed accordingly;

(b) "*long-range transboundary air pollution*" means air pollution whose physical origin is situated wholly or in part within the area under the national

b. *But see* Basic Documents 3.15, 3.19 and 3.26, *infra.*

jurisdiction of one State and which has adverse effects in the area under the jurisdiction of another State at such a distance that it is not generally possible to distinguish the contribution of individual emission sources or groups of sources.

FUNDAMENTAL PRINCIPLES

Article 2

The Contracting Parties, taking due account of the facts and problems involved, are determined to protect man and his environment against air pollution and shall endeavour to limit and, as far as possible, gradually reduce and prevent air pollution including long-range transboundary air pollution.

Article 3

The Contracting Parties, within the framework of the present Convention, shall by means of exchanges of information, consultation, research and monitoring, develop without undue delay policies and strategies which shall serve as a means of combating the discharge of air pollutants, taking into account efforts already made at national and international levels.

Article 4

The Contracting Parties shall exchange information on and review their policies, scientific activities and technical measures aimed at combating, as far as possible, the discharge of air pollutants which may have adverse effects, thereby contributing to the reduction of air pollution including long-range transboundary air pollution.

Article 5

Consultations shall be held, upon request, at an early stage between, on the one hand, Contracting Parties which are actually affected by or exposed to a significant risk of long-range transboundary air pollution and, on the other hand, Contracting Parties within which and subject to whose jurisdiction a significant contribution to long-range transboundary air pollution originates, or could originate, in connexion with activities carried on or contemplated therein.

AIR QUALITY MANAGEMENT

Article 6

Taking into account articles 2 to 5, the ongoing research, exchange of information and monitoring and the results thereof, the cost and effectiveness of local and other remedies and, in order to combat air pollution, in particular that originating from new or rebuilt installations, each Contracting Party undertakes to develop the best policies and strategies including air quality management systems and, as part of them, control measures compatible with balanced development, in particular by using the best available technology which is economically feasible and low-and non-waste technology.

RESEARCH AND DEVELOPMENT

Article 7

The Contracting Parties, as appropriate to their needs, shall initiate and co-operate in the conduct of research into and/or development of:

(a) existing and proposed technologies for reducing emissions of sulphur compounds and other major air pollutants, including technical and economic feasibility, and environmental consequences;

(b) instrumentation and other techniques for monitoring and measuring emission rates and ambient concentrations of air pollutants;

(c) improved models for a better understanding of the transmission of long-range transboundary air pollutants;

(d) the effects of sulphur compounds and other major air pollutants on human health and the environment, including agriculture, forestry, materials, aquatic and other natural ecosystems and visibility, with a view to establishing a scientific basis for dose/effect relationships designed to protect the environment;

(e) the economic, social and environmental assessment of alternative measures for attaining environmental objectives including the reduction of long-range transboundary air pollution;

(f) education and training programmes related to the environmental aspects of pollution by sulphur compounds and other major air pollutants.

EXCHANGE OF INFORMATION

Article 8

The Contracting Parties, within the framework of the Executive Body referred to in article 10 and bilaterally, shall, in their common interests, exchange available information on:

(a) data on emissions at periods of time to be agreed upon, of agreed air pollutants, starting with sulphur dioxide, coming from grid-units of agreed size; or on the fluxes of agreed air pollutants, starting with sulphur dioxide, across national borders, at distances and at periods of time to be agreed upon;

(b) major changes in national policies and in general industrial development, and their potential impact, which would be likely to cause significant changes in long-range transboundary air pollution;

(c) control technologies for reducing air pollution relevant to long-range transboundary air pollution;

(d) the projected cost of the emission control of sulphur compounds and other major air pollutants on a national scale;

(e) meteorological and physico-chemical data relating to the processes during transmission;

(f) physico-chemical and biological data relating to the effects of long-range transboundary air pollution and the extent of the damage which these data indicate can be attributed to long-range transboundary air pollution;

(g) national, subregional and regional policies and strategies for the control of sulphur compounds and other major air pollutants.

IMPLEMENTATION AND FURTHER DEVELOPMENT OF THE CO-OPERATIVE PROGRAMME FOR THE MONITORING AND EVALUATION OF THE LONG-RANGE TRANSMISSION OF AIR POLLUTANTS IN EUROPE

Article 9

The Contracting Parties stress the need for the implementation of the existing "Co-operative programme for the monitoring and evaluation of the long-range transmission of air pollutants in Europe" (hereinafter referred to as EMEP) and, with regard to the further development of this programme, agree to emphasize:

(a) the desirability of Contracting Parties joining in and fully implementing EMEP which, as a first step, is based on the monitoring of sulphur dioxide and related substances;

(b) the need to use comparable or standardized procedures for monitoring whenever possible;

(c) the desirability of basing the monitoring programme on the framework of both national and international programmes. The establishment of monitoring stations and the collection of data shall be carried out under the national jurisdiction of the country in which the monitoring stations are located;

(d) the desirability of establishing a framework for a co-operative environmental monitoring programme, based on and taking into account present and future national, subregional, regional and other international programmes;

(e) the need to exchange data on emissions at periods of time to be agreed upon, of agreed air pollutants, starting with sulphur dioxide, coming from grid-units of agreed size; or on the fluxes of agreed air pollutants, starting with sulphur dioxide, across national borders, at distances and at periods of time to be agreed upon. The method, including the model, used to determine the fluxes, as well as the method, including the model, used to determine the transmission of air pollutants based on the emissions per grid-unit, shall be made available and periodically reviewed, in order to improve the methods and the models;

(f) their willingness to continue the exchange and periodic updating of national data on total emissions of agreed air pollutants, starting with sulphur dioxide;

(g) the need to provide meteorological and physico-chemical data relating to processes during transmission;

(h) the need to monitor chemical components in other media such as water, soil and vegetation, as well as a similar monitoring programme to record effects on health and environment;

(i) the desirability of extending the national EMEP networks to make them operational for control and surveillance purposes.

EXECUTIVE BODY

Article 10

1. The representatives of the Contracting Parties shall, within the framework of the Senior Advisers to ECE Governments on Environmental Problems, constitute the Executive Body of the present Convention, and shall meet at least annually in that capacity.

2. The Executive Body shall:

(a) review the implementation of the present Convention;

(b) establish, as appropriate, working groups to consider matters related to the implementation and development of the present Convention and to this end to prepare appropriate studies and other documentation and to submit recommendations to be considered by the Executive Body;

(c) fulfil such other functions as may be appropriate under the provisions of the present Convention.

3. The Executive Body shall utilize the Steering Body for the EMEP to play an integral part in the operation of the present Convention, in particular with regard to data collection and scientific co-operation.

4. The Executive Body, in discharging its functions, shall, when it deems appropriate, also make use of information from other relevant international organizations.

SECRETARIAT

Article 11

The Executive Secretary of the Economic Commission for Europe shall carry out, for the Executive Body, the following secretariat functions:

(a) to convene and prepare the meetings of the Executive Body;

(b) to transmit to the Contracting Parties reports and other information received in accordance with the provisions of the present Convention;

(c) to discharge the functions assigned by the Executive Body.

AMENDMENTS TO THE CONVENTION

Article 12

1. Any Contracting Party may propose amendments to the present Convention.

2. The text of proposed amendments shall be submitted in writing to the Executive Secretary of the Economic Commission for Europe, who shall communicate them to all Contracting Parties. The Executive Body shall discuss proposed amendments at its next annual meeting provided that such proposals have been circulated by the Executive Secretary of the Economic Commission for Europe to the Contracting Parties at least ninety days in advance.

3. An amendment to the present Convention shall be adopted by consensus of the representatives of the Contracting Parties, and shall enter into force for the Contracting Parties which have accepted it on the ninetieth day after the date on which two-thirds of the Contracting Parties have deposited their instruments of acceptance with the depositary. Thereafter, the amendment shall enter into force for any other Contracting Party on the ninetieth day after the date on which that Contracting Party deposits its instrument of acceptance of the amendment.

SETTLEMENT OF DISPUTES

Article 13

If a dispute arises between two or more Contracting Parties to the present Convention as to the interpretation or application of the Convention, they shall seek a solution by negotiation or by any other method of dispute settlement acceptable to the parties to the dispute.

SIGNATURE

Article 14

1. The present Convention shall be open for signature at the United Nations Office at Geneva from 13 to 16 November 1979 on the occasion of the High-level Meeting within the framework of the Economic Commission for Europe on the Protection of the Environment, by the member States of the Economic Commission for Europe as well as States having consultative status with the Economic Commission for Europe, pursuant to paragraph 8 of Economic and Social Council resolution 36 (IV) of 28 March 1947, and by regional economic integration organizations, constituted by sovereign States members of the Economic Commission for Europe, which have competence in respect of the negotiation, conclusion and application of international agreements in matters covered by the present Convention.

2. In matters within their competence, such regional economic integration organizations shall, on their own behalf, exercise the rights and fulfil the responsibilities which the present Convention attributes to their member States. In such cases, the member States of these organizations shall not be entitled to exercise such rights individually.

RATIFICATION, ACCEPTANCE, APPROVAL AND ACCESSION

Article 15

1. The present Convention shall be subject to ratification, acceptance or approval.

2. The present Convention shall be open for accession as from 17 November 1979 by the States and organizations referred to in article 14, paragraph 1.

3. The instruments of ratification, acceptance, approval or accession shall be deposited with the Secretary-General of the United Nations, who will perform the functions of the depositary.

ENTRY INTO FORCE

Article 16

1. The present Convention shall enter into force on the ninetieth day after the date of deposit of the twenty-fourth instrument of ratification, acceptance, approval or accession.

2. For each Contracting Party which ratifies, accepts or approves the present Convention or accedes thereto after the deposit of the twenty-fourth instrument of ratification, acceptance, approval or accession, the Convention shall enter into force on the ninetieth day after the date of deposit by such Contracting Party of its instrument of ratification, acceptance, approval or accession.

WITHDRAWAL

Article 17

At any time after five years from the date on which the present Convention has come into force with respect to a Contracting Party, that Contracting Party may withdraw from the Convention by giving written notification to the depositary. Any such withdrawal shall take effect on the ninetieth day after the date of its receipt by the depositary.

AUTHENTIC TEXTS

Article 18

The original of the present Convention, of which the English, French and Russian texts are equally authentic, shall be deposited with the Secretary–General of the United Nations.

3.9 Agreement Governing the Activities of States on the Moon and Other Celestial Bodies. Concluded at New York, 5 December 1979. Entered into force, 11 July 1984. G.A.Res. 34/68, U.N. GAOR, 34th Sess., Supp. No. 46, at 77, U.N. Doc. A/Res/34/68 (1979), 1363 U.N.T.S. 3; *reprinted in* 18 I.L.M. 1434 (1979) & 5 Weston V.E.23

Article 1

1. The provisions of this Agreement relating to the moon shall also apply to other celestial bodies within the solar system, other than the earth, except in so far as specific legal norms enter into force with respect to any of these celestial bodies.

2. For the purposes of this Agreement reference to the moon shall include orbits around or other trajectories to or around it.

3. This Agreement does not apply to extraterrestrial materials which reach the surface of the earth by natural means.

Article 2

All activities on the moon, including its exploration and use, shall be carried out in accordance with international law, in particular the Charter of the United Nations, and taking into account the Declaration on Principles of International Law concerning Friendly Relations and Co-operation among States in accordance with the Charter of the United Nations, adopted by the General Assembly on 24 October 1970, in the interests of maintaining international peace and security and promoting international co-operation and mutual understanding, and with due regard to the corresponding interests of all other States Parties.

Article 3

1. The moon shall be used by all States Parties exclusively for peaceful purposes.

2. Any threat or use of force or any other hostile act or threat of hostile act on the moon is prohibited. It is likewise prohibited to use the moon in order to commit any such act or to engage in any such threat in relation to the earth, the moon, spacecraft, the personnel of spacecraft or man-made space objects.

3. States Parties shall not place in orbit around or other trajectory to or around the moon objects carrying nuclear weapons or any other kinds of weapons of mass destruction or place or use such weapons on or in the moon.

4. The establishment of military bases, installations and fortifications, the testing of any type of weapons and the conduct of military manoeuvres on the moon shall be forbidden. The use of military personnel for scientific research or for any other peaceful purposes shall not be prohibited. The use of any equipment or facility necessary for peaceful exploration and use of the moon shall also not be prohibited.

Article 4

1. The exploration and use of the moon shall be the province of all mankind and shall be carried out for the benefit and in the interests of all countries, irrespective of their degree of economic or scientific development. Due regard shall be paid to the interests of present and future generations as well as to the need to promote higher standards of living and conditions of economic and social progress and development in accordance with the Charter of the United Nations.

2. States Parties shall be guided by the principle of co-operation and mutual assistance in all their activities concerning the exploration and use of the moon. International co-operation in pursuance of this Agreement should be as wide as possible and may take place on a multilateral basis, on a bilateral basis or through international intergovernmental organizations.

Article 5

1. States Parties shall inform the Secretary–General of the United Nations as well as the public and the international scientific community, to the greatest extent feasible and practicable, of their activities concerned with the exploration and use of the moon. Information on the time, purposes, locations, orbital parameters and duration shall be given in respect of each mission to the moon as soon as possible after launching, while information on the results of each mission, including scientific results, shall be furnished upon completion of the mission. In the case of a mission lasting more than thirty days, information on conduct of the mission, including any scientific results, shall be given periodically at thirty-day intervals. For missions lasting more than six months, only significant additions to such information need be reported thereafter.

2. If a State Party becomes aware that another State Party plans to operate simultaneously in the same area of or in the same orbit around or trajectory to or around the moon, it shall promptly inform the other State of the timing of and plans for its own operations.

3. In carrying out activities under this Agreement, States Parties shall promptly inform the Secretary–General, as well as the public and the international scientific community, of any phenomena they discover in outer space, including the moon, which could endanger human life or health, as well as of any indication of organic life.

Article 6

1. There shall be freedom of scientific investigation on the moon by all States Parties without discrimination of any kind, on the basis of equality and in accordance with international law.

2. In carrying out scientific investigations and in furtherance of the provisions of this Agreement, the States Parties shall have the right to collect on and remove from the moon samples of its mineral and other substances. Such samples shall remain at the disposal of those States Parties which caused them to be collected and may be used by them for scientific purposes. States Parties shall have regard to the desirability of making a portion of such samples available to other interested States Parties and the international scientific community for scientific investigation. States Parties may in the course of scientific investigations also use mineral and other substances of the moon in quantities appropriate for the support of their missions.

3. States Parties agree on the desirability of exchanging scientific and other personnel on expeditions to or installations on the moon to the greatest extent feasible and practicable.

Article 7

1. In exploring and using the moon, States Parties shall take measures to prevent the disruption of the existing balance of its environment whether by introducing adverse changes in that environment, by its harmful contamination through the introduction of extra-environmental matter or otherwise. States Parties shall also take measures to avoid harmfully affecting the environment of the earth through the introduction of extraterrestrial matter or otherwise.

2. States Parties shall inform the Secretary–General of the United Nations of the measures being adopted by them in accordance with paragraph 1 of this article and shall also, to the maximum extent feasible, notify him in advance of all placements by them of radio-active materials on the moon and of the purposes of such placements.

3. States Parties shall report to other States Parties and to the Secretary–General concerning areas of the moon having special scientific interest in order that, without prejudice to the rights of other States Parties, consideration may be given to

the designation of such areas as international scientific preserves for which special protective arrangements are to be agreed upon in consultation with the competent bodies of the United Nations.

Article 8

1. States Parties may pursue their activities in the exploration and use of the moon anywhere on or below its surface, subject to the provisions of this Agreement.

2. For these purposes States Parties may, in particular:

(a) Land their space objects on the moon and launch them from the moon;

(b) Place their personnel, space vehicles, equipment, facilities, stations and installations anywhere on or below the surface of the moon.

Personnel, space vehicles, equipment, facilities, stations and installations may move or be moved freely over or below the surface of the moon.

3. Activities of States Parties in accordance with paragraphs 1 and 2 of this article shall not interfere with the activities of other States Parties on the moon. Where such interference may occur, the States Parties concerned shall undertake consultations in accordance with article 15, paragraphs 2 and 3 of this Agreement.

Article 9

1. States Parties may establish manned and unmanned stations on the moon. A State Party establishing a station shall use only that area which is required for the needs of the station and shall immediately inform the Secretary–General of the United Nations of the location and purposes of that station. Subsequently, at annual intervals that State shall likewise inform the Secretary–General whether the station continues in use and whether its purposes have changed.

2. Stations shall be installed in such a manner that they do not impede the free access to all areas of the moon by personnel, vehicles and equipment of other States Parties conducting activities on the moon in accordance with the provisions of this Agreement or of article I of the Treaty on Principles Governing the Activities of States in the Exploration and Use of Outer Space, including the Moon and Other Celestial Bodies.

Article 10

1. States Parties shall adopt all practicable measures to safeguard the life and health of persons on the moon. For this purpose they shall regard any person on the moon as an astronaut within the meaning of article V of the Treaty on Principles Governing the Activities of States in the Exploration and Use of Outer Space, including the Moon and Other Celestial Bodies and as part of the personnel of a spacecraft within the meaning of the Agreement on the Rescue of Astronauts, the Return of Astronauts and the Return of Objects Launched into Outer Space.

2. States Parties shall offer shelter in their stations, installations, vehicles and other facilities to persons in distress on the moon.

Article 11

1. The moon and its natural resources are the common heritage of mankind, which finds its expression in the provisions of this Agreement and in particular in paragraph 5 of this article.

2. The moon is not subject to national appropriation by any claim of sovereignty, by means of use or occupation, or by any other means.

3. Neither the surface nor the subsurface of the moon, nor any part thereof or natural resources in place, shall become property of any State, international intergov-

ernmental or non-governmental organization, national organization or non-governmental entity or of any natural person. The placement of personnel, space vehicles, equipment, facilities, stations and installations on or below the surface of the moon, including structures connected with its surface or subsurface, shall not create a right of ownership over the surface or the subsurface of the moon or any areas thereof. The foregoing provisions are without prejudice to the international régime referred to in paragraph 5 of this article.

4. States Parties have the right to exploration and use of the moon without discrimination of any kind, on a basis of equality and in accordance with international law and the terms of this Agreement.

5. States Parties to this Agreement hereby undertake to establish an international régime, including appropriate procedures, to govern the exploitation of the natural resources of the moon as such exploitation is about to become feasible. This provision shall be implemented in accordance with article 18 of this Agreement.

6. In order to facilitate the establishment of the international régime referred to in paragraph 5 of this article, States Parties shall inform the Secretary–General of the United Nations as well as the public and the international scientific community, to the greatest extent feasible and practicable, of any natural resources they may discover on the moon.

7. The main purposes of the international régime to be established shall include:

(a) The orderly and safe development of the natural resources of the moon;

(b) The rational management of those resources;

(c) The expansion of opportunities in the use of those resources;

(d) An equitable sharing by all States Parties in the benefits derived from those resources, whereby the interests and needs of the developing countries, as well as the efforts of those countries which have contributed either directly or indirectly to the exploration of the moon, shall be given special consideration.

8. All the activities with respect to the natural resources of the moon shall be carried out in a manner compatible with the purposes specified in paragraph 7 of this article and the provisions of article 6, paragraph 2, of this Agreement.

Article 12

1. States Parties shall retain jurisdiction and control over their personnel, vehicles, equipment, facilities, stations and installations on the moon. The ownership of space vehicles, equipment, facilities, stations and installations shall not be affected by their presence on the moon.

2. Vehicles, installations and equipment or their component parts found in places other than their intended location shall be dealt with in accordance with article 5 of the Agreement on Rescue of Astronauts, the Return of Astronauts and the Return of Objects Launched into Outer Space.

3. In the event of an emergency involving a threat to human life, States Parties may use the equipment, vehicles, installations, facilities or supplies of other States Parties on the moon. Prompt notification of such use shall be made to the Secretary–General of the United Nations or the State Party concerned.

Article 13

A State Party which learns of the crash landing, forced landing or other unintended landing on the moon of a space object, or its component parts, that were not launched by it, shall promptly inform the launching State Party and the Secretary–General of the United Nations.

Article 14

1. States Parties to this Agreement shall bear international responsibility for national activities on the moon, whether such activities are carried on by governmental agencies or by non-governmental entities, and for assuring that national activities are carried out in conformity with the provisions set forth in this Agreement. States Parties shall ensure that non-governmental entities under their jurisdiction shall engage in activities on the moon only under the authority and continuing supervision of the appropriate State Party.

2. States Parties recognize that detailed arrangements concerning liability for damage caused on the moon, in addition to the provisions of the Treaty on Principles Governing the Activities of States in the Exploration and Use of Outer Space, including the Moon and Other Celestial Bodies and the Convention on International Liability for Damage Caused by Space Objects, may become necessary as a result of more extensive activities on the moon. Any such arrangements shall be elaborated in accordance with the procedure provided for in article 18 of this Agreement.

Article 15

1. Each State Party may assure itself that the activities of other States Parties in the exploration and use of the moon are compatible with the provisions of this Agreement. To this end, all space vehicles, equipment, facilities, stations and installations on the moon shall be open to other States Parties. Such States Parties shall give reasonable advance notice of a projected visit, in order that appropriate consultations may be held and that maximum precautions may be taken to assure safety and to avoid interference with normal operations in the facility to be visited. In pursuance of this article, any State Party may act on its own behalf or with the full or partial assistance of any other State Party or through appropriate international procedures within the framework of the United Nations and in accordance with the Charter.

2. A State Party which has reason to believe that another State Party is not fulfilling the obligations incumbent upon it pursuant to this Agreement or that another State Party is interfering with the rights which the former State has under this Agreement may request consultations with that State Party. A State Party receiving such a request shall enter into such consultations without delay. Any other State Party which requests to do so shall be entitled to take part in the consultations. Each State Party participating in such consultations shall seek a mutually acceptable resolution of any controversy and shall bear in mind the rights and interests of all States Parties. The Secretary–General of the United Nations shall be informed of the results of the consultations and shall transmit the information received to all States Parties concerned.

3. If the consultations do not lead to a mutually acceptable settlement which has due regard for the rights and interests of all States Parties, the parties concerned shall take all measures to settle the dispute by other peaceful means of their choice appropriate to the circumstances and the nature of the dispute. If difficulties arise in connexion with the opening of consultations or if consultations do not lead to a mutually acceptable settlement, any State Party may seek the assistance of the Secretary–General, without seeking the consent of any other State Party concerned, in order to resolve the controversy. A State Party which does not maintain diplomatic relations with another State Party concerned shall participate in such consultations, at its choice, either itself or through another State Party or the Secretary–General as intermediary.

Article 16

With the exception of articles 17 to 21, references in this Agreement to States shall be deemed to apply to any international intergovernmental organization which conducts space activities if the organization declares its acceptance of the rights and obligations provided for in this Agreement and if a majority of the States members of the organization are States Parties to this Agreement and to the Treaty on Principles Governing the Activities of States in the Exploration and Use of Outer Space, including the Moon and Other Celestial Bodies. States members of any such organization which are States Parties to this Agreement shall take all appropriate steps to ensure that the organization makes a declaration in accordance with the foregoing.

Article 17

Any State Party to this Agreement may propose amendments to the Agreement. Amendments shall enter into force for each State Party to the Agreement accepting the amendments upon their acceptance by a majority of the States Parties to the Agreement and thereafter for each remaining State Party to the Agreement on the date of acceptance by it.

Article 18

Ten years after the entry into force of this Agreement, the question of the review of the Agreement shall be included in the provisional agenda of the General Assembly of the United Nations in order to consider, in the light of past application of the Agreement, whether it requires revision. However, at any time after the Agreement has been in force for five years, the Secretary–General of the United Nations, as depository, shall, at the request of one third of the States Parties to the Agreement and with the concurrence of the majority of the States Parties, convene a conference of the States Parties to review this Agreement. A review conference shall also consider the question of the implementation of the provisions of article 11, paragraph 5, on the basis of the principle referred to in paragraph 1 of that article and taking into account in particular any relevant technological developments.

Article 19

1. This Agreement shall be open for signature by all States at United Nations Headquarters in New York.

2. This Agreement shall be subject to ratification by signatory States. Any State which does not sign this Agreement before its entry into force in accordance with paragraph 3 of this article may accede to it at any time. Instruments of ratification or accession shall be deposited with the Secretary–General of the United Nations.

3. This Agreement shall enter into force on the thirtieth day following the date of deposit of the fifth instrument of ratification.

4. For each State depositing its instrument of ratification or accession after the entry into force of this Agreement, it shall enter into force on the thirtieth day following the date of deposit of any such instrument.

5. The Secretary–General shall promptly inform all signatory and acceding States of the date of each signature, the date of deposit of each instrument of ratification or accession to this Agreement, the date of its entry into force and other notices.

Article 20

Any State Party to this Agreement may give notice of its withdrawal from the Agreement one year after its entry into force by written notification to the Secretary–General of the United Nations. Such withdrawal shall take effect one year from the date of receipt of this notification.

3.10 European Communities Council Directive No. 80/779 on Air Quality Limit Values (Without Annexes but as Amended). Adopted at Brussels, 15 July 1980. L229 O.J.E.C. 30 (1980)

THE COUNCIL OF THE EUROPEAN COMMUNITIES,

Having regard to the Treaty establishing the European Economic Community, and in particular Articles 100 and 235 thereof,

Having regard to the proposal from the Commission,

Having regard to the opinion of the European Parliament,

Having regard to the opinion of the Economic and Social Committee,

Whereas the European Communities' programmes of action on the environment of 1973 and 1977 provide that priority is to be given to measures against sulphur dioxide and suspended particulates because of their toxicity and the current state of knowledge of their effects on human health and the environment;

Whereas, since any discrepancy between the provisions already applicable or being prepared in the various Member States with regard to sulphur dioxide and suspended particulates could give rise to unequal conditions of competition and could consequently directly affect the functioning of the common market, the legislative provisions in this area should be harmonized as prescribed in Article 100 of the Treaty;

Whereas one of the basic tasks of the European Economic Community is to promote throughout the Community a harmonious development of economic activities and a continued and balanced expansion; whereas such an achievement is inconceivable without measures to combat pollution, improve the quality of life and protect the environment; whereas, since the Treaty has not provided the necessary powers in this field, Article 235 of the Treaty must be invoked;

Whereas, in order to protect human health in particular, it is necessary to set for these two pollutants limit values which must not be exceeded in the territory of the Member States during specified periods; whereas these values should be based on the findings reached in the framework of the WHO, particularly with regard to the dose/effect relationships established for sulphur dioxide and suspended particulates taken together;

Whereas, despite the measures taken, it may not be possible to comply with these limit values in certain zones; whereas the Member States must therefore be allowed temporary derogations on condition that they forward to the Commission plans for the progressive improvement of the quality of the air in those zones;

Whereas guide values should also be set to serve as long-term precautions for health and the environment and as reference points for the establishment of specific schemes within zones determined by the Member States;

Whereas the measures taken pursuant to this Directive must be economically feasible and compatible with balanced development;

Whereas it is necessary to establish suitable monitoring of air quality and particularly of observance of the limit values; whereas the Member States should therefore be obliged to establish measuring stations to supply the data necessary for the application of the Directive;

Whereas, since different sampling and analysis methods are applied in the Member States, it is necessary to permit, under certain conditions, the use of sampling and measurement methods other than the reference methods laid down in the Directive;

Whereas, since some Member States use particular methods of sampling and analysis which cannot easily be correlated with the reference methods, it is necessary that the Directive specify different limit values which are to be respected where such methods are used; whereas the Member States concerned should also carry out parallel measurements at a series of representative stations using the reference methods in addition to their own methods of measurement; whereas the Commission must make further proposals in the light of these parallel measurements and of the need to avoid discriminatory provisions;

Whereas the subsequent development of reference methods of sampling and analysis referred to in this Directive may be desirable in the light of technical and scientific progress in this area; whereas in order to facilitate implementation of the work necessary to this end, a procedure should be set up to establish close cooperation between the Member States and the Commission within a Committee on Adaptation to Scientific and Technical Progress,

HAS ADOPTED THIS DIRECTIVE:

Article 1

The purpose of this Directive is to fix limit values (Annex I) and guide values (Annex II) for sulphur dioxide and suspended particulates in the atmosphere and the conditions for their application in order to improve:

— the protection of human health,

— the protection of the environment.

Article 2

1. 'Limit values' means:

— the concentrations of sulphur dioxide and suspended particulates considered simultaneously in accordance with Table A in Annex I, and

— the concentrations of suspended particulates considered separately in accordance with Table B in Annex I,

which, in order to protect human health in particular, must not be exceeded throughout the territory of the Member States during specified periods and under the conditions laid down in the following Articles.

2. 'Guide values' means the concentrations of sulphur dioxide and suspended particulates over specified periods which are given in Annex II and are intended to serve as:

— long-term precautions for health and the environment,

— reference points for the establishment of specific schemes within zones determined by the Member States.

Article 3

1. Member States shall take appropriate measures to ensure that as from 1 April 1983 the concentrations of sulphur dioxide and suspended particulates in the atmosphere are not greater than the limit values given in Annex I, without prejudice to the following provisions.

2. Where a Member State considers that there is a likelihood that, despite the measures taken, the concentrations of sulphur dioxide and suspended particulates in the atmosphere might, after 1 April 1983, exceed in certain zones the limit values given in Annex I, it shall inform the Commission thereof before 1 October 1982.

It shall at the same time forward to the Commission plans for the progressive improvement of the quality of the air in those zones. These plans, drawn up on the basis of relevant information on the nature, origin and evolution of the pollution, shall describe in particular the measures taken or to be taken and the procedures implemented or to be implemented by the Member State concerned. These measures and procedures must bring the concentrations of sulphur dioxide and suspended particulates in the atmosphere within these zones to values below or equal to the limit values given in Annex I as soon as possible and by 1 April 1993 at the latest.

Article 4

1. In the zones in which the Member State concerned considers it necessary to limit or prevent a foreseeable increase in pollution by sulphur dioxide and suspended particulates in the wake of development, in particular urban or industrial development, the Member State shall, taking the guide values in Annex II as a reference point, fix values which must be lower than the limit values in Annex I.

2. In zones on its territory which the Member State concerned considers should be afforded special environmental protection, the Member State shall fix values which are generally lower than the guide values in Annex II.

3. Member States shall inform the Commission of the values, deadlines and timetables they have laid down for the zones referred to in paragraphs 1 and 2, and of any appropriate measures they have taken.

Article 5

In addition to the provisions referred to in Article 3(1) and Article 4(1), Member States shall, with the object of taking further precautions for the protection of health and the environment, endeavour to move towards the guide values in Annex II wherever the measured concentrations are higher than these values.

Article 6

Member States shall establish measuring stations designed to supply the data necessary for the application of this Directive, in particular in zones where the limit values referred to in Article 3(1) are likely to be approached or exceeded and in the zones referred to in Article 3(2); the stations must be located at sites where pollution is thought to be greatest and where the measured concentrations are representative of local conditions.

Article 7

1. Following the entry into force of this Directive, Member States shall inform the Commission, not later than six months after the end (31 March) of the annual reference period, of instances in which the limit values laid down in Annex I have been exceeded and of the concentrations recorded.

2. They shall also notify the Commission, not later than one year after the end of the annual reference period, of the reasons for such instances and of the measures they have taken to avoid their recurrence.

3. In addition, Member States shall forward information to the Commission, at its request, on the concentrations of sulphur dioxide and suspended particulates in any zones they have designated pursuant to Article 4(1) and (2).

Article 8

The Commission shall each year publish a summary report on the application of this Directive.

Article 9

Application of the measures taken pursuant to this Directive must not bring about a significant deterioration in the quality of the air where the level of pollution by sulphur dioxide and suspended particulates at the time of implementation of this Directive is low in relation to the limit values set out in Annex I.

Article 10

1. For the purposes of applying this Directive, the Member States shall use either the reference methods of sampling and analysis referred to in Annex III or any other method of sampling and analysis in respect of which they demonstrate to the Commission at regular intervals:

— either that it ensures satisfactory correlation of results with those obtained using the reference method;

— or that measurements taken in parallel with the reference method at a series of representative stations chosen in accordance with the requirements laid down in Article 6 show that there is a reasonably stable relationship between the results obtained using that method and those obtained using the reference method.

2. Without prejudice to the provisions of this Directive, a Member State may also use, pending the decision of the Council on the proposals from the Commission referred to in paragraph 4, the sampling and analysis methods laid down in Annex IV and the values associated with these methods also laid down in Annex IV in substitution for the limit values set out in Annex I.

3. A Member State which decides to avail itself of the provisions of paragraph 2 must however take measurements in parallel at a series of representative measuring stations, chosen in accordance with the requirements of Article 6, in order to verify the corresponding stringency of the limit values set out in Annex IV and Annex I. The results of these parallel measurements, including in particular instances in which the limit values laid down in Annex I have been exceeded and the concentrations recorded, shall be forwarded to the Commission at regular intervals, and at least twice a year, for incorporation in the annual report provided for in Article 8.

4. The Commission shall, after five years, but within six years of the expiry of the limit of 24 months specified in Article 15(1), submit a report to the Council on the results of the parallel measurements carried out under paragraph 3 and shall, having regard in particular to these results and to the need to avoid discriminatory provisions, make proposals relating to paragraph 2 and Annex IV. In the report provided for in Article 8 the Commission will indicate whether it has noted instances in which the limit values fixed in Annex I have been exceeded to a significant extent on repeated occasions.

5. The Commission shall, in selected locations in the Member States and in cooperation with the latter, carry out studies on the sampling and analysis of sulphur dioxide, and of black smoke and suspended particulates. These studies shall be designed in particular to promote the harmonization of methods of sampling and analysis of these pollutants.

Article 11

1. Where Member States fix in border regions values for concentrations of sulphur dioxide and suspended particulates in the atmosphere in accordance with Article 4(1) and (2), they shall hold prior consultations. The Commission may attend such consultations.

2. Where the limit values given in Annex I or the values referred to in Article 4(1) and (2), inasmuch as the latter values have been the subject of consultations in accordance with paragraph 1, are or might be exceeded following significant pollution which originates or may have originated in another Member State, the Member States concerned shall hold consultations with a view to remedying the situation. The Commission may attend such consultations.

Article 12

The procedure laid down in Articles 13 and 14 for the adaptation on this Directive to technical progress shall cover the subsequent development of the reference methods of sampling and analysis referred to in Annex III. This adaptation must not result in any direct or indirect modification of effective concentration values given in Annexes I and II.

Article 13

1. For the purpose of Article 12 a Committee on the adaptation of this Directive to scientific and technical progress, hereinafter called 'the Committee', shall be set up; it shall consist of representatives of the Member States, with a Commission representative as chairman.

2. The Committee shall adopt its own rules of procedure.

Article 14

1. Where the procedure laid down in this Article is invoked, the Committee shall be convened by the chairman, either on his own initiative or at the request of the representative of a Member State.

2. The Commission representative shall submit a draft of the measures to be taken to the Committee. The Committee shall give its opinion on the draft within a time limit set by the chairman having regard to the urgency of the matter. Decisions shall be taken by a majority of 41 votes, the votes of the Member States being weighted as provided in Article 148(2) of the Treaty. The chairman shall not vote.

3. The Commission shall adopt the proposed measures if they are consistent with the opinion of the Committee.

Where the proposed measures are not consistent with the opinion of the Committee, or if no opinion is delivered, the Commission shall without delay submit to the Council a proposal on the measures to be taken. The Council shall decide by a qualified majority.

If within three months of the proposal being submitted to it the Council has not acted, the proposed measures shall be adopted by the Commission.

Article 15

1. Member States shall bring into force the laws, regulations and administrative provisions necessary to comply with this Directive within 24 months of its notification and shall forthwith inform the Commission thereof.

2. Member States shall communicate to the Commission the texts of the provisions of national law which they adopt in the field covered by this Directive.

Article 16

This Directive is addressed to the Member States.

AMENDMENT TO DIRECTIVE NO. 80/779/EEC (89/427/EEC, 14 July 1989)

THE COUNCIL OF THE EUROPEAN COMMUNITIES,

Having regard to the Treaty establishing the European Economic Community, and in particular Article 130s thereof,

Having regard to the proposal from the Commission,

Having regard to the opinion of the European Parliament,

Having regard to the opinion of the Economic and Social Committee,

Whereas the European Communities' 1973, 1977, 1983 and 1987 action programmes on the environment put the accent on harmonization of the action taken to protect the environment and on the need to reduce the concentrations of the principal pollutants in the air to levels considered acceptable for protecting sensitive ecosystems;

Whereas Council Directive 80/779/EEC, as last amended by the 1985 Act of Accession, offers a choice between two methods of sampling and analysis and two sets of associated limit values;

Whereas Article 10(4) of the abovementioned Directive requires the submission between July 1987 and July 1988, of proposals on this parallel application of two different sets of measurement methods and limit values;

Whereas these proposals must take account of the results of the parallel measurements referred to in Article 10(3) and of the need to avoid discriminatory provisions;

Whereas the results of the parallel measurements have shown that the limit values set out in Annex I and Annex IV to this Directive do not correspond as regards their stringency;

Whereas some Member States apply the limit values in Annex I and others those in Annex IV;

Whereas this has led to the use of different methods of sampling which are difficult to compare;

Whereas it is essential to harmonize the measurement methods and whereas, therefore, reference methods or technical specifications for the analysis and sampling of sulphur dioxide and suspended particulates in the air must be defined and finalized;

Whereas the Member States have taken measures to observe the limit values in the exempted zones as soon as possible and by 1 April 1993 at the latest;

Whereas these measures are based on one or other of the two measurement methods and associated values laid down by Directive 80/779/EEC;

Whereas the dual approach for measuring suspended particulates in the air causes discrimination between Member States;

Whereas a two-stage review is needed to draft proposals to avoid this dual approach without calling into question completion of the measures already taken by the Member States to observe the limit values;

Whereas these amendments must be taken into account in the obligations imposed by Article 3 of the said Directive on Member States applying Annex IV thereof,

HAS ADOPTED THIS DIRECTIVE:

Article 1

Directive 80/779/EEC is hereby amended as follows:

1. Article 10(1), (3) and (4) is replaced by the following:

'1. For the purposes of applying this Directive, Member States shall use either the reference methods of sampling and analysis referred to in Annex III for sulphur dioxide and for suspended particulates measured by the black smoke method or in Annex IV for suspended particulates measured by the gravimetric method, or any other method of sampling and analysis in respect of which they demonstrate to the Commission at regular intervals:

— either that it ensures satisfactory correlation of results with those obtained using the reference method,

— or that measurements taken in parallel with the reference method at a series of representative stations chosen in accordance with the requirements laid down in

Article 6 show that there is a reasonably stable relationship between the results obtained using that method and those obtained using the reference method.'

'3. By way of derogation from Article 3, Member States which decide to avail themselves of the provisions of paragraph 2 shall:

— inform the Commission, before 1 January 1991, of any zones where they consider that there is a likelihood that the concentrations of sulphur dioxide and suspended particulates in the air might exceed the limit values set out in Annex IV after 1 January 1991,

— forward to the Commission, as from 1 April 1991, plans for the progressive improvement of air quality in those zones. These plans, drawn up on the basis of relevant information on the nature, origin and development of the pollution, shall describe in particular the measures taken or to be taken and the procedures implemented or to be implemented by the Member States concerned. These measures and procedures must bring the concentrations of sulphur dioxide and suspended particulates in the air in these zones to values below or equal to the limit values set out in Annex IV as soon as possible and by 1 April 1993 at the latest.'

'4. To overcome the disadvantages of the dual approach currently laid down in Annexes I and IV, which are not completely equivalent, by 31 December 1992 the Commission shall submit to the Council a proposal for a general review of this Directive. The proposal shall take account of the experience acquired from the studies referred to in paragraph 5 and of the results of subsequent measurements taken using technical specifications or reference methods for determining suspended particulates and sulphur dioxide. These technical specifications or reference methods must be finalized by the Commission, in agreement with the Member States, by 31 December 1990.

This proposal shall cover any other aspects in need of review in the light of scientific knowledge and of the experience acquired over the period of application of this Directive. It shall take account of, *inter alia,* aspects connected with the design of the networks for measuring air pollution and with the installation of measuring equipment as well as the quality and comparability of the measurements taken.'

2. Annex IV shall be amended in accordance with the Annex to this Directive.

Article 2

1. Member States shall bring into force the laws, regulations and administrative provisions necessary to comply with this Directive within 18 months of its notification. They shall forthwith inform the Commission thereof.

2. Member States shall see to it that they communicate to the Commission the texts of the provisions of national law which they adopt in the field covered by this Directive.

Article 3

This Directive is addressed to the Member States.

3.11 Memorandum of Intent Between Canada and the United States Concerning Transboundary Air Pollution (Without Annex). Concluded at Washington, 5 August 1980. Entered into force, 5 August 1980. 32 U.S.T. 2521, T.I.A.S. No. 9856; *reprinted in* 20 I.L.M. 690 (1981)

The Government of the United States of America and the Government of Canada,

Share a concern about actual and potential damage resulting from transboundary air pollution, (which is the short and long range transport of air pollutants between their countries), including the already serious problem of acid rain;

Recognize this is an important and urgent bilateral problem as it involves the flow of air pollutants in both directions across the international boundary, especially the long range transport of air pollutants;

Share also a common determination to combat transboundary air pollution in keeping with their existing international rights, obligations, commitments and cooperative practices, including those set forth in the 1909 Boundary Waters Treaty, the 1972 Stockholm Declaration on the Human Environment, the 1978 Great Lakes Water Quality Agreement, and the 1979 ECE Convention on Long Range Transboundary Air Pollution;

Undertook in July 1979 to develop a bilateral cooperative agreement on air quality which would deal effectively with transboundary air pollution;

Are resolved as a matter of priority both to improve scientific understanding of the long range transport of air pollutants and its effects and to develop and implement policies, practices and technologies to combat its impact;

Are resolved to protect the environment in harmony with measures to meet energy needs and other national objectives;

Note scientific findings which indicate that continued pollutant loadings will result in extensive acidification in geologically sensitive areas during the coming years, and that increased pollutant loadings will accelerate this process;

Are concerned that environmental stress could be increased if action is not taken to reduce transboundary air pollution;

Are convinced that the best means to protect the environment from the effects of transboundary air pollution is through the achievement of necessary reductions in pollutant loadings;

Are convinced also that this common problem requires cooperative action by both countries;

Intend to increase bilateral cooperative action to deal effectively with transboundary air pollution, including acid rain.

In particular, the Government of the United States of America and the Government of Canada intend:

1. to develop a bilateral agreement which will reflect and further the development of effective domestic control programs and other measures to combat transboundary air pollution;

2. to facilitate the conclusion of such an agreement as soon as possible; and,

3. pending conclusion of such an agreement, to take interim actions available under current authority to combat transboundary air pollution.

The specific undertakings of both Governments at this time are outlined below.

INTERIM ACTIONS

1. *Transboundary Air Pollution Agreement*

Further to their Joint Statement of July 26, 1979, and subsequent bilateral discussions, both Governments shall take all necessary steps forthwith:

(a) to establish a United States/Canada Coordinating Committee which will undertake preparatory discussions immediately and commence formal negotiations no later than June 1, 1981, of a cooperative agreement on transboundary air pollution; and

(b) to provide the necessary resources for the Committee to carry out its work, including the working group structure as set forth in the Annex. Members will be appointed to the work groups by each Government as soon as possible.

2. *Control Measures*

To combat transboundary air pollution both Governments shall:

(a) develop domestic air pollution control policies and strategies, and as necessary and appropriate, seek legislative or other support to give effect to them;

(b) promote vigorous enforcement of existing laws and regulations as they require limitation of emissions from new, substantially modified and existing facilities in a way which is responsive to the problems of transboundary air pollution; and

(c) share information and consult on actions being taken pursuant to (a) and (b) above.

3. *Notification and Consultation*

Both Governments shall continue and expand their long-standing practice of advance notification and consultation on proposed actions involving a significant risk or potential risk of causing or increasing transboundary air pollution, including:

(a) proposed major industrial development or other actions which may cause significant increases in transboundary air pollution; and

(b) proposed changes of policy, regulations or practices which may significantly affect transboundary air pollution.

4. *Scientific Information, Research and Development*

In order to improve understanding of their common problem and to increase their capability for controlling transboundary air pollution both Governments shall:

(a) exchange information generated in research programs being undertaken in both countries on the atmospheric aspects of the transport of air pollutants and on their effects on aquatic and terrestrial ecosystems and on human health and property;

(b) maintain and further develop a coordinated program for monitoring and evaluation of the impacts of transboundary air pollution, including the maintenance of a United States/Canada sampling network and exchange of data on current and projected emissions of major air pollutants; and

(c) continue to exchange information on research to develop improved technologies for reducing emissions of major air pollutants of concern.

The Memorandum of Intent will become effective on signature and will remain in effect until revised by mutual agreement.

3.12 MEXICO-UNITED STATES AGREEMENT TO CO-OPERATE IN THE SOLUTION OF ENVIRONMENTAL PROBLEMS IN THE BORDER AREA (Without Annexes). Concluded at La Paz (Mexico), 14 August 1983. Entered into force, 16 February 1984. *Reprinted in* 22 I.L.M. 1025 (1983)

Whereas, the Governments of Mexico and the United States share many environmental problems related to large and expanding urban populations, substantial industrial activity, and a common border between the two countries; and both countries possess many areas of natural and man-made scenic and recreational value; and

Whereas, the Subsecretariat for Environmental Improvement of Mexico (SMA) and the Environmental Protection Agency (EPA) of the United States share a concern for protecting and improving the human and natural environments of their respective nations, and a common interest in the cause of global as well as common border environmental protection and improvement; and

Whereas, the Governments of Mexico and the U.S. have pledged increased cooperation through the Consultative Mechanism set up by the two Presidents to include environmental cooperation;

It is Hereby AGREED that:

1. The SMA and EPA will initiate a cooperative effort to resolve environmental problems of mutual concern in border areas as well as any environmental protection matter through exchanges of information and personnel, and the establishment of parallel projects which the two parties consider appropriate to adopt.

2. The SMA and EPA will accomplish parallel activities, while allowing for the possibility that, at any given time, through special agreement, joint actions tending to resolve specific problems, may be conducted.

3. SMA and EPA senior officials will meet annually, unless they mutually agree otherwise, to discuss overall policies, programs and problems which are of common concern. The annual meeting will be held, alternately in each country, at a mutually agreeable time and site.

4. Experts designated by SMA and EPA will meet periodically or as necessary to review technical issues and plan parallel projects, including pollution abatement and control, regulations, quality assurance, research, and monitoring, that are of common interest or concern to both Mexico and the United States. An annual meeting of designated experts will be held at a site mutually agreed to by both parties and may coincide with the U.S./Mexico Border Health Association annual meetings or with other meetings. The SMA and EPA experts may make policy recommendations for consideration by the respective heads of SMA and EPA.

5. The meetings of the SMA and EPA representatives will not be limited to consideration of border problems alone but may include discussions of all areas of environmental protection and enhancement. It is understood that the Water Treaty of 1944 between the two Governments entrusted the solution of border sanitation problems to the International Boundary and Water Commission.

6. Each Party will name one person to act as coordinator to facilitate exchanges of information and other cooperation under this Memorandum of Understanding. The coordinators will establish procedures and details for the meetings of the senior officials as well as experts, including the time, place and agenda.

7. The coordinators may invite representatives of federal, state and local government agencies, international organizations, members of private organizations or other private citizens to participate in meetings, conferences, and other parallel activities as deemed appropriate.

8. Parallel activities may be conducted when approved by appropriate authorities of the respective governments and may include but will not be limited to the following:

— Development of pollution abatement and control programs directed toward specific pollution problems affecting either or both countries along the border.

— Development of an early warning system to alert the two Governments to potential environmental problems.

— Review and consultation regarding national environmental policies and strategies of Mexico and the United States.

— Development of data gathering, processing and mechanisms for the exchanges of information of common interest.

9. The coordinators will be responsible for the general management of programs, workshops, projects and activities undertaken pursuant to this Memorandum of Understanding. This includes definition of each program, workshop or project as to scope, priority, and completion schedules. The coordinators may delegate work on a special problem area to a special subcommittee which shall examine the problem in detail and make recommendations to the Governments through the SMA and EPA, respectively.

10. Unless otherwise agreed, each Party will bear the cost of its participation, including personnel costs, in activities undertaken pursuant to this Memorandum of Understanding.

11. Work under this Memorandum of Understanding is subject to the availability of funds and other resources to each Party, and to the laws and regulations of Mexico and the United States.

12. Results of work accomplished under this Memorandum of Understanding will be fully available to both parties and either Party may release information in its possession to the public on 10 days notice to the other Party.

13. This Memorandum of Understanding will enter into force when signed by both Parties and approved by the two Governments through an exchange of notes. The Memorandum of Understanding will remain in force indefinitely until either Party notifies the other of its intent to terminate the agreement, with 90 days notification.

3.13 European Communities Council Directive No. 85/203 on Air Quality Standards for Nitrogen Dioxide. Adopted at Brussels, 7 March 1985. L87 O.J.E.C. (1985)

THE COUNCIL OF THE EUROPEAN COMMUNITIES,

Having regard to the Treaty establishing the European Economic Community, and in particular Articles 100 and 235 thereof,

Having regard to the proposal from the Commission,

Having regard to the opinion of the European Parliament,

Having regard to the opinion of the Economic and Social Committee,

Whereas the programmes of action of the European Communities on the environment of 1973, 1977 and 1982 provide that priority is to be given to measures against nitrogen dioxide because of its noxiousness and having regard to the current state of knowledge of its effects on human health and the environment;

Whereas insufficient technical and scientific information is available to enable the Council to lay down specific standards for the environment generally and whereas the adoption of limit values for the protection of human health will contribute to the protection of the environment as well;

Whereas any discrepancy between the provisions already applicable or being drawn up in the various Member States with regard to nitrogen dioxide in the air could give rise to unequal conditions of competition and could in consequence directly affect the functioning of the common market; whereas, therefore, the approximation of laws prescribed in Article 100 of the Treaty should be carried out in this area;

Whereas one of the basic tasks of the Community is to promote throughout the Community a harmonious development of economic activities and a continued and balanced expansion, which is inconceivable without an attack on pollution and nuisance or an improvement in the quality of life and the protection of the environment; whereas, since the Treaty has not provided the necessary powers, recourse must be had to Article 235 of the Treaty;

Whereas, in order to protect in particular human health and the environment, it is necessary to set for nitrogen dioxide a limit value which must not be exceeded in the territory of the Member States during specified periods and whereas this value should be based on the results of work carried out for the World Health Organization, particularly with regard to the dose/effect relationships established for this pollutant;

Whereas, despite the measures taken, it may not be possible to comply with the limit value in certain zones; whereas the Member States may be allowed temporary derogations on condition that they forward to the Commission plans for the gradual improvement of the quality of the air in these zones;

Whereas it is expected that the Council will shortly establish a further legal act enabling Member States to impose significantly lower limit values for exhaust gases from motor vehicles;

Whereas the measures taken pursuant to this Directive must be economically feasible and compatible with balanced development;

Whereas nitrogen dioxide is also a precursor in the formation of photochemical oxidants which can be harmful to man and the environment and whereas preventive action can help reduce their formation;

Whereas it is necessary to establish measuring stations to monitor compliance with the limit value for nitrogen dioxide and whereas it is desirable that these stations also measure nitric oxide which is an intermediary step in the formation of nitrogen dioxide;

Whereas, in view of the existence of different methods of analysis in the Member States, it is necessary to permit, under certain conditions, the use of methods of analysis other than the reference method laid down in the Directive;

Whereas, in addition to the limit value, there is a need to provide for guide values to improve the protection of human health and contribute to the long-term protection of the environment;

Whereas subsequent changes in the reference method of analysis referred to in this Directive may be desirable in the light of technical and scientific progress in this area; whereas, in order to facilitate the implementation of the work necessary to this end, a procedure should be set up to establish close cooperation between Member States and the Commission within a Committee on Adaptation to Scientific and Technical Progress,

HAS ADOPTED THIS DIRECTIVE:

Article 1

1. The purpose of this Directive is to:

— fix a limit value (Annex I) for nitrogen dioxide in the atmosphere specifically to help protect human beings against the effects of nitrogen dioxide in the environment,

— lay down guide values (Annex II) for nitrogen dioxide in the atmosphere in order to improve the protection of human health and contribute to the long-term protection of the environment.

2. This Directive shall not apply to exposure at work or inside buildings.

Article 2

For the purposes of this Directive:

— 'limit value' means the concentration of nitrogen dioxide as defined in the table in Annex I which must not be exceeded throughout the territory of the Member States during specified periods and under the conditions laid down in the following Articles,

— 'guide values' means the concentrations of nitrogen dioxide as given in Annex II considered over specified periods and intended, in particular, to serve as reference points for the establishment of specific schemes within zones determined by the Member States.

Article 3

1. Member States shall take the necessary measures to ensure that as from 1 July 1987 the concentrations of nitrogen dioxide in the atmosphere measured in accordance with Annex III are not greater than the limit value given in Annex I.

2. However, when in particular circumstances the nitrogen dioxide concentrations in the atmosphere in certain zones are likely, despite the measures taken, to exceed the limit value in Annex I after 1 July 1987, the Member State concerned shall inform the Commission thereof before 1 July 1987.

It shall forward plans for the gradual improvement of the quality of the air in these zones to the Commission as soon as possible. These plans, drawn up on the basis of relevant information on the nature, origin and development of this pollution, shall describe, in particular, the measures taken or to be taken and the procedures implemented or to be implemented by the Member State concerned. These measures and procedures must aim at reducing the nitrogen dioxide concentrations in the atmosphere within these zones to values not exceeding the limit value given in Annex I as rapidly as possible and by 1 January 1994 at the latest.

Article 4

1. In the zones in which the Member State concerned considers it necessary to limit or prevent a foreseeable increase in pollution by nitrogen dioxide in the wake of urban or industrial development in particular, it may fix values lower than the limit value in Annex I.

2. In zones which the Member State concerned considers should be afforded special environmental protection, it may fix values which are generally lower than the guide values in Annex II.

Article 5

Member States may, at any time, fix values more stringent than those laid down in this Directive.

Article 6

Member States shall establish measuring stations to supply the data necessary for the application of this Directive in accordance with the specifications in Annex III, in particular in zones where the limit value is exceeded or likely to be exceeded and in the zones referred to in Article 4.

Such stations may also measure concentrations of nitric oxide.

Article 7

1. From 1 July 1987 Member States shall inform the Commission, not later than six months after the end (31 December) of the annual reference period, of instances in which the limit value laid down in Annex I has been exceeded and of the concentrations recorded.

2. Member States shall also notify the Commission, not later than one year after the end of the annual reference period, of the reasons for such instances and of the measures they have taken to deal with them.

3. In addition, Member States shall inform the Commission, at its request, of:

— the concentrations they have measured,

— the limit values, deadlines and timetables they have laid down,

— any appropriate measures they have taken, concerning the zones referred to in Article 4(1) and (2).

This information must also be made available to the public.

Article 8

The Commission shall publish periodically a summary report on the application of this Directive.

Article 9

The application of the measures taken pursuant to this Directive must not lead to a significant deterioration in the quality of the air in zones, outside urban areas, where the level of pollution by nitrogen dioxide at the time of implementation of this Directive is low in relation to the limit value laid down in Annex I.

Article 10

In applying this Directive, Member States shall use:

— either the reference method of analysis referred to in Annex IV,

— or any other method of analysis which the Commission has been shown is equivalent to the reference method.

Article 11

1. Where a Member State intends to fix, in a region near the border with one or more other Member States, values for concentrations of nitrogen dioxide in the atmosphere in accordance with Article 4(1) and (2), it shall hold prior consultations with the Member States concerned. The Commission shall be informed and may attend such consultations.

2. Where the limit value given in Annex I or the values referred to in Article 4(1) and (2)—provided that the latter values have been the subject of consultations in accordance with paragraph 1—are or are likely to be exceeded following significant pollution which originates or may originate in another Member State, the Member States concerned shall hold consultations with a view to remedying the situation. The Commission shall be informed and may attend such consultations.

Article 12

The amendments necessary to adapt the specifications in Annex IV to technical progress shall be adopted in accordance with the procedure described in Article 14. These amendments shall not be such as to alter, directly or indirectly, the limit value laid down in Annex I.

Article 13

1. For the purposes of Article 12, a Committee on the Adaptation of this Directive to Scientific and Technical Progress, hereinafter called 'the Committee', shall be set up, composed of representatives of the Member States with a Commission representative as Chairman.

2. The Committee shall adopt its own rules of procedure.

Article 14

1. Where the procedure laid down in this Article is to be followed, matters shall be referred to the Committee by its Chairman, either on his own initiative or at the request of the representative of a Member State.

2. The Commission representative shall submit a draft of the measures to be taken to the Committee. The Committee shall give its opinion on the draft within a time limit set by the Chairman having regard to the urgency of the matter. Decisions shall be taken by a majority of 54 votes, the votes of the Member States being weighted as provided in Article 148(2) of the Treaty. The Chairman shall not vote.

3. The Commission shall adopt the proposed measures if they are consistent with the opinion of the Committee.

Where the proposed measures are not consistent with the opinion of the Committee, or if no opinion is delivered, the Commission shall without delay submit to the Council a proposal on the measures to be taken. The Council shall decide by a qualified majority.

If, within three months of the proposal being submitted to it, the Council has not acted, the proposed measures shall be adopted by the Commission.

Article 15

1. Member States shall bring into force the laws, regulations and administrative provisions necessary to comply with this Directive by 1 January 1987 at the latest and shall forthwith inform the Commission thereof.

2. Member States shall communicate to the Commission the texts of the provisions of national law which they adopt in the field covered by this Directive.

Article 16

This Directive is addressed to the Member States.

3.14 VIENNA CONVENTION FOR THE PROTECTION OF THE OZONE LAYER (With Annexes I & II).[c] Concluded at Vienna, 22 March 1985. Entered into force, 22 September 1988. UNEP Doc. IG.53/5; *reprinted in* 26 I.L.M. 1529 (1987) & 5 Weston V.E.5

Article 1

Definitions

For the purposes of this Convention:

1. 'The ozone layer' means the layer of atmospheric ozone above the planetary boundary layer.

2. 'Adverse effects' means changes in the physical environment or biota, including changes in climate, which have significant deleterious effects on human health or on the composition, resilience and productivity of natural and managed ecosystems, or on materials useful to mankind.

3. 'Alternative technologies or equipment' means technologies or equipment the use of which makes it possible to reduce or effectively eliminate emissions of substances which have or are likely to have adverse effects on the ozone layer.

4. 'Alternative substances' means substances which reduce, eliminate or avoid adverse effects on the ozone layer.

5. 'Parties' means, unless the text otherwise indicates, Parties to this Convention.

6. 'Regional economic integration organization' means an organization constituted by sovereign States of a given region which has competence in respect of matters governed by this Convention or its protocols and has been duly authorized, in accordance with its internal procedures, to sign, ratify, accept, approve or accede to the instruments concerned.

7. 'Protocols' means protocols to this Convention.

Article 2

General Obligations

1. The Parties shall take appropriate measures in accordance with the provisions of this Convention and of those protocols in force to which they are party to protect human health and the environment against adverse effects resulting or likely to result from human activities which modify or are likely to modify the ozone layer.

2. To this end the Parties shall, in accordance with the means at their disposal and their capabilities:

(a) Co-operate by means of systematic observations, research and information exchange in order to better understand and assess the effects of human activities on the ozone layer and the effects on human health and the environment from modification of the ozone layer;

(b) Adopt appropriate legislative or administrative measures and co-operate in harmonizing appropriate policies to control, limit, reduce or prevent human activities under their jurisdiction or control should it be found that these activities have or are likely to have adverse effects resulting from modification or likely modification of the ozone layer;

(c) Co-operate in the formulation of agreed measures, procedures and standards for the implementation of this Convention, with a view to the adoption of protocols and annexes;

c. *See also* Basic Document 3.18, *infra*.

(d) Co-operate with competent international bodies to implement effectively this Convention and protocols to which they are party.

3. The provisions of this Convention shall in no way affect the right of Parties to adopt, in accordance with international law, domestic measures additional to those referred to in paragraphs 1 and 2 above, nor shall they affect additional domestic measures already taken by a Party, provided that these measures are not incompatible with their obligations under this Convention.

4. The application of this article shall be based on relevant scientific and technical considerations.

Article 3

Research and Systematic Observations

1. The Parties undertake, as appropriate, to initiate and co-operate in, directly or through competent international bodies, the conduct of research and scientific assessments on:

(a) The physical and chemical processes that may affect the ozone layer;

(b) The human health and other biological effects deriving from any modifications of the ozone layer, particularly those resulting from changes in ultra-violet solar radiation having biological effects (UV–B);

(c) Climatic effects deriving from any modifications of the ozone layer;

(d) Effects deriving from any modifications of the ozone layer and any consequent change in UV–B radiation on natural and synthetic materials useful to mankind;

(e) Substances, practices, processes and activities that may affect the ozone layer, and their cumulative effects;

(f) Alternative substances and technologies;

(g) Related socio-economic matters;

and as further elaborated in annexes I and II.

2. The Parties undertake to promote or establish, as appropriate, directly or through competent international bodies and taking fully into account national legislation and relevant ongoing activities at both the national and international levels, joint or complementary programmes for systematic observation of the state of the ozone layer and other relevant parameters, as elaborated in annex I.

3. The Parties undertake to co-operate, directly or through competent international bodies, in ensuring the collection, validation and transmission of research and observational data through appropriate world data centres in a regular and timely fashion.

Article 4

Co-operation in the Legal, Scientific and Technical Fields

1. The Parties shall facilitate and encourage the exchange of scientific, technical, socio-economic, commercial and legal information relevant to this Convention as further elaborated in annex II. Such information shall be supplied to bodies agreed upon by the Parties. Any such body receiving information regarded as confidential by the supplying Party shall ensure that such information is not disclosed and shall aggregate it to protect its confidentiality before it is made available to all Parties.

2. The Parties shall co-operate, consistent with their national laws, regulations and practices and taking into account in particular the needs of the developing countries, in promoting, directly or through competent international bodies, the

development and transfer of technology and knowledge. Such co-operation shall be carried out particularly through:

(a) Facilitation of the acquisition of alternative technologies by other Parties;

(b) Provision of information on alternative technologies and equipment, and supply of special manuals or guides to them;

(c) The supply of necessary equipment and facilities for research and systematic observations;

(d) Appropriate training of scientific and technical personnel.

Article 5

Transmission of Information

The Parties shall transmit, through the secretariat, to the Conference of the Parties established under article 6 information on the measures adopted by them in implementation of this Convention and of protocols to which they are party in such form and at such intervals as the meetings of the parties to the relevant instruments may determine.

Article 6

Conference of the Parties

1. A Conference of the Parties is hereby established. The first meeting of the Conference of the Parties shall be convened by the secretariat designated on an interim basis under article 7 not later than one year after entry into force of this Convention. Thereafter, ordinary meetings of the Conference of the Parties shall be held at regular intervals to be determined by the Conference at its first meeting.

2. Extraordinary meetings of the Conference of the Parties shall be held at such other times as may be deemed necessary by the Conference, or at the written request of any Party, provided that, within six months of the request being communicated to them by the secretariat, it is supported by at least one third of the Parties.

3. The Conference of the Parties shall by consensus agree upon and adopt rules of procedure and financial rules for itself and for any subsidiary bodies it may establish, as well as financial provisions governing the functioning of the secretariat.

4. The Conference of the Parties shall keep under continuous review the implementation of this Convention, and, in addition, shall:

(a) Establish the form and the intervals for transmitting the information to be submitted in accordance with article 5 and consider such information as well as reports submitted by any subsidiary body;

(b) Review the scientific information on the ozone layer, on its possible modification and on possible effects of any such modification;

(c) Promote, in accordance with article 2, the harmonization of appropriate policies, strategies and measures for minimizing the release of substances causing or likely to cause modification of the ozone layer, and make recommendations on any other measures relating to this Convention;

(d) Adopt, in accordance with articles 3 and 4, programmes for research, systematic observations, scientific and technological co-operation, the exchange of information and the transfer of technology and knowledge;

(e) Consider and adopt, as required, in accordance with articles 9 and 10, amendments to this Convention and its annexes;

(f) Consider amendments to any protocol, as well as to any annexes thereto, and, if so decided, recommend their adoption to the parties to the protocol concerned;

(g) Consider and adopt, as required, in accordance with article 10, additional annexes to this Convention;

(h) Consider and adopt, as required, protocols in accordance with article 8;

(i) Establish such subsidiary bodies as are deemed necessary for the implementation of this Convention;

(j) Seek, where appropriate, the services of competent international bodies and scientific committees, in particular the World Meteorological Organization and the World Health Organization, as well as the Co-ordinating Committee on the Ozone Layer, in scientific research, systematic observations and other activities pertinent to the objectives of this Convention, and make use as appropriate of information from these bodies and committees;

(k) Consider and undertake any additional action that may be required for the achievement of the purposes of this Convention.

5. The United Nations, its specialized agencies and the International Atomic Energy Agency, as well as any State not party to this Convention, may be represented at meetings of the Conference of the Parties by observers. Any body or agency, whether national or international, governmental or non-governmental, qualified in fields relating to the protection of the ozone layer which has informed the secretariat of its wish to be represented at a meeting of the Conference of the Parties as an observer may be admitted unless at least one-third of the Parties present object. The admission and participation of observers shall be subject to the rules of procedure adopted by the Conference of the Parties.

Article 7

Secretariat

1. The functions of the secretariat shall be:

(a) To arrange for and service meetings provided for in articles 6, 8, 9 and 10;

(b) To prepare and transmit reports based upon information received in accordance with articles 4 and 5, as well as upon information derived from meetings of subsidiary bodies established under article 6;

(c) To perform the functions assigned to it by any protocol;

(d) To prepare reports on its activities carried out in implementation of its functions under this Convention and present them to the Conference of the Parties;

(e) To ensure the necessary co-ordination with other relevant international bodies, and in particular to enter into such administrative and contractual arrangements as may be required for the effective discharge of its functions;

(f) To perform such other functions as may be determined by the Conference of the Parties.

2. The secretariat functions will be carried out on an interim basis by the United Nations Environment Programme until the completion of the first ordinary meeting of the Conference of the Parties held pursuant to article 6. At its first ordinary meeting, the Conference of the Parties shall designate the secretariat from amongst those existing competent international organizations which have signified their willingness to carry out the secretariat functions under this Convention.

Article 8

Adoption of Protocols

1. The Conference of the Parties may at a meeting adopt protocols pursuant to article 2.

2. The text of any proposed protocol shall be communicated to the Parties by the secretariat at least six months before such a meeting.

Article 9

Amendment of the Convention or Protocols

1. Any Party may propose amendments to this Convention or to any protocol. Such amendments shall take due account, *inter alia,* of relevant scientific and technical considerations.

2. Amendments to this Convention shall be adopted at a meeting of the Conference of the Parties. Amendments to any protocol shall be adopted at a meeting of the Parties to the protocol in question. The text of any proposed amendment to this Convention or to any protocol, except as may otherwise be provided in such protocol, shall be communicated to the Parties by the secretariat at least six months before the meeting at which it is proposed for adoption. The secretariat shall also communicate proposed amendments to the signatories to this Convention for information.

3. The Parties shall make every effort to reach agreement on any proposed amendment to this Convention by consensus. If all efforts at consensus have been exhausted, and no agreement reached, the amendment shall as a last resort be adopted by a three-fourths majority vote of the Parties present and voting at the meeting, and shall be submitted by the Depositary to all Parties for ratification, approval or acceptance.

4. The procedure mentioned in paragraph 3 above shall apply to amendments to any protocol, except that a two-thirds majority of the parties to that protocol present and voting at the meeting shall suffice for their adoption.

5. Ratification, approval or acceptance of amendments shall be notified to the Depositary in writing. Amendments adopted in accordance with paragraph 3 or 4 above shall enter into force between parties having accepted them on the ninetieth day after the receipt by the Depositary of notification of their ratification, approval or acceptance by at least three-fourths of the Parties to this Convention or by at least two-thirds of the parties to the protocol concerned, except as may otherwise be provided in such protocol. Thereafter the amendments shall enter into force for any other Party on the ninetieth day after that Party deposits its instrument of ratification, approval or acceptance of the amendments.

6. For the purposes of this article, "Parties present and voting" means Parties present and casting an affirmative or negative vote.

Article 10

Adoption and Amendment of Annexes

1. The annexes to this Convention or to any protocol shall form an integral part of this Convention or of such protocol, as the case may be, and, unless expressly provided otherwise, a reference to this Convention or its protocols constitutes at the same time a reference to any annexes thereto. Such annexes shall be restricted to scientific, technical and administrative matters.

2. Except as may be otherwise provided in any protocol with respect to its annexes, the following procedure shall apply to the proposal, adoption and entry into force of additional annexes to this Convention or of annexes to a protocol:

(a) Annexes to this Convention shall be proposed and adopted according to the procedure laid down in article 9, paragraphs 2 and 3, while annexes to any protocol shall be proposed and adopted according to the procedure laid down in article 9, paragraphs 2 and 4;

(b) Any party that is unable to approve an additional annex to this Convention or an annex to any protocol to which it is party shall so notify the Depositary, in writing, within six months from the date of the communication of the adoption by the Depositary. The Depositary shall without delay notify all Parties of any such notification received. A Party may at any time substitute an acceptance for a previous declaration of objection and the annexes shall thereupon enter into force for that Party;

(c) On the expiry of six months from the date of the circulation of the communication by the Depositary, the annex shall become effective for all Parties to this Convention or to any protocol concerned which have not submitted a notification in accordance with the provision of subparagraph (b) above.

3. The proposal, adoption and entry into force of amendments to annexes to this Convention or to any protocol shall be subject to the same procedure as for the proposal, adoption and entry into force of annexes to the Convention or annexes to a protocol. Annexes and amendments thereto shall take due account, *inter alia,* of relevant scientific and technical considerations.

4. If an additional annex or an amendment to an annex involves an amendment to this Convention or to any protocol, the additional annex or amended annex shall not enter into force until such time as the amendment to this Convention or to the protocol concerned enters into force.

Article 11

Settlement of Disputes

1. In the event of a dispute between Parties concerning the interpretation or application of this Convention, the parties concerned shall seek solution by negotiation.

2. If the parties concerned cannot reach agreement by negotiation, they may jointly seek the good offices of, or request mediation by, a third party.

3. When ratifying, accepting, approving or acceding to this Convention, or at any time thereafter, a State or regional economic integration organization may declare in writing to the Depositary that for a dispute not resolved in accordance with paragraph 1 or paragraph 2 above, it accepts one or both of the following means of dispute settlement as compulsory:

(a) Arbitration in accordance with procedures to be adopted by the Conference of the Parties at its first ordinary meeting;

(b) Submission of the dispute to the International Court of Justice.

4. If the parties have not, in accordance with paragraph 3 above, accepted the same or any procedure, the dispute shall be submitted to conciliation in accordance with paragraph 5 below unless the parties otherwise agree.

5. A conciliation commission shall be created upon the request of one of the parties to the dispute. The commission shall be composed of an equal number of members appointed by each party concerned and a chairman chosen jointly by the members appointed by each party. The commission shall render a final and recommendatory award, which the parties shall consider in good faith.

6. The provisions of this article shall apply with respect to any protocol except as otherwise provided in the protocol concerned.

Article 12

Signature

This Convention shall be open for signature by States and by regional economic integration organizations at the Federal Ministry for Foreign Affairs of the Republic of Austria in Vienna from 22 March 1985 to 21 September 1985, and at United Nations Headquarters in New York from 22 September 1985 to 21 March 1986.

Article 13

Ratification, Acceptance or Approval

1. This Convention and any protocol shall be subject to ratification, acceptance or approval by States and by regional economic integration organizations. Instruments of ratification, acceptance or approval shall be deposited with the Depositary.

2. Any organization referred to in paragraph 1 above which becomes a Party to this Convention or any protocol without any of its member States being a Party shall be bound by all the obligations under the Convention or the protocol, as the case may be. In the case of such organizations, one or more of whose member States is a Party to the Convention or relevant protocol, the organization and its member States shall decide on their respective responsibilities for the performance of their obligation under the Convention or protocol, as the case may be. In such cases, the organization and the member States shall not be entitled to exercise rights under the Convention or relevant protocol concurrently.

3. In their instruments of ratification, acceptance or approval, the organizations referred to in paragraph 1 above shall declare the extent of their competence with respect to the matters governed by the Convention or the relevant protocol. These organizations shall also inform the Depositary of any substantial modification in the extent of their competence.

Article 14

Accession

1. This Convention and any protocol shall be open for accession by States and by regional economic integration organizations from the date on which the Convention or the protocol concerned is closed for signature. The instruments of accession shall be deposited with the Depositary.

2. In their instruments of accession, the organizations referred to in paragraph 1 above shall declare the extent of their competence with respect to the matters governed by the Convention or the relevant protocol. These organizations shall also inform the Depositary of any substantial modification in the extent of their competence.

3. The provisions of article 13, paragraph 2, shall apply to regional economic integration organizations which accede to this Convention or any protocol.

Article 15

Right to Vote

1. Each Party to this Convention or to any protocol shall have one vote.

2. Except as provided for in paragraph 1 above, regional economic integration organizations, in matters within their competence, shall exercise their right to vote with a number of votes equal to the number of their member States which are Parties to the Convention or the relevant protocol. Such organizations shall not exercise their right to vote if their member States exercise theirs, and vice versa.

Article 16

Relationship between the Convention and its Protocols

1. A State or a regional economic integration organization may not become a party to a protocol unless it is, or becomes at the same time, a Party to the Convention.

2. Decisions concerning any protocol shall be taken only by the parties to the protocol concerned.

Article 17

Entry into Force

1. This Convention shall enter into force on the ninetieth day after the date of deposit of the twentieth instrument of ratification, acceptance, approval or accession.

2. Any protocol, except as otherwise provided in such protocol, shall enter into force on the ninetieth day after the date of deposit of the eleventh instrument of ratification, acceptance or approval of such protocol or accession thereto.

3. For each Party which ratifies, accepts or approves this Convention or accedes thereto after the deposit of the twentieth instrument of ratification, acceptance, approval or accession, it shall enter into force on the ninetieth day after the date of deposit by such Party of its instrument of ratification, acceptance, approval or accession.

4. Any protocol, except as otherwise provided in such protocol, shall enter into force for a party that ratifies, accepts or approves that protocol or accedes thereto after its entry into force pursuant to paragraph 2 above, on the ninetieth day after the date on which that party deposits its instrument of ratification, acceptance, approval or accession, or on the date on which the Convention enters into force for that Party, whichever shall be the later.

5. For the purposes of paragraphs 1 and 2 above, any instrument deposited by a regional economic integration organization shall not be counted as additional to those deposited by member States of such organization.

Article 18

Reservations

No reservations may be made to this Convention.

Article 19

Withdrawal

1. At any time after four years from the date on which this Convention has entered into force for a Party, that Party may withdraw from the Convention by giving written notification to the Depositary.

2. Except as may be provided in any protocol, at any time after four years from the date on which such protocol has entered into force for a party, that party may withdraw from the protocol by giving written notification to the Depositary.

3. Any such withdrawal shall take effect upon expiry of one year after the date of its receipt by the Depositary, or on such later date as may be specified in the notification of the withdrawal.

4. Any Party which withdraws from this Convention shall be considered as also having withdrawn from any protocol to which it is party.

Article 20

Depositary

1. The Secretary–General of the United Nations shall assume the functions of Depositary of this Convention and any protocols.

2. The Depositary shall inform the Parties, in particular, of:

(a) The signature of this Convention and of any protocol, and the deposit of instruments of ratification, acceptance, approval or accession in accordance with articles 13 and 14;

(b) The date on which the Convention and any protocol will come into force in accordance with article 17;

(c) Notifications of withdrawal made in accordance with article 19;

(d) Amendments adopted with respect to the Convention and any protocol, their acceptance by the parties and their date of entry into force in accordance with article 9;

(e) All communications relating to the adoption and approval of annexes and to the amendment of annexes in accordance with article 10;

(f) Notifications by regional economic integration organizations of the extent of their competence with respect to matters governed by this Convention and any protocols, and of any modifications thereof;

(g) Declarations made in accordance with article 11, paragraph 3.

Article 21

Authentic Texts

The original of this Convention, of which the Arabic, Chinese, English, French, Russian and Spanish texts are equally authentic, shall be deposited with the Secretary–General of the United Nations.

Annex I

Research and Systematic Observations

1. The Parties to the Convention recognize that the major scientific issues are:

(a) Modification of the ozone layer which would result in a change in the amount of solar ultra-violet radiation having biological effects (UV–B) that reaches the Earth's surface and the potential consequences for human health, for organisms, ecosystems and materials useful to mankind;

(b) Modification of the vertical distribution of ozone, which could change the temperature structure of the atmosphere and the potential consequences for weather and climate.

2. The Parties to the Convention, in accordance with article 3, shall co-operate in conducting research and systematic observations and in formulating recommendations for future research and observation in such areas as:

(a) *Research into the physics and chemistry of the atmosphere*

(i) Comprehensive theoretical models: further development of models which consider the interaction between radiative, dynamic and chemical processes; studies of the simultaneous effects of various man-made and naturally occurring species upon atmospheric ozone; interpretation of satellite and non-satellite measurement data sets; evaluation of trends in atmospheric and geophysical parameters, and the development of methods for attributing changes in these parameters to specific causes;

(ii) Laboratory studies of: rate coefficients, absorption cross-sections and mechanisms of tropospheric and stratospheric chemical and photochemical processes; spectroscopic data to support field measurements in all relevant spectral regions;

(iii) Field measurements: the concentration and fluxes of key source gases of both natural and anthropogenic origin; atmospheric dynamics studies; simultaneous measurements of photochemically-related species down to the planetary boundary layer, using *in situ* and remote sensing instruments; intercomparison of different sensors, including co-ordinated correlative measurements for satellite instrumentation; three-dimensional fields of key atmospheric trace constituents, solar spectral flux and meteorological parameters;

(iv) Instrument development, including satellite and non-satellite sensors for atmospheric trace constituents, solar flux and meteorological parameters;

(b) *Research into health, biological and photodegradation effects*

(i) The relationship between human exposure to visible and ultra-violet solar radiation and (a) the development of both non-melanoma and melanoma skin cancer and (b) the effects on the immunological system;

(ii) Effects of UV–B radiation, including the wavelength dependence, upon (a) agricultural crops, forests and other terrestrial ecosystems and (b) the aquatic food web and fisheries, as well as possible inhibition of oxygen production by marine phytoplankton;

(iii) The mechanisms by which UV–B radiation acts on biological materials, species and ecosystems, including: the relationship between dose, dose rate, and response; photorepair, adaptation, and protection;

(iv) Studies of biological action spectra and the spectral response using polychromatic radiation in order to include possible interactions of the various wavelength regions;

(v) The influence of UV–B radiation on: the sensitivities and activities of biological species important to the biospheric balance; primary processes such as photosynthesis and biosynthesis;

(vi) The influence of UV–B radiation on the photodegradation of pollutants, agricultural chemicals and other materials;

(c) *Research on effects on climate*

(i) Theoretical and observational studies of the radiative effects of ozone and other trace species and the impact on climate parameters, such as land and ocean surface temperatures, precipitation patterns, the exchange between the troposphere and stratosphere;

(ii) The investigation of the effects of such climate impacts on various aspects of human activity;

(d) *Systematic observations on:*

(i) The status of the ozone layer (i.e. the spatial and temporal variability of the total column content and vertical distribution) by making the Global Ozone Observing System, based on the integration of satellite and ground-based systems, fully operational;

(ii) The tropospheric and stratospheric concentrations of source gases for the HO_x, NO_x, $C10_x$ and carbon families;

(iii) The temperature from the ground to the mesosphere, utilizing both ground-based and satellite systems;

(iv) Wavelength-resolved solar flux reaching, and thermal radiation leaving, the Earth's atmosphere, utilizing satellite measurements;

(v) Wavelength-resolved solar flux reaching the Earth's surface in the ultra-violet range having biological effects (UV–B);

(vi) Aerosol properties and distribution from the ground to the mesosphere, utilizing ground-based, airborne and satellite systems;

(vii) Climatically important variables by the maintenance of programmes of high-quality meteorological surface measurements;

(viii) Trace species, temperatures, solar flux and aerosols utilizing improved methods for analysing global data.

3. The Parties to the Convention shall co-operate, taking into account the particular needs of the developing countries, in promoting the appropriate scientific and technical training required to participate in the research and systematic observations outlined in this annex. Particular emphasis should be given to the intercalibration of observational instrumentation and methods with a view to generating comparable or standardized scientific data sets.

4. The following chemical substances of natural and anthropogenic origin, not listed in order of priority, are thought to have the potential to modify the chemical and physical properties of the ozone layer.

(a) Carbon substances

(i) *Carbon monoxide (CO)*

Carbon monoxide has significant natural and anthropogenic sources, and is thought to play a major direct role in tropospheric photochemistry, and an indirect role in stratospheric photochemistry.

(ii) *Carbon dioxide (CO_2)*

Carbon dioxide has significant natural and anthropogenic sources, and affects stratospheric ozone by influencing the thermal structure of the atmosphere.

(iii) *Methane (CH_4)*

Methane has both natural and anthropogenic sources, and affects both tropospheric and stratospheric ozone.

(iv) *Non-methane hydrocarbon species*

Non-methane hydrocarbon species, which consist of a large number of chemical substances, have both natural and anthropogenic sources, and play a direct role in tropospheric photochemistry and an indirect role in stratospheric photochemistry.

(b) Nitrogen substances

(i) *Nitrous oxide (N_2O)*

The dominant sources of N_2O are natural, but anthropogenic contributions are becoming increasingly important. Nitrous oxide is the primary source of stratospheric NO_x, which play a vital role in controlling the abundance of stratospheric ozone.

(ii) *Nitrogen oxides (NO_x)*

Ground-level sources of NO_x play a major direct role only in tropospheric photochemical processes and an indirect role in stratospheric photochemistry, whereas injection of NO_x close to the tropopause may lead directly to a change in upper tropospheric and stratospheric ozone.

(c) Chlorine substances

(i) *Fully halogenated alkanes, e.g.* CCl_4, $CFCl_3$ *(CFC–11)*, CF_2Cl_2 *(CFC–12)*, $C_2F_3Cl_3$ *(CFC–113)*, $C_2F_4Cl_2$ *(CFC–114)*

Fully halogenated alkanes are anthropogenic and act as a source of $C10_x$, which plays a vital role in ozone photochemistry, especially in the 30–50 km altitude region.

(ii) *Partially halogenated alkanes, e.g.* CH_3Cl, CHF_2Cl *(CFC–22)*, CH_3CCl_3, $CHFCl_2$ *(CFC–21)*

The sources of CH_3Cl are natural, whereas the other partially halogenated alkanes mentioned above are anthropogenic in origin. These gases also act as a source of stratospheric $C10_x$.

(d) Bromine substances

Fully halogenated alkanes, e.g. CF_3Br

These gases are anthropogenic and act as a source of BrO_x, which behaves in a manner similar to ClO_x.

(e) Hydrogen substances

(i) *Hydrogen* (H_2)

Hydrogen, the source of which is natural and anthropogenic, plays a minor role in stratospheric photochemistry.

(ii) *Water* (H_2O)

Water, the source of which is natural, plays a vital role in both tropospheric and stratospheric photochemistry. Local sources of water vapour in the stratosphere include the oxidation of methane and, to a lesser extent, of hydrogen.

Annex II

Information Exchange

1. The Parties to the Convention recognize that the collection and sharing of information is an important means of implementing the objectives of this Convention and of assuring that any actions that may be taken are appropriate and equitable. Therefore, Parties shall exchange scientific, technical, socio-economic, business, commercial and legal information.

2. The Parties to the Convention, in deciding what information is to be collected and exchanged, should take into account the usefulness of the information and the costs of obtaining it. The Parties further recognize that co-operation under this annex has to be consistent with national laws, regulations and practices regarding patents, trade secrets, and protection of confidential and proprietary information.

3. *Scientific information*

This includes information on:

(a) Planned and ongoing research, both governmental and private, to facilitate the co-ordination of research programmes so as to make the most effective use of available national and international resources;

(b) The emission data needed for research;

(c) Scientific results published in peer-reviewed literature on the understanding of the physics and chemistry of the Earth's atmosphere and of its susceptibility to change, in particular on the state of the ozone layer and effects on human health, environment and climate which would result from changes on all time-scales in either the total column content or the vertical distribution of ozone;

(d) The assessment of research results and the recommendations for future research.

4. *Technical information*

This includes information on:

(a) The availability and cost of chemical substitutes and of alternative technologies to reduce the emissions of ozone-modifying substances and related planned and ongoing research;

(b) The limitations and any risks involved in using chemical or other substitutes and alternative technologies.

5. *Socio-economic and commercial information on the substances referred to in annex I*

This includes information on:

(a) Production and production capacity;

(b) Use and use patterns;

(c) Imports/exports;

(d) The costs, risks and benefits of human activities which may indirectly modify the ozone layer and of the impacts of regulatory actions taken or being considered to control these activities.

6. *Legal information*

This includes information on:

(a) National laws, administrative measures and legal research relevant to the protection of the ozone layer;

(b) International agreements, including bilateral agreements, relevant to the protection of the ozone layer;

(c) Methods and terms of licensing and availability of patents relevant to the protection of the ozone layer.

3.15 Protocol to the 1979 Convention on Long-range Transboundary Air Pollution on the Reduction of Sulphur Emissions or Their Transboundary Fluxes by at Least 30 Per Cent.[d] Done in Helsinki, 8 July 1985. Entered into force, 2 September 1987. EB.AIR/12; *reprinted in* 27 I.L.M. 707 (1988) & 5 Weston V.E.6

The Parties,

Determined to implement the Convention on Long-range Transboundary Air Pollution,

Concerned that the present emissions of air pollutants are causing widespread damage, in exposed parts of Europe and North America, to natural resources of vital environmental and economic importance, such as forests, soils and waters, and to materials (including historical monuments) and, under certain circumstances, have harmful effects on human health,

Aware of the fact that the predominant sources of air pollution contributing to the acidification of the environment are the combustion of fossil fuels for energy production, and the main technological processes in various industrial sectors, as well as transport, which lead to emissions of sulphur dioxide, nitrogen oxides, and other pollutants,

Considering that high priority should be given to reducing sulphur emissions, which will have positive results environmentally, on the overall economic situation and on human health,

Recalling the decision of the United Nations Economic Commission for Europe (ECE) at its thirty-ninth session, which stresses the urgency of intensifying efforts to arrive at co-ordinated national strategies and policies in the ECE region to reduce sulphur emissions effectively a national levels,

Recalling the recognition by the Executive Body for the Convention at its first session of the need to decrease effectively the total annual emissions of sulphur compounds or their transboundary fluxes by 1993–1995, using 1980 levels as the basis for calculations of reductions,

Recalling that the Multilateral Conference on the Causes and Prevention of Damage to Forests and Water by Air Pollution in Europe (Munich, 24–27 June 1984) had requested that the Executive Body for the Convention, as a matter of highest priority, adopt a proposal for a specific agreement on the reduction of annual national sulphur emissions or their transboundary fluxes by 1993 at the latest,

Noting that a number of Contracting Parties to the Convention have decided to implement reductions of their national annual sulphur emissions or their transboundary fluxes by at least 30 per cent as soon as possible and at the latest by 1993, using 1980 levels as the basis for calculation of reductions,

Recognizing, on the other hand, that some Contracting Parties to the Convention, while not signing the present Protocol at the time of its opening for signature, will nevertheless contribute significantly to the reduction of transboundary air pollution, or will continue to make efforts to control sulphur emissions, as stated in the document annexed to the report of the Executive Body at its third session,

Have agreed as follows:

Article 1

Definitions

For the purposes of the present Protocol,

d. *See* Basic Document 3.8, *supra*.

1. "Convention" means the Convention on Long-range Transboundary Air Pollution, adopted in Geneva on 13 November 1979,

2. "EMEP" means the Co-operative Programme for Monitoring and Evaluation of the Long-range Transmission of Air Pollutants in Europe,

3. "Executive Body" means the Executive Body for the Convention constituted under article 10, paragraph 1 of the Convention,

4. "Geographical scope of EMEP" means the area defined in article 1, paragraph 4 of the Protocol to the 1979 Convention on Long-range Transboundary Air Pollution on Long-term Financing of the Co-operative Programme for Monitoring and Evaluation of the Long-range Transmission of Air Pollutants in Europe (EMEP), adopted in Geneva on 28 September 1984,

5. "Parties" means, unless the context otherwise requires, the Parties to the present Protocol.

Article 2

Basic provisions

The Parties shall reduce their national annual sulphur emissions or their transboundary fluxes by at least 30 per cent as soon as possible and at the latest by 1993, using 1980 levels as the basis for calculation of reductions.

Article 3

Further reductions

The Parties recognize the need for each of them to study at the national level the necessity for further reductions, beyond those referred to in article 2, of sulphur emissions or their transboundary fluxes when environmental conditions warrant.

Article 4

Reporting of annual emissions

Each Party shall provide annually to the Executive Body its levels of national annual sulphur emissions, and the basis upon which they have been calculated.

Article 5

Calculations of transboundary fluxes

EMEP shall in good time before the annual meetings of the Executive Body provide to the Executive Body calculations of sulphur budgets and also of transboundary fluxes and depositions of sulphur compounds for each previous year within the geographical scope of EMEP, utilizing appropriate models. In areas outside the geographical scope of EMEP, models appropriate to the particular circumstances of Parties therein shall be used.

Article 6

National programmes, policies and strategies

The Parties shall, within the framework of the Convention, develop without undue delay national programmes, policies and strategies which shall serve as a means of reducing sulphur emissions or their transboundary fluxes, by at least 30 per cent as soon as possible and at the latest by 1993, and shall report thereon as well as on progress towards achieving the goal to the Executive Body.

Article 7

Amendments to the Protocol

1. Any Party may propose amendments to the present Protocol.

2. Proposed amendments shall be submitted in writing to the Executive Secretary of the Economic Commission for Europe who shall communicate them to all Parties. The Executive Body shall discuss the proposed amendments at its next annual meeting provided that such proposals have been circulated by the Executive Secretary of the Economic Commission for Europe to the Parties at least 90 days in advance.

3. An amendment to the present Protocol shall be adopted by consensus of the representatives of the Parties, and shall enter into force for the Parties which have accepted it on the ninetieth day after the date on which two-thirds of the Parties have deposited their instruments of acceptance of the amendment. The amendment shall enter into force for any other Party on the ninetieth day after the date on which that Party deposits its instrument of acceptance of the amendment.

Article 8

Settlement of disputes

If a dispute arises between two or more Parties as to the interpretation or application of the present Protocol, they shall seek a solution by negotiation or by any other method of dispute settlement acceptable to the parties to the dispute.

Article 9

Signature

1. The present Protocol shall be open for signature at Helsinki (Finland) from 8 July 1985 until 12 July 1985 inclusive, by the member States of the Economic Commission for Europe as well as States having consultative status with the Economic Commission for Europe, pursuant to paragraph 8 of Economic and Social Council resolution 36 (IV) of 28 March 1947, and by regional economic integration organizations, constituted by sovereign States members of the Economic Commission for Europe, which have competence in respect of the negotiation, conclusion and application of international agreements in matters covered by the present Protocol, provided that the States and organizations concerned are Parties to the Convention.

2. In matters within their competence, such regional economic integration organizations shall, on their own behalf, exercise the rights and fulfil the responsibilities which the present Protocol attributes to their member States. In such cases, the member States of these organizations shall not be entitled to exercise such rights individually.

Article 10

Ratification, acceptance, approval and accession

1. The present Protocol shall be subject to ratification, acceptance or approval by Signatories.

2. The present Protocol shall be open for accession as from 13 July 1985 by the States and organizations referred to in article 9, paragraph 1.

3. A State or organization acceding to the present Protocol after its entry into force shall implement Article 2 at the latest by 1993. However, if the Protocol is acceded to after 1990, Article 2 may be implemented later than 1993 by the Party concerned but not later than 1995, and such a Party shall implement Article 6 correspondingly.

4. The instruments of ratification, acceptance, approval or accession shall be deposited with the Secretary–General of the United Nations, who will perform the functions of depositary.

Article 11

Entry into force

1. The present Protocol shall enter into force on the ninetieth day following the date on which the sixteenth instrument of ratification, acceptance, approval or accession has been deposited.

2. For each State and organization referred to in article 9, paragraph 1, which ratifies, accepts or approves the present Protocol or accedes thereto after the deposit of the sixteenth instrument of ratification, acceptance, approval, or accession, the Protocol shall enter into force on the ninetieth day after the date of deposit by such Party of its instrument of ratification, acceptance, approval, or accession.

Article 12

Withdrawal

At any time after five years from the date on which the present Protocol has come into force with respect to a Party, that Party may withdraw from it by giving written notification to the depositary. Any such withdrawal shall take effect on the ninetieth day after the date of its receipt by the depositary.

Article 13

Authentic texts

The original of the present Protocol, of which the English, French and Russian texts are equally authentic, shall be deposited with the Secretary-General of the United Nations.

IN WITNESS WHEREOF the undersigned, being duly authorized thereto, have signed the present Protocol.

DONE at Helsinki this eighth day of July one thousand nine hundred and eighty-five.

3.16 IAEA Convention on Early Notification of a Nuclear Accident. Concluded at Vienna and New York, 26 September 1986. Entered into force, 27 October 1986. IAEA INFCIRC 335, IAEA Leg. Ser. No. 14; *reprinted in* 25 I.L.M. 1369 (1986) & 5 Weston V.E.7

Article 1

Scope of application

1. This Convention shall apply in the event of any accident involving facilities or activities of a State Party or of persons or legal entities under its jurisdiction or control, referred to in paragraph 2 below, from which a release of radioactive material occurs or is likely to occur and which has resulted or may result in an international transboundary release that could be of radiological safety significance for another State.

2. The facilities and activities referred to in paragraph 1 are the following:

(a) any nuclear reactor wherever located;

(b) any nuclear fuel cycle facility;

(c) any radioactive waste management facility;

(d) the transport and storage of nuclear fuels or radioactive wastes;

(e) the manufacture, use, storage, disposal and transport of radioisotopes for agricultural, industrial, medical and related scientific and research purposes; and

(f) the use of radioisotopes for power generation in space objects.

Article 2

Notification and information

In the event of an accident specified in article 1 (hereinafter referred to as a "nuclear accident"), the State Party referred to in that article shall:

(a) forthwith notify, directly or through the International Atomic Energy Agency (hereinafter referred to as the "Agency"), those States which are or may be physically affected as specified in article 1 and the Agency of the nuclear accident, its nature, the time of its occurrence and its exact location where appropriate; and

(b) promptly provide the States referred to in sub-paragraph (a), directly or through the Agency, and the Agency with such available information relevant to minimizing the radiological consequences in those States, as specified in article 5.

Article 3

Other Nuclear Accidents

With a view to minimizing the radiological consequences, States Parties may notify in the event of nuclear accidents other than those specified in article 1.

Article 4

Functions of the Agency

The Agency shall:

(a) forthwith inform States Parties, Member States, other States which are or may be physically affected as specified in article 1 and relevant international intergovernmental organizations (hereinafter referred to as "international organizations") of a notification received pursuant to sub-paragraph (a) of article 2; and

(b) promptly provide any State Party, Member State or relevant international organization, upon request, with the information received pursuant to sub-paragraph (b) of article 2.

Article 5

Information to be provided

1. The information to be provided pursuant to sub-paragraph (b) of article 2 shall comprise the following data as then available to the notifying State Party:

(a) the time, exact location where appropriate, and the nature of the nuclear accident;

(b) the facility or activity involved;

(c) the assumed or established cause and the foreseeable development of the nuclear accident relevant to the transboundary release of the radioactive materials;

(d) the general characteristics of the radioactive release, including, as far as is practicable and appropriate, the nature, probable physical and chemical form and the quantity, composition and effective height of the radioactive release;

(e) information on current and forecast meteorological and hydrological conditions, necessary for forecasting the transboundary release of the radioactive materials;

(f) the results of environmental monitoring relevant to the transboundary release of the radioactive materials;

(g) the off-site protective measures taken or planned;

(h) the predicted behaviour over time of the radioactive release.

2. Such information shall be supplemented at appropriate intervals by further relevant information on the development of the emergency situation, including its foreseeable or actual termination.

3. Information received pursuant to sub-paragraph (b) of article 2 may be used without restriction, except when such information is provided in confidence by the notifying State Party.

Article 6

Consultations

A State Party providing information pursuant to sub-paragraph (b) of article 2 shall, as far as is reasonably practicable, respond promptly to a request for further information or consultations sought by an affected State Party with a view to minimizing the radiological consequences in that State.

Article 7

Competent authorities and points of contact

1. Each State Party shall make known to the Agency and to other States Parties, directly or through the Agency, its competent authorities and point of contact responsible for issuing and receiving the notification and information referred to in article 2. Such points of contact and a focal point within the Agency shall be available continuously.

2. Each State Party shall promptly inform the Agency of any changes that may occur in the information referred to in paragraph 1.

3. The Agency shall maintain an up-to-date list of such national authorities and points of contact as well as points of contact of relevant international organizations

and shall provide it to States Parties and Member States and to relevant international organizations.

Article 8

Assistance to States Parties

The Agency shall, in accordance with its Statute and upon a request of a State Party which does not have nuclear activities itself and borders on a State having an active nuclear programme but not Party, conduct investigations into the feasibility and establishment of an appropriate radiation monitoring system in order to facilitate the achievement of the objectives of this Convention.

Article 9

Bilateral and multilateral arrangements

In furtherance of their mutual interests, States Parties may consider, where deemed appropriate, the conclusion of bilateral or multilateral arrangements relating to the subject matter of this Convention.

Article 10

Relationship to other international agreements

This Convention shall not affect the reciprocal rights and obligations of States Parties under existing international agreements which relate to the matters covered by this Convention, or under future international agreements concluded in accordance with the object and purpose of this Convention.

Article 11

Settlement of disputes

1. In the event of a dispute between States Parties, or between a State Party and the Agency, concerning the interpretation or application of this Convention, the parties to the dispute shall consult with a view to the settlement of the dispute by negotiation or by any other peaceful means of settling disputes acceptable to them.

2. If a dispute of this character between States Parties cannot be settled within one year from the request for consultation pursuant to paragraph 1, it shall, at the request of any party to such dispute, be submitted to arbitration or referred to the International Court of Justice for decision. Where a dispute is submitted to arbitration, if, within six months from the date of the request, the parties to the dispute are unable to agree on the organization of the arbitration, a party may request the President of the International Court of Justice or the Secretary–General of the United Nations to appoint one or more arbitrators. In cases of conflicting requests by the parties to the dispute, the request to the Secretary–General of the United Nations shall have priority.

3. When signing, ratifying, accepting, approving or acceding to this Convention, a State may declare that it does not consider itself bound by either or both of the dispute settlement procedures provided for in paragraph 2. The other States Parties shall not be bound by a dispute settlement procedure provided for in paragraph 2 with respect to a State Party for which such a declaration is in force.

4. A State Party which has made a declaration in accordance with paragraph 3 may at any time withdraw it by notification to the depositary.

Article 12

Entry into force

1. This Convention shall be open for signature by all States and Namibia, represented by the United Nations Council for Namibia, at the headquarters of the

International Atomic Energy Agency in Vienna and at the headquarters of the United Nations in New York, from 26 September 1986 and 6 October 1986 respectively, until its entry into force or for twelve months, whichever period is longer.

2. A State and Namibia, represented by the United Nations Council for Namibia, may express its consent to be bound by this Convention either by signature, or by deposit of an instrument of ratification, acceptance or approval following signature made subject to ratification, acceptance or approval, or by deposit of an instrument of accession. The instruments of ratification, acceptance, approval or accession shall be deposited with the depositary.

3. This Convention shall enter into force thirty days after consent to be bound has been expressed by three States.

4. For each State expressing consent to be bound by this Convention after its entry into force, this Convention shall enter into force for that State thirty days after the date of expression of consent.

5. (a) This Convention shall be open for accession, as provided for in this article, by international organizations and regional integration organizations constituted by sovereign States, which have competence in respect of the negotiation, conclusion and application of international agreements in matters covered by this Convention.

(b) In matters within their competence such organizations shall, on their own behalf, exercise the rights and fulfil the obligations which this Convention attributes to States Parties.

(c) When depositing its instrument of accession, such an organization shall communicate to the depositary a declaration indicating the extent of its competence in respect of matters covered by this Convention.

(d) Such an organization shall not hold any vote additional to those of its Member States.

Article 13

Provisional application

A State may, upon signature or at any later date before this Convention enters into force for it, declare that it will apply this Convention provisionally.

Article 14

Amendments

1. A State Party may propose amendments to this Convention. The proposed amendment shall be submitted to the depositary who shall circulate it immediately to all other States Parties.

2. If a majority of the States Parties request the depositary to convene a conference to consider the proposed amendments, the depositary shall invite all States Parties to attend such a conference to begin not sooner than thirty days after the invitations are issued. Any amendment adopted at the conference by a two-thirds majority of all States Parties shall be laid down in a protocol which is open to signature in Vienna and New York by all States Parties.

3. The protocol shall enter into force thirty days after consent to be bound has been expressed by three States. For each State expressing consent to be bound by the protocol after its entry into force, the protocol shall enter into force for that State thirty days after the date of expression of consent.

Article 15

Denunciation

1. A State Party may denounce this Convention by written notification to the depositary.

2. Denunciation shall take effect one year following the date on which the notification is received by the depositary.

Article 16

Depositary

1. The Director General of the Agency shall be the depositary of this Convention.

2. The Director General of the Agency shall promptly notify States Parties and all other States of:

(a) each signature of this Convention or any protocol of amendment;

(b) each deposit of an instrument of ratification, acceptance, approval or accession concerning this Convention or any protocol of amendment;

(c) any declaration or withdrawal thereof in accordance with article 11;

(d) any declaration of provisional application of this Convention in accordance with article 13;

(e) the entry into force of this Convention and of any amendment thereto; and

(f) any denunciation made under article 15.

Article 17

Authentic texts and certified copies

The original of this Convention, of which the Arabic, Chinese, English, French, Russian and Spanish texts are equally authentic, shall be deposited with the Director General of the International Atomic Energy Agency who shall send certified copies to States Parties and all other States.

* * *

3.17 IAEA Convention on Assistance in the Case of a Nuclear Accident or Radiological Emergency. Concluded at Vienna and New York, 26 September 1986. Entered into force, 26 February 1987. IAEA INFCIRC 336, IAEA Leg.Ser.No. 14; *reprinted in* 25 I.L.M. 1377 (1986) & 5 Weston V.E.8

Article 1

General provisions

1. The States Parties shall cooperate between themselves and with the International Atomic Energy Agency (hereinafter referred to as the "Agency") in accordance with the provisions of this Convention to facilitate prompt assistance in the event of a nuclear accident or radiological emergency to minimize its consequences and to protect life, property and the environment from the effects of radioactive releases.

2. To facilitate such cooperation States Parties may agree on bilateral or multilateral arrangements or, where appropriate, a combination of these, for preventing or minimizing injury and damage which may result in the event of a nuclear accident or radiological emergency.

3. The States Parties request the Agency, acting within the framework of its Statute, to use its best endeavours in accordance with the provisions of this Convention to promote, facilitate and support the cooperation between States Parties provided for in this Convention.

Article 2

Provision of assistance

1. If a State Party needs assistance in the event of a nuclear accident or radiological emergency, whether or not such accident or emergency originates within its territory, jurisdiction or control, it may call for such assistance from any other State Party, directly or through the Agency, and from the Agency, or, where appropriate, from other international intergovernmental organizations (hereinafter referred to as "international organizations").

2. A State Party requesting assistance shall specify the scope and type of assistance required and, where practicable, provide the assisting party with such information as may be necessary for that party to determine the extent to which it is able to meet the request. In the event that it is not practicable for the requesting State Party to specify the scope and type of assistance required, the requesting State Party and the assisting party shall, in consultation, decide upon the scope and type of assistance required.

3. Each State Party to which a request for such assistance is directed shall promptly decide and notify the requesting State Party, directly or through the Agency, whether it is in a position to render the assistance requested, and the scope and terms of the assistance that might be rendered.

4. States Parties shall, within the limits of their capabilities, identify and notify the Agency of experts, equipment and materials which could be made available for the provision of assistance to other States Parties in the event of a nuclear accident or radiological emergency as well as the terms, especially financial, under which such assistance could be provided.

5. Any State Party may request assistance relating to medical treatment or temporary relocation into the territory of another State Party of people involved in a nuclear accident or radiological emergency.

6. The Agency shall respond, in accordance with its Statute and as provided for in this Convention, to a requesting State Party's or a Member State's request for assistance in the event of a nuclear accident or radiological emergency by:

(a) making available appropriate resources allocated for this purpose;

(b) transmitting promptly the request to other States and international organizations which, according to the Agency's information, may possess the necessary resources; and

(c) if so requested by the requesting State, co-ordinating the assistance at the international level which may thus become available.

Article 3

Direction and control of assistance

Unless otherwise agreed:

(a) the overall direction, control, co-ordination and supervision of the assistance shall be the responsibility within its territory of the requesting State. The assisting party should, where the assistance involves personnel, designate in consultation with the requesting State, the person who should be in charge of and retain immediate operational supervision over the personnel and the equipment provided by it. The designated person should exercise such supervision in cooperation with the appropriate authorities of the requesting State;

(b) the requesting State shall provide, to the extent of its capabilities, local facilities and services for the proper and effective administration of the assistance. It shall also ensure the protection of personnel, equipment and materials brought into its territory by or on behalf of the assisting party for such purpose;

(c) ownership of equipment and materials provided by either party during the periods of assistance shall be unaffected, and their return shall be ensured;

(d) a State Party providing assistance in response to a request under paragraph 5 of article 2 shall co-ordinate that assistance within its territory.

Article 4

Competent authorities and points of contact

1. Each State Party shall make known to the Agency and to other States Parties, directly or through the Agency, its competent authorities and point of contact authorized to make and receive requests for and to accept offers of assistance. Such points of contact and a focal point within the Agency shall be available continuously.

2. Each State Party shall promptly inform the Agency of any changes that may occur in the information referred to in paragraph 1.

3. The Agency shall regularly and expeditiously provide to States Parties, Member States and relevant international organizations the information referred to in paragraphs 1 and 2.

Article 5

Functions of the Agency

The States Parties request the Agency, in accordance with paragraph 3 of article 1 and without prejudice to other provisions of this Convention, to:

(a) collect and disseminate to States Parties and Member States information concerning:

(i) experts, equipment and materials which could be made available in the event of nuclear accidents or radiological emergencies;

(ii) methodologies, techniques and available results of research relating to response to nuclear accidents or radiological emergencies;

(b) assist a State Party or a Member State when requested in any of the following or other appropriate matters:

(i) preparing both emergency plans in the case of nuclear accidents and radiological emergencies and the appropriate legislation;

(ii) developing appropriate training programs for personnel to deal with nuclear accidents and radiological emergencies;

(iii) transmitting requests for assistance and relevant information in the event of a nuclear accident or radiological emergency;

(iv) developing appropriate radiation monitoring programmes, procedures and standards;

(v) conducting investigations into the feasibility of establishing appropriate radiation monitoring systems;

(c) make available to a State Party or a Member State requesting assistance in the event of a nuclear accident or radiological emergency appropriate resources allocated for the purpose of conducting an initial assessment of the accident or emergency;

(d) offer its good offices to the States Parties and Member States in the event of a nuclear accident or radiological emergency;

(e) establish and maintain liaison with relevant international organizations for the purposes of obtaining and exchanging relevant information and data, and make a list of such organizations available to States Parties, Member States and the aforementioned organizations.

Article 6

Confidentiality and public statements

1. The requesting State and the assisting party shall protect the confidentiality of any confidential information that becomes available to either of them in connection with the assistance in the event of a nuclear accident or radiological emergency. Such information shall be used exclusively for the purpose of the assistance agreed upon.

2. The assisting party shall make every effort to coordinate with the requesting State before releasing information to the public on the assistance provided in connection with a nuclear accident or radiological emergency.

Article 7

Reimbursement of costs

1. An assisting party may offer assistance without costs to the requesting State. When considering whether to offer assistance on such a basis, the assisting party shall take into account:

(a) the nature of the nuclear accident or radiological emergency;

(b) the place of origin of the nuclear accident or radiological emergency;

(c) the needs of developing countries;

(d) the particular needs of countries without nuclear facilities; and

(e) any other relevant factors.

2. When assistance is provided wholly or partly on a reimbursement basis, the requesting State shall reimburse the assisting party for the costs incurred for the services rendered by persons or organizations acting on its behalf, and for all expenses

in connection with the assistance to the extent that such expenses are not directly defrayed by the requesting State. Unless otherwise agreed, reimbursement shall be provided promptly after the assisting party has presented its request for reimbursement to the requesting State, and in respect of costs other than local costs, shall be freely transferrable.

3. Notwithstanding paragraph 2, the assisting party may at any time waive, or agree to the postponement of, the reimbursement in whole or in part. In considering such waiver or postponement, assisting parties shall give due consideration to the needs of developing countries.

Article 8

Privileges, immunities and facilities

1. The requesting State shall afford to personnel of the assisting party and personnel acting on its behalf the necessary privileges, immunities and facilities for the performance of their assistance functions.

2. The requesting State shall afford the following privileges and immunities to personnel of the assisting party or personnel acting on its behalf who have been duly notified to and accepted by the requesting State:

(a) immunity from arrest, detention and legal process, including criminal, civil and administrative jurisdiction, of the requesting State, in respect of acts or omissions in the performance of their duties; and

(b) exemption from taxation, duties or other charges, except those which are normally incorporated in the price of goods or paid for services rendered, in respect of the performance of their assistance functions.

3. The requesting State shall:

(a) afford the assisting party exemption from taxation, duties or other charges on the equipment and property brought into the territory of the requesting State by the assisting party for the purpose of the assistance; and

(b) provide immunity from seizure, attachment or requisition of such equipment and property.

4. The requesting State shall ensure the return of such equipment and property. If requested by the assisting party, the requesting State shall arrange, to the extent it is able to do so, for the necessary decontamination of recoverable equipment involved in the assistance before its return.

5. The requesting State shall facilitate the entry into, stay in and departure from its national territory of personnel notified pursuant to paragraph 2 and of equipment and property involved in the assistance.

6. Nothing in this article shall require the requesting State to provide its nationals or permanent residents with the privileges and immunities provided for in the foregoing paragraphs.

7. Without prejudice to the privileges and immunities, all beneficiaries enjoying such privileges and immunities under this article have a duty to respect the laws and regulations of the requesting State. They shall also have the duty not to interfere in the domestic affairs of the requesting State.

8. Nothing in this article shall prejudice rights and obligations with respect to privileges and immunities afforded pursuant to other international agreements or the rules of customary international law.

9. When signing, ratifying, accepting, approving or acceding to this Convention, a State may declare that it does not consider itself bound in whole or in part by paragraphs 2 and 3.

10. A State Party which has made a declaration in accordance with paragraph 9 may at any time withdraw it by notification to the depositary.

Article 9

Transit of personnel, equipment and property

Each State Party shall, at the request of the requesting State or the assisting party, seek to facilitate the transit through its territory of duly notified personnel, equipment and property involved in the assistance to and from the requesting State.

Article 10

Claims and compensation

1. The States Parties shall closely cooperate in order to facilitate the settlement of legal proceedings and claims under this article.

2. Unless otherwise agreed, a requesting State shall in respect of death or of injury to persons, damage to or loss of property, or damage to the environment caused within its territory or other area under its jurisdiction or control in the course of providing the assistance requested:

(a) not bring any legal proceedings against the assisting party or persons or other legal entities acting on its behalf;

(b) assume responsibility for dealing with legal proceedings and claims brought by third parties against the assisting party or against persons or other legal entities acting on its behalf;

(c) hold the assisting party or persons or other legal entities acting on its behalf harmless in respect of legal proceedings and claims referred to in sub-paragraph (b); and

(d) compensate the assisting party or persons or other legal entities acting on its behalf for:

(i) death of or injury to personnel of the assisting party or persons acting on its behalf;

(ii) loss of or damage to non-consumable equipment or materials related to the assistance;

except in cases of wilful misconduct by the individuals who caused the death, injury, loss or damage.

3. This article shall not prevent compensation or indemnity available under any applicable international agreement or national law of any State.

4. Nothing in this article shall require the requesting State to apply paragraph 2 in whole or in part to its nationals or permanent residents.

5. When signing, ratifying, accepting, approving or acceding to this Convention, a State may declare:

(a) that it does not consider itself bound in whole or in part by paragraph 2;

(b) that it will not apply paragraph 2 in whole or in part in cases of gross negligence by the individuals who caused the death, injury, loss or damage.

6. A State Party which has made a declaration in accordance with paragraph 5 may at any time withdraw it by notification to the depositary.

Article 11

Termination of assistance

The requesting State or the assisting party may at any time, after appropriate consultations and by notification in writing, request the termination of assistance received or provided under this Convention. Once such a request has been made, the parties involved shall consult with each other to make arrangements for the proper conclusion of the assistance.

Article 12

Relationship to other international agreements

This Convention shall not affect the reciprocal rights and obligations of States Parties under existing international agreements which relate to the matters covered by this Convention, or under future international agreements concluded in accordance with the object and purpose of this Convention.

Article 13

Settlement of disputes

1. In the event of a dispute between States Parties, or between a State Party and the Agency, concerning the interpretation or application of this Convention, the parties to the dispute shall consult with a view to the settlement of the dispute by negotiation or by any other peaceful means of settling disputes acceptable to them.

2. If a dispute of this character between States Parties cannot be settled within one year from the request for consultation pursuant to paragraph 1, it shall, at the request of any party to such dispute, be submitted to arbitration or referred to the International Court of Justice for decision. Where a dispute is submitted to arbitration, if, within six months from the date of the request, the parties to the dispute are unable to agree on the organization of the arbitration, a party may request the President of the International Court of Justice or the Secretary–General of the United Nations to appoint one or more arbitrators. In cases of conflicting requests by the parties to the dispute, the request to the Secretary–General of the United Nations shall have priority.

3. When signing, ratifying, accepting, approving or acceding to this Convention, a State may declare that it does not consider itself bound by either or both of the dispute settlement procedures provided for in paragraph 2. The other States Parties shall not be bound by a dispute settlement procedure provided for in paragraph 2 with respect to a State Party for which such a declaration is in force.

4. A State Party which has made a declaration in accordance with paragraph 3 may at any time withdraw it by notification to the depositary.

Article 14

Entry into force

1. This Convention shall be open for signature by all States and Namibia, represented by the United Nations Council for Namibia, at the Headquarters of the International Atomic Energy Agency in Vienna and at the Headquarters of the United Nations in New York, from 26 September 1986 and 6 October 1986 respectively, until its entry into force or for twelve months, whichever period is longer.

2. A State and Namibia, represented by the United Nations Council for Namibia, may express its consent to be bound by this Convention either by signature, or by deposit of an instrument of ratification, acceptance or approval following signature made subject to ratification, acceptance or approval, or by deposit of an instrument of accession. The instruments of ratification, acceptance, approval or accession shall be deposited with the depositary.

3. This Convention shall enter into force thirty days after consent to be bound has been expressed by three States.

4. For each State expressing consent to be bound by this Convention after its entry into force, this Convention shall enter into force for that State thirty days after the date of expression of consent.

5. (a) This Convention shall be open for accession, as provided for in this article, by international organizations and regional integration organizations constituted by sovereign States, which have competence in respect of the negotiation, conclusion and application of international agreements in matters covered by this Convention.

(b) In matters within their competence such organizations shall, on their own behalf, exercise the rights and fulfil the obligations which this Convention attributes to States Parties.

(c) When depositing its instrument of accession, such an organization shall communicate to the depositary a declaration indicating the extent of its competence in respect of matters covered by this Convention.

(d) Such an organization shall not hold any vote additional to those of its Member States.

Article 15

Provisional application

A State may, upon signature or at any later date before this Convention enters into force for it, declare that it will apply this Convention provisionally.

Article 16

Amendments

1. A State Party may propose amendments to this Convention. The proposed amendment shall be submitted to the depositary who shall circulate it immediately to all other States Parties.

2. If a majority of the States Parties request the depositary to convene a conference to consider the proposed amendments, the depositary shall invite all States Parties to attend such a conference to begin not sooner than thirty days after the invitations are issued. Any amendment adopted at the conference by a two-thirds majority of all States Parties shall be laid down in a protocol which is open to signature in Vienna and New York by all States Parties.

3. The protocol shall enter into force thirty days after consent to be bound has been expressed by three States. For each State expressing consent to be bound by the protocol after its entry into force, the protocol shall enter into force for that State thirty days after the date of expression of consent.

Article 17

Denunciation

1. A State Party may denounce this Convention by written notification to the depositary.

2. Denunciation shall take effect one year following the date on which the notification is received by the depositary.

Article 18

Depositary

1. The Director General of the Agency shall be the depositary of this Convention.

2. The Director General of the Agency shall promptly notify States Parties and all other States of:

(a) each signature of this Convention or any protocol of amendment;

(b) each deposit of an instrument of ratification, acceptance, approval or accession concerning this Convention or any protocol of amendment;

(c) any declaration or withdrawal thereof in accordance with articles 8, 10 and 13;

(d) any declaration of provisional application of this Convention in accordance with article 15;

(e) the entry into force of this Convention and of any amendment thereto; and

(f) any denunciation made under article 17.

Article 19

Authentic texts and certified copies

The original of this Convention, of which the Arabic, Chinese, English, French, Russian and Spanish texts are equally authentic, shall be deposited with the Director General of the International Atomic Energy Agency who shall send certified copies to States Parties and all other States.

3.18 Montreal Protocol on Substances That Deplete the Ozone Layer (as Amended and Adjusted).[e] Adopted on 16 September 1987. Entered into force, 1 January 1989. *Reprinted in* 26 I.L.M. 1550 (1987) & 5 Weston V.E.9. Amended and adjusted by the Second Meeting of the Parties (London, 27–29 June 1990), U.N.Doc. UNEP/OzL.Pro.2/3, *reprinted in* 30 I.L.M. 537 (1991) & 5 Weston V.E.17; by the Fourth Meeting of the Parties (Copenhagen, 23–25 November 1992), *reprinted in* 32 I.L.M 874 (1993) & 5 Weston V.E.20; by the Seventh Meeting of the Parties (Vienna, 5–7 December 1995), U.N. Doc. UNEP/OzL.Pro.7/12, 1996 WL 806145 (Treaty), and by the Ninth Meeting of the Parties (Montreal, 15–17 September 1997), U.N. Doc. UNEP/OzL.Pro.9/12, 1998 WL 428304 (Treaty)

Preamble

The Parties to this Protocol,

Being Parties to the Vienna Convention for the Protection of the Ozone Layer,

Mindful of their obligation under that Convention to take appropriate measures to protect human health and the environment against adverse effects resulting or likely to result from human activities which modify or are likely to modify the ozone layer,

Recognizing that world-wide emissions of certain substances can significantly deplete and otherwise modify the ozone layer in a manner that is likely to result in adverse effects on human health and the environment,

Conscious of the potential climatic effects of emissions of these substances,

Aware that measures taken to protect the ozone layer from depletion should be based on relevant scientific knowledge, taking into account technical and economic considerations,

Determined to protect the ozone layer by taking precautionary measures to control equitably total global emissions of substances that deplete it, with the ultimate objective of their elimination on the basis of developments in scientific knowledge, taking into account technical and economic considerations and bearing in mind the developmental needs of developing countries,

Acknowledging that special provision is required to meet the needs of developing countries, including the provision of additional financial resources and access to relevant technologies, bearing in mind that the magnitude of funds necessary is predictable, and the funds can be expected to make a substantial difference in the world's ability to address the scientifically established problem of ozone depletion and its harmful effects,

Noting the precautionary measures for controlling emissions of certain chlorofluorocarbons that have already been taken at national and regional levels,

Considering the importance of promoting international co-operation in the research, development and transfer of alternative technologies relating to the control and reduction of emissions of substances that deplete the ozone layer, bearing in mind in particular the needs of developing countries,

HAVE AGREED AS FOLLOWS:

ARTICLE 1. DEFINITIONS

For the purposes of this Protocol:

1. "Convention" means the Vienna Convention for the Protection of the Ozone Layer, adopted on 22 March 1985.

e. *See* Basic Document 3.14, *supra*.

2. "Parties" means, unless the text otherwise indicates, Parties to this Protocol.

3. "Secretariat" means the Secretariat of the Convention.

4. "Controlled substance" means a substance in Annex A, Annex B, Annex C or Annex E to this Protocol, whether existing alone or in a mixture. It includes the isomers of any such substance, except as specified in the relevant Annex, but excludes any controlled substance or mixture which is in a manufactured product other than a container used for the transportation or storage of that substance.

5. "Production" means the amount of controlled substances produced, minus the amount destroyed by technologies to be approved by the Parties and minus the amount entirely used as feedstock in the manufacture of other chemicals. The amount recycled and reused is not to be considered as "production".

6. "Consumption" means production plus imports minus exports of controlled substances.

7. "Calculated levels" of production, imports, exports and consumption means levels determined in accordance with Article 3.

8. "Industrial rationalization" means the transfer of all or a portion of the calculated level of production of one Party to another, for the purpose of achieving economic efficiencies or responding to anticipated shortfalls in supply as a result of plant closures.

ARTICLE 2. CONTROL MEASURES

1. Incorporated in Article 2A.

2. Replaced by Article 2B.

3. Replaced by Article 2A.

4. Replaced by Article 2A.

5. Any Party may, for one or more control periods, transfer to another Party any portion of its calculated level of production set out in Articles 2A to 2E, and Article 2H, provided that the total combined calculated levels of production of the Parties concerned for any group of controlled substances do not exceed the production limits set out in those Articles for that group.

Such transfer of production shall be notified to the Secretariat by each of the Parties concerned, stating the terms of such transfer and the period for which it is to apply.

> 5 bis. Any Party not operating under paragraph 1 of Article 5 may, for one or more control periods, transfer to another such Party any portion of its calculated level of consumption set out in Article 2F, provided that the calculated level of consumption of controlled substances in Group I of Annex A of the Party transferring the portion of its calculated level of consumption did not exceed 0.25 kilograms per capita in 1989 and that the total combined calculated levels of consumption of the Parties concerned do not exceed the consumption limits set out in Article 2F. Such transfer of consumption shall be notified to the Secretariat by each of the Parties concerned, stating the terms of such transfer and the period for which it is to apply.

6. Any Party not operating under Article 5, that has facilities for the production of Annex A or Annex B controlled substances under construction, or contracted for, prior to 16 September 1987, and provided for in national legislation prior to 1 January 1987, may add the production from such facilities to its 1986 production of such substances for the purposes of determining its calculated level of production for 1986, provided that such facilities are completed by 31 December 1990 and that such

production does not raise that Party's annual calculated level of consumption of the controlled substances above 0.5 kilograms per capita.

7. Any transfer of production pursuant to paragraph 5 or any addition of production pursuant to paragraph 6 shall be notified to the Secretariat, no later than the time of the transfer or addition.

8. (a) Any Parties which are Member States of a regional economic integration organization as defined in Article 1 (6) of the Convention may agree that they shall jointly fulfil their obligations respecting consumption under this Article and Articles 2A to 2H provided that their total combined calculated level of consumption does not exceed the levels required by this Article and Articles 2A to 2H.

(b) The Parties to any such agreement shall inform the Secretariat of the terms of the agreement before the date of the reduction in consumption with which the agreement is concerned.

(c) Such agreement will become operative only if all Member States of the regional economic integration organization and the organization concerned are Parties to the Protocol and have notified the Secretariat of their manner of implementation.

9. (a) Based on the assessments made pursuant to Article 6, the Parties may decide whether:

(i) Adjustments to the ozone depleting potentials specified in Annex A, Annex B, Annex C and/or Annex E should be made and, if so, what the adjustments should be; and

(ii) Further adjustments and reductions of production or consumption of the controlled substances should be undertaken and, if so, what the scope, amount and timing of any such adjustments and reductions should be;

(b) Proposals for such adjustments shall be communicated to the Parties by the Secretariat at least six months before the meeting of the Parties at which they are proposed for adoption;

(c) In taking such decisions, the Parties shall make every effort to reach agreement by consensus. If all efforts at consensus have been exhausted, and no agreement reached, such decisions shall, as a last resort, be adopted by a two-thirds majority vote of the Parties present and voting representing a majority of the Parties operating under Paragraph 1 of Article 5 present and voting and a majority of the Parties not so operating present and voting;

(d) The decisions, which shall be binding on all Parties, shall forthwith be communicated to the Parties by the Depositary. Unless otherwise provided in the decisions, they shall enter into force on the [expiration] of six months from the date of the circulation of the communication by the Depositary.

10. Based on the assessments made pursuant to Article 6 of this Protocol and in accordance with the procedure set out in Article 9 of the Convention, the Parties may decide:

(a) whether any substances, and if so which, should be added to or removed from any annex to this Protocol, and

(b) the mechanism, scope and timing of the control measures that should apply to those substances;

11. Notwithstanding the provisions contained in this Article and Articles 2A to 2H Parties may take more stringent measures than those required by this Article and Articles 2A to 2H.

Introduction to The Adjustments

The Second, Fourth, Seventh and Ninth Meetings of the Parties to the Montreal Protocol on Substances that Deplete the Ozone Layer decided, on the basis of assessments made pursuant to Article 6 of the Protocol, to adopt adjustments and reductions of production and consumption of the controlled substances in Annexes A, B, C and E to the Protocol as follows (the text here shows the cumulative effect of all the adjustments):

ARTICLE 2A. CFCs

1. Each Party shall ensure that for the twelve-month period commencing on the first day of the seventh month following the date of entry into force of this Protocol, and in each twelve-month period thereafter, its calculated level of consumption of the controlled substances in Group I of Annex A does not exceed its calculated level of consumption in 1986. By the end of the same period, each Party producing one or more of these substances shall ensure that its calculated level of production of the substances does not exceed its calculated level of production in 1986, except that such level may have increased by no more than ten per cent based on the 1986 level. Such increase shall be permitted only so as to satisfy the basic domestic needs of the Parties operating under Article 5 and for the purposes of industrial rationalization between Parties.

2. Each Party shall ensure that for the period from 1 July 1991 to 31 December 1992 its calculated levels of consumption and production of the controlled substances in Group I of Annex A do not exceed 150 [percent] of its calculated levels of production and consumption of those substances in 1986; with effect from 1 January 1993, the twelve-month control period for these controlled substances shall run from 1 January to 31 December each year.

3. Each Party shall ensure that for the twelve-month period commencing on 1 January 1994, and in each twelve-month period thereafter, its calculated level of consumption of the controlled substances in Group I of Annex A does not exceed, annually, twenty-five per cent of its calculated level of consumption in 1986. Each Party producing one or more of these substances shall, for the same periods, ensure that its calculated level of production of the substances does not exceed, annually, twenty-five [percent] of its calculated level of production in 1986. However, in order to satisfy the basic domestic needs of the Parties operating under paragraph 1 of Article 5, its calculated level of production may exceed that limit by up to ten per cent of its calculated level of production in 1986.

4. Each Party shall ensure that for the twelve-month period commencing on 1 January 1996, and in each twelve-month period thereafter, its calculated level of consumption of the controlled substances in Group I of Annex A does not exceed zero.

Each Party producing one or more of these substances shall, for the same periods, ensure that its calculated level of production of the substances does not exceed zero. However, in order to satisfy the basic domestic needs of the Parties operating under paragraph 1 of Article 5, its calculated level of production may exceed that limit by up to fifteen per cent of its calculated level of production in 1986. This paragraph will apply save to the extent that the Parties decide to permit the level of production or consumption that is necessary to satisfy uses agreed by them to be essential.

ARTICLE 2B. HALONS

1. Each Party shall ensure that for the twelve-month period commencing on 1 January 1992, and in each twelve-month period thereafter, its calculated level of consumption of the controlled substances in Group II of Annex A does not exceed, annually, its calculated level of consumption in 1986. Each Party producing one or more of these substances shall, for the same periods, ensure that its calculated level of production of the substances does not exceed, annually, its calculated level of produc-

tion in 1986. However, in order to satisfy the basic domestic needs of the Parties operating under paragraph 1 of Article 5, its calculated level of production may exceed that limit by up to ten per cent of its calculated level of production in 1986.

2. Each Party shall ensure that for the twelve-month period commencing on 1 January 1994, and in each twelve-month period thereafter, its calculated level of consumption of the controlled substances in Group II of Annex A does not exceed zero.

Each Party producing one or more of these substances shall, for the same periods, ensure that its calculated level of production of the substances does not exceed zero. However, in order to satisfy the basic domestic needs of the Parties operating under paragraph 1 of Article 5, its calculated level of production may exceed that limit by up to fifteen per cent of its calculated level of production in 1986. This paragraph will apply save to the extent that the Parties decide to permit the level of production or consumption that is necessary to satisfy uses agreed by them to be essential.

ARTICLE 2C. OTHER FULLY HALOGENATED CFCs

1. Each Party shall ensure that for the twelve-month period commencing on 1 January 1993, its calculated level of consumption of the controlled substances in Group I of Annex B does not exceed, annually, eighty per cent of its calculated level of consumption in 1989. Each Party producing one or more of these substances shall, for the same period, ensure that its calculated level of production of the substances does not exceed, annually, eighty [percent] of its calculated level of production in 1989. However, in order to satisfy the basic domestic needs of the Parties operating under paragraph 1 of Article 5, its calculated level of production may exceed that limit by up to ten [percent] of its calculated level of production in 1989.

2. Each Party shall ensure that for the twelve-month period commencing on 1 January 1994, and in each twelve-month period thereafter, its calculated level of consumption of the controlled substances in Group I of Annex B does not exceed, annually, twenty-five per cent of its calculated level of consumption in 1989. Each Party producing one or more of these substances shall, for the same periods, ensure that its calculated level of production of the substances does not exceed, annually, twenty-five [percent] of its calculated level of production in 1989. However, in order to satisfy the basic domestic needs of the Parties operating under paragraph 1 of Article 5, its calculated level of production may exceed that limit by up to ten [percent] of its calculated level of production in 1989.

3. Each Party shall ensure that for the twelve-month period commencing on 1 January 1996, and in each twelve-month period thereafter, its calculated level of consumption of the controlled substances in Group I of Annex B does not exceed zero.

Each Party producing one or more of these substances shall, for the same periods, ensure that its calculated level of production of the substances does not exceed zero. However, in order to satisfy the basic domestic needs of the Parties operating under paragraph 1 of Article 5, its calculated level of production may exceed that limit by up to fifteen per cent of its calculated level of production in 1989. This paragraph will apply save to the extent that the Parties decide to permit the level of production or consumption that is necessary to satisfy uses agreed by them to be essential.

ARTICLE 2D. CARBON TETRACHLORIDE

1. Each Party shall ensure that for the twelve-month period commencing on 1 January 1995, its calculated level of consumption of the controlled substance in Group II of Annex B does not exceed, annually, fifteen [percent] of its calculated level of consumption in 1989. Each Party producing the substance shall, for the same period, ensure that its calculated level of production of the substance does not exceed, annually, fifteen [percent] of its calculated level of production in 1989. However, in order to satisfy the basic domestic needs of the Parties operating under paragraph 1 of

Article 5, its calculated level of production may exceed that limit by up to ten per cent of its calculated level of production in 1989.

2. Each Party shall ensure that for the twelve-month period commencing on 1 January 1996, and in each twelve-month period thereafter, its calculated level of consumption of the controlled substance in Group II of Annex B does not exceed zero. Each Party producing the substance shall, for the same periods, ensure that its calculated level of production of the substance does not exceed zero. However, in order to satisfy the basic domestic needs of the Parties operating under paragraph 1 of Article 5, its calculated level of production may exceed that limit by up to fifteen [percent] of its calculated level of production in 1989. This paragraph will apply save to the extent that the Parties decide to permit the level of production or consumption that is necessary to satisfy uses agreed by them to be essential.

ARTICLE 2E. 1,1,1–TRICHLOROETHANE (METHYL CHLOROFORM)

1. Each Party shall ensure that for the twelve-month period commencing on 1 January 1993, its calculated level of consumption of the controlled substance in Group III of Annex B does not exceed, annually, its calculated level of consumption in 1989.

Each Party producing the substance shall, for the same period, ensure that its calculated level of production of the substance does not exceed, annually, its calculated level of production in 1989. However, in order to satisfy the basic domestic needs of the Parties operating under paragraph 1 of Article 5, its calculated level of production may exceed that limit by up to ten [percent] of its calculated level of production in 1989.

2. Each Party shall ensure that for the twelve-month period commencing on 1 January 1994, and in each twelve-month period thereafter, its calculated level of consumption of the controlled substance in Group III of Annex B does not exceed, annually, fifty [percent] of its calculated level of consumption in 1989. Each Party producing the substance shall, for the same periods, ensure that its calculated level of production of the substance does not exceed, annually, fifty [percent] of its calculated level of production in 1989. However, in order to satisfy the basic domestic needs of the Parties operating under paragraph 1 of Article 5, its calculated level of production may exceed that limit by up to ten [percent] of its calculated level of production in 1989.

3. Each Party shall ensure that for the twelve-month period commencing on 1 January 1996, and in each twelve-month period thereafter, its calculated level of consumption of the controlled substance in Group III of Annex B does not exceed zero.

Each Party producing the substance shall, for the same periods, ensure that its calculated level of production of the substance does not exceed zero. However, in order to satisfy the basic domestic needs of the Parties operating under paragraph 1 of Article 5, its calculated level of production may exceed that limit by up to fifteen [percent] of its calculated level of production for 1989. This paragraph will apply save to the extent that the Parties decide to permit the level of production or consumption that is necessary to satisfy uses agreed by them to be essential.

ARTICLE 2F: HYDROCHLOROFLUOROCARBONS

1. Each Party shall ensure that for the twelve-month period commencing on 1 January 1996, and in each twelve-month period thereafter, its calculated level of consumption of the controlled substances in Group I of Annex C does not exceed, annually, the sum of:

(a) Two point eight [percent] of its calculated level of consumption in 1989 of the controlled substances in Group I of Annex A; and

(b) Its calculated level of consumption in 1989 of the controlled substances in Group I of Annex C.

2. Each Party shall ensure that for the twelve month period commencing on 1 January 2004, and in each twelve-month period thereafter, its calculated level of consumption of the controlled substances in Group I of Annex C does not exceed, annually, sixty-five per cent of the sum referred to in paragraph 1 of this Article.

3. Each Party shall ensure that for the twelve-month period commencing on 1 January 2010, and in each twelve-month period thereafter, its calculated level of consumption of the controlled substances in Group I of Annex C does not exceed, annually, thirty-five per cent of the sum referred to in paragraph 1 of this Article.

4. Each Party shall ensure that for the twelve-month period commencing on 1 January 2015, and in each twelve-month period thereafter, its calculated level of consumption of the controlled substances in Group I of Annex C does not exceed, annually, ten per cent of the sum referred to in paragraph 1 of this Article.

5. Each Party shall ensure that for the twelve-month period commencing on 1 January 2020, and in each twelve-month period thereafter, its calculated level of consumption of the controlled substances in Group I of Annex C does not exceed, annually, zero point five per cent of the sum referred to in paragraph 1 of this Article. Such consumption shall, however, be restricted to the servicing of refrigeration and air conditioning equipment existing at that date.

6. Each Party shall ensure that for the twelve-month period commencing on 1 January 2030, and in each twelve-month period thereafter, its calculated level of consumption of the controlled substances in Group I of Annex C does not exceed zero.

7. As of 1 January 1996, each Party shall [endeavor] to ensure that:

(a) The use of controlled substances in Group I of Annex C is limited to those applications where other more environmentally suitable alternative substances or technologies are not available;

(b) The use of controlled substances in Group I of Annex C is not outside the areas of application currently met by controlled substances in Annexes A, B and C, except in rare cases for the protection of human life or human health; and

(c) Controlled substances in Group I of Annex C are selected for use in a manner that minimizes ozone depletion, in addition to meeting other environmental, safety and economic considerations.

ARTICLE 2G. HYDROBROMOFLUOROCARBONS

Each Party shall ensure that for the twelve-month period commencing on 1 January 1996, and in each twelve-month period thereafter, its calculated level of consumption of the controlled substances in Group II of Annex C does not exceed zero. Each Party producing the substances shall, for the same periods, ensure that its calculated level of production of the substances does

not exceed zero. This paragraph will apply save to the extent that the Parties decide to permit the level of production or consumption that is necessary to satisfy uses agreed by them to be essential.

ARTICLE 2H. METHYL BROMIDE

1. Each Party shall ensure that for the twelve-month period commencing on 1 January 1995, and in each twelve-month period thereafter, its calculated level of consumption of the controlled substance in Annex E does not exceed, annually, its calculated level of consumption in 1991. Each Party producing the substance shall, for the same period, ensure that its calculated level of production of the substance does not exceed, annually, its calculated level of production in 1991.

However, in order to satisfy the basic domestic needs of the Parties operating under paragraph 1 of Article 5, its calculated level of production may exceed that limit by up to ten per cent of its calculated level of production in 1991.

2. Each Party shall ensure that for the twelve-month period commencing on 1 January 1999, and in the twelve-month period thereafter, its calculated level of consumption of the controlled substance in Annex E does not exceed, annually, seventy-five [percent] of its calculated level of consumption in 1991. Each Party producing the substance shall, for the same periods, ensure that its calculated level of production of the substance does not exceed, annually, seventy-five [percent] of its calculated level of production in 1991. However, in order to satisfy the basic domestic needs of the Parties operating under paragraph 1 of Article 5, its calculated level of production may exceed that limit by up to ten [percent] of its calculated level of production in 1991.

3. Each Party shall ensure that for the twelve-month period commencing on 1 January 2001, and in the twelve-month period thereafter, its calculated level of consumption of the controlled substance in Annex E does not exceed, annually, fifty percent of its calculated level of consumption in 1991. Each Party producing the substance shall, for the same periods, ensure that its calculated level of production of the substance does not exceed, annually, fifty [percent] of its calculated level of production in 1991. However, in order to satisfy the basic domestic needs of the Parties operating under paragraph 1 of Article 5, its calculated level of production may exceed that limit by up to ten [percent] of its calculated level of production in 1991.

4. Each Party shall ensure that for the twelve-month period commencing on 1 January 2003, and in the twelve-month period thereafter, its calculated level of consumption of the controlled substance in Annex E does not exceed, annually, thirty [percent] of its calculated level of consumption in 1991. Each Party producing the substance shall, for the same periods, ensure that its calculated level of production of the substance does not exceed, annually, thirty [percent] of its calculated level of production in 1991. However, in order to satisfy the basic domestic needs of the Parties operating under paragraph 1 of Article 5, its calculated level of production may exceed that limit by up to ten [percent] of its calculated level of production in1991.

5. Each Party shall ensure that for the twelve-month period commencing on 1 January 2005, and in each twelve-month period thereafter, its calculated level of consumption of the controlled substance in Annex E does not exceed zero. Each Party producing the substance shall, for the same periods, ensure that its calculated level of production of the substance does not exceed zero. However, in order to satisfy the basic domestic needs of the Parties operating under paragraph 1 of Article 5, its calculated level of production may exceed that limit by up to fifteen [percent] of its calculated level of production in 1991.This paragraph will apply save to the extent that the Parties decide to permit the level of production or consumption that is necessary to satisfy uses agreed by them to be critical uses.

6. The calculated levels of consumption and production under this Article shall not include the amounts used by the Party for quarantine and pre-shipment applications.

ARTICLE 3. CALCULATION OF CONTROL LEVELS

For the purposes of Articles 2, 2A to 2H and 5, each Party shall, for each group of substances in Annex A, Annex B, Annex C or Annex E determine its calculated levels of:

(a) Production by:

(i) multiplying its annual production of each controlled substance by the ozone depleting potential specified in respect if it [is] in Annex A, Annex B, Annex C or Annex E;

(ii) adding together, for each such Group, the resulting figures;

(b) Imports and exports, respectively, by following, mutatis mutandis, the procedure set out in subparagraph (a); and

(c) Consumption by adding together its calculated levels of production and imports and subtracting its calculated level of exports as determined in accordance with subparagraphs (a) and (b). However, beginning on 1 January 1993, any export of controlled substances to non-Parties shall not be subtracted in calculating the consumption level of the exporting Party.

[The underlined text printed below in Articles 4, 4A and 4B derives from the Amendment adopted by the Parties at the Ninth Conference of the Parties (the "Montreal Amendment"). At the date of printing, this Amendment is not in force. It will enter into force, only for those Parties which ratify it, on 1 January 1999, subject to the conditions set out on page U3.]

ARTICLE 4. CONTROL OF TRADE WITH NON-PARTIES

1. As of 1 January 1990, each party shall ban the import of the controlled substances in Annex A from any State not party to this Protocol.

1 bis. Within one year of the date of the entry into force of this paragraph, each Party shall ban the import of the controlled substances in Annex B from any State not party to this Protocol.

1 ter. Within one year of the date of entry into force of this paragraph, each Party shall ban the import of any controlled substances in Group II of Annex C from any State not party to this Protocol.

1 qua. Within one year of the date of entry into force of this paragraph, each Party shall ban the import of the controlled substance in Annex E from any State not party to this Protocol.

2. As of 1 January 1993, each Party shall ban the export of any controlled substances in Annex A to any State not party to this Protocol.

2 bis. Commencing one year after the date of entry into force of this paragraph, each Party shall ban the export of any controlled substances in Annex B to any State not party to this Protocol.

2 ter. Commencing one year after the date of entry into force of this paragraph, each Party shall ban the export of any controlled substances in Group II of Annex C to any State not party to this Protocol.

2 qua. Within one year of the date of entry into force of this paragraph, each Party shall ban the export of the controlled substance in Annex E to any State not party to this Protocol.

3. By 1 January 1992, the Parties shall, following the procedures in Article 10 of the Convention, elaborate in an annex a list of products containing controlled substances in Annex A. Parties that have not objected to the annex in accordance with those procedures shall ban, within one year of the annex having become effective, the import of those products from any State not party to this Protocol.

3 bis. Within three years of the date of the entry into force of this paragraph, the Parties shall, following the procedures in Article 10 of the Convention, elaborate in an annex a list of products containing controlled substances in Annex B. Parties that have not objected to the annex in accordance with those procedures

shall ban, within one year of the annex having become effective, the import of those products from any State not party to this Protocol.

3 ter. Within three years of the date of entry into force of this paragraph, the Parties shall, following the procedures in Article10 of the Convention, elaborate in an annex a list of products containing controlled substances in Group II of Annex C. Parties that have not objected to the annex in accordance with those procedures shall ban, within one year of the annex having become effective, the import of those products from any State not party to this Protocol.

4. By 1 January 1994, the Parties shall determine the feasibility of banning or restricting, from States not party to this Protocol, the import of products produced with, but not containing, controlled substances in Annex A. If determined feasible, the Parties shall, following the procedures in Article 10 of the Convention, elaborate in an annex a list of such products. Parties that have not objected to the annex in accordance with those procedures shall ban, within one year of the annex having become effective, the import of those products from any State not party to this Protocol.

4 bis. Within five years of the date of the entry into force of this paragraph, the Parties shall determine the feasibility of banning or restricting, from States not party to this Protocol, the import of products produced with, but not containing, controlled substances in Annex B. If determined feasible, the Parties shall, following the procedures in Article 10 of the Convention, elaborate in an annex a list of such products. Parties that have not objected to the annex in accordance with those procedures shall ban or restrict, within one year of the annex having become effective, the import of those products from any State not party to this Protocol.

4 ter. Within five years of the date of entry into force of this paragraph, the Parties shall determine the feasibility of banning or restricting, from States not party to this Protocol, the import of products produced with, but not containing, controlled substances in Group II of Annex C. If determined feasible, the Parties shall, following the procedures in Article 10 of the Convention, elaborate in an annex a list of such products. Parties that have not objected to the annex in accordance with those procedures shall ban or restrict, within one year of the annex having become effective, the import of those products from any State not party to this Protocol.

5. Each Party undertakes to the fullest practicable extent to discourage the export to any State not party to this Protocol of technology for producing and for utilizing controlled substances in Annexes A and B, Group II of Annex C and Annex E.

6. Each Party shall refrain from providing new subsidies, aid, credits, guarantees or insurance programmes for the export to States not party to this Protocol of products, equipment, plants or technology that would facilitate the production of controlled substances in Annexes A and B, Group II of Annex C and Annex E.

7. Paragraphs 5 and 6 shall not apply to products, equipment, plants or technology that improve the containment, recovery, recycling or destruction of controlled substances, promote the development of alternative substances, or otherwise contribute to the reduction of emissions of controlled substances in Annexes A and B, Group II of Annex C and Annex E.

8. Notwithstanding the provisions of this Article, imports and exports referred to in paragraphs 1 to 4 ter of this Article may be permitted from, or to, any State not party to this Protocol, if that State is determined, by a meeting of the Parties, to be in full compliance with Article 2, Articles 2A to 2E, Articles 2G and 2H and this Article, and have submitted data to that effect as specified in Article 7.

9. For the purposes of this Article, the term "State not party to this Protocol" shall include, with respect to a particular controlled substance, a State or regional

economic integration organization that has not agreed to be bound by the control measures in effect for that substance.

10. By 1 January 1996, the Parties shall consider whether to amend this Protocol in order to extend the measures in this Article to trade in controlled substances in Group I of Annex C and in Annex E with States not party to the Protocol.

ARTICLE 4A. CONTROL OF TRADE WITH PARTIES

1. Where, after the phase-out date applicable to it for a controlled substance, a Party is unable, despite having taken all practicable steps to comply with its obligation under the Protocol, to cease production of that substance for domestic consumption, other than for uses agreed by the Parties to be essential, it shall ban the export of used, recycled and reclaimed quantities of that substance, other than for the purpose of destruction.

2. Paragraph 1 of this Article shall apply without prejudice to the operation of Article 11 of the Convention and then on-compliance procedure developed under Article 8 of the Protocol.

ARTICLE 4B. LICENSING

1. Each Party shall, by 1 January 2000 or within three months of the date of entry into force of this Article for it, whichever is the later, establish and implement a system for licensing the import and export of new, used, recycled and reclaimed controlled substances in Annexes A, B, C and E.

2. Notwithstanding paragraph 1 of this Article, any Party operating under paragraph 1 of Article 5 which decides it is not in a position to establish and implement a system for licensing the import and export of controlled substances in Annexes C and E, may delay taking those actions until 1 January 2005 and 1 January 2002, respectively.

3. Each Party shall, within three months of the date of introducing its licensing system, report to the Secretariat on the establishment and operation of that system.

4. The Secretariat shall periodically prepare and circulate to all Parties a list of the Parties that have reported to it on their licensing systems and shall forward this information to the Implementation Committee for consideration and appropriate recommendations to the Parties.

ARTICLE 5. SPECIAL SITUATION OF DEVELOPING COUNTRIES

1. Any Party that is a developing country and whose annual calculated level of consumption of the controlled substances in Annex A is less than 0.3 kilograms per capita on the date of the entry into force of the Protocol for it, or any time thereafter until 1 January 1999, shall, in order to meet its basic domestic needs, be entitled to delay for ten years its compliance with the control measures set out in Articles 2A to 2E, provided that any further amendments to the adjustments or Amendment adopted at the Second Meeting of the Parties in London, 29 June 1990, shall apply to the Parties operating under this paragraph after the review provided for in paragraph 8 of this Article has taken place and shall be based on the conclusions of that review.

1 bis. The Parties shall, taking into account the review referred to in paragraph 8 of this Article, the assessments made pursuant to Article 6 and any other relevant information, decide by 1 January 1996, through the procedure set forth in paragraph 9 of Article 2:

(a) With respect to paragraphs 1 to 6 of Article 2F, what base year, initial levels, control schedules and phase-out date for consumption of the controlled substances in Group I of Annex C will apply to Parties operating under paragraph 1 of this Article;

(b) With respect to Article 2G, what phase-out date for production and consumption of the controlled substances in Group II of Annex C will apply to Parties operating under paragraph 1 of this Article; and

(c) With respect to Article 2H, what base year, initial levels and control schedules for consumption and production of the controlled substance in Annex E will apply to Parties operating under paragraph 1 of this Article.

2. However, any Party operating under paragraph 1 of this Article shall exceed neither an annual calculated level of consumption of the controlled substances in Annex A of 0.3 kilograms per capita nor an annual calculated level of consumption of controlled substances of Annex B of 0.2 kilograms per capita.

3. When implementing the control measures set out in Articles 2A to 2E, any Party operating under paragraph 1 of this Article shall be entitled to use:

(a) For controlled substances under Annex A, either the average of its annual calculated level of consumption for the period 1995 to 1997 inclusive or a calculated level of consumption of 0.3 kilograms per capita, whichever is the lower, as the basis for determining its compliance with the control measures relating to consumption.

(b) For controlled substances under Annex B, the average of its annual calculated level of consumption for the period 1998 to 2000 inclusive or a calculated level of consumption of 0.2 kilograms per capita, whichever is the lower, as the basis for determining its compliance with the control measures relating to consumption.

(c) For controlled substances under Annex A, either the average of its annual calculated level of production for the period 1995 to 1997 inclusive or a calculated level of production of 0.3 kilograms per capita, whichever is the lower, as the basis for determining its compliance with the control measures relating to production.

(d) For controlled substances under Annex B, either the average of its annual calculated level of production for the period 1998 to 2000 inclusive or a calculated level of production of 0.2 kilograms per capita, whichever is the lower, as the basis for determining its compliance with the control measures relating to production.

4. If a Party operating under paragraph 1 of this Article, at any time before the control measures obligations in Articles 2A to 2H become applicable to it, finds itself unable to obtain an adequate supply of controlled substances, it may notify this to the Secretariat. The Secretariat shall forthwith transmit a copy of such notification to the Parties, which shall consider the matter at their next Meeting, and decide upon appropriate action to be taken.

5. Developing the capacity to fulfil the obligations of the Parties operating under paragraph 1 of this Article to comply with the control measures set out in Articles 2A to 2E, and any control measures in Articles 2F to 2H that are decided pursuant to paragraph 1 bis of this Article, and their implementation by those same Parties will depend upon the effective implementation of the financial co-operation as provided by Article 10 and the transfer of technology as provided by Article 10A.

6. Any Party operating under paragraph 1 of this Article may, at any time, notify the Secretariat in writing that, having taken all practicable steps it is unable to implement any or all of the obligations laid down in Articles 2A to 2E, or any or all obligations in Articles 2F to 2H that are decided pursuant to paragraph 1 bis of this Article, due to the inadequate implementation of Articles 10 and 10A. The Secretariat shall forthwith transmit a copy of the notification to the Parties, which shall consider the matter at their next Meeting, giving due recognition to paragraph 5 of this Article and shall decide upon appropriate action to be taken.

7. During the period between notification and the Meeting of the Parties at which the appropriate action referred to in paragraph 6 above is to be decided, or for a further period if the Meeting of the Parties so decides, the non-compliance procedures referred to in Article 8 shall not be invoked against the notifying Party.

8. A Meeting of the Parties shall review, not later than 1995, the situation of the Parties operating under paragraph 1 of this Article, including the effective implementation of financial co-operation and transfer of technology to them, and adopt such revisions that may be deemed necessary regarding the schedule of control measures applicable to those Parties.

8 bis. Based on the conclusions of the review referred to in paragraph 8 above:

(a) With respect to the controlled substances in Annex A, a Party operating under paragraph 1 of this Article shall, in order to meet its basic domestic needs, be entitled to delay for ten years its compliance with the control measures adopted by the Second Meeting of the Parties in London, 29 June 1990, and reference by the Protocol to Articles 2A and 2B shall be read accordingly;

(b) With respect to the controlled substances in Annex B, a Party operating under paragraph 1 of this Article shall, in order to meet its basic domestic needs, be entitled to delay for ten years its compliance with the control measures adopted by the Second Meeting of the Parties in London, 29 June 1990, and reference by the Protocol to Articles 2C to 2E shall be read accordingly.

8 ter. Pursuant to paragraph 1 bis above:

(a) Each Party operating under paragraph 1 of this Article shall ensure that for the twelve-month period commencing on 1 January 2016, and in each twelve-month period thereafter, its calculated level of consumption of the controlled substances in Group I of Annex C does not exceed, annually, its calculated level of consumption in 2015;

(b) Each Party operating under paragraph 1 of this Article shall ensure that for the twelve-month period commencing on 1 January 2040, and in each twelve-month period thereafter, its calculated level of consumption of the controlled substances in Group I of Annex C does not exceed zero;

(c) Each Party operating under paragraph 1 of this Article shall comply with Article 2G;

(d) With regard to the controlled substance contained in Annex E:

(i) As of 1 January 2002 each Party operating under paragraph 1 of this Article shall comply with the control measures set out in paragraph 1 of Article 2H and, as the basis for its compliance with these control measures, it shall use the average of its annual calculated level of consumption and production, respectively, for the period of 1995 to 1998 inclusive;

(ii) Each Party operating under paragraph 1 of this Article shall ensure that for the twelve-month period commencing on 1 January 2005, and in each twelve-month period thereafter, its calculated levels of consumption and production of the controlled substance in Annex E do not exceed, annually, eighty [percent] of the average of its annual calculated levels of consumption and production, respectively, for the period of 1995 to 1998 inclusive;

(iii) Each Party operating under paragraph 1 of this Article shall ensure that for the twelve-month period commencing on 1 January 2015 and in each twelve-month period thereafter, its calculated levels of consumption and production of the controlled substance in Annex E do not exceed zero. This paragraph will apply save to the extent that the Parties decide to permit the level of production or consumption that is necessary to satisfy uses agreed by them to be critical uses;

(iv) The calculated levels of consumption and production under this subparagraph shall not include the amounts used by the Party for quarantine and pre-shipment applications.

9. Decisions of the Parties referred to in paragraph 4, 6 and 7 of this Article shall be taken according to the same procedure applied to decision-making under Article 10.

ARTICLE 6. ASSESSMENT AND REVIEW OF CONTROL MEASURES

Beginning in 1990, and at least every four years thereafter, the Parties shall assess the control measures provided for in Article 2 and Articles 2A to 2H on the basis of available scientific, environmental, technical and economic information. At least one year before each assessment, the Parties shall convene appropriate panels of experts qualified in the fields mentioned and determine the composition and terms of reference of any such panels. Within one year of being convened, the panels will report their conclusions, through the Secretariat, to the Parties.

ARTICLE 7. REPORTING OF DATA

1. Each Party shall provide to the Secretariat, within three months of becoming a Party, statistical data on its production, imports and exports of each of the controlled substances in Annex A for the year 1986, or the best possible estimates of such data where actual data are not available.

2. Each Party shall provide to the Secretariat statistical data on its production, imports and exports of each of the controlled substances

— in Annexes B and C, for the year 1989;

— in Annex E, for the year 1991,

or the best possible estimates of such data where actual data are not available, not later than three months after the date when the provisions set out in the Protocol with regard to the substances in Annexes B, C and E respectively enter into force for that Party.

3. Each Party shall provide to the Secretariat statistical data on its annual production (as defined in paragraph 5 of Article 1) of each of the controlled substances listed in Annexes A, B, C and E and, separately, for each substance,

— Amounts used for feedstocks,

— Amounts destroyed by technologies approved by the Parties, and

— Imports from and exports to Parties and non-Parties respectively, for the year during which provisions concerning the substances in Annexes A, B, C and E respectively entered into force for that Party and for each year thereafter. Data shall be forwarded not later than nine months after the end of the year to which the data relate.

3 bis. Each Party shall provide to the Secretariat separate statistical data of its annual imports and exports of each of the controlled substances listed in Group II of Annex A and Group I of Annex C that have been recycled.

4. For Parties operating under the provisions of paragraph 8 (a) of Article 2, the requirements in paragraphs 1, 2, 3 and 3 bis of this Article in respect of statistical data on imports and exports shall be satisfied if the regional economic integration organization concerned provides data on imports and exports between the organization and States that are not members of that organization.

ARTICLE 8. NON-COMPLIANCE

The Parties, at their first meeting, shall consider and approve procedures and institutional mechanisms for determining non-compliance with the provisions of this Protocol and for treatment of Parties found to be in non-compliance.

ARTICLE 9. RESEARCH, DEVELOPMENT, PUBLIC AWARENESS AND EXCHANGE OF INFORMATION

1. The Parties shall co-operate, consistent with their national laws, regulations and practices and taking into account in particular the needs of developing countries, in promoting, directly or through competent international bodies, research, development and exchange of information on:

(a) best technologies for improving the containment, recovery, recycling, or destruction of controlled substances or otherwise reducing their emissions;

(b) possible alternatives to controlled substances, to products containing such substances, and to products manufactured with them; and

(c) costs and benefits of relevant control strategies.

2. The Parties, individually, jointly or through competent international bodies, shall co-operate in promoting public awareness of the environmental effects of the emissions of controlled substances and other substances that deplete the ozone layer.

3. Within two years of the entry into force of this Protocol and every two years thereafter, each Party shall submit to the Secretariat a summary of the activities it has conducted pursuant to this Article.

ARTICLE 10. FINANCIAL MECHANISM

1. The Parties shall establish a mechanism for the purposes of providing financial and technical co-operation, including the transfer of technologies, to Parties operating under paragraph 1 of Article 5 of this Protocol to enable their compliance with the control measures set out in Articles 2A to 2E, and any control measures in Articles 2F to 2H that are decided pursuant to paragraph 1 bis of Article 5 of the Protocol. The mechanism, contributions to which shall be additional to other financial transfers to Parties operating under that paragraph, shall meet all agreed incremental costs of such Parties in order to enable their compliance with the control measures of the Protocol. An indicative list of the categories of incremental costs shall be decided by the meeting of the Parties.

2. The mechanism established under paragraph 1 shall include a Multilateral Fund. It may also include other means of multilateral, regional and bilateral co-operation.

3. The Multilateral Fund shall:

(a) Meet, on a grant or concessional basis as appropriate, and according to criteria to be decided upon by the Parties, the agreed incremental costs;

(b) Finance clearing-house functions to:

(i) Assist Parties operating under paragraph 1 of Article 5, through country specific studies and other technical co-operation, to identify their needs for co-operation;

(ii) Facilitate technical co-operation to meet these identified needs;

(iii) Distribute, as provided for in Article 9, information and relevant materials, and hold workshops, training sessions, and other related activities, for the benefit of Parties that are developing countries; and

(iv) Facilitate and monitor other multilateral, regional and bilateral co-operation available to Parties that are developing countries;

(c) Finance the secretarial services of the Multilateral Fund and related support costs.

4. The Multilateral Fund shall operate under the authority of the Parties who shall decide on its overall policies.

5. The Parties shall establish an Executive Committee to develop and monitor the implementation of specific operational policies, guidelines and administrative arrangements, including the disbursement of resources, for the purpose of achieving the objectives of the Multilateral Fund. The Executive Committee shall discharge its tasks and responsibilities, specified in its terms of reference as agreed by the Parties, with the co-operation and assistance of the International Bank for Reconstruction and Development (World Bank), the United Nations Environment Programme, the United Nations Development Programme or other appropriate agencies depending on their respective areas of expertise. The members of the Executive Committee, which shall be selected on the basis of a balanced representation of the Parties operating under paragraph 1 of Article 5 and of the Parties not so operating, shall be endorsed by the Parties.

6. The Multilateral Fund shall be financed by contributions from Parties not operating under paragraph 1 of Article 5 in convertible currency or, in certain circumstances, in kind and/or in national currency, on the basis of the United Nations scale of assessments. Contributions by other Parties shall be encouraged. Bilateral and, in particular cases agreed by a decision of the Parties, regional co-operation may, up to a percentage and consistent with any criteria to be specified by decision of the Parties, be considered as a contribution to the Multilateral Fund, provided that such co-operation, as a minimum:

(a) Strictly relates to compliance with the provisions of this Protocol;

(b) Provides additional resources; and

(c) Meets agreed incremental costs.

7. The Parties shall decide upon the programme budget of the Multilateral Fund for each fiscal period and upon the percentage of contributions of the individual Parties thereto.

8. Resources under the Multilateral Fund shall be disbursed with the concurrence of the beneficiary Party.

9. Decisions by the Parties under this Article shall be taken by consensus whenever possible. If all efforts at consensus have been exhausted and no agreement reached, decisions shall be adopted by a two-thirds majority vote of the Parties present and voting, representing a majority of the Parties operating under paragraph 1 of Article 5 present and voting and a majority of the Parties not so operating present and voting.

10. The financial mechanism set out in this Article is without prejudice to any future arrangements that may be developed with respect to other environmental issues.

ARTICLE 10A. TRANSFER OF TECHNOLOGY

Each Party shall take every practicable step, consistent with the programmes supported by the financial mechanism, to ensure:

(a) that the best available, environmentally safe substitutes and related technologies are expeditiously transferred to Parties operating under paragraph 1 of Article 5; and

(b) that the transfers referred to in subparagraph (a) occur under fair and most favourable conditions.

ARTICLE 11. MEETINGS OF THE PARTIES

1. The Parties shall hold meetings at regular intervals. The Secretariat shall convene the first meeting of the Parties not later than one year after the date of the entry into force of this Protocol and in conjunction with a meeting of the Conference of

the Parties to the Convention, if a meeting of the latter is scheduled within that period.

2. Subsequent ordinary meetings of the parties shall be held, unless the Parties otherwise decide, in conjunction with meetings of the Conference of the Parties to the Convention. Extraordinary meetings of the Parties shall be held at such other times as may be deemed necessary by a meeting of the Parties, or at the written request of any Party, provided that within six months of such a request being communicated to them by the Secretariat, it is supported by at least one third of the Parties.

3. The Parties, at their first meeting, shall:

(a) adopt by consensus rules of procedure for their meetings;

(b) adopt by consensus the financial rules referred to in paragraph 2 of Article 13;

(c) establish the panels and determine the terms of reference referred to in Article 6;

(d) consider and approve the procedures and institutional mechanisms specified in Article 8; and

(e) begin preparation of work plans pursuant to paragraph 3 of Article 10. [The Article 10 in question is that of the original Protocol adopted in 1987.]

4. The functions of the meetings of the Parties shall be to:

(a) review the implementation of this Protocol;

(b) decide on any adjustments or reductions referred to in paragraph 9 of Article 2;

(c) decide on any addition to, insertion in or removal from any annex of substances and on related control measures in accordance with paragraph 10 of Article 2;

(d) establish, where necessary, guidelines or procedures for reporting of information as provided for in Article 7 and paragraph 3 of Article 9;

(e) review requests for technical assistance submitted pursuant to paragraph 2 of Article 10;

(f) review reports prepared by the secretariat pursuant to subparagraph (c) of Article 12;

(g) assess, in accordance with Article 6, the control measures;

(h) consider and adopt, as required, proposals for amendment of this Protocol or any annex and for any new annex;

(i) consider and adopt the budget for implementing this Protocol; and

(j) consider and undertake any additional action that may be required for the achievement of the purposes of this Protocol.

5. The United Nations, its specialized agencies and the International Atomic Energy Agency, as well as any State not party to this Protocol, may be represented at meetings of the Parties as observers. Any body or agency, whether national or international, governmental or non-governmental, qualified in fields relating to the protection of the ozone layer which has informed the secretariat of its wish to be represented at a meeting of the Parties as an observer may be admitted unless at least one third of the Parties present object. The admission and participation of observers shall be subject to the rules of procedure adopted by the Parties.

ARTICLE 12. SECRETARIAT

For the purposes of this Protocol, the Secretariat shall:

(a) arrange for and service meetings of the Parties as provided for in Article 11;

(b) receive and make available, upon request by a Party, data provided pursuant to Article 7;

(c) prepare and distribute regularly to the Parties reports based on information received pursuant to Articles 7 and 9;

(d) notify the Parties of any request for technical assistance received pursuant to Article 10 so as to facilitate the provision of such assistance;

(e) encourage non-Parties to attend the meetings of the Parties as observers and to act in accordance with the provisions of this Protocol;

(f) provide, as appropriate, the information and requests referred to in subparagraphs (c) and (d) to such non-party observers; and

(g) perform such other functions for the achievement of the purposes of this Protocol as may be assigned to it by the Parties.

ARTICLE 13. FINANCIAL PROVISIONS

1. The funds required for the operation of this Protocol, including those for the functioning of the Secretariat related to this Protocol, shall be charged exclusively against contributions from the Parties.

2. The Parties, at their first meeting, shall adopt by consensus financial rules for the operation of this Protocol.

ARTICLE 14. RELATIONSHIP OF THIS PROTOCOL TO THE CONVENTION

Except as otherwise provided in this Protocol, the provisions of the Convention relating to its protocols shall apply to this Protocol.

ARTICLE 15. SIGNATURE

This Protocol shall be open for signature by States and by regional economic integration organizations in Montreal on 16 September 1987, in Ottawa from 17 September 1987 to 16 January 1988, and at United Nations Headquarters in New York from 17 January 1988 to 15 September 1988.

ARTICLE 16. ENTRY INTO FORCE

1. This Protocol shall enter into force on 1 January 1989, provided that at least eleven instruments of ratification, acceptance, approval of the Protocol or accession thereto have been deposited by States or regional economic integration organizations representing at least two-thirds of 1986 estimated global consumption of the controlled substances, and the provisions of paragraph 1 of Article 17 of the Convention have been fulfilled. In the event that these conditions have not been fulfilled by that date, the Protocol shall enter into force on the ninetieth day following the date on which the conditions have been fulfilled.

2. For the purposes of paragraph 1, any such instrument deposited by a regional economic integration organization shall not be counted as additional to those deposited by member States of such organization.

3. After the entry into force of this Protocol, any State or regional economic integration organization shall become a Party to it on the ninetieth day following the date of deposit of its instrument of ratification, acceptance, approval or accession.

ARTICLE 17. PARTIES JOINING AFTER ENTRY INTO FORCE

Subject to Article 5, any State or regional economic integration organization which becomes a Party to this Protocol after the date of its entry into force, shall fulfil forthwith the sum of the obligations under Article 2, as well as under Articles 2A to 2H and Article 4, that apply at that date to the States and regional economic integration organizations that became Parties on the date the Protocol entered into force.

ARTICLE 18. RESERVATIONS

No reservations may be made to this Protocol.

ARTICLE 19. WITHDRAWAL

Any Party may withdraw from this Protocol by giving written notification to the Depositary at any time after four years of assuming the obligations specified in paragraph 1 of Article 2A. Any such withdrawal shall take effect upon expir[ation] of one year after the date of its receipt by the Depositary, or on such later date as may be specified in the notification of the withdrawal.

ARTICLE 20. AUTHENTIC TEXTS

The original of this Protocol, of which the Arabic, Chinese, English, French, Russian and Spanish texts are equally authentic, shall be deposited with the Secretary-General of the United Nations.

IN WITNESS WHEREOF THE UNDERSIGNED, BEING DULY AUTHORIZED TO THAT EFFECT, HAVE SIGNED THIS PROTOCOL DONE AT MONTREAL THIS SIXTEENTH DAY OF SEPTEMBER, ONE THOUSAND NINE HUNDRED AND EIGHTY SEVEN.

ANNEX A
CONTROLLED SUBSTANCES

Group	Substance	Ozone depleting Potential *
Group I		
$CFCl_3$	(CFC–11)	1.0
CF_2Cl_2	(CFC–12)	1.0
$C_2F_3Cl_3$	(CFC–113)	0.8
$C_2F_4Cl_2$	(CFC–114)	1.0
C_2F_5Cl	(CFC–115)	0.6
Group II		
CF_2BrCl	(halon–1211)	3.0
CF_3Br	(halon–1301)	10.0
$C_2F_4Br_2$	(halon–2402)	6.0

* These ozone depleting potentials are estimates based on existing knowledge and will be reviewed and revised periodically.

ANNEX B
CONTROLLED SUBSTANCES

Group	Substance	Ozone–Depleting Potential
Group I		
CF_3Cl	(CFC–13)	1.0
C_2FCl_5	(CFC–111)	1.0
$C_2F_2Cl_4$	(CFC–112)	1.0
C_3FCl_7	(CFC–211)	1.0
$C_3F_2Cl_6$	(CFC–212)	1.0
$C_3F_3Cl_5$	(CFC–213)	1.0
$C_3F_4Cl_4$	(CFC–214)	1.0
$C_3F_5Cl_3$	(CFC–215)	1.0
$C_3F_6Cl_2$	(CFC–216)	1.0
C_3F_7Cl	(CFC–217)	1.0
Group II		

Group	Substance	Ozone–Depleting Potential
Ccl4	carbon tetrachloride	1.1
Group III		
C2H3Cl3 *	1,1,1–trichloroethane *	(methyl chloroform) 0.1

* This formula does not refer to 1,1,2–trichloroethane.

ANNEX C
CONTROLLED SUBSTANCES

Group	Substance	Number of isomers	Ozone–Depleting Potential *
Group I			
CHFCl2	(HCFC–21) **	1	0.04
CHF2Cl	(HCFC–22) **	1	0.055
CH2FCl	(HCFC–31)	1	0.02
C2HFCl4	(HCFC–121)	2	0.01–0.04
C2HF2Cl3	(HCFC–122)	3	0.02–0.08
C2HF3Cl2	(HCFC–123)	3	0.02–0.06
CHCl2CF3	(HCFC–123) **	–	0.02
C2HF4Cl	(HCFC–124)	2	0.02–0.04
CHFClCF3	(HCFC–124) **	–	0.022
C2H2FCl3	(HCFC–131)	3	0.007–0.05
C2H2F2Cl2	(HCFC–132)	4	0.008–0.05
C2H2F3Cl	(HCFC–133)	3	0.02–0.06
C2H3FCl2	(HCFC–141)	3	0.005–0.07
CH3CFCl2	(HCFC–141b) **		0.11
C2H3F2Cl	(HCFC–142)	3	0.008–0.07
CH3CF2Cl	(HCFC–142b) **	–	0.065
C2H4FCl	(HCFC–151)	2	0.003–0.005
C3HFCl6	(HCFC–221)	5	0.015–0.07
C3HF2Cl5	(HCFC–222)	9	0.01–0.09
C3HF3Cl4	(HCFC–223)	12	0.01–0.08
C3HF4Cl3	(HCFC–224)	12	0.01–0.09
C3HF5Cl2	(HCFC–225)	9	0.02–0.07
CF3CF2CHCl2	(HCFC–225ca) **	–	0.025
CF2ClCF2CHClF	(HCFC–225cb) **	–	0.033
C3HF6Cl	(HCFC–226)	5	0.02–0.10
C3H2FCl5	(HCFC–231)	9	0.05–0.09
C3H2F2Cl4	(HCFC–232)	16	0.008–0.10
C3H2F3Cl3	(HCFC–233)	18	0.007–0.23
C3H2F4Cl2	(HCFC–234)	16	0.01–0.28
C3H2F5Cl	(HCFC–235)	9	0.03–0.52
C3H3FCl4	(HCFC–241)	12	0.004–0.09
C3H3F2Cl3	(HCFC–242)	18	0.005–0.13
C3H3F3Cl2	(HCFC–243)	18	0.007–0.12
C3H3F4Cl	(HCFC–244)	12	0.009–B0.14
C3H4FCl3	(HCFC–251)	12	0.001–0.01
C3H4F2Cl2	(HCFC–252)	16	0.005–0.04
C3H4F3Cl	(HCFC–253)	12	0.003–0.03
C3H5FCl2	(HCFC–261)	9	0.002–0.02
C3H5F2Cl	(HCFC–262)	9	0.002–0.02
C3H6FCl	(HCFC–271)	5	0.001–0.03
Group II			
CHF Br2		1	1.00
CHF2Br	(HBFC–22B1)	1	0.74
CH2FBr		1	0.73
C2HFBr4		2	0.3–0.8
C2HF2Br3		3	0.5–1.8
C2HF3Br2		3	0.4–1.6
C2HF4Br		2	0.7–1.2
C2H2FBr3		3	0.1–1.1

Group	Substance	Number of isomers	Ozone–Depleting Potential *
C2H2F2Br2		4	0.2–1.5
C2H2F3Br		3	0.7–1.6
C2H3FBr2		3	0.1–1.7
C2H3F2Br		3	0.2–1.1
C2H4FBr		2	0.07–0.1
C3HFBr6		5	0.3–1.5
C3HF2Br5		9	0.2–1.9
C3HF3Br4		12	0.3–1.8
C3HF4Br3		12	0.5–2.2
C3HF5Br2		9	0.9–2.0
C3HF6Br		5	0.7–3.3
C3H2FBr5		9	0.1–1.9
C3H2F2Br4		16	0.2–2.1
C3H2F3Br3		18	0.2–5.6
C3H2F4Br2		16	0.3–7.5
C3H2F5Br		8	0.9–1.4
C3H3FBr4		12	0.08–1.9
C3H3F2Br3		18	0.1–3.1
C3H3F3Br2		18	0.1–2.5
C3H3F4Br		12	0.3–4.4
C3H4FBr3		12	0.03–0.3
C3H4F2Br2		16	0.1–1.0
C3H4F3Br		12	0.07–0.8
C3H5FBr2		9	0.04–0.4
C3H5F2Br		9	.07–0.8
C3H6FBr		5	0.02–0.7

* Where a range of ODPs is indicated, the highest value in that range shall be used for the purposes of the Protocol. The ODPs listed as a single value have been determined from calculations based on laboratory measurements. Those listed as a range are based on estimates and are less certain. The range pertains to an isomeric group. The upper value is the estimate of the ODP of the isomer with the highest ODP, and the lower value is the estimate of the ODP of the isomer with the lowest ODP.

** Identifies the most commercially viable substances with ODP values listed against them to be used for the purposes of the Protocol.

ANNEX D *:
A LIST OF PRODUCTS ** CONTAINING CONTROLLED SUBSTANCES SPECIFIED IN ANNEX A

Products	Customs code number
1. Automobile and truck air conditioning units (whether incorporated in vehicles or not)	______________
2. Domestic and commercial refrigeration and air conditioning/heat pump equipment ***	______________
e.g.	______________
Refrigerators	______________
Freezers	______________
Dehumidifiers	______________
Water coolers	______________
Ice machines	______________
Air conditioning and heat pump units	______________
3. Aerosol products, except medical aerosols	______________
4. Portable fire extinguisher	______________
5. Insulation boards, panels and pipe covers	______________
6. Pre-polymers	______________

* This Annex was adopted by the Third Meeting of the Parties in Nairobi, 21 June 1991 as required by paragraph 3 of Article 4 of the Protocol.

** Though not when transported in consignments of personal or household effects or in similar non-commercial situations normally exempted from customs attention.

*** When containing controlled substances in Annex A as a refrigerant and/or in insulating material of the product.

ANNEX E
CONTROLLED SUBSTANCE

Group	Substance	Ozone–Depleting Potential
Group I		
CH3Br	methyl bromide	0.6

3.19 Protocol to the 1979 Convention on Long-range Transboundary Air Pollution Concerning the Control of Emissions of Nitrogen Oxides or Their Transboundary Fluxes.[f] Concluded at Sofia, 31 October 1988. Entered into force, 14 February 1991. EB.AIR/21; *reprinted in* 28 I.L.M. 212 (1989) & 5 Weston V.E.10

Article 1

Definitions

For the purposes of the present Protocol,

1. "Convention" means the Convention on Long-range Transboundary Air Pollution, adopted in Geneva on 13 November 1979;

2. "EMEP" means the Co-operative Programme for Monitoring and Evaluation of the Long-range Transmission of Air Pollutants in Europe;

3. "Executive Body" means the Executive Body for the Convention constituted under article 10, paragraph 1 of the Convention;

4. "Geographical scope of EMEP" means the area defined in article 1, paragraph 4 of the Protocol to the 1979 Convention on Long-range Transboundary Air Pollution on Long-term Financing of the Co-operative Programme for Monitoring and Evaluation of the Long-range Transmission of Air Pollutants in Europe (EMEP), adopted in Geneva on 28 September 1984;

5. "Parties" means, unless the context otherwise requires, the Parties to the present Protocol;

6. "Commission" means the United Nations Economic Commission for Europe;

7. "Critical load" means a quantitative estimate of the exposure to one or more pollutants below which significant harmful effects on specified sensitive elements of the environment do not occur according to present knowledge;

8. "Major existing stationary source" means any existing stationary source the thermal input of which is at least 100 MW;

9. "Major new stationary source" means any new stationary source the thermal input of which is at least 50 MW;

10. "Major source category" means any category of sources which emit or may emit air pollutants in the form of nitrogen oxides, including the categories described in the Technical Annex, and which contribute at least 10 per cent of the total national emissions of nitrogen oxides on an annual basis as measured or calculated in the first calendar year after the date of entry into force of the present Protocol, and every fourth year thereafter;

11. "New stationary source" means any stationary source the construction or substantial modification of which is commenced after the expiration of two years from the date of entry into force of this Protocol;

12. "New mobile source" means a motor vehicle or other mobile source which is manufactured after the expiration of two years from the date of entry into force of the present Protocol.

Article 2

Basic obligations

1. The Parties shall, as soon as possible and as a first step, take effective measures to control and/or reduce their national annual emissions of nitrogen oxides or their transboundary fluxes so that these, at the latest by 31 December 1994, do not

f. *See* Basic Document 3.8, *supra.*

exceed their national annual emissions of nitrogen oxides or transboundary fluxes of such emissions for the calendar year 1987 or any previous year to be specified upon signature of, or accession to, the Protocol, provided that in addition, with respect to any Party specifying such a previous year, its national average annual transboundary fluxes or national average annual emissions of nitrogen oxides for the period from 1 January 1987 to 1 January 1996 do not exceed its transboundary fluxes or national emissions for the calendar year 1987.

2. Furthermore, the Parties shall in particular, and no later than two years after the date of entry into force of the present Protocol:

(a) Apply national emissions standards to major new stationary sources and/or source categories, and to substantially modified stationary sources in major source categories, based on the best available technologies which are economically feasible, taking into consideration the Technical Annex;

(b) Apply national emission standards to new mobile sources in all major source categories based on the best available technologies which are economically feasible, taking into consideration the Technical Annex and the relevant decisions taken within the framework of the Inland Transport Committee of the Commission; and

(c) Introduce pollution control measures for major existing stationary sources, taking into consideration the Technical Annex and the characteristics of the plant, its age and its rate of utilization and the need to avoid undue operational disruption.

3. (a) The Parties shall, as a second step, commence negotiations, no later than six months after the date of entry into force of the present Protocol, on further steps to reduce national annual emissions of nitrogen oxides or transboundary fluxes of such emissions, taking into account the best available scientific and technological developments, internationally accepted critical loads and other elements resulting from the work programme undertaken under article 6.

(b) To this end, the Parties shall co-operate in order to establish:

(i) Critical loads;

(ii) Reductions in national annual emissions of nitrogen oxides or transboundary fluxes of such emissions as required to achieve agreed objectives based on critical loads; and

(iii) Measures and a time-table commencing no later than 1 January 1996 for achieving such reductions.

4. Parties may take more stringent measures than those required by the present article.

Article 3

Exchange of technology

1. The Parties shall, consistent with their national laws, regulations and practices, facilitate the exchange of technology to reduce emissions of nitrogen oxides, particularly through the promotion of:

(a) Commercial exchange of available technology;

(b) Direct industrial contacts and co-operation, including joint ventures;

(c) Exchange of information and experience; and

(d) Provision of technical assistance.

2. In promoting the activities specified in subparagraphs (a) to (d) above, the Parties shall create favourable conditions by facilitating contacts and co-operation

among appropriate organizations and individuals in the private and public sectors that are capable of providing technology, design and engineering services, equipment or finance.

3. The Parties shall, no later than six months after the date of entry into force of the present Protocol, commence consideration of procedures to create more favourable conditions for the exchange of technology to reduce emissions of nitrogen oxides.

Article 4

Unleaded fuel

The Parties shall, as soon as possible and no later than two years after the date of entry into force of the present Protocol, make unleaded fuel sufficiently available, in particular cases as a minimum along main international transit routes, to facilitate the circulation of vehicles equipped with catalytic converters.

Article 5

Review process

1. The Parties shall regularly review the present Protocol, taking into account the best available scientific substantiation and technological development.

2. The first review shall take place no later than one year after the date of entry into force of the present Protocol.

Article 6

Work to be undertaken

The Parties shall give high priority to research and monitoring related to the development and application of an approach based on critical loads to determine, on a scientific basis, necessary reductions in emissions of nitrogen oxides. The Parties shall, in particular, through national research programmes, in the work plan of the Executive Body and through other co-operative programmes within the framework of the Convention, seek to:

(a) Identify and quantify effects of emissions of nitrogen oxides on humans, plant and animal life, waters, soils and materials, taking into account the impact on these of nitrogen oxides from sources other than atmospheric deposition;

(b) Determine the geographical distribution of sensitive areas;

(c) Develop measurements and model calculations including harmonized methodologies for the calculation of emissions, to quantify the long-range transport of nitrogen oxides and related pollutants;

(d) Improve estimates of the performance and costs of technologies for control of emissions of nitrogen oxides and record the development of improved and new technologies; and

(e) Develop, in the context of an approach based on critical loads, methods to integrate scientific, technical and economic data in order to determine appropriate control strategies.

Article 7

National programmes, policies and strategies

The Parties shall develop without undue delay national programmes, policies and strategies to implement the obligations under the present Protocol that shall serve as a means of controlling and reducing emissions of nitrogen oxides or their transboundary fluxes.

Article 8

Information exchange and annual reporting

1. The Parties shall exchange information by notifying the Executive Body of the national programmes, policies and strategies that they develop in accordance with article 7 and by reporting to it annually on progress achieved under, and any changes to, those programmes, policies and strategies, and in particular on:

(a) The levels of national annual emissions of nitrogen oxides and the basis upon which they have been calculated;

(b) Progress in applying national emission standards required under article 2, subparagraphs 2(a) and 2(b), and the national emission standards applied or to be applied, and the sources and/or source categories concerned;

(c) Progress in introducing the pollution control measures required under article 2, subparagraph 2(c), the sources concerned and the measures introduced or to be introduced;

(d) Progress in making unleaded fuel available;

(e) Measures taken to facilitate the exchange of technology; and

(f) Progress in establishing critical loads.

2. Such information shall, as far as possible, be submitted in accordance with a uniform reporting framework.

Article 9

Calculations

EMEP shall, utilizing appropriate models and in good time before the annual meetings of the Executive Body, provide to the Executive Body calculations of nitrogen budgets and also of transboundary fluxes and deposition of nitrogen oxides within the geographical scope of EMEP. In areas outside the geographical scope of EMEP, models appropriate to the particular circumstances of Parties to the Convention therein shall be used.

Article 10

Technical Annex

The Technical Annex to the present Protocol is recommendatory in character. It shall form an integral part of the Protocol.

Article 11

Amendments to the Protocol

1. Any Party may propose amendments to the present Protocol.

2. Proposed amendments shall be submitted in writing to the Executive Secretary of the Commission who shall communicate them to all Parties. The Executive Body shall discuss the proposed amendments at its next annual meeting provided that these proposals have been circulated by the Executive Secretary to the Parties at least ninety days in advance.

3. Amendments to the Protocol, other than amendments to its Technical Annex, shall be adopted by consensus of the Parties present at a meeting of the Executive Body, and shall enter into force for the Parties which have accepted them on the ninetieth day after the date on which two-thirds of the Parties have deposited their instruments of acceptance thereof. Amendments shall enter into force for any Party which has accepted them after two-thirds of the Parties have deposited their instruments of acceptance of the amendment, on the ninetieth day after the date on which that Party deposited its instrument of acceptance of the amendments.

4. Amendments to the Technical Annex shall be adopted by consensus of the Parties present at a meeting of the Executive Body and shall become effective thirty days after the date on which they have been communicated in accordance with paragraph 5 below.

5. Amendments under paragraphs 3 and 4 above shall, as soon as possible after their adoption, be communicated by the Executive Secretary to all Parties.

Article 12

Settlement of disputes

If a dispute arises between two or more Parties as to the interpretation or application of the present Protocol, they shall seek a solution by negotiation or by any other method of dispute settlement acceptable to the parties to the dispute.

Article 13

Signature

1. The present Protocol shall be open for signature at Sofia from 1 November 1988 until 4 November 1988 inclusive, then at the Headquarters of the United Nations in New York until 5 May 1989, by the member States of the Commission as well as States having consultative status with the Commission, pursuant to paragraph 8 of Economic and Social Council resolution 36 (IV) of 28 March 1947, and by regional economic integration organizations, constituted by sovereign States members of the Commission, which have competence in respect of the negotiation, conclusion and application of international agreements in matters covered by the Protocol, provided that the States and organizations concerned are Parties to the Convention.

2. In matters within their competence, such regional economic integration organizations shall, on their own behalf, exercise the rights and fulfil the responsibilities which the present Protocol attributes to their member States. In such cases, the member States of these organizations shall not be entitled to exercise such rights individually.

Article 14

Ratification, acceptance, approval and accession

1. The present Protocol shall be subject to ratification, acceptance or approval by Signatories.

2. The present Protocol shall be open for accession as from 6 May 1989 by the States and organizations referred to in article 13, paragraph 1.

3. A State or organization which accedes to the present Protocol after 31 December 1993 may implement articles 2 and 4 no later than 31 December 1995.

4. The instruments of ratification, acceptance, approval or accession shall be deposited with the Secretary-General of the United Nations, who will perform the functions of depositary.

Article 15

Entry into force

1. The present Protocol shall enter into force on the ninetieth day following the date on which the sixteenth instrument of ratification, acceptance, approval or accession has been deposited.

2. For each State and organization referred to in article 13, paragraph 1, which ratifies, accepts or approves the present Protocol or accedes thereto after the deposit of the sixteenth instrument of ratification, acceptance, approval, or accession, the Proto-

col shall enter into force on the ninetieth day following the date of deposit by such Party of its instrument of ratification, acceptance, approval, or accession.

Article 16

Withdrawal

At any time after five years from the date on which the present Protocol has come into force with respect to a Party, that Party may withdraw from it by giving written notification to the depositary. Any such withdrawal shall take effect on the ninetieth day following the date of its receipt by the depositary, or on such later date as may be specified in the notification of the withdrawal.

Article 17

Authentic texts

The original of the present Protocol, of which the English, French and Russian texts are equally authentic, shall be deposited with the Secretary–General of the United Nations.

3.20 CONVENTION ON THE TRANSBOUNDARY EFFECTS OF INDUSTRIAL ACCIDENTS (With Annexes). Done at Helsinki, 17 March 1992. Not yet in force. Doc. ENVWA/R.54 and Add.1; *reprinted in* 31 I.L.M. 1330 (1992)

PREAMBLE

The Parties to this Convention,

Mindful of the special importance, in the interest of present and future generations, of protecting human beings and the environment against the effects of industrial accidents,

Recognizing the importance and urgency of preventing serious adverse effects of industrial accidents on human beings and the environment, and of promoting all measures that stimulate the rational, economic and efficient use of preventive, preparedness and response measures to enable environmentally sound and sustainable economic development,

Taking into account the fact that the effects of industrial accidents may make themselves felt across borders, and require cooperation among States,

Affirming the need to promote active international cooperation among the States concerned before, during and after an accident, to enhance appropriate policies and to reinforce and coordinate action at all appropriate levels for promoting the prevention of, preparedness for and response to the transboundary effects of industrial accidents,

Noting the importance and usefulness of bilateral and multilateral arrangements for the prevention of, preparedness for and response to the effects of industrial accidents,

Conscious of the role played in this respect by the United Nations Economic Commission for Europe (ECE) and recalling, inter alia, the ECE Code of Conduct on Accidental Pollution of Transboundary Inland Waters and the Convention on Environmental Impact Assessment in a Transboundary Context,

Having regard to the relevant provisions of the Final Act of the Conference on Security and Cooperation in Europe (CSCE), the Concluding Document of the Vienna Meeting of Representatives of the Participating States of the CSCE, and the outcome of the Sofia Meeting on the Protection of the Environment of the CSCE, as well as to pertinent activities and mechanisms in the United Nations Environment Programme (UNEP), in particular the APELL programme, in the International Labour Organisation (ILO), in particular the Code of Practice on the Prevention of Major Industrial Accidents, and in other relevant international organizations,

Considering the pertinent provisions of the Declaration of the United Nations Conference on the Human Environment, and in particular principle 21, according to which States have, in accordance with the Charter of the United Nations and the principles of international law, the sovereign right to exploit their own resources pursuant to their own environmental policies, and the responsibility to ensure that activities within their jurisdiction or control do not cause damage to the environment of other States or of areas beyond the limits of national jurisdiction,

Taking account of the polluter-pays principle as a general principle of international environmental law,

Underlining the principles of international law and custom, in particular the principles of good-neighbourliness, reciprocity, non-discrimination and good faith,

Have agreed as follows:

Article 1

DEFINITIONS

For the purposes of this Convention,

(a) "Industrial accident" means an event resulting from an uncontrolled development in the course of any activity involving hazardous substances either:

(i) In an installation, for example during manufacture, use, storage, handling, or disposal; or

(ii) During transportation in so far as it is covered by paragraph 2(d) of Article 2;

(b) "Hazardous activity" means any activity in which one or more hazardous substances are present or may be present in quantities at or in excess of the threshold quantities listed in Annex I hereto, and which is capable of causing transboundary effects;

(c) "Effects" means any direct or indirect, immediate or delayed adverse consequences caused by an industrial accident on, inter alia:

(i) Human beings, flora and fauna;

(ii) Soil, water, air and landscape;

(iii) The interaction between the factors in (i) and (ii);

(iv) Material assets and cultural heritage, including historical monuments;

(d) "Transboundary effects" means serious effects within the jurisdiction of a Party as a result of an industrial accident occurring within the jurisdiction of another Party;

(e) "Operator" means any natural or legal person, including public authorities, in charge of an activity, e.g. supervising, planning to carry out or carrying out an activity;

(f) "Party" means, unless the text otherwise indicates, a Contracting Party to this Convention;

(g) "Party of origin" means any Party or Parties under whose jurisdiction an industrial accident occurs or is capable of occurring;

(h) "Affected Party" means any Party or Parties affected or capable of being affected by transboundary effects of an industrial accident;

(i) "Parties concerned" means any Party of origin and any affected Party;

(j) "The public" means one or more natural or legal persons.

Article 2

SCOPE

1. This Convention shall apply to the prevention of, preparedness for and response to industrial accidents capable of causing transboundary effects, including the effects of such accidents caused by natural disasters, and to international cooperation concerning mutual assistance, research and development, exchange of information and exchange of technology in the area of prevention of, preparedness for and response to industrial accidents.

2. This Convention shall not apply to:

(a) Nuclear accidents or radiological emergencies;

(b) Accidents at military installations;

(c) Dam failures, with the exception of the effects of industrial accidents caused by such failures;

(d) Land-based transport accidents with the exception of:

(i) Emergency response to such accidents;

(ii) Transportation on the site of the hazardous activity;

(e) Accidental release of genetically modified organisms;

(f) Accidents caused by activities in the marine environment, including seabed exploration or exploitation;

(g) Spills of oil or other harmful substances at sea.

Article 3

GENERAL PROVISIONS

1. The Parties shall, taking into account efforts already made at national and international levels, take appropriate measures and cooperate within the framework of this Convention, to protect human beings and the environment against industrial accidents by preventing such accidents as far as possible, by reducing their frequency and severity and by mitigating their effects. To this end, preventive, preparedness and response measures, including restoration measures, shall be applied.

2. The Parties shall, by means of exchange of information, consultation and other cooperative measures and without undue delay, develop and implement policies and strategies for reducing the risks of industrial accidents and improving preventive, preparedness and response measures, including restoration measures, taking into account, in order to avoid unnecessary duplication, efforts already made at national and international levels.

3. The Parties shall ensure that the operator is obliged to take all measures necessary for the safe performance of the hazardous activity and for the prevention of industrial accidents.

4. To implement the provisions of this Convention, the Parties shall take appropriate legislative, regulatory, administrative and financial measures for the prevention of, preparedness for and response to industrial accidents.

5. The provisions of this Convention shall not prejudice any obligations of the Parties under international law with regard to industrial accidents and hazardous activities.

Article 4

IDENTIFICATION, CONSULTATION AND ADVICE

1. For the purpose of undertaking preventive measures and setting up preparedness measures, the Party of origin shall take measures, as appropriate, to identify hazardous activities within its jurisdiction and to ensure that affected Parties are notified of any such proposed or existing activity.

2. Parties concerned shall, at the initiative of any such Party, enter into discussions on the identification of those hazardous activities that are, reasonably, capable of causing transboundary effects. If the Parties concerned do not agree on whether an activity is such a hazardous activity, any such Party may, unless the Parties concerned agree on another method of resolving the question, submit that question to an inquiry commission in accordance with the provisions of Annex II hereto for advice,

3. The Parties shall, with respect to proposed or existing hazardous activities, apply the procedures set out in Annex III hereto.

4. When a hazardous activity is subject to an environmental impact assessment in accordance with the Convention on Environmental Impact Assessment in a Transboundary Context and that assessment includes an evaluation of the transboundary effects of industrial accidents from the hazardous activity which is performed in conformity with the terms of this Convention, the final decision taken for the purposes

of the Convention on Environmental Impact Assessment in a Transboundary Context shall fulfil the relevant requirements of this Convention.

Article 5

VOLUNTARY EXTENSION

Parties concerned should, at the initiative of any of them, enter into discussions on whether to treat an activity not covered by Annex I as a hazardous activity. Upon mutual agreement, they may use an advisory mechanism of their choice, or an inquiry commission in accordance with Annex II, to advise them. Where the Parties concerned so agree, this Convention, or any part thereof, shall apply to the activity in question as if it were a hazardous activity.

Article 6

PREVENTION

1. The Parties shall take appropriate measures for the prevention of industrial accidents, including measures to induce action by operators to reduce the risk of industrial accidents. Such measures may include, but are not limited to those referred to in Annex IV hereto.

2. With regard to any hazardous activity, the Party of origin shall require the operator to demonstrate the safe performance of the hazardous activity by the provision of information such as basic details of the process, including but not limited to, analysis and evaluation as detailed in Annex V hereto.

Article 7

DECISION–MAKING ON SITING

Within the framework of its legal system, the Party of origin shall, with the objective of minimizing the risk to the population and the environment of all affected Parties, seek the establishment of policies on the siting of new hazardous activities and on significant modifications to existing hazardous activities. Within the framework of their legal systems, the affected Parties shall seek the establishment of policies on significant developments in areas which could be affected by transboundary effects of an industrial accident arising out of a hazardous activity so as to minimize the risks involved. In elaborating and establishing these policies, the Parties should consider the matters set out in Annex V, paragraph 2, subparagraphs (1) to (8), and Annex VI hereto.

Article 8

EMERGENCY PREPAREDNESS

1. The Parties shall take appropriate measures to establish and maintain adequate emergency preparedness to respond to industrial accidents. The Parties shall ensure that preparedness measures are taken to mitigate transboundary effects of such accidents, on-site duties being undertaken by operators. These measures may include, but are not limited to those referred to in Annex VII hereto. In particular, the Parties concerned shall inform each other of their contingency plans.

2. The Party of origin shall ensure for hazardous activities the preparation and implementation of on-site contingency plans, including suitable measures for response and other measures to prevent and minimize transboundary effects. The Party of origin shall provide to the other Parties concerned the elements it has for the elaboration of contingency plans.

3. Each Party shall ensure for hazardous activities the preparation and implementation of off-site contingency plans covering measures to be taken within its

territory to prevent and minimize transboundary effects. In preparing these plans, account shall be taken of the conclusions of analysis and evaluation, in particular the matters set out in Annex V, paragraph 2, subparagraphs (1) to (5). Parties concerned shall endeavour to make such plans compatible. Where appropriate, joint off-site contingency plans shall be drawn up in order to facilitate the adoption of adequate response measures.

4. Contingency plans should be reviewed regularly, or when circumstances so require, taking into account the experience gained in dealing with actual emergencies.

Article 9

INFORMATION TO, AND PARTICIPATION OF THE PUBLIC

1. The Parties shall ensure that adequate information is given to the public in the areas capable of being affected by an industrial accident arising out of a hazardous activity. This information shall be transmitted through such channels as the Parties deem appropriate, shall include the elements contained in Annex VIII hereto and should take into account matters set out in Annex V, paragraph 2, subparagraphs (1) to (4) and (9).

2. The Party of origin shall, in accordance with the provisions of this Convention and whenever possible and appropriate, give the public in the areas capable of being affected an opportunity to participate in relevant procedures with the aim of making known its views and concerns on prevention and preparedness measures, and shall ensure that the opportunity given to the public of the affected Party is equivalent to that given to the public of the Party of origin.

3. The Parties shall, in accordance with their legal systems and, if desired, on a reciprocal basis provide natural or legal persons who are being or are capable of being adversely affected by the transboundary effects of an industrial accident in the territory of a Party, with access to, and treatment in the relevant administrative and judicial proceedings, including the possibilities of starting a legal action and appealing a decision affecting their rights, equivalent to those available to persons within their own jurisdiction.

Article 10

INDUSTRIAL ACCIDENT NOTIFICATION SYSTEMS

1. The Parties shall, with the aim of obtaining and transmitting industrial accident notifications containing information needed to counteract transboundary effects, provide for the establishment and operation of compatible and efficient industrial accident notification systems at appropriate levels.

2. In the event of an industrial accident, or imminent threat thereof, which causes or is capable of causing transboundary effects, the Party of origin shall ensure that affected Parties are, without delay, notified at appropriate levels through the industrial accident notification systems. Such notification shall include the elements contained in Annex IX hereto.

3. The Parties concerned shall ensure that, in the event of an industrial accident or imminent threat thereof, the contingency plans prepared in accordance with Article 8 are activated as soon as possible and to the extent appropriate to the circumstances.

Article 11

RESPONSE

1. The Parties shall ensure that, in the event of an industrial accident, or imminent threat thereof, adequate response measures are taken, as soon as possible and using the most efficient practices, to contain and minimize effects.

2. In the event of an industrial accident, or imminent threat thereof, which causes or is capable of causing transboundary effects, the Parties concerned shall ensure that the effects are assessed—where appropriate, jointly for the purpose of taking adequate response measures. The Parties concerned shall endeavour to coordinate their response measures.

Article 12

MUTUAL ASSISTANCE

1. If a Party needs assistance in the event of an industrial accident, it may ask for assistance from other Parties, indicating the scope and type of assistance required. A Party to whom a request for assistance is directed shall promptly decide and inform the requesting Party whether it is in a position to render the assistance required and indicate the scope and terms of the assistance that might be rendered.

2. The Parties concerned shall cooperate to facilitate the prompt provision of assistance agreed to under paragraph 1 of this Article, including, where appropriate, action to minimize the consequences and effects of the industrial accident, and to provide general assistance. Where Parties do not have bilateral or multilateral agreements which cover their arrangements for providing mutual assistance, the assistance shall be rendered in accordance with Annex X hereto, unless the Parties agree otherwise.

Article 13

RESPONSIBILITY AND LIABILITY

The Parties shall support appropriate international efforts to elaborate rules, criteria and procedures in the field of responsibility and liability.

Article 14

RESEARCH AND DEVELOPMENT

The Parties shall, as appropriate, initiate and cooperate in the conduct of research into, and in the development of methods and technologies for the prevention of, preparedness for and response to industrial accidents. For these purposes, the Parties shall encourage and actively promote scientific and technological cooperation, including research into less hazardous processes aimed at limiting accident hazards and preventing and limiting the consequences of industrial accidents.

Article 15

EXCHANGE OF INFORMATION

The Parties shall, at the multilateral or bilateral level, exchange reasonably obtainable information, including the elements contained in Annex XI hereto.

Article 16

EXCHANGE OF TECHNOLOGY

1. The Parties shall, consistent with their laws, regulations and practices, facilitate the exchange of technology for the prevention of, preparedness for and response to the effects of industrial accidents, particularly through the promotion of:

(a) Exchange of available technology on various financial bases;

(b) Direct industrial contacts and cooperation;

(c) Exchange of information and experience;

(d) Provision of technical assistance.

2. In promoting the activities specified in paragraph 1, subparagraphs (a) to (d) of this Article, the Parties shall create favourable conditions by facilitating contacts and cooperation among appropriate organizations and individuals in both the private and the public sectors that are capable of providing technology, design and engineering services, equipment or finance.

Article 17

COMPETENT AUTHORITIES AND POINTS OF CONTACT

1. Each Party shall designate or establish one or more competent authorities for the purposes of this Convention.

2. Without prejudice to other arrangements at the bilateral or multilateral level, each Party shall designate or establish one point of contact for the purpose of industrial accident notifications pursuant to Article 10, and one point of contact for the purpose of mutual assistance pursuant to Article 12. These points of contact should preferably be the same.

3. Each Party shall, within three months of the date of entry into force of this Convention for that Party, inform the other Parties, through the secretariat referred to in Article 20, which body or bodies it has designated as its point(s) of contact and as its competent authority or authorities.

4. Each Party shall, within one month of the date of decision, inform the other Parties, through the secretariat, of any changes regarding the designation(s) it has made under paragraph 3 of this Article.

5. Each Party shall keep its point of contact and industrial accident notification systems pursuant to Article 10 operational at all times.

6. Each Party shall keep its point of contact and the authorities responsible for making and receiving requests for, and accepting offers of assistance pursuant to Article 12 operational at all times.

Article 18

CONFERENCE OF THE PARTIES

1. The representatives of the Parties shall constitute the Conference of the Parties of this Convention and hold their meetings on a regular basis. The first meeting of the Conference of the Parties shall be convened not later than one year after the date of the entry into force of this Convention. Thereafter, a meeting of the Conference of the Parties shall be held at least once a year or at the written request of any Party, provided that, within six months of the request being communicated to them by the secretariat, it is supported by at least one third of the Parties.

2. The Conference of the Parties shall:

(a) Review the implementation of this Convention;

(b) Carry out advisory functions aimed at strengthening the ability of Parties to prevent, prepare for and respond to the transboundary effects of industrial accidents, and at facilitating the provision of technical assistance and advice at the request of Parties faced with industrial accidents;

(c) Establish, as appropriate, working groups and other appropriate mechanisms to consider matters related to the implementation and development of this Convention and, to this end, to prepare appropriate studies and other documentation and submit recommendations for consideration by the Conference of the Parties;

(d) Fulfil such other functions as may be appropriate under the provisions of this Convention;

(e) At its first meeting, consider and, by consensus, adopt rules of procedure for its meetings.

3. The Conference of the Parties, in discharging its functions, shall, when it deems appropriate, also cooperate with other relevant international organizations.

4. The Conference of the Parties shall, at its first meeting, establish a programme of work, in particular with regard to the items contained in Annex XII hereto. The Conference of the Parties shall also decide on the method of work, including the use of national centres and cooperation with relevant international organizations and the establishment of a system with a view to facilitating the implementation of this Convention, in particular for mutual assistance in the event of an industrial accident, and building upon pertinent existing activities within relevant international organizations. As part of the programme of work, the Conference of the Parties shall review existing national, regional and international centres, and other bodies and programmes aimed at coordinating information and efforts in the prevention of, preparedness for and response to industrial accidents, with a view to determining what additional international institutions or centres may be needed to carry out the tasks listed in Annex XII.

5. The Conference of the Parties shall, at its first meeting, commence consideration of procedures to create more favourable conditions for the exchange of technology for the prevention of, preparedness for and response to the effects of industrial accidents.

6. The Conference of the Parties shall adopt guidelines and criteria to facilitate the identification of hazardous activities for the purposes of this Convention.

Article 19

RIGHT TO VOTE

1. Except as provided for in paragraph 2 of this Article, each Party to this Convention shall have one vote.

2. Regional economic integration organizations as defined in Article 27 shall, in matters within their competence, exercise their right to vote with a number of votes equal to the number of their member States which are Parties to this Convention. Such organizations shall not exercise their right to vote if their member States exercise theirs, and vice versa.

Article 20

SECRETARIAT

The Executive Secretary of the Economic Commission for Europe shall carry out the following secretariat functions:

(a) Convene and prepare meetings of the Parties;

(b) Transmit to the Parties reports and other information received in accordance with the provisions of this Convention;

(c) Such other functions as may be determined by the Parties.

Article 21

SETTLEMENT OF DISPUTES

1. If a dispute arises between two or more Parties about the interpretation or application of this Convention, they shall seek a solution by negotiation or by any other method of dispute settlement acceptable to the parties to the dispute.

2. When signing, ratifying, accepting, approving or acceding to this Convention, or at any time thereafter, a Party may declare in writing to the Depositary that, for a

dispute not resolved in accordance with paragraph 1 of this Article, it accepts one or both of the following means of dispute settlement as compulsory in relation to any Party accepting the same obligation:

(a) Submission of the dispute to the International Court of Justice;

(b) Arbitration in accordance with the procedure set out in Annex XIII hereto.

3. If the parties to the dispute have accepted both means of dispute settlement referred to in paragraph 2 of this Article, the dispute may be submitted only to the International Court of Justice, unless the parties to the dispute agree otherwise.

Article 22

LIMITATIONS ON THE SUPPLY OF INFORMATION

1. The provisions of this Convention shall not affect the rights or the obligations of Parties in accordance with their national laws, regulations, administrative provisions or accepted legal practices and applicable international regulations to protect information related to personal data, industrial and commercial secrecy, including intellectual property, or national security.

2. If a Party nevertheless decides to supply such protected information to another Party, the Party receiving such protected information shall respect the confidentiality of the information received and the conditions under which it is supplied, and shall only use that information for the purposes for which it was supplied.

Article 23

IMPLEMENTATION

The Parties shall report periodically on the implementation of this Convention.

Article 24

BILATERAL AND MULTILATERAL AGREEMENTS

1. The Parties may, in order to implement their obligations under this Convention, continue existing or enter into new bilateral or multilateral agreements or other arrangements.

2. The provisions of this Convention shall not affect the right of Parties to take, by bilateral or multilateral agreement where appropriate, more stringent measures than those required by this Convention.

Article 25

STATUS OF ANNEXES

The Annexes to this Convention form an integral part of the Convention.

Article 26

AMENDMENTS TO THE CONVENTION

1. Any Party may propose amendments to this Convention.

2. The text of any proposed amendment to this Convention shall be submitted in writing to the Executive Secretary of the Economic Commission for Europe, who shall circulate it to all Parties. The Conference of the Parties shall discuss proposed amendments at its next annual meeting, provided that such proposals have been circulated to the Parties by the Executive Secretary of the Economic Commission for Europe at least ninety days in advance.

3. For amendments to this Convention—other than those to Annex I, for which the procedure is described in paragraph 4 of this Article:

(a) Amendments shall be adopted by consensus of the Parties present at the meeting and shall be submitted by the Depositary to all Parties for ratification, acceptance or approval;

(b) Instruments of ratification, acceptance or approval of amendments shall be deposited with the Depositary. Amendments adopted in accordance with this Article shall enter into force for Parties that have accepted them on the ninetieth day following the day of receipt by the Depositary of the sixteenth instrument of ratification, acceptance or approval;

(c) Thereafter, amendments shall enter into force for any other Party on the ninetieth day after that Party deposits its instruments of ratification, acceptance or approval of the amendments.

4. For amendments to Annex I:

(a) The Parties shall make every effort to reach agreement by consensus. If all efforts at consensus have been exhausted and no agreement reached, the amendments shall, as a last resort, be adopted by a nine-tenths majority vote of the Parties present and voting at the meeting. If adopted by the Conference of the Parties, the amendments shall be communicated to the Parties and recommended for approval;

(b) On the expiry of twelve months from the date of their communication by the Executive Secretary of the Economic Commission for Europe, the amendments to Annex I shall become effective for those Parties to this Convention which have not submitted a notification in accordance with the provisions of paragraph 4(c) of this Article, provided that at least sixteen Parties have not submitted such a notification;

(c) Any Party that is unable to approve an amendment to Annex I of this Convention shall so notify the Executive Secretary of the Economic Commission for Europe in writing within twelve months from the date of the communication of the adoption. The Executive Secretary shall without delay notify all Parties of any such notification received. A Party may at any time substitute an acceptance for its previous notification and the amendment to Annex I shall thereupon enter into force for that Party.

(d) For the purpose of this paragraph "Parties present and voting" means Parties present and casting an affirmative or negative vote.

Article 27

SIGNATURE

This Convention shall be open for signature at Helsinki from 17 to 18 March 1992 inclusive, and thereafter at United Nations Headquarters in New York until 18 September 1992, by States members of the Economic Commission for Europe, as well as States having consultative status with the Economic Commission for Europe pursuant to paragraph 8 of Economic and Social Council resolution 36 (IV) of 28 March 1947, and by regional economic integration organizations constituted by sovereign States members of the Economic Commission for Europe to which their member States have transferred competence in respect of matters governed by this Convention, including the competence to enter into treaties in respect of these matters.

Article 28

DEPOSITARY

The Secretary–General of the United Nations shall act as the Depositary of this Convention.

Article 29

RATIFICATION, ACCEPTANCE, APPROVAL AND ACCESSION

1. This Convention shall be subject to ratification, acceptance or approval by the signatory States and regional economic integration organizations referred to in Article 27.

2. This Convention shall be open for accession by the States and organizations referred to in Article 27.

3. Any organization referred to in Article 27 which becomes Party to this Convention without any of its member States being a Party shall be bound by all the obligations under this Convention. In the case of such organizations, one or more of whose member States is a Party to this Convention, the organization and its member States shall decide on their respective responsibilities for the performance of their obligations under this Convention. In such cases, the organization and the member States shall not be entitled to exercise rights under this Convention concurrently.

4. In their instruments of ratification, acceptance, approval or accession, the regional economic integration organizations referred to in Article 27 shall declare the extent of their competence with respect to the matters governed by this Convention. These organizations shall also inform the Depositary of any substantial modification to the extent of their competence.

Article 30

ENTRY INTO FORCE

1. This Convention shall enter into force on the ninetieth day after the date of deposit of the sixteenth instrument of ratification, acceptance, approval or accession.

2. For the purposes of paragraph 1 of this Article, any instrument deposited by an organization referred to in Article 27 shall not be counted as additional to those deposited by States members of such an organization.

3. For each State or organization referred to in Article 27 which ratifies, accepts or approves this Convention or accedes thereto after the deposit of the sixteenth instrument of ratification, acceptance, approval or accession, this Convention shall enter into force on the ninetieth day after the date of deposit by such State or organization of its instrument of ratification, acceptance, approval or accession.

Article 31

WITHDRAWAL

1. At any time after three years from the date on which this Convention has come into force with respect to a Party, that Party may withdraw from this Convention by giving written notification to the Depositary. Any such withdrawal shall take effect on the ninetieth day after the date of the receipt of the notification by the Depositary.

2. Any such withdrawal shall not affect the application of Article 4 to an activity in respect of which a notification has been made pursuant to Article 4, paragraph 1, or a request for discussions has been made pursuant to Article 4, paragraph 2.

Article 32

AUTHENTIC TEXTS

The original of this Convention, of which the English, French and Russian texts are equally authentic, shall be deposited with the Secretary-General of the United Nations.

IN WITNESS WHEREOF the undersigned, being duly authorized thereto, have signed this Convention.

DONE at Helsinki, this seventeenth day of March one thousand nine hundred and ninety-two.

ANNEX I

HAZARDOUS SUBSTANCES FOR THE PURPOSES OF DEFINING HAZARDOUS ACTIVITIES

The quantities set out below relate to each activity or group of activities. Where a range of quantities is given in Part I, the threshold quantities are the maximum quantities given in each range. Five years after the entry into force of this Convention, the lowest quantity given in each range shall become the threshold quantity, unless amended.

Where a substance or preparation named in Part II also falls within a category in Part I, the threshold quantity set out in Part II shall be used.

For the identification of hazardous activities, Parties shall take into consideration the foreseeable possibility of aggravation of the hazards involved and the quantities of the hazardous substances and their proximity, whether under the charge of one or more operators.

PART I. Categories of substances and preparations not specifically named in Part II

Category	Threshold Quantity (Tonnes)
1. Flammable gases . . . including LPG	200
2. Highly flammable liquids	50,000
3. Very toxic	20
4. Toxic	500–200
5. Oxidizing	500–200
6. Explosive	200–50
7. Flammable liquids (handled under special conditions of pressure and temperature)	200
8. Dangerous for the environment	200

FLAMMABLE GASES: substances which in the gaseous state at normal pressure and mixed with air become flammable and the boiling point of which at normal pressure is 20° C or below;

HIGHLY FLAMMABLE LIQUIDS: substances which have a flash point lower than 21° C and the boiling point of which at normal pressure is above 20° C;

VERY TOXIC: substances . . . owing to their physical and chemical properties, are capable of creating industrial accident hazards.

OXIDIZING: substances which give rise to highly exothermic reaction when in contact with other substances, particularly flammable substances.

EXPLOSIVE: substances which may explode under the effect of flame or which are more sensitive to shocks or friction than dinitrobenzene.

FLAMMABLE LIQUIDS: substances which have a flash point lower than 55° C and which remain liquid under pressure, where particular processing conditions, such as high pressure and high temperature, may create industrial accident hazards.

DANGEROUS FOR THE ENVIRONMENT: substances showing the values for acute toxicity to the aquatic environment. . . .

PART II. Named substances

	Substance	Threshold Quantity (Tonnes)
1.	Ammonia	500
2a.	Ammonium nitrate	2,500
2b.	Ammonium nitrate in the form of fertilizers	10,000
3.	Acrylonitrile	200
4.	Chlorine	25
5.	Ethylene oxide	50
6.	Hydrogen cyanide	20
7.	Hydrogen fluoride	50
8.	Hydrogen sulphide	50
9.	Sulphur dioxide	250
10.	Sulphur trioxide	75
11.	Lead alkyls	50
12.	Phosgene	0.75
13.	Methyl isocyanate	0.15

ANNEX II

INQUIRY COMMISSION PROCEDURE PURSUANT TO ARTICLES 4 AND 5

1. The requesting Party or Parties shall notify the secretariat that it or they is (are) submitting question(s) to an inquiry commission established in accordance with the provisions of this Annex. The notification shall state the subject-matter of the inquiry. The secretariat shall immediately inform all Parties to the Convention of this submission.

2. The inquiry commission shall consist of three members. Both the requesting party and the other party to the inquiry procedure shall appoint a scientific or technical expert and the two experts so appointed shall designate by common agreement a third expert, who shall be the president of the inquiry commission. The latter shall not be a national of one of the parties to the inquiry procedure, nor have his or her usual place of residence in the territory of one of these parties, nor be employed by any of them, nor have dealt with the case in any other capacity.

3. If the president of the inquiry commission has not been designated within two months of the appointment of the second expert, the Executive Secretary of the Economic Commission for Europe shall, at the request of either party, designate the president within a further two-month period.

4. If one of the parties to the inquiry procedure does not appoint an expert within one month of its receipt of the notification by the secretariat, the other party may inform the Executive Secretary of the Economic Commission for Europe, who shall designate the president of the inquiry commission within a further two-month period. Upon designation, the president of the inquiry commission shall request the party which has not appointed an expert to do so within one month. If it fails to do so within that period, the president shall inform the Executive Secretary of the Economic Commission for Europe who shall make this appointment within a further two-month period.

5. The inquiry commission shall adopt its own rules of procedure.

6. The inquiry commission may take all appropriate measures in order to carry out its functions.

7. The parties to the inquiry procedure shall facilitate the work of the inquiry commission and in particular shall, using all means at their disposal:

(a) Provide the inquiry commission with all relevant documents, facilities and information;

(b) Enable the inquiry commission, where necessary, to call witnesses or experts and receive their evidence.

8. The parties and the experts shall protect the confidentiality of any information they receive in confidence during the work of the inquiry commission.

9. If one of the parties to the inquiry procedure does not appear before the inquiry commission or fails to present its case, the other party may request the inquiry commission to continue the proceedings and to complete its work. Absence of a party or failure of a party to present its case shall not constitute a bar to the continuation and completion of the work of the inquiry commission.

10. Unless the inquiry commission determines otherwise because of the particular circumstances of the matter, the expenses of the inquiry commission, including the remuneration of its members, shall be borne equally by the parties to the inquiry procedure. The inquiry commission shall keep a record of all its expenses and shall furnish a final statement thereof to the parties.

11. Any Party which has an interest of a factual nature in the subject-matter of the inquiry procedure and which may be affected by an opinion in the matter may intervene in the proceedings with the consent of the inquiry commission.

12. The decisions of the inquiry commission on matters of the procedure shall be taken by majority vote of its members. The final opinion of the inquiry commission shall reflect the view of the majority of its members and shall include any dissenting view.

13. The inquiry commission shall present its final opinion within two months of the date on which it was established, unless it finds it necessary to extend this time-limit for a period which should not exceed two months.

14. The final opinion of the inquiry commission shall be based on accepted scientific principles. The final opinion shall be transmitted by the inquiry commission to the parties to the inquiry procedure and to the secretariat.

ANNEX III

PROCEDURES PURSUANT TO ARTICLE 4

1. A Party of origin may request consultations with another Party, in accordance with paragraphs 2 to 5 of this Annex, in order to determine whether that Party is an affected Party.

2. For a proposed or existing hazardous activity, the Party of origin shall, for the purposes of ensuring adequate and effective consultations, provide for the notification at appropriate levels of any Party that it considers may be an affected Party as early as possible and no later than when informing its own public about that proposed or existing activity. For existing hazardous activities such notification shall be provided no later than two years after the entry into force of this Convention for a Party of origin.

3. The notification shall contain, inter alia:

(a) Information on the hazardous activity, including any available information or report, such as information produced in accordance with Article 6, on its possible transboundary effects in the event of an industrial accident;

(b) An indication of a reasonable time within which a response under paragraph 4 of this Annex is required, taking into account the nature of the activity; and may include the information set out in paragraph 6 of this Annex.

4. The notified Parties shall respond to the Party of origin within the time specified in the notification, acknowledging receipt of the notification and indicating whether they intend to enter into consultation.

5. If a notified Party indicates that it does not intend to enter into consultation, or if it does not respond within the time specified in the notification, the provisions set down in the following paragraphs of this Annex shall not apply. In such circumstances, the right of a Party of origin to determine whether to carry out an assessment and analysis on the basis of its national law and practice is not prejudiced.

6. Upon receipt of a response from a notified Party indicating its desire to enter into consultation, the Party of origin shall, if it has not already done so, provide to the notified Party:

(a) Relevant information regarding the time schedule for analysis, including an indication of the time schedule for the transmittal of comments;

(b) Relevant information on the hazardous activity and its transboundary effects in the event of an industrial accident;

(c) The opportunity to participate in evaluations of the information or any report demonstrating possible transboundary effects.

7. An affected Party shall, at the request of the Party of origin, provide the latter with reasonably obtainable information relating to the area under the jurisdiction of the affected Party capable of being affected, where such information is necessary for the preparation of the assessment and analysis and measures. The information shall be furnished promptly and, as appropriate, through a joint body where one exists.

8. The Party of origin shall furnish the affected Party directly, as appropriate, or, where one exists, through a joint body with the analysis and evaluation documentation as described in Annex V, paragraphs 1 and 2.

9. The Parties concerned shall inform the public in areas reasonably capable of being affected by the hazardous activity and shall arrange for the distribution of the analysis and evaluation documentation to it and to authorities in the relevant areas. The Parties shall ensure them an opportunity for making comments on, or objections to, the hazardous activity and shall arrange for their views to be submitted to the competent authority of the Party of origin, either directly to that authority or, where appropriate, through the Party of origin, within a reasonable time.

10. The Party of origin shall, after completion of the analysis and evaluation documentation, enter without undue delay into consultations with the affected Party concerning, inter alia, the transboundary effects of the hazardous activity in the event of an industrial accident, and measures to reduce or eliminate its effects. The consultations may relate to:

(a) Possible alternatives to the hazardous activity, including the no-action alternative, and possible measures to mitigate transboundary effects at the expense of the Party of origin;

(b) Other forms of possible mutual assistance for reducing any transboundary effects;

(c) Any other appropriate matters.

The Parties concerned shall, on the commencement of such consultations, agree on a reasonable time-frame for the duration of the consultation period. Any such consultations may be conducted through an appropriate joint body, where one exists.

11. The Parties concerned shall ensure that due account is taken of the analysis and evaluation, as well as of the comments received pursuant to paragraph 9 of this Annex and of the outcome of the consultations referred to in paragraph 10 of this Annex.

12. The Party of origin shall notify the affected Parties of any decision on the activity, along with the reasons and considerations on which it was based.

13. If, after additional and relevant information concerning the transboundary effects of a hazardous activity and which was not available at the time consultations were held with respect to that activity, becomes available to a Party concerned, that Party shall immediately inform the other Party or Parties concerned. If one of the Parties concerned so requests, renewed consultations shall be held.

ANNEX IV

PREVENTIVE MEASURES PURSUANT TO ARTICLE 6

The following measures may be carried out, depending on national laws and practices, by Parties, competent authorities, operators, or by joint efforts:

1. The setting of general or specific safety objectives;

2. The adoption of legislative provisions or guidelines concerning safety measures and safety standards;

3. The identification of those hazardous activities which require special preventive measures, which may include a licensing or authorization system;

4. The evaluation of risk analyses or of safety studies for hazardous activities and an action plan for the implementation of necessary measures,

5. The provision to the competent authorities of the information needed to assess risks;

6. The application of the most appropriate technology in order to prevent industrial accidents and protect human beings and the environment;

7. The undertaking, in order to prevent industrial accidents, of the appropriate education and training of all persons engaged in hazardous activities on-site under both normal and abnormal conditions;

8. The establishment of internal managerial structures and practices designed to implement and maintain safety regulations effectively;

9. The monitoring and auditing of hazardous activities and the carrying out of inspections.

ANNEX V

ANALYSIS AND EVALUATION

1. The analysis and evaluation of the hazardous activity should be performed with a scope and to a depth which vary depending on the purpose for which they are carried out.

2. The following table illustrates, for the purposes of the related Articles, matters which should be considered in the analysis and evaluation, for the purposes listed: Purpose of analysis Emergency planning under Article 8

Matters to be considered:

(1) The quantities and properties of hazardous substances on the site;

(2) Brief descriptive scenarios of a representative sample of industrial accidents possibly arising from the hazardous activity, including an indication of the likelihood of each;

(3) For each scenario:

(a) The approximate quantity of a release;

(b) The extent and severity of the resulting consequences both for people and for the non-human environment in favourable and unfavourable conditions, including the extent of resulting hazard zones;

(c) The time-scale within which the industrial accident could develop from the initiating event;

(d) Any action which could be taken to minimize the likelihood of escalation.

(4) The size and distribution of the population in the vicinity, including any large concentrations of people potentially in the hazard zone;

(5) The age, mobility and susceptibility of that population.

Decision-making on siting under Article 7

In addition to items (1) to (5) above:

(6) The severity of the harm inflicted on people and the environment, depending on the nature and circumstances of the release;

(7) The distance from the location of the hazardous activity at which harmful effects on people and the environment may reasonably occur in the event of an industrial accident;

(8) The same information not only for the present situation but also for planned or reasonably foreseeable future developments.

Information to the public under Article 9

In addition to items (1) to (4) above:

(9) The people who may be affected by an industrial accident.

Preventive measures under Article 6

In addition to items (4) to (9) above, more detailed versions of the descriptions and assessments set out in items (1) to (3) will be needed for preventive measures. In addition to those descriptions and assessments, the following matters should also be covered:

(10) The conditions and quantities in which hazardous materials are handled;

(11) A list of the scenarios for the types of industrial accidents with serious effects, to include examples covering the full range of incident size and the possibility of effects from adjacent activities;

(12) For each scenario, a description of the events which could initiate an industrial accident and the steps whereby it could escalate;

(13) An assessment, at least in general terms, of the likelihood of each step occurring, taking into account the arrangements in (14);

(14) A description of the preventive measures in terms of both equipment and procedures designed to minimize the likelihood of each step occurring;

(15) An assessment of the effects that deviations from normal operating conditions could have, and the consequent arrangements for safe shut-down of the hazardous activity or any part thereof in an emergency, and of the need for staff training to ensure that potentially serious deviations are recognized at an early stage and appropriate action taken;

(16) An assessment of the extent to which modifications, repair work and maintenance work on the hazardous activity could place the control measures at risk, and the consequent arrangements to ensure that control is maintained.

ANNEX VI

DECISION–MAKING ON SITING PURSUANT TO ARTICLE 7

The following illustrates the matters which should be considered pursuant to Article 7:

1. The results of risk analysis and evaluation, including an evaluation pursuant to Annex V of the physical characteristics of the area in which the hazardous activity is being planned;

2. The results of consultations and public participation processes;

3. An analysis of the increase or decrease of the risk caused by any development in the territory of the affected Party in relation to an existing hazardous activity in the territory of the Party of origin;

4. The evaluation of the environmental risks, including any transboundary effects;

5. An evaluation of the new hazardous activities which could be a source of risk;

6. A consideration of the siting of new, and significant modifications to existing hazardous activities at a safe distance from existing centres of population, as well as the establishment of a safety area around hazardous activities, within such areas, developments which would increase the populations at risk, or otherwise increase the severity of the risk, should be closely examined.

ANNEX VII

EMERGENCY PREPAREDNESS MEASURES PURSUANT TO ARTICLE 8

1. All contingency plans, both on-and off-site, should be coordinated to provide a comprehensive and effective response to industrial accidents.

2. The contingency plans should include the actions necessary to localize emergencies and to prevent or minimize their transboundary effects. They should also include arrangements for warning people and, where appropriate, arrangements for their evacuation, other protective or rescue actions and health services.

3. Contingency plans should give on-site personnel, people who might be affected off site and rescue forces, details of technical and organizational procedures which are appropriate for response in the event of an industrial accident capable of having transboundary effects and to prevent and minimize effects on people and the environment, both on and off site.

4. Examples of matters which could be covered by on-site contingency plans include:

(a) Organizational roles and responsibilities on site for dealing with an emergency;

(b) A description of the action which should be taken in the event of an industrial accident, or an imminent threat thereof, in order to control the condition or event, or details of where such a description can be found;

(c) A description of the equipment and resources available;

(d) Arrangements for providing early warning of industrial accidents to the public authority responsible for the off-site emergency response, including the type of information which should be included in an initial warning and the arrangements for providing more detailed information as it becomes available;

(e) Arrangements for training personnel in the duties they will be expected to perform.

5. Examples of matters which could be covered by off-site contingency plans include:

(a) Organizational roles and responsibilities off-site for dealing with an emergency, including how integration with on-site plans is to be achieved;

(b) Methods and procedures to be followed by emergency and medical personnel;

(c) Methods for rapidly determining the affected area;

(d) Arrangements for ensuring that prompt industrial accident notification is made to affected or potentially affected Parties and that that liaison is maintained subsequently;

(e) Identification of resources necessary to implement the plan and the arrangements for coordination;

(f) Arrangements for providing information to the public including, where appropriate, the arrangements for reinforcing and repeating the information provided to the public pursuant to article 9;

(g) Arrangements for training and exercises.

6. Contingency plans could include the measures for: treatment; collection; clean-up; storage; removal and safe disposal of hazardous substances and contaminated material; and restoration.

ANNEX VIII

INFORMATION TO THE PUBLIC PURSUANT TO ARTICLE 9

1. The name of the company, address of the hazardous activity and identification by position held of the person giving the information;

2. An explanation in simple terms of the hazardous activity, including the risks;

3. The common names or the generic names or the general danger classification of the substances and preparations which are involved in the hazardous activity, with an indication of their principal dangerous characteristics;

4. General information resulting from an environmental impact assessment, if available and relevant;

5. The general information relating to the nature of an industrial accident that could possibly occur in the hazardous activity, including its potential effects on the population and the environment;

6. Adequate information on how the affected population will be warned and kept informed in the event of an industrial accident;

7. Adequate information on the actions the affected population should take and on the behaviour they should adopt in the event of an industrial accident;

8. Adequate information on arrangements made regarding the hazardous activity, including liaison with the emergency services, to deal with industrial accidents, to reduce the severity of the industrial accidents and to mitigate their effects;

9. General information on the emergency services' off-site contingency plan, drawn up to cope with any off-site effects, including the transboundary effects of an industrial accident;

10. General information on special requirements and conditions to which the hazardous activity is subject according to the relevant national regulations and/or administrative provisions, including licensing or authorization systems;

11. Details of where further relevant information can be obtained.

ANNEX IX

INDUSTRIAL ACCIDENT NOTIFICATION SYSTEMS PURSUANT TO ARTICLE 10

1. The industrial accident notification systems shall enable the speediest possible transmission of data and forecasts according to previously determined codes using compatible data-transmission and data-treatment systems for emergency warning and response, and for measures to minimize and contain the consequences of transboundary effects, taking account of different needs at different levels.

2. The industrial accident notification shall include the following:

(a) The type and magnitude of the industrial accident, the hazardous substances involved (if known), and the severity of its possible effects;

(b) The time of occurrence and exact location of the accident;

(c) Such other available information as necessary for an efficient response to the industrial accident.

3. The industrial accident notification shall be supplemented at appropriate intervals, or whenever required, by further relevant information on the development of the situation concerning transboundary effects.

4. Regular tests and reviews of the effectiveness of the industrial accident notification systems shall be undertaken, including the regular training of the personnel involved. Where appropriate, such tests, reviews and training shall be performed jointly.

ANNEX X

MUTUAL ASSISTANCE PURSUANT TO ARTICLE 12

1. The overall direction, control, coordination and supervision of the assistance is the responsibility of the requesting Party. The personnel involved in the assisting operation shall act in accordance with the relevant laws of the requesting Party. The appropriate authorities of the requesting Party shall cooperate with the authority designated by the assisting Party, pursuant to Article 17, as being in charge of the immediate operational supervision of the personnel and the equipment provided by the assisting Party.

2. The requesting Party shall, to the extent of its capabilities, provide local facilities and services for the proper and effective administration of the assistance, and shall ensure the protection of personnel, equipment and materials brought into its territory by, or on behalf of, the assisting Party for such a purpose.

3. Unless otherwise agreed by the Parties concerned, assistance shall be provided at the expense of the requesting Party. The assisting Party may at any time waive wholly or partly the reimbursement of costs.

4. The requesting Party shall use its best efforts to afford to the assisting Party and persons acting on its behalf the privileges, immunities or facilities necessary for the expeditious performance of their assistance functions. The requesting Party shall not be required to apply this provision to its own nationals or permanent residents or to afford them the privileges and immunities referred to above.

5. A Party shall, at the request of the requesting or assisting Party, endeavour to facilitate the transit through its territory of duly notified personnel, equipment and property involved in the assistance to and from the requesting Party.

6. The requesting Party shall facilitate the entry into, stay in and departure from its national territory of duly notified personnel and of equipment and property involved in the assistance.

7. With regard to acts resulting directly from the assistance provided, the requesting Party shall, in respect of the death of or injury to persons, damage to or loss of property, or damage to the environment caused within its territory in the course of the provision of the assistance requested, hold harmless and indemnify the assisting Party or persons acting on its behalf and compensate them for death or injury suffered by them and for loss of or damage to equipment or other property involved in the assistance. The requesting Party shall be responsible for dealing with claims brought by third parties against the assisting Party or persons acting on its behalf.

8. The Parties concerned shall cooperate closely in order to facilitate the settlement of legal proceedings and claims which could result from assistance operations.

9. Any Party may request assistance relating to the medical treatment or the temporary relocation in the territory of another Party of persons involved in an accident.

10. The affected or requesting Party may at any time, after appropriate consultations and by notification, request the termination of assistance received or provided under this Convention. Once such a request has been made, the Parties concerned shall consult one another with a view to making arrangements for the proper termination of the assistance.

ANNEX XI

EXCHANGE OF INFORMATION PURSUANT TO ARTICLE 15

Information shall include the following elements, which can also be the subject of multilateral and bilateral cooperation:

(a) Legislative and administrative measures, policies, objectives and priorities for prevention, preparedness and response, scientific activities and technical measures to reduce the risk of industrial accidents from hazardous activities, including the mitigation of transboundary effects;

(b) Measures and contingency plans at the appropriate level affecting other Parties;

(c) Programmes for monitoring, planning, research and development, including their implementation and surveillance;

(d) Measures taken regarding prevention of, preparedness for and response to industrial accidents;

(e) Experience with industrial accidents and cooperation in response to industrial accidents with transboundary effects;

(f) The development and application of the best available technologies for improved environmental protection and safety;

(g) Emergency preparedness and response;

(h) Methods used for the prediction of risks, including criteria for the monitoring and assessment of transboundary effects.

ANNEX XII

TASKS FOR MUTUAL ASSISTANCE PURSUANT TO ARTICLE 18, PARAGRAPH 4

1. Information and data collection and dissemination

(a) Establishment and operation of an industrial accident notification system that can provide information on industrial accidents and on experts, in order to involve the experts as rapidly as possible in providing assistance;

(b) Establishment and operation of a data bank for the reception, processing and distribution of necessary information on industrial accidents, including their effects, and also on measures applied and their effectiveness;

(c) Elaboration and maintenance of a list of hazardous substances, including their relevant characteristics, and of information on how to deal with those in the event of an industrial accident;

(d) Establishment and maintenance of a register of experts to provide consultative and other kinds of assistance regarding preventive, preparedness and response measures, including restoration measures;

(e) Maintenance of a list of hazardous activities;

(f) Production and maintenance of a list of hazardous substances covered by the provisions of Annex I, Part I.

2. Research, training and methodologies

(a) Development and provision of models based on experience from industrial accidents, and scenarios for preventive, preparedness and response measures;

(b) Promotion of education and training, organization of international symposia and promotion of cooperation in research and development.

3. Technical assistance

(a) Fulfillment of advisory functions aimed at strengthening the ability to apply preventive, preparedness and response measures;

(b) Undertaking, at the request of a Party, of inspections of its hazardous activities and the provision of assistance in organizing its national inspections according to the requirements of this Convention.

4. Assistance in the case of an emergency

Provision, at the request of a Party, of assistance by, inter alia, sending experts to the site of an industrial accident to provide consultative and other kinds of assistance in response to the industrial accident.

ANNEX XIII

ARBITRATION

1. The claimant Party or Parties shall notify the secretariat that the Parties have agreed to submit the dispute to arbitration pursuant to Article 21, paragraph 2 of this Convention. The notification shall state the subject-matter of arbitration and include, in particular, the Articles of this Convention, the interpretation or application of which is at issue. The secretariat shall forward the information received to all Parties to this Convention.

2. The arbitral tribunal shall consist of three members. Both the claimant Party or Parties and the other Party or Parties to the dispute shall appoint an arbitrator, and the two arbitrators so appointed shall designate by common agreement the third arbitrator, who shall be the president of the arbitral tribunal. The latter shall not be a national of one of the parties to the dispute, nor have his or her usual place of residence in the territory of one of these parties, nor be employed by any of them, nor have dealt with the case in any other capacity.

3. If the president of the arbitral tribunal has not been designated within two months of the appointment of the second arbitrator, the Executive Secretary of the Economic Commission for Europe shall, at the request of either party to the dispute, designate the president within a further two-month period.

4. If one of the parties to the dispute does not appoint an arbitrator within two months of the receipt of the request, the other party may so inform the Executive

Secretary of the Economic Commission for Europe, who shall designate the president of the arbitral tribunal within a further two-month period. Upon designation, the president of the arbitral tribunal shall request the party which has not appointed an arbitrator to do so within two months. If it fails to do so within that period, the president shall inform the Executive Secretary of the Economic Commission for Europe, who shall make this appointment within a further two-month period.

5. The arbitral tribunal shall render its decision in accordance with international law and in accordance with the provisions of this Convention.

6. Any arbitral tribunal constituted under the provisions set out herein shall draw up its own rules of procedure.

7. The decisions of the arbitral tribunal, both on procedure and on substance, shall be taken by majority vote of its members.

8. The tribunal may take all appropriate measures to establish the facts.

9. The parties to the dispute shall facilitate the work of the arbitral tribunal and, in particular shall, using all means at their disposal:

(a) Provide the tribunal with all relevant documents, facilities and information;

(b) Enable the tribunal, where necessary, to call witnesses or experts and receive their evidence.

10. The parties to the dispute and the arbitrators shall protect the confidentiality of any information they receive in confidence during the proceedings of the arbitral tribunal.

11. The arbitral tribunal may, at the request of one of the parties, recommend interim measures of protection.

12. If one of the parties to the dispute does not appear before the arbitral tribunal or fails to defend its case, the other party may request the tribunal to continue the proceedings and to render its final decision. Absence of a party or failure of a party to defend its case shall not constitute a bar to the proceedings.

13. The arbitral tribunal may hear and determine counter-claims arising directly out of the subject-matter of the dispute.

14. Unless the arbitral tribunal determines otherwise because of the particular circumstances of the case, the expenses of the tribunal, including the remuneration of its members, shall be borne equally by the parties to the dispute. The tribunal shall keep a record of all its expenses and shall furnish a final statement thereof to the parties to the dispute.

15. Any Party to this Convention which has an interest of a legal nature in the subject-matter of the dispute and which may be affected by a decision in the case, may intervene in the proceedings with the consent of the tribunal.

16. The arbitral tribunal shall render its award within five months of the date on which it is established unless it finds it necessary to extend the time-limit for a period which should not exceed five months.

17. The award of the arbitral tribunal shall be accompanied by a statement of reasons. It shall be final and binding upon all parties to the dispute. The award will be transmitted by the arbitral tribunal to the parties to the dispute and to the secretariat. The secretariat will forward the information received to all Parties to this Convention.

18. Any dispute which may arise between the parties concerning the interpretation or execution of the award may be submitted by either party to the arbitral tribunal which made the award or, if the latter cannot be seized thereof, to another tribunal constituted for this purpose in the same manner as the first.

3.21 UNITED NATIONS FRAMEWORK CONVENTION ON CLIMATE CHANGE (Without Annexes I & II).[g] Concluded at Rio De Janeiro, 9 May 1992. Entered into force, 21 March 1994. U.N.Doc. A/CONF.151/26; *reprinted in* 31 I.L.M. 849 (1992) & 5 Weston V.E.19

The Parties to this Convention,

Acknowledging that change in the Earth's climate and its adverse effects are a common concern of humankind,

Concerned that human activities have been substantially increasing the atmospheric concentrations of greenhouse gases, that these increases enhance the natural greenhouse effect, and that this will result on average in an additional warming of the Earth's surface and atmosphere and may adversely affect natural ecosystems and humankind,

Noting that the largest share of historical and current global emissions of greenhouse gases has originated in developed countries, that per capita emissions in developing countries are still relatively low and that the share of global emissions originating in developing countries will grow to meet their social and development needs,

Aware of the role and importance in terrestrial and marine ecosystems of sinks and reservoirs of greenhouse gases,

Noting that there are many uncertainties in predictions of climate change, particularly with regard to the timing, magnitude and regional patterns thereof,

Acknowledging that the global nature of climate change calls for the widest possible cooperation by all countries and their participation in an effective and appropriate international response, in accordance with their common but differentiated responsibilities and respective capabilities and their social and economic conditions,

Recalling the pertinent provisions of the Declaration of the United Nations Conference on the Human Environment, adopted at Stockholm on 16 June 1972,

Recalling also that States have, in accordance with the Charter of the United Nations and the principles of international law, the sovereign right to exploit their own resources pursuant to their own environmental and developmental policies, and the responsibility to ensure that activities within their jurisdiction or control do not cause damage to the environment of other States or of areas beyond the limits of national jurisdiction,

Reaffirming the principle of sovereignty of States in international cooperation to address climate change,

Recognizing that States should enact effective environmental legislation, that environmental standards, management objectives and priorities should reflect the environmental and developmental context to which they apply, and that standards applied by some countries may be inappropriate and of unwarranted economic and social cost to other countries, in particular developing countries,

Recalling the provisions of General Assembly resolution 44/228 of 22 December 1989 on the United Nations Conference on Environment and Development, and resolutions 43/53 of 6 December 1988, 44/207 of 22 December 1989, 45/212 of 21 December 1990 and 46/169 of 19 December 1991 on protection of global climate for present and future generations of mankind,

Recalling also the provisions of General Assembly resolution 44/206 of 22 December 1989 on the possible adverse effects of sealevel rise on islands and coastal areas, particularly low-lying coastal areas and the pertinent provisions of General Assembly

g. *See also* Basic Document 3.25, *infra*.

resolution 44/172 of 19 December 1989 on the implementation of the Plan of Action to Combat Desertification,

Recalling further the Vienna Convention for the Protection of the Ozone Layer, 1985, and the Montreal Protocol on Substances that Deplete the Ozone Layer, 1987, as adjusted and amended on 29 June 1990,

Noting the Ministerial Declaration of the Second World Climate Conference adopted on 7 November 1990,

Conscious of the valuable analytical work being conducted by many States on climate change and of the important contributions of the World Meteorological Organization, the United Nations Environment Programme and other organs, organizations and bodies of the United Nations system, as well as other international and intergovernmental bodies, to the exchange of results of scientific research and the coordination of research,

Recognizing that steps required to understand and address climate change will be environmentally, socially and economically most effective if they are based on relevant scientific, technical and economic considerations and continually re-evaluated in the light of new findings in these areas,

Recognizing that various actions to address climate change can be justified economically in their own right and can also help in solving other environmental problems,

Recognizing also the need for developed countries to take immediate action in a flexible manner on the basis of clear priorities, as a first step towards comprehensive response strategies at the global, national and, where agreed, regional levels that take into account all greenhouse gases, with due consideration of their relative contributions to the enhancement of the greenhouse effect,

Recognizing further that low-lying and other small island countries, countries with low-lying coastal, arid and semi-arid areas or areas liable to floods, drought and desertification, and developing countries with fragile mountainous ecosystems are particularly vulnerable to the adverse effects of climate change,

Recognizing the special difficulties of those countries, especially developing countries, whose economies are particularly dependent on fossil fuel production, use and exportation, as a consequence of action taken on limiting greenhouse gas emissions,

Affirming that responses to climate change should be coordinated with social and economic development in an integrated manner with a view to avoiding adverse impacts on the latter, taking into full account the legitimate priority needs of developing countries for the achievement of sustained economic growth and the eradication of poverty,

Recognizing that all countries, especially developing countries, need access to resources required to achieve sustainable social and economic development and that, in order for developing countries to progress towards that goal, their energy consumption will need to grow taking into account the possibilities for achieving greater energy efficiency and for controlling greenhouse gas emissions in general, including through the application of new technologies on terms which make such an application economically and socially beneficial,

Determined to protect the climate system for present and future generations,

Have agreed as follows:

ARTICLE 1
DEFINITIONS

For the purposes of this Convention:

1. "Adverse effects of climate change" means changes in the physical environment or biota resulting from climate change which have significant deleterious effects on the composition, resilience or productivity of natural and managed ecosystems or on the operation of socio-economic systems or on human health and welfare.

2. "Climate change" means a change of climate which is attributed directly or indirectly to human activity that alters the composition of the global atmosphere and which is in addition to natural climate variability observed over comparable time periods.

3. "Climate system" means the totality of the atmosphere, hydrosphere, biosphere and geosphere and their interactions.

4. "Emissions" means the release of greenhouse gases and/or their precursors into the atmosphere over a specified area and period of time.

5. "Greenhouse gases" means those gaseous constituents of the atmosphere, both natural and anthropogenic, that absorb and re-emit infrared radiation.

6. "Regional economic integration organization" means an organization constituted by sovereign States of a given region which has competence in respect of matters governed by this Convention or its protocols and has been duly authorized, in accordance with its internal procedures, to sign, ratify, accept, approve or accede to the instruments concerned.

7. "Reservoir" means a component or components of the climate system where a greenhouse gas or a precursor of a greenhouse gas is stored.

8. "Sink" means any process, activity or mechanism which removes a greenhouse gas, an aerosol or a precursor of a greenhouse gas from the atmosphere.

9. "Source" means any process or activity which releases a greenhouse gas, an aerosol or a precursor of a greenhouse gas into the atmosphere.

ARTICLE 2

OBJECTIVE

The ultimate objective of this Convention and any related legal instruments that the Conference of the Parties may adopt is to achieve, in accordance with the relevant provisions of the Convention, stabilization of greenhouse gas concentrations in the atmosphere at a level that would prevent dangerous anthropogenic interference with the climate system. Such a level should be achieved within a time-frame sufficient to allow ecosystems to adapt naturally to climate change, to ensure that food production is not threatened and to enable economic development to proceed in a sustainable manner.

ARTICLE 3

PRINCIPLES

In their actions to achieve the objective of the Convention and to implement its provisions, the Parties shall be guided, *inter alia,* by the following:

1. The Parties should protect the climate system for the benefit of present and future generations of humankind, on the basis of equity and in accordance with their common but differentiated responsibilities and respective capabilities. Accordingly, the developed country Parties should take the lead in combating climate change and the adverse effects thereof.

2. The specific needs and special circumstances of developing country Parties, especially those that are particularly vulnerable to the adverse effects of climate change, and of those Parties, especially developing country Parties, that

would have to bear a disproportionate or abnormal burden under the Convention, should be given full consideration.

3. The Parties should take precautionary measures to anticipate, prevent or minimize the causes of climate change and mitigate its adverse effects. Where there are threats of serious or irreversible damage, lack of full scientific certainty should not be used as a reason for postponing such measures, taking into account that policies and measures to deal with climate change should be cost-effective so as to ensure global benefits at the lowest possible cost. To achieve this, such policies and measures should take into account different socio-economic contexts, be comprehensive, cover all relevant sources, sinks and reservoirs of greenhouse gases and adaptation, and comprise all economic sectors. Efforts to address climate change may be carried out cooperatively by interested Parties.

4. The Parties have a right to, and should, promote sustainable development. Policies and measures to protect the climate system against human-induced change should be appropriate for the specific conditions of each Party and should be integrated with national development programmes, taking into account that economic development is essential for adopting measures to address climate change.

5. The Parties should cooperate to promote a supportive and open international economic system that would lead to sustainable economic growth and development in all Parties, particularly developing country Parties, thus enabling them better to address the problems of climate change. Measures taken to combat climate change, including unilateral ones, should not constitute a means of arbitrary or unjustifiable discrimination or a disguised restriction on international trade.

ARTICLE 4

COMMITMENTS

1. All Parties, taking into account their common but differentiated responsibilities and their specific national and regional development priorities, objectives and circumstances, shall:

(a) Develop, periodically update, publish and make available to the Conference of the Parties, in accordance with Article 12, national inventories of anthropogenic emissions by sources and removals by sinks of all greenhouse gases not controlled by the Montreal Protocol, using comparable methodologies to be agreed upon by the Conference of the Parties;

(b) Formulate, implement, publish and regularly update national and, where appropriate, regional programmes containing measures to mitigate climate change by addressing anthropogenic emissions by sources and removals by sinks of all greenhouse gases not controlled by the Montreal Protocol, and measures to facilitate adequate adaptation to climate change;

(c) Promote and cooperate in the development, application and diffusion, including transfer, of technologies, practices and processes that control, reduce or prevent anthropogenic emissions of greenhouse gases not controlled by the Montreal Protocol in all relevant sectors, including the energy, transport, industry, agriculture, forestry and waste management sectors;

(d) Promote sustainable management, and promote and cooperate in the conservation and enhancement, as appropriate, of sinks and reservoirs of all greenhouse gases not controlled by the Montreal Protocol, including biomass, forests and oceans as well as other terrestrial, coastal and marine ecosystems;

(e) Cooperate in preparing for adaptation to the impacts of climate change; develop and elaborate appropriate and integrated plans for coastal zone management, water resources and agriculture, and for the protection and rehabilitation of areas, particularly in Africa, affected by drought and desertification, as well as floods;

(f) Take climate change considerations into account, to the extent feasible, in their relevant social, economic and environmental policies and actions, and employ appropriate methods, for example impact assessments, formulated and determined nationally, with a view to minimizing adverse effects on the economy, on public health and on the quality of the environment, of projects or measures undertaken by them to mitigate or adapt to climate change;

(g) Promote and cooperate in scientific, technological, technical, socio-economic and other research, systematic observation and development of data archives related to the climate system and intended to further the understanding and to reduce or eliminate the remaining uncertainties regarding the causes, effects, magnitude and timing of climate change and the economic and social consequences of various response strategies;

(h) Promote and cooperate in the full, open and prompt exchange of relevant scientific, technological, technical, socio-economic and legal information related to the climate system and climate change, and to the economic and social consequences of various response strategies;

(i) Promote and cooperate in education, training and public awareness related to climate change and encourage the widest participation in this process, including that of non-governmental organizations; and

(j) Communicate to the Conference of the Parties information related to implementation, in accordance with Article 12.

2. The developed country Parties and other Parties included in annex I commit themselves specifically as provided for in the following:

(a) Each of these Parties shall adopt national policies and take corresponding measures on the mitigation of climate change, by limiting its anthropogenic emissions of greenhouse gases and protecting and enhancing its greenhouse gas sinks and reservoirs. These policies and measures will demonstrate that developed countries are taking the lead in modifying longer-term trends in anthropogenic emissions consistent with the objective of the Convention, recognizing that the return by the end of the present decade to earlier levels of anthropogenic emissions of carbon dioxide and other greenhouse gases not controlled by the Montreal Protocol would contribute to such modification, and taking into account the differences in these Parties' starting points and approaches, economic structures and resource bases, the need to maintain strong and sustainable economic growth, available technologies and other individual circumstances, as well as the need for equitable and appropriate contributions by each of these Parties to the global effort regarding that objective. These Parties may implement such policies and measures jointly with other Parties and may assist other Parties in contributing to the achievement of the objective of the Convention and, in particular, that of this subparagraph;

(b) In order to promote progress to this end, each of these Parties shall communicate, within six months of the entry into force of the Convention for it and periodically thereafter, and in accordance with Article 12, detailed information on its policies and measures referred to in subparagraph (a) above, as well as on its resulting projected anthropogenic emissions by sources and removals by sinks of greenhouse gases not controlled by the Montreal Protocol for the period referred to in subparagraph (a), with the aim of returning individually or jointly to their 1990 levels these anthropogenic emissions of carbon dioxide and other greenhouse gases not controlled by the Montreal Protocol. This information will be reviewed by the Conference of the Parties, at its first session and periodically thereafter, in accordance with Article 7;

(c) Calculations of emissions by sources and removals by sinks of greenhouse gases for the purposes of subparagraph (b) above should take into account the best available scientific knowledge, including the effective capacity of sinks and the respective contributions of such gases to climate change. The Conference of the Parties shall consider and agree on methodologies for these calculations at its first session and review them regularly thereafter;

(d) The Conference of the Parties shall, at its first session, review the adequacy of subparagraphs (a) and (b) above. Such review shall be carried out in the light of the best available scientific information and assessment on climate change and its impacts, as well as relevant technical, social and economic information. Based on this review, the Conference of the Parties shall take appropriate action, which may include the adoption of amendments to the commitments in subparagraphs (a) and (b) above. The Conference of the Parties, at its first session, shall also take decisions regarding criteria for joint implementation as indicated in subparagraph (a) above. A second review of subparagraphs (a) and (b) shall take place not later than 31 December 1998, and thereafter at regular intervals determined by the Conference of the Parties, until the objective of the Convention is met;

(e) Each of these Parties shall:

(i) coordinate as appropriate with other such Parties, relevant economic and administrative instruments developed to achieve the objective of the Convention; and

(ii) identify and periodically review its own policies and practices which encourage activities that lead to greater levels of anthropogenic emissions of greenhouse gases not controlled by the Montreal Protocol than would otherwise occur;

(f) The Conference of the Parties shall review, not later than 31 December 1998, available information with a view to taking decisions regarding such amendments to the lists in annexes I and II as may be appropriate, with the approval of the Party concerned;

(g) Any Party not included in annex I may, in its instrument of ratification, acceptance, approval or accession, or at any time thereafter, notify the Depositary that it intends to be bound by subparagraphs (a) and (b) above. The Depositary shall inform the other signatories and Parties of any such notification.

3. The developed country Parties and other developed Parties included in annex II shall provide new and additional financial resources to meet the agreed full costs incurred by developing country Parties in complying with their obligations under Article 12, paragraph 1. They shall also provide such financial resources, including for the transfer of technology, needed by the developing country Parties to meet the agreed full incremental costs of implementing measures that are covered by paragraph 1 of this Article and that are agreed between a developing country Party and the international entity or entities referred to in Article 11, in accordance with that Article. The implementation of these commitments shall take into account the need for adequacy and predictability in the flow of funds and the importance of appropriate burden sharing among the developed country Parties.

4. The developed country Parties and other developed Parties included in annex II shall also assist the developing country Parties that are particularly vulnerable to the adverse effects of climate change in meeting costs of adaptation to those adverse effects.

5. The developed country Parties and other developed Parties included in annex II shall take all practicable steps to promote, facilitate and finance, as appropriate, the transfer of, or access to, environmentally sound technologies and know-how to other Parties, particularly developing country Parties, to enable them to implement the provisions of the Convention. In this process, the developed country Parties shall support the development and enhancement of endogenous capacities and technologies of developing country Parties. Other Parties and organizations in a position to do so may also assist in facilitating the transfer of such technologies.

6. In the implementation of their commitments under paragraph 2 above, a certain degree of flexibility shall be allowed by the Conference of the Parties to the Parties included in annex I undergoing the process of transition to a market economy, in order to enhance the ability of these Parties to address climate change, including with regard to the historical level of anthropogenic emissions of greenhouse gases not controlled by the Montreal Protocol chosen as a reference.

7. The extent to which developing country Parties will effectively implement their commitments under the Convention will depend on the effective implementation by developed country Parties of their commitments under the Convention related to financial resources and transfer of technology and will take fully into account that economic and social development and poverty eradication are the first and overriding priorities of the developing country Parties.

8. In the implementation of the commitments in this Article, the Parties shall give full consideration to what actions are necessary under the Convention, including actions related to funding, insurance and the transfer of technology, to meet the specific needs and concerns of developing country Parties arising from the adverse effects of climate change and/or the impact of the implementation of response measures, especially on:

(a) Small island countries;

(b) Countries with low-lying coastal areas;

(c) Countries with arid and semi-arid areas, forested areas and areas liable to forest decay;

(d) Countries with areas prone to natural disasters;

(e) Countries with areas liable to drought and desertification;

(f) Countries with areas of high urban atmospheric pollution;

(g) Countries with areas with fragile ecosystems, including mountainous ecosystems;

(h) Countries whose economies are highly dependent on income generated from the production, processing and export, and/or on consumption of fossil fuels and associated energy-intensive products; and

(i) Land-locked and transit countries.

Further, the Conference of the Parties may take actions, as appropriate, with respect to this paragraph.

9. The Parties shall take full account of the specific needs and special situations of the least developed countries in their actions with regard to funding and transfer of technology.

10. The Parties shall, in accordance with Article 10, take into consideration in the implementation of the commitments of the Convention the situation of Parties, particularly developing country Parties, with economies that are vulnerable to the adverse effects of the implementation of measures to respond to climate change. This applies notably to Parties with economies that are highly dependent on income generated from the production, processing and export, and/or consumption of fossil

fuels and associated energy-intensive products and/or the use of fossil fuels for which such Parties have serious difficulties in switching to alternatives.

ARTICLE 5

RESEARCH AND SYSTEMATIC OBSERVATION

In carrying out their commitments under Article 4, paragraph 1(g), the Parties shall:

(a) Support and further develop, as appropriate, international and intergovernmental programmes and networks or organizations aimed at defining, conducting, assessing and financing research, data collection and systematic observation, taking into account the need to minimize duplication of effort;

(b) Support international and intergovernmental efforts to strengthen systematic observation and national scientific and technical research capacities and capabilities, particularly in developing countries, and to promote access to, and the exchange of, data and analyses thereof obtained from areas beyond national jurisdiction; and

(c) Take into account the particular concerns and needs of developing countries and cooperate in improving their endogenous capacities and capabilities to participate in the efforts referred to in subparagraphs (a) and (b) above.

ARTICLE 6

EDUCATION, TRAINING AND PUBLIC AWARENESS

In carrying out their commitments under Article 4, paragraph 1(i), the Parties shall:

(a) Promote and facilitate at the national and, as appropriate, subregional and regional levels, and in accordance with national laws and regulations, and within their respective capacities:

(i) the development and implementation of educational and public awareness programmes on climate change and its effects;

(ii) public access to information on climate change and its effects;

(iii) public participation in addressing climate change and its effects and developing adequate responses; and

(iv) training of scientific, technical and managerial personnel.

(b) Cooperate in and promote, at the international level, and, where appropriate, using existing bodies:

(i) the development and exchange of educational and public awareness material on climate change and its effects; and

(ii) the development and implementation of education and training programmes, including the strengthening of national institutions and the exchange or secondment of personnel to train experts in this field, in particular for developing countries.

ARTICLE 7

CONFERENCE OF THE PARTIES

1. A Conference of the Parties is hereby established.

2. The Conference of the Parties, as the supreme body of this Convention, shall keep under regular review the implementation of the Convention and any related legal instruments that the Conference of the Parties may adopt, and shall make, within its

mandate, the decisions necessary to promote the effective implementation of the Convention. To this end, it shall:

(a) Periodically examine the obligations of the Parties and the institutional arrangements under the Convention, in the light of the objective of the Convention, the experience gained in its implementation and the evolution of scientific and technological knowledge;

(b) Promote and facilitate the exchange of information on measures adopted by the Parties to address climate change and its effects, taking into account the differing circumstances, responsibilities and capabilities of the Parties and their respective commitments under the Convention;

(c) Facilitate, at the request of two or more Parties, the coordination of measures adopted by them to address climate change and its effects, taking into account the differing circumstances, responsibilities and capabilities of the Parties and their respective commitments under the Convention;

(d) Promote and guide, in accordance with the objective and provisions of the Convention, the development and periodic refinement of comparable methodologies, to be agreed on by the Conference of the Parties, *inter alia,* for preparing inventories of greenhouse gas emissions by sources and removals by sinks, and for evaluating the effectiveness of measures to limit the emissions and enhance the removals of these gases;

(e) Assess, on the basis of all information made available to it in accordance with the provisions of the Convention, the implementation of the Convention by the Parties, the overall effects of the measures taken pursuant to the Convention, in particular environmental, economic and social effects as well as their cumulative impacts and the extent to which progress towards the objective of the Convention is being achieved;

(f) Consider and adopt regular reports on the implementation of the Convention and ensure their publication;

(g) Make recommendations on any matters necessary for the implementation of the Convention;

(h) Seek to mobilize financial resources in accordance with Article 4, paragraphs 3, 4 and 5, and Article 11;

(i) Establish such subsidiary bodies as are deemed necessary for the implementation of the Convention;

(j) Review reports submitted by its subsidiary bodies and provide guidance to them;

(k) Agree upon and adopt, by consensus, rules of procedure and financial rules for itself and for any subsidiary bodies;

(*l*) Seek and utilize, where appropriate, the services and cooperation of, and information provided by, competent international organizations and intergovernmental and non-governmental bodies; and

(m) Exercise such other functions as are required for the achievement of the objective of the Convention as well as all other functions assigned to it under the Convention.

3. The Conference of the Parties shall, at its first session, adopt its own rules of procedure as well as those of the subsidiary bodies established by the Convention, which shall include decision-making procedures for matters not already covered by decision-making procedures stipulated in the Convention. Such procedures may include specified majorities required for the adoption of particular decisions.

4. The first session of the Conference of the Parties shall be convened by the interim secretariat referred to in Article 21 and shall take place not later than one year after the date of entry into force of the Convention. Thereafter, ordinary sessions of the Conference of the Parties shall be held every year unless otherwise decided by the Conference of the Parties.

5. Extraordinary sessions of the Conference of the Parties shall be held at such other times as may be deemed necessary by the Conference, or at the written request of any Party, provided that, within six months of the request being communicated to the Parties by the secretariat, it is supported by at least one-third of the Parties.

6. The United Nations, its specialized agencies and the International Atomic Energy Agency, as well as any State member thereof or observers thereto not Party to the Convention, may be represented at sessions of the Conference of the Parties as observers. Any body or agency, whether national or international, governmental or non-governmental, which is qualified in matters covered by the Convention, and which has informed the secretariat of its wish to be represented at a session of the Conference of the Parties as an observer, may be so admitted unless at least one-third of the Parties present object. The admission and participation of observers shall be subject to the rules of procedure adopted by the Conference of the Parties.

ARTICLE 8

SECRETARIAT

1. A secretariat is hereby established.

2. The functions of the secretariat shall be:

(a) To make arrangements for sessions of the Conference of the Parties and its subsidiary bodies established under the Convention and to provide them with services as required;

(b) To compile and transmit reports submitted to it;

(c) To facilitate assistance to the Parties, particularly developing country Parties, on request, in the compilation and communication of information required in accordance with the provisions of the Convention;

(d) To prepare reports on its activities and present them to the Conference of the Parties;

(e) To ensure the necessary coordination with the secretariats of other relevant international bodies;

(f) To enter, under the overall guidance of the Conference of the Parties, into such administrative and contractual arrangements as may be required for the effective discharge of its functions; and

(g) To perform the other secretariat functions specified in the Convention and in any of its protocols and such other functions as may be determined by the Conference of the Parties.

3. The Conference of the Parties, at its first session, shall designate a permanent secretariat and make arrangements for its functioning.

ARTICLE 9

SUBSIDIARY BODY FOR SCIENTIFIC AND TECHNOLOGICAL ADVICE

1. A subsidiary body for scientific and technological advice is hereby established to provide the Conference of the Parties and, as appropriate, its other subsidiary bodies with timely information and advice on scientific and technological matters relating to the Convention. This body shall be open to participation by all Parties and shall be multidisciplinary. It shall comprise government representatives competent in

the relevant field of expertise. It shall report regularly to the Conference of the Parties on all aspects of its work.

2. Under the guidance of the Conference of the Parties, and drawing upon existing competent international bodies, this body shall:

(a) Provide assessments of the state of scientific knowledge relating to climate change and its effects;

(b) Prepare scientific assessments on the effects of measures taken in the implementation of the Convention;

(c) Identify innovative, efficient and state-of-the-art technologies and know-how and advise on the ways and means of promoting development and/or transferring such technologies;

(d) Provide advice on scientific programmes, international cooperation in research and development related to climate change, as well as on ways and means of supporting endogenous capacity-building in developing countries; and

(e) Respond to scientific, technological and methodological questions that the Conference of the Parties and its subsidiary bodies may put to the body.

3. The functions and terms of reference of this body may be further elaborated by the Conference of the Parties.

ARTICLE 10

SUBSIDIARY BODY FOR IMPLEMENTATION

1. A subsidiary body for implementation is hereby established to assist the Conference of the Parties in the assessment and review of the effective implementation of the Convention. This body shall be open to participation by all Parties and comprise government representatives who are experts on matters related to climate change. It shall report regularly to the Conference of the Parties on all aspects of its work.

2. Under the guidance of the Conference of the Parties, this body shall:

(a) Consider the information communicated in accordance with Article 12, paragraph 1, to assess the overall aggregated effect of the steps taken by the Parties in the light of the latest scientific assessments concerning climate change;

(b) Consider the information communicated in accordance with Article 12, paragraph 2, in order to assist the Conference of the Parties in carrying out the reviews required by Article 4, paragraph 2(d); and

(c) Assist the Conference of the Parties, as appropriate, in the preparation and implementation of its decisions.

ARTICLE 11

FINANCIAL MECHANISM

1. A mechanism for the provision of financial resources on a grant or concessional basis, including for the transfer of technology, is hereby defined. It shall function under the guidance of and be accountable to the Conference of the Parties, which shall decide on its policies, programme priorities and eligibility criteria related to this Convention. Its operation shall be entrusted to one or more existing international entities.

2. The financial mechanism shall have an equitable and balanced representation of all Parties within a transparent system of governance.

3. The Conference of the Parties and the entity or entities entrusted with the operation of the financial mechanism shall agree upon arrangements to give effect to the above paragraphs, which shall include the following:

(a) Modalities to ensure that the funded projects to address climate change are in conformity with the policies, programme priorities and eligibility criteria established by the Conference of the Parties;

(b) Modalities by which a particular funding decision may be reconsidered in light of these policies, programme priorities and eligibility criteria;

(c) Provision by the entity or entities of regular reports to the Conference of the Parties on its funding operations, which is consistent with the requirement for accountability set out in paragraph 1 above; and

(d) Determination in a predictable and identifiable manner of the amount of funding necessary and available for the implementation of this Convention and the conditions under which that amount shall be periodically reviewed.

4. The Conference of the Parties shall make arrangements to implement the above-mentioned provisions at its first session, reviewing and taking into account the interim arrangements referred to in Article 21, paragraph 3, and shall decide whether these interim arrangements shall be maintained. Within four years thereafter, the Conference of the Parties shall review the financial mechanism and take appropriate measures.

5. The developed country Parties may also provide and developing country Parties avail themselves of, financial resources related to the implementation of the Convention through bilateral, regional and other multilateral channels.

ARTICLE 12

COMMUNICATION OF INFORMATION RELATED TO IMPLEMENTATION

1. In accordance with Article 4, paragraph 1, each Party shall communicate to the Conference of the Parties, through the secretariat, the following elements of information:

(a) A national inventory of anthropogenic emissions by sources and removals by sinks of all greenhouse gases not controlled by the Montreal Protocol, to the extent its capacities permit, using comparable methodologies to be promoted and agreed upon by the Conference of the Parties;

(b) A general description of steps taken or envisaged by the Party to implement the Convention; and

(c) Any other information that the Party considers relevant to the achievement of the objective of the Convention and suitable for inclusion in its communication, including, if feasible, material relevant for calculations of global emission trends.

2. Each developed country Party and each other Party included in annex I shall incorporate in its communication the following elements of information:

(a) A detailed description of the policies and measures that it has adopted to implement its commitment under Article 4, paragraphs 2(a) and 2(b); and

(b) A specific estimate of the effects that the policies and measures referred to in subparagraph (a) immediately above will have on anthropogenic emissions by its sources and removals by its sinks of greenhouse gases during the period referred to in Article 4, paragraph 2(a).

3. In addition, each developed country Party and each other developed Party included in annex II shall incorporate details of measures taken in accordance with Article 4, paragraphs 3, 4 and 5.

4. Developing country Parties may, on a voluntary basis, propose projects for financing, including specific technologies, materials, equipment, techniques or practices that would be needed to implement such projects, along with, if possible, an

estimate of all incremental costs, of the reductions of emissions and increments of removals of greenhouse gases, as well as an estimate of the consequent benefits.

5. Each developed country Party and each other Party included in annex I shall make its initial communication within six months of the entry into force of the Convention for that Party. Each Party not so listed shall make its initial communication within three years of the entry into force of the Convention for that Party, or of the availability of financial resources in accordance with Article 4, paragraph 3. Parties that are least developed countries may make their initial communication at their discretion. The frequency of subsequent communications by all Parties shall be determined by the Conference of the Parties, taking into account the differentiated timetable set by this paragraph.

6. Information communicated by Parties under this Article shall be transmitted by the secretariat as soon as possible to the Conference of the Parties and to any subsidiary bodies concerned. If necessary, the procedures for the communication of information may be further considered by the Conference of the Parties.

7. From its first session, the Conference of the Parties shall arrange for the provision to developing country Parties of technical and financial support, on request, in compiling and communicating information under this Article, as well as in identifying the technical and financial needs associated with proposed projects and response measures under Article 4. Such support may be provided by other Parties, by competent international organizations and by the secretariat, as appropriate.

8. Any group of Parties may, subject to guidelines adopted by the Conference of the Parties, and to prior notification to the Conference of the Parties, make a joint communication in fulfilment of their obligations under this Article, provided that such a communication includes information on the fulfilment by each of these Parties of its individual obligations under the Convention.

9. Information received by the secretariat that is designated by a Party as confidential, in accordance with criteria to be established by the Conference of the Parties, shall be aggregated by the secretariat to protect its confidentiality before being made available to any of the bodies involved in the communication and review of information.

10. Subject to paragraph 9 above, and without prejudice to the ability of any Party to make public its communication at any time, the secretariat shall make communications by Parties under this Article publicly available at the time they are submitted to the Conference of the Parties.

ARTICLE 13

RESOLUTION OF QUESTIONS REGARDING IMPLEMENTATION

The Conference of the Parties shall, at its first session, consider the establishment of a multilateral consultative process, available to Parties on their request, for the resolution of questions regarding the implementation of the Convention.

ARTICLE 14

SETTLEMENT OF DISPUTES

1. In the event of a dispute between any two or more Parties concerning the interpretation or application of the Convention, the Parties concerned shall seek a settlement of the dispute through negotiation or any other peaceful means of their own choice.

2. When ratifying, accepting, approving or acceding to the Convention, or at any time thereafter, a Party which is not a regional economic integration organization may declare in a written instrument submitted to the Depositary that, in respect of any

dispute concerning the interpretation or application of the Convention, it recognizes as compulsory *ipso facto* and without special agreement, in relation to any Party accepting the same obligation:

(a) Submission of the dispute to the International Court of Justice, and/or

(b) Arbitration in accordance with procedures to be adopted by the Conference of the Parties as soon as practicable, in an annex on arbitration.

A Party which is a regional economic integration organization may make a declaration with like effect in relation to arbitration in accordance with the procedures referred to in subparagraph (b) above.

3. A declaration made under paragraph 2 above shall remain in force until it expires in accordance with its terms or until three months after written notice of its revocation has been deposited with the Depositary.

4. A new declaration, a notice of revocation or the expiry of a declaration shall not in any way affect proceedings pending before the International Court of Justice or the arbitral tribunal, unless the parties to the dispute otherwise agree.

5. Subject to the operation of paragraph 2 above, if after twelve months following notification by one Party to another that a dispute exists between them, the Parties concerned have not been able to settle their dispute through the means mentioned in paragraph 1 above, the dispute shall be submitted, at the request of any of the parties to the dispute, to conciliation.

6. A conciliation commission shall be created upon the request of one of the parties to the dispute. The commission shall be composed of an equal number of members appointed by each party concerned and a chairman chosen jointly by the members appointed by each party. The commission shall render a recommendatory award, which the parties shall consider in good faith.

7. Additional procedures relating to conciliation shall be adopted by the Conference of the Parties, as soon as practicable, in an annex on conciliation.

8. The provisions of this Article shall apply to any related legal instrument which the Conference of the Parties may adopt, unless the instrument provides otherwise.

ARTICLE 15

AMENDMENTS TO THE CONVENTION

1. Any Party may propose amendments to the Convention.

2. Amendments to the Convention shall be adopted at an ordinary session of the Conference of the Parties. The text of any proposed amendment to the Convention shall be communicated to the Parties by the secretariat at least six months before the meeting at which it is proposed for adoption. The secretariat shall also communicate proposed amendments to the signatories to the Convention and, for information, to the Depositary.

3. The Parties shall make every effort to reach agreement on any proposed amendment to the Convention by consensus. If all efforts at consensus have been exhausted, and no agreement reached, the amendment shall as a last resort be adopted by a three-fourths majority vote of the Parties present and voting at the meeting. The adopted amendment shall be communicated by the secretariat to the Depositary, who shall circulate it to all Parties for their acceptance.

4. Instruments of acceptance in respect of an amendment shall be deposited with the Depositary. An amendment adopted in accordance with paragraph 3 above shall enter into force for those Parties having accepted it on the ninetieth day after the date of receipt by the Depositary of an instrument of acceptance by at least three-fourths of the Parties to the Convention.

5. The amendment shall enter into force for any other Party on the ninetieth day after the date on which that Party deposits with the Depositary its instrument of acceptance of the said amendment.

6. For the purposes of this Article, "Parties present and voting" means Parties present and casting an affirmative or negative vote.

ARTICLE 16

ADOPTION AND AMENDMENT OF ANNEXES TO THE CONVENTION

1. Annexes to the Convention shall form an integral part thereof and, unless otherwise expressly provided, a reference to the Convention constitutes at the same time a reference to any annexes thereto. Without prejudice to the provisions of Article 14, paragraphs 2(b) and 7, such annexes shall be restricted to lists, forms and any other material of a descriptive nature that is of a scientific, technical, procedural or administrative character.

2. Annexes to the Convention shall be proposed and adopted in accordance with the procedure set forth in Article 15, paragraphs 2, 3, and 4.

3. An annex that has been adopted in accordance with paragraph 2 above shall enter into force for all Parties to the Convention six months after the date of the communication by the Depositary to such Parties of the adoption of the annex, except for those Parties that have notified the Depositary, in writing, within that period of their non-acceptance of the annex. The annex shall enter into force for Parties which withdraw their notification of non-acceptance on the ninetieth day after the date on which withdrawal of such notification has been received by the Depositary.

4. The proposal, adoption and entry into force of amendments to annexes to the Convention shall be subject to the same procedure as that for the proposal, adoption and entry into force of annexes to the Convention in accordance with paragraphs 2 and 3 above.

5. If the adoption of an annex or an amendment to an annex involves an amendment to the Convention, that annex or amendment to an annex shall not enter into force until such time as the amendment to the Convention enters into force.

ARTICLE 17

PROTOCOLS

1. The Conference of the Parties may, at any ordinary session, adopt protocols to the Convention.

2. The text of any proposed protocol shall be communicated to the Parties by the secretariat at least six months before such a session.

3. The requirements for the entry into force of any protocol shall be established by that instrument.

4. Only Parties to the Convention may be Parties to a protocol.

5. Decisions under any protocol shall be taken only by the Parties to the protocol concerned.

ARTICLE 18

RIGHT TO VOTE

1. Each Party to the Convention shall have one vote, except as provided for in paragraph 2 below.

2. Regional economic integration organizations, in matters within their competence, shall exercise their right to vote with a number of votes equal to the number of

their member States that are Parties to the Convention. Such an organization shall not exercise its right to vote if any of its member States exercises its right, and vice versa.

ARTICLE 19

DEPOSITARY

The Secretary-General of the United Nations shall be the Depositary of the Convention and of protocols adopted in accordance with Article 17.

ARTICLE 20

SIGNATURE

This Convention shall be open for signature by States Members of the United Nations or of any of its specialized agencies or that are Parties to the Statute of the International Court of Justice and by regional economic integration organizations at Rio de Janeiro, during the United Nations Conference on Environment and Development, and thereafter at United Nations Headquarters in New York from 20 June 1992 to 19 June 1993.

ARTICLE 21

INTERIM ARRANGEMENTS

1. The secretariat functions referred to in Article 8 will be carried out on an interim basis by the secretariat established by the General Assembly of the United Nations in its resolution 45/212 of 21 December 1990, until the completion of the first session of the Conference of the Parties.

2. The head of the interim secretariat referred to in paragraph 1 above will cooperate closely with the Intergovernmental Panel on Climate Change to ensure that the Panel can respond to the need for objective scientific and technical advice. Other relevant scientific bodies could also be consulted.

3. The Global Environment Facility of the United Nations Development Programme, the United Nations Environment Programme and the International Bank for Reconstruction and Development shall be the international entity entrusted with the operation of the financial mechanism referred to in Article 11 on an interim basis. In this connection, the Global Environment Facility should be appropriately restructured and its membership made universal to enable it to fulfil the requirements of Article 11.

ARTICLE 22

RATIFICATION, ACCEPTANCE, APPROVAL OR ACCESSION

1. The Convention shall be subject to ratification, acceptance, approval or accession by States and by regional economic integration organizations. It shall be open for accession from the day after the date on which the Convention is closed for signature. Instruments of ratification, acceptance, approval or accession shall be deposited with the Depositary.

2. Any regional economic integration organization which becomes a Party to the Convention without any of its member States being a Party shall be bound by all the obligations under the Convention. In the case of such organizations, one or more of whose member States is a Party to the Convention, the organization and its member States shall decide on their respective responsibilities for the performance of their obligations under the Convention. In such cases, the organization and the member States shall not be entitled to exercise rights under the Convention concurrently.

3. In their instruments of ratification, acceptance, approval or accession, regional economic integration organizations shall declare the extent of their competence with

respect to the matters governed by the Convention. These organizations shall also inform the Depositary, who shall in turn inform the Parties, of any substantial modification in the extent of their competence.

ARTICLE 23

ENTRY INTO FORCE

1. The Convention shall enter into force on the ninetieth day after the date of deposit of the fiftieth instrument of ratification, acceptance, approval or accession.

2. For each State or regional economic integration organization that ratifies, accepts or approves the Convention or accedes thereto after the deposit of the fiftieth instrument of ratification, acceptance, approval or accession, the Convention shall enter into force on the ninetieth day after the date of deposit by such State or regional economic integration organization of its instrument of ratification, acceptance, approval or accession.

3. For the purposes of paragraphs 1 and 2 above, any instrument deposited by a regional economic integration organization shall not be counted as additional to those deposited by States members of the organization.

ARTICLE 24

RESERVATIONS

No reservations may be made to the Convention.

ARTICLE 25

WITHDRAWAL

1. At any time after three years from the date on which the Convention has entered into force for a Party, that Party may withdraw from the Convention by giving written notification to the Depositary.

2. Any such withdrawal shall take effect upon expiry of one year from the date of receipt by the Depositary of the notification of withdrawal, or on such later date as may be specified in the notification of withdrawal.

3. Any Party that withdraws from the Convention shall be considered as also having withdrawn from any protocol to which it is a Party.

ARTICLE 26

AUTHENTIC TEXTS

The original of this Convention, of which the Arabic, Chinese, English, French, Russian and Spanish texts are equally authentic, shall be deposited with the Secretary–General of the United Nations.

3.22 CONVENTION ON NUCLEAR SAFETY. Adopted on 17 June 1994. Entered into force, 24 October 1996. IAEA INFCIRC/449; *reprinted in* 33 I.L.M. 1514 (1994) & 5 Weston V.I.6a

THE CONTRACTING PARTIES

(i) Aware of the importance to the international community of ensuring that the use of nuclear energy is safe, well regulated and environmentally sound;

(ii) Reaffirming the necessity of continuing to promote a high level of nuclear safety worldwide;

(iii) Reaffirming that responsibility for nuclear safety rests with the State having jurisdiction over a nuclear installation;

(iv) Desiring to promote an effective nuclear safety culture;

(v) Aware that accidents at nuclear installations have the potential for transboundary impacts;

(vi) Keeping in mind the Convention on the Physical Protection of Nuclear Material (1979), the Convention on Early Notification of a Nuclear Accident (1986), and the Convention on Assistance in the Case of a Nuclear Accident or Radiological Emergency (1986);

(vii) Affirming the importance of international co-operation for the enhancement of nuclear safety through existing bilateral and multilateral mechanisms and the establishment of this incentive Convention;

(viii) Recognizing that this Convention entails a commitment to the application of fundamental safety principles for nuclear installations rather than of detailed safety standards and that there are internationally formulated safety guidelines which are updated from time to time and so can provide guidance on contemporary means of achieving a high level of safety;

(ix) Affirming the need to begin promptly the development of an international convention on the safety of radioactive waste management as soon as the ongoing process to develop waste management safety fundamentals has resulted in broad international agreement;

(x) Recognizing the usefulness of further technical work in connection with the safety of other parts of the nuclear fuel cycle, and that this work may, in time, facilitate the development of current or future international instruments;

HAVE AGREED as follows:

CHAPTER 1. OBJECTIVES, DEFINITIONS AND SCOPE OF APPLICATION

ARTICLE 1. OBJECTIVES

The objectives of this Convention are:

(i) to achieve and maintain a high level of nuclear safety worldwide through the enhancement of national measures and international co-operation including, where appropriate, safety-related technical co-operation;

(ii) to establish and maintain effective defences in nuclear installations against potential radiological hazards in order to protect individuals, society and the environment from harmful effects of ionizing radiation from such installations;

(iii) to prevent accidents with radiological consequences and to mitigate such consequences should they occur.

ARTICLE 2. DEFINITIONS

For the purpose of this Convention:

(i) "nuclear installation" means for each Contracting Party any land-based civil nuclear power plant under its jurisdiction including such storage, handling and treatment facilities for radioactive materials as are on the same site and are directly related to the operation of the nuclear power plant. Such a plant ceases to be a nuclear installation when all nuclear fuel elements have been removed permanently from the reactor core and have been stored safely in accordance with approved procedures, and a decommissioning programme has been agreed to by the regulatory body.

(ii) "regulatory body" means for each Contracting Party any body or bodies given the legal authority by that Contracting Party to grant licences and to regulate the siting, design, construction, commissioning, operation or decommissioning of nuclear installations.

(iii) "licence" means any authorization granted by the regulatory body to the applicant to have the responsibility for the siting, design, construction, commissioning, operation or decommissioning of a nuclear installation.

ARTICLE 3. SCOPE OF APPLICATION

This Convention shall apply to the safety of nuclear installations.

CHAPTER 2. OBLIGATIONS

(a) General Provisions

ARTICLE 4. IMPLEMENTING MEASURES

Each Contracting Party shall take, within the framework of its national law, the legislative, regulatory and administrative measures and other steps necessary for implementing its obligations under this Convention.

ARTICLE 5. REPORTING

Each Contracting Party shall submit for review, prior to each meeting referred to in Article 20, a report on the measures it has taken to implement each of the obligations of this Convention.

ARTICLE 6. EXISTING NUCLEAR INSTALLATIONS

Each Contracting Party shall take the appropriate steps to ensure that the safety of nuclear installations existing at the time the Convention enters into force for that Contracting Party is reviewed as soon as possible. When necessary in the context of this Convention, the Contracting Party shall ensure that all reasonably practicable improvements are made as a matter of urgency to upgrade the safety of the nuclear installation. If such upgrading cannot be achieved, plans should be implemented to shut down the nuclear installation as soon as practically possible. The timing of the shut-down may take into account the whole energy context and possible alternatives as well as the social, environmental and economic impact.

(b) Legislation and regulation

ARTICLE 7. LEGISLATIVE AND REGULATORY FRAMEWORK

1. Each Contracting Party shall establish and maintain a legislative and regulatory framework to govern the safety of nuclear installations.

2. The legislative and regulatory framework shall provide for:

(i) the establishment of applicable national safety requirements and regulations;

(ii) a system of licensing with regard to nuclear installations and the prohibition of the operation of a nuclear installation without a licence;

(iii) a system of regulatory inspection and assessment of nuclear installations to ascertain compliance with applicable regulations and the terms of licences;

(iv) the enforcement of applicable regulations and of the terms of licences, including suspension, modification or revocation.

ARTICLE 8. REGULATORY BODY

1. Each Contracting Party shall establish or designate a regulatory body entrusted with the implementation of the legislative and regulatory framework referred to in Article 7, and provided with adequate authority, competence and financial and human resources to fulfil its assigned responsibilities.

2. Each Contracting Party shall take the appropriate steps to ensure an effective separation between the functions of the regulatory body and those of any other body or organization concerned with the promotion or utilization of nuclear energy.

ARTICLE 9. RESPONSIBILITY OF THE LICENCE HOLDER

Each Contracting Party shall ensure that prime responsibility for the safety of a nuclear installation rests with the holder of the relevant licence and shall take the appropriate steps to ensure that each such licence holder meets its responsibility.

(c) General Safety Considerations

ARTICLE 10. PRIORITY TO SAFETY

Each Contracting Party shall take the appropriate steps to ensure that all organizations engaged in activities directly related to nuclear installations shall establish policies that give due priority to nuclear safety.

ARTICLE 11. FINANCIAL AND HUMAN RESOURCES

1. Each Contracting Party shall take the appropriate steps to ensure that adequate financial resources are available to support the safety of each nuclear installation throughout its life.

2. Each Contracting Party shall take the appropriate steps to ensure that sufficient numbers of qualified staff with appropriate education, training and retraining are available for all safety-related activities in or for each nuclear installation, throughout its life.

ARTICLE 12. HUMAN FACTORS

Each Contracting Party shall take the appropriate steps to ensure that the capabilities and limitations of human performance are taken into account throughout the life of a nuclear installation.

ARTICLE 13. QUALITY ASSURANCE

Each Contracting Party shall take the appropriate steps to ensure that quality assurance programmes are established and implemented with a view to providing confidence that specified requirements for all activities important to nuclear safety are satisfied throughout the life of a nuclear installation.

ARTICLE 14. ASSESSMENT AND VERIFICATION OF SAFETY

Each Contracting Party shall take the appropriate steps to ensure that:

(i) comprehensive and systematic safety assessments are carried out before the construction and commissioning of a nuclear installation and throughout its life. Such assessments shall be well documented, subsequently updated in the light of operating experience and significant new safety information, and reviewed under the authority of the regulatory body;

(ii) verification by analysis, surveillance, testing and inspection is carried out to ensure that the physical state and the operation of a nuclear installation continue to be in accordance with its design, applicable national safety requirements, and operational limits and conditions.

ARTICLE 15. RADIATION PROTECTION

Each Contracting Party shall take the appropriate steps to ensure that in all operational states the radiation exposure to the workers and the public caused by a nuclear installation shall be kept as low as reasonably achievable and that no individual shall be exposed to radiation doses which exceed prescribed national dose limits.

ARTICLE 16. EMERGENCY PREPAREDNESS

1. Each Contracting Party shall take the appropriate steps to ensure that there are on-site and off-site emergency plans that are routinely tested for nuclear installations and cover the activities to be carried out in the event of an emergency.

For any new nuclear installation, such plans shall be prepared and tested before it commences operation above a low power level agreed by the regulatory body.

2. Each Contracting Party shall take the appropriate steps to ensure that, insofar as they are likely to be affected by a radiological emergency, its own population and the competent authorities of the States in the vicinity of the nuclear installation are provided with appropriate information for emergency planning and response.

3. Contracting Parties which do not have a nuclear installation on their territory, insofar as they are likely to be affected in the event of a radiological emergency at a nuclear installation in the vicinity, shall take the appropriate steps for the preparation and testing of emergency plans for their territory that cover the activities to be carried out in the event of such an emergency.

(d) Safety of Installations

ARTICLE 17. SITING

Each Contracting Party shall take the appropriate steps to ensure that appropriate procedures are established and implemented:

(i) for evaluating all relevant site-related factors likely to affect the safety of a nuclear installation for its projected lifetime;

(ii) for evaluating the likely safety impact of a proposed nuclear installation on individuals, society and the environment;

(iii) for re-evaluating as necessary all relevant factors referred to in sub-paragraphs (i) and (ii) so as to ensure the continued safety acceptability of the nuclear installation;

(iv) for consulting Contracting Parties in the vicinity of a proposed nuclear installation, insofar as they are likely to be affected by that installation and, upon request providing the necessary information to such Contracting Parties, in order to enable them to evaluate and make their own assessment of the likely safety impact on their own territory of the nuclear installation.

ARTICLE 18. DESIGN AND CONSTRUCTION

Each Contracting Party shall take the appropriate steps to ensure that:

(i) the design and construction of a nuclear installation provides for several reliable levels and methods of protection (defense in depth) against the release of radioactive materials, with a view to preventing the occurrence of accidents and to mitigating their radiological consequences should they occur;

(ii) the technologies incorporated in the design and construction of a nuclear installation are proven by experience or qualified by testing or analysis;

(iii) the design of a nuclear installation allows for reliable, stable and easily manageable operation, with specific consideration of human factors and the manmachine interface.

ARTICLE 19. OPERATION

Each Contracting Party shall take the appropriate steps to ensure that:

(i) the initial authorization to operate a nuclear installation is based upon an appropriate safety analysis and a commissioning programme demonstrating that the installation, as constructed, is consistent with design and safety requirements;

(ii) operational limits and conditions derived from the safety analysis, tests and operational experience are defined and revised as necessary for identifying safe boundaries for operation;

(iii) operation, maintenance, inspection and testing of a nuclear installation are conducted in accordance with approved procedures;

(iv) procedures are established for responding to anticipated operational occurrences and to accidents;

(v) necessary engineering and technical support in all safety-related fields is available throughout the lifetime of a nuclear installation;

(vi) incidents significant to safety are reported in a timely manner by the holder of the relevant licence to the regulatory body;

(vii) programmes to collect and analyse operating experience are established, the results obtained and the conclusions drawn are acted upon and that existing mechanisms are used to share important experience with international bodies and with other operating organizations and regulatory bodies;

(viii) the generation of radioactive waste resulting from the operation of a nuclear installation is kept to the minimum practicable for the process concerned, both in activity and in volume, and any necessary treatment and storage of spent fuel and waste directly related to the operation and on the same site as that of the nuclear installation take into consideration conditioning and disposal.

CHAPTER 3. MEETINGS OF THE CONTRACTING PARTIES

ARTICLE 20. REVIEW MEETINGS

1. The Contracting Parties shall hold meetings (hereinafter referred to as "review meetings") for the purpose of reviewing the reports submitted pursuant to Article 5 in accordance with the procedures adopted under Article 22.

2. Subject to the provisions of Article 24 sub-groups comprised of representatives of Contracting Parties may be established and may function during the review meetings as deemed necessary for the purpose of reviewing specific subjects contained in the reports.

3. Each Contracting Party shall have a reasonable opportunity to discuss the reports submitted by other Contracting Parties and to seek clarification of such reports.

ARTICLE 21. TIMETABLE

1. A preparatory meeting of the Contracting Parties shall be held not later than six months after the date of entry into force of this Convention.

2. At this preparatory meeting, the Contracting Parties shall determine the date for the first review meeting. This review meeting shall be held as soon as possible, but not later than thirty months after the date of entry into force of this Convention.

3. At each review meeting, the Contracting Parties shall determine the date for the next such meeting. The interval between review meetings shall not exceed three years.

ARTICLE 22. PROCEDURAL ARRANGEMENTS

1. At the preparatory meeting held pursuant to Article 21 the Contracting Parties shall prepare and adopt by consensus Rules of Procedure and Financial Rules. The Contracting Parties shall establish in particular and in accordance with the Rules of Procedure:

(i) guidelines regarding the form and structure of the reports to be submitted pursuant to Article 5;

(ii) a date for the submission of such reports;

(iii) the process for reviewing such reports.

2. At review meetings the Contracting Parties may, if necessary, review the arrangements established pursuant to sub-paragraphs (i)-(iii) above, and adopt revisions by consensus unless otherwise provided for in the Rules of Procedure. They may also amend the Rules of Procedure and the Financial Rules, by consensus.

ARTICLE 23. EXTRAORDINARY MEETINGS

An extraordinary meeting of the Contracting Parties shall be held:

(i) if so agreed by a majority of the Contracting Parties present and voting at a meeting, abstentions being considered as voting; or

(ii) at the written request of a Contracting Party, within six months of this request having been communicated to the Contracting Parties and notification having been received by the secretariat referred to in Article 28, that the request has been supported by a majority of the Contracting Parties.

ARTICLE 24. ATTENDANCE

1. Each Contracting Party shall attend meetings of the Contracting Parties and be represented at such meetings by one delegate, and by such alternates, experts and advisers as it deems necessary.

2. The Contracting Parties may invite, by consensus, any intergovernmental organization which is competent in respect of matters governed by this Convention to attend, as an observer, any meeting, or specific sessions thereof. Observers shall be required to accept in writing, and in advance, the provisions of Article 27.

ARTICLE 25. SUMMARY REPORTS

The Contracting Parties shall adopt, by consensus, and make available to the public a document addressing issues discussed and conclusions reached during a meeting.

ARTICLE 26. LANGUAGES

1. The languages of meetings of the Contracting Parties shall be Arabic, Chinese, English, French, Russian and Spanish unless otherwise provided in the Rules of Procedure.

2. Reports submitted pursuant to Article 5 shall be prepared in the national language of the submitting Contracting Party or in a single designated language to be agreed in the Rules of Procedure. Should the report be submitted in a national language other than the designated ***1523** language, a translation of the report into the designated language shall be provided by the Contracting Party.

3. Notwithstanding the provisions of paragraph 2, if compensated, the secretariat will assume the translation into the designated language of reports submitted in any other language of the meeting.

ARTICLE 27. CONFIDENTIALITY

1. The provisions of this Convention shall not affect the rights and obligations of the Contracting Parties under their law to protect information from disclosure. For the purposes of this Article, "information" includes, inter alia, (i) personal data; (ii) information protected by intellectual property rights or by industrial or commercial confidentiality; and (iii) information relating to national security or to the physical protection of nuclear materials or nuclear installations.

2. When, in the context of this Convention, a Contracting Party provides information identified by it as protected as described in paragraph 1, such information shall be used only for the purposes for which it has been provided and its confidentiality shall be respected.

3. The content of the debates during the reviewing of the reports by the Contracting Parties at each meeting shall be confidential.

ARTICLE 28. SECRETARIAT

1. The International Atomic Energy Agency, (hereinafter referred to as the "Agency") shall provide the secretariat for the meetings of the Contracting Parties.

2. The secretariat shall:

(i) convene, prepare and service the meetings of the Contracting Parties;

(ii) transmit to the Contracting Parties information received or prepared in accordance with the provisions of this Convention.

The costs incurred by the Agency in carrying out the functions referred to in subparagraphs i) and (ii) above shall be borne by the Agency as part of its regular budget.

3. The Contracting Parties may, by consensus, request the Agency to provide other services in support of meetings of the Contracting Parties. The Agency may provide such services if they can be undertaken within its programme and regular budget. Should this not be possible, the Agency may provide such services if voluntary funding is provided from another source.

CHAPTER 4. FINAL CLAUSES AND OTHER PROVISIONS

ARTICLE 29. RESOLUTION OF DISAGREEMENTS

In the event of a disagreement between two or more Contracting Parties concerning the interpretation or application of this Convention, the Contracting Parties shall consult within the framework of a meeting of the Contracting Parties with a view to resolving the disagreement.

ARTICLE 30. SIGNATURE, RATIFICATION, ACCEPTANCE, APPROVAL, ACCESSION

1. This Convention shall be open for signature by all States at the Headquarters of the Agency in Vienna from 20 September 1994 until its entry into force.

2. This Convention is subject to ratification, acceptance or approval by the signatory States.

3. After its entry into force, this Convention shall be open for accession by all States.

4. (i) This Convention shall be open for signature or accession by regional organizations of an integration or other nature, provided that any such organization is constituted by sovereign States and has competence in respect of the negotiation, conclusion and application of international agreements in matters covered by this Convention.

(ii) In matters within their competence, such organizations shall, on their own behalf, exercise the rights and fulfil the responsibilities which this Convention attributes to States Parties.

(iii) When becoming party to this Convention, such an organization shall communicate to the Depositary referred to in Article 34, a declaration indicating which States are members thereof, which articles of this Convention apply to it, and the extent of its competence in the field covered by those articles.

(iv) Such an organization shall not hold any vote additional to those of its Member States.

5. Instruments of ratification, acceptance, approval or accession shall be deposited with the Depositary.

ARTICLE 31. ENTRY INTO FORCE

1. This Convention shall enter into force on the ninetieth day after the date of deposit with the Depositary of the twenty-second instrument of ratification, acceptance or approval, including the instruments of seventeen States, each having at least one nuclear installation which has achieved criticality in a reactor core.

2. For each State or regional organization of an integration or other nature which ratifies, accepts, approves or accedes to this Convention after the date of deposit of the last instrument required to satisfy the conditions set forth in paragraph 1, this Convention shall enter into force on the ninetieth day after the date of deposit with the Depositary of the appropriate instrument by such a State or organization.

ARTICLE 32. AMENDMENTS TO THE CONVENTION

1. Any Contracting Party may propose an amendment to this Convention. Proposed amendments shall be considered at a review meeting or an extraordinary meeting.

2. The text of any proposed amendment and the reasons for it shall be provided to the Depositary who shall communicate the proposal to the Contracting Parties promptly and at least ninety days before the meeting for which it is submitted for consideration. Any comments received on such a proposal shall be circulated by the Depositary to the Contracting Parties.

3. The Contracting Parties shall decide after consideration of the proposed amendment whether to adopt it by consensus, or, in the absence of consensus, to submit it to a Diplomatic Conference. A decision to submit a proposed amendment to a Diplomatic Conference shall require a two-thirds majority vote of the Contracting Parties present and voting at the meeting, provided that at least one half of the Contracting Parties are present at the time of voting. Abstentions shall be considered as voting.

4. The Diplomatic Conference to consider and adopt amendments to this Convention shall be convened by the Depositary and held no later than one year after the appropriate decision taken in accordance with paragraph 3 of this Article. The

Diplomatic Conference shall make every effort to ensure amendments are adopted by consensus. Should this not be possible, amendments shall be adopted with a two-thirds majority of all Contracting Parties.

5. Amendments to this Convention adopted pursuant to paragraphs 3 and 4 above shall be subject to ratification, acceptance, approval, or confirmation by the Contracting Parties and shall enter into force for those Contracting Parties which have ratified, accepted, approved or confirmed them on the ninetieth day after the receipt by the Depositary of the relevant instruments by at least three fourths of the Contracting Parties. For a Contracting Party which subsequently ratifies, accepts, approves or confirms the said amendments, the amendments will enter into force on the ninetieth day after that Contracting Party has deposited its relevant instrument.

ARTICLE 33. DENUNCIATION

1. Any Contracting Party may denounce this Convention by written notification to the Depositary.

2. Denunciation shall take effect one year following the date of the receipt of the notification by the Depositary, or on such later date as may be specified in the notification.

ARTICLE 34. DEPOSITARY

1. The Director General of the Agency shall be the Depositary of this Convention.

2. The Depositary shall inform the Contracting Parties of:

(i) the signature of this Convention and of the deposit of instruments of ratification, acceptance, approval or accession, in accordance with Article 30;

(ii) the date on which the Convention enters into force, in accordance with Article 31;

(iii) the notifications of denunciation of the Convention and the date thereof, made in accordance with Article 33;

(iv) the proposed amendments to this Convention submitted by Contracting Parties, the amendments adopted by the relevant Diplomatic Conference or by the meeting of the Contracting Parties, and the date of entry into force of the said amendments, in accordance with Article 32.

ARTICLE 35. AUTHENTIC TEXTS

The original of this Convention of which the Arabic, Chinese, English, French, Russian and Spanish texts are equally authentic, shall be deposited with the Depositary, who shall send certified copies thereof to the Contracting Parties.

3.23 1997 VIENNA CONVENTION ON CIVIL LIABILITY FOR NUCLEAR DAMAGE. Done in Vienna, 21 May 1963 (original convention) & 12 September 1997 (amending protocol). Original (1963) convention entered into force, 12 November 1977. Amending protocol is not yet in force. 1063 U.N.T.S. 265, IAEA INFCIRC 500 (1996)(original); *reprinted in* 27 I.L.M. 727 (1963) & 5 Weston V.J.3; protocol *reprinted in* 36 I.L.M. 1462 (1997)

The Contracting Parties,

Having recognized the desirability of establishing some minimum standards to provide financial protection against damage resulting from certain peaceful uses of nuclear energy,

Believing that a convention on civil liability for nuclear damage would also contribute to the development of friendly relations among nations, irrespective of their differing constitutional and social systems,

Have decided to conclude a convention for such purposes, and thereto have agreed as follows—

ARTICLE I

1. For the purposes of this Convention—

(a) "Person" means any individual, partnership, any private or public body whether corporate or not, any international organization enjoying legal personality under the law of the Installation State, and any State or any of its constituent sub-divisions.

(b) "National of a Contracting Party" includes a Contracting Party or any of its constituent sub-divisions, a partnership, or any private or public body whether corporate or not established within the territory of a Contracting Party.

(c) "Operator", in relation to a nuclear installation, means the person designated or recognized by the Installation State as the operator of that installation.

(d) "Installation State", in relation to a nuclear installation, means the Contracting Party within whose territory that installation is situated or, if it is not situated within the territory of any State, the Contracting Party by which or under the authority of which the nuclear installation is operated.

(e) "Law of the competent court" means the law of the court having jurisdiction under this Convention, including any rules of such law relating to conflict of laws.

(f) "Nuclear fuel" means any material which is capable of producing energy by a self-sustaining chain process of nuclear fission.

(g) "Radioactive products or waste" means any radioactive material produced in, or any material made radioactive by exposure to the radiation incidental to, the production or utilization of nuclear fuel, but does not include radioisotopes which have reached the final stage of fabrication so as to be usable for any scientific, medical, agricultural, commercial or industrial purpose.

(h) "Nuclear material" means-

(i) nuclear fuel, other than natural uranium and depleted uranium, capable of producing energy by a self-sustaining chain process of nuclear fission outside a nuclear reactor, either alone or in combination with some other material; and

(ii) radioactive products or waste.

(i) "Nuclear reactor" means any structure containing nuclear fuel in such an arrangement that a self-sustaining chain process of nuclear fission can occur therein without an additional source of neutrons.

(j) "Nuclear installation" means-

(i) any nuclear reactor other than one with which a means of sea or air transport is equipped for use as a source of power, whether for propulsion thereof or for any other purpose;

(ii) any factory using nuclear fuel for the production of nuclear material, or any factory for the processing of nuclear material, including any factory for the re-processing of irradiated nuclear fuel;

(iii) any facility where nuclear material is stored other than storage incidental to the carriage of such material; provided that the Installation State may determine that several nuclear installations of one operator which are located at the same site shall be considered as a single nuclear installation, and

(iv) such other installations in which there are nuclear fuel or radioactive products or waste as the Board of Governors of the International Atomic Energy Agency shall from time to time determine.

(k) "Nuclear Damage" means-

(i) loss of life or personal injury;

(ii) loss of or damage to property;

and each of the following to the extent determined by the law of the competent court—

(iii) economic loss arising from loss or damage referred to in sub-paragraph (i) or (ii), insofar as not included in those sub-paragraphs, if incurred by a person entitled to claim in respect of such loss or damage;

(iv) the costs of measures of reinstatement of impaired environment, unless such impairment is insignificant, if such measures are actually taken or to be taken, and insofar as not included in sub-paragraph (ii);

(v) loss of income deriving from an economic interest in any use or enjoyment of the environment, incurred as a result of a significant impairment of that environment, and insofar as not included in sub-paragraph (ii);

(vi) the costs of preventive measures, and further loss or damage caused by such measures;

(vii) any other economic loss, other than any caused by the impairment of the environment, if permitted by the general law on civil liability of the competent court, in the case of subparagraphs (i) to (v) and (vii) above, to the extent that the loss or damage arises out of or results from ionizing radiation emitted by any source of radiation inside a nuclear installation, or emitted from nuclear fuel or radioactive products or waste in, or of nuclear material coming from, originating in, or sent to, a nuclear installation, whether so arising from the radioactive properties of such matter, or from a combination of radioactive properties with toxic, explosive or other hazardous properties of such matter.

(*l*) "Nuclear incident" means any occurrence or series of occurrences having the same origin which causes nuclear damage or, but only with respect to preventive measures, creates a grave and imminent threat of causing such damage.

(m) "Measures of reinstatement" means any reasonable measures which have been approved by the competent authorities of the State where the measures were taken, and which aim to reinstate or restore damaged or destroyed components of the environment, or to introduce, where reasonable, the equivalent of these components into the environment. The law of the State where the damage is suffered shall determine who is entitled to take such measures.

(n) "Preventive measures" means any reasonable measures taken by any person after a nuclear incident has occurred to prevent or minimize damage referred to in sub-paragraphs (k)(i) to (v) or (vii), subject to any approval of the competent authorities required by the law of the State where the measures were taken.

(*o*) "Reasonable measures" means measures which are found under the law of the competent court to be appropriate and proportionate having regard to all the circumstances, for example-

(i) the nature and extent of the damage incurred or, in the case of preventive measures, the nature and extent of the risk of such damage;

(ii) the extent to which, at the time they are taken, such measures are likely to be effective; and

(iii) relevant scientific and technical expertise.

(p) "Special Drawing Right", hereinafter referred to as SDR, means the unit of account defined by the International Monetary Fund and used by it for its own operations and transactions.

2. An Installation State may, if the small extent of the risks involved so warrants, exclude any nuclear installation or small quantities of nuclear material from the application of this Convention, provided that-

(a) with respect to nuclear installations, criteria for such exclusion have been established by the Board of Governors of the International Atomic Energy Agency and any exclusion by an Installation State satisfies such criteria; and

(b) with respect to small quantities of nuclear material, maximum limits for the exclusion of such quantities have been established by the Board of Governors of the International Atomic Energy Agency and any exclusion by an Installation State is within such established limits.

The criteria for the exclusion of nuclear installations and the maximum limits for the exclusion of small quantities of nuclear material shall be reviewed periodically by the Board of Governors.

ARTICLE I A

1. This Convention shall apply to nuclear damage wherever suffered.

2. However, the legislation of the Installation State may exclude from the application of this Convention damage suffered—

(a) in the territory of a non-Contracting State; or

(b) in any maritime zones established by a non-Contracting State in accordance with the international law of the sea.

3. An exclusion pursuant to paragraph 2 of this Article may apply only in respect of a non-Contracting State which at the time of the incident-

(a) has a nuclear installation in its territory or in any maritime zones established by it in accordance with the international law of the sea; and

(b) does not afford equivalent reciprocal benefits.

4. Any exclusion pursuant to paragraph 2 of this Article shall not affect the rights referred to in sub-paragraph (a) of paragraph 2 of Article IX and any exclusion

pursuant to paragraph 2(b) of this Article shall not extend to damage on board or to a ship or an aircraft.

ARTICLE I B

This Convention shall not apply to nuclear installations used for non-peaceful purposes.

ARTICLE II

1. The operator of a nuclear installation shall be liable for nuclear damage upon proof that such damage has been caused by a nuclear incident—

(a) in his nuclear installation; or

(b) involving nuclear material coming from or originating in his nuclear installation, and occurring-

(i) before liability with regard to nuclear incidents involving the nuclear material has been assumed, pursuant to the express terms of a contract in writing, by the operator of another nuclear installation;

(ii) in the absence of such express terms, before the operator of another nuclear installation has taken charge of the nuclear material; or

(iii) where the nuclear material is intended to be used in a nuclear reactor with which a means of transport is equipped for use as a source of power, whether for propulsion thereof or for any other purpose, before the person duly authorized to operate such reactor has taken charge of the nuclear material; but

(iv) where the nuclear material has been sent to a person within the territory of a non-Contracting State, before it has been unloaded from the means of transport by which it has arrived in the territory of that non-Contracting State;

(c) involving nuclear material sent to his nuclear installation, and occurring-

(i) after liability with regard to nuclear incidents involving the nuclear material has been assumed by him, pursuant to the express terms of a contract in writing, from the operator of another nuclear installation;

(ii) in the absence of such express terms, after he has taken charge of the nuclear material; or

(iii) after he has taken charge of the nuclear material from a person operating a nuclear reactor with which a means of transport is equipped for use as a source of power, whether for propulsion thereof or for any other purpose; but

(iv) where the nuclear material has, with the written consent of the operator, been sent from a person within the territory of a non-Contracting State, only after it has been loaded on the means of transport by which it is to be carried from the territory of that State; provided that, if nuclear damage is caused by a nuclear incident occurring in a nuclear installation and involving nuclear material stored therein incidentally to the carriage of such material, the provisions of sub-paragraph (a) of this paragraph shall not apply where another operator or person is solely liable pursuant to the provisions of sub-paragraph (b) or (c) of this paragraph.

2. The Installation State may provide by legislation that, in accordance with such terms as may be specified therein, a carrier of nuclear material or a person handling radioactive waste may, at his request and with the consent of the operator concerned, be designated or recognized as operator in the place of that operator in respect of such

nuclear material or radioactive waste respectively. In this case such carrier or such person shall be considered, for all the purposes of this Convention, as an operator of a nuclear installation situated within the territory of that State.

3. (a) Where nuclear damage engages the liability of more than one operator, the operators involved shall, in so far as the damage attributable to each operator is not reasonably separable, be jointly and severally liable. The Installation State may limit the amount of public funds made available per incident to the difference, if any, between the amounts hereby established and the amount established pursuant to paragraph 1 of Article V.

(b) Where a nuclear incident occurs in the course of carriage of nuclear material, either in one and the same means of transport, or, in the case of storage incidental to the carriage, in one and the same nuclear installation, and causes nuclear damage which engages the liability of more than one operator, the total liability shall not exceed the highest amount applicable with respect to any one of them pursuant to Article V.

(c) In neither of the cases referred to in sub-paragraphs (a) and (b) of this paragraph shall the liability of any one operator exceed the amount applicable with respect to him pursuant to Article V.

4. Subject to the provisions of paragraph 3 of this Article, where several nuclear installations of one and the same operator are involved in one nuclear incident, such operator shall be liable in respect of each nuclear installation involved up to the amount applicable with respect to him pursuant to Article V. The Installation State may limit the amount of public funds made available as provided for in sub-paragraph (a) of paragraph 3 of this Article.

5. Except as otherwise provided in this Convention, no person other than the operator shall be liable for nuclear damage. This, however, shall not affect the application of any international convention in the field of transport in force or open for signature, ratification or accession at the date on which this Convention is opened for signature.

6. No person shall be liable for any loss or damage which is not nuclear damage pursuant to sub-paragraph (k) of paragraph 1 of Article I but which could have been determined as such pursuant to the provisions of that sub-paragraph. could have been included as such pursuant to sub-paragraph (k) (ii) of that paragraph.

7. Direct action shall lie against the person furnishing financial security pursuant to Article VII, if the law of the competent court so provides.

ARTICLE III

The operator liable in accordance with this Convention shall provide the carrier with a certificate issued by or on behalf of the insurer or other financial guarantor furnishing the financial security required pursuant to Article VII. However, the Installation State may exclude this obligation in relation to carriage which takes place wholly within its own territory. The certificate shall state the name and address of that operator and the amount, type and duration of the security, and these statements may not be disputed by the person by whom or on whose behalf the certificate was issued. The certificate shall also indicate the nuclear material in respect of which the security applies and shall include a statement by the competent public authority of the Installation State that the person named is an operator within the meaning of this Convention.

ARTICLE IV

1. The liability of the operator for nuclear damage under this Convention shall be absolute.

2. If the operator proves that the nuclear damage resulted wholly or partly either from the gross negligence of the person suffering the damage or from an act or omission of such person done with intent to cause damage, the competent court may, if its law so provides, relieve the operator wholly or partly from his obligation to pay compensation in respect of the damage suffered by such person.

3. No liability under this Convention shall attach to an operator if he proves that the nuclear damage is directly due to an act of armed conflict, hostilities, civil war or insurrection.

4. Whenever both nuclear damage and damage other than nuclear damage have been caused by a nuclear incident or jointly by a nuclear incident and one or more other occurrences, such other damage shall, to the extent that it is not reasonably separable from the nuclear damage, be deemed, for the purposes of this Convention, to be nuclear damage caused by that nuclear incident. Where, however, damage is caused jointly by a nuclear incident covered by this Convention and by an emission of ionizing radiation not covered by it, nothing in this Convention shall limit or otherwise affect the liability, either as regards any person suffering nuclear damage or by way of recourse or contribution, of any person who may be held liable in connection with that emission of ionizing radiation.

5. The operator shall not be liable under this Convention for nuclear damage—

(a) to the nuclear installation itself and any other nuclear installation, including a nuclear installation under construction, on the site where that installation is located; and

(b) to any property on that same site which is used or to be used in connection with any such installation.

6. Compensation for damage caused to the means of transport upon which the nuclear material involved was at the time of the nuclear incident shall not have the effect of reducing the liability of the operator in respect of other damage to an amount less than either 150 million SDRs, or any higher amount established by the legislation of a Contracting Party, or an amount established pursuant to sub-paragraph (c) of paragraph 1 of Article V.

7. Nothing in this Convention shall affect the liability of any individual for nuclear damage for which the operator, by virtue of paragraph 3 or 5 of this Article, is not liable under this Convention and which that individual caused by an act or omission done with intent to cause damage.

ARTICLE V

1. The liability of the operator may be limited by the Installation State for any one nuclear incident, either-

(a) to not less than 300 million SDRs; or

(b) to not less than 150 million SDRs provided that in excess of that amount and up to at least 300 million SDRs public funds shall be made available by that State to compensate nuclear damage; or

(c) for a maximum of 15 years from the date of entry into force of this Protocol, to a transitional amount of not less than 100 million SDRs in respect of a nuclear incident occurring within that period. An amount lower than 100 million SDRs may be established, provided that public funds shall be made available by that State to compensate nuclear damage between that lesser amount and 100 million SDRs.

2. Notwithstanding paragraph 1 of this Article, the Installation State, having regard to the nature of the nuclear installation or the nuclear substances involved and to the likely consequences of an incident originating therefrom, may establish a lower

amount of liability of the operator, provided that in no event shall any amount so established be less than 5 million SDRs, and provided that the Installation State ensures that public funds shall be made available up to the amount established pursuant to paragraph 1.

3. The amounts established by the Installation State of the liable operator in accordance with paragraphs 1 and 2 of this Article and paragraph 6 of Article IV shall apply wherever the nuclear incident occurs.

ARTICLE V A

1. Interest and costs awarded by a court in actions for compensation of nuclear damage shall be payable in addition to the amounts referred to in Article V.

2. The amounts mentioned in Article V and paragraph 6 of Article IV may be converted into national currency in round figures.

ARTICLE V B

Each Contracting Party shall ensure that persons suffering damage may enforce their rights to compensation without having to bring separate proceedings according to the origin of the funds provided for such compensation.

ARTICLE V C

1. If the courts having jurisdiction are those of a Contracting Party other than the Installation State, the public funds required under sub-paragraphs (b) and (c) of paragraph 1 of Article V and under paragraph 1 of Article VII, as well as interest and costs awarded by a court, may be made available by the first-named Contracting Party. The Installation State shall reimburse to the other Contracting Party any such sums paid. These two Contracting Parties shall agree on the procedure for reimbursement.

2. If the courts having jurisdiction are those of a Contracting Party other than the Installation State, the Contracting Party whose courts have jurisdiction shall take all measures necessary to enable the Installation State to intervene in proceedings and to participate in any settlement concerning compensation.

ARTICLE V D

1. A meeting of the Contracting Parties shall be convened by the Director General of the International Atomic Energy Agency to amend the limits of liability referred to in Article V if one-third of the Contracting Parties express a desire to that effect.

2. Amendments shall be adopted by a two-thirds majority of the Contracting Parties present and voting, provided that at least one-half of the Contracting Parties shall be present at the time of the voting.

3. When acting on a proposal to amend the limits, the meeting of the Contracting Parties shall take into account, inter alia, the risk of damage resulting from a nuclear incident, changes in the monetary values, and the capacity of the insurance market.

4. (a) Any amendment adopted in accordance with paragraph 2 of this Article shall be notified by the Director General of the IAEA to all Contracting Parties for acceptance. The amendment shall be considered accepted at the end of a period of 18 months after it has been notified provided that at least one-third of the Contracting Parties at the time of the adoption of the amendment by the meeting have communicated to the Director General of the IAEA that they accept the amendment. An amendment accepted in accordance with this paragraph shall enter into force 12 months after its acceptance for those Contracting Parties which have accepted it.

(b) If, within a period of 18 months from the date of notification for acceptance, an amendment has not been accepted in accordance with sub-paragraph (a), the amendment shall be considered rejected.

5. For each Contracting Party accepting an amendment after it has been accepted but not entered into force or after its entry into force in accordance with paragraph 4 of this Article, the amendment shall enter into force 12 months after its acceptance by that Contracting Party.

6. A State which becomes a Party to this Convention after the entry into force of an amendment in accordance with paragraph 4 of this Article shall, failing an expression of a different intention by that State—

(a) be considered as a Party to this Convention as so amended; and

(b) be considered as a Party to the unamended Convention in relation to any State Party not bound by the amendment.

ARTICLE VI

1. (a) Rights of compensation under this Convention shall be extinguished if an action is not brought within-

(i) with respect to loss of life and personal injury, thirty years from the date of the nuclear incident;

(ii) with respect to other damage, ten years from the date of the nuclear incident.

(b) If, however, under the law of the Installation State, the liability of the operator is covered by insurance or other financial security including State funds for a longer period, the law of the competent court may provide that rights of compensation against the operator shall only be extinguished after such a longer period which shall not exceed the period for which his liability is so covered under the law of the Installation State.

(c) Actions for compensation with respect to loss of life and personal injury or, pursuant to an extension under sub-paragraph (b) of this paragraph with respect to other damage, which are brought after a period of ten years from the date of the nuclear incident shall in no case affect the rights of compensation under this Convention of any person who has brought an action against the operator before the expiry of that period.

2. (Deleted–1997)

3. Rights of compensation under the Convention shall be subject to prescription or extinction, as provided by the law of the competent court, if an action is not brought within three years from the date on which the person suffering damage had knowledge or ought reasonably to have had knowledge of the damage and of the operator liable for the damage, provided that the periods established pursuant to sub-paragraphs (a) and (b) of paragraph 1 of this Article shall not be exceeded.

4. Unless the law of the competent court otherwise provides, any person who claims to have suffered nuclear damage and who has brought an action for compensation within the period applicable pursuant to this Article may amend his claim to take into account any aggravation of the damage, even after the expiry of that period, provided that final judgment has not been entered.

5. Where jurisdiction is to be determined pursuant to sub-paragraph (b) of paragraph 3 of Article XI and a request has been made within the period applicable pursuant to this Article to any one of the Contracting Parties empowered so to determine, but the time remaining after such determination is less than six months, the period within which an action may be brought shall be six months, reckoned from the date of such determination.

ARTICLE VII

1. (a) The operator shall be required to maintain insurance or other financial security covering his liability for nuclear damage in such amount, of such type and in such terms as the Installation State shall specify. The Installation State shall ensure the payment of claims for compensation for nuclear damage which have been established against the operator by providing the necessary funds to the extent that the yield of insurance or other financial security is inadequate to satisfy such claims, but not in excess of the limit, if any, established pursuant to Article V. Where the liability of the operator is unlimited, the Installation State may establish a limit of the financial security of the operator liable, provided that such limit is not lower than 300 million SDRs. The Installation State shall ensure the payment of claims for compensation for nuclear damage which have been established against the operator to the extent that the yield of the financial security is inadequate to satisfy such claims, but not in excess of the amount of the financial security to be provided under this paragraph.

(b) Notwithstanding sub-paragraph (a) of this paragraph, where the liability of the operator is unlimited, the Installation State, having regard to the nature of the nuclear installation or the nuclear substances involved and to the likely consequences of an incident originating therefrom, may establish a lower amount of financial security of the operator, provided that in no event shall any amount so established be less than 5 million SDRs, and provided that the Installation State ensures the payment of claims for compensation for nuclear damage which have been established against the operator by providing necessary funds to the extent that the yield of insurance or other financial security is inadequate to satisfy such claims, and up to the limit provided pursuant to sub-paragraph (a) of this paragraph.

2. Nothing in paragraph 1 of this Article or sub-paragraphs (b) and (c) of paragraph 1 of Article V shall require a Contracting Party or any of its constituent sub-divisions, such as States or Republics, to maintain insurance or other financial security to cover their liability as operators.

3. The funds provided by insurance, by other financial security or by the Installation State pursuant to paragraph 1 of this Article or sub-paragraphs (b) and (c) of paragraph 1 of Article V shall be exclusively available for compensation due under this Convention.

4. No insurer or other financial guarantor shall suspend or cancel the insurance or other financial security provided pursuant to paragraph 1 of this Article or sub-paragraphs (b) and (c) of paragraph 1 of Article V without giving notice in writing of at least two months to the competent public authority or, in so far as such insurance or other financial security relates to the carriage of nuclear material, during the period of the carriage in question.

ARTICLE VIII

1. Subject to the provisions of this Convention, the nature, form and extent of the compensation, as well as the equitable distribution thereof, shall be governed by the law of the competent court.

2. Subject to application of the rule of sub-paragraph (c) of paragraph 1 of Article VI, where in respect of claims brought against the operator the damage to be compensated under this Convention exceeds, or is likely to exceed, the maximum amount made available pursuant to paragraph 1 of Article V, priority in the distribution of the compensation shall be given to claims in respect of loss of life or personal injury.

ARTICLE IX

1. Where provisions of national or public health insurance, social insurance, social security, workmen's compensation or occupational disease compensation systems include compensation for nuclear damage, rights of beneficiaries of such systems to obtain compensation under this Convention and rights of recourse by virtue of such systems against the operator liable shall be determined, subject to the provisions of this Convention, by the law of the Contracting Party in which such systems have been established, or by the regulations of the intergovernmental organization which has established such systems.

2. (a) If a person who is a national of a Contracting Party, other than the operator, has paid compensation for nuclear damage under an international convention or under the law of a non-Contracting State, such person shall, up to the amount which he has paid, acquire by subrogation the rights under this Convention of the person so compensated. No rights shall be so acquired by any person to the extent that the operator has a right of recourse against such person under this Convention.

(b) Nothing in this Convention shall preclude an operator who has paid compensation for nuclear damage out of funds other than those provided pursuant to paragraph 1 of Article VII from recovering from the person providing financial security pursuant to that paragraph or from the Installation State, up to the amount he has paid, the sum which the person so compensated would have obtained under this Convention.

ARTICLE X

The operator shall have a right of recourse only—

(a) if this is expressly provided for by a contract in writing; or

(b) if the nuclear incident results from an act or omission done with intent to cause damage, against the individual who has acted or omitted to act with such intent. The right of recourse provided for under this Article may also be extended to benefit the Installation State insofar as it has provided public funds pursuant to this Convention.

ARTICLE XI

1. Except as otherwise provided in this Article, jurisdiction over actions under Article II shall lie only with the courts of the Contracting Party within whose territory the nuclear incident occurred.

1bis. Where a nuclear incident occurs within the area of the exclusive economic zone of a Contracting Party or, if such a zone has not been established, in an area not exceeding the limits of an exclusive economic zone, were one to be established, jurisdiction over actions concerning nuclear damage from that nuclear incident shall, for the purposes of this Convention, lie only with the courts of that Party. The preceding sentence shall apply if that Contracting Party has notified the Depositary of such area prior to the nuclear incident. Nothing in this paragraph shall be interpreted as permitting the exercise of jurisdiction in a manner which is contrary of the international law of the sea, including the United Nations Convention on the Law of the Sea.

2. Where a nuclear incident does not occur within the territory of any Contracting Party, or within an area notified pursuant to paragraph 1bis, or where the place of the nuclear incident cannot be determined with certainty, jurisdiction over such actions shall lie with the courts of the Installation State of the operator liable.

3. Where under paragraph 1, 1bis or 2 of this Article, jurisdiction would lie with the courts of more than one Contracting Party, jurisdiction shall lie—

(a) if the nuclear incident occurred partly outside the territory of any Contracting Party, and partly within the territory of a single Contracting Party, with the courts of the latter; and

(b) in any other case, with the courts of that Contracting Party which is determined by agreement between the Contracting Parties whose courts would be competent under paragraph 1 or 2 of this Article.

4. The Contracting Party whose courts have jurisdiction shall ensure that only one of its courts shall have jurisdiction in relation to any one nuclear incident.

ARTICLE XI A

The Contracting Party whose courts have jurisdiction shall ensure that in relation to actions for compensation of nuclear damage—

(a) any State may bring an action on behalf of persons who have suffered nuclear damage, who are nationals of that State or have their domicile or residence in its territory, and who have consented thereto; and

(b) any person may bring an action to enforce rights under this Convention acquired by subrogation or assignment.

ARTICLE XII

1. A judgment that is no longer subject to ordinary forms of review entered by a court of a Contracting Party having jurisdiction shall be recognized, except—

(a) where the judgment was obtained by fraud;

(b) where the party against whom the judgment was pronounced was not given a fair opportunity to present his case; or

(c) where the judgment is contrary to the public policy of the Contracting Party within the territory of which recognition is sought, or is not in accord with fundamental standards of justice.

2. A judgment which is recognized under paragraph 1 of this Article shall, upon being presented for enforcement in accordance with the formalities required by the law of the Contracting Party where enforcement is sought, be enforceable as if it were a judgment of a court of that Contracting Party. The merits of a claim on which the judgment has been given shall not be subject to further proceedings.

ARTICLE XIII

1. This Convention and the national law applicable thereunder shall be applied without any discrimination based upon nationality, domicile or residence.

2. Notwithstanding paragraph 1 of this Article, insofar as compensation for nuclear damage is in excess of 150 million SDRs, the legislation of the Installation State may derogate from the provisions of this Convention with respect to nuclear damage suffered in the territory, or in any maritime zone established in accordance with the international law of the sea, of another State which at the time of the incident, has a nuclear installation in such territory, to the extent that it does not afford reciprocal benefits of an equivalent amount.

ARTICLE XIV

Except in respect of measures of execution, jurisdictional immunities under rules of national or international law shall not be invoked in actions under this Convention before the courts competent pursuant to Article XI.

ARTICLE XV

The Contracting Parties shall take appropriate measures to ensure that compensation for nuclear damage, interest and costs awarded by a court in connection therewith, insurance and reinsurance premiums and funds provided by insurance, reinsurance or other financial security, or funds provided by the Installation State, pursuant to this Convention, shall be freely transferable into the currency of the Contracting Party within whose territory the damage is suffered, and of the Contracting Party within whose territory the claimant is habitually resident, and, as regards insurance or reinsurance premiums and payments, into the currencies specified in the insurance or reinsurance contract.

ARTICLE XVI

No person shall be entitled to recover compensation under this Convention to the extent that he has recovered compensation in respect of the same nuclear damage under another international convention on civil liability in the field of nuclear energy.

ARTICLE XVII

This Convention shall not, as between the parties to them, affect the application of any international agreements or international conventions on civil liability in the field of nuclear energy in force, or open for signature, ratification or accession at the date on which this Convention is opened for signature.

ARTICLE XVIII

This Convention shall not affect the rights and obligations of a Contracting Party under the general rules of public international law.

ARTICLE XIX

Any Contracting Party entering into an agreement pursuant to subparagraph (b) of paragraph 3 of Article XI shall furnish without delay to the Director General of the International Atomic Energy Agency for information and dissemination to the other Contracting Parties a copy of such agreement.

The Contracting Parties shall furnish to the Director General for information and dissemination to the other Contracting Parties copies of their respective laws and regulations relating to matters covered by this Convention.

ARTICLE XX

Notwithstanding the termination of the application of this Convention to any Contracting Party, either by termination pursuant to Article XXV or by denunciation pursuant to Article XXVI, the provisions of this Convention shall continue to apply to any nuclear damage caused by a nuclear incident occurring before such termination.

ARTICLE XX A

1. In the event of a dispute between Contracting Parties concerning the interpretation or application of this Convention, the parties to the dispute shall consult with a view to the settlement of the dispute by negotiation or by any other peaceful means of settling disputes acceptable to them.

2. If a dispute of this character referred to in paragraph 1 of this Article cannot be settled within six months from the request for consultation pursuant to paragraph 1 of this Article, it shall, at the request of any party to such dispute, be submitted to arbitration or referred to the International Court of Justice for decision. Where a dispute is submitted to arbitration, if, within six months from the date of the request, the parties to the dispute are unable to agree on the organization of the arbitration, a

party may request the President of the International Court of Justice or the Secretary–General of the United Nations to appoint one or more arbitrators. In cases of conflicting requests by the parties to the dispute, the request to the Secretary–General of the United Nations shall have priority.

3. When ratifying, accepting, approving or acceding to this Convention, a State may declare that it does not consider itself bound by either or both of the dispute settlement procedures provided for in paragraph 2 of this Article. The other Contracting Parties shall not be bound by a dispute settlement procedure provided for in paragraph 2 of this Article with respect to a Contracting Party for which such a declaration is in force.

4. A Contracting Party which has made a declaration in accordance with paragraph 3 of this Article may at any time withdraw it by notification to the depositary.

ARTICLE XXVI

(deleted)

ARTICLE XXVIII

This Convention shall be registered by the Director General of the International Atomic Energy Agency in accordance with Article 102 of the Charter of the United Nations.

ARTICLE XXIX

The original of this Convention, of which the English, French, Russian and Spanish texts are equally authentic, shall be deposited with the Director General of the International Atomic Energy Agency, who shall issue certified copies.

IN WITNESS WHEREOF, the undersigned Plenipotentiaries, duly authorized thereto, have signed this Convention.

DONE in Vienna, this twenty-first day of May, one thousand nine hundred and sixty-three.

3.24 Convention on Supplementary Compensation for Nuclear Damage. Adopted in Vienna, 12 September 1997. Not yet in force. *Reprinted in* 36 I.L.M. 1454 (1997)

The Contracting Parties,

Recognizing the importance of the measures provided in the Vienna Convention on Civil Liability for Nuclear Damage and the Paris Convention on Third Party Liability in the Field of Nuclear Energy as well as in national legislation on compensation for nuclear damage consistent with the principles of these Conventions;

Desirous of establishing a worldwide liability regime to supplement and enhance these measures with a view to increasing the amount of compensation for nuclear damage;

Recognizing further that such a worldwide liability regime would encourage regional and global co-operation to promote a higher level of nuclear safety in accordance with the principles of international partnership and solidarity;

Have Agreed as follows:

CHAPTER I

GENERAL PROVISIONS

Article I

Definitions

For the purposes of this Convention:

(a) "Vienna Convention" means the Vienna Convention on Civil Liability for Nuclear Damage of 21 May 1963 and any amendment thereto which is in force for a Contracting Party to this Convention.

(b) "Paris Convention" means the Paris Convention on Third Party Liability in the Field of Nuclear Energy of 29 July 1960 and any amendment thereto which is in force for a Contracting Party to this Convention.

(c) "Special Drawing Right", hereinafter referred to as SDR, means the unit of account defined by the International Monetary Fund and used by it for its own operations and transactions.

(d) "Nuclear reactor" means any structure containing nuclear fuel in such an arrangement that a self-sustaining chain process of nuclear fission can occur therein without an additional source of neutrons.

(e) "Installation State", in relation to a nuclear installation, means the Contracting Party within whose territory that installation is situated or, if it is not situated within the territory of any State, the Contracting Party by which or under the authority of which the nuclear installation is operated.

(f) "Nuclear Damage" means:

(i) loss of life or personal injury;

(ii) loss of or damage to property;

and each of the following to the extent determined by the law of the competent court:

(iii) economic loss arising from loss or damage referred to in sub-paragraph (i) or (ii), insofar as not included in those sub-paragraphs, if incurred by a person entitled to claim in respect of such loss or damage;

(iv) the costs of measures of reinstatement of impaired environment, unless such impairment is insignificant, if such measures are actually taken or to be taken, and insofar as not included in sub-paragraph (ii);

(v) loss of income deriving from an economic interest in any use or enjoyment of the environment, incurred as a result of a significant impairment of that environment, and insofar as not included in sub-paragraph (ii);

(vi) the costs of preventive measures, and further loss or damage caused by such measures;

(vii) any other economic loss, other than any caused by the impairment of the environment, if permitted by the general law on civil liability of the competent court,

in the case of sub-paragraphs (i) to (v) and (vii) above, to the extent that the loss or damage arises out of or results from ionizing radiation emitted by any source of radiation inside a nuclear installation, or emitted from nuclear fuel or radioactive products or waste in, or of nuclear material coming from, originating in, or sent to, a nuclear installation, whether so arising from the radioactive properties of such matter, or from a combination of radioactive properties with toxic, explosive or other hazardous properties of such matter.

(g) "Measures of reinstatement" means any reasonable measures which have been approved by the competent authorities of the State where the measures were taken, and which aim to reinstate or restore damaged or destroyed components of the environment, or to introduce, where reasonable, the equivalent of these components into the environment. The law of the State where the damage is suffered shall determine who is entitled to take such measures.

(h) "Preventive measures" means any reasonable measures taken by any person after a nuclear incident has occurred to prevent or minimize damage referred to in sub-paragraphs (f)(i) to (v) or (vii), subject to any approval of the competent authorities required by the law of the State where the measures were taken.

(i) "Nuclear incident" means any occurrence or series of occurrences having the same origin which causes nuclear damage or, but only with respect to preventive measures, creates a grave and imminent threat of causing such damage.

(j) "Installed nuclear capacity" means for each Contracting Party the total of the number of units given by the formula set out in Article IV.2; and "thermal power" means the maximum thermal power authorized by the competent national authorities.

(k) "Law of the competent court" means the law of the court having jurisdiction under this Convention, including any rules of such law relating to conflict of laws.

(*l*) "Reasonable measures" means measures which are found under the law of the competent court to be appropriate and proportionate, having regard to all the circumstances, for example:

(i) the nature and extent of the damage incurred or, in the case of preventive measures, the nature and extent of the risk of such damage;

(ii) the extent to which, at the time they are taken, such measures are likely to be effective; and

(iii) relevant scientific and technical expertise.

Article II

Purpose and Application

1. The purpose of this Convention is to supplement the system of compensation provided pursuant to national law which:

(a) implements one of the instruments referred to in Article I (a) and (b); or

(b) complies with the provisions of the Annex to this Convention.

2. The system of this Convention shall apply to nuclear damage for which an operator of a nuclear installation used for peaceful purposes situated in the territory of a Contracting Party is liable under either one of the Conventions referred to in Article I or national law mentioned in paragraph 1(b) of this Article.

3. The Annex referred to in paragraph 1(b) shall constitute an integral part of this Convention.

CHAPTER II

COMPENSATION

Article III

Undertaking

1. Compensation in respect of nuclear damage per nuclear incident shall be ensured by the following means:

(a) (i) the Installation State shall ensure the availability of 300 million SDRs or a greater amount that it may have specified to the Depositary at any time prior to the nuclear incident, or a transitional amount pursuant to sub-paragraph (ii);

(ii) a Contracting Party may establish for the maximum of 10 years from the date of the opening for signature of this Convention, a transitional amount of at least 150 million SDRs in respect of a nuclear incident occurring within that period.

(b) beyond the amount made available under sub-paragraph (a), the Contracting Parties shall make available public funds according to the formula specified in Article IV.

2. (a) Compensation for nuclear damage in accordance with paragraph 1(a) shall be distributed equitably without discrimination on the basis of nationality, domicile or residence, provided that the law of the Installation State may, subject to obligations of that State under other conventions on nuclear liability, exclude nuclear damage suffered in a non-Contracting State.

(b) Compensation for nuclear damage in accordance with paragraph 1(b), shall, subject to Articles V and XI.1(b), be distributed equitably without discrimination on the basis of nationality, domicile or residence.

3. If the nuclear damage to be compensated does not require the total amount under paragraph 1(b), the contributions shall be reduced proportionally.

4. The interest and costs awarded by a court in actions for compensation of nuclear damage are payable in addition to the amounts awarded pursuant to paragraphs 1(a) and (b) and shall be proportionate to the actual contributions made pursuant to paragraphs 1(a) and (b), respectively, by the operator liable, the Contracting Party in whose territory the nuclear installation of that operator is situated, and the Contracting Parties together.

Article IV

Calculation of Contributions

1. The formula for contributions according to which the Contracting Parties shall make available the public funds referred to in Article III.1(b) shall be determined as follows:

(a) (i) the amount which shall be the product of the installed nuclear capacity of that Contracting Party multiplied by 300 SDRs per unit of installed capacity; and

(ii) the amount determined by applying the ratio between the United Nations rate of assessment for that Contracting Party as assessed for the year preceding the year in which the nuclear incident occurs, and the total of such rates for all Contracting Parties to 10% of the sum of the amounts calculated for all Contracting Parties under sub-paragraph (i).

(b) Subject to sub-paragraph (c), the contribution of each Contracting Party shall be the sum of the amounts referred to in sub-paragraphs (a)(i) and (ii), provided that States on the minimum United Nations rate of assessment with no nuclear reactors shall not be required to make contributions.

(c) The maximum contribution which may be charged per nuclear incident to any Contracting Party, other than the Installation State, pursuant to sub-paragraph (b) shall not exceed its specified percentage of the total of contributions of all Contracting Parties determined pursuant to sub-paragraph (b). For a particular Contracting Party, the specified percentage shall be its UN rate of assessment expressed as a percentage plus 8 percentage points. If, at the time an incident occurs, the total installed capacity represented by the Parties to this Convention is at or above a level of 625,000 units, this percentage shall be increased by one percentage point. It shall be increased by one additional percentage point for each increment of 75,000 units by which the capacity exceeds 625,000 units.

2. The formula is for each nuclear reactor situated in the territory of the Contracting Party, 1 unit for each MW of thermal power. The formula shall be calculated on the basis of the thermal power of the nuclear reactors shown at the date of the nuclear incident in the list established and kept up to date in accordance with Article VIII.

3. For the purpose of calculating the contributions, a nuclear reactor shall be taken into account from that date when nuclear fuel elements have been first loaded into the nuclear reactor. A nuclear reactor shall be excluded from the calculation when all fuel elements have been removed permanently from the reactor core and have been stored safely in accordance with approved procedures.

Article V

Geographical Scope

1. The funds provided for under Article III.1(b) shall apply to nuclear damage which is suffered:

(a) in the territory of a Contracting Party; or

(b) in or above maritime areas beyond the territorial sea of a Contracting Party:

(i) on board or by a ship flying the flag of a Contracting Party, or on board or by an aircraft registered in the territory of a Contracting Party, or on or by an artificial island, installation or structure under the jurisdiction of a Contracting Party; or

(ii) by a national of a Contracting Party;

excluding damage suffered in or above the territorial sea of a State not Party to this Convention; or

(c) in or above the exclusive economic zone of a Contracting Party or on the continental shelf of a Contracting Party in connection with the exploitation or the exploration of the natural resources of that exclusive economic zone or continental shelf;

provided that the courts of a Contracting Party have jurisdiction pursuant to Article XIII.

2. Any signatory or acceding State may, at the time of signature of or accession to this Convention or on the deposit of its instrument of ratification, declare that for the purposes of the application of paragraph 1(b)(ii), individuals or certain categories thereof, considered under its law as having their habitual residence in its territory, are assimilated to its own nationals.

3. In this article, the expression "a national of a Contracting Party" shall include a Contracting Party or any of its constituent sub-divisions, or a partnership, or any public or private body whether corporate or not established in the territory of a Contracting Party.

CHAPTER III

ORGANIZATION OF SUPPLEMENTARY FUNDING

Article VI

Notification of Nuclear Damage

Without prejudice to obligations which Contracting Parties may have under other international agreements, the Contracting Party whose courts have jurisdiction shall inform the other Contracting Parties of a nuclear incident as soon as it appears that the damage caused by such incident exceeds, or is likely to exceed, the amount available under Article III.1(a) and that contributions under Article III.1(b) may be required. The Contracting Parties shall without delay make all the necessary arrangements to settle the procedure for their relations in this connection.

Article VII

Call for Funds

1. Following the notification referred to in Article VI, and subject to Article X.3, the Contracting Party whose courts have jurisdiction shall request the other Contracting Parties to make available the public funds required under Article III.1(b) to the extent and when they are actually required and shall have exclusive competence to disburse such funds.

2. Independently of existing or future regulations concerning currency or transfers, Contracting Parties shall authorize the transfer and payment of any contribution provided pursuant to Article III.1(b) without any restriction.

Article VIII

List of Nuclear Installations

1. Each Contracting State shall, at the time when it deposits its instrument of ratification, acceptance, approval or accession, communicate to the Depositary a complete listing of all nuclear installations referred to in Article IV.3. The listing shall contain the necessary particulars for the purpose of the calculation of contributions.

2. Each Contracting State shall promptly communicate to the Depositary all modifications to be made to the list. Where such modifications include the addition of a nuclear installation, the communication must be made at least three months before the expected date when nuclear material will be introduced into the installation.

3. If a Contracting Party is of the opinion that the particulars, or any modification to be made to the list communicated by a Contracting State pursuant to paragraphs 1 and 2, do not comply with the provisions, it may raise objections thereto

by addressing them to the Depositary within three months from the date on which it has received notice pursuant to paragraph 5. The Depositary shall forthwith communicate this objection to the State to whose information the objection has been raised. Any unresolved differences shall be dealt with in accordance with the dispute settlement procedure laid down in Article XVI.

4. The Depositary shall maintain, update and annually circulate to all Contracting States the list of nuclear installations established in accordance with this Article. Such list shall consist of all the particulars and modifications referred to in this Article, it being understood that objections submitted under this Article shall have effect retrospective to the date on which they were raised, if they are sustained.

5. The Depositary shall give notice as soon as possible to each Contracting Party of the communications and objections which it has received pursuant to this Article.

Article IX

Rights of Recourse

1. Each Contracting Party shall enact legislation in order to enable both the Contracting Party in whose territory the nuclear installation of the operator liable is situated and the other Contracting Parties who have paid contributions referred to in Article III.1(b), to benefit from the operator's right of recourse to the extent that he has such a right under either one of the Conventions referred to in Article I or national legislation mentioned in Article II.1(b) and to the extent that contributions have been made by any of the Contracting Parties.

2. The legislation of the Contracting Party in whose territory the nuclear installation of the operator liable is situated may provide for the recovery of public funds made available under this Convention from such operator if the damage results from fault on his part.

3. The Contracting Party whose courts have jurisdiction may exercise the rights of recourse provided for in paragraphs 1 and 2 on behalf of the other Contracting Parties which have contributed.

Article X

Disbursements, Proceedings

1. The system of disbursements by which the funds required under Article III.1 are to be made available and the system of apportionment thereof shall be that of the Contracting Party whose courts have jurisdiction.

2. Each Contracting Party shall ensure that persons suffering damage may enforce their rights to compensation without having to bring separate proceedings according to the origin of the funds provided for such compensation and that Contracting Parties may intervene in the proceedings against the operator liable.

3. No Contracting Party shall be required to make available the public funds referred to in Article III.1(b) if claims for compensation can be satisfied out of the funds referred to in Article III.1(a).

Article XI

Allocation of Funds

The funds provided under Article III.1(b) shall be distributed as follows:

1. (a) 50% of the funds shall be available to compensate claims for nuclear damage suffered in or outside the Installation State;

(b) 50% of the funds shall be available to compensate claims for nuclear damage suffered outside the territory of the Installation State to the extent that such claims are uncompensated under sub-paragraph (a).

(c) In the event the amount provided pursuant to Article III.1(a) is less than 300 million SDRs:

(i) the amount in paragraph 1(a) shall be reduced by the same percentage as the percentage by which the amount provided pursuant to Article III.1(a) is less than 300 million SDRs; and

(ii) the amount in paragraph 1(b) shall be increased by the amount of the reduction calculated pursuant to sub-paragraph (i).

2. If a Contracting Party, in accordance with Article III.1(a), has ensured the availability without discrimination of an amount not less than 600 million SDRs, which has been specified to the Depositary prior to the nuclear incident, all funds referred to in Article III.1(a) and (b) shall, notwithstanding paragraph 1, be made available to compensate nuclear damage suffered in and outside the Installation State.

CHAPTER IV

EXERCISE OF OPTIONS

Article XII

1. Except insofar as this Convention otherwise provides, each Contracting Party may exercise the powers vested in it by virtue of the Vienna Convention or the Paris Convention, and any provisions made thereunder may be invoked against the other Contracting Parties in order that the public funds referred to in Article III.1(b) be made available.

2. Nothing in this Convention shall prevent any Contracting Party from making provisions outside the scope of the Vienna or the Paris Convention and of this Convention, provided that such provision shall not involve any further obligation on the part of the other Contracting Parties, and provided that damage in a Contracting Party having no nuclear installations within its territory shall not be excluded from such further compensation on any grounds of lack of reciprocity.

3. (a) Nothing in this Convention shall prevent Contracting Parties from entering into regional or other agreements with the purpose of implementing their obligations under Article III.1(a) or providing additional funds for the compensation of nuclear damage, provided that this shall not involve any further obligation under this Convention for the other Contracting Parties.

(b) A Contracting Party intending to enter into any such agreement shall notify all other Contracting Parties of its intention. Agreements concluded shall be notified to the Depositary.

CHAPTER V

JURISDICTION AND APPLICABLE LAW

Article XIII

Jurisdiction

1. Except as otherwise provided in this article, jurisdiction over actions concerning nuclear damage from a nuclear incident shall lie only with the courts of the Contracting Party within which the nuclear incident occurs.

2. Where a nuclear incident occurs within the area of the exclusive economic zone of a Contracting Party or, if such a zone has not been established, in an area not exceeding the limits of an exclusive economic zone, were one to be established by that

party, jurisdiction over actions concerning nuclear damage from that nuclear incident shall, for the purposes of this Convention, lie only with the courts of that party. The preceding sentence shall apply if that Contracting Party has notified the Depositary of such area prior to the nuclear incident. Nothing in this paragraph shall be interpreted as permitting the exercise of jurisdiction in a manner which is contrary to the international law of the sea, including the United Nations Convention on the Law of the Sea. However, if the exercise of such jurisdiction is inconsistent with the obligations of that Party under Article XI of the Vienna Convention or Article 13 of the Paris Convention in relation to a State not Party to this Convention jurisdiction shall be determined according to those provisions.

3. Where a nuclear incident does not occur within the territory of any Contracting Party or within an area notified pursuant to paragraph 2, or where the place of a nuclear incident cannot be determined with certainty, jurisdiction over actions concerning nuclear damage from the nuclear incident shall lie only with the courts of the Installation State.

4. Where jurisdiction over actions concerning nuclear damage would lie with the courts of more than one Contracting Party, these Contracting Parties shall determine by agreement which Contracting Party's courts shall have jurisdiction.

5. A judgment that is no longer subject to ordinary forms of review entered by a court of a Contracting Party having jurisdiction shall be recognized except:

(a) where the judgment was obtained by fraud;

(b) where the party against whom the judgment was pronounced was not given a fair opportunity to present his case; or

(c) where the judgment is contrary to the public policy of the Contracting Party within the territory of which recognition is sought, or is not in accord with fundamental standards of justice.

6. A judgment which is recognized under paragraph 5 shall, upon being presented for enforcement in accordance with the formalities required by the law of the Contracting Party where enforcement is sought, be enforceable as if it were a judgment of a court of that Contracting Party. The merits of a claim on which the judgment has been given shall not be subject to further proceedings.

7. Settlements effected in respect of the payment of compensation out of the public funds referred to in Article III.1(b) in accordance with the conditions established by national legislation shall be recognized by the other Contracting Parties.

Article XIV

Applicable Law

1. Either the Vienna Convention or the Paris Convention or the Annex to this Convention, as appropriate, shall apply to a nuclear incident to the exclusion of the others.

2. Subject to the provisions of this Convention, the Vienna Convention or the Paris Convention, as appropriate, the applicable law shall be the law of the competent court.

Article XV

Public International Law

This Convention shall not affect the rights and obligations of a Contracting Party under the general rules of public international law.

CHAPTER VI

DISPUTE SETTLEMENT

Article XVI

1. In the event of a dispute between Contracting Parties concerning the interpretation or application of this Convention, the parties to the dispute shall consult with a view to the settlement of the dispute by negotiation or by any other peaceful means of settling disputes acceptable to them.

2. If a dispute of this character referred to in paragraph 1 cannot be settled within six months from the request for consultation pursuant to paragraph 1, it shall, at the request of any party to such dispute, be submitted to arbitration or referred to the International Court of Justice for decision. Where a dispute is submitted to arbitration, if, within six months from the date of the request, the parties to the dispute are unable to agree on the organization of the arbitration, a party may request the President of the International Court of Justice or the Secretary–General of the United Nations to appoint one or more arbitrators. In cases of conflicting requests by the parties to the dispute, the request to the Secretary–General of the United Nations shall have priority.

3. When ratifying, accepting, approving or acceding to this Convention, a State may declare that it does not consider itself bound by either or both of the dispute settlement procedures provided for in paragraph 2. The other Contracting Parties shall not be bound by a dispute settlement procedure provided for in paragraph 2 with respect to a Contracting Party for which such a declaration is in force.

4. A Contracting Party which has made a declaration in accordance with paragraph 3 may at any time withdraw it by notification to the Depositary.

ANNEX

A Contracting Party which is not a Party to any of the Conventions mentioned in Article I(a) or (b) of this Convention shall ensure that its national legislation is consistent with the provisions laid down in this Annex insofar as those provisions are not directly applicable within that Contracting Party. A Contracting Party having no nuclear installation on its territory is required to have only that legislation which is necessary to enable such a Party to give effect to its obligations under this Convention.

Article 1

Definitions

1. In addition to the definitions in Article I of this Convention, the following definitions apply for the purposes of this Annex:

(a) "Nuclear Fuel" means any material which is capable of producing energy by a self-sustaining chain process of nuclear fission.

(b) "Nuclear Installation" means:

(i) any nuclear reactor other than one with which a means of sea or air transport is equipped for use as a source of power, whether for propulsion thereof or for any other purpose;

(ii) any factory using nuclear fuel for the production of nuclear material, or any factory for the processing of nuclear material, including any factory for the re-processing of irradiated nuclear fuel; and

(iii) any facility where nuclear material is stored, other than storage incidental to the carriage of such material;

provided that the Installation State may determine that several nuclear installations of one operator which are located at the same site shall be considered as a single nuclear installation.

(c) "Nuclear material" means:

(i) nuclear fuel, other than natural uranium and depleted uranium, capable of producing energy by a self-sustaining chain process of nuclear fission outside a nuclear reactor, either alone or in combination with some other material; and

(ii) radioactive products or waste.

(d) "Operator", in relation to a nuclear installation, means the person designated or recognized by the Installation State as the operator of that installation.

(e) "Radioactive products or waste" means any radioactive material produced in, or any material made radioactive by exposure to the radiation incidental to, the production or utilization of nuclear fuel, but does not include radioisotopes which have reached the final stage of fabrication so as to be usable for any scientific, medical, agricultural, commercial or industrial purpose.

2. An Installation State may, if the small extent of the risks involved so warrants, exclude any nuclear installation or small quantities of nuclear material from the application of this Convention, provided that:

(a) with respect to nuclear installations, criteria for such exclusion have been established by the Board of Governors of the International Atomic Energy Agency and any exclusion by an Installation State satisfies such criteria; and

(b) with respect to small quantities of nuclear material, maximum limits for the exclusion of such quantities have been established by the Board of Governors of the International Atomic Energy Agency and any exclusion by an Installation State is within such established limits.

The criteria for the exclusion of nuclear installations and the maximum limits for the exclusion of small quantities of nuclear material shall be reviewed periodically by the Board of Governors.

Article 2

Conformity of Legislation

1. The national law of a Contracting Party is deemed to be in conformity with the provisions of Articles 3, 4, 5 and 7 if it contained on 1 January 1995 and continues to contain provisions that:

(a) provide for strict liability in the event of a nuclear incident where there is substantial nuclear damage off the site of the nuclear installation where the incident occurs;

(b) require the indemnification of any person other than the operator liable for nuclear damage to the extent that person is legally liable to provide compensation; and

(c) ensure the availability of at least 1000 million SDRs in respect of a civil nuclear power plant and at least 300 million SDRs in respect of other civil nuclear installations for such indemnification.

2. If in accordance with paragraph 1, the national law of a Contracting Party is deemed to be in conformity with the provision of Articles 3, 4, 5 and 7, then that Party:

(a) may apply a definition of nuclear damage that covers loss or damage set forth in Article I(f) of this Convention and any other loss or damage to the extent that the loss or damage arises out of or results from the radioactive properties, or a combination of radioactive properties with toxic, explosive or other hazardous properties of nuclear fuel or radioactive products or waste in, or of nuclear material coming from, originating in, or sent to, a nuclear installation; or other ionizing radiation emitted by any source of radiation inside a nuclear installation, provided that such application does not affect the undertaking by that Contracting Party pursuant to Article III of this Convention; and

(b) may apply the definition of nuclear installation in paragraph 3 of this Article to the exclusion of the definition in Article 1.1(b) of this Annex.

3. For the purpose of paragraph 2 (b) of this Article, "nuclear installation" means:

(a) any civil nuclear reactor other than one with which a means of sea or air transport is equipped for use as a source of power, whether for propulsion thereof or any other purpose; and

(b) any civil facility for processing, reprocessing or storing:

(i) irradiated nuclear fuel; or

(ii) radioactive products or waste that:

(1) result from the reprocessing of irradiated nuclear fuel and contain significant amounts of fission products; or

(2) contain elements that have an atomic number greater than 92 in concentrations greater than 10 nano-curies per gram.

(c) any other civil facility for processing, reprocessing or storing nuclear material unless the Contracting Party determines the small extent of the risks involved with such an installation warrants the exclusion of such a facility from this definition.

4. Where that national law of a Contracting Party which is in compliance with paragraph 1 of this Article does not apply to a nuclear incident which occurs outside the territory of that Contracting Party, but over which the courts of that Contracting Party have jurisdiction pursuant to Article XIII of this Convention, Articles 3 to 11 of the Annex shall apply and prevail over any inconsistent provisions of the applicable national law.

Article 3

Operator Liability

1. The operator of a nuclear installation shall be liable for nuclear damage upon proof that such damage has been caused by a nuclear incident:

(a) in that nuclear installation; or

(b) involving nuclear material coming from or originating in that nuclear installation, and occurring:

(i) before liability with regard to nuclear incidents involving the nuclear material has been assumed, pursuant to the express terms of a contract in writing, by the operator of another nuclear installation;

(ii) in the absence of such express terms, before the operator of another nuclear installation has taken charge of the nuclear material; or

(iii) where the nuclear material is intended to be used in a nuclear reactor with which a means of transport is equipped for use as a source of power, whether for propulsion thereof or for any other purpose, before the person duly authorized to operate such reactor has taken charge of the nuclear material; but

(iv) where the nuclear material has been sent to a person within the territory of a non-Contracting State, before it has been unloaded from the means of transport by which it has arrived in the territory of that non-Contracting State;

(c) involving nuclear material sent to that nuclear installation, and occurring:

(i) after liability with regard to nuclear incidents involving the nuclear material has been assumed by the operator pursuant to the express terms of a contract in writing, from the operator of another nuclear installation;

(ii) in the absence of such express terms, after the operator has taken charge of the nuclear material; or

(iii) after the operator has taken charge of the nuclear material from a person operating a nuclear reactor with which a means of transport is equipped for use as a source of power, whether for propulsion thereof or for any other purpose; but

(iv) where the nuclear material has, with the written consent of the operator, been sent from a person within the territory of a non-Contracting State, only after it has been loaded on the means of transport by which it is to be carried from the territory of that State;

provided that, if nuclear damage is caused by a nuclear incident occurring in a nuclear installation and involving nuclear material stored therein incidentally to the carriage of such material, the provisions of sub-paragraph (a) shall not apply where another operator or person is solely liable pursuant to sub-paragraph (b) or (c).

2. The Installation State may provide by legislation that, in accordance with such terms as may be specified in that legislation, a carrier of nuclear material or a person handling radioactive waste may, at such carrier or such person's request and with the consent of the operator concerned, be designated or recognized as operator in the place of that operator in respect of such nuclear material or radioactive waste respectively. In this case such carrier or such person shall be considered, for all the purposes of this Convention, as an operator of a nuclear installation situated within the territory of that State.

3. The liability of the operator for nuclear damage shall be absolute.

4. Whenever both nuclear damage and damage other than nuclear damage have been caused by a nuclear incident or jointly by a nuclear incident and one or more other occurrences, such other damage shall, to the extent that it is not reasonably separable from the nuclear damage, be deemed to be nuclear damage caused by that nuclear incident. Where, however, damage is caused jointly by a nuclear incident covered by the provisions of this Annex and by an emission of ionizing radiation not covered by it, nothing in this Annex shall limit or otherwise affect the liability, either as regards any person suffering nuclear damage or by way of recourse or contribution, of any person who may be held liable in connection with that emission of ionizing radiation.

5. (a) No liability shall attach to an operator for nuclear damage caused by a nuclear incident directly due to an act of armed conflict, hostilities, civil war or insurrection.

(b) Except insofar as the law of the Installation State may provide to the contrary, the operator shall not be liable for nuclear damage caused by a nuclear incident caused directly due to a grave natural disaster of an exceptional character.

6. National law may relieve an operator wholly or partly from the obligation to pay compensation for nuclear damage suffered by a person if the operator proves the

nuclear damage resulted wholly or partly from the gross negligence of that person or an act or omission of that person done with the intent to cause damage.

7. The operator shall not be liable for nuclear damage:

(a) to the nuclear installation itself and any other nuclear installation, including a nuclear installation under construction, on the site where that installation is located; and

(b) to any property on that same site which is used or to be used in connection with any such installation;

(c) unless otherwise provided by national law, to the means of transport upon which the nuclear material involved was at the time of the nuclear incident. If national law provides that the operator is liable for such damage, compensation for that damage shall not have the effect of reducing the liability of the operator in respect of other damage to an amount less than either 150 million SDRs, or any higher amount established by the legislation of a Contracting Party.

8. Nothing in this Convention shall affect the liability outside this Convention of the operator for nuclear damage for which by virtue of paragraph 7(c) he is not liable under this Convention.

9. The right to compensation for nuclear damage may be exercised only against the operator liable, provided that national law may permit a direct right of action against any supplier of funds that are made available pursuant to provisions in national law to ensure compensation through the use of funds from sources other than the operator.

10. The operator shall incur no liability for damage caused by a nuclear incident outside the provisions of national law in accordance with this Convention.

Article 4

Liability amounts

1. Subject to Article III.1(a)(ii), the liability of the operator may be limited by the Installation State for any one nuclear incident, either:

(a) to not less than 300 million SDRs; or

(b) to not less then 150 million SDRs provided that in excess of that amount and up to at least 300 million SDRs public funds shall be made available by that State to compensate nuclear damage.

2. Notwithstanding paragraph 1, the Installation State, having regard to the nature of the nuclear installation or the nuclear substances involved and to the likely consequences of an incident originating therefrom, may establish a lower amount of liability of the operator, provided that in no event shall any amount so established be less than 5 million SDRs, and provided that the Installation State ensures that public funds shall be made available up to the amount established pursuant to paragraph 1.

3. The amounts established by the Installation State of the liable operator in accordance with paragraphs 1 and 2, as well as the provisions of any legislation of a Contracting Party pursuant to Article 3.7(c) shall apply wherever the nuclear incident occurs.

Article 5

Financial Security

1. (a) The operator shall be required to have and maintain insurance or other financial security covering his liability for nuclear damage in such amount, of such type and in such terms as the Installation State shall specify. The Installation State shall ensure the payment of claims for compensation for nuclear damage which have

been established against the operator by providing the necessary funds to the extent that the yield of insurance or other financial security is inadequate to satisfy such claims, but not in excess of the limit, if any, established pursuant to Article 4. Where the liability of the operator is unlimited, the Installation State may establish a limit of the financial security of the operator liable provided that such limit is not lower than 300 million SDRs. The Installation State shall ensure the payment of claims for compensation for nuclear damage which have been established against the operator to the extent that yield of the financial security is inadequate to satisfy such claims, but not in excess of the amount of the financial security to be provided under this paragraph.

(b) Notwithstanding sub-paragraph (a), the Installation State, having regard to the nature of the nuclear installation or the nuclear substances involved and to the likely consequences of an incident originating therefrom, may establish a lower amount of financial security of the operator, provided that in no event shall any amount so established be less than 5 million SDRs, and provided that the Installation State ensures the payment of claims for compensation for nuclear damage which have been established against the operator by providing necessary funds to the extent that the yield of insurance or other financial security is inadequate to satisfy such claims, and up to the limit provided in sub-paragraph (a).

2. Nothing in paragraph 1 shall require a Contracting Party or any of its constituent sub-divisions to maintain insurance or other financial security to cover their liability as operators.

3. The funds provided by insurance, by other financial security or by the Installation State pursuant to paragraph 1 or Article 4.1(b) shall be exclusively available for compensation due under this Annex.

4. No insurer or other financial guarantor shall suspend or cancel the insurance or other financial security provided pursuant to paragraph 1 without giving notice in writing of at least two months to the competent public authority or, in so far as such insurance or other financial security relates to the carriage of nuclear material, during the period of the carriage in question.

Article 6

Carriage

1. With respect to a nuclear incident during carriage, the maximum amount of liability of the operator shall be governed by the national law of the Installation State.

2. A Contracting Party may subject carriage of nuclear material through its territory to the condition that the amount of liability of the operator be increased to an amount not to exceed the maximum amount of liability of the operator of a nuclear installation situated in its territory.

3. The provisions of paragraph 2 shall not apply to:

(a) carriage by sea where, under international law, there is a right of entry in cases of urgent distress into ports of a Contracting Party or a right of innocent passage through its territory;

(b) carriage by air where, by agreement or under international law, there is a right to fly over or land on the territory of a Contracting Party.

Article 7

Liability of More Than One Operator

1. Where nuclear damage engages the liability of more than one operator, the operators involved shall, in so far as the damage attributable to each operator is not

reasonably separable, be jointly and severally liable. The Installation State may limit the amount of public funds made available per incident to the difference, if any, between the amounts hereby established and the amount established pursuant to Article 4.1.

2. Where a nuclear incident occurs in the course of carriage of nuclear material, either in one and the same means of transport, or, in the case of storage incidental to the carriage, in one and the same nuclear installation, and causes nuclear damage which engages the liability of more than one operator, the total liability shall not exceed the highest amount applicable with respect to any one of them pursuant to Article 4.

3. In neither of the cases referred to in paragraphs 1 and 2 shall the liability of any one operator exceed the amount applicable with respect to him pursuant to Article 4.

4. Subject to the provisions of paragraphs 1 to 3, where several nuclear installations of one and the same operator are involved in one nuclear incident, such operator shall be liable in respect of each nuclear installation involved up to the amount applicable with respect to him pursuant to Article 4. The Installation State may limit the amount of public funds made available as provided for in paragraph 1.

Article 8

Compensation Under National Law

1. For purposes of this Convention, the amount of compensation shall be determined without regard to any interest or costs awarded in a proceeding for compensation of nuclear damage.

2. Compensation for damage suffered outside the Installation State shall be provided in a form freely transferable among Contracting Parties.

3. Where provisions of national or public health insurance, social insurance, social security, workmen's compensation or occupational disease compensation systems include compensation for nuclear damage, rights of beneficiaries of such systems and rights of recourse by virtue of such systems shall be determined by the national law of the Contracting Party in which such systems have been established or by the regulations of the intergovernmental organization which has established such systems.

Article 9

Period of Extinction

1. Rights of compensation under this Convention shall be extinguished if an action is not brought within ten years from the date of the nuclear incident. If, however, under the law of the Installation State the liability of the operator is covered by insurance or other financial security or by State funds for a period longer than ten years, the law of the competent court may provide that rights of compensation against the operator shall only be extinguished after a period which may be longer than ten years, but shall not be longer than the period for which his liability is so covered under the law of the Installation State.

2. Where nuclear damage is caused by a nuclear incident involving nuclear material which at the time of the nuclear incident was stolen, lost, jettisoned or abandoned, the period established pursuant to paragraph 1 shall be computed from the date of that nuclear incident, but the period shall in no case, subject to legislation pursuant to paragraph 1, exceed a period of twenty years from the date of the theft, loss, jettison or abandonment.

3. The law of the competent court may establish a period of extinction or prescription of not less than three years from the date on which the person suffering

nuclear damage had knowledge or should have had knowledge of the damage and of the operator liable for the damage, provided that the period established pursuant to paragraphs 1 and 2 shall not be exceeded.

4. If the national law of a Contracting Party provides for a period of extinction or prescription greater than ten years from the date of a nuclear incident, it shall contain provisions for the equitable and timely satisfaction of claims for loss of life or personal injury filed within ten years from the date of the nuclear incident.

Article 10

Right of Recourse

National law may provide that the operator shall have a right of recourse only:

(a) if this is expressly provided for by a contract in writing; or

(b) if the nuclear incident results from an act or omission done with intent to cause damage, against the individual who has acted or omitted to act with such intent.

Article 11

Applicable Law

Subject to the provisions of this Convention, the nature, form, extent and equitable distribution of compensation for nuclear damage caused by a nuclear incident shall be governed by the law of the competent court.

3.25 KYOTO PROTOCOL TO THE UNITED NATIONS FRAMEWORK CONVENTION ON CLIMATE CHANGE.[h] Done at Kyoto, Japan, 10 December 1997. Not yet in force. FCCC/CP/1997/7/Add.1; *reprinted in* 37 I.L.M. 32 (1998)

The Parties to this Protocol,

Being Parties to the United Nations Framework Convention on Climate Change, hereinafter referred to as "the Convention",

In pursuit of the ultimate objective of the Convention as stated in its Article 2,

Recalling the provisions of the Convention,

Being guided by Article 3 of the Convention,

Pursuant to the Berlin Mandate adopted by decision 1/CP.1 of the Conference of the Parties to the Convention at its first session,

Have agreed as follows:

Article 1

For the purposes of this Protocol, the definitions contained in Article 1 of the Convention shall apply. In addition:

1. "Conference of the Parties" means the Conference of the Parties to the Convention.

2. "Convention" means the United Nations Framework Convention on Climate Change, adopted in New York on 9 May 1992.

3. "Intergovernmental Panel on Climate Change" means the Intergovernmental Panel on Climate Change established in 1988 jointly by the World Meteorological Organization and the United Nations Environment Programme.

4. "Montreal Protocol" means the Montreal Protocol on Substances that Deplete the Ozone Layer, adopted in Montreal on 16 September 1987 and as subsequently adjusted and amended.

5. "Parties present and voting" means Parties present and casting an affirmative or negative vote.

6. "Party" means, unless the context otherwise indicates, a Party to this Protocol.

7. "Party included in Annex I" means a Party included in Annex I to the Convention, as may be amended, or a Party which has made a notification under Article 4, paragraph 2(g), of the Convention.

Article 2

1. Each Party included in Annex I in achieving its quantified emission limitation and reduction commitments under Article 3, in order to promote sustainable development, shall:

(a) Implement and/or further elaborate policies and measures in accordance with its national circumstances, such as:

(i) Enhancement of energy efficiency in relevant sectors of the national economy;

(ii) Protection and enhancement of sinks and reservoirs of greenhouse gases not controlled by the Montreal Protocol, taking into account its commitments under relevant international environmental agreements; promotion of sustainable forest management practices, afforestation and—reforestation;

h. *See* Basic Document 3.21, *supra*.

(iii) Promotion of sustainable forms of agriculture in light of climate change considerations;

(iv) Promotion, research, development and increased use of new and renewable forms of energy, of carbon dioxide sequestration technologies and of advanced and innovative environmentally sound technologies;

(v) Progressive reduction or phasing out of market imperfections, fiscal incentives, tax and duty exemptions and subsidies in all greenhouse gas emitting sectors that run counter to the objective of the Convention and apply market instruments;

(vi) Encouragement of appropriate reforms in relevant sectors aimed at promoting policies and measures which limit or reduce emissions of greenhouse gases not controlled by the Montreal Protocol;

(vii) Measures to limit and/or reduce emissions of greenhouse gases not controlled by the Montreal Protocol in the transport sector;

(viii) Limitation and/or reduction of methane through recovery and use in waste management, as well as in the production, transport and distribution of energy;

(b) Cooperate with other such Parties to enhance the individual and combined effectiveness of their policies and measures adopted under this Article, pursuant to Article 4, paragraph 2(e)(i), of the Convention. To this end, these Parties shall take steps to share their experience and exchange information on such policies and measures, including developing ways of improving their comparability, transparency and effectiveness. The Conference of the Parties serving as the meeting of the Parties to this Protocol shall, at its first session or as soon as practicable thereafter, consider ways to facilitate such cooperation, taking into account all relevant information.

2. The Parties included in Annex I shall pursue limitation or reduction of emissions of greenhouse gases not controlled by the Montreal Protocol from aviation and marine bunker fuels, working through the International Civil Aviation Organization and the International Maritime Organization, respectively.

3. The Parties included in Annex I shall strive to implement policies and measures under this Article in such a way as to minimize adverse effects, including the adverse effects of climate change, effects on international trade, and social, environmental and economic impacts on other Parties, especially developing country Parties and in particular those identified in Article 4, paragraphs 8 and 9 of the Convention, taking into account Article 3 of the Convention. The Conference of the Parties serving as the meeting of the Parties to this Protocol may take further action, as appropriate, to promote the implementation of the provisions of this paragraph.

4. The Conference of the Parties serving as the meeting of the Parties to this Protocol, if it decides that it would be beneficial to coordinate any of the policies and measures in paragraph 1(a) above, taking into account different national circumstances and potential effects, shall consider ways and means to elaborate the coordination of such policies and measures.

Article 3

1. The Parties included in Annex I shall, individually or jointly, ensure that their aggregate anthropogenic carbon dioxide equivalent emissions of the greenhouse gases listed in Annex A do not exceed their assigned amounts, calculated pursuant to their quantified emission limitation and reduction commitments inscribed in Annex B and in accordance with the provisions of this Article, with a view to reducing their overall emissions of such gases by at least 5 per cent below 1990 levels in the commitment period 2008 to 2012.

2. Each Party included in Annex I shall, by 2005, have made demonstrable progress in achieving its commitments under this Protocol.

3. The net changes in greenhouse gas emissions from sources and removals by sinks resulting from direct human-induced land use change and forestry activities, limited to afforestation, reforestation, and deforestation since 1990, measured as verifiable changes in stocks in each commitment period shall be used to meet the commitments in this Article of each Party included in Annex I. The greenhouse gas emissions from sources and removals by sinks associated with those activities shall be reported in a transparent and verifiable manner and reviewed in accordance with Articles 7 and 8.

4. Prior to the first session of the Conference of the Parties serving as the meeting of the Parties to this Protocol, each Party included in Annex I shall provide for consideration by the Subsidiary Body for Scientific and Technological Advice data to establish its level of carbon stocks in 1990 and to enable an estimate to be made of its changes in carbon stocks in subsequent years. The Conference of the Parties serving as the meeting of the Parties to this Protocol shall, at its first session or as soon as practicable thereafter, decide upon modalities, rules and guidelines as to how and which additional human-induced activities related to changes in greenhouse gas emissions and removals in the agricultural soil and land use change and forestry categories, shall be added to, or subtracted from, the assigned amount for Parties included in Annex I, taking into account uncertainties, transparency in reporting, verifiability, the methodological work of the Intergovernmental Panel on Climate Change, the advice provided by the Subsidiary Body for Scientific and Technological Advice in accordance with Article 5 and the decisions of the Conference of the Parties. Such a decision shall apply in the second and subsequent commitment periods. A Party may choose to apply such a decision on these additional human-induced activities for its first commitment period, provided that these activities have taken place since 1990.

5. The Parties included in Annex I undergoing the process of transition to a market economy whose base year or period was established pursuant to decision 9/CP.2 of the Conference of the Parties at its second session, shall use that base year or period for the implementation of their commitments under this Article. Any other Party included in Annex I undergoing the process of transition to a market economy which has not yet submitted its first national communication under Article 12 of the Convention may also notify the Conference of the Parties serving as the meeting of the Parties to this Protocol that it intends to use a historical base year or period other than 1990 for the implementation of its commitments under this Article. The Conference of the Parties serving as the meeting of the Parties to this Protocol shall decide on the acceptance of such notification.

6. Taking into account Article 4, paragraph 6, of the Convention, in the implementation of their commitments under this Protocol other than those in this Article, a certain degree of flexibility shall be allowed by the Conference of the Parties serving as the meeting of the Parties to this Protocol to the Parties included in Annex I undergoing the process of transition to a market economy.

7. In the first quantified emission limitation and reduction commitment period, from 2008 to 2012, the assigned amount for each Party included in Annex I shall be equal to the percentage inscribed for it in Annex B of its aggregate anthropogenic carbon dioxide equivalent emissions of the greenhouse gases listed in Annex A in 1990, or the base year or period determined in accordance with paragraph 5 above, multiplied by five. Those Parties included in Annex I for whom land use change and forestry constituted a net source of greenhouse gas emissions in 1990 shall include in their 1990 emissions base year or period the aggregate anthropogenic carbon dioxide equivalent emissions minus removals in 1990 from land use change for the purposes of calculating their assigned amount.

8. Any Party included in Annex I may use 1995 as its base year for hydrofluorocarbons, perfluorocarbons and sulphur hexafluoride, for the purposes of the calculation referred to in paragraph 7 above.

9. Commitments for subsequent periods for Parties included in Annex I shall be established in amendments to Annex B to this Protocol, which shall be adopted in accordance with the provisions of Article 20, paragraph 7. The Conference of the Parties serving as the meeting of the Parties to this Protocol shall initiate the consideration of such commitments at least seven years before the end of the first commitment period mentioned in paragraph 7 above.

10. Any emission reduction units, or any part of an assigned amount, which a Party acquires from another Party in accordance with the provisions of Article 6 and of Article 16 bis shall be added to the assigned amount for that Party.

11. Any emission reduction units, or any part of an assigned amount, which a Party transfers to another Party in accordance with the provisions of Article 6 and of Article 16 bis shall be subtracted from the assigned amount for that Party.

12. Any certified emission reductions which a Party acquires from another Party in accordance with the provisions of Article 12 shall be added to the assigned amount for that Party.

13. If the emissions of a Party included in Annex I during a commitment period are less than its assigned amount under this Article, this difference shall, on request of that Party, be added to the assigned amount for that Party for subsequent commitment periods.

14. Each Party included in Annex I shall strive to implement the commitments mentioned in paragraph 1 above in such a way as to minimize adverse social, environmental and economic impacts on developing country Parties, particularly those identified in Article 4, paragraphs 8 and 9, of the Convention. In line with relevant decisions of the Conference of the Parties on the implementation of those paragraphs, the Conference of the Parties serving as the meeting of the Parties to this Protocol shall, at its first session, consider what actions are necessary to minimize the adverse effects of climate change and/or the impacts of response measures on Parties referred to in those paragraphs. Among the issues to be considered shall be the establishment of funding, insurance and transfer of technology.

Article 4

1. Any Parties included in Annex I that have agreed to jointly fulfil their commitments under Article 3 shall be deemed to have met those commitments provided that their total combined aggregate anthropogenic carbon dioxide equivalent emissions of the greenhouse gases listed in Annex A do not exceed their assigned amounts calculated pursuant to their quantified emission limitation and reduction commitments inscribed in Annex B and in accordance with the provisions of Article 3. The respective emission level allocated to each of the Parties to the agreement shall be set out in that agreement.

2. The Parties to any such agreement shall notify the secretariat of the terms of the agreement on the date of deposit of their instruments of ratification, acceptance, approval or accession. The secretariat shall in turn inform the Parties and signatories to the Convention of the terms of the agreement.

3. The agreement shall remain in operation for the duration of the commitment period specified in Article 3, paragraph 7.

4. If Parties acting jointly do so in the framework of, and together with, a regional economic integration organization, any alteration in the composition of the organization after adoption of this Protocol shall not affect existing commitments under this Protocol. Any alteration in the composition of the organization shall only

apply for the purposes of those commitments under Article 3 that are adopted subsequent to that revision.

5. In the event of failure by the Parties to such an agreement to achieve their total combined level of emission reductions, each Party to such an agreement shall be responsible for its own level of emissions set out in the agreement.

6. If Parties acting jointly do so in the framework of, and together with, a regional economic integration organization which is itself a Party to this Protocol, each member State of that regional economic integration organization individually, and together with the regional economic integration organization acting in accordance with Article 23, shall, in the event of failure to achieve the total combined level of emission reductions, be responsible for its level of emissions as notified in accordance with this Article.

Article 5

1. Each Party included in Annex I shall have in place, no later than one year prior to the start of the first commitment period, a national system for the estimation of anthropogenic emissions by sources and removals by sinks of all greenhouse gases not controlled by the Montreal Protocol. Guidelines for such national systems, which shall incorporate the methodologies specified in paragraph 2 below, shall be decided upon by the Conference of the Parties serving as the meeting of the Parties to this Protocol at its first session.

2. Methodologies for estimating anthropogenic emissions by sources and removals by sinks of all greenhouse gases not controlled by the Montreal Protocol shall be those accepted by the Intergovernmental Panel on Climate Change and agreed upon by the Conference of the Parties at its third session. Where such methodologies are not used, appropriate adjustments shall be applied according to methodologies agreed upon by the Conference of the Parties serving as the meeting of the Parties to this Protocol at its first session. Based on the work of, inter alia, the Intergovernmental Panel on Climate Change and advice provided by the Subsidiary Body for Scientific and Technological Advice, the Conference of the Parties serving as the meeting of the Parties to this Protocol shall regularly review and, as appropriate, revise such methodologies and adjustments, taking fully into account any relevant decisions by the Conference of the Parties. Any revision to methodologies or adjustments shall be used only for the purposes of ascertaining compliance with commitments under Article 3 in respect of any commitment period adopted subsequent to that revision.

3. The global warming potentials used to calculate the carbon dioxide equivalence of anthropogenic emissions by sources and removals by sinks of greenhouse gases not controlled by the Montreal Protocol listed in Annex A shall be those accepted by the Intergovernmental Panel on Climate Change and agreed upon by the Conference of the Parties at its third session. Based on the work of, inter alia, the Intergovernmental Panel on Climate Change and advice provided by the Subsidiary Body for Scientific and Technological Advice, the Conference of the Parties serving as the meeting of the Parties to this Protocol shall regularly review and, as appropriate, revise the global warming potential of each such greenhouse gas, taking fully into account any relevant decisions by the Conference of the Parties. Any revision to a global warming potential shall apply only to those commitments under Article 3 in respect of any commitment period adopted subsequent to that revision.

Article 6

1. For the purpose of meeting its commitments under Article 3, any Party included in Annex I may transfer to, or acquire from, any other such Party emission reduction units resulting from projects aimed at reducing anthropogenic emissions by

sources or enhancing anthropogenic removals by sinks of greenhouse gases in any sector of the economy, provided that:

(a) Any such project has the approval of the Parties involved;

(b) Any such project provides a reduction in emissions by sources, or an enhancement of removals by sinks, that is additional to any that would otherwise occur;

(c) It does not acquire any emission reduction units if it is not in compliance with its obligations under Articles 5 and 7; and

(d) The acquisition of emission reduction units shall be supplemental to domestic actions for the purposes of meeting commitments under Article 3.

2. The Conference of the Parties serving as the meeting of the Parties to this Protocol may, at its first session or as soon as practicable thereafter, further elaborate guidelines for the implementation of this Article, including for verification and reporting.

3. A Party included in Annex I may authorize legal entities to participate, under its responsibility, in actions leading to the generation, transfer or acquisition under this Article of emission reduction units.

4. If a question of implementation by a Party included in Annex I of the requirements referred to in this paragraph is identified in accordance with the relevant provisions of Article 8, transfers and acquisitions of emission reduction units may continue to be made after the question has been identified, provided that any such units may not be used by a Party to meet its commitments under Article 3 until any issue of compliance is resolved.

Article 7

1. Each Party included in Annex I shall incorporate in its annual inventory of anthropogenic emissions by sources and removals by sinks of greenhouse gases not controlled by the Montreal Protocol, submitted in accordance with the relevant decisions of the Conference of the Parties, the necessary supplementary information for the purposes of ensuring compliance with Article 3, to be determined in accordance with paragraph 4 below.

2. Each Party included in Annex I shall incorporate in its national communication, submitted under Article 12 of the Convention, the supplementary information necessary to demonstrate compliance with its commitments under this Protocol, to be determined in accordance with paragraph 4 below.

3. Each Party included in Annex I shall submit the information required under paragraph 1 above annually, beginning with the first inventory due under the Convention for the first year of the commitment period after this Protocol has entered into force for it. Each such Party shall submit the information required under paragraph 2 above as part of the first national communication due under the Convention after this Protocol has entered into force for it and after the adoption of guidelines as provided for in paragraph 4 below. The frequency of subsequent submission of information required under this Article shall be determined by the Conference of the Parties serving as the meeting of the Parties to this Protocol, taking into account any timetable for the submission of national communications decided upon by the Conference of the Parties.

4. The Conference of the Parties serving as the meeting of the Parties to this Protocol shall adopt at its first session, and review periodically thereafter, guidelines for the preparation of the information required under this Article, taking into account guidelines for the preparation of national communications by Parties included in Annex I adopted by the Conference of the Parties. The Conference of the Parties

serving as the meeting of the Parties to this Protocol shall also, prior to the first commitment period, decide upon modalities for the accounting of assigned amounts.

Article 8

1. The information submitted under Article 7 by each Party included in Annex I shall be reviewed by expert review teams pursuant to the relevant decisions of the Conference of the Parties and in accordance with guidelines adopted for this purpose by the Conference of the Parties serving as the meeting of the Parties to this Protocol under paragraph 4 below. The information submitted under Article 7, paragraph 1, by each Party included in Annex I shall be reviewed as part of the annual compilation and accounting of emissions inventories and assigned amounts. Additionally, the information submitted under Article 7, paragraph 2, by each Party included in Annex I shall be reviewed as part of the review of communications.

2. Expert review teams shall be coordinated by the secretariat and shall be composed of experts selected from those nominated by Parties to the Convention and, as appropriate, by intergovernmental organizations, in accordance with guidance provided for this purpose by the Conference of the Parties.

3. The review process shall provide a thorough and comprehensive technical assessment of all aspects of the implementation by a Party of this Protocol. The expert review teams shall prepare a report to the Conference of the Parties serving as the meeting of the Parties to this Protocol, assessing the implementation of the commitments of the Party and identifying any potential problems in, and factors influencing, the fulfilment of commitments. Such reports shall be circulated by the secretariat to all Parties to the Convention. The secretariat shall list those questions of implementation indicated in such reports for further consideration by the Conference of the Parties serving as the meeting of the Parties to this Protocol.

4. The Conference of the Parties serving as the meeting of the Parties to this Protocol shall adopt at its first session, and review periodically thereafter, guidelines for the review of implementation by expert review teams taking into account the relevant decisions of the Conference of the Parties.

5. The Conference of the Parties serving as the meeting of the Parties to this Protocol shall, with the assistance of the Subsidiary Body for Implementation and, as appropriate, the Subsidiary Body for Scientific and Technological Advice, consider:

(a) The information submitted by the Parties under Article 7 and the reports of the expert reviews thereon conducted under this Article; and

(b) Those questions of implementation listed by the secretariat under paragraph 3 above, as well as any questions raised by Parties.

6. Pursuant to its consideration of the information referred to in paragraph 5 above, the Conference of the Parties serving as the meeting of the Parties to this Protocol shall take decisions on any matter required for the implementation of this Protocol.

Article 9

1. The Conference of the Parties serving as the meeting of the Parties to this Protocol shall periodically review this Protocol in the light of the best available scientific information and assessments on climate change and its impacts, as well as relevant technical, social and economic information. Such reviews shall be coordinated with pertinent reviews under the Convention, in particular those required by Article 4, paragraph 2(d), and Article 7, paragraph 2(a), of the Convention. Based on these reviews, the Conference of the Parties serving as the meeting of the Parties to this Protocol shall take appropriate action.

2. The first review shall take place at the second session of the Conference of the Parties serving as the meeting of the Parties to this Protocol. Further reviews shall take place at regular intervals and in a timely manner.

Article 10

All Parties, taking into account their common but differentiated responsibilities and their specific national and regional development priorities, objectives and circumstances, without introducing any new commitments for Parties not included in Annex I, but reaffirming existing commitments in Article 4, paragraph 1, of the Convention, and continuing to advance the implementation of these commitments in order to achieve sustainable development, taking into account Article 4, paragraphs 3, 5 and 7, of the Convention, shall:

(a) Formulate, where relevant and to the extent possible, cost-effective national, and where appropriate regional programmes to improve the quality of local emission factors, activity data and/or models which reflect the socio-economic conditions of each Party for the preparation and periodic updating of national inventories of anthropogenic emissions by sources and removals by sinks of all greenhouse gases not controlled by the Montreal Protocol, using comparable methodologies to be agreed upon by the Conference of the Parties, and consistent with the guidelines for national communications adopted by the Conference of the Parties;

(b) Formulate, implement, publish and regularly update national and, where appropriate, regional programmes containing measures to mitigate climate change and measures to facilitate adequate adaptation to climate change:

(i) Such programmes would, inter alia, concern the energy, transport and industry sectors as well as agriculture, forestry and waste management. Furthermore, adaptation technologies and methods for improving spatial planning would improve adaptation to climate change; and

(ii) Parties included in Annex I shall submit information on action under this Protocol, including national programmes, according to the guidelines laid down in Article 8; and other Parties shall seek to include in their national communications, as appropriate, information on programmes which contain measures that the Party believes contribute to addressing climate change and its adverse impacts, including the abatement of increase in greenhouse gas emissions, and enhancement of and removals by sinks, capacity building and adaptation measures.

(c) Cooperate in the promotion of effective modalities for the development, application and diffusion of, and take all practicable steps to promote, facilitate and finance, as appropriate, the transfer of, or access to, environmentally sound technologies, know-how, practices and processes pertinent to climate change, in particular to developing countries, including the formulation of policies and programmes for the effective transfer of environmentally sound technologies that are publicly owned or in the public domain and the creation of an enabling environment for the private sector, to promote and enhance access to, and transfer of, environmentally sound technologies;

(d) Cooperate in scientific and technical research and promote the maintenance and the development of systematic observation systems and development of data archives to reduce uncertainties related to the climate system, the adverse impacts of climate change and the economic and social consequences of various response strategies, and promote the development and strengthening of endogenous capacities and capabilities to participate in international and intergovernmental efforts, programmes and networks on research and systematic observation, taking into account Article 5 of the Convention;

(e) Cooperate in and promote at the international level, and, where appropriate, using existing bodies, the development and implementation of education and training programmes, including the strengthening of national capacity building, in particular human and institutional capacities and the exchange or secondment of personnel to train experts in this field, in particular for developing countries, and facilitate at the national level public awareness and public access to information on climate change. Suitable modalities should be developed to implement these activities through the relevant bodies of the Convention taking into account Article 6 of the Convention;

(f) Include in their national communications information on programmes and activities undertaken pursuant to this Article in accordance with relevant decisions of the Conference of the Parties; and

(g) Give full consideration, in implementing the commitments in this Article, to Article 4, paragraph 8, of the Convention.

Article 11

1. In the implementation of Article 10, Parties shall take into account the provisions of Article 4, paragraphs 4, 5, 7, 8 and 9 of the Convention.

2. In the context of the implementation of Article 4, paragraph 1, of the Convention, in accordance with the provisions of Article 4, paragraph 3, and Article 11 of the Convention, and through the operating entity or entities of the financial mechanism of the Convention, the developed country Parties and other developed Parties included in Annex II to the Convention shall:

(a) Provide new and additional financial resources to meet the agreed full costs incurred by developing country Parties in advancing the implementation of existing commitments under Article 4, paragraph 1(a), of the Convention that are covered in Article 10, subparagraph (a); and

(b) Also provide such financial resources, including for the transfer of technology, needed by the developing country Parties to meet the agreed full incremental costs of advancing the implementation of existing commitments in Article 4, paragraph 1, of the Convention that are covered by Article 10 and that are agreed between a developing country Party and the international entity or entities referred to in Article 11 of the Convention, in accordance with that Article.

The implementation of these existing commitments shall take into account the need for adequacy and predictability in the flow of funds and the importance of appropriate burden sharing among developed country Parties. The guidance to the financial mechanism of the Convention in relevant decisions of the Conference of the Parties, including those agreed before the adoption of this Protocol, shall apply mutatis mutandis to the provisions of this paragraph.

3. The developed country Parties and other developed Parties in Annex II to the Convention may also provide, and developing country Parties avail themselves of, financial resources for the implementation of Article 10, through bilateral, regional and other multilateral channels.

Article 12

1. A clean development mechanism is hereby defined.

2. The purpose of the clean development mechanism shall be to assist Parties not included in Annex I in achieving sustainable development and in contributing to the ultimate objective of the Convention, and to assist Parties included in Annex I in achieving compliance with their quantified emission limitation and reduction commitments under Article 3.

3. Under the clean development mechanism:

(a) Parties not included in Annex I will benefit from project activities resulting in certified emission reductions; and

(b) Parties included in Annex I may use the certified emission reductions accruing from such project activities to contribute to compliance with part of their quantified emission limitation and reduction commitments under Article 3, as determined by the Conference of the Parties serving as the meeting of the Parties to this Protocol.

4. The clean development mechanism shall be subject to the authority and guidance of the Conference of the Parties serving as the meeting of the Parties to this Protocol and be supervised by an executive board of the clean development mechanism.

5. Emission reductions resulting from each project activity shall be certified by operational entities to be designated by the Conference of the Parties serving as the meeting of the Parties to this Protocol, on the basis of:

(a) Voluntary participation approved by each Party involved;

(b) Real, measurable, and long-term benefits related to the mitigation of climate change; and

(c) Reductions in emissions that are additional to any that would occur in the absence of the certified project activity.

6. The clean development mechanism shall assist in arranging funding of certified project activities as necessary.

7. The Conference of the Parties serving as the meeting of the Parties to this Protocol shall, at its first session, elaborate modalities and procedures with the objective of ensuring transparency, efficiency and accountability through independent auditing and verification of project activities.

8. The Conference of the Parties serving as the meeting of the Parties to this Protocol shall ensure that a share of the proceeds from certified project activities is used to cover administrative expenses as well as to assist developing country Parties that are particularly vulnerable to the adverse effects of climate change to meet the costs of adaptation.

9. Participation under the clean development mechanism, including in activities mentioned in paragraph 3(a) above and acquisition of certified emission reductions, may involve private and/or public entities, and is to be subject to whatever guidance may be provided by the executive board of the clean development mechanism.

10. Certified emission reductions obtained during the period from the year 2000 up to the beginning of the first commitment period can be used to assist in achieving compliance in the first commitment period.

Article 13

1. The Conference of the Parties, the supreme body of the Convention, shall serve as the meeting of the Parties to this Protocol.

2. Parties to the Convention that are not Parties to this Protocol may participate as observers in the proceedings of any session of the Conference of the Parties serving as the meeting of the Parties to this Protocol. When the Conference of the Parties serves as the meeting of the Parties to this Protocol, decisions under this Protocol shall be taken only by those that are Parties to it.

3. When the Conference of the Parties serves as the meeting of the Parties to this Protocol, any member of the Bureau of the Conference of the Parties representing a Party to the Convention but, at that time, not a Party to this Protocol, shall be

substituted by an additional member to be elected by and from amongst the Parties to this Protocol.

4. The Conference of the Parties serving as the meeting of the Parties to this Protocol shall keep under regular review the implementation of this Protocol and shall make, within its mandate, the decisions necessary to promote its effective implementation. It shall perform the functions assigned to it by this Protocol and shall:

(a) Assess, on the basis of all information made available to it in accordance with the provisions of this Protocol, the implementation of this Protocol by the Parties, the overall effects of the measures taken pursuant to this Protocol, in particular environmental, economic and social effects as well as their cumulative impacts and the extent to which progress towards the objective of the Convention is being achieved;

(b) Periodically examine the obligations of the Parties under this Protocol, giving due consideration to any reviews required by Article 4, paragraph 2(d), and Article 7, paragraph 2, of the Convention, in the light of the objective of the Convention, the experience gained in its implementation and the evolution of scientific and technological knowledge, and in this respect consider and adopt regular reports on the implementation of this Protocol;

(c) Promote and facilitate the exchange of information on measures adopted by the Parties to address climate change and its effects, taking into account the differing circumstances, responsibilities and capabilities of the Parties and their respective commitments under this Protocol;

(d) Facilitate, at the request of two or more Parties, the coordination of measures adopted by them to address climate change and its effects, taking into account the differing circumstances, responsibilities and capabilities of the Parties and their respective commitments under this Protocol;

(e) Promote and guide, in accordance with the objective of the Convention and the provisions of this Protocol, and taking fully into account the relevant decisions by the Conference of the Parties, the development and periodic refinement of comparable methodologies for the effective implementation of this Protocol, to be agreed on by the Conference of the Parties serving as the meeting of the Parties to this Protocol;

(f) Make recommendations on any matters necessary for the implementation of this Protocol;

(g) Seek to mobilize additional financial resources in accordance with Article 11, paragraph 2;

(h) Establish such subsidiary bodies as are deemed necessary for the implementation of this Protocol;

(i) Seek and utilize, where appropriate, the services and cooperation of, and information provided by, competent international organizations and intergovernmental and non-governmental bodies; and

(j) Exercise such other functions as may be required for the implementation of this Protocol, and consider any assignment resulting from a decision by the Conference of the Parties.

5. The rules of procedure of the Conference of the Parties and financial procedures of the Convention shall be applied mutatis mutandis under this Protocol, except as may be otherwise decided by consensus by the Conference of the Parties serving as the meeting of the Parties to this Protocol.

6. The first session of the Conference of the Parties serving as the meeting of the Parties to this Protocol shall be convened by the secretariat in conjunction with the

first session of the Conference of the Parties that is scheduled after the date of the entry into force of this Protocol. Subsequent ordinary sessions of the Conference of the Parties serving as the meeting of the Parties to this Protocol shall be held every year and in conjunction with ordinary sessions of the Conference of the Parties unless otherwise decided by the Conference of the Parties serving as the meeting of the Parties to this Protocol.

7. Extraordinary sessions of the Conference of the Parties serving as the meeting of the Parties to this Protocol shall be held at such other times as may be deemed necessary by the Conference of the Parties serving as the meeting of the Parties to this Protocol, or at the written request of any Party, provided that, within six months of the request being communicated to the Parties by the secretariat, it is supported by at least one third of the Parties.

8. The United Nations, its specialized agencies and the International Atomic Energy Agency, as well as any State member thereof or observers thereto not party to the Convention, may be represented at sessions of the Conference of the Parties serving as the meeting of the Parties to this Protocol as observers. Any body or agency, whether national or international, governmental or non-governmental, which is qualified in matters covered by this Protocol and which has informed the secretariat of its wish to be represented at a session of the Conference of the Parties serving as the meeting of the Parties to this Protocol as an observer, may be so admitted unless at least one third of the Parties present object. The admission and participation of observers shall be subject to the rules of procedure, as referred to in paragraph 5 above.

Article 14

1. The secretariat established by Article 8 of the Convention shall serve as the secretariat of this Protocol.

2. Article 8, paragraph 2, of the Convention on the functions of the secretariat, and Article 8, paragraph 3, of the Convention on arrangements made for the functioning of the secretariat, shall apply mutatis mutandis to this Protocol. The secretariat shall, in addition, exercise the functions assigned to it under this Protocol.

Article 15

1. The Subsidiary Body for Scientific and Technological Advice and the Subsidiary Body for Implementation established by Articles 9 and 10 of the Convention shall serve as, respectively, the Subsidiary Body for Scientific and Technological Advice and the Subsidiary Body for Implementation of this Protocol. The provisions relating to the functioning of these two bodies under the Convention shall apply mutatis mutandis to this Protocol. Sessions of the meetings of the Subsidiary Body for Scientific and Technological Advice and the Subsidiary Body for Implementation of this Protocol shall be held in conjunction with the meetings of, respectively, the Subsidiary Body for Scientific and Technological Advice and the Subsidiary Body for Implementation of the Convention.

2. Parties to the Convention that are not Parties to this Protocol may participate as observers in the proceedings of any session of the subsidiary bodies. When the subsidiary bodies serve as the subsidiary bodies of this Protocol, decisions under this Protocol shall be taken only by the Parties to this Protocol.

3. When the subsidiary bodies established by Articles 9 and 10 of the Convention exercise their functions with regard to matters concerning this Protocol, any member of the Bureaux of those subsidiary bodies representing a Party to the Convention but, at that time, not a party to this Protocol, shall be substituted by an additional member to be elected by and from amongst the Parties to this Protocol.

Article 16

The Conference of the Parties serving as the meeting of the Parties to this Protocol shall, as soon as practicable, consider the application to this Protocol of, and modify as appropriate, the multilateral consultative process referred to in Article 13 of the Convention, in the light of any relevant decisions that may be taken by the Conference of the Parties. Any multilateral consultative process that may be applied to this Protocol shall operate without prejudice to the procedures and mechanisms established in accordance with Article 17.

Article 16 bis

The Conference of the Parties shall define the relevant principles, modalities, rules and guidelines, in particular for verification, reporting and accountability for emissions trading. The Parties included in Annex B may participate in emissions trading for the purposes of fulfilling their commitments under Article 3 of this Protocol. Any such trading shall be supplemental to domestic actions for the purpose of meeting quantified emission limitation and reduction commitments under that Article.

Article 17

The Conference of the Parties serving as the meeting of the Parties to this Protocol shall, at its first session, approve appropriate and effective procedures and mechanisms to determine and to address cases of non-compliance with the provisions of this Protocol, including through the development of an indicative list of consequences, taking into account the cause, type, degree and frequency of non-compliance. Any procedures and mechanisms under this Article entailing binding consequences shall be adopted by means of an amendment to this Protocol.

Article 18

The provisions of Article 14 of the Convention on settlement of disputes shall apply mutatis mutandis to this Protocol.

Article 19

1. Any Party may propose amendments to this Protocol.

2. Amendments to this Protocol shall be adopted at an ordinary session of the Conference of the Parties serving as the meeting of the Parties to this Protocol. The text of any proposed amendment to this Protocol shall be communicated to the Parties by the secretariat at least six months before the meeting at which it is proposed for adoption. The secretariat shall also communicate the text of any proposed amendments to the Parties and signatories to the Convention and, for information, to the Depositary.

3. The Parties shall make every effort to reach agreement on any proposed amendment to this Protocol by consensus. If all efforts at consensus have been exhausted, and no agreement reached, the amendment shall as a last resort be adopted by a three-fourths majority vote of the Parties present and voting at the meeting. The adopted amendment shall be communicated by the secretariat to the Depositary, who shall circulate it to all Parties for their acceptance.

4. Instruments of acceptance in respect of an amendment shall be deposited with the Depositary. An amendment adopted in accordance with paragraph 3 above shall enter into force for those Parties having accepted it on the ninetieth day after the date of receipt by the Depositary of an instrument of acceptance by at least three fourths of the Parties to this Protocol.

5. The amendment shall enter into force for any other Party on the ninetieth day after the date on which that Party deposits with the Depositary its instrument of acceptance of the said amendment.

Article 20

1. Annexes to this Protocol shall form an integral part thereof and, unless otherwise expressly provided, a reference to this Protocol constitutes at the same time a reference to any annexes thereto. Any annexes adopted after the entry into force of this Protocol shall be restricted to lists, forms and any other material of a descriptive nature that is of a scientific, technical, procedural or administrative character.

2. Any Party may make proposals for an annex to this Protocol and may propose amendments to annexes to this Protocol.

3. Annexes to this Protocol and amendments to annexes to this Protocol shall be adopted at an ordinary session of the Conference of the Parties serving as the meeting of the Parties to this Protocol. The text of any proposed annex or amendment to an annex shall be communicated to the Parties by the secretariat at least six months before the meeting at which it is proposed for adoption. The secretariat shall also communicate the text of any proposed annex or amendment to an annex to the Parties and signatories to the Convention and, for information, to the Depositary.

4. The Parties shall make every effort to reach agreement on any proposed annex or amendment to an annex by consensus. If all efforts at consensus have been exhausted, and no agreement reached, the annex or amendment to an annex shall as a last resort be adopted by a three-fourths majority vote of the Parties present and voting at the meeting. The adopted annex or amendment to an annex shall be communicated by the secretariat to the Depositary, who shall circulate it to all Parties for their acceptance.

5. An annex, other than Annex A or B, that has been adopted or amended in accordance with paragraphs 3 and 4 above shall enter into force for all Parties to this Protocol six months after the date of the communication by the Depositary to such Parties of the adoption or amendment of the annex, except for those Parties that have notified the Depositary in writing within that period of their non-acceptance of the annex or amendment to the annex. The annex or amendment to an annex shall enter into force for Parties which withdraw their notification of non-acceptance on the ninetieth day after the date on which withdrawal of such notification has been received by the Depositary.

6. If the adoption of an annex or an amendment to an annex involves an amendment to this Protocol, that annex or amendment to an annex shall not enter into force until such time as the amendment to this Protocol enters into force.

7. Amendments to Annexes A and B to this Protocol shall be adopted and enter into force in accordance with the procedure set out in Article 19, provided that any amendments to Annex B shall be adopted only with the written consent of the Party concerned.

Article 21

1. Each Party shall have one vote, except as provided for in paragraph 2 below.

2. Regional economic integration organizations, in matters within their competence, shall exercise their right to vote with a number of votes equal to the number of their member States which are Parties to this Protocol. Such an organization shall not exercise its right to vote if any of its member States exercises its right, and vice versa.

Article 22

The Secretary–General of the United Nations shall be the Depositary of this Protocol.

Article 23

1. This Protocol shall be open for signature and subject to ratification, acceptance or approval by States and regional economic integration organizations which are Parties to the Convention. It shall be open for signature at United Nations Headquarters in New York from 16 March 1998 to 15 March 1999. This Protocol shall be open for accession from the day after the date on which it is closed for signature. Instruments of ratification, acceptance, approval or accession shall be deposited with the Depositary.

2. Any regional economic integration organization which becomes a Party to this Protocol without any of its member States being a Party shall be bound by all the obligations under this Protocol. In the case of such organizations, one or more of whose member States is a Party to this Protocol, the organization and its member States shall decide on their respective responsibilities for the performance of their obligations under this Protocol. In such cases, the organization and the member States shall not be entitled to exercise rights under this Protocol concurrently.

3. In their instruments of ratification, acceptance, approval or accession, regional economic integration organizations shall declare the extent of their competence with respect to the matters governed by this Protocol. These organizations shall also inform the Depositary, who shall in turn inform the Parties, of any substantial modification in the extent of their competence.

Article 24

1. This Protocol shall enter into force on the ninetieth day after the date on which not less than 55 Parties to the Convention, incorporating Parties included in Annex I which accounted in total for at least 55 per cent of the total carbon dioxide emissions for 1990 of the Parties included in Annex I, have deposited their instruments of ratification, acceptance, approval or accession.

2. For the purposes of this Article, "the total carbon dioxide emissions for 1990 of the Parties included in Annex I" means the amount communicated on or before the date of adoption of this Protocol by the Parties included in Annex I in their first national communications submitted in accordance with Article 12 of the Convention.

3. For each State or regional economic integration organization that ratifies, accepts or approves this Protocol or accedes thereto after the conditions set out in paragraph 1 above for the entry into force have been fulfilled, this Protocol shall enter into force on the ninetieth day following the date of deposit of its instrument of ratification, acceptance, approval or accession.

4. For the purposes of this Article, any instrument deposited by a regional economic integration organization shall not be counted as additional to those deposited by States members of the organization.

Article 25

No reservations may be made to this Protocol.

Article 26

1. At any time after three years from the date on which this Protocol has entered into force for a Party, that Party may withdraw from this Protocol by giving written notification to the Depositary.

2. Any such withdrawal shall take effect upon expiry of one year from the date of receipt by the Depositary of the notification of withdrawal, or on such later date as may be specified in the notification of withdrawal.

3. Any Party that withdraws from the Convention shall be considered as also having withdrawn from this Protocol.

Article 27

The original of this Protocol, of which the Arabic, Chinese, English, French, Russian and Spanish texts are equally authentic, shall be deposited with the Secretary–General of the United Nations.

Done at Kyoto this tenth day of December one thousand nine hundred and ninety-seven.

Annex A

Greenhouse gases

Carbon dioxide (CO sub2)
Methane (CH sub4)
Nitrous oxide (N sub2 O)
Hydrofluorocarbons (HFCs)
Perfluorocarbons (PFCs)
Sulphur hexafluoride (SF sub6)

Sectors/source categories

Energy

Fuel combustion
Energy industries
Manufacturing industries and construction
Transport
Other sectors
Other
Fugitive emissions from fuels
Solid fuels
Oil and natural gas
Other

Industrial processes

Mineral products
Chemical industry
Metal production
Other production
Production of halocarbons and sulphur hexafluoride
Consumption of halocarbons and sulphur hexafluoride
Other

Solvent and other product use

Agriculture

Enteric fermentation
Manure management
Rice cultivation
Agricultural soils
Prescribed burning of savannas
Field burning of agricultural residues
Other

Waste Solid waste disposal on land

Wastewater handling
Waste incineration
Other

Annex B

Party	Quantified emission limitation or reduction commitment (percentage of base year or period)
Australia	108
Austria	92
Belgium	92
Bulgaria	92
Canada	94
Croatia	95
Czech Republic	92
Denmark	92

Party	Quantified emission limitation or reduction commitment (percentage of base year or period)
Estonia	92
European Community	92
Finland	92
France	92
Germany	92
Greece	92
Hungary	94
Iceland	110
Ireland	92
Italy	92
Japan	94
Latvia	92
Liechtenstein	92
Lithuania	92
Luxembourg	92
Monaco	92
Netherlands	92
New Zealand	100
Norway	101
Poland	94
Portugal	92
Romania	92
Russian Federation	100
Slovakia	92
Slovenia	92
Spain	92
Sweden	92
Switzerland	92
Ukraine	100
United Kingdom	92
United States of America	93

3.26 Protocol to the Convention on Long-Range Transboundary Air Pollution on Persistent Organic Pollutants (Without Annexes).[i] Concluded at Aarhus (Denmark), 24 June 1998. Not yet in force. EB.AIR/1998/2; *reprinted in* 37 I.L.M. 505 (1998)

The Parties,

Determined to implement the Convention on Long-range Transboundary Air Pollution,

Recognizing that emissions of many persistent organic pollutants are transported across international boundaries and are deposited in Europe, North America and the Arctic, far from their site of origin, and that the atmosphere is the dominant medium of transport,

Aware that persistent organic pollutants resist degradation under natural conditions and have been associated with adverse effects on human health and the environment,

Concerned that persistent organic pollutants can biomagnify in upper trophic levels to concentrations which might affect the health of exposed wildlife and humans,

Acknowledging that the Arctic ecosystems and especially its indigenous people, who subsist on Arctic fish and mammals, are particularly at risk because of the biomagnification of persistent organic pollutants,

Mindful that measures to control emissions of persistent organic pollutants would also contribute to the protection of the environment and human health in areas outside the United Nations Economic Commission for Europe's region, including the Arctic and international waters,

Resolved to take measures to anticipate, prevent or minimize emissions of persistent organic pollutants, taking into account the application of the precautionary approach, as set forth in principle 15 of the Rio Declaration on Environment and Development,

Reaffirming that States have, in accordance with the Charter of the United Nations and the principles of international law, the sovereign right to exploit their own resources pursuant to their own environmental and development policies, and the responsibility to ensure that activities within their jurisdiction or control do not cause damage to the environment of other States or of areas beyond the limits of national jurisdiction,

Noting the need for global action on persistent organic pollutants and recalling the role envisaged in chapter 9 of Agenda 21 for regional agreements to reduce global transboundary air pollution and, in particular, for the United Nations Economic Commission for Europe to share its regional experience with other regions of the world,

Recognizing that there are subregional, regional and global regimes in place, including international instruments governing the management of hazardous wastes, their transboundary movement and disposal, in particular the Basel Convention on the Control of Transboundary Movements of Hazardous Wastes and their Disposal,

Considering that the predominant sources of air pollution contributing to the accumulation of persistent organic pollutants are the use of certain pesticides, the manufacture and use of certain chemicals, and the unintentional formation of certain substances in waste incineration, combustion, metal production and mobile sources,

Aware that techniques and management practices are available to reduce emissions of persistent organic pollutants into the air,

i. *See also* Basic Document 3.8.

Conscious of the need for a cost-effective regional approach to combating air pollution,

Noting the important contribution of the private and non-governmental sectors to knowledge of the effects associated with persistent organic pollutants, available alternatives and abatement techniques, and their role in assisting in the reduction of emissions of persistent organic pollutants,

Bearing in mind that measures taken to reduce persistent organic pollutant emissions should not constitute a means of arbitrary or unjustifiable discrimination or a disguised restriction on international competition and trade,

Taking into consideration existing scientific and technical data on emissions, atmospheric processes and effects on human health and the environment of persistent organic pollutants, as well as on abatement costs, and acknowledging the need to continue scientific and technical cooperation to further the understanding of these issues,

Recognizing the measures on persistent organic pollutants already taken by some of the Parties on a national level and/or under other international conventions,

Have agreed as follows:

Article 1

DEFINITIONS

For the purposes of the present Protocol,

1. "Convention" means the Convention on Long-range Transboundary Air Pollution, adopted in Geneva on 13 November 1979;

2. "EMEP" means the Cooperative Programme for Monitoring and Evaluation of the Long-range Transmission of Air Pollutants in Europe;

3. "Executive Body" means the Executive Body for the Convention constituted under article 10, paragraph 1, of the Convention;

4. "Commission" means the United Nations Economic Commission for Europe;

5. "Parties" means, unless the context otherwise requires, the Parties to the present Protocol;

6. "Geographical scope of EMEP" means the area defined in article 1, paragraph 4, of the Protocol to the 1979 Convention on Long-range Transboundary Air Pollution on Long-term Financing of the Cooperative Programme for Monitoring and Evaluation of the Long-range Transmission of Air Pollutants in Europe (EMEP), adopted in Geneva on 28 September 1984;

7. "Persistent organic pollutants" (POPs) are organic substances that: (i) possess toxic characteristics; (ii) are persistent; (iii) bioaccumulate; (iv) are prone to long-range transboundary atmospheric transport and deposition; and (v) are likely to cause significant adverse human health or environmental effects near to and distant from their sources;

8. "Substance" means a single chemical species, or a number of chemical species which form a specific group by virtue of (a) having similar properties and being emitted together into the environment; or (b) forming a mixture normally marketed as a single article;

9. "Emission" means the release of a substance from a point or diffuse source into the atmosphere;

10. "Stationary source" means any fixed building, structure, facility, installation, or equipment that emits or may emit any persistent organic pollutant directly or indirectly into the atmosphere;

11. "Major stationary source category" means any stationary source category listed in annex VIII;

12. "New stationary source" means any stationary source of which the construction or substantial modification is commenced after the expiry of two years from the date of entry into force of: (i) this Protocol; or (ii) an amendment to annex III or VIII, where the stationary source becomes subject to the provisions of this Protocol only by virtue of that amendment. It shall be a matter for the competent national authorities to decide whether a modification is substantial or not, taking into account such factors as the environmental benefits of the modification.

Article 2

OBJECTIVE

The objective of the present Protocol is to control, reduce or eliminate discharges, emissions and losses of persistent organic pollutants.

Article 3

BASIC OBLIGATIONS

1. Except where specifically exempted in accordance with article 4, each Party shall take effective measures:

(a) To eliminate the production and use of the substances listed in annex I in accordance with the implementation requirements specified therein;

(b)(i) To ensure that, when the substances listed in annex I are destroyed or disposed of, such destruction or disposal is undertaken in an environmentally sound manner, taking into account relevant subregional, regional and global regimes governing the management of hazardous wastes and their disposal, in particular the Basel Convention on the Control of Transboundary Movements of Hazardous Wastes and their Disposal;

(ii) To endeavour to ensure that the disposal of substances listed in annex I is carried out domestically, taking into account pertinent environmental considerations;

(iii) To ensure that the transboundary movement of the substances listed in annex I is conducted in an environmentally sound manner, taking into consideration applicable subregional regional, and global regimes governing the transboundary movement of hazardous wastes, in particular the Basel Convention on the Control of Transboundary Movements of Hazardous Wastes and their Disposal;

(c) To restrict the substances listed in annex II to the uses described, in accordance with the implementation requirements specified therein.

2. The requirements specified in paragraph 1 (b) above shall become effective for each substance upon the date that production or use of that substance is eliminated, whichever is later.

3. For substances listed in annex I, II, or III, each Party should develop appropriate strategies for identifying articles still in use and wastes containing such substances, and shall take appropriate measures to ensure that such wastes and such articles, upon becoming wastes, are destroyed or disposed of in an environmentally sound manner.

4. For the purposes of paragraphs 1 to 3 above, the terms waste, disposal, and environmentally sound shall be interpreted in a manner consistent with the use of those terms under the Basel Convention on the Control of Transboundary Movements of Hazardous Wastes and their Disposal.

5. Each Party shall:

(a) Reduce its total annual emissions of each of the substances listed in annex III from the level of the emission in a reference year set in accordance with that annex by taking effective measures, appropriate in its particular circumstances;

(b) No later than the timescales specified in annex VI, apply:

(i) The best available techniques, taking into consideration annex V, to each new stationary source within a major stationary source category for which annex V identifies best available techniques;

(ii) Limit values at least as stringent as those specified in annex IV to each new stationary source within a category mentioned in that annex, taking into consideration annex V. A Party may, as an alternative, apply different emission reduction strategies that achieve equivalent overall emission levels;

(iii) The best available techniques, taking into consideration annex V, to each existing stationary source within a major stationary source category for which annex V identifies best available techniques, insofar as this is technically and economically feasible. A Party may, as an alternative, apply different emission reduction strategies that achieve equivalent overall emission reductions;

(iv) Limit values at least as stringent as those specified in annex IV to each existing stationary source within a category mentioned in that annex, insofar as this is technically and economically feasible, taking into consideration annex V. A Party may, as an alternative, apply different emission reduction strategies that achieve equivalent overall emission reductions;

(v) Effective measures to control emissions from mobile sources, taking into consideration annex VII.

6. In the case of residential combustion sources, the obligations set out in paragraph 5 (b) (i) and (iii) above shall refer to all stationary sources in that category taken together.

7. Where a Party, after the application of paragraph 5 (b) above, cannot achieve the requirements of paragraph 5 (a) above for a substance specified in annex III, it shall be exempted from its obligations in paragraph 5 (a) above for that substance.

8. Each Party shall develop and maintain emission inventories for the substances listed in annex III, and shall collect available information relating to the production and sales of the substances listed in annexes I and II, for those Parties within the geographical scope of EMEP, using, as a minimum, the methodologies and the spatial and temporal resolution specified by the Steering Body of EMEP, and, for those Parties outside the geographical scope of EMEP, using as guidance the methodologies developed through the work plan of the Executive Body. It shall report this information in accordance with the reporting requirements set out in article 9 below.

Article 4

EXEMPTIONS

1. Article 3, paragraph 1, shall not apply to quantities of a substance to be used for laboratory-scale research or as a reference standard.

2. A Party may grant an exemption from article 3, paragraphs 1 (a) and (c), in respect of a particular substance, provided that the exemption is not granted or used in a manner that would undermine the objectives of the present Protocol, and only for the following purposes and under the following conditions:

(a) For research other than that referred to in paragraph 1 above, if:

(i) No significant quantity of the substance is expected to reach the environment during the proposed use and subsequent disposal;

(ii) The objectives and parameters of such research are subject to assessment and authorization by the Party; and

(iii) In the event of a significant release of a substance into the environment, the exemption will terminate immediately, measures will be taken to mitigate the release as appropriate, and an assessment of the containment measures will be conducted before research may resume;

(b) To manage as necessary a public health emergency, if:

(i) No suitable alternative measures are available to the Party to address the situation;

(ii) The measures taken are proportional to the magnitude and severity of the emergency;

(iii) Appropriate precautions are taken to protect human health and the environment and to ensure that the substance is not used outside the geographical area subject to the emergency;

(iv) The exemption is granted for a period of time that does not exceed the duration of the emergency; and

(v) Upon termination of the emergency, any remaining stocks of the substance are subject to the provisions of article 3, paragraph 1 (b);

(c) For a minor application judged to be essential by the Party, if:

(i) The exemption is granted for a maximum of five years;

(ii) The exemption has not previously been granted by it under this article;

(iii) No suitable alternatives exist for the proposed use;

(iv) The Party has estimated the emissions of the substance resulting from the exemption and their contribution to the total emissions of the substance from the Parties;

(v) Adequate precautions are taken to ensure that the emissions to the environment are minimized; and

(vi) Upon termination of the exemption, any remaining stocks of the substance are subject to the provisions of article 3, paragraph 1 (b).

3. Each Party shall, no later than ninety days after granting an exemption under paragraph 2 above, provide the secretariat with, as a minimum, the following information:

(a) The chemical name of the substance subject to the exemption;

(b) The purpose for which the exemption has been granted;

(c) The conditions under which the exemption has been granted;

(d) The length of time for which the exemption has been granted;

(e) Those to whom, or the organization to which, the exemption applies; and

(f) For an exemption granted under paragraphs 2 (a) and (c) above, the estimated emissions of the substance as a result of the exemption and an assessment of their contribution to the total emissions of the substance from the Parties.

4. The secretariat shall make available to all Parties the information received under paragraph 3 above.

Article 5

EXCHANGE OF INFORMATION AND TECHNOLOGY

The Parties shall, in a manner consistent with their laws, regulations and practices, create favourable conditions to facilitate the exchange of information and technology designed to reduce the generation and emission of persistent organic pollutants and to develop cost-effective alternatives, by promoting, inter alia:

(a) Contacts and cooperation among appropriate organizations and individuals in the private and public sectors that are capable of providing technology, design and engineering services, equipment or finance;

(b) The exchange of and access to information on the development and use of alternatives to persistent organic pollutants as well as on the evaluation of the risks that such alternatives pose to human health and the environment, and information on the economic and social costs of such alternatives;

(c) The compilation and regular updating of lists of their designated authorities engaged in similar activities in other international forums;

(d) The exchange of information on activities conducted in other international forums.

Article 6

PUBLIC AWARENESS

The Parties shall, consistent with their laws, regulations and practices, promote the provision of information to the general public, including individuals who are direct users of persistent organic pollutants. This information may include, inter alia:

(a) Information, including labelling, on risk assessment and hazard;

(b) Information on risk reduction;

(c) Information to encourage the elimination of persistent organic pollutants or a reduction in their use, including, where appropriate, information on integrated pest management, integrated crop management and the economic and social impacts of this elimination or reduction; and

(d) Information on alternatives to persistent organic pollutants, as well as an evaluation of the risks that such alternatives pose to human health and the environment, and information on the economic and social impacts of such alternatives.

Article 7

STRATEGIES, POLICIES, PROGRAMMES, MEASURES AND INFORMATION

1. Each Party shall, no later than six months after the date on which this Protocol enters into force for it, develop strategies, policies and programmes in order to discharge its obligations under the present Protocol.

2. Each Party shall:

(a) Encourage the use of economically feasible, environmentally sound management techniques, including best environmental practices, with respect to all aspects of the use, production, release, processing, distribution, handling, transport and reprocessing of substances subject to the present Protocol and manufactured articles, mixtures or solutions containing such substances;

(b) Encourage the implementation of other management programmes to reduce emissions of persistent organic pollutants, including voluntary programmes and the use of economic instruments;

(c) Consider the adoption of additional policies and measures as appropriate in its particular circumstances, which may include non-regulatory approaches;

(d) Make determined efforts that are economically feasible to reduce levels of substances subject to the present Protocol that are contained as contaminants in other substances, chemical products or manufactured articles, as soon as the relevance of the source has been established;

(e) Take into consideration in its programmes for evaluating substances, the characteristics specified in paragraph 1 of Executive Body decision 1998/2 on information to be submitted and procedures for adding substances to annex I, II or III, including any amendments thereto.

3. The Parties may take more stringent measures than those required by the present Protocol.

Article 8

RESEARCH, DEVELOPMENT AND MONITORING

The Parties shall encourage research, development, monitoring and cooperation related, but not limited, to:

(a) Emissions, long-range transport and deposition levels and their modelling, existing levels in the biotic and abiotic environment, the elaboration of procedures for harmonizing relevant methodologies;

(b) Pollutant pathways and inventories in representative ecosystems;

(c) Relevant effects on human health and the environment, including quantification of those effects;

(d) Best available techniques and practices, including agricultural practices, and emission control techniques and practices currently employed by the Parties or under development;

(e) Methodologies permitting consideration of socio-economic factors in the evaluation of alternative control strategies;

(f) An effects-based approach which integrates appropriate information, including information obtained under subparagraphs (a) to (e) above, on measured or modelled environmental levels, pathways, and effects on human health and the environment, for the purpose of formulating future control strategies which also take into account economic and technological factors;

(g) Methods for estimating national emissions and projecting future emissions of individual persistent organic pollutants and for evaluating how such estimates and projections can be used to structure future obligations;

(h) Levels of substances subject to the present Protocol that are contained as contaminants in other substances, chemical products or manufactured articles and the significance of these levels for long-range transport, as well as techniques to reduce levels of these contaminants, and, in addition, levels of persistent organic pollutants generated during the life cycle of timber treated with pentachlorophenol.

Priority should be given to research on substances considered to be the most likely to be submitted under the procedures specified in article 14, paragraph 6.

Article 9

REPORTING

1. Subject to its laws governing the confidentiality of commercial information:

(a) Each Party shall report, through the Executive Secretary of the Commission, to the Executive Body, on a periodic basis as determined by the Parties meeting within the Executive Body, information on the measures that it has taken to implement the present Protocol;

(b) Each Party within the geographical scope of EMEP shall report, through the Executive Secretary of the Commission, to EMEP, on a periodic basis to be determined by the Steering Body of EMEP and approved by the Parties at a session of the Executive Body, information on the levels of emissions of persistent organic pollutants using, as a minimum, the methodologies and the temporal and spatial resolution specified by the Steering Body of EMEP. Parties in areas outside the geographical scope of EMEP shall make available similar information to the Executive Body if requested to do so. Each Party shall also provide information on the levels of emissions of the substances listed in annex III for the reference year specified in that annex.

2. The information to be reported in accordance with paragraph 1 (a) above shall be in conformity with a decision regarding format and content to be adopted by the Parties at a session of the Executive Body. The terms of this decision shall be reviewed as necessary to identify any additional elements regarding the format or the content of the information that is to be included in the reports.

3. In good time before each annual session of the Executive Body, EMEP shall provide information on the long-range transport and deposition of persistent organic pollutants.

Article 10

REVIEWS BY THE PARTIES AT SESSIONS OF THE EXECUTIVE BODY

1. The Parties shall, at sessions of the Executive Body, pursuant to article 10, paragraph 2 (a), of the Convention, review the information supplied by the Parties, EMEP and other subsidiary bodies, and the reports of the Implementation Committee referred to in article 11 of the present

Protocol.

2. The Parties shall, at sessions of the Executive Body, keep under review the progress made towards achieving the obligations set out in the present Protocol.

3. The Parties shall, at sessions of the Executive Body, review the sufficiency and effectiveness of the obligations set out in the present Protocol. Such reviews will take into account the best available scientific information on the effects of the deposition of persistent organic pollutants, assessments of technological developments, changing economic conditions and the fulfilment of the obligations on emission levels. The procedures, methods and timing for such reviews shall be specified by the Parties at a session of the Executive Body. The first such review shall be completed no later than three years after the present Protocol enters into force.

Article 11

COMPLIANCE Compliance by each Party with its obligations under the present Protocol shall be reviewed regularly. The Implementation Committee established by decision 1997/2 of the Executive Body at its fifteenth session shall carry out such reviews and report to the Parties meeting within the Executive Body in accordance with the terms of the annex to that decision, including any amendments thereto.

Article 12

SETTLEMENT OF DISPUTES

1. In the event of a dispute between any two or more Parties concerning the interpretation or application of the present Protocol, the Parties concerned shall seek a

settlement of the dispute through negotiation or any other peaceful means of their own choice. The parties to the dispute shall inform the Executive Body of their dispute.

2. When ratifying, accepting, approving or acceding to the present Protocol, or at anytime thereafter, a Party which is not a regional economic integration organization may declare in a written instrument submitted to the Depositary that, in respect of any dispute concerning the interpretation or application of the Protocol, it recognizes one or both of the following means of dispute settlement as compulsory ipso facto and without special agreement, in relation to any Party accepting the same obligation:

(a) Submission of the dispute to the International Court of Justice;

(b) Arbitration in accordance with procedures to be adopted by the Parties at a session of the Executive Body, as soon as practicable, in an annex on arbitration.

A Party which is a regional economic integration organization may make a declaration with like effect in relation to arbitration in accordance with the procedures referred to in subparagraph (b) above.

3. A declaration made under paragraph 2 above shall remain in force until it expires in accordance with its terms or until three months after written notice of its revocation has been deposited with the Depositary.

4. A new declaration, a notice of revocation or the expiry of a declaration shall not in any way affect proceedings pending before the International Court of Justice or the arbitral tribunal, unless the parties to the dispute agree otherwise.

5. Except in a case where the parties to a dispute have accepted the same means of dispute settlement under paragraph 2, if after twelve months following notification by one Party to another that a dispute exists between them, the Parties concerned have not been able to settle their dispute through the means mentioned in paragraph 1 above, the dispute shall be submitted, at the request of any of the parties to the dispute, to conciliation.

6. For the purpose of paragraph 5, a conciliation commission shall be created. The commission shall be composed of equal numbers of members appointed by each Party concerned or, where the Parties in conciliation share the same interest, by the group sharing that interest, and a chairperson chosen jointly by the members so appointed. The commission shall render a recommendatory award, which the Parties shall consider in good faith.

Article 13

ANNEXES

The annexes to the present Protocol shall form an integral part of the Protocol. Annexes V and VII are recommendatory in character.

Article 14

AMENDMENTS

1. Any Party may propose amendments to the present Protocol.

2. Proposed amendments shall be submitted in writing to the Executive Secretary of the Commission, who shall communicate them to all Parties. The Parties meeting within the Executive Body shall discuss the proposed amendments at its next session, provided that the proposals have been circulated by the Executive Secretary to the Parties at least ninety days in advance.

3. Amendments to the present Protocol and to annexes I to IV, VI and VIII shall be adopted by consensus of the Parties present at a session of the Executive Body, and shall enter into force for the Parties which have accepted them on the ninetieth day after the date on which two thirds of the Parties have deposited with the Depositary

their instruments of acceptance thereof. Amendments shall enter into force for any other Party on the ninetieth day after the date on which that Party has deposited its instrument of acceptance thereof.

4. Amendments to annexes V and VII shall be adopted by consensus of the Parties present at a session of the Executive Body. On the expiry of ninety days from the date of its communication to all Parties by the Executive Secretary of the Commission, an amendment to any such annex shall become effective for those Parties which have not submitted to the Depositary a notification in accordance with the provisions of paragraph 5 below, provided that at least sixteen Parties have not submitted such a notification.

5. Any Party that is unable to approve an amendment to annex V or VII shall so notify the Depositary in writing within ninety days from the date of the communication of its adoption. The Depositary shall without delay notify all Parties of any such notification received. A Party may at any time substitute an acceptance for its previous notification and, upon deposit of an instrument of acceptance with the Depositary, the amendment to such an annex shall become effective for that Party.

6. In the case of a proposal to amend annex I, II, or III by adding a substance to the present Protocol:

(a) The proposer shall provide the Executive Body with the information specified in Executive Body decision 1998/2, including any amendments thereto; and

(b) The Parties shall evaluate the proposal in accordance with the procedures set forth in Executive Body decision 1998/2, including any amendments thereto.

7. Any decision to amend Executive Body decision 1998/2 shall be taken by consensus of the Parties meeting within the Executive Body and shall take effect sixty days after the date of adoption.

Article 15

SIGNATURE

1. The present Protocol shall be open for signature at Aarhus (Denmark) from 24 to 25 June 1998, then at United Nations Headquarters in New York until 21 December 1998, by States members of the Commission as well as States having consultative status with the Commission pursuant to paragraph 8 of Economic and Social Council resolution 36 (IV) of 28 March 1947, and by regional economic integration organizations, constituted by sovereign States members of the Commission, which have competence in respect of the negotiation, conclusion and application of international agreements in matters covered by the Protocol, provided that the States and organizations concerned are Parties to the Convention.

2. In matters within their competence, such regional economic integration organizations shall, on their own behalf, exercise the rights and fulfil the responsibilities which the present Protocol attributes to their member States. In such cases, the member States of these organizations shall not be entitled to exercise such rights individually.

Article 16

RATIFICATION, ACCEPTANCE, APPROVAL AND ACCESSION

1. The present Protocol shall be subject to ratification, acceptance or approval by Signatories.

2. The present Protocol shall be open for accession as from 21 December 1998 by the States and organizations that meet the requirements of article 15, paragraph 1.

Article 17

DEPOSITARY

The instruments of ratification, acceptance, approval or accession shall be deposited with the Secretary–General of the United Nations, who will perform the functions of Depositary.

Article 18

ENTRY INTO FORCE

1. The present Protocol shall enter into force on the ninetieth day following the date on which the sixteenth instrument of ratification, acceptance, approval or accession has been deposited with the Depositary.

2. For each State and organization referred to in article 15, paragraph 1, which ratifies, accepts or approves the present Protocol or accedes thereto after the deposit of the sixteenth instrument of ratification, acceptance, approval or accession, the Protocol shall enter into force on the ninetieth day following the date of deposit by such Party of its instrument of ratification, acceptance, approval or accession.

Article 19

WITHDRAWAL

At any time after five years from the date on which the present Protocol has come into force with respect to a Party, that Party may withdraw from it by giving written notification to the Depositary. Any such withdrawal shall take effect on the ninetieth day following the date of its receipt by the Depositary, or on such later date as may be specified in the notification of the withdrawal.

Article 20

AUTHENTIC TEXTS

The original of the present Protocol, of which the English, French and Russian texts are equally authentic, shall be deposited with the Secretary–General of the United Nations.

IN WITNESS WHEREOF the undersigned, being duly authorized thereto, have signed the present Protocol.

Done at Aarhus (Denmark), this twenty-fourth day of June, one thousand nine hundred and ninety-eight.

* * *

4. Hydrosphere

4.1 Treaty Between Canada and the United States of America Relating to Boundary Waters and Questions Arising Along the Boundary Between the United States and Canada.[a] Concluded at Washington, 11 January 1909. Entered into force, 5 May 1910. 36 Stat. 2448, T.S. No. 548

The United States of America and His Majesty the King of the United Kingdom of Great Britain and Ireland and of the British Dominions beyond the Seas, Emperor of India, being equally desirous to prevent disputes regarding the use of boundary waters and to settle all questions which are now pending between the United States and the Dominion of Canada involving the rights, obligations, or interests of either in relation to the other or to the inhabitants of the other, along their common frontier, and to make provision for the adjustment and settlement of all such questions as may hereafter arise, have resolved to conclude a treaty in furtherance of these ends, and for that purpose have appointed as their respective plenipotentiaries:

The President of the United States of America, Elihu Root, Secretary of State of the United States; and

His Britannic Majesty, the Right Honorable James Bryce, O.M., His Ambassador Extraordinary and Plenipotentiary at Washington;

Who, after having communicated to one another their full powers, found in good and due form, have agreed upon the following articles:

Preliminary Article

For the purposes of this treaty boundary waters are defined as the waters from main shore to main shore of the lakes and rivers and connecting waterways, or the portions thereof, along which the international boundary between the United States and the Dominion of Canada passes, including all bays, arms, and inlets thereof, but not including tributary waters which in their natural channels would flow into such lakes, rivers, and waterways, or waters flowing from such lakes, rivers, and waterways, or the waters of rivers flowing across the boundary.

Article I

The High Contracting Parties agree that the navigation of all navigable boundary waters shall forever continue free and open for the purposes of commerce to the inhabitants and to the ships, vessels, and boats of both countries equally, subject, however, to any laws and regulations of either country, within its own territory, not inconsistent with such privilege of free navigation and applying equally and without discrimination to the inhabitants, ships, vessels, and boats of both countries.

It is further agreed that so long as this treaty shall remain in force, this same right of navigation shall extend to the waters of Lake Michigan and to all canals connecting boundary waters, and now existing or which may hereafter be constructed on either side of the line. Either of the High Contracting Parties may adopt rules and regulations governing the use of such canals within its own territory and may charge tolls for the use thereof, but all such rules and regulations and all tolls charged shall apply alike to the subjects or citizens of the High Contracting Parties and the ships, vessels, and boats of both of the High Contracting Parties, and they shall be placed on terms of equality in the use thereof.

a. Article 5 terminated by treaty of 27 February 1950.

Article II

Each of the High Contracting Parties reserves to itself or to the several State Governments on the one side and the Dominion or Provincial Governments on the other as the case may be, subject to any treaty provisions now existing with respect thereto, the exclusive jurisdiction and control over the use and diversion, whether temporary or permanent, of all waters on its own side of the line which in their natural channels would flow across the boundary or into boundary waters; but it is agreed that any interference with or diversion from their natural channel of such waters on either side of the boundary, resulting in any injury on the other side of the boundary, shall give rise to the same rights and entitle the injured parties to the same legal remedies as if such injury took place in the country where such diversion or interference occurs; but this provision shall not apply to cases already existing or to cases expressly covered by special agreement between the parties hereto.

It is understood, however, that neither of the High Contracting Parties intends by the foregoing provision to surrender any right, which it may have, to object to any interference with or diversions of waters on the other side of the boundary the effect of which would be productive of material injury to the navigation interests on its own side of the boundary.

Article III

It is agreed that, in addition to the uses, obstructions, and diversions heretofore permitted or hereafter provided for by special agreement between the Parties hereto, no further or other uses or obstructions or diversions, whether temporary or permanent, of boundary waters on either side of the line, affecting the natural level or flow of boundary waters on the other side of the line, shall be made except by authority of the United States or the Dominion of Canada within their respective jurisdictions and with the approval, as hereinafter provided, of a joint commission, to be known as the International Joint Commission.

The foregoing provisions are not intended to limit or interfere with the existing rights of the Government of the United States on the one side and the Government of the Dominion of Canada on the other, to undertake and carry on governmental works in boundary waters for the deepening of channels, the construction of breakwaters, the improvement of harbors, and other governmental works for the benefit of commerce and navigation, provided that such works are wholly on its own side of the line and do not materially affect the level or flow of the boundary waters on the other, nor are such provisions intended to interfere with the ordinary use of such waters for domestic and sanitary purposes.

Article IV

The High Contracting Parties agree that, except in cases provided for by special agreement between them, they will not permit the construction or maintenance on their respective sides of the boundary of any remedial or protective works or any dams or other obstructions in waters flowing from boundary waters or in waters at a lower level than the boundary in rivers flowing across the boundary, the effect of which is to raise the natural level of waters on the other side of the boundary unless the construction or maintenance thereof is approved by the aforesaid International Joint Commission.

It is further agreed that the waters herein defined as boundary waters and waters flowing across the boundary shall not be polluted on either side to the injury of health or property on the other.

Article V

The High Contracting Parties agree that it is expedient to limit the diversion of waters from the Niagara River so that the level of Lake Erie and the flow of the stream shall not be appreciably affected. It is the desire of both Parties to accomplish this object with the least possible injury to investments which have already been made in the construction of power plants on the United States side of the river under grants of authority from the State of New York, and on the Canadian side of the river under licenses authorized by the Dominion of Canada and the Province of Ontario.

So long as this treaty shall remain in force, no diversion of the waters of the Niagara River above the Falls from the natural course and stream thereof shall be permitted except for the purposes and to the extent hereinafter provided.

The United States may authorize and permit the diversion within the State of New York of the waters of said river above the Falls of Niagara, for power purposes, not exceeding in the aggregate a daily diversion at the rate of twenty thousand cubic feet of water per second.

The United Kingdom, by the Dominion of Canada, or the Province of Ontario, may authorize and permit the diversion within the Province of Ontario of the waters of said river above the Falls of Niagara, for power purposes, not exceeding in the aggregate a daily diversion at the rate of thirty-six thousand cubic feet of water per second.

The prohibitions of this article shall not apply to the diversion of water for sanitary or domestic purposes, or for the service of canals for the purposes of navigation.

Article VI

The High Contracting Parties agree that the St. Mary and Milk Rivers and their tributaries (in the State of Montana and the Provinces of Alberta and Saskatchewan) are to be treated as one stream for the purposes of irrigation and power, and the waters thereof shall be apportioned equally between the two countries, but in making such equal apportionment more than half may be taken from one river and less than half from the other by either country so as to afford a more beneficial use to each. It is further agreed that in the division of such waters during the irrigation season, between the 1st of April and 31st of October, inclusive, annually, the United States is entitled to a prior appropriation of 500 cubic feet per second of the waters of the Milk River, or so much of such amount as constitutes three-fourths of its natural flow, and that Canada is entitled to a prior appropriation of 500 cubic feet per second of the flow of the St. Mary River, or so much of such amount as constitutes three-fourths of its natural flow.

The channel of the Milk River in Canada may be used at the convenience of the United States for the conveyance, while passing through Canadian territory, of waters diverted from the St. Mary River. The provisions of Article II of this treaty shall apply to any injury resulting to property in Canada from the conveyance of such waters through the Milk River.

The measurement and apportionment of the water to be used by each country shall from time to time be made jointly by the properly constituted reclamation officers of the United States and the properly constituted irrigation officers of His Majesty under the direction of the International Joint Commission.

Article VII

The High Contracting Parties agree to establish and maintain an International Joint Commission of the United States and Canada composed of six commissioners, three on the part of the United States appointed by the President thereof, and three on the part of the United Kingdom appointed by His Majesty on the recommendation of the Governor in Council of the Dominion of Canada.

Article VIII

This International Joint Commission shall have jurisdiction over and shall pass upon all cases involving the use or obstruction or diversion of the waters with respect to which under Articles III and IV of this treaty the approval of this Commission is required, and in passing upon such cases the Commission shall be governed by the following rules or principles which are adopted by the High Contracting Parties for this purpose:

The High Contracting Parties shall have, each on its own side of the boundary, equal and similar rights in the use of the waters hereinbefore defined as boundary waters.

The following order of precedence shall be observed among the various uses enumerated hereinafter for these waters, and no use shall be permitted which tends materially to conflict with or restrain any other use which is given preference over it in this order of precedence:

(1) Uses for domestic and sanitary purposes;

(2) Uses for navigation, including the service of canals for the purposes of navigation;

(3) Uses for power and for irrigation purposes.

The foregoing provisions shall not apply to or disturb any existing uses of boundary waters on either side of the boundary.

The requirement for an equal division may in the discretion of the Commission be suspended in cases of temporary diversions along boundary waters at points where such equal division can not be made advantageously on account of local conditions, and where such diversion does not diminish elsewhere the amount available for use on the other side.

The Commission in its discretion may make its approval in any case conditional upon the construction of remedial or protective works to compensate so far as possible for the particular use or diversion proposed, and in such cases may require that suitable and adequate provision, approved by the Commission, be made for the protection and indemnity against injury of any interests on either side of the boundary.

In cases involving the elevation of the natural level of waters on either side of the line as a result of the construction or maintenance on the other side of remedial or protective works or dams or other obstructions in boundary waters or in waters flowing therefrom or in waters below the boundary in rivers flowing across the boundary, the Commission shall require, as a condition of its approval thereof, that suitable and adequate provision, approved by it, be made for the protection and indemnity of all interests on the other side of the line which may be injured thereby.

The majority of the Commissioners shall have power to render a decision. In case the Commission is evenly divided upon any question or matter presented to it for decision, separate reports shall be made by the Commissioners on each side to their own Government. The High Contracting Parties shall thereupon endeavor to agree upon an adjustment of the question or matter of difference, and if an agreement is reached between them, it shall be reduced to writing in the form of a protocol, and shall be communicated to the Commissioners, who shall take such further proceedings as may be necessary to carry out such agreement.

Article IX

The High Contracting Parties further agree that any other questions or matters of difference arising between them involving the rights, obligations, or interests of either in relation to the other or to the inhabitants of the other along the common frontier between the United States and the Dominion of Canada, shall be referred from time to time to the International Joint Commission for examination and report, whenever either the Government of the United States or the Government of the Dominion of Canada shall request that such questions or matters of difference be so referred.

The International Joint Commission is authorized in each case so referred to examine into and report upon the facts and circumstances of the particular questions and matters referred, together with such conclusions and recommendations as may be appropriate, subject, however, to any restrictions or exceptions which may be imposed with respect thereto by the terms of the reference.

Such reports of the Commission shall not be regarded as decisions of the questions or matters so submitted either on the facts or the law, and shall in no way have the character of an arbitral award.

The Commission shall make a joint report to both Governments in all cases in which all or a majority of the Commissioners agree, and in case of disagreement the minority may make a joint report to both Governments, or separate reports to their respective Governments.

In case the Commission is evenly divided upon any question or matter referred to it for report, separate reports shall be made by the Commissioners on each side to their own Government.

Article X

Any questions or matters of difference arising between the High Contracting Parties involving the rights, obligations, or interests of the United States or of the Dominion of Canada either in relation to each other or to their respective inhabitants, may be referred for decision to the International Joint Commission by the consent of the two Parties, it being understood that on the part of the United States any such action will be by and with the advice and consent of the Senate, and on the part of His Majesty's Government with the consent of the Governor General in Council. In each case so referred, the said Commission is authorized to examine into and report upon the facts and circumstances of the particular questions and matters referred, together with such conclusions and recommendations as may be appropriate, subject, however, to any restrictions or exceptions which may be imposed with respect thereto by the terms of the reference.

A majority of the said Commission shall have power to render a decision or finding upon any of the questions or matters so referred.

If the said Commission is equally divided or otherwise unable to render a decision or finding as to any questions or matters so referred, it shall be the duty of the Commissioners to make a joint report to both Governments, or separate reports to their respective Governments, showing the different conclusions arrived at with regard to the matters or questions so referred, which questions or matters shall thereupon be referred for decision by the High Contracting Parties to an umpire chosen in accordance with the procedure prescribed in the fourth, fifth, and sixth paragraphs of Article XLV of The Hague Convention for the pacific settlement of international disputes, dated October 18, 1907. Such umpire shall have power to render a final decision with respect to those matters and questions so referred on which the Commission failed to agree.

Article XI

A duplicate original of all decisions rendered and joint reports made by the Commission shall be transmitted to and filed with the Secretary of State of the United States and the Governor General of the Dominion of Canada, and to them shall be addressed all communications of the Commission.

Article XII

The International Joint Commission shall meet and organize at Washington promptly after the members thereof are appointed, and when organized the Commission may fix such times and places for its meetings as may be necessary, subject at all times to special call or direction by the two Governments. Each Commissioner, upon the first joint meeting of the Commission after his appointment, shall, before proceeding with the work of the Commission, make and subscribe a solemn declaration in writing that he will faithfully and impartially perform the duties imposed upon him under this treaty, and such declaration shall be entered on the records of the proceedings of the Commission.

The United States and Canadian sections of the Commission may each appoint a secretary, and these shall act as joint secretaries of the Commission at its joint sessions, and the Commission may employ engineers and clerical assistants from time to time as it may deem advisable. The salaries and personal expenses of the Commission and of the secretaries shall be paid by their respective Governments, and all reasonable and necessary joint expenses of the Commission, incurred by it, shall be paid in equal moieties by the High Contracting Parties.

The Commission shall have power to administer oaths to witnesses, and to take evidence on oath whenever deemed necessary in any proceeding, or inquiry, or matter within its jurisdiction under this treaty, and all parties interested therein shall be given convenient opportunity to be heard, and the High Contracting Parties agree to adopt such legislation as may be appropriate and necessary to give the Commission the powers above mentioned on each side of the boundary, and to provide for the issue of subpoenas and for compelling the attendance of witnesses in proceedings before the Commission. The Commission may adopt such rules of procedure as shall be in accordance with justice and equity, and may make such examination in person and through agents or employees as may be deemed advisable.

Article XIII

In all cases where special agreements between the High Contracting Parties hereto are referred to in the foregoing articles, such agreements are understood and intended to include not only direct agreements between the High Contracting Parties, but also any mutual arrangement between the United States and the Dominion of Canada expressed by concurrent or reciprocal legislation on the part of Congress and the Parliament of the Dominion.

Article XIV

The present treaty shall be ratified by the President of the United States of America, by and with the advice and consent of the Senate thereof, and by His Britannic Majesty. The ratifications shall be exchanged at Washington as soon as possible and the treaty shall take effect on the date of the exchange of its ratifications. It shall remain in force for five years, dating from the day of exchange of ratifications, and thereafter until terminated by twelve months' written notice given by either High Contracting Party to the other.

4.2 Convention on the High Seas.[b] Concluded at Geneva, 29 April 1958. Entered into force, 30 September 1962. 450 U.N.T.S. 82, 13 U.S.T. 2312, T.I.A.S. No. 5200; *reprinted in* 5 Weston V.F.3

Article 1

The term "high seas" means all parts of the sea that are not included in the territorial sea or in the internal waters of a State.

Article 2

The high seas being open to all nations, no State may validly purport to subject any part of them to its sovereignty. Freedom of the high seas is exercised under the conditions laid down by these articles and by the other rules of international law. It comprises, *inter alia,* both for coastal and non-coastal States:

(1) Freedom of navigation;

(2) Freedom of fishing;

(3) Freedom to lay submarine cables and pipelines;

(4) Freedom to fly over the high seas.

These freedoms, and others which are recognized by the general principles of international law, shall be exercised by all States with reasonable regard to the interests of other States in their exercise of the freedom of the high seas.

Article 3

1. In order to enjoy the freedom of the seas on equal terms with coastal States, States having no sea-coast should have free access to the sea. To this end States situated between the sea and a State having no sea-coast shall by common agreement with the latter, and in conformity with existing international conventions, accord:

(*a*) To the State having no sea-coast, on a basis of reciprocity, free transit through their territory; and

(*b*) To ships flying the flag of that State treatment equal to that accorded to their own ships, or to the ships of any other States, as regards access to seaports and the use of such ports.

2. States situated between the sea and a State having no sea-coast shall settle, by mutual agreement with the latter, and taking into account the rights of the coastal State or State of transit and the special conditions of the State having no sea-coast, all matters relating to freedom of transit and equal treatment in ports, in case such States are not already parties to existing international conventions.

Article 4

Every State, whether coastal or not, has the right to sail ships under its flag on the high seas.

Article 5

1. Each State shall fix the conditions for the grant of its nationality to ships, for the registration of ships in its territory, and for the right to fly its flag. Ships have the nationality of the State whose flag they are entitled to fly. There must exist a genuine link between the State and the ship; in particular, the State must effectively exercise

b. *See also* Optional Protocol to the 1958 Law of the Sea Conventions Concerning the Compulsory Settlement of Disputes (which provides for reference to the International Court of Justice of disputes arising out of this agreement), concluded 29 April 1958 and entered into force 30 September 1962 (450 UNTS 169).

its jurisdiction and control in administrative, technical and social matters over ships flying its flag.

2. Each State shall issue to ships to which it has granted the right to fly its flag documents to that effect.

Article 6

1. Ships shall sail under the flag of one State only and, save in exceptional cases expressly provided for in international treaties or in these articles, shall be subject to its exclusive jurisdiction on the high seas. A ship may not change its flag during a voyage or while in a port of call, save in the case of a real transfer of ownership or change of registry.

2. A ship which sails under the flags of two or more States, using them according to convenience, may not claim any of the nationalities in question with respect to any other State, and may be assimilated to a ship without nationality.

Article 7

The provisions of the preceding articles do not prejudice the question of ships employed on the official service of an inter-governmental organization flying the flag of the organization.

Article 8

1. Warships on the high seas have complete immunity from the jurisdiction of any State other than the flag State.

2. For the purposes of these articles, the term "warship" means a ship belonging to the naval forces of a State and bearing the external marks distinguishing warships of its nationality, under the command of an officer duly commissioned by the government and whose name appears in the Navy List, and manned by a crew who are under regular naval discipline.

Article 9

Ships owned or operated by a State and used only on government non-commercial service shall, on the high seas, have complete immunity from the jurisdiction of any State other than the flag State.

Article 10

1. Every State shall take such measures for ships under its flag as are necessary to ensure safety at sea with regard *inter alia* to:

(*a*) The use of signals, the maintenance of communications and the prevention of collisions;

(*b*) The manning of ships and labour conditions for crews taking into account the applicable international labour instruments;

(*c*) The construction, equipment and seaworthiness of ships.

2. In taking such measures each State is required to conform to generally accepted international standards and to take any steps which may be necessary to ensure their observance.

Article 11

1. In the event of a collision or of any other incident of navigation concerning a ship on the high seas, involving the penal or disciplinary responsibility of the master or of any other person in the service of the ship, no penal or disciplinary proceedings may

be instituted against such persons except before the judicial or administrative authorities either of the flag State or of the State of which such person is a national.

2. In disciplinary matters, the State which has issued a master's certificate or a certificate of competence or license shall alone be competent, after due legal process, to pronounce the withdrawal of such certificates, even if the holder is not a national of the State which issued them.

3. No arrest or detention of the ship, even as a measure of investigation, shall be ordered by any authorities other than those of the flag State.

Article 12

1. Every State shall require the master of a ship sailing under its flag, in so far as he can do so without serious danger to the ship, the crew or the passengers,

(*a*) To render assistance to any person found at sea in danger of being lost;

(*b*) To proceed with all possible speed to the rescue of persons in distress if informed of their need of assistance, in so far as such action may reasonably be expected of him;

(*c*) After a collision, to render assistance to the other ship, her crew and her passengers and, where possible, to inform the other ship of the name of his own ship, her port of registry and the nearest port at which she will call.

2. Every coastal State shall promote the establishment and maintenance of an adequate and effective search and rescue service regarding safety on and over the sea and—where circumstances so require—by way of mutual regional arrangements co-operate with neighbouring States for this purpose.

Article 13

Every State shall adopt effective measures to prevent and punish the transport of slaves in ships authorized to fly its flag, and to prevent the unlawful use of its flag for that purpose. Any slave taking refuge on board any ship, whatever its flag, shall *ipso facto* be free.

Article 14

All States shall co-operate to the fullest possible extent in the repression of piracy on the high seas or in any other place outside the jurisdiction of any State.

Article 15

Piracy consists of any of the following acts:

(1) Any illegal acts of violence, detention or any act of depredation, committed for private ends by the crew or the passengers of a private ship or a private aircraft, and directed:

(*a*) On the high seas, against another ship or aircraft, or against persons or property on board such ship or aircraft;

(*b*) Against a ship, aircraft, persons or property in a place outside the jurisdiction of any State;

(2) Any act of voluntary participation in the operation of a ship or of an aircraft with knowledge of facts making it a pirate ship or aircraft;

(3) Any act of inciting or of intentionally facilitating an act described in sub-paragraph 1 or sub-paragraph 2 of this article.

Article 16

The acts of piracy, as defined in article 15, committed by a warship, government ship or government aircraft whose crew has mutinied and taken control of the ship or aircraft are assimilated to acts committed by a private ship.

Article 17

A ship or aircraft is considered a pirate ship or aircraft if it is intended by the persons in dominant control to be used for the purpose of committing one of the acts referred to in article 15. The same applies if the ship or aircraft has been used to commit any such act, so long as it remains under the control of the persons guilty of that act.

Article 18

A ship or aircraft may retain its nationality although it has become a pirate ship or aircraft. The retention or loss of nationality is determined by the law of the State from which such nationality was derived.

Article 19

On the high seas, or in any other place outside the jurisdiction of any State, every State may seize a pirate ship or aircraft, or a ship taken by piracy and under the control of pirates, and arrest the persons and seize the property on board. The courts of the State which carried out the seizure may decide upon the penalties to be imposed, and may also determine the action to be taken with regard to the ships, aircraft or property, subject to the rights of third parties acting in good faith.

Article 20

Where the seizure of a ship or aircraft on suspicion of piracy has been effected without adequate grounds, the State making the seizure shall be liable to the State the nationality of which is possessed by the ship or aircraft, for any loss or damage caused by the seizure.

Article 21

A seizure on account of piracy may only be carried out by warships or military aircraft, or other ships or aircraft on government service authorized to that effect.

Article 22

1. Except where acts of interference derive from powers conferred by treaty, a warship which encounters a foreign merchant ship on the high seas is not justified in boarding her unless there is reasonable ground for suspecting:

(*a*) That the ship is engaged in piracy; or

(*b*) That the ship is engaged in the slave trade; or

(*c*) That though flying a foreign flag or refusing to show its flag, the ship is, in reality, of the same nationality as the warship.

2. In the cases provided for in sub-paragraphs (*a*), (*b*) and (*c*) above, the warship may proceed to verify the ship's right to fly its flag. To this end, it may send a boat under the command of an officer to the suspected ship. If suspicion remains after the documents have been checked, it may proceed to a further examination on board the ship, which must be carried out with all possible consideration.

3. If the suspicions prove to be unfounded, and provided that the ship boarded has not committed any act justifying them, it shall be compensated for any loss or damage that may have been sustained.

Article 23

1. The hot pursuit of a foreign ship may be undertaken when the competent authorities of the coastal State have good reason to believe that the ship has violated the laws and regulations of that State. Such pursuit must be commenced when the foreign ship or one of its boats is within the internal waters or the territorial sea or the contiguous zone of the pursuing State, and may only be continued outside the territorial sea or the contiguous zone if the pursuit has not been interrupted. It is not necessary that, at the time when the foreign ship within the territorial sea or the contiguous zone receives the order to stop, the ship giving the order should likewise be within the territorial sea or the contiguous zone. If the foreign ship is within a contiguous zone, as defined in article 24 of the Convention on the Territorial Sea and the Contiguous Zone, the pursuit may only be undertaken if there has been a violation of the rights for the protection of which the zone was established.

2. The right of hot pursuit ceases as soon as the ship pursued enters the territorial sea of its own country or of a third State.

3. Hot pursuit is not deemed to have begun unless the pursuing ship has satisfied itself by such practicable means as may be available that the ship pursued or one of its boats or other craft working as a team and using the ship pursued as a mother ship are within the limits of the territorial sea, or as the case may be within the contiguous zone. The pursuit may only be commenced after a visual or auditory signal to stop has been given at a distance which enables it to be seen or heard by the foreign ship.

4. The right of hot pursuit may be exercised only by warships or military aircraft, or other ships or aircraft on government service specially authorized to that effect.

5. Where hot pursuit is effected by an aircraft:

(*a*) The provisions of paragraph 1 to 3 of this article shall apply *mutatis mutandis;*

(*b*) The aircraft giving the order to stop must itself actively pursue the ship until a ship or aircraft of the coastal State, summoned by the aircraft, arrives to take over the pursuit, unless the aircraft is itself able to arrest the ship. It does not suffice to justify an arrest on the high seas that the ship was merely sighted by the aircraft as an offender or suspected offender, if it was not both ordered to stop and pursued by the aircraft itself or other aircraft or ship which continue the pursuit without interruption.

6. The release of a ship arrested within the jurisdiction of a State and escorted to a port of that State for the purposes of an enquiry before the competent authorities may not be claimed solely on the ground that the ship, in the course of its voyage, was escorted across a portion of the high seas, if the circumstances rendered this necessary.

7. Where a ship has been stopped or arrested on the high seas in circumstances which do not justify the exercise of the right of hot pursuit, it shall be compensated for any loss or damage that may have been thereby sustained.

Article 24

Every State shall draw up regulations to prevent pollution of the seas by the discharge of oil from ships or pipelines or resulting from the exploitation and exploration of the seabed and its subsoil, taking account of existing treaty provisions on the subject.

Article 25

1. Every State shall take measures to prevent pollution of the seas from the dumping of radio-active waste, taking into account any standards and regulations which may be formulated by the competent international organizations.

2. All States shall co-operate with the competent international organizations in taking measures for the prevention of pollution of the seas or air space above, resulting from any activities with radio-active materials or other harmful agents.

Article 26

1. All States shall be entitled to lay submarine cables and pipelines on the bed of the high seas.

2. Subject to its right to take reasonable measures for the exploration of the continental shelf and the exploitation of its natural resources, the coastal State may not impede the laying or maintenance of such cables or pipelines.

3. When laying such cables or pipelines the State in question shall pay due regard to cables or pipelines already in position on the seabed. In particular, possibilities of repairing existing cables or pipelines shall not be prejudiced.

Article 27

Every State shall take the necessary legislative measures to provide that the breaking or injury by a ship flying its flag or by a person subject to its jurisdiction of a submarine cable beneath the high seas done wilfully or through culpable negligence, in such a manner as to be liable to interrupt or obstruct telegraphic or telephonic communications, and similarly the breaking or injury of a submarine pipeline or high-voltage power cable shall be a punishable offence. This provision shall not apply to any break or injury caused by persons who acted merely with the legitimate object of saving their lives or their ships, after having taken all necessary precautions to avoid such break or injury.

Article 28

Every State shall take the necessary legislative measures to provide that, if persons subject to its jurisdiction who are the owners of a cable or pipeline beneath the high seas, in laying or repairing that cable or pipeline, cause a break in or injury to another cable or pipeline, they shall bear the cost of the repairs.

Article 29

Every State shall take the necessary legislative measures to ensure that the owners of ships who can prove that they have sacrificed an anchor, a net or any other fishing gear, in order to avoid injuring a submarine cable or pipeline, shall be indemnified by the owner of the cable or pipeline, provided that the owner of the ship has taken all reasonable precautionary measures beforehand.

Article 30

The provisions of this Convention shall not affect conventions or other international agreements already in force, as between States Parties to them.

Article 31

This Convention shall, until 31 October 1958, be open for signature by all States Members of the United Nations or of any of the specialized agencies, and by any other State invited by the General Assembly of the United Nations to become a Party to the Convention.

Article 32

This Convention is subject to ratification. The instruments of ratification shall be deposited with the Secretary–General of the United Nations.

Article 33

This Convention shall be open for accession by any States belonging to any of the categories mentioned in article 31. The instruments of accession shall be deposited with the Secretary–General of the United Nations.

Article 34

1. This Convention shall come into force on the thirtieth day following the date of deposit of the twenty-second instrument of ratification or accession with the Secretary–General of the United Nations.

2. For each State ratifying or acceding to the Convention after the deposit of the twenty-second instrument of ratification or accession, the Convention shall enter into force on the thirtieth day after deposit by such State of its instrument of ratification or accession.

Article 35

1. After the expiration of a period of five years from the date on which this Convention shall enter into force, a request for the revision of this Convention may be made at any time by any Contracting Party by means of a notification in writing addressed to the Secretary–General of the United Nations.

2. The General Assembly of the United Nations shall decide upon the steps, if any, to be taken in respect of such request.

Article 36

The Secretary–General of the United Nations shall inform all States Members of the United Nations and the other States referred to in article 31:

(*a*) Of signatures to this Convention and of the deposit of instruments of ratification or accession, in accordance with articles 31, 32 and 33;

(*b*) Of the date on which this Convention will come into force, in accordance with article 34;

(*c*) Of requests for revision in accordance with article 35.

Article 37

The original of this Convention, of which the Chinese, English, French, Russian and Spanish texts are equally authentic, shall be deposited with the Secretary–General of the United Nations, who shall send certified copies thereof to all States referred to in article 31.

4.3 Convention on the Continental Shelf.[c] Concluded at Geneva, 29 April 1958. Entered into force, 10 June 1964. 499 U.N.T.S. 311, 15 U.S.T. 471, T.I.A.S. No. 5578; *reprinted in* 5 Weston V.F.4

Article 1

For the purpose of these articles, the term "continental shelf" is used as referring (*a*) to the seabed and subsoil of the submarine areas adjacent to the coast but outside the area of the territorial sea, to a depth of 200 metres or, beyond that limit, to where the depth of the superjacent waters admits of the exploitation of the natural resources of the said areas; (*b*) to the seabed and subsoil of similar submarine areas adjacent to the coasts of islands.

Article 2

1. The coastal State exercises over the continental shelf sovereign rights for the purpose of exploring it and exploiting its natural resources.

2. The rights referred to in paragraph 1 of this article are exclusive in the sense that if the coastal State does not explore the continental shelf or exploit its natural resources, no one may undertake these activities, or make a claim to the continental shelf, without the express consent of the coastal State.

3. The rights of the coastal State over the continental shelf do not depend on occupation, effective or notional, or on any express proclamation.

4. The natural resources referred to in these articles consist of the mineral and other non-living resources of the seabed and subsoil together with living organisms belonging to sedentary species, that is to say, organisms which, at the harvestable stage, either are immobile on or under the seabed or are unable to move except in constant physical contact with the seabed or the subsoil.

Article 3

The rights of the coastal State over the continental shelf do not affect the legal status of the superjacent waters as high seas, or that of the airspace above those waters.

Article 4

Subject to its right to take reasonable measures for the exploration of the continental shelf and the exploitation of its natural resources, the coastal State may not impede the laying or maintenance of submarine cables or pipe lines on the continental shelf.

Article 5

1. The exploration of the continental shelf and the exploitation of its natural resources must not result in any unjustifiable interference with navigation, fishing or the conservation of the living resources of the sea, nor result in any interference with fundamental oceanographic or other scientific research carried out with the intention of open publication.

2. Subject to the provisions of paragraphs 1 and 6 of this article, the coastal State is entitled to construct and maintain or operate on the continental shelf installations and other devices necessary for its exploration and the exploitation of its natural

c. *See also* Optional Protocol to the 1958 Law of the Sea Conventions Concerning the Compulsory Settlement of Disputes (which provides for reference to the International Court of Justice of disputes arising out of this agreement), concluded 29 April 1958 and entered into force 30 September 1962 (450 UNTS 169).

resources, and to establish safety zones around such installations and devices and to take in those zones measures necessary for their protection.

3. The safety zones referred to in paragraph 2 of this article may extend to a distance of 500 metres around the installations and other devices which have been erected, measured from each point of their outer edge. Ships of all nationalities must respect these safety zones.

4. Such installations and devices, though under the jurisdiction of the coastal State, do not possess the status of islands. They have no territorial sea of their own, and their presence does not affect the delimitation of the territorial sea of the coastal State.

5. Due notice must be given of the construction of any such installations, and permanent means for giving warning of their presence must be maintained. Any installations which are abandoned or disused must be entirely removed.

6. Neither the installations or devices, nor the safety zones around them, may be established where interference may be caused to the use of recognized sea lanes essential to international navigation.

7. The coastal State is obliged to undertake, in the safety zones, all appropriate measures for the protection of the living resources of the sea from harmful agents.

8. The consent of the coastal State shall be obtained in respect of any research concerning the continental shelf and undertaken there. Nevertheless the coastal State shall not normally withhold its consent if the request is submitted by a qualified institution with a view to purely scientific research into the physical or biological characteristics of the continental shelf, subject to the proviso that the coastal State shall have the right, if it so desires, to participate or to be represented in the research, and that in any event the results shall be published.

Article 6

1. Where the same continental shelf is adjacent to the territories of two or more States whose coasts are opposite each other, the boundary of the continental shelf appertaining to such States shall be determined by agreement between them. In the absence of agreement, and unless another boundary line is justified by special circumstances, the boundary is the median line, every point of which is equidistant from the nearest points of the baselines from which the breadth of the territorial sea of each State is measured.

2. Where the same continental shelf is adjacent to the territories of two adjacent States, the boundary of the continental shelf shall be determined by agreement between them. In the absence of agreement, and unless another boundary line is justified by special circumstances, the boundary shall be determined by application of the principle of equidistance from the nearest points of the baselines from which the breadth of the territorial sea of each State is measured.

3. In delimiting the boundaries of the continental shelf, any lines which are drawn in accordance with the principles set out in paragraphs 1 and 2 of this article should be defined with reference to charts and geographical features as they exist at a particular date, and reference should be made to fixed permanent identifiable points on the land.

Article 7

The provisions of these articles shall not prejudice the right of the coastal State to exploit the subsoil by means of tunnelling irrespective of the depth of water above the subsoil.

Article 8

This Convention shall, until 31 October 1958, be open for signature by all States Members of the United Nations or of any of the specialized agencies, and by any other State invited by the General Assembly of the United Nations to become a Party to the Convention.

Article 9

This Convention is subject to ratification. The instruments of ratification shall be deposited with the Secretary–General of the United Nations.

Article 10

This Convention shall be open for accession by any States belonging to any of the categories mentioned in article 8. The instruments of accession shall be deposited with the Secretary–General of the United Nations.

Article 11

1. This Convention shall come into force on the thirtieth day following the date of deposit of the twenty-second instrument of ratification or accession with the Secretary–General of the United Nations.

2. For each State ratifying or acceding to the Convention after the deposit of the twenty-second instrument of ratification or accession, the Convention shall enter into force on the thirtieth day after deposit by such State of its instrument of ratification or accession.

Article 12

1. At the time of signature, ratification or accession, any State may make reservations to articles of the Convention other than to articles 1 to 3 inclusive.

2. Any Contracting State making a reservation in accordance with the preceding paragraph may at any time withdraw the reservation by a communication to that effect addressed to the Secretary–General of the United Nations.

Article 13

1. After the expiration of a period of five years from the date on which this Convention shall enter into force, a request for the revision of this Convention may be made at any time by any Contracting Party by means of a notification in writing addressed to the Secretary–General of the United Nations.

2. The General Assembly of the United Nations shall decide upon the steps, if any, to be taken in respect of such request.

Article 14

The Secretary–General of the United Nations shall inform all States Members of the United Nations and the other States referred to in article 8:

(*a*) Of signatures to this Convention and of the deposit of instruments of ratification or accession, in accordance with articles 8, 9 and 10;

(*b*) Of the date on which this Convention will come into force, in accordance with article 11;

(*c*) Of requests for revision in accordance with article 13;

(*d*) Of reservations to this Convention, in accordance with article 12.

Article 15

The original of this Convention, of which the Chinese, English, French, Russian and Spanish texts are equally authentic, shall be deposited with the Secretary–General of the United Nations, who shall send certified copies thereof to all States referred to in article 8.

4.4 Convention on the Territorial Sea and Contiguous Zone.[d] Concluded at Geneva, 29 April 1958. Entered into Force, 10 September 1964. 516 U.N.T.S. 205, 15 U.S.T. 1606, T.I.A.S. No. 5639; *reprinted in* 5 Weston V.F.5

Part I

TERRITORIAL SEA

Section I. General

Article 1

1. The sovereignty of a State extends, beyond its land territory and its internal waters, to a belt of sea adjacent to its coast, described as the territorial sea.

2. This sovereignty is exercised subject to the provisions of these articles and to other rules of international law.

Article 2

The sovereignty of a coastal State extends to the air space over the territorial sea as well as to its bed and subsoil.

Section II. Limits of the Territorial Sea

Article 3

Except where otherwise provided in these articles, the normal baseline for measuring the breadth of the territorial sea is the low-water line along the coast as marked on large-scale charts officially recognized by the coastal State.

Article 4

1. In localities where the coast line is deeply indented and cut into, or if there is a fringe of islands along the coast in its immediate vicinity, the method of straight baselines joining appropriate points may be employed in drawing the baseline from which the breadth of the territorial sea is measured.

2. The drawing of such baselines must not depart to any appreciable extent from the general direction of the coast, and the sea areas lying within the lines must be sufficiently closely linked to the land domain to be subject to the régime of internal waters.

3. Baselines shall not be drawn to and from low-tide elevations, unless lighthouses or similar installations which are permanently above sea level have been built on them.

4. Where the method of straight baselines is applicable under the provisions of paragraph 1, account may be taken, in determining particular baselines, of economic interests peculiar to the region concerned, the reality and the importance of which are clearly evidenced by a long usage.

5. The system of straight baselines may not be applied by a State in such a manner as to cut off from the high seas the territorial sea of another State.

6. The coastal State must clearly indicate straight baselines on charts, to which due publicity must be given.

d. *See also* Optional Protocol to the 1958 Law of the Sea Conventions Concerning the Compulsory Settlement of Disputes (which provides for reference to the International Court of Justice of disputes arising out of this agreement), concluded 29 April 1958 and entered into force 30 September 1962 (450 UNTS 169).

Article 5

1. Waters on the landward side of the baseline of the territorial sea form part of the internal waters of the State.

2. Where the establishment of a straight baseline in accordance with article 4 has the effect of enclosing as internal waters areas which previously had been considered as part of the territorial sea or of the high seas, a right of innocent passage, as provided in articles 14 to 23, shall exist in those waters.

Article 6

The outer limit of the territorial sea is the line every point of which is at a distance from the nearest point of the baseline equal to the breadth of the territorial sea.

Article 7

1. This article relates only to bays the coasts of which belong to a single State.

2. For the purposes of these articles, a bay is a well-marked indentation whose penetration is in such proportion to the width of its mouth as to contain landlocked waters and constitute more than a mere curvature of the coast. An indentation shall not, however, be regarded as a bay unless its area is as large as, or larger than, that of the semi-circle whose diameter is a line drawn across the mouth of that indentation.

3. For the purpose of measurement, the area of an indentation is that lying between the low-water mark around the shore of the indentation and a line joining the low-water marks of its natural entrance points. Where, because of the presence of islands, an indentation has more than one mouth, the semi-circle shall be drawn on a line as long as the sum total of the lengths of the lines across the different mouths. Islands within an indentation shall be included as if they were part of the water areas of the indentation.

4. If the distance between the low-water marks of the natural entrance points of a bay does not exceed twenty-four miles, a closing line may be drawn between these two low-water marks, and the waters enclosed thereby shall be considered as internal waters.

5. Where the distance between the low-water marks of the natural entrance points of a bay exceeds twenty-four miles, a straight baseline of twenty-four miles shall be drawn within the bay in such a manner as to enclose the maximum area of water that is possible with a line of that length.

6. The foregoing provisions shall not apply to so-called "historic" bays, or in any case where the straight baseline system provided for in article 4 is applied.

Article 8

For the purpose of delimiting the territorial sea, the outermost permanent harbour works which form an integral part of the harbour system shall be regarded as forming part of the coast.

Article 9

Roadsteads which are normally used for the loading, unloading and anchoring of ships, and which would otherwise be situated wholly or partly outside the outer limit of the territorial sea, are included in the territorial sea. The coastal State must clearly demarcate such roadsteads and indicate them on charts together with their boundaries, to which due publicity must be given.

Article 10

1. An island is a naturally-formed area of land, surrounded by water, which is above water at high-tide.

2. The territorial sea of an island is measured in accordance with the provisions of these articles.

Article 11

1. A low-tide elevation is a naturally-formed area of land which is surrounded by and above water at low-tide but submerged at high-tide. Where a low-tide elevation is situated wholly or partly at a distance not exceeding the breadth of the territorial sea from the mainland or an island, the low-water line on that elevation may be used as the baseline for measuring the breadth of the territorial sea.

2. Where a low-tide elevation is wholly situated at a distance exceeding the breadth of the territorial sea from the mainland or an island, it has no territorial sea of its own.

Article 12

1. Where the coasts of two States are opposite or adjacent to each other, neither of the two States is entitled, failing agreement between them to the contrary, to extend its territorial sea beyond the median line every point of which is equidistant from the nearest points on the baselines from which the breadth of the territorial seas of each of the two States is measured. The provisions of this paragraph shall not apply, however, where it is necessary by reason of historic title or other special circumstances to delimit the territorial seas of the two States in a way which is at variance with this provision.

2. The line of delimitation between the territorial seas of two States lying opposite to each other or adjacent to each other shall be marked on large-scale charts officially recognized by the coastal States.

Article 13

If a river flows directly into the sea, the baseline shall be a straight line across the mouth of the river between points on the low-tide line of its banks.

SECTION III. RIGHT OF INNOCENT PASSAGE

SUB-SECTION A. RULES APPLICABLE TO ALL SHIPS

Article 14

1. Subject to the provisions of these articles, ships of all States, whether coastal or not, shall enjoy the right of innocent passage through the territorial sea.

2. Passage means navigation through the territorial sea for the purpose either of traversing that sea without entering internal waters, or of proceeding to internal waters, or of making for the high seas from internal waters.

3. Passage includes stopping and anchoring, but only in so far as the same are incidental to ordinary navigation or are rendered necessary by *force majeure* or by distress.

4. Passage is innocent so long as it is not prejudicial to the peace, good order or security of the coastal State. Such passage shall take place in conformity with these articles and with other rules of international law.

5. Passage of foreign fishing vessels shall not be considered innocent if they do not observe such laws and regulations as the coastal State may make and publish in order to prevent these vessels from fishing in the territorial sea.

6. Submarines are required to navigate on the surface and to show their flag.

Article 15

1. The coastal State must not hamper innocent passage through the territorial sea.

2. The coastal State is required to give appropriate publicity to any dangers to navigation, of which it has knowledge, within its territorial sea.

Article 16

1. The coastal State may take the necessary steps in its territorial sea to prevent passage which is not innocent.

2. In the case of ships proceeding to internal waters, the coastal State shall also have the right to take the necessary steps to prevent any breach of the conditions to which admission of those ships to those waters is subject.

3. Subject to the provisions of paragraph 4, the coastal State may, without discrimination amongst foreign ships, suspend temporarily in specified areas of its territorial sea the innocent passage of foreign ships if such suspension is essential for the protection of its security. Such suspension shall take effect only after having been duly published.

4. There shall be no suspension of the innocent passage of foreign ships through straits which are used for international navigation between one part of the high seas and another part of the high seas or the territorial sea of a foreign State.

Article 17

Foreign ships exercising the right of innocent passage shall comply with the laws and regulations enacted by the coastal State in conformity with these articles and other rules of international law and, in particular, with such laws and regulations relating to transport and navigation.

SUB-SECTION B. RULES APPLICABLE TO MERCHANT SHIPS

Article 18

1. No charge may be levied upon foreign ships by reason only of their passage through the territorial sea.

2. Charges may be levied upon a foreign ship passing through the territorial sea as payment only for specific services rendered to the ship. These charges shall be levied without discrimination.

Article 19

1. The criminal jurisdiction of the coastal State should not be exercised on board a foreign ship passing through the territorial sea to arrest any person or to conduct any investigation in connexion with any crime committed on board the ship during its passage, save only in the following cases:

(*a*) If the consequences of the crime extend to the coastal State; or

(*b*) If the crime is of a kind to disturb the peace of the country or the good order of the territorial sea; or

(*c*) If the assistance of the local authorities has been requested by the captain of the ship or by the consul of the country whose flag the ship flies; or

(*d*) If it is necessary for the suppression of illicit traffic in narcotic drugs.

2. The above provisions do not affect the right of the coastal State to take any steps authorized by its laws for the purpose of an arrest or investigation on board a foreign ship passing through the territorial sea after leaving internal waters.

3. In the cases provided for in paragraphs 1 and 2 of this article, the coastal State shall, if the captain so requests, advise the consular authority of the flag State before taking any steps, and shall facilitate contact between such authority and the ship's crew. In cases of emergency this notification may be communicated while the measures are being taken.

4. In considering whether or how an arrest should be made, the local authorities shall pay due regard to the interests of navigation.

5. The coastal State may not take any steps on board a foreign ship passing through the territorial sea to arrest any person or to conduct any investigation in connexion with any crime committed before the ship entered the territorial sea, if the ship, proceeding from a foreign port, is only passing through the territorial sea without entering internal waters.

Article 20

1. The coastal State should not stop or divert a foreign ship passing through the territorial sea for the purpose of exercising civil jurisdiction in relation to a person on board the ship.

2. The coastal State may not levy execution against or arrest the ship for the purpose of any civil proceedings, save only in respect of obligations or liabilities assumed or incurred by the ship itself in the course or for the purpose of its voyage through the waters of the coastal State.

3. The provisions of the previous paragraph are without prejudice to the right of the coastal State, in accordance with its laws, to levy execution against or to arrest, for the purpose of any civil proceedings, a foreign ship lying in the territorial sea, or passing through the territorial sea after leaving internal waters.

Sub-Section C. Rules Applicable to Government Ships Other Than Warships

Article 21

The rules contained in sub-sections A and B shall also apply to government ships operated for commercial purposes.

Article 22

1. The rules contained in sub-section A and in article 18 shall apply to government ships operated for non-commercial purposes.

2. With such exceptions as are contained in the provisions referred to in the preceding paragraph, nothing in these articles affects the immunities which such ships enjoy under these articles or other rules of international law.

Sub-Section D. Rule Applicable to Warships

Article 23

If any warship does not comply with the regulations of the coastal State concerning passage through the territorial sea and disregards any request for compliance which is made to it, the coastal State may require the warship to leave the territorial sea.

Part II

CONTIGUOUS ZONE

Article 24

1. In a zone of the high seas contiguous to its territorial sea, the coastal State may exercise the control necessary to:

(*a*) Prevent infringement of its customs, fiscal, immigration or sanitary regulations within its territory or territorial sea;

(*b*) Punish infringement of the above regulations committed within its territory or territorial sea.

2. The contiguous zone may not extend beyond twelve miles from the baseline from which the breadth of the territorial sea is measured.

3. Where the coasts of two States are opposite or adjacent to each other, neither of the two States is entitled, failing agreement between them to the contrary, to extend its contiguous zone beyond the median line every point of which is equidistant from the nearest points on the baselines from which the breadth of the territorial seas of the two States is measured.

Part III

FINAL ARTICLES

Article 25

The provisions of this Convention shall not affect conventions or other international agreements already in force, as between States Parties to them.

Article 26

This Convention shall, until 31 October 1958, be open for signature by all States Members of the United Nations or of any of the specialized agencies, and by any other State invited by the General Assembly of the United Nations to become a Party to the Convention.

Article 27

This Convention is subject to ratification. The instruments of ratification shall be deposited with the Secretary–General of the United Nations.

Article 28

This Convention shall be open for accession by any States belonging to any of the categories mentioned in article 26. The instruments of accession shall be deposited with the Secretary–General of the United Nations.

Article 29

1. This Convention shall come into force on the thirtieth day following the date of deposit of the twenty-second instrument of ratification or accession with the Secretary–General of the United Nations.

2. For each State ratifying or acceding to the Convention after the deposit of the twenty-second instrument of ratification or accession, the Convention shall enter into force on the thirtieth day after deposit by such State of its instrument of ratification or accession.

Article 30

1. After the expiration of a period of five years from the date on which this Convention shall enter into force, a request for the revision of this Convention may be made at any time by any Contracting Party by means of a notification in writing addressed to the Secretary–General of the United Nations.

2. The General Assembly of the United Nations shall decide upon the steps, if any, to be taken in respect of such request.

Article 31

The Secretary–General of the United Nations shall inform all States Members of the United Nations and the other States referred to in article 26:

(*a*) Of signatures to this Convention and of the deposit of instruments of ratification or accession, in accordance with articles 26, 27 and 28;

(*b*) Of the date on which this Convention will come into force, in accordance with article 29;

(*c*) Of requests for revision in accordance with article 30.

Article 32

The original of this Convention, of which the Chinese, English, French, Russian and Spanish texts are equally authentic, shall be deposited with the Secretary–General of the United Nations, who shall send certified copies thereof to all States referred to in article 26.

4.5 Convention on the Liability of Operators of Nuclear Ships. Concluded at Brussels, 25 May 1962. Not yet in force. IAEA Leg.Ser. No. 4 at 34, 57 A.J.I.L. 268 (1963)

The contracting Parties,

Having recognized the desirability of determining by agreement certain uniform rules concerning the liability of operators of nuclear ships,

Have decided to conclude a Convention for this purpose, and thereto agreed as follows:

Article I

For the purpose of this Convention:

1. "Nuclear ship" means any ship equipped with a nuclear power plant.

2. "Licensing State" means the Contracting State which operates or which has authorized the operation of a nuclear ship under its flag.

3. "Person" means any individual or partnership, or any public or private body whether corporate or not, including a State or any of its constituent subdivisions.

4. "Operator" means the person authorized by the licensing State to operate a nuclear ship, or where a Contracting State operates a nuclear ship, that State.

5. "Nuclear fuel" means any material which is capable of producing energy by a self-sustaining process of nuclear fission and which is used or intended for use in a nuclear ship.

6. "Radioactive products or waste" means any material, including nuclear fuel, made radioactive by neutron irradiation incidental to the utilization of nuclear fuel in a nuclear ship.

7. "Nuclear damage" means loss of life or personal injury and loss or damage to property which arises out of or results from the radioactive properties or a combination of radioactive properties with toxic, explosive or other hazardous properties of nuclear fuel or of radioactive products or waste; any other loss, damage or expense so arising or resulting shall be included only if and to the extent that the applicable national law so provides.

8. "Nuclear incident" means any occurrence or series of occurrences having the same origin which causes nuclear damage.

9. "Nuclear power plant" means any power plant in which a nuclear reactor is, or is to be used as, the source of power, whether for propulsion of the ship or for any other purpose.

10. "Nuclear reactor" means any installation containing nuclear fuel in such an arrangement that a self-sustained chain process of nuclear fission can occur therein without an additional source of neutrons.

11. "Warship" means any ship belonging to the naval forces of a State and bearing the external marks distinguishing warships of its nationality, under the command of an officer duly commissioned by the Government of such State and whose name appears in the Navy List, and manned by a crew who are under regular naval discipline.

12. "Applicable national law" means the national law of the court having jurisdiction under the Convention including any rules of such national law relating to conflict of laws.

Article II

1. The operator of a nuclear ship shall be absolutely liable for any nuclear damage upon proof that such damage has been caused by a nuclear incident involving the nuclear fuel of, or radioactive products or waste produced in such ship.

2. Except as otherwise provided in this Convention no person other than the operator shall be liable for such nuclear damage.

3. Nuclear damage suffered by the nuclear ship itself, its equipment, fuel or stores shall not be covered by the operator's liability as defined in this Convention.

4. The operator shall not be liable with respect to nuclear incidents occurring before the nuclear fuel has been taken in charge by him or after the nuclear fuel or radioactive products or waste have been taken in charge by another person duly authorized by law and liable for any nuclear damage that may be caused by them.

5. If the operator proves that the nuclear damage resulted wholly or partially from an act or omission done with intent to cause damage by the individual who suffered the damage, the competent courts may exonerate the operator wholly or partially from his liability to such individual.

6. Notwithstanding the provisions of paragraph 1 of this Article, the operator shall have a right of recourse:

a) If the nuclear incident results from a personal act or omission done with intent to cause damage, in which event recourse shall lie against the individual who has acted, or omitted to act, with such intent;

b) If the nuclear incident occurred as a consequence of any wreck-raising operation, against the person or persons who carried out such operation without the authority of the operator or of the State having licensed the sunken ship or of the State in whose waters the wreck is situated;

c) If recourse is expressly provided for by contract.

Article III

1. The liability of the operator as regards one nuclear ship shall be limited to 1500 million francs in respect of any one nuclear incident, notwithstanding that the nuclear incident may have resulted from any fault of privity of that operator; such limit shall include neither any interest nor costs awarded by a court in actions for compensation under this Convention.

2. The operator shall be required to maintain insurance, or other financial security covering his liability for nuclear damage, in such amount, of such type and in such terms as the licensing State shall specify. The licensing State shall ensure the payment of claims for compensation for nuclear damage established against the operator by providing the necessary funds up to the limit laid down in paragraph 1 of this Article to the extent that the yield of the insurance or the financial security is inadequate to satisfy such claims.

3. However, nothing in paragraph 2 of this Article shall require any Contracting State or any of its constituent subdivisions, such as States, Republics or Cantons, to maintain insurance or other financial security to cover their liability as operators of nuclear ships.

4. The franc mentioned in paragraph 1 of this Article is a unit of account constituted by sixty-five and one half milligrams of gold of millesimal fineness nine hundred. The amount awarded may be converted into each national currency in round figures. Conversion into national currencies other than gold shall be effected on the basis of their gold at the date of payment.

Article IV

Whenever both nuclear damage and damage other than nuclear damage have been caused by a nuclear incident or jointly by a nuclear incident and one or more other occurrences and the nuclear damage and such other damage are not reasonably separable, the entire damage shall, for the purposes of this Convention, be deemed to be nuclear damage exclusively caused by the nuclear incident. However, where damage is caused jointly by a nuclear incident covered by this Convention and by an emission of ionizing radiation or by an emission of ionizing radiation in combination with the toxic, explosive or other hazardous properties of the source of radiation not covered by it, nothing in this Convention shall limit or otherwise affect the liability, either as regards the victims or by way of recourse or contribution, of any person who may be held liable in connection with the emission of ionizing radiation or by the toxic explosive or other hazardous properties of the source of radiation not covered by this Convention.

Article V

1. Rights of compensation under this Convention shall be extinguished if an action is not brought within ten years from the date of the nuclear incident. If, however, under the law of the licensing State the liability of the operator is covered by insurance or other financial security or State indemnification for a period longer than ten years, the applicable national law may provide that rights of compensation against the operator shall only be extinguished after a period which may be longer than ten years but shall not be longer than the period for which his liability is so covered under the law of the licensing State. However, such extension of the extinction period shall in no case affect the right of compensation under this Convention of any person who has brought an action for loss of life or personal injury against the operator before the expiry of the aforesaid period of ten years.

2. Where nuclear damage is caused by nuclear fuel, radioactive products or waste which were stolen, lost, jettisoned, or abandoned, the period established under paragraph 1 of this Article shall be computed from the date of the nuclear incident causing the nuclear damage, but the period shall in no case exceed a period of twenty years from the date of the theft, loss, jettison or abandonment.

3. The applicable national law may establish a period of extinction or prescription of not less than three years from the date on which the person who claims to have suffered nuclear damage had knowledge or ought reasonably to have had knowledge of the damage and of the person responsible for the damage, provided that the period established under paragraphs 1 and 2 of this Article shall not be exceeded.

4. Any person who claims to have suffered nuclear damage and who has brought an action for compensation within the period applicable under this Article may amend his claim to take into account any aggravation of the damage, even after the expiry of that period, provided that final judgment has not been entered.

Article VI

Where provisions of national health insurance, social security, workmen's compensation or occupational disease compensation systems include compensation for nuclear damage, rights of beneficiaries under such systems and rights of subrogation, or of recourse against the operator, by virtue of such systems, shall be determined by the law of the Contracting State having established such systems. However, if the law of such Contracting State allows claims of beneficiaries of such systems and such rights of subrogation and recourse to be brought against the operator in conformity with the terms of this Convention, this shall not result in the liability of the operator exceeding the amount specified in paragraph 1 of Article III.

Article VII

1. Where nuclear damage engages the liability of more than one operator and the damage attributable to each operator is not reasonably separable, the operators involved shall be jointly and severally liable for such damage. However, the liability of any one operator shall not exceed the limit laid down in Article III.

2. In the case of a nuclear incident where the nuclear damage arises out of or results from nuclear fuel or radioactive products or waste of more than one nuclear ship of the same operator, that operator shall be liable in respect of each ship up to the limit laid down in Article III.

3. In case of joint and several liability, and subject to the provisions of paragraph 1 of this Article:

a) Each operator shall have a right of contribution against the others in proportion to the fault attaching to each of them;

b) Where circumstances are such that the degree of fault cannot be apportioned, the total liability shall be borne in equal parts.

Article VIII

No liability under this Convention shall attach to an operator in respect to nuclear damage caused by a nuclear incident directly due to an act of war, hostilities, civil war or insurrection.

Article IX

The sums provided by insurance, by other financial security or by State indemnification in conformity with paragraph 2 of this Article III shall be exclusively available for compensation due under this Convention.

Article X

1. Any action for compensation shall be brought, at the option of the claimant, either before the courts of the licensing State or before the courts of the Contracting State or States in whose territory nuclear damage has been sustained.

2. If the licensing State has been or might be called upon to ensure the payment of claims for compensation in accordance with paragraph 2 of Article III of this Convention, it may intervene as party in any proceedings brought against the operator.

3. Any immunity from legal processes pursuant to rules of national or international law shall be waived with respect to duties or obligations arising under, or for the purpose of, this Convention. Nothing in this Convention shall make warships or other State-owned or State-operated ships on non-commercial service liable to arrest, attachment or seizure or confer jurisdiction in respect of warships on the courts of any foreign State.

Article XI

1. When, having regard to the likelihood of any claims arising out of a nuclear incident exceeding the amount specified in Article III of this Convention, a court of the licensing State, at the request of the operator, a claimant or the licensing State, so certifies, the operator or the licensing State shall make that amount available in that court to pay any such claims; that amount shall be regarded as constituting the limitation fund in respect of that incident.

2. The amount may be made available for the purposes of the preceding paragraph by payment into court or by the provision of security or guarantees sufficient to satisfy the court that the money will be available when required to meet any established claim.

3. After the fund has been constituted in accordance with paragraph 1 of this Article the court of the licensing State shall be exclusively competent to determine all matters relating to the apportionment and distribution of the fund.

4. a) A final judgment entered by a court having jurisdiction under Article X shall be recognized in the territory of any other Contracting State, except:

i) where the judgment was obtained by fraud; or

ii) the operator was not given a fair opportunity to present his case;

b) A final judgment which is recognized shall, upon being presented for enforcement in accordance with the formalities required by the law of the Contracting State where enforcement is sought, be enforceable as if it were a judgment of a court of that State;

c) The merits of a claim on which the judgment has been given shall not be subject to further proceedings.

5. a) If a person who is a national of a Contracting State, other than the operator, has paid compensation for nuclear damage under an International Convention or under the law of a non-Contracting State, such person shall, up to the amount which he has paid, acquire by subrogation the rights which the person so compensated would have enjoyed under this Convention. However, no rights shall be so acquired by any person if and to the extent that the operator has a right of recourse or contribution against such person under this Convention;

b) If a limitation fund has been set up and

i) the operator has paid, prior to its being set up, compensation for nuclear damage; or

ii) the operator has paid, after it has been set up, compensation for nuclear damage under an International Convention or the law of a non-Contracting State,

he shall be entitled to recover from the fund, up to the amount which he has paid, the amount which the person so compensated would have obtained in the distribution of the fund;

c) If no limitation fund is set up, nothing in this Convention shall preclude an operator, who has paid compensation for nuclear damage out of funds other than those provided pursuant to paragraph 2 of Article III, from recovering from the person providing financial security under paragraph 2 of Article III or from the licensing State, up to the amount he has paid, the sum which the person so compensated would have obtained under this Convention;

d) In this paragraph the expression "a national of a Contracting State" shall include a Contracting State or any of its constituent subdivisions or a partnership or any public or private body whether corporate or not established in a Contracting State.

6. Where no fund has been constituted under the provisions of this Article, the licensing State shall adopt such measures as are necessary to ensure that adequate sums provided by it or by insurance or other financial security in accordance with paragraph 2 of Article III, shall be available for the satisfaction of any claim established by a judgment of a court of any other Contracting State which would be recognized under paragraph 4 of this Article; the sums shall be made available, at the option of the claimant, either in the licensing State or in the Contracting State in which the damage was sustained or in the Contracting State in which the claimant is habitually resident.

7. After the limitation fund has been constituted in accordance with paragraph 1 of this Article or, where no such fund has been constituted, if the sums provided by the

licensing State, or by insurance, or other financial security are available in accordance with paragraph 6 of this Article to meet a claim for compensation, the claimant shall not be entitled to exercise any right against any other asset of the operator in respect of his claim for nuclear damage, and any bail or security (other than security for costs) given by or on behalf of that operator in any Contracting State shall be released.

Article XII

1. The Contracting States undertake to adopt such measures as are necessary to ensure implementation of the provisions of this Convention, including any appropriate measures for the prompt and equitable distribution of the sums available for compensation for nuclear damage.

2. The Contracting States undertake to adopt such measures as are necessary to ensure that insurance and reinsurance premiums and sums provided by insurance, reinsurance or other financial security, or provided by them in accordance with paragraph 2 of Article III, shall be freely transferable into the currency of the Contracting State in which the damage was sustained, of the Contracting State in which the claimant is habitually resident or, as regards insurance and reinsurance premiums and payments, in the currencies specified in the insurance or reinsurance contract.

3. This Convention shall be applied without discrimination based upon nationality, domicile or residence.

Article XIII

This Convention applies to nuclear damage caused by a nuclear incident occurring in any part of the world and involving the nuclear fuel of, or radioactive products or waste produced in, a nuclear ship flying the flag of a Contracting State.

Article XIV

This Convention shall supersede any International Conventions in force or open for signature, ratification or accession at the date on which this Convention is opened for signature, but only to the extent that such Conventions would be in conflict with it; however, nothing in this Article shall affect the obligations of Contracting States to non-Contracting States arising under such International Conventions.

Article XV

1. Each Contracting State undertakes to take all measures necessary to prevent a nuclear ship flying its flag from being operated without a licence or authority granted by it.

2. In the event of nuclear damage involving the nuclear fuel of, or radioactive products or waste produced in a nuclear ship flying the flag of a Contracting State, the operation of which was not at the time of the nuclear incident licensed or authorized by such Contracting State, the owner of the nuclear ship at the time of the nuclear incident shall be deemed to be the operator of the nuclear ship for all the purposes of this Convention, except that his liability shall not be limited in amount.

3. In such an event, the Contracting State whose flag the nuclear ship flies shall be deemed to be the licensing State for all the purposes of this Convention and shall, in particular, be liable for compensation for victims in accordance with the obligations imposed on a licensing State by Article III and up to the limit laid down therein.

4. Each Contracting State undertakes not to grant a licence or authority to operate a nuclear ship flying the flag of another State. However, nothing in this paragraph shall prevent a Contracting State from implementing the requirements of

its national law concerning the operation of a nuclear ship within its internal waters and territorial sea.

Article XVI

This Convention shall apply to a nuclear ship from the date of her launching. Between her launching and the time she is authorized to fly a flag, the nuclear ship shall be deemed to be operated by the owner and to be flying the flag of the State in which she was built.

Article XVII

Nothing in this Convention shall affect any right which a Contracting State may have under international law to deny access to its waters and harbours to nuclear ships licensed by another Contracting State, even when it has formally complied with all the provisions of this Convention.

Article XVIII

An action for compensation for nuclear damage shall be brought against the operator; it may also be brought against the insurer or any person other than the licensing State who has provided financial security to the operator pursuant to paragraph 2 of Article III, if the right to bring an action against the insurer or such other person is provided under the applicable national law.

Article XIX

Notwithstanding the termination of this Convention or the termination of its application to any Contracting State pursuant to Article XXVII, the provisions of the Convention shall continue to apply with respect to any nuclear damage caused by a nuclear incident involving the nuclear fuel of, or radioactive products or waste produced in, a nuclear ship licensed or otherwise authorized for operation by any Contracting State prior to the date of such termination, provided the nuclear incident occurred prior to the date of such termination or, in the event of a nuclear incident occurring subsequent to the date of such termination, prior to the expiry of a period of twenty-five years after the date of such licensing or other authorization to operate such ship.

Article XX

Without prejudice to Article X, any dispute between two or more Contracting Parties concerning the interpretation or application of this Convention which cannot be settled through negociation, shall, at the request of one of them, be submitted to arbitration. If within six months from the date of the request for arbitration the Parties are unable to agree on the organization of the arbitration, any one of those Parties may refer the dispute to the International Court of Justice by request in conformity with the Statute of the Court.

Article XXI

1. Each Contracting Party may at the time of signature or ratification of this Convention or accession thereto, declare that it does not consider itself bound by Article XX of the Convention. The other Contracting Parties shall not be bound by this Article with respect to any Contracting Party having made such a reservation.

2. Any Contracting Party having made a reservation in accordance with paragraph 1 may at any time withdraw this reservation by notification to the Belgian Government.

Article XXII

This Convention shall be open for signature by the States represented at the eleventh session (1961–1962) of the Diplomatic Conference on Maritime Law.

Article XXIII

This Convention shall be ratified and the instruments of ratification shall be deposited with the Belgian Government.

Article XXIV

1. This Convention shall come into force three months after the deposit of an instrument of ratification by at least one licencing State and one other State.

2. This Convention shall come into force, in respect of each signatory State which ratifies it after its entry into force as provided in paragraph 1 of this Article, three months after the date of deposit of the instrument of ratification of that State.

Article XXV

1. States Members of the United Nations Members of the specialized agencies and of the International Atomic Energy Agency not represented at the eleventh session of the Diplomatic Conference on Maritime Law, may accede to this Convention.

2. The instruments of accession shall be deposited with the Belgian Government.

3. The Convention shall come into force in respect of the acceding State three months after the date of deposit of the instrument of accession of that State, but not before the date of entry into force of the Convention as established by Article XXIV.

Article XXVI

1. A conference for the purpose of revising this Convention shall be convened by the Belgian Government and the International Atomic Energy Agency after the Convention has been in force five years.

2. Such a conference shall also be convened by the Belgian Government and the International Atomic Energy Agency before the expiry of this term or thereafter, if one third of the Contracting States express a desire to that effect.

Article XXVII

1. Any Contracting State may denounce this Convention by notification to the Belgian Government at any time after the first revision Conference held in accordance with the provisions of Article XXVI 1.

2. This denunciation shall take effect one year after the date on which the notification has been received by the Belgian Government.

Article XXVIII

The Belgian Government shall notify the States represented at the eleventh session of the Diplomatic Conference on Maritime Law, and the States acceding to this Convention, of the following:

1. Signatures, ratifications and accessions received in accordance with Article XXII, XXIII and XXV.

2. The date on which the Convention will come into force in accordance with Article XXIV.

3. Denunciations received in accordance with Article XXVII.

4.6 Helsinki Rules on the Uses of the Waters of International Rivers (Without Comments and Annex). Adopted by the International Law Association at Helsinki, 20 August 1966. 52 I.L.A. 484 (1967); *reprinted in* 5 Weston V.F.32

CHAPTER 1

GENERAL

Article I

The general rules of international law as set forth in these chapters are applicable to the use of the waters of an international drainage basin except as may be provided otherwise by convention, agreement or binding custom among the basin States.

Article II

An international drainage basin is a geographical area extending over two or more States determined by the watershed limits of the system of waters, including surface and underground waters, flowing into a common terminus.

Article III

A "basin State" is a state the territory of which includes a portion of an international drainage basin.

CHAPTER 2

EQUITABLE UTILIZATION OF THE WATERS OF AN INTERNATIONAL DRAINAGE BASIN

Article IV

Each basin State is entitled, within its territory, to a reasonable and equitable share in the beneficial uses of the waters of an international drainage basin.

Article V

(1) What is a reasonable and equitable share within the meaning of Article IV is to be determined in the light of all the relevant factors in each particular case.

(2) Relevant factors which are to be considered include, but are not limited to:

(a) the geography of the basin, including in particular the extent of the drainage area in the territory of each basin State;

(b) the hydrology of the basin, including in particular the contribution of water by each basin State;

(c) the climate affecting the basin;

(d) the past utilization of the waters of the basin, including in particular existing utilization;

(e) the economic and social needs of each basin State;

(f) the population dependent on the waters of the basin in each basin State;

(g) the comparative costs of alternative means of satisfying the economic and social needs of each basin State;

(h) the availability of other resources;

(i) the avoidance of unnecessary waste in the utilization of waters of the basin;

(j) the practicability of compensation to one or more of the co-basin States as a means of adjusting conflicts among uses; and

(k) the degree to which the needs of a basin State may be satisfied, without causing substantial injury to a co-basin State.

(3) The weight to be given to each factor is to be determined by its importance in comparison with that of other relevant factors. In determining what is a reasonable and equitable share, all relevant factors are to be considered together and a conclusion reached on the basis of the whole.

Article VI

A use or category of uses is not entitled to any inherent preference over any other use or category of uses.

Article VII

A basin State may not be denied the present reasonable use of the waters of an international drainage basin to reserve for a co-basin State a future use of such waters.

Article VIII

1. An existing reasonable use may continue in operation unless the factors justifying its continuance are outweighed by other factors leading to the conclusion that it be modified or terminated so as to accommodate a competing incompatible use.

2. (a) A use that is in fact operational is deemed to have been an existing use from the time of the initiation of construction directly related to the use or, where such construction is not required, the undertaking of comparable acts of actual implementation.

(b) Such a use continues to be an existing use until such time as it is discontinued with the intention that it be abandoned.

3. A use will not be deemed an existing use if at the time of becoming operational it is incompatible with an already existing reasonable use.

CHAPTER 3

POLLUTION

Article IX

As used in this Chapter, the term "water pollution" refers to any detrimental change resulting from human conduct in the natural composition, content, or quality of the waters of an international drainage basin.

Article X

1. Consistent with the principle of equitable utilization of the waters of an international drainage basin, a State

(a) must prevent any new form of water pollution or any increase in the degree of existing water pollution in an international drainage basin which would cause substantial injury in the territory of a co-basin State, and

(b) should take all reasonable measures to abate existing water pollution in an international drainage basin to such an extent that no substantial damage is caused in the territory of a co-basin State.

2. The rule stated in paragraph 1 of this Article applies to water pollution originating

(a) within a territory of the State, or

(b) outside the territory of the State, if it is caused by the State's conduct.

Article XI

1. In the case of a violation of the rule stated in paragraph 1(a) of Article X of this Chapter, the State responsible shall be required to cease the wrongful conduct and compensate the injured co-basin State for the injury that has been caused to it.

2. In a case falling under the rule stated in paragraph 1(b) of Article X, if a State fails to take reasonable measures, it shall be required promptly to enter into negotiations with the injured State with a view toward reaching a settlement equitable under the circumstances.

CHAPTER 4

NAVIGATION

Article XII

1. This Chapter refers to those rivers and lakes portions of which are both navigable and separate or traverse the territories of two or more States.

2. Rivers or lakes are "navigable" if in their natural or canalized state they are currently used for commercial navigation or are capable by reason of their natural condition of being so used.

3. In this Chapter the term "riparian State" refers to a State through or along which the navigable portion of a river flows or a lake lies.

Article XIII

Subject to any limitations or qualifications referred to in these Chapters, each riparian State is entitled to enjoy rights of free navigation on the entire course of a river or lake.

Article XIV

"Free navigation", as the term is used in this Chapter, includes the following freedoms for vessels of a riparian State on a basis of equality:

(a) freedom of movement on the entire navigable course of the river or lake;

(b) freedom to enter ports and to make use of plants and docks; and

(c) freedom to transport goods and passengers, either directly or through trans-shipment, between the territory of one riparian State and the territory of another riparian State and between the territory of a riparian State and the open sea.

Article XV

A riparian State may exercise rights of police, including but not limited to the protection of public safety and health, over that portion of the river or lake subject to its jurisdiction, provided the exercise of such rights does not unreasonably interfere with the enjoyment of the rights of free navigation defined in Articles XIII and XIV.

Article XVI

Each riparian State may restrict or prohibit the loading by vessels of a foreign State of goods and passengers in its territory for discharge in such territory.

Article XVII

A riparian State may grant rights of navigation to non-riparian State on rivers or lakes within its territory.

Article XVIII

Each riparian State is, to the extent of the means available or made available to it, required to maintain in good order that portion of the navigable course of a river or lake within its jurisdiction.

Article XIX

The rules stated in this Chapter are not applicable to the navigation of vessels of war or of vessels performing police or administrative functions, or, in general, exercising any other form of public authority.

Article XX

In time of war, other armed conflict, or public emergency constituting a threat to the life of the State, a riparian State may take measures derogating from its obligations under this Chapter to the extent strictly required by the exigencies of the situation, provided that such measures are not inconsistent with its other obligations under international law. The riparian State shall in any case facilitate navigation for humanitarian purposes.

CHAPTER 5

TIMBER FLOATING

Article XXI

The floating of timber on a watercourse which flows through or between the territories of two or more States is governed by the following Articles except in cases in which floating is governed by rules of navigation according to applicable law or custom binding upon the riparians.

Article XXII

The States riparian to an international watercourse utilized for navigation may determine by common consent whether and under what conditions timber floating may be permitted upon the watercourse.

Article XXIII

1. It is recommended that each State riparian to an international watercourse not used for navigation should, with due regard to other uses of the watercourse, authorise the co-riparian States to use the watercourse and its banks within the territory of each riparian State for the floating of timber.

2. This authorization should extend to all necessary work along the banks by the floating crew and to the installation of such facilities as may be required for the timber floating.

Article XXIV

If a riparian State requires permanent installation for floating inside a territory of a co-riparian State or if it is necessary to regulate the flow of the watercourse, all questions connected with these installations and measures should be determined by agreement between the States concerned.

Article XXV

Co-riparian States of a watercourse which is, or is to be used for floating timber should negotiate in order to come to an agreement governing the administrative regime of floating, and if necessary to establish a joint agency or commission in order to facilitate the regulation of floating in all aspects.

CHAPTER 6

PROCEDURES FOR THE PREVENTION AND SETTLEMENT OF DISPUTES

Article XXVI

This Chapter relates to procedures for the prevention and settlement of international disputes as to the legal rights or other interests of basin States and of other States in the waters of an international drainage basin.

Article XXVII

1. Consistently with the Charter of the United Nations, States are under an obligation to settle international disputes as to their legal rights or other interests by peaceful means in such a manner that international peace and security, and justice are not endangered.

2. It is recommended that States resort progressively to the means of prevention and settlement of disputes stipulated in Articles XXIX to XXXIV of this Chapter.

Article XXVIII

1. States are under a primary obligation to resort to means of prevention and settlement of disputes stipulated in the applicable treaties binding upon them.

2. States are limited to the means of prevention and settlement of disputes stipulated in treaties binding upon them only to the extent provided by the applicable treaties.

Article XXIX

1. With a view to preventing disputes from arising between basin States as to their legal rights or other interest, it is recommended that each basin State furnish relevant and reasonably available information to the other basin States concerning the waters of a drainage basin within its territory and its use of, and activities with respect to such waters.

2. A State, regardless of its location in a drainage basin, should in particular furnish to any other basin State, the interests of which may be substantially affected, notice of any proposed construction or installation which would alter the regime of the basin in a way which might give rise to a dispute as defined in Article XXVI. The notice should include such essential facts as will permit the recipient to make an assessment of the probable effect of the proposed alteration.

3. A State providing the notice referred to in paragraph 2 of this Article should afford to the recipient a reasonable period of time to make an assessment of the probable effect of the proposed construction or installation and to submit its views thereon to the State furnishing the notice.

4. If a State has failed to give the notice referred to in paragraph 2 of this Article, the alteration by the State in the regime of the drainage basin shall not be given the weight normally accorded to temporal priority in use in the event of a determination of what is a reasonable and equitable share of the waters of the basin.

Article XXX

In case of a dispute between States as to their legal rights or other interests, as defined in Article XXVI, they should seek a solution by negotiation.

Article XXXI

1. If a question or dispute arises which relates to the present or future utilization of the waters of an international drainage basin, it is recommended that the basin States refer the question or dispute to a joint agency and that they request the agency

to survey the international drainage basin and to formulate plans or recommendations for the fullest and most efficient use thereof in the interests of all such States.

2. It is recommended that the joint agency be instructed to submit reports on all matters within its competence to the appropriate authorities of the member States concerned.

3. It is recommended that the member States of the joint agency in appropriate cases invite non-basin States which by treaty enjoy a right in the use of the waters and an international drainage basin to associate themselves with the work of the joint agency or that they be permitted to appear before the agency.

Article XXXII

If a question or a dispute is one which is considered by the States concerned to be incapable of resolution in the manner set forth in Article XXXI, it is recommended that they seek the good offices, or jointly request the mediation of a third State, of a qualified international organisation or of a qualified person.

Article XXXIII

1. If the States concerned have not been able to resolve their dispute through negotiation or have been unable to agree on the measures described in Article XXXI and XXXII, it is recommended that they form a commission of inquiry or an ad hoc conciliation commission, which shall endeavour to find a solution, likely to be accepted by the States concerned, of any dispute as to their legal rights.

2. It is recommended that the conciliation commission be constituted in the manner set forth in the Annex.

Article XXXIV

It is recommended that the States concerned agree to submit their legal disputes to an *ad hoc* arbitral tribunal, to a permanent arbitral tribunal or to the International Court of Justice if:

(a) A commission has not been formed as provided in Article XXXIII, or

(b) The commission has not been able to find a solution to be recommended, or

(c) A solution recommended has not been accepted by the States concerned, and

(d) An agreement has not been otherwise arrived at.

Article XXXV

It is recommended that in the event of arbitration the States concerned have recourse to the Model Rules on Arbitral Procedure prepared by the International Law Commission of the United Nations at its tenth session in 1958.

Article XXXVI

Recourse to arbitration implies the undertaking by the States concerned to consider the award to be given as final and to submit in good faith to its execution.

Article XXXVII

The means of settlement referred to in the preceding Articles of this Chapter are without prejudice to the utilization of means of settlement recommended to, or required of, members of regional arrangements or agencies and of other international organizations.

4.7 International Convention Relating to Intervention on the High Seas in Cases of Oil Pollution Casualties (Without Annex and Protocol). Concluded at Brussels, 29 November 1969. Entered into force, 6 May 1975. 970 U.N.T.S. 211, 26 U.S.T. 765, T.I.A.S. No. 8068; *reprinted in* 9 I.L.M. 25 (1986) & 5 Weston V.F.7

Article I. 1. Parties to the present Convention may take such measures on the high seas as may be necessary to prevent, mitigate or eliminate grave and imminent danger to their coastline or related interests from pollution or threat of pollution of the sea by oil, following upon a maritime casualty or acts related to such a casualty, which may reasonably be expected to result in major harmful consequences.

2. However, no measures shall be taken under the present Convention against any warship or other ship owned or operated by a State and used, for the time being, only on government non-commercial service.

Article II. For the purposes of the present Convention:

1. "Maritime casualty" means a collision of ships, stranding or other incident of navigation, or other occurrence on board a ship or external to it resulting in material damage or imminent threat of material damage to a ship or cargo.

2. "Ship" means:

(*a*) any sea-going vessel of any type whatsoever, and

(*b*) any floating craft, with the exception of an installation or device engaged in the exploration and exploitation of the resources of the sea-bed and the ocean floor and the subsoil thereof.

3. "Oil" means crude oil, fuel oil, diesel oil and lubricating oil.

4. "Related interests" means the interests of a coastal State directly affected or threatened by the maritime casualty, such as:

(*a*) maritime coastal, port or estuarine activities, including fisheries activities, constituting an essential means of livelihood of the persons concerned;

(*b*) tourist attractions of the area concerned;

(*c*) the health of the coastal population and the well-being of the area concerned, including conservation of living marine resources and of wildlife.

5. "Organization" means the Inter–Governmental Maritime Consultative Organization.

Article III. When a coastal State is exercising the right to take measures in accordance with Article I, the following provisions shall apply:

(*a*) before taking any measures, a coastal State shall proceed to consultations with other States affected by the maritime casualty, particularly with the flag State or States;

(*b*) the coastal State shall notify without delay the proposed measures to any persons physical or corporate known to the coastal State, or made known to it during the consultations, to have interests which can reasonably be expected to be affected by those measures. The coastal State shall take into account any views they may submit;

(*c*) before any measure is taken, the coastal State may proceed to a consultation with independent experts, whose names shall be chosen from a list maintained by the Organization;

(*d*) in cases of extreme urgency requiring measures to be taken immediately, the coastal State may take measures rendered necessary by the urgency of the situation, without prior notification or consultation or without continuing consultations already begun;

(*e*) a coastal State shall, before taking such measures and during their course, use its best endeavours to avoid any risk to human life, and to afford persons in distress any assistance of which they may stand in need, and in appropriate cases to facilitate the repatriation of ships' crews, and to raise no obstacle thereto;

(*f*) measures which have been taken in application of Article I shall be notified without delay to the States and to the known physical or corporate persons concerned, as well as to the Secretary–General of the Organization.

Article IV. 1. Under the supervision of the Organization, there shall be set up and maintained the list of experts contemplated by Article III of the present Convention, and the Organization shall make necessary and appropriate regulations in connexion therewith, including the determination of the required qualifications.

2. Nominations to the list may be made by Member States of the Organization and by Parties to this Convention. The experts shall be paid on the basis of services rendered by the States utilizing those services.

Article V. 1. Measures taken by the coastal State in accordance with Article I shall be proportionate to the damage actual or threatened to it.

2. Such measures shall not go beyond what is reasonably necessary to achieve the end mentioned in Article I and shall cease as soon as that end has been achieved; they shall not unnecessarily interfere with the rights and interests of the flag State, third States and of any persons, physical or corporate, concerned.

3. In considering whether the measures are proportionate to the damage, account shall be taken of:

(*a*) the extent and probability of imminent damage if those measures are not taken; and

(*b*) the likelihood of those measures being effective; and

(*c*) the extent of the damage which may be caused by such measures.

Article VI. Any Party which has taken measures in contravention of the provisions of the present Convention causing damage to others, shall be obliged to pay compensation to the extent of the damage caused by measures which exceed those reasonably necessary to achieve the end mentioned in Article I.

Article VII. Except as specifically provided, nothing in the present Convention shall prejudice any otherwise applicable right, duty, privilege or immunity or deprive any of the Parties or any interested physical or corporate person of any remedy otherwise applicable.

Article VIII. 1. Any controversy between the Parties as to whether measures taken under Article I were in contravention of the provisions of the present Convention, to whether compensation is obliged to be paid under Article VI, and to the amount of such compensation shall, if settlement by negotiation between the Parties involved or between the Party which took the measures and the physical or corporate claimants has not been possible, and if the Parties do not otherwise agree, be submitted upon request of any of the Parties concerned to conciliation or, if conciliation does not succeed, to arbitration, as set out in the Annex to the present Convention.

2. The Party which took the measures shall not be entitled to refuse a request for conciliation or arbitration under provisions of the preceding paragraph solely on the grounds that any remedies under municipal law in its own courts have not been exhausted.

Article IX. 1. The present Convention shall remain open for signature until 31 December 1970 and shall thereafter remain open for accession.

2. States Members of the United Nations or any of the Specialized Agencies or of the International Atomic Energy Agency or Parties to the Statute of the International Court of Justice may become Parties to this Convention by:

(*a*) signature without reservation as to ratification, acceptance or approval;

(*b*) signature subject to ratification, acceptance or approval followed by ratification, acceptance or approval; or

(*c*) accession.

Article X. 1. Ratification, acceptance, approval or accession shall be effected by the deposit of a formal instrument to that effect with the Secretary–General of the Organization.

2. Any instrument of ratification, acceptance, approval or accession deposited after the entry into force of an amendment to the present Convention with respect to all existing Parties or after the completion of all measures required for the entry into force of the amendment with respect to those Parties shall be deemed to apply to the Convention as modified by the amendment.

Article XI. 1. The present Convention shall enter into force on the ninetieth day following the date on which Governments of fifteen States have either signed it without reservation as to ratification, acceptance or approval or have deposited instruments of ratification, acceptance, approval or accession with the Secretary–General of the Organization.

2. For each State which subsequently ratifies, accepts, approves or accedes to it the present Convention shall come into force on the ninetieth day after deposit by such State of the appropriate instrument.

Article XII. 1. The present Convention may be denounced by any Party at any time after the date on which the Convention comes into force for that State.

2. Denunciation shall be effected by the deposit of an instrument with the Secretary–General of the Organization.

3. A denunciation shall take effect one year, or such longer period as may be specified in the instrument of denunciation, after its deposit with the Secretary–General of the Organization.

Article XIII. 1. The United Nations where it is the administering authority for a territory, or any State Party to the present Convention responsible for the international relations of a territory, shall as soon as possible consult with the appropriate authorities of such territories or take such other measures as may be appropriate, in order to extend the present Convention to that territory and may at any time by notification in writing to the Secretary–General of the Organization declare that the present Convention shall extend to such territory.

2. The present Convention shall, from the date of receipt of the notification or from such other date as may be specified in the notification, extend to the territory named therein.

3. The United Nations, or any Party which has made a declaration under paragraph 1 of this Article may at any time after the date on which the Convention has been so extended to any territory declare by notification in writing to the Secretary–General of the Organization that the present Convention shall cease to extend to any such territory named in the notification.

4. The present Convention shall cease to extend to any territory mentioned in such notification one year, or such longer period as may be specified therein, after the date of receipt of the notification by the Secretary–General of the Organization.

Article XIV. 1. A Conference for the purpose of revising or amending the present Convention may be convened by the Organization.

2. The Organization shall convene a Conference of the States Parties to the present Convention for revising or amending the present Convention at the request of not less than one-third of the Parties.

Article XV. 1. The present Convention shall be deposited with the Secretary–General of the Organization.

2. The Secretary–General of the Organization shall:

(*a*) inform all States which have signed or acceded to the Convention of:

(i) each new signature or deposit of instrument together with the date thereof;

(ii) the deposit of any instrument of denunciation of this Convention together with the date of the deposit;

(iii) the extension of the present Convention to any territory under paragraph 1 of Article XIII and of the termination of any such extension under the provisions of paragraph 4 of that Article stating in each case the date on which the present Convention has been or will cease to be so extended;

(*b*) transmit certified true copies of the present Convention to all Signatory States and to all States which accede to the present Convention.

Article XVI. As soon as the present Convention comes into force, the text shall be transmitted by the Secretary–General of the Organization to the Secretariat of the United Nations for registration and publication in accordance with Article 102 of the Charter of the United Nations.

Article XVII. The present Convention is established in a single copy in the English and French languages, both texts being equally authentic. Official translations in the Russian and Spanish languages shall be prepared and deposited with the signed original.

4.8 DECLARATION OF PRINCIPLES GOVERNING THE SEA-BED AND THE OCEAN FLOOR, AND THE SUBSOIL THEREOF, BEYOND THE LIMITS OF NATIONAL JURISDICTION. Adopted by the U.N. General Assembly, 17 December 1970. U.N. Doc. A/RES/2749(XXV); *reprinted in* 10 I.L.M. 220 (1971) & 5 Weston V.F.10

THE GENERAL ASSEMBLY,

Recalling its resolutions 2340 (XXII) of 18 December 1967, 2467 (XXIII) of 21 December 1968 and 2574 (XXIV) of 15 December 1969, concerning the area to which the title of the item refers.

Affirming that there is an area of the sea-bed and the ocean floor, and the subsoil thereof, beyond the limits of national jurisdiction, the precise limits of which are yet to be determined.

Recognizing that the existing legal régime of the high seas does not provide substantive rules for regulating the exploration of the aforesaid area and the exploitation of its resources.

Convinced that the area shall be reserved exclusively for peaceful purposes and that the exploration of the area and the exploitation of its resources shall be carried out for the benefit of mankind as a whole.

Believing it essential that an international régime applying to the area and its resources and including appropriate international machinery should be established as soon as possible.

Bearing in mind that the development and use of the area and its resources shall be undertaken in such a manner as to foster healthy development of the world economy and balanced growth of international trade, and to minimize any adverse economic effects caused by fluctuation of prices of raw materials resulting from such activities.

Solemnly declares that:

1. The sea-bed and ocean floor, and the subsoil thereof, beyond the limits of national jurisdiction (hereinafter referred to as the area), as well as the resources of the area, are the common heritage of mankind.

2. The area shall not be subject to appropriation by any means by States or persons, natural or juridical, and no State shall claim or exercise sovereignty or sovereign rights over any part thereof.

3. No State or person, natural or juridical, shall claim, exercise or acquire rights with respect to the area or its resources incompatible with the international régime to be established and the principles of this Declaration.

4. All activities regarding the exploration and exploitation of the resources of the area and other related activities shall be governed by the international régime to be established.

5. The area shall be open to use exclusively for peaceful purposes by all States whether coastal or land-locked, without discrimination, in accordance with international régime to be established.

6. States shall act in the area in accordance with the applicable principles and rules of international law including the Charter of the United Nations and the Declaration on Principles of International Law concerning Friendly Relations and Co-operation among States in accordance with the Charter of the United Nations, adopted by the General Assembly on 24 October 1970, in the interests of maintaining international peace and security and promoting international co-operation and mutual understanding.

7. The exploration of the area and the exploitation of its resources shall be carried out for the benefit of mankind as a whole, irrespective of the geographical location of States, whether land-locked or coastal, and taking into particular consideration the interests and needs of the developing countries.

8. The area shall be reserved exclusively for peaceful purposes, without prejudice to any measures which have been or may be agreed upon in the context of international negotiations undertaken in the field of disarmament and which may be applicable to a broader area. One or more international agreements shall be concluded as soon as possible in order to implement effectively this principle and to constitute a step towards the exclusion of the sea-bed, the ocean floor and the subsoil thereof from the arms race.

9. On the basis of the principles of this Declaration, an international régime applying to the area and its resources and including appropriate international machinery to give effect to its provisions shall be established by an international treaty of a universal character, generally agreed upon. The régime shall, *inter alia,* provide for the orderly and safe development and rational management of the area and its resources and for expanding opportunities in the use thereof and ensure the equitable sharing by States in the benefits derived therefrom, taking into particular consideration the interests and needs of the developing countries, whether land-locked or coastal.

10. States shall promote international co-operation in scientific research exclusively for peaceful purposes:

(a) By participation in international programmes and by encouraging co-operation in scientific research by personnel of different countries;

(b) Through effective publication of research programmes and dissemination of the results of research through international channels;

(c) By co-operation in measures to strengthen research capabilities of developing countries, including the participation of their nationals in research programmes. No such activity shall form the legal basis for any claims with respect to any part of the area or its resources.

11. With respect to activities in the area and acting in conformity with the international régime to be established, States shall take appropriate measures for and shall co-operate in the adoption and implementation of international rules, standards and procedures for, *inter alia:*

(a) Prevention of pollution and contamination, and other hazards to the marine environment, including the coastline, and of interference with the ecological balance of the marine environment;

(b) Protection and conservation of the natural resources of the area and prevention of damage to the flora and fauna of the marine environment.

12. In their activities in the area, including those relating to its resources, States shall pay due regard to the rights and legitimate interests of coastal States in the region of such activities, as well as of all other States which may be affected by such activities. Consultations shall be maintained with the coastal States concerned with respect to activities relating to the exploration of the area and the exploitation of its resources with a view to avoiding infringement of such rights and interests.

13. Nothing herein shall affect:

(a) The legal status of the waters superjacent to the area or that of the air space above those waters;

(b) The rights of coastal States with respect to measures to prevent, mitigate or eliminate grave and imminent danger to their coastline or related interests from pollution or threat thereof resulting from, or from other hazardous occurrences caused by, any activities in the area, subject to the international régime to be established.

14. Every State shall have the responsibility to ensure that activities in the area, including those relating to its resources, whether undertaken by governmental agencies, or nongovernmental entities or persons under its jurisdiction, or acting on its behalf, shall be carried out in conformity with the international régime to be established. The same responsibility applies to international organizations and their members for activities undertaken by such organizations or on their behalf. Damage caused by such activities shall entail liability.

15. The parties to any dispute relating to activities in the area and its resources shall resolve such dispute by the measures mentioned in Article 33 of the Charter of the United Nations and such procedures for settling disputes as may be agreed upon in the international régime to be established.

4.9 Convention Relating to Civil Liability in the Field of Maritime Carriage of Nuclear Material (Without Final Act). Concluded at Brussels, 17 December 1971. Entered into force, 15 July 1975. 974 U.N.T.S. 255

The High Contracting Parties,

Considering that the Paris Convention of 29 July 1960 on Third Party Liability in the Field of Nuclear Energy and its Additional Protocol of 28 January 1964 (hereinafter referred to as "the Paris Convention") and the Vienna Convention of 21 May 1963 on Civil Liability for Nuclear Damage (hereinafter referred to as "the Vienna Convention") provide that, in the case of damage caused by a nuclear incident occurring in the course of maritime carriage of nuclear material covered by such Conventions, the operator of a nuclear installation is the person liable for such damage,

Considering that similar provisions exist in the national law in force in certain States,

Considering that the application of any preceding international Convention in the field of maritime transport is however maintained,

Desirous of ensuring that the operator of a nuclear installation will be exclusively liable for damage caused by a nuclear incident occurring in the course of maritime carriage of nuclear material,

Have agreed as follows:

Article 1. Any person who by virtue of an international convention or national law applicable in the field of maritime transport might be held liable for damage caused by a nuclear incident shall be exonerated from such liability:

(*a*) if the operator of a nuclear installation is liable for such damage under either the Paris or the Vienna Convention, or

(*b*) if the operator of a nuclear installation is liable for such damage by virtue of a national law governing the liability for such damage, provided that such law is in all respects as favourable to persons who may suffer damage as either the Paris or the Vienna Convention.

Article 2. 1. The exoneration provided for in Article I shall also apply in respect of damage caused by a nuclear incident:

(*a*) to the nuclear installation itself or to any property on the site of that installation which is used or to be used in connexion with that installation, or

(*b*) to the means of transport upon which the nuclear material involved was at the time of the nuclear incident,

for which the operator of the nuclear installation is not liable because his liability for such damage has been excluded pursuant to the provisions of either the Paris or the Vienna Convention, or, in cases referred to in Article 1(*b*), by equivalent provisions of the national law referred to therein.

2. The provisions of paragraph 1 shall not, however, affect the liability of any individual who has caused the damage by an act or omission done with intent to cause damage.

Article 3. No provision of the present Convention shall affect the liability of the operator of a nuclear ship in respect of damage caused by a nuclear incident involving the nuclear fuel of or radioactive products or waste produced in such ship.

Article 4. The present Convention shall supersede any international Conventions in the field of maritime transport which, at the date on which the present Convention is opened for signature, are in force or open for signature, ratification or accession but only to the extent that such Conventions would be in conflict with it; however, nothing in this Article shall affect the obligations of the Contracting Parties to the present Convention to non-Contracting States arising under such international Conventions.

Article 5. 1. The present Convention shall be opened for signature in Brussels and shall remain open for signature in London at the Headquarters of the Inter-Governmental Maritime Consultative Organization (hereinafter referred to as "the Organization") until 31 December 1972 and shall thereafter remain open for accession.

2. States Members of the United Nations or any of the Specialized Agencies or of the International Atomic Energy Agency or Parties to the Statute of the International Court of Justice may become Parties to the present Convention by:

(*a*) signature without reservation as to ratification, acceptance or approval;

(*b*) signature subject to ratification, acceptance or approval followed by ratification, acceptance or approval; or

(*c*) accession.

3. Ratification, acceptance, approval or accession shall be effected by the deposit of a formal instrument to that effect with the Secretary-General of the Organization.

Article 6. 1. The present Convention shall enter into force on the ninetieth day following the date on which five States have either signed it without reservation as to ratification, acceptance or approval or have deposited instruments of ratification, acceptance, approval or accession with the Secretary-General of the Organization.

2. For any State which subsequently signs the present Convention without reservation as to ratification, acceptance or approval, or deposits its instrument of ratification, acceptance, approval or accession, the Convention shall come into force on the ninetieth day after the date of such signature or deposit.

Article 7. 1. The present Convention may be denounced by any Contracting Party to it at any time after the date on which the Convention comes into force for that State.

2. Denunciation shall be effected by a notification in writing delivered to the Secretary-General of the Organization.

3. A denunciation shall take effect one year, or such longer period as may be specified in the notification, after its receipt by the Secretary-General of the Organization.

4. Notwithstanding a denunciation by a Contracting Party pursuant to this Article the provisions of the present Convention shall continue to apply to any damage caused by a nuclear incident occurring before the denunciation takes effect.

Article 8. 1. The United Nations where it is the administering authority for a territory, or any Contracting Party to the present Convention responsible for the international relations of a territory, may at any time by notification in writing to the Secretary-General of the Organization declare that the present Convention shall extend to such territory.

2. The present Convention shall, from the date of receipt of the notification or from such other date as may be specified in the notification, extend to the territory named therein.

3. The United Nations, or any Contracting Party which had made a declaration under paragraph 1 of this Article may at any time after the date on which the Convention has been so extended to any territory declare by notification in writing to the Secretary-General of the Organization that the present Convention shall cease to extend to any such territory named in the notification.

4. The present Convention shall cease to extend to any territory mentioned in such notification one year, or such longer period as may be specified therein, after the date of receipt of the notification by the Secretary–General of the Organization.

Article 9. 1. A Conference for the purpose of revising or amending the present Convention may be convened by the Organization.

2. The Organization shall convene a Conference of the Contracting Parties to the present Convention for revising or amending it at the request of not less than one-third of the Contracting Parties.

Article 10. A Contracting Party may make reservations corresponding to those which it has validly made to the Paris or Vienna Convention. A reservation may be made at the time of signature, ratification, acceptance, approval or accession.

Article 11. 1. The present Convention shall be deposited with the Secretary–General of the Organization.

2. The Secretary–General of the Organization shall:

(*a*) inform all States which have signed or acceded to the present Convention of:

(i) each new signature and each deposit of an instrument together with the date thereof;

(ii) any reservation made in conformity with the present Convention;

(iii) the date of entry into force of the present Convention;

(iv) any denunciation of the present Convention and the date on which it takes effect;

(v) the extension of the present Convention to any territory under paragraph 1 of Article 8 and of the termination of any such extension under the provisions of paragraph 4 of that Article stating in each case the date on which the present Convention has been or will cease to be so extended;

(*b*) transmit certified true copies of the present Convention to all Signatory States and to all States which have acceded to the present Convention.

3. As soon as the present Convention comes into force, a certified true copy thereof shall be transmitted by the Secretary–General of the Organization to the Secretariat of the United Nations for registration and publication in accordance with Article 102 of the Charter of the United Nations.

Article 12. The present Convention is established in a single original in the English and French languages, both texts being equally authentic. Official translations in the Russian and Spanish languages shall be prepared by the Secretariat of the Organization and deposited with the signed original.

4.10 ILA Draft Articles on Marine Pollution of Continental Origin (Without Comments). Adopted 26 August 1972. 55 I.L.A. XVII 97 (1972); *reprinted in* 5 Weston V.F.13

Article I

As used in this chapter "Continental sea-water pollution" means any detrimental change in the natural composition, content or quality of sea water resulting from human conduct taking place within the limits of the national jurisdiction of a State.

This conduct shall include, *inter alia,* the discharge or introduction of substances directly into the sea from pipelines, extended outlets, or ships, or indirectly through rivers or other watercourses whether natural or artificial, or through atmospheric fall-out.

Article II

Taking into account all relevant factors referred to in Article III, a State

(a) shall prevent any new form of continental sea-water pollution or any increase in the degree of existing continental sea-water pollution which would cause substantial injury in the territory of another State or to any of its rights under international law or to the marine environment, and

(b) shall take all reasonable measures to abate existing continental sea-water pollution to such an extent that no substantial injury of the kind referred to in paragraph (a) is caused.

Article III

(a) States should establish, as soon as possible, international standards for the control of sea-water pollution, having regard to all relevant factors, including the following:—

—the geography and hydrography of the area (inland waters, territorial sea, contiguous zone and continental shelf);

—climatological conditions;

—quality and composition of affected sea waters;

—the conservation of the maritime environment (flora and fauna);

—the resources of the sea-bed and the subsoil and their economic value for present and potential users;

—the recreational facilities of the coastal area;

—the past, present and future utilization of the coastal area and sea water;

—the economic and social needs of the (coastal) States involved;

—the existence of alternative means for waste disposal;

—the adaptation of detrimental changes to beneficial human uses;

—the avoidance of unnecessary waste-disposal;

(b) Until such standards are established, the existence of substantial injury from pollution shall be determined by taking into consideration all relevant factors, including those referred to in paragraph (a).

(c) The weight to be given to each factor is to be determined by its importance in comparison with that of other relevant factors.

Article IV

When it is contended that the conduct of a State is not in accordance with its obligations under these Articles, that State shall promptly enter into negotiations with the complainant with a view to reaching a solution that is equitable under the circumstances.

Article V

In the case of violation of the rules in Article II, the State responsible shall cease the wrongful conduct and shall compensate the injured State for the injury that has been caused to it.

Article VI

In case of a dispute, Articles XXXI to XXXVII of the Helsinki Rules are, so far as may be, applicable.

4.11 CONVENTION ON THE PREVENTION OF MARINE POLLUTION BY DUMPING OF WASTES AND OTHER MATTER (With Annexes and as Amended to 1989 but Without Addendum). Concluded at Washington, 29 December 1972. Entered into force, 30 August 1975. 1046 U.N.T.S. 120, 26 U.S.T. 2403, T.I.A.S. No. 8165; *reprinted in* 11 I.L.M. 1294 (1973) & 5 Weston V.I.7

The Contracting Parties to this Convention,

Recognizing that the marine environment and the living organisms which it supports are of vital importance to humanity, and all people have an interest in assuring that it is so managed that its quality and resources are not impaired;

Recognizing that the capacity of the sea to assimilate wastes and render them harmless, and its ability to regenerate natural resources is not unlimited;

Recognizing that States have, in accordance with the Charter of the United Nations and the principles of international law, the sovereign right to exploit their own resources pursuant to their own environmental policies, and the responsibility to ensure that activities within their jurisdiction or control do not cause damage to the environment of other States or of areas beyond the limits of national jurisdiction;

Recognizing resolution 2749 (XXV) of the General Assembly of the United Nations on the principles governing the sea-bed and the ocean floor and the subsoil thereof, beyond the limits of national jurisdiction;

Noting that marine pollution originates in many sources, such as dumping and discharges through the atmosphere, rivers, estuaries, outfalls and pipelines, and that it is important that States use the best practicable means to prevent such pollution and develop products and processes which will reduce the amount of harmful wastes to be disposed of;

Being convinced that international action to control the pollution of the sea by dumping can and must be taken without delay but that this action should not preclude discussion of measures to control other sources of marine pollution as soon as possible; and

Wishing to improve protection of the marine environment by encouraging States with a common interest in particular geographical areas to enter into appropriate agreements supplementary to this Convention;

Have agreed as follows:

Article I. Contracting Parties shall individually and collectively promote the effective control of all sources of pollution of the marine environment, and pledge themselves especially to take all practicable steps to prevent the pollution of the sea by the dumping of waste and other matter that is liable to create hazards to human health, to harm living resources and marine life, to damage amenities or to interfere with other legitimate uses of the sea.

Article II. Contracting Parties shall, as provided for in the following Articles, take effective measures individually, according to their scientific, technical and economic capabilities, and collectively, to prevent marine pollution caused by dumping and shall harmonize their policies in this regard.

Article III. For the purposes of this Convention:

1. (*a*) "Dumping" means:

(i) any deliberate disposal at sea of wastes or other matter from vessels, aircraft, platforms or other man-made structures at sea;

(ii) any deliberate disposal at sea of vessels, aircraft, platforms or other man-made structures at sea.

(*b*) "Dumping" does not include:

(i) the disposal at sea of wastes or other matter incidental to, or derived from the normal operations of vessels, aircraft, platforms or other man-made structures at sea and their equipment, other than wastes or other matter transported by or to vessels, aircraft, platforms or other man-made structures at sea, operating for the purpose of disposal of such matter or derived from the treatment of such wastes or other matter on such vessels, aircraft, platforms or structures;

(ii) placement of matter for a purpose other than the mere disposal thereof, provided that such placement is not contrary to the aims of this Convention.

(*c*) The disposal of wastes or other matter directly arising from, or related to the exploration, exploitation and associated off-shore processing of sea-bed mineral resources will not be covered by the provisions of this Convention.

2. "Vessels and aircraft" means waterborne or airborne craft of any type whatsoever. This expression includes air-cushioned craft and floating craft, whether self-propelled or not.

3. "Sea" means all marine waters other than the internal waters of States.

4. "Wastes or other matter" means material and substance of any kind, form or description.

5. "Special permit" means permission granted specifically on application in advance and in accordance with Annex II and Annex III.

6. "General permit" means permission granted in advance and in accordance with Annex III.

7. The "Organisation" means the Organisation designated by the Contracting Parties in accordance with Article XIV(2).

Article IV. 1. In accordance with the provisions of this Convention, Contracting Parties shall prohibit the dumping of any wastes or other matter in whatever form or condition except as otherwise specified below:

(*a*) the dumping of wastes or other matter listed in Annex I is prohibited;

(*b*) the dumping of wastes or other matter listed in Annex II requires a prior special permit;

(*c*) the dumping of all other wastes or matter requires a prior general permit.

2. Any permit shall be issued only after careful consideration of all the factors set forth in Annex III, including prior studies of the characteristics of the dumping site, as set forth in Sections B and C of that Annex.

3. No provision of this Convention is to be interpreted as preventing a Contracting Party from prohibiting, insofar as that Party is concerned, the dumping of wastes or other matter not mentioned in Annex I. That Party shall notify such measures to the Organisation.

Article V. 1. The provisions of Article IV shall not apply when it is necessary to secure the safety of human life or of vessels, aircraft, platforms or other man-made structures at sea in cases of *force majeure* caused by stress of weather, or in any case which constitutes a danger to human life or a real threat to vessels, aircraft, platforms or other man-made structures at sea, if dumping appears to be the only way of averting the threat and if there is every probability that the damage consequent upon such dumping will be less than would otherwise occur. Such dumping shall be so conducted as to minimise the likelihood of damage to human or marine life and shall be reported forthwith to the Organisation.

2. A Contracting Party may issue a special permit as an exception to Article IV(1)(*a*), in emergencies, posing unacceptable risk relating to human health and admitting no other feasible solution. Before doing so the Party shall consult any other country or countries that are likely to be affected and the Organisation which, after consulting other Parties, and international organisations as appropriate, shall, in accordance with Article XIV promptly recommend to the Party the most appropriate procedures to adopt. The Party shall follow these recommendations to the maximum extent feasible consistent with the time within which action must be taken and with the general obligation to avoid damage to the marine environment and shall inform the Organisation of the action it takes. The Parties pledge themselves to assist one another in such situations.

3. Any Contracting Party may waive its rights under paragraph (2) at the time of, or subsequent to ratification of, or accession to this Convention.

Article VI. 1. Each Contracting Party shall designate an appropriate authority or authorities to:

(*a*) issue special permits which shall be required prior to, and for, the dumping of matter listed in Annex II and in the circumstances provided for in Article V(2);

(*b*) issue general permits which shall be required prior to, and for, the dumping of all other matter;

(*c*) keep records of the nature and quantities of all matter permitted to be dumped and the location, time and method of dumping;

(*d*) monitor individually, or in collaboration with other Parties and competent international organisations, the condition of the seas for the purposes of this Convention.

2. The appropriate authority or authorities of a Contracting Party shall issue prior special or general permits in accordance with paragraph (1) in respect of matter intended for dumping:

(*a*) loaded in its territory;

(*b*) loaded by a vessel or aircraft registered in its territory or flying its flag, when the loading occurs in the territory of a State not party to this Convention.

3. In issuing permits under sub-paragraphs (1)(*a*) and (*b*) above, the appropriate authority or authorities shall comply with Annex III, together with such additional criteria, measures and requirements as they may consider relevant.

4. Each Contracting Party, directly or through a Secretariat established under a regional agreement, shall report to the Organisation, and where appropriate to other Parties, the information specified in sub-paragraphs (*c*) and (*d*) of paragraph (1) above, and the criteria, measures and requirements it adopts in accordance with paragraph (3) above. The procedure to be followed and the nature of such reports shall be agreed by the Parties in consultation.

Article VII. 1. Each Contracting Party shall apply the measures required to implement the present Convention to all:

(*a*) vessels and aircraft registered in its territory or flying its flag;

(*b*) vessels and aircraft loading in its territory or territorial seas matter which is to be dumped;

(*c*) vessels and aircraft and fixed or floating platforms under its jurisdiction believed to be engaged in dumping.

2. Each Party shall take in its territory appropriate measures to prevent and punish conduct in contravention of the provisions of this Convention.

3. The Parties agree to co-operate in the development of procedures for the effective application of this Convention particularly on the high seas, including procedures for the reporting of vessels and aircraft observed dumping in contravention of the Convention.

4. This Convention shall not apply to those vessels and aircraft entitled to sovereign immunity under international law. However, each Party shall ensure by the adoption of appropriate measures that such vessels and aircraft owned or operated by it act in a manner consistent with the object and purpose of this Convention, and shall inform the Organisation accordingly.

5. Nothing in this convention shall affect the right of each Party to adopt other measures, in accordance with the principles of international law, to prevent dumping at sea.

Article VIII. In order to further the objectives of this Convention, the Contracting Parties with common interests to protect in the marine environment in a given geographical area shall endeavour, taking into account characteristic regional features, to enter into regional agreements consistent with this Convention for the prevention of pollution, especially by dumping. The Contracting Parties to the present Convention shall endeavour to act consistently with the objectives and provisions of such regional agreements, which shall be notified to them by the Organisation. Contracting Parties shall seek to co-operate with the Parties to regional agreements in order to develop harmonized procedures to be followed by Contracting Parties to the different conventions concerned. Special attention shall be given to co-operation in the field of monitoring and scientific research.

Article IX. The Contracting Parties shall promote, through collaboration within the Organisation and other international bodies, support for those Parties which request it for:

(*a*) the training of scientific and technical personnel;

(*b*) the supply of necessary equipment and facilities for research and monitoring;

(*c*) the disposal and treatment of waste and other measures to prevent or mitigate pollution caused by dumping;

preferably within the countries concerned, so furthering the aims and purposes of this Convention.

Article X. In accordance with the principles of international law regarding State responsibility for damage to the environment of oher States or to any other area of the environment, caused by dumping of wastes and other matter of all kinds, the Contracting Parties undertake to develop procedures for the assessment of liability and the settlement of disputes regarding dumping.

Article XI. The Contracting Parties shall at their first consultative meeting consider procedures for the settlement of disputes concerning the interpretation and application of this Convention.

Article XII. The Contracting Parties pledge themselves to promote, within the competent specialised agencies and other international bodies, measures to protect the marine environment against pollution caused by:

(*a*) hydrocarbons, including oil, and their wastes;

(*b*) other noxious or hazardous matter transported by vessels for purposes other than dumping;

(*c*) wastes generated in the course of operation of vessels, aircraft, platforms and other man-made structures at sea;

(*d*) radio-active pollutants from all sources, including vessels;

(*e*) agents of chemical and biological warfare;

(*f*) wastes or other matter directly arising from, or related to the exploration, exploitation and associated off-shore processing of sea-bed mineral resources.

The Parties will also promote, within the appropriate international organisation, the codification of signals to be used by vessels engaged in dumping.

Article XIII. Nothing in this Convention shall prejudice the codification and development of the law of the sea by the United Nations Conference on the Law of the Sea convened pursuant to Resolution 2750 C(XXV) of the General Assembly of the United Nations nor the present or future claims and legal views of any State concerning the law of the sea and the nature and extent of coastal and flag State jurisdiction. The Contracting Parties agree to consult at a meeting to be convened by the Organisation after the Law of the Sea Conference, and in any case not later than 1976, with a view to defining the nature and extent of the right and the responsibility of a coastal State to apply the Convention in a zone adjacent to its coast.

Article XIV. 1. The Government of the United Kingdom of Great Britain and Northern Ireland as a depositary shall call a meeting of the Contracting Parties not later than three months after the entry into force of this Convention to decide on organisational matters.

2. The Contracting Parties shall designate a competent Organisation existing at the time of that meeting to be responsible for Secretariat duties in relation to this Convention. Any Party to this Convention not being a member of this Organisation shall make an appropriate contribution to the expenses incurred by the Organisation in performing these duties.

3. The Secretariat duties of the Organisation shall include:

(*a*) the convening of consultative meetings of the Contracting Parties not less frequently than once every two years and of special meetings of the Parties at any time on the request of two thirds of the Parties;

(*b*) preparing and assisting, in consultation with the Contracting Parties and appropriate International Organisations, in the development and implementation of procedures referred to in sub-paragraph (4)(*e*) of this Article;

(*c*) considering enquiries by, and information from the Contracting Parties, consulting with them and with the appropriate International Organisations, and providing recommendations to the Parties on questions related to, but not specifically covered by the Convention;

(*d*) conveying to the Parties concerned all notifications received by the Organisation in accordance with Articles IV(3), V(1) and (2), VI(4), XV, XX and XXI.

Prior to the designation of the Organisation these functions shall, as necessary, be performed by the depositary, who for this purpose shall be the Government of the United Kingdom of Great Britain and Northern Ireland.

4. Consultative or special meetings of the Contracting Parties shall keep under continuing review the implementation of this Convention and may, *inter alia:*

(*a*) review and adopt amendments to this Convention and its Annexes in accordance with Article XV;

(*b*) invite the appropriate scientific body or bodies to collaborate with and to advise the Parties or the Organisation on any scientific or technical aspect relevant to this Convention, including particularly the content of the Annexes;

(*c*) receive and consider reports made pursuant to Article VI(4);

(*d*) promote co-operation with and between regional organisations concerned with the prevention of marine pollution;

(*e*) develop or adopt, in consultation with appropriate International Organisations, procedures referred to in Article V(2), including basic criteria for determining exceptional and emergency situations, and procedures for consultative advice and the safe disposal of matter in such circumstances, including the designation of appropriate dumping areas, and recommend accordingly;

(*f*) consider any additional action that may be required.

5. The Contracting Parties at their first consultative meeting shall establish rules of procedure as necessary.

Article XV. 1. (*a*) At meetings of the Contracting Parties called in accordance with Article XIV amendments to this Convention may be adopted by a two-thirds majority of those present. An amendment shall enter into force for the Parties which have accepted it on the sixtieth day after two thirds of the Parties shall have deposited an instrument of acceptance of the amendment with the Organisation. Thereafter the amendment shall enter into force for any other Party 30 days after that Party deposits its instrument of acceptance of the amendment.

(*b*) The Organisation shall inform all Contracting Parties of any request made for a special meeting under Article XIV and of any amendments adopted at meetings of the Parties and of the date on which each such amendment enters into force for each Party.

2. Amendments to the Annexes will be based on scientific or technical considerations. Amendments to the Annexes approved by a two-thirds majority of those present at a meeting called in accordance with Article XIV shall enter into force for each Contracting Party immediately on notification of its acceptance to the Organisation and 100 days after approval by the meeting for all other Parties except for those which before the end of the 100 days make a declaration that they are not able to accept the amendment at that time. Parties should endeavour to signify their acceptance of an amendment to the Organisation as soon as possible after approval at a meeting. A Party may at any time substitute an acceptance for a previous declaration of objection and the amendment previously objected to shall thereupon enter into force for that Party.

3. An acceptance or declaration of objection under this Article shall be made by the deposit of an instrument with the Organisation. The Organisation shall notify all Contracting Parties of the receipt of such instruments.

4. Prior to the designation of the Organisation, the Secretarial functions herein attributed to it shall be performed temporarily by the Government of the United Kingdom of Great Britain and Northern Ireland, as one of the depositaries of this Convention.

Article XVI. This Convention shall be open for signature by any State at London, Mexico City, Moscow and Washington from 29 December 1972 until 31 December 1973.

Article XVII. This Convention shall be subject to ratification. The instruments of ratification shall be deposited with the Governments of Mexico, the Union of Soviet Socialist Republics, the United Kingdom of Great Britain and Northern Ireland, and the United States of America.

Article XVIII. After 31 December 1973, this Convention shall be open for accession by any State. The instruments of accession shall be deposited with the Governments of Mexico, the Union of Soviet Socialist Republics, the United Kingdom of Great Britain and Northern Ireland, and the United States of America.

Article XIX. 1. This Convention shall enter into force on the thirtieth day following the date of deposit of the fifteenth instrument of ratification or accession.

2. For each Contracting Party ratifying or acceding to the Convention after the deposit of the fifteenth instrument of ratification or accession, the Convention shall enter into force on the thirtieth day after deposit by such Party of its instrument of ratification or accession.

Article XX. The depositaries shall inform Contracting Parties:

(*a*) of signatures to this Convention and of the deposit of instruments of ratification, accession or withdrawal, in accordance with Articles XVI, XVII, XVIII and XXI, and

(*b*) of the date on which this Convention will enter into force, in accordance with Article XIX.

Article XXI. Any Contracting Party may withdraw from this Convention by giving six months' notice in writing to a depositary, which shall promptly inform all Parties of such notice.

Article XXII. The original of this Convention of which the English, French, Russian and Spanish texts are equally authentic, shall be deposited with the Governments of Mexico, the Union of Soviet Socialist Republics, the United Kingdom of Great Britain and Northern Ireland and the United States of America who shall send certified copies thereof to all States.

ANNEX I

1. Organohalogen compounds.

2. Mercury and mercury compounds.

3. Cadmium and cadmium compounds.

4. Persistent plastics and other persistent synthetic materials, for example, netting and ropes, which may float or may remain in suspension in the sea in such a manner as to interfere materially with fishing, navigation or other legitimate uses of the sea.

5. Crude oil and its wastes, refined petroleum products, petroleum distillate residues, and any mixtures containing any of these, taken on board for the purpose of dumping.

6. High-level radio-active wastes or other high-level radio-active matter, defined on public health, biological or other grounds, by the competent international body in this field, at present the International Atomic Energy Agency, as unsuitable for dumping at sea.

7. Materials in whatever form (e.g. solids, liquids, semi-liquids, gases or in a living state) produced for biological and chemical warfare.

8. The preceding paragraphs of this Annex do not apply to substances which are rapidly rendered harmless by physical, chemical or biological processes in the sea provided they do not:

(i) make edible marine organisms unpalatable, or

(ii) endanger human health or that of domestic animals.

The consultative procedure provided for under Article XIV should be followed by a Party if there is doubt about the harmlessness of the substances.

9. This Annex does not apply to wastes or other materials (e.g. sewage sludges and dredged spoils) containing the matter referred to in paragraphs 1–5 above as trace contaminants. Such wastes shall be subject to the provisions of Annexes II and III as appropriate.

10. Paragraphs 1 and 5 of this annex do not apply to the disposal of wastes or other matter referred to in these paragraphs by means of incineration at sea. Incineration of such wastes or other matter at sea requires a prior special permit. In the issue of special permits for incineration, the Contracting Parties shall apply the regulations for the control of incineration of wastes and other matter at sea set forth in the addendum to this annex (which shall constitute an integral part of this annex) and take full account of the technical guidelines on the control of incineration of wastes and other matter at sea adopted by the Contracting Parties in consultation.

ANNEX II

The following substances and materials requiring special care are listed for the purposes of Article VI(1)(a).

A. Wastes containing significant amounts of the matters listed below:

arsenic)
lead)
copper) and their compounds
zinc)
organosilicon compounds
cyanides
fluorides
pesticides and their by-products not covered in Annex I.

B. In the issue of permits for the dumping of large quantities of acids and alkalis, consideration shall be given to the possible presence in such wastes of the substances listed in paragraph A and to the following additional substances:

beryllium)
chromium)
nickel) and their compounds
vanadium)

C. Containers, scrap metal and other bulky wastes liable to sink to the sea bottom which may present a serious obstacle to fishing or navigation.

D. Radio-active wastes or other radio-active matter not included in Annex I. In the issue of permits for the dumping of this matter, the Contracting Parties should take full account of the recommendations of the competent international body in this field, at present the International Atomic Energy Agency.

E. In the issue of special permits for the incineration of substances and materials listed in this annex, the Contracting Parties shall apply the regulations for the control of incineration of wastes and other matter at sea set forth in the addendum to annex I and take full account of the technical guidelines on the control of incineration of wastes and other matter at sea adopted by the Contracting Parties in consultation, to the extent specified in these regulations and guidelines.

F. Substances which, though of a non-toxic nature, may become harmful due to the quantities in which they are dumped, or which are liable to seriously reduce amenities.

ANNEX III

Provisions to be considered in establishing criteria governing the issue of permits for the dumping of matter at sea, taking into account Article IV(2), include:

A. Characteristics and composition of the matter

1. Total amount and average composition of matter dumped (e.g. per year).

2. Form, e.g. solid, sludge, liquid, or gaseous.

3. Properties: physical (e.g. solubility and density), chemical and biochemical (e.g. oxygen demand, nutrients) and biological (e.g. presence of viruses, bacteria, yeasts, parasites).

4. Toxicity.

5. Persistence: physical, chemical and biological.

6. Accumulation and biotransformation in biological materials or sediments.

7. Susceptibility to physical, chemical and biochemical changes and interaction in the aquatic environment with other dissolved organic and inorganic materials.

8. Probability of production of taints or other changes reducing marketability of resources (fish, shellfish, etc.).

B. Characteristics of dumping site and method of deposit

1. Location (e.g. co-ordinates of the dumping area, depth and distance from the coast), location in relation to other areas (e.g. amenity areas, spawning, nursery and fishing areas and exploitable resources).

2. Rate of disposal per specific period (e.g. quantity per day, per week, per month).

3. Methods of packaging and containment, if any.

4. Initial dilution achieved by proposed method of release.

5. Dispersal characteristics (e.g. effects of currents, tides and wind on horizontal transport and vertical mixing).

6. Water characteristics (e.g. temperature, pH, salinity, stratification, oxygen indices of pollution—dissolved oxygen (DO), chemical oxygen demand (COD), biochemical oxygen demand (BOD)—nitrogen present in organic and mineral form including ammonia, suspended matter, other nutrients and productivity).

7. Bottom characteristics (e.g. topography, geochemical and geological characteristics and biological productivity).

8. Existence and effects of other dumpings which have been made in the dumping area (e.g. heavy metal background reading and organic carbon content).

9. In issuing a permit for dumping, Contracting Parties should consider whether an adequate scientific basis exists for assessing the consequences of such dumping, as outlined in this Annex, taking into account seasonal variations.

C. General considerations and conditions

1. Possible effects on amenities (e.g. presence of floating or stranded material, turbidity, objectionable odour, discolouration and foaming).

2. Possible effects on marine life, fish and shellfish culture, fish stocks and fisheries, seaweed harvesting and culture.

3. Possible effects on other uses of the sea (e.g. impairment of water quality for industrial use, underwater corrosion of structures, interference with ship operations from floating materials, interference with fishing or navigation through deposit of waste or solid objects on the sea floor and protection of areas of special importance for scientific or conservation purposes).

4. The practical availability of alternative land-based methods of treatment, disposal or elimination, or of treatment to render the matter less harmful for dumping at sea.

4.12 MARPOL 73/78: PROTOCOL OF 1978 RELATING TO THE INTERNATIONAL CONVENTION FOR THE PREVENTION OF POLLUTION FROM SHIPS, 1973 (With Convention Text and Excerpts from Annexes I, II & V),[e] Concluded at London, 17 February, 1978. Entered into force 2 October 1983. I.M.C.O. Doc TSPP/CONF/11, 1341 U.N.T.S. 3; *reprinted in* 5 Weston V.F.20

THE PARTIES TO THE PRESENT PROTOCOL,

RECOGNIZING the significant contribution which can be made by the International Convention for the Prevention of Pollution from Ships, 1973, to the protection of the marine environment from pollution from ships,

RECOGNIZING ALSO the need to improve further the prevention and control of marine pollution from ships, particularly oil tankers,

RECOGNIZING FURTHER the need for implementing the Regulations for the Prevention of Pollution by Oil contained in Annex I of that Convention as early and as widely as possible,

ACKNOWLEDGING HOWEVER the need to defer the application of Annex II of that Convention until certain technical problems have been satisfactorily resolved,

CONSIDERING that these objectives may best be achieved by the conclusion of a Protocol Relating to the International Convention for the Prevention of Pollution from Ships, 1973,

HAVE AGREED as follows:

ARTICLE I

General Obligations

1. The Parties to the present Protocol undertake to give effect to the provisions of:

(a) the present Protocol and the Annex hereto which shall constitute an integral part of the present Protocol; and

(b) the International Convention for the Prevention of Pollution from Ships, 1973 (hereinafter referred to as "the Convention"), subject to the modifications and additions set out in the present Protocol.

2. The provisions of the Convention and the present Protocol shall be read and interpreted together as one single instrument.

3. Every reference to the Protocol constitutes at the same time a reference to the Annex hereto.

ARTICLE II

Implementation of Annex II of the Convention

1. Notwithstanding the provisions of Article 14(1) of the Convention, the Parties to the present Protocol agree that they shall not be bound by the provisions of Annex

e. The 1978 Protocol incorporates, with modifications, the provisions of the International Convention for the Prevention of Pollution from Ships, 1973, *signed at London* Nov. 2, 1973, *reprinted in* 12 I.L.M. 1319 (1978). The 1973 Convention never entered into force on its own. Accordingly, as of October 2, 1983, when the 1978 Protocol entered into force, the regime to be applied by the states parties to the 1978 Protocol was the regime contained in the 1973 Convention as modified by the 1978 Protocol. This document therefore reflects the terms of the 1978 Protocol, *and incorporates the 1973 Convention as modified.* Article I of the 1978 Protocol directs that "the provisions of the Convention and the present Protocol shall be read and interpreted together as one single instrument," and the consolidated text of the two instruments has come to be known as MARPOL 73/78. *See* International Maritime Organization, MARPOL 73/78, Consolidated Edition (IMO 1997).

II of the Convention for a period of three years from the date of entry into force of the present Protocol or for such longer period as may be decided by a two-thirds majority of the Parties to the present Protocol in the Marine Environment Protection Committee (hereinafter referred to as "the Committee") of the Inter–Governmental Maritime Consultative Organization (hereinafter referred to as "the Organization").

2. During the period specified in paragraph 1 of this Article, the Parties to the present Protocol shall not be under any obligations nor entitled to claim any privileges under the Convention in respect of matters relating to Annex II of the Convention and all reference to Parties in the Convention shall not include the Parties to the present Protocol in so far as matters relating to that Annex are concerned.

ARTICLE III

Communication of Information

The text of Article 11(1)(b) of the Convention is replaced by the following:

"a list of nominated surveyors or recognized organizations which are authorized to act on their behalf in the administration of matters relating to the design, construction, equipment and operation of ships carrying harmful substances in accordance with the provisions of the Regulations for circulation to the Parties for information of their officers. The Administration shall therefore notify the Organization of the specific responsibilities and conditions of the authority delegated to nominated surveyors or recognized organizations."

ARTICLE IV

Signature, Ratification, Acceptance, Approval and Accession

1. The present Protocol shall be open for signature at the Headquarters of the Organization from 1 June 1978 to 31 May 1979 and shall thereafter remain open for accession. States may become Parties to the present Protocol by:

(a) signature without reservation as to ratification, acceptance or approval; or

(b) signature, subject to ratification, acceptance or approval, followed by ratification, acceptance or approval; or

(c) accession.

2. Ratification, acceptance, approval or accession shall be effected by the deposit of an instrument to that effect with the Secretary–General of the Organization.

ARTICLE V

Entry into Force

1. The present Protocol shall enter into force twelve months after the date on which not less than fifteen States, the combined merchant fleets of which constitute not less than fifty per cent of the gross tonnage of the world's merchant shipping, have become Parties to it in accordance with Article IV of the present Protocol.

2. Any instrument of ratification, acceptance, approval or accession deposited after the date on which the present Protocol enters into force shall take effect three months after the date of deposit.

3. After the date on which an amendment to the present Protocol is deemed to have been accepted in accordance with Article 16 of the Convention, any instrument of ratification, acceptance, approval or accession deposited shall apply to the present Protocol as amended.

ARTICLE VI

Amendments

The procedures set out in Article 16 of the Convention in respect of amendments to the Articles, an Annex and an Appendix to an Annex of the Convention shall apply respectively to amendments to the Articles, the Annex and an Appendix to the Annex of the present Protocol.

ARTICLE VII

Denunciation

1. The present Protocol may be denounced by any Party to the present Protocol at any time after the expiry of five years from the date on which the Protocol enters into force for that Party.

2. Denunciation shall be effected by the deposit of an instrument of denunciation with the Secretary–General of the Organization.

3. A denunciation shall take effect twelve months after receipt of the notification by the Secretary–General of the Organization or after the expiry of any other longer period which may be indicated in the notification.

ARTICLE VIII

Depositary

1. The present Protocol shall be deposited with the Secretary–General of the Organization (hereinafter referred to as "the Depositary").

2. The Depositary shall:

(a) inform all States which have signed the present Protocol or acceded thereto of:

(i) each new signature or deposit of an instrument of ratification, acceptance, approval or accession, together with the date thereof;

(ii) the date of entry into force of the present protocol;

(iii) the deposit of any instrument of denunciation of the present Protocol together with the date on which it was received and the date on which the denunciation takes effect;

(iv) any decision made in accordance with Article II(1) of the present Protocol;

(b) transmit certified true copies of the present Protocol to all States which have signed the present Protocol or acceded thereto.

3. As soon as the present Protocol enters into force, a certified true copy thereof shall be transmitted by the Depositary to the Secretariat of the United Nations for registration and publication in accordance with Article 102 of the Charter of the United Nations.

ARTICLE IX

Languages

The present Protocol is established in a single original in the English, French, Russian and Spanish languages, each text being equally authentic. Official translations in the Arabic, German, Italian and Japanese languages shall be prepared and deposited with the signed original.

International Convention for the Prevention of Pollution From Ships 1973, as amended

ARTICLE 1

General Obligations under the Convention

(1) The Parties to the Convention undertake to give effect to the provisions of the present Convention and those Annexes thereto by which they are bound, in order to prevent the pollution of the marine environment by the discharge of harmful substances or effluents containing such substances in contravention of the Convention.

(2) Unless expressly provided otherwise, a reference to the present Convention constitutes at the same time a reference to its Protocols and to the Annexes.

ARTICLE 2

Definitions

For the purposes of the present Convention, unless expressly provided otherwise:

(1) "Regulations" means the Regulations contained in the Annexes to the present Convention.

(2) "Harmful substance" means any substance which, if introduced into the sea, is liable to create hazards to human health, to harm living resources and marine life, to damage amenities or to interfere with other legitimate uses of the sea, and includes any substance subject to control by the present Convention.

(3)(a) "Discharge", in relation to harmful substances or effluents containing such substances, means any release howsoever caused from a ship and includes any escape, disposal, spilling, leaking, pumping, emitting or emptying;

(b) "Discharge" does not include:

(i) dumping within the meaning of the Convention on the Prevention of Marine Pollution by Dumping of Wastes and Other Matter, done at London on 13 November 1972; or

(ii) release of harmful substances directly arising from the exploration, exploitation and associated off-shore processing of sea-bed mineral resources; or

(iii) release of harmful substances for purposes of legitimate scientific research into pollution abatement or control.

(4) "Ship" means a vessel of any type whatsoever operating in the marine environment and includes hydrofoil boats, air-cushion vehicles, submersibles, floating craft and fixed or floating platforms.

(5) "Administration" means the Government of the State under whose authority the ship is operating. With respect to a ship entitled to fly a flag of any State, the Administration is the Government of that State. With respect to fixed or floating platforms engaged in exploration and exploitation of the sea-bed and subsoil thereof adjacent to the coast over which the coastal State exercises sovereign rights for the purposes of exploration and exploitation of their natural resources, the Administration is the Government of the coastal State concerned.

(6) "Incident" means an event involving the actual or probable discharge into the sea of a harmful substance, or effluents containing such a substance.

(7) "Organization" means the Inter–Governmental Maritime Consultative Organization.

ARTICLE 3

Application

(1) The present Convention shall apply to:

(a) ships entitled to fly the flag of a Party to the Convention; and

(b) ships not entitled to fly the flag of a Party but which operate under the authority of a Party.

(2) Nothing in the present Article shall be construed as derogating from or extending the sovereign rights of the Parties under international law over the sea-bed and subsoil thereof adjacent to their coasts for the purposes of exploration and exploitation of their natural resources.

(3) The present Convention shall not apply to any warship, naval auxiliary or other ship owned or operated by a State and used, for the time being, only on government non-commercial service. However, each Party shall ensure by the adoption of appropriate measures not impairing the operations or operational capabilities of such ships owned or operated by it, that such ships act in a manner consistent, so far as is reasonable and practicable, with the present Convention.

ARTICLE 4

Violation

(1) Any violation of the requirements of the present Convention shall be prohibited and sanctions shall be established therefor under the law of the Administration of the ship concerned wherever the violation occurs. If the Administration is informed of such a violation and is satisfied that sufficient evidence is available to enable proceedings to be brought in respect of the alleged violation, it shall cause such proceedings to be taken as soon as possible, in accordance with its law.

(2) Any violation of the requirements of the present Convention within the jurisdiction of any Party to the Convention shall be prohibited and sanctions shall be established therefor under the law of that Party. Whenever such a violation occurs, that Party shall either:

(a) cause proceedings to be taken in accordance with its law; or

(b) furnish to the Administration of the ship such information and evidence as may be in its possession that a violation has occurred.

(3) Where information or evidence with respect to any violation of the present Convention by a ship is furnished to the Administration of that ship, the Administration shall promptly inform the Party which has furnished the information or evidence, and the Organization, of the action taken.

(4) The penalties specified under the law of a Party pursuant to the present Article shall be adequate in severity to discourage violations of the present Convention and shall be equally severe irrespective of where the violations occur.

ARTICLE 5

Certificates and Special Rules on Inspection of Ships

(1) Subject to the provisions of paragraph (2) of the present Article a certificate issued under the authority of a Party to the Convention in accordance with the provisions of the Regulations shall be accepted by the other Parties and regarded for all purposes covered by the present Convention as having the same validity as a certificate issued by them.

(2) A ship required to hold a certificate in accordance with the provisions of the Regulations is subject, while in the ports or off-shore terminals under the jurisdiction

of a Party, to inspection by officers duly authorized by that Party. Any such inspection shall be limited to verifying that there is on board a valid certificate, unless there are clear grounds for believing that the condition of the ship or its equipment does not correspond substantially with the particulars of that certificate. In that case, or if the ship does not carry a valid certificate, the Party carrying out the inspection shall take such steps as will ensure that the ship shall not sail until it can proceed to sea without presenting an unreasonable threat of harm to the marine environment. That Party may, however, grant such a ship permission to leave the port or off-shore terminal for the purpose of proceeding to the nearest appropriate repair yard available.

(3) If a Party denies a foreign ship entry to the ports or off-shore terminals under its jurisdiction or takes any action against such a ship for the reason that the ship does not comply with the provisions of the present Convention, the Party shall immediately inform the consul or diplomatic representative of the Party whose flag the ship is entitled to fly, or if this is not possible, the Administration of the ship concerned. Before denying entry or taking such action the Party may request consultation with the Administration of the ship concerned. Information shall also be given to the Administration when a ship does not carry a valid certificate in accordance with the provisions of the Regulations.

(4) With respect to the ships of non-Parties to the Convention, Parties shall apply the requirements of the present Convention as may be necessary to ensure that no more favorable treatment is given to such ships.

ARTICLE 6

Detection of Violations and Enforcement of the Convention

(1) Parties to the Convention shall co-operate in the detection of violations and the enforcement of the provisions of the present Convention, using all appropriate and practicable measures of detection and environmental monitoring, adequate procedures for reporting and accumulation of evidence.

(2) A ship to which the present Convention applies may, in any port or off-shore terminal of a Party, be subject to inspection by officers appointed or authorized by that Party for the purpose of verifying whether the ship has discharged any harmful substances in violation of the provisions of the Regulations. If an inspection indicates a violation of the Convention, a report shall be forwarded to the Administration for any appropriate action.

(3) Any Party shall furnish to the Administration evidence, if any, that the ship has discharged harmful substances or effluents containing such substances in violation of the provisions of the Regulations. If it is practicable to do so, the competent authority of the former Party shall notify the Master of the ship of the alleged violation.

(4) Upon receiving such evidence, the Administration so informed shall investigate the matter, and may request the other party to furnish further or better evidence of the alleged contravention. If the Administration is satisfied that sufficient evidence is available to enable proceedings to be brought in respect of the alleged violation, it shall cause such proceedings to be taken in accordance with its law as soon as possible. The Administration shall promptly inform the Party which has reported the alleged violation, as well as the Organization, of the action taken.

(5) A Party may also inspect a ship to which the present Convention applies when it enters the ports or off-shore terminals under its jurisdiction, if a request for an investigation is received from any Party together with sufficient evidence that the ship has discharged harmful substances or effluents containing such substances in any place. The report of such investigation shall be sent to the Party requesting it and to

the Administration so that the appropriate action may be taken under the present Convention.

ARTICLE 7

Undue Delay to Ships

(1) All possible efforts shall be made to avoid a ship being unduly detained or delayed under Articles 4, 5 or 6 of the present Convention.

(2) When a ship is unduly detained or delayed under Articles 4, 5 or 6 of the present Convention, it shall be entitled to compensation for any loss or damage suffered.

ARTICLE 8

Reports on Incidents Involving Harmful Substances

(1) A report of an incident shall be made without delay to the fullest extent possible in accordance with the provisions of Protocol I to the present Convention.

(2) Each Party to the Convention shall:

(a) make all arrangements necessary for an appropriate officer or agency to receive and process all reports on incidents; and

(b) notify the Organization with complete details of such arrangements for circulation to other Parties and Member States of the Organization.

(3) Whenever a Party receives a report under the provisions of the present Article, that Party shall relay the report without delay to:

(a) the Administration of the ship involved; and

(b) any other State which may be affected.

(4) Each Party to the Convention undertakes to issue instructions to its maritime inspection vessels and aircraft and to other appropriate services, to report to its authorities any incident referred to in Protocol I to the present Convention. That Party shall, if it considers it appropriate, report accordingly to the Organization and to any other party concerned.

ARTICLE 9

Other Treaties and Interpretation

(1) Upon its entry into force, the present Convention supersedes the International Convention for the Prevention of Pollution of the Sea by Oil, 1954, as amended, as between Parties to that Convention.

(2) Nothing in the present Convention shall prejudice the codification and development of the law of the sea by the United Nations Conference on the Law of the Sea convened pursuant to Resolution 2750 C(XXV) of the General Assembly of the United Nations nor the present or future claims and legal views of any State concerning the law of the sea and the nature and extent of coastal and flag State jurisdiction.

(3) The term "jurisdiction" in the present Convention shall be construed in the light of international law in force at the time of application or interpretation of the present Convention.

ARTICLE 10

Settlement of Disputes

Any dispute between two or more Parties to the Convention concerning the interpretation or application of the present Convention shall, if settlement by negotiation between the Parties involved has not been possible, and if these Parties do not

otherwise agree, be submitted upon request of any of them to arbitration as set out in Protocol II to the present Convention.

ARTICLE 11

Communication of Information

(1) The Parties to the Convention undertake to communicate to the Organization:

(a) the text of laws, orders, decrees and regulations and other instruments which have been promulgated on the various matters within the scope of the present Convention;

(b) a list of nominated surveyors or recognized organizations which are authorized to act on their behalf in the administration of matters relating to the design, construction, equipment and operation of ships carrying harmful substances in accordance with the provisions of the Regulations for circulation to the Parties for information of their officers. The Administration shall therefore notify the Organization of the specific responsibilities and conditions of the authority delegated to nominated surveyors or recognized organizations;

(c) a sufficient number of specimens of their certificates issued under the provisions of the Regulations;

(d) a list of reception facilities including their location, capacity and available facilities and other characteristics;

(e) official reports or summaries of official reports in so far as they show the results of the application of the present Convention; and

(f) an annual statistical report, in a form standardized by the Organization, of penalties actually imposed for infringement of the present Convention.

(2) The Organization shall notify Parties of the receipt of any communications under the present Article and circulate to all Parties any information communicated to it under sub-paragraphs (1)(b) to (f) of the present Article.

ARTICLE 12

Casualties to Ships

(1) Each Administration undertakes to conduct an investigation of any casualty occurring to any of its ships subject to the provisions of the Regulations if such casualty has produced a major deleterious effect upon the marine environment.

(2) Each Party to the Convention undertakes to supply the Organization with information concerning the findings of such investigation, when it judges that such information may assist in determining what changes in the present Convention might be desirable.

ARTICLE 13

Signature, Ratification, Acceptance, Approval and Accession

(1) The present Convention shall remain open for signature at the Headquarters of the Organization from 15 January 1974 until 31 December 1974 and shall thereafter remain open for accession. States may become Parties to the present Convention by:

(a) signature without reservation as to ratification, acceptance or approval; or

(b) signature subject to ratification, acceptance or approval, followed by ratification, acceptance or approval; or

(c) accession.

(2) Ratification, acceptance, approval or accession shall be effected by the deposit of an instrument to that effect with the Secretary–General of the Organization.

(3) The Secretary–General of the Organization shall inform all States which have signed the present Convention or acceded to it of any signature or of the deposit of any new instrument of ratification, acceptance, approval or accession and the date of its deposit.

ARTICLE 14

Optional Annexes

(1) A State may at the time of signing, ratifying, accepting, approving or acceding to the present Convention declare that it does not accept any one or all of Annexes III, IV and V (hereinafter referred to as "Optional Annexes") of the present Convention. Subject to the above, Parties to the Convention shall be bound by any Annex in its entirety.

(2) A State which has declared that it is not bound by an Optional Annex may at any time accept such Annex by depositing with the Organization an instrument of the kind referred to in Article 13(2).

(3) A State which makes a declaration under paragraph (1) of the present Article in respect of an Optional Annex and which has not subsequently accepted that Annex in accordance with paragraph (2) of the present Article shall not be under any obligation nor entitled to claim any privileges under the present Convention in respect of matters related to such Annex and all references to Parties in the present Convention shall not include that State in so far as matters related to such Annex are concerned.

(4) The Organization shall inform the States which have signed or acceded to the present Convention of any declaration under the present Article as well as the receipt of any instrument deposited in accordance with the provisions of paragraph (2) of the present Article.

ARTICLE 15

Entry into Force

(1) The present Convention shall enter into force twelve months after the date on which not less than 15 States, the combined merchant fleets of which constitute not less than fifty per cent of the gross tonnage of the world's merchant shipping, have become parties to it in accordance with Article 13.

(2) An Optional Annex shall enter into force twelve months after the date on which the conditions stipulated in paragraph (1) of the present Article have been satisfied in relation to that Annex.

(3) The Organization shall inform the States which have signed the present Convention or acceded to it of the date on which it enters into force and of the date on which an Optional Annex enters into force in accordance with paragraph (2) of the present Article.

(4) For States which have deposited an instrument of ratification, acceptance, approval or accession in respect of the present Convention or any Optional Annex after the requirements for entry into force thereof have been met but prior to the date of entry into force, the ratification, acceptance, approval or accession shall take effect on the date of entry into force of the Convention or such Annex or three months after the date of deposit of the instrument whichever is the later date.

(5) For States which have deposited an instrument of ratification, acceptance, approval or accession after the date on which the Convention or an Optional Annex entered into force, the Convention or the Optional Annex shall become effective three months after the date of deposit of the instrument.

(6) After the date on which all the conditions required under Article 16 to bring an amendment to the present Convention or an Optional Annex into force have been fulfilled, any instrument of ratification, acceptance, approval or accession deposited shall apply to the Convention or Annex as amended.

ARTICLE 16

Amendments

(1) The present Convention may be amended by any of the procedures specified in the following paragraphs.

(2) Amendments after consideration by the Organization:

(a) any amendment proposed by a Party to the Convention shall be submitted to the Organization and circulated by its Secretary–General to all Members of the Organization and all Parties at least six months prior to its consideration;

(b) any amendment proposed and circulated as above shall be submitted to an appropriate body by the Organization for consideration;

(c) Parties to the Convention, whether or not Members of the Organization, shall be entitled to participate in the proceedings of the appropriate body;

(d) amendments shall be adopted by a two-thirds majority of only the Parties to the Convention present and voting;

(e) if adopted in accordance with sub-paragraph (d) above, amendments shall be communicated by the Secretary–General of the Organization to all the Parties to the Convention for acceptance;

(f) an amendment shall be deemed to have been accepted in the following circumstances:

(i) an amendment to an Article of the Convention shall be deemed to have been accepted on the date on which it is accepted by two-thirds of the Parties, the combined merchant fleets of which constitute not less than fifty per cent of the gross tonnage of the world's merchant fleet;

(ii) an amendment to an Annex to the Convention shall be deemed to have been accepted in accordance with the procedure specified in sub-paragraph (f)(iii) unless the appropriate body, at the time of its adoption, determines that the amendment shall be deemed to have been accepted on the date on which it is accepted by two-thirds of the Parties, the combined merchant fleets of which constitute not less than fifty per cent of the gross tonnage of the world's merchant fleet. Nevertheless, at any time before the entry into force of an amendment to an Annex to the Convention, a Party may notify the Secretary–General of the Organization that its express approval will be necessary before the amendment enters into force for it. The latter shall bring such notification and the date of its receipt to the notice of Parties;

(iii) an amendment to an Appendix to an Annex to the Convention shall be deemed to have been accepted at the end of a period to be determined by the appropriate body at the time of its adoption, which period shall be not less than ten months, unless within that period an objection is communicated to the Organization by not less than one-third of the Parties or by the Parties the combined merchant fleets of which constitute not less than fifty per cent of the gross tonnage of the world's merchant fleet whichever condition is fulfilled;

(iv) an amendment to Protocol I to the Convention shall be subject to the same procedures as for the amendments to the Annexes to the Convention, as provided for in sub-paragraphs (f)(ii) or (f)(iii) above;

(v) an amendment to Protocol II to the Convention shall be subject to the same procedures as for the amendments to an Article of the Convention, as provided for in sub-paragraph (f)(i) above;

(g) the amendment shall enter into force under the following conditions:

(i) in the case of an amendment to an Article of the Convention, to Protocol II, or to Protocol I or to an Annex to the Convention not under the procedure specified in sub-paragraph (f)(iii), the amendment accepted in conformity with the foregoing provisions shall enter into force six months after the date of its acceptance with respect to the Parties which have declared that they have accepted it;

(ii) in the case of an amendment to Protocol I, to an Appendix to an Annex or to an Annex to the Convention under the procedure specified in sub-paragraph (f)(iii), the amendment deemed to have been accepted in accordance with the foregoing conditions shall enter into force six months after its acceptance for all the Parties with the exception of those which, before that date, have made a declaration that they do not accept it or a declaration under subparagraph (f)(ii), that their express approval is necessary.

(3) Amendment by a Conference:

(a) Upon the request of a Party, concurred in by at least one-third of the Parties, the Organization shall convene a Conference of Parties to the Convention to consider amendments to the present Convention.

(b) Every amendment adopted by such a Conference by a two-thirds majority of those present and voting of the Parties shall be communicated by the Secretary–General of the Organization to all Contracting Parties for their acceptance.

(c) Unless the Conference decides otherwise, the amendment shall be deemed to have been accepted and to have entered into force in accordance with the procedures specified for that purpose in paragraph (2)(f) and (g) above.

(4)(a) In the case of an amendment to an Optional Annex, a reference in the present Article to a "Party to the Convention" shall be deemed to mean a reference to a Party bound by that Annex.

(b) Any Party which has declined to accept an amendment to an Annex shall be treated as a non-Party only for the purpose of application of that amendment.

(5) The adoption and entry into force of a new Annex shall be subject to the same procedures as for the adoption and entry into force of an amendment to an Article of the Convention.

(6) Unless expressly provided otherwise, any amendment to the present Convention made under this Article, which relates to the structure of a ship, shall apply only to ships for which the building contract is placed, or in the absence of a building contract, the keel of which is laid, on or after the date on which the amendment comes into force.

(7) Any amendment to a Protocol or to an Annex shall relate to the substance of that Protocol or Annex and shall be consistent with the Articles of the present Convention.

(8) The Secretary–General of the Organization shall inform all Parties of any amendments which enter into force under the present Article, together with the date on which each such amendment enters into force.

(9) Any declaration of acceptance or of objection to an amendment under the present article shall be notified in writing to the Secretary–General of the Organization. The latter shall bring such notification and the date of its receipt to the notice of the Parties to the Convention.

ARTICLE 17

Promotion of Technical Co-operation

The Parties to the Convention shall promote, in consultation with the Organization and other international bodies, with assistance and co-ordination by the Executive Director of the United Nations Environment Programme, support for those Parties which request technical assistance for:

(a) the training of scientific and technical personnel;

(b) the supply of necessary equipment and facilities for reception and monitoring;

(c) the facilitation of other measures and arrangements to prevent or mitigate pollution of the marine environment by ships; and

(d) the encouragement of research;

preferably within the countries concerned, so furthering the aims and purposes of the present Convention.

ARTICLE 18

Denunciation

(1) The present Convention or any Optional Annex may be denounced by any Parties to the Convention at any time after the expiry of five years from the date on which the Convention or such Annex enters into force for that Party.

(2) Denunciation shall be effected by notification in writing to the Secretary–General of the Organization who shall inform all the other Parties of any such notification received and of the date of its receipt as well as the date on which such denunciation takes effect.

(3) A denunciation shall take effect twelve months after receipt of the notification of denunciation by the Secretary–General of the Organization or after the expiry of any other longer period which may be indicated in the notification.

ARTICLE 19

Deposit and Registration

(1) The present Convention shall be deposited with the Secretary–General of the Organization who shall transmit certified true copies thereof to all States which have signed the present Convention or acceded to it.

(2) As soon as the present Convention enters into force, the text shall be transmitted by the Secretary–General of the Organization to the Secretary–General of the United Nations for registration and publication, in accordance with Article 102 of the Charter of the United Nations.

ARTICLE 20

Languages

The present Convention is established in a single copy in the English, French, Russian and Spanish languages, each text being equally authentic. Official translations in the Arabic, German, Italian and Japanese languages shall be prepared and deposited with the signed original.

Protocol I

Provisions Concerning Reports on Incidents Involving Harmful Substances (in accordance with Article 8 of the Convention)

* * *

Protocol II

Arbitration *(in accordance with Article 10 of the Convention)*

* * *

Annex I of MARPOL 73/78 (including amendments):

Regulations For the Prevention of Pollution By Oil

CHAPTER I—GENERAL

Regulation 1

Definitions

For the purposes of this Annex:

(1) "Oil" means petroleum in any form including crude oil, fuel oil, sludge, oil refuse and refined products (other than petrochemicals which are subject to the provisions of Annex II of the present Convention) and, without limiting the generality of the foregoing, includes the substances listed in Appendix I to this Annex.

(2) "Oily mixture" means a mixture with any oil content.

(3) "Oil fuel" means any oil used as fuel in connection with the propulsion and auxiliary machinery of the ship in which such oil is carried.

(4) "Oil tanker" means a ship constructed or adapted primarily to carry oil in bulk in its cargo spaces and includes combination carriers and any "chemical tanker" as defined in Annex II of the present Convention when it is carrying a cargo or part cargo of oil in bulk.

(5) "Combination carrier" means a ship designed to carry either oil or solid cargoes in bulk.

(6) "New ship" means a ship:

(a) for which the building contract is placed after 31 December 1975; or

(b) in the absence of a building contract, the keel of which is laid or which is at a similar stage of construction after 30 June 1976; or

(c) the delivery of which is after 31 December 1979; or

(d) which has undergone a major conversion:

(i) for which the contract is placed after 31 December 1975; or

(ii) in the absence of a contract, the construction work of which is begun after 30 June 1976; or

(iii) which is completed after 31 December 1979.

(7) "Existing ship" means a ship which is not a new ship.

(8)(a) "Major conversion" means a conversion of an existing ship:

(i) which substantially alters the dimensions or carrying capacity of the ship; or

(ii) which changes the type of the ship; or

(iii) the intent of which in the opinion of the Administration is substantially to prolong its life; or

(iv) which otherwise so alters the ship that, if it were a new ship, it would become subject to relevant provisions of the present Convention not applicable to it as an existing ship.

(b) Notwithstanding the provisions of sub-paragraph (a) of this paragraph, conversion of an existing oil tanker of 20,000 tons deadweight and above to meet the requirements of Regulation 13 of this Annex shall not be deemed to constitute a major conversion for the purposes of this Annex.

(9) "Nearest land". The term "from the nearest land" means from the baseline from which the territorial sea of the territory in question is established in accordance with international law, except that, for the purposes of the present Convention "from the nearest land" off the north eastern coast of Australia shall mean from a line drawn from a point on the coast of Australia in

latitude 11°00′ South, longitude 142°08′ East to a point in latitude 10°35′ South,

longitude 141°55′ East, thence to a point latitude 10°00′ South,

longitude 142°00′ East, thence to a point latitude 9°10′ South,

longitude 143°52′ East, thence to a point latitude 9°00′ South,

longitude 144°30′ East, thence to a point latitude 13°00′ South,

longitude 144°00′ East, thence to a point latitude 15°00′ South,

longitude 146°00′ East, thence to a point latitude 18°00′ South,

longitude 147°00′ East, thence to a point latitude 21°00′ South,

longitude 153°00′ East, thence to a point on the coast of Australia in latitude 24°42′ South, longitude 153°15′ East.

(10) "Special area" means a sea area where for recognized technical reasons in relation to its oceanographical and ecological condition and to the particular character of its traffic the adoption of special mandatory methods for the prevention of sea pollution by oil is required. Special areas shall include those listed in Regulation 10 of this Annex.

(11) "Instantaneous rate of discharge of oil content" means the rate of discharge of oil in litres per hour at any instant divided by the speed of the ship in knots at the same instant.

(12) "Tank" means an enclosed space which is formed by the permanent structure of a ship and which is designed for the carriage of liquid in bulk.

(13) "Wing tank" means any tank adjacent to the side shell plating.

(14) "Centre tank" means any tank inboard of a longitudinal bulkhead.

(15) "Slop tank" means a tank specifically designated for the collection of tank drainings, tank washings and other oily mixtures.

(16) "Clean ballast" means the ballast in a tank which since oil was last carried therein, has been so cleaned that effluent therefrom if it were discharged from a ship which is stationary into clean calm water on a clear day would not produce visible traces of oil on the surface of the water or on adjoining shorelines or cause a sludge or emulsion to be deposited beneath the surface of the water or upon adjoining shorelines. If the ballast is discharged through an oil discharge monitoring and control system approved by the Administration, evidence based on such a system to the effect that the oil content of the effluent did not exceed 15 parts per million shall be determinative that the ballast was clean, notwithstanding the presence of visible traces.

(17) "Segregated ballast" means the ballast water introduced into a tank which is completely separated from the cargo oil and oil fuel system and which is permanently allocated to the carriage of ballast or to the carriage of ballast or cargoes other than oil or noxious substances as variously defined in the Annexes of the present Convention.

* * *

(26) Notwithstanding the provisions of paragraph (6) of this Regulation, for the purposes of Regulations 13, 13B, 13E and 18(4) of this Annex, "new oil tanker" means an oil tanker:

(a) for which the building contract is placed after 1 June 1979; or

(b) in the absence of a building contract, the keel of which is laid or which is at a similar stage of construction after 1 January 1980; or

(c) the delivery of which is after 1 June 1982; or

(d) which has undergone a major conversion:

(i) for which the contract is placed after 1 June 1979; or

(ii) in the absence of a contract, the construction work of which is begun after 1 January 1980; or

(iii) which is completed after 1 June 1982;

except that, for oil tankers of 70,000 tons deadweight and above, the definition in paragraph (6) of this Regulation shall apply for the purposes of Regulation 13(1) of this Annex.

(27) Notwithstanding the provisions of paragraph (7) of this Regulation, for the purposes of Regulations 13, 13A, 13B, 13C, 13D, 18(5) and 18(6)(c) of this Annex, "existing oil tanker" means an oil tanker which is not a new oil tanker as defined in paragraph (26) of this Regulation.

(28) "Crude oil" means any liquid hydrocarbon mixture occurring naturally in the earth whether or not treated to render it suitable for transportation and includes:

(a) crude oil from which certain distillate fractions may have been removed; and

(b) crude oil to which certain distillate fractions may have been added.

(29) "Crude oil tanker" means an oil tanker engaged in the trade of carrying crude oil.

(30) "Product carrier" means an oil tanker engaged in the trade of carrying oil other than crude oil.

Regulation 2

Application

(1) Unless expressly provided otherwise, the provisions of this Annex shall apply to all ships.

(2) In ships other than oil tankers fitted with cargo spaces which are constructed and utilized to carry oil in bulk of an aggregate capacity of 200 cubic metres or more, the requirements of Regulations 9, 10, 14, 15(1), (2) and (3), 18, 20 and 24(4) of this Annex for oil tankers shall also apply to the construction and operation of those spaces, except that where such aggregate capacity is less than 1,000 cubic metres the requirements of Regulation 15(4) of this Annex may apply in lieu of Regulation 15(1), (2) and (3).

(3) Where a cargo subject to the provisions of Annex II of the present Convention is carried in a cargo space of an oil tanker, the appropriate requirements of Annex II of the present Convention shall also apply.

(4)(a) Any hydrofoil, air-cushion vehicle and other new type of vessel (near-surface craft, submarine craft, etc.) whose constructional features are such as to render the application of any of the provisions of Chapters II and III of this Annex relating to construction and equipment unreasonable or impracticable may be exempted by the Administration from such provisions, provided that the construction and equipment of that ship provides equivalent protection against pollution by oil, having regard to the service for which it is intended.

(b) Particulars of any such exemption granted by the Administration shall be indicated in the Certificate referred to in Regulation 5 of this Annex.

(c) The Administration which allows any such exemption shall, as soon as possible, but not more than ninety days thereafter, communicate to the Organization particulars of same and the reasons, therefor, which the Organization shall circulate to the Parties to the Convention for their information and appropriate action, if any.

Regulation 3

Equivalents

(1) The Administration may allow any fitting, material, appliance or apparatus to be fitted in a ship as an alternative to that required by this Annex if such fitting, material, appliance or apparatus is at least as effective as that required by this Annex. This authority of the Administration shall not extend to substitution of operational methods to effect the control of discharge of oil as equivalent to those design and construction features which are prescribed by Regulations in this Annex.

(2) The Administration which allows a fitting, material, appliance or apparatus, as an alternative to that required by this Annex shall communicate to the Organization for circulation to the Parties to the Convention particulars thereof, for their information and appropriate action, if any.

Regulation 4

Surveys and Inspections

(1) Every oil tanker of 150 tons gross tonnage and above, and every other ship of 400 tons gross tonnage and above shall be subject to the surveys specified below:

(a) An initial survey before the ship is put in service or before the Certificate required under Regulation 5 of this Annex is issued for the first time, which shall include a complete survey of its structure, equipment, systems, fittings, arrangements and material in so far as the ship is covered by this Annex. This survey shall be such as to ensure that the structure, equipment, systems, fittings, arrangements and material fully comply with the applicable requirements of this Annex.

(b) Periodical surveys at intervals specified by the Administration, but not exceeding five years, which shall be such as to ensure that the structure, equipment, systems, fittings, arrangements and material fully comply with the requirements of this Annex.

(c) A minimum of one intermediate survey during the period of validity of the Certificate which shall be such as to ensure that the equipment and associated pump and piping systems, including oil discharge monitoring and control systems, crude oil washing systems, oily-water separating equipment and oil filtering systems, fully comply with the applicable requirements of this Annex and are in good working order. In cases where only one such intermediate survey is carried out in any one Certificate validity period, it shall be held not before six months prior to, nor later than six months after the half-way date of the Certificate's period of validity. Such intermediate surveys shall be endorsed on the Certificate issued under Regulation 5 of this Annex.

(2) The Administration shall establish appropriate measures for ships which are not subject to the provisions of paragraph (1) of this Regulation in order to ensure that the applicable provisions of this Annex are complied with.

(3)(a) Surveys of ships as regards the enforcement of the provisions of this Annex shall be carried out by officers of the Administration. The Administration may, however, entrust the surveys either to surveyors nominated for the purpose or to organizations recognized by it.

(b) The Administration shall institute arrangements for unscheduled inspections to be carried out during the period of validity of the Certificate. Such inspections shall ensure that the ship and its equipment remain in all respects satisfactory for the service for which the ship is intended. These inspections may be carried out by their own inspection services, or by nominated surveyors or by recognized organizations, or by other Parties upon request of the Administration. Where the Administration, under the provisions of paragraph (1) of this Regulation, establishes mandatory annual surveys, the above unscheduled inspections shall not be obligatory.

(c) An Administration nominating surveyors or recognizing organizations to conduct surveys and inspections as set forth in sub-paragraphs (a) and (b) of this paragraph, shall as a minimum empower any nominated surveyor or recognized organization to:

(i) require repairs to a ship; and

(ii) carry out surveys and inspections if requested by the appropriate authorities of a Port State.

The Administration shall notify the Organization of the specific responsibilities and conditions of the authority delegated to the nominated surveyors or recognized organizations, for circulation to Parties to the present Protocol for the information of their officers.

(d) When a nominated surveyor or recognized organization determines that the condition of the ship or its equipment does not correspond substantially with the particulars of the Certificate or is such that the ship is not fit to proceed to sea without presenting an unreasonable threat of harm to the marine environment, such surveyor or organization shall immediately ensure that corrective action is taken and shall in due course notify the Administration. If such corrective action is not taken the Certificate should be withdrawn and the Administration shall be notified immediately; and if the ship is in a port of another Party, the appropriate authorities of the Port State shall also be notified immediately. When an officer of the Administration, a nominated surveyor or recognized organization has notified the appropriate authorities of the Port State, the Government of the Port State concerned shall give such officer, surveyor or organization any necessary assistance to carry out their obligations under this Regulation. When applicable, the Government of the Port State concerned shall take such steps as will ensure that the ship shall not sail until it can proceed to sea or leave the port for the purpose of proceeding to the nearest appropriate repair yard available without presenting an unreasonable threat of harm to the marine environment.

(e) In every case, the Administration concerned shall fully guarantee the completeness and efficiency of the survey and inspection and shall undertake to ensure the necessary arrangements to satisfy this obligation.

(4)(a) The condition of the ship and its equipment shall be maintained to conform with the provisions of the present Convention to ensure that the ship in all respects will remain fit to proceed to sea without presenting an unreasonable threat of harm to the marine environment.

(b) After any survey of the ship under paragraph (1) of this Regulation has been completed, no change shall be made in the structure, equipment, systems, fittings, arrangements or material covered by the survey, without the sanction of the Administration, except the direct replacement of such equipment and fittings.

(c) Whenever an accident occurs to a ship or a defect is discovered which substantially affects the integrity of the ship or the efficiency or completeness of its equipment covered by this Annex the master or owner of the ship shall report at the earliest opportunity to the Administration, the recognized organization or the nominated surveyor responsible for issuing the relevant Certificate, who shall cause investigations to be initiated to determine whether a survey as required by paragraph (1) of this Regulation is necessary. If the ship is in a port of another Party, the master or owner shall also report immediately to the appropriate authorities of the Port State and the nominated surveyor or recognized organization shall ascertain that such report has been made.

Regulation 5

Issue of Certificate

(1) An International Oil Pollution Prevention Certificate shall be issued, after survey in accordance with the provisions of Regulation 4 of this Annex, to any oil tanker of 150 tons gross tonnage and above and any other ships of 400 tons gross tonnage and above which are engaged in voyages to ports or off-shore terminals under the jurisdiction of other Parties to the Convention. In the case of existing ships this requirement shall apply twelve months after the date of entry into force of the present Convention.

(2) Such Certificate shall be issued either by the Administration or by any persons or organization duly authorized by it. In every case the Administration assumes full responsibility for the Certificate.

Regulation 6

Issue of a Certificate by another Government

(1) The Government of a Party to the Convention may, at the request of the Administration, cause a ship to be surveyed and, if satisfied that the provisions of this Annex are complied with, shall issue or authorize the issue of an International Oil Pollution Prevention Certificate to the ship in accordance with this Annex.

(2) A copy of the Certificate and a copy of the survey report shall be transmitted as soon as possible to the requesting Administration.

(3) A Certificate so issued shall contain a statement to the effect that it has been issued at the request of the Administration and it shall have the same force and receive the same recognition as the Certificate issued under Regulation 5 of this Annex.

(4) No International Oil Pollution Prevention Certificate shall be issued to a ship which is entitled to fly the flag of a State which is not a Party.

Regulation 7

Form of Certificate

The International Oil Pollution Prevention Certificate shall be drawn up in an official language of the issuing country in the form corresponding to the model given in Appendix II to this Annex. If the language used is neither English nor French, the text shall include a translation into one of these languages.

Regulation 8

Duration of Certificate

(1) An International Oil Pollution Prevention Certificate shall be issued for a period specified by the Administration, which shall not exceed five years from the date of issue, provided that in the case of an oil tanker operating with dedicated clean

ballast tanks for a limited period specified in Regulation 13(9) of this Annex, the period of validity of the Certificate shall not exceed such specified period.

(2) A Certificate shall cease to be valid if significant alterations have taken place in the construction, equipment, systems, fittings, arrangements or material required without the sanction of the Administration, except the direct replacement of such equipment or fittings, or if intermediate surveys as specified by the Administration under Regulation 4(1)(c) of this Annex are not carried out.

(3) A Certificate issued to a ship shall also cease to be valid upon transfer of the ship to the flag of another State. A new Certificate shall only be issued when the Government issuing the new Certificate is fully satisfied that the ship is in full compliance with the requirements of Regulation 4(4)(a) and (b) of this Annex. In the case of a transfer between Parties, if requested within three months after the transfer has taken place, the Government of the Party whose flag the ship was formerly entitled to fly shall transmit as soon as possible to the Administration a copy of the Certificate carried by the ship before the transfer and, if available, a copy of the relevant survey report.

CHAPTER II—REQUIREMENTS FOR CONTROL OF OPERATIONAL POLLUTION

Regulation 9

Control of Discharge of Oil

(1) Subject to the provisions of Regulations 10 and 11 of this Annex and paragraph (2) of this Regulation, any discharge into the sea of oil or oily mixtures from ships to which this Annex applies shall be prohibited except when all the following conditions are satisfied:

(a) for an oil tanker, except as provided for in sub-paragraph (b) of this paragraph:

(i) the tanker is not within a special area;

(ii) the tanker is more than 50 nautical miles from the nearest land;

(iii) the tanker is proceeding en route;

(iv) the instantaneous rate of discharge of oil content does not exceed 30 litres per nautical mile;

(v) the total quantity of oil discharged into the sea does not exceed for existing tankers 1/15,000 of the total quantity of the particular cargo of which the residue formed a part, and for new tankers 1/30,000 of the total quantity of the particular cargo of which the residue formed a part; and

(vi) the tanker has in operation an oil discharge monitoring and control system and a slop tank arrangement as required by Regulation 15 of this Annex.

(b) from a ship of 400 tons gross tonnage and above other than an oil tanker and from machinery space bilges excluding cargo pump room bilges of an oil tanker unless mixed with oil cargo residue:

(i) the ship is not within a special area;

(ii) the ship is the ship is proceeding en route;

(iii) the oil content of the effluent without dilution does not exceed 15 parts per million; and

(iv) the ship has in operation equipment as required by regulation 16 of this Annex;

(2) In the case of a ship of less than 400 tons gross tonnage other than an oil tanker whilst outside the special area, the Administration shall ensure that it is equipped as far as practicable and reasonable with installations to ensure the storage of oil residues on board and their discharge to reception facilities or into the sea in compliance with the requirements of paragraph (1)(b) of this Regulation.

(3) Whenever visible traces of oil are observed on or below the surface of the water in the immediate vicinity of a ship or its wake, Governments of Parties to the Convention should, to the extent they are reasonably able to do so, promptly investigate the facts bearing on the issue of whether there has been a violation of the provisions of this Regulation or Regulation 10 of this Annex. The investigation should include, in particular, the wind and sea conditions, the track and speed of the ship, other possible sources of the visible traces in the vicinity, and any relevant oil discharge records.

(4) The provisions of paragraph (1) of this Regulation shall not apply to the discharge of clean or segregated ballast or unprocessed oily mixtures which without dilution have an oil content not exceeding 15 parts per million and which do not originate from cargo pump-room bilges and are not mixed with oil cargo residues.

(5) No discharge into the sea shall contain chemicals or other substances in quantities or concentrations which are hazardous to the marine environment or chemicals or other substances introduced for the purpose of circumventing the conditions of discharge specified in this Regulation.

(6) The oil residues which cannot be discharged into the sea in compliance with paragraphs (1), (2) and (4) of this Regulation shall be retained on board or discharged to reception facilities.

(7) In the case of a ship, referred to in regulation 16(6) of this Annex, not fitted with equipment as required by regulation 16(1) or 16(2) of this Annex, the provisions of paragraph 1(b) of this regulation will not apply until 6 July 1998 or the date on which the ship is fitted with such equipment, whichever is the earlier. Until this date any discharge from machinery space bilges into the sea of oil or oily mixtures from such a ship shall be prohibited except when all the following conditions are satisfied:

(a) the oily mixture does not originate from the cargo pump-room bilges;

(b) the oily mixture is not mixed with oil cargo residues;

(c) the ship is not within a special area;

(d) the ship is more than 12 nautical miles from the nearest land;

(e) the ship is proceeding en route;

(f) the oil content of the effluent is less than 100 parts per million; and

(g) the ship has in operation oily-water separating equipment of a design approved by the Administration, taking into account the specification recommended by the Organization.

Regulation 10

Methods for the Prevention of Oil Pollution from Ships while operating in Special Areas

(1) For the purposes of this Annex, the special areas are the Mediterranean Sea area, the Baltic Sea area, the Black Sea area, the Red Sea area, the "Gulfs area", the Gulf of Aden and the Antarctic area, which are defined as follows:

(a) The Mediterranean Sea area means the Mediterranean Sea proper including the gulfs and seas therein with the boundary between the Mediterranean and the Black Sea constituted by the 41°N parallel and bounded to the west by the Straits of Gibraltar at the meridian of 5°3652CW.

(b) The Baltic Sea area means the Baltic Sea proper with the Gulf of Bothnia, the Gulf of Finland and the entrance to the Baltic Sea bounded by the parallel of the Skaw in the Skagerrak at 57°44.8′N.

(c) The Black Sea area means the Black Sea proper with the boundary between the Mediterranean and the Black Sea constituted by the parallel 41°N.

(d) The Red Sea area means the Red Sea proper including the Gulfs of Suez and Aqaba bounded at the south by the rhumb line between Ras si Ane (12°8.5′N, 43°19.6′E) and Husn Murad (12°40.4′N, 43°30.2′E).

(e) The Gulfs area means the sea area located north west of the rhumb line between Ras al Hadd (22°30′N, 59°48′E) and Ras Al Fasteh (25°04′N, 61°25′E).

(f) The Antarctic area means the sea area south of 60° S.

(2) Subject to the provisions of Regulation 11 of this Annex:

(a) Any discharge into the sea of oil or oily mixture from any oil tanker, or any ship of 400 tons gross tonnage and above other than an oil tanker, shall be prohibited, while in a special area. In respect of the Antarctic area, any discharge into the sea of oil or oily mixture from any ship shall be prohibited.

(b) Except as provided for in respect of the Antarctic area under paragraph 2(a) of this Regulation, any discharge into the sea of oil or oily mixture from a ship of less than 400 tons gross tonnage, other than an oil tanker, shall be prohibited while in a special area.

(3) (a) The provisions of paragraph (2) of this Regulation shall not apply to the discharge of clean or segregated ballast.

(b) The provisions of sub-paragraph (2)(a) of this Regulation shall not apply to the discharge of processed bilge water from machinery spaces, provided that all of the following conditions are satisfied:

(i) the bilge water does not originate from cargo pump room bilges;

(ii) the bilge water is not mixed with oil cargo residues;

(iii) the ship is proceeding en route;

(iv) the oil content of the effluent without dilution does not exceed 15 parts per million;

(v) the ship has in operation oil filtering equipment complying with Regulation 16(5) of this Annex; and

(vi) the filtering system is equipped with a stopping device which will ensure that the discharge is automatically stopped when the oil content of the effluent exceeds 15 parts per million.

(4)(a) No discharge into the sea shall contain chemicals or other substances in quantities or concentrations which are hazardous to the marine environment or chemicals or other substances introduced for the purpose of circumventing the conditions of discharge specified in this Regulation.

(b) The oil residues which cannot be discharged into the sea in compliance with paragraph (2) or (3) of this Regulation shall be retained on board or discharged to reception facilities.

(5) Nothing in this Regulation shall prohibit a ship on a voyage only part of which is in a special area from discharging outside the special area in accordance with Regulation 9 of this Annex.

(6) Whenever visible traces of oil are observed on or below the surface of the water in the immediate vicinity of a ship or its wake, the Governments of Parties to the Convention should, to the extent they are reasonably able to do so, promptly

investigate the facts bearing on the issue of whether there has been a violation of the provisions of this Regulation or Regulation 9 of this Annex. The investigation should include, in particular, the wind and sea conditions, the track and speed of the ship, other possible sources of the visible traces in the vicinity, and any relevant oil discharge records.

(7) Reception facilities within special areas:

(a) Mediterranean Sea, Black Sea and Baltic Sea areas:

(i) The Government of each Party to the Convention, the coastline of which borders on any given special area undertakes to ensure that not later than 1 January 1977 all oil loading terminals and repair ports within the special area are provided with facilities adequate for the reception and treatment of all the dirty ballast and tank washing water from oil tankers. In addition all ports within the special area shall be provided with adequate reception facilities for other residues and oily mixtures from all ships. Such facilities shall have adequate capacity to meet the needs of the ships using them without causing undue delay.

(ii) The Government of each Party having under its jurisdiction entrances to seawater courses with low depth contour which might require a reduction of draught by the discharge of ballast undertakes to ensure the provision of the facilities referred to in sub-paragraph (a)(i) of this paragraph but with the proviso that ships required to discharge slops or dirty ballast could be subject to some delay.

(iii) During the period between the entry into force of the present Convention (if earlier than 1 January 1977) and 1 January 1977 ships while navigating in the special areas shall comply with the requirements of Regulation 9 of this Annex. However, the Governments of Parties the coastlines of which border any of the special areas under this sub-paragraph may establish a date earlier than 1 January 1977, but after the date of entry into force of the present Convention, from which the requirements of this Regulation in respect of the special areas in question shall take effect:

(1) if all the reception facilities required have been provided by the date so established; and

(2) provided that the Parties concerned notify the Organization of the date so established at least six months in advance, for circulation to other Parties.

(iv) After 1 January 1977, or the date established in accordance with sub-paragraph (a)(iii) of this paragraph if earlier, each Party shall notify the Organization for transmission to the Contracting Governments concerned of all cases where the facilities are alleged to be inadequate.

(b) Red Sea area, Gulfs area and Gulf of Arden area:

(i) The Government of each Party the coastline of which borders on the special areas undertakes to ensure that as soon as possible all oil loading terminals and repair ports within these special areas are provided with facilities adequate for the reception and treatment of all the dirty ballast and tank washing water from tankers. In addition all ports within the special area shall be provided with adequate reception facilities for other residues and oily mixtures from all ships. Such facilities shall have adequate capacity to meet the needs of the ships using them without causing undue delay.

(ii) The Government of each Party having under its jurisdiction entrances to seawater courses with low depth contour which might require a reduction of draught by the discharge of ballast shall undertake to ensure the provision of the facilities referred to in sub-paragraph (b)(i) of this paragraph but with the proviso that ships required to discharge slops or dirty ballast could be subject to some delay.

(iii) Each Party concerned shall notify the Organization of the measures taken pursuant to provisions of sub-paragraph (b)(i) and (ii) of this paragraph. Upon receipt of sufficient notifications the Organization shall establish a date from which the requirements of this Regulation in respect of the area in question shall take effect. The Organization shall notify all Parties of the date so established no less than twelve months in advance of that date.

(iv) During the period between the entry into force of the present Convention and the date so established, ships while navigating in the special area shall comply with the requirements of Regulation 9 of this Annex.

(v) After such date oil tankers loading in ports in these special areas where such facilities are not yet available shall also fully comply with the requirements of this Regulation. However, oil tankers entering these special areas for the purpose of loading shall make every effort to enter the area with only clean ballast on board.

(vi) After the date on which the requirements for the special area in question take effect, each Party shall notify the Organization for transmission to the Parties concerned of all cases where the facilities are alleged to be inadequate.

(vii) At least the reception facilities as prescribed in Regulation 12 of this Annex shall be provided by 1 January 1977 or one year after the date of entry into force of the present Convention, whichever occurs later.

(8) Notwithstanding paragraph (7) of this Regulation, the following rules apply to the Antarctic area:

(a) The Government of each Party to the Convention whose ports are used by ships departing en route to or arrive from the Antarctic area undertakes to ensure that as soon as practicable adequate facilities are provided for the reception of all sludge, dirty ballast, tank washing water, and other oily residues and mixtures from all ships, without causing undue delay, and according to the needs of the ships using them.

(b) The Government of each Party to the Convention shall ensure that all ships entitled to fly its flag, before entering the Antarctic area, are fitted with a tank or tanks of sufficient capacity on board for the retention of all sludge, dirty ballast, tank washing water and other oily residues and mixtures while operating in the area and have concluded arrangements to discharge such oily residues at a reception facility after leaving the area.

Regulation 11

Exceptions

Regulations 9 and 10 of this Annex shall not apply to:

(a) the discharge into the sea of oil or oily mixture necessary for the purpose of securing the safety of a ship or saving life at sea; or

(b) the discharge into the sea of oil or oily mixture resulting from damage to a ship or its equipment:

(i) provided that all reasonable precautions have been taken after the occurrence of the damage or discovery of the discharge for the purpose of preventing or minimizing the discharge; and

(ii) except if the owner or the Master acted either with intent to cause damage, or recklessly and with knowledge that damage would probably result; or

(c) the discharge into the sea of substances containing oil, approved by the Administration, when being used for the purpose of combating specific pollution incidents in order to minimize the damage from pollution. Any such discharge shall be subject to the approval of any Government in whose jurisdiction it is contemplated the discharge will occur.

Regulation 12

Reception Facilities

(1) Subject to the provisions of Regulation 10 of this Annex, the Government of each Party undertakes to ensure the provision at oil loading terminals, repair ports, and in other ports in which ships have oily residues to discharge, of facilities for the reception of such residues and oily mixtures as remain from oil tankers and other ships adequate to meet the needs of the ships using them without causing undue delay to ships.

(2) Reception facilities in accordance with paragraph (1) of this Regulation shall be provided in:

(a) all ports and terminals in which crude oil is loaded into oil tankers where such tankers have immediately prior to arrival completed a ballast voyage of not more than 72 hours or not more than 1,200 nautical miles;

(b) all ports and terminals in which oil other than crude oil in bulk is loaded at an average quantity of more than 1,000 metric tons per day;

(c) all ports having ship repair yards or tank cleaning facilities;

(d) all ports and terminals which handle ships provided with the sludge tank(s) required by Regulation 17 of this Annex;

(e) all ports in respect of oily bilge waters and other residues, which cannot be discharged in accordance with Regulation 9 of this Annex; and

(f) all loading ports for bulk cargoes in respect of oil residues from combination carriers which cannot be discharged in accordance with Regulation 9 of this Annex.

(3) The capacity for the reception facilities shall be as follows:

(a) Crude oil loading terminals shall have sufficient reception facilities to receive oil and oily mixtures which cannot be discharged in accordance with the provisions of Regulation 9(1)(a) of this Annex from all oil tankers on voyages as described in paragraph (2)(a) of this Regulation.

(b) Loading ports and terminals referred to in paragraph (2)(b) of this Regulation shall have sufficient reception facilities to receive oil and oily mixtures which cannot be discharged in accordance with the provisions of Regulation 9(1)(a) of this Annex from oil tankers which load oil other than crude oil in bulk.

(c) All ports having ship repair yards or tank cleaning facilities shall have sufficient reception facilities to receive all residues and oily mixtures which remain on board for disposal from ships prior to entering such yards or facilities.

(d) All facilities provided in ports and terminals under paragraph (2)(d) of this Regulation shall be sufficient to receive all residues retained according to Regulation 17 of this Annex from all ships that may reasonably be expected to call at such ports and terminals.

(e) All facilities provided in ports and terminals under this Regulation shall be sufficient to receive only bilge waters and other residues which cannot be discharged in accordance with Regulation 9 of this Annex.

(f) The facilities provided in loading ports for bulk cargoes shall take into account the special problems of combination carriers as appropriate.

(4) The reception facilities prescribed in paragraphs (2) and (3) of this Regulation shall be made available no later than one year from the date of entry into force of the present Convention or by 1 January 1977, whichever occurs later.

(5) Each Party shall notify the Organization for transmission to the Parties concerned of all cases where the facilities provided under this Regulation are alleged to be inadequate.

Regulation 13

Segregated Ballast Tanks, Dedicated Clean Ballast Tanks and Crude Oil Washing

Subject to the provisions of Regulations 13C and 13D of this Annex, oil tankers shall comply with the requirements of this Regulation.

New oil tankers of 20,000 tons deadweight and above

(1) Every new crude oil tanker of 20,000 tons deadweight and above and every new product carrier of 30,000 tons deadweight and above shall be provided with segregated ballast tanks and shall comply with paragraphs (2), (3) and (4), or paragraph (5) as appropriate, of this Regulation.

(2) The capacity of the segregated ballast tanks shall be so determined that the ship may operate safely on ballast voyages without recourse to the use of cargo tanks for water ballast except as provided for in paragraph (3) or (4) of this Regulation.

* * *

(3) In no case shall ballast water be carried in cargo tanks, except:

(a) on those rare voyages when weather conditions are so severe that, in the opinion of the master, it is necessary to carry additional ballast water in cargo tanks for the safety of the ship;

(b) in exceptional cases where the particular character of the operation of an oil tanker renders it necessary to carry ballast water in excess of the quantity required under paragraph (2) of this Regulation, provided that such operation of the oil tanker falls under the category of exceptional cases as established by the Organization.

Such additional ballast water shall be processed and discharged in compliance with Regulation 9 of this Annex and in accordance with the requirements of Regulation 15 of this Annex and an entry shall be made in the Oil Record Book referred to in Regulation 20 of this Annex.

(4) In the case of new crude oil tankers, the additional ballast permitted in paragraph (3) of this Regulation shall be carried in cargo tanks only if such tanks have been crude oil washed in accordance with Regulation 13B of this Annex before departure from an oil unloading port or terminal.

(5) Notwithstanding the provisions of paragraph (2) of this Regulation, the segregated ballast conditions for oil tankers less than 150 metres in length shall be to the satisfaction of the Administration.

(6) Every new crude oil tanker of 20,000 tons deadweight and above shall be fitted with a cargo tank cleaning system using crude oil washing. The Administration shall undertake to ensure that the system fully complies with the requirements of Regulation 13B of this Annex within one year after the tanker was first engaged in the trade

of carrying crude oil or by the end of the third voyage carrying crude oil suitable for crude oil washing, whichever occurs later. Unless such oil tanker carries crude oil which is not suitable for crude oil washing, the oil tanker shall operate the system in accordance with the requirements of that Regulation.

Existing crude oil tankers of 40,000 tons deadweight and above

(7) Subject to the provisions of paragraphs (8) and (9) of this Regulation every existing crude oil tanker of 40,000 tons deadweight and above shall be provided with segregated ballast tanks and shall comply with the requirements of paragraphs (2) and (3) of this Regulation from the date of entry into force of the present Convention.

(8) Existing crude oil tankers referred to in paragraph (7) of this Regulation may, in lieu of being provided with segregated ballast tanks, operate with a cargo tank cleaning procedure using crude oil washing in accordance with Regulation 13B of this Annex unless the crude oil tanker is intended to carry crude oil which is not suitable for crude oil washing.

(9) Existing crude oil tankers referred to in paragraph (7) or (8) of this Regulation may, in lieu of being provided with segregated ballast tanks or operating with a cargo tank cleaning procedure using crude oil washing, operate with dedicated clean ballast tanks in accordance with the provisions of Regulation 13A of this Annex for the following period:

(a) for crude oil tankers of 70,000 tons deadweight and above, until two years after the date of entry into force of the present Convention; and

(b) for crude oil tankers of 40,000 tons deadweight and above but below 70,000 tons deadweight, until four years after the date of entry into force of the present Convention.

Existing product carriers of 40,000 tons deadweight and above

(10) From the date of entry into force of the present Convention, every existing product carrier of 40,000 tons deadweight and above shall be provided with segregated ballast tanks and shall comply with the requirements of paragraphs (2) and (3) of this Regulation, or, alternatively, operate with dedicated clean ballast tanks in accordance with the provisions of Regulation 13A of this Annex.

An oil tanker qualified as a segregated ballast oil tanker

(11) Any oil tanker which is not required to be provided with segregated ballast tanks in accordance with paragraph (1), (7) or (10) of this Regulation may, however, be qualified as a segregated ballast tanker, provided that it complies with the requirements of paragraphs (2) and (3), or paragraph (5) as appropriate, of this Regulation.

Regulation 13A

Requirements for Oil Tankers with Dedicated Clean Ballast Tanks

(1) An oil tanker operating with dedicated clean ballast tanks in accordance with the provisions of Regulation 13(9) or (10) of this Annex, shall have adequate tank capacity, dedicated solely to the carriage of clean ballast as defined in Regulation 1(16) of this Annex, to meet the requirements of Regulation 13(2) and (3) of this Annex.

(2) The arrangements and operational procedures for dedicated clean ballast tanks shall comply with the requirements established by the Administration. Such requirements shall contain at least all the provisions of the Specifications for Oil Tankers with Dedicated Clean Ballast Tanks adopted by the International Conference on Tanker Safety and Pollution Prevention, 1978, in Resolution 14 and as may be revised by the Organization.

(3) An oil tanker operating with dedicated clean ballast tanks shall be equipped with an oil content meter, approved by the Administration on the basis of specifica-

tions recommended by the Organization, to enable supervision of the oil content in ballast water being discharged. The oil content meter shall be installed no later than at the first scheduled shipyard visit of the tanker following the entry into force of the present Convention. Until such time as the oil content meter is installed, it shall immediately before discharge of ballast be established by examination of the ballast water from dedicated tanks that no contamination with oil has taken place.

(4) Every oil tanker operating with dedicated clean ballast tanks shall be provided with a Dedicated Clean Ballast Tank Operation Manual detailing the system and specifying operational procedures. Such a Manual shall be to the satisfaction of the Administration and shall contain all the information set out in the Specifications referred to in paragraph (2) of this Regulation. If an alteration affecting the dedicated clean ballast tank system is made, the Operation Manual shall be revised accordingly.

Regulation 13B

Requirements for Crude Oil Washing

(1) Every crude oil washing system required to be provided in accordance with Regulation 13(6) and (8) of this Annex shall comply with the requirements of this Regulation.

(2) The crude oil washing installation and associated equipment and arrangements shall comply with the requirements established by the Administration. Such requirements shall contain at least all the provisions of the Specifications for the Design, Operation and Control of Crude Oil Washing Systems adopted by the International Conference on Tanker Safety and Pollution Prevention, 1978, in Resolution 15 and as may be revised by the Organization.

(3) An inert gas system shall be provided in every cargo tank and slop tank in accordance with the appropriate Regulations of Chapter II–2 of the International Convention for the Safety of Life at Sea, 1974, as modified and added to by the Protocol of 1978 Relating to the International Convention for the Safety of Life at Sea, 1974 and as may be further amended.

(4) With respect to the ballasting of cargo tanks, sufficient cargo tanks shall be crude oil washed prior to each ballast voyage in order that, taking into account the tanker's trading pattern and expected weather conditions, ballast water is put only into cargo tanks which have been crude oil washed.

(5) Every oil tanker operating with crude oil washing systems shall be provided with an Operations and Equipment Manual detailing the system and equipment and specifying operational procedures. Such a Manual shall be to the satisfaction of the Administration and shall contain all the information set out in the Specifications referred to in paragraph (2) of this Regulation. If an alteration affecting the crude oil washing system is made, the Operations and Equipment Manual shall be revised accordingly.

Regulation 13C

Existing Tankers Engaged in Specific Trades

* * *

Regulation 13D

Existing Oil Tankers Having Special Ballast Arrangements

* * *

Regulation 13E

Protective Location of Segregated Ballast Spaces

(1) In every new crude oil tanker of 20,000 tons deadweight and above and every new product carrier of 30,000 tons deadweight and above, the segregated ballast tanks required to provide the capacity to comply with the requirements of Regulation 13 of this Annex which are located within the cargo tank length, shall be arranged in accordance with the requirements of paragraphs (2), (3) and (4) of this Regulation to provide a measure of protection against oil outflow in the event of grounding or collision.

* * *

Regulation 14

Segregation of Oil and Water Ballast and Carriage of Oil in Forepeak Tanks

* * *

Regulation 15

Retention of Oil on Board

* * *

Regulation 16

Oil Discharge Monitoring and Control System and Oil Filtering Equipment

* * *

Regulation 17

Tanks for Oil Residues (Sludge)

* * *

Regulation 18

Pumping, Piping and Discharge Arrangements of Oil Tankers

* * *

Regulation 19

Standard Discharge Connection

* * *

Regulation 20

Oil Record Book

(1) Every oil tanker of 150 tons gross tonnage and above and every ship of 400 tons gross tonnage and above other than an oil tanker shall be provided with an Oil Record Book Part I (Machinery Space Operations). Every oil tanker of 150 tons gross tonnage and above shall also be provided with an Oil Record Book Part II (Cargo Ballast Operations). The Oil Record Book(s), whether as a part of the ship's official log book or otherwise, shall be in the Form(s) specified in Appendix III to this Annex.

(2) The Oil Record Book shall be completed on each occasion, on a tank to tank basis if appropriate, whenever any of the following operations take place in the ship:

(a) for machinery space operations (all ships):

(i) ballasting or cleaning of oil fuel tanks;

(ii) discharge of dirty ballast or cleaning water from tanks referred to under (i) of the sub-paragraph;

(iii) disposal of oily residues (sludge);

(iv) discharge overboard or disposal otherwise of bilge water which has accumulated in machinery spaces.

(b) for cargo/ballast operations (oil tankers):

(i) loading of oil cargo;

(ii) internal transfer of oil cargo during voyage;

(iii) unloading of oil cargo;

(iv) ballasting of cargo tanks and dedicated clean ballast tanks;

(v) cleaning of cargo tanks including crude oil washing;

(vi) discharge of ballast except from segregated ballast tanks;

(vii) discharge of water from slop tanks;

(viii) closing of all applicable valves or similar devices after slop tank discharge operations;

(ix) closing of valves necessary for isolation of dedicated clean ballast tanks from cargo and stripping lines after slop tank discharge operations;

(x) disposal of residues.

(3) In the event of such discharge of oil or oily mixture as is referred to in Regulation 11 of this Annex or in the event of accidental or other exceptional discharge of oil not excepted by that Regulation, a statement shall be made in the Oil Record Book of the circumstances of, and the reasons for, the discharge.

(4) Each operation described in paragraph (2) of this Regulation shall be fully recorded without delay in the Oil Record Book so that all the entries in the book appropriate to that operation are completed. Each completed operation shall be signed by the officer or officers in charge of the operations concerned and each completed page shall be signed by the master of the ship. The entries in the Oil Record Book shall be in an official language of the State whose flag the ship is entitled to fly, and, for ships holding an International Oil Pollution Prevention Certificate, in English or French. The entries in an official national language of the State whose flag the ship is entitled to fly shall prevail in case of a dispute or discrepancy.

(5) The Oil Record Book shall be kept in such a place as to be readily available for inspection at all reasonable times and, except in the case of unmanned ships under tow, shall be kept on board the ship. It shall be preserved for a period of three years after the last entry has been made.

(6) The competent authority of the Government of a Party to the Convention may inspect the Oil Record Book on board any ship to which this Annex applies while the ship is in its port or offshore terminals and may make a copy of any entry in that book and may require the Master of the ship to certify that the copy is a true copy of such entry. Any copy so made which has been certified by the Master of the ship as a true copy of an entry in the ship's Oil Record Book shall be made admissible in any judicial proceedings as evidence of the facts stated in the entry. The inspection of an Oil Record Book and the taking of a certified copy by the competent authority under this paragraph shall be performed as expeditiously as possible without causing the ship to be unduly delayed.

(7) For oil tankers of less than 150 tons gross tonnage operating in accordance with Regulation 15(4) of this Annex an appropriate Oil Record Book should be developed by the Administration.

Regulation 21

Special Requirements for Drilling Rigs and other Platforms

* * *

CHAPTER III—REQUIREMENTS FOR MINIMIZING OIL POLLUTION FROM OIL TANKERS DUE TO SIDE AND BOTTOM DAMAGES

Regulation 22

Damage Assumptions

(1) For the purpose of calculating hypothetical oil outflow from oil tankers, three dimensions of the extent of damage of a parallelepiped on the side and bottom of the ship are assumed as follows. In the case of bottom damages two conditions are set forth to be applied individually to the stated portions of the oil tanker. * * *

Regulation 23

Hypothetical Outflow of Oil

(1) The hypothetical outflow of oil in the case of side damage (O_c) and bottom damage (O_s) shall be calculated by the following formulae with respect to compartments breached by damage to all conceivable locations along the length of the ship to the extent as defined in Regulation 22 of this Annex.

* * *

(5) An Administration may credit as reducing oil outflow in case of bottom damage, an installed cargo transfer system having an emergency high suction in each cargo oil tank, capable of transferring from a breached tank or tanks to segregated ballast tanks or to available cargo tankage if it can be assured that such tanks will have sufficient ullage. Credit for such a system would be governed by ability to transfer in two hours of operation oil equal to one half of the largest of the breached tanks involved and by availability of equivalent receiving capacity in ballast or cargo tanks. The credit shall be confined to permitting calculation of O_s according to formula (III). The pipes for such suctions shall be installed at least at a height not less than the vertical extent of the bottom damage v_s. The Administration shall supply the Organization with the information concerning the arrangements accepted by it, for circulation to other Parties to the Convention.

Regulation 24

Limitation of Size and Arrangement of Cargo Tanks

(1) Every new oil tanker shall comply with the provisions of this Regulation. Every existing oil tanker shall be required, within two years after the date of entry into force of the present Convention, to comply with the provisions of this Regulation if such a tanker falls into either of the following categories:

(a) a tanker, the delivery of which is after 1 January 1977; or

(b) a tanker to which both the following conditions apply:

(i) delivery is not later than 1 January 1977; and

(ii) the building contract is placed after 1 January 1974, or in cases where no building contract has previously been placed, the keel is laid or the tanker is at a similar stage of construction after 30 June 1974.

(2) Cargo tanks of oil tankers shall be of such size and arrangements that the hypothetical outflow O_c or O_s calculated in accordance with the provisions of Regulation 23 of this Annex anywhere in the length of the ship does not exceed 30,000 cubic metres or 400 $\sqrt[3]{DW}$, whichever is the greater, but subject to a maximum of 40,000 cubic metres.

* * *

Regulation 25

Subdivision and Stability

(1) Every new oil tanker shall comply with the subdivision and damage stability criteria as specified in paragraph (3) of this Regulation, after the assumed side or bottom damage as specified in paragraph (2) of this Regulation, for any operating draught reflecting actual partial or full load conditions consistent with trim and strength of the ship as well as specific gravities of the cargo. . . .

* * *

CHAPTER IV—PREVENTION OF POLLUTION ARISING FROM AN OIL POLLUTION INCIDENT

Regulation 26

Shipboard Oil Pollution Emergency Plan

(1) Every oil tanker of 150 tons gross tonnage and above and every ship other than an oil tanker of 400 tons gross tonnage and above shall carry on board a shipboard oil pollution emergency plan approved by the Administration. In the case of ships built before 4 April 1993 this requirement shall apply 24 months after that date.

(2) Such a plan shall be in accordance with Guidelines developed by the Organization and written in the working language of the master and officers. The plan shall consist at least of:

(a) the procedure to be followed by the master or other persons having charge of the ship to report an oil pollution incident, as required in article 8 and Protocol I of the present Convention, based on the guidelines developed by the Organization;

(b) the list of authorities or persons to be contacted in the event of an oil pollution incident;

(c) a detailed description of the action to be taken immediately by persons on board to reduce or control the discharge of oil following the incident; and

(d) the procedures and point of contact on the ship for co-ordinating shipboard action with national and local authorities in combating the pollution.

Appendix I

List of Oils (this list of oils shall not be considered as comprehensive)

Asphalt solutions

Blending Stocks
Roofers Flux
Straight Run Residue

Oils

Clarified
Crude Oil

Oils

Mixtures containing crude oil
Diesel Oil
Fuel Oil No. 4
Fuel Oil No. 5
Fuel Oil No. 6
Residual Fuel Oil
Road Oil
Transformer Oil

Oils

Aromatic Oil (excluding vegetable oil)
Lubricating Oils and Blending Stocks
Mineral Oil
Motor Oil
Penetrating Oil
Spindle Oil
Turbine Oil

Distillates

Straight Run
Flashed Feed Stocks

Gas Oil

Cracked

Gasoline Blending Stocks

Alkylates—fuel
Reformates
Polymer—fuel

Gasolines

Casinghead (natural)
Automotive
Aviation
Straight Run
Fuel Oil No. 1 (Kerosene)
Fuel Oil No. 1–D
Fuel Oil No. 2
Fuel Oil No. 2–D

Jet Fuels

JP–1 (Kerosene)
JP–3
JP–4
JP–5 (Kerosene, Heavy)
Turbo Fuel
Kerosene
Mineral Spirit

Naphtha

Solvent
Petroleum
Heartcut Distillate Oil

Appendix II

Form of IOPP Certificate

* * *

Appendix III

Form of Oil Record Book

* * *

Annex II of MARPOL 73/78 (including amendments):

Regulations For the Control of Pollution by Noxious Liquid Substances in Bulk

Regulation 1

Definitions

For the purposes of this Annex:

(1) "Chemical tanker" means a ship constructed or adapted primarily to carry a cargo of noxious liquid substances in bulk and includes an "oil tanker" as defined in Annex I of the present Convention when carrying a cargo or part cargo of noxious liquid substances in bulk.

(2) "Clean ballast" means ballast carried in a tank which, since it was last used to carry a cargo containing a substance in Category A, B, C or D has been thoroughly cleaned and the residues resulting therefrom have been discharged and the tank emptied in accordance with the appropriate requirements of this Annex.

(3) "Segregated ballast" means ballast water introduced into a tank permanently allocated to the carriage of ballast or to the carriage of ballast or cargoes other than oil or noxious liquid substances as variously defined in the Annexes of the present Convention, and which is completely separated from the cargo and oil fuel system.

(4) "Nearest land" is as defined in Regulation 1(9) of Annex I of the present Convention.

(5) "Liquid substances" are those having a vapour pressure not exceeding 2.8 kp/cm^2 at a temperature of 37.8°C.

(6) "Noxious liquid substance" means any substance designated in Appendix II to this Annex or provisionally assessed under the provisions of Regulation 3(4) as falling into Category A, B, C or D.

(7) "Special area" means a sea area where for recognized technical reasons in relation to its oceanographic and ecological condition and to its peculiar transportation traffic the adoption of special mandatory methods for the prevention of sea pollution by noxious liquid substances is required.

Special areas shall be:

(a) The Baltic Sea Area, and

(b) The Black Sea Area, and

(c) The Antarctic area.

(8) "Baltic Sea Area" is as defined in Regulation 10(1)(b) of Annex I of the present Convention.

(9) "Black Sea Area" is as defined in Regulation 10(1)(c) of Annex I of the present Convention.

(9A) The Antarctic area means the sea area south of latitude 60 degrees S.

(10) "International Bulk Chemical Code" means the International Code for the Construction and Equipment of Ships Carrying Dangerous Chemicals in Bulk adopted by the Marine Environment Protection Committee of the Organization by resolution MEPC 19(22), as may be amended by the Organization, provided that such amendments are adopted and brought into force in accordance with the provisions of Article 16 of the present Convention concerning amendment procedures applicable to an Appendix to an Annex.

(11) "Bulk Chemical Code" means the Code for the Construction and Equipment of Ships Carrying Dangerous Chemicals in Bulk adopted by the Marine Environment Protection Committee of the Organization by resolution MEPC 20(22), as may be amended by the Organization, provided that such amendments are adopted and brought into force in accordance with the provisions of Article 16 of the present Convention concerning amendment procedures applicable to an Appendix to an Annex.

(12) "Ship constructed" means a ship the keel of which is laid or which is at a similar stage of construction. A ship converted to a chemical tanker, irrespective of the date of construction, shall be treated as a chemical tanker constructed on the date on which such conversion commenced. This conversion provision shall not apply to the modification of a ship which complies with all of the following conditions:

(a) the ship is constructed before 1 July 1986; and

(b) the ship is certified under the Bulk Chemical Code to carry only those products identified by the Code as substances with pollution hazards only.

(13) "Similar stage of construction" means the stage at which:

(a) construction identifiable with a specific ship begins; and

(b) assembly of that ship has commenced comprising at least 50 tons or one per cent of the estimated mass of all structural material, whichever is less.

Regulation 2

Application

(1) Unless expressly provided otherwise the provisions of this Annex shall apply to all ships carrying noxious liquid substances in bulk.

(2) Where a cargo subject to the provisions of Annex I of the present Convention is carried in a cargo space of a chemical tanker, the appropriate requirements of Annex I of the present Convention shall also apply.

(3) Regulation 13 of this Annex shall apply only to ships carrying substances which are categorized for discharge control purposes in Category A, B or C.

(4) For ships constructed before 1 July 1986, the provisions of Regulation 5 of this Annex in respect of the requirement to discharge below the waterline and maximum concentration in the wake astern of the ship shall apply as from 1 January 1988.

(5) The Administration may allow any fitting, material, appliance or apparatus to be fitted in a ship as an alternative to that required by this Annex if such fitting, material, appliance or apparatus is at least as effective as that required by this Annex. This authority of the Administration shall not extend to the substitution of operational methods to effect the control of discharge of noxious liquid substances as equivalent to those design and construction features which are prescribed by Regulations in this Annex.

(6) The Administration which allows a fitting, material, appliance or apparatus as alternative to that required by this Annex, under paragraph (5) of this Regulation, shall communicate to the Organization for circulation to the Parties to the Convention, particulars thereof, for their information and appropriate action, if any.

(7) (a) Where an amendment to this Annex and to the International Bulk Chemical Code and the Bulk Chemical Code involves changes to the structure or equipment and fittings due to the upgrading of the requirements for the carriage of certain substances, the Administration may modify or delay for a specified period the application of such an amendment to ships constructed before the date of entry into force of that amendment, if the immediate application of such an amendment is considered unreasonable or impracticable. Such relaxation shall be determined with respect to each substance, having regard to the guidelines developed by the Organization.

(b) The Administration allowing a relaxation of the application of an amendment under this paragraph shall submit to the Organization a report giving details of the ship or ships concerned, the cargoes carried, the trade in which each ship is engaged and the justification for the relaxation, for circulation to the Parties to the Convention for their information and appropriate action, if any.

Regulation 3

Categorization and Listing of Noxious Liquid Substances

(1) For the purpose of the Regulations of this Annex, noxious liquid substances shall be divided into four categories as follows:

(a) Category A—Noxious liquid substances which if discharged into the sea from tank cleaning or deballasting operations would present a major hazard to either marine resources or human health or cause serious harm to amenities or other legitimate uses of the sea and therefore justify the application of stringent anti-pollution measures.

(b) Category B—Noxious liquid substances which if discharged into the sea from tank cleaning or deballasting operations would present a hazard to either marine resources or human health or cause harm to amenities or other legitimate uses of the sea and therefore justify the application of special anti-pollution measures.

(c) Category C—Noxious liquid substances which if discharged into the sea from tank cleaning or deballasting operations would present a minor hazard to either marine resources or human health or cause minor harm to amenities or other legitimate uses of the sea and therefore require special operational conditions.

(d) Category D—Noxious liquid substances which if discharged into the sea from tank cleaning or deballasting operations would present a recognizable hazard to either marine resources or human health or cause minimal harm to amenities or other legitimate uses of the sea and therefore require some attention in operational conditions.

(2) Guidelines for use in the categorization of noxious liquid substances are given in Appendix I to this Annex.

(3) Noxious liquid substances carried in bulk which are presently categorized as category A, B, C or D and subject to the provisions of this Annex are referred to in appendix II to this Annex.

(4) Where it is proposed to carry a liquid substance in bulk which has not been categorized under paragraph (1) of this Regulation or evaluated as referred to in Regulation 4(1) of this Annex, the Governments of Parties to the Convention involved in the proposed operation shall establish and agree on a provisional assessment for the proposed operation on the basis of the guidelines referred to in paragraph (2) of this Regulation. Until full agreement between the Governments involved has been reached, the substance shall be carried under the most severe conditions proposed. As soon as possible, but not later than ninety days after its first carriage, the Administration concerned shall notify the Organization and provide details of the substance and the provisional assessment for prompt circulation to all Parties for their information and consideration. The Government of each Party shall have a period of ninety days in which to forward its comments to the Organization, with a view to the assessment of the substance.

Regulation 4

Other Liquid Substances

(1) The substance referred to in appendix III to this Annex have been evaluated and found to fall outside category A, B, C and D, as defined in regulation 3(1) of this Annex because they are at present considered to present no harm to human health, marine resources, amenities or other legitimate uses of the sea, when discharged into the sea from tank cleaning or deballasting operation.

(2) The discharge of bilge or ballast water or other residues or mixtures containing only substances referred to in appendix III to this Annex shall not be subject to any requirement of this Annex.

(3) The discharge into the sea of clean ballast or segregated ballast shall not be subject to any requirement of this Annex.

Regulation 5

Discharge of Noxious Liquid Substances

Subject to the provisions of paragraph (14) of t his regulation and of regulation 6 of this Annex,

(1) The discharge into the sea of substances in Category A as defined in Regulation 3(1)(a) of this Annex or of those provisionally assessed as such, or ballast water, tank washings, or other residues or mixtures containing such substances shall be

prohibited. If tanks containing such substances or mixtures are to be washed, the resulting residues shall be discharged to a reception facility until the concentration of the substance in the effluent to such facility is at or below 0.1% by weight and until the tank is empty, with the exception of phosphorus, yellow or white for which the residual concentration shall be at 0.01% by weight. Any water subsequently added to the tank may be discharged into the sea when all the following conditions are satisfied:

(a) the ship is proceeding en route at a speed of at least 7 knots in the case of self-propelled ships or at least 4 knots in the case of ships which are not self-propelled;

(b) the discharge is made below the waterline, taking into account the location of the seawater intakes; and

(c) the discharge is made at a distance of not less than 12 nautical miles from the nearest land and in a depth of water of not less than 25 metres.

(2) The discharge into the sea of substances in Category B as defined in Regulation 3(1)(b) of this Annex or of those provisionally assessed as such, or ballast water, tank washings, or other residues or mixtures containing such substances shall be prohibited except when all the following conditions are satisfied:

(a) the ship is proceeding en route at a speed of at least 7 knots in the case of self-propelled ships or at least 4 knots in the case of ships which are not self-propelled;

(b) the procedures and arrangements for discharge are approved by the Administration. Such procedures and arrangements shall be based upon standards developed by the Organization and shall ensure that the concentration and rate of discharge of the effluent is such that the concentration of the substance in the wake astern of the ship does not exceed 1 part per million;

(c) the maximum quantity of cargo discharged from each tank and its associated piping system does not exceed the maximum quantity approved in accordance with the procedures referred to in sub-paragraph (b) of this paragraph, which shall in no case exceed the greater of 1 cubic metre or 1/3,000 of the tank capacity in cubic metres;

(d) the discharge is made below the waterline, taking into account the location of the seawater intakes; and

(e) the discharge is made at a distance of not less than 12 nautical miles from the nearest land and in a depth of water of not less than 25 metres.

(3) The discharge into the sea of substances in Category C as defined in Regulation 3(1)(c) of this Annex or of those provisionally assessed as such, or ballast water, tank washings, or other residues or mixtures containing such substances shall be prohibited except when all the following conditions are satisfied:

(a) the ship is proceeding en route at a speed of at least 7 knots in the case of self-propelled ships or at least 4 knots in the case of ships which are not self-propelled;

(b) the procedures and arrangements for discharge are approved by the Administration. Such procedures and arrangements shall be based upon standards developed by the Organization and shall ensure that the concentration and rate of discharge of the effluent is such that the concentration of the substance in the wake astern of the ship does not exceed 10 parts per million;

(c) the maximum quantity of cargo discharged from each tank and its associated piping system does not exceed the maximum quantity approved in accordance with the procedures referred to in sub-paragraph (b) of this paragraph, which shall in no case exceed the greater of 3 cubic metres or 1/1,000 of the tank capacity in cubic metres;

(d) the discharge is made below the waterline, taking into account the location of the seawater intakes; and

(e) the discharge is made at a distance of not less than 12 nautical miles from the nearest land and in a depth of water of not less than 25 metres.

(4) The discharge into the sea of substances in Category D as defined in Regulation 3(1)(d) of this Annex, or of those provisionally assessed as such, or ballast water, tank washings, or other residues or mixtures containing such substances shall be prohibited except when all the following conditions are satisfied:

(a)2 the ship is proceeding en route at a speed of at least 7 knots in the case of self-propelled ships or at least 4 knots in the case of ships which are not self-propelled;

(b) such mixtures are of a concentration not greater than one part of the substance in ten parts of water; and

(c) the discharge is made at a distance of not less than 12 nautical miles from the nearest land.

(5) Ventilation procedures approved by the Administration may be used to remove cargo residues from a tank. Such procedures shall be based upon standards developed by the Organization. Any water subsequently introduced into the tank shall be regarded as clean and shall not be subject to paragraph (1), (2), (3) or (4) of this Regulation.

(6) The discharge into the sea of substances which have not been categorized, provisionally assessed, or evaluated as referred to in Regulation 4(1) of this Annex, or of ballast water, tank washings, or other residues or mixtures containing such substances shall be prohibited.

Categories A, B and C Substances within Special Areas

Subject to the provisions of Regulation 6 of this Annex,

(7) The discharge into the sea of substances in Category A as defined in Regulation 3(1)(a) of this Annex or of those provisionally assessed as such, or ballast water, tank washings, or other residues or mixtures containing such substances shall be prohibited. If tanks containing such substances or mixtures are to be washed the resulting residues shall be discharged to a reception facility which the States bordering the special area shall provide in accordance with Regulation 7 of this Annex, until the concentration of the substance in the effluent to such facility is at or below the residual concentration prescribed for that substance in column IV of Appendix II to this Annex and until the tank is empty. Any water subsequently added to the tank may be discharged into the sea when all the following conditions are satisfied:

(a) the ship is proceeding en route at a speed of at least 7 knots in the case of self-propelled ships or at least 4 knots in the case of ships which are not self-propelled;

(b) the discharge is made below the waterline, taking into account the location of the seawater intakes; and

(c) the discharge is made at a distance of not less than 12 nautical miles from the nearest land and in a depth of water of not less than 25 metres.

(8) The discharge into the sea of substances in Category B as defined in Regulation 3(1)(b) of this Annex or of those provisionally assessed as such, or ballast water, tank washings, or other residues or mixtures containing such substances shall be prohibited except when all the following conditions are satisfied:

(a) the tank has been prewashed in accordance with the procedure approved by the Administration and based on standards developed by the Organization and the resulting tank washings have been discharged to a reception facility;

(b) the ship is proceeding en route at a speed of at least 7 knots in the case of self-propelled ships or at least 4 knots in the case of ships which are not self-propelled;

(c) the procedures and arrangements for discharge and washings are approved by the Administration. Such procedures and arrangements shall be based upon standards developed by the Organization and shall ensure that the concentration and rate of discharge of the effluent is such that the concentration of the substance in the wake astern of the ship does not exceed 1 part per million;

(d) the discharge is made below the waterline, taking into account the location of the seawater intakes; and

(e) the discharge is made at a distance of not less than 12 nautical miles from the nearest land and in a depth of water of not less than 25 metres.

(9) The discharge into the sea of substances in Category C as defined in Regulation 3(1)(c) of this Annex or of those provisionally assessed as such, or ballast water, tank washings, or other residues or mixtures containing such substances shall be prohibited except when all the following conditions are satisfied:

(a) the ship is proceeding en route at a speed of at least 7 knots in the case of self-propelled ships or at least 4 knots in the case of ships which are not self-propelled;

(b) the procedures and arrangements for discharge are approved by the Administration. Such procedures and arrangements shall be based upon standards developed by the Organization and shall ensure that the concentration and rate of discharge of the effluent is such that the concentration of the substance in the wake astern of the ship does not exceed 1 part per million;

(c) the maximum quantity of cargo discharged from each tank and its associated piping system does not exceed the maximum quantity approved in accordance with the procedures referred to in sub-paragraph (b) of this paragraph which shall in no case exceed the greater of 1 cubic metre or 1/3,000 of the tank capacity in cubic metres;

(d) the discharge is made below the waterline, taking into account the location of the seawater intakes; and

(e) the discharge is made at a distance of not less than 12 nautical miles from the nearest land and in a depth of water of not less than 25 metres.

(10) Ventilation procedures approved by the Administration may be used to remove cargo residues from a tank. Such procedures shall be based upon standards developed by the Organization. Any water subsequently introduced into the tank shall be regarded as clean and shall not be subject to paragraph (7), (8) or (9) of this Regulation.

(11) The discharge into the sea of substances which have not been categorized, provisionally assessed or evaluated as referred to in Regulation 4(1) of this Annex, or of ballast water, tank washings, or other residues or mixtures containing such substances shall be prohibited.

(12) Nothing in this Regulation shall prohibit a ship from retaining on board the residues from a Category B or C cargo and discharging such residues into the sea outside a special area in accordance with paragraph (2) or (3) of this Regulation, respectively.

(13)(a) The Governments of Parties to the Convention, the coastlines of which border on any given special area, shall collectively agree and establish a date by which time the requirement of Regulation 7(1) of this Annex will be fulfilled and from which the requirements of paragraphs (7), (8), (9) and (10) of this Regulation in respect of that area shall take effect and notify the Organization of the date so established at least six months in advance of that date. The Organization shall then promptly notify all Parties of that date.

(b) If the date of entry into force of the present Convention is earlier than the date established in accordance with sub-paragraph (a) of this paragraph, the requirements of paragraphs (1), (2) and (3) of this Regulation shall apply during the interim period.

(14) In respect of the Antarctic area any discharge into the sea of noxious liquid substances or mixtures containing such substances shall be prohibited.

Regulation 5A

Pumping, Piping and Unloading Arrangements

* * *

Regulation 6

Exceptions

Regulation 5 of this Annex shall not apply to:

(a) the discharge into the sea of noxious liquid substances or mixtures containing such substances necessary for the purpose of securing the safety of a ship or saving life at sea; or

(b) the discharge into the sea of noxious liquid substances or mixtures containing such substances resulting from damage to a ship or its equipment:

(i) provided that all reasonable precautions have been taken after the occurrence of the damage or discovery of the discharge for the purpose of preventing or minimizing the discharge; and

(ii) except if the owner or the Master acted either with intent to cause damage, or recklessly and with knowledge that damage would probably result; or

(c) the discharge into the sea of noxious liquid substances or mixtures containing such substances, approved by the Administration, when being used for the purpose of combating specific pollution incidents in order to minimize the damage from pollution. Any such discharge shall be subject to the approval of any Government in whose jurisdiction it is contemplated the discharge will occur.

Regulation 7

Reception Facilities and Cargo Unloading Terminal Arrangements

* * *

Regulation 8

Measures of Control

(1)(a) The Government of each Party to the Convention shall appoint or authorize surveyors for the purpose of implementing this Regulation. The surveyors shall execute control in accordance with control procedures developed by the Organization.

* * *

Regulation 9

Cargo Record Book

(1) Every ship to which this Annex applies shall be provided with a Cargo Record Book, whether as part of the ship's official log book or otherwise, in the form specified in Appendix IV to this Annex.

(2) The Cargo Record Book shall be completed, on a tank-to-tank basis, whenever any of the following operations with respect to a noxious liquid substance take place in the ship:

(i) loading of cargo;

(ii) internal transfer of cargo;

(iii) unloading of cargo;

(iv) cleaning of cargo tanks;

(v) ballasting of cargo tanks;

(vi) discharge of ballast from cargo tanks;

(vii) disposal of residues to reception facilities;

(viii) discharge into the sea or removal by ventilation of residues in accordance with Regulation 5 of this Annex.

(3) In the event of any discharge of the kind referred to in Article 8 of the present Convention and Regulation 6 of this Annex of any noxious liquid substance or mixture containing such substance, whether intentional or accidental, an entry shall be made in the Cargo Record Book stating the circumstances of, and the reason for, the discharge.

(4) When a surveyor appointed or authorized by the Government of the Party to the Convention to supervise any operations under this Annex has inspected a ship, then that surveyor shall make an appropriate entry in the Cargo Record Book.

(5) Each operation referred to in paragraphs (2) and (3) of this Regulation shall be fully recorded without delay in the Cargo Record Book so that all the entries in the Book appropriate to that operation are completed. Each entry shall be signed by the officer or officers in charge of the operation concerned and each page shall be signed by the Master of the ship. The entries in the Cargo Record Book shall be in an official language of the State whose flag the ship is entitled to fly, and, for ships holding an International Pollution Prevention Certificate for the Carriage of Noxious Liquid Substances in Bulk or a Certificate referred to in Regulation 12A of this Annex in English or French. The entries in an official national language of the State whose flag the ship is entitled to fly shall prevail in case of a dispute or discrepancy.

(6) The Cargo Record Book shall be kept in such a place as to be readily available for inspection and, except in the case of unmanned ships under tow, shall be kept on board the ship. It shall be retained for a period of three years after the last entry has been made.

(7) The competent authority of the Government of a Party may inspect the Cargo Record Book on board any ship to which this Annex applies while the ship is in its port, and may make a copy of any entry in that book and may require the Master of the ship to certify that the copy is a true copy of such entry. Any copy so made which has been certified by the Master of the ship as a true copy of an entry in the ship's Cargo Record Book shall be made admissible in any judicial proceedings as evidence of the facts stated in the entry. The inspection of a Cargo Record Book and the taking of a certified copy by the competent authority under this paragraph shall be performed as expeditiously as possible without causing the ship to be unduly delayed.

Regulation 10

Surveys

(1) Ships carrying noxious liquid substances in bulk shall be subject to the surveys specified below:

(a) An initial survey before the ship is put in service or before the Certificate required under Regulation 11 of this Annex is issued for the first time, and which shall include a complete survey of its structure, equipment, systems, fittings, arrangements and material in so far as the ship is covered by this Annex. This survey shall be such as to ensure that the structure, equipment, systems, fittings, arrangements and material fully comply with the applicable requirements of this Annex.

(b) Periodical surveys at intervals specified by the Administration, but not exceeding five years, and which shall be such as to ensure that the structure, equipment, systems, fittings, arrangements and material fully comply with the requirements of this Annex.

(c) A minimum of one intermediate survey during the period of validity of the Certificate and which shall be such as to ensure that the equipment and associated pump and piping systems fully comply with the applicable requirements of this Annex and are in good working order. In cases where only one such intermediate survey is carried out in any one Certificate validity period, it shall be held not before six months prior to, nor later than six months after the half-way date of the Certificate's period of validity. Such intermediate surveys shall be endorsed on the Certificate issued under Regulation 11 of this Annex.

(d) An annual survey within 3 months before or after the day and the month of the date of issue of the Certificate and which shall include a general examination to ensure that the structure, fittings, arrangements and materials remain in all respects satisfactory for the service for which the ship is intended. Such annual surveys shall be endorsed on the Certificate issued under Regulation 11 of this Annex.

(2)(a) Surveys of ships as regards the enforcement of the provisions of this Annex shall be carried out by officers of the Administration. The Administration may, however, entrust the surveys either to surveyors nominated for the purpose or to organizations recognized by it.

(b) An Administration nominating surveyors or recognizing organizations to conduct surveys and inspections as set forth in sub-paragraph (a) of this paragraph, shall as a minimum empower any nominated surveyor or recognized organization to:

(i) require repairs to a ship; and

(ii) carry out surveys and inspections if requested by the appropriate authorities of a port State.

The Administration shall notify the Organization of the specific responsibilities and conditions of the authority delegated to the nominated surveyors or recognized organizations, for circulation to Parties to the present Convention for the information of their officers.

(c) When a nominated surveyor or recognized organization determines that the condition of the ship or its equipment does not correspond substantially with the particulars of the Certificate, or is such that the ship is not fit to proceed to sea without presenting an unreasonable threat of harm to the marine environment, such surveyor or organization shall immediately ensure that corrective action is taken and shall in due course notify the Administration. If such corrective action is not taken the Certificate should be withdrawn and the

Administration shall be notified immediately; and if the ship is in a port of another Party, the appropriate authorities of the port State shall also be notified immediately. When an officer of the Administration, a nominated surveyor or recognized organization has notified the appropriate authorities of the port State, the Government of the port State concerned shall give such officer, surveyor, or organization any necessary assistance to carry out their obligations under this Regulation. When applicable, the Government of the port State concerned shall take such steps as will ensure that the ship shall not sail until it can proceed to sea or leave the port for the purpose of proceeding to the nearest appropriate repair yard available without presenting an unreasonable threat of harm to the marine environment.

(d) In every case, the Administration concerned shall fully guarantee the completeness and efficiency of the survey and inspection and shall undertake to ensure the necessary arrangements to satisfy this obligation.

(3)(a) The condition of the ship and its equipment shall be maintained to conform with the provisions of the present Convention to ensure that the ship in all respects will remain fit to proceed to sea without presenting an unreasonable threat of harm to the marine environment.

(b) After any survey of the ship under paragraph (1) of this Regulation has been completed, no change shall be made in the structure, equipment, systems, fittings, arrangements or material covered by the survey, without the sanction of the Administration, except the direct replacement of such equipment and fittings.

(c) Whenever an accident occurs to a ship or a defect is discovered which substantially affects the integrity of the ship or the efficiency or completeness of its equipment covered by this Annex, the master or owner of the ship shall report at the earliest opportunity to the Administration, the recognized organization or the nominated surveyor responsible for issuing the relevant Certificate, who shall cause investigations to be initiated to determine whether a survey as required by paragraph (1) of this Regulation is necessary. If the ship is in a port of another Party, the master or owner shall also report immediately to the appropriate authorities of the port State and the nominated surveyor or recognized organization shall ascertain that such report has been made.

Regulation 11

Issue of Certificate

(1) An International Pollution Prevention Certificate for the Carriage of Noxious Liquid Substances in Bulk shall be issued, after survey in accordance with the provisions of Regulation 10 of this Annex, to any ship carrying noxious liquid substances in bulk and which is engaged in voyages to ports or terminals under the jurisdiction of other Parties to the Convention.

(2) Such Certificate shall be issued either by the Administration or by any person or organization duly authorized by it. In every case, the Administration assumes full responsibility for the Certificate.

(3)(a) The Government of a Party to the Convention may, at the request of the Administration, cause a ship to be surveyed and, if satisfied that the provisions of this Annex are complied with, shall issue or authorize the issue of an International Pollution Prevention Certificate for the Carriage of Noxious Liquid Substances in Bulk to the ship in accordance with this Annex.

(b) A copy of the Certificate and a copy of the survey report shall be transmitted as soon as possible to the requesting Administration.

(c) A Certificate so issued shall contain a statement to the effect that it has been issued at the request of the Administration and it shall have the same force and receive the same recognition as the Certificate issued under paragraph (1) of this Regulation.

(d) No International Pollution Prevention Certificate for the Carriage of Noxious Liquid Substances in Bulk shall be issued to a ship which is entitled to fly the flag of a State which is not a Party.

(4) The International Pollution Prevention Certificate for the Carriage of Noxious Liquid Substances in Bulk shall be drawn up in an official language of the issuing country in the form corresponding to the model given in Appendix V to this Annex. If the language used is neither English nor French, the text shall include a translation into one of these languages.

Regulation 12

Duration of Certificate

(1) An International Pollution Prevention Certificate for the Carriage of Noxious Liquid Substances in Bulk shall be issued for a period specified by the Administration, which shall not exceed five years from the date of issue.

(2) A Certificate shall cease to be valid if significant alterations have taken place in the construction, equipment, systems, fittings, arrangements or material required without the sanction of the Administration, except the direct replacement of such equipment or fittings, or if intermediate or annual surveys as specified by the Administration under Regulation 10(1)(c) or (d) of this Annex are not carried out.

(3) A Certificate issued to a ship shall also cease to be valid upon transfer of the ship to the flag of another State. A new Certificate shall be issued only when the Government issuing the new Certificate is fully satisfied that the ship is in full compliance with the requirements of Regulation 10(3)(a) and (b) of this Annex. In the case of a transfer between Parties, if requested within three months after the transfer has taken place, the Government of the Party whose flag the ship was formerly entitled to fly shall transmit as soon as possible to the Administration a copy of the Certificate carried by the ship before the transfer and, if available, a copy of the relevant survey report.

Regulation 12A

Survey and Certification of Chemical Tankers

Notwithstanding the provisions of Regulations 10, 11 and 12 of this Annex, chemical tankers which have been surveyed and certified by States Parties to the present Convention in accordance with the provisions of the International Bulk Chemical Code or the Bulk Chemical Code, as applicable, shall be deemed to have complied with the provisions of the said Regulations, and the Certificate issued under that Code shall have the same force and receive the same recognition as the Certificate issued under Regulation 11 of this Annex.

Regulation 13

Requirements for Minimizing Accidental Pollution

(1) The design, construction, equipment and operation of ships carrying noxious liquid substances of Category A, B or C in bulk, shall be such as to minimize the uncontrolled discharge into the sea of such substances.

(2) Chemical tankers constructed on or after 1 July 1986 shall comply with the requirements of the International Bulk Chemical Code.

(3) Chemical tankers constructed before 1 July 1986 shall comply with the following requirements:

(a) The following chemical tankers shall comply with the requirements of the Bulk Chemical Code as applicable to ships referred to in 1.7.2 of that Code:

(i) ships for which the building contract is placed on or after 2 November 1973 and which are engaged on voyages to ports or terminals under the jurisdiction of other States Parties to the Convention; and

(ii) ships constructed on or after 1 July 1983 which are engaged solely on voyages between ports or terminals within the State the flag of which the ship is entitled to fly;

(b) The following chemical tankers shall comply with the requirements of the Bulk Chemical Code as applicable to ships referred to in 1.7.3 of that Code:

(i) ships for which the building contract is placed before 2 November 1973 and which are engaged on voyages to ports or terminals under the jurisdiction of other States Parties to the Convention; and

(ii) ships constructed before 1 July 1983 which are engaged on voyages between ports or terminals within the State the flag of which the ship is entitled to fly, except that for ships of less than 1,600 tons gross tonnage compliance with the Code in respect of construction and equipment shall take effect not later than 1 July 1994.

(4) In respect of ships other than chemical tankers carrying noxious liquid substances of Category A, B or C in bulk, the Administration shall establish appropriate measures based on the Guidelines developed by the Organization in order to ensure that the provisions of paragraph (1) of this Regulation are complied with.

Regulation 14

Carriage and Discharge of Oil-like Substances

Notwithstanding the provisions of other Regulations of this Annex, noxious liquid substances referred to in Appendix II of this Annex as falling under Category C or D and identified by the Organization as oil-like substances under the criteria developed by the Organization, may be carried on an oil tanker as defined in Annex I of the Convention and discharged in accordance with the provisions of Annex I of the present Convention, provided that all of the following conditions are complied with:

(a) the ship complies with the provisions of Annex I of the present Convention as applicable to product carriers as defined in that Annex;

(b) the ship carries an International Oil Pollution Prevention Certificate and its Supplement B and the Certificate is endorsed to indicate that the ship may carry oil-like substances in conformity with this Regulation and the endorsement includes a list of oil-like substances the ship is allowed to carry;

(c) in the case of Category C substances the ship complies with the ship type 3 damage stability requirements of:

(i) the International Bulk Chemical Code in the case of a ship constructed on or after 1 July 1986; or

(ii) the Bulk Chemical Code, as applicable under Regulation 13 of this Annex, in the case of a ship constructed before 1 July 1986; and

(d) the oil content meter in the oil discharge monitoring and control system of the ship is approved by the Administration for use in monitoring the oil-like substances to be carried.

Appendix I

Guidelines for the Categorization of Noxious Liquid Substances

* * *

Appendix II

List of Noxious Liquid Substances Carried in Bulk

* * *

Appendix III

List of Other Liquid Substances

* * *

Appendix IV

Cargo Record Book for Ships Carrying Noxious Liquid Substances in Bulk

* * *

Annex III of MARPOL 73/78

Regulations for the Prevention of Pollution by Harmful Substances Carried by Sea in Packaged Form

* * *

Annex IV of MARPOL 73/78

Regulations for the Prevention of Pollution by Sewage From Ships (not yet in force)

* * *

Annex V of MARPOL 73/78 (including amendments):

Regulations for the Prevention of Pollution by Garbage From Ships

Regulation 1

Definitions

For the purposes of this Annex:

(1) "Garbage" means all kinds of victual, domestic and operational waste excluding fresh fish and parts thereof, generated during the normal operation of the ship and liable to be disposed of continuously or periodically except those substances which are defined or listed in other Annexes to the present Convention.

(2) "Nearest land". The term "from the nearest land" means from the baseline from which the territorial sea of the territory in question is established in accordance with international law except that, for the purposes of the present Convention "from the nearest land" off the north eastern coast of Australia shall mean from a line drawn from a point on the coast of Australia in latitude 11° South, longitude 142°08' East to a point in latitude 10°35' South,

longitude 141°55′ East, thence to a point latitude 10°00′ South,

longitude 142°00′ East, thence to a point latitude 9°10′ South,

longitude 143°52′ East, thence to a point latitude 9°00′ South,

longitude 144°30′ East, thence to a point latitude 13°00′ South,

longitude 144°00′ East, thence to a point latitude 15°00′ South,

longitude 146°00′ East, thence to a point latitude 18°00′ South,

longitude 147°00′ East, thence to a point latitude 21°00′ South, longitude 153°00′ East, thence to a point on the coast of Australia in latitude 24°42′ South, longitude 153°15′ East.

(3) "Special area" means a sea area where for recognized technical reasons in relation to its oceanographical and ecological condition and to the particular character of its traffic the adoption of special mandatory methods for the prevention of sea pollution by garbage is required. Special areas shall include those listed in Regulation 5 of this Annex.

Regulation 2

Application

Unless expressly provided otherwise, the provisions of this Annex shall apply to all ships.

Regulation 3

Disposal of Garbage Outside Special Areas

(1) Subject to the provisions of Regulations 4, 5 and 6 of this Annex:

(a) the disposal into the sea of all plastics, including but not limited to synthetic ropes, synthetic fishing nets and plastic garbage bags is prohibited;

(b) the disposal into the sea of the following garbage shall be made as far as practicable from the nearest land but in any case is prohibited if the distance from the nearest land is less than:

(i) 25 nautical miles for dunnage, lining and packing materials which will float;

(ii) 12 nautical miles for food wastes and all other garbage including paper products, rags, glass, metal, bottles, crockery and similar refuse;

(c) disposal into the sea of garbage specified in sub-paragraph (b)(ii) of this Regulation may be permitted when it is passed through a comminuter or grinder and made as far as practicable from the nearest land but in any case is prohibited if the distance from the nearest land is less than 3 nautical miles. Such comminuted or ground garbage shall be capable of passing through a screen with openings no greater than 25 millimetres.

(2) When the garbage is mixed with other discharges having different disposal or discharge requirements the more severe requirements shall apply.

Regulation 4

Disposals from Drilling Rigs

(1) Fixed or floating platforms engaged in the exploration, exploitation and associated offshore processing of sea-bed mineral resources, and all other ships when alongside such platforms or within 500 metres of such platforms, are forbidden to dispose of any materials regulated by this Annex, except as permitted by paragraph (2) of this Regulation.

(2) The disposal into the sea of food wastes when passed through a comminuter or grinder from such fixed or floating drilling rigs located more than 12 nautical miles from land and all other ships when positioned as above. Such comminuted or ground food wastes shall be capable of passing through a screen with openings no greater than 25 millimetres.

Regulation 5

Disposal of Garbage Within Special Areas

(1) For the purpose of this Annex the special areas are the Mediterranean Sea area, the Baltic Sea area, the Black Sea area, the Red Sea area, the "Gulfs area", the

North Sea area, the Antarctic area and the Wider Caribbean Region, including the Gulf of Mexico and the Caribbean Sea, which are defined as follows:

(a) The Mediterranean Sea area means the Mediterranean Sea proper including the gulfs and seas therein with the boundary between the Mediterranean and the Black Sea constituted by the 41°N parallel and bounded to the west by the Straits of Gibraltar at the meridian of 5°36′W.

(b) The Baltic Sea area means the Baltic Sea proper with the Gulf of Bothnia and the Gulf of Finland and the entrance to the Baltic Sea bounded by the parallel of the Skaw in the Skagerrak at 57°44.8'N.

(c) The Black Sea area means the Black Sea proper with the boundary between the Mediterranean and the Black Sea constituted by the parallel 41°N.

(d) The Red Sea area means the Red Sea proper including the Gulfs of Suez and Aqaba bounded at the south by the rhumb line between Ras si Ane (12°8.5′N, 43°19.6′E) and Husn Murad (12°40.4′N, 43°30.2′E).

(e) The "Gulfs area" means the sea area located north west of the rhumb line between Ras al Hadd (22°30′N, 59°48′E) and Ras al Fasteh (25°04′N, 61°25′E).

(f) The "North Sea Area" means the North Sea proper including seas therein with the boundary between:

(i) the North Sea southwards of latitude 62° N and eastwards of longitude 4° W;

(ii) the Skagerrak, the southern limit of which is determined east of the Skaw by latitude 57°44.8′ N; and

(iii) the English Channel and its approaches eastwards of longitude 5° W and northwards of latitude 48°30′ N.

(g) the "Antarctic area" means the sea area south of latitude 60° S.

(h) the "Wider Caribbean Region", as defined in article 2, paragraph 1 of the Convention for the Protection and Development of the Marine Environment of the Wider Caribbean Region (Cartagena de Indias, 1983), means the Gulf of Mexico and Caribbean Sea proper including the bays and seas therein and that portion of the Atlantic Ocean ithin the boundary constituted by the 30° N parallel from Florida eastward to 77°30' W eridian, thence a rhumb line to the intersection of 20° N parallel and 50° W meridian, thence a rhumb line drawn south-westerly to the eastern boundary of French Guiana.

(2) Subject to the provisions of Regulation 6 of this Annex:

(a) disposal into the sea of the following is prohibited:

(i) all plastics, including but not limited to synthetic ropes, synthetic fishing nets and plastic garbage bags;

(ii) all other garbage, including paper products, rags, glass, metal, bottles, crockery, dunnage, lining and packing materials;

(b) except as provided in subparagraph (c) of this paragraph, disposal into the sea of food wastes shall be made as far as practicable from land, but in any case not less than 12 nautical miles from the nearest land,

(c) disposal into the Wider Caribbean Region of food wastes which have been passed through a comminuter or grinder shall be made as far as practicable from land, but in any case not subject to regulation 4 not less than 3 nautical miles from the nearest land. Such comminuted or ground food wastes shall be capable of passing through a screen with openings no greater than 25 millimetres.

(3) When the garbage is mixed with other discharges having different disposal or discharge requirements the more stringent requirements shall apply.

(4) Reception facilities within special areas.

(a) The Government of each party to the Convention, the coast line of which borders a special area undertakes to ensure that as soon as possible in all ports within a special area, adequate reception facilities are provided in accordance with Regulation 7 of this Annex, taking into account the special needs of ships operating in these areas.

(b) The Government of each party concerned shall notify the Organization of the measures taken pursuant to sub-paragraph (a) of this Regulation. Upon receipt of sufficient notifications the Organization shall establish a date from which the requirements of this Regulation in respect of the area in question shall take effect. The Organization shall notify all parties of the date so established no less than twelve months in advance of that date.

(c) After date so established, ships calling also at ports in these special areas where such facilities are not yet available, shall fully comply with the requirements of this Regulation.

(5) Notwithstanding paragraph 4 of this Regulation, the following rules apply to the Antarctic area:

(a) The Government of each Party to the Convention at whose ports ships depart en route to or arriving from the Antarctic area undertakes to ensure that as soon as practicable adequate facilities are provided for the reception of all garbage from all ships, without causing undue delay, and according to the needs of the ships using them.

(b) The Government of each Party to the Convention shall ensure that all ships entitled to fly its flag, before entering the Antarctic area, have sufficient capacity on board for the retention of all garbage while operating in the area and have concluded arrangements to discharge such garbage at a reception facility after leaving the area.

Regulation 6

Exception

Regulations 3, 4 and 5 of this Annex shall not apply to:

(a) the disposal of garbage from a ship necessary for the purpose of securing the safety of a ship, the health of its personnel, or saving life at sea;

(b) the escape of garbage resulting from damage to a ship or its equipment provided all reasonable precautions have been taken before and after the occurrence of the damage, for the purpose of preventing or minimizing the escape;

(c) the accidental loss of synthetic fishing nets or synthetic material incidental to the repair of such nets, provided that all reasonable precautions have been taken to prevent such loss.

Regulation 7

Reception Facilities

(1) The Government of each party to the Convention undertakes to ensure the provisions of facilities at ports and terminals for the reception of garbage, without causing undue delay to ships, and according to the needs of the ships using them.

(2) The Government of each party shall notify the Organization for transmission to the parties concerned of all cases where the facilities provided under this Regulation are alleged to be inadequate.

Regulation 8

Port State Control on Operational requirements

(1) A ship when in a port of another Party is subject to inspection by officers duly authorized by such Party concerning operational requirements under this Annex, where there are clear grounds for believing that the master or crew are not familiar with essential shipboard procedures relating to the prevention of pollution by garbage.

(2) In the circumstances given in paragraph (1) of this regulation, the Party shall take such steps as will ensure that the ship shall not sail until the situation has been brought to order in accordance with the requirements of this Annex.

(3) Procedures relating to the port State control prescribed in article 5 of the present Convention shall apply to this regulation.

(4) Nothing in this regulation shall be construed to limit the rights and obligations of a Party carrying out control over operational requirements specifically provided for in the present Convention.

Regulation 9

Placards, Garbage Management Plans and Garbage Record–Keeping

(1) (a) Every ship of 12 meters or more in length shall display placards which notify the crew and passengers of the disposal requirements of regulations 3 and 5 of this Annex, as applicable.

(b) The placards shall be written in the official language of the State whose flag the ship is entitled to fly and, for ships engaged in voyages to ports or offshore terminals under the jurisdiction of other Parties to the Convention, in English or French.

(2) Every ship of 400 tons gross tonnage and above, and every ship which is certified to carry 15 persons or more, shall carry a garbage management plan which the crew shall follow. This plan shall provide written procedures for collecting, storing, processing and disposing of garbage, including the use of the equipment on board. It shall also designate the person in charge of carrying out the plan. Such a plan shall be in accordance with the guidelines developed by the Organization and written in the working language of the crew.

(3) Every ship of 400 tons gross tonnage and above and every ship which is certified to carry 15 persons or more engaged in voyages to ports or offshore terminals under the jurisdiction of other Parties to the Convention and every fixed and floating platform engaged in exploration and exploitation of the sea-bed, shall be provided with a Garbage Record Book. The Garbage Record Book, whether as a part of the ship's official logbook or otherwise, shall be in the form specified in the Appendix to this Annex;

(a) each discharge operation, or completed incineration, shall be recorded in the Garbage Record Book and signed for on the date of the incineration or discharge by the officer in charge. Each completed page of the Garbage Record Book shall be signed by the master of the ship. The entries in the Garbage Record Book shall be both in an official language of the State whose flag the ship is entitled to fly, and in English or French. The entries in an official national language of the State whose flag the ship is entitled to fly shall prevail in case of a dispute or discrepancy;

(b) the entry for each incineration or discharge shall include date and time, position of the ship, description of the garbage and the estimated amount incinerated or discharged;

(c) the Garbage Record Book shall be kept on board the ship and in such a place as to be available for inspection in a reasonable time. This document shall be preserved for a period of two years after the last entry is made on the record;

(d) in the event of discharge, escape or accidental loss referred to in regulation 6 of this Annex an entry shall be made in the Garbage Record Book of the circumstances of, and the reasons for, the loss.

(4) The Administration may waive the requirements for Garbage Record Books for:

(i) any ship engaged on voyages of 1 hour or less in duration which is certified to carry 15 persons or more; or

(ii) fixed or floating platforms while engaged in exploration and exploitation of the sea-bed.

(5) The competent authority of the Government of a Party to the Convention may inspect the Garbage Record Book on board any ship to which this regulation applies while the ship is in its ports or offshore terminals and may make a copy of any entry in that book, and may require the master of the ship to certify that the copy is a true copy of such an entry. Any copy so made, which has been certified by the master of the ship as a true copy of an entry in the ship's Garbage Record Book, shall be admissible in any judicial proceedings as evidence of the facts stated in the entry. The inspection of a Garbage Record Book and the taking of a certified copy by the competent authority under this paragraph shall be performed as expeditiously as possible without causing the ship to be unduly delayed.

(6) In the case of ships built before 1 July 1997, this regulation shall apply as from 1 July 1998.

APPENDIX

Form of Garbage Record Book

* * *

4.13 Convention on the Protection of the Marine Environment of the Baltic Sea Area (Without Annexes). Concluded at Helsinki, 22 March 1974. Entered into force, 3 May 1980. *Reprinted in* 13 I.L.M. 546 (1974) & 5 Weston V.F.17

THE STATES PARTIES TO THIS CONVENTION,

CONSCIOUS of the indispensable economic, social and cultural values of the marine environment of the Baltic Sea Area and its living resources for the peoples of the Contracting Parties;

BEARING IN MIND the exceptional hydrographic and ecological characteristics of the Baltic Sea Area and the sensitivity of its living resources to changes in the environment;

NOTING the rapid development of human activities at the Baltic Sea Area, the considerable population living within its catchment area and the highly urbanized and industrialized state of the Contracting Parties as well as their intensive agriculture and forestry;

NOTING with deep concern the increasing pollution of the Baltic Sea Area, originating from many sources such as discharges through rivers, estuaries, outfalls and pipelines, dumping and normal operations of vessels as well as through airborne pollutants;

CONSCIOUS of the responsibility of the Contracting Parties to protect and enhance the values of the marine environment of the Baltic Sea Area for the benefit of their peoples;

RECOGNIZING that the protection and enhancement of the marine environment of the Baltic Sea Area are tasks that cannot effectively be accomplished by national efforts only but that also close regional co-operation and other appropriate international measures aiming at fulfilling these tasks are urgently needed;

NOTING that the relevant recent international conventions even after having entered into force for the respective Contracting Parties do not cover all special requirements to protect and enhance the marine environment of the Baltic Sea Area;

NOTING the importance of scientific and technological co-operation in the protection and enhancement of the marine environment of the Baltic Sea Area, particularly between the Contracting Parties;

DESIRING to develop further regional co-operation in the Baltic Sea Area, the possibilities and requirements of which were confirmed by the signing of the Convention on Fishing and Conservation of the Living Resources in the Baltic Sea and the Belts, Gdansk 1973;

CONSCIOUS of the importance of regional intergovernmental co-operation in the protection of the marine environment of the Baltic Sea Area as an integral part of the peaceful co-operation and mutual understanding between all European States;

HAVE AGREED as follows:

Article 1

Convention area

For the purposes of the present Convention "the Baltic Sea Area" shall be the Baltic Sea proper with the Gulf of Bothnia, the Gulf of Finland and the entrance to the Baltic Sea bounded by the parallel of the Skaw in the Skagerrak at 57°44′8″N. It does not include internal waters of the Contracting Parties.

Article 2

Definitions

For the purposes of the present Convention:

1. "Pollution" means introduction by man, directly or indirectly, of substances or energy into the marine environment, including estuaries, resulting in such deleterious effects as hazard to human health, harm to living resources and marine life, hindrance to legitimate uses of the sea including fishing, impairment of the quality for use of sea water, and reduction of amenities;

2. "Land-based pollution" means pollution of the sea caused by discharges from land reaching the sea waterborne, airborne or directly from the coast, including outfalls from pipelines;

3. a) "Dumping" means:

(i) any deliberate disposal at sea of wastes or other matter from vessels, aircraft, platforms or other man-made structures at sea;

(ii) any deliberate disposal at sea of vessels, aircraft, platforms or other man-made structures at sea;

b) "Dumping" does not include:

(i) the disposal at sea of wastes or other matter incidental to, or derived from the normal operations of vessels, aircraft, platforms or other man-made structures at sea and their equipment, other than wastes or other matter transported by or to vessels, aircraft, platforms or other man-made structures at sea, operating for the purpose of disposal of such matter or derived from the treatment of such wastes or other matter on such vessels, aircraft, platforms or structures;

(ii) placement of matter for a purpose other than the mere disposal thereof, provided that such placement is not contrary to the aims of the present Convention;

4. "Vessels and aircraft" means waterborne or airborne craft of any type whatsoever. This expression includes hydrofoil boats, air-cushion vehicles, submersibles, floating craft whether self-propelled or not, and fixed or floating platforms;

5. "Oil" means petroleum in any form including crude oil, fuel oil, sludge, oil refuse and refined products;

6. "Harmful substance" means any hazardous, noxious, or other substance, which, if introduced into the sea, is liable to cause pollution;

7. "Incident" means an event involving the actual or probable discharge into the sea of a harmful substance, or effluents containing such a substance.

Article 3

Fundamental principles and obligations

1. The Contracting Parties shall individually or jointly take all appropriate legislative, administrative or other relevant measures in order to prevent and abate pollution and to protect and enhance the marine environment of the Baltic Sea Area.

2. The Contracting Parties shall use their best endeavours to ensure that the implementation of the present Convention shall not cause an increase in the pollution of sea areas outside the Baltic Sea Area.

Article 4

Application

1. The present Convention shall apply to the protection of the marine environment of the Baltic Sea Area which comprises the water-body and the sea-bed including their living resources and other forms of marine life.

2. Without prejudice to the sovereign rights in regard to their territorial sea, each Contracting Party shall implement the provisions of the present Convention within its territorial sea through its national authorities.

3. While the provisions of the present Convention do not apply to internal waters, which are under the sovereignty of each Contracting Party, the Contracting Parties undertake, without prejudice to their sovereign rights, to ensure that the purposes of the present Convention will be obtained in these waters.

4. The present Convention shall not apply to any warship, naval auxiliary, military aircraft or other ship and aircraft owned or operated by a State and used, for the time being, only on government non-commercial service.

However, each Contracting Party shall ensure, by the adoption of appropriate measures not impairing the operations or operational capabilities of such ships and aircraft owned or operated by it, that such ships and aircraft act in a manner consistent, so far as is reasonable and practicable, with the present Convention.

Article 5

Hazardous substances

The Contracting Parties undertake to counteract the introduction, whether airborne, waterborne or otherwise, into the Baltic Sea Area of hazardous substances as specified in Annex I of the present Convention.

Article 6

Principles and obligations concerning land-based pollution

1. The Contracting Parties shall take all appropriate measures to control and minimize land-based pollution of the marine environment of the Baltic Sea Area.

2. In particular, the Contracting Parties shall take all appropriate measures to control and strictly limit pollution by noxious substances and materials in accordance with Annex II of the present Convention. To this end they shall, inter alia, as appropriate co-operate in the development and adoption of specific programmes, guidelines, standards or regulations concerning discharges, environmental quality, and products containing such substances and materials and their use.

3. The substances and materials listed in Annex II of the present Convention shall not be introduced into the marine environment of the Baltic Sea Area in significant quantities without a prior special permit, which may be periodically reviewed, by the appropriate national authority.

4. The appropriate national authority will inform the Commission referred to in Article 12 of the present Convention of the quantity, quality and way of discharge if it considers that significant quantities of substances and materials listed in Annex II of the present Convention were discharged.

5. The Contracting Parties shall endeavor to establish and adopt common criteria for issuing permits for discharges.

6. To control and minimize pollution of the Baltic Sea Area by harmful substances the Contracting Parties shall, in addition to the provisions of Article 5 of the present Convention, aim at attaining the goals and applying the criteria enumerated in Annex III of the present Convention.

7. If the discharge from a watercourse, flowing through the territories of two or more Contracting Parties or forming a boundary between them, is liable to cause pollution of the marine environment of the Baltic Sea Area, the Contracting Parties concerned shall in common take appropriate measures in order to prevent and abate such pollution.

8. The Contracting Parties shall endeavour to use best practicable means in order to minimize the airborne pollution of the Baltic Sea Area by noxious substances.

Article 7

Prevention of pollution from ships

1. In order to protect the Baltic Sea Area from pollution by deliberate, negligent or accidental release of oil, harmful substances other than oil, and by the discharge of sewage and garbage from ships, the Contracting Parties shall take measures as set out in Annex IV of the present Convention.

2. The Contracting Parties shall develop and apply uniform requirements for the capacity and location of facilities for the reception of residues of oil, harmful substances other than oil, including sewage and garbage, taking into account inter alia the special needs of passenger ships and combination carriers.

Article 8

Pleasure craft

The Contracting Parties shall, in addition to implementing those provisions of the present Convention which can appropriately be applied to pleasure craft, take special measures in order to abate harmful effects on the marine environment of the Baltic Sea Area of pleasure craft activities. The measures shall inter alia deal with adequate reception facilities for wastes from pleasure craft.

Article 9

Prevention of dumping

1. The Contracting Parties shall, subject to Paragraphs 2 and 4 of this Article, prohibit dumping in the Baltic Sea Area.

2. Dumping of dredged spoils shall be subject to a prior special permit by the appropriate national authority in accordance with the provisions of Annex V of the present Convention.

3. Each Contracting Party undertakes to ensure compliance with the provisions of this Article by vessels and aircraft:

a) registered in its territory or flying its flag;

b) loading, within its territory or territorial sea, matter which is to be dumped; or

c) believed to be engaged in dumping within its territorial sea.

4. The provisions of this Article shall not apply when the safety of human life or of a vessel or aircraft at sea is threatened by the complete destruction or total loss of the vessel or aircraft, or in any case which constitutes a danger to human life, if dumping appears to be the only way of averting the threat and if there is every probability that the damage consequent upon such dumping will be less than would otherwise occur. Such dumping shall be so conducted as to minimize the likelihood of damage to human or marine life.

5. Dumping made under the provisions of Paragraph 4 of this Article shall be reported and dealt with in accordance with Annex VI of the present Convention and shall also be reported forthwith to the Commission referred to in Article 12 of the

present Convention in accordance with the provisions of Regulation 4 of Annex V of the present Convention.

6. In case of dumping suspected to be in contravention of the provisions of this Article the Contracting Parties shall co-operate in investigating the matter in accordance with Regulation 2 of Annex IV of the present Convention.

Article 10

Exploration and exploitation of the sea-bed and its subsoil

Each Contracting Party shall take all appropriate measures in order to prevent pollution of the marine environment of the Baltic Sea Area resulting from exploration or exploitation of its part of the sea-bed and its subsoil or from any associated activities thereon. It shall also ensure that adequate equipment is at hand to start an immediate abatement of pollution in that area.

Article 11

Co-operation in combatting marine pollution

The Contracting Parties shall take measures and co-operate as set out in Annex VI of the present Convention in order to eliminate or minimize pollution of the Baltic Sea Area by oil or other harmful substances.

Article 12

Institutional and organizational framework

1. The Baltic Marine Environment Protection Commission, hereinafter referred to as "the Commission", is hereby established for the purposes of the present Convention.

2. The chairmanship of the Commission shall be given to each Contracting Party in turn in alphabetical order of the names of the States in the English language.

The Chairman shall serve for a period of two years, and cannot during the period of his chairmanship serve as representative of his country.

Should the chairmanship fall vacant, the Contracting Party chairing the Commission shall nominate a successor to remain in office until the term of chairmanship of that Contracting Party expires.

3. Meetings of the Commission shall be held at least once a year upon convocation by the Chairman. Upon the request of a Contracting Party, provided it is endorsed by another Contracting Party, the Chairman shall, as soon as possible, summon an extraordinary meeting at such time and place as the Chairman determines, however, not later than ninety days from the date of the submission of the request.

4. The first meeting of the Commission shall be called by the Depositary Government and shall take place within a period of ninety days from the date following the entry into force of the present Convention.

5. Each Contracting Party shall have one vote in the Commission. Unless otherwise provided under the present Convention, the Commission shall take its decisions unanimously.

Article 13

The duties of the Commission

The duties of the Commission shall be:

a) To keep the implementation of the present Convention under continuous observation;

b) To make recommendations on measures relating to the purposes of the present Convention;

c) To keep under review the contents of the present Convention including its Annexes and to recommend to the Contracting Parties such amendments to the present Convention including its Annexes as may be required including changes in the lists of substances and materials as well as the adoption of new Annexes;

d) To define pollution control criteria, objectives for the reduction of pollution, and objectives concerning measures, particularly according to Annex III of the present Convention;

e) To promote in close co-operation with appropriate governmental bodies, taking into consideration Sub–Paragraph f) of this Article, additional measures to protect the marine environment of the Baltic Sea Area and for this purpose:

(i) to receive, process, summarize and disseminate from available sources relevant scientific, technological and statistical information; and

(ii) to promote scientific and technological research;

f) To seek, when appropriate, the services of competent regional and other international organizations to collaborate in scientific and technological research as well as other relevant activities pertinent to the objectives of the present Convention;

g) To assume such other functions as may be appropriate under the terms of the present Convention.

Article 14

Administrative provisions for the Commission

1. The working language of the Commission shall be English.

2. The Commission shall adopt its Rules of Procedure.

3. The office of the Commission, hereafter referred to as the "Secretariat", shall be in Helsinki.

4. The Commission shall appoint an Executive Secretary and make provisions for the appointment of such other personnel as may be necessary, and determine the duties, terms and conditions of the Executive Secretary.

5. The Executive Secretary shall be the chief administrative official of the Commission and shall perform the functions that are necessary for the administration of the present Convention, the work of the Commission and other tasks entrusted to the Executive Secretary by the Commission and its Rules of Procedure.

Article 15

Financial provisions for the Commission

1. The Commission shall adopt its Financial Rules.

2. The Commission shall adopt an annual or biennial budget of proposed expenditures and budget estimates for the fiscal period following thereafter.

3. The total amount of the budget, including any supplementary budget adopted by the Commission, shall be contributed by the Contracting Parties in equal parts, unless the Commission unanimously decides otherwise.

4. Each Contracting Party shall pay the expenses related to the participation in the Commission of its representatives, experts and advisers.

Article 16

Scientific and technological co-operation

1. The Contracting Parties undertake directly, or when appropriate through competent regional or other international organizations, to co-operate in the fields of science, technology and other research, and to exchange data as well as other scientific information for the purposes of the present Convention.

2. Without prejudice to Paragraphs 1, 2 and 3 of Article 4 of the present Convention the Contracting Parties undertake directly, or when appropriate through competent regional or other international organizations, to promote studies, undertake, support or contribute to programmes aimed at developing ways and means for the assessment of the nature and extent of pollution, pathways, exposures, risks and remedies in the Baltic Sea Area, and particularly to develop alternative methods of treatment, disposal and elimination of such matter and substances that are likely to cause pollution of the marine environment of the Baltic Sea Area.

3. The Contracting Parties undertake directly, or when appropriate through competent regional or other international organizations, and, on the basis of the information and data acquired pursuant to Paragraphs 1 and 2 of this Article, to co-operate in developing inter-comparable observation methods, in performing baseline studies and in establishing complementary or joint programmes for monitoring.

4. The organization and scope of work connected with the implementation of tasks referred to in the preceding Paragraphs should primarily be outlined by the Commission.

Article 17

Responsibility for damage

The Contracting Parties undertake, as soon as possible, jointly to develop and accept rules concerning responsibility for damage resulting from acts or omissions in contravention of the present Convention, including, inter alia, limits of responsibility, criteria and procedures for the determination of liability and available remedies.

Article 18

Settlement of disputes

1. In case of a dispute between Contracting Parties as to the interpretation or application of the present Convention, they should seek a solution by negotiation. If the Parties concerned cannot reach agreement they should seek the good offices of or jointly request the mediation by a third Contracting Party, a qualified international organization or a qualified person.

2. If the Parties concerned have not been able to resolve their dispute through negotiation or have been unable to agree on measures as described above, such disputes shall be, upon common agreement, submitted to an ad-hoc arbitration tribunal, to a permanent arbitration tribunal, or to the International Court of Justice.

Article 19

Safeguard of certain freedoms

Nothing in the present Convention shall be construed as infringing upon the freedom of navigation, fishing, marine scientific research and other legitimate uses of the high seas, as well as upon the right of innocent passage through the territorial sea.

Article 20

Status of Annexes

The Annexes attached to the present Convention form an integral part of the Convention.

Article 21

Relation to other Conventions

The provisions of the present Convention shall be without prejudice to the rights and obligations of the Contracting Parties under treaties concluded previously as well as under treaties which may be concluded in the future, furthering and developing the general principles of the Law of the Sea that the present Convention is based upon and in particular provisions concerning the prevention of pollution of the marine environment.

Article 22

Revision of the Convention

A conference for the purpose of a general revision of the present Convention may be convened with the consent of the Contracting Parties or at the request of the Commission.

Article 23

Amendments to the Articles of the Convention

1. Each Contracting Party may propose amendments to the Articles of the present Convention. Any such proposed amendment shall be submitted to the Depositary Government and communicated by it to all Contracting Parties, which shall inform the Depositary Government of either their acceptance or rejection of the amendment as soon as possible after the receipt of the communication.

The amendment shall enter into force ninety days after the Depositary Government has received notifications of acceptance of that amendment from all Contracting Parties.

2. With the consent of the Contracting Parties or at the request of the Commission a conference may be convened for the purpose of amending the present Convention.

Article 24

Amendments to the Annexes and the adoption of Annexes

1. Any amendment to the Annexes proposed by a Contracting Party shall be communicated to the other Contracting Parties by the Depositary Government and considered in the Commission. If adopted by the Commission, the amendment shall be communicated to the Contracting Parties and recommended for acceptance.

2. Such amendment shall be deemed to have been accepted at the end of a period determined by the Commission unless within that period any one of the Contracting Parties has objected to the amendment. The accepted amendment shall enter into force on a date determined by the Commission.

The period determined by the Commission shall be prolonged for an additional period of six months and the date of entry into force of the amendment postponed accordingly, if, in exceptional cases, any Contracting Party before the expiring of the period determined by the Commission informs the Depositary Government, that, although it intends to accept the proposal, the constitutional requirements for such an acceptance are not yet fulfilled in its State.

3. An Annex to the present Convention may be adopted in accordance with the provisions of this Article.

4. The Depositary Government shall inform all Contracting Parties of any amendments or the adoption of a new Annex which enter into force under this Article and of the date on which such amendment or new Annex enters into force.

5. Any objection under this Article shall be made by notification in writing to the Depositary Government which shall notify all Contracting Parties and the Executive Secretary of any such notification and the date of its receipt.

Article 25

Reservations

1. The provisions of the present Convention shall not be subject to reservations.

2. The provision of Paragraph 1 of this Article does not prevent a Contracting Party from suspending for a period not exceeding one year the application of an Annex of the present Convention or part thereof or an amendment thereto after the Annex in question or the amendment thereto has entered into force.

3. If after the entry into force of the present Convention a Contracting Party invokes the provisions of Paragraph 2 of this Article it shall inform the other Contracting Parties, at the time of the adoption by the Commission of an amendment to an Annex or a new Annex, of those provisions which will be suspended in accordance with Paragraph 2 of this Article.

Article 26

Signature, ratification, approval, and accession

1. The present Convention shall be open for signature in Helsinki on 22 March 1974 by the Baltic Sea States participating in the Diplomatic Conference on the Protection of the Marine Environment of the Baltic Sea Area, held in Helsinki from 18 to 22 March 1974. The present Convention shall be open for accession to any other State interested in fulfilling the aims and purposes of the present Convention, provided that this State is invited by all the Contracting Parties.

2. The present Convention shall be subject to ratification or approval by the States which have signed it.

3. The instruments of ratification, approval, or accession shall be deposited with the Government of Finland, which will perform the duties of the Depositary Government.

Article 27

Entry into force

The present Convention shall enter into force two months after the deposit of the seventh instrument of ratification or approval.

Article 28

Withdrawal

1. At any time after the expiry of five years from the date of entry into force of the present Convention any Contracting Party may, by giving written notification to the Depositary Government, withdraw from the present Convention. The withdrawal shall take effect for such Contracting Party on the thirty-first day of December of the year which follows the year in which the Depositary Government was notified of the withdrawal.

2. In case of notification of withdrawal by a Contracting Party the Depositary Government shall convene a meeting of the Contracting Parties for the purpose of considering the effect of the withdrawal.

Article 29

Language

The present Convention has been drawn up in a single copy in the English language. Official translations into the Danish, Finnish, German, Polish, Russian, and Swedish languages shall be prepared and deposited with the signed original.

4.14 CONVENTION FOR THE PREVENTION OF MARINE POLLUTION FROM LAND-BASED SOURCES (Without Annexes but as Amended). Concluded at Paris, 4 June 1974. Entered into force, 6 May 1978. *Reprinted in* 13 I.L.M. 352 (1974) & Weston V.F.18

THE CONTRACTING PARTIES:

RECOGNIZING that the marine environment and the living resources which it supports are of vital importance to all nations;

MINDFUL that the ecological equilibrium and the legitimate uses of the sea are increasingly threatened by pollution;

CONSIDERING the recommendations of the United Nations Conference on the Human Environment, held in Stockholm in June 1972;

RECOGNIZING that concerted action at national, regional and global levels is essential to prevent and combat marine pollution;

CONVINCED that international action to control the pollution of the sea from land-based sources can and should be taken without delay, as part of progressive and coherent measures to protect the marine environment from pollution, whatever its origin, including current efforts to combat the pollution of international waterways;

CONSIDERING that the common interests of States concerned with the same marine area should induce them to cooperate at regional or sub-regional levels;

RECALLING the Convention for the Prevention of Marine Pollution by Dumping from Ships and Air-craft concluded in Oslo on 15 February 1972;

Have agreed as follows:

ARTICLE I

1. The Contracting Parties pledge themselves to take all possible steps to prevent pollution of the sea, by which is meant the introduction by man, directly or indirectly, of substances or energy into the marine environment (including estuaries) resulting in such deleterious effects as hazards to human health, harm to living resources and to marine eco-systems, damage to amenities or interference with other legitimate uses of the sea.

2. The Contracting Parties shall adopt individually and jointly measures to combat marine pollution from land-based sources in accordance with the provisions of the present convention and shall harmonize their policies in this regard.

ARTICLE 2

The present Convention shall apply to the maritime area within the following limits:

a) those parts of the Atlantic and Arctic Oceans and the dependent seas which lie North of 36° north latitude and between 42° west longitude and 51° east longitude, but excluding:

i) the Baltic Sea and Belts lying to the south and east of lines drawn from Hasenore Head to Gniben Point, from Korshage to Spodsbierg and from Gilbierg Head to Kulien, and

ii) the Mediterranean Sea and its dependent seas as far as the point of intersection of the parallel of 36° north latitude and the meridian of 5°36′ west longitude;

b) that part of the Atlantic Ocean north of 59° north latitude and between 44° west longitude and 42° west longitude.

ARTICLE 3

For the purpose of the present Convention:

a) "*Maritime area*"—means the high seas, the territorial seas of Contracting Parties and waters on the landward side of the base lines from which the breadth of the territorial sea is measured, extending, in the case of watercourses up to the freshwater limit unless otherwise decided under Article 16 of the present Convention;

b) "*Freshwater limit*"—means the place in the watercourse where, at low tide and in a period of low freshwater flow, there is an appreciable increase in salinity due to the presence of sea-water;

c) "*Pollution from land-based sources*"—means the pollution of the maritime area:

i) through watercourses,

ii) from the coast, including introduction through underwater or other pipelines,

iii) from man-made structures placed under the jurisdiction of a Contracting Party within the limits of the area to which the present Convention applies.

iv) by emissions into the atmosphere from land or from man-made structures as defined in subparagraph iii, above.

ARTICLE 4

1. The Contracting Parties undertake:

a) to eliminate, if necessary by stages, pollution of the maritime area from land-based sources of substances listed in Part I of Annex A to the present Convention;

b) to limit strictly pollution of the maritime area from land-based sources of the substances listed in Part II of Annex A to the present Convention.

2. In order to carry out the undertakings in paragraph 1 of this Article, the Contracting Parties, jointly or individually as appropriate, shall implement programmes and measures:

a) for the elimination, as a matter of urgency, of pollution of the maritime area from land-based sources by substances listed in Part I of Annex A to the present Convention;

b) for the reduction or, as appropriate, elimination of pollution of the maritime area from land-based sources by substances listed in Part II of Annex A to the present Convention. These substances shall be discharged only after approval has been granted by the appropriate Authorities within each contracting State. Such approval shall be periodically reviewed.

3. The programmes and measures adopted under paragraph 2 above shall include, as appropriate, specific regulations or standards governing the quality of the environment, discharges into the maritime area, such discharges into watercourses and emissions into the atmosphere as affect the maritime area, and the composition and use of substances and products and shall take into account the latest technical developments.

The programmes shall contain time-limits for their completion.

4. Furthermore, the Contracting Parties may, jointly or individually as appropriate, implement programmes or measures to forestall, reduce or eliminate pollution of the maritime area from land-based sources by a substance not then listed in Annex A

to the present Convention, if scientific evidence has established that a serious hazard may be created in the maritime area by that substance and if urgent action is necessary.

ARTICLE 5

1. The Contracting Parties undertake to adopt measures to forestall and, as appropriate, eliminate pollution of the maritime area from land-based sources by radio-active substances referred to in Part III of Annex A of the present Convention.

2. Without prejudice to their obligations under other Treaties and Conventions, in implementing this undertaking the Contracting Parties shall:

a) take full account of the recommendations of the appropriate international Organizations and Agencies;

b) take account of the monitoring procedures recommended by these international Organisations and Agencies;

c) coordinate their monitoring and study of radio-active substances in accordance with Article 10 and 11 of the present Convention.

ARTICLE 6

1. With a view to preserving and enhancing the quality of the marine environment, the Contracting Parties, without prejudice to the provisions of Article 4, shall endeavour:

a) to reduce existing pollution from land-based sources;

b) to forestall any new pollution from land-based sources, including that which derives from new substances.

2. In implementing this undertaking, the Contracting Parties shall take account of:

a) the nature and quantities of the pollutants under consideration;

b) the level of existing pollution;

c) the quality and absorptive capacity of the receiving waters of the maritime area;

d) the need for an integrated planning policy, consistent with the requirement of environmental protection.

ARTICLE 7

The Contracting Parties agree to apply the measures they adopt in such a way as to avoid increasing pollution:

—in the seas outside the area to which the present Convention applies;

—in the maritime area covered by the present Convention, originating otherwise than from land-based sources.

ARTICLE 8

No provision of the present Convention may be interpreted as preventing the Contracting Parties from taking more stringent measures to combat marine pollution from land-based sources.

ARTICLE 9

1. When pollution from land-based sources originating from the territory of a Contracting Party by substances not listed in Part 1 of Annex A of the present Convention is likely to prejudice the interests of one or more of the other Parties to the

Convention, the Contracting Parties concerned undertake to enter into consultation, at the request of any one of them, with a view to negotiating a co-operation agreement.

2. At the request of any Contracting Party concerned, the Commission referred to in Article 15 of the present Convention shall consider the question and may make recommendations with a view to reaching a satisfactory solution.

3. The special agreements specified in Paragraph 1 of this Article may, among other things, define the areas to which they shall apply, the quality objectives to be achieved, and the methods for achieving these objectives including methods for the application of appropriate standards, and the scientific and technical information to be collected.

4. The Contracting Parties signatory to these agreements shall, through the medium of the Commission, inform the other Contracting Parties of their purport and of the progress made in putting them into effect.

ARTICLE 10

The Contracting Parties agree to establish complementary or joint programmes of scientific and technical research, including research into the best methods of eliminating or replacing noxious substances so as to reduce marine pollution from land-based sources, and to transmit to each other the information so obtained. In doing so they will have regard to the work carried out, in these fields, by the appropriate international Organizations and Agencies.

ARTICLE 11

The Contracting Parties agree to set up progressively, and to operate within the area covered by the present Convention, a permanent monitoring system allowing of:

—the earliest possible assessment of the existing level of marine pollution;

—the assessment of the effectiveness of measures for the reduction of marine pollution from land-based sources taken under the terms of the present Convention.

For this purpose the Contracting Parties shall lay down the ways and means of pursuing individually or jointly systematic and ad hoc monitoring programmes. These programmes shall take into account the deployment of research vessels and other facilities in the monitoring area.

The programmes will take into account similar programmes pursued in accordance with Conventions already in force and by the appropriate international Organisations and Agencies.

ARTICLE 12

1. Each Contracting Party undertakes to ensure compliance with the provisions of this Convention and to take in its territory appropriate measures to prevent and punish conduct in contravention of the provisions of the present Convention.

2. The Contracting Parties shall inform the Commission of the legislative and administrative measures they have taken to implement the provisions of the above paragraph.

ARTICLE 13

The Contracting Parties undertake to assist one another as appropriate to prevent incidents which may result in pollution from land-based sources, to minimize and eliminate the consequences of such incidents, and to exchange information to that end.

ARTICLE 14

1. The provisions of the present Convention may not be invoked against a Contracting Party to the extent that the latter is prevented, as a result of pollution having its origin in the territory of a non-Contracting State, from ensuring their full application.

2. However, the said Contracting Party shall endeavour to co-operate with the non-Contracting State so as to make possible the full application of the present Convention.

ARTICLE 15

A Commission made of representatives of each of the Contracting Parties is hereby established. The Commission shall meet at regular intervals and at any time, when due to special circumstances it is so decided in accordance with the rules of procedure.

ARTICLE 16

It shall be the duty of the Commission:

a) to exercise overall supervision over the implementation of the present Convention;

b) to review generally the condition of the seas within the area to which the present Convention applies, the effectiveness of the control measures being adopted and the need for any additional or different measures;

c) to examine the feasibility of and, as appropriate to fix, if necessary, in accordance with Article 3(a), on the proposal of the Contracting Party or Parties bordering on the same watercourse and following a standard procedure, the limit to which the maritime area shall extend in this watercourse;

d) to draw up, in accordance with Article 4 of the present Convention, programmes and measures for the elimination or reduction of pollution from land-based sources;

e) to make recommendations in accordance with the provisions of Article 9;

f) to receive and review information and distribute it to the Contracting Parties in accordance with the provisions of Article 11, 12, and 17 of the present Convention;

g) to make, in accordance with Article 13, recommendations regarding any amendment to the lists of substances included in Annex A of the present Convention;

h) to discharge such other functions, as may be appropriate, under the terms of the present Convention.

ARTICLE 17

The Contracting Parties, in accordance with a standard procedure, shall transmit to the Commission:

a) the results of monitoring pursuant to Article (11).

b) the most detailed information available on the substances listed in the Annexes to the present Convention and liable to find their way into the maritime area.

The Contracting Parties shall endeavour to improve progressively techniques for gathering such information which can contribute to the revision of the pollution reduction programmes adopted in accordance with Article 4.

ARTICLE 18

1. The Commission shall draw up its own Rules of Procedure which shall be adopted by unanimous vote.

2. The Commission shall draw up its own Financial Regulations which shall be adopted by unanimous vote.

3. The Commission shall adopt, by unanimous vote, programmes and measures for the reduction or elimination of pollution from land-based sources as provided for in Article 4, and for scientific research and monitoring as provided for in Articles 10 and 11 and the decisions under Article 16c.

Such programmes and measures shall commence for, and be applied by, all Contracting Parties two hundred days after adoption, unless the Commission specifies another date.

Should unanimity not be attainable, the Commission may nonetheless adopt a programme or measures by a three quarters majority vote of its members. Such programmes or measures shall commence for those Contracting Parties which voted for them two hundred days after their adoption, unless the Commission specifies another date, and for any other Contracting Party after it has explicitly accepted the programme or measures which it may do at any time.

The Commission may adopt, in accordance with Article 16g, recommendations for amendments to Annex A to the present Convention by a three quarters majority vote of its members and shall submit them for the approval of the Governments of the Contracting Parties. Any Government of a Contracting Party that is unable to approve an amendment shall notify the Depositary Government in writing within a period of two hundred days after the adoption of the Recommendation of amendment in the Commission. Should no such notification be received, the amendment shall enter into force for all Contracting Parties two hundred and thirty days after the vote in the Commission. The Depositary Government shall notify the Contracting Parties as soon as possible of the receipt of any notification.

ARTICLE 19

Within its competences, the European Economic Community is entitled to a number of votes equal to the number of its member States which are Contracting Parties to the present Convention.

The European Economic Community shall not exercise its right to vote in cases where its member States exercise theirs and conversely.

ARTICLE 20

The depositary Government shall convene the first meeting of the Commission as soon as possible after the coming into force of the present Convention.

ARTICLE 21

Any dispute between Contracting Parties relating to the interpretation or application of the present Convention, which cannot be settled otherwise by the parties concerned, for instance by means of inquiry or conciliation within the Commission, shall, at the request of any of those Parties be submitted to arbitration under the conditions laid down in Annex B to the Convention.

ARTICLE 22

The present Convention shall be open at Paris, from 4th June 1974 to 30th June 1975, for signature by the States invited to the Diplomatic Conference on the Convention for the prevention of Marine Pollution from Land–Based Sources held at Paris and by the European Economic Community.

ARTICLE 23

The present Convention shall be subject to ratification, acceptance or approval. The instruments of ratification, acceptance or approval shall be deposited with the Government of the French Republic.

ARTICLE 24

1. After 30th June 1975, the present Convention shall be open for accession by States referred to in Article 22 and by the European Economic Community.

2. The present Convention shall also be open for accession from the same date by any other Contracting Party to the Convention for the prevention of Marine Pollution by Dumping from Ships and Aircraft opened for signature at Oslo on 15th February 1972.

3. From the date of its entry into force, the present Convention shall be open for accession by any State not referred to in Article 22 located upstream on watercourses crossing the territory of one or more Contracting Parties to the present Convention and reaching the maritime area defined in Article 2.

4. The Contracting Parties may, by unanimous vote, invite other States to accede to the present Convention. In that case the maritime area defined in Article 2 may, if necessary, be amended in accordance with Article 27 of the present Convention.

5. The instruments of accession shall be deposited with the Government of the French Republic.

ARTICLE 25

1. The present Convention shall come into force on the thirtieth day following the date of deposit of the seventh instrument of ratification, approval, acceptance or accession.

2. For each Party ratifying, accepting or approving the present Convention or acceding to it after the deposit of the seventh instrument of ratification, approval, acceptance or accession, the present Convention shall enter into force on the thirtieth day after deposit by that Party of its instrument of ratification, acceptance, approval or accession.

ARTICLE 26

At any time after the expiry of two years from the date of coming into force of the present Convention in relation to any Contracting Party such Party may withdraw from the Convention by notice in writing to the depositary Government. Such notice shall take effect one year after the date on which it is received.

ARTICLE 27

1. The depositary Government shall, at the request of the Commission on a decision taken by a two-thirds majority of its members, call a Conference for the purpose of revising or amending the present Convention.

2. Upon accession by a State as provided for in Paragraphs 2, 3, and 4 of Article 24, the maritime area defined in Article 2 may be amended upon a proposal by the Commission adopted by a unanimous vote. Such amendments shall enter into force after unanimous approval by the Contracting Parties.

ARTICLE 28

The depositary Government shall inform the Contracting Parties and those referred to in Article 22:

(a) of signatures to the present Convention, of the deposit of instruments or ratification, acceptance, approval or accession, and of notices of withdrawal in accordance with Articles 22, 23, 24 and 26;

(b) of the date on which the present Convention comes into force in accordance with Article 25;

(c) of the receipt of notifications of approval or of objection to the present Convention and its annexes, and of the entry into force of amendments thereto, in accordance with Articles 18 and 27 of the present Convention.

ARTICLE 29

The original of the present Convention of which the French and English texts shall be equally authentic, shall be deposited with the Government of the French Republic which shall send certified copies thereof to the Contracting Parties and the States referred to in Article 22 and shall deposit a certified copy with the Secretary General of the United Nations for registration and publication in accordance with Article 102 of the United Nations Charter.

4.15 Convention for the Protection of the Mediterranean Sea Against Pollution (Without Protocols and Annex). Concluded at Barcelona, 16 February 1976. Entered into force, 12 February 1978. *Reprinted in* 15 I.L.M. 290 (1976) & 5 Weston V.F.19

THE CONTRACTING PARTIES,

Conscious of the economic, social, health and cultural value of the marine environment of the Mediterranean Sea Area,

Fully aware of their responsibility to preserve this common heritage for the benefit and enjoyment of present and future generations,

Recognizing the threat posed by pollution to the marine environment, its ecological equilibrium, resources and legitimate uses,

Mindful of the special hydrographic and ecological characteristics of the Mediterranean Sea Area and its particular vulnerability to pollution,

Noting that existing international conventions on the subject do not cover, in spite of the progress achieved, all aspects and sources of marine pollution and do not entirely meet the special requirements of the Mediterranean Sea Area,

Realizing fully the need for close co-operation among the States and international organizations concerned in a co-ordinated and comprehensive regional approach for the protection and enhancement of the marine environment in the Mediterranean Sea Area,

HAVE AGREED AS FOLLOWS:

Article 1

Geographical coverage

1. For the purposes of this Convention, the Mediterranean Sea Area shall mean the maritime waters of the Mediterranean Sea proper, including its gulfs and seas bounded to the west by the meridian passing through Cape Spartel lighthouse, at the entrance of the Straits of Gibraltar, and to the East by the southern limits of the Straits of the Dardanelles between Mehmetcik and Kumkale lighthouses.

2. Except as may be otherwise provided in any protocol to this Convention the Mediterranean Sea Area shall not include internal waters of the Contracting Parties.

Article 2

Definitions

For the purposes of this Convention:

a) "pollution" means the introduction by man, directly or indirectly, of substances or energy into the marine environment resulting in such deleterious effects as harm to living resources, hazards to human health, hindrance to marine activities including fishing, impairment of quality for use of sea water and reduction of amenities.

b) "organization" means the body designated as responsible for carrying out secretariat functions pursuant to article 13 of this Convention.

Article 3

General provisions

1. The Contracting Parties may enter into bilateral or multilateral agreements, including regional or sub-regional agreements, for the protection of the marine environment of the Mediterranean Sea against pollution, provided that such agreements are consistent with this Convention and conform to international law. Copies of

such agreements between Contracting Parties to this Convention shall be communicated to the Organization.

2. Nothing in this Convention shall prejudice the codification and development of the Law of the Sea by the United Nations Conference on the Law of the Sea convened pursuant to Resolution 2750 C (XXV) of the General Assembly of the United Nations, nor the present or future claims and legal views of any State concerning the law of the sea and nature and extent of coastal and flag State jurisdiction.

Article 4

General undertakings

1. The Contracting Parties shall individually or jointly take all appropriate measures in accordance with the provisions of this Convention and those protocols in force to which they are party, to prevent, abate and combat pollution of the Mediterranean Sea Area and to protect and enhance the marine environment in that Area.

2. The Contracting Parties shall co-operate in the formulation and adoption of protocols, in addition to the protocols opened for signature at the same time as this Convention, prescribing agreed measures, procedures and standards for the implementation of this Convention.

3. The Contracting Parties further pledge themselves to promote, within the international bodies considered to be competent by the Contracting Parties, measures concerning the protection of the marine environment in the Mediterranean Sea Area from all types and sources of pollution.

Article 5

Pollution caused by dumping from ships and aircraft

The Contracting Parties shall take all appropriate measures to prevent and abate pollution of the Mediterranean Sea Area caused by dumping from ships and aircraft.

Article 6

Pollution from ships

The Contracting Parties shall take all measures in conformity with international law to prevent, abate and combat pollution of the Mediterranean Sea Area caused by discharges from ships and to ensure the effective implementation in that Area of the rules which are generally recognized at the international level relating to the control of this type of pollution.

Article 7

Pollution resulting from exploration and exploitation of the continental shelf and the seabed and its subsoil

The Contracting Parties shall take all appropriate measures to prevent, abate and combat pollution of the Mediterranean Sea Area resulting from exploration and exploitation of the continental shelf and the seabed and its subsoil.

Article 8

Pollution from land-based sources

The Contracting Parties shall take all appropriate measures to prevent, abate and combat pollution of the Mediterranean Sea Area caused by discharges from rivers, coastal establishments or outfalls, or emanating from any other land-based sources within their territories.

Article 9

Co-operation in dealing with pollution emergencies

1. The Contracting Parties shall co-operate in taking the necessary measures for dealing with pollution emergencies in the Mediterranean Sea Area, whatever the causes of such emergencies, and reducing or eliminating damage resulting therefrom.

2. Any Contracting Party which becomes aware of any pollution emergency in the Mediterranean Sea Area shall without delay notify, the Organization and, either through the Organization or directly, any Contracting Party likely to be affected by such emergency.

Article 10

Monitoring

1. The Contracting Parties shall endeavor to establish, in close co-operation with the international bodies which they consider competent, complementary or joint programmes including, as appropriate, programmes at the bilateral or multilateral levels, for pollution monitoring in the Mediterranean Sea Area and shall endeavor to establish a pollution monitoring system for that Area.

2. For this purpose, the Contracting Parties shall designate the competent authorities responsible for pollution monitoring within areas under their national jurisdiction and participate as far as practicable in international arrangements for pollution monitoring in areas beyond national jurisdiction.

3. The Contracting Parties undertake to co-operate in the formulation, adoption and implementation of such annexes to this Convention as may be required to prescribe common procedures and standards for pollution monitoring.

Article 11

Scientific and technological co-operation

1. The Contracting Parties undertake as far as possible to co-operate directly, or when appropriate through competent regional or other international organizations, in the fields of science and technology, and to exchange data as well as other scientific information for the purpose of this Convention.

2. The Contracting Parties undertake as far as possible to develop and co-ordinate their national research programmes relating to all types of marine pollution in the Mediterranean Sea Area and to co-operate in the establishment and implementation of regional and other international research programmes for the purposes of this Convention.

3. The Contracting Parties undertake to co-operate in the provision of technical and other possible assistance in fields relating to marine pollution, with priority to be given to the special needs of developing countries in the Mediterranean region.

Article 12

Liability and compensation

The Contracting Parties undertake to co-operate as soon as possible in the formulation and adoption of appropriate procedures for the determination of liability and compensation for damage resulting from the pollution of the marine environment deriving from violations of the provisions of this Convention and applicable protocols.

Article 13

Institutional arrangements

The Contracting Parties designate the United Nations Environment Programme as responsible for carrying out the following secretariat functions:

(i) To convene and prepare the meetings of Contracting Parties and conferences provided for in articles 14, 15, and 16;

(ii) To transmit to the Contracting Parties notifications, reports and other information received in accordance with articles 3, 9, and 20;

(iii) To consider inquiries by, and information from, the Contracting Parties, and to consult with them on questions relating to this Convention and the protocols and annexes thereto;

(iv) To perform the functions assigned to it by the protocols to this Convention;

(v) To perform such other functions as may be assigned to it by the Contracting Parties;

(vi) To ensure the necessary co-ordination with other international bodies which the Contracting Parties consider competent, and in particular to enter into such administrative arrangements as may be required for the effective discharge of the secretariat functions.

Article 14

Meetings of the Contracting Parties

1. The Contracting Parties shall hold ordinary meetings once every two years, and extraordinary meetings at any other time deemed necessary, upon the request of the Organization or at the request of any Contracting Party, provided that such requests are supported by at least two Contracting Parties.

2. It shall be the function of the meetings of the Contracting Parties to keep under review the implementation of this Convention and the protocols and, in particular:

(i) To review generally the inventories carried out by Contracting Parties and competent international organizations on the state of marine pollution and its effects in the Mediterranean Sea Area;

(ii) To consider reports submitted by the Contracting Parties under article 20;

(iii) To adopt, review and amend as required the annexes to this Convention and to the protocols, in accordance with the procedure established in article 17;

(iv) To make recommendations regarding the adoption of any additional protocols or any amendments to this Convention or the protocols in accordance with the provisions of articles 15 and 16;

(v) To establish working groups as required to consider any matters related to this Convention and the protocols and annexes;

(vi) To consider and undertake any additional action that may be required for the achievement of the purposes of this Convention and the protocols.

Article 15

Adoption of additional protocols

1. The Contracting Parties, at a diplomatic conference, may adopt additional protocols to this Convention pursuant to paragraph 2 of article 4.

2. A diplomatic conference for the purpose of adopting additional protocols shall be convened by the Organization at the request of two thirds of the Contracting Parties.

3. Pending the entry into force of this Convention the Organization may, after consulting with the signatories to this Convention, convene a diplomatic conference for the purpose of adopting additional protocols.

Article 16

Amendment of the Convention or protocols

1. Any Contracting Party to this Convention may propose amendments to the Convention. Amendments shall be adopted by a diplomatic conference which shall be convened by the Organization at the request of two thirds of the Contracting Parties.

2. Any Contracting Party to this Convention may propose amendments to any protocol. Such amendments shall be adopted by a diplomatic conference which shall be convened by the Organization at the request of two thirds of the Contracting Parties to the protocol concerned.

3. Amendments to this Convention shall be adopted by a three-fourths majority vote of the Contracting Parties to the Convention which are represented at the diplomatic conference, and shall be submitted by the Depositary for acceptance by all Contracting Parties to the Convention. Amendments to any protocol shall be adopted by a three-fourths majority vote of the Contracting Parties to such protocol which are represented at the diplomatic conference, and shall be submitted by the Depositary for acceptance by all Contracting Parties to such protocol.

4. Acceptance of amendments shall be notified to the Depositary in writing. Amendments adopted in accordance with paragraph 3 of this article shall enter into force between Contracting Parties having accepted such amendments on the thirtieth day follow the receipt by the Depositary of notification of their acceptance by at least three fourths of the Contracting Parties to this Convention or to the protocol concerned, as the case may be.

5. After the entry into force of an amendment to this Convention or to a protocol, any new Contracting Party to this Convention or such protocol shall become a Contracting Party to the instrument as amended.

Article 17

Annexes and amendments to annexes

1. Annexes to this Convention or to any protocol shall form an integral part of the Convention or such protocol, as the case may be.

2. Except as may be otherwise provided in any protocol, the following procedure shall apply to the adoption and entry into force of any amendments to annexes to this Convention or to any protocol, with the exception of amendments to the annex on arbitration:

(i) Any Contracting Party may propose amendments to the annexes to this Convention or to protocols at the meetings referred to in article 14:

(ii) Such amendments shall be adopted by a three-fourths majority vote of the Contracting Parties to the instrument in question;

(iii) The Depositary shall without delay communicate the amendments so adopted to all Contracting Parties;

(iv) Any Contracting Party that is unable to approve an amendment to the annexes to this Convention or to any protocol shall so notify in writing the Depositary within a period determined by the Contracting Parties concerned when adopting the amendment;

(v) The Depositary shall without delay notify all Contracting Parties of any notification received pursuant to the preceding sub-paragraph;

(vi) On expiry of the period referred to in sub-paragraph (iv) above, the amendment to the annex shall become effective for all Contracting Parties to this Convention or to the protocol concerned which have not submitted a notification in accordance with the provisions of that sub-paragraph.

3. The adoption and entry into force of a new annex to this Convention or to any protocol shall be subject to the same procedure as for the adoption and entry into force, provided that, if any amendment to the Convention or the protocol concerned is involved the new annex shall not enter into force until such time as the amendment to the Convention or the protocol concerned enters into force.

4. Amendments to the annex on arbitration shall be considered to be amendments to this Convention and shall be proposed and adopted in accordance with the procedures set out in article 16 above.

Article 18

Rules of procedure and financial rules

1. The Contracting Parties shall adopt rules of procedure for their meetings and conferences envisaged in articles 14, 15, and 16 above.

2. The Contracting Parties shall adopt financial rules, prepared in consultation with the Organization, to determine, in particular, their financial participation.

Article 19

Special exercise of voting right

Within the areas of their competence, the European Economic Community and any regional economic grouping referred to in article 24 of this Convention shall exercise their right to vote with a number of votes equal to the number of their member States which are Contracting Parties to this Convention and to one or more protocols; the European Economic Community and any grouping as referred to above shall not exercise their right to vote in cases where the member States concerned exercise theirs, and conversely.

Article 20

Reports

The Contracting Parties shall transmit to the Organization reports on the measures adopted in implementation of this Convention and of protocols to which they are Parties, in such form and at such intervals as the meetings of Contracting Parties may determine.

Article 21

Compliance control

The Contracting Parties undertake to co-operate in the development of procedures enabling them to control the application of this Convention and the protocols.

Article 22

Settlement of disputes

1. In case of a dispute between Contracting Parties as to the interpretation or application of this Convention or the protocols, they shall seek a settlement of the dispute through negotiation or any other peaceful means of their own choice.

2. If the parties concerned cannot settle their dispute through the means mentioned in the preceding paragraph, the dispute shall upon common agreement be submitted to arbitration under the conditions laid down in Annex A to this Convention.

3. Nevertheless, the Contracting Parties may at any time declare that they recognize as compulsory *ipso-facto* and without special agreement, in relation to any other Party accepting the same obligation, the application of the arbitration procedure

in conformity with the provisions of Annex A. Such declaration shall be notified in writing to the Depositary, who shall communicate it to the other Parties.

Article 23

Relationship between the Convention and protocols

1. No one may become a Contracting Party to this Convention unless it becomes at the same time a Contracting Party to at least one of the protocols. No one may become a Contracting Party to a protocol unless it is, or becomes at the same time a Contracting Party to this Convention.

2. Any protocol to this Convention shall be binding only on the Contracting Parties to the protocol in question.

3. Decisions concerning any protocol pursuant to articles 14, 16 and 17 of this Convention shall be taken only by the Parties to the protocol concerned.

Article 24

Signature

This Convention, the Protocol for the Prevention of Pollution of the Mediterranean Sea by Dumping from Ships and Aircraft and the Protocol Concerning Co-operation in Combating Pollution of the Mediterranean Sea by Oil and Other Harmful Substances in Cases of Emergency shall be open for signature in Barcelona on 16 February 1976 and in Madrid from 17 February 1976 to 16 February 1977 by any State invited as a participant in the Conference of Plenipotentiaries of the Coastal States of the Mediterranean Region on the Protection of the Mediterranean Sea, held in Barcelona from 2 to 16 February 1976, and by any State entitled to sign any protocol in accordance with the provisions of such protocol. They shall also be open until the same date for signature by the European Economic Community and by any similar regional economic grouping at least one member of which is a coastal State of the Mediterranean Sea Area and which exercise competences in fields covered by this Convention, as well as by any protocol affecting them.

Article 25

Ratification, acceptance or approval

This Convention and any protocol thereto shall be subject to ratification, acceptance, or approval. Instruments of ratification, acceptance or approval shall be deposited with the Government of Spain, which will assume the functions of Depositary.

Article 26

Accession

1. As from 17 February 1977, the present Convention, the Protocol for the Prevention of Pollution of the Mediterranean Sea by Dumping from Ships and Aircraft, and the Protocol Concerning Co-operation in Combating Pollution of the Mediterranean Sea by Oil and Other Harmful Substances in Cases of Emergency shall be open for accession by the States, by the European Economic Community and by any grouping as referred to in article 24.

2. After the entry into force of the Convention and of any protocol, any State not referred to in article 24 may accede to this Convention and to any protocol, subject to prior approval by three-fourths of the Contracting Parties to the protocol concerned.

3. Instruments of accession shall be deposited with the Depositary.

Article 27

Entry into force

1. This Convention shall enter into force on the same date as the protocol first entering into force.

2. The Convention shall also enter into force with regard to the States, the European Economic Community and any regional economic grouping referred to in article 24 if they have complied with the formal requirements for becoming Contracting Parties to any other protocol not yet entered into force.

3. Any protocol to this Convention, except as otherwise provided in such protocol, shall enter into force on the thirtieth day following the date of deposit of at least six instruments of ratification, acceptance, or approval of, or accession to, such protocol by the Parties referred to in article 24.

4. Thereafter, this Convention and any protocol shall enter into force with respect to any State, the European Economic Community and any regional economic grouping referred to in article 24 on the thirtieth day following the date of deposit of the instruments of ratification, acceptance, approval or accession.

Article 28

Withdrawal

1. At any time after three years from the date of entry into force of this Convention, any Contracting Party may withdraw from this Convention by giving written notification of withdrawal.

2. Except as may be otherwise provided in any protocol to this Convention, any Contracting Party may, at any time after three years from the date of entry into force of such protocol, withdraw from such protocol by giving written notification of withdrawal.

3. Withdrawal shall take effect 90 days after the date on which notification of withdrawal is received by the Depositary.

4. Any Contracting Party which withdraws from this Convention shall be considered as also having withdrawn from any protocol to which it was a Party.

5. Any Contracting Party which, upon its withdrawal from a protocol, is no longer a Party to any protocol to this Convention, shall be considered as also having withdrawn from this Convention.

Article 29

Responsibilities of the Depository

1. The Depositary shall inform the Contracting Parties, any other Party referred in article 24, and the Organizations:

(i) Of the signature of this Convention and of any protocol thereto, and of the deposit of instruments of ratification, acceptance, approval or accession in accordance with articles 24, 25 and 26;

(ii) Of the date on which the Convention and any protocol will come into force in accordance with the provisions of article 27;

(iii) Of notifications of withdrawal made in accordance with article 28;

(iv) Of the amendments adopted with respect to the Convention and to any protocol, their acceptance by the Contracting Parties and the date of entry into force of those amendments in accordance with the provisions of article 16;

(v) Of the adoption of new annexes and of the amendment of any annex in accordance with article 17;

(vi) Of declarations recognizing as compulsory the application of the arbitration procedure mentioned in paragraph 3 of article 22.

2. The original of this Convention and of any protocol thereto shall be deposited with the Depositary, the Government of Spain, which shall send certified copies thereof to the Contracting Parties, to the Organization, and to the Secretary–General of the United Nations for registration and publication in accordance with Article 102 of the United Nations Charter.

4.16 CONVENTION FOR THE PROTECTION OF THE RHINE RIVER AGAINST POLLUTION BY CHEMICAL POLLUTION (Without Annexes). Concluded at Bonn, 3 December 1976. Entered into force, 2 January 1979. 1124 U.N.T.S. 375; *reprinted in* 6 I.L.M. 242 (1967)

The Government of the Federal Republic of Germany, the Government of the French Republic, the Government of the Grand Duchy of Luxembourg, the Government of the Kingdom of the Netherlands, the Government of the Swiss Confederation and the European Economic Community,

Referring to the Agreement of 29 April 1963 and the Additional Agreement of 3 December 1976 on the International Commission for the Protection of the Rhine against Pollution,

Considering that chemical pollution of the waters of the Rhine is a threat to its flora and fauna and also has undesirable effects on sea water,

Conscious of the dangers for certain uses of the waters of the Rhine that may result from such pollution,

Desiring to improve the quality of the waters of the Rhine with these uses in mind,

Considering that the Rhine is also used for other purposes, in particular for shipping and for receiving effluents,

Convinced that international action to protect the waters of the Rhine against chemical pollution must be evaluated in conjunction with other efforts to protect these waters, in particular efforts aimed at the conclusion of agreements to counter pollution by chlorides and thermal pollution, and that such action forms part of the continuing and interrelated measures to protect both fresh water and sea water against pollution,

Considering the action taken by the European Economic Community to protect the waters, in particular under the Council's directive of 4 May 1976 concerning pollution resulting from specific dangerous substances discharged into the water environment of the Community,

Referring to the results of the ministerial conferences held on 25 and 26 October 1972 in The Hague, 4 and 5 December 1973 in Bonn and 1 April 1976 in Paris, on protection of the Rhine against pollution,

Have agreed as follows:

Article 1. (1) In order to improve the quality of the waters of the Rhine, the Contracting Parties, in accordance with the following provisions, shall take appropriate action:

(*a*) To eliminate pollution of the surface waters of the Rhine basin by the dangerous substances included in the families and groupings of substances specified in annex I (hereinafter referred to as "substances listed in annex I"); they shall aim gradually to eliminate discharges of these substances, taking into account the findings of research carried out by specialists on each of these substances, as well as the technical means available;

(*b*) To reduce pollution of the waters of the Rhine by those dangerous substances included in the families and groups of substances listed in annex II (hereinafter referred to as "substances listed in annex II").

(2) When taking the action referred to in paragraph 1, reasonable consideration shall be given to the fact that the waters of the Rhine are used for the following purposes:

(*a*) Supplying drinking water for human consumption,

(*b*) Consumption by domestic and wild animals,

(c) Conserving and developing the natural flora and fauna, and maintaining the self-purifying capacity of the waters,

(d) Fishing,

(e) Recreation, taking hygienic and aesthetic requirements into consideration,

(f) Direct or indirect supply of fresh water to agricultural land,

(g) Production of water for industrial uses, and the need to preserve an acceptable quality of sea water.

(3) The provisions of this Agreement are only the first step towards achieving the aim referred to in paragraph 1 of this article.

(4) Annex A of this Agreement provides a description of what the Contracting Parties understand by the term "Rhine" for purposes of implementing the Agreement.

Article 2. (1) The Governments Parties to this Agreement shall, in accordance with the provisions of annex III, paragraph 1, draw up a national list of those discharges into the surface waters of the Rhine basin that may contain substances covered in annex I to which emission standards may be applicable.

(2) The Governments shall, in accordance with the provisions of annex III, paragraph 2, inform the International Commission for the Protection of the Rhine against Pollution (hereinafter referred to as "the International Commission"), of the items on this list, which shall be updated regularly and at least once every three years.

(3) The proposals made by the International Commission, referred to in article 6, paragraph 3, may, if necessary, contain a list of various substances listed in annex II.

Article 3. (1) Every discharge into the surface waters of the Rhine basin that may contain one of the substances listed in annex I shall require prior approval by the competent authority of the Government concerned.

(2) In the case of discharges of those substances into the surface waters of the Rhine basin and when required for the implementation of this Agreement, in the case of discharges of those substances into drains, the approval shall specify emission standards which shall not exceed the limits set in article 5.

(3) So far as current discharges of those substances are concerned, the approval shall set a deadline for compliance with its terms. This deadline shall not exceed the limits set in article 5, paragraph 3.

(4) Approval shall be given only for a limited period. It may be renewed in the light of any changes made in the limits referred to in article 5.

Article 4. (1) The emission standards specified in the approval granted under article 3 shall determine:

(a) The permissible maximum concentration of a substance in discharges; in cases of dilution, the limits referred to in article 5, paragraph 2, subparagraph *(a)*, shall be divided by the dilution factor;

(b) The permissible maximum quantity of a substance in discharges over one or more fixed periods of time; if necessary, this maximum may also be expressed as a unit of weight of the pollutant per unit of the characteristic component of the polluting action (for instance, per unit of weight of raw material or per unit of product).

(2) If the discharger declares that he cannot comply with the prescribed emission standards, or if the competent authority of the Government concerned confirms this, permission shall be refused.

(3) If the emission standards are not being adhered to, the competent authority of the Government concerned shall take all appropriate steps to ensure that the terms of the approval are complied with and, where necessary, that the discharge is forbidden.

Article 5. (1) The International Commission shall propose the limits referred to in article 3, paragraph 2, and, where necessary, their applicability to discharges into drains. These limits shall be set in accordance with the procedure laid down in article 14. Once adopted, they shall be included in annex IV.

(2) These limits shall be determined:

(a) By the permissible maximum concentration of a substance in the discharges; and

(b) Where appropriate, by the permissible maximum quantity of such a substance, expressed as a unit of weight of the pollutant per unit of the component characteristic of the polluting action (for instance, per unit of weight of raw material or per unit of product).

Where appropriate, the limits applicable to industrial effluents shall be determined by sector and by product type.

The limits applicable to the substances listed in annex I shall be determined primarily on the basis of:

—Toxicity,

—Persistence,

—Bio-accumulation,

taking into consideration the best technical facilities available.

(3) The International Commission shall propose to the Parties to the Agreement the deadlines referred to in article 3, paragraph 3, taking into account the distinctive characteristics of the industrial sectors concerned and, where appropriate, of product types. These deadlines shall be established in accordance with the procedure laid down in article 14.

(4) The International Commission shall use the findings obtained at the international measurement points in order to establish to what extent the content of substances listed in annex I in the waters of the Rhine has changed after implementation of the foregoing provisions.

(5) The International Commission, if this is required from the point of view of the quality of the waters of the Rhine, may propose other measures aimed at reducing the pollution of the waters of the Rhine, particularly with regard to toxicity, persistence and bio-accumulation of the substance concerned. These proposals shall be adopted in accordance with the procedure laid down in article 14.

Article 6. (1) Every discharge of one of the substances listed in annex II which could detrimentally affect the quality of the waters of the Rhine shall be regulated by the national authorities with a view to introducing rigorous restrictions.

(2) The Governments Parties to this Agreement shall endeavour, within a period of two years from the entry into force of this Agreement, to establish national programmes reducing pollution of the waters of the Rhine by the substances listed in annex II; for their implementation they shall apply in particular the measures indicated in paragraphs 1, 4, 6 and 7 of this article.

(3) Before establishing these national programmes, the Contracting Parties shall confer in the International Commission in order to co-ordinate them. To this end, the International Commission shall regularly compare the draft national programmes in order to ensure their compatibility in terms of aims and means, and shall make proposals, in particular for the achievement of common aims relating to reducing the pollution of the waters of the Rhine. These proposals shall be adopted in accordance with the procedure laid down in article 14 of this Agreement. Comparison of national draft programmes shall not be allowed to cause delays in the implementation, at the

national or regional level, of measures intended to reduce the pollution of the waters of the Rhine.

(4) For each discharge that may contain one of the substances listed in annex II, prior authorization shall be required from the competent authority of the Government concerned which establishes the emission standards. The standards shall be determined in terms of the quality goals indicated in paragraph 5.

(5) The programmes referred to in paragraph 2 of this article shall prescribe quality goals for the waters of the Rhine.

(6) The programmes may also include specific provisions concerning the composition and use of substances or groups of substances and of products, and shall take account of the latest economically viable technical developments.

(7) The programmes shall set deadlines for their implementation.

(8) The International Commission shall be provided with a summary of the programmes and the results of their implementation.

Article 7. (1) The Contracting Parties shall take all necessary statutory and administrative action in order to guarantee that storage of the substances listed in annexes I and II is organized so as to avoid any danger of polluting the waters of the Rhine.

(2) The International Commission shall, as necessary, propose to the Contracting Parties appropriate measures for protecting groundwater in order to prevent pollution of the waters of the Rhine by the substances covered in annexes I and II.

Article 8. (1) The Contracting Parties shall ensure that discharges are regulated in accordance with this Agreement.

(2) They shall inform the International Commission annually of their experiences.

Article 9. Implementation of the measures adopted under this Agreement shall in no case lead to a direct or indirect increase in the pollution of the waters of the Rhine.

Article 10. (1) In order to monitor the proportion of substances covered in annexes I and II in the waters of the Rhine, each Government concerned shall be responsible for the installation and operation of measuring instruments and systems, at the agreed measurement stations on the Rhine, which shall serve to determine the concentration of these substances.

(2) Each Government concerned shall inform the International Commission regularly, and at least once annually, of the results of this monitoring process.

(3) The International Commission shall prepare an annual report which summarizes the results of the monitoring process and makes it possible to keep track of the changes in the quality of the waters of the Rhine.

Article 11. When a Government Party to this Agreement discovers in the waters of the Rhine a sudden and large increase of substances listed in annexes I and II, or becomes aware of an accident which may result in a serious threat to the quality of those waters, it shall immediately inform the International Commission and those Contracting Parties which may be affected, using a procedure to be established by the International Commission.

Article 12. (1) The Contracting Parties shall regularly inform the International Commission of the experience they have acquired through implementation of this Agreement.

(2) The International Commission shall draw up, as necessary, recommendations for progressive improvement in the implementation of this Agreement.

Article 13. The International Commission shall draw up recommendations for achieving comparability of results through the use of appropriate methods of measurement and analysis.

Article 14. (1) Annexes I to IV, which form an integral part of this Agreement, may be amended and supplemented in order to bring them into line with scientific and technical developments or to make the efforts to counter chemical pollution of the waters of the Rhine more effective.

(2) To this end, the International Commission shall recommend such amendments or additions as it deems useful.

(3) The amended or supplemented texts shall enter into force after their unanimous adoption by the Contracting Parties.

Article 15. Any dispute between the Contracting Parties, relating to the interpretation or implementation of this Agreement, which cannot be settled by negotiation shall, unless the Parties to the dispute decide otherwise, be submitted, at the request of either of them, to arbitration in accordance with the provisions of annex B which forms an integral part of this Agreement.

Article 16. In implementing this Agreement the European Economic Community and its member States shall take action with regard to those areas which fall within their respective jurisdictions.

Article 17. (1) Each signatory Party shall notify the Government of the Swiss Confederation of the completion of the procedures incumbent on such Party for the entry into force of this Agreement.

(2) Subject to notification by all Parties of the completion of the procedures required for the entry into force of the Additional Agreement to the Agreement on the International Commission for the Protection of the Rhine against Pollution, the present Agreement shall enter into force on the first day of the second month following receipt of the last notification specified in the previous paragraph.

Article 18. Upon the expiry of a period of three years after its entry into force, this Agreement may be denounced at any time by any of the Contracting Parties by means of a declaration addressed to the Government of the Swiss Confederation. The denunciation shall enter into force, for the denouncing Party, six months after receipt of the declaration by the Government of the Swiss Confederation.

Article 19. The Government of the Swiss Confederation shall inform the Contracting Parties of the date of receipt of each notification or declaration received in pursuance of articles 14, 17 and 18.

Article 20. (1) If the Agreement on the International Commission for the Protection of the Rhine against Pollution of 29 April 1963 is denounced by one of the Parties to that Agreement, the Contracting Parties shall immediately consult each other concerning the measures required to ensure the continuing discharge of the functions incumbent upon the International Commission under this Agreement.

(2) If no agreement has been reached within six months after the start of these consultations, each of the Contracting Parties may at any time denounce this Agreement in accordance with article 18, without waiting for the expiry of the three-year period.

Article 21. This Agreement, prepared in a single original in the German, French and Dutch languages, all three texts being equally authentic, shall be deposited in the archives of the Government of the Swiss Confederation, which shall transmit an authenticated copy thereof to each of the Contracting Parties.

* * *

4.17 Convention for the Protection of the Rhine River Against Pollution by Chlorides (Without Annexes). Concluded at Bonn, 3 December 1976. Entered into force, 5 July 1985. *Reprinted in* 16 I.L.M. 265 (1977)

The Government of the Federal Republic of Germany,
The Government of the French Republic,
The Government of the Grand Duchy of Luxembourg,
The Government of the Kingdom of the Netherlands,
and the Government of the Swiss Confederation,

Referring to the Agreement of April 29, 1963 concerning the International Commission for the Protection of the Rhine against Pollution,

Considering the present amount of chloride ions in the Rhine,

Aware of the damage that could result therefrom,

Referring to the findings and results of the Conference of Ministers on the Pollution of the Rhine, which took place at The Hague on October 25–26, 1972, during the course of which the desire was expressed to improve progressively the quality of the waters of the Rhine so that at the German–Netherlands border the chloride ion content will not be greater than 200 mg/l, Have agreed on the following:

Article 1

1. The Contracting Parties will strengthen their cooperation for the purpose of fighting against the pollution of the Rhine by chloride ions on the basis, during an initial stage, of the provisions of this Convention.

2. Annex A to the Convention specifies what the Contracting Parties understand by the term "Rhine" for the purposes of the application of the aforementioned Convention.

Article 2

1. The discharge of chloride ions into the Rhine will be reduced by at least 60 kg/s of chloride ions (annual average). This objective will be achieved gradually and in French territory.

2. In order to achieve the objective indicated in the preceding paragraph, the French Government will, under the conditions set forth in Annex I of this Convention, install an injection system in the subsoil of Alsace in order to reduce over a period of ten years the discharges from the Alsace Potassium Mines by an initial quantity of 20 kg/s of chloride ions. The installation shall be constructed as soon as possible, no later than 18 months after the entry into force of the Convention. The French Government will report regularly to the International Commission for the Protection of the Rhine against Pollution (hereinafter designated "the International Commission").

3. The Contracting Parties are agreed that the French Government will, after consideration of the results obtained during the initial stage described in paragraph 2, take all steps necessary to achieve before January 1, 1980 the objective set forth in paragraph 1, by injection into the Alsatian sub-soil or by other means, subject to an agreement on the technical terms and conditions of the project and on the financing of the costs relating thereto.

4. The French Government will present an over-all plan on the technical terms and conditions and the costs of the measures to be taken pursuant to paragraph 3.

Article 3

1. The Contracting Parties will take in their own territory, the necessary measures to prevent an increase in the amounts of chloride ions discharged into the Rhine basin. The national concentration figures are shown in Annex II.

2. An increase in the amounts of chloride ions from isolated discharges shall be admissible only to the extent that the Contracting Parties concerned will offset such concentration in their respective territories or if a general method of offsetting it is found within the framework of the International Commission. This provision shall not hinder the application of Article 6.

3. A Contracting Party may, in exceptional cases and for imperative reasons, after having requested the opinion of the International Commission, authorize an increase in concentration without immediately offsetting it.

4. The Contracting Parties will control all discharges of chloride ions greater than 1 kg/s in the basin of the Rhine in their territory.

5. Each Contracting Party will send an annual report to the International Commission which shall indicate as precisely as possible the increase in the chloride-ion concentration in the waters of the Rhine. This report shall be based on all significant data from pertinent national programs and shall distinguish discharges greater than 1 Kg/s from other discharges. Should such a distinction be impossible to make, it must be reported to the International Commission.

6. The Annex mentioned previously in paragraph 1 as well as the maximum concentration of 1 kg/s of chloride ions shall be reviewed each year by the International Commission as the situation develops. If necessary, the International Commission shall propose changes in the Annex to the Governments.

Article 4

1. The French Government, on its own initiative or at the request of another Contracting Party, may have the process of injection or resorption of chloride ions halted when there is evidence of serious danger to the environment and particularly to the water table.

2. The French Government, or any other requesting Party, will immediately inform the International Commission of the situation and will provide data on the extent and nature of the danger.

3. The French Government will immediately take the steps rendered necessary by the situation and will report them to the International Commission. When the situation is no longer considered dangerous, the chloride-ion injection or resorption process is to be resumed without delay.

4. The Contracting Parties will, at the request of one of them, consult among themselves within the International Commission if the need for additional measures should arise.

Article 5

If the process of injection or resorption of chloride ions causes damage for which compensation cannot be guaranteed fully or in part by the constructors of the works or by third parties, the Contracting Parties will consult among themselves at the request of one among them regarding a possible contribution that may be paid to the French Government.

Article 6

The International Commission shall present to the Contracting Parties within four years of the entry into force of the Convention proposals concerning the means to achieve progressively a new chloride-ion concentration limitation over the entire course of the Rhine.

Article 7

1. The expenses resulting from injection as provided in Article 2 paragraph 2 and from the preparatory works will be assumed by the French Party.

2. The Contracting Parties mentioned below will contribute to the total cost of 132 million French francs by means of a lump sum payment, prorated as follows:

Federal Republic of Germany	30%
Kingdom of the Netherlands	34%
Swiss Confederation	6%

The payments shall be made no later than three months after the entry into force of this Convention.

3. The Contracting Parties will deliberate, following the presentation of the overall plan provided for in Article 2(4) and at the request of the French Government, on the financing of the measures to be carried out in application of Article 2(3) on the basis of the prorating given in paragraph 2 above. The costs of preliminary research, particularly relating to studies and exploration, and, in addition, the unforeseen expenses not covered by the financing of the first stage shall likewise be included in the financing plan.

Article 8

The payments specified in Article 7(2) shall be made in French francs to account No. 440–09/line 1 in the Central Accounting Agency of the French Treasury.

Article 9

When, following the entry into force of this Convention, the International Commission ascertains that at one of the measuring points the load and concentration of chloride ions shows a continuing tendency to increase, it shall request each Contracting Party in whose territory the cause of this increase is located to take the necessary steps to halt it.

Article 10

1. If any difficulties should result from the application of Article 9, and a period of six months has gone by since such difficulties were noted by the International Commission, the latter, in order to present a report to the Governments, may call upon the services of an independent expert at the request of a Contracting Party.

2. The expenses relating to the inquiry, including the expert's fee shall be divided among the Contracting Parties mentioned below, as follows:

Federal Republic of Germany	two sevenths
French Republic	two sevenths
Kingdom of the Netherlands	two sevenths
Swiss Confederation	one seventh

The International Commission may, in certain cases, establish a different method for dividing the expenses.

Article 11

When a Contracting Party notes a sudden and sizeable increase in chloride ions in the waters of the Rhine or has knowledge of an accident that may seriously endanger the quality of those waters, it will report it without delay to the International Commission and to the Contracting Parties likely to be affected, according to a procedure to be established by the International Commission.

Article 12

1. Each Contracting Party concerned will be responsible at the appropriate measuring stations, for the installation and operation of the measuring equipment and systems serving to check the concentration of chloride ions in the waters of the Rhine.

2. The chloride-ion concentrations shall be determined on the basis of the measurements carried out according to the recommendations of the International Commission.

3. The Contracting Parties will report to the International Commission regularly and at least every six months the results of the checks carried out pursuant to paragraph 1 above.

Any dispute between the Contracting Parties regarding the interpretation or application of the present Convention that cannot be settled by negotiation shall, except when the Parties to the dispute decide otherwise, be subject, at the request of one of them, to arbitration in accordance with the provisions of Annex B. The latter, as well as Annexes A, I, and II shall form an integral part of this Convention.

Article 14

Each Signatory Party will notify the Government of the Swiss Confederation of the execution of the procedures required for the entry into force of this Convention. It shall enter into force on the first day of the second month following receipt of the last notification.

Article 15

At the end of three years following its entry into force, this Convention may be denounced at any time by any of the Contracting Parties by means of a statement addressed to the Government of the Swiss Confederation. The denunciation shall take effect, for the denouncing Party, six months following receipt of the statement by the Government of the Swiss Confederation. This shall not have the effect of compromising the continued execution of tasks for which international financing has been obtained.

Article 16

The Government of the Swiss Confederation will inform the Contracting Parties of the date of receipt of any notification or statement received pursuant to Articles 14 and 15.

Article 17

1. If the April 29, 1963 Agreement concerning the International Commission for the Protection of the Rhine Against Pollution is denounced by one of the Parties to the aforementioned Agreement, the Contracting Parties will consult without delay on the measures necessary to ensure the continued execution of the tasks that, according to this Convention, are the responsibility of the International Commission.

2. If an agreement is not reached in the six months following the opening of discussions, each of the Contracting Parties may denounce this Convention at anytime in accordance with Article 15, without waiting for the three-year period to elapse.

Article 18

This Convention, drawn up in a single copy in German, French and Dutch, the three texts being equally authentic shall be deposited in the Archives of the Government of the Swiss Confederation, which shall transmit a certified copy to each of the Contracting Parties.

4.18 Kuwait Regional Convention for Co-operation on the Protection of the Marine Environment From Pollution (Without Protocols). Concluded at Kuwait, 24 April 1978. Entered into force, 30 June 1979. 1140 U.N.T.S. 133; *reprinted in* 17 I.L.M. 511 (1978)

* * *

The Government of the State of Bahrain, the Imperial Government of Iran, the Government of the Republic of Iraq, the Government of the State of Kuwait, the Government of the Sultanate of Oman, the Government of the State of Qatar, the Government of the Kingdom of Saudi Arabia, the Government of the United Arab Emirates,

Realizing that pollution of the marine environment in the Region shared by Bahrain, Iran, Iraq, Kuwait, Oman, Qatar, Saudi Arabia and the United Arab Emirates, by oil and other harmful or noxious materials arising from human activities on land or at sea, especially through indiscriminate and uncontrolled discharge of these substances, presents a growing threat to marine life, fisheries, human health, recreational uses of beaches and other amenities,

Mindful of the special hydrographic and ecological characteristics of the marine environment of the Region and its particular vulnerability to pollution,

Conscious of the need to ensure that the processes of urban and rural development and resultant land use should be carried out in such a manner as to preserve, as far as possible, marine resources and coastal amenities, and that such development should not lead to deterioration of the marine environment,

Convinced of the need to ensure that the processes of industrial development should not, in any way, cause damage to the marine environment of the Region, jeopardize its living resources or create hazards to human health,

Recognizing the need to develop an integrated management approach to the use of the marine environment and the coastal areas which will allow the achievement of environmental and development goals in a harmonious manner,

Recognizing also the need for a carefully planned research, monitoring and assessment programme in view of the scarcity of scientific information on marine pollution in the Region,

Considering that the States sharing the Region have a special responsibility to protect its marine environment,

Aware of the importance of co-operation and co-ordination of action on a regional basis with the aim of protecting the marine environment of the Region for the benefit of all concerned, including future generations,

Bearing in mind the existing international conventions relevant to the present Convention,

Have agreed as follows:

Article I. Definitions

For the purpose of the present Convention:

(*a*) "Marine pollution" means the introduction by man, directly or indirectly, of substances or energy into the marine environment resulting or likely to result in such deleterious effects as harm to living resources, hazards to human health, hindrance to marine activities including fishing, impairment of quality for use of sea water and reduction of amenities;

(*b*) "National Authority" means the authority designated by each Contracting State as responsible for the co-ordination of national efforts for implementing the Convention and its protocols;

(*c*) "Organization" means the organization established by the Contracting States in accordance with article XVI;

(*d*) "Secretariat" means the organ of the Organization established in accordance with article XVI;

(*e*) "Action Plan" means the Action Plan for the Development and Protection of the Marine Environment and the Coastal Areas of Bahrain, Iran, Iraq, Kuwait, Oman, Qatar, Saudi Arabia and the United Arab Emirates adopted at the Kuwait Regional Conference of Plenipotentiaries on the Protection and Development of the Marine Environment and the Coastal Areas, convened from 15 to 23 April 1978.

Article II. Geographical Coverage

(*a*) The present Convention shall apply to the sea area in the Region bounded in the south by the following rhumb lines: from Ras Dharbat Ali in (16°39′ N, 53°3′30″ E) then to a position in (16°00′ N, 53°25′ E) then to a position in (17°00′ N, 56°30′ E) then to a position in (20°30′ N, 60°00′ E) then to Ras AlFasteh in (25°04′ N, 61°25′ E) (hereinafter referred to as the "Sea Area");

(*b*) The Sea Area shall not include internal waters of the Contracting States unless it is otherwise stated in the present Convention or in any of its protocols.

Article III. General Obligations

(*a*) The Contracting States shall, individually and/or jointly, take all appropriate measures in accordance with the present Convention and those protocols in force to which they are party to prevent, abate and combat pollution of the marine environment in the Sea Area;

(*b*) In addition to the Protocol Concerning Regional Co-operation in Combating Pollution by Oil and Other Harmful Substances in Cases of Emergency opened for signature at the same time as the present Convention, the Contracting States shall co-operate in the formulation and adoption of other protocols prescribing agreed measures, procedures and standards for the implementation of the Convention;

(*c*) The Contracting States shall establish national standards, laws and regulations as required for the effective discharge of the obligation prescribed in paragraph (*a*) of this article, and shall endeavour to harmonise their national policies in this regard and for this purpose appoint the National Authority;

(*d*) The Contracting States shall co-operate with the competent international, regional and sub-regional organizations to establish and adopt regional standards, recommended practices and procedures to prevent, abate and combat pollution from all sources in conformity with the objectives of the present Convention, and to assist each other in fulfilling their obligations under the present Convention;

(*e*) The Contracting States shall use their best endeavour to ensure that the implementation of the present Convention shall not cause transformation of one type of pollution to another which could be more detrimental to the environment.

Article IV. Pollution From Ships

The Contracting States shall take all appropriate measures in conformity with the present Convention and the applicable rules of international law to prevent, abate and combat pollution in the Sea Area caused by intentional or accidental discharges from ships, and shall ensure effective compliance in the Sea Area with applicable international rules relating to the control of this type of pollution, including load-on-top, segregated ballast and crude oil washing procedures for tankers.

Article V. POLLUTION CAUSED BY DUMPING FROM SHIPS AND AIRCRAFT

The Contracting States shall take all appropriate measures to prevent, abate and combat pollution in the Sea Area caused by dumping of wastes and other matter from ships and aircraft, and shall ensure effective compliance in the Sea Area with applicable international rules relating to the control of this type of pollution as provided for in relevant international conventions.

Article VI. POLLUTION FROM LAND-BASED SOURCES

The Contracting States shall take all appropriate measures to prevent, abate and combat pollution caused by discharges from land reaching the Sea Area whether waterborne, air-borne, or directly from the coast including outfalls and pipelines.

Article VII. POLLUTION RESULTING FROM EXPLORATION AND EXPLOITATION OF THE BED OF THE TERRITORIAL SEA AND ITS SUB-SOIL AND THE CONTINENTAL SHELF

The Contracting States shall take all appropriate measures to prevent, abate and combat pollution in the Sea Area resulting from exploration and exploitation of the bed of the territorial sea and its sub-soil and the continental shelf, including the prevention of accidents and the combating of pollution emergencies resulting in damage to the marine environment.

Article VIII. POLLUTION FROM OTHER HUMAN ACTIVITIES

The Contracting States shall take all appropriate measures to prevent, abate and combat pollution of the Sea Area resulting from land reclamation and associated suction dredging and coastal dredging.

Article IX. CO-OPERATION IN DEALING WITH POLLUTION EMERGENCIES

(*a*) The Contracting States shall, individually and/or jointly, take all necessary measures, including those to ensure that adequate equipment and qualified personnel are readily available, to deal with pollution emergencies in the Sea Area, whatever the cause of such emergencies, and to reduce or eliminate damage resulting therefrom;

(*b*) Any Contracting State which becomes aware of any pollution emergency in the Sea Area shall, without delay, notify the Organization referred to under article XVI and, through the secretariat, any Contracting State likely to be affected by such emergency.

Article X. SCIENTIFIC AND TECHNOLOGICAL CO-OPERATION

(*a*) The Contracting States shall co-operate directly, or, where appropriate, through competent international and regional organizations, in the field of scientific research, monitoring and assessment concerning pollution in the Sea Area, and shall exchange data as well as other scientific information for the purpose of the present Convention and any of its protocols;

(*b*) The Contracting States shall co-operate further to develop and co-ordinate national research and monitoring programmes relating to all types of pollution in the Sea Area and to establish in co-operation with competent regional or international organizations, a regional network of such programmes to ensure compatible results. For this purpose, each Contracting State shall designate the National Authority responsible for pollution research and monitoring within the areas under its national jurisdiction. The Contracting States shall participate in international arrangements for pollution research and monitoring in areas beyond their national jurisdiction.

Article XI. ENVIRONMENTAL ASSESSMENT

(*a*) Each Contracting State shall endeavour to include an assessment of the potential environmental effects in any planning activity entailing projects within its territory, particularly in the coastal areas, which may cause significant risks of pollution in the Sea Area;

(*b*) The Contracting States may, in consultation with the secretariat, develop procedures for dissemination of information of the assessment of the activities referred to in paragraph (*a*) above;

(*c*) The Contracting States undertake to develop, individually or jointly, technical and other guidelines in accordance with standard scientific practice to assist the planning of their development projects in such a way as to minimize their harmful impact on the marine environment. In this regard international standards may be used where appropriate.

Article XII. TECHNICAL AND OTHER ASSISTANCE

The Contracting States shall co-operate directly or through competent regional or international organizations in the development of programmes of technical and other assistance in fields relating to marine pollution in co-ordination with the Organization referred to in article XVI.

Article XIII. LIABILITY AND COMPENSATION

The Contracting States undertake to co-operate in the formulation and adoption of appropriate rules and procedures for the determination of:

(*a*) Civil liability and compensation for damage resulting from pollution of the marine environment, bearing in mind applicable international rules and procedures relating to those matters; and

(*b*) Liability and compensation for damage resulting from violation of obligations under the present Convention and its protocols.

Article XIV. SOVEREIGN IMMUNITY

Warships or other ships owned or operated by a State, and used only on Government non-commercial service, shall be exempted from the application of the provisions of the present Convention. Each Contracting State shall, as far as possible, ensure that its warships or other ships owned or operated by that State, and used only on Government non-commercial service, shall comply with the present Convention in the prevention of pollution to the marine environment.

Article XV. DISCLAIMER

Nothing in the present Convention shall prejudice or affect the rights or claims of any Contracting State in regard to the nature or extent of its maritime jurisdiction which may be established in conformity with international law.

Article XVI. REGIONAL ORGANIZATION FOR THE PROTECTION OF THE MARINE ENVIRONMENT

(*a*) The Contracting States hereby establish a Regional Organization for the Protection of the Marine Environment, the permanent headquarters of which shall be located in Kuwait;

(*b*) The Organization shall consist of the following organs:

(i) A Council which shall be comprised of the Contracting States and shall perform the functions set forth in paragraph (*d*) of article XVII;

(ii) A Secretariat which shall perform the functions set forth in paragraph (*a*) of article XVIII; and

(iii) A Judicial Commission for the Settlement of Disputes whose composition, terms of reference and rules of procedure shall be established at the first meeting of the Council.

Article XVII. Council

(*a*) The meetings of the Council shall be convened in accordance with paragraph (*a*) of article XVIII and paragraph (*b*) of article XXX. The Council shall hold ordinary meetings once a year. Extraordinary meetings of the Council shall be held upon the request of at least one Contracting State endorsed by at least one other Contracting State, or upon the request of the Executive Secretary endorsed by at least two Contracting States. Meetings of the Council shall be convened at the headquarters of the Organization or at any other place agreed upon by consultation amongst the Contracting States. Three fourths of the Contracting States shall constitute a quorum;

(*b*) The Chairmanship of the Council shall be given to each Contracting State in turn in alphabetical order of the names of the States in the English language. The Chairman shall serve for a period of one year and cannot during the period of chairmanship serve as a representative of his State. Should the chairmanship fall vacant, the Contracting State chairing the Council shall designate a successor to remain in office until the term of chairmanship of that Contracting State expires;

(*c*) The voting procedure in the Council shall be as follows:

(i) Each Contracting State shall have one vote;

(ii) Decisions on substantive matters shall be taken by a unanimous vote of the Contracting States present and voting;

(iii) Decisions on procedural matters shall be taken by three-fourths majority vote of the Contracting States present and voting.

(*d*) The functions of the Council shall be:

(i) To keep under review the implementation of the Convention and its protocols, and the Action Plan referred to in paragraph (*e*) of article I;

(ii) To review and evaluate the state of marine pollution and its effects on the Sea Area on the basis of reports provided by the Contracting States and the competent international or regional organizations;

(iii) To adopt, review and amend as required in accordance with procedures established in article XXI, the annexes to the Convention and to its protocols;

(iv) To receive and to consider reports submitted by the Contracting States under articles IX and XXIII;

(v) To consider reports prepared by the Secretariat on questions relating to the Convention and to matters relevant to the administration of the Organization;

(vi) To make recommendations regarding the adoption of any additional protocols or any amendments to the Convention or to its protocols in accordance with articles XIX and XX;

(vii) To establish subsidiary bodies and *ad hoc* working groups as required to consider any matters related to the Convention and its protocols and annexes to the Convention and its protocols;

(viii) To appoint an Executive Secretary and to make provision for the appointment by the Executive Secretary of such other personnel as may be necessary;

(ix) To review periodically the functions of the Secretariat;

(x) To consider and to undertake any additional action that may be required for the achievement of the purposes of the Convention and its protocols.

Article XVIII. SECRETARIAT

(*a*) The Secretariat shall be comprised of an Executive Secretary and the personnel necessary to perform the following functions:

(i) To convene and to prepare the meetings of the Council and its subsidiary bodies and *ad hoc* working groups as referred to in article XVII, and conferences as referred to in articles XIX and XX;

(ii) To transmit to the Contracting States notifications, reports and other information received in accordance with articles IX and XXIII;

(iii) To consider enquiries by, and information from, the Contracting States and to consult with them on questions relating to the Convention and its protocols and annexes thereto;

(iv) To prepare reports on matters relating to the Convention and to the administration of the Organization;

(v) To establish, maintain and disseminate an up-to-date collection of national laws of all States concerned relevant to the protection of the marine environment;

(vi) To arrange, upon request, for the provision of technical assistance and advice for the drafting of appropriate national legislation for the effective implementation of the Convention and its protocols;

(vii) To arrange for training programmes in areas related to the implementation of the Convention and its protocols;

(viii) To carry out its assignments under the protocols to the Convention;

(ix) To perform such other functions as may be assigned to it by the Council for the implementation of the Convention and its protocols.

(*b*) The Executive Secretary shall be the chief administrative official of the Organization and shall perform the functions that are necessary for the administration of the present Convention, the work of the Secretariat and other tasks entrusted to the Executive Secretary by the Council and as provided for in its rules of procedure and financial rules.

Article XIX. ADOPTION OF ADDITIONAL PROTOCOLS

Any Contracting State may propose additional protocols to the present Convention pursuant to paragraph (*b*) of article III at a diplomatic conference of the Contracting States to be convened by the Secretariat at the request of at least three Contracting States. Additional protocols shall be adopted by a unanimous vote of the Contracting States present and voting.

Article XX. AMENDMENTS TO THE CONVENTION AND ITS PROTOCOLS

(*a*) Any Contracting State to the present Convention or to any of its protocols may propose amendments to the Convention or to the protocol concerned at a diplomatic conference to be convened by the Secretariat at the request of at least three Contracting States. Amendments to the Convention and its protocols shall be adopted by a unanimous vote of the Contracting States present and voting;

(*b*) Amendments to the Convention or any protocol adopted by a diplomatic conference shall be submitted by the Depositary for acceptance by all Contracting States. Acceptance of amendments to the Convention or to any protocol shall be notified to the Depositary in writing. Amendments adopted in accordance with this article shall enter into force for all Contracting States, except those which have notified the Depositary of a different intention, on the thirtieth day following the receipt by the Depositary of notification of their acceptance by at least three-fourths of the Contracting States to the Convention or any protocol concerned as the case may be;

(*c*) After the entry into force of an amendment to the Convention or to a protocol, any new Contracting State to the Convention or such protocol shall become a Contracting State to the instrument as amended.

Article XXI. ANNEXES AND AMENDMENTS TO ANNEXES

(*a*) Annexes to the Convention or to any protocol shall form an integral part of the Convention or such protocol;

(*b*) Except as may be otherwise provided in any protocol, the following procedure shall apply to the adoption and entry into force of any amendments to annexes to the Convention or to any protocol:

(i) Any Contracting State to the Convention or to a protocol may propose amendments to the annexes to the instrument in question at the meetings of the Council referred to in article XVII;

(ii) Such amendments shall be adopted at such meetings by a unanimous vote;

(iii) The Depositary referred to in article XXX shall communicate amendments so adopted to all Contracting States without delay;

(iv) Any Contracting State which has a different intention with respect to an amendment to the annexes to the Convention or to any protocol shall notify the Depositary in writing within a period determined by the Contracting States concerned when adopting the amendment;

(v) The Depositary shall notify all Contracting States without delay of any notification received pursuant to the preceding sub-paragraph;

(vi) On the expiry of the period referred to in sub-paragraph (iv) above, the amendment to the annex shall become effective for all Contracting States to the Convention or to the protocol concerned which have not submitted a notification in accordance with the provisions of that sub-paragraph;

(*c*) The adoption and entry into force of a new annex to the Convention or to any protocol shall be subject to the same procedure as for the adoption and entry into force of an amendment to an annex in accordance with the provisions of this article, provided that, if any amendment to the Convention or the protocol concerned is involved, the new annex shall not enter into force until such time as the amendment to the Convention or the protocol concerned enters into force.

Article XXII. RULES OF PROCEDURE AND FINANCIAL RULES

(*a*) The Council shall, at its first meeting, adopt its own rules;

(*b*) The Council shall adopt financial rules to determine, in particular, the financial participation of the Contracting States.

Article XXIII. Reports

Each Contracting State shall submit to the Secretariat reports on measures adopted in implementation of the provisions of the Convention and its protocols in such form and at such intervals as may be determined by the Council.

Article XXIV. Compliance Control

The Contracting States shall co-operate in the development of procedures for the effective application of the Convention and its protocols, including detection of violations, using all appropriate and practicable measures of detection and environmental monitoring, including adequate procedures for reporting and accumulation of evidence.

Article XXV. Settlement of Disputes

(*a*) In case of a dispute as to the interpretation or application of this Convention or its protocols, the Contracting States concerned shall seek a settlement of the dispute through negotiation or any other peaceful means of their own choice.

(*b*) If the Contracting States concerned cannot settle the dispute through the means mentioned in paragraph (*a*) of this article, the dispute shall be submitted to the Judicial Commission for the Settlement of Disputes referred to in paragraph (*b*)(iii) of article XVI.

Article XXVI. Signature

The present Convention together with the Protocol Concerning Regional Co-operation in Combating Pollution by Oil and other Harmful Substances in Cases of Emergency shall be open for signature in Kuwait from 24 April to 23 July 1978 by any State invited as a participant in the Kuwait Regional Conference of Plenipotentiaries on the Protection and Development of the Marine Environment and the Coastal Areas, convened from 15 to 23 April 1978 for the purpose of adopting the Convention and the Protocol.

Article XXVII. Ratification, Acceptance, Approval or Accession

(*a*) The present Convention together with the Protocol concerning Regional Co-operation in Combating Pollution by Oil and other Harmful Substances in Cases of Emergency and any other protocol thereto shall be subject to ratification, acceptance, or approval by the States referred to in article XXVI.

(*b*) As from 24 July 1978, this Convention together with the Protocol Concerning Regional Co-operation in Combating Pollution by Oil and other Harmful Substances in Cases of Emergency shall be open for accession by the States referred to in article XXVI;

(*c*) Any State which has ratified, accepted, approved or acceded to the present Convention shall be considered as having ratified, accepted, approved or acceded to the Protocol Concerning Regional Co-operation in Combating Pollution by Oil and other Harmful Substances in Cases of Emergency;

(*d*) Instruments of ratification, acceptance, approval or accession shall be deposited with the Government of Kuwait which will assume the functions of Depositary.

Article XXVIII. Entry Into Force

(*a*) The present Convention together with the Protocol Concerning Regional Co-operation in Combating Pollution by Oil and other Harmful Substances in Cases of Emergency shall enter into force on the ninetieth day following the date of deposit of at least five instruments of ratification, acceptance or approval of, or accession to, the Convention;

(*b*) Any other protocol to this Convention, except as otherwise provided in such protocol, shall enter into force on the ninetieth day following the date of deposit of at least five instruments of ratification, acceptance or approval of, or accession to, such protocol;

(*c*) After the date of deposit of five instruments of ratification, acceptance or approval of, or accession to, this Convention or any other protocol, this Convention or any such protocol shall enter into force with respect to any State on the ninetieth day following the date of deposit by that State of the instrument of ratification, acceptance, approval or accession.

Article XXIX. Withdrawal

(*a*) At any time after five years from the date of entry into force of this Convention, any Contracting State may withdraw from this Convention by giving written notification of withdrawal to the Depositary;

(*b*) Except as may be otherwise provided in any other protocol to the Convention, any Contracting State may, at any time after five years from the date of entry into force of such protocol, withdraw from such protocol by giving written notification of withdrawal to the Depositary;

(*c*) Withdrawal shall take effect ninety days after the date on which notification of withdrawal is received by the Depositary;

(*d*) Any Contracting State which withdraws from the Convention shall be considered as also having withdrawn from any protocol to which it was a party;

(*e*) Any Contracting State which withdraws from the Protocol concerning Regional Co-operation in Combating Pollution by Oil and other Harmful Substances in Cases of Emergency shall be considered as also having withdrawn from the Convention.

Article XXX. Responsibilities of the Depositary

(*a*) The Depositary shall inform the Contracting States and the Secretariat of the following:

(i) Signature of this Convention and of any protocol thereto, and of the deposit of the instruments of ratification, acceptance, approval or accession in accordance with article XXVII;

(ii) Date on which Convention and any protocol will enter into force in accordance with the provisions of article XXVIII;

(iii) Notification of a different intention made in accordance with articles XX and XXI;

(iv) Notification of withdrawal made in accordance with article XXIX;

(v) Amendments adopted with respect to the Convention and to any protocol, their acceptance by the Contracting State and the date of entry into force of those amendments in accordance with the provisions of article XX;

(vi) Adoption of new annexes and of the amendment of any annex in accordance with article XXI;

(*b*) The Depositary shall call the first meeting of the Council within six months of the date on which the Convention enters into force.

The original of this Convention, of any protocol thereto, of any annex to the Convention or to a protocol, or of any amendment to the Convention, to a protocol or to an annex of the Convention or of a protocol shall be deposited with the Depositary, the Government of Kuwait who shall send copies thereof to all States concerned and shall register all such instruments and all subsequent actions in respect of them with the Secretariat of the United Nations in accordance with Article 102 of the Charter of the United Nations.

4.19 PROTOCOL FOR THE PROTECTION OF THE MEDITERRANEAN SEA AGAINST POLLUTION FROM LAND-BASED SOURCES (Without Annexes). Concluded at Athens, 17 May 1980. Entered into force, 17 June 1983. *Reprinted in* 19 I.L.M. 869 (1980) & 5 Weston V.F.21

The Contracting Parties to the present Protocol,

Being Parties to the Convention for the Protection of the Mediterranean Sea against Pollution, adopted at Barcelona on 16 February 1976,

Desirous of implementing article 4, paragraph 2, and articles 8 and 15 of the said Convention,

Noting the rapid increase of human activities in the Mediterranean Sea Area, particularly in the fields of industrialization and urbanization, as well as the seasonal increase in the coastal population due to tourism,

Recognizing the danger posed to the marine environment and to human health by pollution from land-based sources and the serious problems resulting therefrom in many coastal waters and river estuaries of the Mediterranean Sea, primarily due to the release of untreated, insufficiently treated or inadequately disposed domestic or industrial discharges,

Recognizing the differences in levels of development between the coastal States, and taking account of the economic and social imperatives of the developing countries,

Determined to take in close co-operation the necessary measures to protect the Mediterranean Sea against pollution from land-based sources,

Have agreed as follows:

Article 1

The Contracting Parties to this Protocol (hereinafter referred to as "the Parties") shall take all appropriate measures to prevent, abate, combat and control pollution of the Mediterranean Sea Area caused by discharges from rivers, coastal establishments or outfalls, or emanating from any other land-based sources within their territories.

Article 2

For the purposes of this Protocol:

(a) "The Convention" means the Convention for the Protection of the Mediterranean Sea against Pollution, adopted at Barcelona on 16 February 1976;

(b) "Organization" means the body referred to in article 13 of the Convention;

(c) "Freshwater limit" means the place in watercourses where, at low tides and in a period of low freshwater flow, there is an appreciable increase in salinity due to the presence of sea water.

Article 3

The area to which this Protocol applies (hereinafter referred to as the "Protocol Area") shall be:

(a) the Mediterranean Sea Area as defined in article 1 of the Convention;

(b) waters on the landward side of the baselines from which the breadth of the territorial sea is measured and extending, in the case of watercourses, up to the freshwater limit;

(c) saltwater marshes communicating with the sea.

Article 4

1. This Protocol shall apply:

(a) to polluting discharges reaching the Protocol Area from land-based sources within the territories of the Parties, in particular:

—directly, from outfalls discharging into the sea or through coastal disposal;

—indirectly, through rivers, canals or other watercourses, including underground watercourses, or through run-off;

(b) to pollution from land-based sources transported by the atmosphere, under conditions to be defined in an additional annex to this Protocol and accepted by the Parties in conformity with the provisions of article 17 of the Convention.

2. This Protocol shall also apply to polluting discharges from fixed man-made off-shore structures which are under the jurisdiction of a Party and which serve purposes other than exploration and exploitation of mineral resources of the continental shelf and the sea-bed and its sub-soil.

Article 5

1. The Parties undertake to eliminate pollution of the Protocol Area from land-based sources by substances listed in annex I to this Protocol.

2. To this end they shall elaborate and implement, jointly or individually, as appropriate, the necessary programmes and measures.

3. These programmes and measures shall include, in particular, common emission standards and standards for use.

4. The standards and the time-tables for the implementation of the programmes and measures aimed at eliminating pollution from land-based sources shall be fixed by the Parties and periodically reviewed, if necessary every two years, for each of the substances listed in annex I, in accordance with the provisions of article 15 of this Protocol.

Article 6

1. The Parties shall strictly limit pollution from land-based sources in the Protocol Area by substances or sources listed in annex II to this Protocol.

2. To this end they shall elaborate and implement, jointly or individually, as appropriate, suitable programmes and measures.

3. Discharges shall be strictly subject to the issue, by the competent national authorities, of an authorization taking due account of the provisions of annex III to this Protocol.

Article 7

1. The Parties shall progressively formulate and adopt, in co-operation with the competent international organizations, common guidelines and, as appropriate, standards or criteria dealing in particular with:

(a) the length, depth and position of pipelines for coastal outfalls, taking into account, in particular, the methods used for pretreatment of effluents;

(b) special requirements for effluents necessitating separate treatment;

(c) the quality of sea water used for specific purposes that is necessary for the protection of human health, living resources and ecosystems;

(d) the control and progressive replacement of products, installations and industrial and other processes causing significant pollution of the marine environment;

(e) specific requirements concerning the quantities of the substances listed in annexes I and II discharged, their concentration in effluents and methods of discharging them.

2. Without prejudice to the provisions of article 5 of this Protocol, such common guidelines, standards or criteria shall take into account local ecological, geographical and physical characteristics, the economic capacity of the Parties and their need for development, the level of existing pollution and the real absorptive capacity of the marine environment.

3. The programmes and measures referred to in articles 5 and 6 shall be adopted by taking into account, for their progressive implementation, the capacity to adapt and reconvert existing installations, the economic capacity of the Parties and their need for development.

Article 8

Within the framework of the provisions of, and the monitoring programmes provided for in, article 10 of the Convention, and if necessary in co-operation with the competent international organizations, the Parties shall carry out at the earliest possible date monitoring activities in order:

(a) systematically to assess, as far as possible, the levels of pollution along their coasts, in particular with regard to the substances or sources listed in annexes I and II, and periodically to provide information in this respect;

(b) to evaluate the effects of measures taken under this Protocol to reduce pollution of the marine environment.

Article 9

In conformity with article 11 of the Convention, the Parties shall co-operate as far as possible in scientific and technological fields related to pollution from land-based sources, particularly research on inputs, pathways and effects of pollutants and on the development of new methods for their treatment, reduction or elimination. To this end the Parties shall, in particular, endeavour to:

(a) exchange scientific and technical information;

(b) co-ordinate their research programmes.

Article 10

1. The Parties shall, directly or with the assistance of competent regional or other international organizations or bilaterally, co-operate with a view to formulating and, as far as possible, implementing programmes of assistance to developing countries, particularly in the fields of science, education and technology, with a view to preventing pollution from land-based sources and its harmful effects in the marine environment.

2. Technical assistance would include, in particular, the training of scientific and technical personnel, as well as the acquisition, utilization and production by those countries of appropriate equipment on advantageous terms to be agreed upon among the Parties concerned.

Article 11

1. If discharges from a watercourse which flows through the territories of two or more Parties or forms a boundary between them are likely to cause pollution of the marine environment of the Protocol Area, the Parties in question, respecting the provisions of this Protocol in so far as each of them is concerned, are called upon to co-operate with a view to ensuring its full application.

2. A Party shall not be responsible for any pollution originating on the territory of a non-contracting State. However, the said Party shall endeavour to co-operate with the said State so as to make possible full application of the Protocol.

Article 12

1. Taking into account article 22, paragraph 1, of the Convention, when land-based pollution originating from the territory of one Party is likely to prejudice directly the interests of one or more of the other Parties, the Parties concerned shall, at the request of one or more of them, undertake to enter into consultation with a view to seeking a satisfactory solution.

2. At the request of any Party concerned, the matter shall be placed on the agenda of the next meeting of the Parties held in accordance with article 14 of this Protocol; the meeting may make recommendations with a view to reaching a satisfactory solution.

Article 13

1. The Parties shall inform one another through the Organization of measures taken, of results achieved and, if the case arises, of difficulties encountered in the application of this Protocol. Procedures for the collection and submission of such information shall be determined at the meetings of the Parties.

2. Such information shall include, *inter alia:*

(a) statistical data on the authorizations granted in accordance with article 6 of this Protocol;

(b) data resulting from monitoring as provided for in article 8 of this Protocol;

(c) quantities of pollutants discharged from their territories;

(d) measures taken in accordance with articles 5 and 6 of this Protocol.

Article 14

1. Ordinary meetings of the Parties shall take place in conjunction with ordinary meetings of the Contracting Parties to the Convention held pursuant to article 14 of the Convention. The Parties may also hold extraordinary meetings in accordance with article 14 of the Convention.

2. The functions of the meetings of the Parties to this Protocol shall be, *inter alia:*

(a) to keep under review the implementation of this Protocol and to consider the efficacy of the measures adopted and the advisability of any other measures, in particular in the form of annexes;

(b) to revise and amend any annex to this Protocol, as appropriate;

(c) to formulate and adopt programmes and measures in accordance with articles 5, 6 and 15 of this Protocol;

(d) to adopt, in accordance with article 7 of this Protocol, common guidelines, standards or criteria, in any form decided upon by the Parties;

(e) to make recommendations in accordance with article 12, paragraph 2, of this Protocol;

(f) to consider the information submitted by the Parties under article 13 of this Protocol;

(g) to discharge such other functions as may be appropriate for the application of this Protocol.

Article 15

1. The meeting of the Parties shall adopt, by a two-thirds majority, the programmes and measures for the abatement or the elimination of pollution from land-based sources which are provided for in articles 5 and 6 of this Protocol.

2. The Parties which are not able to accept a programme or measures shall inform the meeting of the Parties of the action they intend to take as regards the programme or measures concerned, it being understood that these Parties may, at any time, give their consent to the programme or measures that have been adopted.

Article 16

1. The provisions of the Convention relating to any Protocol shall apply with respect to this Protocol.

2. The rules of procedure and the financial rules adopted pursuant to article 18 of the Convention shall apply with respect to this Protocol, unless the Parties to this Protocol agree otherwise.

3. This Protocol shall be open for signature, at Athens from 17 May 1980 to 16 June 1980, and at Madrid from 17 June 1980 to 16 May 1981, by any State invited to the Conference of Plenipotentiaries of the Coastal States of the Mediterranean Region for the Protection of the Mediterranean Sea against Pollution from Land–Based Sources held at Athens from 12 May to 17 May 1980. It shall also be open until the same dates for signature by the European Economic Community and by any similar regional economic grouping of which at least one member is a coastal State of the Mediterranean Sea Area and which exercises competence in fields covered by this Protocol.

4. This Protocol shall be subject to ratification, acceptance or approval. Instruments of ratification, acceptance or approval shall be deposited with the Government of Spain, which will assume the functions of Depositary.

5. As from 17 May 1981, this Protocol shall be open for accession by the States referred to in paragraph 3 above, by the European Economic Community and by any grouping referred to in that paragraph.

6. This Protocol shall enter into force on the thirtieth day following the deposit of at least six instruments of ratification, acceptance or approval of, or accession to, the Protocol by the Parties referred to in paragraph 3 of this article.

4.20 UNITED NATIONS CONVENTION ON THE LAW OF THE SEA (With Annex V).[f] Concluded at Montego Bay, 10 December 1982. Entered into force, 16 November 1994. U.N. Doc. A/CONF.62/122; *reprinted in* 21 I.L.M. 1261 (1982) & 5 Weston V.F.22

The States Parties to this Convention,

Prompted by the desire to settle, in a spirit of mutual understanding and co-operation, all issues relating to the law of the sea and aware of the historic significance of this Convention as an important contribution to the maintenance of peace, justice and progress for all peoples of the world,

Noting that developments since the United Nations Conferences on the Law of the Sea held at Geneva in 1958 and 1960 have accentuated the need for a new and generally acceptable Convention on the law of the sea,

Conscious that the problems of ocean space are closely interrelated and need to be considered as a whole,

Recognizing the desirability of establishing through this Convention, with due regard for the sovereignty of all States, a legal order for the seas and oceans which will facilitate international communication, and will promote the peaceful uses of the seas and oceans, the equitable and efficient utilization of their resources, the conservation of their living resources, and the study, protection and preservation of the marine environment,

Bearing in mind that the achievement of these goals will contribute to the realization of a just and equitable international economic order which takes into account the interests and needs of mankind as a whole and, in particular, the special interests and needs of developing countries, whether coastal or land-locked,

Desiring by this Convention to develop the principles embodied in resolution 2749 (XXV) of 17 December 1970 in which the General Assembly of the United Nations solemnly declared *inter alia* that the area of the sea-bed and ocean floor and the subsoil thereof, beyond the limits of national jurisdiction, as well as its resources, are the common heritage of mankind, the exploration and exploitation of which shall be carried out for the benefit of mankind as a whole, irrespective of the geographical location of States,

Believing that the codification and progressive development of the law of the sea achieved in this Convention will contribute to the strengthening of peace, security, co-operation and friendly relations among all nations in conformity with the principles of justice and equal rights and will promote the economic and social advancement of all peoples of the world, in accordance with the Purposes and Principles of the United Nations as set forth in the Charter,

Affirming that matters not regulated by this Convention continue to be governed by the rules and principles of general international law,

Have agreed as follows:

PART I

INTRODUCTION

Article 1

Use of terms and scope

1. For the purposes of this Convention:

(1) "Area" means the sea-bed and ocean floor and subsoil thereof, beyond the limits of national jurisdiction;

f. This Convention supersedes the 1958 Geneva law of the sea conventions (Basic Documents 4.2, 4.3, 4.4, *supra*, and 6.3, *infra*) upon entry into force for the parties.

(2) "Authority" means the International Sea–Bed Authority;

(3) "activities in the Area" means all activities of exploration for, and exploitation of, the resources of the Area;

(4) "pollution of the marine environment" means the introduction by man, directly or indirectly, of substances or energy into the marine environment, including estuaries, which results or is likely to result in such deleterious effects as harm to living resources and marine life, hazards to human health, hindrance to marine activities, including fishing and other legitimate uses of the sea, impairment of quality for use of sea water and reduction of amenities;

(5)(a) "dumping" means:

(i) any deliberate disposal of wastes or other matter from vessels, aircraft, platforms or other man-made structures at sea;

(ii) any deliberate disposal of vessels, aircraft, platforms or other man-made structures at sea;

(b) "dumping" does not include:

(i) the disposal of wastes or other matter incidental to, or derived from the normal operations of vessels, aircraft, platforms or other man-made structures at sea and their equipment, other than wastes or other matter transported by or to vessels, aircraft, platforms or other man-made structures at sea, operating for the purpose of disposal of such matter or derived from the treatment of such wastes or other matter on such vessels, aircraft, platforms or structures;

(ii) placement of matter for a purpose other than the mere disposal thereof, provided that such placement is not contrary to the aims of this Convention.

2. (1) "States Parties" means States which have consented to be bound by this Convention and for which this Convention is in force.

(2) This Convention applies *mutatis mutandis* to the entities referred to in article 305, paragraph 1(b), (c), (d), (e) and (f), which become Parties to this Convention in accordance with the conditions relevant to each, and to that extent "States Parties" refers to those entities.

PART II

TERRITORIAL SEA AND CONTIGUOUS ZONE

SECTION 1. GENERAL PROVISIONS

Article 2

Legal status of the territorial sea, of the air space over the territorial sea and of its bed and subsoil

1. The sovereignty of a coastal State extends, beyond its land territory and internal waters and, in the case of an archipelagic State, its archipelagic waters, to an adjacent belt of sea, described as the territorial sea.

2. This sovereignty extends to the air space over the territorial sea as well as to its bed and subsoil.

3. The sovereignty over the territorial sea is exercised subject to this Convention and to other rules of international law.

SECTION 2. LIMITS OF THE TERRITORIAL SEA

Article 3

Breadth of the territorial sea

Every State has the right to establish the breadth of its territorial sea up to a limit not exceeding 12 nautical miles, measured from baselines determined in accordance with this Convention.

Article 4

Outer limit of the territorial sea

The outer limit of the territorial sea is the line every point of which is at a distance from the nearest point of the baseline equal to the breadth of the territorial sea.

Article 5

Normal baseline

Except where otherwise provided in this Convention, the normal baseline for measuring the breadth of the territorial sea is the low-water line along the coast as marked on large-scale charts officially recognized by the coastal State.

Article 6

Reefs

In the case of islands situated on atolls or of islands having fringing reefs, the baseline for measuring the breadth of the territorial sea is the seaward low-water line of the reef, as shown by the appropriate symbol on charts officially recognized by the coastal State.

Article 7

Straight baselines

1. [*See* Basic Document 4.4, Art. 4(1).]

2. Where because of the presence of a delta and other natural conditions the coastline is highly unstable, the appropriate points may be selected along the furthest seaward extent of the low-water line and, notwithstanding subsequent regression of the low-water line, the straight baselines shall remain effective until changed by the coastal State in accordance with this Convention.

3. [*See* Basic Document 4.4, Art. 4(2).]

4. Straight baselines shall not be drawn to and from low-tide elevations, unless lighthouses or similar installations which are permanently above sea level have been built on them or except in instances where the drawing of baselines to and from such elevations has received general international recognition.

5. [*See* Basic Document 4.4, Art. 4(4).]

6. The system of straight baselines may not be applied by a State in such a manner as to cut off the territorial sea of another State from the high seas or an exclusive economic zone.

Article 8

Internal waters

1. Except as provided in Part IV, waters on the landward side of the baseline of the territorial sea form part of the internal waters of the State.

2. Where the establishment of a straight baseline in accordance with the method set forth in article 7 has the effect of enclosing as internal waters areas which had not previously been considered as such, a right of innocent passage as provided in this Convention shall exist in those waters.

Article 9

Mouths of rivers

[*See* Basic Document 4.4, Art. 13.]

Article 10

Bays

1. [*See* Basic Document 4.4, Art. 7(1).]

2. [*See* Basic Document 4.4, Art. 7(2).]

3. [*See* Basic Document 4.4, Art. 7(3).]

4. [*See* Basic Document 4.4, Art. 7(4).]

5. [*See* Basic Document 4.4, Art. 7(5).]

6. The foregoing provisions do not apply to so-called "historic" bays, or in any case where the system of straight baselines provided for in article 7 is applied.

Article 11

Ports

For the purpose of delimiting the territorial sea, the outermost permanent harbour works which form an integral part of the harbour system are regarded as forming part of the coast. Off-shore installations and artificial islands shall not be considered as permanent harbour works.

Article 12

Roadsteads

Roadsteads which are normally used for the loading, unloading and anchoring of ships, and which would otherwise be situated wholly or partly outside the outer limit of the territorial sea, are included in the territorial sea.

Article 13

Low-tide elevations

[*See* Basic Document 4.4, Art. 11.]

Article 14

Combination of methods for determining baselines

The coastal State may determine baselines in turn by any of the methods provided for in the foregoing articles to suit different conditions.

Article 15

Delimitation of the territorial sea between States with opposite or adjacent coasts

[*See* Basic Document 4.4, Art. 12(1).]

Article 16

Charts and lists of geographical co-ordinates

1. The baselines for measuring the breadth of the territorial sea determined in accordance with articles 7, 9 and 10, or the limits derived therefrom, and the lines of

delimitation drawn in accordance with articles 12 and 15 shall be shown on charts of a scale or scales adequate for ascertaining their position. Alternatively, a list of geographical co-ordinates of points, specifying the geodetic datum, may be substituted.

2. The coastal State shall give due publicity to such charts or lists of geographical co-ordinates and shall deposit a copy of each such chart or list with the Secretary-General of the United Nations.

SECTION 3. INNOCENT PASSAGE IN THE TERRITORIAL SEA

SUBSECTION A. RULES APPLICABLE TO ALL SHIPS

Article 17

Right of innocent passage

[*See* Basic Document 4.4, Art. 14(1).]

Article 18

Meaning of passage

1. Passage means navigation through the territorial sea for the purpose of:

(a) traversing that sea without entering internal waters or calling at a roadstead or port facility outside internal waters; or

(b) proceeding to or from internal waters or a call at such roadstead or port facility.

2. Passage shall be continuous and expeditious. However, passage includes stopping and anchoring, but only in so far as the same are incidental to ordinary navigation or are rendered necessary by *force majeure* or distress or for the purpose of rendering assistance to persons, ships or aircraft in danger or distress.

Article 19

Meaning of innocent passage

1. [*See* Basic Document 4.4, Art. 14(4).]

2. Passage of a foreign ship shall be considered to be prejudicial to the peace, good order or security of the coastal State if in the territorial sea it engages in any of the following activities:

(a) any threat or use of force against the sovereignty, territorial integrity or political independence of the coastal State, or in any other manner in violation of the principles of international law embodied in the Charter of the United Nations;

(b) any exercise or practice with weapons of any kind;

(c) any act aimed at collecting information to the prejudice of the defence or security of the coastal State;

(d) any act of propaganda aimed at affecting the defence or security of the coastal State;

(e) the launching, landing or taking on board of any aircraft;

(f) the launching, landing or taking on board of any military device;

(g) the loading or unloading of any commodity, currency or person contrary to the customs, fiscal, immigration or sanitary laws and regulations of the coastal State;

(h) any act of wilful and serious pollution contrary to this Convention;

(i) any fishing activities;

(j) the carrying out of research or survey activities;

(k) any act aimed at interfering with any systems of communication or any other facilities or installations of the coastal State;

(*l*) any other activity not having a direct bearing on passage.

Article 20

Submarines and other underwater vehicles

In the territorial sea, submarines and other underwater vehicles are required to navigate on the surface and to show their flag.

Article 21

Laws and regulations of the coastal State relating to innocent passage

1. The coastal State may adopt laws and regulations, in conformity with the provisions of this Convention and other rules of international law, relating to innocent passage through the territorial sea, in respect of all or any of the following:

(a) the safety of navigation and the regulation of maritime traffic;

(b) the protection of navigational aids and facilities and other facilities or installations;

(c) the protection of cables and pipelines;

(d) the conservation of the living resources of the sea;

(e) the prevention of infringement of the fisheries laws and regulations of the coastal State;

(f) the preservation of the environment of the coastal State and the prevention, reduction and control of pollution thereof;

(g) marine scientific research and hydrographic surveys;

(h) the prevention of infringement of the customs, fiscal, immigration or sanitary laws and regulations of the coastal State.

2. Such laws and regulations shall not apply to the design, construction, manning or equipment of foreign ships unless they are giving effect to generally accepted international rules or standards.

3. The coastal State shall give due publicity to all such laws and regulations.

4. Foreign ships exercising the right of innocent passage through the territorial sea shall comply with all such laws and regulations and all generally accepted international regulations relating to the prevention of collisions at sea.

Article 22

Sea lanes and traffic separation schemes in the territorial sea

1. The coastal State may, where necessary, having regard to the safety of navigation, require foreign ships exercising the right of innocent passage through its territorial sea to use such sea lanes and traffic separation schemes as it may designate or prescribe for the regulation of the passage of ships.

2. In particular, tankers, nuclear-powered ships and ships carrying nuclear or other inherently dangerous or noxious substances or materials may be required to confine their passage to such sea lanes.

3. In the designation of sea lanes and the prescription of traffic separation schemes under this article, the coastal State shall take into account:

(a) the recommendations of the competent international organization;

(b) any channels customarily used for international navigation;

(c) the special characteristics of particular ships and channels; and

(d) the density of traffic.

4. The coastal State shall clearly indicate such sea lanes and traffic separation schemes on charts to which due publicity shall be given.

Article 23

Foreign nuclear-powered ships and ships carrying nuclear or other inherently dangerous or noxious substances

Foreign nuclear-powered ships and ships carrying nuclear or other inherently dangerous or noxious substances shall, when exercising the right of innocent passage through the territorial sea, carry documents and observe special precautionary measures established for such ships by international agreements.

Article 24

Duties of the coastal State

1. The coastal State shall not hamper the innocent passage of foreign ships through the territorial sea except in accordance with this Convention. In particular, in the application of this Convention or of any laws or regulations adopted in conformity with this Convention, the coastal State shall not:

(a) impose requirements on foreign ships which have the practical effect of denying or impairing the right of innocent passage; or

(b) discriminate in form or in fact against the ships of any State or against ships carrying cargoes to, from or on behalf of any State.

2. [*See* Basic Document 4.4, Art. 15(2).]

Article 25

Rights of protection of the coastal State

1. [*See* Basic Document 4.4, Art. 16(1).]

2. In the case of ships proceeding to internal waters or a call at a port facility outside internal waters, the coastal State also has the right to take the necessary steps to prevent any breach of the conditions to which admission of those ships to internal waters or such a call is subject.

3. The coastal State may, without discrimination in form or in fact among foreign ships, suspend temporarily in specified areas of its territorial sea the innocent passage of foreign ships if such suspension is essential for the protection of its security, including weapons exercises. Such suspension shall take effect only after having been duly published.

Article 26

Charges which may be levied upon foreign ships

[*See* Basic Document 4.4, Art. 18.]

SUBSECTION B. RULES APPLICABLE TO MERCHANT SHIPS AND GOVERNMENT SHIPS OPERATED FOR COMMERCIAL PURPOSES

Article 27

Criminal jurisdiction on board a foreign ship

1. The criminal jurisdiction of the coastal State should not be exercised on board a foreign ship passing through the territorial sea to arrest any person or to conduct

any investigation in connection with any crime committed on board the ship during its passage, save only in the following cases:

(a) if the consequences of the crime extend to the coastal State;

(b) if the crime is of a kind to disturb the peace of the country or the good order of the territorial sea;

(c) if the assistance of the local authorities has been requested by the master of the ship or by a diplomatic agent or consular officer of the flag State; or

(d) if such measures are necessary for the suppression of illicit traffic in narcotic drugs or psychotropic substances.

2. [*See* Basic Document 4.4, Art. 19(2).]

3. [*See* Basic Document 4.4, Art. 19(3).]

4. [*See* Basic Document 4.4, Art. 19(4).]

5. Except as provided in Part XII or with respect to violations of laws and regulations adopted in accordance with Part V, the coastal State may not take any steps on board a foreign ship passing through the territorial sea to arrest any person or to conduct any investigation in connection with any crime committed before the ship entered the territorial sea, if the ship, proceeding from a foreign port, is only passing through the territorial sea without entering internal waters.

Article 28

Civil jurisdiction in relation to foreign ships

[*See* Basic Document 4.4, Art. 20.]

SUBSECTION C. RULES APPLICABLE TO WARSHIPS AND OTHER GOVERNMENT SHIPS OPERATED FOR NON–COMMERCIAL PURPOSES

Article 29

Definition of warships

For the purposes of this Convention, "warship" means a ship belonging to the armed forces of a State bearing the external marks distinguishing such ships of its nationality, under the command of an officer duly commissioned by the government of the State and whose name appears in the appropriate service list or its equivalent, and manned by a crew which is under regular armed forces discipline.

Article 30

Non-compliance by warships with the laws and regulations of the coastal State

If any warship does not comply with the laws and regulations of the coastal State concerning passage through the territorial sea and disregards any request for compliance therewith which is made to it, the coastal State may require it to leave the territorial sea immediately.

Article 31

Responsibility of the flag State for damage caused by a warship or other government ship operated for non-commercial purposes

The flag State shall bear international responsibility for any loss or damage to the coastal State resulting from the non-compliance by a warship or other government ship operated for non-commercial purposes with the laws and regulations of the coastal State concerning passage through the territorial sea or with the provisions of this Convention or other rules of international law.

Article 32

Immunities of warships and other government ships operated for non-commercial purposes

With such exceptions as are contained in subsection A and in articles 30 and 31, nothing in this Convention affects the immunities of warships and other government ships operated for non-commercial purposes.

SECTION 4. CONTIGUOUS ZONE

Article 33

Contiguous zone

1. [*See* Basic Document 4.4, Art. 24(1).]

2. The contiguous zone may not extend beyond 24 nautical miles from the baselines from which the breadth of the territorial sea is measured.

PART III

STRAITS USED FOR INTERNATIONAL NAVIGATION

SECTION 1. GENERAL PROVISIONS

Article 34

Legal status of waters forming straits used for international navigation

1. The régime of passage through straits used for international navigation established in this Part shall not in other respects affect the legal status of the waters forming such straits or the exercise by the States bordering the straits of their sovereignty or jurisdiction over such waters and their air space, bed and subsoil.

2. The sovereignty or jurisdiction of the States bordering the straits is exercised subject to this Part and to other rules of international law.

Article 35

Scope of this Part

Nothing in this Part affects:

(a) any areas of internal waters within a strait, except where the establishment of a straight baseline in accordance with the method set forth in article 7 has the effect of enclosing as internal waters areas which had not previously been considered as such;

(b) the legal status of the waters beyond the territorial seas of States bordering straits as exclusive economic zones or high seas; or

(c) the legal régime in straits in which passage is regulated in whole or in part by long-standing international conventions in force specifically relating to such straits.

Article 36

High seas routes or routes through exclusive economic zones through straits used for international navigation

This Part does not apply to a strait used for international navigation if there exists through the strait a route through the high seas or through an exclusive economic zone of similar convenience with respect to navigational and hydrographical characteristics; in such routes, the other relevant Parts of this Convention, including the provisions regarding the freedoms of navigation and overflight, apply.

SECTION 2. TRANSIT PASSAGE

Article 37

Scope of this section

This section applies to straits which are used for international navigation between one part of the high seas or an exclusive economic zone and another part of the high seas or an exclusive economic zone.

Article 38

Right of transit passage

1. In straits referred to in article 37, all ships and aircraft enjoy the right of transit passage, which shall not be impeded; except that, if the strait is formed by an island of a State bordering the strait and its mainland, transit passage shall not apply if there exists seaward of the island a route through the high seas or through an exclusive economic zone of similar convenience with respect to navigational and hydrographical characteristics.

2. Transit passage means the exercise in accordance with this Part of the freedom of navigation and overflight solely for the purpose of continuous and expeditious transit of the strait between one part of the high seas or an exclusive economic zone and another part of the high seas or an exclusive economic zone. However, the requirement of continuous and expeditious transit does not preclude passage through the strait for the purpose of entering, leaving or returning from a State bordering the strait, subject to the conditions of entry to that State.

3. Any activity which is not an exercise of the right of transit passage through a strait remains subject to the other applicable provisions of this Convention.

Article 39

Duties of ships and aircraft during transit passage

1. Ships and aircraft, while exercising the right of transit passage, shall:

(a) proceed without delay through or over the strait;

(b) refrain from any threat or use of force against the sovereignty, territorial integrity or political independence of States bordering the strait, or in any other manner in violation of the principles of international law embodied in the Charter of the United Nations;

(c) refrain from any activities other than those incident to their normal modes of continuous and expeditious transit unless rendered necessary by *force majeure* or by distress;

(d) comply with other relevant provisions of this Part.

* * *

Article 40

Research and survey activities

During transit passage, foreign ships, including marine scientific research and hydrographic survey ships, may not carry out any research or survey activities without the prior authorization of the States bordering straits.

Article 41

Sea lanes and traffic separation schemes in straits used for international navigation

1. In conformity with this Part, States bordering straits may designate sea lanes and prescribe traffic separation schemes for navigation in straits where necessary to promote the safe passage of ships.

2. Such States may, when circumstances require, and after giving due publicity thereto, substitute other sea lanes or traffic separation schemes for any sea lanes or traffic separation schemes previously designated or prescribed by them.

3. Such sea lanes and traffic separation schemes shall conform to generally accepted international regulations.

4. Before designating or substituting sea lanes or prescribing or substituting traffic separation schemes, States bordering straits shall refer proposals to the competent international organization with a view to their adoption. The organization may adopt only such sea lanes and traffic separation schemes as may be agreed with the States bordering the straits, after which the States may designate, prescribe or substitute them.

5. In respect of a strait where sea lanes or traffic separation schemes through the waters of two or more States bordering the strait are being proposed, the States concerned shall co-operate in formulating proposals in consultation with the competent international organization.

6. States bordering straits shall clearly indicate all sea lanes and traffic separation schemes designated or prescribed by them on charts to which due publicity shall be given.

7. Ships in transit passage shall respect applicable sea lanes and traffic separation schemes established in accordance with this article.

Article 42

Laws and regulations of States bordering straits relating to transit passage

1. Subject to the provisions of this section, States bordering straits may adopt laws and regulations relating to transit passage through straits, in respect of all or any of the following:

(a) the safety of navigation and the regulation of maritime traffic, as provided in article 41;

(b) the prevention, reduction and control of pollution, by giving effect to applicable international regulations regarding the discharge of oil, oily wastes and other noxious substances in the strait;

(c) with respect to fishing vessels, the prevention of fishing, including the stowage of fishing gear;

(d) the loading or unloading of any commodity, currency or person in contravention of the customs, fiscal, immigration or sanitary laws and regulations of States bordering straits.

2. Such laws and regulations shall not discriminate in form or in fact among foreign ships or in their application have the practical effect of denying, hampering or impairing the right of transit passage as defined in this section.

3. States bordering straits shall give due publicity to all such laws and regulations.

4. Foreign ships exercising the right of transit passage shall comply with such laws and regulations.

5. The flag State of a ship or the State of registry of an aircraft entitled to sovereign immunity which acts in a manner contrary to such laws and regulations or other provisions of this Part shall bear international responsibility for any loss or damage which results to States bordering straits.

Article 43

Navigational and safety aids and other improvements and the prevention, reduction and control of pollution

User States and States bordering a strait should by agreement co-operate:

(a) in the establishment and maintenance in a strait of necessary navigational and safety aids or other improvements in aid of international navigation; and

(b) for the prevention, reduction and control of pollution from ships.

Article 44

Duties of States bordering straits

States bordering straits shall not hamper transit passage and shall give appropriate publicity to any danger to navigation or overflight within or over the strait of which they have knowledge. There shall be no suspension of transit passage.

SECTION 3. INNOCENT PASSAGE

Article 45

Innocent passage

1. The régime of innocent passage, in accordance with Part II, section 3, shall apply in straits used for international navigation:

(a) excluded from the application of the régime of transit passage under article 38, paragraph 1; or

(b) between a part of the high seas or an exclusive economic zone and the territorial sea of a foreign State.

2. There shall be no suspension of innocent passage through such straits.

PART IV

ARCHIPELAGIC STATES

Article 46

Use of terms

For the purposes of this Convention:

(a) "archipelagic State" means a State constituted wholly by one or more archipelagos and may include other islands;

(b) "archipelago" means a group of islands, including parts of islands, interconnecting waters and other natural features which are so closely interrelated that such islands, waters and other natural features form an intrinsic geographical, economic and political entity, or which historically have been regarded as such.

Article 47

Archipelagic baselines

1. An archipelagic State may draw straight archipelagic baselines joining the outermost points of the outermost islands and drying reefs of the archipelago provided that within such baselines are included the main islands and an area in which the ratio of the area of the water to the area of the land, including atolls, is between 1 to 1 and 9 to 1.

2. The length of such baselines shall not exceed 100 nautical miles, except that up to 3 per cent of the total number of baselines enclosing any archipelago may exceed that length, up to a maximum length of 125 nautical miles.

3. The drawing of such baselines shall not depart to any appreciable extent from the general configuration of the archipelago.

4. Such baselines shall not be drawn to and from low-tide elevations, unless lighthouses or similar installations which are permanently above sea level have been built on them or where a low-tide elevation is situated wholly or partly at a distance not exceeding the breadth of the territorial sea from the nearest island.

5. The system of such baselines shall not be applied by an archipelagic State in such a manner as to cut off from the high seas or the exclusive economic zone the territorial sea of another State.

6. If a part of the archipelagic waters of an archipelagic State lies between two parts of an immediately adjacent neighbouring State, existing rights and all other legitimate interests which the latter State has traditionally exercised in such waters and all rights stipulated by agreement between those States shall continue and be respected.

* * *

Article 48

Measurement of the breadth of the territorial sea, the contiguous zone, the exclusive economic zone and the continental shelf

The breadth of the territorial sea, the contiguous zone, the exclusive economic zone and the continental shelf shall be measured from archipelagic baselines drawn in accordance with article 47.

Article 49

Legal status of archipelagic waters, of the air space over archipelagic waters and of their bed and subsoil

1. The sovereignty of an archipelagic State extends to the waters enclosed by the archipelagic baselines drawn in accordance with article 47, described as archipelagic waters, regardless of their depth or distance from the coast.

2. This sovereignty extends to the air space over the archipelagic waters, as well as to their bed and subsoil, and the resources contained therein.

* * *

Article 50

Delimitation of internal waters

Within its archipelagic waters, the archipelagic State may draw closing lines for the delimitation of internal waters, in accordance with articles 9, 10 and 11.

Article 51

Existing agreements, traditional fishing rights and existing submarine cables

1. Without prejudice to article 49, an archipelagic State shall respect existing agreements with other States and shall recognize traditional fishing rights and other legitimate activities of the immediately adjacent neighbouring States in certain areas falling within archipelagic waters. The terms and conditions for the exercise of such rights and activities, including the nature, the extent and the areas to which they apply, shall, at the request of any of the States concerned, be regulated by bilateral agreements between them. Such rights shall not be transferred to or shared with third States or their nationals.

2. An archipelagic State shall respect existing submarine cables laid by other States and passing through its waters without making a landfall. An archipelagic State shall permit the maintenance and replacement of such cables upon receiving due notice of their location and the intention to repair or replace them.

Article 52

Right of innocent passage

1. Subject to article 53 and without prejudice to article 50, ships of all States enjoy the right of innocent passage through archipelagic waters, in accordance with Part II, section 3.

2. The archipelagic State may, without discrimination in form or in fact among foreign ships, suspend temporarily in specified areas of its archipelagic waters the innocent passage of foreign ships if such suspension is essential for the protection of its security. Such suspension shall take effect only after having been duly published.

Article 53

Right of archipelagic sea lanes passage

1. An archipelagic State may designate sea lanes and air routes thereabove, suitable for the continuous and expeditious passage of foreign ships and aircraft through or over its archipelagic waters and the adjacent territorial sea.

2. All ships and aircraft enjoy the right of archipelagic sea lanes passage in such sea lanes and air routes.

* * *

6. An archipelagic State which designates sea lanes under this article may also prescribe traffic separation schemes for the safe passage of ships through narrow channels in such sea lanes.

* * *

8. Such sea lanes and traffic separation schemes shall conform to generally accepted international regulations.

Article 54

Duties of ships and aircraft during their passage, research and survey activities, duties of the archipelagic State and laws and regulations of the archipelagic State relating to archipelagic sea lanes passage

Articles 39, 40, 42 and 44 apply *mutatis mutandis* to archipelagic sea lanes passage.

PART V

EXCLUSIVE ECONOMIC ZONE

Article 55

Specific legal régime of the exclusive economic zone

The exclusive economic zone is an area beyond and adjacent to the territorial sea, subject to the specific legal régime established in this Part, under which the rights and jurisdiction of the coastal State and the rights and freedoms of other States are governed by the relevant provisions of this Convention.

Article 56

Rights, jurisdiction and duties of the coastal State in the exclusive economic zone

1. In the exclusive economic zone, the coastal State has:

(a) sovereign rights for the purpose of exploring and exploiting, conserving and managing the natural resources, whether living or non-living, of the waters superjacent to the sea-bed and of the sea-bed and its subsoil, and with regard to other activities for the economic exploitation and exploration of the zone, such as the production of energy from the water, currents and winds;

(b) jurisdiction as provided for in the relevant provisions of this Convention with regard to:

(i) the establishment and use of artificial islands, installations and structures;

(ii) marine scientific research;

(iii) the protection and preservation of the marine environment;

(c) other rights and duties provided for in this Convention.

2. In exercising its rights and performing its duties under this Convention in the exclusive economic zone, the coastal State shall have due regard to the rights and duties of other States and shall act in a manner compatible with the provisions of this Convention.

3. The rights set out in this article with respect to the sea-bed and subsoil shall be exercised in accordance with Part VI.

Article 57

Breadth of the exclusive economic zone

The exclusive economic zone shall not extend beyond 200 nautical miles from the baselines from which the breadth of the territorial sea is measured.

Article 58

Rights and duties of other States in the exclusive economic zone

1. In the exclusive economic zone, all States, whether coastal or land-locked, enjoy, subject to the relevant provisions of this Convention, the freedoms referred to in article 87 of navigation and overflight and of the laying of submarine cables and pipelines, and other internationally lawful uses of the sea related to these freedoms, such as those associated with the operation of ships, aircraft and submarine cables and pipelines, and compatible with the other provisions of this Convention.

2. Articles 88 to 115 and other pertinent rules of international law apply to the exclusive economic zone in so far as they are not incompatible with this Part.

3. In exercising their rights and performing their duties under this Convention in the exclusive economic zone, States shall have due regard to the rights and duties of the coastal State and shall comply with the laws and regulations adopted by the coastal State in accordance with the provisions of this Convention and other rules of international law in so far as they are not incompatible with this Part.

Article 59

Basis for the resolution of conflicts regarding the attribution of rights and jurisdiction in the exclusive economic zone

In cases where this Convention does not attribute rights or jurisdiction to the coastal State or to other States within the exclusive economic zone, and a conflict arises between the interests of the coastal State and any other State or States, the conflict should be resolved on the basis of equity and in the light of all the relevant circumstances, taking into account the respective importance of the interests involved to the parties as well as to the international community as a whole.

Article 60

Artificial islands, installations and structures in the exclusive economic zone

1. In the exclusive economic zone, the coastal State shall have the exclusive right to construct and to authorize and regulate the construction, operation and use of:

(a) artificial islands;

(b) installations and structures for the purposes provided for in article 56 and other economic purposes;

(c) installations and structures which may interfere with the exercise of the rights of the coastal State in the zone.

2. The coastal State shall have exclusive jurisdiction over such artificial islands, installations and structures, including jurisdiction with regard to customs, fiscal, health, safety and immigration laws and regulations.

3. Due notice must be given of the construction of such artificial islands, installations or structures, and permanent means for giving warning of their presence must be maintained. * * *

* * *

7. Artificial islands, installations and structures and the safety zones around them may not be established where interference may be caused to the use of recognized sea lanes essential to international navigation.

8. Artificial islands, installations and structures do not possess the status of islands. They have no territorial sea of their own, and their presence does not affect the delimitation of the territorial sea, the exclusive economic zone or the continental shelf.

Article 61

Conservation of the living resources

1. The coastal State shall determine the allowable catch of the living resources in its exclusive economic zone.

2. The coastal State, taking into account the best scientific evidence available to it, shall ensure through proper conservation and management measures that the maintenance of the living resources in the exclusive economic zone is not endangered by over-exploitation. As appropriate, the coastal State and competent international organizations, whether subregional, regional or global, shall co-operate to this end.

3. Such measures shall also be designed to maintain or restore populations of harvested species at levels which can produce the maximum sustainable yield, as qualified by relevant environmental and economic factors, including the economic needs of coastal fishing communities and the special requirements of developing States, and taking into account fishing patterns, the interdependence of stocks and any generally recommended international minimum standards, whether subregional, regional or global.

4. In taking such measures the coastal State shall take into consideration the effects on species associated with or dependent upon harvested species with a view to maintaining or restoring populations of such associated or dependent species above levels at which their reproduction may become seriously threatened.

5. Available scientific information, catch and fishing effort statistics, and other data relevant to the conservation of fish stocks shall be contributed and exchanged on a regular basis through competent international organizations, whether subregional, regional or global, where appropriate and with participation by all States concerned, including States whose nationals are allowed to fish in the exclusive economic zone.

Article 62

Utilization of the living resources

1. The coastal State shall promote the objective of optimum utilization of the living resources in the exclusive economic zone without prejudice to article 61.

2. The coastal State shall determine its capacity to harvest the living resources of the exclusive economic zone. Where the coastal State does not have the capacity to harvest the entire allowable catch, it shall, through agreements or other arrangements and pursuant to the terms, conditions, laws and regulations referred to in paragraph 4, give other States access to the surplus of the allowable catch, having particular regard to the provisions of articles 69 and 70, especially in relation to the developing States mentioned therein.

3. In giving access to other States to its exclusive economic zone under this article, the coastal State shall take into account all relevant factors, including, *inter alia,* the significance of the living resources of the area to the economy of the coastal State concerned and its other national interests, the provisions of articles 69 and 70, the requirements of developing States in the subregion or region in harvesting part of the surplus and the need to minimize economic dislocation in States whose nationals have habitually fished in the zone or which have made substantial efforts in research and identification of stocks.

4. Nationals of other States fishing in the exclusive economic zone shall comply with the conservation measures and with the other terms and conditions established in the laws and regulations of the coastal State. These laws and regulations shall be consistent with this Convention. * * *

5. Coastal States shall give due notice of conservation and management laws and regulations.

Article 63

Stocks occurring within the exclusive economic zones of two or more coastal States or both within the exclusive economic zone and in an area beyond and adjacent to it

1. Where the same stock or stocks of associated species occur within the exclusive economic zones of two or more coastal States, these States shall seek, either directly or through appropriate subregional or regional organizations, to agree upon the measures necessary to co-ordinate and ensure the conservation and development of such stocks without prejudice to the other provisions of this Part.

2. Where the same stock or stocks of associated species occur both within the exclusive economic zone and in an area beyond and adjacent to the zone, the coastal State and the States fishing for such stocks in the adjacent area shall seek, either directly or through appropriate subregional or regional organizations, to agree upon the measures necessary for the conservation of these stocks in the adjacent area.

Article 64

Highly migratory species

1. The coastal State and other States whose nationals fish in the region for the highly migratory species listed in Annex I shall co-operate directly or through appropriate international organizations with a view to ensuring conservation and promoting the objective of optimum utilization of such species throughout the region, both within and beyond the exclusive economic zone. In regions for which no appropriate international organization exists, the coastal State and other States whose nationals harvest these species in the region shall co-operate to establish such an organization and participate in its work.

2. The provisions of paragraph 1 apply in addition to the other provisions of this Part.

Article 65

Marine mammals

Nothing in this Part restricts the right of a coastal State or the competence of an international organization, as appropriate, to prohibit, limit or regulate the exploitation of marine mammals more strictly than provided for in this Part. States shall cooperate with a view to the conservation of marine mammals and in the case of cetaceans shall in particular work through the appropriate international organizations for their conservation, management and study.

Article 66

Anadromous stocks

1. States in whose rivers anadromous stocks originate shall have the primary interest in and responsibility for such stocks.

* * *

Article 67

Catadromous species

1. A coastal State in whose waters catadromous species spend the greater part of their life cycle shall have responsibility for the management of these species and shall ensure the ingress and egress of migrating fish.

* * *

Article 68

Sedentary species

This Part does not apply to sedentary species as defined in article 77, paragraph 4.

Article 69

Right of land-locked States

1. Land-locked States shall have the right to participate, on an equitable basis, in the exploitation of an appropriate part of the surplus of the living resources of the exclusive economic zones of coastal States of the same subregion or region, taking into account the relevant economic and geographical circumstances of all the States concerned and in conformity with the provisions of this article and of articles 61 and 62.

2. The terms and modalities of such participation shall be established by the States concerned through bilateral, subregional or regional agreements taking into account, *inter alia:*

(a) the need to avoid effects detrimental to fishing communities or fishing industries of the coastal State;

(b) the extent to which the land-locked State, in accordance with the provisions of this article, is participating or is entitled to participate under existing bilateral, subregional or regional agreements in the exploitation of living resources of the exclusive economic zones of other coastal States;

(c) the extent to which other land-locked States and geographically disadvantaged States are participating in the exploitation of the living resources of the exclusive economic zone of the coastal State and the consequent need to avoid a particular burden for any single coastal State or a part of it;

(d) the nutritional needs of the populations of the respective States.

3. When the harvesting capacity of a coastal State approaches a point which would enable it to harvest the entire allowable catch of the living resources in its exclusive economic zone, the coastal State and other States concerned shall cooperate in the establishment of equitable arrangements on a bilateral, subregional or regional basis to allow for participation of developing land-locked States of the same subregion or region in the exploitation of the living resources of the exclusive economic zones of coastal States of the subregion or region, as may be appropriate in the circumstances and on terms satisfactory to all parties. In the implementation of this provision the factors mentioned in paragraph 2 shall also be taken into account.

4. Developed land-locked States shall, under the provisions of this article, be entitled to participate in the exploitation of living resources only in the exclusive economic zones of developed coastal States of the same subregion or region having regard to the extent to which the coastal State, in giving access to other States to the living resources of its exclusive economic zone, has taken into account the need to minimize detrimental effects on fishing communities and economic dislocation in States whose nationals have habitually fished in the zone.

5. The above provisions are without prejudice to arrangements agreed upon in subregions or regions where the coastal States may grant to land-locked States of the same subregion or region equal or preferential rights for the exploitation of the living resources in the exclusive economic zones.

Article 70

Right of geographically disadvantaged States

[This article is in all essential respects identical to Article 69, supra.]

Article 71

Non-applicability of articles 69 and 70

The provisions of articles 69 and 70 do not apply in the case of a coastal State whose economy is overwhelmingly dependent on the exploitation of the living resources of its exclusive economic zone.

Article 72

Restrictions on transfer of rights

* * *

Article 73

Enforcement of laws and regulations of the coastal State

1. The coastal State may, in the exercise of its sovereign rights to explore, exploit, conserve and manage the living resources in the exclusive economic zone, take such measures, including boarding, inspection, arrest and judicial proceedings, as may be necessary to ensure compliance with the laws and regulations adopted by it in conformity with this Convention.

2. Arrested vessels and their crews shall be promptly released upon the posting of reasonable bond or other security.

3. Coastal State penalties for violations of fisheries laws and regulations in the exclusive economic zone may not include imprisonment, in the absence of agreements to the contrary by the States concerned, or any other form of corporal punishment.

4. In cases of arrest or detention of foreign vessels the coastal State shall promptly notify the flag State, through appropriate channels, of the action taken and of any penalties subsequently imposed.

Article 74

Delimitation of the exclusive economic zone between States with opposite or adjacent coasts

1. The delimitation of the exclusive economic zone between States with opposite or adjacent coasts shall be effected by agreement on the basis of international law, as referred to in Article 38 of the Statute of the International Court of Justice, in order to achieve an equitable solution.

2. If no agreement can be reached within a reasonable period of time, the States concerned shall resort to the procedures provided for in Part XV.

* * *

Article 75

Charts and lists of geographical co-ordinates

* * *

PART VI

CONTINENTAL SHELF

Article 76

Definition of the continental shelf

1. The continental shelf of a coastal State comprises the sea-bed and subsoil of the submarine areas that extend beyond its territorial sea throughout the natural prolongation of its land territory to the outer edge of the continental margin, or to a distance of 200 nautical miles from the baselines from which the breadth of the territorial sea is measured where the outer edge of the continental margin does not extend up to that distance.

2. The continental shelf of a coastal State shall not extend beyond the limits provided for in paragraphs 4 to 6.

3. The continental margin comprises the submerged prolongation of the land mass of the coastal State, and consists of the sea-bed and subsoil of the shelf, the slope and the rise. It does not include the deep ocean floor with its oceanic ridges or the subsoil thereof.

4. (a) For the purposes of this Convention, the coastal State shall establish the outer edge of the continental margin wherever the margin extends beyond 200 nautical miles from the baselines from which the breadth of the territorial sea is measured, by either:

(i) a line delineated in accordance with paragraph 7 by reference to the outermost fixed points at each of which the thickness of sedimentary rocks is at least 1 per cent of the shortest distance from such point to the foot of the continental slope; or

(ii) a line delineated in accordance with paragraph 7 by reference to fixed points not more than 60 nautical miles from the foot of the continental slope.

(b) In the absence of evidence to the contrary, the foot of the continental slope shall be determined as the point of maximum change in the gradient at its base.

5. The fixed points comprising the line of the outer limits of the continental shelf on the sea-bed, drawn in accordance with paragraph 4(a)(i) and (ii), either shall not exceed 350 nautical miles from the baselines from which the breadth of the territorial sea is measured or shall not exceed 100 nautical miles from the 2,500 metre isobath, which is a line connecting the depths of 2,500 metres.

6. Notwithstanding the provisions of paragraph 5, on submarine ridges, the outer limit of the continental shelf shall not exceed 350 nautical miles from the baselines from which the breadth of the territorial sea is measured. This paragraph does not apply to submarine elevations that are natural components of the continental margin, such as its plateaux, rises, caps, banks and spurs.

7. The coastal State shall delineate the outer limits of its continental shelf, where that shelf extends beyond 200 nautical miles from the baselines from which the breadth of the territorial sea is measured, by straight lines not exceeding 60 nautical miles in length, connecting fixed points, defined by coordinates of latitude and longitude.

* * *

Article 77

Rights of the coastal State over the continental shelf

1. [*See* Basic Document 4.4, Art. 2(1).]

2. The rights referred to in paragraph 1 are exclusive in the sense that if the coastal State does not explore the continental shelf or exploit its natural resources, no one may undertake these activities without the express consent of the coastal State.

3. [*See* Basic Document 4.4, Art. 2(3).]

4. [*See* Basic Document 4.4, Art. 2(4).]

Article 78

Legal status of the superjacent waters and air space and the rights and freedoms of other States

1. The rights of the coastal State over the continental shelf do not affect the legal status of the superjacent waters or of the air space above those waters.

2. The exercise of the rights of the coastal State over the continental shelf must not infringe or result in any unjustifiable interference with navigation and other rights and freedoms of other States as provided for in this Convention.

Article 79

Submarine cables and pipelines on the continental shelf

1. All States are entitled to lay submarine cables and pipelines on the continental shelf, in accordance with the provisions of this article.

2. Subject to its right to take reasonable measures for the exploration of the continental shelf, the exploitation of its natural resources and the prevention, reduction and control of pollution from pipelines, the coastal State may not impede the laying or maintenance of such cables or pipelines.

3. The delineation of the course for the laying of such pipelines on the continental shelf is subject to the consent of the coastal State.

4. Nothing in this Part affects the right of the coastal State to establish conditions for cables or pipelines entering its territory or territorial sea, or its jurisdiction over cables and pipelines constructed or used in connection with the exploration of its continental shelf or exploitation of its resources or the operations of artificial islands, installations and structures under its jurisdiction.

5. When laying submarine cables or pipelines, States shall have due regard to cables or pipelines already in position. In particular, possibilities of repairing existing cables or pipelines shall not be prejudiced.

Article 80

Artificial islands, installations and structures on the continental shelf

Article 60 applies *mutatis mutandis* to artificial islands, installations and structures on the continental shelf.

Article 81

Drilling on the continental shelf

The coastal State shall have the exclusive right to authorize and regulate drilling on the continental shelf for all purposes.

Article 82

Payments and contributions with respect to the exploitation of the continental shelf beyond 200 nautical miles

1. The coastal State shall make payments or contributions in kind in respect of the exploitation of the non-living resources of the continental shelf beyond 200 nautical miles from the baselines from which the breadth of the territorial sea is measured.

2. The payments and contributions shall be made annually with respect to all production at a site after the first five years of production at that site. For the sixth year, the rate of payment or contribution shall be 1 per cent of the value or volume of production at the site. The rate shall increase by 1 per cent for each subsequent year until the twelfth year and shall remain at 7 per cent thereafter. Production does not include resources used in connection with exploitation.

3. A developing State which is a net importer of a mineral resource produced from its continental shelf is exempt from making such payments or contributions in respect of that mineral resource.

4. The payments or contributions shall be made through the Authority, which shall distribute them to States Parties to this Convention, on the basis of equitable sharing criteria, taking into account the interests and needs of developing States, particularly the least developed and the land-locked among them.

Article 83

Delimitation of the continental shelf between States with opposite or adjacent coasts

1. The delimitation of the continental shelf between States with opposite or adjacent coasts shall be effected by agreement on the basis of international law, as referred to in Article 38 of the Statute of the International Court of Justice, in order to achieve an equitable solution.

2. If no agreement can be reached within a reasonable period of time, the States concerned shall resort to the procedures provided for in Part XV.

Article 84

Charts and lists of geographical co-ordinates

* * *

Article 85

Tunnelling

This Part does not prejudice the right of the coastal State to exploit the subsoil by means of tunnelling, irrespective of the depth of water above the subsoil.

PART VII

HIGH SEAS

SECTION 1. GENERAL PROVISIONS

Article 86

Application of the provisions of this Part

The provisions of this Part apply to all parts of the sea that are not included in the exclusive economic zone, in the territorial sea or in the internal waters of a State, or in the archipelagic waters of an archipelagic State. This article does not entail any abridgement of the freedoms enjoyed by all States in the exclusive economic zone in accordance with article 58.

Article 87

Freedom of the high seas

1. The high seas are open to all States, whether coastal or land-locked. Freedom of the high seas is exercised under the conditions laid down by this Convention and by other rules of international law. It comprises, *inter alia,* both for coastal and land-locked States:

(a) freedom of navigation;

(b) freedom of overflight;

(c) freedom to lay submarine cables and pipelines, subject to Part VI;

(d) freedom to construct artificial islands and other installations permitted under international law, subject to Part VI;

(e) freedom of fishing, subject to the conditions laid down in section 2;

(f) freedom of scientific research, subject to Parts VI and XIII.

2. These freedoms shall be exercised by all States with due regard for the interests of other States in their exercise of the freedom of the high seas, and also with due regard for the rights under this Convention with respect to activities in the Area.

Article 88

Reservation of the high seas for peaceful purposes

The high seas shall be reserved for peaceful purposes.

Article 89

Invalidity of claims of sovereignty over the high seas

No State may validly purport to subject any part of the high seas to its sovereignty.

Article 90

Right of navigation

[*See* Basic Document 4.2, Art. 4.]

Article 91

Nationality of ships

[*See* Basic Document 4.2, Art. 5.]

Article 92

Status of ships

[*See* Basic Document 4.2, Art. 6.]

Article 93

Ships flying the flag of the United Nations, its specialized agencies and the International Atomic Energy Agency

The preceding articles do not prejudice the question of ships employed on the official service of the United Nations, its specialized agencies or the International Atomic Energy Agency, flying the flag of the organization.

Article 94

Duties of the flag State

1. Every State shall effectively exercise its jurisdiction and control in administrative, technical and social matters over ships flying its flag.

2. In particular every State shall:

(a) maintain a register of ships containing the names and particulars of ships flying its flag, except those which are excluded from generally accepted international regulations on account of their small size; and

(b) assume jurisdiction under its internal law over each ship flying its flag and its master, officers and crew in respect of administrative, technical and social matters concerning the ship.

3. Every State shall take such measures for ships flying its flag as are necessary to ensure safety at sea with regard, *inter alia,* to:

(a) the construction, equipment and seaworthiness of ships;

(b) the manning of ships, labour conditions and the training of crews, taking into account the applicable international instruments;

(c) the use of signals, the maintenance of communications and the prevention of collisions.

4. Such measures shall include those necessary to ensure:

(a) that each ship, before registration and thereafter at appropriate intervals, is surveyed by a qualified surveyor of ships, and has on board such charts, nautical publications and navigational equipment and instruments as are appropriate for the safe navigation of the ship;

(b) that each ship is in the charge of a master and officers who possess appropriate qualifications, in particular in seamanship, navigation, communications and marine engineering, and that the crew is appropriate in qualification and numbers for the type, size, machinery and equipment of the ship;

(c) that the master, officers and, to the extent appropriate, the crew are fully conversant with and required to observe the applicable international regulations concerning the safety of life at sea, the prevention of collisions, the prevention, reduction and control of marine pollution, and the maintenance of communications by radio.

5. In taking the measures called for in paragraphs 3 and 4 each State is required to conform to generally accepted international regulations, procedures and practices and to take any steps which may be necessary to secure their observance.

6. A State which has clear grounds to believe that proper jurisdiction and control with respect to a ship have not been exercised may report the facts to the flag State. Upon receiving such a report, the flag State shall investigate the matter and, if appropriate, take any action necessary to remedy the situation.

7. Each State shall cause an inquiry to be held by or before a suitably qualified person or persons into every marine casualty or incident of navigation on the high seas involving a ship flying its flag and causing loss of life or serious injury to nationals of another State or serious damage to ships or installations of another State or to the marine environment. The flag State and the other State shall co-operate in the conduct of any inquiry held by that other State into any such marine casualty or incident of navigation.

Article 95

Immunity of warships on the high seas

[*See* Basic Document 4.2, Art. 8(1).]

Article 96

Immunity of ships used only on government non-commercial service

[*See* Basic Document 4.2, Art. 9.]

Article 97

Penal jurisdiction in matters of collision or in any other incident of navigation

[*See* Basic Document 4.2, Art. 11.]

Article 98

Duty to render assistance

[*See* Basic Document 4.2, Art. 12.]

Article 99

Prohibition of the transport of slaves

[*See* Basic Document 4.2, Art. 13.]

Article 100

Duty to co-operate in the repression of piracy

[*See* Basic Document 4.2, Art. 14.]

Article 101

Definition of piracy

[*See* Basic Document 4.2, Art. 15.]

Article 102

Piracy by a warship, government ship or government aircraft whose crew has mutinied

The acts of piracy, as defined in article 101, committed by a warship, government ship or government aircraft whose crew has mutinied and taken control of the ship or aircraft are assimilated to acts committed by a private ship or aircraft.

Article 103

Definition of a pirate ship or aircraft

A ship or aircraft is considered a pirate ship or aircraft if it is intended by the persons in dominant control to be used for the purpose of committing one of the acts referred to in article 101. The same applies if the ship or aircraft has been used to commit any such act, so long as it remains under the control of the persons guilty of that act.

Article 104

Retention or loss of the nationality of a pirate ship or aircraft

[*See* Basic Document 4.2, Art. 18.]

Article 105

Seizure of a pirate ship or aircraft

[*See* Basic Document 4.2, Art. 19.]

Article 106

Liability for seizure without adequate grounds

[*See* Basic Document 4.2, Art. 20.]

Article 107

Ships and aircraft which are entitled to seize on account of piracy

[*See* Basic Document 4.2, Art. 21.]

Article 108

Illicit traffic in narcotic drugs or psychotropic substances

1. All States shall co-operate in the suppression of illicit traffic in narcotic drugs and psychotropic substances engaged in by ships on the high seas contrary to international conventions.

2. Any State which has reasonable grounds for believing that a ship flying its flag is engaged in illicit traffic in narcotic drugs or psychotropic substances may request the co-operation of other States to suppress such traffic.

Article 109

Unauthorized broadcasting from the high seas

1. All States shall co-operate in the suppression of unauthorized broadcasting from the high seas.

2. For the purposes of this Convention, "unauthorized broadcasting" means the transmission of sound radio or television broadcasts from a ship or installation on the high seas intended for reception by the general public contrary to international regulations, but excluding the transmission of distress calls.

3. Any person engaged in unauthorized broadcasting may be prosecuted before the court of:

(a) the flag State of the ship;

(b) the State of registry of the installation;

(c) the State of which the person is a national;

(d) any State where the transmissions can be received; or

(e) any State where authorized radio communication is suffering interference.

4. On the high seas, a State having jurisdiction in accordance with paragraph 3 may, in conformity with article 110, arrest any person or ship engaged in unauthorized broadcasting and seize the broadcasting apparatus.

Article 110

Right of visit

1. Except where acts of interference derive from powers conferred by treaty, a warship which encounters on the high seas a foreign ship, other than a ship entitled to complete immunity in accordance with articles 95 and 96, is not justified in boarding it unless there is reasonable ground for suspecting that:

(a) the ship is engaged in piracy;

(b) the ship is engaged in the slave trade;

(c) the ship is engaged in unauthorized broadcasting and the flag State of the warship has jurisdiction under article 109;

(d) the ship is without nationality; or

(e) though flying a foreign flag or refusing to show its flag, the ship is, in reality, of the same nationality as the warship.

2. In the cases provided for in paragraph 1, the warship may proceed to verify the ship's right to fly its flag. To this end, it may send a boat under the command of an officer to the suspected ship. If suspicion remains after the documents have been checked, it may proceed to a further examination on board the ship, which must be carried out with all possible consideration.

3. If the suspicions prove to be unfounded, and provided that the ship boarded has not committed any act justifying them, it shall be compensated for any loss or damage that may have been sustained.

4. These provisions apply *mutatis mutandis* to military aircraft.

5. These provisions also apply to any other duly authorized ships or aircraft clearly marked and identifiable as being on government service.

Article 111

Right of hot pursuit

1. The hot pursuit of a foreign ship may be undertaken when the competent authorities of the coastal State have good reason to believe that the ship has violated the laws and regulations of that State. Such pursuit must be commenced when the foreign ship or one of its boats is within the internal waters, the archipelagic waters, the territorial sea or the contiguous zone of the pursuing State, and may only be continued outside the territorial sea or the contiguous zone if the pursuit has not been interrupted. It is not necessary that, at the time when the foreign ship within the territorial sea or the contiguous zone receives the order to stop, the ship giving the order should likewise be within the territorial sea or the contiguous zone. If the foreign ship is within a contiguous zone, as defined in article 33, the pursuit may only be undertaken if there has been a violation of the rights for the protection of which the zone was established.

2. The right of hot pursuit shall apply *mutatis mutandis* to violations in the exclusive economic zone or on the continental shelf, including safety zones around continental shelf installations, of the laws and regulations of the coastal State applicable in accordance with this Convention to the exclusive economic zone or the continental shelf, including such safety zones.

3. [*See* Basic Document 4.2, Art. 23(2).]

4. Hot pursuit is not deemed to have begun unless the pursuing ship has satisfied itself by such practicable means as may be available that the ship pursued or one of its boats or other craft working as a team and using the ship pursued as a mother ship is within the limits of the territorial sea, or, as the case may be, within the contiguous zone or the exclusive economic zone or above the continental shelf. The pursuit may only be commenced after a visual or auditory signal to stop has been given at a distance which enables it to be seen or heard by the foreign ship.

5. The right of hot pursuit may be exercised only by warships or military aircraft, or other ships or aircraft clearly marked and identifiable as being on government service and authorized to that effect.

6. Where hot pursuit is effected by an aircraft:

(a) the provisions of paragraphs 1 to 4 shall apply *mutatis mutandis;*

(b) [See Basic Document 4.2, Art. 23(5)(b).]

7. The release of a ship arrested within the jurisdiction of a State and escorted to a port of that State for the purposes of an inquiry before the competent authorities may not be claimed solely on the ground that the ship, in the course of its voyage, was escorted across a portion of the exclusive economic zone or the high seas, if the circumstances rendered this necessary.

8. Where a ship has been stopped or arrested outside the territorial sea in circumstances which do not justify the exercise of the right of hot pursuit, it shall be compensated for any loss or damage that may have been thereby sustained.

Article 112

Right to lay submarine cables and pipelines

1. All States are entitled to lay submarine cables and pipelines on the bed of the high seas beyond the continental shelf.

2. Article 79, paragraph 5, applies to such cables and pipelines.

Article 113

Breaking or injury of a submarine cable or pipeline

[*See* Basic Document 4.2, Art. 27.]

Article 114

Breaking or injury by owners of a submarine cable or pipeline of another submarine cable or pipeline

[*See* Basic Document 4.2, Art. 28.]

Article 115

Indemnity for loss incurred in avoiding injury to a submarine cable or pipeline

[*See* Basic Document 4.2, Art. 29.]

SECTION 2. CONSERVATION AND MANAGEMENT OF THE LIVING RESOURCES OF THE HIGH SEAS

Article 116

Right to fish on the high seas

All States have the right for their nationals to engage in fishing on the high seas subject to:

(a) their treaty obligations;

(b) the rights and duties as well as the interests of coastal States provided for, *inter alia,* in article 63, paragraph 2, and articles 64 to 67; and

(c) the provisions of this section.

Article 117

Duty of States to adopt with respect to their nationals measures for the conservation of the living resources of the high seas

[*See* Basic Document 6.3, Art. 1(2).]

Article 118

Co-operation of States in the conservation and management of living resources

States shall co-operate with each other in the conservation and management of living resources in the areas of the high seas. States whose nationals exploit identical living resources, or different living resources in the same area, shall enter into negotiations with a view to taking the measures necessary for the conservation of the living resources concerned. They shall, as appropriate, co-operate to establish subregional or regional fisheries organizations to this end.

Article 119

Conservation of the living resources of the high seas

1. In determining the allowable catch and establishing other conservation measures for the living resources in the high seas, States shall:

(a) take measures which are designed, on the best scientific evidence available to the States concerned, to maintain or restore populations of harvested species at levels which can produce the maximum sustainable yield, as qualified by relevant environmental and economic factors, including the special requirements of developing States, and taking into account fishing patterns, the interdependence of stocks and any generally recommended international minimum standards, whether subregional, regional or global;

(b) take into consideration the effects on species associated with or dependent upon harvested species with a view to maintaining or restoring populations of such associated or dependent species above levels at which their reproduction may become seriously threatened.

2. Available scientific information, catch and fishing effort statistics, and other data relevant to the conservation of fish stocks shall be contributed and exchanged on a regular basis through competent international organizations, whether subregional, regional or global, where appropriate and with participation by all States concerned.

3. States concerned shall ensure that conservation measures and their implementation do not discriminate in form or in fact against the fishermen of any State.

Article 120

Marine mammals

Article 65 also applies to the conservation and management of marine mammals in the high seas.

PART VIII

REGIME OF ISLANDS

Article 121

Régime of islands

1. An island is a naturally formed area of land, surrounded by water, which is above water at high tide.

2. Except as provided for in paragraph 3, the territorial sea, the contiguous zone, the exclusive economic zone and the continental shelf of an island are determined in accordance with the provisions of this Convention applicable to other land territory.

3. Rocks which cannot sustain human habitation or economic life of their own shall have no exclusive economic zone or continental shelf.

PART IX

ENCLOSED OR SEMI-ENCLOSED SEAS

Article 122

Definition

For the purposes of this Convention, "enclosed or semi-enclosed sea" means a gulf, basin or sea surrounded by two or more States and connected to another sea or the ocean by a narrow outlet or consisting entirely or primarily of the territorial seas and exclusive economic zones of two or more coastal States.

Article 123

Co-operation of States bordering enclosed or semi-enclosed seas

States bordering an enclosed or semi-enclosed sea should co-operate with each other in the exercise of their rights and in the performance of their duties under this Convention. * * *

PART X

RIGHT OF ACCESS OF LAND-LOCKED STATES TO AND FROM THE SEA AND FREEDOM OF TRANSIT

Article 124

Use of terms

1. For the purposes of this Convention:

(a) "land-locked State" means a State which has no sea-coast;

(b) "transit State" means a State, with or without a sea-coast, situated between a land-locked State and the sea, through whose territory traffic in transit passes;

(c) "traffic in transit" means transit of persons, baggage, goods and means of transport across the territory of one or more transit States, when the passage across such territory, with or without trans-shipment, warehousing, breaking bulk or change in the mode of transport, is only a portion of a complete journey which begins or terminates within the territory of the land-locked State;

(d) "means of transport" means:

(i) railway rolling stock, sea, lake and river craft and road vehicles;

(ii) where local conditions so require, porters and pack animals.

2. Land-locked States and transit States may, by agreement between them, include as means of transport pipelines and gas lines and means of transport other than those included in paragraph 1.

Article 125

Right of access to and from the sea and freedom of transit

1. Land-locked States shall have the right of access to and from the sea for the purpose of exercising the rights provided for in this Convention including those relating to the freedom of the high seas and the common heritage of mankind. To this

end, land-locked States shall enjoy freedom of transit through the territory of transit States by all means of transport.

2. The terms and modalities for exercising freedom of transit shall be agreed between the land-locked States and transit States concerned through bilateral, subregional or regional agreements.

3. Transit States, in the exercise of their full sovereignty over their territory, shall have the right to take all measures necessary to ensure that the rights and facilities provided for in this Part for land-locked States shall in no way infringe their legitimate interests.

Article 126

Exclusion of application of the most-favoured-nation clause

* * *

Article 127

Customs duties, taxes and other charges

1. Traffic in transit shall not be subject to any customs duties, taxes or other charges except charges levied for specific services rendered in connection with such traffic.

2. Means of transport in transit and other facilities provided for and used by land-locked States shall not be subject to taxes or charges higher than those levied for the use of means of transport of the transit State.

Article 128

Free zones and other customs facilities

* * *

Article 129

Co-operation in the construction and improvement of means of transport

* * *

Article 130

Measures to avoid or eliminate delays or other difficulties of a technical nature in traffic in transit

* * *

Article 131

Equal treatment in maritime ports

* * *

Article 132

Grant of greater transit facilities

* * *

PART XI

THE AREA

SECTION 1. GENERAL PROVISIONS

Article 133

Use of terms

For the purposes of this Part:

(a) "resources" means all solid, liquid or gaseous mineral resources in situ in the Area at or beneath the sea-bed, including polymetallic nodules;

(b) resources, when recovered from the Area, are referred to as "minerals".

Article 134

Scope of this Part

1. This Part applies to the Area.

2. Activities in the Area shall be governed by the provisions of this Part.

3. The requirements concerning deposit of, and publicity to be given to, the charts or lists of geographical co-ordinates showing the limits referred to in article 1, paragraph 1(1), are set forth in Part VI.

4. Nothing in this article affects the establishment of the outer limits of the continental shelf in accordance with Part VI or the validity of agreements relating to delimitation between States with opposite or adjacent coasts.

Article 135

Legal status of the superjacent waters and air space

Neither this Part nor any rights granted or exercised pursuant thereto shall affect the legal status of the waters superjacent to the Area or that of the air space above those waters.

SECTION 2. PRINCIPLES GOVERNING THE AREA

Article 136

Common heritage of mankind

The Area and its resources are the common heritage of mankind.

Article 137

Legal status of the Area and its resources

1. No State shall claim or exercise sovereignty or sovereign rights over any part of the Area or its resources, nor shall any State or natural or juridical person appropriate any part thereof. No such claim or exercise of sovereignty or sovereign rights nor such appropriation shall be recognized.

2. All rights in the resources of the Area are vested in mankind as a whole, on whose behalf the Authority shall act. These resources are not subject to alienation. The minerals recovered from the Area, however, may only be alienated in accordance with this Part and the rules, regulations and procedures of the Authority.

3. No State or natural or juridical person shall claim, acquire or exercise rights with respect to the minerals recovered from the Area except in accordance with this Part. Otherwise, no such claim, acquisition or exercise of such rights shall be recognized.

Article 138

General conduct of States in relation to the Area

The general conduct of States in relation to the Area shall be in accordance with the provisions of this Part, the principles embodied in the Charter of the United Nations and other rules of international law in the interests of maintaining peace and security and promoting international co-operation and mutual understanding.

Article 139

Responsibility to ensure compliance and liability for damage

1. States Parties shall have the responsibility to ensure that activities in the Area, whether carried out by States Parties, or state enterprises or natural or juridical persons which possess the nationality of States Parties or are effectively controlled by them or their nationals, shall be carried out in conformity with this Part. The same responsibility applies to international organizations for activities in the Area carried out by such organizations.

* * *

Article 140

Benefit of mankind

1. Activities in the Area shall, as specifically provided for in this Part, be carried out for the benefit of mankind as a whole, irrespective of the geographical location of States, whether coastal or land-locked, and taking into particular consideration the interests and needs of developing States and of peoples who have not attained full independence or other self-governing status recognized by the United Nations in accordance with General Assembly resolution 1514 (XV) and other relevant General Assembly resolutions.

2. The Authority shall provide for the equitable sharing of financial and other economic benefits derived from activities in the Area through any appropriate mechanism, on a non-discriminatory basis, in accordance with article 160, paragraph 2(f)(i).

Article 141

Use of the Area exclusively for peaceful purposes

The Area shall be open to use exclusively for peaceful purposes by all States, whether coastal or land-locked, without discrimination and without prejudice to the other provisions of this Part.

Article 142

Rights and legitimate interests of coastal States

1. Activities in the Area, with respect to resource deposits in the Area which lie across limits of national jurisdiction, shall be conducted with due regard to the rights and legitimate interests of any coastal State across whose jurisdiction such deposits lie.

* * *

Article 143

Marine scientific research

1. Marine scientific research in the Area shall be carried out exclusively for peaceful purposes and for the benefit of mankind as a whole, in accordance with Part XIII.

2. The Authority may carry out marine scientific research concerning the Area and its resources, and may enter into contracts for that purpose. The Authority shall promote and encourage the conduct of marine scientific research in the Area, and shall co-ordinate and disseminate the results of such research and analysis when available.

3. States Parties may carry out marine scientific research in the Area. States Parties shall promote international co-operation in marine scientific research in the Area by:

(a) participating in international programmes and encouraging co-operation in marine scientific research by personnel of different countries and of the Authority;

(b) ensuring that programmes are developed through the Authority or other international organizations as appropriate for the benefit of developing States and technologically less developed States with a view to:

(i) strengthening their research capabilities;

(ii) training their personnel and the personnel of the Authority in the techniques and applications of research;

(iii) fostering the employment of their qualified personnel in research in the Area;

(c) effectively disseminating the results of research and analysis when available, through the Authority or other international channels when appropriate.

Article 144

Transfer of technology

1. The Authority shall take measures in accordance with this Convention:

(a) to acquire technology and scientific knowledge relating to activities in the Area; and

(b) to promote and encourage the transfer to developing States of such technology and scientific knowledge so that all States Parties benefit therefrom.

2. To this end the Authority and States Parties shall co-operate in promoting the transfer of technology and scientific knowledge relating to activities in the Area so that the Enterprise and all States Parties may benefit therefrom. In particular they shall initiate and promote:

(a) programmes for the transfer of technology to the Enterprise and to developing States with regard to activities in the Area, including, *inter alia,* facilitating the access of the Enterprise and of developing States to the relevant technology, under fair and reasonable terms and conditions;

(b) measures directed towards the advancement of the technology of the Enterprise and the domestic technology of developing States, particularly by providing opportunities to personnel from the Enterprise and from developing States for training in marine science and technology and for their full participation in activities in the Area.

Article 145

Protection of the marine environment

Necessary measures shall be taken in accordance with this Convention with respect to activities in the Area to ensure effective protection for the marine environment from harmful effects which may arise from such activities. To this end the Authority shall adopt appropriate rules, regulations and procedures for *inter alia:*

(a) the prevention, reduction and control of pollution and other hazards to the marine environment, including the coastline, and of interference with the ecological balance of the marine environment, particular attention being paid to the need for protection from harmful effects of such activities as drilling, dredging, excavation, disposal of waste, construction and operation or maintenance of installations, pipelines and other devices related to such activities;

(b) the protection and conservation of the natural resources of the Area and the prevention of damage to the flora and fauna of the marine environment.

Article 146

Protection of human life

With respect to activities in the Area, necessary measures shall be taken to ensure effective protection of human life. * * *

Article 147

Accommodation of activities in the Area and in the marine environment

1. Activities in the Area shall be carried out with reasonable regard for other activities in the marine environment.

2. Installations used for carrying out activities in the Area shall be subject to the following conditions:

(a) such installations shall be erected, emplaced and removed solely in accordance with this Part and subject to the rules, regulations and procedures of the Authority. Due notice must be given of the erection, emplacement and removal of such installations, and permanent means for giving warning of their presence must be maintained;

(b) such installations may not be established where interference may be caused to the use of recognized sea lanes essential to international navigation or in areas of intense fishing activity;

(c) safety zones shall be established around such installations with appropriate markings to ensure the safety of both navigation and the installations. The configuration and location of such safety zones shall not be such as to form a belt impeding the lawful access of shipping to particular maritime zones or navigation along international sea lanes;

(d) such installations shall be used exclusively for peaceful purposes;

(e) such installations do not possess the status of islands. They have no territorial sea of their own, and their presence does not affect the delimitation of the territorial sea, the exclusive economic zone or the continental shelf.

3. Other activities in the marine environment shall be conducted with reasonable regard for activities in the Area.

Article 148

Participation of developing States in activities in the Area

The effective participation of developing States in activities in the Area shall be promoted as specifically provided for in this Part, having due regard to their special interests and needs, and in particular to the special need of the land-locked and geographically disadvantaged among them to overcome obstacles arising from their disadvantaged location, including remoteness from the Area and difficulty of access to and from it.

Article 149

Archaeological and historical objects

All objects of an archaeological and historical nature found in the Area shall be preserved or disposed of for the benefit of mankind as a whole, particular regard being paid to the preferential rights of the State or country of origin, or the State of cultural origin, or the State of historical and archaeological origin.

SECTION 3. DEVELOPMENT OF RESOURCES OF THE AREA

Article 150

Policies relating to activities in the Area

Activities in the Area shall, as specifically provided for in this Part, be carried out in such a manner as to foster healthy development of the world economy and balanced growth of international trade, and to promote international co-operation for the over-all development of all countries, especially developing States, and with a view to ensuring:

(a) the development of the resources of the Area;

(b) orderly, safe and rational management of the resources of the Area, including the efficient conduct of activities in the Area and, in accordance with sound principles of conservation, the avoidance of unnecessary waste;

(c) the expansion of opportunities for participation in such activities consistent in particular with articles 144 and 148;

(d) participation in revenues by the Authority and the transfer of technology to the Enterprise and developing States as provided for in this Convention;

(e) increased availability of the minerals derived from the Area as needed in conjunction with minerals derived from other sources, to ensure supplies to consumers of such minerals;

(f) the promotion of just and stable prices remunerative to producers and fair to consumers for minerals derived both from the Area and from other sources, and the promotion of long-term equilibrium between supply and demand;

(g) the enhancement of opportunities for all States Parties, irrespective of their social and economic systems or geographical location, to participate in the development of the resources of the Area and the prevention of monopolization of activities in the Area;

(h) the protection of developing countries from adverse effects on their economies or on their export earnings resulting from a reduction in the price of an affected mineral, or in the volume of exports of that mineral, to the extent that such reduction is caused by activities in the Area, as provided in article 151;

(i) the development of the common heritage for the benefit of mankind as a whole; and

(j) conditions of access to markets for the imports of minerals produced from the resources of the Area and for imports of commodities produced from such minerals shall not be more favourable than the most favourable applied to imports from other sources.

Article 151

Production policies

1. (a) Without prejudice to the objectives set forth in article 150 and for the purpose of implementing subparagraph (h) of that article, the Authority, acting through existing forums or such new arrangements or agreements as may be appropriate, in which all interested parties, including both producers and consumers, participate, shall take measures necessary to promote the growth, efficiency and stability of markets for those commodities produced from the minerals derived from the Area, at prices remunerative to producers and fair to consumers. All States Parties shall co-operate to this end.

* * *

2. (a) During the interim period specified in paragraph 3, commercial production shall not be undertaken pursuant to an approved plan of work until the operator has applied for and has been issued a production authorization by the Authority. Such production authorizations may not be applied for or issued more than five years prior to the planned commencement of commercial production under the plan of work

unless, having regard to the nature and timing of project development, the rules, regulations and procedures of the Authority prescribe another period.

* * *

3. The interim period shall begin five years prior to 1 January of the year in which the earliest commercial production is planned to commence under an approved plan of work. If the earliest commercial production is delayed beyond the year originally planned, the beginning of the interim period and the production ceiling originally calculated shall be adjusted accordingly. The interim period shall last 25 years or until the end of the Review Conference referred to in article 155 or until the day when such new arrangements or agreements as are referred to in paragraph 1 enter into force, whichever is earliest. The Authority shall resume the power provided in this article for the remainder of the interim period if the said arrangements or agreements should lapse or become ineffective for any reason whatsoever.

4. [This provision establishes the production ceiling for any one year of the interim period and the manner of its calculation.]

5. The Authority shall reserve to the Enterprise for its initial production a quantity of 38,000 metric tonnes of nickel from the available production ceiling calculated pursuant to paragraph 4.

6. [This provision authorizes supplementing production subject to certain conditions.]

7. The levels of production of other metals such as copper, cobalt and manganese extracted from the polymetallic nodules that are recovered pursuant to a production authorization should not be higher than those which would have been produced had the operator produced the maximum level of nickel from those nodules pursuant to this article. The Authority shall establish rules, regulations and procedures pursuant to Annex III, article 17, to implement this paragraph.

8. Rights and obligations relating to unfair economic practices under relevant multilateral trade agreements shall apply to the exploration for and exploitation of minerals from the Area. In the settlement of disputes arising under this provision, States Parties which are Parties to such multilateral trade agreements shall have recourse to the dispute settlement procedures of such agreements.

9. The Authority shall have the power to limit the level of production of minerals from the Area, other than minerals from polymetallic nodules, under such conditions and applying such methods as may be appropriate by adopting regulations in accordance with article 161, paragraph 8.

10. Upon the recommendation of the Council on the basis of advice from the Economic Planning Commission, the Assembly shall establish a system of compensation or take other measures of economic adjustment assistance including co-operation with specialized agencies and other international organizations to assist developing countries which suffer serious adverse effects on their export earnings or economies resulting from a reduction in the price of an affected mineral or in the volume of exports of that mineral, to the extent that such reduction is caused by activities in the Area. The Authority on request shall initiate studies on the problems of those States which are likely to be most seriously affected with a view to minimizing their difficulties and assisting them in their economic adjustment.

Article 152

Exercise of powers and functions by the Authority

1. The Authority shall avoid discrimination in the exercise of its powers and functions, including the granting of opportunities for activities in the Area.

2. Nevertheless, special consideration for developing States, including particular consideration for the land-locked and geographically disadvantaged among them, specifically provided for in this Part shall be permitted.

Article 153

System of exploration and exploitation

1. Activities in the Area shall be organized, carried out and controlled by the Authority on behalf of mankind as a whole in accordance with this article as well as other relevant provisions of this Part and the relevant Annexes, and the rules, regulations and procedures of the Authority.

2. Activities in the Area shall be carried out as prescribed in paragraph 3:

(a) by the Enterprise, and

(b) in association with the Authority by States Parties, or state enterprises or natural or juridical persons which possess the nationality of States Parties or are effectively controlled by them or their nationals, when sponsored by such States, or any group of the foregoing which meets the requirements provided in this Part and in Annex III.

3. Activities in the Area shall be carried out in accordance with a formal written plan of work drawn up in accordance with Annex III and approved by the Council after review by the Legal and Technical Commission. In the case of activities in the Area carried out as authorized by the Authority by the entities specified in paragraph 2(b), the plan of work shall, in accordance with Annex III, article 3, be in the form of a contract. Such contracts may provide for joint arrangements in accordance with Annex III, article 11.

* * *

Article 154

Periodic review

Every five years from the entry into force of this Convention, the Assembly shall undertake a general and systematic review of the manner in which the international régime of the Area established in this Convention has operated in practice. In the light of this review the Assembly may take, or recommend that other organs take, measures in accordance with the provisions and procedures of this Part and the Annexes relating thereto which will lead to the improvement of the operation of the régime.

Article 155

The Review Conference

1. Fifteen years from 1 January of the year in which the earliest commercial production commences under an approved plan of work, the Assembly shall convene a conference for the review of those provisions of this Part and the relevant Annexes which govern the system of exploration and exploitation of the resources of the Area.
* * *

* * *

SECTION 4. THE AUTHORITY

SUBSECTION A. GENERAL PROVISIONS

Article 156

Establishment of the Authority

1. There is hereby established the International Sea-Bed Authority, which shall function in accordance with this Part.

2. All States Parties are ipso facto members of the Authority.

3. Observers at the Third United Nations Conference on the Law of the Sea who have signed the Final Act and who are not referred to in article 305, paragraph 1(c), (d), (e) or (f), shall have the right to participate in the Authority as observers, in accordance with its rules, regulations and procedures.

4. The seat of the Authority shall be in Jamaica.

5. The Authority may establish such regional centres or offices as it deems necessary for the exercise of its functions.

Article 157

Nature and fundamental principles of the Authority

1. The Authority is the organization through which States Parties shall, in accordance with this Part, organize and control activities in the Area, particularly with a view to administering the resources of the Area.

2. The powers and functions of the Authority shall be those expressly conferred upon it by this Convention. The Authority shall have such incidental powers, consistent with this Convention, as are implicit in and necessary for the exercise of those powers and functions with respect to activities in the Area.

3. The Authority is based on the principle of the sovereign equality of all its members.

4. All members of the Authority shall fulfil in good faith the obligations assumed by them in accordance with this Part in order to ensure to all of them the rights and benefits resulting from membership.

Article 158

Organs of the Authority

1. There are hereby established, as the principal organs of the Authority, an Assembly, a Council and a Secretariat.

2. There is hereby established the Enterprise, the organ through which the Authority shall carry out the functions referred to in article 170, paragraph 1.

3. Such subsidiary organs as may be found necessary may be established in accordance with this Part.

4. Each principal organ of the Authority and the Enterprise shall be responsible for exercising those powers and functions which are conferred upon it. In exercising such powers and functions each organ shall avoid taking any action which may derogate from or impede the exercise of specific powers and functions conferred upon another organ.

SUBSECTION B. THE ASSEMBLY

Article 159

Composition, procedure and voting

1. The Assembly shall consist of all the members of the Authority. Each member shall have one representative in the Assembly, who may be accompanied by alternates and advisers.

2. The Assembly shall meet in regular annual sessions and in such special sessions as may be decided by the Assembly, or convened by the Secretary–General at the request of the Council or of a majority of the members of the Authority.

3. Sessions shall take place at the seat of the Authority unless otherwise decided by the Assembly.

4. The Assembly shall adopt its rules of procedure. At the beginning of each regular session, it shall elect its President and such other officers as may be required. They shall hold office until a new President and other officers are elected at the next regular session.

5. A majority of the members of the Assembly shall constitute a quorum.

6. Each member of the Assembly shall have one vote.

* * *

Article 160

Powers and functions

1. The Assembly, as the sole organ of the Authority consisting of all the members, shall be considered the supreme organ of the Authority to which the other principal organs shall be accountable as specifically provided for in this Convention. The Assembly shall have the power to establish general policies in conformity with the relevant provisions of this Convention on any question or matter within the competence of the Authority.

* * *

SUBSECTION C. THE COUNCIL

Article 161

Composition, procedure and voting

1. The Council shall consist of 36 members of the Authority elected by the Assembly in the following order:

(a) four members from among those States Parties which, during the last five years for which statistics are available, have either consumed more than 2 per cent of total world consumption or have had net imports of more than 2 per cent of total world imports of the commodities produced from the categories of minerals to be derived from the Area, and in any case one State from the Eastern European (Socialist) region, as well as the largest consumer;

(b) four members from among the eight States Parties which have the largest investments in preparation for and in the conduct of activities in the Area, either directly or through their nationals, including at least one State from the Eastern European (Socialist) region;

(c) four members from among States Parties which on the basis of production in areas under their jurisdiction are major net exporters of the categories of minerals to be derived from the Area, including at least two developing States whose exports of such minerals have a substantial bearing upon their economies;

(d) six members from among developing States Parties, representing special interests. The special interests to be represented shall include those of States with large populations, States which are land-locked or geographically disadvantaged, States which are major importers of the categories of minerals to be derived from the Area, States which are potential producers of such minerals, and least developed States;

(e) eighteen members elected according to the principle of ensuring an equitable geographical distribution of seats in the Council as a whole, provided that each geographical region shall have at least one member elected under this subparagraph. For this purpose, the geographical regions shall be Africa, Asia, Eastern European (Socialist), Latin America and Western European and Others.

2. In electing the members of the Council in accordance with paragraph 1, the Assembly shall ensure that:

(a) land-locked and geographically disadvantaged States are represented to a degree which is reasonably proportionate to their representation in the Assembly;

(b) coastal States, especially developing States, which do not qualify under paragraph 1(a), (b), (c) or (d) are represented to a degree which is reasonably proportionate to their representation in the Assembly;

(c) each group of States Parties to be represented on the Council is represented by those members, if any, which are nominated by that group.

3. Elections shall take place at regular sessions of the Assembly. Each member of the Council shall be elected for four years. At the first election, however, the term of one half of the members of each group referred to in paragraph 1 shall be two years.

4. Members of the Council shall be eligible for re-election, but due regard should be paid to the desirability of rotation of membership.

5. The Council shall function at the seat of the Authority, and shall meet as often as the business of the Authority may require, but not less than three times a year.

6. A majority of the members of the Council shall constitute a quorum.

7. Each member of the Council shall have one vote.

* * *

Article 162

Powers and functions

1. The Council is the executive organ of the Authority. The Council shall have the power to establish, in conformity with this Convention and the general policies established by the Assembly, the specific policies to be pursued by the Authority on any question or matter within the competence of the Authority.

* * *

Article 163

Organs of the Council

1. There are hereby established the following organs of the Council:

(a) an Economic Planning Commission;

(b) a Legal and Technical Commission.

2. Each Commission shall be composed of 15 members, elected by the Council from among the candidates nominated by the States Parties. However, if necessary, the Council may decide to increase the size of either Commission having due regard to economy and efficiency.

3. Members of a Commission shall have appropriate qualifications in the area of competence of that Commission. States Parties shall nominate candidates of the highest standards of competence and integrity with qualifications in relevant fields so as to ensure the effective exercise of the functions of the Commissions.

* * *

Article 164

The Economic Planning Commission

1. Members of the Economic Planning Commission shall have appropriate qualifications such as those relevant to mining, management of mineral resource activities,

international trade or international economics. The Council shall endeavour to ensure that the membership of the Commission reflects all appropriate qualifications. The Commission shall include at least two members from developing States whose exports of the categories of minerals to be derived from the Area have a substantial bearing upon their economies.

* * *

Article 165

The Legal and Technical Commission

1. Members of the Legal and Technical Commission shall have appropriate qualifications such as those relevant to exploration for and exploitation and processing of mineral resources, oceanology, protection of the marine environment, or economic or legal matters relating to ocean mining and related fields of expertise. The Council shall endeavour to ensure that the membership of the Commission reflects all appropriate qualifications.

* * *

SUBSECTION D. THE SECRETARIAT

Article 166

The Secretariat

1. The Secretariat of the Authority shall comprise a Secretary–General and such staff as the Authority may require.

2. The Secretary–General shall be elected for four years by the Assembly from among the candidates proposed by the Council and may be re-elected.

3. The Secretary–General shall be the chief administrative officer of the Authority, and shall act in that capacity in all meetings of the Assembly, of the Council and of any subsidiary organ, and shall perform such other administrative functions as are entrusted to the Secretary–General by these organs.

4. The Secretary–General shall make an annual report to the Assembly on the work of the Authority.

Article 167

The staff of the Authority

* * *

Article 168

International character of the Secretariat

1. In the performance of their duties the Secretary–General and the staff shall not seek or receive instructions from any government or from any other source external to the Authority. They shall refrain from any action which might reflect on their position as international officials responsible only to the Authority. * * *

* * *

Article 169

Consultation and co-operation with international and non-governmental organizations

* * *

SUBSECTION E. THE ENTERPRISE

Article 170

The Enterprise

1. The Enterprise shall be the organ of the Authority which shall carry out activities in the Area directly, pursuant to article 153, paragraph 2(a), as well as the transporting, processing and marketing of minerals recovered from the Area.

2. The Enterprise shall, within the framework of the international legal personality of the Authority, have such legal capacity as is provided for in the Statute set forth in Annex IV. The Enterprise shall act in accordance with this Convention and the rules, regulations and procedures of the Authority, as well as the general policies established by the Assembly, and shall be subject to the directives and control of the Council.

* * *

SUBSECTION F. FINANCIAL ARRANGEMENTS OF THE AUTHORITY

Article 171

Funds of the Authority

The funds of the Authority shall include:

(a) assessed contributions made by members of the Authority in accordance with article 160, paragraph 2(e);

(b) funds received by the Authority pursuant to Annex III, article 13, in connection with activities in the Area;

(c) funds transferred from the Enterprise in accordance with Annex IV, article 10;

(d) funds borrowed pursuant to article 174;

(e) voluntary contributions made by members or other entities; and

(f) payments to a compensation fund, in accordance with article 151, paragraph 10, whose sources are to be recommended by the Economic Planning Commission.

Article 172

Annual budget of the Authority

* * *

Article 173

Expenses of the Authority

* * *

Article 174

Borrowing power of the Authority

* * *

Article 175

Annual audit

* * *

SUBSECTION G. LEGAL STATUS, PRIVILEGES AND IMMUNITIES

Article 176

Legal status

The Authority shall have international legal personality and such legal capacity as may be necessary for the exercise of its functions and the fulfilment of its purposes.

Article 177

Privileges and immunities

To enable the Authority to exercise its functions, it shall enjoy in the territory of each State Party the privileges and immunities set forth in this subsection. The privileges and immunities relating to the Enterprise shall be those set forth in Annex IV, article 13.

Article 178

Immunity from legal process

The Authority, its property and assets, shall enjoy immunity from legal process except to the extent that the Authority expressly waives this immunity in a particular case.

Article 179

Immunity from search and any form of seizure

* * *

Article 180

Exemption from restrictions, regulations, controls and moratoria

* * *

Article 181

Archives and official communications of the Authority

* * *

Article 182

Privileges and immunities of certain persons connected with the Authority

* * *

Article 183

Exemption from taxes and customs duties

* * *

SUBSECTION H. SUSPENSION OF THE EXERCISE OF RIGHTS AND PRIVILEGES OF MEMBERS

Article 184

Suspension of the exercise of voting rights

A State Party which is in arrears in the payment of its financial contributions to the Authority shall have no vote if the amount of its arrears equals or exceeds the amount of the contribution due from it for the preceding two full years. The Assembly may, nevertheless, permit such a member to vote if it is satisfied that the failure to pay is due to conditions beyond the control of the member.

Article 185

Suspension of exercise of rights and privileges of membership

1. A State Party which has grossly and persistently violated the provisions of this Part may be suspended from the exercise of the rights and privileges of membership by the Assembly upon the recommendation of the Council.

2. No action may be taken under paragraph 1 until the Sea–Bed Disputes Chamber has found that a State Party has grossly and persistently violated the provisions of this Part.

SECTION 5. SETTLEMENT OF DISPUTES AND ADVISORY OPINIONS

Article 186

Sea–Bed Disputes Chamber of the International Tribunal for the Law of the Sea

The establishment of the Sea–Bed Disputes Chamber and the manner in which it shall exercise its jurisdiction shall be governed by the provisions of this section, of Part XV and of Annex VI.

Article 187

Jurisdiction of the Sea–Bed Disputes Chamber

The Sea–Bed Disputes Chamber shall have jurisdiction under this Part and the Annexes relating thereto in disputes with respect to activities in the Area falling within the following categories:

(a) disputes between States Parties concerning the interpretation or application of this Part and the Annexes relating thereto;

(b) disputes between a State Party and the Authority concerning:

(i) acts or omissions of the Authority or of a State Party alleged to be in violation of this Part or the Annexes relating thereto or of rules, regulations and procedures of the Authority adopted in accordance therewith; or

(ii) acts of the Authority alleged to be in excess of jurisdiction or a misuse of power;

(c) disputes between parties to a contract, being States Parties, the Authority or the Enterprise, state enterprises and natural or juridical persons referred to in article 153, paragraph 2(b), concerning:

(i) the interpretation or application of a relevant contract or a plan of work; or

(ii) acts or omissions of a party to the contract relating to activities in the Area and directed to the other party or directly affecting its legitimate interests;

(d) disputes between the Authority and a prospective contractor who has been sponsored by a State as provided in article 153, paragraph 2(b), and has duly fulfilled the conditions referred to in Annex III, article 4, paragraph 6, and article 13, paragraph 2, concerning the refusal of a contract or a legal issue arising in the negotiation of the contract;

(e) disputes between the Authority and a State Party, a state enterprise or a natural or juridical person sponsored by a State Party as provided for in article 153, paragraph 2(b), where it is alleged that the Authority has incurred liability as provided in Annex III, article 22;

(f) any other disputes for which the jurisdiction of the Chamber is specifically provided in this Convention.

Article 188

Submission of disputes to a special chamber of the International Tribunal for the Law of the Sea or an ad hoc chamber of the Sea–Bed Disputes Chamber or to binding commercial arbitration

* * *

Article 189

Limitation on jurisdiction with regard to decisions of the Authority

* * *

Article 190

Participation and appearance of sponsoring States Parties in proceedings

* * *

Article 191

Advisory opinions

The Sea–Bed Disputes Chamber shall give advisory opinions at the request of the Assembly or the Council on legal questions arising within the scope of their activities. Such opinions shall be given as a matter of urgency.

PART XII

PROTECTION AND PRESERVATION OF THE MARINE ENVIRONMENT

SECTION 1. GENERAL PROVISIONS

Article 192

General obligation

States have the obligation to protect and preserve the marine environment.

Article 193

Sovereign right of States to exploit their natural resources

States have the sovereign right to exploit their natural resources pursuant to their environmental policies and in accordance with their duty to protect and preserve the marine environment.

Article 194

Measures to prevent, reduce and control pollution of the marine environment

1. States shall take, individually or jointly as appropriate, all measures consistent with this Convention that are necessary to prevent, reduce and control pollution of the marine environment from any source, using for this purpose the best practicable means at their disposal and in accordance with their capabilities, and they shall endeavour to harmonize their policies in this connection.

2. States shall take all measures necessary to ensure that activities under their jurisdiction or control are so conducted as not to cause damage by pollution to other States and their environment, and that pollution arising from incidents or activities under their jurisdiction or control does not spread beyond the areas where they exercise sovereign rights in accordance with this Convention.

3. The measures taken pursuant to this Part shall deal with all sources of pollution of the marine environment. These measures shall include, *inter alia,* those designed to minimize to the fullest possible extent:

(a) the release of toxic, harmful or noxious substances, especially those which are persistent, from land-based sources, from or through the atmosphere or by dumping;

(b) pollution from vessels, in particular measures for preventing accidents and dealing with emergencies, ensuring the safety of operations at sea, preventing intentional and unintentional discharges, and regulating the design, construction, equipment, operation and manning of vessels;

(c) pollution from installations and devices used in exploration or exploitation of the natural resources of the sea-bed and subsoil, in particular measures for preventing accidents and dealing with emergencies, ensuring the safety of operations at sea, and regulating the design, construction, equipment, operation and manning of such installations or devices;

(d) pollution from other installations and devices operating in the marine environment, in particular measures for preventing accidents and dealing with emergencies, ensuring the safety of operations at sea, and regulating the design, construction, equipment, operation and manning of such installations or devices.

4. In taking measures to prevent, reduce or control pollution of the marine environment, States shall refrain from unjustifiable interference with activities carried out by other States in the exercise of their rights and in pursuance of their duties in conformity with this Convention.

5. The measures taken in accordance with this Part shall include those necessary to protect and preserve rare or fragile ecosystems as well as the habitat of depleted, threatened or endangered species and other forms of marine life.

Article 195

Duty not to transfer damage or hazards or transform one type of pollution into another

* * *

Article 196

Use of technologies or introduction of alien or new species

1. States shall take all measures necessary to prevent, reduce and control pollution of the marine environment resulting from the use of technologies under their jurisdiction or control, or the intentional or accidental introduction of species, alien or new, to a particular part of the marine environment, which may cause significant and harmful changes thereto.

2. This article does not affect the application of this Convention regarding the prevention, reduction and control of pollution of the marine environment.

SECTION 2. GLOBAL AND REGIONAL CO-OPERATION

Article 197

Co-operation on a global or regional basis

States shall co-operate on a global basis and, as appropriate, on a regional basis, directly or through competent international organizations, in formulating and elaborating international rules, standards and recommended practices and procedures consistent with this Convention, for the protection and preservation of the marine environment, taking into account characteristic regional features.

Article 198

Notification of imminent or actual damage

When a State becomes aware of cases in which the marine environment is in imminent danger of being damaged or has been damaged by pollution, it shall immediately notify other States it deems likely to be affected by such damage, as well as the competent international organizations.

Article 199

Contingency plans against pollution

In the cases referred to in article 198, States in the area affected, in accordance with their capabilities, and the competent international organizations shall co-operate, to the extent possible, in eliminating the effects of pollution and preventing or minimizing the damage. To this end, States shall jointly develop and promote contingency plans for responding to pollution incidents in the marine environment.

Article 200

Studies, research programmes and exchange of information and data

States shall co-operate, directly or through competent international organizations, for the purpose of promoting studies, undertaking programmes of scientific research and encouraging the exchange of information and data acquired about pollution of the marine environment. They shall endeavour to participate actively in regional and global programmes to acquire knowledge for the assessment of the nature and extent of pollution, exposure to it, and its pathways, risks and remedies.

Article 201

Scientific criteria for regulations

In the light of the information and data acquired pursuant to article 200, States shall co-operate, directly or through competent international organizations, in establishing appropriate scientific criteria for the formulation and elaboration of rules, standards and recommended practices and procedures for the prevention, reduction and control of pollution of the marine environment.

SECTION 3. TECHNICAL ASSISTANCE

Article 202

Scientific and technical assistance to developing States

States shall, directly or through competent international organizations:

(a) promote programmes of scientific, educational, technical and other assistance to developing States for the protection and preservation of the marine environment and the prevention, reduction and control of marine pollution. Such assistance shall include, *inter alia:*

(i) training of their scientific and technical personnel;

(ii) facilitating their participation in relevant international programmes;

(iii) supplying them with necessary equipment and facilities;

(iv) enhancing their capacity to manufacture such equipment;

(v) advice on and developing facilities for research, monitoring, educational and other programmes;

(b) provide appropriate assistance, especially to developing States, for the minimization of the effects of major incidents which may cause serious pollution of the marine environment;

(c) provide appropriate assistance, especially to developing States, concerning the preparation of environmental assessments.

Article 203

Preferential treatment for developing States

Developing States shall, for the purposes of prevention, reduction and control of pollution of the marine environment or minimization of its effects, be granted preference by international organizations in:

(a) the allocation of appropriate funds and technical assistance; and

(b) the utilization of their specialized services.

SECTION 4. MONITORING AND ENVIRONMENTAL ASSESSMENT

Article 204

Monitoring of the risks or effects of pollution

1. States shall, consistent with the rights of other States, endeavour, as far as practicable, directly or through the competent international organizations, to observe, measure, evaluate and analyse, by recognized scientific methods, the risks or effects of pollution of the marine environment.

2. In particular, States shall keep under surveillance the effects of any activities which they permit or in which they engage in order to determine whether these activities are likely to pollute the marine environment.

Article 205

Publication of reports

States shall publish reports of the results obtained pursuant to article 204 or provide such reports at appropriate intervals to the competent international organizations, which should make them available to all States.

Article 206

Assessment of potential effects of activities

When States have reasonable grounds for believing that planned activities under their jurisdiction or control may cause substantial pollution of or significant and harmful changes to the marine environment, they shall, as far as practicable, assess the potential effects of such activities on the marine environment and shall communicate reports of the results of such assessments in the manner provided in article 205.

SECTION 5. INTERNATIONAL RULES AND NATIONAL LEGISLATION TO PREVENT, REDUCE AND CONTROL POLLUTION OF THE MARINE ENVIRONMENT

Article 207

Pollution from land-based sources

1. States shall adopt laws and regulations to prevent, reduce and control pollution of the marine environment from land-based sources, including rivers, estuaries, pipelines and outfall structures, taking into account internationally agreed rules, standards and recommended practices and procedures.

2. States shall take other measures as may be necessary to prevent, reduce and control such pollution.

3. States shall endeavour to harmonize their policies in this connection at the appropriate regional level.

4. States, acting especially through competent international organizations or diplomatic conference, shall endeavour to establish global and regional rules, standards and recommended practices and procedures to prevent, reduce and control pollution of the marine environment from land-based sources, taking into account characteristic regional features, the economic capacity of developing States and their need for economic development. Such rules, standards and recommended practices and procedures shall be re-examined from time to time as necessary.

5. Laws, regulations, measures, rules, standards and recommended practices and procedures referred to in paragraphs 1, 2 and 4 shall include those designed to minimize, to the fullest extent possible, the release of toxic, harmful or noxious substances, especially those which are persistent, into the marine environment.

Article 208

Pollution from sea-bed activities subject to national jurisdiction

[This article is in all essential respects identical to article 207, *supra.*]

Article 209

Pollution from activities in the Area

1. International rules, regulations and procedures shall be established in accordance with Part XI to prevent, reduce and control pollution of the marine environment from activities in the Area. Such rules, regulations and procedures shall be re-examined from time to time as necessary.

2. Subject to the relevant provisions of this section, States shall adopt laws and regulations to prevent, reduce and control pollution of the marine environment from activities in the Area undertaken by vessels, installations, structures and other devices flying their flag or of their registry or operating under their authority, as the case may be. The requirements of such laws and regulations shall be no less effective than the international rules, regulations and procedures referred to in paragraph 1.

Article 210

Pollution by dumping

1. States shall adopt laws and regulations to prevent, reduce and control pollution of the marine environment by dumping.

2. States shall take other measures as may be necessary to prevent, reduce and control such pollution.

3. Such laws, regulations and measures shall ensure that dumping is not carried out without the permission of the competent authorities of States.

4. States, acting especially through competent international organizations or diplomatic conference, shall endeavour to establish global and regional rules, standards and recommended practices and procedures to prevent, reduce and control such pollution. Such rules, standards and recommended practices and procedures shall be re-examined from time to time as necessary.

5. Dumping within the territorial sea and the exclusive economic zone or onto the continental shelf shall not be carried out without the express prior approval of the coastal State, which has the right to permit, regulate and control such dumping after due consideration of the matter with other States which by reason of their geographical situation may be adversely affected thereby.

6. National laws, regulations and measures shall be no less effective in preventing, reducing and controlling such pollution than the global rules and standards.

Article 211
Pollution from vessels

1. States, acting through the competent international organization or general diplomatic conference, shall establish international rules and standards to prevent, reduce and control pollution of the marine environment from vessels and promote the adoption, in the same manner, wherever appropriate, of routing systems designed to minimize the threat of accidents which might cause pollution of the marine environment, including the coastline, and pollution damage to the related interests of coastal States. Such rules and standards shall, in the same manner, be re-examined from time to time as necessary.

2. States shall adopt laws and regulations for the prevention, reduction and control of pollution of the marine environment from vessels flying their flag or of their registry. Such laws and regulations shall at least have the same effect as that of generally accepted international rules and standards established through the competent international organization or general diplomatic conference.

3. States which establish particular requirements for the prevention, reduction and control of pollution of the marine environment as a condition for the entry of foreign vessels into their ports or internal waters or for a call at their off-shore terminals shall give due publicity to such requirements and shall communicate them to the competent international organization. Whenever such requirements are established in identical form by two or more coastal States in an endeavour to harmonize policy, the communication shall indicate which States are participating in such co-operative arrangements. Every State shall require the master of a vessel flying its flag or of its registry, when navigating within the territorial sea of a State participating in such co-operative arrangements, to furnish, upon the request of that State, information as to whether it is proceeding to a State of the same region participating in such co-operative arrangements and, if so, to indicate whether it complies with the port entry requirements of that State. This article is without prejudice to the continued exercise by a vessel of its right of innocent passage or to the application of article 25, paragraph 2.

4. Coastal States may, in the exercise of their sovereignty within their territorial sea, adopt laws and regulations for the prevention, reduction and control of marine pollution from foreign vessels, including vessels exercising the right of innocent passage. Such laws and regulations shall, in accordance with Part II, section 3, not hamper innocent passage of foreign vessels.

5. Coastal States, for the purpose of enforcement as provided for in section 6, may in respect of their exclusive economic zones adopt laws and regulations for the prevention, reduction and control of pollution from vessels conforming to and giving effect to generally accepted international rules and standards established through the competent international organization or general diplomatic conference.

6. (a) Where the international rules and standards referred to in paragraph 1 are inadequate to meet special circumstances and coastal States have reasonable grounds for believing that a particular, clearly defined area of their respective exclusive economic zones is an area where the adoption of special mandatory measures for the prevention of pollution from vessels is required for recognized technical reasons in relation to its oceanographical and ecological conditions, as well as its utilization or the protection of its resources and the particular character of its traffic, the coastal States, after appropriate consultations through the competent international organization with any other States concerned, may, for that area, direct a communication to that organization, submitting scientific and technical evidence in support and information on necessary reception facilities. Within 12 months after receiving such a communication, the organization shall determine whether the conditions in that area correspond to the requirements set out above. If the organization so determines, the coastal States

may, for that area, adopt laws and regulations for the prevention, reduction and control of pollution from vessels implementing such international rules and standards or navigational practices as are made applicable, through the organization, for special areas. These laws and regulations shall not become applicable to foreign vessels until 15 months after the submission of the communication to the organization.

(b) The coastal States shall publish the limits of any such particular, clearly defined area.

(c) If the coastal States intend to adopt additional laws and regulations for the same area for the prevention, reduction and control of pollution from vessels, they shall, when submitting the aforesaid communication, at the same time notify the organization thereof. Such additional laws and regulations may relate to discharges or navigational practices but shall not require foreign vessels to observe design, construction, manning or equipment standards other than generally accepted international rules and standards; they shall become applicable to foreign vessels 15 months after the submission of the communication to the organization, provided that the organization agrees within 12 months after the submission of the communication.

7. The international rules and standards referred to in this article should include *inter alia* those relating to prompt notification to coastal States, whose coastline or related interests may be affected by incidents, including maritime casualties, which involve discharges or probability of discharges.

Article 212

Pollution from or through the atmosphere

1. States shall adopt laws and regulations to prevent, reduce and control pollution of the marine environment from or through the atmosphere, applicable to the air space under their sovereignty and to vessels flying their flag or vessels or aircraft of their registry, taking into account internationally agreed rules, standards and recommended practices and procedures and the safety of air navigation.

2. States shall take other measures as may be necessary to prevent, reduce and control such pollution.

3. States, acting especially through competent international organizations or diplomatic conference, shall endeavour to establish global and regional rules, standards and recommended practices and procedures to prevent, reduce and control such pollution.

SECTION 6. ENFORCEMENT

Article 213

Enforcement with respect to pollution from land-based sources

States shall enforce their laws and regulations adopted in accordance with article 207 and shall adopt laws and regulations and take other measures necessary to implement applicable international rules and standards established through competent international organizations or diplomatic conference to prevent, reduce and control pollution of the marine environment from land-based sources.

Article 214

Enforcement with respect to pollution from sea-bed activities

States shall enforce their laws and regulations adopted in accordance with article 208 and shall adopt laws and regulations and take other measures necessary to implement applicable international rules and standards established through competent international organizations or diplomatic conference to prevent, reduce and control pollution of the marine environment arising from or in connection with sea-bed activities subject to their jurisdiction and from artificial islands, installations and structures under their jurisdiction, pursuant to articles 60 and 80.

Article 215

Enforcement with respect to pollution from activities in the Area

Enforcement of international rules, regulations and procedures established in accordance with Part XI to prevent, reduce and control pollution of the marine environment from activities in the Area shall be governed by that Part.

Article 216

Enforcement with respect to pollution by dumping

1. Laws and regulations adopted in accordance with this Convention and applicable international rules and standards established through competent international organizations or diplomatic conference for the prevention, reduction and control of pollution of the marine environment by dumping shall be enforced:

(a) by the coastal State with regard to dumping within its territorial sea or its exclusive economic zone or onto its continental shelf;

(b) by the flag State with regard to vessels flying its flag or vessels or aircraft of its registry;

(c) by any State with regard to acts of loading of wastes or other matter occurring within its territory or at its off-shore terminals.

2. No State shall be obliged by virtue of this article to institute proceedings when another State has already instituted proceedings in accordance with this article.

Article 217

Enforcement by flag States

1. States shall ensure compliance by vessels flying their flag or of their registry with applicable international rules and standards, established through the competent international organization or general diplomatic conference, and with their laws and regulations adopted in accordance with this Convention for the prevention, reduction and control of pollution of the marine environment from vessels and shall accordingly adopt laws and regulations and take other measures necessary for their implementation. Flag States shall provide for the effective enforcement of such rules, standards, laws and regulations, irrespective of where a violation occurs.

2. States shall, in particular, take appropriate measures in order to ensure that vessels flying their flag or of their registry are prohibited from sailing, until they can proceed to sea in compliance with the requirements of the international rules and standards referred to in paragraph 1, including requirements in respect of design, construction, equipment and manning of vessels.

3. States shall ensure that vessels flying their flag or of their registry carry on board certificates required by and issued pursuant to international rules and standards referred to in paragraph 1. States shall ensure that vessels flying their flag are periodically inspected in order to verify that such certificates are in conformity with the actual condition of the vessels. These certificates shall be accepted by other States as evidence of the condition of the vessels and shall be regarded as having the same force as certificates issued by them, unless there are clear grounds for believing that the condition of the vessel does not correspond substantially with the particulars of the certificates.

4. If a vessel commits a violation of rules and standards established through the competent international organization or general diplomatic conference, the flag State,

without prejudice to articles 218, 220 and 228, shall provide for immediate investigation and where appropriate institute proceedings in respect of the alleged violation irrespective of where the violation occurred or where the pollution caused by such violation has occurred or has been spotted.

5. Flag States conducting an investigation of the violation may request the assistance of any other State whose co-operation could be useful in clarifying the circumstances of the case. States shall endeavour to meet appropriate requests of flag States.

6. States shall, at the written request of any State, investigate any violation alleged to have been committed by vessels flying their flag. If satisfied that sufficient evidence is available to enable proceedings to be brought in respect of the alleged violation, flag States shall without delay institute such proceedings in accordance with their laws.

7. Flag States shall promptly inform the requesting State and the competent international organization of the action taken and its outcome. Such information shall be available to all States.

8. Penalties provided for by the laws and regulations of States for vessels flying their flag shall be adequate in severity to discourage violations wherever they occur.

Article 218

Enforcement by port States

1. When a vessel is voluntarily within a port or at an off-shore terminal of a State, that State may undertake investigations and, where the evidence so warrants, institute proceedings in respect of any discharge from that vessel outside the internal waters, territorial sea or exclusive economic zone of that State in violation of applicable international rules and standards established through the competent international organization or general diplomatic conference.

2. No proceedings pursuant to paragraph 1 shall be instituted in respect of a discharge violation in the internal waters, territorial sea or exclusive economic zone of another State unless requested by that State, the flag State, or a State damaged or threatened by the discharge violation, or unless the violation has caused or is likely to cause pollution in the internal waters, territorial sea or exclusive economic zone of the State instituting the proceedings.

3. When a vessel is voluntarily within a port or at an off-shore terminal of a State, that State shall, as far as practicable, comply with requests from any State for investigation of a discharge violation referred to in paragraph 1, believed to have occurred in, caused, or threatened damage to the internal waters, territorial sea or exclusive economic zone of the requesting State. It shall likewise, as far as practicable, comply with requests from the flag State for investigation of such a violation, irrespective of where the violation occurred.

4. The records of the investigation carried out by a port State pursuant to this article shall be transmitted upon request to the flag State or to the coastal State. Any proceedings instituted by the port State on the basis of such an investigation may, subject to section 7, be suspended at the request of the coastal State when the violation has occurred within its internal waters, territorial sea or exclusive economic zone. The evidence and records of the case, together with any bond or other financial security posted with the authorities of the port State, shall in that event be transmitted to the coastal State. Such transmittal shall preclude the continuation of proceedings in the port State.

Article 219

Measures relating to seaworthiness of vessels to avoid pollution

Subject to section 7, States which, upon request or on their own initiative, have ascertained that a vessel within one of their ports or at one of their off-shore terminals is in violation of applicable international rules and standards relating to seaworthiness of vessels and thereby threatens damage to the marine environment shall, as far as practicable, take administrative measures to prevent the vessel from sailing. Such States may permit the vessel to proceed only to the nearest appropriate repair yard and, upon removal of the causes of the violation, shall permit the vessel to continue immediately.

Article 220

Enforcement by coastal States

1. When a vessel is voluntarily within a port or at an off-shore terminal of a State, that State may, subject to section 7, institute proceedings in respect of any violation of its laws and regulations adopted in accordance with this Convention or applicable international rules and standards for the prevention, reduction and control of pollution from vessels when the violation has occurred within the territorial sea or the exclusive economic zone of that State.

2. Where there are clear grounds for believing that a vessel navigating in the territorial sea of a State has, during its passage therein, violated laws and regulations of that State adopted in accordance with this Convention or applicable international rules and standards for the prevention, reduction and control of pollution from vessels, that State, without prejudice to the application of the relevant provisions of Part II, section 3, may undertake physical inspection of the vessel relating to the violation and may, where the evidence so warrants, institute proceedings, including detention of the vessel, in accordance with its laws, subject to the provisions of section 7.

3. Where there are clear grounds for believing that a vessel navigating in the exclusive economic zone or the territorial sea of a State has, in the exclusive economic zone, committed a violation of applicable international rules and standards for the prevention, reduction and control of pollution from vessels or laws and regulations of that State conforming and giving effect to such rules and standards, that State may require the vessel to give information regarding its identity and port of registry, its last and its next port of call and other relevant information required to establish whether a violation has occurred.

4. States shall adopt laws and regulations and take other measures so that vessels flying their flag comply with requests for information pursuant to paragraph 3.

5. Where there are clear grounds for believing that a vessel navigating in the exclusive economic zone or the territorial sea of a State has, in the exclusive economic zone, committed a violation referred to in paragraph 3 resulting in a substantial discharge causing or threatening significant pollution of the marine environment, that State may undertake physical inspection of the vessel for matters relating to the violation if the vessel has refused to give information or if the information supplied by the vessel is manifestly at variance with the evident factual situation and if the circumstances of the case justify such inspection.

6. Where there is clear objective evidence that a vessel navigating in the exclusive economic zone or the territorial sea of a State has, in the exclusive economic zone, committed a violation referred to in paragraph 3 resulting in a discharge causing major damage or threat of major damage to the coastline or related interests of the coastal State, or to any resources of its territorial sea or exclusive economic zone, that State may, subject to section 7, provided that the evidence so warrants, institute proceedings, including detention of the vessel, in accordance with its laws.

7. Notwithstanding the provisions of paragraph 6, whenever appropriate procedures have been established, either through the competent international organization or as otherwise agreed, whereby compliance with requirements for bonding or other appropriate financial security has been assured, the coastal State if bound by such procedures shall allow the vessel to proceed.

8. The provisions of paragraphs 3, 4, 5, 6 and 7 also apply in respect of national laws and regulations adopted pursuant to article 211, paragraph 6.

Article 221

Measures to avoid pollution arising from maritime casualties

1. Nothing in this Part shall prejudice the right of States, pursuant to international law, both customary and conventional, to take and enforce measures beyond the territorial sea proportionate to the actual or threatened damage to protect their coastline or related interests, including fishing, from pollution or threat of pollution following upon a maritime casualty or acts relating to such a casualty, which may reasonably be expected to result in major harmful consequences.

2. For the purposes of this article, "maritime casualty" means a collision of vessels, stranding or other incident of navigation, or other occurrence on board a vessel or external to it resulting in material damage or imminent threat of material damage to a vessel or cargo.

Article 222

Enforcement with respect to pollution from or through the atmosphere

States shall enforce, within the air space under their sovereignty or with regard to vessels flying their flag or vessels or aircraft of their registry, their laws and regulations adopted in accordance with article 212, paragraph 1, and with other provisions of this Convention and shall adopt laws and regulations and take other measures necessary to implement applicable international rules and standards established through competent international organizations or diplomatic conference to prevent, reduce and control pollution of the marine environment from or through the atmosphere, in conformity with all relevant international rules and standards concerning the safety of air navigation.

SECTION 7. SAFEGUARDS

Article 223

Measures to facilitate proceedings

In proceedings instituted pursuant to this Part, States shall take measures to facilitate the hearing of witnesses and the admission of evidence submitted by authorities of another State, or by the competent international organization, and shall facilitate the attendance at such proceedings of official representatives of the competent international organization, the flag State and any State affected by pollution arising out of any violation. The official representatives attending such proceedings shall have such rights and duties as may be provided under national laws and regulations or international law.

Article 224

Exercise of powers of enforcement

The powers of enforcement against foreign vessels under this Part may only be exercised by officials or by warships, military aircraft, or other ships or aircraft clearly marked and identifiable as being on government service and authorized to that effect.

Article 225

Duty to avoid adverse consequences in the exercise of the powers of enforcement

In the exercise under this Convention of their powers of enforcement against foreign vessels, States shall not endanger the safety of navigation or otherwise create any hazard to a vessel, or bring it to an unsafe port or anchorage, or expose the marine environment to an unreasonable risk.

Article 226

Investigation of foreign vessels

1. (a) States shall not delay a foreign vessel longer than is essential for purposes of the investigations provided for in articles 216, 218 and 220. Any physical inspection of a foreign vessel shall be limited to an examination of such certificates, records or other documents as the vessel is required to carry by generally accepted international rules and standards or of any similar documents which it is carrying; further physical inspection of the vessel may be undertaken only after such an examination and only when:

(i) there are clear grounds for believing that the condition of the vessel or its equipment does not correspond substantially with the particulars of those documents;

(ii) the contents of such documents are not sufficient to confirm or verify a suspected violation; or

(iii) the vessel is not carrying valid certificates and records.

(b) If the investigation indicates a violation of applicable laws and regulations or international rules and standards for the protection and preservation of the marine environment, release shall be made promptly subject to reasonable procedures such as bonding or other appropriate financial security.

(c) Without prejudice to applicable international rules and standards relating to the seaworthiness of vessels, the release of a vessel may, whenever it would present an unreasonable threat of damage to the marine environment, be refused or made conditional upon proceeding to the nearest appropriate repair yard. Where release has been refused or made conditional, the flag State of the vessel must be promptly notified, and may seek release of the vessel in accordance with Part XV.

2. States shall co-operate to develop procedures for the avoidance of unnecessary physical inspection of vessels at sea.

Article 227

Non-discrimination with respect to foreign vessels

* * *

Article 228

Suspension and restrictions on institution of proceedings

* * *

Article 229

Institution of civil proceedings

* * *

Article 230

Monetary penalties and the observance of recognized rights of the accused

* * *

Article 231

Notification to the flag State and other States concerned

* * *

Article 232

Liability of States arising from enforcement measures

States shall be liable for damage or loss attributable to them arising from measures taken pursuant to section 6 when such measures are unlawful or exceed those reasonably required in the light of available information. States shall provide for recourse in their courts for actions in respect of such damage or loss.

Article 233

Safeguards with respect to straits used for international navigation

* * *

SECTION 8. ICE-COVERED AREAS

Article 234

Ice-covered areas

Coastal States have the right to adopt and enforce non-discriminatory laws and regulations for the prevention, reduction and control of marine pollution from vessels in ice-covered areas within the limits of the exclusive economic zone, where particularly severe climatic conditions and the presence of ice covering such areas for most of the year create obstructions or exceptional hazards to navigation, and pollution of the marine environment could cause major harm to or irreversible disturbance of the ecological balance. Such laws and regulations shall have due regard to navigation and the protection and preservation of the marine environment based on the best available scientific evidence.

SECTION 9. RESPONSIBILITY AND LIABILITY

Article 235

Responsibility and liability

1. States are responsible for the fulfilment of their international obligations concerning the protection and preservation of the marine environment. They shall be liable in accordance with international law.

2. States shall ensure that recourse is available in accordance with their legal systems for prompt and adequate compensation or other relief in respect of damage caused by pollution of the marine environment by natural or juridical persons under their jurisdiction.

3. With the objective of assuring prompt and adequate compensation in respect of all damage caused by pollution of the marine environment, States shall co-operate in the implementation of existing international law and the further development of international law relating to responsibility and liability for the assessment of and compensation for damage and the settlement of related disputes, as well as, where appropriate, development of criteria and procedures for payment of adequate compensation, such as compulsory insurance or compensation funds.

SECTION 10. SOVEREIGN IMMUNITY

Article 236

Sovereign immunity

The provisions of this Convention regarding the protection and preservation of the marine environment do not apply to any warship, naval auxiliary, other vessels or aircraft owned or operated by a State and used, for the time being, only on government non-commercial service. However, each State shall ensure, by the adoption of appropriate measures not impairing operations or operational capabilities of such vessels or aircraft owned or operated by it, that such vessels or aircraft act in a manner consistent, so far as is reasonable and practicable, with this Convention.

SECTION 11. OBLIGATIONS UNDER OTHER CONVENTIONS ON THE PROTECTION AND PRESERVATION OF THE MARINE ENVIRONMENT

Article 237

Obligations under other conventions on the protection and preservation of the marine environment

1. The provisions of this Part are without prejudice to the specific obligations assumed by States under special conventions and agreements concluded previously which relate to the protection and preservation of the marine environment and to agreements which may be concluded in furtherance of the general principles set forth in this Convention.

2. Specific obligations assumed by States under special conventions, with respect to the protection and preservation of the marine environment, should be carried out in a manner consistent with the general principles and objectives of this Convention.

PART XIII

MARINE SCIENTIFIC RESEARCH

SECTION 1. GENERAL PROVISIONS

Article 238

Right to conduct marine scientific research

All States, irrespective of their geographical location, and competent international organizations have the right to conduct marine scientific research subject to the rights and duties of other States as provided for in this Convention.

Article 239

Right to conduct marine scientific research

States and competent international organizations shall promote and facilitate the development and conduct of marine scientific research in accordance with this Convention.

Article 240

General principles for the conduct of marine scientific research

In the conduct of marine scientific research the following principles shall apply:

(a) marine scientific research shall be conducted exclusively for peaceful purposes;

(b) marine scientific research shall be conducted with appropriate scientific methods and means compatible with this Convention;

(c) marine scientific research shall not unjustifiably interfere with other legitimate uses of the sea compatible with this Convention and shall be duly respected in the course of such uses;

(d) marine scientific research shall be conducted in compliance with all relevant regulations adopted in conformity with this Convention including those for the protection and preservation of the marine environment.

Article 241

Non-recognition of marine scientific research activities as the legal basis for claims

Marine scientific research activities shall not constitute the legal basis for any claim to any part of the marine environment or its resources.

SECTION 2. INTERNATIONAL CO–OPERATION

Article 242

Promotion of international co-operation

1. States and competent international organizations shall, in accordance with the principle of respect for sovereignty and jurisdiction and on the basis of mutual benefit, promote international co-operation in marine scientific research for peaceful purposes.

2. In this context, without prejudice to the rights and duties of States under this Convention, a State, in the application of this Part, shall provide, as appropriate, other States with a reasonable opportunity to obtain from it, or with its co-operation, information necessary to prevent and control damage to the health and safety of persons and to the marine environment.

Article 243

Creation of favourable conditions

States and competent international organizations shall co-operate, through the conclusion of bilateral and multilateral agreements, to create favourable conditions for the conduct of marine scientific research in the marine environment and to integrate the efforts of scientists in studying the essence of phenomena and processes occurring in the marine environment and the interrelations between them.

Article 244

Publication and dissemination of information and knowledge

* * *

SECTION 3. CONDUCT AND PROMOTION OF MARINE SCIENTIFIC RESEARCH

Article 245

Marine scientific research in the territorial sea

Coastal States, in the exercise of their sovereignty, have the exclusive right to regulate, authorize and conduct marine scientific research in their territorial sea. Marine scientific research therein shall be conducted only with the express consent of and under the conditions set forth by the coastal State.

Article 246

Marine scientific research in the exclusive economic zone and on the continental shelf

1. Coastal States, in the exercise of their jurisdiction, have the right to regulate, authorize and conduct marine scientific research in their exclusive economic zone and

on their continental shelf in accordance with the relevant provisions of this Convention.

2. Marine scientific research in the exclusive economic zone and on the continental shelf shall be conducted with the consent of the coastal State.

3. Coastal States shall, in normal circumstances, grant their consent for marine scientific research projects by other States or competent international organizations in their exclusive economic zone or on their continental shelf to be carried out in accordance with this Convention exclusively for peaceful purposes and in order to increase scientific knowledge of the marine environment for the benefit of all mankind. To this end, coastal States shall establish rules and procedures ensuring that such consent will not be delayed or denied unreasonably.

4. For the purposes of applying paragraph 3, normal circumstances may exist in spite of the absence of diplomatic relations between the coastal State and the researching State.

5. Coastal States may however in their discretion withhold their consent to the conduct of a marine scientific research project of another State or competent international organization in the exclusive economic zone or on the continental shelf of the coastal State if that project:

(a) is of direct significance for the exploration and exploitation of natural resources, whether living or non-living;

(b) involves drilling into the continental shelf, the use of explosives or the introduction of harmful substances into the marine environment;

(c) involves the construction, operation or use of artificial islands, installations and structures referred to in articles 60 and 80;

(d) contains information communicated pursuant to article 248 regarding the nature and objectives of the project which is inaccurate or if the researching State or competent international organization has outstanding obligations to the coastal State from a prior research project.

6. Notwithstanding the provisions of paragraph 5, coastal States may not exercise their discretion to withhold consent under subparagraph (a) of that paragraph in respect of marine scientific research projects to be undertaken in accordance with the provisions of this Part on the continental shelf, beyond 200 nautical miles from the baselines from which the breadth of the territorial sea is measured, outside those specific areas which coastal States may at any time publicly designate as areas in which exploitation or detailed exploratory operations focused on those areas are occurring or will occur within a reasonable period of time. Coastal States shall give reasonable notice of the designation of such areas, as well as any modifications thereto, but shall not be obliged to give details of the operations therein.

7. The provisions of paragraph 6 are without prejudice to the rights of coastal States over the continental shelf as established in article 77.

8. Marine scientific research activities referred to in this article shall not unjustifiably interfere with activities undertaken by coastal States in the exercise of their sovereign rights and jurisdiction provided for in this Convention.

Article 247

Marine scientific research projects undertaken by or under the auspices of international organizations

* * *

Article 248

Duty to provide information to the coastal State

States and competent international organizations which intend to undertake marine scientific research in the exclusive economic zone or on the continental shelf of a coastal State shall, not less than six months in advance of the expected starting date of the marine scientific research project, provide that State with a full description of:

(a) the nature and objectives of the project;

(b) the method and means to be used, including name, tonnage, type and class of vessels and a description of scientific equipment;

(c) the precise geographical areas in which the project is to be conducted;

(d) the expected date of first appearance and final departure of the research vessels, or deployment of the equipment and its removal, as appropriate;

(e) the name of the sponsoring institution, its director, and the person in charge of the project; and

(f) the extent to which it is considered that the coastal State should be able to participate or to be represented in the project.

Article 249

Duty to comply with certain conditions

1. States and competent international organizations when undertaking marine scientific research in the exclusive economic zone or on the continental shelf of a coastal State shall comply with the following conditions:

(a) ensure the right of the coastal State, if it so desires, to participate or be represented in the marine scientific research project, especially on board research vessels and other craft or scientific research installations, when practicable, without payment of any remuneration to the scientists of the coastal State and without obligation to contribute towards the costs of the project;

(b) provide the coastal State, at its request, with preliminary reports, as soon as practicable, and with the final results and conclusions after the completion of the research;

(c) undertake to provide access for the coastal State, at its request, to all data and samples derived from the marine scientific research project and likewise to furnish it with data which may be copied and samples which may be divided without detriment to their scientific value;

(d) if requested, provide the coastal State with an assessment of such data, samples and research results or provide assistance in their assessment or interpretation;

(e) ensure, subject to paragraph 2, that the research results are made internationally available through appropriate national or international channels, as soon as practicable;

(f) inform the coastal State immediately of any major change in the research programme;

(g) unless otherwise agreed, remove the scientific research installations or equipment once the research is completed.

2. This article is without prejudice to the conditions established by the laws and regulations of the coastal State for the exercise of its discretion to grant or withhold consent pursuant to article 246, paragraph 5, including requiring prior agreement for making internationally available the research results of a project of direct significance for the exploration and exploitation of natural resources.

Article 250

Communications concerning marine scientific research projects

Communications concerning the marine scientific research projects shall be made through appropriate official channels, unless otherwise agreed.

Article 251

General criteria and guidelines

States shall seek to promote through competent international organizations the establishment of general criteria and guidelines to assist States in ascertaining the nature and implications of marine scientific research.

Article 252

Implied consent

States or competent international organizations may proceed with a marine scientific research project six months after the date upon which the information required pursuant to article 248 was provided to the coastal State unless within four months of the receipt of the communication containing such information the coastal State has informed the State or organization conducting the research that:

(a) it has withheld its consent under the provisions of article 246; or

(b) the information given by that State or competent international organization regarding the nature or objectives of the project does not conform to the manifestly evident facts; or

(c) it requires supplementary information relevant to conditions and the information provided for under articles 248 and 249; or

(d) outstanding obligations exist with respect to a previous marine scientific research project carried out by that State or organization, with regard to conditions established in article 249.

Article 253

Suspension or cessation of marine scientific research activities

1. A coastal State shall have the right to require the suspension of any marine scientific research activities in progress within its exclusive economic zone or on its continental shelf if:

(a) the research activities are not being conducted in accordance with the information communicated as provided under article 248 upon which the consent of the coastal State was based; or

(b) the State or competent international organization conducting the research activities fails to comply with the provisions of article 249 concerning the rights of the coastal State with respect to the marine scientific research project.

* * *

Article 254

Rights of neighbouring land-locked and geographically disadvantaged States

1. States and competent international organizations which have submitted to a coastal State a project to undertake marine scientific research referred to in article 246, paragraph 3, shall give notice to the neighbouring land-locked and geographically disadvantaged States of the proposed research project, and shall notify the coastal State thereof.

2. After the consent has been given for the proposed marine scientific research project by the coastal State concerned, in accordance with article 246 and other relevant provisions of this Convention, States and competent international organizations undertaking such a project shall provide to the neighbouring land-locked and geographically disadvantaged States, at their request and when appropriate, relevant information as specified in article 248 and article 249, paragraph 1(f).

3. The neighbouring land-locked and geographically disadvantaged States referred to above shall, at their request, be given the opportunity to participate, whenever feasible, in the proposed marine scientific research project through qualified experts appointed by them and not objected to by the coastal State, in accordance with the conditions agreed for the project, in conformity with the provisions of this Convention, between the coastal State concerned and the State or competent international organizations conducting the marine scientific research.

* * *

Article 255

Measures to facilitate marine scientific research and assist research vessels

States shall endeavour to adopt reasonable rules, regulations and procedures to promote and facilitate marine scientific research conducted in accordance with this Convention beyond their territorial sea and, as appropriate, to facilitate, subject to the provisions of their laws and regulations, access to their harbours and promote assistance for marine scientific research vessels which comply with the relevant provisions of this Part.

Article 256

Marine scientific research in the Area

All States, irrespective of their geographical location, and competent international organizations have the right, in conformity with the provisions of Part XI, to conduct marine scientific research in the Area.

Article 257

Marine scientific research in the water column beyond the exclusive economic zone

All States, irrespective of their geographical location, and competent international organizations have the right, in conformity with this Convention, to conduct marine scientific research in the water column beyond the limits of the exclusive economic zone.

SECTION 4. SCIENTIFIC RESEARCH INSTALLATIONS OR EQUIPMENT IN THE MARINE ENVIRONMENT

Article 258

Deployment and use

The deployment and use of any type of scientific research installations or equipment in any area of the marine environment shall be subject to the same conditions as are prescribed in this Convention for the conduct of marine scientific research in any such area.

Article 259

Legal status

The installations or equipment referred to in this section do not possess the status of islands. They have no territorial sea of their own, and their presence does not affect the delimitation of the territorial sea, the exclusive economic zone or the continental shelf.

Article 260

Safety zones

Safety zones of a reasonable breadth not exceeding a distance of 500 metres may be created around scientific research installations in accordance with the relevant provisions of this Convention. All States shall ensure that such safety zones are respected by their vessels.

Article 261

Non-interference with shipping routes

The deployment and use of any type of scientific research installations or equipment shall not constitute an obstacle to established international shipping routes.

Article 262

Identification markings and warning signals

Installations or equipment referred to in this section shall bear identification markings indicating the State of registry or the international organization to which they belong and shall have adequate internationally agreed warning signals to ensure safety at sea and the safety of air navigation, taking into account rules and standards established by competent international organizations.

SECTION 5. RESPONSIBILITY AND LIABILITY

Article 263

Responsibility and liability

1. States and competent international organizations shall be responsible for ensuring that marine scientific research, whether undertaken by them or on their behalf, is conducted in accordance with this Convention.

2. States and competent international organizations shall be responsible and liable for the measures they take in contravention of this Convention in respect of marine scientific research conducted by other States, their natural or juridical persons or by competent international organizations, and shall provide compensation for damage resulting from such measures.

3. States and competent international organizations shall be responsible and liable pursuant to article 235 for damage caused by pollution of the marine environment arising out of marine scientific research undertaken by them or on their behalf.

SECTION 6. SETTLEMENT OF DISPUTES AND INTERIM MEASURES

Article 264

Settlement of disputes

Disputes concerning the interpretation or application of the provisions of this Convention with regard to marine scientific research shall be settled in accordance with Part XV, sections 2 and 3.

Article 265

Interim measures

Pending settlement of a dispute in accordance with Part XV, sections 2 and 3, the State or competent international organization authorized to conduct a marine scientific research project shall not allow research activities to commence or continue without the express consent of the coastal State concerned.

PART XIV

DEVELOPMENT AND TRANSFER OF MARINE TECHNOLOGY

SECTION 1. GENERAL PROVISIONS

Article 266

Promotion of the development and transfer of marine technology

1. States, directly or through competent international organizations, shall cooperate in accordance with their capabilities to promote actively the development and transfer of marine science and marine technology on fair and reasonable terms and conditions.

2. States shall promote the development of the marine scientific and technological capacity of States which may need and request technical assistance in this field, particularly developing States, including land-locked and geographically disadvantaged States, with regard to the exploration, exploitation, conservation and management of marine resources, the protection and preservation of the marine environment, marine scientific research and other activities in the marine environment compatible with this Convention, with a view to accelerating the social and economic development of the developing States.

3. States shall endeavour to foster favourable economic and legal conditions for the transfer of marine technology for the benefit of all parties concerned on an equitable basis.

Article 267

Protection of legitimate interests

States, in promoting co-operation pursuant to article 266, shall have due regard for all legitimate interests including, *inter alia,* the rights and duties of holders, suppliers and recipients of marine technology.

Article 268

Basic objectives

States, directly or through competent international organizations, shall promote:

(a) the acquisition, evaluation and dissemination of marine technological knowledge and facilitate access to such information and data;

(b) the development of appropriate marine technology;

(c) the development of the necessary technological infrastructure to facilitate the transfer of marine technology;

(d) the development of human resources through training and education of nationals of developing States and countries and especially the nationals of the least developed among them;

(e) international co-operation at all levels, particularly at the regional, subregional and bilateral levels.

Article 269

Measures to achieve the basic objectives

In order to achieve the objectives referred to in article 268, States, directly or through competent international organizations, shall endeavour, *inter alia,* to:

(a) establish programmes of technical co-operation for the effective transfer of all kinds of marine technology to States which may need and request technical assistance in this field, particularly the developing land-locked and geographically disadvantaged States, as well as other developing States which have not been able either to establish or develop their own technological capacity in marine science and in the exploration and exploitation of marine resources or to develop the infrastructure of such technology;

(b) promote favourable conditions for the conclusion of agreements, contracts and other similar arrangements, under equitable and reasonable conditions;

(c) hold conferences, seminars and symposia on scientific and technological subjects, in particular on policies and methods for the transfer of marine technology;

(d) promote the exchange of scientists and of technological and other experts;

(e) undertake projects and promote joint ventures and other forms of bilateral and multilateral co-operation.

SECTION 2. INTERNATIONAL CO–OPERATION

Article 270

Ways and means of international co-operation

International co-operation for the development and transfer of marine technology shall be carried out, where feasible and appropriate, through existing bilateral, regional or multilateral programmes, and also through expanded and new programmes in order to facilitate marine scientific research, the transfer of marine technology, particularly in new fields, and appropriate international funding for ocean research and development.

Article 271

Guidelines, criteria and standards

States, directly or through competent international organizations, shall promote the establishment of generally accepted guidelines, criteria and standards for the transfer of marine technology on a bilateral basis or within the framework of international organizations and other fora, taking into account, in particular, the interests and needs of developing States.

Article 272

Co-ordination of international programmes

In the field of transfer of marine technology, States shall endeavour to ensure that competent international organizations co-ordinate their activities, including any regional or global programmes, taking into account the interests and needs of developing States, particularly land-locked and geographically disadvantaged States.

Article 273

Co-operation with international organizations and the Authority

States shall co-operate actively with competent international organizations and the Authority to encourage and facilitate the transfer to developing States, their nationals and the Enterprise of skills and marine technology with regard to activities in the Area.

Article 274

Objectives of the Authority

Subject to all legitimate interests including, *inter alia,* the rights and duties of holders, suppliers and recipients of technology, the Authority, with regard to activities in the Area, shall ensure that:

(a) on the basis of the principle of equitable geographical distribution, nationals of developing States, whether coastal, land-locked or geographically disadvantaged, shall be taken on for the purposes of training as members of the managerial, research and technical staff constituted for its undertakings;

(b) the technical documentation on the relevant equipment, machinery, devices and processes is made available to all States, in particular developing States which may need and request technical assistance in this field;

(c) adequate provision is made by the Authority to facilitate the acquisition of technical assistance in the field of marine technology by States which may need and request it, in particular developing States, and the acquisition by their nationals of the necessary skills and know-how, including professional training;

(d) States which may need and request technical assistance in this field, in particular developing States, are assisted in the acquisition of necessary equipment, processes, plant and other technical know-how through any financial arrangements provided for in this Convention.

SECTION 3. NATIONAL AND REGIONAL MARINE SCIENTIFIC AND TECHNOLOGICAL CENTRES

Article 275

Establishment of national centres

1. States, directly or through competent international organizations and the Authority, shall promote the establishment, particularly in developing coastal States, of national marine scientific and technological research centres and the strengthening of existing national centres, in order to stimulate and advance the conduct of marine scientific research by developing coastal States and to enhance their national capabilities to utilize and preserve their marine resources for their economic benefit.

* * *

Article 276

Establishment of regional centres

* * *

Article 277

Functions of regional centres

* * *

SECTION 4. CO-OPERATION AMONG INTERNATIONAL ORGANIZATIONS

Article 278

Co-operation among international organizations

The competent international organizations referred to in this Part and in Part XIII shall take all appropriate measures to ensure, either directly or in close co-operation among themselves, the effective discharge of their functions and responsibilities under this Part.

PART XV

SETTLEMENT OF DISPUTES

SECTION 1. GENERAL PROVISIONS

Article 279

Obligation to settle disputes by peaceful means

States Parties shall settle any dispute between them concerning the interpretation or application of this Convention by peaceful means in accordance with Article 2, paragraph 3, of the Charter of the United Nations and, to this end, shall seek a solution by the means indicated in Article 33, paragraph 1, of the Charter.

Article 280

Settlement of disputes by any peaceful means chosen by the parties

Nothing in this Part impairs the right of any States Parties to agree at any time to settle a dispute between them concerning the interpretation or application of this Convention by any peaceful means of their own choice.

Article 281

Procedure where no settlement has been reached by the parties

1. If the States Parties which are parties to a dispute concerning the interpretation or application of this Convention have agreed to seek settlement of the dispute by a peaceful means of their own choice, the procedures provided for in this Part apply only where no settlement has been reached by recourse to such means and the agreement between the parties does not exclude any further procedure.

2. If the parties have also agreed on a time-limit, paragraph 1 applies only upon the expiration of that time-limit.

Article 282

Obligations under general, regional or bilateral agreements

If the States Parties which are parties to a dispute concerning the interpretation or application of this Convention have agreed, through a general, regional or bilateral agreement or otherwise, that such dispute shall, at the request of any party to the dispute, be submitted to a procedure that entails a binding decision, that procedure shall apply in lieu of the procedures provided for in this Part, unless the parties to the dispute otherwise agree.

Article 283

Obligation to exchange views

1. When a dispute arises between States Parties concerning the interpretation or application of this Convention, the parties to the dispute shall proceed expeditiously to an exchange of views regarding its settlement by negotiation or other peaceful means.

2. The parties shall also proceed expeditiously to an exchange of views where a procedure for the settlement of such a dispute has been terminated without a settlement or where a settlement has been reached and the circumstances require consultation regarding the manner of implementing the settlement.

Article 284

Conciliation

1. A State Party which is a party to a dispute concerning the interpretation or application of this Convention may invite the other party or parties to submit the dispute to conciliation in accordance with the procedure under Annex V, section 1, or another conciliation procedure.

2. If the invitation is accepted and if the parties agree upon the conciliation procedure to be applied, any party may submit the dispute to that procedure.

3. If the invitation is not accepted or the parties do not agree upon the procedure, the conciliation proceedings shall be deemed to be terminated.

4. Unless the parties otherwise agree, when a dispute has been submitted to conciliation, the proceedings may be terminated only in accordance with the agreed conciliation procedure.

Article 285

Application of this section to disputes submitted pursuant to Part XI

This section applies to any dispute which pursuant to Part XI, section 5, is to be settled in accordance with procedures provided for in this Part. If an entity other than a State Party is a party to such a dispute, this section applies *mutatis mutandis.*

SECTION 2. COMPULSORY PROCEDURES ENTAILING BINDING DECISIONS

Article 286

Application of procedures under this section

Subject to section 3, any dispute concerning the interpretation or application of this Convention shall, where no settlement has been reached by recourse to section 1, be submitted at the request of any party to the dispute to the court or tribunal having jurisdiction under this section.

Article 287

Choice of procedure

1. When signing, ratifying or acceding to this Convention or at any time thereafter, a State shall be free to choose, by means of a written declaration, one or more of the following means for the settlement of disputes concerning the interpretation or application of this Convention:

(a) the International Tribunal for the Law of the Sea established [in Hamburg, West Germany] in accordance with Annex VI;

(b) the International Court of Justice;

(c) an arbitral tribunal constituted in accordance with Annex VII;

(d) a special arbitral tribunal constituted in accordance with Annex VIII for one or more of the categories of disputes specified therein.

2. A declaration made under paragraph 1 shall not affect or be affected by the obligation of a State Party to accept the jurisdiction of the Sea–Bed Disputes Chamber of the International Tribunal for the Law of the Sea to the extent and in the manner provided for in Part XI, section 5.

3. A State Party, which is a party to a dispute not covered by a declaration in force, shall be deemed to have accepted arbitration in accordance with Annex VII.

4. If the parties to a dispute have accepted the same procedure for the settlement of the dispute, it may be submitted only to that procedure, unless the parties otherwise agree.

5. If the parties to a dispute have not accepted the same procedure for the settlement of the dispute, it may be submitted only to arbitration in accordance with Annex VII, unless the parties otherwise agree.

6. A declaration made under paragraph 1 shall remain in force until three months after notice of revocation has been deposited with the Secretary–General of the United Nations.

7. A new declaration, a notice of revocation or the expiry of a declaration does not in any way affect proceedings pending before a court or tribunal having jurisdiction under this article, unless the parties otherwise agree.

8. Declarations and notices referred to in this article shall be deposited with the Secretary–General of the United Nations, who shall transmit copies thereof to the States Parties.

Article 288

Jurisdiction

1. A court or tribunal referred to in article 287 shall have jurisdiction over any dispute concerning the interpretation or application of this Convention which is submitted to it in accordance with this Part.

2. A court or tribunal referred to in article 287 shall also have jurisdiction over any dispute concerning the interpretation or application of an international agreement related to the purposes of this Convention, which is submitted to it in accordance with the agreement.

3. The Sea–Bed Disputes Chamber of the International Tribunal for the Law of the Sea established in accordance with Annex VI, and any other chamber or arbitral tribunal referred to in Part XI, section 5, shall have jurisdiction in any matter which is submitted to it in accordance therewith.

4. In the event of a dispute as to whether a court or tribunal has jurisdiction, the matter shall be settled by decision of that court or tribunal.

Article 289

Experts

In any dispute involving scientific or technical matters, a court or tribunal exercising jurisdiction under this section may, at the request of a party or *proprio motu,* select in consultation with the parties no fewer than two scientific or technical experts chosen preferably from the relevant list prepared in accordance with Annex VII, article 2, to sit with the court or tribunal but without the right to vote.

Article 290

Provisional measures

1. If a dispute has been duly submitted to a court or tribunal which considers that *prima facie* it has jurisdiction under this Part or Part XI, section 5, the court or tribunal may prescribe any provisional measures which it considers appropriate under the circumstances to preserve the respective rights of the parties to the dispute or to prevent serious harm to the marine environment, pending the final decision.

* * *

6. The parties to the dispute shall comply promptly with any provisional measures prescribed under this article.

Article 291

Access

1. All the dispute settlement procedures specified in this Part shall be open to States Parties.

2. The dispute settlement procedures specified in this Part shall be open to entities other than States Parties only as specifically provided for in this Convention.

Article 292

Prompt release of vessels and crews

1. Where the authorities of a State Party have detained a vessel flying the flag of another State Party and it is alleged that the detaining State has not complied with the provisions of this Convention for the prompt release of the vessel or its crew upon the posting of a reasonable bond or other financial security, the question of release from detention may be submitted to any court or tribunal agreed upon by the parties or, failing such agreement within 10 days from the time of detention, to a court or

tribunal accepted by the detaining State under article 287 or to the International Tribunal for the Law of the Sea, unless the parties otherwise agree.

2. The application for release may be made only by or on behalf of the flag State of the vessel.

3. The court or tribunal shall deal without delay with the application for release and shall deal only with the question of release, without prejudice to the merits of any case before the appropriate domestic forum against the vessel, its owner or its crew. The authorities of the detaining State remain competent to release the vessel or its crew at any time.

4. Upon the posting of the bond or other financial security determined by the court or tribunal, the authorities of the detaining State shall comply promptly with the decision of the court or tribunal concerning the release of the vessel or its crew.

Article 293

Applicable law

1. A court or tribunal having jurisdiction under this section shall apply this Convention and other rules of international law not incompatible with this Convention.

2. Paragraph 1 does not prejudice the power of the court or tribunal having jurisdiction under this section to decide a case *ex aequo et bono,* if the parties so agree.

Article 294

Preliminary proceedings

1. A court or tribunal provided for in article 287 to which an application is made in respect of a dispute referred to in article 297 shall determine at the request of a party, or may determine *proprio motu,* whether the claim constitutes an abuse of legal process or whether *prima facie* it is well founded. If the court or tribunal determines that the claim constitutes an abuse of legal process or is *prima facie* unfounded, it shall take no further action in the case.

* * *

Article 295

Exhaustion of local remedies

Any dispute between States Parties concerning the interpretation or application of this Convention may be submitted to the procedures provided for in this section only after local remedies have been exhausted where this is required by international law.

Article 296

Finality and binding force of decisions

1. Any decision rendered by a court or tribunal having jurisdiction under this section shall be final and shall be complied with by all the parties to the dispute.

2. Any such decision shall have no binding force except between the parties and in respect of that particular dispute.

SECTION 3. LIMITATIONS AND EXCEPTIONS TO APPLICABILITY OF SECTION 2

Article 297

Limitations on applicability of section 2

1. Disputes concerning the interpretation or application of this Convention with regard to the exercise by a coastal State of its sovereign rights or jurisdiction provided

for in this Convention shall be subject to the procedures provided for in section 2 in the following cases:

(a) when it is alleged that a coastal State has acted in contravention of the provisions of this Convention in regard to the freedoms and rights of navigation, overflight or the laying of submarine cables and pipelines, or in regard to other internationally lawful uses of the sea specified in article 58;

(b) when it is alleged that a State in exercising the aforementioned freedoms, rights or uses has acted in contravention of this Convention or of laws or regulations adopted by the coastal State in conformity with this Convention and other rules of international law not incompatible with this Convention; or

(c) when it is alleged that a coastal State has acted in contravention of specified international rules and standards for the protection and preservation of the marine environment which are applicable to the coastal State and which have been established by this Convention or through a competent international organization or diplomatic conference in accordance with this Convention.

2. (a) Disputes concerning the interpretation or application of the provisions of this Convention with regard to marine scientific research shall be settled in accordance with section 2, except that the coastal State shall not be obliged to accept the submission to such settlement of any dispute arising out of:

(i) the exercise by the coastal State of a right or discretion in accordance with article 246; or

(ii) a decision by the coastal State to order suspension or cessation of a research project in accordance with article 253.

(b) A dispute arising from an allegation by the researching State that with respect to a specific project the coastal State is not exercising its rights under articles 246 and 253 in a manner compatible with this Convention shall be submitted, at the request of either party, to conciliation under Annex V, section 2, provided that the conciliation commission shall not call in question the exercise by the coastal State of its discretion to designate specific areas as referred to in article 246, paragraph 6, or of its discretion to withhold consent in accordance with article 246, paragraph 5.

3. (a) Disputes concerning the interpretation or application of the provisions of this Convention with regard to fisheries shall be settled in accordance with section 2, except that the coastal State shall not be obliged to accept the submission to such settlement of any dispute relating to its sovereign rights with respect to the living resources in the exclusive economic zone or their exercise, including its discretionary powers for determining the allowable catch, its harvesting capacity, the allocation of surpluses to other States and the terms and conditions established in its conservation and management laws and regulations.

(b) Where no settlement has been reached by recourse to section 1 of this Part, a dispute shall be submitted to conciliation under Annex V, section 2, at the request of any party to the dispute, when it is alleged that:

(i) a coastal State has manifestly failed to comply with its obligations to ensure through proper conservation and management measures that the maintenance of the living resources in the exclusive economic zone is not seriously endangered;

(ii) a coastal State has arbitrarily refused to determine, at the request of another State, the allowable catch and its capacity to harvest living resources with respect to stocks which that other State is interested in fishing; or

(iii) a coastal State has arbitrarily refused to allocate to any State, under articles 62, 69 and 70 and under the terms and conditions established by the coastal State consistent with this Convention, the whole or part of the surplus it has declared to exist.

(c) In no case shall the conciliation commission substitute its discretion for that of the coastal State.

(d) The report of the conciliation commission shall be communicated to the appropriate international organizations.

(e) In negotiating agreements pursuant to articles 69 and 70, States Parties, unless they otherwise agree, shall include a clause on measures which they shall take in order to minimize the possibility of a disagreement concerning the interpretation or application of the agreement, and on how they should proceed if a disagreement nevertheless arises.

Article 298

Optional exceptions to applicability of section 2

1. When signing, ratifying or acceding to this Convention or at any time thereafter, a State may, without prejudice to the obligations arising under section 1, declare in writing that it does not accept any one or more of the procedures provided for in section 2 with respect to one or more of the following categories of disputes:

(a)(i) disputes concerning the interpretation or application of articles 15, 74 and 83 relating to sea boundary delimitations, or those involving historic bays or titles, provided that a State having made such a declaration shall, when such a dispute arises subsequent to the entry into force of this Convention and where no agreement within a reasonable period of time is reached in negotiations between the parties, at the request of any party to the dispute, accept submission of the matter to conciliation under Annex V, section 2; and provided further that any dispute that necessarily involves the concurrent consideration of any unsettled dispute concerning sovereignty or other rights over continental or insular land territory shall be excluded from such submission;

(ii) after the conciliation commission has presented its report, which shall state the reasons on which it is based, the parties shall negotiate an agreement on the basis of that report; if these negotiations do not result in an agreement, the parties shall, by mutual consent, submit the question to one of the procedures provided for in section 2, unless the parties otherwise agree;

(iii) this subparagraph does not apply to any sea boundary dispute finally settled by an arrangement between the parties, or to any such dispute which is to be settled in accordance with a bilateral or multilateral agreement binding upon those parties;

(b) disputes concerning military activities, including military activities by government vessels and aircraft engaged in non-commercial service, and disputes concerning law enforcement activities in regard to the exercise of sovereign rights or jurisdiction excluded from the jurisdiction of a court or tribunal under article 297, paragraph 2 or 3;

(c) disputes in respect of which the Security Council of the United Nations is exercising the functions assigned to it by the Charter of the United Nations, unless the Security Council decides to remove the matter from its agenda or calls upon the parties to settle it by the means provided for in this Convention.

2. A State Party which has made a declaration under paragraph 1 may at any time withdraw it, or agree to submit a dispute excluded by such declaration to any procedure specified in this Convention.

3. A State Party which has made a declaration under paragraph 1 shall not be entitled to submit any dispute falling within the excepted category of disputes to any

procedure in this Convention as against another State Party, without the consent of that party.

4. If one of the States Parties has made a declaration under paragraph 1(a), any other State Party may submit any dispute falling within an excepted category against the declarant party to the procedure specified in such declaration.

5. A new declaration, or the withdrawal of a declaration, does not in any way affect proceedings pending before a court or tribunal in accordance with this article, unless the parties otherwise agree.

6. Declarations and notices of withdrawal of declarations under this article shall be deposited with the Secretary–General of the United Nations, who shall transmit copies thereof to the States Parties.

Article 299

Right of the parties to agree upon a procedure

1. A dispute excluded under article 297 or excepted by a declaration made under article 298 from the dispute settlement procedures provided for in section 2 may be submitted to such procedures only by agreement of the parties to the dispute.

2. Nothing in this section impairs the right of the parties to the dispute to agree to some other procedure for the settlement of such dispute or to reach an amicable settlement.

PART XVI

GENERAL PROVISIONS

Article 300

Good faith and abuse of rights

States Parties shall fulfil in good faith the obligations assumed under this Convention and shall exercise the rights, jurisdiction and freedoms recognized in this Convention in a manner which would not constitute an abuse of right.

Article 301

Peaceful uses of the seas

In exercising their rights and performing their duties under this Convention, States Parties shall refrain from any threat or use of force against the territorial integrity or political independence of any State, or in any other manner inconsistent with the principles of international law embodied in the Charter of the United Nations.

Article 302

Disclosure of information

Without prejudice to the right of a State Party to resort to the procedures for the settlement of disputes provided for in this Convention, nothing in this Convention shall be deemed to require a State Party, in the fulfilment of its obligations under this Convention, to supply information the disclosure of which is contrary to the essential interests of its security.

Article 303

Archaeological and historical objects found at sea

1. States have the duty to protect objects of an archaeological and historical nature found at sea and shall co-operate for this purpose.

2. In order to control traffic in such objects, the coastal State may, in applying article 33, presume that their removal from the sea-bed in the zone referred to in that

article without its approval would result in an infringement within its territory or territorial sea of the laws and regulations referred to in that article.

3. Nothing in this article affects the rights of identifiable owners, the law of salvage or other rules of admiralty, or laws and practices with respect to cultural exchanges.

4. This article is without prejudice to other international agreements and rules of international law regarding the protection of objects of an archaeological and historical nature.

Article 304

Responsibility and liability for damage

The provisions of this Convention regarding responsibility and liability for damage are without prejudice to the application of existing rules and the development of further rules regarding responsibility and liability under international law.

PART XVII

FINAL PROVISIONS

* * *

Article 309

Reservations and exceptions

No reservations or exceptions may be made to this Convention unless expressly permitted by other articles of this Convention.

Article 310

Declarations and statements

Article 309 does not preclude a State, when signing, ratifying or acceding to this Convention, from making declarations or statements, however phrased or named, with a view, *inter alia,* to the harmonization of its laws and regulations with the provisions of this Convention, provided that such declarations or statements do not purport to exclude or to modify the legal effect of the provisions of this Convention in their application to that State.

Article 311

Relation to other conventions and international agreements

1. This Convention shall prevail, as between States Parties, over the Geneva Conventions on the Law of the Sea of 29 April 1958.

2. This Convention shall not alter the rights and obligations of States Parties which arise from other agreements compatible with this Convention and which do not affect the enjoyment by other States Parties of their rights or the performance of their obligations under this Convention.

3. Two or more States Parties may conclude agreements modifying or suspending the operation of provisions of this Convention, applicable solely to the relations between them, provided that such agreements do not relate to a provision derogation from which is incompatible with the effective execution of the object and purpose of this Convention, and provided further that such agreements shall not affect the application of the basic principles embodied herein, and that the provisions of such agreements do not affect the enjoyment by other States Parties of their rights or the performance of their obligations under this Convention.

4. States Parties intending to conclude an agreement referred to in paragraph 3 shall notify the other States Parties through the depositary of this Convention of their intention to conclude the agreement and of the modification or suspension for which it provides.

5. This article does not affect international agreements expressly permitted or preserved by other articles of this Convention.

6. State Parties agree that there shall be no amendments to the basic principle relating to the common heritage of mankind set forth in article 136 and that they shall not be party to any agreement in derogation thereof.

* * *

Article 317

Denunciation

1. A State Party may, by written notification addressed to the Secretary–General of the United Nations, denounce this Convention and may indicate its reasons. Failure to indicate reasons shall not affect the validity of the denunciation. The denunciation shall take effect one year after the date of receipt of the notification, unless the notification specifies a later date.

2. A State shall not be discharged by reason of the denunciation from the financial and contractual obligations which accrued while it was a Party to this Convention, nor shall the denunciation affect any right, obligation or legal situation of that State created through the execution of this Convention prior to its termination for that State.

3. The denunciation shall not in any way affect the duty of any State Party to fulfil any obligation embodied in this Convention to which it would be subject under international law independently of this Convention.

Article 318

Status of Annexes

The Annexes form an integral part of this Convention and, unless expressly provided otherwise, a reference to this Convention or to one of its Parts includes a reference to the Annexes relating thereto.

* * *

ANNEX V. CONCILIATION

SECTION 1. CONCILIATION PROCEDURE PURSUANT TO SECTION 1 OF PART XV

Article 1

Institution of proceedings

If the parties to a dispute have agreed, in accordance with article 284, to submit it to conciliation under this section, any such party may institute the proceedings by written notification addressed to the other party or parties to the dispute.

Article 2

List of conciliators

A list of conciliators shall be drawn up and maintained by the Secretary–General of the United Nations. Every State Party shall be entitled to nominate four conciliators, each of whom shall be a person enjoying the highest reputation for fairness, competence and integrity. The names of the persons so nominated shall constitute the list. If at any time the conciliators nominated by a State Party in the list so constituted shall be fewer than four, that State Party shall be entitled to make further nominations as necessary. The name of a conciliator shall remain on the list until withdrawn by the State Party which made the nomination, provided that such conciliator shall continue to serve on any conciliation commission to which that conciliator has been appointed until the completion of the proceedings before that commission.

Article 3

Constitution of conciliation commission

The conciliation commission shall, unless the parties otherwise agree, be constituted as follows:

(a) Subject to subparagraph (g), the conciliation commission shall consist of five members.

(b) The party instituting the proceedings shall appoint two conciliators to be chosen preferably from the list referred to in article 2 of this Annex, one of whom may be its national, unless the parties otherwise agree. Such appointments shall be included in the notification referred to in article 1 of this Annex.

(c) The other party to the dispute shall appoint two conciliators in the manner set forth in subparagraph (b) within 21 days of receipt of the notification referred to in article 1 of this Annex. If the appointments are not made within that period, the party instituting the proceedings may, within one week of the expiration of that period, either terminate the proceedings by notification addressed to the other party or request the Secretary–General of the United Nations to make the appointments in accordance with subparagraph (e).

(d) Within 30 days after all four conciliators have been appointed, they shall appoint a fifth conciliator chosen from the list referred to in article 2 of this Annex, who shall be chairman. If the appointment is not made within that period, either party may, within one week of the expiration of that period, request the Secretary–General of the United Nations to make the appointment in accordance with subparagraph (e).

(e) Within 30 days of the receipt of a request under subparagraph (c) or (d), the Secretary–General of the United Nations shall make the necessary appointments from the list referred to in article 2 of this Annex in consultation with the parties to the dispute.

(f) Any vacancy shall be filled in the manner prescribed for the initial appointment.

(g) Two or more parties which determine by agreement that they are in the same interest shall appoint two conciliators jointly. Where two or more parties have separate interests or there is a disagreement as to whether they are of the same interest, they shall appoint conciliators separately.

(h) In disputes involving more than two parties having separate interests, or where there is disagreement as to whether they are of the same interest, the parties shall apply subparagraphs (a) to (f) in so far as possible.

Article 4

Procedure

The conciliation commission shall, unless the parties otherwise agree, determine its own procedure. The commission may, with the consent of the parties to the dispute, invite any State Party to submit to it its views orally or in writing. Decisions of the commission regarding procedural matters, the report and recommendations shall be made by a majority vote of its members.

Article 5

Amicable settlement

The commission may draw the attention of the parties to any measures which might facilitate an amicable settlement of the dispute.

Article 6

Functions of the commission

The commission shall hear the parties, examine their claims and objections, and make proposals to the parties with a view to reaching an amicable settlement.

Article 7

Report

1. The commission shall report within 12 months of its constitution. Its report shall record any agreements reached and, failing agreement, its conclusions on all questions of fact or law relevant to the matter in dispute and such recommendations as the commission may deem appropriate for an amicable settlement. The report shall be deposited with the Secretary–General of the United Nations and shall immediately be transmitted by him to the parties to the dispute.

2. The report of the commission, including its conclusions or recommendations, shall not be binding upon the parties.

Article 8

Termination

The conciliation proceedings are terminated when a settlement has been reached, when the parties have accepted or one party has rejected the recommendations of the report by written notification addressed to the Secretary–General of the United Nations, or when a period of three months has expired from the date of transmission of the report to the parties.

Article 9

Fees and expenses

The fees and expenses of the commission shall be borne by the parties to the dispute.

Article 10

Right of parties to modify procedure

The parties to the dispute may by agreement applicable solely to that dispute modify any provision of this Annex.

SECTION 2. COMPULSORY SUBMISSION TO CONCILIATION PROCEDURE PURSUANT TO SECTION 3 OF PART XV

Article 11

Institution of proceedings

1. Any party to a dispute which, in accordance with Part XV, section 3, may be submitted to conciliation under this section, may institute the proceedings by written notification addressed to the other party or parties to the dispute.

2. Any party to the dispute, notified under paragraph 1, shall be obliged to submit to such proceedings.

Article 12

Failure to reply or to submit to conciliation

The failure of a party or parties to the dispute to reply to notification of institution of proceedings or to submit to such proceedings shall not constitute a bar to the proceedings.

Article 13

Competence

A disagreement as to whether a conciliation commission acting under this section has competence shall be decided by the commission.

Article 14

Application of section 1

Articles 2 to 10 of section 1 of this Annex apply subject to this section.

4.21 Montreal Guidelines for the Protection of the Marine Environment Against Pollution From Land-Based Sources (Without Annexes). Adopted at Montreal, 24 May 1985. UNEP/GC.13/9/Add.3, UNEP/GC/DEC/13/1811, UNEP ELPG No.7; *reprinted in* 5 Weston V.F.24

1. *Definitions*

For the purposes of these guidelines:

(a) "Pollution" means the introduction by man, directly or indirectly, of substances or energy into the marine environment which results or is likely to result in such deleterious effects as harm to living resources and marine ecosystems, hazards to human health, hindrance to marine activities, including fishing and other legitimate uses of the sea, impairment of quality for use of sea water and reduction of amenities;

(b) "Land-based sources" means:

(i) Municipal, industrial or agricultural sources, both fixed and mobile, on land, discharges from which reach the marine environment, in particular:

a. From the coast, including from outfalls discharging directly into the marine environment and through run-off;

b. Through rivers, canals of other watercourses, including underground watercourses; and

c. Via the atmosphere;

(ii) Sources of marine pollution from activities conducted on offshore fixed or mobile facilities within the limits of national jurisdiction, save to the extent that these sources are governed by appropriate international agreements.

(c) "Marine environment" means the maritime area extending, in the case of watercourses, up to the freshwater limit and including inter-tidal zones and salt-water marshes;

(d) "Freshwater limit" means the place in watercourses where, at low tide and in a period of low freshwater flow, there is an appreciable increase in salinity due to the presence of sea water.

2. *Basic obligation*

States have the obligation to protect and preserve the marine environment. In exercising their sovereign right to exploit their natural resources, all States have the duty to prevent, reduce and control pollution of the marine environment.

3. *Discharges affecting other States or areas beyond the limits of national jurisdiction*

States have the duty to ensure that discharges from land-based sources within their territories do not cause pollution to the marine environment of other States or of areas beyond the limits of national jurisdiction.

4. *Adoption of measures against pollution from land-based sources*

(a) States should adopt, individually or jointly, and in accordance with their capabilities, all measures necessary to prevent, reduce and control pollution from land-based sources, including those designed to minimize to the fullest possible extent the release of toxic, harmful or noxious substances; especially those which are persistent, into the marine environment. States should ensure that such measures take into account internationally agreed rules, criteria, standards and recommended practices and procedures.

(b) In taking measures to prevent, reduce and control pollution from land-based sources, States should refrain, in accordance with international law, from unjustifiable interference with activities carried out by other States in the exercise of their sovereign rights and in pursuance of their duties in conformity with internationally agreed rules, criteria, standards and recommended practices and procedures.

5. *Co-operation on a global, regional or bilateral basis*

(a) States should undertake, as appropriate, to establish internationally agreed rules, criteria, standards and recommended practices and procedures to prevent, reduce and control pollution from land-based sources, with a view to co-ordinating their policies in this connection, particularly at the local and regional level. Such rules, criteria, standards and recommended practices and procedures should take into account local ecological, geographical and physical characteristics, the economic capacity of States and their need for sustainable development and environmental protection, and the assimilative capacity of the marine environment, and should be reviewed from time to time as necessary;

(b) States not bordering on the marine environment should co-operate in preventing, reducing and controlling pollution of the marine environment originating or partially originating from releases within their territory into or reaching water basins or watercourses flowing into the marine environment or via the atmosphere. To this end, States concerned should as far as possible, and, as appropriate, in co-operation with competent international organizations, take necessary measures to prevent, reduce and control pollution of the marine environment from land-based sources;

(c) If discharges from a watercourse which flows through the territories of two or more States or forms a boundary between them are likely to cause pollution of the marine environment, the States concerned should co-operate in taking necessary measures to prevent, reduce and control such pollution.

6. *Duty not to transfer or transform pollution from land-based sources*

In taking measures to prevent, reduce and control pollution from land-based sources, States have the duty to act so as not to transfer directly or indirectly, damage or hazards from one area to another or transform such pollution into another type of pollution.

7. *Specially protected areas*

(a) States should, in a manner consistent with international law, take all appropriate measures, such as the establishment of marine sanctuaries and reserves, to protect certain areas to the fullest possible extent from pollution, including that from land-based sources, taking into account the relevant provisions of annex I;

(b) States should, as practicable, undertake to develop, jointly or individually, environmental quality objectives for specially protected areas, conforming with the intended uses, and strive to maintain or ameliorate existing conditions by comprehensive environmental management practices.

8. *Scientific and technical co-operation*

States should co-operate, directly and/or through competent international organizations, in the field of science and technology related to pollution from land-based sources, and exchange data and other scientific information for the purpose of preventing, reducing and controlling such pollution, taking into account national regulations regarding the protection of confidential information. They should, in particular, undertake to develop and co-ordinate to the fullest possible extent their national research programmes and to co-operate in the establishment and implementation of regional and other international research programmes.

9. *Assistance to developing countries*

(a) States should, directly and/or through competent international organizations, promote programmes of assistance to developing countries in the fields of education, environmental and pollution awareness, training, scientific research and transfer of technology and know-how, for the purpose of improving the capacity of the developing countries to prevent, reduce and control pollution from land-based sources and to assess its effects on the marine environment;

(b) Such assistance should include:

(i) Training of scientific and technical personnel;

(ii) Facilitation of the participation of developing countries in relevant international programmes;

(iii) Acquisition, utilization, maintenance and production by those countries of appropriate equipment; and

(iv) Advice on, and development of, facilities for education, training, research, monitoring and other programmes;

(c) States should, directly and/or through competent international organizations, promote programmes of assistance to developing countries for the establishment, as necessary, of infrastructure for the effective implementation of applicable internationally agreed rules, criteria, standards and recommended practices and procedures related to the protection of the marine environment against pollution from land-based sources, including the provision of expert advice on the development of the necessary legal and administrative measures.

10. *Development of a comprehensive environmental management approach*

States should undertake to develop, as far as practicable, a comprehensive environmental management approach to the prevention, reduction and control of pollution from land-based sources, taking into account relevant existing programmes at the bilateral, regional or global level and the provisions of annex I. Such a comprehensive approach should include the identification of desired and attainable water use objectives for the specific marine environments.

11. *Monitoring and data management*

States should endeavour to establish directly or, whenever necessary, through competent international organizations, complementary or joint programmes for monitoring, storage and exchange of data, based, when possible, on compatible procedures and methods, taking into account relevant existing programmes at the bilateral, regional or global level and the provisions of annex III, in order to:

(a) Collect data on natural conditions in the region concerned as regards its physical, biological and chemical characteristics;

(b) Collect data on inputs of substances or energy that cause or potentially cause pollution emanating from land-based sources, including information on the distribution of sources and the quantities introduced to the region concerned;

(c) Assess systematically the levels of pollution along their coasts emanating from land-based sources and the fates and effects of pollution in the region concerned; and

(d) Evaluate the effectiveness of measures in meeting the environmental objectives for specific marine environments.

12. *Environmental assessment*

States should assess the potential effects/impacts, including possible transboundary effects/impacts, of proposed major projects under their jurisdiction or control, particularly in coastal areas, which may cause pollution from land-based sources, so that appropriate measures may be taken to prevent or mitigate such pollution.

13. *Development of control strategies*

(a) States should develop, adopt and implement programmes and measures for the prevention, reduction and control of pollution from land-based sources. They should employ an appropriate control strategy or combination of control strategies, taking into account relevant international or national experience, as described in annex I;

(b) States should, as appropriate, progressively formulate and adopt, in co-operation with competent international organizations, standards based on marine quality or on emissions, as well as recommended practices and procedures, taking into account the provisions of annex I;

(c) Where appropriate, States should undertake to establish priorities for action, based on lists of substances pollution by which should be eliminated and of substances pollution by which should be strictly limited on the basis of their toxicity, persistence, bioaccumulation and other criteria as elaborated in annex II, or in relevant international agreements.

14. *Pollution emergencies arising from land-based sources*

States and, as appropriate, competent international organizations should take all necessary measures for preventing and dealing with marine pollution emergencies from land-based sources, however caused, and for reducing or eliminating damage or the threat of damage therefrom. To this end States should, as appropriate, individually or jointly, develop and promote national and international contingency plans for responding to incidents of pollution from land-based sources and should co-operate with one another and, whenever necessary, through competent international organizations.

15. *Notification, information exchange and consultation*

Whenever releases originating or likely to originate from land-based sources within the territory of a State are likely to cause pollution to the marine environment of one or more other States or of areas beyond the limits of national jurisdiction, that State should immediately notify such other State or States, as well as competent international organizations, and provide them with timely information that will enable them, where necessary, to take appropriate action to prevent, reduce and control such pollution. Furthermore, consultations deemed appropriate by States concerned should be undertaken with a view to preventing, reducing and controlling such pollution.

16. *National laws and procedures*

(a) Each State should adopt and implement national laws and regulations for the protection and preservation of the marine environment against pollution from land-based sources, taking into account internationally agreed rules, criteria, standards and recommended practices and procedures, and take appropriate measures to ensure compliance with such laws and regulations;

(b) Paragraph (a) above is without prejudice to the right of States to take more stringent measures nationally or in co-operation with each other to prevent, reduce and control pollution from land-based sources under their jurisdiction or control;

(c) Each State should, on a reciprocal basis, grant equal access to and non-discriminatory treatment in its courts, tribunals and administrative proceedings to persons in other States who are or may be affected by pollution from land-based sources under its jurisdiction or control.

17. *Liability and compensation for pollution damage emanating from land-based sources*

(a) States should ensure that recourse is available in accordance with their legal systems for prompt and adequate compensation or other relief in respect of damage caused by pollution of the marine environment by natural or juridical persons under their jurisdiction;

(b) To this end, States should formulate and adopt appropriate procedures for the determination of liability for damage resulting from pollution from land-based sources. Such procedures should include measures for addressing damage caused by releases of a significant scale or by the substances referred to in guideline 13(c).

18. *Implementation reports*

States should report, as appropriate, to other States concerned, directly or through competent international organizations, on measures taken, on results achieved and, if the case arises, on difficulties encountered in the implementation of applicable internationally agreed rules, criteria, standards and recommended practices and procedures. To this end, States should designate national authorities as focal points for the reporting of such measures, results and difficulties.

19. *Institutional arrangements*

(a) States should ensure that adequate institutional arrangements are made at the appropriate regional or global level, for the purpose of achieving the objectives of these guidelines, and in particular for promoting the formulation, adoption and application of international rules, criteria, standards and recommended practices and procedures, and for monitoring the condition of the marine environment;

(b) The functions of such institutional arrangements should include:

(i) Periodic assessment of the state of the specific marine environment concerned;

(ii) Formulation and adoption, as appropriate, of a comprehensive environmental management approach consistent with the provisions of guidelines 7 and 10;

(iii) Adoption, review and revision, as necessary, of the lists referred to in guideline 13;

(iv) Development and adoption, as appropriate, of programmes and measures consistent with the provisions of guidelines 10 and 13;

(v) Consideration, where necessary, of the reports and information submitted in accordance with guidelines 15 and 18;

(vi) Recommendation of appropriate measures to be taken for the prevention, reduction and control of pollution from land-based sources, such as assistance to developing countries, the strengthening of regional co-operation mechanisms, consideration of aspects of transboundary pollution, and the difficulties encountered in the implementation of agreed rules; and

(vii) Review of the implementation of relevant internationally agreed rules, criteria, standards and recommended practices and procedures, and of the efficacy of the measures adopted and the advisability of any other measures.

4.22 Convention for the Protection of the Natural Resources and Environment of the South Pacific Region (SREP Convention) (Without Protocols). Concluded at Noumea, 25 November 1986. Entered into force, 22 August 1990. *Reprinted in* 26 I.L.M. 38 (1987) & 5 Weston V.C.6

Article 1

GEOGRAPHICAL COVERAGE

1. This Convention shall apply to the South Pacific Region, hereinafter referred to as "the Convention Area" as defined in paragraph (a) of article 2.

2. Except as may be otherwise provided in any Protocol to this Convention, the Convention Area shall not include internal waters or archipelagic waters of the Parties as defined in accordance with international law.

Article 2

DEFINITIONS

For the purpose of this Convention and its Protocols unless otherwise defined in any such Protocol:

(a) the "Convention Area" shall comprise:

(i) the 200 nautical mile zones established in accordance with international law off:

American Samoa
Australia (East Coast and Islands to eastward including Macquarie Island)
Cook Islands
Federated States of Micronesia
Fiji
French Polynesia
Guam
Kiribati
Marshall Islands
Nauru
New Caledonia and Dependencies
New Zealand
Niue
Northern Mariana Islands
Palau
Papua New Guinea
Pitcairn Islands
Solomon Islands
Tokelau
Tonga
Tuvalu
Vanuatu
Wallis and Futuna
Western Samoa

(ii) those areas of high seas which are enclosed from all sides by the 200 nautical mile zones referred to in sub-paragraph (i);

(iii) areas of the Pacific Ocean which have been included in the Convention Area pursuant to article 3;

(b) "dumping" means:

—any deliberate disposal at sea of wastes or other matter from vessels, aircraft, platforms or other man-made structures at sea;

—any deliberate disposal at sea of vessels, aircraft, platforms or other man-made structures at sea;

"dumping" does not include:

—the disposal of wastes or other matter incidental to, or derived from the normal operations of vessels, aircraft, platforms or other man-made structures at sea and their equipment, other than wastes or other matter transported by or to vessels, aircraft, platforms or other man-made structures at sea, operating for the purpose of disposal of such matter or derived from the treatment of such wastes or other matter on such vessels, aircraft, platforms or structures;

—placement of matter for a purpose other than the mere disposal thereof, provided that such placement is not contrary to the aims of this Convention;

(c) "wastes or other matter" means material and substances of any kind, form or description;

(d) the following wastes or other matter shall be considered to be non-radioactive: sewage sludge, dredge spoil, fly ash, agricultural wastes, construction materials, vessels, artificial reef building materials and other such materials, provided that they have not been contaminated with radio nuclides of anthropogenic origin (except dispersed global fallout from nuclear weapons testing), nor are potential sources of naturally occurring radio nuclides for commercial purposes, nor have been enriched in natural or artificial radio nuclides;

if there is a question as to whether the material to be dumped should be considered non-radioactive, for the purposes of this Convention, such material shall not be dumped unless the appropriate national authority of the proposed dumper confirms that such dumping would not exceed the individual and collective dose limits of the International Atomic Energy Agency general principles for the exemption of radiation sources and practices from regulatory control. The national authority shall also take into account the relevant recommendations, standards and guidelines developed by the International Atomic Energy Agency;

(e) "vessels" and "aircraft" means waterborne or airborne craft of any type whatsoever. This expression includes air cushioned craft and floating craft, whether self-propelled or not;

(f) "pollution" means the introduction by man, directly or indirectly, of substances or energy into the marine environment (including estuaries) which results or is likely to result in such deleterious effects as harm to living resources and marine life, hazards to human health, hindrance to marine activities, including fishing and other legitimate uses of the sea, impairment of quality for use of sea water and reduction of amenities;

in applying this definition to the Convention obligations, the Parties shall use their best endeavours to comply with the appropriate standards and recommendations established by competent international organisations, including the International Atomic Energy Agency;

(g) "Organisation" means the South Pacific Commission;

(h) "Director" means the Director of the South Pacific Bureau for Economic Co-operation.

Article 3
ADDITION TO THE CONVENTION AREA

Any Party may add areas under its jurisdiction within the Pacific Ocean between the Tropic of Cancer and 60 degrees South latitude and between 130 degrees East longitude and 120 degrees West longitude to the Convention Area. Such addition shall be notified to the Depositary who shall promptly notify the other Parties and the Organisation. Such areas shall be incorporated within the Convention Area ninety days after notification to the Parties by the Depositary, provided there has been no objection to the proposal to add new areas by any Party affected by that proposal. If there is any such objection the Parties concerned will consult with a view to resolving the matter.

Article 4
GENERAL PROVISIONS

1. The Parties shall endeavour to conclude bilateral or multilateral agreements, including regional or sub-regional agreements, for the protection, development and

management of the marine and coastal environment of the Convention Area. Such agreements shall be consistent with this Convention and in accordance with international law. Copies of such agreements shall be communicated to the Organisation and through it to all Parties to this Convention.

2. Nothing in this Convention or its Protocols shall be deemed to affect obligations assumed by a Party under agreements previously concluded.

3. Nothing in this Convention and its Protocols shall be construed to prejudice or affect the interpretation and application of any provision or term in the Convention on the Prevention of Marine Pollution by Dumping of Wastes and Other Matter, 1972.

4. This Convention and its Protocols shall be construed in accordance with international law relating to their subject matter.

5. Nothing in this Convention and its Protocols shall prejudice the present or future claims and legal views of any Party concerning the nature and extent of maritime jurisdiction.

6. Nothing in this Convention shall affect the sovereign right of States to exploit, develop and manage their own natural resources pursuant to their own policies, taking into account their duty to protect and preserve the environment. Each Party shall ensure that activities within its jurisdiction or control do not cause damage to the environment of other States or of areas beyond the limits of its national jurisdiction.

Article 5

GENERAL OBLIGATIONS

1. The Parties shall endeavour, either individually or jointly, to take all appropriate measures in conformity with international law and in accordance with this Convention and those Protocols in force to which they are party to prevent, reduce and control pollution of the Convention Area, from any source, and to ensure sound environmental management and development of natural resources, using for this purpose the best practicable means at their disposal, and in accordance with their capabilities. In doing so the Parties shall endeavor to harmonize their policies at the regional level.

2. The Parties shall use their best endeavors to ensure that the implementation of this Convention shall not result in an increase in pollution in the marine environment outside the Convention Area.

3. In addition to the Protocol for the Prevention of Pollution of the South Pacific Region by Dumping and the Protocol Concerning Co-operation in Combating Pollution Emergencies in the South Pacific Region, the Parties shall co-operate in the formulation and adoption of other Protocols prescribing agreed measures, procedures and standards to prevent, reduce and control pollution from all sources or in promoting environmental management in conformity with the objectives of this Convention.

4. The Parties shall, taking into account existing internationally recognized rules, standards, practices and procedures, co-operate with competent global, regional and sub-regional organisations to establish and adopt recommended practices, procedures and measures to prevent, reduce and control pollution from all sources and to promote sustained resource management and to ensure the sound development of natural resources in conformity with the objectives of this Convention and its Protocols, and to assist each other in fulfilling their obligations under this Convention and its Protocols.

5. The Parties shall endeavor to establish laws and regulations for the effective discharge of the obligations prescribed in this Convention. Such laws and regulations shall be no less effective than international rules, standards and recommended practices and procedures.

Article 6

POLLUTION FROM VESSELS

The Parties shall take all appropriate measures to prevent, reduce and control pollution in the Convention Area caused by discharges from vessels, and to ensure the effective application in the Convention Area of the generally accepted international rules and standards established through the competent international organisation or general diplomatic conference relating to the control of pollution from vessels.

Article 7

POLLUTION FROM LAND-BASED SOURCES

The Parties shall take all appropriate measures to prevent, reduce and control pollution in the Convention Area caused by coastal disposal or by discharges emanating from rivers, estuaries, coastal establishments, outfall structures, or any other sources in their territory.

Article 8

POLLUTION FROM SEA-BED ACTIVITIES

The Parties shall take all appropriate measures to prevent, reduce and control pollution in the Convention Area resulting directly or indirectly from exploration and exploitation of the sea-bed and its subsoil.

Article 9

AIRBORNE POLLUTION

The Parties shall take all appropriate measures to prevent, reduce and control pollution in the Convention Area resulting from discharges into the atmosphere from activities under their jurisdiction.

Article 10

DISPOSAL OF WASTES

1. The Parties shall take all appropriate measures to prevent, reduce and control pollution in the Convention Area caused by dumping from vessels, aircraft, or man-made structures at sea, including the effective application of the relevant internationally recognized rules and procedures relating to the control of dumping of wastes and other matter. The Parties agree to prohibit the dumping of radioactive wastes or other radioactive matter in the Convention area. Without prejudice to whether or not disposal into the seabed and subsoil of wastes or other matter is "dumping", the Parties agree to prohibit the disposal into the seabed and subsoil of the Convention area of radioactive wastes or other radioactive matter.

2. This article shall also apply to the continental shelf of a Party where it extends, in accordance with international law, outward beyond the Convention Area.

Article 11

STORAGE OF TOXIC AND HAZARDOUS WASTES

The Parties shall take all appropriate measures to prevent, reduce and control pollution in the Convention Area resulting from the storage of toxic and hazardous wastes. In particular, the Parties shall prohibit the storage of radioactive wastes or other radioactive matter in the Convention Area.

Article 12

TESTING OF NUCLEAR DEVICES

The Parties shall take all appropriate measures to prevent, reduce and control pollution in the Convention Area which might result from the testing of nuclear devices.

Article 13

MINING AND COASTAL EROSION

The Parties shall take all appropriate measures to prevent, reduce and control environmental damage in the Convention Area, in particular coastal erosion caused by coastal engineering, mining activities, sand removal, land reclamation and dredging.

Article 14

SPECIALLY PROTECTED AREAS AND PROTECTION OF WILD FLORA AND FAUNA

The Parties shall, individually or jointly, take all appropriate measures to protect and preserve rare or fragile ecosystems and depleted, threatened or endangered flora and fauna as well as their habitat in the Convention Area. To this end, the Parties shall, as appropriate, establish protected areas, such as parks and reserves, and prohibit or regulate any activity likely to have adverse effects on the species, ecosystems or biological processes that such areas are designed to protect. The establishment of such areas shall not affect the rights of other Parties or third States under international law. In addition, the Parties shall exchange information concerning the administration and management of such areas.

Article 15

CO-OPERATION IN COMBATING POLLUTION IN CASES OF EMERGENCY

1. The Parties shall co-operate in taking all necessary measures to deal with pollution emergencies in the Convention Area, whatever the cause of such emergencies, and to prevent, reduce and control pollution or the threat of pollution resulting therefrom. To this end, the Parties shall develop and promote individual contingency plans and joint contingency plans for responding to incidents involving pollution or the threat thereof in the Convention Area.

2. When a Party becomes aware of a case in which the Convention Area is in imminent danger of being polluted or has been polluted, it shall immediately notify other countries and territories it deems likely to be affected by such pollution, as well as the Organisation. Furthermore it shall inform, as soon as feasible, such other countries and territories and the Organisation of any measures it has itself taken to reduce or control pollution or the threat thereof.

Article 16

ENVIRONMENTAL IMPACT ASSESSMENT

1. The Parties agree to develop and maintain, with the assistance of competent global, regional and sub-regional organisations as requested, technical guidelines and legislation giving adequate emphasis to environmental and social factors to facilitate balanced development of their natural resources and planning of their major projects which might affect the marine environment in such a way as to prevent or minimize harmful impacts on the Convention Area.

2. Each Party shall, within its capabilities, assess the potential effects of such projects on the marine environment, so that appropriate measures can be taken to prevent any substantial pollution of, or significant and harmful changes within, the Convention Area.

3. With respect to the assessment referred to in paragraph 2, each Party shall, where appropriate, invite:

(a) public comment according to its national procedures,

(b) other Parties that may be affected to consult with it and submit comments.

The results of these assessments shall be communicated to the Organisation, which shall make them available to interested Parties.

Article 17

SCIENTIFIC AND TECHNICAL CO–OPERATION

1. The Parties shall co-operate, either directly or with the assistance of competent global, regional and sub-regional organisations, in scientific research, environmental monitoring, and the exchange of data and other scientific and technical information related to the purposes of the Convention.

2. In addition, the Parties shall, for the purposes of this Convention, develop and co-ordinate research and monitoring programmes relating to the Convention Area and co-operate, as far as practicable, in the establishment and implementation of regional, sub-regional and international research programmes.

Article 18

TECHNICAL AND OTHER ASSISTANCE

The Parties undertake to co-operate, directly and when appropriate through the competent global, regional and sub-regional organisations, in the provision to other Parties of technical and other assistance in fields relating to pollution and sound environmental management of the Convention Area, taking into account the special needs of the island developing countries and territories.

Article 19

TRANSMISSION OF INFORMATION

The Parties shall transmit to the Organisation information on the measures adopted by them in the implementation of this Convention and of Protocols to which they are Parties, in such form and at such intervals as the Parties may determine.

Article 20

LIABILITY AND COMPENSATION

The Parties shall co-operate in the formulation and adoption of appropriate rules and procedures in conformity with international law in respect of liability and compensation for damage resulting from pollution of the Convention Area.

Article 21

INSTITUTIONAL ARRANGEMENTS

1. The Organisation shall be responsible for carrying out the following secretariat functions:

(a) to prepare and convene the meetings of Parties;

(b) to transmit to the Parties notifications, reports and other information received in accordance with this Convention and its Protocols;

(c) to perform the functions assigned to it by the Protocols to this Convention;

(d) to consider enquiries by, and information from, the Parties and to consult with them on questions relating to this Convention and the Protocols;

(e) to co-ordinate the implementation of co-operative activities agreed upon by the Parties;

(f) to ensure the necessary co-ordination with other competent global, regional and sub-regional bodies;

(g) to enter into such administrative arrangements as may be required for the effective discharge of the secretariat functions;

(h) to perform such other functions as may be assigned to it by the Parties; and

(i) to transmit to the South Pacific Conference and the South Pacific Forum the reports of ordinary and extraordinary meetings of the Parties.

2. Each Party shall designate an appropriate national authority to serve as the channel of communication with the Organisation for the purposes of this Convention.

Article 22

MEETINGS OF THE PARTIES

1. The Parties shall hold ordinary meetings once every two years. Ordinary meetings shall review the implementation of this Convention and its Protocols and, in particular, shall:

(a) assess periodically the state of the environment in the Convention Area;

(b) consider the information submitted by the Parties under article 19;

(c) adopt, review and amend as required annexes to this Convention and to its Protocols, in accordance with the provisions of article 25;

(d) make recommendations regarding the adoption of any Protocols or any amendments to this Convention or its Protocols in accordance with the provisions of articles 23 and 24;

(e) establish working groups as required to consider any matters concerning this Convention and its Protocols;

(f) consider co-operative activities to be undertaken within the framework of this Convention and its Protocols, including their financial and institutional implications and to adopt decisions relating thereto;

(g) consider and undertake any additional action that may be required for the achievement of the purposes of this Convention and its Protocols; and

(h) adopt by consensus financial rules and budget, prepared in consultation with the Organization, to determine, *inter alia,* the financial participation of the Parties under this Convention and those Protocols to which they are party.

2. The Organisation shall convene the first ordinary meeting of the Parties not later than one year after the date on which the Convention enters into force in accordance with article 31.

3. Extraordinary meetings shall be convened at the request of any Party or upon the request of the Organisation, provided that such requests are supported by at least two-thirds of the Parties. It shall be the function of an extraordinary meeting of the Parties to consider those items proposed in the request for the holding of the extraordinary meeting and any other items agreed to by all the Parties attending the meeting.

4. The Parties shall adopt by consensus at their first ordinary meeting, rules of procedure for their meetings.

Article 23

ADOPTION OF PROTOCOLS

1. The Parties may, at a conference of plenipotentiaries, adopt Protocols to this Convention pursuant to paragraph 3 of article 5.

2. If so requested by a majority of the Parties, the Organisation shall convene a conference of plenipotentiaries for the purpose of adopting Protocols to this Convention.

Article 24

AMENDMENT OF THE CONVENTION AND ITS PROTOCOLS

1. Any Party may propose amendments to this Convention. Amendments shall be adopted by a conference of plenipotentiaries which shall be convened by the Organisation at the request of two-thirds of the Parties.

2. Any Party to this Convention may propose amendments to any Protocol. Such amendments shall be adopted by a conference of plenipotentiaries which shall be convened by the Organisation at the request of two-thirds of the Parties to the Protocol concerned.

3. A proposed amendment to the Convention or any Protocol shall be communicated to the Organisation, which shall promptly transmit such proposal for consideration to all the other Parties.

4. A conference of plenipotentiaries to consider a proposed amendment to the Convention or any Protocol shall be convened not less than ninety days after the requirements for the convening of the Conference have been met pursuant to paragraphs 1 or 2, as the case may be.

5. Any amendment to this Convention shall be adopted by a three-fourths majority vote of the Parties to the Convention which are represented at the conference of plenipotentiaries and shall be submitted by the Depositary for acceptance by all Parties to the Convention. Amendments to any Protocol shall be adopted by a three-fourths majority vote of the Parties to the Protocol which are represented at the conference of plenipotentiaries and shall be submitted by the Depositary for acceptance by all Parties to the Protocol.

6. Instruments of ratification, acceptance or approval of amendments shall be deposited with the Depositary. Amendments shall enter into force between Parties having accepted such amendments on the thirtieth day following the date of receipt by the Depositary of the instruments of at least three-fourths of the Parties to this Convention or to the Protocol concerned, as the case may be. Thereafter the amendments shall enter into force for any other Party on the thirtieth day after the date on which that Party deposits its instrument.

7. After the entry into force of an amendment to this Convention or to a Protocol, any new Party to the Convention or such protocol shall become a Party to the Convention or Protocol as amended.

Article 25

ANNEXES AND AMENDMENT OF ANNEXES

1. Annexes to this Convention or to any Protocol shall form an integral part of the Convention or such Protocol respectively.

2. Except as may be otherwise provided in any Protocol with respect to its annexes, the following procedures shall apply to the adoption and entry into force of any amendments to annexes to this Convention or to annexes to any Protocol:

(a) any Party may propose amendments to the annexes to this Convention or annexes to any Protocol;

(b) any proposed amendment shall be notified by the Organisation to the Parties not less than sixty days before the convening of a meeting of the Parties unless this requirement is waived by the meeting;

(c) such amendments shall be adopted at a meeting of the Parties by a three-fourths majority vote of the Parties to the instrument in question;

(d) the Depositary shall without delay communicate the amendments so adopted to all Parties;

(e) any Party that is unable to approve an amendment to the annexes to this Convention or to annexes to any Protocol shall so notify in writing to the Depositary within one hundred days from the date of the communication of the amendment by the Depositary. A Party may at any time substitute an acceptance for a previous declaration of objection, and the amendment shall thereupon enter into force for that Party;

(f) the Depositary shall without delay notify all Parties of any notification received pursuant to the preceding sub-paragraph; and

(g) on expiry of the period referred to in sub-paragraph (e) above, the amendment to the annex shall become effective for all Parties to this Convention or to the Protocol concerned which have not submitted a notification in accordance with the provisions of that sub-paragraph.

3. The adoption and entry into force of a new annex shall be subject to the same procedure as that for the adoption and entry into force of an amendment to an annex as set out in the provisions of paragraph 2, provided that, if any amendment to the Convention or the Protocol concerned is involved, the new annex shall not enter into force until such time as that amendment enters into force.

4. Amendments to the Annex on Arbitration shall be considered to be amendments to this Convention or its Protocols and shall be proposed and adopted in accordance with the procedures set out in article 24.

Article 26

SETTLEMENT OF DISPUTES

1. In case of a dispute between Parties as to the interpretation or application of this Convention or its Protocols, they shall seek a settlement of the dispute through negotiation or any other peaceful means of their own choice. If the Parties concerned cannot reach agreement, they should seek the good offices of, or jointly request mediation by, a third Party.

2. If the Parties concerned cannot settle their dispute through the means mentioned in paragraph 1, the dispute shall, upon common agreement, except as may be otherwise provided in any Protocol to this Convention, be submitted to arbitration under conditions laid down in the Annex on Arbitration to this Convention. However, failure to reach common agreement on submission of the dispute to arbitration shall not absolve the Parties from the responsibility of continuing to seek to resolve it by means referred to in paragraph 1.

3. A Party may at any time declare that it recognizes as compulsory *ipso facto* and without special agreement, in relation to any other Party accepting the same obligation, the application of the arbitration procedure set out in the Annex on Arbitration. Such declaration shall be notified in writing to the Depositary who shall promptly communicate it to the other Parties.

Article 27

RELATIONSHIP BETWEEN THIS CONVENTION AND ITS PROTOCOLS

1. No State may become a Party to this Convention unless it becomes at the same time a Party to one or more Protocols. No State may become a Party to a Protocol unless it is, or becomes at the same time, a Party to this Convention.

2. Decisions concerning any Protocol pursuant to articles 22, 24 and 25 of this Convention shall be taken only by the Parties to the Protocol concerned.

Article 28

SIGNATURE

This Convention, the Protocol Concerning Co-operation in Combating Pollution Emergencies in the South Pacific Region, and the Protocol for the Prevention of Pollution of the South Pacific Region by Dumping shall be open for signature at the South Pacific Commission Headquarters in Noumea, New Caledonia on 25 November 1986 and at the South Pacific Bureau for Economic Co-operation Headquarters, Suva, Fiji from 26 November 1986 to 25 November 1987 by States which were invited to participate in the Plenipotentiary Meeting of the High Level Conference on the Protection of the Natural Resources and Environment of the South Pacific Region held at Noumea, New Caledonia from 24 November 1986 to 25 November 1986.

Article 29

RATIFICATION, ACCEPTANCE OR APPROVAL

This Convention and any Protocol thereto shall be subject to ratification, acceptance or approval by States referred to in article 28. Instruments of ratification, acceptance or approval shall be deposited with the Director who shall be the Depositary.

Article 30

ACCESSION

1. This Convention and any Protocol thereto shall be open to accession by the States referred to in article 28 as from the day following the date on which the Convention or Protocol concerned was closed for signature.

2. Any State not referred to in paragraph 1 may accede to the Convention and to any Protocol subject to prior approval by three-fourths of the Parties to the Convention or the Protocol concerned.

3. Instruments of accession shall be deposited with the Depositary.

Article 31

ENTRY INTO FORCE

1. This Convention shall enter into force on the thirtieth day following the date of deposit of at least ten instruments of ratification, acceptance, approval or accession.

2. Any Protocol to this Convention, except as otherwise provided in such Protocol, shall enter into force on the thirtieth day following the date of deposit of at least five instruments of ratification, acceptance or approval of such Protocol, or of accession thereto, provided that no Protocol shall enter into force before the Convention. Should the requirements for entry into force of a Protocol be met prior to those for entry into force of the Convention pursuant to paragraph 1, such Protocol shall enter into force on the same date as the Convention.

3. Thereafter, this Convention and any Protocol shall enter into force with respect to any State referred to in articles 28 or 30 on the thirtieth day following the date of deposit of its instrument of ratification, acceptance, approval or accession.

Article 32

DENUNCIATION

1. At any time after two years from the date of entry into force of this Convention with respect to a Party, that Party may denounce the Convention by giving written notification to the Depositary.

2. Except as may be otherwise provided in any Protocol to this Convention, any Party may, at any time after two years from the date of entry into force of such Protocol with respect to that Party, denounce the Protocol by giving written notification to the Depositary.

3. Denunciation shall take effect ninety days after the date on which notification of denunciation is received by the Depositary.

4. Any Party which denounces this Convention shall be considered as also having denounced any Protocol to which it was a Party.

5. Any Party which, upon its denunciation of a Protocol, is no longer a Party to any Protocol to this Convention, shall be considered as also having denounced this Convention.

Article 33

RESPONSIBILITIES OF THE DEPOSITARY

1. The Depositary shall inform the Parties, as well as the Organisation:

(a) of the signature of this Convention and of any Protocol thereto and of the deposit of instruments of ratification, acceptance, approval, or accession in accordance with articles 29 and 30;

(b) of the date on which the Convention and any Protocol will come into force in accordance with the provisions of article 31;

(c) of notification of denunciation made in accordance with article 32;

(d) of notification of any addition to the Convention Area in accordance with article 3;

(e) of the amendments adopted with respect to the Convention and to any Protocol, their acceptance by the Parties and the date of their entry into force in accordance with the provisions of article 24; and

(f) of the adoption of new annexes and of the amendments of any annex in accordance with article 25.

2. The original of this Convention and of any Protocol thereto shall be deposited with the Depositary who shall send certified copies thereof to the Signatories, the Parties, to the Organisation and to the Secretary–General of the United Nations for registration and publication in accordance with article 102 of the United Nations Charter.

4.23 Bellagio Draft Treaty Concerning the Use of Transboundary Groundwaters, 1989. *Reprinted in* 1 Basic Documents of International Environmental Law 42 (H. Hohmann ed. 1992)

Agreement Concerning the Use of Transboundary Groundwaters

The High Contracting Parties, ______ and ______,

Motivated by the spirit of cordiality and cooperation which characterizes the relations between them;

Desirous of expanding the scope of their concerted actions with respect to the problems confronting their Peoples along their common frontier;

Recognizing the critical importance of their transboundary water resources and the need to enhance the rational use and conservation of the said resources on a long-term basis;

Noting especially the present unsatisfactory state of protection and control of their transboundary groundwaters as well as the prospects of crisis conditions in some areas because of increasing demands upon, and the decreasing quality of, those groundwaters;

Seeking to provide for the utilization, protection and control of those groundwaters on an equitable basis and, to that end, for the creation and maintenance of an adequate data base;

Recognizing that the optimum and efficient use of their transboundary water resources is essential to the interests of both Parties;

Resolving to protect the quality of the transboundary groundwaters for present and future generations;

Wishing to resolve amicably any differences that may arise in connection with the use, protection or control of the said transboundary groundwaters and, for that purpose, to utilize a joint agency; and

Concluding that the best means to achieve the rational management of their transboundary water resources and the protection of the underground environment is to adopt, in principle, an integrated approach including, where appropriate, the conjunctive use of surface water and groundwater in their border region,

Have agreed as follows:

Article I

Definitions

As used in this Agreement:

1. "Aquifer" means a subsurface waterbearing geologic formation from which significant quantities of water may be extracted.

2. "Border region" means the area within approximately ______ kilometers from each side of the mutual boundary as set forth on the annexed map.

3. "The Commission" means the agency designated in Article III, para. 1, of this Agreement.

4. "Conjunctive Use" means the integrated development and management of surface and groundwater as a total water supply system.

5. "Contaminant" means any substance, species or energy which detrimentally affects directly, indirectly, cumulatively or in combination with other substances, human health or safety or agricultural or industrial products or processes, or flora, fauna or an ecosystem.

6. "Contamination" means any detrimental chemical, physical, biological, or temperature change in the content or characteristics of a body of water.

7. "Depletion" means the withdrawal of water from an aquifer at a rate faster than it is recharged, otherwise known as "mining" the water.

8. "Drought" means a condition of abnormal water scarcity in a specific area resulting from natural conditions.

9. "Drought Alert" means the declared condition provided for in Article XII.

10. "Drought Emergency" means the declared emergency provided for in Article XII.

11. "Drought Management Plan" means the plan provided for pursuant to Article XII.

12. "Environmental sensitivity" means vulnerability or susceptibility to changes detrimentally affecting the quality of life or one or more biological or physical systems.

13. "Government(s)" means the governments of the Parties to this Agreement.

14. "Groundwater" means the water in aquifers.

15. "Impairment" means any physical change in an aquifer or its recharge area which significantly reduces or restricts the potential for use of the waters of the aquifer.

16. "Interrelated surface water" means those surface waters in the territory of either Party, the quantity or quality of which is affected by the outflows from, or the inflows to, transboundary groundwater.

17. "Pollution" means the introduction of any contaminant by man, directly or indirectly, into groundwaters or surface waters.

18. "Public Health Emergency" means the declared emergency provided for in Article IX.

19. "Recharge" means the addition of water to an aquifer by infiltration of precipitation through the soil or of water from surface streams, lakes, or reservoirs, by discharges of water to the land surface, or by injection of water into the aquifer through wells.

20. "Transboundary aquifer" means an aquifer intersected by a common boundary.

21. "Transboundary Groundwater Conservation Area" means an area declared by the Commission pursuant to Article VII.

22. "Transboundary groundwaters" means waters in transboundary aquifers.

Article II

General Purposes

1. The Parties recognize their common interest and responsibility in ensuring the reasonable and equitable development and management of groundwaters in the border region for the well being of their Peoples.

2. Accordingly, the Parties have entered into this Agreement in order to attain the optimum utilization and conservation of transboundary groundwaters and to protect the underground environment. It is also the purpose of the Parties to develop and maintain reliable data and information concerning transboundary aquifers and their waters in order to use and protect these waters in a rational and informed manner.

Article III

The Commission Responsible Under this Agreement

1. The ______ Commission is designated as the Parties' agency to carry out the functions and responsibilities provided for by this Agreement.

2. The Commission shall be authorized a technical staff, which, in collaboration with the technical staffs of the Governments, shall assist the Commission in the accomplishment of its functions and responsibilities.

3. The Commission is authorized to declare Transboundary Groundwater Conservation Areas, Drought Alerts, Drought Emergencies and Public Health Emergencies, and to promulgate the corresponding plans and Depletion Plans, in accordance with the provisions of this Agreement.

4. The Commission shall have jurisdiction over such additional matters concerning the border region as are from time to time referred to it by the Governments jointly.

5. The Commission shall prepare and propose to the Governments a budget, conforming insofar as practicable to the budget cycles and procedures of the Governments, covering the projected expenses and capital costs of the Commission's joint operations, plant and staff. The total amount of each budget shall be divided between the Governments in the proportions agreed upon by the Commission and approved by the Governments.

6. The budget for the separate operating costs of each national section shall be the responsibility of the respective Government.

7. The Governments may jointly refer a specific matter relating to transboundary groundwater to the Commission for investigation or action. Individually Governments may request the Commission's advice relating to transboundary groundwaters on matters originating within the requesting Government's portion of the order region.

8. The Commission shall cause each such referral and request to be taken up and investigated, studied or acted upon, as appropriate. The Commission shall render a report to the Governments on every referral and request taken up.

Article IV

Enforcement and Oversight Responsibilities

1. The enforcement of water quality and quantity measures and related land use controls within the territory of each Party shall be the responsibility of that Party or of its political subdivisions, as appropriate.

2. The Commission shall biennially conduct a review of the water quality and quantity control measures taken within each Party's territory affecting the border region and shall issue a Report containing its assessment of the adequacy and effectiveness of programs for the protection and improvement of the transboundary aquifers and their waters and withdrawal and land use controls, including with respect to any Transboundary Groundwater Conservation Areas, Depletion Plans, Drought Emergency Plans and Health Emergencies. To that end, each Government shall furnish the Commission with the relevant data, information, and studies for use by the Commission in preparing its Report, in accordance with the reporting formats provided by the Commission.

3. In addition to facilitating, as needed, the Commission's oversight responsibilities under paragraph 2, each Government shall make a biennial Report to the Commission specifying the water quality and conservation measures taken; quantities withdrawn, transferred and exchanged, and any problems encountered in carrying out the provisions of this Agreement or in implementation of any of the conservation, depletion and drought management plans and health emergency measures adopted.

Article V

Establishment and Maintenance of the Database

1. The Commission is charged with the creation and maintenance of a comprehensive and unified database pertaining to transboundary groundwaters, in the languages of the Parties. The database shall include an inventory of all transboundary groundwater resources taking into account quantity, quality, aquifer geometry, recharge rates, interaction with surface waters, and other pertinent data and shall identify all transboundary aquifers.

2. The Commission shall carry out studies directly, or through research programs conducted by or with other bodies, public or private:

(a) to identify inadequacies in available data and to propose remedial action;

(b) to examine present and potential future uses of said groundwaters, taking into account demographic projections and socio-economic development plans;

(c) to assess the impact of present and potential development on transboundary groundwaters and related resources;

(d) to study possible alternative sources of surface water and groundwater for use in the border region, taking into account the quantity and quality of the waters and the potential for the conjunctive use of the available waters; and

(e) to examine the potential for, and the consequences of, drought, floods, and contamination in the border region.

3. The Parties undertake to facilitate the acquisition of information and data by the Commission on a timely basis in accordance with the Commission's requirements.

4. The Commission shall compile, analyze, and disseminate the data, information and studies and provide the results to the Governments.

Article VI

Water Quality Protection

1. The Parties undertake cooperatively to protect and to improve, insofar as practicable, the quality of transboundary aquifers and their waters in conjunction with their programs for surface water quality control, and to avoid appreciable harm in or to the territories of the Parties.

2. The Governments shall promptly inform the Commission of any actual or planned, significantly polluting discharge into transboundary groundwaters or recharge areas, or of other activity with the potential for significant leaching into transboundary groundwaters.

3. The Commission shall without delay consider the gravity of any situation indicating significant groundwater contamination, or the threat thereof, in any part of the border region in accordance with the provisions of Article VII.

Article VII

Transboundary Groundwater Conservation Areas

1. The Commission shall determine the desirability of declaring any area within the border region containing transboundary groundwaters to be a Transboundary Groundwater Conservation Area.

2. In the event that the Commission determines that a Transboundary Groundwater Conservation Area is desirable, such determination shall be reported to the Governments with a draft of the proposed declaration and justification therefore, including the delineation of the area and its aquifer(s)

3. If no Government files an objection with the Commission within one hundred eighty (180) days, the Commission shall issue the formal declaration. Any objection(s) filed shall specify, with an explanation, the objectionable section(s) of the proposed declaration or justification or both.

4. Unless an objection requires termination of consideration, the Commission shall within ninety (90) days of receipt of objections, report to the Governments a revised proposed declaration, to be effective within ninety (90) days, unless a Government files a subsequent objection with the Commission. If no subsequent objection is filed within the said ninety (90) day period, the formal declaration shall be issued by the Commission. If a subsequent objection is filed within the ninety (90) day period, the Commission shall refer the matter, together with the entire record, to the Governments for resolution by consultation.

5. In making its determination, the Commission shall consider whether:

(a) groundwater withdrawals exceed or are likely to exceed recharge so as to endanger yield or water quality or are likely to diminish the quantity or quality of interrelated surface waters;

(b) recharge has been or may become impaired;

(c) the use of the included aquifer(s) as an important source of drinking water has been, or may become impaired;

(d) the aquifer(s) have been or may become contaminated; and

(e) recurring or persistent drought conditions necessitate management of all or some water supplies in the particular area.

6. In making its determination, the Commission shall take into account the impact of the implementation of the declaration under consideration on the sources and uses of water previously allocated by agreements between the Parties or under the Drought Management Plan.

7. The Commission shall periodically review the appropriateness of continuing or modifying Transboundary Groundwater Conservation Areas.

Article VIII

Comprehensive Management Plans

1. For each declared Transboundary Groundwater Conservation Area, the Commission shall prepare a Comprehensive Management Plan for the rational development, use, protection and control of the waters in the Transboundary Groundwater Conservation Area.

2. A Comprehensive Management Plan may:

(a) prescribe measures to prevent, eliminate or mitigate degradation of transboundary groundwater quality, and for that purpose may:

(1) classify transboundary groundwaters according to use and coordinate the formulation of water quality standards;

(2) identify toxic and hazardous contaminants in the Area and require a continuing record of such substances from origin to disposal;

(3) establish criteria for the safe storage of wastes and maintain an inventory of dumpsites, abandoned as well as active, that have caused or may cause transboundary aquifer pollution;

(4) propose a scheme for monitoring water quality conditions including the placement and operation of test wells and for remedial actions where required, including pretreatment and effluent discharge limitations and charges; and

(5) provide for the establishment, where required, of protective zones in which land use must be regulated.

(b) allocate the uses of groundwaters and interrelated surface waters taking into account any other allocation(s) previously made applicable within the Transboundary Groundwater Conservation Area.

(c) prescribe measures including pumping limitations, criteria for well placement and number of new wells, retirement of existing wells, imposition of extraction fees, planned depletion regimes or reservations of groundwaters for future use.

(d) arrange, where conditions are favorable, programs of transboundary aquifer recharge.

(e) articulate programs of conjunctive use where appropriate.

(f) prescribe the integration and coordination of water quality and quantity control programs.

(g) include other measures and actions as may be deemed appropriate by the Commission.

3. In making any allocations of water uses within a Comprehensive Management Plan, the Commission shall consider all relevant factors such as:

(a) hydrogeology and meteorology;

(b) existing and planned uses;

(c) environmental sensitivity;

(d) quality control requirements;

(e) socio-economic implications (including dependency);

(f) water conservation practices (including efficiency of water use);

(g) artificial recharge potential; and

(h) comparative costs and implications of alternative sources of supply.

The weight to be given to each factor is to be determined by its importance in comparison with that of the other relevant factors.

4. The Commission shall submit proposed Comprehensive Management Plans to the Governments.

(a) If no Government files an objection with the Commission within one hundred eighty (180) days, the Commission shall adopt the Plan and monitor its implementation.

(b) A Government's objections shall specify with an explanation the objectionable portions of the proposed Comprehensive Management Plan.

(c) Within ninety (90) days of receipt of objections, the Commission shall submit to the Governments a revised proposed Comprehensive Management Plan to be effective within ninety (90) days unless a subsequent objection is filed. If no subsequent objection is filed with the ninety (90) day period, the proposed Comprehensive Management Plan shall be adopted and the Commission shall monitor its implementation. If subsequent objections are filed within the ninety (90) day period, the Commission shall refer the matter, together with the entire record, to the Governments for resolution by consultation.

5. The Commission is authorized to approve advances and exchanges of water consistent with the objectives of the applicable Comprehensive Management Plan.

6. The Commission shall monitor and evaluate the measures taken under the Comprehensive Management Plan and shall propose, as appropriate, modifications thereto.

Article IX

Public Health Emergencies

1. Upon a determination by the Commission or any Government that there is an imminent or actual public health hazard involving the contamination of transboundary groundwaters, the Commission shall notify the respective Governments, and may declare a Public Health Emergency for a stated period.

2. In the event that the Public Health Emergency is not mitigated or abated within the initial stated period, the Commission may extend the emergency for such additional period as may be deemed necessary under the circumstances.

3. On the basis of the declaration, the Commission shall have authority to investigate the area of imminent or actual contamination and to prescribe measures to prevent, eliminate or mitigate the public health hazard.

4. The Governments shall provide the indicated information, data, studies and reports concerning public health emergencies as set forth in Paragraphs 2 and 3 of Article IV.

Article X

Planned Depletion

1. The Commission, after evaluation of all relevant considerations, may prepare and, with the consent of the Governments, may approve a plan for the depletion of an aquifer over a calculated period. The plan may apportion the uses and specify the rates and means of extraction of the transboundary groundwaters, and may authorize advances, exchanges and transboundary transfers of water consistent with the objectives of the Depletion Plan.

2. The Governments shall provide the indicated information, data, studies and reports concerning depletion as set forth in Paragraphs 2 and 3 of Article IV.

Article XI

Transboundary Transfers

Nothing in this Agreement shall be so construed as to preclude either short-term or long-term transfers of waters between the Parties under terms and conditions approved by the Commission.

Article XII

Planning for Drought

1. The Commission shall, within two (2) years of the coming into force of this Agreement, complete the preparation of a Drought Management Plan applicable to the border region for activation in the region, or in parts thereof, in the event of drought. The completed Plan shall be submitted to the Governments for standby approval.

2. The Drought Management Plan shall:

(a) specify the hydrometeorological preconditions for the declaration of a Drought Alert and, thereunder, the conservation measures to be observed by all water users within the border region;

(b) specify the hydrometeorological preconditions for the declaration of a Drought Emergency and, thereunder, the specific measures to be observed by all water users within the border region;

(c) provide for the monitoring of the hydrometeorological conditions generally in the border region, and compliance with prescribed conservation or other specific measures under any Drought Alert or Drought Emergency; and

(d) provide for periodic reports to the Governments during any Drought Alert or Drought Emergency, to include any proposed modifications to the Drought Emergency Plan and any modifications made to the prescribed measures under any Drought Alert or Drought Emergency.

3. The Drought Management Plan may:

(a) designate and reserve certain transboundary aquifers or specific well sites for use in times of drought;

(b) provide, for the duration of any declared Drought Emergency:

(1) the conjunctive management of groundwater and surface water supplies within or made available to the border region or part(s) thereof governed by the declaration;

(2) increases and reductions in the normal allowable withdrawals and at variance with allocations made under a Comprehensive Management Plan for a Transboundary Groundwater Conservation Area or by prior agreements between the Parties, maintaining to the extent practicable the established withdrawal ratios between the Parties and an equitable balance of all emergency obligations.

(3) authorization to use designated and reserved groundwaters within the border region.

(c) include other structural and nonstructural measures deemed likely to be needed under various drought conditions.

4. The conservation and other specific measures provided in the Plan for Drought Alert declarations or Drought Emergency declarations may be modified or suspended by the Commission to meet the specific requirements of the situation at the time of such declarations and during the time such declarations remain in force.

5. The authority to determine the existence of the preconditions specified in the approved Drought Management Plan and to declare drought alerts and drought emergencies thereunder, in any portion of the border region, is vested in the Commission.

6. The Commission is authorized to modify or terminate a declaration of Drought alert or of Drought Emergency when the hydrometeorological conditions so warrant.

7. Declarations of Drought Alert and Drought Emergency, and modifications to or termination of the same, shall be immediately communicated to the Governments and published so as to come to the attention of all water users in the border region.

8. The Governments shall provide the indicated information, data, studies and reports concerning drought as set forth in Paragraphs 2 and 3 of Article IV.

Article XIII

Inquiry in the Public Interest

1. The Commission shall by general notice invite written statements and information from all persons professing interest in the groundwater-related conditions and activities in the portion of the border region for which a Transboundary Groundwater Conservation Area declaration, a Comprehensive Management Plan, a Depletion Plan, a transboundary transfer, or a Drought Alert or Emergency declaration is under consideration.

2. All submissions received pursuant to Paragraph 1 shall be taken into account by the Commission.

3. Whenever the Commission deems that public interest warrants, it shall schedule and conduct hearings open to the public in appropriate places and facilities in the border region, and shall make and publish a record of such hearings.

4. Any person professing an interest may also petition the Commission at any time requesting the Commission to schedule a hearing or to invite written statements and information concerning groundwater conditions in the border region, or urging the Commission to take a particular action under this Agreement.

5. When deemed useful by the Commission, technical meetings, workshops and briefings relating to transboundary groundwater matters may be held under the auspices of the Commission or in cooperation with authorities and organizations concerned with the welfare of the border region.

Article XIV

Existing Rights and Obligations

The rights and obligations of the Parties as set forth in prior agreements between the Parties shall not be permanently altered by this Agreement or any measures taken hereunder.

Article XV

Accommodation of Differences

1. The Commission shall expend its best efforts to resolve differences within the Commission with respect to the facts and circumstances of a situation within the purview of this Agreement. Failure to resolve such differences within six (6) months at the technical level of the Commission shall result in the submission of the difference(s), together with the entire record, to the Governments for resolution by consultation.

2. If after good faith consultations during a period of twelve (12) months the Governments are unable to reach an accommodation of a difference or differences between them concerning the facts and circumstances of a situation within the purview of this Agreement, or with respect to which the Commission has been unable to reach agreement,

(a) any Government is entitled to invoke this Article to the effect that a commission of inquiry be appointed and charged with a full and impartial study for the purpose of verification of the facts of the situation;

(b) the Governments shall appoint and instruct the commissioner(s), and defray the expenses of such commissions equally, unless otherwise agreed; and

(c) in the event the Governments fail to agree upon the implementation of this Paragraph within six (6) months from the date of its formal invocation, the ______, at the request of any Government shall, after consultation with each Government, appoint the commissioner(s), instruct the same, and apportion the expenses of the commission, as may be required to render the commission operational.

3. A commission of inquiry appointed under this Article shall render a report to the Governments within the terms of its instructions and on the basis of independent and detailed examination of the data and information made available to it by the Governments and the Commission, and may request such additional data and information as the commission of inquiry deems significant for its deliberations and findings.

4. On the basis of the report of a commission of inquiry, the Parties undertake promptly to enter into consultations for the purpose of reaching an agreed accommodation of the difference(s).

5. The Commission shall expend its best efforts to resolve differences within the Commission with respect to the interpretation of this Agreement, of any declaration, plan or prescribed measure, or of any other relevant document, referral, request or decision. Failure to resolve such differences within six (6) months by the Commission shall result in the submission of such difference(s), together with the record of deliberations, to the Governments for resolution by consultation.

6. Should the Governments, after six (6) months of consultations fail to agree upon a questioned interpretation submitted to them by the Commission, pursuant to Paragraph 5, or that has otherwise arisen, including with respect to the validity or interpretation of any binding decision by the Commission, the provisions of Article XVI of this Agreement shall apply.

Article XVI

Resolution of Disputes

1. If the consultations called for under Article XV do not achieve an agreed accommodation, the Governments shall promptly enter into formal, direct negotiations for the purpose of resolving the disagreement.

2. Should the Governments not achieve agreement after six (6) months of direct negotiations, the Parties shall refer the matter to mediation, conciliation, arbitration, the International Court of Justice or any other means of peaceful settlement, absent a previously agreed, applicable means of dispute settlement binding upon the Parties.

3. In resolving differences and questions affecting the implementation of this Agreement and decisions taken thereunder, the Parties undertake to avoid delay and to facilitate the process of resolution as between themselves and, as appropriate, before any mediator, conciliator, tribunal or other settlement forum, taking into account the importance of timely resolution with respect to critical transboundary groundwater situations.

Article XVII

Amendment

This Agreement may be amended by agreement of the Parties.

4.24 Convention for the Protection of the Marine Environment of the North-East Atlantic ("OSPAR Convention"). Done at Paris, 22 September 1992. Entered into force, 25 March 1998. *Reprinted in* 32 I.L.M. 1069 (1993)

The Contracting Parties,

Recognising that the marine environment and the fauna and flora which it supports are of vital importance to all nations;

Recognising the inherent worth of the marine environment of the North–East Atlantic and the necessity for providing coordinated protection for it;

Recognising that concerted action at national, regional and global levels is essential to prevent and eliminate marine pollution and to achieve sustainable management of the maritime area, that is, the management of human activities in such a manner that the marine ecosystem will continue to sustain the legitimate uses of the sea and will continue to meet the needs of present and future generations;

Mindful that the ecological equilibrium and the legitimate uses of the sea are threatened by pollution;

Considering the recommendations of the United Nations Conference on the Human Environment, held in Stockholm in June 1972;

Considering also the results of the United Nations Conference on the Environment and Development held in Rio de Janeiro in June 1992;

Recalling the relevant provisions of customary international law reflected in Part XII of the United Nations Law of the Sea Convention and, in particular, Article 197 on global and regional cooperation for the protection and preservation of the marine environment;

Considering that the common interests of States concerned with the same marine area should induce them to cooperate at regional or sub-regional levels;

Recalling the positive results obtained within the context of the Convention for the prevention of marine pollution by dumping from ships and aircraft signed in Oslo on 15th February 1972, as amended by the protocols of 2nd March 1983 and 5th December 1989, and the Convention for the prevention of marine pollution from land-based sources signed in Paris on 4th June 1974, as amended by the protocol of 26th March 1986;

Convinced that further international action to prevent and eliminate pollution of the sea should be taken without delay, as part of progressive and coherent measures to protect the marine environment;

Recognising that it may be desirable to adopt, on the regional level, more stringent measures with respect to the prevention and elimination of pollution of the marine environment or with respect to the protection of the marine environment against the adverse effects of human activities than are provided for in international conventions or agreements with a global scope;

Recognising that questions relating to the management of fisheries are appropriately regulated under international and regional agreements dealing specifically with such questions;

Considering that the present Oslo and Paris Conventions do not adequately control some of the many sources of pollution, and that it is therefore justifiable to replace them with the present Convention, which addresses all sources of pollution of the marine environment and the adverse effects of human activities upon it, takes into account the precautionary principle and strengthens regional cooperation;

Have Agreed as follows:

Article 1

DEFINITIONS

For the purposes of the Convention:

(a) "Maritime area" means the internal waters and the territorial seas of the Contracting Parties, the sea beyond and adjacent to the territorial sea under the jurisdiction of the coastal state to the extent recognised by international law, and the high seas, including the bed of all those waters and its sub-soil, situated within the following limits:

(i) those parts of the Atlantic and Arctic Oceans and their dependent seas which lie north of 36 degrees north latitude and between 42 degrees west longitude and 51 degrees east longitude, but excluding:

(1) the Baltic Sea and the Belts lying to the south and east of lines drawn from Hasenore Head to Gniben Point, from Korshage to Spodsbjerg and from Gilbjerg Head to Kullen,

(2) the Mediterranean Sea and its dependent seas as far as the point of intersection of the parallel of 36 degrees north latitude and the meridian of 5 degrees 36' west longitude;

(ii) that part of the Atlantic Ocean north of 59 degrees north latitude and between 44 degrees west longitude and 42 degrees west longitude.

(b) "Internal waters" means the waters on the landward side of the baselines from which the breadth of the territorial sea is measured, extending in the case of watercourses up to the freshwater limit.

(c) "Freshwater limit" means the place in a watercourse where, at low tide and in a period of low freshwater flow, there is an appreciable increase in salinity due to the presence of seawater.

(d) "Pollution" means the introduction by man, directly or indirectly, of substances or energy into the maritime area which results, or is likely to result, in hazards to human health, harm to living resources and marine ecosystems, damage to amenities or interference with other legitimate uses of the sea.

(e) "Land-based sources" means point and diffuse sources on land from which substances or energy reach the maritime area by water, through the air, or directly from the coast. It includes sources associated with any deliberate disposal under the sea-bed made accessible from land by tunnel, pipeline or other means and sources associated with man-made structures placed, in the maritime area under the jurisdiction of a Contracting Party, other than for the purpose of offshore activities.

(f) "Dumping" means

(i) any deliberate disposal in the maritime area of wastes or other matter

(1) from vessels or aircraft;

(2) from offshore installations;

(ii) any deliberate disposal in the maritime area of

(1) vessels or aircraft;

(2) offshore installations and offshore pipelines.

(g) "Dumping" does not include:

(i) the disposal in accordance with the International Convention for the Prevention of Pollution from Ships, 1973, as modified by the Protocol of 1978 relating thereto, or other applicable international law, of wastes or other matter incidental to, or derived from, the normal operations of vessels or aircraft or offshore installations other than wastes or other matter transported by or to vessels or aircraft or offshore installations for the purpose of disposal of such wastes or other matter or derived from the treatment of such wastes or other matter on such vessels or aircraft or offshore installations;

(ii) placement of matter for a purpose other than the mere disposal thereof, provided that, if the placement is for a purpose other than that for which the matter was originally designed or constructed, it is in accordance with the relevant provisions of the Convention; and

(iii) for the purposes of Annex III, the leaving wholly or partly in place of a disused offshore installation or disused offshore pipeline, provided that any such operation takes place in accordance with any relevant provision of the Convention and with other relevant international law.

(h) "Incineration" means any deliberate combustion of wastes or other matter in the maritime area for the purpose of their thermal destruction.

(i) "Incineration" does not include the thermal destruction of wastes or other matter in accordance with applicable international law incidental to, or derived from the normal operation of vessels or aircraft, or offshore installations other than the thermal destruction of wastes or other matter on vessels or aircraft or offshore installations operating for the purpose of such thermal destruction.

(j) "Offshore activities" means activities carried out in the maritime area for the purposes of the exploration, appraisal or exploitation of liquid and gaseous hydrocarbons.

(k) "Offshore sources" means offshore installations and offshore pipelines from which substances or energy reach the maritime area.

(*l*) "Offshore installation" means any man-made structure, plant or vessel or parts thereof, whether floating or fixed to the seabed, placed within the maritime area for the purpose of offshore activities.

(m) "Offshore pipeline" means any pipeline which has been placed in the maritime area for the purpose of offshore activities.

(n) "Vessels or aircraft" means waterborne or airborne craft of any type whatsoever, their parts and other fittings. This expression includes air-cushion craft, floating craft whether self-propelled or not, and other man-made structures in the maritime area and their equipment, but excludes offshore installations and offshore pipelines.

(*o*) "Wastes or other matter" does not include:

(i) human remains;

(ii) offshore installations;

(iii) offshore pipelines;

(iv) unprocessed fish and fish offal discarded from fishing vessels.

(p) "Convention" means, unless the text otherwise indicates, the Convention for the Protection of the Marine Environment of the North–East Atlantic, its Annexes and Appendices.

(q) "Oslo Convention" means the Convention for the Prevention of Marine Pollution by Dumping from Ships and Aircraft signed in Oslo on 15th February 1972, as amended by the protocols of 2nd March 1983 and 5th December 1989.

(r) "Paris Convention" means the Convention for the Prevention of Marine Pollution from Land-based Sources, signed in Paris on 4th June 1974, as amended by the protocol of 26th March 1986. [13 I.L.M. 352 (1974); 27 I.L.M. 625 (1988)]

(s) "Regional economic integration organisation" means an organisation constituted by sovereign States of a given region which has competence in respect of matters governed by the Convention and has been duly authorised, in accordance with its internal procedures, to sign, ratify, accept, approve or accede to the Convention.

Article 2

GENERAL OBLIGATIONS

1. (a) The Contracting Parties shall, in accordance with the provisions of the Convention, take all possible steps to prevent and eliminate pollution and shall take the necessary measures to protect the maritime area against the adverse effects of human activities so as to safeguard human health and to conserve marine ecosystems and, when practicable, restore marine areas which have been adversely affected.

(b) To this end Contracting Parties shall, individually and jointly, adopt programmes and measures and shall harmonise their policies and strategies.

2. The Contracting Parties shall apply:

(a) the precautionary principle, by virtue of which preventive measures are to be taken when there are reasonable grounds for concern that substances or energy introduced, directly or indirectly, into the marine environment may bring about hazards to human health, harm living resources and marine ecosystems, damage amenities or interfere with other legitimate uses of the sea, even when there is no conclusive evidence of a causal relationship between the inputs and the effects;

(b) the polluter pays principle, by virtue of which the costs of pollution prevention, control and reduction measures are to be borne by the polluter.

3. (a) In implementing the Convention, Contracting Parties shall adopt programmes and measures which contain, where appropriate, time-limits for their completion and which take full account of the use of the latest technological developments and practices designed to prevent and eliminate pollution fully.

(b) To this end they shall:

(i) taking into account the criteria set forth in Appendix 1, define with respect to programmes and measures the application of, inter alia,

—best available techniques

—best environmental practice

including, where appropriate, clean technology;

(ii) in carrying out such programmes and measures, ensure the application of best available techniques and best environmental practice as so defined, including, where appropriate, clean technology.

4. The Contracting Parties shall apply the measures they adopt in such a way as to prevent an increase in pollution of the sea outside the maritime area or in other parts of the environment.

5. No provision of the Convention shall be interpreted as preventing the Contracting Parties from taking, individually or jointly, more stringent measures with respect to the prevention and elimination of pollution of the maritime area or with respect to the protection of the maritime area against the adverse effects of human activities.

Article 3

POLLUTION FROM LAND–BASED SOURCES

The Contracting Parties shall take, individually and jointly, all possible steps to prevent and eliminate pollution from land-based sources in accordance with the provisions of the Convention, in particular as provided for in Annex I.

Article 4

POLLUTION BY DUMPING OR INCINERATION

The Contracting Parties shall take, individually and jointly, all possible steps to prevent and eliminate pollution by dumping or incineration of wastes or other matter in accordance with the provisions of the Convention, in particular as provided for in Annex II.

Article 5

POLLUTION FROM OFFSHORE SOURCES

The Contracting Parties shall take, individually and jointly, all possible steps to prevent and eliminate pollution from offshore sources in accordance with the provisions of the Convention, in particular as provided for in Annex III.

Article 6

ASSESSMENT OF THE QUALITY OF THE MARINE ENVIRONMENT

The Contracting Parties shall, in accordance with the provisions of the Convention, in particular as provided for in Annex IV:

(a) undertake and publish at regular intervals joint assessments of the quality status of the marine environment and of its development, for the maritime area or for regions or subregions thereof;

(b) include in such assessments both an evaluation of the effectiveness of the measures taken and planned for the protection of the marine environment and the identification of priorities for action.

Article 7

POLLUTION FROM OTHER SOURCES

The Contracting Parties shall cooperate with a view to adopting Annexes, in addition to the Annexes mentioned in Articles 3, 4, 5 and 6 above, prescribing measures, procedures and standards to protect the maritime area against pollution from other sources, to the extent that such pollution is not already the subject of effective measures agreed by other international organisations or prescribed by other international conventions.

Article 8

SCIENTIFIC AND TECHNICAL RESEARCH

1. To further the aims of the Convention, the Contracting Parties shall establish complementary or joint programmes of scientific or technical research and, in accordance with a standard procedure, to transmit to the Commission:

(a) the results of such complementary, joint or other relevant research;

(b) details of other relevant programmes of scientific and technical research.

2. In so doing, the Contracting Parties shall have regard to the work carried out, in these fields, by the appropriate international organisations and agencies.

Article 9

ACCESS TO INFORMATION

1. The Contracting Parties shall ensure that their competent authorities are required to make available the information described in paragraph 2 of this Article to any natural or legal person, in response to any reasonable request, without that

person's having to prove an interest, without unreasonable charges, as soon as possible and at the latest within two months.

2. The information referred to in paragraph 1 of this Article is any available information in written, visual, aural or data-base form on the state of the maritime area, on activities or measures adversely affecting or likely to affect it and on activities or measures introduced in accordance with the Convention.

3. The provisions of this Article shall not affect the right of Contracting Parties, in accordance with their national legal systems and applicable international regulations, to provide for a request for such information to be refused where it affects:

(a) the confidentiality of the proceedings of public authorities, international relations and national defence;

(b) public security;

(c) matters which are, or have been, sub judice, or under enquiry (including disciplinary enquiries), or which are the subject of preliminary investigation proceedings;

(d) commercial and industrial confidentiality, including intellectual property;

(e) the confidentiality of personal data and/or files;

(f) material supplied by a third party without that party being under a legal obligation to do so;

(g) material, the disclosure of which would make it more likely that the environment to which such material related would be damaged.

4. The reasons for a refusal to provide the information requested must be given.

Article 10

COMMISSION

1. A Commission, made up of representatives of each of the Contracting Parties, is hereby established. The Commission shall meet at regular intervals and at any time when, due to special circumstances, it is so decided in accordance with the Rules of Procedure.

2. It shall be the duty of the Commission:

(a) to supervise the implementation of the Convention;

(b) generally to review the condition of the maritime area, the effectiveness of the measures being adopted, the priorities and the need for any additional or different measures;

(c) to draw up, in accordance with the General Obligations of the Convention, programmes and measures for the prevention and elimination of pollution and for the control of activities which may, directly or indirectly, adversely affect the maritime area; such programmes and measure may, when appropriate, include economic instruments;

(d) to establish at regular intervals its programme of work;

(e) to set up such subsidiary bodies as it considers necessary and to define their terms of reference;

(f) to consider and, where appropriate, adopt proposals for the amendment of the Convention in accordance with Articles 15, 16, 17, 18, 19 and 27;

(g) to discharge the functions conferred by Articles 21 and 23 and such other functions as may be appropriate under the terms of the Convention;

3. To these ends the Commission may, inter alia, adopt decisions and recommendations in accordance with Article 13.

4. The Commission shall draw up its Rules of Procedure which shall be adopted by unanimous vote of the Contracting Parties.

5. The Commission shall draw up its Financial Regulations which shall be adopted by unanimous vote of the Contracting Parties.

Article 11

OBSERVERS

1. The Commission may, by unanimous vote of the Contracting Parties, decide to admit as an observer:

(a) any State which is not a Contracting Party to the Convention;

(b) any international governmental or any non-governmental organisation the activities of which are related to the Convention.

2. Such observers may participate in meetings of the Commission but without the right to vote and may present to the Commission any information or reports relevant to the objectives of the Convention.

3. The conditions for the admission and the participation of observers shall be set in the Rules of Procedure of the Commission.

Article 12

SECRETARIAT

1. A permanent Secretariat is hereby established.

2. The Commission shall appoint an Executive Secretary and determine the duties of that post and the terms and conditions upon which it is to be held.

3. The Executive Secretary shall perform the functions that are necessary for the administration of the Convention and for the work of the Commission as well as the other tasks entrusted to the Executive Secretary by the Commission in accordance with its Rules of Procedure and its Financial Regulations.

Article 13

DECISIONS AND RECOMMENDATIONS

1. Decisions and recommendations shall be adopted by unanimous vote of the Contracting Parties. Should unanimity not be attainable, and unless otherwise provided in the Convention, the Commission may nonetheless adopt decisions or recommendations by a three-quarters majority vote of the Contracting Parties.

2. A decision shall be binding on the expiry of a period of two hundred days after its adoption for those Contracting Parties that voted for it and have not within that period notified the Executive Secretary in writing that they are unable to accept the decision, provided that at the expiry of that period three-quarters of the Contracting Parties have either voted for the decision and not withdrawn their acceptance or notified the Executive Secretary in writing that they are able to accept the decision. Such a decision shall become binding on any other Contracting Party which has notified the Executive Secretary in writing that it is able to accept the decision from the moment of that notification or after the expiry of a period of two hundred days after the adoption of the decision, whichever is later.

3. A notification under paragraph 2 of this Article to the Executive Secretary may indicate that a Contracting Party is unable to accept a decision insofar as it relates to one or more of its dependent or autonomous territories to which the Convention applies.

4. All decisions adopted by the Commission shall, where appropriate, contain provisions specifying the timetable by which the decision shall be implemented.

5. Recommendations shall have no binding force.

6. Decisions concerning any Annex or Appendix shall be taken only by the Contracting Parties bound by the Annex or Appendix concerned.

Article 14

STATUS OF ANNEXES AND APPENDICES

1. The Annexes and Appendices form an integral part of the Convention.

2. The Appendices shall be of a scientific, technical or administrative nature.

Article 15

AMENDMENT OF THE CONVENTION

1. Without prejudice to the provisions of paragraph 2 of Article 27 and to specific provisions applicable to the adoption or amendment of Annexes or Appendices, an amendment to the Convention shall be governed by the present Article.

2. Any Contracting Party may propose an amendment to the Convention. The text of the proposed amendment shall be communicated to the Contracting Parties by the Executive Secretary of the Commission at least six months before the meeting of the Commission at which it is proposed for adoption. The Executive Secretary shall also communicate the proposed amendment to the signatories to the Convention for information.

3. The Commission shall adopt the amendment by unanimous vote of the Contracting Parties.

4. The adopted amendment shall be submitted by the Depositary Government to the Contracting Parties for ratification, acceptance or approval. Ratification, acceptance or approval of the amendment shall be notified to the Depositary Government in writing.

5. The amendment shall enter into force for those Contracting Parties which have ratified, accepted or approved it on the thirtieth day after receipt by the Depositary Government of notification of its ratification, acceptance or approval by at least seven Contracting Parties. Thereafter the amendment shall enter into force for any other Contracting Party on the thirtieth day after that Contracting Party has deposited its instrument of ratification, acceptance or approval of the amendment.

Article 16

ADOPTION OF ANNEXES

The provisions of Article 15 relating to the amendment of the Convention shall also apply to the proposal, adoption and entry into force of an Annex to the Convention, except that the Commission shall adopt any Annex referred to in Article 7 by a three-quarters majority vote of the Contracting Parties.

Article 17

AMENDMENT OF ANNEXES

1. The provisions of Article 15 relating to the amendment of the Convention shall also apply to an amendment to an Annex to the Convention, except that the Commission shall adopt amendments to any Annex referred to in Articles 3, 4, 5, 6 or 7 by a three-quarters majority vote of the Contracting Parties bound by that Annex.

2. If the amendment of an Annex is related to an amendment to the Convention, the amendment of the Annex shall be governed by the same provisions as apply to the amendment to the Convention.

Article 18

ADOPTION OF APPENDICES

1. If a proposed Appendix is related to an amendment to the Convention or an Annex, proposed for adoption in accordance with Article 15 or Article 17, the proposal, adoption and entry into force of that Appendix shall be governed by the same provisions as apply to the proposal, adoption and entry into force of that amendment.

2. If a proposed Appendix is related to an Annex to the Convention, proposed for adoption in accordance with Article 16, the proposal, adoption and entry into force of that Appendix shall be governed by the same provisions as apply to the proposal, adoption and entry into force of that Annex.

Article 19

AMENDMENT OF APPENDICES

1. Any Contracting Party bound by an Appendix may propose an amendment to that Appendix. The text of the proposed amendment shall be communicated to all Contracting Parties to the Convention by the Executive Secretary of the Commission as provided for in paragraph 2 of Article 15.

2. The Commission shall adopt the amendment to an Appendix by a three-quarters majority vote of the Contracting Parties bound by that Appendix.

3. An amendment to an Appendix shall enter into force on the expiry of a period of two hundred days after its adoption for those Contracting Parties which are bound by that Appendix and have not within that period notified the Depositary Government in writing that they are unable to accept that amendment, provided that at the expiry of that period three-quarters of the Contracting Parties bound by that Appendix have either voted for the amendment and not withdrawn their acceptance or have notified the Depositary Government in writing that they are able to accept the amendment.

4. A notification under paragraph 3 of this Article to the Depositary Government may indicate that a Contracting Party is unable to accept the amendment insofar as it relates to one or more of its dependent or autonomous territories to which the Convention applies.

5. An amendment to an Appendix shall become binding on any other Contracting Party bound by the Appendix which has notified the Depositary Government in writing that it is able to accept the amendment from the moment of that notification or after the expiry of a period of two hundred days after the adoption of the amendment, whichever is later.

6. The Depositary Government shall without delay notify all Contracting Parties of any such notification received.

7. If the amendment of an Appendix is related to an amendment to the Convention or an Annex, the amendment of the Appendix shall be governed by the same provisions as apply to the amendment to the Convention or that Annex.

Article 20

RIGHT TO VOTE

1. Each Contracting Party shall have one vote in the Commission.

2. Notwithstanding the provisions of paragraph 1 of this Article, the European Economic Community and other regional economic integration organisations, within

the areas of their competence, are entitled to a number of votes equal to the number of their Member States which are Contracting Parties to the Convention. Those organisations shall not exercise their right to vote in cases where their Member States exercise theirs and conversely.

Article 21

TRANSBOUNDARY POLLUTION

1. When pollution originating from a Contracting Party is likely to prejudice the interests of one or more of the other Contracting Parties to the Convention, the Contracting Parties concerned shall enter into consultation, at the request of any one of them, with a view to negotiating a cooperation agreement.

2. At the request of any Contracting Party concerned, the Commission shall consider the question and may make recommendations with a view to reaching a satisfactory solution.

3. An agreement referred to in paragraph 1 of this Article may, inter alia, define the areas to which it shall apply, the quality objectives to be achieved and the methods for achieving these objectives, including methods for the application of appropriate standards and the scientific and technical information to be collected.

4. The Contracting Parties signatory to such an agreement shall, through the medium of the Commission, inform the other Contracting Parties of its purport and of the progress made in putting it into effect.

Article 22

REPORTING TO THE COMMISSION

The Contracting Parties shall report to the Commission at regular intervals on:

(a) the legal, regulatory, or other measures taken by them for the implementation of the provisions of the Convention and of decisions and recommendations adopted thereunder, including in particular measures taken to prevent and punish conduct in contravention of those provisions;

(b) the effectiveness of the measures referred to in subparagraph (a) of this Article;

(c) problems encountered in the implementation of the provisions referred to in subparagraph (a) of this Article.

Article 23

COMPLIANCE

The Commission shall:

(a) on the basis of the periodical reports referred to in Article 22 and any other report submitted by the Contracting Parties, assess their compliance with the Convention and the decisions and recommendations adopted thereunder;

(b) when appropriate, decide upon and call for steps to bring about full compliance with the Convention, and decisions adopted thereunder, and promote the implementation of recommendations, including measures to assist a Contracting Party to carry out its obligations.

Article 24

REGIONALISATION

The Commission may decide that any decision or recommendation adopted by it shall apply to all, or a specified part, of the maritime area and may provide for different timetables to be applied, having regard to the differences between ecological and economic conditions in the various regions and sub-regions covered by the Convention.

Article 25

SIGNATURE

The Convention shall be open for signature at Paris from 22nd September 1992 to 30th June 1993 by:

(a) the Contracting Parties to the Oslo Convention or the Paris Convention;

(b) any other coastal State bordering the maritime area;

(c) any State located upstream on watercourses reaching the maritime area;

(d) any regional economic integration organisation having as a member at least one State to which any of the subparagraphs (a) to (c) of this Article applies.

Article 26

RATIFICATION, ACCEPTANCE OR APPROVAL

The Convention shall be subject to ratification, acceptance or approval. The instruments of ratification, acceptance or approval shall be deposited with the Government of the French Republic.

Article 27

ACCESSIONS

1. After 30th June 1993, the Convention shall be open for accession by the States and regional economic integration organisations referred to in Article 25.

2. The Contracting Parties may unanimously invite States or regional economic integration organisations not referred to in Article 25 to accede to the Convention. In the case of such an accession, the definition of the maritime area shall, if necessary, be amended by a decision of the Commission adopted by unanimous vote of the Contracting Parties. Any such amendment shall enter into force after unanimous approval of all the Contracting Parties on the thirtieth day after the receipt of the last notification by the Depositary Government.

3. Any such accession shall relate to the Convention including any Annex and any Appendix that have been adopted at the date of such accession, except when the instrument of accession contains an express declaration of non-acceptance of one or several Annexes other than Annexes I, II, III and IV.

4. The instruments of accession shall be deposited with the Government of the French Republic.

Article 28

RESERVATIONS

No reservation to the Convention may be made.

Article 29

ENTRY INTO FORCE

1. The Convention shall enter into force on the thirtieth day following the date on which all Contracting Parties to the Oslo Convention and all Contracting Parties to the Paris Convention have deposited their instrument of ratification, acceptance, approval or accession.

2. For any State or regional economic integration organisation not referred to in paragraph 1 of this Article, the Convention shall enter into force in accordance with paragraph 1 of this Article, or on the thirtieth day following the date of the deposit of the instrument of ratification, acceptance, approval or accession by that State or regional economic integration organisations, whichever is later.

Article 30

WITHDRAWAL

1. At any time after the expiry of two years from the date of entry into force of the Convention for a Contracting Party, that Contracting Party may withdraw from the Convention by notification in writing to the Depositary Government.

2. Except as may be otherwise provided in an Annex other than Annexes I to IV to the Convention, any Contracting Party may at any time after the expiry of two years from the date of entry into force of such Annex for that Contracting Party withdraw from such Annex by notification in writing to the Depositary Government.

3. Any withdrawal referred to in paragraphs 1 and 2 of this Article shall take effect one year after the date on which the notification of that withdrawal is received by the Depositary Government.

Article 31

REPLACEMENT OF THE OSLO AND PARIS CONVENTIONS

1. Upon its entry into force, the Convention shall replace the Oslo and Paris Conventions as between the Contracting Parties.

2. Notwithstanding paragraph 1 of this Article, decisions, recommendations and all other agreements adopted under the Oslo Convention or the Paris Convention shall continue to be applicable, unaltered in their legal nature, to the extent that they are compatible with, or not explicitly terminated by, the Convention, any decisions or, in the case of existing recommendations, any recommendations adopted thereunder.

Article 32

SETTLEMENT OF DISPUTES

1. Any disputes between Contracting Parties relating to the interpretation or application of the Convention, which cannot be settled otherwise by the Contracting Parties concerned, for instance by means of inquiry or conciliation within the Commission, shall at the request of any of those Contracting Parties, be submitted to arbitration under the conditions laid down in this Article.

2. Unless the parties to the dispute decide otherwise, the procedure of the arbitration referred to in paragraph 1 of this Article shall be in accordance with paragraphs 3 to 10 of this Article.

3. (a) At the request addressed by one Contracting Party to another Contracting Party in accordance with paragraph 1 of this Article, an arbitral tribunal shall be constituted. The request for arbitration shall state the subject matter of the application including in particular the Articles of the Convention, the interpretation or application of which is in dispute.

(b) The applicant party shall inform the Commission that it has requested the setting up of an arbitral tribunal, stating the name of the other party to the dispute and the Articles of the Convention the interpretation or application of which, in its opinion, is in dispute. The Commission shall forward the information thus received to all Contracting Parties to the Convention.

4. The arbitral tribunal shall consist of three members: each of the parties to the dispute shall appoint an arbitrator; the two arbitrators so appointed shall designate by common agreement the third arbitrator who shall be the chairman of the tribunal. The latter shall not be a national of one of the parties to the dispute, nor have his usual place of residence in the territory of one of these parties, nor be employed by any of them, nor have dealt with the case in any other capacity.

5. (a) If the chairman of the arbitral tribunal has not been designated within two months of the appointment of the second arbitrator, the President of the International Court of Justice shall, at the request of either party, designate him within a further two months' period.

(b) If one of the parties to the dispute does not appoint an arbitrator within two months of receipt of the request, the other party may inform the President of the International Court of Justice who shall designate the chairman of the arbitral tribunal within a further two months' period. Upon designation, the chairman of the arbitral tribunal shall request the party which has not appointed an arbitrator to do so within two months. After such period, he shall inform the President of the International Court of Justice who shall make this appointment within a further two months' period.

6. (a) The arbitral tribunal shall decide according to the rules of international law and, in particular, those of the Convention.

(b) Any arbitral tribunal constituted under the provisions of this Article shall draw up its own rules of procedure.

(c) In the event of a dispute as to whether the arbitral tribunal has jurisdiction, the matter shall be decided by the decision of the arbitral tribunal.

7. (a) The decisions of the arbitral tribunal, both on procedure and on substance, shall be taken by majority voting of its members.

(b) The arbitral tribunal may take all appropriate measures in order to establish the facts. It may, at the request of one of the parties, recommend essential interim measures of protection.

(c) If two or more arbitral tribunals constituted under the provisions of this Article are seized of requests with identical or similar subjects, they may inform themselves of the procedures for establishing the facts and take them into account as far as possible.

(d) The parties to the dispute shall provide all facilities necessary for the effective conduct of the proceedings.

(e) The absence or default of a party to the dispute shall not constitute an impediment to the proceedings.

8. Unless the arbitral tribunal determines otherwise because of the particular circumstances of the case, the expenses of the tribunal, including the remuneration of its members, shall be borne by the parties to the dispute in equal shares. The tribunal shall keep a record of all its expenses, and shall furnish a final statement thereof to the parties.

9. Any Contracting Party that has an interest of a legal nature in the subject matter of the dispute which may be affected by the decision in the case, may intervene in the proceedings with the consent of the tribunal.

10. (a) The award of the arbitral tribunal shall be accompanied by a statement of reasons. It shall be final and binding upon the parties to the dispute.

(b) Any dispute which may arise between the parties concerning the interpretation or execution of the award may be submitted by either party to the arbitral tribunal which made the award or, if the latter cannot be seized thereof, to another arbitral tribunal constituted for this purpose in the same manner as the first.

Article 33

DUTIES OF THE DEPOSITARY GOVERNMENT

The Depositary Government shall inform the Contracting Parties and the signatories to the Convention:

(a) of the deposit of instruments of ratification, acceptance, approval or accession, of declarations of non-acceptance and of notifications of withdrawal in accordance with Articles 26, 27 and 30;

(b) of the date on which the Convention comes into force in accordance with Article 29;

(c) of the receipt of notifications of acceptance, of the deposit of instruments of ratification, acceptance, approval or accession and of the entry into force of amendments to the Convention and of the adoption and amendment of Annexes or Appendices, in accordance with Articles 15, 16, 17, 18 and

Article 34

ORIGINAL TEXT

The original of the Convention, of which the French and English texts shall be equally authentic, shall be deposited with the Government of the French Republic which shall send certified copies thereof to the Contracting Parties and the signatories to the Convention and shall deposit a certified copy with the Secretary General of the United Nations for registration and publication in accordance with Article 102 of the United Nations Charter.

IN WITNESS WHEREOF, the undersigned, being duly authorised by their respective Governments, have signed this Convention.

DONE at Paris, on the twenty-second day of September 1992

ANNEX I

ON THE PREVENTION AND ELIMINATION OF POLLUTION FROM LAND-BASED SOURCES

Article 1

1. When adopting programmes and measures for the purpose of this Annex, the Contracting Parties shall require, either individually or jointly, the use of

—best available techniques for point sources

—best environmental practice for point and diffuse sources

including, where appropriate, clean technology.

2. When setting priorities and in assessing the nature and extent of the programmes and measures and their time scales, the Contracting Parties shall use the criteria given in Appendix 2.

3. The Contracting Parties shall take preventive measures to minimise the risk of pollution caused by accidents.

4. When adopting programmes and measures in relation to radioactive substances, including waste, the Contracting Parties shall also take account of:

(a) the recommendations of the other appropriate international organisations and agencies;

(b) the monitoring procedures recommended by these international organisations and agencies.

Article 2

1. Point source discharges to the maritime area, and releases into water or air which reach and may affect the maritime area, shall be strictly subject to authorisation or regulation by the competent authorities of the Contracting Parties. Such authorisation or regulation shall, in particular, implement relevant decisions of the Commission which bind the relevant Contracting Party.

2. The Contracting Parties shall provide for a system of regular monitoring and inspection by their competent authorities to assess compliance with authorisations and regulations of releases into water or air.

Article 3

For the purposes of this Annex, it shall, inter alia, be the duty of the Commission to draw up:

(a) plans for the reduction and phasing out of substances that are toxic, persistent and liable to bioaccumulate arising from land-based sources;

(b) when appropriate, programmes and measures for the reduction of inputs of nutrients from urban, municipal, industrial, agricultural and other sources.

ANNEX II

ON THE PREVENTION AND ELIMINATION OF POLLUTION BY DUMPING OR INCINERATION

Article 1

This Annex shall not apply to any deliberate disposal in the maritime area of:

(a) wastes or other matter from offshore installations;

(b) offshore installations and offshore pipelines.

Article 2

Incineration is prohibited.

Article 3

1. The dumping of all wastes or other matter is prohibited, except for those wastes or other matter listed in paragraphs 2 and 3 of this Article.

2. The list referred to in paragraph 1 of this Article is as follows:

(a) dredged material;

(b) inert materials of natural origin, that is solid, chemically unprocessed geological material the chemical constituents of which are unlikely to be released into the marine environment;

(c) sewage sludge until 31st December 1998;

(d) fish waste from industrial fish processing operations;

(e) vessels or aircraft until, at the latest, 31st December 2004.

3. (a) The dumping of low and intermediate level radioactive substances, including wastes, is prohibited.

(b) As an exception to subparagraph 3(a) of this Article, those Contracting Parties, the United Kingdom and France, who wish to retain the option of an exception to subparagraph 3(a) in any case not before the expiry of a period of 15 years from 1st January 1993, shall report to the meeting of the Commission at Ministerial level in 1997 on the steps taken to explore alternative land-based options.

(c) Unless, at or before the expiry of this period of 15 years, the Commission decides by a unanimous vote not to continue the exception provided in subparagraph 3(b), it shall take a decision pursuant to Article 13 of the Convention on the prolongation for a period of 10 years after 1st January 2008 of the prohibition, after which another meeting of the Commission at Ministerial level shall be held. Those Contracting Parties mentioned in subparagraph 3(b) of this Article still wishing to retain the option mentioned in subparagraph 3(b) shall report to the Commission meetings to be held at Ministerial level at two yearly intervals from 1999 onwards about the progress in establishing alternative land-based options and on the results of scientific studies which show that any potential dumping operations would not result in hazards to human health, harm to living resources or marine ecosystems, damage to amenities or interference with other legitimate uses of the sea.

Article 4

The Contracting Parties shall ensure that:

(a) no wastes or other matter listed in paragraph 2 of Article 3 of this Annex shall be dumped without authorisation by their competent authorities, or regulation;

(b) such authorisation or regulation is in accordance with the relevant applicable criteria, guidelines and procedures adopted by the Commission in accordance with Article 6 of this Annex;

(c) with the aim of avoiding situations in which the same dumping operation is authorised or regulated by more than one Contracting Party, their competent authorities shall, as appropriate, consult before granting an authorisation or applying regulation.

2. Any authorisation or regulation under paragraph 1 of this Article shall not permit the dumping of vessels or aircraft containing substances which result or are likely to result in hazards to human health, harm to living resources and marine ecosystems, damage to amenities or interference with other legitimate uses of the sea.

3. Each Contracting Party shall keep, and report to the Commission records of the nature and the quantities of wastes or other matter dumped in accordance with paragraph 1 of this Article, and of the dates, places and methods of dumping.

Article 5

No placement of matter in the maritime area for a purpose other than that for which it was originally designed or constructed shall take place without authorisation or regulation by the competent authority of the relevant Contracting Party. Such authorisation or regulation shall be in accordance with the relevant applicable criteria, guidelines and procedures adopted by the Commission in accordance with Article 6 of this Annex. This provision shall not be taken to permit the dumping of wastes or other matter otherwise prohibited under this Annex.

Article 6

For the purposes of this Annex, it shall, inter alia, be the duty of the Commission to draw up and adopt criteria, guidelines and procedures relating to the dumping of wastes or other matter listed in paragraph 2 of Article 3, and to the placement of matter referred to in Article 5, of this Annex, with a view to preventing and eliminating pollution.

Article 7

The provisions of this Annex concerning dumping shall not apply in case of force majeure, due to stress of weather or any other cause, when the safety of human life or of a vessel or aircraft is threatened. Such dumping shall be so conducted as to minimise the likelihood of damage to human or marine life and shall immediately be reported to the Commission, together with full details of the circumstances and of the nature and quantities of the wastes or other matter dumped.

Article 8

The Contracting Parties shall take appropriate measures, both individually and within relevant international organisations, to prevent and eliminate pollution resulting from the abandonment of vessels or aircraft in the maritime area caused by accidents. In the absence of relevant guidance from such international organisations, the measures taken by individual Contracting Parties should be based on such guidelines as the Commission may adopt.

Article 9

In an emergency, if a Contracting Party considers that wastes or other matter the dumping of which is prohibited under this Annex cannot be disposed of on land without unacceptable danger or damage, it shall forthwith consult other Contracting Parties with a view to finding the most satisfactory methods of storage or the most satisfactory means of destruction or disposal under the prevailing circumstances. The Contracting Party shall inform the Commission of the steps adopted following this consultation. The Contracting Parties pledge themselves to assist one another in such situations.

Article 10

1. Each Contracting Party shall ensure compliance with the provisions of this Annex:

(a) by vessels or aircraft registered in its territory;

(b) by vessels or aircraft loading in its territory the wastes or other matter which are to be dumped or incinerated;

(c) by vessels or aircraft believed to be engaged in dumping or incineration within its internal waters or within its territorial sea or within that part of the sea beyond and adjacent to the territorial sea under the jurisdiction of the coastal state to the extent recognised by international law.

2. Each Contracting Party shall issue instructions to its maritime inspection vessels and aircraft and to other appropriate services to report to its authorities any incidents or conditions in the maritime area which give rise to suspicions that dumping in contravention of the provisions of the present Annex has occurred or is about to occur. Any Contracting Party whose authorities receive such a report shall, if it considers it appropriate, accordingly inform any other Contracting Party concerned.

3. Nothing in this Annex shall abridge the sovereign immunity to which certain vessels are entitled under international law.

ANNEX III

ON THE PREVENTION AND ELIMINATION OF POLLUTION FROM OFFSHORE SOURCES

Article 1

This Annex shall not apply to any deliberate disposal in the maritime area of:

(a) wastes or other matter from vessels or aircraft;

(b) vessels or aircraft.

Article 2

1. When adopting programmes and measures for the purpose of this Annex, the Contracting Parties shall require, either individually or jointly, the use of:

(a) best available techniques

(b) best environmental practice including, where appropriate, clean technology.

2. When setting priorities and in assessing the nature and extent of the programmes and measures and their time scales, the Contracting Parties shall use the criteria given in Appendix 2.

Article 3

1. Any dumping of wastes or other matter from offshore installations is prohibited.

2. This prohibition does not relate to discharges or emissions from offshore sources.

Article 4

1. The use on, or the discharge or emission from, offshore sources of substances which may reach and affect the maritime area shall be strictly subject to authorisation or regulation by the competent authorities of the Contracting Parties. Such authorisation or regulation shall, in particular, implement the relevant applicable decisions, recommendations and all other agreements adopted under the Convention.

2. The competent authorities of the Contracting Parties shall provide for a system of monitoring and inspection to assess compliance with authorisation or regulation as provided for in paragraph 1 of Article 4 of this Annex.

Article 5

1. No disused offshore installation or disused offshore pipeline shall be dumped and no disused offshore installation shall be left wholly or partly in place in the maritime area without a permit issued by the competent authority of the relevant Contracting Party on a case-by-case basis. The Contracting Parties shall ensure that their authorities, when granting such permits, shall implement the relevant applicable decisions, recommendations and all other agreements adopted under the Convention.

2. No such permit shall be issued if the disused offshore installation or disused offshore pipeline contains substances which result or are likely to result in hazards to human health, harm to living resources and marine ecosystems, damage to amenities or interference with other legitimate uses of the sea.

3. Any Contracting Party which intends to take the decision to issue a permit for the dumping of a disused offshore installation or a disused offshore pipeline placed in the maritime area after 1st January 1998 shall, through the medium of the Commission, inform the other Contracting Parties of its reasons for accepting such dumping, in order to make consultation possible.

4. Each Contracting Party shall keep, and report to the Commission, records of the disused offshore installations and disused offshore pipelines dumped and of the disused offshore installations left in place in accordance with the provisions of this Article, and of the dates, places and methods of dumping.

Article 6

Articles 3 and 5 of this Annex shall not apply in case of force majeure, due to stress of weather or any other cause, when the safety of human life or of an offshore installation is threatened. Such dumping shall be so conducted as to minimise the likelihood of damage to human or marine life and shall immediately be reported to the Commission, together with full details of the circumstances and of the nature and quantities of the matter dumped.

Article 7

The Contracting Parties shall take appropriate measures, both individually and within relevant international organisations, to prevent and eliminate pollution resulting from the abandonment of offshore installations in the maritime area caused by accidents. In the absence of relevant guidance from such international organisations, the measures taken by individual Contracting Parties should be based on such guidelines as the Commission may adopt.

Article 8

No placement of a disused offshore installation or a disused offshore pipeline in the maritime area for a purpose other than that for which it was originally designed or constructed shall take place without authorisation or regulation by the competent authority of the relevant Contracting Party. Such authorisation or regulation shall be in accordance with the relevant applicable criteria, guidelines and procedures adopted by the Commission in accordance with subparagraph (d) of Article 10 of this Annex. This provision shall not be taken to permit the dumping of disused offshore installations or disused offshore pipelines in contravention of the provisions of this Annex.

Article 9

1. Each Contracting Party shall issue instructions to its maritime inspection vessels and aircraft and to other appropriate services to report to its authorities any incidents or conditions in the maritime area which give rise to suspicions that a contravention of the provisions of the present Annex has occurred or is about to occur. Any Contracting Party whose authorities receive such a report shall, if it considers it appropriate, accordingly inform any other Contracting Party concerned.

2. Nothing in this Annex shall abridge the sovereign immunity to which certain vessels are entitled under international law.

Article 10

For the purposes of this Annex, it shall, inter alia, be the duty of the Commission:

(a) to collect information about substances which are used in offshore activities and, on the basis of that information, to agree lists of substances for the purposes of paragraph 1 of Article 4 of this Annex;

(b) to list substances which are toxic, persistent and liable to bioaccumulate and to draw up plans for the reduction and phasing out of their use on, or discharge from, offshore sources;

(c) to draw up criteria, guidelines and procedures for the prevention of pollution from dumping of disused offshore installations and of disused offshore pipelines, and the leaving in place of offshore installations, in the maritime area;

(d) to draw up criteria, guidelines and procedures relating to the placement of disused offshore installations and disused offshore pipelines referred to in Article 8 of this Annex, with a view to preventing and eliminating pollution.

ANNEX IV

ON THE ASSESSMENT OF THE QUALITY OF THE MARINE ENVIRONMENT

Article 1

1. For the purposes of this Annex "monitoring" means the repeated measurement of:

(a) the quality of the marine environment and each of its compartments, that is, water, sediments and biota;

(b) activities or natural and anthropogenic inputs which may affect the quality of the marine environment;

(c) the effects of such activities and inputs.

2. Monitoring may be undertaken either for the purposes of ensuring compliance with the Convertion, with the objective of identifying patterns and trends or for research purposes.

Article 2

For the purposes of this Annex, the Contracting Parties shall:

(a) cooperate in carrying out monitoring programmes and submit the resulting data to the Commission;

(b) comply with quality assurance prescriptions and participate in intercalibration exercises;

(c) use and develop, individually or preferably jointly, other duly validated scientific assessment tools, such as modelling, remote sensing and progressive risk assessment strategies;

(d) carry out, individually or preferably jointly, research which is considered necessary to assess the quality of the marine environment, and to increase knowledge and scientific understanding of the marine environment and, in particular, of the relationship between inputs, concentration and effects;

(e) take into account scientific progress which is considered to be useful for such assessment purposes and which has been made elsewhere either on the initiative of individual researchers and research institutions, or through other national and international research programmes or under the auspices of the European Economic Community or other regional economic integration organisations.

Article 3

For the purposes of this Annex, it shall, inter alia, be the duty of the Commission:

(a) to define and impiement programmes of collaborative monitoring and assessment-related research, to draw up codes of practice for the guidance of participants in carrying out these monitoring programmes and to approve the presentation and interpretation of their results;

(b) to carry out assessments taking into account the results of relevant monitoring and research and the data relating to inputs of substances or energy into the maritime area which are provided by virtue of other Annexes to the Convention, as well as other relevant information;

(c) to seek, where appropriate, the advice or services of competent regional organisations and other competent international organisations and competent bodies with a view to incorporating the latest results of scientific research;

(d) to cooperate with competent regional organisations and other competent international organisations in carrying out quality status assessments.

APPENDIX 1 CRITERIA FOR THE DEFINITION OF PRACTICES AND TECHNIQUES MENTIONED IN PARAGRAPH 3(b)(i) OF ARTICLE 2 OF THE CONVENTION

BEST AVAILABLE TECHNIQUES

1. The use of the best available techniques shall emphasise the use of non-waste technology, if available.

2. The term "best available techniques" means the latest stage of development (state of the art) of processes, of facilities or of methods of operation which indicate the practical suitability of a particular measure for limiting discharges, emissions and waste. In determining whether a set of processes, facilities and methods of operation constitute the best available techniques in general or individual cases, special consideration shall be given to:

(a) comparable processes, facilities or methods of operation which have recently been successfully tried out;

(b) technological advances and changes in scientific knowledge and understanding;

(c) the economic feasibility of such techniques;

(d) time limits for installation in both new and existing plants;

(e) the nature and volume of the discharges and emissions concerned.

3. It therefore follows that what is "best available techniques" for a particular process will change with time in the light of technological advances, economic and social factors, as well as changes in scientific knowledge and understanding.

4. If the reduction of discharges and emissions resulting from the use of best available techniques does not lead to environmentally acceptable results, additional measures have to be applied.

5. "Techniques" include both the technology used and the way in which the installation is designed, built, maintained, operated and dismantled.

BEST ENVIRONMENTAL PRACTICE

6. The term "best environmental practice" means the application of the most appropriate combination of environmental control measures and strategies. In making a selection for individual cases, at least the following graduated range of measures should be considered:

(a) the provision of information and education to the public and to users about the environmental consequences of choice of particular activities and choice of products, their use and ultimate disposal;

(b) the development and application of codes of good environmental practice which covers all aspect of the activity in the product's life;

(c) the mandatory application of labels informing users of environmental risks related to a product, its use and ultimate disposal;

(d) saving resources, including energy;

(e) making collection and disposal systems available to the public;

(f) avoiding the use of hazardous substances or products and the generation of hazardous waste;

(g) recycling, recovery and re-use;

(h) the application of economic instruments to activities, products or groups of products;

(i) establishing a system of licensing, involving a range of restrictions or a ban.

7. In determining what combination of measures constitute best environmental practice, in general or individual cases, particular consideration should be given to:

(a) the environmental hazard of the product and its production, use and ultimate disposal;

(b) the substitution by less polluting activities or substances;

(c) the scale of use;

(d) the potential environmental benefit or penalty of substitute materials or activities;

(e) advances and changes in scientific knowledge and understanding;

(f) time limits for implementation;

(g) social and economic implications.

8. It therefore follows that best environmental practice for a particular source will change with time in the light of technological advances, economic and social factors, as well as changes in scientific knowledge and understanding.

9. If the reduction of inputs resulting from the use of best environmental practice does not lead to environmentally acceptable results, additional measures have to be applied and best environmental practice redefined.

APPENDIX 2 CRITERIA MENTIONED IN PARAGRAPH 2 OF ARTICLE 1 OF ANNEX I AND IN PARAGRAPH 2 OF ARTICLE 2 OF ANNEX III

1. When setting priorities and in assessing the nature and extent of the programmes and measures and their time scales, the Contracting Parties shall use the criteria given below:

(a) persistency;

(b) toxicity or other noxious properties;

(c) tendency to bioaccumulation;

(d) radioactivity;

(e) the ratio between observed or (where the results of observations are not yet available) predicted concentrations and no observed effect concentrations;

(f) anthropogenically caused risk of eutrophication;

(g) transboundary significance;

(h) risk of undesirable changes in the marine ecosystem and irreversibility or durability of effects;

(i) interference with harvesting of sea-foods or with other legitimate uses of the sea;

(j) effects on the taste and/or smell of products for human consumption from the sea, or effects on smell, colour, transparency or other characteristics of the water in the marine environment;

(k) distribution pattern (i.e., quantities involved, use pattern and liability to reach the marine environment);

(*l*) non-fulfilment of environmental quality objectives.

2. These criteria are not necessarily of equal importance for the consideration of a particular substance or group of substances.

3. The above criteria indicate that substances which shall be subject to programmes and measures include:

(a) heavy metals and their compounds;

(b) organohalogen compounds (and substances which may form such compounds in the marine environment);

(c) organic compounds of phosphorus and silicon;

(d) biocides such as pesticides, fungicides, herbicides, insecticides, slimicides and chemicals used, inter alia, for the preservation of wood, timber, wood pulp, cellulose, paper, hides and textiles;

(e) oils and hydrocarbons of petroleum origin;

(f) nitrogen and phosphorus compounds;

(g) radioactive substances, including wastes;

(h) persistent synthetic materials which may float, remain in suspension or sink.

4.25 International Convention on Civil Liability for Oil Pollution Damage, 1992.[g] Concluded at London, 27 November 1992. Entered into force 30 May 1996. *Reprinted in* Civil Liability for Oil Pollution Damage, at 47 (IMO 1996) & 5 Weston V.J.12 (1969 Convention)

Article I

For the purposes of this Convention:

1. "Ship" means any sea-going vessel and seaborne craft of any type whatsoever constructed or adapted for the carriage of oil in bulk as cargo, provided that a ship capable of carrying oil and other cargoes shall be regarded as a ship only when it is actually carrying oil in bulk as cargo and during any voyage following such carriage unless it is proved that it has no residues of such carriage of oil in bulk aboard.

2. "Person" means any individual or partnership or any public or private body, whether corporate or not, including a State or any of its constituent subdivisions.

3. "Owner" means the person or persons registered as the owner of the ship or, in the absence of registration, the person or persons owning the ship. However in the case of a ship owned by a State and operated by a company which in that State is registered as the ship's operator, "owner" shall mean such company.

4. "State of the ship's registry" means in relation to registered ships the State of registration of the ship, and in relation to unregistered ships the State whose flag the ship is flying.

5. "Oil" means any persistent hydrocarbon mineral oil such as crude oil, fuel oil, heavy diesel oil and lubricating oil, whether carried on board a ship as cargo or in the bunkers of such a ship.

6. "Pollution damage" means:

(a) loss or damage caused outside the ship by contamination resulting from the escape or discharge of oil from the ship, wherever such escape or discharge may occur, provided that compensation for impairment of the environment other than loss of profit from such impairment shall be limited to costs of reasonable measures of reinstatement actually undertaken or to be undertaken;

(b) the costs of preventive measures and further loss or damage caused by preventive measures.

7. "Preventive measures" means any reasonable measures taken by any person after an incident has occurred to prevent or minimize pollution damage.

8. "Incident" means any occurrence, or series of occurrences having the same origin, which causes pollution damage or creates a grave and imminent threat of causing such damage.

9. "Organization" means the International Maritime Organization.

10. "1969 Liability Convention" means the International Convention on Civil Liability for Oil Pollution Damage, 1969. For States Parties to the Protocol of 1976 to that Convention, the term shall be deemed to include the 1969 Liability Convention as amended by that Protocol.

g. This document reproduces the consolidated text of the International Convention on Civil Liability for Oil Pollution Damage, *concluded at Brussels on* Nov. 29, 1969, 973 U.N.T.S. 3, 9 I.L.M. 45 (1970), as amended by the 1976 and 1992 Protocols to that Convention. The 1992 Protocol provides that the 1969 Liability Convention and the Protocol shall be "read and interpreted together as one single instrument" and that the consolidated text shall be known as the "International Convention on Civil Liability for Oil Pollution Damage, 1992."

Article II

This Convention shall apply exclusively:

(a) to pollution damage caused:

(i) in the territory, including the territorial sea, of a Contracting State, and

(ii) in the exclusive economic zone of a Contracting State, established in accordance with international law, or, if a Contracting State has not established such a zone, in an area beyond and adjacent to the territorial sea of that State determined by that State in accordance with international law and extending not more than 200 nautical miles from the baselines from which the breadth of its territorial sea is measured;

(b) to preventive measures, wherever taken, to prevent or minimize such damage.

Article III

1. Except as provided in paragraphs 2 and 3 of this Article, the owner of a ship at the time of an incident, or, where the incident consists of a series of occurrences, at the time of the first such occurrence, shall be liable for any pollution damage caused by the ship as a result of the incident.

2. No liability for pollution damage shall attach to the owner if he proves that the damage:

(a) resulted from an act of war, hostilities, civil war, insurrection or a natural phenomenon of an exceptional, inevitable and irresistible character, or

(b) was wholly caused by an act or omission done with intent to cause damage by a third party, or

(c) was wholly caused by the negligence or other wrongful act of any Government or other authority responsible for the maintenance of lights or other navigational aids in the exercise of that function.

3. If the owner proves that the pollution damage resulted wholly or partially either from an act or omission done with intent to cause damage by the person who suffered the damage or from the negligence of that person, the owner may be exonerated wholly or partially from his liability to such person.

4. No claim for compensation for pollution damage may be made against the owner otherwise than in accordance with this Convention. Subject to paragraph 5 of this Article, no claim for compensation for pollution damage under this Convention or otherwise may be made against:

(a) the servants or agents of the owner or the members of the crew;

(b) the pilot or any other person who, without being a member of the crew, performs services for the ship;

(c) any charterer (howsoever described, including a bareboat charterer), manager or operator of the ship;

(d) any person performing salvage operations with the consent of the owner or on the instructions of a competent public authority;

(e) any person taking preventive measures;

(f) all servants or agents of persons mentioned in subparagraphs (c), (d) and (e); unless the damage resulted from their personal act or omission, committed with the intent to cause such damage, or recklessly and with knowledge that such damage would probably result.

5. Nothing in this Convention shall prejudice any right of recourse of the owner against third parties.

Article IV

When an incident involving two or more ships occurs and pollution damage results therefrom, the owners of all the ships concerned, unless exonerated under Article III, shall be jointly and severally liable for all such damage which is not reasonably separable.

Article V

1. The owner of a ship shall be entitled to limit his liability under this Convention in respect of any one incident to an aggregate amount calculated as follows:

(a) 3 million units of account for a ship not exceeding 5,000 units of tonnage;

(b) for a ship with a tonnage in excess thereof, for each additional unit of tonnage, 420 units of account in addition to the amount mentioned in subparagraph (a); provided, however, that this aggregate amount shall not in any event exceed 59.7 million units of account.

2. The owner shall not be entitled to limit his liability under this Convention if it is proved that the pollution damage resulted from his personal act or omission, committed with the intent to cause such damage, or recklessly and with knowledge that such damage would probably result.

3. For the purpose of availing himself of the benefit of limitation provided for in paragraph 1 of this Article the owner shall constitute a fund for the total sum representing the limit of his liability with the Court or other competent authority of any one of the Contracting States in which action is brought under Article IX or, if no action is brought, with any Court or other competent authority in any one of the Contracting States in which an action can be brought under Article IX. The fund can be constituted either by depositing the sum or by producing a bank guarantee or other guarantee, acceptable under the legislation of the Contracting State where the fund is constituted, and considered to be adequate by the Court or other competent authority.

4. The fund shall be distributed among the claimants in proportion to the amounts of their established claims.

5. If before the fund is distributed the owner or any of his servants or agents or any person providing him insurance or other financial security has as a result of the incident in question, paid compensation for pollution damage, such person shall, up to the amount he has paid, acquire by subrogation the rights which the person so compensated would have enjoyed under this Convention.

6. The right of subrogation provided for in paragraph 5 of this Article may also be exercised by a person other than those mentioned therein in respect of any amount of compensation for pollution damage which he may have paid but only to the extent that such subrogation is permitted under the applicable national law.

7. Where the owner or any other person establishes that he may be compelled to pay at a later date in whole or in part any such amount of compensation, with regard to which such person would have enjoyed a right of subrogation under paragraph 5 or 6 of this Article, had the compensation been paid before the fund was distributed, the Court or other competent authority of the State where the fund has been constituted may order that a sufficient sum shall be provisionally set aside to enable such person at such later date to enforce his claim against the fund.

8. Claims in respect of expenses reasonably incurred or sacrifices reasonably made by the owner voluntarily to prevent or minimize pollution damage shall rank equally with other claims against the fund.

9. (a) The "unit of account" referred to in paragraph 1 of this Article is the Special Drawing Right as defined by the International Monetary Fund. The amounts mentioned in paragraph 1 shall be converted into national currency on the basis of the value of that currency by reference to the Special Drawing Right on the date of the constitution of the fund referred to in paragraph 3. The value of the national currency, in terms of the Special Drawing Right, of a Contracting State which is a member of the International Monetary Fund shall be calculated in accordance with the method of valuation applied by the International Monetary Fund in effect on the date in question for its operations and transactions. The value of the national currency, in terms of the Special Drawing Right, of a Contracting State which is not a member of the International Monetary Fund shall be calculated in a manner determined by that State.

(b) Nevertheless, a Contracting State which is not a member of the International Monetary Fund and whose law does not permit the application of the provisions of paragraph 9(a) may, at the time of ratification, acceptance, approval of or accession to this Convention or at any time thereafter, declare that the unit of account referred to in paragraph 9(a) shall be equal to 15 gold francs. The gold franc referred to in this paragraph corresponds to sixty-five and a half milligrammes of gold of millesimal fineness nine hundred. The conversion of the gold franc into the national currency shall be made according to the law of the State concerned.

(c) The calculation mentioned in the last sentence of paragraph 9(a) and the conversion mentioned in paragraph 9(b) shall be made in such manner as to express in the national currency of the Contracting State as far as possible the same real value for the amounts in paragraph 1 as would result from the application of the first three sentences of paragraph 9(a). Contracting States shall communicate to the depositary the manner of calculation pursuant to paragraph 9(a), or the result of the conversion in paragraph 9(b) as the case may be, when depositing an instrument of ratification, acceptance, approval of or accession to this Convention and whenever there is a change in either.

10. For the purpose of this Article the ships tonnage shall be the gross tonnage calculated in accordance with the tonnage measurement regulations contained in Annex I of the International Convention on Tonnage Measurement of Ships, 1969.

11. The insurer or other person providing financial security shall be entitled to constitute a fund in accordance with this Article on the same conditions and having the same effect as if it were constituted by the owner. Such a fund may be constituted even if, under the provisions of paragraph 2, the owner is not entitled to limit his liability, but its constitution shall in that case not prejudice the rights of any claimant against the owner.

Article VI

1. Where the owner, after an incident, has constituted a fund in accordance with Article V, and is entitled to limit his liability,

(a) no person having a claim for pollution damage arising out of that incident shall be entitled to exercise any right against any other assets of the owner in respect of such claim;

(b) the Court or other competent authority of any Contracting State shall order the release of any ship or other property belonging to the owner which has been arrested in respect of a claim for pollution damage arising out of that incident, and shall similarly release any bail or other security furnished to avoid such arrest.

2. The foregoing shall, however, only apply if the claimant has access to the Court administering the fund and the fund is actually available in respect or his claim.

Article VII

1. The owner of a ship registered in a Contracting State and carrying more than 2,000 tons of oil in bulk as cargo shall be required to maintain insurance or other financial security, such as the guarantee of a bank or a certificate delivered by an international compensation fund, in the sums fixed by applying the limits of liability prescribed in Article V, paragraph 1 to cover his liability for pollution damage under this Convention.

2. A certificate attesting that insurance or other financial security is in force in accordance with the provisions of this Convention shall be issued to each ship after the appropriate authority of a Contracting State has determined that the requirements of paragraph 1 have been complied with. With respect to a ship registered in a Contracting State such certificate shall be issued or certified by the appropriate authority of the State of the ship's registry; with respect to at ship not registered in a Contracting State it may be issued or certified by the appropriate authority of any Contracting State. This certificate shall be in the form of the annexed model and shall contain the following particulars:

(a) name of ship and port of registration;

(b) name and principal place of business of owner;

(c) type of security;

(d) name and principal place of business of insurer or other person giving security and, where appropriate, place of business where the insurance or security is established;

(e) period of validity of certificate which shall not be longer than the period of validity of the insurance or other security.

3. The certificate shall be in the official language or languages of the issuing State. If the language used is neither English nor French, the text shall include a translation into one of these languages.

4. The certificate shall be carried on board the ship and a copy shall be deposited with the authorities who keep the record of the ship's registry or, if the ship is not registered in a Contracting State, with the authorities of the State issuing or certifying the certificate.

5. An insurance or other financial security shall not satisfy the requirements of this Article if it can cease, for reasons other than the expiry of the period of validity of the insurance or security specified in the certificate under paragraph 2 of this Article, before three months have elapsed from the date on which notice of its termination is given to the authorities referred to in paragraph 4 of this Article, unless the certificate has been surrendered to these authorities or a new certificate has been issued within the said period. The foregoing provisions shall similarly apply to any modification which results in the insurance or security no longer satisfying the requirements of this Article.

6. The State of registry shall, subject to the provisions of this Article, determine the conditions of issue and validity of the certificate.

7. Certificates issued or certified under the authority of a Contracting State in accordance with paragraph 2 shall be accepted by other Contracting States for the purposes of this Convention and shall be regarded by other Contracting States as having the same force as certificates issued or certified by them even if issued or certified in respect of a ship not registered in a Contracting State. A Contracting State may at any time request consultation with the issuing or certifying State should it believe that the insurer or guarantor named in the certificate is not financially capable of meeting the obligations imposed by this Convention.

8. Any claim for compensation for pollution damage may be brought directly against the insurer or other person providing financial security for the owner's liability for pollution damage. In such case the defendant may, even if the owner is not entitled to limit his liability according to Article V, paragraph 2, avail himself of the limits of liability prescribed in Article V, paragraph 1. He may further avail himself of the defenses (other than the bankruptcy or winding up of the owner)which the owner himself would have been entitled to invoke. Furthermore, the defendant may avail himself of the defense that the pollution damage resulted from the wilful misconduct of the owner himself, but the defendant shall not avail himself of any other defence which he might have been entitled to invoke in proceedings brought by the owner against him. The defendant shall in any event have the right to require the owner to be joined in the proceedings.

9. Any sums provided by insurance or by other financial security maintained in accordance with paragraph 1 of this Article shall be available exclusively for the satisfaction of claims under this Convention.

10. A Contracting State shall not permit a ship under its flag to which this Article applies to trade unless a certificate has been issued under paragraph 2 or 12 of this Article.

11. Subject to the provisions of this Article, each Contracting State shall ensure, under its national legislation, that insurance or other security to the extent specified in paragraph 1 of this Article is in force in respect of any ship, wherever registered, entering or leaving a port in its territory, or arriving at or leaving an off-shore terminal in its territorial sea, if the ship actually carries more than 2,000 tons of oil in bulk as cargo.

12. If insurance or other financial security is not maintained in respect of a ship owned by a Contracting State, the provisions of this Article relating thereto shall not be applicable to such ship, but the ship shall carry a certificate issued by the appropriate authorities of the State of the ship's registry stating that the ship is owned by that State and that the ship's liability is covered within the limits prescribed by Article V, paragraph 1. Such a certificate shall follow as closely as practicable the model prescribed by paragraph 2 of this Article.

Article VIII

Rights of compensation under this Convention shall be extinguished unless an action is brought thereunder within three years from the date when the damage occurred. However, in no case shall an action be brought after six years from the date of the incident which caused the damage. Where this incident consists of a series of occurrences, the six-years period shall run from the date of the first such occurrence.

Article IX

1. Where an incident has caused pollution damage in the territory, including the territorial sea or an area referred to in Article II, of one or more Contracting States or preventive measures have been taken to prevent or minimize pollution damage in such territory including the territorial sea or area, actions for compensation may only be brought in the Courts of any such Contracting State or States. Reasonable notice of any such action shall be given to the defendant.

2. Each Contracting State shall ensure that its Courts possess the necessary jurisdiction to entertain such actions for compensation.

3. After the fund has been constituted in accordance with Article V the Courts of the State in which the fund is constituted shall be exclusively competent to determine all matters relating to the apportionment and distribution of the fund.

Article X

1. Any judgment given by a Court with jurisdiction in accordance with Article IX which is enforceable in the State of origin where it is no longer subject to ordinary forms of review, shall be recognized in any Contracting State, except:

(a) where the judgment was obtained by fraud; or

(b) where the defendant was not given reasonable notice and a fair opportunity to present his case.

2. A judgment recognized under paragraph 1 of this Article shall be enforceable in each Contracting State as soon as the formalities required in that State have been complied with. The formalities shall not permit the merits of the case to be re-opened.

Article XI

1. The provisions of this Convention shall not apply to warships or other ships owned or operated by a State and used, for the time being, only on government non-commercial service.

2. With respect to ships owned by a Contracting State and used for commercial purposes, each State shall be subject to suit in the jurisdictions set forth in Article IX and shall waive all defences based on its status as a sovereign State.

Article XII

This Convention shall supersede any International Conventions in force or open for signature, ratification or accession at the date on which the Convention is opened for signature, but only to the extent that such Conventions would be in conflict with it; however, nothing in this Article shall affect the obligations of Contracting States to non-Contracting States arising under such International Conventions.

Article XII bis

Transitional provisions

The following transitional provisions shall apply in the case of a State which at the time of an incident is a Party both to this Convention and to the 1969 Liability Convention:

(a) where an incident has caused pollution damage within the scope of this Convention, liability under this Convention shall be deemed to be discharged if, and to the extent that, it also arises under the 1969 Liability Convention;

(b) where an incident has caused pollution damage within the scope of this Convention, and the State is a Party both to this Convention and to the International Convention on the Establishment of an International Fund for Compensation for Oil Pollution Damage, 1971, liability remaining to be discharged after the application of subparagraph (a) of this Article shall arise under this Convention only to the extent that pollution damage remains uncompensated after application of the said 1971 Convention;

(c) in the application of Article III, Paragraph 4, of this Convention the expression "this Convention" shall be interpreted as referring to this Convention or the 1969 Liability Convention, as appropriate;

(d) in the application of Article V, paragraph 3, of this Convention the total sum of the fund to be constituted shall be reduced by the amount by which liability has been deemed to be discharged in accordance with subparagraph (a) of this Article.

Article XII ter

Final clauses

The final clauses of this Convention shall be Articles 12 to 18 of the Protocol of 1992 to amend the 1969 Liability Convention. References in this Convention to Contracting States shall be taken to mean references to the Contracting States of that Protocol.

FINAL CLAUSES

[Articles 12–18 of the 1992 Protocol to Amend the 1969 Liability Convention]

Article 12

Signature, ratification, acceptance, approval and accession

1. This Protocol shall be open for signature at London from 15 January 1993 to 14 January 1994 by all States.

2. Subject to paragraph 4, any State may become a Party to this Protocol by:

(a) signature subject to ratification, acceptance or approval followed by ratification, acceptance or approval; or

(b) accession.

3. Ratification, acceptance, approval or accession shall be effected by the deposit of a formal instrument to that effect with the Secretary–General of the Organization.

4. Any Contracting State to the International Convention on the Establishment of an International Fund for Compensation for Oil Pollution Damage, 1971, hereinafter referred to as the 1971 Fund Convention, may ratify, accept, approve or accede to this Protocol only if it ratifies, accepts, approves or accedes to the Protocol of 1992 to amend that Convention at the same time, unless it denounces the 1971 Fund Convention to take effect on the date when this Protocol enters into force for that State.

5. A State which is a Party to this protocol but not a Party to the 1969 Liability Convention shall be bound by the provisions of the 1969 Liability Convention as amended by this Protocol in relation to other States Parties hereto, but shall not be bound by the provisions of the 1969 Liability Convention in relation to States Parties thereto.

6. Any instrument of ratification, acceptance, approval or accession deposited after the entry into force of an amendment to the 1969 Liability Convention as amended by this Protocol shall be deemed to apply to the Convention so amended, as modified by such amendment.

Article 13

Entry into force

1. This Protocol shall enter into force twelve months following the date on which ten States including four States each with not less than one million units of gross tanker tonnage have deposited instruments of ratification, acceptance, approval or accession with the Secretary–General of the Organization.

2. However, any Contracting State to the 1971 Fund Convention may, at the time of the deposit of its instrument of ratification, acceptance, approval or accession in respect of this Protocol, declare that such instrument shall be deemed not to be effective for the purposes of this Article until the end of the six-month period in Article 31 of the Protocol of 1992 to amend the 1971 Fund Convention. A State which is not a Contracting State to the 1971 Fund Convention but which deposits an instrument of ratification, acceptance, approval or accession in respect of the Protocol of 1992 to

amend the 1971 Fund Convention may also make a declaration in accordance with this paragraph at the same time.

3. Any State which has made a declaration in accordance with the preceding paragraph may withdraw it at any time by means of a notification addressed to the Secretary–General of the Organization. Any such withdrawal shall take effect on the date the notification is received, provided that such State shall be deemed to have deposited its instrument of ratification, acceptance, approval or accession in respect of this Protocol on that date.

4. For any State which ratifies, accepts, approves or accedes to it after the conditions in paragraph 1 for entry into force have been met, this Protocol shall enter into force twelve months following the date of deposit by such State of the appropriate instrument.

Article 14

Revision and amendment

1. A Conference for the purpose of revising or amending the 1992 Liability Convention may be convened by the Organization.

2. The Organization shall convene a Conference of Contracting States for the purpose of revising or amending the 1992 Liability Convention at the request of not less than one third of the Contracting States.

Article 15

Amendments of limitation amounts

1. Upon the request of at least one quarter of the Contracting States any proposal to amend the limits of liability laid down in Article V, paragraph 1, of the 1969 Liability Convention as amended by this Protocol shall be circulated by the Secretary–General to all Members of the Organization and to all Contracting States.

2. Any amendment proposed and circulated as above shall be submitted to the Legal Committee of the Organization for consideration at a date at least six months after the date of its circulation.

3. All Contracting States to the 1969 Liability Convention as amended by this Protocol, whether or not Members of the Organization, shall be entitled to participate in the proceeding of the Legal Committee for the consideration and adoption of amendments.

4. Amendments shall be adopted by a two-thirds majority of the Contracting States present and voting in the Legal Committee, expanded as provided for in paragraph 3, on condition that at least one half of the Contracting States shall be present at the time of voting.

5. When acting on a proposal to amend the limits, the Legal Committee shall take into account the experience of incidents and in particular the amount of damage resulting therefrom, changes in the monetary values and the effect of the proposed amendment on the cost of insurance. It shall also take into account the relationship between the limits in Article V, paragraph 1, of the 1969 Liability Convention as amended by this Protocol and those in Article 4, paragraph 4, of the International Convention on the Establishment of an International Fund for Compensation for Oil Pollution Damage, 1992.

6. (a) No amendment of the limits of liability under this Article may be considered before 15 January 1998 nor less than five years from the date of entry into force of a previous amendment under this Article. No amendment under this Article shall be considered before this Protocol has entered into force.

(b) No limit may be increased so as to exceed an amount which corresponds to the limit laid down in the 1969 Liability Convention as amended by this Protocol increased by 6 per cent per year calculated on a compound basis from 15 January 1993.

(c) No limit may be increased so as to exceed an amount which corresponds to the limit laid down in the 1969 Liability Convention as amended by this Protocol multiplied by 3.

7. Any amendment adopted in accordance with paragraph 4 shall be notified by the Organization to all Contracting States. The amendment shall be deemed to have been accepted at the end of a period of eighteen months after the date of notification, unless within that period not less than one quarter of the States that were Contracting States at the time of the adoption of the amendment by the Legal Committee have communicated to the Organization that they do not accept the amendment in which case the amendment is rejected and shall have no effect.

8. An amendment deemed to have been accepted in accordance with paragraph 7 shall enter into force eighteen months after its acceptance.

9. All Contracting States shall be bound by the amendment, unless they denounce this Protocol in accordance with Article 16, paragraphs 1 and 2, at least six months before the amendment enters into force. Such denunciation shall take effect when the amendment enters into force.

10. When an amendment has been adopted by the Legal Committee but the eighteen-month period for its acceptance has not yet expired, a State which becomes a Contracting State during that period shall be bound by the amendment if it enters into force. A State which becomes a Contracting State after that period shall be bound by an amendment which has been accepted in accordance with paragraph 7. In the case referred to in this paragraph, a State becomes bound by an amendment when that amendment enters into force, or when this Protocol enters into force for that State, if later.

Article 16
Denunciation

1. This Protocol may be denounced by any Party at any time after the date on which it enters into force for that Party.

2. Denunciation shall be effected by the deposit of an instrument with the Secretary–General of the Organization.

3. A denunciation shall take effect twelve months, or such longer period as may be specified in the instrument of denunciation, after its deposit with the Secretary–General of the Organization.

4. As between the Parties to this Protocol, denunciation by any of them of the 1969 Liability Convention in accordance with Article XVI thereof shall not be construed in any way as a denunciation of the 1969 Liability Convention as amended by this Protocol.

5. Denunciation of the Protocol of 1992 to amend the 1971 Fund Convention by a State which remains a Party to the 1971 Fund Convention shall be deemed to be a denunciation of this Protocol. Such denunciation shall take effect on the date on which denunciation of the Protocol of 1992 to amend the 1971 Fund Convention takes effect according to Article 34 of that Protocol.

Article 17
Depositary

1. This Protocol and any amendments accepted under Article 15 shall be deposited with the Secretary–General of the Organization.

2. The Secretary–General of the Organization shall:

(a) inform all States which have signed or acceded to this protocol of:

(i) each new signature or deposit of an instrument together with the date thereof;

(ii) each declaration and notification under Article 13 and each declaration and communication under Article 13 and each declaration and communication under Article V, paragraph 9, of the 1992 Liability Convention;

(iii) the date of entry into force of this Protocol;

(iv) any proposal to amend limits of liability which has been made in accordance with Article 15, paragraph 1;

(v) any amendment which has been adopted in accordance with Article 15, paragraph 4;

(vi) any amendment deemed to have been accepted under Article 15, paragraph 7, together with the date on which that amendment shall enter into force in accordance with paragraphs 8 and 9 of that Article;

(vii) the deposit of any instrument of denunciation of this Protocol together with the date of the deposit and the date on which it takes effect;

(viii) any denunciation deemed to have been made under Article 16, paragraph 5;

(ix) any communication called for by any Article of this Protocol;

(b) transmit certified true copies of this Protocol to all Signatory States and to all States which accede to this Protocol.

3. As soon as this Protocol enters into force, the text shall be transmitted by the Secretary–General of the Organization to the Secretariat of the United Nations for registration and publication in accordance with Article 102 of the Charter of the United Nations.

Article 18

Languages

This Protocol is established in a single original in the Arabic, Chinese, English, French, Russian and Spanish languages, each text being equally authentic.

DONE AT LONDON, this twenty-seventh day of November one thousand nine hundred and ninety-two.

IN WITNESS WHEREOF the undersigned, being duly authorized by their respective Governments for that purpose, have signed this Protocol.

ANNEX

Certificate of Insurance or Other Financial Security in Respect of Civil Liability for Oil Pollution Damage

Issued in accordance with the provisions of Article VII of the International Convention on Civil Liability for Oil Pollution Damage, 1992.

Name of ship	Distinctive number or letters	Port of Registry	Name and address of owner

This is to certify that there is in force in respect of the above-named ship a policy of insurance or other financial security satisfying the requirements of Article VII of the International Convention on Civil Liability for Oil Pollution Damage, 1992.

Type of Security ______________________________

Duration of Security ______________________________

Name and Address of the Insurer(s) and/or Guarantor(s) ______________________________

____

Name ______________________________

Address ______________________________

____

This certificate is valid until ______________________________

Issued or certified by the Government of ______________________________

(Full designation of the State)

At ______________________________ On ______________________________ ______________

(Place) *(Date)*

____

Signature and Title of issuing or certifying official

Explanatory Notes:

1. If desired, the designation of the State may include a reference to the competent public authority of the country where the certificate is issued.

2. If the total amount of security has been furnished by more than one source, the amount of each of them should be indicated.

3. If security is furnished in several forms, these should be enumerated.

4. The entry "Duration of Security" must stipulate the date on which such security takes effect.

4.26 International Convention on the Establishment of an International Fund for Compensation for Oil Pollution Damage, 1992 (Without Annex and Protocols).[h] Concluded at London, 27 November 1992. Entered into force, 30 May 1996. *Reprinted in* Civil Liability for Oil Pollution Damage, at 67 (IMO 1996) & 5 Weston V.F.30 (1971 Convention)

* * *

General Provisions

Article 1. For the purposes of this Convention:

1. "1992 Liability Convention" means the International Convention on Civil Liability for Oil Pollution Damage, 1992.

1. *bis* "1971 Fund Convention" means the International Convention on the Establishment of an International fund for Compensation for Oil Pollution Damage, 1971. For States Parties to the Protocol of 1976 to that Convention, the term shall be deemed to include the 1971 Fund Convention as amended by that Protocol.

2. "Ship", "Person", "Owner", "Oil", "Pollution Damage", "Preventive Measures", "Incident", and "Organization" have the same meaning as in Article I of the 1992 Liability Convention.

3. "Contributing Oil" means crude oil and fuel oil as defined in sub-paragraphs (*a*) and (*b*) below:

(*a*) "Crude Oil" means any liquid hydrocarbon mixture occurring naturally in the earth whether or not treated to render it suitable for transportation. It also includes crude oils from which certain distillate fractions have been removed (sometimes referred to as "topped crudes") or to which certain distillate fractions have been added (sometimes referred to as "spiked" or "reconstituted" crudes).

(*b*) "Fuel Oil" means heavy distillates or residues from crude oil or blends of such materials intended for use as a fuel for the production of heat or power of a quality equivalent to the "American Society for Testing and Materials' Specification for Number Four Fuel Oil (Designation D 396–69)", or heavier.

4. "Unit of account" has the same meaning as in Article V, paragraph 9, of the 1992 Liability Convention.

5. "Ship's tonnage" has the same meaning as in Article V, paragraph 10, of the 1992 Liability Convention.

6. "Ton", in relation to oil, means a metric ton.

7. "Guarantor" means any person providing insurance or other financial security to cover an owner's liability in pursuance of Article VII, paragraph 1, of the 1992 Liability Convention.

8. "Terminal installation" means any site for the storage of oil in bulk which is capable of receiving oil from waterborne transportation, including any facility situated off-shore and linked to such site.

9. Where an incident consists of a series of occurrences, it shall be treated as having occurred on the date of the first such occurrence.

h. This document reproduces the consolidated text of the International Convention on the Establishment of an International Fund for Compensation for Oil Pollution Damage (without annex and protocols), *concluded at Brussels,* 1971 U.N.J.Y.B. 103, as amended by the 1976 and 1992 Protocols to that Convention. The 1992 Protocol provides that the 1971 Fund Convention and the Protocol shall be "read and interpreted together as one single instrument" and that the consolidated text shall be known as the "International Fund for Compensation for Oil Pollution Damage, 1992."

Article 2. 1. An International Fund for compensation for pollution damage, to be named "The International Oil Pollution Compensation Fund 1992" and hereinafter referred to as "the Fund", is hereby established with the following aims:

(a) to provide compensation for pollution damage to the extent that the protection afforded by the 1992 Liability Convention is inadequate;

(b) to give effect to the related purposes set out in this Convention.

2. The Fund shall in each Contracting State be recognized as a legal person capable under the laws of that State of assuming rights and obligations and of being a party in legal proceedings before the courts of that State. Each Contracting State shall recognize the Director of the Fund (hereinafter referred to as "the Director") as the legal representative of the Fund.

Article 3. This Convention shall apply exclusively:

(a) to pollution damage caused:

(i) in the territory, including the territorial sea, of a Contracting State, and

(ii) in the exclusive economic zone of a Contracting State, established in accordance with international law, or, if a Contracting State has not established such a zone, in an area beyond and adjacent to the territorial sea of that State determined by that State in accordance with international law baselines from which the breadth of its territorial sea is measured;

(b) to preventive measures, wherever taken, to prevent or minimize such damage.

Compensation

Article 4. 1. For the purpose of fulfilling its function under Article 2, paragraph 1(*a*), the Fund shall pay compensation to any person suffering pollution damage if such person has been unable to obtain full and adequate compensation for the damage under the terms of the 1992 Liability Convention,

(*a*) Because no liability for the damage arises under the 1992 Liability Convention;

(*b*) Because the owner liable for the damage under the 1992 Liability Convention is financially incapable of meeting his obligations in full and any financial security that may be provided under Article VII of that Convention does not cover or is insufficient to satisfy the claims for compensation for the damage; an owner being treated as financially incapable of meeting his obligations and a financial security being treated as insufficient if the person suffering the damage has been unable to obtain full satisfaction of the amount of compensation due under the 1992 Liability Convention after having taken all reasonable steps to pursue the legal remedies available to him;

(*c*) Because the damage exceeds the owner's liability under the 1992 Liability Convention as limited pursuant to Article V, paragraph 1, of that Convention or under the terms of any other international Convention in force or open for signature, ratification or accession at the date of this Convention.

Expenses reasonably incurred or sacrifices reasonably made by the owner voluntarily to prevent or minimize pollution damage shall be treated as pollution damage for the purposes of this Article.

2. The Fund shall incur no obligation under the preceding paragraph if:

(*a*) It proves that the pollution damage resulted from an act of war, hostilities, civil war or insurrection or was caused by oil which has escaped or been discharged from a warship or other ship owned or operated by a State and used, at the time of the incident, only on Government non-commercial service; or

(*b*) The claimant cannot prove that the damage resulted from an incident involving one or more ships.

3. If the Fund proves that the pollution damage resulted wholly or partially either from an act or omission done with the intent to cause damage by the person who suffered the damage or from the negligence of that person, the Fund may be exonerated wholly or partially from its obligation to pay compensation to such person. The Fund shall in any event be exonerated to the extent that the shipowner may have been exonerated under Article III, paragraph 3, of the 1992 Liability Convention. However, there shall be no such exoneration of the Fund with regard to preventive measures.

4. (a) Except as otherwise provided in subparagraphs (b) and (c) of this paragraph, the aggregate amount of compensation payable by the Fund under this Article shall in respect of any one incident be limited, so that the total sum of that amount and the amount of compensation actually paid under the 1992 Liability Convention for pollution damage within the scope of application of this Convention as defined in Article 3 shall not exceed 135 million units of account.

(b) Except as otherwise provided in subparagraph (c), the aggregate amount of compensation payable by the Fund under this Article for pollution damage resulting from a natural phenomenon of an exceptional inevitable and irresistible character shall not exceed 135 million units of account.

(c) The maximum amount of compensation referred to in subparagraphs (a) and (b) shall be 200 million units of account with respect to any incident occurring during any period when there are three Parties to this Convention in respect of which the combined relevant quantity of contributing oil received by persons in the territories of such Parties, during the preceding calendar year, equaled or exceeded 600 million tons.

(d) Interest accrued on a fund constituted in accordance with Article V, paragraph 3, of the 1992 Liability Convention, if any, shall not be taken into account for the computation of the maximum compensation payable by the Fund under this Article.

(e) The amounts mentioned in this Article shall be converted into national currency on the basis of the value of that currency by reference to the Special Drawing Right on the date of the decision of the Assembly of the Fund as to the first date of payment of compensation.

5. Where the amount of established claims against the Fund exceeds the aggregate amount of compensation payable under paragraph 4, the amount available shall be distributed in such a manner that the proportion between any established claim and the amount of compensation actually recovered by the claimant under this Convention shall be the same for all claimants.

6. The Assembly of the Fund may decide that, in exceptional cases, compensation in accordance with this Convention can be paid even if the owner of the ship has not constituted a fund in accordance with Article V, paragraph 3, of the 1992 Liability Convention. In such case paragraph 4 (e) of this Article applies accordingly.

7. The Fund shall, at the request of a Contracting State, use its good offices as necessary to assist that State to secure promptly such personnel, material and services as are necessary to enable the State to take measures to prevent or mitigate pollution damage arising from an incident in respect of which the Fund may be called upon to pay compensation under this Convention.

8. The Fund may, on conditions to be laid down in the Internal Regulations, provide credit facilities with a view to the taking of preventive measures against pollution damage arising from a particular incident in respect of which the Fund may be called upon to pay compensation under this Convention.

Article 5. [*deleted*]

Article 6. Rights to compensation under Article 4 shall be extinguished unless an action is brought thereunder or a notification has been made pursuant to Article 7, paragraph 6, within three years from the date when the damage occurred. However, in no case shall an action be brought after six years from the date of the incident which caused the damage.

Article 7. 1. Subject to the subsequent provisions of this Article, any action against the Fund for compensation under Article 4 or indemnification under Article 5 of this Convention shall be brought only before a court competent under Article IX of the 1992 Liability Convention in respect of actions against the owner who is or who would, but for the provisions of Article III, paragraph 2, of that Convention, have been liable for pollution damage caused by the relevant incident.

2. Each Contracting State shall ensure that its courts possess the necessary jurisdiction to entertain such actions against the Fund as are referred to in paragraph 1.

3. Where an action for compensation for pollution damage has been brought before a court competent under Article IX of the 1992 Liability Convention against the owner of a ship or his guarantor, such court shall have exclusive jurisdictional competence over any action against the Fund for compensation or indemnification under the provisions of Article 4 of this Convention in respect of the same damage. However, where an action for compensation for pollution damage under the 1992 Liability Convention has been brought before a court in a State Party to the 1992 Liability Convention but not to this Convention, any action against the Fund under Article 4 of this Convention shall at the option of the claimant be brought either before a court of the State where the Fund has its headquarters or before any court of a State Party to this Convention competent under Article IX of the 1992 Liability Convention.

4. Each Contracting State shall ensure that the Fund shall have the right to intervene as a party to any legal proceedings instituted in accordance with Article IX of the 1992 Liability Convention before a competent court of that State against the owner of a ship or his guarantor.

5. Except as otherwise provided in paragraph 6, the Fund shall not be bound by any judgment or decision in proceedings to which it has not been a party or by any settlement to which it is not a party.

6. Without prejudice to the provisions of paragraph 4, where an action under the 1992 Liability Convention for compensation for pollution damage has been brought against an owner or his guarantor before a competent court in a Contracting State, each party to the proceedings shall be entitled under the national law of that State to notify the Fund of the proceedings. Where such notification has been made in accordance with the formalities required by the law of the court seized and in such time and in such a manner that the Fund has in fact been in a position effectively to intervene as a party to the proceedings, any judgment rendered by the court in such proceedings shall, after it has become final and enforceable in the State where the judgment was given, become binding upon the Fund in the sense that the facts and findings in that judgment may not be disputed by the Fund even if the Fund has not actually intervened in the proceedings.

Article 8. Subject to any decision concerning the distribution referred to in Article 4, paragraph 5, any judgment given against the Fund by a court having jurisdiction in accordance with Article 7, paragraphs 1 and 3, shall, when it has become enforceable in the State of origin and is in that State no longer subject to ordinary forms of review, be recognized and enforceable in each Contracting State on the same conditions as are prescribed in Article X of the 1992 Liability Convention.

Article 9. 1. The Fund shall, in respect of any amount of compensation for pollution damage paid by the Fund in accordance with Article 4, paragraph 1, of this Convention, acquire by subrogation the rights that the person so compensated may enjoy under the 1992 Liability Convention against the owner or his guarantor.

2. Nothing in this Convention shall prejudice any right of recourse or subrogation of the Fund against persons other than those referred to in the preceding paragraph. In any event the right of the Fund to subrogation against such person shall not be less favourable than that of an insurer of the person to whom compensation has been paid.

3. Without prejudice to any other rights of subrogation or recourse against the Fund which may exist, a Contracting State or agency thereof which has paid compensation for pollution damage in accordance with provisions of national law shall acquire by subrogation the rights which the person so compensated would have enjoyed under this Convention.

Contributions

Article 10. 1. Annual contributions to the Fund shall be made in respect of each Contracting State by any person who, in the calendar year referred to in Article 12, paragraph 2(a) or (b), has received in total quantities exceeding 150,000 tons:

(*a*) In the ports or terminal installations in the territory of that State contributing oil carried by sea to such ports or terminal installations; and

(*b*) In any installations situated in the territory of that Contracting State contributing oil which has been carried by sea and discharged in a port or terminal installation of a non-Contracting State, provided that contributing oil shall only be taken into account by virtue of this sub-paragraph on first receipt in a Contracting State after its discharge in that non-Contracting State.

2. (*a*) For the purposes of paragraph 1, where the quantity of contributing oil received in the territory of a Contracting State by any person in a calendar year when aggregated with the quantity of contributing oil received in the same Contracting State in that year by any associated person or persons exceeds 150,000 tons, such person shall pay contributions in respect of the actual quantity received by him notwithstanding that that quantity did not exceed 150,000 tons.

(*b*) "Associated person" means any subsidiary or commonly controlled entity. The question whether a person comes within this definition shall be determined by the national law of the State concerned.

Article 11. [*deleted*]

Article 12. 1. With a view to assessing the amount of annual contributions due, if any, and taking account of the necessity to maintain sufficient liquid funds, the Assembly shall for each calendar year make an estimate in the form of a budget of:

(i) Expenditure

(*a*) Costs and expenses of the administration of the Fund in the relevant year and any deficit from operations in preceding years;

(*b*) Payments to be made by the Fund in the relevant year for the satisfaction of claims against the Fund due under Article 4, including repayment on loans previously taken by the Fund for the satisfaction of such claims, to the extent that the aggregate amount of such claims in respect of any one incident does not exceed four million units of account;

(*c*) Payments to be made by the Fund in the relevant year for the satisfaction of claims against the Fund due under Article 4, including repayments on loans previously taken by the Fund for the satisfaction of such claims, to the extent that the aggregate amount of such claims in respect of any one incident is in excess of four million units of account;

(ii) Income

(*a*) Surplus funds from operations in preceding years, including any interest;

(*b*) annual contributions, if required to balance the budget;

(*c*) Any other income.

2. The Assembly shall decide the total amount of contributions to be levied. On the basis of that decision, the Director shall, in respect of each Contracting State, calculate for each person referred to in Article 10 the amount of his annual contribution:

(*a*) In so far as the contribution is for the satisfaction of payments referred to in paragraph 1(i)(*a*) and (*b*) on the basis of a fixed sum for each ton of contributing oil received in the relevant State by such persons during the preceding calendar year; and

(*b*) In so far as the contribution is for the satisfaction of payments referred to in paragraph 1(i)(*c*) of this article on the basis of a fixed sum for each ton of contributing oil received by such person during the calendar year preceding that in which the incident in question occurred, provided that State was a party to this Convention at the date of the incident.

3. The sums referred to in paragraph 2 above shall be arrived at by dividing the relevant total amount of contributions required by the total amount of contributing oil received in all Contracting States in the relevant year.

4. The annual contribution shall be due on the date to be laid down in the Internal Regulations of the Fund. The Assembly may decide on a different date of payment.

5. The Assembly may decide, under the conditions to be laid down in the Financial Regulations of the Fund, to make transfers between funds received in accordance with article 12.2(a) and funds received in accordance with article 12.2(b).

Article 13. 1. The amount of any contribution due under Article 12 and which is in arrears shall bear interest at a rate which shall be determined in accordance with the Internal Regulations of the Fund, provided that different rates may be fixed for different circumstances.

2. Each Contracting State shall ensure that any obligation to contribute to the Fund arising under this Convention in respect of oil received within the territory of that State is fulfilled and shall take any appropriate measures under its law, including the imposing of such sanctions as it may deem necessary, with a view to the effective execution of any such obligation; provided, however, that such measures shall only be directed against those persons who are under an obligation to contribute to the Fund.

3. Where a person who is liable in accordance with the provisions of Articles 10 and 12 to make contributions to the Fund does not fulfil his obligations in respect of any such contribution or any part thereof and is in arrears, the Director shall take all appropriate action against such person on behalf of the Fund with a view to the recovery of the amount due. However, where the defaulting contributor is manifestly insolvent or the circumstances otherwise so warrant, the Assembly may, upon recommendation of the Director, decide that no action shall be taken or continued against the contributor.

Article 14. 1. Each Contracting State may at the time when it deposits its instrument of ratification or accession or at any time thereafter declare that it assumes itself obligations that are incumbent under this Convention on any person who is liable to contribute to the Fund in accordance with Article 10, paragraph 1, in respect of oil received within the territory of that State. Such declaration shall be made in writing and shall specify which obligations are assumed.

2. Where a declaration under paragraph 1 is made prior to the entry into force of this Convention in accordance with Article 40, it shall be deposited with the Secretary–General of the Organization who shall after the entry into force of the Convention communicate the declaration to the Director.

3. A declaration under paragraph 1 which is made after the entry into force of this Convention shall be deposited with the Director.

4. A declaration made in accordance with this article may be withdrawn by the relevant State giving notice thereof in writing to the Director. Such notification shall take effect three months after the Director's receipt thereof.

5. Any State which is bound by a declaration made under this article shall, in any proceedings brought against it before a competent court in respect of any obligation specified in the declaration, waive any immunity that it would otherwise be entitled to invoke.

Article 15. 1. Each Contracting State shall ensure that any person who receives contributing oil within its territory in such quantities that he is liable to contribute to the Fund appears on a list to be established and kept up to date by the Director in accordance with the subsequent provisions of this article.

2. For the purposes set out in paragraph 1, each Contracting State shall communicate, at a time and in the manner to be prescribed in the Internal Regulations, to the Director the name and address of any person who in respect of that State is liable to contribute to the Fund pursuant to Article 10, as well as data on the relevant quantities of contributing oil received by any such person during the preceding calendar year.

3. For the purposes of ascertaining who are, at any given time, the persons liable to contribute to the Fund in accordance with Article 10, paragraph 1, and of establishing, where applicable, the quantities of oil to be taken into account for any such person when determining the amount of his contribution, the list shall be *prima facie* evidence of the facts stated therein.

4. Where a Contracting State does not fulfill its obligations to submit to the Director the communication referred to in paragraph 2 and this results in a financial loss for the Fund, that Contracting State shall be liable of compensate the Fund for such loss. The Assembly shall, on the recommendation of the Director, decide whether such compensation shall be payable by that Contracting State.

Organization and administration

Article 16. The Fund shall have an Assembly and a Secretariat headed by a Director.

Assembly

Article 17. The Assembly shall consist of all Contracting States to this Convention.

Article 18. The functions of the Assembly shall be:

1. To elect at each regular session its Chairman and two Vice–Chairmen who shall hold office until the next regular session;

2. To determine its own rules of procedure, subject to the provisions of this Convention;

3. To adopt Internal Regulations necessary for the proper functioning of the Fund;

4. To appoint the Director and make provisions for the appointment of such other personnel as may be necessary and determine the terms and conditions of service of the Director and other personnel;

5. To adopt the annual budget and fix the annual contributions;

6. To appoint auditors and approve the accounts of the Fund;

7. To approve settlements of claims against the Fund, to take decisions in respect of the distribution among claimants of the available amount of compensation in accordance with Article 4, paragraph 5, and to determine the terms and conditions according to which provisional payments in respect of claims shall be made with a view to ensuring that victims of pollution damage are compensated as promptly as possible;

8. [*deleted*]

9. To establish any temporary or permanent subsidiary body it may consider to be necessary, to define its terms of reference and to give it the authority needed to perform the functions entrusted to it; when appointing the members of such body, the Assembly shall endeavour to secure an equitable geographical distribution of members and to ensure that the Contracting States, in respect of which the largest quantities of contributing oil are being received, are appropriately represented; the Rules of Procedure of the Assembly may be applied, mutatis mutandis, for the work of such subsidiary body;

10. To determine which non-Contracting States and which inter-governmental and international non-governmental organizations shall be admitted to take part, without voting rights, in meetings of the Assembly, and subsidiary bodies;

11. To give instructions concerning the administration of the Fund to the Director and subsidiary bodies;

12. [*deleted*]

13. To supervise the proper execution of the Convention and of its own decisions;

14. To perform such other functions as are allocated to it under the Convention or are otherwise necessary for the proper operation of the Fund.

Article 19. 1. Regular sessions of the Assembly shall take place once every calendar year upon convocation by the Director.

2. Extraordinary sessions of the Assembly shall be convened by the Director at the request of at least one third of the members of the Assembly and may be convened on the Director's own initiative after consultation with the Chairman of the Assembly. The Director shall give members at least thirty days' notice of such sessions.

Article 20. A majority of the members of the Assembly shall constitute a quorum for its meetings.

Article 21 to 27 [*deleted*]

Secretariat

Article 28. 1. The Secretariat shall comprise the Director and such staff as the administration of the Fund may require.

2. The Director shall be the legal representative of the Fund.

Article 29. 1. The Director shall be the chief administrative officer of the Fund. Subject to the instructions given to him by the Assembly, he shall perform those functions which are assigned to him by this Convention, the Internal Regulations of the Fund and the Assembly.

2. The Director shall in particular:

(*a*) Appoint the personnel required for the administration of the Fund;

(*b*) Take all appropriate measures with a view to the proper administration of the Fund's assets;

(*c*) Collect the contributions due under this Convention while observing in particular the provisions of Article 13, paragraph 3;

(*d*) To the extent necessary to deal with claims against the Fund and carry out the other functions of the Fund, employ the services of legal, financial and other experts;

(*e*) Take all appropriate measures for dealing with claims against the Fund within the limits and on conditions to be laid down in the Internal Regulations, including the final settlement of claims without the prior approval of the Assembly where these Regulations so provide;

(*f*) Prepare and submit to the Assembly the financial statements and budget estimates for each calendar year;

(*g*) Prepare in consultation with the Chairman of the Assembly, and publish a report of the activities of the Fund during the previous calendar year;

(*h*) Prepare, collect and circulate the papers, documents, agenda, minutes and information that may be required for the work of the Assembly and subsidiary bodies.

Article 30. In the performance of their duties the Director and the staff and experts appointed by him shall not seek or receive instructions from any Government or from any authority external to the Fund. They shall refrain from any action which might reflect on their position as international officials. Each Contracting State on its part undertakes to respect the exclusively international character of the responsibilities of the Director and the staff and experts appointed by him, and not to seek to influence them in the discharge of their duties.

Finances

Article 31. 1. Each Contracting State shall bear the salary, travel and other expenses of its own delegation to the Assembly and of its representatives on subsidiary bodies.

2. Any other expenses incurred in the operation of the Fund shall be borne by the Fund.

Voting

Article 32. The following provisions shall apply to voting in the Assembly:

(*a*) Each member shall have one vote;

(*b*) Except as otherwise provided in Article 33, decisions of the Assembly shall be by a majority vote of the members present and voting;

(*c*) Decisions where a three-fourths or a two-thirds majority is required shall be by a three-fourths or two-thirds majority vote, as the case may be, of those present;

(*d*) For the purpose of this article the phrase "members present" means "members present at the meeting at the time of the vote", and the phrase "members present and voting" means "members present and casting an affirmative or negative vote". Members who abstain from voting shall be considered as not voting.

Article 33. The following decisions of the Assembly shall require a two-thirds majority:

(*a*) A decision under Article 13, paragraph 3, not to take or continue action against a contributor;

(*b*) The appointment of the Director under Article 18, paragraph 4;

(*c*) The establishment of subsidiary bodies, under Article 18, paragraph 9, and matters relating to such establishment.

Article 34. 1. The Fund, its assets, income, including contributions, and other property shall enjoy in all Contracting States exemption from all direct taxation.

2. When the Fund makes substantial purchases of movable or immovable property, or has important work carried out which is necessary for the exercise of its official activities and the cost of which includes indirect taxes or sales taxes, the Governments of Member States shall take, whenever possible, appropriate measures for the remission or refund of the amount of such duties and taxes.

3. No exemption shall be accorded in the case of duties, taxes or dues which merely constitute payment for public utility services.

4. The Fund shall enjoy exemption from all customs duties, taxes and other related taxes on articles imported or exported by it or on its behalf for its official use. Articles thus imported shall not be transferred either for consideration or gratis on the territory of the country into which they have been imported except on conditions agreed by the government of that country.

5. Persons contributing to the Fund and victims and owners of ships receiving compensation from the Fund shall be subject to the fiscal legislation of the State where they are taxable, no special exemption or other benefit being conferred on them in this respect.

6. Information relating to individual contributors supplied for the purpose of this Convention shall not be divulged outside the Fund except in so far as it may be strictly necessary to enable the Fund to carry out its functions including the bringing and defending of legal proceedings.

7. Independently of existing or future regulations concerning currency or transfers, Contracting States shall authorize the transfer and payment of any contribution to the Fund and of any compensation paid by the Fund without any restriction.

Transitional Provisions

Article 35. Claims for compensation under Article 4 arising from incidents occurring after the date of entry into force of this Convention may not be brought against the Fund earlier than the one hundred and twentieth day after that date.

Article 36. The Secretary–General of the Organization shall convene the first session of the Assembly. This session shall take place as soon as possible after entry into force of this Convention and, in any case, not more than thirty days after such entry into force.

Article 36 bis. The following transitional provisions shall apply in the period, hereinafter referred to as the transitional period, commencing with the date of entry into force of this Convention and ending with the date on which the denunciations provided for in Article 31 of the 1992 Protocol to amend the 1971 Fund Convention take effect:

(a) In the application of paragraph 1 (a) of Article 2 of this Convention, the reference to the 1992 Liability Convention shall include reference to the International Convention on Civil Liability for Oil Pollution Damage, 1969, either in its original version or as amended by the Protocol thereto of 1976 (referred to in this article as "the 1969 Liability Convention"), and also the 1971 Fund Convention.

(b) Where an incident has caused pollution damage within the scope of this Convention, the Fund shall pay compensation to any person suffering pollution damage only if, and to the extent that, such person has been unable to obtain full and adequate compensation for the damage under the terms of the 1969 Liability Convention, the 1971 Fund Convention and the 1992 Liability Convention, provided that, in respect of pollution damage within the scope of this Convention in respect of a Party to this Convention but not a Party to the 1971 Fund Convention, the Fund shall pay compensation to any person suffering pollution damage only if, and to the extent that, such person would have been unable to obtain full and adequate compensation had that State been party to each of the above-mentioned Conventions.

(c) In the application of Article 4 of this Convention, the amount to be taken into account in determining the aggregate amount of compensation payable by the Fund shall also include the amount of compensation actually paid under the 1969 Liability Convention, if any, and the amount of compensation actually paid or deemed to have been paid under the 1971 Fund Convention.

(d) Paragraph 1 of Article 9 of this Convention shall also apply to the rights enjoyed under the 1969 Liability Convention.

Article 36 ter. 1. Subject to paragraph 4 of this article, the aggregate amount of the annual contributions payable in respect of contributing oil received in a single Contraction State during a calendar year shall not exceed 27.5% of the total amount of annual contributions pursuant to the 1992 Protocol to amend the 1971 Fund Convention, in respect of that calendar year.

2. If the application of the provisions in paragraphs 2 and 3 of Article 12 would result in the aggregate amount of the contributions payable by contributors in a single Contracting State in respect of a given calendar year exceeding 27.5% of the total annual contributions, the contributions payable by all contributors in that State shall be reduced pro rata so that their aggregate contributions equal 27.5% of the total annual contributions to the Fund in respect of that year.

3. If the contributions payable by persons in a given Contracting State shall be reduced pursuant to paragraph 2 of this article, the contributions payable by persons in all other Contracting States shall be increased pro rata so as to ensure that the total amount of contributions payable by all persons liable to contribute to the Fund in respect of the calendar year in question will reach the total amount of contributions decided by the Assembly.

4. The provisions in paragraphs 1 to 3 of this article shall operate until the total quantity of contributing oil received in all Contracting States in a calendar year has reached 750 million tons or until a period of 5 years after the date of entry into force of the said 1992 Protocol has elapsed, whichever occurs earlier.

Article 36 quater. Notwithstanding the provisions of this Convention, the following provisions shall apply to the administration of the Fund during the period in which both the 1971 Fund Convention and this Convention are in force:

(a) The Secretariat of the Fund, established by the 1971 Convention (hereinafter referred to as "the 1971 Fund"), headed by the Director, may also function as the Secretariat and the Director of the Fund.

(b) If, in accordance with subparagraph (a), the Secretariat and the Director of the 1971 Fund also perform the function of Secretariat and Director of the Fund, the Fund shall be represented, in cases of conflict of interests between the 1971 Fund and the Fund, by the Chairman of the Assembly of the Fund.

(c) The Director and the staff and experts appointed by him, performing their duties under this Convention and the 1971 Fund Convention, shall not be regarded as contravening the provisions of Article 30 of this Convention in so far as they discharge their duties in accordance with this article.

(d) The Assembly of the Fund shall endeavour not to take decisions which are incompatible with decisions taken by the Assembly of the 1971 Fund. If differences of opinion with respect to common administrative issues arise, the Assembly of the Fund shall try to reach a consensus with the Assembly of the 1971 Fund, in a spirit of mutual co-operation and with the common aims of both organizations in mind.

(e) The Fund may succeed to the rights, obligations and assets of the 1971 Fund if the Assembly of the 1971 Fund so decides, in accordance with Article 44, paragraph 2, of the 1971 Fund Convention.

(f) The Fund shall reimburse to the 1971 Fund all costs and expenses arising from administrative services performed by the 1971 Fund on behalf of the Fund.

Article 36 quinquies. Final clauses

The final clauses of this Convention shall be Articles 28 to 39 of the Protocol of 1992 to amend the 1971 Fund Convention. References in this Convention to Contracting States shall be taken to mean references to the Contracting States of that Protocol.

FINAL CLAUSES

[Articles 28–39 of the Protocol of 1992 to Amend the 1991 Fund Convention]

Article 28

Signature, ratification, acceptance, approval and accession

1. This Protocol shall be open for signature at London from 15 January 1993 to 14 January 1994 by any State which has signed the 1992 Liability Convention.

2. Subject to paragraph 4, this Protocol shall be ratified, accepted or approved by States which have signed it.

3. Subject to paragraph 4, this Protocol is open for accession by States which did not sign it.

4. This Protocol may be ratified, accepted, approved or acceded to only by States which have ratified, accepted, approved or acceded to the 1992 Liability Convention.

5. Ratification, acceptance, approval or accession shall be effected by the deposit of a formal instrument to that effect with the Secretary–General of the Organization.

6. A State which is a Party to this Protocol but is not a Party to the 1971 Fund Convention shall be bound by the provisions of the 1971 Fund Convention as amended by this Protocol in relation to other Parties hereto, but shall not be bound by the provisions of the 1971 Fund Convention in relation to Parties thereto.

7. Any instrument of ratification, acceptance, approval or accession deposited after the entry into force of an amendment to the 1971 Fund Convention as amended by this Protocol shall be deemed to apply to the Convention so amended, as modified by such amendment.

Article 29

Information on contributing oil

1. Before this Protocol comes into force for a State, that State shall, when depositing an instrument referred to in Article 28, paragraph 5, and annually thereafter at a date to be determined by the Secretary–General of the Organization, communicate to him the name and address of any person who in respect of that State would be

liable to contribute to the Fund pursuant to Article 10 of the 1971 Fund Convention as amended by this Protocol as well as data on the relevant quantities of contributing oil received by any such person in the territory of that State during the preceding calendar year.

2. During the transitional period, the Director shall, for Parties, communicate annually to the Secretary–General of the Organization data on quantities of contributing oil received by persons liable to contribute to the Fund pursuant to Article 10 of the 1971 Fund Convention as amended by this Protocol.

Article 30

Entry into force

1. This Protocol shall enter into force twelve months following the date on which the following requirements are fulfilled:

(a) at least eight States have deposited instruments of ratification, acceptance, approval or accession with the Secretary–General of the Organization; and

(b) the Secretary–General of the Organization has received information in accordance with Article 29 that those persons who would be liable to contribute pursuant to Article 10 of the 1971 Fund Convention as amended by this Protocol have received during the preceding calendar year a total quantity of at least 450 million tons of contributing oil.

2. However, this Protocol shall not enter into force before the 1992 Liability Convention has entered into force.

3. For each State which ratifies, accepts, approves or accedes to this Protocol after the conditions in paragraph 1 for entry into force have been met, the Protocol shall enter into force twelve months following the date of the deposit by such State of the appropriate instrument.

4. Any State may, at the time of the deposit of its instrument of ratification, acceptance, approval or accession in respect of this Protocol declare that such instrument shall not take effect for the purpose of this article until the end of the six-month period in Article 31.

5. Any State which has made a declaration in accordance with the preceding paragraph may withdraw it at any time by means of a notification addressed to the Secretary–General of the Organization. Any such withdrawal shall take effect on the date the notification is received, and any State making such a withdrawal shall be deemed to have deposited its instrument of ratification, acceptance, approval or accession in respect of this Protocol on that date.

6. Any State which has made a declaration under Article 13, paragraph 2, of the Protocol of 1992 to amend the 1969 Liability Convention shall be deemed to have also made a declaration under paragraph 4 of this article. Withdrawal of a declaration under the said Article 13, paragraph 2, shall be deemed to constitute withdrawal also under paragraph 5 of this article.

Article 31

Denunciation of the 1969 and 1971 Conventions

Subject to Article 30, within six months following the date on which the following requirements are fulfilled:

(a) at least eight States have become Parties to this Protocol or have deposited instruments of ratification, acceptance, approval or accession with the Secretary–General of the Organization, whether or not subject to Article 30, paragraph 4, and

(b) the Secretary–General of the Organization has received information in accordance with Article 29 that those persons who are or would be liable to contribute pursuant to Article 10 of the 1971 Fund Convention as amended by this Protocol have received during the preceding calendar year a total quantity of at least 750 million tons of contributing oil;

each Party to this Protocol and each State which has deposited an instrument of ratification, acceptance, approval or accession, whether or not subject to Article 30, paragraph 4, shall, if Party thereto, denounce the 1971 Fund Convention and the 1969 Liability Convention with effect twelve months after the expiry of the above-mentioned six-month period.

Article 32

Revision and amendment

1. A conference for the purpose of revising or amending the 1992 Fund Convention may be convened by the Organization.

2. The Organization shall convene a Conference of Contracting States for the purpose of revising or amending the 1992 Fund Convention at the request of not less than one third of all Contracting States.

Article 33

Amendment of compensation limits

1. Upon the request of at least one quarter of the Contracting States, any proposal to amend the limits of amounts of compensation laid down in Article 4, paragraph 4, of the 1971 Fund Convention as amended by this Protocol shall be circulated by the Secretary–General to all Members of the Organization and to all Contracting States.

2. Any amendment proposed and circulated as above shall be submitted to the legal Committee of the Organization for consideration at a date at least six months after the date of its circulation.

3. All Contracting States to the 1971 Fund Convention as amended by this Protocol, whether or not Members of the Organization, shall be entitled to participate in the proceedings of the Legal Committee for the consideration and adoption of amendments.

4. Amendments shall be adopted by a two-thirds majority of the Contracting States present and voting in the Legal Committee, expanded as provided for in paragraph 3, on condition that at least one half of the Contracting States shall be present at the time of voting.

5. When acting on a proposal to amend the limits, the Legal Committee shall take into account the experience of incidents and in particular the amount of damage resulting therefrom and changes in the monetary values. It shall also take into account the relationship between the limits in Article 4, paragraph 4, of the 1971 Fund Convention as amended by this Protocol and those in Article V, paragraph 1, of the International Convention on Civil Liability for Oil Pollution Damage, 1992.

6. (a) No amendment of the limits under this article may be considered before 15 January 1998 nor less than five years from the date of entry into force of a previous amendment under this article. No amendment under this article shall be considered before this Protocol has entered into force.

(b) No limit may be increased so as to exceed an amount which corresponds to the limit laid down in the 1971 Fund Convention as amended by this Protocol increased by six per cent per year calculated on a compound basis for 15 January 1993.

(c) No limit may be increased so as to exceed an amount which corresponds to the limit laid down in the 1971 Fund Convention as amended by this Protocol multiplied by three.

7. Any amendment adopted in accordance with paragraph 4 shall be notified by the Organization to all Contracting States. The amendment shall be deemed to have been accepted at the end of a period of eighteen months after the date of notification unless within that period not less than one quarter of the States that were Contracting States at the time of the adoption of the amendment by the Legal Committee have communicated to the Organization that they do not accept the amendment in which case the amendment is rejected and shall have no effect.

8. An amendment deemed to have been accepted in accordance with paragraph 7 shall enter into force eighteen months after its acceptance.

9. All Contracting States shall be bound by the amendment, unless they denounce this Protocol in accordance with Article 34, paragraphs 1 and 2, at least six months before the amendment enters into force. Such denunciation shall take effect when the amendment enters into force.

10. When an amendment has been adopted by the Legal Committee but the eighteen-month period for its acceptance has not yet expired, a State which becomes a Contracting State during that period shall be bound by the amendment if it enters into force. A State which becomes a Contracting State after that period shall be bound by an amendment which has been accepted in accordance with paragraph 7. In the cases referred to in this paragraph, a State becomes bound by an amendment when that amendment enters into force, or when this Protocol enters into force for that State, if later.

Article 34

Denunciation

1. This Protocol may be denounced by any Party at any time after the date on which it enters into force for that Party.

2. Denunciation shall be effected by the deposit of an instrument with the Secretary–General of the Organization.

3. A denunciation shall take effect twelve months, or such longer period as may be specified in the instrument of denunciation, after its deposit with the Secretary–General of the Organization.

4. Denunciation of the 1992 Liability Convention shall be deemed to be a denunciation of this Protocol. Such denunciation shall take effect on the date on which denunciation of the Protocol of 1992 to amend the 1969 Liability Convention takes effect according to Article 16 of that Protocol.

5. Any Contracting State to this Protocol which has not denounced the 1971 Fund Convention and the 1969 Liability Convention as required by Article 31 shall be deemed to have denounced this Protocol with effect twelve months after the expiry of the six-month period mentioned in that article. As from the date on which the denunciations provided for in Article 31 take effect, any Party to this Protocol which deposits an 1969 Liability Convention shall be deemed to have denounced this Protocol with effect from the date on which such instrument takes effect.

6. As between the Parties to this Protocol, denunciation by any of them of the 1971 Fund Convention in accordance with Article 41 thereof shall not be construed in any way as a denunciation of the 1971 Fund Convention as amended by this Protocol.

7. Notwithstanding a denunciation of this Protocol by a Party pursuant to this article, any provisions of this Protocol relating to the obligations to make contributions under Article 10 of the 1971 Fund Convention as amended by this Protocol with

respect to an incident referred to in Article 12, paragraph 2(b), of that amended Convention and occurring before the denunciation takes effect shall continue to apply.

Article 35

Extraordinary sessions of the Assembly

1. Any Contracting State may, within ninety days after the deposit of an instrument of denunciation the result of which it considers will significantly increase the level of contributions for the remaining Contracting States, request the Director to convene an extraordinary session of the Assembly. The Director shall convene the Assembly to meet not later than sixty days after receipt of the request.

2. The Director may convene, on his own initiative, an extraordinary session of the Assembly to meet within sixty days after the deposit of any instrument of denunciation, if he considers that such denunciation will result in a significant increase in the level of contributions of the remaining Contracting States.

3. If the Assembly at an extraordinary session convened in accordance with paragraph 1 or 2 decides that the denunciation will result in a significant increase in the level of contributions for the remaining Contracting States, any such State may, not later than one hundred and twenty days before the date on which the denunciation takes effect, denounce this Protocol with effect from the same date.

Article 36

Termination

1. This Protocol shall cease to be in force on the date when the number of Contracting States falls below three.

2. States which are bound by this Protocol on the day before the date it ceases to be in force shall enable the Fund to exercise its functions as described under Article 37 of this Protocol and shall, for that purpose only, remain bound by this Protocol.

Article 37

Winding up of the Fund

1. If this Protocol ceases to be in force, the Fund shall nevertheless:

(a) meet its obligations in respect of any incident occurring before the Protocol ceased to be in force;

(b) be entitled to exercise its rights to contributions to the extent that these contributions are necessary to meet the obligations under subparagraph (a), including expenses for the administration of the Fund necessary for this purpose.

2. The Assembly shall take all appropriate measures to complete the winding up of the Fund including the distribution in an equitable manner of any remaining assets among those persons who have contributed to the Fund.

3. For the purposes of this article the Fund shall remain a legal person.

Article 38

Depositary

1. This Protocol and any amendments accepted under Article 33 shall be deposited with the Secretary–General of the Organization.

2. The Secretary–General of the Organization shall:

(a) inform all States which have signed or acceded to this Protocol of:

(i) each new signature or deposit of an instrument together with the date thereof,

(ii) each declaration and notification under Article 30 including declarations and withdrawals deemed to have been made in accordance with that Article;

(iii) the date of entry into force of this Protocol;

(iv) the date by which denunciations provided for in Article 31 are required to be made;

(v) any proposal to amend limits of amounts of compensation which has been made in accordance with Article 33, paragraph 1;

(vi) any amendment which has been adopted in accordance with Article 33, paragraph 4;

(vii) any amendment deemed to have been accepted under Article 33, paragraph 7, together with the date on which that amendment shall enter into force in accordance with paragraphs 8 and 9 of that article;

(viii) the deposit of an instrument of denunciation of this Protocol together with the date of the deposit and the date on which it takes effect;

(ix) any denunciation deemed to have been made under Article 34, paragraph 5;

(x) any communication called for by any article in this Protocol;

(b) transmit certified true copies of this Protocol to all Signatory States and to all States which accede to the Protocol.

3. As soon as this Protocol enters into force, the text shall be transmitted by the Secretary-General of the Organization to the Secretariat of the United Nations for registration and publication in accordance with Article 102 of the Charter of the United Nations.

Article 39

Languages

This protocol is established in a single original in the Arabic, Chinese, English, French, Russian and Spanish languages, each text being equally authentic.

DONE AT LONDON this twenty-seventh day of November one thousand nine hundred and ninety-two.

IN WITNESS WHEREOF the undersigned being duly authorized for that purpose have signed this Protocol.

4.27 1997 Ships' Routeing Amendment to the International Convention for the Safety of Life at Sea, 1974. Concluded at London, 16 May 1995. Entered into force, 1 January 1997. I.M.O. Resolution MSC.46(65)

Regulation V/8—Routeing

Ships' routeing

(a) Ships' routeing systems contribute to safety of life at sea, safety and efficiency of navigation, and/or protection of the marine environment. Ships' routeing systems are recommended for use by, and may be made mandatory for, all ships, certain categories of ships or ships carrying certain cargoes, when adopted and implemented in accordance with the guidelines and criteria developed by the Organization.

(b) The Organization is recognized as the only international body for developing guidelines, criteria and regulations on an international level for ships' routeing systems. Contracting Governments shall refer proposals for the adoption of ships' routeing systems to the Organization. The Organization will collate and disseminate to Contracting Governments all relevant information with regard to any adopted ships' routeing systems.

(c) This regulation, and its associated guidelines and criteria, does not apply to warships, naval auxiliary or other vessels owned or operated by a Contracting Government and used, for the time being, only on government non-commercial service; however, such ships are encouraged to participate in ships' routeing systems adopted in accordance with this regulation.

(d) The initiation of action for establishing a ships' routeing system is the responsibility of the Government or Governments concerned. In developing such systems for adoption by the Organization, the guidelines and criteria developed by the Organization shall be taken into account.

(e) Ships' routeing systems should be submitted to the Organization for adoption. However, a Government or Governments implementing ships' routeing systems not intended to be submitted to the Organization for adoption or which have not been adopted by the Organization are encouraged to follow, wherever possible, the guidelines and criteria developed by the Organization.

(f) Where two or more Governments have a common interest in a particular area, they should formulate joint proposals for the delineation and use of a routeing system therein on the basis of an agreement between them. Upon receipt of such proposal and before proceeding with the consideration of it for adoption, the Organization shall ensure details of the proposal are disseminated to the Governments which have a common interest in the area, including countries in the vicinity of the proposed ships' routeing system.

(g) Contracting Governments shall adhere to the measures adopted by the Organization concerning ships' routeing. They shall promulgate all information necessary for the safe and effective use of adopted ships' routeing systems. A Government or Governments concerned may monitor traffic in those systems. Contracting Governments will do everything in their power to secure the appropriate use of ships' routeing systems adopted by the Organization.

(h) A ship shall use a mandatory ships' routeing system adopted by the Organization as required for its category or cargo carried and in accordance with the relevant provisions in force unless there are compelling reasons not to use a particular ships' routeing system. Any such reason shall be recorded in the ship's log.

(i) Mandatory ships' routeing systems shall be reviewed by the Contracting Government or Governments concerned in accordance with the guidelines and criteria developed by the Organization.

(j) All adopted ships' routeing systems and actions taken to enforce compliance with those systems shall be consistent with international law, including the relevant provisions of the 1982 United Nations Convention on the Law of the Sea.

(k) Nothing in this regulation nor its associated guidelines and criteria shall prejudice the rights and duties of Governments under international law or the legal regime of international straits.

4.28 Global Programme of Action for the Protection of the Marine Environment From Land-Based Activities. Concluded at Washington, 3 November 1995. UNEP(OCA)/LBA/IG.2/7

I. INTRODUCTION

A. The Need for Action

1. The major threats to the health and productivity and biodiversity of the marine environment result from human activities on land-in coastal areas and further inland. Most of the pollution load of the oceans, including municipal, industrial and agricultural wastes and run-off, as well as atmospheric deposition, emanates from such land-based activities and affects the most productive areas of the marine environment, including estuaries and near-shore coastal waters. These areas are likewise threatened by physical alteration of the coastal environment, including destruction of habitats of vital importance for ecosystem health. Moreover, contaminants which pose risks to human health and living resources are transported long distances by watercourses, ocean currents and atmospheric processes.

2. The bulk of the world's population lives in coastal areas, and there is a continuing trend towards its concentration in these regions. The health, well-being and, in some cases, the very survival of coastal populations depend upon the health and well-being of coastal systems–estuaries and wetlands–as well as their associated watersheds and drainage basins and near-shore coastal waters. Ultimately, sustainable patterns of human activity in coastal areas depend upon a healthy marine environment, and vice versa.

B. Aims of the Global Programme of Action

3. The Global Programme of Action aims at preventing the degradation of the marine environment from land-based activities by facilitating the realization of the duty of States to preserve and protect the marine environment. It is designed to assist States in taking actions individually or jointly within their respective policies, priorities and resources, which will lead to the prevention, reduction, control and/or elimination of the degradation of the marine environment, as well as to its recovery from the impacts of land-based activities. Achievement of the aims of the Programme of Action will contribute to maintaining and, where appropriate, restoring the productive capacity and biodiversity of the marine environment, ensuring the protection of human health, as well as promoting the conservation and sustainable use of marine living resources.

C. Legal and Institutional Framework

4. International law, as reflected in the provisions of the United Nations Convention on the Law of the Sea (UNCLOS) and elsewhere, sets forth rights and obligations of States and provides the international basis upon which to pursue the protection and sustainable development of the marine and coastal environment and its resources.

5. In accordance with general international law, while States have the sovereign right to exploit their natural resources pursuant to their environmental policies, the enjoyment of such right shall be in accordance with the duty to protect and preserve the marine environment. This fundamental duty is to protect and preserve the marine environment from all sources of pollution, including land-based activities. Of particular significance for the Global Programme of Action are the provisions contained in articles 207 and 213 of UNCLOS.

6. Also of particular importance for the Programme of Action is the emphasis, in parts XII, XIII and XIV of the Convention, dealing, respectively, with protection and preservation of the marine environment, marine scientific research and the development and transfer of marine technology, on the obligation of States to cooperate in the

development of the marine scientific and technological capacity of developing States and to provide them with scientific and technical assistance.

7. The duty of States to preserve and protect the marine environment has been reflected and elaborated upon in numerous global conventions and regional instruments (e.g. the Convention on the Prevention of Marine Pollution by Dumping of Wastes and Other Matter; Basel Convention on the Control of Transboundary Movements of Hazardous Wastes and their Disposal; Convention on Biological Diversity; United Nations Framework Convention on Climate Change; Regional Seas Conventions; International Convention for the Prevention of Pollution from Ships (MARPOL 73/78), etc.). Innovative new principles and approaches applicable to the prevention of the degradation of the marine environment from land-based activities have been included in a number of such agreements.

8. In 1982, the United Nations Environment Programme (UNEP) took the initiative to develop advice to Governments on addressing impacts on the marine environment from land-based activities. This initiative resulted in the preparation of the Montreal Guidelines for the Protection of the Marine Environment Against Pollution from Land-based Sources in 1985.

9. The duty to protect the marine environment from land-based activities was placed squarely in the context of sustainable development by the United Nations Conference on Environment and Development in 1992. Therein, States agreed it is necessary:

(a) To apply preventive, precautionary, and anticipatory approaches so as to avoid degradation of the marine environment, as well as to reduce the risk of long-term or irreversible adverse effects upon it;

(b) To ensure prior assessment of activities that may have significant adverse impacts upon the marine environment;

(c) To integrate protection of the marine environment into relevant general environmental, social and economic development policies;

(d) To develop economic incentives, where appropriate, to apply clean technologies and other means consistent with the internalization of environmental costs, such as the "polluter pays" principle, so as to avoid degradation of the marine environment;

(e) To improve the living standards of coastal populations, particularly in developing countries, so as to contribute to reducing the degradation of the coastal and marine environment.

10. As set out in paragraph 17.23 of Agenda 21, States agree that provision of additional financial resources, through appropriate international mechanisms, as well as access to cleaner technologies and relevant research, would be necessary to support action by developing countries to implement this commitment.

11. Agenda 21 linked the implementation of those duties with action to implement commitments to integrated management and sustainable development of the marine environment, including coastal areas under national jurisdiction. In this regard, States agreed to implement the provisions of the programme of action adopted at the World Coast Conference in Noordwijk in 1993 and to further develop those provisions in order to make them more operational.

12. Agenda 21 also linked action to combat marine degradation caused by land-based activities to action to address the specific problems of small island developing States. In this regard, States agreed to implement the provisions of the priority areas of the Programme of Action for the Sustainable Development of Small Island Developing States, adopted in Barbados in 1994.

13. In order to promote, facilitate and finance implementation of Agenda 21 by developing countries, an objective of Agenda 21 is to provide additional financial resources that are both adequate and predictable. Another objective in this context is to promote, facilitate and finance, as appropriate, the access to and the transfer of environmentally sound technologies and corresponding know-how, in particular to developing countries, on favourable terms, including concessional and preferential terms, as mutually agreed, taking into account the need to protect intellectual property rights as well as the special needs of developing countries for the implementation of Agenda 21.

D. The Global Programme of Action

14. The Programme of Action, therefore, is designed to be a source of conceptual and practical guidance to be drawn upon by national and/or regional authorities in devising and implementing sustained action to prevent, reduce, control and/or eliminate marine degradation from land-based activities. Effective implementation of this Programme of Action is a crucial and essential step forward in the protection of the marine environment and will promote the objectives and goals of sustainable development.

15. The Global Programme of Action reflects the fact that States face a growing number of commitments flowing from Agenda 21 and related conventions. Its implementation will require new approaches by, and new forms of collaboration among, Governments, organizations and institutions with responsibilities and expertise relevant to marine and coastal areas, at all levels–national, regional and global. These include the promotion of innovative financial mechanisms to generate needed resources.

II. ACTIONS AT THE NATIONAL LEVEL

Basis for Action

16. Sustainable use of the oceans depends on the maintenance of ecosystem health, public health, food security, and economic and social benefits including cultural values. Many countries depend on sources of income from activities that would be directly threatened by degradation of the marine environment: industries such as fishing and tourism are obvious examples. The subsistence economy of large coastal populations, in particular in the developing countries, is based on marine living resources that would also be threatened by such degradation. Also to be considered are the impacts of such degradation on maritime culture and traditional lifestyles.

17. Food security is threatened, in particular in developing countries, by the loss of marine living resources that are vital for the adequate provision of food and for combating poverty. Public health considerations from a degraded marine environment manifest themselves through the contamination of seafood, direct contact, such as through bathing, and the use of sea water in desalination and food-processing plants.

Objectives

18. To develop comprehensive, continuing and adaptive programmes of action within the framework of integrated coastal area management which should include provisions for:

(a) Identification and assessment of problems;

(b) Establishment of priorities;

(c) Setting management objectives for priority problems;

(d) Identification, evaluation and selection of strategies and measures, including management approaches;

(e) Criteria for evaluating the effectiveness of strategies and programmes;

(f) Programme support elements.

Actions

19. States should, in accordance with their policies, priorities and resources, develop or review national programmes of action within a few years and take forward action to implement these programmes with the assistance of the international cooperation identified in chapter IV, in particular to developing countries, especially the least developed countries, countries with economies in transition and small island developing States (hereinafter referred to as "countries in need of assistance"). The effective development and implementation of national programmes of action should focus on sustainable, pragmatic and integrated environmental management approaches and processes, such as integrated coastal area management, harmonized, as appropriate, with river basin management and land-use plans.

* * *

III. REGIONAL COOPERATION

Basis for action

29. Regional and subregional cooperation and arrangements are crucial for successful actions to protect the marine environment from land-based activities. This is particularly so where a number of countries have coasts in the same marine and coastal area, most notably in enclosed or semi-enclosed seas. Such cooperation allows for more accurate identification and assessment of the problems in particular geographic areas and more appropriate establishment of priorities for action in these areas. Such cooperation also strengthens regional and national capacity-building and offers an important avenue for harmonizing and adjusting measures to fit the particular environmental and socio-economic circumstances. It, moreover, supports a more efficient and cost-effective implementation of the programmes of action.

Objectives

30. To strengthen and, where necessary, create new regional cooperative arrangements and joint actions to support effective action, strategies and programmes for:

(a) Identification and assessment of problems;

(b) Establishment of targets and priorities for action;

(c) Development and implementation of pragmatic and comprehensive management approaches and processes;

(d) Development and implementation of strategies to mitigate and remediate land-based sources of harm to the coastal and marine environment.

Activities

A. Participation in Regional and Subregional Arrangements

31. States should:

(a) Pursue more active participation, including accession or ratification, as appropriate, in regional seas and other international marine and freshwater agreements, conventions and related arrangements;

(b) Strengthen existing regional conventions and programmes, and their institutional arrangements;

(c) Negotiate as, appropriate, new regional conventions and programmes.

* * *

IV. INTERNATIONAL COOPERATION

Basis for action

36. Effective international cooperation is important for the successful and cost-effective implementation of the Programme of Action. International cooperation serves a central role in enhancing capacity-building, technology transfer and cooperation, and financial support. Moreover, effective implementation of the Programme of Action requires efficient support from appropriate international agencies. Furthermore, international cooperation is required to ensure regular review of the implementation of the Programme and its further development and adjustment.

37. At the global level, there is a need for regular reviews of the state of the world marine environment, as well as dialogues, based on reports from relevant regional organizations, on implementation of regional action programmes, including exchange of experiences, the flow of financial resources in support of the implementation, in particular by countries in need of assistance, of national action to prevent and reduce marine degradation caused by land-based activities as well as scientific and technological cooperation and transfer of cleaner technology, in particular, to countries in need of assistance.

Objective

38. To strengthen existing international cooperation and institutional mechanisms and, where appropriate, to establish new arrangements, in order to support States and regional groups to undertake sustained action to address impacts upon the marine environment from land-based activities. Such actions should be based on the commitments with respect to financial resources contained in chapter 33 of Agenda 21, including paragraph 33.11, and those with respect to transfer of environmentally sound technology, cooperation and capacity-building contained in chapter 34 of Agenda 21, including paragraphs 34.4 and 34.14, as well as the commitments contained in paragraphs 17.23 and 17.48.

Activities

39. Recommended actions to give effect to these objectives in support of national and regional action to prevent and reduce marine degradation caused by land-based activities fall into four general categories:

(a) Capacity-building;

(b) The mobilization of financial resources;

(c) The international institutional framework;

(d) Additional areas of international cooperation.

* * *

V. RECOMMENDED APPROACHES BY SOURCE CATEGORY

91. This chapter provides guidance as to the actions that States should consider at national, regional and global levels, in accordance with their national capacities, priorities and available resources, and with the cooperation of the United Nations and other relevant organizations, as appropriate, and with the international cooperation for building capacities and mobilizing resources identified in chapter IV.

92. In the light of the differences between regions and States and the national priorities referred to in paragraphs 53 and 54 above, each State and each regional

grouping should develop its own programme of action. This may or may not be a separate document but it should include specific targets and a clear timetable showing the dates by which the State or States involved commit themselves at a political level to achieve these targets.

93. In addition, action will be needed on certain matters at the global level, either to address global effects or to facilitate action at the national or regional levels. Specific targets for these matters are set out in this chapter.

A. Sewage

1. *Basis for action*

94. Recognizing variation in local conditions, domestic waste water improperly discharged to freshwater and coastal environments may present a variety of concerns. These are associated with: (a) pathogens that may result in human health problems through exposure via bathing waters or through contaminated shellfish, (b) suspended solids, (c) significant nutrient inputs, (d) biochemical oxygen demand (BOD), (e) cultural issues such as taboos in some areas, (f) plastics and other marine debris, (g) ecosystem population effects, and (h) heavy metals and other toxic substances, e.g. hydrocarbons, in those cases where industrial sources may have discharged effluent to municipal collection systems.

95. Environmental effects associated with domestic waste-water discharges are generally local with transboundary implications in certain geographic areas. The commonality of sewage-related problems throughout coastal areas of the world is significant. Consequently, domestic waste-water discharges are considered one of the most significant threats to coastal environments worldwide.

2. *Objective/proposed target*

96. With regard to objectives and targets, paragraph 21.29 of Agenda 21 states:

"Governments, according to their capacities and available resources and with the cooperation of the United Nations and other relevant organizations, as appropriate, should:

"(a) By the year 2000, establish waste treatment and disposal quality criteria, objectives and standards based on the nature and assimilative capacity of the receiving environment;

"(b) By the year 2000, establish sufficient capacity to undertake waste-related pollution impact monitoring and conduct regular surveillance, including epidemiological surveillance, where appropriate;

"(c) By the year 1995, in industrialized countries, and by the year 2005, in developing countries, ensure that at least 50 per cent of all sewage, waste waters and solid wastes are treated or disposed of in conformity with national or international environmental and health quality guidelines;

"(d) By the year 2025, dispose of all sewage, waste waters and solid wastes in conformity with national or international environmental quality guidelines."

* * *

B. Persistent Organic Pollutants (Pops)

1. *Basis for action*

100. Persistent organic pollutants (POPs) are a set of organic compounds that: (i) possess toxic characteristics; (ii) are persistent; (iii) are liable to bioaccumulate; (iv) are prone to long-range transport and deposition; and (v) can result in adverse environmental and human health effects at locations near and far from their source.

POPs are typically characterized as having low water solubility and high fat solubility. Most POPs are anthropogenic in origin. Anthropogenic emissions, both point and diffuse, are associated with industrial processes, product use and applications, waste disposal, leaks and spills, and combustion of fuels and waste materials. Once dispersed, clean-up is rarely possible. Because many POPs are relatively volatile, their remobilization and long-distance redistribution through atmospheric pathways often complicates the identification of specific sources.

101. POPs have long environmental half-lives. Accordingly, successive releases over time result in continued accumulation and the ubiquitous presence of POPs in the global environment.

102. The primary transport routes into the marine and coastal environment include atmospheric deposition and surface run-off. Regional and global transport is predominately mediated by atmospheric circulation, but also occurs through sediment transport and oceanic circulation. Movement may also occur through a successive migration of short-range movements that result from a sequence of volatilization, deposition, and revolatilization. Due to these transport patterns and chemical characteristics, there is a growing body of evidence demonstrating the systematic migration of these substances to cooler latitudes.

2. *Objective/proposed target*

103. The objective/proposed target is:

(a) To reduce and/or eliminate emissions and discharges of POPs that threaten to accumulate to dangerous levels in the marine and coastal environment;

(b) To give immediate attention to finding and introducing preferable substitutes for chemicals that pose unreasonable and otherwise unmanageable risks to human health and the environment;

(c) To use cleaner production processes, including best available techniques, to reduce and/or eliminate hazardous by-products associated with production, incineration and combustion (e.g. dioxins, furans, hexaclorobenzene, poycyclic aromatic hydrocarbons (PAHs));

(d) To promote best environmental practice for pest control in agriculture and aquaculture.

* * *

C. Radioactive Substances

1. *Basis for action*

107. Radioactive substances (i.e., materials containing radionuclides) have entered and/or are entering the marine and coastal environment, directly or indirectly, as a result of a variety of human activities and practices. These activities include production of energy, reprocessing of spent fuel, military operations, nuclear testing, medical applications and other operations associated with the management and disposal of radioactive wastes and the processing of natural materials by industrial processes. Other activities, such as the transport of radioactive material, pose risks of such releases.

108. Radioactive materials can present hazards to human health and to the environment. Suspected radioactive contamination of foodstuffs can also have negative effects on marketing of such foodstuffs.

2. *Objective/proposed target*

109. The objective/proposed target is to reduce and/or eliminate emissions and discharges of radioactive substances in order to prevent, reduce and eliminate pollution

of the marine and coastal environment by human-enhanced levels of radioactive substances.

* * *

D. Heavy metals

1. *Basis for action*

114. Heavy metals are natural constituents of the Earth's crust. Human activities have drastically altered the biochemical and geochemical cycles and balance of some heavy metals. Heavy metals are stable and persistent environmental contaminants since they cannot be degraded or destroyed. Therefore, they tend to accumulate in the soils and sediments. Excessive levels of metals in the marine environment can affect marine biota and pose risk to human consumers of seafood.

115. Metals and their compounds, both inorganic and organic, are released to the environment as a result of a variety of human activities. A wide range of metals and metallic compounds found in the marine environment pose risks to human health through the consumption of seafood where contaminant content and exposure are significant. Many metals are essential to life and only become toxic when exposures to biota become excessive (i.e., exceed some threshold for the introduction of adverse effects). While certain non-essential metals do not have explicit exposure thresholds for the introduction of effects, the nature of biological responses to metal exposure are a direct consequence of exposure and are defined through dose-effect relationships. This differs from the dose-response relationship associated with many synthetic organic contaminants and radionuclides where risk of adverse effects is assumed to be proportional to exposure. Accordingly, it is desirable to minimize such exposures. In contrast, the predominant challenge in the case of heavy metals is one of limiting exposure to levels that do not cause adverse effects.

116. The main anthropogenic sources of heavy metals are various industrial point sources, including present and former mining activities, foundries and smelters, and diffuse sources such as piping, constituents of products, combustion by-products, traffic, etc. Relatively volatile heavy metals and those that become attached to airborne particles can be widely dispersed on very large scales. Heavy metals conveyed in aqueous and sedimentary transport (e.g., river run-off) enter the normal coastal biogeochemical cycle and are largely retained within near-shore and shelf regions.

2. *Objective/proposed target*

117. The objective/proposed target is to reduce and/or eliminate anthropogenic emissions and discharges in order to prevent, reduce and eliminate pollution caused by heavy metals.

* * *

E. Oils (Hydrocarbons)

1. *Basis for action*

121. Many oils are liquid and gaseous hydrocarbons of geological origin. While some oils are naturally occurring, a significant proportion of those in the marine and coastal environment have been derived from anthropogenic sources. Most oils from land-based sources are refined petroleum products or their derivatives. Some oils are volatile or easily degraded and disappear rapidly from aquatic systems, but some may persist in the water column or in sediments. Oils may be toxic to aquatic life when ingested or absorbed through skin or gills, interfere with respiratory systems, foul fur and feathers, smother aquatic communities, habitats and bathing beaches, taint seafood and contaminate water supplies.

122. Land-based sources of oils include operational and accidental discharges and emissions from oil exploration, exploitation, refining and storage facilities; urban, industrial and agricultural run-off; transport; and the inappropriate disposal of used lubricating oils. The main pathways to the marine environment include atmospheric dispersion of volatile fractions; storm sewers and sewage treatment works; and rivers. Impacts from land-derived oils will be regional for the more volatile fractions, and local (occasionally regional) for more refractory components.

2. *Objective/proposed target*

123. The objective is to prevent, reduce and/or eliminate anthropogenic emissions and discharges in order to prevent, reduce and eliminate pollution caused by oil.

* * *

F. Nutrients

1. *Basis for action*

127. Eutrophication can result from augmentation of nutrient inputs to coastal and marine areas as a consequence of human activities. In general, such eutrophication is usually confined to the vicinity of coastal discharges but, because of both the multiplicity of such discharges and regional atmospheric transport of nutrients, such affected coastal areas can be extensive.

128. The effects of the enhanced mobilization of nutrients are enhanced productivity but these can also result in changes in species diversity, excessive algal growth, dissolved oxygen reductions and associated fish kills and, it is suspected, the increased prevalence or frequency of toxic algal blooms.

2. *Objective/proposed target*

129. The objective/proposed target is:

(a) To identify, in broad terms, marine areas where nutrient inputs are causing or are likely to cause pollution, directly or indirectly;

(b) To reduce nutrient inputs into the areas identified;

(c) To reduce the number of marine areas where eutrophication is evident;

(d) To protect and, where appropriate, to restore areas of natural denitrification.

* * *

G. Sediment Mobilization

1. *Basis for action*

133. Natural sedimentation and siltation are important in the development and maintenance of numerous coastal habitats. Habitats requiring sediment input include coastal wetlands, lagoons, estuaries and mangroves. Reduction in natural rates of sedimentation can compromise the integrity of these habitats, as can excessive sediment loads, which may bury benthic communities and threaten sensitive habitats such as coral reefs, mangroves, seagrass beds, and rocky substrates.

134. Contaminated sediments, whether they are fresh inputs or dredged, may also lead to pollution, the latter through resuspension or improper disposal.

135. Anthropogenic modifications to sediment mobilization and sedimentation are made by, inter alia, construction activities, forestry operations, agricultural practices, mining practices, hydrological modifications, dredging activities, and coastal erosion. Effects are generally local in nature, but transboundary implications may

occur in some areas where major river systems form a common border and where littoral currents carry inputs across international boundaries.

2. *Objective/proposed target*

136. The objective/proposed target is to reduce, control and prevent the degradation of the marine environment due to changes in coastal erosion and siltation caused by human activities.

* * *

H. Litter

1. *Basis for action*

140. Litter threatens marine life through entanglement, suffocation and ingestion and is widely recognized to degrade the visual amenities of marine and coastal areas with negative effects on tourism and general aesthetics. Litter is any persistent manufactured or processed solid material which is discarded, disposed of, or abandoned in the marine and coastal environment, sometimes called marine debris. Litter in the marine environment can also destroy coastal habitats and in some situations interfere with biological production in coastal areas.

141. Litter entering the marine and coastal environment has multiple sources. Sources include poorly managed or illegal waste dumps adjacent to rivers and coastal areas, windblown litter from coastal communities, resin pellets used as industrial feedstocks, and litter that is channelled to the marine and coastal environment through municipal stormwater systems and rivers. Marine litter is also caused by dumping of garbage into the marine and coastal environment by municipal authorities as well as recreational and commercial vessels.

142. While international action has been taken to prevent the discharge of plastics and other persistent wastes from vessels, it has been estimated that approximately 80 per cent of persistent wastes originate from land. Floatable litter is known to travel considerable distances with regional and sometimes broader implications. Resin pellets used as industrial feedstock circulate and deposit on oceanic scales.

143. Uncontrolled burning of litter containing plastics may generate significant quantities of POPs, metals and hydrocarbons which can reach the marine and coastal environment.

2. *Objective/proposed target*

144. The objective/proposed target is:

(a) To establish controlled and environmentally sound facilities for receiving, collecting, handling and disposing of litter from coastal area communities;

(b) To reduce significantly the amount of litter reaching the marine and coastal environment by the prevention or reduction of the generation of solid waste and improvements in its management, including collection and recycling of litter.a. In this context, paragraph 21.39 of Agenda 21 states:

"The overall objective of this programme is to provide health-protecting environmentally safe waste collection and disposal services to all people. Governments, according to their capacities and available resources and with the cooperation of the United Nations and other relevant organizations, as appropriate, should:

"(a) By the year 2000, have the necessary technical, financial and human resource capacity to provide waste collection services commensurate with needs;

"(b) By the year 2025, provide all urban populations with adequate waste services;

"(c) By the year 2025, ensure that full urban waste service coverage is maintained and sanitation coverage achieved in all rural areas."

* * *

I. Physical Alterations and Destruction of Habitats

1. *Basis for action*

149. The increase of populations and economic activities in coastal areas is leading to an expansion of construction and alterations to coastal areas and waters. Excavation, oil and gas exploration and exploitation, mining, such as sand and aggregate extraction, the building of ports and marinas and building of coastal defences and other activities linked to urban expansion are giving rise to alterations of coral reefs, shorelands, beachfronts and the seafloor. Important habitats are being destroyed. Wetlands are being transformed into agricultural lands and through coastal development. Tourism, unrestricted and uncontrolled aquaculture, clearance of mangroves and destructive fishing practices, such as the use of dynamite and chemicals, are also causing the physical destruction of important habitats. The introduction of alien species can also have serious effects upon marine ecosystem integrity. Spawning grounds, nurseries and feeding grounds of major living marine resources of crucial importance to world food security are being destroyed. This destruction of habitat exacerbates overharvesting of these living marine resources leading to a growing risk that they are being depleted. This is an increasing threat to the food security of coastal populations, in particular in developing countries.

150. The damming of river systems can result in upstream sedimentation, possible changes in estuarine conditions and interference with fish migration. These adversely affect biological diversity and biological productivity. The practice of saltwinning from saltpan construction in coastal areas can also affect salt concentration levels and biological diversity.

2. *Objective/proposed target*

151. The objective/proposed target is to:

(a) Safeguard the ecosystem function, maintain the integrity and biological diversity of habitats which are of major socio-economic and ecological interest through integrated management of coastal areas;

(b) Where practicable, restore marine and coastal habitats that have been adversely affected by anthropogenic activities.

4.29 Washington Declaration on Protection of the Marine Environment From Land-Based Activities. Adopted on 5 December 1995. Annex II to the Intergovernmental Conference to Adopt a Global Programme of Action for the Protection of the Marine Environment From Land-Based Activities, UNEP(OCA)/LBA/IG.2/6

The representatives of Governments and the European Commission participating in the Conference held in Washington from 23 October to 3 November 1995,

Affirming the need and will to protect and preserve the marine environment for present and future generations,

Reaffirming the relevant provisions of chapters 17, 33 and 34 of Agenda 21 and the Rio Declaration on Environment and Development,

Recognizing the interdependence of human populations and the coastal and marine environment, and the growing and serious threat from land-based activities, to both human health and well-being and the integrity of coastal and marine ecosystems and biodiversity,

Further recognizing the importance of integrated coastal area management and the catchment-area-based approach as means of coordinating programmes aimed at preventing marine degradation from land-based activities with economic and social development programmes,

Also recognizing that the alleviation of poverty is an essential factor in addressing the impacts of land-based activities on coastal and marine areas,

Noting that there are major differences among the different regions of the world, and the States which they comprise, in terms of environmental, economic and social conditions and level of development which will lead to different judgments on priorities in addressing problems related to the degradation of the marine environment by land-based activities,

Acknowledging the need to involve major groups in national, regional and international activities to address degradation of the marine environment by land-based activities,

Strongly supporting the processes set forth in decisions 18/31 and 18/32 of 25 May 1995 of the Governing Council of the United Nations Environment Programme for addressing at the global level the priority issues of persistent organic pollutants and adequate treatment of waste water,

Having therefore adopted the Global Programme of Action for the Protection of the Marine Environment from Land-based Activities,

Hereby declare their commitment to protect and preserve the marine environment from the impacts of land-based activities, and

Declare their intention to do so by:

1. Setting as their common goal sustained and effective action to deal with all land-based impacts upon the marine environment, specifically those resulting from sewage, persistent organic pollutants, radioactive substances, heavy metals, oils (hydrocarbons), nutrients, sediment mobilization, litter, and physical alteration and destruction of habitat;
2. Developing or reviewing national action programmes within a few years on the basis of national priorities and strategies;
3. Taking forward action to implement these programmes in accordance with national capacities and priorities;
4. Cooperating to build capacities and mobilize resources for the development and implementation of such programmes, in particular for developing countries,

especially the least developed countries, countries with economies in transition and small island developing States (hereinafter referred to as "countries in need of assistance");

5. Taking immediate preventive and remedial action, wherever possible, using existing knowledge, resources, plans and processes;

6. Promoting access to cleaner technologies, knowledge and expertise to address land-based activities that degrade the marine environment, in particular for countries in need of assistance;

7. Cooperating on a regional basis to coordinate efforts for maximum efficiency and to facilitate action at the national level, including, where appropriate, becoming parties to and strengthening regional cooperative agreements and creating new agreements where necessary;

8. Encouraging cooperative and collaborative action and partnerships, among governmental institutions and organizations, communities, the private sector and non-governmental organizations which have relevant responsibilities and/or experience;

9. Encouraging and/or making available external financing, given that funding from domestic sources and mechanisms for the implementation of the Global Programme of Action by countries in need of assistance may be insufficient;

10. Promoting the full range of available management tools and financing options in implementing national or regional programmes of action, including innovative managerial and financial techniques, while recognizing the differences between countries in need of assistance and developed States;

11. Urging national and international institutions and the private sector, bilateral donors and multilateral funding agencies to accord priority to projects within national and regional programmes to implement the Global Programme of Action and encouraging the Global Environment Facility to support these projects;

12. Calling upon the United Nations Environment Programme, the United Nations Development Programme, the World Bank, the regional development banks, as well as the agencies within the United Nations system to ensure that their programmes support (through, inter alia, financial cooperation, capacity-building and institutional-strengthening mechanisms) the regional structures in place for the protection of the marine environment;

13. According priority to implementation of the Global Programme of Action within the United Nations system, as well as in other global and regional institutions and organizations with responsibilities and capabilities for addressing marine degradation from land-based activities, and specifically:

    (a) Securing formal endorsement of those parts of the Global Programme of Action that are relevant to such institutions and organizations and incorporating the relevant provisions into their work programmes;

    (b) Establishing a clearing-house mechanism to provide decision makers in all States with direct access to relevant sources of information, practical experience and scientific and technical expertise and to facilitate effective scientific, technical and financial cooperation as well as capacity-building; and

    (c) Providing for periodic intergovernmental review of the Global Programme of Action, taking into account regular assessments of the state of the marine environment;

14. Promoting action to deal with the consequences of sea-based activities, such as shipping, offshore activities and ocean dumping, which require national and/or

regional actions on land, including establishing adequate reception and recycling facilities;

15. Giving priority to the treatment and management of waste water and industrial effluents, as part of the overall management of water resources, especially through the installation of environmentally and economically appropriate sewage systems, including studying mechanisms to channel additional resources for this purpose expeditiously to countries in need of assistance;

16. Requesting the Executive Director of the United Nations Environment Programme, in close partnership with the World Health Organization, the United Nations Centre for Human Settlements (Habitat), the United Nations Development Programme and other relevant organizations, to prepare proposals for a plan to address the global nature of the problem of inadequate management and treatment of waste water and its consequences for human health and the environment, and to promote the transfer of appropriate and affordable technology drawn from the best available techniques;

17. Acting to develop, in accordance with the provisions of the Global Programme of Action, a global, legally binding instrument for the reduction and/or elimination of emissions, discharges and, where appropriate, the elimination of the manufacture and use of the persistent organic pollutants identified in decision 18/32 of the Governing Council of the United Nations Environment Programme.

The nature of the obligations undertaken must be developed recognizing the special circumstances of countries in need of assistance. Particular attention should be devoted to the potential need for the continued use of certain persistent organic pollutants to safeguard human health, sustain food production and to alleviate poverty in the absence of alternatives and the difficulty of acquiring substitutes and transferring of technology for the development and/or production of those substitutes; and

18. Elaborating the steps relating to institutional follow-up, including the clearing-house mechanism, in a resolution of the United Nations General Assembly at its fifty-first session, and in that regard, States should coordinate with the United Nations Environment Programme, as secretariat of the Global Programme of Action, and other relevant agencies within the United Nations system in the development of the resolution and include it on the agenda of the Commission on Sustainable Development at its inter-sessional meeting in February 1996 and its session in April 1996.

4.30 Convention on the Law of the Non-navigational Uses of International Watercourses (With Annex and Statement of Understanding). Adopted on 21 May 1997. Not yet in force. UN Doc. A/51/869; *reprinted in* 36 I.L.M. 700 (1997) & 5 Weston V.F.37

The Parties to the present Convention,

Conscious of the importance of international watercourses and the non-navigational uses thereof in many regions of the world,

Having in mind Article 13, paragraph 1 (a), of the Charter of the United Nations, which provides that the General Assembly shall initiate studies and make recommendations for the purpose of encouraging the progressive development of international law and its codification,

Considering that successful codification and progressive development of rules of international law regarding non-navigational uses of international watercourses would assist in promoting and implementing the purposes and principles set forth in Articles 1 and 2 of the Charter of the United Nations,

Taking into account the problems affecting many international watercourses resulting from, among other things, increasing demands and pollution,

Expressing the conviction that a framework convention will ensure the utilization, development, conservation, management and protection of international watercourses and the promotion of the optimal and sustainable utilization thereof for present and future generations,

Affirming the importance of international cooperation and good-neighbourliness in this field,

Aware of the special situation and needs of developing countries,

Recalling the principles and recommendations adopted by the United Nations Conference on Environment and Development of 1992 in the Rio Declaration and Agenda 21,

Recalling also the existing bilateral and multilateral agreements regarding the non-navigational uses of international watercourses,

Mindful of the valuable contribution of international organizations, both governmental and non-governmental, to the codification and progressive development of international law in this field,

Appreciative of the work carried out by the International Law Commission on the law of the non-navigational uses of international watercourses,

Bearing in mind United Nations General Assembly resolution 49/52 of 9 December 1994,

Have agreed as follows:

PART I. INTRODUCTION

Article 1

Scope of the present Convention

1. The present Convention applies to uses of international watercourses and of their waters for purposes other than navigation and to measures of protection, preservation and management related to the uses of those watercourses and their waters.

2. The uses of international watercourses for navigation is not within the scope of the present Convention except insofar as other uses affect navigation or are affected by navigation.

Article 2

Use of terms

For the purposes of the present Convention:

(a) "Watercourse" means a system of surface waters and groundwaters constituting by virtue of their physical relationship a unitary whole and normally flowing into a common terminus;

(b) "International watercourse" means a watercourse, parts of which are situated in different States;

(c) "Watercourse State" means a State Party to the present Convention in whose territory part of an international watercourse is situated, or a Party that is a regional economic integration organization, in the territory of one or more of whose Member States part of an international watercourse is situated;

(d) "Regional economic integration organization" means an organization constituted by sovereign States of a given region, to which its member States have transferred competence in respect of matters governed by this Convention and which has been duly authorized in accordance with its internal procedures, to sign, ratify, accept, approve or accede to it.

Article 3

Watercourse agreements

1. In the absence of an agreement to the contrary, nothing in the present Convention shall affect the rights or obligations of a watercourse State arising from agreements in force for it on the date on which it became a party to the present Convention.

2. Notwithstanding the provisions of paragraph 1, parties to agreements referred to in paragraph 1 may, where necessary, consider harmonizing such agreements with the basic principles of the present Convention.

3. Watercourse States may enter into one or more agreements, hereinafter referred to as "watercourse agreements", which apply and adjust the provisions of the present Convention to the characteristics and uses of a particular international watercourse or part thereof.

4. Where a watercourse agreement is concluded between two or more watercourse States, it shall define the waters to which it applies. Such an agreement may be entered into with respect to an entire international watercourse or any part thereof or a particular project, programme or use except insofar as the agreement adversely affects, to a significant extent, the use by one or more other watercourse States of the waters of the watercourse, without their express consent.

5. Where a watercourse State considers that adjustment and application of the provisions of the present Convention is required because of the characteristics and uses of a particular international watercourse, watercourse States shall consult with a view to negotiating in good faith for the purpose of concluding a watercourse agreement or agreements.

6. Where some but not all watercourse States to a particular international watercourse are parties to an agreement, nothing in such agreement shall affect the rights or obligations under the present Convention of watercourse States that are not parties to such an agreement.

Article 4

Parties to watercourse agreements

1. Every watercourse State is entitled to participate in the negotiation of and to become a party to any watercourse agreement that applies to the entire international watercourse, as well as to participate in any relevant consultations.

2. A watercourse State whose use of an international watercourse may be affected to a significant extent by the implementation of a proposed watercourse agreement that applies only to a part of the watercourse or to a particular project, programme or use is entitled to participate in consultations on such an agreement and, where appropriate, in the negotiation thereof in good faith with a view to becoming a party thereto, to the extent that its use is thereby affected.

PART II. GENERAL PRINCIPLES

Article 5

Equitable and reasonable utilization and participation

1. Watercourse States shall in their respective territories utilize an international watercourse in an equitable and reasonable manner. In particular, an international watercourse shall be used and developed by watercourse States with a view to attaining optimal and sustainable utilization thereof and benefits therefrom, taking into account the interests of the watercourse States concerned, consistent with adequate protection of the watercourse.

2. Watercourse States shall participate in the use, development and protection of an international watercourse in an equitable and reasonable manner. Such participation includes both the right to utilize the watercourse and the duty to cooperate in the protection and development thereof, as provided in the present Convention.

Article 6

Factors relevant to equitable and reasonable utilization

1. Utilization of an international watercourse in an equitable and reasonable manner within the meaning of article 5 requires taking into account all relevant factors and circumstances, including:

(a) Geographic, hydrographic, hydrological, climatic, ecological and other factors of a natural character;

(b) The social and economic needs of the watercourse States concerned;

(c) The population dependent on the watercourse in each watercourse State;

(d) The effects of the use or uses of the watercourses in one watercourse State on other watercourse States;

(e) Existing and potential uses of the watercourse;

(f) Conservation, protection, development and economy of use of the water resources of the watercourse and the costs of measures taken to that effect;

(g) The availability of alternatives, of comparable value, to a particular planned or existing use.

2. In the application of article 5 or paragraph 1 of this article, watercourse States concerned shall, when the need arises, enter into consultations in a spirit of cooperation.

3. The weight to be given to each factor is to be determined by its importance in comparison with that of other relevant factors. In determining what is a reasonable and equitable use, all relevant factors are to be considered together and a conclusion reached on the basis of the whole.

Article 7

Obligation not to cause significant harm

1. Watercourse States shall, in utilizing an international watercourse in their territories, take all appropriate measures to prevent the causing of significant harm to other watercourse States.

2. Where significant harm nevertheless is caused to another watercourse State, the States whose use causes such harm shall, in the absence of agreement to such use, take all appropriate measures, having due regard for the provisions of articles 5 and 6, in consultation with the affected State, to eliminate or mitigate such harm and, where appropriate, to discuss the question of compensation.

Article 8

General obligation to cooperate

1. Watercourse States shall cooperate on the basis of sovereign equality, territorial integrity, mutual benefit and good faith in order to attain optimal utilization and adequate protection of an international watercourse.

2. In determining the manner of such cooperation, watercourse States may consider the establishment of joint mechanisms or commissions, as deemed necessary by them, to facilitate cooperation on relevant measures and procedures in the light of experience gained through cooperation in existing joint mechanisms and commissions in various regions.

Article 9

Regular exchange of data and information

1. Pursuant to article 8, watercourse States shall on a regular basis exchange readily available data and information on the condition of the watercourse, in particular that of a hydrological, meteorological, hydrogeological and ecological nature and related to the water quality as well as related forecasts.

2. If a watercourse State is requested by another watercourse State to provide data or information that is not readily available, it shall employ its best efforts to comply with the request but may condition its compliance upon payment by the requesting State of the reasonable costs of collecting and, where appropriate, processing such data or information.

3. Watercourse States shall employ their best efforts to collect and, where appropriate, to process data and information in a manner which facilitates its utilization by the other watercourse States to which it is communicated.

Article 10

Relationship between different kinds of uses

1. In the absence of agreement or custom to the contrary, no use of an international watercourse enjoys inherent priority over other uses.

2. In the event of a conflict between uses of an international watercourse, it shall be resolved with reference to articles 5 to 7, with special regard being given to the requirements of vital human needs.

PART III. PLANNED MEASURES

Article 11

Information concerning planned measures

Watercourse States shall exchange information and consult each other and, if necessary, negotiate on the possible effects of planned measures on the condition of an international watercourse.

Article 12

Notification concerning planned measures with possible adverse effects

Before a watercourse State implements or permits the implementation of planned measures which may have a significant adverse effect upon other watercourse States, it shall provide those States with timely notification thereof. Such notification shall be accompanied by available technical data and information, including the results of any environmental impact assessment, in order to enable the notified States to evaluate the possible effects of the planned measures.

Article 13

Period for reply to notification

Unless otherwise agreed:

(a) A watercourse State providing a notification under article 12 shall allow the notified States a period of six months within which to study and evaluate the possible effects of the planned measures and to communicate the findings to it;

(b) This period shall, at the request of a notified State for which the evaluation of the planned measures poses special difficulty, be extended for a period of six months.

Article 14

Obligations of the notifying State during the period for reply

During the period referred to in article 13, the notifying State:

(a) Shall cooperate with the notified States by providing them, on request, with any additional data and information that is available and necessary for an accurate evaluation; and

(b) Shall not implement or permit the implementation of the planned measures without the consent of the notified States.

Article 15

Reply to notification

The notified States shall communicate their findings to the notifying State as early as possible within the period applicable pursuant to article 13. If a notified State finds that implementation of the planned measures would be inconsistent with the provisions of articles 5 or 7, it shall attach to its finding a documented explanation setting forth the reasons for the finding.

Article 16

Absence of reply to notification

1. If, within the period applicable pursuant to article 13, the notifying State receives no communication under article 15, it may, subject to its obligations under articles 5 and 7, proceed with the implementation of the planned measures, in accordance with the notification and any other data and information provided to the notified States.

2. Any claim to compensation by a notified State which has failed to reply within the period applicable pursuant to article 13 may be offset by the costs incurred by the notifying State for action undertaken after the expiration of the time for a reply which would not have been undertaken if the notified State had objected within that period.

Article 17

Consultations and negotiations concerning planned measures

1. If a communication is made under article 15 that implementation of the planned measures would be inconsistent with the provisions of articles 5 or 7, the notifying State and the State making the communication shall enter into consultations

and, if necessary, negotiations with a view to arriving at an equitable resolution of the situation.

2. The consultations and negotiations shall be conducted on the basis that each State must in good faith pay reasonable regard to the rights and legitimate interests of the other State.

3. During the course of the consultations and negotiations, the notifying State shall, if so requested by the notified State at the time it makes the communication, refrain from implementing or permitting the implementation of the planned measures for a period of six months unless otherwise agreed.

Article 18

Procedures in the absence of notification

1. If a watercourse State has reasonable grounds to believe that another watercourse State is planning measures that may have a significant adverse effect upon it, the former State may request the latter to apply the provisions of article 12. The request shall be accompanied by a documented explanation setting forth its grounds.

2. In the event that the State planning the measures nevertheless finds that it is not under an obligation to provide a notification under article 12, it shall so inform the other State, providing a documented explanation setting forth the reasons for such finding. If this finding does not satisfy the other State, the two States shall, at the request of that other State, promptly enter into consultations and negotiations in the manner indicated in paragraphs 1 and 2 of article 17.

3. During the course of the consultations and negotiations, the State planning the measures shall, if so requested by the other State at the time it requests the initiation of consultations and negotiations, refrain from implementing or permitting the implementation of those measures for a period of six months unless otherwise agreed.

Article 19

Urgent implementation of planned measures

1. In the event that the implementation of planned measures is of the utmost urgency in order to protect public health, public safety or other equally important interests, the State planning the measures may, subject to articles 5 and 7, immediately proceed to implementation, notwithstanding the provisions of article 14 and paragraph 3 of article 17.

2. In such case, a formal declaration of the urgency of the measures shall be communicated without delay to the other watercourse States referred to in article 12 together with the relevant data and information.

3. The State planning the measures shall, at the request of any of the States referred to in paragraph 2, promptly enter into consultations and negotiations with it in the manner indicated in paragraphs 1 and 2 of article 17.

PART IV. PROTECTION, PRESERVATION AND MANAGEMENT

Article 20

Protection and preservation of ecosystems

Watercourse States shall, individually and, where appropriate, jointly, protect and preserve the ecosystems of international watercourses.

Article 21

Prevention, reduction and control of pollution

1. For the purpose of this article, "pollution of an international watercourse" means any detrimental alteration in the composition or quality of the waters of an international watercourse which results directly or indirectly from human conduct.

2. Watercourse States shall, individually and, where appropriate, jointly, prevent, reduce and control the pollution of an international watercourse that may cause significant harm to other watercourse States or to their environment, including harm to human health or safety, to the use of the waters for any beneficial purpose or to the living resources of the watercourse. Watercourse States shall take steps to harmonize their policies in this connection.

3. Watercourse States shall, at the request of any of them, consult with a view to arriving at mutually agreeable measures and methods to prevent, reduce and control pollution of an international watercourse, such as:

(a) Setting joint water quality objectives and criteria;

(b) Establishing techniques and practices to address pollution from point and non-point sources;

(c) Establishing lists of substances the introduction of which into the waters of an international watercourse is to be prohibited, limited, investigated or monitored.

Article 22

Introduction of alien or new species

Watercourse States shall take all measures necessary to prevent the introduction of species, alien or new, into an international watercourse which may have effects detrimental to the ecosystem of the watercourse resulting in significant harm to other watercourse States.

Article 23

Protection and preservation of the marine environment

Watercourse States shall, individually and, where appropriate, in cooperation with other States, take all measures with respect to an international watercourse that are necessary to protect and preserve the marine environment, including estuaries, taking into account generally accepted international rules and standards.

Article 24

Management

1. Watercourse States shall, at the request of any of them, enter into consultations concerning the management of an international watercourse, which may include the establishment of a joint management mechanism.

2. For the purposes of this article, "management" refers, in particular, to:

(a) Planning the sustainable development of an international watercourse and providing for the implementation of any plans adopted; and

(b) Otherwise promoting the rational and optimal utilization, protection and control of the watercourse.

Article 25

Regulation

1. Watercourse States shall cooperate, where appropriate, to respond to needs or opportunities for regulation of the flow of the waters of an international watercourse.

2. Unless otherwise agreed, watercourse States shall participate on an equitable basis in the construction and maintenance or defrayal of the costs of such regulation works as they may have agreed to undertake.

3. For the purposes of this article, "regulation" means the use of hydraulic works or any other continuing measure to alter, vary or otherwise control the flow of the waters of an international watercourse.

Article 26

Installations

1. Watercourse States shall, within their respective territories, employ their best efforts to maintain and protect installations, facilities and other works related to an international watercourse.

2. Watercourse States shall, at the request of any of them which has reasonable grounds to believe that it may suffer significant adverse effects, enter into consultations with regard to:

(a) The safe operation and maintenance of installations, facilities or other works related to an international watercourse; and

(b) The protection of installations, facilities or other works from wilful or negligent acts or the forces of nature.

PART V. HARMFUL CONDITIONS AND EMERGENCY SITUATIONS

Article 27

Prevention and mitigation of harmful conditions

Watercourse States shall, individually and, where appropriate, jointly, take all appropriate measures to prevent or mitigate conditions related to an international watercourse that may be harmful to other watercourse States, whether resulting from natural causes or human conduct, such as flood or ice conditions, water-borne diseases, siltation, erosion, salt-water intrusion, drought or desertification.

Article 28

Emergency situations

1. For the purposes of this article, "emergency" means a situation that causes, or poses an imminent threat of causing, serious harm to watercourse States or other States and that results suddenly from natural causes, such as floods, the breaking up of ice, landslides or earthquakes, or from human conduct, such as industrial accidents.

2. A watercourse State shall, without delay and by the most expeditious means available, notify other potentially affected States and competent international organizations of any emergency originating within its territory.

3. A watercourse State within whose territory an emergency originates shall, in cooperation with potentially affected States and, where appropriate, competent international organizations, immediately take all practicable measures necessitated by the circumstances to prevent, mitigate and eliminate harmful effects of the emergency.

4. When necessary, watercourse States shall jointly develop contingency plans for responding to emergencies, in cooperation, where appropriate, with other potentially affected States and competent international organizations.

PART VI. MISCELLANEOUS PROVISIONS

Article 29

International watercourses and installations in time of armed conflict

International watercourses and related installations, facilities and other works shall enjoy the protection accorded by the principles and rules of international law applicable in international and non-international armed conflict and shall not be used in violation of those principles and rules.

Article 30

Indirect procedures

In cases where there are serious obstacles to direct contacts between watercourse States, the States concerned shall fulfil their obligations of cooperation provided for in the present Convention, including exchange of data and information, notification, communication, consultations and negotiations, through any indirect procedure accepted by them.

Article 31

Data and information vital to national defence or security

Nothing in the present Convention obliges a watercourse State to provide data or information vital to its national defence or security. Nevertheless, that State shall cooperate in good faith with the other watercourse States with a view to providing as much information as possible under the circumstances.

Article 32

Non-discrimination

Unless the watercourse States concerned have agreed otherwise for the protection of the interests of persons, natural or juridical, who have suffered or are under a serious threat of suffering significant transboundary harm as a result of activities related to an international watercourse, a watercourse State shall not discriminate on the basis of nationality or residence or place where the injury occurred, in granting to such persons, in accordance with its legal system, access to judicial or other procedures, or a right to claim compensation or other relief in respect of significant harm caused by such activities carried on in its territory.

Article 33

Settlement of disputes

1. In the event of a dispute between two or more Parties concerning the interpretation or application of the present Convention, the Parties concerned shall, in the absence of an applicable agreement between them, seek a settlement of the dispute by peaceful means in accordance with the following provisions.

2. If the Parties concerned cannot reach agreement by negotiation requested by one of them, they may jointly seek the good offices of, or request mediation or conciliation by, a third party, or make use, as appropriate, of any joint watercourse institutions that may have been established by them or agree to submit the dispute to arbitration or to the International Court of Justice.

3. Subject to the operation of paragraph 10, if after six months from the time of the request for negotiations referred to in paragraph 2, the Parties concerned have not been able to settle their dispute through negotiation or any other means referred to in paragraph 2, the dispute shall be submitted, at the request of any of the parties to the dispute, to impartial fact-finding in accordance with paragraphs 4 to 9, unless the Parties otherwise agree.

4. A Fact-finding Commission shall be established, composed of one member nominated by each Party concerned and in addition a member not having the nationality of any of the Parties concerned chosen by the nominated members who shall serve as Chairman.

5. If the members nominated by the Parties are unable to agree on a Chairman within three months of the request for the establishment of the Commission, any Party concerned may request the Secretary–General of the United Nations to appoint the Chairman who shall not have the nationality of any of the parties to the dispute or of any riparian State of the watercourse concerned. If one of the Parties fails to nominate a member within three months of the initial request pursuant to paragraph 3, any other Party concerned may request the Secretary–General of the United Nations to appoint a person who shall not have the nationality of any of the parties to the dispute or of any riparian State of the watercourse concerned. The person so appointed shall constitute a single-member Commission.

6. The Commission shall determine its own procedure.

7. The Parties concerned have the obligation to provide the Commission with such information as it may require and, on request, to permit the Commission to have access to their respective territory and to inspect any facilities, plant, equipment, construction or natural feature relevant for the purpose of its inquiry.

8. The Commission shall adopt its report by a majority vote, unless it is a single-member Commission, and shall submit that report to the Parties concerned setting forth its findings and the reasons therefor and such recommendations as it deems appropriate for an equitable solution of the dispute, which the Parties concerned shall consider in good faith.

9. The expenses of the Commission shall be borne equally by the Parties concerned.

10. When ratifying, accepting, approving or acceding to the present Convention, or at any time thereafter, a Party which is not a regional economic integration organization may declare in a written instrument submitted to the Depositary that, in respect of any dispute not resolved in accordance with paragraph 2, it recognizes as compulsory ipso facto and without special agreement in relation to any Party accepting the same obligation:

(a) Submission of the dispute to the International Court of Justice; and/or

(b) Arbitration by an arbitral tribunal established and operating, unless the parties to the dispute otherwise agreed, in accordance with the procedure laid down in the annex to the present Convention.

A Party which is a regional economic integration organization may make a declaration with like effect in relation to arbitration in accordance with subparagraph (b).

PART VII. FINAL CLAUSES

Article 34

Signature

The present Convention shall be open for signature by all States and by regional economic integration organizations from . . . until . . . at United Nations Headquarters in New York.

Article 35

Ratification, acceptance, approval or accession

1. The present Convention is subject to ratification, acceptance, approval or accession by States and by regional economic integration organizations. The instruments of ratification, acceptance, approval or accession shall be deposited with the Secretary–General of the United Nations.

2. Any regional economic integration organization which becomes a Party to this Convention without any of its member States being a Party shall be bound by all the

obligations under the Convention. In the case of such organizations, one or more of whose member States is a Party to this Convention, the organization and its member States shall decide on their respective responsibilities for the performance of their obligations under the Convention. In such cases, the organization and the member States shall not be entitled to exercise rights under the Convention concurrently.

3. In their instruments of ratification, acceptance, approval or accession, the regional economic integration organizations shall declare the extent of their competence with respect to the matters governed by the Convention. These organizations shall also inform the Secretary–General of the United Nations of any substantial modification in the extent of their competence.

Article 36

Entry into force

1. The present Convention shall enter into force on the ninetieth day following the date of deposit of the thirty-fifth instrument of ratification, acceptance, approval or accession with the Secretary–General of the United Nations.

2. For each State or regional economic integration organization that ratifies, accepts or approves the Convention or accedes thereto after the deposit of the thirty-fifth instrument of ratification, acceptance, approval or accession, the Convention shall enter into force on the ninetieth day after the deposit by such State or regional economic integration organization of its instrument of ratification, acceptance, approval or accession.

3. For the purposes of paragraphs 1 and 2, any instrument deposited by a regional economic integration organization shall not be counted as additional to those deposited by States.

Article 37

Authentic texts

The original of the present Convention, of which the Arabic, Chinese, English, French, Russian and Spanish texts are equally authentic, shall be deposited with the Secretary–General of the United Nations.

IN WITNESS WHEREOF the undersigned plenipotentiaries, being duly authorized thereto, have signed this Convention.

DONE at New York, this ______ day of ______ one thousand nine hundred and ninety-seven.

ANNEX

ARBITRATION

Article 1

Unless the parties to the dispute otherwise agree, the arbitration pursuant to article 33 of the Convention shall take place in accordance with articles 2 to 14 of the present annex.

Article 2

The claimant party shall notify the respondent party that it is referring a dispute to arbitration pursuant to article 33 of the Convention. The notification shall state the subject matter of arbitration and include, in particular, the articles of the Convention, the interpretation or application of which are at issue. If the parties do not agree on the subject matter of the dispute, the arbitral tribunal shall determine the subject matter.

Article 3

1. In disputes between two parties, the arbitral tribunal shall consist of three members. Each of the parties to the dispute shall appoint an arbitrator and the two arbitrators so appointed shall designate by common agreement the third arbitrator, who shall be the Chairman of the tribunal. The latter shall not be a national of one of the parties to the dispute or of any riparian State of the watercourse concerned, nor have his or her usual place of residence in the territory of one of these parties or such riparian State, nor have dealt with the case in any other capacity.

2. In disputes between more than two parties, parties in the same interest shall appoint one arbitrator jointly by agreement.

3. Any vacancy shall be filled in the manner prescribed for the initial appointment.

Article 4

1. If the Chairman of the arbitral tribunal has not been designated within two months of the appointment of the second arbitrator, the President of the International Court of Justice shall, at the request of a party, designate the Chairman within a further two-month period.

2. If one of the parties to the dispute does not appoint an arbitrator within two months of receipt of the request, the other party may inform the President of the International Court of Justice, who shall make the designation within a further two-month period.

Article 5

The arbitral tribunal shall render its decisions in accordance with the provisions of this Convention and international law.

Article 6

Unless the parties to the dispute otherwise agree, the arbitral tribunal shall determine its own rules of procedure.

Article 7

The arbitral tribunal may, at the request of one of the Parties, recommend essential interim measures of protection.

Article 8

1. The parties to the dispute shall facilitate the work of the arbitral tribunal and, in particular, using all means at their disposal, shall:

(a) Provide it with all relevant documents, information and facilities; and

(b) Enable it, when necessary, to call witnesses or experts and receive their evidence.

2. The parties and the arbitrators are under an obligation to protect the confidentiality of any information they receive in confidence during the proceedings of the arbitral tribunal.

Article 9

Unless the arbitral tribunal determines otherwise because of the particular circumstances of the case, the costs of the tribunal shall be borne by the parties to the dispute in equal shares. The tribunal shall keep a record of all its costs, and shall furnish a final statement thereof to the parties.

Article 10

Any Party that has an interest of a legal nature in the subject matter of the dispute which may be affected by the decision in the case, may intervene in the proceedings with the consent of the tribunal.

Article 11

The tribunal may hear and determine counterclaims arising directly out of the subject matter of the dispute.

Article 12

Decisions both on procedure and substance of the arbitral tribunal shall be taken by a majority vote of its members.

Article 13

If one of the parties to the dispute does not appear before the arbitral tribunal or fails to defend its case, the other party may request the tribunal to continue the proceedings and to make its award. Absence of a party or a failure of a party to defend its case shall not constitute a bar to the proceedings. Before rendering its final decision, the arbitral tribunal must satisfy itself that the claim is well founded in fact and law.

Article 14

1. The tribunal shall render its final decision within five months of the date on which it is fully constituted unless it finds it necessary to extend the time limit for a period which should not exceed five more months.

2. The final decision of the arbitral tribunal shall be confined to the subject matter of the dispute and shall state the reasons on which it is based. It shall contain the names of the members who have participated and the date of the final decision. Any member of the tribunal may attach a separate or dissenting opinion to the final decision.

3. The award shall be binding on the parties to the dispute. It shall be without appeal unless the parties to the dispute have agreed in advance to an appellate procedure.

4. Any controversy which may arise between the parties to the dispute as regards the interpretation or manner of implementation of the final decision may be submitted by either party for decision to the arbitral tribunal which rendered it.

[STATEMENTS OF UNDERSTANDING PERTAINING TO CERTAIN ARTICLES OF THE CONVENTION]

8. During the elaboration of the draft Convention on the Law of the Non-navigational Uses of International Watercourses, the Chairman of the Working Group of the Whole took note of the following statements of understanding pertaining to the texts of the draft Convention:

As regards article 1:

(a) The concept of "preservation" referred to in this article and the Convention includes also the concept of "conservation";

(b) The present Convention does not apply to the use of living resources that occur in international watercourses, except to the extent provided for in part IV and except insofar as other uses affect such resources.

As regards article 2 (c):

The term "watercourse State" is used in this Convention as a term of art. Although this provision provides that States and regional economic integration organizations can both fall within this definition, it was recognized that nothing in this paragraph could be taken to imply that regional economic integration organizations have the status of States in international law.

As regards article 3:

(a) The present Convention will serve as a guideline for future watercourse agreements and, once such agreements are concluded, it will not alter the rights and obligations provided therein, unless such agreements provide otherwise;

(b) The term "significant" is not used in this article or elsewhere in the present Convention in the sense of "substantial". What is to be avoided are localized agreements, or agreements concerning a particular project, programme or use, which have a significant adverse effect upon third watercourse States. While such an effect must be capable of being established by objective evidence and not be trivial in nature, it need not rise to the level of being substantial.

As regards article 6 (1) (e):

In order to determine whether a particular use is equitable and reasonable, the benefits as well as the negative consequences of a particular use should be taken into account.

As regards article 7 (2):

In the event such steps as are required by article 7 (2) do not eliminate the harm, such steps as are required by article 7 (2) shall then be taken to mitigate the harm.

As regards article 10:

In determining "vital human needs", special attention is to be paid to providing sufficient water to sustain human life, including both drinking water and water required for production of food in order to prevent starvation.

As regards articles 21, 22 and 23:

As reflected in the commentary of the International Law Commission, these articles impose a due diligence standard on watercourse States.

As regards article 28:

The specific reference to "international organizations" is by no means intended to undermine the importance of cooperation, where appropriate, with competent international organizations on matters dealt with in other articles and, in particular, dealt with in the articles in part IV.

As regards article 29:

This article serves as a reminder that the principles and rules of international law applicable in international and non-international armed conflict contain important provisions concerning international watercourses and related works. The principles and rules of international law that are applicable in a particular case are those that are binding on the States concerned. Just as article 29 does not alter or amend existing law, it also does not purport to extend the applicability of any instrument to States not parties to that instrument.

* * *

Throughout the elaboration of the draft Convention, reference had been made to the commentaries to the draft articles prepared by the International Law Commission to clarify the contents of the articles.

5. Lithosphere

5.1 FAO International Code of Conduct on the Distribution and Use of Pesticides (As Amended in 1989). Adopted 28 November 1985. 23 FAO Conf.Res. 10/85; *reprinted in* 5 Weston V.H.17

Article 1.

Objectives of the Code

1.1 The objectives of this Code are to set forth responsibilities and establish voluntary standards of conduct for all public and private entities engaged in or affecting the distribution and use of pesticides, particularly where there is no or an inadequate national law to regulate pesticides.

1.2 The Code describes the shared responsibility of many segments of society, including governments, individually or in regional groupings, industry, trade and international institutions, to work together so that the benefits to be derived from the necessary and acceptable use of pesticides are achieved without significant adverse effects on people or the environment. To this end, all references in this Code to a government or governments shall be deemed to apply equally to regional groupings of governments for matters falling within their areas of competence.

1.3 The Code addresses the need for a cooperative effort between governments of exporting and importing countries to promote practices which ensure efficient and safe use while minimizing health and environmental concerns due to improper handling or use.

1.4 The entities which are addressed by this Code include international organizations; governments of exporting and importing countries; industry, including manufacturers, trade associations, formulators and distributors; users; and public-sector organizations such as environmental groups, consumer groups and trade unions.

1.5 The standards of conduct set forth by this Code:

1.5.1 encourage responsible and generally accepted trade practices;

1.5.2 assist countries which have not yet established controls designed to regulate the quality and suitability of pesticide products needed in that country and to address the safe handling and use of such products;

1.5.3 promote practices which encourage the safe and efficient use of pesticides, including minimizing adverse effects on humans and the environment and preventing accidental poisoning from improper handling;

1.5.4 ensure that pesticides are used effectively for the improvement of agricultural production and of human, animal and plant health.

1.6 The Code is designed to be used, within the context of national law, as a basis whereby government authorities, pesticide manufacturers, those engaged in trade and any citizens concerned may judge whether their proposed actions and the actions of others constitute acceptable practices.

Article 2.

Definitions

For the purpose of this Code:

Active ingredient means the biologically active part of the pesticide present in a formulation.

Advertising means the promotion of the sale and use of pesticides by print and electronic media, signs, displays, gift, demonstration or word of mouth.

Banned means a pesticide for which all registered uses have been prohibited by final government regulatory action, or for which all requests for registration or equivalent action for all uses have, for health or environmental reasons, not been granted.

Common name means the name assigned to a pesticide active ingredient by the International Standards Organization or adopted by national standards authorities to be used as a generic or non proprietary name for that particular active ingredient only.

Distinguishing name means the name under which the pesticide is labelled, registered and promoted by the manufacturer and which, if protected under national legislation, can be used exclusively by the manufacturer to distinguish the product from other pesticides containing the same active ingredient.

Distribution means the process by which pesticides are supplied through trade channels on local or international markets.

Environment means surroundings, including water, air, soil and their interrelationship as well as all relationships between them and any living organisms.

Extension service means those entities in the country concerned responsible for the transfer of information and advice to farmers regarding the improvement of agricultural practices, including production, handling, storage and marketing.

Formulation means the combination of various ingredients designed to render the product useful and effective for the purpose claimed; the form of the pesticide as purchased by users.

Hazard means the likelihood that a pesticide will cause an adverse effect (injury) under the conditions in which it is used.

Integrated pest management means a pest management system that, in the context of the associated environment and the population dynamics of the pest species, utilizes all suitable techniques and methods in as compatible a manner as possible and maintains the pest populations at levels below those causing economically unacceptable damage or loss.

Label means the written, printed or graphic matter on, or attached to, the pesticide; or the immediate container thereof and the outside container or wrapper of the retail package of the pesticide.

Manufacturer means a corporation or other entity in the public or private sector or any individual engaged in the business or function (whether directly or through an agent or through an entity controlled by or under contract with it) of manufacturing a pesticide active ingredient or preparing its formulation or product.

Marketing means the overall process of product promotion, including advertising, product public relations and information services as well as distribution and selling on local or international markets.

Maximum residue limit (MRL) means the maximum concentration of a residue that is legally permitted or recognized as acceptable in or on a food, agricultural commodity or animal feedstuff.

Packaging means the container together with the protective wrapping used to carry pesticide products via wholesale or retail distribution to users.

Pesticide means any substance or mixture of substances intended for preventing, destroying or controlling any pest, including vectors of human or animal disease, unwanted species of plants or animals causing harm during or otherwise interfering with the production, processing, storage, transport, or marketing of food, agricultural commodities, wood and wood products or animal feedstuffs, or which may be administered to animals for the control of insects, arachnids or other pests in or on their bodies. The term includes substances intended for use as a plant growth regulator, defoliant, desiccant, or agent for thinning fruit or preventing the premature fall of fruit, and substances applied to crops either before or after harvest to protect the commodity from deterioration during storage and transport.

Pesticide industry means all those organizations and individuals engaged in manufacturing, formulating or marketing pesticides and pesticide products.

Pesticide legislation means any laws or regulations introduced to regulate the manufacture, marketing, storage, labelling, packaging and use of pesticides in their qualitative, quantitative and environmental aspects.

Poison means a substance that can cause disturbance of structure or function, leading to injury or death when absorbed in relatively small amounts by human beings, plants or animals.

Poisoning means occurrence of damage or disturbance caused by a poison, and includes intoxication.

Prior Information Consent (PIC) refers to the principle that international shipment of a pesticide that is banned or severely restricted in order to protect human health or the environment should not proceed without the agreement, where such agreement exists, or contrary to the decision of the designated national authority in the participating importing country.

Prior Informed Consent Procedure (PIC procedure) means the procedure for formally obtaining and disseminating the decisions of importing countries as to whether they wish to receive further shipments of pesticides that have been banned or severely restricted. A specific procedure was established for selecting pesticides for initial implementation of the PIC procedures. These include pesticides that have been previously banned or severely restricted as well as certain pesticide formulations that are acutely toxic. This procedure is described in the Guidelines on the Operation of Prior Informed Consent.

Product means the pesticide in the form in which it is packaged and sold; it usually contains an active ingredient plus adjuvants and may require dilution prior to use.

Protective clothing means any clothes, materials or devices that are designed to provide protection from pesticides when they are handled or applied.

Public sector groups means (but is not limited to) scientific associations; farmer groups; citizens' organizations; environmental, consumer and health organizations; and labour unions.

Registration means the process whereby the responsible national government authority approves the sale and use of a pesticide following the evaluation of comprehensive scientific data demonstrating that the product is effective for the purposes intended and not unduly hazardous to human or animal health or the environment.

Repackaging means the transfer of pesticide from any commercial package into any other, usually smaller, container for subsequent sale.

Residue means any specified substance in food, agricultural commodities, or animal feed resulting from the use of a pesticide. The term includes any derivatives of a pesticide, such as conversion products, metabolites, reaction products, and impurities considered to be of toxicological significance. The term "pesticide residue" includes residues from unknown or unavoidable sources (e.g., environmental) as well as known uses of the chemical.

Responsible authority means the government agency or agencies responsible for regulating the manufacture, distribution or use of pesticides and more generally for implementing pesticide legislation.

Risk means the expected frequency of undesirable effects of exposure to the pesticide.

Severely restricted—a limited ban—means a pesticide for which virtually all registered uses have been prohibited by final government regulatory action but certain specific registered use or uses remain authorized.

Toxicity means a physiological or biological property which determines the capacity of a chemical to do harm or produce injury to a living organism by other than mechanical means.

Trader means anyone engaged in trade, including export, import, formulation and domestic distribution.

Use pattern embodies the combination of all factors involved in the use of a pesticide, including the concentration of active ingredient in the preparation being applied, rate of application, time of treatment, number of treatments, use of adjuvants and methods and sites of application which determine the quantity applied, timing of treatment and interval before harvest, etc.

Article 3.

Pesticide management

3.1 Governments have the overall responsibility and should take the specific powers to regulate the distribution and use of pesticides in their countries.

3.2 The pesticide industry should adhere to the provisions of this Code as a standard for the manufacture, distribution and advertising of pesticides, particularly in countries lacking appropriate legislation and advisory services.

3.3 Governments of exporting countries should help to the extent possible, directly or through their pesticide industries, to:

3.3.1 provide technical assistance to other countries, especially those with shortages of technical expertise, in the assessment of the relevant data on pesticides, including those provided by industry (see also Article 4);

3.3.2 ensure that good trading practices are followed in the export of pesticides, especially to those countries with no or limited regulatory schemes (see also Articles 8 and 9).

3.4 Manufacturers and traders should observe the following practices in pesticide management, especially in countries without legislation or means of implementing regulations:

3.4.1 supply only pesticides of adequate quality, packaged and labelled as appropriate for each specific market;

3.4.2 pay special attention to formulations, presentation, packaging and labelling in order to reduce hazard to users, to the maximum extent possible consistent with the effective functioning of the pesticide in the particular circumstances in which it is to be used;

3.4.3 provide, with each package of pesticide, information and instructions in a form and language adequate to ensure safe and effective use;

3.4.4 retain an active interest in following their products to the ultimate consumer, keeping track of major uses and the occurrence of any problems arising in the actual use of their products as a basis for determining the need for changes in labelling, directions for use, packaging, formulation or product availability.

3.5 Pesticides whose handling and application require the use of uncomfortable and expensive protective clothing and equipment should be avoided, especially in the case of small scale users in tropical climates.

3.6 National and international organizations, governments, and pesticide industries should take action in coordinated efforts to disseminate educational materials of all types to pesticide users, farmers, farmers' organizations, agricultural workers, unions and other interested parties. Similarly, affected parties should seek and understand educational materials before using pesticides and should follow proper procedures.

3.7 Governments should allocate high priority and adequate resources to the task of effectively managing the availability, distribution and use of pesticides in their countries.

3.8 Concerted efforts should be made by governments and pesticide industries to develop and promote integrated pest management systems and the use of safe, efficient, cost-effective application methods. Public-sector groups and international organizations should actively support such activities.

3.9 International organizations should provide information on specific pesticides and give guidance on methods of analysis through the provision of criteria documents, fact sheets, training sessions, etc.

3.10 It is recognized that the development of resistance of pests to pesticides can be a major problem. Therefore, governments, industry, national institutions, international organizations and public sector groups should collaborate in developing strategies which will prolong the useful life of valuable pesticides and reduce the adverse effects of the development of resistant species.

Article 4.

Testing of Pesticides

4.1 Pesticide manufacturers are expected to:

4.1.1 ensure that each pesticide and pesticide product is adequately and effectively tested by well recognized procedures and test methods so as to fully evaluate its safety, efficacy and fate with regard to the various anticipated conditions in regions or countries of use;

4.1.2 ensure that such tests are conducted in accordance with sound scientific procedures and good laboratory practice the data produced by such tests, when evaluated by competent experts, must be capable of showing whether the product can be handled and used safely without unacceptable hazard to human health, plants, animals, wildlife and the environment;

4.1.3 make available copies or summaries of the original reports of such tests for assessment by responsible government authorities in all countries where the pesticide is to be offered for sale. Evaluation of the data should be referred to qualified experts;

4.1.4 take care to see that the proposed use pattern, label claims and directions, packages, technical literature and advertising truly reflect the outcome of these scientific tests and assessments;

4.1.5 provide, at the request of a country, advice on methods for the analysis of any active ingredient of formulation that they manufacture, and provide the necessary analytical standards;

4.1.6 provide advice and assistance for training technical staff in relevant analytical work. Formulators should actively support this effort;

4.1.7 conduct residue trials prior to marketing in accordance with FAO guidelines on good analytical practice and on crop residue data in order to provide a basis for establishing appropriate maximum residue limits (MRLs).

4.2 Each country should possess or have access to facilities to verify and exercise control over the quality of pesticides offered for sale, to establish the quantity of the active ingredient or ingredients and the suitability of their formulation.

4.3 International organizations and other interested bodies should, within available resources, consider assisting in the establishment of analytical laboratories in pesticide importing countries, either on a country or on a multilateral regional basis; these laboratories should be capable of carrying out product and residue analysis and should have adequate supplies of analytical standards, solvents and reagents.

4.4 Exporting governments and international organizations must play an active role in assisting developing countries in training personnel in the interpretation and evaluation of test data.

4.5 Industry and governments should collaborate in conducting post-registration surveillance or monitoring studies to determine the fate and environmental effect of pesticides under field conditions.

Article 5.

Reducing health hazards

5.1 Governments which have not already done so should:

5.1.1 implement a pesticide registration and control scheme along the lines set out in Article 6;

5.1.2 decide, and from time to time review, the pesticides to be marketed in their country, their acceptable uses and their availability to each segment of the public;

5.1.3 provide guidance and instructions for the treatment of suspected pesticide poisoning for their basic health workers, physicians and hospital staff;

5.1.4 establish national or regional poisoning information and control centres at strategic locations to provide immediate guidance on first aid and medical treatment, accessible at all times by telephone or radio. Governments should collect reliable information about the health aspects of pesticides. Suitably trained people with adequate resources must be made available to ensure information is collected.

5.1.5 keep extension and advisory services, as well as farmers' organizations, adequately informed about the range of pesticide products available for use in each area;

5.1.6 ensure, with the cooperation of industry, that where pesticides are available through outlets which also deal in food, medicines, other products for internal consumption or topical application, or clothing, they are physically segregated from other merchandise, so as to avoid any possibility of contamination or of mistaken identity. Where appropriate, they should be clearly marked as hazardous materials. Every effort should be made to publicize the dangers of storing foodstuffs and pesticides together.

5.2 Even where a control scheme is in operation, industry should:

5.2.1 cooperate in the periodic reassessment of the pesticides which are marketed and in providing the poison control centres and other medical practitioners with information about hazards;

5.2.2 make every reasonable effort to reduce hazard by:

5.2.2.1 making less toxic formulations available;

5.2.2.2 introducing products in ready-to-use packages and otherwise developing safer and more efficient methods of application;

5.2.2.3 using containers that are not attractive for subsequent reuse and promoting programmes to discourage their reuse;

5.2.2.4 using containers that are safe (e.g., not attractive to or easily opened by children), particularly for the more toxic home use products;

5.2.2.5 using clear and concise labelling;

5.2.3 halt sale, and recall products, when safe use does not seem possible under any use directions or restrictions.

5.3 Government and industry should further reduce hazards by making provision for safe storage and disposal of pesticides and containers at both warehouse and farm level, and through proper siting and control of wastes from formulating plants.

5.4 To avoid unjustified confusion and alarm among the public, public-sector groups should consider all available facts and try to distinguish between major differences in levels of risk among pesticides and uses.

5.5 In establishing production facilities in developing countries, manufacturers and governments should cooperate to:

5.5.1 adopt engineering standards and safe operating practices appropriate to the nature of the manufacturing operations and the hazards involved;

5.5.2 take all necessary precautions to protect the health and safety of operatives, bystanders and the environment;

5.5.3 maintain quality-assurance procedures to ensure that the products manufactured comply to the relevant standards of purity, performance, stability and safety.

Article 6.

Regulatory and technical requirements

6.1 Governments should:

6.1.1 take action to introduce the necessary legislation for the regulation, including registration, of pesticides and make provisions for its effective enforcement, including the establishment of appropriate educational, advisory, extension and health-care services; the FAO guidelines for the registration and control of pesticides should be followed, as far as possible, taking full account of local needs, social and economic conditions, levels of literacy, climatic conditions and availability of pesticide application equipment;

6.1.2 strive to establish pesticide registration schemes and infrastructures under which products can be registered prior to domestic use and, accordingly, ensure that each pesticide product is registered under the laws or regulations of the country of use before it can be made available there:

6.1.3 protect the proprietary rights to use of data;

6.1.4 collect and record data on the actual import, formulation and use of pesticides in each country in order to assess the extent of any possible effects on human health or the environment, and to follow trends in use levels for economic and other purposes.

6.2 The pesticides industry should:

6.2.1 provide an objective appraisal together with the necessary supporting data on each product;

6.2.2 ensure that the active ingredient and other ingredients of pesticide preparations marketed correspond in identity, quality, purity and composition to the substances tested, evaluated and cleared for toxicological and environmental acceptability;

6.2.3 ensure that active ingredients and formulated products for pesticides for which international specifications have been developed conform with the specifications of FAO, where intended for use in agriculture; and with WHO pesticide specifications, where intended for use in public health;

6.2.4 verify the quality and purity of the pesticides offered for sale;

6.2.5 when problems occur, voluntarily take corrective action, and when requested by governments, help find solutions to difficulties.

Article 7.

Availability and Use

7.1 Responsible authorities should give special attention to drafting rules and regulations on the availability of pesticides. These should be compatible with existing levels of training and expertise in handling pesticides on the part of the intended users. The parameters on which such decisions are based vary widely and must be left to the discretion of each government, bearing in mind the situation prevailing in the country.

7.2 In addition, governments should take note of and, where appropriate, follow the WHO classifications of pesticides by hazard and associate the hazard class with well-recognized hazard symbols as the basis for their own regulatory measures. In any event, the type of formulation and method of application should be taken into account in determining the risk and degree of restriction appropriate to the product.

7.3 Two methods of restricting availability can be exercised by the responsible authority: not registering a product; or, as a condition of registration, restricting the availability to certain groups of users in accordance with national assessments of hazards involved in the use of the product in the particular country.

7.4 All pesticides made available to the general public should be packaged and labelled in a manner which is consistent with the FAO guidelines on packaging and labelling and with appropriate national regulations.

7.5 Prohibition of the importation, sale and purchase of an extremely toxic product may be desirable if control measures or good marketing practices are insufficient to ensure that the product can be used safely. However, this is a matter for decision in the light of national circumstances.

Article 8.

Distribution and Trade

8.1 Industry should:

8.1.1 test all pesticide products to evaluate safety with regard to human health and the environment prior to marketing, as provided for in Article 4, and ensure that all pesticide products are likewise adequately tested for efficacy and stability and crop tolerance, under procedures that will predict performance under the conditions prevailing in the region where the product is to be used, before they are offered there for sale;

8.1.2 submit the results of all such tests to the local responsible authority for independent evaluation and approval before the products enter trade channels in that country;

8.1.3 take all necessary steps to ensure that pesticides entering international trade conform to relevant FAO, WHO or equivalent specifications for composition and quality (where such specifications have been developed) and to the principles embodied in pertinent FAO guidelines, and in rules and regulations on classification and packaging, marketing, labelling and documentation laid down by international organizations concerned with modes of transport (ICAO, IMO, RID and IATA in particular);

8.1.4 undertake to see that pesticides which are manufactured for export are subject to the same quality requirements and standards as those applied by the manufacturer to comparable domestic products;

8.1.5 ensure that pesticides manufactured or formulated by a subsidiary company meet appropriate quality requirements and standards which should be consistent with the requirements of the host country and of the parent company;

8.1.6 encourage importing agencies, national or regional formulators and their respective trade organizations to cooperate in order to achieve fair practices and safe marketing and distribution practices and to collaborate with authorities in stamping out any malpractices within the industry;

8.1.7 recognize that the recall of a pesticide by a manufacturer and distributor may be desirable when faced with a pesticide which represents an unacceptable hazard to human and animal health and the environment when used as recommended, and cooperate accordingly;

8.1.8 endeavour to ensure that pesticides are traded by and purchased from reputable traders, who should preferably be members of a recognized trade organization;

8.1.9 see that persons involved in the sale of any pesticide are trained adequately to ensure that they are capable of providing the buyer with advice on safe and efficient use;

8.1.10 provide a range of pack sizes and types which are appropriate for the needs of small-scale farmers and other local users to avoid handling hazards and the risk that resellers will repackage products into unlabelled or inappropriate containers.

8.2 Governments and responsible authorities should take the necessary regulatory measures to prohibit the repackaging, decanting or dispensing of any pesticide in food or beverage containers and should rigidly enforce punitive measures that effectively deter such practices.

8.3 Governments of countries importing food and agricultural commodities should recognize good agricultural practices in countries with which they trade and, in accordance with recommendations of the Codex Alimentarius Commission, should establish a legal basis for the acceptance of pesticide residues resulting from such good agricultural practices.

Article 9.

Information Exchange and Prior Informed Consent

9.1 The government of any country that takes action to ban or severely restrict the use or handling of a pesticide in order to protect health or the environment should notify FAO as soon a possible of the action it has taken. FAO will notify the designated national authorities in other countries of the action of the notifying government.

9.2 The purpose of notification regarding control action is to give competent authorities in other countries the opportunity to assess the risks associated with the pesticides, and to make timely and informed decisions as to the importation and use of the pesticides concerned, after taking into account local, public health, economic, environmental and administrative conditions. The minimum information to be provided for this purpose should be:

9.2.1 the identity (common name, distinguishing name and chemical name);

9.2.2 a summary of the control action taken and of the reasons for itif the control action bans or restricts certain uses but allows other uses, such information should be included:

9.2.3 an indication of the additional information that is available, and the name and address of the contact point in the country to which a request for further information should be addressed.

Information Exchange Among Countries

9.3 If export of a pesticide banned or severely restricted in the country of export occurs, the country of export should ensure that necessary steps are taken to provide the designated national authority of the country of import with relevant information.

9.4 The purpose of information regarding exports is to remind the country of import of the original notification regarding control action and to alert it to the fact that an export is expected or is about to occur. The minimum information to be provided for this purpose should be:

9.4.1 a copy of, or reference to, the information provided at the time of the notification of control action;

9.4.2 indication that an export of the chemical concerned is expected or is about to occur.

9.5 Provision of information regarding exports should take place at the time of the first export following the control action, and should recur in the case of any significant development of new information or condition surrounding the control action. It is the intention that the information should be provided prior to export.

9.6 The provision to individual countries of any additional information on the reasons for control actions taken by any country must take into account protection of any proprietary data from unauthorized use.

Prior Informed Consent

9.7 Pesticides that are banned or severely restricted for reasons of health or the environment are subject to the Prior Informed Consent procedure. No pesticide in these categories should be exported to an importing country participating in the PIC procedure contrary to that country's decision made in accordance with the FAO operational procedures for PIC.

9.8 FAO will:

9.8.1 review notifications of control actions to ensure conformity with definitions in Article 2 of the Code, and will develop the relevant guidance documents;

9.8.2 in cooperation with UNEP, develop and maintain a data base of control actions and decisions taken by all Member Governments;

9.8.3 inform all designated national authorities and relevant international organizations of, and publicize in such form as may be appropriate, notifications received under Article 9.1 and decisions communicated to it regarding the use and importation of a pesticide that has been included in the PIC procedure;

9.8.4 FAO will seek advice at regular intervals and review the criteria for inclusion of pesticides in the Prior Informed Consent procedure and the operation of the Prior Informed Consent scheme and will report to Member Governments on its findings.

9.9 Governments of importing countries should establish internal procedures and designate the appropriate authority for the receipt and handling of information.

9.10 Governments of importing countries participating in the PIC procedure, when advised by FAO of control action within this procedure, should:

9.10.1 decide on future acceptability of that pesticide in their country and advise FAO as soon as that decision has been made;

9.10.2 ensure that governmental measures or actions taken with regard to an imported pesticide for which information has been received are not more restrictive than those applied to the same pesticide produced domestically or imported from a country other than the one that supplied the information;

9.10.3 ensure that such a decision is not used inconsistently with the provisions of the General Agreement on Tariffs and Trade (GATT).

9.11 Governments of pesticide exporting countries should:

9.11.1 advise their pesticide exporters and industry of the decisions of participating importing countries;

9.11.2 take appropriate measures, within their authority and legislative competence, designed to ensure that exports do not occur contrary to the decision of participating importing countries.

Article 10.

Labelling, Packaging, Storage and Disposal

10.1 All pesticide containers should be clearly labelled in accordance with applicable international guidelines, such as the FAO guidelines on good labelling practice.

10.2 Industry should use labels that:

10.2.1 include recommendations consistent with those of the recognized research and advisory agencies in the country of sale;

10.2.2 include appropriate symbols and pictograms whenever possible, in addition to written instructions, warnings and precautions;

10.2.3 in international trade, clearly show appropriate WHO hazard classification of the contents or, if this is inappropriate or inconsistent with national regulations, use the relevant classification;

10.2.4 include, in the appropriate language or languages, a warning against the reuse of containers, and instructions for the safe disposal or decontamination of empty containers;

10.2.5 identify each lot or batch of the product in numbers or letters that can be read, transcribed and communicated by anyone without the need for codes or other means of deciphering;

10.2.6 are marked with the date (month and year) of formulation of the lot or batch and with relevant information on the storage stability of the product.

10.3 Industry should ensure that:

10.3.1 packaging, storage and disposal of pesticides conform in principle to the FAO guidelines for packaging and storage, the FAO guidelines for the disposal of waste pesticides and containers, and WHO specifications for pesticides used in public health;

10.3.2 in cooperation with governments, packaging or repackaging is carried out only on licensed premises where the responsible authority is convinced that staff are adequately protected against toxic hazards, that the resulting product will be properly packaged and labelled, and that the content will conform to the relevant quality standards.

10.4 Governments should take the necessary regulatory measures to prohibit the repacking, decanting or dispensing of any pesticide into food or beverage containers in trade channels and rigidly enforce punitive measures that effectively deter such practices.

Article 11.

Advertising

11.1 Industry should ensure that:

11.1.1 all statements used in advertising are capable of technical substantiation;

11.1.2 advertisements do not contain any statement or visual presentation which, directly or by implication, omission, ambiguity or exaggerated claim, is likely to mislead the buyer, in particular with regard to the safety of the product, its nature, composition, or suitability for use, or official recognition or approval;

11.1.3 pesticides which are legally restricted to use by trained or registered operators are not publicly advertised through journals other than those catering for such operations, unless the restricted availability is clearly and prominently shown:

11.1.4 no firm or individual in any one country simultaneously markets different pesticide active ingredients or combinations of ingredients under a single distinguishing name;

11.1.5 advertising does not encourage uses other than those specified on the approved label;

11.1.6 promotional material does not include use recommendations at variance with those of the recognized research and advisory agencies;

11.1.7 advertisements do not misuse research results or quotations from technical and scientific literature; and scientific jargon and irrelevancies are not used to make claims appear to have a scientific basis they do not possess;

11.1.8 claims as to safety, including statements such as "safe", "non-poisonous", "harmless", "non-toxic", are not made, with or without a qualifying phrase such as "when used as directed";

11.1.9 statements comparing the safety of different products are not made;

11.1.10 misleading statements are not made concerning the effectiveness of the product;

11.1.11 no guarantees or implied guarantees—e.g. "more profits with * * * ", "guarantees high yields"—are given unless definite evidence to substantiate such claims is available;

11.1.12 advertisements do not contain any visual representation of potentially dangerous practices, such as mixing or application without sufficient protective clothing, use near food, or use by or near children;

11.1.13 advertising or promotional material draws attention to the appropriate warning phrases and symbols as laid down in the labeling guidelines;

11.1.14 technical literature provides adequate information on correct practices, including the observance of recommended rates, frequency of applications, and safe pre-harvest intervals;

11.1.15 false or misleading comparisons with other pesticides are not made;

11.1.16 all staff involved in sales promotion are adequately trained and possess sufficient technical knowledge to present complete, accurate and valid information on the products sold;

11.1.17 advertisements encourage purchasers and users to read the label carefully, or have the label read to them if they cannot read.

11.2 International organizations and public-sector groups should call attention to departures from this Article.

11.3 Governments are encouraged to work with manufacturers to take advantage of their marketing skills and infrastructure, in order to provide public-service advertising regarding the safe and effective use of pesticides. This advertising could focus on such factors as proper maintenance and use of equipment, special precautions for children and pregnant women, the danger of reusing containers, and the importance of following label directions.

Article 12.

Monitoring the Observance of the Code

12.1 The Code should be published and should be observed through collaborative action on the part of governments, individually or in regional groupings, appropriate organizations and bodies of the United Nations system, international governmental organizations and the pesticide industry.

12.2 The Code should be brought to the attention of all concerned in the manufacture, marketing and use of pesticides and in the control of such activities, so that governments, individually or in regional groupings, industry and international institutions understand their shared responsibilities in working together to ensure that the objectives of the Code are achieved.

12.3 All parties addressed by this Code should observe this Code and should promote the principles and ethics expressed by the Code, irrespective of other parties' ability to observe the Code. The pesticide industry should cooperate fully in the observance of the Code and promote the principles and ethics expressed by the Code, irrespective of a government's ability to observe the Code.

12.4 Independently of any measures taken with respect to the observance of this Code, all relevant legal rules, whether legislative, administrative, judicial or customary, dealing with liability, consumer protection, conservation, pollution control and other related subjects should be strictly applied.

12.5 FAO and other competent international organizations should give full support to the observance of the Code, as adopted.

12.6 Governments should monitor the observance of the Code and report on progress made to the Director General of FAO.

12.7 Governing Bodies should periodically review the relevance and effectiveness of the Code. The Code should be considered a dynamic text which must be brought up to date as required, taking into account technical, economic and social progress.

5.2 OECD Council Decision/Recommendation on Exports of Hazardous Wastes From the OECD Area (With Measures Concerning the Control of Exports of Hazardous Wastes and Appended Definitions). Adopted 5 June 1986. 1986 O.E.C.D. C(86)64 (Final), O.E.C.D. 86; *reprinted* in 5 Weston V.I.9

The Council

Having regard to Articles 5(*a*) and 5(*b*) of the Convention on the Organisation for Economic Co-operation and Development of 14th December 1960;

Having regard to the Decision and Recommendation of the Council of 1st February 1984 on Transfrontier Movements of Hazardous Waste [C(83)180(Final)] and without prejudice to that Decision and Recommendation;

Having regard to the Resolution of the Council of 20th June, 1985 on International Co-operation Concerning Transfrontier Movements of Hazardous Wastes [C(85)100], by which it has been decided to develop an international system for effective control of transfrontier movements of hazardous wastes, including an international agreement of a legally binding character;

Considering the European Communities Council Directive of 6th December, 1984 on the Supervision and Control within the European Community of the Transfrontier Shipment of Hazardous Waste [84/631/EEC], supplemented by the Decision of the Council of the European Communities of 6th March, 1986;

Considering the work carried out within the United Nations Environment Programme on the environmentally sound management of hazardous wastes;

Considering the particular nature of wastes and the distinction between wastes and products which are traded internationally;

Convinced that the exports of hazardous wastes may, if not properly monitored and controlled, result in serious risks to health and the environment;

On the proposal of the Environment Committee:

I. Decides that Member countries shall:

(*i*) Monitor and control exports of hazardous wastes to a final destination which is outside the OECD area; and for this purpose shall ensure that their competent authorities are empowered to prohibit such exports in appropriate instances;

(*ii*) Apply no less strict controls on transfrontier movements of hazardous wastes involving non-Member countries than they would on movements involving only Member countries;

(*iii*) Prohibit movements of hazardous wastes to a final destination in a non-Member country without the consent of that country and the prior notification to any transit countries of the proposed movements;

(*iv*) Prohibit movements of hazardous wastes to a non-Member country unless the wastes are directed to an adequate disposal facility in that country.

II. Recommends that, to implement this Decision, Member countries should:

(*i*) Seek to conclude bilateral or multilateral agreements with non-Member countries to which frequent exports of hazardous wastes are taking place or are foreseen to take place;

(*ii*) Apply the measures set out below concerning the control of exports of hazardous wastes to a final destination outside the OECD area.

III. Instructs the Environment Committee to take account of the elements of this Decision/Recommendation in developing the draft international agreement referred to in the resolution of the Council of International Co-operation Concerning Transfrontier Movements of Hazardous Wastes [C(85)100].

MEASURES CONCERNING THE CONTROL OF EXPORTS OF HAZARDOUS WASTES

1. The following measures are designed to facilitate the harmonization of policies concerning transfrontier movements of hazardous wastes to a final destination outside the OECD area. They do not prejudice the implementation of stricter measures which have been or might be adopted at national, regional or world level to reduce the dangers associated with the transport and disposal of hazardous wastes.

2. These measures should apply in the absence of a bilateral or multilateral agreement concerning transfrontier movements of hazardous wastes between the exporting Member country and the importing non-Member country concerned, and should be taken into account in the negotiation of such an agreement.

3. Member countries should require, with respect to any export of hazardous wastes to a final destination outside the OECD area, that the measures set out below be taken by the exporter or by the competent authorities of the exporting country.

4. The exporter should:

(*a*) provide the competent authorities of the importing country (and of any transit countries) with at least the same information that he would provide them if they were Member countries;

(*b*) inform the competent authorities of the importing country of any specific disposal methods legally required or forbidden for such wastes in the exporting country;

(*c*) provide to the competent authorities of the exporting country:

(*i*) the information used by the exporter to assure himself that the proposed disposal operation can be performed in an environmentally sound manner;

(*ii*) certification that the proposed disposal facility may, under the laws and regulations of the importing country, dispose of the kinds of wastes whose export is proposed;

(*iii*) a copy of an undertaking by the operator of the proposed disposal facility that he will dispose of the wastes as foreseen in the disposal contract, and in the facility specified therein;

(*iv*) a copy of the information transmitted to the competent authorities of the importing country to obtain their written consent to the import and disposal of the wastes;

(*v*) a copy of the written consent of the competent authorities of the importing country, and confirmation that the competent authorities of any transit countries have received delivery of notification;

(*d*) demand and receive from the disposer documents confirming that the wastes have been handed over to the disposer and disposed of as foreseen, and put these documents at the disposition of the competent authorities of the exporting country.

5. Member countries may choose to charge their competent authorities instead of the exporter with some of the tasks listed above.

6. The competent authorities of the exporting country should:

(*a*) before any final decision is taken, inform the competent authorities of the importing country when they have specific environmental concerns regarding the proposed disposal operation;

(*b*) prohibit the export of the hazardous wastes whenever:

(*i*) they are not satisfied with the information provided under 4(*c*) above;

(*ii*) an objection is made by any country of transit and no appropriate alternative route can be found by the exporter;

(*iii*) the proposed disposal operation is not in conformity with applicable international law;

(*c*) prohibit additional exports of hazardous waste to a given destination when the documents specified in 4(*d*) above were not provided to the exporter by the disposer after a previous export to the same destination;

(*d*) notify the exporter promptly whether or not they object to the proposed transfrontier movement;

(*e*) notify the competent authorities of the importing country if they have prohibited the export of the wastes.

APPENDIX

DEFINITIONS

For the purpose of this Decision/Recommendation:

(*a*) "Waste" means any material considered as waste or legally defined as waste in the country where it is situated or through or to which it is conveyed;

(*b*) "Hazardous waste" means any waste other than radioactive waste considered as hazardous or legally defined as hazardous in the country where it is situated or through or to which it is conveyed, because of the potential risk to man or the environment likely to result from an accident or from improper transport or disposal;

(*c*) "Transfrontier movement of hazardous wastes" means any shipment of wastes from one country to another, where the wastes are considered as being hazardous wastes in at least one of the countries concerned. Hazardous wastes arising from the normal operation of ships, including slopes and residues, shall not be considered a transfrontier movement covered by this Decision/Recommendation;

(*d*) "Exporting country" means any country from which a transfrontier movement of hazardous wastes is initiated or is envisaged;

(*e*) "Importing country" means any country to which a transfrontier movement of hazardous wastes takes place or is envisaged for purpose of disposal (treatment, landfill, storage, dumping or incineration at sea);

(*f*) "Transit country" means any country other than the exporting or importing country across which a transfrontier movement of hazardous waste takes place or is envisaged;

(*g*) "Exporter" means the generator of the wastes or the person in the exporting country who arranges for exporting the wastes at the request and on behalf of the generator;

(*h*) "OECD area" means all land or marine areas under the national jurisdiction of any OECD Member country.

5.3 UNEP Governing Council Decision on Cairo Guidelines and Principles for the Environmentally Sound Management of Hazardous Wastes (Without Annex). Adopted by the UNEP Governing Council at Cairo, 17 June 1987. UNEP/GC/DEC/14/30, UNEP ELPG No. 8; *reprinted in* 5 Weston V.I.10

Introduction

This set of guidelines and principles is addressed to Governments with a view to assisting them in the process of developing policies for the environmentally sound management of hazardous wastes. They have been prepared on the basis of common elements and principles derived from relevant existing bilateral, regional and global agreements and national regulations, drawing upon experience already gained through their preparation and implementation. Special importance is attached to respect for the balance achieved in principle 21 of the Stockholm Declaration on the Human Environment between the rights and duties of States concerning their natural resources and the environment.

These general guidelines cover the management of hazardous wastes from their generation to their final disposal and, in particular, the problem of transfrontier movements of such wastes, which calls for international co-operation between exporting and importing countries in the light of their joint responsibility for the protection of the global environment.

These guidelines are without prejudice to the provisions of particular systems arising from international agreements in the field of hazardous waste management. They have been developed with a view to assisting States in the process of developing appropriate bilateral, regional and multilateral agreements and national legislation for the environmentally sound management of hazardous wastes. The guidelines deal mainly with the administrative aspects of the environmentally sound management of hazardous wastes, and do not claim to give specific guidance on the more technical aspects of dealing with hazardous wastes.

At the present time, waste management differs substantially in different regions of the world, particularly according to their state of economic development. This imbalance necessitates co-operation to improve the management of hazardous wastes in the interest of the environment, especially as regards actual and potential transfrontier movements of such wastes.

Although the guidelines have not been prepared specifically to address the situation of developing countries, they nevertheless provide a framework for effective and environmentally sound hazardous waste management policies in those countries. Implementation of the guidelines should thus help them to avoid serious and costly environmental problems due to mismanagement of hazardous wastes. By implementing the guidelines, countries could incorporate a sound waste management policy into their national economic development policies.

PART 1

GENERAL PROVISIONS

1. *Definitions*

For the purposes of the present guidelines and principles:

(a) "Wastes" means any materials considered as wastes or legally defined as wastes in the State where they are situated or through or to which they are conveyed;

(b) "Hazardous wastes" means wastes other than radioactive wastes which, by reason of their chemical reactivity or toxic, explosive, corrosive or other characteristics causing danger or likely to cause danger to health or the environment, whether alone or when coming into contact with other wastes, are legally defined as hazardous in the State in which they are generated or in which they are disposed of or through which they are transported;

(c) "Management" means the collection, transport (including transfrontier movements), storage (including storage at transfer stations), treatment and disposal of hazardous wastes;

(d) "Transport" means the movement of hazardous wastes from the place at which they are generated until they arrive at an approved site or facility for disposal;

(e) "Disposal" means final disposal;

(f) "Approved site or facility" means a site or facility for the storage, treatment or disposal of hazardous wastes which has been the subject of a prior written authorization or operating permit for this purpose from a competent authority in the State where the site or facility is located.

(g) "Competent authority" means a governmental authority with appropriate qualifications designated or established by a State to be responsible, within such geographical area and with such jurisdiction as the State may think fit, for the planning, organization, authorization and supervision of the management of hazardous wastes;

(h) "Pollution" means the introduction by man, directly or indirectly, of any hazardous wastes into the environment as a result of which there arises any hazard to human health, plant or animal life, harm to living resources or to ecosystems, damage to amenities or interference with other legitimate uses of the environment;

(i) "Contingency" means any accident or other event occurring during the management of hazardous wastes which gives rise to or presents a threat of pollution;

(j) "Territory" means areas over which a State has jurisdiction for the protection of the environment;

(k) "Export" means the movement of hazardous wastes beyond the territory of the State in which they were generated;

(*l*) "State of export" means a State in which hazardous wastes which are the subject of an export are generated;

(m) "State of import" means a State in which hazardous wastes are received for disposal;

(n) "Transit State" means a State, not being the State of export or of import, through the territory of which a movement of hazardous wastes takes place.

2. *General Principles*

(a) States should take such steps as are necessary, whether by legislation or otherwise, to ensure the protection of health and the environment from damage arising from the generation and management of hazardous wastes. To this end, States should, *inter alia,* ensure that transfrontier movements of hazardous wastes are kept to the minimum compatible with the efficient and environmentally sound management of such wastes.

(b) States should take all practicable steps to ensure that the management of hazardous wastes is conducted in accordance with international law applicable in matters of environmental protection.

3. *Non–Discriminatory Control of Hazardous Wastes*

Each State should ensure that, within its jurisdiction, hazardous wastes to be exported are controlled no less stringently than those remaining within its territory.

4. *International Cooperation*

Without prejudice to the other provisions of these guidelines and principles, States should, in a manner appropriate to their needs and capabilities, initiate and co-operate in:

(a) The achievement and improvement of the environmentally sound management of hazardous wastes;

(b) The development and implementation of new environmentally sound low-waste technologies and the improvement of existing technologies with a view to reducing the generation of hazardous wastes and achieving more effective and efficient methods of ensuring their management in an environmentally sound manner, including the study of the economic, social and environmental effects of the adoption of such new or improved technologies;

(c) Monitoring the effects of the management of hazardous wastes on health and the environment;

(d) Exchanges of information, whether on a bilateral or multilateral basis, with a view to promoting the environmentally sound management of hazardous wastes.

5. *Transfer of Technology*

States should, in a manner appropriate to their needs and capabilities, whether directly or through the appropriate international organizations, promote actively and in accordance with their legitimate interests the transfer of fair and reasonable conditions of technology related to the environmentally sound management of hazardous wastes. They should also promote the technical capacity of States, especially of developing States, which may need and request technical assistance in this field.

6. *Transfer or Transformation of Pollution*

States and persons involved in the management of hazardous wastes should recognize that protection of health and the environment is not achieved by the mere transformation of one form of pollution into another, nor by the mere transfer of the effects of pollution from one location to another, but only by the use of the waste treatment option (which may include transformation or transfer) which minimizes the environmental impact.

PART II

GENERATION AND MANAGEMENT OF HAZARDOUS WASTES

7. *Preventive Measures*

(a) States should take such steps as are appropriate to ensure that the generation of hazardous wastes within their territories is reduced to a minimum.

(b) States should ensure that persons involved in the management of hazardous wastes take such steps as are necessary to prevent pollution arising from such management and, if pollution should occur, to minimize the consequences thereof for health and the environment.

(c) In particular, States should take such steps as are necessary to promote the development and employment of low-waste technologies applicable to activities generating hazardous wastes and the recycling and reuse of hazardous wastes unavoidably produced by such activities.

8. *Establishment of Competent Authorities*

Each State should designate or establish one or more competent authorities as defined in guideline 1.

PART III

CONTROL OVER DISPOSAL OF HAZARDOUS WASTES

9. *Disposal Plans for Hazardous Wastes*

(a) States should ensure that each competent authority prepares, in its area of responsibility, in consultation with the other public authorities concerned and with the participation of the public as appropriate, a plan for the management of hazardous wastes describing the arrangements for implementing that plan.

(b) Such plans should be reviewed by the competent authorities to ensure their continuing adequacy in the light of experience in the operation of the plans and of changes in circumstances, including changes in the state of scientific knowledge.

10. *Separation of Hazardous Wastes*

The competent authorities should ensure that persons concerned in the management of hazardous wastes keep them separate from other wastes where it is necessary to do so for their environmentally sound management.

11. *Collection of Hazardous Wastes*

States should promote the establishment of a system of collection of hazardous wastes, including those that are generated in small quantities.

12. *Duty to Ensure Safe Disposal*

States should ensure that persons engaged in activities in the course of which hazardous wastes are generated are required to make appropriate arrangements for the disposal of those wastes in an environmentally sound manner. In particular, they should satisfy themselves as to the capability and reliability of persons and facilities involved in the management of such wastes.

13. *Use of Best Practicable Means*

States should ensure that persons involved in the management of hazardous wastes employ the best practicable means in all aspects of such management.

14. *Approved Sites and Facilities*

(a) States should take such steps as are necessary to require that the storage, treatment and disposal of hazardous wastes take place only at approved sites or facilities.

(b) An authorization or operating permit for approved sites or facilities should be granted only if:

(i) An assessment undertaken by or at the request of the competent authority has established that no significant adverse effects on health or the environment are to be expected as a result of such storage, treatment or disposal;

(ii) The competent authority is satisfied as to the suitability of the operator of the facility at which such storage, treatment or disposal is to be carried out, including the technical knowledge and financial means of that operator to carry out the operations in respect of which the authorization or operating permit is sought to be granted and to take the appropriate safety measures in respect thereof.

15. *International Listing of Approved Sites and Facilities*

For the guidance of their competent authorities and to ensure the optimal use of their disposal facilities in conformity with guideline 2, States should consider the establishment, on a bilateral or multilateral basis, of lists of approved sites and facilities in their respective territories.

16. *Transfrontier Effects of Approved Sites and Facilities Pre–Authorization Information*

(a) States should ensure that, where it is proposed to grant an authorization or operating permit under guideline 14 in respect of activities which may have significant effects on health or the environment in another State (hereinafter referred to as "the State concerned"), the State concerned is provided in a timely manner by the State entitled to grant the authorization or operating permit (hereinafter referred to as "the authorizing State") with sufficient information, in conformity with the laws and regulations of the latter State, to enable it to evaluate accurately the likely effects of those activities.

(b) The State concerned should respect the confidentiality of the information transmitted to it under paragraph (a) above.

17. *Transfrontier Effects Consultation*

In the circumstances described in guideline 16, the authorizing State and the State concerned should, prior to the adoption of any decision in the authorizing State as to the granting of the authorization or operating permit, enter into consultations which shall be conducted in good faith. These consultations should take place promptly and should be concluded within a reasonable time.

18. *Transfrontier Effects Equal Access and Treatment*

In the circumstances described in guideline 16, the authorizing State should accord to the public authorities and nationals of the State concerned the same rights of participation in the administrative and judicial proceedings related to the granting of authorizations or operating permits and in any appeal or review thereof as those which are accorded to its own public authorities and nationals.

PART IV

MONITORING, REMEDIAL ACTION AND RECORD KEEPING

19. *Monitoring*

(a) States should ensure that the operators of sites or facilities at which hazardous wastes are managed are required, as appropriate, to monitor the effects of those activities on health and the environment and to supply the competent authorities with the results of such monitoring, either periodically or on demand. States should ensure that the protection of abandoned sites or closed facilities against the subsequent unauthorized disposal of hazardous wastes, and the monitoring of such sites or facilities for effects on health and the environment, continue after their abandonment or closure.

(b) States should ensure that the competent authorities have the power to enter upon the sites or facilities mentioned in paragraph (a) above and upon such other premises as may be necessary for the purposes of monitoring the effects upon health and the environment of the activities carried out at those sites or facilities. States should also ensure that the competent authorities have the power to order the cessation, limitation or modification of those activities if it is determined that adverse effects on health and the environment are taking place, or are likely to take place.

(c) States should ensure that appropriate remedial action is taken in cases where monitoring gives indications that management of hazardous wastes has resulted in adverse effects on health or the environment.

(d) States should ensure that persons involved in the management of hazardous wastes keep accurate and precise records, as appropriate, of the relevant information concerning wastes, including the type, quantity, physical and chemical characteristics, origin and location within the site or facility of such wastes.

20. *Public Access to Information*

States should ensure that competent authorities keep a record of the authorizations or operating permits issued by them under guideline 14, and that the public have access to information concerning the number and types of those authorizations or permits and the conditions attached thereto.

PART V

SAFETY AND CONTINGENCY PLANNING

21. *Instruction of Workers*

States should ensure that persons employed at sites or facilities at which hazardous wastes are managed receive, on a continuing basis, information on the conditions attached to authorizations or permits, and full and appropriate instruction as to the safety precautions necessary to ensure the protection of health and the environment, including the actions to be taken by them in any contingency.

22. *Contingency Plans*

States within whose territories hazardous wastes are managed should recognize the need for studies on the risks of sites or facilities, and contingency plans prepared by operators of sites or facilities, or by the competent authorities, as appropriate, and the application of such plans as and when necessary. These plans should take into account any potential adverse effects on health and the environment in other States.

23. *Contingency Plans Transfrontier Effects*

(a) If a State has reason to believe that a contingency which has arisen within its territory is likely to have significant adverse effects on health and the environment in another State, that State should as soon as practicable supply the other State with the information necessary to enable it to adopt effective countermeasures.

(b) States should provide such assistance as they can reasonably make available to other States in which a contingency has occurred.

PART VI

TRANSPORT OF HAZARDOUS WASTES

24. *Transport Rules*

States should ensure that the transport of hazardous wastes is conducted in a manner compatible with international conventions and other international instruments governing the transport of hazardous materials or wastes.

25. *Transport Documentation*

To ensure that hazardous wastes are safely transported for disposal, and to maintain records of the transport and disposal of such wastes, States should establish a system by which all transport of such wastes should be accompanied by a hazardous wastes movement document from the point of generation to the point of disposal. This document should be available to the competent authorities and to all parties involved in the management of such wastes.

26. *Notification and Consent Procedure in Respect of Transfrontier Movements of Hazardous Wastes*

(a) States should establish a system which ensures that all States involved in a transfrontier movement of hazardous wastes receive full information sufficiently in advance to enable them to assess the proposed movement properly.

(b) A State of export should take such steps as are necessary to ensure that a request from a State of import or transit State for relevant information concerning the transfrontier movement in question elicits a constructive and timely response.

(c) In the absence of bilateral, regional or multilateral arrangements, States should provide that it shall not be lawful for any person to initiate a transfrontier movement of hazardous wastes until the State of import and any transit State have given their consent to that movement.

(d) The consent of the State of import referred to in paragraph (c) above should take the form of an explicit consent, provided always that States may by bilateral or multilateral arrangements adopt a tacit consent procedure.

(e) Any transit State should be notified in a timely manner of a proposed movement, and may object to it within a reasonable time in accordance with its national laws and regulations. The consent of a transit State referred to in paragraph (c) above may also take the form of a tacit consent.

(f) The State of export should not permit a transfrontier movement of hazardous wastes to be initiated unless it is not satisfied that the wastes in question can be managed in an environmentally sound manner, at an approved site or facility and with the consent of the State of import.

(g) In order to facilitate implementation of this guideline, each State should designate an agency which shall be the focal point to which the notifications and inquiries mentioned in the foregoing paragraphs may be addressed.

(h) Nothing in this guideline shall be so construed as to affect the sovereign right of a State to refuse to accept within its territory hazardous wastes originating elsewhere.

27. *States of Export to Readmit Exports*

Where a State of import or transit State, in conformity with its laws and regulations, opposes a transfrontier movement of hazardous wastes into its territory, and where the hazardous wastes which are the subject of the transfrontier movement have already left the State of export, the latter should not object to reimport any of the wastes.

28. *States to Cooperate in the Management of Hazardous Wastes*

States should, in pursuance of guideline 2, enter into bilateral, regional or multilateral agreements for the management of their hazardous wastes in order to ensure the optimal use of their treatment and disposal facilities.

PART VII

LIABILITY AND COMPENSATION

29. *Liability, Insurance and Compensation for Damage caused by hazardous wastes*

States should ensure that provision is made in their national laws and regulations for (a) liability, (b) insurance and (c) compensation and/or other remedies for damage arising from the management of hazardous wastes, and they should take such steps as are necessary to ensure the compatibility and, where appropriate, the harmonization of such laws and regulations.

5.4 UNEP Governing Council Decision on London Guidelines for the Exchange of Information on Chemicals in International Trade (With Annexes II & III and as Amended in 1989). Adopted by the UNEP Governing Council at London, 19 June 1987. UNEP/PIC/WG.2/2, at 9, UNEP ELPG No. 10, UNEP/GC/DEC/15/30; *reprinted in* 5 Weston V.I.24

Introduction to the Guidelines

1. This set of Guidelines is addressed to Governments with a view to assisting them in the process of increasing chemical safety in all countries through the exchange of information on chemicals in international trade. They have been developed on the basis of common elements and principles derived from relevant existing bilateral, regional and global instruments and national regulations, drawing upon experience already gained through their preparation and implementation.

2. The Guidelines are general in nature and are aimed at enhancing the sound management of chemicals through the exchange of scientific, technical, economic and legal information. Special provisions have been included regarding the exchange of information on banned or severely restricted chemicals in international trade, which call for co-operation between exporting and importing countries in the light of their joint responsibility for the protection of human health and the environment at the global level. To this end, all references in these Guidelines to a Government or Governments shall be deemed to apply equally to regional economic integration organizations for matters falling within their areas of competence.

3. The Guidelines are without prejudice to the provisions of particular systems or procedures included in existing or future national legislation and bilateral, regional and multilateral instruments for the exchange of information on chemicals; rather, they have been prepared with a view to assisting States in the process of developing such arrangements.

4. These Guidelines do not preclude States from instituting broader and more frequent information exchange or other systems involving consultation with importing countries on banned or severely restricted chemicals designed to gain experience with alternative procedures.

5. These Guidelines provide a mechanism for importing countries to formally record and disseminate their decisions regarding the future importation of chemicals which have been banned or severely restricted and outlines the shared responsibilities of importing and exporting countries and exporting industries in ensuring that these decisions are heeded.

6. The importance of technical and financial assistance to enhance decision-making and training in the safe use of chemicals is recognized by the Guidelines.

7. These Guidelines are complementary to existing instruments developed by the United Nations and the World Health Organization and to the International Code of Conduct on the Distribution and Use of Pesticides of the Food and Agriculture Organization of the United Nations, which is the primary guidance for the management of pesticides internationally. These Guidelines should be implemented in a non-duplicative manner for the different classes of chemicals covered by existing instruments.

8. Although the Guidelines have not been prepared specifically to address the situation of developing countries, they nevertheless provide a framework for the establishment of procedures for the effective use of information on chemicals in these countries. Implementation of the Guidelines should thus help them to avoid serious and costly health and environmental problems due to ignorance about the risks associated with the use of chemicals, particularly those that have been banned or severely restricted in other States.

PART I

GENERAL PROVISIONS

1. *Definitions*

For the purposes of the Guidelines:

(a) "Chemical" means a chemical substance whether by itself or in a mixture or preparation, whether manufactured or obtained from nature and includes such substances used as industrial chemicals and pesticides;

(b) "Banned chemical" means a chemical which has, for health or environmental reasons, been prohibited for all uses by final governmental regulatory action;

(c) "Severely restricted chemical" means a chemical for which, for health or environmental reasons, virtually all uses have been prohibited nationally by final government regulatory action, but for which certain specific uses remain authorized;

(d) "International trade" means export or import of chemicals;

(e) "Export" and "import" mean, in their respective connotations, the movement of a chemical from one State to another State, but exclude mere transit operations;

(f) "Management" means the handling, supply, transport, storage, treatment, application, or other use of a chemical subsequent to its initial manufacture or formulation;

(g) "Prior informed consent" (PIC) refers to the *principle* that international shipment of a chemical that is banned or severely restricted in order to protect human health or the environment should not proceed without the agreement, where such agreement exists, or contrary to the decision, of the designated national authority in the importing country;

(h) "Prior informed consent procedure" (PIC procedure) means the *procedure* for formally obtaining and disseminating the decisions of importing countries as to whether they wish to receive future shipments of chemicals which have been banned or severely restricted. A specific procedure was established for selecting chemicals for initial implementation of the PIC procedures. These include chemicals which have been previously banned or severely restricted as well as certain pesticide formulations which are acutely toxic. This is explained in annex II.

2. *General Principles*

(a) Both States of export and States of import should protect human health and the environment against potential harm by exchanging information on chemicals in international trade;

(b) In their activities with regard to chemicals, States should act, in so far as is applicable, in accordance with principle 21 of the Declaration of the United Nations Conference on the Human Environment;

(c) States taking measures to regulate chemicals with a view to protecting human, animal or plant life or health, or the environment, should ensure that regulations and standards for this purpose do not create unnecessary obstacles to international trade;

(d) States should ensure that governmental control measures or actions taken with regard to an imported chemical for which information has been received in implementation of the Guidelines are not more restrictive than those applied to the same chemical produced for domestic use or imported from a State other than the one that supplied the information;

(e) States with more advanced systems for the safe management of chemicals should share their experience with those countries in need of improved systems;

(f) Both States of import and States of export should, as appropriate, strengthen their existing infrastructures and institutions in the following ways:

(i) Establishing and strengthening legislative and regulatory systems and other mechanisms for improving control and management of chemicals. This may include development of model legislation or regulations, in light of these Guidelines and other relevant guidelines prepared by other organizations;

(ii) Creating national registers of toxic chemicals, including both industrial chemicals and pesticides;

(iii) Preparing and updating manuals, directories and documentation for better utilization of facilities for information collection and dissemination at the country level and to on-line facilities at the regional level.

3. *Exemptions*

These Guidelines should not apply to:

(a) Pharmaceuticals, including narcotics, drugs and psychotropic substances;

(b) Radioactive materials;

(c) Chemicals imported for the purpose of research or analysis in quantities not likely to affect the environment or human health;

(d) Chemicals imported as personal or household effects, in quantities reasonable for these uses;

(e) Food additives.

4. *Effects on Other Instruments*

(a) States should take the necessary measures with regard to implementation of these Guidelines;

(b) The provisions of these Guidelines do not affect the obligations of States deriving from any relevant international agreement to which they are or may become party.

5. *Institutional Arrangements*

5.1 UNEP and FAO should develop an information exchange system to ensure that designated national authorities of importing and exporting countries have a single contact point for obtaining information and communicating decisions on chemicals subject to the PIC procedure;

5.2 UNEP should share with FAO the operational responsibility for the implementation of the PIC procedure and jointly manage and implement common elements including the selection of chemicals to be included in the PIC procedure, preparation of the PIC guidance documents, mechanisms for information sharing, and creation of data bases;

5.3 UNEP should collaborate with FAO in reviewing the implementation of the PIC procedure, including participation, responses, and violations of importing country decisions;

5.4 For purposes of international communications, each State should designate a national governmental authority (or authorities) competent to perform the administrative functions related to the exchange of information and decisions regarding importation of chemicals included in the PIC procedure;

5.5 The designated national authority should be authorized to communicate, directly or as provided by national law or regulation, with designated national authorities of other States and with international organizations concerned to exchange information, to make and communicate decisions regarding chemicals included in the PIC procedure and to submit reports at the request of such States or organizations or on its own initiative;

5.6 States should ensure that designated national authorities have sufficient national resources to assume responsibility with regard to implementation of these Guidelines;

5.7 States should as soon as possible make available the name and address of their designated national authority to the International Register of Potentially Toxic Chemicals (IRPTC), as well as subsequent changes;

5.8 A register of designated national authorities should be maintained, regularly updated, and disseminated by IRPTC;

5.9 IRPTC should, in addition:

(a) Co-ordinate the network of designated national authorities;

(b) Develop recommendations on practices and procedures, and such joint programmes and measures as may be required to make the Guidelines effective;

(c) Maintain liaison with other concerned intergovernmental and non-governmental organizations;

(d) Keep under review the implementation of these Guidelines, on the basis of periodic reports from designated national authorities and provide biennial reports on the effectiveness of the Guidelines and suggestions for their improvement.

PART II

NOTIFICATION AND INFORMATION REGARDING BANNED AND SEVERELY RESTRICTED CHEMICALS AND OPERATION OF THE PIC PROCEDURE

6. *Notification of Control Action*

(a) States having taken control action to ban or severely restrict a chemical as defined in these Guidelines should notify IRPTC. IRPTC will disseminate these notifications as provided in these Guidelines;

(b) The purpose of the notification regarding control action is to give competent authorities in other States the opportunity to assess the risks associated with the chemical, and to make timely and informed decisions thereon, taking into account local environmental, public health, economic and administrative conditions, and with regard to existing information on toxicology, safety and regulatory aspects;

(c) The minimum information to be provided for this purpose should be:

(i) The chemical identification/specification of the chemical;

(ii) A summary of the control action taken and of the reasons for it. If the control action bans or restricts certain uses but allows other uses, such information should be included;

(iii) The fact that additional information is available, and the indication of the contact point in the State of export to which a request for further information should be addressed;

(d) To the extent practicable, the designated national authority issuing the notification should provide information concerning alternative measures, such as, for example, integrated pest management procedures, non-chemical alternatives and impact mitigation measures;

(e) Notification of control action should be provided as soon as practicable after the control action is taken. For chemicals banned or severely restricted before the implementation of these Guidelines, an inventory of prior control actions should be provided to IRPTC, unless such information has already been provided and circulated by IRPTC to all designated national authorities.

7. *Operation of the PIC Procedure*

7.1 *Determination of Participation in the PIC Procedure*

PIC is a procedure which operates in addition to information exchange and export notification. Those countries which elect to participate in the PIC procedure will have the opportunity to record their decisions regarding future imports of banned or severely restricted chemicals in a formal way.

(a) Countries may participate in the information exchange procedures under these Guidelines without participating in the PIC procedure;

(b) All exporting countries are expected to participate in the PIC procedure by respecting the decisions of importing countries;

(c) IRPTC should invite countries to participate in the PIC procedure with respect to imports. Designated national authorities should reply indicating whether their country will participate. If there is no reply a follow-up letter should be sent 60 days after the first invitation. If there is no response, IRPTC should take additional steps to obtain a decision. If after that, there is still no response then it will be assumed that the country does not wish to participate in the procedure;

(d) A country may designate one competent body to handle both industrial chemicals and pesticides or may designate separate competent bodies for each;

(e) A country may elect at any time to participate or not participate in the PIC procedure by communicating its decision to IRPTC;

(f) IRPTC should make available on request a list of countries who have elected to participate, countries which have elected not to participate and countries which did not respond.

7.2 *Identification of Chemicals for Inclusion in the PIC Procedure*

(a) As provided in paragraph 9, IRPTC will notify each participating country of each chemical that is the subject of a notification of a final government control action and that meets the definitions as being banned or severely restricted for environmental or human health reasons for a decision under its conditions of use as to whether that country wishes to permit use and importation of the chemical. An informal consultative process may be used to assist IRPTC in determining whether the control action meets the definitions of the Guidelines;

(b) As provided in paragraph 9, IRPTC should send qualifying control actions, along with PIC decision guidance documents, to the appropriate designated national authority or authorities in each participating country for decision.

7.3 *Response to Notification of Control Action for Chemicals Identified for Inclusion in the PIC Procedure*

(a) The designated national authority in each participating importing country shall make an initial response to IRPTC within 90 days. A response may take either of two forms:

(i) A final decision to permit use and importation, to prohibit use and importation or to permit importation only under specified stated conditions;

(ii) An interim response which may be:

a. A statement that importation is under active review but that final decision has not yet been reached;

b. A request for further information; and/or

c. A request for assistance in evaluating the chemical.

An interim response may also contain a statement permitting importation with or without stated specified conditions or prohibiting importation during the interim period until a final decision is made;

(b) The designated national authority shall use the form provided to make such response;

(c) IRPTC should send reminders to countries as necessary to encourage a response and should facilitate the provision of technical assistance where requested;

(d) If a participating importing country does not make a response or responds with an interim decision that does not address importation, the *status quo* with respect to importation of the chemical should continue. This means that the chemical should not be exported without the explicit consent of the importing country, unless it is a pesticide which is registered in the importing country or is a chemical the use or importation of which has been allowed by other governmental action of the importing country;

(e) If a country takes a unilateral action which affects the *status quo* with respect to a chemical, it must so notify IRPTC to make IRPTC aware of the decision. Such a unilateral action will be interpreted as superseding any previous decision it has made with respect to the chemical;

(f) When an importing country takes a final or interim decision which affects the *status quo,* it should also communicate this decision to the national competent authority responsible for controlling imports so that it can take appropriate import control actions under its authority.

7.4 *Dissemination of Information*

(a) IRPTC will inform designated national authorities of decisions taken by participating importing countries in a timely fashion and should also make these available to industry and other interested parties on request, preferably through a computer data base. This information should also be included in the regular updates of the United Nations Consolidated List of Products whose Consumption and/or Sale have been Banned, Withdrawn or Severely Restricted by Governments. Semi-annually, IRPTC will notify all Governments in writing of the status of the decisions by importing countries;

(b) Governments of exporting countries shall, upon receipt of importing countries' decisions, transmit them to their industry.

8. *Information regarding exports*

(a) If an export of a chemical banned or severely restricted in the State of export occurs, the State of export should ensure that necessary steps are taken to provide the designated national authority of the State of import with relevant information;

(b) The purpose of information regarding exports is to remind the State of import of the original notification regarding control action and to alert it to the fact that an export will occur or is occurring;

(c) The minimum information to be provided for this purpose should be:

(i) A copy of, or reference to, the information provided at the time of notification of control action;

(ii) Indication that an export of the chemical concerned will occur or is occurring;

(iii) An estimate of the quantity to be exported annually as well as any shipment-specific information that might be available;

(d) States should endeavor to ensure that, to the extent possible, information regarding exports provided or received in implementation of these guidelines is forwarded to the State of final destination and to IRPTC;

(e) Provision of information regarding exports should take place when the first export following the control action occurs, and should recur periodically or in the case of any significant development of new information or condition surrounding the control action. It is the intention that, in so far as possible, the information should be provided prior to export. Where the chemical has been banned or severely restricted before the adoption of these Guidelines, the "first export following the control action" should be considered to be the first export after adoption of these Guidelines.

9. *Channels of Notification and Information*

(a) Notifications of control actions should be addressed to IRPTC for transmission to designated national authorities;

(b) Participating importing countries should send their response on the prescribed forms to IRPTC for appropriate dissemination;

(c) PIC decision guidance documents will be transmitted by IRPTC to designated national authorities in participating importing countries for their decision and response and to designated national authorities in other countries for their information;

(d) Information on exports should be addressed to the national authority designated for this purpose in the State of import.

10. *Feedback*

Designated national authorities of States of import should provide to IRPTC, for the purpose of periodic review pursuant to paragraph 5.9(d), a summary of action taken as a result of notifications and information received pursuant to paragraphs 6, 7.3 and 8 and information on any difficulties which they have experienced in using these Guidelines.

11. *Confidential Data*

(a) States undertaking information exchange in implementation of these Guidelines should establish internal procedures for the receipt, handling and protection of confidential and proprietary information received from other States;

(b) States receiving notifications and information regarding exports should be responsible for the protection of proprietary rights and the confidentiality of data received under these Guidelines when claimed by the State supplying the information.

12. *Functions of Designated National Authorities*

(a) *Control action.* It should be the function of designated national authorities, with regard to control action taken by States to ban or severely restrict a chemical:

(i) To provide notification to IRPTC, in accordance with these Guidelines, that such control action has been taken;

(ii) To receive from IRPTC notification that such action has been taken in other States, and to ensure its prompt transmittal to all other national authorities concerned;

(iii) To receive from the United Nations the regular updates of the United Nations Consolidated List of Products Whose Consumption and/or Sale have been Banned, Withdrawn or Severely Restricted by Governments;

(iv) To reply to the request for participation in the PIC procedures in accordance with paragraph 7.1 of these Guidelines;

(v) To respond to notifications of control action in accordance with paragraph 7.3 of these Guidelines, including response to the lists to be circulated in accordance with paragraph 7.2 and Annex II;

(b) *Imports.* It should be the function of designated national authorities, with regard to imports of banned or severely restricted chemicals:

(i) To receive from States of export information on exports, and to ensure the prompt transmittal of such information to all other authorities concerned in the State of import;

(ii) To transmit to States of export requests for further information as required;

(iii) To provide feedback information to IRPTC on action taken as a result of notifications and information received and on any difficulties experienced in the exchange of data with States of exports;

(iv) To advise and assist import control authorities so that they can take appropriate import control actions under their authority;

(v) To strengthen national decision-making procedures and import control mechanisms;

(vi) To ensure that decisions apply uniformly to all sources of import and to domestic production of chemicals for domestic use;

(vii) To encourage that chemicals subject to PIC be purchased only from sources in exporting countries which are participants in that procedure;

(c) *Exports.* It should be the function of designated national authorities, with regard to exports of banned or severely restricted chemicals:

(i) To ensure the issuance or transmittal of information on exports;

(ii) To respond to requests for information from other States, especially as regards sources of precautionary information on safe use and handling of the chemicals concerned;

(iii) To communicate PIC decisions to their export industry;

(iv) To implement appropriate procedures, within their authority, designed to ensure that exports do not occur contrary to the PIC decisions of participating importing countries;

(d) *Other functions.* Designated national authorities should also consider the need:

(i) To provide information regarding applicable national regulations for the management of banned or severely restricted chemicals;

(ii) To ensure the provision of appropriate precautionary information to persons using or handling the chemicals concerned;

(iii) To keep records of notifications and information received, issued and transmitted which could be open for public inspection in accordance with national law, except for information classified as confidential or proprietary;

(iv) To keep records of imports and exports of banned and severely restricted chemicals.

PART III

GENERAL INFORMATION EXCHANGE AND PROVISION OF TECHNICAL ASSISTANCE REGARDING CHEMICALS

13. *Information, Advice and Assistance*

(a) For the protection of human health and the environment, States should facilitate:

(i) The exchange of scientific information (including toxicological and safety data) and technical, economic and legal information concerning the management of chemicals, particularly through designated national governmental authorities and through intergovernmental organizations as appropriate;

(ii) The provision upon request of technical advice and assistance concerning the management of chemicals to other States, on a bilateral or multilateral basis, taking into account the special needs of developing countries.

(b) With regard to the export of chemicals, States of export should ensure that, where appropriate, information, advice and assistance is provided to States of import concerned regarding the sound management of such chemicals, including appropriate precautionary information;

(c) With regard to the use of imported chemicals, States of import should, on the basis of notification and information provided by States of export, take the necessary measures to ensure that users are provided with information, advice and assistance for the sound management of such chemicals, including appropriate precautionary information;

(d) As far as practicable, precautionary information should be provided in the principal language or languages of the State of import and of the area of intended use, and should be accompanied by suitable pictorial and/or tactile aids and labels.

14. Classification, Packaging and Labeling

(a) States should recognize that classification, packaging and labelling are important elements in information exchange on chemicals in international trade, and that it is desirable that chemicals exported from their territories are subject to no less stringent requirements of classification, packaging and labelling than comparable products destined for use in the State of export;

(b) In the development and implementation of existing and future internationally harmonized procedures for the classification, packaging and labelling of chemicals in international trade, States should take into account the special circumstances surrounding the management of chemicals in developing countries;

(c) In the absence of other standards in the State of import, States should ensure that the classification, packaging and labelling of chemicals exported from their territories conform to recognized and, where appropriate, internationally harmonized procedures and practices for ensuring the protection of human health and the environment during use of these chemicals.

15. Technical Assistance

(a) IRPTC should encourage funding agencies, such as the development banks and the United Nations Development Programme, and bilateral donors to provide training, technical assistance and funding for institutional strengthening and should further encourage other United Nations organizations to strengthen their activities related to safe management of chemicals;

(b) States with more advanced chemical regulatory programmes should provide technical assistance to other countries in developing infrastructure and capacity to manage chemicals within their countries, including implementation of the provisions of these Guidelines. Developing countries with more advanced systems should be particularly encouraged to provide technical assistance to other developing countries with no, or less advanced, systems of chemical management.

To the extent possible, donor countries and institutions and recipient countries should inform IRPTC of all such technical assistance activities;

(c) Special attention should be devoted by technical assistance and funding authorities to those countries without any regulatory procedures on chemicals in developing a régime for their control;

(d) Essential elements of technical assistance needed by developing countries for the management of chemicals include:

(i) Strengthening existing infrastructure and institutions;

(ii) Provision for the interchange of experts, including short missions, from developed countries to developing countries and vice versa and in particular from one developing country to another for the purposes of:

a. Sharing each other's experience and exchanging ideas;

b. Advising on analysis of information on chemical risks and benefits, conducting environmental impact assessment, and disposing of unusable products safely;

c. Sharing information on new products and alternatives;

d. Ascertaining research and development requirements for local pesticide efficacy studies and development of alternatives;

e. Assisting one another in dealing with practical difficulties in implementing these Guidelines;

(iii) Training to include:

a. Technical workshops on a local, regional and international level;

b. Awareness campaigns on the safe management of chemicals for industrial and agricultural workers, customs officials and doctors;

c. Opportunities for decision makers in developing countries to study systems in countries which have been successfully implementing these Guidelines.

* * *

ANNEX II

PROCEDURE FOR INITIAL IDENTIFICATION OF CHEMICALS FOR INCLUSION IN THE PRIOR INFORMED CONSENT PROCEDURE

1. Control actions have been taken prior to the adoption of the prior informed consent (PIC) procedure in the London Guidelines for the Exchange of Information on Chemicals in International Trade. Some have been notified to the International Register of Potentially Toxic Chemicals (IRPTC) and some have not been submitted. It is necessary to take these into account in starting up the PIC procedures. The following approach will be used to incorporate previous control actions:

(a) Designated national authorities in all States should submit inventories of control actions in accordance with paragraph 6 of these Guidelines, including all information specified in that paragraph, to IRPTC if they have not already done so. Submissions should be made as soon as possible to be available in IRPTC prior to the date of implementation of the PIC procedures;

(b) On the basis of these submissions, IRPTC will identify all chemicals banned or severely restricted by five or more countries. These will be introduced into the PIC process according to the following criteria:

(i) All chemicals banned or severely restricted as defined in these Guidelines by 10 or more countries should be immediately placed on a list and circulated, with PIC decision guidance documents, to countries participating in these Guidelines for determination regarding future use and importation;

(ii) Chemicals banned or severely restricted by 5 or more countries, but by less than 10, should be submitted to an informal consultation to determine whether they meet the definitions of banned and severely restricted for human health or environmental reasons. This determination should be made as expeditiously as possible. Those chemicals that meet the definitions will be circulated as an addition to the list referred to in subparagraph (i) above, with PIC decision guidance documents, for a determination by participating importing countries regarding their future use and importation;

(c) Should additional inventories of past control actions be received by IRPTC subsequent to the implementation date of the PIC procedures, they will be added to the original inventory. This updated inventory should be assessed annually in the same manner as the original inventory under step (b) above and incorporated into the PIC procedure as appropriate. These additional chemicals should be circulated to participating importing countries for their consideration and determinations regarding future use and importation under the PIC procedures. This annual reappraisal of the inventory of past control actions should continue until IRPTC has received adequate information from Governments that these reappraisals are no longer essential to the operation of the PIC procedures.

2. Additionally, an Expert Group will consider the problem of acutely hazardous pesticide formulations to determine if there exists a need for a list of such products to supplement the chemicals already subject to the PIC procedure.

3. This Expert Group should be made up of representatives from the World Health Organization (WHO), the Food and Agriculture Organization of the United Nations (FAO), the United Nations Environment Programme (UNEP) and national pesticide registrars. They may call upon the expertise of industry and non-governmental organizations and other experts as they deem necessary and will review formulations based on the WHO Class 1A compounds.

4. If the Group concludes that there are acutely hazardous pesticide formulations of concern to developing countries which are not already included in the PIC procedure, a supplemental list of such formulations will be recommended for inclusion.

ANNEX III

INFORMATION TO BE INCLUDED IN A PRIOR INFORMED CONSENT (PIC) DECISION GUIDANCE DOCUMENT

A prior informed consent (PIC) decision guidance document will be prepared for each chemical placed into the PIC procedures. The document should consist of three parts, containing the following information to the extent it is available. In the case of the initial list, a summary of all control actions to date will be provided. For subsequent control actions, each national action will be provided as received with appropriate references to previous actions for the second and following notifications by additional countries.

(a) *A summary of the control action:*

(i) The common and trade names of the chemical, its specification and numerical identification, using widely recognized chemical numbering systems;

(ii) Whether a pesticide or industrial chemical, or both;

(iii) Nature of the control action and date taken;

(iv) Reasons for the control action;

(v) Uses banned;

(vi) Uses continued in effect, if any;

(vii) Alternatives considered effective replacements by the country taking the control action, including, e.g., integrated pest management and non-chemical alternatives;

(viii) A contact for further information in the country taking the control action, including telephone, telefax and telex numbers, in addition to a mailing address;

(ix) Relevant references supporting the action;

(b) *Summary information on the chemical, including:*

(i) Description of the chemical;

(ii) Uses and formulations;

(iii) Chemical and physical properties;

(iv) Toxicological characteristics;

(v) Environmental characteristics, including effects on fish and wildlife, mechanisms of transport and fate.

(vi) Exposure potential, including:

a. Dietary, through food and water;

b. Occupational, both chronic and acute, including manufacture and use;

c. Environmental;

d. Product use, storage, transport and disposal;

e. Accidental poisoning;

(vii) Protective measures to reduce exposure;

(viii) Packaging and labelling recommendations;

(ix) Storage recommendations;

(x) Waste disposal methods;

(xi) Maximum residue limits assessment (for pesticides);

(xii) References;

(c) *Response form(s)* to provide a convenient way for a participating importing country to register its decision with the International Register of Potentially Toxic Chemicals (IRPTC). (In the case of the initial list one form will be necessary for each chemical.)

5.5 OAU Council of Ministers Resolution on Dumping of Nuclear and Industrial Waste in Africa. Adopted at Addis Ababa, 23 May 1988. *Reprinted in* 28 I.L.M. 567 (1989) & 5 Weston V.I.10a

The Council of Ministers of the Organization of African Unity, meeting in its Forty-eighth Ordinary Session, in Addis Ababa, Ethiopia, from 19 to 23 May 1988,

Aware of the growing practice of dumping nuclear and industrial wastes in African countries by transnational corporations and other enterprises from industrialized countries, which they cannot dispose of within their territories,

Gravely concerned about the growing tendency of some African countries to conclude agreements or arrangements with such corporations and enterprises which facilitate the dumping of nuclear and industrial wastes in their territorial boundaries,

Bearing in mind the harmful effects of radiation from nuclear and other hazardous industrial wastes to human and marine life as well as to the ecosystems on which they depend for their existence:

1. DECLARES that the dumping of nuclear and industrial wastes in Africa is a crime against Africa and the African people;

2. CONDEMNS all transnational corporations and enterprises involved in the introduction, in any form, of nuclear and industrial wastes in Africa; and DEMANDS that they clean up the areas that have already been contaminated by them;

3. CALLS UPON African countries which have concluded or are in the process of concluding agreements or arrangements for dumping nuclear and industrial wastes in their territories to put an end to these transactions;

4. REQUESTS Member States of the OAU to carry out information campaigns among their people about the danger of Nuclear and Industrial Wastes;

5. REQUESTS the Secretary-General of the Organization of African Unity (OAU), in close collaboration with the Director-General of the International Atomic Energy Agency (IAEA), the Executive Secretary of the United Nations Economic Commission for Africa (ECA), the Executive Director of the United Nations Environment Programme (UNEP), and other concerned organizations, to assist African countries to establish appropriate mechanisms for monitoring and control of the movement and disposal of Nuclear and Industrial Wastes in Africa;

6. REQUESTS ALSO the Secretary-General of the Organization of African Unity (OAU) to take appropriate steps to ensure the inscription of The Dumping of Nuclear and Industrial Wastes in Africa as an item on the Agenda of the Forty-third Session of the U.N. General Assembly;

7. REQUESTS FURTHER the Secretary-General of the Organization of African Unity (OAU) to report to the Council of Ministers at its Fiftieth Session, on the implementation of this resolution;

8. CALLS UPON Member States to adhere to the guidelines and principles of Cairo on the dumping of dangerous wastes using ecologically rational methods;

9. INVITES Member States to participate in the Working Group charged with the drafting of the Convention on the Control of the Movement of Dangerous Wastes across Borders.

5.6 Basel Convention on the Control of Transboundary Movements of Hazardous Wastes and Their Disposal (as Amended and With Annexes). Concluded at Basel, 22 March 1989. Entered into force, 5 May 1992. *Reprinted* in 28 I.L.M. 657 (1989) & 5 Weston V.I.11

Preamble

The Parties to this Convention,

Aware of the risk of damage to human health and the environment caused by hazardous wastes and other wastes and the transboundary movement thereof,

Mindful of the growing threat to human health and the environment posed by the increased generation and complexity, and transboundary movement of hazardous wastes and other wastes,

Mindful also that the most effective way of protecting human health and the environment from the dangers posed by such wastes is the reduction of their generation to a minimum in terms of quantity and/or hazard potential,

Convinced that States should take necessary measures to ensure that the management of hazardous wastes and other wastes including their transboundary movement and disposal is consistent with the protection of human health and the environment whatever the place of their disposal,

Noting that States should ensure that the generator should carry out duties with regard to the transport and disposal of hazardous wastes and other wastes in a manner that is consistent with the protection of the environment, whatever the place of disposal.

Fully recognizing that any State has the sovereign right to ban the entry or disposal of foreign hazardous wastes and other wastes in its territory.

Recognizing also the increasing desire for the prohibition of transboundary movements of hazardous wastes and their disposal in other States, especially developing countries,

Recognizing that transboundary movements of hazardous wastes, especially to developing countries, have a high risk of not constituting an environmentally sound management of hazardous wastes as required by this Convention;

Convinced that hazardous wastes and other wastes should, as far as is compatible with environmentally sound and efficient management, be disposed of in the State where they were generated,

Aware also that transboundary movements of such wastes from the State of their generation to any other State should be permitted only when conducted under conditions which do not endanger human health and the environment, and under conditions in conformity with the provisions of this Convention,

Considering that enhanced control of transboundary movement of hazardous wastes and other wastes will act as an incentive for their environmentally sound management and for the reduction of the volume of such transboundary movement,

Convinced that States should take measures for the proper exchange of information on and control of the transboundary movement of hazardous wastes and other wastes from and to those States,

Noting that a number of international and regional agreements have addressed the issue of protection and preservation of the environment with regard to the transit of dangerous goods.

Taking into account the Declaration of the United Nations Conference on the Human Environment (Stockholm, 1972), the Cairo Guidelines and Principles for the Environmentally Sound Management of Hazardous Wastes adopted by the Governing Council of the United Nations Environment Programme (UNEP) by decision 14/30 of 17 June 1987, the Recommendations of the United Nations Committee of Experts on the Transport of Dangerous Goods (formulated in 1957 and updated biennially), relevant recommendations, declarations, instruments and regulations adopted within the United Nations system and the work and studies done within other international and regional organizations,

Mindful of the spirit, principles, aims and functions of the World Charter for Nature adopted by the General Assembly of the United Nations at its thirty-seventh session (1982) as the rule of ethics in respect of the protection of the human environment and the conservation of natural resources,

Affirming that States are responsible for the fulfilment of their international obligations concerning the protection of human health and protection and preservation of the environment, and are liable in accordance with international law,

Recognizing that in the case of a material breach of the provisions of this Convention or any protocol thereto the relevant international law of treaties shall apply,

Aware of the need to continue the development and implementation of environmentally sound low-waste technologies, recycling options, good house-keeping and management systems with a view to reducing to a minimum the generation of hazardous wastes and other wastes,

Aware also of the growing international concern about the need for stringent control of transboundary movement of hazardous wastes and other wastes, and of the need as far as possible to reduce such movement to a minimum,

Concerned about the problem of illegal transboundary traffic in hazardous wastes and other wastes,

Taking into account also the limited capabilities of the developing countries to manage hazardous wastes and other wastes,

Recognizing the need to promote the transfer of technology for the sound management of hazardous wastes and other wastes produced locally, particularly to the developing countries in accordance with the spirit of the Cairo Guidelines and decision 14/16 of the Governing Council of UNEP on Promotion of the transfer of environmental protection technology,

Recognizing also that hazardous wastes and other wastes should be transported in accordance with relevant international conventions and recommendations,

Convinced also that the transboundary movement of hazardous wastes and other wastes should be permitted only when the transport and the ultimate disposal of such wastes is environmentally sound, and

Determined to protect, by strict control, human health and the environment against the adverse effects which may result from the generation and management of hazardous wastes and other wastes,

HAVE AGREED AS FOLLOWS:

Article 1
Scope of the Convention

1. The following wastes that are subject to transboundary movement shall be "hazardous wastes" for the purposes of this Convention:

(a) Wastes that belong to any category contained in Annex I, unless they do not possess any of the characteristics contained in Annex III; and

(b) Wastes that are not covered under paragraph (a) but are defined as, or are considered to be, hazardous wastes by the domestic legislation of the Party of export, import or transit.

2. Wastes that belong to any category contained in Annex II that are subject to transboundary movement shall be "other wastes" for the purposes of this Convention.

3. Wastes which, as a result of being radioactive, are subject to other international control systems, including international instruments, applying specifically to radioactive materials, are excluded from the scope of this Convention.

4. Wastes which derive from the normal operations of a ship, the discharge of which is covered by another international instrument, are excluded from the scope of this Convention.

Article 2
Definitions

For the purposes of this Convention:

1. "Wastes" are substances or objects which are disposed of or are intended to be disposed of or are required to be disposed of by the provisions of national law;

2. "Management" means the collection, transport and disposal of hazardous wastes or other wastes, including after-care of disposal sites;

3. "Transboundary movement" means any movement of hazardous wastes or other wastes from an area under the national jurisdiction of one State to or through an area under the national jurisdiction of another State or to or through an area not under the national jurisdiction of any State, provided at least two States are involved in the movement;

4. "Disposal" means any operation specified in Annex IV to this Convention;

5. "Approved site or facility" means a site or facility for the disposal of hazardous wastes or other wastes which is authorized or permitted to operate for this purpose by a relevant authority of the State where the site or facility is located;

6. "Competent authority" means one governmental authority designated by a Party to be responsible, within such geographical areas as the Party may think fit, for receiving the notification of a transboundary movement of hazardous wastes or other wastes, and any information related to it, and for responding to such a notification, as provided in Article 6;

7. "Focal point" means the entity of a Party referred to in Article 5 responsible for receiving and submitting information as provided for in Articles 13 and 16;

8. "Environmentally sound management of hazardous wastes or other wastes" means taking all practicable steps to ensure that hazardous wastes or other wastes are managed in a manner which will protect human health and the environment against the adverse effects which may result from such wastes;

9. "Area under the national jurisdiction of a State" means any land, marine area or airspace within which a State exercises administrative and regulatory responsibility in accordance with international law in regard to the protection of human health or the environment;

10. "State of export" means a Party from which a transboundary movement of hazardous wastes or other wastes is planned to be initiated or is initiated;

11. "State of import" means a Party to which a transboundary movement of hazardous wastes or other wastes is planned or takes place for the purpose of disposal therein or for the purpose of loading prior to disposal in an area not under the national jurisdiction of any State;

12. "State of transit" means any State, other than the State of export or import, through which a movement of hazardous wastes or other wastes is planned or takes place;

13. "States concerned" means Parties which are States of export or import, or transit States, whether or not Parties;

14. "Person" means any natural or legal person;

15. "Exporter" means any person under the jurisdiction of the State of export who arranges for hazardous wastes or other wastes to be exported;

16. "Importer" means any person under the jurisdiction of the State of import who arranges for hazardous wastes or other wastes to be imported;

17. "Carrier" means any person who carries out the transport of hazardous wastes or other wastes;

18. "Generator" means any person whose activity produces hazardous wastes or other wastes or, if that person is not known, the person who is in possession and/or control of those wastes;

19. "Disposer" means any person to whom hazardous wastes or other wastes are shipped and who carries out the disposal of such wastes;

20. "Political and/or economic integration organization" means an organization constituted by sovereign States to which its member States have transferred competence in respect of matters governed by this Convention and which has been duly authorized, in accordance with its internal procedures, to sign, ratify, accept, approve, formally confirm or accede to it;

21. "Illegal traffic" means any transboundary movement of hazardous wastes or other wastes as specified in Article 9.

Article 3

National Definitions of Hazardous Wastes

1. Each Party shall, within six months of becoming a Party to this Convention, inform the Secretariat of the Convention of the wastes, other than those listed in Annexes I and II, considered or defined as hazardous under its national legislation and of any requirements concerning transboundary movement procedures applicable to such wastes.

2. Each Party shall subsequently inform the Secretariat of any significant changes to the information it has provided pursuant to paragraph 1.

3. The Secretariat shall forthwith inform all Parties of the information it has received pursuant to paragraphs 1 and 2.

4. Parties shall be responsible for making the information transmitted to them by the Secretariat under paragraph 3 available to their exporters.

Article 4

General Obligations

1. (a) Parties exercising their right to prohibit the import of hazardous wastes or other wastes for disposal shall inform the other Parties of their decision pursuant to Article 13.

(b) Parties shall prohibit or shall not permit the export of hazardous wastes and other wastes to the Parties which have prohibited the import of such wastes, when notified pursuant to subparagraph (a) above.

(c) Parties shall prohibit or shall not permit the export of hazardous wastes and other wastes if the State of import does not consent in writing to the specific import, in the case where that State of import has not prohibited the import of such wastes.

2. Each Party shall take the appropriate measures to:

(a) Ensure that the generation of hazardous wastes and other wastes within it is reduced to a minimum, taking into account social, technological and economic aspects;

(b) Ensure the availability of adequate disposal facilities, for the environmentally sound management of hazardous wastes and other wastes, that shall be located, to the extent possible, within it, whatever the place of their disposal;

(c) Ensure that persons involved in the management of hazardous wastes or other wastes within it take such steps as are necessary to prevent pollution due to hazardous wastes and other wastes arising from such management and, if such pollution occurs, to minimize the consequences thereof for human health and the environment;

(d) Ensure that the transboundary movement of hazardous wastes and other wastes is reduced to the minimum consistent with the environmentally sound and efficient management of such wastes, and is conducted in a manner which will protect human health and the environment against the adverse effects which may result from such movement;

(e) Not allow the export of hazardous wastes or other wastes to a State or group of States belonging to an economic and/or political integration organization that are Parties, particularly developing countries, which have prohibited by their legislation all imports, or if it has reason to believe that the wastes in question will not be managed in an environmentally sound manner, according to criteria to be decided on by the Parties at their first meeting.

(f) Require that information about a proposed transboundary movement of hazardous wastes and other wastes be provided to the States concerned, according to Annex V A, to state clearly the effects of the proposed movement on human health and the environment;

(g) Prevent the import of hazardous wastes and other wastes if it has reason to believe that the wastes in question will not be managed in an environmentally sound manner;

(h) Co-operate in activities with other Parties and interested organizations, directly and through the Secretariat, including the dissemination of information on the transboundary movement of hazardous wastes and other wastes, in order to improve the environmentally sound management of such wastes and to achieve the prevention of illegal traffic;

3. The Parties consider that illegal traffic in hazardous wastes or other wastes is criminal.

4. Each Party shall take appropriate legal, administrative and other measures to implement and enforce the provisions of this Convention, including measures to prevent and punish conduct in contravention of the Convention.

5. A Party shall not permit hazardous wastes or other wastes to be exported to a non-Party or to be imported from a non-Party.

6. The Parties agree not to allow the export of hazardous wastes or other wastes for disposal within the area south of 60 South latitude, whether or not such wastes are subject to transboundary movement.

7. Furthermore, each Party shall:

(a) Prohibit all persons under its national jurisdiction from transporting or disposing of hazardous wastes or other wastes unless such persons are authorized or allowed to perform such types of operations;

(b) Require that hazardous wastes and other wastes that are to be the subject of a transboundary movement be packaged, labelled, and transported in conformity with generally accepted and recognized international rules and standards in the field of packaging, labelling, and transport, and that due account is taken of relevant internationally recognized practices;

(c) Require that hazardous wastes and other wastes be accompanied by a movement document from the point at which a transboundary movement commences to the point of disposal.

8. Each Party shall require that hazardous wastes or other wastes, to be exported, are managed in an environmentally sound manner in the State of import or elsewhere. Technical guidelines for the environmentally sound management of wastes subject to this Convention shall be decided by the Parties at their first meeting.

9. Parties shall take the appropriate measures to ensure that the transboundary movement of hazardous wastes and other wastes only be allowed if:

(a) The State of export does not have the technical capacity and the necessary facilities, capacity or suitable disposal sites in order to dispose of the wastes in question in an environmentally sound and efficient manner; or

(b) The wastes in question are required as a raw material for recycling or recovery industries in the State of import; or

(c) The transboundary movement in question is in accordance with other criteria to be decided by the Parties, provided those criteria do not differ from the objectives of this Convention.

10. The obligation under this Convention of States in which hazardous wastes and other wastes are generated to require that those wastes are managed in an environmentally sound manner may not under any circumstances be transferred to the States of import or transit.

11. Nothing in this Convention shall prevent a Party from imposing additional requirements that are consistent with the provisions of this Convention, and are in accordance with the rules of international law, in order better to protect human health and the environment.

12. Nothing in this Convention shall affect in any way the sovereignty of States over their territorial sea established in accordance with international law, and the sovereign rights and the jurisdiction which States have in their exclusive economic zones and their continental shelves in accordance with international law, and the exercise by ships and aircraft of all States of navigational rights and freedoms as provided for in international law and as reflected in relevant international instruments.

13. Parties shall undertake to review periodically the possibilities for the reduction of the amount and/or the pollution potential of hazardous wastes and other wastes which are exported to other States, in particular to developing countries.

Article 4A

1. Each Party listed in Annex VII shall prohibit all transboundary movements of hazardous wastes which are destined for operations according to Annex IV A, to States not listed in Annex VII.

2. Each Party listed in Annex VII shall phase out by 31 December 1997, and prohibit as of that date, all transboundary movements of hazardous wastes under Article 1(i)(a) of the Convention which are destined for operations according to Annex IV B to States not listed in Annex VII. Such transboundary movement shall not be prohibited unless the wastes in question are characterised as hazardous under the Convention.

Article 5

Designation of Competent Authorities and Focal Point

To facilitate the implementation of this Convention, the Parties shall:

1. Designate or establish one or more competent authorities and one focal point. One competent authority shall be designated to receive the notification in case of a State of transit.

2. Inform the Secretariat, within three months of the date of the entry into force of this Convention for them, which agencies they have designated as their focal point and their competent authorities.

3. Inform the Secretariat, within one month of the date of decision, of any changes regarding the designation made by them under paragraph 2 above.

Article 6

Transboundary Movement between Parties

1. The State of export shall notify, or shall require the generator or exporter to notify, in writing, through the channel of the competent authority of the State of export, the competent authority of the States concerned of any proposed transboundary movement of hazardous wastes or other wastes. Such notification shall contain the declarations and information specified in Annex V A, written in a language acceptable to the State of import. Only one notification needs to be sent to each State concerned.

2. The State of import shall respond to the notifier in writing, consenting to the movement with or without conditions, denying permission for the movement, or requesting additional information. A copy of the final response of the State of import shall be sent to the competent authorities of the States concerned which are Parties.

3. The State of export shall not allow the generator or exporter to commence the transboundary movement until it has received written confirmation that:

(a) The notifier has received the written consent of the State of import; and

(b) The notifier has received from the State of import confirmation of the existence of a contract between the exporter and the disposer specifying environmentally sound management of the wastes in question.

4. Each State of transit which is a Party shall promptly acknowledge to the notifier receipt of the notification. It may subsequently respond to the notifier in writing, within 60 days, consenting to the movement with or without conditions, denying permission for the movement, or requesting additional information. The State of export shall not allow the transboundary movement to commence until it has received the written consent of the State of transit. However, if at any time a Party decides not to require prior written consent, either generally or under specific conditions, for transit transboundary movements of hazardous wastes or other wastes, or modifies its requirements in this respect, it shall forthwith inform the other Parties of its decision pursuant to Article 13. In this latter case, if no response is received by the State of export within 60 days of the receipt of a given notification by the State of transit, the State of export may allow the export to proceed through the State of transit.

5. In the case of a transboundary movement of wastes where the wastes are legally defined as or considered to be hazardous wastes only:

(a) By the State of export, the requirements of paragraph 9 of this Article that apply to the importer or disposer and the State of import shall apply *mutatis mutandis* to the exporter and State of export, respectively:

(b) By the State of import, or by the States of import and transit which are Parties, the requirements of paragraphs 1, 3, 4 and 6 of this Article that apply to the exporter and State of export shall apply *mutatis mutandis* to the importer or disposer and State of import, respectively; or

(c) By any State of transit which is a Party, the provisions of paragraph 4 shall apply to such State.

6. The State of export may, subject to the written consent of the States concerned, allow the generator or the exporter to use a general notification where hazardous wastes or other wastes having the same physical and chemical characteristics are shipped regularly to the same disposer via the same customs office of exit of the State of export via the same customs office of entry of the State of import, and, in the case of transit, via the same customs office of entry and exist of the State or States of transit.

7. The States concerned may make their written consent to the use of the general notification referred to in paragraph 6 subject to the supply of certain information, such as the exact quantities or periodical lists of hazardous wastes or other wastes to be shipped.

8. The general notification and written consent referred to in paragraphs 6 and 7 may cover multiple shipments of hazardous wastes or other wastes during a maximum period of 12 months.

9. The Parties shall require that each person who takes charge of a transboundary movement of hazardous wastes or other wastes sign the movement document either upon delivery or receipt of the wastes in question. They shall also require that the disposer inform both the exporter and the competent authority of the State of export of receipt by the disposer of the wastes in question and, in due course, of the completion of disposal as specified in the notification. If no such information is received within the State of export, the competent authority of the State of export or the exporter shall so notify the State of import.

10. The notification and response required by this Article shall be transmitted to the competent authority of the Parties concerned or to such governmental authority as may be appropriate in the case of non-Parties.

11. Any transboundary movement of hazardous wastes or other wastes shall be covered by insurance, bond or other guarantee as may be required by the State of import or any State of transit which is a Party.

Article 7

Transboundary Movement from a Party through States which are not Parties

Paragraph 2 of Article 6 of the Convention shall apply *mutatis mutandis* to transboundary movement of hazardous wastes or other wastes from a Party through a State or States which are not Parties.

Article 8

Duty to Re-import

When a transboundary movement of hazardous wastes or other wastes to which the consent of the States concerned has been given, subject to the provisions of this Convention, cannot be completed in accordance with the terms of the contract, the State of export shall ensure that the wastes in question are taken back into the State of export, by the exporter, if alternative arrangements cannot be made for their disposal in an environmentally sound manner, within 90 days from the time that the importing State informed the State of export and the Secretariat, or such other period of time as the States concerned agree. To this end, the State of export and any Party of transit shall not oppose, hinder or prevent the return of those wastes to the State of export.

Article 9

Illegal Traffic

1. For the purpose of this Convention, any transboundary movement of hazardous wastes or other wastes:

(a) without notification pursuant to the provisions of this Convention to all States concerned; or

(b) without the consent pursuant to the provisions of this Convention of a State concerned; or

(c) with consent obtained from States concerned through falsification, misrepresentation or fraud; or

(d) that does not conform in a material may with the documents; or

(e) that results in deliberate disposal (e.g. dumping) of hazardous wastes or other wastes in contravention of this Convention and of general principles of international law, shall be deemed to be illegal traffic.

2. In case of a transboundary movement of hazardous wastes or other wastes deemed to be illegal traffic as the result of conduct on the part of the exporter or generator, the State of export shall ensure that the wastes in question are:

(a) taken back by the exporter or the generator or, if necessary, by itself into the State of export, or, if impracticable,

(b) are otherwise disposed of in accordance with the provisions of this Convention, within 30 days from the time the State of export has been informed about the illegal traffic or such other period of time as States concerned may agree. To this end the Parties concerned shall not oppose, hinder or prevent the return of those wastes to the State of export.

3. In the case of a transboundary movement of hazardous wastes or other wastes deemed to be illegal traffic as the result of conduct on the part of the importer or disposer, the State of import shall ensure that the wastes in question are disposed of in an environmentally sound manner by the importer or disposer or, if necessary, by itself within 30 days from the time the illegal traffic has come to the attention of the State of import or such other period of time as the States concerned may agree. To this end, the Parties concerned shall co-operate, as necessary, in the disposal of the wastes in an environmentally sound manner.

4. In cases where the responsibility for the illegal traffic cannot be assigned either to the exporter or generator or to the importer or disposer, the Parties concerned or other Parties, as appropriate, shall ensure, through co-operation, that the wastes in question are disposed of as soon as possible in an environmentally sound manner either in the State of export or the State of import or elsewhere as appropriate.

5. Each Party shall introduce appropriate national/domestic legislation to prevent and punish illegal traffic. The Parties shall co-operate with a view to achieving the objects of this Article.

Article 10

International Co-operation

1. The Parties shall co-operate with each other in order to improve and achieve environmentally sound management of hazardous wastes and other wastes.

2. To this end, the Parties shall:

(a) Upon request, make available information, whether on a bilateral or multilateral basis, with a view to promoting the environmentally sound management of hazardous wastes and other wastes, including harmonization of technical standards and practices for the adequate management of hazardous wastes and other wastes;

(b) Co-operate in monitoring the effects of the management of hazardous wastes on human health and the environment;

(c) Co-operate, subject to their national laws, regulations and policies, in the development and implementation of new environmentally sound low-waste technologies and the improvement of existing technologies with a view to eliminating, as far as practicable, the generation of hazardous wastes and other wastes and achieving more effective and efficient methods of ensuring their management in an environmentally sound manner, including the study of the economic, social and environmental effects of the adoption of such new or improved technologies;

(d) Co-operate actively, subject to their national laws, regulations and policies, in the transfer of technology and management systems related to the environmentally sound management of hazardous wastes and other wastes. They shall also co-operate in developing the technical capacity among Parties, especially those which may need and request technical assistance in this field;

(e) Co-operate in developing appropriate technical guidelines and/or codes of practice.

3. The Parties shall employ appropriate means to co-operate in order to assist developing countries in the implementation of subparagraphs a, b, c and d of paragraph 2 of Article 4.

4. Taking into account the needs of developing countries, co-operation between Parties and the competent international organizations is encouraged to promote, *inter alia,* public awareness, the development of sound management of hazardous wastes and other wastes and the adoption of new low-waste technologies.

Article 11

Bilateral, Multilateral and Regional Agreements

1. Notwithstanding the provisions of Article 4, paragraph 5, Parties may enter into bilateral, multilateral, or regional agreements or arrangements regarding transboundary movement of hazardous wastes or other wastes with Parties or non-Parties provided that such agreements or arrangements do not derogate from the environmentally sound management of hazardous wastes and other wastes as required by this Convention. These agreements or arrangements shall stipulate provisions which are not less environmentally sound than those provided for by this Convention in particular taking into account the interests of developing countries.

2. Parties shall notify the Secretariat of any bilateral, multilateral or regional agreements or arrangements referred to in paragraph 1 and those which they have entered into prior to the entry into force of this Convention for them, for the purpose of controlling transboundary movements of hazardous wastes and other wastes which take place entirely among the Parties to such agreements. The provisions of this Convention shall not affect transboundary movements which take place pursuant of such agreements provided that such agreements are compatible with the environmentally sound management of hazardous wastes and other wastes as required by this Convention.

Article 12

Consultations on Liability

The Parties shall co-operate with a view to adopting, as soon as practicable, a protocol setting out appropriate rules and procedures in the field of liability and compensation for damage resulting from the transboundary movement and disposal of hazardous wastes and other wastes.

Article 13

Transmission of Information

1. The Parties shall, whenever it comes to their knowledge, ensure that, in the case of an accident occurring during the transboundary movement of hazardous wastes or other wastes or their disposal, which are likely to present risks to human health and the environment in other States, those states are immediately informed.

2. The Parties shall inform each other, through the Secretariat, of:

(a) Changes regarding the designation of competent authorities and/or focal points, pursuant to Article 5;

(b) Changes in their national definition of hazardous wastes, pursuant to Article 3; and, as soon as possible,

(c) Decisions made by them not to consent totally or partially to the import of hazardous wastes or other wastes for disposal within the area under their national jurisdiction;

(d) Decisions taken by them to limit or ban the export of hazardous wastes or other wastes;

(e) Any other information required pursuant to paragraph 4 of this Article.

3. The Parties, consistent with national laws and regulations, shall transmit, through the Secretariat, to the Conference of the Parties established under Article 15, before the end of each calendar year, a report on the previous calendar year, containing the following information:

(a) Competent authorities and focal points that have been designated by them pursuant to Article 5;

(b) Information regarding transboundary movements of hazardous wastes or other wastes in which they have been involved, including:

(i) The amount of hazardous wastes and other wastes exported, their category, characteristics, destination, any transit country and disposal method as stated on the response to notification;

(ii) The amount of hazardous wastes and other wastes imported, their category, characteristics, origin, and disposal methods;

(iii) Disposals which did not proceed as intended;

(iv) Efforts to achieve a reduction of the amount of hazardous wastes or other wastes subject to transboundary movement;

(c) Information on the measures adopted by them in implementation of this Convention;

(d) Information on available qualified statistics which have been complied by them on the effects on human health and the environment of the generation, transportation and disposal of hazardous wastes or other wastes;

(e) Information concerning bilateral, multilateral and regional agreements and arrangements entered into pursuant to Article 11 of this Convention;

(f) Information on accidents occurring during the transboundary movement and disposal of hazardous wastes and other wastes and on the measures undertaken to deal with them;

(g) Information on disposal options operated within the area of their national jurisdiction;

(h) Information on measures undertaken for development of technologies for the reduction and/or elimination of production of hazardous wastes and other wastes; and

(i) Such other matters as the Conference of the Parties shall deem relevant.

4. The Parties, consistent with national laws and regulations, shall ensure that copies of each notification concerning any given transboundary movement of hazardous wastes or other wastes, and the response to it, are sent to the Secretariat when a Party considers that its environment may be affected by that transboundary movement has requested that this should be done.

Article 14

Financial Aspects

1. The Parties agree that, according to the specific needs of different regions and subregions, regional or sub-regional centres for training and technology transfers regarding the management of hazardous wastes and other wastes and the minimization of their generation should be established. The Parties shall decide on the establishment of appropriate funding mechanisms of a voluntary nature.

2. The Parties shall consider the establishment of a revolving fund to assist on an interim basis in case of emergency situations to minimize damage from accidents arising from transboundary movement of hazardous wastes and other wastes or during the disposal of those wastes.

Article 15

Conference of the Parties

1. A Conference of the Parties is hereby established. The first meeting of the Conference of the Parties shall be convened by the Executive Director of UNEP not later than one year after the entry into force of this Convention. Thereafter, ordinary meetings of the Conference of the Parties shall be held at regular intervals to be determined by the Conference at its first meeting.

2. Extraordinary meetings of the Conference of the Parties shall be held at such other times as may be deemed necessary by the Conference, or at the written request of any Party, provided that, within six months of the request being communicated to them by the Secretariat, it is supported by at least one third of the Parties.

3. The Conference of the Parties shall by consensus agree upon and adopt rules of procedure for itself and for any subsidiary body it may establish, as well as financial rules to determine in particular the financial participation of the Parties under this Convention.

4. The Parties at their first meeting shall consider any additional measures needed to assist them in fulfilling their responsibilities with respect to the protection and the preservation of the marine environment in the context of this Convention.

5. The Conference of the Parties shall keep under continuous review and evaluation the effective implementation of this Convention, and, in addition, shall:

(a) Promote the harmonization of appropriate policies, strategies and measures for minimizing harm to human health and the environment by hazardous wastes and other wastes;

(b) Consider and adopt, as required, amendments to this Convention and its annexes, taking into consideration, *inter alia,* available scientific, technical, economic and environmental information;

(c) Consider and undertake any additional action that may be required for the achievement of the purposes of this Convention in the light of experience gained in its operation and in the operation of the agreements and arrangements envisaged in Article 11;

(d) Consider and adopt protocols as required; and

(e) Establish such subsidiary bodies as are deemed necessary for the implementation of this Convention.

6. The United Nations, its specialized agencies, as well as any State not party to this Convention, may be represented as observers at meetings of the Conference of the Parties. Any other body or agency, whether national or international, governmental or non-governmental, qualified in fields relating to hazardous wastes or other wastes which has informed the Secretariat of its wish to be represented as an observer at a meeting of the Conference of the Parties, may be admitted unless at least one third of the Parties present object. The admission and participation of observers shall be subject to the rules of procedure adopted by the Conference of the Parties.

7. The Conference of the Parties shall undertake three years after the entry into force of this Convention, and at least every six years thereafter, an evaluation of its effectiveness and, if deemed necessary, to consider the adoption of a complete or partial ban of transboundary movements of hazardous wastes and other wastes in light of the latest scientific, environmental, technical and economic information.

Article 16

Secretariat

1. The functions of the Secretariat shall be:

(a) To arrange for and service meetings provided for in Article 15 and 17;

(b) To prepare and transmit reports based upon information received in accordance with Articles 3, 4, 6, 11 and 13 as well as upon information derived from meetings of subsidiary bodies established upon Article 15 as well as upon, as appropriate, information provided by relevant intergovernmental and nongovernmental entities;

(c) To prepare reports on its activities carried out in implementation of its functions under this Convention and present them to the Conference of the Parties;

(d) To ensure the necessary coordination with relevant international bodies, and in particular to enter into such administrative and contractual arrangements as may be required for the effective discharge of its functions;

(e) To communicate with focal points and competent authorities established by the Parties in accordance with Article 5 of this Convention;

(f) To compile information concerning authorized national sites and facilities of Parties available for the disposal of their hazardous wastes and other wastes and to circulate this information among Parties;

(g) To receive and convey information from and to Parties on:

sources of technical assistance and training;

available technical and scientific know-how;

sources of advice and expertise; and

availability of resources

with a view to assisting them, upon request, in such areas as:

the handling of the notification system of this Convention;

the management of hazardous wastes and other wastes;

environmentally sound technologies relating to hazardous wastes and other wastes, such as low-and non-waste technology;

the assessment of disposal capabilities and sites;

the monitoring of hazardous wastes and other wastes; and

emergency responses;

(h) To provide Parties, upon request, with information on consultants or consulting firms having the necessary technical competence in the field, which can assist them to examine a notification for a transboundary movement, the concurrence of a shipment of hazardous wastes or other wastes with the relevant notification, and/or the fact that the proposed disposal facilities for hazardous wastes or other wastes are environmentally sound, when they have reason to believe that the wastes in question will not be managed in an environmentally sound manner. Any such examination would not be at the expense of the Secretariat;

(i) To assist Parties upon request in their identification of cases of illegal traffic and to circulate immediately to the Parties concerned any information it has received regarding illegal traffic;

(j) To co-operate with Parties and with relevant and competent international organizations and agencies in the provision of experts and equipment for the purpose of rapid assistance to States in the event of an emergency situation; and

(k) To perform such other functions relevant to the purposes of this Convention as may be determined by the Conference of the Parties.

2. The Secretariat functions will be carried out on an interim basis by UNEP until the completion of the first meeting of the Conference of the Parties held pursuant to Article 15.

3. At its first meeting, the Conference of the Parties shall designate the Secretariat from among those existing competent intergovernmental organizations which have signified their willingness to carry out the Secretariat functions under this Convention. At this meeting, the Conference of the Parties shall also evaluate the implementation by the interim Secretariat of the functions assigned to it, in particular under paragraph 1 above, and decide upon the structures appropriate for those functions.

Article 17

Amendment of the Convention

1. Any Party may propose amendments to this Convention and any Party to a protocol may propose amendments to that protocol. Such amendments shall take due account, *inter alia,* of relevant scientific and technical considerations.

2. Amendments to this Convention shall be adopted at a meeting of the Conference of the Parties. Amendments to any protocol shall be adopted at a meeting of the Parties to the protocol in question. The text of any proposed amendment to this Convention or to any protocol, except as may otherwise be provided in such protocol, shall be communicated to the Parties by the Secretariat at least six months before the meeting at which it is proposed for adoption. The Secretariat shall also communicate proposed amendments to the Signatories to this Convention for information.

3. The Parties shall make every effort to reach agreement on any proposed amendment to this Convention by consensus. If all efforts at consensus have been exhausted, and no agreement reached, the amendment shall as a last resort be adopted by a three-fourths majority vote of the Parties present and voting at the meeting, and shall be submitted by the Depositary to all Parties for ratification, approval, formal confirmation or acceptance.

4. The procedure mentioned in paragraph 3 above shall apply to amendments to any protocol, except that a two-thirds majority of the Parties to that protocol present and voting at the meeting shall suffice for their adoption.

5. Instruments of ratification, approval, formal confirmation or acceptance of amendments shall be deposited with the Depositary. Amendments adopted in accordance with paragraphs 3 or 4 above shall enter into force between Parties having accepted them on the ninetieth day after the receipt by the Depositary of their instrument of ratification, approval, formal confirmation or acceptance by at least three-fourths of the Parties who accepted the amendments to the protocol concerned, except as may otherwise be provided in such protocol. The amendments shall enter into force for any other Party on the ninetieth day after that Party deposits its instrument of ratification, approval, formal confirmation or acceptance of the amendments.

6. For the purpose of this Article, "Parties present and voting" means Parties present and casting an affirmative or negative vote.

Article 18

Adoption and Amendment of Annexes

1. The annexes of this Convention or to any protocol shall form an integral part of this Convention or of such protocol, as the case may be and, unless expressly provided otherwise, a reference to this Convention or its protocols constitutes at the same time a reference to any annexes thereto. Such annexes shall be restricted to scientific, technical and administrative matters.

2. Except as may be otherwise provided in any protocol with respect to its annexes, the following procedure shall apply to the proposal, adoption and entry into force of additional annexes to this Convention or of annexes to a protocol:

(a) Annexes to this Convention and its protocols shall be proposed and adopted according to the procedure laid down in Article 17, paragraphs 2, 3 and 4;

(b) Any Party that is unable to accept an additional annex to this Convention or an annex to any protocol to which it is party shall so notify the Depositary, in writing, within six months from the date of the communication of the adoption by the Depositary. The Depositary shall without delay notify all Parties of any such notification received. A Party may at any time substitute an acceptance for a previous declaration of objection and the annexes shall thereupon enter into force for that Party;

(c) On the expiry of six months from the date of the circulation of the communication by the Depositary, the annex shall become effective for all Parties to this Convention or to any protocol concerned, which have not submitted a notification in accordance with the provision of subparagraph (b) above.

3. The proposal, adoption and entry into force of amendments to annexes to this Convention or to any protocol shall be subject to the same procedure as for the proposal, adoption and entry into force of annexes to the Convention or annexes to a protocol. Annexes and amendments thereto shall take due account, *inter alia,* of relevant scientific and technical considerations.

4. If an additional annex or an amendment to an annex involves an amendment to this Convention or to any protocol, the additional annex or amended annex shall not enter into force until such time as the amendment to this Convention or to the protocol enters into force.

Article 19

Verification

Any Party which has reason to believe that another Party is acting or has acted in breach of its obligations under this Convention may inform the Secretariat thereof, and in such an event, shall simultaneously and immediately inform, directly or through the Secretariat, the Party against whom the allegations are made. All relevant information should be submitted by the Secretariat to the Parties.

Article 20

Settlement of Disputes

1. In case of a dispute between Parties as to the interpretation or application of, or compliance with, this Convention or any protocol thereto, they shall seek a settlement of the dispute through negotiation or any other peaceful means of their own choice.

2. If the Parties concerned cannot settle their dispute through the means mentioned in the preceding paragraph, the dispute, if the parties to the dispute agree, shall be submitted to the International Court of Justice or to arbitration under the conditions set out in Annex VI on Arbitration. However, failure to reach common agreement on submission of the dispute to the International Court of Justice or to arbitration shall not absolve the Parties from the responsibility of continuing to seek to resolve it by the means referred to in paragraph 1.

3. When ratifying, accepting, approving, formally confirming or acceding to this Convention, or at any time thereafter, a State or political and/or economic integration organization may declare that it recognizes as compulsory *ipso facto* and without special agreement, in relation to any Party accepting the same obligation:

(a) submission of the dispute to the International Court of Justice; and/or

(b) arbitration in accordance with the procedures set out in Annex VI.

Such declaration shall be notified in writing to the Secretariat which shall communicate it to the Parties.

Article 21

Signature

This Convention shall be open for signature by States, by Namibia, represented by the United Nations Council for Namibia, and by political and/or economic integration organizations, in Basel on 22 March 1989, at the Federal Department of Foreign Affairs of Switzerland in Berne from 23 March 1989 to 30 June 1989 and at United Nations Headquarters in New York from 1 July 1989 to 22 March 1990.

Article 22

Ratification, Acceptance, Formal Confirmation or Approval

1. This Convention shall be subject to ratification, acceptance or approval by States and by Namibia, represented by the United Nations Council for Namibia, and to formal confirmation or approval by political and/or economic integration organizations. Instruments of ratification, acceptance, formal confirmation, or approval shall be deposited with the Depositary.

2. Any organization referred to in paragraph 1 above which becomes a Party to this Convention without any of its member States being a party shall be bound by all the obligations under the Convention. In the case of such organizations, one or more of whose member States is a Party to the Convention, the organization and its member States shall decide on their respective responsibilities for the performance of their obligations under the Convention. In such cases, the organization and the member States shall not be entitled to exercise rights under the Convention concurrently.

3. In their instruments of formal confirmation or approval, the organizations referred to in paragraph 1 above shall declare the extent of their competence with respect to the matters governed by the Convention. These organizations shall also

inform the Depositary, who will inform the Parties of any substantial modification in the extent of their competence.

Article 23

Accession

1. This Convention shall be open for accession by States, by Namibia, represented by the United Nations Council for Namibia, and by political and/or economic integration organizations from the day after the date on which the Convention is closed for signature. The instruments of accession shall be deposited with the Depositary.

2. In their instruments of accession, the organizations referred to in paragraph 1 above shall declare the extent of their competence with respect to the matters governed by the Convention. These organizations shall also inform the Depositary of any substantial modification in the extent of their competence.

3. The provisions of Article 22, paragraph 2, shall apply to political and/or economic integration organizations which accede to this Convention.

Article 24

Right to Vote

1. Except as provided for in paragraph 2 below, each Contracting Party to this Convention shall have one vote.

2. Political and/or economic integration organizations, in matters within their competence, in accordance with Article 22, paragraph 3, and Article 23, paragraph 2, shall exercise their right to vote with a number of votes equal to the number of their member States which are Parties to the Convention or the relevant protocol. Such organizations shall not exercise their right to vote if their member States exercise theirs, and vice versa.

Article 25

Entry into Force

1. This Convention shall enter into force on the ninetieth day after the date of deposit of the twentieth instrument of ratification, acceptance, formal confirmation, approval or accession.

2. For each State or political and/or economic integration organization which ratifies, accepts, approves or formally confirms this Convention or accedes thereto after the date of the deposit of the twentieth instrument of ratification, acceptance, approval, formal confirmation or accession, it shall enter into force on the ninetieth day after the date of deposit by such State or political and/or economic integration organization of its instrument of ratification, acceptance, approval, formal confirmation or accession.

3. For the purposes of paragraphs 1 and 2 above, any instrument deposited by a political and/or economic integration organization shall not be counted as additional to those deposited by member States of such organization.

Article 26

Reservations and Declarations

1. No reservation or exception may be made to this Convention.

2. Paragraph 1 of this Article does not preclude a State or political and/or economic integration organization, when signing, ratifying, accepting, approving, formally confirming or acceding to this Convention, from making declarations or statements, however phrased or named, with a view, *inter alia,* to the harmonization of its

laws and regulations with the provisions of this Convention, provided that such declarations or statements do not purport to exclude or to modify the legal effects of the provisions of the Convention in their application to that State.

Article 27

Withdrawal

1. At any time after three years from the date on which this Convention has entered into force for a Party, that Party may withdraw from the Convention by giving written notification to the Depositary.

2. Withdrawal shall be effective one year from receipt of notification by the Depositary, or on such later date as may be specified in the notification.

Article 28

Depositary

The Secretary-General of the United Nations shall be the Depository of this Convention and of any protocol thereto.

Article 29

Authentic Texts

The original Arabic, Chinese, English, French, Russian and Spanish texts of this Convention are equally authentic.

* * *

ANNEX I

CATEGORIES OF WASTES TO BE CONTROLLED

Waste Streams

Y1 Clinical wastes from medical care in hospitals, medical centers and clinics
Y2 Wastes from the production and preparation of pharmaceutical products
Y3 Waste pharmaceuticals, drugs and medicines
Y4 Wastes from the production, formulation and use of biocides and phytopharmaceuticals
Y5 Wastes from the manufacture, formulation and use of wood preserving chemicals
Y6 Wastes from the production, formulation and use of organic solvents
Y7 Wastes from heat treatment and tempering operations containing cyanides
Y8 Waste mineral oils unfit for their originally intended use
Y9 Waste oils/water, hydrocarbons/water mixtures, emulsions
Y10 Waste substances and articles containing or contaminated with polychlorinated biphenyls (PCBs) and/or polychlorinated terphenyls (PCTs) and/or polybrominated biphenyls (PBBs)
Y11 Waste tarry residues arising from refining, distillation and any pyrolytic treatment
Y12 Wastes from production, formulation and use of inks, dyes, pigments, paints, lacquers, varnish
Y13 Wastes from production, formulation and use of resins, latex, plasticizers, glues/adhesives
Y14 Waste chemical substances arising from research and development or teaching activities which are not identified and/or are new and whose effects on man and/or the environment are not known
Y15 Wastes of an explosive nature not subject to other legislation

Y16 Wastes from production, formulation and use of photographic chemicals and processing materials
Y17 Wastes resulting from surface treatment of metals and plastics
Y18 Residues arising from industrial waste disposal operations

Wastes Having as Constituents:

Y19 Metal carbonyls
Y20 Beryllium; beryllium compounds
Y21 Hexavalent chromium compounds
Y22 Cooper compounds
Y23 Zinc compounds
Y24 Arsenic; arsenic compounds
Y25 Selenium; selenium compounds
Y26 Cadmium; cadmium compounds
Y27 Antimony; antimony compounds
Y28 Tellurium; tellurium compounds
Y29 Mercury; mercury compounds
Y30 Thallium; thallium compounds
Y31 Lead; lead compounds
Y32 Inorganic fluorine compounds excluding calcium fluoride
Y33 Inorganic cyanides
Y34 Acidic solutions or acids in solid form
Y35 Basic solutions or bases in solid form
Y36 Asbestos (dust and fibres)
Y37 Organic phosphorous compounds
Y38 Organic cyanides
Y39 Phenols; phenol compounds including chlorophenols
Y40 Ethers
Y41 Halogenated organic solvents
Y42 Organic solvents excluding halogenated solvents
Y43 Any congenor of polychlorinated dibenzo-furan
Y44 Any congenor of polychlorinated dibenzo-p-dioxin
Y45 Organohalogen compounds other than substances referred to in this Annex (e.g. Y39, Y41, Y42, Y43, Y44).

ANNEX II

CATEGORIES OF WASTES REQUIRING SPECIAL CONSIDERATION

Y46 Wastes collected from households
Y47 Residues arising from the incineration of household wastes

ANNEX III

LIST OF HAZARDOUS CHARACTERISTICS

UN Class	*Code*	*Characteristics*
1	**H1**	**Explosive** An explosive substance or waste is a solid or liquid substance or waste (or mixture of substances or wastes) which is in itself capable by chemical reaction of producing gas at such a temperature and pressure and at such a speed as to cause damage to the surroundings.
3	**H3**	**Flammable liquids** The word "flammable" has the same meaning as "inflammable". Flammable liquids are liquids, or mixtures of liquids, or liquids containing solids in solution or suspension (for example, paints,

UN Class	*Code*	*Characteristics*
		varnishes, lacquers, etc., but not including substances or wastes otherwise classified on account of their dangerous characteristics) which give off a flammable vapour at temperatures of not more than 60.5C, closed-cup test, or not more than 65.6C, open-cup test. (Since the results of open-cup tests and of closed-cup tests are not strictly comparable and even individual results by the same test are often variable, regulations varying from the above figures to make allowance for such differences would be within the spirit of this definition.)
4.1	H4.1	**Flammable solids** Solids, or waste solids, other than those classed as explosives, which under conditions encountered in transport are readily combustible, or may cause or contribute to fire through friction.
4.2	H4.2	**Substances or wastes liable to spontaneous combustion** Substances or wastes which are liable to spontaneous heating under normal conditions encountered in transport, or to heating upon contact with air, and being then liable to catch fire.
4.3	H4.3	**Substances or wastes which, in contact with water emit flammable gases** Substances or wastes which, by interaction with water, are liable to become spontaneously flammable or to give off flammable gases in dangerous quantities.
5.1	H5.1	**Oxidizing** Substances or wastes which, while in themselves not necessarily combustible, may, generally by yielding oxygen cause, or contribute to, the combustion of other materials.
5.2	H5.2	**Organic Peroxides** Organic substances or wastes which contain the bivalent-O-O-structure are thermally unstable substances which may undergo exothermic self-accelerating decomposition.
6.1	H6.1	**Poisonous (Acute)** Substances or wastes liable either to cause death or serious injury or to harm human health if swallowed or inhaled or by skin contact.
6.2	H6.2	**Infectious substances** Substances or wastes containing viable microorganisms or their toxins which are known or suspected to cause disease in animals or humans.
8	H8	**Corrosives** Substances or wastes which, by chemical action, will cause severe damage when in contact with living tissue, or, in the case of leakage, will materially damage, or even destroy, other goods or the means of transport; they may also cause other hazards.
9	H10	**Liberation of toxic gases in contact with air or water** Substances or wastes which, by interaction with air or water, are liable to give off toxic gases in dangerous quantities.
9	H11	**Toxic (Delayed or chronic)** Substances or wastes which, if they are inhaled or ingested or if they penetrate the skin, may involve delayed or chronic effects, including carcinogenicity.
9	H12	**Ecotoxic** Substances or wastes which if released present or may present immediate or delayed adverse impacts to the environment by means of bioaccumulation and/or toxic effects upon biotic systems.
9	H13	**Capable, by any means, after disposal, of yielding another material, e.g., leachate, which possesses any of the characteristics listed above.**

Tests

The potential hazards posed by certain types of wastes are not yet fully documented; tests to define quantitatively these hazards do not exist. Further research is necessary in order to develop means to characterize potential hazards posed to man and/or the environment by these wastes. Standardized tests have been derived with respect to pure substances and materials. Many countries have developed national tests which can be applied to materials listed in Annex I, in order to decide if these materials exhibit any of the characteristics listed in this Annex.

ANNEX IV

DISPOSAL OPERATIONS

A. Operations which do not lead to the Possibility of Resource Recovery, Recycling, Reclamation, Direct re-use or Alternative Users

Section A encompasses all such disposal operations which occur in practice.

D1 Deposit into or onto land, (e.g., landfill, etc.)
D2 Land treatment, (e.g., biodegradation of liquid or sludgy discards in soils, etc.)
D3 Deep injection, (e.g. injection of pumpable discards into wells, salt domes or naturally occurring repositories, etc.)
D4 Surface impoundment, (e.g., placement of liquid or sludge discards into pits, ponds or lagoons, etc.)
D5 Specially engineered landfill, (e.g., placement into lined discrete cells which are capped and isolated from one another and the environment, etc.)
D6 Release into a water body except seas/oceans
D7 Release into seas/oceans including sea-bed insertion
D8 Biological treatment not specified elsewhere in this Annex which results in final compounds or mixtures which are discarded by means of any of the operations in Section A
D9 Physico chemical treatment not specified elsewhere in this Annex which results in final compounds or mixtures which are discarded by means of any of the operations in Section A, (e.g., evaporation, drying, calcination, neutralization, precipitation, etc.)
D10 Incineration on land
D11 Incineration at sea
D12 Permanent storage (e.g., emplacement of containers in a mine, etc.)
D13 Blending or mixing prior to submission to any of the operations in Section A
D14 Repackaging prior to submission to any of the operations in Section A
D15 Storage pending any of the operations in Section A

B. Operations which may lead to Resource Recovery, Recycling, Reclamation, Direct re-use or Alternative Uses

Section B encompasses all such operations with respect to materials legally defined as or considered to be hazardous waste and which otherwise would have been destined for operations included in Section A

R1 Use as a fuel (other than in direct incineration) or other means to generate energy

R2 Solvent reclamation/regeneration
R3 Recycling/reclamation of organic substances which are not used as solvents

R4 Recycling/reclamation of metals and metal compounds
R5 Recycling/reclamation of other inorganic materials
R6 Regeneration of acids or bases
R7 Recovery of components used for pollution abatement
R8 Recovery of components from catalysts
R9 Used oil-refining or other uses of previously used oil
R10 Land treatment resulting in benefit to agriculture or ecological improvement
R11 Uses of residual materials obtained from any of the operations numbered R1R10
R12 Exchange of wastes for submission to any of the operations numbered R1R11
R13 Accumulation of material intended for any operation in Section B

ANNEX V A

INFORMATION TO BE PROVIDED ON NOTIFICATION

1. Reason for waste export
2. Exporter of the waste
3. Generator(s) of the waste and site of generation
4. Disposer of the waste and actual site of disposal
5. Intended carrier(s) of the waste of their agents, if known
6. Country of export of the waste Competent authority
7. Expected countries of transit Competent authority
8. Country of import of the waste Competent authority
9. General or single notification
10. Projected date(s) of shipment(s) and period of time over which waste is to be exported and proposed itinerary (including point of entry and exit)
11. Means of transport envisaged (road, rail, sea, air, inland waters)
12. Information relating to insurance
13. Designation and physical description of the wastes including Y number and UN number and its composition and information on any special handling requirements including emergency provisions in case of accidents
14. Type of packaging envisaged (e.g. bulk, drummed, tanker)
15. Estimated quantity in weight/volume
16. Process by which the waste is generated
17. For wastes listed in Annex I, classifications from Annex III: hazardous characteristic, H number, and UN class.
18. Method of disposal as per Annex IV
19. Declaration by the generator and exporter that the information is correct
20. Information transmitted (including technical description of the plant) to the exporter or generator from the disposer of the waste upon which the latter has based his assessment that there was no reason to believe that the wastes will not be managed in an environmentally sound manner in accordance with the laws and regulations of the country of import.
21. Information concerning the contract between the exporter and disposer.

ANNEX V B

INFORMATION TO BE PROVIDED ON THE MOVEMENT DOCUMENT

1. Exporter of the waste
2. Generator(s) of the waste and site of generation
3. Disposer of the waste and actual site of disposal

4. Carrier(s) of the waste or his agent(s)
5. Subject of general or single notification
6. The date the transboundary movement started and date(s) and signature on receipt by each person who takes charge of the waste
7. Means of transport (road, rail, inland, waterway, sea, air) including countries of export, transit and import, also point of entry and exit where these have been designated
8. General description of the waste (physical state, proper UN shipping name and class, UN number, Y number and H number as applicable)
9. Information on special handling requirements including emergency provision in case of accidents
10. Type and number of packages
11. Quantity in weight/volume
12. Declaration by the generator or exporter that the information is correct
13. Declaration by the generator or exporter indicating no objection from the component authorities of all States concerned which are Parties
14. Certification by disposer of receipt at designated disposal facility and indication of method of disposal and of the approximate date of disposal

ANNEX VI

ARBITRATION

Article 1

Unless the agreement referred to in Article 20 of the Convention provides otherwise, the arbitration procedure shall be conducted in accordance with Articles 2 to 10 below.

Article 2

The claimant party shall notify the Secretariat that the parties have agreed to submit the dispute to arbitration pursuant to paragraph 2 or paragraph 3 of Article 20 and include, in particular, the Articles of the Convention the interpretation or application of which are at issue. The Secretariat shall forward the information thus received to all Parties to the Convention.

Article 3

The arbitral tribunal shall consist of three members. Each of the Parties to the dispute shall appoint an arbitrator, and the two arbitrators so appointed shall designate by common agreement the third arbitrator, who shall be the chairman of the tribunal. The latter shall not be a national of one of the parties to the dispute, nor have his usual place of residence in the territory of one of these parties, nor be employed by any of them, nor have dealt with the case in any other capacity.

Article 4

1. If the chairman of the arbitral tribunal has not been designated within two months of the appointment of the second arbitrator, the Secretary-General of the United Nations shall, at the request of either party, designate him within a further two months period.

2. If one of the parties to the dispute does not appoint an arbitrator within two months of the receipt of the request, the other party may inform the Secretary-General of the United Nations who shall designate the chairman of the arbitral tribunal within a further two months' period. Upon designation, the chairman of the arbitral shall request the party which has not appointed an arbitration to do so within two months.

After such period, he shall inform the Secretary-General of the United Nations, who shall make this appointment within a further two months' period.

Article 5

1. The arbitral tribunal shall render its decision in accordance with international law and in accordance with the provisions of this Convention.

2. Any arbitral tribunal constituted under the provisions of this Annex shall draw up its own rules of procedure.

Article 6

1. The decisions of the arbitral tribunal both on procedure and on substance, shall be taken by majority vote of its members.

2. The tribunal may take all appropriate measures in order to establish the facts. It may, at the request of one of the parties, recommend essential interim measures of protection.

3. The parties to the dispute shall provide all facilities necessary for the effective conduct of the proceedings.

4. The absence or default of a party in the dispute shall not constitute an impediment to the proceedings.

Article 7

The tribunal may hear and determine counter-claims arising directly out of the subject-matter of the dispute.

Article 8

Unless the arbitral tribunal determines otherwise because of the particular circumstances of the case, the expenses of the tribunal, including the remuneration of its members, shall be borne by the parties to the dispute in equal shares. The tribunal shall keep a record of all its expenses, and shall furnish a final statement thereof to the parties.

Article 9

Any Party that has an interest of a legal nature in the subject-matter of the dispute which may be affected by the decision in the case, may intervene in the proceedings with the consent of the tribunal.

Article 10

1. The tribunal shall render its award within five months of the date on which it is established unless it finds it necessary to extend the time-limit for a period which should not exceed five months.

2. The award of the arbitral tribunal shall be accompanied by a statement of reasons. It shall be final and binding upon the parties to the dispute.

3. Any dispute which may arise between the parties concerning the interpretation or execution of the award may be submitted by either party to the arbitral tribunal which made the award or, if the latter cannot be seized thereof, to another tribunal constituted for this purpose in the same manner as the first.

5.7 Bamako Convention on the Ban of Import Into Africa and the Control of Transboundary Movement and Management of Hazardous Wastes Within Africa (With Annexes). Concluded at Bamako, 29 January 1991. Not in force. *Reprinted in* 30 I.L.M. 775 (1991) & Weston V.I.14

PREAMBLE

The Parties to this Convention,

1. *Mindful* of the growing threat to human health and the environment posed by the increased generation and the complexity of hazardous wastes,

2. *Further mindful* that the most effective way of protecting human health and the environment from the dangers posed by such wastes is the reduction of their generation to a minimum in terms of quantity and/or hazard potential,

3. *Aware* of the risk of damage to human health and the environment caused by transboundary movements of hazardous wastes,

4. *Reiterating* that States should ensure that the generator should carry out his responsibilities with regard to the transport and disposal of hazardous wastes in a manner that is consistent with the protection of human health and environment, whatever the place of disposal,

5. *Recalling* relevant Chapter of the Charter of the Organization of African Unity (OAU) on environmental protection, the African Charter for Human and Peoples' Rights, chapter IX of the Lagos Plan of Action and other Recommendations adopted by the Organization of African Unity on the environment,

6. *Further recognizing* the sovereignty of States to ban the importation into, and the transit through, their territory, of hazardous wastes and substances for human health and environmental reasons,

7. *Recognizing also* the increasing mobilization in Africa for the prohibition of transboundary movements of hazardous wastes and their disposal in African countries,

8. *Convinced* that hazardous wastes should, as far as is compatible with environmentally sound and efficient management, be disposed in the State where they were generated,

9. *Convinced* that the effective control and minimization of transboundary movements of hazardous wastes will act as an incentive, in Africa and elsewhere, for the reduction of the volume of the generation of such wastes,

10. *Noting* that a number of international and regional agreements deal with the problem of the protection and preservation of the environment with regard to the transit of dangerous goods,

11. *Taking into account* the Declaration of the United Nations Conference on the Human Environment (Stockholm, 1972), the Cairo Guidelines and Principles for the Environmentally Sound Management of Hazardous Wastes adopted by the Governing Council of the United Nations Environment Programme (UNEP) by Decision 14/30 of 17 June, 1987, the Recommendations of the United Nations Committee of Experts on the Transport of Dangerous Goods (formulated in 1957 and updated biennially), the Charter of Human Rights, relevant recommendations, declarations, instruments and regulations adopted within the United Nations System, the relevant Articles of the 1989 Basel Convention on the Control of Transboundary Movements of Hazardous Wastes and their Disposal, allows for the establishment of regional agreements which may be equal to or stronger than its own provisions, Article 39 of the Lome IV Convention relating to the international movement of hazardous wastes and radioactive wastes, African intergovernmental organizations and the work and studies done within other international and regional organizations,

12. *Mindful* of the spirit, principles, aims and functions of the African Convention on the Conservation of Nature and Natural Resources adopted by the African Heads of State and Government in Algiers (1968) and the World Charter for Nature adopted by the General Assembly of the United Nations at its thirty-seventh session (1982) as the rule of ethics in respect of the protection of human environment and the conservation of natural resources,

13. *Concerned* by the problems of the transboundary traffic in hazardous wastes,

14. *Recognizing* the need to promote the development of clean production methods, including clean technologies, for the sound management of hazardous wastes produced in Africa, in particular, to avoid, minimize and eliminate the generation of such wastes,

15. *Recognizing* also that when necessary hazardous wastes should be transported in accordance with relevant international conventions and recommendations,

16. *Determined* to protect, by strict control, the human health of the African population and the environment against the adverse effects which may result from the generation of hazardous wastes,

17. *Affirming* a commitment also to responsibly address the problem of hazardous wastes originating within the Continent of Africa,

HAVE AGREED AS FOLLOWS:

ARTICLE 1
DEFINITIONS

For the purpose of this Convention:

1. "Wastes" are substances or materials which are disposed of, or are intended to be disposed of, or are required to be disposed of by the provisions of national law;

2. "Hazardous wastes" shall mean wastes as specified in Article 2 of this Convention.

3. "Management" means the prevention and reduction of hazardous wastes and the collection, transport, storage, treatment either for re-use or disposal of hazardous wastes including after-care of disposal sites;

4. "Transboundary movement" means any movement of hazardous wastes from an area under the national jurisdiction of any state to or through an area under the national jurisdiction of another State, or to or through an area not under the national jurisdiction of another State, provided at least two States are involved in the movement;

5. "Clean production methods" means production or industrial systems which avoid or eliminate the generation of hazardous wastes and hazardous products in conformity with Article 4, Section 3(f) and (g) of this Convention;

6. "Disposal" means any operation specified in Annex III to this Convention;

7. "Approved site or facility" means a site or facility for the disposal of hazardous wastes which is authorised or permitted to operate for this purpose by a relevant authority of the State where the site or facility is located;

8. "Competent authority" means one governmental authority designated by a Party to be responsible, within such geographical areas as the Party may think fit, for receiving the notification of a transboundary movement of hazardous wastes and any information related to it, and for responding to such a notification, as provided in Article 6;

9. "Focal point" means the entity of a Party referred to in Article 5 responsible for receiving and submitting information as provided for in Articles 13 and 16;

10. "Environmentally sound management of hazardous wastes" means taking all practicable steps to ensure that hazardous wastes are managed in a manner which will protect human health and the environment against the adverse effects which may result from such wastes;

11. "Area under the national jurisdiction of a State" means any land, marine area or airspace within which a State exercises administrative and regulatory responsibility in accordance with international law in regard to the protection of human health or the environment;

12. "State of export" means a State from which a transboundary movement of hazardous wastes is planned to be initiated or is initiated;

13. "State of import" means a State to which a transboundary movement is planned or takes place for the purpose of disposal therein or for the purpose of loading prior to disposal in an area not under the national jurisdiction of any State;

14. "State of transit" means any State, other than the State of export or import, through which a movement of hazardous wastes is planned or takes place;

15. "States concerned" means Parties which are States of export or import, or transit States whether or not Parties;

16. "Person" means any natural or legal person;

17. "Exporter" means any person under the jurisdiction of the State of export who arranges for hazardous wastes to be exported;

18. "Importer" means any person under the jurisdiction of the State of import who arranges for hazardous wastes to be imported;

19. "Carrier" means any person who carries out the transport of hazardous wastes;

20. "Generator" means any person whose activity produces hazardous wastes, or, if that person is not known, the person who is in possession and/or control of those wastes;

21. "Disposer" means any person to whom hazardous wastes are shipped and who carries out the disposal of such wastes;

22. "Illegal traffic" means any transboundary movement of hazardous wastes as specified in Article 9;

22. "Dumping at sea" means the deliberate disposal of hazardous wastes at sea from vessels, aircraft, platforms or other man-made structures at sea, and includes ocean incineration and disposal into the seabed and sub-seabed.

ARTICLE 2

SCOPE OF THE CONVENTION

1. The following substances shall be "hazardous wastes" for the purposes of this convention:

(a) Wastes that belong to any category contained in Annex I of this Convention;

(b) Wastes that are not covered under paragraph (a) above but are defined as, or are considered to be, hazardous wastes by the domestic legislation of the State of export, import or transit;

(c) Wastes which possess any of the characteristics contained in Annex II of this Convention;

(d) Hazardous substances which have been banned, cancelled or refused registration by government regulatory action, or voluntarily withdrawn from registration, in the country of manufacture, for human health and environmental reasons.

2. Wastes which, as a result of being radioactive, are subject to any international control systems, including international instruments, applying specifically to radioactive materials, are included in the scope of this Convention.

3. Wastes which derive from the normal operations of a ship, the discharge of which is covered by another international instrument, shall not fall within the scope of this Convention.

ARTICLE 3

NATIONAL DEFINITIONS OF HAZARDOUS WASTES

1. Each State shall, within six months of becoming a Party to this Convention, inform the Secretariat of the Convention of the wastes, other than those listed in Annex 1 of this Convention, considered or defined as hazardous under its national legislation and of any requirements concerning transboundary movement procedures applicable to such wastes.

2. Each Party shall subsequently inform the Secretariat of any significant changes to the information it has provided pursuant to Paragraph 1 of this Convention.

3. The Secretariat shall forthwith inform all Parties of the information it has received pursuant to Paragraphs 1 and 2 of this Article.

4. Parties shall be responsible for making the information transmitted to them by the Secretariat under Paragraph 3 of this Article, available to their exporters and other appropriate bodies.

ARTICLE 4

GENERAL OBLIGATIONS

1. Hazardous Waste Import Ban

All Parties shall take appropriate legal, administrative and other measures within the area under their jurisdiction to prohibit the import of all hazardous wastes, for any reason, into Africa from non-Contracting Parties. Such import shall be deemed illegal and a criminal act. All Parties shall:

(a) Forward as soon as possible, all information relating to such illegal hazardous waste import activity to the Secretariat who shall distribute the information to all Contracting Parties;

(b) Co-operate to ensure that no imports of hazardous wastes from a non-Party enter to this Convention. To this end, the Parties shall, at the Conference of the Contracting Parties consider other enforcement mechanisms.

2. Ban on Dumping of Hazardous Wastes at Sea, Internal Waters and Waterways

(a) Parties in conformity with related international conventions and instruments shall, in the exercise of their jurisdiction within their internal waters, territorial seas, exclusive economic zones and continental shelf, adopt legal, administrative and other appropriate measures to control all carriers from non-Parties, and prohibit the dumping at sea of hazardous wastes, including their incineration at sea and their disposal in the seabed and sub-seabed; any dumping of hazardous wastes at sea, including incineration at sea as well as seabed and sub-seabed disposal, by Contracting Parties, whether in internal waters, territorial seas, exclusive economic zones or high seas shall be deemed to be illegal;

(b) Parties shall forward, as soon as possible, all information relating to dumping of hazardous wastes to the Secretariat which shall distribute the information to all Contracting Parties.

3. Waste Generation in Africa

Each Party shall:

(a) Ensure that hazardous waste generators submit to the Secretariat reports regarding the wastes that they generate in order to enable the Secretariat of the Convention to produce a complete hazardous waste audit;

(b) Impose unlimited liability as well as joint and several liability on hazardous waste generators;

(c) Ensure that the generation of hazardous wastes within the area under its jurisdiction is reduced to a minimum taking into account social, technological and economic aspects;

(d) Ensure the availability of adequate treatment and/or disposal facilities, for the environmentally sound management of hazardous wastes which shall be located, to the extent possible, within its jurisdiction;

(e) Ensure that persons involved in the management of hazardous wastes within its jurisdiction take such steps as are necessary to prevent pollution arising from such wastes and, if such pollution occurs, to minimize the consequence thereof for human health and the environment;

The Adoption of Precautionary Measures:

(f) Each Party shall strive to adopt and implement the preventive, precautionary approach to pollution problems which entails, inter-alia, preventing the release into the environment of substances which may cause harm to humans or the environment without waiting for scientific proof regarding such harm. The Parties shall co-operate with each other in taking the appropriate measures to implement the precautionary principle to pollution prevention through the application of clean production methods, rather than the pursuit of a permissible emissions approach based on assimilative capacity assumptions;

(g) In this respect Parties shall promote clean production methods applicable to entire product life cycles including:

raw material selection, extraction and processing;

product conceptualisation, design, manufacture and assemblage;

materials transport during all phases;

industrial and household usage;

reintroduction of the product into industrial systems or nature when it no longer serves a useful function;

Clean production shall not include "end-of-pipe" pollution controls such as filters and scrubbers, or chemical, physical or biological treatment. Measures which reduce the volume of waste by incineration or concentration, mask the hazard by dilution, or transfer pollutants from one environmental medium to another, are also excluded.

(h) The issue of the transfer to Africa of polluting technologies shall be kept under systematic review by the Secretariat of the Conference and periodic reports made to the Conference of the Parties.

Obligations in the Transport and Transboundary Movement of Hazardous Wastes from Contracting Parties:

(i) Each Party shall prevent the export of hazardous wastes to States which have prohibited by their legislation or international agreements all such imports, or if it has reason to believe that the wastes in question will not be managed in an environmentally sound manner, according to criteria to be decided on by the Parties at their first meeting;

(j) A Party shall not permit hazardous wastes to be exported to a State which does not have the facilities for disposing of them in an environmentally sound manner;

(k) Each Party shall ensure that hazardous wastes to be exported are managed in an environmentally sound manner in the State of import and of transit. Technical guidelines for the environmentally sound management of wastes subject to this Convention shall be decided by the Parties at their first meeting;

(*l*) The Parties agree not to allow the export of hazardous wastes for disposal within the area South of 60 degrees South Latitude, whether or not such wastes are subject to transboundary movement;

(m) Furthermore, each Party shall:

(i) prohibit all persons under its national jurisdiction from transporting or disposing of hazardous wastes unless such persons are authorized or allowed to perform such operations;

(ii) ensure that hazardous wastes that are to be the subject of a transboundary movement are packaged, labelled, and transported in conformity with generally accepted and recognized international rules and standards in the field of packaging, labelling and transport, and that due account is taken of relevant internationally recognized practices;

(iii) ensure that hazardous wastes be accompanied by a movement document, containing information specified in Annex IV B, from the point at which a transboundary movement commences to the point of disposal;

(n) Parties shall take the appropriate measures to ensure that the transboundary movements of hazardous wastes only are allowed if:

(i) the State of export does not have the technical capacity and the necessary facilities, capacity or suitable disposal sites in order to dispose of the wastes in question in an environmentally sound and efficient manner, or

(ii) the transboundary movement in question is in accordance with other criteria to be decided by the Parties, provided those criteria do not differ from the objectives of this Convention;

(*o*) Under this Convention, the obligation of States in which hazardous wastes are generated, requiring that those wastes are managed in an environmentally sound manner, may not under any circumstances be transferred to the States of import or transit;

(p) Parties shall undertake to review periodically the possibilities for the reduction of the amount and/or the pollution potential of hazardous wastes which are exported to other States;

(q) Parties exercising their right to prohibit the import of hazardous wastes for disposal shall inform the other Parties of their decision pursuant to Article 13;

(r) Parties shall prohibit or shall not permit the export of hazardous wastes to States which have prohibited the import of such wastes when notified by the Secretariat or any competent authority pursuant to sub-paragraph (q) above;

(s) Parties shall prohibit or shall not permit the export of hazardous wastes if the State of import does not consent in writing to the specific import, in the case where that State of import has not prohibited the import of such wastes;

(t) Parties shall ensure that the transboundary movement of hazardous wastes is reduced to the minimum consistent with the environmentally sound and efficient management of such wastes, and is conducted in a manner which will protect human health and the environment against the adverse effects which may result from such movements;

(u) Parties shall require that information about a proposed transboundary movement of hazardous wastes be provided to the States concerned, according to Annex IV A, and state clearly the potential effects of the proposed movement on human health and the environment.

4. Furthermore

(a) Parties shall undertake to enforce the obligation of this Convention against offenders and infringements according to relevant national laws and/or order to better protect human health and the environment;

(b) Nothing in this Convention shall prevent a Party from imposing additional requirements that are consistent with the provisions of this Convention, and are in accordance with the rules of international law, in order to better protect human health and the environment;

(c) This Convention recognizes the sovereignty of States over their territorial seas, waterways and air space established in accordance with international law, and jurisdiction which States have in their exclusive economic zone and their continental shelves in accordance with international law, and the exercise by ships and aircraft of all States of navigation rights and freedoms as provided for in international law and as reflected in relevant international instruments.

ARTICLE 5

DESIGNATION OF COMPETENT AUTHORITIES FOCAL POINT AND DUMPWATCH

To facilitate the implementation of this Convention, the Parties shall:

1. Designate or establish one or more competent authorities and one focal point. One competent authority shall be designated to receive the notification in case of a State of transit.

2. Inform the Secretariat, within three months of the date of the entry into force of this Convention for them, which agencies they have designated as their focal point and their competent authorities.

3. Inform the Secretariat, within one month of the date of decision, of any changes regarding the designations made by them under paragraph 2 above.

4. Appoint a national body to act as a Dumpwatch. In such capacity as a Dumpwatch, the designated national body only will be required to co-ordinate with the concerned governmental and non-governmental bodies.

ARTICLE 6

TRANSBOUNDARY MOVEMENT AND NOTIFICATION PROCEDURES

1. The State of export shall notify, or shall require the generator or exporter to notify, in writing, through the channel of the competent authority of the State of export, the competent authority of the States concerned of any proposed transboundary movement of hazardous wastes. Such notification shall contain the declaration and information specified in Annex IV A, of this Convention, written in a language acceptable to the State of import. Only one notification needs to be sent to each State concerned.

2. The State of import shall respond to the notifier in writing consenting to the movement with or without conditions, denying permission for the movement, or requesting additional information. A copy of the final response of the State of import shall be sent to the competent authorities of the States concerned that are Parties to this Convention.

3. The State of export shall not allow the transboundary movement until it has received:

(a) written consent of the State of import, and

(b) from the State of import written confirmation of the existence of a contract between the exporter and the disposer specifying environmentally sound management of the wastes in question.

4. Each State of transit which is a Party to this Convention shall promptly acknowledge to the notifier receipt of the notification. It may subsequently respond to the notifier in writing within 60 days consenting to the movement with or without conditions, denying permission for the movement, or requesting additional information. The State of export shall not allow the transboundary movement to commence until it has received the written consent of the State of transit.

5. In the case of a transboundary movement of hazardous wastes where the wastes are legally defined as or considered to be hazardous wastes only:

(a) by the State of export, the requirements of paragraph 8 of this Article that apply to the importer or disposer and the State of import shall apply *mutatis mutandis* to the exporter and State of export respectively;

(b) by the State of import or by the States of import and transit which are Parties to this Convention, the requirements of paragraphs 1, 3, 4 and 6 of this Article that apply to the exporter and State of export shall apply *mutatis mutandis* to the importer or disposer and State of import, respectively; or

(c) by any State of transit which is Party to this Convention, the provisions of paragraph 4 shall apply to such State.

6. The State shall use a shipment specific notification even where hazardous wastes having the same physical and chemical characteristics are shipped regularly to the same disposer via the same customs office of entry of the State of import, and in the case of transit via the same customs office of entry and exit of the State or States of transit; specific notification of each and every shipment shall be required and contain the information in Annex IV A of this Convention.

7. Each Party to this Convention shall limit their points or ports of entry and notify the Secretariat to this effect for distribution to all Contracting Parties. Such points and ports shall be the only ones permitted for the transboundary movement of hazardous wastes.

8. The Parties to this Convention shall require that each person who takes charge of a transboundary movement of hazardous wastes sign the movement document either upon delivery or receipt of the wastes in question. They shall also require that the disposer inform both the exporter and the competent authority of the State of export of receipt by the disposer of the wastes in question and, in due course, of the completion of disposal as specified in the notification. If no such information is received within the State of export, the competent authority of the State of export or the exporter shall so notify the State of import.

9. The notification and response by this Article shall be transmitted to the competent authority of the States concerned.

10. Any transboundary movement of hazardous wastes shall be covered by insurance, bond or other guarantee as may be required by the State of import or any State of transit which is a Party of this Convention.

ARTICLE 7

TRANSBOUNDARY MOVEMENT FROM A PARTY THROUGH STATES WHICH ARE NOT PARTIES

Paragraph 2 of Article 6 of the Convention shall apply *mutatis mutandis* to transboundary movements of hazardous wastes from a Party through a State or States which are not Parties.

ARTICLE 8

DUTY TO REIMPORT

When a transboundary movement of hazardous wastes to which the consent of the States concerned has been given, subject to the provisions of this Convention, cannot be completed in accordance with the terms of the contract, the State of export shall ensure that the wastes in question are taken back into the State of export, by the exporter, if alternative arrangements cannot be made for their disposal in an environmentally sound manner within a maximum of 90 days from the time that the importing State informed the State of export and the Secretariat. To this end, the State of export and any State of transit shall not oppose, hinder or prevent the return of those wastes to the State of export.

ARTICLE 9

ILLEGAL TRAFFIC

1. For the purpose of this Convention, any transboundary movement of hazardous wastes under the following situations shall be deemed to be illegal traffic:

(a) if carried out without notification, pursuant to the provisions of this Convention, to all States concerned, or

(b) if carried out without the consent, pursuant to the provisions of this Convention, of a State concerned; or

(c) if consent is obtained from States concerned through falsification, misrepresentation or fraud; or

(d) if it does not conform in a material way with the documents; or

(e) if it results in deliberate disposal of hazardous wastes in contravention of this Convention and of general principles of international law.

2. Each State shall introduce appropriate national legislation for imposing criminal penalties on all persons who have planned, carried out, or assisted in such illegal imports. Such penalties shall be sufficiently high to both punish and deter such conduct.

3. In case of a transboundary movement of hazardous wastes deemed to be illegal traffic as the result of conduct on the part of the exporter or generator the State of export shall ensure that the wastes in question are taken back by the exporter or generator or if necessary by itself into the State of export, within 30 days from the time the State of export has been informed about the illegal traffic. To this end the States concerned shall not oppose, hinder or prevent the return of those wastes to the State of export and appropriate legal action shall be taken against the contravenor(s).

4. In the case of a transboundary movement of hazardous wastes deemed to be illegal traffic as the result of conduct on the part of the importer or disposer, the State of import shall ensure that the wastes in question are returned to the exporter by the

importer and that legal proceedings according to the provisions of this Convention are taken against the contravenor(s).

ARTICLE 10

INTRAAFRICAN COOPERATION

1. The Parties to this Convention shall co-operate with one another and with relevant African organizations, to improve and achieve the environmentally sound management of hazardous wastes.

2. To this end, the Parties shall:

(a) Make available information, whether on a bilateral or multilateral basis, with a view to promoting clean production methods and the environmentally sound management of hazardous wastes, including harmonization of technical standards and practices for the adequate management of hazardous wastes;

(b) Co-operate in monitoring the effects of the management of hazardous wastes on human health and the environment;

(c) Co-operate, subject to their national laws, regulations and policies, in the development and implementation of new environmentally sound clean production technologies and the improvement of existing technologies with a view to eliminating, as far as practicable, the generation of hazardous wastes and achieving more effective and efficient methods of ensuring their management in an environmentally sound manner, including the study of the economic, social and environmental effects of the adoption of such new and improved technologies;

(d) Co-operate actively to their national laws, regulations and policies, in the transfer of technology and management systems related to the environmentally sound management of hazardous wastes. They shall also co-operate in developing the technical capacity among Parties, especially those which may need and request technical assistance in this field;

(e) Co-operate in developing appropriate technical guidelines and/or codes of practice;

(f) Co-operate in the exchange and dissemination of information on the movement of hazardous wastes in conformity with Article 13 of this Convention.

ARTICLE 11

INTERNATIONAL COOPERATION

BILATERAL, MULTILATERAL AND REGIONAL AGREEMENTS

1. Parties to this Convention may enter into bilateral, multilateral, or regional agreements or arrangements regarding the transboundary movement and management of hazardous wastes generated in Africa with Parties or non-Parties provided that such agreements or arrangements do not derogate from the environmentally sound management of hazardous wastes as required by this Convention. These agreements or arrangements shall stipulate provisions which are no less environmentally sound than those provided for by this Convention.

2. Parties shall notify the Secretariat of any bilateral, multilateral or regional agreements or arrangements referred to in paragraph 1 of this Article and those which they have entered into prior to the entry into force of this Convention for them, for purpose of controlling transboundary movements of hazardous wastes which take place entirely among the Parties to such agreements. The provisions of this Convention shall not affect transboundary movements of hazardous wastes generated in Africa which take place pursuant to such agreements provided that such agreements are compatible with the environmentally sound management of hazardous wastes as required by this Convention.

3. Each Contracting Party shall prohibit vessels flying its flag or aircraft registered in its territory from carrying out activities in contravention of this Convention.

4. Parties shall use appropriate measures to promote SouthSouth cooperation in the implementation of this Convention.

5. Taking into account the needs of developing countries, cooperation between international organizations is encouraged in order to promote, among other things, public awareness, the development of the rational management of hazardous wastes and the adoption of new and less polluting technologies.

ARTICLE 12
LIABILITIES AND COMPENSATION

The Conference of Parties shall set up an Ad Hoc expert organ to prepare a draft protocol setting out appropriate rules and procedures in the field of liabilities and compensation for damage resulting from the transboundary movement of hazardous wastes.

ARTICLE 13
TRANSMISSION OF INFORMATION

1. The Parties shall ensure that in the case of an accident occurring during the transboundary movement of hazardous wastes or their disposal which is likely to present risks to human health and the environment in other States, those States are immediately informed.

2. The States shall inform each other, through the Secretariat, of:

(a) Changes regarding the designation of competent authorities and/or focal points, pursuant to Article 5 of the present Convention.

(b) Changes in their national definition of hazardous wastes, pursuant to article 3 of the present Convention;

(c) Decisions made by them to limit or ban the import of hazardous wastes;

(d) Any other information required pursuant to paragraph 4 of this Article.

3. The Parties, consistent with national laws and regulations, shall set up information collection and dissemination mechanisms for hazardous wastes. They shall transmit such information through the Secretariat, to the Conference of the Parties established under Article 15 of the present Convention, before the end of each calendar year, in a report on the previous calendar year, containing the following information:

(a) Competent authorities, Dumpwatch, and focal points that have been designated by them pursuant to Article 5 of the present Convention.

(b) Information regarding transboundary movements of hazardous wastes in which they have been involved including:

(i) The quantity of hazardous wastes exported, their category, characteristics, destination, any transit country and disposal methods as stated in the notification;

(ii) The amount of hazardous wastes imported, their category, characteristics, origin, and disposal methods;

(iii) Disposals which did not proceed as intended;

(iv) Efforts to achieve a reduction of the amount of hazardous wastes subject to transboundary movements.

(c) Information on the measures adopted by them in the implementation of this Convention;

(d) Information on available qualified statistics which have been compiled by them on the effects on human health and the environment of the generation, transportation, and disposal of hazardous wastes as part of the information required in conformity with Article 4 Section 3(a) of this Convention;

(e) Information concerning bilateral, multilateral and regional agreements and arrangements entered into pursuant to Article 11 of this Convention;

(f) Information on accidents occurring during the transboundary movements and disposal of hazardous wastes and on the measures undertaken to deal with them;

(g) Information on disposal options operated within the area under their national jurisdiction;

(h) Information on measures undertaken for the development of clean production methods, including clean production technologies, for the reduction and/or elimination of the production of hazardous wastes; and

(i) Such other matters as the Conference of the Parties shall deem relevant.

4. The Parties, consistent with national laws and regulations, shall ensure that copies of each notification concerning any given transboundary movement of hazardous wastes, and the response to it, are sent to the Secretariat.

ARTICLE 14
FINANCIAL ASPECTS

1. The regular budget of the Conference of the Parties, as required in Articles 15 and 16 of this Convention, shall be prepared by the Secretariat and approved by the Conference.

2. Parties shall, at the first meeting of the Conference of the Parties, agree on a scale of contributions to the recurrent budget of the Secretariat.

3. The Parties shall also consider the establishment of a revolving fund to assist on an interim basis, in case of emergency situations to minimize damage from disasters or accidents arising from transboundary movements of hazardous wastes or during the disposal of such wastes.

4. The Parties agree that, according to the specific needs of different regions and sub-regions, regional or sub-regional centres for training and technology transfers regarding the management of hazardous wastes and the minimization of their generation should be established as well as appropriate funding mechanisms of a voluntary nature.

ARTICLE 15
CONFERENCE OF THE PARTIES

1. A Conference of the Parties, made up of Ministers having the environment as their mandate, is hereby established. The first meeting of the Conference of the Parties shall be convened by the Secretary-General of the OAU not later than one year after the entry into force of this Convention. Thereafter, ordinary meetings of the Conference of the Parties shall be held at regular intervals to be determined by the Conference at its first meeting.

2. The Conference of the Parties to this Convention shall adopt Rules of Procedure for itself and for any subsidiary body it may establish, as well as financial rules to determine in particular the financial participation of the Parties under this Convention.

3. The Parties to this Convention at their first meeting shall consider any additional measures needed to assist them in fulfilling their responsibilities with

respect to the protection and the preservation of the marine and inland waters environments in the context of this Convention.

4. The Conference of the Parties shall keep under continuous review and evaluation the effective implementation of this Convention, and in addition, shall:

(a) promote the harmonization of appropriate policies, strategies and measures for minimizing harm to human health and the environment by hazardous wastes;

(b) consider and adopt, as required, amendments to this Convention and its annexes, taking into consideration, inter alia, available scientific, technical, economic and environmental information;

(c) consider and undertake any additional action that may be required for the achievement of the purpose of this Convention in the light of experience gained in its operation and in the operation of the agreements and arrangements envisaged in Article 11 of the present Convention;

(d) consider and adopt protocols as required;

(e) establish such subsidiary bodies as are deemed necessary for the implementation of this Convention; and

(f) make decisions for the peaceful settlement of disputes arising from the transboundary movement of hazardous wastes, if need be, according to international law.

5. Organisations may be represented as observers at meetings of the Conference of the Parties to this Convention. Any body or agency, whether national or international, governmental or non-governmental, qualified in fields relating to hazardous wastes which has informed the Secretariat, may be represented as an observer at a meeting of the Conference of the Parties to this Convention. The admission and participation of observers shall be subject to the rules of procedures adopted by the Conference of the Parties.

ARTICLE 16

SECRETARIAT

1. The functions of the secretariat shall be:

(a) to arrange for, and service, meetings provided for in Articles 15 and 17 of the present Convention.

(b) to prepare and transmit reports based upon information received in accordance with Articles 3, 4, 6, 11, and 13 of the present Convention as well as upon information derived from meetings of subsidiary bodies established under Article 15 of the present Convention as well as upōn, as appropriate, information provided by relevant inter-governmental and non-governmental entities;

(c) to prepare reports on its activities carried out in the implementation of its functions under this Convention and present them to the Conference of the Parties;

(d) to ensure the necessary co-ordination with relevant international bodies, and in particular to enter into such administrative and contractual arrangements as may be required for the effective discharge of its functions;

(e) to communicate with focal points, competent authorities and Dumpwatch established by the Parties in accordance with Article 5 of this Convention as well as appropriate inter-governmental and non-governmental organizations which may provide assistance in the implementation of this Convention.

(f) to compile information concerning approved national sites and facilities of Parties to this Convention available for the disposal an treatment of their hazardous wastes and to circulate this information;

(g) to receive and convey information from and to Parties to this Convention on:

sources of technical assistance and training;

available technical and scientific know-how;

sources of advice and expertise; and

availability of resources.

This information will assist them in:

the management of the notification system of this Convention;

environmentally sound clean production methods relating to hazardous wastes, such as clean production technologies;

the assessment of disposal capabilities and sites;

the monitoring of hazardous wastes; and

emergency responses;

(h) to provide the Parties to this Convention with information on consultants or consulting firms having the necessary technical competence in the field, which can assist them with examining a notification for a transboundary movement, the concurrence of a shipment of hazardous wastes with the relevant notification, and/or whether the proposed disposal facilities for hazardous wastes are environmentally sound, when they have reason to believe that the wastes in question will not be managed in an environmentally sound manner. Any such examinations would not be at the expense of the Secretariat;

(i) to assist Parties to this Convention in their identification of cases of illegal traffic and to circulate immediately to the Parties concerned any information it has received regarding illegal traffic;

(j) to co-operate with Parties to this Convention and with relevant and competent international organizations and agencies in the provision of experts and equipment for the purpose of rapid assistance to States in the event of an emergency situation; and

(k) to perform such other functions relevant to the purposes of this Convention as may be determined by the Conference of the Parties to this Convention.

2. The Secretariat's functions shall be carried out on an interim basis by the Organization of African Unity (OAU) jointly with the United Nations Economic Commission for Africa (ECA) until the completion of the first meeting of the Conference of the Parties held pursuant to Article 15 of the present Convention. At this meeting, the Conference of the Parties shall also evaluate the implementation by the interim Secretariat of the functions assigned to it, in particular under paragraph 1 above, and decide upon the structures appropriate for those functions.

ARTICLE 17

AMENDMENT OF THE CONVENTION AND OF PROTOCOLS

1. Any Party may propose amendments to this Convention and any Party to a Protocol may propose amendments to that Protocol. Such amendments shall take due account, *inter alia,* of relevant scientific, technical, environmental and social considerations.

2. Amendments to this Convention shall be adopted at a meeting of the Conference of the Parties. Amendments to any Protocol shall be adopted at a meeting of the Parties to the Protocol in question. The text of any proposed amendment to this Convention or to any Protocol, except as may otherwise be provided in such Protocol, shall be communicated to the Parties by the Secretariat at least six months before the meeting at which it is proposed for adoption. The Secretariat shall also communicate proposed amendments to the Signatories to this Convention for their information.

3. The Parties shall make every effort to reach agreement on any proposed amendment to this Convention by consensus. If all efforts at consensus have been exhausted, and no agreement reached, the amendment shall, as a last resort, be adopted by a two-thirds majority vote of the Parties present and voting at the meeting. It shall then be submitted by the Depository to all Parties for ratification, approval, formal confirmation or acceptance.

Amendments of Protocols to this Convention

4. The procedure specified in paragraph 3 above shall apply to amendments to any Protocol, except that a two-thirds majority of the Parties to that Protocol present and voting at the meeting shall suffice for their adoption.

GENERAL PROVISIONS

5. Instruments of ratification, approval, formal confirmation or acceptance of amendments shall be deposited with the Depository. Amendments adopted in accordance with paragraph 3 or 4 above shall enter into force between Parties having accepted them, on the ninetieth day after the receipt by the Depository of the instrument of ratification, approval, formal confirmation or acceptance by at least two-thirds of the Parties who accepted the amendments to the Protocol concerned, except as may otherwise be provided in such Protocol. The amendments shall enter into force for any other Party on the ninetieth day after that Party deposits its instrument of ratification, approval, formal confirmation or acceptance of the amendments.

6. For the purpose of this Article, "Parties present and voting" means Parties present and casting an affirmative or negative vote.

ARTICLE 18

ADOPTION AND AMENDMENT OF ANNEXES

1. The annexes to this Convention or to any Protocol shall form an integral part of this Convention or of such Protocol, as the case may be and, unless expressly provided otherwise, a reference to this Convention or its Protocols constitutes at the same time a reference to any annexes thereto. Such annexes shall be restricted to scientific, technical and administrative matters.

2. Except as may be otherwise provided in any Protocol with respect to its annexes, the following procedures shall apply to the proposal, adoption and entry into force of additional annexes to this Convention or of annexes to a protocol:

(a) Annexes to this Convention and its Protocols shall be proposed and adopted according to the procedures laid down in Article 17, paragraphs 1, 2, 3, and 4 of the present Convention;

(b) Any Party that is unable to accept an additional annex to this Convention or an annex to any Protocol to which it is Party shall so notify the Depository, in writing, within six months from the date of the communication of the adoption by the Depository. The Depository shall without delay notify all Parties of any such notification received. A Party may at any time substitute an acceptance for a previous declaration of objection and the annexes shall thereupon enter into force for that Party;

(c) Upon the expiration of six months from the date of the circulation of the communication by the Depository, the annex shall become effective for all Parties to this Convention or to any Protocol concerned, which have not submitted a notification in accordance with the provision of subparagraph (b) above.

3. The proposal, adoption and entry into force of amendments to annexes to this Convention or to any Protocol shall be subject to the same procedure as for the proposal, adoption and entry into force of annexes to the Convention or annexes to a Protocol. Annexes and amendments thereto shall take due account, *inter alia,* of relevant scientific and technical considerations.

4. If an additional annex or an amendment to an annex involves an amendment to this Convention or to any Protocol, the additional annex or amended annex shall not enter into force until such time as the amendment to this Convention or to the Protocol enters into force.

ARTICLE 19

VERIFICATION

Any Party which has reason to believe that another Party is acting or has acted in breach of its obligations under this Convention must inform the Secretariat thereof, and in such an event, shall simultaneously and immediately inform, directly or through the Secretariat, the Party against whom the allegations are made. The Secretariat shall carry out a verification of the substance of the allegation and submit a report thereof to all the Parties to this convention.

ARTICLE 20

SETTLEMENT OF DISPUTES

1. In case of dispute between Parties as to the interpretation or application of, or compliance with, this Convention or any Protocol thereto, the Parties shall seek a settlement of the dispute through negotiations or any other peaceful means of their own choice.

2. If the Parties concerned cannot settle their dispute as provided in paragraph 1 of this Article, the dispute shall be submitted either to an Ad Hoc organ set up by the Conference for this purpose or to the International Court of Justice.

3. The conduct of arbitration of disputes between Parties by the Ad Hoc organ provided for in paragraph 2 of this Article shall be as provided in Annex V of this Convention.

ARTICLE 21

SIGNATURE

This Convention shall be open for signature by Member States of the OAU in Bamako and Addis Ababa for a period of six months from 30 January 1991 to 31 July 1991.

ARTICLE 22

RATIFICATION, ACCEPTANCE, FORMAL CONFIRMATION OR APPROVAL

1. This Convention shall be subject to ratification, acceptance, formal confirmation or approval by Member States of the OAU. Instruments of ratification, acceptance, formal confirmation, or approval shall be deposited with the Depository.

2. Parties shall be bound by all obligations of this Convention.

ARTICLE 23

ACCESSION

This Convention shall be open for accession by Member States of the OAU from the date after the day on which the Convention is closed for signature. The instruments of accession shall be deposited with the Depository.

ARTICLE 24

RIGHT TO VOTE

Each Contracting Party to this Convention shall have one vote.

ARTICLE 25

ENTRY INTO FORCE

1. This Convention shall enter into force on the ninetieth day after the date of deposit of the tenth instrument of ratification from Parties signatory to this Convention.

2. For each State which ratifies this Convention or accedes thereto after the date of the deposit of the tenth instrument of ratification, it shall enter into force on the ninetieth day after the date of deposit by such State of its instrument of accession or ratification.

ARTICLE 26

RESERVATIONS AND DECLARATIONS

1. No reservations or exception may be made to this Convention.

2. Paragraph 1 of this Article does not preclude a State when signing, ratifying, or acceding to this Convention, from making declarations or statements, however phrased or named, with a view, inter alia, to the harmonization of its laws and regulations with the provisions of this Convention, provided that such declarations or statements do not purport to exclude or to modify the legal effects of the provisions of the Convention in their application to that State.

ARTICLE 27

WITHDRAWAL

1. At any time after three years from the date on which this Convention has entered into force for a Party, that Party may withdraw from the Convention by giving written notification to the Depository.

2. Withdrawal shall be effective one year after receipt of notification by the Depository, or on such later date as may be specified in the notification.

3. Withdrawal shall not exempt the withdrawing Party from fulfilling any obligations it might have incurred under this Convention.

ARTICLE 28

DEPOSITORY

The Secretary-General of the Organization of African Unity shall be the Depository for this Convention and of any Protocol thereto.

ARTICLE 29

REGISTRATION

This Convention, as soon as it enters into force, shall be registered with the Secretary-General of the United Nations Organization in conformity with Article 102 of the Charter of the United Nations.

ARTICLE 30

AUTHENTIC TEXTS

The Arabic, English, French and Portuguese texts of this Convention are equally authentic.

* * *

ANNEX I

CATEGORIES OF WASTES WHICH ARE HAZARDOUS WASTES

Waste Streams

Y0 All wastes containing or contaminated by radionuclides, the concentration or properties of which result from human activity.

Y1 Clinical wastes from medical care in hospitals, medical centres and clinics.

Y2 Wastes from the production and preparation of pharmaceutical products.

Y3 Wastes pharmaceuticals, drugs and medicines.

Y4 Wastes from the production, formulation and use of biocides and phytopharmaceuticals.

Y5 Wastes from the manufacture, formulation and use of wood preserving chemicals.

Y6 Wastes from the production, formulation and use of organic solvents.

Y7 Wastes from heat treatment and tempering operations containing cyanides.

Y8 Waste mineral oils unfit for their originally intended use.

Y9 Waste oils/water, hydrocarbons/water mixtures, emulsions.

Y10 Waste substances and articles containing or contaminated with polychlorinated biphenyls (PCBs) and/or polychlorinated terphenyls (PCTs) and/or polybrominated biphenyls (PBBs).

Y11 Waste tarry residues arising from refining, distillation and any pyrolytic treatment.

Y12 Wastes from production, formulation and use of inks, dyes, pigments, paints, lacquers, varnish.

Y13 Wastes from production, formulation and use of resins, latex, plasticizers, glues/adhesives.

Y14 Waste chemical substances arising from research and development or teaching activities which are not identified and/or are new and whose effects on man and/or the environment are not known.

Y15 Wastes of an explosive nature not subject to other legislation.

Y16 Wastes from production, formulation and use of photographic chemicals and processing materials.

Y17 Wastes resulting from surface treatment of metals and plastics.

Y18 Residues arising from industrial waste disposal operations.

Y46 Wastes collected from households, including sewage and sewage sludges.

Y47 Residues arising from the incineration of household wastes.

Wastes having as constituents:

Y19 Metal carbonyls.

Y20 Beryllium; beryllium compounds.

Y21 Hexavalant chromium compounds.

Y22 Copper compounds.

Y23 Zinc compounds.

Y24 Arsenic; arsenic compounds.

Y25 Selenium; selenium compounds.

Y26 Cadmium; cadmium compounds.

Y27 Antimony; antimony compounds.

Y28 Tellurium; tellurium compounds.
Y29 Mercury; mercury compounds.
Y30 Thallium; thallium compounds.
Y31 Lead; lead compounds.
Y32 Inorganic fluorine compounds excluding calcium fluoride.
Y33 Inorganic cyanides.
Y34 Acidic solutions or acids in solid form.
Y35 Basic solutions or bases in solid form.
Y36 Asbestos (dust and fibres).
Y37 Organic phosphorous compounds.
Y38 Organic cyanides.
Y39 Phenols; phenol compounds including chlorophenols.
Y40 Ethers.
Y41 Halogenated organic solvents.
Y42 Organic solvents excluding halogenated solvents.
Y43 Any congenor of polychlorinated dibenzo-furan.
Y44 Any congenor of polychlorinated dibenzo-p-dioxin.
Y45 Organohalogen compounds other than substances referred to in this Annex (e.g., Y39, Y41, Y42, Y43, Y44).

ANNEX II

LIST OF HAZARDOUS CHARACTERISTICS

UN Class	*Code*	*Characteristics*
1	H1	**Explosive** An explosive substance or waste is a solid or liquid substance or waste (or mixture of substances or wastes) which is in itself capable by chemical reaction or producing gas at such a temperature and pressure and at such a speed as to cause damage to the surroundings.
3	H3	**Flammable liquids** The word "flammable" has the same meaning as "inflammable". Flammable liquids are liquids, or mixtures of liquids, or liquids containing solids in solution or suspension (for example paints, varnishes, lacquers, etc .., but not including substances or wastes otherwise classified on account of their dangerous characteristics) which give off a flammable vapour at temperatures of not more than 60.5 degrees C, closed up test, or not more than 65.6 degrees C, open-cup test. (Since the results of open-cup tests and of closed-up tests are not strictly comparable and even individual results by the same test are often variable, regulations varying from the above figures to make allowance for such difference would be within the spirit of this definition).
4.1	H4.1	**Flammable solids** Solids, or waste solids, other than those classed as explosives, which under conditions encountered in transport are readily combustible, or may cause or contribute to fire through friction.
4.2	H4.2	**Substances or wastes liable to spontaneous combustion** Substances or wastes which are liable to spontaneous heating under normal conditions encountered in transport, or to heating up on contact with air, and being then liable to catch fire.
4.3	H4.3	**Substances or wastes which, in contact with water emit flammable gases** Substances or wastes which, by interaction with water, are liable to become spontaneously flammable or to give off flammable gases in dangerous quantities.
5.1	H5.1	**Oxidizing**

UN Class	Code	Characteristics
		Substances or wastes which, while in themselves not necessarily combustible, may, generally by yielding oxygen, cause or contribute to the combustion of other materials.
5.2	**H5.2**	**Organic peroxides** Organic substances or wastes which contain the bivalent-O–O-structure are thermally unstable substances which may undergo exothermic self-accelerating decomposition.
6.1	**H6.1**	**Poisonous (Acute)** Substances or wastes liable either to cause death or serious injury or to harm human health if swallowed or inhaled or by skin contact.
6.2	**H6.2**	**Infectious substances** Substances or wastes containing viable micro organisms or their toxins which are known or suspected to cause disease in animals or humans.
8	**H8**	**Corrosives** Substances or wastes which, by chemical action, will cause severe damage when in contact with living tissue, or in the case of leakage, will materially damage, or even destroy, other goods or the means of transport; they may also cause other hazards.
9	**H10**	**Liberation of toxic gases in contact with air or water** Substances or wastes which, by interaction with air or water, are liable to give off toxic gases in dangerous quantities.
9	**H11**	**Toxic (Delayed or chronic)** Substances or wastes which, if they are inhaled or ingested or if they penetrate the skin, may involve delayed or chronic effects, including carcinogenicity.
9	**H12**	**Ecotoxic** Substances or wastes which if released present or may present immediate or delayed adverse impacts to the environment by means of bioaccumulation and/or toxic effects upon biotic systems.
9	**H13**	**Capable, by any means, after disposal, of yielding another material, e.g., leachate, which possesses any of the characteristics listed above.**

ANNEX III

DISPOSAL OPERATIONS

D1 Deposit into or onto land, (e.g., landfill, etc ..).

D2 Land treatment, (e.g. biodegradation of liquid or sludgy discards in soils, etc ..).

D3 Deep injection, (e.g., injection of pumpable discards into wells, salt domes or naturally occurring repositories, etc ..).

D4 Surface impoundment, (e.g., placement of liquid into lined discrete cells which are capped and isolated from one another and the environment, etc ..).

D6 Release into a water body except seas/oceans.

D7 Release into seas/oceans including sea-bed insertion.

D8 Biological treatment not specified elsewhere in this Annex which results in final compounds or mixtures which are discarded by means of any of the operations in Annex III.

D9 Physico-chemical treatment not specified elsewhere in the Annex which results in final compounds or mixtures which are discarded by means of any of the operations in Annex III (e.g., evaporation, drying, calcination, neutralisation, precipitation, etc ..).

D10 Incineration on land.
D11 Incineration at sea.
D12 Permanent storage, (e.g., emplacement of containers in a mine, etc ..).
D13 Blending or mixing prior to submission to any of the operations in Annex III.
D14 Repackaging prior to submission to any of the operations in Annex III.
D15 Storage pending any of the operations in Annex III.
D16 Use of a fuel (other than in direct incineration) or other means to generate energy.
D17 Solvent reclamation/regeneration.
D18 Recycling/reclamation of organic substances which are not used as solvents.
D19 Recycling/reclamation of metals and metal compounds.
D20 Recycling/reclamation of other inorganic materials.
D21 Regeneration of acids and bases.
D22 Recovery of components used for pollution abatement.
D23 Recovery of components from catalysts.
D24 Used oil re-refining or other reuses of previously used oil,
D25 Land treatment resulting in benefit to agriculture or ecological improvement.
D26 Uses of residual materials obtained from any of the operations numbered D1D25.
D27 Exchange of wastes for submission to any of the operations numbered D1D26.
D28 Accumulation of material intended for any operation in Annex III.

ANNEX IV A

INFORMATION TO BE PROVIDED ON NOTIFICATION

1. Reason for waste export
2. Exporter of the waste
3. Generator(s) of the waste and site of generation
4. Importer and disposer of the waste and actual site of disposal
5. Intended carrier(s) of the waste or their agents, if known
6. Country of export of the waste. Competent authority
7. Countries of transit. Competent authority
8. [omitted]
9. Projected date of shipment and period of time over which waste is to be exported and proposed itinerary (including point of entry and exit).
10. Means of transport envisaged (road, rail, sea, air, inland waters).
11. Information relating to insurance
12. Designation and physical description of the waste including Y number and UN number and its composition and information on any special handling requirements including emergency provisions in case of accidents.
13. Type of packaging envisaged (e.g., bulk, drummer, tanker).
14. Estimated quantity in weight/volume
15. Process by which the waste is generated
16. Waste classification from Annex II: Hazardous characteristics, H number, and UN class.
17. Method of disposal as per Annex III.
18. Declaration by the generator and exporter that the information is correct.
19. Information transmitted (including technical description of the plant) to the exporter or generator from the disposer of the waste upon which

the latter has based his assessment that there was no reason to believe that the wastes will not be managed in an environmentally sound manner in accordance with the laws and regulations of the country of import.

20. Information concerning the contract between the exporter and disposer.

* * *

ANNEX IV B

INFORMATION TO BE PROVIDED ON THE MOVEMENT DOCUMENT

1. Exporter of the waste
2. Generator(s) of the waste and site of generation
3. Importer and disposer of the waste and actual site of disposal
4. Carrier(s) of the waste or his agent(s)
5. The date the transboundary movement started and date(s) and signature on receipt by each person who takes charge of the waste.
6. Means of transport (road, rail, inland waterway, sea, air) including countries of export, transit and import, also point of entry and exit where these have been designated.
7. General description of the waste (physical state, proper UN shipping name and class, UN number, Y number and H number as applicable).
8. Information on special handling requirements including emergency provisions in case of accidents.
9. Type and number of packages.
10. Quantity in weight/volume.
11. Declaration by the generator or exporter that the information is correct.
12. Declaration by disposer or exporter indicating no objection from the competent authorities of all States concerned.
13. Certification by disposer of receipt at designated disposal facility and indication of method of disposal and of the appropriate date of disposal.

* * *

ANNEX V

ARBITRATION

Article 1

Unless the agreement referred to in Article 20 of the Convention provides otherwise, the arbitration procedure shall be conducted in accordance with Articles 2 to 10 below.

Article 2

The claimant Party shall notify the Secretariat that the Parties have agreed to submit the dispute to arbitration pursuant to paragraph 1 or paragraph 2 of Article 20 of the Convention and include, in particular, the Articles of the Convention, and the interpretation or application of which are at issue. The Secretariat shall forward the information thus received to all Parties to the Convention.

Article 3

The arbitral tribunal shall consist of three members. Each of the Parties to the dispute shall appoint an arbitrator, and the two arbitrators so appointed shall designate by common agreement the third arbitrator, who shall be the chairman of the tribunal. The latter shall not be a national of one of the parties to the dispute, nor have his usual place of residence in one of the Parties, nor be employed by any of them, nor have dealt with the case in any other capacity.

Article 4

1. If the Chairman of the arbitral tribunal has not been designated within two months of the appointment of the second arbitrator, the Secretary-General of the OAU shall, at the request of either Party, designate him within a further two months period.

2. If one of the Parties to the dispute does not appoint an arbitrator within two months of the receipt of the request, the other Party may inform the Secretary-General of the OAU who shall designate the chairman of the arbitral tribunal within a further two months period. Upon designation, the chairman of the arbitral tribunal shall request the Party which has not appointed an arbitrator to do so within two months. After such period, he shall inform the Secretary-General of the OAU who shall make this appointment within a further two month's period.

Article 5

1. The arbitral tribunal shall render its decision in accordance with international law and in accordance with the provisions of this Convention.

2. Any arbitral tribunal constituted under the provisions of this Annex shall draw up its own rules of procedure.

Article 6

1. The decision of the arbitral tribunal both on procedure and on substance, shall be taken by majority vote of its members.

2. The tribunal may take all appropriate measures in order to establish the facts. It may, at the request of one of the Parties, recommend essential interim measures of protection.

3. The Parties to the dispute shall provide all facilities necessary for the effective conduct of the proceedings.

4. The absence or default of a Party in the dispute shall not constitute an impediment to the proceedings.

Article 7

The tribunal may hear and determine counter-claims arising directly out of the subject-matter of the dispute.

Article 8

Unless the arbitral tribunal determines otherwise because of the particular circumstances of the case, the expenses of the tribunal, including the remuneration of its members, shall be borne by the Parties to the dispute in equal shares. The tribunal shall keep a record of all its expenses, and shall furnish a final statement thereof to the Parties.

Article 9

Any Party that has an interest of a legal nature in the subject-matter of the dispute which may be affected by the decision in the case, may intervene in the proceedings with the consent of the tribunal.

Article 10

1. The tribunal shall render its award within five months of the date on which it is established unless it finds it necessary to extend the time-limit for a period which should not exceed five months.

2. The award of the arbitral tribunal shall be accompanied by a statement of reasons. It shall be final and binding upon the Parties to the dispute.

3. Any dispute which may arise between the Parties concerning the interpretation or execution of the award may be submitted by either Party to the arbitral tribunal which made the award or, if the latter cannot be seized thereof, to another tribunal constituted for this purpose in the same manner as the first.

5.8 CONVENTION TO COMBAT DESERTIFICATION IN THOSE COUNTRIES EXPERIENCING SERIOUS DROUGHT AND/OR DESERTIFICATION, PARTICULARLY IN AFRICA. Adopted on 17 June 1994. Entered into force, 26 December 1996. U.N. Doc. No. A/AC.241/15/Rev.7; *reprinted in* 33 I.L.M. 1328 (1994) & 5 Weston V.G.4

The Parties to this Convention,

Affirming that human beings in affected or threatened areas are at the centre of concerns to combat desertification and mitigate the effects of drought,

Reflecting the urgent concern of the international community, including States and international organizations, about the adverse impacts of desertification and drought,

Aware that arid, semi-arid and dry sub-humid areas together account for a significant proportion of the Earth's land area and are the habitat and source of livelihood for a large segment of its population,

Acknowledging that desertification and drought are problems of global dimension in that they affect all regions of the world and that joint action of the international community is needed to combat desertification and/or mitigate the effects of drought,

Noting the high concentration of developing countries, notably the least developed countries, among those experiencing serious drought and/or desertification, and the particularly tragic consequences of these phenomena in Africa,

Noting also that desertification is caused by complex interactions among physical, biological, political, social, cultural and economic factors,

Considering the impact of trade and relevant aspects of international economic relations on the ability of affected countries to combat desertification adequately,

Conscious that sustainable economic growth, social development and poverty eradication are priorities of affected developing countries, particularly in Africa, and are essential to meeting sustainability objectives,

Mindful that desertification and drought affect sustainable development through their interrelationships with important social problems such as poverty, poor health and nutrition, lack of food security, and those arising from migration, displacement of persons and demographic dynamics,

Appreciating the significance of the past efforts and experience of States and international organizations in combatting desertification and mitigating the effects of drought, particularly in implementing the Plan of Action to Combat Desertification which was adopted at the United Nations Conference on Desertification in 1977,

Realizing that, despite efforts in the past, progress in combatting desertification and mitigating the effects of drought has not met expectations and that a new and more effective approach is needed at all levels within the framework of sustainable development,

Recognizing the validity and relevance of decisions adopted at the United Nations Conference on Environment and Development, particularly of Agenda 21 and its chapter 12, which provide a basis for combatting desertification,

Reaffirming in this light the commitments of developed countries as contained in paragraph 13 of chapter 33 of Agenda 21,

Recalling General Assembly resolution 47/188, particularly the priority in it prescribed for Africa, and all other relevant United Nations resolutions, decisions and programmes on desertification and drought, as well as relevant declarations by African countries and those from other regions,

Reaffirming the Rio Declaration on Environment and Development which states, in its Principle 2, that States have, in accordance with the Charter of the United Nations and the principles of international law, the sovereign right to exploit their own resources pursuant to their own environmental and developmental policies, and the responsibility to ensure that activities within their jurisdiction or control do not cause damage to the environment of other States or of areas beyond the limits of national jurisdiction,

Recognizing that national Governments play a critical role in combating desertification and mitigating the effects of drought and that progress in that respect depends on local implementation of action programmes in affected areas,

Recognizing also the importance and necessity of international cooperation and partnership in combatting desertification and mitigating the effects of drought,

Recognizing the importance of the provision to affected developing countries, particularly in Africa, of effective means, inter alia substantial financial resources, including new and additional funding, and access to technology, without which it will be difficult for them to implement fully their commitments under this Convention,

Expressing concern over the impact of desertification and drought on affected countries in Central Asia and the Transcaucasus,

Stressing the important role played by women in regions affected by desertification and/or drought, particularly in rural areas of developing countries, and the importance of ensuring the full participation of both men and women at all levels in programmes to combat desertification and mitigate the effects of drought,

Emphasizing the special role of non-governmental organizations and other major groups in programmes to combat desertification and mitigate the effects of drought,

Bearing in mind the relationship between desertification and other environmental problems of global dimension facing the international and national communities,

Bearing also in mind the contribution that combating desertification can make to achieving the objectives of the United Nations Framework Convention on Climate Change, the Convention on Biological Diversity and other related environmental conventions,

Believing that strategies to combat desertification and mitigate the effects of drought will be most effective if they are based on sound systematic observation and rigorous scientific knowledge and if they are continuously reevaluated,

Recognizing the urgent need to improve the effectiveness and coordination of international cooperation to facilitate the implementation of national plans and priorities,

Determined to take appropriate action in combating desertification and mitigating the effects of drought for the benefit of present and future generations,

Have agreed as follows:

PART I

INTRODUCTION

Article 1

Use of terms

For the purposes of this Convention:

(a) "desertification" means land degradation in arid, semi-arid and dry sub-humid areas resulting from various factors, including climatic variations and human activities;

(b) "combating desertification" includes activities which are part of the integrated development of land in arid, semi-arid and dry sub-humid areas for sustainable development which are aimed at:

(i) prevention and/or reduction of land degradation;

(ii) rehabilitation of partly degraded land; and

(iii) reclamation of desertified land;

(c) "drought" means the naturally occurring phenomenon that exists when precipitation has been significantly below normal recorded levels, causing serious hydrological imbalances that adversely affect land resource production systems;

(d) "mitigating the effects of drought" means activities related to the prediction of drought and intended to reduce the vulnerability of society and natural systems to drought as it relates to combating desertification;

(e) "land" means the terrestrial bio-productive system that comprises soil, vegetation, other biota, and the ecological and hydrological processes that operate within the system;

(f) "land degradation" means reduction or loss, in arid, semi-arid and dry sub-humid areas, of the biological or economic productivity and complexity of rainfed cropland, irrigated cropland, or range, pasture, forest and woodlands resulting from land uses or from a process or combination of processes, including processes arising from human activities and habitation patterns, such as:

(i) soil erosion caused by wind and/or water;

(ii) deterioration of the physical, chemical and biological or economic properties of soil; and

(iii) long-term loss of natural vegetation;

(g) "arid, semi-arid and dry sub-humid areas" means areas, other than polar and sub-polar regions, in which the ratio of annual precipitation to potential evapotranspiration falls within the range from 0.05 to 0.65;

(h) "affected areas" means arid, semi-arid and/or dry sub-humid areas affected or threatened by desertification;

(i) "affected countries" means countries whose lands include, in whole or in part, affected areas;

(j) "regional economic integration organization" means an organization constituted by sovereign States of a given region which has competence in respect of matters governed by this Convention and has been duly authorized, in accordance with its internal procedures, to sign, ratify, accept, approve or accede to this Convention;

(k) "developed country Parties" means developed country Parties and regional economic integration organizations constituted by developed countries;

Article 2

Objective

1. The objective of this Convention is to combat desertification and mitigate the effects of drought in countries experiencing serious drought and/or desertification, particularly in Africa, through effective action at all levels, supported by international cooperation and partnership arrangements, in the framework of an integrated approach which is consistent with Agenda 21, with a view to contributing to the achievement of sustainable development in affected areas.

2. Achieving this objective will involve long-term integrated strategies that focus simultaneously, in affected areas, on improved productivity of land, and the rehabilita-

tion, conservation and sustainable management of land and water resources, leading to improved living conditions, in particular at the community level.

Article 3

Principles

In order to achieve the objective of this Convention and to implement its provisions, the Parties shall be guided, inter alia, by the following:

(a) the Parties should ensure that decisions on the design and implementation of programmes to combat desertification and/or mitigate the effects of drought are taken with the participation of populations and local communities and that an enabling environment is created at higher levels to facilitate action at national and local levels;

(b) the Parties should, in a spirit of international solidarity and partnership, improve cooperation and coordination at subregional, regional and international levels, and better focus financial, human, organizational and technical resources where they are needed;

(c) the Parties should develop, in a spirit of partnership, cooperation among all levels of government, communities, non-governmental organizations and landholders to establish a better understanding of the nature and value of land and scarce water resources in affected areas and to work towards their sustainable use; and

(d) the Parties should take into full consideration the special needs and circumstances of affected developing country Parties, particularly the least developed among them.

PART II

GENERAL PROVISIONS

Article 4

General obligations

1. The Parties shall implement their obligations under this Convention, individually or jointly, either through existing or prospective bilateral and multilateral arrangements or a combination thereof, as appropriate, emphasizing the need to coordinate efforts and develop a coherent long-term strategy at all levels.

2. In pursuing the objective of this Convention, the Parties shall:

(a) adopt an integrated approach addressing the physical, biological and socio-economic aspects of the processes of desertification and drought;

(b) give due attention, within the relevant international and regional bodies, to the situation of affected developing country Parties with regard to international trade, marketing arrangements and debt with a view to establishing an enabling international economic environment conducive to the promotion of sustainable development;

(c) integrate strategies for poverty eradication into efforts to combat desertification and mitigate the effects of drought;

(d) promote cooperation among affected country Parties in the fields of environmental protection and the conservation of land and water resources, as they relate to desertification and drought;

(e) strengthen subregional, regional and international cooperation;

(f) cooperate within relevant intergovernmental organizations;

(g) determine institutional mechanisms, if appropriate, keeping in mind the need to avoid duplication; and

(h) promote the use of existing bilateral and multilateral financial mechanisms and arrangements that mobilize and channel substantial financial resources to affected developing country Parties in combatting desertification and mitigating the effects of drought.

3. Affected developing country Parties are eligible for assistance in the implementation of the Convention.

Article 5

Obligations of affected country Parties

In addition to their obligations pursuant to Article 4, affected country Parties undertake to:

(a) give due priority to combating desertification and mitigating the effects of drought, and allocate adequate resources in accordance with their circumstances and capabilities;

(b) establish strategies and priorities, within the framework of sustainable development plans and/or policies, to combat desertification and mitigate the effects of drought;

(c) address the underlying causes of desertification and pay special attention to the socio-economic factors contributing to desertification processes;

(d) promote awareness and facilitate the participation of local populations, particularly women and youth, with the support of non-governmental organizations, in efforts to combat desertification and mitigate the effects of drought; and

(e) provide an enabling environment by strengthening, as appropriate, relevant existing legislation and, where they do not exist, enacting new laws and establishing long-term policies and action programmes.

Article 6

Obligations of developed country Parties

In addition to their general obligations pursuant to Article 4, developed country Parties undertake to:

(a) actively support, as agreed, individually or jointly, the efforts of affected developing country Parties, particularly those in Africa, and the least developed countries, to combat desertification and mitigate the effects of drought;

(b) provide substantial financial resources and other forms of support to assist affected developing country Parties, particularly those in Africa, effectively to develop and implement their own long-term plans and strategies to combat desertification and mitigate the effects of drought;

(c) promote the mobilization of new and additional funding pursuant to Article 20, paragraph 2 (b);

(d) encourage the mobilization of funding from the private sector and other non-governmental sources; and

(e) promote and facilitate access by affected country Parties, particularly affected developing country Parties, to appropriate technology, knowledge and know-how.

Article 7

Priority for Africa

In implementing this Convention, the Parties shall give priority to affected African country Parties, in the light of the particular situation prevailing in that region, while not neglecting affected developing country Parties in other regions.

Article 8

Relationship with other conventions

1. The Parties shall encourage the coordination of activities carried out under this Convention and, if they are Parties to them, under other relevant international agreements, particularly the United Nations Framework Convention on Climate Change and the Convention on Biological Diversity, in order to derive maximum benefit from activities under each agreement while avoiding duplication of effort. The Parties shall encourage the conduct of joint programmes, particularly in the fields of research, training, systematic observation and information collection and exchange, to the extent that such activities may contribute to achieving the objectives of the agreements concerned.

2. The provisions of this Convention shall not affect the rights and obligations of any Party deriving from a bilateral, regional or international agreement into which it has entered prior to the entry into force of this Convention for it.

PART III

ACTION PROGRAMMES, SCIENTIFIC AND TECHNICAL COOPERATION AND SUPPORTING MEASURES

Section 1: Action programmes

Article 9

Basic approach

1. In carrying out their obligations pursuant to Article 5, affected developing country Parties and any other affected country Party in the framework of its regional implementation annex or, otherwise, that has notified the Permanent Secretariat in writing of its intention to prepare a national action programme, shall, as appropriate, prepare, make public and implement national action programmes, utilizing and building, to the extent possible, on existing relevant successful plans and programmes, and subregional and regional action programmes, as the central element of the strategy to combat desertification and mitigate the effects of drought. Such programmes shall be updated through a continuing participatory process on the basis of lessons from field action, as well as the results of research. The preparation of national action programmes shall be closely interlinked with other efforts to formulate national policies for sustainable development.

2. In the provision by developed country Parties of different forms of assistance under the terms of Article 6, priority shall be given to supporting, as agreed, national, sub-regional and regional action programmes of affected developing country Parties, particularly those in Africa, either directly or through relevant multilateral organizations or both.

3. The Parties shall encourage organs, funds and programmes of the United Nations system and other relevant intergovernmental organizations, academic institutions, the scientific community and non-governmental organizations in a position to cooperate, in accordance with their mandates and capabilities, to support the elaboration, implementation and follow-up of action programmes.

Article 10

National action programmes

1. The purpose of national action programmes is to identify the factors contributing to desertification and practical measures necessary to combat desertification and mitigate the effects of drought.

2. National action programmes shall specify the respective roles of government, local communities and land users and the resources available and needed. They shall, inter alia:

(a) incorporate long-term strategies to combat desertification and mitigate the effects of drought, emphasize implementation and be integrated with national policies for sustainable development;

(b) allow for modifications to be made in response to changing circumstances and be sufficiently flexible at the local level to cope with different socio-economic, biological and geo-physical conditions;

(c) give particular attention to the implementation of preventive measures for lands that are not yet degraded or which are only slightly degraded;

(d) enhance national climatological, meteorological and hydrological capabilities and the means to provide for drought early warning;

(e) promote policies and strengthen institutional frameworks which develop cooperation and coordination, in a spirit of partnership, between the donor community, governments at all levels, local populations and community groups, and facilitate access by local populations to appropriate information and technology;

(f) provide for effective participation at the local, national and regional levels of non-governmental organizations and local populations, both women and men, particularly resource users, including farmers and pastoralists and their representative organizations, in policy planning, decision-making, and implementation and review of national action programmes; and

(g) require regular review of, and progress reports on, their implementation.

3. National action programmes may include, inter alia, some or all of the following measures to prepare for and mitigate the effects of drought:

(a) establishment and/or strengthening, as appropriate, of early warning systems, including local and national facilities and joint systems at the subregional and regional levels, and mechanisms for assisting environmentally displaced persons;

(b) strengthening of drought preparedness and management, including drought contingency plans at the local, national, subregional and regional levels, which take into consideration seasonal to interannual climate predictions;

(c) establishment and/or strengthening, as appropriate, of food security systems, including storage and marketing facilities, particularly in rural areas;

(d) establishment of alternative livelihood projects that could provide incomes in drought prone areas; and

(e) development of sustainable irrigation programmes for both crops and livestock.

4. Taking into account the circumstances and requirements specific to each affected country Party, national action programmes include, as appropriate, inter alia, measures in some or all of the following priority fields as they relate to combating desertification and mitigating the effects of drought in affected areas and to their populations: promotion of alternative livelihoods and improvement of national econom-

ic environments with a view to strengthening programmes aimed at the eradication of poverty and at ensuring food security, demographic dynamics, sustainable management of natural resources, sustainable agricultural practices, development and efficient use of various energy sources, institutional and legal frameworks, strengthening of capabilities for assessment and systematic observation, including hydrological and meteorological services, and capacity building, education and public awareness.

Article 11

Subregional and regional action programmes

Affected country Parties shall consult and cooperate to prepare, as appropriate, in accordance with relevant regional implementation annexes, subregional and/or regional action programmes to harmonize, complement and increase the efficiency of national programmes. The provisions of Article 10 shall apply mutatis mutandis to subregional and regional programmes. Such cooperation may include agreed joint programmes for the sustainable management of transboundary natural resources, scientific and technical cooperation, and strengthening of relevant institutions.

Article 12

International cooperation

Affected country Parties, in collaboration with other Parties and the international community, should cooperate to ensure the promotion of an enabling international environment in the implementation of the Convention. Such cooperation should also cover fields of technology transfer as well as scientific research and development, information collection and dissemination and financial resources.

Article 13

Support for the elaboration and implementation of action programmes

1. Measures to support action programmes pursuant to Article 9 include, inter alia:

(a) financial cooperation to provide predictability for action programmes, allowing for necessary long-term planning;

(b) elaboration and use of cooperation mechanisms which better enable support at the local level, including action through non-governmental organizations, in order to promote the replicability of successful pilot programme activities where relevant;

(c) increased flexibility in project design, funding and implementation in keeping with the experimental, iterative approach indicated for participatory action at the local community level; and

(d) as appropriate, administrative and budgetary procedures that increase the efficiency of cooperation and of support programmes.

2. In providing such support to affected developing country Parties, priority shall be given to African country Parties and to least developed country Parties.

Article 14

Coordination in the elaboration and implementation of action programmes

1. The Parties shall work closely together, directly and through relevant intergovernmental organizations, in the elaboration and implementation of action programmes.

2. The Parties shall develop operational mechanisms, particularly at the national and field levels, to ensure the fullest possible coordination among developed country

Parties, developing country Parties and relevant intergovernmental and non-governmental organizations, in order to avoid duplication, harmonize interventions and approaches, and maximize the impact of assistance. In affected developing country Parties, priority will be given to coordinating activities related to international cooperation in order to maximize the efficient use of resources, to ensure responsive assistance, and to facilitate the implementation of national action programmes and priorities under this Convention.

Article 15

Regional implementation annexes

Elements for incorporation in action programmes shall be selected and adapted to the socio-economic, geographical and climatic factors applicable to affected country Parties or regions, as well as to their level of development. Guidelines for the preparation of action programmes and their exact focus and content for particular subregions and regions are set out in the regional implementation annexes.

Section 2: Scientific and technical cooperation

Article 16

Information collection, analysis and exchange

The Parties agree, according to their respective capabilities, to integrate and coordinate the collection, analysis and exchange of relevant short term and long term data and information to ensure systematic observation of land degradation in affected areas and to understand better and assess the processes and effects of drought and desertification. This would help accomplish, inter alia, early warning and advance planning for periods of adverse climatic variation in a form suited for practical application by users at all levels, including especially local populations. To this end, they shall, as appropriate:

(a) facilitate and strengthen the functioning of the global network of institutions and facilities for the collection, analysis and exchange of information, as well as for systematic observation at all levels, which shall, inter alia:

(i) aim to use compatible standards and systems;

(ii) encompass relevant data and stations, including in remote areas;

(iii) use and disseminate modern technology for data collection, transmission and assessment on land degradation; and

(iv) link national, subregional and regional data and information centres more closely with global information sources;

(b) ensure that the collection, analysis and exchange of information address the needs of local communities and those of decision makers, with a view to resolving specific problems, and that local communities are involved in these activities;

(c) support and further develop bilateral and multilateral programmes and projects aimed at defining, conducting, assessing and financing the collection, analysis and exchange of data and information, including, inter alia, integrated sets of physical, biological, social and economic indicators;

(d) make full use of the expertise of competent intergovernmental and non-governmental organizations, particularly to disseminate relevant information and experiences among target groups in different regions;

(e) give full weight to the collection, analysis and exchange of socioeconomic data, and their integration with physical and biological data;

(f) exchange and make fully, openly and promptly available information from all publicly available sources relevant to combating desertification and mitigating the effects of drought; and

(g) subject to their respective national legislation and/or policies, exchange information on local and traditional knowledge, ensuring adequate protection for it and providing appropriate return from the benefits derived from it, on an equitable basis and on mutually agreed terms, to the local populations concerned.

Article 17

Research and development

1. The Parties undertake, according to their respective capabilities, to promote technical and scientific cooperation in the fields of combatting desertification and mitigating the effects of drought through appropriate national, subregional, regional and international institutions. To this end, they shall support research activities that:

(a) contribute to increased knowledge of the processes leading to desertification and drought and the impact of, and distinction between, causal factors, both natural and human, with a view to combatting desertification and mitigating the effects of drought, and achieving improved productivity as well as sustainable use and management of resources;

(b) respond to well defined objectives, address the specific needs of local populations and lead to the identification and implementation of solutions that improve the living standards of people in affected areas;

(c) protect, integrate, enhance and validate traditional and local knowledge, know-how and practices, ensuring, subject to their respective national legislation and/or policies, that the owners of that knowledge will directly benefit on an equitable basis and on mutually agreed terms from any commercial utilization of it or from any technological development derived from that knowledge;

(d) develop and strengthen national, subregional and regional research capabilities in affected developing country Parties, particularly in Africa, including the development of local skills and the strengthening of appropriate capacities, especially in countries with a weak research base, giving particular attention to multidisciplinary and participative socio-economic research;

(e) take into account, where relevant, the relationship between poverty, migration caused by environmental factors, and desertification;

(f) promote the conduct of joint research programmes between national, subregional, regional and international research organizations, in both the public and private sectors, for the development of improved, affordable and accessible technologies for sustainable development through effective participation of local populations and communities; and

(g) enhance the availability of water resources in affected areas, by means of, inter alia, cloud-seeding.

2. Research priorities for particular regions and subregions, reflecting different local conditions, should be included in action programmes. The Conference of the Parties shall review research priorities periodically on the advice of the Committee on Science and Technology.

Article 18

Transfer, acquisition, adaptation and development of technology

1. The Parties undertake, as mutually agreed and in accordance with their respective national legislation and/or policies, to promote, finance and/or facilitate the

financing of the transfer, acquisition, adaptation and development of environmentally sound, economically viable and socially acceptable technologies relevant to combatting desertification and/or mitigating the effects of drought, with a view to contributing to the achievement of sustainable development in affected areas. Such cooperation shall be conducted bilaterally or multilaterally, as appropriate, making full use of the expertise of intergovernmental and non-governmental organizations. The Parties shall, in particular:

(a) fully utilize relevant existing national, subregional, regional and international information systems and clearing-houses for the dissemination of information on available technologies, their sources, their environmental risks and the broad terms under which they may be acquired;

(b) facilitate access, in particular by affected developing country Parties, on favourable terms, including on concessional and preferential terms, as mutually agreed, taking into account the need to protect intellectual property rights, to technologies most suitable to practical application for specific needs of local populations, paying special attention to the social, cultural, economic and environmental impact of such technology;

(c) facilitate technology cooperation among affected country Parties through financial assistance or other appropriate means;

(d) extend technology cooperation with affected developing country Parties, including, where relevant, joint ventures, especially to sectors which foster alternative livelihoods; and

(e) take appropriate measures to create domestic market conditions and incentives, fiscal or otherwise, conducive to the development, transfer, acquisition and adaptation of suitable technology, knowledge, know-how and practices, including measures to ensure adequate and effective protection of intellectual property rights.

2. The Parties shall, according to their respective capabilities, and subject to their respective national legislation and/or policies, protect, promote and use in particular relevant traditional and local technology, knowledge, know-how and practices and, to that end, they undertake to:

(a) make inventories of such technology, knowledge, know-how and practices and their potential uses with the participation of local populations, and disseminate such information, where appropriate, in cooperation with relevant intergovernmental and non-governmental organizations;

(b) ensure that such technology, knowledge, know-how and practices are adequately protected and that local populations benefit directly, on an equitable basis and as mutually agreed, from any commercial utilization of them or from any technological development derived therefrom;

(c) encourage and actively support the improvement and dissemination of such technology, knowledge, know-how and practices or of the development of new technology based on them; and

(d) facilitate, as appropriate, the adaptation of such technology, knowledge, know-how and practices to wide use and integrate them with modern technology, as appropriate.

Section 3: Supporting measures

Article 19

Capacity building, education and public awareness

1. The Parties recognize the significance of capacity building—that is to say, institution building, training and development of relevant local and national capaci-

ties—in efforts to combat desertification and mitigate the effects of drought. They shall promote, as appropriate, capacity-building:

(a) through the full participation at all levels of local people, particularly at the local level, especially women and youth, with the cooperation of non-governmental and local organizations;

(b) by strengthening training and research capacity at the national level in the field of desertification and drought;

(c) by establishing and/or strengthening support and extension services to disseminate relevant technology methods and techniques more effectively, and by training field agents and members of rural organizations in participatory approaches for the conservation and sustainable use of natural resources;

(d) by fostering the use and dissemination of the knowledge, know-how and practices of local people in technical cooperation programmes, wherever possible;

(e) by adapting, where necessary, relevant environmentally sound technology and traditional methods of agriculture and pastoralism to modern socio-economic conditions;

(f) by providing appropriate training and technology in the use of alternative energy sources, particularly renewable energy resources, aimed particularly at reducing dependence on wood for fuel;

(g) through cooperation, as mutually agreed, to strengthen the capacity of affected developing country Parties to develop and implement programmes in the field of collection, analysis and exchange of information pursuant to Article 16;

(h) through innovative ways of promoting alternative livelihoods, including training in new skills;

(i) by training of decision makers, managers, and personnel who are responsible for the collection and analysis of data for the dissemination and use of early warning information on drought conditions and for food production;

(j) through more effective operation of existing national institutions and legal frameworks and, where necessary, creation of new ones, along with strengthening of strategic planning and management; and

(k) by means of exchange visitor programmes to enhance capacity building in affected country Parties through a long-term, interactive process of learning and study.

2. Affected developing country Parties shall conduct, in cooperation with other Parties and competent intergovernmental and non-governmental organizations, as appropriate, an interdisciplinary review of available capacity and facilities at the local and national levels, and the potential for strengthening them.

3. The Parties shall cooperate with each other and through competent intergovernmental organizations, as well as with non-governmental organizations, in undertaking and supporting public awareness and educational programmes in both affected and, where relevant, unaffected country Parties to promote understanding of the causes and effects of desertification and drought and of the importance of meeting the objective of this Convention. To that end, they shall:

(a) organize awareness campaigns for the general public;

(b) promote, on a permanent basis, access by the public to relevant information, and wide public participation in education and awareness activities;

(c) encourage the establishment of associations that contribute to public awareness;

(d) develop and exchange educational and public awareness material, where possible in local languages, exchange and second experts to train personnel of affected developing country Parties in carrying out relevant education and awareness programmes, and fully utilize relevant educational material available in competent international bodies;

(e) assess educational needs in affected areas, elaborate appropriate school curricula and expand, as needed, educational and adult literacy programmes and opportunities for all, in particular for girls and women, on the identification, conservation and sustainable use and management of the natural resources of affected areas; and

(f) develop interdisciplinary participatory programmes integrating desertification and drought awareness into educational systems and in non-formal, adult, distance and practical educational programmes.

4. The Conference of the Parties shall establish and/or strengthen networks of regional education and training centres to combat desertification and mitigate the effects of drought. These networks shall be coordinated by an institution created or designated for that purpose, in order to train scientific, technical and management personnel and to strengthen existing institutions responsible for education and training in affected country Parties, where appropriate, with a view to harmonizing programmes and to organizing exchanges of experience among them. These networks shall cooperate closely with relevant intergovernmental and non-governmental organizations to avoid duplication of effort.

Article 20

Financial resources

1. Given the central importance of financing to the achievement of the objective of the Convention, the Parties, taking into account their capabilities, shall make every effort to ensure that adequate financial resources are available for programmes to combat desertification and mitigate the effects of drought.

2. In this connection, developed country Parties, while giving priority to affected African country Parties without neglecting affected developing country Parties in other regions, in accordance with Article 7, undertake to:

(a) mobilize substantial financial resources, including grants and concessional loans, in order to support the implementation of programmes to combat desertification and mitigate the effects of drought;

(b) promote the mobilization of adequate, timely and predictable financial resources, including new and additional funding from the Global Environment Facility of the agreed incremental costs of those activities concerning desertification that relate to its four focal areas, in conformity with the relevant provisions of the Instrument establishing the Global Environment Facility;

(c) facilitate through international cooperation the transfer of technology, knowledge and know-how; and

(d) explore, in cooperation with affected developing country Parties, innovative methods and incentives for mobilizing and channeling resources, including those of foundations, non-governmental organizations and other private sector entities, particularly debt swaps and other innovative means which increase financing by reducing the external debt burden of affected developing country Parties, particularly those in Africa.

3. Affected developing country Parties, taking into account their capabilities, undertake to mobilize adequate financial resources for the implementation of their national action programmes.

4. In mobilizing financial resources, the Parties shall seek full use and continued qualitative improvement of all national, bilateral and multilateral funding sources and mechanisms, using consortia, joint programmes and parallel financing, and shall seek to involve private sector funding sources and mechanisms, including those of non-governmental organizations. To this end, the Parties shall fully utilize the operational mechanisms developed pursuant to Article 14.

5. In order to mobilize the financial resources necessary for affected developing country Parties to combat desertification and mitigate the effects of drought, the Parties shall:

(a) rationalize and strengthen the management of resources already allocated for combating desertification and mitigating the effects of drought by using them more effectively and efficiently, assessing their successes and shortcomings, removing hindrances to their effective use and, where necessary, reorienting programmes in light of the integrated long-term approach adopted pursuant to this Convention;

(b) give due priority and attention within the governing bodies of multilateral financial institutions, facilities and funds, including regional development banks and funds, to supporting affected developing country Parties, particularly those in Africa, in activities which advance implementation of the Convention, notably action programmes they undertake in the framework of regional implementation annexes; and

(c) examine ways in which regional and sub-regional cooperation can be strengthened to support efforts undertaken at the national level.

6. Other country Parties are encouraged to provide, on a voluntary basis, knowledge, know-how and techniques related to desertification and/or financial resources to affected developing country Parties.

7. The full implementation by affected developing country Parties, particularly those in Africa, of their obligations under the Convention will be greatly assisted by the fulfilment by developed country Parties of their obligations under the Convention, including in particular those regarding financial resources and transfer of technology. In fulfilling their obligations, developed country Parties should take fully into account that economic and social development and poverty eradication are the first priorities of affected developing country Parties, particularly those in Africa.

Article 21

Financial mechanisms

1. The Conference of the Parties shall promote the availability of financial mechanisms and shall encourage such mechanisms to seek to maximize the availability of funding for affected developing country Parties, particularly those in Africa, to implement the Convention. To this end, the Conference of the Parties shall consider for adoption inter alia approaches and policies that:

(a) facilitate the provision of necessary funding at the national, subregional, regional and global levels for activities pursuant to relevant provisions of the Convention;

(b) promote multiple-source funding approaches, mechanisms and arrangements and their assessment, consistent with Article 20;

(c) provide on a regular basis, to interested Parties and relevant intergovernmental and non-governmental organizations, information on available sources of funds and on funding patterns in order to facilitate coordination among them;

(d) facilitate the establishment, as appropriate, of mechanisms, such as national desertification funds, including those involving the participation of non-governmental organizations, to channel financial resources rapidly and efficiently to the local level in affected developing country Parties; and

(e) strengthen existing funds and financial mechanisms at the sub-regional and regional levels, particularly in Africa, to support more effectively the implementation of the Convention.

2. The Conference of the Parties shall also encourage the provision, through various mechanisms within the United Nations system and through multilateral financial institutions, of support at the national, sub-regional and regional levels to activities that enable developing country Parties to meet their obligations under the Convention.

3. Affected developing country Parties shall utilize, and where necessary, establish and/or strengthen, national coordinating mechanisms, integrated in national development programmes, that would ensure the efficient use of all available financial resources. They shall also utilize participatory processes involving non-governmental organizations, local groups and the private sector, in raising funds, in elaborating as well as implementing programmes and in assuring access to funding by groups at the local level. These actions can be enhanced by improved coordination and flexible programming on the part of those providing assistance.

4. In order to increase the effectiveness and efficiency of existing financial mechanisms, a Global Mechanism to promote actions leading to the mobilization and channeling of substantial financial resources, including for the transfer of technology, on a grant basis, and/or on concessional or other terms, to affected developing country Parties, is hereby established. This Global Mechanism shall function under the authority and guidance of the Conference of the Parties and be accountable to it.

5. The Conference of the Parties shall identify, at its first ordinary session, an organization to house the Global Mechanism. The Conference of the Parties and the organization it has identified shall agree upon modalities for this Global Mechanism to ensure inter alia that such Mechanism:

(a) identifies and draws up an inventory of relevant bilateral and multilateral cooperation programmes that are available to implement the Convention;

(b) provides advice, on request, to Parties on innovative methods of financing and sources of financial assistance and on improving the coordination of cooperation activities at the national level;

(c) provides interested Parties and relevant intergovernmental and non-governmental organizations with information on available sources of funds and on funding patterns in order to facilitate coordination among them; and

(d) reports to the Conference of the Parties, beginning at its second ordinary session, on its activities.

6. The Conference of the Parties shall, at its first session, make appropriate arrangements with the organization it has identified to house the Global Mechanism for the administrative operations of such Mechanism, drawing to the extent possible on existing budgetary and human resources.

7. The Conference of the Parties shall, at its third ordinary session, review the policies, operational modalities and activities of the Global Mechanism accountable to it pursuant to paragraph 4, taking into account the provisions of Article 7. On the basis of this review, it shall consider and take appropriate action.

PART IV

INSTITUTIONS

Article 22

Conference of the Parties

1. A Conference of the Parties is hereby established.

2. The Conference of the Parties is the supreme body of the Convention. It shall make, within its mandate, the decisions necessary to promote its effective implementation. In particular, it shall:

(a) regularly review the implementation of the Convention and the functioning of its institutional arrangements in the light of the experience gained at the national, subregional, regional and international levels and on the basis of the evolution of scientific and technological knowledge;

(b) promote and facilitate the exchange of information on measures adopted by the Parties, and determine the form and timetable for transmitting the information to be submitted pursuant to Article 26, review the reports and make recommendations on them;

(c) establish such subsidiary bodies as are deemed necessary for the implementation of the Convention;

(d) review reports submitted by its subsidiary bodies and provide guidance to them;

(e) agree upon and adopt, by consensus, rules of procedure and financial rules for itself and any subsidiary bodies;

(f) adopt amendments to the Convention pursuant to Articles 30 and 31;

(g) approve a programme and budget for its activities, including those of its subsidiary bodies, and undertake necessary arrangements for their financing;

(h) as appropriate, seek the cooperation of, and utilize the services of and information provided by, competent bodies or agencies, whether national or international, intergovernmental or non-governmental;

(i) promote and strengthen the relationship with other relevant conventions while avoiding duplication of effort; and

(j) exercise such other functions as may be necessary for the achievement of the objective of the Convention.

3. The Conference of the Parties shall, at its first session, adopt its own rules of procedure, by consensus, which shall include decision-making procedures for matters not already covered by decision-making procedures stipulated in the Convention. Such procedures may include specified majorities required for the adoption of particular decisions.

4. The first session of the Conference of the Parties shall be convened by the interim secretariat referred to in Article 35 and shall take place not later than one year after the date of entry into force of the Convention. Unless otherwise decided by the Conference of the Parties, the second, third and fourth ordinary sessions shall be held yearly, and thereafter, ordinary sessions shall be held every two years.

5. Extraordinary sessions of the Conference of the Parties shall be held at such other times as may be decided either by the Conference of the Parties in ordinary session or at the written request of any Party, provided that, within three months of the request being communicated to the Parties by the Permanent Secretariat, it is supported by at least one-third of the Parties.

6. At each ordinary session, the Conference of the Parties shall elect a Bureau. The structure and functions of the Bureau shall be determined in the rules of procedure. In appointing the Bureau, due regard shall be paid to the need to ensure equitable geographical distribution and adequate representation of affected country Parties, particularly those in Africa.

7. The United Nations, its specialized agencies and any State member thereof or observers thereto not Party to the Convention, may be represented at sessions of the Conference of the Parties as observers. Any body or agency, whether national or

international, governmental or non-governmental, which is qualified in matters covered by the Convention, and which has informed the Permanent Secretariat of its wish to be represented at a session of the Conference of the Parties as an observer, may be so admitted unless at least one-third of the Parties present object. The admission and participation of observers shall be subject to the rules of procedure adopted by the Conference of the Parties.

8. The Conference of the Parties may request competent national and international organizations which have relevant expertise to provide it with information relevant to Article 16, paragraph (g), Article 17, paragraph 1 (c) and Article 18, paragraph 2(b).

Article 23

Permanent Secretariat

1. A Permanent Secretariat is hereby established.

2. The functions of the Permanent Secretariat shall be:

(a) to make arrangements for sessions of the Conference of the Parties and its subsidiary bodies established under the Convention and to provide them with services as required;

(b) to compile and transmit reports submitted to it;

(c) to facilitate assistance to affected developing country Parties, on request, particularly those in Africa, in the compilation and communication of information required under the Convention;

(d) to coordinate its activities with the secretariats of other relevant international bodies and conventions;

(e) to enter, under the guidance of the Conference of the Parties, into such administrative and contractual arrangements as may be required for the effective discharge of its functions;

(f) to prepare reports on the execution of its functions under this Convention and present them to the Conference of the Parties; and

(g) to perform such other secretariat functions as may be determined by the Conference of the Parties.

3. The Conference of the Parties, at its first session, shall designate a Permanent Secretariat and make arrangements for its functioning.

Article 24

Committee on Science and Technology

1. A Committee on Science and Technology is hereby established as a subsidiary body of the Conference of the Parties to provide it with information and advice on scientific and technological matters relating to combating desertification and mitigating the effects of drought. The Committee shall meet in conjunction with the ordinary sessions of the Conference of the Parties and shall be multidisciplinary and open to the participation of all Parties. It shall be composed of government representatives competent in the relevant fields of expertise. The Conference of the Parties shall decide, at its first session, on the terms of reference of the Committee.

2. The Conference of the Parties shall establish and maintain a roster of independent experts with expertise and experience in the relevant fields. The roster shall be based on nominations received in writing from the Parties, taking into account the need for a multidisciplinary approach and broad geographical representation.

3. The Conference of the Parties may, as necessary, appoint ad hoc panels to provide it, through the Committee, with information and advice on specific issues regarding the state of the art in fields of science and technology relevant to combating desertification and mitigating the effects of drought. These panels shall be composed of experts whose names are taken from the roster, taking into account the need for a multidisciplinary approach and broad geographical representation. These experts shall have scientific backgrounds and field experience and shall be appointed by the Conference of the Parties on the recommendation of the Committee. The Conference of the Parties shall decide on the terms of reference and the modalities of work of these panels.

Article 25

Networking of institutions, agencies and bodies

1. The Committee on Science and Technology shall, under the supervision of the Conference of the Parties, make provision for the undertaking of a survey and evaluation of the relevant existing networks, institutions, agencies and bodies willing to become units of a network. Such a network shall support the implementation of the Convention.

2. On the basis of the results of the survey and evaluation referred to in paragraph 1, the Committee on Science and Technology shall make recommendations to the Conference of the Parties on ways and means to facilitate and strengthen networking of the units at the local, national and other levels, with a view to ensuring that the thematic needs set out in Articles 16 to 19 are addressed.

3. Taking into account these recommendations, the Conference of the Parties shall:

(a) identify those national, subregional, regional and international units that are most appropriate for networking, and recommend operational procedures, and a time frame, for them; and

(b) identify the units best suited to facilitating and strengthening such networking at all levels.

PART V

PROCEDURES

Article 26

Communication of information

1. Each Party shall communicate to the Conference of the Parties for consideration at its ordinary sessions, through the Permanent Secretariat, reports on the measures which it has taken for the implementation of the Convention. The Conference of the Parties shall determine the timetable for submission and the format of such reports.

2. Affected country Parties shall provide a description of the strategies established pursuant to Article 5 and of any relevant information on their implementation.

3. Affected country Parties which implement action programmes pursuant to Articles 9 to 15 shall provide a detailed description of the programmes and of their implementation.

4. Any group of affected country Parties may make a joint communication on measures taken at the subregional and/or regional levels in the framework of action programmes.

5. Developed country Parties shall report on measures taken to assist in the preparation and implementation of action programmes, including information on the financial resources they have provided, or are providing, under the Convention.

6. Information communicated pursuant to paragraphs 1 to 4 shall be transmitted by the Permanent Secretariat as soon as possible to the Conference of the Parties and to any relevant subsidiary body.

7. The Conference of the Parties shall facilitate the provision to affected developing countries, particularly those in Africa, on request, of technical and financial support in compiling and communicating information in accordance with this Article, as well as identifying the technical and financial needs associated with action programmes.

Article 27

Measures to resolve questions on implementation

The Conference of the Parties shall consider and adopt procedures and institutional mechanisms for the resolution of questions that may arise with regard to the implementation of the Convention.

Article 28

Settlement of disputes

1. Parties shall settle any dispute between them concerning the interpretation or application of the Convention through negotiation or other peaceful means of their own choice.

2. When ratifying, accepting, approving, or acceding to the Convention, or at any time thereafter, a Party which is not a regional economic integration organization may declare in a written instrument submitted to the Depositary that, in respect of any dispute concerning the interpretation or application of the Convention, it recognizes one or both of the following means of dispute settlement as compulsory in relation to any Party accepting the same obligation:

(a) arbitration in accordance with a procedure adopted by the Conference of the Parties in an annex as soon as practicable;

(b) submission of the dispute to the International Court of Justice.

3. A Party which is a regional economic integration organization may make a declaration with like effect in relation to arbitration in accordance with the procedure referred to in paragraph 2 (a).

4. A declaration made pursuant to paragraph 2 shall remain in force until it expires in accordance with its terms or until three months after written notice of its revocation has been deposited with the Depositary.

5. The expiry of a declaration, a notice of revocation or a new declaration shall not in any way affect proceedings pending before an arbitral tribunal or the International Court of Justice unless the Parties to the dispute otherwise agree.

6. If the Parties to a dispute have not accepted the same or any procedure pursuant to paragraph 2 and if they have not been able to settle their dispute within twelve months following notification by one Party to another that a dispute exists between them, the dispute shall be submitted to conciliation at the request of any Party to the dispute, in accordance with procedure adopted by the Conference of the Parties in an Annex as soon as practicable.

Article 29

Status of annexes

1. Annexes form an integral part of the Convention and, unless expressly provided otherwise, a reference to the Convention also constitutes a reference to its Annexes.

2. The Parties shall interpret the provisions of the Annexes in a manner that is in conformity with their rights and obligations under the Articles of this Convention.

Article 30

Amendments to the Convention

1. Any Party may propose amendments to the Convention.

2. Amendments to the Convention shall be adopted at an ordinary session of the Conference of the Parties. The text of any proposed amendment shall be communicated to the Parties by the Permanent Secretariat at least six months before the meeting at which it is proposed for adoption. The Permanent Secretariat shall also communicate proposed amendments to the signatories to the Convention.

3. The Parties shall make every effort to reach agreement on any proposed amendment to the Convention by consensus. If all efforts at consensus have been exhausted and no agreement reached, the amendment shall, as a last resort, be adopted by a two-thirds majority vote of the Parties present and voting at the meeting. The adopted amendment shall be communicated by the Permanent Secretariat to the Depositary, who shall circulate it to all Parties for their ratification, acceptance, approval or accession.

4. Instruments of ratification, acceptance, approval or accession in respect of an amendment shall be deposited with the Depositary. An amendment adopted pursuant to paragraph 3 shall enter into force for those Parties having accepted it on the ninetieth day after the date of receipt by the Depositary of an instrument of ratification, acceptance, approval or accession by at least two-thirds of the Parties to the Convention which were Parties at the time of the adoption of the amendment.

5. The amendment shall enter into force for any other Party on the ninetieth day after the date on which that Party deposits with the Depositary its instrument of ratification, acceptance or approval of, or accession to the said amendment.

6. For the purposes of this Article and Article 31, "Parties present and voting" means Parties present and casting an affirmative or negative vote.

Article 31

Adoption and amendment of annexes

1. Any additional annex to the Convention and any amendment to an annex shall be proposed and adopted in accordance with the procedure for amendment of the Convention set forth in Article 30, provided that, in adopting an additional regional implementation annex or amendment to any regional implementation annex, the majority provided for in that Article shall include a two thirds majority vote of the Parties of the region concerned present and voting. The adoption or amendment of an annex shall be communicated by the Depositary to all Parties.

2. An annex, other than an additional regional implementation annex, or an amendment to an annex, other than an amendment to any regional implementation annex, that has been adopted in accordance with paragraph 1, shall enter into force for all Parties to the Convention six months after the date of communication by the Depositary to such Parties of the adoption of such annex or amendment, except for those Parties that have notified the Depositary in writing within that period of their

non-acceptance of such annex or amendment. Such annex or amendment shall enter into force for Parties which withdraw their notification of non-acceptance on the ninetieth day after the date on which withdrawal of such notification has been received by the Depositary.

3. An additional regional implementation annex or amendment to any regional implementation annex that has been adopted in accordance with paragraph 1, shall enter into force for all Parties to the Convention six months after the date of the communication by the Depositary to such Parties of the adoption of such annex or amendment, except with respect to:

(a) any Party that has notified the Depositary in writing, within such six month period, of its non-acceptance of that additional regional implementation annex or of the amendment to the regional implementation annex, in which case such annex or amendment shall enter into force for Parties which withdraw their notification of non-acceptance on the ninetieth day after the date on which withdrawal of such notification has been received by the Depositary; and

(b) any Party that has made a declaration with respect to additional regional implementation annexes or amendments to regional implementation annexes in accordance with Article 34, paragraph 4, in which case any such annex or amendment shall enter into force for such a Party on the ninetieth day after the date of deposit with the Depositary of its instrument of ratification, acceptance, approval or accession with respect to such annex or amendment.

4. If the adoption of an annex or an amendment to an annex involves an amendment to the Convention, that annex or amendment to an annex shall not enter into force until such time as the amendment to the Convention enters into force.

Article 32

Right to vote

1. Except as provided for in paragraph 2, each Party to the Convention shall have one vote.

2. Regional economic integration organizations, in matters within their competence, shall exercise their right to vote with a number of votes equal to the number of their member States that are Parties to the Convention. Such an organization shall not exercise its right to vote if any of its member States exercises its right, and vice versa.

PART VI

FINAL PROVISIONS

Article 33

Signature

This Convention shall be opened for signature at Paris, on 14 October, 1994, by States Members of the United Nations or any of its specialized agencies or that are Parties to the Statute of the International Court of Justice and by regional economic integration organizations. It shall remain open for signature, thereafter, at the United Nations Headquarters in New York until 26 December, 1996.

Article 34

Ratification, acceptance, approval and accession

1. The Convention shall be subject to ratification, acceptance, approval or accession by States and by regional economic integration organizations. It shall be open for accession from the day after the date on which the Convention is closed for signature.

Instruments of ratification, acceptance, approval or accession shall be deposited with the Depositary.

2. Any regional economic integration organization which becomes a Party to the Convention without any of its member States being a Party to the Convention shall be bound by all the obligations under the Convention. Where one or more member States of such an organization are also Party to the Convention, the organization and its member States shall decide on their respective responsibilities for the performance of their obligations under the Convention. In such cases, the organization and the member States shall not be entitled to exercise rights under the Convention concurrently.

3. In their instruments of ratification, acceptance, approval or accession, regional economic integration organizations shall declare the extent of their competence with respect to the matters governed by the Convention. They shall also promptly inform the Depositary, who shall in turn inform the Parties, of any substantial modification in the extent of their competence.

4. In its instrument of ratification, acceptance, approval or accession, any Party may declare that, with respect to it, any additional regional implementation annex or any amendment to any regional implementation annex shall enter into force only upon the deposit of its instrument of ratification, acceptance, approval or accession with respect thereto.

Article 35

Interim arrangements

The secretariat functions referred to in Article 23 will be carried out on an interim basis by the secretariat established by the General Assembly of the United Nations in its resolution 47/188 of 22 December 1992, until the completion of the first session of the Conference of the Parties.

Article 36

Entry into force

1. The Convention shall enter into force on the ninetieth day after the date of deposit of the fiftieth instrument of ratification, acceptance, approval or accession.

2. For each State or regional economic integration organization ratifying, accepting, approving or acceding to the Convention after the deposit of the fiftieth instrument of ratification, acceptance, approval or accession, the Convention shall enter into force on the ninetieth day after the date of deposit by such State or regional economic integration organization of its instrument of ratification, acceptance, approval or accession.

3. For the purposes of paragraphs 1 and 2, any instrument deposited by a regional economic integration organization shall not be counted as additional to those deposited by States members of the organization.

Article 37

Reservations

No reservations may be made to this Convention.

Article 38

Withdrawal

1. At any time after three years from the date on which the Convention has entered into force for a Party, that Party may withdraw from the Convention by giving written notification to the Depositary.

2. Any such withdrawal shall take effect upon expiry of one year from the date of receipt by the Depositary of the notification of withdrawal, or on such later date as may be specified in the notification of withdrawal.

Article 39

Depositary

The Secretary–General of the United Nations shall be the Depositary of the Convention.

Article 40

Authentic texts

The original of the present Convention, of which the Arabic, Chinese, English, French, Russian and Spanish texts are equally authentic, shall be deposited with the Secretary–General of the United Nations.

IN WITNESS WHEREOF the undersigned, being duly authorized to that effect, have signed the present Convention.

DONE AT Paris, this 17th day of June one thousand nine hundred and ninety-four.

ANNEX I

REGIONAL IMPLEMENTATION ANNEX FOR AFRICA

Article 1

Scope

This Annex applies to Africa, in relation to each Party and in conformity with the Convention, in particular its Article 7, for the purpose of combating desertification and/or mitigating the effects of drought in its arid, semi-arid and dry sub-humid areas.

Article 2

Purpose

The purpose of this Annex, at the national, subregional and regional levels in Africa and in the light of its particular conditions, is to:

(a) identify measures and arrangements, including the nature and processes of assistance provided by developed country Parties, in accordance with the relevant provisions of the Convention;

(b) provide for the efficient and practical implementation of the Convention to address conditions specific to Africa; and

(c) promote processes and activities relating to combating desertification and/or mitigating the effects of drought within the arid, semi-arid and dry sub-humid areas of Africa.

Article 3

Particular conditions of the African region

In carrying out their obligations under the Convention, the Parties shall, in the implementation of this Annex, adopt a basic approach that takes into consideration the following particular conditions of Africa:

(a) the high proportion of arid, semi-arid and dry sub-humid areas;

(b) the substantial number of countries and populations adversely affected by desertification and by the frequent recurrence of severe drought;

(c) the large number of affected countries that are landlocked;

(d) the widespread poverty prevalent in most affected countries, the large number of least developed countries among them, and their need for significant amounts of external assistance, in the form of grants and loans on concessional terms, to pursue their development objectives;

(e) the difficult socio-economic conditions, exacerbated by deteriorating and fluctuating terms of trade, external indebtedness and political instability, which induce internal, regional and international migrations;

(f) the heavy reliance of populations on natural resources for subsistence which, compounded by the effects of demographic trends and factors, a weak technological base and unsustainable production practices, contributes to serious resource degradation;

(g) the insufficient institutional and legal frameworks, the weak infrastructural base and the insufficient scientific, technical and educational capacity, leading to substantial capacity building requirements; and

(h) the central role of actions to combat desertification and/or mitigate the effects of drought in the national development priorities of affected African countries.

Article 4

Commitments and obligations of African country Parties

1. In accordance with their respective capabilities, African country Parties undertake to:

(a) adopt the combating of desertification and/or the mitigation of the effects of drought as a central strategy in their efforts to eradicate poverty;

(b) promote regional cooperation and integration, in a spirit of solidarity and partnership based on mutual interest, in programmes and activities to combat desertification and/or mitigate the effects of drought;

(c) rationalize and strengthen existing institutions concerned with desertification and drought and involve other existing institutions, as appropriate, in order to make them more effective and to ensure more efficient use of resources;

(d) promote the exchange of information on appropriate technology, knowledge, know-how and practices between and among them; and

(e) develop contingency plans for mitigating the effects of drought in areas degraded by desertification and/or drought.

2. Pursuant to the general and specific obligations set out in Articles 4 and 5 of the Convention, affected African country Parties shall aim to:

(a) make appropriate financial allocations from their national budgets consistent with national conditions and capabilities and reflecting the new priority Africa has accorded to the phenomenon of desertification and/or drought;

(b) sustain and strengthen reforms currently in progress toward greater decentralization and resource tenure as well as reinforce participation of local populations and communities; and

(c) identify and mobilize new and additional national financial resources, and expand, as a matter of priority, existing national capabilities and facilities to mobilize domestic financial resources.

Article 5

Commitments and obligations of developed country Parties

1. In fulfilling their obligations pursuant to Articles 4, 6 and 7 of the Convention, developed country Parties shall give priority to affected African country Parties and, in this context, shall:

(a) assist them to combat desertification and/or mitigate the effects of drought by, inter alia, providing and/or facilitating access to financial and/or other resources, and promoting, financing and/or facilitating the financing of the transfer, adaptation and access to appropriate environmental technologies and know-how, as mutually agreed and in accordance with national policies, taking into account their adoption of poverty eradication as a central strategy;

(b) continue to allocate significant resources and/or increase resources to combat desertification and/or mitigate the effects of drought; and

(c) assist them in strengthening capacities to enable them to improve their institutional frameworks, as well as their scientific and technical capabilities, information collection and analysis, and research and development for the purpose of combating desertification and/or mitigating the effects of drought.

2. Other country Parties may provide, on a voluntary basis, technology, knowledge and know-how relating to desertification and/or financial resources, to affected African country Parties. The transfer of such knowledge, know-how and techniques is facilitated by international cooperation.

Article 6

Strategic planning framework for sustainable development

1. National action programmes shall be a central and integral part of a broader process of formulating national policies for the sustainable development of affected African country Parties.

2. A consultative and participatory process involving appropriate levels of government, local populations, communities and non-governmental organizations shall be undertaken to provide guidance on a strategy with flexible planning to allow maximum participation from local populations and communities. As appropriate, bilateral and multilateral assistance agencies may be involved in this process at the request of an affected African country Party.

Article 7

Timetable for preparation of action programmes

Pending entry into force of this Convention, the African country Parties, in cooperation with other members of the international community, as appropriate, shall, to the extent possible, provisionally apply those provisions of the Convention relating to the preparation of national, subregional and regional action programmes.

Article 8

Content of national action programmes

1. Consistent with Article 10 of the Convention, the overall strategy of national action programmes shall emphasize integrated local development programmes for affected areas, based on participatory mechanisms and on integration of strategies for poverty eradication into efforts to combat desertification and mitigate the effects of drought. The programmes shall aim at strengthening the capacity of local authorities and ensuring the active involvement of local populations, communities and groups, with emphasis on education and training, mobilization of non-governmental organiza-

tions with proven expertise and strengthening of decentralized governmental structures.

2. National action programmes shall, as appropriate, include the following general features:

(a) the use, in developing and implementing national action programmes, of past experiences in combatting desertification and/or mitigating the effects of drought, taking into account social, economic and ecological conditions;

(b) the identification of factors contributing to desertification and/or drought and the resources and capacities available and required, and the setting up of appropriate policies and institutional and other responses and measures necessary to combat those phenomena and/or mitigate their effects; and

(c) the increase in participation of local populations and communities, including women, farmers and pastoralists, and delegation to them of more responsibility for management.

3. National action programmes shall also, as appropriate, include the following:

(a) measures to improve the economic environment with a view to eradicating poverty:

(i) increasing incomes and employment opportunities, especially for the poorest members of the community, by:

—developing markets for farm and livestock products;

—creating financial instruments suited to local needs;

—encouraging diversification in agriculture and the setting-up of agricultural enterprises; and

—developing economic activities of a para-agricultural or non-agricultural type;

(ii) improving the long-term prospects of rural economies by the creation of:

—incentives for productive investment and access to the means of production; and

—price and tax policies and commercial practices that promote growth;

(iii) defining and applying population and migration policies to reduce population pressure on land; and

(iv) promoting the use of drought resistant crops and the application of integrated dry-land farming systems for food security purposes;

(b) measures to conserve natural resources:

(i) ensuring integrated and sustainable management of natural resources, including:

—agricultural land and pastoral land;

—vegetation cover and wildlife;

—forests;

—water resources; and

—biological diversity;

(ii) training with regard to, and strengthening, public awareness and environmental education campaigns and disseminating knowledge of techniques relating to the sustainable management of natural resources; and

(iii) ensuring the development and efficient use of diverse energy sources, the promotion of alternative sources of energy, particularly solar energy, wind energy and biogas, and specific arrangements for the transfer, acquisition and adaptation of relevant technology to alleviate the pressure on fragile natural resources;

(c) measures to improve institutional organization:

(i) defining the roles and responsibilities of central government and local authorities within the framework of a land use planning policy;

(ii) encouraging a policy of active decentralization, devolving responsibility for management and decision-making to local authorities, and encouraging initiatives and the assumption of responsibility by local communities and the establishment of local structures; and

(iii) adjusting, as appropriate, the institutional and regulatory framework of natural resource management to provide security of land tenure for local populations;

(d) measures to improve knowledge of desertification:

(i) promoting research and the collection, processing and exchange of information on the scientific, technical and socio-economic aspects of desertification;

(ii) improving national capabilities in research and in the collection, processing, exchange and analysis of information so as to increase understanding and to translate the results of the analysis into operational terms; and

(iii) encouraging the medium and long term study of:

—socio-economic and cultural trends in affected areas;

—qualitative and quantitative trends in natural resources; and

—the interaction between climate and desertification; and

(e) measures to monitor and assess the effects of drought:

(i) developing strategies to evaluate the impacts of natural climate variability on regional drought and desertification and/or to utilize predictions of climate variability on seasonal to interannual time scales in efforts to mitigate the effects of drought;

(ii) improving early warning and response capacity, efficiently managing emergency relief and food aid, and improving food stocking and distribution systems, cattle protection schemes and public works and alternative livelihoods for drought prone areas; and

(iii) monitoring and assessing ecological degradation to provide reliable and timely information on the process and dynamics of resource degradation in order to facilitate better policy formulations and responses.

Article 9

Preparation of national action programmes and implementation and evaluation indicators

Each affected African country Party shall designate an appropriate national coordinating body to function as a catalyst in the preparation, implementation and evaluation of its national action programme. This coordinating body shall, in the light of Article 3 and as appropriate:

(a) undertake an identification and review of actions, beginning with a locally driven consultation process, involving local populations and communities and with the cooperation of local administrative authorities, developed country Parties and intergovernmental and non-governmental organizations, on the basis of initial consultations of those concerned at the national level;

(b) identify and analyze the constraints, needs and gaps affecting development and sustainable land use and recommend practical measures to avoid duplication by making full use of relevant ongoing efforts and promote implementation of results;

(c) facilitate, design and formulate project activities based on interactive, flexible approaches in order to ensure active participation of the population in affected areas, to minimize the negative impact of such activities, and to identify and prioritize requirements for financial assistance and technical cooperation;

(d) establish pertinent, quantifiable and readily verifiable indicators to ensure the assessment and evaluation of national action programmes, which encompass actions in the short, medium and long terms, and of the implementation of such programmes; and

(e) prepare progress reports on the implementation of the national action programmes.

Article 10

Organizational framework of subregional action programmes

1. Pursuant to Article 4 of the Convention, African country Parties shall cooperate in the preparation and implementation of subregional action programmes for central, eastern, northern, southern and western Africa and, in that regard, may delegate the following responsibilities to relevant subregional intergovernmental organizations:

(a) acting as focal points for preparatory activities and coordinating the implementation of the subregional action programmes;

(b) assisting in the preparation and implementation of national action programmes;

(c) facilitating the exchange of information, experience and know-how as well as providing advice on the review of national legislation; and

(d) any other responsibilities relating to the implementation of subregional action programmes.

2. Specialized subregional institutions may provide support, upon request, and/or be entrusted with the responsibility to coordinate activities in their respective fields of competence.

Article 11

Content and preparation of subregional action programmes

Subregional action programmes shall focus on issues that are better addressed at the subregional level. They shall establish, where necessary, mechanisms for the management of shared natural resources. Such mechanisms shall effectively handle transboundary problems associated with desertification and/or drought and shall provide support for the harmonious implementation of national action programmes. Priority areas for subregional action programmes shall, as appropriate, focus on:

(a) joint programmes for the sustainable management of transboundary natural resources through bilateral and multilateral mechanisms, as appropriate;

(b) coordination of programmes to develop alternative energy sources;

(c) cooperation in the management and control of pests as well as of plant and animal diseases;

(d) capacity building, education and public awareness activities that are better carried out or supported at the subregional level;

(e) scientific and technical cooperation, particularly in the climatological, meteorological and hydrological fields, including networking for data collection and assessment, information sharing and project monitoring, and coordination and prioritization of research and development activities;

(f) early warning systems and joint planning for mitigating the effects of drought, including measures to address the problems resulting from environmentally induced migrations;

(g) exploration of ways of sharing experiences, particularly regarding participation of local populations and communities, and creation of an enabling environment for improved land use management and for use of appropriate technologies;

(h) strengthening of the capacity of subregional organizations to coordinate and provide technical services, as well as establishment, reorientation and strengthening of subregional centres and institutions; and

(i) development of policies in fields, such as trade, which have impact upon affected areas and populations, including policies for the coordination of regional marketing regimes and for common infrastructure.

Article 12

Organizational framework of the regional action programme

1. Pursuant to Article 11 of the Convention, African country Parties shall jointly determine the procedures for preparing and implementing the regional action programme.

2. The Parties may provide appropriate support to relevant African regional institutions and organizations to enable them to assist African country Parties to fulfil their responsibilities under the Convention.

Article 13

Content of the regional action programme

The regional action programme includes measures relating to combating desertification and/or mitigating the effects of drought in the following priority areas, as appropriate:

(a) development of regional cooperation and coordination of sub-regional action programmes for building regional consensus on key policy areas, including through regular consultations of sub-regional organizations;

(b) promotion of capacity building in activities which are better implemented at the regional level;

(c) the seeking of solutions with the international community to global economic and social issues that have an impact on affected areas taking into account Article 4, paragraph 2 (b) of the Convention;

(d) promotion among the affected country Parties of Africa and its subregions, as well as with other affected regions, of exchange of information and appropriate techniques, technical know-how and relevant experience;

(e) promotion of scientific and technological cooperation particularly in the fields of climatology, meteorology, hydrology, water resource development and alternative energy sources;

(f) coordination of sub-regional and regional research activities and identification of regional priorities for research and development;

(g) coordination of networks for systematic observation and assessment and information exchange, as well as their integration into world wide networks; and

(h) coordination of and reinforcement of sub-regional and regional early warning systems and drought contingency plans.

Article 14

Financial resources

1. Pursuant to Article 20 of the Convention and Article 4, paragraph 2, affected African country Parties shall endeavour to provide a macroeconomic framework conducive to the mobilization of financial resources and shall develop policies and establish procedures to channel resources more effectively to local development programmes, including through non-governmental organizations, as appropriate.

2. Pursuant to Article 21, paragraphs 4 and 5 of the Convention, the Parties agree to establish an inventory of sources of funding at the national, subregional, regional and international levels to ensure the rational use of existing resources and to identify gaps in resource allocation, to facilitate implementation of the action programmes. The inventory shall be regularly reviewed and up-dated.

3. Consistent with Article 7 of the Convention, the developed country Parties shall continue to allocate significant resources and/or increased resources and other forms of assistance to affected African country Parties on the basis of partnership agreements and arrangements referred to in Article 18, giving, inter alia, due attention to matters related to debt, international trade and marketing arrangements in accordance with Article 4, paragraph 2 (b) of the Convention.

Article 15

Financial Mechanisms

1. Consistent with Article 7 of the Convention and considering the particular situation prevailing in this region, the Parties shall pay special attention to the implementation in Africa of the provisions of Article 21, paragraph 1 (d) and (e) of the Convention, notably by:

(a) facilitating the establishment of mechanisms, such as national desertification funds, to channel financial resources to the local level; and

(b) strengthening existing funds and financial mechanisms at the subregional and regional levels.

2. Consistent with Articles 20 and 21 of the Convention, the Parties which are also members of the governing bodies of relevant regional and subregional financial institutions, including the African Development Bank and the African Development Fund, shall promote efforts to give due priority and attention to the activities of those institutions that advance the implementation of this Annex.

3. The Parties shall streamline, to the extent possible, procedures for channeling funds to affected African country Parties.

Article 16

Technical assistance and cooperation

The Parties undertake, in accordance with their respective capabilities, to rationalize technical assistance to, and cooperation with, African country Parties with a view to increasing project and programme effectiveness by, inter alia:

(a) limiting the costs of support measures and backstopping, especially overhead costs, so that, in any case, such costs shall only represent an appropriately low percentage of the total cost of the project so as to maximize project efficiency;

(b) giving preference to the utilization of competent national experts or, where necessary, competent experts from within the subregion and/or region, in project design, preparation and implementation, and to the building of local expertise where it does not exist; and

(c) effectively managing and coordinating, as well as efficiently utilizing, technical assistance to be provided.

Article 17

Transfer, acquisition, adaptation and access to environmentally sound technology

In implementing Article 18 of the Convention relating to transfer, acquisition, adaptation and development of technology, the Parties undertake to give priority to African country Parties and, as necessary, to develop with them new models of partnership and cooperation with a view to strengthening capacity building in the fields of scientific research and development and information collection and dissemination to enable them to implement their strategies to combat desertification and mitigate the effects of drought.

Article 18

Coordination and partnership agreements

1. African country Parties shall coordinate the preparation, negotiation and implementation of national, subregional and regional action programmes. They may involve, as appropriate, other Parties and relevant intergovernmental and non-governmental organizations in this process.

2. The objectives of such coordination shall be to ensure that financial and technical cooperation is consistent with the Convention and to provide the necessary continuity in the use and administration of resources.

3. African country Parties shall organize consultative processes at the national, subregional and regional levels. These consultative processes may:

(a) serve as a forum to negotiate and conclude partnership agreements based on national, subregional and regional action programmes; and

(b) specify the contribution of African country Parties and other members of the consultative groups to the programmes and identify priorities and agreements on implementation and evaluation indicators, as well as funding arrangements for implementation.

4. The Permanent Secretariat may, at the request of African country Parties, pursuant to Article 23 of the Convention, facilitate the convocation of such consultative processes by:

(a) providing advice on the organization of effective consultative arrangements, drawing on experiences from other such arrangements;

(b) providing information to relevant bilateral and multilateral agencies concerning consultative meetings or processes, and encouraging their active involvement; and

(c) providing other information that may be relevant in establishing or improving consultative arrangements.

5. The subregional and regional coordinating bodies shall, inter alia:

(a) recommend appropriate adjustments to partnership agreements;

(b) monitor, assess and report on the implementation of the agreed subregional and regional programmes; and

(c) aim to ensure efficient communication and cooperation among African country Parties.

6. Participation in the consultative groups shall, as appropriate, be open to Governments, interested groups and donors, relevant organs, funds and programmes of the United Nations system, relevant subregional and regional organizations, and representatives of relevant non-governmental organizations. Participants of each consultative group shall determine the modalities of its management and operation.

7. Pursuant to Article 14 of the Convention, developed country Parties are encouraged to develop, on their own initiative, an informal process of consultation and coordination among themselves, at the country, subregional and regional levels, and, at the request of an affected African country Party or of an appropriate subregional or regional organization, to participate in a national, subregional or regional consultative process that would evaluate and respond to assistance needs in order to facilitate implementation.

Article 19

Follow-up arrangements

Follow-up of this annex shall be carried out by African country Parties in accordance with the Convention as follows:

(a) at the national level, by a mechanism the composition of which should be determined by each affected African country Party and which shall include representatives of local communities and shall function under the supervision of the national coordinating body referred to in Article 9;

(b) at the subregional level, by a multidisciplinary scientific and technical consultative committee, the composition and modalities of operation of which shall be determined by the African country Parties of the subregion concerned; and

(c) at the regional level, by mechanisms defined in accordance with the relevant provisions of the Treaty establishing the African Economic Community, and by an African Scientific and Technical Advisory Committee.

5.9 Rotterdam Convention on the Prior Informed Consent Procedure for Certain Hazardous Chemicals and Pesticides in International Trade. Adopted on 10 September 1998. UNEP/FAO/PIC/CONF/2

The Parties to this Convention,

Aware of the harmful impact on human health and the environment from certain hazardous chemicals and pesticides in international trade,

Recalling the pertinent provisions of the Rio Declaration on Environment and Development and chapter 19 of Agenda 21 on "Environmentally sound management of toxic chemicals, including prevention of illegal international traffic in toxic and dangerous products",

Mindful of the work undertaken by the United Nations Environment Programme (UNEP) and the Food and Agriculture Organization of the United Nations (FAO) in the operation of the voluntary Prior Informed Consent procedure, as set out in the UNEP Amended London Guidelines for the Exchange of Information on Chemicals in International Trade (hereinafter referred to as the "Amended London Guidelines") and the FAO International Code of Conduct on the Distribution and Use of Pesticides (hereinafter referred to as the "International Code of Conduct"),

Taking into account the circumstances and particular requirements of developing countries and countries with economies in transition, in particular the need to strengthen national capabilities and capacities for the management of chemicals, including transfer of technology, providing financial and technical assistance and promoting cooperation among the Parties,

Noting the specific needs of some countries for information on transit movements,

Recognizing that good management practices for chemicals should be promoted in all countries, taking into account, *inter alia*, the voluntary standards laid down in the International Code of Conduct and the UNEP Code of Ethics on the International Trade in Chemicals,

Desiring to ensure that hazardous chemicals that are exported from their territory are packaged and labelled in a manner that is adequately protective of human health and the environment, consistent with the principles of the Amended London Guidelines and the International Code of Conduct,

Recognizing that trade and environmental policies should be mutually supportive with a view to achieving sustainable development,

Emphasizing that nothing in this Convention shall be interpreted as implying in any way a change in the rights and obligations of a Party under any existing international agreement applying to chemicals in international trade or to environmental protection,

Understanding that the above recital is not intended to create a hierarchy between this Convention and other international agreements,

Determined to protect human health, including the health of consumers and workers, and the environment against potentially harmful impacts from certain hazardous chemicals and pesticides in international trade,

HAVE AGREED AS FOLLOWS:

Article 1

Objective

The objective of this Convention is to promote shared responsibility and cooperative efforts among Parties in the international trade of certain hazardous chemicals in order to protect human health and the environment from potential harm and to contribute to their environmentally sound use, by facilitating information exchange about their characteristics, by providing for a national decision-making process on their import and export and by disseminating these decisions to Parties.

Article 2

Definitions

For the purposes of this Convention:

(a) "Chemical" means a substance whether by itself or in a mixture or preparation and whether manufactured or obtained from nature, but does not include any living organism. It consists of the following categories: pesticide (including severely hazardous pesticide formulations) and industrial;

(b) "Banned chemical" means a chemical all uses of which within one or more categories have been prohibited by final regulatory action, in order to protect human health or the environment. It includes a chemical that has been refused approval for first-time use or has been withdrawn by industry either from the domestic market or from further consideration in the domestic approval process and where there is clear evidence that such action has been taken in order to protect human health or the environment;

(c) "Severely restricted chemical" means a chemical virtually all use of which within one or more categories has been prohibited by final regulatory action in order to protect human health or the environment, but for which certain specific uses remain allowed. It includes a chemical that has, for virtually all use, been refused for approval or been withdrawn by industry either from the domestic market or from further consideration in the domestic approval process, and where there is clear evidence that such action has been taken in order to protect human health or the environment;

(d) "Severely hazardous pesticide formulation" means a chemical formulated for pesticidal use that produces severe health or environmental effects observable within a short period of time after single or multiple exposure, under conditions of use;

(e) "Final regulatory action" means an action taken by a Party, that does not require subsequent regulatory action by that Party, the purpose of which is to ban or severely restrict a chemical;

(f) "Export" and "import" mean, in their respective connotations, the movement of a chemical from one Party to another Party, but exclude mere transit operations;

(g) "Party" means a State or regional economic integration organization that has consented to be bound by this Convention and for which the Convention is in force;

(h) "Regional economic integration organization" means an organization constituted by sovereign States of a given region to which its member States have transferred competence in respect of matters governed by this Convention and which has been duly authorized, in accordance with its internal procedures, to sign, ratify, accept, approve or accede to this Convention;

(i) "Chemical Review Committee" means the subsidiary body referred to in paragraph 6 of Article 18.

Article 3

Scope of the Convention

1. This Convention applies to:

(a) Banned or severely restricted chemicals; and

(b) Severely hazardous pesticide formulations.

2. This Convention does not apply to:

(a) Narcotic drugs and psychotropic substances;

(b) Radioactive materials;

(c) Wastes;

(d) Chemical weapons;

(e) Pharmaceuticals, including human and veterinary drugs;

(f) Chemicals used as food additives;

(g) Food;

(h) Chemicals in quantities not likely to affect human health or the environment provided they are imported:

(i) For the purpose of research or analysis; or

(ii) By an individual for his or her own personal use in quantities reasonable for such use.

Article 4

Designated national authorities

1. Each Party shall designate one or more national authorities that shall be authorized to act on its behalf in the performance of the administrative functions required by this Convention.

2. Each Party shall seek to ensure that such authority or authorities have sufficient resources to perform their tasks effectively.

3. Each Party shall, no later than the date of the entry into force of this Convention for it, notify the name and address of such authority or authorities to the Secretariat. It shall forthwith notify the Secretariat of any changes in the name and address of such authority or authorities.

4. The Secretariat shall forthwith inform the Parties of the notifications it receives under paragraph 3.

Article 5

Procedures for banned or severely restricted chemicals

1. Each Party that has adopted a final regulatory action shall notify the Secretariat in writing of such action. Such notification shall be made as soon as possible, and in any event no later than ninety days after the date on which the final regulatory action has taken effect, and shall contain the information required by Annex I, where available.

2. Each Party shall, at the date of entry into force of this Convention for it, notify the Secretariat in writing of its final regulatory actions in effect at that time, except that each Party that has submitted notifications of final regulatory actions under the Amended London Guidelines or the International Code of Conduct need not resubmit those notifications.

3. The Secretariat shall, as soon as possible, and in any event no later than six months after receipt of a notification under paragraphs 1 and 2, verify whether the notification contains the information required by Annex I. If the notification contains the information required, the Secretariat shall forthwith forward to all Parties a summary of the information received. If the notification does not contain the information required, it shall inform the notifying Party accordingly.

4. The Secretariat shall every six months communicate to the Parties a synopsis of the information received pursuant to paragraphs 1 and 2, including information regarding those notifications which do not contain all the information required by Annex I.

5. When the Secretariat has received at least one notification from each of two Prior Informed Consent regions regarding a particular chemical that it has verified meet the requirements of Annex I, it shall forward them to the Chemical Review Committee. The composition of the Prior Informed Consent regions shall be defined in a decision to be adopted by consensus at the first meeting of the Conference of the Parties.

6. The Chemical Review Committee shall review the information provided in such notifications and, in accordance with the criteria set out in Annex II, recommend to the Conference of the Parties whether the chemical in question should be made subject to the Prior Informed Consent procedure and, accordingly, be listed in Annex III.

Article 6

Procedures for severely hazardous pesticide formulations

1. Any Party that is a developing country or a country with an economy in transition and that is experiencing problems caused by a severely hazardous pesticide formulation under conditions of use in its territory, may propose to the Secretariat the listing of the severely hazardous pesticide formulation in Annex III. In developing a proposal, the Party may draw upon technical expertise from any relevant source. The proposal shall contain the information required by part 1 of Annex IV.

2. The Secretariat shall, as soon as possible, and in any event no later than six months after receipt of a proposal under paragraph 1, verify whether the proposal contains the information required by part 1 of Annex IV. If the proposal contains the information required, the Secretariat shall forthwith forward to all Parties a summary of the information received. If the proposal does not contain the information required, it shall inform the proposing Party accordingly.

3. The Secretariat shall collect the additional information set out in part 2 of Annex IV regarding the proposal forwarded under paragraph 2.

4. When the requirements of paragraphs 2 and 3 above have been fulfilled with regard to a particular severely hazardous pesticide formulation, the Secretariat shall forward the proposal and the related information to the Chemical Review Committee.

5. The Chemical Review Committee shall review the information provided in the proposal and the additional information collected and, in accordance with the criteria set out in part 3 of Annex IV, recommend to the Conference of the Parties whether the severely hazardous pesticide formulation in question should be made subject to the Prior Informed Consent procedure and, accordingly, be listed in Annex III.

Article 7

Listing of chemicals in Annex III

1. For each chemical that the Chemical Review Committee has decided to recommend for listing in Annex III, it shall prepare a draft decision guidance document. The decision guidance document should, at a minimum, be based on the information specified in Annex I, or, as the case may be, Annex IV, and include information on uses of the chemical in a category other than the category for which the final regulatory action applies.

2. The recommendation referred to in paragraph 1 together with the draft decision guidance document shall be forwarded to the Conference of the Parties. The Conference of the Parties shall decide whether the chemical should be made subject to

the Prior Informed Consent procedure and, accordingly, list the chemical in Annex III and approve the draft decision guidance document.

3. When a decision to list a chemical in Annex III has been taken and the related decision guidance document has been approved by the Conference of the Parties, the Secretariat shall forthwith communicate this information to all Parties.

Article 8

Chemicals in the voluntary Prior Informed Consent procedure

For any chemical, other than a chemical listed in Annex III, that has been included in the voluntary Prior Informed Consent procedure before the date of the first meeting of the Conference of the Parties, the Conference of the Parties shall decide at that meeting to list the chemical in Annex III, provided that it is satisfied that all the requirements for listing in that Annex have been fulfilled.

Article 9

Removal of chemicals from Annex III

1. If a Party submits to the Secretariat information that was not available at the time of the decision to list a chemical in Annex III and that information indicates that its listing may no longer be justified in accordance with the relevant criteria in Annex II or, as the case may be, Annex IV, the Secretariat shall forward the information to the Chemical Review Committee.

2. The Chemical Review Committee shall review the information it receives under paragraph 1. For each chemical that the Chemical Review Committee decides, in accordance with the relevant criteria in Annex II or, as the case may be, Annex IV, to recommend for removal from Annex III, it shall prepare a revised draft decision guidance document.

3. A recommendation referred to in paragraph 2 shall be forwarded to the Conference of the Parties and be accompanied by a revised draft decision guidance document. The Conference of the Parties shall decide whether the chemical should be removed from Annex III and whether to approve the revised draft decision guidance document.

4. When a decision to remove a chemical from Annex III has been taken and the revised decision guidance document has been approved by the Conference of the Parties, the Secretariat shall forthwith communicate this information to all Parties.

Article 10

Obligations in relation to imports of chemicals listed in Annex III

1. Each Party shall implement appropriate legislative or administrative measures to ensure timely decisions with respect to the import of chemicals listed in Annex III.

2. Each Party shall transmit to the Secretariat, as soon as possible, and in any event no later than nine months after the date of dispatch of the decision guidance document referred to in paragraph 3 of Article 7, a response concerning the future import of the chemical concerned. If a Party modifies this response, it shall forthwith submit the revised response to the Secretariat.

3. The Secretariat shall, at the expiration of the time period in paragraph 2, forthwith address to a Party that has not provided such a response, a written request to do so. Should the Party be unable to provide a response, the Secretariat shall, where appropriate, help it to provide a response within the time period specified in the last sentence of paragraph 2 of Article 11.

4. A response under paragraph 2 shall consist of either:

(a) A final decision, pursuant to legislative or administrative measures:

(i) To consent to import;

(ii) Not to consent to import; or

(iii) To consent to import only subject to specified conditions; or

(b) An interim response, which may include:

(i) An interim decision consenting to import with or without specified conditions, or not consenting to import during the interim period;

(ii) A statement that a final decision is under active consideration;

(iii) A request to the Secretariat, or to the Party that notified the final regulatory action, for further information;

(iv) A request to the Secretariat for assistance in evaluating the chemical.

5. A response under subparagraphs (a) or (b) of paragraph 4 shall relate to the category or categories specified for the chemical in Annex III.

6. A final decision should be accompanied by a description of any legislative or administrative measures upon which it is based.

7. Each Party shall, no later than the date of entry into force of this Convention for it, transmit to the Secretariat responses with respect to each chemical listed in Annex III. A Party that has provided such responses under the Amended London Guidelines or the International Code of Conduct need not resubmit those responses.

8. Each Party shall make its responses under this Article available to those concerned within its jurisdiction, in accordance with its legislative or administrative measures.

9. A Party that, pursuant to paragraphs 2 and 4 above and paragraph 2 of Article 11, takes a decision not to consent to import of a chemical or to consent to its import only under specified conditions shall, if it has not already done so, simultaneously prohibit or make subject to the same conditions:

(a) Import of the chemical from any source; and

(b) Domestic production of the chemical for domestic use.

10. Every six months the Secretariat shall inform all Parties of the responses it has received. Such information shall include a description of the legislative or administrative measures on which the decisions have been based, where available. The Secretariat shall, in addition, inform the Parties of any cases of failure to transmit a response.

Article 11

Obligations in relation to exports of chemicals listed in Annex III

1. Each exporting Party shall:

(a) Implement appropriate legislative or administrative measures to communicate the responses forwarded by the Secretariat in accordance with paragraph 10 of Article 10 to those concerned within its jurisdiction;

(b) Take appropriate legislative or administrative measures to ensure that exporters within its jurisdiction comply with decisions in each response no later than six months after the date on which the Secretariat first informs the Parties of such response in accordance with paragraph 10 of Article 10;

(c) Advise and assist importing Parties, upon request and as appropriate:

(i) To obtain further information to help them to take action in accordance with paragraph 4 of Article 10 and paragraph 2 (c) below; and

(ii) To strengthen their capacities and capabilities to manage chemicals safely during their life-cycle.

2. Each Party shall ensure that a chemical listed in Annex III is not exported from its territory to any importing Party that, in exceptional circumstances, has failed to transmit a response or has transmitted an interim response that does not contain an interim decision, unless:

(a) It is a chemical that, at the time of import, is registered as a chemical in the importing Party; or

(b) It is a chemical for which evidence exists that it has previously been used in, or imported into, the importing Party and in relation to which no regulatory action to prohibit its use has been taken; or

(c) Explicit consent to the import has been sought and received by the exporter through a designated national authority of the importing Party. The importing Party shall respond to such a request within sixty days and shall promptly notify the Secretariat of its decision.

The obligations of exporting Parties under this paragraph shall apply with effect from the expiration of a period of six months from the date on which the Secretariat first informs the Parties, in accordance with paragraph 10 of Article 10, that a Party has failed to transmit a response or has transmitted an interim response that does not contain an interim decision, and shall apply for one year.

Article 12

Export notification

1. Where a chemical that is banned or severely restricted by a Party is exported from its territory, that Party shall provide an export notification to the importing Party. The export notification shall include the information set out in Annex V.

2. The export notification shall be provided for that chemical prior to the first export following adoption of the corresponding final regulatory action. Thereafter, the export notification shall be provided before the first export in any calendar year. The requirement to notify before export may be waived by the designated national authority of the importing Party.

3. An exporting Party shall provide an updated export notification after it has adopted a final regulatory action that results in a major change concerning the ban or severe restriction of that chemical.

4. The importing Party shall acknowledge receipt of the first export notification received after the adoption of the final regulatory action. If the exporting Party does not receive the acknowledgement within thirty days of the dispatch of the export notification, it shall submit a second notification. The exporting Party shall make reasonable efforts to ensure that the importing Party receives the second notification.

5. The obligations of a Party set out in paragraph 1 shall cease when:

(a) The chemical has been listed in Annex III;

(b) The importing Party has provided a response for the chemical to the Secretariat in accordance with paragraph 2 of Article 10; and

(c) The Secretariat has distributed the response to the Parties in accordance with paragraph 10 of Article 10.

Article 13

Information to accompany exported chemicals

1. The Conference of the Parties shall encourage the World Customs Organization to assign specific Harmonized System customs codes to the individual chemicals or

groups of chemicals listed in Annex III, as appropriate. Each Party shall require that, whenever a code has been assigned to such a chemical, the shipping document for that chemical bears the code when exported.

2. Without prejudice to any requirements of the importing Party, each Party shall require that both chemicals listed in Annex III and chemicals banned or severely restricted in its territory are, when exported, subject to labelling requirements that ensure adequate availability of information with regard to risks and/or hazards to human health or the environment, taking into account relevant international standards.

3. Without prejudice to any requirements of the importing Party, each Party may require that chemicals subject to environmental or health labelling requirements in its territory are, when exported, subject to labelling requirements that ensure adequate availability of information with regard to risks and/or hazards to human health or the environment, taking into account relevant international standards.

4. With respect to the chemicals referred to in paragraph 2 that are to be used for occupational purposes, each exporting Party shall require that a safety data sheet that follows an internationally recognized format, setting out the most up-to-date information available, is sent to each importer.

5. The information on the label and on the safety data sheet should, as far as practicable, be given in one or more of the official languages of the importing Party.

Article 14

Information exchange

1. Each Party shall, as appropriate and in accordance with the objective of this Convention, facilitate:

(a) The exchange of scientific, technical, economic and legal information concerning the chemicals within the scope of this Convention, including toxicological, ecotoxicological and safety information;

(b) The provision of publicly available information on domestic regulatory actions relevant to the objectives of this Convention; and

(c) The provision of information to other Parties, directly or through the Secretariat, on domestic regulatory actions that substantially restrict one or more uses of the chemical, as appropriate.

2. Parties that exchange information pursuant to this Convention shall protect any confidential information as mutually agreed.

3. The following information shall not be regarded as confidential for the purposes of this Convention:

(a) The information referred to in Annexes I and IV, submitted pursuant to Articles 5 and 6 respectively;

(b) The information contained in the safety data sheet referred to in paragraph 4 of Article 13;

(c) The expiry date of the chemical;

(d) Information on precautionary measures, including hazard classification, the nature of the risk and the relevant safety advice; and

(e) The summary results of the toxicological and ecotoxicological tests.

4. The production date of the chemical shall generally not be considered confidential for the purposes of this Convention.

5. Any Party requiring information on transit movements through its territory of chemicals listed in Annex III may report its need to the Secretariat, which shall inform all Parties accordingly.

Article 15

Implementation of the Convention

1. Each Party shall take such measures as may be necessary to establish and strengthen its national infrastructures and institutions for the effective implementation of this Convention. These measures may include, as required, the adoption or amendment of national legislative or administrative measures and may also include:

(a) The establishment of national registers and databases including safety information for chemicals;

(b) The encouragement of initiatives by industry to promote chemical safety; and

(c) The promotion of voluntary agreements, taking into consideration the provisions of Article 16.

2. Each Party shall ensure, to the extent practicable, that the public has appropriate access to information on chemical handling and accident management and on alternatives that are safer for human health or the environment than the chemicals listed in Annex III.

3. The Parties agree to cooperate, directly or, where appropriate, through competent international organizations, in the implementation of this Convention at the subregional, regional and global levels.

4. Nothing in this Convention shall be interpreted as restricting the right of the Parties to take action that is more stringently protective of human health and the environment than that called for in this Convention, provided that such action is consistent with the provisions of this Convention and is in accordance with international law.

Article 16

Technical assistance

The Parties shall, taking into account in particular the needs of developing countries and countries with economies in transition, cooperate in promoting technical assistance for the development of the infrastructure and the capacity necessary to manage chemicals to enable implementation of this Convention. Parties with more advanced programmes for regulating chemicals should provide technical assistance, including training, to other Parties in developing their infrastructure and capacity to manage chemicals throughout their life-cycle.

Article 17

Non-Compliance

The Conference of the Parties shall, as soon as practicable, develop and approve procedures and institutional mechanisms for determining non-compliance with the provisions of this Convention and for treatment of Parties found to be in non-compliance.

Article 18

Conference of the Parties

1. A Conference of the Parties is hereby established.

2. The first meeting of the Conference of the Parties shall be convened by the Executive Director of UNEP and the Director–General of FAO, acting jointly, no later than one year after the entry into force of this Convention. Thereafter, ordinary meetings of the Conference of the Parties shall be held at regular intervals to be determined by the Conference.

3. Extraordinary meetings of the Conference of the Parties shall be held at such other times as may be deemed necessary by the Conference, or at the written request of any Party provided that it is supported by at least one third of the Parties.

4. The Conference of the Parties shall by consensus agree upon and adopt at its first meeting rules of procedure and financial rules for itself and any subsidiary bodies, as well as financial provisions governing the functioning of the Secretariat.

5. The Conference of the Parties shall keep under continuous review and evaluation the implementation of this Convention. It shall perform the functions assigned to it by the Convention and, to this end, shall:

(a) Establish, further to the requirements of paragraph 6 below, such subsidiary bodies as it considers necessary for the implementation of the Convention;

(b) Cooperate, where appropriate, with competent international organizations and intergovernmental and non-governmental bodies; and

(c) Consider and undertake any additional action that may be required for the achievement of the objectives of the Convention.

6. The Conference of the Parties shall, at its first meeting, establish a subsidiary body, to be called the Chemical Review Committee, for the purposes of performing the functions assigned to that Committee by this Convention. In this regard:

(a) The members of the Chemical Review Committee shall be appointed by the Conference of the Parties. Membership of the Committee shall consist of a limited number of government-designated experts in chemicals management. The members of the Committee shall be appointed on the basis of equitable geographical distribution, including ensuring a balance between developed and developing Parties;

(b) The Conference of the Parties shall decide on the terms of reference, organization and operation of the Committee;

(c) The Committee shall make every effort to make its recommendations by consensus. If all efforts at consensus have been exhausted, and no consensus reached, such recommendation shall as a last resort be adopted by a two-thirds majority vote of the members present and voting.

7. The United Nations, its specialized agencies and the International Atomic Energy Agency, as well as any State not Party to this Convention, may be represented at meetings of the Conference of the Parties as observers. Any body or agency, whether national or international, governmental or non-governmental, qualified in matters covered by the Convention, and which has informed the Secretariat of its wish to be represented at a meeting of the Conference of the Parties as an observer may be admitted unless at least one third of the Parties present object. The admission and participation of observers shall be subject to the rules of procedure adopted by the Conference of the Parties.

Article 19

Secretariat

1. A Secretariat is hereby established.

2. The functions of the Secretariat shall be:

(a) To make arrangements for meetings of the Conference of the Parties and its subsidiary bodies and to provide them with services as required;

(b) To facilitate assistance to the Parties, particularly developing Parties and Parties with economies in transition, on request, in the implementation of this Convention;

(c) To ensure the necessary coordination with the secretariats of other relevant international bodies;

(d) To enter, under the overall guidance of the Conference of the Parties, into such administrative and contractual arrangements as may be required for the effective discharge of its functions; and

(e) To perform the other secretariat functions specified in this Convention and such other functions as may be determined by the Conference of the Parties.

3. The secretariat functions for this Convention shall be performed jointly by the Executive Director of UNEP and the Director–General of FAO, subject to such arrangements as shall be agreed between them and approved by the Conference of the Parties.

4. The Conference of the Parties may decide, by a three-fourths majority of the Parties present and voting, to entrust the secretariat functions to one or more other competent international organizations, should it find that the Secretariat is not functioning as intended.

Article 20

Settlement of disputes

1. Parties shall settle any dispute between them concerning the interpretation or application of this Convention through negotiation or other peaceful means of their own choice.

2. When ratifying, accepting, approving or acceding to this Convention, or at any time thereafter, a Party that is not a regional economic integration organization may declare in a written instrument submitted to the Depositary that, with respect to any dispute concerning the interpretation or application of the Convention, it recognizes one or both of the following means of dispute settlement as compulsory in relation to any Party accepting the same obligation:

(a) Arbitration in accordance with procedures to be adopted by the Conference of the Parties in an annex as soon as practicable; and

(b) Submission of the dispute to the International Court of Justice.

3. A Party that is a regional economic integration organization may make a declaration with like effect in relation to arbitration in accordance with the procedure referred to in paragraph 2 (a).

4. A declaration made pursuant to paragraph 2 shall remain in force until it expires in accordance with its terms or until three months after written notice of its revocation has been deposited with the Depositary.

5. The expiry of a declaration, a notice of revocation or a new declaration shall not in any way affect proceedings pending before an arbitral tribunal or the International Court of Justice unless the parties to the dispute otherwise agree.

6. If the parties to a dispute have not accepted the same or any procedure pursuant to paragraph 2, and if they have not been able to settle their dispute within twelve months following notification by one party to another that a dispute exists between them, the dispute shall be submitted to a conciliation commission at the request of any party to the dispute. The conciliation commission shall render a report with recommendations. Additional procedures relating to the conciliation commission

shall be included in an annex to be adopted by the Conference of the Parties no later than the second meeting of the Conference.

Article 21

Amendments to the Convention

1. Amendments to this Convention may be proposed by any Party.

2. Amendments to this Convention shall be adopted at a meeting of the Conference of the Parties. The text of any proposed amendment shall be communicated to the Parties by the Secretariat at least six months before the meeting at which it is proposed for adoption. The Secretariat shall also communicate the proposed amendment to the signatories to this Convention and, for information, to the Depositary.

3. The Parties shall make every effort to reach agreement on any proposed amendment to this Convention by consensus. If all efforts at consensus have been exhausted, and no agreement reached, the amendment shall as a last resort be adopted by a three-fourths majority vote of the Parties present and voting at the meeting.

4. The amendment shall be communicated by the Depositary to all Parties for ratification, acceptance or approval.

5. Ratification, acceptance or approval of an amendment shall be notified to the Depositary in writing. An amendment adopted in accordance with paragraph 3 shall enter into force for the Parties having accepted it on the ninetieth day after the date of deposit of instruments of ratification, acceptance or approval by at least three fourths of the Parties. Thereafter, the amendment shall enter into force for any other Party on the ninetieth day after the date on which that Party deposits its instrument of ratification, acceptance or approval of the amendment.

Article 22

Adoption and amendment of annexes

1. Annexes to this Convention shall form an integral part thereof and, unless expressly provided otherwise, a reference to this Convention constitutes at the same time a reference to any annexes thereto.

2. Annexes shall be restricted to procedural, scientific, technical or administrative matters.

3. The following procedure shall apply to the proposal, adoption and entry into force of additional annexes to this Convention:

(a) Additional annexes shall be proposed and adopted according to the procedure laid down in paragraphs 1, 2 and 3 of Article 21;

(b) Any Party that is unable to accept an additional annex shall so notify the Depositary, in writing, within one year from the date of communication of the adoption of the additional annex by the Depositary. The Depositary shall without delay notify all Parties of any such notification received. A Party may at any time withdraw a previous notification of non-acceptance in respect of an additional annex and the annex shall thereupon enter into force for that Party subject to subparagraph (c) below; and

(c) On the expiry of one year from the date of the communication by the Depositary of the adoption of an additional annex, the annex shall enter into force for all Parties that have not submitted a notification in accordance with the provisions of subparagraph (b) above.

4. Except in the case of Annex III, the proposal, adoption and entry into force of amendments to annexes to this Convention shall be subject to the same procedures as for the proposal, adoption and entry into force of additional annexes to the Convention.

5. The following procedure shall apply to the proposal, adoption and entry into force of amendments to Annex III:

(a) Amendments to Annex III shall be proposed and adopted according to the procedure laid down in Articles 5 to 9 and paragraph 2 of Article 21;

(b) The Conference of the Parties shall take its decisions on adoption by consensus;

(c) A decision to amend Annex III shall forthwith be communicated to the Parties by the Depositary. The amendment shall enter into force for all Parties on a date to be specified in the decision.

6. If an additional annex or an amendment to an annex is related to an amendment to this Convention, the additional annex or amendment shall not enter into force until such time as the amendment to the Convention enters into force.

Article 23

Voting

1. Each Party to this Convention shall have one vote, except as provided for in paragraph 2 below.

2. A regional economic integration organization, on matters within its competence, shall exercise its right to vote with a number of votes equal to the number of its member States that are Parties to this Convention. Such an organization shall not exercise its right to vote if any of its member States exercises its right to vote, and vice versa.

3. For the purposes of this Convention, "Parties present and voting" means Parties present and casting an affirmative or negative vote.

Article 24

Signature

This Convention shall be open for signature at Rotterdam by all States and regional economic integration organizations from ___ to ___, and at United Nations Headquarters in New York from ___ to ___.

Article 25

Ratification, acceptance, approval or accession

1. This Convention shall be subject to ratification, acceptance or approval by States and by regional economic integration organizations. It shall be open for accession by States and by regional economic integration organizations from the day after the date on which the Convention is closed for signature. Instruments of ratification, acceptance, approval or accession shall be deposited with the Depositary.

2. Any regional economic integration organization that becomes a Party to this Convention without any of its member States being a Party shall be bound by all the obligations under the Convention. In the case of such organizations, one or more of whose member States is a Party to this Convention, the organization and its member States shall decide on their respective responsibilities for the performance of their obligations under the Convention. In such cases, the organization and the member States shall not be entitled to exercise rights under the Convention concurrently.

3. In its instrument of ratification, acceptance, approval or accession, a regional economic integration organization shall declare the extent of its competence in respect of the matters governed by this Convention. Any such organization shall also inform the Depositary, who shall in turn inform the Parties, of any relevant modification in the extent of its competence.

Article 26

Entry into force

1. This Convention shall enter into force on the ninetieth day after the date of deposit of the fiftieth instrument of ratification, acceptance, approval or accession.

2. For each State or regional economic integration organization that ratifies, accepts or approves this Convention or accedes thereto after the deposit of the fiftieth instrument of ratification, acceptance, approval or accession, the Convention shall enter into force on the ninetieth day after the date of deposit by such State or regional economic integration organization of its instrument of ratification, acceptance, approval or accession.

3. For the purpose of paragraphs 1 and 2, any instrument deposited by a regional economic integration organization shall not be counted as additional to those deposited by member States of that organization.

Article 27

Reservations

No reservations may be made to this Convention.

Article 28

Withdrawal

1. At any time after three years from the date on which this Convention has entered into force for a Party, that Party may withdraw from the Convention by giving written notification to the Depositary.

2. Any such withdrawal shall take effect upon expiry of one year from the date of receipt by the Depositary of the notification of withdrawal, or on such later date as may be specified in the notification of withdrawal.

Article 29

Depositary

The Secretary–General of the United Nations shall be the Depositary of this Convention.

Article 30

Authentic texts

The original of this Convention, of which the Arabic, Chinese, English, French, Russian and Spanish texts are equally authentic, shall be deposited with the Secretary–General of the United Nations.

IN WITNESS WHEREOF the undersigned, being duly authorized to that effect, have signed this Convention.

Done at Rotterdam on this __ day of __, one thousand nine hundred and ninety-eight.

Annex I

INFORMATION REQUIREMENTS FOR NOTIFICATIONS MADE PURSUANT TO ARTICLE 5

Notifications shall include:

1. *Properties, identification and uses*

(a) Common name;

(b) Chemical name according to an internationally recognized nomenclature (for example, International Union of Pure and Applied Chemistry (IUPAC)), where such nomenclature exists;

(c) Trade names and names of preparations;

(d) Code numbers: Chemicals Abstract Service (CAS) number, Harmonized System customs code and other numbers;

(e) Information on hazard classification, where the chemical is subject to classification requirements;

(f) Use or uses of the chemical;

(g) Physico-chemical, toxicological and ecotoxicological properties.

2. *Final regulatory action*

(a) Information specific to the final regulatory action:

(i) Summary of the final regulatory action;

(ii) Reference to the regulatory document;

(iii) Date of entry into force of the final regulatory action;

(iv) Indication of whether the final regulatory action was taken on the basis of a risk or hazard evaluation and, if so, information on such evaluation, covering a reference to the relevant documentation;

(v) Reasons for the final regulatory action relevant to human health, including the health of consumers and workers, or the environment;

(vi) Summary of the hazards and risks presented by the chemical to human health, including the health of consumers and workers, or the environment and the expected effect of the final regulatory action;

(b) Category or categories where the final regulatory action has been taken, and for each category:

(i) Use or uses prohibited by the final regulatory action;

(ii) Use or uses that remain allowed;

(iii) Estimation, where available, of quantities of the chemical produced, imported, exported and used;

(c) An indication, to the extent possible, of the likely relevance of the final regulatory action to other States and regions;

(d) Other relevant information that may cover:

(i) Assessment of socio-economic effects of the final regulatory action;

(ii) Information on alternatives and their relative risks, where available, such as:

—Integrated pest management strategies;

—Industrial practices and processes, including cleaner technology.

Annex II

CRITERIA FOR LISTING BANNED OR SEVERELY RESTRICTED CHEMICALS IN ANNEX III

In reviewing the notifications forwarded by the Secretariat pursuant to paragraph 5 of Article 5, the Chemical Review Committee shall:

(a) Confirm that the final regulatory action has been taken in order to protect human health or the environment;

(b) Establish that the final regulatory action has been taken as a consequence of a risk evaluation. This evaluation shall be based on a review of scientific data in the context of the conditions prevailing in the Party in question. For this purpose, the documentation provided shall demonstrate that:

(i) Data have been generated according to scientifically recognized methods;

(ii) Data reviews have been performed and documented according to generally recognized scientific principles and procedures;

(iii) The final regulatory action was based on a risk evaluation involving prevailing conditions within the Party taking the action;

(c) Consider whether the final regulatory action provides a sufficiently broad basis to merit listing of the chemical in Annex III, by taking into account:

(i) Whether the final regulatory action led, or would be expected to lead, to a significant decrease in the quantity of the chemical used or the number of its uses;

(ii) Whether the final regulatory action led to an actual reduction of risk or would be expected to result in a significant reduction of risk for human health or the environment of the Party that submitted the notification;

(iii) Whether the considerations that led to the final regulatory action being taken are applicable only in a limited geographical area or in other limited circumstances;

(iv) Whether there is evidence of ongoing international trade in the chemical;

(d) Take into account that intentional misuse is not in itself an adequate reason to list a chemical in Annex III.

Annex III

CHEMICALS SUBJECT TO THE PRIOR INFORMED CONSENT PROCEDURE

Chemical	Relevant CAS number(s)	Category
2,4,5–T	93–76–5	Pesticide
Aldrin	309–00–2	Pesticide
Captafol	2425–06–1	Pesticide
Chlordane	57–74–9	Pesticide
Chlordimeform	6164–98–3	Pesticide
Chlorobenzilate	510–15–6	Pesticide
DDT	50–29–3	Pesticide
Dieldrin	60–57–1	Pesticide
Dinoseb and dinoseb salts	88–85–7	Pesticide
1,2–dibromoethane (EDB)	106–93–4	Pesticide
Fluoroacetamide	640–19–7	Pesticide
HCH (mixed isomers)	608–73–1	Pesticide
Heptachlor	76–44–8	Pesticide
Hexachlorobenzene	118–74–1	Pesticide
Lindane	58–89–9	Pesticide
Mercury compounds, including inorganic mercury compounds, alkyl		Pesticide

Chemical	Relevant CAS number(s)	Category
mercury compounds and alkyloxyalkyl and aryl mercury compounds		
Pentachlorophenol	87–86–5	Pesticide
Monocrotophos (Soluble liquid formulations of the substance that exceed 600 g active ingredient/l)	6923–22–4	Severely hazardous pesticide formulation
Methamidophos (Soluble liquid formulations of the substance that exceed 600 g active ingredient/l)	10265–92–6	Severely hazardous pesticide formulation
Phosphamidon (Soluble liquid formulations of the substance that exceed 1000 g active ingredient/l)	13171–21–6 (mixture, (E) & (Z) isomers) 23783–98–4 ((Z)-isomer) 297–99–4 ((E)-isomer)	Severely hazardous pesticide formulation
Methyl-parathion (emulsifiable concentrates (EC) with 19.5%, 40%, 50%, 60% active ingredient and dusts containing 1.5%, 2% and 3% active ingredient)	298–00–0	Severely hazardous pesticide formulation
Parathion (all formulations—aerosols, dustable powder (DP), emulsifiable concentrate (EC), granules (GR) and wettable powders (WP)—of this substance are included, except capsule suspensions (CS))	56–38–2	Severely hazardous pesticide formulation
Crocidolite	12001–28–4	Industrial
Polybrominated biphenyls (PBB)	36355–01–8(hexa-) 27858–07–7 (octa-) 13654–09–6 (deca-)	Industrial
Polychlorinated biphenyls (PCB)	1336–36–3	Industrial
Polychlorinated terphenyls (PCT)	61788–33–8	Industrial
Tris (2,3–dibromopropyl) phosphate	126–72–7	Industrial

Annex IV

INFORMATION AND CRITERIA FOR LISTING SEVERELY HAZARDOUS PESTICIDE FORMULATIONS IN ANNEX III

Part 1. Documentation required from a proposing Party

Proposals submitted pursuant to paragraph 1 of Article 6 shall include adequate documentation containing the following information:

(a) Name of the hazardous pesticide formulation;

(b) Name of the active ingredient or ingredients in the formulation;

(c) Relative amount of each active ingredient in the formulation;

(d) Type of formulation;

(e) Trade names and names of the producers, if available;

(f) Common and recognized patterns of use of the formulation within the proposing Party;

(g) A clear description of incidents related to the problem, including the adverse effects and the way in which the formulation was used;

(h) Any regulatory, administrative or other measure taken, or intended to be taken, by the proposing Party in response to such incidents.

Part 2. Information to be collected by the Secretariat

Pursuant to paragraph 3 of Article 6, the Secretariat shall collect relevant information relating to the formulation, including:

(a) The physico-chemical, toxicological and ecotoxicological properties of the formulation;

(b) The existence of handling or applicator restrictions in other States;

(c) Information on incidents related to the formulation in other States;

(d) Information submitted by other Parties, international organizations, non-governmental organizations or other relevant sources, whether national or international;

(e) Risk and/or hazard evaluations, where available;

(f) Indications, if available, of the extent of use of the formulation, such as the number of registrations or production or sales quantity;

(g) Other formulations of the pesticide in question, and incidents, if any, relating to these formulations;

(h) Alternative pest-control practices;

(i) Other information which the Chemical Review Committee may identify as relevant.

Part 3. Criteria for listing severely hazardous pesticide formulations in Annex III

In reviewing the proposals forwarded by the Secretariat pursuant to paragraph 5 of Article 6, the Chemical Review Committee shall take into account:

(a) The reliability of the evidence indicating that use of the formulation, in accordance with common or recognized practices within the proposing Party, resulted in the reported incidents;

(b) The relevance of such incidents to other States with similar climate, conditions and patterns of use of the formulation;

(c) The existence of handling or applicator restrictions involving technology or techniques that may not be reasonably or widely applied in States lacking the necessary infrastructure;

(d) The significance of reported effects in relation to the quantity of the formulation used;

(e) That intentional misuse is not in itself an adequate reason to list a formulation in Annex III.

Annex V

INFORMATION REQUIREMENTS FOR EXPORT NOTIFICATION

1. Export notifications shall contain the following information:

(a) Name and address of the relevant designated national authorities of the exporting Party and the importing Party;

(b) Expected date of export to the importing Party;

(c) Name of the banned or severely restricted chemical and a summary of the information specified in Annex I that is to be provided to the Secretariat in accordance with Article 5. Where more than one such chemical is included in a mixture or preparation, such information shall be provided for each chemical;

(d) A statement indicating, if known, the foreseen category of the chemical and its foreseen use within that category in the importing Party;

(e) Information on precautionary measures to reduce exposure to, and emission of, the chemical;

(f) In the case of a mixture or a preparation, the concentration of the banned or severely restricted chemical or chemicals in question;

(g) Name and address of the importer;

(h) Any additional information that is readily available to the relevant designated national authority of the exporting Party that would be of assistance to the designated national authority of the importing Party.

2. In addition to the information referred to in paragraph 1, the exporting Party shall provide such further information specified in Annex I as may be requested by the importing Party.

6. Biosphere

6.1 Convention on Nature Protection and Wildlife Preservation in the Western Hemisphere (Without Annex). Concluded at Washington, 12 October 1940. Entered into force, 1 May 1942. 161 U.N.T.S. 193, 56 Stat. 1354, T.S. No. 981; *reprinted in* 5A Weston V.H.1

Preamble

The Governments of the American Republics, wishing to protect and preserve in their natural habitat representatives of all species and genera of their native flora and fauna, including migratory birds, in sufficient numbers and over areas extensive enough to assure them from becoming extinct through any agency within man's control; and

Wishing to protect and preserve scenery of extraordinary beauty, unusual and striking geologic formations, regions and natural objects of aesthetic, historic or scientific value, and areas characterized by primitive conditions in those cases covered by this Convention; and

Wishing to conclude a convention on the protection of nature and the preservation of flora and fauna to effectuate the foregoing purposes, have agreed upon the following Articles:

Article I

Description of terms used in the wording of this Convention

1. The expression NATIONAL PARKS shall denote:

   Areas established for the protection and preservation of superlative scenery, flora and fauna of national significance which the general public may enjoy and from which it may benefit when placed under public control.

2. The expression NATIONAL RESERVES shall denote:

   Regions established for conservation and utilization of natural resources under government control, on which protection of animal and plant life will be afforded in so far as this may be consistent with the primary purpose of such reserves.

3. The expression NATURE MONUMENTS shall denote:

   Regions, objects, or living species of flora or fauna of aesthetic, historic or scientific interest to which strict protection is given. The purpose of nature monuments is the protection of a specific object, or a species of flora or fauna, and setting aside an area, an object, or a single species, as an inviolate nature monument, except for duly authorized scientific investigations or government inspection.

4. The expression STRICT WILDERNESS RESERVES shall denote:

   A region under public control characterized by primitive conditions of flora, fauna, transportation and habitation wherein there is no provision for the passage of motorized transportation and all commercial developments are included.

5. The expression MIGRATORY BIRDS shall denote:

   Birds of those species, all or some of whose individual members, may in any season cross any of the boundaries between the American countries. Some of the species of the following families are examples of birds characterized as migratory: Charadriidae, Scolopacidae, Caprimulgidae, Hirundinidae.

Article II

1. The Contracting Governments will explore at once the possibility of establishing in their territories national parks, national reserves, nature monuments, and strict wilderness reserves as defined in the preceding article. In cases where such establishment is feasible, the creation thereof shall be begun as soon as possible after the effective date of the present Convention.

2. If in any country the establishment of national parks, national reserves, nature monuments, or strict wilderness reserves is found to be impractical at present, suitable areas, objects or living species of fauna or flora, as the case may be, shall be selected as early as possible to be transformed into national parks, national reserves, nature monuments or strict wilderness reserves as soon as, in the opinion of the authorities concerned, circumstances will permit.

3. The Contracting Governments shall notify the Pan American Union of the establishment of any national parks, national reserves, nature monuments, or strict wilderness reserves, and of the legislation, including the methods of administrative control, adopted in connection therewith.

Article III

The Contracting Governments agree that the boundaries of national parks shall not be altered, or any portion thereof be capable of alienation, except by the competent legislative authority. The resources of these reserves shall not be subject to exploitation for commercial profit.

The Contracting Governments agree to prohibit hunting, killing and capturing of members of the fauna and destruction or collection of representatives of the flora in national parks except by or under the direction or control of the park authorities, or for duly authorized scientific investigations.

The Contracting Governments further agree to provide facilities for public recreation and education in national parks consistent with the purposes of this Convention.

Article IV

The Contracting Governments agree to maintain the strict wilderness reserves inviolate, as far as practicable, except for duly authorized scientific investigations or government inspection, or such uses as are consistent with the purposes for which the area was established.

Article V

1. The Contracting Governments agree to adopt, or to propose such adoption to their respective appropriate law-making bodies, suitable laws and regulations for the protection and preservation of flora and fauna within their national boundaries, but not included in the national parks, national reserves, nature monuments, or strict wilderness reserves referred to in Article II hereof. Such regulations shall contain proper provisions for the taking of specimens of flora and fauna for scientific study and investigation by properly accredited individuals and agencies.

2. The Contracting Governments agree to adopt, or to recommend that their respective legislatures adopt, laws which will assure the protection and preservation of the natural scenery, striking geological formations, and regions and natural objects of aesthetic interest or historic or scientific value.

Article VI

The Contracting Governments agree to cooperate among themselves in promoting the objectives of the present Convention. To this end they will lend proper assistance, consistent with national laws, to scientists of the American Republics engaged in research and field study; they may, when circumstances warrant, enter into agreements with one another or with scientific institutions of the Americas in order to increase the effectiveness of this collaboration; and they shall make available to all the American Republics equally through publication or otherwise the scientific knowledge resulting from such cooperative effort.

Article VII

The Contracting Governments shall adopt appropriate measures for the protection of migratory birds of economic or aesthetic value or to prevent the threatened extinction of any given species. Adequate measures shall be adopted which will permit, in so far as the respective governments may see fit, a rational utilization of migratory birds for the purpose of sports as well as for food, commerce, and industry, and for scientific study and investigation.

Article VIII

The protection of the species mentioned in the Annex to the present Convention is declared to be of special urgency and importance. Species included therein shall be protected as completely as possible, and their hunting, killing, capturing, or taking, shall be allowed only with the permission of the appropriate government authorities in the country. Such permission shall be granted only under special circumstances, in order to further scientific purposes, or when essential for the administration of the area in which the animal or plant is found.

Article IX

Each Contracting Government shall take the necessary measures to control and regulate the importation, exportation and transit of protected fauna or flora or any part thereof by the following means:

1. The issuing of certificates authorizing the exportation or transit of protected species of flora or fauna, or parts thereof.

2. The prohibition of the importation of any species of fauna or flora or any part thereof protected by the country of origin unless accompanied by a certificate of lawful exportation as provided for in Paragraph 1 of this Article.

Article X

1. The terms of this convention shall in no way be interpreted as replacing international agreements previously entered into by one or more of the High Contracting Powers.

2. The Pan American Union shall notify the Contracting Parties of any information relevant to the purposes of the present Convention communicated to it by any national museums or by any organizations, national or international, established within their jurisdiction and interested in the purposes of the Convention.

Article XI

1. The original of the present Convention in Spanish, English, Portuguese and French shall be deposited with the Pan American Union and opened for signature by the American Governments on October 12, 1940.

2. The present Convention shall remain open for signature by the American Governments. The instruments of ratification shall be deposited with the Pan Ameri-

can Union, which shall notify their receipt and the dates thereof, and the terms of any accompanying declarations or reservations, to all participating Governments.

3. The present Convention shall come into force three months after the deposit of not less than five ratifications with the Pan American Union.

4. Any ratification received after the date of the entry into force of the Convention, shall take effect three months after the date of its deposit with the Pan American Union.

Article XII

1. Any Contracting Government may at any time denounce the present Convention by a notification in writing addressed to the Pan American Union. Such denunciation shall take effect one year after the date of the receipt of the notification by the Pan American Union, provided, however, that no denunciation shall take effect until the expiration of five years from the date of the entry into force of this Convention.

2. If, as the result of simultaneous or successive denunciations, the number of Contracting Governments is reduced to less than three, the Convention shall cease to be in force from the date on which the last of such denunciations takes effect in accordance with the provisions of the preceding Paragraph.

3. The Pan American Union shall notify all of the American Governments of any denunciations and the date on which they take effect.

4. Should the Convention cease to be in force under the provisions of Paragraph 2 of this article, the Pan American Union shall notify all of the American Governments, indicating the date on which this will become effective.

IN WITNESS WHEREOF, the undersigned Plenipotentiaries, having deposited their full powers found to be in due and proper form, sign this Convention at the Pan American Union, Washington, D.C., on behalf of their respective Governments and affix thereto their seals on the dates appearing opposite their signatures.

* * *

6.2 INTERNATIONAL CONVENTION FOR THE REGULATION OF WHALING (Without Schedule but as Amended by 1956 Protocol). Concluded at Washington, 2 December 1946. Entered into force, 10 November 1948. 161 U.N.T.S. 72, T.I.A.S. No. 1849; 338 U.N.T.S. 366, 10 U.S.T. 952, T.I.A.S. No. 4228; *reprinted in* 5A Weston V.H.2

The Governments whose duly authorized representatives have subscribed hereto,

Recognizing the interest of the nations of the world in safeguarding for future generations the great natural resources represented by the whale stocks;

Considering that the history of whaling has seen overfishing of one area after another and of one species of whale after another to such a degree that it is essential to protect all species of whales from further overfishing;

Recognizing that the whale stocks are susceptible of natural increases if whaling is properly regulated, and that increases in the size of whale stocks will permit increases in the numbers of whales which may be captured without endangering these natural resources;

Recognizing that it is in the common interest to achieve the optimum level of whale stocks as rapidly as possible without causing wide-spread economic and nutritional distress;

Recognizing that in the course of achieving these objectives, whaling operations should be confined to those species best able to sustain exploitation in order to give an interval for recovery to certain species of whales now depleted in numbers;

Desiring to establish a system of international regulation for the whale fisheries to ensure proper and effective conservation and development of whale stocks on the basis of the principles embodied in the provisions of the International Agreement for the Regulation of Whaling signed in London on June 8, 1937 and the protocols to that Agreement signed in London on June 24, 1938 and November 26, 1945; and

Having decided to conclude a convention to provide for the proper conservation of whale stocks and thus make possible the orderly development of the whaling industry;

Have agreed as follows:

Article I

1. This Convention includes the Schedule attached thereto which forms an integral part thereof. All references to "Convention" shall be understood as including the said Schedule either in its present terms or as amended in accordance with the provisions of Article V.

2. This Convention applies to factory ships, land stations, and whale catchers under the jurisdiction of the Contracting Governments, and to all waters in which whaling is prosecuted by such factory ships, land stations, and whale catchers.

Article II

As used in this Convention

1. "factory ship" means a ship in which or on which whales are treated whether wholly or in part;

2. "land station" means a factory on the land at which whales are treated whether wholly or in part;

3. "whale catcher" means a helicopter, or other aircraft, or a ship, used for the purpose of hunting, taking, killing, towing, holding on to, or scouting for whales;

4. "Contracting Government" means any Government which has deposited an instrument of ratification or has given notice of adherence to this Convention.

Article III

1. The Contracting Governments agree to establish an International Whaling Commission, hereinafter referred to as the Commission, to be composed of one member of each Contracting Government. Each member shall have one vote and may be accompanied by one or more experts and advisers.

2. The Commission shall elect from its own members a Chairman and Vice Chairman and shall determine its own Rules of Procedure. Decisions of the Commission shall be taken by a simple majority of those members voting except that a three-fourths majority of those members voting shall be required for action in pursuance of Article V. The Rules of Procedure may provide for decisions otherwise than at meetings of the Commission.

3. The Commission may appoint its own Secretary and staff.

4. The Commission may set up, from among its own members and experts or advisers, such committees as it considers desirable to perform such functions as it may authorize.

5. The expenses of each member of the Commission and of his experts and advisers shall be determined and paid by his own Government.

6. Recognizing that specialized agencies related to the United Nations will be concerned with the conservation and development of whale fisheries and the products arising therefrom and desiring to avoid duplication of functions, the Contracting Governments will consult among themselves within two years after the coming into force of this Convention to decide whether the Commission shall be brought within the framework of a specialized agency related to the United Nations.

7. In the meantime the Government of the United Kingdom of Great Britain and Northern Ireland shall arrange, in consultation with the other Contracting Governments, to convene the first meeting of the Commission, and shall initiate the consultation referred to in paragraph 6 above.

8. Subsequent meetings of the Commission shall be convened as the Commission may determine.

Article IV

1. The Commission may either in collaboration with or through independent agencies of the Contracting Governments or other public or private agencies, establishments, or organizations, or independently

(*a*) encourage, recommend, or if necessary, organize studies and investigations relating to whales and whaling;

(*b*) collect and analyze statistical information concerning the current condition and trend of the whale stocks and the effects of whaling activities thereon;

(*c*) study, appraise, and disseminate information concerning methods of maintaining and increasing the populations of whale stocks.

2. The Commission shall arrange for the publication of reports of its activities, and it may publish independently or in collaboration with the International Bureau for Whaling Statistics at Sandefjord in Norway and other organizations and agencies such reports as it deems appropriate, as well as statistical, scientific, and other pertinent information relating to whales and whaling.

Article V

1. The Commission may amend from time to time the provisions of the Schedule by adopting regulations with respect to the conservation and utilization of whale resources, fixing (*a*) protected and unprotected species; (*b*) open and closed seasons; (*c*)

open and closed waters, including the designation of sanctuary areas; (*d*) size limits for each species; (*e*) time, methods, and intensity of whaling (including the maximum catch of whales to be taken in any one season); (*f*) types and specifications of gear and apparatus and appliances which may be used; (*g*) methods of measurement; (*h*) catch returns and other statistical and biological records; and (*i*) methods of inspection.

2. These amendments of the Schedule (*a*) shall be such as are necessary to carry out the objectives and purposes of this Convention and to provide for the conservation, development, and optimum utilization of the whale resources; (*b*) shall be based on scientific findings; (*c*) shall not involve restrictions on the number or nationality of factory ships or land stations, nor allocate specific quotas to any factory ship or land station or to any group of factory ships or land stations; and (*d*) shall take into consideration the interests of the consumers of whale products and the whaling industry.

3. Each of such amendments shall become effective with respect to the Contracting Governments ninety days following notification of the amendment by the Commission to each of the Contracting Governments, except that (*a*) if any Government presents to the Commission objection to any amendment prior to the expiration of this ninety-day period, the amendment shall not become effective with respect to any of the Governments for an additional ninety days; (*b*) thereupon, any other Contracting Government may present objection to the amendment at any time prior to the expiration of the additional ninety-day period, or before the expiration of thirty days from the date of receipt of the last objection received during such additional ninety-day period, whichever date shall be the later; and (*c*) thereafter, the amendment shall become effective with respect to all Contracting Governments which have not presented objection but shall not become effective with respect to any Government which has so objected until such date as the objection is withdrawn. The Commission shall notify each Contracting Government immediately upon receipt of each objection and withdrawal and each Contracting Government shall acknowledge receipt of all notification of amendments, objections, and withdrawals.

4. No amendments shall become effective before July 1, 1949.

Article VI

The Commission may from time to time make recommendations to any or all Contracting Governments on any matters which relate to whales or whaling and to the objectives and purposes of this Convention.

Article VII

The Contracting Governments shall ensure prompt transmission to the International Bureau for Whaling Statistics at Sandefjord in Norway, or to such other body as the Commission may designate, of notifications and statistical and other information required by this Convention in such form and manner as may be prescribed by the Commission.

Article VIII

1. Notwithstanding anything contained in this Convention, any Contracting Government may grant to any of its nationals a special permit authorizing that national to kill, take, and treat whales for purposes of scientific research subject to such restrictions as to number and subject to such other conditions as the Contracting Government thinks fit, and the killing, taking, and treating of whales in accordance with the provisions of this Article shall be exempt from the operation of this Convention. Each Contracting Government shall report at once to the Commission all such authorizations which it has granted. Each Contracting Government may at any time revoke any such special permit which it has granted.

2. Any whales taken under these special permits shall so far as practicable be processed and the proceeds shall be dealt with in accordance with directions issued by the Government by which the permit was granted.

3. Each Contracting Government shall transmit to such body as may be designated by the Commission, in so far as practicable, and at intervals of not more than one year, scientific information available to that Government with respect to whales and whaling, including the results of research conducted pursuant to paragraph 1 of this Article and to Article IV.

4. Recognizing that continuous collection and analysis of biological data in connection with the operations of factory ships and land stations are indispensable to sound and constructive management of the whale fisheries, the Contracting Governments will take all practicable measures to obtain such data.

Article IX

1. Each Contracting Government shall take appropriate measures to ensure the application of the provisions of this Convention and the punishment of infractions against the said provisions in operations carried out by persons or by vessels under its jurisdiction.

2. No bonus or other remuneration calculated with relation to the results of their work shall be paid to the gunners and crews of whale catchers in respect of any whales the taking of which is forbidden by this Convention.

3. Prosecution for infractions against or contraventions of this Convention shall be instituted by the Government having jurisdiction over the offense.

4. Each Contracting Government shall transmit to the Commission full details of each infraction of the provisions of this Convention by persons or vessels under the jurisdiction of that Government as reported by its inspectors. This information shall include a statement of measures taken for dealing with the infraction and of penalties imposed.

Article X

1. This Convention shall be ratified and the instruments of ratification shall be deposited with the Government of the United States of America.

2. Any Government which has not signed this Convention may adhere thereto after it enters into force by a notification in writing to the Government of the United States of America.

3. The Government of the United States of America shall inform all other signatory Governments and all adhering Governments of all ratifications deposited and adherences received.

4. This Convention shall, when instruments of ratification have been deposited by at least six signatory Governments, which shall include the Governments of the Netherlands, Norway, the Union of Soviet Socialist Republics, the United Kingdom of Great Britain and Northern Ireland, and the United States of America, enter into force with respect to those Governments and shall enter into force with respect to each Government which subsequently ratifies or adheres on the date of the deposit of its instrument of ratification or the receipt of its notification of adherence.

5. The provisions of the Schedule shall not apply prior to July 1, 1948. Amendments to the Schedule adopted pursuant to Article V shall not apply prior to July 1, 1949.

Article XI

Any Contracting Government may withdraw from this Convention on June thirtieth of any year by giving notice on or before January first of the same year to the depositary Government, which upon receipt of such a notice shall at once communicate it to the other Contracting Governments. Any other Contracting Government may, in like manner, within one month of the receipt of a copy of such notice from the depositary Government, give notice of withdrawal, so that the Convention shall cease to be in force on June thirtieth of the same year with respect to the Government giving notice of withdrawal.

This Convention shall bear the date on which it is opened for signature and shall remain open for signature for a period of fourteen days thereafter.

6.3 Convention on Fishing and Conservation of the Living Resources of the High Seas.[a] Concluded at Geneva, 29 April 1958. Entered into force, 20 March 1966. 559 U.N.T.S. 285, 17 U.S.T. 138, T.I.A.S. No. 5969[b]; *reprinted in* 5A Weston V.H.5

Article 1

1. All States have the right for their nationals to engage in fishing on the high seas, subject (*a*) to their treaty obligations, (*b*) to the interests and rights of coastal States as provided for in this Convention, and (*c*) to the provisions contained in the following articles concerning conservation of the living resources of the high seas.

2. All States have the duty to adopt, or to co-operate with other States in adopting, such measures for their respective nationals as may be necessary for the conservation of the living resources of the high seas.

Article 2

As employed in this Convention, the expression "conservation of the living resources of the high seas" means the aggregate of the measures rendering possible the optimum sustainable yield from those resources so as to secure a maximum supply to food and other marine products. Conservation programmes should be formulated with a view to securing in the first place a supply of food for human consumption.

Article 3

A State whose nationals are engaged in fishing any stock or stocks of fish or other living marine resources in any area of the high seas where the nationals of other States are not thus engaged shall adopt, for its own nationals, measures in that area when necessary for the purpose of the conservation of the living resources affected.

Article 4

1. If the nationals of two or more States are engaged in fishing the same stock or stocks of fish or other living marine resources in any area or areas of the high seas, these States shall, at the request of any of them, enter into negotiations with a view to prescribing by agreement for their nationals the necessary measures for the conservation of the living resources affected.

2. If the States concerned do not reach agreement within twelve months, any of the parties may initiate the procedure contemplated by article 9.

Article 5

1. If, subsequent to the adoption of the measures referred to in articles 3 and 4, nationals of other States engage in fishing the same stock or stocks of fish or other living marine resources in any area or areas of the high seas, the other States shall apply the measures, which shall not be discriminatory in form or in fact, to their own nationals not later than seven months after the date on which the measures shall have been notified to the Director-General of the Food and Agriculture Organization of the United Nations. The Director-General shall notify such measures to any State which so requests and, in any case, to any State specified by the State initiating the measure.

2. If these other States do not accept the measures so adopted and if no agreement can be reached within twelve months, any of the interested parties may

a. *See also* Basic Documents 4.2, 4.3, and 4.4, *supra.*

b. *See also* Optional Protocol to the 1958 Law of the Sea Conventions Concerning the Compulsory Settlement of Disputes (which provides for reference to the International Court of Justice of disputes arising out of this agreement), concluded 29 April 1958 and entered into force 30 September 1962 (450 UNTS 169).

initiate the procedure contemplated by article 9. Subject to paragraph 2 of article 10, the measures adopted shall remain obligatory pending the decision of the special commission.

Article 6

1. A coastal State has a special interest in the maintenance of the productivity of the living resources in any area of the high seas adjacent to its territorial sea.

2. A coastal State is entitled to take part on an equal footing in any system of research and regulation for purposes of conservation of the living resources of the high seas in that area, even though its nationals do not carry on fishing there.

3. A state whose nationals are engaged in fishing in any area of the high seas adjacent to the territorial sea of a State shall, at the request of that coastal State, enter into negotiations with a view to prescribing by agreement the measures necessary for the conservation of the living resources of the high seas in that area.

4. A State whose nationals are engaged in fishing in any area of the high seas adjacent to the territorial sea of a coastal State shall not enforce conservation measures in that area which are opposed to those which have been adopted by the coastal State, but may enter into negotiations with the coastal State with a view to prescribing by agreement the measures necessary for the conservation of the living resources of the high seas in that area.

5. If the States concerned do not reach agreement with respect to conservation measures within twelve months, any of the parties may initiate the procedure contemplated by article 9.

Article 7

1. Having regard to the provisions of paragraph 1 of article 6, any coastal State may, with a view to the maintenance of the productivity of the living resources of the sea, adopt unilateral measures of conservation appropriate to any stock of fish or other marine resources in any area of the high seas adjacent to its territorial sea, provided that negotiations to that effect with the other States concerned have not led to an agreement within six months.

2. The measures which the coastal State adopts under the previous paragraph shall be valid as to other States only if the following requirements are fulfilled:

(*a*) That there is a need for urgent application of conservation measures in the light of the existing knowledge of the fishery;

(*b*) That the measures adopted are based on appropriate scientific findings;

(*c*) That such measures do not discriminate in form or in fact against foreign fishermen.

3. These measures shall remain in force pending the settlement, in accordance with the relevant provisions of this Convention, of any disagreement as to their validity.

4. If the measures are not accepted by the other States concerned, any of the parties may initiate the procedure contemplated by article 9. Subject to paragraph 2 of article 10, the measures adopted shall remain obligatory pending the decision of the special commission.

5. The principles of geographical demarcation as defined in article 12 of the Convention on the Territorial Sea and the Contiguous Zone shall be adopted when coasts of different States are involved.

Article 8

1. Any State which, even if its nationals are not engaged in fishing in an area of the high seas not adjacent to its coast, has a special interest in the conservation of the living resources of the high seas in that area, may request the State or States whose nationals are engaged in fishing there to take the necessary measures of conservation under articles 3 and 4 respectively, at the same time mentioning the scientific reasons which in its opinion make such measures necessary, and indicating its special interest.

2. If no agreement is reached within twelve months, such State may initiate the procedure contemplated by article 9.

Article 9

1. Any dispute which may arise between States under articles 4, 5, 6, 7 and 8 shall, at the request of any of the parties, be submitted for settlement to a special commission of five members, unless the parties agree to seek a solution by another method of peaceful settlement, as provided for in Article 33 of the Charter of the United Nations.

2. The members of the commission, one of whom shall be designated as chairman, shall be named by agreement between the States in dispute within three months of the request for settlement in accordance with the provisions of this article. Failing agreement they shall, upon the request of any State party, be named by the Secretary–General of the United Nations, within a further three-month period, in consultation with the States in dispute and with the President of the International Court of Justice and the Director-General of the Food and Agriculture Organization of the United Nations, from amongst well-qualified persons being nationals of States not involved in the dispute and specializing in legal, administrative or scientific questions relating to fisheries, depending upon the nature of the dispute to be settled. Any vacancy arising after the original appointment shall be filled in the same manner as provided for the initial selection.

3. Any State party to proceedings under these articles shall have the right to name one of its nationals to the special commission, with the right to participate fully in the proceedings on the same footing as a member of the commission, but without the right to vote or to take part in the writing of the commission's decision.

4. The commission shall determine its own procedure, assuring each party to the proceedings a full opportunity to be heard and to present its case. It shall also determine how the costs and expenses shall be divided between the parties to the dispute, failing agreement by the parties on this matter.

5. The special commission shall render its decision within a period of five months from the time it is appointed unless it decides, in case of necessity, to extend the time limit for a period not exceeding three months.

6. The special commission shall, in reaching its decisions, adhere to these articles and to any special agreements between the disputing parties regarding settlement of the dispute.

7. Decisions of the commission shall be by majority vote.

Article 10

1. The special commission shall, in disputes arising under article 7, apply the criteria listed in paragraph 2 of that article. In disputes under articles 4, 5, 6 and 8, the commission shall apply the following criteria, according to the issues involved in the dispute:

(*a*) Common to the determination of disputes arising under articles 4, 5 and 6 are the requirements:

(i) That scientific findings demonstrate the necessity of conservation measures;

(ii) That the specific measures are based on scientific findings and are practicable; and

(iii) That the measures do not discriminate, in form or in fact, against fishermen of other States;

(*b*) Applicable to the determination of disputes arising under article 8 is the requirement that scientific findings demonstrate the necessity for conservation measures, or that the conservation programme is adequate, as the case may be.

2. The special commission may decide that pending its award the measures in dispute shall not be applied, provided that, in the case of disputes under article 7, the measures shall only be suspended when it is apparent to the commission on the basis of *prima facie* evidence that the need for the urgent application of such measures does not exist.

Article 11

The decisions of the special commission shall be binding on the States concerned and the provisions of paragraph 2 of Article 94 of the Charter of the United Nations shall be applicable to those decisions. If the decisions are accompanied by any recommendations, they shall receive the greatest possible consideration.

Article 12

1. If the factual basis of the award of the special commission is altered by substantial changes in the conditions of the stock or stocks of fish or other living marine resources or in methods of fishing, any of the States concerned may request the other States to enter into negotiations with a view to prescribing by agreement the necessary modifications in the measures of conservation.

2. If no agreement is reached within a reasonable period of time, any of the States concerned may again resort to the procedure contemplated by article 9 provided that at least two years have elapsed from the original award.

Article 13

1. The regulation of fisheries conducted by means of equipment embedded in the floor of the sea in areas of the high seas adjacent to the territorial sea of a State may be undertaken by that State where such fisheries have long been maintained and conducted by its nationals, provided that non-nationals are permitted to participate in such activities on an equal footing with nationals except in areas where such fisheries have by long usage been exclusively enjoyed by such nationals. Such regulations will not, however, affect the general status of the areas as high seas.

2. In this article, the expression "fisheries conducted by means of equipment embedded in the floor of the sea" means those fisheries using gear with supporting members embedded in the sea floor, constructed on a site and left there to operate permanently or, if removed, restored each season on the same site.

Article 14

In articles 1, 3, 4, 5, 6 and 8, the term "nationals" means fishing boats or craft of any size having the nationality of the State concerned, according to the law of that State, irrespective of the nationality of the members of their crews.

Article 15

This Convention shall, until 31 October 1958, be open for signature by all States Members of the United Nations or of any of the specialized agencies, and by any other

State invited by the General Assembly of the United Nations to become a Party to the Convention.

Article 16

This Convention is subject to ratification. The instruments of ratification shall be deposited with the Secretary–General of the United Nations.

Article 17

This Convention shall be open for accession by any States belonging to any of the categories mentioned in article 15. The instruments of accession shall be deposited with the Secretary–General of the United Nations.

Article 18

1. This Convention shall come into force on the thirtieth day following the date of deposit of the twenty-second instrument of ratification or accession with the Secretary–General of the United Nations.

2. For each State ratifying or acceding to the Convention after the deposit of the twenty-second instrument of ratification or accession, the Convention shall enter into force on the thirtieth day after deposit by such State of its instrument of ratification or accession.

Article 19

1. At the time of signature, ratification or accession, any State may make reservations to articles of the Convention other than to articles 6, 7, 9, 10, 11 and 12.

2. Any contracting State making a reservation in accordance with the preceding paragraph may at any time withdraw the reservation by a communication to that effect addressed to the Secretary–General of the United Nations.

Article 20

1. After the expiration of a period of five years from the date on which this Convention shall enter into force, a request for the revision of this Convention may be made at any time by any contracting party by means of a notification in writing addressed to the Secretary–General of the United Nations.

2. The General Assembly of the United Nations shall decide upon the steps, if any, to be taken in respect of such request.

Article 21

The Secretary–General of the United Nations shall inform all States Members of the United Nations and the other States referred to in article 15:

(*a*) Of signatures to this Convention and of the deposit of instruments of ratification or accession, in accordance with articles 15, 16 and 17;

(*b*) Of the date on which this Convention will come into force, in accordance with article 18;

(*c*) Of requests for revision in accordance with article 20;

(*d*) Of reservations to this Convention, in accordance with article 19.

Article 22

The original of this Convention, of which the Chinese, English, French, Russian and Spanish texts are equally authentic, shall be deposited with the Secretary–General of the United Nations, who shall send certified copies thereof to all States referred to in article 15.

6.4 African Convention on the Conservation of Nature and Natural Resources (Without List of Protected Species). Concluded at Algiers, 15 September 1968. Entered into force, 16 June 1969. 1001 U.N.T.S. 3; *reprinted in* 5A Weston V.H.7

Preamble

We, the Heads of State and Government of Independent African States,

Fully conscious that soil, water, flora and faunal resources constitute a capital of vital importance to mankind;

Confirming, as we accepted upon declaring our adherence to the Charter of the Organization of African Unity, that we know that it is our duty "to harness the natural and human resources of our continent for the total advancement of our peoples in spheres of human endeavour";

Fully conscious of the ever-growing importance of natural resources from an economic, nutritional, scientific, educational, cultural and aesthetic point of view;

Conscious of the dangers which threaten some of these irreplaceable assets;

Accepting that the utilization of the natural resources must aim at satisfying the needs of man according to the carrying capacity of the environment;

Desirous of undertaking individual and joint action for the conservation, utilization and development of these assets by establishing and maintaining their rational utilization for the present and future welfare of mankind;

Convinced that one of the most appropriate means of achieving this end is to bring into force a convention;

Have agreed as follows:

Article I

The Contracting States hereby establish an African Convention on the Conservation of nature and natural resources.

Article II. Fundamental principle

The Contracting States shall undertake to adopt the measures necessary to ensure conservation, utilization and development of soil, water, flora and faunal resources in accordance with scientific principles and with due regard to the best interests of the people.

Article III. Definitions

For purposes of the present Convention, the meaning of the following expressions shall be as defined below:

1. "Natural Resources" means renewable resources; that is soil, water, flora and fauna.

2. "Specimen" means an individual example of a species of wild animal or wild plant or part of a wild plant.

3. "Trophy" means any dead animal specimen or part thereof whether included in a manufactured or processed object or otherwise dealt with, unless it has lost its original identity; also nests, eggs and eggshells.

4. "Conservation area" means any protected natural resource area, whether it be a strict natural reserve, a national park or a special reserve;

(*a*) "strict nature reserve" means an area:

(1) under State control and the boundaries of which may not be altered nor any portion alienated except by the competent legislative authority,

(2) throughout which any form of hunting or fishing, any undertaking connected with forestry, agriculture or mining, any grazing, any excavation or prospecting, drilling, levelling of the ground or construction, any work tending to alter the configuration of the soil or the character of the vegetation, any water pollution and, generally, any act likely to harm or disturb the fauna or flora, including introduction of zoological or botanical species, whether indigenous or imported, wild or domesticated, are strictly forbidden,

(3) where it shall be forbidden to reside, enter, traverse or camp, and where it shall be forbidden to fly over at low altitude, without a special written permit from the competent authority, and in which scientific investigations (including removal of animals and plants in order to maintain an ecosystem) may only be undertaken by permission of the competent authority;

(*b*) "national park" means an area:

(1) under State control and the boundaries of which may not be altered or any portion alienated except by the competent legislative authority,

(2) exclusively set aside for the propagation, protection, conservation and management of vegetation and wild animals as well as for the protection of sites, land-scapes or geological formations of particular scientific or aesthetic value, for the benefit and enjoyment of the general public, and

(3) in which the killing, hunting and capture of animals and the destruction or collection of plants are prohibited except for scientific and management purposes and on the condition that such measures are taken under the direction or control of the competent authority,

(4) covering any aquatic environment to which all of the provisions of section (*b*)(13) above are applicable.

The activities prohibited in strict nature reserve under the provisions of section (*a*)(2) of paragraph 4 of this article are equally prohibited in national parks except in so far as they are necessary to enable the park authorities to implement the provisions of section (2) of this paragraph, by applying, for example, appropriate management practices, and to enable the public to visit these parks; however, sport fishing may be practiced with the authorization and under the control of the competent authority.

(*c*) "special reserve" means other protected areas such as:

(1) "game reserve" which shall denote an area

(*a*) set aside for the conservation, management and propagation of wild animal life and the protection and management of its habitat,

(*b*) within which the hunting, killing or capture of fauna shall be prohibited except by or under the direction or control of the reserve authorities,

(*c*) where settlement and other human activities shall be controlled or prohibited;

(2) "partial reserve" or "sanctuary" which shall denote an area

(*a*) set aside to protect characteristic wildlife and especially bird communities, or to protect particularly threatened animal or plant species and especially those listed in the Annex to this Convention, together with the biotopes essential for their survival,

(*b*) in which all other interests and activities shall be subordinated to this end;

(3) "soil", "water" or "forest" reserve shall denote areas set aside to protect such resources.

Article IV. SOIL

The Contracting States shall take effective measures for conservation and improvement of the soil and shall in particular combat erosion and misuse of the soil. To this end:

(*a*) they shall establish land-use plans based on scientific investigations (ecological, pedological, economic, and sociological) and, in particular, classification of land-use capability;

(*b*) they shall, when implementing agricultural practices and agrarian reforms,

(1) improve soil-conservation and introduce improved farming methods, which ensure long-term productivity of the land,

(2) control erosion caused by various forms of land-use which may lead to loss of vegetation cover.

Article V. WATER

1. The Contracting States shall establish policies for conservation, utilization and development of underground and surface water, and shall endeavour to guarantee for their populations a sufficient and continuous supply of suitable water, taking appropriate measures with due regard to

(1) the study of water cycles and the investigation of each catchment area,

(2) the co-ordination and planning of water resources development projects,

(3) the administration and control of all water utilization, and

(4) prevention and control of water pollution.

2. Where surface or underground water resources are shared by two or more of the Contracting States, the latter shall act in consultation, and if the need arises, set up inter-State Commissions to study and resolve problems arising from the joint use of these resources, and for the joint development and conservation thereof.

Article VI. FLORA

1. The Contracting States shall take all necessary measures for the protection of flora and to ensure its best utilization and development. To this end the Contracting States shall:

(*a*) adopt scientifically-based conservation, utilization and management plans of forests and rangeland, taking into account the social and economic needs of the States concerned, the importance of the vegetation cover for the maintenance of the water balance of an area, the productivity of soils and the habitat requirements of the fauna;

(*b*) observe section (*a*) above by paying particular attention to controlling bush fires, forest exploitation, land clearing for cultivation, and over-grazing by domestic and wild animals;

(*c*) set aside areas for forest reserves and carry out afforestation programmes where necessary;

(*d*) limitation of forest grazing to season and intensities that will not prevent forest regeneration; and

(*e*) establish botanical gardens to perpetuate plant species of particular interest.

2. The Contracting States also shall undertake the conservation of plant species or communities, which are threatened and/or of special scientific or aesthetic value by ensuring that they are included in conservation areas.

Article VII. FAUNAL RESOURCES

1. The Contracting States shall ensure conservation, wise use and development of faunal resources and their environment, within the framework of land-use planning and of economic and social development. Management shall be carried out in accordance with plans based on scientific principles, and to that end the Contracting States shall:

(*a*) manage wildlife populations inside designated areas according to the objectives of such areas and also manage exploitable wildlife populations outside such areas for an optimum sustained yield, compatible with and complementary to other land uses; and

(*b*) manage aquatic environments, whether in fresh, brackish or coastal water, with a view to minimize deleterious effects of any water and land use practice which might adversely affect aquatic habitats.

2. The Contracting States shall adopt adequate legislation on hunting, capture and fishing, under which:

(*a*) the issue of permits is properly regulated;

(*b*) unauthorized methods are prohibited;

(*c*) the following methods of hunting, capture and fishing are prohibited:

(1) any methods liable to cause a mass destruction of wild animals,

(2) the use of drugs, poisons, poisoned weapons or poisoned baits,

(3) the use of explosives,

(4) the following methods of hunting and capture are particularly prohibited:

(a) the use of mechanically propelled vehicles,

(b) the use of fire,

(c) the use of fire arms capable of firing more than one round at each pull of the trigger,

(d) hunting or capture at night,

(e) the use of missiles containing detonators;

(*d*) the following methods of hunting or capture are as far as possible prohibited:

(1) the use of nets and stockades,

(2) the use of concealed traps, pits, snares, set-gun traps, deadfalls, and hunting from a blind or hide;

(*e*) with a view to as rational use as possible of game meat the abandonment by hunters of carcasses of animals, which represent a food resource, is prohibited.

Capture of animals with the aid of drugs or mechanically-propelled vehicles, or hunting or capture by night if carried out by, or under the control of, the competent authority shall nevertheless be exempted from the prohibitions under (*c*) above.

Article VIII. PROTECTED SPECIES

1. The Contracting States recognize that it is important and urgent to accord a special protection to those animal and plant species that are threatened with extinction, or which may become so, and to the habitat necessary to their survival. Where such a species is represented only in the territory of one Contracting State, that State has a particular responsibility for its protection. These species which are, or may be listed, according to the degree of protection that shall be given to them are placed in Class A or B of the annex to this Convention, and shall be protected by Contracting States as follows:

(1) species in Class A shall be totally protected throughout the entire territory of the Contracting States; the hunting, killing, capture or collection of specimens shall be permitted only on the authorization in each case of the highest competent authority and only if required in the national interest or for scientific purposes; and

(2) species in Class B shall be totally protected, but may be hunted, killed, captured or collected under special authorization granted by the competent authority.

2. The competent authority of each Contracting State shall examine the necessity of applying the provisions of this article to species not listed in the annex, in order to conserve the indigenous flora and fauna of their respective countries. Such additional species shall be placed in Class A or B by the State concerned, according to its specific requirements.

Article IX. TRAFFIC IN SPECIMENS AND TROPHIES

1. In the case of animal species to which Article VIII does not apply the Contracting States shall:

(*a*) regulate trade in and transport of specimens and trophies;

(*b*) control the application of these regulations in such a way as to prevent trade in specimens and trophies which have been illegally captured or killed or obtained.

2. In the case of plant and animal species to which Article VIII, paragraph (1), applies, the Contracting States shall:

(*a*) take all measures similar to those in paragraph (1);

(*b*) make the export of such specimens and trophies subject to an authorization:

(1) additional to that required for their capture, killing or collection by Article VIII

(2) which indicates their destination,

(3) which shall not be given unless the specimens or trophies have been obtained legally,

(4) which shall be examined prior to exportation;

(5) which shall be on a standard form, as may be arranged under Article XVI;

(*c*) make the import and transit of such specimens and trophies subject to the presentation of the authorization required under section (*b*) above, with due provision for the confiscation of specimens and trophies exported illegally, without prejudice to the application of other penalties.

Article X. CONSERVATION AREAS

1. The Contracting States shall maintain and extend where appropriate, within their territory and where applicable in their territorial waters, the conservation areas existing at the time of entry into force of the present Convention and, preferably within the framework of land-use planning programmes, assess the necessity of establishing additional conservation areas in order to:

(1) protect those ecosystems which are most representative of and particularly those which are in any respect peculiar to their territories;

(2) ensure conservation of all species and more particularly of those listed or may be listed in the annex to this Convention;

2. The Contracting States shall establish where necessary, around the borders of conservation areas, zones within which the competent authorities shall control activities detrimental to the protected natural resources.

Article XI. CUSTOMARY RIGHTS

The Contracting States shall take all necessary legislative measures to reconcile customary rights with the provisions of this Convention.

Article XII. RESEARCH

The Contracting States shall encourage and promote research in conservation, utilization and management of natural resources and shall pay particular attention to ecological and sociological factors.

Article XIII. CONSERVATION EDUCATION

1. (*a*) The Contracting States shall ensure that their peoples appreciate their close dependence on natural resources and that they understand the need, and rules for, the rational utilization of these resources.

(*b*) For this purpose they shall ensure that the principles indicated in paragraph (1):

(1) are included in educational programmes at all levels,

(2) form the object of information campaigns capable of acquainting the public with, and winning it over to, the idea of conservation.

2. In order to put into effect paragraph (1) above, the Contracting States shall make maximum use of the educational value of conservation areas.

Article XIV. DEVELOPMENT PLANS

1. The Contracting States shall ensure that conservation and management of natural resources are treated as an integral part of national and/or regional development plans.

2. In the formulation of all development plans, full consideration shall be given to ecological, as well as to economic and social factors.

3. Where any development plan is likely to affect the natural resources of another State, the latter shall be consulted.

Article XV. ORGANIZATION OF NATIONAL CONSERVATION SERVICES

Each Contracting State shall establish, if it has not already done so, a single agency empowered to deal with all matters covered by this Convention, but, where this is not possible a co-ordinating machinery shall be established for this purpose.

Article XVI. INTER-STATE CO-OPERATION

1. The Contracting States shall co-operate:

(*a*) whenever such co-operation is necessary to give effect to the provisions of this Convention, and

(*b*) whenever any national measure is likely to affect the natural resources of any other State.

2. The Contracting States shall supply the Organization of African Unity with:

(*a*) the text of laws, decrees, regulations and instructions in force in their territories, which are intended to ensure the implementation of this Convention,

(*b*) reports on the results achieved in applying the provisions of this Convention, and

(*c*) all the information necessary for the complete documentation of matters dealt with by this Convention if requested.

3. If so requested by Contracting States, the Organization of African Unity shall organize any meeting which may be necessary to dispose of any matters covered by this Convention. Requests for such meetings must be made by at least three of the Contracting States and be approved by two thirds of the States which it is proposed should participate in such meetings.

4. Any expenditure arising from this Convention, which devolves upon the Organization of African Unity shall be included in its regular budget, unless shared by the Contracting States or otherwise defrayed.

Article XVII. PROVISION FOR EXCEPTIONS

1. The provisions of this Convention shall not affect the responsibilities of Contracting States concerning:

(1) the paramount interest of the State,

(2) "force majeure",

(3) defence of human life.

2. The provisions of this Convention shall not prevent Contracting States:

(1) in time of famine,

(2) for the protection of public health,

(3) in defence of property,

to enact measures contrary to the provisions of the Convention, provided their application is precisely defined in respect of aim, time and place.

Article XVIII. SETTLEMENT OF DISPUTES

Any dispute between the Contracting States relating to the interpretation or application of this Convention, which cannot be settled by negotiation, shall at the request of any party be submitted to the Commission of Mediation, Conciliation and Arbitration of the Organization of African Unity.

Article XIX. SIGNATURE AND RATIFICATION

1. This Convention shall be open for signature immediately after being approved by the Assembly of Heads of State and Government of the Organization of African Unity.

2. This Convention shall be ratified by each of the Contracting States. The instruments of ratification shall be deposited with the Administrative Secretary–General of the Organization of African Unity.

Article XX. Reservations

1. At the time of signature, ratification or accession, any State may declare its acceptance of this Convention in part only, provided that such reservation may not apply to the provisions of Articles II to XI.

2. Reservations made in conformity with the preceding paragraph shall be deposited together with the instruments of ratification or accession.

3. Any Contracting State which has formulated a reservation in conformity with the preceding paragraph may at any time withdraw it by notifying the Administrative Secretary–General of the Organization of African Unity.

Article XXI. Entry into force

1. This Convention shall come into force on the thirtieth day following the date of deposit of the fourth instrument of ratification or accession with the Administrative Secretary–General of the Organization of African Unity, who shall inform participating States accordingly.

2. In the case of a State ratifying or acceding to the Convention after the depositing of the fourth instrument of ratification or accession, the Convention shall come into force on the thirtieth day after the deposit by such State of its instrument of ratification or accession.

3. The London Convention of 1933 or any other Convention on the conservation of flora and fauna in their natural state shall cease to have effect in States in which this Convention has come into force.

Article XXII. Accession

1. After the date of approval specified in Article XIX, paragraph (1), this Convention shall be open to accession by any independent and sovereign African State.

2. The instruments of accession shall be deposited with the Administrative Secretary–General of the Organization of African Unity.

Article XXIII. Denunciation

1. Any Contracting State may denounce this Convention by notification in writing addressed to the Administrative Secretary–General of the Organization of African Unity.

2. Such denunciation shall take effect, for such a State, one year after the date of receipt of its notification by the Administrative Secretary–General of the Organization of African Unity.

3. No denunciation shall, however, be made before the expiry of a period of five years from the date at which for the State concerned this Convention comes into force.

Article XXIV. Revision

1. After the expiry of a period of five years from the date of entry into force of this Convention, any Contracting State may at any time make a request for the revision of part or the whole of this Convention by notification in writing addressed to the Administrative Secretary–General of the Organization of African Unity.

2. In the event of such a request the appropriate organ of the Organization of African Unity shall deal with the matter in accordance with the provision of sections 3 and 4 of Article XVI of this Convention.

3. (a) At the request of one or more Contracting States and notwithstanding the provisions of paragraphs (1) and (2) of this Article, the annex to this Convention may be revised or added to by the appropriate organ of the Organization of African Unity.

(b) Such revision or addition shall come into force three months after the approval by the appropriate organ of the Organization of African Unity.

Article XXV. Final Provisions

The original of this Convention of which both the English and the French texts are authentic, shall be deposited with the Administrative Secretary–General of the Organization of African Unity.

List of protected species

* * *

6.5 Convention on International Trade in Endangered Species of Wild Fauna and Flora (CITES) (With Appendices and as Amended). Concluded at Washington, 3 March 1973. Entered into force, 1 July 1975. 993 U.N.T.S. 243, 27 U.S.T. 1087, T.I.A.S. No. 8249; *reprinted in* 12 I.L.M. 1085 (1973) & 5A Weston V.H.10

The Contracting States,

RECOGNIZING that wild fauna and flora in their many beautiful and varied forms are an irreplaceable part of the natural systems of the earth which must be protected for this and the generations to come;

CONSCIOUS of the ever-growing value of wild fauna and flora from aesthetic, scientific, cultural, recreational and economic points of view;

RECOGNIZING that peoples and States are and should be the best protectors of their own wild fauna and flora;

RECOGNIZING, in addition, that international cooperation is essential for the protection of certain species of wild fauna and flora against over-exploitation through international trade;

CONVINCED of the urgency of taking appropriate measures to this end;

HAVE AGREED as follows:

Article I

Definitions

For the purpose of the present Convention, unless the context otherwise requires:

(a) "Species" means any species, sub-species, or geographically separate population thereof;

(b) "Specimen" means:

(i) any animal or plant, whether alive or dead;

(ii) in the case of an animal: for species included in Appendices I and II, any readily recognizable part or derivative thereof; and for species included in Appendix III, any readily recognizable part or derivative thereof specified in Appendix III in relation to the species; and

(iii) in the case of a plant: for species included in Appendix I, any readily recognizable part or derivative thereof; and for species included in Appendices II and III, any readily recognizable part or derivative thereof specified in Appendices II and III in relation to the species;

(c) "Trade" means export, re-export, import and introduction from the sea;

(d) "Re-export" means export of any specimen that has previously been imported;

(e) "Introduction from the sea" means transportation into a State of specimens of any species which were taken in the marine environment not under the jurisdiction of any State;

(f) "Scientific Authority" means a national scientific authority designated in accordance with Article IX;

(g) "Management Authority" means a national management authority designated in accordance with Article IX;

(h) "Party" means a State for which the present Convention has entered into force.

Article II

Fundamental Principles

1. Appendix I shall include all species threatened with extinction which are or may be affected by trade. Trade in specimens of these species must be subject to particularly strict regulation in order not to endanger further their survival and must only be authorized in exceptional circumstances.

2. Appendix II shall include:

(a) all species which although not necessarily now threatened with extinction may become so unless trade in specimens of such species is subject to strict regulation in order to avoid utilization incompatible with their survival; and

(b) other species which must be subject to regulation in order that trade in specimens of certain species referred to in sub-paragraph (a) of this paragraph may be brought under effective control.

3. Appendix III shall include all species which any Party identifies as being subject to regulation within its jurisdiction for the purpose of preventing or restricting exploitation, and as needing the cooperation of other parties in the control of trade.

4. The Parties shall not allow trade in specimens of species included in Appendices I, II and III except in accordance with the provisions of the present Convention.

Article III

Regulation of Trade in Specimens of Species included in Appendix I

1. All trade in specimens of species included in Appendix I shall be in accordance with the provisions of this Article.

2. The export of any specimen of a species included in Appendix I shall require the prior grant and presentation of an export permit. An export permit shall only be granted when the following conditions have been met:

(a) a Scientific Authority of the State of export has advised that such export will not be detrimental to the survival of that species;

(b) a Management Authority of the State of export is satisfied that the specimen was not obtained in contravention of the laws of that State for the protection of fauna and flora;

(c) a Management Authority of the State of export is satisfied that any living specimen will be so prepared and shipped as to minimize the risk of injury, damage to health or cruel treatment; and

(d) a Management Authority of the State of export is satisfied that an import permit has been granted for the specimen.

3. The import of any specimen of a species included in Appendix I shall require the prior grant and presentation of an import permit and either an export permit or a re-export certificate. An import permit shall only be granted when the following conditions have been met:

(a) a Scientific Authority of the State of import has advised that the import will be for purposes which are not detrimental to the survival of the species involved;

(b) a Scientific Authority of the State of import is satisfied that the proposed recipient of a living specimen is suitably equipped to house and care for it; and

(c) a Management Authority of the State of import is satisfied that the specimen is not to be used for primarily commercial purposes.

4. The re-export of any specimen of a species included in Appendix I shall require the prior grant and presentation of a re-export certificate. A re-export certificate shall only be granted when the following conditions have been met:

(a) a Management Authority of the State of re-export is satisfied that the specimen was imported into that State in accordance with the provisions of the present Convention;

(b) a Management Authority of the State of re-export is satisfied that any living specimen will be so prepared and shipped as to minimize the risk of injury, damage to health or cruel treatment; and

(c) a Management Authority of the State of re-export is satisfied that an import permit has been granted for any living specimen.

5. The introduction from the sea of any specimen of a species included in Appendix I shall require the prior grant of a certificate from a Management Authority of the State of introduction. A certificate shall only be granted when the following conditions have been met:

(a) a Scientific Authority of the State of introduction advises that the introduction will not be detrimental to the survival of the species involved;

(b) a Management Authority of the State of introduction is satisfied that the proposed recipient of a living specimen is suitably equipped to house and care for it; and

(c) a Management Authority of the State of introduction is satisfied that the specimen is not to be used for primarily commercial purposes.

Article IV

Regulation of Trade in Specimens of Species included in Appendix II

1. All trade in specimens of species included in Appendix II shall be in accordance with the provisions of this Article.

2. The export of any specimen of a species included in Appendix II shall require the prior grant and presentation of an export permit. An export permit shall only be granted when the following conditions have been met:

(a) a Scientific Authority of the State of export has advised that such export will not be detrimental to the survival of that species;

(b) a Management Authority of the State of export is satisfied that the specimen was not obtained in contravention of the laws of that State for the protection of fauna and flora; and

(c) a Management Authority of the State of export is satisfied that any living specimen will be so prepared and shipped as to minimize the risk of injury, damage to health or cruel treatment.

3. A Scientific Authority in each Party shall monitor both the export permits granted by that State for specimens of species included in Appendix II and the actual exports of such specimens. Whenever a Scientific Authority determines that the export of specimens of any such species should be limited in order to maintain that species throughout its range at a level consistent with its role in the ecosystems in which it occurs and well above the level at which that species might become eligible for inclusion in Appendix I, the Scientific Authority shall advise the appropriate Management Authority of suitable measures to be taken to limit the grant of export permits for specimens of that species.

4. The import of any specimen of a species included in Appendix II shall require the prior presentation of either an export permit or a re-export certificate.

5. The re-export of any specimen of a species included in Appendix II shall require the prior grant and presentation of a re-export certificate. A re-export certificate shall only be granted when the following conditions have been met:

(a) a Management Authority of the State of re-export is satisfied that the specimen was imported into that State in accordance with the provisions of the present Convention; and

(b) a Management Authority of the State of re-export is satisfied that any living specimen will be so prepared and shipped as to minimize the risk of injury, damage to health or cruel treatment.

6. The introduction from the sea of any specimen of a species included in Appendix II shall require the prior grant of a certificate from a Management Authority of the State of introduction. A certificate shall only be granted when the following conditions have been met:

(a) a Scientific Authority of the State of introduction advises that the introduction will not be detrimental to the survival of the species involved; and

(b) a Management Authority of the State of introduction is satisfied that any living specimen will be so handled as to minimize the risk of injury, damage to health or cruel treatment.

7. Certificates referred to in paragraph 6 of this Article may be granted on the advice of a Scientific Authority, in consultation with other national scientific authorities or, when appropriate, international scientific authorities, in respect of periods not exceeding one year for total numbers of specimens to be introduced in such periods.

Article V

Regulation of Trade in Specimens of Species included in Appendix III

1. All trade in specimens of species included in Appendix III shall be in accordance with the provisions of this Article.

2. The export of any specimen of a species included in Appendix III from any State which has included that species in Appendix III shall require the prior grant and presentation of an export permit. An export permit shall only be granted when the following conditions have been met:

(a) a Management Authority of the State of export is satisfied that the specimen was not obtained in contravention of the laws of that State for the protection of fauna and flora; and

(b) a Management Authority of the State of export is satisfied that any living specimen will be so prepared and shipped as to minimize the risk of injury, damage to health or cruel treatment.

3. The import of any specimen of a species included in Appendix III shall require, except in circumstances to which paragraph 4 of this Article applies, the prior presentation of a certificate of origin and, where the import is from a State which has included that species in Appendix III, an export permit.

4. In the case of re-export, a certificate granted by the Management Authority of the State of re-export that the specimen was processed in that State or is being re-exported shall be accepted by the State of import as evidence that the provisions of the present Convention have been complied with in respect of the specimen concerned.

Article VI

Permits and Certificates

1. Permits and certificates granted under the provisions of Articles III, IV, and V shall be in accordance with the provisions of this Article.

2. An export permit shall contain the information specified in the model set forth in Appendix IV, and may only be used for export within a period of six months from the date on which it was granted.

3. Each permit or certificate shall contain the title of the present Convention, the name and any identifying stamp of the Management Authority granting it and a control number assigned by the Management Authority.

4. Any copies of a permit or certificate issued by a Management Authority shall be clearly marked as copies only and no such copy may be used in place of the original, except to the extent endorsed thereon.

5. A separate permit or certificate shall be required for each consignment of specimens.

6. A Management Authority of the State of import of any specimen shall cancel and retain the export permit or re-export certificate and any corresponding import permit presented in respect of the import of that specimen.

7. Where appropriate and feasible a Management Authority may affix a mark upon any specimen to assist in identifying the specimen. For these purposes "mark" means any indelible imprint, lead seal or other suitable means of identifying a specimen, designed in such a way as to render its imitation by unauthorized persons as difficult as possible.

Article VII

Exemptions and Other Special Provisions Relating to Trade

1. The provisions of Articles III, IV and V shall not apply to the transit or transshipment of specimens through or in the territory of a Party while the specimens remain in Customs control.

2. Where a Management Authority of the State of export or re-export is satisfied that a specimen was acquired before the provisions of the present Convention applied to that specimen, the provisions of Articles III, IV and V shall not apply to that specimen where the Management Authority issues a certificate to that effect.

3. The provisions of Articles III, IV and V shall not apply to specimens that are personal or household effects. This exemption shall not apply where:

(a) in the case of specimens of a species included in Appendix I, they were acquired by the owner outside his State of usual residence, and are being imported into that State; or

(b) in the case of specimens of species included in Appendix II:

(i) they were acquired by the owner outside his State of usual residence and in a State where removal from the wild occurred;

(ii) they are being imported into the owner's State of usual residence; and

(iii) the State where removal from the wild occurred requires the prior grant of export permits before any export of such specimens;

unless a Management Authority is satisfied that the specimens were acquired before the provisions of the present Convention applied to such specimens.

4. Specimens of an animal species included in Appendix I bred in captivity for commercial purposes, or of a plant species included in Appendix I artificially propagated for commercial purposes, shall be deemed to be specimens of species included in Appendix II.

5. Where a Management Authority of the State of export is satisfied that any specimen of an animal species was bred in captivity or any specimen of a plant species was artificially propagated, or is a part of such an animal or plant or was derived

therefrom, a certificate by that Management Authority to that effect shall be accepted in lieu of any of the permits or certificates required under the provisions of Articles III, IV or V.

6. The provisions of Articles III, IV and V shall not apply to the non-commercial loan, donation or exchange between scientists or scientific institutions registered by a Management Authority of their State, of herbarium specimens, other preserved, dried or embedded museum specimens, and live plant material which carry a label issued or approved by a Management Authority.

7. A Management Authority of any State may waive the requirements of Articles III, IV and V and allow the movement without permits or certificates of specimens which form part of a travelling zoo, circus, menagerie, plant exhibition or other travelling exhibition provided that:

(a) the exporter or importer registers full details of such specimens with that Management Authority;

(b) the specimens are in either of the categories specified in paragraphs 2 or 5 of this Article; and

(c) the Management Authority is satisfied that any living specimen will be so transported and cared for as to minimize the risk of injury, damage to health or cruel treatment.

Article VIII

Measures to be Taken by the Parties,

1. The Parties shall take appropriate measures to enforce the provisions of the present Convention and to prohibit trade in specimens in violation thereof. These shall include measures:

(a) to penalize trade in, or possession of, such specimens, or both; and

(b) to provide for the confiscation or return to the State of export of such specimens.

2. In addition to the measures taken under paragraph 1 of this Article a Party may, when it deems it necessary, provide for any method of internal reimbursement for expenses incurred as a result of the confiscation of a specimen traded in violation of the measures taken in the application of the provisions of the present Convention.

3. As far as possible, the Parties shall ensure that specimens shall pass through any formalities required for trade with a minimum of delay. To facilitate such passage, a Party may designate ports of exit and ports of entry at which specimens must be presented for clearance. The Parties shall ensure further that all living specimens, during any period of transit, holding or shipment, are properly cared for so as to minimize the risk of injury, damage to health or cruel treatment.

4. Where a living specimen is confiscated as a result of measures referred to in paragraph 1 of this Article:

(a) the specimen shall be entrusted to a Management Authority of the State of confiscation;

(b) the Management Authority shall, after consultation with the State of export, return the specimen to that State at the expense of that State, or to a rescue centre or such other place as the Management Authority deems appropriate and consistent with the purposes of the present Convention; and

(c) the Management Authority may obtain the advice of a Scientific Authority, or may, whenever it considers it desirable, consult the Secretariat in order to facilitate the decision under sub-paragraph (b) of this paragraph, including the choice of a rescue centre or other place.

5. A rescue centre as referred to in paragraph 4 of this Article means an institution designated by a Management Authority to look after the welfare of living specimens, particularly those that have been confiscated.

6. Each Party shall maintain records of trade in specimens of species included in Appendices I, II and III which shall cover:

(a) the names and addresses of exporters and importers; and

(b) the number and type of permits and certificates granted; the States with which such trade occurred; the numbers or quantities and types of specimens, names of species as included in Appendices I, II and III and, where applicable, the size and sex of the specimens in question.

7. Each Party shall prepare periodic reports on its implementation of the present Convention and shall transmit to the Secretariat:

(a) an annual report containing a summary of the information specified in sub-paragraph (b) of paragraph 6 of this Article; and

(b) a biennial report on legislative, regulatory and administrative measures taken to enforce the provisions of the present Convention.

8. The information referred to in paragraph 7 of this Article shall be available to the public where this is not inconsistent with the law of the Party concerned.

Article IX

Management and Scientific Authorities

1. Each Party shall designate for the purposes of the present Convention:

(a) one or more Management Authorities competent to grant permits or certificates on behalf of that Party; and

(b) one or more Scientific Authorities.

2. A State depositing an instrument of ratification, acceptance, approval or accession shall at that time inform the Depositary Government of the name and address of the Management Authority authorized to communicate with other Parties and with the Secretariat.

3. Any changes in the designations or authorizations under the provisions of this Article shall be communicated by the Party concerned to the Secretariat for transmission to all other Parties.

4. Any Management Authority referred to in paragraph 2 of this Article shall if so requested by the Secretariat or the Management Authority of another Party, communicate to it impression of stamps, seals or other devices used to authenticate permits or certificates.

Article X

Trade with States not Party to the Convention

Where export or re-export is to, or import is from, a State not a Party to the present Convention, comparable documentation issued by the competent authorities in that State which substantially conforms with the requirements of the present Convention for permits and certificates may be accepted in lieu thereof by any Party.

Article XI

Conference of the Parties

1. The Secretariat shall call a meeting of the Conference of the Parties not later than two years after the entry into force of the present Convention.

2. Thereafter the Secretariat shall convene regular meetings at least once every two years, unless the Conference decides otherwise, and extraordinary meetings at any time on the written request of at least one-third of the Parties.

3. At meetings, whether regular or extraordinary, the Parties shall review the implementation of the present Convention and may:

(a) make such provision as may be necessary to enable the Secretariat to carry out its duties and adopt financial provisions;

(b) consider and adopt amendments to Appendices I and II in accordance with Article XV;

(c) review the progress made towards the restoration and conservation of the species included in Appendices I, II and III;

(d) receive and consider any reports presented by the Secretariat or by any Party; and

(e) where appropriate, make recommendations for improving the effectiveness of the present Convention.

4. At each regular meeting, the Parties may determine the time and venue of the next regular meeting to be held in accordance with the provisions of paragraph 2 of this Article.

5. At any meeting, the Parties may determine and adopt rules of procedure for the meeting.

6. The United Nations, its Specialized Agencies and the International Atomic Energy Agency, as well as any State not a Party to the present Convention, may be represented at meetings of the Conference by observers, who shall have the right to participate but not to vote.

7. Any body or agency technically qualified in protection, conservation or management of wild fauna and flora, in the following categories, which has informed the Secretariat of its desire to be represented at meetings of the Conference by observers, shall be admitted unless at least one-third of the Parties present object:

(a) international agencies or bodies, either governmental or non-governmental, and national governmental agencies and bodies; and

(b) national non-governmental agencies or bodies which have been approved for this purpose by the State in which they are located. Once admitted, these observers shall have the right to participate but not to vote.

Article XII

The Secretariat

1. Upon entry into force of the present Convention, a Secretariat shall be provided by the Executive Director of the United Nations Environment Programme. To the extent and in the manner he considers appropriate, he may be assisted by suitable inter-governmental or non-governmental international or national agencies and bodies technically qualified in protection, conservation and management of wild fauna and flora.

2. The functions of the Secretariat shall be:

(a) to arrange for and service meetings of the Parties;

(b) to perform the functions entrusted to it under the provisions of Articles XV and XVI of the present Convention;

(c) to undertake scientific and technical studies in accordance with programmes authorized by the Conference of the parties as will contribute to the implementation of the present Convention, including studies concerning standards for appropriate preparation and shipment of living specimens and the means of identifying specimens;

(d) to study the reports of Parties and to request from Parties such further information with respect thereto as it deems necessary to ensure implementation of the present Convention;

(e) to invite the attention of the Parties to any matter pertaining to the aims of the present Convention;

(f) to publish periodically and distribute to the Parties current editions of Appendices I, II and III together with any information which will facilitate identification of specimens of species included in those Appendices;

(g) to prepare annual reports to the Parties on its work and on the implementation of the present Convention and such other reports as meetings of the Parties may request;

(h) to make recommendations for the implementation of the aims and provisions of the present Convention, including the exchange of information of a scientific or technical nature;

(i) to perform any other function as may be entrusted to it by the Parties.

Article XIII

International Measures

1. When the Secretariat in the light of information received is satisfied that any species included in Appendices I or II is being affected adversely by trade in specimens of that species or that the provisions of the present Convention are not being effectively implemented, it shall communicate such information to the authorized Management Authority of the Party or Parties concerned.

2. When any Party receives a communication as indicated in paragraph 1 of this Article, it shall, as soon as possible, inform the Secretariat of any relevant facts insofar as its laws permit and, where appropriate, propose remedial action. Where the Party considers that an inquiry is desirable, such inquiry may be carried out by one or more persons expressly authorized by the Party.

3. The information provided by the Party or resulting from any inquiry as specified in paragraph 2 of this Article shall be reviewed by the next Conference of the Parties which may make whatever recommendations it deems appropriate.

Article XIV

Effect on Domestic Legislation and International Conventions

1. The provisions of the present Convention shall in no way affect the right of Parties to adopt:

(a) stricter domestic measures regarding the conditions for trade, taking, possession or transport of specimens of species included in Appendices I, II and III, or the complete prohibition thereof; or

(b) domestic measures restricting or prohibiting trade, taking, possession, or transport of species not included in Appendices I, II or III.

2. The provisions of the present Convention shall in no way affect the provisions of any domestic measures or the obligations of Parties deriving from any treaty, convention, or international agreement relating to other aspects of trade, taking, possession, or transport of specimens which is in force or subsequently may enter into force for any Party including any measure pertaining to the Customs, public health, veterinary or plant quarantine fields.

3. The provisions of the present Convention shall in no way affect the provisions of, or the obligations deriving from, any treaty, convention or international agreement concluded or which may be concluded between States creating a union or regional trade agreement establishing or maintaining a common external customs control and removing customs control between the parties thereto insofar as they relate to trade among the States members of that union or agreement.

4. A State Party to the present Convention, which is also a Party to any other treaty, convention or international agreement which is in force at the time of the coming into force of the present Convention and under the provisions of which protection is afforded to marine species included in Appendix II, shall be relieved of the obligations imposed on it under the provisions of the present Convention with respect to trade in specimens of species included in Appendix II that are taken by ships registered in that State and in accordance with the provisions of such other treaty, convention or international agreement.

5. Notwithstanding the provisions of Articles III, IV and V, any export of a specimen taken in accordance with paragraph 4 of this Article shall only require a certificate from a Management Authority of the State of introduction to the effect that the specimen was taken in accordance with the provisions of the other treaty, convention or international agreement in question.

6. Nothing in the present Convention shall prejudice the codification and development of the law of the sea by the United Nations Conference on the Law of the Sea convened pursuant to Resolution 2750 C(XXV) of the General Assembly of the United Nations nor the present or future claims and legal views of any State concerning the law of the sea and the nature and extent of coastal and flag State jurisdiction.

Article XV

Amendments to Appendices I and II

1. The following provisions shall apply in relation to amendments to Appendices I and II at meetings of the Conference of the Parties:

(a) Any Party may propose an amendment to Appendix I or II for consideration at the next meeting. The text of the proposed amendment shall be communicated to the Secretariat at least 150 days before the meeting. The Secretariat shall consult the other Parties and interested bodies on the amendment in accordance with the provisions of sub-paragraphs (b) and (c) of paragraph 2 of this Article and shall communicate the response to all Parties not later than 30 days before the meeting.

(b) Amendments shall be adopted by a two-thirds majority of Parties present and voting. For these purposes "Parties present and voting" means Parties present and casting an affirmative or negative vote. Parties abstaining from voting shall not be counted among the two-thirds required for adopting an amendment.

(c) Amendments adopted at a meeting shall enter into force 90 days after that meeting for all Parties except those which make a reservation in accordance with paragraph 3 of this Article.

2. The following provisions shall apply in relation to amendments to Appendices I and II between meetings of the Conference of the Parties:

(a) Any Party may propose an amendment to Appendix I or II for consideration between meetings by the postal procedures set forth in this paragraph.

(b) For marine species, the Secretariat shall, upon receiving the text of the proposed amendment, immediately communicate it to the Parties. It shall also consult inter-governmental bodies having a function in relation to those species especially with a view to obtaining scientific data these bodies may be able to provide and to ensuring co-ordination with any conservation measures enforced by such bodies. The Secretariat shall communicate the views expressed and data provided by these bodies and its own findings and recommendations to the Parties as soon as possible.

(c) For species other than marine species, the Secretariat shall, upon receiving the text of the proposed amendment, immediately communicate it to the Parties, and, as soon as possible thereafter, its own recommendations.

(d) Any Party may, within 60 days of the date on which the Secretariat communicated its recommendations to the Parties under sub-paragraphs (b) or (c) of this paragraph, transmit to the Secretariat any comments on the proposed amendment together with any relevant scientific data and information.

(e) The Secretariat shall communicate the replies received together with its own recommendations to the Parties as soon as possible.

(f) If no objection to the proposed amendment is received by the Secretariat within 30 days of the date the replies and recommendations were communicated under the provisions of sub-paragraph (e) of this paragraph, the amendment shall enter into force 90 days later for all Parties except those which make a reservation in accordance with paragraph 3 of this Article.

(g) If an objection by any Party is received by the Secretariat, the proposed amendment shall be submitted to a postal vote in accordance with the provisions of sub-paragraphs (h), (i) and (j) of this paragraph.

(h) The Secretariat shall notify the Parties that notification of objection has been received.

(i) Unless the Secretariat receives the votes for, against or in abstention from at least one-half of the Parties within 60 days of the date of notification under sub-paragraph (h) of this paragraph, the proposed amendment shall be referred to the next meeting of the Conference for further consideration.

(j) Provided that votes are received from one-half of the Parties, the amendment shall be adopted by a two-thirds majority of Parties casting an affirmative or negative vote.

(k) The Secretariat shall notify all Parties of the result of the vote.

(*l*) If the proposed amendment is adopted it shall enter into force 90 days after the date of the notification by the Secretariat of its acceptance for all Parties except those which make a reservation in accordance with paragraph 3 of this Article.

3. During the period of 90 days provided for by sub-paragraph (c) of paragraph 1 or sub-paragraph (*l*) of paragraph 2 of this Article any Party may by notification in writing to the Depositary Government make a reservation with respect to the amendment. Until such reservation is withdrawn the Party shall be treated as a State not a Party to the present Convention with respect to trade in the species concerned.

Article XVI

Appendix III and Amendments thereto

1. Any Party may at any time submit to the Secretariat a list of species which it identifies as being subject to regulation within its jurisdiction for the purpose mentioned in paragraph 3 of Article II. Appendix III shall include the names of the Parties submitting the species for inclusion therein, the scientific names of the species so submitted, and any parts or derivatives of the animals or plants concerned that are specified in relation to the species for the purposes of sub-paragraph (b) of Article I.

2. Each list submitted under the provisions of paragraph 1 of this Article shall be communicated to the Parties by the Secretariat as soon as possible after receiving it. The list shall take effect as part of Appendix III 90 days after the date of such communication. At any time after the communication of such list, any Party may by notification in writing to the Depositary Government enter a reservation with respect to any species or any parts or derivatives, and until such reservation is withdrawn, the State shall be treated as a State not a Party to the present Convention with respect to trade in the species or part or derivative concerned.

3. A Party which has submitted a species for inclusion in Appendix III may withdraw it at any time by notification to the Secretariat which shall communicate the withdrawal to all Parties. The withdrawal shall take effect 30 days after the date of such communication.

4. Any Party submitting a list under the provisions of paragraph 1 of this Article shall submit to the Secretariat a copy of all domestic laws and regulations applicable to the protection of such species, together with any interpretations which the Party may deem appropriate or the Secretariat may request. The Party shall, for as long as the species in question is included in Appendix III, submit any amendments of such laws and regulations or any new interpretations as they are adopted.

Article XVII

Amendment of the Convention

1. An extraordinary meeting of the Conference of the Parties shall be convened by the Secretariat on the written request of at least one-third of the Parties to consider and adopt amendments to the present Convention. Such amendments shall be adopted by a two-thirds majority of Parties present and voting. For these purposes "Parties present and voting" means Parties present and casting an affirmative or negative vote. Parties abstaining from voting shall not be counted among the two-thirds required for adopting an amendment.

2. The text of any proposed amendment shall be communicated by the Secretariat to all Parties at least 90 days before the meeting.

3. An amendment shall enter into force for the Parties which have accepted it 60 days after two-thirds of the Parties have deposited an instrument of acceptance of the amendment with the Depositary Government. Thereafter, the amendment shall enter into force for any other Party 60 days after that Party deposits its instrument of acceptance of the amendment.

Article XVIII

Resolution of Disputes

1. Any dispute which may arise between two or more Parties with respect to the interpretation or application of the provisions of the present Convention shall be subject to negotiation between the Parties involved in the dispute.

2. If the dispute cannot be resolved in accordance with paragraph 1 of this Article, the Parties may, by mutual consent, submit the dispute to arbitration, in particular that of the Permanent Court of Arbitration at The Hague, and the Parties submitting the dispute shall be bound by the arbitral decision.

Article XIX

Signature

The present Convention shall be open for signature at Washington until 30th April 1973 and thereafter at Berne until 31st December 1974.

Article XX

Ratification, Acceptance, Approval

The present Convention shall be subject to ratification, acceptance or approval. Instruments of ratification, acceptance or approval shall be deposited with the Government of the Swiss Confederation which shall be the Depositary Government.

Article XXI

Accession

The present Convention shall be open indefinitely for accession. Instruments of accession shall be deposited with the Depositary Government.[c]

Article XXII

Entry into Force

1. The present Convention shall enter into force 90 days after the date of deposit of the tenth instrument of ratification, acceptance, approval or accession, with the Depositary Government.

2. For each State which ratifies, accepts or approves the present Convention or accedes thereto after the deposit of the tenth instrument of ratification, acceptance, approval or accession, the present Convention shall enter into force 90 days after the deposit by such State of its instrument of ratification, acceptance, approval or accession.

Article XXIII

Reservations

1. The provisions of the present Convention shall not be subject to general reservations. Specific reservations may be entered in accordance with the provisions of this Article and Articles XV and XVI.

2. Any State may, on depositing its instrument of ratification, acceptance, approval or accession, enter a specific reservation with regard to:

c. The Amendments to the Convention adopted in Gaborone further adds to Article XXI, after the words "Depositary Government," the following 5 paragraphs:

1. This Convention shall be open for accession by regional economic integration organizations constituted by sovereign States which have competence in respect of the negotiation, conclusion and implementation of international agreements in matters transferred to them by their Member States and covered by this Convention.

2. In their instruments of accession, such organizations shall declare the extent of their competence with respect to the matters governed by the Convention. These organizations shall also inform the Depositary Government of any substantial modification in the extent of their competence. Notifications by regional economic integration organizations concerning their competence with respect to matters governed by this Convention and modifications thereto shall be distributed to the Parties by the Depositary Government.

3. In matters within their competence, such regional economic organizations shall exercise the rights and fulfill the obligations which this Convention attributes to their Member States, which are Parties to the Convention. In such cases the Member States of the organization shall not be entitled to exercise such rights individually.

4. In the fields of their competence, regional economic integration organizations shall exercise their right to vote with a number of votes equal to the number of their Member States which are Parties to the Convention. Such organizations shall not exercise their right to vote if their Member States exercise theirs, and vice versa.

5. Any reference to 'Party' in the sense used in Article 1(h) of this Convention to 'State'/'States' or to 'State Party'/'States Parties' to the Convention shall be construed as including a reference to any regional economic organization having competence in respect of the negotiation, conclusion and application of international agreements in matters covered by this Convention.

(a) any species included in Appendix I, II or III; or

(b) any parts or derivatives specified in relation to a species included in Appendix III.

3. Until a Party withdraws its reservation entered under the provisions of this Article, it shall be treated as a State not a Party to the present Convention with respect to trade in the particular species or parts or derivatives specified in such reservation.

Article XXIV

Denunciation

Any Party may denounce the present Convention by written notification to the Depositary Government at any time. The denunciation shall take effect twelve months after the Depositary Government has received the notification.

Article XXV

Depositary

1. The original of the present Convention, in the Chinese, English, French, Russian and Spanish languages, each version being equally authentic, shall be deposited with the Depositary Government, which shall transmit certified copies thereof to all States that have signed it or deposited instruments of accession to it.

2. The Depositary Government shall inform all signatory and acceding States and the Secretariat of signatures, deposit of instruments of ratification, acceptance, approval or accession, entry into force of the present Convention, amendments thereto, entry and withdrawal of reservations and notifications of denunciation.

3. As soon as the present Convention enters into force, a certified copy thereof shall be transmitted by the Depositary Government to the Secretariat of the United Nations for registration and publication in accordance with Article 102 of the Charter of the United Nations.

APPENDICES I, II AND III TO THE CONVENTION ON INTERNATIONAL TRADE IN ENDANGERED SPECIES OF WILD FAUNA AND FLORA

The list of endangered species provided here is reproduced from information published by the United States government at 50 C.F.R. s 23.23 (1999). The official list is maintained by the CITES secretariat.

The list of species is organized as follows:

Major group	Subgroups
Mammals	Orders, in taxonomic sequence.
Birds	Orders, in taxonomic sequence.
Reptiles	Orders, in taxonomic sequence.
Amphibians	Orders, in taxonomic sequence.
Fishes	Orders, in taxonomic sequence.
Molluscs	Classes.
Arthropods	Classes.
Plants	Families, in alphabetical sequence.

Within each Subgroup, lower taxonomic units (mainly genera, but sometimes families or subfamilies) are listed in alphabetical sequence. Within genera, the scientific names of the species are listed in alphabetical sequence. The scientific name takes precedence over the common name in determining if a species is listed.

The appendix column of the list includes the annotation "pe" (=possibly extinct) for certain species. It also contains the names of Parties including species in Appendix III.

Species	Common name	Appendix	First listing date (month/day/year)
CLASS MAMMALIA:	MAMMALS:		
Order Monotremata:	Monotremes:		
Zaglossus spp.	Spiny anteaters	II	2/4/77
Order Dasyuromorphia:	Dunnarts (Marsupial-mice), Tasmanian wolf:		
Sminthopsis longicaudata	Long-tailed marsupial-mouse, Long-tailed dunnart	I	7/1/75
S. psammophila	Large desert marsupial-mouse, Sandhill dunnart	I	7/1/75
Thylacinus cynocephalus	Tasmanian wolf, Thylacine	I pe	7/1/75
Order Peramelemorphia:	Bandicoots:		
Chaeropus ecaudatus	Pig-footed bandicoot	I pe	7/1/75
Macrotis lagotis	Rabbit bandicoot, Bilby	I	7/1/75
M. leucura	Lesser rabbit bandicoot, Yallara	I	7/1/75
Perameles bougainville	Barred bandicoot, Long-nosed bandicoot, Mari	I	7/1/75
Order Diprotodontia:	Kangaroos, Wombats, Wallabies, Cuscuses, Rat-kangaroos, etc.:		
Bettongia spp. (except species listed below)	Rat-kangaroo	I	6/28/79
B. lesueur	Lesueur's rat-kangaroo, Boodie	I	7/1/75
B. penicillata (=tropica)	Brush-tailed rat-kangaroo, Woylie	I	7/1/75
Caloprymnus campestris	Desert rat-kangaroo	I pe	7/1/75
D. inustus	Grizzled tree kangaroo	II	7/1/75
D. ursinus	Vogelkop tree kangaroo	II	7/1/75
Lagorchestes hirsutus	Western hare wallaby, Wurrup	I	7/1/75
Lagostrophus fasciatus	Banded hare wallaby, Munning	I	7/1/75
Lasiorhinus krefftii	Queensland hairy-nosed wombat	I	7/1/75
Onychogalea fraenata	Bridled nail-tailed wallaby	I	7/1/75
O. lunata	Crescent nail-tailed wallaby	I	7/1/75
Phalanger maculatus (see Spilocuscus maculatus)			
P. orientalis	Gray cuscus	II	6/28/79
Spilocuscus maculatus	Spotted cuscus	II	6/28/79
Order Scandentia	Tree shrews	II	2/4/77
Tupaiidae spp.	Tree shrews	II	2/4/77
Order Chiroptera:	Bats:		
Acerodon spp. (all species except those in App. I)	Flying foxes	II	1/18/90

Species	Common name	Appendix	Date
A. jubatus	Golden-capped fruit bat	I	1/18/90
A. lucifer	Panay giant fruit bat	I pe	1/18/90
Pteropus spp. (all species except those in App. I or with earlier date in App. II)	Flying foxes	II	1/18/90
P. insularis	Truk flying fox	I	10/22/87
P. macrotis	Big-eared flying fox	II	10/22/87
P. mariannus	Mariana flying fox, Mariana fruit bat	I	10/22/87
P. molossinus	Ponape flying fox	I	10/22/87
P. phaeocephalus	Mortlock flying fox	I	10/22/87
P. pilosus	Palau flying fox	I	10/22/87
P. samoensis	Samoa flying fox	I	10/22/87
P. tokudae	Little Mariana fruit bat, Tokuda's flying fox	II	10/22/87
P. tonganus	Insular flying fox, Tonga fruit bat	I	10/22/87
Vampyrops lineatus	White-lined bat	III (Uruguay)	7/14/76
Order Primates (formerly including order Scandentia, above):	Primates: Monkeys, Apes, etc.:		
All species of primates except those in App. I or with earlier date in App. II	A4/77.		
Allocebus spp	Hairy-eared dwarf lemur	I	7/1/75
Alouatta palliata (=villosa)	Mantled howler monkey	I	7/1/75
A. pigra	Black howler monkey	I	7/1/75
Ateles geoffroyi frontatus	Black-handed spider monkey	I	7/1/75
A. geoffroyi panamensis	Black-handed spider monkey	I	7/1/75
Avahi spp	Avahis, Woolly lemurs	I	7/1/75
Brachyteles arachnoides	Woolly spider monkey	I	7/1/75
Cacajao spp	Uakaris	I	7/1/75
Callimico goeldii	Goeldi's monkey, Callimico	I	7/1/75
Callithrix aurita (=C. jacchus aurita)	White-eared marmoset	I	2/4/77
C. flaviceps (=C. jacchus flaviceps)	Buff-headed marmoset	I	2/4/77
Cebus capucinus	White-throated capuchin	II	7/1/75
Cercocebus galeritus galeritus	Tana River mangabey, Agile mangabey	I	7/1/75
Cercopithecus diana (=C. roloway)	Diana monkey	I	2/4/77
Cheirogaleus spp	Dwarf lemurs	I	7/1/75
Chiropotes albinasus	White-nosed saki	I	7/1/75
Colobus (see Procolobus)			
Daubentonia madagascariensis	Aye-aye	I	7/1/75

Eulemur spp	Lemurs	I	7/1/75
Gorilla gorilla	Gorilla	I	7/1/75
Hapalemur spp	Gentle lemurs	I	7/1/75
Hylobates spp	Gibbons, Siamang	I	7/1/75
Indri spp	Indri	I	7/1/75
Lagothrix flavicauda	Yellow-tailed woolly monkey	I	2/4/77
Lemur spp	Lemurs	I	7/1/75
Leontopithecus (=Leontideus) spp	Golden lion tamarin	I	7/1/75
Lepilemur spp	Sportive lemur, Weasel lemur	I	7/1/75
Loris tardigradus	Slender loris	II	7/1/75
Macaca silenus	Lion-tailed macaque	I	7/1/75
M. sylvanus	Barbary ape	II	7/1/75
Mandrillus leucophaeus	Drill	I	2/4/77
M. sphinx	Mandrill	I	2/4/77
Microcebus spp	Mouse lemurs	I	7/1/75
Nasalis (=Simias) concolor	Pagi Island langur	I	7/1/75
N. larvatus	Proboscis monkey	I	7/1/75
Nycticebus coucang	Slow loris	II	7/1/75
Pan spp	Chimpanzee, Bonobo	I	7/1/75
Papio (see Mandrillus)			
Phaner sp	Fork-marked mouse lemurs	I	7/1/75
Pongo pygmaeus	Orangutan	I	7/1/75
Presbytis entellus (see Semnopithecus entellus)			
P. pileata (see Trachypithecus pileatus)			
P. potenziani	Long-tailed langur, Mentawai leaf monkey	I	2/4/77
Presbytis (other species) (see Trachypithecus)			
Procolobus badius gordonorum	Uhehe red colobus	II	7/1/75
P. pennantii kirki (=C. badius kirkii)	Zanzibar red colobus	I	7/1/75
P. rufomitratus (=C. badius rufomitratus)	Tana River red colobus	I	7/1/75
P. verus	Olive colobus	II	7/1/75
Propithecus spp	Sifakas	I	7/1/75
Pygathrix (=Rhinopithecus) spp. (except those species with earlier date)	Snub-nosed langurs	I	2/4/77
P. nemaeus	Douc langur	I	7/1/75
P. roxellana	Sichuan snub-nosed langur	I	7/1/75
Saguinus bicolor	Pied tamarin	I	2/4/77
S. geoffroyi	Geoffroy's marmoset	I	2/4/77
S. leucopus	White-footed tamarin, Silvery-brown bare-face tamarin	I	2/4/77
S. oedipus (including S. oedipus geoffroyi)	Cotton-top tamarin	I	2/4/77
Saimiri oerstedii	Red-backed squirrel monkey	I	7/1/75

Semnopithecus entellus	Gray langur, Common Indian langur	I	7/1/75
Symphalangus (see Hylobates)	....	....	....
Trachypithecus geei	Golden langur	I	7/1/75
T. johnii	Nilgiri langur ..	II	7/1/75
T. pileatus	Capped langur ...	I	7/1/75
Tupaiidae spp. (see order Scandentia, above)	....	....	....
Varecia spp................	Lemurs	I	7/1/75
Order Xenarthra:	Anteaters, Sloths, Armadillos:	....	....
Bradypus variegatus (=boliviensis or griseus)	Three-toed sloth	II	7/1/75
Cabassous centralis	Five-toed armadillo	III (Costa Rica)	10/28/76
C. tatouay (=gymnurus)	Naked-tailed armadillo	III (Uruguay)	7/14/76
Chaetophractus nationi (subject to a zero export quota)	Hairy armadillo .	II	9/18/97
Choloepus hoffmanni	Two-toed sloth ..	III (Costa Rica)	10/28/76
Myrmecophaga tridactyla ...	Giant anteater ..	II	7/1/75
Priodontes maximus (=giganteus)	Giant armadillo .	I	7/1/75
Tamandua tetradactyla (=T. mexicana)	Tamandua, Collared anteater	III (Guatemala)	4/23/81
Order Pholidota:	Pangolins, Scaly Anteaters:	....	....
Manis spp..................	Pangolins	II	7/1/75
Order Lagomorpha:	Rabbits, Hares: ..	....	....
Caprolagus hispidus	Hispid hare, Assam rabbit ...	I	7/1/75
Romerolagus diazi	Mexican volcano rabbit	I	7/1/75
Order Rodentia:	Rodents:	....	....
Agouti (=Cuniculus) paca ..	Greater paca, Spotted cavy ...	III (Honduras)	4/13/87
Anomalurus beecrofti	Beecroft's scaly-tailed flying squirrel	III (Ghana)	2/26/76
A. derbianus	Lord Derby's scaly-tailed flying squirrel	III (Ghana)	2/26/76
A. pelii	Pel's scaly-tailed flying squirrel	III (Ghana)	2/26/76
Chinchilla spp. (populations of South America, except domesticated specimens) .	Chinchillas	I	2/4/77
Cynomys mexicanus	Mexican prairie dog	I	7/1/75
Dasyprocta punctata	Common agouti ...	III (Honduras)	4/13/87
Epixerus ebii	African palm squirrel	III (Ghana)	2/26/76
Hystrix cristata	Crested porcupine	III (Ghana)	2/26/76
Idiurus macrotis	Long-eared pygmy flying squirrel	III (Ghana) .	2/26/76
Leporillus conditor	Australian stick-nest rat .	I	7/1/75
Marmota caudata	Long-tailed marmot	III (India)	3/16/89
M. himalayana	Himalayan marmot	III (India)	3/16/89

Pseudomys praeconis	Shark Bay mouse	I	7/1/75
Ratufa spp	Giant squirrels	II	7/1/75
Sciurus deppei	Deppe's squirrel	III (Costa Rica)	10/28/76
Sphiggurus (=Coendou) mexicanus	Middle American prehensile-tailed porcupine, Coendou	III (Honduras)	4/13/87
S. (=Coendou) spinosus	Prehensile-tailed porcupine	III (Uruguay)	7/14/76
Xeromys myoides	False water rat	I	7/1/75
Zyzomys pedunculatus	Australian native mouse, McDonnell Range rock rat	I	7/1/75
Order Cetacea:	Whales, Porpoises, Dolphins:		
All species except those in App. I or with earlier date in App. II	All whales, porpoises, and dolphins not listed below	II	6/28/79
Balaena mysticetus	Bowhead whale	I	7/1/75
Balaenoptera acutorostrata (all populations except that of West Greenland: entry into force as App. I on 1/1/86)	Minke whale	I	6/28/79
B. borealis	Sei whale	I	2/4/77
B. edeni	Bryde's whale	I	6/28/79
B. musculus	Blue whale	I	7/1/75
B. physalus	Fin whale	I	2/4/77
Berardius spp	Beaked whales	I	6/28/79
Caperea marginata (entry into force as App. I on 1/1/86)	Pygmy right whale	I	6/28/79
Eschrichtius robustus (=glaucus)	Gray whale	I	7/1/75
Eubalaena (=Balaena) spp	Right whales	I	7/1/75
Hyperoodon spp	Bottle-nosed whales	I	6/28/79
Lipotes vexillifer	White flag dolphin, Chinese river dolphin	I	6/28/79
Megaptera novaeangliae	Humpback whale	I	7/1/75
Monodon monoceros	Narwhal	II	11/16/75
Neophocaena phocaenoides	Finless porpoise	I	6/28/79
Phocoena sinus	Gulf of California harbor porpoise, Cochita	I	6/28/79
Physeter catodon (=macrocephalus)	Sperm whale	I	2/4/77
Platanista spp	Ganges and Indus River dolphins	I	7/1/75
Pontoporia (=Stenodelphis) blainvillei	La Plata River dolphin	II	7/14/76
Sotalia spp	Humpbacked dolphins	I	6/28/79
Sousa spp	Humpbacked dolphins	I	6/28/79
Order Carnivora:	Carnivores: Cats, Bears, etc.:		
Acinonyx jubatus	Cheetah	I	7/1/75
Ailuropoda melanoleuca	Giant panda	I	3/14/84
Ailurus fulgens	Lesser panda	I	7/1/75
Aonyx congicus (=microdon) (populations of Cameroon and Nigeria)	West African "clawless" otter	I	7/1/75

Arctictis binturong	Binturong	III (India)	3/16/89
Bassaricyon gabbii	Bushy-tailed olingo	III (Costa Rica)	10/28/76
Bassariscus sumichrasti	Cacomistle	III (Costa Rica)	10/28/76
Canis aureus	Golden jackal	III (India)	3/16/89
C. lupus (all subspecies and populations except those listed below)	Gray wolf	II	2/4/77
C. lupus (India, Pakistan, Bhutan, and Nepal populations)	Gray wolf	I	2/4/77
C. lupus crassodon	Gray wolf, Vancouver Island gray wolf	II	7/1/75
C. lupus irremotus	Gray wolf, Rocky Mountain gray wolf	II	7/1/75
C. lupus monstrabilis	Gray wolf	II	7/1/75
C. lupus pallipes	Gray wolf, Middle East gray wolf	II	7/1/75
Caracal (=Felis) caracal (Asian population)	Caracal	I	7/1/75
Catopuma (=Felis) temminckii	Asian golden cat	I	7/1/75
Cerdocyon thous	Crab-eating fox	II	6/11/92
Chrysocyon brachyurus	Maned wolf	II	7/1/75
Civettictis (=Viverra) civetta	African civet	III (Botswana)	4/24/78
Conepatus humboldtii	Humboldt's hognose skunk	II	6/28/79
Cryptoprocta ferox	Fossa	II	2/4/77
Cuon alpinus	Dhole	II	7/1/75
Cynogale bennettii	Otter civet	II	7/1/75
Dusicyon thous (see Cerdocyon thous)			
Dusicyon (other species) (see Pseudalopex)			
Eira barbara	Tayra	III (Honduras)	4/13/87
Enhydra lutris nereis	Southern sea otter	I	7/1/75
Eupleres goudotii (=major)	Malagasy mongoose	II	2/4/77
Felidae spp. (all species in family except Felis catus or those in App. I or with earlier date in App. II)	Cats (not including House cats)	II	2/4/77
Felis (see also the following genera, formerly included in Felis: Caracal, Catopuma, Herpailurus, Leopardus, Lynx, Oncifelis, Oreailurus, Pardofelis, Prionailurus, and Puma)			
F. nigripes	Black-footed cat	I	7/1/75
Fossa fossana (=fossa)	Fanaloka	II	2/4/77
Galictis vittata (=allamandi)	Grison	III (Costa Rica)	10/28/76
Helarctos malayanus	Sun bear	I	7/1/75
Hemigalus derbyanus	Banded palm civet	II	2/4/77
Herpailurus (=Felis) yaguarondi (North and Central American populations)	Jaguarundi	I	7/1/75
H. yaguarondi (South American populations)	Jaguarundi	II	7/1/75

Herpestes brachyurus fusca (=H. fuscus)	Indian brown mongoose	III (India)	3/16/89
H. edwardsii	Indian gray mongoose	III (India)	3/16/89
H. javanicus auropunctata (=H. auropunctatus)	Small Indian mongoose	III (India)	3/16/89
H. smithii	Ruddy mongoose	III (India)	3/16/89
H. urva	Crab-eating mongoose	III (India)	3/16/89
H. vitticollis	Stripe-necked mongoose	III (India)	3/16/89
Hyaena (see Parahyaena)			
Leopardus (=Felis) pardalis (except subspecies with earlier date)	Ocelot	I	2/4/77
L. pardalis mearnsi	Ocelot	I	7/1/75
L. pardalis mitis	Brazilian ocelot	I	7/1/75
L. tigrinus (=Felis tigrina) (except subspecies with earlier date)	Tiger cat, Little spotted cat	I	2/4/77
L. tigrinus oncilla	Tiger cat	I	7/1/75
L. wiedii (except subspecies with earlier date)	Margay	I	2/4/77
L. wiedii nicaraguae	Central American margay	I	7/1/75
L. wiedii salvinia	Guatemalan margay	I	7/1/75
Lontra felina	Marine otter	I	7/1/75
L. longicaudis	Long-tailed otter, Neotropical otter	I	7/1/75
L. provocax	Southern river otter, South American river otter	I	7/1/75
Lutra lutra	European river otter	I	2/4/77
Lutra (other species) (see Lontra)			
Lutrinae spp. (all species except those in App. I)	Otters	II	2/4/77
Lynx pardinus (=Felis pardina)	Spanish lynx, Iberian lynx	I	2/4/77
L. rufus (=Felis rufa) escuinapae	Mexican bobcat	II	7/1/75
Martes flavigula (including M. gwatkinsi)	Yellow-throated marten	III (India)	3/16/89
M. foina intermedia	Beech marten	III (India)	3/16/89
Mellivora capensis	Honey badger, Ratel	III (Ghana and Botswana)	2/26/76
Melursus (=Ursus) ursinus	Sloth bear	I	9/21/88
Mustela altaica	Mountain weasel	III (India)	3/16/89
M. erminea ferghanae	Ermine	III (India)	3/16/89
M. kathiah	Yellow-bellied weasel	III (India)	3/16/89
M. nigripes	Black-footed ferret	I	7/1/75
M. sibirica	Siberian weasel	III (India)	3/16/89
Nasua narica	Common coati, Coatimundi	III (Honduras)	4/13/87
N. nasua solitaria	Coatimundi	III (Uruguay)	7/14/76
Neofelis nebulosa	Clouded leopard	I	7/1/75

Species	Common name	Appendix	Date
Oncifelis (=Felis) geoffroyi	Geoffroy's cat	I	2/4/77
Oreailurus (=Felis) jacobita	Andean cat	I	7/1/75
Paguma larvata	Masked palm civet	III (India)	3/16/89
Panthera leo persica	Asiatic lion, Indian lion	I	7/1/75
P. onca	Jaguar	I	7/1/75
P. pardus	Leopard	I	7/1/75
P. tigris	Tiger	I	7/1/75
P. uncia (see Uncia uncia)			
Paradoxurus hermaphroditus	Common palm civet	III (India)	3/16/89
P. jerdoni	Jerdon's palm civet	III (India)	3/16/89
Parahyaena brunnea	Brown hyaena	II	7/1/75
Pardofelis (=Felis) marmorata	Marbled cat	I	7/1/75
Potos flavus	Kinkajou	III (Honduras)	4/13/87
Prionailurus (=Felis) bengalensis bengalensis (Bangladesh, India, and Thailand populations)	Leopard cat	I	7/1/75
P. bengalensis bengalensis (all other populations)	Leopard cat	II	7/1/75
P. planiceps	Flat-headed cat	I	7/1/75
P. rubiginosus (=Felis rubiginosa) (Indian population)	Rusty-spotted cat	I	2/4/77
Prionodon linsang	Banded linsang	II	7/1/75
P. pardicolor	Spotted linsang	I	7/1/75
Proteles cristatus	Aardwolf	III (Botswana)	4/24/78
Pseudalopex culpaeus	Culpeo fox	II	6/28/79
P. griseus (=fulvipes)	Argentine gray fox	II	6/28/79
P. gymnocercus	Pampas fox	II	10/22/87
Pteronura brasiliensis	Giant otter	I	7/1/75
Puma (=Felis) concolor coryi	Florida panther, Florida puma	I	7/1/75
P. concolor costaricensis	Costa Rican puma	I	7/1/75
P. concolor couguar	Eastern puma, Adirondack cougar	I	7/1/75
Selenarctos thibetanus (see Ursus thibetanus)			
Speothos venaticus	Bush dog	I	2/4/77
Tremarctos ornatus	Spectacled bear	I	2/4/77
Uncia uncia	Snow leopard	I	7/1/75
Ursidae spp. (all species in family except those in App. I or with earlier date in App. II; includes Baltic States and former USSR populations)	Bears	II	6/11/92
Ursus americanus	American black bear	II	9/18/91
U. arctos (all Asian populations, including populations of Iran, Iraq, Syria, Turkey, and the former USSR, except populations and subspecies listed in App. I)	Brown bear	II	1/18/90
U. arctos (all European populations except Italian population and former USSR populations)	European brown Bear	II	7/29/83

Ursus arctos (all North American populations except U. a. nelsoni) ...	Brown bear, Grizzly bear ...	II	7/1/75
U. arctos (all populations of Bhutan, Mongolia, and China except subspecies with earlier date)	Brown bear	I	1/18/90
U. arctos (Italian population)	European brown bear	I	7/1/75
U. arctos isabellinus	Red bear	I	6/28/79
U. arctos nelsoni	Mexican grizzly bear	I	7/1/75
U. arctos pruinosus	Tibetan blue bear	I	7/1/75
U. (=Thalarctos) maritimus	Polar bear	II	7/1/75
U. thibetanus (except subspecies listed below)	Asiatic black bear	I	6/28/79
U. thibetanus gedrosianus .	Baluchistan black bear	I	2/4/77
Viverra civettina (=megaspila)	Malabar large-spotted civet	III (India)	3/16/89
V. zibetha	Large Indian civet	III (India)	3/16/89
Viverricula indica	Lesser oriental civet, Small Indian civet ...	III (India)	3/16/89
Vulpes bengalensis	Bengal fox	III (India)	3/16/89
V. cana	Blanford's fox ..	II	2/4/77
V. vulpes griffithi	Griffith's red fox	III (India)	3/16/89
V. vulpes montana	Montane red fox .	III (India)	3/16/89
V. vulpes pusilla (=leucopus)	Little red fox ..	III (India)	3/16/89
V. (=Fennecus) zerda	Fennec fox	II	4/22/76
Order Pinnipedia:	Seals, Sea lions:		
Arctocephalus spp. (except species listed below) ...	Southern fur seals	II	2/4/77
A. australis	Southern fur seal	II	7/1/75
A. galapagoensis	Galapagos fur seal	II	7/1/75
A. philippii	Juan Fernandez fur seal	II	7/1/75
A. townsendi	Guadalupe fur seal	I	7/1/75
Mirounga leonina	Southern elephant seal	II	7/1/75
Monachus spp.	Monk seals	I	7/1/75
Odobenus rosmarus	Walrus	III (Canada)	11/16/75
Order Proboscidea:	Elephants:		
Elephas maximus	Asian elephant ..	I	7/1/75
Loxodonta africana (except the populations of Botswana, Namibia, and Zimbabwe)	African elephant	I	2/4/77
L. africana [only the populations of Botswana, Namibia, and Zimbabwe, to allow: (1) export of hunting trophies for non-commercial purposes; (2) export of live animals to appropriate and acceptable destinations (Namibia: for non-commercial purposes only); (3) export of hides (Zimbabwe			

only); (4) export of leather goods and ivory carvings for non-commercial purposes (Zimbabwe only). No international trade in ivory is permitted before 18 months after the transfer to Appendix II comes into effect (i.e., March 18, 1999). Thereafter, under experimental quotas for raw ivory not exceeding 25.3 tons (Botswana), 13.8 tons (Namibia) and 20 tons (Zimbabwe), raw ivory may be exported only to Japan, subject to the conditions established in Decision of the Conference of the Parties regarding ivory No. 10.1. Specimens not meeting any of the above conditions shall be deemed to be specimens of species included in Appendix I and the trade in them shall be regulated accordingly] ..	African elephant	II	2/4/77
Order Sirenia:	Dugongs, Manatees:		
Dugong dugon (except for Australian population) ..	Dugong	I	7/1/75
D. dugon (Australian population)	Dugong	II	7/1/75
Trichechus inunguis	South American manatee, Amazonian manatee	I	7/1/75
T. manatus	West Indian manatee	I	7/1/75
T. senegalensis	West African manatee	II	7/1/75
Order Perissodactyla:	Odd-toed ungulates:		
Ceratotherium simum cottoni	Northern white rhinoceros	I	7/1/75
C. s. simum (population of South Africa) (no trade allowed, except for hunting trophies and for the sale of live animals to appropriate and acceptable destinations)	Southern white rhinoceros	II	2/4/77
Dicerorhinus (=Didermocerus) sumatrensis	Sumatran rhinoceros	I	7/1/75
Diceros bicornis	Black rhinoceros	I	7/1/75
Equus africanus (=E. asinus)	African wild ass	I	7/29/83
E. grevyi	Grevy's zebra ...	I	6/28/79
E. hemionus (except subspecies listed below)	Asian wild ass ..	II	7/1/75
E. hemionus hemionus	Asian wild ass ..	I	7/1/75
E. hemionus khur (see E. onager khur)			
E. kiang (=hemionus) (except subspecies listed below)	Kiang	II	7/1/75

Species	Common name	Appendix	Date
E. kiang khur (see E. onager khur)			
E. onager (=hemionus) (except subspecies listed below)	Onager	II	7/1/75
E. onager khur	Onager	I	7/1/75
E. przewalskii	Przewalski's horse	I	7/1/75
E. zebra hartmannae	Hartmann's mountain zebra	II	6/28/79
E. zebra zebra	Cape mountain zebra	I	7/1/75
Rhinocerotidae spp. (all species and populations in the family except those in App. II or with earlier date in App. I)	Rhinoceroses	I	2/4/77
Rhinoceros sondaicus	Javan rhinoceros	I	7/1/75
R. unicornis	Great Indian one-horned rhinoceros	I	7/1/75
Tapirus spp. (except for species listed below)	Tapirs	I	7/1/75
T. terrestris	South American tapir	II	7/1/75
Order Artiodactyla:	Even-toed ungulates:		
Addax nasomaculatus	Addax	I	7/1/75
Ammotragus lervia	Barbary sheep, Aoudad	II	4/22/76
Antilocapra americana (Mexican population)	Mexican pronghorn	I	7/1/75
Antilope cervicapra	Blackbuck antelope	III (Nepal)	11/16/75
Axis porcinus annamiticus	Indochina hog deer	I	7/1/75
A. porcinus calamianensis	Calamianes deer	I	7/1/75
A. porcinus kuhli	Kuhl's deer, Bawean hog deer	I	7/1/75
Babyrousa babyrussa	Babirusa	I	7/1/75
Bison bison athabascae	Wood bison	II	7/1/75
Blastocerus dichotomus	Marsh deer	I	7/1/75
Boocercus (see Tragelaphus)			
Bos frontalis (see B. gaurus)			
B. gaurus	Seladang, Gaur	I	7/1/75
B. grunniens (see B. mutus)			
Bos mutus (excluding domestic forms)	Wild yak	I	7/1/75
B. (=Novibos) sauveli	Kouprey	I	7/1/75
Bubalus arnee (formerly listed as B. bubalis, a non-protected, domesticated form)	Water buffalo	III (Nepal)	11/16/75
B. (=Anoa) depressicornis	Lowland anoa	I	7/1/75
B. (=Anoa) mindorensis	Tamaraw	I	7/1/75
B. (=Anoa) quarlesi	Mountain anoa	I	7/1/75
Budorcas taxicolor	Takin	II	8/1/85
Capra falconeri	Markhor	I	7/1/75
Capricornis sumatraensis (see Naemorhedus sumatraensis)			
Catagonus wagneri	Chacoan peccary, Giant peccary	I	10/22/87
Cephalophus dorsalis	Bay duiker	II	7/29/83
C. jentinki	Jentink's duiker	I	7/29/83
C. monticola	Blue duiker	II	7/1/75
C. ogilbyi	Ogilby's duiker	II	7/29/83
C. sylvicultor	Yellow-backed duiker	II	7/29/83
C. zebra	Zebra-banded duiker	II	7/29/83

Cervus dama mesopotamicus (see Dama mesopotamica)			
C. duvaucelii	Swamp deer	I	7/1/75
C. elaphus bactrianus	Bactrian deer	II	7/1/75
C. elaphus barbarus	Barbary deer	III (Tunisia)	4/22/76
C. elaphus hanglu	Kashmir stag	I	7/1/75
C. eldii	Eld's brow-antlered deer	I	7/1/75
C. porcinus (see Axis porcinus)			
Choeropsis liberiensis (see Hexaprotodon liberiensis)			
Dama mesopotamica	Persian fallow deer	I	2/4/77
Damaliscus dorcas dorcas (see D. pygargus dorcas)			
D. lunatus	Sassaby antelope, Korrigum	III (Ghana)	2/26/76
D. pygargus dorcas	Bontebok	II	7/1/75
Gazella cuvieri (=G. gazella cuvieri)	Mountain gazelle	III (Tunisia)	4/22/76
G. dama	Dama gazelle	I	7/29/83
G. dorcas	Dorcas gazelle	III (Tunisia)	4/22/76
G. leptoceros	Slender-horned gazelle	III (Tunisia)	4/22/76
Hexaprotodon liberiensis	Pygmy hippopotamus	II	7/1/75
Hippocamelus spp.	Huemals	I	7/1/75
Hippopotamus amphibius	Hippopotamus	II	2/26/76
Hippotragus niger variani	Giant sable antelope	I	7/1/75
Hyemoschus aquaticus	Water chevrotain	III (Ghana)	2/26/76
Kobus leche	Lechwe	II	7/1/75
Lama guanicoe	Guanaco	II	8/12/78
Mazama americana cerasina	Red brocket deer	III (Guatemala)	4/23/81
Megamuntiacus vuquanghensis	Giant muntjac	I	2/16/95
Moschus spp. (all except populations in App. I)	Musk deer	II	2/16/79
Moschus spp. (populations of Afghanistan, Bhutan, India, Myanmar, Nepal, and Pakistan)	Musk deer	I	7/1/75
Muntiacus crinifrons	Black muntjac	I	8/1/85
Naemorhedus baileyi	Goral	I	7/1/75
N. caudatus	Goral	I	7/1/75
N. sumatraensis	Serow	I	7/1/75
N. goral	Goral	I	7/1/75
Nemorhaedus (see Naemorhedus)			
Odocoileus virginianus mayensis	Whitetail deer	III (Guatemala)	4/23/81
Oryx dammah (=O. tao)	Scimitar-horned oryx	I	7/1/75
O. leucoryx	Arabian oryx	I	7/1/75
Ovis ammon (except subspecies listed below)	Argali	II	7/1/75
O. ammon hodgsonii	Tibetan argali	I	7/1/75
Ovis ammon nigrimontana	Kara Tau argali	I	7/1/75
O. aries ophion (=O. musimon ophion) (see O. orientalis ophion)			
O. canadensis (Mexican population)	Mexican bighorn sheep	II	7/1/75
O. orientalis ophion	Cyprian red sheep	I	7/1/75
O. vignei vignei	Shapo	I	7/1/75
Ozotoceros bezoarticus	Pampas deer	I	7/1/75
Pantholops hodgsonii	Tibetan antelope	I	7/1/75

Scientific name	Common name	Appendix	Date
Pecari tajacu (except populations of the United States and Mexico)	Collared peccary	II	10/22/87
Pseudoryx nghetinhensis	Vu Quang ox	I	2/16/95
Pudu mephistophiles	Northern pudu	II	7/1/75
P. puda (=P. pudu)	Pudu	I	7/1/75
Rupicapra pyrenaica (=rupicapra) ornata	Apennian chamois	I	7/1/75
Saiga tatarica	Saiga antelope	II	2/16/95
Sus salvanius	Pygmy hog	I	7/1/75
Tayassu pecari	White-lipped peccary	II	10/22/87
T. tajacu (see Pecari tajacu)			
Tetracerus quadricornis	Four-horned antelope	III (Nepal)	11/16/75
Tragelaphus (=Taurotragus) eurycerus	Bongo antelope	III (Ghana)	2/26/76
T. spekii	Sitatunga antelope	III (Ghana)	2/26/76
Vicugna vicugna (except populations listed below, under the conditions specified)	Vicun6a	I	7/1/75
V. vicugna [Argentina: wild populations of the Province of Jujuy and the semi-captive populations of the Provinces of Jujuy, Salta, Catamarca, La Rioja and San Juan (export limited to wool sheared from live animals and to cloth and items made thereof, including luxury handicrafts and knitted articles; the reverse side of cloth and cloth products must bear the logo adopted by countries signatory to the Convenio para la Conservacion y Manejo de la Vicuna and the words, "VICUNA-ARGENTINA"; all specimens not meeting any of the above conditions shall be deemed to be specimens of species included in Appendix I and the trade in them shall be regulated accordingly)]	Vicuna	II	7/1/75
V. vicugna [Bolivia: populations of the Conservation Units of Mauri-Desaguadero, Ulla Ulla and Lipez-Chichas (export limited to wool sheared from live animals and to cloth and items made thereof, including luxury handicrafts and knitted articles, but with a zero annual export quota; the reverse side of cloth and cloth products must bear the logo adopted by countries signatory to the Convenio para la Conservacion y Manejo de la Vicuna and			

the words, "VICUNA-BOLIVIA"; all specimens not meeting any of the above conditions shall be deemed to be specimens of species included in Appendix I and the trade in them shall be regulated accordingly)]	Vicuna	II	7/1/75
V. vicugna [Chile: populations of Paranicota Province, la. Region of Tarapaca (export limited to wool sheared from live animals and to cloth and items made thereof, including luxury handicrafts and knitted articles; the reverse side of cloth and cloth products must bear the logo adopted by countries signatory to the Convenio para la Conservacion y Manejo de la Vicuna and the words, "VICUNA-CHILE"; all specimens not meeting any of the above conditions shall be deemed to be specimens of species included in Appendix I and the trade in them shall be regulated accordingly)]	Vicuna	II	7/1/75
V. vicugna [Peru: all populations (export limited to the stock of 3249 kg. extant in November, 1994, to wool sheared from live animals, and to cloth and items made thereof, including luxury handicrafts and knitted articles; the reverse side of cloth and cloth products must bear the logo adopted by countries signatory to the Convenio para la Conservacion y Manejo de la Vicuna and the words, "VICUNA-PERU"; all specimens not meeting any of the above conditions shall be deemed to be specimens of species included in Appendix I and the trade in them shall be regulated accordingly)] .	Vicuna	II	7/1/75*
CLASS AVES:	BIRDS:		
Order Struthioniformes: ...	Ostriches:	....	....
Struthio camelus (populations of Algeria, Burkina Faso, Cameroon, Central African Republic, Chad, Mali, Mauritania, Morocco, Niger, Nigeria, Senegal, and Sudan)	Ostrich	I	7/29/83
Order Rheiformes	Rheas:	....	....

Species	Common name	Appendix	Date
Pterocnemia pennata (see Rhea pennata)			
Rhea americana (all subspecies except that with earlier date in App. II)	Greater rhea, Common rhea	II	7/14/76
R. americana albescens	Greater rhea	II	7/1/75
R. pennata (except subspecies listed below)	Lesser rhea	I	6/28/79
R. pennata garleppi	Lesser rhea	I	7/1/75
R. pennata pennata	Darwin's rhea	I	7/1/75
Order Tinamiformes:	Tinamous:		
Tinamus solitarius	Solitary tinamou	I	7/1/75
Order Sphenisciformes:	Penguins:		
Spheniscus demersus	Jackass penguin, Blackfooted Cape penguin	II	7/1/75
S. humboldti	Humboldt penguin	I	6/6/81
Order Podicipediformes:	Grebes:		
Podilymbus gigas	Atitlan grebe	I	7/1/75
Order Procellariiformes:	Albatrosses, Shearwaters, Petrels:		
Diomedea albatrus	Short-tailed albatross	I	7/1/75
Order Pelecaniformes:	Tropicbirds, Pelicans, Frigatebirds:		
Fregata andrewsi	Andrew's frigatebird	I	7/1/75
Papasula abbotti	Abbott's booby	I	7/1/75
Pelecanus crispus	Dalmatian pelican	I	7/1/75
Sula abbotti (see Papasula abbotti)			
Order Ciconiiformes:	Herons, Storks, Ibises, Flamingos:		
Ardea goliath	Goliath heron	III (Ghana)	2/26/76
Balaeniceps rex	Whale-headed stork	II	10/22/87
Bostrychia hagedash	Hadada ibis	III (Ghana)	2/26/76
B. rara	Spotted-breasted ibis	III (Ghana)	2/26/76
Bubulcus (=Ardeola) ibis	Cattle egret	III (Ghana)	2/26/76
Casmerodius (=Egretta) albus	Great white egret	III (Ghana)	2/26/76
Ciconia boyciana	Oriental white stork	I	7/1/75
C. ciconia boyciana (see C. boyciana)			
C. nigra	Black stork	II	7/1/75
Egretta garzetta	Little egret	III (Ghana)	2/26/76
Ephippiorhynchus senegalensis	Saddlebill stork	III (Ghana)	2/26/76
Eudocimus ruber	Scarlet ibis	II	10/22/87
Geronticus calvus	Southern bald ibis	II	7/1/75
G. eremita	Northern bald ibis, Hermit ibis	I	6/28/79
Hagedashia hagedash (see Bostrychia hagedash)			
Jabiru mycteria	Jabiru	I	8/1/85
Lampribis rara (see Bostrychia rara)			
Leptoptilos crumeniferus	Marabou stork	III (Ghana)	2/26/76
Mycteria cinerea	Milky wood stork	I	10/22/87
Nipponia nippon	Japanese crested ibis	I	7/1/75

Phoenicopteridae spp. (except species or populations with an earlier date in App. II)	Flamingos	II	7/29/83
Phoenicopterus andinus	Andean flamingo	II	7/1/75
P. chilensis	Chilean flamingo	II	7/1/75
P. jamesi	James flamingo	II	7/1/75
P. ruber ruber	American flamingo	II	6/28/79
Platalea leucorodia	White spoonbill	II	7/1/75
Threskiornis aethiopicus	Sacred ibis	III (Ghana)	2/26/76
Order Anseriformes:	Ducks, Geese, Swans, Screamers:		
Alopochen aegyptiacus	Egyptian goose	III (Ghana)	2/26/76
Anas acuta	Northern pintail	III (Ghana)	2/26/76
A. aucklandica (=chlorotis, =nesiotis)	Brown teal	I	7/1/75
A. bernieri	Madagascar teal	II	7/1/75
A. capensis	Cape wigeon	III (Ghana)	2/26/76
A. chlorotis (see A. aucklandica)			
A. clypeata	Northern shoveler	III (Ghana)	2/26/76
A. crecca	Green-winged teal	III (Ghana)	2/26/76
A. formosa	Baikal teal	II	6/11/92
A. laysanensis (=A. platyrhynchos laysanensis)	Laysan duck	I	7/1/75
A. nesiotis (see A. aucklandica)			
A. oustaleti (=A. platyrhynchos oustaleti)	Marianas mallard	I	7/1/75
A. penelope	Europeon wigeon	III (Ghana)	2/26/76
A. querquedula	Garganey	III (Ghana)	2/26/76
Aythya nyroca	White-eyed pochard	III (Ghana)	2/26/76
Branta canadensis leucopareia	Aleutian Canada goose	I	7/1/75
B. ruficollis	Red-breasted goose	II	7/1/75
B. (=Nesochen) sandvicensis	Hawaiian goose, Nene	I	7/1/75
Cairina moschata	Muscovy duck	III (Honduras)	4/13/87
C. scutulata	White-winged duck	I	7/1/75
Coscoroba coscoroba	Coscoroba swan	II	7/1/75
Cygnus melanocorypha	Black-necked swan	II	7/1/75
Dendrocygna arborea	Cuban tree duck, West Indian whistling-duck	II	7/1/75
D. autumnalis	Black-bellied whistling-duck	III (Honduras)	4/13/87
D. bicolor (=fulva)	Fulvous whistling-duck	III (Ghana and Honduras)	2/26/76
D. viduata	White-faced whistling-duck	III (Ghana)	2/26/76
Nettapus auritus	African pygmy goose	III (Ghana)	2/26/76
Oxyura leucocephala	White-headed duck	II	7/29/83
Plectropterus gambensis	Spur-winged goose	III (Ghana)	2/26/76
Pteronetta hartlaubii	Hartlaub's duck	III (Ghana)	2/26/76
Rhodonessa caryophyllacea	Pink-headed duck	I pe	7/1/75
Sarkidiornis melanotos	Comb duck	II	7/1/75
Order Falconiformes:	Hawks, Falcons, Vultures, Eagles:		
All species except those in App. I, or with earlier date in App. II, and except Cathartidae			

species not specifically listed below	All species except New World vultures not specifically listed below	II	6/28/79
Accipitridae spp. (all South American populations)	Hawks, Harriers	II	10/28/76
Accipiter gentilis	Northern goshawk	II	2/4/77
A. gundlachi	Gundlach's hawk	II	2/4/77
A. nisus	European sparrow hawk	II	2/4/77
Aegypius monachus	European black vulture, Cinerous vulture	II	2/4/77
Aquila spp. (all species except those in App. I or with earlier date in App. II)	Eagles	II	2/4/77
A. adalberti (=A. heliaca adalberti)	Imperial eagle	I	2/4/77
A. chrysaetos	Golden eagle	II	7/1/75
A. heliaca	Imperial eagle	I	2/4/77
Chondrohierax uncinatus wilsonii	Cuban hook-billed kite	I	2/4/77
Circaetus spp	Snake-eagles	II	2/4/77
Circus spp	Harriers	II	2/4/77
Falconidae spp. (all species in family except those in App. I)	Falcons, Caracaras	II	7/1/75
Falco araea	Seychelles kestrel	I	7/1/75
F. jugger	Laggar falcon	I	7/1/75
F. newtoni (Seychelles population) (=F.newtoni aldabranus)	Aldabra kestrel	I	7/1/75
F. pelegrinoides (=F. peregrinus pelegrinoides)	Barbary falcon	I	7/1/75
F. peregrinus	Peregrine falcon	I	7/1/75
F. punctatus	Mauritius kestrel	I	7/1/75
F. rusticolus	Gyrfalcon	I	7/1/75
Gymnogyps californianus	California condor	I	7/1/75
Gypaetus barbatus	Lammergeier	II	2/4/77
Gyps fulvus	Griffon vulture	II	2/4/77
Haliaeetus spp. (except species in App. I)	Sea-eagles, Fish-eagles	II	2/4/77
H. albicilla (except subspecies listed below)	White-tailed eagle	I	2/4/77
H. albicilla greenlandicus	Greenland white-tailed sea-eagle	I	7/1/75
H. leucocephalus (except subspecies listed below)	Bald eagle	I	2/4/77
H. leucocephalus leucocephalus	Southern bald eagle	I	7/1/75
Harpia harpyja	Harpy eagle	I	7/1/75
Harpyopsis novaeguineae	New Guinea harpy eagle	II	2/4/77
Milvus milvus	Red kite	II	2/4/77
Pandion haliaetus	Osprey	II	2/4/77
Pithecophaga jefferyi	Monkey-eating eagle	I	7/1/75
Sagittarius serpentarius	Secretary bird	II	2/26/76
Sarcoramphus papa	King vulture	III (Honduras)	4/13/87
Vultur gryphus	Andean condor	I	7/1/75

Species	Common name	Appendix	Country	Date
Order Galliformes:	Pheasants, Curassows, Megapodes, Hoatzin:			
Aburria (see Pipile)				
Agelastes meleagrides	White-breasted guineafowl	III	(Ghana)	2/26/76
Agriocharis ocellata	Ocellated turkey	III	(Guatemala)	4/23/81
Arborophila orientalis (=brunneopectus)	Bar-backed partridge, Bare-throated tree-partridge	III	(Malaysia)	11/13/86
A. (=Tropicoperdix) charltonii	Scaly-breasted partridge, Chestnut-breasted tree-partridge	III	(Malaysia)	11/13/86
Argusianus argus	Great argus pheasant	II		7/1/75
Caloperdix oculea	Ferruginous wood-partridge	III	(Malaysia)	11/13/86
Catreus wallichi	Cheer pheasant	I		7/1/75
Colinus virginianus ridgwayi	Masked bobwhite	I		7/1/75
Crax alberti	Blue-knobbed curassow	III	(Colombia)	9/21/88
C. blumenbachii	Red-billed curassow	I		7/1/75
C. daubentoni	Yellow-knobbed curassow	III	(Colombia)	9/21/88
C. globulosa	Wattled curassow	III	(Colombia)	9/21/88
C. mitu mitu (see Mitu mitu mitu)				
C. pauxi (see Pauxi pauxi)				
C. rubra	Great curassow	III	(Colombia, Costa Rica, Guatemala, and Honduras)	10/28/76
Crossoptilon crossoptilon	White-eared pheasant	I		7/1/75
C. harmani (=C. crossoptilon harmani)	Elwes's eared-pheasant	I		7/1/75
C. mantchuricum	Brown-eared pheasant	I		7/1/75
Gallus sonneratii	Gray jungle fowl	II		7/1/75
Ithaginis cruentus	Blood pheasant	II		7/1/75
Lophophorus impejanus	Himalayan monal	I		7/1/75
L. lhuysii	Chinese monal	I		7/1/75
L. sclateri	Sclater's monal	I		7/1/75
Lophura edwardsi	Edward's pheasant	I		7/1/75
L. erythrophthalma	Crestless fireback	III	(Malaysia)	11/13/86
L. ignita	Crested fireback	III	(Malaysia)	11/13/86
L. imperialis	Imperial pheasant	I		7/1/75
L. swinhoii	Swinhoe's pheasant	I		7/1/75
Macrocephalon maleo	Maleo megapode	I		7/1/75
Melanoperdix nigra	Black wood-partridge	III	(Malaysia)	11/13/86

Species	Common name	Appendix	Date
Mitu mitu mitu	Mitu, Razor-billed curassow	I	7/1/75
Oreophasis derbianus	Horned guan	I	7/1/75
Ortalis vetula	Plain chachalaca	III (Guatemala, Honduras)	4/23/81
Pauxi pauxi	Northern helmeted curassow	III (Colombia)	9/21/88
Pavo muticus	Green peafowl	II	2/4/77
Penelope albipennis	White-winged guan	I	6/6/81
P. purpurascens	Northern crested guan	III (Honduras)	4/13/87
Penelopina nigra	Black chachalaca, Highland guan	III (Guatemala)	4/23/81
Pipile jacutinga	Black-fronted piping-guan	I	7/1/75
P. pipile pipile	Trinidad white-headed curassow	I	7/1/75
Polyplectron bicalcaratum	Gray peacock-pheasant	II	7/1/75
P. emphanum	Palawan peacock-pheasant	I	7/1/75
P. germaini	Germain's peacock-pheasant	II	7/1/75
P. inopinatum	Rothschild's pea-cock-pheasant, Mountain peacock pheasant	III (Malaysia)	11/13/86
P. malacense	Malaysian peacock-pheasant	II	7/1/75
P. schleiermacheri (=P. malacense schleiermacheri)	Bornean peacock-pheasant	II	7/1/75
Rheinardia ocellata (=R. nigrescens)	Rheinard's crested argus, Crested argus pheasant	I	11/13/86
Rhizothera longirostris	Long-billed wood-partridge	III (Malaysia)	11/13/86
Rollulus roulroul	Crested wood-partridge, Roulroul, Green-winged wood partridge	III (Malaysia)	11/13/86
Syrmaticus ellioti	Elliot's pheasant	I	7/1/75
S. humiae	Bar-tailed pheasant	I	7/1/75
S. mikado	Mikado pheasant	I	7/1/75
Tetraogallus caspius	Caspian snowcock	I	7/1/75
T. tibetanus	Tibetan snowcock	I	7/1/75
Tragopan blythii	Blyth's tragopan	I	7/1/75
T. caboti	Cabot's tragopan	I	7/1/75
T. melanocephalus	Western tragopan	I	7/1/75
T. satyra	Satyr tragopan	III (Nepal)	11/16/75
Tympanuchus cupido attwateri	Attwater's greater prairie chicken	I	7/1/75
Order Gruiformes:	Cranes, Rails, Bustards:		
Anthropoides (see Grus)			
Ardeotis nigriceps	Great Indian bustard	I	7/1/75

Balearica regulorum	Crowned crane	II	7/1/75
Chlamydotis undulata	Houbara bustard	I	7/1/75
Choriotis (see Ardeotis)			
Eupodotis bengalensis	Bengal florican	I	7/1/75
G. sylvestris	Lord Howe wood rail	I	7/1/75
Gruidae spp. (all species and subspecies except those in App. I and those with earlier date in App. II)	Cranes	II	8/1/85
Grus americana	Whooping Crane	I	7/1/75
G. canadensis nesiotes	Cuba sandhill crane	I	7/1/75
G. canadensis pratensis	Florida sandhill crane	II	7/1/75
G. canadensis pulla	Mississippi sandhill crane	I	7/1/75
G. japonensis	Manchurian crane	I	7/1/75
G. leucogeranus	Siberian white crane	I	7/1/75
G. monacha	Hooded crane	I	7/1/75
G. nigricollis	Black-necked crane	I	7/1/75
G. vipio	White-naped crane	I	7/1/75
G. virgo	Demoiselle crane	II	7/29/83
Houbaropsis (see Eupodotis)			
Otididae spp. (all species except those in App. I or with earlier date in App. II)	Bustards	II	10/22/87
Otis tarda	Great bustard	II	7/1/75
Rhynochetos jubatus	Kagu	I	7/1/75
Tricholimnas sylvestris (see Gallirallus sylvestris)			
Order Charadriiformes:	Shorebirds, Gulls, Terns, Skimmers, Auks:		
Burhinus bistriatus	Double-striped thick-knee, Mexican stone curlew	III (Guatemala)	4/23/81
Larus relictus	Relict gull	I	7/1/75
Numenius borealis	Eskimo curlew	I	7/1/75
N. tenuirostris	Slender-billed curlew	I	7/1/75
Tringa guttifer	Nordmann's greenshank	I	7/1/75
Order Columbifomes:	Pigeons, Doves, Sand-grouse:		
Caloenas nicobarica	Nicobar pigeon	I	6/28/79
Columba guinea	Speckled pigeon	III (Ghana)	2/26/76
C. iriditorques	Bronze-necked pigeon, Bronze-naped pigeon	III (Ghana)	2/26/76
C. livia	Rock dove	III (Ghana)	2/26/76
C. mayeri	Pink pigeon	III (Mauritius)	12/4/75
C. unicincta	African wood pigeon	III (Ghana)	2/26/76
Ducula mindorensis	Mindoro imperial pigeon	I	7/1/75
Gallicolumba luzonica	Bleeding-heart pigeon	II	7/1/75
Goura spp.	Crowned pigeons	II	7/1/75
Nesoenas mayeri (see Columba mayeri)			
Oena capensis	Namaqua dove, Masked dove	III (Ghana)	2/26/76

Streptopelia decipiens	African mourning dove, Mourning collared dove ..	III (Ghana)	2/26/76
S. roseogrisea	African turtle dove, African collared dove ..	III (Ghana)	2/26/76
S. semitorquata	Red-eyed dove ...	III (Ghana)	2/26/76
S. senegalensis	Laughing dove ...	III (Ghana)	2/26/76
S. turtur	Turtle dove	III (Ghana)	2/26/76
S. vinacea	Vinaceous dove ..	III (Ghana)	2/26/76
Treron calva	African green pigeon	III (Ghana)	2/26/76
T. waalia	Yellow-bellied green pigeon ...	III (Ghana)	2/26/76
Turtur abyssinicus	Black-billed wood dove	III (Ghana)	2/26/76
T. afer	Blue-spotted wood dove	III (Ghana)	2/26/76
T. brehmeri	Blue-headed wood dove	III (Ghana)	2/26/76
T. tympanistria	Tambourine dove .	III (Ghana)	2/26/76
Order Psittaciformes:	Parrots, Parakeets, Macaws, Lories:	....	
All species in order except those in App. I or with earlier date in App. II, and except Melopsittacus undulatus, Nymphicus hollandicus, and Psittacula krameri. However, the latter is listed separately in App. III	All Parrots, Parakeets, Macaws, Lories, Cockatoos, etc. not listed below (not including the Budgerigar, Cockatiel, and Rose-ringed parakeet)	II	6/6/81
Amazona arausiaca	Red-necked parrot	I	6/6/81
A. barbadensis	Yellow-shouldered parrot	I	6/6/81
A. brasiliensis	Red-tailed parrot	I	6/6/81
A. dufresniana rhodocorytha (see A. rhodocorytha) ...	....	....	
A. guildingii	St. Vincent parrot	I	7/1/75
A. imperialis	Imperial parrot, Sisserou	I	7/1/75
A. leucocephala	Cuban parrot	I	7/1/75
A. pretrei	Red-spectacted parrot	I	7/1/75
A. rhodocorytha	Red-browed parrot	I	7/1/75
A. tucumana	Tucuman parrot ..	I	6/6/81
A. versicolor	St. Lucia parrot	I	7/1/75
A. vinacea	Vinaceous parrot	I	7/1/75
Amazona viridigenalis	Red-crowned (= Green-cheeked) parrot	I	6/6/81
A. vittata	Puerto Rican parrot	I	7/1/75
Anodorhynchus glaucus	Glaucous macaw ..	I	7/1/75
A. hyacinthinus	Hyacinth macaw ..	I	6/6/81
A. leari	Lear's macaw, Indigo macaw ...	I	7/1/75
Ara ambigua	Buffon's macaw, Great green macaw	I	10/28/76

A. glaucogularis	Caninde macaw	I	6/6/81
A. macao	Scarlet macaw	I	10/28/76
A. maracana	Illiger's macaw	I	6/6/81
A. militaris	Military macaw	I	6/6/81
A. rubrogenys	Red-fronted macaw	I	6/6/81
Aratinga guarouba	Golden parakeet	I	7/1/75
Cacatua goffini	Goffin's cockatoo	I	6/6/81
C. haematuropygia	Red-vented cockatoo	I	6/6/81
C. moluccensis	Moluccan cockatoo	I	6/6/81
C. (=Kakatoe) tenuirostris	Long-billed corella, Slender-billed cockatoo	II	2/4/77
Calyptorhynchus lathami	Glossy black cockatoo	II	2/4/77
Coracopsis nigra (Seychelles population)	Seychelles vasa parrot	II	7/1/75
Cyanoliseus patagonus byroni	Burrowing parakeet	II	6/28/79
Cyanopsitta spixii	Spix's macaw	I	7/1/75
Cyanoramphus auriceps forbesi	Forbes' parakeet, Yellow-fronted parakeet	I	7/1/75
C. auriceps malherbi	Orange-fronted parakeet	II	7/1/75
C. cookii	Norfolk parakeet	I	7/1/75
C. malherbi (see C. auriceps malherbi)			
C. novaezelandiae	New Zealand parakeet, Red-fronted parakeet	I	7/1/75
C. unicolor	Antipodes green parakeet	II	7/1/75
Cyclopsitta diophthalma coxeni	Coxen's fig parrot	I	2/4/77
Eos histrio	Red and blue lory	I	6/6/81
Eunymphicus cornutus	Horned parakeet	II	7/1/75
Geopsittacus occidentalis (see Pezoporus occidentalis)			
Neophema chrysogaster	Orange-bellied parakeet	I	7/1/75
N. splendida	Scarlet-chested parakeet	II	7/1/75
Northiella haematogaster narethae	Blue-bonnet parrot	II	2/4/77
Ognorhynchus icterotis	Yellow-eared parrot	I	6/6/81
Opopsitta (see Cyclopsitta)			
Pezoporus occidentalis	Night parrot, Australian night parrot	I pe	7/1/75
P. wallicus	Ground parrot	I	2/4/77
Pionopsitta pileata	Red-capped parrot, Pileated parrot	I	7/1/75
Poicephalus robustus	Cape parrot	II	7/1/75
Polytelis alexandrae	Princess parrot	II	2/4/77
Probosciger aterrimus	Great black cockatoo, Palm cockatoo	I	7/1/75
Prosopeia personata	Masked shining parrot, Yellow-breasted musk parrot	II	7/1/75

Species	Common name	Appendix	Date
Psepnotus chrysopterygius	Golden-shouldered parakeet	I	7/1/75
P. dissimilis	Hooded parrot	I	7/1/75
P. pulcherrimus	Paradise parakeet	I pe	7/1/75
P. haematogaster narethae (see Northiella)			
Psittacula echo (=P. krameri echo)	Rose-ringed parakeet	I	7/1/75
P. krameri	Ring-neck parakeet	III (Ghana)	2/26/76
Psittacus erithacus princeps	Principe parrot	II	7/1/75
Pyrrhura cruentata	Blue-throated parakeet, Ochre-marked parakeet	I	7/1/75
Rhynchopsitta pachyrhyncha	Thick-billed parrot	I	7/1/75
R. terrisi (=R. pachyrhyncha terrisi)	Maroon-fronted parrot	I	6/6/81
Strigops habroptilus	Kakapo, Owl parrot	I	7/1/75
Tanygnathus lucionensis	Blue-naped parrot	II	2/4/77
Vini ultramarina	Ultramarine lorikeet	I	6/6/81
Order Cuculiformes:	Cuckoos, Plantain-eaters, Turacos:		
Corythaeola cristata	Great blue turaco	III (Ghana)	2/4/77
Crinifer piscator	Gray plantain eater	III (Ghana)	2/4/77
Musophaga (=Tauraco, =Gallirex) porphyreolopha	Violet-crested turaco	II	7/1/75
M. violacea	Violet turaco	III (Ghana)	2/4/77
Tauraco spp. (except those with earlier date in App. II or III)	Turacos, Louries	II	2/16/95
T. corythaix	Knysna turaco	II	2/4/77
T. macrorhynchus	Yellow-billed turaco	II	2/4/77
Order Strigiformes:	Owls:		
All species except those in App. I or with earlier date in App. II	All Owls not listed below	II	6/28/79
Athene blewitti	Forest little owl, Forest spotted owlet	I	6/28/79
Bubo ascalaphus	Pharaoh eagle owl	II	2/4/77
B. bengalensis	Rock eagle owl	II	2/4/77
B. bubo	Eurasian eagle owl	II	2/4/77
Mimizuku gurneyi	Giant scops owl	I	7/1/75
Ninox novaeseelandiae undulata	Great hawk-owl	I	2/4/77
N. squamipila natalis	Great hawk-owl, Moluccan hawk-owl	I	2/4/77
Nyctea scandiaca	Snowy owl	II	2/4/77
Otus gurneyi (see Mimizuku gurneyi)			
O. nudipes newtoni	Virgin Island screech owl	II	7/1/75
Strigidae (all species native to Ghana)	Owls	II	2/26/76
Strix butleri	Hume's wood owl	II	2/4/77
S. nebulosa	Great gray owl	II	11/16/75
Tytonidae (all species native to Ghana)	Barn owls	II	2/26/76

Scientific name	Common name	App.	Date
Tyto soumagnei	Madagascar red owl	I	2/4/77
Order Apodiformes:	Swifts, Hummingbirds:		
Glaucis (see Ramphodon)			
Ramphodon dohrnii	Hook-billed hermit	I	7/1/75
Trochilidae spp.	Hummingbirds	II	10/22/87
Order Trogoniformes:	Trogons:		
Pharomachrus mocinno	Resplendent quetzal	I	7/1/75
Order Coraciiformes:	Hornbills, Kingfishers, Rollers, Bee-eaters, Motmots:		
Aceros spp. (all species except those in App. I or with earlier date in App. II)	Hornbills	II	6/11/92
A. narcondami	Narcondam hornbill	II	7/1/75
A. nipalensis	Rufous-necked hornbill	I	6/11/92
A. subruficollis	Plain-pouched hornbill	I	6/11/92
Anorrhinus (=Ptilolaemus) spp.	Hornbills	II	6/11/92
Anthracoceros spp.	Hornbills, Pied hornbills	II	6/11/92
Buceros spp. (all species and subspecies except those in App. I or with earlier date in App. II)	Giant hornbills	II	6/11/92
B. bicornis	Great hornbill	I	7/1/75
B. hydrocorax hydrocorax	Luzon-Marinduque rufous hornbill	II	7/1/75
B. rhinoceros (except subspecies with earlier date)	Rhinoceros hornbill	II	1/18/90
B. rhinoceros rhinoceros	Malay rhinoceros hornbill	II	7/1/75
B. (=Rhinoplax) vigil	Helmeted hornbill	I	7/1/75
Penelopides spp.	Hornbills	II	6/11/92
Order Piciformes:	Woodpeckers, Toucans, Jacamars, Barbets:		
Baillonius bailloni	Saffron toucanet	III (Argentina)	6/11/92
Campephilus imperialis	Imperial woodpecker	I	7/1/75
Dryocopus javensis richardsi	Tristam's white-bellied woodpecker	I	7/1/75
Pteroglossus aracari	Black-necked aracari	II	6/11/92
P. castanotis	Chestnut-eared aracari	III (Argentina)	6/11/92
P. viridis	Green aracari	II	6/11/92
Ramphastos dicolorus	Red-breasted toucan	III (Argentina)	6/11/92
R. sulphuratus	Keel-billed toucan	II	4/23/81
R. toco	Toco toucan	II	6/11/92
R. tucanus	Red-billed toucan	II	6/11/92
R. vitellinus	Channel-billed toucan	II	6/11/92

Scientific name	Common name	Appendix	Date
Selenidera maculirostris	Spot-billed toucanet	III (Argentina)	6/11/92
Semnornis ramphastinus	Toucan barbet	III (Colombia)	5/28/89
Order Passeriformes:	Perching birds, Songbirds:		
Agelaius (=Xanthopsar) flavus	Saffron-cowled blackbird	I	7/14/76
Amadina fasciata	Cut-throat	III (Ghana)	2/26/76
Amandava formosa	Green avadavat	II	9/18/97
Amandava subflava	Zebra waxbill	III (Ghana)	2/26/76
Amblyospiza albifrons	Grosbeak weaver	III (Ghana)	2/26/76
Anaplectes rubriceps	Red-headed malimbe	III (Ghana)	2/26/76
Anomalospiza imberbis	Parasitic weaver	III (Ghana)	2/26/76
Atrichornis clamosus	Noisy scrub-bird	I	7/1/75
Bebrornis rodericanus	Rodriquez Island warbler	III (Mauritius)	12/4/75
Bubalornis albirostris	Buffalo weaver	III (Ghana)	2/26/76
Carduelis (=Spinus) cucullata	Red siskin	I	7/1/75
C. (=Spinus) yarrellii	Yellow-faced siskin	II	7/1/75
Cephalopterus ornatus	Amazonian umbrellabird	III (Colombia)	9/21/88
C. penduliger	Long-wattled umbrellabird	III (Colombia)	9/21/88
Cotinga maculata	Banded cotinga	I	7/1/75
Cyornis ruckii	Rueck's blue flycatcher, Niltava	II	7/1/75
Dasyornis broadbenti litoralis	Western rufous bristlebird	I pe	7/1/75
D. longirostris (=D. brachypterus longirostris)	Western bristlebird	I	7/1/75
Estrilda astrild	Common waxbill	III (Ghana)	2/26/76
E. caerulescens	Lavender waxbill, Lavender fire-finch	III (Ghana)	2/26/76
E. melpoda	Orange-cheeked waxbill	III (Ghana)	2/26/76
E. troglodytes	Black-rumped waxbill	III (Ghana)	2/26/76
Euplectes afer	Yellow-crowned bishop	III (Ghana)	2/26/76
E. ardens	Red-collared whydah	III (Ghana)	2/26/76
E. franciscanus	Red bishop, Orange bishop	III (Ghana)	2/26/76
E. hordeaceus	Black-winged red bishop	III (Ghana)	2/26/76
E. macrourus	Yellow-mantled whydah	III (Ghana)	2/26/76
E. orix (see E. franciscanus)			
Gracula religiosa	Hill myna	II	6/11/92
Gubernatrix cristata	Yellow cardinal	II	7/14/76
Lagonosticta larvata (see L. vinacea)			
L. rara	Black-bellied waxbill	III (Ghana)	2/26/76
L. rubricata	African waxbill	III (Ghana)	2/26/76
L. rufopicta	Bar-breasted waxbill	III (Ghana)	2/26/76

L. senegala	Red-billed fire finch, Red-billed waxbill	III (Ghana)	2/26/76
L. vinacea	Vinaceous waxbill	III (Ghana)	2/26/76
Leiothrix argentaurius	Silver-eared mesia	II	9/18/97
L. lutea	Pekin robin	II	9/18/97
Leucopsar rothschildi	Rothschild's starling, Myna	I	7/1/75
Lichenostomus melanops cassidix	Helmeted honeyeater	I	7/1/75
Liocichla omeiensis	Omei Shan liocichla	II	9/18/97
Lonchura bicolor	Black-and white mannikin	III (Ghana)	2/26/76
L. cantans	White-throated munia, African silverbill	III (Ghana)	2/26/76
L. cucullata	Bronze mannikin	III (Ghana)	2/26/76
L. fringilloides	Magpie mannikin, Pied mannikin	III (Ghana)	2/26/76
L. malabarica (see L. cantans)			
Malimbus cassini	Cassin's malimbe	III (Ghana)	2/26/76
M. malimbicus	Crested malimbe	III (Ghana)	2/26/76
M. nitens	Gray's malimbe	III (Ghana)	2/26/76
M. rubriceps (see Anaplectes rubriceps)			
M. rubricollis	Red-headed weaver	III (Ghana)	2/26/76
M. scutatus	Red-vented malimbe	III (Ghana)	2/26/76
Mandingoa nitidula	Green-backed twin-spot	III (Ghana)	2/26/76
Meliphaga cassidix (see Lichenostomus melanops cassidix)			
Nesocharis capistrata	Gray-headed olive-back	III (Ghana)	2/26/76
Nigrita bicolor	Chestnut-breasted negro-finch	III (Ghana)	2/26/76
N. canicapilla	Gray-headed negro-finch	III (Ghana)	2/26/76
N. fusconota	White-breasted negro-finch	III (Ghana)	2/26/76
N. luteifrons	Pale-fronted negro-finch	III (Ghana)	2/26/76
Niltava (=Muscicapa) (see Cyornis)			
Ortygospiza atricollis	Common quail-finch	III (Ghana)	2/26/76
Pachyphantes superciliosus	Compact weaver	III (Ghana)	2/26/76
Padda oryzivora	Java sparrow	II	9/18/97
Paradiseidae spp. (all species in family)	Birds of paradise	II	7/1/75
Parmoptila rubrifrons (=woodhousei)	Jameson's antpecker, Flowerpecker weaver-finch	III (Ghana)	2/26/76
Paroaria capitata	Yellow-billed cardinal	II	10/22/87
P. coronata	Red-crested cardinal	II	10/22/87
Passer griseus	Gray-headed sparrow	III (Ghana)	2/26/76
Petronia dentata	Bush petronia	III (Ghana)	2/26/76
Pholidornis rushiae	Tit-hylia	III (Ghana)	2/26/76
Picathartes gymnocephalus	Bare-headed rockfowl, White-necked rockfowl	I	7/1/75

P. oreas	Gray-necked rockfowl, Red-headed rockfowl	I	7/1/75
Pitta brachyura nympha (see P. nympha)			
P. guajana	Blue-tailed pitta, Banded pitta	II	12/7/87
P. gurneyi	Gurney's pitta	I	12/7/87
P. kochi	Koch's pitta	I	7/1/75
P. nympha	Fairy pitta, Blue-winged pitta	II	7/1/75
Plocepasser superciliosus	Chestnut-crowned sparrow-weaver	III (Ghana)	2/26/76
Ploceus albinucha	White-naped black weaver	III (Ghana)	2/26/76
P. aurantius	Orange weaver	III (Ghana)	2/26/76
P. cucullatus	Black-headed weaver	III (Ghana)	2/26/76
P. heuglini	Heuglin's masked weaver	III (Ghana)	2/26/76
P. luteolus	Little weaver	III (Ghana)	2/26/76
P. melanocephalus	Yellow-backed weaver	III (Ghana)	2/26/76
P. nigerrimus	Viellot's weaver	III (Ghana)	2/26/76
P. nigricollis	Black-necked weaver	III (Ghana)	2/26/76
P. pelzelni	Slender-billed weaver	III (Ghana)	2/26/76
P. preussi	Golden-backed weaver	III (Ghana)	2/26/76
P. superciliosus (see Pachyphantes superciliosus)			
P. tricolor	Yellow-mantled weaver	III (Ghana)	2/26/76
P. vitellinus (=P. velatus)	Vitelline masked weaver	III (Ghana)	2/26/76
Poephila cincta cincta	Black-throated finch, Parson finch	II	10/17/80
Pseudochelidon sirintarae	White-eyed river martin	I	7/1/75
Pycnonotus zeylanicus	Straw-headed bulbul	II	9/18/97
Pyrenestes ostrinus	Black-bellied seedcracker	III (Ghana)	2/26/76
Pytilia hypogrammica	Yellow-winged pytilia	III (Ghana)	2/26/76
P. phoenicoptera	Red-winged pytilia	III (Ghana)	2/26/76
Quelea erythrops	Red-headed quelea	III (Ghana)	2/26/76
Rupicola spp.	Cocks-of-the-rock	II	7/1/75
Serinus canicapillus (=gularis)	West African seedeater	III (Ghana)	2/26/76
S. leucopygius	White-rumped seedeater	III (Ghana)	2/26/76
S. mozambicus	Yellow-fronted canary	III (Ghana)	2/26/76
Spermophaga haematina	Blue-bill	III (Ghana)	2/26/76
Sporopipes frontalis	Speckled-fronted weaver	III (Ghana)	2/26/76
Tangara fastuosa	Seven-colored tanager	II	9/18/97
Tchitrea (see Terpsiphone)			
Terpsiphone bourbonnensis	Coq de Boise, Mascarene paradise flycatcher	III (Mauritius)	12/4/75

Scientific name	Common name	Appendix	Date
Uraeginthus bengalus	Red-cheeked cordon-bleu	III (Ghana)	2/26/76
Vidua (=Hypochera) chalybeata	Village indigobird	III (Ghana)	2/26/76
V. interjecta	Uelle paradise whydah	III (Ghana)	2/26/76
V. larvaticola	Bako indigobird	III (Ghana)	2/26/76
V. macroura	Pin-tailed whydah	III (Ghana)	2/26/76
V. orientalis (=paradisaea)	Northern paradise whydah	III (Ghana)	2/26/76
V. raricola	Jambandu indigobird	III (Ghana)	2/26/76
V. togoensis	Togo paradise whydah	III (Ghana)	2/26/76
V. wilsoni	Wilson's indigobird	III (Ghana)	2/26/76
Xanthopsar (see Agelaius)			
Xipholena atropurpurea	White-winged cotinga	I	7/1/75
Zosterops albogularis	White-chested white-eye, Norfolk Island white-eye	I	7/1/75
CLASS REPTILIA:	REPTILES:		
Order Testudinata:	Turtles, Tortoises:		
Batagur baska	River terrapin, Tuntong	I	7/1/75
Callagur borneoensis	Painted terrapin	II	9/18/97
Cheloniidae spp. (all species in family)	Sea turtles	I	7/1/75
Chersina (=Testudo) spp.	Bow-sprit tortoises	II	7/1/75
Clemmys insculpta	Wood turtle	II	6/11/92
C. muhlenbergi	Bog turtle	I	7/1/75
Dermatemys mawii	Central American river turtle	II	6/6/81
Dermochelys coriacea	Leatherback sea turtle	I	7/1/75
Erymnochelys madagascariensis	Madagascar turtle	II	7/1/75
Geochelone spp. (except species listed below)	Land tortoises	II	7/1/75
G. (=Testudo) nigra (=elephantopus)	Galapagos tortoise	I	7/1/75
G. (=Testudo) radiata	Madagascar radiated tortoise	I	7/1/75
G. (=Testudo) yniphora	Angulated tortoise	I	7/1/75
Geoclemys (=Damonia) hamiltonii	Spotted pond turtle	I	7/1/75
Gopherus spp. (except species listed below)	Gopher tortoises	II	7/1/75
G. flavomarginatus	Bolson tortoise	I	7/1/75
Homopus spp.	African parrot-beaked tortoises	II	7/1/75
Kachuga tecta	Indian sawback turtle	I	7/1/75
Kinixys spp.	Hinged-back tortoise	II	7/1/75
Lissemys punctata (all subspecies except punctata)	Indian flap-shell tortoise	II	2/16/95
L. p. punctata	Indian flap-shell tortoise	II	7/1/75
Malacochersus spp.	Pancake tortoises	II	7/1/75

Melanochelys (=Geoemyda) tricarinata	Three-keeled Asian turtle	I	7/1/75
Morenia ocellata	Burmese peacock turtle	I	7/1/75
Pelomedusa subrufa	Helmeted terrapin	III (Ghana)	2/26/76
Peltocephalus dumeriliana	Big-headed Amazon River turtle	II	7/1/75
Pelusios adansonii	Adanson's hinged terrapin	III (Ghana)	2/26/76
P. castaneus	Brown hinged terrapin, Swamp hinged terrapin	III (Ghana)	2/26/76
P. gabonensis	Gabon hinged terrapin	III (Ghana)	2/26/76
P. niger	Black hinged terrapin	III (Ghana)	2/26/76
Podocnemis spp.	South American turtles	II	7/1/75
Psammobates (=Testudo) geometricus	Geometric turtle	I	2/4/77
Pseudemydura umbrina	Short-necked swamp turtle	I	7/1/75
Pyxis spp.	Madagascar spider tortoises	II	7/1/75
Terrapene spp. (all species except those in App. I)	Box turtles	II	2/16/95
T. coahuila	Aquatic box turtle	I	7/1/75
Testudinidae spp. (all species except those in App. I or with earlier date in App. II)	Land tortoises	II	2/4/77
Testudo spp. (all species except those in App. I)	Land tortoises	II	7/1/75
T. kleinmanni	Egyptian tortoise	I	2/4/77
Trionyx ater	Cuatro Cienegas softshell turtle	I	7/1/75
T. gangeticus	Indian softshell turtle	I	7/1/75
T. hurum	Peacock softshell turtle	I	7/1/75
T. nigricans	Black softshell turtle	I	7/1/75
T. triunguis	Three-clawed turtle	III (Ghana)	2/26/76
Order Crocodylia:	Crocodiles, Alligators, Caimans, Gavials:		
Alligatoridae spp. (all species in family except those in App. I or with earlier date in App. II)	All Alligators and Caimans not listed below	II	2/4/77
Alligator mississippiensis	American alligator	II	7/1/75
A. sinensis	Chinese alligator	I	7/1/75
Caiman crocodilus apaporiensis	Apaporis River caiman	I	7/1/75
C. crocodilus crocodilus	Common caiman, Spectacled caiman	II	7/1/75
C. crocodilus fuscus (including C. crocodilus chiapasius)	Brown caiman	II	7/1/75
C. crocodilus yacare (=C. yacare)	Yacare	II	7/1/75
Caiman latirostris (except population of Argentina)	Broad-snouted caiman	I	7/1/75

Crocodylidae spp. (all species in family except those in App. I or with earlier date in App. II)	All Crocodiles not listed below	II	2/4/77
Crocodylus acutus	American crocodile	I	7/1/75
C. cataphractus	African slender-snouted crocodile	I	7/1/75
C. intermedius	Orinoco crocodile	I	7/1/75
C. johnsoni	Johnson's crocodile	II	7/1/75
C. moreletii	Morelet's crocodile	I	7/1/75
C. niloticus (except those populations in App. II)	Nile crocodile	I	7/1/75
Crocodylus niloticus (populations of Botswana, Kenya, Malawi, South Africa, Zambia, and Zimbabwe, subject to ranching provisions)	Nile crocodile	II	7/1/75
C. niloticus (population of Ethiopia, Madagascar, Mozambique, Tanzania, and Uganda, subject to an annual export quota)	Nile crocodile	II	7/1/75
C. novaeguineae (except subspecies listed below)	New Guinea crocodile, Freshwater crocodile	II	7/1/75
C. novaeguineae mindorensis	Philippine crocodile	I	7/1/75
C. palustris	Mugger crocodile	I	7/1/75
C. porosus (except populations of Australia, Papua New Guinea, and Indonesia)	Saltwater crocodile	I	7/1/75
C. porosus (Australia and Papua New Guinea populations)	Saltwater crocodile	II	7/1/75
C. porosus (Indonesian population subject to ranching provisions)	Saltwater crocodile	II	7/1/75
C. rhombifer	Cuban crocodile	I	7/1/75
C. siamensis	Siamese crocodile	I	7/1/75
Gavialis gangeticus	Gavial, Gharial	I	7/1/75
Melanosuchus niger (except for population of Ecuador)	Black caiman	I	7/1/75
Melanosuchus niger (population of Ecuador, subject to a zero annual export quota until a different quota has been approved by the Secretariat)	Black caiman	II	7/1/75
Osteolaemus tetraspis (except subspecies listed below)	Dwarf crocodile	I	2/4/77
O. tetraspis osborni	Dwarf crocodile	I	7/1/75
O. tetraspis tetraspis	Dwarf crocodile	I	7/1/75
Paleosuchus trigonatus	Smooth-fronted caiman	II	7/1/75
Tomistoma schlegelii	Tomistoma, False gavial	I	7/1/75
Order Rhynchocephalia:	Tuatara:		

Sphenodon spp	Tuataras	I	7/1/75
Order Sauria:	Lizards:		
Amblyrhynchus cristatus	Galapagos marine iguana	II	7/1/75
Brachylophus spp	Fiji iguanas	I	6/6/81
Bradypodion spp	Chameleons	II	2/4/77
Chamaeleo spp	Chameleons	II	2/4/77
Cnemidophorus hyperythrus	Orange-throated whiptail lizard	II	7/1/75
Conolophus spp. (except species listed below)	Land lizards	II	2/4/77
C. pallidus	Barrington Island land lizard	II	7/1/75
C. subcristatus	Galapagos land iguana	II	7/1/75
Cordylus spp	Girdled lizards	II	6/6/81
Corucia zebrata	Prehensile-tailed skink	II	6/11/92
Crocodilurus lacertinus	Dragon lizardet	II	2/4/77
Cyclura spp	Ground iguanas	I	2/4/77
Cyrtodactylus serpensinsula	Serpent Island gecko	II	2/4/77
Dracaena spp	Caiman lizards	II	2/4/77
Gallotia simonyi	Hierro giant lizard	I	10/22/87
Heloderma spp	Beaded lizards, Gila monster	II	7/1/75
Iguana spp	Iguanas	II	2/4/77
Phelsuma spp	Day geckos	II	2/4/77
Phrynosoma coronatum (except subspecies with earlier date in App. II)	Coastal horned lizards	II	6/11/92
P. coronatum blainvillei	San Diego horned lizard	II	7/1/75
Podarcis lilfordi	Lilford's wall lizard	II	10/22/87
P. pityusensis	Ibiza wall lizard	II	10/22/87
Pseudocordylus spp	Crag lizards	II	6/6/81
Sauromalus varius	San Esteban Island chuckwalla	I	6/6/81
Shinisaurus crocodilurus	Chinese crocodile lizard	II	1/18/90
Tupinambis spp	Tegu lizards	II	2/4/77
Uromastyx spp	Spiny-tailed lizards	II	2/4/77
Varanus spp. (all species except those in App. I)	Monitor lizards	II	7/1/75
V. bengalensis	Indian monitor, Bengal monitor	I	7/1/75
V. flavescens	Yellow monitor	I	7/1/75
V. griseus	Desert monitor	I	7/1/75
V. komodoensis	Komodo Island monitor, Komodo dragon	I	7/1/75
Order Serpentes:	Snakes:		
Acrantophis spp	Madagascar boas	I	2/4/77
Agkistrodon bilineatus	Cantil	III (Honduras)	4/13/87
Atretium schistosum	Olive keelback water snake	III (India)	2/12/84
Boa (=Constrictor) constrictor	Boa constrictor	II	7/1/75
Boa constrictor occidentalis	Argentine boa constrictor	I	2/4/77
Boidae spp. (all species except those in App. I or with earlier date in App. II)	All Boa constrictors, Pythons not listed below	II	2/4/77

Scientific name	Common name	Appendix	Date
Bolyeria multocarinata	Round Island boa	I	2/4/77
Bothrops asper	Terciopelo	III (Honduras)	4/13/87
B. nasutus	Rainforest hognosed pit-viper	III (Honduras)	4/13/87
B. nummifer	Jumping pit-viper	III (Honduras)	4/13/87
B. ophryomegas	Slender hognosed pit-viper	III (Honduras)	4/13/87
B. schlegelii	Eyelash palm pit-viper	III (Honduras)	4/13/87
Casarea dussumieri	Round Island boa	I	2/4/77
Cerberus rhynchops	Dog-faced water snake	III (India)	2/12/84
Clelia (=Pseudoboa) clelia	Mussurana snake	II	7/1/75
Crotalus durissus	Tropical rattlesnake, Cascabel	III (Honduras)	4/13/87
Cyclagras (=Hydrodynastes) gigas	South American false water cobra	II	7/1/75
Elachistodon westermanni	Indian egg-eating snake	II	7/1/75
Epicrates cenchria cenchria	Rainbow boa	II	7/1/75
E. inornatus	Puerto Rican boa	I	2/4/77
E. monensis	Mona boa	I	2/4/77
E. subflavus	Jamaican boa	I	7/1/75
Eunectes notaeus	Yellow anaconda	II	7/1/75
Hoplocephalus bungaroides	Broad-headed snake	II	8/1/85
Micrurus diastema	Atlanta coral snake	III (Honduras)	4/13/87
M. nigrocinctus	Black-banded coral snake	III (Honduras)	4/13/87
Naja kaouthia (see Naja naja)			
Naja naja	Indian cobra	II	2/12/84
Naja oxiana (see Naja naja)			
Ophiophagus hannah	King cobra	II	2/12/84
Ptyas mucosus	Oriental rat snake, Whipsnake	II	2/12/84
Python spp. (except subspecies listed below)	Pythons	II	7/1/75
P. molurus molurus	Indian python	I	7/1/75
Sanzinia madagascariensis	Tree boa	I	2/4/77
Vipera russellii	Russell's viper	III (India)	2/12/84
V. ursinii (except USSR populations)	Orsini's viper	I	10/22/87
V. wagneri	Wagner's viper	II	6/11/92
Xenochrophis (=Natrix) piscator	Checkered keelback water snake	III (India)	2/12/84
CLASS AMPHIBIA:	AMPHIBIANS:		
Order Caudata:	Salamanders:		
Ambystoma dumerilii	Lake Patzcuaro salamander	II	7/1/75
A. mexicanum	Axolotl	II	7/1/75
Andrias spp.	Giant salamanders	I	7/1/75
Order Anura:	Frogs, Toads:		
Atelopus varius zeteki	Panamanian golden frog	I	7/1/75
Bufo periglenes	Monte Verde golden toad	I	7/1/75

Species	Common name	Appendix	Date
B. retiformis	Sonoran green toad	II	7/1/75
B. superciliaris	Cameroon toad	I	7/1/75
Dendrobates spp.	Poison dart frogs, Poison arrow frogs	II	10/22/87
Dyscophus antongilii	Tomato frog	I	10/22/87
Epipedobates spp. (see Dendrobates spp.)			
Mantella aurantiaca	Malagasy golden mantella	II	2/16/95
Minyobates spp. (see Dendrobates spp.)			
Nectophrynoides spp.	African viviparous toads	I	7/1/75
Phyllobates spp.	Poison arrow frogs	II	10/22/87
Rana hexadactyla	Asian bullfrog	II	8/1/85
R. tigerina	Indian bullfrog	II	8/1/85
Rheobatrachus spp.	Platypus frog	II	8/1/85
CLASS OSTEICHTHYES:	BONY FISHES:		
Order Ceratodontiformes (=Ceratodiformes):	Lungfishes:		
Neoceratodus forsteri	Australian lungfish	II	7/1/75
Order Coelacanthiformes:	Coelacanth:		
Latimeria chalumnae	Coelacanth, Gombessa	I	7/1/75
Order Acipenseriformes (all species except those in App. I or with earlier date in App. II)	All Sturgeons and Paddlefish not listed below	II	4/1/98
Acipenser brevirostrum	Short-nosed sturgeon	I	7/1/75
A. oxyrhynchus	Atlantic sturgeon	II	7/1/75
A. sturio	Baltic sturgeon	I	7/1/75
Polyodon spathula	Paddlefish	II	6/11/92
Order Osteoglossiformes:	Bonytongues:		
Arapaima gigas	Arapaima	II	7/1/75
Scleropages formosus	Asian bonytongue	I	7/1/75
Order Cypriniformes:			
Caecobarbus geertsi	African blind barb, Congo blind barb	II	6/6/81
Chasmistes cujus	Cui-ui	I	7/1/75
Probarbus jullieni	Ikan temolek, Pla eesok	I	7/1/75
Order Siluriformes:	Catfishes:		
Pangasianodon gigas	Thailand giant catfish	I	7/1/75
Order Perciformes:	Perch-like fishes:		
Cynoscion macdonaldi	Totoaba	I	2/4/77
PHYLUM ARTHROPODA:	ARTHROPODS:		
CLASS Insecta:	Insects:		
Bhutanitis spp.	Bhutan glory swallowtails	II	10/22/87
Ornithoptera spp. (all species except those in App. I or with earlier date in App. II)	All Birdwing butterflies not listed below	II	2/16/79
O. alexandrae	Queen Alexandra's birdwing butterfly	I	2/4/77
O. allotei	Birdwing butterfly	II	2/4/77
O. chimaera	Birdwing butterfly	II	2/4/77
O. goliath	Birdwing butterfly	II	2/4/77

O. meridionalis	Birdwing butterfly	II	2/4/77
O. paradisea	Paradise birdwing butterfly	II	2/4/77
O. victoriae	Queen Victoria's birdwing butterfly	II	2/4/77
Papilio chikae	Luzon peacock swallowtail	I	10/22/87
P. homerus	Homerus swallowtail	I	10/22/87
P. hospiton	Corsican swallowtail	I	10/22/87
Parnassius apollo	Mountain apollo butterfly	II	2/4/77
P. apollo apollo	Mountain apollo butterfly	II	7/1/75
Teinopalpus spp............	Kaiser-I-Hind butterflies	II	10/22/87
Trogonoptera spp...........	Birdwing butterflies	II	2/16/79
Troides spp................	Birdwing butterflies	II	2/16/79
CLASS Arachnida:	Arachnids:		
Brachypelma (=Euathlus) spp. (except species with earlier date in App. II)	Red-kneed tarantulas	II	2/16/95
B. smithi	Red-kneed tarantula	II	8/1/85
Pandinus dictator	Emperor scorpion	II	2/16/95
P. gambiensis	Emperor scorpion	II	2/16/95
P. imperator	Emperor scorpion	II	2/16/95
PHYLUM ANNELIDA:	ANNELID WORMS:		
CLASS Hirudinea:	Leeches:		
Order Arhynchobdelliformes:	Rhynchobedellids:		
Hirudo medicinalis	Medicinal leech .	II	10/22/87
PHYLUM MOLLUSCA:	MOLLUSCS:		
CLASS Pelecypoda (=Bivalvia):	Clams, Mussels:		
Conradilla caelata	Birdwing pearly mussel	I	7/1/75
Cyprogenia aberti	Edible pearly mussel	II	7/1/75
Dromus dromas	Dromedary pearly mussel	I	7/1/75
Epioblasma (=Dysnomia) curtisi (=E. florentina curtisi)	Curtis' pearly mussel	I	7/1/75
E. florentina (=E. florentina florentina) ..	Yellow-blossom pearly mussel ..	I	7/1/75
E. sampsoni	Sampson's pearly mussel	I	7/1/75
E. sulcata perobliqua	White cat's paw mussel	I	7/1/75
E. torulosa gubernaculum ..	Green-blossom pearly mussel ..	I	7/1/75
E. torulosa rangiana	Tan-blossom pearly mussel ..	II	7/1/75
E. torulosa torulosa	Tuberculed-blossom pearly mussel	I	7/1/75
E. turgidula	Turgid-blossom pearly mussel ..	I	7/1/75
E. walkeri	Brown-blossom pearly mussel ..	I	7/1/75
Fusconaia cuneolus	Fine-rayed pigtoe mussel	I	7/1/75
F. edgariana	Shiny pigtoe mussel	I	7/1/75

Hippopus spp. (see

Tridacnidae spp.)			
L. higginsii	Higgin's eye mussel	I	7/1/75
L. orbiculata orbiculata	Pink mucket mussel	I	7/1/75
L. satur	Plain pocketbook mussel	I	7/1/75
L. virescens	Alabama lamp pearly mussel	I	7/1/75
Plethobasus cicatricosus	White wartyback mussel	I	7/1/75
P. cooperianus	Orange-footed pimpleback mussel	I	7/1/75
Pleurobema clava	Club pearly mussel	II	7/1/75
P. plenum	Rough pigtoe mussel	I	7/1/75
Potamilus (=Proptera) capax	Fat pocketbook mussel	I	7/1/75
Quadrula intermedia	Cumberland monkey-face mussel	I	7/1/75
Q. sparsa	Appalachian monkey-face mussel	I	7/1/75
Toxolasma (=Carunculina) cylindrella	Pale lilliput pearly mussel	I	7/1/75
Tridacna derasa	Giant clam	II	5/29/83
T. gigas	Giant clam	II	5/29/83
Tridacnidae spp. (includes all species in genera Hippopus and Tridacna except those with earlier date in App. II)	Giant clams	II	8/1/85
Unio (=Megalonaias) nickliniana	Nicklin's pearly mussel	I	7/1/75
U. (=Lampsilis or Cyrtonaias) tampicoensis tecomatensis	Tampico pearly mussel	I	7/1/75
Villosa (=Micromya) trabalis	Cumberland bean mussel	I	7/1/75
CLASS Gastropoda:	Snails:		
Achatinella spp.	Oahu tree snails	I	10/22/87
Papustyla (=Papuina) pulcherrima	Manus Island tree snail	II	7/1/75
Strombus gigas	Queen conch	II	6/11/92
PHYLUM CNIDARIA (=COELENTERATA):	CORAL-LIKE ANIMALS:		
CLASS Anthozoa:	Corals, Sea anemones:		
Order Coenothecalia:			
All species in the Order (except those in genus with earlier date)		II	1/18/90
Heliopora spp.	Blue corals	II	8/1/85
Order Stolonifera:			
Tubiporidae spp. (all species in family except genus with earlier date)		II	1/18/90
Tubipora spp.	Organ-pipe corals	II	8/1/85
Order Antipatharia:	Black corals:		
All species in the Order		II	6/6/81
Order Scleractinia:	Stony corals:		
All species in the Order (except the following genera with earlier date)		II	1/18/90

Acropora spp	Staghorn corals	II	8/1/85
Euphyllia spp	Trumpet corals	II	8/1/85
Favia spp	Brain corals	II	8/1/85
Fungia spp	Mushroom corals	II	8/1/85
Halomitra spp	Bowl corals	II	8/1/85
Lobophyllia spp	Brain corals	II	8/1/85
Merulina spp	Merulinas	II	8/1/85
Pavona spp	Cactus corals	II	8/1/85
Pectinia spp	Lettuce corals	II	8/1/85
Platygyra spp	Brain corals	II	8/1/85
Pocillopora spp	Brush corals	II	8/1/85
Polyphyllia spp	Feather corals	II	8/1/85
Seriatopora spp	Birds nest corals	II	8/1/85
Stylophora spp	Cauliflower corals	II	8/1/85
CLASS Hydrozoa:	Sea ferns, Fire corals, Stinging medusae:		
Order Milleporina (=Athecata):			
Milleporidae spp. (all species in family except genus with earlier date)		II	1/18/90
Millepora spp	Fire corals	II	8/1/85
Order Stylasterina:			
Stylasteridae spp. (all species in family)		II	1/18/90
Plant Kingdom (note general exclusions and exceptions in introductory text):	Plants		
Family Agavaceae:	Agave family:		
Agave arizonica	New River agave	I	7/29/83
A. parviflora	Santa Cruz striped agave	I	7/29/83
Agave victoriae-reginae (=A. ferninandi-regis)	Queen Victoria agave	II	7/29/83
Nolina interrata	Dehesa bear-grass	I	7/29/83
Family Amaryllidaceae:	Amaryllis family:		
Galanthus spp. (and their natural hybrids)	Snowdrops	II	1/18/90
Sternbergia spp	Sternbergias	II	1/18/90
Family Apocynaceae:	Dogbane family:		
Pachypodium spp. (except species listed in App. I)	Pachypodiums	II	7/1/75
P. ambongense (and its natural hybrids)		I	7/1/75
P. baronii (and its natural hybrids)		I	7/1/75
Pachypodium brevicaule (and its natural hybrids)		II	7/1/75
P. decaryi (and its natural hybrids)		I	7/1/75
Rauvolfia serpentina (except chemical derivatives)	Snake-root devil-pepper	II	1/18/90
Family Araliaceae:	Ginseng family:		
Panax quinquefolius (whole and sliced roots and parts of roots, excluding manufactured parts or derivatives such as powders, pills, extracts, tonics, teas, and confectionery)	American ginseng	II	7/1/75
Family Araucariaceae:	Monkey-puzzle tree family:		
Araucaria araucana (all populations except that of Chile)	Monkey-puzzle tree	II	7/1/75

Scientific name	Common name	App.	Date
A. araucana (population of Chile)	Monkey-puzzle tree	I	7/1/75
Family Asclepiadaceae:	Milkweed family:		
Ceropegia spp.	Ceropegias	II	6/28/79
Frerea indica		II	6/28/79
Family Berberidaceae:	Barberry family:		
Podophyllum hexandrum (=P. emodi, =Sinopodophyllum hexandrum) (except chemical derivatives)	Himalayan may-apple	II	1/18/90
Family Bromeliaceae:	Pineapple family:		
Tillandsia harrisii	Harris tillandsia	II	6/11/92
T. kammii	Kamm tillandsia	II	6/11/92
T. kautskyi	Kautsky tillandsia	II	6/11/92
T. mauryana	Maury tillandsia	II	6/11/92
T. sprengeliana	Sprengel tillandsia	II	6/11/92
T. sucrei	Sucre tillandsia	II	6/11/92
T. xerographica	Xerographic tillandsia	II	6/11/92
Family Byblidaceae:	Byblis family:		
Byblis spp.	Byblis, Rainbow plants	II	6/28/79
Family Cactaceae (note general exclusions and exceptions in introductory text):	Cactus family:		
All species except those in App. I, and except artificially propagated specimens of the following hybrids and/or cultivars: (1) Hatiora x graeseri (=H. gaertneri x H. rosea); (2) Schlumbergera (=Zygocactus) truncata cultivars and its hybrids with S. opuntoides (=S.x exotica), S. orssichiana, and S. russelliana (=S.x buckleyi); (3) Gymnocalycium mihanovichii cultivars lacking chlorophyll, grafted on Hatiora "Jusbertii", Hylocereus trigonus or H. undatus; and (4)Opuntia microdasys	Cacti	II	7/1/75
Ariocarpus spp. (includes Neogomesia sp. and Roseocactus spp.)	Living-rock cacti	I	7/1/75
Astrophytum (=Echinocactus) asterias	Sea-urchin cactus, Star cactus	I	7/1/75
Aztekium ritteri	Aztec cactus	I	7/1/75
Coryphantha (other than C. werdermannii) (see Escobaria)			
Coryphantha werdermannii (=C. densispina; Mammillaria w.)	Jabali pincushion cactus	I	7/1/75
Discocactus spp.	Discocacti	I	7/1/75
Disocactus (=Lobeira, =Nopalxochia) macdougallii	MacDougall's cactus	I	7/1/75

Echinocereus ferreirianus var. lindsayi (=E. lindsayi)	Lindsay's hedgehog cactus	I	7/1/75
Echinocereus (=Cereus, =Wilcoxia) schmollii	Lamb's-tail cactus	I	7/1/75
Escobaria leei (=E. sneedii var. leei)	Lee pincushion cactus	I	7/1/75
Escobaria minima (=Coryphantha m., not Mammillaria m.; =C. nelliae, E. n., =Mammillaria n.)	Nellie's corycactus	I	7/1/75
E. sneedii, including E. s. var. leei (=Coryphantha s. var. l., =E. leei, =Mammillaria l.) and E. s. var. sneedii (=Coryphantha s., =Mammillaria s.)	Sneed pincushion cactus	I	7/1/75
Mammillaria pectinifera (=Solisia pectinata)	Conchilinque	I	7/1/75
M. solisioides	Pitayita	I	7/1/75
Melocactus conoideus	Conelike Turk's-cap cactus	I	7/1/75
M. deinacanthus	Wonderfully bristled Turk's-cap cactus	I	7/1/75
M. glaucescens	Wooly waxy-stemmed Turk's-cap cactus	I	7/1/75
M. paucispinus	Few-spined Turk's-cap cactus	I	7/1/75
Obregonia denegrii	Artichoke cactus	I	7/1/75
Pachycereus militaris (=Backebergia m., =Cephalocereus m., =Mitrocereus m., =Pachycereus chrysomallus)	Teddy-bear cactus, Military cap	I	7/1/75
Pediocactus (=Toumeya) bradyi	Brady's pincushion cactus	I	7/1/75
Pediocactus knowltonii (=P. bradyi var. k., =Toumeya k.)	Knowlton cactus	I	7/1/75
P. despainii	San Rafael cactus	I	7/1/75
P. paradinei (=Pilocanthus p.)	Houserock Valley cactus	I	7/1/75
P. peeblesianus, including P. p. var. fickeiseniae (=Navajoa f., =Toumeya f.) and P. p. var. peeblesianus (=Echinocactus p., =Navajoa p., =Toumeya p., =Utahia p.)	Fickeisen Navajo cactus, Peeble's Navajo cactus	I	7/1/75

Scientific name	Common name	Appendix	Date
P. sileri (=Echinocactus s., =Utahia s.)	Siler's pincushion cactus	I	7/1/75
P. winkleri	Winkler's cactus	I	7/1/75
Pelecyphora (=Encephalocarpus) spp.	Hatchet cactus, Pinecone cactus, Peyotillo	I	7/1/75
Sclerocactus brevihamatus subsp. tobuschii (=Ancistrocactus t., =Echinocactus t., =Ferocactus t., =Mammillaria t.)	Tobusch fishhook cactus	I	7/1/75
S. erectocentrus (=Echinocactus e., =Echinomastus e., =Neolloydia e., =Thelocactus e.; =Echinomastus acunensis, =Echinomastus e. var a., =Neolloydia e. var a.; =Echinocactus krausei, =Echinomastus k.)	Redspine fishhook cactus	I	7/1/75
S. glaucus (=S. franklinii; =Echinocactus g., =Ferocactus g., =Pediocactus g., =S. whipplei var. g.; =E. subglaucus; =S. wetlandicus; =S. w. var. ilseae)	Uinta Basin hookless cactus	I	7/1/75
S. (=Echinomastus, =Neolloydia) mariposensis	Mariposa cactus	I	7/1/75
S. mesae-verdae	Mesa Verde cactus	I	7/1/75
S. papyracanthus (=Echinocactus p., =Mammillaria p., =Pediocactus p., =Toumeya p.)	Grama-grass cactus	I	7/1/75
S. pubispinus	Great Basin fishhook cactus	I	7/1/75
S. wrightiae	Wright's fishhook cactus	I	7/1/75
Strombocactus spp. (=S. disciformis in broad sense)	Disc cactus, Top cactus	I	7/1/75
Turbinicarpus spp. (includes Gymnocactus spp., most Neolloydia spp. (in sense of E.F. Anderson 1986), Normanbokea spp., and Rapicactus spp.)	Turbinicarps	I	7/1/75
Uebelmannia spp.	Uebelmann cacti	I	7/1/75
Family Caryocaraceae:	Souari family:		
Caryocar costaricense	Ajo	II	7/1/75
Family Cephalotaceae:	Australian pitcher-plant family:		
Cephalotus follicularis	West Australian pitcher plant	II	6/28/79
Family Compositae (=Asteraceae):	Aster family:		
Saussurea costus (=lappa)	Costus, Kuth root	I	7/1/75
Family Crassulaceae:	Stonecrop family:		

Dudleya stolonifera	Laguna Beach dudleya	I	7/29/83
D. traskiae	Santa Barbara Island dudleya .	I	7/29/83
Family Cupressaceae:	Cypress family: ..		
Fitz-Roya cupressoides	Fitzroya, Alerce	I	7/1/75
Pilgerodendron uviferum ...	Pilgerodendron ..	I	7/1/75
Family Cyatheaceae:	Tree-fern family:		
All species in the family except those with earlier date		II	2/4/77
Cyathea (=Hemitelia) capensis		II	7/1/75
C. dredgei		II	7/1/75
C. mexicana		II	7/1/75
C. (=Alsophila) salvinii ..		II	7/1/75
Family Cycadaceae:	Old World cycad family (see families Stangeriaceae and Zamiaceae for other cycads):		
All species in the family except species in App. I		II	2/4/77
Cycas beddomei	Beddome cycad ...	I	2/4/77
Family Diapensiaceae:	Diapensia family:		
Shortia galacifolia	Oconee bells	II	7/29/83
Family Dicksoniaceae:	Tree-fern family:		
All species in the family .		II	2/4/77
Family Didiereaceae:	Alluaudia family:		
All species in the family .		II	2/4/77
Family Dioscoreaceae:	Yam family:		
Dioscorea deltoidea	Kniss, Kurta	II	7/1/75
Family Droseraceae:	Sundew family: ...		
Dionaea muscipula	Venus flytrap ...	II	6/11/92
Family Ericaceae:	Heath family:		
Kalmia cuneata	White wicky	II	7/29/83
Family Euphorbiaceae:	Spurge family: ...		
Euphorbia spp., except those species in App. I, and excluding non-succulent species and artificially propagated specimens of Euphorbia trigona cultivars	Euphorbias	II	7/1/75
E. capsaintemariensis (= E. decaryi var. c.) (and its natural hybrids)		I	7/1/75
E. decaryi (and its natural hybrids) (see also E. capsaintemariensis, formerly included in E. decaryi)		I	7/1/75
E. subgenus Lacanthis dwarf species in Madagascar and their natural hybrids as given below:	Malagasy dwarf euphorbias as shown:		
E. ambovombensis (and its natural hybrids)		I	7/1/75
E. cremersii		I	7/1/75
E. cylindrifolia (including subsp. tuberifera) (and its natural hybrids)		I	7/1/75
E. francoisii (and its natural hybrids)		I	7/1/75
E. moratii (and its natural hybrids)		I	7/1/75
E. parvicyathophora (and its natural hybrids)		I	7/1/75

E. quartziticola (and its natural hybrids)		I	7/1/75
E. tulearensis (= E. capsaintemariensis var. tulearensis) (and its natural hybrids)		I	7/1/75
Family Fouquieriaceae:	Ocotillo family:		
Fouquieria columnaris	Boojum tree	II	7/29/83
F. fasciculata	Arbol del barril	I	7/29/83
F. purpusii		I	7/29/83
Family Gnetaceae:	Gnetum family:		
Gnetum montanum		III (Nepal)	11/16/75
Family Juglandaceae:	Walnut family:		
Oreomunnea (=Engelhardia) pterocarpa	Gavilaln	II	7/1/75
Family Leguminosae (=Fabaceae):	Pea family:		
Dalbergia nigra	Brazilian rosewood	I	6/11/92
Pericopsis elata (including logs, sawn wood, and veneer sheets, but not other parts or derivatives)	Afrormosia	II	6/11/92
Platymiscium pleiostachyum	Cristobal, Granadillo	II	7/1/75
Pterocarpus santalinus (only logs, wood-chips, and unprocessed broken material)	Red sandalwood, Redsanders	II	2/16/95
Family Liliaceae:	Lily family:		
Aloe spp. (all except those in App. I, and excluding A. vera [=barbadensis] except A. vera var. chinensis)	Aloes	II	7/1/75
A. albida		I	7/1/75
A. albiflora		I	7/1/75
A. alfredii		I	7/1/75
A. bakeri		I	7/1/75
A. bellatula		I	7/1/75
A. calcairophila		I	7/1/75
A. compressa (incl. var. rugosquamosa, var. schistophila)		I	7/1/75
A. delphinensis		I	7/1/75
A. descoingsii		I	7/1/75
A. fragilis		I	7/1/75
A. haworthioides (incl. var. aurantiaca)		I	7/1/75
A. helenae		I	7/1/75
A. laeta (incl. var. maniensis)		I	7/1/75
A. parallelifolia		I	7/1/75
A. parvula		I	7/1/75
A. pillansii	Boomaalwyn	I	7/1/75
A. polyphylla	Spiral aloe	I	7/1/75
A. rauhii		I	7/1/75
A. suzannae		I	7/1/75
A. thorncroftii		I	7/1/75
A. versicolor		I	7/1/75
A. vossii		I	7/1/75
Family Magnoliaceae:	Magnolia family:		
Magnolia (=Talauma) hodgsonii		III (Nepal)	11/16/75
Family Meliaceae:	Mahogany family:		
Swietenia humilis	Pacific Coast mahogany	II	7/1/75
Swietenia macrophylla (populations in the			

Americas, including logs, sawn wood, and veneer sheets, but not other parts or derivatives ...	Bigleaf mahogany	III (Costa Rica)	11/16/95
S. mahagoni (including logs, sawn wood, and veneer sheets, but not other parts or derivatives)	Caribbean mahogany	II	6/11/92
Family Nepenthaceae:	Old World pitcher-plant family:		
Nepenthes spp. (all species except those in App. I)	Tropical pitcher plants	II	10/22/87
N. khasiana	Indian tropical pitcher plant	I	10/22/87
N. rajah	Giant tropical pitcher plant	I	6/6/81
Family Orchidaceae (= Apostasiaceae, Cypripediaceae) (note general exclusions and exceptions in introductory text):	Orchid family: ...		
All species except those in App. I	Orchids	II	7/1/75
Cattleya trianae	Christmas orchid	I	7/1/75
Dendrobium cruentum		I	7/1/75
Laelia jongheana		I	7/1/75
L. lobata		I	7/1/75
Paphiopedilum spp.	Asian tropical lady's slippers	I	7/1/75
Peristeria elata	Holy Ghost, Dove orchid	I	7/1/75
Phragmipedium spp. (includes Mexipedium sp.)	New World tropical lady's slippers	I	7/1/75
Renanthera imschootiana		I	7/1/75
Vanda coerulea	Blue vanda	I	7/1/75
Family Palmae (=Arecaceae):	Palm family:		
Chrysalidocarpus decipiens		II	2/4/77
Neodypsis decaryi	Triangle palm	II	7/1/75
Family Papaveraceae:	Poppy family:		
Meconopsis regia		III (Nepal)	11/16/75
Family Pinaceae:	Pine family:		
Abies guatemalensis	Guatemalan fir	I	7/1/75
Family Podocarpaceae:	Podocarp family:		
Podocarpus neriifolius		III (Nepal)	11/16/75
P. parlatorei	Parlatore's podocarp, Monteromero	I	7/1/75
Family Podophyllaceae (see Berberidaceae)			
Family Portulacaceae:	Portulaca family:		
Anacampseros spp. (including A. [= Grahamia] australiana, A. [=G.] kurtzii)		II	7/1/75
Avonia spp. (formerly a part of Anacampseros spp.)		II	7/1/75
Lewisia cotyledon	Siskiyou lewisia	II	7/29/83
L. maguirei	Maguire's lewisia	II	7/29/83
L. serrata	Saw-toothed lewisia	II	7/29/83
Family Primulaceae:	Primrose family:		
Cyclamen spp., excluding artificially propagated specimens of the			

cultivars of Cyclamen persicum (except when traded as dormant tubers)	Cyclamens	II	7/1/75
Family Proteaceae:	Protea family:		
Orothamnus zeyheri	Marsh-rose	II	7/1/75
Protea odorata	Ground-rose	II	7/1/75
Family Ranunculaceae:	Buttercup family:		
Hydrastis canadensis (whole and sliced roots and parts of roots, excluding manufactured parts or derivatives such as powders, pills, extracts, tonics, teas, and confectionery)	Goldenseal	II	9/18/97
Family Rosaceae:	Rose family:		
Prunus africana	African cherry	II	2/16/95
Family Rubiaceae:	Coffee family:		
Balmea stormiae	Ayuque	I	7/1/75
Family Sarraceniaceae:	New World pitcher-plant family:		
Darlingtonia californica	Western pitcher plant, Cobra-lily	II	6/6/81
Sarracenia spp. (all species and natural hybrids except species in App. I)	Trumpet pitcher plants	II	10/22/87
S. alabamensis subsp. alabamensis (=S. rubra subsp. alabamensis)	Alabama canebrake pitcher plant	I	6/6/81
S. jonesii (=S. rubra subsp. jonesii)	Mountain sweet pitcher plant	I	6/6/81
S. oreophila	Green pitcher plant	I	6/6/81
Family Scrophulariaceae:	Figwort family:		
Picrorhiza kurrooa (whole and sliced roots and parts of roots, excluding manufactured parts or derivatives such as powders, pills, extracts, tonics, teas, and confectionery)	Kutki	II	9/18/97
Family Stangeriaceae:	Stangeria family:		
Bowenia spp. (formerly in Zamiaceae)	Bipinnate cycads	II	2/4/77
Stangeria eriopus (=paradoxa)	Stangeria, Fern-leafed cycad	I	7/1/75
Family Taxaceae:	Yew family:		
Taxus wallichiana (=T. baccata subsp. wallichiana) (except finished pharmaceutical products)	Himalayan yew	II	2/16/95
Family Tetracentraceae:	Tetracentron family:		
Tetracentron sinense	Tetracentron	III (Nepal)	11/16/75
Family Thymelaeaceae (=Aquilariaceae):	Mezereon family:		
Aquilaria malaccensis	Agarwood, Aloewood	II	2/16/95
Family Valerianaceae:	Valerian family:		
Nardostachys grandiflora (=Nardostachys jatamansi misapplied) (whole and			

sliced roots and parts of roots, excluding manufactured parts or derivatives such as powders, pills, extracts, tonics, teas, and confectionery)	Himalayan nard or spikenard	II	9/18/97
Family Welwitschiaceae: ...	Welwitschia family:	....	
Welwitschia mirabilis (=bainesii)	Welwitschia	II	7/1/75
Family Zamiaceae:	Cycad family:	....	
All species except those in App. I	....	II	2/4/77
Ceratozamia spp............	Ceratozamias, Horncones	I	2/4/77
Chigua spp..................	....	I	2/4/77
Encephalartos spp...........	Bread palms, African cycads .	I	7/1/75
Microcycas calocoma	Palma corcho, Microcycas	I	7/1/75
Family Zingiberaceae:	Ginger family: ...	....	
Hedychium philippinense ...	Philippine garland flower .	II	7/1/75
Family Zygophyllaceae:	Cresote-bush family:	....	
Guaiacum officinale	Commoner lignum vitae	II	6/11/92
G. sanctum	Holywood lignum vitae	II	7/1/75

6.6 Endangered Species Act of 1973 (As Amended). 16 U.S.C. 1531 & 1537 (1976 & Supp. V 1981)

1531. Congressional findings and declaration of purposes and policy

(a). Findings

The Congress finds and declares that

(1). various species of fish, wildlife, and plants in the United States have been rendered extinct as a consequence of economic growth and development untempered by adequate concern and conservation;

(2). other species of fish, wildlife, and plants have been so depleted in numbers that they are in danger of or threatened with extinction;

(3). these species of fish, wildlife, and plants are of esthetic, ecological, educational, historical, recreational, and scientific value to the Nation and its people;

(4). the United States has pledged itself as a sovereign state in the international community to conserve to the extent practicable the various species of fish or wildlife and plants facing extinction, pursuant to

(A) migratory bird treaties with Canada and Mexico;

(B) the Migratory and Endangered Bird Treaty with Japan;

(C) the Convention on Nature Protection and Wildlife Preservation in the Western Hemisphere;

(D) the International Convention for the Northwest Atlantic Fisheries;

(E) the International Convention for the High Seas Fisheries of the North Pacific Ocean;

(F) the Convention on International Trade in Endangered Species of Wild Fauna and Flora; and

(G) other international agreements.

(5). encouraging the States and other interested parties, through Federal financial assistance and a system of incentives, to develop and maintain conservation programs which meet national and international standards is a key to meeting the Nation's international commitments and to better safeguarding, for the benefit of all citizens, the Nation's heritage in fish and wildlife.

(b). Purposes

The purposes of this chapter are to provide a means whereby the ecosystems upon which endangered species and threatened species depend may be conserved, to provide a program for the conservation of such endangered species and threatened species, and to take such steps as may be appropriate to achieve the purposes of the treaties and conventions set forth in subsection (a) of this section.

(c). Policy

It is further declared to be the policy of Congress that all Federal departments and agencies shall seek to conserve endangered species and threatened species and shall utilize their authorities in furtherance of the purposes of this chapter.

(Pub.L. 93205, 2, Dec. 28, 1973, 87 Stat. 884.)

* * *

1537. International cooperation

(a). Financial assistance

As a demonstration of the commitment of the United States to the worldwide protection of endangered species and threatened species, the President may, subject to the provisions of section 724 of title 31, use foreign currencies accruing to the United States Government under the Agricultural Trade Development and Assistance Act of 1954 [7 U.S.C. 1691 et seq.] or any other law to provide to any foreign country (with its consent) assistance in the development and management of programs in that country which the Secretary determines to be necessary or useful for the conservation of any endangered species or threatened species listed by the Secretary pursuant to section 1533 of this title. The President shall provide assistance (which includes, but is not limited to, the acquisition, by lease or otherwise, of lands, waters, or interests therein) to foreign countries under this section under such terms and conditions as he deems appropriate. Whenever foreign currencies are available for the provision of assistance under this section, such currencies shall be used in preference to funds appropriated under the authority of section 1542 of this title.

(b). Encouragement of foreign programs

In order to carry out further the provisions of this chapter, the Secretary, through the Secretary of State, shall encourage

(1) foreign countries to provide for the conservation of fish or wildlife including endangered species and threatened species listed pursuant to section 1533 of this title;

(2) the entering into of bilateral or multilateral agreements with foreign countries to provide for such conservation; and

(3) foreign persons who directly or indirectly take fish or wildlife in foreign countries or on the high seas for importation into the United States for commercial or other purposes to develop and carry out with such assistance as he may provide, conservation practices designed to enhance such fish or wildlife and their habitat.

(c). Personnel

After consultation with the Secretary of State, the Secretary may

(1) assign or otherwise make available any officer or employee of his department for the purpose of cooperating with foreign countries and international organizations in developing personnel resources and programs which promote the conservation of fish or wildlife; and

(2) conduct or provide financial assistance for the educational training of foreign personnel, in this country or abroad, in fish, wildlife, or plant management, research and law enforcement and to render professional assistance abroad in such matters.

(d). Investigations

After consultation with the Secretary of State and the Secretary of the Treasury, as appropriate, the Secretary may conduct or cause to be conducted such law enforcement investigations and research abroad as he deems necessary to carry out the purposes of this chapter.

(e). Convention implementation

The President is authorized and directed to designate agencies to act as the Management Authority or Authorities and the Scientific Authority or Authorities pursuant to the Convention. The agencies so designated shall thereafter be authorized to do all things assigned to them under the Convention, including the issuance of permits and certificates. The agency designated by the President to communicate with other parties to the Convention and with the Secretariat shall also be empowered, where appropriate, in consultation with the State Department, to act on behalf of and represent the United States in all regards as required by the Convention. The President shall also designate those agencies which shall act on behalf of and represent the United States in all regards as required by the Convention on Nature Protection and Wildlife Preservation in the Western Hemisphere.

(Pub.L. 93205, 8, Dec. 28, 1973, 87 Stat. 892.)

6.7 Convention on the Conservation of Migratory Species of Wild Animals (Without Appendices) (As Amended 1985, 1988). Signed at Bonn, 23 June 1979. Entered into force, 1 November 1983. *Reprinted in* 19 I.L.M. 15 (1980) & 5A Weston V.H.11

The Contracting Parties,

RECOGNIZING that wild animals in their innumerable forms are an irreplaceable part of the earth's natural system which must be conserved for the good of mankind;

AWARE that each generation of man holds the resources of the earth for future generations and has an obligation to ensure that this legacy is conserved and, where utilized, is used wisely;

CONSCIOUS of the ever-growing value of wild animals from environmental, ecological, genetic, scientific, aesthetic, recreational, cultural, educational, social and economic points of view;

CONCERNED particularly with those species of wild animals that migrate across or outside national jurisdictional boundaries;

RECOGNIZING that the States are and must be the protectors of the migratory species of wild animals that live within or pass through their national jurisdictional boundaries;

CONVINCED that conservation and effective management of migratory species of wild animals require the concerted action of all States within the national jurisdictional boundaries of which such species spend any part of their life cycle;

RECALLING Recommendation 32 of the Action Plan adopted by the United Nations Conference on the Human Environment (Stockholm, 1972) and noted with satisfaction at the Twenty-seventh Session of the General Assembly of the United Nations,

HAVE AGREED as follows:

Article I

Interpretation

1. For the purpose of this Convention:

a) "Migratory species" means the entire population or any geographically separate part of the population of any species or lower taxon of wild animals, a significant proportion of whose members cyclically and predictably cross one or more national jurisdictional boundaries;

b) "Conservation status of a migratory species" means the sum of the influences acting on the migratory species that may affect its long-term distribution and abundance;

c) "Conservation status" will be taken as "favourable" when:

(1) population dynamics data indicate that the migratory species is maintaining itself on a long-term basis as a viable component of its ecosystems;

(2) the range of the migratory species is neither currently being reduced, nor is likely to be reduced, on a long-term basis;

(3) there is, and will be in the foreseeable future sufficient habitat to maintain the population of the migratory species on a long-term basis; and

(4) the distribution and abundance of the migratory species approach historic coverage and levels to the extent that potentially suitable ecosystems exist and to the extent consistent with wise wildlife management;

d) "Conservation status" will be taken as "unfavourable" if any of the conditions set out in sub-paragraph (c) of this paragraph is not met;

e) "Endangered" in relation to a particular migratory species means that the migratory species is in danger of extinction throughout all or a significant portion of its range;

f) "Range" means all the areas of land or water that a migratory species inhabits, stays in temporarily, crosses or overflies at any time on its normal migration route;

g) "Habitat" means any area in the range of a migratory species which contains suitable living conditions for that species;

h) "Range State" in relation to a particular migratory species means any State (and where appropriate any other Party referred to under subparagraph (k) of this paragraph) that exercises jurisdiction over any part of the range of that migratory species, or a State, flag vessels of which are engaged outside national jurisdictional limits in taking that migratory species;

i) "Taking" means taking, hunting, fishing capturing, harassing, deliberate killing, or attempting to engage in any such conduct;

j) "Agreement" means an international agreement relating to the conservation of one or more migratory species as provided for in Articles IV and V of this Convention; and

k) "Party" means a State or any regional economic integration organization constituted by sovereign States which has competence in respect of the negotiation, conclusion and application of international Agreements in matters covered by this Convention for which this Convention is in force.

2. In matters within their competence, the regional economic integration organizations which are Parties to this Convention shall in their own name exercise the rights and fulfil the responsibilities which this Convention attributes to their member States. In such cases the member States of these organizations shall not be entitled to exercise such rights individually.

3. Where this Convention provides for a decision to be taken by either a two-thirds majority or a unanimous decision of "the Parties present and voting" this shall mean "the Parties present and casting an affirmative or negative vote". Those abstaining from voting shall not be counted amongst "the Parties present and voting" in determining the majority.

Article II

Fundamental principles

1. The Parties acknowledge the importance of migratory species being conserved and of Range States agreeing to take action to this end whenever possible and appropriate, paying special attention to migratory species the conservation status of which is unfavourable, and taking individually or in co-operation appropriate and necessary steps to conserve such species and their habitat.

2. The Parties acknowledge the need to take action to avoid any migratory species becoming endangered.

3. In particular, the Parties:

a) should promote, co-operate in and support research relating to migratory species;

b) shall endeavour to provide immediate protection for migratory species included in Appendix I; and

c) shall endeavour to conclude Agreements covering the conservation and management of migratory species included in Appendix II.

Article III

Endangered migratory species: Appendix I

1. Appendix I shall list migratory species which are endangered.

2. A migratory species may be listed in Appendix I provided that reliable evidence, including the best scientific evidence available, indicates that the species is endangered.

3. A migratory species may be removed from Appendix I when the Conference of the Parties determines that:

a) reliable evidence, including the best scientific evidence available, indicates that the species is no longer endangered, and

b) the species is not likely to become endangered again because of loss of protection due to its removal from Appendix I.

4. Parties that are Range States of a migratory species listed in Appendix I shall endeavour:

a) to conserve and, where feasible and appropriate, restore those habitats of the species which are of importance in removing the species from danger of extinction;

b) to prevent, remove, compensate for or minimize, as appropriate, the adverse effects of activities or obstacles that seriously impede or prevent the migration of the species; and

c) to the extent feasible and appropriate, to prevent, reduce or control factors that are endangering or are likely to further endanger the species, including strictly controlling the introduction of, or controlling or eliminating, already introduced exotic species.

5. Parties that are Range States of a migratory species listed in Appendix I shall prohibit the taking of animals belonging to such species. Exceptions may be made to this prohibition only if:

a) the taking is for scientific purposes;

b) the taking is for the purpose of enhancing the propagation or survival of the affected species;

c) the taking is to accommodate the needs of traditional subsistence users of such species; or

d) extraordinary circumstances so require; provided that such exceptions are precise as to content and limited in space and time. Such taking should not operate to the disadvantage of the species.

6. The Conferences of the Parties may recommend to the Parties that are Range States of a migratory species listed in Appendix I that they take further measures considered appropriate to benefit the species.

7. The Parties shall as soon as possible inform the Secretariat of any exceptions made pursuant to paragraph 5 of this Article.

Article IV

Migratory species to be the subject of agreements: Appendix II

1. Appendix II shall list migratory species which have an unfavourable conservation status and which require international agreements for their conservation and management, as well as those which have a conservation status which would signifi-

cantly benefit from the international cooperation that could be achieved by an international agreement.

2. If the circumstances so warrant, a migratory species may be listed both in Appendix I and Appendix II.

3. Parties that are Range States of migratory species listed in Appendix II shall endeavour to conclude Agreements where these should benefit the species and should give priority to those species in an unfavourable conservation status.

4. Parties are encouraged to take action with a view to concluding agreements for any population or any geographically separate part of the population of any species or lower taxon of wild animals, members of which periodically cross one or more national jurisdiction boundaries.

5. The Secretariat shall be provided with a copy of each Agreement concluded pursuant to the provisions of this Article.

Article V

Guidelines for agreements

1. The object of each Agreement shall be to restore the migratory species concerned to a favourable conservation status or to maintain it in such a status. Each Agreement should deal with those aspects of the conservation and management of the migratory species concerned which serve to achieve that object.

2. Each Agreement should cover the whole of the range of the migratory species concerned and should be open to accession by all Range States of that species, whether or not they are Parties to this Convention.

3. An Agreement should, wherever possible, deal with more than one migratory species.

4. Each Agreement should:

a) identify the migratory species covered;

b) describe the range and migration route of the migratory species;

c) provide for each Party to designate its national authority concerned with the implementation of the Agreement,

d) establish, if necessary, appropriate machinery to assist in carrying out the aims of the Agreement, to monitor its effectiveness, and to prepare reports for the Conference of the Parties;

e) provide for procedures for the settlement of disputes between Parties to the Agreement; and

f) at a minimum, prohibit, in relation to a migratory species of the Order Cetacea, any taking that is not permitted for that migratory species under any other multilateral Agreement and provide for accession to the Agreement by States that are not Range States of that migratory species.

5. Where appropriate and feasible, each Agreement should provide for but not be limited to:

a) periodic review of the conservation status of the migratory species concerned and the identification of the factors which may be harmful to that status;

b) co-ordinated conservation and management plans;

c) research into the ecology and population dynamics of the migratory species concerned, with special regard to migration;

d) the exchange of information on the migratory species concerned, special regard being paid to the exchange of the results of research and of relevant statistics;

e) conservation and, where required and feasible, restoration of the habitats of importance in maintaining a favourable conservation status, and protection of such habitats from disturbances, including strict control of the introduction of, or control of already introduced, exotic species detrimental to the migratory species;

f) maintenance of a network of suitable habitats appropriately disposed in relation to the migration routes;

g) where it appears desirable, the provision of new habitats favourable to the migratory species or reintroduction of the migratory species into favourable habitats;

h) elimination of, to the maximum extent possible, or compensation for activities and obstacles which hinder or impede migration;

i) prevention, reduction or control of the release into the habitat of the migratory species of substances harmful to that migratory species;

j) measures based on sound ecological principles to control and manage the taking of the migratory species;

k) procedures for co-ordinating action to suppress illegal taking;

l) exchange of information on substantial threats to the migratory species;

m) emergency procedures whereby conservation action would be considerably and rapidly strengthened when the conservation status of the migratory species is seriously affected; and

n) making the general public aware of the contents and aims of the Agreement.

Article VI

Range states

1. A list of the Range States of migratory species listed in Appendices I and II shall be kept up to date by the Secretariat using information it has received from the Parties.

2. The Parties shall keep the Secretariat informed in regard to which of the migratory species listed in Appendices I and II they consider themselves to be Range States, including provision of information on their flag vessels engaged outside national jurisdictional limits in taking the migratory species concerned and, where possible, future plans in respect of such taking.

3. The Parties which are Range States for migratory species listed in Appendix I or Appendix II should inform the Conference of the Parties through the Secretariat, at least six months prior to each ordinary meeting of the Conference, on measures that they are taking to implement the provisions of this Convention for these species.

Article VII

The conference of the parties

1. The Conference of the Parties shall be the decision-making organ of this Convention.

2. The Secretariat shall call a meeting of the Conference of the Parties not later than two years after the entry into force of this Convention.

3. Thereafter the Secretariat shall convene ordinary meetings of the Conference of the Parties at intervals of not more than three years, unless the Conference decides

otherwise, and extraordinary meetings at any time on the written request of at least one-third of the Parties.

4. The Conference of the Parties shall establish and keep under review the financial regulations of this Convention. The Conference of the Parties shall, at each of its ordinary meetings, adopt the budget for the next financial period. Each Party shall contribute to this budget according to a scale to be agreed upon by the Conference. Financial regulations, including the provisions on the budget and the scale of contributions as well as their modifications, shall be adopted by unanimous vote of the Parties present and voting.

5. At each of its meetings the Conference of the Parties shall review the implementation of this Convention and may in particular:

a) review and assess the conservation status of migratory species;

b) review the progress made towards the conservation of migratory species, especially those listed in Appendices I and II;

c) make such provision and provide such guidance as may be necessary to enable the Scientific Council and the Secretariat to carry out their duties;

d) receive and consider any reports presented by the Scientific Council, the Secretariat, any Party or any standing body established pursuant to an Agreement;

e) make recommendations to the Parties for improving the conservation status of migratory species and review the progress being made under Agreements;

f) in those cases where an Agreement has not been concluded, make recommendations for the convening of meetings of the Parties that are Range States of a migratory species or group of migratory species to discuss measures to improve the conservation status of the species;

g) make recommendations to the Parties for improving the effectiveness of this Convention; and

h) decide on any additional measure that should be taken to implement the objectives of this Convention.

6. Each meeting of the Conference of the Parties should determine the time and venue of the next meeting.

7. Any meeting of the Conference of the Parties shall determine and adopt rules of procedure for that meeting. Decisions at a meeting of the Conference of the Parties shall require a two-thirds majority of the Parties present and voting, except where otherwise provided for by this Convention.

8. The United Nations, its Specialized Agencies, the International Atomic Energy Agency, as well as any State not a party to this Convention and, for each Agreement, the body designated by the parties to that Agreement, may be represented by observers at meetings of the Conference of the Parties.

9. Any agency or body technically qualified in protection, conservation and management of migratory species, in the following categories, which has informed the Secretariat of its desire to be represented at meetings of the Conference of the Parties by observers, shall be admitted unless at least one-third of the Parties present object:

a) international agencies or bodies, either governmental or non-governmental, and national governmental agencies and bodies; and

b) national non-governmental agencies or bodies which have been approved for this purpose by the State in which they are located.

Once admitted, these observers shall have the right to participate but not to vote.

Article VIII

The scientific council

1. At its first meeting, the Conference of the Parties shall establish a Scientific Council to provide advice on scientific matters.

2. Any Party may appoint a qualified expert as a member of the Scientific Council. In addition, the Scientific Council shall include as members qualified experts selected and appointed by the Conference of the Parties; the number of these experts, the criteria for their selection and the terms of their appointments shall be as determined by the Conference of the Parties.

3. The Scientific Council shall meet at the request of the Secretariat as required by the Conference of the Parties.

4. Subject to the approval of the Conference of the Parties, the Scientific Council shall establish its own rules of procedure.

5. The Conference of the Parties shall determine the functions of the Scientific Council, which may include:

a) providing scientific advice to the Conference of the Parties, to the Secretariat, and, if approved by the Conference of the Parties, to any body set up under this Convention or an Agreement or to any Party;

b) recommending research and the co-ordination of research on migratory species, evaluating the results of such research in order to ascertain the conservation status of migratory species and reporting to the Conference of the Parties on such status and measures for its improvement;

c) making recommendations to the Conference of the Parties as to the migratory species to be included in Appendices I and II, together with an indication of the range of such migratory species;

d) making recommendations to the Conference of the Parties as to specific conservation and management measures to be included in Agreements on migratory species; and

e) recommending to the Conference of the Parties solutions to problems relating to the scientific aspects of the implementation of this Convention, in particular with regard to the habitats of migratory species.

Article IX

The secretariat

1. For the purposes of this Convention a Secretariat shall be established.

2. Upon entry into force of this Convention, the Secretariat is provided by the Executive Director of the United Nations Environment Programme. To the extent and in the manner he considers appropriate, he may be assisted by suitable intergovernmental or non-governmental, international or national agencies and bodies technically qualified in protection, conservation and management of wild animals.

3. If the United Nations Environment Programme is no longer able to provide the Secretariat, the Conference of the Parties shall make alternative arrangements for the Secretariat.

4. The functions of the Secretariat shall be:

a) to arrange for and service meetings: (i) of the Conference of the Parties, and (ii) of the Scientific Council;

b) to maintain liaison with and promote liaison between the Parties, the standing bodies set up under Agreements and other international organizations concerned with migratory species;

c) to obtain from any appropriate source reports and other information which will further the objectives and implementation of this Convention and to arrange for the appropriate dissemination of such information;

d) to invite the attention of the Conference of the Parties to any matter pertaining to the objectives of this Convention;

e) to prepare for the Conference of the Parties reports on the work of the Secretariat and on the implementation of this Convention;

f) to maintain and publish a list of Range States of all migratory species included in Appendices I and II;

g) to promote, under the direction of the Conference of the Parties, the conclusion of Agreements,

h) to maintain and make available to the Parties a list of Agreements and, if so required by the Conference of the Parties, to provide any information on such Agreements;

i) to maintain and publish a list of the recommendations made by the Conference of the Parties pursuant to sub-paragraphs (e), (f) and (g) of paragraph 5 of Article VII or of decisions made pursuant to sub-paragraph (h) of that paragraph;

j) to provide for the general public information concerning this Convention and its objectives; and

k) to perform any other function entrusted to it under this Convention or by the Conference of the Parties.

Article X

Amendment of the convention

1. This Convention may be amended at any ordinary or extraordinary meeting of the Conference of the Parties.

2. Proposals for amendment may be made by any Party.

3. The text of any proposed amendment and the reasons for it shall be communicated to the Secretary at least one hundred and fifty days before the meeting at which it is to be considered and shall promptly be communicated by the Secretary to all Parties. Any comments on the text by the Parties shall be communicated to the Secretariat not less than sixty days before the meeting begins. The Secretariat shall, immediately after the last day for submission of comments, communicate to the Parties all comments submitted by that day.

4. Amendments shall be adopted by a two-thirds majority of Parties present and voting.

5. An amendment adopted shall enter into force for all Parties which have accepted it on the first day of the third month following the date on which two-thirds of the Parties have deposited an instrument of acceptance with the Depositary. For each Party which deposits an instrument of acceptance after the date on which two-thirds of the Parties have deposited an instrument of acceptance, the amendment shall enter into force for that Party on the first day of the third month following the deposit of its instrument of acceptance.

Article XI

Amendment of the appendices

1. Appendices I and II may be amended at any ordinary or extraordinary meeting of the Conference of the Parties.

2. Proposals for amendment may be made by any Party.

3. The text of any proposed amendment and the reasons for it, based on the best scientific evidence available, shall be communicated to the Secretariat at least one hundred and fifty days before the meeting and shall promptly be communicated by the Secretariat to all Parties. Any comments on the text by the Parties shall be communicated to the Secretariat not less than sixty days before the meeting begins. The Secretariat shall, immediately after the last day for submission of comments, communicate to the Parties all comments submitted by that day.

4. Amendments shall be adopted by a two-thirds majority of Parties present and voting.

5. An amendment to the Appendices shall enter into force for all Parties ninety days after the meeting of the Conference of the Parties at which it was adopted, except for those Parties which make a reservation in accordance with paragraph 6 of this Article.

6. During the period of ninety days provided for in paragraph 5 of this Article, any Party may by notification in writing to the Depositary make a reservation with respect to the amendment. A reservation to an amendment may be withdrawn by written notification to the Depositary and thereupon the amendment shall enter into force for that Party ninety days after the reservation is withdrawn.

Article XII

Effect on international conventions and other legislation

1. Nothing in this Convention shall prejudice the codification and development of the law of the sea by the United Nations Conference on the Law of the Sea convened pursuant to Resolution 2750 C (XXV) of the General Assembly of the United Nations nor the present or future claims and legal views of any State concerning the law of the sea and the nature and extent of coastal and flag State jurisdiction.

2. The provisions of this Convention shall in no way affect the rights or obligations of any Party deriving from any existing treaty, convention or Agreement.

3. The provisions of this Convention shall in no way affect the right of Parties to adopt stricter domestic measures concerning the conservation of migratory species listed in Appendices I and II or to adopt domestic measures concerning the conservation of species not listed in Appendices I and II.

Article XIII

Settlement of disputes

1. Any dispute which may arise between two or more Parties with respect to the interpretation or application of the provisions of this Convention shall be subject to negotiation between the Parties involved in the dispute.

2. If the dispute cannot be resolved in accordance with paragraph 1 of this Article, the Parties may, by mutual consent, submit the dispute to arbitration, in particular that of the Permanent Court of Arbitration at The Hague, and the Parties submitting the dispute shall be bound by the arbitral decision.

Article XIV

Reservations

1. The provisions of this Convention shall not be subject to general reservations. Specific reservations may be entered in accordance with the provisions of this Article and Article XI.

2. Any State or regional economic integration organization may, on depositing its instrument of ratification, acceptance, approval or accession, enter a specific reserva-

tion with regard to the presence on either Appendix I or Appendix II or both, of any migratory species and shall then not be regarded as a Party in regard to the subject of that reservation until ninety days after the Depositary has transmitted to the Parties notification that such reservation has been withdrawn.

Article XV

Signature

This Convention shall be open for signature at Bonn for all States and any regional economic integration organization until the twenty-second day of June, 1980.

Article XVI

Ratification, acceptance, approval

This Convention shall be subject to ratification, acceptance or approval. Instruments of ratification, acceptance or approval shall be deposited with the Government of the Federal Republic of Germany, which shall be the Depositary.

Article XVII

Accession

After the twenty-second day of June 1980 this Convention shall be open for accession by all non-signatory States and any regional economic integration organization. Instruments of accession shall be deposited with the Depositary.

Article XVIII

Entry into force

1. This Convention shall enter into force on the first day of the third month following the date of deposit of the fifteenth instrument of ratification, acceptance, approval or accession with the Depositary.

2. For each State or each regional economic integration organization which ratifies, accepts or approves this Convention or accedes thereto after the deposit of the fifteenth instrument of ratification, acceptance, approval or accession, this Convention shall enter into force on the first day of the third month following the deposit by such State or such organization of its instrument of ratification, acceptance, approval or accession.

Article XIX

Denunciation

Any Party may denounce this Convention by written notification to the Depositary at any time. The denunciation shall take effect twelve months after the Depositary has received the notification.

Article XX

Depositary

1. The original of this Convention, in the English, French, German, Russian and Spanish languages, each version being equally authentic, shall be deposited with the Depositary. The Depositary shall transmit certified copies of each of these versions to all States and all regional economic integration organizations that have signed the Convention or deposited instruments of accession to it.

2. The Depositary shall, after consultation with the Governments concerned, prepare official versions of the text of this Convention in the Arabic and Chinese languages.

3. The Depositary shall inform all signatory and acceding States and all signatory and acceding regional economic integration organizations and the Secretariat of signatures, deposit of instruments of ratification, acceptance, approval or accession, entry into force of this Convention, amendments thereto, specific reservations and notifications of denunciation.

4. As soon as this Convention enters into force, a certified copy thereof shall be transmitted by the Depositary to the Secretariat of the United Nations for registration and publication in accordance with Article 102 of the Charter of the United Nations. In witness whereof the undersigned, being duly authorized to that effect, have signed this Convention.

Done at Bonn on 23 June 1979.

6.8 Convention for the Prohibition of Fishing With Long Driftnets in the South Pacific (Without Protocols). Concluded at Wellington, 23 November 1989. Entered into force, 17 May 1991. *Reprinted in* 29 I.L.M. 1454 (1990) & 5A Weston V.H.18

The Parties to this Convention,

RECOGNISING the importance of marine living resources to the people of the South Pacific region;

PROFOUNDLY CONCERNED at the damage now being done by pelagic drift-net fishing to the albacore tuna resource and to the environment and economy of the South Pacific region;

CONCERNED ALSO for the navigational threat posed by drift-net fishing;

NOTING that the increasing fishing capacity induced by large scale drift-net fishing threatens the fish stocks in the South Pacific;

MINDFUL OF the relevant rules of international law, including the provisions of the United Nations Convention on the Law of the Sea, done at Montego Bay on 10 December 1982, in particular Parts V, VII and XVI;

RECALLING the Declaration of the South Pacific Forum at Tarawa, 11 July 1989, that a Convention should be adopted to ban the use of drift nets in the South Pacific region;

RECALLING ALSO the Resolution of the 29th South Pacific Conference at Guam, which called for an immediate ban on the practice of drift-net fishing in the South Pacific Commission region;

HAVE AGREED as follows:

Article 1

DEFINITIONS

For the purpose of this Convention and its Protocols:

(a) The "Convention Area",

(i) Subject to subparagraph (ii) of this paragraph, shall be the area lying within 10 degrees North latitude and 50 degrees South latitude and 130 degrees East longitude and 120 degrees West longitude, and shall also include all waters under the fisheries jurisdiction of any Party to this Convention;

(ii) In the case of a State or Territory which is Party to the Convention by virtue of paragraph 1(b) or 1(c) of article 10, it shall include only waters under the fisheries jurisdiction of that Party, adjacent to the Territory referred to in paragraph 1(b) or 1(c) of article 10.

(b) "drift net" means a gillnet or other net or a combination of nets which is more than 2.5 kilometres in length the purpose of which is to enmesh, entrap or entangle fish by drifting on the surface of or in the water;

(c) "drift net fishing activities" means:

(i) catching, taking or harvesting fish with the use of a drift net;

(ii) attempting to catch, take or harvest fish with the use of a drift net;

(iii) engaging in any other activity which can reasonably be expected to result in the catching, taking or harvesting of fish with the use of a drift net, including searching for and locating fish to be taken by that method;

(iv) any operations at sea in support of, or in preparation for, any activity described in this paragraph, including operations of placing, searching for or recovering fish aggregating devices or associated electronic equipment such as radio beacons;

(v) aircraft use, relating to the activities described in this paragraph, except for flights in emergencies involving the health or safety of crew members or the safety of a vessel; or

(vi) transporting, transshipping and processing any drift-net catch, and cooperation in the provision of food, fuel and other supplies for vessels equipped for or engaged in drift-net fishing.

(d) the "FFA" means the South Pacific Forum Fisheries Agency; and

(e) "fishing vessel" means any vessel or boat equipped for or engaged in searching for, catching, processing or transporting fish or other marine organisms.

Article 2

MEASURES REGARDING NATIONALS AND VESSELS

Each Party undertakes to prohibit its nationals and vessels documented under its laws from engaging in drift-net fishing activities within the Convention Area.

Article 3

MEASURES AGAINST DRIFTNET FISHING ACTIVITIES

1. Each Party undertakes:

(a) not to assist or encourage the use of driftnets within the Convention Area; and

(b) to take measures consistent with international law to restrict drift-net fishing activities within the Convention Area, including but not limited to:

(i) prohibiting the use of driftnets within areas under its fisheries jurisdiction; and

(ii) prohibiting the transshipment of drift-net catches within areas under its jurisdiction.

2. Each Party may also take measures consistent with international law to:

(a) prohibit the landing of drift-net catches within its territory;

(b) prohibit the processing of drift-net catches in facilities under its jurisdiction;

(c) prohibit the importation of any fish or fish product, whether processed or not, which was caught using a driftnet.

(d) restrict port access and port servicing facilities for drift-net fishing vessels; and

(e) prohibit the possession of drift nets on board any fishing vessel within areas under its fisheries jurisdiction.

3. Nothing in this Convention shall prevent a Party from taking measures against drift-net fishing activities which are stricter than those required by the Convention.

Article 4

ENFORCEMENT

1. Each Party shall take appropriate measures to ensure the application of the provisions of this Convention.

2. The Parties undertake to collaborate to facilitate surveillance and enforcement of measures taken by Parties pursuant to this Convention.

3. The Parties undertake measures leading to the withdrawal of good standing on the Regional Register of Foreign Fishing Vessels maintained by the FFA against any vessel engaging in drift-net fishing activities.

Article 5

CONSULTATION WITH NONPARTIES

1. The Parties shall seek to consult with any State which is eligible to become a Party to this Convention on any matter relating to drift-net fishing activities which appear to affect adversely the conservation of marine living resources within the Convention Area or the implementation of the Convention and its protocols.

2. The Parties shall seek to reach agreement with any State referred to in paragraph 1 of this article, concerning the prohibitions established pursuant to articles 2 and 3.

Article 6

INSTITUTIONAL ARRANGEMENTS

1. The FFA shall be responsible for carrying out the following functions:

(a) the collection, preparation and dissemination of information on drift-net fishing activities within the Convention Area;

(b) the facilitation of scientific analyses on the effects of drift-net fishing activities within the Convention Area, including consultations with appropriate regional and international organizations; and

(c) the preparation and transmission to the Parties of the annual report on any drift-net fishing activities within the Convention Area and the measures taken to implement this Convention or its Protocols.

2. Each Party shall expeditiously convey to the FFA:

(a) information on the measures adopted by it pursuant to the implementation of the Convention; and

(b) information on, and scientific analyses on the effects of, drift-net fishing activities relevant to the Convention Area.

3. All Parties, including States or Territories not members of the FFA, and the FFA shall cooperate to promote the effective implementation of this article.

Article 7

REVIEW AND CONSULTATION AMONG PARTIES

1. Without prejudice to the conduct of consultations among Parties by other means, the FFA, at the request of three Parties, shall convene meetings of the Parties to review the implementation of this Convention and its Protocols.

2. Parties to the Protocols shall be invited to any such meeting and to participate in a manner to be determined by the Parties to the Convention.

Article 8

CONSERVATION AND MANAGEMENT MEASURES

Parties to this Convention shall co-operate with each other and with appropriate distant water fishing nations and other entities or organizations in the development of conservation and management measures for South Pacific albacore tuna within the Convention Area.

Article 9

PROTOCOLS

This Convention may be supplemented by Protocols or associated instruments to further its objectives.

Article 10

SIGNATURE, RATIFICATION AND ACCESSION

1. This Convention shall be open for signature by:

(a) any member of the FFA; and

(b) any State in respect of any Territory situated within the Convention Area for which it is internationally responsible; or

(c) any Territory situated within the Convention Area which has been authorized to sign the Convention and to assume rights and obligations under it by the Government of the State which is internationally responsible for it.

2. This Convention is subject to ratification by members of the FFA and the other States and Territories referred to in paragraph 1 of this article. The instruments of ratification shall be deposited with the Government of New Zealand which shall be the depositary.

3. This Convention shall remain open for accession by the members of the FFA and the other States and Territories referred to in paragraph 1 of this article. The instruments of accession shall be deposited with the Depositary.

Article 11

RESERVATIONS

This Convention shall not be subject to reservations.

Article 12

AMENDMENTS

1. Any Party may propose amendments to this Convention.

2. Amendments shall be adopted by consensus among the Parties.

3. Any amendments adopted shall be submitted by the Depositary to all Parties for ratification, approval or acceptance.

4. An amendment shall enter into force thirty days after receipt by the Depositary of instruments of ratification, approval or acceptance from all Parties.

Article 13

ENTRY INTO FORCE

1. This Convention shall enter into force on the date of deposit of the fourth instrument of ratification or accession.

2. For any member of the FFA or a State or Territory which ratifies or accedes to this Convention after the date of deposit of the fourth instrument of ratification or accession, the Convention shall enter into force on the date of deposit of its instruments of ratification or accession.

Article 14

CERTIFICATION AND REGISTRATION

1. The original of this Convention and its Protocols shall be deposited with the Depositary, which shall transmit certified copies to all States and Territories eligible to become Party to Convention and to all States eligible to become Party to a Protocol to the Convention.

2. The Depositary shall register this Convention and its Protocols in accordance with Article 102 of the Charter of the United Nations.

6.9 Resolution on Large-scale Pelagic Driftnet Fishing and Its Impact on the Living Marine Resources of the World's Oceans and Seas. Adopted by the U.N. General Assembly, 22 December 1989. U.N. Doc. A/RES/44/225; *reprinted in* 29 I.L.M. 1555 (1990) & 5A Weston V.H.19

The General Assembly,

Noting that many countries are disturbed by the increase in the use of large-scale pelagic driftnets, which can reach or exceed 30 miles (48 kilometres) in total length, to catch living marine resources on the high seas of the world's oceans and seas,

Mindful that large-scale pelagic driftnet fishing, a method of fishing with a net or a combination of nets intended to be held in a more or less vertical position by floats and weights, the purpose of which is to enmesh fish by drifting on the surface of or in the water, can be a highly indiscriminate and wasteful fishing method that is widely considered to threaten the effective conservation of living marine resources, such as highly migratory and anadromous species of fish, birds and marine mammals,

Drawing attention to the fact that the present resolution does not address the question of small-scale driftnet fishing traditionally conducted in coastal waters, especially by developing countries, which provides an important contribution to their subsistence and economic development,

Expressing concern that, in addition to targeted species of fish, non-targeted fish, marine mammals, seabirds and other living marine resources of the world's oceans and seas can become entangled in large-scale pelagic driftnets, either in those in active use or in those that are lost or discarded, and as a result of such entanglement are often either injured or killed,

Recognizing that more than one thousand fishing vessels use large-scale pelagic driftnets in the Pacific, Atlantic and Indian Oceans and in other areas of the high seas,

Recognizing also that any regulatory measure to be taken for the conservation and management of living marine resources should take account of the best available scientific data and analysis,

Recalling the relevant principles elaborated in the United Nations Convention on the Law of the Sea,

Affirming that, in accordance with the relevant articles of the Convention, all members of the international community have a duty to co-operate globally and regionally in the conservation and management of living resources on the high seas, and a duty to take, or to co-operate with others in taking, such measures for their nationals as may be necessary for the conservation of those resources,

Recalling that, in accordance with the relevant articles of the Convention, it is the responsibility of all members of the international community to ensure the conservation and management of living marine resources and the protection and preservation of the living marine environment within their exclusive economic zones,

Noting the serious concern, particularly among coastal States and States with fishing interests, that the overexploitation of living marine resources of the high seas adjacent to the exclusive economic zones of coastal States is likely to have an adverse impact on the same resources within such zones, and noting also, in this regard, the responsibility for co-operation in accordance with the relevant articles of the Convention,

Noting further that the countries of the South Pacific Forum and the South Pacific Commission, in recognition of the importance of living marine resources to the people of the South Pacific region, have called for a cessation of such fishing in the South Pacific and the implementation of effective management programmes,

Taking note of the adoption of the Tarawa Declaration on this subject by the Twentieth South Pacific Forum at Tarawa, Kiribati, on 11 July 1989 and the adoption by South Pacific States and territories of the Convention on the Prohibition of Driftnet Fishing in the South Pacific, at Wellington on 24 November 1989,

Noting that some members of the international community have entered into co-operative enforcement and monitoring programmes for the immediate evaluation of the impact of large-scale pelagic driftnet fishing,

Recognizing that some members of the international community have taken steps to reduce their driftnet operations in some regions in response to regional concerns,

1. *Calls upon* all members of the international community, particularly those with fishing interests, to strengthen their co-operation in the conservation and management of living marine resources;

2. *Calls upon* all those involved in large-scale pelagic driftnet fishing to co-operate fully with the international community, and especially with coastal States and the relevant international and regional organizations, in the enhanced collection and sharing of statistically sound scientific data in order to continue to assess the impact of such fishing methods and to secure conservation of the world's living marine resources;

3. *Recommends* that all interested members of the international community, particularly within regional organizations, continue to consider and, by 30 June 1991, review the best available scientific data on the impact of large-scale pelagic driftnet fishing and agree upon further co-operative regulation and monitoring measures, as needed;

4. *Also recommends* that all members of the international community, bearing in mind the special role of regional organizations and regional and bilateral co-operation in the conservation and management of living marine resources as reflected in the relevant articles of the United Nations Convention on the Law of the Sea, agree to the following measures:

(*a*) Moratoria should be imposed on all large-scale pelagic driftnet fishing by 30 June 1992, with the understanding that such a measure will not be imposed in a region or, if implemented, can be lifted, should effective conservation and management measures be taken based upon statistically sound analysis to be jointly made by concerned parties of the international community with an interest in the fishery resources of the region, to prevent unacceptable impact of such fishing practices on that region and to ensure the conservation of the living marine resources of that region;

(*b*) Immediate action should be taken to reduce progressively large-scale pelagic driftnet fishing activities in the South Pacific region with a view to the cessation of such activities by 1 July 1991, as an interim measure, until appropriate conservation and management arrangements for South Pacific albacore tuna resources are entered into by the parties concerned;

(*c*) Further expansion of large-scale pelagic driftnet fishing on the high seas of the North Pacific and all the other high seas outside the Pacific Ocean should cease immediately, with the understanding that this measure will be reviewed subject to the conditions in paragraph 4(*a*) of the present resolution;

5. *Encourages* those coastal countries which have exclusive economic zones adjacent to the high seas to take appropriate measures and to co-operate in the collection and submission of scientific information on driftnet fishing in their own exclusive economic zones, taking into account the measures taken for the conservation of living marine resources of the high seas;

6. *Requests* specialized agencies, particularly the Food and Agriculture Organization of the United Nations, and other appropriate organs, organizations and programmes of the United Nations system, as well as the various regional and subregional fisheries organizations, urgently to study large-scale pelagic driftnet fishing and its impact on living marine resources and to report their views to the Secretary–General;

7. *Requests* the Secretary–General to bring the present resolution to the attention of all members of the international community, intergovernmental organizations, non-governmental organizations in consultative status with the Economic and Social Council, and well-established scientific institutions with expertise in relation to living marine resources;

8. *Requests* the Secretary–General to submit to the General Assembly at its forty-fifth session a report on the implementation of the present resolution.

6.10 Resolution 46/215 on Large-scale Pelagic Driftnet Fishing and Its Impact on the Living Marine Resources of the World's Oceans and Seas. Adopted by the UN General Assembly, 20 December 1991. U.N.Doc. A/RES/46/215; *reprinted in* 31 I.L.M. 241 (1992) & 5A Weston V.H.21

The General Assembly,

Recalling its resolutions 44/225 and 45/197, concerning large-scale pelagic drift-net fishing and its impact on the living marine resources of the world's oceans and seas, including enclosed and semi-enclosed seas, which took into account the concerns of the developing countries and were adopted by consensus on 22 December 1989 and 21 December 1990, respectively,

Also recalling, in particular, that the General Assembly recommended that all members of the international community agree to certain measures specified in the operative paragraphs of resolution 44/225,

Further recalling the relevant principles elaborated in the United Nations Convention on the Law of the Sea, which are referred to in the seventh to tenth preambular paragraphs of resolution 44/225,

Expressing deep concern about reports of expansion of large-scale pelagic drift-net fishing activities on the high seas in contravention of resolutions 44/225 and 45/197, including attempts to expand large-scale pelagic drift-net fishing in the high seas areas of the Indian Ocean,

Commending the unilateral, regional and international efforts that have been undertaken by members of the international community and international organizations to implement and support the objectives of resolutions 44/225 and 45/197,

Noting that at the Twenty-second South Pacific Forum, held at Palikir on 29 and 30 July 1991, the heads of Government reaffirmed their opposition to large-scale pelagic drift-net fishing, and in this regard, *inter alia,* welcomed the entry into force on 17 May 1991 of the Convention for the Prohibition of Fishing with Long Drift-nets in the South Pacific,

Recalling the Castries Declaration, in which the Authority of the Organization of Eastern Caribbean States resolved to establish a regional regime for the regulation and management of the pelagic resources in the Lesser Antilles region that would outlaw the use of drift-nets and called upon other States in the region to cooperate in this regard,

Welcoming the actions taken that have resulted in the cessation of all large-scale pelagic drift-net fishing activities in the South Pacific in advance of the date stipulated in paragraph 4(*b*) of resolution 44/225 for the termination of such activities,

Also welcoming the decision of other members of the international community to cease large-scale pelagic drift-net fishing on the high seas,

Commending the efforts of many members of the international community to compile data on large-scale pelagic drift-net fishing and to submit their findings to the Secretary–General,

Noting the contributions to the report of the Secretary–General made by some members of the international community and by intergovernmental and non-governmental organizations,

Noting also the significant concerns expressed by members of the international community and competent regional fisheries bodies regarding the impact of large-scale pelagic drift-net fishing on the marine environment,

Noting further that, in accordance with paragraph 3 of resolution 44/225, some members of the international community have reviewed the best available scientific data on the impact of large-scale pelagic drift-net fishing and have failed to conclude that this practice has no adverse impact which threatens the conservation and sustainable management of living marine resources,

Noting that the grounds for concerns expressed about the unacceptable impact of large-scale pelagic drift-net fishing in resolutions 44/225 and 45/197 have been confirmed and that evidence has not demonstrated that the impact can be fully prevented,

Recognizing that a moratorium on large-scale pelagic drift-net fishing is required, notwithstanding that it will have adverse socio-economic effects on the communities involved in high seas pelagic drift-net fishing operations,

1. *Recalls* its resolutions 44/225 and 45/197;

2. *Commends* the efforts jointly to collect statistically sound data regarding large-scale pelagic drift-net fishing in the North Pacific Ocean, which were reviewed at the meeting of scientists held at Sidney, Canada, in June 1991, and presented at the symposium on the high seas drift-net fisheries in the North Pacific Ocean, held at Tokyo in November 1991 under the auspices of the International North Pacific Fisheries Commission;

3. *Calls upon* all members of the international community to implement resolutions 44/225 and 45/197 by, *inter alia,* taking the following actions:

(*a*) Beginning on 1 January 1992, reduce fishing effort in existing large-scale pelagic high seas drift-net fisheries by, *inter alia,* reducing the number of vessels involved, the length of the nets and the area of operation, so as to achieve, by 30 June 1992, a 50 per cent reduction in fishing effort;

(*b*) Continue to ensure that the areas of operation of large-scale pelagic high seas drift-net fishing are not expanded and, beginning on 1 January 1992, are further reduced in accordance with paragraph 3(*a*) of the present resolution;

(*c*) Ensure that a global moratorium on all large-scale pelagic drift-net fishing is fully implemented on the high seas of the world's oceans and seas, including enclosed seas and semi-enclosed seas, by 31 December 1992;

4. *Reaffirms* the importance it attaches to compliance with the present resolution and encourages all members of the international community to take measures, individually and collectively, to prevent large-scale pelagic drift-net fishing operations on the high seas of the world's oceans and seas, including enclosed seas and semi-enclosed seas;

5. *Requests* the Secretary–General to bring the present resolution to the attention of all members of the international community, intergovernmental and non-governmental organizations and well-established scientific institutions with expertise in relation to living marine resources;

6. *Requests* the members and organizations referred to above to submit to the Secretary–General information concerning activities or conduct inconsistent with the terms of the present resolution;

7. *Also requests* the Secretary–General to submit to the General Assembly at its forty-seventh session a report on the implementation of the present resolution.

6.11 Convention on Biological Diversity (With Annexes). Concluded at Rio De Janeiro, 5 June 1992. Entered into force, 29 December 1993. *Reprinted in* 31 I.L.M. 818 (1992) & 5A Weston V.H.22

Preamble

The Contracting Parties,

Conscious of the intrinsic value of biological diversity and of the ecological, genetic, social, economic, scientific, educational, cultural, recreational and aesthetic values of biological diversity and its components,

Conscious also of the importance of biological diversity for evolution and for maintaining life sustaining systems of the biosphere,

Affirming that the conservation of biological diversity is a common concern of humankind,

Reaffirming that States have sovereign rights over their own biological resources,

Reaffirming also that States are responsible for conserving their biological diversity and for using their biological resources in a sustainable manner,

Concerned that biological diversity is being significantly reduced by certain human activities,

Aware of the general lack of information and knowledge regarding biological diversity and of the urgent need to develop scientific, technical and institutional capacities to provide the basic understanding upon which to plan and implement appropriate measures,

Noting that it is vital to anticipate, prevent and attack the causes of significant reduction or loss of biological diversity at source,

Noting also that where there is a threat of significant reduction or loss of biological diversity, lack of full scientific certainty should not be used as a reason for postponing measures to avoid or minimize such a threat,

Noting further that the fundamental requirement for the conservation of biological diversity is the *in-situ* conservation of ecosystems and natural habitats and the maintenance and recovery of viable populations of species in their natural surroundings,

Noting further that *ex-situ* measures, preferably in the country of origin, also have an important role to play,

Recognizing the close and traditional dependence of many indigenous and local communities embodying traditional lifestyles on biological resources, and the desirability of sharing equitably benefits arising from the use of traditional knowledge, innovations and practices relevant to the conservation of biological diversity and the sustainable use of its components,

Recognizing also the vital role that women play in the conservation and sustainable use of biological diversity and affirming the need for the full participation of women at all levels of policy-making and implementation for biological diversity conservation,

Stressing the importance of, and the need to promote, international, regional and global cooperation among States and intergovernmental organizations and the non-governmental sector for the conservation of biological diversity and the sustainable use of its components,

Acknowledging that the provision of new and additional financial resources and appropriate access to relevant technologies can be expected to make a substantial difference in the world's ability to address the loss of biological diversity,

Acknowledging further that special provision is required to meet the needs of developing countries, including the provision of new and additional financial resources and appropriate access to relevant technologies,

Noting in this regard the special conditions of the least developed countries and small island States,

Acknowledging that substantial investments are required to conserve biological diversity and that there is the expectation of a broad range of environmental, economic and social benefits from those investments,

Recognizing that economic and social development and poverty eradication are the first and overriding priorities of developing countries,

Aware that conservation and sustainable use of biological diversity is of critical importance for meeting the food, health and other needs of the growing world population, for which purpose access to and sharing of both genetic resources and technologies are essential,

Noting that, ultimately, the conservation and sustainable use of biological diversity will strengthen friendly relations among States and contribute to peace for humankind,

Desiring to enhance and complement existing international arrangements for the conservation of biological diversity and sustainable use of its components, and

Determined to conserve and sustainably use biological diversity for the benefit of present and future generations.

Have agreed as follows:

Article 1. Objectives

The objectives of this Convention, to be pursued in accordance with its relevant provisions, are the conservation of biological diversity, the sustainable use of its components and the fair and equitable sharing of the benefits arising out of the utilization of genetic resources, including by appropriate access to genetic resources and by appropriate transfer of relevant technologies, taking into account all rights over those resources and to technologies, and by appropriate funding.

Article 2. Use of Terms

For the purposes of this Convention:

"*Biological diversity* "means the variability among living organisms from all sources including, *inter alia,* terrestrial, marine and other aquatic ecosystems and the ecological complexes of which they are part; this includes diversity within species, between species and of ecosystems.

"*Biological resources* "includes genetic resources, organisms or parts thereof, populations, or any other biotic component of ecosystems with actual or potential use or value for humanity.

"*Biotechnology* "means any technological application that uses biological systems, living organisms, or derivatives thereof, to make or modify products or processes for specific use.

"*Country of origin of genetic resources* "means the country which possesses those genetic resources in *in-situ* conditions.

"*Country providing genetic resources* "means the country supplying genetic resources collected from *in-situ* sources, including populations of both wild and domesticated species, or taken from *ex-situ* sources, which may or may not have originated in that country.

"*Domesticated or cultivated species* "means species in which the evolutionary process has been influenced by humans to meet their needs.

"*Ecosystem* "means a dynamic complex of plant, animal and micro-organism communities and their non-living environment interacting as a functional unit.

"*Ex-situ conservation* "means the conservation of components of biological diversity outside their natural habitats.

"*Genetic material* "means any material of plant, animal, microbial or other origin containing functional units of heredity.

"*Genetic resources* "means genetic material of actual or potential value.

"*Habitat* "means the place or type of site where an organism or population naturally occurs.

"*In-situ conditions* "means conditions where genetic resources exist within ecosystems and natural habitats, and, in the case of domesticated or cultivated species, in the surroundings where they have developed their distinctive properties.

"*In-situ conservation* "means the conservation of ecosystems and natural habitats and the maintenance and recovery of viable populations of species in their natural surroundings and, in the case of domesticated or cultivated species, in the surroundings where they have developed their distinctive properties.

"*Protected area* "means a geographically defined area which is designated or regulated and managed to achieve specific conservation objectives.

"*Regional economic integration organization* "means an organization constituted by sovereign States of a given region, to which its member States have transferred competence in respect of matters governed by this Convention and which has been duly authorized, in accordance with its internal procedures, to sign, ratify, accept, approve or accede to it.

"*Sustainable use* "means the use of components of biological diversity in a way and at a rate that does not lead to the long-term decline of biological diversity, thereby maintaining its potential to meet the needs and aspirations of present and future generations.

"*Technology* "includes biotechnology.

Article 3. Principle

States have, in accordance with the Charter of the United Nations and the principles of international law, the sovereign right to exploit their own resources pursuant to their own environmental policies, and the responsibility to ensure that activities within their jurisdiction or control do not cause damage to the environment of other States or of areas beyond the limits of national jurisdiction.

Article 4. Jurisdictional Scope

Subject to the rights of other States, and except as otherwise expressly provided in this Convention, the provisions of this Convention apply, in relation to each Contracting Party:

(a) In the case of components of biological diversity, in areas within the limits of its national jurisdiction; and

(b) In the case of processes and activities, regardless of where their effects occur, carried out under its jurisdiction or control, within the area of its national jurisdiction or beyond the limits of national jurisdiction.

Article 5. Cooperation

Each Contracting Party shall, as far as possible and as appropriate, cooperate with other Contracting Parties, directly or, where appropriate, through competent international organizations, in respect of areas beyond national jurisdiction and on other matters of mutual interest, for the conservation and sustainable use of biological diversity.

Article 6. General Measures for Conservation and Sustainable Use

Each Contracting Party shall, in accordance with its particular conditions and capabilities:

(a) Develop national strategies, plans or programmes for the conservation and sustainable use of biological diversity or adapt for this purpose existing strategies, plans or programmes which shall reflect, inter alia, the measures set out in this Convention relevant to the Contracting Party concerned; and

(b) Integrate, as far as possible and as appropriate, the conservation and sustainable use of biological diversity into relevant sectoral or cross-sectoral plans, programmes and policies.

Article 7. Identification and Monitoring

Each Contracting Party shall, as far as possible and as appropriate, in particular for the purposes of Articles 8 to 10:

(a) Identify components of biological diversity important for its conservation and sustainable use having regard to the indicative list of categories set down in Annex I;

(b) Monitor, through sampling and other techniques, the components of biological diversity identified pursuant to subparagraph (a) above, paying particular attention to those requiring urgent conservation measures and those which offer the greatest potential for sustainable use;

(c) Identify processes and categories of activities which have or are likely to have significant adverse impacts on the conservation and sustainable use of biological diversity, and monitor their effects through sampling and other techniques; and

(d) Maintain and organize, by any mechanism data, derived from identification and monitoring activities pursuant to subparagraphs (a), (b) and (c) above.

Article 8. In-situ Conservation

Each Contracting Party shall, as far as possible and as appropriate:

(a) Establish a system of protected areas or areas where special measures need to be taken to conserve biological diversity;

(b) Develop, where necessary, guidelines for the selection, establishment and management of protected areas or areas where special measures need to be taken to conserve biological diversity;

(c) Regulate or manage biological resources important for the conservation of biological diversity whether within or outside protected areas, with a view to ensuring their conservation and sustainable use;

(d) Promote the protection of ecosystems, natural habitats and the maintenance of viable populations of species in natural surroundings;

(e) Promote environmentally sound and sustainable development in areas adjacent to protected areas with a view to furthering protection of these areas;

(f) Rehabilitate and restore degraded ecosystems and promote the recovery of threatened species, *inter alia,* through the development and implementation of plans or other management strategies;

(g) Establish or maintain means to regulate, manage or control the risks associated with the use and release of living modified organisms resulting from biotechnology which are likely to have adverse environmental impacts that could affect the conservation and sustainable use of biological diversity, taking also into account the risks to human health;

(h) Prevent the introduction of, control or eradicate those alien species which threaten ecosystems, habitats or species;

(i) Endeavour to provide the conditions needed for compatibility between present uses and the conservation of biological diversity and the sustainable use of its components;

(j) Subject to its national legislation, respect, preserve and maintain knowledge, innovations and practices of indigenous and local communities embodying traditional lifestyles relevant for the conservation and sustainable use of biological diversity and promote their wider application with the approval and involvement of the holders of such knowledge, innovations and practices and encourage the equitable sharing of the benefits arising from the utilization of such knowledge, innovations and practices;

(k) Develop or maintain necessary legislation and/or other regulatory provisions for the protection of threatened species and populations;

(*l*) Where a significant adverse effect on biological diversity has been determined pursuant to Article 7, regulate or manage the relevant processes and categories of activities; and

(m) Cooperate in providing financial and other support for *in-situ* conservation outlined in subparagraphs (a) to (*l*) above, particularly to developing countries.

Article 9. Ex-situ Conservation

Each Contracting Party shall, as far as possible and as appropriate, and predominantly for the purpose of complementing *in-situ* measures:

(a) Adopt measures for the *ex-situ* conservation of components of biological diversity, preferably in the country of origin of such components;

(b) Establish and maintain facilities for *ex-situ* conservation of and research on plants, animals and micro-organisms, preferably in the country of origin of genetic resources;

(c) Adopt measures for the recovery and rehabilitation of threatened species and for their reintroduction into their natural habitats under appropriate conditions;

(d) Regulate and manage collection of biological resources from natural habitats for *ex-situ* conservation purposes so as not to threaten ecosystems and *in-situ* populations of species, except where special temporary *ex-situ* measures are required under subparagraph (c) above; and

(e) Cooperate in providing financial and other support for *ex-situ* conservation outlined in subparagraphs (a) to (d) above and in the establishment and maintenance of *ex-situ* conservation facilities in developing countries.

Article 10. Sustainable Use of Components of Biological Diversity

Each Contracting Party shall, as far as possible and as appropriate:

(a) Integrate consideration of the conservation and sustainable use of biological resources into national decision-making;

(b) Adopt measures relating to the use of biological resources to avoid or minimize adverse impacts on biological diversity;

(c) Protect and encourage customary use of biological resources in accordance with traditional cultural practices that are compatible with conservation or sustainable use requirements;

(d) Support local populations to develop and implement remedial action in degraded areas where biological diversity has been reduced; and

(e) Encourage cooperation between its governmental authorities and its private sector in developing methods for sustainable use of biological resources.

Article 11. Incentive Measures

Each Contracting Party shall, as far as possible and as appropriate, adopt economically and socially sound measures that act as incentives for the conservation and sustainable use of components of biological diversity.

Article 12. Research and Training

The Contracting Parties, taking into account the special needs of developing countries, shall:

(a) Establish and maintain programmes for scientific and technical education and training in measures for the identification, conservation and sustainable use of biological diversity and its components and provide support for such education and training for the specific needs of developing countries;

(b) Promote and encourage research which contributes to the conservation and sustainable use of biological diversity, particularly in developing countries, *inter alia,* in accordance with decisions of the Conference of the Parties taken in consequence of recommendations of the Subsidiary Body on Scientific, Technical and Technological Advice; and

(c) In keeping with the provisions of Articles 16, 18 and 20, promote and cooperate in the use of scientific advances in biological diversity research in developing methods for conservation and sustainable use of biological resources.

Article 13. Public Education and Awareness

The Contracting Parties shall:

(a) Promote and encourage understanding of the importance of, and the measures required for, the conservation of biological diversity, as well as its propagation through media, and the inclusion of these topics in educational programmes; and

(b) Cooperate, as appropriate, with other States and international organizations in developing educational and public awareness programmes, with respect to conservation and sustainable use of biological diversity.

Article 14. Impact Assessment and Minimizing Adverse Impacts

1. Each Contracting Party, as far as possible and as appropriate, shall:

(a) Introduce appropriate procedures requiring environmental impact assessment of its proposed projects that are likely to have significant adverse effects on biological diversity with a view to avoiding or minimizing such effects and, where appropriate, allow for public participation in such procedures;

(b) Introduce appropriate arrangements to ensure that the environmental consequences of its programmes and policies that are likely to have significant adverse impacts on biological diversity are duly taken into account;

(c) Promote, on the basis of reciprocity, notification, exchange of information and consultation on activities under their jurisdiction or control which are likely to significantly affect adversely the biological diversity of other States or areas beyond the limits of national jurisdiction, by encouraging the conclusion of bilateral, regional or multilateral arrangements, as appropriate;

(d) In the case of imminent or grave danger or damage, originating under its jurisdiction or control, to biological diversity within the area under jurisdiction of other States or in areas beyond the limits of national jurisdiction, notify immediately the potentially affected States of such danger or damage, as well as initiate action to prevent or minimize such danger or damage; and

(e) Promote national arrangements for emergency responses to activities or events, whether caused naturally or otherwise, which present a grave and imminent danger to biological diversity and encourage international cooperation to supplement such national efforts and, where appropriate and agreed by the States or regional economic integration organizations concerned, to establish joint contingency plans.

2. The Conference of the Parties shall examine, on the basis of studies to be carried out, the issue of liability and redress, including restoration and compensation, for damage to biological diversity, except where such liability is a purely internal matter.

Article 15. Access to Genetic Resources

1. Recognizing the sovereign rights of States over their natural resources, the authority to determine access to genetic resources rests with the national governments and is subject to national legislation.

2. Each Contracting Party shall endeavour to create conditions to facilitate access to genetic resources for environmentally sound uses by other Contracting Parties and not to impose restrictions that run counter to the objectives of this Convention.

3. For the purpose of this Convention, the genetic resources being provided by a Contracting Party, as referred to in this Article and Articles 16 and 19, are only those that are provided by Contracting Parties that are countries of origin of such resources or by the Parties that have acquired the genetic resources in accordance with this Convention.

4. Access, where granted, shall be on mutually agreed terms and subject to the provisions of this Article.

5. Access to genetic resources shall be subject to prior informed consent of the Contracting Party providing such resources, unless otherwise determined by that Party.

6. Each Contracting Party shall endeavour to develop and carry out scientific research based on genetic resources provided by other Contracting Parties with the full participation of, and where possible in, such Contracting Parties.

7. Each Contracting Party shall take legislative, administrative or policy measures, as appropriate, and in accordance with Articles 16 and 19 and, where necessary, through the financial mechanism established by Articles 20 and 21 with the aim of sharing in a fair and equitable way the results of research and development and the benefits arising from the commercial and other utilization of genetic resources with

the Contracting Party providing such resources. Such sharing shall be upon mutually agreed terms.

Article 16. Access to and Transfer of Technology

1. Each Contracting Party, recognizing that technology includes biotechnology, and that both access to and transfer of technology among Contracting Parties are essential elements for the attainment of the objectives of this Convention, undertakes subject to the provisions of this Article to provide and/or facilitate access for and transfer to other Contracting Parties of technologies that are relevant to the conservation and sustainable use of biological diversity or make use of genetic resources and do not cause significant damage to the environment.

2. Access to and transfer of technology referred to in paragraph 1 above to developing countries shall be provided and/or facilitated under fair and most favourable terms, including on concessional and preferential terms where mutually agreed, and, where necessary, in accordance with the financial mechanism established by Articles 20 and 21. In the case of technology subject to patents and other intellectual property rights, such access and transfer shall be provided on terms which recognize and are consistent with the adequate and effective protection of intellectual property rights. The application of this paragraph shall be consistent with paragraphs 3, 4 and 5 below.

3. Each Contracting Party shall take legislative, administrative or policy measures, as appropriate, with the aim that Contracting Parties, in particular those that are developing countries, which provide genetic resources are provided access to and transfer of technology which makes use of those resources, on mutually agreed terms, including technology protected by patents and other intellectual property rights, where necessary, through the provisions of Articles 20 and 21 and in accordance with international law and consistent with paragraphs 4 and 5 below.

4. Each Contracting Party shall take legislative, administrative or policy measures, as appropriate, with the aim that the private sector facilitates access to, joint development and transfer of technology referred to in paragraph 1 above for the benefit of both governmental institutions and the private sector of developing countries and in this regard shall abide by the obligations included in paragraphs 1, 2 and 3 above.

5. The Contracting Parties, recognizing that patents and other intellectual property rights may have an influence on the implementation of this Convention, shall cooperate in this regard subject to national legislation and international law in order to ensure that such rights are supportive of and do not run counter to its objectives.

Article 17. Exchange of Information

1. The Contracting Parties shall facilitate the exchange of information, from all publicly available sources, relevant to the conservation and sustainable use of biological diversity, taking into account the special needs of developing countries.

2. Such exchange of information shall include exchange of results of technical, scientific and socio-economic research, as well as information on training and surveying programmes, specialized knowledge, indigenous and traditional knowledge as such and in combination with the technologies referred to in Article 16, paragraph 1. It shall also, where feasible, include repatriation of information.

Article 18. Technical and Scientific Cooperation

1. The Contracting Parties shall promote international technical and scientific cooperation in the field of conservation and sustainable use of biological diversity, where necessary, through the appropriate international and national institutions.

2. Each Contracting Party shall promote technical and scientific cooperation with other Contracting Parties, in particular developing countries, in implementing this Convention, inter alia, through the development and implementation of national policies. In promoting such cooperation, special attention should be given to the development and strengthening of national capabilities, by means of human resources development and institution building.

3. The Conference of the Parties, at its first meeting, shall determine how to establish a clearing-house mechanism to promote and facilitate technical and scientific cooperation.

4. The Contracting Parties shall, in accordance with national legislation and policies, encourage and develop methods of cooperation for the development and use of technologies, including indigenous and traditional technologies, in pursuance of the objectives of this Convention. For this purpose, the Contracting Parties shall also promote cooperation in the training of personnel and exchange of experts.

5. The Contracting Parties shall, subject to mutual agreement, promote the establishment of joint research programmes and joint ventures for the development of technologies relevant to the objectives of this Convention.

Article 19. Handling of Biotechnology and Distribution of its Benefits

1. Each Contracting Party shall take legislative, administrative or policy measures, as appropriate, to provide for the effective participation in biotechnological research activities by those Contracting Parties, especially developing countries, which provide the genetic resources for such research, and where feasible in such Contracting Parties.

2. Each Contracting Party shall take all practicable measures to promote and advance priority access on a fair and equitable basis by Contracting Parties, especially developing countries, to the results and benefits arising from biotechnologies based upon genetic resources provided by those Contracting Parties. Such access shall be on mutually agreed terms.

3. The Parties shall consider the need for and modalities of a protocol setting out appropriate procedures, including, in particular, advance informed agreement, in the field of the safe transfer, handling and use of any living modified organism resulting from biotechnology that may have adverse effect on the conservation and sustainable use of biological diversity.

4. Each Contracting Party shall, directly or by requiring any natural or legal person under its jurisdiction providing the organisms referred to in paragraph 3 above, provide any available information about the use and safety regulations required by that Contracting Party in handling such organisms, as well as any available information on the potential adverse impact of the specific organisms concerned to the Contracting Party into which those organisms are to be introduced.

Article 20. Financial Resources

1. Each Contracting Party undertakes to provide, in accordance with its capabilities, financial support and incentives in respect of those national activities which are intended to achieve the objectives of this Convention, in accordance with its national plans, priorities and programmes.

2. The developed country Parties shall provide new and additional financial resources to enable developing country Parties to meet the agreed full incremental costs to them of implementing measures which fulfil the obligations of this Convention and to benefit from its provisions and which costs are agreed between a developing country Party and the institutional structure referred to in Article 21, in accordance with policy, strategy, programme priorities and eligibility criteria and an indicative list

of incremental costs established by the Conference of the Parties. Other Parties, including countries undergoing the process of transition to a market economy, may voluntarily assume the obligations of the developed country Parties. For the purpose of this Article, the Conference of the Parties, shall at its first meeting establish a list of developed country Parties and other Parties which voluntarily assume the obligations of the developed country Parties. The Conference of the Parties shall periodically review and if necessary amend the list. Contributions from other countries and sources on a voluntary basis would also be encouraged. The implementation of these commitments shall take into account the need for adequacy, predictability and timely flow of funds and the importance of burden-sharing among the contributing Parties included in the list.

3. The developed country Parties may also provide, and developing country Parties avail themselves of, financial resources related to the implementation of this Convention through bilateral, regional and other multilateral channels.

4. The extent to which developing country Parties will effectively implement their commitments under this Convention will depend on the effective implementation by developed country Parties of their commitments under this Convention related to financial resources and transfer of technology and will take fully into account the fact that economic and social development and eradication of poverty are the first and overriding priorities of the developing country Parties.

5. The Parties shall take full account of the specific needs and special situation of least developed countries in their actions with regard to funding and transfer of technology.

6. The Contracting Parties shall also take into consideration the special conditions resulting from the dependence on, distribution and location of, biological diversity within developing country Parties, in particular small island States.

7. Consideration shall also be given to the special situation of developing countries, including those that are most environmentally vulnerable, such as those with arid and semi-arid zones, coastal and mountainous areas.

Article 21. Financial Mechanism

1. There shall be a mechanism for the provision of financial resources to developing country Parties for purposes of this Convention on a grant or concessional basis the essential elements of which are described in this Article. The mechanism shall function under the authority and guidance of, and be accountable to, the Conference of the Parties for purposes of this Convention. The operations of the mechanism shall be carried out by such institutional structure as may be decided upon by the Conference of the Parties at its first meeting. For purposes of this Convention, the Conference of the Parties shall determine the policy, strategy, programme priorities and eligibility criteria relating to the access to and utilization of such resources. The contributions shall be such as to take into account the need for predictability, adequacy and timely flow of funds referred to in Article 20 in accordance with the amount of resources needed to be decided periodically by the Conference of the Parties and the importance of burden-sharing among the contributing Parties included in the list referred to in Article 20, paragraph 2. Voluntary contributions may also be made by the developed country Parties and by other countries and sources. The mechanism shall operate within a democratic and transparent system of governance.

2. Pursuant to the objectives of this Convention, the Conference of the Parties shall at its first meeting determine the policy, strategy and programme priorities, as well as detailed criteria and guidelines for eligibility for access to and utilization of the financial resources including monitoring and evaluation on a regular basis of such utilization. The Conference of the Parties shall decide on the arrangements to give

effect to paragraph 1 above after consultation with the institutional structure entrusted with the operation of the financial mechanism.

3. The Conference of the Parties shall review the effectiveness of the mechanism established under this Article, including the criteria and guidelines referred to in paragraph 2 above, not less than two years after the entry into force of this Convention and thereafter on a regular basis. Based on such review, it shall take appropriate action to improve the effectiveness of the mechanism if necessary.

4. The Contracting Parties shall consider strengthening existing financial institutions to provide financial resources for the conservation and sustainable use of biological diversity.

Article 22. Relationship with Other International Conventions

1. The provisions of this Convention shall not affect the rights and obligations of any Contracting Party deriving from any existing international agreement, except where the exercise of those rights and obligations would cause a serious damage or threat to biological diversity.

2. Contracting Parties shall implement this Convention with respect to the marine environment consistently with the rights and obligations of States under the law of the sea.

Article 23. Conference of the Parties

1. A Conference of the Parties is hereby established. The first meeting of the Conference of the Parties shall be convened by the Executive Director of the United Nations Environment Programme not later than one year after the entry into force of this Convention. Thereafter, ordinary meetings of the Conference of the Parties shall be held at regular intervals to be determined by the Conference at its first meeting.

2. Extraordinary meetings of the Conference of the Parties shall be held at such other times as may be deemed necessary by the Conference, or at the written request of any Party, provided that, within six months of the request being communicated to them by the Secretariat, it is supported by at least one third of the Parties.

3. The Conference of the Parties shall by consensus agree upon and adopt rules of procedure for itself and for any subsidiary body it may establish, as well as financial rules governing the funding of the Secretariat. At each ordinary meeting, it shall adopt a budget for the financial period until the next ordinary meeting.

4. The Conference of the Parties shall keep under review the implementation of this Convention, and, for this purpose, shall:

(a) Establish the form and the intervals for transmitting the information to be submitted in accordance with Article 26 and consider such information as well as reports submitted by any subsidiary body;

(b) Review scientific, technical and technological advice on biological diversity provided in accordance with Article 25;

(c) Consider and adopt, as required, protocols in accordance with Article 28;

(d) Consider and adopt, as required, in accordance with Articles 29 and 30, amendments to this Convention and its annexes;

(e) Consider amendments to any protocol, as well as to any annexes thereto, and, if so decided, recommend their adoption to the Parties to the protocol concerned;

(f) Consider and adopt, as required, in accordance with Article 30, additional annexes to this Convention;

(g) Establish such subsidiary bodies, particularly to provide scientific and technical advice, as are deemed necessary for the implementation of this Convention;

(h) Contact, through the Secretariat, the executive bodies of conventions dealing with matters covered by this Convention with a view to establishing appropriate forms of cooperation with them; and

(i) Consider and undertake any additional action that may be required for the achievement of the purposes of this Convention in the light of experience gained in its operation.

5. The United Nations, its specialized agencies and the International Atomic Energy Agency, as well as any State not Party to this Convention, may be represented as observers at meetings of the Conference of the Parties. Any other body or agency, whether governmental or nongovernmental, qualified in fields relating to conservation and sustainable use of biological diversity, which has informed the Secretariat of its wish to be represented as an observer at a meeting of the Conference of the Parties, may be admitted unless at least one third of the Parties present object. The admission and participation of observers shall be subject to the rules of procedure adopted by the Conference of the Parties.

Article 24. Secretariat

1. A secretariat is hereby established. Its functions shall be:

(a) To arrange for and service meetings of the Conference of the Parties provided for in Article 23;

(b) To perform the functions assigned to it by any protocol;

(c) To prepare reports on the execution of its functions under this Convention and present them to the Conference of the Parties;

(d) To coordinate with other relevant international bodies and, in particular to enter into such administrative and contractual arrangements as may be required for the effective discharge of its functions; and

(e) To perform such other functions as may be determined by the Conference of the Parties.

2. At its first ordinary meeting, the Conference of the Parties shall designate the secretariat from amongst those existing competent international organizations which have signified their willingness to carry out the secretariat functions under this Convention.

Article 25. Subsidiary Body on Scientific, Technical and Technological Advice

1. A subsidiary body for the provision of scientific, technical and technological advice is hereby established to provide the Conference of the Parties and, as appropriate, its other subsidiary bodies with timely advice relating to the implementation of this Convention. This body shall be open to participation by all Parties and shall be multidisciplinary. It shall comprise government representatives competent in the relevant field of expertise. It shall report regularly to the Conference of the Parties on all aspects of its work.

2. Under the authority of and in accordance with guidelines laid down by the Conference of the Parties, and upon its request, this body shall:

(a) Provide scientific and technical assessments of the status of biological diversity;

(b) Prepare scientific and technical assessments of the effects of types of measures taken in accordance with the provisions of this Convention;

(c) Identify innovative, efficient and state-of-the-art technologies and know-how relating to the conservation and sustainable use of biological diversity and advise on the ways and means of promoting development and/or transferring such technologies;

(d) Provide advice on scientific programmes and international cooperation in research and development related to conservation and sustainable use of biological diversity; and

(e) Respond to scientific, technical, technological and methodological questions that the Conference of the Parties and its subsidiary bodies may put to the body.

3. The functions, terms of reference, organization and operation of this body may be further elaborated by the Conference of the Parties.

Article 26. Reports

Each Contracting Party shall, at intervals to be determined by the Conference of the Parties, present to the Conference of the Parties, reports on measures which it has taken for the implementation of the provisions of this Convention and their effectiveness in meeting the objectives of this Convention.

Article 27. Settlement of Disputes

1. In the event of a dispute between Contracting Parties concerning the interpretation or application of this Convention, the parties concerned shall seek solution by negotiation.

2. If the parties concerned cannot reach agreement by negotiation, they may jointly seek the good offices of, or request mediation by, a third party.

3. When ratifying, accepting, approving or acceding to this Convention, or at any time thereafter, a State or regional economic integration organization may declare in writing to the Depositary that for a dispute not resolved in accordance with paragraph 1 or paragraph 2 above, it accepts one or both of the following means of dispute settlement as compulsory:

(a) Arbitration in accordance with the procedure laid down in Part 1 of Annex II;

(b) Submission of the dispute to the International Court of Justice.

4. If the parties to the dispute have not, in accordance with paragraph 3 above, accepted the same or any procedure, the dispute shall be submitted to conciliation in accordance with Part 2 of Annex II unless the parties otherwise agree.

5. The provisions of this Article shall apply with respect to any protocol except as otherwise provided in the protocol concerned.

Article 28. Adoption of Protocols

1. The Contracting Parties shall cooperate in the formulation and adoption of protocols to this Convention.

2. Protocols shall be adopted at a meeting of the Conference of the Parties.

3. The text of any proposed protocol shall be communicated to the Contracting Parties by the Secretariat at least six months before such a meeting.

Article 29. Amendment of the Convention or Protocols

1. Amendments to this Convention may be proposed by any Contracting Party. Amendments to any protocol may be proposed by any Party to that protocol.

2. Amendments to this Convention shall be adopted at a meeting of the Conference of the Parties. Amendments to any protocol shall be adopted at a meeting of the Parties to the Protocol in question. The text of any proposed amendment to this Convention or to any protocol, except as may otherwise be provided in such protocol, shall be communicated to the Parties to the instrument in question by the Secretariat at least six months before the meeting at which it is proposed for adoption. The Secretariat shall also communicate proposed amendments to the signatories to this Convention for information.

3. The Parties shall make every effort to reach agreement on any proposed amendment to this Convention or to any protocol by consensus. If all efforts at consensus have been exhausted, and no agreement reached, the amendment shall as a last resort be adopted by a two-thirds majority vote of the Parties to the instrument in question present and voting at the meeting, and shall be submitted by the Depositary to all Parties for ratification, acceptance or approval.

4. Ratification, acceptance or approval of amendments shall be notified to the Depositary in writing. Amendments adopted in accordance with paragraph 3 above shall enter into force among Parties having accepted them on the ninetieth day after the deposit of instruments of ratification, acceptance or approval by at least two thirds of the Contracting Parties to this Convention or of the Parties to the protocol concerned, except as may otherwise be provided in such protocol. Thereafter the amendments shall enter into force for any other Party on the ninetieth day after that Party deposits its instrument of ratification, acceptance or approval of the amendments.

5. For the purposes of this Article, "Parties present and voting" means Parties present and casting an affirmative or negative vote.

Article 30. Adoption and Amendment of Annexes

1. The annexes to this Convention or to any protocol shall form an integral part of the Convention or of such protocol, as the case may be, and, unless expressly provided otherwise, a reference to this Convention or its protocols constitutes at the same time a reference to any annexes thereto. Such annexes shall be restricted to procedural, scientific, technical and administrative matters.

2. Except as may be otherwise provided in any protocol with respect to its annexes, the following procedure shall apply to the proposal, adoption and entry into force of additional annexes to this Convention or of annexes to any protocol:

(a) Annexes to this Convention or to any protocol shall be proposed and adopted according to the procedure laid down in Article 29;

(b) Any Party that is unable to approve an additional annex to this Convention or an annex to any protocol to which it is Party shall so notify the Depositary, in writing, within one year from the date of the communication of the adoption by the Depositary. The Depositary shall without delay notify all Parties of any such notification received. A Party may at any time withdraw a previous declaration of objection and the annexes shall thereupon enter into force for that Party subject to subparagraph (c) below;

(c) On the expiry of one year from the date of the communication of the adoption by the Depositary, the annex shall enter into force for all Parties to this Convention or to any protocol concerned which have not submitted a notification in accordance with the provisions of subparagraph (b) above.

3. The proposal, adoption and entry into force of amendments to annexes to this Convention or to any protocol shall be subject to the same procedure as for the proposal, adoption and entry into force of annexes to the Convention or annexes to any protocol.

4. If an additional annex or an amendment to an annex is related to an amendment to this Convention or to any protocol, the additional annex or amendment shall not enter into force until such time as the amendment to the Convention or to the protocol concerned enters into force.

Article 31. Right to Vote

1. Except as provided for in paragraph 2 below, each Contracting Party to this Convention or to any protocol shall have one vote.

2. Regional economic integration organizations, in matters within their competence, shall exercise their right to vote with a number of votes equal to the number of their member States which are Contracting Parties to this Convention or the relevant protocol. Such organizations shall not exercise their right to vote if their member States exercise theirs, and vice versa.

Article 32. Relationship between this Convention and Its Protocols

1. A State or a regional economic integration organization may not become a Party to a protocol unless it is, or becomes at the same time, a Contracting Party to this Convention.

2. Decisions under any protocol shall be taken only by the Parties to the protocol concerned. Any Contracting Party that has not ratified, accepted or approved a protocol may participate as an observer in any meeting of the parties to that protocol.

Article 33. Signature

This Convention shall be open for signature at Rio de Janeiro by all States and any regional economic integration organization from 5 June 1992 until 14 June 1992, and at the United Nations Headquarters in New York from 15 June 1992 to 4 June 1993.

Article 34. Ratification, Acceptance or Approval

1. This Convention and any protocol shall be subject to ratification, acceptance or approval by States and by regional economic integration organizations. Instruments of ratification, acceptance or approval shall be deposited with the Depositary.

2. Any organization referred to in paragraph 1 above which becomes a Contracting Party to this Convention or any protocol without any of its member States being a Contracting Party shall be bound by all the obligations under the Convention or the protocol, as the case may be. In the case of such organizations, one or more of whose member States is a Contracting Party to this Convention or relevant protocol, the organization and its member States shall decide on their respective responsibilities for the performance of their obligations under the Convention or protocol, as the case may be. In such cases, the organization and the member States shall not be entitled to exercise rights under the Convention or relevant protocol concurrently.

3. In their instruments of ratification, acceptance or approval, the organizations referred to in paragraph 1 above shall declare the extent of their competence with respect to the matters governed by the Convention or the relevant protocol. These organizations shall also inform the Depositary of any relevant modification in the extent of their competence.

Article 35. Accession

1. This Convention and any protocol shall be open for accession by States and by regional economic integration organizations from the date on which the Convention or the protocol concerned is closed for signature. The instruments of accession shall be deposited with the Depositary.

2. In their instruments of accession, the organizations referred to in paragraph 1 above shall declare the extent of their competence with respect to the matters governed by the Convention or the relevant protocol. These organizations shall also inform the Depositary of any relevant modification in the extent of their competence.

3. The provisions of Article 34, paragraph 2, shall apply to regional economic integration organizations which accede to this Convention or any protocol.

Article 36. Entry Into Force

1. This Convention shall enter into force on the ninetieth day after the date of deposit of the thirtieth instrument of ratification, acceptance, approval or accession.

2. Any protocol shall enter into force on the ninetieth day after the date of deposit of the number of instruments of ratification, acceptance, approval or accession, specified in that protocol, has been deposited.

3. For each Contracting Party which ratifies, accepts or approves this Convention or accedes thereto after the deposit of the thirtieth instrument of ratification, acceptance, approval or accession, it shall enter into force on the ninetieth day after the date of deposit by such Contracting Party of its instrument of ratification, acceptance, approval or accession.

4. Any protocol, except as otherwise provided in such protocol, shall enter into force for a Contracting Party that ratifies, accepts or approves that protocol or accedes thereto after its entry into force pursuant to paragraph 2 above, on the ninetieth day after the date on which that Contracting Party deposits its instrument of ratification, acceptance, approval or accession, or on the date on which this Convention enters into force for that Contracting Party, whichever shall be the later.

5. For the purposes of paragraphs 1 and 2 above, any instrument deposited by a regional economic integration organization shall not be counted as additional to those deposited by member States of such organization.

Article 37. Reservations

No reservations may be made to this Convention.

Article 38. Withdrawals

1. At any time after two years from the date on which this Convention has entered into force for a Contracting Party, that Contracting Party may withdraw from the Convention by giving written notification to the Depositary.

2. Any such withdrawal shall take place upon expiry of one year after the date of its receipt by the Depositary, or on such later date as may be specified in the notification of the withdrawal.

3. Any Contracting Party which withdraws from this Convention shall be considered as also having withdrawn from any protocol to which it is party.

Article 39. Financial Interim Arrangements

Provided that it has been fully restructured in accordance with the requirements of Article 21, the Global Environment Facility of the United Nations Development Programme, the United Nations Environment Programme and the International Bank for Reconstruction and Development shall be the institutional structure referred to in Article 21 on an interim basis, for the period between the entry into force of this Convention and the first meeting of the Conference of the Parties or until the Conference of the Parties decides which institutional structure will be designated in accordance with Article 21.

Article 40. Secretariat Interim Arrangements

The secretariat to be provided by the Executive Director of the United Nations Environment Programme shall be the secretariat referred to in Article 24, paragraph 2, on an interim basis for the period between the entry into force of this Convention and the first meeting of the Conference of the Parties.

Article 41. Depositary

The Secretary–General of the United Nations shall assume the functions of Depositary of this Convention and any protocols.

Article 42. Authentic Texts

The original of this Convention, of which the Arabic, Chinese, English, French, Russian and Spanish texts are equally authentic, shall be deposited with the Secretary–General of the United Nations.

Annex I

IDENTIFICATION AND MONITORING

1. Ecosystems and habitats: containing high diversity, large numbers of endemic or threatened species, or wilderness; required by migratory species; of social, economic, cultural or scientific importance; or, which are representative, unique or associated with key evolutionary or other biological processes;

2. Species and communities which are: threatened; wild relatives of domesticated or cultivated species; of medicinal, agricultural or other economic value; or social, scientific or cultural importance; or importance for research into the conservation and sustainable use of biological diversity, such as indicator species; and

3. Described genomes and genes of social, scientific or economic importance.

Annex II

Part 1

ARBITRATION

Article 1

The claimant party shall notify the Secretariat that the parties are referring a dispute to arbitration pursuant to Article 27. The notification shall state the subject-matter of arbitration and include, in particular, the articles of the Convention or the protocol, the interpretation or application of which are at issue. If the parties do not agree on the subject matter of the dispute before the President of the tribunal is designated, the arbitral tribunal shall determine the subject matter. The Secretariat shall forward the information thus received to all Contracting Parties to this Convention or to the protocol concerned.

Article 2

1. In disputes between two parties, the arbitral tribunal shall consist of three members. Each of the parties to the dispute shall appoint an arbitrator and the two arbitrators so appointed shall designate by common agreement the third arbitrator who shall be the President of the tribunal. The latter shall not be a national of one of the parties to the dispute, nor have his or her usual place of residence in the territory of one of these parties, nor be employed by any of them, nor have dealt with the case in any other capacity.

2. In disputes between more than two parties, parties in the same interest shall appoint one arbitrator jointly by agreement.

3. Any vacancy shall be filled in the manner prescribed for the initial appointment.

Article 3

1. If the President of the arbitral tribunal has not been designated within two months of the appointment of the second arbitrator, the Secretary–General of the United Nations shall, at the request of a party, designate the President within a further two-month period.

2. If one of the parties to the dispute does not appoint an arbitrator within two months of receipt of the request, the other party may inform the Secretary–General who shall make the designation within a further two-month period.

Article 4

The arbitral tribunal shall render its decisions in accordance with the provisions of this Convention, any protocols concerned, and international law.

Article 5

Unless the parties to the dispute otherwise agree, the arbitral tribunal shall determine its own rules of procedure.

Article 6

The arbitral tribunal may, at the request of one of the parties, recommend essential interim measures of protection.

Article 7

The parties to the dispute shall facilitate the work of the arbitral tribunal and, in particular, using all means at their disposal, shall:

(a) Provide it with all relevant documents, information and facilities; and

(b) Enable it, when necessary, to call witnesses or experts and receive their evidence.

Article 8

The parties and the arbitrators are under an obligation to protect the confidentiality of any information they receive in confidence during the proceedings of the arbitral tribunal.

Article 9

Unless the arbitral tribunal determines otherwise because of the particular circumstances of the case, the costs of the tribunal shall be borne by the parties to the dispute in equal shares. The tribunal shall keep a record of all its costs, and shall furnish a final statement thereof to the parties.

Article 10

Any Contracting Party that has an interest of a legal nature in the subject-matter of the dispute which may be affected by the decision in the case, may intervene in the proceedings with the consent of the tribunal.

Article 11

The tribunal may hear and determine counterclaims arising directly out of the subject-matter of the dispute.

Article 12

Decisions both on procedure and substance of the arbitral tribunal shall be taken by a majority vote of its members.

Article 13

If one of the parties to the dispute does not appear before the arbitral tribunal or fails to defend its case, the other party may request the tribunal to continue the proceedings and to make its award. Absence of a party or a failure of a party to defend its case shall not constitute a bar to the proceedings. Before rendering its final decision, the arbitral tribunal must satisfy itself that the claim is well founded in fact and law.

Article 14

The tribunal shall render its final decision within five months of the date on which it is fully constituted unless it finds it necessary to extend the time-limit for a period which should not exceed five more months.

Article 15

The final decision of the arbitral tribunal shall be confined to the subject-matter of the dispute and shall state the reasons on which it is based. It shall contain the names of the members who have participated and the date of the final decision. Any member of the tribunal may attach a separate or dissenting opinion to the final decision.

Article 16

The award shall be binding on the parties to the dispute. It shall be without appeal unless the parties to the dispute have agreed in advance to an appellate procedure.

Article 17

Any controversy which may arise between the parties to the dispute as regards the interpretation or manner of implementation of the final decision may be submitted by either party for decision to the arbitral tribunal which rendered it.

Part 2

CONCILIATION

Article 1

A conciliation commission shall be created upon the request of one of the parties to the dispute. The commission shall, unless the parties otherwise agree, be composed of five members, two appointed by each Party concerned and a President chosen jointly by those members.

Article 2

In disputes between more than two parties, parties in the same interest shall appoint their members of the commission jointly by agreement. Where two or more parties have separate interests or there is a disagreement as to whether they are of the same interest, they shall appoint their members separately.

Article 3

If any appointments by the parties are not made within two months of the date of the request to create a conciliation commission, the Secretary–General of the United Nations shall, if asked to do so by the party that made the request, make those appointments within a further two-month period.

Article 4

If a President of the conciliation commission has not been chosen within two months of the last of the members of the commission being appointed, the Secretary-General of the United Nations shall, if asked to do so by a party, designate a President within a further two-month period.

Article 5

The conciliation commission shall take its decisions by majority vote of its members. It shall, unless the parties to the dispute otherwise agree, determine its own procedure. It shall render a proposal for resolution of the dispute, which the parties shall consider in good faith.

Article 6

A disagreement as to whether the conciliation commission has competence shall be decided by the commission.

6.12 Nonlegally Binding Authoritative Statement of Principles for a Global Consensus on the Management, Conservation and Sustainable Development of All Types of Forests. **Adopted by the UN Conference on Environment and Development at Rio De Janeiro, 13 June 1992. U.N. Doc. A/Conf. 151/26 (Vol. III) (1992); *reprinted in* 31 I.L.M. 881 (1992) & 5A Weston V.H.23**

PREAMBLE

(a) The subject of forests is related to the entire range of environmental and development issues and opportunities, including the right to socio-economic development on a sustainable basis.

(b) The guiding objective of these principles is to contribute to the management, conservation and sustainable development of forests and to provide for their multiple and complementary functions and uses.

(c) Forestry issues and opportunities should be examined in a holistic and balanced manner within the overall context of environment and development, taking into consideration the multiple functions and uses of forests, including traditional uses, and the likely economic and social stress when these uses are constrained or restricted, as well as the potential for development that sustainable forest management can offer.

(d) These principles reflect a first global consensus on forests. In committing themselves to the prompt implementation of these principles, countries also decide to keep them under assessment for their adequacy with regard to further international cooperation on forest issues.

(e) These principles should apply to all types of forests, both natural and planted, in all geographic regions and climatic zones, including austral, boreal, subtemperate, temperate, subtropical and tropical.

(f) All types of forests embody complex and unique ecological processes which are the basis for their present and potential capacity to provide resources to satisfy human needs as well as environmental values, and as such their sound management and conservation is of concern to the Governments of the countries to which they belong and are of value to local communities and to the environment as a whole.

(g) Forests are essential to economic development and the maintenance of all forms of life.

(h) Recognizing that the responsibility for forest management, conservation and sustainable development is in many States allocated among federal/national, state/provincial and local levels of government, each State, in accordance with its constitution and/or national legislation, should pursue these principles at the appropriate level of government.

PRINCIPLES/ELEMENTS

1. (a) States have, in accordance with the Charter of the United Nations and the principles of international law, the sovereign right to exploit their own resources pursuant to their own environmental policies and have the responsibility to ensure that activities within their jurisdiction or control do not cause damage to the environment of other States or of areas beyond the limits of national jurisdiction.

(b) The agreed full incremental cost of achieving benefits associated with forest conservation and sustainable development requires increased international cooperation and should be equitably shared by the international community.

2. (a) States have the sovereign and inalienable right to utilize, manage and develop their forests in accordance with their development needs and level of socio-economic development and on the basis of national policies consistent with sustainable development and legislation, including the conversion of such areas for other uses within the overall socio-economic development plan and based on rational land-use policies.

(b) Forest resources and forest lands should be sustainably managed to meet the social, economic, ecological, cultural and spiritual human needs of present and future generations. These needs are for forest products and services, such as wood and wood products, water, food, fodder, medicine, fuel, shelter, employment, recreation, habitats for wildlife, landscape diversity, carbon sinks and reservoirs, and for other forest products. Appropriate measures should be taken to protect forests against harmful effects of pollution, including air-borne pollution, fires, pests and diseases in order to maintain their full multiple value.

(c) The provision of timely, reliable and accurate information on forests and forest ecosystems is essential for public understanding and informed decision-making and should be ensured.

(d) Governments should promote and provide opportunities for the participation of interested parties, including local communities and indigenous people, industries, labour, non-governmental organizations and individuals, forest dwellers and women, in the development, implementation and planning of national forest policies.

3. (a) National policies and strategies should provide a framework for increased efforts, including the development and strengthening of institutions and programmes for the management, conservation and sustainable development of forests and forest lands.

(b) International institutional arrangements, building on those organizations and mechanisms already in existence, as appropriate, should facilitate international cooperation in the field of forests.

(c) All aspects of environmental protection and social and economic development as they relate to forests and forest lands should be integrated and comprehensive.

4. The vital role of all types of forests in maintaining the ecological processes and balance at the local, national, regional and global levels through, *inter alia,* their role in protecting fragile ecosystems, watersheds and freshwater resources and as rich storehouses of biodiversity and biological resources and sources of genetic material for biotechnology products, as well as photosynthesis, should be recognized.

5. (a) National forest policies should recognize and duly support the identity, culture and the rights of indigenous people, their communities and other communities and forest dwellers. Appropriate conditions should be promoted for these groups to enable them to have an economic stake in forest use, perform economic activities, and achieve and maintain cultural identity and social organization, as well as adequate levels of livelihood and well-being, through, *inter alia,* those land tenure arrangements which serve as incentives for the sustainable management of forests.

(b) The full participation of women in all aspects of the management, conservation and sustainable development of forests should be actively promoted.

6. (a) All types of forests play an important role in meeting energy requirements through the provision of a renewable source of bio-energy, particularly in developing countries, and the demands for fuelwood for household and industrial needs should be met through sustainable forest management, afforestation and reforestation. To this end, the potential contribution of plantations of both indigenous and introduced species for the provision of both fuel and industrial wood should be recognized.

(b) National policies and programmes should take into account the relationship, where it exists, between the conservation, management and sustainable development of forests and all aspects related to the production, consumption, recycling and/or final disposal of forest products.

(c) Decisions taken on the management, conservation and sustainable development of forest resources should benefit, to the extent practicable, from a comprehensive assessment of economic and non-economic values of forest goods and services and of the environmental costs and benefits. The development and improvement of methodologies for such evaluations should be promoted.

(d) The role of planted forests and permanent agricultural crops as sustainable and environmentally sound sources of renewable energy and industrial raw material should be recognized, enhanced and promoted. Their contribution to the maintenance of ecological processes, to offsetting pressure on primary/old-growth forest and to providing regional employment and development with the adequate involvement of local inhabitants should be recognized and enhanced.

(e) Natural forests also constitute a source of goods and services, and their conservation, sustainable management and use should be promoted.

7. (a) Efforts should be made to promote a supportive international economic climate conducive to sustained and environmentally sound development of forests in all countries, which include, *inter alia,* the promotion of sustainable patterns of production and consumption, the eradication of poverty and the promotion of food security.

(b) Specific financial resources should be provided to developing countries with significant forest areas which establish programmes for the conservation of forests including protected natural forest areas. These resources should be directed notably to economic sectors which would stimulate economic and social substitution activities.

8. (a) Efforts should be undertaken towards the greening of the world. All countries, notably developed countries, should take positive and transparent action towards reforestation, afforestation and forest conservation, as appropriate.

(b) Efforts to maintain and increase forest cover and forest productivity should be undertaken in ecologically, economically and socially sound ways through the rehabilitation, reforestation and re-establishment of trees and forests on unproductive, degraded and deforested lands, as well as through the management of existing forest resources.

(c) The implementation of national policies and programmes aimed at forest management, conservation and sustainable development, particularly in developing countries, should be supported by international financial and technical cooperation, including through the private sector, where appropriate.

(d) Sustainable forest management and use should be carried out in accordance with national development policies and priorities and on the basis of environmentally sound national guidelines. In the formulation of such guidelines, account should be taken, as appropriate and if applicable, of relevant internationally agreed methodologies and criteria.

(e) Forest management should be integrated with management of adjacent areas so as to maintain ecological balance and sustainable productivity.

(f) National policies and/or legislation aimed at management, conservation and sustainable development of forests should include the protection of ecologically viable representative or unique examples of forests, including primary/old-growth forests, cultural, spiritual, historical, religious and other unique and valued forests of national importance.

(g) Access to biological resources, including genetic material, shall be with due regard to the sovereign rights of the countries where the forests are located and to the sharing on mutually agreed terms of technology and profits from biotechnology products that are derived from these resources.

(h) National policies should ensure that environmental impact assessments should be carried out where actions are likely to have significant adverse impacts on important forest resources, and where such actions are subject to a decision of a competent national authority.

9. (a) The efforts of developing countries to strengthen the management, conservation and sustainable development of their forest resources should be supported by the international community, taking into account the importance of redressing external indebtedness, particularly where aggravated by the net transfer of resources to developed countries, as well as the problem of achieving at least the replacement value of forests through improved market access for forest products, especially processed products. In this respect, special attention should also be given to the countries undergoing the process of transition to market economies.

(b) The problems that hinder efforts to attain the conservation and sustainable use of forest resources and that stem from the lack of alternative options available to local communities, in particular the urban poor and poor rural populations who are economically and socially dependent on forests and forest resources, should be addressed by Governments and the international community.

(c) National policy formulation with respect to all types of forests should take account of the pressures and demands imposed on forest ecosystems and resources from influencing factors outside the forest sector, and intersectoral means of dealing with these pressures and demands should be sought.

10. New and additional financial resources should be provided to developing countries to enable them to sustainably manage, conserve and develop their forest resources, including through afforestation, reforestation and combating deforestation and forest and land degradation.

11. In order to enable, in particular, developing countries to enhance their endogenous capacity and to better manage, conserve and develop their forest resources, the access to and transfer of environmentally sound technologies and corresponding know-how on favourable terms, including on concessional and preferential terms, as mutually agreed, in accordance with the relevant provisions of Agenda 21, should be promoted, facilitated and financed, as appropriate.

12. (a) Scientific research, forest inventories and assessments carried out by national institutions which take into account, where relevant, biological, physical, social and economic variables, as well as technological development and its application in the field of sustainable forest management, conservation and development, should be strengthened through effective modalities, including international cooperation. In this context, attention should also be given to research and development of sustainably harvested non-wood products.

(b) National and, where appropriate, regional and international institutional capabilities in education, training, science, technology, economics, anthropology and social aspects of forests and forest management are essential to the conservation and sustainable development of forests and should be strengthened.

(c) International exchange of information on the results of forest and forest management research and development should be enhanced and broadened, as appropriate, making full use of education and training institutions, including those in the private sector.

(d) Appropriate indigenous capacity and local knowledge regarding the conservation and sustainable development of forests should, through institutional and financial support, and in collaboration with the people in local communities concerned, be recognized, respected, recorded, developed and, as appropriate, introduced in the implementation of programmes. Benefits arising from the utilization of indigenous knowledge should therefore be equitably shared with such people.

13. (a) Trade in forest products should be based on non-discriminatory and multilaterally agreed rules and procedures consistent with international trade law and practices. In this context, open and free international trade in forest products should be facilitated.

(b) Reduction or removal of tariff barriers and impediments to the provision of better market access and better prices for higher value-added forest products and their local processing should be encouraged to enable producer countries to better conserve and manage their renewable forest resources.

(c) Incorporation of environmental costs and benefits into market forces and mechanisms, in order to achieve forest conservation and sustainable development, should be encouraged both domestically and internationally.

(d) Forest conservation and sustainable development policies should be integrated with economic, trade and other relevant policies.

(e) Fiscal, trade, industrial, transportation and other policies and practices that may lead to forest degradation should be avoided. Adequate policies, aimed at management, conservation and sustainable development of forests, including where appropriate, incentives, should be encouraged.

14. Unilateral measures, incompatible with international obligations or agreements, to restrict and/or ban international trade in timber or other forest products should be removed or avoided, in order to attain long-term sustainable forest management.

15. Pollutants, particularly air-borne pollutants, including those responsible for acidic deposition, that are harmful to the health of forest ecosystems at the local, national, regional and global levels should be controlled.

6.13 Agreement to Promote Compliance With International Conservation and Management Measures by Fishing Vessels on the High Seas. Adopted by the Twenty-seventh Session of the Food and Agriculture Organization of the United Nations Conference, 24 November 1993. Not yet in force. *Reprinted in* 33 I.L.M. 968 (1994)

Preamble

The Parties to this Agreement,

Recognizing that all States have the right for their nationals to engage in fishing on the high seas, subject to the relevant rules of international law, as reflected in the United Nations Convention on the Law of the Sea,

Further recognizing that, under international law as reflected in the United Nations Convention on the Law of the Sea, all States have the duty to take, or to cooperate with other States in taking, such measures for their respective nationals as may be necessary for the conservation of the living resources of the high seas,

Acknowledging the right and interest of all States to develop their fishing sectors in accordance with their national policies, and the need to promote cooperation with developing countries to enhance their capabilities to fulfil their obligations under this Agreement,

Recalling that Agenda 21, adopted by the United Nations Conference on Environment and Development, calls upon States to take effective action, consistent with international law, to deter reflagging of vessels by their nationals as a means of avoiding compliance with applicable conservation and management rules for fishing activities on the high seas,

Further recalling that the Declaration of Cancun, adopted by the International Conference on Responsible Fishing, also calls on States to take action in this respect,

Bearing in mind that under Agenda 21, States commit themselves to the conservation and sustainable use of marine living resources on the high seas,

Calling upon States which do not participate in global, regional or subregional fisheries organizations or arrangements to join or, as appropriate, to enter into understandings with such organizations or with parties to such organizations or arrangements with a view to achieving compliance with international conservation and management measures,

Conscious of the duties of every State to exercise effectively its jurisdiction and control over vessels flying its flag, including fishing vessels and vessels engaged in the transhipment of fish,

Mindful that the practice of flagging or reflagging fishing vessels as a means of avoiding compliance with international conservation and management measures for living marine resources, and the failure of flag States to fulfil their responsibilities with respect to fishing vessels entitled to fly their flag, are among the factors that seriously undermine the effectiveness of such measures,

Realizing that the objective of this Agreement can be achieved through specifying flag States' responsibility in respect of fishing vessels entitled to fly their flags and operating on the high seas, including the authorization by the flag State of such operations, as well as through strengthened international cooperation and increased transparency through the exchange of information on high seas fishing,

Noting that this Agreement will form an integral part of the International Code of Conduct for Responsible Fishing called for in the Declaration of Cancun,

Desiring to conclude an international agreement within the framework of the Food and Agriculture Organization of the United Nations, hereinafter referred to as FAO, under Article XIV of the FAO Constitution,

Have agreed as follows:

Article I

Definitions

For the purposes of this Agreement:

(a) "fishing vessel" means any vessel used or intended for use for the purposes of the commercial exploitation of living marine resources, including mother ships and any other vessels directly engaged in such fishing operations;

(b) "international conservation and management measures" means measures to conserve or manage one or more species of living marine resources that are adopted and applied in accordance with the relevant rules of international law as reflected in the 1982 United Nations Convention on the Law of the Sea. Such measures may be adopted either by global, regional or subregional fisheries organizations, subject to the rights and obligations of their members, or by treaties or other international agreements;

(c) "length" means

(i) for any fishing vessel built after 18 July 1982, 96 percent of the total length on a waterline at 85 percent of the least moulded depth measured from the top of the keel, or the length from the foreside of the stem to the axis of the rudder stock on that waterline, if that be greater. In ships designed with a rake of keel the waterline on which this length is measured shall be parallel to the designed waterline;

(ii) for any fishing vessel built before 18 July 1982, registered length as entered on the national register or other record of vessels;

(d) "record of fishing vessels" means a record of fishing vessels in which are recorded pertinent details of the fishing vessel. It may constitute a separate record for fishing vessels or form part of a general record of vessels;

(e) "regional economic integration organization" means a regional economic integration organization to which its member States have transferred competence over matters covered by this Agreement, including the authority to make decisions binding on its member States in respect of those matters;

(f) "vessels entitled to fly its flag" and "vessels entitled to fly the flag of a State", includes vessels entitled to fly the flag of a member State of a regional economic integration organization.

Article II

Application

1. Subject to the following paragraphs of this Article, this Agreement shall apply to all fishing vessels that are used or intended for fishing on the high seas.

2. A Party may exempt fishing vessels of less than 24 metres in length entitled to fly its flag from the application of this Agreement unless the Party determines that such an exemption would undermine the object and purpose of this Agreement, provided that such exemptions:

(a) shall not be granted in respect of fishing vessels operating in fishing regions referred to in paragraph 3 below, other than fishing vessels that are entitled to fly the flag of a coastal State of that fishing region; and

(b) shall not apply to the obligations undertaken by a Party under paragraph 1 of Article III, or paragraph 7 of Article VI of this Agreement.

3. Without prejudice to the provisions of paragraph 2 above, in any fishing region where bordering coastal States have not yet declared exclusive economic zones, or

equivalent zones of national jurisdiction over fisheries, such coastal States as are Parties to this Agreement may agree, either directly or through appropriate regional fisheries organizations, to establish a minimum length of fishing vessels below which this Agreement shall not apply in respect of fishing vessels flying the flag of any such coastal State and operating exclusively in such fishing region.

Article III
Flag state responsibility

1. (a) Each Party shall take such measures as may be necessary to ensure that fishing vessels entitled to fly its flag do not engage in any activity that undermines the effectiveness of international conservation and management measures.

(b) In the event that a Party has, pursuant to paragraph 2 of Article II, granted an exemption for fishing vessels of less than 24 metres in length entitled to fly its flag from the application of other provisions of this Agreement, such Party shall nevertheless take effective measures in respect of any such fishing vessel that undermines the effectiveness of international conservation and management measures. These measures shall be such as to ensure that the fishing vessel ceases to engage in activities that undermine the effectiveness of the international conservation and management measures.

2. In particular, no Party shall allow any fishing vessel entitled to fly its flag to be used for fishing on the high seas unless it has been authorized to be so used by the appropriate authority or authorities of that Party. A fishing vessel so authorized shall fish in accordance with the conditions of the authorization.

3. No Party shall authorize any fishing vessel entitled to fly its flag to be used for fishing on the high seas unless the Party is satisfied that it is able, taking into account the links that exist between it and the fishing vessel concerned, to exercise effectively its responsibilities under this Agreement in respect of that fishing vessel.

4. Where a fishing vessel that has been authorized to be used for fishing on the high seas by a Party ceases to be entitled to fly the flag of that Party, the authorization to fish on the high seas shall be deemed to have been cancelled.

5. (a) No Party shall authorize any fishing vessel previously registered in the territory of another Party that has undermined the effectiveness of international conservation and management measures to be used for fishing on the high seas, unless it is satisfied that

(i) any period of suspension by another Party of an authorization for such fishing vessel to be used for fishing on the high seas has expired; and

(ii) no authorization for such fishing vessel to be used for fishing on the high seas has been withdrawn by another Party within the last three years.

(b) The provisions of subparagraph (a) above shall also apply in respect of fishing vessels previously registered in the territory of a State which is not a Party to this Agreement, provided that sufficient information is available to the Party concerned on the circumstances in which the authorization to fish was suspended or withdrawn.

(c) The provisions of subparagraphs (a) and (b) shall not apply where the ownership of the fishing vessel has subsequently changed, and the new owner has provided sufficient evidence demonstrating that the previous owner or operator has no further legal, beneficial or financial interest in, or control of, the fishing vessel.

(d) Notwithstanding the provisions of subparagraphs (a) and (b) above, a Party may authorize a fishing vessel, to which those subparagraphs would otherwise apply, to be used for fishing on the high seas, where the Party concerned, after having taken into account all relevant facts, including the circumstances in which the fishing authorization has been withdrawn by the other Party or State, has determined that to grant an authorization to use the vessel for fishing on the high seas would not undermine the object and purpose of this Agreement.

6. Each Party shall ensure that all fishing vessels entitled to fly its flag that it has entered in the record maintained under Article IV are marked in such a way that they can be readily identified in accordance with generally accepted standards, such as the FAO Standard Specifications for the Marking and Identification of Fishing Vessels.

7. Each Party shall ensure that each fishing vessel entitled to fly its flag shall provide it with such information on its operations as may be necessary to enable the Party to fulfil its obligations under this Agreement, including in particular information pertaining to the area of its fishing operations and to its catches and landings.

8. Each Party shall take enforcement measures in respect of fishing vessels entitled to fly its flag which act in contravention of the provisions of this Agreement, including, where appropriate, making the contravention of such provisions an offence under national legislation. Sanctions applicable in respect of such contraventions shall be of sufficient gravity as to be effective in securing compliance with the requirements of this Agreement and to deprive offenders of the benefits accruing from their illegal activities. Such sanctions shall, for serious offences, include refusal, suspension or withdrawal of the authorization to fish on the high seas.

Article IV

Records of fishing vessels

Each Party shall, for the purposes of this Agreement, maintain a record of fishing vessels entitled to fly its flag and authorized to be used for fishing on the high seas, and shall take such measures as may be necessary to ensure that all such fishing vessels are entered in that record.

Article V

International cooperation

1. The Parties shall cooperate as appropriate in the implementation of this Agreement, and shall, in particular, exchange information, including evidentiary material, relating to activities of fishing vessels in order to assist the flag State in identifying those fishing vessels flying its flag reported to have engaged in activities undermining international conservation and management measures, so as to fulfil its obligations under Article III.

2. When a fishing vessel is voluntarily in the port of a Party other than its flag State, that Party, where it has reasonable grounds for believing that the fishing vessel has been used for an activity that undermines the effectiveness of international conservation and management measures, shall promptly notify the flag State accordingly. Parties may make arrangements regarding the undertaking by port States of such investigatory measures as may be considered necessary to establish whether the fishing vessel has indeed been used contrary to the provisions of this Agreement.

3. The Parties shall, when and as appropriate, enter into cooperative agreements or arrangements of mutual assistance on a global, regional, subregional or bilateral basis so as to promote the achievement of the objectives of this Agreement.

Article VI

Exchange of information

1. Each Party shall make readily available to FAO the following information with respect to each fishing vessel entered in the record required to be maintained under Article IV:

(a) name of fishing vessel, registration number, previous names (if known), and port of registry;

(b) previous flag (if any);

(c) International Radio Call Sign (if any);

(d) name and address of owner or owners;

(e) where and when built;

(f) type of vessel;

(g) length.

2. Each Party shall, to the extent practicable, make available to FAO the following additional information with respect to each fishing vessel entered in the record required to be maintained under Article IV:

(a) name and address of operator (manager) or operators (managers) (if any);

(b) type of fishing method or methods;

(c) moulded depth;

(d) beam;

(e) gross register tonnage;

(f) power of main engine or engines.

3. Each Party shall promptly notify to FAO any modifications to the information listed in paragraphs 1 and 2 of this Article.

4. FAO shall circulate periodically the information provided under paragraphs 1, 2, and 3 of this Article to all Parties, and, on request, individually to any Party. FAO shall also, subject to any restrictions imposed by the Party concerned regarding the distribution of information, provide such information on request individually to any global, regional or subregional fisheries organization.

5. Each Party shall also promptly inform FAO of-

(a) any additions to the record;

(b) any deletions from the record by reason of-

(i) the voluntary relinquishment or non-renewal of the fishing authorization by the fishing vessel owner or operator;

(ii) the withdrawal of the fishing authorization issued in respect of the fishing vessel under paragraph 8 of Article III;

(iii) the fact that the fishing vessel concerned is no longer entitled to fly its flag;

(iv) the scrapping, decommissioning or loss of the fishing vessel concerned; or

(v) any other reason.

6. Where information is given to FAO under paragraph 5 (b) above, the Party concerned shall specify which of the reasons listed in that paragraph is applicable.

7. Each Party shall inform FAO of

(a) any exemption it has granted under paragraph 2 of Article II, the number and type of fishing vessel involved and the geographical areas in which such fishing vessels operate; and

(b) any agreement reached under paragraph 3 of Article II.

8. (a) Each Party shall report promptly to FAO all relevant information regarding any activities of fishing vessels flying its flag that undermine the effectiveness of

international conservation and management measures, including the identity of the fishing vessel or vessels involved and measures imposed by the Party in respect of such activities. Reports on measures imposed by a Party may be subject to such limitations as may be required by national legislation with respect to confidentiality, including, in particular, confidentiality regarding measures that are not yet final.

(b) Each Party, where it has reasonable grounds to believe that a fishing vessel not entitled to fly its flag has engaged in any activity that undermines the effectiveness of international conservation and management measures, shall draw this to the attention of the flag State concerned and may, as appropriate, draw it to the attention of FAO. It shall provide the flag State with full supporting evidence and may provide FAO with a summary of such evidence. FAO shall not circulate such information until such time as the flag State has had an opportunity to comment on the allegation and evidence submitted, or to object as the case may be.

9. Each Party shall inform FAO of any cases where the Party, pursuant to paragraph 5 (d) of Article III, has granted an authorization notwithstanding the provisions of paragraph 5 (a) or 5 (b) of Article III. The information shall include pertinent data permitting the identification of the fishing vessel and the owner or operator and, as appropriate, any other information relevant to the Party's decision.

10. FAO shall circulate promptly the information provided under paragraphs 5, 6, 7, 8 and 9 of this Article to all Parties, and, on request, individually to any Party. FAO shall also, subject to any restrictions imposed by the Party concerned regarding the distribution of information, provide such information promptly on request individually to any global, regional or subregional fisheries organization.

11. The Parties shall exchange information relating to the implementation of this Agreement, including through FAO and other appropriate global, regional and subregional fisheries organizations.

Article VII

Cooperation with developing countries

The Parties shall cooperate, at a global, regional, subregional or bilateral level, and, as appropriate, with the support of FAO and other international or regional organizations, to provide assistance, including technical assistance, to Parties that are developing countries in order to assist them in fulfilling their obligations under this Agreement.

Article VIII

Non-parties

1. The Parties shall encourage any State not party to this Agreement to accept this Agreement and shall encourage any non-Party to adopt laws and regulations consistent with the provisions of this Agreement.

2. The Parties shall cooperate in a manner consistent with this Agreement and with international law to the end that fishing vessels entitled to fly the flags of non-Parties do not engage in activities that undermine the effectiveness of international conservation and management measures.

3. The Parties shall exchange information amongst themselves, either directly or through FAO, with respect to activities of fishing vessels flying the flags of non-Parties that undermine the effectiveness of international conservation and management measures.

Article IX

Settlement of disputes

1. Any Party may seek consultations with any other Party or Parties on any dispute with regard to the interpretation or application of the provisions of this Agreement with a view to reaching a mutually satisfactory solution as soon as possible.

2. In the event that the dispute is not resolved through these consultations within a reasonable period of time, the Parties in question shall consult among themselves as soon as possible with a view to having the dispute settled by negotiation, inquiry, mediation, conciliation, arbitration, judicial settlement or other peaceful means of their own choice.

3. Any dispute of this character not so resolved shall, with the consent of all Parties to the dispute, be referred for settlement to the International Court of Justice, to the International Tribunal for the Law of the Sea upon entry into force of the 1982 United Nations Convention on the Law of the Sea or to arbitration. In the case of failure to reach agreement on referral to the International Court of Justice, to the International Tribunal for the Law of the Sea or to arbitration, the Parties shall continue to consult and cooperate with a view to reaching settlement of the dispute in accordance with the rules of international law relating to the conservation of living marine resources.

Article X

Acceptance

1. This Agreement shall be open to acceptance by any Member or Associate Member of FAO, and to any non-member State that is a member of the United Nations, or of any of the specialized agencies of the United Nations or of the International Atomic Energy Agency.

2. Acceptance of this Agreement shall be effected by the deposit of an instrument of acceptance with the Director–General of FAO, hereinafter referred to as the Director–General.

3. The Director–General shall inform all Parties, all Members and Associate Members of FAO and the Secretary–General of the United Nations of all instruments of acceptance received.

4. When a regional economic integration organization becomes a Party to this Agreement, such regional economic integration organization shall, in accordance with the provisions of Article II.7 of the FAO Constitution, as appropriate, notify such modifications or clarifications to its declaration of competence submitted under Article II.5 of the FAO Constitution as may be necessary in light of its acceptance of this Agreement. Any Party to this Agreement may, at any time, request a regional economic integration organization that is a Party to this Agreement to provide information as to which, as between the regional economic integration organization and its Member States, is responsible for the implementation of any particular matter covered by this Agreement. The regional economic integration organization shall provide this information within a reasonable time.

Article XI

Entry into force

1. This Agreement shall enter into force as from the date of receipt by the Director–General of the twenty-fifth instrument of acceptance.

2. For the purpose of this Article, an instrument deposited by a regional economic integration organization shall not be counted as additional to those deposited by member States of such an organization.

Article XII

Reservations

Acceptance of this Agreement may be made subject to reservations which shall become effective only upon unanimous acceptance by all Parties to this Agreement. The Director–General shall notify forthwith all Parties of any reservation. Parties not having replied within three months from the date of the notification shall be deemed to have accepted the reservation. Failing such acceptance, the State or regional economic integration organization making the reservation shall not become a Party to this Agreement.

Article XIII

Amendments

1. Any proposal by a Party for the amendment of this Agreement shall be communicated to the Director–General.

2. Any proposed amendment of this Agreement received by the Director–General from a Party shall be presented to a regular or special session of the Conference for approval and, if the amendment involves important technical changes or imposes additional obligations on the Parties, it shall be considered by an advisory committee of specialists convened by FAO prior to the Conference.

3. Notice of any proposed amendment of this Agreement shall be transmitted to the Parties by the Director–General not later than the time when the agenda of the session of the Conference at which the matter is to be considered is dispatched.

4. Any such proposed amendment of this Agreement shall require the approval of the Conference and shall come into force as from the thirtieth day after acceptance by two-thirds of the Parties. Amendments involving new obligations for Parties, however, shall come into force in respect of each Party only on acceptance by it and as from the thirtieth day after such acceptance. Any amendment shall be deemed to involve new obligations for Parties unless the Conference, in approving the amendment, decides otherwise by consensus.

5. The instruments of acceptance of amendments involving new obligations shall be deposited with the Director–General, who shall inform all Parties of the receipt of acceptance and the entry into force of amendments.

6. For the purpose of this Article, an instrument deposited by a regional economic integration organization shall not be counted as additional to those deposited by member States of such an organization.

Article XIV

Withdrawal

Any Party may withdraw from this Agreement at any time after the expiry of two years from the date upon which the Agreement entered into force with respect to that Party, by giving written notice of such withdrawal to the Director–General who shall immediately inform all the Parties and the Members and Associate Members of FAO of such withdrawal. Withdrawal shall become effective at the end of the calendar year following that in which the notice of withdrawal has been received by the Director–General.

Article XV

Duties of the depositary

The Director–General shall be the Depositary of this Agreement. The Depositary shall:

(a) send certified copies of this Agreement to each Member and Associate Member of FAO and to such non-member States as may become party to this Agreement;

(b) arrange for the registration of this Agreement, upon its entry into force, with the Secretariat of the United Nations in accordance with Article 102 of the Charter of the United Nations;

(c) inform each Member and Associate Member of FAO and any non-member States as may become Party to this Agreement of:

(i) instruments of acceptance deposited in accordance with Article X;

(ii) the date of entry into force of this Agreement in accordance with Article XI;

(iii) proposals for and the entry into force of amendments to this Agreement in accordance with Article XIII;

(iv) withdrawals from this Agreement pursuant to Article XIV.

6.14 Agreement for the Implementation of the Provisions of the United Nations Convention of the Law of the Sea of 10 December 1982 Relating to the Conservation and Management of Straddling Fish Stocks and Highly Migratory Fish Stocks. Adopted by the U.N. Conference on Straddling Fish Stocks and Highly Migratory Fish Stocks, 4 August 1995. Opened for signature, 4 December 1995. Not yet in force. U.N. Doc. A/CONF.164/38 (1995); *reprinted in* 34 I.L.M. 1542 (1995) & 5A Weston V.H.24

The States Parties to this Agreement,

Recalling the relevant provisions of the United Nations Convention on the Law of the Sea of 10 December 1982,

Determined to ensure the long-term conservation and sustainable use of straddling fish stocks and highly migratory fish stocks,

Resolved to improve cooperation between States to that end,

Calling for more effective enforcement by flag States, port States and coastal States of the conservation and management measures adopted for such stocks,

Seeking to address in particular the problems identified in chapter 17, programme area C, of Agenda 21 adopted by the United Nations Conference on Environment and Development, namely, that the management of high seas fisheries is inadequate in many areas and that some resources are overutilized, and noting that there are problems of unregulated fishing, over-capitalization, excessive fleet size, vessel reflagging to escape controls, insufficiently selective gear, unreliable databases and lack of sufficient cooperation between States,

Committing themselves to responsible fisheries,

Conscious of the need to avoid adverse impacts on the marine environment, preserve biodiversity, maintain the integrity of marine ecosystems and minimize the risk of long-term or irreversible effects of fishing operations,

Recognizing the need for specific assistance, including financial, scientific and technological assistance, in order that developing States can participate effectively in the conservation, management and sustainable use of straddling fish stocks and highly migratory fish stocks,

Convinced that an agreement for the implementation of the relevant provisions of the Convention would best serve these purposes and contribute to the maintenance of international peace and security,

Affirming that matters not regulated by the Convention or by this Agreement continue to be governed by the rules and principles of general international law,

Have agreed as follows:

PART I

GENERAL PROVISIONS

Article 1

Use of terms and scope

1. For the purposes of this Agreement:

(a) "Convention" means the United Nations Convention on the Law of the Sea of 10 December 1982;

(b) "conservation and management measures" means measures to conserve and manage one or more species of living marine resources that are adopted and applied consistent with the relevant rules of international law as reflected in the Convention and this Agreement;

(c) "fish" includes molluscs and crustaceans except those belonging to sedentary species as defined in article 77 of the Convention; and

(d) "arrangement" means a cooperative mechanism established in accordance with the Convention and this Agreement by two or more States for the purpose, inter alia, of establishing conservation and management measures in a subregion or region for one or more straddling fish stocks or highly migratory fish stocks.

2. (a) "States Parties" means States which have consented to be bound by this Agreement and for which the Agreement is in force.

(b) This Agreement applies mutatis mutandis:

(i) to any entity referred to in article 305, paragraph 1 (c), (d) and (e), of the Convention and

(ii) subject to article 47, to any entity referred to as an "international organization" in Annex IX, article 1, of the Convention which becomes a Party to this Agreement, and to that extent "States Parties" refers to those entities.

3. This Agreement applies mutatis mutandis to other fishing entities whose vessels fish on the high seas.

Article 2

Objective

The objective of this Agreement is to ensure the long-term conservation and sustainable use of straddling fish stocks and highly migratory fish stocks through effective implementation of the relevant provisions of the Convention.

Article 3

Application

1. Unless otherwise provided, this Agreement applies to the conservation and management of straddling fish stocks and highly migratory fish stocks beyond areas under national jurisdiction, except that articles 6 and 7 apply also to the conservation and management of such stocks within areas under national jurisdiction, subject to the different legal regimes that apply within areas under national jurisdiction and in areas beyond national jurisdiction as provided for in the Convention.

2. In the exercise of its sovereign rights for the purpose of exploring and exploiting, conserving and managing straddling fish stocks and highly migratory fish stocks within areas under national jurisdiction, the coastal State shall apply mutatis mutandis the general principles enumerated in article 5.

3. States shall give due consideration to the respective capacities of developing States to apply articles 5, 6 and 7 within areas under national jurisdiction and their need for assistance as provided for in this Agreement. To this end, Part VII applies mutatis mutandis in respect of areas under national jurisdiction.

Article 4

Relationship between this Agreement and the Convention

Nothing in this Agreement shall prejudice the rights, jurisdiction and duties of States under the Convention. This Agreement shall be interpreted and applied in the context of and in a manner consistent with the Convention.

PART II

CONSERVATION AND MANAGEMENT OF STRADDLING FISH STOCKS AND HIGHLY MIGRATORY FISH STOCKS

Article 5

General principles

In order to conserve and manage straddling fish stocks and highly migratory fish stocks, coastal States and States fishing on the high seas shall, in giving effect to their duty to cooperate in accordance with the Convention:

(a) adopt measures to ensure long-term sustainability of straddling fish stocks and highly migratory fish stocks and promote the objective of their optimum utilization;

(b) ensure that such measures are based on the best scientific evidence available and are designed to maintain or restore stocks at levels capable of producing maximum sustainable yield, as qualified by relevant environmental and economic factors, including the special requirements of developing States, and taking into account fishing patterns, the interdependence of stocks and any generally recommended international minimum standards, whether subregional, regional or global;

(c) apply the precautionary approach in accordance with article 6;

(d) assess the impacts of fishing, other human activities and environmental factors on target stocks and species belonging to the same ecosystem or associated with or dependent upon the target stocks;

(e) adopt, where necessary, conservation and management measures for species belonging to the same ecosystem or associated with or dependent upon the target stocks, with a view to maintaining or restoring populations of such species above levels at which their reproduction may become seriously threatened;

(f) minimize pollution, waste, discards, catch by lost or abandoned gear, catch of non-target species, both fish and non-fish species (hereinafter referred to as non-target species) and impacts on associated or dependent species, in particular endangered species, through measures including, to the extent practicable, the development and use of selective, environmentally safe and cost-effective fishing gear and techniques;

(g) protect biodiversity in the marine environment;

(h) take measures to prevent or eliminate overfishing and excess fishing capacity and to ensure that levels of fishing effort do not exceed those commensurate with the sustainable use of fishery resources;

(i) take into account the interests of artisanal and subsistence fishers;

(j) collect and share, in a timely manner, complete and accurate data concerning fishing activities on, inter alia, vessel position, catch of target and non-target species and fishing effort, as set out in Annex I, as well as information from national and international research programmes;

(k) promote and conduct scientific research and develop appropriate technologies in support of fishery conservation and management; and

(*l*) implement and enforce conservation and management measures through effective monitoring, control and surveillance.

Article 6

Application of the precautionary approach

1. States shall apply the precautionary approach widely to conservation, management and exploitation of straddling fish stocks and highly migratory fish stocks in order to protect the living marine resources and preserve the marine environment.

2. States shall be more cautious when information is uncertain, unreliable or inadequate. The absence of adequate scientific information shall not be used as a reason for postponing or failing to take conservation and management measures.

3. In implementing the precautionary approach, States shall:

(a) improve decision-making for fishery resource conservation and management by obtaining and sharing the best scientific information available and implementing improved techniques for dealing with risk and uncertainty;

(b) apply the guidelines set out in Annex II and determine, on the basis of the best scientific information available, stock-specific reference points and the action to be taken if they are exceeded;

(c) take into account, inter alia, uncertainties relating to the size and productivity of the stocks, reference points, stock condition in relation to such reference points, levels and distribution of fishing mortality and the impact of fishing activities on non-target and associated or dependent species, as well as existing and predicted oceanic, environmental and socio-economic conditions; and

(d) develop data collection and research programmes to assess the impact of fishing on non-target and associated or dependent species and their environment, and adopt plans which are necessary to ensure the conservation of such species and to protect habitats of special concern.

4. States shall take measures to ensure that, when reference points are approached, they will not be exceeded. In the event that they are exceeded, States shall, without delay, take the action determined under paragraph 3 (b) to restore the stocks.

5. Where the status of target stocks or non-target or associated or dependent species is of concern, States shall subject such stocks and species to enhanced monitoring in order to review their status and the efficacy of conservation and management measures. They shall revise those measures regularly in the light of new information.

6. For new or exploratory fisheries, States shall adopt as soon as possible cautious conservation and management measures, including, inter alia, catch limit and effort limit. Such measures shall remain in force until there are sufficient data to allow assessment of the impact of the fisheries on the long-term sustainability of the stocks, whereupon conservation and management measures based on that assessment shall be implemented. The latter measures shall, if appropriate, allow for the gradual development of the fisheries.

7. If a natural phenomenon has a significant adverse impact on the status of straddling fish stocks or highly migratory fish stocks, States shall adopt conservation and management measures on an emergency basis to ensure that fishing activity does not exacerbate such adverse impact. States shall also adopt such measures on an emergency basis where fishing activity presents a serious threat to the sustainability of such stocks. Measures taken on an emergency basis shall be temporary and shall be based on the best scientific evidence available.

Article 7

Compatibility of conservation and management measures

1. Without prejudice to the sovereign rights of coastal States for the purpose of exploring and exploiting, conserving and managing the living marine resources within areas under national jurisdiction as provided for in the Convention, and the right of all States for their nationals to engage in fishing on the high seas in accordance with the Convention:

(a) with respect to straddling fish stocks, the relevant coastal States and the States whose nationals fish for such stocks in the adjacent high seas area shall seek, either directly or through the appropriate mechanisms for cooperation provided for in Part III, to agree upon the measures necessary for the conservation of these stocks in the adjacent high seas area;

(b) with respect to highly migratory fish stocks, the relevant coastal States and other States whose nationals fish for such stocks in the region shall cooperate, either directly or through the appropriate mechanisms for cooperation provided for in Part III, with a view to ensuring conservation and promoting the objective of optimum utilization of such stocks throughout the region, both within and beyond the areas under national jurisdiction.

2. Conservation and management measures established for the high seas and those adopted for areas under national jurisdiction shall be compatible in order to ensure conservation and management of the straddling fish stocks and highly migratory fish stocks in their entirety. To this end, coastal States and States fishing on the high seas have a duty to cooperate for the purpose of achieving compatible measures in respect of such stocks. In determining compatible conservation and management measures, States shall:

(a) take into account the conservation and management measures adopted and applied in accordance with article 61 of the Convention in respect of the same stocks by coastal States within areas under national jurisdiction and ensure that measures established in respect of such stocks for the high seas do not undermine the effectiveness of such measures;

(b) take into account previously agreed measures established and applied for the high seas in accordance with the Convention in respect of the same stocks by relevant coastal States and States fishing on the high seas;

(c) take into account previously agreed measures established and applied in accordance with the Convention in respect of the same stocks by a subregional or regional fisheries management organization or arrangement;

(d) take into account the biological unity and other biological characteristics of the stocks and the relationships between the distribution of the stocks, the fisheries and the geographical particularities of the region concerned, including the extent to which the stocks occur and are fished in areas under national jurisdiction;

(e) take into account the respective dependence of the coastal States and the States fishing on the high seas on the stocks concerned; and

(f) ensure that such measures do not result in harmful impact on the living marine resources as a whole.

3. In giving effect to their duty to cooperate, States shall make every effort to agree on compatible conservation and management measures within a reasonable period of time.

4. If no agreement can be reached within a reasonable period of time, any of the States concerned may invoke the procedures for the settlement of disputes provided for in Part VIII.

5. Pending agreement on compatible conservation and management measures, the States concerned, in a spirit of understanding and cooperation, shall make every effort to enter into provisional arrangements of a practical nature. In the event that they are unable to agree on such arrangements, any of the States concerned may, for the purpose of obtaining provisional measures, submit the dispute to a court or tribunal in accordance with the procedures for the settlement of disputes provided for in Part VIII.

6. Provisional arrangements or measures entered into or prescribed pursuant to paragraph 5 shall take into account the provisions of this Part, shall have due regard to the rights and obligations of all States concerned, shall not jeopardize or hamper the reaching of final agreement on compatible conservation and management measures and shall be without prejudice to the final outcome of any dispute settlement procedure.

7. Coastal States shall regularly inform States fishing on the high seas in the subregion or region, either directly or through appropriate subregional or regional fisheries management organizations or arrangements, or through other appropriate

means, of the measures they have adopted for straddling fish stocks and highly migratory fish stocks within areas under their national jurisdiction.

8. States fishing on the high seas shall regularly inform other interested States, either directly or through appropriate subregional or regional fisheries management organizations or arrangements, or through other appropriate means, of the measures they have adopted for regulating the activities of vessels flying their flag which fish for such stocks on the high seas.

PART III

MECHANISMS FOR INTERNATIONAL COOPERATION CONCERNING STRADDLING FISH STOCKS AND HIGHLY MIGRATORY FISH STOCKS

Article 8

Cooperation for conservation and management

1. Coastal States and States fishing on the high seas shall, in accordance with the Convention, pursue cooperation in relation to straddling fish stocks and highly migratory fish stocks either directly or through appropriate subregional or regional fisheries management organizations or arrangements, taking into account the specific characteristics of the subregion or region, to ensure effective conservation and management of such stocks.

2. States shall enter into consultations in good faith and without delay, particularly where there is evidence that the straddling fish stocks and highly migratory fish stocks concerned may be under threat of over-exploitation or where a new fishery is being developed for such stocks. To this end, consultations may be initiated at the request of any interested State with a view to establishing appropriate arrangements to ensure conservation and management of the stocks. Pending agreement on such arrangements, States shall observe the provisions of this Agreement and shall act in good faith and with due regard to the rights, interests and duties of other States.

3. Where a subregional or regional fisheries management organization or arrangement has the competence to establish conservation and management measures for particular straddling fish stocks or highly migratory fish stocks, States fishing for the stocks on the high seas and relevant coastal States shall give effect to their duty to cooperate by becoming members of such organization or participants in such arrangement, or by agreeing to apply the conservation and management measures established by such organization or arrangement. States having a real interest in the fisheries concerned may become members of such organization or participants in such arrangement. The terms for participation in such organization or arrangement shall not preclude such States from membership or participation; nor shall they be applied in a manner which discriminates against any State or group of States having a real interest in the fisheries concerned.

4. Only those States which are members of such an organization or participants in such an arrangement, or which agree to apply the conservation and management measures established by such organization or arrangement, shall have access to the fishery resources to which those measures apply.

5. Where there is no subregional or regional fisheries management organization or arrangement to establish conservation and management measures for a particular straddling fish stock or highly migratory fish stock, relevant coastal States and States fishing on the high seas for such stock in the subregion or region shall cooperate to establish such an organization or enter into other appropriate arrangements to ensure conservation and management of such stock and shall participate in the work of the organization or arrangement.

6. Any State intending to propose that action be taken by an intergovernmental organization having competence with respect to living resources should, where such action would have a significant effect on conservation and management measures already established by a competent subregional or regional fisheries management organization or arrangement, consult through that organization or arrangement with its members or participants. To the extent practicable, such consultation should take place prior to the submission of the proposal to the intergovernmental organization.

Article 9

Subregional and regional fisheries management organizations and arrangements

1. In establishing subregional or regional fisheries management organizations or in entering into subregional or regional fisheries management arrangements for straddling fish stocks and highly migratory fish stocks, States shall agree, inter alia, on:

(a) the stocks to which conservation and management measures apply, taking into account the biological characteristics of the stocks concerned and the nature of the fisheries involved;

(b) the area of application, taking into account article 7, paragraph 1, and the characteristics of the subregion or region, including socio-economic, geographical and environmental factors;

(c) the relationship between the work of the new organization or arrangement and the role, objectives and operations of any relevant existing fisheries management organizations or arrangements; and

(d) the mechanisms by which the organization or arrangement will obtain scientific advice and review the status of the stocks, including, where appropriate, the establishment of a scientific advisory body.

2. States cooperating in the formation of a subregional or regional fisheries management organization or arrangement shall inform other States which they are aware have a real interest in the work of the proposed organization or arrangement of such cooperation.

Article 10

Functions of subregional and regional fisheries management organizations and arrangements

In fulfilling their obligation to cooperate through subregional or regional fisheries management organizations or arrangements, States shall:

(a) agree on and comply with conservation and management measures to ensure the long-term sustainability of straddling fish stocks and highly migratory fish stocks;

(b) agree, as appropriate, on participatory rights such as allocations of allowable catch or levels of fishing effort;

(c) adopt and apply any generally recommended international minimum standards for the responsible conduct of fishing operations;

(d) obtain and evaluate scientific advice, review the status of the stocks and assess the impact of fishing on non-target and associated or dependent species;

(e) agree on standards for collection, reporting, verification and exchange of data on fisheries for the stocks;

(f) compile and disseminate accurate and complete statistical data, as described in Annex I, to ensure that the best scientific evidence is available, while maintaining confidentiality where appropriate;

(g) promote and conduct scientific assessments of the stocks and relevant research and disseminate the results thereof;

(h) establish appropriate cooperative mechanisms for effective monitoring, control, surveillance and enforcement;

(i) agree on means by which the fishing interests of new members of the organization or new participants in the arrangement will be accommodated;

(j) agree on decision-making procedures which facilitate the adoption of conservation and management measures in a timely and effective manner;

(k) promote the peaceful settlement of disputes in accordance with Part VIII;

(*l*) ensure the full cooperation of their relevant national agencies and industries in implementing the recommendations and decisions of the organization or arrangement; and

(m) give due publicity to the conservation and management measures established by the organization or arrangement.

Article 11

New members or participants

In determining the nature and extent of participatory rights for new members of a subregional or regional fisheries management organization, or for new participants in a subregional or regional fisheries management arrangement, States shall take into account, inter alia:

(a) the status of the straddling fish stocks and highly migratory fish stocks and the existing level of fishing effort in the fishery;

(b) the respective interests, fishing patterns and fishing practices of new and existing members or participants;

(c) the respective contributions of new and existing members or participants to conservation and management of the stocks, to the collection and provision of accurate data and to the conduct of scientific research on the stocks;

(d) the needs of coastal fishing communities which are dependent mainly on fishing for the stocks;

(e) the needs of coastal States whose economies are overwhelmingly dependent on the exploitation of living marine resources; and

(f) the interests of developing States from the subregion or region in whose areas of national jurisdiction the stocks also occur.

Article 12

Transparency in activities of subregional and regional fisheries management organizations and arrangements

1. States shall provide for transparency in the decision-making process and other activities of subregional and regional fisheries management organizations and arrangements.

2. Representatives from other intergovernmental organizations and representatives from non-governmental organizations concerned with straddling fish stocks and highly migratory fish stocks shall be afforded the opportunity to take part in meetings of subregional and regional fisheries management organizations and arrangements as observers or otherwise, as appropriate, in accordance with the procedures of the organization or arrangement concerned. Such procedures shall not be unduly restrictive in this respect. Such intergovernmental organizations and non-governmental

organizations shall have timely access to the records and reports of such organizations and arrangements, subject to the procedural rules on access to them.

Article 13

Strengthening of existing organizations and arrangements

States shall cooperate to strengthen existing subregional and regional fisheries management organizations and arrangements in order to improve their effectiveness in establishing and implementing conservation and management measures for straddling fish stocks and highly migratory fish stocks.

Article 14

Collection and provision of information and cooperation in scientific research

1. States shall ensure that fishing vessels flying their flag provide such information as may be necessary in order to fulfil their obligations under this Agreement. To this end, States shall in accordance with Annex I:

(a) collect and exchange scientific, technical and statistical data with respect to fisheries for straddling fish stocks and highly migratory fish stocks;

(b) ensure that data are collected in sufficient detail to facilitate effective stock assessment and are provided in a timely manner to fulfil the requirements of subregional or regional fisheries management organizations or arrangements; and

(c) take appropriate measures to verify the accuracy of such data.

2. States shall cooperate, either directly or through subregional or regional fisheries management organizations or arrangements:

(a) to agree on the specification of data and the format in which they are to be provided to such organizations or arrangements, taking into account the nature of the stocks and the fisheries for those stocks; and

(b) to develop and share analytical techniques and stock assessment methodologies to improve measures for the conservation and management of straddling fish stocks and highly migratory fish stocks.

3. Consistent with Part XIII of the Convention, States shall cooperate, either directly or through competent international organizations, to strengthen scientific research capacity in the field of fisheries and promote scientific research related to the conservation and management of straddling fish stocks and highly migratory fish stocks for the benefit of all. To this end, a State or the competent international organization conducting such research beyond areas under national jurisdiction shall actively promote the publication and dissemination to any interested States of the results of that research and information relating to its objectives and methods and, to the extent practicable, shall facilitate the participation of scientists from those States in such research.

Article 15

Enclosed and semi-enclosed seas

In implementing this Agreement in an enclosed or semi-enclosed sea, States shall take into account the natural characteristics of that sea and shall also act in a manner consistent with Part IX of the Convention and other relevant provisions thereof.

Article 16

Areas of high seas surrounded entirely by an area under the national jurisdiction of a single State

1. States fishing for straddling fish stocks and highly migratory fish stocks in an area of the high seas surrounded entirely by an area under the national jurisdiction of

a single State and the latter State shall cooperate to establish conservation and management measures in respect of those stocks in the high seas area. Having regard to the natural characteristics of the area, States shall pay special attention to the establishment of compatible conservation and management measures for such stocks pursuant to article 7. Measures taken in respect of the high seas shall take into account the rights, duties and interests of the coastal State under the Convention, shall be based on the best scientific evidence available and shall also take into account any conservation and management measures adopted and applied in respect of the same stocks in accordance with article 61 of the Convention by the coastal State in the area under national jurisdiction. States shall also agree on measures for monitoring, control, surveillance and enforcement to ensure compliance with the conservation and management measures in respect of the high seas.

2. Pursuant to article 8, States shall act in good faith and make every effort to agree without delay on conservation and management measures to be applied in the carrying out of fishing operations in the area referred to in paragraph 1. If, within a reasonable period of time, the fishing States concerned and the coastal State are unable to agree on such measures, they shall, having regard to paragraph 1, apply article 7, paragraphs 4, 5 and 6, relating to provisional arrangements or measures. Pending the establishment of such provisional arrangements or measures, the States concerned shall take measures in respect of vessels flying their flag in order that they do not engage in fisheries which could undermine the stocks concerned.

PART IV

NON–MEMBERS AND NON–PARTICIPANTS

Article 17

Non-members of organizations and non-participants in arrangements

1. A State which is not a member of a subregional or regional fisheries management organization or is not a participant in a subregional or regional fisheries management arrangement, and which does not otherwise agree to apply the conservation and management measures established by such organization or arrangement, is not discharged from the obligation to cooperate, in accordance with the Convention and this Agreement, in the conservation and management of the relevant straddling fish stocks and highly migratory fish stocks.

2. Such State shall not authorize vessels flying its flag to engage in fishing operations for the straddling fish stocks or highly migratory fish stocks which are subject to the conservation and management measures established by such organization or arrangement.

3. States which are members of a subregional or regional fisheries management organization or participants in a subregional or regional fisheries management arrangement shall, individually or jointly, request the fishing entities referred to in article 1, paragraph 3, which have fishing vessels in the relevant area to cooperate fully with such organization or arrangement in implementing the conservation and management measures it has established, with a view to having such measures applied de facto as extensively as possible to fishing activities in the relevant area. Such fishing entities shall enjoy benefits from participation in the fishery commensurate with their commitment to comply with conservation and management measures in respect of the stocks.

4. States which are members of such organization or participants in such arrangement shall exchange information with respect to the activities of fishing vessels flying the flags of States which are neither members of the organization nor participants in the arrangement and which are engaged in fishing operations for the relevant stocks. They shall take measures consistent with this Agreement and international law

to deter activities of such vessels which undermine the effectiveness of subregional or regional conservation and management measures.

PART V

DUTIES OF THE FLAG STATE

Article 18

Duties of the flag State

1. A State whose vessels fish on the high seas shall take such measures as may be necessary to ensure that vessels flying its flag comply with subregional and regional conservation and management measures and that such vessels do not engage in any activity which undermines the effectiveness of such measures.

2. A State shall authorize the use of vessels flying its flag for fishing on the high seas only where it is able to exercise effectively its responsibilities in respect of such vessels under the Convention and this Agreement.

3. Measures to be taken by a State in respect of vessels flying its flag shall include:

(a) control of such vessels on the high seas by means of fishing licences, authorizations or permits, in accordance with any applicable procedures agreed at the subregional, regional or global level;

(b) establishment of regulations:

(i) to apply terms and conditions to the licence, authorization or permit sufficient to fulfil any subregional, regional or global obligations of the flag State;

(ii) to prohibit fishing on the high seas by vessels which are not duly licensed or authorized to fish, or fishing on the high seas by vessels otherwise than in accordance with the terms and conditions of a licence, authorization or permit;

(iii) to require vessels fishing on the high seas to carry the licence, authorization or permit on board at all times and to produce it on demand for inspection by a duly authorized person; and

(iv) to ensure that vessels flying its flag do not conduct unauthorized fishing within areas under the national jurisdiction of other States;

(c) establishment of a national record of fishing vessels authorized to fish on the high seas and provision of access to the information contained in that record on request by directly interested States, taking into account any national laws of the flag State regarding the release of such information;

(d) requirements for marking of fishing vessels and fishing gear for identification in accordance with uniform and internationally recognizable vessel and gear marking systems, such as the Food and Agriculture Organization of the United Nations Standard Specifications for the Marking and Identification of Fishing Vessels;

(e) requirements for recording and timely reporting of vessel position, catch of target and non-target species, fishing effort and other relevant fisheries data in accordance with subregional, regional and global standards for collection of such data;

(f) requirements for verifying the catch of target and non-target species through such means as observer programmes, inspection schemes, unloading reports, supervision of transshipment and monitoring of landed catches and market statistics;

(g) monitoring, control and surveillance of such vessels, their fishing operations and related activities through, inter alia:

(i) the implementation of national inspection schemes and subregional and regional schemes for cooperation in enforcement pursuant to articles 21 and 22, including requirements for such vessels to permit access by duly authorized inspectors from other States;

(ii) the implementation of national observer programmes and subregional and regional observer programmes in which the flag State is a participant, including requirements for such vessels to permit access by observers from other States to carry out the functions agreed under the programmes; and

(iii) the development and implementation of vessel monitoring systems, including, as appropriate, satellite transmitter systems, in accordance with any national programmes and those which have been subregionally, regionally or globally agreed among the States concerned;

(h) regulation of transshipment on the high seas to ensure that the effectiveness of conservation and management measures is not undermined; and

(i) regulation of fishing activities to ensure compliance with subregional, regional or global measures, including those aimed at minimizing catches of non-target species.

4. Where there is a subregionally, regionally or globally agreed system of monitoring, control and surveillance in effect, States shall ensure that the measures they impose on vessels flying their flag are compatible with that system.

PART VI

COMPLIANCE AND ENFORCEMENT

Article 19

Compliance and enforcement by the flag State

1. A State shall ensure compliance by vessels flying its flag with subregional and regional conservation and management measures for straddling fish stocks and highly migratory fish stocks. To this end, that State shall:

(a) enforce such measures irrespective of where violations occur;

(b) investigate immediately and fully any alleged violation of subregional or regional conservation and management measures, which may include the physical inspection of the vessels concerned, and report promptly to the State alleging the violation and the relevant subregional or regional organization or arrangement on the progress and outcome of the investigation;

(c) require any vessel flying its flag to give information to the investigating authority regarding vessel position, catches, fishing gear, fishing operations and related activities in the area of an alleged violation;

(d) if satisfied that sufficient evidence is available in respect of an alleged violation, refer the case to its authorities with a view to instituting proceedings, without delay, in accordance with its laws and, where appropriate, detain the vessel concerned; and

(e) ensure that, where it has been established, in accordance with its laws, a vessel has been involved in the commission of a serious violation of such measures, the vessel does not engage in fishing operations on the high seas until such time as all outstanding sanctions imposed by the flag State in respect of the violation have been complied with.

2. All investigations and judicial proceedings shall be carried out expeditiously. Sanctions applicable in respect of violations shall be adequate in severity to be effective in securing compliance and to discourage violations wherever they occur and shall deprive offenders of the benefits accruing from their illegal activities. Measures

applicable in respect of masters and other officers of fishing vessels shall include provisions which may permit, inter alia, refusal, withdrawal or suspension of authorizations to serve as masters or officers on such vessels.

Article 20

International cooperation in enforcement

1. States shall cooperate, either directly or through subregional or regional fisheries management organizations or arrangements, to ensure compliance with and enforcement of subregional and regional conservation and management measures for straddling fish stocks and highly migratory fish stocks.

2. A flag State conducting an investigation of an alleged violation of conservation and management measures for straddling fish stocks or highly migratory fish stocks may request the assistance of any other State whose cooperation may be useful in the conduct of that investigation. All States shall endeavour to meet reasonable requests made by a flag State in connection with such investigations.

3. A flag State may undertake such investigations directly, in cooperation with other interested States or through the relevant subregional or regional fisheries management organization or arrangement. Information on the progress and outcome of the investigations shall be provided to all States having an interest in, or affected by, the alleged violation.

4. States shall assist each other in identifying vessels reported to have engaged in activities undermining the effectiveness of subregional, regional or global conservation and management measures.

5. States shall, to the extent permitted by national laws and regulations, establish arrangements for making available to prosecuting authorities in other States evidence relating to alleged violations of such measures.

6. Where there are reasonable grounds for believing that a vessel on the high seas has been engaged in unauthorized fishing within an area under the jurisdiction of a coastal State, the flag State of that vessel, at the request of the coastal State concerned, shall immediately and fully investigate the matter. The flag State shall cooperate with the coastal State in taking appropriate enforcement action in such cases and may authorize the relevant authorities of the coastal State to board and inspect the vessel on the high seas. This paragraph is without prejudice to article 111 of the Convention.

7. States Parties which are members of a subregional or regional fisheries management organization or participants in a subregional or regional fisheries management arrangement may take action in accordance with international law, including through recourse to subregional or regional procedures established for this purpose, to deter vessels which have engaged in activities that undermine the effectiveness of or otherwise violate the conservation and management measures established by that organization or arrangement from fishing on the high seas in the subregion or region until such time as appropriate action is taken by the flag State.

Article 21

Subregional and regional cooperation in enforcement

1. In any high seas area covered by a subregional or regional fisheries management organization or arrangement, a State Party which is a member of such organization or a participant in such arrangement may, through its duly authorized inspectors, board and inspect, in accordance with paragraph 2, fishing vessels flying the flag of another State Party to this Agreement, whether or not such State Party is also a member of the organization or a participant in the arrangement, for the purpose of ensuring compliance with conservation and management measures for straddling fish

stocks and highly migratory fish stocks established by that organization or arrangement.

2. States shall establish, through subregional or regional fisheries management organizations or arrangements, procedures for boarding and inspection pursuant to paragraph 1, as well as procedures to implement other provisions of this article. Such procedures shall be consistent with this article and the basic procedures set out in article 22 and shall not discriminate against non-members of the organization or non-participants in the arrangement. Boarding and inspection as well as any subsequent enforcement action shall be conducted in accordance with such procedures. States shall give due publicity to procedures established pursuant to this paragraph.

3. If, within two years of the adoption of this Agreement, any organization or arrangement has not established such procedures, boarding and inspection pursuant to paragraph 1, as well as any subsequent enforcement action, shall, pending the establishment of such procedures, be conducted in accordance with this article and the basic procedures set out in article 22.

4. Prior to taking action under this article, inspecting States shall, either directly or through the relevant subregional or regional fisheries management organization or arrangement, inform all States whose vessels fish on the high seas in the subregion or region of the form of identification issued to their duly authorized inspectors. The vessels used for boarding and inspection shall be clearly marked and identifiable as being on government service. At the time of becoming a Party to this Agreement, a State shall designate an appropriate authority to receive notifications pursuant to this article and shall give due publicity of such designation through the relevant subregional or regional fisheries management organization or arrangement.

5. Where, following boarding and inspection, there are clear grounds for believing that a vessel has engaged in any activity contrary to the conservation and management measures referred to in paragraph 1, the inspecting State shall, where appropriate, secure evidence and shall promptly notify the flag State of the alleged violation.

6. The flag State shall respond to the notification referred to in paragraph 5 within three working days of its receipt, or such other period as may be prescribed in procedures established in accordance with paragraph 2, and shall either:

(a) fulfil, without delay, its obligations under article 19 to investigate and, if evidence so warrants, take enforcement action with respect to the vessel, in which case it shall promptly inform the inspecting State of the results of the investigation and of any enforcement action taken; or

(b) authorize the inspecting State to investigate.

7. Where the flag State authorizes the inspecting State to investigate an alleged violation, the inspecting State shall, without delay, communicate the results of that investigation to the flag State. The flag State shall, if evidence so warrants, fulfil its obligations to take enforcement action with respect to the vessel. Alternatively, the flag State may authorize the inspecting State to take such enforcement action as the flag State may specify with respect to the vessel, consistent with the rights and obligations of the flag State under this Agreement.

8. Where, following boarding and inspection, there are clear grounds for believing that a vessel has committed a serious violation, and the flag State has either failed to respond or failed to take action as required under paragraphs 6 or 7, the inspectors may remain on board and secure evidence and may require the master to assist in further investigation including, where appropriate, by bringing the vessel without delay to the nearest appropriate port, or to such other port as may be specified in procedures established in accordance with paragraph 2. The inspecting State shall immediately inform the flag State of the name of the port to which the vessel is to

proceed. The inspecting State and the flag State and, as appropriate, the port State shall take all necessary steps to ensure the well-being of the crew regardless of their nationality.

9. The inspecting State shall inform the flag State and the relevant organization or the participants in the relevant arrangement of the results of any further investigation.

10. The inspecting State shall require its inspectors to observe generally accepted international regulations, procedures and practices relating to the safety of the vessel and the crew, minimize interference with fishing operations and, to the extent practicable, avoid action which would adversely affect the quality of the catch on board. The inspecting State shall ensure that boarding and inspection is not conducted in a manner that would constitute harassment of any fishing vessel.

11. For the purposes of this article, a serious violation means:

(a) fishing without a valid licence, authorization or permit issued by the flag State in accordance with article 18, paragraph 3 (a);

(b) failing to maintain accurate records of catch and catch-related data, as required by the relevant subregional or regional fisheries management organization or arrangement, or serious misreporting of catch, contrary to the catch reporting requirements of such organization or arrangement;

(c) fishing in a closed area, fishing during a closed season or fishing without, or after attainment of, a quota established by the relevant subregional or regional fisheries management organization or arrangement;

(d) directed fishing for a stock which is subject to a moratorium or for which fishing is prohibited;

(e) using prohibited fishing gear;

(f) falsifying or concealing the markings, identity or registration of a fishing vessel;

(g) concealing, tampering with or disposing of evidence relating to an investigation;

(h) multiple violations which together constitute a serious disregard of conservation and management measures; or

(i) such other violations as may be specified in procedures established by the relevant subregional or regional fisheries management organization or arrangement.

12. Notwithstanding the other provisions of this article, the flag State may, at any time, take action to fulfil its obligations under article 19 with respect to an alleged violation. Where the vessel is under the direction of the inspecting State, the inspecting State shall, at the request of the flag State, release the vessel to the flag State along with full information on the progress and outcome of its investigation.

13. This article is without prejudice to the right of the flag State to take any measures, including proceedings to impose penalties, according to its laws.

14. This article applies mutatis mutandis to boarding and inspection by a State Party which is a member of a subregional or regional fisheries management organization or a participant in a subregional or regional fisheries management arrangement and which has clear grounds for believing that a fishing vessel flying the flag of another State Party has engaged in any activity contrary to relevant conservation and management measures referred to in paragraph 1 in the high seas area covered by such organization or arrangement, and such vessel has subsequently, during the same fishing trip, entered into an area under the national jurisdiction of the inspecting State.

15. Where a subregional or regional fisheries management organization or arrangement has established an alternative mechanism which effectively discharges the obligation under this Agreement of its members or participants to ensure compliance with the conservation and management measures established by the organization or arrangement, members of such organization or participants in such arrangement may agree to limit the application of paragraph 1 as between themselves in respect of the conservation and management measures which have been established in the relevant high seas area.

16. Action taken by States other than the flag State in respect of vessels having engaged in activities contrary to subregional or regional conservation and management measures shall be proportionate to the seriousness of the violation.

17. Where there are reasonable grounds for suspecting that a fishing vessel on the high seas is without nationality, a State may board and inspect the vessel. Where evidence so warrants, the State may take such action as may be appropriate in accordance with international law.

18. States shall be liable for damage or loss attributable to them arising from action taken pursuant to this article when such action is unlawful or exceeds that reasonably required in the light of available information to implement the provisions of this article.

Article 22

Basic procedures for boarding and inspection pursuant to article 21

1. The inspecting State shall ensure that its duly authorized inspectors:

(a) present credentials to the master of the vessel and produce a copy of the text of the relevant conservation and management measures or rules and regulations in force in the high seas area in question pursuant to those measures;

(b) initiate notice to the flag State at the time of the boarding and inspection;

(c) do not interfere with the master's ability to communicate with the authorities of the flag State during the boarding and inspection;

(d) provide a copy of a report on the boarding and inspection to the master and to the authorities of the flag State, noting therein any objection or statement which the master wishes to have included in the report;

(e) promptly leave the vessel following completion of the inspection if they find no evidence of a serious violation; and

(f) avoid the use of force except when and to the degree necessary to ensure the safety of the inspectors and where the inspectors are obstructed in the execution of their duties. The degree of force used shall not exceed that reasonably required in the circumstances.

2. The duly authorized inspectors of an inspecting State shall have the authority to inspect the vessel, its licence, gear, equipment, records, facilities, fish and fish products and any relevant documents necessary to verify compliance with the relevant conservation and management measures.

3. The flag State shall ensure that vessel masters:

(a) accept and facilitate prompt and safe boarding by the inspectors;

(b) cooperate with and assist in the inspection of the vessel conducted pursuant to these procedures;

(c) do not obstruct, intimidate or interfere with the inspectors in the performance of their duties;

(d) allow the inspectors to communicate with the authorities of the flag State and the inspecting State during the boarding and inspection;

(e) provide reasonable facilities, including, where appropriate, food and accommodation, to the inspectors; and

(f) facilitate safe disembarkation by the inspectors.

4. In the event that the master of a vessel refuses to accept boarding and inspection in accordance with this article and article 21, the flag State shall, except in circumstances where, in accordance with generally accepted international regulations, procedures and practices relating to safety at sea, it is necessary to delay the boarding and inspection, direct the master of the vessel to submit immediately to boarding and inspection and, if the master does not comply with such direction, shall suspend the vessel's authorization to fish and order the vessel to return immediately to port. The flag State shall advise the inspecting State of the action it has taken when the circumstances referred to in this paragraph arise.

Article 23

Measures taken by a port State

1. A port State has the right and the duty to take measures, in accordance with international law, to promote the effectiveness of subregional, regional and global conservation and management measures. When taking such measures a port State shall not discriminate in form or in fact against the vessels of any State.

2. A port State may, inter alia, inspect documents, fishing gear and catch on board fishing vessels, when such vessels are voluntarily in its ports or at its offshore terminals.

3. States may adopt regulations empowering the relevant national authorities to prohibit landings and transshipments where it has been established that the catch has been taken in a manner which undermines the effectiveness of subregional, regional or global conservation and management measures on the high seas.

4. Nothing in this article affects the exercise by States of their sovereignty over ports in their territory in accordance with international law.

PART VII

REQUIREMENTS OF DEVELOPING STATES

Article 24

Recognition of the special requirements of developing States

1. States shall give full recognition to the special requirements of developing States in relation to conservation and management of straddling fish stocks and highly migratory fish stocks and development of fisheries for such stocks. To this end, States shall, either directly or through the United Nations Development Programme, the Food and Agriculture Organization of the United Nations and other specialized agencies, the Global Environment Facility, the Commission on Sustainable Development and other appropriate international and regional organizations and bodies, provide assistance to developing States.

2. In giving effect to the duty to cooperate in the establishment of conservation and management measures for straddling fish stocks and highly migratory fish stocks, States shall take into account the special requirements of developing States, in particular:

(a) the vulnerability of developing States which are dependent on the exploitation of living marine resources, including for meeting the nutritional requirements of their populations or parts thereof;

(b) the need to avoid adverse impacts on, and ensure access to fisheries by, subsistence, small-scale and artisanal fishers and women fishworkers, as well as indigenous people in developing States, particularly small island developing States; and

(c) the need to ensure that such measures do not result in transferring, directly or indirectly, a disproportionate burden of conservation action onto developing States.

Article 25

Forms of cooperation with developing States

1. States shall cooperate, either directly or through subregional, regional or global organizations:

(a) to enhance the ability of developing States, in particular the least-developed among them and small island developing States, to conserve and manage straddling fish stocks and highly migratory fish stocks and to develop their own fisheries for such stocks;

(b) to assist developing States, in particular the least-developed among them and small island developing States, to enable them to participate in high seas fisheries for such stocks, including facilitating access to such fisheries subject to articles 5 and 11; and

(c) to facilitate the participation of developing States in subregional and regional fisheries management organizations and arrangements.

2. Cooperation with developing States for the purposes set out in this article shall include the provision of financial assistance, assistance relating to human resources development, technical assistance, transfer of technology, including through joint venture arrangements, and advisory and consultative services.

3. Such assistance shall, inter alia, be directed specifically towards:

(a) improved conservation and management of straddling fish stocks and highly migratory fish stocks through collection, reporting, verification, exchange and analysis of fisheries data and related information;

(b) stock assessment and scientific research; and

(c) monitoring, control, surveillance, compliance and enforcement, including training and capacity-building at the local level, development and funding of national and regional observer programmes and access to technology and equipment.

Article 26

Special assistance in the implementation of this Agreement

1. States shall cooperate to establish special funds to assist developing States in the implementation of this Agreement, including assisting developing States to meet the costs involved in any proceedings for the settlement of disputes to which they may be parties.

2. States and international organizations should assist developing States in establishing new subregional or regional fisheries management organizations or arrangements, or in strengthening existing organizations or arrangements, for the conservation and management of straddling fish stocks and highly migratory fish stocks.

PART VIII

PEACEFUL SETTLEMENT OF DISPUTES

Article 27

Obligation to settle disputes by peaceful means

States have the obligation to settle their disputes by negotiation, inquiry, mediation, conciliation, arbitration, judicial settlement, resort to regional agencies or arrangements, or other peaceful means of their own choice.

Article 28

Prevention of disputes

States shall cooperate in order to prevent disputes. To this end, States shall agree on efficient and expeditious decision-making procedures within subregional and regional fisheries management organizations and arrangements and shall strengthen existing decision-making procedures as necessary.

Article 29

Disputes of a technical nature

Where a dispute concerns a matter of a technical nature, the States concerned may refer the dispute to an ad hoc expert panel established by them. The panel shall confer with the States concerned and shall endeavour to resolve the dispute expeditiously, without recourse to binding procedures for the settlement of disputes.

Article 30

Procedures for the settlement of disputes

1. The provisions relating to the settlement of disputes set out in Part XV of the Convention apply mutatis mutandis to any dispute between States Parties to this Agreement concerning the interpretation or application of this Agreement, whether or not they are also Parties to the Convention.

2. The provisions relating to the settlement of disputes set out in Part XV of the Convention apply mutatis mutandis to any dispute between States Parties to this Agreement concerning the interpretation or application of a subregional, regional or global fisheries agreement relating to straddling fish stocks or highly migratory fish stocks to which they are parties, including any dispute concerning the conservation and management of such stocks, whether or not they are also Parties to the Convention.

3. Any procedure accepted by a State Party to this Agreement and the Convention pursuant to article 287 of the Convention shall apply to the settlement of disputes under this Part, unless that State Party, when signing, ratifying or acceding to this Agreement, or at any time thereafter, has accepted another procedure pursuant to article 287 for the settlement of disputes under this Part.

4. A State Party to this Agreement which is not a Party to the Convention, when signing, ratifying or acceding to this Agreement, or at any time thereafter, shall be free to choose, by means of a written declaration, one or more of the means set out in article 287, paragraph 1, of the Convention for the settlement of disputes under this Part. Article 287 shall apply to such a declaration, as well as to any dispute to which such State is a party which is not covered by a declaration in force. For the purposes of conciliation and arbitration in accordance with Annexes V, VII and VIII to the Convention, such State shall be entitled to nominate conciliators, arbitrators and experts to be included in the lists referred to in Annex V, article 2, Annex VII, article 2, and Annex VIII, article 2, for the settlement of disputes under this Part.

5. Any court or tribunal to which a dispute has been submitted under this Part shall apply the relevant provisions of the Convention, of this Agreement and of any relevant subregional, regional or global fisheries agreement, as well as generally accepted standards for the conservation and management of living marine resources and other rules of international law not incompatible with the Convention, with a view to ensuring the conservation of the straddling fish stocks and highly migratory fish stocks concerned.

Article 31

Provisional measures

1. Pending the settlement of a dispute in accordance with this Part, the parties to the dispute shall make every effort to enter into provisional arrangements of a practical nature.

2. Without prejudice to article 290 of the Convention, the court or tribunal to which the dispute has been submitted under this Part may prescribe any provisional measures which it considers appropriate under the circumstances to preserve the respective rights of the parties to the dispute or to prevent damage to the stocks in question, as well as in the circumstances referred to in article 7, paragraph 5, and article 16, paragraph 2.

3. A State Party to this Agreement which is not a Party to the Convention may declare that, notwithstanding article 290, paragraph 5, of the Convention, the International Tribunal for the Law of the Sea shall not be entitled to prescribe, modify or revoke provisional measures without the agreement of such State.

Article 32

Limitations on applicability of procedures for the settlement of disputes

Article 297, paragraph 3, of the Convention applies also to this Agreement.

PART IX

NON–PARTIES TO THIS AGREEMENT

Article 33

Non-parties to this agreement

1. States Parties shall encourage non-parties to this Agreement to become parties thereto and to adopt laws and regulations consistent with its provisions.

2. States Parties shall take measures consistent with this Agreement and international law to deter the activities of vessels flying the flag of non-parties which undermine the effective implementation of this Agreement.

PART X

GOOD FAITH AND ABUSE OF RIGHTS

Article 34

Good faith and abuse of rights

States Parties shall fulfil in good faith the obligations assumed under this Agreement and shall exercise the rights recognized in this Agreement in a manner which would not constitute an abuse of right.

Part XI

RESPONSIBILITY AND LIABILITY

Article 35

Responsibility and liability

States Parties are liable in accordance with international law for damage or loss attributable to them in regard to this Agreement.

PART XII

REVIEW CONFERENCE

Article 36

Review conference

1. Four years after the date of entry into force of this Agreement, the Secretary–General of the United Nations shall convene a conference with a view to assessing the effectiveness of this Agreement in securing the conservation and management of straddling fish stocks and highly migratory fish stocks. The Secretary–General shall invite to the conference all States Parties and those States and entities which are entitled to become parties to this Agreement as well as those intergovernmental and non-governmental organizations entitled to participate as observers.

2. The conference shall review and assess the adequacy of the provisions of this Agreement and, if necessary, propose means of strengthening the substance and methods of implementation of those provisions in order better to address any continuing problems in the conservation and management of straddling fish stocks and highly migratory fish stocks.

PART XIII

FINAL PROVISIONS

Article 37

Signature

This Agreement shall be open for signature by all States and the other entities referred to in article 1, paragraph 2(b), and shall remain open for signature at United Nations Headquarters for twelve months from the fourth of December 1995.

Article 38

Ratification

This Agreement is subject to ratification by States and the other entities referred to in article 1, paragraph 2(b). The instruments of ratification shall be deposited with the Secretary–General of the United Nations.

Article 39

Accession

This Agreement shall remain open for accession by States and the other entities referred to in article 1, paragraph 2(b). The instruments of accession shall be deposited with the Secretary–General of the United Nations.

Article 40

Entry into force

1. This Agreement shall enter into force 30 days after the date of deposit of the thirtieth instrument of ratification or accession.

2. For each State or entity which ratifies the Agreement or accedes thereto after the deposit of the thirtieth instrument of ratification or accession, this Agreement shall enter into force on the thirtieth day following the deposit of its instrument of ratification or accession.

Article 41

Provisional application

1. This Agreement shall be applied provisionally by a State or entity which consents to its provisional application by so notifying the depositary in writing. Such

provisional application shall become effective from the date of receipt of the notification.

2. Provisional application by a State or entity shall terminate upon the entry into force of this Agreement for that State or entity or upon notification by that State or entity to the depositary in writing of its intention to terminate provisional application.

Article 42

Reservations and exceptions

No reservations or exceptions may be made to this Agreement.

Article 43

Declarations and statements

Article 42 does not preclude a State or entity, when signing, ratifying or acceding to this Agreement, from making declarations or statements, however phrased or named, with a view, inter alia, to the harmonization of its laws and regulations with the provisions of this Agreement, provided that such declarations or statements do not purport to exclude or to modify the legal effect of the provisions of this Agreement in their application to that State or entity.

Article 44

Relation to other agreements

1. This Agreement shall not alter the rights and obligations of States Parties which arise from other agreements compatible with this Agreement and which do not affect the enjoyment by other States Parties of their rights or the performance of their obligations under this Agreement.

2. Two or more States Parties may conclude agreements modifying or suspending the operation of provisions of this Agreement, applicable solely to the relations between them, provided that such agreements do not relate to a provision derogation from which is incompatible with the effective execution of the object and purpose of this Agreement, and provided further that such agreements shall not affect the application of the basic principles embodied herein, and that the provisions of such agreements do not affect the enjoyment by other States Parties of their rights or the performance of their obligations under this Agreement.

3. States Parties intending to conclude an agreement referred to in paragraph 2 shall notify the other States Parties through the depositary of this Agreement of their intention to conclude the agreement and of the modification or suspension for which it provides.

Article 45

Amendment

1. A State Party may, by written communication addressed to the Secretary-General of the United Nations, propose amendments to this Agreement and request the convening of a conference to consider such proposed amendments. The Secretary–General shall circulate such communication to all States Parties. If, within six months from the date of the circulation of the communication, not less than one half of the States Parties reply favourably to the request, the Secretary–General shall convene the conference.

2. The decision-making procedure applicable at the amendment conference convened pursuant to paragraph 1 shall be the same as that applicable at the United Nations Conference on Straddling Fish Stocks and Highly Migratory Fish Stocks, unless otherwise decided by the conference. The conference should make every effort

to reach agreement on any amendments by way of consensus and there should be no voting on them until all efforts at consensus have been exhausted.

3. Once adopted, amendments to this Agreement shall be open for signature by States Parties for twelve months from the date of adoption at United Nations Headquarters, unless otherwise provided in the amendment itself.

4. Articles 38, 39, 47 and 50 apply to all amendments to this Agreement.

5. Amendments to this Agreement shall enter into force for the States Parties ratifying or acceding to them on the thirtieth day following the deposit of instruments of ratification or accession by two thirds of the States Parties. Thereafter, for each State Party ratifying or acceding to an amendment after the deposit of the required number of such instruments, the amendment shall enter into force on the thirtieth day following the deposit of its instrument of ratification or accession.

6. An amendment may provide that a smaller or a larger number of ratifications or accessions shall be required for its entry into force than are required by this article.

7. A State which becomes a Party to this Agreement after the entry into force of amendments in accordance with paragraph 5 shall, failing an expression of a different intention by that State:

(a) be considered as a Party to this Agreement as so amended; and

(b) be considered as a Party to the unamended Agreement in relation to any State Party not bound by the amendment.

Article 46

Denunciation

1. A State Party may, by written notification addressed to the Secretary-General of the United Nations, denounce this Agreement and may indicate its reasons. Failure to indicate reasons shall not affect the validity of the denunciation. The denunciation shall take effect one year after the date of receipt of the notification, unless the notification specifies a later date.

2. The denunciation shall not in any way affect the duty of any State Party to fulfil any obligation embodied in this Agreement to which it would be subject under international law independently of this Agreement.

Article 47

Participation by international organizations

1. In cases where an international organization referred to in Annex IX, article 1, of the Convention does not have competence over all the matters governed by this Agreement, Annex IX to the Convention shall apply mutatis mutandis to participation by such international organization in this Agreement, except that the following provisions of that Annex shall not apply:

(a) article 2, first sentence; and

(b) article 3, paragraph 1.

2. In cases where an international organization referred to in Annex IX, article 1, of the Convention has competence over all the matters governed by this Agreement, the following provisions shall apply to participation by such international organization in this Agreement:

(a) at the time of signature or accession, such international organization shall make a declaration stating:

(i) that it has competence over all the matters governed by this Agreement;

(ii) that, for this reason, its member States shall not become States Parties, except in respect of their territories for which the international organization has no responsibility; and

(iii) that it accepts the rights and obligations of States under this Agreement;

(b) participation of such an international organization shall in no case confer any rights under this Agreement on member States of the international organization;

(c) in the event of a conflict between the obligations of an international organization under this Agreement and its obligations under the agreement establishing the international organization or any acts relating to it, the obligations under this Agreement shall prevail.

Article 48

Annexes

1. The Annexes form an integral part of this Agreement and, unless expressly provided otherwise, a reference to this Agreement or to one of its Parts includes a reference to the Annexes relating thereto.

2. The Annexes may be revised from time to time by States Parties. Such revisions shall be based on scientific and technical considerations. Notwithstanding the provisions of article 45, if a revision to an Annex is adopted by consensus at a meeting of States Parties, it shall be incorporated in this Agreement and shall take effect from the date of its adoption or from such other date as may be specified in the revision. If a revision to an Annex is not adopted by consensus at such a meeting, the amendment procedures set out in article.45 shall apply.

Article 49

Depositary

The Secretary–General of the United Nations shall be the depositary of this Agreement and any amendments or revisions thereto.

Article 50

Authentic texts

The Arabic, Chinese, English, French, Russian and Spanish texts of this Agreement are equally authentic.

IN WITNESS WHEREOF, the undersigned Plenipotentiaries, being duly authorized thereto, have signed this Agreement.

OPENED FOR SIGNATURE at New York, this fourth day of December, one thousand nine hundred and ninety-five, in a single original, in the Arabic, Chinese, English, French, Russian and Spanish languages.

ANNEX I

STANDARD REQUIREMENTS FOR THE COLLECTION AND SHARING OF DATA

Article 1

General principles

1. The timely collection, compilation and analysis of data are fundamental to the effective conservation and management of straddling fish stocks and highly migratory fish stocks. To this end, data from fisheries for these stocks on the high seas and those in areas under national jurisdiction are required and should be collected and compiled in such a way as to enable statistically meaningful analysis for the purposes of fishery

resource conservation and management. These data include catch and fishing effort statistics and other fishery-related information, such as vessel-related and other data for standardizing fishing effort. Data collected should also include information on non-target and associated or dependent species. All data should be verified to ensure accuracy. Confidentiality of non-aggregated data shall be maintained. The dissemination of such data shall be subject to the terms on which they have been provided.

2. Assistance, including training as well as financial and technical assistance, shall be provided to developing States in order to build capacity in the field of conservation and management of living marine resources. Assistance should focus on enhancing capacity to implement data collection and verification, observer programmes, data analysis and research projects supporting stock assessments. The fullest possible involvement of developing State scientists and managers in conservation and management of straddling fish stocks and highly migratory fish stocks should be promoted.

Article 2

Principles of data collection, compilation and exchange

The following general principles should be considered in defining the parameters for collection, compilation and exchange of data from fishing operations for straddling fish stocks and highly migratory fish stocks:

(a) States should ensure that data are collected from vessels flying their flag on fishing activities according to the operational characteristics of each fishing method (e.g., each individual tow for trawl, each set for long-line and purse-seine, each school fished for pole-and-line and each day fished for troll) and in sufficient detail to facilitate effective stock assessment;

(b) States should ensure that fishery data are verified through an appropriate system;

(c) States should compile fishery-related and other supporting scientific data and provide them in an agreed format and in a timely manner to the relevant subregional or regional fisheries management organization or arrangement where one exists. Otherwise, States should cooperate to exchange data either directly or through such other cooperative mechanisms as may be agreed among them;

(d) States should agree, within the framework of subregional or regional fisheries management organizations or arrangements, or otherwise, on the specification of data and the format in which they are to be provided, in accordance with this Annex and taking into account the nature of the stocks and the fisheries for those stocks in the region. Such organizations or arrangements should request non-members or non-participants to provide data concerning relevant fishing activities by vessels flying their flag;

(e) such organizations or arrangements shall compile data and make them available in a timely manner and in an agreed format to all interested States under the terms and conditions established by the organizations or arrangements; and

(f) scientists of the flag State and from the relevant subregional or regional fisheries management organization or arrangement should analyse the data separately or jointly, as appropriate.

Article 3

Basic fishery data

1. States shall collect and make available to the relevant subregional or regional fisheries management organization or arrangement the following types of data in

sufficient detail to facilitate effective stock assessment in accordance with agreed procedures:

(a) time series of catch and effort statistics by fishery and fleet;

(b) total catch in number, nominal weight or both by species (both target and non-target) as is appropriate to each fishery. [Nominal weight is defined by the Food and Agriculture Organization of the United Nations as the live-weight equivalent of the landings];

(c) discard statistics, including estimates where necessary, reported as number or nominal weight by species, as is appropriate to each fishery;

(d) effort statistics appropriate to each fishing method; and

(e) fishing location, date and time fished and other statistics on fishing operations as appropriate.

2. States shall also collect where appropriate and provide to the relevant subregional or regional fisheries management organization or arrangement information to support stock assessment, including:

(a) composition of the catch according to length, weight and sex;

(b) other biological information supporting stock assessments, such as information on age, growth, recruitment, distribution and stock identity; and

(c) other relevant research, including surveys of abundance, biomass surveys, hydro-acoustic surveys, research on environmental factors affecting stock abundance, and oceanographic and ecological studies.

Article 4

Vessel data and information

1. States should collect the following types of vessel-related data for standardizing fleet composition and vessel fishing power and for converting between different measures of effort in the analysis of catch and effort data:

(a) vessel identification, flag and port of registry;

(b) vessel type;

(c) vessel specifications (e.g., material of construction, date built, registered length, gross registered tonnage, power of main engines, hold capacity and catch storage methods); and

(d) fishing gear description (e.g., types, gear specifications and quantity).

2. The flag State will collect the following information:

(a) navigation and position fixing aids;

(b) communication equipment and international radio call sign; and

(c) crew size.

Article 5

Reporting

A State shall ensure that vessels flying its flag send to its national fisheries administration and, where agreed, to the relevant subregional or regional fisheries management organization or arrangement, logbook data on catch and effort, including data on fishing operations on the high seas, at sufficiently frequent intervals to meet national requirements and regional and international obligations. Such data shall be transmitted, where necessary, by radio, telex, facsimile or satellite transmission or by other means.

Article 6

Data verification

States or, as appropriate, subregional or regional fisheries management organizations or arrangements should establish mechanisms for verifying fishery data, such as:

(a) position verification through vessel monitoring systems;

(b) scientific observer programmes to monitor catch, effort, catch composition (target and non-target) and other details of fishing operations;

(c) vessel trip, landing and transshipment reports; and

(d) port sampling.

Article 7

Data exchange

1. Data collected by flag States must be shared with other flag States and relevant coastal States through appropriate subregional or regional fisheries management organizations or arrangements. Such organizations or arrangements shall compile data and make them available in a timely manner and in an agreed format to all interested States under the terms and conditions established by the organizations or arrangements, while maintaining confidentiality of non-aggregated data, and should, to the extent feasible, develop database systems which provide efficient access to data.

2. At the global level, collection and dissemination of data should be effected through the Food and Agriculture Organization of the United Nations. Where a subregional or regional fisheries management organization or arrangement does not exist, that organization may also do the same at the subregional or regional level by arrangement with the States concerned.

ANNEX II

GUIDELINES FOR THE APPLICATION OF PRECAUTIONARY REFERENCE POINTS IN CONSERVATION AND MANAGEMENT OF STRADDLING FISH STOCKS AND HIGHLY MIGRATORY FISH STOCKS

1. A precautionary reference point is an estimated value derived through an agreed scientific procedure, which corresponds to the state of the resource and of the fishery, and which can be used as a guide for fisheries management.

2. Two types of precautionary reference points should be used: conservation, or limit, reference points and management, or target, reference points. Limit reference points set boundaries which are intended to constrain harvesting within safe biological limits within which the stocks can produce maximum sustainable yield. Target reference points are intended to meet management objectives.

3. Precautionary reference points should be stock-specific to account, inter alia, for the reproductive capacity, the resilience of each stock and the characteristics of fisheries exploiting the stock, as well as other sources of mortality and major sources of uncertainty.

4. Management strategies shall seek to maintain or restore populations of harvested stocks, and where necessary associated or dependent species, at levels consistent with previously agreed precautionary reference points. Such reference points shall be used to trigger pre-agreed conservation and management action. Management strategies shall include measures which can be implemented when precautionary reference points are approached.

5. Fishery management strategies shall ensure that the risk of exceeding limit reference points is very low. If a stock falls below a limit reference point or is at risk of falling below such a reference point, conservation and management action should be

initiated to facilitate stock recovery. Fishery management strategies shall ensure that target reference points are not exceeded on average.

6. When information for determining reference points for a fishery is poor or absent, provisional reference points shall be set. Provisional reference points may be established by analogy to similar and better-known stocks. In such situations, the fishery shall be subject to enhanced monitoring so as to enable revision of provisional reference points as improved information becomes available.

7. The fishing mortality rate which generates maximum sustainable yield should be regarded as a minimum standard for limit reference points. For stocks which are not overfished, fishery management strategies shall ensure that fishing mortality does not exceed that which corresponds to maximum sustainable yield, and that the biomass does not fall below a predefined threshold. For overfished stocks, the biomass which would produce maximum sustainable yield can serve as a rebuilding target.

6.15 CODE OF CONDUCT FOR RESPONSIBLE FISHERIES. Adopted by the Twenty-eighth Session of the Food and Agriculture Organization of the United Nations, 31 October 1995.

* * *

INTRODUCTION

Fisheries, including aquaculture, provide a vital source of food, employment, recreation, trade and economic well being for people throughout the world, both for present and future generations and should therefore be conducted in a responsible manner. This Code sets out principles and international standards of behaviour for responsible practices with a view to ensuring the effective conservation, management and development of living aquatic resources, with due respect for the ecosystem and biodiversity. The Code recognizes the nutritional, economic, social, environmental and cultural importance of fisheries, and the interests of all those concerned with the fishery sector. The Code takes into account the biological characteristics of the resources and their environment and the interests of consumers and other users. States and all those involved in fisheries are encouraged to apply the Code and give effect to it.

1-NATURE AND SCOPE OF THE CODE

1.1 This Code is voluntary. However, certain parts of it are based on relevant rules of international law, including those reflected in the United Nations Convention on the Law of the Sea of 10 December 1982. The Code also contains provisions that may be or have already been given binding effect by means of other obligatory legal instruments amongst the Parties, such as the Agreement to Promote Compliance with International Conservation and Management Measures by Fishing Vessels on the High Seas, 1993, which, according to FAO Conference resolution 15/93, paragraph 3, forms an integral part of the Code.

1.2 The Code is global in scope, and is directed toward members and non-members of FAO, fishing entities, subregional, regional and global organizations, whether governmental or non-governmental, and all persons concerned with the conservation of fishery resources and management and development of fisheries, such as fishers, those engaged in processing and marketing of fish and fishery products and other users of the aquatic environment in relation to fisheries.

* * *

2-OBJECTIVES OF THE CODE

The objectives of the Code are to:

1. establish principles, in accordance with the relevant rules of international law, for responsible fishing and fisheries activities, taking into account all their relevant biological, technological, economic, social, environmental and commercial aspects;

2. establish principles and criteria for the elaboration and implementation of national policies for responsible conservation of fisheries resources and fisheries management and development;

* * *

10. provide standards of conduct for all persons involved in the fisheries sector.

3-RELATIONSHIP WITH OTHER INTERNATIONAL INSTRUMENTS

3.1 The Code is to be interpreted and applied in conformity with the relevant rules of international law, as reflected in the United Nations Convention on the Law of the Sea, 1982. Nothing in this Code prejudices the rights, jurisdiction and duties of States under international law as reflected in the Convention.

3.2 The Code is also to be interpreted and applied:

a. in a manner consistent with the relevant provisions of the Agreement for the Implementation of the Provisions of the United Nations Convention on the Law of the Sea of 10 December 1982 Relating to the Conservation and Management of Straddling Fish Stocks and Highly Migratory Fish Stocks;

b. in accordance with other applicable rules of international law, including the respective obligations of States pursuant to international agreements to which they are party; and

c. in the light of the 1992 Declaration of Cancun, the 1992 Rio Declaration on Environment and Development, and Agenda 21 adopted by the United Nations Conference on Environment and Development (UNCED), in particular Chapter 17 of Agenda 21, and other relevant declarations and international instruments.

4-Implementation, Monitoring and Updating

4.1 All members and non-members of FAO, fishing entities and relevant subregional, regional and global organizations, whether governmental or non-governmental, and all persons concerned with the conservation, management and utilization of fisheries resources and trade in fish and fishery products should collaborate in the fulfilment and implementation of the objectives and principles contained in this Code.

* * *

6-General Principles

6.1 States and users of living aquatic resources should conserve aquatic ecosystems. The right to fish carries with it the obligation to do so in a responsible manner so as to ensure effective conservation and management of the living aquatic resources.

6.2 Fisheries management should promote the maintenance of the quality, diversity and availability of fishery resources in sufficient quantities for present and future generations in the context of food security, poverty alleviation and sustainable development. Management measures should not only ensure the conservation of target species but also of species belonging to the same ecosystem or associated with or dependent upon the target species.

6.3 States should prevent overfishing and excess fishing capacity and should implement management measures to ensure that fishing effort is commensurate with the productive capacity of the fishery resources and their sustainable utilization. States should take measures to rehabilitate populations as far as possible and when appropriate.

6.4 Conservation and management decisions for fisheries should be based on the best scientific evidence available, also taking into account traditional knowledge of the resources and their habitat, as well as relevant environmental, economic and social factors. States should assign priority to undertake research and data collection in order to improve scientific and technical knowledge of fisheries including their interaction with the ecosystem. In recognizing the transboundary nature of many aquatic ecosystems, States should encourage bilateral and multilateral cooperation in research, as appropriate.

6.5 States and subregional and regional fisheries management organizations should apply a precautionary approach widely to conservation, management and exploitation of living aquatic resources in order to protect them and preserve the aquatic environment, taking account of the best scientific evidence available. The absence of adequate scientific information should not be used as a reason for postponing or failing to take measures to conserve target species, associated or dependent species and non-target species and their environment.

6.6 Selective and environmentally safe fishing gear and practices should be further developed and applied, to the extent practicable, in order to maintain biodiversity and to conserve the population structure and aquatic ecosystems and protect fish quality. Where proper selective and environmentally safe fishing gear and practices exist, they should be recognized and accorded a priority in establishing conservation and management measures for fisheries. States and users of aquatic ecosystems should minimize waste, catch of non-target species, both fish and non-fish species, and impacts on associated or dependent species.

* * *

6.10 Within their respective competences and in accordance with international law, including within the framework of subregional or regional fisheries conservation and management organizations or arrangements, States should ensure compliance with and enforcement of conservation and management measures and establish effective mechanisms, as appropriate, to monitor and control the activities of fishing vessels and fishing support vessels.

6.11 States authorizing fishing and fishing support vessels to fly their flags should exercise effective control over those vessels so as to ensure the proper application of this Code. They should ensure that the activities of such vessels do not undermine the effectiveness of conservation and management measures taken in accordance with international law and adopted at the national, subregional, regional or global levels. States should also ensure that vessels flying their flags fulfil their obligations concerning the collection and provision of data relating to their fishing activities.

6.12 States should, within their respective competences and in accordance with international law, cooperate at subregional, regional and global levels through fisheries management organizations, other international agreements or other arrangements to promote conservation and management, ensure responsible fishing and ensure effective conservation and protection of living aquatic resources throughout their range of distribution, taking into account the need for compatible measures in areas within and beyond national jurisdiction.

* * *

6.14 International trade in fish and fishery products should be conducted in accordance with the principles, rights and obligations established in the World Trade Organization (WTO) Agreement and other relevant international agreements. States should ensure that their policies, programmes and practices related to trade in fish and fishery products do not result in obstacles to this trade, environmental degradation or negative social, including nutritional, impacts.

6.15 States should cooperate in order to prevent disputes. All disputes relating to fishing activities and practices should be resolved in a timely, peaceful and cooperative manner, in accordance with applicable international agreements or as may otherwise be agreed between the parties. Pending settlement of a dispute, the States concerned should make every effort to enter into provisional arrangements of a practical nature which should be without prejudice to the final outcome of any dispute settlement procedure.

* * *

7-*Fisheries Management*

7.1 General

7.1.1 States and all those engaged in fisheries management should, through an appropriate policy, legal and institutional framework, adopt measures for the long-term conservation and sustainable use of fisheries resources. Conservation and management measures, whether at local, national, subregional or regional levels, should be based on the best scientific evidence available and be designed to ensure the long-term sustainability of fishery resources at levels which promote the objective of their optimum utilization and maintain their availability for present and future generations; short term considerations should not compromise these objectives.

* * *

7.1.3 For transboundary fish stocks, straddling fish stocks, highly migratory fish stocks and high seas fish stocks, where these are exploited by two or more States, the States concerned, including the relevant coastal States in the case of straddling and highly migratory stocks, should cooperate to ensure effective conservation and management of the resources. This should be achieved, where appropriate, through the establishment of a bilateral, subregional or regional fisheries organization or arrangement.

7.1.4 A subregional or regional fisheries management organization or arrangement should include representatives of States in whose jurisdictions the resources occur, as well as representatives from States which have a real interest in the fisheries on the resources outside national jurisdictions. Where a subregional or regional fisheries management organization or arrangement exists and has the competence to establish conservation and management measures, those States should cooperate by becoming a member of such organization or a participant in such arrangement, and actively participate in its work.

7.1.5 A State which is not a member of a subregional or regional fisheries management organization or is not a participant in a subregional or regional fisheries management arrangement should nevertheless cooperate, in accordance with relevant international agreements and international law, in the conservation and management of the relevant fisheries resources by giving effect to any conservation and management measures adopted by such organization or arrangement.

* * *

7.1.7 States should establish, within their respective competences and capacities, effective mechanisms for fisheries monitoring, surveillance, control and enforcement to ensure compliance with their conservation and management measures, as well as those adopted by subregional or regional organizations or arrangements.

* * *

7.2 Management objectives

7.2.1 Recognizing that long-term sustainable use of fisheries resources is the overriding objective of conservation and management, States and subregional or regional fisheries management organizations and arrangements should, inter alia, adopt appropriate measures, based on the best scientific evidence available, which are designed to maintain or restore stocks at levels capable of producing maximum sustainable yield, as qualified by relevant environmental and economic factors, including the special requirements of developing countries.

7.2.2 Such measures should provide inter alia that:

a. excess fishing capacity is avoided and exploitation of the stocks remains economically viable;

b. the economic conditions under which fishing industries operate promote responsible fisheries;

c. the interests of fishers, including those engaged in subsistence, small-scale and artisanal fisheries, are taken into account;

d. biodiversity of aquatic habitats and ecosystems is conserved and endangered species are protected;

e. depleted stocks are allowed to recover or, where appropriate, are actively restored;

f. adverse environmental impacts on the resources from human activities are assessed and, where appropriate, corrected; and

g. pollution, waste, discards, catch by lost or abandoned gear, catch of non-target species, both fish and non-fish species, and impacts on associated or dependent species are minimized, through measures including, to the extent practicable, the development and use of selective, environmentally safe and cost-effective fishing gear and techniques.

7.2.3 States should assess the impacts of environmental factors on target stocks and species belonging to the same ecosystem or associated with or dependent upon the target stocks, and assess the relationship among the populations in the ecosystem.

* * *

7.5 Precautionary approach

7.5.1 States should apply the precautionary approach widely to conservation, management and exploitation of living aquatic resources in order to protect them and preserve the aquatic environment. The absence of adequate scientific information should not be used as a reason for postponing or failing to take conservation and management measures.

7.5.2 In implementing the precautionary approach, States should take into account, inter alia, uncertainties relating to the size and productivity of the stocks, reference points, stock condition in relation to such reference points, levels and distribution of fishing mortality and the impact of fishing activities, including discards, on non-target and associated or dependent species, as well as environmental and socio-economic conditions.

7.5.3 States and subregional or regional fisheries management organizations and arrangements should, on the basis of the best scientific evidence available, inter alia, determine:

a. stock specific target reference points, and, at the same time, the action to be taken if they are exceeded; and

b. stock-specific limit reference points, and, at the same time, the action to be taken if they are exceeded; when a limit reference point is approached, measures should be taken to ensure that it will not be exceeded.

7.5.4 In the case of new or exploratory fisheries, States should adopt as soon as possible cautious conservation and management measures, including, inter alia, catch limits and effort limits. Such measures should remain in force until there are sufficient data to allow assessment of the impact of the fisheries on the long-term sustainability of the stocks, whereupon conservation and management measures based on that assessment should be implemented. The latter measures should, if appropriate, allow for the gradual development of the fisheries.

7.5.5 If a natural phenomenon has a significant adverse impact on the status of living aquatic resources, States should adopt conservation and management measures on an emergency basis to ensure that fishing activity does not exacerbate such adverse impact. States should also adopt such measures on an emergency basis where fishing activity presents a serious threat to the sustainability of such resources. Measures taken on an emergency basis should be temporary and should be based on the best scientific evidence available.

7.6 Management measures

7.6.1 States should ensure that the level of fishing permitted is commensurate with the state of fisheries resources.

7.6.2 States should adopt measures to ensure that no vessel be allowed to fish unless so authorized, in a manner consistent with international law for the high seas or in conformity with national legislation within areas of national jurisdiction.

7.6.3 Where excess fishing capacity exists, mechanisms should be established to reduce capacity to levels commensurate with the sustainable use of fisheries resources so as to ensure that fishers operate under economic conditions that promote responsible fisheries. Such mechanisms should include monitoring the capacity of fishing fleets.

7.6.4 The performance of all existing fishing gear, methods and practices should be examined and measures taken to ensure that fishing gear, methods and practices which are not consistent with responsible fishing are phased out and replaced with more acceptable alternatives. In this process, particular attention should be given to the impact of such measures on fishing communities, including their ability to exploit the resource.

7.6.5 States and fisheries management organizations and arrangements should regulate fishing in such a way as to avoid the risk of conflict among fishers using different vessels, gear and fishing methods.

7.6.6 When deciding on the use, conservation and management of fisheries resources, due recognition should be given, as appropriate, in accordance with national laws and regulations, to the traditional practices, needs and interests of indigenous people and local fishing communities which are highly dependent on fishery resources for their livelihood.

7.6.7 In the evaluation of alternative conservation and management measures, their cost-effectiveness and social impact should be considered.

7.6.8 The efficacy of conservation and management measures and their possible interactions should be kept under continuous review. Such measures should, as appropriate, be revised or abolished in the light of new information.

7.6.9 States should take appropriate measures to minimize waste, discards, catch by lost or abandoned gear, catch of non-target species, both fish and non-fish species, and negative impacts on associated or dependent species, in particular endangered species. Where appropriate, such measures may include technical measures related to fish size, mesh size or gear, discards, closed seasons and areas and zones reserved for selected fisheries, particularly artisanal fisheries. Such measures should be applied, where appropriate, to protect juveniles and spawners. States and subregional or regional fisheries management organizations and arrangements should promote, to the extent practicable, the development and use of selective, environmentally safe and cost effective gear and techniques.

7.6.10 States and subregional and regional fisheries management organizations and arrangements, in the framework of their respective competences, should introduce measures for depleted resources and those resources threatened with depletion that facilitate the sustained recovery of such stocks. They should make every effort to ensure that resources and habitats critical to the well-being of such resources which have been adversely affected by fishing or other human activities are restored.

* * *

8-Fishing Operations

8.1 Duties of all States

8.1.1 States should ensure that only fishing operations allowed by them are conducted within waters under their jurisdiction and that these operations are carried out in a responsible manner.

8.1.2 States should maintain a record, updated at regular intervals, on all authorizations to fish issued by them.

8.1.3 States should maintain, in accordance with recognized international standards and practices, statistical data, updated at regular intervals, on all fishing operations allowed by them.

8.1.4 States should, in accordance with international law, within the framework of subregional or regional fisheries management organizations or arrangements, cooperate to establish systems for monitoring, control, surveillance and enforcement of applicable measures with respect to fishing operations and related activities in waters outside their national jurisdiction.

8.1.5 States should ensure that health and safety standards are adopted for everyone employed in fishing operations. Such standards should be not less than the minimum requirements of relevant international agreements on conditions of work and service.

8.1.6 States should make arrangements individually, together with other States or with the appropriate international organization to integrate fishing operations into maritime search and rescue systems.

8.1.7 States should enhance through education and training programmes the education and skills of fishers and, where appropriate, their professional qualifications. Such programmes should take into account agreed international standards and guidelines.

8.1.8 States should, as appropriate, maintain records of fishers which should, whenever possible, contain information on their service and qualifications, including certificates of competency, in accordance with their national laws.

8.1.9 States should ensure that measures applicable in respect of masters and other officers charged with an offence relating to the operation of fishing vessels should include provisions which may permit, inter alia, refusal, withdrawal or suspension of authorizations to serve as masters or officers of a fishing vessel.

8.1.10 States, with the assistance of relevant international organizations, should endeavour to ensure through education and training that all those engaged in fishing operations be given information on the most important provisions of this Code, as well as provisions of relevant international conventions and applicable environmental and other standards that are essential to ensure responsible fishing operations.

8.2 Flag State duties

8.2.1 Flag States should maintain records of fishing vessels entitled to fly their flag and authorized to be used for fishing and should indicate in such records details of the vessels, their ownership and authorization to fish.

8.2.2 Flag States should ensure that no fishing vessels entitled to fly their flag fish on the high seas or in waters under the jurisdiction of other States unless such vessels have been issued with a Certificate of Registry and have been authorized to fish by the competent authorities. Such vessels should carry on board the Certificate of Registry and their authorization to fish.

8.2.3 Fishing vessels authorized to fish on the high seas or in waters under the jurisdiction of a State other than the flag State, should be marked in accordance with uniform and internationally recognizable vessel marking systems such as the FAO

Standard Specifications and Guidelines for Marking and Identification of Fishing Vessels.

8.2.4 Fishing gear should be marked in accordance with national legislation in order that the owner of the gear can be identified. Gear marking requirements should take into account uniform and internationally recognizable gear marking systems.

8.2.5 Flag States should ensure compliance with appropriate safety requirements for fishing vessels and fishers in accordance with international conventions, internationally agreed codes of practice and voluntary guidelines. States should adopt appropriate safety requirements for all small vessels not covered by such international conventions, codes of practice or voluntary guidelines.

8.2.6 States not party to the Agreement to Promote Compliance with International Conservation and Management Measures by Vessels Fishing in the High Seas should be encouraged to accept the Agreement and to adopt laws and regulations consistent with the provisions of the Agreement.

8.2.7 Flag States should take enforcement measures in respect of fishing vessels entitled to fly their flag which have been found by them to have contravened applicable conservation and management measures, including, where appropriate, making the contravention of such measures an offence under national legislation. Sanctions applicable in respect of violations should be adequate in severity to be effective in securing compliance and to discourage violations wherever they occur and should deprive offenders of the benefits accruing from their illegal activities. Such sanctions may, for serious violations, include provisions for the refusal, withdrawal or suspension of the authorization to fish.

8.2.8 Flag States should promote access to insurance coverage by owners and charterers of fishing vessels. Owners or charterers of fishing vessels should carry sufficient insurance cover to protect the crew of such vessels and their interests, to indemnify third parties against loss or damage and to protect their own interests.

8.2.9 Flag States should ensure that crew members are entitled to repatriation, taking account of the principles laid down in the "Repatriation of Seafarers Convention (Revised), 1987, (No.166)".

8.2.10 In the event of an accident to a fishing vessel or persons on board a fishing vessel, the flag State of the fishing vessel concerned should provide details of the accident to the State of any foreign national on board the vessel involved in the accident. Such information should also, where practicable, be communicated to the International Maritime Organization.

* * *

8.5 Fishing gear selectivity

8.5.1 States should require that fishing gear, methods and practices, to the extent practicable, are sufficiently selective so as to minimize waste, discards, catch of non-target species, both fish and non-fish species, and impacts on associated or dependent species and that the intent of related regulations is not circumvented by technical devices. In this regard, fishers should cooperate in the development of selective fishing gear and methods. States should ensure that information on new developments and requirements is made available to all fishers.

8.5.2 In order to improve selectivity, States should, when drawing up their laws and regulations, take into account the range of selective fishing gear, methods and strategies available to the industry.

8.5.3 States and relevant institutions should collaborate in developing standard methodologies for research into fishing gear selectivity, fishing methods and strategies.

8.5.4 International cooperation should be encouraged with respect to research programmes for fishing gear selectivity, and fishing methods and strategies, dissemination of the results of such research programmes and the transfer of technology.

* * *

11-Post-harvest Practices and Trade

* * *

11.2 Responsible international trade

11.2.1 The provisions of this Code should be interpreted and applied in accordance with the principles, rights and obligations established in the World Trade Organization (WTO) Agreement.

11.2.2 International trade in fish and fishery products should not compromise the sustainable development of fisheries and responsible utilization of living aquatic resources.

11.2.3 States should ensure that measures affecting international trade in fish and fishery products are transparent, based, when applicable, on scientific evidence, and are in accordance with internationally agreed rules.

11.2.4 Fish trade measures adopted by States to protect human or animal life or health, the interests of consumers or the environment, should not be discriminatory and should be in accordance with internationally agreed trade rules, in particular the principles, rights and obligations established in the Agreement on the Application of Sanitary and Phytosanitary Measures and the Agreement on Technical Barriers to Trade of the WTO.

11.2.5 States should further liberalize trade in fish and fishery products and eliminate barriers and distortions to trade such as duties, quotas and non-tariff barriers in accordance with the principles, rights and obligations of the WTO Agreement.

11.2.6 States should not directly or indirectly create unnecessary or hidden barriers to trade which limit the consumer's freedom of choice of supplier or that restrict market access.

11.2.7 States should not condition access to markets to access to resources. This principle does not preclude the possibility of fishing agreements between States which include provisions referring to access to resources, trade and access to markets, transfer of technology, scientific research, training and other relevant elements.

11.2.8 States should not link access to markets to the purchase of specific technology or sale of other products.

11.2.9 States should cooperate in complying with relevant international agreements regulating trade in endangered species.

11.2.10 States should develop international agreements for trade in live specimens where there is a risk of environmental damage in importing or exporting States.

11.2.11 States should cooperate to promote adherence to, and effective implementation of relevant international standards for trade in fish and fishery products and living aquatic resource conservation.

11.2.12 States should not undermine conservation measures for living aquatic resources in order to gain trade or investment benefits.

11.2.13 States should cooperate to develop internationally acceptable rules or standards for trade in fish and fishery products in accordance with the principles, rights, and obligations established in the WTO Agreement.

11.2.14 States should cooperate with each other and actively participate in relevant regional and multilateral fora, such as the WTO, in order to ensure equitable, non-discriminatory trade in fish and fishery products as well as wide adherence to multilaterally agreed fishery conservation measures.

11.2.15 States, aid agencies, multilateral development banks and other relevant international organizations should ensure that their policies and practices related to the promotion of international fish trade and export production do not result in environmental degradation or adversely impact the nutritional rights and needs of people for whom fish is critical to their health and well being and for whom other comparable sources of food are not readily available or affordable.

* * *

6.16 Jakarta Ministerial Statement on the Implementation of the Convention on Biological Diversity. Adopted by the Second Session of the Conference of the Parties to the Convention on Biological Diversity on 17 November 1995. UNEP/CBD/COP/2/19

WE, THE MINISTERS PARTICIPATING IN THE MINISTERIAL SEGMENT OF THE SECOND MEETING OF THE CONFERENCE OF THE PARTIES TO THE CONVENTION ON BIOLOGICAL DIVERSITY, HELD IN JAKARTA, INDONESIA, ON 14 AND 15 NOVEMBER 1995;

1. REALIZE that biological diversity that comprises variability of genes, species and ecosystems is the world's most valuable resource for the sustainability and welfare of all humankind;

2. NOTE that this second meeting of the Conference of the Parties coincides with the commemoration of the fiftieth anniversary of the Republic of Indonesia's independence and of the creation of the United Nations Organization, and RECOGNIZE that such a historic moment offers an unequalled opportunity to further strengthen multilateral cooperation for promoting the objectives of the Convention on Biological Diversity for the benefit of present and future generations;

3. REAFFIRM the Convention as the legal instrument to advance the conservation of biological diversity, the sustainable use of its components and the fair and equitable sharing of the benefits arising out of the use of genetic resources;

4. REGARD the Convention as a treaty with a global vision based on common concern and mutual assistance, recognition and articulation of national sovereignty over their own biological resources, particularly genetic resources, and recognition of national responsibility for conservation of biological diversity and for using biological resources sustainably and for creating conditions to facilitate access to genetic resources;

5. FURTHER RECOGNIZE that the Convention is based on mutual reliance and fair and equitable sharing of benefits for the prosperity of humankind;

6. REAFFIRM that, by becoming Parties to the Convention, our Governments have committed themselves to the Convention's objectives and its provisions;

7. REAFFIRM the Convention as a global partnership, based on mutual assistance and international cooperation to achieve the conservation of biological diversity, the sustainable use of its components and the fair and equitable sharing of the benefits arising out of the utilization of genetic resources, for the benefit of present and future generations;

8. REAFFIRM ALSO that the second meeting of the Conference of the Parties to the Convention on Biological Diversity provides the momentum for global agreement relating to the implementation of Article 19, paragraph 3, of the Convention on the consideration of the need for and modalities of a protocol on the safe transfer, handling and use of any living modified organism resulting from biotechnology that may have adverse effects on the conservation and sustainable use of biological diversity;

9. RECOGNIZE the urgency of the task we face, and the individual and collective responsibilities of Parties to the Convention for the implementation of biological diversity conservation, sustainable use and sharing of benefits for the equitable welfare of all people;

10. AWARE of the need for more information and knowledge regarding biological diversity at all levels, and the need to implant the value of biological diversity in the minds and hearts of all people, STRESS the importance of promoting education on biological diversity at all levels of formal and non-formal education systems;

11. FURTHER REAFFIRM the importance of the clearing-house mechanism for technical and scientific cooperation in support of the implementation of the Convention at national level and emphasize the need for its accessibility to all countries;

12. ENCOURAGE the Convention, through its relevant organs, to strengthen relationships with other relevant conventions and processes, including the Commission on Sustainable Development and its Intergovernmental Panel on Forests;

13. WELCOME the establishment of a position within the Secretariat of the Convention on Biological Diversity on all issues pertaining to the implementation of Article 8(j) of the Convention related to indigenous and local communities;

14. REAFFIRM that there is a critical need for the Conference of the Parties to address the conservation and sustainable use of marine and coastal biological diversity, and urge Parties to initiate immediate action to implement the decisions adopted on this issue. In this context, WELCOME the commitment of the Government of the Republic of Indonesia to play a major role in facilitating such implementation at the global and regional level and the declaration by the Conference of the Parties of the new global consensus on the importance of marine and coastal biological diversity as the "Jakarta Mandate on Marine and Coastal Biological Diversity";

15. FURTHER ENCOURAGE the Conference of the Parties, through its relevant organs, to actively assist Parties to fulfill their obligations, especially through cooperation, collaboration and partnership;

16. URGE the international community to continue to take action and make every effort to assist developing countries to build their own institutional capacity, including human resource development, to conserve and use sustainable biological diversity including through in-situ and ex-situ conservation and to facilitate the transfer of technology in accordance with the provisions of the Convention;

17. URGE States involved in nuclear testing to take note of the views put forward by a significant number of Parties expressing their strong concern over the impacts of nuclear testing on biodiversity, in particular to the coastal and marine ecosystems and CALL on these States to cease nuclear testing and to conclude a comprehensive test ban treaty in 1996;

18. URGE States that have not yet done so to ratify or accede to the Convention and to begin implementing the Convention on Biological Diversity;

19. CALL UPON all Governments and the citizens of our planet to celebrate the International Day for Biological Diversity on 29 December, reflecting our individual and joint responsibility for conserving and using biological diversity sustainably;

20. DECLARE that our Governments will continue to spare no effort in undertaking to fulfil the provisions of the Convention for the benefit of life on Earth, for present and future generations.

7. Miscellaneous

A. Economic Trade/Development

7.1 General Agreement on Tariffs And Trade (GATT) 1947 (Without Annexes, Protocols And Schedules But as Revised to 1994). Concluded at Geneva, 30 October 1947. Currently in effect as part of GATT 1994.[a] 55 U.N.T.S. 187, T.I.A.S. No. 1700; *reprinted in* 4 Weston IV.C.1: *Arts. I, III, IX, XI and XX*

ARTICLE I

General Most-Favoured-Nation Treatment

1. With respect to customs duties and charges of any kind imposed on or in connection with importation or exportation or imposed on the international transfer of payments for imports or exports, and with respect to the method of levying such duties and charges, and with respect to all rules and formalities in connection with importation and exportation, and with respect to all matters referred to in paragraphs 2 and 4 of Article III, any advantage, favour, privilege or immunity granted by any contracting party to any product originating in or destined for any other country shall be accorded immediately and unconditionally to the like product originating in or destined for the territories of all other contracting parties.

2. The provisions of paragraph 1 of this Article shall not require the elimination of any preference in respect of import duties or charges which do not exceed the levels provided for in paragraph 4 of this Article and which fall within the following descriptions:

(a) Preferences in force exclusively between two or more of the territories listed in Annex A, subject to the conditions set forth therein;

(b) Preferences in force exclusively between two or more territories which on July 1, 1939, were connected by common sovereignty or relations of protection or suzerainty and which are listed in Annexes B, C and D, subject to the conditions set forth therein;

(c) Preferences in force exclusively between the United States of America and the Republic of Cuba;

(d) Preferences in force exclusively between neighbouring countries listed in Annexes E and F.

3. The provisions of paragraph 1 shall not apply to preferences between the countries formerly a part of the Ottoman Empire and detached from it on July 24, 1923, provided such preferences are approved under paragraph 5 of Article XXV, which shall be applied in this respect in the light of paragraph 1 of Article XXIX.

4. The margin of preference on any product in respect of which a preference is permitted under paragraph 2 of this Article but is not specifically set forth as a maximum margin of preference in the appropriate Schedule annexed to this Agreement shall not exceed:

a. This document reproduces portions of the text of the original GATT 1947, as revised through 1 January 1994. GATT 1947 has been superceded and replaced by GATT 1994, which is part of Annex 1A of the Agreement Establishing the World Trade Organization (*see* Basic Document 7.6). Because GATT 1994 incorporates GATT 1947 by reference, we have reproduced relevant sections of GATT 1947 in this Documents Supplement.

(a) in respect of duties or charges on any product described in such schedule, the difference between the most-favoured-nation and preferential rates provided for therein; if no preferential rate is provided for, the preferential rate shall for the purposes of this paragraph be taken to be that in force on April 10, 1947, and, if no most-favoured-nation rate is provided for, the margin shall not exceed the difference between the most-favoured-nation and preferential rates existing on April 10, 1947;

(b) in respect of duties or charges on any product not described in the appropriate Schedule, the difference between the most-favoured-nation and preferential rates existing on April 10, 1947.

In the case of the contracting parties named in Annex G, the date of April 10, 1947, referred to in sub-paragraph (a) and (b) of this paragraph shall be replaced by the respective dates set forth in that Annex.

* * *

ARTICLE III

National Treatment on Internal Taxation and Regulation

1. The contracting parties recognize that internal taxes and other internal charges, and laws, regulations and requirements affecting the internal sale, offering for sale, purchase, transportation, distribution or use of products, and internal quantitative regulations requiring the mixture processing or use of products in specified amounts or proportions, should not be applied to imported or domestic products so as to afford protection to domestic production.

2. The products of the territory of any contracting party imported into the territory of any other contracting party shall not be subject, directly or indirectly, to internal taxes or other internal charges of any kind in excess of those applied, directly or indirectly, to like domestic products. Moreover, no contracting party shall otherwise apply internal taxes or other internal charges to imported or domestic products in a manner contrary to the principles set forth in paragraph 1.

3. With respect to any existing internal tax which is inconsistent with the provisions of paragraph 2, but which is specifically authorized under a trade agreement, in force on April 10, 1947, in which the import duty on the taxed product is bound against increase, the contracting party imposing the tax shall be free to postpone the application of the provisions of paragraph 2 to such tax until such time as it can obtain release from the obligations of such trade agreement in order to permit the increase of such duty to the extent necessary to compensate for the elimination of the protective element of the tax.

4. The products of the territory of any contracting party imported into the territory of any other contracting party shall be accorded treatment no less favourable than that accorded to like products of national origin in respect of all laws, regulations and requirements affecting their internal sale, offering for sale, purchase, transportation, distribution or use. The provisions of this paragraph shall not prevent the applications of differential internal transportation charges which are based exclusively on the economic operation of the means of transport and not on the nationality of the product.

5. No contracting party shall establish or maintain any internal quantitative regulation relating to the mixture, processing or use of products in specified amounts or proportions which requires, directly or indirectly, that any specified amount or proportion of any product which is the subject of the regulation must be supplied from domestic sources. Moreover, no contracting party shall otherwise apply internal quantitative regulations in an manner contrary to the principles set forth in paragraph 1.

6. The provisions of paragraph 5 shall not apply to any internal quantitative regulation in force in the territory of any contracting party on July 1, 1939, April 10, 1947, or March 24, 1948, at the option of that contracting party; *Provided* that any such regulation which is contrary to the provisions of paragraph 5 shall not be modified to the detriment of imports and shall be treated as a customs duty for the purpose of negotiation.

7. No internal quantitative regulation relating to the mixture, processing or use of products in specified amounts or proportions shall be applied in such a manner as to allocate any such amount or proportion among external sources of supply.

8. (a) The provisions of this Article shall not apply to laws, regulations or requirements governing the procurement by governmental agencies of products purchased for governmental purposes and not with a view to commercial resale or with a view to use in the production of goods for commercial sale.

(b) The provisions of this Article shall not prevent the payment of subsidies exclusively to domestic producers, including payments to domestic producers derived from the proceeds of internal taxes or charges applied consistently with the provisions of this Article and subsidies effected through governmental purchases of domestic products.

9. The contracting parties recognize that internal maximum price control measures, even though conforming to the other provisions of this Article, can have effects prejudicial to the interests of contracting parties supplying imported products. Accordingly, contracting parties applying such measures shall take account of the interests of exporting contracting parties with a view to avoiding to the fullest practicable extent such prejudicial effects.

10. The provisions of this Article shall not prevent any contracting party from establishing or maintaining internal quantitative regulations relating to exposed cinematograph films and meeting the requirements of Article IV.

* * *

ARTICLE IX

Marks of Origin

1. Each contracting party shall accord to the products of the territories of their contracting parties treatment with regard to marking requirements no less favourable than the treatment accorded to like products of any third country.

2. The contracting parties recognize that, in adopting and enforcing laws and regulations relating to marks of origin, the difficulties and inconveniences which such measures may cause to the commerce and industry of exporting countries should be reduced to a minimum, due regard being had to the necessity of protecting consumers against fraudulent or misleading indications.

3. Whenever it is administratively practicable to do so, contracting parties should permit required marks of origin to be affixed at the time of importation.

4. The laws and regulations of contracting parties relating to the marking of imported products shall be such as to permit compliance without seriously damaging the products, or materially reducing their value, or unreasonably increasing their cost.

5. As a general rule, no special duty or penalty should be imposed by any contracting party for failure to comply with marking requirements prior to importation unless corrective marking is unreasonably delayed or deceptive marks have been affixed or the required marking has been intentionally omitted.

6. The contracting parties shall co-operate with each other with a view to preventing the use of trade names in such manner as to misrepresent the true origin of

a product, to the detriment of such distinctive regional or geographical names of products of the territory of a contracting party as are protected by its legislation. Each contracting party shall accord full and sympathetic consideration to such requests or representations as may be made by any other contracting party regarding the application of the undertaking set forth in the preceding sentence to names of products which have been communicated to it by the other contracting party.

* * *

ARTICLE XI

General Elimination of Quantitative Restrictions

1. No prohibitions or restrictions other than duties, taxes or other charges, whether made effective through quotas, import or export licences or other measures, shall be instituted or maintained by any contracting party on the importation of any product of the territory of any other contracting party or on the exportation or sale for export of any product destined for the territory of any other contracting party.

2. The provisions of paragraph 1 of this Article shall not extend to the following:

(a) Export prohibitions or restrictions temporarily applied to prevent or relieve critical shortages of foodstuffs or other products essential to the exporting contracting party;

(b) Import and export prohibitions or restrictions necessary to the application of standards or regulations for the classification, grading or marketing of commodities in international trade;

(c) Import restrictions on any agricultural or fisheries product, imported in any form, necessary to the enforcement of governmental measures which operate:

(i) to restrict the quantities of the like domestic product permitted to be marketed or produced, or, if there is no substantial domestic production of the like product, of a domestic product for which the imported product can be directly substituted; or

(ii) to remove a temporary surplus of the like domestic product or, if there is no substantial domestic production of the like product, of a domestic product for which the imported product can be directly substituted, by making the surplus available to certain groups of domestic consumers free of charge or at prices below the current market level; or

(iii) to restrict the quantities permitted to be produced of any animal product the production of which is directly dependent, wholly or mainly, on the imported commodity, if the domestic production of that commodity is relatively negligible.

Any contracting party applying restrictions on the importation of any product pursuant to sub-paragraph (c) of this paragraph shall give public notice of the total quantity or value of the product permitted to be imported during a specified future period and of any change in such quantity or value. Moreover, any restrictions applied under (i) above shall not be such as will reduce the total of imports relative to the total of domestic production, as compared with the proportion which might reasonably be expected to rule between the two in the absence of restrictions. In determining this proportion, the contracting party shall pay due regard to the proportion prevailing during a previous representative period and to any special factors which may have affected or may be affecting the trade in the product concerned.

* * *

ARTICLE XX

General Exceptions

Subject to the requirement that such measures are not applied in a manner which would constitute a means of arbitrary or unjustifiable discrimination between countries where the same conditions prevail, or a disguised restriction on international trade, nothing in this Agreement shall be construed to prevent the adoption or enforcement by any contracting party of measures:

(a) necessary to protect public morals;

(b) necessary to protect human, animal or plant life or health;

(c) relating to the importation or exportation of gold or silver;

(d) necessary to secure compliance with laws or regulations which are not inconsistent with the provisions of this Agreement, including those relating to customs enforcement, the enforcement of monopolies operated under paragraph 4 of Article II and Article XVII, the protection of patents, trade marks and copyrights, and the prevention of deceptive practices;

(e) relating to the products of prison labour;

(f) imposed for the protection of national treasures of artistic, historic or archaeological value;

(g) relating to the conservation of exhaustible natural resources if such measures are made effective in conjunction with restrictions on domestic production or consumption;

(h) undertaken in pursuance of obligations under any intergovernmental commodity agreement which conforms to criteria submitted to the contracting parties and not disapproved by them or which is itself so submitted and not so disapproved;

(i) involving restrictions on exports of domestic materials necessary to ensure essential quantities of such materials to a domestic processing industry during periods when the domestic price of such materials is held below the world price as part of a governmental stabilization plan; *Provided* that such restrictions shall not operate to increase the exports of or the protection afforded to such domestic industry, and shall not depart from the provisions of this Agreement relating to nondiscrimination;

(j) essential to the acquisition or distribution of products in general or local short supply; *Provided* that any such measures shall be consistent with the principle that all contracting parties are entitled to an equitable share of the international supply of such products, and that any such measures which are inconsistent with the other provisions of this Agreement shall be discontinued as soon as the conditions giving rise to them have ceased to exist. The contracting parties shall review the need for this sub-paragraph not later than 30 June 1960.

7.2 CHARTER OF ECONOMIC RIGHTS AND DUTIES OF STATES. Adopted by the U.N. General Assembly, 12 December 1974. G.A. Res. 3281, U.N. GAOR, 29th Sess., Supp. No. 31, at 50, UN Doc. A/9631 (1975); *reprinted in* 14 I.L.M. 251 (1975) & 4 Weston IV.F.5: *Arts. 3, 30*

Article 3. In the exploitation of natural resources shared by two or more countries, each State must co-operate on the basis of a system of information and prior consultations in order to achieve optimum use of such resources without causing damage to the legitimate interest of others.

* * *

Article 30. The protection, preservation and enhancement of the environment for the present and future generations is the responsibility of all States. All States shall endeavour to establish their own environmental and developmental policies in conformity with such responsibility. The environmental policies of all States shall enhance and not adversely affect the present and future development potential of developing countries. All States have the responsibility to ensure that activities within their jurisdiction or control do not cause damage to the environment of other States or of areas beyond the limits of national jurisdiction. All States should co-operate in evolving international norms and regulations in the field of the environment.

7.3 DRAFT CODE OF CONDUCT ON TRANSNATIONAL CORPORATIONS. Adopted by the U.N. Economic and Social Council, 1 February 1988. U.N. Doc. E/1988/39/Add. 1 (1988); *reprinted in* 4 Weston IV.D.9: *Paras. 43–45*

Environmental protection

43. Transnational corporations shall carry out their activities in accordance with national laws, regulations, established administrative practices and policies relating to the preservation of the environment of the countries in which they operate and with due regard to relevant international standards. Transnational corporations should, in performing their activities, take steps to protect the environment and where damaged to rehabilitate it and should make efforts to develop and apply adequate technologies for this purpose.

44. Transnational corporations shall, in respect of the products, processes and services they have introduced or propose to introduce in any country, supply to the competent authorities of that country on request or on a regular basis, as specified by these authorities, all relevant information concerning:

Characteristics of these products, processes and other activities including experimental uses and related aspects which may harm the environment and the measures and costs necessary to avoid or at least to mitigate their harmful effects;

Prohibitions, restrictions, warnings and other public regulatory measures imposed in other countries on grounds of protection of the environment on these products, processes and services.

45. Transnational corporations should be responsive to requests from Governments of the countries in which they operate and be prepared where appropriate to co-operate with international organizations in their efforts to develop and promote national and international standards for the protection of the environment.

7.4 NORTH AMERICAN AGREEMENT ON ENVIRONMENTAL COOPERATION (With Annexes). Concluded at Mexico City, Washington and Ottawa, 8, 9, 12 & 14 September 1993. Entered into force, 1 January 1994. *Reprinted in* 32 I.L.M. 1480 (1993)

PREAMBLE

The Government of the United States of America, the Government of Canada and the Government of the United Mexican States:

CONVINCED of the importance of the conservation, protection and enhancement of the environment in their territories and the essential role of cooperation in these areas in achieving sustainable development for the well-being of present and future generations;

REAFFIRMING the sovereign right of States to exploit their own resources pursuant to their own environmental and development policies and their responsibility to ensure that activities within their jurisdiction or control do not cause damage to the environment of other States or of areas beyond the limits of national jurisdiction;

RECOGNIZING the interrelationship of their environments;

ACKNOWLEDGING the growing economic and social links between them, including the North American Free Trade Agreement (NAFTA);

RECONFIRMING the importance of the environmental goals and objectives of the NAFTA, including enhanced levels of environmental protection;

EMPHASIZING the importance of public participation in conserving, protecting and enhancing the environment;

NOTING the existence of differences in their respective natural endowments, climatic and geographical conditions, and economic, technological and infrastructural capabilities;

REAFFIRMING the Stockholm Declaration on the Human Environment of 1972 and the Rio Declaration on Environment and Development of 1992;

RECALLING their tradition of environmental cooperation and expressing their desire to support and build on international environmental agreements and existing policies and laws, in order to promote cooperation between them; and

CONVINCED of the benefits to be derived from a framework, including a Commission, to facilitate effective cooperation on the conservation, protection and enhancement of the environment in their territories;

HAVE AGREED AS FOLLOWS:

PART ONE

OBJECTIVES

Article 1: Objectives

The objectives of this Agreement are to:

(a) foster the protection and improvement of the environment in the territories of the Parties for the well-being of present and future generations;

(b) promote sustainable development based on cooperation and mutually supportive environmental and economic policies;

(c) increase cooperation between the Parties to better conserve, protect, and enhance the environment, including wild flora and fauna;

(d) support the environmental goals and objectives of the NAFTA;

(e) avoid creating trade distortions or new trade barriers;

(f) strengthen cooperation on the development and improvement of environmental laws, regulations, procedures, policies and practices;

(g) enhance compliance with, and enforcement of, environmental laws and regulations;

(h) promote transparency and public participation in the development of environmental laws, regulations and policies;

(i) promote economically efficient and effective environmental measures; and

(j) promote pollution prevention policies and practices.

PART TWO

OBLIGATIONS

Article 2: General Commitments

1. Each Party shall, with respect to its territory:

(a) periodically prepare and make publicly available reports on the state of the environment;

(b) develop and review environmental emergency preparedness measures;

(c) promote education in environmental matters, including environmental law;

(d) further scientific research and technology development in respect of environmental matters;

(e) assess, as appropriate, environmental impacts; and

(f) promote the use of economic instruments for the efficient achievement of environmental goals.

2. Each Party shall consider implementing in its law any recommendation developed by the Council under Article 10(5)(b).

3. Each Party shall consider prohibiting the export to the territories of the other Parties of a pesticide or toxic substance whose use is prohibited within the Party's territory. When a Party adopts a measure prohibiting or severely restricting the use of a pesticide or toxic substance in its territory, it shall notify the other Parties of the measure, either directly or through an appropriate international organization.

Article 3: Levels of Protection

Recognizing the right of each Party to establish its own levels of domestic environmental protection and environmental development policies and priorities, and to adopt or modify accordingly its environmental laws and regulations, each Party shall ensure that its laws and regulations provide for high levels of environmental protection and shall strive to continue to improve those laws and regulations.

Article 4: Publication

1. Each Party shall ensure that its laws, regulations, procedures and administrative rulings of general application respecting any matter covered by this Agreement are promptly published or otherwise made available in such a manner as to enable interested persons and Parties to become acquainted with them.

2. To the extent possible, each Party shall:

(a) publish in advance any such measure that it proposes to adopt; and

(b) provide interested persons and Parties a reasonable opportunity to comment on such proposed measures.

Article 5: Government Enforcement Action

1. With the aim of achieving high levels of environmental protection and compliance with its environmental laws and regulations, each Party shall effectively enforce its environmental laws and regulations through appropriate governmental action, subject to Article 37, such as:

(a) appointing and training inspectors;

(b) monitoring compliance and investigating suspected violations, including through on-site inspections;

(c) seeking assurances of voluntary compliance and compliance agreements;

(d) publicly releasing non-compliance information;

(e) issuing bulletins or other periodic statements on enforcement procedures;

(f) promoting environmental audits;

(g) requiring record keeping and reporting;

(h) providing or encouraging mediation and arbitration services;

(i) using licenses, permits or authorizations;

(j) initiating, in a timely manner, judicial, quasi-judicial or administrative proceedings to seek appropriate sanctions or remedies for violations of its environmental laws and regulations;

(k) providing for search, seizure or detention; or

(*l*) issuing administrative orders, including orders of a preventative, curative or emergency nature.

2. Each Party shall ensure that judicial, quasi-judicial or administrative enforcement proceedings are available under its law to sanction or remedy violations of its environmental laws and regulations.

3. Sanctions and remedies provided for a violation of a Party's environmental laws and regulations shall, as appropriate:

(a) take into consideration the nature and gravity of the violation, any economic benefit derived from the violation by the violator, the economic condition of the violator, and other relevant factors; and

(b) include compliance agreements, fines, imprisonment, injunctions, the closure of facilities, and the cost of containing or cleaning up pollution.

Article 6: Private Access to Remedies

1. Each Party shall ensure that interested persons may request the Party's competent authorities to investigate alleged violations of its environmental laws and regulations and shall give such requests due consideration in accordance with law.

2. Each Party shall ensure that persons with a legally recognized interest under its law in a particular matter have appropriate access to administrative, quasi-judicial or judicial proceedings for the enforcement of the Party's environmental laws and regulations.

3. Private access to remedies shall include rights, in accordance with the Party's law, such as:

(a) to sue another person under that Party's jurisdiction for damages;

(b) to seek sanctions or remedies such as monetary penalties, emergency closures or orders to mitigate the consequences of violations of its environmental laws and regulations;

(c) to request the competent authorities to take appropriate action to enforce that Party's environmental laws and regulations in order to protect the environment or to avoid environmental harm; or

(d) to seek injunctions where a person suffers, or may suffer, loss, damage or injury as a result of conduct by another person under that Party's jurisdiction contrary to that Party's environmental laws and regulations or from tortious conduct.

Article 7: Procedural Guarantees

1. Each Party shall ensure that its administrative, quasi-judicial and judicial proceedings referred to in Articles 5(2) and 6(2) are fair, open and equitable, and to this end shall provide that such proceedings:

(a) comply with due process of law;

(b) are open to the public, except where the administration of justice otherwise requires;

(c) entitle the parties to the proceedings to support or defend their respective positions and to present information or evidence; and

(d) are not unnecessarily complicated and do not entail unreasonable charges or time limits or unwarranted delays.

2. Each Party shall provide that final decisions on the merits of the case in such proceedings are:

(a) in writing and preferably state the reasons on which the decisions are based;

(b) made available without undue delay to the parties to the proceedings and, consistent with its law, to the public; and

(c) based on information or evidence in respect of which the parties were offered the opportunity to be heard.

3. Each Party shall provide, as appropriate, that parties to such proceedings have the right, in accordance with its law, to seek review and, where warranted, correction of final decisions issued in such proceedings.

4. Each Party shall ensure that tribunals that conduct or review such proceedings are impartial and independent and do not have any substantial interest in the outcome of the matter.

PART THREE

COMMISSION FOR ENVIRONMENTAL COOPERATION

Article 8: The Commission

1. The Parties hereby establish the Commission for Environmental Cooperation.

2. The Commission shall comprise a Council, a Secretariat and a Joint Public Advisory Committee.

Section A: The Council

Article 9: Council Structure and Procedures

1. The Council shall comprise cabinet-level or equivalent representatives of the Parties, or their designees.

2. The Council shall establish its rules and procedures.

3. The Council shall convene:

(a) at least once a year in regular session; and

(b) in special session at the request of any Party.

Regular sessions shall be chaired successively by each Party.

4. The Council shall hold public meetings in the course of all regular sessions. Other meetings held in the course of regular or special sessions shall be public where the Council so decides.

5. The Council may:

(a) establish, and assign responsibilities to, ad hoc or standing committees, working groups or expert groups;

(b) seek the advice of non-governmental organizations or persons, including independent experts; and

(c) take such other action in the exercise of its functions as the Parties may agree.

6. All decisions and recommendations of the Council shall be taken by consensus, except as the Council may otherwise decide or as otherwise provided in this Agreement.

7. All decisions and recommendations of the Council shall be made public, except as the Council may otherwise decide or as otherwise provided in this Agreement.

Article 10: Council Functions

1. The Council shall be the governing body of the Commission and shall:

(a) serve as a forum for the discussion of environmental matters within the scope of this Agreement;

(b) oversee the implementation and develop recommendations on the further elaboration of this Agreement and, to this end, the Council shall, within four years after the date of entry into force of this Agreement, review its operation and effectiveness in the light of experience;

(c) oversee the Secretariat;

(d) address questions and differences that may arise between the Parties regarding the interpretation or application of this Agreement;

(e) approve the annual program and budget of the Commission; and

(f) promote and facilitate cooperation between the Parties with respect to environmental matters.

2. The Council may consider, and develop recommendations regarding:

(a) comparability of techniques and methodologies for data gathering and analysis, data management and electronic data communications on matters covered by this Agreement;

(b) pollution prevention techniques and strategies;

(c) approaches and common indicators for reporting on the state of the environment;

(d) the use of economic instruments for the pursuit of domestic and internationally agreed environmental objectives;

(e) scientific research and technology development in respect of environmental matters;

(f) promotion of public awareness regarding the environment;

(g) transboundary and border environmental issues, such as the long-range transport of air and marine pollutants;

(h) exotic species that may be harmful;

(i) the conservation and protection of wild flora and fauna and their habitat, and specially protected natural areas;

(j) the protection of endangered and threatened species;

(k) environmental emergency preparedness and response activities;

(*l*) environmental matters as they relate to economic development;

(m) the environmental implications of goods throughout their life cycles;

(n) human resource training and development in the environmental field;

(*o*) the exchange of environmental scientists and officials;

(p) approaches to environmental compliance and enforcement;

(q) ecologically sensitive national accounts;

(r) eco-labelling; and

(s) other matters as it may decide.

3. The Council shall strengthen cooperation on the development and continuing improvement of environmental laws and regulations, including by:

(a) promoting the exchange of information on criteria and methodologies used in establishing domestic environmental standards; and

(b) without reducing levels of environmental protection, establishing a process for developing recommendations on greater compatibility of environmental technical regulations, standards and conformity assessment procedures in a manner consistent with the NAFTA.

4. The Council shall encourage:

(a) effective enforcement by each Party of its environmental laws and regulations;

(b) compliance with those laws and regulations; and

(c) technical cooperation between the Parties.

5. The Council shall promote and, as appropriate, develop recommendations regarding:

(a) public access to information concerning the environment that is held by public authorities of each Party, including information on hazardous materials and activities in its communities, and opportunity to participate in decision-making processes related to such public access; and

(b) appropriate limits for specific pollutants, taking into account differences in ecosystems.

6. The Council shall cooperate with the NAFTA Free Trade Commission to achieve the environmental goals and objectives of the NAFTA by:

(a) acting as a point of inquiry and receipt for comments from non-governmental organizations and persons concerning those goals and objectives;

(b) providing assistance in consultations under Article 1114 of the NAFTA where a Party considers that another Party is waiving or derogating from, or offering to waive or otherwise derogate from, an environmental measure as an encouragement to establish, acquire, expand or retain an investment of an investor, with a view to avoiding any such encouragement;

(c) contributing to the prevention or resolution of environment-related trade disputes by:

(i) seeking to avoid disputes between the Parties,

(ii) making recommendations to the Free Trade Commission with respect to the avoidance of such disputes, and

(iii) identifying experts able to provide information or technical advice to NAFTA committees, working groups and other NAFTA bodies;

(d) considering on an ongoing basis the environmental effects of the NAFTA; and

(e) otherwise assisting the Free Trade Commission in environment-related matters.

7. Recognizing the significant bilateral nature of many transboundary environmental issues, the Council shall, with a view to agreement between the Parties pursuant to this Article within three years on obligations, consider and develop recommendations with respect to:

(a) assessing the environmental impact of proposed projects subject to decisions by a competent government authority and likely to cause significant adverse transboundary effects, including a full evaluation of comments provided by other Parties and persons of other Parties;

(b) notification, provision of relevant information and consultation between Parties with respect to such projects; and

(c) mitigation of the potential adverse effects of such projects.

8. The Council shall encourage the establishment by each Party of appropriate administrative procedures pursuant to its environmental laws to permit another Party to seek the reduction, elimination or mitigation of transboundary pollution on a reciprocal basis.

9. The Council shall consider and, as appropriate, develop recommendations on the provision by a Party, on a reciprocal basis, of access to and rights and remedies before its courts and administrative agencies for persons in another Party's territory who have suffered or are likely to suffer damage or injury caused by pollution originating in its territory as if the damage or injury were suffered in its territory.

Section B: The Secretariat

Article 11: Secretariat Structure and Procedures

1. The Secretariat shall be headed by an Executive Director, who shall be chosen by the Council for a three-year term, which may be renewed by the Council for one additional three-year term. The position of Executive Director shall rotate consecutively between nationals of each Party. The Council may remove the Executive Director solely for cause.

2. The Executive Director shall appoint and supervise the staff of the Secretariat, regulate their powers and duties and fix their remuneration in accordance with general standards to be established by the Council. The general standards shall provide that:

(a) staff shall be appointed and retained, and their conditions of employment shall be determined, strictly on the basis of efficiency, competence and integrity;

(b) in appointing staff, the Executive Director shall take into account lists of candidates prepared by the Parties and by the Joint Public Advisory Committee;

(c) due regard shall be paid to the importance of recruiting an equitable proportion of the professional staff from among the nationals of each Party; and

(d) the Executive Director shall inform the Council of all appointments.

3. The Council may decide, by a two-thirds vote, to reject any appointment that does not meet the general standards. Any such decision shall be made and held in confidence.

4. In the performance of their duties, the Executive Director and the staff shall not seek or receive instructions from any government or any other authority external to the Council. Each Party shall respect the international character of the responsibili-

ties of the Executive Director and the staff and shall not seek to influence them in the discharge of their responsibilities.

5. The Secretariat shall provide technical, administrative and operational support to the Council and to committees and groups established by the Council, and such other support as the Council may direct.

6. The Executive Director shall submit for the approval of the Council the annual program and budget of the Commission, including provision for proposed cooperative activities and for the Secretariat to respond to contingencies.

7. The Secretariat shall, as appropriate, provide the Parties and the public information on where they may receive technical advice and expertise with respect to environmental matters.

8. The Secretariat shall safeguard:

(a) from disclosure information it receives that could identify a non-governmental organization or person making a submission if the person or organization so requests or the Secretariat otherwise considers it appropriate; and

(b) from public disclosure any information it receives from any non-governmental organization or person where the information is designated by that non-governmental organization or person as confidential or proprietary.

Article 12: Annual Report of the Commission

1. The Secretariat shall prepare an annual report of the Commission in accordance with instructions from the Council. The Secretariat shall submit a draft of the report for review by the Council. The final report shall be released publicly.

2. The report shall cover:

(a) activities and expenses of the Commission during the previous year;

(b) the approved program and budget of the Commission for the subsequent year;

(c) the actions taken by each Party in connection with its obligations under this Agreement, including data on the Party's environmental enforcement activities;

(d) relevant views and information submitted by non-governmental organizations and persons, including summary data regarding submissions, and any other relevant information the Council deems appropriate;

(e) recommendations made on any matter within the scope of this Agreement; and

(f) any other matter that the Council instructs the Secretariat to include.

3. The report shall periodically address the state of the environment in the territories of the Parties.

Article 13: Secretariat Reports

1. The Secretariat may prepare a report for the Council on any matter within the scope of the annual program. Should the Secretariat wish to prepare a report on any other environmental matter related to the cooperative functions of this Agreement, it shall notify the Council and may proceed unless, within 30 days of such notification, the Council objects by a two-thirds vote to the preparation of the report. Such other environmental matters shall not include issues related to whether a Party has failed to enforce its environmental laws and regulations. Where the Secretariat does not have specific expertise in the matter under review, it shall obtain the assistance of one or more independent experts of recognized experience in the matter to assist in the preparation of the report.

2. In preparing such a report, the Secretariat may draw upon any relevant technical, scientific or other information, including information:

(a) that is publicly available;

(b) submitted by interested non-governmental organizations and persons;

(c) submitted by the Joint Public Advisory Committee;

(d) furnished by a Party;

(e) gathered through public consultations, such as conferences, seminars and symposia; or

(f) developed by the Secretariat, or by independent experts engaged pursuant to paragraph 1.

3. The Secretariat shall submit its report to the Council, which shall make it publicly available, normally within 60 days following its submission, unless the Council otherwise decides.

Article 14: Submissions on Enforcement Matters

1. The Secretariat may consider a submission from any non-governmental organization or person asserting that a Party is failing to effectively enforce its environmental law, if the Secretariat finds that the submission:

(a) is in writing in a language designated by that Party in a notification to the Secretariat;

(b) clearly identifies the person or organization making the submission;

(c) provides sufficient information to allow the Secretariat to review the submission, including any documentary evidence on which the submission may be based;

(d) appears to be aimed at promoting enforcement rather than at harassing industry;

(e) indicates that the matter has been communicated in writing to the relevant authorities of the Party and indicates the Party's response, if any; and

(f) is filed by a person or organization residing or established in the territory of a Party.

2. Where the Secretariat determines that a submission meets the criteria set out in paragraph 1, the Secretariat shall determine whether the submission merits requesting a response from the Party. In deciding whether to request a response, the Secretariat shall be guided by whether:

(a) the submission alleges harm to the person or organization making the submission;

(b) the submission, alone or in combination with other submissions, raises matters whose further study in this process would advance the goals of this Agreement;

(c) private remedies available under the Party's law have been pursued; and

(d) the submission is drawn exclusively from mass media reports.

Where the Secretariat makes such a request, it shall forward to the Party a copy of the submission and any supporting information provided with the submission.

3. The Party shall advise the Secretariat within 30 days or, in exceptional circumstances and on notification to the Secretariat, within 60 days of delivery of the request:

(a) whether the matter is the subject of a pending judicial or administrative proceeding, in which case the Secretariat shall proceed no further; and

(b) of any other information that the Party wishes to submit, such as

i) whether the matter was previously the subject of a judicial or administrative proceeding, and

ii) whether private remedies in connection with the matter are available to the person or organization making the submission and whether they have been pursued.

Article 15: Factual Record

1. If the Secretariat considers that the submission, in the light of any response provided by the Party, warrants developing a factual record, the Secretariat shall so inform the Council and provide its reasons.

2. The Secretariat shall prepare a factual record if the Council, by a two-thirds vote, instructs it to do so.

3. The preparation of a factual record by the Secretariat pursuant to this Article shall be without prejudice to any further steps that may be taken with respect to any submission.

4. In preparing a factual record, the Secretariat shall consider any information furnished by a Party and may consider any relevant technical, scientific or other information:

(a) that is publicly available;

(b) submitted by interested non-governmental organizations or persons;

(c) submitted by the Joint Public Advisory Committee; or

(d) developed by the Secretariat or by independent experts.

5. The Secretariat shall submit a draft factual record to the Council. Any Party may provide comments on the accuracy of the draft within 45 days thereafter.

6. The Secretariat shall incorporate, as appropriate, any such comments in the final factual record and submit it to the Council.

7. The Council may, by a two-thirds vote, make the final factual record publicly available, normally within 60 days following its submission.

Section C: Advisory Committees

Article 16: Joint Public Advisory Committee

1. The Joint Public Advisory Committee shall comprise 15 members, unless the Council otherwise decides. Each Party or, if the Party so decides, its National Advisory Committee convened under Article 17, shall appoint an equal number of members.

2. The Council shall establish the rules of procedure for the Joint Public Advisory Committee, which shall choose its own chair.

3. The Joint Public Advisory Committee shall convene at least once a year at the time of the regular session of the Council and at such other times as the Council, or the Committee's chair with the consent of a majority of its members, may decide.

4. The Joint Public Advisory Committee may provide advice to the Council on any matter within the scope of this Agreement, including on any documents provided to it under paragraph 6, and on the implementation and further elaboration of this Agreement, and may perform such other functions as the Council may direct.

5. The Joint Public Advisory Committee may provide relevant technical, scientific or other information to the Secretariat, including for purposes of developing a factual record under Article 15. The Secretariat shall forward to the Council copies of any such information.

6. The Secretariat shall provide to the Joint Public Advisory Committee at the time they are submitted to the Council copies of the proposed annual program and budget of the Commission, the draft annual report, and any report the Secretariat prepares pursuant to Article 13.

7. The Council may, by a two-thirds vote, make a factual record available to the Joint Public Advisory Committee.

Article 17: National Advisory Committees

Each Party may convene a national advisory committee, comprising members of its public, including representatives of non-governmental organizations and persons, to advise it on the implementation and further elaboration of this Agreement.

Article 18: Governmental Committees

Each Party may convene a governmental committee, which may comprise or include representatives of federal and state or provincial governments, to advise it on the implementation and further elaboration of this Agreement.

Section D: Official Languages

Article 19: Official Languages

The official languages of the Commission shall be English, French and Spanish. All annual reports under Article 12, reports submitted to the Council under Article 13, factual records submitted to the Council under Article 15(6) and panel reports under Part Five shall be available in each official language at the time they are made public. The Council shall establish rules and procedures regarding interpretation and translation.

PART FOUR

COOPERATION AND PROVISION OF INFORMATION

Article 20: Cooperation

1. The Parties shall at all times endeavor to agree on the interpretation and application of this Agreement, and shall make every attempt through cooperation and consultations to resolve any matter that might affect its operation.

2. To the maximum extent possible, each Party shall notify any other Party with an interest in the matter of any proposed or actual environmental measure that the Party considers might materially affect the operation of this Agreement or otherwise substantially affect that other Party's interests under this Agreement.

3. On request of any other Party, a Party shall promptly provide information and respond to questions pertaining to any such actual or proposed environmental measure, whether or not that other Party has been previously notified of that measure.

4. Any Party may notify any other Party of, and provide to that Party, any credible information regarding possible violations of its environmental law, specific and sufficient to allow the other Party to inquire into the matter. The notified Party shall take appropriate steps in accordance with its law to so inquire and to respond to the other Party.

Article 21: Provision of Information

1. On request of the Council or the Secretariat, each Party shall, in accordance with its law, provide such information as the Council or the Secretariat may require, including:

(a) promptly making available any information in its possession required for the preparation of a report or factual record, including compliance and enforcement data; and

(b) taking all reasonable steps to make available any other such information requested.

2. If a Party considers that a request for information from the Secretariat is excessive or otherwise unduly burdensome, it may so notify the Council. The Secretariat shall revise the scope of its request to comply with any limitations established by the Council by a two-thirds vote.

3. If a Party does not make available information requested by the Secretariat, as may be limited pursuant to paragraph 2, it shall promptly advise the Secretariat of its reasons in writing.

PART FIVE

CONSULTATION AND RESOLUTION OF DISPUTES

Article 22: Consultations

1. Any Party may request in writing consultations with any other Party regarding whether there has been a persistent pattern of failure by that other Party to effectively enforce its environmental law.

2. The requesting Party shall deliver the request to the other Parties and to the Secretariat.

3. Unless the Council otherwise provides in its rules and procedures established under Article 9(2), a third Party that considers it has a substantial interest in the matter shall be entitled to participate in the consultations on delivery of written notice to the other Parties and to the Secretariat.

4. The consulting Parties shall make every attempt to arrive at a mutually satisfactory resolution of the matter through consultations under this Article.

Article 23: Initiation of Procedures

1. If the consulting Parties fail to resolve the matter pursuant to Article 22 within 60 days of delivery of a request for consultations, or such other period as the consulting Parties may agree, any such Party may request in writing a special session of the Council.

2. The requesting Party shall state in the request the matter complained of and shall deliver the request to the other Parties and to the Secretariat.

3. Unless it decides otherwise, the Council shall convene within 20 days of delivery of the request and shall endeavor to resolve the dispute promptly.

4. The Council may:

(a) call on such technical advisers or create such working groups or expert groups as it deems necessary.

(b) have recourse to good offices, conciliation, mediation or such other dispute resolution procedures, or

(c) make recommendations.

as may assist the consulting Parties to reach a mutually satisfactory resolution of the dispute. Any such recommendations shall be made public if the Council, by a two-thirds vote, so decides.

5. Where the Council decides that a matter is more properly covered by another agreement or arrangement to which the consulting Parties are party, it shall refer the matter to those Parties for appropriate action in accordance with such other agreement or arrangement.

Article 24: Request for an Arbitral Panel

1. If the matter has not been resolved within 60 days after the Council has convened pursuant to Article 23, the Council shall, on the written request of any consulting Party and by a two-thirds vote, convene an arbitral panel to consider the matter where the alleged persistent pattern of failure by the Party complained against to effectively enforce its environmental law relates to a situation involving workplaces, firms, companies or sectors that produce goods or provide services:

(a) traded between the territories of the Parties; or

(b) that compete, in the territory of the Party complained against, with goods or services produced or provided by persons of another Party.

2. A third Party that considers it has a substantial interest in the matter shall be entitled to join as a complaining Party on delivery of written notice of its intention to participate to the disputing Parties and the Secretariat. The notice shall be delivered at the earliest possible time, and in any event no later than seven days after the date of the vote of the Council to convene a panel.

3. Unless otherwise agreed by the disputing Parties, the panel shall be established and perform its functions in a manner consistent with the provisions of this Part.

Article 25: Roster

1. The Council shall establish and maintain a roster of up to 45 individuals who are willing and able to serve as panelists. The roster members shall be appointed by consensus for terms of three years, and may be reappointed.

2. Roster members shall:

(a) have expertise or experience in environmental law or its enforcement, or in the resolution of disputes arising under international agreements, or other relevant scientific, technical or professional expertise or experience;

(b) be chosen strictly on the basis of objectivity, reliability and sound judgment;

(c) be independent of, and not be affiliated with or take instructions from, any Party, the Secretariat or the Joint Public Advisory Committee; and

(d) comply with a code of conduct to be established by the Council.

Article 26: Qualifications of Panelists

1. All panelists shall meet the qualifications set out in Article 25(2).

2. Individuals may not serve as panelists for a dispute in which:

(a) they have participated pursuant to Article 23(4); or

(b) they have, or a person or organization with which they are affiliated has, an interest, as set out in the code of conduct established under Article 25(2)(d).

Article 27: Panel Selection

1. Where there are two disputing Parties, the following procedures shall apply:

(a) The panel shall comprise five members.

(b) The disputing Parties shall endeavor to agree on the chair of the panel within 15 days after the Council votes to convene the panel. If the disputing Parties are unable to agree on the chair within this period, the disputing Party chosen by lot shall select within five days a chair who is not a citizen of that Party.

(c) Within 15 days of selection of the chair, each disputing Party shall select two panelists who are citizens of the other disputing Party.

(d) If a disputing Party fails to select its panelists within such period, such panelists shall be selected by lot from among the roster members who are citizens of the other disputing Party.

2. Where there are more than two disputing Parties, the following procedures shall apply:

(a) The panel shall comprise five members.

(b) The disputing Parties shall endeavor to agree on the chair of the panel within 15 days after the Council votes to convene the panel. If the disputing Parties are unable to agree on the chair within this period, the Party or Parties on the side of the dispute chosen by lot shall select within 10 days a chair who is not a citizen of such Party or Parties.

(c) Within 30 days of selection of the chair, the Party complained against shall select two panelists, one of whom is a citizen of a complaining Party, and the other of whom is a citizen of another complaining Party. The complaining Parties shall select two panelists who are citizens of the Party complained against.

(d) If any disputing Party fails to select a panelist within such period, such panelist shall be selected by lot in accordance with the citizenship criteria of subparagraph (c).

3. Panelists shall normally be selected from the roster. Any disputing Party may exercise a peremptory challenge against any individual not on the roster who is proposed as a panelist by a disputing Party within 30 days after the individual has been proposed.

4. If a disputing Party believes that a panelist is in violation of the code of conduct, the disputing Parties shall consult and, if they agree, the panelist shall be removed and a new panelist shall be selected in accordance with this Article.

Article 28: Rules of Procedure

1. The Council shall establish Model Rules of Procedure. The procedures shall provide:

(a) a right to at least one hearing before the panel;

(b) the opportunity to make initial and rebuttal written submissions; and

(c) that no panel may disclose which panelists are associated with majority or minority opinions.

2. Unless the disputing Parties otherwise agree, panels convened under this Part shall be established and conduct their proceedings in accordance with the Model Rules of Procedure.

3. Unless the disputing Parties otherwise agree within 20 days after the Council votes to convene the panel, the terms of reference shall be:

"To examine, in light of the relevant provisions of the Agreement, including those contained in Part Five, whether there has been a persistent pattern of failure by the Party complained against to effectively enforce its environmental law, and to make findings, determinations and recommendations in accordance with Article 31(2)."

Article 29: Third Party Participation

A Party that is not a disputing Party, on delivery of a written notice to the disputing Parties and to the Secretariat, shall be entitled to attend all hearings, to make written and oral submissions to the panel and to receive written submissions of the disputing Parties.

Article 30: Role of Experts

On request of a disputing Party, or on its own initiative, the panel may seek information and technical advice from any person or body that it deems appropriate, provided that the disputing Parties so agree and subject to such terms and conditions as such Parties may agree.

Article 31: Initial Report

1. Unless the disputing Parties otherwise agree, the panel shall base its report on the submissions and arguments of the Parties and on any information before it pursuant to Article 30.

2. Unless the disputing Parties otherwise agree, the panel shall, within 180 days after the last panelist is selected, present to the disputing Parties an initial report containing:

(a) findings of fact;

(b) its determination as to whether there has been a persistent pattern of failure by the Party complained against to effectively enforce its environmental law, or any other determination requested in the terms of reference; and

(c) in the event the panel makes an affirmative determination under subparagraph (b), its recommendations, if any, for the resolution of the dispute, which normally shall be that the Party complained against adopt and implement an action plan sufficient to remedy the pattern of non-enforcement.

3. Panelists may furnish separate opinions on matters not unanimously agreed.

4. A disputing Party may submit written comments to the panel on its initial report within 30 days of presentation of the report.

5. In such an event, and after considering such written comments, the panel, on its own initiative or on the request of any disputing Party, may:

(a) request the views of any participating Party:

(b) reconsider its report; and

(c) make any further examination that it considers appropriate.

Article 32: Final Report

1. The panel shall present to the disputing Parties a final report, including any separate opinions on matters not unanimously agreed, within 60 days of presentation of the initial report, unless the disputing Parties otherwise agree.

2. The disputing Parties shall transmit to the Council the final report of the panel, as well as any written views that a disputing Party desires to be appended, on a confidential basis within 15 days after it is presented to them.

3. The final report of the panel shall be published five days after it is transmitted to the Council.

Article 33: Implementation of Final Report

If, in its final report, a panel determines that there has been a persistent pattern of failure by the Party complained against to effectively enforce its environmental law, the disputing Parties may agree on a mutually satisfactory action plan, which normally shall conform with the determinations and recommendations of the panel. The disputing Parties shall promptly notify the Secretariat and the Council of any agreed resolution of the dispute.

Article 34: Review of Implementation

1. If, in its final report, a panel determines that there has been a persistent pattern of failure by the Party complained against to effectively enforce its environmental law, and:

(a) the disputing Parties have not agreed on an action plan under Article 33 within 60 days of the date of the final report, or

(b) the disputing Parties cannot agree on whether the Party complained against is fully implementing

(i) an action plan agreed under Article 33.

(ii) an action plan deemed to have been established by a panel under paragraph 2, or

(iii) an action plan approved or established by a panel under paragraph 4,

any disputing Party may request that the panel be reconvened. The requesting Party shall deliver the request in writing to the other Parties and to the Secretariat. The Council shall reconvene the panel on delivery of the request to the Secretariat.

2. No Party may make a request under paragraph 1(a) earlier than 60 days, or later than 120 days, after the date of the final report. If the disputing Parties have not agreed to an action plan and if no request was made under paragraph 1(a), the last action plan, if any, submitted by the Party complained against to the complaining Party or Parties within 60 days of the date of the final report, or such other period as the disputing Parties may agree, shall be deemed to have been established by the panel 120 days after the date of the final report.

3. A request under paragraph 1(b) may be made no earlier than 180 days after an action plan has been:

(a) agreed under Article 33;

(b) deemed to have been established by a panel under paragraph 2; or

(c) approved or established by a panel under paragraph 4;

and only during the term of any such action plan.

4. Where a panel has been reconvened under paragraph 1(a), it:

(a) shall determine whether any action plan proposed by the Party complained against is sufficient to remedy the pattern of non-enforcement and

(i) if so, shall approve the plan, or

(ii) if not, shall establish such a plan consistent with the law of the Party complained against, and

(b) may, where warranted, impose a monetary enforcement assessment in accordance with Annex 34,

within 90 days after the panel has been reconvened or such other period as the disputing Parties may agree.

5. Where a panel has been reconvened under paragraph 1(b), it shall determine either that:

(a) the Party complained against is fully implementing the action plan, in which case the panel may not impose a monetary enforcement assessment, or

(b) the Party complained against is not fully implementing the action plan, in which case the panel shall impose a monetary enforcement assessment in accordance with Annex 34.

within 60 days after it has been reconvened or such other period as the disputing Parties may agree.

6. A panel reconvened under this Article shall provide that the Party complained against shall fully implement any action plan referred to in paragraph 4(a)(ii) or 5(b), and pay any monetary enforcement assessment imposed under paragraph 4(b) or 5(b), and any such provision shall be final.

Article 35: Further Proceeding

A complaining Party may, at any time beginning 180 days after a panel determination under Article 34(5)(b), request in writing that a panel be reconvened to determine whether the Party complained against is fully implementing the action plan. On delivery of the request to the other Parties and the Secretariat, the Council shall reconvene the panel. The panel shall make the determination within 60 days after it has been reconvened or such other period as the disputing Parties may agree.

Article 36: Suspension of Benefits

1. Subject to Annex 36A, where a Party fails to pay a monetary enforcement assessment within 180 days after it is imposed by a panel:

(a) under Article 34(4)(b), or

(b) under Article 34(5)(b), except where benefits may be suspended under paragraph 2(a).

any complaining Party or Parties may suspend, in accordance with Annex 36B, the application to the Party complained against of NAFTA benefits in an amount no greater than that sufficient to collect the monetary enforcement assessment.

2. Subject to Annex 36A, where a panel has made a determination under Article 34(5)(b) and the panel:

(a) has previously imposed a monetary enforcement assessment under Article 34(4)(b) or established an action plan under Article 34(4)(a)(ii); or

(b) has subsequently determined under Article 35 that a Party is not fully implementing an action plan;

the complaining Party or Parties may, in accordance with Annex 36B, suspend annually the application to the Party complained against of NAFTA benefits in an amount no greater than the monetary enforcement assessment imposed by the panel under Article 34(5)(b).

3. Where more than one complaining Party suspends benefits under paragraph 1 or 2, the combined suspension shall be no greater than the amount of the monetary enforcement assessment.

4. Where a Party has suspended benefits under paragraph 1 or 2, the Council shall, on the delivery of a written request by the Party complained against to the other Parties and the Secretariat, reconvene the panel to determine whether the monetary enforcement assessment has been paid or collected, or whether the Party complained against is fully implementing the action plan, as the case may be. The panel shall submit its report within 45 days after it has been reconvened. If the panel determines that the assessment has been paid or collected, or that the Party complained against is fully implementing the action plan, the suspension of benefits under paragraph 1 or 2, as the case may be, shall be terminated.

5. On the written request of the Party complained against, delivered to the other Parties and the Secretariat, the Council shall reconvene the panel to determine whether the suspension of benefits by the complaining Party or Parties pursuant to paragraph 1 or 2 is manifestly excessive. Within 45 days of the request, the panel shall present a report to the disputing Parties containing its determination.

PART SIX

GENERAL PROVISIONS

Article 37: Enforcement Principle

Nothing in this Agreement shall be construed to empower a Party's authorities to undertake environmental law enforcement activities in the territory of another Party.

Article 38: Private Rights

No Party may provide for a right of action under its law against any other Party on the ground that another Party has acted in a manner inconsistent with this Agreement.

Article 39: Protection of Information

1. Nothing in this Agreement shall be construed to require a Party to make available or allow access to information:

(a) the disclosure of which would impede its environmental law enforcement; or

(b) that is protected from disclosure by its law governing business or proprietary information, personal privacy or the confidentiality of governmental decision making.

2. If a Party provides confidential or proprietary information to another Party, the Council, the Secretariat or the Joint Public Advisory Committee, the recipient shall treat the information on the same basis as the Party providing the information.

3. Confidential or proprietary information provided by a Party to a panel under this Agreement shall be treated in accordance with the rules of procedure established under Article 28.

Article 40: Relation to Other Environmental Agreements

Nothing in this Agreement shall be construed to affect the existing rights and obligations of the Parties under other international environmental agreements, including conservation agreements, to which such Parties are party.

Article 41: Extent of Obligations

Annex 41 applies to the Parties specified in that Annex.

Article 42: National Security

Nothing in this Agreement shall be construed:

(a) to require any Party to make available or provide access to information the disclosure of which it determines to be contrary to its essential security interests; or

(b) to prevent any Party from taking any actions that it considers necessary for the protection of its essential security interests relating to

(i) arms, ammunition and implements of war, or

(ii) the implementation of national policies or international agreements respecting the non-proliferation of nuclear weapons or other nuclear explosive devices.

Article 43: Funding of the Commission

Each Party shall contribute an equal share of the annual budget of the Commission, subject to the availability of appropriated funds in accordance with the Party's legal procedures. No Party shall be obligated to pay more than any other Party in respect of an annual budget.

Article 44: Privileges and Immunities

The Executive Director and staff of the Secretariat shall enjoy in the territory of each Party such privileges and immunities as are necessary for the exercise of their functions.

Article 45: Definitions

1. For purposes of this Agreement:

A Party has not failed to "effectively enforce its environmental law" or to comply with Article 5(1) in a particular case where the action or inaction in question by agencies or officials of that Party:

(a) reflects a reasonable exercise of their discretion in respect of investigatory, prosecutorial, regulatory or compliance matters; or

(b) results from bona fide decisions to allocate resources to enforcement in respect of other environmental matters determined to have higher priorities;

"non-governmental organization" means any scientific, professional, business, non-profit, or public interest organization or association which is neither affiliated with, nor under the direction of, a government:

"persistent pattern" means a sustained or recurring course of action or inaction beginning after the date of entry into force of this Agreement;

"province" means a province of Canada, and includes the Yukon Territory and the Northwest Territories and their successors; and

"territory" means for a Party the territory of that Party as set out in Annex 45.

2. For purposes of Article 14(1) and Part Five:

(a) "environmental law" means any statute or regulation of a Party, or provision thereof, the primary purpose of which is the protection of the environment, or the prevention of a danger to human life or health, through

(i) the prevention, abatement or control of the release, discharge, or emission of pollutants or environmental contaminants.

(ii) the control of environmentally hazardous or toxic chemicals, substances, materials and wastes, and the dissemination of information related thereto, or

(iii) the protection of wild flora or fauna, including endangered species, their habitat, and specially protected natural areas

in the Party's territory, but does not include any statute or regulation, or provision thereof, directly related to worker safety or health.

(b) For greater certainty, the term "environmental law" does not include any statute or regulation, or provision thereof, the primary purpose of which is managing the commercial harvest or exploitation, or subsistence or aboriginal harvesting, of natural resources.

(c) The primary purpose of a particular statutory or regulatory provision for purposes of subparagraphs (a) and (b) shall be determined by reference to its primary purpose, rather than to the primary purpose of the statute or regulation of which it is part.

3. For purposes of Article 14(3). "judicial or administrative proceeding" means:

(a) a domestic judicial, quasi-judicial or administrative action pursued by the Party in a timely fashion and in accordance with its law. Such actions comprise; mediation; arbitration; the process of issuing a license, permit, or authorization; seeking an assurance of voluntary compliance or a compliance agreement; seeking sanctions or remedies in an administrative or judicial forum; and the process of issuing an administrative order; and

(b) an international dispute resolution proceeding to which the Party is party.

PART SEVEN

FINAL PROVISIONS

Article 46: Annexes

The Annexes to this Agreement constitute an integral part of the Agreement.

Article 47: Entry into Force

This Agreement shall enter into force on January 1, 1994, immediately after entry into force of the NAFTA, on an exchange of written notifications certifying the completion of necessary legal procedures.

Article 48: Amendments

1. The Parties may agree on any modification of or addition to this Agreement.

2. When so agreed, and approved in accordance with the applicable legal procedures of each Party, a modification or addition shall constitute an integral part of this Agreement.

Article 49: Accession

Any country or group of countries may accede to this Agreement subject to such terms and conditions as may be agreed between such country or countries and the Council and following approval in accordance with the applicable legal procedures of each country.

Article 50: Withdrawal

A Party may withdraw from this Agreement six months after it provides written notice of withdrawal to the other Parties. If a Party withdraws, the Agreement shall remain in force for the remaining Parties.

Article 51: Authentic Texts

The English, French, and Spanish texts of this Agreement are equally authentic.

* * *

ANNEX 34

MONETARY ENFORCEMENT ASSESSMENTS

1. For the first year after the date of entry into force of this Agreement, any monetary enforcement assessment shall be no greater than 20 million dollars (U.S.) or its equivalent in the currency of the Party complained against. Thereafter, any monetary enforcement assessment shall be no greater than .007 percent of total trade in goods between the Parties during the most recent year for which data are available.

2. In determining the amount of the assessment, the panel shall take into account:

(a) the pervasiveness and duration of the Party's persistent pattern of failure to effectively enforce its environmental law;

(b) the level of enforcement that could reasonably be expected of a Party given its resource constraints;

(c) the reasons, if any, provided by the Party for not fully implementing an action plan;

(d) efforts made by the Party to begin remedying the pattern of non-enforcement after the final report of the panel; and

(e) any other relevant factors.

3. All monetary enforcement assessments shall be paid in the currency of the Party complained against into a fund established in the name of the Commission by

the Council and shall be expended at the direction of the Council to improve or enhance the environment or environmental law enforcement in the Party complained against, consistent with its law.

ANNEX 36A

CANADIAN DOMESTIC ENFORCEMENT AND COLLECTION

1. For the purposes of this Annex, "panel determination" means:

(a) a determination by a panel under Article 34(4)(b) or 5(b) that provides that Canada shall pay a monetary enforcement assessment; and

(b) a determination by a panel under Article 34(5)(b) that provides that Canada shall fully implement an action plan where the panel:

(i) has previously established an action plan under Article 34(4)(a)(ii) or imposed a monetary enforcement assessment under Article 34(4)(b); or

(ii) has subsequently determined under Article 35 that Canada is not fully implementing an action plan.

2. Canada shall adopt and maintain procedures that provide that:

(a) subject to subparagraph (b), the Commission, at the request of a complaining Party, may in its own name file in a court of competent jurisdiction a certified copy of a panel determination;

(b) the Commission may file in court a panel determination that is a panel determination described in paragraph 1(a) only if Canada has failed to comply with the determination within 180 days of when the determination was made;

(c) when filed, the panel determination, for purposes of enforcement, shall become an order of the court;

(d) the Commission may take proceedings for enforcement of a panel determination that is made an order of the court, in that court, against the person against whom the panel determination is addressed in accordance with paragraph 6 of Annex 41;

(e) proceedings to enforce a panel determination that has been made an order of the court shall be conducted by way of summary proceedings;

(f) in proceedings to enforce a panel determination that is a panel determination described in paragraph 1(b) and that has been made an order of the court, the court shall promptly refer any question of fact or any question of interpretation of the panel determination to the panel that made the panel determination, and the decision of the panel shall be binding on the court;

(g) a panel determination that has been made an order of the court shall not be subject to domestic review or appeal; and

(h) an order made by the court in proceedings to enforce a panel determination that has been made an order of the court shall not be subject to review or appeal.

3. Where Canada is the Party complained against, the procedures adopted and maintained by Canada under this Annex shall apply and the procedures set out in Article 36 shall not apply.

4. Any change by Canada to the procedures adopted and maintained by Canada under this Annex that have the effect of undermining the provisions of this Annex shall be considered a breach of this Agreement.

ANNEX 36B

SUSPENSION OF BENEFITS

1. Where a complaining Party suspends NAFTA tariff benefits in accordance with this Agreement, the Party may increase the rates of duty on originating goods of the Party complained against to levels not to exceed the lesser of:

(a) the rate that was applicable to those goods immediately prior to the date of entry into force of the NAFTA, and

(b) the Most–Favored–Nation rate applicable to those goods on the date the Party suspends such benefits,

and such increase may be applied only for such time as is necessary to collect, through such increase, the monetary enforcement assessment.

2. In considering what tariff or other benefits to suspend pursuant to Article 36(1) or (2):

(a) a complaining Party shall first seek to suspend benefits in the same sector or sectors as that in respect of which there has been a persistent pattern of failure by the Party complained against to effectively enforce its environmental law; and

(b) a complaining Party that considers it is not practicable or effective to suspend benefits in the same sector or sectors may suspend benefits in other sectors.

ANNEX 41

EXTENT OF OBLIGATIONS

1. On the date of signature of this Agreement, or of the exchange of written notifications under Article 47, Canada shall set out in a declaration a list of any provinces for which Canada is to be bound in respect of matters within their jurisdiction. The declaration shall be effective on delivery to the other Parties, and shall carry no implication as to the internal distribution of powers within Canada. Canada shall notify the other Parties six months in advance of any modification to its declaration.

2. When considering whether to instruct the Secretariat to prepare a factual record pursuant to Article 15, the Council shall take into account whether the submission was made by a non-governmental organization or enterprise incorporated or otherwise organized under the laws of a province included in the declaration made under paragraph 1.

3. Canada may not request consultations under Article 22 or a Council meeting under Article 23 or request the establishment of a panel or join as a complaining Party under Article 24 against another Party at the instance, or primarily for the benefit, of any government of a province not included in the declaration made under paragraph 1.

4. Canada may not request a Council meeting under Article 23, or request the establishment of a panel or join as a complaining Party under Article 24 concerning whether there has been a persistent pattern of failure by another Party to effectively enforce its environmental law, unless Canada states in writing that the matter would be under federal jurisdiction if it were to arise within the territory of Canada, or:

(a) Canada states in writing that the matter would be under provincial jurisdiction if it were to arise within the territory of Canada; and

(b) the provinces included in the declaration account for at least 55 percent of Canada's Gross Domestic Product (GDP) for the most recent year in which data are available, and

(c) where the matter concerns a specific industry or sector, at least 55 percent of total Canadian production in that industry or sector is accounted for by the provinces included in the declaration for the most recent year in which data are available.

5. No other Party may request a Council meeting under Article 23 or request the establishment of a panel or join as a complaining Party under Article 24 concerning whether there has been a persistent failure to effectively enforce an environmental law of a province unless that province is included in the declaration made under paragraph 1 and the requirements of subparagraphs 4(b) and (c) have been met.

6. Canada shall, no later than the date on which an arbitral panel is convened pursuant to Article 24 respecting a matter within the scope of paragraph 5 of this Annex, notify in writing the complaining Parties and the Secretariat of whether any monetary enforcement assessment or action plan imposed by a panel under Article 34(4) or 34(5) against Canada shall be addressed to Her Majesty in right of Canada or Her Majesty in right of the province concerned.

7. Canada shall use its best efforts to make this Agreement applicable to as many of its provinces as possible.

8. Two years after the date of entry into force of this Agreement, the Council shall review the operation of this Annex and, in particular, shall consider whether the Parties should amend the thresholds established in paragraph 4.

ANNEX 45

COUNTRY–SPECIFIC DEFINITIONS

For purposes of this Agreement:

"territory" means:

(a) with respect to Canada, the territory to which its customs laws apply, including any areas beyond the territorial seas of Canada within which, in accordance with international law and its domestic law, Canada may exercise rights with respect to the seabed and subsoil and their natural resources;

(b) with respect to Mexico,

(i) the states of the Federation and the Federal District,

(ii) the islands, including the reefs and keys, in adjacent seas,

(iii) the islands of Guadalupe and Revillagigedo situated in the Pacific Ocean,

(iv) the continental shelf and the submarine shelf of such islands, keys and reefs,

(v) the waters of the territorial seas, in accordance with international law, and its interior maritime waters,

(vi) the space located above the national territory, in accordance with international law, and

(vii) any areas beyond the territorial seas of Mexico within which, in accordance with international law, including the United Nations Convention on the Law of the Sea, and its domestic law, Mexico may exercise rights with respect to the seabed and subsoil and their natural resources; and

(c) with respect to the United States.

(i) the customs territory of the United States, which includes the 50 states, the District of Columbia and Puerto Rico,

(ii) the foreign trade zones located in the United States and Puerto Rico, and

(iii) any areas beyond the territorial seas of the United States within which, in accordance with international law and its domestic law, the United States may exercise rights with respect to the seabed and subsoil and their natural resources.

7.5 Marrakesh Ministerial Decision on Trade and Environment. Adopted by the Trade Negotiations Committee of the Uruguay Round of Multilateral Trade Negotiations at Marrakesh, 14 April 1994. MTN/TNC/W/141; *reprinted in* 33 I.L.M. 1267 (1994)

TRADE AND ENVIRONMENT

Decision of 14 April 1994

Ministers, meeting on the occasion of signing the Final Act embodying the results of the Uruguay Round of Multilateral Trade Negotiations at Marrakesh on 15 April 1994,

Recalling the preamble of the Agreement establishing the World Trade Organization (WTO), which states that members' "relations in the field of trade and economic endeavour should be conducted with a view to raising standards of living, ensuring full employment and a large and steadily growing volume of real income and effective demand, and expanding the production of and trade in goods and services, while allowing for the optimal use of the world's resources in accordance with the objective of sustainable development, seeking both to protect and preserve the environment and to enhance the means for doing so in a manner consistent with their respective needs and concerns at different levels of economic development,"

Noting:

—the Rio Declaration on Environment and Development, Agenda 21, and its follow-up in GATT, as reflected in the statement of the Chairman of the Council of Representatives to the CONTRACTING PARTIES at their 48th Session in December 1992, as well as the work of the Group on Environmental Measures and International Trade, the Committee on Trade and Development, and the Council of Representatives;

—the work programme envisaged in the Decision on Trade in Services and the Environment; and

—the relevant provisions of the Agreement on Trade–Related Aspects of Intellectual Property Rights,

Considering that there should not be, nor need be, any policy contradiction between upholding and safeguarding an open, non-discriminatory and equitable multilateral trading system on the one hand, and acting for the protection of the environment, and the promotion of sustainable development on the other,

Desiring to coordinate the policies in the field of trade and environment, and this without exceeding the competence of the multilateral trading system, which is limited to trade policies and those trade-related aspects of environmental policies which may result in significant trade effects for its members,

Decide:

—to direct the first meeting of the General Council of the WTO to establish a Committee on Trade and Environment open to all members of the WTO to report to the first biennial meeting of the Ministerial Conference after the entry into force of the WTO when the work and terms of reference of the Committee will be reviewed, in the light of recommendations of the Committee,

—that the TNC Decision of 15 December 1993 which reads, in part, as follows:

"(a) to identify the relationship between trade measures and environmental measures, in order to promote sustainable development;

(b) to make appropriate recommendations on whether any modifications of the provisions of the multilateral trading system are required, compatible with the open, equitable and non-discriminatory nature of the system, as regards, in particular:

—the need for rules to enhance positive interaction between trade and environmental measures, for the promotion of sustainable development, with special consideration to the needs of developing countries, in particular those of the least developed among them; and

—the avoidance of protectionist trade measures, and the adherence to effective multilateral disciplines to ensure responsiveness of the multilateral trading system to environmental objectives set forth in Agenda 21 and the Rio Declaration, in particular Principle 12; and

—surveillance of trade measures used for environmental purposes, of trade-related aspects of environmental measures which have significant trade effects, and of effective implementation of the multilateral disciplines governing those measures;"

constitutes, along with the preambular language above, the terms of reference of the Committee on Trade and Environment,

—that, within these terms of reference, and with the aim of making international trade and environmental policies mutually supportive, the Committee will initially address the following matters, in relation to which any relevant issue may be raised:

—the relationship between the provisions of the multilateral trading system and trade measures for environmental purposes, including those pursuant to multilateral environmental agreements;

—the relationship between environmental policies relevant to trade and environmental measures with significant trade effects and the provisions of the multilateral trading system;

—the relationship between the provisions of the multilateral trading system and:

(a) charges and taxes for environmental purposes

(b) requirements for environmental purposes relating to products, including standards and technical regulations, packaging, labelling and recycling;

—the provisions of the multilateral trading system with respect to the transparency of trade measures used for environmental purposes and environmental measures and requirements which have significant trade effects;

—the relationship between the dispute settlement mechanisms in the multilateral trading system and those found in multilateral environmental agreements;

—the effect of environmental measures on market access, especially in relation to developing countries, in particular to the least developed among them, and environmental benefits of removing trade restrictions and distortions;

—the issue of exports of domestically prohibited goods,

—that the Committee on Trade and Environment will consider the work programme envisaged in the Decision on Trade in Services and the Environment and the relevant provisions of the Agreement on Trade-Related Aspects of Intellectual Property Rights as an integral part of its work, within the above terms of reference,

—that, pending the first meeting of the General Council of the WTO, the work of the Committee on Trade and Environment should be carried out by a Sub-Committee of the Preparatory Committee of the World Trade Organization (PCWTO), open to all members of the PCWTO,

—to invite the Sub–Committee of the Preparatory Committee, and the Committee on Trade and Environment when it is established, to provide input to the relevant bodies in respect of appropriate arrangements for relations with inter-governmental and non-governmental organizations referred to in Article V of the WTO.

7.6 Agreement Establishing the World Trade Organization. Adopted on 15 April 1994. Entered into force, 1 January 1995. *Reprinted in* 33 I.L.M. 1125 (1994) & 4 Weston IV.C.2A: *Preamble, Articles II, III:3, IV:2,3*

The *Parties* to this Agreement,

Recognizing that their relations in the field of trade and economic endeavour should be conducted with a view to raising standards of living, ensuring full employment and a large and steadily growing volume of real income and effective demand, and expanding the production of and trade in goods and services, while allowing for the optimal use of the world's resources in accordance with the objective of sustainable development, seeking both to protect and preserve the environment and to enhance the means for doing so in a manner consistent with their respective needs and concerns at different levels of economic development,

Recognizing further that there is need for positive efforts designed to ensure that developing countries, and especially the least developed among them, secure a share in the growth in international trade commensurate with the needs of their economic development,

Being desirous of contributing to these objectives by entering into reciprocal and mutually advantageous arrangements directed to the substantial reduction of tariffs and other barriers to trade and to the elimination of discriminatory treatment in international trade relations,

Resolved, therefore, to develop an integrated, more viable and durable multilateral trading system encompassing the General Agreement on Tariffs and Trade, the results of past trade liberalization efforts, and all of the results of the Uruguay Round of Multilateral Trade Negotiations,

Determined to preserve the basic principles and to further the objectives underlying this multilateral trading system,

Agree as follows:

* * *

Article II

Scope of the WTO

1. The WTO shall provide the common institutional framework for the conduct of trade relations among its Members in matters related to the agreements and associated legal instruments included in the Annexes to this Agreement.

2. The agreements and associated legal instruments included in Annexes 1, 2 and 3 (hereinafter referred to as "Multilateral Trade Agreements") are integral parts of this Agreement, binding on all Members.

3. The agreements and associated legal instruments included in Annex 4 (hereinafter referred to as "Plurilateral Trade Agreements") are also part of this Agreement for those Members that have accepted them, and are binding on those Members. The Plurilateral Trade Agreements do not create either obligations or rights for Members that have not accepted them.

4. The General Agreement on Tariffs and Trade 1994 as specified in Annex 1A (hereinafter referred to as "GATT 1994") is legally distinct from the General Agreement on Tariffs and Trade, dated 30 October 1947, annexed to the Final Act Adopted at the Conclusion of the Second Session of the Preparatory Committee of the United Nations Conference on Trade and Employment, as subsequently rectified, amended or modified (hereinafter referred to as "GATT 1947").

Article III

Functions of the WTO

* * *

3. The WTO shall administer the Understanding on Rules and Procedures Governing the Settlement of Disputes (hereinafter referred to as the "Dispute Settlement Understanding" or "DSU") in Annex 2 to this Agreement.

* * *

Article IV

Structure of the WTO

* * *

2. There shall be a General Council composed of representatives of all the Members, which shall meet as appropriate. In the intervals between meetings of the Ministerial Conference, its functions shall be conducted by the General Council. The General Council shall also carry out the functions assigned to it by this Agreement. The General Council shall establish its rules of procedure and approve the rules of procedure for the Committees provided for in paragraph 7.

3. The General Council shall convene as appropriate to discharge the responsibilities of the Dispute Settlement Body provided for in the Dispute Settlement Understanding. The Dispute Settlement Body may have its own chairman and shall establish such rules of procedure as it deems necessary for the fulfilment of those responsibilities.

* * *

7.7 Agreement on Technical Barriers to Trade. Concluded at Marrakesh, 15 April 1994. Entered into force, 1 January 1995. Marrakesh Agreement Establishing the World Trade Organization, Annex 1A. *Reprinted in* Uruguay Round Trade Agreements, Text of Agreements, Implementing Bill, H.R. Doc. No. 103–316, Vol.1, 103d Cong., 2d Sess. 1427 & 33 I.L.M. 81 (1994)

Members,

Having regard to the Uruguay Round of Multilateral Trade Negotiations;

Desiring to further the objectives of GATT 1994;

Recognizing the important contribution that international standards and conformity assessment systems can make in this regard by improving efficiency of production and facilitating the conduct of international trade;

Desiring therefore to encourage the development of such international standards and conformity assessment systems;

Desiring however to ensure that technical regulations and standards, including packaging, marking and labelling requirements, and procedures for assessment of conformity with technical regulations and standards do not create unnecessary obstacles to international trade;

Recognizing that no country should be prevented from taking measures necessary to ensure the quality of its exports, or for the protection of human, animal or plant life or health, of the environment, or for the prevention of deceptive practices, at the levels it considers appropriate, subject to the requirement that they are not applied in a manner which would constitute a means of arbitrary or unjustifiable discrimination between countries where the same conditions prevail or a disguised restriction on international trade, and are otherwise in accordance with the provisions of this Agreement;

Recognizing that no country should be prevented from taking measures necessary for the protection of its essential security interest;

Recognizing the contribution which international standardization can make to the transfer of technology from developed to developing countries;

Recognizing that developing countries may encounter special difficulties in the formulation and application of technical regulations and standards and procedures for assessment of conformity with technical regulations and standards, and desiring to assist them in their endeavours in this regard;

Hereby agree as follows:

Article 1

General Provisions

1.1 General terms for standardization and procedures for assessment of conformity shall normally have the meaning given to them by definitions adopted within the United Nations system and by international standardizing bodies taking into account their context and in the light of the object and purpose of this Agreement.

1.2 However, for the purposes of this Agreement the meaning of the terms given in Annex 1 applies.

1.3 All products, including industrial and agricultural products, shall be subject to the provisions of this Agreement.

1.4 Purchasing specifications prepared by governmental bodies for production or consumption requirements of governmental bodies are not subject to the provisions of this Agreement but are addressed in the Agreement on Government Procurement, according to its coverage.

1.5 The provisions of this Agreement do not apply to sanitary and phytosanitary measures as defined in Annex A of the Agreement on the Application of Sanitary and Phytosanitary Measures.

1.6 All references in this Agreement to technical regulations, standards and conformity assessment procedures shall be construed to include any amendments thereto and any additions to the rules or the product coverage thereof, except amendments and additions of an insignificant nature.

TECHNICAL REGULATIONS AND STANDARDS

Article 2

Preparation, Adoption and Application of Technical Regulations by Central Government Bodies

With respect to their central government bodies:

2.1 Members shall ensure that in respect of technical regulations, products imported from the territory of any Member shall be accorded treatment no less favourable than that accorded to like products of national origin and to like products originating in any other country.

2.2 Members shall ensure that technical regulations are not prepared, adopted or applied with a view to or with the effect of creating unnecessary obstacles to international trade. For this purpose, technical regulations shall not be more trade-restrictive than necessary to fulfil a legitimate objective, taking account of the risks non-fulfilment would create. Such legitimate objectives are, inter alia: national security requirements; the prevention of deceptive practices; protection of human health or safety, animal or plant life or health, or the environment. In assessing such risks, relevant elements of consideration are, inter alia: available scientific and technical information, related processing technology or intended end-uses of products.

2.3 Technical regulations shall not be maintained if the circumstances or objectives giving rise to their adoption no longer exist or if the changed circumstances or objectives can be addressed in a less trade-restrictive manner.

2.4 Where technical regulations are required and relevant international standards exist or their completion is imminent, Members shall use them, or the relevant parts of them, as a basis for their technical regulations except when such international standards or relevant parts would be an ineffective or inappropriate means for the fulfilment of the legitimate objectives pursued, for instance because of fundamental climatic or geographical factors or fundamental technological problems.

2.5 A Member preparing, adopting or applying a technical regulation which may have a significant effect on trade of other Members shall, upon the request of another Member, explain the justification for that technical regulation in terms of the provisions of paragraphs 2 to 4. Whenever a technical regulation is prepared, adopted or applied for one of the legitimate objectives explicitly mentioned in paragraph 2, and is in accordance with relevant international standards, it shall be rebuttably presumed not to create an unnecessary obstacle to international trade.

2.6 With a view to harmonizing technical regulations on as wide a basis as possible, Members shall play a full part, within the limits of their resources, in the preparation by appropriate international standardizing bodies of international standards for products for which they either have adopted, or expect to adopt, technical regulations.

2.7 Members shall give positive consideration to accepting as equivalent technical regulations of other Members, even if these regulations differ from their own, provided they are satisfied that these regulations adequately fulfil the objectives of their own regulations.

2.8 Wherever appropriate, Members shall specify technical regulations based on product requirements in terms of performance rather than design or descriptive characteristics.

2.9 Whenever a relevant international standard does not exist or the technical content of a proposed technical regulation is not in accordance with the technical content of relevant international standards, and if the technical regulation may have a significant effect on trade of other Members, Members shall:

2.9.1 publish a notice in a publication at an early appropriate stage, in such a manner as to enable interested parties in other Members to become acquainted with it, that they propose to introduce a particular technical regulation;

2.9.2 notify other Members through the Secretariat of the products to be covered by the proposed technical regulation, together with a brief indication of its objective and rationale. Such notifications shall take place at an early appropriate stage, when amendments can still be introduced and comments taken into account;

2.9.3 upon request, provide to other Members particulars or copies of the proposed technical regulation and, whenever possible, identify the parts which in substance deviate from relevant international standards;

2.9.4 without discrimination, allow reasonable time for other Members to make comments in writing, discuss these comments upon request, and take these written comments and the results of these discussions into account.

2.10 Subject to the provisions in the lead-in to paragraph 9, where urgent problems of safety, health, environmental protection or national security arise or threaten to arise for a Member, that Member may omit such of the steps enumerated in paragraph 9 as it finds necessary, provided that the Member, upon adoption of a technical regulation, shall:

2.10.1 notify immediately other Members through the Secretariat of the particular technical regulation and the products covered, with a brief indication of the objective and the rationale of the technical regulation, including the nature of the urgent problems;

2.10.2 upon request, provide other Members with copies of the technical regulation;

2.10.3 without discrimination, allow other Members to present their comments in writing, discuss these comments upon request, and take these written comments and the results of these discussions into account.

2.11 Members shall ensure that all technical regulations which have been adopted are published promptly or otherwise made available in such a manner as to enable interested parties in other Members to become acquainted with them.

2.12 Except in those urgent circumstances referred to in paragraph 10, Members shall allow a reasonable interval between the publication of technical regulations and their entry into force in order to allow time for producers in exporting Members, and particularly in developing country Members, to adapt their products or methods of production to the requirements of the importing Member.

Article 3

Preparation, Adoption and Application of Technical Regulations by Local Government Bodies and Non-Governmental Bodies

With respect to their local government and non-governmental bodies within their territories:

3.1 Members shall take such reasonable measures as may be available to them to ensure compliance by such bodies with the provisions of Article 2, with the exception of the obligation to notify as referred to in paragraphs 9.2 and 10.1 of Article 2.

3.2 Members shall ensure that the technical regulations of local governments on the level directly below that of the central government in Members are notified in accordance with the provisions of paragraphs 9.2 and 10.1 of Article 2, noting that notification shall not be required for technical regulations the technical content of which is substantially the same as that of previously notified technical regulations of central government bodies of the Member concerned.

3.3 Members may require contact with other Members, including the notifications, provision of information, comments and discussions referred to in paragraphs 9 and 10 of Article 2, to take place through the central government.

3.4 Members shall not take measures which require or encourage local government bodies or non-governmental bodies within their territories to act in a manner inconsistent with the provisions of Article 2.

3.5 Members are fully responsible under this Agreement for the observance of all provisions of Article 2. Members shall formulate and implement positive measures and mechanisms in support of the observance of the provisions of Article 2 by other than central government bodies.

Article 4

Preparation, Adoption and Application of Standards

4.1 Members shall ensure that their central government standardizing bodies accept and comply with the Code of Good Practice for the Preparation, Adoption and Application of Standards in Annex 3 to this Agreement (referred to in this Agreement as the "Code of Good Practice"). They shall take such reasonable measures as may be available to them to ensure that local government and non-governmental standardizing bodies within their territories, as well as regional standardizing bodies of which they or one or more bodies within their territories are members, accept and comply with this Code of Good Practice. In addition, Members shall not take measures which have the effect of, directly or indirectly, requiring or encouraging such standardizing bodies to act in a manner inconsistent with the Code of Good Practice. The obligations of Members with respect to compliance of standardizing bodies with the provisions of the Code of Good Practice shall apply irrespective of whether or not a standardizing body has accepted the Code of Good Practice.

4.2 Standardizing bodies that have accepted and are complying with the Code of Good Practice shall be acknowledged by the Members as complying with the principles of this Agreement.

CONFORMITY WITH TECHNICAL REGULATIONS AND STANDARDS

Article 5

Procedures for Assessment of Conformity by Central Government Bodies

5.1 Members shall ensure that, in cases where a positive assurance of conformity with technical regulations or standards is required, their central government bodies apply the following provisions to products originating in the territories of other Members:

5.1.1 conformity assessment procedures are prepared, adopted and applied so as to grant access for suppliers of like products originating in the territories of other Members under conditions no less favourable than those accorded to suppliers of like products of national origin or originating in any other country, in a comparable situation; access entails suppliers' right to an assessment of conformity under the rules of the procedure, including, when foreseen by this procedure, the possibility to have conformity assessment activities undertaken at the site of facilities and to receive the mark of the system;

5.1.2 conformity assessment procedures are not prepared, adopted or applied with a view to or with the effect of creating unnecessary obstacles to international trade. This means, inter alia, that conformity assessment procedures shall not be more strict or be applied more strictly than is necessary to give the importing Member adequate confidence that products conform with the applicable technical regulations or standards, taking account of the risks non-conformity would create.

5.2 When implementing the provisions of paragraph 1, Members shall ensure that:

5.2.1 conformity assessment procedures are undertaken and completed as expeditiously as possible and in a no less favourable order for products originating in the territories of other Members than for like domestic products;

5.2.2 the standard processing period of each conformity assessment procedure is published or that the anticipated processing period is communicated to the applicant upon request; when receiving an application, the competent body promptly examines the completeness of the documentation and informs the applicant in a precise and complete manner of all deficiencies; the competent body transmits as soon as possible the results of the assessment in a precise and complete manner to the applicant so that corrective action may be taken if necessary; even when the application has deficiencies, the competent body proceeds as far as practicable with the conformity assessment if the applicant so requests; and that, upon request, the applicant is informed of the stage of the procedure, with any delay being explained;

5.2.3 information requirements are limited to what is necessary to assess conformity and determine fees;

5.2.4 the confidentiality of information about products originating in the territories of other Members arising from or supplied in connection with such conformity assessment procedures is respected in the same way as for domestic products and in such a manner that legitimate commercial interests are protected;

5.2.5 any fees imposed for assessing the conformity of products originating in the territories of other Members are equitable in relation to any fees chargeable for assessing the conformity of like products of national origin or originating in any other country, taking into account communication, transportation and other costs arising from differences between location of facilities of the applicant and the conformity assessment body;

5.2.6 the siting of facilities used in conformity assessment procedures and the selection of samples are not such as to cause unnecessary inconvenience to applicants or their agents;

5.2.7 whenever specifications of a product are changed subsequent to the determination of its conformity to the applicable technical regulations or standards, the conformity assessment procedure for the modified product is limited to what is necessary to determine whether adequate confidence exists that the product still meets the technical regulations or standards concerned;

5.2.8 a procedure exists to review complaints concerning the operation of a conformity assessment procedure and to take corrective action when a complaint is justified.

5.3 Nothing in paragraphs 1 and 2 shall prevent Members from carrying out reasonable spot checks within their territories.

5.4 In cases where a positive assurance is required that products conform with technical regulations or standards, and relevant guides or recommendations issued by international standardizing bodies exist or their completion is imminent, Members shall ensure that central government bodies use them, or the relevant parts of them, as a basis for their conformity assessment procedures, except where, as duly explained upon request, such guides or recommendations or relevant parts are inappropriate for the Members concerned, for, inter alia, such reasons as: national security requirements; the prevention of deceptive practices; protection of human health or safety, animal or plant life or health, or the environment; fundamental climatic or other geographical factors; fundamental technological or infrastructural problems.

5.5 With a view to harmonizing conformity assessment procedures on as wide a basis as possible, Members shall play a full part, within the limits of their resources, in the preparation by appropriate international standardizing bodies of guides and recommendations for conformity assessment procedures.

5.6 Whenever a relevant guide or recommendation issued by an international standardizing body does not exist or the technical content of a proposed conformity assessment procedure is not in accordance with relevant guides and recommendations issued by international standardizing bodies, and if the conformity assessment procedure may have a significant effect on trade of other Members, Members shall:

5.6.1 publish a notice in a publication at an early appropriate stage, in such a manner as to enable interested parties in other Members to become acquainted with it, that they propose to introduce a particular conformity assessment procedure;

5.6.2 notify other Members through the Secretariat of the products to be covered by the proposed conformity assessment procedure, together with a brief indication of its objective and rationale. Such notifications shall take place at an early appropriate stage, when amendments can still be introduced and comments taken into account;

5.6.3 upon request, provide to other Members particulars or copies of the proposed procedure and, whenever possible, identify the parts which in substance deviate from relevant guides or recommendations issued by international standardizing bodies;

5.6.4 without discrimination, allow reasonable time for other Members to make comments in writing, discuss these comments upon request, and take these written comments and the results of these discussions into account.

5.7 Subject to the provisions in the lead-in to paragraph 6, where urgent problems of safety, health, environmental protection or national security arise or threaten to arise for a Member, that Member may omit such of the steps enumerated in paragraph 6 as it finds necessary, provided that the Member, upon adoption of the procedure, shall:

5.7.1 notify immediately other Members through the Secretariat of the particular procedure and the products covered, with a brief indication of the objective and the rationale of the procedure, including the nature of the urgent problems;

5.7.2 upon request, provide other Members with copies of the rules of the procedure;

5.7.3 without discrimination, allow other Members to present their comments in writing, discuss these comments upon request, and take these written comments and the results of these discussions into account.

5.8 Members shall ensure that all conformity assessment procedures which have been adopted are published promptly or otherwise made available in such a manner as to enable interested parties in other Members to become acquainted with them.

5.9 Except in those urgent circumstances referred to in paragraph 7, Members shall allow a reasonable interval between the publication of requirements concerning conformity assessment procedures and their entry into force in order to allow time for producers in exporting Members, and particularly in developing country Members, to adapt their products or methods of production to the requirements of the importing Member.

Article 6

Recognition of Conformity Assessment by Central Government Bodies

With respect to their central government bodies:

6.1 Without prejudice to the provisions of paragraphs 3 and 4, Members shall ensure, whenever possible, that results of conformity assessment procedures in other Members are accepted, even when those procedures differ from their own, provided they are satisfied that those procedures offer an assurance of conformity with applicable technical regulations or standards equivalent to their own procedures. It is recognized that prior consultations may be necessary in order to arrive at a mutually satisfactory understanding regarding, in particular:

6.1.1 adequate and enduring technical competence of the relevant conformity assessment bodies in the exporting Member, so that confidence in the continued reliability of their conformity assessment results can exist; in this regard, verified compliance, for instance through accreditation, with relevant guides or recommendations issued by international standardizing bodies shall be taken into account as an indication of adequate technical competence;

6.1.2 limitation of the acceptance of conformity assessment results to those produced by designated bodies in the exporting Member.

6.2 Members shall ensure that their conformity assessment procedures permit, as far as practicable, the implementation of the provisions in paragraph 1.

6.3 Members are encouraged, at the request of other Members, to be willing to enter into negotiations for the conclusion of agreements for the mutual recognition of results of each other's conformity assessment procedures. Members may require that such agreements fulfil the criteria of paragraph 1 and give mutual satisfaction regarding their potential for facilitating trade in the products concerned.

6.4 Members are encouraged to permit participation of conformity assessment bodies located in the territories of other Members in their conformity assessment procedures under conditions no less favourable than those accorded to bodies located within their territory or the territory of any other country.

Article 7

Procedures for Assessment of Conformity by Local Government Bodies

With respect to their local government bodies within their territories:

7.1 Members shall take such reasonable measures as may be available to them to ensure compliance by such bodies with the provisions of Articles 5 and 6, with the exception of the obligation to notify as referred to in paragraphs 6.2 and 7.1 of Article 5.

7.2 Members shall ensure that the conformity assessment procedures of local governments on the level directly below that of the central government in Members are notified in accordance with the provisions of paragraphs 6.2 and 7.1 of Article 5, noting that notifications shall not be required for conformity assessment procedures the technical content of which is substantially the same as that of previously notified conformity assessment procedures of central government bodies of the Members concerned.

7.3 Members may require contact with other Members, including the notifications, provision of information, comments and discussions referred to in paragraphs 6 and 7 of Article 5, to take place through the central government.

7.4 Members shall not take measures which require or encourage local government bodies within their territories to act in a manner inconsistent with the provisions of Articles 5 and 6.

7.5 Members are fully responsible under this Agreement for the observance of all provisions of Articles 5 and 6. Members shall formulate and implement positive measures and mechanisms in support of the observance of the provisions of Articles 5 and 6 by other than central government bodies.

Article 8

Procedures for Assessment of Conformity by Non–Governmental Bodies

8.1 Members shall take such reasonable measures as may be available to them to ensure that non-governmental bodies within their territories which operate conformity assessment procedures comply with the provisions of Articles 5 and 6, with the exception of the obligation to notify proposed conformity assessment procedures. In addition, Members shall not take measures which have the effect of, directly or indirectly, requiring or encouraging such bodies to act in a manner inconsistent with the provisions of Articles 5 and 6.

8.2 Members shall ensure that their central government bodies rely on conformity assessment procedures operated by non-governmental bodies only if these latter bodies comply with the provisions of Articles 5 and 6, with the exception of the obligation to notify proposed conformity assessment procedures.

Article 9

International and Regional Systems

9.1 Where a positive assurance of conformity with a technical regulation or standard is required, Members shall, wherever practicable, formulate and adopt international systems for conformity assessment and become members thereof or participate therein.

9.2 Members shall take such reasonable measures as may be available to them to ensure that international and regional systems for conformity assessment in which relevant bodies within their territories are members or participants comply with the provisions of Articles 5 and 6. In addition, Members shall not take any measures which have the effect of, directly or indirectly, requiring or encouraging such systems to act in a manner inconsistent with any of the provisions of Articles 5 and 6.

9.3 Members shall ensure that their central government bodies rely on international or regional conformity assessment systems only to the extent that these systems comply with the provisions of Articles 5 and 6, as applicable.

INFORMATION AND ASSISTANCE

Article 10

Information About Technical Regulations, Standards and Conformity Assessment Procedures

10.1 Each Member shall ensure that an enquiry point exists which is able to answer all reasonable enquiries from other Members and interested parties in other Members as well as to provide the relevant documents regarding:

10.1.1 any technical regulations adopted or proposed within its territory by central or local government bodies, by non-governmental bodies which have legal power to enforce a technical regulation, or by regional standardizing bodies of which such bodies are members or participants;

10.1.2 any standards adopted or proposed within its territory by central or local government bodies, or by regional standardizing bodies of which such bodies are members or participants;

10.1.3 any conformity assessment procedures, or proposed conformity assessment procedures, which are operated within its territory by central or local government bodies, or by non-governmental bodies which have legal power to enforce a technical regulation, or by regional bodies of which such bodies are members or participants;

10.1.4 the membership and participation of the Member, or of relevant central or local government bodies within its territory, in international and regional standardizing bodies and conformity assessment systems, as well as in bilateral and multilateral arrangements within the scope of this Agreement; it shall also be able to provide reasonable information on the provisions of such systems and arrangements;

10.1.5 the location of notices published pursuant to this Agreement, or the provision of information as to where such information can be obtained; and

10.1.6 the location of the enquiry points mentioned in paragraph 3.

10.2 If, however, for legal or administrative reasons more than one enquiry point is established by a Member, that Member shall provide to the other Members complete and unambiguous information on the scope of responsibility of each of these enquiry points. In addition, that Member shall ensure that any enquiries addressed to an incorrect enquiry point shall promptly be conveyed to the correct enquiry point.

10.3 Each Member shall take such reasonable measures as may be available to it to ensure that one or more enquiry points exist which are able to answer all reasonable enquiries from other Members and interested parties in other Members as well as to provide the relevant documents or information as to where they can be obtained regarding:

10.3.1 any standards adopted or proposed within its territory by non-governmental standardizing bodies, or by regional standardizing bodies of which such bodies are members or participants; and

10.3.2 any conformity assessment procedures, or proposed conformity assessment procedures, which are operated within its territory by non-governmental bodies, or by regional bodies of which such bodies are members or participants;

10.3.3 the membership and participation of relevant non-governmental bodies within its territory in international and regional standardizing bodies and conformity assessment systems, as well as in bilateral and multilateral arrangements within the scope of this Agreement; they shall also be able to provide reasonable information on the provisions of such systems and arrangements.

10.4 Members shall take such reasonable measures as may be available to them to ensure that where copies of documents are requested by other Members or by interested parties in other Members, in accordance with the provisions of this Agreement, they are supplied at an equitable price (if any) which shall, apart from the real cost of delivery, be the same for the nationals of the Member concerned or of any other Member.

10.5 Developed country Members shall, if requested by other Members, provide, in English, French or Spanish, translations of the documents covered by a specific notification or, in case of voluminous documents, of summaries of such documents.

10.6 The Secretariat shall, when it receives notifications in accordance with the provisions of this Agreement, circulate copies of the notifications to all Members and interested international standardizing and conformity assessment bodies, and draw the attention of developing country Members to any notifications relating to products of particular interest to them.

10.7 Whenever a Member has reached an agreement with any other country or countries on issues related to technical regulations, standards or conformity assessment procedures which may have a significant effect on trade, at least one Member party to the agreement shall notify other Members through the Secretariat of the products to be covered by the agreement and include a brief description of the agreement. Members concerned are encouraged to enter, upon request, into consultations with other Members for the purposes of concluding similar agreements or of arranging for their participation in such agreements.

10.8 Nothing in this Agreement shall be construed as requiring:

10.8.1 the publication of texts other than in the language of the Member;

10.8.2 the provision of paniculars or copies of drafts other than in the language of the Member except as stated in paragraph 5; or

10.8.3 Members to furnish any information, the disclosure of which they consider contrary to their essential security interests.

10.9 Notifications to the Secretariat shall be in English, French or Spanish.

10.10 Members shall designate a single central government authority that is responsible for the implementation on the national level of the provisions concerning notification procedures under this Agreement except those included in Annex 3.

10.11 If, however, for legal or administrative reasons the responsibility for notification procedures is divided among two or more central government authorities, the Member concerned shall provide to the other Members complete and unambiguous information on the scope of responsibility of each of these authorities.

Article 11

Technical Assistance to Other Members

11.1 Members shall, if requested, advise other Members, especially the developing country Members, on the preparation of technical regulations.

11.2 Members shall, if requested, advise other Members, especially the developing country Members, and shall grant them technical assistance on mutually agreed terms and conditions regarding the establishment of national standardizing bodies, and participation in the international standardizing bodies, and shall encourage their national standardizing bodies to do likewise.

11.3 Members shall, if requested, take such reasonable measures as may be available to them to arrange for the regulatory bodies within their territories to advise other Members, especially the developing country Members, and shall grant them technical assistance on mutually agreed terms and conditions regarding:

11.3.1 the establishment of regulatory bodies, or bodies for the assessment of conformity with technical regulations; and

11.3.2 the methods by which their technical regulations can best be met.

11.4 Members shall, if requested, take such reasonable measures as may be available to them to arrange for advice to be given to other Members, especially the developing country Members, and shall grant them technical assistance on mutually agreed terms and conditions regarding the establishment of bodies for the assessment of conformity with standards adopted within the territory of the requesting Member.

11.5 Members shall, if requested, advise other Members, especially the developing country Members, and shall grant them technical assistance on mutually agreed terms and conditions regarding the steps that should be taken by their producers if they wish to have access to systems for conformity assessment operated by governmental or non-governmental bodies within the territory of the Member receiving the request.

11.6 Members which are members or participants of international or regional systems for conformity assessment shall, if requested, advise other Members, especially the developing country Members, and shall grant them technical assistance on mutually agreed terms and conditions regarding the establishment of the institutions and legal framework which would enable them to fulfil the obligations of membership or participation in such systems.

11.7 Members shall, if so requested, encourage bodies within their territories which are members or participants of international or regional systems for conformity assessment to advise other Members, especially the developing country Members, and should consider requests for technical assistance from them regarding the establishment of the institutions which would enable the relevant bodies within their territories to fulfil the obligations of membership or participation.

11.8 In providing advice and technical assistance to other Members in terms of paragraphs 1 to 7, Members shall give priority to the needs of the least-developed country Members.

Article 12

Special and Differential Treatment of Developing Country Members

12.1 Members shall provide differential and more favourable treatment to developing country Members to this Agreement, through the following provisions as well as through the relevant provisions of other Articles of this Agreement.

12.2 Members shall give particular attention to the provisions of this Agreement concerning developing country Members' rights and obligations and shall take into account the special development, financial and trade needs of developing country Members in the implementation of this Agreement, both nationally and in the operation of this Agreement's institutional arrangements.

12.3 Members shall, in the preparation and application of technical regulations, standards and conformity assessment procedures, take account of the special development, financial and trade needs of developing country Members, with a view to ensuring that such technical regulations, standards and conformity assessment procedures do not create unnecessary obstacles to exports from developing country Members.

12.4 Members recognize that, although international standards, guides or recommendations may exist, in their particular technological and socio-economic conditions, developing country Members adopt certain technical regulations, standards or conformity assessment procedures aimed at preserving indigenous technology and production methods and processes compatible with their development needs. Members therefore recognize that developing country Members should not be expected to use international standards as a basis for their technical regulations or standards, including test methods, which are not appropriate to their development, financial and trade needs.

12.5 Members shall take such reasonable measures as may be available to them to ensure that international standardizing bodies and international systems for conformity assessment are organized and operated in a way which facilitates active and representative participation of relevant bodies in all Members, taking into account the special problems of developing country Members.

12.6 Members shall take such reasonable measures as may be available to them to ensure that international standardizing bodies, upon request of developing country Members, examine the possibility of, and, if practicable, prepare international standards concerning products of special interest to developing country Members.

12.7 Members shall, in accordance with the provisions of Article 11, provide technical assistance to developing country Members to ensure that the preparation and application of technical regulations, standards and conformity assessment procedures do not create unnecessary obstacles to the expansion and diversification of exports from developing country Members. In determining the terms and conditions of the technical assistance, account shall be taken of the stage of development of the requesting Members and in particular of the least-developed country Members.

12.8 It is recognized that developing country Members may face special problems, including institutional and infrastructural problems, in the field of preparation and application of technical regulations, standards and conformity assessment procedures. It is further recognized that the special development and trade needs of developing country Members, as well as their stage of technological development, may hinder their ability to discharge fully their obligations under this Agreement. Members, therefore, shall take this fact fully into account. Accordingly, with a view to ensuring that developing country Members are able to comply with this Agreement, the Committee on Technical Barriers to Trade provided for in Article 13 (referred to in this Agreement as the "Committee") is enabled to grant, upon request, specified, time-limited exceptions in whole or in part from obligations under this Agreement. When considering such requests the Committee shall take into account the special problems, in the field of preparation and application of technical regulations, standards and conformity assessment procedures, and the special development and trade needs of the developing country Member, as well as its stage of technological development, which may hinder its ability to discharge fully its obligations under this Agreement. The Committee shall, in particular, take into account the special problems of the least-developed country Members.

12.9 During consultations, developed country Members shall bear in mind the special difficulties experienced by developing country Members in formulating and implementing standards and technical regulations and conformity assessment procedures, and in their desire to assist developing country Members with their efforts in this direction, developed country Members shall take account of the special needs of the former in regard to financing, trade and development.

12.10 The Committee shall examine periodically the special and differential treatment, as laid down in this Agreement, granted to developing country Members on national and international levels.

INSTITUTIONS, CONSULTATION AND DISPUTE SETTLEMENT

Article 13

The Committee on Technical Barriers to Trade

13.1 A Committee on Technical Barriers to Trade is hereby established, and shall be composed of representatives from each of the Members. The Committee shall elect its own Chairman and shall meet as necessary, but no less than once a year, for the purpose of affording Members the opportunity of consulting on any matters relating to the operation of this Agreement or the furtherance of its objectives, and shall carry out such responsibilities as assigned to it under this Agreement or by the Members.

13.2 The Committee shall establish working parties or other bodies as may be appropriate, which shall carry out such responsibilities as may be assigned to them by the Committee in accordance with the relevant provisions of this Agreement.

13.3 It is understood that unnecessary duplication should be avoided between the work under this Agreement and that of governments in other technical bodies. The Committee shall examine this problem with a view to minimizing such duplication.

Article 14

Consultation and Dispute Settlement

14.1 Consultations and the settlement of disputes with respect to any matter affecting the operation of this Agreement shall take place under the auspices of the Dispute Settlement Body and shall follow, mutatis mutandis, the provisions of Articles XXII and XXIII of GATT 1994, as elaborated and applied by the Dispute Settlement Understanding.

14.2 At the request of a party to a dispute, or at its own initiative, a panel may establish a technical expert group to assist in questions of a technical nature, requiring detailed consideration by experts.

14.3 Technical expert groups shall be governed by the procedures of Annex 2.

14.4 The dispute settlement provisions set out above can be invoked in cases where a Member considers that another Member has not achieved satisfactory results under Articles 3, 4, 7, 8 and 9 and its trade interests are significantly affected. In this respect, such results shall be equivalent to those as if the body in question were a Member.

FINAL PROVISIONS

Article 15

Final Provisions

Reservations

15.1 Reservations may not be entered in respect of any of the provisions of this Agreement without the consent of the other Members.

Review

15.2 Each Member shall, promptly after the date on which the WTO Agreement enters into force for it, inform the Committee of measures in existence or taken to ensure the implementation and administration of this Agreement. Any changes of such measures thereafter shall also be notified to the Committee.

15.3 The Committee shall review annually the implementation and operation of this Agreement taking into account the objectives thereof.

15.4 Not later than the end of the third year from the date of entry into force of the WTO Agreement and at the end of each three-year period thereafter, the Committee shall review the operation and implementation of this Agreement, including the provisions relating to transparency, with a view to recommending an adjustment of the rights and obligations of this Agreement where necessary to ensure mutual economic advantage and balance of rights and obligations, without prejudice to the provisions of Article 12. Having regard, inter alia, to the experience gained in the implementation of the Agreement, the Committee shall, where appropriate, submit proposals for amendments to the text of this Agreement to the Council for Trade in Goods.

7.8 UNDERSTANDING ON RULES AND PROCEDURES GOVERNING THE SETTLEMENT OF DISPUTES. Concluded at Marrakesh, 15 April 1994. Entered into force 1 January 1995. Marrakesh Agreement Establishing the World Trade Organization, Annex 2; *reprinted in* 33 I.L.M. 1226 (1994) & 4 Weston IV.C.3

* * *

Article 2

Administration

1. The Dispute Settlement Body is hereby established to administer these rules and procedures and, except as otherwise provided in a covered agreement, the consultation and dispute settlement provisions of the covered agreements. Accordingly, the DSB shall have the authority to establish panels, adopt panel and Appellate Body reports, maintain surveillance of implementation of rulings and recommendations, and authorize suspension of concessions and other obligations under the covered agreements. With respect to disputes arising under a covered agreement which is a Plurilateral Trade Agreement, the term "Member" as used herein shall refer only to those Members that are parties to the relevant Plurilateral Trade Agreement. Where the DSB administers the dispute settlement provisions of a Plurilateral Trade Agreement, only those Members that are parties to that Agreement may participate in decisions or actions taken by the DSB with respect to that dispute.

* * *

Article 11

Function of Panels

The function of panels is to assist the DSB in discharging its responsibilities under this Understanding and the covered agreements. Accordingly, a panel should make an objective assessment of the matter before it, including an objective assessment of the facts of the case and the applicability of and conformity with the relevant covered agreements, and make such other findings as will assist the DSB in making the recommendations or in giving the rulings provided for in the covered agreements. Panels should consult regularly with the parties to the dispute and give them adequate opportunity to develop a mutually satisfactory solution.

* * *

Article 16

Adoption of Panel Reports

* * *

4. Within 60 days after the date of circulation of a panel report to the Members, the report shall be adopted at a DSB meeting[1] unless a party to the dispute formally notifies the DSB of its decision to appeal or the DSB decides by consensus not to adopt the report. If a party has notified its decision to appeal, the report by the panel shall not be considered for adoption by the DSB until after completion of the appeal. This adoption procedure is without prejudice to the right of Members to express their views on a panel report.

1. If a meeting of the DSB is not scheduled within this period at a time that enables the requirements of paragraphs 1 and 4 of Article 16 to be met, a meeting of the DSB shall be held for this purpose.

Article 17

Appellate Review

Standing Appellate Body

1. A standing Appellate Body shall be established by the DSB. The Appellate Body shall hear appeals from panel cases. It shall be composed of seven persons, three of whom shall serve on any one case. Persons serving on the Appellate Body shall serve in rotation. Such rotation shall be determined in the working procedures of the Appellate Body.

* * *

Adoption of Appellate Body Reports

14. An Appellate Body report shall be adopted by the DSB and unconditionally accepted by the parties to the dispute unless the DSB decides by consensus not to adopt the Appellate Body report within 30 days following its circulation to the Members.[2] This adoption procedure is without prejudice to the right of Members to express their views on an Appellate Body report.

* * *

Article 21

Surveillance of Implementation of Recommendations and Rulings

1. Prompt compliance with recommendations or rulings of the DSB is essential in order to ensure effective resolution of disputes to the benefit of all Members.

2. If a meeting of the DSB is not scheduled during this period, such a meeting of the DSB shall be held for this purpose.

7.9 WTO Decision on Trade in Services and the Environment. Adopted by the WTO Council for Trade in Services, 1 March 1995. WTO Doc. No. S/L/4 (4 April 1995)

The Council for Trade in Services,

Acknowledging that measures necessary to protect the environment may conflict with the provisions of the Agreement; and

Noting that since measures necessary to protect the environment typically have as their objective the protection of human, animal or plant life or health, it is not clear that there is a need to provide for more than is contained in paragraph (b) of Article XIV;

Decides as follows:

1. In order to determine whether any modification of Article XIV of the Agreement is required to take account of such measures, to request the Committee on Trade and Environment to examine and report, with recommendations if any, on the relationship between services trade and the environment including the issue of sustainable development. The Committee shall also examine the relevance of intergovernmental agreements on the environment and their relationship to the Agreement.

2. The Committee shall report the results of its work to the first biennial meeting of the Ministerial Conference after the entry into force of the Agreement Establishing the World Trade Organization.

B. Human Rights/Social Justice

7.10 Convention on the Prevention and Punishment of the Crime of Genocide. Concluded at New York, 9 December 1948. Entered into force, 12 January 1951. 78 U.N.T.S. 277; *reprinted in* 3 Weston III.J.2: *Arts. II-IV*

Article II. In the present Convention, genocide means any of the following acts committed with intent to destroy, in whole or in part, a national, ethnical, racial or religious group, as such:

(a) Killing members of the group;

(b) Causing serious bodily or mental harm to members of the group;

(c) Deliberately inflicting on the group conditions of life calculated to bring about its physical destruction in whole or in part;

(d) Imposing measures intended to prevent births within the group;

(e) Forcibly transferring children of the group to another group.

Article III. The following acts shall be punishable:

(a) Genocide;

(b) Conspiracy to commit genocide;

(c) Direct and public incitement to commit genocide;

(d) Attempt to commit genocide;

(e) Complicity in genocide.

Article IV. Persons committing genocide or any of the other acts enumerated in Article III shall be punished, whether they are constitutionally responsible rulers, public officials or private individuals.

7.11 UNIVERSAL DECLARATION OF HUMAN RIGHTS. Adopted by the U.N. General Assembly, 10 December 1948. G.A.Res. 217A, U.N. GAOR, 3rd Sess., Pt. I, Resolutions, at 71, U.N. Doc. A/810; *reprinted in* 3 Weston III.A.1

PREAMBLE

Whereas recognition of the inherent dignity and of the equal and inalienable rights of all members of the human family is the foundation of freedom, justice and peace in the world,

Whereas disregard and contempt for human rights have resulted in barbarous acts which have outraged the conscience of mankind, and the advent of a world in which human beings shall enjoy freedom of speech and belief and freedom from fear and want has been proclaimed as the highest aspiration of the common people,

Whereas it is essential, if man is not to be compelled to have recourse, as a last resort, to rebellion against tyranny and oppression, that human rights should be protected by the rule of law,

Whereas it is essential to promote the development of friendly relations between nations,

Whereas the peoples of the United Nations have in the Charter reaffirmed their faith in fundamental human rights, in the dignity and worth of the human person and in the equal rights of men and women and have determined to promote social progress and better standards of life in larger freedom,

Whereas Member States have pledged themselves to achieve, in co-operation with the United Nations, the promotion of universal respect for and observance of human rights and fundamental freedoms,

Whereas a common understanding of these rights and freedoms is of the greatest importance for the full realization of this pledge,

Now, therefore,

The General Assembly

Proclaims this Universal Declaration of Human Rights as a common standard of achievement for all peoples and all nations, to the end that every individual and every organ of society, keeping this Declaration constantly in mind, shall strive by teaching and education to promote respect for these rights and freedoms and by progressive measures, national and international, to secure their universal and effective recognition and observance, both among the peoples of Member States themselves and among the peoples of territories under their jurisdiction.

Article 1. All human beings are born free and equal in dignity and rights. They are endowed with reason and conscience and should act towards one another in a spirit of brotherhood.

Article 2. Everyone is entitled to all the rights and freedoms set forth in this Declaration, without distinction of any kind, such as race, colour, sex, language, religion, political or other opinion, national or social origin, property, birth or other status.

Furthermore, no distinction shall be made on the basis of the political, jurisdictional or international status of the country or territory to which a person belongs, whether it be independent, trust, non-self-governing or under any other limitation of sovereignty.

Article 3. Everyone has the right to life, liberty and the security of person.

Article 4. No one shall be held in slavery or servitude; slavery and the slave trade shall be prohibited in all their forms.

Article 5. No one shall be subjected to torture or to cruel, inhuman or degrading treatment or punishment.

Article 6. Everyone has the right to recognition everywhere as a person before the law.

Article 7. All are equal before the law and are entitled without any discrimination to equal protection of the law. All are entitled to equal protection against any discrimination in violation of this Declaration and against any incitement to such discrimination.

Article 8. Everyone has the right to an effective remedy by the competent national tribunals for acts violating the fundamental rights granted him by the constitution or by law.

Article 9. No one shall be subjected to arbitrary arrest, detention or exile.

Article 10. Everyone is entitled in full equality to a fair and public hearing by an independent and impartial tribunal, in the determination of his rights and obligations and of any criminal charge against him.

Article 11. (1) Everyone charged with a penal offence has the right to be presumed innocent until proved guilty according to law in a public trial at which he has had all the guarantees necessary for his defence.

(2) No one shall be held guilty of any penal offence on account of any act or omission which did not constitute a penal offence, under national or international law, at the time when it was committed. Nor shall a heavier penalty be imposed than the one that was applicable at the time the penal offence was committed.

Article 12. No one shall be subjected to arbitrary interference with his privacy, family, home or correspondence, nor to attacks upon his honour and reputation. Everyone has the right to the protection of the law against such interference or attacks.

Article 13. (1) Everyone has the right to freedom of movement and residence within the borders of each State.

(2) Everyone has the right to leave any country, including his own, and to return to his country.

Article 14. (1) Everyone has the right to seek and to enjoy in other countries asylum from persecution.

(2) This right may not be invoked in the case of prosecutions genuinely arising from nonpolitical crimes or from acts contrary to the purposes and principles of the United Nations.

Article 15. (1) Everyone has the right to a nationality.

(2) No one shall be arbitrarily deprived of his nationality nor denied the right to change his nationality.

Article 16. (1) Men and women of full age, without any limitation due to race, nationality or religion, have the right to marry and to found a family. They are entitled to equal rights as to marriage, during marriage and at its dissolution.

(2) Marriage shall be entered into only with the free and full consent of the intending spouses.

(3) The family is the natural and fundamental group unit of society and is entitled to protection by society and the State.

Article 17. (1) Everyone has the right to own property alone as well as in association with others.

(2) No one shall be arbitrarily deprived of his property.

Article 18. Everyone has the right to freedom of thought, conscience and religion; this right includes freedom to change his religion or belief, and freedom, either alone or in community with others and in public or private, to manifest his religion or belief in teaching, practice, worship and observance.

Article 19. Everyone has the right to freedom of opinion and expression; this right includes freedom to hold opinions without interference and to seek, receive and impart information and ideas through any media and regardless of frontiers.

Article 20. (1) Everyone has the right to freedom of peaceful assembly and association.

(2) No one may be compelled to belong to an association.

Article 21. (1) Everyone has the right to take part in the government of his country, directly or through freely chosen representatives.

(2) Everyone has the right of equal access to public service in his country.

(3) The will of the people shall be the basis of the authority of government; this will shall be expressed in periodic and genuine elections which shall be by universal and equal suffrage and shall be held by secret vote or by equivalent free voting procedures.

Article 22. Everyone, as a member of society, has the right to social security and is entitled to realization, through national effort and international co-operation and in accordance with the organization and resources of each State, of the economic, social and cultural rights indispensable for his dignity and the free development of his personality.

Article 23. (1) Everyone has the right to work, to free choice of employment, to just and favourable conditions of work and to protection against unemployment.

(2) Everyone, without any discrimination, has the right to equal pay for equal work.

(3) Everyone who works has the right to just and favourable remuneration ensuring for himself and his family an existence worthy of human dignity, and supplemented, if necessary, by other means of social protection.

(4) Everyone has the right to form and to join trade unions for the protection of his interests.

Article 24. Everyone has the right to rest and leisure, including reasonable limitation of working hours and periodic holidays with pay.

Article 25. (1) Everyone has the right to a standard of living adequate for the health and well-being of himself and of his family, including food, clothing, housing and medical care and necessary social services, and the right to security in the event of unemployment, sickness, disability, widowhood, old age or other lack of livelihood in circumstances beyond his control.

(2) Motherhood and childhood are entitled to special care and assistance. All children, whether born in or out of wedlock, shall enjoy the same social protection.

Article 26. (1) Everyone has the right to education. Education shall be free, at least in the elementary and fundamental stages. Elementary education shall be compulsory. Technical and professional education shall be made generally available and higher education shall be equally accessible to all on the basis of merit.

(2) Education shall be directed to the full development of the human personality and to the strengthening of respect for human rights and fundamental freedoms. It shall promote understanding, tolerance and friendship among all nations, racial or religious groups, and shall further the activities of the United Nations for the maintenance of peace.

(3) Parents have a prior right to choose the kind of education that shall be given to their children.

Article 27. (1) Everyone has the right freely to participate in the cultural life of the community, to enjoy the arts and to share in scientific advancement and its benefits.

(2) Everyone has the right to the protection of the moral and material interests resulting from any scientific, literary or artistic production of which he is the author.

Article 28. Everyone is entitled to a social and international order in which the rights and freedoms set forth in this Declaration can be fully realized.

Article 29. (1) Everyone has duties to the community in which alone the free and full development of his personality is possible.

(2) In the exercise of his rights and freedoms, everyone shall be subject only to such limitations as are determined by law solely for the purpose of securing due recognition and respect for the rights and freedoms of others and of meeting the just requirements of morality, public order and the general welfare in a democratic society.

(3) These rights and freedoms may in no case be exercised contrary to the purposes and principles of the United Nations.

Article 30. Nothing in this Declaration may be interpreted as implying for any State, group or person any right to engage in any activity or to perform any act aimed at the destruction of any of the rights and freedoms set forth herein.

7.12 UNESCO Declaration on the Principles of International Cultural Co-operation. Adopted on 4 November 1966. *Reprinted in* Human Rights: A Compilation of International Instruments 409 (United Nations 1988)

The General Conference of the United Nations Educational, Scientific and Cultural Organization, met in Paris for its fourteenth session, this fourth day of November 1966, being the twentieth anniversary of the foundation of the Organization,

Recalling that the Constitution of the Organization declares that "since wars begin in the minds of men, it is in the minds of men that the defences of peace must be constructed" and that the peace must be founded, if it is not to fail, upon the intellectual and moral solidarity of mankind,

Recalling that the Constitution also states that the wide diffusion of culture and the education of humanity for justice and liberty and peace are indispensable to the dignity of man and constitute a sacred duty which all the nations must fulfil in a spirit of mutual assistance and concern,

Considering that the Organization's Member States, believing in the pursuit of truth and the free exchange of ideas and knowledge, have agreed and determined to develop and to increase the means of communication between their peoples,

Considering that, despite the technical advances which facilitate the development and dissemination of knowledge and ideas, ignorance of the way of life and customs of peoples still presents an obstacle to friendship among the nations, to peaceful co-operation and to the progress of mankind,

Taking account of the Universal Declaration of Human Rights, the Declaration of the Rights of the Child, the Declaration on the Granting of Independence to Colonial Countries and Peoples, the United Nations Declaration on the Elimination of All Forms of Racial Discrimination, the Declaration on the Promotion among Youth of the Ideals of Peace, Mutual Respect and Understanding between Peoples, and the Declaration on the Inadmissibility of Intervention in the Domestic Affairs of States and the Protection of their Independence and Sovereignty, proclaimed successively by the General Assembly of the United Nations,

Convinced by the experience of the Organization's first twenty years that, if international cultural co-operation is to be strengthened, its principles require to be affirmed,

Proclaims this Declaration of the principles of international cultural co-operation, to the end that governments, authorities, organizations, associations and institutions responsible for cultural activities may constantly be guided by these principles; and for the purpose, as set out in the Constitution of the Organization, of advancing, through the educational, scientific and cultural relations of the peoples of the world, the objectives of peace and welfare that are defined in the Charter of the United Nations:

Article 1

1. Each culture has a dignity and value which must be respected and preserved.

2. Every people has the right and the duty to develop its culture.

3. In their rich variety and diversity, and in the reciprocal influences they exert on one another, all cultures form part of the common heritage belonging to all mankind.

Article II

Nations shall endeavour to develop the various branches of culture side by side and, as far as possible, simultaneously, so as to establish a harmonious balance between technical progress and the intellectual and moral advancement of mankind.

Article III

International cultural co-operation shall cover all aspects of intellectual and creative activities relating to education, science and culture.

Article IV

The aims of international cultural co-operation in its various forms, bilateral or multilateral, regional or universal, shall be:

1. To spread knowledge, to stimulate talent and to enrich cultures;

2. To develop peaceful relations and friendship among the peoples and bring about a better understanding of each other's way of life;

3. To contribute to the application of the principles set out in the United Nations Declarations that are recalled in the Preamble to this Declaration;

4. To enable everyone to have access to knowledge, to enjoy the arts and literature of all peoples, to share in advances made in science in all parts of the world and in the resulting benefits, and to contribute to the enrichment of cultural life;

5. To raise the level of the spiritual and material life of man in all parts of the world.

Article V

Cultural co-operation is a right and a duty for all peoples and all nations, which should share with one another their knowledge and skills.

Article VI

International co-operation, while promoting the enrichment of all cultures through its beneficent action, shall respect the distinctive character of each.

Article VII

1. Broad dissemination of ideas and knowledge, based on the freest exchange and discussion, is essential to creative activity, the pursuit of truth and the development of the personality.

2. In cultural co-operation, stress shall be laid on ideas and values conducive to the creation of a climate of friendship and peace. Any mark of hostility in attitudes and in expression of opinion shall be avoided. Every effort shall be made, in presenting and disseminating information, to ensure its authenticity.

Article VIII

Cultural co-operation shall be carried on for the mutual benefit of all the nations practising it. Exchanges to which it gives rise shall be arranged in a spirit of broad reciprocity.

Article IX

Cultural co-operation shall contribute to the establishment of stable, long-term relations between peoples, which should be subjected as little as possible to the strains which may arise in international life.

Article X

Cultural co-operation shall be specially concerned with the moral and intellectual education of young people in a spirit of friendship, international understanding and peace and shall foster awareness among States of the need to stimulate talent and promote the training of the rising generations in the most varied sectors.

Article XI

1. In their cultural relations, States shall bear in mind the principles of the United Nations. In seeking to achieve international co-operation, they shall respect the sovereign equality of States and shall refrain from intervention in matters which are essentially within the domestic jurisdiction of any State.

2. The principles of this Declaration shall be applied with due regard for human rights and fundamental freedoms.

7.13 INTERNATIONAL COVENANT ON ECONOMIC, SOCIAL AND CULTURAL RIGHTS. Concluded at New York, 16 December 1966. Entered into force, 3 January 1976. 993 U.N.T.S. 3; *reprinted in* 3 Weston III.A.2: *Arts. 1, 2, 10, 15, 25*

* * *

Article 1. (1) All peoples have the right of self-determination. By virtue of that right they freely determine their political status and freely pursue their economic, social and cultural development.

(2) All peoples may, for their own ends, freely dispose of their natural wealth and resources without prejudice to any obligations arising out of international economic co-operation, based upon the principle of mutual benefit, and international law. In no case may a people be deprived of its own means of subsistence.

(3) The States Parties to the present Covenant, including those having responsibility for the administration of Non-Self-Governing and Trust Territories, shall promote the realization of the right of self-determination, and shall respect that right, in conformity with the provisions of the Charter of the United Nations.

* * *

Article 2. (1) Each State Party to the present Covenant undertakes to take steps, individually and through international assistance and co-operation, especially economic and technical, to the maximum of its available resources, with a view to achieving progressively the full realization of the rights recognized in the present Covenant by all appropriate means, including particularly the adoption of legislative measures.

(2) The States Parties to the present Covenant undertake to guarantee that the rights enunciated in the present Covenant will be exercised without discrimination of any kind as to race, colour, sex, language, religion, political or other opinion, national or social origin, property, birth or other status.

(3) Developing countries, with due regard to human rights and their national economy, may determine to what extent they would guarantee the economic rights recognized in the present Covenant to non-nationals.

* * *

Article 10. The States Parties to the present Covenant recognize that:

(1) The widest possible protection and assistance should be accorded to the family, which is the natural and fundamental group unit of society, particularly for its establishment and while it is responsible for the care and education of dependent children. Marriage must be entered into with the free consent of the intending spouses.

(2) Special protection should be accorded to mothers during a reasonable period before and after childbirth. During such period working mothers should be accorded paid leave or leave with adequate social security benefits.

(3) Special measures of protection and assistance should be taken on behalf of all children and young persons without any discrimination for reasons of parentage or other conditions. Children and young persons should be protected from economic and social exploitation. Their employment in work harmful to their morals or health or dangerous to life or likely to hamper their normal development should be punishable by law. States should also set age limits below which the paid employment of child labour should be prohibited and punishable by law.

* * *

Article 15. (1) The States Parties to the present Covenant recognize the right of everyone:

(a) To take part in cultural life;

(b) To enjoy the benefits of scientific progress and its applications;

(c) To benefit from the protection of the moral and material interests resulting from any scientific, literary or artistic production of which he is the author.

(2) The steps to be taken by the States Parties to the present Covenant to achieve the full realization of this right shall include those necessary for the conservation, the development and the diffusion of science and culture.

(3) The States Parties to the present Covenant undertake to respect the freedom indispensable for scientific research and creative activity.

(4) The States Parties to the present Covenant recognize the benefits to be derived from the encouragement and development of international contacts and co-operation in the scientific and cultural fields.

* * *

Article 25. Nothing in the present Covenant shall be interpreted as impairing the inherent right of all peoples to enjoy and utilize fully and freely their natural wealth and resources.

7.14 INTERNATIONAL COVENANT ON CIVIL AND POLITICAL RIGHTS. **Concluded at New York, 16 December 1966. Entered into force, 23 March 1976. 999 U.N.T.S. 171; *reprinted in* 3 Weston III.A.3: *Arts. 1, 2, 6, 14, 23, 24, 27, 47***

* * *

Article 1. (1) All peoples have the right of self-determination. By virtue of that right they freely determine their political status and freely pursue their economic, social and cultural development.

(2) All peoples may, for their own ends, freely dispose of their natural wealth and resources without prejudice to any obligations arising out of international economic co-operation, based upon the principle of mutual benefit, and international law. In no case may a people be deprived of its own means of subsistence.

(3) The States Parties to the present Covenant, including those having responsibility for the administration of Non-Self-Governing and Trust Territories, shall promote the realization of the right of self-determination, and shall respect that right, in conformity with the provisions of the Charter of the United Nations.

* * *

Article 2. (1) Each State Party to the present Covenant undertakes to respect and to ensure to all individuals within its territory and subject to its jurisdiction the rights recognized in the present Covenant, without distinction of any kind, such as race, colour, sex, language, religion, political or other opinion, national or social origin, property, birth or other status.

(2) Where not already provided for by existing legislative or other measures, each State Party to the present Covenant undertakes to take the necessary steps, in accordance with its constitutional processes and with the provisions of the present Covenant, to adopt such legislative or other measures as may be necessary to give effect to the rights recognized in the present Covenant.

(3) Each State Party to the present Covenant undertakes:

(a) To ensure that any person whose rights or freedoms as herein recognized are violated shall have an effective remedy, notwithstanding that the violation has been committed by persons acting in an official capacity;

(b) To ensure that any person claiming such a remedy shall have his right thereto determined by competent judicial, administrative or legislative authorities, or by any other competent authority provided for by the legal system of the State, and to develop the possibilities of judicial remedy;

(c) To ensure that the competent authorities shall enforce such remedies when granted.

* * *

Article 6. (1) Every human being has the inherent right to life. This right shall be protected by law. No one shall be arbitrarily deprived of his life.

(2) In countries which have not abolished the death penalty, sentence of death may be imposed only for the most serious crimes in accordance with the law in force at the time of the commission of the crime and not contrary to the provisions of the present Covenant and to the Convention on the Prevention and Punishment of the Crime of Genocide. This penalty can only be carried out pursuant to a final judgment rendered by a competent court.

(3) When deprivation of life constitutes the crime of genocide, it is understood that nothing in this article shall authorize any State Party to the present Covenant to derogate in any way from any obligation assumed under the provi-

sions of the Convention on the Prevention and Punishment of the Crime of Genocide.

(4) Anyone sentenced to death shall have the right to seek pardon or commutation of the sentence. Amnesty, pardon or commutation of the sentence of death may be granted in all cases.

(5) Sentence of death shall not be imposed for crimes committed by persons below eighteen years of age and shall not be carried out on pregnant women.

(6) Nothing in this article shall be invoked to delay or to prevent the abolition of capital punishment by any State Party to the present Covenant.

* * *

Article 14. (1) All persons shall be equal before the courts and tribunals. In the determination of any criminal charge against him, or of his rights and obligations in a suit at law, everyone shall be entitled to a fair and public hearing by a competent, independent and impartial tribunal established by law. The Press and the public may be excluded from all or part of a trial for reasons of morals, public order (*ordre public*) or national security in a democratic society, or when the interest of the private lives of the parties so requires, or to the extent strictly necessary in the opinion of the court in special circumstances where publicity would prejudice the interests of justice; but any judgment rendered in a criminal case or in a suit at law shall be made public except where the interest of juvenile persons otherwise requires or the proceedings concern matrimonial disputes or the guardianship of children.

(2) Everyone charged with a criminal offence shall have the right to be presumed innocent until proved guilty according to law.

(3) In the determination of any criminal charge against him, everyone shall be entitled to the following minimum guarantees, in full equality:

(a) To be informed promptly and in detail in a language which he understands of the nature and cause of the charge against him;

(b) To have adequate time and facilities for the preparation of his defence and to communicate with counsel of his own choosing;

(c) To be tried without undue delay;

(d) To be tried in his presence, and to defend himself in person or through legal assistance of his own choosing; to be informed, if he does not have legal assistance, of this right; and to have legal assistance assigned to him, in any case where the interests of justice so require, and without payment by him in any such case if he does not have sufficient means to pay for it;

(e) To examine, or have examined, the witnesses against him and to obtain the attendance and examination of witnesses on his behalf under the same conditions as witnesses against him;

(f) To have the free assistance of an interpreter if he cannot understand or speak the language used in court;

(g) Not to be compelled to testify against himself or to confess guilt.

(4) In the case of juvenile persons, the procedure shall be such as will take account of their age and the desirability of promoting their rehabilitation.

(5) Everyone convicted of a crime shall have the right to his conviction and sentence being reviewed by a higher tribunal according to law.

(6) When a person has by a final decision been convicted of a criminal offense and when subsequently his conviction has been reversed or he has been pardoned on the ground that a new or newly discovered fact shows conclusively that there

has been a miscarriage of justice, the person who has suffered punishment as a result of such conviction shall be compensated according to law, unless it is proved that the non-disclosure of the unknown fact in time is wholly or partly attributable to him.

(7) No one shall be liable to be tried or punished again for an offence for which he has already been finally convicted or acquitted in accordance with the law and penal procedure of each country.

* * *

Article 23. (1) The family is the natural and fundamental group unit of society and is entitled to protection by society and the State.

(2) The right of men and women of marriageable age to marry and to found a family shall be recognized.

(3) No marriage shall be entered into without the free and full consent of the intending spouses.

(4) States Parties to the present Covenant shall take appropriate steps to ensure equality of rights and responsibilities of spouses as to marriage, during marriage and at its dissolution. In the case of dissolution, provision shall be made for the necessary protection of any children.

Article 24. (1) Every child shall have, without any discrimination as to race, colour, sex, language, religion, national or social origin, property or birth, the right to such measures of protection as are required by his status as a minor, on the part of his family, society and the State.

(2) Every child shall be registered immediately after birth and shall have a name.

(3) Every child has the right to acquire a nationality.

* * *

Article 27. In those States in which ethnic, religious or linguistic minorities exist, persons belonging to such minorities shall not be denied the right, in community with the other members of their group, to enjoy their own culture, to profess and practise their own religion, or to use their own language.

* * *

Article 47. Nothing in the present Covenant shall be interpreted as impairing the inherent right of all peoples to enjoy and utilize fully and freely their natural wealth and resources.

7.15 FINAL ACT OF THE UNITED NATIONS INTERNATIONAL CONFERENCE ON HUMAN RIGHTS. Concluded at Teheran, 13 May 1968. *Reprinted in* Human Rights: A Compilation of International Instruments 43 (United Nations 1988) & 3 Weston III.U.1

The International Conference on Human Rights,

Having met at Teheran from April 22 to May 13, 1968 to review the progress made in the twenty years since the adoption of the Universal Declaration of Human Rights and to formulate a programme for the future,

Having considered the problems relating to the activities of the United Nations for the promotion and encouragement of respect for human rights and fundamental freedoms,

Bearing in mind the resolutions adopted by the Conference,

Noting that the observance of the International Year for Human Rights takes place at a time when the world is undergoing a process of unprecedented change,

Having regard to the new opportunities made available by the rapid progress of science and technology,

Believing that, in an age when conflict and violence prevail in many parts of the world, the fact of human interdependence and the need for human solidarity are more evident than ever before,

Recognizing that peace is the universal aspiration of mankind and that peace and justice are indispensable to the full realization of human rights and fundamental freedoms,

Solemnly proclaims that:

1. It is imperative that the members of the international community fulfil their solemn obligations to promote and encourage respect for human rights and fundamental freedoms for all without distinctions of any kind such as race, colour, sex, language, religion, political or other opinions;

2. The Universal Declaration of Human Rights states a common understanding of the peoples of the world concerning the inalienable and inviolable rights of all members of the human family and constitutes an obligation for the members of the international community;

3. The International Covenant on Civil and Political Rights, the International Covenant on Economic, Social and Cultural Rights, the Declaration on the Granting of Independence to Colonial Countries and Peoples, the International Convention on the Elimination of All Forms of Racial Discrimination as well as other conventions and declarations in the field of human rights adopted under the auspices of the United Nations, the specialized agencies and the regional intergovernmental organizations, have created new standards and obligations to which States should conform;

4. Since the adoption of the Universal Declaration of Human Rights the United Nations has made substantial progress in defining standards for the enjoyment and protection of human rights and fundamental freedoms. During this period many important international instruments were adopted but much remains to be done in regard to the implementation of those rights and freedoms;

5. The primary aim of the United Nations in the sphere of human rights is the achievement by each individual of the maximum freedom and dignity. For the realization of this objective, the laws of every country should grant each individual, irrespective of race, language, religion or political belief, freedom of expression, of information, of conscience and of religion, as well as the right to participate in the political, economic, cultural and social life of his country;

6. States should reaffirm their determination effectively to enforce the principles enshrined in the Charter of the United Nations and in other international instruments that concern human rights and fundamental freedoms;

7. Gross denials of human rights under the repugnant policy of *apartheid* is a matter of the gravest concern to the international community. This policy of *apartheid,* condemned as a crime against humanity, continues seriously to disturb international peace and security. It is therefore imperative for the international community to use every possible means to eradicate this evil. The struggle against *apartheid* is recognized as legitimate;

8. The peoples of the world must be made fully aware of the evils of racial discrimination and must join in combating them. The implementation of this principle of non-discrimination, embodied in the Charter of the United Nations, the Universal Declaration of Human Rights, and other international instruments in the field of human rights, constitutes a most urgent task of mankind at the international as well as at the national level. All ideologies based on racial superiority and intolerance must be condemned and resisted;

9. Eight years after the General Assembly's Declaration on the Granting of Independence to Colonial Countries and Peoples the problems of colonialism continue to preoccupy the international community. It is a matter of urgency that all Member States should co-operate with the appropriate organs of the United Nations so that effective measures can be taken to ensure that the Declaration is fully implemented;

10. Massive denials of human rights, arising out of aggression or any armed conflict with their tragic consequences, and resulting in untold human misery, engender reactions which could engulf the world in ever growing hostilities. It is the obligation of the international community to co-operate in eradicating such scourges;

11. Gross denials of human rights arising from discrimination on grounds of race, religion, belief or expressions of opinion outrage the conscience of mankind and endanger the foundations of freedom, justice and peace in the world;

12. The widening gap between the economically developed and developing countries impedes the realization of human rights in the international community. The failure of the Development Decade to reach its modest objectives makes it all the more imperative for every nation, according to its capacities, to make the maximum possible effort to close this gap;

13. Since human rights and fundamental freedoms are indivisible, the full realization of civil and political rights without the enjoyment of economic, social and cultural rights is impossible. The achievement of lasting progress in the implementation of human rights is dependent upon sound and effective national and international policies of economic and social development;

14. The existence of over seven hundred million illiterates throughout the world is an enormous obstacle to all efforts at realizing the aims and purposes of the Charter of the United Nations and the provisions of the Universal Declaration of Human Rights. International action aimed at eradicating illiteracy from the face of the earth and promoting education at all levels requires urgent attention;

15. The discrimination of which women are still victims in various regions of the world must be eliminated. An inferior status for women is contrary to the Charter of the United Nations as well as the provisions of the Universal Declaration of Human Rights. The full implementation of the Declaration on the Elimination of Discrimination against Women is a necessity for the progress of mankind;

16. The protection of the family and of the child remains the concern of the international community. Parents have a basic human right to determine freely and responsibly the number and the spacing of their children;

17. The aspirations of the younger generation for a better world, in which human rights and fundamental freedoms are fully implemented, must be given the highest encouragement. It is imperative that youth participate in shaping the future of mankind;

18. While recent scientific discoveries and technological advances have opened vast prospects for economic, social and cultural progress, such developments may nevertheless endanger the rights and freedoms of individuals and will require continuing attention;

19. Disarmament would release immense human and material resources now devoted to military purposes. These resources should be used for the promotion of human rights and fundamental freedoms. General and complete disarmament is one of the highest aspirations of all peoples;

Therefore,

The International Conference on Human Rights,

1. *Affirming* its faith in the principles of the Universal Declaration of Human Rights and other international instruments in this field,

2. *Urges* all peoples and governments to dedicate themselves to the principles enshrined in the Universal Declaration of Human Rights and to redouble their efforts to provide for all human beings a life consonant with freedom and dignity and conducive to physical, mental, social and spiritual welfare.

7.16 American Convention on Human Rights. Concluded at San José, 22 November 1969. Entered into force, 18 July 1978. O.A.S.T.S. No. 36, O.A.S. Off.Rec. O.E.A./Ser. L/V/II.23 Doc. 21 Rev. 6 (1979); *reprinted in* 9 I.L.M. 673 (1970) & 3 Weston III.B.24: *Arts. 1, 4, 16, 21, 27*

* * *

Article 1. Obligation to Respect Rights

1. The States Parties to this Convention undertake to respect the rights and freedoms recognized herein and to ensure to all persons subject to their jurisdiction the free and full exercise of those rights and freedoms, without any discrimination for reasons of race, color, sex, language, religion, political or other opinion, national or social origin, economic status, birth, or any other social condition.

2. For the purposes of this Convention, "person" means every human being.

* * *

Article 4. Right to Life

1. Every person has the right to have his life respected. This right shall be protected by law and, in general, from the moment of conception. No one shall be arbitrarily deprived of his life.

2. In countries that have not abolished the death penalty, it may be imposed only for the most serious crimes and pursuant to a final judgment rendered by a competent court and in accordance with a law establishing such punishment, enacted prior to the commission of the crime. The application of such punishment shall not be extended to crimes to which it does not presently apply.

3. The death penalty shall not be reestablished in states that have abolished it.

4. In no case shall capital punishment be inflicted for political offenses or related common crimes.

5. Capital punishment shall not be imposed upon persons who, at the time the crime was committed, were under 18 years of age or over 70 years of age; nor shall it be applied to pregnant women.

6. Every person condemned to death shall have the right to apply for amnesty, pardon, or commutation of sentence, which may be granted in all cases. Capital punishment shall not be imposed while such a petition is a pending decision by the competent authority.

* * *

Article 16. Freedom of Association

1. Everyone has the right to associate freely for ideological, religious, political, economic, labor, social, cultural, sports, or other purposes.

2. The exercise of this right shall be subject only to such restrictions established by law as may be necessary in a democratic society, in the interest of national security, public safety or public order, or to protect public health or morals or the rights and freedoms of others.

3. The provisions of this article do not bar the imposition of legal restrictions, including even deprivation of the exercise of the right of association, on members of the armed forces and the police.

* * *

Article 21. Right to Property

1. Everyone has the right to the use and enjoyment of his property. The law may subordinate such use and enjoyment to the interest of society.

2. No one shall be deprived of his property except upon payment of just compensation, for reasons of public utility or social interest, and in the cases and according to the forms established by law.

3. Usury and any other form of exploitation of man by man shall be prohibited by law.

* * *

Article 27. Suspension of Guarantees

1. In time of war, public danger, or other emergency that threatens the independence or security of a State Party, it may take measures derogating from its obligations under the present Convention to the extent and for the period of time strictly required by the exigencies of the situation, provided that such measures are not inconsistent with its other obligations under international law and do not involve discrimination on the ground of race, color, sex, language, religion, or social origin.

2. The foregoing provision does not authorize any suspension of the following articles: Article 3 (Right to Juridical Personality), Article 4 (Right to Life), Article 5 (Right to Humane Treatment), Article 6 (Freedom from Slavery), Article 9 (Freedom from Ex Post Facto Laws), Article 12 (Freedom of Conscience and Religion), Article 17 (Rights of the Family), Article 18 (Right to a Name), Article 19 (Rights of the Child), Article 20 (Right to Nationality), and Article 23 (Right to Participate in Government), or of the judicial guarantees essential for the protection of such rights.

3. Any State Party availing itself of the right of suspension shall immediately inform the other States Parties, through the Secretary General of the Organization of American States, of the provisions the application of which it has suspended, the reasons that gave rise to the suspension, and the date set for the termination of such suspension.

* * *

7.17 DECLARATION ON SOCIAL PROGRESS AND DEVELOPMENT. Adopted by the U.N. General Assembly, 11 December 1969. G.A. Res. 2542, U.N. GAOR, 24th Sess., Supp. No. 30, at 49, U.N. Doc. A/7630 (1970); *reprinted in* 3 Weston III.R.1

The General Assembly,

Mindful of the pledge of Members of the United Nations under the Charter to take joint and separate action in co-operation with the Organization to promote higher standards of living, full employment and conditions of economic and social progress and development,

Reaffirming faith in human rights and fundamental freedoms and in the principles of peace, of the dignity and worth of the human person, and of social justice proclaimed in the Charter,

Recalling the principles of the Universal Declaration of Human Rights, the International Covenants on Human Rights, the Declaration of the Rights of the Child, the Declaration on the Granting of Independence to Colonial Countries and Peoples, the International Convention on the Elimination of All Forms of Racial Discrimination, the United Nations Declaration on the Elimination of All Forms of Racial Discrimination, the Declaration on the Promotion among Youth of the Ideals of Peace, Mutual Respect and Understanding between Peoples, the Declaration on the Elimination of Discrimination against Women and of resolutions of the United Nations,

Bearing in mind the standards already set for social progress in the constitutions, conventions, recommendations and resolutions of the International Labour Organisation, the Food and Agriculture Organization of the United Nations, the United Nations Educational, Scientific and Cultural Organization, the World Health Organization, the United Nations Children's Fund and of other organizations concerned,

Convinced that man can achieve complete fulfilment of his aspirations only within a just social order and that it is consequently of cardinal importance to accelerate social and economic progress everywhere, thus contributing to international peace and solidarity,

Convinced that international peace and security on the one hand, and social progress and economic development on the other, are closely interdependent and influence each other,

Persuaded that social development can be promoted by peaceful coexistence, friendly relations and co-operation among States with different social, economic or political systems,

Emphasizing the interdependence of economic and social development in the wider process of growth and change, as well as the importance of a strategy of integrated development which takes full account at all stages of its social aspects,

Regretting the inadequate progress achieved in the world social situation despite the efforts of States and the international community,

Recognizing that the primary responsibility for the development of the developing countries rests on those countries themselves and acknowledging the pressing need to narrow and eventually close the gap in the standards of living between economically more advanced and developing countries and, to that end, that Member States shall have the responsibility to pursue internal and external policies designed to promote social development throughout the world, and in particular to assist developing countries to accelerate their economic growth,

Recognizing the urgency of devoting to works of peace and social progress resources being expended on armaments and wasted on conflict and destruction,

Conscious of the contribution that science and technology can render towards meeting the needs common to all humanity,

Believing that the primary task of all States and international organizations is to eliminate from the life of society all evils and obstacles to social progress, particularly such evils as inequality, exploitation, war, colonialism and racism,

Desirous of promoting the progress of all mankind towards these goals and of overcoming all obstacles to their realization,

Solemnly proclaims this Declaration on Social Progress and Development and calls for national and international action for its use as a common basis for social development policies:

PART I

Principles

Article 1

All peoples and all human beings, without distinction as to race, colour, sex, language, religion, nationality, ethnic origin, family or social status, or political or other conviction, shall have the right to live in dignity and freedom and to enjoy the fruits of social progress and should, on their part, contribute to it.

Article 2

Social progress and development shall be founded on respect for the dignity and value of the human person and shall ensure the promotion of human rights and social justice, which requires:

(*a*) The immediate and final elimination of all forms of inequality, exploitation of peoples and individuals, colonialism and racism, including nazism and *apartheid,* and all other policies and ideologies opposed to the purposes and principles of the United Nations;

(*b*) The recognition and effective implementation of civil and political rights as well as of economic, social and cultural rights without any discrimination.

Article 3

The following are considered primary conditions of social progress and development:

(*a*) National independence based on the right of peoples to self-determination;

(*b*) The principle of non-interference in the internal affairs of States;

(*c*) Respect for the sovereignty and territorial integrity of States;

(*d*) Permanent sovereignty of each nation over its natural wealth and resources;

(*e*) The right and responsibility of each State and, as far as they are concerned, each nation and people to determine freely its own objectives of social development, to set its own priorities and to decide in conformity with the principles of the Charter of the United Nations the means and methods of their achievement without any external interference;

(*f*) Peaceful coexistence, peace, friendly relations and co-operation among States irrespective of differences in their social, economic or political systems.

Article 4

The family as a basic unit of society and the natural environment for the growth and well-being of all its members, particularly children and youth, should be assisted and protected so that it may fully assume its responsibilities within the community. Parents have the exclusive right to determine freely and responsibly the number and spacing of their children.

Article 5

Social progress and development require the full utilization of human resources, including, in particular:

(*a*) The encouragement of creative initiative under conditions of enlightened public opinion;

(*b*) The dissemination of national and international information for the purpose of making individuals aware of changes occurring in society as a whole;

(*c*) The active participation of all elements of society, individually or through associations, in defining and in achieving the common goals of development with full respect for the fundamental freedoms embodied in the Universal Declaration of Human Rights;

(*d*) The assurance to disadvantaged or marginal sectors of the population of equal opportunities for social and economic advancement in order to achieve an effectively integrated society.

Article 6

Social development requires the assurance to everyone of the right to work and the free choice of employment.

Social progress and development require the participation of all members of society in productive and socially useful labour and the establishment, in conformity with human rights and fundamental freedoms and with the principles of justice and the social function of property, of forms of ownership of land and of the means of production which preclude any kind of exploitation of man, ensure equal rights to property for all and create conditions leading to genuine equality among people.

Article 7

The rapid expansion of national income and wealth and their equitable distribution among all members of society are fundamental to all social progress, and they should therefore be in the forefront of the preoccupations of every State and Government.

The improvement in the position of the developing countries in international trade resulting, among other things, from the achievement of favourable terms of trade and of equitable and remunerative prices at which developing countries market their products is necessary in order to make it possible to increase national income and in order to advance social development.

Article 8

Each Government has the primary role and ultimate responsibility of ensuring the social progress and well-being of its people, of planning social development measures as part of comprehensive development plans, of encouraging and co-ordinating or integrating all national efforts towards this end and of introducing necessary changes in the social structure. In planning social development measures, the diversity of the needs of developing and developed areas, and of urban and rural areas, within each country, shall be taken into due account.

Article 9

Social progress and development are the common concerns of the international community, which shall supplement, by concerted international action, national efforts to raise the living standards of peoples.

Social progress and economic growth require recognition of the common interest of all nations in the exploration, conservation, use and exploitation, exclusively for peaceful purposes and in the interests of all mankind, of those areas of the environment such as outer space and the sea-bed and ocean floor and the subsoil thereof, beyond the limits of national jurisdiction, in accordance with the purposes and principles of the Charter of the United Nations.

PART II

Objectives

Social progress and development shall aim at the continuous raising of the material and spiritual standards of living of all members of society, with respect for and in compliance with human rights and fundamental freedoms, through the attainment of the following main goals:

Article 10

(*a*) The assurance at all levels of the right to work and the right of everyone to form trade unions and workers' associations and to bargain collectively; promotion of full productive employment and elimination of unemployment and under-employment; establishment of equitable and favourable conditions of work for all, including the improvement of health and safety conditions; assurance of just remuneration for labour without any discrimination as well as a sufficiently high minimum wage to ensure a decent standard of living; the protection of the consumer;

(*b*) The elimination of hunger and malnutrition and the guarantee of the right to proper nutrition;

(*c*) The elimination of poverty; the assurance of a steady improvement in levels of living and of a just and equitable distribution of income;

(*d*) The achievement of the highest standards of health and the provision of health protection for the entire population, if possible free of charge;

(*e*) The eradication of illiteracy and the assurance of the right to universal access to culture, to free compulsory education at the elementary level and to free education at all levels; the raising of the general level of life-long education;

(*f*) The provision for all, particularly persons in low-income groups and large families, of adequate housing and community services.

Social progress and development shall aim equally at the progressive attainment of the following main goals:

Article 11

(*a*) The provision of comprehensive social security schemes and social welfare services; the establishment and improvement of social security and insurance schemes for all persons who, because of illness, disability or old age, are temporarily or permanently unable to earn a living, with a view to ensuring a proper standard of living for such persons and for their families and dependents;

(*b*) The protection of the rights of the mother and child; concern for the upbringing and health of children; the provision of measures to safeguard the health and welfare of women and particularly of working mothers during pregnancy and the infancy of their children, as well as of mothers whose earnings are the sole source of livelihood for the family; the granting to women of pregnancy and maternity leave and allowances without loss of employment or wages;

(*c*) The protection of the rights and the assuring of the welfare of children, the aged and the disabled; the provision of protection for the physically or mentally disadvantaged;

(*d*) The education of youth in, and promotion among them of, the ideals of justice and peace, mutual respect and understanding among peoples; the promotion of full participation of youth in the process of national development;

(*e*) The provision of social defence measures and the elimination of conditions leading to crime and delinquency, especially juvenile delinquency;

(*f*) The guarantee that all individuals, without discrimination of any kind, are made aware of their rights and obligations and receive the necessary aid in the exercise and safeguarding of their rights.

Social progress and development shall further aim at achieving the following main objectives:

Article 12

(*a*) The creation of conditions for rapid and sustained social and economic development, particularly in the developing countries; change in international economic relations; new and effective methods of international cooperation in which equality of opportunity should be as much a prerogative of nations as of individuals within a nation;

(*b*) The elimination of all forms of discrimination and exploitation and all other practices and ideologies contrary to the purposes and principles of the Charter of the United Nations;

(*c*) The elimination of all forms of foreign economic exploitation, particularly that practiced by international monopolies, in order to enable the people of every country to enjoy in full the benefits of their national resources.

Social progress and development shall finally aim at the attainment of the following main goals:

Article 13

(*a*) Equitable sharing of scientific and technological advances by developed and developing countries, and a steady increase in the use of science and technology for the benefit of the social development of society;

(*b*) The establishment of a harmonious balance between scientific, technological and material progress and the intellectual, spiritual, cultural and moral advancement of humanity;

(*c*) The protection and improvement of the human environment.

PART III

Means and Methods

On the basis of the principles set forth in this Declaration, the achievement of the objectives of social progress and development requires the mobilization of the necessary resources by national and international action, with particular attention to such means and methods as:

Article 14

(*a*) Planning for social progress and development, as an integrated part of balanced over-all development planning;

(*b*) The establishment, where necessary, of national systems for framing and carrying out social policies and programmes, and the promotion by the countries concerned of planned regional development, taking into account differing regional conditions and needs, particularly the development of regions which are less favoured or under-developed by comparison with the rest of the country;

(*c*) The promotion of basic and applied social research, particularly comparative international research applied to the planning and execution of social development programmes.

Article 15

(*a*) The adoption of measures to ensure the effective participation, as appropriate, of all the elements of society in the preparation and execution of national plans and programmes of economic and social development;

(*b*) The adoption of measures for an increasing rate of popular participation in the economic, social, cultural and political life of countries through national governmental bodies, non-governmental organizations, co-operatives, rural associations, workers' and employers' organizations and women's and youth organizations, by such methods as national and regional plans for social and economic progress and community development, with a view to achieving a fully integrated national society, accelerating the process of social mobility and consolidating the democratic system;

(*c*) Mobilization of public opinion, at both national and international levels, in support of the principles and objectives of social progress and development;

(*d*) The dissemination of social information, at the national and the international level, to make people aware of changing circumstances in society as a whole, and to educate the consumer.

Article 16

(*a*) Maximum mobilization of all national resources and their rational and efficient utilization; promotion of increased and accelerated productive investment in social and economic fields and of employment; orientation of society towards the development process;

(*b*) Progressively increasing provision of the necessary budgetary and other resources required for financing the social aspects of development;

(*c*) Achievement of equitable distribution of national income, utilizing, *inter alia,* the fiscal system and government spending as an instrument for the equitable distribution and redistribution of income in order to promote social progress;

(*d*) The adoption of measures aimed at prevention of such an outflow of capital from developing countries as would be detrimental to their economic and social development.

Article 17

(*a*) The adoption of measures to accelerate the process of industrialization, especially in developing countries, with due regard for its social aspects, in the interests of the entire population; development of an adequate organizational and legal framework conducive to an uninterrupted and diversified growth of the industrial sector; measures to overcome the adverse social effects which may result from urban development and industrialization, including automation; maintenance of a proper balance between rural and urban development, and in particular, measures designed to ensure healthier living conditions, especially in large industrial centres;

(*b*) Integrated planning to meet the problems of urbanization and urban development;

(*c*) Comprehensive rural development schemes to raise the levels of living of the rural populations and to facilitate such urban-rural relationships and population distribution as will promote balanced national development and social progress;

(*d*) Measures for appropriate supervision of the utilization of land in the interests of society.

The achievement of the objectives of social progress and development equally requires the implementation of the following means and methods:

Article 18

(*a*) The adoption of appropriate legislative, administrative and other measures ensuring to everyone not only political and civil rights, but also the full realization of economic, social and cultural rights without any discrimination;

(*b*) The promotion of democratically based social and institutional reforms and motivation for change basic to the elimination of all forms of discrimination and exploitation and conducive to high rates of economic and social progress, to include land reform, in which the ownership and use of land will be made to serve best the objectives of social justice and economic development;

(*c*) The adoption of measures to boost and diversify agricultural production through, *inter alia,* the implementation of democratic agrarian reforms, to ensure an adequate and well-balanced supply of food, its equitable distribution among the whole population and the improvement of nutritional standards;

(*d*) The adoption of measures to introduce, with the participation of the Government, low-cost housing programmes in both rural and urban areas;

(*e*) Development and expansion of the system of transportation and communications, particularly in developing countries.

Article 19

(*a*) The provision of free health services to the whole population and of adequate preventive and curative facilities and welfare medical services accessible to all;

(*b*) The enactment and establishment of legislative measures and administrative regulations with a view to the implementation of comprehensive programmes of social security schemes and social welfare services and to the improvement and co-ordination of existing services;

(*c*) The adoption of measures and the provision of social welfare services to migrant workers and their families, in conformity with the provisions of Convention No. 97 of the International Labour Organisation and other international instruments relating to migrant workers;

(*d*) The institution of appropriate measures for the rehabilitation of mentally or physically disabled persons, especially children and youth, so as to enable them to the fullest possible extent to be useful members of society-these measures shall include the provision of treatment and technical appliances, education, vocational and social guidance, training and selective placement, and other assistance required-and the creation of social conditions in which the handicapped are not discriminated against because of their disabilities.

Article 20

(*a*) The provision of full democratic freedoms to trade unions; freedom of association for all workers, including the right to bargain collectively and to strike, recognition of the right to form other organizations of working people; the provision for the growing participation of trade unions in economic and social development; effective participation of all members of trade unions in the deciding of economic and social issues which affect their interests;

(*b*) The improvement of health and safety conditions for workers, by means of appropriate technological and legislative measures and the provision of the material prerequisites for the implementation of those measures, including the limitation of working hours;

(*c*) The adoption of appropriate measures for the development of harmonious industrial relations.

Article 21

(*a*) The training of national personnel and cadres, including administrative, executive, professional and technical personnel needed for social development and for over-all development plans and policies;

(*b*) The adoption of measures to accelerate the extension and improvement of general, vocational and technical education and of training and retraining, which should be provided free at all levels;

(*c*) Raising the general level of education; development and expansion of national information media, and their rational and full use towards continuing education of the whole population and towards encouraging its participation in social development activities; the constructive use of leisure, particularly that of children and adolescents;

(*d*) The formulation of national and international policies and measures to avoid the "brain drain" and obviate its adverse effects.

Article 22

(*a*) The development and co-ordination of policies and measures designed to strengthen the essential functions of the family as a basic unit of society;

(*b*) The formulation and establishment, as needed, of programmes in the field of population, within the framework of national demographic policies and as part of the welfare medical services, including education, training of personnel and the provision to families of the knowledge and means necessary to enable them to exercise their right to determine freely and responsibly the number and spacing of their children;

(*c*) The establishment of appropriate child-care facilities in the interest of children and working parents.

The achievement of the objectives of social progress and development finally requires the implementation of the following means and methods:

Article 23

(*a*) The laying down of economic growth rate targets for the developing countries within the United Nations policy for development, high enough to lead to a substantial acceleration of their rates of growth;

(*b*) The provision of greater assistance on better terms; the implementation of the aid volume target of a minimum of 1 per cent of the gross national product at market prices of economically advanced countries; the general easing of the terms of lending to the developing countries through low interest rates on loans and long grace periods for the repayment of loans, and the assurance that the allocation of such loans will be based strictly on socio-economic criteria free of any political considerations;

(*c*) The provision of technical, financial and material assistance, both bilateral and multilateral, to the fullest possible extent and on favourable terms, and improved co-ordination of international assistance for the achievement of the social objectives of national development plans;

(*d*) The provision to the developing countries of technical, financial and material assistance and of favourable conditions to facilitate the direct exploitation of their national resources and natural wealth by those countries with a view to enabling the peoples of those countries to benefit fully from their national resources;

(*e*) The expansion of international trade based on principles of equality and non-discrimination, the rectification of the position of developing countries in international trade by equitable terms of trade, a general non-reciprocal and non-discriminatory system of preferences for the exports of developing countries to the developed countries, the establishment and implementation of general and comprehensive commodity agreements, and the financing of reasonable buffer stocks by international institutions.

Article 24

(*a*) Intensification of international co-operation with a view to ensuring the international exchange of information, knowledge and experience concerning social progress and development;

(*b*) The broadest possible international technical, scientific and cultural co-operation and reciprocal utilization of the experience of countries with different economic and social systems and different levels of development, on the basis of mutual advantage and strict observance of and respect for national sovereignty;

7.18 CONVENTION FOR THE PROTECTION OF THE WORLD CULTURAL AND NATURAL HERITAGE. Concluded at Paris, 16 November 1972. Entered into force, 17 December 1975. 1037 U.N.T.S. 151, 27 U.S.T. 37; *reprinted in* 11 I.L.M. 1358 (1972) & 5 Weston V.B.4

The General Conference of the United Nations Educational, Scientific and Cultural Organization meeting in Paris from 17 October to 21 November 1972, at its seventeenth session,

Noting that the cultural heritage and the natural heritage are increasingly threatened with destruction not only by the traditional causes of decay, but also by changing social and economic conditions which aggravate the situation with even more formidable phenomena of damage or destruction,

Considering that deterioration or disappearance of any item of the cultural or natural heritage constitutes a harmful impoverishment of the heritage of all the nations of the world,

Considering that protection of this heritage at the national level often remains incomplete because of the scale of the resources which it requires and of the insufficient economic, scientific and technical resources of the country where the property to be protected is situated,

Recalling that the Constitution of the Organization provides that it will maintain, increase and diffuse knowledge, by assuring the conservation and protection of the world's heritage, and recommending to the nations concerned the necessary international conventions,

Considering that the existing international conventions, recommendations and resolutions concerning cultural and natural property demonstrate the importance, for all the peoples of the world, of safeguarding this unique and irreplaceable property, to whatever people it may belong,

Considering that parts of the cultural or natural heritage are of outstanding interest and therefore need to be preserved as part of the world heritage of mankind as a whole,

Considering that, in view of the magnitude and gravity of the new dangers threatening them, it is incumbent on the international community as a whole to participate in the protection of the cultural and natural heritage of outstanding universal value, by the granting of collective assistance which, although not taking the place of action by the State concerned, will serve as an effective complement thereto,

Considering that it is essential for this purpose to adopt new provisions in the form of a convention establishing an effective system of collective protection of the cultural and natural heritage of outstanding universal value, organized on a permanent basis and in accordance with modern scientific methods,

Having decided, at its sixteenth session, that this question should be made the subject of an international convention,

Adopts this sixteenth day of November 1972 this Convention.

I. DEFINITIONS OF THE CULTURAL AND THE NATURAL HERITAGE

Article 1

For the purposes of this Convention, the following shall be considered as "cultural heritage":

monuments: architectural works, works of monumental sculpture and painting, elements or structures of an archaeological nature, inscriptions, cave dwellings and combinations of features, which are of outstanding universal value from the point of view of history, art or science;

groups of buildings: groups of separate or connected buildings which, because of their architecture, their homogeneity or their place in the landscape, are of outstanding universal value from the point of view of history, art or science;

sites: works of man or the combined works of nature and of man, and areas including archaeological sites which are of outstanding universal value from the historical, aesthetic, ethnological or anthropological points of view.

Article 2

For the purposes of this Convention, the following shall be considered as "natural heritage":

natural features consisting of physical and biological formations or groups of such formations, which are of outstanding universal value from the aesthetic or scientific point of view;

geological and physiographical natural sites or precisely delineated natural areas of outstanding universal value from the point of view of science, conservation or natural beauty.

Article 3

It is for each State Party to this Convention to identify and delineate the different properties situated on its territory mentioned in Article 1 and 2 above.

II. NATIONAL PROTECTION AND INTERNATIONAL PROTECTION OF THE CULTURAL AND NATURAL HERITAGE

Article 4

Each State Party to this Convention recognizes that the duty of ensuring the identification, protection, conservation, presentation and transmission to future generations of the cultural and natural heritage referred to in Articles 1 and 2 and situated on its territory, belongs primarily to that State. It will do all it can to this end, to the utmost of its own resources and, where appropriate, with any international assistance and co-operation, in particular, financial, artistic, scientific and technical, which it may be able to obtain.

Article 5

To ensure that effective and active measures are taken for the protection, conservation and presentation of the cultural and natural heritage situated on its territory, each State Party to this Convention shall endeavour, in so far as possible, and as appropriate for each country:

(a) to adopt a general policy which aims to give the cultural and natural heritage a function in the life of the community and to integrate the protection of that heritage into comprehensive planning programmes;

(b) to set up within its territories, where such services do not exist, one or more services for the protection, conservation and presentation of the cultural and natural heritage with an appropriate staff and possessing the means to discharge their functions;

(c) to develop scientific and technical studies and research and to work out such operating methods as will make the State capable of counteracting the dangers that threaten its cultural or natural heritage;

(d) to take the appropriate legal, scientific, technical, administrative and financial measures necessary for the identification, protection, conservation, presentation and rehabilitation of this heritage; and

(e) to foster the establishment or development of national or regional centres for training in the protection, conservation and presentation of the cultural and natural heritage and to encourage scientific research in this field.

Article 6

1. Whilst fully respecting the sovereignty of the States on whose territory the cultural and natural heritage mentioned in Articles 1 and 2 is situated, and without prejudice to property rights provided by national legislation, the States Parties to this Convention recognize that such heritage constitutes a world heritage for whose protection it is the duty of the international community as a whole to co-operate.

2. The States Parties undertake, in accordance with the provisions of this Convention, to give their help in the identification, protection, conservation and preservation of the cultural and natural heritage referred to in paragraphs 2 and 4 of Article 11 if the States on whose territory it is situated so request.

3. Each State Party to this Convention undertakes not to take any deliberate measures which might damage directly or indirectly the cultural and natural heritage referred to in Articles 1 and 2 situated on the territory of other States Parties to this Convention.

Article 7

For the purpose of this Convention, international protection of the world cultural and natural heritage shall be understood to mean the establishment of a system of international co-operation and assistance designed to support States Parties to the Convention in their efforts to conserve and identify that heritage.

III. INTERGOVERNMENTAL COMMITTEE FOR THE PROTECTION OF THE WORLD CULTURAL AND NATURAL HERITAGE

Article 8

1. An Intergovernmental Committee for the Protection of the Cultural and Natural Heritage of Outstanding Universal Value, called "the World Heritage Committee", is hereby established within the United Nations Educational, Scientific and Cultural Organization. It shall be composed of 15 States Parties to the Convention, elected by States Parties to the Convention meeting in general assembly during the ordinary session of the General Conference of the United Nations Educational, Scientific and Cultural Organization. The number of States members of the Committee shall be increased to 21 as from the date of the ordinary session of the General Conference following the entry into force of this Convention for at least 40 States.

2. Election of members of the Committee shall ensure an equitable representation of the different regions and cultures of the world.

3. A representative of the International Centre for the Study of the Preservation and Restoration of Cultural Property (Rome Centre), a representative of the International Council of Monuments and Sites (ICOMOS) and a representative of the International Union for Conservation of Nature and Natural Resources (IUCN), to whom may be added, at the request of States Parties to the Convention meeting in general assembly during the ordinary sessions of the General Conference of the United Nations Educational, Scientific and Cultural Organization, representatives of other intergovernmental or non-governmental organizations, with similar objectives, may attend the meetings of the Committee in an advisory capacity.

Article 9

1. The term of office of States members of the World Heritage Committee shall extend from the end of the ordinary session of the General Conference during which they are elected until the end of its third subsequent ordinary session.

2. The term of office of one-third of the members designated at the time of the first election shall, however, cease at the end of the first ordinary session of the General Conference following that at which they were elected; and the term of office of a further third of the members designated at the same time shall cease at the end of the second ordinary session of the General Conference following that at which they were elected. The names of these members shall be chosen by lot by the President of the General Conference of the United Nations Educational, Scientific and Cultural Organization after the first election.

3. States members of the Committee shall choose as their representatives persons qualified in the field of the cultural or natural heritage.

Article 10

1. The World Heritage Committee shall adopt its Rules of Procedure.

2. The Committee may at any time invite public or private organizations or individuals to participate in its meetings for consultation on particular problems.

3. The Committee may create such consultative bodies as it deems necessary for the performance of its functions.

Article 11

1. Every State Party to this Convention shall, in so far as possible, submit to the World Heritage Committee an inventory of property forming part of the cultural and natural heritage, situated in its territory and suitable for inclusion in the list provided for in paragraph 2 of this Article. This inventory, which shall not be considered exhaustive, shall include documentation about the location of the property in question and its significance.

2. On the basis of the inventories submitted by States in accordance with paragraph 1, the Committee shall establish, keep up to date and publish, under the title of "World Heritage List, a list of properties forming part of the cultural heritage and natural heritage, as defined in Articles 1 and 2 of this Convention, which it considers as having outstanding universal value in terms of such criteria as it shall have established. An updated list shall be distributed at least every two years.

3. The inclusion of a property in the World Heritage List requires the consent of the State concerned. The inclusion of a property situated in a territory, sovereignty or jurisdiction over which is claimed by more than one State shall in no way prejudice the rights of the parties to the dispute.

4. The Committee shall establish, keep up to date and publish, whenever circumstances shall so require, under the title of "List of World Heritage in Danger", a list of the property appearing in the World Heritage List for the conservation of which major operations are necessary and for which assistance has been requested under this Convention. This list shall contain an estimate of the cost of such operations. The list may include only such property forming part of the cultural and natural heritage as is threatened by serious and specific dangers, such as the threat of disappearance caused by accelerated deterioration, large-scale public or private projects or rapid urban or tourist development projects; destruction caused by changes in the use or ownership of the land; major alterations due to unknown causes; abandonment for any reason whatsoever; the outbreak or the threat of an armed conflict; calamities and cataclysms; serious fires, earthquakes, landslides; volcanic eruptions; changes in water level, floods, and tidal waves. The Committee may at any time, in case of urgent need, make a new entry in the List of World Heritage in Danger and publicize such entry immediately.

5. The Committee shall define the criteria on the basis of which a property belonging to the cultural or natural heritage may be included in either of the lists mentioned in paragraphs 2 and 4 of this article.

6. Before refusing a request for inclusion in one of the two lists mentioned in paragraphs 2 and 4 of this article, the Committee shall consult the State Party in whose territory the cultural or natural property in question is situated.

7. The Committee shall, with the agreement of the States concerned, co-ordinate and encourage the studies and research needed for the drawing up of the lists referred to in paragraphs 2 and 4 of this article.

Article 12

The fact that a property belonging to the cultural or natural heritage has not been included in either of the two lists mentioned in paragraphs 2 and 4 of Article 11 shall in no way be construed to mean that it does not have an outstanding universal value for purposes other than those resulting from inclusion in these lists.

Article 13

1. The World Heritage Committee shall receive and study requests for international assistance formulated by States Parties to this Convention with respect to property forming part of the cultural or natural heritage, situated in their territories, and included or potentially suitable for inclusion in the lists referred to in paragraphs 2 and 4 of Article 11. The purpose of such requests may be to secure the protection, conservation, presentation or rehabilitation of such property.

2. Requests for international assistance under paragraph 1 of this article may also be concerned with identification of cultural or natural property defined in Articles 1 and 2, when preliminary investigations have shown that further inquiries would be justified.

3. The Committee shall decide on the action to be taken with regard to these requests, determine where appropriate, the nature and extent of its assistance, and authorize the conclusion, on its behalf, of the necessary arrangements with the government concerned.

4. The Committee shall determine an order of priorities for its operations. It shall in so doing bear in mind the respective importance for the world cultural and natural heritage of the property requiring protection, the need to give international assistance to the property most representative of a natural environment or of the genius and the history of the peoples of the world, the urgency of the work to be done, the resources available to the States on whose territory the threatened property is situated and in particular the extent to which they are able to safeguard such property by their own means.

5. The Committee shall draw up, keep up to date and publicize a list of property for which international assistance has been granted.

6. The Committee shall decide on the use of the resources of the Fund established under Article 15 of this Convention. It shall seek ways of increasing these resources and shall take all useful steps to this end.

7. The Committee shall co-operate with international and national governmental and nongovernmental organizations having objectives similar to those of this Convention. For the implementation of its programmes and projects, the Committee may call on such organizations, particularly the International Centre for the Study of the Preservation and Restoration of Cultural Property (the Rome Centre), the International Council of Monuments and Sites (ICOMOS) and the International Union for Conservation of Nature and Natural Resources (IUCN), as well as on public and private bodies and individuals.

8. Decisions of the Committee shall be taken by a majority of two-thirds of its members present and voting. A majority of the members of the Committee shall constitute a quorum.

Article 14

1. The World Heritage Committee shall be assisted by a Secretariat appointed by the Director–General of the United Nations Educational, Scientific and Cultural Organization.

2. The Director–General of the United Nations Educational, Scientific and Cultural Organization, utilizing to the fullest extent possible the services of the International Centre for the Study of the Preservation and the Restoration of Cultural Property (the Rome Centre), the International Council of Monuments and Sites (ICOMOS) and the International Union for Conservation of Nature and Natural Resources (IUCN) in their respective areas of competence and capability, shall prepare the Committee's documentation and the agenda of its meetings and shall have the responsibility for the implementation of its decisions.

IV. FUND FOR THE PROTECTION OF THE WORLD CULTURAL AND NATURAL HERITAGE

Article 15

1. A Fund for the Protection of the World Cultural and Natural Heritage of Outstanding Universal Value, called "the World Heritage Fund", is hereby established.

2. The Fund shall constitute a trust fund, in conformity with the provisions of the Financial Regulations of the United Nations Educational, Scientific and Cultural Organization.

3. The resources of the Fund shall consist of:

(a) compulsory and voluntary contributions made by the States Parties to this Convention,

(b) contributions, gifts or bequests which may be made by:

(i) other States;

(ii) the United Nations Educational, Scientific and Cultural Organization, other organizations of the United Nations system, particularly the United Nations Development Programme or other intergovernmental organizations;

(iii) public or private bodies or individuals;

(c) any interest due on the resources of the Fund;

(d) funds raised by collections and receipts from events organized for the benefit of the Fund; and

(e) all other resources authorized by the Fund's regulations, as drawn up by the World Heritage Committee.

4. Contributions to the Fund and other forms of assistance made available to the Committee may be used only for such purposes as the Committee shall define. The Committee may accept contributions to be used only for a certain programme or project, provided that the Committee shall have decided on the implementation of such programme or project. No political conditions may be attached to contributions made to the Fund.

Article 16

1. Without prejudice to any supplementary voluntary contribution, the States Parties to this Convention undertake to pay regularly, every two years, to the World Heritage Fund, contributions, the amount of which, in the form of a uniform percentage applicable to all States, shall be determined by the General Assembly of States Parties to the Convention, meeting during the sessions of the General Conference of the United Nations Educational, Scientific and Cultural Organization. This decision of

the General Assembly requires the majority of the States Parties present and voting, which have not made the declaration referred to in paragraph 2 of this Article. In no case shall the compulsory contribution of States Parties to the Convention exceed 1% of the contribution to the Regular Budget of the United Nations Educational, Scientific and Cultural Organization.

2. However, each State referred to in Article 31 or in Article 32 of this Convention may declare, at the time of the deposit of its instruments of ratification, acceptance or accession, that it shall not be bound by the provisions of paragraph 1 of this Article.

3. A State Party to the Convention which has made the declaration referred to in paragraph 2 of this Article may at any time withdraw the said declaration by notifying the Director–General of the United Nations Educational, Scientific and Cultural Organization. However, the withdrawal of the declaration shall not take effect in regard to the compulsory contribution due by the State until the date of the subsequent General Assembly of States Parties to the Convention.

4. In order that the Committee may be able to plan its operations effectively, the contributions of States Parties to this Convention which have made the declaration referred to in paragraph 2 of this Article, shall be paid on a regular basis, at least every two years, and should not be less than the contributions which they should have paid if they had been bound by the provisions of paragraph 1 of this Article.

5. Any State Party to the Convention which is in arrears with the payment of its compulsory or voluntary contribution for the current year and the calendar year immediately preceding it shall not be eligible as a Member of the World Heritage Committee, although this provision shall not apply to the first election.

The terms of office of any such State which is already a member of the Committee shall terminate at the time of the elections provided for in Article 8, paragraph 1 of this Convention.

Article 17

The States Parties to this Convention shall consider or encourage the establishment of national, public and private foundations or associations whose purpose is to invite donations for the protection of the cultural and natural heritage as defined in Articles 1 and 2 of this Convention.

Article 18

The States Parties to this Convention shall give their assistance to international fund-raising campaigns organized for the World Heritage Fund under the auspices of the United Nations Educational, Scientific and Cultural Organization. They shall facilitate collections made by the bodies mentioned in paragraph 3 of Article 15 for this purpose.

V. CONDITIONS AND ARRANGEMENTS FOR INTERNATIONAL ASSISTANCE

Article 19

Any State Party to this Convention may request international assistance for property forming part of the cultural or natural heritage of outstanding universal value situated within its territory. It shall submit with its request such information and documentation provided for in Article 21 as it has in its possession and as will enable the Committee to come to a decision.

Article 20

Subject to the provisions of paragraph 2 of Article 13, sub-paragraph (c) of Article 22 and Article 23, international assistance provided for by this Convention may be granted only to property forming part of the cultural and natural heritage which the World Heritage Committee has decided, or may decide, to enter in one of the lists mentioned in paragraphs 2 and 4 of Article 11.

Article 21

1. The World Heritage Committee shall define the procedure by which requests to it for international assistance shall be considered and shall specify the content of the request, which should define the operation contemplated, the work that is necessary, the expected cost thereof, the degree of urgency and the reasons why the resources of the State requesting assistance do not allow it to meet all the expenses. Such requests must be supported by experts' reports whenever possible.

2. Requests based upon disasters or natural calamities should, by reasons of the urgent work which they may involve, be given immediate, priority consideration by the Committee, which should have a reserve fund at its disposal against such contingencies.

3. Before coming to a decision, the Committee shall carry out such studies and consultations as it deems necessary.

Article 22

Assistance granted by the World Heritage Committee may take the following forms:

(a) studies concerning the artistic, scientific and technical problems raised by the protection, conservation, presentation and rehabilitation of the cultural and natural heritage, as defined in paragraphs 2 and 4 of Article 11 of this Convention;

(b) provision of experts, technicians and skilled labour to ensure that the approved work is correctly carried out;

(c) training of staff and specialists at all levels in the field of identification, protection, conservation, presentation and rehabilitation of the cultural and natural heritage;

(d) supply of equipment which the State concerned does not possess or is not in a position to acquire;

(e) low-interest or interest-free loans which might be repayable on a long-term basis;

(f) the granting, in exceptional cases and for special reasons, of non-repayable subsidies.

Article 23

The World Heritage Committee may also provide international assistance to national or regional centres for the training of staff and specialists at all levels in the field of identification, protection, conservation, presentation and rehabilitation of the cultural and natural heritage.

Article 24

International assistance on a large scale shall be preceded by detailed scientific, economic and technical studies. These studies shall draw upon the most advanced techniques for the protection, conservation, presentation and rehabilitation of the natural and cultural heritage and shall be consistent with the objectives of this Convention. The studies shall also seek means of making rational use of the resources available in the State concerned.

Article 25

As a general rule, only part of the cost of work necessary shall be borne by the international community. The contribution of the State benefiting from international assistance shall constitute a substantial share of the resources devoted to each programme or project, unless its resources do not permit this.

Article 26

The World Heritage Committee and the recipient State shall define in the agreement they conclude the conditions in which a programme or project for which international assistance under the terms of this Convention is provided, shall be carried out. It shall be the responsibility of the State receiving such international assistance to continue to protect, conserve and present the property so safeguarded, in observance of the conditions laid down by the agreement.

VI. EDUCATIONAL PROGRAMMES

Article 27

1. The States Parties to this Convention shall endeavour by all appropriate means, and in particular by educational and information programmes, to strengthen appreciation and respect by their peoples of the cultural and natural heritage defined in Articles 1 and 2 of the Convention.

2. They shall undertake to keep the public broadly informed of the dangers threatening this heritage and of activities carried on in pursuance of this Convention.

Article 28

States Parties to this Convention which receive international assistance under the Convention shall take appropriate measures to make known the importance of the property for which assistance has been received and the role played by such assistance.

VII. REPORTS

Article 29

1. The States Parties to this Convention shall, in the reports which they submit to the General Conference of the United Nations Educational, Scientific and Cultural Organization on dates and in a manner to be determined by it, give information on the legislative and administrative provisions which they have adopted and other action which they have taken for the application of this Convention, together with details of the experience acquired in this field.

2. These reports shall be brought to the attention of the World Heritage Committee.

3. The Committee shall submit a report on its activities at each of the ordinary sessions of the General Conference of the United Nations Educational, Scientific and Cultural Organization.

VIII. FINAL CLAUSES

Article 30

This Convention is drawn up in Arabic, English, French, Russian and Spanish, the five texts being equally authoritative.

Article 31

1. This Convention shall be subject to ratification or acceptance by States members of the United Nations Educational, Scientific and Cultural Organization in accordance with their respective constitutional procedures.

2. The instruments of ratification or acceptance shall be deposited with the Director–General of the United Nations Educational, Scientific and Cultural Organization.

Article 32

1. This Convention shall be open to accession by all States not members of the United Nations Educational, Scientific and Cultural Organization which are invited by the General Conference of the Organization to accede to it.

2. Accession shall be effected by the deposit of an instrument of accession with the Director–General of the United Nations Educational, Scientific and Cultural Organization.

Article 33

This Convention shall enter into force three months after the date of the deposit of the twentieth instrument of ratification, acceptance or accession, but only with respect to those States which have deposited their respective instruments of ratification, acceptance or accession on or before that date. It shall enter into force with respect to any other State three months after the deposit of its instrument of ratification, acceptance or accession.

Article 34

The following provisions shall apply to those States Parties to this Convention which have a federal or non-unitary constitutional system:

(a) with regard to the provisions of this Convention, the implementation of which comes under the legal jurisdiction of the federal or central legislative power, the obligations of the federal or central government shall be the same as for those States Parties which are not federal States;

(b) with regard to the provisions of this Convention, the implementation of which comes under the legal jurisdiction of individual constituent States, countries, provinces or cantons that are not obliged by the constitutional system of the federation to take legislative measures, the federal government shall inform the competent authorities of such States, countries, provinces or cantons of the said provisions, with its recommendation for their adoption.

Article 35

1. Each State Party to this Convention may denounce the Convention.

2. The denunciation shall be notified by an instrument in writing, deposited with the Director–General of the United Nations Educational, Scientific and Cultural Organization.

3. The denunciation shall take effect twelve months after the receipt of the instrument of denunciation. It shall not affect the financial obligations of the denouncing State until the date on which the withdrawal takes effect.

Article 36

The Director–General of the United Nations Educational, Scientific and Cultural Organization shall inform the States members of the Organization, the States not members of the Organization which are referred to in Article 32, as well as the United Nations, of the deposit of all the instruments of ratification, acceptance, or accession provided for in Articles 31 and 32, and of the denunciations provided for in Article 35.

Article 37

1. This Convention may be revised by the General Conference of the United Nations Educational, Scientific and Cultural Organization. Any such revision shall, however, bind only the States which shall become Parties to the revising convention.

2. If the General Conference should adopt a new convention revising this Convention in whole or in part, then, unless the new convention otherwise provides, this Convention shall cease to be open to ratification, acceptance or accession, as from the date on which the new revising convention enters into force.

Article 38

In conformity with Article 102 of the Charter of the United Nations, this Convention shall be registered with the Secretariat of the United Nations at the request of the Director–General of the United Nations Educational, Scientific and Cultural Organization.

Done in Paris, this twenty-third day of November 1972, in two authentic copies bearing the signature of the President of the seventeenth session of the General Conference and of the Director–General of the United Nations Educational, Scientific and Cultural Organization, which shall be deposited in the archives of the United Nations Educational, Scientific and Cultural Organization, and certified true copies of which shall be delivered to all the States referred to in Article 31 and 32 as well as to the United Nations.

7.19 CONVENTION ON THE ELIMINATION OF ALL FORMS OF DISCRIMINATION AGAINST WOMEN. Concluded at New York, 18 December 1979. Entered into force, 3 September 1981. 1249 U.N.T.S. 13; *reprinted in* 19 I.L.M. 33 (1980) & 3 Weston III.C.12: *Art. 12*

Article 12. (1) States Parties shall take all appropriate measures to eliminate discrimination against women in the field of health care in order to ensure, on a basis of equality of men and women, access to health care services, including those related to family planning.

(2) Notwithstanding the provisions of paragraph 1 above, States Parties shall ensure to women appropriate services in connexion with pregnancy, confinement and the post-natal period, granting free services where necessary, as well as adequate nutrition during pregnancy and lactation.

7.20 Declaration on the Right to Development. Adopted by the U.N. General Assembly, 4 December 1986. G.A. Res. 41/128 (Annex), U.N. GAOR, 41st Sess., Supp. No. 53, at 186, U.N. Doc. A/41/53 (1987); *reprinted in* 3 Weston III.R.2

The General Assembly,

Bearing in mind the purposes and principles of the Charter of the United Nations relating to the achievement of international co-operation in solving international problems of an economic, social, cultural or humanitarian nature, and in promoting and encouraging respect for human rights and fundamental freedoms for all without distinction as to race, sex, language or religion,

Recognizing that development is a comprehensive economic, social, cultural and political process, which aims at the constant improvement of the well-being of the entire population and of all individuals on the basis of their active, free and meaningful participation in development and in the fair distribution of benefits resulting therefrom,

Considering that under the provisions of the Universal Declaration of Human Rights everyone is entitled to a social and international order in which the rights and freedoms set forth in that Declaration can be fully realized,

Recalling the provisions of the International Covenant on Economic, Social and Cultural Rights and the International Covenant on Civil and Political Rights,

Recalling further the relevant agreements, conventions, resolutions, recommendations and other instruments of the United Nations and its specialized agencies concerning the integral development of the human being, economic and social progress and development of all peoples, including those instruments concerning decolonization, the prevention of discrimination, respect for, and observance of, human rights and fundamental freedoms, the maintenance of international peace and security and the further promotion of friendly relations and co-operation among States in accordance with the Charter,

Recalling the right of peoples to self-determination, by virtue of which they have the right freely to determine their political status and to pursue their economic, social and cultural development,

Recalling further the right of peoples to exercise, subject to relevant provisions of both International Covenants on Human Rights, their full and complete sovereignty over all their natural wealth and resources,

Mindful of the obligation of States under the Charter to promote universal respect for and observance of human rights and fundamental freedoms for all without distinction of any kind such as race, colour, sex, language, religion, political or other opinion, national or social origin, property, birth or other status,

Considering that the elimination of the massive and flagrant violations of the human rights of the peoples and individuals affected by situations such as those resulting from colonialism, neo-colonialism, *apartheid,* all forms of racism and racial discrimination, foreign domination and occupation, aggression and threats against national sovereignty, national unity and territorial integrity and threats of war would contribute to the establishment of circumstances propitious to the development of a great part of mankind,

Concerned at the existence of serious obstacles to development, as well as to the complete fulfilment of human beings and of peoples, constituted, *inter alia,* by the denial of civil, political, economic, social and cultural rights, and considering that all human rights and fundamental freedoms are indivisible and interdependent and that, in order to promote development, equal attention and urgent consideration should be given to the implementation, promotion and protection of civil, political, economic, social and cultural rights and that, accordingly, the promotion of, respect for, and enjoyment of certain human rights and fundamental freedoms cannot justify the denial of other human rights and fundamental freedoms,

Considering that international peace and security are essential elements for the realization of the right to development,

Reaffirming that there is a close relationship between disarmament and development and that progress in the field of disarmament would considerably promote progress in the field of development and that resources released through disarmament measures should be devoted to the economic and social development and well-being of all peoples and, in particular, those of the developing countries,

Recognizing that the human person is the central subject of the development process and that development policy should therefore make the human being the main participant and beneficiary of development,

Recognizing that the creation of conditions favourable to the development of peoples and individuals is the primary responsibility of their States,

Aware that efforts to promote and protect human rights at the international level should be accompanied by efforts to establish a new international economic order,

Confirming that the right to development is an inalienable human right and that equality of opportunity for development is a prerogative both of nations and of individuals who make up nations,

Proclaims the following Declaration on the right to development:

ARTICLE 1

1. The right to development is an inalienable human right by virtue of which every human person and all peoples are entitled to participate in, contribute to, and enjoy economic, social, cultural and political development, in which all human rights and fundamental freedoms can be fully realized.

2. The human right to development also implies the full realization of the right of peoples to self-determination, which includes, subject to relevant provisions of both International Covenants on Human Rights, the exercise of their inalienable right to full sovereignty over all their natural wealth and resources.

ARTICLE 2

1. The human person is the central subject of development and should be the active participant and beneficiary of the right to development.

2. All human beings have a responsibility for development, individually and collectively, taking into account the need for full respect of their human rights and fundamental freedoms as well as their duties to the community, which alone can ensure the free and complete fulfilment of the human being, and they should therefore promote and protect an appropriate political, social and economic order for development.

3. States have the right and the duty to formulate appropriate national development policies that aim at the constant improvement of the well-being of the entire population and of all individuals, on the basis of their active, free and meaningful participation in development and in the fair distribution of the benefits resulting therefrom.

ARTICLE 3

1. States have the primary responsibility for the creation of national and international conditions favourable to the realization of the right to development.

2. The realization of the right to development requires full respect for the principles of international law concerning friendly relations and co-operation among States in accordance with the Charter of the United Nations.

3. States have the duty to co-operate with each other in ensuring development and eliminating obstacles to development. States should fulfil their rights and duties in such a manner as to promote a new international economic order based on sovereign equality, interdependence, mutual interest and co-operation among all States, as well as to encourage the observance and realization of human rights.

ARTICLE 4

1. States have the duty to take steps, individually and collectively, to formulate international development policies with a view to facilitating the full realization of the right to development.

2. Sustained action is required to promote more rapid development of developing countries. As a complement to the efforts of developing countries effective international co-operation is essential in providing these countries with appropriate means and facilities to foster their comprehensive development.

ARTICLE 5

States shall take resolute steps to eliminate the massive and flagrant violations of the human rights of peoples and human beings affected by situations such as those resulting from *apartheid*, all forms of racism and racial discrimination, colonialism, foreign domination and occupation, aggression, foreign interference and threats against national sovereignty, national unity and territorial integrity, threats of war and refusal to recognize the fundamental right of peoples to self-determination.

ARTICLE 6

1. All States should co-operate with a view to promoting, encouraging and strengthening universal respect for and observance of all human rights and fundamental freedoms for all without any distinction as to race, sex, language and religion.

2. All human rights and fundamental freedoms are indivisible and interdependent, equal attention and urgent consideration should be given to the implementation, promotion and protection of civil, political, economic, social and cultural rights.

3. States should take steps to eliminate obstacles to development resulting from failure to observe civil and political rights as well as economic, social and cultural rights.

ARTICLE 7

All States should promote the establishment, maintenance and strengthening of international peace and security and, to that end, should do their utmost to achieve general and complete disarmament under effective international control as well as to ensure that the resources released by effective disarmament measures are used for comprehensive development, in particular that of the developing countries.

ARTICLE 8

1. States should undertake, at the national level, all necessary measures for the realization of the right to development and shall ensure, *inter alia,* equality of opportunity for all in their access to basic resources, education, health services, food, housing, employment and the fair distribution of income. Effective measures should be undertaken to ensure that women have an active role in the development process. Appropriate economic and social reforms should be made with a view to eradicating all social injustices.

2. States should encourage popular participation in all spheres as an important factor in development and in the full realization of all human rights.

ARTICLE 9

1. All the aspects of the right to development set forth in this Declaration are indivisible and interdependent and each of them should be considered in the context of the whole.

2. Nothing in this Declaration shall be construed as being contrary to the purposes and principles of the United Nations, or as implying that any State, group or person has a right to engage in any activity or to perform any act aimed at the violation of the rights set forth in the Universal Declaration of Human Rights and in the International Covenants on Human Rights.

ARTICLE 10

Steps should be taken to ensure the full exercise and progressive enhancement of the right to development, including the formulation, adoption and implementation of policy, legislative and other measures at the national and international levels.

7.21 INTERNATIONAL LABOUR ORGANIZATION CONVENTION (NO. 169) CONCERNING INDIGENOUS AND TRIBAL PEOPLES IN INDEPENDENT COUNTRIES. Concluded at Geneva, 27 June 1989. Entered into force, 5 September 1991. *Reprinted in* 28 I.L.M. 1382 (1989) & 3 Weston III.F.2

The General Conference of the International Labour Organization,

Having been convened at Geneva by the Governing Body of the International Labour Office, and having met in its 76th Session on 7 June 1989, and

Noting the international standards contained in the Indigenous and Tribal Populations Convention and Recommendation, 1957, and

Recalling the terms of the Universal Declaration of Human Rights, the International Covenant on Economic, Social and Cultural Rights, the International Covenant on Civil and Political Rights, and the many international instruments on the prevention of discrimination, and

Considering that the developments which have taken place in international law since 1957, as well as developments in the situation of indigenous and tribal peoples in all regions of the world, have made it appropriate to adopt new international standards on the subject with a view to removing the assimilationist orientation of the earlier standards, and

Recognising the aspirations of these peoples to exercise control over their own institutions, ways of life and economic development and to maintain and develop their identities, languages and religions, within the framework of the States in which they live, and

Noting that in many parts of the world these peoples are unable to enjoy their fundamental human rights to the same degree as the rest of the population of the States within which they live, and that their laws, values, customs and perspectives have often been eroded, and

Calling attention to the distinctive contributions of indigenous and tribal peoples to the cultural diversity and social and ecological harmony of humankind and to international co-operation and understanding, and

Noting that the following provisions have been framed with the co-operation of the United Nations, the Food and Agriculture Organisation of the United Nations, the United Nations Educational, Scientific and Cultural Organisation and the World Health Organisation, as well as of the Inter-American Indian Institute, at appropriate levels and in their respective fields, and that it is proposed to continue this co-operation in promoting and securing the application of these provisions, and

Having decided upon the adoption of certain proposals with regard to the partial revision of the Indigenous and Tribal Populations Convention, 1957 (No. 107), which is the fourth item on the agenda of the session, and

Having determined that these proposals shall take the form of an international Convention revising the Indigenous and Tribal Populations Convention, 1957;

adopts this twenty-seventh day of June of the year one thousand nine hundred and eighty-nine the following Convention, which may be cited as the Indigenous and Tribal Peoples Convention, 1989:

Part I. General Policy

Article 1

1. This Convention applies to:

(a) tribal peoples in independent countries whose social, cultural and economic conditions distinguish them from other sections of the national community, and

whose status is regulated wholly or partially by their own customs or traditions or by special laws or regulations;

(b) peoples in independent countries who are regarded as indigenous on account of their descent from the populations which inhabited the country, or a geographical region to which the country belongs, at the time of conquest or colonisation or the establishment of present state boundaries and who, irrespective of their legal status, retain some or all of their own social, economic, cultural and political institutions.

2. Self-identification as indigenous or tribal shall be regarded as a fundamental criterion for determining the groups to which the provisions of this Convention apply.

3. The use of the term "peoples" in this Convention shall not be construed as having any implications as regards the rights which may attach to the term under international law.

Article 2

1. Governments shall have the responsibility for developing, with the participation of the peoples concerned, co-ordinated and systematic action to protect the rights of these peoples and to guarantee respect for their integrity.

2. Such action shall include measures for:

(a) ensuring that members of these peoples benefit on an equal footing from the rights and opportunities which national laws and regulations grant to other members of the population;

(b) promoting the full realisation of the social, economic and cultural rights of these peoples with respect for their social and cultural identity, their customs and traditions and their institutions;

(c) assisting the members of the peoples concerned to eliminate socio-economic gaps that may exist between indigenous and other members of the national community, in a manner compatible with their aspirations and ways of life.

Article 3

1. Indigenous and tribal peoples shall enjoy the full measure of human rights and fundamental freedoms without hindrance or discrimination. The provisions of the Convention shall be applied without discrimination to male and female members of these peoples.

2. No form of force or coercion shall be used in violation of the human rights and fundamental freedoms of the peoples concerned, including the rights contained in this Convention.

Article 4

1. Special measures shall be adopted as appropriate for safeguarding the persons, institutions, property, labour, cultures and environment of the peoples concerned.

2. Such special measures shall not be contrary to the freely-expressed wishes of the peoples concerned.

3. Enjoyment of the general rights of citizenship, without discrimination, shall not be prejudiced in any way by such special measures.

Article 5

In applying the provisions of this Convention:

(a) the social, cultural, religious and spiritual values and practices of these peoples shall be recognised and protected, and due account shall be taken of the nature of the problems which face them both as groups and as individuals;

(b) the integrity of the values, practices and institutions of these peoples shall be respected;

(c) policies aimed at mitigating the difficulties experienced by these peoples in facing new conditions of life and work shall be adopted, with the participation and co-operation of the peoples affected.

Article 6

1. In applying the provisions of this Convention, governments shall:

(a) consult the peoples concerned, through appropriate procedures and in particular through their representative institutions, whenever consideration is being given to legislative or administrative measures which may affect them directly;

(b) establish means by which these peoples can freely participate, to at least the same extent as other sectors of the population, at all levels of decision-making in elective institutions and administrative and other bodies responsible for policies and programmes which concern them;

(c) establish means for the full development of these peoples' own institutions and initiatives, and in appropriate cases provide the resources necessary for this purpose.

2. The consultations carried out in application of this Convention shall be undertaken, in good faith and in a form appropriate to the circumstances, with the objective of achieving agreement or consent to the proposed measures.

Article 7

1. The peoples concerned shall have the right to decide their own priorities for the process of development as it affects their lives, beliefs, institutions and spiritual well-being and the lands they occupy or otherwise use, and to exercise control, to the extent possible, over their own economic, social and cultural development. In addition, they shall participate in the formulation, implementation and evaluation of plans and programmes for national and regional development which may affect them directly.

2. The improvement of the conditions of life and work and levels of health and education of the peoples concerned, with their participation and co-operation, shall be a matter of priority in plans for the overall economic development of areas they inhabit. Special projects for development of the areas in question shall also be so designed as to promote such improvement.

3. Governments shall ensure that, whenever appropriate, studies are carried out, in co-operation with the peoples concerned, to assess the social, spiritual, cultural and environmental impact on them of planned development activities. The results of these studies shall be considered as fundamental criteria for the implementation of these activities.

4. Governments shall take measures, in co-operation with the peoples concerned, to protect and preserve the environment of the territories they inhabit.

Article 8

1. In applying national laws and regulations to the peoples concerned, due regard shall be had to their customs or customary laws.

2. These peoples shall have the right to retain their own customs and institutions, where these are not incompatible with fundamental rights defined by the

national legal system and with internationally recognised human rights. Procedures shall be established, whenever necessary, to resolve conflicts which may arise in the application of this principle.

3. The application of paragraphs 1 and 2 of this Article shall not prevent members of these peoples from exercising the rights granted to all citizens and from assuming the corresponding duties.

Article 9

1. To the extent compatible with the national legal system and internationally recognised human rights, the methods customarily practised by the peoples concerned for dealing with offences committed by their members shall be respected.

2. The customs of these peoples in regard to penal matters shall be taken into consideration by the authorities and courts dealing with such cases.

Article 10

1. In imposing penalties laid down by general law on members of these peoples account shall be taken of their economic, social and cultural characteristics.

2. Preference shall be given to methods of punishment other than confinement in prison.

Article 11

The exaction from members of the peoples concerned of compulsory personal services in any form, whether paid or unpaid, shall be prohibited and punishable by law, except in cases prescribed by law for all citizens.

Article 12

The peoples concerned shall be safeguarded against the abuse of their rights and shall be able to take legal proceedings, either individually or through their representative bodies, for the effective protection of these rights. Measures shall be taken to ensure that members of these peoples can understand and be understood in legal proceedings, where necessary through the provision of interpretation or by other effective means.

Part II. Land

Article 13

1. In applying the provisions of this Part of the Convention governments shall respect the special importance for the cultures and spiritual values of the peoples concerned of their relationship with the lands or territories, or both as applicable, which they occupy or otherwise use, and in particular the collective aspects of this relationship.

2. The use of the term "lands" in Articles 15 and 16 shall include the concept of territories, which covers the total environment of the areas which the peoples concerned occupy or otherwise use.

Article 14

1. The rights of ownership and possession of the peoples concerned over the lands which they traditionally occupy shall be recognised. In addition, measures shall be taken in appropriate cases to safeguard the right of the peoples concerned to use lands not exclusively occupied by them, but to which they have traditionally had access for their subsistence and traditional activities. Particular attention shall be paid to the situation of nomadic peoples and shifting cultivators in this respect.

2. Governments shall take steps as necessary to identify the lands which the peoples concerned traditionally occupy, and to guarantee effective protection of their rights of ownership and possession.

3. Adequate procedures shall be established within the national legal system to resolve land claims by the peoples concerned.

Article 15

1. The rights of the peoples concerned to the natural resources pertaining to their lands shall be specially safeguarded. These rights include the right of these peoples to participate in the use, management and conservation of these resources.

2. In cases in which the State retains the ownership of mineral or sub-surface resources or rights to other resources pertaining to lands, governments shall establish or maintain procedures through which they shall consult these peoples, with a view to ascertaining whether and to what degree their interests would be prejudiced, before undertaking or permitting any programmes for the exploration or exploitation of such resources pertaining to their lands. The peoples concerned shall wherever possible participate in the benefits of such activities, and shall receive fair compensation for any damages which they may sustain as a result of such activities.

Article 16

1. Subject to the following paragraphs of this Article, the peoples concerned shall not be removed from the lands which they occupy.

2. Where the relocation of these peoples is considered necessary as an exceptional measure, such relocation shall take place only with their free and informed consent. Where their consent cannot be obtained, such relocation shall take place only following appropriate procedures established by national laws and regulations, including public inquiries where appropriate, which provide the opportunity for effective representation of the peoples concerned.

3. Whenever possible, these peoples shall have the right to return to their traditional lands, as soon as the grounds for relocation cease to exist.

4. When such return is not possible, as determined by agreement or, in the absence of such agreement, through appropriate procedures, these peoples shall be provided in all possible cases with lands of quality and legal status at least equal to that of the lands previously occupied by them, suitable to provide for their present needs and future development. Where the peoples concerned express a preference for compensation in money or in kind, they shall be so compensated under appropriate guarantees.

5. Persons thus relocated shall be fully compensated for any resulting loss or injury.

Article 17

1. Procedures established by the peoples concerned for the transmission of land rights among members of these peoples shall be respected.

2. The peoples concerned shall be consulted whenever consideration is being given to their capacity to alienate their lands or otherwise transmit their rights outside their own community.

3. Persons not belonging to these peoples shall be prevented from taking advantage of their customs or of lack of understanding of the laws on the part of their members to secure the ownership, possession or use of land belonging to them.

Article 18

Adequate penalties shall be established by law for unauthorised intrusion upon, or use of, the lands of the peoples concerned, and governments shall take measures to prevent such offences.

Article 19

National agrarian programmes shall secure to the peoples concerned treatment equivalent to that accorded to other sectors of the population with regard to:

(a) the provision of more land for these peoples when they have not the area necessary for providing the essentials of a normal existence, or for any possible increase in their numbers;

(b) the provision of the means required to promote the development of the lands which these peoples already possess.

Part III. Recruitment and Conditions of Employment

Article 20

1. Governments shall, within the framework of national laws and regulations, and in co-operation with the peoples concerned, adopt special measures to ensure the effective protection with regard to recruitment and conditions of employment of workers belonging to these peoples, to the extent that they are not effectively protected by laws applicable to workers in general.

2. Governments shall do everything possible to prevent any discrimination between workers belonging to the peoples concerned and other workers, in particular as regards:

(a) admission to employment, including skilled employment, as well as measures for promotion and advancement;

(b) equal remuneration for work of equal value;

(c) medical and social assistance, occupational safety and health, all social security benefits and any other occupationally related benefits, and housing;

(d) the right of association and freedom for all lawful trade union activities, and the right to conclude collective agreements with employers or employers' organisations.

3. The measures taken shall include measures to ensure:

(a) that workers belonging to the peoples concerned, including seasonal, casual and migrant workers in agricultural and other employment, as well as those employed by labour contractors, enjoy the protection afforded by national law and practice to other such workers in the same sectors, and that they are fully informed of their rights under labour legislation and of the means of redress available to them;

(b) that workers belonging to these peoples are not subjected to working conditions hazardous to their health, in particular through exposure to pesticides or other toxic substances;

(c) that workers belonging to these peoples are not subjected to coercive recruitment systems, including bonded labour and other forms of debt servitude;

(d) that workers belonging to these peoples enjoy equal opportunities and equal treatment in employment for men and women, and protection from sexual harassment.

4. Particular attention shall be paid to the establishment of adequate labour inspection services in areas where workers belonging to the peoples concerned under-

take wage employment, in order to ensure compliance with the provisions of this Part of this Convention.

Part IV. Vocational Training, Handicrafts and Rural Industries

Article 21

Members of the peoples concerned shall enjoy opportunities at least equal to those of other citizens in respect of vocational training measures.

Article 22

1. Measures shall be taken to promote the voluntary participation of members of the peoples concerned in vocational training programmes of general application.

2. Whenever existing programmes of vocational training of general application do not meet the special needs of the peoples concerned, governments shall, with the participation of these peoples, ensure the provision of special training programmes and facilities.

3. Any special training programmes shall be based on the economic environment, social and cultural conditions and practical needs of the peoples concerned. Any studies made in this connection shall be carried out in co-operation with these peoples, who shall be consulted on the organisation and operation of such programmes. Where feasible, these peoples shall progressively assume responsibility for the organisation and operation of such special training programmes, if they so decide.

Article 23

1. Handicrafts, rural and community-based industries, and subsistence economy and traditional activities of the peoples concerned, such as hunting, fishing, trapping and gathering, shall be recognised as important factors in the maintenance of their cultures and in their economic self-reliance and development. Governments shall, with the participation of these people and whenever appropriate, ensure that these activities are strengthened and promoted.

2. Upon the request of the peoples concerned, appropriate technical and financial assistance shall be provided wherever possible, taking into account the traditional technologies and cultural characteristics of these peoples, as well as the importance of sustainable and equitable development.

Part V. Social Security and Health

Article 24

Social security schemes shall be extended progressively to cover the peoples concerned, and applied without discrimination against them.

Article 25

1. Governments shall ensure that adequate health services are made available to the peoples concerned, or shall provide them with resources to allow them to design and deliver such services under their own responsibility and control, so that they may enjoy the highest attainable standard of physical and mental health.

2. Health services shall, to the extent possible, be community-based. These services shall be planned and administered in co-operation with the peoples concerned and take into account their economic, geographic, social and cultural conditions as well as their traditional preventive care, healing practices and medicines.

3. The health care system shall give preference to the training and employment of local community health workers, and focus on primary health care while maintaining strong links with other levels of health care services.

4. The provision of such health services shall be co-ordinated with other social, economic and cultural measures in the country.

Part VI. Education and Means of Communication

Article 26

Measures shall be taken to ensure that members of the peoples concerned have the opportunity to acquire education at all levels on at least an equal footing with the rest of the national community.

Article 27

1. Education programmes and services for the peoples concerned shall be developed and implemented in co-operation with them to address their special needs, and shall incorporate their histories, their knowledge and technologies, their value systems and their further social, economic and cultural aspirations.

2. The competent authority shall ensure the training of members of these peoples and their involvement in the formulation and implementation of education programmes, with a view to the progressive transfer of responsibility for the conduct of these programmes to these peoples as appropriate.

3. In addition, governments shall recognise the right of these peoples to establish their own educational institutions and facilities, provided that such institutions meet minimum standards established by the competent authority in consultation with these peoples. Appropriate resources shall be provided for this purpose.

Article 28

1. Children belonging to the peoples concerned shall, wherever practicable, be taught to read and write in their own indigenous language or in the language most commonly used by the group to which they belong. When this is not practicable, the competent authorities shall undertake consultations with these peoples with a view to the adoption of measures to achieve this objective.

2. Adequate measures shall be taken to ensure that these peoples have the opportunity to attain fluency in the national language or in one of the official languages of the country.

3. Measures shall be taken to preserve and promote the development and practice of the indigenous languages of the peoples concerned.

Article 29

The imparting of general knowledge and skills that will help children belonging to the peoples concerned to participate fully and on an equal footing in their own community and in the national community shall be an aim of education for these peoples.

Article 30

1. Governments shall adopt measures appropriate to the traditions and cultures of the peoples concerned, to make known to them their rights and duties, especially in regard to labour, economic opportunities, education and health matters, social welfare and their rights deriving from this Convention.

2. If necessary, this shall be done by means of written translations and through the use of mass communications in the languages of these peoples.

Article 31

Educational measures shall be taken among all sections of the national community, and particularly among those that are in most direct contact with the peoples concerned, with the object of eliminating prejudices that they may harbour in respect of these peoples. To this end, efforts shall be made to ensure that history textbooks and other educational materials provide a fair, accurate and informative portrayal of the societies and cultures of these peoples.

Part VII. Contacts and Co-operation Across Borders

Article 32

Governments shall take appropriate measures, including by means of international agreements, to facilitate contacts and co-operation between indigenous and tribal peoples across borders, including activities in the economic, social, cultural, spiritual and environmental fields.

Part VIII. Administration

Article 33

1. The governmental authority responsible for the matters covered in this Convention shall ensure that agencies or other appropriate mechanisms exist to administer the programmes affecting the peoples concerned, and shall ensure that they have the means necessary for the proper fulfilment of the functions assigned to them.

2. These programmes shall include:

(a) the planning, co-ordination, execution and evaluation, in co-operation with the peoples concerned, of the measures provided for in this Convention;

(b) the proposing of legislative and other measures to the competent authorities and supervision of the application of the measures taken, in co-operation with the peoples concerned.

Part IX. General Provisions

Article 34

The nature and scope of the measures to be taken to give effect to this Convention shall be determined in a flexible manner, having regard to the conditions characteristic of each country.

Article 35

The application of the provisions of this Convention shall not adversely affect rights and benefits of the peoples concerned pursuant to other Conventions and Recommendations, international instruments, treaties, or national laws, awards, custom or agreements.

Part X. Final Provisions

Article 36

This Convention revises the Indigenous and Tribal Populations Convention, 1957.

Article 37

The formal ratifications of this Convention shall be communicated to the Director-General of the International Labour Office for registration.

7.22 CONVENTION ON THE RIGHTS OF THE CHILD. Concluded at New York, 20 November 1989. Entered into force, 2 September 1990. G.A.RES. 44/25 (Annex), U.N. GAOR, 44th Sess., Supp. No. 49, at 166, U.N.Doc. A/Res/44/25 (1990); *reprinted in* 28 I.L.M. 1448 (1989) & 3 Weston III.D.3: *Art. 2*

Article 2

1. States Parties shall respect and ensure the rights set forth in the present Convention to each child within their jurisdiction without discrimination of any kind, irrespective of the child's or his or her parent's or legal guardian's race, colour, sex, language, religion, political or other opinion, national, ethnic or social origin, property, disability, birth or other status.

2. States Parties shall take all appropriate measures to ensure that the child is protected against all forms of discrimination or punishment on the basis of the status, activities, expressed opinions, or beliefs of the child's parents, legal guardians, or family members.

7.23 International Convention on the Protection of the Rights of All Migrant Workers and Members of Their Families. Adopted by the General Assembly, 18 December 1990. Not yet in force. *Reprinted in* 30 I.L.M. 1517 (1991) & 3 Weston III.O.6

The States Parties to the present Convention,

Taking into account the principles embodied in the basic instruments of the United Nations concerning human rights, in particular the Universal Declaration of Human Rights, the International Covenant on Economic, Social and Cultural Rights, the International Covenant on Civil and Political Rights, the International Convention on the Elimination of All Forms of Racial Discrimination, the Convention on the Elimination of All Forms of Discrimination against Women and the Convention on the Rights of the Child,

Taking into account also the principles and standards set forth in the relevant instruments elaborated within the framework of the International Labour Organisation, especially the Convention concerning Migration for Employment (No. 97), the Convention concerning Migrations in Abusive Conditions and the Promotion of Equality of Opportunity and Treatment of Migrant Workers (No. 143), the Recommendation concerning Migration for Employment (No. 86), the Recommendation concerning Migrant Workers (No. 151), the Convention concerning Forced or Compulsory Labour (No. 29) and the Convention concerning Abolition of Forced Labour (No. 105),

Reaffirming the importance of the principles contained in the Convention against Discrimination in Education of the United Nations Educational, Scientific and Cultural Organization,

Recalling the Convention against Torture and Other Cruel, Inhuman or Degrading Treatment or Punishment, the Declaration of the Fourth United Nations Congress on the Prevention of Crime and the Treatment of Offenders, the Code of Conduct for Law Enforcement Officials, and the Slavery Conventions,

Recalling that one of the objectives of the International Labour Organisation, as stated in its Constitution, is the protection of the interests of workers when employed in countries other than their own, and bearing in mind the expertise and experience of that organization in matters related to migrant workers and members of their families,

Recognizing the importance of the work done in connection with migrant workers and members of their families in various organs of the United Nations, in particular in the Commission on Human Rights and the Commission for Social Development, and in the Food and Agriculture Organization of the United Nations, the United Nations Educational, Scientific and Cultural Organization and the World Health Organization, as well as in other international organizations,

Recognizing also the progress made by certain States on a regional or bilateral basis towards the protection of the rights of migrant workers and members of their families, as well as the importance and usefulness of bilateral and multilateral agreements in this field,

Realizing the importance and extent of the migration phenomenon, which involves millions of people and affects a large number of States in the international community,

Aware of the impact of the flows of migrant workers on States and people concerned, and desiring to establish norms which may contribute to the harmonization of the attitudes of States through the acceptance of basic principles concerning the treatment of migrant workers and members of their families,

Considering the situation of vulnerability in which migrant workers and members of their families frequently find themselves owing, among other things, to their absence from their State of origin and to the difficulties they may encounter arising from their presence in the State of employment,

Convinced that the rights of migrant workers and members of their families have not been sufficiently recognized everywhere and therefore require appropriate international protection,

Taking into account the fact that migration is often the cause of serious problems for the members of the families of migrant workers as well as for the workers themselves, in particular because of the scattering of the family,

Bearing in mind that the human problems involved in migration are even more serious in the case of irregular migration and convinced therefore that appropriate action should be encouraged in order to prevent and eliminate clandestine movements and trafficking in migrant workers, while at the same time assuring the protection of their fundamental human rights,

Considering that workers who are non-documented or in an irregular situation are frequently employed under less favourable conditions of work than other workers and that certain employers find this an inducement to seek such labour in order to reap the benefits of unfair competition,

Considering also that recourse to the employment of migrant workers who are in an irregular situation will be discouraged if the fundamental human rights of all migrant workers are more widely recognized and, moreover, that granting certain additional rights to migrant workers and members of their families in a regular situation will encourage all migrants and employers to respect and comply with the laws and procedures established by the States concerned,

Convinced, therefore, of the need to bring about the international protection of the rights of all migrant workers and members of their families, reaffirming and establishing basic norms in a comprehensive convention which could be applied universally,

Have agreed as follows:

PART I

Scope and definitions

Article 1

1. The present Convention is applicable, except as otherwise provided hereafter, to all migrant workers and members of their families without distinction of any kind such as sex, race colour, language, religion or conviction, political or other opinion, national, ethnic or social origin, nationality, age, economic position, property, marital status, birth or other status.

2. The present Convention shall apply during the entire migration process of migrant workers and members of their families, which comprises preparation for migration, departure, transit and the entire period of stay and remunerated activity in the State of employment as well as return to the State of origin or the State of habitual residence.

Article 2

For the purposes of the present Convention:

1. The term "migrant worker" refers to a person who is to be engaged, is engaged or has been engaged in a remunerated activity in a State of which he or she is not a national.

2. (a) The term "frontier worker" refers to a migrant worker who retains his or her habitual residence in a neighbouring State to which he or she normally returns every day or at least once a week;

(b) The term "seasonal worker" refers to a migrant worker whose work by its character is dependent on seasonal conditions and is performed only during part of the year;

(c) The term "seafarer", which includes a fisherman, refers to a migrant worker employed on board a vessel registered in a State of which he or she is not a national;

(d) The term "worker on an offshore installation" refers to a migrant worker employed on an offshore installation that is under the jurisdiction of a State of which he or she is not a national;

(e) The term "itinerant worker" refers to a migrant worker who, having his or her habitual residence in one State, has to travel to another State or States for short periods, owing to the nature of his or her occupation;

(f) The term "project-tied worker" refers to a migrant worker admitted to a State of employment for a defined period to work solely on a specific project being carried out in that State by his or her employer;

(g) The term "specified-employment worker" refers to a migrant worker:

(i) Who has been sent by his or her employer for a restricted and defined period of time to a State of employment to undertake a specific assignment or duty; or

(ii) Who engages for a restricted and defined period of time in work that requires professional, commercial, technical or other highly specialized skill; or

(iii) Who, upon the request of his or her employer in the State of employment, engages for a restricted and defined period of time in work whose nature is transitory or brief;

and who is required to depart from the State of employment either at the expiration of his or her authorized period of stay, or earlier if he or she no longer undertakes that specific assignment or duty or engages in that work;

(h) The term "self-employed worker" refers to a migrant worker who is engaged in a remunerated activity otherwise than under a contract of employment and who earns his or her living through this activity normally working alone or together with members of his or her family, and to any other migrant worker recognized as self-employed by applicable legislation of the State of employment or bilateral or multilateral agreements.

Article 3

The present Convention shall not apply to:

(a) Persons sent or employed by international organizations and agencies or persons sent or employed by a State outside its territory to perform official functions, whose admission and status are regulated by general international law or by specific international agreements or conventions;

(b) Persons seat or employed by a State or on its behalf outside its territory who participate in development programmes and other co-operation programmes, whose admission and status are regulated by agreement with the State of employment and who, in accordance with that agreement, are not considered migrant workers;

(c) Persons taking up residence in a State different from their State of origin as investors;

(d) Refugees and stateless persons, unless such application is provided for in the relevant national legislation of, or international instruments in force for, the State Party concerned;

(e) Students and trainees;

(f) Seafarers and workers on an offshore installation who have not been admitted to take up residence and engage in a remunerated activity in the State of employment.

Article 4

For the purposes of the present Convention the term "members of the family" refers to persons married to migrant workers or having with them a relationship that, according to applicable law, produces effects equivalent to marriage, as well as their dependent children and other dependent persons who are recognized as members of the family by applicable legislation or applicable bilateral or multilateral agreements between the States concerned.

Article 5

For the purposes of the present Convention, migrant workers and members of their families:

(a) Are considered as documented or in a regular situation if they are authorized to enter, to stay and to engage in a remunerated activity in the State of employment pursuant to the law of that State and to international agreements to which that State is a party;

(b) Are considered as non-documented or in an irregular situation if they do not comply with the conditions provided for in subparagraph (a) of the present article.

Article 6

For the purposes of the present Convention:

(a) The term "State of origin" means the State of which the person concerned is a national;

(b) The term "State of employment" means a State where the migrant worker is to be engaged, is engaged or has been engaged in a remunerated activity, as the case may be;

(c) The term "State of transit" means any State through which the person concerned passes on any journey to the State of employment or from the State of employment to the State of origin or the State of habitual residence.

PART II

Non-discrimination with respect to rights

Article 7

States Parties undertake, in accordance with the international instruments concerning human rights, to respect and to ensure to all migrant workers and members of their families within their territory or subject to their jurisdiction the rights provided for in the present Convention without distinction of any kind such as sex, race, colour, language, religion or conviction, political or other opinion, national, ethnic or social origin, nationality, age, economic position, property, marital status, birth or other status.

PART III

Human rights of all migrant workers and members of their families

Article 8

1. Migrant workers and members of their families shall be free to leave any State, including their State of origin. This right shall not be subject to any restrictions except those that are provided by law, are necessary to protect national security, public order (ordre public), public health or morals or the rights and freedoms of others and are consistent with the other rights recognized in the present part of the Convention.

2. Migrant workers and members of their families shall have the right at any time to enter and remain in their State of origin.

Article 9

The right to life of migrant workers and members of their families shall be protected by law.

* * *

Article 15

No migrant worker or member of his or her family shall be arbitrarily deprived of property, whether owned individually or in association with others. Where, under the legislation in force in the State of employment, the assets of a migrant worker or a member of his or her family are expropriated in whole or in part, the person concerned shall have the right to fair and adequate compensation.

* * *

Article 22

1. Migrant workers and members of their families shall not be subject to measures of collective expulsion. Each case of expulsion shall be examined and decided individually.

2. Migrant workers and members of their families may be expelled from the territory of a State Party only in pursuance of a decision taken by the competent authority in accordance with law.

3. The decision shall be communicated to them in a language they understand. Upon their request where not otherwise mandatory, the decision shall be communicated to them in writing and, save in exceptional circumstances on account of national security, the reasons for the decision likewise stated. The persons concerned shall be informed of these rights before or at the latest at the time the decision is rendered.

4. Except where a final decision is pronounced by a judicial authority, the person concerned shall have the right to submit the reason he or she should not be expelled and to have his or her case reviewed by the competent authority, unless compelling reasons of national security require otherwise. Pending such review, the person concerned shall have the right to seek a stay of the decision of expulsion.

5. If a decision of expulsion that has already been executed is subsequently annulled, the person concerned shall have the right to seek compensation according to law and the earlier decision shall not be used to prevent him or her from re-entering the State concerned.

6. In case of expulsion, the person concerned shall have a reasonable opportunity before or after departure to settle any claims for wages and other entitlements due to him or her and any pending liabilities.

7. Without prejudice to the execution of a decision of expulsion, a migrant worker or a member of his or her family who is subject to such a decision may seek entry into a State other than his or her State of origin.

8. In case of expulsion of a migrant worker or a member of his or her family the costs of expulsion shall not be borne by him or her. The person concerned may be required to pay his or her own travel costs.

9. Expulsion from the State of employment shall not in itself prejudice any rights of a migrant worker or a member of his or her family acquired in accordance with the law of that State, including the right to receive wages and other entitlements due to him or her.

Article 23

Migrant workers and members of their families shall have the right to have recourse to the protection and assistance of the consular or diplomatic authorities of their State of origin or of a State representing the interests of that State whenever the rights recognized in the present Convention are impaired. In particular, in case of expulsion, the person concerned shall be informed of this right without delay and the authorities of the expelling State shall facilitate the exercise of such right.

* * *

Article 55

Migrant, workers who have been granted permission to engage in a remunerated activity, subject to the conditions attached to such permission, shall be entitled to equality of treatment with nationals of the State of employment in the exercise of that remunerated activity.

Article 56

1. Migrant workers and members of their families referred to in the present part of the Convention may not be expelled from a State of employment, except for reasons defined in the national legislation of that State, and subject to the safeguards established in part III.

2. Expulsion shall not be resorted to for the purpose of depriving a migrant worker or a member of his or her family of the rights arising out of the authorization of residence and the work permit.

3. In considering whether to expel a migrant worker or a member of his or her family, account should be taken of humanitarian considerations and of the length of time that the person concerned has already resided in the State of employment.

* * *

PART VIII

General provisions

Article 79

Nothing in the present Convention shall affect the right of each State Party to establish the criteria governing admission of migrant workers and members of their families. Concerning other matters related to their legal situation and treatment as migrant workers and members of their families, States Parties shall be subject to the limitations set forth in the present Convention.

Article 80

Nothing in the present Convention shall be interpreted as impairing the provisions of the Charter of the United Nations and of the constitutions of the specialized agencies which define the respective responsibilities of the various organs of the United Nations and of the specialized agencies in regard to the matters dealt with in the present Convention.

Article 81

1. Nothing in the present Convention shall affect more favourable rights or freedoms granted to migrant workers and members of their families by virtue of:

(a) The law or practice of a State Party; or

(b) Any bilateral or multilateral treaty in force for the State Party concerned.

2. Nothing in the present Convention may be interpreted as implying for any State, group or person any right to engage in any activity or perform any act that would impair any of the rights and freedoms as set forth in the present Convention.

Article 82

The rights of migrant workers and members of their families provided for in the present Convention may not be renounced. It shall not be permissible to exert any form of pressure upon migrant workers and members of their families with a view to their relinquishing or foregoing any of the said rights. It shall not be possible to derogate by contract from rights recognized in the present Convention. States Parties shall take appropriate measures to ensure that these principles are respected.

Article 83

Each State Party to the present Convention undertakes:

(a) To ensure that any person whose rights or freedoms as herein recognized are violated shall have an effective remedy, notwithstanding that the violation has been committed by persons acting in an official capacity;

(b) To ensure that any persons seeking such a remedy shall have his or her claim reviewed and decided by competent judicial, administrative or legislative authorities, or by any other competent authority provided for by the legal system of the State, and to develop the possibilities of judicial remedy;

(c) To ensure that the competent authorities shall enforce such remedies when granted.

* * *

Article 92

1. Any dispute between two or more States Parties concerning the interpretation or application of the present Convention that is not settled by negotiation shall, at the request of one of them, be submitted to arbitration. If within six months from the date of the request for arbitration the Parties are unable to agree on the organization of the arbitration, any one of those Parties may refer the dispute to the International Court of Justice by request in conformity with the Statute of the Court.

2. Each State Party may at the time of signature or ratification of the present Convention or accession thereto declare that it does not consider itself bound by paragraph 1 of the present article. The other States Parties shall not be bound by that paragraph with respect to any State Party that has made such a declaration.

3. Any State Party that has made a declaration in accordance with paragraph 2 of the present article may at any time withdraw that declaration by notification to the Secretary–General of the United Nations.

* * *

7.24 DRAFT DECLARATION ON THE RIGHTS OF INDIGENOUS PEOPLES AS AGREED UPON BY THE MEMBERS OF THE WORKING GROUP ON INDIGENOUS PEOPLES AT ITS ELEVENTH SESSION. Adopted on 23 August 1993. UN Doc. E/CN. 4/Sub. 2/1993/29; *reprinted in* 3 Weston III.V.3

Affirming that indigenous peoples are equal in dignity and rights to all other peoples, while recognizing the right of all peoples to be different, to consider themselves different, and to be respected as such,

Affirming also that all peoples contribute to the diversity and richness of civilizations and cultures, which constitute the common heritage of humankind,

Affirming further that all doctrines, policies and practices based on or advocating superiority of peoples or individuals on the basis of national origin, racial, religious, ethnic or cultural differences are racist, scientifically false, legally invalid, morally condemnable and socially unjust,

Reaffirming also that indigenous peoples, in the exercise of their rights, should be free from discrimination of any kind,

Concerned that indigenous peoples have been deprived of their human rights and fundamental freedoms, resulting, *inter alia,* in their colonization and dispossession of their lands, territories and resources, thus preventing them from exercising, in particular, their right to development in accordance with their own needs and interests,

Recognizing the urgent need to respect and promote the inherent rights and characteristics of indigenous peoples, especially their rights to their lands, territories and resources, which derive from their political, economic and social structures, and from their cultures, spiritual traditions, histories and philosophies,

Welcoming the fact that indigenous peoples are organizing themselves for political, economic, social and cultural enhancement and in order to bring an end to all forms of discrimination and oppression wherever they occur,

Convinced that control by indigenous peoples over developments affecting them and their lands, territories and resources will enable them to maintain and strengthen their institutions, cultures and traditions, and to promote their development in accordance with their institutions, cultures and traditions, and to promote their development in accordance with their aspirations and needs,

Recognizing also that respect for indigenous knowledge, cultures and traditional practices contributes to sustainable and equitable development and proper management of the environment,

Emphasizing the need for demilitarization of the lands and territories of indigenous peoples, which will contribute to peace, economic and social progress and development, understanding and friendly relations among nations and peoples of the world,

Recognizing in particular the right of indigenous families and communities to retain shared responsibility for the upbringing, training, education and well-being of their children,

Recognizing also that indigenous peoples have the right freely to determine their relationships with States in a spirit of coexistence, mutual benefit and full respect,

Considering that treaties, agreements and other arrangements between States and indigenous peoples are properly matters of international concern and responsibility,

Acknowledging that the Charter of the United Nations, the International Covenant on Economic, Social and Cultural Rights and the International Covenant on

Civil and Political Rights affirm the fundamental importance of the right of self-determination of all peoples, by virtue of which they freely determine their political status and freely pursue their economic, social and cultural development,

Bearing in mind that nothing in this Declaration may be used to deny any peoples their right of self-determination,

Encouraging States to comply with and effectively implement all international instruments, in particular those related to human rights, as they apply to indigenous peoples, in consultation and cooperation with the peoples concerned,

Emphasizing that the United Nations has an important and continuing role to play in promoting and protecting the rights of indigenous peoples,

Believing that this Declaration is a further important step forward for the recognition, promotion and protection of the rights and freedoms of indigenous peoples United Nations system in this field,

Solemnly proclaims the following United Nations Declaration on the Rights of Indigenous Peoples:

ARTICLES

PART I

1. Indigenous peoples have the right to the full and effective enjoyment of all human rights and fundamental freedoms recognized in the Charter of the United Nations, the Universal Declaration of Human Rights and international human rights law.

2. Indigenous individuals and peoples are free and equal to all other individuals and peoples in dignity and rights, and have the right to be free from any kind of adverse discrimination, in particular that based on their indigenous origin or identity.

3. Indigenous peoples have the right of self-determination. By virtue of that right they freely determine their political status and freely pursue their economic, social and cultural development.

4. Indigenous peoples have the right to maintain and strengthen their distinct political, economic, social and cultural characteristics, as well as their legal systems, while retaining their rights to participate fully, if they so choose, in the political, economic, social and cultural life of the State.

5. Every indigenous individual has the right to a nationality.

PART II

6. Indigenous peoples have the collective right to live in freedom, peace and security as distinct peoples and to full guarantees against genocide or any other act of violence, including the removal of indigenous children from their families and communities under any pretext.

In addition, they have the individual rights to life, physical and mental integrity, liberty and security of person.

7. Indigenous peoples have the collective and individual right not to be subjected to ethnocide and cultural genocide, including prevention of and redress for:

(a) Any action which has the aim or effect of depriving them of their integrity as distinct peoples, or of their cultural values or ethnic identities;

(b) Any action which has the aim or effect of dispossessing them of their lands, territories or resources;

(c) Any form of population transfer which has the aim or effect of violating or undermining any of their rights;

(d) Any form of assimilation or integration by other cultures or ways of life imposed on them by legislative, administrative or other measures;

(e) Any form of propaganda directed against them.

8. Indigenous peoples have the collective and individual right to maintain and develop their distinct identities and characteristics, including the right to identify themselves as indigenous and to be recognized as such.

9. Indigenous peoples and individuals have the right to belong to an indigenous community or nation, in accordance with the traditions and customs of the community or nation concerned. No disadvantage of any kind may arise from the exercise of such a right.

10. Indigenous peoples shall not be forcibly removed from their lands or territories. No relocation shall take place without the free and informed consent of the indigenous peoples concerned and after agreement on just and fair compensation and, where possible, with the option of return.

11. Indigenous peoples have the right to special protection and security in periods of armed conflict.

States shall observe international standards, in particular the Fourth Geneva Convention of 1949, for the protection of civilian populations in circumstances of emergency and armed conflict, and shall not:

(a) Recruit indigenous individuals against their will into the armed forces and, in particular, for use against other indigenous peoples;

(b) Recruit indigenous children into the armed forces under any circumstances;

(c) Force indigenous individuals to abandon their lands, territories or means of subsistence, or relocate them in special centres for military purposes;

(d) Force indigenous individuals to work for military purposes under any discriminatory conditions.

PART III

12. Indigenous peoples have the right to practise and revitalize their cultural traditions and customs. This includes the right to maintain, protect and develop the past, present and future manifestations of their cultures, such as archaeological and historical sites, artifacts, designs, ceremonies, technologies and visual and performing arts and literature, as well as the right to the restitution of cultural, intellectual, religious and spiritual property taken without their free and informed consent or in violation of their laws, traditions and customs.

13. Indigenous peoples have the right to manifest, practise, develop and teach their spiritual and religious traditions, customs and ceremonies; the right to maintain, protect, and have access in privacy to their religious and cultural sites; the right to the use and control of ceremonial objects; and the right to the repatriation of human remains.

States shall take effective measures, in conjunction with the indigenous peoples concerned, to ensure that indigenous sacred places, including burial sites, be preserved, respected and protected.

14. Indigenous peoples have the right to revitalize, use, develop and transmit to future generations their histories, languages, oral traditions, philosophies, writing systems and literatures, and to designate and retain their own names for communities, places and persons.

States shall take effective measures, whenever any right of indigenous peoples may be threatened, to ensure this right is protected and also to ensure that they can understand and be understood in political, legal and administrative proceedings, where necessary through the provision of interpretation or by other appropriate means.

PART IV

15. Indigenous children have the right to all levels and forms of education of the State. All indigenous peoples also have this right and the right to establish and control their educational systems and institutions providing education in their own languages, in a manner appropriate to their cultural methods of teaching and learning.

Indigenous children living outside their communities have the right to be provided access to education in their own culture and language.

States shall take effective measures to provide appropriate resources for these purposes.

16. Indigenous peoples have the right to have the dignity and diversity of their cultures, traditions, histories and aspirations appropriately reflected in all forms of education and public information.

States shall take effective measures, in consultation with the indigenous peoples concerned, to eliminate prejudice and discrimination and to promote tolerance, understanding and good relations among indigenous peoples and all segments of society.

17. Indigenous peoples have the right to establish their own media in their own languages. They also have the right to equal access to all forms of non-indigenous media.

States shall take effective measures to ensure that State-owned media duly reflect indigenous cultural diversity.

18. Indigenous peoples have the right to enjoy fully all rights established under international labour law and national labour legislation.

Indigenous individuals have the right not to be subjected to any discriminatory conditions of labour, employment or salary.

PART V

19. Indigenous peoples have the right to participate fully, if they so choose, at all levels of decision-making in matters which may affect their rights, lives and destinies through representatives chosen by themselves in accordance with their own procedures, as well as to maintain and develop their own indigenous decision-making institutions.

20. Indigenous peoples have the right to participate fully, if they so choose, through procedures determined by them, in devising legislative or administrative measures that may affect them.

States shall obtain the free and informed consent of the peoples concerned before adopting and implementing such measures.

21. Indigenous peoples have the right to maintain and develop their political, economic and social systems, to be secure in the enjoyment of their own means of subsistence and development, and to engage freely in all their traditional and other economic activities. Indigenous peoples who have been deprived of their means of subsistence and development are entitled to just and fair compensation.

22. Indigenous peoples have the right to special measures for the immediate, effective and continuing improvement of their economic and social conditions, including in the areas of employment, vocational training and retraining, housing, sanitation, health and social security.

Particular attention shall be paid to the rights and special needs of indigenous elders, women, youth, children and disabled persons.

23. Indigenous peoples have the right to determine and develop priorities and strategies for exercising their right to development. In particular, indigenous peoples have the right to determine and develop all health, housing and other economic and social programmes affecting them and, as far as possible, to administer such programmes through their own institutions.

24. Indigenous peoples have the right to their traditional medicines and health practices, including the right to the protection of vital medicinal plants, animals and minerals.

They also have the right to access, without any discrimination, to all medical institutions, health services and medical care.

PART VI

25. Indigenous peoples have the right to maintain and strengthen their distinctive spiritual and material relationship with the lands, territories, waters and coastal seas and other resources which they have traditionally owned or otherwise occupied or used, and to uphold their responsibilities to future generations in this regard.

26. Indigenous peoples have the right to own, develop, control and use the lands and territories, including the total environment of the lands, air, waters, coastal seas, sea-ice, flora and fauna and other resources which they have traditionally owned or otherwise occupied or used. This includes the right to the full recognition of their laws, traditions and customs, land-tenure systems and institutions for the development and management of resources, and the right to effective measures by States to prevent any interference with, alienation of or encroachment upon these rights.

27. Indigenous peoples have the right to the restitution of the lands, territories and resources which they have traditionally owned or otherwise occupied or used; and which have been confiscated, occupied, used or damaged without their free and informed consent. Where this is not possible, they have the right to just and fair compensation. Unless otherwise freely agreed upon by the peoples concerned, compensation shall take the form of lands, territories and resources equal in quality, size and legal status.

28. Indigenous peoples have the right to the conservation, restoration and protection of the total environment and the productive capacity of their lands, territories and resources, as well as to assistance for this purpose from States and through international cooperation. Military activities shall not take place in the lands and territories of indigenous peoples, unless otherwise freely agreed upon by the peoples concerned.

States shall take effective measures to ensure that no storage or disposal of hazardous materials shall take place in the lands and territories of indigenous peoples.

States shall also take effective measures to ensure, as needed, that programmes for monitoring, maintaining and restoring the health of indigenous peoples, as developed and implemented by the peoples affected by such materials, are duly implemented.

29. Indigenous peoples are entitled to the recognition of the full ownership, control and protection of their cultural and intellectual property.

They have the right to special measures to control, develop and protect their sciences, technologies and cultural manifestations, including human and other genetic resources, seeds, medicines, knowledge of the properties of fauna and flora, oral traditions, literatures, designs and visual and performing arts.

30. Indigenous peoples have the right to determine and develop priorities and strategies for the development or use of their lands, territories and other resources, including the right to require that States obtain their free and informed consent prior to the approval of any project affecting their lands, territories and other resources,

particularly in connection with the development, utilization or exploitation of mineral, water or other resources. Pursuant to agreement with the indigenous peoples concerned, just and fair compensation shall be provided for any such activities and measures taken to mitigate adverse environmental, economic, social, cultural or spiritual impact.

PART VII

31. Indigenous peoples, as a specific form of exercising their right to self-determination, have the right to autonomy or self-government in matters relating to their internal and local affairs, including culture, religion, education, information, media, health, housing, employment, social welfare, economic activities, land and resources management, environment and entry by non-members, as well as ways and means for financing these autonomous functions.

32. Indigenous peoples have the collective right to determine their own citizenship in accordance with their customs and traditions. Indigenous citizenship does not impair the right of indigenous individuals to obtain citizenship of the States in which they live.

Indigenous peoples have the right to determine the structures and to select the membership of their institutions in accordance with their own procedures.

33. Indigenous peoples have the right to promote, develop and maintain their institutional structures and their distinctive juridical customs, traditions, procedures and practices, in accordance with internationally recognized human rights standards.

34. Indigenous peoples have the collective right to determine the responsibilities of individuals to their communities.

35. Indigenous peoples, in particular those divided by international borders, have the right to maintain and develop contracts, relations and cooperation, including activities for spiritual, cultural, political, economic and social purposes, with other peoples across borders.

States shall take effective measures to ensure the exercise and implementation of this right.

36. Indigenous peoples have the right to the recognition, observance and enforcement of treaties, agreements and other constructive arrangements concluded with States or their successors, according to their original spirit and intent, and to have States honour and respect such treaties, agreements and other constructive arrangements. Conflicts and disputes which cannot otherwise be settled should be submitted to competent international bodies agreed to by all parties concerned.

PART VIII

37. States shall take effective and appropriate measures, in consultation with the indigenous peoples concerned, to give full effect to the provisions of this Declaration. The rights recognized herein shall be adopted and included in national legislation in such a manner that indigenous peoples can avail themselves of such rights in practice.

38. Indigenous peoples have the right to have access to adequate financial and technical assistance, from States and through international cooperation, to pursue freely their political, economic, social, cultural and spiritual development and for the enjoyment of the rights and freedoms recognized in this Declaration.

39. Indigenous peoples have the right to have access to and prompt decision through mutually acceptable and fair procedures for the resolution of conflicts and disputes with States, as well as to effective remedies for all infringements of their individual and collective rights. Such a decision shall take into consideration the customs, traditions, rules and legal systems of the indigenous peoples concerned.

40. The organs and specialized agencies of the United Nations system and other intergovernmental organizations shall contribute to the full realization of the provisions of this Declaration through the mobilization, *inter alia,* of financial cooperation and technical assistance. Ways and means of ensuring participation of indigenous peoples on issues affecting them shall be established.

41. The United Nations shall take the necessary steps to ensure the implementation of this Declaration including the creation of a body at the highest level with special competence in this field and with the direct participation of indigenous peoples. All United Nations bodies shall promote respect for and full application of the provisions of this Declaration.

PART IX

42. The rights recognized herein constitute the minimum standards for the survival, dignity and well-being of the indigenous peoples of the world.

43. All the rights and freedoms recognized herein are equally guaranteed to male and female indigenous individuals.

44. Nothing in this Declaration may be construed as diminishing or extinguishing existing or future rights indigenous peoples may have or acquire.

45. Nothing in this Declaration may be interpreted as implying for any State, group or person any right to engage in any activity or to perform any act contrary to the Charter of the United Nations.

C. WAR/PEACE

7.25 CONVENTION (NO. IV) RESPECTING THE LAWS AND CUSTOMS OF WAR ON LAND, WITH ANNEX OF REGULATIONS.[b] Concluded at The Hague, 18 October 1907. Entered into force, 26 January 1910. 36 Stat. 2277, T.S. No. 539; *reprinted in* 2 Weston II.B.1

* * *

Article 1

The Contracting Powers shall issue instructions to their armed land forces which shall be in conformity with the Regulations respecting the Laws and Customs of War on Land, annexed to the present Convention.

Article 2

The provisions contained in the Regulations referred to in Article 1, as well as in the present Convention, do not apply except between Contracting Powers, and then only if all the belligerents are parties to the Convention.

Article 3

A belligerent party which violates the provisions of the said Regulations shall, if the case demands, be liable to pay compensation. It shall be responsible for all acts committed by persons forming part of its armed forces.

Article 4

The present Convention, duly ratified, shall as between the Contracting Powers, be substituted for the Convention of the 29th July, 1899, respecting the Laws and Customs of War on Land.

The Convention of 1899 remains in force as between the Powers which signed it, and which do not also ratify the present Convention.

Article 5

The present Convention shall be ratified as soon as possible.

The ratifications shall be deposited at The Hague.

The first deposit of ratifications shall be recorded in a procès-verbal signed by the Representatives of the Powers which take part therein and by the Netherlands Minister for Foreign Affairs.

The subsequent deposits of ratifications shall be made by means of a written notification, addressed to the Netherlands Government and accompanied by the instrument of ratification.

A duly certified copy of the procès-verbal relative to the first deposit of ratifications, of the notifications mentioned in the preceding paragraph, as well as of the instruments of ratifications, shall be immediately sent by the Netherlands Government, through the diplomatic channel, to the Powers invited to the Second Peace

b. The Preamble to this Convention (No. IV) which contains the famous "De Martens clause," after its author Feodor de Martens, the principle Russian delegate to the First and Second Hague Peace Conferences of 1899 and 1907 has been omitted. The "De Martens Clause" provides:

Until a more complete code of the laws of war has been issued, the High Contracting Parties deem it expedient to declare that, in cases not included in the Regulations adopted by them, the inhabitants and the belligerents remain under the protection and the rule of the principles of the law of nations, as they result from the usages established among civilized peoples, from the laws of humanity, and from the dictates of the public conscience.

Conference, as well as to the other Powers which have adhered to the Convention. In the cases contemplated in the preceding paragraph the said Government shall at the same time inform them of the date on which it received the notification.

Article 6

Non–Signatory Powers may adhere to the present Convention.

The Power which desires to adhere notifies in writing its intention to the Netherlands Government, forwarding to it the act of adhesion, which shall be deposited in the archives of the said Government.

This Government shall at once transmit to all the other Powers a duly certified copy of the notification as well as the act of adhesion, mentioning the date on which it received the notification.

Article 7

The present Convention shall come into force, in the case of the Powers which were a party to the first deposit of ratifications, sixty days after the date of the procès-verbal of this deposit, and, in the case of the Powers which ratify subsequently or which adhere, sixty days after the notification of their ratification or of their adhesion has been received by the Netherlands Government.

Article 8

In the event of one of the Contracting Powers wishing to denounce the present Convention, the denunciation shall be notified in writing to the Netherlands Government, which shall at once communicate a duly certified copy of the notification to all the other Powers, informing them of the date on which it was received.

The denunciation shall only have effect in regard to the notifying Power, and one year after the notification has reached the Netherlands Government.

Article 9

A register kept by the Netherlands Ministry for Foreign Affairs shall give the date of the deposit of ratifications made in virtue of Article 5, paragraphs 3 and 4, as well as the date on which the notifications of adhesion (Article 6, paragraph 2) or of denunciation (Article 8, paragraph 1) were received.

Each Contracting Power is entitled to have access to this register and to be supplied with duly certified extracts.

ANNEX TO THE CONVENTION

Regulations Respecting the Laws and Customs of War on Land

SECTION 1. ON BELLIGERENTS

CHAPTER I. *The Qualifications of Belligerents*

Article 1

The laws, rights, and duties of war apply not only to armies, but also to militia and volunteer corps fulfilling the following conditions:

1. To be commanded by a person responsible for his subordinates;
2. To have a fixed distinctive emblem recognizable at a distance;
3. To carry arms openly; and
4. To conduct their operations in accordance with the laws and customs of war.

In countries where militia or volunteer corps constitute the army, or form part of it, they are included under the denomination "army".

* * *

SECTION II. HOSTILITIES

CHAPTER I. *Means of Injuring the Enemy, Sieges, and Bombardments*

Article 22

The right of belligerents to adopt means of injuring the enemy is not unlimited.

Article 23

In addition to the prohibitions provided by special Conventions, it is especially forbidden:

(a) To employ poison or poisoned weapons;

(b) To kill or wound treacherously individuals belonging to the hostile nation or army;

(c) To kill or wound an enemy who, having laid down his arms, or having no longer means of defence, has surrendered at discretion;

(d) To declare that no quarter will be given;

(e) To employ arms, projectiles, or material calculated to cause unnecessary suffering;

(f) To make improper use of a flag of truce, of the national flag, or of the military insignia and uniform of the enemy, as well as the distinctive badges of the Geneva Convention;

(g) To destroy or seize the enemy's property, unless such destruction or seizure be imperatively demanded by the necessities of war;

(h) To declare abolished, suspended, or inadmissible in a Court of law the rights and actions of the nationals of the hostile party.

A belligerent is likewise forbidden to compel the nationals of the hostile party to take part in the operations of war directed against their own country, even if they were in the belligerent's service before the commencement of the war.

Article 24

Ruses of war and the employment of measures necessary for obtaining information about the enemy and the country are considered permissible.

Article 25

The attack or bombardment, by whatever means, of towns, villages, dwellings, or buildings which are undefended is prohibited.

Article 26

The officer in command of an attacking force must, before commencing a bombardment, except in cases of assault, do all in his power to warn the authorities.

Article 27

In sieges and bombardments all necessary steps must be taken to spare, as far as possible, buildings dedicated to religion, art, science, or charitable purposes, historic monuments, hospitals, and places where the sick and wounded are collected, provided they are not being used at the time for military purposes.

It is the duty of the besieged to indicate the presence of such buildings or places by distinctive and visible signs, which shall be notified to the enemy beforehand.

Article 28

The pillage of a town or place, even when taken by assault, is prohibited.

* * *

7.26 GENEVA CONVENTION (NO. IV) RELATIVE TO THE PROTECTION OF CIVILIAN PERSONS IN TIME OF WAR (Without Annexes).[c] Concluded at Geneva, 12 August 1949. Entered into force, 21 October 1950. 75 U.N.T.S. 287, 6 T.S. No. 3114, T.I.A.S. No. 3362; *reprinted in* 2 Weston II.B.14: *Arts. 2, 53, 146, 147, 158*

* * *

Article 2

In addition to the provisions which shall be implemented in peacetime, the present Convention shall apply to all cases of declared war or of any other armed conflict which may arise between two or more of the High Contracting Parties, even if the state of war is not recognized by one of them.

The Convention shall also apply to all cases of partial or total occupation of the territory of a High Contracting Party, even if the said occupation meets with no armed resistance.

Although one of the Powers in conflict may not be a party to the present Convention, the Powers who are parties thereto shall remain bound by it in their mutual relations. They shall furthermore be bound by the Convention in relation to the said Power, if the latter accepts and applies the provisions thereof.

* * *

Article 53

Any destruction by the Occupying Power of real or personal property belonging individually or collectively to private persons, or to the State, or to other public authorities, or to social or cooperative organizations, is prohibited, except where such destruction is rendered absolutely necessary by military operations.

* * *

Article 146

The High Contracting Parties undertake to enact any legislation necessary to provide effective penal sanctions for persons committing, or ordering to be committed, any of the grave breaches of the present Convention defined in the following Article.

Each High Contracting Party shall be under the obligation to search for persons alleged to have committed, or to have ordered to be committed, such grave breaches, and shall bring such persons, regardless of their nationality, before its own courts. It may also, if it prefers, and in accordance with the provisions of its own legislation, hand such persons over for trial to another High Contracting Party concerned, provided such High Contracting Party has made out a prima facie case.

Each High Contracting Party shall take measures necessary for the suppression of all acts contrary to the provisions of the present Convention other than the grave breaches defined in the following Article.

In all circumstances, the accused persons shall benefit by safeguards of proper trial and defence, which shall not be less favourable than those provided by Article 105 and those following of the Geneva Convention relative to the Treatment of Prisoners of War of August 12, 1949.

c. *See also* Basic Document 7.31, *infra*

Article 147

Grave breaches to which the preceding Article relates shall be those involving any of the following acts, if committed against persons or property protected by the present Convention: wilful killing, torture or inhuman treatment, including biological experiments, wilfully causing great suffering or serious injury to body or health, unlawful deportation or transfer or unlawful confinement of a protected person, compelling a protected person to serve in the forces of a hostile Power, or wilfully depriving a protected person of the right of fair and regular trial prescribed in the present Convention, taking of hostages and extensive destruction and appropriation of property, not justified by military necessity and carried out unlawfully and wantonly.

* * *

Article 158

Each of the High Contracting Parties shall be at liberty to denounce the present Convention.

The denunciation shall be notified in writing to the Swiss Federal Council, which shall transmit it to the Governments of all the High Contracting Parties.

The denunciation shall take effect one year after the notification thereof has been made to the Swiss Federal Council. However, a denunciation of which notification has been made at a time when the denouncing Power is involved in a conflict shall not take effect until peace has been concluded, and until after operations connected with the release, repatriation and re-establishment of the person protected by the present Convention have been terminated.

The denunciation shall have effect only in respect of the denouncing Power. It shall in no way impair the obligations which the Parties to the conflict shall remain bound to fulfil by virtue of the principles of the law of nations, as they result from the usages established among civilized peoples, from the laws of humanity and the dictates of the public conscience.

7.27 Principles of International Law Recognized in the Charter of the Nuremberg Tribunal and in the Judgment of the Tribunal.[d] Adopted by the U.N. International Law Commission, 2 August 1950. 2 Y.B.I.L.C. 374 (1950); *reprinted in* 2 Weston II.E.4

PRINCIPLE I

Any person who commits an act which constitutes a crime under international law is responsible therefor and liable to punishment.

98. This principle is based on the first paragraph of article 6 of the Charter of the Nuremberg Tribunal which established the competence of the Tribunal to try and punish persons who, acting in the interests of the European Axis countries, whether as individuals or as members of organizations, committed any of the crimes defined in sub-paragraphs (a), (b) and (c) of article 6. The text of the Charter declared punishable only persons "acting in the interests of the European Axis countries" but, as a matter of course, Principle I is now formulated in general terms.

99. The general rule underlying Principle I is that international law may impose duties on individuals directly without any interposition of internal law. The findings of the Tribunal were very definite on the question whether rules of international law may apply to individuals. "That international law imposes duties and liabilities upon individuals as well as upon States", said the judgment of the Tribunal, "has long been recognized". It added: "Crimes against international law are committed by men, not by abstract entities, and only by punishing individuals who commit such crimes can the provision of international law be enforced."

PRINCIPLE II

The fact that internal law does not impose a penalty for an act which constitutes a crime under international law does not relieve the person who committed the act from responsibility under international law.

100. This principle is a corollary to Principle I. Once it is admitted that individuals are responsible for crimes under international law, it is obvious that they are not relieved from their international responsibility by the fact that their acts are not held to be crimes under the law of any particular country.

101. The Charter of the Nuremberg Tribunal referred, in express terms, to this relation between international and national responsibility only with respect to crimes against humanity. Sub-paragraph (c) of article 6 of the Charter defined as crimes against humanity certain acts "whether or not [committed] in violation of the domestic law of the country where perpetrated". The Commission has formulated Principle II in general terms.

102. The principle that a person who has committed an international crime is responsible therefore and liable to punishment under international law, independently of the provisions of internal law, implies what is commonly called the "supremacy" of international law over national law. The Tribunal considered that international law can bind individuals even if national law does not direct them to observe the rules of international law, as shown by the following statement of the judgment: "* * * the very essence of the Charter is that individuals have international duties which transcend the national obligations of obedience imposed by the individual State".

PRINCIPLE III

The fact that a person who committed an act which constitutes a crime under international law acted as Head of State or responsible Government official does not relieve him from responsibility under international law.

d. *See also* Affirmation of the Principles of International Law Recognized by the Charter of the Nuremberg Tribunal, GA Res. 95, 1st Sess., Supp. for 23 Oct.–15 Dec. 1946, at 188, UN Doc. A/236 (1946).

103. This principle is based on article 7 of the Charter of the Nuremberg Tribunal. According to the Charter and the judgment, the act that an individual acted as Head of State or responsible government official did not relieve him from international responsibility. "The principle of international law which, under certain circumstances, protects the representatives of a State", said the Tribunal, "cannot be applied to acts which are condemned as criminal by international law. The authors of these acts cannot shelter themselves behind their official position in order to be freed from punishment.... " The same idea was also expressed in the following passage of the findings: "He who violates the laws of war cannot obtain immunity while acting in pursuance of the authority of the State if the State in authorizing action moves outside its competence under international law."

104. The last phrase of article 7 of the Charter, "or mitigating punishment", has not been retained in the formulation of Principle III. The Commission considers that the question of mitigating punishment is a matter for the competent court to decide.

PRINCIPLE IV

The fact that a person acted pursuant to order of his Government or of a superior does not relieve him from responsibility under international law, provided a moral choice was in fact possible to him.

105. This text is based on the principle contained in article 88 of the Charter of the Nuremberg Tribunal as interpreted in the judgment. The idea expressed in Principle IV is that superior orders are not a defence provided a moral choice was possible to the accused. In conformity with this conception, the Tribunal rejected the argument of the defence that there could not be any responsibility since most of the defendants acted under the orders of Hitler. The Tribunal declared: "The provisions of this article [article 8] are in conformity with the law of all nations. That a soldier was ordered to kill or torture in violation of the international law of war has never been recognized as a defence to such acts of brutality, though, as the Charter here provides, the order may be urged in mitigation of the punishment. The true test, which is found in varying degrees in the criminal law of most nations, is not the existence of the order but whether moral choice was in fact possible."

106. The last phrase of article 88 of the Charter "but may be considered in mitigation of punishment, if the Tribunal determines that justice so requires", has not been retained for the reason stated under Principle III, in paragraph 104 above.

PRINCIPLE V

Any person charged with a crime under international law has the right to a fair trial on the facts and law.

107. The principle that a defendant charged with a crime under international law must have the right to a fair trial was expressly recognized and carefully developed by the Charter of the Nuremberg Tribunal. The Charter contained a chapter entitled: "Fair Trial for Defendants," which for the purpose of ensuring such fair trial provided the following procedure:

> "a The indictment shall include full particulars specifying in details the charges against the defendants. A copy of the indictment and of all the documents lodged with the indictment, translated into a language which he understands, shall be furnished to the defendant at a reasonable time before the trial.
>
> "b During any preliminary examination or trial of a defendant he shall have the right to give any explanation relevant to the charges made against him.
>
> "c A preliminary examination of a defendant and his trial shall be conducted in, or translated into, a language which the defendant understands.

"d A defendant shall have the right to conduct his own defence before the Tribunal or to have the assistance of counsel.

"e A defendant shall have the right through himself or through his counsel to present evidence at the trial in support of his defence, and to cross-examine any witness called by the prosecution."

108. The right to a fair trial was also referred to in the judgment itself. The Tribunal said in this respect: "With regard to the constitution of the Court all that the defendants are entitled to ask is to receive a fair trial on the facts and law."

109. In the view of the Commission, the expression "fair trial" should be understood in the light of the above-quoted provisions of the Charter of the Nuremberg Tribunal.

PRINCIPLE VI

The crimes hereinafter set out are punishable as crimes under international law:

(a) *Crimes against peace:*

(i) *Planning, preparation, initiation or waging of a war of aggression or a war in violation of international treaties, agreements or assurances;*

(ii) *Participation in a common plan or conspiracy for the accomplishment of any of the acts mentioned under (i).*

110. Both categories of crimes are characterized by the fact that they are connected with "war of aggression or war in violation of international treaties, agreements or assurances".

111. The Tribunal made a general statement to the effect that its Charter was "the expression of international law existing at the time to its creation". It, in particular, refuted the argument of the defence that aggressive war was not an international crime. For this refutation the Tribunal relied primarily on the General Treaty for the Renunciation of War of 27 August 1928 (Kellogg-Briand Pact) which in 1939 was in force between sixty-three States. "The nations who signed the Pact or adhered to it unconditionally", said the Tribunal, "condemned recourse to war for the future as an instrument of policy, and expressly renounced it. After the signing of the Pact, any nation resorting to war as an instrument of national policy breaks the Pact. In the opinion of the Tribunal, the solemn renunciation of war as an instrument of national policy necessarily involves the proposition that such a war is illegal in international law; and that those who planned and waged such a war, with its inevitable and terrible consequences, are committing a crime in so doing. War for the solution of international controversies undertaken as an instrument of national policy certainly includes a war of aggression, and such a war is therefore outlawed by the Pact".

112. In support of its interpretation of the Kellogg-Briand Pact, the Tribunal cited some other international instruments which condemned war of aggression as an international crime. The draft of a Treaty of Mutual Assistance sponsored by the League of Nations in 1923 declared, in its article 1, "that aggressive war is an international crime". The Preamble to the League of Nations Protocol for the Pacific Settlement of International disputes (Geneva Protocol), of 1924, "recognizing the solidarity of the members of the International Community", stated that "a war of aggression constitutes a violation of this solidarity, and is an international crime", and that the contracting parties were "desirous of facilitating the complete application of the system provided in the Covenant of the League of Nations for the pacific settlement of disputes between the States and of ensuring the repression of international crimes". The declaration concerning wars of aggression adopted on 24 September 1927 by the Assembly of the League of Nations declared, in its preamble, that war was an "international crime". The resolution unanimously adopted on 18 February

1928 by twenty-one American Republics at the Sixth (Havana) International Conference of American States, provided that "war of aggression constitutes an international crime against the human species".

113. The Charter of the Nuremberg Tribunal did not contain any definition of "war of aggression", nor was there any such definition in the judgment of the Tribunal. It was by reviewing the historical events before and during the war that it found that certain of the defendants planned and waged aggressive wars against twelve nations and were therefore guilty of a series of crimes.

114. According to the Tribunal, this made it unnecessary to discuss the subject in further detail, or to consider at any length the extent to which these aggressive wars were also "wars in violation of international treaties, agreements, or assurances".

115. The term "assurances" is understood by the Commission as including any pledge or guarantee of peace given by a State, even unilaterally.

116. The terms "planning" and "preparation" of a war of aggression were considered by the Tribunal as comprising all the stages in the bringing about of a war of aggression from the planning to the actual initiation of the war. In view of that, the Tribunal did not make any clear distinction between planning and preparation. As stated in the judgment, "planning and preparation are essential to the making of war".

117. The meaning of the expression "waging of a war of aggression" was discussed in the Commission during the consideration of the definition of "crimes against peace". Some members of the Commission feared that everyone in uniform who fought in a war of aggression might be charged with the "waging" of such a war. The Commission understands the expression to refer only to high ranking military personnel and high State officials, and believes that this was also the view of the Tribunal.

118. A legal notion of the Charter to which the defence objected was the one concerning "conspiracy". The Tribunal recognized that "conspiracy is not defined in the Charter". However, it stated the meaning of the term, though only in a restricted way. "But in the opinion of the Tribunal", it was said in the judgment, "the conspiracy must be clearly outlined in its criminal purpose. It must not be too far removed from the time of decision and of action. The planning, to be criminal, must not rest merely on the declarations of a party programme such as are found in the twenty-five points of the Nazi Party, announced in 1920, or the political affirmations expressed in *Mein Kampf* in later years. The Tribunal must examine whether a concrete plan to wage war existed, and determine the participants in that concrete plan".

(b) *War crimes:*

Violations of the laws or customs of war which include, but are not limited to, murder, ill-treatment or deportation to slave-labour or for any other purpose of civilian population of or in occupied territory, murder or ill-treatment of prisoners of war, of persons on the seas, killing of hostages, plunder of public or private property, wanton destruction of cities, towns, or villages, or devastation not justified by military necessity.

119. The Tribunal emphasized that before the last war the crimes defined by article 6(b) of its Charter were already recognized as crimes under international law. The Tribunal stated that such crimes were covered by specific provisions of the Regulations annexed to The Hague Convention of 1907 respecting the Laws and Customs of War on Land and of the Geneva Convention of 1929 on the Treatment of Prisoners of War. After enumerating the said provisions, the Tribunal stated: "That violation of these provisions constituted crimes for which the guilty individuals were punishable is too well settled to admit or argument."

(c) *Crimes against humanity:*

Murder, extermination, enslavement, deportation and other inhuman acts done against any civilian population, or persecutions on political, racial or religious grounds, when such acts are done or such persecutions are carried on in execution of or in connexion with any crime against peace or any war crime.

120. Article 6(c) of the Charter of the Nuremberg Tribunal distinguished two categories of punishable acts, to wit: first, murder, extermination, enslavement, deportation and other inhuman acts committed against any civilian population, before or during the war, and second, persecution on political, racial or religious grounds. Acts within these categories, according to the Charter, constituted international crimes only when committed "in execution of or in connexion with any crimes within the jurisdiction of the Tribunal". The crimes referred to as falling, within the jurisdiction of the Tribunal were crimes against peace and war crimes.

121. Though it found that "political opponents were murdered in Germany before the war, and that many of them were kept in concentration camps in circumstances of great horror and cruelty", that "the policy of persecution, repression and murder of civilians in Germany before the war of 1939, who were likely to be hostile to the Government, was most ruthlessly carried out", and that "the persecution of Jews during the same period is established beyond all doubt", the Tribunal considered that it had not been satisfactorily proved that before the outbreak of war these acts had been committed in execution of, or in connexion with, any crime within the jurisdiction of the Tribunal. For this reason the Tribunal declared itself unable to "make a general declaration that the acts before 1939 were crimes against humanity within the meaning of the Charter".

122. The Tribunal did not, however, thereby exclude the possibility that crimes against humanity might be committed also before a war.

123. In its definition of crimes against humanity the Commission has omitted the phrase "before or during the war" contained in article 6(c) of the Charter of the Nuremberg Tribunal because this phrase referred to a particular war, the war of 1939. The omission of the phrase does not mean that the Commission considers that crimes against humanity can be committed only during a War. On the contrary, the Commission is of the opinion that such crimes may take place also before a war in connexion with crimes against peace.

124. In accordance with article 6(c) of the Charter, the above formulation characterizes as crimes against humanity murder, extermination, enslavement, etc., committed against "any" civilian population. This means that these acts may be crimes against humanity even if they are committed by the perpetrator against his own population.

PRINCIPLE VII

Complicity in the commission of a crime against peace, a war crime, or a crime against humanity as set forth in Principle VI is a crime under international law.

125. The only provision in the Charter of the Nuremberg Tribunal regarding responsibility for complicity was that of the last paragraph of article 6 which reads as follows: "Leaders, organizers, instigators and accomplices participating in the formulation or execution of a common plan or conspiracy to commit any of the foregoing crimes are responsible for all acts performed by any persons in execution of such a plan."

126. The Tribunal, commenting on this provision in connexion with its discussion of count one of the indictment, which charged certain defendants with conspiracy to commit aggressive war, war crimes and crimes against humanity, said that, in its opinion, the provision did not "add a new and separate crime to those already listed". In the view of the Tribunal, the provision was designed to "establish the responsibility

of persons participating in a common plan'' to prepare, initiate and wage aggressive war. Interpreted literally, this statement would seem to imply that the complicity rule did not apply to crimes perpetrated by individual action.

127. On the other hand, the Tribunal convicted several of the defendants of war crimes and crimes against humanity because they gave orders resulting in atrocious and criminal acts which they did not commit themselves. In practice, therefore, the Tribunal seems to have applied general principles of criminal law regarding complicity. This view is corroborated by expressions used by the Tribunal in assessing the guilt of particular defendants.

7.28 Draft Articles on the Draft Code of Crimes Against the Peace and Security of Mankind (as Revised Through 1991). First adopted by the U.N. International Law Commission, 4 December 1954. G.A. Res. 46/405, U.N. GAOR, 46th Sess., Supp. No. 10, at 198, U.N. Doc. A/46/405 (1991); *reprinted in* 30 I.L.M. 1554 (1991) & 2 Weston II.E.5

PART I

CHAPTER 1. DEFINITION AND CHARACTERIZATION

Article 1

Definition

The crimes [under international law] defined in this Code constitute crimes against the peace and security of mankind.

Article 2

Characterization

The characterization of an act or omission as a crime against the peace and security of mankind is independent of internal law. The fact that an act or omission is or is not punishable under internal law does not affect this characterization.

CHAPTER 2. GENERAL PRINCIPLES

Article 3

Responsibility and punishment

1. An individual who commits a crime against the peace and security of mankind is responsible therefore and is liable to punishment.

2. An individual who aids, abets or provides the means for the commission of a crime against the peace and security of mankind or conspires in or directly incites the commission of such a crime is responsible therefore and is liable to punishment.

3. An individual who commits an act constituting an attempt to commit a crime against the peace and security of mankind [as set out in articles * * *] is responsible therefore and is liable to punishment. Attempt means any commencement of execution of a crime that failed or was halted only because of circumstances independent of the perpetrator's intention.

Article 4

Motives

Responsibility for a crime against the peace and security of mankind is not affected by any motives invoked by the accused which are not covered by the definition of the crime.

Article 5

Responsibility of States

Prosecution of an individual for a crime against the peace and security of mankind does not relieve a State of any responsibility under international law for an act or omission attributable to it.

Article 6

Obligation to try or extradite

1. A State in whose territory an individual alleged to have committed a crime against the peace and security of mankind is present shall either try or extradite him.

2. If extradition is requested by several States, special consideration shall be given to the request of the State in whose territory the crime was committed.

3. The provisions of paragraphs 1 and 2 do not prejudge the establishment and the jurisdiction of an international criminal court.

Article 7

Non-applicability of statutory limitations

No statutory limitation shall apply to crimes against the peace and security of mankind.

Article 8

Judicial guarantees

An individual charged with a crime against the peace and security of mankind shall be entitled without discrimination to the minimum guarantees due to all human beings with regard to the law and the facts. In particular, he shall have the right to be presumed innocent until proved guilty and have the rights:

(a) in the determination of any charge against him, to have a fair and public hearing by a competent, independent and impartial tribunal duly established by law or by treaty;

(b) to be informed promptly and in detail in a language which he understands of the nature and cause of the charge against him;

(c) to have adequate time and facilities for the preparation of his defence and to communicate with counsel of his own choosing;

(d) to be tried without undue delay;

(e) to be tried in his presence, and to defend himself in person or through legal assistance of his own choosing; to be informed, if he does not have legal assistance, of this right; and to have legal assistance assigned to him and without payment by him in any such case if he does not have sufficient means to pay for it;

(f) to examine, or have examined, the witnesses against him and to obtain the attendance and examination of witnesses on his behalf under the same conditions as witnesses against him;

(g) to have the free assistance of an interpreter if he cannot understand or speak the language used in court;

(h) not to be compelled to testify against himself or to confess guilt.

Article 9

Non bis in idem

1. No one shall be tried or punished for a crime under this Code for which he has already been finally convicted or acquitted by an international criminal court.

2. Subject to paragraphs 3, 4 and 5, no one shall be tried or punished for a crime under this Code in respect of an act for which he has already been finally convicted or acquitted by a national court, provided that, if a punishment was imposed, it has been enforced or is in the process of being.

3. Notwithstanding the provisions of paragraph 2, an individual may be tried and punished by an international criminal court or by a national court for a crime under this Code if the act which was the subject of a trial and judgement as an ordinary crime corresponds to one of the crimes characterized in this Code.

4. Notwithstanding the provisions of paragraph 2, an individual may be tried and punished by a national court of another State for a crime under the Code:

(a) if the act which was the subject of the previous judgement took place in the territory of that State; or

(b) if that State has been the main victim of the crime.

5. In the case of a subsequent conviction under this Code, the court, in passing sentence, shall deduct any penalty imposed and implemented as a result of a previous conviction for the same act.

Article 10

Non-retroactivity

1. No one shall be convicted under this Code for acts committed before its entry into force.

2. Nothing in this article shall preclude the trial and punishment of anyone for any act which, at the time when it was committed, was criminal in accordance with international law or domestic law applicable in conformity with international law.

Article 11

Order of a Government or a superior

The fact that an individual charged with a crime against the peace and security of mankind acted pursuant to an order of a Government or a superior does not relieve him of criminal responsibility if, in the circumstances at the time, it was possible for him not to comply with that order.

Article 12

Responsibility of the superior

The fact that a crime against the peace and security of mankind was committed by a subordinate does not relieve his superiors of criminal responsibility, if they knew or had information enabling them to conclude, in the circumstances at the time, that the subordinate was committing or was going to commit such a crime and if they did not take all feasible measures within their power to prevent or repress the crime.

Article 13

Official position and responsibility

The official position of an individual who commits a crime against the peace and security of mankind, and particularly the fact that he acts as head of State or Government, does not relieve him of criminal responsibility.

Article 14

Defences and extenuating circumstances

1. The competent court shall determine the admissibility of defences under the general principles of law, in the light of the character of each crime.

2. In passing sentence, the court shall, where appropriate, take into account extenuating circumstances.

PART II

CRIMES AGAINST THE PEACE AND SECURITY OF MANKIND

Article 15

Aggression

1. An individual who as leader or organizer plans, commits, or orders the commission of an act of aggression shall, on conviction thereof, be sentenced [to * * *].

2. Aggression is the use of armed force by a State against the sovereignty, territorial integrity or political independence of another State, or in any other manner inconsistent with the Charter of the United Nations.

3. The first use of armed force by a State in contravention of the Charter shall constitute prima facie evidence of an act of aggression, although the Security Council may, in conformity with the Charter, conclude that a determination that an act of aggression has been committed would not be justified in the light of other relevant circumstances, including the fact that the acts concerned or their consequences are not of sufficient gravity.

4. Any of the following acts, regardless of a declaration of war, constitutes an act of aggression, due regard being paid to paragraphs 2 and 3:

(a) the invasion or attack by the armed forces of a State of the territory of another State, or any military occupation, however temporary, resulting from such invasion or attack, or any annexation by the use of force of the territory of another State or part thereof;

(b) bombardment by the armed forces of a State against the territory of another State or the use of any weapons by a State against the territory of another State;

(c) the blockade of the port or coasts of a State by the armed forces of another State;

(d) an attack by the armed forces of a State on the land, sea or air forces, or marine and air fleets of another State;

(e) the use of armed forces of one State which are within the territory of another State with the agreement of the receiving State, in contravention of the conditions provided for in the agreement, or any extension of their presence in such territory beyond the termination of the agreement;

(f) the action of a State in allowing its territory, which it has placed at the disposal of another State, to be used by that other State for perpetrating an act of aggression against a third State;

(g) the sending by or on behalf of a State of armed bands, groups, irregulars or mercenaries, which carry out acts of armed force against another State of such gravity as to amount to the acts listed above, or its substantial involvement therein;

(h) any other acts determination by the Security Council as constituting acts of aggression under the provisions of the Charter;

[5. Any determination by the Security Council as to the existence of an act of aggression is binding on national courts.]

6. Nothing in this article shall be interpreted as in any way enlarging or diminishing the scope of the Charter of the United Nations including its provisions concerning cases in which the use of force is lawful.

7. Nothing in this article could in any way prejudice the right to self-determination, freedom and independence, as derived from the Charter, of peoples forcibly deprived of that right and referred to in the Declaration on Principles of International Law concerning Friendly Relations and Cooperation among States in accordance with the Charter of the United Nations, particularly peoples under colonial and racist regimes or other forms of alien domination, nor the right of these peoples to struggle to that end and to seek and receive support, in accordance with the principles of the Charter and in conformity with the above-mentioned Declaration.

Article 16

Threat of aggression

1. An individual who as leader or organizer commits or orders the commission of a threat of aggression shall, on conviction thereof, be sentenced [to * * *].

2. Threat of aggression consists of declarations, communications, demonstrations of force or any other measures which would give good reason to the Government of a State to believe that aggression is being seriously contemplated against that State.

Article 17

Intervention

1. An individual who as leader or organizer commits or orders the commission of an act of intervention in the internal or external affairs of a State shall, on conviction thereof, be sentenced [to * * *].

2. Intervention in the internal or external affairs of a State consists of fomenting [armed] subversive or terrorist activities or by organizing, assisting or financing such activities, or supplying arms for the purpose of such activities, thereby [seriously] undermining the free exercise by that State of its sovereign rights.

3. Nothing in this article shall in any way prejudice the right of peoples to self-determination as enshrined in the Charter of the United Nations.

Article 18

Colonial domination and other forms of alien domination

An individual who as leader or organizer establishes or maintains by force or orders the establishment or maintenance by force of colonial domination or any other form of alien domination contrary to the right of peoples to self-determination as enshrined in the Charter of the United Nations, shall, on conviction thereof, be sentenced [to * * *].

Article 19

Genocide

1. An individual who commits or orders the commission of an act of genocide shall, on conviction thereof, be sentenced [to * * *].

2. Genocide means any of the following acts committed with intent to destroy, in whole or in part, a national, ethnic, racial or religious group as such:

(a) killing members of the group;

(b) causing serious bodily or mental harm to members of the group;

(c) deliberately inflicting on the group conditions of life calculated to bring about its physical destruction in whole or in part;

(d) imposing measures intended to prevent births within the group.

Article 20

Apartheid

1. An individual who as leader or organizer commits or orders the commission of the crime of apartheid shall, on conviction thereof, be sentenced [to * * *].

2. Apartheid consists of any of the following acts based on policies and practices of racial segregation and discrimination committed for the purpose of establishing or maintaining domination by one racial group over any other racial group and systematically oppressing it:

(a) denial to a member or members of a racial group of the right to life and liberty of person;

(b) deliberate imposition on a racial group of living conditions calculated to cause its physical destruction in whole or in part;

(c) any legislative measures and other measures calculated to prevent a racial group from participating in the political, social, economic and cultural life of the country and the deliberate creation of conditions preventing the full development of such a group;

(d) any measures, including legislative measures, designated to divide the population along racial lines, in particular by the creation of separate reserves and ghettos for the members of a racial group, the prohibition of marriages among members of various racial groups or the expropriation of landed property belonging to a racial group or to members thereof;

(e) exploitation of the labour of the members of a racial group, in particular by submitting them to forced labour;

(f) persecution of organizations and persons, by depriving them of fundamental rights and freedoms, because they oppose apartheid.

Article 21

Systematic or mass violations of human rights

An individual who commits or orders the commission of any of the following violations of human rights:

—murder

—torture

—establishing or maintaining over persons a status of slavery, servitude or forced labour

—persecution on social, political, racial, religious or cultural grounds in a systematic manner or on a mass scale; or

—deportation or forcible transfer of population

shall, on conviction thereof, be sentenced [to * * *].

Article 22

Exceptionally serious war crimes

1. An individual who commits or orders the commission of an exceptionally serious war crime shall, on conviction thereof, be sentenced [to * * *].

2. For the purposes of this Code, an exceptionally serious war crime is an exceptionally serious violation of principles and rules of international law applicable in armed conflict consisting of any of the following acts:

(a) acts of inhumanity, cruelty or barbarity directed against the life, dignity or physical or mental integrity of persons[, in particular wilful killing, torture, mutilation, biological experiments, taking of hostages, compelling a protected person to serve in the forces of a hostile Power, unjustifiable delay in the repatriation of prisoners of war after the cessation of active hostilities, deportation or transfer of the civilian population and collective punishment];

(b) establishment of settlers in an occupied territory and changes to the demographic composition of an occupied territory;

(c) use of unlawful weapons;

(d) employing methods or means of warfare which are intended or may be expected to cause widespread, long-term and severe damage to the natural environment;

(e) large-scale destruction of civilian property;

(f) wilful attacks on property of exceptional religious, historical or cultural value.

Article 23

Recruitment, use, financing and training of mercenaries

1. An individual who as an agent or representative of a State commits or orders the commission of any of the following acts:

—recruitment, use, financing or training of mercenaries for activities directed against another State or for the purpose of opposing the legitimate exercise of the inalienable right of peoples to self-determination as recognized under international law

shall, on conviction thereof, be sentenced [to * * *].

2. A mercenary is any individual who:

(a) is specially recruited locally or abroad in order to fight in an armed conflict;

(b) is motivated to take part in the hostilities essentially by the desire for private gain and, in fact, is promised, by or on behalf of a party to the conflict, material compensation substantially in excess of that promised or paid to combatants of similar rank and functions in the armed forces of that party;

(c) is neither a national or a party to the conflict nor a resident of territory controlled by a party to the conflict;

(d) is not a member of the armed forces of a party to the conflict; and

(e) has not been sent by a State which is not a party to the conflict on official duty as a member of its armed forces.

3. A mercenary is also any individual who, in any other situation:

(a) is specially recruited locally or abroad for the purpose of participating in a concerted act of violence aimed at:

(i) overthrowing a Government or otherwise undermining the constitution order of a State; or

(ii) undermining the territorial integrity of a State;

(b) is motivated to take part therein essentially by the desire for significant private gain and is prompted by the promise or payment of material compensation;

(c) is neither a national nor a resident of the State against which such an act is directed;

(d) has not been sent by a State on official duty; and

(e) is not a member of the armed forces of the State is whose territory the act is undertaken.

Article 24

International terrorism

An individual who as an agent or representative of a State commits or orders the commission of any of the following acts:

—undertaking, organizing, assisting, financing, encouraging or tolerating act against another State directed at persons or property and of such a nature as to create a state of terror in the minds of public figures, groups of persons or the general public

shall, on conviction thereof, be sentenced [to * * *].

Article 25

Illicit traffic in narcotic drugs

1. An individual who commits or orders the commission of any of the following acts:

—undertaking, organizing, facilitating, financing or encouraging illicit traffic in narcotic drugs on a large scale, whether within the confines of a State or in a transboundary context

shall, on conviction thereof, be sentenced [to * * *].

2. For the purposes of paragraph 1, facilitating or encouraging illicit traffic in narcotic drugs includes the acquisition, holding, conversion or transfer of property by an individual who knows that such property is derived from the crime described in this article in order to conceal or disguise the illicit origin of the property.

3. Illicit traffic in narcotic drugs means any production, manufacture, extraction, preparation, offering, offering for sale, distribution, sale, delivery on any terms whatsoever, brokerage, dispatch, dispatch in transit, transport, importation or exportation of any narcotic drug or any psychotropic substance contrary to international law.

Article 26

Wilful and severe damage to the environment

An individual who wilfully causes or orders the causing of widespread, long-term and severe damage to the natural environment shall, on conviction thereof, be sentenced [to * * *].

7.29 Treaty on the Non-proliferation of Nuclear Weapons. Concluded at London, Moscow, and Washington, 1 July 1968. Entered into force, 5 March 1970. 729 U.N.T.S. 161, 21 T.S. 483, T.I.A.S. No. 6839; *Reprinted in* 7 I.L.M. 809 (1968) & 2 Weston II.C.17: *Arts. III, VI*

Article III

1. Each non-nuclear-weapon State Party to the Treaty undertakes to accept safeguards, as set forth in an agreement to be negotiated and concluded with the International Atomic Energy Agency in accordance with the Statute of the International Atomic Energy Agency and the Agency's safeguards system, for the exclusive purpose of verification of the fulfilment of its obligations assumed under this Treaty with a view to preventing diversion of nuclear energy from peaceful uses to nuclear weapons or other nuclear explosive devices. Procedures for the safeguards required by this Article shall be followed with respect to source or special fissionable material whether it is being produced, processed or used in any principal nuclear facility or is outside any such facility. The safeguards required by this Article shall be applied on all source or special fissionable material in all peaceful nuclear activities within the territory of such State, under its jurisdiction, or carried out under its control anywhere.

2. Each State Party to the Treaty undertakes not to provide: (a) source or special fissionable material, or (b) equipment or material especially designed or prepared for the processing, use or production of special fissionable material, to any non-nuclear-weapon State for peaceful purposes, unless the source or special fissionable material shall be subject to the safeguards required by this Article.

3. The safeguards required by this Article shall be implemented in a manner designed to comply with Article IV of this Treaty, and to avoid hampering the economic or technological development of the Parties or international co-operation in the field of peaceful nuclear activities, including the international exchange of nuclear material and equipment for the processing, use or production of nuclear material for peaceful purposes in accordance with the provisions of this Article and the principle of safeguarding set forth in the Preamble of the Treaty.

4. Non-nuclear-weapon States Party to the Treaty shall conclude agreements with the International Atomic Energy Agency to meet the requirements of this Article either individually or together with other States in accordance with the Statute of the International Atomic Energy Agency. Negotiation of such agreements shall commence within 180 days from the original entry into force of this Treaty. For States depositing their instruments of ratification or accession after the 180-day period, negotiation of such agreements shall commence not later than the date of such deposit. Such agreements shall enter into force not later than eighteen months after the date of initiation of negotiations.

* * *

Article VI

Each of the Parties to the Treaty undertakes to pursue negotiations in good faith on effective measures relating to cessation of the nuclear arms race at an early date and to nuclear disarmament, and on a treaty on general and complete disarmament under strict and effective international control.

7.30 Convention on the Prohibition of Military or Any Other Hostile Use of Environmental Modification Techniques (ENMOD) (Without Annex). Adopted by the U.N. General Assembly, 10 December 1976. Entered into force, 5 October 1978. 1108 U.N.T.S. 151, 31 T.S. 333, T.I.A.S No. 9614; *reprinted in* 16 I.L.M. 88 (1977) & 2 Weston II.B.19

The States Parties to this Convention,

Guided by the interest of consolidating peace, and wishing to contribute to the cause of halting the arms race, and of bringing about general and complete disarmament under strict and effective international control, and of saving mankind from the danger of using new means of warfare,

Determined to continue negotiations with a view to achieving effective progress towards further measures in the field of disarmament,

Recognizing that scientific and technical advances may open new possibilities with respect to modification of the environment,

Recalling the Declaration of the United Nations Conference on the Human Environment, adopted at Stockholm on 16 June 1972,

Realizing that the use of environmental modification techniques for peaceful purposes could improve the interrelationship of man and nature and contribute to the preservation and improvement of the environment for the benefit of present and future generations,

Recognizing, however, that military or any other hostile use of such techniques could have effects extremely harmful to human welfare,

Desiring to prohibit effectively military or any other hostile use of environmental modification techniques in order to eliminate the dangers to mankind from such use, and affirming their willingness to work towards the achievement of this objective,

Desiring also to contribute to the strengthening of trust among nations and to the further improvement of the international situation in accordance with the purposes and principles of the Charter of the United Nations,

Have agreed on the following:

Article I

1. Each State Party to this Convention undertakes not to engage in military or any other hostile use of environmental modification techniques having widespread, long-lasting or severe effects as the means of destruction, damage or injury to any other State Party.

2. Each State Party to this Convention undertakes not to assist, encourage or induce any State, group of States or international organization to engage in activities contrary to the provisions of paragraph 1 of this article.

Article II

As used in article I, the term "environmental modification techniques" refers to any technique for changing—through the deliberate manipulation of natural processes-the dynamics, composition or structure of the earth, including its biota, lithosphere, hydrosphere and atmosphere, or of outer space.

Article III

1. The provisions of this Convention shall not hinder the use of environmental modification techniques for peaceful purposes and shall be without prejudice to the generally recognized principles and applicable rules of international law concerning such use.

2. The States Parties to this Convention undertake to facilitate, and have the right to participate in, the fullest possible exchange of scientific and technological information on the use of environmental modification techniques for peaceful purposes. States Parties in a position to do so shall contribute, alone or together with other States or international organizations, to international economic and scientific co-operation in the preservation, improvement and peaceful utilization of the environment, with due consideration for the needs of the developing areas of the world.

Article IV

Each State Party to this Convention undertakes to take any measures it considers necessary in accordance with its constitutional processes to prohibit and prevent any activity in violation of the provisions of the Convention anywhere under its jurisdiction or control.

Article V

1. The States Parties to this Convention undertake to consult one another and to co-operate in solving any problems which may arise in relation to the objectives of, or in the application of the provisions of, the Convention. Consultation and co-operation pursuant to this article may also be undertaken through appropriate international procedures within the framework of the United Nations and in accordance with its Charter. These international procedures may include the services of appropriate international organizations, as well as of a Consultative Committee of Experts as provided for in paragraph 2 of this article.

2. For the purposes set forth in paragraph 1 of this article, the Depositary shall, within one month of the receipt of a request from any State Party to this Convention, convene a Consultative Committee of Experts. Any State Party may appoint an expert to this Committee whose functions and rules of procedure are set out in the annex, which constitutes an integral part of the Convention. The committee shall transmit to the Depositary a summary of its findings of fact, incorporating all views and information presented to the Committee during its proceedings. The Depositary shall distribute the summary to all States Parties.

3. Any State Party to this Convention which has reasons to believe that any other State Party is acting in breach of obligations deriving from the provisions of the Convention may lodge a complaint with the Security Council of the United Nations. Such a complaint should include all relevant information as well as all possible evidence supporting its validity.

4. Each State Party to this Convention undertakes to co-operate in carrying out any investigation which the Security Council may initiate, in accordance with the provisions of the Charter of the United Nations, on the basis of the complaint received by the Council. The Security Council shall inform the States Parties of the results of the investigation.

5. Each State Party to this Convention undertakes to provide or support assistance, in accordance with the provisions of the Charter of the United Nations, to any State Party which so requests, if the Security Council decides that such Party has been harmed or is likely to be harmed as a result of violation of the Convention.

Article VI

1. Any State Party may propose amendments to this Convention. The text of any proposed amendment shall be submitted to the Depositary, who shall promptly circulate it to all States Parties.

2. An amendment shall enter into force for all States Parties which have accepted it, upon the deposit with the Depositary of instruments of acceptance by a

majority of States Parties. Thereafter it shall enter into force for any remaining State Party on the date of deposit of its instrument of acceptance.

Article VII

This Convention shall be of unlimited duration.

Article VIII

1. Five years after the entry into force of this Convention, a conference of the States Parties to the Convention shall be convened by the Depositary at Geneva. The conference shall review the operation of the Convention with a view to ensuring that its purposes and provisions are being realized, and shall in particular examine the effectiveness of the provisions of article I, paragraph 1, in eliminating the dangers of military or any other hostile use of environmental modification techniques.

2. At intervals of not less than five years thereafter, a majority of the States Parties to this Convention may obtain, by submitting a proposal to this effect to the Depositary, the convening of a conference with the same objectives.

3. If no review conference has been convened pursuant to paragraph 2 of this article within ten years following the conclusion of a previous review conference, the Depositary shall solicit the views of all States Parties to this Convention on the holding of such a conference. If one third or ten of the States Parties, whichever number is less, respond affirmatively, the Depositary shall take immediate steps to convene the conference.

Article IX

1. This Convention shall be open to all States for signature. Any State which does not sign the Convention before its entry into force in accordance with paragraph 3 of this article may accede to it at any time.

2. This Convention shall be subject to ratification by signatory States. Instruments of ratification and of accession shall be deposited with the Secretary-General of the United Nations.

3. This Convention shall enter into force upon the deposit with the Depositary of instruments of ratification by twenty Governments in accordance with paragraph 2 of this article.

4. For those States whose instruments of ratification or accession are deposited after the entry into force of this Convention, it shall enter into force on the date of the deposit of their instruments of ratification or accession.

5. The Depositary shall promptly inform all signatory and acceding States of the date of each signature, the date of deposit of each instrument of ratification or accession and the date of the entry into force of this Convention and of any amendments thereto, as well as of the receipt of other notices.

6. This Convention shall be registered by the Depositary in accordance with Article 102 of the Charter of the United Nations.

Article X

This Convention, of which the Arabic, Chinese, English, French, Russian and Spanish texts are equally authentic, shall be deposited with the Secretary-General of the United Nations who shall send certified copies thereof to the Governments of the signatory and acceding States.

7.31 PROTOCOL ADDITIONAL (NO. I) TO THE GENEVA CONVENTIONS OF AUGUST 12, 1949, AND RELATING TO THE PROTECTION OF VICTIMS OF INTERNATIONAL ARMED CONFLICTS.[e] Concluded at Geneva, 8 June 1977. Entered into force, 7 December 1978. 1125 U.N.T.S. 3; *reprinted in* 16 I.L.M. 1391 (1977) & 2 Weston II.B.20: *Arts. 1, 35, 36, 51, 54–58, 85*

Article 1—General principles and scope of application

1. The High Contracting Parties undertake to respect and to ensure respect for this Protocol in all circumstances.

2. In cases not covered by this Protocol or by other international agreements, civilians and combatants remain under the protection and authority of the principles of international law derived from established custom, from the principles of humanity and from dictates of public conscience.

3. This Protocol, which supplements the Geneva Conventions of 12 August 1949 for the protection of war victims, shall apply in the situations referred to in Article 2 common to those Conventions.

4. The situations referred to in the preceding paragraph include armed conflicts in which peoples are fighting against colonial domination and alien occupation and against racist regimes in the exercise of their right of self-determination, as enshrined in the Charter of the United Nations and Declaration of Principles of International Law concerning Friendly Relations and Co-operation among States in accordance with the Charter of the United Nations.

* * *

Article 35—Basic rules

1. In any armed conflict, the right of the Parties to the conflict to choose methods or means of warfare is not unlimited.

2. It is prohibited to employ weapons, projectiles and material and methods of warfare of a nature to cause superfluous injury or unnecessary suffering.

3. It is prohibited to employ methods or means of warfare which are intended, or may be expected, to cause widespread, long-term and severe damage to the natural environment.

Article 36—New weapons

In the study, development, acquisition or adoption of a new weapon, means or method of warfare, a High Contracting Party is under an obligation to determine whether its employment would, in some or all circumstances, be prohibited by this Protocol or by any other rule of international law applicable to the High Contracting Party.

* * *

Article 51—Protection of the civilian population

1. The civilian population and individual civilians shall enjoy general protection against dangers arising from military operations. To give effect to this protection, the following rules, which are additional to other applicable rules of international law, shall be observed in all circumstances.

2. The civilian population as such, as well as individual civilians, shall not be the object of attack. Acts or threats of violence the primary purpose of which is to spread terror among the civilian population are prohibited.

e. *See* Basic Document 7.26, *supra*.

3. Civilians shall enjoy the protection afforded by this section, unless and for such time as they take a direct part in hostilities.

4. Indiscriminate attacks are prohibited. Indiscriminate attacks are:

(a) those which are not directed at a specific military objective;

(b) those which employ a method or means of combat which cannot be directed at a specific military objective; or

(c) those which employ a method or means of combat the effects of which cannot be limited as required by this Protocol;

and consequently, in each such case, are of a nature to strike military objectives and civilians or civilian objects without distinction.

5. Among others, the following types of attacks are to be considered as indiscriminate:

(a) an attack by bombardment by any methods or means which treats as a single military objective a number of clearly separated and distinct military objectives located in a city, town, village or other area containing a similar concentration of civilians or civilian objects; and

(b) an attack which may be expected to cause incidental loss of civilian life, injury to civilians, damage to civilian objects, or a combination thereof, which would be excessive in relation to the concrete and direct military advantage anticipated.

6. Attacks against the civilian population or civilians by way of reprisals are prohibited.

7. The presence or movements of the civilian population or individual civilians shall not be used to render certain points or areas immune from military operations, in particular in attempts to shield military objectives from attacks or to shield, favour or impede military operations. The Parties to the conflict shall not direct the movement of the civilian population or individual civilians in order to attempt to shield military objectives from attacks or to shield military operations.

8. Any violation of these prohibitions shall not release the Parties to the conflict from their legal obligations with respect to the civilian population and civilians, including the obligation to take the precautionary measures provided for in Article 57.

* * *

Article 54—Protection of objects indispensable to the survival of the civilian population

1. Starvation of civilians as a method of warfare is prohibited.

2. It is prohibited to attack, destroy, remove or render useless objects indispensable to the survival of the civilian population, such as food-stuffs, agricultural areas for the production of food-stuffs, crops, livestock, drinking water installations and supplies and irrigation works, for the specific purpose of denying them for their sustenance value to the civilian population or to the adverse Party, whatever the motive, whether in order to starve out civilians, to cause them to move away, or for any other motive.

3. The prohibitions in paragraph 2 shall not apply to such of the objects covered by it as are used by an adverse Party:

(a) as sustenance solely for the members of its armed forces; or

(b) if not as sustenance, then in direct support of military action, provided, however, that in no event shall actions against these objects be taken which may be expected to leave the civilian population with such inadequate food or water as to cause its starvation or force its movement.

4. These objects shall not be made the object of reprisals.

5. In recognition of the vital requirements of any Party to the conflict in the deference of its national territory against invasion, derogation from the prohibitions contained in paragraph 2 may be made by a Party to the conflict within such territory under its own control where required by imperative military necessity.

Article 55—Protection of the natural environment

1. Care shall be taken in warfare to protect the natural environment against widespread, long-term and severe damage. This protection includes a prohibition of the use of methods or means of warfare which are intended or may be expected to cause such damage to the natural environment and thereby to prejudice the health or survival of the population.

2. Attacks against the natural environment by way of reprisals are prohibited.

Article 56—Protection of works and installations containing dangerous forces

1. Works or installations containing dangerous forces, namely dams, dykes and nuclear electrical generating stations, shall not be made the object of attack, even where these objects are military objectives, if such attack may cause the release of dangerous forces and consequent severe losses among the civilian population. Other military objectives located at or in the vicinity of these works or installations shall not be made the object of attack if such attack may cause the release of dangerous forces from the works or installations and consequent severe losses among the civilian population.

2. The special protection against attack provided by paragraph 1 shall cease:

(a) for a dam or a dyke only if it is used for other than its normal function and in regular, significant and direct support of military operations and if such attack is the only feasible way to terminate such support;

(b) for a nuclear electrical generating station only if it provides electric power in regular, significant and direct support of military operations and if such attack is the only feasible way to terminate such support;

(c) for other military objectives located at or in the vicinity of these works or installations only if they are used in regular, significant and direct support of military operations and if such attack is the only feasible way to terminate such support.

3. In all cases, the civilian population and individual civilians shall remain entitled to all the protection accorded them by international law, including the protection of the precautionary measures provided for in Article 57. If the protection ceases and any of the works, installations or military objectives mentioned in paragraph 1 is attacked, all practical precautions shall be taken to avoid the release of dangerous forces.

4. It is prohibited to make any of the works, installations or military objectives mentioned in paragraph 1 the object of reprisals.

5. The Parties to the conflict shall endeavour to avoid locating any military objectives in the vicinity of the works or installations mentioned in paragraph 1. Nevertheless, installations erected for the sole purpose of defending the protected works or installations from attack are permissible and shall not themselves be made the object of attack, provided that they are not used in hostilities except for defensive actions necessary to respond to attacks against the protected works or installations and that their armament is limited to weapons capable only of repelling hostile action against the protected works or installations.

6. The High Contracting Parties and the Parties to the conflict are urged to conclude further agreements among themselves to provide additional protection for objects containing dangerous forces.

7. In order to facilitate the identification of the objects protected by this article, the Parties to the conflict may mark them with a special sign consisting of a group of three bright orange circles placed on the same axis, as specified in Article 16 of Annex I to this Protocol. The absence of such marking in no way relieves any Party to the conflict of its obligations under this Article.

CHAPTER IV
PRECAUTIONARY MEASURES

Article 57—Precautions in attack

1. In the conduct of military operations, constant care shall be taken to spare the civilian population, civilians and civilian objects.

2. With respect to attacks, the following precautions shall be taken:

(a) those who plan or decide upon an attack shall:

(i) do everything feasible to verify that the objectives to be attacked are neither civilians nor civilian objects and are not subject to special protection but are military objectives within the meaning of paragraph 2 of Article 52 and that it is not prohibited by the provisions of this Protocol to attack them;

(ii) take all feasible precautions in the choice of means and methods of attack with a view to avoiding, and in any event to minimizing, incidental loss of civilian life, injury to civilians and damage to civilian objects;

(iii) refrain from deciding to launch any attack which may be expected to cause incidental loss of civilian life, injury to civilians, damage to civilian objects, or a combination thereof, which would be excessive in relation to the concrete and direct military advantage anticipated.

(b) an attack shall be cancelled or suspended if it becomes apparent that the objective is not a military one or is subject to special protection or that the attack may be expected to cause incidental loss of civilian life, injury to civilians, damage to civilian objects, or a combination thereof, which would be excessive in relation to the concrete and direct military advantage anticipated;

(c) effective advance warning shall be given of attacks which may affect the civilian population, unless circumstances do not permit.

3. When a choice is possible between several military objectives for obtaining a similar military advantage; the objective to be selected shall be that the attack on which may be expected to cause the least danger to civilian lives and to civilian objects.

4. In the conduct of military operations at sea or in the air, each Party to the conflict shall, in conformity with its rights and duties under the rules of international law applicable in armed conflict, take all reasonable precautions to avoid losses of civilian lives and damage to civilian objects.

5. No provision of this article may be constructed as authorizing any attacks against the civilian population, civilians or civilian objects.

Article 58—Precautions against the effects of attacks

The Parties to the conflict shall, to the maximum extent feasible:

(a) without prejudice to Article 49 of the Fourth Convention, endeavour to remove the civilian population, individual civilians and civilian objects under their control from the vicinity of military objectives;

(b) avoid locating military objectives within or near densely populated areas;

(c) take the other necessary precautions to protect the civilian population, individual civilians and civilian objects under their control against the dangers resulting from military operations.

* * *

Article 85—Repression of breaches of this protocol

1. The provisions of the Conventions relating to the repression of breaches and grave breaches, supplemented by this Section, shall apply to the repression of breaches and grave breaches of this Protocol.

2. Acts described as grave breaches in the Conventions are grave breaches of this Protocol if committed against persons in the power of an adverse Party protected by Articles 44, 45 and 73 of this Protocol, or against the wounded, sick and shipwrecked of the adverse Party who are protected by this Protocol, or against those medical or religious personnel, medical units or medical transports which are under the control of the adverse Party and are protected by this Protocol.

3. In addition to the grave breaches defined in Article 11, the following acts shall be regarded as grave breaches of this Protocol, when committed wilfully, in violation of the relevant provisions of this Protocol, and causing death or serious injury to body or health:

(a) making the civilian population or individual civilians the object of attack;

(b) launching an indiscriminate attack affecting the civilian population or civilian objects in the knowledge that such attack will cause excessive loss of life, injury to civilians or damage to civilian objects, as defined in Article 57, paragraph 2(a)(iii);

(c) launching an attack against works or installations containing dangerous forces in the knowledge that such attack will cause excessive loss of life, injury to civilians or damage to civilian objects, as defined in Article 57, paragraph 2(a)(iii);

(d) making non-defended localities and demilitarized zones the object of attack;

(e) making a person the object of attack in the knowledge that he is *hors de combat;*

(f) the perfidious use, in violation of Article 37, of the distinctive emblem of the red cross, red crescent or red lion and sun or of other protective signs recognized by the Conventions or this Protocol.

4. In addition to the grave breaches defined in the preceding paragraphs and in the Conventions, the following shall be regarded as grave breaches of this Protocol, when committed wilfully and in violation of the Conventions or the Protocol.

(a) the transfer by the occupying Power of parts of its own civilian populations into the territory it occupies, or the deportation or transfer of all or parts of the population of the occupied territory within or outside this territory, in violation of Article 49 of the Fourth Convention;

(b) unjustifiable delay in the repatriation of prisoners of war or civilians;

(c) practices of *apartheid* and other inhuman and degrading practices involving outrages upon personal dignity, based on racial discrimination.

(d) making the clearly-recognized historic monuments, works of art or places of worship which constitute the cultural or spiritual heritage of peoples and to which special protection has been given by special arrangement, for example, within the framework of a competent international organization, the object of attack, causing as a result extensive destruction thereof, where there is no evidence of the violation by the adverse Party of Article 53, subparagraph (b), and when such historic monuments, works of art and places of worship are not located in the immediate proximity of military objectives;

(e) depriving a person protected by the Conventions or referred to in paragraph 2 of this Article of the rights of fair and regular trial.

5. Without prejudice to the application of the Conventions and of this Protocol, grave breaches of these instruments shall be regarded as war crimes.

7.32 United Nations Security Council Resolution 687 (Concerning the Restoration of Peace and Security in Iraq and Kuwait). Adopted at the 2981st Mtg., 3 April 1991. U.N. Doc. S/Res/687 (1991); *reprinted in* 30 I.L.M. 846 (1991) & 2 Weston II.D.25

The Security Council.

Recalling its resolutions 660 (1990) of 2 August 1990, 661 (1990) of 6 August 1990, 662 (1990) of 9 August 1990, 664 (1990) of 18 August 1990, 665 (1990) of 25 August 1990, 666 (1990) of 13 September 1990, 667 (1990) of 16 September 1990, 669 (1990) of 24 September 1990, 670 (1990) of 25 September 1990, 674 (1990) of 29 October 1990, 677 (1990) of 28 November 1990, 678 (1990) of 29 November 1990 and 686 (1991) of 2 March 1991,

Welcoming the restoration to Kuwait of its sovereignty, independence and territorial integrity and the return of its legitimate Government,

Affirming the commitment of all Member States to the sovereignty, territorial integrity and political independence of Kuwait and Iraq, and noting the intention expressed by the Member States cooperating with Kuwait under paragraph 2 of resolution 678 (1990) to bring their military presence in Iraq to an end as soon as possible consistent with paragraph 8 of resolution 686 (1991),

Reaffirming the need to be assured to Iraq's peaceful intentions in the light of its unlawful invasion and occupation of Kuwait,

Taking note of the letter sent by the Minister for Foreign Affairs of Iraq on 27 February 1991 and those sent pursuant to resolution 686 (1991),

Noting that Iraq and Kuwait, as independent sovereign States, signed at Baghdad on 4 October 1963 "Agreed Minutes Between the State of Kuwait and the Republic of Iraq Regarding the Restoration of Friendly Relations, Recognition and Related Matters", thereby recognizing formally the boundary between Iraq and Kuwait and the allocation of islands, which were registered with the United Nations in accordance with Article 102 of the Charter of the United Nations and in which Iraq recognized the independence and complete sovereignty of the State of Kuwait within its borders as specified and accepted in the letter of the Prime Minister of Iraq dated 21 July 1932, and as accepted by the Ruler of Kuwait in his letter dated 10 August 1932,

Conscious of the need for demarcation of the said boundary,

Conscious also of the statements by Iraq threatening to use weapons in violation of its obligations under the Geneva Protocol for the Prohibition of the Use of War of Asphyxiating, Poisonous or Other Gases, and of Bacteriological Methods of Warfare, signed at Geneva on 17 June 1925, and of its prior use of chemical weapons and affirming that grave consequences would follow any further use by Iraq of such weapons,

Recalling that Iraq has subscribed to the Declaration adopted by all States participating in the Conference of States Parties to the 1925 Geneva Protocol and Other Interested States, held in Paris from 7 to 11 January 1989, establishing the objective of universal elimination of chemical and biological weapons,

Recalling also that Iraq has signed the Convention on the Prohibition of the Development, Production and Stockpiling of Bacteriological (Biological) and Toxin Weapons and on Their Destruction, of 10 April 1972,

Noting the importance of Iraq ratifying this Convention,

Noting moreover the importance of all States adhering to this Convention and encouraging its forthcoming Review Conference to reinforce the authority, efficiency and universal scope of the convention,

Stressing the importance of an early conclusion by the Conference on Disarmament of its work on a Convention on the Universal Prohibition of Chemical Weapons and of universal adherence thereto,

Aware of the use by Iraq of ballistic missiles in unprovoked attacks and therefore of the need to take specific measures in regard to such missiles located in Iraq,

Concerned by the reports in the hands of Member States that Iraq has attempted to acquire materials for a nuclear-weapons programme contrary to its obligations under the Treaty on the Non-Proliferation of Nuclear Weapons of 1 July 1968,

Recalling the objective of the establishment of a nuclear-weapons-free zone in the region of the Middle East,

Conscious of the threat that all weapons of mass destruction pose to peace and security in the area and of the need to work towards the establishment in the Middle East of a zone free of such weapons,

Conscious also of the objective of achieving balanced and comprehensive control of armaments in the region,

Conscious further of the importance of achieving the objectives noted above using all available means, including a dialogue among the States of the region,

Noting that resolution 686 (1991) marked the lifting of the measures imposed by resolution 661 (1990) in so far as they applied to Kuwait,

Noting that despite the progress being made in fulfilling the obligations of resolution 686 (1991), many Kuwait and third country nations are still not accounted for and property remains unreturned,

Recalling the International Convention against the Taking of Hostages, opened for signature at New York on 18 December 1979, which categorizes all acts of taking hostages as manifestations of international terrorism,

Deploring threats made by Iraq during the recent conflict to make use of terrorism against targets outside Iraq and the taking of hostages by Iraq,

Taking note with grave concern of the reports of the Secretary-General of 20 March 1991 and 28 March 1991, and conscious of the necessity to meet urgently the humanitarian needs in Kuwait and Iraq,

Bearing in mind its objective of restoring international peace and security in the area as set out in recent resolutions of the Security Council,

Conscious of the need to take the following measures acting under Chapter VII of the Charter,

1. *Affirms* all thirteen resolutions noted above, except as expressly changed below to achieve the goals of this resolution, including a formal cease-fire;

A

2. *Demands* that Iraq and Kuwait respect the inviolability of the international boundary and the allocation of islands set out in the "Agreed Minutes Between the State of Kuwait and the Republic of Iraq Regarding the Restoration of Friendly Relations, Recognition and Related Matters", signed by them in the exercise of their sovereignty at Baghdad on 4 October 1963 and registered with the United Nations and published by the United Nations in document 7063, United Nations, Treaty Series, 1964;

3. *Calls upon* the Secretary-General to lend his assistance to make arrangements with Iraq and Kuwait to demarcate the boundary between Iraq and Kuwait, drawing on appropriate material, including the map transmitted by Security Council document S/22412 and to report back to the Security Council within one month;

4. *Decides* to guarantee the inviolability of the above-mentioned international boundary and to take as appropriate all necessary measures to that end in accordance with the Charter of the United Nations;

B

5. *Requests* the Secretary-General, after consulting with Iraq and Kuwait, to submit within three days to the Security Council for its approval a plan for the immediate deployment of a United Nations observer unit to monitor the Khor Abdullah and a demilitarized zone, which is hereby established, extending ten kilometres into Iraq and five kilometres into Kuwait from the boundary referred to in the "Agreed Minutes Between the State of Kuwait and the Republic of Iraq Regarding the Restoration of Friendly Relations, Recognition and Related Matters" of 4 October 1963; to deter violations of the boundary through its presence in and surveillance of the demilitarized zone; to observe any hostile or potentially hostile action mounted from the territory of one State to the other; and for the Secretary-General to report regularly to the Security Council on the operations of the unit, and immediately if there are serious violations of the zone or potential threats to peace;

6. *Notes* that as soon as the Secretary-General notifies the Security Council of the completion of the deployment of the United Nations observer unit, the conditions will be established for the Member States cooperating with Kuwait in accordance with resolution 678 (1990) to bring their military presence in Iraq to an end consistent with resolution 686 (1991);

C

7. *Invites* Iraq to reaffirm unconditionally its obligations under the Geneva Protocol for the Prohibition of the Use in War of Asphyxiating, Poisonous or Other Gases, and of Bacteriological Methods of Warfare, signed at Geneva on 17 June 1925, and to ratify the Convention on the Prohibition of the Development, Production and Stockpiling of Bacteriological (Biological) and Toxin Weapons and on Their Destruction, of 10 April 1972;

8. *Decides* that Iraq shall unconditionally accept the destruction, removal, or rendering harmless, under international supervision, of:

(a) All chemical and biological weapons and all stocks of agents and all related subsystems and components and all research, development, support and manufacturing facilities;

(b) All ballistic missiles with range greater than 150 kilometres and related major parts, and repair and production facilities;

9. *Decides,* for the implementation of paragraph 8 above, the following:

(a) Iraq shall submit to the Secretary-General, within fifteen days of the adoption of the present resolution, a declaration of the locations, amounts and types of all items specified in paragraph 8 and agree to urgent, on-site inspection as specified below;

(b) The Secretary-General, in consultation with the appropriate Governments and, where appropriate, with the Director-General of the World Health Organization, within forty-five days of the passage of the present resolution, shall develop, and submit to the Council for approval, a plan calling for the completion of the following acts within forty-five days of such approval:

(i) The forming of a Special Commission, which shall carry out immediate on-site inspection of Iraq's biological, chemical and missile capabilities, based on Iraq's declarations and the designation of any additional locations by the Special Commission itself;

(ii) The yielding by Iraq of possession to the Special Commission for destruction, removal or rendering harmless, taking into account the requirements of public safety, of all items specified under paragraph 8(a) above, including items at the additional locations designated by the Special Commission under paragraph 9(b)(i) above and the destruction by Iraq, under the supervision of the Special Commission, of all its missile capabilities, including launchers, as specified under paragraph 8(b) above;

(iii) The provision by the Special Commission of the assistance and cooperation to the Director-General of the International Atomic Energy Agency required in paragraphs 12 and 13 below;

10. *Decides* that Iraq shall unconditionally undertake not to use, develop, construct or acquire any of the items specified in paragraphs 8 and 9 above and requests the Secretary-General, in consultation with the Special Commission, to develop a plan for the future ongoing monitoring and verification of Iraq's compliance with this paragraph, to be submitted to the Security Council for approval within one hundred and twenty days of the passage of this resolution;

11. *Invites* Iraq to reaffirm unconditionally its obligations under the Treaty on the Non-Proliferation of Nuclear Weapons of 1 July 1968;

12. *Decides* that Iraq shall unconditionally agree not to acquire or develop nuclear weapons or nuclear-weapons-usable material or any subsystems or components or any research, development, support or manufacturing facilities related to the above; to submit to the Secretary-General and the Director-General of the International Atomic Energy Agency within fifteen days of the adoption of the present resolution a declaration of the locations, amounts, and types of all items specified above; to place all of its nuclear-weapons-usable materials under the exclusive control, for custody and removal, of the International Atomic Energy Agency, with the assistance and cooperation of the Special Commission as provided for in the plan of the Secretary-General discussed in paragraph 9(b) above; to accept, in accordance with the arrangements provided for in paragraph 13 below, urgent on-site inspection and the destruction, removal or rendering harmless as appropriate of all items specified above; and to accept the plan discussed in paragraph 13 below for the future ongoing monitoring and verification of its compliance with these undertakings;

13. *Requests* the Director-General of the International Atomic Energy Agency, through the Secretary-General, with the assistance and cooperation of the Special Commission as provided for in the plan of the Secretary-General in paragraph 9(b) above, to carry out immediate on-site inspection of Iraq's nuclear capabilities based on Iraq's declarations and the designation of any additional locations by the Special Commission; to develop a plan for submission to the Security Council within forty-five days calling for the destruction, removal, or rendering harmless as appropriate of all items listed in paragraph 12 above; to carry out the plan within forty-five days following approval by the Security Council; and to develop a plan, taking into account the rights and obligations of Iraq under the Treaty on the Non—Proliferation of Nuclear Weapons of 1 July 1968, for the future ongoing monitoring and verification of Iraq's compliance with paragraph 12 above, including an inventory of all nuclear material in Iraq subject to the Agency's verification and inspections to confirm that Agency safeguards cover all relevant nuclear activities in Iraq, to be submitted to the Security Council for approval within one hundred and twenty days of the passage of the present resolution;

14. *Takes note* that the actions to be taken by Iraq in paragraphs 8, 9, 10, 11, 12 and 13 of the present resolution represent steps towards the goal of establishing in the Middle East a zone free from weapons of mass destruction and all missiles for their delivery and the objective of a global ban on chemical weapons;

D

15. *Requests* the Secretary-General to report to the Security Council on the steps taken to facilitate the return of all Kuwait property seized by Iraq, including a list of any property that Kuwait claims has not been returned or which has not been returned intact;

E

16. *Reaffirms* that Iraq, without prejudice to the debts and obligations of Iraq arising prior to 2 August 1990, which will be addressed through the normal mechanisms, is liable under international law for any direct loss, damage, including environmental damage and the depletion of natural resources, or injury to foreign Governments, nationals and corporations, as a result of Iraq's unlawful invasion and occupation of Kuwait;

17. *Decides* that all Iraqi statements made since 2 August 1990 repudiating its foreign debt are null and void, and demands that Iraq adhere scrupulously to all of its obligations concerning servicing and repayment of its foreign debt;

18. *Decides* also to create a fund to pay compensation for claims that fall within paragraph 16 above and to establish a Commission that will administer the fund;

19. *Directs* the Secretary-General to develop and present to the Security Council for decision, no later than thirty days following the adoption of the present resolution, recommendations for the fund to meet the requirement for the payment of claims established in accordance with paragraph 18 above and for a programme to implement the decisions in paragraphs 16, 17 and 18 above, including: administration of the fund; mechanisms for determining the appropriate level of Iraq's contribution to the fund based on a percentage of the value of the exports of petroleum and petroleum products from Iraq not to exceed a figure to be suggested to the Council by the Secretary-General, taking into account the requirements of the people of Iraq, Iraq's payment capacity as assessed in conjunction with the international financial institutions taking into consideration external debt service, and the needs of the Iraqi economy; arrangements for ensuring that payments are made to the fund; the process by which funds will be allocated and claims paid; appropriate procedures for evaluating losses, listing claims and verifying their validity and resolving disputed claims in respect of Iraq's liability as specified in paragraph 16 above; and the composition of the Commission designated above;

F

20. *Decides,* effective immediately, that the prohibition against the sale or supply to Iraq of commodities or products, other than medicine and health supplies, and prohibitions against financial transactions related thereto contained in resolution 661 (1990) shall not apply to foodstuffs notified to the Security Council Committee established by resolution 661 (1990) concerning the situations between Iraq and Kuwait or, with the approval of that Committee, under the simplified and accelerated "no-objection" procedure, to materials and supplies for essential civilian needs as identified in the report of the Secretary-General dated essential civilian needs as identified in the report of the Secretary-General dated 20 March 1991, and in any further findings of humanitarian need by the Committee;

21. *Decides* that the Security Council shall review the provisions of paragraph 20 above every sixty days in the light of the policies and practices of the Government of Iraq, including the implementation of all relevant resolutions of the Security Council, for the purpose of determining whether to reduce or lift the prohibitions referred to therein;

22. *Decides* that upon the approval by the Security Council of the programme called for in paragraph 19 above and upon Council agreement that Iraq has completed all actions contemplated in paragraphs 8, 9, 10, 11, 12 and 13 above, the prohibitions against the import of commodities and products originating in Iraq and the prohibitions against financial transactions related thereto contained in resolution 661 (1990) shall have no further force or effect;

23. *Decides* that, pending action by the Security Council under paragraph 22 above, the Security Council Committee established by resolution 661 (1990) shall be empowered to approve, when required to assure adequate financial resources on the part of Iraq to carry out the activities under paragraph 20 above, exceptions to the prohibition against the import of commodities and products originating in Iraq;

24. *Decides* that, in accordance with resolution 661 (1990) and subsequent related resolutions and until a further decision is taken by the Security Council, all States shall continue to prevent the sale or supply, or the promotion or facilitation of such sale or supply, to Iraq by their nationals, or from their territories or using their flag vessels or aircraft, of:

(a) Arms and related *materiel* of all types, specifically including the sale or transfer through other means of all forms of conventional military equipment, including for paramilitary forces, and spare parts and components and their means of production, for such equipment;

(b) Items specified and defined in paragraphs 8 and 12 above not otherwise covered above;

(c) Technology under licensing or other transfer arrangements used in the production, utilization or stockpiling of items specified in subparagraphs (a) and (b) above;

(d) Personnel or materials for training or technical support services relating to the design, development, manufacture, use, maintenance or support of items specified in subparagraphs (a) and (b) above;

25. *Calls upon* all States and international organizations to act strictly in accordance with paragraph 24 above, notwithstanding the existence of any contracts, agreements, licences or any other arrangements;

26. *Requests* the Secretary-General, in consultation with appropriate Governments, to develop within sixty days, for the approval of the Security Council, guidelines to facilitate full international implementation of paragraphs 24 and 25 above and paragraph 27 below, and to make them available to all States and to establish procedure for updating these guidelines periodically;

27. *Calls upon* all states to maintain such national controls and procedures and to take such other actions consistent with the guidelines to be established by the Security Council under paragraph 26 above as may be necessary to ensure compliance with the terms of paragraph 24 above, and calls upon international organizations to take all appropriate steps to assist in ensuring such full compliance;

28. *Agrees* to review its decisions in paragraphs 22, 23, 24 and 25 above, except for the items specified and defined in paragraphs 8 and 12 above, on a regular basis and in any case one hundred and twenty days following passage of the present resolution, taking into account Iraq's compliance with the resolution and general progress towards the control of armaments in the region;

29. *Decides* that all States, including Iraq, shall take the necessary measures to ensure that no claim shall lie at the instance of the Government of Iraq, or of any person or body in Iraq, or of any person claiming through or for the benefit of any such person or body, in connection with any contract or other transaction where its

performance was affected by reason of the measures taken by the Security Council in resolution 661 (1990) and related resolutions;

G

30. *Decides* that, in furtherance of its commitment to facilitate the repatriation of all Kuwaiti and third country national, Iraq shall extend all necessary cooperation to the International Committee of the Red Cross, providing lists of such persons, facilitating the access of the International Committee of the Red Cross to all such persons wherever located or detained and facilitating the search by the International Committee of the Red Cross for those Kuwaiti and third country nationals still unaccounted for;

31. *Invites* the International Committee of the Red Cross to keep the Secretary-General apprised as appropriate of all activities undertaken in connection with facilitating the repatriation or return of all Kuwaiti and third country nationals or their remains present in Iraq on or after 2 August 1990;

H

32. Requires Iraq to inform the Security Council that it will not commit or support any act of international terrorism or allow any organization directed towards commission of such acts to operate within its territory and to condemn unequivocally and renounce all acts, methods and practices of terrorism;

I

33. *Declares* that, upon official notification by Iraq to the Secretary-General and to the Security Council of its acceptance of the provisions above, a formal cease-fire is effective between Iraq and Kuwait and the Member States cooperating with Kuwait in accordance with resolution 678 (1990);

34. *Decides* to remain seized of the matter and to take such further steps as may be required for the implementation of the present resolution and to secure peace and security in the area.

8. Arbitral/Judicial Decisions

8.1 Summary of Case Relating to the Territorial Jurisdiction of the International Commission of the River Oder (Czech., Den., Fr., Ger., Swed., U.K./Pol.), 1929 P.C.I.J. (ser. A) No. 23, at 5

In this case, the Permanent Court of International Justice was called upon to decide whether the jurisdiction of the International Commission of the River Oder, established under the Versailles Peace Treaty of June 28, 1919 to facilitate the internationalization of the navigable sections of the Oder, extended as well to the navigable sections of the Warta and Note rivers, tributaries of the Oder situated in Polish territory. The Court held that the Oder Commission's jurisdiction was defined in Article 331 of the Versailles Treaty. To reach this conclusion, however, the P.C.I.J. was obliged to interpret Article 331, and in so doing it invoked two clusters of customary international law principles: first, the canons of treaty interpretation, in particular the canon that insists upon an interpretation "which is most favourable to the freedom of States" when, as in this instance, the intentions of the Parties are in doubt; and second, "the principles governing international fluvial law in general". The Court reasoned, at 2728:

> * * * [W]hen consideration is given to the manner in which States have regarded the concrete situations arising out of the fact that a single waterway traverses or separates the territory of more than one State, and the possibility of fulfilling the requirements of justice and the considerations of utility which this fact places in relief, it is at once seen that a solution of the problem has been sought not in the idea of a right of passage in favour of upstream States, but in that of a community of interest of riparian States. This community of interest in a navigable river becomes the basis of a common legal right, the essential features of which are the perfect equality of all riparian States in the user of the whole course of the river and the exclusion of any preferential privilege of any one riparian State in relation to the others.
>
> It is on this conception that international river law * * * is undoubtedly based. * * * If the common legal right is based on the existence of a navigable waterway separating or traversing several States, it is evident that this common right extends to the whole navigable course of the river and does not stop short at the last frontier; no instance of a treaty in which the upstream limit of an internationalization of a river is determined by such frontier rather than by certain conditions of navigability has been brought to the attention of the Court.

8.2 Summary of Diversion of Water From the Meuse Case (Neth. v. Belg.), 1937 P.C.I.J. (ser. A/B) No. 70, at 4

In this case, pitting The Netherlands against Belgium for diversions of canal and irrigation water from the River Meuse allegedly in violation of Belgium's international obligations, the Permanent Court of International Justice had to interpret an 1863 treaty between the two countries, the purpose of which was to prevent the excessive speed of the current of the ZuidWillemsvaart, a canal running from Maastrich in The Netherlands to Bois-le-Duc in Belgium. Finding no violation of the 1863 treaty but faced with the taking of water not regulated by the treaty, the Court was forced to look to customary State practice and general principles of law. In so doing, it announced the following rule:

> As regards [canals which are situated entirely in Dutch or Belgian territory], each of the two States is at liberty, in its own territory, to modify them, to enlarge them, to transform them, to fill them in and even to increase the volume of water in them from new sources, provided that the diversion of water at the treaty feeder and the volume of water to be discharged therefrom to maintain the normal level and flow in the ZuidWillemsvaart is not affected.

Thus the P.C.I.J. invoked and formalized the customary rule that a State is at liberty to do what it wants in its own territory as long as it does not endanger the physical well-being of its neighbors.

8.3 Summary of Lac Lanoux Arbitration (Spain v. Fr.), 12 U.N.R.I.A.A. 281 (1957)

In this dispute, wherein Spain unsuccessfully objected to a French hydroelectric power plan on the grounds that, if effectuated, it would alter the natural flow of a river crossing from France into Spain, the decision turned, as noted above, on the interpretation of an 1866 treaty. However, because Spain claimed, beyond the treaty, that customary international law requires prior agreement among co-riparians whenever a substantial alteration of a transboundary system of waters is contemplated, the Tribunal considered itself obliged to take "international common law" into account. It did so, at 308 and 316, echoing all the above-summarized cases, as follows:

> International practice reflects the conviction that States ought to strive to conclude * * * agreements [regarding the industrial use of international rivers] * * *. But international practice does not so far permit more than the following conclusion: the rule that States may utilize the hydraulic power of international watercourses only on condition of a *prior* agreement between the interested States cannot be established as a custom, even less a general principle of law * * *.
>
> * * *
>
> As a matter of form, the upstream State has, procedurally, a right of initiative; it is not obliged to associate the downstream State in the elaboration of its schemes. If, in the course of discussions, the downstream State submits schemes to it, the upstream State must examine them, but it has the right to give preference to the solution contained in its own scheme provided that it takes into consideration in a reasonable manner the interests of the downstream State.

The Tribunal then held that, although the State Parties had failed to reach agreement, France had sufficiently involved Spain in the preparation of its hydroelectric scheme.

8.4 Trail Smelter Arbitration (U.S. v. Can.) (1941), 3 U.N.R.I.A.A. 1938 (1949)

[*Eds.*This case resulted from sulphur dioxide (SO_2) fumes emitted into the atmosphere by a smelter plant owned by a Canadian corporation (the Consolidated Mining and Smelting Company of Canada, Limited), located on the Columbia River at Trail, British Columbia, seven miles from the State of Washington. The Trail smelter plant was alleged to have caused environmental damage in that United States jurisdiction (Washington). It was decided by a special Arbitral Tribunal composed of one American chosen by the United States, one Canadian chosen by Canada, and a Belgian chosen by the United States and Canada jointly. The convention establishing the Tribunal called for the application of the "law and practice followed in dealing with cognate questions in the United States of America as well as international law and practice." 3 U.N.R.I.A.A. 1905, 1908 (1949). In a prior decision, the Tribunal had determined that the air pollution created by the smelter had caused damage in the State of Washington over a 12year period, from 1925 to 1937. In the instant decision, reported on March 11, 1941, the Tribunal held Canada responsible and directed injunctive relief and payment of an indemnity, as follows:]

[1]. This Tribunal is constituted under, and its powers are derived from and limited by, the Convention between the United States of America and the Dominion of Canada signed at Ottawa, April, 15, 1935, duly ratified by the two parties, and ratifications exchanged at Ottawa, August 3, 1935 (hereinafter termed "the Convention").

* * *

[4]. The Tribunal herewith reports its final decisions.

[5]. The controversy is between two Governments involving damage occurring, or having occurred, in the territory of one of them (the United States of America) and alleged to be due to an agency situated in the territory of the other (the Dominion of Canada). In this controversy, the Tribunal did not sit and is not sitting to pass upon claims presented by individuals or on behalf of one or more individuals by their Government, although individuals may come within the meaning of "parties concerned", in Article IV and of "interested parties", in Article VIII of the Convention and although the damage suffered by individuals did, in part, "afford a convenient scale for the calculation of the reparation due to the State" * * *

[6]. As between the two countries involved, each has an equal interest that if a nuisance is proved, the indemnity to damaged parties for proven damage shall be just and adequate and each has also an equal interest that unproven or unwarranted claims shall not be allowed. For, while the United States' interests may now be claimed to be injured by the operations of a Canadian corporation, it is equally possible that at some time in the future Canadian interests might be claimed to be injured by an American corporation. As has well been said: "It would not be to the advantage of the two countries concerned that industrial effort should be prevented by exaggerating the interests of the agricultural community. Equally, it would not be to the advantage of the two countries that the agricultural community should be oppressed to advance the interest of industry."

[7]. Considerations like the above are reflected in the provisions of the Convention in Article IV, that "the desire of the high contracting parties" is "to reach a solution just to all parties concerned". And the phraseology of the questions submitted to the Tribunal clearly evinces a desire and an intention that, to some extent, in making its answers to the questions, the Tribunal should endeavor to adjust the conflicting interests by some "just solution" which would allow the continuance of the operation of the Trail Smelter but under such restrictions and limitations as would, as far as foreseeable, prevent damage in the United States, and as would enable indemnity to be

obtained, if in spite of such restrictions and limitations, damage should occur in the future in the United States.

[8]. In arriving at its decision, the Tribunal has had always to bear in mind the further fact that in the preamble to the Convention, it is stated that it is concluded with the recognition of "the desirability and necessity of effecting a permanent settlement".

[9]. The duty imposed upon the Tribunal by the Convention was to "finally decide" the following questions:

> (1) Whether damage caused by the Trail Smelter in the State of Washington has occurred since the first day of January, 1932, and, if so, what indemnity should be paid therefor?
>
> (2) In the event of the answer to the first part of the preceding question being in the affirmative, whether the Trail Smelter should be required to refrain from causing damage in the State of Washington in the future and, if so, to what extent?
>
> (3) In the light of the answer to the preceding question, what measures or régime, if any, should be adopted or maintained by the Trail Smelter?
>
> (4) What indemnity or compensation, if any, should be paid on account of any decision or decisions rendered by the Tribunal pursuant to the next two preceding questions?

* * *

[13]. On April 16, 1938, the Tribunal reported its "final decision" on Question No. 1, as well as its temporary decisions on Questions No. 2 and No. 3, and provided for a temporary régime thereunder. The decision reported on April 16, 1938, will be referred to hereinafter as the "previous decision".

[14]. Concerning Question No. 1, in the statement presented by the Agent for the Government of the United States, claims for damages of $1,849,156.16 with interest of $250,855.01 (total $2,100,011.17) were presented, divided into seven categories, in respect of (*a*) cleared land and improvements; (*b*) of uncleared land and improvements; (*c*) live stock; (*d*) property in the town of Northport; (*e*) wrong done the United States in violation of sovereignty, measured by cost of investigation from January 1, 1932, to June 30, 1936; (*f*) interest on $350,000 accepted in satisfaction of damage to January 1, 1932, but not paid on that date; (*g*) business enterprises. The area claimed to be damaged contained "more than 140,000 acres", including the town of Northport.

[15]. The Tribunal disallowed the claims of the United States with reference to items (*c*), (*d*), (*e*), (*f*) and (*g*) but allowed them, in part, with respect to the remaining items (*a*) and (*b*).

[16]. In conclusion (end of Part Two of the previous decision), the Tribunal answered Question No. 1 as follows:

> Damage caused by the Trail Smelter in the State of Washington has occurred since the first day of January, 1932, and up to October 1, 1937, and the indemnity to be paid therefor is seventy-eight thousand dollars ($78,000), and is to be complete and final indemnity and compensation for all damage which occurred between such dates. Interest at the rate of six per centum per year will be allowed on the above sum of seventy-eight thousand dollars ($78,000) from the date of the filing of this report and decision until date of payment. This decision is not subject to alteration or modification by the Tribunal hereafter. The fact of existence of damage, if any, occurring after October 1, 1937, and the indemnity to be paid therefor, if any, the Tribunal will determine in its final decision.

[17]. Answering Questions No. 2 and No. 3, the Tribunal decided that, until a final decision should be made, the Trail Smelter should be subject to a temporary régime (described more in detail in Part Four of the present decision) and a trial period was established to a date not later than October 1, 1940, in order to enable the Tribunal to establish a permanent régime based on a "more adequate and intensive study", since the Tribunal felt that the information that had been placed before it did not enable it to determine at that time with sufficient certainty upon a permanent régime.

* * *

[19]. It had been provided in the previous decision that a final decision on the outstanding questions would be rendered within three months from the termination of the trial period therein prescribed, i.e., from October 1, 1940, unless the trial period was ended sooner. The trial period was not terminated before October 1, 1940, * * *.

* * *

[21]. The period within which the Tribunal shall report its final decisions was extended by agreement of the two Governments until March 12, 1941.

* * *

[57]. The first question under Article III of the Convention is: "(1) Whether damage caused by the Trail Smelter in the State of Washington has occurred since the first day of January, 1932, and, if so, what indemnity should be paid therefor."

[58]. This question has been answered by the Tribunal in its previous decision, as to the period from January 1, 1932 to October 1, 1937, as set forth above.

* * *

[113]. The Tribunal is requested to say that damage has occurred in the State of Washington since October 1, 1937, as a consequence of the emission of sulphur dioxide by the smelters of the Consolidated Mining and Smelting Company at Trail, B.C., and that an indemnity in the sum of $34,807 should be paid therefor.

* * *

[137]. Since the Tribunal has, in its previous decision, answered Question No. 1 with respect to the period from the first day of January, 1932, to the first day of October, 1937, it now answers Question No. 1 with respect to the period from the first day of October, 1937, to the first day of October, 1940, as follows:

> (1) No damage caused by the Trail Smelter in the State of Washington has occurred since the first day of October, 1937, and prior to the first day of October, 1940, and hence no indemnity shall be paid therefor.

* * *

[138]. The second question under Article III of the Convention is as follows:

> In the event of the answer to the first part of the preceding question being in the affirmative, whether the Trail Smelter should be required to refrain from causing damage in the State of Washington in the future and, if so, to what extent?

[139]. Damage has occurred since January 1, 1932, as fully set forth in the previous decision. To that extent, the first part of the preceding question has thus been answered in the affirmative.

* * *

[142]. The first problem which arises is whether the question should be answered on the basis of the law followed in the United States or on the basis of international

law. The Tribunal, however, finds that this problem need not be solved here as the law followed in the United States in dealing with the quasi-sovereign rights of the States of the Union, in the matter of air pollution, whilst more definite, is in conformity with the general rules of international law.

[143]. Particularly in reaching its conclusions as regards this question as well as the next, the Tribunal has given consideration to the desire of the high contracting parties "to reach a solution just to all parties concerned".

[144]. As Professor Eagleton puts in (*Responsibility of States in International Law,* 1928, p. 80): "A State owes at all times a duty to protect other States against injurious acts by individuals from within its jurisdiction." A great number of such general pronouncements by leading authorities concerning the duty of a State to respect other States and their territory have been presented to the Tribunal. These and many others have been carefully examined. International decisions, in various matters, from the Alabama case onward, and also earlier ones, are based on the same general principle, and, indeed, this principle, as such, has not been questioned by Canada. But the real difficulty often arises rather when it comes to determine what, *pro subjecta materie,* is deemed to constitute an injurious act.

* * *

[146]. No case of air pollution dealt with by an international tribunal has been brought to the attention of the Tribunal nor does the Tribunal know of any such case. The nearest analogy is that of water pollution. But, here also, no decision of an international tribunal has been cited or has been found.

[147]. There are, however, as regards both air pollution and water pollution, certain decisions of the Supreme Court of the United States which may legitimately be taken as a guide in this field of international law, for it is reasonable to follow by analogy, in international cases, precedents established by that court in dealing with controversies between States of the Union or with other controversies concerning the quasi-sovereign rights of such States, where no contrary rule prevails in international law and no reason for rejecting such precedents can be adduced from the limitations of sovereignty inherent in the Constitution of the United States.

[148]. In the suit of the *State of Missouri v. the State of Illinois* (200 U.S. 496, 521) concerning the pollution, within the boundaries of Illinois, of the Illinois River, an affluent of the Mississippi flowing into the latter where it forms the boundary between that State and Missouri, an injunction was refused. "Before this court ought to intervene", said the court, "the case should be of serious magnitude, clearly and fully proved, and the principle to be applied should be one which the court is prepared deliberately to maintain against all considerations on the other side. (See *Kansas v. Colorado,* 185 U.S. 125.)" The court found that the practice complained of was general along the shores of the Mississippi River at that time, that it was followed by Missouri itself and that thus a standard was set up by the defendant which the claimant was entitled to invoke.

[149]. As the claims of public health became more exacting and methods for removing impurities from the water were perfected, complaints ceased. It is significant that Missouri sided with Illinois when the other riparians of the Great Lakes' system sought to enjoin it to desist from diverting the waters of that system into that of the Illinois and Mississippi for the very purpose of disposing of the Chicago sewage.

[150]. In the more recent suit of the State of New York against the State of New Jersey (256 U.S. 296, 309), concerning the pollution of New York Bay, the injunction was also refused for lack of proof, some experts believing that the plans which were in dispute would result in the presence of "offensive odors and unsightly deposits", other equally reliable experts testifying that they were confidently of the opinion that the waters would be sufficiently purified. The court, referring to *Missouri v. Illinois,* said:

"* * * the burden upon the State of New York of sustaining the allegations of its bill is much greater than that imposed upon a complainant in an ordinary suit between private parties. Before this court can be moved to exercise its extraordinary power under the Constitution to control the conduct of one State at the suit of another, the threatened invasion of rights must be of serious magnitude and it must be established by clear and convincing evidence."

[151]. What the Supreme Court says there of its power under the Constitution equally applies to the extraordinary power granted this Tribunal under the Convention. What is true between States of the Union is, at least, equally true concerning the relations between the United States and the Dominion of Canada.

[152]. In another recent case concerning water pollution (283 U.S. 473), the complainant was successful. The City of New York was enjoined, at the request of the State of New Jersey, to desist, within a reasonable time limit, from the practice of disposing of sewage by dumping it into the sea, a practice which was injurious to the coastal waters of New Jersey in the vicinity of her bathing resorts.

[153]. In the matter of air pollution itself, the leading decisions are those of the Supreme Court in the *State of Georgia v. Tennessee Copper Company and Ducktown Sulphur, Copper and Iron Company, Limited.* Although dealing with a suit against private companies, the decisions were on questions cognate to those here at issue. Georgia stated that it had in vain sought relief from the State of Tennessee, on whose territory the smelters were located, and the court defined the nature of the suit by saying: "This is a suit by a State for an injury to it in its capacity of quasi-sovereign. In that capacity, the State has an interest independent of and behind the titles of its citizens, in all the earth and air within its domain."

[154]. On the question whether an injunction should be granted or not, the court said (206 U.S. 230):

> It (the State) has the last word as to whether its mountains shall be stripped of their forests and its inhabitants shall breathe pure air * * *. It is not lightly to be presumed to give up quasi-sovereign rights for pay and * * * if that be its choice, it may insist that an infraction of them shall be stopped. This court has not quite the same freedom to balance the harm that will be done by an injunction against that of which the plaintiff complains, that it would have in deciding between two subjects of a single political power. Without excluding the considerations that equity always takes into account * * * it is a fair and reasonable demand on the part of a sovereign that the air over its territory should not be polluted on a great scale by sulphurous acid gas, that the forests on its mountains, be they better or worse, and whatever domestic destruction they may have suffered, should not be further destroyed or threatened by the act of persons beyond its control, that the crops and orchards on its hills should not be endangered from the same source * * *. Whether Georgia, by insisting upon this claim, is doing more harm than good to her own citizens, is for her to determine. The possible disaster to those outside the State must be accepted as a consequence of her standing upon her extreme rights.

[155]. Later on, however, when the court actually framed an injunction, in the case of the *Ducktown Company* (237 U.S. 474, 477) (an agreement on the basis of an annual compensation was reached with the most important of the two smelters, the Tennessee Copper Company), they did not go beyond a decree "adequate to diminish materially the present probability of damage to its (Georgia's) citizens".

[156]. Great progress in the control of fumes has been made by science in the last few years and this progress should be taken into account.

[157]. The Tribunal, therefore, finds that the above decisions, taken as a whole, constitute an adequate basis for its conclusions, namely, that, under the principles of

international law, as well as of the law of the United States, no State has the right to use or permit the use of its territory in such a manner as to cause injury by fumes in or to the territory of another or the properties or persons therein, when the case is of serious consequence and the injury is established by clear and convincing evidence.

[158]. The decisions of the Supreme Court of the United States which are the basis of these conclusions are decisions in equity and a solution inspired by them, together with the régime hereinafter prescribed, will, in the opinion of the Tribunal, be "just to all parties concerned", as long, at least, as the present conditions in the Columbia River Valley continue to prevail.

[159]. Considering the circumstances of the case, the Tribunal holds that the Dominion of Canada is responsible in international law for the conduct of the Trail Smelter. Apart from the undertakings in the Convention, it is, therefore, the duty of the Government of the Dominion of Canada to see to it that this conduct should be in conformity with the obligation of the Dominion under international law as herein determined.

[160]. The Tribunal, therefore, answers Question No. 2 as follows: (2) So long as the present conditions in the Columbia River Valley prevail, the Trail Smelter shall be required to refrain from causing any damage through fumes in the State of Washington; the damage herein referred to and its extent being such as would be recoverable under the decisions of the courts of the United States in suits between private individuals. The indemnity for such damage should be fixed in such manner as the Governments, acting under Article XI of the Convention, should agree upon.

Part Four

[161]. The third question under Article III of the Convention is as follows: "In the light of the answer to the preceding question, what measures or régime, if any, should be adopted and maintained by the Trail Smelter?"

[162]. Answering this question in the light of the preceding one, since the Tribunal has, in its previous decision, found that damage caused by the Trail Smelter has occurred in the State of Washington since January 1, 1932, and since the Tribunal is of opinion that damage may occur in the future unless the operations of the Smelter shall be subject to some control, in order to avoid damage occurring, the Tribunal now decides that a régime or measure of control shall be applied to the operations of the Smelter and shall remain in full force unless and until modified in accordance with the provisions hereinafter set forth in Section 3, Paragraph VI of the present part of this decision.

* * *

Part Five

[227]. The fourth question under Article III of the Convention is as follows:

> What indemnity or compensation, if any, should be paid on account of any decision or decisions rendered by the Tribunal pursuant to the next two preceding Questions?

[228]. The Tribunal is of opinion that the prescribed régime will probably remove the causes of the present controversy and, as said before, will probably result in preventing any damage of a material nature occurring in the State of Washington in the future.

[229]. But since the desirable and expected result of the régime or measure of control hereby required to be adopted and maintained by the Smelter may not occur, and since in its answer to Question No. 2, the Tribunal has required the Smelter to refrain from causing damage in the State of Washington in the future, as set forth

therein, the Tribunal answers Question No. 4 and decides that on account of decisions rendered by the Tribunal in its answers to Question No. 2 and Question No. 3 there shall be paid as follows: (*a*) if any damage as defined under Question No. 2 shall have occurred since October 1, 1940, or shall occur in the future, whether through failure on the part of the Smelter to comply with the regulations herein prescribed or notwithstanding the maintenance of the régime, an indemnity shall be paid for such damage but only when and if the two Governments shall make arrangements for the disposition of claims for indemnity under the provisions of Article XI of the Convention; (*b*) if as a consequence of the decision of the Tribunal in its answers to Question No. 2 and Question No. 3, the United States shall find it necessary to maintain in the future an agent or agents in the area in order to ascertain whether damage shall have occurred in spite of the régime prescribed herein, the reasonable cost of such investigations not in excess of $7,500 in any one year shall be paid to the United States as a compensation, but only if and when the two Governments determine under Article XI of the Convention that damage has occurred in the year in question, due to the operation of the Smelter, and "disposition of claims for indemnity for damage" has been made by the two Governments; but in no case shall the aforesaid compensation be payable in excess of the indemnity for damage; and further it is understood that such payment is hereby directed by the Tribunal only as a compensation to be paid on account of the answers of the Tribunal to Question No. 2 and Question No. 3 (as provided for in Question No. 4) and *not* as any part of indemnity for the damage to be ascertained and to be determined upon by the two Governments under Article XI of the Convention.

Part Six

[230]. Since further investigations in the future may be possible under the provisions of Part Four and of Part Five of this decision, the Tribunal finds it necessary to include in its report, the following provision:

[231]. Investigators appointed by or on behalf of either Government, whether jointly or severally, and the members of the Commission provided for in Paragraph VI of Section 3 of Part Four of this decision, shall be permitted at all reasonable times to inspect the operations of the Smelter and to enter upon and inspect any of the properties in the State of Washington which may be claimed to be affected by fumes. This provision shall also apply to any localities where instruments are operated under the present régime or under any amended régime. Wherever under the present régime or any amended régime, instruments have to be maintained and operated by the Smelter on the territory of the United States, the Government of the United States shall undertake to secure for the Government of the Dominion of Canada the facilities reasonably required to that effect.

[232]. The Tribunal expresses the strong hope that any investigations which the Governments may undertake in the future, in connection with the matters dealt with in this decision, shall be conducted jointly.

8.5 Corfu Channel Case (U.K. v. Alb.), 1949 I.C.J. 4

[*Eds.*On May 15, 1946, British warships passing through the Corfu Channel, in Albanian territorial waters, were fired upon by Albanian coastal batteries; and on October 22, 1946, two British warships passing through that Channel struck mines, which caused damage to the vessels and loss of lives among the crews. On November 1213, 1946, without Albanian consent, units of the Royal British Navy swept for mines that part of the Corfu Channel that was situated in Albanian waters. The United Kingdom raised the issue in the Security Council, which recommended that the two Parties refer the matter to the International Court of Justice. When the case first came up for hearing, Albania unsuccessfully raised a Preliminary Objection to the Court's jurisdiction (1948 I.C.J. 4, 15). At the hearing on the merits, pursuant to a Special Agreement between the State parties, the Court had to consider the following two questions:

> "(1) Is Albania responsible under international law for the explosions which occurred on the 22nd October 1946 in Albanian waters and for the damage and loss of human life which resulted from them and is there any duty to pay compensation?"
>
> "(2) Has the United Kingdom under international law violated the sovereignty of the Albanian People's Republic by reason of the acts of the Royal Navy in Albanian waters on the 22nd October and on the 12th and 13th November 1946 and is there any duty to give satisfaction?"

On April 9, 1949, by 11 votes to 5, the Court held that Albania was responsible for the explosions and the ensuing damage, and, unanimously, that the United Kingdom had violated Albanian sovereignty in November. In so holding, the Court reasoned as follows:]

[16]. By the first part of the Special Agreement, the following question is submitted to the Court:

> "(1) Is Albania responsible under international law for the explosions which occurred on the 22nd October 1946 in Albanian waters and for the damage and loss of human life which resulted from them and is there any duty to pay compensation?"

[17]. On October 22nd, 1946, a squadron of British warships, the cruisers *Mauritius* and *Leander* and the destroyers *Saumarez* and *Volage,* left the port of Corfu and proceeded northward through a channel previously swept for mines in the North Corfu Strait. The cruiser *Mauritius* was leading, followed by the destroyer *Saumarez;* at a certain distance thereafter came the cruiser *Leander* followed by the destroyer *Volage.* Outside the Bay of Saranda, *Saumarez* struck a mine and was heavily damaged. *Volage* was ordered to give her assistance and to take her in tow. Whilst towing the damaged ship, *Volage* struck a mine and was much damaged. Nevertheless, she succeeded in towing the other ship back to Corfu.

[18]. Three weeks later, on November 13th, the North Corfu Channel was swept by British minesweepers and twenty-two moored mines were cut. Two mines were taken to Malta for expert examination. During the minesweeping operation it was thought that the mines were of the German GR type, but it was subsequently established that they were of the German GY type.

* * *

[28]. The Court consequently finds that the following facts are established. The two ships were mined in Albanian territorial waters in a previously swept and check-swept channel just at the place where a newly laid minefield consisting of moored contact German GY mines was discovered three weeks later. The damage sustained by the ships was inconsistent with damage which could have been caused by floating

mines, magnetic ground mines, magnetic moored mines, or German GR mines, but its nature and extent were such as would be caused by mines of the type found in the minefield. In such circumstances the Court arrives at the conclusion that the explosions were due to mines belonging to that minefield.

[29]. Such are the facts upon which the Court must, in order to reply to the first question of the Special Agreement, give judgment as to Albania's responsibility for the explosions on October 22nd, 1946, and for the damage and loss of human life which resulted, and for the compensation, if any, due in respect of such damage and loss.

[30]. To begin with, the foundation for Albania's responsibility, as alleged by the United Kingdom, must be considered. On this subject, the main position of the United Kingdom is to be found in its submission No. 2: that the minefield which caused the explosions was laid between May 15th, 1946, and October 22nd, 1946, by or with the connivance or knowledge of the Albanian Government.

[31]. The Court considered first the various grounds for responsibility alleged in this submission.

[32]. In fact, although the United Kingdom Government never abandoned its contention that Albania herself laid the mines, very little attempt was made by the Government to demonstrate this point. In the written Reply, the United Kingdom Government takes note of the Albanian Government's formal statement that it did not lay the mines, and was not in a position to do so, as Albania possessed no navy; and that, on the whole Albanian littoral, the Albanian authorities only had a few launches and motor boats. In the light of these statements, the Albanian Government was called upon, in the Reply, to disclose the circumstances in which two Yugoslav war vessels, the *Mljet* and the *Meljine,* carrying contact mines of the GY type, sailed southward from the port of Sibenik on or about October 18th, and proceeded to the Corfu Channel. The United Kingdom Government, having thus indicated the argument upon which it was thenceforth to concentrate, stated that it proposed to show that the said warships, with the knowledge and connivance of the Albanian Government, laid mines in the Corfu Channel just before October 22nd, 1946. The facts were presented in the same light and in the same language in the oral reply by Counsel for the United Kingdom Government at the sittings on January 17th and 18th, 1949.

[33]. Although the suggestion that the minefield was laid by Albania was repeated in the United Kingdom statement in Court on January 18th, 1949, and in the final submissions read in Court on the same day, this suggestion was in fact hardly put forward at that time except *pro memoria,* and no evidence in support was furnished.

[34]. In these circumstances, the Court need pay no further attention to this matter.

[35]. The Court now comes to the second alternative argument of the United Kingdom Government, namely, that the minefield was laid with the connivance of the Albanian Government. According to this argument, the minelaying operation was carried out by two Yugoslav warships at a date prior to October 22nd, but very near that date. This would imply collusion between the Albanian and the Yugoslav Governments, consisting either of a request by the Albanian Government to the Yugoslav Government for assistance, or of acquiescence by the Albanian authorities in the laying of the mines.

* * *

[42]. In the light of the information now available to the Court, the authors of the minelaying remain unknown. In any case, the task of the Court, as defined by the Special Agreement, is to decide whether Albania is responsible, under international law, for the explosions which occurred on October 22nd, 1946, and to give judgment as to the compensation, if any.

[43]. Finally, the United Kingdom Government put forward the argument that, whoever the authors of the minelaying were, it could not have been done without the Albanian Government's knowledge.

[44]. It is clear that knowledge of the minelaying cannot be imputed to the Albanian Government by reason merely of the fact that a minefield discovered in Albanian territorial waters caused the explosions of which the British warships were the victims. It is true, as international practice shows, that a State on whose territory or in whose waters an act contrary to international law has occurred, may be called upon to give an explanation. It is also true that that State cannot evade such a request by limiting itself to a reply that it is ignorant of the circumstances of the act and of its authors. The State may, up to a certain point, be bound to supply particulars of the use made by it of the means of information and inquiry at its disposal. But it cannot be concluded from the mere fact of the control exercised by a State over its territory and waters that that State necessarily knew, or ought to have known, of any unlawful act perpetrated therein, nor yet that it necessarily knew, or should have known, the authors. This fact, by itself and apart from other circumstances, neither involves *prima facie* responsibility nor shifts the burden of proof.

[45]. On the other hand, the fact of this exclusive territorial control exercised by a State within its frontiers has a bearing upon the methods of proof available to establish the knowledge of that State as to such events. By reason of this exclusive control, the other State, the victim of a breach of international law, is often unable to furnish direct proof of facts giving rise to responsibility. Such a State should be allowed a more liberal recourse to inferences of fact and circumstantial evidence. This indirect evidence is admitted in all systems of law, and its use is recognized by international decisions. It must be regarded as of special weight when it is based on a series of facts linked together and leading logically to a single conclusion.

[46]. The Court must examine therefore whether it has been established by means of indirect evidence that Albania has knowledge of minelaying in her territorial waters independently of any connivance on her part in this operation. The proof may be drawn from inferences of fact, provided that they leave *no room* for reasonable doubt. The elements of fact on which these inferences can be based may differ from those which are relevant to the question of connivance.

[47]. In the present case, two series of facts, which corroborate one another, have to be considered: the first relates to Albania's attitude before and after the disaster of October 22nd, 1946; the other concerns the feasibility of observing minelaying from the Albanian coast.

[48]. 1. It is clearly established that the Albanian Government constantly kept a close watch over the waters of the North Corfu Channel, at any rate after May 1946.... This vigilance sometimes went so far as to involve the use of force....

* * *

[53]. Another indication of the Albanian Government's knowledge consists in the fact that that Government did not notify the presence of mines in its waters, at the moment when it must have known this, at the latest after the sweep on November 13th, and further, whereas the Greek Government immediately appointed a Commission to inquire into the events of October 22nd, the Albanian Government took no decision of such a nature, nor did it proceed to the judicial investigation incumbent, in such a case, on the territorial sovereign.

[54]. This attitude does not seem reconcilable with the alleged ignorance of the Albanian authorities that the minefield had been laid in Albanian territorial waters. It could be explained if the Albanian Government, while knowing of the minelaying, desired the circumstances of the operation to remain secret.

[55]. 2. As regards the possibility of observing minelaying from the Albanian coast, the Court regards the following facts, relating to the technical conditions of a secret minelaying and to the Albanian surveillance, as particularly important.

[56]. The Bay of Saranda and the channel used by shipping through the Strait are, from their geographical configuration, easily watched; the entrance of the bay is dominated by heights offering excellent observation points, both over the bay and over the Strait; whilst the channel throughout is close to the Albanian coast. The laying of a minefield in these waters could hardly fail to have been observed by the Albanian coastal defences.

[57]. On this subject, it must first be said that the minelaying operation itself must have required a certain time. The method adopted required, according to the Experts of the Court, the methodical and well thought-out laying of two rows of mines that had clearly a combined offensive and defensive purpose: offensive, to prevent the passage, through the Channel, of vessels drawing ten feet of water or more; defensive, to prevent vessels of the same draught from entering the Bay of Saranda. The report of the Experts reckons the time that the minelayers would have been in the waters, between Cape Kiephali and St. George's Monastery, at between two and two and a half hours. This is sufficient time to attract the attention of the observation posts, placed, as the Albanian Government stated, at Cape Kiephali and St. George's Monastery.

* * *

[62]. The Court cannot fail to give great weight to the opinion of the Experts who examined the locality in a manner giving every guarantee of correct and impartial information. Apart from the existence of a look-out post at Cape Denta, which has not been proved, the Court, basing itself on the declarations of the Albanian Government that look-out posts were stationed at Cape Kiephali and St. George's Monastery, refers to the following conclusions in the Experts' Report: (1) that in the case of minelaying from the North towards the South, the minelayers would have been seen from Cape Kiephali; (2) in the case of minelaying from the South, the minelayers would have been seen from Cape Kiephali and St. George's Monastery.

[63]. From all the facts and observations mentioned above, the Court draws the conclusion that the laying of the minefield which caused the explosions on October 22nd, 1946, could not have been accomplished without the knowledge of the Albanian Government.

[64]. The obligations resulting for Albania from this knowledge are not disputed between the Parties. Counsel for the Albanian Government expressly recognized that [*translation*] "if Albania had been informed of the operation before the incidents of October 22nd, and in time to warn the British vessels and shipping in general of the existence of mines in the Corfu Channel, her responsibility would be involved * * *.".

[65]. The obligations incumbent upon the Albanian authorities consisted in notifying, for the benefit of shipping in general, the existence of a minefield in Albanian territorial waters and in warning the approaching British warships of the imminent danger to which the minefield exposed them. Such obligations are based, not on the Hague Convention of 1907, No. VIII, which is applicable in time of war, but on certain general and well-recognized principles, namely: elementary considerations of humanity, even more exacting in peace than in war; the principle of the freedom of maritime communication; and every State's obligation not to allow knowingly its territory to be used for acts contrary to the rights of other States.

[66]. In fact, Albania neither notified the existence of the minefield, nor warned the British warships of the danger they were approaching.

[67]. But Albania's obligation to notify shipping of the existence of mines in her waters depends on her having obtained knowledge of that fact in sufficient time before October 22nd; and the duty of the Albanian coastal authorities to warn the British

ships depends on the time that elapsed between the moment that these ships were reported and the moment of the first explosion.

[68]. On this subject, the Court makes the following observations. As has already been stated, the Parties agree that the mines were recently laid. It must be concluded that the minelaying, whatever may have been its exact date, was done at a time when there was a close Albanian surveillance over the Strait. If it be supposed that it took place at the last possible moment, i.e., in the night of October 21st-22nd, the only conclusion to be drawn would be that a general notification to the shipping of all States before the time of the explosions would have been difficult, perhaps even impossible. But this would certainly not have prevented the Albanian authorities from taking, as they should have done, all necessary steps immediately to warn ships near the danger zone, more especially those that were approaching that zone. When on October 22nd about 13.00 hours the British warships were reported by the look-out post at St. George's Monastery to the Commander of the Coastal Defences as approaching Cape Long, it was perfectly possible for the Albanian authorities to use the interval of almost two hours that elapsed before the explosion affecting *Saumarez* (14.53 hours or 14.55 hours) to warn the vessels of the danger into which they were running.

[69]. In fact, nothing was attempted by the Albanian authorities to prevent the disaster. These grave omissions involve the international responsibility of Albania.

[70]. The Court therefore reaches the conclusion that Albania is responsible under international law for the explosions which occurred on October 22nd, 1946, in Albanian waters, and for the damage and loss of human life which resulted from them, and that there is a duty upon Albania to pay compensation to the United Kingdom.

* * *

[84]. In the second part of the Special Agreement, the following question is submitted to the Court:

> "(2). Has the United Kingdom under international law violated the sovereignty of the Albanian People's Republic by reason of the acts of the Royal Navy in Albanian waters on the 22nd October and on the 12th and 13th November 1946 and is there any duty to give satisfaction?"

[85]. The Court will first consider whether the sovereignty of Albania was violated by reason of the acts of the British Navy in Albanian waters on October 22nd, 1946.

* * *

[91]. It is, in the opinion of the Court, generally recognized and in accordance with international custom that States in time of peace have a right to send their warships through straits used for international navigation between two parts of the high seas without the previous authorization of a coastal State, provided that the passage is *innocent*. Unless otherwise prescribed in an international convention, there is no right for a coastal State to prohibit such passage through straits in time of peace.

[92]. The Albanian Government does not dispute that the North Corfu Channel is a strait in the geographical sense; but it denies that this Channel belongs to the class of international highways through which a right of passage exists, on the grounds that it is only of secondary importance and not even a necessary route between two parts of the high seas, and that it is used almost exclusively for local traffic to and from the ports of Corfu and Saranda.

* * *

[94]. One fact of particular importance is that the North Corfu Channel constitutes a frontier between Albania and Greece, that a part of it is wholly within the

territorial waters of these States, and that the Strait is of special importance to Greece by reason of the traffic to and from the port of Corfu.

[95]. Having regard to these various considerations, the Court has arrived at the conclusion that the North Corfu Channel should be considered as belonging to the class of international highways through which passage cannot be prohibited by a coastal State in time of peace.

[96]. On the other hand, it is a fact that the two coastal States did not maintain normal relations, that Greece had made territorial claims precisely with regard to a part of Albanian territory bordering on the Channel, that Greece had declared that she considered herself technically in a state of war with Albania, and that Albania, invoking the danger of Greek incursions, had considered it necessary to take certain measures of vigilance in this region. The Court is of opinion that Albania, in view of these exceptional circumstances, would have been justified in issuing regulations in respect of the passage of warships through the Strait, but not in prohibiting such passage or in subjecting it to the requirement of special authorization.

[97]. For these reasons the Court is unable to accept the Albanian contention that the Government of the United Kingdom has violated Albanian sovereignty by sending the warships through the Strait without having obtained the previous authorization of the Albanian Government.

[98]. In these circumstances, it is unnecessary to consider the more general question, much debated by the Parties, whether States under international law have a right to send warships in time of peace through territorial waters not included in a strait.

* * *

[101]. It remains, therefore, to consider whether the *manner* in which the passage was carried out was consistent with the principle of innocent passage and to examine the various contentions of the Albanian Government in so far as they appear to be relevant.

* * *

[108]. Having examined the various contentions of the Albanian Government in so far as they appear to be relevant, the Court has arrived at the conclusion that the United Kingdom did not violate the sovereignty of Albania by reason of the acts of the British Navy in Albanian waters on October 22nd, 1946.

[109]. In addition to the passage of the United Kingdom warships on October 22nd, 1946, the second question in the Special Agreement relates to the acts of the Royal Navy in Albanian waters on November 12th and 13th, 1946. This is the minesweeping operation called "Operation Retail" by the Parties during the proceedings. This name will be used in the present Judgment.

* * *

[112]. The United Kingdom Government does not dispute that "Operation Retail" was carried out against the clearly expressed wish of the Albanian Government. It recognizes that the operation had not the consent of the international mine clearance organizations, that it could not be justified as the exercise of a right of innocent passage, and lastly that, in principle, international law does not allow a State to assemble a large number of warships in the territorial waters of another State and to carry out minesweeping in those waters. The United Kingdom Government states that the operation was one of extreme urgency, and that it considered itself entitled to carry it out without anybody's consent.

* * *

[118]. The Court cannot accept such a line of defence. The Court can only regard the alleged right of intervention as the manifestation of a policy of force, such as has, in the past, given rise to most serious abuses and such as cannot, whatever be the present defects in international organization, find a place in international law. Intervention is perhaps still less admissible in the particular form it would take here; for, from the nature of things, it would be reserved for the most powerful States, and might easily lead to perverting the administration of international justice itself.

8.6 Nuclear Tests Cases (N.Z. v. Fr.), 1974 I.C.J. 457[a]

[*Eds.*In 1973, both Australia and New Zealand protested announced French atmospheric nuclear tests to be held in the South Pacific at France's Mururoa atoll. Additionally, they instituted proceedings before the International Court of Justice, by unilateral application in accordance with the General Act for the Pacific Settlement of International Disputes[b] as well as Article 36 of the Court's Statute **(Basic Document 1.4, supra)**. France denied the Court's competence and refused to appear. Australia and New Zealand also requested the Court to indicate interim measures of protection, on the ground that radioactive fallout from any tests held before the final judgment of the Court on the legality of such tests would prejudice the interests of the two countries concerned. In 1973, the Court, by 8 votes to 6, issued the requested order (1973 I.C.J. 99, 135). France ignored the Order and announced a further series of tests. Australia and New Zealand then asked the Court to declare such atmospheric tests to be illegal and to order France to abstain in the future. The Court considered the present hearing as related to preliminary matters and stated that it would avoid decisions on the substance. After the institution of proceedings, the French Government issued a number of statements intimating that no further tests would be held, and the Court decided, by 9 votes to 6, that the claims no longer had any object and that it was therefore not called upon to give a decision. The Court reasoned as follows:]

15. It is to be regretted that the French Government has failed to appear in order to put forward its arguments on the issues arising in the present phase of the proceedings, and the Court has thus not had the assistance it might have derived from such arguments or from any evidence adduced in support of them. The Court nevertheless has to proceed and reach a conclusion, and in doing so must have regard not only to the evidence brought before it and the arguments addressed to it by the Applicant, but also to any documentary or other evidence which may be relevant. It must on this basis satisfy itself, first that there exists no bar to the exercise of its judicial function, and secondly, if no such bar exists, that the Application is well founded in fact and in law.

16. The present case relates to a dispute between the Government of New Zealand and the French Government concerning the legality of atmospheric nuclear tests conducted by the latter Government in the South Pacific region. Since in the present phase of the proceedings the Court has to deal only with preliminary matters, it is appropriate to recall that its approach to a phase of this kind must be, as it was expressed in the *Fisheries Jurisdiction* cases, as follows:

> "The issue being thus limited, the Court will avoid not only all expressions of opinion on matters of substance, but also any pronouncement which might prejudge or appear to prejudge any eventual decision on the merits." (*I.C.J. Reports 1973,* pp. 7 and 54.)

It will however be necessary to give a summary of the principal facts underlying the case.

17. Prior to the filing of the Application instituting proceedings in this case, the French Government had carried out atmospheric tests of nuclear devices at its Centre d'expérimentations du Pacifique in the territory of French Polynesia, in the years 1966, 1967, 1968, 1970, 1971 and 1972. The main firing site used has been Mururoa atoll, some 2,500 nautical miles from the nearest point of the North Island of New Zealand and approximately 1,050 nautical miles from the nearest point of the Cook

a. The case of Australia v. France, identical in all essential respects, is omitted due to space limitations.

b. Concluded 26 September 1928, entered into force 16 August 1929, 93 L.N.T.S. 343. The General Act was superseded in 1949 by the Revised General Act for the Pacific Settlement of International Disputes, concluded 28 April 1949, entered into force 20 September 1950, 71 UNTS 101, *reprinted as* Basic Document I.H.4 in 1 *International Law and World Order: Basic Documents* (B. Weston ed.1994).

Islands, a self-governing State linked in free association with New Zealand. The French Government has created "Prohibited Zones" for aircraft and "Dangerous Zones" for aircraft and shipping, in order to exclude aircraft and shipping from the area of the tests centre; these "zones" have been put into effect during the period of testing in each year in which tests have been carried out.

18. As the United Nations Scientific Committee on the Effects of Atomic Radiation has recorded in its successive reports to the General Assembly, the testing of nuclear devices in the atmosphere has entailed the release into the atmosphere and the consequent dissipation, in varying degrees throughout the world, of measurable quantities of radio-active matter. It is asserted by New Zealand that the French atmospheric tests have caused some fall-out of this kind to be deposited, *inter alia,* on New Zealand territory; France has maintained, in particular, that the radio-active matter produced by its tests has been so infinitesimal that it may be regarded as negligible and that any fall-out on New Zealand territory has never involved any danger to the health of the population of New Zealand. These disputed points are clearly matters going to the merits of the case, and the Court must therefore refrain, for the reasons given above, from expressing any view on them.

19. By letters of 21 September 1973 and 1 November 1974, the Government of New Zealand informed the Court that subsequent to the Court's Order of 22 June 1973 indicating, as interim measures under Article 41 of the Statute, *(inter alia)* that the French Government should avoid nuclear tests causing the deposit of radio-active fall-out on New Zealand territory, two further series of atmospheric tests, in the months of July and August 1973 and June to September 1974, had been carried out at the Centre d'expérimentations du Pacifique. The letters also stated that fall-out had been recorded on New Zealand territory, analysis of samples of which, according to the New Zealand Government, established conclusively the presence of fall-out from these tests, and that it was "the view of the New Zealand Government that there has been a clear breach by the French Government of the Court's Order of 22 June 1973".

20. Recently a number of authoritative statements have been made on behalf of the French Government concerning its intentions as to future nuclear testing in the South Pacific region. The significance of these statements, and their effect for the purposes of the present proceedings, will be examined in detail later in the present Judgment.

* * *

33. At the hearing of 10 July 1974 the Court was presented by counsel for New Zealand with an interpretation of certain expressions of intention communicated to the New Zealand Government by the French Government and the French President. In particular he referred to a communiqué of 8 June 1974 (paragraph 35 below) and a diplomatic Note of 10 June 1974 (paragraph 36 below), and after quoting from that Note, he said:

> "I emphasize two points: first, the most France is offering is that in her own time she will cease to disregard an existing Order of the Court; and second, even that offer is qualified by the phrase 'in the normal course of events'. New Zealand has not been given anything in the nature of an unqualified assurance that 1974 will see the end of atmospheric nuclear testing in the South Pacific."

Since that time, certain French authorities have made a number of consistent public statements concerning future tests which provide material facilitating the Court's task of assessing the Applicant's interpretation of the earlier documents, and which indeed require to be examined in order to discern whether they embody any modification of intention as to France's future conduct. It is true that these statements have not been made before the Court, but they are in the public domain, are known to the New Zealand Government, and were commented on by its Prime Minister in his statement of 1 November 1974. It will clearly be necessary to consider all these statements, both those drawn to the Court's attention in July 1974 and those subsequently made.

* * *

35. It will be convenient to take the statements referred to above in chronological order. The first statement is contained in the communiqué issued by the Office of the President of the French Republic on 8 June 1974, shortly before the commencement of the 1974 series of French nuclear tests:

> "The Decree reintroducing the security measures in the South Pacific nuclear test zone has been published in the Official Journal of 8 June 1974.
>
> The Office of the President of the Republic takes this opportunity of stating that in view of the stage reached in carrying out the French nuclear defence programme France will be in a position to pass on to the stage of underground explosions as soon as the series of tests planned for this summer is completed."

36. The second is contained in a Note of 10 June 1974 from the French Embassy in Wellington to the New Zealand Ministry of Foreign Affairs:

> "It should * * * be pointed out that the decision taken by the Office of the President of the French Republic to have the opening of the nuclear test series preceded by a press communiqué represents a departure from the practice of previous years. This procedure has been chosen in view of the fact that a new element has intervened in the development of the programme for perfecting the French deterrent force. This new element is as follows: France, at the point which has been reached in the execution of its programme of defence by nuclear means, will be in a position to move to the stage of underground firings as soon as the test series planned for this summer is completed.
>
> Thus the atmospheric tests which will be carried out shortly will, in the normal course of events, be the last of this type.
>
> The French authorities express the hope that the New Zealand Government will find this information of some interest and will wish to take it into consideration."

37. As indicated by counsel for the Applicant at the hearing of 10 July 1974, the reaction of the New Zealand Prime Minister to this second statement was expressed in a letter to the President of the French Republic dated 11 June 1974, from which the following are two extracts:

> "* * * I have noted that the terms of the announcement do not represent an unqualified renunciation of atmospheric testing for the future."
>
> "I would hope that even at this stage you would be prepared to weigh the implications of any further atmospheric testing in the Pacific and resolve to put an end to this activity which has been the source of grave anxiety to the people in the Pacific region for more than a decade."

Thus the phrase "in the normal course of events" was regarded by New Zealand as qualifying the statement made, so that it did not meet the expectations of the Applicant, which evidently regarded those words as a form of escape clause. This is clear from the observations of counsel for New Zealand at the hearing of 10 July 1974. In a Note of 17 June 1974, the New Zealand Embassy in Paris stated that it had good reason to believe that France had carried out an atmospheric nuclear test on 16 June and made this further comment:

> "The announcement that France will proceed to underground tests in 1975, while presenting a new development, does not affect New Zealand's fundamental opposition to all nuclear testing, nor does it in any way reduce New Zealand's opposition to the atmospheric tests set down for this year: the more so since the

French Government is unable to give firm assurances that no atmospheric testing will be undertaken after 1974."

38. The third French statement is contained in a reply made on 1 July 1974 by the President of the Republic to the New Zealand Prime Minister's letter of 11 June:

> "In present circumstances, it is at least gratifying for me to note the positive reaction in your letter to the announcement in the communiqué of 8 June 1974 that we are going over to underground tests. There is in this a new element whose importance will not, I trust, escape the New Zealand Government."

39. These three statements were all drawn to the notice of the Court by the Applicant at the time of the oral proceedings. As already indicated, the Court will also have to consider the relevant statements subsequently made by the French authorities: on 25 July 1974 by the President of the Republic; on 16 August 1974 by the Minister of Defence; on 25 September 1974 by the Minister for Foreign Affairs in the United Nations General Assembly; and on 11 October 1974 by the Minister of Defence.

40. The next statement to be considered, therefore, will be that made on 25 July at a press conference given by the President of the Republic, when he said:

> "* * * on this question of nuclear tests, you know that the Prime Minister had publicly expressed himself in the National Assembly in his speech introducing the Government's programme. He had indicated that French nuclear testing would continue. I had myself made it clear that this round of atmospheric tests would be the last, and so the members of the Government were completely informed of our intentions in this respect * * *"

41. On 16 August 1974, in the course of an interview on French television, the Minister of Defence said that the French Government had done its best to ensure that the 1974 nuclear tests would be the last atmospheric tests.

42. On 25 September 1974, the French Minister for Foreign Affairs, addressing the United Nations General Assembly, said:

> "We have now reached a stage in our nuclear technology that makes it possible for us to continue our programme by underground testing, and we have taken steps to do so as early as next year."

43. On 11 October 1974, the Minister of Defence held a press conference during which he stated twice, in almost identical terms, that there would not be any atmospheric tests in 1975 and that France was ready to proceed to underground tests. When the comment was made that he had not added "in the normal course of events", he agreed that he had not. This latter point is relevant in view of the Note of 10 June 1974 from the French Embassy in Wellington to the Ministry of Foreign Affairs of New Zealand (paragraph 36 above), to the effect that the atmospheric tests contemplated "will, in the normal course of events, be the last of this type". The Minister also mentioned that, whether or not other governments had been officially advised of the decision, they could become aware of it through the press and by reading the communiqués issued by the Office of the President of the Republic.

44. In view of the foregoing, the Court finds that the communiqué issued on 8 June 1974 (paragraph 35 above), the French Embassy's Note of 10 June 1974 (paragraph 36 above) and the President's letter of 1 July 1974 (paragraph 38) conveyed to New Zealand the announcement that France, following the conclusion of the 1974 series of tests, would cease the conduct of atmospheric nuclear tests. Special attention is drawn to the hope expressed in the Note of 10 June 1974 "that the New Zealand Government will find this information of some interest and will wish to take it into consideration", and the reference in that Note and in the letter of 1 July 1974 to "a new element" whose importance is urged upon the New Zealand Government. The Court must consider in particular the President's statement of 25 July 1974 (paragraph 40 above) followed by the Defence Minister's statement of 11 October 1974

(paragraph 43). These reveal that the official statements made on behalf of France concerning future nuclear testing are not subject to whatever proviso, if any, was implied by the expression "in the normal course of events *[normalement]*".

45. Before considering whether the declarations made by the French authorities meet the object of the claim by the Applicant that no further atmospheric nuclear tests should be carried out in the South Pacific, it is first necessary to determine the status and scope on the international plane of these declarations.

46. It is well recognized that declarations made by way of unilateral acts, concerning legal or factual situations, may have the effect of creating legal obligations. Declarations of this kind may be, and often are, very specific. When it is the intention of the State making the declaration that it should become bound according to its terms, that intention confers on the declaration the character of a legal undertaking, the State being thenceforth legally required to follow a course of conduct consistent with the declaration. An undertaking of this kind, if given publicly, and with an intent to be bound, even though not made within the context of international negotiations, is binding. In these circumstances, nothing in the nature of a *quid pro quo,* nor any subsequent acceptance of the declaration, nor even any reply or reaction from other States, is required for the declaration to take effect, since such a requirement would be inconsistent with the strictly unilateral nature of the juridical act by which the pronouncement by the State was made.

47. Of course, not all unilateral acts imply obligation; but a State may choose to take up a certain position in relation to a particular matter with the intention of being bound—the intention is to be ascertained by interpretation of the act. When States make statements by which their freedom of action is to be limited, a restrictive interpretation is called for.

48. With regard to the question of form, it should be observed that this is not a domain in which international law imposes any special or strict requirements. Whether a statement is made orally or in writing makes no essential difference, for such statements made in particular circumstances may create commitments in international law, which does not require that they should be couched in written form. Thus the question of form is not decisive. As the Court said in its Judgment on the preliminary objections in the case concerning the *Temple of Preah Vihear:*

> "Where * * * as is generally the case in international law, which places the principal emphasis on the intention of the parties, the law prescribes no particular form, parties are free to choose what form they please provided their intention clearly results from it." (*I.C.J. Reports 1961,* p. 31.)

The Court further stated in the same case: "* * * the sole relevant question is whether the language employed in any given declaration does reveal a clear intention * * * "(*ibid.,* p. 32).

49. One of the basic principles governing the creation and performance of legal obligations, whatever their source, is the principle of good faith. Trust and confidence are inherent in international co-operation, in particular in an age when this co-operation in many fields is becoming increasingly essential. Just as the very rule of *pacta sunt servanda* in the law of treaties is based on good faith, so also is the binding character of an international obligation assumed by unilateral declaration. Thus interested States may take cognizance of unilateral declarations and place confidence in them, and are entitled to require that the obligation thus created be respected.

50. Having examined the legal principles involved, the Court will now turn to the particular statements made by the French Government. The Government of New Zealand has made known to the Court its own interpretation of some of these statements at the oral proceedings (paragraph 27 above). As to subsequent statements, reference may be made to what was said by the Prime Minister of New Zealand on 1

November 1974 (paragraph 28 above). It will be observed that New Zealand has recognized the possibility of the dispute being resolved by a unilateral declaration, of the kind specified above, on the part of France. In the public statement of 1 November 1974, it is stated that "Until we have an assurance that nuclear testing of this kind is finished for good, the dispute between New Zealand and France persists". This is based on the view that "the option of further atmospheric tests have been left open". The Court must however form its own view of the meaning and scope intended by the author of a unilateral declaration which may create a legal obligation, and cannot in this respect be bound by the view expressed by another State which is in no way a party to the text.

51. Of the statements by the French Government now before the Court, the most essential are clearly those made by the President of the Republic. There can be no doubt, in view of his functions, that his public communications or statements, oral or written, as Head of State, are in international relations acts of the French State. His statements, and those of members of the French Government acting under his authority, up to the last statement made by the Minister of Defence (of 11 October 1974), constitute a whole. Thus, in whatever form these statements were expressed, they must be held to constitute an engagement of the State, having regard to their intention and to the circumstances in which they were made.

52. The unilateral statements of the French authorities were made outside the Court, publicly and *erga omnes,* even if some of them were communicated to the Government of New Zealand. As was observed above, to have legal effect, there was no need for these statements to be addressed to a particular State, nor was acceptance by any other State required. The general nature and characteristics of these statements are decisive for the evaluation of the legal implications, and it is to the interpretation of the statements that the Court must now proceed. The Court is entitled to presume, at the outset, that these statements were made *in vacuo,* but in relation to the tests which constitute the very object of the present proceedings, although France has not appeared in the case.

53. In announcing that the 1974 series of atmospheric tests would be the last, the French Government conveyed to the world at large, including the Applicant, its intention effectively to terminate these tests. It was bound to assume that other States might take note of these statements and rely on their being effective. The validity of these statements and their legal consequences must be considered within the general framework of the security of international intercourse, and the confidence and trust which are so essential in the relations among States. It is from the actual substance of these statements and from the circumstances attending their making, that the legal implications of the unilateral act must be deduced. The objects of these statements are clear and they were addressed to the international community as a whole, and the Court holds that they constitute an undertaking possessing legal effect. The Court considers that the President of the Republic, in deciding upon the effective cessation of atmospheric tests, gave an undertaking to the international community to which his words were addressed. It is true that the French Government has consistently maintained that its nuclear experiments do not contravene any subsisting provision of international law, nor did France recognize that it was bound by any rule of international law to terminate its tests, but this does not affect the legal consequences of the statements examined above. The Court finds that the unilateral undertaking resulting from these statements cannot be interpreted as having been made in implicit reliance on an arbitrary power of reconsideration. The Court finds further that the French Government has undertaken an obligation the precise nature and limits of which must be understood in accordance with the actual terms in which they have been publicly expressed.

54. The Court will now confront the commitment entered into by France with the claim advanced by the Applicant. Though the latter has formally requested from

the Court a finding on the rights and obligations of the Parties, it has throughout the dispute maintained as its final objective the termination of the tests. It has sought from France an assurance that the French programme of atmospheric nuclear testing would come to an end. While expressing its opposition to the 1974 tests, the Government of New Zealand made specific reference to an assurance that "1974 will see the end of atmospheric nuclear testing in the South Pacific" (paragraph 33 above). On more than one occasion it has indicated that it would be ready to accept such an assurance. Since the Court now finds that a commitment in this respect has been entered into by France, there is no occasion for a pronouncement in respect of rights and obligations of the Parties concerning the past—which in other circumstances the Court would be entitled and even obliged to make—whatever the date by reference to which such pronouncement might be made.

55. Thus the Court faces a situation in which the objective of the Applicant has in effect been accomplished, inasmuch as the Court finds that France has undertaken the obligation to hold no further nuclear tests in the atmosphere in the South Pacific.

* * *

58. The Court, as a court of law, is called upon to resolve existing disputes between States. Thus the existence of a dispute is the primary condition for the Court to exercise its judicial function; it is not sufficient for one party to assert that there is a dispute, since "whether there exists an international dispute is a matter for objective determination" by the Court (*Interpretation of Peace Treaties with Bulgaria, Hungary and Romania (First Phase), Advisory Opinion, I.C.J. Reports 1950,* p. 74). The dispute brought before it must therefore continue to exist at the time when the Court makes its decision. It must not fail to take cognizance of a situation in which the dispute has disappeared because the final objective which the Applicant has maintained throughout has been achieved by other means. If the declarations of France concerning the effective cessation of the nuclear tests have the significance described by the Court, that is to say if they have caused the dispute to disappear, all the necessary consequences must be drawn from this finding.

59. It may be argued that although France may have undertaken such an obligation, by a unilateral declaration, not to carry out atmospheric nuclear tests in the South Pacific region, a judgment of the Court on this subject might still be of value because, if the Judgment upheld the Applicant's contentions, it would reinforce the position of the Applicant by affirming the obligation of the Respondent. However, the Court having found that the Respondent has assumed an obligation as to conduct, concerning the effective cessation of nuclear tests, no further judicial action is required. The Applicant has repeatedly sought from the Respondent an assurance that the tests would cease, and the Respondent has, on its own initiative, made a series of statements to the effect that they will cease. Thus the Court concludes that, the dispute having disappeared, the claim advanced by New Zealand no longer has any object. It follows that any further finding would have no *raison d'être.*

* * *

62. Thus the Court finds that no further pronouncement is required in the present case. It does not enter into the adjudicatory functions of the Court to deal with issues *in abstracto,* once it has reached the conclusion that the merits of the case no longer fall to be determined. The object of the claim having clearly disappeared, there is nothing on which to give judgment.

8.7 GATT Panel Report on United States Restrictions on Imports of Tuna (Tuna I). Submitted to the GATT Council, 16 August 1991. Not adopted. GATT Doc. No. DS21/R, GATT B.I.S.D. (39th Supp) at 155 (1993); *reprinted in* 30 I.L.M. 1594 (1991)

* * *

5. FINDINGS

A. Introduction

5.1. The Panel noted that the issues before it arose essentially from the following facts: the Marine Mammal Protection Act (MMPA) regulates, inter alia, the harvesting of tuna by United States fishermen and others who are operating within the jurisdiction of the United States. The MMPA requires that such fishermen use certain fishing techniques to reduce the taking of dolphin incidental to the harvesting of fish. The United States authorities have licensed fishing of yellowfin tuna by United States vessels in the ETP on the condition that the domestic fleet not exceed an incidental taking of 20,500 dolphins per year in the ETP.

5.2. The MMPA also requires that the United States Government ban the importation of commercial fish or products from fish caught with commercial fishing technology which results in the incidental killing or incidental serious injury of ocean mammals in excess of United States standards. Under United States customs law, fish caught by a vessel registered in a country is deemed to originate in that country. As a condition of access to the United States market for the yellowfin tuna or yellowfin tuna products caught by its fleet, each country of registry of vessels fishing yellowfin tuna in the ETP must prove to the satisfaction of the United States authorities that its overall regulatory regime regarding the taking of marine mammals is comparable to that of the United States. To meet this requirement, the country in question must prove that the average rate of incidental taking of marine mammals by its tuna fleet operating in the ETP is not in excess of 1.25 times the average incidental taking rate of United States vessels operating in the ETP during the same period. The exact methods of calculating and comparing these average incidental taking rates have been specified by regulation.

5.3. The MMPA also provides that ninety days after imports of yellowfin tuna and yellowfin tuna products from a country have been prohibited as above, importation of such tuna and tuna products from any "intermediary nation" shall also be prohibited, unless the intermediary nation proves that it too has acted to ban imports of such tuna and tuna products from the country subject to the direct import embargo.

5.4. Six months after either the direct embargo or the "intermediary nations" embargo goes into effect, the United States authorities are required to take action which triggers Section 8 of the Fishermen's Protective Act (the Pelly Amendment). This provision enables the President in his discretion to prohibit imports of all fish or wildlife products from the country in question, "for such duration as the President determines appropriate and to the extent that such prohibition is sanctioned by the General Agreement on Tariffs and Trade".

5.5. Under the MMPA, the United States currently prohibits importation into its customs territory of yellowfin tuna and yellowfin tuna products from Mexico which were caught with purse-seine nets in the ETP. A predecessor embargo was imposed on such tuna and tuna products on 28 August 1990; the embargo in its present form has been in place since 26 March 1991. Since 24 May 1991 the United States has also implemented the "intermediary nations" embargo provisions of the MMPA by prohibiting the importation of yellowfin tuna or yellowfin tuna products from any other country if the tuna was harvested with purse-seine nets in the ETP by vessels of Mexico. If either of these prohibitions is in effect six months after its inception, then as of that date the President will have the discretionary authority under the Pelly Amendment to prohibit imports of all fish products of Mexico or of any "intermediary nation" for such duration as he determines appropriate and to the extent that such action is "sanctioned by the General Agreement".

5.6. The Dolphin Protection Consumer Information Act (DPCIA) provides that when a tuna product exported from or offered for sale in the United States bears the optional label "Dolphin Safe" or any similar label indicating it was fished in a manner not harmful to dolphins, this tuna product may not contain tuna harvested on the high seas by a vessel engaged in driftnet fishing, or harvested in the ETP by a vessel using a purse-seine net unless it is accompanied by documentary evidence showing that the purse-seine net was not intentionally deployed to encircle dolphins. The use of the label "Dolphin Safe" is not a requirement but is voluntary. The labelling provisions of the DPCIA took effect on 28 May 1991.

5.7. The Panel decided to examine successively:

(a) the prohibition of imports of certain yellowfin tuna and certain yellowfin tuna products from Mexico imposed by the United States and the provisions of the MMPA on which it is based;

(b) the prohibition of imports of certain yellowfin tuna and certain yellowfin tuna products from "intermediary nations" imposed by the United States and the provisions of the MMPA on which it is based;

(c) the possible extension of each of these import prohibitions to all fish products from Mexico and the "intermediary nations", under the MMPA and Section 8 of the Fishermen's Protective Act (the Pelly Amendment); and

(d) the application to tuna and tuna products from Mexico of the labelling provisions of the DPCIA, as well as these provisions as such.

In accordance with the established practice, the Panel further decided that it would examine each of the above issues first in the light of the provisions of the General Agreement which Mexico claims to have been violated by the United States and then, if it were to find an inconsistency with any of the provisions invoked by Mexico, in the light of the exceptions in the General Agreement raised by the United States.

* * *

Article XX

General

5.22. The Panel noted that the United States had argued that its direct embargo under the MMPA could be justified under Article XX(b) or Article XX(g), and that Mexico had argued that a contracting party could not simultaneously argue that a measure is compatible with the general rules of the General Agreement and invoke Article XX for that measure. The Panel recalled that previous panels had established that Article XX is a limited and conditional exception from obligations under other provisions of the General Agreement, and not a positive rule establishing obligations in itself. Therefore, the practice of panels has been to interpret Article XX narrowly, to place the burden on the party invoking Article XX to justify its invocation, and not to examine Article XX exceptions unless invoke. Nevertheless, the Panel considered that a party to a dispute could argue in the alternative that Article XX might apply, without this argument constituting ipso facto an admission that the measures in question would otherwise be inconsistent with the General Agreement. Indeed, the efficient operation of the dispute settlement process required that such arguments in the alternative be possible.

5.23. The Panel proceeded to examine whether Article XX(b) or Article XX(g) could justify the MMPA provisions on imports of certain yellowfin tuna and yellowfin tuna products, and the import ban imposed under these provisions. The Panel noted that Article XX provides that:

> "Subject to the requirement that such measures are not applied in a manner which would constitute a means of arbitrary or unjustifiable discrimination between countries where the same conditions prevail, or a disguised restriction on international trade, nothing in this Agreement shall be construed to prevent the adoption or enforcement by any contracting party of measures . . .
>
> (b) necessary to protect human, animal or plant life or health; . . .
>
> (g) relating to the conservation of exhaustible natural resources if such measures are made effective in conjunction with restrictions on domestic production or consumption; . . .".

Article XX(b)

5.24. The Panel noted that the United States considered the prohibition of imports of certain yellowfin tuna and certain yellowfin tuna products from Mexico, and the provisions of the MMPA on which this prohibition is based, to be justified by Article XX(b) because they served solely the purpose of protecting dolphin life and health and were "necessary" within the meaning of that provision because, in respect of the protection of dolphin life and health outside its jurisdiction, there was no alternative measure reasonably available to the United States to achieve this objective. Mexico considered that Article XX(b) was not applicable to a measure imposed to protect the life or health of animals outside the jurisdiction of the contracting party taking it and that the import prohibition imposed by the United States was not necessary because alternative means consistent with the General Agreement were available to it to protect dolphin lives or health, namely international co-operation between the countries concerned.

5.25. The Panel noted that the basic question raised by these arguments, namely whether Article XX(b) covers measures necessary to protect human, animal or plant life or health outside the jurisdiction of the contracting party taking the measure, is not clearly answered by the text of that provision. It refers to life and health protection generally without expressly limiting that protection to the jurisdiction of the contracting party concerned. The Panel therefore decided to analyze this issue in the light of the drafting history of Article XX(b), the purpose of this provision, and the consequences that the interpretations proposed by the parties would have for the operation of the General Agreement as a whole.

5.26. The Panel noted that the proposal for Article XX(b) dated from the Draft Charter of the International Trade Organization (ITO) proposed by the United States, which stated in Article 32, "Nothing in Chapter IV [on commercial policy] of this Charter shall be construed to prevent the adoption or enforcement by any Member of measures; . . . (b) necessary to protect human, animal or plant life or health". In the New York Draft of the ITO Charter, the preamble had been revised to read as it does at present, and exception (b) read: "For the purpose of protecting human, animal or plant life or health, if corresponding domestic safeguards under similar conditions exist in the importing country". This added proviso reflected concerns regarding the abuse of sanitary regulations by importing countries. Later, Commission A of the Second Session of the Preparatory Committee in Geneva agreed to drop this proviso as unnecessary. Thus, the record indicates that the concerns of the drafters of Article XX(b) focused on the use of sanitary measures to safeguard life or health of humans, animals or plants within the jurisdiction of the importing country.

5.27. The Panel further noted that Article XX(b) allows each contracting party to set its human, animal or plant life or health standards. The conditions set out in Article XX(b) which limit resort to this exception, namely that the measure taken must be "necessary" and not "constitute a means of arbitrary or unjustifiable discrimination or a disguised restriction on international trade", refer to the trade measure requiring justification under Article XX(b), not however to the life or health standard chosen by the contracting party. The Panel recalled the finding of a previous panel that this paragraph of Article XX was intended to allow contracting parties to impose trade restrictive measures inconsistent with the General Agreement to pursue overriding public policy goals to the extent that such inconsistencies were unavoidable. The Panel considered that if the broad interpretation of Article XX(b) suggested by the United States were accepted, each contracting party could unilaterally determine the life or health protection policies from which other contracting parties could not deviate without jeopardizing their rights under the General Agreement. The General Agreement would then no longer constitute a multilateral framework for trade among all contracting parties but would provide legal security only in respect of trade between a limited number of contracting parties with identical internal regulations.

5.28. The Panel considered that the United States' measures, even if Article XX(b) were interpreted to permit extrajurisdictional protection of life and health, would not meet the requirement of necessity set out in that provision. The United States had not demonstrated to the Panel—as required of the party invoking an Article XX exception—that it had exhausted all options reasonably available to it to pursue its dolphin protection objectives through measures consistent with the General Agreement, in particular through the negotiation of international cooperative arrangements, which would seem to be desirable in view of the fact that dolphins roam the waters of many states and the high seas. Moreover, even assuming that an import prohibition were the only resort reasonably available to the United States, the particular measure chosen by the United States could in the Panel's view not be considered to be necessary within the meaning of Article XX(b). The United States linked the maximum incidental dolphin taking rate which Mexico had to meet during a particular period in order to be able to export tuna to the United States to the taking rate actually recorded for United States fishermen during the same period. Consequently, the Mexican authorities could not know whether, at a given point of time, their policies conformed to the United States' dolphin protection standards. The Panel considered that a limitation on trade based on such unpredictable conditions could not be regarded as necessary to protect the health or life of dolphins.

5.29. On the basis of the above considerations, the Panel found that the United States' direct import prohibition imposed on certain yellowfin tuna and certain yellowfin tuna products of Mexico and the provisions of the MMPA under which it is imposed could not be justified under the exception in Article XX(b).

Article XX(g)

5.30. The Panel proceeded to examine whether the prohibition on imports of certain yellowfin tuna and certain yellowfin tuna products from Mexico and the MMPA provisions under which it was imposed could be justified under the exception in Article XX(g). The Panel noted that the United States, in invoking Article XX(g) with respect to its direct import prohibition under the MMPA, had argued that the measures taken under the MMPA are measures primarily aimed at the conservation of dolphin, and that the import restrictions on certain tuna and tuna products under the MMPA are "primarily aimed at rendering effective restrictions on domestic production or consumption" of dolphin. The Panel also noted that Mexico had argued that the United States measures were not justified under the exception in Article XX(g) because, inter alia, this provision could not be applied extrajurisdictionally.

5.31. The Panel noted that Article XX(g) required that the measures relating to the conservation of exhaustible natural resources be taken "in conjunction with restrictions on domestic production or consumption". A previous panel had found that a measure could only be considered to have been taken "in conjunction with" production restrictions "if it was primarily aimed at rendering effective these restrictions''. A country can effectively control the production or consumption of an exhaustible natural resource only to the extent that the production or consumption is under its jurisdiction. This suggests that Article XX(g) was intended to permit contracting parties to take trade measures primarily aimed at rendering effective restrictions on production or consumption within their jurisdiction.

5.32. The Panel further noted that Article XX(g) allows each contracting party to adopt its own conservation policies. The conditions set out in Article XX(g) which limit resort to this exception, namely that the measures taken must be related to the conservation of exhaustible natural resources, and that they not ''constitute a means of arbitrary or unjustifiable discrimination ... or a disguised restriction on international trade'' refer to the trade measure requiring justification under Article XX(g), not however to the conservation policies adopted by the contracting party. The Panel considered that if the extrajurisdictional interpretation of Article XX(g) suggested by the United States were accepted, each contracting party could unilaterally determine the conservation policies from which other contracting parties could not deviate without jeopardizing their rights under the General Agreement. The considerations that led the Panel to reject an extrajurisdictional application of Article XX(b) therefore apply also to Article XX(g).

5.33. The Panel did not consider that the United States measures, even if Article XX(g) could be applied extrajurisdictionally, would meet the conditions set out in that provision. A previous panel found that a measure could be considered as ''relating to the conservation of exhaustible natural resources'' within the meaning of Article XX(g) only if it was primarily aimed at such conservation. The Panel recalled that the United States linked the maximum incidental dolphin-taking rate which Mexico had to meet during a particular period in order to be able to export tuna to the United States to the taking rate actually recorded for United States fishermen during the same period. Consequently, the Mexican authorities could not know whether, at a given point of time, their conservation policies conformed to the United States conservation standards. The Panel considered that a limitation on trade based on such unpredictable conditions could not be regarded as being primarily aimed at the conservation of dolphins.

5.34. On the basis of the above considerations, the Panel found that the United States direct import prohibition on certain yellowfin tuna and certain yellowfin tuna products of Mexico directly imported from Mexico, and the provisions of the MMPA under which it is imposed, could not be justified under Article XX(g).

C. Secondary embargo on imports of certain yellowfin tuna and certain yellowfin tuna products from ''intermediary nations'' under the MMPA

Articles III and XI

5.35. The Panel noted that Mexico had claimed that the ''intermediary nations'' embargo was inconsistent with Articles XI and XIII. The United States considered that these measures fell instead under Article III and the Note Ad Article III as they provided for enforcement of requirements for yellowfin tuna harvested in the ETP using purse-seine nets. The Panel found that since the United States domestic regulations on tuna harvesting were not applied to tuna as a product, the ''intermediary nations'' embargo did not fall within the scope of the Note Ad Article III, and was therefore a quantitative restriction subject to Article XI.

5.36. The Panel further noted that the MMPA required that the United States authorities implement a prohibition on imports of yellowfin tuna and yellowfin tuna products from ''intermediary nations'', and that the United States was refusing entry to yellowfin tuna unless the importer declared that no yellowfin tuna or yellowfin tuna product in the shipment were harvested with purse-seine nets in the ETP by vessels of Mexico. The Panel therefore found that these measures and the provisions of the

MMPA mandating such an embargo were import restrictions or prohibitions inconsistent with Article XI:1. The United States did not present to the Panel any arguments to support a different legal conclusion regarding Article XI.

5.37. The Panel recalled its finding on the Pelly Amendment in paragraph 5.21 above, namely that this provision as such was not inconsistent with the obligations of the United States under the General Agreement because the Pelly Amendment does not require trade measures to be taken. The Panel considered that this finding was equally valid in the case of the "intermediary nations" embargo.

Article XX(b) and XX(g)

5.38. The Panel noted that the United States had argued that the intermediary nations embargo was justified as a measure under Articles XX(b) and XX(g) to protect and conserve dolphin, and that the intermediary country measures were necessary to protect animal life or health and related to the conservation of exhaustible natural resources. The Panel recalled its findings with regard to the consistency of the direct embargo with Articles XX(b) and XX(g) in paragraphs 5.29 and 5.34 above, and found that the considerations that led the Panel to reject the United States invocation of these provisions in that instance applied to the "intermediary nations" embargo as well.

Article XX(d)

5.39. The Panel then proceeded to examine the consistency of the "intermediary nations" embargo with Article XX(d), which the United States had invoked. The relevant part of Article XX(d) reads as follows:

> "Subject to the requirement that such measures are not applied in a manner which would constitute a means of arbitrary or unjustifiable discrimination between countries where the same conditions prevail, or a disguised restriction on international trade, nothing in this Agreement shall be construed to prevent the adoption or enforcement by any contracting party of measures . . .
>
> (d) necessary to secure compliance with laws or regulations which are not inconsistent with the provisions of this Agreement . . . ".

5.40. The Panel noted that Article XX(d) requires that the "laws or regulations" with which compliance is being secured be themselves "not inconsistent" with the General Agreement. The Panel noted that the United States had argued that the "intermediary nations" embargo was necessary to support the direct embargo because countries whose exports were subject to such an embargo should not be able to nullify the embargo's effect by exporting to the United States indirectly through third countries. The Panel found that, given its finding that the direct embargo was inconsistent with the General Agreement, the "intermediary nations" embargo and the provisions of the MMPA under which it is imposed could not be justified under Article XX(d) as a measure to secure compliance with "laws or regulations not inconsistent with the provisions of this Agreement".

D. Dolphin Protection Consumer Information Act (DPCIA)

5.41. The Panel noted that Mexico considered the labelling provisions of the DPCIA to be marking requirements falling under Article IX:1, which reads:

> "Each contracting party shall accord to the products of the territories of other contracting parties treatment with regard to marking requirements no less favourable than the treatment accorded to like products of any third country".

The United States considered that the labelling provisions were subject not to Article IX but to the most-favoured-nation and national-treatment provisions of Articles I:1 and III:4. The Panel noted that the title of Article IX is "Marks of Origin" and its text refers to marking of origin of imported products. The Panel further noted that Article

IX does not contain a national-treatment but only a most-favoured-nation requirement, which indicates that this provision was intended to regulate marking of origin of imported products but not marking of products generally. The Panel therefore found that the labelling provisions of the DPCIA did not fall under Article IX:1.

5.42. The Panel proceeded to examine the subsidiary argument by Mexico that the labelling provisions of the DPCIA were inconsistent with Article I:1 because they discriminated against Mexico as a country fishing in the ETP. The Panel noted that the labelling provisions of the DPCIA do not restrict the sale of tuna products; tuna products can be sold freely both with and without the "Dolphin Safe" label. Nor do these provisions establish requirements that have to be met in order to obtain an advantage from the government. Any advantage which might possibly result from access to this label depends on the free choice by consumers to give preference to tuna carrying the "Dolphin Safe" label. The labelling provisions therefore did not make the right to sell tuna or tuna products, nor the access to a government-conferred advantage affecting the sale of tuna or tuna products, conditional upon the use of tuna harvesting methods. The only issue before the Panel was therefore whether the provisions of the DPCIA governing the right of access to the label met the requirements of Article I:1.

5.43. The Panel noted that the DPCIA is based inter alia on a finding that dolphins are frequently killed in the course of tuna-fishing operations in the ETP through the use of purse-seine nets intentionally deployed to encircle dolphins. The DPCIA therefore accords the right to use the label "Dolphin Safe" for tuna harvested in the ETP only if such tuna is accompanied by documentary evidence showing that it was not harvested with purse-seine nets intentionally deployed to encircle dolphins. The Panel examined whether this requirement applied to tuna from the ETP was consistent with Article I:1. According to the information presented to the Panel, the harvesting of tuna by intentionally encircling dolphins with purse-seine nets was practised only in the ETP because of the particular nature of the association between dolphins and tuna observed only in that area. By imposing the requirement to provide evidence that this fishing technique had not been used in respect of tuna caught in the ETP the United States therefore did not discriminate against countries fishing in this area. The Panel noted that, under United States customs law, the country of origin of fish was determined by the country or registry of the vessel that had caught the fish; the geographical area where the fish was caught was irrelevant for the determination of origin. The labelling regulations governing tuna caught in the ETP thus applied to all countries whose vessels fished in this geographical area and thus did not distinguish between products originating in Mexico and products originating in other countries.

5.44. The Panel found for these reasons that the tuna products labelling provisions of the DPCIA relating to tuna caught in the ETP were not inconsistent with the obligations of the United States under Article I:1 of the General Agreement.

6. CONCLUDING REMARKS

6.1. The Panel wished to underline that its task was limited to the examination of this matter "in the light of the relevant GATT provisions", and therefore did not call for a finding on the appropriateness of the United States' and Mexico's conservation policies as such.

6.2. The Panel wished to note the fact, made evident during its consideration of this case, that the provisions of the General Agreement impose few constraints on a contracting party's implementation of domestic environmental policies. The Panel recalled its findings in paragraphs 5.10—5.16 above that under these provisions, a contracting party is free to tax or regulate imported products and like domestic products as long as its taxes or regulations do not discriminate against imported products or afford protection to domestic producers, and a contracting party is also free to tax or regulate domestic production for environmental purposes. As a corollary to these rights, a contracting party may not restrict imports of a product merely because it originates in a country with environmental policies different from its own.

6.3. The Panel further recalled its finding that the import restrictions examined in this dispute, imposed to respond to differences in environmental regulation of producers, could not be justified under the exceptions in Articles XX(b) or XX(g). These exceptions did not specify criteria limiting the range of life or health protection policies, or resource conservation policies, for the sake of which they could be invoked. It seemed evident to the Panel that, if the CONTRACTING PARTIES were to permit import restrictions in response to differences in environmental policies under the General Agreement, they would need to impose limits on the range of policy differences justifying such responses and to develop criteria so as to prevent abuse. If the CONTRACTING PARTIES were to decide to permit trade measures of this type in particular circumstances it would therefore be preferable for them to do so not by interpreting Article XX, but by amending or supplementing the provisions of the General Agreement or waiving obligations thereunder. Such an approach would enable the CONTRACTING PARTIES to impose such limits and develop such criteria.

6.4. These considerations led the Panel to the view that the adoption of its report would affect neither the rights of individual contracting parties to pursue their internal environmental policies and to co-operate with one another in harmonizing such policies, nor the right of the CONTRACTING PARTIES acting jointly to address international environmental problems which can only be resolved through measures in conflict with the present rules of the General Agreement.

7. CONCLUSIONS

7.1. (a) The prohibition of imports of certain yellowfin tuna and certain yellowfin tuna products of Mexico and the provisions of the Marine Mammal Protection Act under which it is imposed are contrary to Article XI:1 and are not justified by Article XX(b) or Article XX(g).

(b) The import prohibitions imposed by the United States with regard to certain yellowfin tuna and certain yellowfin tuna products of "intermediary nations" and the provisions of the Marine Mammal Protection Act under which they are imposed are contrary to Article XI:1 and are not justified by Article XX(b), XX(d) or XX(g).

(c) The Panel recommends that the CONTRACTING PARTIES request the United States to bring the above measures into conformity with its obligations under the General Agreement.

7.2. The provisions of Section 8 of the Fishermen's Protective Act (the Pelly Amendment) as such are not inconsistent with the obligations of the United States under the General Agreement.

7.3. The tuna products labelling provisions of the Dolphin Protection Consumer Information Act relating to tuna caught in the Eastern Tropical Pacific Ocean are not inconsistent with the obligations of the United States under Article I:1 of the General Agreement.

8.8 GATT Panel Report on United States-restrictions on Imports of Tuna (Tuna II). Submitted to the GATT Council, 16 June 1994. Not adopted. GATT Doc. No. DS 29/R; *reprinted in* 33 I.L.M. 839 (1994)

I. INTRODUCTION

1.1 On 11 March 1992, the European Economic Community ("EEC") requested the United States to hold consultations under Article XXIII:1 on restrictions maintained by the United States on the importation of certain tuna products (DS29/1). The consultations were held on 10 April 1992. As they did not result in a satisfactory adjustment of the matter, the EEC, in a communication dated 5 June 1992, requested the CONTRACTING PARTIES to establish a panel to examine the matter under Article XXIII:2 (DS29/2). On 3 July 1992, the Kingdom of the Netherlands ("the Netherlands"), on behalf of the Netherlands Antilles, requested the United States to hold consultations pursuant to Article XXIII:1 concerning the same restrictions (DS33/1). These consultations were held on 13 July 1992. Since they did not result in a satisfactory adjustment of the matter, the Netherlands, in a communication dated 14 July 1992, requested to be joined, as a co-complainant, in the panel to be established pursuant to the request of the EEC (DS29/3).

* * *

V. FINDINGS

A. Introduction

5.1 Since tuna are often found swimming below dolphins in the eastern tropical Pacific Ocean, fishing vessels in that region commonly encircle dolphins with purse-seine nets in order to capture tuna. In 1986, this practice resulted in the death of an estimated 133,000 dolphins. By 1991, changes in fishing equipment and methods reduced total deaths to less than 27,500. National efforts to reduce dolphin mortality have led to specific legislation in some countries. International efforts have taken place under the auspices of the Inter–American Tropical Tuna Commission ("IATTC"), which operates a research and development, training and observer program intended to reduce dolphin mortality. In 1992, the governments of major tuna fishing countries signed an agreement under the auspices of the IATTC aimed at reducing dolphin mortality to under 5,000 by 1999.

1. United States restrictions affecting domestic tuna and tuna fishing

5.2 The Marine Mammal Protection Act of 1972 prohibits any person or vessel under United States jurisdiction from taking any marine mammal in connection with the harvesting of fish. The Act further prohibits the use of any fishing method contrary to regulations issued under the Act, and imposes civil penalties for violations. Persons or vessels under the jurisdiction of the United States may however take marine mammals incidental to commercial fishing operations, subject to the conditions of a permit granted under the Act. The only permit issued by the United States has been to the American Tunaboat Association. This permit specifically requires that: vessels not deploy purse seine nets on, or encircle, any school of dolphin in which eastern spinner dolphin or coastal spotted dolphin are observed; total dolphin mortalities not exceed 800 for the period 1 January 1993 through 1 March 1994; purse seine nets not be deployed after sunset; explosive devices not generally be used; and vessels carry an official observer certified by the United States or by the IATTC. The permit expires on 1 March 1994. If by that date no major purse seine tuna fishing country has entered into an agreement with the United States on yellowfin tuna harvesting practices in the eastern tropical Pacific Ocean, the permit is extended to 31 December 1999, on the condition that the permit holder reduce dolphin mortality by a significant amount each year to levels approaching zero by the expiry of the permit.

2. United States restrictions affecting direct imports of tuna ("primary nation embargo")

5.3 The Act also prohibits the import into the United States of tuna or tuna products harvested by a method that results in the incidental killing or serious injury of marine mammals in excess of United States standards. In order to meet this requirement, the tuna exporting country must prove that it has fishing technology and a rate of incidental taking comparable to those of the United States. In the case of exports of yellowfin tuna from the eastern tropical Pacific, the following requirements must be met. First, the exporting country nation must have adopted a regulatory program governing the incidental taking of marine mammals in the course of harvesting that is comparable to that of the United States, and that includes regulations on activities such as encircling marine mammals and setting nets at sundown. Second, the vessels of the harvesting nation must have a rate of incidental taking of marine mammals comparable to that of United States vessels. This comparability is defined as an average rate of incidental taking by vessels of the harvesting nation of no more than 1.25 times that of United States vessels during the same period. Third, the vessels of the harvesting nation must not incidentally take in a given year more than 15% of eastern spinner dolphin and not more than 2% of coastal spotted dolphin as a proportion of the total number of marine mammals taken by such vessels. Fourth, the rate of incidental taking by the harvesting nation must be monitored by the IATTC or by others under an equivalent approved program. Fifth, the harvesting nation must comply with all reasonable requests by the United States for cooperation in specified research programs.

5.4 The primary nation embargo does not apply if the harvesting country opts to enter into a formal agreement with the United States, containing certain specific commitments. These require that the country: ban the practice of harvesting tuna through the use of purse seine nets deployed on, or to encircle, dolphins or other marine mammals, beginning 1 March 1994 for a period of five years, unless terminated earlier under prescribed conditions; require an observer on each vessel engaging in purse seine fishing in the eastern tropical Pacific, subject to certain conditions; and reduce dolphin mortality resulting from purse seine net operations conducted by its vessels in the period 1 January 1993 through 28 February 1994 to a level that is lower than such mortality in 1992, by a statistically significant margin. The Act provides that the United States will periodically determine whether each country having made commitments is in fact fully implementing them. If the Secretary to the Treasury determines that such country is not implementing its commitments then, fifteen days after having notified the President and Congress of this determination, the Secretary will prohibit the import from that country of all yellowfin tuna and yellowfin tuna products. Unless the country concerned certifies and provides reasonable proof within 60 days of the import ban that it has fully complied with its commitments, the President will direct the Secretary of the Treasury to prohibit the import from that country of one or more other fish and fish product categories that together amount to at least 40% of total fish and fish product imports from that country.

3. United States restrictions affecting indirect imports of tuna ("intermediary nation embargo")

5.5 The Act provides that any nation ("intermediary nation") that exports yellowfin tuna or yellowfin tuna products to the United States, and that imports yellowfin tuna or yellowfin tuna products that are subject to a direct prohibition on import into the United States, must certify and provide reasonable proof that it has not imported products subject to the direct prohibition within the preceding six months. This provision, effective 26 October 1992, is an amendment of an earlier provision, interpreted by a United States court to require that proof be made that each country identified as an intermediary nation had itself prohibited the import of any tuna that was barred from direct importation into the United States. Subsequent to the entry into force of the new provision France, the Netherlands Antilles and the United Kingdom were withdrawn from the list of intermediary nations. Costa Rica, Italy, Japan and Spain remained on the list.

B. Articles III and XI

5.6 The Panel noted the arguments of the EEC and the Netherlands that the primary nation trade embargoes, while not currently applied to exports of tuna from their territories, could nonetheless be examined under the General Agreement as mandatory measures. The United States disagreed, arguing that measures could not be challenged under the General Agreement unless the trade of the challenging contracting party was affected, and that this was not the case for trade in tuna from the EEC and the Netherlands. The Panel observed that the CONTRACTING PARTIES had accepted that commitments which contracting parties exchanged in tariff negotiations were commitments on conditions of competition for trade, not on volume of trade. It further observed that the CONTRACTING PARTIES had also decided in previous cases that legislation requiring the executive to act contrary to obligations under the General Agreement was inconsistent with the General Agreement, whether or not the legislation had actually been applied in a particular case. The Panel noted that the legislation providing for the primary nation embargo left no discretion to the United States executive as to whether, in the cases in which the legislative requirements were not met, a trade embargo would in fact be applied. The Panel therefore found that the primary nation embargo was mandatory legislation, and that the EEC and the Netherlands could thus challenge its consistency with the General Agreement.

5.7 The Panel then noted the argument of the EEC and the Netherlands that measures taken under the primary and intermediary nation embargoes were not justifiable as measures relating to the enforcement at the time or point of importation of an internal law, regulation or requirement that applied equally to the imported product and the like domestic product, under the terms of the Note ad Article III. The measures constituted a quantitative restriction which was not permitted under the terms of Article XI:1. The United States did not refute these claims, other than to state that the EEC and the Netherlands, as the complainants, bore the burden of proof.

5.8 The Panel proceeded first to examine whether the United States measures, although applied at the border, should nonetheless be examined under the national treatment provisions of Article III. The Panel observed that a Note to Article III extends the scope of Article III to domestic measures enforced at the time or point of importation as follows:

> "any law, regulation or requirement ... which applies to an imported product and to the like domestic product and is ... enforced in the case of the imported product at the time or point of importation, is nevertheless to be regarded as ... a law, regulation or requirement ... subject to the provisions of Article III".

The Panel observed however that this provision can only be invoked in respect of a measure which "applies to an imported product and to the like domestic product". The Panel also noted that the national treatment standard, as it relates to laws, regulations and requirements, is specified in Article III:4:, which states:

> "The products of the territory of any contracting party imported into the territory of any other contracting party shall be accorded treatment no less favourable than that accorded to like products of national origin in respect of all laws, regulations and requirements affecting their internal sale, offering for sale, transportation, distribution or use.... " (emphasis added)

The Panel noted that Article III calls for a comparison between the treatment accorded to domestic and imported like products, not for a comparison of the policies or practices of the country of origin with those of the country of importation. The Panel found therefore that the Note ad Article III could only permit the enforcement, at the time or point of importation, of those laws, regulations and requirements that affected or were applied to the imported and domestic products considered as products. The Note therefore could not apply to the enforcement at the time or point of importation of laws, regulations or requirements that related to policies or practices that could not affect the product as such, and that accorded less favourable treatment to like products not produced in conformity with the domestic policies of the importing country.

5.9 The Panel then examined in this light the measures taken by the United States. It noted that the import embargoes distinguished between tuna products according to harvesting practices and tuna import policies of the exporting countries; that the measures imposed by the United States in respect of domestic tuna similarly distinguished between tuna and tuna products according to tuna harvesting methods; and that none of these practices, policies and methods could have any impact on the inherent character of tuna as a product. The Panel therefore concluded that the Note ad Article III was not applicable.

5.10 The Panel then examined whether the United States measures were consistent with Article XI:1, which reads in part:

> "No prohibitions or restrictions other than duties, taxes or other charges, whether made effective through quotas, import or export licences or other measures, shall be instituted or maintained by any contracting party on the importation of any product of the territory of any other contracting party".

The Panel noted that the embargoes imposed by the United States were "prohibitions or restrictions" in the terms of Article XI, since they banned the import of tuna or tuna products from any country not meeting certain policy conditions. They were not "duties, taxes or other charges". The Panel therefore concluded that the measures were inconsistent with Article XI:1.

C. Article XX(g)

5.11 The Panel noted the United States argument that both the primary and intermediary nation embargoes, even if inconsistent with Articles III or XI, were justified by Article XX (g) as measures relating to the conservation of dolphins, an exhaustible natural resource. The United States argued that there was no requirement in Article XX (g) for the resources to be within the territorial jurisdiction of the country taking the measure. The United States further argued that the measures were taken in conjunction with restrictions on domestic production and consumption. Finally, it argued that the measures met the requirement of the preamble to Article XX. The EEC and the Netherlands disagreed, stating that the resource to be conserved had to be within the territorial jurisdiction of the country taking the measure. The EEC and the Netherlands were further of the view that the United States measures were not related to the conservation of an exhaustible natural resource under Article XX (g), and were not taken in conjunction with domestic restrictions on production or consumption.

5.12 The Panel proceeded first to examine the text of Article XX(g), which, together with its preamble, states:

> "Subject to the requirement that such measures are not applied in a manner which would constitute a means of arbitrary or unjustifiable discrimination between countries where the same conditions prevail, or a disguised restriction on international trade, nothing in this Agreement shall be construed to prevent the adoption or enforcement by any contracting party of measures:

* * *

(g) relating to the conservation of exhaustible natural resources if such measures are made effective in conjunction with restrictions on domestic production or consumption;"

The Panel observed that the text of Article XX(g) suggested a three-step analysis:

—First, it had to be determined whether the policy in respect of which these provisions were invoked fell within the range of policies to conserve exhaustible natural resources.

—Second, it had to be determined whether the measure for which the exception was being invoked—that is the particular trade measure inconsistent with the obligations under the General Agreement—was "related to" the conservation of exhaustible natural resources, and whether it was made effective "in conjunction" with restrictions on domestic production or consumption.

—Third, it had to be determined whether the measure was applied in conformity with the requirement set out in the preamble to Article XX, namely that the measure not be applied in a manner which would constitute a means of arbitrary or unjustifiable discrimination between countries where the same conditions prevail or in a manner which would constitute a disguised restriction on international trade.

1. Conservation of an exhaustible natural resource

5.13 Concerning the first of the above three questions, the Panel noted that the United States maintained that dolphins were an exhaustible natural resource. The EEC disagreed. The Panel, noting that dolphin stocks could potentially be exhausted, and that the basis of a policy to conserve them did not depend on whether at present their stocks were depleted, accepted that a policy to conserve dolphins was a policy to conserve an exhaustible natural resource.

5.14 The Panel noted that the EEC and the Netherlands argued that the exhaustible natural resource to be conserved under Article XX (g) could not be located outside the territorial jurisdiction of the country taking the measure. It based this view on an examination of the Article XX (g) in its context, and in light of the object and purpose of the General Agreement. The United States disagreed, pointing out that there was no textual or other basis for reading such a requirement into Article XX (g).

5.15 The Panel observed, first, that the text of Article XX (g) does not spell out any limitation on the location of the exhaustible natural resources to be conserved. It noted that the conditions set out in the text of Article XX (g) and the preamble qualify only the trade measure requiring justification ("related to") or the manner in which the trade measure is applied ("in conjunction with", "arbitrary or unjustifiable discrimination", "disguised restriction on international trade"). The nature and precise scope of the policy area named in the Article, the conservation of exhaustible natural resources, is not spelled out or specifically conditioned by the text of the Article, in particular with respect to the location of the exhaustible natural resource to be conserved. The Panel noted that two previous panels have considered Article XX (g) to be applicable to policies related to migratory species of fish, and had made no distinction between fish caught within or outside the territorial jurisdiction of the contracting party that had invoked this provision.

5.16 The Panel then observed that measures providing different treatment to products of different origins could in principle be taken under other paragraphs of Article XX and other Articles of the General Agreement with respect to things located, or actions occurring, outside the territorial jurisdiction of the party taking the measure. An example was the provision in Article XX (e) relating to products of prison labour. It could not therefore be said that the General Agreement proscribed in an absolute manner measures that related to things or actions outside the territorial jurisdiction of the party taking the measure.

5.17 The Panel further observed that, under general international law, states are not in principle barred from regulating the conduct of their nationals with respect to persons, animals, plants and natural resources outside of their territory. Nor are states barred, in principle, from regulating the conduct of vessels having their nationality, or any persons on these vessels, with respect to persons, animals, plants and natural resources outside their territory. A state may in particular regulate the conduct of its fishermen, or of vessels having its nationality or any fishermen on these vessels, with respect to fish located in the high seas.

5.18 The Panel noted that the parties based many of their arguments on the location of the exhaustible natural resource in Article XX (g) on environmental and trade treaties other than the General Agreement. However, it was first of all necessary to determine the extent to which these treaties were relevant to the interpretation of the text of the General Agreement. The Panel recalled that it is generally accepted that the Vienna Convention on the Law of Treaties expresses the basic rules of treaty interpretation (see Annex B attached), and that the parties to the dispute shared this view. It therefore proceeded to examine the treaties in this light.

5.19 The Panel recalled that the Vienna Convention provides for a general rule of interpretation (Article 31) and a supplementary means of interpretation (Article 32). The Panel first examined whether, under the general rule of interpretation of the Vienna Convention, the treaties referred to might be taken into account for the purposes of interpreting the General Agreement. The general rule provides that "any subsequent agreement between the parties regarding the interpretation of the treaty or the application of its provisions" is one of the elements relevant to the interpretation of a treaty. However the Panel observed that the agreements cited by the parties to the dispute were bilateral or plurilateral agreements that were not concluded among the contracting parties to the General Agreement, and that they did not apply to the interpretation of the General Agreement or the application of its provisions. Indeed, many of the treaties referred to could not have done so, since they were concluded prior to the negotiation of the General Agreement. The Panel also observed that under the general rule of interpretation in the Vienna Convention account should be taken of "any subsequent practice in the application of the treaty which established the agreement of the parties regarding its interpretation." However, the Panel noted that practice under the bilateral and plurilateral treaties cited could not be taken as practice under the General Agreement, and therefore could not affect the interpretation of it. The Panel therefore found that under the general rule contained in Article 31 of the Vienna Convention, these treaties were not relevant as a primary means of interpretation of the text of the General Agreement.

5.20 The Panel then examined whether the treaties referred to might be relevant as a supplementary means of interpretation of the General Agreement under the Vienna Convention. The Panel noted that the supplementary means permitted by Article 32 of the Vienna Convention include "the preparatory work of the treaty and the circumstances of its conclusion". However, the terms of this provision make clear that its applicability is limited. Preparatory work and other supplementary means of interpretation may only be used "to confirm" an interpretation reached under the general rule of interpretation, or when application of the general rule "leaves the meaning ambiguous or obscure", or "leads to a result which is manifestly absurd or unreasonable." Even if interpretation according to the general rule had led to this result, the Panel considered that those cited treaties that were concluded prior to the conclusion of the General Agreement were of little assistance in interpreting the text of Article XX (g), since it appeared to the Panel on the basis of the material presented to it that no direct references were made to these treaties in the text of the General Agreement, the Havana Charter, or in the preparatory work to these instruments. The Panel also found that the statements and drafting changes made during the negotiation of the Havana Charter and the General Agreement cited by the parties did not provide clear support for any particular contention of the parties on the question of the location of the exhaustible natural resource in Article XX(g). In view of the above, the Panel could see no valid reason supporting the conclusion that the provisions of Article XX (g) apply only to policies related to the conservation of exhaustible natural resources located within the territory of the contracting party invoking the provision. The Panel consequently found that the policy to conserve dolphins in the eastern tropical Pacific Ocean, which the United States pursued within its jurisdiction over its nationals and vessels, fell within the range of policies covered by Article XX (g).

2. "Related to" the conservation of an exhaustible natural resource; made effective "in conjunction" with restrictions on domestic production or consumption

5.21 The Panel then examined the second of the above three questions, namely whether the primary and intermediary nation embargoes imposed by the United States on yellowfin tuna could be considered to be "related to" the conservation of an exhaustible natural resource within the meaning of Article XX (g), and whether they were made effective "in conjunction with" restrictions on domestic production or consumption. The United States argued that its measures met both requirements. The EEC disagreed, stating the measures had to be "primarily aimed" at the conservation of the exhaustible natural resource, and at rendering effective the restrictions on domestic production or consumption.

5.22 The Panel proceeded first to examine the relationship established by Article XX (g) between the trade measure and the policy of conserving an exhaustible natural resource, and between the trade measure and the restrictions on domestic production or consumption. It noted that a previous panel had stated that the scope of the terms "relating to" and "in conjunction with" had to be interpreted in a way that ensured that the scope of provisions under Article XX (g) corresponded to the purposes for which it was included in the General Agreement. That panel had stated that

> " ... the purpose of including Article XX(g) in the General Agreement was not to widen the scope for measures serving trade policy purposes but merely to ensure that the commitments under the General Agreement do not hinder the pursuit of policies aimed at the conservation of exhaustive natural resources".

The previous panel had concluded that the term "relating to" should be taken to mean "primarily aimed" at the conservation of natural resources, and that the term "in conjunction with" should be taken to mean "primarily aimed" at rendering effective the restrictions on domestic production or consumption. The Panel agreed with the reasoning of the previous panel, on the understanding that the words "primarily aimed at" referred not only to the purpose of the measure, but also to its effect on the conservation of the natural resource.

5.23 The Panel then proceeded to examine whether the embargoes imposed by the United States could be considered to be primarily aimed at the conservation of an exhaustible natural resource, and primarily aimed at rendering effective restrictions on domestic production or consumption. In particular, the Panel examined the relationship of the United States measures with the expressed goal of dolphin conservation. The Panel noted that measures taken under the intermediary nation embargo prohibited imports from a country of any tuna, whether or not the particular tuna was harvested in a manner that harmed or could harm dolphins, and whether or not the country had tuna harvesting practices and policies that harmed or could harm dolphins, as long as it was from a country that imported tuna from countries maintaining tuna harvesting practices and policies not comparable to those of the United States. The Panel then observed that the prohibition on imports of tuna into the United States taken under the intermediary nation embargo could not, by itself, further the United States conservation objectives. The intermediary nation embargo could achieve its intended effect only if it were followed by changes in policies or practices, not in the country exporting tuna to the United States, but in third countries from which the exporting country imported tuna.

5.24 The Panel noted also that measures taken under the primary nation embargo prohibited imports from a country of any tuna, whether or not the particular tuna was harvested in a way that harmed or could harm dolphins, as long as the country's tuna harvesting practices and policies were not comparable to those of the United States. The Panel observed that, as in the case of the intermediary nation embargo, the prohibition on imports of tuna into the United States taken under the primary nation embargo could not possibly, by itself, further the United States conservation objectives. The primary nation embargo could achieve its desired effect only if it were followed by changes in policies and practices in the exporting countries. In view of the foregoing, the Panel observed that both the primary and intermediary nation embargoes on tuna implemented by the United States were taken so as to force other countries to change their policies with respect to persons and things within their own jurisdiction, since the embargoes required such changes in order to have any effect on the conservation of dolphins.

5.25 The Panel then examined whether, under Article XX (g), measures primarily aimed at the conservation of exhaustible natural resources, or primarily aimed at rendering effective domestic restrictions on their production or consumption, could include measures taken so as to force other countries to change their policies with respect to persons or things within their own jurisdictions, and requiring such changes in order to be effective. The Panel noted that the text of Article XX does not provide a clear answer to this question. It therefore proceeded to examine the text of Article XX (g) in the light of the object and purpose of the General Agreement.

5.26 The Panel observed that Article XX provides for an exception to obligations under the General Agreement. The long-standing practice of panels has accordingly been to interpret this provision narrowly, in a manner that preserves the basic objectives and principles of the General Agreement. If Article XX were interpreted to permit contracting parties to deviate from the obligations of the General Agreement by taking trade measures to implement policies, including conservation policies, within their own jurisdiction, the basic objectives of the General Agreement would be maintained. If however Article XX were interpreted to permit contracting parties to take trade measures so as to force other contracting parties to change their policies within their jurisdiction, including their conservation policies, the balance of rights and obligations among contracting parties, in particular the right of access to markets, would be seriously impaired. Under such an interpretation the General Agreement could no longer serve as a multilateral framework for trade among contracting parties.

5.27 The Panel concluded that measures taken so as to force other countries to change their policies, and that were effective only if such changes occurred, could not be primarily aimed either at the conservation of an exhaustible natural resource, or at rendering effective restrictions on domestic production or consumption, in the meaning of Article XX (g). Since an essential condition of Article XX (g) had not been met, the Panel did not consider it necessary to examine whether the United States measures had also met the other requirements of Article XX. The Panel accordingly found that the import prohibitions on tuna and tuna products maintained by the United States inconsistently with Article XI:1 were not justified by Article XX (g).

D. Article XX (b)

5.28 The Panel noted the United States argument that both the primary and intermediary nation embargoes, even if inconsistent with Articles III or XI, were justified by Article XX (b) as measures necessary to protect the life and health of dolphins. The United States argued that there was no requirement in Article XX (b) that the animals whose life or health was to be protected had to be within the jurisdiction of the country taking the measure. The United States further argued that the measures were necessary to fulfil the policy goal of protecting the life and health of dolphins. Finally, it argued that the measures met the requirement of the preamble to Article XX. The EEC and the Netherlands disagreed, stating that the animals whose life or health was to be protected had to be within the jurisdiction of the country taking the measure. The EEC and the Netherlands were further of the view that the United States measures were not necessary within the meaning of Article XX (b).

5.29 The Panel proceeded first to examine the text of Article XX(b), which, together with its preamble, states:

> "Subject to the requirement that such measures are not applied in a manner which would constitute a means of arbitrary or unjustifiable discrimination between countries where the same conditions prevail, or a disguised restriction on international trade, nothing in this Agreement shall be construed to prevent the adoption or enforcement by any contracting party of measures:
>
> * * *
>
> (b) necessary to protect the human, animal, or plant life or health"

The Panel observed that the text of Article XX(b) suggested a three-step analysis:

—First, it had to be determined whether the policy in respect of which these provisions were invoked fell within the range of policies referred to in these provisions, that is policies to protect human, animal or plant life or health;

—Second, it had to be determined whether the measure for which the exception was being invoked—that is the particular trade measure inconsistent with the obligations under the General Agreement—was "necessary" to protect human, animal or plant life or health;

—Third, it had to be determined whether the measure was applied in a manner consistent with the requirement set out in the preamble to Article XX, namely that the measure not be applied in a manner which would constitute a means of arbitrary or unjustifiable discrimination between countries where the same conditions prevail or in a manner which would constitute a disguised restriction on international trade.

1. To protect human, animal or plant life and health

5.30 Turning to the first of the above three questions, the Panel noted that the parties did not disagree that the protection of dolphin life or health was a policy that could come within Article XX (b). The EEC argued, however, that Article XX (b) could not justify measures taken to protect living things located outside the territorial jurisdiction of the party taking the measure. The United States disagreed. The arguments on this issue advanced by the parties were similar to those made under Article XX (g).

5.31 The Panel recalled its reasoning under Article XX (g). It observed that the text of Article XX (b) does not spell out any limitation on the location of the living things to be protected. It noted that the conditions set out in the text of Article XX (b) and the preamble qualify only the trade measure requiring justification ("necessary to") or the manner in which the trade measure is applied ("arbitrary or unjustifiable discrimination", "disguised restriction on international trade"). The nature and precise scope of the policy area named in the Article, the protection of living things, is not specified in the text of the Article, in particular with respect to the location of the living things to be protected.

5.32 The Panel further recalled its observation that elsewhere in the General Agreement measures according different treatment to products of different origins could in principle be taken with respect to things located, or actions occurring, outside the territorial jurisdiction of the party taking the measure. It could not therefore be said that the General Agreement prescribed in an absolute manner such measures. The Panel further recalled its observation that, under general international law, states are not in principle barred from regulating the conduct of their nationals with respect to persons, animals, plants and natural resources outside of their territory (see paragraph 5.17 above).

5.33 The Panel noted that the United States and the EEC, as under Article XX (g), based many of their arguments regarding the location of the living things to protected under Article XX (b) on environmental and trade treaties other than the General Agreement. However, for the reasons advanced under its discussion of Article XX (g), the Panel did not consider that the treaties were relevant for the interpretation of the text of the General Agreement (see paragraphs 5.19–5.20). The Panel also noted that the statements and drafting changes made during the negotiation of the Havana Charter and the General Agreement did not clearly support any particular contention of the parties with respect to the location of the living thing to be protected under Article XX (b). The Panel did not see the need to settle the issue argued by the parties as to whether the intent of the drafters was to restrict measures justifiable under Article XX to sanitary measures. The Panel therefore found that the policy to protect the life and health of dolphins in the eastern tropical Pacific Ocean, which the United States pursued within its jurisdiction over its nationals and vessels, fell within the range of policies covered by Article XX (b).

2. "Necessary"

5.34 The Panel then examined the second of the above three questions, namely whether the primary and intermediary nation embargoes imposed by the United States on yellowfin tuna could be considered to be "necessary" for the protection of the living things within the meaning of Article XX (b). The United States argued that its measures met this requirement, since "necessary" in this sense simply meant "needed". The EEC disagreed, stating that the normal meaning of the term "necessary" was "indispensable" or "unavoidable". The EEC further argued that adopted panel reports had stated that a measure otherwise inconsistent with the General Agreement could only be justified as necessary under Article XX (b) if no other consistent measure, or more consistent measure, were reasonably available to fulfil the policy objective.

5.35 The Panel proceeded first to examine the relationship established by Article XX (b) between the trade measure and the policy of protecting living things. It noted that, in the ordinary meaning of the term, "necessary" meant that no alternative existed. A previous panel, in discussing the use of the same term in Article XX (d), stated that

> "a contracting party cannot justify a measure inconsistent with another GATT provision as 'necessary' in terms of Article XX(d) if an alternative measure which it could reasonably be expected to employ and which is not inconsistent with other GATT provisions is available to it. By the same token, in cases where a measure consistent with other GATT provisions is not reasonably available, a contracting party is bound to use, among the measures reasonably available to it, that which entails the least degree of inconsistency with other GATT provisions."

This interpretation had also been accepted by another panel specifically examining Article XX (b). The Panel agreed with the reasoning of these previous panels. The Panel then proceeded to examine whether the trade embargoes imposed by the United States could be considered to be "necessary" in this sense to protect the life or health of dolphins.

5.36 The Panel noted that measures taken under the intermediary nation embargo prohibited imports from a country of any tuna, whether or not the particular tuna was harvested in a manner that harmed or could harm dolphins, and whether or not the country had tuna harvesting practices and policies that harmed or could harm dolphin, as long as it was from a country that imported tuna from countries maintaining tuna harvesting practices and policies not comparable to those of the United States. The Panel observed that the prohibition on imports of tuna into the United States taken under the intermediary nation embargo could not, by itself, further the United States conservation objectives. The intermediary nation embargo would achieve its intended effect only if it were followed by changes in policies or practices, not in the country exporting tuna to the United States, but in third countries from which the exporting country imported tuna.

5.37 The Panel also recalled that measures taken under the primary nation embargo prohibited imports from a country of any tuna, whether or not the particular tuna was harvested in a way that harmed or could harm dolphins, as long as the country's tuna harvesting practices and policies were not comparable to those of the United States. The Panel observed that, as in the case of the intermediary nation embargo, the prohibition on imports of tuna into the United States taken under the primary nation embargo could not possibly, by itself, further the United States objective of protecting the life and health of dolphins. The primary nation embargo could achieve its desired effect only if it were followed by changes in policies and practices in the exporting countries. In view of the foregoing, the Panel observed that both the primary and intermediary nation embargoes on tuna were taken by the United States so as to force other countries to change their policies with respect to persons and things within their own jurisdiction, since the embargoes required such changes in order to have any effect on the protection of the life or health of dolphins.

5.38 The Panel then examined whether, under Article XX (b), measures necessary to protect the life or health of animals could include measures taken so as to force other countries to change their policies within their own jurisdictions, and requiring such changes in order to be effective. The Panel noted that the text of Article XX is not explicit on this question. The Panel then recalled its reasoning under its examination of Article XX (g) that Article XX, as a provision for exceptions, should be interpreted narrowly and in a way that preserves the basic objectives and principles of the General Agreement. If Article XX (b) were interpreted to permit contracting parties to deviate from the basic obligations of the General Agreement by taking trade measures to implement policies within their own jurisdiction, including policies to protect living things, the objectives of the General Agreement would be maintained. If however Article XX (b) were interpreted to permit contracting parties to impose trade embargoes so as to force other countries to change their policies within their jurisdiction, including policies to protect living things, and which required such changes to be effective, the objectives of the General Agreement would be seriously impaired.

5.39 The Panel concluded that measures taken so as to force other countries to change their policies, and that were effective only if such changes occurred, could not be considered "necessary" for the protection of animal life or health in the sense of Article XX (b). Since an essential condition of Article XX (b) had not been met, the Panel did not consider it necessary to examine the further issue of whether the United States measures had also met the other requirements of Article XX. The Panel accordingly found that the import prohibitions on tuna and tuna products maintained by the United States inconsistently with Article XI: 1 were not justified by Article XX (b).

E. Article XX (d)

5.40 The Panel noted the United States argument that the import prohibitions taken under the intermediary nation embargo were justified by Article XX (d), since they were necessary to secure compliance with import prohibitions under the primary nation embargo provisions. The EEC and the Netherlands disagreed. They stated that, since the measures taken under the primary nation embargo were inconsistent with the General Agreement, they could not serve as the basis for an invocation of Article XX (d).

5.41 The Panel examined the text of Article XX(d) which, together with its preamble, stated:

"Subject to the requirement that such measures are not applied in a manner which would constitute a means of arbitrary or unjustifiable discrimination between countries where the same conditions prevail, or a disguised restriction on international trade, nothing in this Agreement shall be construed to prevent the adoption or enforcement by any contracting party of measures:

* * *

(d) necessary to secure compliance with laws or regulations which are not inconsistent with the provisions of this Agreement . . . "

The Panel, recalling its finding that the measures taken under the primary nation embargo were inconsistent with Article XI:1 of the General Agreement, concluded that the primary nation embargo could not, by the explicit terms of Article XX (d), serve as a basis for the justification of the intermediary nation embargo.

F. Concluding observations

5.42 The Panel noted that the objective of sustainable development, which includes the protection and preservation of the environment, has been widely recognized by the contracting parties to the General Agreement. The Panel observed that the issue in this dispute was not the validity of the environmental objectives of the United States to protect and conserve dolphins. The issue was whether, in the pursuit of its environmental objectives, the United States could impose trade embargoes to secure changes in the policies which other contracting parties pursued within their own jurisdiction. The Panel therefore had to resolve whether the contracting parties, by agreeing to give each other in Article XX the right to take trade measures necessary to protect the health and life of plants, animals and persons or aimed at the conservation of exhaustible natural resources, had agreed to accord each other the right to impose trade embargoes for such purposes. The Panel had examined this issue in the light of the recognized methods of interpretation and had found that none of them lent any support to the view that such an agreement was reflected in Article XX.

5.43 The Panel further observed that the dispute settlement procedures cannot add to or diminish rights of contracting parties under the General Agreement. It noted that other procedures existed under the General Agreement that permit the obligations of a contracting party to be waived. The Panel noted that the relationship between environmental and trade measures would be considered in the context of preparations for the World Trade Organization.

VI. CONCLUSIONS

6.1 In the light of its findings above, the Panel concluded that the United States import prohibitions on tuna and tuna products under Section 101 (a)(2) and Section 305 (a)(1) and (2) of the Marine Mammal Protection Act (the "primary nation embargo") and under Section 101 (a)(2)(C) of the Marine Mammal Protection Act (the "intermediary nation embargo") did not meet the requirements of the Note ad Article III, were contrary to Article XI: 1, and were not covered by the exceptions in Article XX (b), (g) or (d) of the General Agreement.

6.2 The Panel recommends that the CONTRACTING PARTIES request the United States to bring the above measures into conformity with its obligations under the General Agreement.

8.9 WTO Appellate Body Report on United States Standards for Reformulated and Conventional Gasoline. Adopted on 20 May 1996. WTO Doc. No. WT/DS2/AB/R; *reprinted in* 35 I.L.M. 603 (1996)

* * *

C. The Panel Report: Its Findings and Conclusions

The Panel's overall conclusions and its recommendation are set out in the following terms:

8.1 In the light of the findings above, the Panel concluded that the baseline establishment methods contained in Part 80 of Title 40 of the Code of Federal Regulations are not consistent with Article III:4 of the General Agreement, and cannot be justified under paragraphs (b), (d) and (g) of Article XX of the General Agreement.

8.2 The Panel recommends that the Dispute Settlement Body request the United States to bring this part of the Gasoline Rule into conformity with its obligations under the General Agreement.

On route to its overall conclusions, the Panel made the following principal findings:

(i) that the Panel's terms of reference were established after the 75 per cent rule had ceased to have any effect, and the rule had not been mentioned in the terms of reference, and that, in any case, it was unnecessary, in view of findings (ii), (iv), (v) and (vii) below, to determine whether the measure at issue was inconsistent with Article I:1 of the General Agreement on Tariffs and Trade 1994 (the "General Agreement");

(ii) that imported and domestic gasoline were "like products" and that since, under the baseline establishment rules of the Gasoline Rule, imported gasoline was effectively prevented from benefitting from as favourable sales conditions as were afforded domestic gasoline by an individual baseline tied to the producer of a product, imported gasoline was treated "less favourably" than domestic gasoline. The baseline establishment rules of the Gasoline Rule were accordingly inconsistent with Article III:4 of the General Agreement;

(iii) that, in view of finding (ii), it was necessary to examine the consistency of the Gasoline Rule with Article III:1;

(iv) that the "aspect of the baseline establishment methods" found inconsistent with Article III:4 was not justified under Article XX(b) of the General Agreement as "necessary to protect human, animal or plant life or health";

(v) that the "maintenance of discrimination between imported and domestic gasoline" contrary to Article III:4 was not justified under Article XX(d) as "necessary to secure compliance with laws or regulations which are not inconsistent with the provisions of [the General] Agreement";

(vi) that clean air was an exhaustible natural resource within the meaning of Article XX(g) of the General Agreement;

(vii) that the baseline establishment rules found to be inconsistent with Article III:4 could not be justified under Article XX(g) as a measure "relating to" the conservation of exhaustible natural resources;

(viii) that it was unnecessary, in the light of finding (vii), to determine whether the measure at issue was "made effective in conjunction with restrictions on domestic production or consumption";

(ix) that it was unnecessary, in the light of finding (vii), to determine whether the measure at issue met the conditions in the introductory clause of Article XX (sometimes referred to as the chapeau of Article XX);

(x) that it was unnecessary, in view of findings (ii), (iv), (v) and (vii), to determine whether the measure at issue was inconsistent with Article XXIII:1(b) as having nullified and impaired benefits accruing under the General Agreement; and

(xi) that it was unnecessary, in the light of findings (ii), (iv), (v) and (vii), to determine whether the measure at issue was inconsistent with Articles 2.1 and 2.2 of the Agreement on Technical Barriers to Trade (the "TBT Agreement").

* * *

III. THE ISSUE OF JUSTIFICATION UNDER ARTICLE XX(G) OF THE GENERAL AGREEMENT

Article XX(g) needs to be set out in full:

Article XX

General Exceptions

Subject to the requirement that such measures are not applied in a manner which would constitute a means of arbitrary or unjustifiable discrimination between countries where the same conditions prevail, or a disguised restriction on international trade, nothing in this Agreement shall be construed to prevent the adoption or enforcement by any contracting party of measures:

* * *

(g) relating to the conservation of exhaustible natural resources if such measures are made effective in conjunction with restrictions on domestic production or consumption;

* * *

A. "Measures"

The initial issue we are asked to look at relates to the proper meaning of the term "measures" as used both in the chapeau of Article XX and in Article XX(g). The question is whether "measures" refers to the entire Gasoline Rule or, alternatively, only to the particular provisions of the Gasoline Rule which deal with the establishment of baselines for domestic refiners, blenders and importers.

Cast in the foregoing terms, the issue does not appear to be a live one. True enough the Panel Report used differing terms, or terms of shifting reference, in designating the "measures" in different parts of the Report. The Panel Report, however, held only the baseline establishment rules of the Gasoline Rule to be inconsistent with Article III:4, to the extent that such rules provided "less favourable treatment" for imported than for domestic gasoline. These are the same provisions which the Panel evaluated, and found wanting, under the justifying provisions of Article XX(g). The Panel Report did not purport to find the Gasoline Rule itself as a whole, or any part thereof other than the baseline establishment rules, to be inconsistent with Article III:4; accordingly, there was no need at all to examine whether the whole of the Gasoline Rule or any of its other rules, was saved or justified by Article XX(g). The Panel here was following the practice of earlier panels in applying Article XX to provisions found to be inconsistent with Article III:4: the "measures" to be analyzed under Article XX are the same provisions infringing Article III:4. These earlier panels had not interpreted "measures" more broadly under Article XX to include provisions not themselves found inconsistent with Article III:4. In the present appeal, no one has suggested in their final submissions that the Appellate Body should examine under Article XX any portion of the Gasoline Rule other than the baseline establishment rules held to be in conflict with Article III:4. No one has urged an interpretation of "measures" which would encompass the Gasoline Rule in its totality.

At the oral hearing and in its Post–Hearing Memorandum, the United States complained about the designation of the baseline establishment rules in the Panel Report and by the Appellees Venezuela and Brazil, in such terms as "the difference in treatment", "the less favourable treatment" or "the discrimination." It is, of course, true that the baseline establishment rules had been found by the Panel to be inconsistent with Article III:4 of the General Agreement. The frequent designation of those provisions by the Panel in terms of its legal conclusion in respect of Article III:4, in the Appellate Body's view, did not serve the cause of clarity in analysis when it came to evaluating the same baseline establishment rules under Article XX(g).

B. "relating to the conservation of exhaustible natural resources"

The Panel Report took the view that clean air was a "natural resource" that could be "depleted." Accordingly, as already noted earlier, the Panel concluded that a policy to reduce the depletion of clean air was a policy to conserve an exhaustible natural resource within the meaning of Article XX(g). Shortly thereafter, however, the Panel Report also concluded that "the less favourable baseline establishments methods" were not primarily aimed at the conservation of exhaustible natural resources and thus fell outside the justifying scope of Article XX(g).

The Panel, addressing the task of interpreting the words "relating to", quoted with approval the following passage from the panel report in the 1987 Herring and Salmon case:

> as the preamble of Article XX indicates, the purpose of including Article XX:(g) in the General Agreement was not to widen the scope for measures serving trade policy purposes but merely to ensure that the commitments under the General Agreement do not hinder the pursuit of policies aimed at the conservation of exhaustive natural resources. The Panel concluded for these reasons that, while a trade measure did not have to be necessary or essential to the conservation of an exhaustible natural resource, it had to be primarily aimed at the conservation of an exhaustible natural resource to be considered as "relating to" conservation within the meaning of Article XX: (g). (emphasis added by the Panel)

The Panel Report then went on to apply the 1987 Herring and Salmon reasoning and conclusion to the baseline establishment rules of the Gasoline Rule in the following manner:

> The Panel then considered whether the precise aspects of the Gasoline Rule that it had found to violate Article III—the less favourable baseline establishments methods that adversely affected the conditions of competition for imported gasoline—were primarily aimed at the conservation of natural resources. The Panel saw no direct connection between less favourable treatment of imported gasoline that was chemically identical to domestic gasoline, and the US objective of improving air quality in the United States. Indeed, in the view of the Panel, being consistent with the obligation to provide no less favourable treatment would not prevent the attainment of the desired level of conservation of natural resources under the Gasoline Rule. Accordingly, it could not be said that the baseline establishment methods that afforded less favourable treatment to imported gasoline were primarily aimed at the conservation of natural resources. In the Panel's view, the above-noted lack of connection was underscored by the fact that affording treatment of imported gasoline consistent with its Article III:4 obligations would not in any way hinder the United States in its pursuit of its conservation policies under the Gasoline Rule. Indeed, the United States remained free to regulate in order to obtain whatever air quality it wished. The Panel therefore concluded that the less favourable baseline

establishments methods at issue in this case were not primarily aimed at the conservation of natural resources.

It is not easy to follow the reasoning in the above paragraph of the Panel Report. In our view, there is a certain amount of opaqueness in that reasoning. The Panel starts with positing that there was "no direct connection" between the baseline establishment rules which it characterized as "less favourable treatment" of imported gasoline that was chemically identical to the domestic gasoline and "the US objective of improving air quality in the United States." Shortly thereafter, the Panel went on to conclude that "accordingly, it could not be said that the baseline establishment rules that afforded less favourable treatment to imported gasoline were primarily aimed at the conservation of natural resources" (emphasis added). The Panel did not try to clarify whether the phrase "direct connection" was being used as a synonym for "primarily aimed at" or whether a new and additional element (on top of "primarily aimed at") was being demanded.

One problem with the reasoning in that paragraph is that the Panel asked itself whether the "less favourable treatment" of imported gasoline was "primarily aimed at" the conservation of natural resources, rather than whether the "measure", i.e. the baseline establishment rules, were "primarily aimed at" conservation of clean air. In our view, the Panel here was in error in referring to its legal conclusion on Article III:4 instead of the measure in issue. The result of this analysis is to turn Article XX on its head. Obviously, there had to be a finding that the measure provided "less favourable treatment" under Article III:4 before the Panel examined the "General Exceptions" contained in Article XX. That, however, is a conclusion of law. The chapeau of Article XX makes it clear that it is the "measures" which are to be examined under Article XX(g), and not the legal finding of "less favourable treatment."

Furthermore, the Panel Report appears to have utilized a conclusion it had reached earlier in holding that the baseline establishment rules did not fall within the justifying terms of Articles XX(b); i.e. that the baseline establishment rules were not "necessary" for the protection of human, animal or plant life. The Panel Report, it will be recalled, found that the baseline establishment rules had not been shown by the United States to be "necessary" under Article XX(b) since alternative measures either consistent or less inconsistent with the General Agreement were reasonably available to the United States for achieving its aim of protecting human, animal or plant life. In other words, the Panel Report appears to have applied the "necessary" test not only in examining the baseline establishment rules under Article XX(b), but also in the course of applying Article XX(g).

A principal difficulty, in the view of the Appellate Body, with the Panel Report's application of Article XX(g) to the baseline establishment rules is that the Panel there overlooked a fundamental rule of treaty interpretation. This rule has received its most authoritative and succinct expression in the Vienna Convention on the Law of Treaties (the "Vienna Convention") which provides in relevant part:

ARTICLE 31

General rule of interpretation

1. A treaty shall be interpreted in good faith in accordance with the ordinary meaning to be given to the terms of the treaty in their context and in the light of its object and purpose.

The "general rule of interpretation" set out above has been relied upon by all of the participants and third participants, although not always in relation to the same issue. That general rule of interpretation has attained the status of a rule of customary or general international law. As such, it forms part of the "customary rules of interpretation of public international law" which the Appellate Body has been directed, by Article 3(2) of the DSU, to apply in seeking to clarify the provisions of the General

Agreement and the other "covered agreements" of the Marrakesh Agreement Establishing the World Trade Organization (the "WTO Agreement"). That direction reflects a measure of recognition that the General Agreement is not to be read in clinical isolation from public international law.

Applying the basic principle of interpretation that the words of a treaty, like the General Agreement, are to be given their ordinary meaning, in their context and in the light of the treaty's object and purpose, the Appellate Body observes that the Panel Report failed to take adequate account of the words actually used by Article XX in its several paragraphs. In enumerating the various categories of governmental acts, laws or regulations which WTO Members may carry out or promulgate in pursuit of differing legitimate state policies or interests outside the realm of trade liberalization, Article XX uses different terms in respect of different categories:

"necessary"—in paragraphs (a), (b) and (d);

"relating to"—in paragraphs (c), (e) and (g);

"in pursuance of"—in paragraph (h); and

"essential"—in paragraph (j);

"for the protection of"—in paragraph (f);

"involving"—in paragraph (i).

It does not seem reasonable to suppose that the WTO Members intended to require, in respect of each and every category, the same kind or degree of connection or relationship between the measure under appraisal and the state interest or policy sought to be promoted or realized.

At the same time, Article XX(g) and its phrase, "relating to the conservation of exhaustible natural resources," need to be read in context and in such a manner as to give effect to the purposes and objects of the General Agreement. The context of Article XX(g) includes the provisions of the rest of the General Agreement, including in particular Articles I, III and XI; conversely, the context of Articles I and III and XI includes Article XX. Accordingly, the phrase "relating to the conservation of exhaustible natural resources" may not be read so expansively as seriously to subvert the purpose and object of Article III:4. Nor may Article III:4 be given so broad a reach as effectively to emasculate Article XX(g) and the policies and interests it embodies. The relationship between the affirmative commitments set out in, e.g., Articles I, III and XI, and the policies and interests embodied in the "General Exceptions" listed in Article XX, can be given meaning within the framework of the General Agreement and its object and purpose by a treaty interpreter only on a case-to-case basis, by careful scrutiny of the factual and legal context in a given dispute, without disregarding the words actually used by the WTO Members themselves to express their intent and purpose.

The 1987 Herring and Salmon report, and the Panel Report itself, gave some recognition to the foregoing considerations of principle. As earlier noted, the Panel Report quoted the following excerpt from the Herring and Salmon report:

> as the preamble of Article XX indicates, the purpose of including Article XX(g) in the General Agreement was not to widen the scope for measures serving trade policy purposes but merely to ensure that the commitments under the General Agreement do not hinder the pursuit of policies aimed at the conservation of exhaustible natural resources. (emphasis added)

All the participants and the third participants in this appeal accept the propriety and applicability of the view of the Herring and Salmon report and the Panel Report that a measure must be "primarily aimed at" the conservation of exhaustible natural resources in order to fall within the scope of Article XX(g). Accordingly, we see no need to examine this point further, save, perhaps, to note that the phrase "primarily aimed at'' is not itself treaty language and was not designed as a simple litmus test for inclusion or exclusion from Article XX(g).

Against this background, we turn to the specific question of whether the baseline establishment rules are appropriately regarded as "primarily aimed at" the conservation of natural resources for the purposes of Article XX(g). We consider that this question must be answered in the affirmative.

The baseline establishment rules, taken as a whole (that is, the provisions relating to establishment of baselines for domestic refiners, along with the provisions relating to baselines for blenders and importers of gasoline), need to be related to the "non-degradation" requirements set out elsewhere in the Gasoline Rule. Those provisions can scarcely be understood if scrutinized strictly by themselves, totally divorced from other sections of the Gasoline Rule which certainly constitute part of the context of these provisions. The baseline establishment rules whether individual or statutory, were designed to permit scrutiny and monitoring of the level of compliance of refiners, importers and blenders with the "non-degradation" requirements. Without baselines of some kind, such scrutiny would not be possible and the Gasoline Rule's objective of stabilizing and preventing further deterioration of the level of air pollution prevailing in 1990, would be substantially frustrated. The relationship between the baseline establishment rules and the "non-degradation" requirements of the Gasoline Rule is not negated by the inconsistency, found by the Panel, of the baseline establishment rules with the terms of Article III:4. We consider that, given that substantial relationship, the baseline establishment rules cannot be regarded as merely incidentally or inadvertently aimed at the conservation of clean air in the United States for the purposes of Article XX(g).

C. "if such measures are made effective in conjunction with restrictions on domestic production or consumption"

The Panel did not find it necessary to deal with the issue of whether the baseline establishment rules "are made effective in conjunction with restrictions on domestic production or consumption", since it had earlier concluded that those rules had not even satisfied the preceding requirement of "relating to" in the sense of being "primarily aimed at" the conservation of clean air. Having been unable to concur with that earlier conclusion of the Panel, we must now address this second requirement of Article XX(g), the United States having, in effect, appealed from the failure of the Panel to proceed further with its inquiry into the availability of Article XX(g) as a justification for the baseline establishment rules.

The claim of the United States is that the second clause of Article XX(g) requires that the burdens entailed by regulating the level of pollutants in the air emitted in the course of combustion of gasoline, must not be imposed solely on, or in respect of, imported gasoline.

On the other hand, Venezuela and Brazil refer to prior panel reports which include statements to the effect that to be deemed as "made effective in conjunction with restrictions on domestic production or consumption", a measure must be "primarily aimed at" making effective certain restrictions on domestic production or consumption. Venezuela and Brazil also argue that the United States has failed to show the existence of restrictions on domestic production or consumption of a natural resource under the Gasoline Rule since clean air was not an exhaustible natural resource within the meaning of Article XX(g). Venezuela contends, finally, that the United States has not discharged its burden of showing that the baseline establishment rules make the United States' regulatory scheme "effective." The claim of Venezuela is, in effect, that to be properly regarded as "primarily aimed at" the conservation of natural resources, the baseline establishment rules must not only "reflect a conservation purpose" but also be shown to have had "some positive conservation effect."

The Appellate Body considers that the basic international law rule of treaty interpretation, discussed earlier, that the terms of a treaty are to be given their ordinary meaning, in context, so as to effectuate its object and purpose, is applicable here, too. Viewed in this light, the ordinary or natural meaning of "made effective" when used in connection with a measure—a governmental act or regulation-may be seen to refer to such measure being "operative", as "in force", or as having "come into effect." Similarly, the phrase "in conjunction with" may be read quite plainly as "together with" or "jointly with." Taken together, the second clause of Article XX(g) appears to us to refer to governmental measures like the baseline establishment rules being promulgated or brought into effect together with restrictions on domestic production or consumption of natural resources. Put in a slightly different manner, we believe that the clause "if such measures are made effective in conjunction with restrictions on domestic product or consumption" is appropriately read as a requirement that the measures concerned impose restrictions, not just in respect of imported gasoline but also with respect to domestic gasoline. The clause is a requirement of even-handedness in the imposition of restrictions, in the name of conservation, upon the production or consumption of exhaustible natural resources.

There is, of course, no textual basis for requiring identical treatment of domestic and imported products. Indeed, where there is identity of treatment—constituting real, not merely formal, equality of treatment—it is difficult to see how inconsistency with Article III:4 would have arisen in the first place. On the other hand, if no restrictions on domestically-produced like products are imposed at all, and all limitations are placed upon imported products alone, the measure cannot be accepted as primarily or even substantially designed for implementing conservationist goals. The measure would simply be naked discrimination for protecting locally-produced goods.

In the present appeal, the baseline establishment rules affect both domestic gasoline and imported gasoline, providing for—generally speaking—individual baselines for domestic refiners and blenders and statutory baselines for importers. Thus, restrictions on the consumption or depletion of clean air by regulating the domestic production of "dirty" gasoline are established jointly with corresponding restrictions with respect to imported gasoline. That imported gasoline has been determined to have been accorded "less favourable treatment" than the domestic gasoline in terms of Article III:4, is not material for purposes of analysis under Article XX(g). It might also be noted that the second clause of Article XX(g) speaks disjunctively of "domestic production or consumption."

We do not believe, finally, that the clause "if made effective in conjunction with restrictions on domestic production or consumption" was intended to establish an empirical "effects test" for the availability of the Article XX(g) exception. In the first place, the problem of determining causation, well-known in both domestic and international law, is always a difficult one. In the second place, in the field of conservation of exhaustible natural resources, a substantial period of time, perhaps years, may have to elapse before the effects attributable to implementation of a given measure may be observable. The legal characterization of such a measure is not reasonably made contingent upon occurrence of subsequent events. We are not, however, suggesting that consideration of the predictable effects of a measure is never relevant. In a particular case, should it become clear that realistically, a specific measure cannot in any possible situation have any positive effect on conservation goals, it would very probably be because that measure was not designed as a conservation regulation to begin with. In other words, it would not have been "primarily aimed at" conservation of natural resources at all.

IV. THE INTRODUCTORY PROVISIONS OF ARTICLE XX OF THE GENERAL AGREEMENT: APPLYING THE CHAPEAU OF THE GENERAL EXCEPTIONS

Having concluded, in the preceding section, that the baseline establishment rules of the Gasoline Rule fall within the terms of Article XX(g), we come to the question of whether those rules also meet the requirements of the chapeau of Article XX. In order that the justifying protection of Article XX may be extended to it, the measure at issue must not only come under one or another of the particular exceptions—paragraphs (a) to (j)—listed under Article XX; it must also satisfy the requirements imposed by the opening clauses of Article XX. The analysis is, in other words, two-tiered: first, provisional justification by reason of characterization of the measure under XX(g); second, further appraisal of the same measure under the introductory clauses of Article XX.

The chapeau by its express terms addresses, not so much the questioned measure or its specific contents as such, but rather the manner in which that measure is applied. It is, accordingly, important to underscore that the purpose and object of the introductory clauses of Article XX is generally the prevention of "abuse of the exceptions of [what was later to become] Article [XX]." This insight drawn from the drafting history of Article XX is a valuable one. The chapeau is animated by the principle that while the exceptions of Article XX may be invoked as a matter of legal right, they should not be so applied as to frustrate or defeat the legal obligations of the holder of the right under the substantive rules of the General Agreement. If those exceptions are not to be abused or misused, in other words, the measures falling within the particular exceptions must be applied reasonably, with due regard both to the legal duties of the party claiming the exception and the legal rights of the other parties concerned.

The burden of demonstrating that a measure provisionally justified as being within one of the exceptions set out in the individual paragraphs of Article XX does not, in its application, constitute abuse of such exception under the chapeau, rests on the party invoking the exception. That is, of necessity, a heavier task than that involved in showing that an exception, such as Article XX(g), encompasses the measure at issue.

The enterprise of applying Article XX would clearly be an unprofitable one if it involved no more than applying the standard used in finding that the baseline establishment rules were inconsistent with Article III:4. That would also be true if the finding were one of inconsistency with some other substantive rule of the General Agreement. The provisions of the chapeau cannot logically refer to the same standard(s) by which a violation of a substantive rule has been determined to have occurred. To proceed down that path would be both to empty the chapeau of its contents and to deprive the exceptions in paragraphs (a) to (j) of meaning. Such recourse would also confuse the question of whether inconsistency with a substantive rule existed, with the further and separate question arising under the chapeau of Article XX as to whether that inconsistency was nevertheless justified. One of the corollaries of the "general rule of interpretation" in the Vienna Convention is that interpretation must give meaning and effect to all the terms of a treaty. An interpreter is not free to adopt a reading that would result in reducing whole clauses or paragraphs of a treaty to redundancy or inutility.

The chapeau, it will be seen, prohibits such application of a measure at issue (otherwise falling within the scope of Article XX(g)) as would constitute

(a) "arbitrary discrimination" (between countries where the same conditions prevail);

(b) "unjustifiable discrimination" (with the same qualifier); or

(c) "disguised restriction" on international trade.

The text of the chapeau is not without ambiguity, including one relating to the field of application of the standards its contains: the arbitrary or unjustifiable discrimination standards and the disguised restriction on international trade standard. It may be asked whether these standards do not have different fields of application. Such a question was put to the United States in the course of the oral hearing. It was asked whether the words incorporated into the first two standards "between countries where the same conditions prevail" refer to conditions in importing and exporting countries, or only to conditions in exporting countries. The reply of the United States was to the effect that it interpreted that phrase as referring to both the exporting countries and importing countries and as between exporting countries. It also said that the language spoke for itself, but there was no reference to third parties; while some thought that this was only between exporting countries inter se, there is no support in the text for that view. No such question was put to the United States concerning the field of application of the third standard—disguised restriction on international trade. But the United States put forward arguments designed to show that in the case under appeal, it had met all the standards set forth in the chapeau. In doing so, it clearly proceeded on the assumption that, whatever else they might relate to in another case, they were relevant to a case of national treatment where the Panel had found a violation of Article III:4. At no point in the appeal was that assumption challenged by Venezuela or Brazil. Venezuela argued that the United States had failed to meet all the standards contained in the chapeau. So did Norway and the European Communities as third participants. In short, the field of application of these standards was not at issue.

The assumption on which all the participants proceeded is buttressed by the fact that the chapeau says that "nothing in this Agreement shall be construed to prevent the adoption or enforcement by any contracting party of measures . . ." The exceptions listed in Article XX thus relate to all of the obligations under the General Agreement: the national treatment obligation and the most-favoured-nation obligation, of course, but others as well. Effect is more easily given to the words "nothing in this Agreement", and Article XX as a whole including its chapeau more easily integrated into the remainder of the General Agreement, if the chapeau is taken to mean that the standards it sets forth are applicable to all of the situations in which an allegation of a violation of a substantive obligation has been made and one of the exceptions contained in Article XX has in turn been claimed.

Against this background, we see no need to decide the matter of the field of application of the standards set forth in the chapeau nor to make a ruling at variance with the common understanding of the participants.

"Arbitrary discrimination", "unjustifiable discrimination" and "disguised restriction" on international trade may, accordingly, be read side-by-side; they impart meaning to one another. It is clear to us that "disguised restriction" includes disguised discrimination in international trade. It is equally clear that concealed or unannounced restriction or discrimination in international trade does not exhaust the meaning of "disguised restriction." We consider that "disguised restriction", whatever else it covers, may properly be read as embracing restrictions amounting to arbitrary or unjustifiable discrimination in international trade taken under the guise of a measure formally within the terms of an exception listed in Article XX. Put in a somewhat different manner, the kinds of considerations pertinent in deciding whether the application of a particular measure amounts to "arbitrary or unjustifiable discrimination", may also be taken into account in determining the presence of a "disguised restriction" on international trade. The fundamental theme is to be found in the purpose and object of avoiding abuse or illegitimate use of the exceptions to substantive rules available in Article XX.

There was more than one alternative course of action available to the United States in promulgating regulations implementing the CAA. These included the imposition of statutory baselines without differentiation as between domestic and imported gasoline. This approach, if properly implemented, could have avoided any discrimination at all. Among the other options open to the United States was to make available individual baselines to foreign refiners as well as domestic refiners. The United States has put forward a series of reasons why either of these courses was not, in its view, realistically open to it and why, instead, it had to devise and apply the baseline establishment rules contained in the Gasoline Rule.

In explaining why individual baselines for foreign refiners had not been put in place, the United States laid heavy stress upon the difficulties which the EPA would have had to face. These difficulties related to anticipated administrative problems that individual baselines for foreign refiners would have generated. This argument was made succinctly by the United States in the following terms:

> Verification on foreign soil of foreign baselines, and subsequent enforcement actions, present substantial difficulties relating to problems arising whenever a country exercises enforcement jurisdiction over foreign persons. In addition, even if individual baselines were established for several foreign refiners, the importer would be tempted to claim the refinery of origin that presented the most benefits in terms of baseline restrictions, and tracking the refinery or origin would be very difficult because gasoline is a fungible commodity. The United States should not have to prove that it cannot verify information and enforce its regulations in every instance in order to show that the same enforcement conditions do not prevail in the United States and other countries ... The impracticability of verification and enforcement of foreign refiner baselines in this instance shows that the "discrimination" is based on serious, not arbitrary or unjustifiable, concerns stemming from different conditions between enforcement of its laws in the United States and abroad.

Thus, according to the United States, imported gasoline was relegated to the more exacting statutory baseline requirement because of these difficulties of verification and enforcement. The United States stated that verification and enforcement of the Gasoline Rule's requirements for imported gasoline are "much easier when the statutory baseline is used" and that there would be a "dramatic difference" in the burden of administering requirements for imported gasoline if individual baselines were allowed.

While the anticipated difficulties concerning verification and subsequent enforcement are doubtless real to some degree, the Panel viewed them as insufficient to justify the denial to foreign refiners of individual baselines permitted to domestic refiners. The Panel said:

> While the Panel agreed that it would be necessary under such a system to ascertain the origin of gasoline, the Panel could not conclude that the United States had shown that this could not be achieved by other measures reasonably available to it and consistent or less inconsistent with the General Agreement. Indeed, the Panel noted that a determination of origin would often be feasible. The Panel examined, for instance, the case of a direct shipment to the United States. It considered that there was no reason to believe that, given the usual measures available in international trade for determination of origin and tracking of goods (including documentary evidence and third party verification) there was any particular difficulty sufficient to warrant the demands of the baseline establishment methods applied by the United States.

* * *

In the view of the Panel, the United States had reasonably available to it data for, and measures of, verification and assessment which were consistent or less inconsistent with Article III:4. For instance, although foreign data may be formally less subject to complete control by US authorities, this did not amount to establishing that foreign data could not in any circumstances be sufficiently reliable to serve U.S. purposes. This, however, was the practical effect of the application of the Gasoline Rule. In the Panel's view, the United States had not demonstrated that data available from foreign refiners was inherently less susceptible to established techniques of checking, verification, assessment and enforcement than data for other trade in goods subject to US regulation. The nature of the data in this case was similar to data relied upon by the United States in other contexts, including, for example, under the application of antidumping laws. In an antidumping case, only when the information was not supplied or deemed unverifiable did the United States turn to other information. If a similar practice were to be applied in the case of the Gasoline Rule, then importers could, for instance, be permitted to use the individual baselines of foreign refiners for imported gasoline from those refiners, with the statutory baseline being applied only when the source of imported gasoline could not be determined or a baseline could not be established because of an absence of data.

We agree with the finding above made in the Panel Report. There are, as the Panel Report found, established techniques for checking, verification, assessment and enforcement of data relating to imported goods, techniques which in many contexts are accepted as adequate to permit international trade—trade between territorial sovereigns—to go on and grow. The United States must have been aware that for these established techniques and procedures to work, cooperative arrangements with both foreign refiners and the foreign governments concerned would have been necessary and appropriate. At the oral hearing, in the course of responding to an enquiry as to whether the EPA could have adapted, for purposes of establishing individual refinery baselines for foreign refiners, procedures for verification of information found in U.S. antidumping laws, the United States said that "in the absence of refinery cooperation and the possible absence of foreign government cooperation as well", it was unlikely that the EPA auditors would be able to conduct the on-site audit reviews necessary to establish even the overall quality of refineries' 1990 gasoline. From this statement, there arises a strong implication, it appears to the Appellate Body, that the United States had not pursued the possibility of entering into cooperative arrangements with the governments of Venezuela and Brazil or, if it had, not to the point where it encountered governments that were unwilling to cooperate. The record of this case sets out the detailed justifications put forward by the United States. But it does not reveal what, if any, efforts had been taken by the United States to enter into appropriate procedures in cooperation with the governments of Venezuela and Brazil so as to mitigate the administrative problems pleaded by the United States. The fact that the United States Congress might have intervened, as it did later intervene, in the process by denying funding, is beside the point: the United States, of course, carries responsibility for actions of both the executive and legislative departments of government.

In its submissions, the United States also explained why the statutory baseline requirement was not imposed on domestic refiners as well. Here, the United States stressed the problems that domestic refineries would have faced had they been required to comply with the statutory baseline. The Panel Report summarized the United States' argument in the following terms:

> The United States concluded that, contrary to Venezuela's and Brazil's claim, Article XX did not require adoption of the statutory baseline as a national standard even if the difficulties associated with the establishment of individual baselines for importers were insurmountable. Application of the statutory baseline to domestic producers of reformulated and conventional gasoline in 1995 would have been physically and financially impossible because of the magnitude of the changes required in almost all US refineries; it thus would have caused a substantial delay in the programme.

Weighing the feasibility of policy options in economic or technical terms in order to meet an environmental objective was a legitimate consideration, and did not, in itself, constitute protectionism, as alleged by Venezuela and Brazil. Article XX did not require a government to choose the most expensive possible way to regulate its environment.

Clearly, the United States did not feel it feasible to require its domestic refiners to incur the physical and financial costs and burdens entailed by immediate compliance with a statutory baseline. The United States wished to give domestic refiners time to restructure their operations and adjust to the requirements in the Gasoline Rule. This may very well have constituted sound domestic policy from the viewpoint of the EPA and U.S. refiners. At the same time we are bound to note that, while the United States counted the costs for its domestic refiners of statutory baselines, there is nothing in the record to indicate that it did other than disregard that kind of consideration when it came to foreign refiners.

We have above located two omissions on the part of the United States: to explore adequately means, including in particular cooperation with the governments of Venezuela and Brazil, of mitigating the administrative problems relied on as justification by the United States for rejecting individual baselines for foreign refiners; and to count the costs for foreign refiners that would result from the imposition of statutory baselines. In our view, these two omissions go well beyond what was necessary for the Panel to determine that a violation of Article III:4 had occurred in the first place. The resulting discrimination must have been foreseen, and was not merely inadvertent or unavoidable. In the light of the foregoing, our conclusion is that the baseline establishment rules in the Gasoline Rule, in their application, constitute "unjustifiable discrimination" and a "disguised restriction on international trade." We hold, in sum, that the baseline establishment rules, although within the terms of Article XX(g), are not entitled to the justifying protection afforded by Article XX as a whole.

V. FINDINGS AND CONCLUSIONS

For the reasons set out in the preceding sections of this report, the Appellate Body has reached the following conclusions:

(a) the Panel erred in law in its conclusion that the baseline establishment rules contained in Part 80 of Title 40 of the Code of Federal Regulations did not fall within the terms of Article XX(g) of the General Agreement;

(b) the Panel accordingly also erred in law in failing to decide whether the baseline establishment rules contained in Part 80 of Title 40 of the Code of Federal Regulations fell within the ambit of the chapeau of Article XX of the General Agreement;

(c) the baseline establishment rules contained in Part 80 of Title 40 of the Code of Federal Regulations fail to meet the requirements of the chapeau of Article XX of the General Agreement, and accordingly are not justified under Article XX of the General Agreement.

The foregoing legal conclusions modify the conclusions of the Panel as set out in paragraph 8.1 of its Report. The Appellate Body's conclusions leave intact the conclusions of the Panel that were not the subject of appeal.

The Appellate Body recommends that the Dispute Settlement Body request the United States to bring the baseline establishment rules contained in Part 80 of Title 40 of the Code of Federal Regulations into conformity with its obligations under the General Agreement.

It is of some importance that the Appellate Body point out what this does not mean. It does not mean, or imply, that the ability of any WTO Member to take measures to control air pollution or, more generally, to protect the environment, is at issue. That would be to ignore the fact that Article XX of the General Agreement contains provisions designed to permit important state interests—including the protection of human health, as well as the conservation of exhaustible natural resources—to find expression. The provisions of Article XX were not changed as a result of the Uruguay Round of Multilateral Trade Negotiations. Indeed, in the preamble to the WTO Agreement and in the Decision on Trade and Environment, there is specific acknowledgement to be found about the importance of coordinating policies on trade and the environment. WTO Members have a large measure of autonomy to determine their own policies on the environment (including its relationship with trade), their environmental objectives and the environmental legislation they enact and implement. So far as concerns the WTO, that autonomy is circumscribed only by the need to respect the requirements of the General Agreement and the other covered agreements.

* * *

8.10 Summary of Advisory Opinion on the Legality of the Threat or Use of Nuclear Weapons. Issued by the International Court of Justice, 8 July 1996. U.N. Doc. A/51/218; *reprinted in* 35 I.L.M. 809 (1996) & 35 I.L.M. 1343 (1996)

Editor's note: The Court handed down its Advisory Opinion on the request made by the General Assembly of the United Nations on the question concerning the Legality of the Threat or Use of Nuclear Weapons.

The Court was composed as follows: *President* Bedjaoui, *Vice-President* Schwebel; *Judges* Oda, Guillaume, Shahabuddeen, Weeramantry, Ranjeva, Herczegh, Shi, Fleischhauer, Koroma, Vereshchetin, Ferrari Bravo, Higgins; *Registrar* Valencia-Ospina. *President* Bedjaoui, *Judges* Herczegh, Shi, Vereshchetin and Ferrari Bravo appended declarations to the Advisory Opinion of the Court; *Judges* Guillaume, Ranjeva and Fleischhauer appended separate opinions; *Vice-President* Schwebel, *Judges* Oda Shahabuddeen, Weeramantry, Koroma and Higgins appended dissenting opinions.

The various opinions, declarations and separate opinions cover over 200 pages, and are reprinted in 35 I.L.M. 809. The following summary was prepared by the Registrar of the ICJ.

Summary of the Advisory Opinion

Submission of the request and subsequent procedure (paras. 1–9)

The Court begins by recalling that by a letter dated 19 December 1994, filed in the Registry on 6 January 1995, the Secretary-General of the United Nations officially communicated to the Registrar the decision taken by the General Assembly to submit a question to the Court for an advisory opinion. The final paragraph of Resolution 49/75 K, adopted by the General Assembly on 15 December 1994, which sets forth the question, provides that the General Assembly

> "*Decides*, pursuant to Article 96, paragraph 1, of the Charter of the United Nations, to request the International Court of Justice urgently to render its advisory opinion on the following question: 'Is the threat or use of nuclear weapons in any circumstance permitted under international law?'."

The Court then recapitulates the various stages of the proceedings.

Jurisdiction of the Court (paras. 10–18)

The Court first considers whether it has the jurisdiction to give a reply to the request of the General Assembly for an Advisory Opinion and whether, should the answer be in the affirmative, there is any reason it should decline to exercise any such jurisdiction.

The Court observes that it draws its competence in respect of advisory opinions from Article 65, paragraph 1, of its Statute, while Article 96, paragraph 1 of the Charter provides that:

"The General Assembly or the Security Council may request the International Court of Justice to give an advisory opinion on any legal question."

Some States which oppose the giving of an opinion by the Court argued that the General Assembly and Security Council may ask for an advisory opinion on any legal question only within the scope of their activities. In the view of the Court, it matters little whether this interpretation of Article 96, paragraph 1, is or is not correct; in the present case, the General Assembly has competence in any event to seise the Court. Referring to Articles 10, 11 and 13 of the Charter, the Court finds that, indeed, the question put to the Court has a relevance to many aspects of the activities and concerns of the General Assembly including those relating to the threat or use of force in international relations, the disarmament process, and the progressive development of international law.

"Legal Question" (para. 13)

The Court observes that it has already had occasion to indicate that questions

> "framed in terms of law and rais[ing] problems of international law . . . are by their very nature susceptible of a reply based on law . . . [and] appear . . . to be questions of a legal character"

(*Western Sahara, Advisory Opinion, I.C.J. Reports 1975*, p. 18, para. 15).

It finds that the question put to the Court by the General Assembly is indeed a legal one, since the Court is asked to rule on the compatibility of the threat or use of nuclear weapons with the relevant principles and rules of international law. To do this, the Court must identify the existing principles and rules, interpret them and apply them to the threat or use of nuclear weapons, thus offering a reply to the question posed based on law.

The fact that this question also has political aspects, as, in the nature of things, is the case with so many questions which arise in international life, does not suffice to deprive it of its character as a "legal question" and to "deprive the Court of a competence expressly conferred on it by its Statute". Nor are the political nature of the motives which may be said to have inspired the request or the political implications that the opinion given might have of relevance in the establishment of the Court's jurisdiction to give such an opinion.

Discretion of the Court to give an advisory opinion (paras. 14–19)

Article 65, paragraph 1, of the Statute provides: "The Court *may* give an advisory opinion . . ." (Emphasis added.) This is more than an enabling provision. As the Court has repeatedly emphasized, the Statute leaves a discretion as to whether or not it will give an advisory opinion that has been requested of it, once it has established its competence to do so. In this context, the Court has previously noted as follows:

"The Court's Opinion is given not to the States, but to the organ which is entitled to request it; the reply of the Court, itself an 'organ of the United Nations', represents its participation in the activities of the Organization, and, in principle, should not be refused." (*Interpretation of Peace Treaties with Bulgaria, Hungary and Romania, First Phase, Advisory Opinion, I.C.J. Reports 1950*, p. 71; . . .)"

In the history of the present Court there has been no refusal, based on the discretionary power of the Court, to act upon a request for advisory opinion; in the case concerning the *Legality of the Use by a State of Nuclear Weapons in Armed Conflict* the refusal to give the World Health Organization the advisory opinion requested by it was justified by the Court's lack of jurisdiction in that case.

Several reasons were adduced in these proceedings in order to persuade the Court that in the exercise of its discretionary power it should decline to render the opinion requested by the General Assembly. Some States, in contending that the question put to the Court is vague and abstract, appeared to mean by this that there exists no specific dispute on the subject-matter of the question. In order to respond to this argument, it is necessary to distinguish between requirements governing contentious procedure and those applicable to advisory opinions. The purpose of the advisory function is not to settle—at least directly—disputes between States, but to offer legal advice to the organs and institutions requesting the opinion. The fact that the question put to the Court does not relate to a specific dispute should consequently not lead the Court to decline to give the opinion requested. Other arguments concerned the fear that the abstract nature of the question might lead the Court to make hypothetical or speculative declarations outside the scope of its judicial function; the fact that the General Assembly has not explained to the Court for what precise purposes it seeks the advisory opinion; that a reply from the Court in this case might adversely affect disarmament negotiations and would, therefore, be contrary to the interest of the United Nations; and that in answering the question posed, the Court would be going beyond its judicial role and would be taking upon itself a law-making capacity.

The Court does not accept those arguments and concludes that it has the authority to deliver an opinion on the question posed by the General Assembly, and that there exist no "compelling reasons" which would lead the Court to exercise its discretion not to do so. It points out, however, that it is an entirely different question whether, under the constraints placed upon it as a judicial organ, it will be able to give a complete answer to the question asked of it. But that is a different matter from a refusal to answer at all.

Formulation of the question posed (paras. 20 and 22)

The Court finds it unnecessary to pronounce on the possible divergences between the English and French texts of the question put. Its real objective is clear: to determine the legality or illegality of the threat or use of nuclear weapons. And the argument concerning the legal conclusions to be drawn from the use of the word "permitted", and the questions of burden of proof to which it was said to give rise, are found by the Court to be without particular significance for the disposition of the issues before it.

The Applicable Law (paras. 23–34)

In seeking to answer the question put to it by the General Assembly, the Court must decide, after consideration of the great corpus of international law norms available to it, what might be the relevant applicable law.

The Court considers that the question whether a particular loss of life, through the use of a certain weapon in warfare, is to be considered an arbitrary deprivation of life contrary to Article 6 of the International Covenant on Civil and Political Rights, as argued by some of the proponents of the illegality of the use of nuclear weapons, can only be decided by reference to the law applicable in armed conflict and not deduced from the terms of the Covenant itself. The Court also points out that the prohibition of genocide would be pertinent in this case if the recourse to nuclear weapons did indeed entail the element of intent, towards a group as such, required by Article II of the Convention on the Prevention and Punishment of the Crime of Genocide. In the view of the Court, it would only be possible to arrive at such a conclusion after having taken due account of the circumstances specific to each case. And the Court further finds that while the existing international law relating to the protection and safeguarding of the environment does not specifically prohibit the use of nuclear weapons, it indicates important environmental factors that are properly to be taken into account in the context of the implementation of the principles and rules of the law applicable in armed conflict.

In the light of the foregoing the Court concludes that the most directly relevant applicable law governing the question of which it was seised, is that relating to the use of force enshrined in the United Nations Charter and the law applicable in armed conflict which regulates the conduct of hostilities, together with any specific treaties on nuclear weapons that the Court might determine to be relevant.

Unique characteristics of nuclear weapons (paras. 35 and 36)

The Court notes that in order correctly to apply to the present case the Charter law on the use of force and the law applicable in armed conflict, in particular humanitarian law, it is imperative for it to take account of the unique characteristics of nuclear weapons, and in particular their destructive capacity, their capacity to cause untold human suffering, and their ability to cause damage to generations to come.

Provisions of the Charter relating to the threat or use of force (paras. 37–50)

The Court then addresses the question of the legality or illegality of recourse to nuclear weapons in the light of the provisions of the Charter relating to the threat or use of force.

In Article 2, paragraph 4, of the Charter the use of force against the territorial integrity or political independence of another State or in any other manner inconsistent with the purposes of the United Nations is prohibited.

This prohibition of the use of force is to be considered in the light of other relevant provisions of the Charter. In Article 51, the Charter recognizes the inherent right of individual or collective self-defence if an armed attack occurs. A further lawful use of force is envisaged in Article 42, whereby the Security Council may take military enforcement measures in conformity with Chapter VII of the Charter.

These provisions do not refer to specific weapons. They apply to any use of force, regardless of the weapons employed. The Charter neither expressly prohibits, nor permits, the use of any specific weapon, including nuclear weapons.

The entitlement to resort to self-defence under Article 51 is subject to the conditions of necessity and proportionality. As the Court stated in the case concerning *Military and Paramilitary Activities in and against Nicaragua (Nicaragua* v. *United States of America) (I.C.J. Reports 1986*, p. 94, para. 176): "there is a specific rule whereby self-defence would warrant only measures which are proportional to the armed attack and necessary to respond to it, a rule well established in customary international law".

The proportionality principle may thus not in itself exclude the use of nuclear weapons in self-defence in all circumstances. But at the same time, a use of force that is proportionate under the law of self-defence, must, in order to be lawful, also meet the requirements of the law applicable in armed conflict which comprise in particular the principles and rules of humanitarian law. And the Court notes that the very nature of all nuclear weapons and the profound risks associated therewith are further considerations to be borne in mind by States believing they can exercise a nuclear response in self-defence in accordance with the requirements of proportionality.

In order to lessen or eliminate the risk of unlawful attack, States sometimes signal that they possess certain weapons to use in self-defence against any State violating their territorial integrity or political independence. Whether a signaled intention to use force if certain events occur is or is not a "threat" within Article 2, paragraph 4, of the Charter depends upon various factors. The notions of "threat" and "use" of force under Article 2, paragraph 4, of the Charter stand together in the sense that if the use of force itself in a given case is illegal—for whatever reason—the threat to use such force will likewise be illegal. In short, if it is to be lawful, the declared readiness of a State to use force must be a use of force that is in conformity with the Charter. For the rest, no State—whether or not it defended the policy of deterrence—suggested to the Court that it would be lawful to threaten to use force if the use of force contemplated would be illegal.

Rules on the lawfulness or unlawfulness of nuclear weapons as such (paras. 49–73)

Having dealt with the Charter provisions relating to the threat or use of force, the Court turns to the law applicable in situations of armed conflict. It first addresses the question whether there are specific rules in international law regulating the legality or illegality of recourse to nuclear weapons *per se*; it then examines the question put to it in the light of the law applicable in armed conflict proper, i.e. the principles and rules of humanitarian law applicable in armed conflict, and the law of neutrality.

The Court notes by way of introduction that international customary and treaty law does not contain any specific prescription authorizing the threat or use of nuclear weapons or any other weapon in general or in certain circumstances, in particular those of the exercise of legitimate self-defence. Nor, however, is there any principle or rule of international law which would make the legality of the threat or use of nuclear weapons or of any other weapons dependent on a specific authorization. State practice shows that the illegality of the use of certain weapons as such does not result from an absence of authorization but, on the contrary, is formulated in terms of prohibition.

It does not seem to the Court that the use of nuclear weapons can be regarded as specifically prohibited on the basis of certain provisions of the Second Hague Declaration of 1899, the Regulations annexed to the Hague Convention IV of 1907 or the 1925 Geneva Protocol. The pattern until now has been for weapons of mass destruction to be declared illegal by specific instruments. But the Court does not find any specific prohibition of recourse to nuclear weapons in treaties expressly prohibiting the use of certain weapons of mass destruction; and observes that, although, in the last two decades, a great many negotiations have been conducted regarding nuclear weapons, they have not resulted in a treaty of general prohibition of the same kind as for bacteriological and chemical weapons.

The Court notes that the treaties dealing exclusively with acquisition, manufacture, possession, deployment and testing of nuclear weapons, without specifically addressing their threat or use, certainly point to an increasing concern in the international community with these weapons; It concludes from this that these treaties could therefore be seen as foreshadowing a future general prohibition of the use of such weapons, but that they do not constitute such a prohibition by themselves. As to the treaties of Tlatelolco and Rarotonga and their Protocols, and also the declarations made in connection with the indefinite extension of the Treaty on the Non–Proliferation of Nuclear Weapons, it emerges from these instruments that:

(a) a number of States have undertaken not to use nuclear weapons in specific zones (Latin America; the South Pacific) or against certain other States (non-nuclear-weapon States which are parties to the Treaty on the Non–Proliferation of Nuclear Weapons);

(b) nevertheless, even within this framework, the nuclear-weapon States have reserved the right to use nuclear weapons in certain circumstances; and

(c) these reservations met with no objection from the parties to the Tlatelolco or Rarotonga Treaties or from the Security Council.

The Court then turns to an examination of customary international law to determine whether a prohibition of the threat or use of nuclear weapons as such flows from that source of law.

It notes that the Members of the international community are profoundly divided on the matter of whether non-recourse to nuclear weapons over the past fifty years constitutes the expression of an *opinio juris*. Under these circumstances the Court does not consider itself able to find that there is such an *opinio juris*. It points out that the adoption each year by the General Assembly, by a large majority, of resolutions recalling the content of resolution 1653 (XVI), and requesting the member States to conclude a convention prohibiting the use of nuclear weapons in any circumstance, reveals the desire of a very large section of the international community to take, by a specific and express prohibition of the use of nuclear weapons, a significant step forward along the road to complete nuclear disarmament. The emergence, as *lex lata*, of a customary rule specifically prohibiting the use of nuclear weapons as such is hampered by the continuing tensions between the nascent *opinio juris* on the one hand, and the still strong adherence to the doctrine of deterrence(in which the right to use those weapons in the exercise of the right to self-defence against an armed attack threatening the vital security interests of the State is reserved) on the other.

International humanitarian law (paras. 74–87)

Not having found a conventional rule of general scope, nor a customary rule specifically proscribing the threat or use of nuclear weapons *per se*, the Court then deals with the question whether recourse to nuclear weapons must be considered as illegal in the light of the principles and rules of international humanitarian law applicable in armed conflict and of the law of neutrality.

After sketching the historical development of the body of rules which originally were called "laws and customs of war" and later came to be termed "international humanitarian law", the Court observes that the cardinal principles contained in the texts constituting the fabric of humanitarian law are the following. The first is aimed at the protection of the civilian population and civilian objects and establishes the distinction between combatants and non-combatants; States must never make civilians the object of attack and must consequently never use weapons that are incapable of distinguishing between civilian and military targets. According to the second principle, it is prohibited to cause unnecessary suffering to combatants: it is accordingly prohibited to use weapons causing them such harm or uselessly aggravating their suffering. In application of that second principle, States do not have unlimited freedom of choice of means in the weapons they use.

The Court also refers to the Martens Clause, which was first included in the Hague Convention II with Respect to the Laws and Customs of War on Land of 1899 and which has proved to be an effective means of addressing the rapid evolution of military technology. A modern version of that clause is to be found in Article 1, paragraph 2, of Additional Protocol I of 1977, which reads as follows:

> In cases not covered by this Protocol or by other international agreements, civilians and combatants remain under the protection and authority of the principles of international law derived from established custom, from the principles of humanity and from the dictates of public conscience."

The extensive codification of humanitarian law and the extent of the accession to the resultant treaties, as well as the fact that the denunciation clauses that existed in the codification instruments have never been used, have provided the international community with a corpus of treaty rules the great majority of which had already become customary and which reflected the most universally recognized humanitarian principles. These rules indicate the normal conduct and behaviour expected of States.

Turning to the applicability of the principles and rules of humanitarian law to a possible threat or use of nuclear weapons, the Court notes that nuclear weapons were invented after most of the principles and rules of humanitarian law applicable in armed conflict had already come into existence; the Conferences of 1949 and 1974–1977 left these weapons aside, and there is a qualitative as well as quantitative difference between nuclear weapons and all conventional arms. However, in the Court's view, it cannot be concluded from this that the established principles and rules of humanitarian law applicable in armed conflict did not apply to nuclear weapons. Such a conclusion would be incompatible with the intrinsically humanitarian character of the legal principles in question which permeates the entire law of armed conflict and applies to all forms of warfare and to all kinds of weapons, those of the past, those of the present and those of the future. In this respect it seems significant that the thesis that the rules of humanitarian law do not apply to the new weaponry, because of the newness of the latter, has not been advocated in the present proceedings.

The principle of neutrality (paras. 88 and 89)

The Court finds that as in the case of the principles of humanitarian law applicable in armed conflict, international law leaves no doubt that the principle of neutrality, whatever its content, which is of a fundamental character similar to that of the humanitarian principles and rules, is applicable (subject to the relevant provisions of the United Nations Charter), to all international armed conflict, whatever type of weapons might be used.

Conclusions to be drawn from the applicability of international humanitarian law and the principle of neutrality (paras. 90–97)

The Court observes that, although the applicability of the principles and rules of humanitarian law and of the principle of neutrality to nuclear weapons is hardly disputed, the conclusions to be drawn from this applicability are, on the other hand, controversial.

According to one point of view, the fact that recourse to nuclear weapons is subject to and regulated by the law of armed conflict, does not necessarily mean that such recourse is as such prohibited. Another view holds that recourse to nuclear weapons, in view of the necessarily indiscriminate consequences of their use, could never be compatible with the principles and rules of humanitarian law and is therefore prohibited. A similar view has been expressed with respect to the effects of the principle of neutrality. Like the principles and rules of humanitarian law, that principle has therefore been considered by some to rule out the use of a weapon the effects of which simply cannot be contained within the territories of the contending States.

The Court observes that, in view of the unique characteristics of nuclear weapons, to which the Court has referred above, the use of such weapons in fact seems scarcely reconcilable with respect for the requirements of the law applicable in armed conflict. It considers nevertheless, that it does not have sufficient elements to enable it to conclude with certainty that the use of nuclear weapons would necessarily be at variance with the principles and rules of law applicable in armed conflict in any circumstance. Furthermore, the Court cannot lose sight of the fundamental right of every State to survival, and thus its right to resort to self-defence, in accordance with Article 51 of the Charter, when its survival is at stake. Nor can it ignore the practice referred to as "policy of deterrence", to which an appreciable section of the international community adhered for many years.

Accordingly, in view of the present state of international law viewed as a whole, as examined by the Court, and of the elements of fact at its disposal, the Court is led to observe that it cannot reach a definitive conclusion as to the legality or illegality of the use of nuclear weapons by a State in an extreme circumstance of self-defence, in which its very survival would be at stake.

Obligation to negotiate nuclear disarmament (paras. 98–103)

Given the eminently difficult issues that arise in applying the law on the use of force and above all the law applicable in armed conflict to nuclear weapons, the Court considers that it needs to examine one further aspect of the question before it, seen in a broader context.

In the long run, international law, and with it the stability of the international order which it is intended to govern, are bound to suffer from the continuing difference of views with regard to the legal status of weapons as deadly as nuclear weapons. It is consequently important to put an end to this state of affairs: the long-promised complete nuclear disarmament appears to be the most appropriate means of achieving that result.

In these circumstances, the Court appreciates the full importance of the recognition by Article VI of the Treaty on the Non–Proliferation of Nuclear Weapons of an obligation to negotiate in good faith a nuclear disarmament. The legal import of that obligation goes beyond that of a mere obligation of conduct; the obligation involved here is an obligation to achieve a precise result—nuclear disarmament in all its aspects—by adopting a particular course of conduct, namely, the pursuit of negotiations on the matter in good faith. This twofold obligation to pursue and to conclude negotiations formally concerns the 182 States parties to the Treaty on the Non–Proliferation of Nuclear Weapons, or, in other words, the vast majority of the international community. Indeed, any realistic search for general and complete disarmament, especially nuclear disarmament, necessitates the co-operation of all States.

* * *

The Court finally emphasizes that its reply to the question put to it by the General Assembly rests on the totality of the legal grounds set forth by the Court above (paragraphs 20 to 103), each of which is to be read in the light of the others. Some of these grounds are not such as to form the object of formal conclusions in the final paragraph of the Opinion; they nevertheless retain, in the view of the Court, all their importance.

Declaration of President Bedjaoui

After having pointed out that paragraph E of the operative part was adopted by seven votes to seven, with his own casting vote, President Bedjaoui began by stressing that the Court had been extremely meticulous and had shown an acute sense of its responsibilities when proceeding to consider all the aspects of the complex question put to it by the General Assembly. He indicated that the Court had, however, had to find that in the current state of international law, the question was one to which it was unfortunately not in a position to give a clear answer. In his view, the Advisory Opinion thus rendered does at least have the merit of pointing to the imperfections of international law and inviting the States to correct them.

President Bedjaoui indicated that the fact that the Court was unable to go any further should not "in any way be interpreted as leaving the way open to the recognition of the lawfulness of the threat or use of nuclear weapons". According to him, the Court does no more than place on record the existence of a legal uncertainty. After having observed that the voting of the Members of the Court on paragraph E of the operative part is not the reflection of any geographical dividing line, he gives the reasons that led him to approve the pronouncement of the Court.

To that end, he began by emphasizing the particularly exacting nature of international law and the way in which it is designed to be applied in all circumstances. More specifically, he concluded that

> "*the very nature of this blind weapon therefore has a destabilizing effect on humanitarian law which regulates discernment in the type of weapon used. Nuclear weapons, the ultimate evil, destabilize humanitarian law which is the law of the lesser evil. The existence of nuclear weapons is therefore a challenge to the very existence of humanitarian law*, not to mention their long-term effects of damage to the human environment, in respect to which the *right to life* can be exercised".

President Bedjaoui considered that "self-defence—if exercised under extreme circumstances in which the very survival of a State is in question—cannot engender a situation in which a State would exonerate itself from compliance with the *"intransgressible"* norms of international humanitarian law". According to him it would be very rash to accord, without any hesitation, a higher priority to the survival of a State than to the survival of humanity itself.

As the ultimate objective of any action in the field of nuclear weapons is nuclear disarmament, President Bedjaoui concludes by stressing the importance of the obligation to negotiate in good faith for nuclear disarmament—which the Court has moreover recognized. He considers for his part that it is possible to go beyond the conclusions of the Court in this regard and to assert "that there in fact exists a twofold *general obligation*, opposable *erga omnes*, to negotiate in good faith and to achieve a specified result"; in other words, given the at least formally unanimous support for that object, that obligation has now—in his view—assumed customary force.

Declaration of Judge Herczegh

Judge Herczegh, in his declaration, takes the view that the Advisory Opinion could have included a more accurate summary of the present state of international law with regard to the question of the threat and use of nuclear weapons "in any circumstance". He voted in favour of the Advisory Opinion and, more particularly, in favour of paragraph 105, sub-paragraph E, as he did not wish to disassociate himself from the large number of conclusions that were expressed and integrated into the Advisory Opinion, and which he fully endorses.

Declaration Judge Shi

Judge Shi has voted in favour of the operative paragraphs of the Advisory Opinion of the Court. However, he has reservations with regard to the role which the Court assigns to the policy of deterrence in determining the existence of a customary rule on the use of nuclear weapons.

In his view, "nuclear deterrence" is an instrument of policy to which certain nuclear-weapon States, supported by those States accepting nuclear umbrella protection, adhere in their relations with other States. This practice is within the realm of international politics and has no legal value from the standpoint of the formation of a customary rule prohibiting the use of the weapons as such.

It would be hardly compatible with the Court's judicial function if the Court, in determining a rule of existing law governing the use of the weapons, were to have regard to the "policy of deterrence".

Also, leaving aside the nature of the policy of deterrence, States adhering to the policy of deterrence, though important and powerful members of the international community and playing an important role on the stage of international politics, by no means constitute a large proportion of the membership of the international community.

Besides, the structure of the community of states is built on the principle of sovereign equality. The Court cannot view these nuclear-weapon States and their allies in terms of material power, rather should have regard of them from the standpoint of international law. Any undue emphasis on the practice of these materially powerful States, constituting a fraction of membership of the community of States, would not only be contrary to the principle of sovereign equality of States, but also make it more difficult to give an accurate and proper view of the existence of a customary rule on the use of nuclear weapons.

Declaration of Judge Vereshchetin

In his declaration Judge Vereshchetin explains the reasons which have led him to vote in favour of paragraph 2E of the *dispositif,* which carries the implication of the indecisiveness of the Court. In his view, in advisory procedure, where the Court is requested not to resolve an actual dispute, but to state the law as it finds it, the Court may not try to fill any lacuna or improve the law which is imperfect. The Court cannot be blamed for indecisiveness or evasiveness where the law, upon which it is called to pronounce, is itself inconclusive.

Judge Vereshchetin is of the view that the Opinion adequately reflects the current legal situation and shows the most appropriate means to putting an end to the existence of any "grey areas" in the legal status of nuclear weapons.

Declaration of Judge Ferrari Bravo

Judge Ferrari Bravo regrets that the Court should have arbitrarily divided into two categories the long line of General Assembly resolutions that deal with nuclear weapons. Those resolutions are fundamental. This is the case of resolution 1 (I) of 24

January 1946, which clearly points to the existence of a truly solemn *undertaking* to eliminate all forms of nuclear weapons, whose presence in military arsenals was declared unlawful. The Cold War, which intervened shortly afterwards, prevented the *development* of this concept of illegality, while giving rise to the concept of nuclear deterrence which has *no legal value*. The theory of deterrence, while it has occasioned a practice of the nuclear-weapon States and their allies, has not been able to create a legal practice serving as a basis for the incipient creation of an international custom. It has, moreover, helped to widen the gap between Article 2, paragraph 4 of the Charter and Article 51.

The Court should have proceeded to a constructive analysis of the role of the General Assembly resolutions. These have, from the outset, contributed to the formation of a rule prohibiting nuclear weapons. The theory of deterrence has arrested the development of that rule and, while it has prevented the *implementation* of the prohibition of nuclear weapons, it is nonetheless still the case that that "bare" prohibition has remained unchanged and continues to produce its effects, at least with regard to the burden of proof, by making it more difficult for the nuclear powers to vindicate their policies within the framework of the theory of deterrence.

Separate opinion of Judge Guillaume

After having pondered upon the admissibility of the request for advisory opinion, Judge Guillaume begins by expressing his agreement with the Court with regard to the fact that nuclear weapons, like all weapons, can only be used in the exercise of the right of self-defence recognized by Article 51 of the Charter. On the other hand, he says he has had doubts about the applicability of traditional humanitarian law to the use—and above all the threat of use—of nuclear weapons. He goes on to say, however, that he has no choice in the matter but to defer to the consensus that has emerged before the Court between the States.

Moving on to an analysis of the law applicable to armed conflict, he notes that that law essentially implies comparisons in which humanitarian considerations have to be weighed against military requirements. Thus the collateral damage caused to the civilian population must not be "excessive" as compared to the "military advantage" offered. The harm caused to combatants must not be "greater than that unavoidable to achieve legitimate military objectives". On that account, nuclear weapons of mass destruction can only be used lawfully in extreme cases.

In an attempt to define those cases, Judge Guillaume stresses that neither the Charter of the United Nations, nor any conventional or customary rule can detract from the natural right of self-defence recognized by Article 51 of the Charter. He deduces from this that international law cannot deprive a State of the right to resort to nuclear weaponry if that resort constitutes the ultimate means by which it can ensure its survival.

He regrets that the Court has not explicitly recognized this, but stresses that it has done so implicitly. It has certainly concluded that it could not, in those extreme circumstances, make a definitive finding either of legality of illegality in relation to nuclear weapons. In other words, it has taken the view that, in such circumstances, the law provides no guidance to States. However if the law is silent on that matter, the States, in the exercise of their sovereignty, remain free to act as they think fit.

Consequently, it follows implicitly but necessarily from paragraph 2 E of the Court's Advisory Opinion that the States may resort to "the threat or use of nuclear weapons in an extreme circumstance of self-defence, in which the very survival of a State would be at stake". When recognizing such a right the Court, by so doing, has recognized the legality of policies of deterrence.

Separate opinion of Judge Ranjeva

In his separate opinion, Judge Ranjeva has made a point of emphasizing that, for the first time, the Court has unambiguously stated that the use or threat of use of nuclear weapons is contrary to the rules of international law applicable *inter alia* to armed conflict and, more particularly, to the principles and rules of humanitarian law. That indirect response to the question of the General Assembly is, in his view, justified by the very nature of the law of armed conflict, applicable without regard to the status of victim or of aggressor, and that explains why the Court has not gone so far as to uphold the exception of extreme self-defence when the very survival of the State is at stake, as a condition for the suspension of illegality. In his view, the State practice shows that a point of no return has been reached: the principle of the legality of the use or threat of use of nuclear weapons has not been asserted; it is on the basis of a justification of an exception to that principle, accepted as being legal, that the nuclear-weapon States attempt to give the reasons for their policies, and the increasingly closer-knit legal régimes of nuclear weapons have come about in the context of the consolidation and implementation of the final obligation to produce a specific result, i.e., generalized nuclear disarmament. These "givens" thus represent the advent of a consistent and uniform practice: an emergent *opinio juris*.

Judge Ranjeva considers, however, that the equal treatment that the Advisory Opinion has given to the principles of legality and illegality cannot be justified. The General Assembly gave a very clear definition of the object of its question: does international law authorize the use or threat of use of nuclear weapons in any circumstance? By dealing at the same time and, above all, on the same level with both legality and illegality, the Court has been led to adopt a liberal acceptation of the concept of a "legal question" in an advisory proceeding, as henceforth any question whose object is to ask the Court to look into matters that some people do not seek to understand, will be seen as admissible.

In conclusion, Judge Ranjeva, while being aware of the criticisms that specialists in law and judicial matters will be bound to level at the Advisory Opinion, ultimately considers that it does declare the law as it is, while laying down boundaries the exceeding of which is a matter for the competence of States. He nonetheless hopes that no Court will ever have to reach a decision along the lines of the second sub-paragraph of paragraph E.

Separate opinion of Judge Fleischhauer

Judge Fleischhauer's separate opinion highlights that international law is still grappling with and has not yet overcome the dichotomy that is created by the very existence of nuclear weapons between the law applicable in armed conflict, and in particular the rules and principles of humanitarian law on the one side, and the inherent right of self-defence on the other. The known qualities of nuclear weapons let their use appear scarcely reconcilable with humanitarian law, while the right to self-defence would be severely curtailed if for a State, victim of an attack with nuclear, chemical or bacteriological weapons or otherwise constituting a deadly menace for its very existence, nuclear weapons were totally ruled out as an ultimate legal option.

The separate opinion endorses the Court's finding that international law applicable in armed conflict, and particularly the rules and principles of humanitarian law, apply to nuclear weapons. It goes on to agree with the Court's Conclusion that the threat or use of nuclear weapons would generally be contrary to the rules applicable in armed conflict, and in particular the principles and rules of humanitarian law. The separate opinion then welcomes that the Court did not stop there, but that the Court admitted that there can be qualifications to that finding. Had the Court not done so, then it would have given prevalence to one set of the principles involved over the other. The principles involved are, however, all legal principles of equal rank.

The separate opinion continues that the Court could and should have gone further and that it could and should have stated, that in order to reconcile the conflicting principles, their smallest common denominator would apply. That means that recourse to nuclear weapons could remain a justified legal option in an extreme case of individual or collective self-defence as the last resort of a State victim of an attack with nuclear, bacteriological or chemical weapons or otherwise threatening its very existence. The separate opinion sees a confirmation of this view in the legally relevant State practice relating to matters of self-defence.

For a recourse to nuclear weapons to be considered justified, however, not only would the situation have to be extreme, but all the conditions on which the lawfulness of the exercise of the right of self-defence depends in international law, including the requirement of proportionality, would have to be met. Therefore the margin for considering that a particular threat or use of nuclear weapons could be legal, is extremely narrow.

Finally, the separate opinion endorses the existence of a general obligation of States to pursue in good faith, and bring to a conclusion, negotiations leading to nuclear disarmament in all its aspects under strict and effective international control.

Dissenting opinion of Vice–President Schwebel

Vice–President Schwebel, while agreeing with much of the body of the Court's Opinion, dissented because of his "profound" disagreement with its principal operative conclusion: "The Court cannot conclude definitively whether the threat or use of nuclear weapons would be lawful or unlawful an extreme circumstance of self-defence, in which the very survival of a State would be at stake." The Court thereby concluded "on the supreme issue of the threat or use of force of our age that it has no opinion ... that international law and hence the Court have nothing to say. After many months of agonizing appraisal of the law, the Court discovers that there is none. When it comes to the supreme interests of State, the Court discards the legal progress of the Twentieth Century, puts aside the provisions of the United Nations Charter of which it is 'the principal judicial organ', and proclaims, in terms redolent of *Realpolitik*, its ambivalence about the most important provisions of modern international law. If this was to be its ultimate holding, the Court would have done better to have drawn on its undoubted discretion not to render an Opinion at all."

The Court's inconclusiveness was in accordance neither with its Statute, nor its precedent, nor with events which demonstrate the legality of the threat or use of nuclear weapons in extraordinary circumstances. E.g., the threat which Iraq took as a nuclear threat that may have deterred it from using chemical and biological weapons against coalition forces in the Gulf War was "not only eminently lawful but intensely desirable".

While the principles of international humanitarian law govern the use of nuclear weapons, and while "it is extraordinarily difficult to reconcile the use ... of nuclear weapons with the application of those principles", it does not follow that the use of nuclear weapons necessarily and invariably will contravene those principles. But it cannot be accepted that the use of nuclear weapons on a scale which would—or could—result in the deaths of "many millions in indiscriminate inferno and by far-reaching fallout ... and render uninhabitable much or all of the earth, could be lawful." The Court's conclusion that the threat or use of nuclear weapons "generally" would be contrary to the rules of international law applicable in armed conflict "is not unreasonable."

The case as a whole presents an unparalleled tension between State practice and legal principle. State practice demonstrates that nuclear weapons have been manufactured and deployed for some 50 years; that in that deployment inheres a threat of possible use ("deterrence"); and that the international community, far from outlawing the threat or use of nuclear weapons in all circumstances, has recognized in effect or in terms that in certain circumstances nuclear weapons may be used or their use threatened. This State practice is not that of a lone and secondary persistent objector, but a practice of the permanent Members of the Security Council, supported by a large and weighty number of other States, who together represent the bulk of the world's power and much of its population.

The Nuclear Non–Proliferation Treaty and the negative and positive security assurances of the nuclear Powers unanimously accepted by the Security Council indicate the acceptance by the international community of the threat or use of nuclear weapons in certain circumstances. Other nuclear treaties equally infer that nuclear weapons are not comprehensively prohibited either by treaty or customary international law.

General Assembly resolutions to the contrary are not law-making or declaratory of existing international law. When faced with continuing and significant opposition, the repetition of General Assembly resolutions is a mark of ineffectuality in law formation as it is in practical effect.

Dissenting opinion of Judge Oda

Judge Oda voted against part one of the Court's Advisory Opinion because of his view that, for the reasons of judicial propriety and judicial economy, the Court should have exercised its discretionary power to refrain from rendering an Opinion in response to the Request.

In the view of Judge Oda, the question in the Request is not adequately drafted and there was a lack of meaningful consensus of the General Assembly with regard to the 1994 Request. After examining the developments of the relevant General Assembly resolutions on a convention on the prohibition of the use of nuclear weapons up to 1994, he notes that the General Assembly is far from having reached an agreement on the preparation of a Convention rendering the use of nuclear weapons illegal. In the light of that history, the Request was prepared and drafted—not in order to ascertain the status of existing international law on the subject but to try to promote the total elimination of nuclear weapons—that is to say, with highly *political* motives.

He notes that the perpetuation of the NPT régime recognizes two groups of States—the five nuclear-weapon States and the non-nuclear-weapon States. As the five nuclear-weapon States have repeatedly given assurances to the non-nuclear-weapon States of their intention not to use nuclear weapons against them, there is almost no probability of any use of nuclear weapons given the current doctrine of nuclear deterrence.

Judge Oda maintains that an advisory opinion should only be given in the event of a real need. In the present instance there is no need and no rational justification for the General Assembly's request that the Court give an advisory opinion on the existing international law relating to the use of nuclear weapons. He also emphasizes that from the standpoint of judicial economy the right to request an advisory opinion should not be abused.

In concluding his Opinion, Judge Oda stresses his earnest hope that nuclear weapons will be eliminated from the world but states that the decision on this matter is a function of political negotiations among States in Geneva (the Conference on Disarmament) or New York (United Nations) but not one which concerns this judicial institution in The Hague.

He voted against sub-paragraph E as the equivocations contained therein serve, in his view, to confirm his point that it would have been prudent for the Court to decline from the outset to give any opinion at all in the present case.

Dissenting opinion of Judge Shahabuddeen

In Judge Shahabuddeen's dissenting opinion, the essence of the General Assembly's question was whether, in the special case of nuclear weapons, it was possible to reconcile the imperative need of a State to defend itself with the no less imperative need to ensure that, in doing so, it did not imperil the survival of the human species. If a reconciliation was not possible, which side should give way? The question was, admittedly, a difficult one; but the responsibility of the Court to answer it was clear. He was not persuaded that there was any deficiency in the law or the facts which prevented the Court from returning a definitive answer to the real point of the General Assembly's question. In his respectful view, the Court should and could have given a definitive answer—one way or another.

Dissenting opinion of Judge Weeramantry

Judge Weeramantry's Opinion is based on the proposition that the use or threat of use of nuclear weapons is illegal *in any circumstances whatsoever*. It violates the fundamental principles of international law, and represents the very negation of the humanitarian concerns which underlie the structure of humanitarian law. It offends conventional law and, in particular, the Geneva Gas Protocol of 1925, and Article 23*(a)* of the Hague Regulations of 1907. It contradicts the fundamental principle of the dignity and worth of the human person on which all law depends. It endangers the human environment in a manner which threatens the entirety of life on the planet.

He regretted that the Court had not so held, directly and categorically.

However, there were some portions of the Court's Opinion which were of value, in that it expressly held that nuclear weapons were subject to limitations flowing from the United Nations Charter, the general principles of international law, the principles of international humanitarian law, and by a variety of treaty obligations. It was the first international judicial determination to this effect and further clarifications were possible in the future.

Judge Weeramantry's Opinion explained that from the time of Henri Dunant, humanitarian law took its origin and inspiration from a realistic perception of the brutalities of war, and the need to restrain them in accordance with the dictates of the conscience of humanity. The brutalities of the nuclear weapon multiplied a thousand-fold all the brutalities of war as known in the pre-nuclear era. It was doubly clear therefore that the principles of humanitarian law governed this situation.

His Opinion examined in some detail the brutalities of nuclear war, showing numerous ways in which the nuclear weapon was unique, even among weapons of mass destruction in injuring human health, damaging the environment, and destroying all the values of civilization.

The nuclear weapon caused death and destruction; induced cancers, leukaemia, keloids and related afflictions; caused gastro intestinal, cardiovascular and related afflictions; continued, for decades after its use, to induce the health-related problems mentioned above; damaged the environmental rights of future generations; caused congenital deformities, mental retardation and genetic damage; carried the potential to cause a nuclear winter; contaminated and destroyed the food chain; imperilled the eco-system; produced lethal levels of heat and blast; produced radiation and radioactive fall-out; produced a disruptive electromagnetic pulse; produced social disintegration; imperilled all civilization; threatened human survival; wreaked cultural devastation; spanned a time range of thousands of years; threatened all life on the planet; irreversibly damaged the rights of future generations; exterminated civilian populations; damaged neighbouring States; produced psychological stress and fear syndromes—*as no other weapons do.*

While it was true that there was no treaty or rule of law which expressly outlawed nuclear weapons by name, there was an abundance of principles of international law, and particularly international humanitarian law, which left no doubt regarding the illegality of nuclear weapons, when one had regard to their known effects.

Among these principles were the prohibition against causing unnecessary suffering, the principle of proportionality, the principle of discrimination between combatants and civilians, the principle against causing damage to neutral states, the prohibition against causing serious and lasting damage to the environment, the prohibition against genocide, and the basic principles of human rights law.

In addition, there were specific treaty provisions contained in the Geneva Gas Protocol (1925), and the Hague Regulations (1907) which were clearly applicable to nuclear weapons as they prohibited the use of poisons. Radiation directly fell within this description, and the prohibition against the use of poisons was indeed one of the oldest rules of the laws of war.

Judge Weeramantry's Opinion also draws attention to the multicultural and ancient origins of the laws of war, referring to the recognition of its basic rules in Hindu, Buddhist, Chinese, Judaic, Islamic, African, and modern European cultural traditions. As such, the humanitarian rules of warfare were not to be regarded as a new sentiment, invented in the nineteenth century, and so slenderly rooted in universal tradition that they may be lightly overridden.

The Opinion also points out that there cannot be two sets of the laws of war applicable simultaneously to the same conflict—one to conventional weapons, and the other to nuclear weapons.

Judge Weeramantry's analysis includes philosophical perspectives showing that no credible legal system could contain a rule within itself which rendered legitimate an act which could destroy the entire civilization of which that legal system formed a part. Modern juristic discussions showed that a rule of this nature, which may find a place in the rules of a suicide club, could not be part of any reasonable legal system—and international law was pre-eminently such a system.

The Opinion concludes with a reference to the appeal in the Russell–Einstein Manifesto to "remember your humanity and forget the rest", without which the risk arises of universal death. In this context, the Opinion points out that international law is equipped with the necessary array of principles with which to respond, and that international law could contribute significantly towards rolling back the shadow of the mushroom cloud, and heralding the sunshine of the nuclear-free age.

The question should therefore have been answered by the Court—convincingly, clearly, and categorically.

Dissenting opinion of Judge Koroma

In his Dissenting Opinion, Judge Koroma stated that he fundamentally disagreed with the Court's finding that:

> "in view of the current state of international law, and of the elements of fact at its disposal, the Court cannot conclude definitively whether the threat or use of nuclear weapons would be lawful or unlawful in an extreme circumstance of self-defence, in which the very survival of a State would be at stake".

Such a finding, he maintained, could not be sustained on the basis of existing international law, nor in the face of the weight and abundance of evidence and material presented to the Court. In his view, on the basis of the existing law, particularly humanitarian law and the material available to the Court, the use of nuclear weapons in any circumstance would at the very least result in the violation of the principles and rules of that law and is therefore unlawful.

Judge Koroma also pointed out that although the views of states are divided on the question of the effects of the use of nuclear weapons, or as to whether the matter should have been brought before the Court, he took the view that once the Court had found that the General Assembly was competent to pose the question, and that no compelling reason existed against rendering an opinion, the Court should have performed its judicial function and decide the case on the basis of existing international law. He expressed his regret that the Court, even after holding that:

> "the threat or use of nuclear weapons would generally be contrary to the rules of international law applicable in armed conflict, and in particular the principles and rules of humanitarian law".

A finding with which he concurred, save for the word "generally"—the Court had flinched from answering the actual question put to it that the threat or use of nuclear weapons in any circumstance would be unlawful under international law.

He maintained that the Court's answer to the question had turned on the "survival of the state", whereas the question posed to the Court was about the lawfulness of the use of nuclear weapons. He therefore found the Court's judgment not only untenable in law, but even potentially destabilizing of the existing international legal order, as it not only made states that might be disposed to use such weapons judges about the lawfulness of the use of the use of such weapons, but it also threw the regime regarding the prohibition of the use of force and self-defence as regulated by the United Nations Charter into doubt, while at the same time albeit unintentionally it made inroads into the legal restraints imposed on nuclear weapon states regarding such weapons.

Judge Koroma, in his Dissenting Opinion, undertook a survey of what, in his view, is the law applicable to the question, analyzed the material before the Court and came to the conclusion that it is wholly unconvincing for the Court to have ruled that in view of the "current state of the law", it could not conclude definitively whether the use of nuclear weapons would be illegal. In his opinion, not only does the law exist in substantial and ample form, but it is also precise and the purported lacuna is entirely unpersuasive. In his opinion, there was no room for a finding of *non liquet* in the matter before the Court.

On the other hand, after analysing the evidence, Judge Koroma came to the conclusion as the Court that nuclear weapons, when used, are incapable of distinguishing between civilians and military personnel, would result in the death of thousands if not millions of civilians, cause superfluous injury and unnecessary suffering to survivors, affect future generations, damage hospitals and contaminate the natural environment, food and drinking water, with radioactivity, thereby depriving survivors of the means of survival contrary to the Geneva Conventions of 1949 and the 1977 Additional Protocol I thereto. It followed, therefore, that the use of such weapons would be unlawful.

His dissent from the Court's main finding notwithstanding, Judge Koroma stated that the Opinion should not be viewed as entirely without legal significance or merit. The normative findings contained in it should be regarded as a step forward in the historic process of imposing legal restraints in armed conflicts and in reaffirming that nuclear weapons are subject to international law and to the rule of law. The Court's Advisory Opinion, in his view, constitutes for the first in history that a tribunal of this standing has declared and reaffirmed that the threat or use of nuclear weapons that is contrary to Article 2, paragraph 4, of the Charter prohibiting the use of force is unlawful and would be incompatible with the requirements of international law applicable in armed conflict. The finding, though qualified, tantamounts to a rejection of the argument that because nuclear weapons were invented after the advent of humanitarian law, they are therefore not subjected to that law.

In conclusion, Judge Koroma regretted that the Court did not follow through with those normative conclusions and make the only and inescapable finding that because of their established characteristics, it is impossible to conceive of any circumstance when the use of nuclear weapons in an armed conflict would not be unlawful. Such a conclusion by the Court would have been a most invaluable contribution by the Court as the guardian of legality of the United Nations system to what has been described as the most important aspect of international law facing humanity today.

Dissenting opinion of Judge Higgins

Judge Higgins appended a dissenting opinion in which she explained that she was not able to support that key finding of the court in paragraph 2E. In her view the Court had not applied the rules of humanitarian law in a systematic and transparent way to show how it reached the conclusion in the first part of paragraph 2E of the *dispositif*. Nor was the meaning of the first part of paragraph 2E clear. Judge Higgins also opposed the *non-liquet* in the second part of paragraph 2E, believing it to be unnecessary and wrong in law.

* * *

8.11 WTO Panel Report on United States Import Prohibition of Certain Shrimp and Shrimp Products. Circulated to the Members of the WTO, 15 May 1998. WTO Doc. No. WT/DS58/AB/R; *reprinted in* 37 I.L.M. 832 (1998).[c]

* * *

VII. FINDINGS

A. INTRODUCTION

7.1 We note that the dispute arose from the following facts. Most sea turtles are distributed around the world, in sub-tropical or tropical areas. Sea turtles are affected by human activity. They have been exploited for their meat, shell and eggs but they are also affected by the pollution of the oceans and the destruction of their habitats. In addition, they are subject to incidental capture in fisheries. Presently, most populations of sea turtles are considered to be endangered or threatened. In this respect, all marine turtles are included in Appendix I to the 1973 Convention on International Trade in Endangered Species (hereafter "CITES") as species threatened with extinction.

7.2 Pursuant to the US Endangered Species Act of 1973 (hereafter "ESA"), all sea turtles that occur in US waters are listed as endangered or threatened species. Research programmes carried out by the United States have led to the conclusion that incidental capture and drowning of sea turtles by shrimp trawlers is a significant source of mortality for sea turtles. The United States National Marine Fisheries Service (hereafter "NMFS") has developed, within a programme aimed at reducing the mortality of sea turtles in shrimp trawls, turtle excluder devices (hereafter "TEDs"). In 1987, the United States issued regulations under the ESA whereby shrimp fishermen are required to use TEDs or tow time restrictions in specified areas where there is a significant mortality of sea turtles in shrimp trawls. Since December 1994, these regulations have eliminated the option for small trawl vessels to restrict tow times in lieu of using TEDs.

7.3 In 1989, the United States enacted Section 609 of Public Law 101–162 (hereafter "Section 609"). Section 609 calls upon the US Secretary of State, in consultation with the US Secretary of Commerce, inter alia to initiate negotiations for the development of bilateral or multilateral agreements for the protection and conservation of sea turtles, in particular with governments of countries engaged in commercial fishing operations likely to have a negative impact on sea turtles. Section 609 further provides that shrimp harvested with technology that may adversely affect certain sea turtles protected under US law may not be imported into the United States, unless the President annually certifies to the Congress that the harvesting country concerned has a regulatory programme governing the incidental taking of such sea turtles in the course of such harvesting that is comparable to that of the United States, that the average rate of that incidental taking by the vessels of the harvesting country is comparable to the average rate of incidental taking of sea turtles by United States vessels in the course of such harvesting, or that the fishing environment of the harvesting country does not pose a threat of incidental taking to sea turtles in the course of such harvesting.

7.4 The United States issued guidelines in 1991 and 1993 for the implementation of Section 609. Pursuant to these guidelines, Section 609 was applied only to countries of the Caribbean/Western Atlantic. In September 1996, the United States concluded

c. The Panel's decision was appealed. The Appellate Body reversed in part and affirmed in part, ultimately agreeing with the Panel that the U.S. import prohibition violated provisions of GATT 1994. *See* Report of the Appellate Body on United States—Import Prohibition of Certain Shrimp and Shrimp Products, 8 October 1998, WTO Doc. No. DS58/AB/R (12 October 1998).

the Inter-American Convention for the Protection and Conservation of Sea Turtles with a number of countries of that region. In December 1995, the US Court of International Trade (hereafter "CIT") found the 1991 and 1993 guidelines illegal insofar as they limited the geographical scope of Section 609 to shrimp harvested in the wider Caribbean/Western Atlantic area. The CIT directed the US Department of State to prohibit, no later than 1 May 1996, the importation of shrimp or products of shrimp wherever harvested in the wild with commercial fishing technology which may affect adversely those species of sea turtles the conservation of which is the subject of regulations of the Secretary of Commerce.

7.5 In April 1996, the Department of State published revised guidelines to comply with the CIT order of December 1995. The new guidelines extended the scope of Section 609 to shrimp harvested in all countries. The Department of State further determined that, as of 1 May 1996, all shipments of shrimp and shrimp products into the United States must be accompanied by a declaration attesting that the shrimp or shrimp product in question has been harvested "either under conditions that do not adversely affect sea turtles ... or in waters subject to the jurisdiction of a nation currently certified pursuant to Section 609." The 1996 guidelines define "shrimp or shrimp products harvested in conditions that do not affect sea turtles" to include: "(a) Shrimp harvested in an aquaculture facility ...; (b) Shrimp harvested by commercial shrimp trawl vessels using TEDs comparable in effectiveness to those required in the United States; (c) Shrimp harvested exclusively by means that do not involve the retrieval of fishing nets by mechanical devices or by vessels using gear that, in accordance with the US programme, would require TEDs; (d) Species of shrimp, such as the pandalid species, harvested in areas in which sea turtles do not occur". The 1996 guidelines provided that certification could be granted by 1 May 1996, and annually thereafter to harvesting countries other than those where turtles do not occur or that exclusively use means that do not pose a threat to sea turtles "only if the government of [each of those countries] has provided documentary evidence of the adoption of a regulatory program governing the incidental taking of sea turtles in the course of commercial shrimp trawl harvesting that is comparable to that of the United States and if the average take rate of that incidental taking by vessels of the harvesting nation is comparable to the average rate of incidental taking of sea turtles by United States vessels in the course of such harvesting." For the purpose of these certifications, a regulatory programme must include, inter alia, a requirement that all commercial shrimp trawl vessels operating in waters in which there is a likelihood of intercepting sea turtles use TEDs at all time. TEDs must be comparable in effectiveness to those used by the United States. Moreover, the average incidental take rate will be deemed comparable to that of the United States if the harvesting country requires the use of TEDs in a manner comparable to that of the US programme.

7.6 In October 1996, the CIT ruled that the embargo on shrimp and shrimp products enacted by Section 609 applies to "all shrimp and shrimp products harvested in the wild by citizens or vessels of nations which have not been certified." The CIT found that the 1996 guidelines are contrary to Section 609 when allowing, with a shrimp exporter declaration form, imports of shrimp from non-certified countries, if the shrimp was harvested with commercial fishing technology that did not adversely affect sea turtles. The CIT later clarified its decision in ruling that shrimp harvested by manual methods which do not harm sea turtles, by aquaculture and in cold water, could continue to be imported even from countries which have not been certified under Section 609.

B. RULINGS MADE BY THE PANEL IN THE COURSE OF THE PROCEEDINGS

7.7 In the course of the proceedings, we received two documents called amicus briefs and submitted by non-governmental organizations. These documents were also communicated by their authors to the parties to the dispute. In a letter dated 1 August 1997 and at the second substantive meeting of the Panel, India, Malaysia, Pakistan and Thailand requested us not to consider the content of these documents in our examination of the matter under dispute. At the second substantive meeting of the Panel, the United States, stressing that the Panel could seek information from any relevant source under Article 13 of the Understanding on Rules and Procedures Governing the Settlement of Disputes (hereafter "DSU"), urged us to avail ourselves of any relevant information in the two documents, as well as in any other similar communications.

7.8 We had not requested such information as was contained in the above-mentioned documents. We note that, pursuant to Article 13 of the DSU, the initiative to seek information and to select the source of information rests with the Panel. In any other situations, only parties and third parties are allowed to submit information directly to the Panel. Accepting non-requested information from non-governmental sources would be, in our opinion, incompatible with the provisions of the DSU as currently applied. We therefore informed the parties that we did not intend to take these documents into consideration. We observed, moreover, that it was usual practice for parties to put forward whatever documents they considered relevant to support their case and that, if any party in the present dispute wanted to put forward these documents, or parts of them, as part of their own submissions to the Panel, they were free to do so. If this were the case, the other parties would have two weeks to respond to the additional material. We noted that the United States availed themselves of this opportunity by designating Section III of the document submitted by the Center for Marine Conservation and the Center for International Environmental Law as an annex to its second submission to the Panel.

7.9 None of the parties to the dispute requested the Panel to consult experts. However, we noted that parties had submitted a number of studies by experts and often quoted the same scientific documents to support opposite views. Under those circumstances, we decided, acting on our own initiative, to seek scientific and technical advice pursuant to paragraph 1 and paragraph 2, first sentence of Article 13 of the DSU.

7.10 Parties to the dispute were given time to comment in writing on the replies of the experts to the questions of the Panel. However, before and during the hearing of the experts, we recalled that parties should limit their intervention to questions and comments strictly related to the issues raised by the experts. Accordingly, we decided not to take into account in our findings any comment or question raised in relation with the consultation of the experts which would not be strictly related to the scientific issues under discussion with the experts.

C. VIOLATION OF ARTICLE XI:1 OF GATT 1994

7.11 We note that all four complainants raise claims regarding the violation of Article XI GATT 1994. India, Pakistan and Thailand submit that the scope of Article XI:1, which provides for general elimination of quantitative restrictions, is comprehensive and applies to all measures instituted or maintained by a Member prohibiting or restricting the importation, exportation or sale for export of products other than measures that take the form of duties, taxes or other charges. Measures prohibited by Article XI:1 include outright quotas and quantitative restrictions made effective through import or export licences. The embargo applied by the United States on the basis of Article 609 constitutes a prohibition or restriction on the importation of shrimp or shrimp products from the complainants and is not in the nature of a "duty, tax, or other charges" within the meaning of Article XI:1. India, Pakistan and Thailand consider that the 1991 and 1994 reports on United States—Restrictions on Imports of Tuna involve a measure virtually identical to the restriction on imports of shrimp and shrimp products at issue in this case. In those cases, the embargo was applied by the United States to imports of tuna from countries that had not implemented conservation programmes comparable to those of the United States to protect dolphins incidentally taken by commercial fishermen harvesting tuna. In both cases, the panels found that the restriction constituted a violation of Article XI.

7.12 Malaysia argues that the import prohibition imposed by the United States under Section 609 falls under Article XI as it bans import of shrimp or shrimp products from any country not meeting certain policy conditions, and are not duties, taxes or other charges. The findings of the Tuna I and Tuna II cases are equally applicable to the facts of this case. The US prohibition on imports of shrimp and shrimp products is therefore contrary to Article XI:1 and cannot be justified under Article XI:2, as this provision does not address the situation at issue.

7.13 The United States argues that since under Article XX nothing in GATT 1994 is to be construed to prevent the adoption or enforcement of the measures at issue, it need not address Article XI. The United States also considers that the complainants have the burden of establishing any alleged violation of GATT 1994. However, the United States does not dispute that, with respect to countries not certified under Section 609, Section 609 amounts to a restriction on the importation of shrimp within the meaning of Article XI:1 of GATT 1994.

7.14 The arguments put forward by the parties raise the general question of the burden of proof, in terms of who bears this burden and in terms of how much has to be proved in the circumstances of this case. Regarding who bears the burden of proof, we recall the well established general principle of law referred to by the Appellate Body in its report on United States—Measure Affecting Imports of Woven Wool Shirts and Blouses from India: "the burden of proof rests upon the party, whether complaining or defending, who asserts the affirmative of a particular claim or defence". We consequently consider that it is up to the complainants to demonstrate that the US measure at issue violates Article XI:1 of GATT 1994. The arguments of the parties also raise the question of when a panel should consider that a party has provided sufficient evidence in support of a particular claim or defence. We recall that the Appellate Body in the Wool Shirts case found that "precisely how much and precisely what kind of evidence will be required to establish [a presumption that a claim is valid] will necessarily vary . . . from case to case". We therefore have to assess the evidence before us in the light of the particular circumstances of this case. This implies that we may consider any type of evidence, and also that we may reach our conclusions regarding a particular claim on the basis of the level of evidence that we consider sufficient.

7.15 In this respect, we note that the United States, in reply to one of our questions, "does not dispute that with respect to countries not certified under Section 609, Section 609 amounts to a restriction on the importation of shrimp within the meaning of Article XI:1 of GATT 1994". This statement of the United States creates a particular situation where the defendant basically admits that a given measure amounts to a restriction prohibited by GATT 1994. It is usual legal practice for domestic and international tribunals, including GATT panels, to consider that, if a party admits a particular fact, the judge may be entitled to consider such fact as accurate.

7.16 Even if the above-mentioned US declaration does not amount to an admission of a violation of Article XI:1, we consider that the evidence made available to the Panel is sufficient to determine that the United States prohibition of imports of shrimp from non-certified Members violates Article XI:1. Article XI:1 reads in part as follows:

"No prohibitions or restrictions other that duties, taxes or other charges, whether made effective through quotas, import or export licences or other measures, shall be instituted or maintained by any contracting party on the importation of any product of the territory of any other contracting party . . .".

We note that Section 609(b)(1) provides that:

"The importation of shrimp or products from shrimp which have been harvested with commercial fishing technology which may affect adversely such species of sea turtles shall be prohibited no later than May 1, 1991, except as provided in paragraph (2) [i.e. the exporting country is certified]".

Thus, Section 609 expressly requires the imposition of an import ban on imports from non-certified countries. We further note that in its judgement of December 1995, the CIT directed the US Department of State to prohibit, no later that 1 May 1996, the importation of shrimp or products of shrimp wherever harvested in the wild with commercial fishing technology which may affect adversely those species of sea turtles the conservation of which is the subject of regulations of the Secretary of Commerce. Furthermore, the CIT ruled that the US Administration has to apply the import ban, including to TED-caught shrimp, as long as the country concerned has not been certified. In other words, the United States bans imports of shrimp or shrimp products from any country not meeting certain policy conditions. We finally note that previous panels have considered similar measures restricting imports to be "prohibitions or restrictions" within the meaning of Article XI.

7.17 Therefore, we find that the United States admits that, with respect to countries not certified under Section 609, the measures imposed in application of Section 609 amount to "prohibitions or restrictions" on the importation of shrimp within the meaning of Article XI:1 of GATT 1994. Even if one were to consider that the United States has not admitted that it imposes an import prohibition or restriction within the meaning of Article XI:1, we find that the wording of Section 609 and the interpretation made of it by the CIT are sufficient evidence that the United States imposes a "prohibition or restriction" within the meaning of Article XI:1. We therefore find that Section 609 violates Article XI:1 of GATT 1994.

D. VIOLATION OF ARTICLE XIII:1 AND OF ARTICLE I:1 OF GATT 1994

7.18 India, Pakistan and Thailand claim that the import prohibition on shrimp and shrimp products from non-certified countries is inconsistent with the most-favoured-nation principle embodied in Article I:1 GATT 1994 because physically identical shrimp and shrimp products from different Members are treated differently by the United States upon importation. This differentiated treatment is based solely on the method of harvest and the conservation policies of the government under whose jurisdiction the shrimp is harvested. Further, even if one were to assume arguendo that the method of harvest does affect the nature of the shrimp, the embargo violates Article I:1 because, pursuant to the embargo, wild shrimp harvested by use of TEDs are forbidden entry into the United States if harvested by a national of a non-certified country, while shrimp harvested by the same method by a national of a certified country is permitted entry into the United States.

7.19 India, Pakistan and Thailand also claim that the embargo as applied is also inconsistent with Articles I:1 and XIII:1 of the GATT 1994 because initially affected countries were given a phase-in period of three years, while newly affected nations were not given a similar period of time. Malaysia further argues that, while newly affected nations generally received only a four month notice, Malaysia actually was given three months (i.e., until 1 April 1996) to adopt a programme complying with the US requirements. For Malaysia, this differential treatment is also discriminatory and inconsistent with Article XIII:1. According to India, Pakistan and Thailand, initially affected countries were given the opportunity to implement the required use of TEDs without substantially interrupting shrimp trade to the United States. Products from these countries have therefore been given an "advantage, favour, privilege or immunity" over like products originating in the territories of other Members, in violation of Article I:1. Likewise, importation of like products from initially affected countries was not similarly prohibited, in violation of Article XIII:1.

7.20 India, Pakistan and Thailand also argue that Section 609 is inconsistent with Article XIII:1 of GATT 1994 because it restricts the importation of shrimp and shrimp products from countries which have not been certified, while like products from other countries which have been certified can be imported freely into the United States. The United States denies entry of shrimp and shrimp products based on the method of harvest, even though it does not affect the nature of the product. Indeed, all foreign shrimp and shrimp products have the same physical characteristics, end-uses and tariff classifications and are perfectly substitutable. Thus, shrimp products which may be imported into the United States pursuant to Section 609 are like shrimp products from non-certified countries which are denied entry. The differential treatment of like products from certified and non-certified countries violates Article XIII:1. Even assuming that the method of harvest does affect the nature of the product, the embargo violates Article XIII because wild shrimp harvested by use of TEDs are forbidden entry into the United States if harvested by a national of a non-certified country, while shrimp harvested by use of TEDs by a national of a certified country are permitted entry into the United States.

7.21 The United States does not agree with the complainants' claims under Articles I and XIII, particularly since, in the US view, the US measure applies equally to all harvesting Members. The United States further argues that, if the Panel makes a finding with respect to Article XI, there will be no need to reach the claims under Articles I and XIII.

7.22 Given our conclusion in paragraph 7.17 above that Section 609 violates Article XI:1, we consider that it is not necessary for us to review the other claims of the complainants with respect to Articles I:1 and XIII:1. This is consistent with GATT and WTO panel practice and has been confirmed by the Appellate Body in its report in the Wool Shirts case, where the Appellate Body mentioned that "A panel need only address those claims which must be addressed in order to resolve the matter in issue in the dispute."

7.23 Therefore we do not find it necessary to review the allegations of the complainants with respect to Articles I:1 and XIII:1. On the basis of our finding of violation of Article XI:1, we move to address the defence of the United States under Article XX.

E. ARTICLE XX OF GATT 1994

1. Preliminary remarks

7.24 The United States claims that the measures at issue adopted pursuant to Section 609, which were found to be inconsistent with Articles XI:1 GATT 1994, are justified under Article XX(b) and (g) of GATT 1994. India, Pakistan and Thailand argue that Article XX(b) and (g) cannot be invoked to justify a measure which applies to animals not within the jurisdiction of the Member enacting the measure. Malaysia contends that, since Section 609 allows the United States to take actions unilaterally to conserve a shared natural resource, it is therefore in breach of the sovereignty principle under international law. The United States responds that Article XX(b) and (g) contain no jurisdictional limitations, nor limitations on the location of the animals or natural resources to be protected and conserved and that, under general principles of international law relating to sovereignty, States have the right to regulate imports within their jurisdiction.

7.25 The relevant parts of Article XX provide as follows:

Article XX

General exceptions

Subject to the requirement that such measures are not applied in a manner that would constitute a means of arbitrary or unjustifiable discrimination between countries where the same conditions prevail, or a disguised restriction on international trade, nothing in this Agreement shall be construed to prevent the adoption or enforcement by any contracting party of measures:

> . . . (b) necessary to protect human, animal or plant life or health; . . .
>
> (g) relating to the conservation of exhaustible natural resources if such measures are made effective in conjunction with restrictions on domestic production or consumption; . . .

7.26 The arguments of the parties raise the general question of whether Article XX(b) and (g) apply at all when a Member has taken a measure conditioning access to its market for a given product on the adoption of certain conservation policies by the exporting Member(s). We note that Article XX can accommodate a broad range of measures aiming at the conservation and preservation of the environment. At the same time, by accepting the WTO Agreement, Members commit themselves to certain obligations which limit their right to adopt certain measures. We therefore consider it important to determine first whether the scope of Article XX encompasses measures whereby a Member conditions access to its market for a given product on the adoption of certain conservation policies by the exporting Member(s).

7.27 Pursuant to Article 3.2 of the DSU and in accordance with Appellate Body decisions, we should, when trying to clarify the scope of Article XX, have recourse to customary rules of interpretation of public international law. We note that Article 31(1) of the Vienna Convention on the Law of Treaties (1969) (hereafter the "Vienna Convention") provides that:

> "A treaty shall be interpreted in good faith in accordance with the ordinary meaning to be given to the terms of the treaty in their context and in the light of its object and purpose".

Therefore, in order to determine the scope of Article XX, it is necessary to consider not only the terms in their ordinary meaning, but also their context and the object and purpose of GATT 1994 and the WTO Agreement itself.

7.28 Article XX contains an introductory provision, or chapeau, and a number of specific requirements contained in successive paragraphs. As mentioned by the Appellate Body in its report in the Gasoline case, in order for the justification of Article XX to be extended to a given measure, it must not only come under one or another of the particular exceptions—paragraphs (a) to (j)—listed under Article XX; it must also satisfy the requirements imposed by the opening clause of Article XX. We note that panels have in the past considered the specific paragraphs of Article XX before reviewing the applicability of the conditions contained in the chapeau. However, as the conditions contained in the introductory provision apply to any of the paragraphs of Article XX, it seems equally appropriate to analyse first the introductory provision of Article XX.

7.29 We also recall that the Appellate Body considered, in the Gasoline case, that the chapeau by its express terms addresses, not so much the questioned measure or its specific contents, but rather the manner in which that measure is applied. The Appellate Body further underscored that "the purpose and object of the introductory clause of Article XX is generally the prevention of 'abuse of the exceptions of [what was later to become] Article [XX]' ". Hence, the chapeau determines to a large extent the context of the specific exceptions contained in the paragraphs of Article XX. Therefore, we shall first determine whether the measure at issue satisfies the conditions contained in the chapeau. If we find this to be the case, we shall then examine whether the US measure is covered by the terms of Article XX(b) or (g).

7.30 Finally, we keep in mind the well-established practice according to which when an affirmative defence, such as Article XX, is invoked, the burden of proof should rest on the party asserting it. We therefore consider that the burden of proving that the measure at issue is justified under Article XX rests on the United States, as the party asserting this affirmative defence.

2. Chapeau of Article XX

7.31 India, Pakistan and Thailand argue that the embargo applied by the United States is implemented in a manner that constitutes a means of arbitrary or unjustifiable discrimination between countries where the same conditions prevail insofar as the newly affected nations, including India, Pakistan and Thailand, have been given substantially less notice than the other countries, whether the United States or initially affected countries, before being forced to comply with TEDs requirements. They maintain that there is not only a discrimination between exporting countries, but also between exporting countries and the United States. Furthermore, India, Pakistan and Thailand consider that, before requiring TEDs application from them, the United States should have demonstrated that the same conditions do not prevail between India, Pakistan or Thailand and the countries with no TEDs requirement. Moreover, for these complainants, the legislative history of Section 609, which includes discussions of this section in terms of the competitive position of the US shrimp industry, further supports the conclusion that the embargo is a disguised restriction on international trade. The effect of the restriction was not so much reduced importation as the additional cost on the foreign industry, making it less competitive, and the risk that the right to export might be revoked. Malaysia claims that disguised restrictions include disguised discrimination in international trade, and that it has been subject to such discrimination because it was given only a few months to comply with the US requirements as opposed to three years in the case of the initially affected countries.

7.32 The United States argues that the measures related to import of shrimp were carefully and justifiably tied to the particular conditions of each country exporting shrimp to the United States. All exporting nations with the same shrimp harvesting conditions are treated equally, with no discrimination. For the United States, the evidence is overwhelming that the conservation measures under Section 609 are not some artifice intended to protect the US fishing industry. The United States argued that the strong and growing international consensus regarding sea turtle conservation and the mandatory use of TEDs belies any claim that the US measures are some sort of disguised restriction on trade. In addition, the United States maintains that the extension of the application of Section 609 to other countries than the United States and the wider Caribbean/Western Atlantic area has not led to a decrease in the quantities imported nor to an increase in prices.

7.33 In order to apply Article XX in this case, we must, as mentioned in paragraph 7.27 above, interpret it in line with Article 31(1) of the Vienna Convention. More particularly, the chapeau of Article XX must be interpreted on the basis of the ordinary meaning of its terms, in their context and in the light of the object and purpose of GATT 1994 and the WTO Agreement. We consider first if the terms of the chapeau of Article XX explicitly address the issue of whether Article XX contains any limitation on a Member's use of measures conditioning market access to the adoption of certain conservation policies by the exporting Member. In this connection, we note that the chapeau prohibits such application of the measure at issue as would constitute "arbitrary or unjustifiable discrimination" between countries where the same conditions prevail. We note that the US measure at issue applies to all Members seeking to export to the United States wild shrimp retrieved mechanically from waters where sea turtles and shrimp occur concurrently. We consider those Members to be "countries where the same conditions prevail", within the meaning of Article XX. We further note that some of those countries have been "certified" and can export shrimp to the United States whereas some have not and are subject to an import ban. Consequently, discriminatory treatment is applied to shrimp from non-certified countries. Pursuant to the chapeau of Article XX, a measure may discriminate, but not in an "arbitrary" or unjustifiable" manner.

7.34 We therefore move to consider whether the US measure conditioning market access on the adoption of certain conservation policies by the exporting Member could be considered as "unjustifiable" discrimination. As was recalled by the Appellate Body in the Gasoline case, "the text of the chapeau of Article XX is not without ambiguity". The word "unjustifiable" has never actually been subject to any precise interpretation. The ordinary meaning of this term is susceptible to both narrow and broad interpretations. While the ordinary meaning of "unjustifiable" confirms that Article XX is to be applied within certain boundaries, it does not explicitly address the issue of whether Article XX should be interpreted to contain any limitation on a Member's use of measures conditioning market access on the adoption of certain conservation policies by the exporting Member. For that reason, it is essential that we interpret the term "unjustifiable" within its context and in the light of the object and purpose of the agreement to which it belongs.

7.35 Turning to an examination of the context of the terms and the object and purpose of the WTO Agreement, we note that the notion of "context", on the one hand, and of "object and purpose", on the other hand, are intimately linked. Indeed, Article 31(2) of the Vienna Convention provides that the context for the purpose of treaty interpretation comprises the text of the agreement, including its preamble and annexes. By the same token, determining the object and purpose of an agreement implies an examination of the text of the agreement and of its preamble. Consequently, we consider that the context of the chapeau of Article XX cannot be distinguished from that of Article XX as a whole. Furthermore, as the WTO Agreement is an integrated system including GATT 1994, we shall consider as the context of the chapeau and of Article XX as a whole not only the other relevant provisions of GATT 1994 together with its preamble and annexes, but also the WTO Agreement, including its preamble and its other annexes. For the same reasons, the object and purpose to be considered is not only that of GATT 1994, but that of the WTO Agreement as a whole.

7.36 GATT panels had the occasion to address the context and the object and purpose of Article XX. The 1989 panel on United States—Section 337 of the Tariff Act of 1930 considered that:

> "... Article XX is entitled 'General Exceptions' ... Article XX(d) thus provides for a limited and conditional exception from obligations under other provisions". Referring, inter alia, to the above-mentioned report, the panel in the Tuna I case found that: " ... previous panels had established that Article XX is a limited and conditional exception from obligations under other provisions of the General Agreement, and not a positive rule establishing obligations in itself. Therefore, the practice of panels has been to interpret Article XX narrowly...."

7.37 The Appellate Body also described Article XX in very similar language. In the Wool Shirts case, it found that:

> "Articles XX and XI:1(2)(c)(i) are limited exceptions from obligations under certain other provisions of the GATT 1994, not positive rules establishing obligations in themselves".

7.38 The Appellate Body has also discussed the relationship of Article XX(g) to GATT as a whole, in terms that would apply to the relationship to GATT of Article XX taken in its entirety:

> "... Article XX(g) and its phrase, 'relating to the conservation of exhaustible natural resources,' need to be read in context and in such a manner as to give effect to the purposes and objects of the General Agreement. The context of Article XX(g) includes the provisions of the rest of the General Agreement, including in particular Articles I, III and XI; conversely, the context of Articles I and III and XI includes

Article XX. Accordingly, the phrase 'relating to the conservation of exhaustible natural resources' may not be read so expansively as seriously to subvert the purpose and object of Article III:4. Nor may Article III:4 be given so broad a reach as effectively to emasculate Article XX(g) and the policies and interests it embodies. The relationship between the affirmative commitments set out in, e.g., Articles I, III and XI, and the policies and interests embodied in the "General Exceptions" listed in Article XX, can be given meaning within the framework of the General Agreement and its object and purpose by a treaty interpreter only on a case-to-case basis, by careful scrutiny of the factual and legal context in a given dispute, without disregarding the words actually used by the WTO Members themselves to express their intent and purpose."

7.39 While the Appellate Body has noted that the rights that Members do have under Article XX must, of course, be respected, it has also noted the existence of limits and conditions on the scope of Article XX. It has expressed those limits and conditions as follows in respect of its analysis of the object and purpose of the chapeau of Article XX: " ... while the exceptions of Article XX may be invoked as a matter of legal right, they should not be so applied as to frustrate or defeat the legal obligations of the holder of the right under the substantive rules of the General Agreement. If those exceptions [contained in Article XX] are not to be abused or misused, in other words, the measures falling within the particular exceptions must be applied reasonably, with due regard both to the legal duties of the party claiming the exception and the legal rights of the other parties concerned."

7.40 We note that the chapeau to Article XX provides that "nothing in [GATT 1994] shall be construed to prevent the adoption or enforcement ... of measures" otherwise in conformity with Article XX conditions. However, we consider that this wording is not affected by the findings quoted above. As the Appellate Body also put it, Article XX "needs to be read in its context and in such a manner as to give effect to the purposes and objects of the General Agreement" and "the purpose and object of the introductory clauses of Article XX is generally the prevention of 'abuse of the exceptions of ... [Article XX]'." We deduce from this that, when invoking Article XX, a Member invokes the right to derogate to certain specific substantive provisions of GATT 1994 but that, in doing so, it must not frustrate or defeat the purposes and objects of the General Agreement and the WTO Agreement or its legal obligations under the substantive rules of GATT by abusing the exception contained in Article XX.

7.41 We consider this finding of the Appellate Body to be an application of the international law principle according to which international agreements must be applied in good faith, in light of the pacta sunt servanda principle. The concept of good faith is explained in Article 18 of the Vienna Convention which states that "A State is obliged to refrain from acts which would defeat the object and purpose of a treaty".

7.42 We consequently turn to the consideration of the object and purpose of the WTO Agreement, of which GATT 1994 and Article XX thereof are an integral part. We note that the preamble of an agreement may assist in determining its object and purpose. On the one hand, the first paragraph of the Preamble of the WTO Agreement acknowledges that the optimal use of the world's resources must be pursued "in accordance with the objective of sustainable development, seeking both to protect and preserve the environment and to enhance the means of doing so in a manner consistent with [Members'] respective needs and concerns at different levels of economic development". On the other hand, the second paragraph of the Preamble of GATT and the third paragraph of the WTO Preamble refer to "entering into reciprocal and mutually advantageous arrangements directed to the substantial reduction of tariffs and other barriers to trade and to the elimination of discriminatory treatment" in international trade relations. While the WTO Preamble confirms that environmental considerations are important for the interpretation of the WTO Agreement, the central focus of that agreement remains the promotion of economic development through trade; and the provisions of GATT are essentially turned toward liberalization of access to markets on a nondiscriminatory basis.

7.43 We also note that, by its very nature, the WTO Agreement favours a multilateral approach to trade issues. The Preamble to the WTO Agreement provides that Members are "resolved ... to develop an integrated, more viable and durable multilateral trading system [and] ... determined to preserve the basic principles and to further the objectives underlying this multilateral trading system" (emphasis added). Article III:2 of the WTO Agreement also mentions that:

> "The WTO shall provide the forum for negotiations among its Members concerning their multilateral trade relations in matters dealt with under the agreements in the Annexes to this Agreement. The WTO may also provide for a forum for further negotiations among its Members concerning their multilateral trade relations ...".

This approach is also expressed in Article 23.1 of the DSU which stresses the primacy of the multilateral system and rejects unilateralism as a substitute for the procedures foreseen in that agreement.

7.44 Therefore, we are of the opinion that the chapeau Article XX, interpreted within its context and in the light of the object and purpose of GATT and of the WTO Agreement, only allows Members to derogate from GATT provisions so long as, in doing so, they do not undermine the WTO multilateral trading system, thus also abusing the exceptions contained in Article XX. Such undermining and abuse would occur when a Member jeopardizes the operation of the WTO Agreement in such a way that guaranteed market access and nondiscriminatory treatment within a multilateral framework would no longer be possible. As was recalled by previous panels, GATT rules "are not only to protect current trade but also to create the predictability needed to plan future trade". The protection of expectations of Members as to the competitive relationship between their products and the products of other Members is therefore an important principle to be taken into account by panels when reviewing a particular measure. We are of the view that a type of measure adopted by a Member which, on its own, may appear to have a relatively minor impact on the multilateral trading system, may nonetheless raise a serious threat to that system if similar measures are adopted by the same or other Members. Thus, by allowing such type of measures even though their individual impact may not appear to be such as to threaten the multilateral trading system, one would affect the security and predictability of the multilateral trading system. We consequently find that when considering a measure under Article XX, we must determine not only whether the measure on its own undermines the WTO multilateral trading system, but also whether such type of measure, if it were to be adopted by other Members, would threaten the security and predictability of the multilateral trading system.

7.45 In our view, if an interpretation of the chapeau of Article XX were to be followed which would allow a Member to adopt measures conditioning access to its market for a given product upon the adoption by the exporting Members of certain policies, including conservation policies, GATT 1994 and the WTO Agreement could no longer serve as a multilateral framework for trade among Members as security and predictability of trade relations under those agreements would be threatened. This follows because, if one WTO Member were allowed to adopt such measures, then other Members would also have the right to adopt similar measures on the same subject but with differing, or even conflicting, requirements. If that happened, it would be impossible for exporting Members to comply at the same time with multiple conflicting policy requirements. Indeed, as each of these requirements would necessitate the adoption of a policy applicable not only to export production (such as specific standards applicable only to goods exported to the country requiring them) but also to domestic production, it would be impossible for a country to adopt one of those policies without running the risk of breaching other Members' conflicting policy requirements for the same product and being refused access to these other markets. We note that, in the present case, there would not even be the possibility of adapting one's export production to the respective requirements of the different Members. Market access for goods could become subject to an increasing number of conflicting policy requirements for the same product and this would rapidly lead to the end of the WTO multilateral trading system.

7.46 We find support for our reasoning in the Tuna II case where the panel considered a similar issue and found as follows:

> "5.26 The Panel observed that Article XX provides for an exception to obligations under the General Agreement. The long-standing practice of panels has accordingly been to interpret this provision narrowly, in a manner that preserves the basic objectives and principles of the General Agreement. If Article XX were interpreted to permit contracting parties to deviate from the obligations of the General Agreement by taking trade measures to implement policies, including conservation policies, within their own jurisdiction, the basic objectives of the General Agreement would be maintained. If however Article XX were interpreted to permit contracting parties to take trade measures so as to force other contracting parties to change their policies within their jurisdiction, including their conservation policies, the balance of rights and obligations among contracting parties, in particular the right of access to markets, would be seriously impaired. Under such an interpretation the General Agreement could no longer serve as a multilateral framework for trade among contracting parties."

The principle underlying our interpretation of Article XX of GATT 1994 was apparently also at the origin of the findings of the 1952 panel on Belgian Family Allowances. This panel addressed a charge imposed by Belgium on imported products purchased by public bodies when these goods originated in a country whose system of family allowances did not meet specific requirements. In that context, the panel considered that "the Belgian legislation on family allowance was not only inconsistent with the provisions of Article I . . . , but was based on a concept which was difficult to reconcile with the spirit of the General Agreement".

7.47 In light of this analysis of the terms and context of the chapeau of Article XX in the light of the object and purpose of the WTO Agreement, we turn to a consideration of whether the US measure challenged in this case falls within the scope of Article XX.

7.48 The United States argues that the intent of Section 609 is to protect and conserve the life and health of sea turtles by requiring that shrimp imported into the United States has not been harvested in a manner that will harm sea turtles. As a result of judgements of the US Court of International Trade (hereafter "CIT"), the US Administration currently has to apply the import ban, including on TED-caught shrimp, as long as the country concerned has not been certified. In addition, certification is only granted if comprehensive requirements regarding use of TEDs by fishing vessels are applied by the exporting country concerned, or if the shrimp trawling operations of the exporting country take place exclusively in waters in which sea turtles do not occur. Consequently, Section 609, as applied, is a measure conditioning access to the US market for a given product on the adoption by exporting Members of conservation policies that the United States considers to be comparable to its own in terms of regulatory programmes and incidental taking.

7.49 Accordingly, it appears to us that, in light of the context of the term "unjustifiable" and the object and purpose of the WTO Agreement, the US measure at issue constitutes unjustifiable discrimination between countries where the same conditions prevail and thus is not within the scope of measures permitted under Article XX. However, before making a definitive finding on this issue, we must consider several arguments put forward by the United States that relate generally to our analysis of Article XX.

7.50 The United States argues that the Panel should consider the many examples of import bans under various international agreements that show that Members may take actions to protect animals, whether they are located within or outside their jurisdiction. We are of the view that these treaties show that environmental protection through international agreement—as opposed to unilateral measures-have for a long time been a recognized course of action for environmental protection. We note that this US argument addresses the issue of a potential jurisdictional scope of Article XX. However, we consider that this argument bears no direct relation to our finding, which rather addresses the inclusion of certain unilateral measures within the scope ratione materiae of Article XX. In addition, in the present case, we are not dealing with measures taken by the United States in application of an agreement to which it is party, as the United States does not claim that it is allowed or required by any international agreement (other than GATT 1994) to impose an import ban on shrimp in order to protect sea turtles. Rather, we are limiting our finding to measures—taken independently of any such international obligation—conditioning access to the US market for a given product on the adoption by the exporting Member of certain conservation policies. In this regard, we note that banning the importation of a particular product does not per se imply that a change in policy is required from the country whose exports are subject to the import prohibition. For instance, a Member may ban a product on the ground that it is dangerous, and accept a similar product that is safe. This is clearly different from adopting a policy pursuant to which only countries that adopt measures restricting all of their production to products considered safe by a particular Member may export to the market of that Member. We note that a judgement of the CIT interpreting Section 609 ruled that the US Administration has to apply the import ban, including on TED-caught shrimp, as long as the country concerned has not been certified. Currently, certification is only granted if comprehensive requirements regarding use of TEDs by fishing vessels are applied by the exporting country concerned.

7.51 The United States further argues that the complainants confuse the difference between extrajurisdictional application of a country's law and the application by a country of its law, within its jurisdiction, in order to protect resources located outside its jurisdiction. However, we note that we are not basing our finding on an extra-jurisdictional application of US law. Many domestic governmental measures can have an effect outside the jurisdiction of the government which takes them. What we found above was that a measure cannot be considered as falling within the scope of Article XX if it operates so as to affect other governments' policies in a way that threatens the multilateral trading system, as described in paragraph 7.45 above. For instance, a US requirement, that US norms regarding the characteristics of a given product be met for that product to be allowed on the US market, would not constitute such a threat. Such types of measures are contemplated by the WTO Agreement on Technical Barriers to Trade and the Agreement on Sanitary and Phytosanitary Measures. However, requiring that other Members adopt policies comparable to the US policy for their domestic markets and all other markets represents a threat to the WTO multilateral trading system. As affirmed by the Appellate Body in its report in the Gasoline case, "Members have a large measure of autonomy to determine their own policies on the environment ..., their environmental objectives and the environmental legislation they enact and implement", circumscribed only, so far as concerns the WTO, by the need to respect the requirements of the General Agreement and the other covered agreements. Therefore, a Member's measure which conditions access to its market on the adoption by the exporting Member of certain conservation policies is a denial of such autonomy.

7.52 The United States argues that the right of WTO Members to take measures under Article XX to conserve and protect natural resources is reaffirmed and reinforced by the Preamble to the WTO Agreement. Although we do not disagree in general with this statement, we are not persuaded that this argument is a reason to change our finding. Whilst the central focus of that Agreement is to promote economic development through trade, we note that the Preamble acknowledges that the optimal use of the world's resources must be pursued "in accordance with the objective of sustainable development, seeking both to protect and preserve the environment and to enhance the means of doing so in a manner consistent with [Members'] respective needs and concerns at different levels of economic development". Thus the Preamble endorses the fact that environmental policies must be designed taking into account the situation of each Member, both in terms of its actual needs and in terms of its economic means. Moreover, the record before us and, in particular, the answers of the experts to the questions of the Panel, strongly suggest that the environmental issues at stake in this case should be evaluated to a large degree in light of local and regional conditions. They also suggest that conservation measures should be adapted, inter alia, to the environmental, social and economic conditions prevailing where they are to be applied. We further note that the 1992 Rio Declaration on Environment and Development recognises the right of States to design their own environmental policies on the basis of their particular environmental and developmental situations and responsibilities. It also stresses the need for international cooperation and for avoiding unilateral measures. In this light, we consider that the Preamble does not justify interpreting Article XX to allow a Member to condition access to its market for a given product on the adoption of certain conservation policies by exporting Members in order to bring them into line with those of the importing Member. On the contrary, the diversity of the environmental and development situations underlined by the Preamble can best be taken into account through international cooperation. The Preamble also implies that attempts to generalize standards of environmental protection would require multilateral discussion, especially when, as here, developing countries are involved. Therefore, we do not consider that the wording of the Preamble referred to by the United States should lead us to a different conclusion than the one reached above.

7.53 The United States further claims that sea turtles are a shared global resource and that, therefore, it has an interest and a right to impose the measures at issue. Firstly, the United States argues that sea turtles are a shared global resource because they are highly migratory creatures which travel through large expanses of sea, within the range of thousands of kilometres, from the jurisdiction of one Member to those of other Members. Secondly, the United States also argues that, even if sea turtles were not migratory at all, they may still represent a shared global resource in terms of biological diversity in the protection of which the United States may have a legitimate interest. Information brought to the attention of the Panel, including documented statements from the experts, tends to confirm the fact that sea turtles, in certain circumstances of their lives, migrate through the waters of several countries and the high sea. This said, even assuming that sea turtles were a shared global resource, we consider that the notion of "shared" resource implies a common interest in the resource concerned. If such a common interest exists, it would be better addressed through the negotiation of international agreements than by measures taken by one Member conditioning access to its market to the adoption by other Members of certain conservation policies. We note in this respect that Article 5 of the 1992 Convention on Biological Diversity provides that:

> "each contracting party shall, as far as possible and as appropriate, cooperate with other contracting parties directly or, where appropriate, through competent international organizations, in respect of areas beyond national jurisdiction and on other matters of mutual interest, for the conservation and sustainable use of biological diversity."

We consider that this provision is evidence that "matters of mutual interest" have normally to be addressed primarily through international cooperation. Therefore, we find that if, as alleged by the United States, sea turtles are shared global resources, that would not call for a change in our finding. Instead, it suggests that the United States should have entered into international cooperation with the aim of developing internationally accepted conservation methods, including with the complainants.

7.54 In addition, the United States argues that nothing in Article XX requires a Member to seek negotiation of an international agreement instead of, or before adopting unilateral measures. In any event, the United States claims it offered to negotiate but the complainants did not reply.

7.55 Regarding whether there is an obligation for a Member to negotiate, we recall our finding in paragraph 7.45 above that the WTO multilateral trading system would be undermined if Members were allowed to adopt measures making access of other Members to their market conditional upon the adoption by the exporting Members of certain conservation policies because it would not be possible for Members to meet conflicting requirements of such a nature. This is clearly a situation where elaboration of international standards would be desirable. We note in that respect that the WTO Agreements on Technical Barriers to Trade and on Sanitary and Phytosanitary Measures promote the use of international standards. We also recall our consideration in paragraph 7.52. The nature of the measures that the United States was seeking to obtain from the exporting countries concerned and the principles recalled in several international environmental agreements imply that a country seeking to promote environmental concerns of such a nature should engage into international negotiations. The negotiation of a multilateral agreement or action under multilaterally defined criteria is clearly a possible way to avoid threatening the multilateral trading system.

7.56 We note that Section 609 contains provisions calling upon the US Secretary of State to initiate negotiations as soon as possible for the development of bilateral or multilateral agreements for the protection and conservation of the species of sea turtles covered by that Section. The judgement of the CIT which was handed over on 29 December 1995 required the US Administration to apply Section 609 on a worldwide basis (and no longer only to the Wider Caribbean/Western Atlantic region) by no later than 1 May 1996. This implied that, unless the exporting countries decided to use TEDs in their shrimp trawling activities—either of their own initiative or through negotiations—the import ban on wild shrimp would be applied to them as of that date. The United States told us of its efforts to have the deadline set in the CIT judgement postponed. However, we have no evidence that the United States actually undertook negotiations on an agreement on sea turtle conservation techniques which would have included the complainants before the imposition of the import ban as a result of the CIT judgement. From the replies of the parties to our question on this subject, in particular that of the United States, we understand that the United States did not propose the negotiation of an agreement to any of the complainants until after the conclusion of negotiations on the Inter–American Convention for the Protection and Conservation of Sea Turtles, in September 1996, i.e. well after the deadline for the imposition of the import ban of 1 May 1996. Even then, it seems that the efforts made merely consisted of an exchange of documents. We therefore conclude that, in spite of the possibility offered by its legislation, the United States did not enter into negotiations before it imposed the import ban. As we consider that the measures sought by the United States were of the type that would normally require international cooperation, we do not find it necessary to examine whether parties entered into negotiations in good faith and whether the United States, absent any result, would have been entitled to adopt unilateral measures.

7.57 Finally, we note that the United States argues that the use of TEDs has become a recognized multilateral environmental standard. In support of this, the

United States firstly contends that the international community has long recognized the need to protect endangered species such as sea turtles. Secondly, several international conventions require parties to adopt conservation policies and urge them to ensure, through proper conservation measures, the maintenance of living resources, including non-target species caught in fishing operations. In support of these statements, the United States refers to the 1982 United Nations Convention on the Law of the Seas and to paragraph17.46(c) of the 1992 Agenda 21. Thirdly, the United States claims that, either as a result of the Inter–American Convention on the Protection and Conservation of Sea Turtles or of their own initiative, 19 countries currently require TEDs on shrimp trawl vessels subject to their jurisdiction.

7.58 Moving to examine whether international obligations exist with regard to the protection of sea turtles, we first note that both the United States and the complainants have elaborated at length on the policies they have developed to protect sea turtles. Both the United States and the complainants have referred to the Convention on International Trade in Endangered Species of Wild Fauna and Flora (CITES). Parties to the dispute are all parties to CITES and the turtles species covered by the US measures at issue are all listed in Appendix I (Species threatened with extinction). The endangered nature of the species of sea turtles mentioned in Annex I as well as the need to protect them are consequently not contested by the parties to the dispute. However, CITES is about trade in endangered species and the subject of the US import prohibition (shrimp) is not the endangered species whose protection is sought through the import ban. We also note that the United States has mentioned that CITES neither authorizes nor prohibits the sea turtles conservation measures which are at issue in this dispute. Therefore, we consider that CITES, even though its object is to contribute to the protection of certain species, does not impose on its members specific methods of conservation such as TEDs.

7.59 We also note that the development of the use of TEDs is the result of regional agreements or voluntary individual practices of States. In our opinion, the existence of regional agreements and individual practices may not as such suffice to reach the conclusion that the use of TEDs has become a recognized multilateral environmental standard applicable to the complainants. We derive from the submissions of the United States that the application of TEDs based on a convention is only regional. Moreover, if the provisions of the multilateral agreements referred to by the United States (the 1982 United Nations Convention on the Law of the Seas and the 1992 Agenda 21) effectively address the objective of limiting by-catches of non-target species in trawling operations, they do not require the application of specific methods nor, a fortiori, the use of TEDs. Finally, even if a number of countries individually require TEDs on their shrimp trawlers, the fact that the complainants and third parties have objected to their use makes it difficult to conclude that the mandatory use of TEDs has been customarily accepted as a multilateral environmental standard applicable to the complainants.

7.60 In conclusion, we do not consider that any of the arguments raised by the United States would justify a finding different from that reached in paragraph 7.49 above. We consider that our findings do not question the legitimacy of environmental policies, including those promoted through multilateral conventions. We consider our findings to be in line with the principles embodied in many international agreements pursuant to which international cooperation is to be sought before having recourse to unilateral measures. Furthermore, the risk of a multiplicity of conflicting requirements clearly is reduced when requirements are decided in multilateral fora. Moreover, we do not suggest that import markets must exist as an incentive for the destruction of natural resources. Rather, we address a particular situation where a Member has taken unilateral measures which, by their nature, could put the multilateral trading system at risk.

7.61 In reaching our conclusions, we based ourselves on the current status of the WTO rules and of international law. As far as the WTO Agreement is concerned, we considered that certain unilateral measures, insofar as they could jeopardize the multilateral trading system, could not be covered by Article XX. Our findings with respect to international norms confirm our reasoning regarding the WTO Agreement and GATT. General international law and international environmental law clearly favour the use of negotiated instruments rather than unilateral measures when addressing transboundary or global environmental problems, particularly when developing countries are concerned. Hence a negotiated solution is clearly to be preferred, both from a WTO and an international environmental law perspective. However, our findings regarding Article XX do not imply that recourse to unilateral measures is always excluded, particularly after serious attempts have been made to negotiate; nor do they imply that, in any given case, they would be permitted. Nevertheless, in the present case, even though the situation of turtles is a serious one, we consider that the United States adopted measures which, irrespective of their environmental purpose, were clearly a threat to the multilateral trading system and were applied without any serious attempt to reach, beforehand, a negotiated solution.

7.62 We therefore find that the US measure at issue is not within the scope of measures permitted under the chapeau of Article XX.

3. Article XX(b) and (g)

7.63 In line with our approach described in para.7.29 above, we do not find it necessary to examine whether the US measure is covered by the terms of Article XX(b) or (g).

F. ARTICLE XXIII:1(a) OF GATT 1994

7.64 We note that India, Pakistan and Thailand claim that the measure at issue represents a clear infringement of Articles I, XI and XIII of GATT 1994 and that it is well established that "in cases where there is a clear infringement of the provisions of the General Agreement, or in other words, where measures are applied in conflict with the provisions of GATT ... the action would, prima facie, constitute a nullification or impairment ..." within the meaning of Article XXIII of GATT.

7.65 We have found that the US measure at issue violates Article XI and is not justified under Article XX. We therefore conclude that there is a presumption of nullification or impairment within the meaning of Article 3.8 of the DSU, and that it is for the United States to rebut it. We do not consider that the United States has succeeded in rebutting the presumption that its breach of GATT has nullified or impaired benefits accruing to the complainants under GATT 1994.

VIII. CONCLUSIONS

8.1 In the light of the findings above, we conclude that the import ban on shrimp and shrimp products as applied by the United States on the basis of Section 609 of Public Law 101–162 is not consistent with Article XI:1 of GATT 1994, and cannot be justified under Article XX of GATT 1994.

8.2 The Panel recommends that the Dispute Settlement Body request the United States to bring this measure into conformity with its obligations under the WTO Agreement.

IX. CONCLUDING REMARKS

9.1 We note that the issue in dispute was not the urgency of protection of sea turtles. The matter we have been asked to review is Section 609 as interpreted by the CIT and as applied by the United States on the date this Panel was established. It was not our task to review generally the desirability or necessity of the environmental objectives of the US policy on sea turtle conservation. In our opinion, Members are free to set their own environmental objectives. However, they are bound to implement these objectives in such a way that is consistent with their WTO obligations, not depriving the WTO Agreement of its object and purpose. We recall the statement contained in the 1996 report of the Committee on Trade and Environment for the Singapore Ministerial Conference to the effect that there should not be nor need be any policy contradiction between upholding and safeguarding an open, equitable and non-discriminatory multilateral trading system on the one hand and acting for the protection of the environment on the other. We also note that we are bound to make findings on the basis of the existing norms, without prejudice to any potential developments in the relevant fora. In our view, and based on the information provided by the experts, the protection of sea turtles throughout their life stages is important and TEDs are one of the recommended means of protection within an integrated conservation strategy. We consider that the best way for the parties to this dispute to contribute effectively to the protection of sea turtles in a manner consistent with WTO objectives, including sustainable development, would be to reach cooperative agreements on integrated conservation strategies, covering, inter alia, the design, implementation and use of TEDs while taking into account the specific conditions in the different geographical areas concerned.

APPENDIX

STATUS OF BASIC DOCUMENTS IN INTERNATIONAL ENVIRONMENTAL LAW AND WORLD ORDER

(CURRENT TO 1 JAN 99 UNLESS OTHERWISE INDICATED)

For the texts of reservations, declarations, and statements of understanding, and objections qualifying the ratification of, or accession or succession to, the multilateral treaties listed herein, see ***United Nations Multilateral Treaties Deposited with the Secretary General****, published each year and on the Internet.*

1. CONSTITUTIVE/ORGANIC

General

1.1 CONSTITUTION OF THE UNITED STATES OF AMERICA

1.2 CONSTITUTION OF THE INTERNATIONAL LABOUR ORGANISATION

Concluded: 28 Jun 19

Entered into force: 10 Jan 20

Note: The ILO Constitution was an integral part of, and came into force with, the Treaty of Peace between the Allied and Associated Powers and Germany (Treaty of Versailles) which was concluded 28 June 1919 and entered into force 10 January 20. Membership in the League of Nations carried with it automatic membership in the ILO.

Members: 173

Afghanistan (27 Sep 34), Albania (1920–67, 1991), Algeria (19 Oct 62), Angola (4 Jun 76), Antigua and Barbuda (16 Feb 82), Argentina (1919), Armenia (1992), Australia (1919), Austria (24 Jun 47), Azerbaijan (1992), Bahamas (25 May 76), Bahrain (18 Apr 77), Bangladesh (22 Jun 72), Barbados (8 May 67), Belarus (12 May 54), Belgium (1919), Belize (17 Nov 81), Benin (12 Dec 60), Bolivia (1919), Bosnia and Herzegovina (1991), Botswana (27 Feb 78), Brazil (1919), Bulgaria (16 Dec 20), Burkina Faso (21 Nov 60), Burundi (11 Mar 63), Cambodia (24 Feb 69), Cameroon (7 Jun 60), Canada (1919), Central African Republic (27 Oct 60), Chad (10 Nov 60), Chile (1919), China (1919), Colombia (1919), Comoros (23 Oct 78), Congo (10 Nov 60), Costa Rica (21 Apr 44), Côte d'Ivoire (21 Nov 60), Croatia (1992), Cuba (1919), Cyprus (23 Sep 60), Czech Republic (1919), Denmark (1919), Djibouti (3 May 78), Dominica (17 Jun 82), Dominican Republic (29 Sep 24), Ecuador (28 Sep 34), Egypt (19 Jun 36), El Salvador (21 Jun 48), Equatorial Guinea (30 Jan 81), Eritrea (1993), Estonia (1991), Ethiopia (28 Sep 23), Fiji (19 Apr 74), Finland (16 Dec 20), France (1919), Gabon (14 Oct 60), Gambia ( ), Georgia (1992), Germany (12 Jun 51), Ghana (20 May 57), Greece (1919), Grenada (1979), Guatemala (1919–38, 1945), Guinea (1959), Guinea-Bissau (1977), Guyana (8 Jun 66), Haiti (1919), Honduras (1 Jan 55), Hungary (18 Sep 22), Iceland (19 Oct 45), India (1919), Indonesia (12 Jun 50), Iran (1919), Iraq (3 Oct 32), Ireland (10 Sep 23), Israel (13 May 49), Italy (19 Oct 45), Jamaica (26 Dec 62), Japan (26 Nov 51), Jordan (26 Jan 56), Kazakhstan (1992), Kenya (13 Jan 64), Korea (South) (1991), Kuwait (13 Jun 61), Kyrgyzstan (1992), Lao People's Democratic Republic (1964), Latvia (1991), Lebanon (1948), Lesotho (1966–71, 1980), Liberia (1919), Libyan Arab Jamihiriya (1952), Lithuania (1991), Luxembourg (16 Dec 20), Madagascar (1 Nov 60), Malawi (22 Mar 65), Malaysia (11 Nov 57), Mali (22 Sep 31), Malta (1965), Mauritania (1961), Mauritius (1969), Mexico (12 Sep 31), Moldova (1992),

Mongolia (24 May 68), Morocco (13 Jun 56), Mozambique (28 May 76), Myanmar (18 May 48), Namibia (3 Oct 78), Nepal (30 Aug 66), Netherlands (1919), New Zealand (1919), Nicaragua (9 Apr 57), Niger (27 Feb 61), Nigeria (17 Oct 60), Norway (1919), Oman (1995), Pakistan (31 Oct 47), Panama (1919), Papua New Guinea (1 May 76), Paraguay (5 Sep 56), Peru (1919), Philippines (15 Jun 48), Poland (1919), Portugal (1919), Qatar (25 Apr 72), Romania (11 May 56), Russian Federation (26 Apr 54), Rwanda (18 Sep 62), St. Lucia (9 Apr 80), Saint Vincent and the Granadines (1995), San Marino (18 Jun 82), São Tomé and Príncipe (1 Jun 82), Saudi Arabia (12 Jan 76), Senegal (4 Nov 60), Seychelles (25 Apr 77), Sierra Leone (13 Jun 61), Singapore (25 Oct 65), Slovakia (1919), Slovenia (1992), Solomon Islands (28 May 84), Somalia (18 Nov 60), South Africa (1919–41, 1956), Spain (28 May 56), Sri Lanka (28 Jun 48), St. Kitts and Nevis (1996), Sudan (12 Jun 56), Suriname (24 Feb 76), Swaziland (20 May 75), Sweden (1919), Switzerland (1919), Syria (4 Dec 47), Tajikistan (1993), Tanzania (30 Jan 62), Thailand (1919), The former Yugoslav Republic of Macedonia (1992), Togo (7 Jun 60), Trinidad and Tobago (24 May 63), Tunisia (12 Jun 56), Turkey (18 Jul 32), Turkmenistan (1992), Uganda (25 Mar 63), Ukraine 12 May 54), United Arab Emirates (25 Apr 72), United Kingdom (1919), United States (18 Feb 80), Uruguay (1919), Uzbekistan (1992), Venezuela (16 Mar 58), Viet Nam ( ), Yemen (1990), Yugoslavia (23 May 51), Zaire (20 Sep 60), Zambia (2 Dec 64), Zimbabwe (6 Jun 80)

1.3 Charter of the United Nations

Concluded: 26 Jun 45
Entered into force: 24 Oct 45
Parties: 185
Original members: 51

Argentina (24 Sep 45), Australia (1 Nov 45), Belarus (Byelorussian SSR) (24 Oct 45), Belgium (27 Dec 45), Bolivia (14 Nov 45), Brazil (21 Sep 45), Canada (9 Nov 45), Chile (11 Oct 45), China (28 Sep 45), Colombia (5 Nov 45), Costa Rica (2 Nov 45), Cuba (15 Oct 45), Czechoslovakia (19 Oct 45), Denmark (9 Oct 45), Dominican Republic (4 Sep 45), Ecuador (21 Dec 45), Egypt (22 Oct 45), El Salvador (26 Sep 45), Ethiopia (13 Nov 45), France (31 Aug 45), Greece (25 Oct 45), Guatemala (21 Nov 45), Haiti (27 Sep 45), Honduras (17 Dec 45), India (30 Oct 45), Iran (16 Oct 45), Iraq (21 Dec 45), Lebanon (17 Oct 45), Liberia (15 Oct 45), Luxembourg (2 Nov 45), Mexico (7 Nov 45), Netherlands (10 Dec 45), New Zealand (10 Sep 45), Nicaragua (6 Sep 45), Norway (27 Nov 45), Panama (13 Nov 45), Paraguay (12 Oct 45), Peru (31 Oct 45), Philippines (11 Oct 45), Poland (24 Oct 45), Russia (USSR) (24 Oct 45), Saudi Arabia (18 Oct 45), South Africa (7 Nov 45), Syria (19 Oct 45), Turkey (28 Sep 45), Ukraine (Ukrainian SSR) (24 Oct 45), United Kingdom (20 Oct 45), United States (8 Aug 45), Uruguay (18 Dec 45), Venezuela (15 Nov 45), Yugoslavia (19 Oct 45)

* China was originally represented in the UN by the Government of the Republic of China (R.O.C.) on Taiwan until 25 October 1971. Since then, China has been represented by the Government of the People's Republic of China. The R.O.C. is not a member of the UN and has no representation.

Non-signatories admitted under Article 4: 135

Afghanistan (9 Nov 46), Albania (14 Dec 55), Algeria (8 Oct 62), Andorra (28 Jul 93), Angola (1 Dec 76), Antigua/Barbuda (11 Nov 81), Armenia (2 Mar 92), Austria (14 Dec 55), Azerbaijan (2 Mar 92), Bahamas (18 Sep 73), Bahrain (21 Sep 71), Bangladesh (17 Sep 74), Barbados (9 Dec 66), Belize (25 Sep 81), Benin (20 Sep 60), Bhutan (21 Sep 71), Bosnia–Herzegovina (22 May 92), Botswana (17 Oct 66), Brunei (21 Sep 84), Bulgaria (14 Dec 55), Burkina Faso (20 Sep 60), Burundi (18 Sep 62), Cambodia (14 Dec 55), Cameroon (20 Sep 60), Cape Verde (16 Sep 75), Central African Republic (20 Sep 60), Chad (20 Sep 60), Comoros (12 Nov 75), Congo (Brazzaville) (20 Sep 60), Congo (Kinshasa) (20 Sep 60), Côte d'Ivoire (20 Sep 60), Croatia (22 May 92), Cyprus (20 Sep 60), Czech Republic* (19 Jan 93), Djibouti (20 Sep 77), Dominica (18 Dec 78), Equatorial Guinea (12 Nov 68), Eritrea (28 May 93), Estonia (17 Sep 91), Fiji (13 Oct 70), Finland (14 Dec 55), Gabon (20 Sep 60), Gambia (21 Sep 65), Georgia (31 Jul 92), Germany (18 Sep 73), Ghana (8 Mar 57), Grenada (17 Sep

74), Guinea (12 Dec 58), Guinea–Bissau (17 Sep 74), Guyana (20 Sep 66), Hungary (14 Dec 55), Iceland (9 Nov 46), Indonesia (28 Sep 50), Ireland (14 Dec 55), Israel (11 May 49), Italy (14 Dec 55), Jamaica (18 Sep 62), Japan (18 Dec 56), Jordan (14 Dec 55), Kazakhstan (2 Mar 92), Kenya (16 Dec 63), Korea (North) (17 Sep 91), Korea (South) (17 Sep 91), Kuwait (14 May 63), Kyrgyzstan (2 Mar 92), Laos (14 Dec 55), Latvia (17 Sep 91), Lesotho (17 Oct 66), Libya (14 Dec 55), Liechtenstein (18 Sep 90), Lithuania (17 Sep 91), Macedonia (8 Apr 93), Madagascar (20 Sep 60), Malawi (1 Dec 64), Malaysia (17 Sep 57), Maldives (21 Sep 65), Mali (28 Sep 60), Malta (1 Dec 64), Marshall Islands (17 Sep 91), Mauritania (27 Oct 61), Mauritius (24 Apr 68), Micronesia (17 Sep 91), Moldova (2 Mar 92), Monaco (28 May 93), Mongolia (27 Oct 61), Morocco (12 Nov 56), Mozambique (16 Sep 75), Myanmar (Burma) (19 Apr 48), Namibia (23 Apr 90), Nepal (14 Dec 55), Niger (20 Sep 60), Nigeria (7 Oct 60), Oman (7 Oct 71), Pakistan (30 Sep 47), Palau (15 Dec 94), Papua New Guinea (10 Oct 75), Portugal (14 Dec 55), Qatar (21 Sep 71), Romania (14 Dec 55), Rwanda (18 Sep 62), St Kitts/Nevis (23 Sep 83), St Lucia (18 Sep 79), St Vincent/Grenadines (16 Sep 80), Samoa (15 Dec 76), San Marino (2 Mar 92), Sao Tomé/Príncipe (16 Sep 75), Senegal (28 Sep 60), Seychelles (21 Sep 76), Siam (Thailand) (15 Dec 46), Sierra Leone (27 Sep 61), Singapore (21 Sep 65), Slovakia* (19 Jan 93), Slovenia (22 May 92), Solomon Islands (19 Sep 78), Somalia (20 Sep 60), Spain (14 Dec 55), Sri Lanka (14 Dec 55), Sudan (12 Nov 56), Suriname (4 Dec 75), Swaziland (24 Sep 68), Sweden (9 Nov 46), Tajikistan (2 Mar 92), Tanzania (14 Dec 61), Togo (20 Sep 60), Trinidad/Tobago (18 Sep 62), Tunisia (12 Nov 56), Turkmenistan (2 Mar 92), Uganda (25 Oct 62), United Arab Emirates (9 Dec 71), Uzbekistan (2 Mar 92), Vanuatu (15 Sep 81), Vietnam (20 Sep 77), Yemen (30 Sep 47), Zambia (1 Dec 64), Zimbabwe (25 Aug 80)

* Czechoslovakia was a founding member of the UN until its dissolution on 1 Jan 93. The Czech and Slovak republics succeeded Czechoslovakia as separate members on 19 Jan 93. Hence a total of 185 rather than 186 parties.

1.4 STATUTE OF THE INTERNATIONAL COURT OF JUSTICE

Concluded: 26 Jun 45

Entered into force: 24 Oct 45

Note: The Statute is part of the UN Charter (Basic Document I.3, *supra*). All members of the UN are parties to the Statute. Non-members may become parties to the Statute on conditions set in each case by the General Assembly on the recommendation of the Security Council. (Charter Article 93)

Non-members who are parties to the Statute: 2

Nauru (29 Jan 88), Switzerland (28 Jun 48)

1.5 STATUTE OF THE INTERNATIONAL ATOMIC ENERGY AGENCY (IAEA)

Concluded: 26 Oct 56

Entered into force: 29 Jul 57

IAEA Members: 129 (as of at least Oct 97)

Afghanistan, Albania, Algeria, Argentina, Armenia, Australia, Austria, Bangladesh, Belarus, Belgium, Bolivia, Bosnia–Herzegovina, Brazil, Bulgaria, Burkina Faso,* Cambodia, Cameroon, Canada, Chile, China, Colombia, Congo (Kinshasa), Costa Rica, Côte d'Ivoire, Croatia, Cuba, Cyprus, Czech Republic, Denmark, Dominican Republic, Ecuador, Egypt, El Salvador, Estonia, Ethiopia, Finland, France, Gabon, Germany, Ghana, Georgia, Greece, Guatemala, Haiti, Hungary, Iceland, India, Indonesia, Iran, Iraq, Ireland, Israel, Italy, Jamaica, Japan, Jordan, Kazakhstan, Kenya, Korea (South), Kuwait, Latvia, Lebanon, Liberia, Libya, Liechtenstein, Lithuania, Luxembourg, Macedonia, Madagascar, Malaysia, Mali, Malta, Marshall Islands, Mauritius, Mexico, Moldova, Monaco, Mongolia, Morocco, Myanmar (Burma), Namibia, Netherlands, New Zealand, Nicaragua, Niger, Nigeria, Norway, Pakistan, Panama, Paraguay, Peru, Philippines, Poland, Portugal, Qatar, Romania, Russia, Saudi Arabia, Senegal, Sierra Leone, Singapore, Slovakia, Slovenia, South Africa, Spain, Sri Lanka, Sudan, Sweden, Switzerland, Syria, Tanzania, Thailand, Tunisia, Turkey, Uganda, Ukraine,

United Arab Emirates, United Kingdom, United States, Uruguay, Uzbekistan, Vatican City, Venezuela, Vietnam, Yemen, Yugoslavia, Zambia, Zimbabwe

* Membership pending deposit of legal instruments

1.6 **European Union: Consolidated Version of the Treaty Establishing the European Economic Community**

Concluded: 25 Mar 57 (Rome), 7 Feb 92 (Maastricht), 2 Oct 97 (Amsterdam)

Entered into force: 1 Jan 58 (Rome), 1 Nov 93 (Maastricht), not in force as of 1 Jan 99 (Amsterdam)

Parties: 15 (dates are for ratification of the Maastricht treaty)

Austria (11 Nov 94), Belgium (10 Dec 92), Denmark (17 Jun 93), Finland (8 Dec 94), France (4 Nov 92), Germany (13 Oct 93), Greece (3 Nov 92), Ireland (23 Nov 92), Italy (5 Dec 92), Luxembourg (28 Aug 92), Netherlands (28 Dec 92), Portugal (16 Feb 93), Spain (31 Dec 92), Sweden (15 Dec 94), United Kingdom (2 Aug 93)

1.7 **Vienna Convention on the Law of Treaties**

Concluded: 23 May 69

Entered into force: 27 Jan 80

Signed but not ratified: 21

Afghanistan (23 May 69), Bolivia (23 May 69), Brazil (23 May 69), Cambodia (23 May 69), Côte d'Ivoire (23 Jul 69), Ecuador (23 May 69), El Salvador (16 Feb 70), Ethiopia (30 Apr 70), Ghana (23 May 69), Guyana (23 May 69), Iran (23 May 69), Kenya (23 May 69), Luxembourg (4 Sep 69), Madagascar (23 May 69), Malawi (23 Aug 83), Nepal (23 May 69), Pakistan (29 Apr 70), Peru (23 May 69), Trinidad/Tobago (23 May 69), United States (24 Apr 70), Zambia (23 May 69)

Ratified/accepted/approved without qualification: 54

Australia (13 Jun 74), Austria (30 Apr 79), Barbados (24 Jun 71), Bosnia–Herzegovina (6 Mar 92), Cameroon (23 Oct 91), Central African Republic (10 Dec 71), Congo (Brazzaville) (12 Apr 82), Congo (Kinshasa) (25 Jul 77), Croatia (12 Oct 92), Cyprus (28 Dec 76), Egypt (11 Feb 82), Estonia (21 Oct 91), Georgia (8 Jun 95), Greece (30 Oct 74), Guatemala (21 May 97), Haiti (25 Aug 80), Honduras (20 Sep 79), Italy (25 Jul 74), Jamaica (28 Jul 70), Japan (2 Jul 81), Kazakhstan (5 Jan 94), Korea (South) (27 Apr 77), Latvia (4 May 93), Lesotho (3 Mar 72), Liberia (29 Aug 85), Liechtenstein (8 Feb 90), Lithuania (15 Jan 92), Mauritius (18 Jan 73), Malaysia (27 Jul 94), Mexico (25 Sep 74), Moldova (26 Jan 93), Nauru (5 May 78), Niger (27 Oct 71), Nigeria (31 Jul 69), Panama (28 Jul 80), Paraguay (3 Feb 72), Philippines (15 Nov 72), Poland (2 Jul 90), Rwanda (3 Jan 80), Senegal (11 Apr 86), Slovakia* (28 May 93), Slovenia (6 Jul 92), Solomon Islands (9 Aug 89), Spain (16 May 72), Sudan (18 Apr 90), Suriname (31 Jan 91), Switzerland (7 May 90), Tajikistan (6 May 96), Togo (28 Dec 79), Turkmenistan (4 Jan 96), Uruguay (5 Mar 82), Uzbekistan (12 Jul 95), Vatican City (25 Feb 77), Yugoslavia (27 Aug 70)

Ratified/accepted/approved with qualification: 28

Algeria (8 Nov 88), Argentina (5 Dec 72), Belarus** (1 May 86), Belgium (1 Sep 92), Bulgaria (21 Apr 87), Canada (14 Oct 70), Chile (9 Apr 81), Colombia (10 Apr 85), China (3 Sep 97), Costa Rica (22 Nov 96), Czech Republic* (22 Feb 93), Denmark (1 Jun 76), Finland (19 Aug 77), Germany (21 Jul 87), Hungary* * * (19 Jun 87), Kuwait (11 Nov 75), Mongolia* * * (16 May 88), Morocco* * * (26 Sep 72), Netherlands (9 Apr 85), New Zealand (4 Aug 71), Oman (18 Oct 90), Russia** (29 Apr 86), Sweden (4 Feb 75), Syria* * ** (2 Oct 70), Tanzania (12 Apr 76), Tunisia** (23 Jun 71), Ukraine** (14 May 86), United Kingdom (25 Jun 71)

* Succeeding Czechoslovakia (29 Jul 87)

** Reservation not accepted by Germany, Japan, New Zealand, Sweden, United Kingdom, United States

*** Reservation not accepted by Algeria, Israel

**** Reservation not accepted by Israel, Japan, Netherlands, New Zealand, Sweden, United Kingdom, United States

1.8 **Declaration on Principles of International Law Concerning Friendly Relations and Co-Operation Among States in Accordance with the Charter of the United Nations**
Adopted without recorded vote: 24 Oct 70

1.9 **International Law Commission Draft Articles on International Liability for Injurious Consequences Arising Out of Acts Not Prohibited by International Law**
Adopted: 30 May 89

1.10 **International Law Commission Draft Articles on State Responsibility**
Adopted: 12 July 1996

Environmental

1.11 **UNGA Resolution 1803 on Permanent Sovereignty over Natural Resources**
Adopted: 14 Dec 62
For: 87
Afghanistan, Algeria, Argentina, Australia, Austria, Belgium, Benin, Bolivia, Brazil, Burkina Faso, Burundi, Cambodia, Cameroon, Canada, Central African Republic, Chad, Chile, China, Colombia, Congo (Leopoldville), Costa Rica, Côte d'Ivoire, Cyprus, Dominican Republic, El Salvador, Ethiopia, Finland, Greece, Guatemala, Guinea, Haiti, Honduras, Iceland, India, Indonesia, Iran, Iraq, Ireland, Israel, Italy, Jamaica, Japan, Jordan, Lebanon, Liberia, Libya, Luxembourg, Madagascar, Malaysia, Mali, Mauritania, Mexico, Morocco, Netherlands, New Zealand, Nicaragua, Niger, Nigeria, Norway, Pakistan, Panama, Paraguay, Peru, Philippines, Rwanda, Saudi Arabia, Senegal, Sierra Leone, Spain, Sri Lanka, Sweden, Syria, Tanzania, Thailand, Togo, Trinidad and Tobago, Tunisia, Turkey, Uganda, United Arab Emirates, United Kingdom, United States, Uruguay, Venezuela, Yemen, Yugoslavia
Against: 2
France, South Africa
Abstain: 12
Belarus (Byelorussian SSR), Bulgaria, Cuba, Czechoslovakia, Ghana, Hungary, Mongolia, Myanmar, Poland, Romania, Ukraine (Ukrainian SSR), Union of Soviet Socialist Republics

1.12 **Stockholm Declaration of the United Nations Conference on the Human Environment**
Adopted: 16 Jun 72
For: 103*
Against: 0
Abstain: 12
* Adopted with no roll call vote recorded

1.13 **UNGA Resolution 2997 on the Institutional and Financial Arrangement for International Environment Cooperation [Establishing the United Nations Environment Programme (UNEP)]**
Adopted: 15 Dec 72
For: 116*
Against: 0
Abstain: 10
* Adopted with no roll call vote recorded

1.14 **UNGA Resolution 3129 on Co-operation in the Field of the Environment Concerning Natural Resources Shared by Two or More States**
Adopted: 13 Dec 73
For: 77
Algeria, Argentina, Australia, Bahrain, Botswana, Burundi, Cameroon, Canada, Central African Republic, Chad, Congo, Cyprus, Dahomey, Egypt, El Salvador, Fiji, Gabon, Gambia, Ghana, Greece, Guatemala, Guinea, Indonesia, Iran, Iraq,

Ireland, Jamaica, Jordan, Kenya, Kuwait, Laos, Lesotho, Liberia, Libya, Madagascar, Malawi, Malaysia, Mali, Mauritania, Mexico, Morocco, Nepal, Netherlands, New Zealand, Niger, Nigeria, Norway, Oman, Pakistan, Peru, Qatar, Romania, Rwanda, Saudi Arabia, Senegal, Sierra Leone, Singapore, Somalia, Sri Lanka, Sudan, Swaziland, Syria, Thailand, Togo, Tunisia, Uganda, United Arab Emirates, Upper Volta, Yemen, Yemen (Democratic), Yugoslavia, Zaire, Zambia
Against: 5
Bolivia, Brazil, Nicaragua, Paraguay, Portugal
Abstain: 43
Afghanistan, Austria, Barbados, Belgium, Bhutan, Bulgaria, Burma, Belarus (Byelorussian SSR), Chile, China, Colombia, Côte d'Ivoire, Costa Rica, Czechoslovakia, Denmark, Ecuador, Ethiopia, Finland, France, Germany (East), Germany (West), Guyana, Hungary, Iceland, India, Israel, Italy, Japan, Lebanon, Luxembourg, Mongolia, Poland, Russia (USSR), South Africa, Spain, Sweden, Trinidad and Tobago, Turkey, Ukraine (Ukrainian SSR), United Kingdom, United States, Uruguay, Venezuela

1.15 UNGA Resolution 3171 on Permanent Sovereignty over Natural Resources
Adopted: 17 Dec 73
For: 108
Afghanistan, Albania, Algeria, Argentina, Australia, Austria, Bahrain, Barbados, Belarus (Byelorussian SSR), Benin, Bhutan, Bolivia, Botswana, Brazil, Bulgaria, Burundi, Cambodia, Cameroon, Canada, Chad, Chile, China, Congo, Costa Rica, Côte d'Ivoire, Cuba, Cyprus, Czechoslovakia, Dominican Republic, Ecuador, Egypt, El Salvador, Equatorial Guinea, Ethiopia, Fiji, Finland, Gabon, Germany (East), Ghana, Guatemala, Guinea, Guyana, Haiti, Honduras, Hungary, Iceland, India, Indonesia, Iran, Iraq, Jamaica, Jordan, Kenya, Kuwait, Lebanon, Lesotho, Liberia, Libya, Madagascar, Malawi, Malaysia, Mali, Malta, Mexico, Mongolia, Morocco, Myanmar, Nepal, New Zealand, Niger, Nigeria, Oman, Pakistan, Panama, Paraguay, Peru, Philippines, Poland, Qatar, Romania, Russia (USSR), Rwanda, Saudi Arabia, Senegal, Sierra Leone, Singapore, Somalia, Spain, Sri Lanka, Sudan, Sweden, Syria, Tanzania, Thailand, Togo, Trinidad and Tobago, Tunisia, Turkey, Uganda, Ukraine (Ukrainian SSR), United Arab Emirates, Uruguay, Venezuela, Yemen, Yemen (Democratic), Yugoslavia, Zaire, Zambia
Against: 1
United Kingdom
Abstain: 16
Belgium, Denmark, France, German Federal Republic, Greece, Ireland, Israel, Italy, Japan, Luxembourg, Netherlands, Nicaragua, Norway, Portugal, South Africa, United States

1.16 Convention on the Protection of the Environment Between Denmark, Finland, Norway, and Sweden
Concluded: 9 Feb 74
Entered into force: 5 Oct 76
Ratified/accepted/approved without qualification: 4
Denmark (9 Sep 74), Finland (5 Apr 76), Norway (26 Mar 75), Sweden (10 May 74)

1.17 Final Act of the Conference on Security and Co-Operation in Europe
Adopted: 1 Aug 75
Conferees: 35
Austria, Belgium, Bulgaria, Canada, Cyprus, Czechoslovakia, Denmark, Finland, France, German Democratic Republic, German Federal Republic, Greece, Holy See, Hungary, Iceland, Ireland, Italy, Liechtenstein, Luxembourg, Malta, Monaco, Netherlands, Norway, Poland, Portugal, Romania, Russia (USSR), San Marino, Spain, Sweden, Switzerland, Turkey, United Kingdom, United States, Yugoslavia
Signed: 35

Austria, Belgium, Bulgaria, Canada, Cyprus, Czechoslovakia, Denmark, Finland, France, German Democratic Republic, German Federal Republic, Greece, Holy See, Hungary, Iceland, Ireland, Italy, Liechtenstein, Luxembourg, Malta, Monaco, Netherlands, Norway, Poland, Portugal, Romania, Russia (USSR), San Marino, Spain, Sweden, Switzerland, Turkey, United Kingdom, United States, Yugoslavia

1.18 Draft Principles of Conduct in the Field of the Environment for Guidance of States in the Conservation and Harmonious Utilization of Natural Resources Shared by Two or More States
Approved by UNEP Governing Council: 19 May 78

1.19 UNGA Resolution 35/48 on Historical Responsibility of States for the Preservation of Nature for Present and Future Generations
Adopted: 30 Oct 80
For: 68*
Against: 0
Abstain: 47
* Adopted with no roll call vote recorded

1.20 ILA Rules on International Law Applicable to Transfrontier Pollution
Adopted: 4 Sep 82

1.21 World Charter for Nature
Adopted: 28 Oct 82
For: 111
Afghanistan, Angola, Australia, Austria, Bahrain, Bangladesh, Barbados, Belarus (Byelorussian SSR), Belgium, Benin, Bulgaria, Burkina Faso, Burundi, Cambodia, Canada, Cape Verde, Central African Republic, Chad, China, Cameroon, Comoros, Congo, Costa Rica, Cuba, Cyprus, Czechoslovakia, Denmark, Djibouti, Egypt, El Salvador, Equatorial Guinea, Ethiopia, Finland, France, Gabon, Gambia, Germany (East), Germany (West), Greece, Guinea, Guinea–Bissau, Honduras, Hungary, Iceland, India, Indonesia, Iran, Iraq, Ireland, Italy, Côte d'Ivoire, Jamaica, Japan, Kenya, Kuwait, Lao People's Democratic Republic, Libya, Luxembourg, Madagascar, Malawi, Malaysia, Maldives, Mali, Malta, Mauitania, Mongolia, Morocco, Mozambique, Nepal, Netherlands, New Zealand, Nicaragua, Niger, Nigeria, Norway, Oman, Pakistan, Papua New Guinea, Poland, Portugal, Qatar, Romania, Russia (USSR), Rwanda, Samoa, São Tomé and Príncipe, Saudi Arabia, Senegal, Seychelles, Singapore, Solomon Islands, Somalia, Spain, Sri Lanka, Sudan, Swaziland, Sweden, Tanzania, Thailand, Togo, Tunisia, Turkey, Uganda, Ukraine (Ukrainian SSR), United Arab Emirates, United Kingdom, Uruguay, Yemen, Yugoslavia, Zaire, Zambia
Against: 1
United States
Abstain: 18
Algeria, Argentina, Bolivia, Brazil, Chile, Colombia, Dominican Republic, Ecuador, Ghana, Guyana, Lebanon, Mexico, Paraguay, Peru, Philippines, Suriname, Trinidad and Tobago, Venezuela

1.22 Experts Group on Environmental Law of the World Commission on Environment and Development, Legal Principles for Environmental Protection and Sustainable Development
Adopted: 18–20 Jun 86

1.23 Restatement (Third) of the Foreign Relations Law of the United States (§§ 601–604)
Adopted: 14 May 87

1.24 Declaration of the Hague
Adopted: 11 Mar 89
Conferees: 24

Australia, Brazil, Canada, Côte d'Ivoire, Egypt, France, Germany (West), Hungary, India, Indonesia, Italy, Japan, Jordan, Kenya, Malta, Norway, New Zealand, Netherlands, Senegal, Spain, Sweden, Tunisia, Venezuela, Zimbabwe

1.25 LANGKAWI COMMONWEALTH HEADS OF GOVERNMENT DECLARATION ON ENVIRONMENT

Unanimously adopted by the Heads of the Commonwealth States (49 at the time): 21 Oct 89

1.26 AFRICAN, CARIBBEAN, AND PACIFIC STATES–EUROPEAN ECONOMIC COMMUNITY CONVENTION (LOMÉ IV)

Concluded: 15 Dec 89

Entered into force: 1 Sep 91

African ACP Members: 48 (as of at least 10 Dec 97)

Angola (1985), Benin (1963), Botswana (1975), Burkina Faso (1963), Burundi (1963), Cameroon (1963), Cape Verde (1980), Central African Republic (1963), Chad (1963), Comoros (1980), Congo (Brazzaville) (1963), Congo (Kinshasa) (19__), Côte d'Ivoire (1963), Djibouti (1980), Equatorial Guinea (1975), Eritrea (1993), Ethiopia (1975), Gabon (1963), Gambia (1975), Ghana (1975), Guinea (19__), Guinea–Bissau (1975), Kenya (1975), Lesotho (1975), Liberia (1975), Madagascar (1963), Malawi (1975), Mali (1963), Mauritania (1963), Mauritius (1972), Mozambique (1985), Namibia (1989), Niger (1963), Nigeria (1975), Rwanda (1963), São Tomé/Príncipe (1980), Senegal (1963), Seychelles (1980), Sierra Leone (1975), Somalia (1963), South Africa (1997)**, Sudan 1975), Swaziland (1975), Tanzania (1975), Togo (1963), Uganda (1975), Zambia (1975), Zimbabwe (1980)

Caribbean ACP Members: 15 (as of at least 10 Dec 97)

Antigua/Barbuda (1985), Bahamas (1975), Barbados (1975), Belize (1985), Dominica (1980), Dominican Republic (1989), Grenada (1975), Guyana (1975), Haiti (1989), Jamaica (1975), St Kitts/Nevis (1985), St Lucia (1980), St Vincent/Grenadines (1985), Suriname (1980), Trinidad/Tobago (1975)

Pacific ACP Members: 8 (as of at least 10 Dec 97)

Fiji (1975), Kiribati (1980), Papua New Guinea (1980), Solomon Islands (1980), Samoa (1975), Tonga (1975), Tuvalu (1980), Vanuatu (1985)

European Parties to Lomé IV: 15 (as of at least 10 Dec 97)

Austria (__95), Belgium (12 Jul 91), Denmark (4 Jul 91), Finland (__95), France (1 Feb 91), Germany (31 Jan 91), Greece (28 May 91), Ireland (7 May 91), Italy (29 May 91), Luxembourg (20 Jan 91), Netherlands (31 May 91), Portugal (24 Jul 91), Spain (31 May 91), Sweden (__95), United Kingdom (30 May 91)

* Superseding Yaoundé I (1963), Yaoundé II (1969), Lomé (1975), Lomé II (1980), and Lomé III (1985).

** Qualified status.

1.27 CONVENTION ON ENVIRONMENTAL IMPACT ASSESSMENT IN A TRANSBOUNDARY CONTEXT

Concluded: 25 Feb 91

Entered into force: 10 Sep 97

Signed but not ratified: 12 (as of at least 5 May 98)

Belarus (26 Feb 91), Belgium (26 Feb 91), Canada (26 Feb 91), France (26 Feb 91), Germany (26 Feb 91), Iceland (26 Feb 91), Ireland (26 Feb 91), Portugal (26 Feb 91), Romania (26 Feb 91), Russia (26 Feb 91), Ukraine (26 Feb 91), United States (26 Feb 91)

Ratified/accepted/approved without qualification: 17 (as of at least 5 May 98)

Albania (4 Oct 91), Armenia (21 Feb 97),Croatia (8 Jul 96), Czech Republic (30 Sep 93), Denmark (14 Mar 97), European Community (24 Jun 97), Finland (10 Aug 95), Greece (24 Feb 98), Hungary (11 Jul 97), Italy (19 Jan 95), Luxembourg (29 Aug 95), Moldova (4 Jan 94), Norway (23 Jun 93), Poland (12 Jun 97), Slovakia (28 May 93), Spain (10 Sep 92), Sweden (24 Jan 92), Switzerland (16 Sep 96), United Kingdom (10 Oct 97)

Ratified/accepted/approved with qualification: 3 (as of at least 5 May 97)

Austria (4 Oct 91), Bulgaria (12 May 95), Netherlands (28 Feb 95),

1.28 **Arctic Environmental Protection Strategy (AEPS)**
Adopted: 14 Jun 91
Conferees: 8
Canada, Denmark, Finland, Iceland, Norway, Sweden, Union of Soviet Socialist Republics, United States of America

1.29 **Rio Declaration on Environment and Development**
Adopted by consensus by the UN Conference on Environment and Development: 13 Jun 92

1.30 **Agenda 21**
***Approved by the UN Conference on Environment and Development*:** 13 Jun 92

1.31 **UNGA Resolution on Institutional Arrangement to Follow Up the United Nations Conference on Environment and Development**
Adopted without recorded vote: 22 Dec 92

1.32 **Nuuk Declaration on Environment and Development in the Arctic**
Adopted by the Ministers of the Arctic Countries: 16 Sep 93
Conferees: 8
Canada, Denmark, Finland, Iceland, Norway, the Russian Federation, Sweden, United States of America

1.33 **Agreement between the Government of the United States and the Government of the Russian Federation on Cooperation in the Field of Protection of the Environment and Natural Resources**
Concluded: 23 Jun 94
Entered into force: 23 Jun 94

1.34 **Agreement between the United States of America and the Russian Federation on Cooperation in the Prevention of Pollution of the Environment in the Arctic**
Concluded: 16 Dec 94
Entered into force: 16 Dec 94

1.35 **Memorandum of Understanding between the Government of the United States and the Russian Federation on Cooperation in Natural and Manmade Technological Emergency Prevention and Response**
Concluded: 16 July 96
Entered into force: 16 July 96

1.36 **Declaration on the Establishment of the Arctic Council**
Adopted unanimously and signed by representatives of the Arctic States: 19 Sep 96
Signatories: 8
Canada, Denmark, Finland, Iceland, Norway, the Russian Federation, Sweden, United States of America

1.37 **Declaration among the Royal Ministry of Defence of the Kingdom of Norway, the Ministry of Defence of the Russian Federation, and the Department of Defense of the United States of America, on Arctic Military Environmental Cooperation (AMEC)**
Adopted: 26 Sep 96

1.38 **Nairobi Declaration and Governing Council Decision on the Role, Mandate and Governance of the United Nations Environment Programme**
Adopted by the UNEP Governing Council: 7 Feb 97

1.39 AGREEMENT BETWEEN THE GOVERNMENT OF THE KINGDOM OF NORWAY AND THE GOVERNMENT OF THE RUSSIAN FEDERATION ON ENVIRONMENTAL COOPERATION WITH THE DISMANTLING OF RUSSIAN NUCLEAR POWERED SUBMARINES WITHDRAWN FROM THE [RUSSIAN] NAVY'S SERVICE IN THE NORTHERN REGION, AND THE ENHANCEMENT OF NUCLEAR AND RADIATION SAFETY
Concluded: 26 May 98
Entered into force: 26 May 98

2. GLOBAL COMMONS: ANTARCTICA

2.1 ANTARCTIC TREATY
Concluded: 1 Dec 59
Entered into force: 23 Jun 61
Ratified/accepted/approved without qualification: 39 (as of at least 1 Mar 97)
Argentina (23 Jun 61), Australia (23 Jun 61), Austria (25 Aug 87), Belgium (26 Jun 60), Brazil (16 May 75), Bulgaria (11 Sep 78), Canada (4 May 88), Chile (23 Jun 61), China (8 Jun 83), Colombia (31 Jan 89), Cuba (16 Aug 84), Czech Republic (1 Jan 93), Denmark (20 May 65), Ecuador (15 Sep 87), Finland (15 May 84), France (16 Sep 60), Germany (5 Feb 79), Greece (8 Jan 87), Guatemala (31 Jul 91), Hungary (27 Jan 84), Italy (18 Mar 81), Japan (4 Aug 60), Korea (North) (21 Jan 87), Korea (South) (28 Nov 86), Netherlands (30 Mar 67), New Zealand (1 Nov 60), Norway (24 Aug 60), Papua New Guinea (16 Mar 81), Peru (10 Apr 81), Poland (8 Jun 61), Russia (2 Nov 60), Slovakia (1 Jan 93), South Africa (21 Jun 60), Spain (31 Mar 82), Sweden (25 Apr 84), Switzerland (15 Nov 90), Ukraine (28 Oct 92), United Kingdom (31 May 60), United States (18 Aug 60)
Ratified/accepted/approved with qualification: 4 (as of at least 1 Mar 97)
India (19 Aug 83), Romania (15 Sep 71), Uruguay (11 Jan 80)

2.2 CERTAIN RECOMMENDATIONS OF THIRD ANTARCTIC TREATY CONSULTATIVE MEETING, ANNEX: AGREED MEASURES FOR THE CONSERVATION OF ANTARCTIC FAUNA AND FLORA
Adopted: 13 Jun 64

2.3 CONVENTION FOR THE CONSERVATION OF ANTARCTIC SEALS
Concluded: 11 Feb 72
Entered into force: 11 Mar 78
Signed but not ratified: 1 (as of at least 1 Mar 97)
New Zealand (9 Jun 72)
Ratified/accepted/approved without qualification: 12 (as of at least 1 Mar 97)
Australia (1 Jul 87), Belgium (9 Feb 78), Brazil (11 Feb 91), Canada (4 Oct 90), France (19 Feb 75), Italy (2 Apr 92), Japan (28 Aug 80), Norway (10 Dec 73), Poland (15 Aug 80), Russia (8 Feb 78), South Africa (15 Aug 72), United Kingdom (10 Sep 74), United States (19 Jan 77)
Ratified/accepted/approved with qualification: 4 (as of at least 1 Mar 97)
Argentina (7 Mar 78), Chile (7 Feb 80), Germany (30 Sep 87)

2.4 CONVENTION ON THE CONSERVATION OF ANTARCTIC MARINE LIVING RESOURCES (CCAMLR)
Concluded: 20 May 80
Entered into force: 7 Apr 82
Ratified/accepted/approved without qualification: 26 (as of at least 1 Mar 97)
Australia (6 May 81), Belgium (22 Feb 84), Brazil (28 Jan 86), Bulgaria (1 Sep 92), Canada (1 Jul 88), Chile (22 Jul 81), European Community (21 Apr 82), Finland (6 Sep 89), Germany (23 Apr 82), Greece (12 Feb 87), India (17 Jun 85), Italy (29 Mar 89), Japan (26 May 81), Korea (South) (29 Mar 85), Netherlands (23 Feb 90), New Zealand (8 Mar 82), Norway (6 Dec 83), Peru (23 Jun 89),

Poland (28 Mar 84), Russia (26 May 81), South Africa (23 Jul 81), Spain (9 Apr 84), Sweden (6 Jun 84), United Kingdom (31 Aug 81), United States (18 Feb 82), Uruguay (22 Mar 85)
Ratified/accepted/approved with qualification: 2 (as of at least 1 Mar 97)
Argentina (28 May 82), France (16 Sep 82)

2.5 UNGA RESOLUTION 38/77 ON THE QUESTION OF ANTARCTICA
Adopted without recorded vote: 15 Dec 83

2.6 UNGA RESOLUTION 39/152 ON THE QUESTION OF ANTARCTICA
Adopted without recorded vote: 17 Dec 84

2.7 CONVENTION ON THE REGULATION OF ANTARCTIC MINERAL RESOURCE ACTIVITIES (CRAMRA)
Concluded: 2 Jun 88
Not in force as of at least 1 Mar 97
Signed but not ratified: 17 (as of at least 1 Mar 97)
Argentina (17 Mar 89), Brazil (25 Nov 88), Chile (17 Mar 89), China (28 Jun 89), Denmark (25 Feb 89), Finland (25 Nov 88), Japan (22 Nov 89, Korea (South) (25 Nov 88), New Zealand (25 Nov 88), Norway (25 Nov 88), Poland (25 Feb 89), Russia (25 Nov 88), South Africa (25 Nov 88), Sweden (25 Nov 88), United Kingdom (22 Mar 89), United States (30 Nov 88), Uruguay (25 Nov 88)

2.8 UNGA RESOLUTION 44/124 ON THE QUESTION OF ANTARCTICA
Adopted: 15 Dec 89
For Part A: 114
Afghanistan, Albania, Algeria, Angola, Antigua and Barbuda, Argentina, Bahamas, Bahrain, Bangladesh, Barbados, Benin, Bhutan, Bolivia, Brazil, Brunei Darussalam, Burkina Faso, Burundi, Cameroon, Cape Verde, Central African Republic, Chad, China, Colombia, Congo, Costa Rica, Côte d'Ivoire, Cuba, Cyprus, Democratic Kampuchea, Democratic Yemen, Djibouti, Dominica, Dominican Republic, Ecuador, Egypt, El Salvador, Ethiopia, Fiji, Gabon, Gambia, Ghana, Grenada, Guatemala, Guinea, Guinea–Bissau, Guyana, Haiti, Honduras, India, Indonesia, Iran, Iraq, Jamaica, Jordan, Kenya, Kuwait, Lao People's Democratic Republic, Lebanon, Lesotho, Liberia, Libya, Madagascar, Malawi, Malaysia, Maldives, Mali, Mauritania, Mexico, Mongolia, Morocco, Mozambique, Myanmar, Nepal, Nicaragua, Niger, Nigeria, Oman, Pakistan, Panama, Peru, Philippines, Qatar, Romania, Rwanda, Saint Kitts and Nevis, Saint Lucia, Saint Vincent and the Grenadines, São Tomé and Príncipe, Saudi Arabia, Senegal, Seychelles, Sierra Leone, Singapore, Solomon Islands, Somalia, Sri Lanka, Sudan, Suriname, Syria, Thailand, Togo, Trinidad and Tobago, Tunisia, Uganda, United Arab Emirates, Tanzania, Vanuatu, Venezuela, Viet Nam, Yemen, Yugoslavia, Zaire, Zambia, Zimbabwe
Against Part A: 0
Abstain Part A: 6
Ireland, Luxembourg, Malta, Mauritius, Portugal, Swaziland
For Part B: 100
Albania, Algeria, Angola, Antigua and Barbuda, Bahamas, Bahrain, Bangladesh, Barbados, Benin, Bhutan, Bolivia, Botswana, Brunei Darussalam, Burkina Faso, Burundi, Cameroon, Cape Verde, Central African Republic, Chad, Congo, Costa Rica, Côte d'Ivoire, Cyprus, Democratic Kampuchea, Djibouti, Dominica, Dominican Republic, Egypt, El Salvador, Ethiopia, Gabon, Gambia, Ghana, Grenada, Guatemala, Guinea, Guinea–Bissau, Guyana, Haiti, Honduras, Indonesia, Iran, Iraq, Jamaica, Jordan, Kenya, Kuwait, Lebanon, Lesotho, Liberia, Libya, Madagascar, Malawi, Malaysia, Maldives, Mali, Mauritiania, Mexico, Morocco, Mozambique, Myanmar, Nepal, Niger, Nigeria, Oman, Pakistan, Panama, Philippines, Qatar, Romania, Rwanda, Saint Kitts and Nevis, Saint Lucia, Saint Vincent and the Grenadines, São Tomé and Príncipe, Saudi Arabia, Senegal, Seychelles, Sierra Leone, Singapore, Solomon Islands, Somalia, Sri Lanka, Sudan, Suriname, Syria, Thailand, Togo, Trinidad and Tobago, Tunisia, Ugan-

da, United Arab Emirates, Tanzania, Vanuatu, Venezuela, Yemen, Yugoslavia, Zaire, Zambia, Zimbabwe
Against Part B: 0
Abstain Part B: 9
China, Fiji, Ireland, Luxembourg, Malta, Mauritius, Portugal, Swaziland, Turkey

2.9 PROTOCOL ON ENVIRONMENTAL PROTECTION TO THE ANTARCTIC TREATY
Concluded: 4 Oct 91
Entered into force: 14 Jan 98
Signed but not ratified: 10
Austria (4 Oct 91), Canada (4 Oct 91), Colombia (4 Oct 91), Czech Republic (1 Jan 93), Denmark (2 Jul 92), Hungary (4 Oct 91), Korea (North) (4 Oct 91), Romania (4 Oct 91), Slovakia (1 Jan 93), Switzerland (4 Oct 91)
Ratified/accepted/approved without qualification: 8 Argentina (28 Oct 93), Australia (6 Apr 94), Ecuador (4 Jan 93), France (5 Feb 93), Norway (16 Jun 93), Peru (8 Mar 93), Spain (1 Jul 92), Sweden (30 Mar 94)
***Ratified/accepted/approved* (qualifications undetermined):** 19 Belgium (26 Apr 96), Brazil (15 Aug 95), Chile (11 Jan 95), China (2 Aug 94), Finland ( ), Germany (25 Nov 94), Greece (23 May 95), India (26 Apr 96), Italy (31 Mar 95), Japan (15 Dec 97), Korea (South) (2 Jan 96), Netherlands (14 Apr 94), New Zealand (22 Dec 94), Poland (1 Nov 95), Russia ( ), South Africa, (3 Aug 95), United Kingdom (25 Apr 95), United States (14 Apr 97), Uruguay (11 Jan 95)

3. ATMOSPHERE/SPACE

3.1 CONVENTION ON THIRD PARTY LIABILITY IN THE FIELD OF NUCLEAR ENERGY
Concluded: 29 Jul 60
Entered into force: 1 Apr 68
Signed but not ratified: 2 (as of at least Mar 98)
Austria (29 Jul 60), Luxembourg (29 Jul 60)
Ratified/accepted/approved without qualification: 10 (as of at least Mar 98)
Belgium (3 Aug 66), Denmark (4 Sep 74), Finland (16 Jun 72), France (9 Mar 66), Italy (17 Sep 75), Netherlands (28 Dec 79), Portugal (29 Sep 77), Spain (31 Oct 61), Turkey (10 Oct 61), United Kingdom (23 Feb 66)
Ratified/accepted/approved with qualification: 4 (as of at least Mar 98)
Germany (30 Sep 75), Greece (12 May 70), Norway (2 Jul 73), Sweden (1 Apr 68)

3.2 CONVENTION SUPPLEMENTARY TO THE 1960 CONVENTION ON THIRD PARTY LIABILITY IN THE FIELD OF NUCLEAR ENERGY
Concluded: 31 Jan 63
Entered into force: 4 Dec 74
Signed but not ratified: 3 (as of at least Mar 98)
Austria (31 Jan 63), Luxembourg (31 Jan 63), Switzerland (31 Jan 63)
Ratified/accepted/approved without qualification: 7 (as of at least Mar 98)
Belgium (20 Aug 85), Denmark (4 Sep 74), France (30 Mar 66), Italy (3 Feb 76), Spain (27 Jul 66), Sweden (3 Apr 68), United Kingdom (24 Mar 66)
Ratified/accepted/approved with qualification: 4 (as of at least Mar 98)
Finland (14 Jan 77), Germany (1 Oct 75), Netherlands (28 Sep 79), Norway (9 Jul 73)

3.3 TREATY ON PRINCIPLES GOVERNING THE ACTIVITIES OF STATES IN THE EXPLORATION AND USE OF OUTER SPACE, INCLUDING THE MOON AND OTHER CELESTIAL BODIES
Concluded: 27 Jan 67
Entered into force: 10 Oct 67
Signed but not ratified: 28 (as of at least at least 1 Jan 94)

Bolivia (27 Jan 67), Botswana (27 Jan 67), Burundi (27 Jan 67), Cameroon (27 Jan 67), Central African Republic (27 Jan 67), Colombia (27 Jan 67), Congo (Kinshasa) (27 Jan 67), Ethiopia (27 Jan 67), Gambia (2 Jun 67), Ghana (27 Jan 67), Guyana (3 Feb 67), Haiti (27 Jan 67), Honduras (27 Jan 67), Indonesia (27 Jan 67), Iran (27 Jan 67), Jordan (2 Feb 67), Lesotho (27 Jan 67), Luxembourg (27 Jan 67), Malaysia (20 Feb 67), Nicaragua (27 Jan 67), Panama (27 Jan 67), Philippines (27 Jan 67), Rwanda (27 Jan 67), Somalia (2 Feb 67), Togo (27 Jan 67), Trindad/Tobago (24 Jul 67), Yugoslavia (27 Jan 67), Vatican City (5 Apr 67)

Ratified/accepted/approved without qualifications: 87 (as of at least at least 1 Jan 94)

Afghanistan (17 Mar 88), Algeria (27 Jan 92), Antigua/Barbuda (26 Jan 89), Argentina (26 Mar 69), Australia (10 Oct 67), Austria (26 Feb 68), Bahamas (11 Aug 76), Bangladesh (14 Jan 86), Barbados (12 Sep 68), Belgium (30 Mar 73), Benin (19 Jun 86), Bulgaria (28 Mar 67), Burma (18 Mar 70), Belarus (31 Oct 67), Canada (10 Oct 67), Chile (8 Oct 81), Cuba (3 Jun 77), Cyprus (5 Jul 72), Denmark (10 Oct 67), Dominican Republic (21 Nov 68), Ecuador (7 Mar 69), Egypt (10 Oct 67), El Salvador (15 Jan 69), Equatorial Guinea (16 Jan 89), Fiji (18 Jul 72), Finland (12 Jul 67), France (5 Aug 70), Germany (10 Dec 71), Greece (19 Jan 71), Guinea–Bissau (20 Aug 76), Hungary (26 Jun 67), Iceland (5 Feb 68), India (18 Jan 82),Iraq (4 Dec 68), Ireland (17 Jul 68), Israel (18 Feb 77), Italy (4 May 72), Jamaica (6 Aug 70), Japan (10 Oct 67), Kenya (19 Jan 84), Korea (South) (13 Oct 67), Laos (27 Nov 72), Lebanon (31 Mar 69), Libya (3 Jul 68), Mali (11 Jun 68), Mauritius (7 Apr 69), Mexico (31 Jan 68), Mongolia (10 Oct 67), Morocco (21 Dec 67), Nepal (10 Oct 67), Netherlands (10 Oct 69), New Zealand (31 May 68), Niger (17 Apr 67), Nigeria (14 Nov 67), Norway (1 Jul 69), Pakistan (8 Apr 68), Papua New Guinea (27 Oct 80), Peru (26 Feb 79), Poland (30 Jan 68), Romania (9 Apr 68), Russia (10 Oct 67), San Marino (29 Oct 68), Saudi Arabia (17 Dec 68), Seychelles (5 Jan 78), Sierra Leone (13 Jul 67), Singapore (10 Sep 76), South Africa (30 Sep 68), Spain (27 Nov 68), Sri Lanka (18 Nov 86), Sweden (11 Oct 67), Switzerland (18 Dec 69), Syria (14 Nov 68),Thailand (5 Sep 68), Tonga (7 Jul 71), Togo (26 Jun 89), Tunisia (28 Mar 68), Turkey (27 Mar 68), Uganda (24 Apr 68), Ukraine (31 Oct 67), United Kingdom (10 Oct 67), United States (10 Oct 67), Burkina Faso (18 Jun 68), Uruguay (31 Aug 70), Venezuela (3 Mar 70), Vietnam (20 Jun 80), Yemen (1 Jul 79), Zambia (20 Aug 73)

Ratified/accepted/approved with qualification: 6 (as of at least at least 1 Jan 94)

Brazil (5 Mar 69), Czech Republic (1 Jan 93), China (30 Dec 83), Kuwait (7 Jun 72), Madagascar (22 Aug 68), Slovakia (1 Jan 93)

3.4 COUNCIL OF EUROPE COMMITTEE OF MINISTERS RESOLUTION ON AIR POLLUTION IN FRONTIER AREAS

Adopted: 26 Mar 71

3.5 CONVENTION ON THE INTERNATIONAL LIABILITY FOR DAMAGE CAUSED BY SPACE OBJECTS

Concluded: 29 Mar 72

Entry into force: 1 Sep 72

Signed but not ratified: 27 (as of at least at least 1 Mar 97)

Algeria (20 Apr 72), Burundi (29 Mar 72), Cambodia (29 Mar 72), Central African Republic (27 Apr 72), Colombia (29 Mar 72), Congo (Kinshasa) (29 Mar 72), Costa Rica (29 Mar 72), Dominican Republic (26 Apr 72), Egypt (19 May 92), El Salvador (29 Mar 72), Gambia (2 Jun 72), Ghana (29 Mar 72), Guatemala (29 Mar 72), Haiti (29 Mar 72), Honduras (29 Mar 72), Iceland (29 Mar 72), Jordan (6 Jun 72), Lebanon (29 Mar 72), Nepal (29 Mar 72), Nicaragua (29 Mar 72), Oman (23 Jun 72), Peru (10 Apr 72), Philippines (22 Aug 72), Rwanda (29 Mar 72), Sierra Leone (14 Jul 72), South Africa (29 Mar 72), Tanzania (31 May 72)

Ratified/accepted/approved without qualification: 64 (as of at least at least 1 Mar 97)

Antigua/Barbuda (1 Nov 88), Argentina (14 Nov 86), Australia (20 Jan 75), Barbados (26 Dec 88), Belarus (27 Dec 73), Belgium (13 Aug 76), Benin (25 Apr 75), Bosnia–Herzegovina (22 Jul 94), Botswana (11 Mar 74), Brazil (9 Mar 73), Bulgaria (14 May 73), Chile (1 Dec 76), Cuba (25 Nov 82), Cyprus (15 May 73), Ecuador (17 Aug 72), Fiji (4 Apr 73), Finland (1 Feb 77), France (31 Dec 75), Gabon (5 Feb 82), Germany (18 Dec 75), Hungary (27 Dec 72), India (9 Jul 79), Iran (13 Feb 74), Iraq (4 Oct 72), Israel (21 Jun 77), Italy (22 Feb 83), Japan (20 Jun 83), Kenya (25 Sep 75), Laos (20 Mar 73), Liechtenstein (9 Jan 80), Luxembourg (18 Oct 83), Mali (9 Jun 72), Malta (13 Jan 78), Mexico (8 Apr 74), Mongolia (5 Sep 72), Morocco (15 Mar 83), Niger (1 Sep 72), Norway (3 Apr 95), Pakistan (10 Apr 73), Panama (5 Jun 74), Papua New Guinea (27 Oct 80), Poland (25 Jan 73), Qatar (11 Jan 74), Romania (5 Mar 80), Russia (9 Oct 73), Saudi Arabia (17 Dec 76), Senegal (26 Mar 75), Seychelles (5 Jan 78), Singapore (19 Aug 75), Slovenia (20 Aug 92), Spain (2 Jan 80), Sri Lanka (9 Apr 73), Switzerland (22 Jan 74), Syria (6 Feb 80), Taiwan (9 Feb 73), Togo (26 Apr 76), Trindad/Tobago (8 Feb 80), Tunisia (6 Jun 73), Ukraine (16 Oct 73), United Kingdom (9 Oct 73), United States (9 Oct 73), Uruguay (7 Jan 77), Venezuela (1 Aug 78), Zambia (20 Aug 73)

Ratified/accepted/approved with qualification: 13 (as of at least at least 1 Mar 97)

Austria (10 Jan 80), Canada (20 Feb 75), China (20 Dec 88), Czech Republic (1 Jan 93), Denmark (1 Apr 77), EUTELSAT (30 Nov 87), Greece (27 Apr 77), Ireland (29 Jun 72), Korea (South) (14 Jan 80), Kuwait (30 Oct 72), Netherlands (17 Feb 81), New Zealand (30 Oct 74), Sweden (15 Jun 76)

3.6 OECD Council Recommendation on Principles Concerning Transfrontier Pollution

Adopted: 14 Nov 74

3.7 OECD Council Recommendation for the Implementation of a Regime of Equal Right of Access and Non-discrimination in relation to Transfrontier Pollution

Adopted: 17 May 77

3.8 Convention on Long-Range Transboundary Air Pollution (LRTAP)

Concluded: 13 Nov 79

Entered into force: 16 Mar 83

Signed but not ratified: 2 (as of at least 5 Mar 98)

San Marino (14 Nov 79), Vatican City (14 Nov 79)

Ratified/accepted/approved without qualification: 37 (as of at least 5 Mar 98)

Armenia (21 Feb 97), Austria (16 Dec 82), Belarus (14 May 80), Belgium (15 Jul 82), Bosnia–Herzegovina (1 Sep 93), Bulgaria (9 Jun 81), Canada (15 Dec 81), Croatia (21 Sep 92), Cyprus (20 Nov 91), Czech Republic (30 Sep 93), Denmark (18 Jun 82), European Community (15 Jul 82), Finland (15 Apr 81), Germany (15 Jul 82), Greece (30 Aug 83), Hungary (22 Sep 80), Iceland (5 May 83), Ireland (15 Jul 82), Italy (15 Jul 82), Latvia (15 Jul 94), Liechtenstein (22 Nov 83), Lithuania (25 Jan 94), Luxembourg (15 Jul 82), Macedonia (30 Dec 97), Malta (14 Mar 97), Moldova (9 Jun 95), Netherlands (15 Jul 82), Norway (13 Feb 81), Portugal (29 Sep 80), Russia (22 May 80), Slovakia (28 May 93), Slovenia (6 Jul 92), Spain (15 Jun 82), Sweden (12 Feb 81), Switzerland (6 May 83), Turkey (18 Apr 83), Ukraine (5 Jun 80)

Ratified/accepted/approved with qualification: 5 (as of at least 5 Mar 98)

France (3 Nov 81), Poland (19 Jul 85), Romania (27 Feb 91), United Kingdom (15 Jul 82), United States (30 Nov 81)

3.9 Agreement Governing the Activities of States on the Moon and Other Celestial Bodies

Concluded: 5 Dec 79

Entered into force: 11 Jul 84

Signed but not ratified: 5 (as of at least 4 Jun 98)

France (29 Jan 80), Guatemala (20 Nov 80), India (18 Jan 82), Peru (23 Jun 81), Romania (17 Apr 80)
Ratified/accepted/approved without qualification: 9 (as of at least 4 Jun 98)
Australia (7 Jul 86), Austria (11 Jun 84), Chile (12 Nov 81), Mexico (11 Oct 91), Morocco (21 Jan 93), Netherlands (17 Feb 83), Pakistan (27 Feb 86), Philippines (26 May 81), Uruguay (9 Nov 81)

3.10 EUROPEAN COMMUNITIES COUNCIL DIRECTIVE NO 80/779ON AIR QUALITY LIMIT VALUES
Adopted: 15 Jul 80

3.11 MEMORANDUM OF INTENT BETWEEN CANADA AND THE UNITED STATES CONCERNING TRANSBOUNDARY AIR POLLUTION
Concluded: 5 Aug 80
Entered into force: 5 Aug 80

3.12 MEXICO-UNITED STATES AGREEMENT TO CO-OPERATE IN THE SOLUTION OF ENVIRONMENTAL PROBLEMS IN THE BORDER AREA
Concluded: 14 Aug 83
Entered into force: 16 Feb 84

3.13 EUROPEAN COMMUNITIES COUNCIL DIRECTIVE NO. 85/203 ON AIR QUALITY STANDARDS FOR NITROGEN DIOXIDE
Adopted: 7 Mar 85

3.14 VIENNA CONVENTION FOR THE PROTECTION OF THE OZONE LAYER
Concluded: 22 Mar 85
Entered into force: 22 Sep 88
Ratified/accepted/approved without qualification: 163
Algeria (20 Oct 92), Antigua/Barbuda (3 Dec 92), Argentina (18 Jan 90), Australia (16 Sep 87), Austria (19 Aug 87), Azerbaijan (12 Jun 96), Bahamas (1 Apr 93), Bangladesh (2 Aug 90), Barbados (16 Oct 92), Belarus (20 Jun 86), Belgium (17 Oct 88), Belize (6 Jun 97), Benin (1 Jul 93), Bolivia (3 Oct 94), Bosnia–Herzegovina (6 Mar 92), Botswana (4 Dec 91), Brazil (19 Mar 90), Brunei (26 Jul 90), Bulgaria (20 Nov 90), Burkina Faso (30 Mar 89), Burundi (6 Jan 97), Cameroon (30 Aug 89), Canada (4 Jun 86), Central African Republic (29 Mar 93), Chad (18 May 89), Chile (6 Mar 90), China (11 Sep 89), Colombia (16 Jul 90), Comoros (31 Oct 94), Congo (Brazzaville) (16 Nov 94), Congo (Kinshasa) (30 Oct 94), Costa Rica (30 Jul 91), Côte d'Ivoire (5 Apr 93), Croatia (21 Sep 92), Cuba (14 Jul 92), Cyprus (28 May 92), Czech Republic (1 Jan 93), Denmark (29 Sep 88), Dominica (31 Mar 93), Dominican Republic (18 May 93), Ecuador (10 Apr 90), Egypt (9 May 88), El Salvador (2 Oct 92), Equatorial Guinea (17 Aug 88), Estonia (17 Oct 96), Ethiopia (11 Oct 94), European Community (17 Oct 88), Fiji (23 Oct 89), France (4 Dec 87), Gabon (9 Feb 94), Gambia (25 Jul 90), Georgia (21 Mar 96), Germany (30 Sep 88), Ghana (24 Jul 89), Greece (29 Dec 88), Grenada (31 Mar 93), Guatemala (11 Sep 87), Guinea (25 Jun 92), Guyana (12 Aug 93), Honduras (14 Oct 93), Hungary (4 May 88), Iceland (29 Aug 89), India (18 Mar 91), Indonesia (26 Jun 92), Iran (3 Oct 90), Ireland (15 Sep 88), Israel (30 Jun 92), Italy (19 Sep 88), Jamaica (31 Mar 93), Japan (30 Sep 88), Jordan (31 May 89), Kazakhstan (26 Aug 98), Kenya (9 Nov 88), Kiribati (7 Jan 93), Korea (North (24 Jan 95), Korea (South) (27 Feb 92), Kuwait (23 Nov 92), Lao People's Democratic Republic (21 Aug 98), Latvia (28 Apr 95), Lebanon (30 Mar 93), Lesotho (25 Mar 94), Liberia (15 Jan 96), Libya (11 Jul 90), Liechtenstein (8 Feb 89), Lithuania (18 Jan 95), Luxembourg (17 Oct 88), Macedonia (10 Mar 94), Madagascar (7 Nov 96), Malawi (9 Jan 91), Malaysia (29 Aug 89), Maldives (26 Apr 88), Mali (28 Oct 94), Malta (15 Sep 88), Marshall Islands (11 Mar 93), Mauritania (26 May 94), Mauritius (18 Aug 92), Mexico (14 Sep 87), Micronesia (3 Aug 94), Moldova (24 Oct 96), Monaco (12 Mar 93), Mongolia (7 Mar 96), Morocco (28 Dec 95), Mozambique (9 Sep 94), Myanmar (Burma) (24 Nov 93), Namibia (20 Sep 93), Nepal (6 Jul 94), New

Zealand (2 Jun 87), Nicaragua (5 Mar 93), Niger (9 Oct 92), Nigeria (31 Oct 88), Pakistan (18 Dec 92), Panama (13 Feb 89), Papua New Guinea (27 Oct 92), Paraguay (3 Dec 92), Peru (7 Apr 89), Philippines (17 Jul 91), Poland (13 Jul 90), Portugal (17 Oct 88), Qatar (22 Jan 96), Romania (27 Jan 93), Russia (18 Jun 86), St Kitts/Nevis (10 Aug 92), St Lucia (28 Jul 93), St Vincent/Grenadines (2 Dec 96), Samoa (21 Dec 92), Saudi Arabia (1 Mar 93), Senegal (19 Mar 93), Seychelles (6 Jan 93), Singapore (5 Jan 89), Slovakia (1 Jan 93), Slovenia (6 Jul 92), Solomon Islands (17 Jun 93), South Africa (15 Jan 90), Spain (25 Jul 88), Sri Lanka (15 Dec 89), Sudan (29 Jan 93), Suriname (14 Oct 97), Swaziland (10 Nov 92), Switzerland (17 Dec 87), Syria (12 Dec 89), Tajikistan (6 May 96), Tanzania (7 Apr 93), Thailand (7 Jul 89), Togo (25 Feb 91), Tonga (29 Jul 98), Trindad/Tobago (28 Aug 89), Tunisia (25 Sep 89), Turkey (20 Sep 91), Turkmenistan (18 Nov 93), Tuvalu (15 Jul 93), Uganda (24 Jun 88), Ukraine (18 Jun 86), United Arab Emirates (22 Dec 89), United Kingdom (15 May 87), United States (27 Aug 86), Uruguay (27 Feb 89), Uzbekistan (18 May 93), Vanuatu (21 Nov 94), Venezuela (1 Sep 88), Vietnam (26 Jan 94), Yemen (21 Feb 96), Yugoslavia (16 Apr 90), Zambia (24 Jan 90), Zimbabwe (3 Nov 92)

Ratified/accepted/approved with qualification: 6

Bahrain (27 Apr 90), European Community (17 Oct 88), Finland (26 Sep 86), Netherlands (28 Sep 88), Norway (23 Sep 86), Sweden (26 Nov 86)

3.15 PROTOCOL TO THE 1979 CONVENTION ON LONG-RANGE TRANSBOUNDARY AIR POLLUTION ON THE REDUCTION OF SULPHUR EMISSIONS OR THEIR TRANSBOUNDARY FLUXES BY AT LEAST 30 PERCENT

Concluded: 8 Jul 85

Entered into force: 2 Sep 87

Ratified/accepted/approved without qualification: 21 (as of at least 4 Jun 98)

Austria (4 Jun 87), Belarus (10 Sep 86), Belgium (9 Jun 89), Bulgaria (26 Sep 86), Canada (4 Dec 85), Czech Republic (30 Sep 93), Denmark (29 Apr 86), Finland (24 Jun 86), France (13 Mar 86), Germany (3 Mar 87), Hungary (11 Sep 86), Italy (5 Feb 90), Liechtenstein (13 Feb 86), Luxembourg (24 Aug 87), Netherlands (30 Apr 86), Norway (4 Nov 86), Russia (10 Sep 86), Slovakia (28 May 93), Sweden (31 Mar 86), Switzerland (21 Sep 87), Ukraine (2 Oct 86)

3.16 IAEA CONVENTION ON EARLY NOTIFICATION OF A NUCLEAR ACCIDENT

Concluded: 26 Sep 86

Entered into force: 27 Oct 86

Signed but not ratified: 20 (as of at least Mar 98)

Afghanistan (26 Sep 86), Algeria (24 Sep 87), Belgium (26 Sep 86), Cameroon (25 Sep 87), Chile (26 Sep 86), Congo (Kinshasa) (30 Sep 86), Côte d'Ivoire (26 Sep 86), Iran (26 Sep 86), Korea (North) (26 Sep 86), Luxembourg (29 Sep 86), Mali (2 Oct 86), Niger (26 Sep 86), Panama (26 Sep 86), Paraguay (2 Oct 86), Senegal (15 Jun 87), Sierra Leone (25 Mar 87), Sudan (26 Sep 86), Syria (2 Jul 87), Vatican City (26 Sep 86), Zimbabwe (26 Sep 86)

Ratified/accepted/approved without qualification: 36 (as of at least Mar 98)

Armenia (24 Sep 93), Austria (18 Feb 88), Bangladesh (7 Jan 88), Brazil (4 Dec 90), Costa Rica (16 Sep 91), Croatia (29 Sep 92), Cyprus (4 Jan 89), Czech Republic (24 Mar 93), Denmark (26 Sep 86), Finland (11 Dec 86), Germany (14 Sep 89), Guatemala (8 Aug 88), Hungary (10 Mar 87), Iceland (27 Sep 89), Japan (9 Jun 87), Jordan (11 Dec 87), Korea (South) (8 Jun 90), Latvia (28 Dec 92), Mauritius (17 Aug 92), Mexico (10 May 88), Morocco (7 Oct 93), Mongolia (11 Jun 87), New Zealand (11 Mar 87), Nigeria (10 Aug 90), Norway (26 Sep 86), Portugal (30 Apr 93), Slovakia (10 Feb 93), Slovenia (7 Jul 92), Sweden (27 Feb 87), Switzerland (31 May 88), Tunisia (24 Feb 89), Uruguay (21 Dec 89), Vietnam (29 Sep 87), Yugoslavia (8 Feb 89 & 28 Apr 92)

Ratified/accepted/approved with qualification: 36 (as of at least Mar 98)

Argentina (17 Jan 90), Australia (22 Sep 87), Belarus (26 Jan 87), Bulgaria (24 Feb 88), Canada (18 Jan 90), China (10 Sep 87), Cuba (8 Jan 91), Egypt (6 Jul 88), FAO (19 Oct 90), France (6 Mar 89), Greece (6 Jun 91), India (28 Jan 88),

Indonesia (12 Nov 93), Iraq (21 Jul 88), Ireland (13 Sep 91), Israel (25 May 89), Italy (8 Feb 90), Malaysia (1 Sep 87), Monaco (19 Jul 89), Netherlands (23 Sep 91), Nicaragua (11 Nov 93), Pakistan (11 Sep 89), Poland (24 Mar 88), Romania (12 Jun 90), Russia (23 Dec 86 & 26 Dec 91), Saudi Arabia (3 Nov 89), South Africa (10 Aug 87), Spain (13 Sep 89), Sri Lanka (11 Jan 91), Thailand (21 Mar 89), Turkey (3 Jan 91), Ukraine (26 Jan 87), United Arab Emirates (2 Oct 87), United Kingdom (9 Feb 90), United States (19 Sep 88), WHO (10 Aug 88), WMO (17 Apr 90)

Ratified/accepted/approved (qualifications undetermined): 10 (as of at least Mar 98)

Estonia (9 May 94), FAO (19 Oct 90), Lebanon (17 Apr 97), Liechtenstein (19 Apr 94), Lithuania (16 Nov 94), Macedonia (20 Sep 96), Myanmar (Burma) (18 Dec 97), Peru (17 Jul 95), Philippines (5 May 97), Singapore (15 Dec 97)

3.17 IAEA CONVENTION ON ASSISTANCE IN THE CASE OF A NUCLEAR ACCIDENT OR RADIOLOGICAL EMERGENCY

Concluded: 26 Sep 86

Entered into force: 26 Feb 87

Signed but not ratified: 23 (as of at least Mar 98)

Afghanistan (26 Sep 86), Algeria (24 Sep 87), Belgium (26 Sep 86), Cameroon (25 Sep 87), Canada (26 Sep 86), Chile (26 Sep 86), Congo (Kinshasa) (30 Sep 86), Côte d'Ivoire (26 Sep 86), Denmark (26 Sep 86), Iceland (26 Sep 86), Iran (26 Sep 86), Korea (North) (26 Sep 86), Mali (2 Oct 86), Niger (26 Sep 86), Panama (26 Sep 86), Paraguay (2 Oct 86), Portugal (26 Sep 86), Senegal (15 Jun 87), Sierra Leone (25 Mar 87), Sudan (26 Sep 86), Syria (2 Jul 87), Vatican City (26 Sep 86), Zimbabwe (26 Sep 86)

Ratified/accepted/approved without qualification: 27 (as of at least Mar 98)

Armenia (24 Aug 93), Bangladesh (7 Jan 88), Brazil (4 Dec 90), Costa Rica (16 Sep 91), Croatia (29 Sep 92), Cyprus (4 Jan 89), Czech Republic (24 Mar 93), Germany (14 Sep 89), Guatemala (8 Aug 88), Hungary (10 Mar 87), Jordan (11 Dec 87), Latvia (28 Dec 92), Libya (27 Jun 90), Mauritius (17 Aug 92), Mexico (10 May 88), Mongolia (11 Jun 87), Morocco (7 Oct 93), Nicaragua (11 Nov 93), Nigeria (10 Aug 90), Slovakia (10 Feb 93), Slovenia (7 Jul 92), Sweden (24 Jun 92), Switzerland (31 May 88), Tunisia (24 Feb 89), Uruguay (21 Dec 89), Vietnam (29 Sep 87), Yugoslavia (9 Apr 91 & 28 Apr 92)

Ratified/accepted/approved with qualification: 41 (as of at least Mar 98)

Argentina (17 Jan 90), Australia (22 Sep 87), Austria (21 Nov 89), Belarus (26 Jan 87), Bulgaria (24 Feb 88), China (10 Sep 87), Cuba (8 Jan 91), Egypt (17 Oct 88), FAO (19 Oct 90), Finland (27 Nov 90), France (6 Mar 89), Greece (6 Jun 91), India (28 Jan 88), Indonesia (12 Nov 93), Iraq (21 Jul 88), Ireland (13 Sep 91), Israel (25 May 89), Italy (25 Oct 90), Japan (9 Jun 87), Korea (South) (8 Jun 90), Malaysia (1 Sep 87), Monaco (19 Jul 89), Netherlands (23 Sep 91), New Zealand (11 Mar 87),Norway (26 Sep 86), Pakistan (11 Sep 89), Poland (24 Mar 88), Romania (12 Jun 90), Russia (23 Dec 86 & 26 Dec 91), Saudi Arabia (3 Nov 89), South Africa (10 Aug 87), Spain (13 Sep 89), Sri Lanka (11 Jan 91), Thailand (21 Mar 89), Turkey (3 Jan 91), Ukraine (26 Jan 87), United Arab Emirates (2 Oct 87), United Kingdom (9 Feb 90), United States (19 Sep 88), WHO (10 Aug 88), WMO (17 Apr 90)

Ratified/accepted/approved (qualifications undetermined): 7 (as of at least Mar 98)

Estonia (9 May 94), Lebanon (17 Apr 97), Liechtenstein (19 Apr 94), Macedonia (20 Sep 96), Peru (17 Jul 95), Philippines (5 May 97), Singapore (15 Dec 97)

3.18 MONTREAL PROTOCOL ON SUBSTANCES THAT DEPLETE THE OZONE LAYER (AS AMENDED)

Concluded: 16 Sep 87

Entered into force: 1 Jan 89

Ratified/accepted/approved without qualification: 162

Algeria (20 Oct 92), Antigua/Barbuda (3 Dec 92), Argentina (18 Sep 90), Australia (19 May 89), Austria (3 May 89), Azerbaijan (12 Jun 96), Bahamas (4

Mar 93), Bangladesh (2 Aug 90), Barbados (16 Oct 92), Belarus (31 Oct 88), Belgium (30 Dec 88), Belize (9 Jan 98), Benin (1 Jul 93), Bolivia (3 Oct 94), Bosnia-Herzegovina (6 Mar 92), Botswana (4 Dec 91), Brazil (19 Mar 90), Brunei (27 May 93), Bulgaria (20 Nov 90), Burkina Faso (20 Jul 89), Burundi (6 Jan 97), Cameroon (30 Aug 89), Canada (30 Jun 88), Central African Republic (29 Mar 93), Chad (7 Jun 94), Chile (26 Mar 90), China (14 Jun 91), Colombia (6 Dec 93), Comoros (31 Oct 94), Congo (Brazzaville) (16 Nov 94), Congo (Kinshasa) (30 Nov 94), Costa Rica (30 Jul 91), Côte d'Ivoire (5 Apr 93), Croatia (8 Oct 91), Cuba (14 Jul 92), Cyprus (28 May 92), Czech Republic (1 Jan 93), Denmark (16 Dec 88), Dominica (31 Mar 93), Dominican Republic (18 May 93), Ecuador (30 Apr 90), Egypt (2 Aug 88), El Salvador (2 Oct 92), Estonia (17 Oct 96), Ethiopia (11 Oct 94), Fiji (23 Oct 89), France (28 Dec 88), Gabon (9 Feb 94), Gambia (25 Jul 90), Georgia (21 Mar 96), Germany (16 Dec 88), Ghana (24 Jul 89), Greece (29 Dec 88), Grenada (31 Mar 93), Guatemala (7 Nov 89), Guinea (25 Jun 92), Guyana (12 Aug 93), Honduras (14 Oct 93), Hungary (20 Apr 89), Iceland (29 Aug 89), India (19 Jun 92), Indonesia (26 Jun 92), Iran (3 Oct 90), Ireland (16 Dec 88), Israel (30 Jun 92), Italy (16 Dec 88), Jamaica (31 Mar 93), Japan (30 Sep 88), Jordan (31 May 89), Kazakhstan (26 Aug 98), Kenya (9 Nov 88), Kiribati (7 Jan 93), Korea (North (24 Jan 95), Korea (South) (27 Feb 92), Kuwait (23 Nov 92), Lao People's Democratic Republic (21 Aug 98), Latvia (28 Apr 95), Lebanon (31 Mar 93), Lesotho (25 Mar 94), Liberia (15 Jan 96), Libya (11 Jul 90), Liechtenstein (8 Feb 89), Lithuania (18 Jan 95), Luxembourg (17 Oct 88), Macedonia (10 Mar 94) , Madagascar (7 Nov 96), Malawi (9 Jan 91), Malaysia (29 Aug 89), Maldives (16 May 89), Mali (28 Oct 94), Malta (29 Dec 88), Marshall Islands (11 Mar 93), Mauritania (26 May 94), Mauritius (18 Aug 92), Mexico (31 Mar 88), Micronesia (6 Sep 95) , Moldova (24 Oct 96), Monaco (12 Mar 93), Mongolia (7 Mar 96), Morocco (28 Dec 95), Mozambique (9 Sep 94), Myanmar (Burma) (24 Nov 93), Namibia (20 Sep 93), Nepal (6 Jul 94), New Zealand (21 Jul 88), Nicaragua (5 Mar 93), Niger (9 Oct 92), Nigeria (31 Oct 88), Pakistan (18 Dec 92), Panama (3 Mar 89), Papua New Guinea (27 Oct 92), Paraguay (3 Dec 92), Peru (31 Mar 93), Philippines (17 Jul 91), Poland (13 Jul 90), Portugal (17 Oct 88), Qatar (22 Jan 96), Romania (27 Jan 93), Russia (10 Nov 88), St Kitts/Nevis (10 Aug 92), St Lucia (28 Jul 93), St Vincent/Grenadines (2 Dec 96), Samoa (21 Dec 92), Saudi Arabia (1 Mar 93), Senegal (6 May 93), Seychelles (6 Jan 93), Singapore (5 Jan 89), Slovakia (28 May 93), Slovenia (6 Jul 92), Solomon Islands (17 Jun 93), South Africa (15 Jan 90), Spain (16 Dec 88), Sri Lanka (15 Dec 89), Sudan (29 Jan 93), Suriname (14 Oct 97), Swaziland (10 Nov 92), Switzerland (28 Dec 88), Syria (12 Dec 89), Tajikistan (7 Jan 98), Tanzania (16 Apr 93), Thailand (7 Jul 89), Togo (25 Feb 91), Tonga (29 Jul 98), Trindad/Tobago (28 Aug 89), Tunisia (25 Sep 89), Turkey (20 Sep 91), Turkmenistan (18 Nov 93), Tuvalu (15 Jul 93), Uganda (15 Sep 88), Ukraine (20 Sep 88), United Arab Emirates (22 Dec 89), United Kingdom (16 Dec 88), United States (21 Apr 88), Uruguay (8 Jan 91), Uzbekistan (18 May 93), Vanuatu (21 Nov 94), Venezuela (6 Feb 89), Vietnam (26 Jan 94), Yemen (21 Feb 96), Yugoslavia (3 Jan 91), Zambia (24 Jan 90), Zimbabwe (3 Nov 92)

Ratified/accepted/approved with qualification: 6

Bahrain (27 Apr 90), European Community (16 Dec 88), Finland (23 Dec 88), Netherlands (16 Dec 88), Norway (24 Jun 88), Sweden (29 Jun 88)

London Amendment to Montreal Protocol entered into force: 10 Aug 92

Ratifying London Amendment: 127

Copenhagen Amendment to Montreal Protocol entered into force: 14 Jun 94

Ratifying Copenhagen Amendment: 86

Montreal Amendment to Montreal Protocol not in force as of 1 January 1999.

Ratifying Montreal Amendment: 5

3.19 PROTOCOL TO THE 1979 LONG-RANGE TRANSBOUNDARY AIR POLLUTION CONCERNING THE CONTROL OF EMISSIONS OF NITROGEN OXIDES OR THEIR TRANSBOUNDARY FLUXES

Concluded: 31 Oct 88

Entered into force: 14 Feb 91
Signed but not ratified: 2 (as of at least 4 Jun 98)
Belgium (1 Nov 88), Poland (1 Nov 88)
Ratified/accepted/approved without qualification: 25 (as of at least 4 Jun 98)
Austria (15 Jan 90), Belarus (8 Jun 89), Bulgaria (30 Mar 89), Canada (25 Jan 91), Czech Republic (1 Jan 93), Denmark (1 Mar 93), European Community (17 Dec 93), Finland (1 Feb 90), France (20 Jul 89), Germany (16 Nov 90), Greece (29 Apr 98), Hungary (12 Nov 91), Ireland (17 Oct 94), Italy (19 May 92), Liechtenstein (24 Mar 94), Luxembourg (4 Oct 90), Netherlands (11 Oct 89), Norway (11 Oct 89), Russia (21 Jun 89), Slovakia (28 May 93), Spain (4 Dec 91), Sweden (27 Jul 90), Switzerland (18 Sep 90), Ukraine (24 Jul 89), United Kingdom (15 Oct 90)
Ratified/accepted/approved with qualification: 1 (as of at least 4 Jun 98)
United States (13 Jul 89)

3.20 CONVENTION ON THE TRANSBOUNDARY EFFECTS OF INDUSTRIAL ACCIDENTS
Concluded: 17 Mar 92
Not in force as of 1 January 1999.
Signed but not ratified: 21
Austria (18 Mar 92), Belgium (18 Mar 92), Canada (18 Mar 92), Denmark (18 Mar 92), Estonia (18 Mar 92), Finland (18 Mar 92), France (18 Mar 92), Germany (18 Mar 92), Greece (18 Mar 92), Italy (18 Mar 92), Latvia (18 Mar 92), Lithuania (18 Mar 92), Netherlands (18 Mar 92), Poland (18 Mar 92), Portugal (9 Jun 92), Spain (18 Mar 92), Sweden (18 Mar 92), Switzerland (18 Mar 92), United Kingdom (18 Mar 92), United States (18 Mar 92), European Community (18 Mar 92)
Ratified/accepted/approved (qualifications unknown): 7
Albania (5 Jan 94), Bulgaria (12 May 95), Hungary (2 Jun 94), Luxembourg (8 Aug 94), Norway (1 Apr 93), Moldova (4 Jan 94), Russian Federation (1 Feb 94)

3.21 UNITED NATIONS FRAMEWORK CONVENTION ON CLIMATE CHANGE
Concluded: 9 May 92
Entered into force: 21 Mar 94
Signed but not ratified: 9 (as of at least 4 Jun 98)
Afghanistan (12 Jun 92), Angola (14 Jun 92), Belarus (11 Jun 92), Dominican Republic (12 Jun 92), Liberia (12 Jun 92), Libya (29 Jun 92), Madagascar (10 Jun 92), Rwanda (10 Jun 92), São Tomé/Príncipe (12 Jun 92)
Ratified/accepted/approved without qualification: 162 (as of at least 4 Jun 98)
Albania (3 Oct 94), Algeria (9 Jun 93), Antigua/Barbuda (2 Feb 93), Argentina (11 Mar 94), Armenia (14 May 93), Australia (30 Dec 92), Austria (28 Feb 94), Azerbaijan (16 May 95), Bahamas (29 Mar 94), Bahrain (28 Dec 94), Bangladesh (15 Apr 94), Barbados (23 Mar 94), Belgium (4 Jun 92), Belize (13 Jun 92), Benin (30 Jun 94), Bhutan (11 Jun 92), Bolivia (3 Oct 94), Botswana (27 Jan 94), Brazil (28 Feb 94), Burkina Faso (2 Sep 93), Burundi (11 Jun 92), Cambodia (18 Dec 95), Cameroon (19 Oct 94), Canada (4 Dec 92), Cape Verde (29 Mar 95), Central African Republic (10 Mar 95), Chad (7 Jun 94), Chile (22 Dec 94), China (5 Jan 93), Colombia (22 Mar 95), Comoros (31 Oct 94), Congo (Brazzaville) (14 Aug 92), Congo (Kinshasa) (9 Jan 95), Cook Islands (20 Apr 93), Costa Rica (26 Aug 94), Côte d'Ivoire (29 Nov 94), Cyprus (15)ct 97), Czech Republic (7 Oct 93), Denmark (21 Dec 93), Djibouti (27 Aug 95), Dominica (21 Jun 93), Ecuador (23 Feb 93), Egypt (5 Dec 94), El Salvador (13 Jun 92), Eritrea (24 Apr 95), Estonia (27 Jul 94), Ethiopia (5 Apr 94), Finland (3 May 94), France (25 Mar 94), Gabon (21 Jan 98), Gambia (10 Jun 94), Georgia (29 Jul 94), Germany (9 Dec 93), Ghana (6 Sep 95), Greece (4 Aug 94), Grenada (11 Aug 94), Guatemala (15 Dec 95), Guinea (7 May 93), Guinea–Bissau (27 Oct 95), Guyana (29 Aug 94), Haiti (25 Sep 96), Honduras (19 Oct 95), Iceland (16 Jun 93), India (1 Nov 93), Indonesia (23 Aug 94), Iran (18 Jul 96), Ireland (20 Apr 94), Israel (4 Jun 96), Italy (15 Apr 94), Jamaica (6 Jan 95), Japan (28 May 93), Jordan (12 Nov 93), Kazakhstan (17 May 95), Kenya (30 Aug 94), Korea (North)

(5 Dec 94), Korea (South) (14 Dec 93), Kuwait (28 Dec 94), Latvia (23 Mar 95), Laos 94 Jan 95), Lebanon (15 Dec 94), Lesotho (7 Feb 95), Liechtenstein (22 Jun 94), Lithuania (24 Mar 95), Luxembourg (9 May 94), Macedonia (28 Jan 98), Malawi (21 Apr 94), Malaysia 13 Jul 94), Maldives (9 Nov 92), Mali (28 Dec 94), Malta (17 Mar 94), Marshall Islands (8 Oct 92), Mauritania (20 Jan 94), Mauritius (4 Sep 92), Mexico (11 Mar 93), Micronesia (18 Nov 93), Moldova (9 Jun 95), Mongolia (30 Sep 93), Morocco (28 Dec 95), Mozambique (25 Aug 95), Myanmar (Burma) (25 Nov 94), Namibia (16 May 95), Nepal (2 May 94), Netherlands (20 Dec 93), New Zealand (16 Sep 93), Nicaragua (31 Oct 95), Niger (25 Jul 95), Nigeria (29 Aug 94), Niue (28 Feb 96), Norway (9 Jul 93), Oman (8 Feb 95), Pakistan (1 Jun 94), Panama (23 May 95), Paraguay (24 Feb 94), Peru (7 Jun 93), Philippines (2 Aug 94), Poland (28 Jul 94), Portugal (21 Dec 93), Qatar (18 Apr 96), Romania (8 Jun 94), Russia (28 Dec 94), St Kitts/Nevis (7 Jan 93), St Lucia (14 Jun 93), St Vincent/Grenadines (2 Dec 96), Samoa (29 Nov 94), San Marino (28 Oct 94), Saudi Arabia (28 Dec 94), Senegal (17 Oct 94), Seychelles (22 Sep 92), Sierra Leone (22 Jun 95),), Singapore (29 May 97), Slovakia (25 Aug 94), Slovenia (1 Dec 95), South Africa (29 May 97), Spain (21 Dec 93), Sri Lanka (23 Nov 93), Sudan (19 Nov 93), Suriname (14 Oct 97), Swaziland (7 Oct 96), Sweden (23 Jun 93), Switzerland (10 Dec 93), Syria (4 Jan 96), Tajikistan (7 Jan 98),Tanzania (17 Apr 96), Thailand (28 Dec 94), Togo (8 Mar 95), Trindad/Tobago (24 Jun 94), Tunisia (15 Jul 93), Turkmenistan (5 Jun 95), Uganda (8 Sep 93), Ukraine (13 May 97), United Arab Emirates (29 Dec 95), United Kingdom (8 Dec 93), United States (15 Oct 92), Uruguay 18 Aug 94), Uzbekistan (20 Jun 93), Vanuatu (25 Mar 93), Venezuela (28 Dec 94), Vietnam (16 Nov 94), Yemen (21 Feb 96), Yugoslavia (3 Sep 97), Zambia (28 May 93), Zimbabwe (3 Nov 92)

Ratified/accepted/approved with qualification: 12 (as of at least 4 Jun 98)
Bulgaria (12 May 95), Croatia (8 Apr 96), Cuba (5 Jan 94), European Community (21 Dec 93), Fiji (25 Feb 93), Hungary (24 Feb 94), Kiribati (7 Feb 95), Monaco (20 Nov 92), Nauru (11 Nov 93), Papua New Guinea (16 Mar 93), Solomon Islands (28 Dec 94), Tuvalu (26 Oct 93)

3.22 IAEA Convention on Nuclear Safety

Concluded: 17 Jun 94
Entered into force: 24 Oct 96
Signed but not ratified: 25 (as of at least Mar 98)
Algeria (20 Sep 94), Armenia (22 Sep 94), Cuba (20 Sep 94), Denmark (20 Sep 94), Egypt (20 Sep 94), Ghana (6 Jul 95), Iceland (21 Sep 95), India (20 Sep 94), Indonesia (20 Sep 94), Israel (22 Sep 94), Italy (27 Sep 94), Jordan (6 Dec 94), Kazakhstan (20 Sep 96), Monaco (16 Sep 96), Morocco (1 Dec 94), Nicaragua (23 Sep 94), Nigeria (21 Sep 94), Philippines (14 Oct 94), Portugal (3 Oct 94), Sudan (20 Sep 94), Syria (23 Sep 94), Tunisia (20 Sep 94), Ukraine (20 Sep 94), United States (20 Sep 94), Uruguay (28 Feb 96)

Ratified/accepted/approved without qualification: 1 (as of at least Mar 98)
Norway (29 Sep 94)

Ratified/accepted/approved (with qualifications undetermined): 41 (as of at least Mar 98)
Argentina 17 Apr 97, Australia (24 Dec 96), Austria (26 Aug 97), Bangladesh (21 Sep 95), Belgium (13 Jan 97), Brazil (4 Mar 97), Bulgaria (8 Nov 95), Canada (12 Dec 95), Chile (20 Dec 96), China (9 Apr 96), Croatia (18 Apr 96), Czech Republic (18 Sep 95), Finland (22 Jan 96), France (13 Sep 95), Germany (20 Jan 97), Greece (20 Jun 97), Hungary (18 Mar 96), Ireland (11 Jul 96), Japan (12 May 95), Korea (South) (19 Sep 95), Latvia (25 Oct 96), Lebanon (5 Jun 96), Lithuania (12 Jun 96), Luxembourg (7 Apr 97), Mali (13 May 96), Mexico 26 Jul 96), Netherlands (15 Oct 96), Pakistan (30 Sep 97), Peru (1 Jul 97), Poland (14 Jun 95), Romania (1 Jun 95), Russia (12 Jul 96), Slovakia (7 Mar 95), Slovenia (20 Nov 96), South Africa (24 Dec 96), Spain (4 Jul 95), Sweden (11 Sep 95), Switzerland (12 Sep 96), Turkey (8 Mar 95), United Kingdom (17 Jan 96)

3.23 **1997 Vienna Convention on Civil Liability for Nuclear Damage**

The 1997 Vienna Convention is the combined text of the 1963 Vienna Convention on Civil Liability for Nuclear Damage and the 1997 Protocol to Amend that Convention. The status information provided below is for both the 1997 Vienna Convention and the original 1963 Convention.

1997 Vienna Convention on Civil Liability for Nuclear Damage:

Concluded: 12 Sep 97

Not in force as of 28 January 1999

Signed but not ratified: 14

Argentina (19 Dec 97), Belarus (14 Sep 98), Czech Republic (18 Jun 98), Hungary (29 Sep 97), Indonesia (6 Oct 97), Italy (26 Jan 98), Lebanon (30 Sep 97), Lithuania (30 Sep 97), Morocco (29 Sep 97), Peru (4 Jun 98), Philippines (10 Mar 98), Poland (3 Oct 97), Ukraine (29 Sep 97)

Ratified/accepted/approved (qualifications unknown): 1

Romania (29 Dec 98)

1963 Vienna Convention on Civil Liability for Nuclear Damage

Concluded: 21 May 63

Entered into force: 12 Nov 77

Signed but not ratified: 5 (as of at least Mar 98)

Colombia (21 May 63), Israel (19 Aug 97), Morocco (30 Nov 84), Spain (6 Sep 63), United Kingdom (11 Nov 64)

Ratified/accepted/approved without qualification: 19 (as of at least Mar 98)

Argentina (25 Apr 67), Armenia (24 Aug 93), Bolivia (10 Apr 68), Brazil (26 Mar 93), Cameroon (6 Mar 64), Croatia (29 Sep 92), Cuba (25 Oct 65), Egypt (5 Nov 65), Hungary (28 Jul 89), Lithuania (15 Sep 92), Mexico (25 Apr 89), Niger (24 Jul 79), Peru (26 Aug 80), Philippines (15 Nov 65), Poland (23 Jan 90), Romania (29 Dec 92), Slovenia (7 Jul 92), Trindad/Tobago (31 Jan 66), Yugoslavia (12 Aug 77 & 28 Apr 92)

Ratified/accepted/approved with qualification: 1 (as of at least Mar 98)

Chile (23 Nov 89)

Ratified/accepted/approved (qualifications undetermined): 10 (as of at least Mar 98)

Belarus (9 Feb 98), Bulgaria (24 Aug 94), Czech Republic (24 Mar 94), Estonia (9 Mar 94), Latvia (15 Mar 95), Lebanon (17 Apr 97), Macedonia (8 Apr 94), Russia (8 May 96), Slovakia (7 Mar 95), Ukraine (20 Sep 96)

3.24 **Convention on Supplementary Compensation for Nuclear Damage**

Concluded: 12 Sep 97

Not in force as of 28 January 1999.

Signed but not ratified: 13

Argentina (19 Dec 97), Australia (1 Oct 97), Czech Republic (18 Jun 98), Indonesia (6 Oct 97), Italy (26 Jan 98), Lebanon (30 Sep 97), Lithuania (30 Sep 97), Morocco (29 Sep 97), Peru (4 Jun 98), Phillipines (10 Mar 98), Romania (30 Sep 97), Ukraine (29 Sep 97), United States (29 Sep 97)

3.25 **Kyoto Protocol to the United Nations Framework Convention on Climate Change**

Adopted: 11 Dec 97

Not in force as of 15 January 1999.

Signed but not ratified: 71

Antigua and Barbuda (16 Mar 98), Argentina (16 Mar 98), Australia (29 Apr 98), Austria (29 Apr 98), Belgium (29 Apr 98), Bolivia (09 Jul 98), Brazil (29 Apr 98), Bulgaria (18 Sep 98), Canada (29 Apr 98), Chile (17 Jun 98), China (29 May 98), Cook Islands (16 Sep 98), Costa Rica (27 Apr 98), Czech Republic (23 Nov 98), Denmark (29 Apr 98), Ecuador (15 Jan 99), El Salvador (8 June 98), Estonia (03 Dec 98), European Community (29 Apr 98), Fiji (17 Sep 98), Finland (29 Apr 98), France (29 Apr 98), Germany (29 Apr 98), Greece (29 Apr 98), Guatemala (10 Jul 98), Indonesia (13 Jul 98), Ireland (29 Apr 98), Israel (16 Dec 98), Italy (29 Apr 98), Japan (28 Apr 98), Latvia (14 Dec 98), Liechtenstein (29 June 98), Lithuania (21 Sep 98), Luxembourg (29 Apr 98), Maldives (16 Mar 98), Malta (17 Apr 98), Marshall Islands (17 Mar 98), Mexico (9 June 98),

Micronesia (17 Mar 98), Monaco (29 Apr 98), Netherlands (29 Apr 98), New Zealand (22 May 98), Nicaragua (07 Jul 98), Niger (23 Oct 98), Niue (11 Dec 98), Norway (29 Apr 98), Panama (08 June 98), Paraguay (25 Aug 98), Peru (13 Nov 98), Philippines (15 Apr 98), Poland (15 Jul 98), Portugal (29 Apr 98), Republic of Korea (25 Sep 98), Romania (05 Jan 99), Saint Lucia (16 Mar 98), SaintVincent and the Grenadines (19 Mar 98), Samoa (16 Mar 98), Seychelles (20 Mar 98), Slovenia (21 Oct 98), Solomon Islands (29 Sep 98), Spain (29 Apr 98), Sweden (29 Apr 98), Switzerland (16 Mar 98), Trinidad and Tobago (07 Jan 99), Turkmenistan (25 Sep 98), Tuvalu (16 Nov 98), United Kingdom of Great Britain and Northern Ireland (29 Apr 98), United States of America (12 Nov 98), Uruguay (29 July 98), Uzbekistan (20 Nov 98), Viet Nam (03 Dec 98), Zambia (05 Aug 98)

3.26 PROTOCOL TO THE CONVENTION ON LONG-RANGE TRANSBOUNDARY AIR POLLUTION ON PERSISTENT ORGANIC POLLUTANTS

Concluded: 24 Jun 98

Not in force as of 1 January 1999.

Signed but not ratified (as of at least 11 Nov 98): 34

Austria (24 Jun 98), Belgium (24 Jun 98), Bulgaria (24 Jun 98), Canada (24 Jun 98), Croatia (24 Jun 98), Cyprus (24 Jun 98), Czech Republic (24 Jun 98), Denmark (24 Jun 98), European Community (24 Jun 98), Finland (24 Jun 98), France (24 Jun 98), Germany (24 Jun 98), Greece (24 Jun 98), Iceland (24 Jun 98), Ireland (24 Jun 98), Italy (24 Jun 98), Latvia (24 Jun 98), Liechtenstein (24 Jun 98), Lithuania (24 Jun 98), Luxembourg (24 Jun 98), Netherlands (24 Jun 98), Norway (24 Jun 98), Poland (24 Jun 98), Portugal (24 Jun 98), Moldova (24 Jun 98), Romania (24 Jun 98), Slovakia (24 Jun 98), Slovenia (24 Jun 98), Spain (25 Jun 98), Sweden (24 Jun 98), Switzerland (24 Jun 98), Ukraine (24 Jun 98), United Kingdom (24 Jun 98), United States (24 Jun 98)

4. HYDROSPHERE

4.1 TREATY BETWEEN CANADA AND THE UNITED STATES RELATING TO BOUNDARY WATERS AND QUESTIONS ARISING ALONG THE BOUNDARY BETWEEN TRHE UNITED STATES AND CANADA

Concluded: 11 Jan 09

Entered into force: 5 May 10

4.2 CONVENTION ON THE HIGH SEAS

Concluded: 29 Apr 58

Entered into force: 30 Sep 62

Signed but not ratified: 19 (as of at least 4 Jun 98)

Argentina (29 Apr 58), Bolivia (17 Oct 58), Canada (29 Apr 58), Colombia (29 Apr 58), Cuba (29 Apr 58), France (30 Oct 58), Ghana (29 Apr 58), Iceland (29 Apr 58), Iran (28 May 58), Ireland (2 Oct 58), Lebanon (29 May 58), Liberia (27 May 58), New Zealand (29 Oct 58), Pakistan (31 Oct 58), Panama (2 May 58), Sri Lanka (30 Oct 58), Tunisia (30 Oct 58), Uruguay (29 Apr 58), Vatican City (30 Apr 58)

Ratified/accepted/approved without qualification: 47 (as of at least 4 Jun 98)

Afghanistan (1 Sep 93), Australia (14 May 63), Austria (10 Jan 74), Belgium (6 Jan 72), Bosnia–Herzegovina (6 May 92), Burkina Faso (4 Oct 65), Cambodia (18 Mar 60), Central African Republic (15 Oct 62), Costa Rica (16 Feb 72), Croatia (3 Aug 92), Cyprus (23 May 88), Denmark (26 Sep 68), Dominican Republic (11 Aug 64), Fiji (25 Mar 71), Finland (16 Feb 65), Germany (26 Jul 73), Guatemala (27 Nov 61), Haiti (29 Mar 60), Israel (6 Sep 61), Italy (17 Dec 64), Jamaica (8 Oct 65), Japan (10 Jun 68), Kenya (20 Jun 69), Latvia (12 Nov 92), Lesotho (23 Oct 73), Madagascar (31 Jul 62), Malawi (3 Nov 65), Malaysia (21 Dec 60), Mauritius (5 Oct 70), Nepal (28 Dec 62), Netherlands (18 Feb 66), Nigeria (26 Jun 61), Portugal (8 Jan 63), Senegal (25 Apr 61), Sierra Leone (13 Mar 62), Slovenia (6 Jul 92), Solomon Islands (3 Sep 81), South Africa (9 Apr

63), Swaziland (16 Oct 70), Switzerland (18 May 66), Thailand (2 Jul 68), Tonga (29 Jun 71), Trindad/Tobago (11 Apr 66), Uganda (14 Sep 64), United States (12 Apr 61), Venezuela (15 Aug 61), Yugoslavia (28 Jan 66)

Ratified/accepted/approved with qualification: 15 (as of at least 4 Jun 98)

Albania (7 Dec 64), Belarus (27 Feb 61), Bulgaria (31 Aug 62), Czech Republic (22 Feb 93),Hungary (6 Dec 61), Indonesia (10 Aug 61), Mexico (2 Aug 66), Mongolia (15 Oct 76), Poland (29 Jun 62), Romania (12 Dec 61), Russia (22 Nov 60), Slovakia (28 May 93), Spain (25 Feb 71), Ukraine (12 Jan 61), United Kingdom (14 Mar 60)

4.3 Convention on the Continental Shelf

Concluded: 29 Apr 58

Entered into force: 10 Jun 64

Signed but not ratified: 21 (as of at least 4 Jun 98)

Afghanistan (30 Oct 58), Argentina (29 Apr 58), Bolivia (17 Oct 58), Chile (31 Oct 58), Cuba (29 Apr 58), Ecuador (31 Oct 58), Germany (30 Oct 58), Ghana (29 Apr 58), Iceland (29 Apr 58), Indonesia (8 May 58), Iran (28 May 58), Ireland (2 Oct 58), Lebanon (29 May 58), Liberia (27 May 58), Nepal (29 Apr 58), Pakistan (31 Oct 58), Panama (2 May 58), Peru (31 Oct 58), Sri Lanka (30 Oct 58), Tunisia (30 Oct 58), Uruguay (29 Apr 58)

Ratified/accepted/approved without qualification: 51 (as of at least 4 Jun 98)

Albania (17 Feb 64), Australia (14 May 63), Belarus (27 Feb 61), Bosnia–Herzegovina (12 Jan 94), Bulgaria (31 Aug 62), Cambodia (18 Mar 60), Colombia (8 Jan 62), Costa Rica (16 Feb 72), Croatia (3 Aug 92), Cyprus (11 Apr 74), Czech Republic (22 Feb 93), Denmark (12 Jun 63), Dominican Republic (11 Aug 64), Fiji (25 Mar 71), Finland (16 Feb 65), Guatemala (27 Nov 61), Haiti (29 Mar 60), Israel (6 Sep 61), Jamaica (8 Oct 65), Kenya (20 Jun 69), Latvia (2 Dec 92), Lesotho (23 Oct 73), Madagascar (31 Jul 62), Malawi (3 Nov 65), Malaysia (21 Dec 60), Malta (19 May 66), Mauritius (5 Oct 70), Mexico (2 Aug 66), Netherlands (18 Feb 66), New Zealand (18 Jan 65), Nigeria (28 Apr 71), Norway (9 Sep 71), Poland (29 Jun 62), Portugal (8 Jan 63), Romania (12 Dec 61), Russia (22 Nov 60), Senegal (25 Apr 61), Sierra Leone (25 Nov 66), Slovakia (28 May 93), Solomon Islands (3 Sep 81), South Africa (9 Apr 63), Swaziland (16 Oct 70), Sweden (1 Jun 66), Switzerland (18 May 66), Thailand (2 Jul 68), Tonga (29 Jun 71), Trindad/Tobago (11 Jul 68), Uganda (14 Sep 64), Ukraine (12 Jan 61), United Kingdom (11 May 64), United States (12 Apr 61)

Ratified/accepted/approved with qualification: 6 (as of at least 4 Jun 98)

Canada (6 Feb 70), France (14 Jun 65), Greece (6 Nov 72), Spain (25 Feb 71), Venezuela (15 Aug 61), Yugoslavia (28 Jan 66)

Denunciation: Senegal* (30 Mar 76)

* Denunciation objected by United Kingdom. Senegal still listed as a party by depositary.

4.4 Convention on the Territorial Sea and Contiguous Zone

Concluded: 29 Apr 58

Entered into force: 10 Sep 64

Signed but not ratified: 22 (as of at least 4 Jun 98)

Afghanistan (30 Oct 58), Argentina (29 Apr 58), Austria (27 Oct 58), Bolivia (17 Oct 58), Canada (29 Apr 58), Colombia (29 Apr 58), Costa Rica (29 Apr 58), Cuba (29 Apr 58), Ghana (29 Apr 58), Guatemala (29 Apr 58), Iceland (29 Apr 58), Iran (28 May 58), Ireland (2 Oct 58), Liberia (27 May 58), Nepal (29 Apr 58), New Zealand (29 Oct 58), Pakistan (31 Oct 58), Panama (2 May 58), Sri Lanka (30 Oct 58), Tunisia (30 Oct 58), Uruguay (29 Apr 58), Vatican City (30 Apr 58)

Ratified/accepted/approved without qualification: 35 (as of at least 4 Jun 98)

Australia (14 May 63), Belgium (6 Jan 72), Bosnia–Herzegovina (1 Sep 93), Cambodia (18 Mar 60), Croatia (3 Aug 92), Denmark (26 Sep 68), Dominican Republic (11 Aug 64), Finland (16 Feb 65), Haiti (29 Mar 60), Israel (6 Sep 61), Jamaica (8 Oct 65), Japan (10 Jun 68), Kenya (20 Jun 69), Latvia (17 Nov 92),

Lesotho (23 Oct 73), Madagascar (31 Jul 62), Malawi (3 Nov 65), Malaysia (21 Dec 60), Malta (19 May 66), Mauritius (5 Oct 70), Netherlands (18 Feb 66), Nigeria (26 Jun 61), Portugal (8 Jan 63), Senegal (25 Apr 61), Sierra Leone (13 Mar 62), Slovenia (6 Jul 92), South Africa (9 Apr 63), Swaziland (16 Oct 70), Switzerland (18 May 66), Thailand (2 Jul 68), Tonga (29 Jun 71), Trindad/Tobago (11 Apr 66), Uganda (14 Sep 64), United States (12 Apr 61), Yugoslavia (28 Jan 66)

Ratified/accepted/approved with qualification: 16 (as of at least 4 Jun 98)
Belarus (27 Feb 61), Bulgaria (31 Aug 62), Czech Republic (22 Feb 93), Fiji (25 Mar 71), Hungary (6 Dec 61), Italy (17 Dec 64), Lithuania (31 Jan 92), Mexico (2 Aug 66), Romania (12 Dec 61), Russia (22 Nov 60), Slovakia (28 May 93), Solomon Islands (3 Sep 81), Spain (25 Feb 71), Ukraine (12 Jan 61), United Kingdom (14 Mar 60), Venezuela (15 Aug 61)

Denunciation: Senegal* (9 Jul 71)

* Denunciation objected by United Kingdom. Senegal still listed as a party by depositary.

4.5 Convention on the Liability of Operators of Nuclear Ships

Concluded: 25 May 62
Not yet entered into force
Signed but not ratified: 14
Belgium (25 May 62), China (25 May 62), Gernmany (25 Oct 74), India (25 May 62), Indonesia (25 May 62), Ireland (25 May 62), Liberia (25 May 62), Malaysia (25 May 62), Monaco (25 May 62), Monaco (25 May 62), Panama (25 May 62), Philippines (25 May 62), Republic of Kora (25 May 62), United Arab Emirates(25 May 62), Yugoslavia (25 May 62)
Ratified/accepted/approved without qualification: 5
Lebanon (3 Jun 75), Madagascar (13 Jul 65), Portugal (31 Jun 68), Syria (1 Aug 74), Zaire (17 Jul 67)
Ratified/accepted/approved with qualification: 2
Netherlands (20 Mar 74), Suriname (20 Mar 74)

4.6 Helsinki Rules on the Uses of the Waters of International Rivers

Adopted: 20 August 1966

4.7 International Convention relating to Intervention on the High Seas in Cases of Oil Pollution Casualties

Concluded: 29 Nov 69
Entered into force: 6 May 75
Signed but not ratified: 6 (as of at least 1 Mar 97)
Brazil (30 Dec 69), Greece (14 Apr 70), Guatemala (29 Nov 69), Korea (South) (29 Nov 69), Madagascar (29 Nov 69), Romania (30 Dec 70)
Ratified/accepted/approved without qualification: 53 (as of at least 1 Mar 97)
Argentina (21 Apr 87), Bahamas (22 Jul 76), Bangladesh (6 Nov 81), Barbados (6 May 94), Belgium (21 Oct 71), Benin (11 Nov 85), Cameroon (14 May 84), China (23 Feb 90), Côte d'Ivoire (8 Jan 88), Croatia (8 Oct 91), Denmark (18 Dec 70), Djibouti (1 Mar 90), Dominican Republic (5 Feb 75), Ecuador (23 Dec 76), Egypt (3 Feb 89), Fiji (15 Aug 72), Finland (6 Sep 76), Gabon (21 Jan 82), Ghana (20 Apr 78), Iceland (17 Jul 80), Ireland (21 Aug 80), Italy (27 Feb 79), Jamaica (13 Mar 91), Kuwait (2 Apr 81), Lebanon (5 Jun 75), Liberia (25 Sep 72), Mexico (8 Apr 76), Monaco (24 Feb 75), Morocco (11 Apr 74), Nicargaua (15 Nov 94), Netherlands (19 Sep 75), New Zealand (26 Mar 75), Norway (12 Jul 72),Oman (24 Jan 85), Panama (7 Jan 76), Papua New Guinea (12 Mar 80), Poland (1 Jun 76), Portugal (15 Feb 80), Qatar (2 Jun 88), Senegal (27 Mar 72), Slovenia (25 Jun 91), South Africa (1 Jul 86), Spain (8 Nov 73), Sri Lanka (12 Apr 83), Suriname (25 Nov 75), Sweden (8 Feb 73), Switzerland (15 Dec 87), Tunisia (4 May 76), Ukraine (17 Dec 93), United Arab Emirates (15 Dec 83), United States (21 Feb 74), Vanuatu (14 Sep 92), Yemen (6 Mar 79)
Ratified/accepted/approved with qualification: 9 (as of at least 1 Mar 97)

Australia (7 Nov 83), Bulgaria (2 Nov 83), Cuba* (5 May 76), France (10 May 72), Germany (7 May 75), Japan (6 Apr 71), Russia (30 Dec 74), Syria (6 Feb 75), United Kingdom (12 Jan 71)
Ratified/accepted/approved (qualifications undetermined): 3 (as of at least 1 Mar 97)
Chile (28 Feb 95), Georgia (25 Aug 95), Marshall Islands (16 Oct 95), Pakistan (13 Jan 95)
* Reservation not accepted by France and Japan.

4.8 **DECLARATION OF PRINCIPLES GOVERNING THE SEA-BED AND THE OCEAN FLOOR, AND THE SUBSOIL THEREOF, BEYOND THE LIMITS OF NATIONAL JURISDICTION**
Adopted: 17 Dec 70
For: 108*
Against: 0
Abstaining: 14
* Adopted with no roll call vote recorded

4.9 **CONVENTION RELATING TO CIVIL LIABILITY IN THE FIELD OF MARITIME CARRIAGE OF NUCLEAR MATERIAL**
Concluded: 17 Dec 71
Entered into force: 15 July 1975
Signed but not ratified: 4
Brazil (17 Dec 71), Portugal (17 Dec 71), United Kingdom (17 Dec 71), Yugoslavia (17 Dec 71)
Ratified/accepted/approved without qualification: 14
Argentina (18 May 81), Belgium (15 Jun 89), Denmark (4 Sep 74), Finland (4 Sep 91), France (2 Feb 73), Gabon (21 Jan 82), Germany (1 Oct 75), Italy (21 Jul 80), Liberia (17 Feb 81), Netherlands (1 Aug 91), Norway (16 Apr 75), Spain (21 May 74), Sweden (22 Nov 74), Yemen (6 Mar 79)

4.10 **ILA DRAFT ARTICLES ON MARINE POLLUTION OF CONTINENTAL ORIGIN**
Adopted: 26 Aug 72

4.11 **CONVENTION ON THE PREVENTION OF MARINE POLLUTION BY DUMPING OF WASTES AND OTHER MATTER**
Concluded: 29 Dec 72
Entered into force: 30 Aug 75
Signed but not ratified: 15 (as of at least 1 Mar 97)
Bolivia (29 Dec 72), Cambodia (2 Jan 73), Chad (29 Dec 72), Colombia (29 Dec 72), Kuwait (1 Mar 73), Lebanon (29 Dec 72), Lesotho (8 Jan 73), Liberia (29 Dec 72), Nepal (29 Dec 72), Senegal (29 Dec 72), Somalia (16 Apr 73), Taiwan (29 Dec 72), Togo (21 Nov 73), Uruguay (29 Dec 72), Venezuela (30 May 73)
Ratified/accepted/approved without qualification: 66 (as of at least 1 Mar 97)
Afghanistan (2 Apr 75), Antigua/Barbuda (6 Jan 89), Argentina (11 Sep 79), Australia (21 Aug 85), Barbados (4 May 94), Belarus (29 Jan 76), Belgium (12 Jun 85), Brazil (26 Jul 82), Canada (13 Nov 75), Cape Verde (26 May 77), Chile (4 Aug 77), Congo (Kinshasa) (16 Sep 75), Costa Rica (16 Jun 86), Côte d'Ivoire (9 Oct 87), Croatia (8 Oct 91), Cuba (1 Dec 75), Cyprus (7 Jun 90), Denmark (23 Oct 74), Dominican Republic (7 Dec 73), Egypt (30 Jun 92), Finland (3 May 79), Gabon (5 Feb 82), Greece (10 Aug 81), Guatemala (14 Jul 75), Haiti (28 Aug 75), Honduras (2 May 80), Hungary (5 Feb 76), Iceland (24 May 73), Ireland (17 Feb 82), Jamaica (22 Mar 91), Japan (15 Oct 75), Jordan (11 Nov 74), Kenya (7 Jan 76), Kiribati (12 May 82), Korea (South) (21 Dec 93), Libya (22 Nov 76), Luxembourg (21 Feb 91), Malta (28 Dec 89), Mexico (7 Apr 75), Monaco (16 May 77), Morocco (18 Feb 77), Nauru (26 Jul 82), Netherlands (2 Dec 77), Nigeria (19 Mar 76), Norway (4 Apr 74), Oman (13 Mar 84), Panama (31 Jul 75), Papua New Guinea (10 Mar 80), Philippines (10 Aug 73), Poland (23 Jan 79), Portugal (14 Apr 78), Russia (30 Dec 75), St Lucia (23 Aug 85), Seychelles (29 Oct 84), Slovenia (25 Jun 91), Solomon Islands (7 Jul 78), South Africa (7 Aug 78), Spain (31 Jul 74), Suriname (21 Oct 80), Sweden (21 Feb 74), Switzerland (31 Jul 79),

Tunisia (13 Apr 76), Ukraine (5 Feb 76), United Arab Emirates (9 Aug 74), United States (29 Apr 74), Vanuatu (22 Sep 92)

Ratified/accepted/approved with qualification: 6 (as of at least 1 Mar 97)

China (5 Nov 85), France (3 Feb 77), Germany (8 Nov 77), Italy (30 Apr 84), New Zealand (30 Apr 75), United Kingdom (17 Nov 75)

Ratified/accepted/approved (qualifications undetermined): 1 (as of at least 1 Mar 97)

Pakistan (9 Mar 95)

4.12 MARPOL 73/78: PROTOCOL OF 1978 RELATING TO THE INTERNATIONAL CONVENTION FOR THE PREVENTION OF POLLUTION FROM SHIPS, 1973

Concluded: 2 Nov 73 (Convention); 17 Feb 78 (Protocol)

Entered into force:

Text, Annex I & Annex 2: 2 Oct 83

Annex V: 31 Dec 88

Ratified/accepted/approved (Text, Annexes I & II) without qualification: 106

Algeria (31 Jan 89), Antigua and Barbuda (29 Jan 88), Argentina (31 Aug 93), Australia (14 Oct 87), Austria (27 May 88), Bahamas (7 Jun 83), Barbados (6 May 94), Belarus (7 Jan 94), Belgium (6 Mar 84), Belize (26 May 95), Brazil (29 Jan 88), Brunei Darussalam (23 Oct 86), Bulgaria (12 Dec 84), Cambodia (28 Nov 94), Canada (16 Nov 92), Chile (10 Oct 94), China (1 Jul 83), Colombia (27 Jul 81), Cote d'Ivoire (5 Oct 87), Croatia (8 Oct 91) (Date of succession to Yugoslavia), Cuba (21 Dec 92), Cyprus (22 Jun 89), Czechoslovakia (2 Jul 84), Czech Republic (1 Jan 93) (Date of succession to Czechoslovakia), Denmark (27 Nov 80), Djibouti (1 Mar 90), Equador (18 May 90), Egypt (7 Aug 86), Estonia (16 Dec 91), Finland (20 Sep 83), France (25 Sep 81), Gabon (26 Apr 83), Gambia (1 Nov 91), Georgia (8 Nov 94), Germany (21 Jan 82), Germany—Democratic Republic (24 Apr 84), Ghana (3 Jun 91), Greece (23 Sep 82), Hungary (14 Jan 85), Iceland (25Jun 85), India (24 Sep 86), Indonesia (21 Oct 86), Ireland (6 Jan 95), Israel (31 Aug 83), Italy (1 Oct 82), Jamaica (13 Mar 91), Japan (9 Jun 83), Kazakhstan (7 Mar 94), Kenya (15 Dec 92), Korea–Democratic Republic of (1 May 85), Korea–Republic of (23 Jul 84), Latvia (20 May 92), Lebanon (18 Jul 83), Liberia (28 Oct 80), Lithuania (4 Dec 91), Luxembourg (14 Feb 91), Malta (21 Jun 91), Marshall Islands (26 Apr 88), Mauritus (6 Apr 95), Mexico (23 Apr 92), Monaco (20 Aug 92), Morocco (12 Oct 93), Myanmar (4 May 88), Netherlands (30 Jun 83), Norway (15 Jul 80), Oman (13 Mar 84), Pakistan (22 Nov 94), Panama (20 Feb 85), Papaua New Guinea (25 Oct 93), Peru (25 Apr 80), Poland (1 Apr 86), Portugal (22 Oct 87), Romania (15 Apr 93), Russian Federation (3 Nov 83), St. Vincent and the Grenadines (28 Oct 83), Seychelles (28 Nov 90), Singapore (1 Nov 90), Slovenia (25 Jun 91) (Date of succession to Yugoslavia), Slovak Republic (1 Jan 93) (Date of succession to Czechoslovakia), South Africa (28 Nov 84), Spain (6 Jul 84), Suriname (4 No 88), Sweeden (9 Jun 80), Switzerland (15 Dec 87), Syria (9 Nov 88), Togo (9 Feb 90), Tunisia (10 Oct 80), Turkey (10 Oct 90), Tuvalu (22 Aug 85), Ukraine (25 Oct 93), United Kingdom (22 May 80), United States (12 Aug 80), Uruguay (30 Apr 79), Vanuatu (13 Apr 89), Venezuela (29 Jul 94), Vietnam (29 May 91), Yugoslavia (31 Oct 80).

Ratified/accepted/approved Annex V without qualification: 91

Algeria (31 Jan 89), Antigua and Barbuda (29 Jan 88), Argentina (31 Aug 93), Australia (14 Oct 90), Austria (27 May 88), Bahamas (12 Aug 90), Barbados (6 May 94), Belarus (7 Jan 94), Belgium (27 Oct 88), Bulgaria (13 May 93), Cambodia (28 Nov 94), China (21 Nov 88), Colombia (27 Jul 81), Cote d'Ivoire (5 Oct 87), Croatia (8 Oct 91) (Date of succession to Yugoslavia), Cyprus (22 Jun 89), Czechoslovakia (2 Jul 84), Czech Republic (1 Jan 93) (Date of succession to Czechoslovakia), Denmark (27 Nov 80), Ecuador (18 May 90), Egypt (7 Aug 86), Estonia (18 Aug 92), Finland (20 Sep 83) , France (25 Sep 81), Gabon (26 Apr 83), Gambia (1 Nov 91), Georgia (8 Nov 94), Germany (21 Jan 82), Germany–Democratic Republic (25 Apr 84), Greece (23 Sep 82), Hungary (14 Jan 85), Iceland (30 Jun 89), Ireland (6 Jan 95), Italy (1 Oct 82), Jamaica (13 Mar 91), Japan (9 June 83), Kazakhstan (7 Mar 94), Kenya (15 Dec 92), Korea–

Democratic People's Republic of (1 May 85), Latvia (20 May 92), Lebanon (18 Jul 83), Liberia (12 Jun 96), Lithuania (4 Dec 91), Luxembourg (14 Feb 91), Marshall Islands (26 Apr 88), Mauritus (6 Apr 95), Monaco (20 Aug 92), Morocco (12 Oct 93), Netherlands (19 Apr 88), Norway (15 Jul 80), Oman (13 Mar 84), Pakistan (22 Nov 94), Panama (20 Feb 85), Papua New Guinea (25 Oct 93), Peru (25 Apr 80), Poland (1 Apr 86), Portugal (22 Oct 87), Romania (15 Apr 93), Russian Federation (14 Aug 87), St. Vincent and the Grenadines (28 Oct 83), Slovak Republic (1 Jan 93) (Date of succession to Czecholsovakia), Slovenia (25 Jun 91), South Africa (13 May 92), Spain (21 Jan 91), Suriname (4 Nov 88), Sweeden (9 Jun 80), Switzerland (30 Apr 90), Togo (9 Feb 90), Tunisia (10 Oct 80), Turkey (10 Oct 90), Tuvalu (22 Aug 85), Ukraine (25 Oct 93), United Kingdom (27 May 86), United States (30 Dec 87), Uruguay (30 Apr 79), Vanuatu (22 Apr 91), Venezuela (29 Jul 94), Yugoslavia (31 Oct 80).

4.13 CONVENTION ON THE PROTECTION OF THE MARINE ENVIRONMENT OF THE BALTIC SEA AREA

Concluded: 22 Mar 74
Entered into force: 30 May 80
Ratified/accepted/approved without qualifications: 9
Denmark (20 Jul 77), Estonia (22 Jan 92), Finland (27 Jun 75), Germany (3 Mar 80), Latvia (27 May 94), Lithuania (8 Apr 92), Poland (19 Nov 79), Russian Federation (2 Nov 78), Sweden (30 Jul 76)

4.14 CONVENTION FOR THE PREVENTION OF MARINE POLLUTION FROM LAND-BASED SOURCES

Concluded: 4 Jun 74
Entered into force: 6 May 78
Signed but not ratified: 1 (as of at least at least 1 Jan 94)
Luxembourg (11 Jun 74)
Ratified/accepted/approved without qualification: 13 (as of at least at least 1 Jan 94)
Belgium (12 Jan 84), Denmark (1 Mar 76), European Community (23 Jun 75), France (19 Jan 77), Germany (2 Mar 82), Greece (22 Jul 91), Iceland (19 Jun 81), Ireland (29 Aug 84), Netherlands (10 Nov 77), Portugal (10 May 78), Spain (17 Apr 80), Sweden (30 Jul 76), United Kingdom (6 Apr 78)

4.15 CONVENTION FOR THE PROTECTION OF THE MEDITERRANEAN SEA AGAINST POLLUTION

Concluded: 16 Feb 76
Entered into force: 12 Feb 78
Ratified/accepted/approved without qualification: 22
Albania (30 May 90), Algeria (16 Feb 81), Bosnia and Herzegovina (1 Mar 92), Croatia (8 Oct 91), Cyprus (19 Nov 79), Egypt (23 Sep 78), European Economic Community (16 Mar 78), France (10 Apr 78), Greece (3 Jan 79), Israel (2 Apr 78), Italy (3 Feb 79), Lebanon (8 Nov 77), Libyan Arab Jamahiriya (31 Jan 29), Malta (30 Dec 77), Monaco (20 Sep 77), Morocco (15 Jan 80), Slovenia (15 Mar 94), Spain (17 Dec 76), Syrian Arab Republic (25 Jan 79), Tunisia (30 Jul 77), Turkey (6 Apr 81), Yugoslavia (13 Jan 78)
Ratified/accepted/approved with qualification: 4
Egypt (24 Aug 78), France (11 Mar 78), Israel (3 Mar 78), Syria (26 Dec 78)

4.16 CONVENTION FOR THE PROTECTION OF THE RHINE RIVER AGAINST POLLUTION BY CHEMICAL POLLUTION

Concluded: 3 Dec 76
Entered into force: 1 Feb 79
Ratified/accepted/approved without qualification: 6
European Economic Community (26 Sep 78), France (28 Dec 77), Germany (7 Dec 78), Luxembourg (3 May 78), Netherlands (18 Sep 78), Switzerland (28 Nov 77)

4.17 CONVENTION FOR THE PROTECTION OF THE RHINE RIVER AGAINST POLLUTION BY CHLORIDES
Concluded: 3 Dec 76
Entered into force: 5 July 85
Ratified/accepted/approved without qualification: 5
France (2 Feb 84), Germany (7 Dec 78), Luxembourg (3 May 78), Netherlands (18 Sep 78), Switzerland (28 Nov 77

4.18 KUWAIT REGIONAL CONVENTION FOR CO-OPERATION ON THE PROTECTION OF THE MARINE ENVIRONMENT FROM POLLUTION
Concluded: 24 Apr 78
Entered into force: 30 Jun 79
Ratified/accepted/approved without qualification: 8
Bahrain (1 Jul 79), Iran (1 Jun 80), Iraq (1 Jul 79), Kuwait (1 Jul 79), Oman (1 Jul 79), Qatar (1 Jul 79), Saudi Arabia (26 Mar 82), United Arab Emirates (1 Mar 80)

4.19 PROTOCOL FOR THE PROTECTION OF THE MEDITERRANEAN SEA AGAINST POLLUTION FROM LAND-BASED SOURCES
Concluded: 17 May 80
Entered into force: 17 Jun 83
Ratified/accepted/approved without qualification: 20 (as of at least 1 Mar 97)
Albania (30 Mar 90), Algeria (2 May 83), Bosnia–Herzegovina (22 Oct 94), Croatia (8 Oct 91), Cyprus (28 Jun 88), Egypt (18 May 83), European Community (7 Oct 83), Greece (26 Jan 87), Israel (21 Feb 91), Italy (4 Jul 85), Lebanon (27 Dec 94), Libya (6 Jun 89), Malta (2 Mar 89), Monaco (12 Jan 83), Morocco (9 Feb 87), Slovenia (12 Dec 93), Spain (6 Jun 84), Syria (1 Dec 93), Tunisia (29 Oct 81), Turkey (21 Feb 83)
Ratified/accepted/approved with qualification: 1 (as of at least 1 Mar 97)
France (13 Jul 82)

4.20 UNITED NATIONS CONVENTION ON THE LAW OF THE SEA
Concluded: 10 Dec 82
Entered into force: 16 Nov 94
Signed but not ratified: 44 (as of at least 4 Jun 98)
Afghanistan (18 Mar 83), Bangladesh (10 Dec 82), Belarus (10 Dec 82), Belgium (5 Dec 84), Bhutan (10 Dec 82), Burkina Faso (10 Dec 82), Burundi (10 Dec 82), Cambodia (1 Jul 83), Canada (10 Dec 82), Central African Republic (4 Dec 84), Chad (10 Dec 82), Colombia (10 Dec 82), Congo (Brazzaville) (10 Dec 82), Denmark (10 Dec 82), Dominican Republic (10 Dec 82), El Salvador (5 Dec 84), Ethiopia (10 Dec 82), Hungary (10 Dec 82), Iran (10 Dec 82), Korea (North) (10 Dec 82), Laos (10 Dec 82), Lesotho (10 Dec 82), Liberia (10 Dec 82), Libya (3 Dec 84), Liechtenstein (30 Nov 84), Luxembourg (5 Dec 84), Madagascar (25 Feb 83), Malawi (7 Dec 84), Maldives (10 Dec 82), Morocco (10 Dec 82), Nepal (10 Dec 82), Nicaragua (9 Dec 84), Niger (10 Dec 82), Niue (5 Dec 84), Poland (10 Dec 82), Qatar (27 Nov 84), Rwanda (10 Dec 82), Suriname (10 Dec 82), Swaziland (18 Jan 84), Switzerland (17 Oct 84), Thailand (10 Dec 82), Tuvalu (10 Dec 82), Ukraine (Ukrainian SSR) (10 Dec 82), United Arab Emirates (10 Dec 82), Vanuatu (10 Dec 82)
Ratified/accepted/approved without qualification: 75 (as of at least 4 Jun 98)
Antigua/Barbuda (2 Feb 89), Australia (5 Oct 94), Bahamas (29 Jul 83), Bahrain (30 May 85), Barbados (12 Oct 93), Belize (13 Aug 83), Benin (16 Oct 97), Bosnia–Herzegovina (12 Jan 94), Botswana (2 May 90), Brunei (5 Nov 96), Bulgaria (15 May 96), Cameroon (19 Nov 85), Comoros (21 Jun 94, Congo (Kinshasa) (17 Feb 89), Cook Islands (15 Feb 95), Costa Rica (21 Sep 92), Côte d'Ivoire (26 Mar 84), Cyprus (12 Dec 88), Czech Republic (21 Jun 96), Djibouti (8 Oct 91), Dominica (24 Oct 91), Equatorial Guinea (21 Jul 97), Fiji (10 Dec 82), Gabon (11 Mar 98), Gambia (22 May 84), Georgia (21 Mar 96), Ghana (7 Jun 83), Grenada (25 Apr 91), Guinea (6 Sep 85), Guyana (16 Nov 93), Haiti (31

Jul 96), Honduras (5 Oct 93), Indonesia (3 Feb 86), Iraq (30 Jul 85), Jamaica (21 Mar 83), Japan (20 Jun 96), Jordan (27 Nov 95), Kenya (2 Mar 89), Korea (South) (29 Jan 96), Lebanon (5 Jan 95), Macedonia (19 Aug 94), Marshall Islands (9 Aug 91), Mauritania (17 Jul 96), Mauritius (4 Nov 94), Mexico (18 Mar 83), Micronesia (29 Apr 91), Monaco (20 Mar 96), Mongolia (13 Aug 96), Mozambique (13 Mar 97), Myanmar (Burma) (21 May 96), Namibia (18 Apr 83), Nauru (23 Jan 96), New Zealand (19 Jul 96), Nigeria (14 Aug 86), Oman (17 Aug 89), Palau (30 Sep 96), Papua New Guinea (14 Jan 97), Paraguay (26 Sep 86), St Kitts/Nevis (7 Jan 93), St Lucia (27 Mar 85), St Vincent/Grenadines (1 Oct 93), Samoa (14 Aug 95), Senegal (25 Oct 84), Seychelles (16 Sep 91), Singapore (17 Nov 94), Slovakia (8 May 96)), Solomon Islands (23 Jun 97), Somalia (24 Jul 89), Sri Lanka (19 Jul 94), Sudan (23 Jan 85), Togo (16 Apr 85), Tonga (2 Aug 95), Trindad/Tobago (25 Apr 86), Uganda (9 Nov 90), Zambia (7 Mar 83), Zimbabwe (24 Feb 93)

Ratified/accepted/approved with qualification: 50 (as of at least 4 Jun 98) Algeria (11 Jun 96), Angola (5 Dec 90), Argentina (1 Dec 95), Austria (14 Jul 95), Bolivia (28 Apr 95), Brazil (22 Dec 88), Cape Verde (10 Aug 87), Chile (25 Aug 97), China (7 Jun 96), Croatia (5 Apr 95), Cuba (15 Aug 84), Egypt (26 Aug 83), European Community (1 Apr 98), Finland (21 Jun 96), France (11 Apr 96), Germany (14 Oct 94), Greece (21 Jul 95), Guatemala (11 Feb 97), Guinea-Bissau (25 Aug 86), India (29 Jun 95), Iceland (21 Jun 85), Ireland (21 Jun 96), Italy (13 Jan 95), Kuwait (2 May 86), Malaysia (14 Oct 96), Malta (20 May 93), Mali (16 Jul 85), Netherlands (28 Jun 96), Norway (24 Jun 96)), Oman (17 Aug 89), Pakistan (26 Feb 97), Panama (1 Jul 96), Philippines (8 May 84), Portugal (3 Nov 97), Romania (17 Dec 96), Russia (12 Mar 97), São Tomé/Príncipe (3 Nov 87), Saudi Arabia (24 Apr 96), Sierra Leone (12 Dec 94), Slovenia (16 Jun 95), South Africa (23 Dec 97), Spain (15 Jun 97), Sudan (23 Jan 85), Sweden (25 Jun 96), Tanzania (30 Sep 85), Tunisia (24 Apr 85), United Kingdom (25 Jul 97), Uruguay (10 Dec 92), Vietnam (25 Jul 94), Yemen (21 Jul 87), Yugoslavia (5 May 86)

4.21 MONTREAL GUIDELINES FOR THE PROTECTION OF THE MARINE ENVIRONMENT AGAINST POLLUTION FROM LAND-BASED SOURCES

Adopted: 24 May 85

4.22 CONVENTION FOR THE PROTECTION OF THE NATURAL RESOURCES AND ENVIRONMENT OF THE SOUTH PACIFIC REGION

Concluded: 25 Nov 86
Entered into force: 22 Aug 90
Signed but not ratified: 4 (as of at least 1 Mar 97)
Nauru (15 Apr 87), Palau (25 Nov 86), Tuvalu (14 Aug 87), United Kingdom (16 Jul 87)
Ratified/accepted/approved without qualification: 9 (as of at least 1 Mar 97)
Australia (19 Jun 89), Cook Islands (9 Sep 87), Fiji (18 Sep 89), Marshall Islands (4 May 87), Micronesia (29 Nov 88), New Zealand (3 May 90), Papua New Guinea (15 Sep 89), Samoa (22 Aug 90), Solomon Islands (10 Aug 89)
Ratified/accepted/approved with qualification: 2 (as of at least 1 Mar 97) France (17 Jul 90), United States (10 Jun 91)

4.23 BELLAGIO DRAFT TREATY CONCERNING THE USE OF TRANSBOUNDARY GROUNDWATERS, 1989

This draft treaty is intended to serve as a model for states which wish to enter into bilateral or regional agreements concerning the use of their transboundary groundwaters. As a model, the draft treaty itself has never been adopted or signed by any state, except insofar as particular states may have borrowed from its provisions in developing other treaties.

4.24 CONVENTION FOR THE PROTECTION OF THE MARINE ENVIRONMENT OF THE NORTH-EAST ATLANTIC ("OSPAR CONVENTION")

Concluded: 22 Sep 92

Entered into force: 25 Mar 98
Ratified/accepted/approved without qualification: 16
Belgium, Denmark, European Community, Finland, France, Germany, Iceland, Ireland, Netherlands, Norway, Protugal, Spain, Sweden, United Kingdom, Luxembourg, Switzerland

4.25 International Convention on Civil Liability for Oil Pollution Damage, 1992

The 1992 Oil Pollution Damage Liability Convention is an updated version of the 1969 International Convention on Civil Liability for Oil Pollution Damage, revised and renamed by a 1992 Protocol. The status information covers both the 1969 Convention and the 1992 Convention.

1969 Convention:
Concluded: 29 Nov 69
Entered into force: 19 Jun 75
1992 Convention:
Concluded: 27 Nov 92
Entered into force: 30 May 96
Ratified/accepted/approved without qualification: 92 (total); 41(1992 Convention)
Albania (5 Jul 94)*, Algeria (19 Jun 75), Australia (5 Feb 84), Bahamas (20 Oct 76), Barbados (4 Aug 94),Belgium (12 Apr 77), Belize (1 Jul 91), Benin (30 Jan 86)*, Brazil (17 Mar 77)*, Brunei Darussalam (28 Dec 92),Cambodia (26 Feb 95)*, Cameroon (12 Aug 84)*, Canada (24 Apr 89), Chile (31 Oct 77)*, China (29 Apr 80)*, Colombia (24 Jun 90)*, Cote D'Ivoire (19 Jun 75)*, Croatia (8 Oct 91), Cyprus (17 Sep 89), Denmark (19 Jun 75), Djibouti (30 May 90), Dominican Republic (19 Jun 75)*, Ecuador (23 Mar 77)*, Egypt (4 May 89), Estonia (1 Mar 93)*, Fiji (19 Jun 75)*, Finland (8 Jan 81), France (19 Jun 75), Gabon (21 Apr 82)*, Gambia (30 Jan 92)*, Georgia (18 Jul 94)*, Germany (18 Aug 75), Ghana (19 Jul 78)*, Greece (27 Sep 76), Guatemala (18 Jan 83)*, Iceland (15 Oct 80), India (30 Jul 87), Indonesia (30 Nov 78)*, Ireland (17 Feb 93), Italy (28 May 79)*, Japan (1 Sep 76), Kazakhstan (5 Jun 94)*, Kenya (15 Mar 93)*, Kuwait (1 Jul 81)*, Latvia (8 Oct 92), Lebanon (19 Jun 75)*, Liberia (19 Jun 75), Luxembourg (15 May 91)*, Malaysia (6 Apr 95)*, Maldives (14 Jun 81)*, Malta (26 Dec 91)*, Marshall Islands (24 Apr 94), Mauritania (15 Feb 96)*, Mauritius (5 Jul 95)*, Mexico (11 Aug 94), Monaco (19 Nov 75), Morocco (19 Jun 75)*, Netherlands (8 Dec 75), New Zealand (26 Jul 76), Nigeria (5 Aug 81)*, Norway (19 Jun 75), Oman (24 Apr 85), Panama (6 Apr 76)*, Papua New Guinea (10 Jun 80)*, Peru (25 May 87), Poland (16 Jun 76)*, Portugal (24 Feb 77)*, Qatar (31 Aug 88)*, Republic of Korea (18 Mar 79), Russian Federation (22 Sep 75)*, Saint Kitts and Nevis (13 Dec 94)*, Saint Vincent and the Grenadines (18 Jul 89)*, Saudi Arabia (14 Jul 93)*, Senegal (19 Jun 75)*, Seychelles (11 Jul 88)*, Sierra Leone (11 Nov 93)*, Singapore (15 Dec 81), Slovenia (25 Jun 91)*, South Africa (15 Jun 76)*, Spain (7 Mar 76) Sri Lanka (11 Jul 83)*, Sweden (19 Jun 75), Switzerland (14 Mar 88), Syrian Arab Republic (19 Jun 75)*, Tonga (1 May 96)*, Tunisia (2 Aug 76), Tuvalu (1 Oct 78)*, United Arab Emirates (14 Mar 84), United Kingdom (19 Jun 75), Vanuatu (3 May 83)*, Venezuela (20 Apr 92), Yemen (04 Jun 79)*

* Party to the 1969 Convention, but not party to the Protocol which amended it and created the 1992 Convention.

4.26 International Convention on the Establishment of an International Fund for Compensation for Oil Pollution Damage, 1992

The 1992 Fund Convention is an updated version of the 1971 International Convention on the Establishment of an International Fund for Compensation for Oil Pollution Damage, as revised and renamed by a 1992 Protocol. The status information provided below covers both the 1971 Convention and the 1992 Convention.

1971 Convention:
Concluded: 18 Dec 71
Entered into force: 16 Oct 78

1992 Convention:
Concluded: 27 Nov 92
Entered into force: 30 May 96
Ratified/accepted/approved without qualification: 68 (total), 39 (1992 Convention)
Albania (5 Jul 94)*, Algeria (16 Oct 78), Australia (8 Jan 95), Austria (8 Jan 95), Bahamas (16 Oct 78), Barbados (4 Aug 94), Belgium (1 Mar 95), Benin (30 Jan 86)*, Brunei Darussalam (28 Dec 92)*, Cameroon (12 Aug 84)*, Canada (24 Apr 89), Cote D'ivoire (3 Jan 88)*, Croatia (8 Oct 91), Cyprus (24 Oct 89), Denmark (16 Oct 78), Djibouti (30 May 90), Estonia (1 Mar 93)*, Fiji (2 Jun 83)*, Finland (8 Jan 81), France (16 Oct 78), Gabon (21 Apr 82)*, Gambia (30 Jan 92), Germany (16 Oct 78), Ghana (16 Oct 78)*, Greece (16 Mar 87), Iceland (15 Oct 80), India (8 Oct 90)*, Indonesia (30 Nov 78)*, Ireland (17 Feb 93), Italy (28 May 79)*, Japan (16 Oct 78), Kenya (15 Mar 93)*, Kuwait (1 Jul 81)*, Liberia (16 Oct 78), Malaysia (6 Apr 95)*, Maldives (14 Jun 81)*, Malta (26 Dec 91)*, Marshall Islands (28 Feb 95), Mauritania (15 Feb 96), Mauritius (5 Jul 95)*, Mexico (11 Aug 94), Monaco (21 Nov 79), Morocco (31 Mar 93)*, Netherlands (1 Nov 82), Nigeria (10 Dec 87), Norway (16 Oct 78)*, Oman (8 Aug 85), Papua New Guinea (10 Jun 80)*, Poland (15 Dec 85)*, Portugal (10 Dec 85)*, Qatar (31 Aug 88), Republic of Korea (8 Mar 93), Russian Federation (15 Sep 87)*, Saint Kitts and Nevis (13 Dec 94)*, Seychelles (11 Jun 88)*, Sierra Leone (11 Nov 93)*, Slovenia (25 Jun 91)*, Spain (6 Jan 82), Sri Lanka (11 Jul 83)*, Sweden (16 Oct 78), Syrian Arab Republic (16 Oct 78)*, Tonga (1 May 96)*, Tunisia (16 Oct 78), Tuvalu (16 Oct 78)*, United Arab Emirates (14 Mar 84), United Kingdom (16 Oct 78), Vanuatu (13 Apr 89),* Venezuela (20 Apr 92)

* Party to the 1971 Convention, but not party to the 1992 Protocol which amended it.

4.27 1997 Ships' Routeing Amendment to the International Convention for the Safety of Life at Sea

The Routeing Amendment was adopted pursuant to the tacit amendment procedure of the Convention for the Safety of Life at Sea (SOLAS). Under the tacit amendment procedure, an amendment of this sort is binding on all parties to SOLAS except those which have formally objected to it. Hence, this amendment bound all non-objecting parties to SOLAS upon its entry into force. We have been unable to determine whether any party formally objected to this amendment. Accordingly, the ratification information below includes all parties to SOLAS and reflects the dates on which they ratified that Convention.
Adopted: 16 May 95
Entered into force: 1 Jan 97
Ratified/accepted/approved without qualification: 138
Algeria (3 Nov 83), Angola (3 Oct 91), Antigua and Barbuda (9 Feb 87), Argentina (12 Dec 74), Australia (17 Aug 83), Austria (27 May 88), Bahamas (16 Feb 79), Bahrain (21 Oct 85), Bangladesh (6 Nov 81), Barbados (1 Sep 82), Belarus (1 Nov 74), Belgium (17 Dec 74), Belize (2 Apr 91), Benin (1 Nov 85), Brazil (22 May 80), Brunei Darussalam (23 Oct 86), Bulgaria (8 Nov 74), Cambodia (28 Nov 94), Cameroon (14 May 84), Canada (8 May 78), Cape Verde (28 Apr 77), Chile (1 Nov 74), China (20 Jun 75), Colombia (31 Oct 80), Congo (1 Nov 74), D'Ivoire (5 Oct 87), Croatia (8 Oct 91), Cuba (19 Jun 92), Cyprus (11 Oct 85), Czech Republic (1 Jan 93), Democratic People'S Rep. Of Korea (1 Aug 85), Denmark (1 Nov 74), Djibouti (1 Mar 84), Dominican Republic (10 Apr 80), Ecuador (28 May 82), Egypt (1 Nov 74), Estonia (16 Dec 91), Ethiopia (18 Jul 85), Fiji (4 Mar 83), Finland (21 Nov 80), France (1 Nov 74), Gabon (21 Apr 82), Gambia (1 Nov 91), Georgia (19 Apr 94), Germany (18 Feb 75), Ghana (1 Nov 74), Greece (1 Nov 74), Guatemala (22 Oct 82), Guinea (19 Apr 81), Haiti (6 Apr 89), Honduras (24 Sep 85), Hungary (1 Nov 74), Iceland (1 Nov 74), India (16 Jun 76), Indonesia (1 Nov 74), Iran (Islamic Republic Of) (1 Nov 74), Iraq (14 Dec 90), Ireland (29 Nov 83), Israel (1 Nov 74), Italy (11 Jun 80), Jamaica (14 Oct 83), Japan (15 May 80), Jordan (7 Aug 85) Kazakhstan (7 Mar 94), Kuwait (29 Jun 79), Latvia (20 May 92), Lebanon (29 Nov 83), Liberia (1 Nov 74), Libyan Arab Jamahiriya (2 Jul 81), Lithuania (4 Dec 91), Luxembourg (14 Feb

91), Madagascar (7 Jun 96), Malawi (9 Mar 93), Malaysia (19 Oct 83), Maldives (14 Jan 81), Malta (8 Aug 86), Marshall Islands (26 Apr 88), Mauritius (1 Feb 88), Mexico (1 Nov 74), Monaco (1 Nov 74), Morocco (28 Jun 90), Myanmar (11 Nov 87), Netherlands (10 Jul 78),New Zealand (23 May 90), Nigeria (7 May 81), Norway (24 Jun 75), Oman (25 Apr 85), Pakistan (10 Apr 85), Panama (9 Mar 78), Papua New Guinea (12 Nov 80), Peru (4 Dec 79), Philippines (15 Dec 81), Poland (10 Jan 75), Portugal (1 Nov 74), Qatar (22 Dec 80), Republic of Korea (1 Nov 74), Romania (24 May 79), Russian Federation (1 Nov 74), Saint Vincent and the Grenadines (28 Oct 83), Saudi Arabia (24 Apr 85), Seychelles (10 May 88), Sierra Leone (13 Aug 93), Singapore (16 Mar 81), Slovakia (1 Jan 93), Slovenia (25 Jun 91), South Africa (23 May 80), Spain (4 Mar 75), Sri Lanka (30 Aug 83), Sudan (15 May 90), Suriname (4 Nov 88), Sweden (1 Nov 74), Switzerland (1 Nov 74), Thailand (18 Dec 84), Togo (19 Jul 89), Tonga (12 Apr 77), Trinidad and Tobago (15 Feb 79), Tunisia (6 Aug 80), Turkey (31 Jul 80), Tuvalu (22 Aug 85), Ukraine (1 Nov 74), United Arab Emirates (15 Dec 83), United Kingdom (1 Nov 74), United States (1 Nov 74), Uruguay (30 Apr 79), Vanuatu (28 Jul 82), Venezuela (1 Nov 74), Viet Nam (18 Dec 90), Yemen (1 Nov 74)

4.28 GLOBAL PROGRAMME OF ACTION FOR THE PROTECTION OF THE MARINE ENVIRONMENT FROM LAND-BASED ACTIVITIES

Adopted by consensus: 3 Nov 95

Conferees: 110

Antigua and Barbuda, Argentina, Australia, Bahrain, Bangladesh, Belarus, Belgium, Belize, Benin, Bhutan, Botswana, Brazi, Bulgaria, Burkina Faso, Burundi, Cambodia, Cameroon, Canada, Chad, Chile, China, Colombia, Comoros, Congo, Costa Rica, Cote D'ivoire, Croatia, Cuba, Denmark, Dominica, Ecuador, Egypt, Estonia, Ethiopia, Finland, France, Gambia, Georgia, Germany, Ghana, Greece, Honduras, Iceland, India, Indonesia, Israel, Italy, Jamaica, Japan, Jordan, Kazakstan, Kenya, Kiribati, Kuwait, Malawi, Malaysia, Maldives, Malta, Marshall Islands, Mauritius, Mexico, Micronesia (Federated States of), Monaco, Mozambique, Nauru, Netherlands, New Zealand, Nicaragua, Niger, Nigeria, Norway, Pakistan, Peru, Philippines, Poland, Republic of Korea, Romania, Russian Federation, Rwanda, Saint Lucia, Samoa, Sao Tome and Principe, Saudi Arabia, Senegal, Seychelles, Sierra Leone, Slovenia, South Africa, Spain, Sri Lanka, Sweden, Switzerland, Thailand, Togo, Tunisia, Turkey, Turkmenistan, Uganda, United Kingdom of Great Britain and Northern Ireland, United Republic of Tanzania, United States of America, Uruguay, Vanuatu, Venezuela, Yemen, Zaire, Zambia, Zimbabwe

4.29 WASHINGTON DECLARATION ON PROTECTION OF THE MARINE ENVIRONMENT FROM LAND-BASED ACTIVITIES

Adopted by consensus: 5 Dec 95

Conferees: *See* Basic Document 4.27, *supra*

4.30 UNITED NATIONS CONVENTION ON THE LAW OF THE NON-NAVIGATIONAL USES OF INTERNATIONAL WATERCOURSES

Concluded: 21 May 97

Not in forces as of 4 Jun 98

Signed but not ratified: 5 (as of at least 4 Jun 98)

Jordan (17 Apr 98), Luxembourg (14 Oct 97), Portugal (11 Nov 97), South Africa (13 Aug 97), Venezuela (22 Sep 97)

Ratified/accepted/approved without qualification: 1 (as of at least 4 Jun 98)

Finland (23 Jan 98)

Ratified/accepted/approved with qualification: 1 (as of at least 4 Jun 98)

Syria (2 Apr 98)

5. LITHOSPHERE

5.1 **FAO International Code of Conduct on the Distribution and Use of Pesticides**
Adopted: 28 Nov 85

5.2 **OECD Council Decision/Recommendation on Exports of Hazardous Wastes from the OECD Area**
Adopted: 5 Jun 86

5.3 **UNEP Governing Council Decision on Cairo Guidelines and principles for the Environmentally Sound Management of Hazardous Wastes**
Adopted: 17 Jun 87

5.4 **UNEP Governing Council Decision on London Guidelines for the Exchange of Information on Chemicals in International Trade**
Adopted: 19 Jun 87

5.5 **OAU Council of Ministers Resolution on Dumping of Nuclear and Industrial Waste in Africa**
Adopted: 23 May 88

5.6 **Basel Convention on the Control of Transboundary Movements of Hazardous Wastes and Their Disposal**
Concluded: 22 Mar 89
Entered into force: 5 May 92
Signed but not ratified: 3 (as of at least 4 Jun 98)
Afghanistan (22 Mar 89), Haiti (22 Mar 89), United States (22 Mar 90)
Ratified/accepted/approved without qualification: 101 (as of at least 4 Jun 98)
Antigua/Barbuda (5 Apr 93), Argentina (27 Jun 91), Australia (5 Feb 92), Austria (12 Jan 93), Bahamas (12 Aug 92), Bahrain (15 Oct 92), Bangladesh (1 Apr 93), Barbados (24 Aug 95), Belgium (1 Nov 93), Belize (23 May 97), Benin (4 Dec 97), Bolivia (15 Nov 96), Brazil (1 Oct 92), Bulgaria (16 Feb 96), Burundi (6 Jan 97), Canada (28 Aug 92), China (17 Dec 91), Comoros (31 Oct 94), Congo (Kinshasa) (6 Oct 94), Costa Rica (7 Mar 95), Côte d'Ivoire (1 Dec 94), Croatia (9 May 94), Cyprus (17 Sep 92), Czech Republic (30 Sep 93), Dominica (5 May 98), Egypt (8 Jan 93), El Salvador (13 Dec 91), Estonia (21 Jul 92), European Community (7 Feb 94), Finland (19 Nov 91), France (7 Jan 91), Gambia (15 Dec 97), Greece (4 Aug 94), Guatemala (15 May 95), Guinea (26 Apr 95), Honduras (26 Mar 96), Hungary (21 May 90), Iceland (28 Jun 95), India (24 Jun 92), Iran (5 Jan 93), Ireland (7 Feb 94), Israel (14 Dec 94), Jordan (22 Jun 89), Korea (South) (28 Feb 94), Kuwait (11 Oct 93), Kyrgyzstan (13 Aug 96), Latvia (14 Apr 92), Lebanon (21 Dec 94), Liechtenstein (27 Jan 92), Macedonia (16 Jul 97), Malawi (21 Apr 94), Malaysia (8 Oct 93), Maldives (28 Apr 92), Mauritania (16 Aug 96), Mauritius (24 Nov 92), Micronesia (6 Sep 95), Monaco (31 Aug 92), Mongolia (15 Apr 97), Morocco (28 Dec 95), Mozambique (13 Mar 97), Namibia (15 May 95), Nepal (15 Oct 96), Netherlands (16 Apr 93), New Zealand (20 Dec 94), Nicaragua (3 Jun 97), Nigeria (13 Mar 91), Oman (8 Feb 95), Pakistan (26 Jul 94), Panama (22 Feb 91), Papua New Guinea (1 Sep 95), Paraguay (28 Sep 95), Peru (23 Nov 93), Philippines (21 Oct 93), Portugal (26 Jan 94), Qatar (9 Aug 95), Russia (31 Jan 95), St Kitts/Nevis (7 Sep 94), St Lucia (9 Dec 93), St Vincent/Grenadines (2 Dec 96), Saudi Arabia (7 Mar 90), Senegal (10 Nov 92), Seychelles (11 May 93), Singapore (2 Jan 96), Slovakia (1 Jan 93), Slovenia (7 Oct 93), South Africa (5 May 94), Sri Lanka (28 Aug 92), Sweden (2 Aug 91), Switzerland (31 Jan 90), Syria (22 Jan 92), Tanzania (7 Apr 93), Thailand (24 Nov 97), Trinidad/Tobago (18 Feb 94), Tunisia (11 Oct 95), Turkey (22 Jun 94), Turkmenistan (25 Sep 96), United Arab Emirates (17 Nov 92), Uzbekistan (7 Feb 96), Vietnam (13 Mar 95), Yemen (21 Feb 96), Zambia (15 Nov 94)

Ratified/accepted/approved with qualification: 18 (as of at least 4 Jun 98) Chile (11 Aug 92), Colombia (31 Dec 96), Cuba (3 Oct 94), Denmark (6 Feb 94), Ecuador (23 Feb 93), Germany (21 Apr 95), Indonesia (20 Sep 93), Italy (7 Feb 94), Japan (17 Sep 93), Luxembourg (7 Feb 94), Mexico (22 Feb 91), Norway (2 Jul 90), Poland (20 Mar 92), Romania (27 Feb 91), Spain (7 Feb 94), United Kingdom (7 Feb 94)), Uruguay (20 Dec 91), Venezuela (3 Mar 98)

5.7 Bamako Convention on the Ban of Import into Africa and the Control of Transboundary Movement and Management of Hazardous Wastes within Africa

Concluded: 30 Jan 91

Not in force as of at least 1 Mar 97

Signed but not ratified: 19 (as of at least 1 Mar 97)

Benin (30 Jan 91), Burkina Faso (30 Jan 91), Burundi (30 Jan 91), Cameroon (1 Mar 91), Central African Republic (30 Jan 91), Chad (27 Jan 92), Côte d'Ivoire (30 Jan 91), Djibouti (20 Dec 91), Egypt (30 Jan 91), Guinea (30 Jan 91), Guinea–Bissau (1 Mar 91), Lesotho (1 Jun 91), Mali (30 Jan 91), Niger (30 Jan 91), Rwanda (26 Aug 91), Senegal (30 Jan 91), Somalia (1 Jun 91), Swaziland (29 Jun 92), Togo (30 Jan 91)

Ratified/accepted/approved (qualifications undetermined): 4 (as of at least 1 Mar 97), Libya (28 Jan 93), Mauritius (26 Nov 92), Tunisia (14 May 92), Zimbabwe (3 Aug 92)

5.8 United Nations Convention to Combat Desertification in those Countries Experiencing Serious Drought and/or Desertification, Particularly in Africa

Adopted: 17 Jun 94

Entered into force: 26 Dec 96

Signed but not ratified: 13 (as of at least 4 Jun 98)

Australia (14 Oct 94), Colombia (14 Oct 94), Congo (Brazzaville) (15 Oct 94), Croatia (15 Oct 94), Georgia (15 Oct 94), Indonesia (15 Oct 94), Japan (14 Oct 94), Korea (South) (14 Oct 94), Philippines (8 Dec 94), Rwanda (22 Jun 95), São Tomé/Príncipe (4 Oct 95), United States (14 Oct 94), Vanuatu (28 Sep 95)

Ratified/accepted/approved without qualification:120 (as of at least 4 Jun 98)

Afghanistan (1 Nov 95), Angola (30 Jun 97), Antigua/Barbuda (6 Jun 97), Argentina (6 Jan 97), Armenia (2 Jul 97), Bahrain (14 Jul 97), Bangladesh (26 Jan 96)), Barbados (14 May 97), Belgium (30 Jun 97), Benin (29 Aug 96), Bolivia (1 Aug 96), Botswana (11 Sep 96), Brazil (25 Jun 97), Burkina Faso (26 Jan 96), Burundi (6 Jan 97), Cambodia (18 Aug 97), Cameroon (29 May 97), Canada (1 Dec 95), Cape Verde (8 May 95), Central African Republic (5 Sep 96), Chad (27 Sep 96), Chile (11 Nov 97), China (18 Feb 97), Comoros (3 Mar 98), Congo (Kinshasa) (12 Sep 97), Costa Rica (5 Jan 98), Côte d'Ivoire (4 Mar 97), Cuba (13 Mar 97), Denmark (22 Dec 95), Djibouti (12 Jun 97), Dominica (8 Dec 97), Dominican Republic (26 Jun 97), Ecuador (6 Sep 95), Egypt (7 Jul 95), El Salvador (27 Jun 97), Equatorial Guinea (27 Jun 97), Eritrea (14 Aug 96), Ethiopia (27 Jun 97), European Community (26 Mar 98), Finland (20 Sep 95), France (12 Jun 97), Gabon (6 Sep 96), Gambia (11 Jun 96), Germany (10 Jul 96), Ghana (27 Dec 96), Greece (5 May 97), Grenada (28 May 97), Guinea (23 Jun 97), Guinea–Bissau (27 Oct 95), Haiti (25 Sep 96), Honduras (25 Jun 97), Iceland (3 Jun 97), India (17 Dec 96), Iran (29 Apr 97), Ireland (31 Jul 97), Israel (26 Mar 96), Italy (23 Jun 97), Jamaica (12 Nov 97), Jordan (21 Oct 96), Kazakhstan (9 Jul 97), Kenya (24 Jun 97), Kyrgyzstan (19 Sep 97), Laos (20 Sep 96), Lebanon (16 May 96), Lesotho (12 Sep 95), Liberia (2 Mar 98), Libya (22 Jul 96), Luxembourg (4 Feb 97), Madagascar (25 Jun 97), Malaysia (25 Jun 97), Malawi (13 Jun 96), Mali (31 Oct 95), Malta (30 Jun 98), Mauritania (7 Aug 96), Mauritius (23 Jan 96), Mexico (3 Apr 95), Micronesia (25 Mar 96), Mongolia (3 Sep 96), Morocco (7 Nov 96), Mozambique (13 Mar 97), Myanmar (Burma) (2 Jan 97), Namibia (16 May 97), Nepal (15 Oct 96), Nicaragua (17 Feb 98), Niger (19 Jan 96), Nigeria (8 Jul 97), Norway (30 Aug 96), Oman (23 Jul 96), Pakistan (24 Feb 97), Panama (4 Apr 96), Paraguay (15 Jan 97), Peru (9 Nov 95),

Portugal (1 Apr 96), St Kitts/Nevis (30 Jan 97), St Lucia (2 Jul 97), St Vincent/Grenadines (16 Mar 98), Saudi Arabia (25 Jun 97), Senegal (26 Jul 95), Seychelles (26 Jun 97), Sierra Leone (25 Sep 97), South Africa (30 Sep 97), Spain (30 Jan 96), Sudan (24 Nov 95), Swaziland (7 Oct 96), Sweden (12 Dec 95), Switzerland (19 Jan 96), Syria (10 Jun 97), Tajikistan (16 Jul 97), Tanzania (19 Jun 97), Togo (4 Oct 95), Tunisia (11 Oct 95), Turkey (31 Mar 98), Turkmenistan (18 Sep 96), Uganda (25 Jun 97), United Kingdom (18 Oct 96), Uzbekistan (31 Oct 95), Yemen (14 Jan 97), Zambia (19 Sep 96), Zimbabwe (23 Sep 97)

Ratified/accepted/approved with qualification: 4 (as of at least 4 Jun 98)
Algeria (22 May 96), Austria (2 Jun 97), Kuwait (27 Jun 97), Netherlands (27 Jun 95)

5.9 ROTTERDAM CONVENTION ON THE PRIOR INFORMED CONSENT PROCEDURE FOR CERTAIN HAZARDOUS CHEMICALS AND PESTICIDES IN INTERNATIONAL TRADE

Concluded: 10 Sep 98
Not in force as of 2 February 1999
Signed but not ratified: 58
Angola (11 Sep 98), Argentina (11 Sep 98), Armenia (11 Sep 98), Austria (11 Sep 98), Barbados (11 Sep 98), Belgium (11 Sep 98), Benin (11 Sep 98), Brazil (11 Sep 98), Burkina Faso (11 Sep 98), Cameroon (11 Sep 98), Chad (11 Sep 98), Chile (11 Sep 98), Colombia (11 Sep 98), Congo (11 Sep 98), Côte d'Ivoire (11 Sep 98), Cuba (11 Sep 98), Cyprus (11 Sep 98), Democratic Republic of the Congo (11 Sep 98), Denmark (11 Sep 98), Ecuador (11 Sep 98), European Community (11 Sep 98), Finland (11 Sep 98), France (11 Sep 98), Germany (11 Sep 98), Ghana (11 Sep 98), Greece (11 Sep 98), Indonesia (11 Sep 98), Italy (11 Sep 98), Kenya (11 Sep 98), Kuwait (11 Sep 98), Luxembourg (11 Sep 98), Madagascar 8 Dec 1998, Mali (11 Sep 98), Mongolia (11 Sep 98), Namibia (11 Sep 98), Netherlands (11 Sep 98). New Zealand (11 Sep 98), Norway (11 Sep 98), Panama (11 Sep 98), Paraguay (11 Sep 98), Peru (11 Sep 98), Philippines (11 Sep 98), Portugal (11 Sep 98), Saint Lucia 25 Jan 1999, Senegal (11 Sep 98), Seychelles (11 Sep 98), Slovenia (11 Sep 98), Spain (11 Sep 98), Sweden (11 Sep 98), Switzerland (11 Sep 98), Syrian Arab Republic (11 Sep 98), Tajikistan 28 Sep 1998, Tunisia (11 Sep 98), Turkey (11 Sep 98), United Kingdom of Great Britain and Northern Ireland (11 Sep 98), United Republic of Tanzania (11 Sep 98), United States of America (11 Sep 98), Uruguay (11 Sep 98)
Ratified/accepted/approved: 0 (as of 2 Feb 99)

6. BIOSPHERE

6.1 CONVENTION ON NATURE PROTECTION AND WILDLIFE PRESERVATION IN THE WESTERN HEMISPHERE

Concluded: 12 Oct 40
Entered into force: 1 May 42
Signed but not ratified: 3 (as of at least 1 Mar 97)
Bolivia (12 Oct 40), Colombia (17 Jan 41), Cuba (12 Oct 40)
Ratified/accepted/approved without qualification: 18 (as of at least 1 Mar 97)
Brazil (26 Aug 65), Chile (4 Dec 67), Costa Rica (12 Jan 67), Dominican Republic (3 Mar 42), Ecuador (20 Oct 44), El Salvador (2 Dec 41), Guatemala (14 Aug 41), Haiti (31 Jan 42), Mexico (27 Mar 42), Nicaragua (22 May 46), Panama (16 Mar 72), Paraguay (30 Jan 81), Peru (22 Sep 46), Suriname (30 Apr 85), Trindad/Tobago (24 Apr 69), United States (28 Apr 41), Uruguay (9 Apr 70), Venezuela (3 Nov 41)
Ratified/accepted/approved with qualification: 1 (as of at least 1 Mar 97)
Argentina (27 Jun 46)

6.2 INTERNATIONAL CONVENTION FOR THE REGULATION OF WHALING

Concluded: 2 Dec 46
Entered into force: 10 Nov 48

Ratified/accepted/approved without qualification: 29 (as of at least 1 Mar 97)

Antigua/Barbuda (21 Jul 82), Australia (1 Dec 47), Brazil (4 Jan 74), Costa Rica (24 Jul 81), Denmark (23 May 50), Dominica (18 Jun 92), Finland (23 Feb 83), Grenada (7 Apr 93), India (9 Mar 81), Ireland (2 Jan 85), Japan (21 Apr 51), Kenya (2 Dec 81), Korea (South) (29 Dec 78), Mexico (30 Jun 49), Monaco (15 Mar 82), Netherlands (14 Jun 77), New Zealand (15 Jun 76), Oman (15 Jul 80), St Kitts/Nevis (24 Jun 92), St Lucia (29 Jun 81), St Vincent/Grenadines (22 Jul 81), Senegal (15 Jul 82), Seychelles (19 Mar 79), Solomon Islands (10 May 93), South Africa (5 May 48), Spain (6 Jul 79), Sweden (15 Jun 79), Switzerland (29 May 80), Venezuela (11 Jul 91)

Ratified/accepted/approved with qualification: 10 (as of at least 1 Mar 97)

Argentina (18 May 60), Chile (6 Jul 79), China (24 Sep 80), France (3 Dec 48), Germany (2 Jul 82), Norway (23 Sep 60), Peru (18 Jun 76), Russia (11 Sep 48), United Kingdom (17 Jun 47), United States (18 Jul 47)

Denunciations: 10 (as of at least 1 Mar 97)

Belize (30 Jun 88), Canada (30 Jun 82), Ecuador (30 Jun 94), Egypt (30 Jun 89), Iceland (30 Jun 92), Jamaica (30 Jun 84), Mauritius (30 Jun 88), Panama (30 Jun 69), Philippines (30 Jun 88), Uruguay (30 Jun 91)

6.3 Convention on Fishing and Conservation of Living Resources of the High Seas

Concluded: 29 Apr 58

Entered into force: 20 Mar 66

Signed but not ratified: 21 (as of at least 4 Jun 98)

Afghanistan (30 Oct 58), Argentina (29 Apr 58), Bolivia (17 Oct 58), Canada (29 Apr 58), Costa Rica (29 Apr 58), Cuba (29 Apr 58), Ghana (29 Apr 58), Iceland (29 Apr 58), Indonesia (8 May 58), Iran (28 May 58), Ireland (2 Oct 58), Israel (29 Apr 58), Lebanon (29 May 58), Liberia (27 May 58), Nepal (29 Apr 58), New Zealand (29 Oct 58), Pakistan (31 Oct 58), Panama (2 May 58), Sri Lanka (30 Oct 58), Tunisia (30 Oct 58), Uruguay (29 Apr 58)

Ratified/accepted/approved without qualification: 33 (as of at least 4 Jun 98)

Australia (14 May 63), Belgium (6 Jan 72), Bosnia–Herzegovina (12 Jan 94), Burkina Faso (4 Oct 65), Cambodia (18 Mar 60), Colombia (3 Jan 63), Dominican Republic (11 Aug 64), Fiji (25 Mar 71), Finland (16 Feb 65), France (18 Sep 70), Haiti (29 Mar 60), Jamaica (16 Apr 64), Kenya (20 Jun 69), Lesotho (23 Oct 73), Madagascar (31 Jul 62), Malawi (3 Nov 65), Malaysia (21 Dec 60), Mauritius (5 Oct 70), Mexico (2 Aug 66), Netherlands (18 Feb 66), Nigeria (26 Jun 61), Portugal (8 Jan 63), Senegal (25 Apr 61), Sierra Leone (13 Mar 62), Solomon Islands (3 Sep 81), South Africa (9 Apr 63), Switzerland (18 May 66), Thailand (2 Jul 68), Tonga (29 Jun 71), Trindad/Tobago (11 Apr 66), Uganda (14 Sep 64), Venezuela (10 Jul 63), Yugoslavia (28 Jan 66)

Ratified/accepted/approved with qualification: 4 (as of at least 4 Jun 98)

Denmark (26 Sep 68), Spain (25 Feb 71), United Kingdom (14 Mar 60), United States (12 Apr 61)

6.4 African Convention on the Conservation of Nature and Natural Resources

Concluded: 15 Sep 68

Entered into force: 16 Jun 69

Signed but not ratified: 14 (as of at least 1 Mar 97)

Benin (15 Sep 68), Botswana (15 Sep 68), Burundi (15 Sep 68), Chad (15 Sep 68), Comoros (15 Sep 68), Ethiopia (15 Sep 68), Gambia (15 Sep 68), Guinea (15 Sep 68), Lesotho (15 Sep 68), Libya (15 Sep 68), Mauritania (15 Sep 68), Mauritius (15 Sep 68), Sierra Leone (15 Sep 68), Somalia (15 Sep 68)

Ratified/accepted/approved without qualification: 29 (as of at least 1 Mar 97)

Algeria (24 May 83), Burkina Faso (29 Aug 69), Cameroon (29 Sep 78), Central African Republic (16 Mar 70), Congo (Brazzaville) (29 Apr 81), Congo (Kinshasa) (14 Oct 76), Côte d'Ivoire (15 Jan 69), Djibouti (17 Apr 78), Egypt (16 Apr

72), Gabon (18 Nov 88), Ghana (17 May 69), Kenya (12 May 69), Liberia (22 Nov 78), Madagascar (23 Sep 71), Malawi (12 Mar 73), Mali (20 Jun 74), Morocco (11 Nov 77), Mozambique (1 Apr 81), Niger (27 Jan 70), Nigeria (7 May 74), Rwanda (4 Feb 80), Senegal (24 Feb 72), Sudan (30 Oct 73), Swaziland (7 Apr 69), Tanzania (15 Nov 74), Togo (20 Nov 79), Tunisia (4 Feb 79), Uganda (30 Nov 77), Zambia (1 May 72)

6.5 International Convention on International Trade in Endangered Species of Wild Fauna and Flora (CITES)

Concluded: 3 Mar 73
Entered into force: 1 Jul 75
Signed but not ratified: 4 (as of at least 1 Mar 97)
Ireland (1 Nov 74), Kuwait (9 Apr 74), Lesotho (17 Jul 74), Taiwan (27 Apr 73)
Ratified/accepted/approved without qualification: 112 (as of at least 1 Mar 97)
Afghanistan (30 Oct 85), Algeria (23 Nov 83), Antigua and Barbuda (06 Jul 97), Argentina (8 Jan 81), Austria (27 Jan 82), Bahamas (20 Jun 79), Bangladesh (20 Nov 81), Barbados (9 Dec 92), Belgium (3 Oct 83), Belize (19 Aug 86), Benin (28 Feb 84), Bolivia (6 Jul 79), Brazil (6 Aug 75), Brunei (4 May 90), Bulgaria (16 Jan 91), Burkina Faso (13 Oct 89), Burundi (8 Aug 88), Cambodia (02 Jul 97), Cameroon (5 Jun 81), Central African Republic (27 Aug 80), Chad (2 Feb 89), China (8 Jan 81), Colombia (31 Aug 81), Comoros (23 Nov 94), Congo (Brazzaville) (31 Jan 83), Congo (Kinshasa) (20 Jul 76), Costa Rica (30 Jun 75), Côte d'Ivoire (21 Nov 94), Cyprus (18 Oct 74), Czech Republic (14 Apr 93), Djibouti (7 Feb 92), Dominican Republic (17 Dec 86), Ecuador (11 Feb 75), Egypt (4 Jan 78), El Salvador (30 Apr 87), Equatorial Guinea (10 Mar 92), Eritrea (24 Oct 94), Estonia (22 Jul 92), Ethiopia (5 Apr 89), Fiji (29 Sep 97), Finland (10 May 76), Gabon (13 Feb 89), Gambia (26 Aug 77), Ghana (14 Nov 75), Greece (8 Oct 92), Guatemala (7 Nov 79), Guinea (21 Sep 81), Guinea–Bissau (16 May 90), Guyana (27 May 77), Honduras (15 Mar 85), Hungary (29 May 85), India (20 Jul 76), Indonesia (28 Dec 78), Iran (3 Aug 76), Israel (18 Dec 79), Italy (2 Oct 79), Jamaica (22 Mar 97), Jordan (14 Dec 78), Kenya (13 Dec 78), Korea (South) (9 Jul 73), Latvia (12 Feb 97), Liberia (11 Mar 81), Luxembourg (13 Dec 83), Madagascar (20 Aug 75), Malawi (5 Feb 82), Malaysia (20 Oct 77), Mali (18 Jul 94), Malta (17 Apr 89), Mauritania (11 Mar 98), Mauritius (28 Apr 75), Mexico (2 Jul 91), Monaco (19 Apr 78), Morocco (16 Oct 75), Mozambique (25 Mar 81), Myanmar (11 Jun 97), Nepal (18 Jun 75), Netherlands (19 Apr 84), New Zealand (10 May 89), Nicaragua (6 Aug 77), Niger (8 Sep 75), Nigeria (9 May 74), Pakistan (20 Apr 76), Panama (17 Aug 78), Papua New Guinea (12 Dec 75), Paraguay (15 Nov 76), Peru (27 Jun 75), Philippines (18 Aug 81), Poland (12 Dec 89), Portugal (11 Feb 80), Romania (18 Aug 94), Rwanda (20 Oct 80), St Kitts/Nevis (14 Feb 94), St Lucia (15 Dec 82), St Vincent/Grenadines (30 Nov 88), Senegal (5 Aug 77), Seychelles (8 Feb 77), Sierra Leone (28 Oct 94), Slovakia (2 Mar 93), Somalia (2 Dec 85), Sri Lanka (4 May 82), Swaziland (27 Feb 97), Sweden (20 Aug 74), Tanzania (29 Nov 79), Togo (23 Oct 78), Trindad/Tobago (19 Jan 84), Tunisia (10 Jul 74), Uganda (18 Jul 91), United Kingdom (2 Aug 76), Uruguay (2 Apr 75), Uzbekistan (08 Jul 97), Vanuatu (17 Jul 89) Venezuela (24 Oct 77), Vietnam (20 Jan 94), Yemen (03 May 97)
Ratified/accepted/approved with qualification: 24 (as of at least 1 Mar 97)
Australia (29 Jul 76), Botswana (14 Nov 77), Canada (10 Apr 75), Chile (14 Feb 75), Cuba (20 Apr 90), Denmark (26 Jul 77), France (11 May 78), Germany (22 Mar 76), Japan (6 Aug 80), Liechtenstein (30 Nov 79), Namibia (18 Dec 90), Norway (27 Jul 76), Russia (13 Jan 92), Singapore (30 Nov 86), South Africa (15 Jul 75), Spain (30 May 86), Sudan (26 Nov 82), Suriname (17 Nov 80), Switzerland (9 Jul 74), Thailand (21 Jan 83), United Arab Emirates (8 Feb 90), United States (14 Jan 74), Zambia (24 Nov 80), Zimbabwe (19 May 81)
Ratified/accepted/approved (qualifications undetermined): 5 (as of at least 1 Mar 97)

6.6 Endangered Species Act of 1973, as amended

Enacted: 28 Dec 73 (amended 10 Nov 78)

6.7 CONVENTION ON THE CONSERVATION OF MIGRATORY SPECIES OF WILD ANIMALS

Concluded: 23 Jun 79
Entered into force: 1 Nov 83
Signed but not ratified: 8 (as of at least 1 Mar 97)
Central African Republic (23 Jun 79), Chad (23 Jun 79), Côte d'Ivoire (23 Jun 79), Greece (23 Jun 79), Jamaica (20 Jun 80), Madagascar (23 Jun 79), Paraguay (23 Jun 79), Uganda (23 Jun 79)
Ratified/accepted/approved without qualification: 38 (as of at least 1 Mar 97)
Belgium (11 Jul 90), Benin (14 Jan 86), Burkina Faso (9 Oct 89), Cameroon (7 Sep 81), Chile (15 Sep 81), Congo (Kinshasa) (22 Jun 90), Czech Republic (8 Feb 94), Denmark (5 Aug 82), European Community (1 Aug 83), Egypt (11 Feb 82), Finland (3 Oct 88), Germany (31 Jul 84), Ghana (19 Jan 88), Hungary (12 Jul 83), India (4 May 82), Ireland (5 Aug 83), Israel (17 May 83), Italy (26 Aug 83), Luxembourg (30 Nov 82), Mali (28 Jul 87), Monaco (23 Mar 87), Morocco (12 Aug 93), Netherlands (5 Jun 81), Niger (3 Jul 80), Nigeria (15 Oct 86), Norway (30 May 85), Pakistan (22 Sep 87), Panama (20 Feb 89), Poland (1 Feb 96), Portugal (21 Jan 81), Senegal (18 Mar 88), Somalia (11 Nov 85), South Africa (27 Sep 91), Spain (12 Feb 85), Sri Lanka (6 Jun 90), Sweden (9 Jun 83), Tunisia (27 May 87), Uruguay (1 Feb 90)
Ratified/accepted/approved with qualification: 4 (as of at least 1 Mar 97)
Australia (1 Jul 86), France (23 Apr 90), Saudi Arabia (17 Dec 90), United Kingdom (23 Jul 85)
Ratified/accepted/approved (qualifications undetermined): 7 (as of at least 1 Mar 97)
Argentina (*date undetermined*), Guinea (*date undetermined*), Guinea–Bissau (19 Jun 95), Liechtenstein (1 Nov 97),* Mauritania (1 Jul 98),* Peru (1 Jun 97),* Philippines (*date undetermined*), Romania (1 Jul 98),* Slovakia (*date undetermined*), Switzerland (7 Apr 95), Togo (9 Nov 95), Uzbekistan (1 Sep 98)*
* Date of entry into force for this state.

6.8 CONVENTION FOR THE PROHIBITION OF FISHING WITH LONG DRIFTNETS IN THE SOUTH PACIFIC

Concluded: 24 Nov 89
Entered into force: 17 May 91
Signed but not ratified: 9 (as of at least 1 Mar 97)
France (30 Apr 90), Marshall Islands (29 Nov 89), Palau (29 Nov 89), Solomon Islands (7 Mar 91), Tuvalu (13 Feb 90), Vanuatu (13 Feb 90)
Ratified/accepted/approved without qualification: 8 (as of at least 1 Mar 97)
Australia (6 Jul 92), Cook Islands (24 Jan 90), Fiji (18 Jan 94), Kiribati (10 Jan 92), Micronesia (20 Dec 90), Nauru (14 Oct 92), New Zealand (17 May 91), Tukalu (17 May 91)
Ratified/accepted/approved with qualification: 1 (as of at least 1 Mar 97)
United States (28 Feb 92)

6.9 UNGA RESOLUTION 44/225 ON LARGE-SCALE PELAGIC DRIFTNET FISHING AND ITS IMPACT ON THE LIVING MARINE RESOURCES OF THE WORLD'S OCEANS AND SEAS

Adopted unanimously: 22 Dec 89

6.10 UNGA RESOLUTION 46/215 ON LARGE-SCALE PELAGIC DRIFTNET FISHING AND ITS IMPACT ON THE LIVING MARINE RESOURCES OF THE WORLD'S OCEANS AND SEAS

Adopted without recorded vote: 20 Dec 91

6.11 CONVENTION ON BIOLOGICAL DIVERSITY

Concluded: 5 Jun 92
Entered into force: 29 Dec 93
Signed but not ratified: 12 (as of at least 4 Jun 98)
Afghanistan (12 Jun 92), Azerbaijan (12 Jun 92), Kuwait (9 Jun 92), Liberia (12 Jun 92), Libya (29 Jun 92), Malta (12 Jun 92), São Tomé/Príncipe (12 Jun 92),

Thailand (12 Jun 92), Tuvalu (8 Jun 92), United Arab Emirates (11 Jun 92), United States (4 Jun 93), Yugoslavia (8 Jun 92)
Ratified/accepted/approved without qualification: 157 (as of at least 4 Jun 98)
Albania (5 Jan 94), Algeria (14 Aug 95), Angola (1 Apr 98), Antigua/Barbuda (9 Mar 93), Armenia (14 May 93), Australia (18 Jun 93), Bahamas (2 Sep 93), Bahrain (30 Aug 96), Bangladesh (3 May 94), Barbados (10 Dec 93), Belarus (8 Sep 93), Belgium (22 Nov 96), Belize (30 Dec 93), Benin (30 Jun 94), Bhutan (25 Aug 95), Bolivia (3 Oct 94), Botswana (12 Oct 95), Brazil (28 Feb 94), Bulgaria (17 Apr 96), Burkina Faso (2 Sep 93), Burundi (15 Aapr 97), Cambodia (9 Feb 95), Cameroon (19 Oct 94), Canada (4 Dec 92), Cape Verde (29 Mar 95), Central African Republic (15 Mar 95), Chad (7 Jun 94), China (5 Jan 93), Colombia (28 Nov 94), Comoros (29 Sep 94), Congo (Brazzaville) (1 Aug 96), Congo (Kinshasa) (3 Dec 94), Cook Islands (20 Apr 93), Costa Rica (26 Aug 94), Côte d'Ivoire (29 Nov 94), Croatia (7 Oct 96), Cyprus (10 Jul 96), Czech Republic (3 Dec 93), Denmark (21 Dec 93), Djibouti (1 Sep 94), Dominica (6 Apr 94), Dominican Republic (25 Nov 96), Ecuador (23 Feb 93), Egypt (2 Jun 94), El Salvador (8 Sep 94), Equatorial Guinea (6 Dec 94), Eritrea (21 Mar 96), Estonia (27 Jul 94), Ethiopia (5 Apr 94), Fiji (25 Feb 93), Finland (27 Jul 94), Gabon (14 Mar 97), Gambia (10 Jun 94), Germany (21 Dec 93), Ghana (29 Aug 94), Greece (4 Aug 94), Grenada (11 Aug 94), Guatemala (10 Jul 95), Guinea (7 May 93), Guinea–Bissau (27 Oct 95), Guyana (29 Aug 94), Haiti (25 Sep 96), Honduras (31 Jul 95), Hungary (24 Feb 94), Iceland (12 Sep 94), India (18 Feb 94), Indonesia (23 Jun 94), Iran (6 Aug 96), Israel (7 Aug 95), Jamaica (6 Jan 95), Japan (28 May 93), Jordan (12 Nov 93), Kazakhstan (6 Sep 94), Kenya (26 Jul 94, Kiribati (16 Aug 94), Korea (North) (26 Oct 94), Korea (South) (3 Oct 94), Kyrgyzstan (6 Aug 96), Laos (20 Sep 96), Latvia (14 Dec 95), Lebanon (15 Dec 94), Lesotho (10 Jan 95), Lithuania (1 Feb 96), Luxembourg (9 May 94), Macedonia (2 Dec 97), Madagascar (4 Mar 96), Malawi (2 Feb 94), Malaysia (24 Jun 94), Maldives (9 Nov 92), Mali (29 Mar 95), Marshall Islands (8 Oct 92), Mauritania (16 Aug 96), Mauritius (4 Sep 92), Mexico (11 Mar 93), Micronesia (20 Jun 94), Monaco (20 Nov 92), Mongolia (30 Sep 93), Moldova (20 Oct 95), Morocco (21 Aug 95), Mozambique (25 Aug 95), Myanmar (Burma) (25 Nov 94), Namibia (16 May 97), Nauru (11 Nov 93), Nepal (23 Nov 93), Netherlands (12 Jun 94), New Zealand (16 Sep 93), Nicaragua (20 Nov 95), Niue (28 Feb 96), Niger (25 Feb 95), Nigeria (29 Aug 94), Norway (9 Jul 93), Oman (8 Feb 95), Pakistan (26 Jul 94), Panama (17 Jan 95), Paraguay (24 Feb 94), Peru (7 Jun 93), Philippines (8 Oct 93), Poland (18 Jan 96), Portugal (21 Dec 93), Qatar (21 Aug 96), Romania (17 Aug 94), Russia (5 Apr 95), Rwanda (29 May 96), St Kitts/Nevis (7 Jan 93), St Lucia (28 Jul 93), St Vincent/Grenadines (3 Jun 96), Samoa (9 Feb 94), San Marino (28 Oct 94), Senegal (17 Oct 94), Seychelles (22 Sep 92), Sierra Leone (12 Dec 94), Singapore (21 Dec 95), Slovakia (25 Aug 94), Slovenia (9 Jul 96), Solomon Islands (3 Oct 95), South Africa (2 Nov 95), Spain (21 Dec 93), Sri Lanka (23 Feb 94), Suriname (12 Jan 96), Swaziland (9 Nov 94), Sweden (16 Dec 93), Tajikistan (29 Oct 97), Tanzania (8 Mar 96), Togo (4 Oct 95), Trindad/Tobago (1 Aug 96), Tunisia (15 Jul 93), Turkey (14 Feb 97), Turkmenistan (18 Sep 96), Uganda (8 Sep 93), Ukraine (7 Feb 95), Uruguay (5 Nov 93), Uzbekistan (19 Jul 95), Vanuatu (25 Mar 93), Venezuela (13 Sep 94), Vietnam (16 Nov 94), Yemen (21 Feb 96), Zambia (28 May 93), Zimbabwe (11 Nov 94)
Ratified/accepted/approved with qualification: 16 (as of at least 4 Jun 98)
Argentina (22 Nov 94), Austria (18 Aug 94), Chile (9 Sep 94), Cuba (8 Mar 94), European Community (21 Dec 93), France (1 Jul 94), Georgia (2 Jun 94), Ireland (22 Mar 96), Italy (15 Apr 94), Latvia (14 Dec 95), Liechtenstein (19 Nov 97), Papua New Guinea (16 Mar 93), Sudan (30 Oct 95), Switzerland (21 Nov 94), Syria (4 Jan 96), United Kingdom (3 Jun 94)

6.12 NON-LEGALLY BINDING AUTHORITATIVE STATEMENT OF PRINCIPLES FOR A GLOBAL CONSENSUS ON THE MANAGEMENT, CONSERVATION AND SUSTAINABLE DEVELOPMENT OF ALL TYPES OF FORESTS
Adopted: 13 Jun 92

6.13 AGREEMENT TO PROMOTE COMPLIANCE WITH INTERNATIONAL CONSERVATION AND MANAGEMENT MEASURES BY FISHING VESSELS ON THE HIGH SEAS
Adopted: 24 Nov 93
Not in force as of 19 Jan 99.
Ratified/accepted/approved without qualifications: 11
Argentina (24 Jun 96), Canada (20 May 94), European Community (6 Aug 96), Georgia (7 Sep 94), Madagascar (20 Oct 94), Myanmar (8 Sep 94), Namibia (7 Aug 98), Norway (28 Dec 94), St. Kitts & Nevis (24 Jun 94), Sweden (25 Oct 94), United States (19 Dec 95)

6.14 AGREEMENT FOR THE IMPLEMENTATION OF THE PROVISIONS OF THE UNITED NATIONS CONVENTION ON THE LAW OF THE SEA OF 10 DECEMBER 1982, RELATING TO THE CONSERVATION AND MANAGEMENT OF STRADDLING FISH STOCKS AND HIGHLY MIGRATORY FISH STOCKS
Concluded: 4 Aug 95
Not in force as of at least 4 Jun 98
Signed but not ratified: 46 (as of at least 4 Jun 98)
Argentina (4 Dec 95), Australia (4 Dec 95), Austria (27 Jun 96), Bangladesh (4 Dec 95), Belgium (3 Oct 96), Belize (4 Dec 95), Brazil (4 Dec 95), Burkina Faso (15 Oct 96), Canada (4 Dec 95), China 6 Nov 96), Côte d'Ivoire (24 Jan 96), Denmark (27 Jun 96), Egypt (5 Dec 95), European Community (27 Jun 96), Finland (27 Jun 96), France (4 Dec 96), Gabon (7 Oct 96), Germany (28 Aug 96), Greece (27 Jun 96), Guinea–Bissau (4 Dec 95), Indonesia (4 Dec 95), Ireland (27 Jun 96), Israel (4 Dec 95), Italy (27 Jun 86), Jamaica (4 Dec 95), Japan (19 Nov 96), Korea (South) (26 Nov 96), Luxembourg (27 Jun 96), Maldives (8 Oct 96), Marshall Islands (4 Dec 95), Mauritania (21 Dec 95), Micronesia (4 Dec 95), Morocco (4 Dec 95), Netherlands (28 Jun 96), New Zealand (4 Dec 95), Niue (4 Dec 95), Pakistan (15 Feb 96), Papua New Guinea (4 Dec 95), Philippines (30 Aug 96), Portugal (27 Jun 96), Spain (3 Dec 96), Sweden (27 Jun 96), Uganda (10 Oct 96), Ukraine (4 Dec 95), United Kingdom (27 Jun 96), Uruguay (16 Jan 96), Vanuatu (23 Jul 96)
Ratified/accepted/approved without qualification: 15 (as of at least 4 Jun 98)
Bahamas (16 Jan 97), Fiji (12 Dec 96), Iceland (14 Feb 97), Mauritius (25 Mar 97), Micronesia (8 Apr 98), Namibia (8 Apr 98), Nauru (10 Jan 97), St Lucia (9 Aug 96), Samoa (25 Oct 96), Senegal (30 Jan 97), Seychelles (20 Mar 98), Solomon Islands (13 Feb 97), Sri Lanka (24 Oct 96), Tonga (31 Jul 96)
Ratified/accepted/approved with qualification: 3 (as of at least 4 Jun 98)
Norway (30 Dec 96), Russia (4 Dec 95), United States (21 Aug 96)

6.15 FAO CODE OF CONDUCT FOR RESPONSIBLE FISHERIES
Adopted: 31 Oct 95

6.16 JAKARTA MINISTERIAL STATEMENT ON THE IMPLEMENTATION OF THE CONVENTION ON BIOLOGICAL DIVERSITY
Adopted: 17 Nov 95

7. MISCELLANEOUS

Economic Trade/Development

7.1 GENERAL AGREEMENT ON TARIFFS AND TRADE (GATT) 1947
Concluded: 30 Oct 47
Entered into force: 1 Jan 48 (through Protocol of Provisional Application)
Terminated: 31 Dec 95
Currently in effect as part of GATT 1994. *See* Basic Document 7.6, *infra* for status information.
Following the entry into force of the Agreement Establishing the World Trade Organization, the parties to GATT 1947 withdrew from that agreement. However, the provisions of GATT 1947 have continued to remain in effect as part of

GATT 1994, a "legally distinct" agreement which nevertheless incorporates GATT 1947 by reference. GATT 1994 is part of Annex 1A to the WTO Agreement (Basic Document 7.6) and is binding on all countries party to that Agreement. Status information on the WTO Agreement is provided below.

7.2 CHARTER OF ECONOMIC RIGHTS AND DUTIES OF STATES
Adopted: 12 Dec 74
For: 120
Afghanistan, Albania, Algeria, Argentina, Australia, Bahamas, Bahrain, Bangladesh, Barbados, Benin, Bhutan, Bolivia, Botswana, Brazil, Bulgaria, Burkina Faso, Burma, Burundi, Byelorussian SSR (Belarus), Cambodia, Cameroon, Central African Republic, Chad, Chile, China, Colombia, Congo, Côte d'Ivoire, Costa Rica, Cuba, Cyprus, Czechoslovakia, Dominican Republic, Ecuador, Egypt, El Salvador, Equatorial Guinea, Ethiopia, Fiji, Finland, Gabon, Gambia, German Democratic Republic, Ghana, Greece, Grenada, Guatemala, Guinea, Guinea-Bissau, Guyana, Haiti, Honduras, Hungary, Iceland, India, Indonesia, Iran, Iraq, Jamaica, Jordan, Kenya, Kuwait, Laos, Lebanon, Lesotho, Liberia, Libya, Madagascar, Malawi, Malaysia, Mali, Malta, Mauritania, Mauritius, Mozambique, Mexico, Mongolia, Morocco, Nepal, New Zealand, Nicaragua, Niger, Nigeria, Oman, Pakistan, Panama, Paraguay, Peru, Philippines, Poland, Portugal, Qatar, Romania, Rwanda, Saudi Arabia, Senegal, Sierra Leone, Singapore, Somalia, Sri Lanka, Sudan, Swaziland, Sweden, Syria, Tanzania, Thailand, Togo, Trinidad/Tobago, Tunisia, Turkey, Uganda, Ukrainian SSR, United Arab Emirates, Uruguay, USSR, Venezuela, Yemen, Yugoslavia, Zaire, Zambia
Against: 7
Belgium, Denmark, Germany, Luxembourg, Norway, United Kingdom, United States
Abstaining: 10
Austria, Canada, France, Ireland, Israel, Italy, Japan, Netherlands, Norway, Spain

7.3 DRAFT CODE OF CONDUCT ON TRANSNATIONAL CORPORATIONS
Adopted: 1 Feb 88

7.4 NORTH AMERICAN AGREEMENT ON ENVIRONMENTAL COOPERATION
Concluded: 8, 9, 12 & 14 Sep 93
Entered into force: 1 Jan 94
Ratified/accepted/approved without qualification: 3
Canada (12 & 14 Sep 93), Mexico (8 & 14 Sep 93), United States of America (9 & 14 Sep 93)

7.5 MARRAKESH MINISTERIAL DECISION ON TRADE AND ENVIRONMENT
Adopted: 14 Apr 94
Conferees: 125
The Decision was adopted by the Trade Negotiations Committee of the Uruguay Round of Multilateral Trade Negotiations, meeting at the ministerial level on the occasion of the signing of the Final Act that concluded the Uruguay Round and adopted the Agreement Establishing the World Trade Organization. For status information on the WTO Agreement, see Basic Document 7.6, infra.

7.6 AGREEMENT ESTABLISHING THE WORLD TRADE ORGANIZATION
Concluded: 15 Apr 94
Entered into force: 1 January 1995
Ratified/accepted/approved without qualifications (date of entry into force for party): 133
Antigua and Barbuda (1 Jan 95), Angola (1 Dec 1996), Argentina (1 Jan 95), Australia (1 Jan 95), Austria (1 Jan 95), Bahrain (1 Jan 95), Bangladesh (1 Jan 95), Barbados (1 Jan 95), Belgium (1 Jan 95), Belize (1 Jan 95), Benin (22 Feb 96), Bolivia (13 Sept 95), Botswana (31 May 95), Brazil (1 Jan 95), Brunei Darussalam (1 Jan 95), Bulgaria (1 Dec 96), Burkina Faso (3 June 95), Burundi (23 July 95), Cameroon (13 Dec 95), Canada (1 Jan 95) Central African Republic

(31 May 95), Chad (19 Oct 96), Chile (1 Jan 95), Colombia (30 April 95), Congo (27 March 97), Costa Rica (1 Jan 95), Côte d'Ivoire (1 Jan 95), Cuba (20 April 95), Cyprus (30 July 95), Czech Republic (1 January 95), Democratic Republic of the Congo (1 Jan 97), Denmark (1 Jan 95), Djibouti (31 May 95), Dominica (1 Jan 95), Dominican Republic (9 March 95), Ecuador (21 Jan 96), Egypt (30 June 95), El Salvador (7 May 95), European Communities (1 Jan 95), Fiji (14 Jan 96), Finland (1 Jan 95), France (1 Jan 95), Gabon (1 Jan 95), Gambia (23 Oct 96), Germany (1 Jan 95), Ghana (1 Jan 95), Greece (1 Jan 95), Grenada (22 Feb 96), Guatemala (21 July 95), Guinea Bissau (31 May 95), Guinea (25 Oct 95), Guyana (1 Jan 95), Haiti (30 Jan 96), Honduras (1 Jan 95), Hong Kong, China (1 Jan 95), Hungary (1 Jan 95), Iceland (1 Jan 95), India (1 Jan 95), Indonesia (1 Jan 95), Ireland (1 Jan 95), Israel (21 April 95), Italy (1 Jan 95), Jamaica (9 March 95), Japan (1 Jan 95), Kenya (1 Jan 95), Korea (1 Jan 95), Kuwait (1 Jan 95), The Kyrgyz Republic (20 Dec 98), Lesotho (31 May 95), Liechtenstein (1 Sept 95), Luxembourg (1 Jan 95), Macau (1 Jan 95), Madagascar (17 Nov 95), Malawi (31 May 95), Malaysia (1 Jan 95), Maldives (31 May 95), Mali (31 May 95), Malta (1 Jan 95), Mauritania (31 May 95), Mauritius (1 Jan 95), Mexico (1 Jan 95), Mongolia (29 Jan 97), Morocco (1 Jan 95), Mozambique (26 Aug 95), Myanmar (1 Jan 95), Namibia (1 Jan 95), Netherlands—For the Kingdom in Europe and for the Netherlands Antilles (1 Jan 95), New Zealand (1 Jan 95), Nicaragua (3 Sept 95), Niger (13 Dec 96), Nigeria (1 Jan 95), Norway (1 Jan 95), Pakistan (1 Jan 95), Panama (6 Sept 97), Papua New Guinea (9 June 96), Paraguay (1 Jan 95), Peru (1 Jan 95), Philippines (1 Jan 95), Poland (1 July 95), Portugal (1 Jan 95), Qatar (13 Jan 96), Romania (1 Jan 95), Rwanda (22 May 96), Saint Kitts and Nevis (21 Feb 96), Saint Lucia (1 Jan 95), Saint Vincent & the Grenadines (1 Jan 95), Senegal (1 Jan 95), Sierra Leone (23 July 95), Singapore (1 Jan 95), Slovak Republic (1 Jan 95), Slovenia (30 July 95), Solomon Islands (26 July 96), South Africa (1 Jan 95), Spain (1 Jan 95), Sri Lanka (1 Jan 95), Suriname (1 Jan 95), Swaziland (1 Jan 95), Sweden (1 Jan 95), Switzerland (1 July 95), Tanzania (1 Jan 95), Thailand (1 Jan 95), Togo (31 May 95), Trinidad and Tobago (1 March 95), Tunisia (29 March 95), Turkey (26 March 95), Uganda (1 Jan 95), United Arab Emirates (10 April 96), United Kingdom (1 Jan 95), United States (1 Jan 95), Uruguay (1 Jan 95), Venezuela (1 Jan 95), Zambia (1 Jan 95), Zimbabwe (3 March 95)

Negotiating membership (as of 1 January 1999): 35

Albania, Algeria, Andorra, Armenia, Azerbaijan, Belarus, Bhutan, Cambodia, Cape Verde, People's Republic of China, Croatia, Estonia, Ethiopia, Former Yugoslav Republic of Macedonia, Georgia, Holy See (Vatican), Jordan, Kazakstan, Lao People's Democratic Republic, Latvia, Lithuania, Moldova, Nepal, Oman, Sultanate of Russian Federation, Samoa, Saudi Arabia, Seychelles, Sudan, Chinese Taipei, Tonga, Ukraine, Uzbekistan, Vanuatu, Vietnam

7.7 Agreement on Technical Barriers to Trade

Concluded: 15 Apr 94

Entered into force: 1 Jan 95

The Agreement on Technical Barriers to Trade is part of Annex 1A to the WTO Agreement and is binding on all parties to that Agreement. For status information, see Basic Document 7.6, supra.

7.8 Understanding on Rules and Procedures Governing the Settlement of Disputes

Concluded: 15 Apr 94

Entered into force: 1 Jan 95

The Dispute Settlement Understanding is Annex 2 to the WTO Agreement and is binding on all parties to that Agreement. For status information, see Basic Document 7.6, supra.

7.9 WTO Decision on Trade in Services and the Environment

Adopted by consensus by the WTO Council on Services: 1 Mar 95

Human Rights/Social Justice

7.10 CONVENTION ON THE PREVENTION AND PUNISHMENT OF THE CRIME OF GENOCIDE

Concluded: 9 Dec 48

Entered into force: 12 Jan 51

Signed but not ratified: 3 (as of at least 9 Apr 98)

Bolivia (11 Dec 48), Dominican Republic (11 Dec 48), Paraguay (11 Dec 48)

Ratified/accepted/approved without qualification: 99 (as of at least 9 Apr 98)

Afghanistan (22 Mar 56), Antigua/Barbuda (25 Oct 88), Armenia (23 Jun 93), Australia (8 Jul 49), Austria (19 Mar 58), Azerbaijan (16 Aug 96), Bahamas (5 Aug 75), Barbados (14 Jan 80), Belgium (5 Sep 51), Belize (10 Mar 98), Bosnia–Herzegovina (29 Dec 92), Brazil (15 Apr 52), Burkina Faso (14 Sep 65), Burundi (6 Jan 97), Cambodia (14 Oct 50), Canada (3 Sep 52), Chile (3 Jun 53), Colombia (27 Oct 59), Congo (Kinshasa) (31 May 62), Costa Rica (14 Oct 50), Côte d'Ivoire (18 Dec 95), Croatia (12 Oct 92), Cuba (4 Mar 53), Cyprus (29 Mar 82), Czech Republic (22 Feb 93), Denmark (15 Jun 51), Ecuador (21 Dec 49), Egypt (8 Feb 52), El Salvador (28 Sep 50), Estonia (21 Oct 91), Ethiopia (1 Jul 49), Fiji (11 Jan 73), Finland (18 Dec 59), France (14 Oct 50), Gabon (21 Jan 83), Gambia (29 Dec 78), Georgia (11 Oct 93), Germany (24 Nov 54), Ghana (24 Dec 58), Greece (8 Dec 54), Guatemala (13 Jan 50), Haiti (14 Oct 50), Honduras (5 Mar 52), Iceland (29 Aug 49), Iran (14 Aug 56), Iraq (20 Jan 59), Ireland (22 Jun 76), Israel (9 Mar 50), Italy (4 Jun 52), Jamaica (23 Sep 68), Jordan (3 Apr 50), Korea (North) (31 Jan 89), Korea (South) (14 Oct 50), Kuwait (7 Mar 95), Kyrgyzstan (5 Sep 97), Laos (8 Dec 50), Latvia (14 Apr 92), Lebanon (17 Dec 53), Lesotho (29 Nov 74), Liberia (9 Jun 50), Libya (16 May 89), Liechtenstein (24 Mar 94), Lithuania (1 Feb 96), Luxembourg (7 Oct 81), Macedonia (18 Jan 94), Maldives (24 Apr 84), Mali (16 Jul 79), Mexico (22 Jul 52), Moldova (26 Jan 93), Monaco (30 Mar 50), Mozambique (18 Apr 83), Namibia (28 Nov 94), Nepal (17 Jan 69), Netherlands (20 Jun 66), New Zealand (28 Dec 78), Nicaragua (29 Jan 52), Norway (22 Jul 49), Pakistan (12 Oct 57), Panama (11 Jan 50), Papua New Guinea (27 Jan 82), Peru (24 Feb 60), St Vincent/Grenadines (9 Nov 81), Saudi Arabia (13 Jul 50), Senegal (4 Aug 83), Seychelles (5 May 92), Slovenia (6 Jul 92), Sri Lanka (12 Oct 50), Sweden (27 May 52), Syria (25 Jun 55), Tanzania (5 Apr 84), Togo (24 May 84), Tonga (16 Feb 72), Tunisia (29 Nov 56), Turkey (31 Jul 50), Uganda (14 Nov 95), United Kingdom (30 Jan 70), Uruguay (11 Jul 67), Yugoslavia (29 Aug 50), Zimbabwe (13 May 91)

Ratified/accepted/approved with qualification: 26 (as of at least 9 Apr 98)

Albania * (12 May 55), Algeria ** (31 Oct 63), Argentina ** (5 Jun 56), Bahrain (27 Mar 90), Belarus *** (11 Aug 54), Bulgaria *** (21 Jul 50), China **** (18 Apr 83), Hungary (7 Jan 52), India **** (27 Aug 59), Malaysia ** (20 Dec 94), Mongolia (5 Jan 67), Morocco **** (24 Jan 58), Myanmar (Burma) * (14 Mar 56), Philippines ***** (7 Jul 50), Poland ****** (14 Nov 50), Romania ******* (2 Nov 50), Russia (3 May 54), Rwanda **** (16 Apr 75), Singapore ** (18 Aug 95), Slovakia (28 May 93), Spain **** (13 Sep 68), Ukraine (15 Nov 54), United States ******** (25 Nov 88), Venezuela **** (12 Jul 60), Vietnam **** (9 Jun 81), Yemen (9 Feb 87)

* Reservations not accepted by China, United Kingdom

** Reservation not accepted by the United Kingdom

*** Reservation not accepted by Australia, Belgium, Brazil, China, Ecuador, United Kingdom

**** Reservation not accepted by the Netherlands

***** Reservation not accepted by Australia, Brazil, Netherlands, Norway, United Kingdom

****** Reservation not accepted by Australia, Belgium, Brazil, China, Netherlands, United Kingdom

******* Reservation not accepted by Australia, Belgium, Brazil, China, Netherlands, Sri Lanka, United Kingdom

******** Reservation not accepted by Denmark, Estonia, Finland, Greece, Ireland, Italy, Mexico, Netherlands, Norway, Spain, Sweden, United Kingdom

7.11 Universal Declaration of Human Rights

Adopted: 10 Dec 48

For: 48

Afghanistan, Argentina, Australia, Belgium, Bolivia, Brazil, Canada, Chile, China, Colombia, Costa Rica, Cuba, Denmark, Dominican Republic, Ecuador, Egypt, El Salvador, Ethiopia, France, Greece, Guatemala, Haiti, Iceland, India, Iran, Iraq, Lebanon, Liberia, Luxembourg, Mexico, Myanmar, Netherlands, New Zealand, Nicaragua, Norway, Pakistan, Panama, Paraguay, Peru, Philippines, Siam (Thailand), Sweden, Syria, Turkey, United Kingdom, United States, Uruguay, Venezuela

Against: 0

Abstain: 8

Belarus (Byelorussian SSR), Czechoslovakia, Poland, Russia (USSR), Saudi Arabia, South Africa, Ukraine (Ukrainian SSR), Yugoslavia

7.12 UNESCO Declaration on the Principles of International Cultural Co-operation

Adopted: 4 Nov 66

7.13 International Covenant on Economic, Social and Cultural Rights

Concluded: 16 Dec 66

Entered into force: 3 Jan 76

Signed but not ratified: 2 (as of at least 9 Apr 98)

Liberia (18 Apr 67), United States (5 Oct 77)

Ratified/accepted/approved without qualification: 100 (as of at least 9 Apr 98)

Albania (4 Oct 91), Angola (10 Jan 92), Argentina (8 Aug 86), Armenia (13 Sep 93), Australia (10 Dec 75), Austria (10 Sep 78), Azerbaijan (13 Aug 92), Benin (12 Mar 92), Bolivia (12 Aug 82), Bosnia–Herzegovina (1 Sep 93), Brazil (24 Jan 92), Burundi (9 May 90), Cambodia (26 May 92), Cameroon (27 Jun 84), Canada (19 May 76), Cape Verde (6 Aug 93), Central African Republic (8 May 81), Chad (9 Jun 95), Chile (10 Feb 72), China (ROC) (5 Oct 67), Colombia (12 Oct 69), Congo (Kinshasa) (11 Nov 76), Costa Rica (29 Nov 68), Côte d'Ivoire (26 Mar 92), Croatia (8 Oct 91), Cyprus (2 Apr 69), Dominica (17 Jun 93), Dominican Republic (4 Jan 78), Ecuador (6 Mar 69), El Salvador (30 Nov 79), Equatorial Guinea (25 Sep 87), Estonia (21 Oct 91), Ethiopia (11 Jun 93), Finland (19 Aug 75), Gabon (21 Jan 83), Gambia (29 Dec 78), Georgia (3 May 94), Germany (17 Dec 73), Greece (16 May 85), Grenada (6 Sep 91), Guatemala (19 May 88), Guinea–Bissau (2 Jul 92), Guyana (15 Feb 77), Honduras (17 Feb 81), Iceland (22 Aug 79), Iran (24 Jun 75), Israel (3 Oct 91), Italy (15 Sep 78), Jamaica (3 Oct 75), Jordan (28 May 75), Korea (North) (14 Sep 81), Korea (South) (10 Apr 90), Kyrgyzstan (7 Oct 94), Latvia (14 Apr 92), Lebanon (3 Nov 72), Lesotho (9 Sep 92), Lithuania (20 Nov 91), Luxembourg (18 Aug 83), Macedonia (18 Jan 94), Malawi (22 Dec 93), Mali (16 Jul 74), Mauritius (12 Dec 73), Moldova (26 Jan 93), Morocco (3 May 79), Namibia (28 Nov 94), Nepal (14 May 91), Nicaragua (12 Mar 80), Niger (7 Mar 86), Nigeria (29 Jul 93), Panama (8 Mar 77), Paraguay (10 Jun 92), Peru (28 Apr 78), Philippines (7 Jun 74), Poland (18 Mar 77), Portugal (31 Jul 78), St Vincent/Grenadines (9 Nov 81), San Marino (18 Oct 85), São Tomé/Príncipe (31 Oct 95), Senegal (13 Feb 78), Seychelles (5 May 92), Sierra Leone (23 Aug 96), Slovenia (6 Jul 92), Solomon Islands (17 Mar 82), Somalia (24 Jan 90), South Africa (3 Oct 94), Spain (27 Apr 77), Sri Lanka (11 Jun 80), Sudan (18 Mar 86), Suriname (28 Dec 76), Switzerland (18 Jun 92), Tanzania (11 Jun 76), Togo (24 May 84), Tunisia (18 Mar 69), Turkmenistan (1 May 97), Uganda (21 Jan 87), Uruguay (1 Apr 70), Uzbekistan (28 Sep 95), Venezuela (10 May 78), Yugoslavia (2 Jun 71), Zimbabwe (13 May 91)

Ratified/accepted/approved with qualification: 41 (as of at least 9 Apr 98)

Afghanistan (24 Jan 83), Algeria* (12 Sep 89), Barbados (5 Jan 73), Belarus (12 Nov 73), Belgium (21 Apr 83), Bulgaria (21 Sep 70), China (PRC) (27 Oct 97), Congo (Brazzaville) (5 Oct 83), Czech Republic (22 Feb 93), Denmark (6 Jan 72), Egypt (14 Jan 82), France (4 Nov 80), Guinea (24 Jan 78), Hungary (17 Jan 74), India** (10 Apr 79), Iraq (25 Jan 71), Ireland (8 Dec 89), Japan (21 Jun 79), Kenya (1 May 72), Kuwait (21 May 96), Libya (15 May 70), Madagascar (22 Sep 71), Malta (13 Sep 90), Mexico (23 Mar 81), Monaco (28 Aug 97),Mongolia (18 Nov 74), Netherlands (11 Dec 78), New Zealand (28 Dec 78), Norway (13 Sep 72), Romania (9 Dec 74), Russia (16 Oct 73), Rwanda (16 Apr 75), Slovakia (28 May 93), Sweden (6 Dec 71), Syria (21 Apr 69), Trinidad/Tobago (8 Dec 78), Ukraine (12 Nov 73), United Kingdom (20 May 76), Vietnam (24 Sep 82), Yemen (9 Feb 87), Zambia (10 Apr 84)

* Reservation not accepted by Netherlands, Portugal

** Reservation not accepted by France, Germany, Netherlands

7.14 INTERNATIONAL COVENANT ON CIVIL AND POLITICAL RIGHTS

Concluded: 16 Dec 66
Entered into force: 23 Mar 76
Signed but not ratified: 1 (as of at least 9 Apr 98)
Liberia (18 Apr 67)
Ratified/accepted/approved without qualification: 88 (as of at least 9 Apr 98)

Albania (4 Oct 91), Angola (10 Jan 92), Armenia (23 Jun 93), Azerbaijan (13 Aug 92), Benin (12 Mar 92), Bolivia (12 Aug 82), Bosnia–Herzegovina (1 Sep 93), Brazil (24 Jan 92), Burundi (9 May 90), Cambodia (26 May 92), Cameroon (27 Jun 84), Canada (19 May 76), Cape Verde (6 Aug 93), Central African Republic (8 May 81), Chad (9 Jun 95), Chile (10 Dec 72), China (ROC) (5 Oct 67), Colombia (29 Oct 69), Congo (Kinshasa) (1 Nov 76), Costa Rica (29 Nov 68), Côte d'Ivoire (26 Mar 92), Croatia (8 Oct 91), Cyprus (2 Apr 69), Dominica (17 Jun 93), Dominican Republic (4 Jan 78), Ecuador (6 Mar 69), El Salvador (30 Nov 79), Equatorial Guinea (25 Sep 87), Estonia (21 Oct 91), Ethiopia (11 Jun 93), Gabon (21 Jan 83), Georgia (3 May 94), Grenada (6 Sep 91), Guatemala (5 May 92), Haiti (6 Feb 91), Honduras (25 Aug 97), Iran (24 Jun 75), Jamaica (3 Oct 75), Jordan (28 May 75), Kenya (1 May 72), Korea (North) (14 Sep 81), Kyrgyzstan (7 Oct 94), Latvia (14 Apr 92), Lebanon (13 Jan 72), Lesotho (9 Sep 92), Lithuania (20 Nov 91), Macedonia (17 Sep 91), Madagascar (21 Jun 71), Malawi (22 Dec 93), Mali (16 Jul 74), Mauritius (12 Dec 73), Moldova (26 Jan 93), Morocco (3 May 79), Mozambique (21 Jul 93), Namibia (28 Nov 94), Nepal (14 May 91), Nicaragua (12 Mar 80), Niger (7 Mar 86), Nigeria (29 Jul 93), Panama (8 Mar 77), Paraguay (10 Jun 92), Peru (28 Apr 78), Philippines (23 Oct 86), Poland (18 Mar 77), Portugal (15 Jun 78), Rwanda (16 Apr 75), St Vincent/Grenadines (9 Nov 81), San Marino (18 Oct 85), São Tomé/Príncipe (31 Oct 95), Senegal (13 Feb 78), Seychelles (5 May 92), Sierra Leone (23 Aug 96), Slovenia (6 Jul 92), Somalia (24 Jan 90), South Africa (3 Oct 94), Spain (27 Apr 77), Sri Lanka (11 Jun 80), Sudan (18 Mar 86), Suriname (28 Dec 76), Tanzania (11 Jun 76), Togo (24 May 84), Tunisia (18 Mar 69), Uganda (21 Jun 95), Uruguay (1 Apr 70), Uzbekistan (28 Sep 95), Yugoslavia (2 Jun 71), Zambia (10 Apr 84), Zimbabwe (13 May 91)

Ratified/accepted/approved with qualification: 53 (as of at least 97Apr 98)

Afghanistan (24 Jan 83), Algeria* (12 Sep 89), Argentina (8 Aug 86), Australia (13 Aug 80), Austria (10 Sep 78), Barbados (5 Jan 73), Belarus (12 Nov 73), Belgium (21 Apr 83), Belize (10 Jun 96), Bulgaria (21 Sep 70), Congo(Brazzaville)** (5 Oct 83), Czech Republic (22 Feb 93), Denmark (6 Jan 72), Egypt (14 Jan 82), Finland (19 Aug 75), France (4 Nov 80), Gambia (22 Mar 79), Germany (17 Dec 73), Guinea (24 Jan 78), Guyana (15 Feb 77), Hungary (17 Jan 74), Iceland (22 Aug 79), India* * * (10 Apr 79), Iraq (25 Jan 71), Ireland (8 Dec 89), Israel (3 Oct 91), Italy (15 Sep 78), Japan (21 Jun 79), Korea (South)* * ** (10 Apr 90), Kuwait (21 May 96), Libya (15 May 70), Luxembourg (18 Aug 83), Malta (13 Sep 90), Mexico (23 Mar 81), Monaco (28 Aug 97), Mongolia (18 Nov 74), Netherlands (11 Dec 78), New Zealand (28 Dec 78), Norway (13 Sep 72), Romania (9 Dec 74), Russia (16 Oct 73), Slovakia (28 May 93), Sweden (6 Dec

71), Switzerland (18 Jun 92), Syria (21 Apr 69), Thailand (29 Oct 96), Trinidad/Tobago* * *** (21 Dec 78), Ukraine (12 Nov 73), United Kingdom (20 May 76), United States (8 Jun 92), Venezuela (10 May 78), Vietnam (24 Sep 82), Yemen (9 Feb 87)

* Reservation not accepted by Portugal
** Reservation not accepted by Belgium
*** Reservation not accepted by France
**** Reservation not accepted by Czechoslovakia, Netherlands, United Kingdom
***** Reservation not accepted by Germany, Netherlands

7.15 FINAL ACT OF THE UNITED NATIONS INTERNATIONAL CONFERENCE ON HUMAN RIGHTS AT TEHERAN

Adopted: 13 May 68

7.16 AMERICAN CONVENTION ON HUMAN RIGHTS

Concluded: 22 Nov 69
Entered into force: 18 Jul 78
Signed but not ratified: 1 (as of at least 19 Dec 96)
United States (1 Jun 77)
Ratified/accepted/approved without qualification: 11 (as of at least 19 Dec 96)
Colombia (31 Jul 73), Costa Rica (8 Apr 70), Grenada (18 Jul 78), Haiti (27 Sep 77), Honduras (8 Sep 77), Jamaica (7 Aug 78), Nicaragua (25 Sep 79), Panama (22 Jun 78), Paraguay (24 Aug 89), Peru (28 Jul 78), Suriname (12 Nov 87)
Ratified/accepted/approved with qualification: 14 (as of at least 19 Dec 96)
Argentina (5 Sep 84), Barbados (5 Nov 81), Bolivia (19 Jul 79), Brazil (25 Sep 92), Chile (21 Aug 90), Dominica (6 Oct 93), Dominican Republic (19 Apr 78), Ecuador (28 Dec 77), El Salvador (23 Jun 78), Guatemala (25 May 78), Mexico (24 Mar 81), Trinidad/Tobago (29 May 91), Uruguay (19 Apr 85), Venezuela (9 Aug 77)

7.17 DECLARATION ON SOCIAL PROGRESS AND DEVELOPMENT

Adopted: 11 Dec 69
For: 119*
Against: 0
Abstain: 2
* Adopted with no roll call vote recorded

7.18 CONVENTION FOR THE PROTECTION OF THE WORLD CULTURAL AND NATURAL HERITAGE

Adopted unanimously by the UNESCO General Conference: 16 Nov 72
Entered into force: 17 Dec 75
Ratified/accepted/approved (qualifications undetermined): 153 (as of at least 15 Apr 98)
Afghanistan (20 Mar 79), Albania (10 Jul 89), Algeria (24 Jun 74), Angola (7 Nov 91), Antigua/Barbuda (1 Nov 83), Argentina (23 Aug 78), Armenia (5 Sep 93), Andorra (3 Jan 97), Australia (22 Aug 74), Austria (18 Dec 92), Azerbaijan (16 Dec 93), Bahrain (28 May 91), Bangladesh (3 Aug 83), Belarus (12 Oct 88), Belgium (24 Jul 96), Belize (6 Nov 90), Benin (14 Jun 82), Bolivia (4 Oct 76), Bosnia–Herzegovina (12 Jul 93), Brazil (1 Sep 77), Bulgaria (7 Mar 74), Burkina Faso (2 Apr 87), Burundi (19 May 82), Cambodia (28 Nov 91), Cameroon (7 Dec 82), Canada (23 Jul 76), Cape Verde (28 Apr 88), Central African Republic (22 Dec 80), Chile (20 Feb 80), China (12 Dec 85), Colombia (24 May 83), Congo (Brazzaville) (10 Dec 87), Congo (Kinshasa) (23 Sep 74), Costa Rica (23 Aug 77), Côte d'Ivoire (9 Jan 81), Croatia (6 Jul 92), Cuba (24 Mar 81), Cyprus (14 Aug 75), Czech Republic (26 Mar 93), Denmark (25 Jul 79), Dominica (4 Apr 95), Dominican Republic (12 Feb 85), Ecuador (16 Jun 75), Egypt (7 Feb 74), El Salvador (8 Oct 91), Estonia (27 Oct 95), Ethiopia (6 Jul 77), Fiji (21 Nov 90), Finland (4 Mar 87), France (27 Jun 75), Gabon (30 Dec 86), Gambia (1 Jul 87), Georgia (4 Nov 92), Germany (23 Aug 76), Ghana (4 Jul 75), Greece (17 Jul 81),

Guatemala (16 Jan 79), Guinea (18 Mar 79), Guyana (20 Jun 77), Haiti (18 Jan 80), Honduras (8 Jun 79), Hungary (15 Jul 85), Iceland (19 Dec 95), India (14 Nov 77), Indonesia (6 Jul 89), Iran (26 Feb 75), Iraq (5 Mar 74), Ireland (16 Sep 91), Italy (23 Jun 78), Jamaica (14 Jun 83), Japan (30 Jun 92), Jordan (5 May 75), Kazakhstan (29 Apr 94), Kenya (5 Jun 91), Korea (South) (14 Sep 88), Kyrgyzstan (3 Jul 95), Laos (20 Mar 87), Latvia (10 Jan 95), Lebanon (3 Feb 83), Libya (13 Oct 78), Lithuania (31 Mar 92), Luxembourg (28 Sep 83), Macedonia (30 Apr 97), Madagascar (19 Jul 83), Malawi (5 Jan 82), Malaysia (7 Dec 88), Maldives (22 May 86), Mali (5 Apr 77), Malta (14 Nov 78), Mauritania (2 Mar 81), Mauritius (19 Sep 95), Mexico (23 Feb 84), Monaco (7 Nov 78), Mongolia (2 Feb 90), Morocco (28 Oct 75), Mozambique (27 Oct 82), Myanmar (Burma) (29 Apr 94), Nepal (20 Jun 78), Netherlands (26 Aug 92), New Zealand (22 Nov 84), Nicaragua (17 Dec 79), Niger (23 Dec 74), Nigeria (23 Oct 74), Norway (12 May 77), Oman (6 Oct 81), Pakistan (23 Jul 76), Panama (3 Mar 78), Papua New Guinea (28 Jul 97), Paraguay (27 Apr 88), Peru (24 Feb 82), Philippines (19 Sep 85), Poland (29 Jun 76), Portugal (30 Sep 80), Qatar (12 Sep 84), Romania (16 May 90), Russia (12 Oct 88), St Kitts/Nevis (10 Jul 86), St Lucia (14 Oct 91), San Marino (18 Oct 91), Saudi Arabia (7 Aug 78), Senegal (13 Feb 76), Seychelles (9 Apr 80), Slovakia (31 Mar 93), Slovenia (5 Nov 92), Solomon Islands (10 Jun 92), South Africa (10 Jul 97), Spain (4 May 82), Sri Lanka (6 Jun 80), Sudan (6 Jun 74), Suriname (23 Oct 97), Sweden (22 Jan 85), Switzerland (17 Sep 75), Syria (13 Aug 75), Tajikistan (28 Aug 92), Tanzania (2 Aug 77), Thailand (17 Sep 87), Togo (15 Apr 98), Tunisia (10 Mar 75), Tur[illegible]y (16 Mar 83), Turkmenistan (30 Sep 94), Uganda (20 Nov 87), Ukraine (1[illegible]ct 88), United Kingdom (29 May 84), United States (7 Dec 73), Uruguay [illegible]ar 89), Uzbekistan (31 Jan 93), Vatican City (7 Oct 82), Venezuela (30 [illegible] 90), Vietnam (19 Oct 87), Yemen (7 Oct 80), Yugoslavia (26 May 75), Zam[illegible] Jun 84), Zimbabwe (16 Aug 82)

7.19 Convention on the Elimination of All Forms of Discrimin[illegible]tion Against Women

Concluded: 18 Dec 79

Entered into force: 3 Sep 81

Signed but not ratified: 2 (as of at least 9 Apr 98)

Afghanistan (14 Aug 80), United States (17 Jul 80)

Ratified/accepted/approved without qualification: 116 (as of at least 9 Apr 98)

Albania (11 May 94), Andorra (15 Jan 97), Angola (17 Sep 86), Antigua/Barbuda (1 Aug 89), Armenia (13 Sep 93), Azerbaijan (10 Jul 95), Barbados (16 Oct 80), Belarus (4 Feb 81), Belize (16 May 90), Benin (12 Mar 92), Bhutan (31 Aug 81), Bolivia (8 Jun 90), Bosnia–Herzegovina (1 Sep 93), Botswana (13 Aug 96), Brazil (1 Feb 84), Bulgaria (8 Feb 82), Burkina Faso (14 Oct 87), Burundi (8 Jan 92), Cambodia (15 Oct 92), Cameroon (23 Aug 94), Canada (10 Dec 81), Cape Verde (5 Dec 80), Central African Republic (21 Jun 91), Chad (9 Jun 95), Colombia (19 Jan 82), Congo (Brazzaville) (26 Jul 82), Congo (Kinshasa) (17 Oct 86), Comoros (31 Oct 94), Costa Rica (4 Apr 86), Côte d'Ivoire (18 Dec 95), Croatia (9 Sep 92), Czech Republic (22 Feb 93), Denmark (21 Apr 83), Dominica (15 Sep 80), Dominican Republic (2 Sep 82), Ecuador (9 Nov 81), Equatorial Guinea (23 Oct 84), Eritrea (5 Sep 95), Estonia (21 Oct 91), France (14 Dec 83), Finland (4 Sep 86), Gabon (21 Jan 83), Gambia (16 Apr 93), Georgia (26 Oct 94), Ghana (2 Jan 86), Greece (7 Jun 83), Grenada (30 Aug 90), Guatemala (12 Aug 82), Guinea (9 Aug 82), Guinea–Bissau (23 Aug 85), Guyana (17 Jul 80), Haiti (20 Jul 81), Honduras (3 Mar 83), Hungary (22 Dec 80), Iceland (18 Jun 85), Ireland (23 Dec 85), Jamaica (19 Oct 84), Japan (25 Jun 85), Kenya (9 Mar 84), Korea (South) (27 Dec 84), Kyrgyzstan (10 Feb 97), Laos (14 Aug 81), Latvia (14 Apr 92), Liberia (17 Jul 84), Liechtenstein (2 Dec 95), Lithuania (18 Jan 94), Macedonia (18 Jan 94), Madagascar (17 Mar 89), Malawi (12 Mar 87), Mali (10 Sep 85), Moldova (1 Jul 94), Mongolia (20 Jul 81), Mozambique (21 Apr 97), Namibia (23 Nov 92), Nepal (22 Apr 91), Netherlands (23 Jul 91), Nicaragua (27 Oct 81), Nigeria (13 Jun 85), Norway (21 May 81), Panama (29 Oct 81), Papua New Guinea (12 Jan 95), Paraguay (6 Apr 87), Peru (13 Sep 82),

Philippines (5 Aug 81), Portugal (30 Jul 80), Romania (7 Jan 82), Russia (23 Jan 81), Rwanda (2 Mar 81), St Kitts/Nevis (25 Apr 85), St Lucia (8 Oct 82), St Vincent/Grenadines (4 Aug 81), Samoa (25 Sep 92), São Tomé/Príncipe (31 Oct 95), Senegal (5 Feb 85), Seychelles (5 May 92), Sierra Leone (11 Nov 88), Slovakia (28 May 93), Slovenia (6 Jul 92), South Africa (15 Dec 95), Sri Lanka (5 Oct 81), Suriname (1 Mar 93), Sweden (2 Jul 80), Tajikistan (26 Oct 93), Tanzania (20 Aug 85), Thailand (9 Aug 85), Togo (26 Sep 83), Turkmenistan (1 May 97), Uganda (22 Jul 85), Ukraine (12 Mar 81), United Kingdom (7 Apr 86), Uruguay (9 Oct 81), Uzbekistan (19 Jul 95), Vanuatu (8 Sep 95), Yugoslavia (26 Feb 82), Zambia (21 Jun 85), Zimbabwe (13 May 91)

Ratified/accepted/approved with qualification: 46 (as of at least 9 Apr 98)
Algeria (22 May 96), Argentina (15 Jul 85), Australia (28 Jul 83), Austria (31 Mar 82), Bahamas (6 Oct 93), Bangladesh* (6 Nov 84), Belgium (10 Jul 85), Chile (7 Dec 89), China (4 Nov 80), Cuba (17 Jul 80), Cyprus** (23 Jul 85), Egypt* (18 Sep 81), El Salvador (19 Aug 81), Ethiopia (10 Sep 81), Fiji (28 Aug 95), Germany (10 Jul 85), India (9 Jul 93), Indonesia (13 Sep 84), Iraq* (13 Aug 86), Israel (3 Oct 91), Italy (10 Jun 85), Jordan (1 Jul 92), Kuwait (2 Sep 94), Lebanon (16 Apr 97), Lesotho (22 Aug 95), Libya* * * (16 May 89), Luxembourg (2 Feb 89), Malaysia (5 Jul 95), Maldives (1 Jul 93), Malta (8 Mar 91), Mauritius* (9 Jul 84), Mexico (23 Mar 81), Morocco (21 Jun 93), Myanmar (Burma) (22 Jul 97), New Zealand* * ** (10 Jan 85), Pakistan (12 Mar 96), Poland (30 Jul 80), Singapore (5 Oct 95), Spain (5 Jan 84), Switzerland (27 Mar 97), Trinidad/Tobago (12 Jan 90), Tunisia* * * (20 Dec 85), Turkey* * *** (12 Feb 85), Venezuela (2 May 83), Vietnam (17 Feb 82), Yemen (30 May 84)

* Reservation not accepted by Germany, Mexico, Netherlands, Sweden
** Reservation not accepted by Mexico
*** Reservation not accepted by Denmark, Finland, Germany, Mexico, Norway, Netherlands, Sweden
**** Reservation not accepted by Mexico, Sweden
***** Reservation not accepted by Mexico, Netherlands

7.20 DECLARATION ON THE RIGHT TO DEVELOPMENT

Adopted: 4 Dec 86

For: 146

Afghanistan, Algeria, Angola, Antigua and Barbuda, Argentina, Australia, Austria, Bahamas, Bahrain, Bangladesh, Barbados, Belarus (Byelorussian SSR), Belgium, Belize, Benin, Bhutan, Bolivia, Botswana, Brazil, Brunei, Bulgaria, Burkina Faso, Burundi, Cambodia, Cameroon, Canada, Cape Verde, Central African Republic, Chad, Chile, China, Colombia, Comoros, Congo, Costa Rica, Côte d'Ivoire, Cuba, Cyprus, Czechoslovakia, Djibouti, Dominican Republic, Ecuador, Egypt, El Salvador, Equatorial Guinea, Ethiopia, Fiji, France, Gabon, Gambia, German Democratic Republic, Ghana, Greece, Grenada, Guatemala, Guinea, Guinea–Bissau, Guyana, Haiti, Honduras, Hungary, India, Indonesia, Iran, Iraq, Ireland, Italy, Jamaica, Jordan, Kenya, Kuwait, Lao People's Democratic Republic, Lebanon, Lesotho, Liberia, Libya, Luxembourg, Madagascar, Malawi, Malaysia, Maldives, Mali, Mauritania, Mauritius, Mexico, Mongolia, Morocco, Mozambique, Myanmar, Nepal, Netherlands, New Zealand, Nicaragua, Niger, Nigeria, Norway, Oman, Pakistan, Panama, Papua New Guinea, Paraguay, Peru, Philippines, Poland, Portugal, Qatar, Romania, Russia (USSR), Rwanda, Samoa, São Tomé and Príncipe, Saudi Arabia, Senegal, Seychelles, Sierra Leone, Singapore, Solomon Islands, Somalia, Spain, Sri Lanka, St. Kitts and Nevis, St. Lucia, St. Vincent and the Grenadines, Sudan, Suriname, Swaziland, Syria, Tanzania, Thailand, Togo, Trinidad and Tobago, Tunisia, Turkey, Uganda, Ukraine (Ukrainian SSR), United Arab Emirates, Uruguay, Vanuatu, Venezuela, Vietnam, Yemen, Yemen (Democratic), Yugoslavia, Zaire, Zambia, Zimbabwe

Against: 1

United States

Abstain: 8

Denmark, Finland, Germany (West), Iceland, Israel, Japan, Sweden, United Kingdom

7.21 **International Labor Organization Convention (No. 169) Concerning Indigenous and Tribal Peoples in Independent Countries**
Concluded: 27 Jun 89
Entered into force: 5 Sep 91
Ratified/accepted/approved without qualification: 13
Bolivia (11 Dec 91), Colombia (7 Aug 91), Costa Rica (2 Apr 93), Denmark (22 Feb 96), Ecuador (15 May 98), Fiji (3 Mar 98), Guatemala (5 Jun 96), Honduras (28 Mar 95), Mexico (5 Sep 90), Netherlands 2 Feb 98), (Norway (19 Jun 90), Paraguay (2 Feb 94), Peru (2 Feb 94)

7.22 **Convention on the Rights of the Child**
Concluded: 20 Nov 89
Entered into force: 2 Sep 90
Signed but not ratified: 1 (as of at least 9 Apr 98)
United States (16 Feb 95)
Ratified/accepted/approved without qualification: 120 (as of at least 9 Apr 98)
Albania (27 Feb 92), Angola (5 Dec 90), Antigua/Barbuda (5 Oct 93), Armenia (23 Jun 93), Azerbaijan (13 Aug 92), Bahrain (13 Feb 92), Barbados (9 Oct 90), Belarus (1 Oct 90), Belize (2 May 90), Benin (3 Aug 90), Bhutan (1 Aug 90), Bolivia (26 Jun 90), Brazil (24 Sep 90), Bulgaria (3 Jun 91), Burkina Faso (31 Aug 90), Burundi (19 Oct 90), Cambodia (15 Oct 92), Cameroon (11 Jan 93), Cape Verde (4 Jun 92), Central African Republic (23 Apr 92), Chad (2 Oct 90), Chile (13 Aug 90), Comoros (22 Jun 93), Congo (Brazzaville) (14 Oct 93), Congo (Kinshasa) (27 Sep 90), Costa Rica (21 Aug 90), Côte d'Ivoire (4 Feb 91), Cyprus (7 Feb 91), Dominica (13 Mar 91), Dominican Republic (11 Jun 91), El Salvador (10 Jul 90), Equatorial Guinea (15 Jul 92), Eritrea (3 Aug 94), Estonia (21 Oct 91), Ethiopia (14 May 91), Fiji (13 Aug 93), Finland (20 Jun 91), Gabon (9 Feb 94), Gambia (8 Aug 90), Georgia (2 Jun 94), Ghana (5 Feb 90), Greece (11 May 93), Grenada (5 Nov 90), Guinea (13 Jul 90), Guinea–Bissau (20 Jul 90), Guyana (14 Jan 91), Haiti (8 Jun 95), Honduras (10 Aug 90), Hungary (7 Oct 91), Israel (3 Oct 91), Italy (5 Sep 91), Jamaica (14 May 91), Kazakstan (12 Aug 94), Kenya (30 Jul 90), Korea (North) (21 Sep 90), Kyrgyzstan (7 Oct 94), Laos (8 May 91), Latvia (14 Apr 92), Lebanon (14 May 91), Lesotho (10 Mar 92), Liberia (4 Jun 93), Libya (15 Apr 93), Lithuania (31 Jan 92), Macedonia (2 Dec 93), Madagascar (19 Mar 91), Malawi (2 Jan 91), Marshall Islands (4 Oct 93), Mexico (21 Sep 90), Micronesia (5 May 93), Moldova (26 Jan 93), Mongolia (5 Jul 90), Mozambique (26 Apr 94), Myanmar (Burma) (15 Jul 91), Namibia (30 Sep 90), Nauru (27 Jul 94), Nepal (14 Sep 90), Nicaragua (5 Oct 90), Niger (30 Sep 90), Nigeria (19 Apr 91), Niue (20 Dec 95), Norway (8 Jan 91), Palau (4 Aug 95), Panama (12 Dec 90), Papua New Guinea (2 Mar 93), Paraguay (25 Sep 90), Peru (4 Sep 90), Philippines (21 Aug 90), Portugal (21 Sep 90), Romania (28 Sep 90), Russia (16 Aug 90), Rwanda (24 Jan 91), St Kitts/Nevis (24 Jul 90), St Lucia (16 Jun 93), St Vincent/Grenadines (26 Oct 93), San Marino (25 Nov 91), São Tomé/Príncipe (14 May 91), Senegal (30 Jul 90), Seychelles (7 Sep 90), Sierra Leone (18 Jun 90), Solomon Islands (10 Apr 95), South Africa (16 Jun 95), Sri Lanka (12 Jul 91), Sudan (3 Aug 90), Suriname (1 Mar 93), Sweden (29 Jun 90), Tajikistan (26 Oct 93), Tanzania (10 Jan 91), Togo (1 Aug 90), Tonga (6 Nov 95), Trinidad/Tobago (5 Dec 91), Turkmenistan (20 Sep 93), Tuvalu (22 Sep 95), Uganda (17 Aug 90), Ukraine (28 Aug 91), Uzbekistan (29 Jan 94), Vanuatu (7 Jul 93), Vietnam (28 Feb 90), Yemen (1 May 91), Zambia (6 Dec 91), Zimbabwe (11 Sep 90)
Ratified/accepted/approved with qualification: 72 (as of at least 9 Apr 98)
Afghanistan (28 Mar 94), Algeria (16 Apr 93), Andorra (2 Jan 96), Argentina (4 Dec 90), Australia (17 Dec 90), Austria (6 Aug 92), Bahamas (20 Feb 91), Bangladesh (3 Aug 90), Belgium (16 Dec 91), Bosnia–Herzegovina (1 Sep 93), Botswana (14 Mar 95), Brunei (27 Dec 95), Canada (13 Dec 91), China (2 Mar 92), Colombia (28 Jan 91), Cook Islands (6 Jun 97), Croatia (8 Oct 91), Cuba (21 Aug 91), Czech Republic (22 Feb 93), Denmark (19 Jul 91), Djibouti* (6 Dec 90), Ecuador (23 Mar 90), Egypt (6 Jul 90), France (7 Aug 90), Germany (6 Mar 92),

Guatemala (6 Jun 90), Iceland (28 Oct 92), India (11 Dec 92), Indonesia (5 Sep 90), Iran (13 Jul 94), Iraq (15 Jun 94), Ireland (28 Sep 92), Japan (22 Apr 94), Jordan (24 May 91), Kiribati (11 Dec 95), Korea (South) (21 Sep 90), Kuwait (21 Oct 91), Liechtenstein (22 Dec 95), Luxembourg (7 Mar 94), Malaysia (17 Feb 95), Maldives (11 Feb 91), Mali (20 Sep 90), Malta (30 Sep 90), Mauritania (16 May 91), Mauritius (26 Jul 90), Monaco (21 Jun 93), Morocco (21 Jun 93), Netherlands (6 Feb 95), New Zealand (6 Apr 93), Oman (9 Dec 96), Pakistan** (12 Nov 90), Poland (7 Jun 91), Qatar (3 Apr 95), Samoa (29 Nov 94), Saudi Arabia (26 Jan 96), Singapore (5 Oct 95), Slovakia (28 May 93), Slovenia (25 Jun 91), Spain (6 Dec 90), Swaziland (7 Sep 95), Sweden (29 Jun 90), Switzerland (24 Feb 97), Syria (15 Jul 93), Thailand (27 Mar 92), Tunisia (30 Jan 92), Turkey (4 Apr 95), United Arab Emirates (3 Jan 97), United Kingdom (16 Dec 91), Uruguay (20 Nov 90), Vatican City (20 Apr 90), Venezuela (13 Sep 90), Yugoslavia (3 Jan 91)

* Reservation not accepted by Norway

** Reservation not accepted by Finland, Norway, Sweden

7.23 INTERNATIONAL CONVENTION ON THE PROTECTION OF THE RIGHTS OF ALL MIGRANT WORKERS AND MEMBERS OF THEIR FAMILIES

Concluded: 18 Dec 90

Not in force as of at least 9 Apr 98

Signed but not ratified: 2 (as of at least 9 Apr 98)

Chile (24 Sep 93), Mexico (22 May 91)

Ratified/accepted/approved without qualification: 4 (as of at least 9 Apr 98)

Bosnia–Herzegovina (13 Dec 96), Cape Verde (16 Sep 97), Philippines (5 Jul 95), Seychelles (15 Dec 94)

Ratified/accepted/approved with qualification: 5 (as of at least 9 Apr 98)

Colombia (24 May 95), Egypt (19 Feb 93), Morocco (21 Jun 93), Sri Lanka (11 Mar 96), Uganda (14 Nov 95)

7.24 DRAFT DECLARATION ON INDIGENOUS PEOPLES AS AGREED UPON BY THE MEMBERS OF THE WORKING GROUP ON INDIGENOUS PEOPLES AT ITS ELEVENTH SESSION

Adopted: 23 Aug 93

War/Peace

7.25 CONVENTION (NO. IV) RESPECTING THE LAWS AND CUSTOMS OF WAR ON LAND, WITH ANNEX OF REGULATIONS

Concluded: 18 Oct 07

Entered into force: 26 Jan 10

Signed but not ratified: 15

Argentina (18 Oct 07), Bulgaria (18 Oct 07), Chile (18 Oct 07), Colombia (18 Oct 07), Ecuador (18 Oct 07), Greece (18 Oct 07), Italy (18 Oct 07), Montenegro (18 Oct 07), Paraguay (18 Oct 07), Persia (Iran) (18 Oct 07), Peru (18 Oct 07), Serbia (18 Oct 07), Turkey (18 Oct 07), Uruguay (18 Oct 07), Venezuela (18 Oct 07)

Ratified/accepted/approved without qualification: 33

Belarus (4 Jun 62), Belgium (8 Aug 10), Bolivia (27 Nov 09), Brazil (5 Jan 14), China (10 May 17), Cuba (22 Feb 12), Denmark (27 Nov 09), Dominican Republic (16 May 58), El Salvador (27 Nov 09), Ethiopia (5 Aug 35), Fiji (2 Apr 73), Finland (30 Dec 18), France (7 Oct 10) Germany (East) (9 Feb 59), Guatemala (15 May 11), Haiti (2 Feb 10), Liberia (4 Feb 14), Luxembourg (5 Sep 12), Mexico (27 Nov 09), Netherlands (27 Nov 09), Nicaragua (16 Dec 09), Norway (19 Sep 10), Panama (11 Sep 11), Poland (9 May 25), Portugal (13 Apr 11), Romania (1 Mar 12), Russia (7 Mar 55)Siam (Thailand) (12 Mar 10), South Africa (10 Mar 78), Sweden (27 Oct 09), Switzerland (12 May 10), United Kingdom (27 Nov 09), United States (27 Nov 09)

Ratified/accepted/approved with qualification: 4

Austria–Hungary (27 Nov 09), Germany (26 Jan 10), Japan (13 Dec 11), Russia (27 Nov 09)

7.26 GENEVA CONVENTION (NO. IV) RELATIVE TO THE PROTECTION OF CIVILIAN PERSONS IN TIME OF WAR

Concluded: 12 Aug 49

Entered into force: 21 Oct 50

Ratified/accepted/approved without qualification: 156 (as of at least 19 Feb 97)

Afghanistan (26 Sep 56), Algeria (20 Jun 60), Andorra (17 Sep 93), Antigua/Barbuda (6 Oct 86), Argentina (18 Sep 56), Armenia (7 Jun 93), Austria (27 Aug 53), Azerbaijan (1 Jun 93), Bahamas (11 Jul 75), Bahrain (30 Nov 71), Bangladesh (4 Apr 72), Belgium (3 Sep 52), Belize (29 Jun 84), Benin (14 Dec 61), Bhutan (10 Jan 91), Bolivia (10 Dec 76), Bosnia–Herzegovina (31 Dec 92), Botswana (29 Mar 68), Brazil (29 Jun 57), Brunei (10 Oct 91), Burkina Faso (7 Nov 61), Burundi (27 Dec 71), Cambodia (8 Dec 58), Cameroon (16 Sep 63), Canada (14 May 65), Cape Verde (15 Jun 84), Central African Republic (1 Aug 66), Chad (5 Aug 70), Chile (12 Oct 50), Colombia (8 Nov 61), Comoros (21 Nov 85), Congo (Brazzaville) (30 Jan 67), Congo (Kinshasa) (20 Feb 61), Costa Rica (15 Oct 69), Côte d'Ivoire (28 Dec 61), Croatia (11 May 92), Cuba (15 Apr 54), Cyprus (23 May 62), Denmark (27 Jun 51), Djibouti (26 Jan 78), Dominica (28 Sep 81), Dominican Republic (22 Jan 58), Ecuador (11 Aug 54), Egypt (10 Nov 52), El Salvador (17 Jun 53), Equatorial Guinea (24 Jul 86), Estonia (18 Jan 93), Ethiopia (2 Oct 69), Fiji (9 Aug 71), Finland (22 Feb 55), France (28 Jun 51), Gabon (20 Feb 65), Gambia (11 Oct 66), Georgia (14 Sep 93), Ghana (2 Aug 58), Greece (5 Jun 56), Grenada (13 Apr 81), Guatemala (14 May 52), Guinea (11 Jul 84), Guyana (22 Jul 68), Haiti (11 Apr 57), Honduras (31 Dec 65), Iceland (10 Aug 65), India (9 Nov 50), Indonesia (30 Sep 58), Iraq (14 Feb 56), Ireland (27 Sep 62), Italy (17 Dec 51), Jamaica (17 Jul 64), Japan (21 Apr 53), Jordan (29 May 51), Kazakhstan (5 May 92), Kenya (20 Sep 66), Kiribati (5 Jan 89), Kyrgyzstan (18 Sep 92), Laos (29 Oct 56), Latvia (24 Dec 91), Lebanon (10 Apr 51), Lesotho (20 May 68), Liberia (29 Mar 54), Libya (22 May 56), Liechtenstein (21 Sep 50), Lithuania (3 Oct 96), Luxembourg (1 Jul 53), Madagascar (13 Jul 63), Malawi (5 Jan 68), Malaysia (24 Aug 62), Maldives (18 Jun 91), Mali (24 May 65), Malta (22 Aug 68), Mauritania (27 Oct 62), Mauritius (18 Aug 70), Mexico (29 Oct 52), Micronesia (19 Sep 95), Moldova (24 May 93), Monaco (5 Jul 50), Mongolia (12 Feb 58), Morocco (26 Jul 56), Mozambique (14 Mar 83), Myanmar (Burma) (25 Aug 92), Namibia* (18 Oct 83), Nepal (7 Feb 64), Netherlands (3 Aug 54), Nicaragua (17 Dec 53), Niger (16 Apr 64), Nigeria (9 Jun 61), Norway (3 Aug 51), Oman (31 Jan 74), Palau (25 Jun 96), Panama (10 Feb 56), Papua New Guinea (26 May 76), Paraguay (23 Oct 61), Peru (15 Feb 56), Philippines (7 Mar 51), Qatar (15 Oct 75), Rwanda (21 Mar 64), St Kitts/Nevis (14 Feb 86), St Lucia (18 Sep 81), St Vincent/Grenadines (1 Apr 81), Samoa (23 Aug 84), San Marino (29 Aug 53), São Tomé/Príncipe (21 May 76), Saudi Arabia (18 May 63), Senegal (23 Apr 63), Seychelles (8 Nov 84), Sierra Leone (31 May 65), Singapore (27 Apr 73), Slovenia (26 Mar 92), Solomon Islands (6 Jul 81), Somalia (12 Jul 62), South Africa (31 Mar 52), Spain (4 Aug 52), Sri Lanka (28 Feb 59), Sudan (23 Sep 57), Swaziland (28 Jun 73), Sweden (28 Dec 53), Switzerland (31 Mar 50), Syria (2 Nov 53), Tajikistan (13 Jan 93), Tanzania (12 Dec 62), Thailand (29 Dec 54), Togo (6 Jan 62), Tonga (13 Apr 78), Trinidad/Tobago (17 May 63), Tunisia (4 May 57), Turkey (10 Feb 54), Turkmenistan (10 Apr 92), Tuvalu (19 Feb 81), Uganda (18 May 64), United Arab Emirates (10 May 72), Uzbekistan (8 Oct 93), Vanuatu (27 Oct 82), Vatican City (22 Feb 51), Venezuela (13 Feb 56), Zambia (19 Oct 66), Zimbabwe (7 Mar 83)

Ratified/accepted/approved with qualification: 32 (as of at least 19 Feb 97)

Albania (27 May 57), Angola (20 Sep 84), Australia (14 Oct 58), Barbados (10 Sep 68), Belarus (3 Aug 54), Bulgaria (22 Jul 54), China (28 Dec 56), Czech Republic (5 Feb 93), Germany (3 Sep 54), Guinea–Bissau (24 Jul 86), Hungary (3 Aug 54), Iran (20 Feb 57), Israel (6 Jul 51), Korea (North) (27 Aug 57), Korea (South) (16 Aug 66), Kuwait (2 Sep 67), Macedonia (1 Sep 93), New Zealand (2

May 59), Pakistan (12 Jun 51), Poland (26 Nov 54), Portugal (14 Mar 61), Romania (1 Jun 54), Russia (10 May 54), Slovakia (2 Apr 93), Suriname (13 Oct 76), Ukraine (3 Aug 54), United Kingdom (23 Sep 57), United States (2 Aug 55), Uruguay (5 Mar 69), Vietnam (28 Jun 57), Yemen (16 Jul 70), Yugoslavia (21 Apr 50)

* The acceptance by Namibia was by the UN Council for Namibia.

7.27 PRINCIPLES OF INTERNATIONAL LAW RECOGNIZED IN THE CHARTER OF THE NUREMBERG TRIBUNAL AND IN THE JUDGMENT OF THE TRIBUNAL

Adopted: 2 Aug 50

7.28 DRAFT ARTICLES ON THE DRAFT CODE OF CRIMES AGAINST THE PEACE AND SECURITY OF MANKIND (AS REVISED THROUGH 1991)

First adopted: 4 Dec 54

7.29 TREATY ON THE NON-PROLIFERATION OF NUCLEAR WEAPONS

Concluded: 1 Jul 68

Entered into force: 5 Mar 70

Ratified/accepted/approved without qualification: 182 (as of at least at least Jun 97)

Afghanistan* (4 Feb 70), Albania** (12 Sep 90), Algeria (12 Jan 95), Andorra (7 Jun 96), Angola (14 Oct 96), Antigua/Barbuda (17 Jun 85), Argentina (10 Feb 95), Armenia (15 Jul 93), Australia* (23 Jan 73), Austria* (27 Jun 69), Azerbaijan (22 Sep 92), Bahamas (11 Aug 76), Bangladesh* (31 Aug 79), Barbados (21 Feb 80), Belarus (23 Jul 93), Belgium* (2 May 75), Belize (9 Aug 85), Benin (31 Oct 72), Bhutan* (23 May 85), Bolivia (26 May 70), Bosnia–Herzegovina (15 Aug 94), Botswana (28 Apr 69), Brunei* (26 Mar 85), Bulgaria* (5 Sep 69), Burkina Faso (3 Mar 70), Burundi (19 Mar 71), Cambodia (2 Jun 72), Cameroon (8 Jan 69), Canada* (8 Jan 69), Cape Verde (24 Oct 79), Central African Republic (25 Oct 70), Chad (10 Mar 71), Chile (25 May 95), Colombia** (8 Apr 86), Comoros (4 Oct 95), Congo (Brazzaville) (23 Oct 78), Congo (Kinshasa)* (4 Aug 70), Costa Rica* (3 Mar 70), Côte d'Ivoire* (6 Mar 73), Croatia (29 Jun 92), Cyprus* (10 Feb 70), Denmark* (3 Jan 69), Djibouti (16 Oct 96), Dominica (10 Aug 84), Dominican Republic* (24 Jul 71), Ecuador* (7 Mar 69), Egypt* (26 Feb 81), El Salvador* (11 Jul 72), Equatorial Guinea (1 Nov 84), Eritrea (16 Mar 95), Estonia (7 Jan 92), Ethiopia* (5 Feb 70), Fiji* (14 Jul 72), Finland* (5 Feb 69), France (3 Aug 92), Gabon (19 Feb 74), Gambia* (12 May 75), Georgia (7 Mar 94), Germany* (2 May 75), Ghana* (4 May 70), Greece* (11 Mar 70), Grenada (2 Sep 75), Guatemala* (22 Sep 70), Guinea (29 Apr 85), Guinea–Bissau (20 Aug 76), Guyana (19 Oct 93), Haiti (2 Jun 70), Honduras* (16 May 73), Hungary* (27 May 69), Iceland* (18 Jul 69), Indonesia* (12 Jul 79), Iran* (2 Feb 70), Iraq* (29 Oct 69), Ireland* (1 Jul 68), Italy* (2 May 75), Jamaica* (5 Mar 70), Japan* (8 Jun 76), Jordan* (11 Feb 70), Kazakhstan (14 Feb 94), Kenya (11 Jun 70), Kiribati* (18 Apr 85), Korea (North) (12 Dec 85), Korea (South) (23 Apr 75), Kyrgyzstan (5 Jul 94), Laos (20 Feb 70), Latvia (31 Jan 92), Lebanon* (15 Jul 70), Lesotho* (20 May 70), Liberia (5 Mar 70), Libya* (26 May 75), Liechtenstein* (20 Apr 78), Lithuania (23 Sep 91), Luxembourg* (2 May 75), Macedonia (12 Apr 95), Madagascar* (8 Oct 70), Malawi* (18 Feb 86), Malaysia* (5 Mar 70), Maldive Islands* (7 Apr 70), Mali (10 Feb 70), Malta* (6 Feb 70), Marshall Islands (30 Jan 95), Mauritania (23 Oct 93), Mauritius* (8 Apr 69), Mexico* (21 Jan 69), Micronesia (14 Apr 95), Moldova (11 Oct 94), Monaco (13 Mar 95), Mongolia* (14 May 69), Morocco* (27 Nov 70), Mozambique (4 Sep 90), Myanmar (Burma) (2 Dec 92), Namibia (2 Oct 92), Nauru* (7 Jun 82), Nepal* (5 Jan 70), Netherlands* (2 May 75), New Zealand* (10 Sep 69), Nicaragua* (6 Mar 73), Niger (9 Oct 92), Nigeria* (27 Sep 68), Norway* (5 Feb 69), Oman (23 Jan 97), Palau (14 Apr 95), Panama (13 Jan 77), Papua New Guinea* (13 Jan 82), Paraguay* (4 Feb 70), Peru* (3 Mar 70), Philippines* (5 Oct 72), Poland* (12 Jun 69), Portugal* (15 Dec 77), Qatar (3 Apr 89), Romania* (4 Feb 70), Russia (5 Mar 70), Rwanda (20 May 75), St Kitts/Nevis* * * (22 Mar 93), St Lucia* (28 Dec 79), St Vincent/Grenadines (6 Nov 84), Samoa* (17 Mar 75), San Marino (10 Aug 70), São

Tomé/Príncipe (20 Jul 83), Saudi Arabia (3 Oct 88), Senegal* (17 Dec 70), Seychelles (12 Mar 85), Sierra Leone (26 Feb 75), Singapore* (10 Mar 76), Slovakia (1 Jan 93), Slovenia (7 Apr 92), Solomon Islands (17 Jun 81), Somalia (5 Mar 70), South Africa* (10 Jul 91), Spain* (5 Nov 87), Sri Lanka* (5 Mar 79), Sudan* (31 Oct 73), Suriname* (30 Jun 76), Swaziland* (11 Dec 69), Sweden* (9 Jan 70), Switzerland* (9 Mar 77), Syria (24 Sep 69), Tajikistan (17 Jan 95), Tanzania (31 May 91), Thailand* (2 Dec 72), Togo (26 Feb 70), Tonga (14 Jun 71), Trinidad/Tobago (30 Oct 86), Tunisia* (26 Feb 70), Turkey* (17 Apr 80), Turkmenistan (29 Sep 94), Tuvalu* (19 Jan 79), Uganda (20 Oct 82), Ukraine (5 Dec 94), United Arab Emirates (26 Sep 95), United Kingdom (27 Nov 68), UnitedStates (5 Mar 70), Uruguay* (31 Aug 70), Uzbekistan* (2 May 92), Vanuatu (24 Aug 95), Vatican City* (25 Feb 71), Venezuela* (25 Sep 75), Vietnam* (14 Jun 82), Yemen (1 Jun 79), Yugoslavia* * ** (4 Mar 70), Zambia (15 May 91), Zimbabwe (26 Sep 91)

Ratified/accepted/approved with qualification: 4 (as of at least at least Jun 97)

Bahrain (13 Jan 88), China (PRC) (9 Mar 92), Czech Republic* (1 Jan 93), Kuwait (11 Nov 89)

* Has NPT safeguard agreement that has entered into force as of at least 31 Oct 92.

** Non–NPT, full-scope safeguards agreement in force.

*** The United States considers St Kitts/Nevis as being "bound by the obligations in the treaty" on the basis of a general declaration of succession deposited with the United Nations Secretary–General.

**** Not included in total for having dissolved.

7.30 Convention on the Prohibition of Military or any other Hostile Use of Environmental Modification Techniques (ENMOD)

Concluded: 10 Dec 76

Entered into force: 5 Oct 78

Signed but not ratified: 17 (as of at least 13 Feb 98)

Bolivia (18 May 77), Congo (Kinshasa) (28 Feb 78), Ethiopia (18 May 77), Iceland (18 May 77), Iran (18 May 77), Iraq (15 Aug 77), Lebanon (18 May 77), Liberia (18 May 77), Luxembourg (18 May 77), Morocco (18 May 77), Nicaragua (11 Aug 77), Portugal (18 May 77), Sierra Leone (12 Apr 78), Syria (4 Aug 77), Turkey (18 May 77), Uganda (18 May 77), Vatican City (27 May 77)

Ratified/accepted/approved without qualification: 55 (as of at least 13 Feb 98)

Afghanistan (22 Oct 85), Algeria (19 Dec 91), Antigua/Barbuda (25 Oct 88), Australia (7 Sep 84), Bangladesh (3 Oct 79), Belarus (7 Jun 78), Belgium (12 Jul 82), Benin (30 Jun 86), Brazil (12 Oct 84), Bulgaria (31 May 78), Canada (11 Jun 81), Cape Verde (3 Oct 79), Chile (26 Apr 94), Costa Rica (7 Feb 96), Cuba (10 Apr 78), Cyprus (12 Apr 78), Czech Republic (22 Feb 93), Denmark (19 Apr 78), Dominica (9 Nov 92), Egypt (1 Apr 82), Finland (12 May 78), Ghana (22 Jun 78), Greece (23 Aug 83), Hungary (19 Apr 78), India (15 Dec 78), Ireland (16 Dec 82), Italy (27 Nov 81), Japan (9 Jun 82), Korea (North) (8 Nov 84), Laos (5 Oct 78), Malawi (5 Oct 78), Mauritius (9 Dec 92), Mongolia (19 May 78), Niger (17 Feb 93), Norway (15 Feb 79), Pakistan (27 Feb 86), Papua New Guinea (28 Oct 80), Poland (8 Jun 78), Romania (6 May 83), Russia (30 May 78), St Lucia (27 May 93), São Tomé/Príncipe (5 Oct 79), Slovakia (28 May 93), Solomon Islands (19 Jun 81), Spain (19 Jul 78), Sri Lanka (25 Apr 78), Sweden (27 Apr 84), Tunisia (11 May 78), Ukraine (13 Jun 78), United Kingdom (16 May 78), United States (17 Jan 80), Uruguay (16 Sep 93), Uzbekistan (26 May 93), Vietnam (26 Aug 80), Yemen (20 Jul 77)

Ratified/accepted/approved with qualification: 9 (as of at least 19 Feb 97)

Argentina (20 Mar 87), Austria (17 Jan 90), Germany (24 May 83), Guatemala (21 Mar 88), Korea (South) (2 Dec 86), Kuwait (2 Jan 80),* Netherlands (15 Apr 83), New Zealand (7 Sep 84), Switzerland (5 Aug 88)

* Reservation not accepted by Israel

7.31 Protocol Additional (No. I) to the Geneva Conventions of August 12, 1949, and Relating to the Protection of Victims of International Armed Conflicts

Concluded: 8 Jun 77

Entered into force: 7 Dec 78

Signed but not ratified: 9 (as of at least 1 Mar 97)

Iran (12 Dec 77), Ireland (12 Dec 77), Morocco (12 Dec 77), Nicaragua (12 Dec 77), Pakistan (12 Dec 77), Philippines (12 Dec 77), San Marino (22 Jul 78), United Kingdom (12 Dec 77), United States (12 Dec 77)

Ratified/accepted/approved without qualification: 115 (as of at least 1 Mar 97)

Albania (16 Jul 93), Antigua/Barbuda (5 Oct 86), Armenia (7 Jun 93), Bahamas (10 Apr 80), Bahrain (30 Oct 86), Bangladesh (8 Sep 80), Barbados (19 Feb 90), Belarus (23 Oct 89), Belize (29 Jun 84), Benin (28 May 86), Bolivia (8 Dec 83), Bosnia–Herzegovina (31 Dec 92), Botswana (23 May 79), Brazil (5 May 92), Brunei (14 Oct 91), Bulgaria (26 Sep 89), Burkina Faso (20 Oct 87), Burundi (10 Jun 93), Cameroon (16 Mar 84), Cape Verde (16 Mar 95), Central African Republic (17 Jul 84), Chad (17 Jan 97), Chile (24 Apr 91), Colombia (1 Sep 93), Comoros (21 Nov 85), Congo (Brazzaville) (10 Nov 83), Congo (Kinshasa) (3 Jun 82), Costa Rica (15 Dec 83), Côte d'Ivoire (20 Sep 89), Croatia (11 May 92), Cuba (25 Nov 82), Cyprus (1 Jun 79), Czech Republic (5 Feb 93), Djibouti (8 Apr 91), Dominica (25 Apr 96), Dominican Republic (26 May 94), Ecuador (10 Apr 79), El Salvador (23 Nov 78), Equatorial Guinea (24 Jul 86), Estonia (18 Jan 93), Ethiopia (8 Apr 94), Gabon (8 Apr 80), Gambia (12 Jan 89), Georgia (14 Sep 93), Ghana (28 Feb 78), Greece (31 Mar 89), Guatemala (19 Oct 87), Guinea (11 Jul 84), Guinea–Bissau (21 Oct 86), Guyana (18 Jan 88), Honduras (16 Feb 95), Hungary (12 Apr 89), Jamaica (29 Jul 86), Jordan (1 May 79), Kazakhstan (5 May 92), Korea (North) (9 Mar 88), Kuwait (17 Jan 85), Kyrgyzstan (18 Sep 92), Laos (18 Nov 80), Latvia (24 Dec 91), Lesotho (20 May 94)), Liberia (30 Jun 88), Libya (7 Jun 78), Luxembourg (29 Aug 89), Madagascar (8 May 92), Malawi (7 Oct 91), Maldives (3 Sep 91), Mali (8 Feb 89), Mauritania (14 Mar 80), Mauritius (22 Mar 82), Mexico (10 Mar 83), Micronesia (19 Sep 95), Moldova (24 May 93), Mozambique (14 Mar 83), Namibia (18 Oct 83), Niger (8 Jun 79), Nigeria (10 Oct 88), Norway (14 Dec 81), Palau (25 Jun 95), Panama (18 Sep 95), Paraguay (30 Nov 90), Peru (14 Jul 89), Poland (23 Oct 91), Portugal (27 May 92), Romania (21 Jun 90), Rwanda (19 Nov 84), St Kitts/Nevis (14 Feb 86), St Lucia (7 Oct 82), St Vincent/Grenadines (8 Apr 83), Samoa (23 Aug 84), San Marino (5 Apr 94), São Tomé/Príncipe (5 Jul 96), Senegal (7 May 85), Seychelles (8 Nov 84), Sierra Leone (21 Oct 86), Slovakia (2 Apr 93), Slovenia (26 Mar 92), Solomon Islands (19 Sep 88), South Africa (21 Nov 95), Suriname (16 Dec 85), Swaziland (2 Nov 95), Tajikistan (13 Jan 93), Tanzania (15 Feb 83), Togo (21 Jun 84), Tunisia (9 Aug 79), Turkmenistan (10 Apr 92), Uganda (13 Mar 91), Ukraine (25 Jan 90), Uruguay (13 Dec 85), Uzbekistan (8 Oct 93), Vanuatu (28 Feb 85), Vietnam (19 Oct 81), Yemen (17 Apr 90), Zambia (4 May 95), Zimbabwe (19 Oct 92)

Ratified/accepted/approved with qualification: 32 (as of at least 19 Feb 97)

Algeria (16 Aug 89), Angola (20 Sep 84), Argentina (26 Nov 86), Australia (21 Jun 91), Austria (13 Aug 82), Belgium (20 May 86), Canada (20 Nov 90), China (14 Sep 83), Denmark (17 Jun 82), Egypt (9 Oct 92), Finland (7 Aug 80), Germany (14 Feb 91), Iceland (10 Apr 87), Italy (27 Feb 86), Korea (South) (15 Jan 82), Liechtenstein (10 Aug 89), Macedonia (1 Sep 93), Malta (17 Apr 89), Mongolia (6 Dec 95), Netherlands (26 Jun 87), New Zealand (8 Feb 88), Oman (29 Mar 84), Qatar (5 Apr 88), Russia (29 Sep 89), Saudi Arabia (21 Aug 87), Spain (21 Apr 89), Sweden (31 Aug 79), Switzerland (17 Feb 82), Syria (14 Nov 83), United Arab Emirates (9 Mar 83), Vatican City (21 Nov 85), Yugoslavia (11 Jun 79)

Note: States Parties declaring their acceptance of the competence of the International Fact–Finding Commission provided for under Article 90 totaled 49 as of at least 19 Feb 97: Algeria, Argentina, Australia, Austria, Belarus, Belgium, Bolivia, Bosnia–Herzegovina, Brazil, Bulgaria, Canada, Cape Verde, Chile, Colombia, Croatia, Czech Republic,

Denmark, Finland, Germany, Guinea, Hungary, Iceland, Italy, Liechtenstein, Luxembourg, Macedonia, Madagascar, Malta, Mongolia, Namibia, Netherlands, New Zealand, Norway, Poland, Portugal, Qatar, Romania, Russia, Rwanda, Seychelles, Slovakia, Slovenia, Spain, Sweden, Switzerland, Togo, Ukraine, United Arab Emirates, Uruguay

Protocol 1 parties: France (25 Mar 96), United Kingdom (25 Mar 96), United States (25 Mar 96)

Protocol 2 and 3 parties: China (21 Oct 88), France (25 Mar 96), Russia (21 Apr 88), United Kingdom (25 Mar 96), United States (25 Mar 96)

7.32 UNSC Resolution 687 (Concerning the Restoration of Peace and Security in Iraq and Kuwait)

Adopted: 3 Apr 91

For: 12

Austria, Belgium, China, Côte d'Ivoire, France, India, Romania, Russia (USSR), United Kingdom, United States, Zaire, Zimbabwe

Against: 1

Cuba

Abstain: 2

Ecuador, Yemen